Isn't It Time You
Got Wired
with Prentice Hall?

Whether you're looking for information for a research paper, a chance to test your knowledge and study for a big exam, or an easy way to stay in touch with your instructor, you'll find it all online at **www.prenhall.com/roberts**. With a click of the keyboard you can:

QUIZ YOURSELF.

Practice makes perfect. At **www.prenhall.com/roberts** you'll find a full range of quizzes that you can take right on your computer screen. Whether you opt for multiple-choice or short answer, there's no need to wait until next week's class for results—you'll get instant scoring and feedback about how you've done, immediately!

CHAT WITH YOUR INSTRUCTOR.

A quick "send" option gets your essays and quizzes right to your instructor, along with any questions or concerns you didn't express in class. And you'll get answers back when you need them most.

STEP BACK IN TIME.

Ever wonder what life was like when Walt Whitman was writing *Leaves of Grass*? What Ralph Ellison faced when he penned *Invisible Man*? Now it's easy to find out. Our **Living Timeline** lets you click on any date and plunge into pages packed with historical and political detail, social and cultural style—everything you need to bring an era to life and a spark to your research.

FIND AN AUTHOR.

From **www.prenhall.com/roberts** you can link directly to the websites of writers you're reading and discussing. Appreciate the opportunity to turn right to the source for the information on character development and inspiration, background information, career paths, and more.

With more insight, more resources, and more exercises to keep you on your toes, what are you waiting for? Step out of the classroom and into a new world of discovery with Prentice Hall and **www.prenhall.com/roberts**.

Learning doesn't stop in your classroom anymore!
www.prenhall.com/roberts

SIXTH EDITION

LITERATURE

An Introduction to Reading and Writing

Edgar V. Roberts
Lehman College
The City University of New York

Henry E. Jacobs

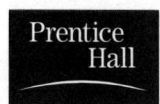
Prentice
Hall

Upper Saddle River, New Jersey 07458

LIBRARY OF CONGRESS CATALOGING-IN-PUBLICATION DATA

ROBERTS, EDGAR V.
    Literature : an introduction to reading and writing / Edgar V. Roberts. — 6th ed.
        p.   cm.
    Includes indexes.
        1. Literature.   2. Exposition (Rhetoric)   3. Literature—Collections.   4. College readers.
        5. Report writing.   I. Title.
        ISBN 0-13-018401-2
    PN45.R575   2000
    808´.0668—dc21   00-039940
                                                                                        CIP

Editor in Chief: Leah Jewell
Senior Acquisitions Editor: Carrie Brandon
Editorial Assistant: Sandy Hrasdzira
Production Editor: Joan E. Foley
Copyeditor: Kathryn Graehl
Prepress and Manufacturing Buyer: Mary Ann Gloriande
Marketing Manager: Rachel Falk
Text Permissions Specialist: Fred Courtright
Image Permissions Coordinator: Carolyn Gauntt
Cover Designer: Ximena Tamvakopoulos
Cover Art: Planet Earth Pictures/FPG International LLC
Insert Design: Maria Lange

This book was set in 10/12 Baskerville by Lithokraft II
and was printed and bound by R. R. Donnelley & Sons Company.
Cover and inserts were printed by Phoenix Color Corp.

For permission to use copyrighted material, grateful
acknowledgment is made to the copyright holders
on pages 2051–2060, which are considered an extension
of this copyright page.

Printed in the United States of America
10 9 8 7 6 5 4 3 2 1

ISBN   0-13-018401-2

Prentice-Hall International (UK) Limited, London
Prentice-Hall of Australia Pty. Limited, Sydney
Prentice-Hall Canada Inc., Toronto
Prentice-Hall Hispanoamerica, S.A., Mexico
Prentice-Hall of India Private Limited, New Delhi
Prentice-Hall of Japan, Inc., Tokyo
Pearson Education Asia Pte. Ltd., Singapore
Editora Prentice-Hall do Brasil, Ltda., Rio de Janeiro

In Loving Memory

Nanette M. Roberts, 1932–2000

"O for the touch of a vanish'd hand,
And the sound of a voice that is still."

Contents

READING AND WRITING ABOUT FICTION

4   CHARACTERS: THE PEOPLE IN FICTION   170

Character Traits,   **170**   •   *How Authors Disclose Character in
Literature,*   **172**   •   *Types of Characters: Round and Flat,*   **174**   •
Reality and Probability: Verisimilitude,   **175**

STORIES FOR STUDY   176

5   POINT OF VIEW: THE POSITION
   OR STANCE OF THE NARRATOR OR SPEAKER   240

An Exercise in Point of View: Reporting an Accident,   **241**   •
Conditions That Affect Point of View,   **243**   •   *Determining a Work's
Point of View,*   **244**   •   *Mingling Points of View,*   **247**   •
Guidelines for Points of View,   **248**

STORIES FOR STUDY   249

12   STORIES FOR ADDITIONAL STUDY

READING AND WRITING ABOUT POETRY

13   MEETING POETRY: AN OVERVIEW   661

15   WORDS: THE BUILDING BLOCKS OF POETRY   719

18   TONE: THE CREATION OF ATTITUDE IN POETRY   808

19 PROSODY: SOUND, RHYTHM, AND RHYME IN POETRY 841

[See also two additional Dickinson poems in this anthology: "Because I Could Not Stop for Death" (Poem 712), p. 671, and "To Hear an Oriole Sing" (Poem 526), p. 859.]

25 POEMS FOR ADDITIONAL STUDY 1115

READING AND WRITING ABOUT **DRAMA**

SPECIAL WRITING TOPICS ABOUT LITERATURE

Thematic
Table of Contents

For analytical purposes, the following alternative table of contents groups the selections into twenty-two separate thematic categories. ("Hope and Renewal" is a new category in the sixth edition.) The subject headings are advisory at best; they are *not* meant to dictate approaches or interpretations. Although many works belong naturally and easily within the niches we have provided, some of the works defy exclusive classification. We have accordingly assigned such works to two or more categories.

Because this table of contents is to be as brief as possible, we use only the last names of authors, eliminate virtually all beginning definite and indefinite articles, and shorten most of the titles. Thus we refer to "Thomas, **Refusal to Mourn**," and to "Shakespeare, **That Time of Year**," and so on, using recognizable short titles whenever possible rather than the full titles that appear in the regular contents, the text itself, and the index. For authors with the same last names (e.g., Phyllis Webb, Charles H. Webb; Flannery O'Connor, Frank O'Connor), we supply the complete name.

CONFORMITY
AND REBELLION

Stories

Poems

Plays

ENDINGS AND BEGINNINGS

Stories

Poems

Plays

FAITH AND DOUBT

Stories

Poems

Play

GOD, INSPIRATION, AND HUMANITY

Stories

Poems

Play

HOPE AND RENEWAL

Stories

Poems

Plays

HUSBANDS AND WIVES

THE INDIVIDUAL AND SOCIETY

INNOCENCE AND EXPERIENCE

NATURE AND HUMANITY

PARENTS AND CHILDREN

SALVATION AND DAMNATION

Stories

Poems

VISIONS OF DEATH

Stories

Poems

Plays

WAR AND VIOLENCE, AND THEIR EFFECTS

Play

WOMEN AND MEN

Preface
to the
Sixth Edition

Like the past editions of *Literature: An Introduction to Reading and Writing,* the sixth edition is a carefully chosen anthology. Most of the works here are by American, British, and Canadian authors, but classical writers from ancient Greece and Rome are also represented, along with more recent writers who lived in or came from Italy, Norway, Germany, Belgium, Ceylon, Indonesia, and Russia. In total, 281 authors are represented, not including anonymous writers. One hundred eighty of the authors—roughly sixty-five percent—were born after 1900. Interestingly, of the writers born since 1935, forty-one are women and thirty-five are men—a number that dramatizes the major importance of women in modern literature. The book includes a total of 491 separate works, not counting portions of critical essays. There are sixty-two stories, 410 poems, and nineteen dramatic works. Each work is suitable for discussion either alone or in comparison. Three plays, seven stories, and forty-one poems are new in this edition.

Readers will note that some of the new stories are classic, like those by Conrad, Forster, and Hardy, and some, such as those by Bambara, Gilchrist, and Oates, are well on their way to becoming classic. The new stories complement the other fifty-five stories, such as those by Atwood, Faulkner, Carver, Crane, Hawthorne, Hodgins, Joyce, Gaines, Gilman, Laurence, Porter, Twain, and Welty, that are retained from earlier editions.

The anthology includes representative poems from late medieval times to our own day, including poets such as Shakespeare, Gray, Wordsworth, Byron, Keats, Tennyson, Rossetti, Pound, and Eliot. The forty-one new poems represent a wide variety of American, British, and Canadian poets. Most of these poets are widely recognized. Berry, Cowper, Queen Elizabeth I, Chief Dan George, Hardy, Jacobsen, Levertov, Longfellow, Lux, Mueller, Van Duyn, and Wilbur come readily to mind. More recent poets, most of them with multiple prizes and awards to their credit, are Collins, Francis, Glück, Merwin, Momaday, and Schnackenberg. Even with the many new poems in the sixth edition of *Literature: An Introduction to Reading and Writing,* the book still retains 369 poems that were included in the fifth edition. A poet new in the fifth edition and retained in the sixth is Michael Ondaatje, who achieved wide recognition because of the many Academy awards received by the film version (1996) of his novel *The English Patient.*

In the drama section, the plays newly included are the medieval *Visitatio Sepulchri,* Wilder's *The Happy Journey to Trenton and Camden,* and Kauffmann's *The More the Merrier.* As in the fifth edition, Ibsen's *An Enemy of the People* is included with *A Dollhouse* to make up a special dramatic career chapter (31) matching the careers chapters for fiction and poetry. Chapter 11, the fiction career chapter, now includes five short stories by Edgar Allan Poe, who is acknowledged as a pioneering theorist of the short story as a genre. Chapter 24, the poetic career chapter, contains Wordsworth, Dickinson, and Frost, as in the fifth edition. Of special note is the inclusion of selected critical essays for special case studies of Poe, Dickinson, and Ibsen. Instructors who choose to do so can use these essays for research-based essays on these writers, and they may wish to use the selected bibliographies for more comprehensive research assignments.

A BRIEF OVERVIEW OF THE SIXTH EDITION

The sixth edition reaffirms a principle to which the book is dedicated—flexibility. Earlier editions have been used for introduction-to-literature courses, genre courses, and both composition and composition-and-literature courses. Adaptability and flexibility have been the keys to this variety. Instructors can use the book for classroom discussions, panel discussions, essay or paragraph-length assignments, and special topics not covered in class. Students will find incentives for understanding and writing about literature through questions, study and writing guides, and also through many suggestions for strengthening their own writing—both on essays and examinations.

FICTION.   The fiction section consists of eleven chapters. Chapter 2 is a general introduction to fiction while Chapters 3–10—the "topical" chapters central to each section of the book—introduce students to such important topics as structure, character, point of view, and theme. Chapter 11 is the career chapter on Poe, and Chapter 12 consists of ten stories for additional study.

POETRY.   The thirteen poetry chapters are arranged similarly to the fiction chapters. Chapter 13 is introductory. Chapters 14–23 deal with topics such as symbolism, imagery, symbolism, and myth. Chapter 24 is the poetic career chapter, consisting of selections by Wordsworth, Dickinson, and Frost. Chapter 25 contains one hundred thirty-nine poems for additional study. In Appendix II we include the biographies of each of the anthologized poets to make the poetry section parallel with the drama and fiction sections.

DRAMA. In the drama section Chapter 26 is introductory. Chapters 27 through 29 concern tragedy, comedy, and realism and nonrealism. At the suggestion of a number of instructors who introduce film in their courses, a unique feature begun in the third edition—Chapter 30, on film—is retained, and the discussion matches those in the other chapters. We have kept the scenes from *Citizen Kane,* by Welles and Mankiewicz, and *The Turning Point,* by Laurents. Chapter 31 is the special chapter on Ibsen. There is no "plays for additional study" chapter to match Chapters 12 and 25 because most plays are quite long, and adding more would extend the book beyond reasonable limits.

Nine of the longer plays from the previous edition have been retained because they are important in an introductory study of drama *(Oedipus the King, Hamlet, A Midsummer Night's Dream, Love is the Doctor, Death of a Salesman, The Glass Menagerie, Mulatto, A Dollhouse, An Enemy of the People).* In an anthology of this scope, the eight short plays *(Am I Blue, The Bear, Before Breakfast, Tea Party, The Visitatio Sepulchri, The More the Merrier, The Happy Journey to Trenton and Camden, Trifles)* are valuable because they may be covered in no more than one or two classroom hours, and also because they may be enlivened by having parts acted out by students. Indeed, the *Visitatio Sepulchri* and Keller's *Tea Party* are brief enough to permit classroom reading and discussion in a single period.

ADDITIONAL FEATURES

SPECIAL WRITING TOPICS. In the sixth edition we have retained the section titled "Special Writing Topics about Literature," which follows the drama section. This section, new in the fifth edition, contains four chapters (32–35) that were formerly appendices, but on the advice of many readers they are now a main part of the book. These chapters, which contain general literary assignments, are newly arranged to place emphasis on research and recent critical theories.

THE GLOSSARY. In the discussions to the various chapters, key terms and concepts are **boldfaced,** and these are gathered alphabetically and explained briefly, with relevant page numbers in the text, in the comprehensive Glossary following Appendix II. The terms in the Glossary are also listed, with page numbers from the text, in the inside back cover. Because *Literature: An Introduction to Reading and Writing* may sometimes serve for reference purposes, the Glossary is intended for general use.

QUESTIONS. Following each anthologized selection in the detailed chapters are study questions designed to help students in their exploration and understanding of literature. Some questions are factual and may be answered quickly. Others provoke extended thought and classroom discussion and may also serve for both in-class and out-of-class writing assignments. At the ends of twenty-six chapters, we include a number of more general "Special Topics for Writing and Argument about (Character, Symbolism, Tragedy, etc.)." Many of these are comparison-contrast topics, and a number of them—at least one in each chapter—are assignments requiring creative writing (for example, "Write a poem" or "Compose a short scene"). What is unique about these topics is that students are asked not only to write creatively and argue cogently, but also to analyze their own creative processes. As already indicated, the sixth edition contains questions designed to add a research component to the study of the chapter topics.

DATES.   To place the various works in historical context, we include the life dates for all authors. Along with the title of each anthologized work, we list the year of publication.

NUMBERING.   For convenient reference, we have adopted a regular style of numbering the selections by fives:

Stories:	every fifth *paragraph*
Poems:	every fifth *line*
Poetic plays:	every fifth *line*, starting at *1* with each new scene and act
Prose plays:	every fifth *speech*, starting at *1* with each new scene and act

GLOSSES.   For the poetry and poetic plays, we provide brief marginal glosses wherever they are needed. For all works, including poetry, we supply explanatory footnotes when necessary. Words and phrases that are glossed or footnoted are highlighted by a small degree sign (°). Footnotes are located according to line, paragraph, or speech numbers.

BOXED DISCUSSIONS WITHIN THE CHAPTERS.   In some of the chapters, particularly Chapters 1, 19, 26, and 32, separately boxed sections contain brief discussions of a number of important and related matters. The topics chosen for this treatment—such as the use of tenses in discussing a work, the use of authorial names, and the concept of decorum—were based on the recommendations of instructors and students.

THEMATIC TABLE OF CONTENTS.   To make *Literature: An Introduction to Reading and Writing* as flexible as possible, we have continued the Thematic Table of Contents that was first added in the fourth edition. In this table, which is located immediately following the organizational Contents, a number of thematic topics are provided, such as *Women and Men; Conformity and Rebellion; Women and Their Roles; Race, Ethnicity, and Nationality; Endings and Beginnings;* and *Innocence and Experience.* Under these topics, generous numbers of stories, poems, and plays are listed (many in a number of categories), so that entire thematic units may be created should instructors wish to use them.

PHOTOGRAPHS AND ART REPRODUCTIONS.   We also include a number of art reproductions and photographs, some within the chapters and some in special colored inserts. We hope that these reproductions, together with others that instructors might add, will encourage comparison-and-contrast discussions and essays about the relationship of literature and art.

FICTION AND DRAMATIZATION.   To strengthen the connection between fiction and dramatization, a number of stories are included that are available on videocassettes, which can be used as teaching tools for support and interpretation. A discussion of the videocassettes is included in the *Instructor's Manual*. In addition, we include two versions of the same subject matter for comparison —a short story and a one-act play—by the same author: Susan Glaspell's "A Jury of Her Peers" (Chapter 4) and *Trifles* (Chapter 26).

Revisions

There is little in the sixth edition that has not been reexamined, revised, or rewritten. Particularly noteworthy are the general introduction (Chapter 1), the introduction to poetry (Chapter 13), and the introduction to drama (Chapter 26), together with the introductory sections on Poe, Wordsworth, Dickinson, and Frost (Chapters 11 and 24), the chapters on figures of speech and prosody (17 and 19), and the chapters on research and taking examinations (32 and 34). Throughout, all subheads are no longer topics but have been fashioned into complete sentences. This change is made in the hope that pointed sentences will enable students to assimilate the following content more easily than before. The Glossary has been corrected and amended in a number of places. Of special importance in each of the main chapters are the sections "Questions for Discovering Ideas" and "Strategies for Organizing Ideas," which have been revised in the light of the continuing goal to help students concentrate on their writing assignments. In the sixth edition the MLA guidelines for the arrangement and dimensions of a typical essay are illustrated in Appendix I, along with the MLA recommendations for the handling of electronic references.

Writing and Reading

The sixth edition of *Literature: An Introduction to Reading and Writing*, like all the previous editions, is dedicated throughout to the interlocking processes of writing and reading. There is no chapter in the book that does not contain essential information and guides for writing. Moreover, we do not simply say what can be done with a topic of literary study, but we also show ways in which it might be done. In most of the chapters there is a demonstrative student essay exemplifying the strategies and methods brought out in the chapter. Following each essay is an analytical commentary showing how the writing principles of the discussion have been carried out. The emphasis throughout these sections is the openness of the writing process along with the unique nature of writing for each topic—while fully acknowledging the need to produce more polished drafts.

Because writing is a major mode of thinking, it is an essential reinforcement of reading. Students who write about what they read learn twice, for as they plan and develop their writing they necessarily grow as thinkers. Such a combined approach is the bedrock idea of this book.

READING AND WRITING NOW AND IN THE FUTURE

A logical extension (and a major hope) of this combined approach is that the techniques students acquire in studying literature as a reading-writing undertaking will help them in every course they may ever take, and in whatever profession they follow. Students will always *read*—if not the authors contained here, then other authors, and certainly newspapers, legal documents, magazine articles, technical reports, business proposals, and much more. Although students may never again be required to write about topics like setting, structure, or prosody, they will certainly find a future need to *write*.

Indeed, the more effectively students learn to write about literature when taking their literature courses, the better they will be able to write later on— no matter what the topic. It is undeniable that the power to analyze problems and make convincing written and oral presentations is a major quality of leadership and success in all fields. To acquire the skills of disciplined reading and strong writing is therefore the best possible preparation that students can make for the future, whatever it may hold.

While we stress the value of our book as a teaching tool, we also emphasize that literature is to be enjoyed and loved. Sometimes we neglect the truth that study and delight are complementary, and that intellectual stimulation and emotional enjoyment develop not only from the immediate responses of pleasure, involvement, and sympathy, but also from the understanding, contemplation, and confidence generated by knowledge and developing skill. We therefore hope that the selections in the sixth edition of *Literature: An Introduction to Reading and Writing* will teach students about humanity, about their own perceptions, feelings, and lives, and about the timeless patterns of human existence. We hope they will take delight in such discoveries and grow as they make them. We see the book as a steppingstone to lifelong understanding and joy in great literature.

ACKNOWLEDGMENTS

As the book goes into the sixth edition, I wish to acknowledge the many people who have offered helpful advice, information, and suggestions. To name them, as Dryden says in *Absalom and Achitophel*, is to praise them. They are Professors Eileen Allman, David Bady, Andrew Brilliant, Rex Butt, Stanley

Coberly, Betty L. Dixon, Elizabeth Keats Flores, Alice Griffin, Robert Halli, Rebecca Heintz, Karen Holt, Claudia Johnson, Matthew Marino, Evan Matthews, Ruth Milberg-Kaye, Nancy Miller, JoAnna Stephens Mink, Ervin Nieves, Michael Paull, Bonnie Ronson, Dan Rubey, Margaret Ellen Sherwood, Beverly J. Slaughter, Keith Walters, Chloe Warner, Scott Westrem, Mardi Valgemae, Matthew Winston, and Ruth Zerner, and also Christel Bell, Linda Bridgers, Catherine Davis, Jim Freund, Edward Hoeppner, Anna F. Jacobs, Eleanor Tubbs, Nanette Roberts, April Roberts, David Roberts, and Eve Zarin. The skilled assistance of Jonathan Roberts has been essential and invaluable at every stage of all the editions.

A number of other people have provided sterling guidance for the preparation of the sixth edition. They are Professors Peggy Cole, Arapahoe Community College; Loren C. Gruber, Missouri Valley College; Edward Martin, Columbus State Community College; and Pearl McHaney, Georgia State University.

I wish especially to thank Carrie Brandon, Senior English Editor at Prentice Hall. Her understanding, creativity, cheerfulness, and helpfulness have made working with her an honor and a pleasure. I also thank Phil Miller, President, Humanities and Social Sciences; Leah Jewell, Editor in Chief, English; and Maggie Barbieri, Nancy Perry, Alison Reeves, Kate Morgan Jackson, Bill Oliver, and Paul O'Connell, earlier Prentice Hall English editors, for their imagination and foresight, and also for their patience with me and support of me over the years. Of major importance was the work of Ray Mullaney, former Editor in Chief, Development, for his pioneering work with the text and for his continued support. I am additionally grateful to Marlane Miriello, Viqi Wagner, Anne Marie Welsh, and (especially) Kathryn Graehl. Special words of thanks are reserved for Joan Foley of Prentice Hall, our Production Editor, who has devoted her knowledge, intelligence, diligence, and skill to the many tasks needed to bring a book of this size to fruition. Additional thanks are due to Fred Courtright for his work on securing permissions, and to Carolyn Gauntt for research into the various photographs and illustrations. I also extend my gratitude to Rachel Falk, Literature Marketing Manager, to her assistant, Chrissy Moodie, and to Literature Assistant, Sandy Hrasdzira. I give final thanks to Gina Sluss, Director of Marketing, of Prentice Hall for her constant support and enthusiasm.

My sorrow is undiminished for the loss of my associate, Professor Henry E. Jacobs (1946–1986) of the University of Alabama. His energy and creativity were essential in planning and writing the first edition, but Fate intervened before we could work together on the later editions, which are nevertheless, in effect, extended collaborations.

Edgar V. Roberts

LITERATURE

LITERATURE

1

Introduction: Reading, Responding to, and Writing about Literature

WHAT IS LITERATURE, AND WHY DO WE STUDY IT?

We use the word **literature,** in a broad sense, to mean compositions that tell stories, dramatize situations, express emotions, and analyze and advocate ideas. Before the invention of writing thousands of years ago, literary works were necessarily spoken or sung, and were retained only as long as living people continued to repeat them. In some societies, the oral tradition of literature still exists, with many poems and stories designed exclusively for spoken delivery. Even in our modern age of writing and printing, much literature is still heard aloud rather than read silently. Parents delight their children with stories and poems; poets and story writers read their works directly before live audiences; plays and scripts are interpreted on stages and before moving-picture cameras for the benefit of a vast public.

No matter how we assimilate literature, we gain much from it. In truth, readers often cannot explain why they enjoy reading, for goals and ideals are not easily articulated. There are, however, areas of general agreement about the value of systematic and extensive reading.

Literature helps us grow, both personally and intellectually. It opens doors for us by providing us with an objective basis for knowledge and understanding. It links us with the cultural, philosophical, and religious world of which we are a part. It enables us to recognize human dreams and struggles in different places and times that we otherwise would never know existed. It helps us develop mature sensibility and compassion for the condition of *all* living things—human, animal, and vegetable. It gives us the knowledge and perception to appreciate the beauty of order and arrangement—gifts that are also bestowed by a well-structured song or a beautifully painted canvas. It provides the comparative basis from which to see worthiness in the aims of all people, and it therefore helps us see beauty in the world around us. It exercises our emotions through interest, concern, sympathy, tension, excitement, regret, fear, laughter, and hope. It encourages us to assist creative and talented people who need recognition and support. Through our cumulative experience in reading, literature shapes our goals and values by clarifying our own identities—both positively, through acceptance of the admirable in human beings, and negatively, through rejection of the sinister. It enables us to develop perspectives on events occurring locally and globally, and thereby it gives us understanding and control. It is one of the shaping influences of life. It makes us human.

TYPES OF LITERATURE: THE GENRES

Literature may be classified into four categories or **genres:** (1) prose fiction, (2) poetry, (3) drama, and (4) nonfiction prose. Usually the first three are classified as **imaginative literature.**

The genres of imaginative literature have much in common, but they also have distinguishing characteristics. **Prose fiction,** or **narrative fiction,** includes **myths, parables, romances, novels,** and **short stories.** Originally, *fiction* meant anything made up, crafted, or shaped, but today the word refers to prose stories based in the imaginations of authors. The essence of fiction is **narration,** the relating or recounting of a sequence of events or actions. Fictional works usually focus on one or a few major characters who change and grow (in their ability to make decisions, awareness and insight, attitude toward others, sensitivity, and moral capacity) as a result of how they deal with other characters and how they attempt to solve their problems. Although fiction, like all imaginative literature, may introduce true historical details, it is not real history, for its main purpose is to interest, stimulate, instruct, and divert, not to create a precise historical record.

If prose is expansive, **poetry** tends toward brevity. It offers us high points of emotion, reflection, thought, and feeling in what the English poet Wordsworth called "narrow room[s]." Yet in this context, it expresses the most powerful and deeply felt experiences of human beings, often awakening deep responses of welcome recognition: "Yes, I know what that's like. I would feel the same way. That's exactly right." Some poems make us think, some make us reflect, and some generally instruct us. Other poems arouse our emotions, surprise us, make us laugh or cry, and inspire us. Many poems become lifelong friends, and we visit them again and again for insight, understanding, laughter, or the quiet reflection of joy or sorrow.

Much poetry depends for its power not only on its words and thoughts but also on its music, using rhyme and a variety of rhythms to emphasize its frequent use of songlike qualities that intensify its emotional content. Many **songs** or **lyrics** have been set to music, and some were written expressly for that purpose. Traditionally important poetic forms are **sonnets** (consisting of fourteen lines) and the increasingly popular **haiku** (only three lines), in addition to **ballads** and **odes, couplets** and **blank verse,** and **villanelles** and **limericks.** Some poems are long and **discursive,** like many poems by the American poet

Whitman. **Epic** poems, such as those by Homer and Milton, contain thousands of lines. Since the time of Whitman, many poets have abandoned rhymes and regular rhythms in favor of **free verse,** a far-ranging type of poetry dependent on content and the natural rhythms of spoken language.

Although poems themselves may vary widely in length, individual lines are often short because poets wring the utmost compression and imaginative power from their words through the devices of **imagery** and **metaphor.** Whatever the poet's method, poetry allows the writer great freedom—sometimes that paradoxical experience of being freest within a restricted verse form.

Drama is literature designed for stage or film presentation by people—actors—for the benefit and delight of other people—an audience. The essence of drama is the development of **character** and **situation** through **speech** and **action.** Like fiction, drama may focus on a single character or a small number of characters, and it enacts fictional (and sometimes historical) events as if they were happening right before our eyes. The audience therefore becomes a direct witness to the ways in which characters are influenced and changed by events and by other characters. Although most modern plays use prose **dialogue** (the conversation of two or more characters), on the principle that the language of drama should resemble the language of ordinary persons as much as possible, many plays from the past, such as those of ancient Greece and Renaissance England, are in poetic form.

Nonfiction prose consists of news reports, feature articles, essays, editorials, textbooks, historical and biographical works, and the like, all of which describe or interpret facts and present judgments and opinions. In nonfiction prose the goal is to present truths and make logical conclusions about the factual world of history, science, and current events. Imaginative literature, although also grounded in facts, is less concerned with the factual record than with the revelation of truths about life and human nature.

READING LITERATURE AND RESPONDING TO IT ACTIVELY

Regrettably, our first readings of works do not provide us with full understanding. After we have finished reading a work, we may find it embarrassingly difficult to answer pointed questions or to say anything intelligent about it at all. But more active and thoughtful readings give us the understanding to develop well-considered answers. Obviously, we need to follow the work and to understand its details, but just as importantly, we need to respond to the words, get at the ideas, and understand the implications of what is happening. We rely on our own fund of knowledge and experience to verify the accuracy and truth of situations and incidents, and we try to articulate our own emotional responses to the characters and their problems.

To illustrate such active responding, the following story, "The Necklace" (1884), by the French writer Guy de Maupassant, is printed with marginal annotations like those that any reader might make during original and follow-up readings. Many observations, particularly at the beginning, are *assimilative;* that is, they do little more than record details about the action. But as the story progresses, the comments begin to reflect conclusions about the story's meaning. Toward the end, the comments are full rather than minimal; they result not only from first responses but also from considered thought. Here, then, is Maupassant's "The Necklace."

Henri-René-Albert-Guy de Maupassant (1850–1893) is considered one of the major nineteenth-century French naturalists. Scion of an aristocratic Norman family, he received his baccalaureate degree from a lycée at LeHavre, after which he began studying law. When the Franco-Prussian War broke out he served in the French army, including battlefield duty. After leaving the military he became a minor bureaucrat, first in Ministry of Marine and then in the Ministry of Education (also the workplace of Loisel, the lackluster husband of "The Necklace").

As a youth Maupassant was a vigorous and powerful oarsman, swimmer, and boatman—a power that he also devoted to his career as a writer. During the 1870s in Paris he had regularly submitted his literary efforts to the novelist Gustave Flaubert (1821–1880), a family friend who regarded him as a son and whose criticism both improved and encourage him. In Maupassant's thirties, after his mentor Flaubert's death, his career flourished. His first published volume was a collection of poems (*De Vers,* 1880), which he had to withdraw after it created a scandal and a lawsuit because of its sexual openness. After this time, until his death in 1893, he produced thirty volumes—novels, poems, articles, travel books, and three hundred short stores. In addition to "The Necklace," a few of his better-known stories are "The Ball of Fat," "Mademoiselle Fifi," and "A Piece of String."

Maupassant was a meticulous writer, devoting great attention to the reality of everyday existence. A number of his stories are about events occurring during the Franco-Prussian War; some are about life among bureaucrats, some about peasant life in Normandy, and a large number, including "The Necklace," about Parisian life. Critics observe that his stories are characterized by strong situational and cosmic irony; human beings are influenced by forces they cannot control, and their wishes are often frustrated by their own defects. Under such circumstances, Maupassant's characters exhibit varying degrees of weakness, hypocrisy, vanity, insensitivity, callousness, and even cruelty, but those who are victimized are viewed with understanding and sympathy.

GUY DE MAUPASSANT   (1850–1893)

The Necklace ("La Parure") _____ *1884*

Translated by Edgar V. Roberts

She was one of those pretty and charming women, born, as if by an error of destiny, into a family of clerks and copyists. She had no dowry, no prospects, no way of getting known, courted, loved, married by a rich and distinguished man. She finally settled for a marriage with a minor clerk in the Ministry of Education.

"She" is pretty but poor. Apparently there is no other life for her than marriage. Without connections, she has no entry into high society, and she marries an insignificant clerk.

She was a simple person, without the money to dress well, but she was as unhappy as if she had gone through bankruptcy, for women have neither rank nor race. In place of high birth or important family connections, they can rely only on their beauty, their grace, and their charm. Their inborn finesse, their elegant taste, their engaging personalities, which are their only power, make working-class women the equals of the grandest ladies.

She suffered constantly, feeling herself destined for all delicacies and luxuries. She suffered because of her grim apartment with its drab walls, threadbare furniture, ugly curtains. All such things, which most other women in her situation would not even have noticed, tortured her and filled her with despair. The sight of the young country girl who did her simple housework awakened in her only a sense of desolation and lost hopes. She daydreamed of large, silent anterooms, decorated with oriental tapestries and lighted by high bronze floor lamps, with two elegant valets in short culottes dozing in large armchairs under the effects of forced-air heaters. She imagined large drawing rooms draped in the most expensive silks, with fine end tables on which were placed knickknacks of inestimable value. She dreamed of the perfume of dainty private rooms, which were designed only for intimate tête-à-têtes with the closest friends, who because of their achievements and fame would make her the envy of all other women.

When she sat down to dinner at her round little table covered with a cloth that had not been washed for three days, in front of her husband who opened the kettle while declaring ecstatically, "Ah, good old boiled beef! I don't know anything better," she dreamed of expensive banquets with shining place settings, and wall hangings portraying ancient heroes and exotic birds in an enchanted forest. She imagined a gourmet-prepared main course carried on the most exquisite trays and served on the most beautiful dishes, with whispered gallantries which she would hear with a sphinxlike smile as she dined on the pink meat of a trout or the delicate wing of a quail.

5 　　She had no decent dresses, no jewels, nothing. And she loved nothing but these; she believed herself born only for these. She burned with the desire to please, to be envied, to be attractive and sought after.

She had a rich friend, a comrade from convent days, whom she did not want to see anymore because she suffered so much when she returned home. She would weep for the entire day afterward with sorrow, regret, despair, and misery.

Well, one evening, her husband came home glowing and carrying a large envelope.

"Here," he said, "this is something for you."

Marginal notes:

She is unhappy.

A view of women that excludes the possibility of a career. In 1884, women had little else than their personalities to get ahead.

She suffers because of her cheap belongings, wanting expensive things. She dreams of wealth and of how other women would envy her if she had all these fine things. But these luxuries are unrealistic and unattainable for her.

Her husband's taste is for plain things, while she dreams of expensive gourmet food. He has adjusted to his status. She has not.

She lives for her unrealistic dreams, and these increase her frustration.

She even thinks of giving up a rich friend because she is so depressed after visiting her.

A new section in the story.

She quickly tore open the envelope and took out a card engraved with these words:

> *The* CHANCELLOR OF EDUCATION *and*
> MRS. GEORGE RAMPONNEAU
> *request that*
> MR. AND MRS. LOISEL
> *do them the honor of coming to dinner*
> *at the Ministry of Education*
> *on the evening of January 8.*

An invitation to dinner at the Ministry of Education. A big plum.

10   Instead of being delighted, as her husband had hoped, she threw the invitation spitefully on the table, muttering:

"What do you expect me to do with this?"

It only upsets her.

"But honey, I thought you'd be glad. You never get to go out, and this is a special occasion! I had a lot of trouble getting the invitation. Everyone wants one. The demand is high and not many clerks get invited. Everyone important will be there."

She looked at him angrily and stated impatiently:

"What do you expect me to wear to go there?"

She declares that she hasn't anything to wear.

15   He had not thought of that. He stammered:

"But your theater dress. That seems nice to me . . ."

He tries to persuade her that her theater dress might do for the occasion.

He stopped, amazed and bewildered, as his wife began to cry. Large tears fell slowly from the corners of her eyes to her mouth. He said falteringly:

"What's wrong? What's the matter?"

But with a strong effort she had recovered, and she answered calmly as she wiped her damp cheeks:

20   "Nothing, except that I have nothing to wear and therefore can't go to the party. Give your invitation to someone else at the office whose wife will have nicer clothes than mine."

She wants something new, and wants to use the occasion to make her dreams come true.

Distressed, he responded:

"Well, all right, Mathilde. How much would a new dress cost, something you could use at other times, but not anything fancy?"

Her name is Mathilde.

He volunteers to pay for a new dress.

She thought for a few moments, adding things up and thinking also of an amount that she could ask without getting an immediate refusal and a frightened outcry from the frugal clerk.

She is manipulating him.

Finally she responded tentatively:

25   "I don't know exactly, but it seems to me that I could get by on four hundred francs."

He blanched slightly at this, because he had set aside just that amount to buy a shotgun for Sunday lark-hunts the next summer with a few friends in the Plain of Nanterre.

The dress will cost him his next summer's vacation. (He doesn't seem to have included her in his plans.)

However, he said:

"All right, you've got four hundred francs, but make it a pretty dress."

As the day of the party drew near, Mrs. Loisel seemed sad, uneasy, anxious, even though her gown was all ready. One evening her husband said to her:

30   "What's the matter? You've been acting funny for several days."

She answered:

"It's awful, but I don't have any jewels to wear, not a single gem, nothing to dress up my outfit. I'll look like a beggar. I'd almost rather not go to the party."

He responded:

"You can wear a corsage of cut flowers. This year it's all the rage. For only ten francs you can get two or three gorgeous roses."

35   She was not convinced.

"No . . . there's nothing more humiliating than looking shabby in the company of rich women."

But her husband exclaimed:

"God, but you're silly! Go to your friend Mrs. Forrestier, and ask her to lend you some jewelry. You know her well enough to do that."

She uttered a cry of joy:

40   "That's right. I hadn't thought of that."

The next day she went to her friend's house and described her problem.

Mrs. Forrestier went to her mirrored wardrobe, took out a large jewel box, opened it, and said to Mrs. Loisel:

"Choose, my dear."

She saw bracelets, then a pearl necklace, then a Venetian cross of finely worked gold and gems. She tried on the jewelry in front of a mirror, and hesitated, unable to make up her mind about each one. She kept asking:

45   "Do you have anything else?"

"Certainly. Look to your heart's content. I don't know what you'd like best."

Suddenly she found a superb diamond necklace in a black satin box, and her heart throbbed with desire for it. Her hands shook as she picked it up. She fastened it around her neck, watched it gleam at her throat, and looked at herself ecstatically.

Then she asked, haltingly and anxiously:

"Could you lend me this, nothing but this?"

50   "Why yes, certainly."

She jumped up, hugged her friend joyfully, then hurried away with her treasure.

Margin notes:

A new section, the third in the story. The day of the party is near.

Now she complains that she doesn't have any nice jewelry. She is manipulating him again.

She has a good point, but there seems to be no way out.

He proposes a solution: borrow jewelry from Mrs. Forrestier, who is apparently the rich friend mentioned earlier.

Mathilde will have her choice of jewels.

A "superb" diamond necklace.

This is what she wants, just this.

She leaves with the "treasure."

The day of the party came. Mrs. Loisel was a success. She was prettier than anyone else, stylish, graceful, smiling and wild with joy. All the men saw her, asked her name, sought to be introduced. All the important administrators stood in line to waltz with her. The Chancellor himself eyed her.

A new section.

The Party. Mathilde is a huge success.

She danced joyfully, passionately, intoxicated with pleasure, thinking of nothing but the moment, in the triumph of her beauty, in the glory of her success, on cloud nine with happiness made up of all the admiration, of all the aroused desire, of this victory so complete and so sweet to the heart of any woman.

Another judgment about women. Does the author mean that only women want to be admired? Don't men want admiration, too?

She did not leave until four o'clock in the morning. Her husband, since midnight, had been sleeping in a little empty room with three other men whose wives had also been enjoying themselves.

Loisel, with other husbands, is bored, while the wives are having a ball.

55   He threw, over her shoulders, the shawl that he had brought for the trip home—a modest everyday wrap, the poverty of which contrasted sharply with the elegance of her evening gown. She felt it and hurried away to avoid being noticed by the other women who luxuriated in rich furs.

Ashamed of her shabby wrap, she rushes away to avoid being seen.

Loisel tried to hold her back:

"Wait a minute. You'll catch cold outdoors. I'll call a cab."

Remember that it is early in January.

But she paid no attention and hurried down the stairs. When they reached the street they found no carriages. They began to look for one, shouting at cabmen passing by at a distance.

They walked toward the Seine, desperate, shivering. Finally, on a quay, they found one of those old night-going buggies that are seen in Paris only after dark, as if they were ashamed of their wretched appearance in daylight.

A comedown after the nice evening. They take a wretched-looking buggy home.

60   It took them to their door, on the Street of Martyrs, and they sadly climbed the stairs to their flat. For her, it was finished. As for him, he could think only that he had to begin work at the Ministry of Education at ten o'clock.

This is a real street in Paris. but is the name significant here?

Loisel is down-to-earth.

She took the shawl off her shoulders, in front of the mirror, to see herself once more in her glory. But suddenly she cried out. The necklace was no longer around her neck!

She has lost the necklace!

Her husband, already half undressed, asked:

"What's wrong?"

She turned toward him frantically:

65   "I . . . I . . . I no longer have Mrs. Forrestier's necklace."

He stood up, bewildered:

"What? . . . How? . . . It's not possible!"

And they looked in the folds of the gown, in the folds of the shawl, in the pockets, everywhere. They found nothing.

They can't find it.

He asked:

70   "You're sure you still had it when you left the party?"

"Yes. I checked it in the vestibule of the Ministry."

"But if you'd lost it in the street, we would've heard it fall. It must be in the cab."

"Yes, probably. Did you notice the number?"

"No. Did you see it?"

75 "No."

Overwhelmed, they looked at each other. Finally, Loisel got dressed again:

"I'm going out to retrace all our steps," he said, "to see if I can find the necklace that way."

And he went out. She stayed in her evening dress, without the energy to get ready for bed, stretched out in a chair, drained of strength and thought.

He goes out to search for the necklace.

Her husband came back at about seven o'clock. He had found nothing.

But is unsuccessful.

80 He went to Police Headquarters and to the newspapers to announce a reward. He went to the small cab companies, and finally he followed up even the slightest hopeful lead.

He really tries. He's doing his best.

She waited the entire day, in the same enervated state, in the face of this frightful disaster.

Loisel came back in the evening, his face pale and haggard. He had found nothing.

"You'll have to write to your friend," he said, "that you broke a clasp on her necklace and that you're having it fixed. That'll give us time to look around."

Loisel's plan to explain delaying the return. He takes charge, is resourceful.

She wrote as he dictated.

85 By the end of a week they had lost all hope.

Things are hopeless.

And Loisel, looking five years older, declared:

"We'll have to see about replacing the jewels."

The next day they took the case which had contained the necklace and went to the jeweler whose name was inside. He looked at his books:

They hunt for a replacement.

"I wasn't the one, Madam, who sold the necklace. I only made the case."

90 Then they went from jeweler to jeweler, searching for a necklace like the other one, racking their memories, both of them sick with worry and anguish.

In a shop in the Palais-Royal, they found a necklace of diamonds that seemed to them exactly like the one they were looking for. It was priced at forty thousand francs. They could buy it for thirty-six thousand.

A new diamond necklace will cost 36,000 francs, a monumental amount.

They got the jeweler to promise not to sell it for three days. And they made an agreement that he would buy it back for thirty-four thousand francs if the original was recovered before the end of February.

They make a deal with the jeweler. (Is Maupassant hinting that things might work out for them?)

Loisel had saved eighteen thousand francs that his father had left him. He would have to borrow the rest.

He borrowed, asking a thousand francs from one, five hundred from another, five louis° here, three louis there. He wrote promissory notes, undertook ruinous obligations, did business with finance companies and the whole tribe of loan sharks. He compromised himself for the remainder of his days, risked his signature without knowing whether he would be able to honor it, and, terrified by anguish over the future, by the black misery that was about to descend on him, by the prospect of all kinds of physical deprivations and moral tortures, he went to get the new necklace, and put down thirty-six thousand francs on the jeweler's counter.

It will take all of Loisel's inheritance plus another 18,000 francs that must be borrowed at enormous rates of interest.

95   Mrs. Loisel took the necklace back to Mrs. Forrestier, who said with an offended tone:

"You should have brought it back sooner; I might have needed it."

Mrs. Forrestier complains about the delay.

She did not open the case, as her friend feared she might. If she had noticed the substitution, what would she have thought? What would she have said? Would she not have taken her for a thief?

Is this enough justification for not telling the truth? It seems to be for the Loisels.

Mrs. Loisel soon discovered the horrible life of the needy. She did her share, however, completely, heroically. That horrifying debt had to be paid. She would pay. They dismissed the maid; they changed their address; they rented an attic flat.

A new section, the fifth.

She learned to do the heavy housework, dirty kitchen jobs. She washed the dishes, wearing away her manicured fingernails on greasy pots and encrusted baking dishes. She hand-washed dirty linen, shirts, and dish towels that she hung out on the line to dry. Each morning, she took the garbage down to the street, and she carried up water, stopping at each floor to catch her breath. And, dressed in cheap house dresses, she went to the fruit dealer, the grocer, the butchers, with her basket under her arms, haggling, insulting, defending her measly cash penny by penny.

They suffer to repay their debts. Loisel works late at night. Mathilde accepts a cheap attic flat, and she does all the heavy housework herself to save on domestic help.

She pinches pennies and haggles with the local tradesmen.

100   They had to make installment payments every month, and, to buy more time, to refinance loans.

They struggle to meet payments.

The husband worked evenings to make fair copies of tradesmen's accounts, and late into the night he made copies at five cents a page.

Mr. Loisel moonlights to make extra money.

And this life lasted ten years.

For ten years they struggle, but they endure.

At the end of ten years, they had paid back everything—everything—including the extra charges imposed by loan sharks and the accumulation of compound interest.

A new section. They have finally paid back the entire debt.

louis: a gold coin worth twenty francs.

Mrs. Loisel looked old now. She had become the strong, hard, and rude woman of poor households. Her hair unkempt, with uneven skirts and rough, red hands, she spoke loudly, washed floors with large buckets of water. But sometimes, when her husband was at work, she sat down near the window, and she dreamed of that evening so long ago, of that party, where she had been so beautiful and so admired.

Mrs. Loisel (how come the narrator does not say "Mathilde"?) is roughened and aged by the work. But she has behaved "heroically" (¶ 98), and has shown her mettle.

105   What would life have been like if she had not lost that necklace? Who knows? Who knows? Life is so peculiar, so uncertain. How little a thing it takes to destroy you or to save you!

The story's moral? Our lives are shaped by small, uncertain things; we hang by a thread.

Well, one Sunday, when she had gone for a stroll along the Champs-Elysées to relax from the cares of the week, she suddenly noticed a woman walking with a child. It was Mrs. Forrestier, still youthful, still beautiful, still attractive.

The final scene on the Champs-Elysées. She sees Jeanne Forrestier, after ten years.

Mrs. Loisel felt moved. Would she speak to her? Yes, certainly. And now that she had paid, she could tell all. Why not?

She walked closer.

"Hello, Jeanne."

110   The other gave no sign of recognition and was astonished to be addressed so familiarly by this working-class woman. She stammered:

They seem to have lost contact with each other totally during the last ten years. Would this have happened in real life?

"But . . . Madam! . . . I don't know. . . . You must have made a mistake."

"No. I'm Mathilde Loisel."

Her friend cried out:

"Oh! . . . My poor Mathilde, you've changed so much."

115   "Yes. I've had some tough times since I saw you last; in fact, hardships . . . and all because of you! . . ."

Jeanne notes Mathilde's changed appearance.

"Of me . . . how so?"

"You remember the diamond necklace that you lent me to go to the party at the Ministry of Education?"

"Yes. What then?"

"Well, I lost it."

120   "How, since you gave it back to me?"

"I returned another exactly like it. And for ten years we've been paying for it. You understand that this wasn't easy for us, who have nothing. . . . Finally it's over, and I'm damned glad."

Mathilde tells Jeanne everything.

Mrs. Forrestier stopped her.

"You say that you bought a diamond necklace to replace mine?"

"Yes, you didn't notice it, eh? It was exactly like yours."

125   And she smiled with proud and childish joy.

Mrs. Forrestier, deeply moved, took both her hands.

"Oh, my poor Mathilde! But mine was only costume jewelry. At most, it was worth only five hundred francs! . . ."

SURPRISE! The lost necklace was **not** real diamonds, and the Loisels slaved for no reason at all. But hard work and sacrifice probably brought out better qualities in Mathilde than she otherwise might have shown. Is this the moral of the story?

READING AND RESPONDING IN A JOURNAL

The marginal comments demonstrate the active reading-responding process you should apply to everything you read. Use the margins in your text similarly to record your comments and questions, but, in addition, plan to keep a **journal** for lengthier responses. Your journal, which may consist of a notebook, note cards, separate sheets of paper, or a computer file, will be immensely useful to you as you move from your initial impressions toward more carefully considered thought.

In keeping your journal, your objective should be to learn assigned works inside and out and then to say perceptive things about them. To achieve this goal, you need to read the work more than once. You will need a good note-taking system so that as you read, you can develop a "memory bank" of your own knowledge about a work. You can draw from this fund of ideas when you begin to write. As an aid in developing your own procedures for reading and "depositing" your ideas, you may wish to begin with the following *Guidelines for Reading*. Of course, you will want to modify these suggestions and to add to them as you become a more experienced, disciplined reader.

GUIDELINES FOR READING

1. **Observations for Basic Understanding**

    a.   Explain words, situations, and concepts. Write down words that are new or not immediately clear. If you find a passage that you do not quickly understand, decide whether the problem arises from unknown words. Use your dictionary, and record the relevant meanings in your journal, but be sure that these meanings clarify your understanding. Make note of special difficulties so that you can ask your instructor about them.

    b.   Determine what is happening. For a story or play, where do the actions take place? What do they show? Who is involved? Who is the major figure? Why is he or she major? What relationships do the characters have with one another? What concerns do the characters have? What do they do? Who says what to whom? How do the speeches advance the action and reveal the characters? For a poem, what is the situation? Who is talking, and to whom? What does the speaker say about the situation? Why does the poem end as it does and where it does?

2. **Notes on First Impressions**

    a.   Make a record of your reactions and responses, which you may derive from your marginal notations. What did you think was memorable, noteworthy, funny, or otherwise striking? Did you worry, get scared, laugh, smile, feel a thrill, learn a great deal, feel proud, find a lot to think about? In your journal, record these responses and explain them more fully.

    b.   Describe interesting characterizations, events, techniques, and ideas. If you like a character or an idea, explain what you like, and do the same for characters and ideas you don't like. Is there anything else in the work that you especially like or dislike? Are parts easy or difficult to understand? Why? Are there any surprises? What was your reaction to them? Be sure to use your own words when writing your explanations.

3. **Development of Ideas and Enlargement of Responses**

   a. Trace developing patterns. Make an outline or a scheme: What conflicts appear? Do these conflicts exist between people, groups, or ideas? How does the author resolve them? Is one force, idea, or side the winner? Why? How do you respond to the winner or to the loser?

   b. Write expanded notes about characters, situations, and actions. What explanations need to be made about the characters? Which actions, scenes, and situations invite interpretation? What assumptions do the characters and speakers reveal about life and humanity generally; about themselves, the people around them, their families, and their friends; and about work, the economy, religion, politics, philosophy, and the state of the world and the universe? What manners or customs do they exhibit? What sort of language do they use? What literary conventions and devices have you noticed, and what do these contribute to the action and ideas of the story?

   c. Write a paragraph or several paragraphs describing your reactions and thoughts. If you have an assignment, your paragraphs may be useful later because you might transfer them directly as early drafts. Even if you are making only a general preparation, however, always write down your thoughts.

   d. Memorize interesting, well-written, and important passages. Use note cards to write them out in full, and keep them in your pocket or purse. When walking to class, riding public transportation, or otherwise not occupying your time, learn them by heart.

   e. Always write down questions that arise as you read. You may raise these in class, and they may also aid your own study.

Sample Journal Entries

The following entries illustrate how you may use the guidelines in your first writing attempts. You should try to develop enough observations and responses to be useful later, both for additional study and for developing essays. Notice that the entries are not only comments but also questions.

JOURNAL ENTRIES ON MAUPASSANT'S
"THE NECKLACE"

Early in the story, Mathilde seems spoiled. She is poor, or at least lower middle class, but is unable to face her own situation.

She is a dreamer and seems harmless. Her daydreams about a fancy home, with all the expensive belongings, are not unusual. Most people dream about being well off.

She is embarrassed by her husband's taste for plain food. The story contrasts her taste for trout and quail with Loisel's cheaper favorites.

When the Loisels get the invitation, Mathilde becomes especially difficult. Her wish for an expensive dress (the cost of Loisel's entire vacation), and then her wanting the jewelry, are problems.

Her success at the party shows that she has the charm the storyteller talks about in paragraph 2. She seems never to have had any other chance to exert her power.

The worst part of her personality is shown when she hurries away from the party because she is ashamed of her everyday shawl. It is Mathilde's unhappiness and unwillingness to adjust to her modest means that cause the financial downfall of the Loisels. This disaster is her fault.

Borrowing the money to replace the necklace shows that both Loisel and Mathilde have a strong sense of honor. Making up for the loss is good, even if it destroys them financially.

There are some nice touches, like Loisel's seeming to be five years older (paragraph 86) and his staying with the other husbands of women enjoying themselves (paragraph 54). These are well done.

It's too bad that Loisel and Mathilde don't confess to Jeanne that the jewels are lost. Their pride or their honor stops them—or perhaps their fear of being accused of theft.

Their ten years of slavish work (paragraphs 98–102) show how they have come down in life. Mathilde does all her work by hand, so she really does pitch in, and she is, as the narrator says, heroic.

Mathilde becomes loud and frumpy when living in the attic flat (paragraph 99), but she also develops strength. She does what she has to. The earlier apartment and the elegance of her imaginary rooms had brought out her limitations.

The setting of the Champs-Elysées also reflects her character, for she feels free there to tell Jeanne about the disastrous loss and sacrifice (paragraph 121), producing the surprise ending.

The narrator's statement "How little a thing it takes to destroy you or to save you!" (paragraph 105) is full of thought. The necklace is little, but it makes a huge problem. This creates the story's irony.

❋   *Questions:* Is this story more about the surprise ending or about the character of Mathilde? Is she to be condemned or admired? Does the outcome stem from the little things that make us or break us, as the narrator suggests, or from the difficulty of rising above one's economic class, which seems true, or both? What do the speaker's remarks about women's status mean? (Remember, the story was published in 1884.) This probably isn't relevant, but wouldn't Jeanne, after hearing about the substitution, give the full value of the necklace to the Loisels, and wouldn't they then be pretty well off?

These are reasonable, if fairly full, remarks and observations about "The Necklace." Use your journal similarly for all reading assignments. If your assignment is simply to learn about a work, general notes like these should be enough. If you are preparing for a test, you might write pointed observations more in line with what is happening in your class, and also write and answer your own questions (see Chapter 34, "Taking Examinations on Literature"). If you have a writing assignment, these entries can help you focus more closely on your topic—such as character, idea, or setting. Whatever your purpose, always use a journal when you read, and put into it as many details and responses as you can. Your journal will then be invaluable in helping you develop your ideas and refresh your memory.

WRITING ESSAYS ON LITERARY TOPICS

Finished writing is the sharpened, focused expression of thought and study. It begins with the search for something to say—an idea. Not all ideas are equal; some are better than others, and getting good ideas is an ability that you will develop the more you think and write. As you discover ideas and write them down, you will also improve your perceptions and increase your critical faculties.

In addition, because literature itself contains the subject material, though not in a systematic way, of philosophy, religion, psychology, sociology, and politics, learning to analyze literature and to write about it will also improve your capacity to deal with these and other disciplines.

Develop an Argument When Writing about Literature

As you write about literature, you should keep two things in mind. Your first goal should be to explain materials in the work. Your second should be to relate your explanations to a specific **argument;** that is, you are writing about a specific work, but you are trying to *prove*—or *demonstrate*—a point or idea about it. This book provides you with a number of separate subjects relating to the study of literature. As you select one of these and begin writing, however, you are not to explain just that such-and-such a story has a first-person point of view or that such-and-such a poem contains a number of similes or metaphors. Rather, you should demonstrate the importance of your topic to the work as a whole in relation to a point or argument. For example, the first-person point of view may be compatible with the need for readers to supply their own interpretations of the story, or the similes and metaphors may expand and deepen the poet's ideas in the poem. Thus you will deal with the approach to the work and will also assert or argue that the approach has a vital bearing on your perception and understanding.

Your writing should therefore always have an argumentative edge—a goal of demonstrating the truth of your conclusions and clarifying and illuminating your idea about the topic and also about the work. It is important that you present your idea or ideas clearly and convincingly by interweaving factual material with reasoned inferences that support a valid conclusion, which you demonstrate to be both true about the work itself (your reading should be accurate) and valid or sound logically (your essay should be correct and coherent).

It is here that the accuracy of your choices of details from the work, the soundness of your conclusions, and the cumulative weight of your evidence are essential. Thus, you cannot allow your main ideas to rest on one detail alone but must support your conclusions by showing that the bulk of material leads to them and that they are linked in a reasonable chain of fact and logic. It is such clarification that is the goal of argumentation.

Writing Does Not Come Easily—for Anyone

The process of creating a successfully argued essay—the actual process itself of writing—is not easy. It is important to admit that writing begins in uncertainty and hesitation, and that it becomes certain and confident—accomplished—only as a result of diligent thought and considerable care. When you read a complete, polished, well-formed piece of writing, you might assume that the writer wrote this successful version in only one draft and never needed to make any changes and improvements in it at all. Nothing could be further from the truth.

If you could see the early drafts of writing you admire, you would be surprised and startled—and also encouraged—to see that good writers are also human and that what they first write is often uncertain, vague, tangential, tentative, incomplete, and messy. Usually, good writers do not like these first drafts, but nevertheless they work with their efforts and build upon them. They discard some details, add others, chop paragraphs in half and reassemble the parts elsewhere, throw out much (and then maybe recover some of it), revise or completely rewrite sentences, change words, correct misspellings, sharpen the thought, and add new material to tie all the parts together and make them flow smoothly.

There Are Three Major Stages in Thinking and Writing

For good and not-so-good writers alike, the writing task follows three basic stages. (1) The first stage—discovering ideas—shares many of the qualities of ordinary conversation. Usually, conversation is random and disorganized. It shifts from topic to topic, often without any apparent cause, and it is repetitive. In discovering ideas for writing, your process is much the same, for you jump from idea to idea and do not necessarily identify the connections or bridges between ideas. (2) By the second step, however—creating an early, rough draft of a critical paper—your thoughts should be less like ordinary conversation and more like classroom discussion. Such discussions generally stick to a point, but they are also free and spontaneous, and digressions often occur. (3) At the third stage—preparing a finished essay—your thinking must be sharply focused, and your writing must be organized, definite, concise, and connected.

If you find that writing an essay gets you into difficulties like false starts, dead ends, total cessation of thought, digressions, despair, hopelessness, and other frustrations, remember that it is important just to start. Jump right in and start writing anything at all—no matter how unacceptable your first efforts may seem—and force yourself to come to grips with the material. Beginning to write does not commit you to your first ideas. They are not untouchable and holy just because they are on paper or on your computer screen. You may throw them out in favor of new ideas. You may also cross out words or move sections around, as you wish. However, if you keep your first thoughts buried in your mind, you will have nothing to work with. It is essential to accept the uncertainties in the writing process and make them work *for* you rather than *against* you.

DISCOVERING IDEAS

You cannot know your own ideas fully until you write them down. Thus, the first thing to do in the writing process is to dig deeply into your mind and drag out all your responses and ideas about the story. Write anything and everything that occurs to you. Don't be embarrassed if things do not look great at first, but keep working toward improvement. If you have questions you can't answer, write them down and plan to answer them later. In your attempts to discover ideas, use the following prewriting techniques.

Brainstorming (Freewriting) Gets Your Mind Going

Brainstorming or **freewriting** is an informal way to describe your own written but private no-holds-barred conversation with yourself. It is your first step in writing. When you begin freewriting, you do not know what is going to happen, so you let your mind play over all the possibilities that you generate as you consider the work, or a particular element of the work, or your own early responses to it. In effect, you are talking to yourself and writing down all your thoughts, whether they fall into patterns or seem disjointed, beside the point, or even foolish. At this time, do not try to organize or criticize your thoughts. Later you can decide which ideas to keep and which to throw out. For now, the goal is to get all your ideas on paper or on the computer screen. As you are developing your essay later on, you may, at any time, return to the brainstorming or freewriting process to initiate and develop new ideas.

Focus on Specific Topics

1. **DEVELOP SUBJECTS YOU CREATE WHEN TAKING NOTES AND BRAINSTORMING.** Although the goal of brainstorming is to be totally free about the topics, you should recognize that you are trying to think creatively. You will therefore need to start directing your mind into specific channels. Once you start focusing on definite topics, your thinking, as we have noted, is analogous to classroom discussion. Let us assume that in freewriting, you produce a topic that you find

especially interesting. You might then start to focus on this topic and to write as much as you can about it. The following examples from early thoughts about Maupassant's "The Necklace" show how a writer may zero in on such a topic—in this case, honor—once the word comes up in freewriting:

> Mathilde could have gone to her friend and told her she had lost the necklace. But she didn't. Did shame overcome her? Would she have felt a loss of honor by confessing the loss of the necklace?
>
> What is honor? Doing what you think you should even if you don't want to, or if it's hard? Or is it pride? Was Mathilde too proud or too honorable to tell her friend? Does having honor mean going a harder way, when either way would probably be okay? Do you have to suffer to be honorable? Does pride or honor produce a choice for suffering?
>
> Mathilde wants others to envy her, to find her attractive. Later she tells Loisel that she would feel humiliated at the party with rich women unless she wore jewelry. Maybe she is more concerned about being admired than about the necklace. Having a high self-esteem has something to do with honor, but more with pride.
>
> Duty. Is it the same as honor? Is it Mathilde's duty to work so hard? Certainly her pride causes her to do her duty and behave honorably, and therefore pride is a step toward honor.
>
> Honor is a major part of life, I think. It seems bigger than any one life or person.
>
> Honor is just an idea or a feeling—can an idea of honor be larger than a life, take over someone's life? Should it?

These paragraphs do not represent finished writing, but they do demonstrate how a writer may attempt to define a term and determine the degree to which it applies to a major character or circumstance. Although the last paragraph departs from the story, this digression is perfectly acceptable because in the freewriting stage, writers treat ideas as they arise. If the ideas amount to something, they may be used in the developing essay; but if they don't, they can be thrown away. The important principle in brainstorming is to record all ideas, with no initial concern about how they might seem to a reader. The results of freewriting are for the eyes of the writer only. (A student once began a freewriting exercise by indicating his desire for a large bowl of ice cream. Although the wish had nothing to do with the topic, it did cause the student to begin writing and to express more germane ideas. Needless to say, the student did not write about dessert in the final essay.)

2. BUILD ON YOUR ORIGINAL NOTES.   An essential way to focus your mind is to mine your journal notes for relevant topics. For example, let us assume that you have made an original note on "The Necklace" about the importance of the attic flat where Mathilde and her husband live after they pay for the replacement necklace. With this note as a start, you can develop a number of ideas, as in the following:

The attic flat is important. Before, in her apartment, Mathilde was dreamy and impractical. She was delicate, but after losing the necklace, no way. She becomes a worker when in the flat. She can do a lot more now.

M. gives up her servant, climbs stairs carrying buckets of water, washes greasy pots, throws water around to clean floors, does all the wash by hand.

While she gets stronger, she also gets loud and frumpy—argues with shopkeepers to get the lowest prices. She stops caring for herself. A reversal here, from incapable and well groomed to coarse but capable. All this change happens in the attic flat.

Notice that even a brief original note can help you discover thoughts that you did not originally have. This act of stretching your mind leads you to put elements of the story together in ways that create support for ideas you may use to build good essays. Even in an assertion as basic as "The attic flat is important," the process itself, which is a form of concentrated thought, leads you creatively forward.

3. RAISE AND ANSWER YOUR OWN QUESTIONS.   A major way to discover ideas about a work is to raise and answer questions as you read. The *Guidelines for Reading* will help you formulate questions (pp. 12–13), but you may also raise specific questions like these (assuming that you are considering a story):

- What explanations are needed for the characters? Which actions, scenes, and situations invite interpretation? Why?
- What assumptions do the characters and speakers reveal about life and humanity generally; about themselves, the people around them, their families, and their friends; and about work, the economy, religion, politics, and the state of the world?
- What are their manners or customs?
- What kinds of words do they use: formal or informal words, slang or profanity?
- What literary conventions and devices have you discovered, and how do these add to the work? (When an author addresses readers directly, for example, that is a convention; when a comparison is used, that is a device, which might be either a metaphor or a simile.)

Of course you may raise other questions as you reread the piece, or you may be left with one or two major questions that you decide to pursue.

4. USE THE PLUS-MINUS, PRO-CON, OR EITHER-OR METHOD FOR PUTTING IDEAS TOGETHER.   A common method of discovering ideas is to develop a set of contrasts: plus-minus, pro-con, either-or. Let us suppose a plus-minus method of considering the character of Mathilde in "The Necklace": Should she be admired (plus) or condemned (minus)?

PLUS: ADMIRED?	*MINUS: CONDEMNED?*
After she cries when they get the invitation, she recovers with a "strong effort"—maybe she doesn't want her husband to feel bad.	She wants to be envied and admired only for being attractive (end of first part), not for more important qualities.
She really scores a great victory at the dance. She does have the power to charm and captivate.	She wastes her time in daydreaming about things she can't have and she whines because she is unhappy.
Once she loses the necklace, she and her husband become impoverished. But she does "her share . . . completely, heroically" (paragraph 98) to make up for the loss.	She manipulates her husband into giving her a lot of money for a party dress, but they live poorly.
Even when she is poor, she still dreams about that marvelous, shining moment. She gets worse than she deserves.	She assumes that her friend would think her a thief if she admitted to returning a different necklace. Shouldn't she have had more confidence in the friend?
At the end, she confesses the loss to her friend.	She becomes loud and coarse and haggles about pennies, thus undergoing a total cheapening of her character.

Once you put contrasting ideas side by side, as in this example, you will get new ideas. Filling the columns almost demands that you list as many contrasting positions as you can and that you think about how material in the work supports each position. It is in this way that true, genuine thinking takes place.

Your notes will therefore be useful regardless of how you finally organize your essay. You may develop either column in a full essay, or you might use the notes to support the idea that Mathilde is too complex to be either wholly admired or wholly condemned. You might even introduce an entirely new idea, such as that Mathilde should be pitied rather than condemned or admired. In short, arranging materials in the plus-minus pattern is a powerful way to discover ideas that can lead to ways of development that you might not otherwise find.

5. TRACE DEVELOPING PATTERNS. You can also discover ideas by making a list or scheme for the story or main idea. What conflicts appear? Do these conflicts exist between people, groups, or ideas? How does the author resolve them? Is one force, idea, or side the winner? Why? How do you respond to the winner or to the loser?

Using this method, you might make a list similar to this one:

Beginning: M. is a fish out of water. She dreams of wealth, but her life is drab and her husband is ordinary.

Fantasies make her even more dissatisfied; she punishes herself by thinking of a wealthy life.

Her character relates to the places in the story: the Street of the Martyrs, the dinner party scene, the attic flat. Also the places she dreams of—she fills them with the most expensive things she can imagine.

They get the dinner invitation—she pouts and whines. Her husband feels discomfort, but she doesn't really harm him. She manipulates him into buying her an expensive party dress, though.

Her dream world hurts her real life when her desire for wealth causes her to borrow the necklace. Losing the necklace is just plain bad luck.

The attic flat brings out coarseness in her. But she also develops a spirit of sacrifice and cooperation. She loses, but she's really a winner.

These observations all focus on Mathilde's character, but you may wish to trace other patterns you find in the story. If you start planning an essay about another pattern, be sure to account for all the actions and scenes that relate to your topic. Otherwise, you may miss a piece of evidence that can lead you to new conclusions.

6. USE YOUR WRITING TO HELP YOU DEVELOP YOUR THINKING.   No matter what method of discovering ideas you use, it is important to realize that *unwritten thought is incomplete thought.* Make a practice of writing your observations about the work in addition to any questions that occur to you. Very likely this practice will lead you to the most startling discoveries that you finally make about a work. This is so because looking at what you have written not only will enable you to correct and improve the writing you have done, but also will lead you to recognize that you need to do more writing. The process goes something like this: "Something needs to be added here—important details that my reader will not have noticed, new support for my argument, a new idea that has just occurred to me, a significant connection to link my thoughts." If you follow such a process, you will be using your own written ideas to create new ideas. You will be advancing your own abilities as a thinker and writer.

DRAFTING YOUR ESSAY

As you use the brainstorming and focusing techniques for discovering ideas, you are also beginning to draft your essay. You will need to revise your ideas as connections among them become more clear, and as you reexamine the work to discover details to support the argument you are developing, but you already have many of the raw materials you need for developing your topic.

Create a Central Idea or Argument

By definition, an essay *is a fully developed and organized set of paragraphs that develop and enlarge a central idea or argument.* All parts of an essay should contribute to the reader's understanding of the idea. To achieve unity and completeness, each paragraph refers to the argument and demonstrates how selected details from the work relate to it and support it. The central idea helps you control and shape your essay, just as it also provides guidance for your reader.

A successful essay about literature is a brief but thorough (not exhaustive) examination of a literary work in light of a particular element, such as *character, point of view,* or *symbolism.* Typical central ideas or arguments might be (1) that a character is strong and tenacious, or (2) that the point of view makes the action seem "distant and objective," or (3) that a major symbol governs the actions and thoughts of the major characters. In essays on these topics, all materials must be tied to such central ideas or arguments. Thus, it is a fact that Mathilde Loisel in "The Necklace" endures ten years of slavish work and sacrifice as her husband accumulates enough money to repay their monumental debt. This fact is not relevant to an essay on her character, however, unless you connect it by an argument showing how it demonstrates one of her major traits—in this case, her growing strength and perseverance.

Look through all of your ideas for one or two that catch your eye for development. If you have used more than one prewriting technique, the chances are that you have already discovered at least a few ideas that are more thought-provoking, or more important, than the others.

WRITING BY HAND, TYPEWRITER, OR WORD PROCESSOR

Writing is an inseparable part of thinking, and unwritten thought is incomplete thought.

Because thinking and writing are interdependent, it is essential to get ideas into a visible form so that you can develop them further. For many students, it is psychologically necessary to carry out this process by writing down ideas by hand or by typewriter. If you are one of these students, make your written or typed responses on only one side of your paper or note cards. This will enable you to spread your materials out and get an actual physical overview of them when you begin writing. Everything will be open to you; none of your ideas will be hidden on the back of the paper.

Today, word processing is thoroughly established as an indispensable tool for writers. The word processor can help you develop ideas, for it enables you to eliminate unworkable thoughts and replace them with others. You can move sentences and paragraphs tentatively into new contexts, test how they look, and move them somewhere else if you choose.

In addition, with the rapid printers available today, you can print drafts even in the initial and tentative stages of writing. Using your printed draft, you can make additional notes, marginal corrections, and suggestions for further development. With the marked-up draft for guidance, you can go back to your word processor and fill in your changes and improvements, repeating this procedure as often as you can. This facility makes the machine an additional incentive for improvement, right up to your final draft.

Word processing also helps you in the final preparation of your essays. Studies have shown that errors and awkward sentences are frequently found at the bottoms of pages prepared by hand or with a conventional typewriter. The reason is that writers hesitate to make improvements when they get near the end of a page because they shun the dreariness of starting the page over. Word processors eliminate this difficulty completely. Changes can be made anywhere in the draft, at any time, without damage to the appearance of the final draft.

Regardless of your writing method, you should always remember that *unwritten thought is incomplete thought.* You cannot lay everything out at once on the word processor's screen. You can see only a small part of what you are writing. Therefore, somewhere in your writing process, prepare a complete draft of what you have written. A clean, readable draft permits you to gather everything together and to make even more improvements through revision.

Once you choose an idea you think you can work with, write it as a complete sentence that is essential to the argument of your essay. A simple phrase, such as "setting and character," does not focus thought the way a sentence does. A sentence moves the topic toward new exploration and discovery because it combines a topic with an outcome, such as "The setting of 'The Necklace' reflects Mathilde's character." You may choose to be even more specific: "Mathilde's strengths and weaknesses are reflected in the real and imaginary places in 'The Necklace.'"

With a single, central idea for your essay, you have a guide by which you can accept, reject, rearrange, and change the ideas you have been developing. You may now draft a few paragraphs to see whether your idea seems valid, or you may decide that it would be more helpful to make an outline or a list before you attempt to support your ideas in a rough draft. In either case, you should use your notes for evidence to connect to your central idea and controlling argument. If you need more ideas, attempt to discover them by using any of the brainstorming-prewriting techniques. If you need to bolster your argument by including more details that are relevant, write them down as you reread the work.

Using the central idea that the changes in the story's settings reflect Mathilde's character might produce a paragraph like the following, which presents an argument about her negative qualities:

> The original apartment in the Street of Martyrs and the dream world of wealthy places both show negative sides of Mathilde's character. The real-life apartment, though livable, is shabby. The furnishings all bring out her discontent. The shabbiness makes her think only of luxuriousness, and her one servant girl causes her to dream of having many servants. The luxury of her dream life heightens her unhappiness with what she actually has.

Even in such a discovery draft, however, where the purpose is to write initial thoughts about the central idea, many details from the story are used in support. In the final draft, this kind of support is absolutely essential.

Create a Thesis Sentence

With your central idea or argument as your focus, you can now decide which of the earlier observations and ideas can be developed further. Your goal is to establish a number of major topics to support your argument and to express them in a **thesis sentence**—an organizing sentence that plans or forecasts the major topics you will treat in your essay. Suppose you choose three ideas from your discovery stage of development. If you put the central idea at the left and the list of topics at the right, you have the shape of the thesis sentence. Note that the first two topics have been taken from the discovery paragraph.

CENTRAL IDEA	*TOPICS*
The setting of "The Necklace" reflects Mathilde's character.	1. Real-life apartment
	2. Dream surroundings
	3. Attic flat

This arrangement leads to the following thesis statement:

> Mathilde's character growth is related to her first apartment, her dream-life mansion rooms, and her attic flat.

You can revise the thesis statement at any stage of the writing process if you find that you do not have enough evidence from the work to support it. Perhaps a new topic may occur to you, and you can include it, appropriately, as a part of your thesis sentence.

As we have seen, the central idea is the *glue* of the essay. The thesis sentence lists the parts to be fastened together—that is, the topics in which the central idea is to be demonstrated and argued. To alert your readers to your essay's structure, the thesis sentence is often placed at the end of the introductory paragraph, just before the body of the essay.

WRITING A FIRST DRAFT

To write a first draft, you support the points of your thesis sentence with your notes and discovery materials. You may alter, reject, and rearrange ideas and details as you wish, as long as you change your thesis sentence to account for the changes (a major reason why most writers write their introductions last). The thesis sentence just shown contains three topics (it could be two, or four, or more) to be used in forming the body of the essay.

BEGIN EACH PARAGRAPH WITH A TOPIC SENTENCE.   Just as the organization of the entire essay is based on the thesis, the form of each paragraph is based on its **topic sentence.** A topic sentence is an assertion about how a topic from the predicate of the thesis statement supports the argument contained in the central idea. The first topic in our example is the relationship of Mathilde's character to her first apartment, and the resulting paragraph should emphasize this relationship. If you choose the coarsening of her character during the ten-year travail, you can then form a topic sentence by connecting the trait with the location, as follows:

> The attic flat reflects the coarsening of Mathilde's character.

Beginning with this sentence, the paragraph will present details that argue how Mathilde's rough, heavy housework has a direct effect on her behavior, appearance, and general outlook.

USE ONLY ONE TOPIC—NO MORE—IN EACH PARAGRAPH.   You should treat each separate topic in a single paragraph—one topic, one paragraph. However, if a topic seems especially difficult, long, and heavily detailed, you may divide it into two or more subtopics, each receiving a separate paragraph of its own—two or more subtopics, two or more separate paragraphs. Should you make this division, your topic then is really a section, and each paragraph in the section should have its own topic sentence.

WRITE SO THAT YOUR PARAGRAPH DEVELOPS OUT OF YOUR TOPIC SENTENCE. Once you choose a topic sentence, you can use it to focus your observations and conclusions. Let us see how our topic about the attic flat may be developed in a paragraph of argument:

> The attic flat reflects the coarsening of Mathilde's character. Maupassant emphasizes the burdens she endures to save money, such as mopping floors, cleaning greasy and encrusted pots and pans, taking out the garbage, and washing clothes and dishes by hand. This work makes her rough and coarse, an effect also shown by her giving up care of her hair and hands, wearing the cheapest dresses possible, haggling with local shopkeepers, and becoming loud and penny-pinching. If at the beginning she is delicate and attractive, at the end she is unpleasant and coarse.

Here, details from the story are introduced to provide support for the topic sentence. All the subjects—the hard work, the lack of personal care, the wearing of cheap dresses, and the haggling with the shopkeepers—are introduced not to retell the story but rather to exemplify the argument the writer is making about Mathilde's character.

USE THE PRESENT TENSE OF VERBS
WHEN REFERRING TO ACTIONS AND IDEAS

Literary works spring into life with each and every reading. You may thus assume that everything happening takes place in the present, and when writing about literature you should use the *present tense of verbs*. It is correct to say "Mathilde and her husband *work* and *economize* [not "*worked* and *economized*"] for ten years to pay off the 18,000-franc debt they *undertake* [not "*undertook*"] to pay for the lost necklace."

When you consider an author's ideas, the present tense is also proper, on the principle that the words of an author are just as alive and current today (and tomorrow) as they were at the moment of writing, even if this same author has been dead for hundreds or even thousands of years.

Because it is incorrect to shift tenses inappropriately, you may encounter a problem when you refer to actions that have occurred prior to the time of the main action. An instance is Hemingway's "Soldier's Home," in which the main character is discontented and unsettled as a result of his combat experiences in Europe during World War I. In such a situation it is important to keep details in order, and thus you may use the past tense as long as you make the relationship clear between past and present, as in this example: "Krebs *cannot settle down* because he *is always thinking* [present tense] about the actions he *went through* [past tense] during the fighting in Europe." This use of the past influencing the present is acceptable because it corresponds to the cause-and-effect relationship brought out in the story.

A problem also arises when you introduce historical or biographical details about a work or author. It is appropriate to use the past tense for such details as long as they actually do belong to the past. Thus it is correct to state that "Shakespeare *lived* from 1564 to 1616" or that "Shakespeare *wrote* his great tragedy Hamlet in about 1600–1601." It is also permissible to mix past and present tenses when you are treating historical facts about a literary work and are also considering it as a living text. Of prime importance is to keep things straight. Here is an example showing how past and present tenses may be used when appropriate:

> Because *Hamlet* **was** first **performed** in about 1601, Shakespeare most probably **wrote** it shortly before this time. In the play, a tragedy, Shakespeare **treats** an act of vengeance, but more importantly he **demonstrates** the difficulty of ever learning the exact truth. The hero, Prince Hamlet, **is** the focus of this difficulty, for the task of revenge **is assigned** to him by the Ghost of his father. Though the Ghost **claims** that his brother, Claudius, **is** his murderer, Hamlet **is** not able to verify this claim.

Here, the historical details are in the past tense, while all details about the play *Hamlet,* including Shakespeare as the creating author whose ideas and words are still alive, are in the present.

As a general principle, you will be right most of the time if you use the present tense exclusively for literary details and the past tense for historical details. When in doubt, however, *consult your instructor.*

DEVELOPING AN OUTLINE

So far we have been developing an outline—that is, a skeletal plan of organization for your essay. Some writers never use formal outlines at all, preferring to make informal lists of ideas, whereas others rely on them constantly. Still other writers insist that they cannot make an outline until they have finished their essays. Regardless of your preference, your finished essay should have a tight structure. Therefore, you should create a guiding outline to develop or to shape your essay.

The outline we have been developing here is the **analytical sentence outline.** This type is easier to create than it sounds. It consists of (1) an introduction, including the central idea and the thesis sentence, together with (2) topic sentences that are to be used in each paragraph of the body, followed by (3) a conclusion.

When applied to the subject we have been developing, such an outline looks like this:

Title: Setting in "The Necklace" Is Connected to Mathilde's Character

1. **Introduction**
   a. *Central idea:* Maupassant uses setting to show Mathilde's character.
   b. *Thesis statement:* Her character growth is brought out by her first apartment, her daydreams about elegant rooms in a mansion, and her attic flat.

2. **Body:** *Topic sentences* a, b, and c (and d, e, and f, if necessary)
   a. Details about her first apartment explain her dissatisfaction and depression.
   b. Her daydreams about mansion rooms are like the apartment because they too make her unhappy.
   c. The attic flat reflects the coarsening of her character.

3. **Conclusion**
   Topic sentence: All details in the story, particularly the setting, are focused on the character of Mathilde.

The *conclusion* may be a summary of the body; it may evaluate the main idea; it may briefly suggest further points of discussion; or it may be a reflection on the details of the body.

Use the Outline in Developing Your Essay

The demonstrative essays included throughout this book are organized according to the principles of the analytical sentence outline. To emphasize the shaping effect of these outlines, all central ideas, thesis sentences, and topic sentences are underlined. In your own writing, you may underline or italicize these "skeletal" sentences as a check on your organization. Unless your instructor requires such markings, however, remove them in your final drafts.

DEMONSTRATIVE STUDENT ESSAY, FIRST DRAFT

The following demonstrative essay is a first draft of the topic we have been developing. It follows the outline presented here, and it includes details from the story in support of the various topics. It is by no means, however, as good a piece of writing as it can be. The draft omits a topic, some additional details, and some new insights that are included in the second draft (pp. 37–39). It therefore reveals the need to make improvements through additional brainstorming and discovery-prewriting techniques.

How Setting in "The Necklace"° Is Related to the Character of Mathilde

[1]
In "The Necklace" Guy de Maupassant does not give much detail about the setting. He does not even describe the necklace itself, which is the central object in his plot; he says only that it is "superb" (paragraph 47). Rather, he uses the setting to reflect the character of the central figure, Mathilde Loisel.* All his details are presented to bring out her traits. Her character growth is related to her first apartment, her daydreams about mansion rooms, and her attic flat.†

[2]
Details about her first apartment explain her dissatisfaction and depression. The walls are "drab," the furniture "threadbare," and the curtains "ugly" (paragraph 3). There is only a simple country girl to do the housework. The tablecloth is not changed daily, and the best dinner dish is boiled beef. Mathilde has no evening clothes, only a theater dress that she does not like. These details show her dissatisfaction about her life with her low-salaried husband.

[3]
Her dream-life images of wealth are like the apartment because they too make her unhappy. In her daydreams about life in a mansion, the rooms are large, filled with expensive furniture and bric-a-brac, and draped in silk. She imagines private rooms for intimate talks, and big dinners with delicacies like trout and quail. With dreams of such a rich home, she feels even more despair about her modest apartment on the Street of Martyrs in Paris.

[4]
The attic flat reflects the coarsening of Mathilde's character. Maupassant emphasizes the burdens she endures to save money, such as mopping floors, cleaning greasy and encrusted pots and pans, taking out the garbage, and washing clothes and dishes by hand. This work makes her rough and coarse, a fact also shown by her giving up care of her hair and hands, wearing the cheapest dresses possible, haggling with local shopkeepers, and becoming loud and penny-pinching. If at the beginning she is delicate and attractive, at the end she is unpleasant and coarse.

° See pp. 4–11 for this story.
* Central idea.
† Thesis sentence.

[5]   In summary, Maupassant focuses everything in the story, including the setting, on the character of Mathilde. Anything extra is not needed, and he does not include it. Thus he says little about the big party scene, but he emphasizes the necessary detail that Mathilde was a great "success" (paragraph 52). It is this detail that brings out some of her early attractiveness and charm (despite her more usual unhappiness). Thus in "The Necklace," Maupassant uses setting as a means to his end--the story of Mathilde and her needless sacrifice.

DEVELOPING AND STRENGTHENING YOUR ESSAY THROUGH REVISION

After finishing a first draft like this one, you may wonder what more you can do. You have read the work several times, discovered ideas to write about through brainstorming techniques, made an outline of your ideas, and written a full draft. How can you do better?

The best way to begin is to observe that a major mistake writers make when writing about literature is to do no more than retell a story or summarize an idea. Retelling a story shows only that you have read it, not that you have thought about it. Writing a good essay requires you to arrange your thoughts into a pattern that can be followed by a perceptive reader.

Use Your Own Order of References

There are many ways to escape the trap of summarizing stories and to set up your own pattern of development. One way is to stress your own order when referring to parts of a work. Do not treat details as they happen, but rearrange them to suit your own thematic plans. Rarely, if ever, should you begin by talking about a work's opening; it is better to talk first about the conclusion or middle. As you examine your first draft, if you find that you have followed the chronological order of the work instead of stressing your own order, you may use one of the prewriting techniques to figure out new ways to connect your materials. The principle is that you should introduce references to the work to support the points you wish to make, and only these points.

Use Literary Material as Evidence to Support an Argument

Whenever you write, your position is like that of a detective using clues as evidence for building a case, or of a lawyer using evidence as support for an argument. Your goal should be to convince your readers of your own knowledge and the reasonableness of your conclusions.

It is vital to use evidence convincingly so that your readers can follow your ideas. Let us look briefly at two drafts of a new example to see how writing can be improved by the pointed use of details. These are from drafts of a longer essay on the character of Mathilde.

PARAGRAPH 1

The major extenuating detail about Mathilde is that she seems to be isolated, locked away from other people. She and her husband do not talk to each other much, except about external things. He speaks about his liking for boiled beef, and she states that she cannot accept the big invitation because she has no nice dresses. Once she gets the dress, she complains because she has no jewelry. Even when borrowing the necklace from Jeanne Forrestier, she does not say much. When she and her husband discover that the necklace is lost, they simply go over the details, and Loisel dictates a letter of explanation, which she writes in her own hand. Even when she meets Jeanne on the Champs-Elysées, Mathilde does not say a great deal about her life but only goes through enough details about the loss and replacement of the necklace to make Jeanne exclaim about the needlessness of the ten-year sacrifice.

PARAGRAPH 2

The major flaw of Mathilde's character is that she is withdrawn and uncommunicative, apparently unwilling or unable to form an intimate relationship. For example, she and her husband do not talk to each other much, except about external things such as his taste for boiled beef and her lack of a party dress and jewelry. With such an uncommunicative marriage, one might suppose that she would be more open with her close friend, Jeanne Forrestier, but Mathilde does not say much even to her. This flaw hurts her greatly, because if she were more open she might have explained the loss and avoided the horrible sacrifice. This lack of openness, along with her self-indulgent dreaminess, is her biggest defect.

A comparison of these paragraphs shows that the first has more words than the second (156 to 119) but that it is more appropriate for a rough than a final draft because the writer does little more than retell the story. The paragraph is cluttered with details that do not support any conclusions. If you try to find what it says about Maupassant's actual use of Mathilde's solitary traits in "The Necklace," you will get little help. The writer needs to consider why these details should be shared, then revise the paragraph according to the central idea.

On the other hand, the details in the right-hand paragraph all support the declared topic. Phrases such as "for example," "with such," and "this lack" show that the writer of paragraph 2 has assumed that the audience knows the story and now wants help in interpretation. Paragraph 2 therefore guides readers by connecting the details to the topic. It uses these details as evidence, not as a retelling of actions. By contrast, paragraph 1 recounts a number of relevant actions but does not connect them to the topic. More details, of course, could have been added to the second paragraph, but they are unnecessary because the paragraph demonstrates the point with the details used. There are many qualities that make good writing good, but one of the most important is shown in a comparison of the two paragraphs: *In good writing, no details are included unless they are used as supporting evidence in a pattern of thought and argument.*

Keep to Your Point

To show another distinction between first- and second-draft writing, let us consider a third example. The following paragraph, in which the writer assumes an audience that is interested in the relationship of economics and politics to literature, is drawn from an essay on "The Idea of Economic Determinism in 'The Necklace.'" In this paragraph the writer argues that economics are related to a number of incidents from the story. The idea is to assert that Mathilde's difficulties result not from character but rather from financial restrictions.

> More important than chance in governing life is the idea that people are controlled by economic circumstances. Mathilde, as is shown at the story's opening, is born poor. Therefore she doesn't get the right doors opened for her, and her marriage is to a minor clerk. With a vivid imagination and a burning desire for luxury, seeming to be born only for the wealthy life, she finds that her poor home brings out her daydreams of expensive surroundings. She taunts her husband, Loisel, when he brings the big invitation, because she does not have a suitable (read "expensive") dress. Once she gets the dress it is jewelry she lacks, and she borrows that and loses it. The loss of the necklace is the greatest trouble because it forces the Loisels to borrow deeply and to lead an impoverished life for ten years.

This paragraph begins with an effective topic sentence, indicating that the writer has a good plan. The remaining part, however, shows how easily writers may be diverted from their objective. The flaw is that the material of the paragraph, while accurate, *is not tied to the topic*. Once the second sentence is under way, the paragraph gets lost in a retelling of events, and the promising topic sentence is forgotten. The paragraph therefore shows that the use of detail alone will not support an intended meaning or argument. Writers must do the connecting themselves, to make sure that all relationships are explicitly clear. *This point cannot be overstressed.*

Let us see how the problem can be treated. If the ideal paragraph can be schematized with line drawings, we might say that the paragraph's topic should be a straight line, moving toward and reaching a specific goal (the topic or argument of the paragraph), with an exemplifying line moving away from the straight line briefly to bring in evidence, but returning to the line to demonstrate the relevance of each new fact. Thus, the ideal scheme looks like this, with a straight line touched a number of times by an undulating line:

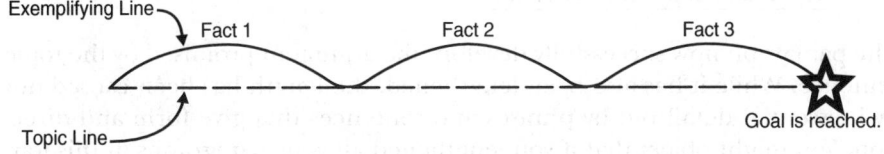

Notice that the exemplifying line, waving to illustrate how documentation or exemplification is to be used, always returns to the topic line. A scheme for the faulty paragraph on "The Necklace," however, would look like this, with the line never returning but flying out into space:

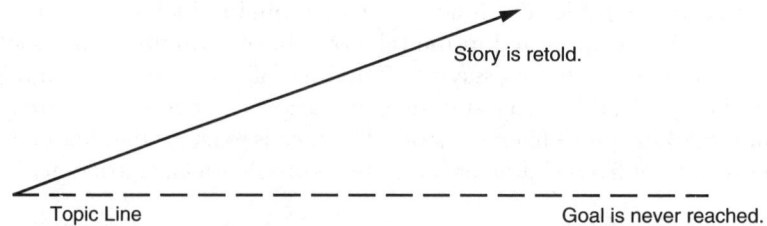

How might the faulty paragraph be improved? The best way is to remind the reader again and again of the topic and to use examples from the text in support.

As our model wavy-line diagram indicates, each time a topic is mentioned, the undulating line merges with the straight, or central-idea line. This relationship of argument to illustrative examples should prevail no matter what subject you write about. If you are analyzing *point of view*, for example, you should keep connecting your material to the speaker, or narrator, and the same applies to topics like character, theme, or setting. According to this principle, we might revise the paragraph on economic determinism in "The Necklace" as follows. (Parts of sentences stressing the relationship of the examples to the topic of the paragraph are underlined.)

> *More important than chance in governing life is the idea that people are controlled by economic circumstances.* As illustration, the speaker begins by emphasizing that Mathilde, the main character, is born poor. Therefore she doesn't get the right doors opened for her, and her marriage is to a minor clerk. In keeping with the idea, her vivid imagination and burning desire for luxury (she seems to have been born only for the wealthy life) feed on her weakness of character as she feels deep unhappiness and depression because of the contrast between her daydreams of expensive surroundings and the poor home she actually has. These straitened economic circumstances inhibit her relationship with her husband, and she taunts him when he brings the big invitation because she does not have a suitable (read "expensive") dress. As a merging of her unrealistic dream life with actual reality, her borrowing of the necklace suggests the impossibility of overcoming economic restrictions. In the context of the idea, the ten-year sacrifice to pay for the lost necklace demonstrates that lack of money keeps people down, destroying their dreams and hopes of a better life.

The paragraph now successfully develops the argument promised by the topic sentence. While it has also been lengthened, the length has been caused not by inessential detail but by phrases and sentences that give form and direction. You might object that if you lengthened all your paragraphs in this way, your essays would grow too bulky. The answer is to reduce the number of major points and paragraphs, on the theory that *it is better to develop a few topics pointedly than to develop many pointlessly.* Revising for the purpose of strengthening central and topic ideas requires that you either throw out some topics or else incorporate them as subpoints in the topics you keep. To control your writing in this way can result only in improvement.

CHECKING THE DEVELOPMENT AND ORGANIZATION OF YOUR IDEAS

It bears repeating over and over again that the first requirement of a good essay is to introduce a point or main idea and then stick to it. Another major step toward excellence is to make your central idea expand and grow. The word *growth* is a metaphor describing the creation of new insights, the disclosure of ideas that were not at first noticeable, and the expression of original, new, and fresh interpretations.

Try to Be Original

In everything you ever write, it is important that you try to be original. You might initially claim that you cannot be original when you are writing about someone else's work. "The author has said everything," might go your argument, "and therefore I can do little more than follow the story." This claim presupposes that you have no choice in selecting material and no opportunity to have individual thoughts and make original contributions.

But you do have choices and opportunities to be original. One obvious area of originality is the development and formulation of your central idea. For example, a natural first response to "The Necklace" is "The story is about a woman who loses a borrowed necklace and endures hardship to help pay for it." Because this response refers only to events in the story and not to any idea, an argument might be introduced if the hardship is called "needless." Just the use of this word alone demands that you explain the differences between needed and unneeded hardships, and your application of these differences to the heroine's plight would produce an original essay. Even better and more original insights could result if the topic of the budding essay were to connect the dreamy, withdrawn traits of the main character to her misfortunes and also to general misfortunes. A resulting central idea might be "People themselves create their own difficulties." Such an argument would require you to define not only the personal but also the representative nature of Mathilde's experiences, an avenue of exploration that could produce much in the way of a fresh, original essay about "The Necklace."

You can also develop your ability to treat your subject freshly and originally if you plan the body of the essay to build up to what you think is your most important and incisive idea. As examples of such planning, the following brief outline suggests how a central idea may be widened and expanded:

Subject: Mathilde Grows as a Character in "The Necklace"
1. She has normal daydreams about a better life.
2. In trying to make her daydreams seem real, she takes a risk but then loses.
3. She develops by facing her mistake and working hard to correct it.

The list shows how a subject can be enlarged if you treat your exemplifying topic in an increasing order of importance. In this case, the order moves from Mathilde's habit of daydreaming to her growing strength of character. The pattern shows how you can meet two primary standards of excellence in writing—organization and growth.

Clearly, you should always try to develop your central idea. Constantly adhere to your topic, and constantly develop it. Nurture it and make it grow. Admittedly, in a short essay you will be able to move only a short distance with an idea or argument, but you should never be satisfied to leave the idea exactly where you found it. To the degree that you can learn to develop your ideas, you will receive recognition for increasingly original writing.

Write with Your Readers in Mind

Whenever you write, you must decide how much detail to discuss. Usually you base this decision on your judgment of your readers. For example, if you assume that they have not read the work, you will need to include a short summary as background. Otherwise, they may not understand your argument.

Consider, too, whether your readers have any special interests or concerns. If they are particularly interested in politics, sociology, religion, or psychology, for example, you may need to select and develop your materials along one of these lines.

Your instructor will let you know who your audience is. Usually, it will be your instructor or your fellow students. They will be familiar with the work and will not expect you to retell a story or summarize an argument. Rather, they will want you to explain and interpret the work in the light of your main assertions about it. Thus, you may omit details that do not exemplify and support your argument, even if these details are otherwise important parts of the work. What you write should always be based on your developing idea together with your assessment of your readers.

USING EXACT, COMPREHENSIVE, AND FORCEFUL LANGUAGE

In addition to being original, organized, and well developed, the best writing is expressed in exact, comprehensive, and forceful language. At any stage of the composition process, you should try to correct your earliest sentences and paragraphs, which usually need to be rethought, reworded, and rearranged.

Try to make your sentences meaningful. First of all, ask yourself whether your sentences really mean what you intend, or whether you can make them more exact and therefore stronger. For example, consider these two sentences from essays about "The Necklace":

> It seems as though the main character's dreams of luxury cause her to respond as she does in the story.

This incident, although it may seem trivial or unimportant, has substantial significance in the creation of the story; by this I mean the incident that occurred is essentially what the story is all about.

These sentences are inexact and vague, and therefore unhelpful; neither of them goes anywhere. The first sentence is satisfactory up to the verb *cause,* but then it falls apart because the writer has lost sight of the essay's purpose. It is best to describe what that response *is,* rather than to be satisfied to say nothing more than that there is a response. To make the sentence more exact, we could make the following revision:

Mathilde's dreams of luxury make it impossible for her to accept her own possessions, and therefore she goes beyond her means in order to attend the party.

With this revision, the writer could readily go on to consider the relationship of the early part of the story to the later parts. Without the revision, it is not clear where the writer might go.

The second sentence is vague because the writer has lost all contact with the main idea or argument. If we adopt the principle of trying to be exact, however, we can bring the dead sentence to life:

The accidental loss of the necklace, which is trivial though costly, supports the narrator's claim that major turns in life are produced not by earthshaking events but rather by minor ones.

In addition to working for exactness, try to make sentences—all sentences, but particularly thesis and topic sentences—complete and comprehensive. Consider the following sentence:

The idea in "The Necklace" is that Mathilde and her husband work hard to pay for the lost necklace.

Although this sentence promises to describe an idea, it does no more than summarize the story's major action. It needs additional rethinking and rephrasing to make it more comprehensive, as in the these two revisions:

In "The Necklace" Maupassant shows that hard work and responsibility are basic and necessary in life.

Maupassant's surprise ending in "The Necklace" symbolizes the need for always being truthful.

Both new sentences are connected to the action described by the original phrasing, "Mathilde and her husband work hard to pay for the lost necklace," although they point toward differing treatments. The first sentence concerns the virtue shown by the Loisels in their sacrifice. Because the second sentence includes the word *symbolizes,* an essay stemming from it would stress the Loisels' mistake in not confessing the loss. In dealing with the symbolic meaning of their failure, an essay developed along the lines of the sentence would focus on the negative aspects of their characters, and an essay developed from the first sentence would stress their positive aspects. Either of the revised sentences, therefore, is more comprehensive than the original sentence and thus would help a writer get on the track toward an accurate and thoughtful essay.

Of course it is never easy to create fine sentences, but as a mode of improvement, you might create some self-testing mechanisms:

- *For treating story materials.* Always relate the materials to an idea or a point. Do not say simply that "Mathilde works constantly for ten years to help pay off the debt." Instead, blend the material into a point, like this: "Mathilde's ten-year effort shows the horror of indebtedness," or "Mathilde's ten-year effort causes her strength of character to emerge."

- *For responses and impressions.* Do not say simply, "The story's ending left me with a definite impression." Your readers want to know what your impression is, and therefore you must describe it, as in the following: "The story's ending surprised me and also made me sympathetic to the major character."

- *For ideas.* Make the idea clear and direct. Do not say, "Mathilde is living in a poor household," but rather use the story material to bring out an idea, as follows: "Mathilde's story shows that living in poverty reduces the quality of life."

- *For critical commentary.* Do not be satisfied with a statement such as "I found 'The Necklace' interesting." Instead try to describe *what* was interesting and *why* it was interesting: "I found 'The Necklace' interesting because it shows how chance and bad luck may either make or destroy people's lives."

Good writing begins with attempts, like these, to rephrase sentences to make them really say something. If you always name and pin down descriptions, responses, and judgments, no matter how difficult the task seems, your sentences can be strong because you will be making them exact.

USING THE NAMES OF AUTHORS

For both men and women writers, you should typically include the author's *full name* in the *first sentence* of your essay. Here are a few model first sentences:

Shirley Jackson's "The Lottery" is a story featuring both suspense and horror.

"The Lottery," by Shirley Jackson, is a story featuring both suspense and horror.

For all later references, use only last names, such as *Jackson, Steinbeck, Munro, Crane,* or *Porter.* However, for the "giants" of literature, you should use the last names exclusively. In referring to writers like Shakespeare and Milton, for example, there is no need to include *William* or *John.*

In spite of today's informal standards, do not use an author's first name, as in "*Shirley* skillfully creates suspense and horror in 'The Lottery.'" Also, do not use a familiar title before the names of dead authors, such as "*Ms.* Jackson's 'The Lottery' is a suspenseful horror story," or "*Mr.* Shakespeare's idea is that information is uncertain." Use the last names alone.

As with all conventions, of course, there are exceptions. If you are referring to a childhood work of a writer, the first name is appropriate, but shift to the last name when referring to the writer's mature works. If your writer has a professional or a noble title, such as *"Judge* O'Connor," *"Governor* Cross," *"Lord* Byron" or *"Queen* Elizabeth," it is not improper to use the title. Even then, however, the titles are commonly omitted for males, so that most references to Lord Byron and Alfred, Lord Tennyson, should be simply to "Byron" and "Tennyson."

Referring to living authors is somewhat problematical. Some journals and newspapers, like the *New York Times,* use the respectful titles *Mr.* and *Ms.* in their reviews. However, scholarly journals, which are likely to remain on library shelves for many decades, follow the general principle of beginning with the entire name and then using only the last name for subsequent references.

DEMONSTRATIVE STUDENT ESSAY, IMPROVED DRAFT

If you refer again to the first draft of the essay about Maupassant's use of setting to illustrate Mathilde's character (pp. 28–29), you might notice that several parts of the draft need extensive reworking and revising. For example, paragraph 2 contains a series of short, unconnected comments, and the last sentence of that paragraph implies that Mathilde's dissatisfaction relates mainly to her husband rather than to her general circumstances. Paragraph 4 focuses too much on Mathilde's coarseness and not enough on her sacrifice and cooperation. The draft also ignores the fact that the story ends in another location, the Champs-Elysées, where Maupassant continues to demonstrate the nature of Mathilde's character. Finally, there is not enough support in this draft for the contention (in paragraph 5) that everything in the story is related to the character of Mathilde.

To discover how these issues can be more fully considered, the following revision of the earlier draft creates more introductory detail, includes an additional paragraph, and reshapes each of the paragraphs to stress the relationship of the central idea or argument to the topics of the various paragraphs. Within the limits of a short assignment, the essay illustrates all the principles of organization and unity that we have been discussing.

Maupassant's Use of Setting in "The Necklace"° to Show the Character of Mathilde

[1] In "The Necklace" Guy de Maupassant uses setting to reflect the character and development of the main character, Mathilde Loisel.* As a result, his setting is not particularly vivid or detailed. He does not even describe the ill-fated neck-lace--the central object in the story--but states only that it is "superb" (paragraph 47). In fact, he includes descriptions of setting only if they illuminate qualities about Mathilde. Her changing character can be related to the first apartment, the dream-life mansion rooms, the attic flat, and the public street.†

° See pp. 4–11 for this story.
* Central idea.
† Thesis sentence.

Details about the modest apartment of the Loisels on the Street of Martyrs indicate Mathilde's peevish lack of adjustment to life. Though everything is serviceable, she is unhappy with the "drab" walls, "threadbare" furniture, and "ugly" curtains (paragraph 3). She has domestic help, but she wants more servants than the simple country girl who does the household chores in the apartment. Her

[2] embarrassment and dissatisfaction are shown by details of her irregularly cleaned tablecloth and the plain and inelegant boiled beef that her husband adores. Even her best theater dress, which is appropriate for apartment life but which is inappropriate for more wealthy surroundings, makes her unhappy. All these details of the apartment establish that Mathilde's major trait at the story's beginning is maladjustment. She therefore seems unpleasant and unsympathetic.

Like the real-life apartment, the impossibly expensive setting of her daydreams about living in a mansion strengthens her unhappiness and her avoidance of reality. All the rooms of her fantasies are large and expensive, draped in silk and filled with nothing but the best furniture and bric-a-brac. Maupassant gives us the following description of her dream world:

[3]

She imagined a gourmet-prepared main course carried on the most exquisite trays and served on the most beautiful dishes, with whispered gallantries which she would hear with a sphinxlike smile as she dined on the pink meat of a trout or the delicate wing of a quail. (paragraph 4)

With such impossible dreams, her despair is complete. Ironically, this despair, together with her inability to live with reality, brings about her undoing. It makes her agree to borrow the necklace (which is just as unreal as her daydreams of wealth), and losing the necklace drives her into the reality of giving up her apartment and moving into the attic flat.

Also ironically, the attic flat is related to the coarsening of her character while at the same time it brings out her best qualities of hard work and honesty. Maupassant emphasizes the drudgery of the work Mathilde endures to maintain the flat, such as walking up many stairs, washing floors with large buckets of water, cleaning greasy and encrusted pots and pans, taking out the garbage, washing clothes by hand, and haggling loudly with local shopkeepers. All this

[4] reflects her coarsening and loss of sensibility, also shown by her giving up hair and hand care and by wearing cheap dresses. The work she performs, however, makes her heroic (paragraph 98). As she cooperates to help her husband pay back the loans, her dreams of a mansion fade, and all she has left is the memory of her triumphant appearance at the Minister of Education's party. Thus the attic flat brings out her physical change for the worse at the same time that it also brings out her psychological and moral change for the better.

Her walk on the Champs-Elysées illustrates another combination of traits-- self-indulgence and frankness. The Champs-Elysées is the most fashionable street in Paris, and her walk to it is similar to her earlier indulgences in her daydreams of upper-class wealth. But it is on this street where she meets Jeanne,

[5] and it is Mathilde's frankness in confessing the loss and replacement to Jeanne that makes Mathilde completely honest. While the walk thus serves as the occasion for the story's concluding surprise and irony, Mathilde's being on the Champs-Elysées is totally in character, in keeping with her earlier reveries about luxury.

[6]

Other details in the story also have a similar bearing on Mathilde's character. For example, the story presents little detail about the party scene beyond the statement that Mathilde is a great "success" (paragraph 52)--a judgment that shows her ability to shine if given the chance. After she and Loisel accept the fact that the necklace cannot be found, Maupassant includes details about the Parisian streets, about the visits to loan sharks, and about the jewelry shops in order to bring out Mathilde's sense of honesty and pride as she "heroically" prepares to live her new life of poverty. Thus, in "The Necklace," Maupassant uses setting to highlight Mathilde's maladjustment, her needless misfortune, her loss of youth and beauty, and finally her growth as a responsible human being.

Commentary on the Essay

Several improvements to the first draft are seen here. The language of paragraph 2 has been revised to show more clearly the inappropriateness of Mathilde's dissatisfaction. In paragraph 3, the irony of the story is brought out, and the writer has connected the details to the central idea in a richer pattern of ideas, showing the effects of Mathilde's despair. Paragraph 5—new in the improved draft—includes additional details about how Mathilde's walk on the Champs-Elysées is related to her character. In paragraph 6, the fact that Mathilde is able "to shine" at the dinner party is interpreted according to the central idea. Finally, the conclusion is now much more specific, summarizing the change in Mathilde's character rather than saying simply that the setting reveals her "needless misfortune." In short, the second draft reflects the complexity of "The Necklace" better than the first draft. Because the writer has revised the first-draft ideas about the story, the final essay is tightly structured, insightful, and forceful.

SUMMARY

Throughout this book, the demonstrative student essays are followed by short commentaries that show how the essays embody the chapter instructions and guidelines. For each essay that has a number of possible approaches, the commentary points out which one is employed, and when an essay uses two or more approaches, the commentary makes this fact clear. In addition, each commentary singles out one of the paragraphs for more detailed analysis of its argument and use of detail. The commentaries will hence help you develop the insights necessary to use the essays as aids in your own study and writing.

To sum up, follow these guidelines whenever you write about a story or any kind of literature:

• Never just retell the story or summarize the work. Bring in story materials only when you can use them as support for your central idea or argument.

• Throughout your essay, keep reminding your reader of your central idea.

• Within each paragraph, make sure that you stress your topic idea.

• Develop your subject. Make it bigger than it was when you began.

- Always make your statements exact, comprehensive, and forceful.
- *And remember, never just retell the story or summarize the work.*

SPECIAL TOPICS FOR WRITING AND ARGUMENT
ABOUT THE WRITING PROCESS

1. Write a brainstorming paragraph on the topic of anything in a literary work that you find especially good or interesting. Write as the thoughts occur to you; do not slow yourself down in an effort to make your writing seem perfect; you can make corrections and improvements later.

2. Using marginal and journal notations, together with any additional thoughts, describe the way in which the author of a particular work has resolved particularly important ideas and difficulties.

3. Create a plus-minus table to list your responses about a character or ideas in a work.

4. Raise questions about the actions of characters in a story or play in order to determine the various customs and manners of the society out of which the work is derived.

5. Analyze and explain the way in which the conflicts in a story or play are developed. What pattern or patterns do you find? Determine the relationship of the conflicts to the work's development, and fashion your idea of this relationship as an argument for a potential essay.

6. Basing your ideas on your marginal and journal notations, select an idea and develop a thesis sentence from it, using your idea and a list of possible topics for the development of an essay.

7. Using the thesis sentence you write for exercise 6, develop a brief topical outline for a full essay.

RESPONDING TO LITERATURE: LIKES AND DISLIKES

People read for many reasons. In the course of daily affairs, they read signs, labels, price tags, recipes, or directions for assembling a piece of furniture or a toy. They read newspapers to learn about national, international, and local events. They might read magazines to learn about important issues, celebrities, political figures, and biographical details about significant persons. Sometimes they might read to pass the time or to take their minds off pressing problems or situations. Also, people regularly read out of necessity—in school and in their work. They study for examinations in chemistry, biology, psychology, and political science. They go over noun paradigms and verb forms in a foreign language. They read to acquire knowledge in many areas, and they read to learn new skills, new information, and new ways to do their jobs better.

But, aside from incidental, leisurely, and obligatory reading, many people turn to imaginative literature, which they read because they like it and find it interesting. Even if they don't like everything they read equally, they nevertheless enjoy reading and usually pick out authors and types of literature that they like.

It is therefore worth considering those qualities of imaginative literature that at the primary level produce responses of pleasure (and also of displeasure). You either like or dislike a story, poem, or play. If you say no more than this, however, you have not said much. Analyzing and explaining your likes and dislikes requires you to describe the reasons for your responses. The goal should be to form your responses as judgments, which are usually *informed* and *informative*, rather than as simple reactions, which may be *uninformed* and *unexplained*.

Sometimes a reader's first responses are that a story or poem is either "okay" or "boring." These reactions usually mask an incomplete and superficial first reading. They are neither informative nor informed. As you study most works, however, you will be drawn into them and become interested and involved. To be interested in a poem, play, or story is to be taken into it emotionally; to be involved suggests that your emotions become almost wrapped up in the characters, problems, outcomes, ideas, and expressions of opinion and emotion. Both "interest" and "involvement" describe genuine responses to reading. Once you get interested and involved, your reading ceases to be a task or an assignment and grows into a pleasure.

Use Your Journal to Record Your Responses

No one can tell you what you should or should not like, for liking is your own concern. While your reading is still fresh, therefore, you should use your journal to record your responses to a work and also your observations about it. Be frank in your judgment. Write down what you like or dislike, and explain the reasons for your responses, even if these are brief and incomplete. If, after later thought and fuller understanding, you change or modify your impressions, write down these changes too. Here is a journal entry that explains a favorable response to Maupassant's "The Necklace":

> I like "The Necklace" because of the surprise ending. It isn't that I like Mathilde's bad luck, but I like the way Maupassant hides the most important fact in the story until the end. Mathilde does all that work and sacrifice for no reason at all, and the surprise ending makes this point strongly.

This paragraph could be developed as part of an essay. It is a clear statement of liking, followed by references to likable things in the story. This response pattern, which can be simply phrased as "I like [dislike] this work because . . . ," is a useful way to begin journal entries because it always requires that you explain your responses. (It is in this way, also, that you can begin to develop an argument about the work.) If at first you cannot explain the causes of your responses, at least make a brief list of the things you like or dislike. If you write nothing, you will probably forget your reactions. Recovering them later, either for discussion or writing, will be difficult.

STATE REASONS FOR YOUR FAVORABLE RESPONSES

Usually you can equate your interest in a work with liking it. You can be more specific about favorable responses by citing one or more of the following:

- You like and admire the characters and what they do and stand for. You get involved with them. When they are in danger, you are concerned; when they succeed, you are happy; when they speak, you like what they say.
- After you have read the last word in a story or play, you are sorry to part with these characters and wish that there were more to read about them and their activities.
- Even if you do not particularly like a character or the characters, you are nevertheless interested in the reasons for and outcomes of their actions.
- You get so interested and involved in the actions or ideas in the work that you do not want to put the work down until you have finished it.
- You like to follow the pattern of action or the development of the author's thoughts, so that you respond with appreciation upon finishing the work.
- You find that reading enables you to relax or to take your mind off a problem or a pressing responsibility.
- You learn something new—something you had never before known or thought about human beings and their ways of handling their problems.
- You learn about customs and ways of life in different places and times.
- You gain new insights into aspects of life that you thought you already understood.
- You feel happy or thrilled because of reading the work.
- You are amused, and you laugh often as you read.
- You like the author's ways of describing scenes, actions, ideas, and feelings.
- You find that many of the expressions are remarkable and beautiful, and are therefore worth remembering.

STATE REASONS FOR YOUR UNFAVORABLE RESPONSES

Although so far we have dismissed "okay" and "boring" and have stressed *interest, involvement,* and *liking,* it is important to know that disliking all or part of a work is normal and acceptable. You do not need to hide this response. Here, for example, are two short journal responses expressing dislike for Maupassant's "The Necklace":

1. I do not like "The Necklace" because Mathilde seems spoiled, and I don't think she is worth reading about.
2. "The Necklace" is not an adventure story, and I like reading only adventure stories.

These are both legitimate responses because they are based on a clear standard of judgment. The first response stems from a distaste for one of the main character's unlikable traits, and the second from a preference for rapidly moving stories that evoke interest in the dangers that main characters face and overcome.

Here is a paragraph-length journal entry that might be developed from the first response. Notice that the reasons for dislike are explained. They would need only slightly more development for use in an essay.

> I dislike "The Necklace" because Mathilde seems spoiled, and I don't think she is worth reading about. She is a phony. She nags her husband because he is not rich. She never tells the truth. I dislike her for hurrying away from the party because she is afraid of being seen in her shabby shawl. She is foolish and dishonest for not telling Jeanne Forrestier about losing the necklace. It's true that she works hard to pay the debt, but she also puts her husband through ten years of hardship. If Mathilde had faced facts, she might have had a better life. I do not like her and cannot like the story because of her.

As long as you include reasons for your dislike, as in the list and in the paragraph, you can use them again in considering the story more fully, when you will surely also expand thoughts, focus your argument, include new details, pick new topics for development as paragraphs, and otherwise modify your journal entry. You might even change your mind. However, even if you do not, it is better to record your original responses and reasons honestly than to force yourself to say you like a story that you do not like.

Put Dislikes into a Larger Context

Although it is important to be honest about disliking a work, it is more important to broaden your perspective and expand your taste. For example, a dislike based on the preference for only mystery or adventure stories, if generally applied, would cause a person to dislike most works of literature. This attitude seems unnecessarily self-limiting.

If negative responses are put in a larger context, however, it is possible to expand the capacity to like and appreciate good literature. For instance, some readers might be preoccupied with their own concerns and therefore be uninterested in remote or "irrelevant" literary figures. However, if by reading about literary characters they can gain insight into general problems of life, and therefore their own concerns, they can find something to like in just about any work. Other readers might like sports and therefore not read anything but the daily sports pages. What probably interests them about sports is competition, however, so if they can follow the competition or *conflict* in a literary work, they will have discovered something to like in that work.

As an example, let us consider again the dislike based on a preference for adventure stories and see whether this preference can be widened. Here are some reasons for liking adventures:

1. Adventure has fast action.
2. It has danger and tension, and therefore interest.

3.   It has daring, active, and successful characters.

4.   It has obstacles that the characters work hard to overcome.

No one could claim that the first three points apply to "The Necklace," but the fourth point is promising. Mathilde, the major character, works hard to overcome an obstacle: She pitches in to help her husband pay the large debt. If you like adventures because the characters try to gain worthy goals, then you can also like "The Necklace" for the same reason. The principle here is clear: If a reason for liking a favorite work or type of work can be found in another work, then there is reason to like that new work.

The following paragraph shows a possible application of this "bridging" process of extending preferences. (The demonstrative essay that begins on p. 46 is also developed along these lines.)

> I usually like only adventure stories, and therefore I disliked "The Necklace" at first because it is not adventure. But one of my reasons for liking adventure is that the characters work hard to overcome difficult obstacles, like finding buried treasure or exploring new places. Mathilde, Maupassant's main character in "The Necklace," also works hard to overcome an obstacle—helping to pay back the money and interest for the borrowed 18,000 francs used as part of the payment for the replacement necklace. I like adventure characters because they stick to things and win out. I see the same toughness in Mathilde. Her problems get more interesting as the story moves on after a slow beginning. I came to like the story.

The principle of "bridging" from like to like is worth restating and emphasizing: If a reason for liking a favorite work or type of work can be found in another work, then there is reason to like that new work. A person who adapts to new reading in this open-minded way can redefine dislikes, no matter how slowly, and may consequently expand the ability to like and appreciate many kinds of literature.

An equally open-minded way to develop understanding and widen taste is to put dislikes in the following light: An author's creation of an unlikable character, situation, attitude, or expression may be deliberate. Your dislike might then result from the author's intentions. A first task of study, therefore, is to understand and explain the intention or plan. As you put the plan into your own words, you may find that you can like a work with unlikable things in it. Here is paragraph that traces this pattern of thinking, based again on "The Necklace":

> Maupassant apparently wants the reader to dislike Mathilde, and I do. At first, he shows her being unrealistic and spoiled. She lies to everyone and nags her husband. Her rushing away from the party so that no one can see her shabby shawl is a form of lying. But I like the story itself because Maupassant makes another kind of point. He does not hide her bad qualities, but he makes it clear that she herself is the cause of her trouble. If people like Mathilde never face the truth, they will get into bad situations. This is a good point, and I like the way Maupassant makes it. The entire story is therefore worth liking even though I still do not like Mathilde.

Both of these "bridging" analyses are consistent with the original negative reactions. In the first paragraph, the writer applies one of his principles of liking to include "The Necklace." In the second, the writer considers her initial dislike in the context of the work, and she discovers a basis for liking the story as a whole while still disliking the main character. The main concern in both responses is to keep an open mind despite initial dislike and then to see whether the unfavorable response can be more fully and broadly considered.

However, if you decide that your dislike overbalances any reasons you can find for liking, then you should explain your dislike. As long as you relate your response to the work accurately and measure it by a clear standard of judgment, your dislike of even a commonly liked work is not unacceptable. The important issue is not so much that you like or dislike a particular work but that you develop your own abilities to analyze and express your ideas.

WRITING ABOUT RESPONSES: LIKES AND DISLIKES

Now that we have looked briefly at the processes of writing, with two drafts of the same essay for illustration, you are ready to apply the principles of the writing process to your own writing—in this case, to an essay about your responses. In developing such an essay, begin by relying on your first reactions. Because it is not easy to reconstruct your first responses after a lapse of time, however, you will need your journal observations to guide you in prewriting. Develop your essay by stressing those characters, incidents, and ideas that interest (or do not interest) you.

As you plan your essay, your challenge will be to connect details from the work to your central idea or argument. That is, once you have begun by stating that you like (or dislike) the story, you might forget to highlight this response as you enumerate details. Therefore you need to stress your involvement in the work as you bring out evidence from it. You can show your attitudes by indicating approval (or disapproval), by commenting favorably (or unfavorably) on the details, by indicating things that seem new (or shopworn) and particularly instructive (or wrong), and by giving assent to (or dissent from) ideas or expressions of feeling.

Strategies for Organizing Ideas

Briefly describe the conditions that influence your response. Your central idea should be why you like or dislike the work. Your thesis sentence should include the major causes of your response, which are to be developed in the body.

The most common approach is to consider specific details that you like or dislike. The list on page 42 may help you articulate your responses. For example, you admired a particular character, or you got so interested in a story that you could not put it down, or you liked a particular passage in a poem or play, or you felt thrilled as you finished reading the work. Also, you may wish to develop a major idea, a fresh insight, or a particular outcome, as in the sample paragraph on page 41, which shows a surprise ending as the cause of a favorable response.

A second approach (see p. 43) is to explain any changes in your responses about the work (i.e., negative to positive and vice versa). This approach requires that you isolate the causes of the change, but it does not require you to retell the story from beginning to end.

1. One way to deal with such a change—the "bridge" method of transferring preference from one type of work to another—is shown in the demonstrative essay.

2. Another way is to explain a change in terms of a new awareness or understanding that you did not have on a first reading. Thus, for example, your first response to "The Necklace" might be unfavorable or neutral because the story may at first seem to move rather slowly. But further consideration might lead you to discover new insights that change your mind, such as the needs to overcome personal pride and to stop minor resentments from growing and festering. Your essay would then explain how these new insights have caused you to like the story.

In your conclusion you might summarize the reasons for your major response. You might also face any issues brought up by a change or modification of your first reactions. For example, if you have always held certain assumptions about your taste but like the work despite these assumptions, you may wish to talk about your own change or development. This topic is personal, but in an essay about your personal responses, discovery about yourself is legitimate and worthy.

DEMONSTRATIVE STUDENT ESSAY, FINAL DRAFT

Some Reasons for Liking Maupassant's "The Necklace"°

[1]
To me, the most likable kind of reading is adventure. There are many reasons for my preference, but an important one is that adventure characters work hard to overcome obstacles. Because Guy de Maupassant's "The Necklace" is not adventure, I did not like it at first. But in one respect the story is like adventure: The major character, Mathilde Loisel, works hard with her husband for ten years to overcome a difficult obstacle (paying an overwhelming debt). Thus, because Mathilde does what adventure characters also do, the story is likable.* Mathilde's appeal results from her hard work, strong character, and sad fate, and also from the way our view of her changes.†

[2]
Mathilde's hard work makes her seem good. Once she and her husband are faced with the huge debt of 18,000 francs, she works like a slave to pay it back. She gives up her servant and moves to a cheaper place. She does the household drudgery, wears cheap clothes, and haggles with shopkeepers. Just like the characters in adventure stories who do hard and unpleasant things, she does what she has to, and this makes her admirable.

° See pp. 4–11 for this story.
* Central idea.
† Thesis sentence.

[3] Her strong character shows her endurance, a likable trait. At first she is nagging and fussy, and she always dreams about wealth and tells lies, but she changes and gets better. She recognizes her blame in losing the necklace, and she has the toughness to help her husband redeem the debt. She sacrifices "heroically" (paragraph 98) by giving up her comfortable way of life, even though in the process she also loses her youth and beauty. Her jobs are not the exotic and glamorous ones of adventure stories, but her force of character makes her as likable as an adventure heroine.

[4] Her sad fate also makes her likable. In adventure stories the characters often suffer as they do their jobs. Mathilde also suffers, but in a different way, because her suffering is permanent while the hardships of adventure characters are temporary. This fact makes her especially pitiable because all her sacrifices are not necessary. This unfairness invites the reader to take her side.

The most important quality promoting admiration is the way in which Maupassant shifts our view of Mathilde. As she goes deeper into her hard life, Maupassant stresses her work and not the innermost thoughts he reveals at the beginning. In other words, the view into her character at the start, when she dreams about wealth, invites dislike; but the focus at the end is on her achievements, with never a complaint--even though she still has golden memories, as the narrator tells us:

[5]
> But sometimes, when her husband was at work, she sat down near the window, and she dreamed of that evening so long ago, of that party, where she had been so beautiful and so admired. (paragraph 104)

A major quality of Maupassant's changed emphasis is that Mathilde's fond memories do not lead to anything unfortunate. His shift in focus, from Mathilde's dissatisfaction to her sharing of responsibility and sacrifice, encourages the reader to like her.

[6] "The Necklace" is not an adventure story, but Mathilde has some of the good qualities of adventure characters. Also, the surprise revelation that the lost necklace was false is an unforgettable twist, and this makes her more deserving than she seems at first. Maupassant has arranged the story so that the reader finally admires Mathilde. "The Necklace" is a skillful and likable story.

Commentary on the Essay

This essay demonstrates how a reader may develop appreciation by transferring a preference for one type of work to a work that does not belong to the type. In the essay, the "bridge" is an already established taste for adventure stories, and the grounds for liking "The Necklace" are that Mathilde, the main character, shares the admirable qualities of adventure heroes and heroines.

In paragraph 1, the introduction, the grounds for transferring preferences are established. Paragraph 2 deals with Mathilde's capacity to work hard, and paragraph 3 considers the equally admirable quality of endurance. The fourth paragraph describes how Mathilde's condition evokes sympathy and pity. These paragraphs hence explain the story's appeal by asserting that the main character is similar to admirable characters from works of adventure.

The fifth paragraph shows that Maupassant, as the story unfolds, alters the reader's perceptions of Mathilde from bad to good. For this reason, paragraph 5 marks a new direction from paragraphs 2, 3, and 4: It moves away from the topic material itself—Mathide's character—to Maupassant's *technique* in handling the topic material.

Paragraph 6, the conclusion, restates the comparison and also introduces the surprise ending as an additional reason for liking "The Necklace." With the body and conclusion together, therefore, the essay establishes five separate reasons as an argument to show the writer's approval of the story. Three of these, derived directly from the main character, constitute the major grounds for liking the story, and two are derived from Maupassant's techniques as an author.

Throughout the essay, the central idea or argument is brought out in words and expressions such as "likable," "Mathilde's appeal," "strong character," "she does what she has to," "pitiable," and "take her side." Many of these expressions were first made in the writer's journal; and, mixed as they are with details from the story, they make for continuity. It is this thematic development, together with details from the story as supporting evidence, that shows how an essay on the responses of liking and disliking may be both informed and informative.

SPECIAL TOPICS FOR WRITING AND ARGUMENT ABOUT RESPONSES TO LITERATURE

1. In the last six months, what literary works did you read which you liked or disliked? Write a brief essay explaining your reasons for your positive or negative responses. To illustrate your arguments, you may make liberal references to these works, and, in addition, you may refer to films or TV shows that you have recently seen.

2. Consider the sample likes/dislikes essay on Maupassant's "The Necklace." Do you accept the arguments in the essay? What other details and arguments can you think of for either liking or disliking the story?

3. Write contrasting paragraphs about a character (whom you know or about whom you have read). In the first, try to make your reader like the character. In the second, try to create a hostile response to the character. Write an additional paragraph explaining the ways in which you tried to create these opposite responses. How fair would it be for a reader to dislike your negative paragraph even though your hostile portrait is successful?

READING
AND
WRITING
ABOUT

FICTION

2

Fiction:
An Overview

Fiction originally meant anything *made up* or *shaped*. As we understand the word now, it refers to *short or long prose stories*—a meaning it has retained since 1599, when this meaning was first recorded. Fiction is distinguished from the works it imitates, such as *historical accounts, reports, biographies, autobiographies, letters,* and *personal memoirs* and *meditations*. While fiction often resembles these forms, it has a separate identity because it originates not in historical facts but in the imaginative and creative powers of the author. Writers of fiction may include historically accurate details, but their overriding goal is to tell a story and say something significant about life.

The essence of fiction, as opposed to drama, is **narration,** the recounting or telling of a sequence of events or actions. The earliest works of fiction relied almost exclusively on narration, with speeches or dialogue being reported rather than quoted directly. Much recent fiction includes extended passages of dialogue, thereby becoming more *dramatic* even though narration is still the primary mode.

Fiction is rooted in ancient legends and myths. Local priests narrated stories about their gods and heroes, as shown in some of the narratives of ancient Egypt. In the course of history, traveling storytellers would appear in a court or village to entertain listeners with tales of adventure in faraway countries. Although many of these were fictionalized accounts of events and people who may not ever have existed, they were largely accepted as fact or history. An especially long tale, an **epic,** was recited over a period of days. To aid their memories and to impress and entertain their listeners, the storytellers chanted their tales in poetry, often accompanying themselves on a stringed instrument.

Legends and epics also reinforced the local religions and power structures. Myths of gods like Zeus and Athena (Greece), Jupiter and Minerva (Rome), and Baal and Ishtar (Mesopotamia) abounded, together with stories of famous men and women like Oedipus, Helen of Troy, Hercules, Achilles, Odysseus, Penelope, Utu-Napishtim, Joseph, David, and Ruth. The ancient Macedonian king and general Alexander the Great (356–323 B.C.E.) developed many of his ideas about nobility and valor from *The Iliad*, Homer's epic about the Trojan War—and, we might add, from discussing the epic with his tutor, the philosopher Aristotle.

Perhaps nowhere is the moralistic-argumentative aspect of ancient storytelling better illustrated than in the **fables** of Aesop, a Greek who wrote in the sixth century B.C.E., and in the **parables** of Jesus as told in the Gospels of the New Testament. In these works, a short narrative provides an illustration of a religious, philosophic, or psychological conclusion.

Starting about eight hundred years ago, storytelling in Western civilization was developed to a fine art by writers such as Marie de France, a Frenchwoman who wrote in England near the end of the twelfth century, Giovanni Boccaccio (Italian, 1313–1375), and Geoffrey Chaucer (English, ca. 1340–1400). William Shakespeare (1564–1616) drew heavily on history and legend for the stories and characters in his plays.

MODERN FICTION

Fiction in the modern sense of the word did not begin to flourish until the seventeenth and eighteenth centuries, when human beings of all social stations and ways of life became important literary topics. As one writer put it in 1709, human nature was not simple, and it could be explained only with reference to many complex motives such as "passion, humor, caprice, zeal, faction, and a thousand other springs."[1] Thus began the individual and psychological concerns that characterize fiction today. Indeed, fiction is strong because it is so real and personal. Most characters have both first and last names; the countries and cities in which they live are modeled on real places; and their actions and interactions are like those which readers themselves have experienced, could experience, or could easily imagine themselves experiencing.

Along with attention to character, fiction is also concerned with the place of individuals in their environments. In the simplest sense, environment is a backdrop or setting within which characters speak, move, and act. But more broadly, environment comprises the social, economic, and political conditions that affect the outcomes of people's lives. Fiction is usually about the interactions among people, but it also involves these larger interactions—either directly or indirectly. Indeed, in a typical work of fiction there are always many forces, both small and large, that influence the ways in which characters meet and deal with their problems.

The first true works of fiction in Europe, however, were less concerned with society or politics than adventure. These were the lengthy Spanish and French **romances** of the sixteenth and seventeenth centuries. In English the word **novel** was borrowed from French and Italian to describe these works and to distinguish them from medieval and classical romances as something that was *new* (the meaning of *novel*). In England the word **story** was used along with *novel* in reference to the new literary form.

---

[1] Anthony Ashley Cooper, Third Earl of Shaftesbury, *Sensus Communis*, Part III, Section iii.

The increased levels of education and literacy in the eighteenth century facilitated the development of fiction. During the times of Shakespeare and John Dryden (1631–1700), the only way a writer could make a living from writing was either to be a member of the nobility or have a subsidy from a member of the nobility, or to have a play accepted at a theater and then receive either a direct payment or the proceeds of an "author's benefit." The paying audiences, however, were limited to people who lived within a short distance of the theater or who had the leisure and money to stay in town during the theater season.

Once great numbers of people could read for themselves, the paying audience for literature expanded. A writer could write a novel and receive money for it from a publisher, who could then profit from a wide sale. Readers could pick up the book when they wished, and they could finish it when they chose. Reading a novel could even be a social event, for people would read to each other as a means of sharing the experience. With this wider audience, authors could make a career out of writing. Fiction had arrived as a major genre of literature.

THE SHORT STORY

Because novels were long, they took a long time to read—hours, days, even weeks. The American writer Edgar Allan Poe (1809–1849) addressed this problem and developed a theory of the **short story,** which he described in a review of Nathaniel Hawthorne's *Twice-Told Tales.* Poe was convinced that "worldly interests" prevented people from gaining the "totality" of comprehension and response that he believed reading should provide. A short, concentrated story (he called it "a brief prose tale" which could be read at a single sitting) was ideal for producing such a strong impression.[2]

In the wake of the taste for short fiction after Poe, many writers have worked in the form. Today, innumerable stories are printed in periodicals, such as *Story* magazine, and collections, such as *American Short Story Masterpieces.* Some of the better-established writers, such as William Faulkner, Ernest Hemingway, Shirley Jackson, Guy de Maupassant, Flannery O'Connor, Alice Walker, and Eudora Welty, to name only a small number, have collected their works and published them in single volumes.

ELEMENTS OF FICTION I:
VERISIMILITUDE AND *DONNÉE*

Fiction, along with drama, has a basis in **realism** or **verisimilitude.** That is, the situations or characters, though they are the **invention** of writers, are similar to those that many human beings experience, know, or think. Even **fantasy,** the creation of events that are dreamlike or fantastic, is anchored in the real world,

[2] For a fuller account of Poe's thought about short fiction, see Chapter 11.

however remotely. This connection of art and life has led some critics to label fiction, and also drama, as an art of **imitation.** Shakespeare's Hamlet states that an actor attempts to portray real human beings in realistic situations (to "hold a mirror up to Nature").

The same may also be said about writers of fiction, with the provisos that reality is not easily defined and that authors can follow many paths in imitating it. What counts in fiction is the way in which authors establish the *ground rules* for their works, whether with realistic or nonrealistic characters, places, actions, and physical and chemical laws. The assumption that authors make about the nature of their story material is called a **postulate** or a **premise**—what Henry James called a **donnée** (something given). The *donnée* of some stories is to resemble the everyday world as much as possible. Eudora Welty's "A Worn Path" (Chapter 3) is such a story. It tells of an elderly woman's walk from her home through a country woods to the streets of a small town, and then to the interior of a building. The events of the story are common; they could happen in life just as Welty presents them.

Once a *donnée* is established, it governs the directions in which the story moves. Jackson's "The Lottery" (Chapter 5), for example, contains a premise or *donnée* that may be phrased like this: "Suppose that a small, ordinary town held a lottery in which the prize was not money but a ritual punishment." Everything in Jackson's story follows from this premise. At first we seem to be reading about innocent actions in a rural American community. By the end, however, in accord with the premise, the story enters the realms of nightmare.

In such ways authors may lead us into remote, fanciful, and symbolic levels of reality, as in Walter Van Tilburg Clark's "The Portable Phonograph" (Chapter 6), where the futuristic *donnée* is that world civilization has been destroyed in a global war. In Poe's "The Masque of the Red Death" (Chapter 11), the phantasmagoric *donnée* is that Death may assume a human shape and claim all the revelers at a bizarre party. Literally nothing is out of bounds as long as the author makes clear the premise for the action.

Scenes and actions such as these, which are not realistic in our ordinary sense of the word, are normal in stories *as long as they follow the author's own stated or implied ground rules.* You may always judge a work by the standard of whether it is consistent with the premise, or the *donnée,* created by the writer.

In addition to referring to various levels of reality, the word *donnée* may also be taken more broadly. In *futuristic* and *science fiction,* for example, there is an assumption or *donnée* of certain situations and technological developments (e.g., interstellar space travel) that are not presently in existence. In a *love story,* the *donnée* is that two people meet and overcome an obstacle of some sort (usually not a serious one) on the way to fulfilling their love. Interesting variations on this type are seen in D. H. Lawrence's "The Horse Dealer's Daughter" (Chapter 10), Alice Munro's "The Found Boat" (Chapter 7), Stephen Dixon's "All Gone" (Chapter 12), and James Joyce's "Araby" (Chapter 10).

There are of course other types. An *apprenticeship* or *growth story,* for example, is about the growth of a major character, such as Jackie in Frank O'Connor's

"First Confession" (Chapter 7), Sarty in William Faulkner's "Barn Burning" (Chapter 4), and Emily in Tillie Olsen's "I Stand Here Ironing" (Chapter 12). In the *detective story,* a mysterious event is posited, and then the detective draws conclusions from the available evidence, as in Poe's "The Purloined Letter" (Chapter 11). A variation on the detective story is seen in Susan Glaspell's "A Jury of Her Peers" (Chapter 4), in which the correct detective work is done by two women, not by the legally sanctioned police investigator.

In addition to setting levels of reality and fictional types, authors may use other controls or springboards as their *données.* Sometimes an initial situation may be the occasion from which the story develops, such as the social worker calling the mother to express concern about the daughter in Olsen's "I Stand Here Ironing." Or the key may be a pattern of behavior (the boy's reactions to the people around him in O'Connor's "First Confession"; or a lie, as in Sherwood Anderson's "I'm a Fool" (Chapter 5); or a lunchtime conversation, as in Margaret Atwood's "Rape Fantasies" (Chapter 8). There is always a shaping force, or a *donnée,* that guides the actions, and often a number of such controls operate at the same time.

ELEMENTS OF FICTION II: CHARACTER, PLOT, STRUCTURE, AND IDEA OR THEME

Works of fiction share a number of common elements. For reference here, the more significant ones are **character, plot, structure,** and **idea** or **theme.**

Character Brings Fiction to Life

Stories, like plays, are about characters, who are *not* real people but who are nevertheless *like* real people. A **character** may be defined as a reasonable facsimile of a human being, with all the good and bad traits of being human. Most stories are concerned with characters who are facing a major problem developing from misunderstanding, misinformation, unfocused ideals and goals, difficult situations, troubled relationships, and generally challenging situations. The characters may win, lose, or tie. They may learn and be the better for the experience or may miss the point and be unchanged.

It is a truism that modern fiction has accompanied the development of a psychological interest in human beings. Psychology itself has grown out of the philosophical and religious idea that people are not evil by nature, but rather that they have many inborn capacities—some for good and others for bad. People are not free of problems, and they make many mistakes in their lives, but they nevertheless are important and interesting, and are therefore worth writing about, whether male or female; young or old; white, black, tan, or yellow; rich or poor; worker or industrialist; traveler or resident; aviator, performer, mother, daughter, homemaker, prince, general, bartender, or checkout clerk.

The range of fictional characters is vast: A married couple struggling to repay an enormous debt, a woman meditating about her daughter's growth, a young man learning about sin and forgiveness, a young woman struggling to overcome the bitter memory of early sexual abuse, a man regretting that he cannot admit a lie, a woman surrounded by her insensitive and self-seeking brothers, a man preserving love in the face of overwhelming difficulties, a woman learning to cope with her son's handicap—all these, and more, may be found in fiction just as they may also be found in all levels and conditions of life. Because as human beings all of us share the same capacities for concern, involvement, sympathy, happiness, sorrow, exhilaration, and disappointment, we are able to find endless interest in such characters and their ways of coping with their circumstances.

Plot Is the Plan of Fiction

Fictional characters, who are drawn from life, go through a series of life-like **actions** or **incidents,** which make up the story. In a well-done story, all the actions or incidents, speeches, thoughts, and observations are linked together to make up an entirety, sometimes called an **organic unity.** The essence of this unity is the development and resolution of a **conflict**—or conflicts—in which the **protagonist,** or central character, is engaged. The interactions of causes and effects as they develop **sequentially** or **chronologically** make up the story's **plot.** That is, a story's actions follow one another in time as the protagonist meets and tries to overcome opposing forces. Sometimes plot has been compared to a story's map, scheme, or blueprint.

Often the protagonist's struggle is directed against another character—an **antagonist.** Just as often, however, the struggle may occur between the protagonist and opposing groups, forces, ideas, and choices—all of which make up a collective antagonist. The conflict may be carried out wherever human beings spend their lives, such as a kitchen, a bedroom, a restaurant, a town square, a farm, an estate, a workshop, or a battlefield. The conflict may also take place internally, within the mind of the protagonist.

Structure Is the Knitting Together of Fiction

Structure refers to the way a story is assembled. Chronologically, all stories are similar because they move from beginning to end in accord with the time needed for *causes* to produce *effects.* But authors choose many different ways to put their stories together. Some stories are told in straightforward sequential order, and a description of the plot of such stories is identical to a description of the structure. Other stories, however, may get pieced together through out-of-sequence and widely separated episodes, speeches, secondhand reports, remembrances, dreams, nightmares, periods of delirium, fragments of letters, overheard conversations, and the like. In such stories, the plot and the structure diverge widely. Therefore, in dealing with the structure of stories, we emphasize not chronological order but the actual *arrangement* and *development* of the stories as they unfold, part by part. Usually we study an entire story, but we may also direct our attention toward a smaller aspect of arrangement such as an episode or passage of dialogue.

Idea or Theme Is the Underlying Thought of Fiction

The word **idea** refers to the result or results of general and abstract thinking. In literary study, the consideration of ideas relates to meaning, interpretation, explanation, and significance. Fiction necessarily embodies issues and ideas. Even stories written for entertainment alone are based in an idea or position. Thus, writers of comic works are committed to the idea that human difficulties can be treated with humor. More serious works may force characters to make difficult moral choices—the thought being that in a losing situation the only winners are those who maintain honor and self-respect. Mystery and suspense stories rest on the belief that problems have solutions, even if they may not at first seem apparent. Writers may deal with the triumphs and defeats of life, the admirable and the despicable, the humorous and the pathetic, but whatever their goal, they are always expressing ideas about human experience. We may therefore raise questions such as these as we look for ideas in fiction: *What does this mean? Why does the author include it? What idea or ideas does it show? Why is it significant?*

Fictional ideas can also be considered as major **themes** that tie individual works together. Often an author makes the theme obvious, as in the Aesop fable in which a man uses an ax to kill a fly on his son's forehead. The theme of this fable might loosely be expressed in a sentence like "The cure should not be worse than the disease." A major theme in Maupassant's "The Necklace" (see pp. 4–11) is that people may be destroyed or saved by unlucky and unforeseeable events. The accidental loss of the borrowed necklace is just such an event, for this misfortune ruins the lives of both Mathilde and her husband.

The process of determining and describing the themes or ideas in stories is never complete; there is always another theme that we can discuss. Thus in "The Necklace," one might note the additional themes that adversity brings out worth, that telling the truth is better than concealing it, that envy often produces ill fortune, and that good fortune is never recognized until it is lost. Indeed, one of the ways in which we may judge stories is to determine the degree to which they embody a number of valid and important ideas.

ELEMENTS OF FICTION III: THE WRITER'S TOOLS

Narration Creates the Sequence and Logic of Fiction

Writers have a number of modes of presentation, or "tools," which they can use in their stories. The principal tool (and the heart of fiction) is **narration,** the reporting of actions in sequential order. The object of narration is to *render* the story, to make it clear and to bring it alive to the reader's imagination through the movement of sentences through time. Unlike works of painting and sculpture, the reading and comprehension of a narration cannot be done in a single view. Jacques-Louis David's painting *Death of Socrates,* for example (p. 59), is like a narrative because it tells a story—an actual historical occurrence. As related by Plato in the dialogue *Phaedo,* Socrates takes the cup of hemlock, which he will drink as the means of carrying out his own execution. But it is *only* this moment of time that David is able to capture in his painting. In contrast, the writer of narrative may include all the events leading up to and following such a moment, for a narration moves in a continuous line, from word to word, scene to scene, action to action, and speech to speech. As a result of this chronological movement, the reader's comprehension must necessarily also be chronological.

Style Is the Author's Skill in Bringing Language to Life

The medium of fiction and of all literature is language, and the manipulation of language—the **style**—is a primary skill of the writer. A mark of a good style is the use of active verbs and nouns that are **specific** and **concrete**. Even with the most active and graphic diction possible, writers can never render their incidents and scenes exactly, but they may be judged on how vividly they tell their stories.

Point of View Guides What We See and Understand in Fiction

One of the most important ways in which writers knit their stories together, and also an important way in which they try to interest and engage readers, is the careful control of **point of view.** Point of view is the **voice** of the story, the speaker who does the narrating. It is the way the reality of a story is made to seem authentic. It may be regarded as the story's *focus,* the *angle of vision* from which things are not only seen and reported but also judged.

Basically, there are two kinds of points of view, but there are many variations, sometimes obvious and sometimes subtle. In the first, the **first-person point of view,** a fictitious observer tells us what he or she saw, heard, concluded, and thought. This viewpoint is characterized by the use of the pronoun *I* as the speaker refers to his or her position as an observer or commentator. The **speaker** or **narrator**—terms that are interchangeable—may sometimes seem to be the author speaking directly using an **authorial voice.** More often, however, the speaker is an independent character—a **persona** with characteristics that separate her or him from the author.

In common with all narrators, the first-person narrator establishes a clearly defined relationship to the story's events. Some narrators are deeply engaged in the action; others are only minor participants or observers; still others have had nothing to do with the action but are transmitting the reports of others more fully involved. Sometimes the narrator uses the *we* pronoun if he or she is represented as part of a group that has witnessed the action or participated in it.

Jacques-Louis David, *The Death of Socrates*. The Metropolitan Museum of Art, Wolfe Fund, 1931.

Often, too, the narrator might use *we* when referring to ideas and interpretations shared with the reader or listener—the idea being to draw readers into the story as much as possible.

The **third-person point of view** uses third-person pronouns (*she, he, it, they, her, him, them,* etc.).[3] The third-person point of view may be (1) **limited,** with the focus being on one particular character and what he or she does, says, hears, thinks, and otherwise experiences; (2) **omniscient,** with the possibility that the activities and thoughts of all the characters are open and fully known by the speaker; or (3) **dramatic,** or **objective,** in which the story is confined *only* to the reporting of actions and speeches, with no commentary and no revelation of the thoughts of any of the characters unless the characters themselves reveal their thoughts dramatically.

Understanding point of view usually requires subtlety of perception—indeed, it may be one of the most difficult of all concepts in the study of fiction. In fuller perspective, therefore, we may think of it as the *total position* from which things are viewed, understood, and communicated. The position might be simply physical: *Where was the speaker located when the events occurred? Does the speaker give us a close or distant view of the events?* The position might also be personal or philosophical: *Do the events illustrate a personal opinion* (Maupassant's "The Necklace"), *embody a philosophical judgment* (Hawthorne's "Young Goodman Brown"), or *argue a theological principle* ("The Parable of the Prodigal Son")?

[3] The possibilities of a second-person point of view are discussed in Chapter 5.

Point of view is one of the major ways by which authors make fiction vital. By controlling point of view, an author helps us make reasonable inferences about the story's actions. Authors use point of view to raise some of the same questions in fiction that perplex us in life. We need to evaluate what fictional narrators as well as real people tell us, for what they say is affected by their limitations, attitudes, opinions, and degree of candidness. The narrator of Mark Twain's "Luck," for example, is convinced that his hero is a total fool, and he tells the story to make us similarly convinced. But could we make a case that he might also be jealous of his boob hero, enough perhaps to omit some of the explanations that might give us a more complete, less biased picture? For readers, the perception of a fictional point of view can be as complex as life itself, and it may be as difficult—in fiction as in life—to evaluate our sources of information.

Description Creates the World of Fiction

Together with narration, a vital aspect of fiction is **description,** which is intended to cause readers to imagine or re-create the scenes and actions of the story. Description can be both physical (places and persons) and psychological (an emotion or set of emotions). Excessive description sometimes interrupts or postpones a story's actions, so many writers include only as much as is necessary to keep the action moving along.

Mood and **atmosphere** are important aspects of descriptive writing, and to the degree that descriptions are evocative, they may reach the level of **metaphor** and **symbolism.** These characteristics of fiction are a property of all literature, and you will also encounter them whenever you read poems and plays.

Dialogue Creates Interactions among Fictional Characters

Another major tool of the writer of fiction is **dialogue.** By definition, dialogue is the conversation of two people, but more than two characters may also participate. It is of course the major medium of the playwright, and it is one of the means by which the fiction writer makes a story vivid and dramatic. Straight narration and description can do no more than make a secondhand assertion ("hearsay") that a character's thoughts and responses exist, but dialogue makes everything firsthand and real.

Dialogue is hence a means of *showing* rather than *reporting*. If characters feel pain or declare love, their own words may be taken as the expression of what is on their minds. Some dialogue may be terse and minimal. Other dialogue may be expanded, depending on the situation, the personalities of the characters, and the author's intent. Dialogue may concern any topic, including personal feelings, reactions to the past, future plans, changing ideas, sudden realizations, and political, social, philosophical, or religious ideas.

The language of dialogue indicates the intelligence, articulateness, educational levels, or emotional states of the speakers. Hence the author might use *grammatical mistakes, faulty pronunciation,* or *slang* to show a character of limited or disadvantaged background or a character who is trying to be seen in that light. *Dialect* shows the region from which the speaker comes, just as an *accent* indicates a place of national origin. *Jargon* and *cliché* suggest self-inflation or intellectual limitations—usually reasons for laughter. The use of *private, intimate expressions* might show people who are close to each other emotionally. Speech that is interrupted by *voiced pauses* (e.g., "er," "ah," "um," "y' know") or speech characterized by *inappropriate words* might show a character who is unsure or not in control. There are many possibilities in dialogue, but no matter what qualities you find, writers include dialogue to enable you to know their characters better.

Tone and Irony Guide Our Perceptions of Fictional Works

In every story we may consider **tone,** that is, the ways in which authors convey attitudes toward readers and also toward the work's subjects. **Irony,** one of the major components of tone, refers to language and situations that seem to reverse normal expectations. *Word choice* is the characteristic of **verbal irony,** in which what is meant is usually the opposite of what is said, as when we *mean* that people are doing badly even though we *say* that they are doing well. Broader forms of irony are *situational* and *dramatic:* **Situational irony** refers to circumstances in which bad things happen to good people, or in which rewards are not earned because forces beyond human comprehension seem to be in total control. In **dramatic irony** characters have only a nonexistent, partial, incorrect, or misguided understanding of what is happening to them, while both readers and other characters understand the situation more fully. Readers hence become concerned about the characters and hope that they will develop understanding quickly enough to avoid the problems bedeviling them and the pitfalls endangering them.

Symbolism and Allegory Show the Relevance of Fiction to the Larger World

In literature, even apparently ordinary things may acquire **symbolic** value; that is, everyday objects may be understood to have meanings that are beyond themselves, bigger than themselves. In fiction, many functional and essential incidents, objects, speeches, and characters may also be construed as symbols. Some symbols are widely recognized and therefore are considered as **cultural** or **universal.** Water, flowers, jewels, the sun, certain stars, the flag, altars, and minarets are examples of cultural symbols. Other symbols are **contextual;** that is, they take on symbolic meaning only in their individual works, as when in Maupassant's "The Necklace" Mathilde and her husband move into an attic flat to save the money that they need to repay their enormous debt. These new quarters may be taken to symbolize the hardship experienced by the poor.

When a complete story, in addition to maintaining its own narrative integrity, can be applied point by point to a parallel set of situations, it is an **allegory.** Many stories are not complete allegories, however, even though they may contain sections having allegorical parallels. Thus, the Loisels' long servitude in Maupassant's "The Necklace" is similar to the lives and activities of many people who perform tasks for mistaken or meaningless reasons. "The Necklace" is therefore allegorical even though it is not an allegory.

Commentary Provides Us with an Author's Thoughts

Writers may also include **commentary, analysis,** or **interpretation,** in the expectation that readers need insight into the characters and actions. When fiction was new, authors often expressed such commentary directly. Henry Fielding (1707–1754) divided his novels into "books" and included a chapter of personal and philosophical commentary at the beginning of each of these. In the next century, George Eliot (1819–1880) included many extensive passages of commentary in her novels.

Later writers have kept commentary at a minimum, preferring instead to concentrate on direct action and dialogue, and allowing readers to draw their own conclusions about meaning. In first-person narrations, however, you may expect the narrators to make their own personal comments. Such observations may be accepted at face value, but you should recognize that anything the speakers say is also a mode of character disclosure and therefore is just as much a part of the story as the narrative incidents.

The Elements Together Are Present in Works of Fiction

These, then, are the major tools of writers of fiction. For analytical purposes, one or another of them may be considered separately so that the artistic achievement of a particular author may be recognized. It is also important to realize that authors may use all the tools simultaneously. The story may be told by a character who is a witness, and thus it has a **first-person point of view.** The major **character,** the **protagonist,** goes through a series of **actions** as a result of a carefully arranged **plot.** Because of this plot, together with the author's chosen method of **narration,** the story will follow a certain kind of arrangement, or **structure,** such as a straightforward **sequence** or a disjointed series of **episodes.** One thing that the action may demonstrate is the **theme** or **central idea.** The writer's **style** may be manifested in **ironic** expressions. The description of the character's actions may reveal **irony of situation,** while at the same time this situation is made vivid through **dialogue** in which the character is a participant. Because the plight of the character is like the plight of many persons in the world, it is an **allegory,** and the character herself or himself may be considered as a **symbol.**

Throughout each story we read, no matter what characteristics we are considering, it is most important to realize that a work of fiction is an entirety, a unity. Any reading of a story should be undertaken not to break things down into parts but to understand and assimilate the work *as a whole.* The separate analysis of various topics is thus a *means* to that end, *not* the end itself. The study of fiction, like the study of all literature, is designed to foster our growth and to increase our understanding of the human condition.

 ## STORIES FOR STUDY

RAYMOND CARVER (1938–1988)

Originally from Oregon, Carver lived in Washington and spent much of his adult life in California. He studied at Chico State and at the Iowa Writers Workshop. After doing blue-collar jobs for a time he worked as an editor and then, finally, as a teacher. Some of his collections are Will You Please Be Quiet, Please? *(1976) and* Cathedral *(1983).* Where I'm Calling From *(1988) collects earlier stories and adds a number of new ones.* Short Cuts *(1993) is a selection of ten stories that were woven together into a film (1993) by Robert Altman. Carver is considered a master of minimalism; that is, fiction that stresses only the essentials of action and description. Generally, his writing is economical, stripped to the bone. Many of his characters seem unusual if not odd or even cruel. For example, one of his brief stories, "Popular Mechanics," takes little more than a single page to depict how a couple breaking up is also about to break up (literally) their child. "Neighbors" is taken from* Where I'm Calling From.

Neighbors ———————————————————————————— *1988*

Bill and Arlene Miller were a happy couple. But now and then they felt they alone among their circle had been passed by somehow, leaving Bill to attend to his bookkeeping duties and Arlene occupied with secretarial chores. They talked about it sometimes, mostly in comparison with the lives of their neighbors, Harriet and Jim Stone. It seemed to the Millers that the Stones lived a fuller and brighter life. The Stones were always going out for dinner, or entertaining at home, or traveling about the country somewhere in connection with Jim's work.

The Stones lived across the hall from the Millers. Jim was a salesman for a machine-parts firm and often managed to combine business with pleasure trips, and on this occasion the Stones would be away for ten days, first to Cheyenne, then on to St. Louis to visit relatives. In their absence, the Millers would look after the Stones' apartment, feed Kitty, and water the plants.

Bill and Jim shook hands beside the car. Harriet and Arlene held each other by the elbows and kissed lightly on the lips.

"Have fun," Bill said to Harriet.

"We will," said Harriet. "You kids have fun too."   5

Arlene nodded.

Jim winked at her. "Bye, Arlene. Take good care of the old man."

"I will," Arlene said.

"Have fun," Bill said.

"You bet," Jim said, clipping Bill lightly on the arm. "And thanks again, you guys."   10
The Stones waved as they drove away, and the Millers waved too.

"Well, I wish it was us," Bill said.

"God knows, we could use a vacation," Arlene said. She took his arm and put it around her waist as they climbed the stairs to their apartment.

After dinner Arlene said, "Don't forget. Kitty gets liver flavor the first night." She stood in the kitchen doorway folding the handmade tablecloth that Harriet had bought for her last year in Santa Fe.

Bill took a deep breath as he entered the Stones' apartment. The air was already   15
heavy and it was vaguely sweet. The sunburst clock over the television said half past eight. He remembered when Harriet had come home with the clock, how she had crossed the hall to show it to Arlene, cradling the brass case in her arms and talking to it through the tissue paper as if it were an infant.

Kitty rubbed her face against his slippers and then turned onto her side, but jumped up quickly as Bill moved to the kitchen and selected one of the stacked cans from the gleaming drainboard. Leaving the cat to pick at her food, he headed for the bathroom. He looked at himself in the mirror and then closed his eyes and then looked again. He opened the medicine chest. He found a container of pills and read the label —*Harriet Stone. One each day as directed*—and slipped it into his pocket. He went back to the kitchen, drew a pitcher of water, and returned to the living room. He finished watering, set the pitcher on the rug, and opened the liquor cabinet. He reached in back for the bottle of Chivas Regal. He took two drinks from the bottle, wiped his lips on his sleeve, and replaced the bottle in the cabinet.

Kitty was on the couch sleeping. He switched off the lights, slowly closing and checking the door. He had the feeling he had left something.

"What kept you?" Arlene said. She sat with her legs turned under her, watching television.

"Nothing. Playing with Kitty," he said, and went over to her and touched her breasts.

"Let's go to bed, honey," he said.   20

The next day Bill took only ten minutes of the twenty-minute break allotted for the afternoon and left at fifteen minutes before five. He parked the car in the lot just as Arlene hopped down from the bus. He waited until she entered the building, then ran up the stairs to catch her as she stepped out of the elevator.

"Bill! God, you scared me. You're early," she said.

He shrugged. "Nothing to do at work," he said.

She let him use her key to open the door. He looked at the door across the hall before following her inside.

"Let's go to bed," he said.   25

"Now?" She laughed. "What's gotten into you?"

"Nothing. Take your dress off." He grabbed for her awkwardly, and she said, "Good God, Bill."

He unfastened his belt.

Later they sent out for Chinese food, and when it arrived they ate hungrily, without speaking, and listened to records.

"Let's not forget to feed Kitty," she said.   30

"I was just thinking about that," he said. "I'll go right over."

* * *

He selected a can of fish flavor for the cat, then filled the pitcher and went to water. When he returned to the kitchen, the cat was scratching in her box. She looked at him steadily before she turned back to the litter. He opened all the cupboards and examined the canned goods, the cereals, the packaged foods, the cocktail and wine glasses, the china, the pots and pans. He opened the refrigerator. He sniffed some celery, took two bites of cheddar cheese, and chewed on an apple as he walked into the bedroom. The bed seemed enormous, with a fluffy white bedspread draped to the floor. He pulled out a nightstand drawer, found a half-empty package of cigarettes and stuffed them into his pocket. Then he stepped to the closet and was opening it when the knock sounded at the front door.

He stopped by the bathroom and flushed the toilet on his way.

"What's been keeping you?" Arlene said. "You've been over here more than an hour."

"Have I really?" he said.   35

"Yes, you have," she said.

"I had to go to the toilet," he said.

"You have your own toilet," she said.

"I couldn't wait," he said.

That night they made love again.   40

In the morning he had Arlene call in for him. He showered, dressed, and made a light breakfast. He tried to start a book. He went out for a walk and felt better. But after a while, hands still in his pockets, he returned to the apartment. He stopped at the Stones' door on the chance he might hear the cat moving about. Then he let himself in at his own door and went to the kitchen for the key.

Inside it seemed cooler than his apartment, and darker too. He wondered if the plants had something to do with the temperature of the air. He looked out the window, and then he moved slowly through each room considering everything that fell under his gaze, carefully, one object at a time. He saw ashtrays, items of furniture, kitchen utensils, the clock. He saw everything. At last he entered the bedroom, and the cat appeared at his feet. He stroked her once, carried her into the bathroom, and shut the door.

He lay down on the bed and stared at the ceiling. He lay for a while with his eyes closed, and then he moved his hand under his belt. He tried to recall what day it was. He tried to remember when the Stones were due back, and then he wondered if they would ever return. He could not remember their faces or the way they talked and dressed. He sighed and with effort rolled off the bed to lean over the dresser and look at himself in the mirror.

He opened the closet and selected a Hawaiian shirt. He looked until he found Bermudas, neatly pressed and hanging over a pair of brown twill slacks. He shed his own clothes and slipped into the shorts and the shirt. He looked in the mirror again. He went to the living room and poured himself a drink and sipped it on his way back to the bedroom. He put on a blue shirt, a dark suit, a blue and white tie, black wing-tip shoes. The glass was empty and he went for another drink.

In the bedroom again, he sat on a chair, crossed his legs, and smiled, observing himself in the mirror. The telephone rang twice and fell silent. He finished the drink and took off the suit. He rummaged through the top drawers until he found a pair of panties and a brassiere. He stepped into the panties and fastened the brassiere, then looked through the closet for an outfit. He put on a black and white checkered skirt and tried to zip it up. He put on a burgundy blouse that buttoned up the front. He considered her shoes, but understood they would not fit. For a long time he looked out the living-room window from behind the curtain. Then he returned to the bedroom and put everything away.

He was not hungry. She did not eat much, either. They looked at each other shyly and smiled. She got up from the table and checked that the key was on the shelf and then she quickly cleared the dishes.

He stood in the kitchen doorway and smoked a cigarette and watched her pick up the key.

"Make yourself comfortable while I go across the hall," she said. "Read the paper or something." She closed her fingers over the key. He was, she said, looking tired.

He tried to concentrate on the news. He read the paper and turned on the television. Finally he went across the hall. The door was locked.

"It's me. Are you still there, honey?" he called.

After a time the lock released and Arlene stepped outside and shut the door. "Was I gone so long?" she said.

"Well, you were," he said.

"Was I?" she said. "I guess I must have been playing with Kitty."

He studied her, and she looked away, her hand still resting on the doorknob.

"It's funny," she said. "You know—to go in someone's place like that."

He nodded, took her hand from the knob, and guided her toward their own door. He let them into their apartment.

"It *is* funny," he said.

He noticed white lint clinging to the back of her sweater, and the color was high in her cheeks. He began kissing her on the neck and hair and she turned and kissed him back.

"Oh, damn," she said. "Damn, damn," she sang, girlishly clapping her hands. "I just remembered. I really and truly forgot to do what I went over there to do. I didn't feed Kitty or do any watering." She looked at him. "Isn't that stupid?"

"I don't think so," he said. "Just a minute. I'll get my cigarettes and go back with you."

She waited until he had closed and locked their door, and then she took his arm at the muscle and said. "I guess I should tell you. I found some pictures."

He stopped in the middle of the hall. "What kind of pictures?"

"You can see for yourself," she said, and she watched him.

"No kidding." He grinned. "Where?"

"In a drawer," she said.

"No kidding," he said.

And then she said, "Maybe they won't come back," and was at once astonished at her words.

"It could happen," he said. "Anything could happen."

"Or maybe they'll come back and . . ." but she did not finish.

They held hands for the short walk across the hall, and when he spoke she could barely hear his voice. 70

"The key," he said. "Give it to me."

"What?" she said. She gazed at the door.

"The key," he said. "You have the key."

"My God," she said, "I left the key inside."

He tried the knob. It was locked. Then she tried the knob. It would not turn. Her 75 lips were parted, and her breathing was hard, expectant. He opened his arms and she moved into them.

"Don't worry," he said into her ear. "For God's sake, don't worry."

They stayed there. They held each other. They leaned into the door as if against a wind, and braced themselves.

QUESTIONS

1.   Who is the speaker of "Neighbors"? On whom is the speaker's attention directed?

2.   Who are the Millers? Do they seem normal at first? As the story progresses, do they seem to get odd? What happens to them?

3.   Should the story be considered as realistic fiction, or would it be more appropriate to consider it as an illustration of life's absurdities?

LAURIE COLWIN   (1944–1992)

Colwin was born in New York and took her higher education at Bard and Columbia. During most of her brief life she worked as an editor and literary agent. Nevertheless she was quite busy as a writer in her own right, writing five novels (including Happy All the Time *[1978] and* Family Happiness *[1982]), two collections of essays, and three collections of stories (*Passion and Affect *[1974];* The Lone Pilgrim *[1981], from which "An Old-Fashioned Story" is taken; and* Another Marvelous Thing *[1986]). Critics have noted her deft and appealing character portrayals, her uniqueness and humor, and her interweaving of the themes of privacy and romantic love.*

An Old-Fashioned Story —————————————————————— *1981*

The Rodkers had a son named Nelson, whom all the world called Nellie. The Leopolds had a daughter named Elizabeth. Marshall Rodker and Roger Leopold had been at college and law school together and courted wives who had been roommates at college. Nelson was two years Elizabeth's senior, and he was a model child in every way.

Elizabeth, on the other hand, began her life as a rebellious, spunky, and passionate child, but she was extraordinarily pretty, and such children are never called difficult: they are called original. It was the ardent hope of these people that their children might be friends and, when they grew up, would like each other well enough to marry.

In order to ensure their happy future, the children were brought together. If Elizabeth looked about to misbehave, Elinor Leopold placed her warm hand on Elizabeth's forearm and, with a little squeeze Elizabeth learned to dread, would say in tones of determined sweetness: "Darling, don't you want to see nice Nellie's chemistry set?" Elizabeth did not want to see it—or Nelson's stamp collection or his perfect math papers or the model city he had built with his Erector set. As she grew older, she did not want to dance with Nelson at dancing class or go to his school reception. But she did these things. That warm pressure on her forearm was as effective as a slap, although her compliance was not gained only by squeezes and horrified looks. Elizabeth had begun to have a secret life: she hated Nelson and she hated the Rodkers with secret fury. While she was too young to wonder if this loathing included her parents, she felt that if they forced Nelson upon her and chose the Rodkers for their dearest friends, they must in some way be against her. At the same time she realized that they were foolable to an amazing extent. If she smiled at Nelson, they were happy and considered her behavior impeccable. If she was rude, she spent weeks in pain—the pain of constant lectures. Thus, she learned to turn a cheerful face while keeping the fires of her dislike properly banked. The fact of the matter was that an afternoon of Nelson's stamp collection was good for two afternoons hanging around the park with her real friends.

Elizabeth's friends came down with measles, chicken pox, and mumps, but Elizabeth considered Nelson her childhood disease. As she got older, she began to feel that he had ruined her early years, but in her twenties she realized what an asset he had been. Without him she would never have learned to shield herself entirely from her parents. She learned from him how little it took to please: Nelson wrapped himself up warm when it was cold. He baked cookies for his mother's birthday. He played chess with his father. That, it appeared, sufficed—a very instructive lesson that was not lost on Elizabeth, who felt that beneath Nelson's clean, wavy hair lived a rat, a suck-up, a traitor to all children.

Nelson had an older brother named James. James was eight years Elizabeth's senior, and she regarded him as veritably ancient. James had been sent away to a progressive school for the brilliant and unmanageable children of the well-to-do. Here he learned to smoke, drive a car without a license, and play cards for money. When these traits became manifest, James was plucked from the libertine environment and sent to one of the nation's oldest and finest establishments for one last crack at making him an eventual leader of men. In this setting he drank beer, set off cherry bombs in trash cans, and hung around with town girls. By the time he was ready to graduate, he added to this sort of hell raising a penchant for seditious literature and came home spouting Marx,° Mao,° and Huysmans.°

Marx: Karl Marx (1818–1883), founder of communism and writer of *The Communist Manifesto* (1848).

Mao: Mao Tse-tung (1893–1976), Chinese communist leader and author of *The Thoughts of Chairman Mao* (1967).

Huysmans: Joris-Karl Huysmans (1848–1907), French novelist, author of *Against the Grain* (1884), a novel about a young man's search for unique and exotic sensations.

At college he learned a great many more bad habits, including how to spend money, drink wine, seduce young women, and break some bone or other right before Thanksgiving vacation called him back to his family. In spite of this, he did extremely well and graduated with honors. The night of his graduation he was arrested with some of his unwholesome friends for disorderly conduct and was made to spend the night in jail. This was meant to scare him. The next morning he was released, his fingerprints in a manila envelope that he might know the kindness doled out by the police to young men who will someday be their elected leaders.

Elizabeth was kept abreast of James's evil career by her parents, who said that James was killing Marshall and breaking poor Harriet's heart. Nelson spoke of his brother as if he were some pathetic sort of animal.

Over a game of Scrabble, which, of course, Nelson was winning, he commented on the arrest.

"Poor Daddy and Mother. Jimmy got arrested, you know. They gave him back his fingerprints, but it will always be on his conscience, and if he's ever asked if he's been arrested, he'll have to say yes."

"Why will he?" Elizabeth said.

"Because it's true," said Nelson. "Besides, it's adolescent and silly. It's just as easy not to get arrested as to get arrested." Nelson at the time was almost sixteen. He was a nice-looking, somewhat expressionless boy whom Elizabeth found more and more repulsive. All his clothes were clean. His hair was combed. Elizabeth knew that he underlined passages in books, a habit she found disgusting. When he read, he sat upright in his leather chair, under proper light with his book held at a proper angle. Elizabeth, who read under the covers with a flashlight, found his posture disgusting as well.

After a brief contemplation of the Scrabble board, Nelson made an ingenious play using the word "vugh," about which Elizabeth was doubtful but did not challenge. It was pointless to challenge Nelson. He was all-knowing and he never cheated. In fact, one of Harriet Rodker's favorite stories about him concerned a point of honor. Nelson, at seven, told his father that he had stolen two gum erasers from Mrs. Williamson's candy store. His father advised him to take them back. "But I can't," Nelson had said. "I was so upset about stealing them that I threw them away." Marshall Rodker then asked his son how he intended to make reparation—*if*, of course, was never at issue. Nelson had said, "I'll go to Mrs. Williamson and tell her what I did and pay her." This he did, and Mrs. Williamson swore she never knew a better boy than Nelson Rodker. Elizabeth was sure this was a true story but for one detail. She was certain that Nelson had not thrown the erasers away; she knew that he had eaten them. She was convinced that when his parents were out he made mashed potatoes from the *Joy of Cooking* so that he could eat them with his hands.

Nelson and Elizabeth went to brother-and-sister schools where Nelson distinguished himself. He won the Latin prize, the good citizen's award, the math medal, and scholar of the year. Meanwhile, James Rodker had dropped out of what little sight he permitted his parents by going to England, where it was thought he was studying economics or history. Only the Leopolds knew how scanty information was about James. At dinner parties his name and the subject of economic history were twined, but during Rodker-Leopold bridge games all was revealed. As Elizabeth stood with her ear to the library door, she learned that whenever the Rodkers went to London to see him, they found that he had just gone abroad, or, if he was in town, he turned up with Hindu or Oriental girls who were clearly his mistresses. Elizabeth longed for these bridge parties. James's career filled her with admiration. With Nelson constantly held over her head, it was hard for her not to have outright affection for anyone who behaved like a punk.

The beautiful daughters of the nervous well-to-do are tended like orchids, especially in a city like New York. Elizabeth was not allowed to take a public bus unaccompanied until she was thirteen. Her friends were carefully picked over. The little O'Connor girl was common; that her father had won a Pulitzer prize was of no matter. The little Jefferson boy was colored. It made no difference that his father was a diplomat. And so on. The only one of Elizabeth's friends Mrs. Leopold approved of was Holly Lukas, whose mother was an old friend. Holly was the only one to be dignified by a first name. Thus, Elizabeth never brought her real friends home, since, with the exception of Holly, they were all wrong: the children of broken homes, the sons and daughters of people with odd political or religious preferences or of blacklisted movie producers. Elizabeth learned the hard way that these children would not be made comfortable in her house. This might have put a crimp in Elizabeth's social life except that none of her friends wanted to entertain at home. They knew early on that the best place to conduct a private life was in public.

And then there was the Fifield Riding Academy incident. Like most girls her age, Elizabeth became horse crazy. She did not want to share this passion with her parents, who felt riding once a week was quite enough, so she made a deal with the stable that, in exchange for a free lesson, she would muck out the stalls on Tuesdays. This, however, was not known by her mother, who had her expensively outfitted. These riding clothes Elizabeth carried in a rucksack along with her real riding clothes—an old pair of blue jeans and a ratty sweater.

It was soon discovered that Elizabeth was coming home late one extra afternoon   1
each week stinking of horse. She was made to remove her jodhpurs at the service entrance and, when these garments were found to be relatively horseless, a search was made and the offending blue jeans rooted out. Mrs. Leopold then sat down to question her daughter. Elizabeth was mute. One word about manure and her riding days were over. But manure was not on Mrs. Leopold's mind and, in fact, when she learned that her spotless baby spent one weekday in the company of a pitchfork, she was much relieved.

She said, "Who works at the stable?"

Elizabeth said, "You know. Mr. Fifield. That girl, Franny Hatch, and some boys."

"What *boys?*"

"Oh, you know. Douglas Fifield and Buddy, the one who takes the little kids around the ring."

The questioning continued until Mrs. Leopold finally asked what she was really   2
after. "Did this Douglas or this Buddy ever try to touch you?"

Elizabeth was fourteen at the time, and it was clear that boys were not what worried Mrs. Leopold. It was Elizabeth herself. What wanton impulse would lead a girl to spend her time working in a stable?

Besides, parents of the time believed in companionship with their children. When Elizabeth discovered bird walking or skating, stationery embossed with birds or skates was ordered in case she wished to write to her relatives. This invasion of privacy, which radical students would later call co-option, looked harmless and well-meant and was practiced by most parents.

When Elizabeth went to college, she had her first taste of freedom. While similarly restrained girls went wild, Elizabeth reveled in being left alone and staying up late at night reading anything she liked. The Leopolds were not against reading, but Elizabeth's reading habits contributed to eyestrain and bad posture and, besides, all that reading made one lopsided. One must also sail, dress well, speak a foreign language, and be good at tennis. Since Elizabeth had never had the luxury to read undisturbed in her own house, she had little time at college to drink to excess or become promiscuous.

At home on holidays she was correctness itself. At twenty, in the middle of her first love affair, she was grown up enough to restrain herself from calling her beloved in Vermont, lest her parents find him on the telephone bill. Elizabeth's parents set great store on adult behavior. Had they known what sort of adult Elizabeth had become, great would have been their dismay. Elizabeth smiled beautifully and behaved in a flawless manner.

Her mother was not entirely happy. She felt, as mothers will, that her daughter   25
was not telling her the sort of things a daughter ought. She was vexed that Elizabeth was far away and none of her college chums could be conned. Mrs. Leopold knew she would have to wait for something to break: Elizabeth would want to go abroad to study, or to go to Africa, or she would turn up engaged to an awful boy. But Elizabeth did none of these things. She was graduated from college, came back to New York, and got a job.

Her decision to live in New York was not easily come by, but she loved New York and she wanted to enjoy it finally on her own terms. She went to her father's bank, and using as collateral a diamond-and-sapphire bracelet left to her by her grandmother, she borrowed enough money to rent an apartment on a little street in Greenwich Village and live until she had a salary. Through a friend of the O'Connor girl's Pulitzer-prize-winning father, she found a job at a publishing company and went to work.

Her parents were puzzled by this. The daughters of their friends were announcing their engagements in the *Times,* and those who joined the Peace Corps or had gone to graduate school were filed under the heading of "Useful Service," as if they had entered convents or dedicated themselves to the poor, following the example of Jane Addams,° who had after all come from a nice, rich family. Elizabeth further puzzled them by refusing to take a cent of their money, although Mrs. Leopold knew the truth: what you dole out to the young binds them to you. To have Elizabeth owing nothing was disconcerting, to say the least.

To even up the side, she called Elizabeth to see if she was comfortable in her little cramped apartment that doubtless had insufficient heat. In the summer she was sure Elizabeth was suffocating and offered an air conditioner. She worried that the cleaners in that part of town did shoddy work and brooded to Elizabeth about what young girls had for dinner.

Elizabeth was in a state of bliss. She could flop down on her bed with no lecture notes or required texts and read. Her friends, who had discovered many dangerous and exotic ways in which to cherish their freedom, found Elizabeth a little pathetic in this respect, but having the power to read what she liked was the ultimate liberty. Staying up all night exhausted her. Drink made her dizzy, drugs either disoriented her or made her sick, and she did not have a promiscuous nature. She did, however, have a lover.

The lover was her next-door neighbor, Roy Wayne Howard, a large man with an   30
Edwardian moustache. Roy was from central Ohio, and he was a fund raiser for the Center for Union Democracy. To this end he tried to hustle money. He found lawyers willing to donate their services. He had once been a hooded witness at the trial of some goons who had threatened an insurgent rank and file. Elizabeth, who was crazy about him, found him heroic.

Jane Addams: Jane Addams (1860–1935), social worker, advocate of women's rights, and founder of Hull House in Chicago.

Elizabeth had run into Roy in the neighborhood: They introduced themselves at the all-night grocery store. One evening Roy appeared at her door with a bottle of whisky and two glasses. He drank most of the whisky while he and Elizabeth sniped at one another. After several evenings of this sort, plus several afternoons watching football games on television and a meal at a crummy Spanish restaurant, they became lovers, and from then on they were on and off. When they were on, they went to prizefights, to bars, and to the jazz clubs Roy loved. After a month of this Roy ceased to appear. Ringing his doorbell and confronting him turned out to be useless. Weeks would go by until they bumped into each other again and were on.

This kept up for a year. Elizabeth was in love with Roy, and this on-again, off-again business upset her. She discussed it with Holly Lukas.

"I can't bear it," Elizabeth wailed. "Why does he do this to me?"

"I would tell you," Holly said, "but you don't want to know."

"Yes, I do."

Holly, who was a great fan of Roy's, explained: "For a smart girl, Elizabeth, you have a very selective intelligence. You're like your mother. You like to see a situation in the light that does you the most good. You think Roy is afraid of intimacy, which is a stylish thing to say, but the truth is that Roy is a little too fond of you, and when it occurs to him that there's nothing in it, he pulls back, for both your sakes."

"What do you mean, both our sakes?" said Elizabeth, who was reaching for her handkerchief.

"Roy is wonderful. Anyone with sense would love Roy. But Roy drinks too much. Roy dresses badly. Roy wants to be a solitary hero. Roy told you that his idea of happiness is to go off to an island in Lake Michigan with a transistor radio and a case of Scotch. You will never marry Roy, and Roy will never marry you. Since you're both old-fashioned, that's bound to catch up with you."

"Yes," said Elizabeth. "It's true. And if I hang around with Roy, I don't have to marry anyone else." Holly had told her this before.

"Absolutely," said Holly. "If you married Roy, both of you would be miserable. Face the fact that you're having a love affair that isn't unhappy but will not lead to anything."

Elizabeth knew the truth when she heard it, but still she went to prizefights and to bars with Roy intermittently.

Meanwhile, once every three weeks or so she had dinner with Nelson so if her mother said, "Aren't you seeing any nice young men?" she could truthfully answer, "I see Nelson."

Nelson called on a Wednesday to ask her out for Saturday. He always appeared in an elegant sports jacket and beautiful trousers. It was hard for Elizabeth to admit that he was good-looking, but he was. One night Nelson, who had been first in his class at law school, mentioned his volunteer prison work.

"You go into prisons looking like that?" she asked.

"Yes, and I wear my watch, too." Said watch was heavy and gold, a Rodker family relic.

"Those cons must really love you."

"Well, as a matter of fact, they do, because they get the services of a first-rate lawyer for free. And why should I change what I wear to go into a prison? I'd feel very condescended to if someone did that to me."

This prison-reform business was hard on Elizabeth. None of Nelson's attitudes were wrong and, worse, he never bragged. How she wished that he had turned out to be

a corporate lawyer, voting Republican and talking about the creeping menace of socialism. Instead, he made a lot of money *and* did good works. There was nothing Elizabeth
could pin on him.

Nelson always took her to a good restaurant and always paid for the meal, but he
explained, "I'm told you're living on what you earn and, since what I earn is about three
times what you earn, it's silly for you to split the check. If you wanted to be fair, you'd
invite me for dinner. Your mother told my mother you're quite a good cook."

This was a sore subject with Elizabeth. She had invited her parents for dinner,   50
after concealing any incriminating thing in the house. Any trace of birth control was
locked away. Any book her mother might pick up and say, "Darling, are you reading
this?," was hidden from view. All but several bottles of liquor were placed under the sink.
No bottles would mean that Elizabeth had no social life. Too many would mean that she
was either drinking to excess or hanging around with those who did.

Mrs. Leopold, who referred to these meals as "Elizabeth's bohemian dinners," said
to her daughter, "I don't know where you learned to use spices in such an original way."
Implying that Elizabeth never could have learned from her—and also that spices were
common, and that real food, eaten by real people, was either plain American or French.

So Elizabeth had no intention of being fair and inviting Nelson for dinner. She
figured he was probably a spy. Still, these dinners with him were not unpleasant, but
after the pleasantest of them Elizabeth made sure that when Nelson left her at her door
she changed her clothes and went next door to Roy Howard.

In early December Roy Howard moved away. He promised he would stay in
touch, but Elizabeth began to cry. Roy said, "I love you in my own way but not in any
way that will do any good." Then he gave her a kiss, and she knew he would continue to
turn up intermittently. However, his moving brought her very low. She saw Nelson
rather more often. He took her for drives in the country, or for walks, or out for dinner.
He talked to her about her work and his own. He was an excellent time filler, and
Elizabeth began to think of him as an old friend, one of those friends who connects
you to your past. During a drive one afternoon he revealed to her that James was
coming home for Christmas.

Coincidental with the departure of Roy Howard was an onslaught by her mother,
who appeared one day at Elizabeth's office to take her out to lunch.

Soon Elizabeth was picking at a salad in a ladies' tearoom while her mother gently   55
grilled her. Why did she look so unwell and tired? Was she having trouble sleeping?
Should she make an appointment with Dr. Goldhauer? Did her employers expect her to
work herself into physical collapse? Mrs. Leopold had the knack of catching her daughter at her most vulnerable.

"I'm perfectly fine. It's just been a hectic week at work," Elizabeth said coldly.

Mrs. Leopold's eyes narrowed—a sign of war. War had once meant prohibition—
of riding lessons and telephone calls. Now war meant a lecture, the only method left to
Mrs. Leopold in her futile search for information. Basically, she wanted to know if
Elizabeth was having romantic troubles, but since she would not ask, she came down
hard on the issue of family loyalty and Elizabeth's lack of interest in the needs of others.

Elizabeth and Holly called these lectures "A Mother's Ten Commandments"—all
of which they broke: Thou shalt tell thy mother everything. Thou shalt live very near
thy mother. Thou shalt bring friends home for thy mother's approval. Thou shalt offer
information about thy love life. Thou shalt dress according to thy mother's style. Thou
shalt constantly be in debt to thy mother for sums large and small. Thou shalt have fierce

family loyalty on all occasions. Thou shalt ask thy mother's opinion. Thou shalt confide thy troubles in thy mother so that thy mother may become hysterical. Thou shalt borrow thy mother's cleaning woman.

The lunch was not a success, and Elizabeth and her mother parted in terrible tempers.

One week later was the Rodkers' annual Christmas party, and Elizabeth was loaded for bear. Her first step was the purchase of a black velvet dress that was low in the back, low in the front, and sleeveless. Next was the gardenia she wore in her hair. She looked quite beautiful, but her mother could not approve of the dress and she found the gardenia excessive. Nelson, however, found her ravishing and told her so. But Nelson's praise was not her goal: she was after James. She had decided that a little public bad behavior was exactly what she needed. It was time to get her mother off her back, outrage the Rodkers, and put to rest once and for all her imitation of a well-composed young woman. She could also blitz what she considered their tidy plans for her: a safe marriage to nice Nelson, or someone very like him.

As soon as she had knocked back several glasses of champagne, she felt up to putting her plan in operation. This was to flirt slowly and blatantly with James. Then, if he was as dashing as she imagined, she would seduce him and then make it known. Before he went back to England, she would dump him. She was about to edge herself over to him when she felt that warm hand on her forearm.

"Darling, Harriet says you haven't said hello to her."

"Harriet can go to hell," said Elizabeth, so fortified by Piper Heidsieck that she ignored the threat of vengeance in her mother's eyes.

She approached James Rodker. Next to him the healthy Nelson palled. James looked haggard, tortured, just the sort of deep and troubled man you find in novels.

"Hello," she said with a big smile. "I haven't seen you since I was a little girl."

"Well, well, well," said James, "aren't you grown-up?" He turned her around and led her to a sofa.

"So you're Nellie's little pal," he said. "I've been hearing so much about you."

"I've always been hearing about you," Elizabeth said.

"Tell you what," said James, "as soon as the whole crowd is here, let's you and me sneak out for a drink and talk about all we've been hearing. What say?"

"All right," said Elizabeth, though this was not quite as she had planned. James had jumped the gun on her.

But things worked out well enough. They made a public exit on the pretext of going out for a bag of ice and had the pleasure of watching Harriet Rodker's lips compress, but before she could speak, Elizabeth and James were out the door and into the elevator.

He took her to a bar around the corner, a dull, wood-paneled place—the sort of bar you can take your son to after a hockey game. They sat in a wooden booth and sipped their drinks in silence. James lit his pipe and smiled a knowing smile.

"So, here you are. The little number they've tucked away for brother Nellie," he said.

"I am not tucked away for anyone."

"No, on second thought, you wouldn't be. Girls like you play for higher stakes. Love or income, or preferably both."

"I don't play for any stakes," Elizabeth said.

"How refreshingly young you are," said James. "Mother implored me to be kind to you."

"As opposed to what?"

"As opposed to dragging you by the hair, knocking you out, and catching a social disease, or giving you one."

"Have you had many social diseases?"

"Oh, several. I have contracted social diseases in Hong Kong, Saigon, and the town of High Wycombe." He set his dead pipe down on the table. "Little girls like you— I beg your pardon—women like you are meant to blush, or don't you blush any more? Probably not."

Elizabeth realized that the romantic James was rather drunk. He then began a long discourse on the subject of the nuclear family, quoting extensively in French from a sociologist Elizabeth had never heard of. Then he launched into an explanation of the English economy, and Elizabeth realized that for all that he was haggard he was extremely dull.

Suddenly he stared directly into Elizabeth's eyes.

"Have you the keys to your apartment?" he said, and, without waiting for an answer, continued, "Give them to me."

Elizabeth was old enough to have been flirted with and propositioned many times. The men she liked best were straightforward, brave enough to state their intentions. The keys James Rodker wanted he wanted to clean his pipe with, she was sure. The easy way with which he made his request indicated to her that this was a well-used ploy. If you forked over your keys, he cleaned his pipe. If you fluttered, James took this as encouragement and ended by using your keys to come and sleep with you. Elizabeth handed over the keys and watched James dig the ashes out of his pipe.

"Clever girl," he said.

"I think we ought to go back," said Elizabeth, who was beginning to feel sleepy. She was profoundly disappointed. James was not a man she wanted to flirt with, and she felt a cold coming on.

"Not so fast," James said. "I'm going to tell you about all those things you've heard about me." And he commenced to describe his college career, the flat he had inhabited in London, the girls he had lived with in Paris, the bar girls he had slept with in Saigon, his position on his paper, and the number of famous friends he had. Elizabeth had to suppress a yawn.

"All right," said James, paying the bill. "Back to the arms of the family. Don't you find it public-spirited of our lovely Nellie to work with the less fortunate?"

Elizabeth swallowed. "Nelson's all right."

"You, of course, are partisan," James said. "Nellie is an insect."

When they returned to the party, Elizabeth realized that they had been gone for two hours and the smug smile James wore announced that they had been up to no good.

Elizabeth spent the next week in her apartment wrapped in a quilt. The cold she had expected materialized. In addition to being ill, she was angry. From Holly she had learned that James Rodker during his stay had not come home several nights and dropped her name frequently. Thus, it was assumed that she and James were up to further evil doings. She said to Holly: "I know I set out to seduce him, but he's just too awful. And besides, look at what he's done! He's set me up! He comes home to rub his parents' nose in it and he used me!"

"Unthinkable," said Holly.

On the afternoon of New Year's Eve Elizabeth was curled up dozing under her quilt. In a few hours she would dress and go to the boozy, happy party Holly gave each New Year's. Elizabeth felt neither happy nor much in the mood for a party. She was brooding heavily but was interrupted by the doorbell. She started—it might be Roy Howard, who sometimes dropped by on whim. But it was not. It was Nelson Rodker.

"Hello," he said. "I was in the neighborhood and I heard you were sick, so I decided to drop by and see you."

This was most unlike Nelson. He was wearing a beautiful suit and gold cuff links. The wind had blown his hair about and made his cheeks blaze. He looked healthy but very serious.

"I guess you came to find out if I was sleeping with your brother," Elizabeth said.

"You're hardly the sort of girl to sleep with Jimmy. He's far too dull for you."

"How would you know?"

"I didn't come to fight with you or to check up on your behavior."

"You came as a kindly gesture to an ill friend."

"I came to see you because I wanted to."

"And to report back to our parents that I'm still alive and that James isn't hiding under my bed?"

"Elizabeth, what is wrong with you? I always think of you as a free spirit and here you chain me to my family."

"You are your family," Elizabeth said sulkily.

"I am most certainly not my family. I don't like my family and I never have. My family is silly, stuffy, and rigid. You're not the only one who behaved yourself and got out fast. What do you think I am?"

"A model boy," said Elizabeth.

Then Nelson did a most un-Nelson thing. He took the quilt from Elizabeth's shoulders, lifted her to her feet and gave her the sort of kiss she had never associated with Nelson or anyone like him.

"I came to tell you that I love you," said Nelson. "I've been wondering for months if I love you because I was told to when I was a child or if I just love you. Well, I just love you."

They stood very close for a long time, the quilt lying at their feet.

"I don't know what to think," Elizabeth said.

"I want to know if you hate me because you expect it of yourself or if you actually hate me."

"I don't hate you," said Elizabeth.

"Do you think you could love me?"

Elizabeth discovered that her head was on his shoulder and that her arms were around his neck.

"It seems to make perfect sense," she said. "But things don't happen this way, do they?"

"Some old friends fall in love, all of a sudden," Nelson said.

"Whatever it is I feel, it seems to have hit me all at once. Or maybe it's crept up on me without my knowing."

"I'd like to take you to Holly's party," said Nelson.

"That's not for hours."

"Oh," said Nelson, "I'm sure we can find a way to pass the time."

"This will certainly amaze everyone," Elizabeth said.

"Only if we tell them," said Nelson. "A secret romance is one thing, but a secret romance worth keeping a secret is quite another. Just the thing for us, don't you think?"

They smiled ravishing smiles. As they stood with their arms entwined, they agreed   125
that it was just the perfect sort of thing for them.

QUESTIONS

1. Describe the situation in the two families. Who is Elizabeth? How completely is she developed as a character? To what degree is she unusual? How does she develop or change? What does she think of her family? What freedom does she covet most? What social conventions does she flaunt?

2. Who is Nelson? What is he like as a child? As an adult? What does Elizabeth think about him? Why is it important in the story's development for Elizabeth to misunderstand Nelson for most of their lives? What does Nelson think of his family? How different is he from his brother James?

3. Is the narrator named? Why or why not? How does the narrator's presentation shape your understanding of situations and characters?

4. What elements in the story are amusing? How does the narrator or speaker contribute to the humor?

5. What surprise occurs at the story's end? What parts of the story might prepare readers for this conclusion? In light of the story's ending, consider the meaning of the title.

TIM O'BRIEN   (b. 1946)

William Timothy O'Brien was born in Minnesota and attended Macalester College in St. Paul. He saw duty in Vietnam during some of the more controversial times of that conflict, and after returning home he did graduate study, worked as a reporter, and became a writer. Among the works he has regularly published since the 1970s are If I Die in a Combat Zone, Box Me Up and Ship Me Home *(1973);* Northern Lights *(1974);* Going After Cacciato *(1978); and* The Things They Carried *(1990). In his stories, which interweave fiction and autobiography, he realistically treats both the horrors of the Vietnam war and the ways in which returning veterans and their loved ones adjust to life after returning home. Because he portrays the lives and feelings of combat soldiers so well, he has been called one of the best American writers about war.*

The Things They Carried _____ *1990*

First Lieutenant Jimmy Cross carried letters from a girl named Martha, a junior at Mount Sebastian College in New Jersey. They were not love letters, but Lieutenant Cross was hoping, so he kept them folded in plastic at the bottom of his rucksack. In the late afternoon, after a day's march, he would dig his foxhole, wash his hands under a canteen, unwrap the letters, hold them with the tips of his fingers, and spend the last hour of light pretending. He would imagine romantic camping trips into the White Mountains in New Hampshire. He would sometimes taste the envelope flaps, knowing her tongue had been there. More than anything, he wanted Martha to love him as he loved her, but the letters were mostly chatty, elusive on the matter of love. She was a virgin, he was almost sure. She was an English major at Mount Sebastian, and she wrote beautifully about her professors and roommates and midterm exams, about her respect for Chaucer and her great affection for Virginia Woolf. She often quoted lines of poetry; she never mentioned the war, except to say, Jimmy, take care of yourself. The letters weighed 10 ounces. They were signed Love, Martha, but Lieutenant Cross understood that Love was only a way of signing and did not mean what he sometimes pretended it meant. At dusk, he would carefully return the letters to his rucksack. Slowly, a bit distracted, he would get up and move among his men, checking the perimeter, then at full dark he would return to his hole and watch the night and wonder if Martha was a virgin.

The things they carried were largely determined by necessity. Among the necessities or near-necessities were P-38 can openers, pocket knives, heat tabs, wristwatches, dog tags, mosquito repellent, chewing gum, candy, cigarettes, salt tablets, packets of Kool-Aid, lighters, matches, sewing kits, Military Payment Certificates, C rations, and two or three canteens of water. Together, these items weighed between 15 and 20 pounds, depending upon a man's habits or rate of metabolism. Henry Dobbins, who was a big man, carried extra rations; he was especially fond of canned peaches in heavy syrup over pound cake. Dave Jensen, who practiced field hygiene, carried a toothbrush, dental floss, and several hotel-sized bars of soap he'd stolen on R&R in Sydney, Australia. Ted Lavender, who was scared, carried tranquilizers until he was shot in the head outside the village of Than Khe in mid-April. By necessity, and because it was SOP, they all carried steel helmets that weighed 5 pounds including the liner and camouflage cover. They carried the standard fatigue jackets and trousers. Very few carried underwear. On their feet they carried jungle boots—2.1 pounds—and Dave Jensen carried three pairs of socks and a can of Dr. Scholl's foot powder as a precaution against trench foot. Until he was shot, Ted Lavender carried six or seven ounces of premium dope, which for him was a necessity. Mitchell Sanders, the RTO, carried condoms. Norman Bowker carried a diary. Rat Kiley carried comic books. Kiowa, a devout Baptist, carried an illustrated New Testament that had been presented to him by his father, who taught Sunday school in Oklahoma City, Oklahoma. As a hedge against bad times, however, Kiowa also carried his grandmother's distrust of the white man, his grandfather's old hunting hatchet. Necessity dictated. Because the land was mined and booby-trapped, it was SOP for each man to carry a steel-centered, nylon-covered flak jacket, which weighed 6.7 pounds, but which on hot days seemed much heavier. Because you could die so quickly, each man carried at least one large compress bandage, usually in the helmet band for easy access. Because the nights were cold, and because the monsoons were wet, each carried a green plastic poncho that could be used as a raincoat or groundsheet or makeshift tent. With its quilted liner, the poncho weighed almost two pounds, but it was worth every ounce. In April, for instance, when Ted Lavender was shot, they used his poncho to wrap him up, then to carry him across the paddy, then to lift him into the chopper that took him away.

They were called legs or grunts.

To carry something was to hump it, as when Lieutenant Jimmy Cross humped his love for Martha up the hills and through the swamps. In its intransitive form, to hump meant to walk, or to march, but it implied burdens far beyond the intransitive.

Almost everyone humped photographs. In his wallet, Lieutenant Cross carried   5
two photographs of Martha. The first was a Kodacolor snapshot signed Love, though he knew better. She stood against a brick wall. Her eyes were gray and neutral, her lips slightly open as she stared straight-on at the camera. At night, sometimes, Lieutenant Cross wondered who had taken the picture, because he knew she had boyfriends, because he loved her so much, and because he could see the shadow of the picture-taker spreading out against the brick wall. The second photograph had been clipped from the 1968 Mount Sebastian yearbook. It was an action shot—women's volleyball—and Martha was bent horizontal to the floor, reaching, the palms of her hands in sharp focus, the tongue taut, the expression frank and competitive. There was no visible sweat. She wore white gym shorts. Her legs, he thought, were almost certainly the legs of a virgin, dry and without hair, the left knee cocked and carrying her entire weight, which was just over one hundred pounds. Lieutenant Cross remembered touching that left knee. A dark theater, he remembered, and the movie was *Bonnie and Clyde,* and Martha wore a tweed skirt, and during the final scene, when he touched her knee, she turned and looked at him in a sad, sober way that made him pull his hand back, but he would always remember the feel of the tweed skirt and the knee beneath it and the sound of the gunfire that killed Bonnie and Clyde, how embarrassing it was, how slow and oppressive. He remembered kissing her good night at the dorm door. Right then, he thought, he should've done something brave. He should've carried her up the stairs to her room and tied her to the bed and touched that left knee all night long. He should've risked it. Whenever he looked at the photographs, he thought of new things he should've done.

What they carried was partly a function of rank, partly of field specialty.

As a first lieutenant and platoon leader, Jimmy Cross carried a compass, maps, code books, binoculars, and a .45-caliber pistol that weighed 2.9 pounds fully loaded. He carried a strobe light and the responsibility for the lives of his men.

As an RTO, Mitchell Sanders carried the PRC-25 radio, a killer, 26 pounds with its battery.

As a medic, Rat Kiley carried a canvas satchel filled with morphine and plasma and malaria tablets and surgical tape and comic books and all the things a medic must carry, including M&M's for especially bad wounds, for a total weight of nearly 20 pounds.

As a big man, therefore a machine gunner, Henry Dobbins carried the M-60,   10
which weighed 23 pounds unloaded, but which was almost always loaded. In addition, Dobbins carried between 10 and 15 pounds of ammunition draped in belts across his chest and shoulders.

As PFCs or Spec 4s, most of them were common grunts and carried the standard M-16 gas-operated assault rifle. The weapon weighed 7.5 pounds unloaded, 8.2 pounds with its full 20-round magazine. Depending on numerous factors, such as topography and psychology, the riflemen carried anywhere from 12 to 20 magazines, usually in cloth bandoliers, adding on another 8.4 pounds at minimum, 14 pounds at maximum. When it was available, they also carried M-16 maintenance gear—rods and steel brushes and swabs and tubes of LSA oil—all of which weighed about a pound. Among the grunts, some carried the M-79 grenade launcher, 5.9 pounds unloaded, a reasonably light weapon except for the ammunition, which was heavy. A single round weighed 10 ounces. The typical load was 25 rounds. But Ted Lavender, who was scared, carried 34 rounds when he was shot and killed outside Than Khe, and he went down under an exceptional burden, more than 20 pounds of ammunition, plus the flak jacket and helmet and rations and water and toilet paper and tranquilizers and all the rest, plus the unweighed fear. He was dead weight. There was no twitching or flopping. Kiowa, who saw it happen, said it was like watching a rock fall, or a big sandbag or something—just boom, then down—not like the movies where the dead guy rolls around and does fancy spins and goes ass over teakettle—not like that, Kiowa said, the poor bastard just flat-fuck fell. Boom. Down. Nothing else. It was a bright morning in mid-April. Lieutenant Cross felt the pain. He blamed himself. They stripped off Lavender's canteens and ammo, all the heavy things, and Rat Kiley said the obvious, the guy's dead, and Mitchell Sanders used his radio to report one U.S. KIA and to request a chopper. Then they wrapped Lavender in his poncho. They carried him out to a dry paddy, established security, and sat smoking the dead man's dope until the chopper came. Lieutenant Cross kept to himself. He pictured Martha's smooth young face, thinking he loved her more than anything, more than his men, and now Ted Lavender was dead because he loved her so much and could not stop thinking about her. When the dustoff arrived, they carried Lavender aboard. Afterward they burned Than Khe. They marched until dusk, then dug their holes, and that night Kiowa kept explaining how you had to be there, how fast it was, how the poor guy just dropped like so much concrete. Boom-down, he said. Like cement.

In addition to the three standard weapons—the M-60, M-16, and M-79—they carried whatever presented itself, or whatever seemed appropriate as a means of killing or staying alive. They carried catch-as-catch-can. At various times, in various situations, they carried M-14s and CAR-15s and Swedish Ks and grease guns and captured AK-47s and Chi-Coms and RPGs and Simonov carbines and black market Uzis and .38-caliber Smith & Wesson handguns and 66 mm LAWs and shotguns and silencers and blackjacks and bayonets and C-4 plastic explosives. Lee Strunk carried a slingshot; a weapon of last resort, he called it. Mitchell Sanders carried brass knuckles. Kiowa carried his grandfather's feathered hatchet. Every third or fourth man carried a Claymore antipersonnel mine—3.5 pounds with its firing device. They all carried fragmentation grenades—14 ounces each. They all carried at least one M-18 colored smoke grenade—24 ounces. Some carried CS or tear gas grenades. Some carried white phosphorus grenades. They carried all they could bear, and then some, including a silent awe for the terrible power of the things they carried.

In the first week of April, before Lavender died, Lieutenant Jimmy Cross received a good-luck charm from Martha. It was a simple pebble, an ounce at most. Smooth to the touch, it was a milky white color with flecks of orange and violet, oval-shaped, like a miniature egg. In the accompanying letter, Martha wrote that she had found the pebble on the Jersey shoreline, precisely where the land touched water at high tide, where things came together but also separated. It was this separate-but-together quality, she wrote, that had inspired her to pick up the pebble and to carry it in her breast pocket for several days, where it seemed weightless, and then to send it through the mail, by air, as a token of her truest feelings for him. Lieutenant Cross found this romantic. But he wondered what her truest feelings were, exactly, and what she meant by separate-but-together. He wondered how the tides and waves had come into play on that afternoon along the Jersey shoreline when Martha saw the pebble and bent down to rescue it from geology. He imagined bare feet. Martha was a poet, with the poet's sensibilities, and her feet would be brown and bare, the toenails unpainted, the eyes chilly and somber like the ocean in March, and though it was painful, he wondered who had been with her that afternoon. He imagined a pair of shadows moving along the strip of sand where things came together but also separated. It was phantom jealousy, he knew, but he couldn't help himself. He loved her so much. On the march, through the hot days of early April, he carried the pebble in his mouth, turning it with his tongue, tasting sea salt and moisture. His mind wandered. He had difficulty keeping his attention on the war. On occasion he would yell at his men to spread out the column, to keep their eyes open, but then he would slip away into daydreams, just pretending, walking barefoot along the Jersey shore, with Martha, carrying nothing. He would feel himself rising. Sun and waves and gentle winds, all love and lightness.

What they carried varied by mission.

When a mission took them to the mountains, they carried mosquito netting,   15
machetes, canvas tarps, and extra bug juice.

If a mission seemed especially hazardous, or if it involved a place they knew to be bad, they carried everything they could. In certain heavily mined AOs, where the land was dense with Toe Poppers and Bouncing Betties, they took turns humping a 28-pound mine detector. With its headphones and big sensing plate, the equipment was a stress on the lower back and shoulders, awkward to handle, often useless because of the shrapnel in the earth, but they carried it anyway, partly for safety, partly for the illusion of safety.

On ambush, or other night missions, they carried peculiar little odds and ends. Kiowa always took along his New Testament and a pair of moccasins for silence. Dave Jensen carried night-sight vitamins high in carotene. Lee Strunk carried his slingshot; ammo, he claimed, would never be a problem. Rat Kiley carried brandy and M&M's candy. Until he was shot, Ted Lavender carried the starlight scope, which weighed 6.3 pounds with its aluminum carrying case. Henry Dobbins carried his girlfriend's pantyhose wrapped around his neck as a comforter. They all carried ghosts. When dark came, they would move out single file across the meadows and paddies to their ambush coordinates, where they would quietly set up the Claymores and lie down and spend the night waiting.

Other missions were more complicated and required special equipment. In mid-April, it was their mission to search out and destroy the elaborate tunnel complexes in the Than Khe area south of Chu Lai. To blow the tunnels, they carried one-pound blocks of pentrite high explosives, four blocks to a man, 68 pounds in all. They carried wiring, detonators, and battery-powered clackers. Dave Jensen carried earplugs. Most often, before blowing the tunnels, they were ordered by higher command to search them, which was considered bad news, but by and large they just shrugged and carried out orders. Because he was a big man, Henry Dobbins was excused from tunnel duty. The others would draw numbers. Before Lavender died there were 17 men in the platoon, and whoever drew the number 17 would strip off his gear and crawl in headfirst with a flashlight and Lieutenant Cross's .45-caliber pistol. The rest of them would fan out as security. They would sit down or kneel, not facing the hole, listening to the ground beneath them, imagining cobwebs and ghosts, whatever was down there—the tunnel walls squeezing in—how the flashlight seemed impossibly heavy in the hand and how it was tunnel vision in the very strictest sense, compression in all ways, even time, and how you had to wiggle in—ass and elbows—a swallowed-up feeling—and how you found yourself worrying about odd things: Will your flashlight go dead? Do rats carry rabies? If you screamed, how far would the sound carry? Would your buddies hear it?

Would they have the courage to drag you out? In some respects, though not many, the waiting was worse than the tunnel itself. Imagination was a killer.

On April 16, when Lee Strunk drew the number 17, he laughed and muttered something and went down quickly. The morning was hot and very still. Not good, Kiowa said. He looked at the tunnel opening, then out across a dry paddy toward the village of Than Khe. Nothing moved. No clouds or birds or people. As they waited, the men smoked and drank Kool-Aid, not talking much, feeling sympathy for Lee Strunk but also feeling the luck of the draw. You win some, you lose some, said Mitchell Sanders, and sometimes you settle for a rain check. It was a tired line and no one laughed.

Henry Dobbins ate a tropical chocolate bar. Ted Lavender popped a tranquilizer and went off to pee.

After five minutes, Lieutenant Jimmy Cross moved to the tunnel, leaned down, and examined the darkness. Trouble, he thought—a cave-in maybe. And then suddenly, without willing it, he was thinking about Martha. The stresses and fractures, the quick collapse, the two of them buried alive under all that weight. Dense, crushing love. Kneeling, watching the hole, he tried to concentrate on Lee Strunk and the war, all the dangers, but his love was too much for him, he felt paralyzed, he wanted to sleep inside her lungs and breathe her blood and be smothered. He wanted her to be a virgin and not a virgin, all at once. He wanted to know her. Intimate secrets: Why poetry? Why so sad? Why that grayness in her eyes? Why so alone? Not lonely, just alone—riding her bike across campus or sitting off by herself in the cafeteria—even dancing, she danced alone—and it was the aloneness that filled him with love. He remembered telling her that one evening. How she nodded and looked away. And how, later, when he kissed her, she received the kiss without returning it, her eyes wide open, not afraid, not a virgin's eyes, just flat and uninvolved.

Lieutenant Cross gazed at the tunnel. But he was not there. He was buried with Martha under the white sand at the Jersey shore. They were pressed together, and the pebble in his mouth was her tongue. He was smiling. Vaguely, he was aware of how quiet the day was, the sullen paddies, yet he could not bring himself to worry about matters of security. He was beyond that. He was just a kid at war, in love. He was twenty-four years old. He couldn't help it.

A few moments later Lee Strunk crawled out of the tunnel. He came up grinning, filthy but alive. Lieutenant Cross nodded and closed his eyes while the others clapped Strunk on the back and made jokes about rising from the dead.

Worms, Rat Kiley said. Right out of the grave. Fuckin' zombie.

The men laughed. They all felt great relief.

Spook city, said Mitchell Sanders.

Lee Strunk made a funny ghost sound, a kind of moaning, yet very happy, and right then, when Strunk made that high happy moaning sound, when he went *Ahhooooo*, right then Ted Lavender was shot in the head on his way back from peeing. He lay with his mouth open. The teeth were broken. There was a swollen black bruise under his left eye. The cheekbone was gone. Oh shit, Rat Kiley said, the guy's dead. The guy's dead, he kept saying, which seemed profound—the guy's dead. I mean really.

The things they carried were determined to some extent by superstition. Lieutenant Cross carried his good-luck pebble. Dave Jensen carried a rabbit's foot. Norman Bowker, otherwise a very gentle person, carried a thumb that had been presented to him as a gift by Mitchell Sanders. The thumb was dark brown, rubbery to the touch, and weighed four ounces at most. It had been cut from a VC corpse, a boy of fifteen or sixteen. They'd found him at the bottom of an irrigation ditch, badly burned, flies in his mouth and eyes. The boy wore black shorts and sandals. At the time of his death he had been carrying a pouch of rice, a rifle and three magazines of ammunition.

You want my opinion, Mitchell Sanders said, there's a definite moral here.

He put his hand on the dead boy's wrist. He was quiet for a time, as if counting a pulse, then he patted the stomach, almost affectionately, and used Kiowa's hunting hatchet to remove the thumb.

Henry Dobbins asked what the moral was.

Moral?

You know. *Moral.*

Sanders wrapped the thumb in toilet paper and handed it across to Norman Bowker. There was no blood. Smiling, he kicked the boy's head, watched the flies scatter, and said, It's like with that old TV show—Paladin. Have gun, will travel.

Henry Dobbins thought about it.

Yeah, well, he finally said. I don't see no moral.

There it *is*, man.

Fuck off.

They carried USO stationery and pencils and pens. They carried Sterno, safety pins, trip flares, signal flares, spools of wire, razor blades, chewing tobacco, liberated joss sticks and statuettes of the smiling Buddha, candles, grease pencils, *The Stars and Stripes,* fingernail clippers, Psy Ops leaflets, bush hats, bolos, and much more. Twice a week, when the resupply choppers came in, they carried hot chow in green mermite cans and large canvas bags filled with iced beer and soda pop. They carried plastic water containers, each with a two-gallon capacity. Mitchell Sanders carried a set of starched tiger fatigues for special occasions. Henry Dobbins carried Black Flag insecticide. Dave Jensen carried empty sandbags that could be filled at night for added protection. Lee Strunk carried tanning lotion. Some things they carried in common. Taking turns, they carried the big PRC-77 scrambler radio, which weighed 30 pounds with its battery. They shared the weight of memory. They took up what others could no longer bear. Often, they carried each other, the wounded or weak. They carried infections. They carried chess sets, basketballs, Vietnamese-English dictionaries, insignia of rank, Bronze Stars and Purple Hearts, plastic cards imprinted with the Code of Conduct. They carried diseases, among them malaria and dysentery. They carried lice and ringworm and leeches and paddy algae and various rots and molds. They carried the land itself—Vietnam, the place, the soil—a powdery orange-red dust that covered their boots and fatigues and faces. They carried the sky. The whole atmosphere, they carried it, the humidity, the monsoons, the stink of fungus and decay, all of it, they carried gravity. They moved like mules. By daylight they took sniper fire, at night they were mortared, but it was not battle, it was just the endless march, village to village, without purpose, nothing won or lost. They marched for the sake of the march. They plodded along slowly, dumbly, leaning forward against the heat, unthinking, all blood and bone, simple grunts, soldiering with their legs, toiling up the hills and down into the paddies and across the rivers and up again and down, just humping, one step and then the next and then another, but no volition, no will, because it was automatic, it was anatomy, and the war was entirely a matter of posture and carriage, the hump was everything, a kind of inertia, a kind of emptiness, a dullness of desire and intellect and conscience and hope and human sensibility. Their principles were in their feet. Their calculations were biological. They had no sense of strategy or mission. They searched the villages without knowing what to look for, not caring, kicking over jars of rice, frisking children and old men, blowing tunnels, sometimes setting fires and sometimes not, then forming up and moving on to the next village, then other villages, where it would always be the same. They carried their own lives. The pressures were enormous. In the heat of early afternoon, they would remove their helmets and flak jackets, walking bare, which was dangerous but which helped ease the strain. They would often discard things along the route of march. Purely for comfort, they would throw away rations, blow their Claymores and grenades, no matter, because by nightfall the resupply choppers would arrive with more of the same, then a day or two later still more, fresh watermelons and crates of ammunition and sunglasses and woolen sweaters—the resources were stunning—sparklers for the Fourth of July, colored eggs for Easter—it was the great American war chest—the fruits of science, the smokestacks, the canneries, the arsenals at Hartford, the Minnesota forests, the machine shops, the vast fields of corn and wheat—they carried like freight trains; they carried it on their backs and shoulders—and for all the ambiguities of Vietnam, all the mysteries and unknowns, there was at least the single abiding certainty that they would never be at a loss for things to carry.

After the chopper took Lavender away. Lieutenant Jimmy Cross led his men into the village of Than Khe. They burned everything. They shot chickens and dogs, they trashed the village well, they called in artillery and watched the wreckage, then they marched for several hours through the hot afternoon, and then at dusk, while Kiowa explained how Lavender died, Lieutenant Cross found himself trembling. 4◦

He tried not to cry. With his entrenching tool, which weighed five pounds, he began digging a hole in the earth.

He felt shame. He hated himself. He had loved Martha more than his men, and as a consequence Lavender was now dead, and this was something he would have to carry like a stone in his stomach for the rest of the war.

All he could do was dig. He used his entrenching tool like an ax, slashing, feeling both love and hate, and then later, when it was full dark, he sat at the bottom of his foxhole and wept. It went on for a long while. In part, he was grieving for Ted Lavender, but mostly it was for Martha, and for himself, because she belonged to another world, which was not quite real, and because she was a junior at Mount Sebastian College in New Jersey, a poet and a virgin and uninvolved, and because he realized she did not love him and never would.

Like cement, Kiowa whispered in the dark. I swear to God—boom, down. Not a word.

I've heard this, said Norman Bowker. 4◦

A pisser, you know? Still zipping himself up. Zapped while zipping.

All right, fine. That's enough.

Yeah, but you had to see it, the guy just—

I *heard*, man. Cement. So why not shut the fuck *up?*

Kiowa shook his head sadly and glanced over at the hole where Lieutenant Jimmy 5◦
Cross sat watching the night. The air was thick and wet. A warm dense fog had settled over the paddies and there was the stillness that precedes rain.

After a time Kiowa sighed.

One thing for sure, he said. The lieutenant's in some deep hurt. I mean that crying jag—the way he was carrying on—it wasn't fake or anything, it was real heavy-duty hurt. The man cares.

Sure, Norman Bowker said.

Say what you want, the man does care.   55

We all got problems.

Not Lavender.

No, I guess not, Bowker said. Do me a favor, though.

Shut up?

That's a smart Indian. Shut up.

Shrugging, Kiowa pulled off his boots. He wanted to say more, just to lighten up   60
his sleep, but instead he opened his New Testament and arranged it beneath his head as a pillow. The fog made things seem hollow and unattached. He tried not to think about Ted Lavender, but then he was thinking how fast it was, no drama, down and dead, and how it was hard to feel anything except surprise. It seemed unchristian. He wished he could find some great sadness, or even anger, but the emotion wasn't there and he couldn't make it happen. Mostly he felt pleased to be alive. He liked the smell of the New Testament under his cheek, the leather and ink and paper and glue, what-ever the chemicals were. He liked hearing the sounds of night. Even his fatigue, it felt fine, the stiff muscles and the prickly awareness of his own body, a floating feeling. He enjoyed not being dead. Lying there, Kiowa admired Lieutenant Jimmy Cross's capac-ity for grief. He wanted to share the man's pain, he wanted to care as Jimmy Cross cared. And yet when he closed his eyes, all he could think was Boom-down, and all he could feel was the pleasure of having his boots off and the fog curling in around him and the damp soil and the Bible smells and the plush comfort of night.

After a moment Norman Bowker sat up in the dark.

What the hell, he said. You want to talk, *talk*. Tell it to me.

Forget it.

No, man, go on. One thing I hate, it's a silent Indian.

For the most part they carried themselves with poise, a kind of dignity. Now and   65
then, however, there were times of panic, when they squealed or wanted to squeal but couldn't, when they twitched and made moaning sounds and covered their heads and said Dear Jesus and flopped around on the earth and fired their weapons blindly and cringed and sobbed and begged for the noise to stop and went wild and made stupid promises to themselves and to God and to their mothers and fathers, hoping not to die. In different ways, it happened to all of them. Afterward, when the firing ended, they would blink and peek up. They would touch their bodies, feeling shame, then quickly hiding it. They would force themselves to stand. As if in slow motion, frame by frame, the world would take on the old logic—absolute silence, then the wind, then sunlight, then voices. It was the burden of being alive. Awkwardly, the men would reassemble them-selves, first in private, then in groups, becoming soldiers again. They would repair the leaks in their eyes. They would check for casualties, call in dust-offs, light cigarettes, try to smile, clear their throats and spit and begin cleaning their weapons. After a time someone would shake his head and say, No lie, I almost shit my pants, and someone else would laugh, which meant it was bad, yes, but the guy had obviously not shit his pants, it wasn't that bad, and in any case nobody would ever do such a thing and then go ahead

and talk about it. They would squint into the dense, oppressive sunlight. For a few moments, perhaps, they would fall silent, lighting a joint and tracking its passage from man to man, inhaling, holding in the humiliation. Scary stuff, one of them might say. But then someone else would grin or flick his eyebrows and say, Roger-dodger, almost cut me a new asshole, *almost.*

There were numerous such poses. Some carried themselves with a sort of wistful resignation, others with pride or stiff soldierly discipline or good humor or macho zeal. They were afraid of dying but they were even more afraid to show it.

They found jokes to tell.

They used a hard vocabulary to contain the terrible softness. *Greased* they'd say. *Offed, lit up, zapped while zipping.* It wasn't cruelty, just stage presence. They were actors. When someone died, it wasn't quite dying, because in a curious way it seemed scripted, and because they had their lines mostly memorized, irony mixed with tragedy, and because they called it by other names, as if to encyst and destroy the reality of death itself. They kicked corpses. They cut off thumbs. They talked grunt lingo. They told stories about Ted Lavender's supply of tranquilizers, how the poor guy didn't feel a thing, how incredibly tranquil he was.

There's a moral here, said Mitchell Sanders.

They were waiting for Lavender's chopper, smoking the dead man's dope.   7

The moral's pretty obvious, Sanders said, and winked. Stay away from drugs. No joke, they'll ruin your day every time.

Cute, said Henry Dobbins.

Mind blower, get it? Talk about wiggy. Nothing left, just blood and brains.

They made themselves laugh.

There it is, they'd say. Over and over—there it is, my friend, there it is—as if the   7 repetition itself were an act of poise, a balance between crazy and almost crazy, knowing without going, there it is, which meant be cool, let it ride, because Oh yeah, man, you can't change what can't be changed, there it is, there it absolutely and positively and fucking well *is.*

They were tough.

They carried all the emotional baggage of men who might die. Grief, terror, love, longing—these were intangibles, but the intangibles had their own mass and specific gravity, they had tangible weight. They carried shameful memories. They carried the common secret of cowardice barely restrained, the instinct to run or freeze or hide, and in many respects this was the heaviest burden of all, for it could never be put down, it required perfect balance and perfect posture. They carried their reputations. They carried the soldier's greatest fear, which was the fear of blushing. Men killed, and died, because they were embarrassed not to. It was what had brought them to the war in the first place, nothing positive, no dreams of glory or honor, just to avoid the blush of dishonor. They died so as not to die of embarrassment. They crawled into tunnels and walked point and advanced under fire. Each morning, despite the unknowns, they made their legs move. They endured. They kept humping. They did not submit to the obvious alternative, which was simply to close the eyes and fall. So easy, really. Go limp and tumble to the ground and let the muscles unwind and not speak and not budge until your buddies picked you up and lifted you into the chopper that would roar and dip its nose and carry you off to the world. A mere matter of falling, yet no one ever fell. It was not courage, exactly; the object was not valor. Rather, they were too frightened to be cowards.

By and large they carried these things inside, maintaining the masks of composure. They sneered at sick call. They spoke bitterly about guys who had found release by shooting off their own toes or fingers. Pussies, they'd say. Candy-asses. It was fierce, mocking talk, with only a trace of envy or awe, but even so the image played itself out behind their eyes.

They imagined the muzzle against flesh. So easy: squeeze the trigger and blow away a toe. They imagined it. They imagined the quick, sweet pain, then the evacuation to Japan, then a hospital with warm beds and cute geisha nurses.

And they dreamed of freedom birds.   80

At night, on guard, staring into the dark, they were carried away by jumbo jets. They felt the rush of takeoff. *Gone!* they yelled. And then velocity—wings and engines— a smiling stewardess—but it was more than a plane, it was a real bird, a big sleek silver bird with feathers and talons and high screeching. They were flying. The weights fell off; there was nothing to bear. They laughed and held on tight, feeling the cold slap of wind and altitude, soaring, thinking *It's over, I'm gone!*—they were naked, they were light and free—it was all lightness, bright and fast and buoyant, light as light, a helium buzz in the brain, a giddy bubbling in the lungs as they were taken up over the clouds and the war, beyond duty, beyond gravity and mortification and global entanglements—*Sin loi!* they yelled. *I'm sorry, motherfuckers, but I'm out of it, I'm goofed, I'm on a space cruise, I'm gone!*—and it was a restful, unencumbered sensation, just riding the light waves, sailing that big silver freedom bird over the mountains and oceans, over America, over the farms and great sleeping cities and cemeteries and highways and the golden arches of McDonald's, it was flight, a kind of fleeing, a kind of falling, falling higher and higher, spinning off the edge of the earth and beyond the sun and through the vast, silent vacuum where there were no burdens and where everything weighed exactly nothing— *Gone!* they screamed. *I'm sorry but I'm gone!*—and so at night, not quite dreaming, they gave themselves over to lightness, they were carried, they were purely borne.

On the morning after Ted Lavender died, First Lieutenant Jimmy Cross crouched at the bottom of his foxhole and burned Martha's letters. Then he burned the two photographs. There was a steady rain falling, which made it difficult, but he used heat tabs and Sterno to build a small fire, screening it with his body, holding the photographs over the tight blue flame with the tips of his fingers.

He realized it was only a gesture. Stupid, he thought. Sentimental, too, but mostly just stupid.

Lavender was dead. You couldn't burn the blame.

Besides, the letters were in his head. And even now, without photographs,   85 Lieutenant Cross could see Martha playing volleyball in her white gym shorts and yellow T-shirt. He could see her moving in the rain.

When the fire died out, Lieutenant Cross pulled his poncho over his shoulders and ate breakfast from a can.

There was no great mystery, he decided.

In those burned letters Martha had never mentioned the war, except to say, Jimmy, take care of yourself. She wasn't involved. She signed the letters Love, but it wasn't love, and all the fine lines and technicalities did not matter. Virginity was no longer an issue. He hated her. Yes, he did. He hated her. Love, too, but it was a hard, hating kind of love.

The morning came up wet and blurry. Everything seemed part of everything else, the fog and Martha and the deepening rain.

He was a soldier, after all.

Half smiling, Lieutenant Jimmy Cross took out his maps. He shook his head hard, as if to clear it, then bent forward and began planning the day's march. In ten minutes, or maybe twenty, he would rouse the men and they would pack up and head west, where the maps showed the country to be green and inviting. They would do what they had always done. The rain might add some weight, but otherwise it would be one more day layered upon all the other days.

He was realistic about it. There was that new hardness in his stomach. He loved her but he hated her.

No more fantasies, he told himself.

Henceforth, when he thought about Martha, it would be only to think that she belonged elsewhere. He would shut down the daydreams. This was not Mount Sebastian, it was another world, where there were no pretty poems or midterm exams, a place where men died because of carelessness and gross stupidity. Kiowa was right. Boom-down, and you were dead, never partly dead.

Briefly, in the rain, Lieutenant Cross saw Martha's gray eyes gazing back at him.

He understood.

It was very sad, he thought. The things men carried inside. The things men did or felt they had to do.

He almost nodded at her, but didn't.

Instead he went back to his maps. He was now determined to perform his duties firmly and without negligence. It wouldn't help Lavender, he knew that, but from this point on he would comport himself as an officer. He would dispose of his good-luck pebble. Swallow it, maybe, or use Lee Strunk's slingshot, or just drop it along the trail. On the march he would impose strict field discipline. He would be careful to send out flank security, to prevent straggling or bunching up, to keep his troops moving at the proper pace and at the proper interval. He would insist on clean weapons. He would confiscate the remainder of Lavender's dope. Later in the day, perhaps, he would call the men together and speak to them plainly. He would accept the blame for what had happened to Ted Lavender. He would be a man about it. He would look them in the eyes, keeping his chin level, and he would issue the new SOPs in a calm, impersonal tone of voice, a lieutenant's voice, leaving no room for argument or discussion. Commencing immediately, he'd tell them, they would no longer abandon equipment along the route of march. They would police up their acts. They would get their shit together, and keep it together, and maintain it neatly and in good working order.

He would not tolerate laxity. He would show strength, distancing himself.

Among the men there would be grumbling, of course, and maybe worse, because their days would seem longer and their loads heavier, but Lieutenant Jimmy Cross reminded himself that his obligation was not to be loved but to lead. He would dispense with love; it was not now a factor. And if anyone quarreled or complained, he would simply tighten his lips and arrange his shoulders in the correct command posture. He might give a curt little nod. Or he might not. He might just shrug and say, Carry on, then they would saddle up and form into a column and move out toward the villages west of Than Khe.

QUESTIONS

1. What do we learn about Lieutenant Jimmy Cross? How do we learn about him? Why does he blame himself for Lavender's death? How does Kiowa

misinterpret his emotions? How do his concerns unify the story? What other unifying elements does the story contain?

2.   What is the effect of the repetitions in the story (the constant descriptions of how much things weigh, the regular need to carry things, the way in which Lavender died)?

3.   Why is Mitchell Sanders unable to put into words the moral of the dead man's thumb? How would you describe the moral?

4.   Analyze paragraph 39. Discuss the various burdens the men of the platoon must carry. What bearing does this paragraph have upon other parts of the story?

ALICE WALKER   (b. 1944)

Walker was born in Georgia and attended Sarah Lawrence College, graduating in 1965. In addition to teaching at Yale, Wellesley, and other schools, she has edited and published fiction, poetry, and biography, and she received a Guggenheim Fellowship in 1977. Her main hobby is gardening. For her collection of poems Revolutionary Petunias *(1973), she received a Wall Book Award nomination. Her best-known novel,* The Color Purple *(1982), was made into a movie that won an Academy Award for 1985.*

Everyday Use _____ *1973*

for your grandmama

I will wait for her in the yard that Maggie and I made so clean and wavy yesterday afternoon. A yard like this is more comfortable than most people know. It is not just a yard. It is like an extended living room. When the hard clay is swept clean as a floor and the fine sand around the edges lined with tiny, irregular grooves, anyone can come and sit and look up into the elm tree and wait for the breezes that never come inside the house.

  Maggie will be nervous until after her sister goes: she will stand hopelessly in corners, homely and ashamed of the burn scars down her arms and legs, eying her sister with a mixture of envy and awe. She thinks her sister has held life always in the palm of one hand, that "no" is a word the world never learned to say to her.

  You've no doubt seen those TV shows° where the child who has "made it" is confronted, as a surprise, by her own mother and father, tottering in weakly from backstage. (A pleasant surprise, of course: What would they do if parent and child came on the show only to curse out and insult each other?) On TV mother and child embrace and smile into each other's faces. Sometimes the mother and father weep, the child wraps them in her arms and leans across the table to tell how she would not have made it without their help. I have seen these programs.

  TV shows: In the early days of television, a popular show was "This Is Your Life," which the narrator describes exactly here.

Sometimes I dream a dream in which Dee and I are suddenly brought together on a TV program of this sort. Out of a dark and soft-seated limousine I am ushered into a bright room filled with many people. There I meet a smiling, gray, sporty man like Johnny Carson who shakes my hand and tells me what a fine girl I have. Then we are on the stage and Dee is embracing me with tears in her eyes. She pins on my dress a large orchid, even though she has told me once that she thinks orchids are tacky flowers.

In real life I am a large, big-boned woman with rough, man-working hands. In the winter I wear flannel nightgowns to bed and overalls during the day. I can kill and clean a hog as mercilessly as a man. My fat keeps me hot in zero weather. I can work outside all day, breaking ice to get water for washing; I can eat pork liver cooked over the open fire minutes after it comes steaming from the hog. One winter I knocked a bull calf straight in the brain between the eyes with a sledge hammer and had the meat hung up to chill before nightfall. But of course all this does not show on television. I am the way my daughter would want me to be: a hundred pounds lighter, my skin like an uncooked barley pancake. My hair glistens in the hot bright lights. Johnny Carson has much to do to keep up with my quick and witty tongue.

But that is a mistake, I know even before I wake up. Who ever knew a Johnson with a quick tongue? Who can even imagine me looking a strange white man in the eye? It seems to me I have talked to them always with one foot raised in flight, with my head turned in whichever way is farthest from them. Dee, though. She would always look anyone in the eye. Hesitation was no part of her nature.

"How do I look, Mama?" Maggie says, showing just enough of her thin body enveloped in pink skirt and red blouse for me to know she's there, hidden by the door.

"Come out into the yard," I say.

Have you ever seen a lame animal, perhaps a dog run over by some careless person rich enough to own a car, sidle up to someone who is ignorant enough to be kind to him? That is the way my Maggie walks. She has been like this, chin on chest, eyes on ground, feet in shuffle, ever since the fire that burned the other house to the ground.

Dee is lighter than Maggie, with nicer hair and a fuller figure. She's a woman now, though sometimes I forget. How long ago was it that the other house burned? Ten, twelve years? Sometimes I can still hear the flames and feel Maggie's arms sticking to me, her hair smoking and her dress falling off her in little black papery flakes. Her eyes seemed stretched open, blazed open by the flames reflected in them. And Dee, I see her standing off under the sweet gum tree she used to dig gum out of; a look of concentration on her face as she watched the last dingy gray board of the house fall in toward the red-hot brick chimney. Why don't you do a dance around the ashes? I'd wanted to ask her. She had hated the house that much.

I used to think she hated Maggie, too. But that was before we raised the money, the church and me, to send her to Augusta° to school. She used to read to us without pity; forcing words, lies, other folks' habits, whole lives upon us two, sitting trapped and ignorant underneath her voice. She washed us in a river of make-believe, burned us with a lot of knowledge we didn't necessarily need to know. Pressed us to her with the serious way she read, to shove us away at just the moment, like dimwits, we seemed about to understand.

Dee wanted nice things. A yellow organdy dress to wear to her graduation from high school; black pumps to match a green suit she'd made from an old suit somebody

Augusta: city in eastern Georgia, the location of Paine College.

gave me. She was determined to stare down any disaster in her efforts. Her eyelids would not flicker for minutes at a time. Often I fought off the temptation to shake her. At sixteen she had a style of her own: and knew what style was.

I never had an education myself. After second grade the school was closed down. Don't ask me why: in 1927 colored asked fewer questions than they do now. Sometimes Maggie reads to me. She stumbles along good-naturedly, but can't see well. She knows she is not bright. Like good looks and money, quickness passed her by. She will marry John Thomas (who has mossy teeth in an earnest face) and then I'll be free to sit here and I guess just sing church songs to myself. Although I never was a good singer. Never could carry a tune. I was always better at a man's job. I used to love to milk till I was hooked in the side° in '49. Cows are soothing and slow and don't bother you, unless you try to milk them the wrong way.

I have deliberately turned my back on the house. It is three rooms, just like the one that burned, except the roof is tin; they don't make shingle roofs any more. There are no real windows, just some holes cut in the sides, like the portholes on a ship, but not round and not square, with rawhide holding the shutters up on the outside. This house is in a pasture, too, like the other one. No doubt when Dee sees it she will want to tear it down. She wrote me once that no matter where we "choose" to live, she will manage to come see us. But she will never bring her friends. Maggie and I thought about this and Maggie asked me, "Mama, when did Dee ever *have* any friends?"

She has a few. Furtive boys in pink shirts hanging about on washday after school. Nervous girls who never laughed. Impressed with her they worshiped the well-turned phrase, the cute shape, the scalding humor that erupted like bubbles in lye. She read to them.   15

When she was courting Jimmy T she didn't have much time to pay to us, but turned all her faultfinding power on him. He *flew* to marry a cheap city girl from a family of ignorant flashy people. She hardly had time to recompose herself.

When she comes I will meet—but there they are!

Maggie attempts to make a dash for the house, in her shuffling way, but I stay her with my hand. "Come back here," I say. And she stops and tries to dig a well in the sand with her toe.

It is hard to see them clearly through the strong sun. But even the first glimpse of leg out of the car tells me it is Dee. Her feet were always neat-looking, as if God himself had shaped them with a certain style. From the other side of the car comes a short, stocky man. Hair is all over his head a foot long and hanging from his chin like a kinky mule tail. I hear Maggie suck in her breath. "Uhnnnh," is what it sounds like. Like when you see the wriggling end of a snake just in front of your foot on the road. "Uhnnnh."

Dee next. A dress down to the ground, in this hot weather. A dress so loud it hurts   20
my eyes. There are yellows and oranges enough to throw back the light of the sun. I feel my whole face warming from the heat waves it throws out. Earrings gold, too, and hanging down to her shoulders. Bracelets dangling and making noises when she moves her arm up to shake the folds of the dress out of her armpits. The dress is loose and flows, and as she walks closer, I like it. I hear Maggie go "Uhnnnh" again. It is her sister's hair. It stands straight up like the wool on a sheep. It is black as night and around the edges are two long pigtails that rope about like small lizards disappearing behind her ears.

hooked in the side: kicked by a cow.

"Wa-su-zo-Tean-o!"° she says, coming on in that gliding way the dress makes her move. The short stocky yellow with the hair to his navel is all grinning and he follows up with "Asalamalakim,° my mother and my sister!" He moves to hug Maggie but she falls back, tight up against the back of my chair. I feel her trembling there and when I look up I see the perspiration falling off her chin.

"Don't get up," says Dee. Since I am stout it takes something of a push. You can see me trying to move a second or two before I make it. She turns, showing white heels through her sandals, and goes back to the car. Out she peeks next with a Polaroid. She stoops down quickly and lines up picture after picture of me sitting there in front of the house with Maggie cowering behind me. She never takes a shot without making sure the house is included. When a cow comes nibbling around the edge of the yard she snaps it and me and Maggie *and* the house. Then she puts the Polaroid in the back seat of the car, and comes up and kisses me on the forehead.

Meanwhile Asalamalakim is going through motions with Maggie's hand. Maggie's hand is as limp as a fish, and probably as cold, despite the sweat, and she keeps trying to pull it back. It looks like Asalamalakim wants to shake hands but wants to do it fancy. Or maybe he don't know how people shake hands. Anyhow, he soon gives up on Maggie.

"Well," I say, "Dee."

"No, Mama," she says. "Not 'Dee,' Wangero Leewanika Kemanjo!"   2⁵

"What happened to 'Dee'?" I wanted to know.

"She's dead," Wangero said. "I couldn't bear it any longer, being named after the people who oppress me."

"You know as well as me you was named after your aunt Dicie," I said. Dicie is my sister. She named Dee. We called her "Big Dee" after Dee was born.

"But who was *she* named after?" asked Wangero.

"I guess after Grandma Dee," I said.   3(

"And who was she named after?" asked Wangero.

"Her mother," I said, and saw Wangero was getting tired. "That's about as far back as I can trace it," I said. Though, in fact, I probably could have carried it back beyond the Civil War through the branches.

"Well," said Asalamalakim, "there you are."

"Uhnnnh," I heard Maggie say.

"There I was not," I said, "before 'Dicie' cropped up in our family, so why should   3⁵
I try to trace it that far back?"

He just stood there grinning, looking down on me like somebody inspecting a Model A car.° Every once in a while he and Wangero sent eye signals over my head.

"How do you pronounce this name?" I asked.

"You don't have to call me by it if you don't want to," said Wangero.

"Why shouldn't I?" I asked. "If that's what you want us to call you, we'll call you."

"I know it might sound awkward at first," said Wangero.

"I'll get used to it," I said. "Ream it out again."   4(

Well, soon we got the name out of the way. Asalamalakim had a name twice as long and three times as hard. After I tripped over it two or three times he told me to just call him Hakim-a-barber. I wanted to ask him was he a barber, but I didn't really think he was, so I didn't ask.

Wa-su-zo-Tean-o: greeting used by black Muslims.
Asalamalakim: Muslim salutation meaning "Peace be with you."
Model A car: the Ford car that replaced the Model T in the late 1920s. The Model A was proverbial for its quality and durability.

"You must belong to those beef-cattle peoples down the road," I said. They said "Asalamalakim" when they met you, too, but they didn't shake hands. Always too busy: feeding the cattle, fixing the fences, putting up salt-lick shelters,° throwing down hay. When the white folks poisoned some of the herd the men stayed up all night with rifles in their hands. I walked a mile and a half just to see the sight.

Hakim-a-barber said, "I accept some of their doctrines, but farming and raising cattle is not my style." (They didn't tell me, and I didn't ask, whether Wangero (Dee) had really gone and married him.)

We sat down to eat and right away he said he didn't eat collards and pork was 45 unclean. Wangero, though, went on through the chitlins and corn bread, the greens and everything else. She talked a blue streak over the sweet potatoes. Everything delighted her. Even the fact that we still used the benches her daddy made for the table when we couldn't afford to buy chairs.

"Oh, Mama!" she cried. Then turned to Hakim-a-barber. "I never knew how lovely these benches are. You can feel the rump prints," she said, running her hands underneath her and along the bench. Then she gave a sigh and her hand closed over Grandma Dee's butter dish. "That's it!" she said. "I knew there was something I wanted to ask you if I could have." She jumped up from the table and went over in the corner where the churn stood, the milk in it clabber° by now. She looked at the churn and looked at it.

"This churn top is what I need," she said. "Didn't Uncle Buddy whittle it out of a tree you all used to have?"

"Yes," I said.

"Uh huh," she said happily. "And I want the dasher, too."

"Uncle Buddy whittle that, too?" asked the barber. 50

Dee (Wangero) looked up at me.

"Aunt Dee's first husband whittled the dash," said Maggie so low you almost couldn't hear her. "His name was Henry, but they called him Stash."

"Maggie's brain is like an elephant's," Wangero said, laughing. "I can use the churn top as a centerpiece for the alcove table," she said, sliding a plate over the churn, "and I'll think of something artistic to do with the dasher."

When she finished wrapping the dasher the handle stuck out. I took it for a moment in my hands. You didn't even have to look close to see where hands pushing the dasher up and down to make butter had left a kind of sink in the wood. In fact, there were a lot of small sinks; you could see where thumbs and fingers had sunk into the wood. It was beautiful light yellow wood, from a tree that grew in the yard where Big Dee and Stash had lived.

After dinner Dee (Wangero) went to the trunk at the foot of my bed and started 55 rifling through it. Maggie hung back in the kitchen over the dishpan. Out came Wangero with two quilts. They had been pieced by Grandma Dee and then Big Dee and me had hung them on the quilt frames on the front porch and quilted them. One was in the Lone Star pattern. The other was Walk Around the Mountain. In both of them were scraps of dresses Grandma Dee had worn fifty and more years ago. Bits and pieces of Grandpa Jarrell's Paisley shirts. And one teeny faded blue piece, about the size of a penny matchbox, that was from Great Grandpa Ezra's uniform that he wore in the Civil War.

---

salt-lick shelters: shelters built to prevent rain from dissolving the large blocks of rock salt set up on poles for cattle.
clabber: curdled, turned sour.

"Mama," Wangero said sweet as a bird. "Can I have these old quilts?"

I heard something fall in the kitchen, and a minute later the kitchen door slammed.

"Why don't you take one or two of the others?" I asked. "These old things was just done by me and Big Dee from some tops your grandma pieced before she died."

"No," said Wangero. "I don't want those. They are stitched around the borders by machine."

"That'll make them last better," I said.

"That's not the point," said Wangero. "These are all pieces of dresses Grandma used to wear. She did all this stitching by hand. Imagine!" She held the quilts securely in her arms, stroking them.

"Some of the pieces, like those lavender ones, come from old clothes her mother handed down to her," I said, moving up to touch the quilts. Dee (Wangero) moved back just enough so that I couldn't reach the quilts. They already belonged to her.

"Imagine!" she breathed again, clutching them closely to her bosom.

"The truth is," I said, "I promised to give them quilts to Maggie, for when she marries John Thomas."

She gasped like a bee had stung her.

"Maggie can't appreciate these quilts!" she said. "She'd probably be backward enough to put them to everyday use."

"I reckon she would," I said. "God knows I been saving 'em for long enough with nobody using 'em. I hope she will!" I didn't want to bring up how I had offered Dee (Wangero) a quilt when she went away to college. Then she had told me they were old-fashioned, out of style.

"But they're *priceless!*" she was saying now, furiously; for she has a temper. "Maggie would put them on the bed and in five years they'd be in rags. Less than that!"

"She can always make some more," I said. "Maggie knows how to quilt."

Dee (Wangero) looked at me with hatred. "You just will not understand. The point is these quilts, *these* quilts!"

"Well," I said, stumped. "What would *you* do with them?"

"Hang them," she said. As if that was the only thing you *could* do with quilts.

Maggie by now was standing in the door. I could almost hear the sound her feet made as they scraped over each other.

"She can have them, Mama," she said, like somebody used to never winning anything, or having anything reserved for her. "I can 'member Grandma Dee without the quilts."

I looked at her hard. She had filled her bottom lip with checkerberry snuff and it gave her face a kind of dopey, hangdog look. It was Grandma Dee and Big Dee who taught her how to quilt herself. She stood there with her scarred hands hidden in the folds of her skirt. She looked at her sister with something like fear but she wasn't mad at her. This was Maggie's portion. This was the way she knew God to work.

When I looked at her like that something hit me in the top of my head and ran down to the soles of my feet. Just like when I'm in church and the spirit of God touches me and I get happy and shout. I did something I never had done before: hugged Maggie to me, then dragged her on into the room, snatched the quilts out of Miss Wangero's hands and dumped them into Maggie's lap. Maggie just sat there on my bed with her mouth open.

"Take one or two of the others," I said to Dee.

But she turned without a word and went out to Hakim-a-barber.

"You just don't understand," she said, as Maggie and I came out to the car.

"What don't I understand?" I wanted to know.   80

"Your heritage," she said. And then she turned to Maggie, kissed her, and said, "You ought to try to make something of yourself, too, Maggie. It's really a new day for us. But from the way you and Mama still live you'd never know it."

She put on some sunglasses that hid everything above the tip of her nose and her chin.

Maggie smiled; maybe at the sunglasses. But a real smile, not scared. After we watched the car dust settle I asked Maggie to bring me a dip of snuff. And then the two of us sat there just enjoying, until it was time to go in the house and go to bed.

QUESTIONS

1. Describe the narrator. Who is she? What is she like? Where and how does she live? What kind of life has she had? How does the story bring out her judgments about her two daughters?

2. Describe the narrator's daughters. How are they different physically and mentally? How have their lives been different?

3. Why did Dee change her name to "Wangero"? How is this change important, and how is it reflected in her attitude toward the family artifacts?

4. Describe the importance of the phrase "everyday use" (paragraph 66). How does this phrase highlight the conflicting values in the story?

JOY WILLIAMS (b. 1944)

Williams was born in Massachusetts and graduated from Marietta College and the University of Iowa. While still in her twenties she published her first stories. Among her novels are State of Grace *(1973),* The Changeling *(1978), and* Breaking and Entering *(1988). Her story collection* Taking Care, *including the title story, appeared in 1982. Her varied interests are shown by the fact that she has published a history and guide to the Keys of Florida, her adopted home state. Among her distinctions are a judgeship of the PEN/Faulkner Award for Fiction, a Wallace Stegner Fellowship, and a Guggenheim Fellowship.*

Taking Care _____ 1982

Jones, the preacher, has been in love all his life. He is baffled by this because as far as he can see, it has never helped anyone, even when they have acknowledged it, which is not often. Jones's love is much too apparent and arouses neglect. He is like an animal in a traveling show who, through some aberration, wears a vital organ outside the skin, awkward and unfortunate, something that shouldn't be seen, certainly something that shouldn't be watched working. Now he sits on a bed beside his wife in the self-care unit of a hospital fifteen miles from their home. She has been committed here for tests. She is so weak, so tired. There is something wrong with her blood. Her arms are covered with bruises where they have gone into the veins. Her hip, too, is blue and swollen where they have drawn out samples of bone marrow. All of this is frightening. The doctors are severe and wise, answering Jones's questions in a way that makes him feel hopelessly deaf. They have told him that there really is no such thing as a disease of the blood, for the blood is not a living tissue but a passive vehicle for the transportation of food, oxygen and waste. They have told him that abnormalities in the blood corpuscles, which his wife seems to have, must be regarded as symptoms of disease elsewhere in the body. They have shown him, upon request, slides and charts of normal and pathological blood cells which look to Jones like canapés. They speak (for he insists) of leukocytosis,° myelocytes° and megaloblasts.° None of this takes into account the love he has for his wife! Jones sits beside her in this dim pleasant room, wearing a grey suit and his clerical collar, for when he leaves her he must visit other parishioners who are patients here. This part of the hospital is like a motel. One may wear one's regular clothes. The rooms have ice-buckets, rugs and colorful bedspreads. How he wishes that they were traveling and staying overnight, this night, in a motel. A nurse comes in with a tiny paper cup full of pills. There are three pills, or rather, capsules, and they are not for his wife but for her blood. The cup is the smallest of its type that Jones has ever seen. All perspective, all sense of time and scale seem abandoned in this hospital. For example, when Jones turns to kiss his wife's hair, he nicks the air instead.

Jones and his wife have one child, a daughter, who, in turn, has a single child, a girl, born one-half year ago. Jones's daughter has fallen in with the stars and is using the heavens, as Jones would be the first to admit, more than he ever has. It has, however, brought her only grief and confusion. She has left her husband and brought the baby to Jones. She has also given him her dog. She is going to Mexico where soon, in the mountains, she will have a nervous breakdown. Jones does not know this, but his daughter has seen it in the stars and is going out to meet it. Jones quickly agrees to care for both the baby and the dog, as this seems to be the only thing his daughter needs from him. The day of the baby's birth is secondary to the position of the planets and the terms of houses, quadrants and gradients.° Her symbol is a bareback rider. To Jones, this is a graceful thought. It signifies audacity. It also means luck. Jones slips a twenty dollar bill in the pocket of his daughter's suitcase and drives her to the airport. The plane taxis down the runway and Jones waves, holding all their luck in his arms.

One afternoon, Jones had come home and found his wife sitting in the garden, weeping. She had been transplanting flowers, putting them in pots before the first frost came. There was dirt on her forehead and around her mouth. Her light clothes felt so heavy. Their weight made her body ache. Each breath was a stone she had to swallow. She cried and cried in the weak autumn sunshine. Jones could see the veins throbbing in her neck. "I'm dying," she said. "It's taking me months to die." But after he had brought her inside, she insisted that she felt better and made them both a cup of tea while Jones potted the rest of the plants and carried them down cellar. She lay on the sofa and Jones sat beside her. They talked quietly with one another. Indeed, they were almost whispering, as though they were in a public place surrounded by strangers instead of in their own house with no one present but themselves. "It's the season," Jones said. "In fall everything slows down, retreats. I'm feeling tired myself. We need

---

leukocytosis: elevated number of white blood cells.
myelocytes: nuclei of nerve cells.
megaloblasts: damaged red blood cells characteristic of anemia and leukemia.
planets . . . gradients: terms used by believers in astrology to determine the future.

iron. I'll go to the druggist right now and buy some iron tablets." His wife agreed. She wanted to go with him, for the ride. Together they ride, through the towns, for miles and miles, even into the next state. She does not want to stop driving. They buy sandwiches and milkshakes and eat in the car. Jones drives. They have to buy more gasoline. His wife sits close to him, her eyes closed, her head tipped back against the seat. He can see the veins beating on in her neck. Somewhere there is a dreadful sound, almost audible. "First I thought it was my imagination," his wife said. "I couldn't sleep. All night I would stay awake, dreaming. But it's not in my head. It's in my ears, my eyes. They ache. Everything. My tongue. My hair. The tips of my fingers are dead." Jones pressed her cold hand to his lips. He thinks of something mad and loving better than he—running out of control, deeply in the darkness of his wife. "Just don't make me go to the hospital," she pleaded. Of course she will go there. The moment has already occurred.

Jones is writing to his daughter. He received a brief letter from her this morning, telling him where she could be reached. The foreign postmark was so large that it almost obliterated Jones's address. She did not mention either her mother or the baby, which makes Jones feel peculiar. His life seems increate as his God's life, perhaps even imaginary. His daughter tells him about the town in which she lives. She does not plan to stay there long. She wants to travel. She will find out exactly what she wants to do and then she will come home again. The town is poor but interesting and there are many Americans there her own age. There is a zoo right on the beach. Almost all the towns, no matter how small, have little zoos. There are primarily eagles and hawks in cages. And what can Jones reply to that? He writes *Everything is fine here. We are burning wood from the old apple tree in the fire place and it smells wonderful. Has the baby had her full series of polio shots? Take care.* Jones uses this expression constantly, usually in totally unwarranted situations, as when he purchases pipe cleaners or drives through toll booths. Distracted, Jones writes off the edge of the paper and onto the blotter. He must begin again. He will mail this on the way to the hospital. They have been taking X-rays for three days now but the pictures are cloudy. They cannot read them. His wife is now in a real sickbed with high metal sides. He sits with her while she eats her dinner. She asks him to take her good nightgown home and wash it with a bar of Ivory. They won't let her do anything now, not even wash out a few things. *You must take care.*

Jones is driving down a country road. It is the first snowfall of the season and he   5
wants to show it to the baby who rides beside him in a small cushioned car seat all her own. Her head is almost on a level with his and she looks earnestly at the landscape, sometimes smiling. They follow the road that winds tightly between fields and deep pine woods. Everything is white and clean. It has been snowing all afternoon and is doing so still, but very very lightly. Fat snowflakes fall solitary against the windshield. Sometimes the baby reaches out for them. Sometimes she gives a brief kick and cry of joy. They have done their errands. Jones has bought milk and groceries and two yellow roses which lie wrapped in tissue and newspaper in the trunk, in the cold. He must buy two on Saturday as the florist is closed on Sunday. He does not like to do this but there is no alternative. The roses do not keep well. Tonight he will give one to his wife. The other he will pack in sugar water and store in the refrigerator. He can only hope that the bud will remain tight until Sunday when he brings it into the terrible heat of the hospital. The baby rocks against the straps of her small carrier. Her lips are pursed as she watches intently the fields, the grey stalks of crops growing out of the snow, the trees. She is warmly dressed and she wears a knitted orange cap. The cap is twenty-three years old, the age of her mother. Jones found it just the other day. It has faded almost to pink on

one side. At one time, it must have been stored in the sun. Jones, driving, feels almost gay. The snow is so beautiful. Everything is white. Jones is an educated man. He has read Melville, who said that white is the colorless all-color of atheism from which we shrink.° Jones does not believe this. He sees a holiness in snow, a promise. He hopes that his wife will know that it is snowing even though she is separated from the window by a curtain. Jones sees something moving across the snow, a part of the snow itself running. Although he is going slowly, he takes his foot completely off the accelerator. "Look, darling, a snowshoe rabbit." At the sound of his voice, the baby stretches open her mouth and narrows her eyes in soundless glee. The hare is splendid. So fast! It flows around invisible obstructions, something out of a kind dream. It flies across the ditch, its paws like paddles, faintly yellow, the color of raw wood. "Look, sweet," cries Jones, "How big he is!" But suddenly the hare is curved and falling, round as a ball, its feet and head tucked closely against its body. It strikes the road and skids upside down for several yards. The car passes around it, avoids it. Jones brakes and stops, amazed. He opens the door and trots back to the animal. The baby twists about in her seat as well as she can and peers after him. It is as though the animal had never been alive at all. Its head is broken in several places. Jones bends to touch its fur, but straightens again, not doing so. A man emerges from the woods, swinging a shotgun. He nods at Jones and picks the hare up by the ears. As he walks away, the hare's legs rub across the ground. There are small crystal stains on the snow. Jones returns to the car. He wants to apologize but he does not know to whom or for what. His life has been devoted to apologetics.° It is his profession. He is concerned with both justification and remorse. He has always acted rightly, but nothing has ever come of it. He gets in the car, starts the engine. "Oh, sweet," he says to the baby. She smiles at him, exposing her tooth. At home that night, after the baby's supper, Jones reads a story to her. She is asleep, panting in her sleep, but Jones tells her the story of al-Boraq,° the milk-white steed of Mohammed, who could stride out of the sight of mankind with a single step.

Jones sorts through a collection of records, none of which have been opened. They are still wrapped in cellophane. The jacket designs are subdued, epic. Names, instruments and orchestras are mentioned confidently. He would like to agree with their importance, for he knows that they have worth, but he is not familiar with the references. His daughter brought these records with her. They had been given to her by an older man, a professor she had been having an affair with. Naturally, this pains Jones. His daughter speaks about the men she has been involved with but no longer cares about. Where did these men come from? Where were they waiting and why have they gone? Jones remembers his daughter when she was a little girl, helping him rake leaves. What can he say? For years on April Fool's Day, she would take tobacco out of his humidor and fill it with corn flakes. Jones is full of remorse and astonishment. When he saw his daughter only a few weeks ago, she was thin and nervous. She had torn out almost all her eyebrows with her fingers from this nervousness. And her lashes. The roots of her eyes were white, like the bulbs of flowers. Her fingernails were crudely bitten, some bleeding below the quick. She was tough and remote, wanting only to go

---

colorless . . . shrink: quotation from Chapter 42, "The Whiteness of the Whale." of *Moby-Dick* (1851) by Herman Melville (1819–1891).

apologetics: the explanation and defense of religion, here, specifically, of Christianity.

al-Boraq: According to the Koran, the angel Gabriel brought the prophet Mohammed to the Islamic Seventh Heaven (made up of divine light) on the mystical horse Borak or al-Borak ("lightning").

on a trip for which she had a ticket. What can he do? He seeks her in the face of the baby but she is not there. All is being both continued and resumed, but the dream is different. The dream cannot be revived. Jones breaks into one of the albums, blows the dust from the needle, plays a record. Outside it is dark. The parsonage is remote and the only buildings nearby are barns. The river cannot be seen. The music is Bruckner's *Te Deum*.° Very nice, Dedicated to God. He plays the other side. A woman, Kathleen Ferrier,° is singing in German. Jones cannot understand the words but the music stuns him. *Kindertotenlieder.*° It is devastating. In college he had studied only scientific German, The vocabulary of submarines, dirigibles and steam engines. Jones plays the record again and again, searching for his old grammar. At last he finds it. The wings of insects are between some of the pages. There are notes in pencil, written in his own young hand.

RENDER:
A. WAS THE TEACHER SATISFIED WITH YOU TODAY?
B. NO. HE IS NOT. MY ESSAY WAS GOOD BUT IT WAS NOT COPIED WELL.
C. I AM SORRY YOU WERE NOT INDUSTRIOUS THIS TIME FOR YOU GENERALLY ARE.

These lessons are neither of life or death. Why was he instructed in them? In the hospital, his wife waits to be translated, no longer a woman, the woman whom he loves, but a situation. Her blood moves mysteriously as constellations. She is under scrutiny and attack and she has abandoned Jones. She is a swimmer waiting to get on with the drowning. Jones is on the shore. In Mexico, his daughter walks along the beach with two men. She is acting out a play that has become her life. Jones is on the mountaintop. The baby cries and Jones takes her from the crib to change her. The dog paws the door. Jones lets him out. He settles down with the baby and listens to the record. He still cannot make out many of the words. The baby wiggles restlessly on his lap. Her eyes are a foal's eyes, navy-blue. She has grown in a few weeks to expect everything from Jones. He props her on one edge of the couch and goes to her small toy box where he keeps a bear, a few rattles and balls. On the way, he opens the door and the dog immediately enters. His heavy coat is cold, fragrant with ice. He noses the baby and she squeals.

Oft denk' ich, sie sind nur ausgegangen:
Bald werden sie wieder nach Hause gelangen!°

Jones selects a bright ball and pushes it gently in her direction.

Bruckner: Anton Bruckner (1824–1896), Austrian composer and organist. His *Te Deum* for chorus, soloists, and orchestra was completed in 1884. The long-play record is Columbia ML 4980.
Kathleen Ferrier: celebrated English contralto (1912–1953), who died of cancer.
Kindertotenlieder: "Songs of the Death of Children" (1902–1904), a cycle of five songs for voice and orchestra by Gustav Mahler (1860–1911), Austrian composer and conductor. Mahler's elder daughter died three years after he completed the work.
Oft . . . gelangen: opening two lines of the fourth song in Mahler's *Kindertotenlieder,* from a poem by Friedrich Rückert (1788–1866): "Often I think they've just gone outside: / They'll get back home again soon!"

It is Sunday morning and Jones is in the pulpit. The church is very old but the walls of the sanctuary have recently been painted a pale blue. In the cemetery adjoining, some of the graves are three hundred years old. It has become a historical landmark and no one has been buried there since World War I. There is a new place, not far away, which the families now use. Plots are marked not with stones but with small tablets, and immediately after any burial, workmen roll grassed sod over the new graves so that there is no blemish on the grounds, not even for a little while. Present for today's service are seventy-eight adults, eleven children and the junior choir. Jones counts them as the offertory is received. The church rolls say that there are three hundred fifty members but as far as Jones can see, everyone is here today. This is the day he baptizes the baby. He has made arrangements with one of the ladies to hold her and bring her up to the font at the end of the first hymn. The baby looks charming in a lacy white dress. Jones has combed her fine hair carefully, slicking it in a curl with water, but now it has dried and it sticks up awkwardly like the crest of a kingfisher. Jones bought the dress in Mammoth Mart, an enormous store which has a large metal elephant dressed in overalls dancing on the roof. He feels foolish at buying it there but he had gone to several stores and that is where he saw the prettiest dress. He blesses the baby with water from the silver bowl. He says, *We are saved not because we are worthy. We are saved because we are loved.* It is a brief ceremony. The baby, looking curiously at Jones, is taken out to the nursery. Jones begins his sermon. He can't remember when he wrote it, but here it is, typed, in front of him. *There is nothing wrong in what one does but there is something wrong in what one becomes.* He finds this questionable but goes on speaking. He has been preaching for thirty-four years. He is gaunt with belief. But his wife has a red cell count of only 2.3 millions. It is not enough! She is not getting enough oxygen! Jones is giving his sermon. Somewhere he has lost what he was looking for. He must have known once, surely. The congregation sways, like the wings of a ray in water. It is Sunday and for patients it is a holiday. The doctors don't visit. There are no tests or diagnoses. Jones would like to leave, to walk down the aisle and out into the winter, where he would read his words into the ground. Why can't he remember his life! He finishes, sits down, stands up to present communion. Tiny cubes of bread lie in a slumped pyramid. They are offered and received. Jones takes his morsel, hacked earlier from a sliced enriched loaf with his own hand. It is so dry, almost wicked. The very thought now sickens him. He chews it over and over again, but it lies unconsumed, like a mussel in his mouth.

Jones is waiting in the lobby for the results of his wife's operation. Has there ever been a time before dread? He would be grateful even to have dread back, but it has been lost, for a long time, in rapid possibility, probability and fact. The baby sits on his knees and plays with his tie. She woke very early this morning for her orange juice and then gravely, immediately, spit it all up. She seems fine now, however, her fingers exploring Jones's tie. Whenever he looks at her, she gives him a dazzling smile. He has spent most of the day fiercely cleaning the house, changing the bed-sheets and the pages of the many calendars that hang in the rooms, things he should have done a week ago. He has dusted and vacuumed and pressed all his shirts. He has laundered all the baby's clothes, soft small sacks and gowns and sleepers which froze in his hands the moment he stepped outside. And now he is waiting and watching his wristwatch. The tumor is precisely this size, they tell him, the size of his clock's face.

Jones has the baby on his lap and he is feeding her. The evening meal is lengthy and complex. First he must give her vitamins, then, because she has a cold, a dropper of liquid aspirin. This is followed by a bottle of milk, eight ounces, and a portion of strained vegetables. He gives her a rest now so that the food can settle. On his hip, she rides through the rooms of the huge house as Jones turns lights off and on. He comes back to the table and gives her a little more milk, a half jar of strained chicken and a few spoonfuls of dessert, usually cobbler, buckle or pudding. The baby enjoys all equally. She is good. She eats rapidly and neatly. Sometimes she grasps the spoon, turns it around and thrusts the wrong end into her mouth. Of course there is nothing that cannot be done incorrectly. Jones adores the baby. He sniffs her warm head. Her birth is a deep error, an abstraction. Born in wedlock but out of love. He puts her in the playpen and tends to the dog. He fills one dish with water and one with horsemeat. He rinses out the empty can before putting it in the wastebasket. The dog eats with great civility. He eats a little meat and then takes some water, then meat, then water. When the dog has finished, the dishes are as clean as though they'd been washed. Jones now thinks about his own dinner. He opens the refrigerator. The ladies of the church have brought brownies, venison, cheese and apple sauce. There are turkey pies, pork chops, steak, haddock and sausage patties. A brilliant light exposes all this food. There is so much of it. It must be used. A crust has formed around the punctures in a can of Pet. There is a clear bag of chicken livers stapled shut. There are large brown eggs in a bowl. Jones stares unhappily at the beads of moisture on cartons and bottles, at the pearls of fat on the cold cooked stew. He sits down. The room is full of lamps and cords. He thinks of his wife, her breathing body deranged in tubes, and begins to shake. All objects here are perplexed by such grief.

Now it is almost Christmas and Jones is walking down by the river, around an abandoned house. The dog wades heavily through the snow, biting it. There are petals of ice on the tree limbs and when Jones lingers under them, the baby puts out her hand and her mouth starts working because she would like to have it, the ice, the branch, everything. His wife will be coming home in a few days, in time for Christmas. Jones has already put up the tree and brought the ornaments down from the attic. He will not trim it until she comes home. He wants very much to make a fine occasion out of opening the boxes of old decorations. The two of them have always enjoyed this greatly in the past. Jones will doubtlessly drop and smash a bauble, for he does every year. He tramps through the snow with his small voyager. She dangles in a shoulder sling, her legs wedged around his hip. They regard the rotting house seriously. Once it was a doctor's home and offices but long before Jones's time, the doctor, who was very respected, had been driven away because a town girl accused him of fathering her child. The story goes that all the doctor said was, "Is that so?" This incensed the town and the girl's parents, who insisted that he take the child as soon as it was born. He did and he cared for the child very well even though his practice was ruined and no one had anything to do with him. A year later the girl told the truth—that the actual father was a young college boy whom she was now going to marry. They wanted the child back, and the doctor willingly returned the infant to them. Of course it is a very old, important story. Jones has always appreciated it, but now he is annoyed at the man's passivity. He wife's sickness has changed everything for Jones. He will continue to accept but he will no longer surrender. Surely things are different for Jones now.

For insurance purposes, Jones's wife is brought out to the car in a wheelchair. She is thin and beautiful. Jones is grateful and confused. He has a mad wish to tip the orderly. Have so many years really passed? Is this not his wife, his love, fresh from giving birth? Isn't everything about to begin? In Mexico, his daughter wanders disinterestedly through a jewelry shop where she picks up a small silver egg. It opens on a hinge and inside are two figures, a bride and groom. Jones puts the baby in his wife's arms. At first the baby is alarmed because she cannot remember this person very well and she reaches for Jones, whimpering. But soon she is soothed by his wife's soft voice and she falls asleep in her arms as they drive. Jones has readied everything carefully for his wife's home-coming. The house is clean and orderly. For days he has restricted himself to only one part of the house so that his clutter will be minimal. Jones helps his wife up the steps to the door. Together they enter the shining rooms.

QUESTIONS

1.   Describe the character of Jones. What is his major trait? How do you learn about it? Why does he continue to practice his profession and care for his family?

2.   On the basis of this story, what can you say about the use of tenses in a narration? Why is the story told mainly in the present tense? What is the relationship here between past and present tense?

3.   Explain why there are so few paragraphs in the story and why they are rather long. Why do you think Williams does not use more dialogue?

4.   Explore the sad or depressing references and situations in the story (e.g., the ill wife, the dead rabbit, the daughter abandoning her child, the songs on the death of children). In the light of such references, how does the story make you think and feel?

THE PRÉCIS OR ABRIDGMENT

A **précis** (*pray-SEE*) is a concise summary, in your own words, of a written work. The closely related word *precise* helps to explain that a précis emphasizes just the most significant details. Other words for précis are *abridgment, paraphrase, abstract, condensation,* and *epitome. Epitome* (*ee-PIT-uh-mee*), from the Greek for a "cutting away" so that only the essential parts remain, is a particularly helpful explanation of the objective of a précis.

Précis Writing Has a Number of Uses

Beyond enabling you to follow a story with accuracy, the précis is important in study, research, and speaking and writing. One of the best ways to study any work is to write a précis of it, for the process forces you to grasp each of the parts. Précis writing can be used in taking notes, preparing for exams, establishing and clarifying facts, studying for classroom discussion, and reinforcing details and ideas learned in the past. The object of a précis should be to retell not all of a story's details but only enough to give the highlights, so that any reader will know the main sections of the work. Although you may sometimes need to condense an entire plot or epitomize an entire argument, most often you will refer to no more than parts of works, because your arguments will depend on a number of separate interpretations of these portions.

GUIDELINES FOR PRÉCIS WRITING

The following guidelines will help you in developing a précis.

1. SELECTION. Only essential details belong in a précis. For example, at the opening of the story "Everyday Use," Walker describes the narrator as a large woman who has lived a very hard life. We learn that she can kill animals for food and survival and that she is fully capable of taking care of herself and her family, but including all these details would needlessly lengthen a précis of "Everyday Use." Instead it is sufficient to say no more than "Mrs. Johnson is a strong woman," because this fact is the most vital one about her. Concentrating on just the essentials enables the shortening required of a précis. Thus a 5,000-word story might be epitomized in 100, 300, or 600 words, with the amount of detail being governed by the desired length. Regardless of the length of your précis, however, base your selection of detail on your judgment of its importance.

2. ACCURACY. All details in a précis should be both correct and accurate. Avoid misstatement, and avoid using words that give a misleading impression of the original. In "The Necklace" (Chapter 1), for example, Mathilde cooperates with her husband for ten years to repay their 18,000-franc debt. In a précis it would be possible to say no more than she "works" during this time. The word *works* is misleading, however, for it may be interpreted to mean that Mathilde gets paid for outside employment. In fact she does not. What Maupassant tells us is that Mathilde gives up her servant girl and then does all the heavy house-work herself in her *own* household, not in the houses of others, as part of her general economizing.

As important as the need to condense long sections of a story accurately is the need to be comprehensive. In reference to Walker's "Everyday Use," there is a concluding dispute between the mother (the narrator) and her visiting daughter about the daughter's request for two homemade quilts. Wangero, the daughter, wants them to adorn a wall, while the mother refuses on the grounds that she has promised them to her other daughter for "everyday use" during her approaching marriage. These details are complex, and they represent the climax of the major conflict in the story. In a précis it is important not only to explain the claims but also to present enough language to highlight the conflict. Thus, accurate and comprehensive language might be: "Mrs. Johnson hesitates, having already promised the quilts to Maggie for use when she gets married. Though Maggie offers to give Wangero the quilts, Mrs. Johnson insists on her original promise. Wangero then objects, claiming that the quilts will be spoiled by 'everyday use' and that her mother misunderstands the value of the family heritage." This language explains the details accurately and comprehensively—the goal of précis writing.

3. DICTION.   A précis should be an original essay and therefore it should be written *in your own words,* not those of the work you are abridging. The best way to ensure original wording is to read the work, take note of the major actions and situations, and then set the work aside as you write. In that way you can avoid the temptation to borrow words.

However, if a number of words from the text find their way into the précis even after you have tried to keep them out, then you must use quotation marks to set them off. As long as direct quotations are kept to a minimum, they are permissible. Too many quoted words, however, indicate that your précis is not original.

4. OBJECTIVITY.   A précis should be scrupulously factual. Avoid explanatory or introductory material unless it is a true part of the story. Just as you need to *include* judgments and interpretations in other kinds of writing about literature, you need to *avoid* them in a précis. Here is a comparative example of what to do and what to avoid:

WHAT TO DO

Mrs. Johnson, a strong woman living on her Southern farm with her younger daughter, Maggie, is waiting for a visit by her elder daughter, Dee. Dee is returning from her home in the city, and the mother has cleaned and swept the house and yard in order to make a good impression.

WHAT TO AVOID

Walker opens the story by building up the contrast that will soon be made apparent. Her narrator, Mrs. Johnson, is a plain, down-to-earth woman who has worked hard all her life and whose basic value is her home and possessions. The contrast is her daughter Dee, whose visit she is waiting for. Dee has left home and lived a sophisticated life in the city. Mrs. Johnson takes pride in her home, while Dee will regard the home and her mother's belongings as being of no more use than to be put on display.

The right-hand column starts with a topic sentence, to which the sentences that follow adhere. Such writing is commendable elsewhere, but not in a précis. The left-hand paragraph is better writing *as a précis,* for it presents a selection of details only as they appear in the story, without introductory sentences. In the story there are no such introductions.

5. SENTENCES.   Because a précis should be concise and factual, it is tempting to write sentences that are like short bursts of machine-gun fire. Sentences of this kind are often called "choppy" or "bumpy." Here is an example of choppy sentences:

Dee comes in a car. She is dressed flamboyantly. She is with a strange man. He is short and bearded. She greets her mother and sister with foreign phrases. The man does, too. She immediately begins taking pictures. She snaps her mother with her sister in the background. She also takes pictures of wandering cows. She makes sure to get the house in all the shots. She kisses her mother then, on the forehead.

An entire essay consisting of sentences like these might make readers feel as though they have been machine-gunned. Although you should include details, you also need to shape and organize your sentences. Here is a more acceptable set of sentences revised to contain the same information:

When Dee comes, she is flamboyantly dressed, and she gets out of the car with a strange, short, and bearded man. Both Dee and the man greet Mrs. Johnson and Maggie with foreign phrases. Before embracing her mother, Dee gets her Polaroid camera and takes pictures of her mother, her sister, and wandering cows, taking care to include the house in all her shots. Only then does she kiss her mother, and then only on the forehead.

This revision blends the shorter sentences together while still attempting to cover the essential details from the story. The phrase "only then" beginning the last sentence gets at Dee's ridiculous behavior without calling it ridiculous. Even though sentences in a précis must be almost rigidly factual, try to make them as graceful as possible.

WRITING A PRÉCIS

Your writing task is to condense the original work with the least possible distortion. Thus it is necessary to keep intact the arrangement and sequence of the original. Let us suppose that a work has a surprise ending, like that in "The Necklace" (Chapter 1). In a précis, it is important to keep the same order and withhold the conclusion until the very end. It is appropriate, however, to introduce essential details of circumstance, such as names and places, at the beginning of the précis, even though these details are not brought out immediately in the story. For example, Maupassant does not name Mathilde right away, and he never says that she is French, but a précis of "The Necklace" would be obscure without these details.

If your assignment is a very short précis, say 100 to 150 words, you might confine everything to only one paragraph. For a longer précis, the normal principle of devoting a separate paragraph to each topic applies. If each major division, episode, scene, action, or section of the story (or play) is considered a topic, then the précis may be divided into paragraphs devoted to each of the divisions.

DEMONSTRATIVE STUDENT ESSAY

A Précis of Alice Walker's "Everyday Use"°

[1] Mrs. Johnson, a strong black woman living on her southern farm with her younger daughter, Maggie, is waiting for a visit by her elder daughter, Dee. Dee is returning from her home in the city, and the mother has cleaned and swept the house and yard in order to make a good impression.

[2] As she waits, she thinks of how independent Dee has been in the past, and of how self-confident and sophisticated she may be now. She contrasts Dee with Maggie, who is awkward, homely, and burn-scarred, and who has never left home. She also contrasts Dee with herself, thinking of Dee's many opportunities for self-improvement while she herself has never had any opportunities at all.

[3] When Dee appears, she is flamboyantly dressed, and she gets out of the car with a strange, short, and bearded man. Both Dee and the man greet Mrs. Johnson with foreign phrases. Before embracing her mother, Dee gets her Polaroid camera and takes pictures of her mother, her sister, and wandering cows, taking care to include the house in all her shots. Only then does she kiss her mother, and then only on the forehead.

[4] Dee soon explains that she no longer wishes to be called "Dee," but that she has taken a new name, "Wangero Leewanika Kemanjo," which she regards as her own, and not the name that previous oppressors had given her. The man she is with has an incomprehensible name, which the family understands as "Hakim-a-Barber," which he has also taken in keeping with his present philosophy.

[5] Once greetings are past, the family sits down to eat. Wangero (Dee) is impressed with the artistic qualities of the homemade furniture, and she asks for the family butter churn and dasher for display in her present home. After dinner, Wangero also asks for two homemade quilts that had been in the family for years. Mrs. Johnson hesitates, having already promised the quilts to Maggie for use when she gets married. Though Maggie offers to give Wangero the quilts, Mrs. Johnson insists on her original promise. Wangero then objects, claiming that the quilts will be spoiled by "everyday use" and that her mother misunderstands the value of the family heritage. Wangero hurriedly leaves with Hakim, while Mrs. Johnson and Maggie remain together, enjoying their snuff, until bedtime.

Commentary on the Essay

This précis, about four hundred words long, illustrates the selection of major actions and the omission of interesting but inessential detail. Thus, the phrase "a strong black woman" contains four words, and it condenses more than one hundred fifty words of detailed description in paragraph 5 of the story. By contrast, paragraph 3 of the demonstrative student essay deals with a relatively short paragraph of the story (paragraph 22). This amount of detail,

° See pp. 89–95 for this story.

however, is important because it indicates, right at Dee's entrance, her confused attitudes about her mother and the farm; the farm seems more to her like something for a scrapbook or for a wall than for real living. It is this confusion on Dee's part that underlies the major conflict of the story.

To demonstrate omissions, some materials that disclose things about Hakim's character and philosophy, to be found in paragraphs 43 through 45 of the story, are left out entirely from the précis because they are not essential to the main characters—namely, the three women.

Each of the five paragraphs in the précis is devoted to comparable sections of "Everyday Use." Paragraphs 1 and 2 describe the story up to the appearance of Dee and her man. Paragraph 3 details Dee's activity at her entrance. Paragraph 4 treats the conversation and narrative from paragraph 24 through paragraph 44 of the story. The last paragraph condenses the dinner and post-dinner scene, featuring Dee's requests to take away family heirlooms, including the vitally important quilts.

The paragraphs of the précis require not only fidelity to the narrative development of the story but also unity of subject matter. Thus, paragraph 1 is unified by the speaker's expectations, while paragraph 2 is unified by her contrast of her two daughters and also her contrast of herself with her returning daughter. Each of the other paragraphs is similarly unified—paragraph 3 by Dee's photography, paragraph 4 by the use of new names, and paragraph 5 by the conflicting attitudes about the disposal of family heirlooms. In any précis, similar attempts should be made to unify paragraphs.

SPECIAL TOPICS FOR WRITING AND ARGUMENT ABOUT FICTION

1. Consider Williams's "Taking Care" as a narrative. To what extent is the author's concern more to reveal a character than to tell a story? If the major quality of a fully developed character in short fiction is adaptation to change, how does the story make Jones's adaptation apparent?

2. Describe the mixture of narration and dialogue in Walker's "Everyday Use." Why is there is a great deal of dialogue from paragraph 24 to the end? On the basis of the mixture of dialogue and narration, what conclusions can you draw about the use that fiction makes of these elements?

3. Love is the major topic in "Taking Care" and "An Old-Fashioned Story." How does each work express its story of love? How may love be compared in the stories? Contrasted? What is the effect of circumstances on the condition of love of the various characters? (See Chapter 35, on comparison and contrast, for ideas about how to develop your essay on this topic.)

4. Suppose that someone has told you that "The Things They Carried" is too detailed and realistic to be considered a story. Explain to this person why the assertion should be considered wrong. What elements of narrative, character, plot, point of view, idea, and description justify calling "The Things They Carried" a story?

5. Consider the narrative of "Neighbors" as an argument. How can you describe the argument? Is Carver arguing that people are civilized as long as they are

being watched or instead that people, when unchecked, are irrational and uncivilized? What does the locked door signify in either argument?

6.   Write a brief episode or story that takes place in a historical period you believe you know well, being as factually accurate as you can. Introduce your own fictional characters as important "movers and shakers," and deal with their public or personal affairs or both. You may model your characters and episodes on historical persons, but you are free to exercise your imagination completely and construct your own characters.

7.   Using standard library reference works (e.g., encyclopedias, biographies of contemporary authors, or comprehensive histories of classical, English, or American literature), gather biographical material about one of the writers included in this chapter. Using this material, write a brief biography of the writer, including references to some of the writer's major works.

3

Plot and Structure: The Development and Organization of Stories

Stories and plays are made up mostly of **actions** or **incidents** that follow one another in chronological order. Finding a sequential or narrative order, however, is only the first step toward the more important consideration—the **plot,** or the controls governing the development of the actions.

PLOT: THE MOTIVATION AND CAUSATION OF FICTION

The English novelist E. M. Forster,[1] in his collection of essays titled *Aspects of the Novel,* presents a memorable illustration of plot. To show a bare set of actions, he uses the following: "The king died, and then the queen died." He points out, however, that this sequence does not form a plot because it lacks *motivation* and *causation*. These he introduces in his next example: "The king died, and then the queen died of grief." The phrase "of grief" shows that one thing (grief) controls or overcomes another (the normal desire to live), and motivation and causation enter the sequence to form a plot. In a well-plotted story or play, a thing precedes or follows another not simply because time ticks away, but more importantly because *effects* follow *causes*. In a good work, nothing is irrelevant or accidental; everything is related and causative.

Determine the Conflict and Conflicts in a Story

The controlling impulse in a connected pattern of causes and effects is **conflict,** which refers to people or circumstances that a character must face and try to overcome. Conflict brings out the extremes of human energy, causing characters to engage in the decisions, actions, responses, and interactions that make up fictional literature.

In its most elemental form, a conflict is the opposition of two people. Their conflict may take the shape of envy, hatred, anger, argument, avoidance,

[1]For Forster's story "The Point of It," see Chapter 12.

gossip, lies, fighting, and many other forms and actions. Conflicts may also exist between groups, although conflicts between individuals are more identifiable and therefore more suitable for stories. Conflicts may also be abstract, such as when an individual opposes larger forces like natural objects, ideas, modes of behavior, or public opinion. A difficult or even impossible *choice*—a **dilemma**—is a natural conflict for an individual person. A conflict may also be brought out in ideas and opinions that clash. In short, conflict shows itself in many ways.

CONFLICT IS DIRECTLY RELATED TO DOUBT, TENSION, AND INTEREST.   Conflict is the major element of plot because opposing forces arouse *curiosity,* cause *doubt,* create *tension,* and produce *interest.* The same responses are the lifeblood of athletic competition. Consider which kind of athletic event is more interesting: (1) One team gets so far ahead that the winner is no longer in doubt, or (2) both teams are so evenly matched that the winner is in doubt even in the final seconds. Obviously, games are uninteresting—as games—unless they are contests between teams of comparable strength. The same principle applies to conflicts in stories and dramas. There should be uncertainty about a protagonist's success: Unless there is doubt, there is no tension, and without tension there is no interest.

FIND THE CONFLICTS TO DETERMINE THE PLOT.   To see a plot in operation, let us build on Forster's description. Here is a simple plot for a story of our own: "John and Jane meet, fall in love, and get married." This is a plot because it shows cause and effect (they get married *because* they fall in love), but with no conflict, the plot is not interesting. However, let us introduce conflicting elements in this common "boy meets girl" story:

> John and Jane meet at school and fall in love. They go together for two years and plan to marry, but a problem arises. Jane wants a career first, and after marriage she wants to be an equal contributor to the family. John understands Jane's wishes, but he wants to get married first and let her finish her studies and have her career after they have children. Jane believes that John's plan is not for her because it constitutes a trap from which she will never escape. This conflict interrupts their plans, and they part in anger and regret. Even though they still love each other, both marry other people and build separate lives and careers. Neither is happy even though they like and respect their spouses. The years pass, and, after children and grandchildren, Jane and John meet again. He is now divorced and she is a widow. Because their earlier conflict is no longer a barrier, they marry and try to make up for the past. Even their new happiness, however, is tinged with regret and reproach because of their earlier conflict, their unhappy solution, their lost years, and their increasing age.

Here we have a true plot because our original "boy meets girl" story outline now contains a major conflict from which a number of related conflicts develop. These conflicts lead to attitudes, choices, and outcomes that make the story interesting. The situation is lifelike; the conflicts rise out of realistic aims and hopes; the outcome is true to life.

THE STRUCTURE OF FICTION

Structure refers to the ways in which writers arrange materials in accord with the general ideas and purposes of their works. Unlike plot, which is concerned with conflict or conflicts, structure defines the layouts of works—the ways the story, play, or poem is shaped. Structure is about matters such as placement, balance, recurring themes, true and misleading conclusions, suspense, and the imitation of models or forms such as reports, letters, conversations, or confessions. A work might be divided into numbered sections or parts, or it might begin in a countryside (or one state) and conclude in a city (or in another state), or it might develop a relationship between two people from their first introduction to their falling in love.

The importance of structure may be seen graphically in the art of the painter. As an example, Claude Lorrain's *Seaport at Sunset* (1639) pictures a lifelike scene comprising a harbor, ships, boats, buildings, and a shore on which people are engaging in activities such as working, chatting, transacting business, and even fighting. Near the horizon, the distant and glowing sun bathes the scene in light and is therefore the center of attention. This structuring of figures and background brings out contrasts between human beings, human artifacts and Nature, and human existence and the cosmos. In short, Claude's painting suggests that, despite temporary human concerns, the source of life is like the sun—remote, vast, mysterious, and beautiful.

Claude Lorrain, *Seaport at Sunset.* Louvre, Paris. Lauros-Giraudon/Art Resource, New York, NY.

In fiction, we find that organization and structure highlight many similar contrasts. To study structure is to study these arrangements and the purposes for which they are made.

FORMAL CATEGORIES OF STRUCTURE

Many aspects of structure are common to all genres of literature. Particularly for stories and plays, however, the following aspects form a skeleton, a pattern of development.

The Exposition Provides the Materials Necessary to Put the Plot into Operation

Exposition is the laying out, the putting forth, of the materials in the story—the main characters, their backgrounds, their characteristics, interests, goals, limitations, potentials, and basic assumptions. It may not be limited to the beginning of the work, where it is most expected, but may be found any-where. Thus, intricacies, twists, turns, false leads, blind alleys, surprises, and other quirks may be introduced to interest, perplex, intrigue, and otherwise please readers. Whenever something new arises, to the degree that it is new it is a part of exposition.

The Complication Marks the Beginning and the Growth of the Conflict

The **complication** is the onset and development of the major conflict—the plot. The major participants are the protagonist and antagonist, together with whatever ideas and values they represent, such as good or evil, freedom or oppression, independence or dependence, love or hate, intelligence or stupid-ity, or knowledge or ignorance.

The Crisis Marks the Decisions Made to End the Conflict

The **crisis** (Greek for "turning point") marks that part of the action where the conflict reaches its greatest tension. During the crisis, a decision or an action to resolve the conflict is undertaken, and therefore the crisis is the point at which curiosity, uncertainty, and tension are greatest. Usually the crisis is fol-lowed closely by the next stage, the *climax*. Often, in fact, the two are so close together that they are considered the same.

The Climax Is the Conclusion of the Conflict

Because the **climax** (Greek for "ladder") is a consequence of the crisis, it is the story's *high point* and may take the shape of a decision, an action, an affir-mation or denial, or an illumination or a realization. It is the logical conclu-sion of the preceding actions; no new major developments follow it. In most stories, the climax occurs at the end or close to it. For example, in Crane's "The Blue Hotel," the climax is the Swede's verbal and physical encounter with the gambler. Everything that happens prior to this confrontation leads to it: the Swede's nervousness and suspicion, his odd behavior at the card table, his drunkenness, his pugnaciousness, his exultation after beating Johnnie, and his defiant exit from the Blue Hotel. The primitive power he thinks he has gained at the hotel causes him to antagonize the gambler—the story's climax—and thus to bring the story to its close.

The Resolution or Dénouement Finishes the Work and Releases the Tension

The **resolution** (a releasing or an untying) or **dénouement** (untying) is the completing of the story or play after the climax, for once the climax has occurred, the work's tension and uncertainty are finished, and most authors conclude quickly to avoid losing their readers' interest. For instance, the dénouement of "The Blue Hotel" comprises a few short details about the gambler's departure, the description of the dead Swede, the news of the gambler's sentence, and the concluding chat between the cowboy and the Easterner. Welty, for example, ends "A Worn Path" with the main character beginning her long and tortuous walk home. In a similarly brief way, Poe ends "The Masque of the Red Death" (Chapter 11) by asserting that the "illimitable" power of the Red Death has overcome the earth and all its occupants. In other words, after the story's major conflilcts are finished, the job of the dénouement is to bring things to a satisfying and rapid ending.

FORMAL AND ACTUAL STRUCTURE

The structure just described is a *formal* one, an ideal pattern that moves directly from beginning to end. Few narratives and dramas follow this pattern exactly, however. Thus a typical mystery story holds back crucial details of exposition (because the goal is to mystify); a suspense story keeps the protagonist ignorant but provides readers with abundant details in order to maximize concern and tension about the outcome.

More realistic, less "artificial" stories might also contain structural variations. For example, Hardy's "The Three Strangers" produces a *double take* because of unique structuring. Toward the story's end, Hardy raises the suspicion that the fugitive prisoner is the third stranger to enter the peasant household. At the end, however, Hardy makes clear that the fugitive is really the first stranger, who is already present when the third stranger enters and leaves. This complication introduces and emphasizes a new understanding of the position of the first stranger as both a righteous person and also a brave one. "The Three Strangers" is just one example of how a structural variation maximizes the impact of a work.

There are many other possible variants in structure. One of these is called **flashback,** or **selective recollection,** in which present circumstances are explained by the selective introduction of past events. The moment at which the flashback is introduced may be a part of the resolution of the plot, and the flashback might lead you into a moment of climax but then go from there to develop the details that are more properly part of the exposition. Let us again consider our brief plot about John and Jane and use the flashback method of structuring the story.

> Jane is now old, and a noise outside causes her to remember the argument that forced her to part with John many years before. They were deeply in love, but their disagreement about her wishes for a career split them apart. Then she pictures in her mind the years she and John have spent happily together after they married. She then contrasts her present happiness with her memory of her earlier, less happy, marriage, and from there she recalls her youthful years of courtship with John before their disastrous conflict developed. Then she looks over at John, reading in a chair, and smiles. John smiles back, and the two embrace. Even then, Jane has tears on her face.

In this structure the action begins and remains in the present. Important parts of the past flood the protagonist's memory in flashback, though not in the order in which they happened. Memory might be used structurally in other ways. An example is Tillie Olsen's "I Stand Here Ironing" (Chapter 12), which is a narrative spoken (or expressed silently) by a mother at her ironing board. The events of the story itself, however, develop through flashbacks—memories of her daughter's growth. In short, the flashback technique creates a unique story that departs significantly from a strictly chronological pattern.

Each narrative or drama has a unique structure. Some stories may be structured according to simple geography, as in Whitecloud's "Blue Winds Dancing" (a ride from California to Wisconsin), Alice Munro's "The Found Boat" (from a spring flood to an exploration on and beside a river [Chapter 7]), and Welty's "A Worn Path" (a walk from country to town). Parts or scenes might be carried on through conversations, as in "The Blue Hotel" and "Everyday Use" (Chapter 2), or through a ceremony witnessed by a major character, as in "Young Goodman Brown" (Chapter 9). A story may unfold in an apparently accidental way, with the characters making vital discoveries about the major characters, as in Glaspell's "A Jury of Her Peers" (Chapter 4). Additionally, parts of a work may be set out as fragments of conversation, as in "A Worn Path," or as a ceremony, as in "Young Goodman Brown," or as an announcement of a party, as in "The Necklace" (Chapter 2). The possible variations in structuring stories are virtually infinite.

STORIES FOR STUDY

STEPHEN CRANE   (1871–1900)

Born in New Jersey, Crane began writing stories at the age of eight, and by the time he was sixteen he was helping his brothers write for newspapers. He attended a number of colleges but did not graduate. While at Syracuse University he completed his first novel, Maggie: A Girl of the Streets, *which he published with borrowed money in 1893. During the remainder of his brief and turbulent life he worked as a writer and war correspondent. He spent a year in the West, and two of his better-known stories, "The Bride Comes to Yellow Sky" and "The Blue Hotel," came out of this experience. His best-known novel,* The Red Badge of Courage, *was published in 1895. "The Blue Hotel" was included in* The Monster and Other Stories *in 1899.*

The Blue Hotel _____ *1899*

I

The Palace Hotel at Fort Romper was painted a light blue, a shade that is on the legs of a kind of heron, causing the bird to declare its position against any background. The Palace Hotel, then, was always screaming and howling in a way that made the dazzling winter landscape of Nebraska seem only a grey swampish hush. It stood alone on the prairie, and when the snow was falling the town two hundred yards away was not visible. But when the traveller alighted at the railway station he was obliged to pass the Palace Hotel before he could come upon the company of low clapboard houses which composed Fort Romper, and it was not to be thought that any traveller could pass the Palace Hotel without looking at it. Pat Scully, the proprietor, had proved himself a master of strategy when he chose his paints. It is true that on clear days, when the great transcontinental expresses, long lines of swaying Pullmans, swept through Fort Romper, passengers were overcome at the sight, and the cult that knows the brown-reds and the subdivisions of the dark greens of the East expressed shame, pity, horror, in a laugh. But to the citizens of this prairie town and to the people who would naturally stop there, Pat Scully had performed a feat. With this opulence and splendour, these creeds, classes, egotisms, that streamed through Romper on the rails day after day, they had no colour in common.

As if the displayed delights of such a blue hotel were not sufficiently enticing, it was Scully's habit to go every morning and evening to meet the leisurely trains that stopped at Romper and work his seductions upon any man that he might see wavering, gripsack in hand.

One morning, when a snow-crusted engine dragged its long string of freight cars and its one passenger coach to the station, Scully performed the marvel of catching three men. One was a shaky and quick-eyed Swede, with a great shining cheap valise; one was a tall bronzed cowboy, who was on his way to a ranch near the Dakota line; one was a little silent man from the East, who didn't look it, and didn't announce it. Scully practically made them prisoners. He was so nimble and merry and kindly that each probably felt it would be the height of brutality to try to escape. They trudged off over the creaking board sidewalks in the wake of the eager little Irishman. He wore a heavy fur cap squeezed tightly down on his head. It caused his two red ears to stick out stiffly, as if they were made of tin.

At last, Scully, elaborately, with boisterous hospitality, conducted them through the portals of the blue hotel. The room which they entered was small. It seemed to be merely a proper temple for an enormous stove, which, in the centre, was humming with godlike violence. At various points on its surface the iron had become luminous and glowed yellow from the heat. Beside the stove Scully's son Johnnie was playing High-Five° with an old farmer who had whiskers both grey and sandy. They were quarreling. Frequently the old farmer turned his face toward a box of sawdust—coloured brown from tobacco juice—that was behind the stove, and spat with an air of great impatience and irritation. With a loud flourish of words Scully destroyed the game of cards, and bustled his son upstairs with part of the baggage of the new guests. He himself conducted them to three basins of the coldest water in the world. The cowboy and the Easterner burnished themselves fiery red with this water, until it seemed to be some kind of metal-polish. The Swede, however, merely dipped his fingers gingerly and with trepidation. It was notable that throughout this series of small ceremonies the three travellers were made to feel that Scully was very benevolent. He was conferring great favours upon them. He handed the towel from one to another with an air of philanthropic impulse.

Afterward they went to the first room, and, sitting about the stove, listened to Scully's officious clamour at his daughters, who were preparing the midday meal. They reflected in the silence of experienced men who tread carefully amid new people. Nevertheless, the old farmer, stationary, invincible in his chair near the warmest part of the stove, turned his face from the sawdust-box frequently and addressed a glowing commonplace to the strangers. Usually he was answered in short but adequate sentences by either the cowboy or the Easterner. The Swede said nothing. He seemed to be occupied in making furtive estimates of each man in the room. One might have thought that he had the sense of silly suspicion which comes to guilt. He resembled a badly frightened man.

Later, at dinner, he spoke a little, addressing his conversation entirely to Scully. He volunteered that he had come from New York, where for ten years he had worked as a tailor. These facts seemed to strike Scully as fascinating, and afterward he volunteered that he had lived at Romper for fourteen years. The Swede asked about the crops and the price of labour. He seemed barely to listen to Scully's extended replies. His eyes continued to rove from man to man.

Finally, with a laugh and a wink, he said that some of these Western communities were very dangerous; and after his statement he straightened his legs under the table, tilted his head, and laughed again, loudly. It was plain that the demonstration had no meaning to the others. They looked at him wondering and in silence.

High-Five: the most commonly played card game in the United States before it was replaced in popularity by poker.

II

As the men trooped heavily back into the front room, the two little windows presented views of a turmoiling sea of snow. The huge arms of the wind were making attempts—mighty, circular, futile—to embrace the flakes as they sped. A gate-post like a still man with a blanched face stood aghast amid this profligate fury. In a hearty voice Scully announced the presence of a blizzard. The guests of the blue hotel, lighting their pipes, assented with grunts of lazy masculine contentment. No island of the sea could be exempt in the degree of this little room with its humming stove. Johnnie, son of Scully, in a tone which defined his opinion of his ability as a card-player, challenged the old farmer of both grey and sandy whiskers to a game of High-Five. The farmer agreed with a contemptuous and bitter scoff. They sat close to the stove, and squared their knees under a wide board. The cowboy and the Easterner watched the game with interest. The Swede remained near the window, aloof, but with a countenance that showed signs of an inexplicable excitement.

The play of Johnnie and the grey-beard was suddenly ended by another quarrel. The old man arose while casting a look of heated scorn at his adversary. He slowly buttoned his coat, and then stalked with fabulous dignity from the room. In the discreet silence of all other men the Swede laughed. His laughter rang somehow childish. Men by this time had begun to look at him askance, as if they wished to inquire what ailed him.

A new game was formed jocosely. The cowboy volunteered to become the part- 10
ner of Johnnie, and they all then turned to ask the Swede to throw in his lot with the little Easterner. He asked some questions about the game, and, learning that it wore many names, and that he had played it when it was under an alias, he accepted the invitation. He strode toward the men nervously, as if he expected to be assaulted. Finally, seated, he gazed from face to face and laughed shrilly. This laugh was so strange that the Easterner looked up quickly, the cowboy sat intent and with his mouth open, and Johnnie paused, holding the cards with still fingers.

Afterward there was a short silence. Then Johnnie said, "Well, let's get at it. Come on now!" They pulled their chairs forward until their knees were bunched under the board. They began to play, and their interest in the game caused the others to forget the manner of the Swede.

The cowboy was a board-whacker. Each time that he held superior cards he whanged them, one by one, with exceeding force, down upon the improvised table, and took the tricks with a glowing air of prowess and pride that sent thrills of indignation into the hearts of his opponents. A game with a board-whacker in it is sure to become intense. The countenances of the Easterner and the Swede were miserable whenever the cowboy thundered down his aces and kings, while Johnnie, his eyes gleaming with joy, chuckled and chuckled.

Because of the absorbing play none considered the strange ways of the Swede. They paid strict heed to the game. Finally, during a lull caused by a new deal, the Swede suddenly addressed Johnnie: "I suppose there have been a good many men killed in this room." The jaws of the others dropped and they looked at him.

"What in hell are you talking about?" said Johnnie.

The Swede laughed again his blatant laugh, full of a kind of false courage and 15
defiance. "Oh, you know what I mean all right," he answered.

"I'm a liar if I do!" Johnnie protested. The card was halted, and the men stared at the Swede. Johnnie evidently felt that as the son of the proprietor he should make a direct inquiry. "Now, what might you be drivin' at, mister?" he asked. The

Swede winked at him. It was a wink full of cunning. His fingers shook on the edge of the board. "Oh, maybe you think I have been to nowheres. Maybe you think I'm a tenderfoot?"

"I don't know nothin' about you," answered Johnnie, "and I don't give a damn where you've been. All I got to say is that I don't know what you're driving at. There hain't never been nobody killed in this room."

The cowboy, who had been steadily gazing at the Swede, then spoke. "What's wrong with you, mister?"

Apparently it seemed to the Swede that he was formidably menaced. He shivered and turned white near the corners of his mouth. He sent an appealing glance in the direction of the little Easterner. During these moments he did not forget to wear his air of advanced pot-valour. "They say they don't know what I mean," he remarked mockingly to the Easterner.

The latter answered after prolonged and cautious reflection. "I don't understand you," he said, impassively.   20

The Swede made a movement then which announced that he thought he had encountered treachery from the only quarter where he had expected sympathy, if not help. "Oh, I see you are all against me. I see—"

The cowboy was in a state of deep stupefaction. "Say," he cried, as he tumbled the deck violently down upon the board, "say, what are you gittin' at, hey?"

The Swede sprang up with the celerity of a man escaping from a snake on the floor. "I don't want to fight!" he shouted, "I don't want to fight!"

The cowboy stretched his long legs indolently and deliberately. His hands were in his pockets. He spat into the sawdust-box. "Well, who the hell thought you did?" he inquired.

The Swede backed rapidly toward a corner of the room. His hands were out pro-   25
tectingly in front of his chest, but he was making an obvious struggle to control his fright. "Gentlemen," he quavered. "I suppose I am going to be killed before I can leave this house! I suppose I am going to be killed before I can leave this house!" In his eyes was the dying-swan° look. Through the windows could be seen the snow turning blue in the shadow of dusk. The wind tore at the house, and some loose thing beat regularly against the clapboards like a spirit tapping.

A door opened, and Scully himself entered. He paused in surprise as he noted the tragic attitude of the Swede. Then he said. "What's the matter here?"

The Swede answered him swiftly and eagerly: "These men are going to kill me."

"Kill you!" ejaculated Scully. "Kill you! What are you talkin'?"

The Swede made the gesture of a martyr.

Scully wheeled sternly upon his son. "What is this, Johnnie?"   30

The lad had grown sullen. "Damned if I know," he answered. "I can't make no sense of it." He began to shuffle the cards, fluttering them together with an angry snap. "He says a good many men have been killed in this room, or something like that. And he says he's goin' to be killed here too. I don't know what ails him. He's crazy, I shouldn't wonder."

Scully then looked for explanation to the cowboy, but the cowboy simply shrugged his shoulders.

"Kill you?" said Scully again to the Swede. "Kill you? Man, you're off your nut."

---

dying swan: Proverbially, a swan sings its most beautiful notes when it is about to die.

"Oh, I know," burst out the Swede. "I know what will happen. Yes, I'm crazy—yes. Yes, of course, I'm crazy—yes. But I know one thing—" There was a sort of sweat of misery and terror upon his face. "I know I won't get out of here alive."

The cowboy drew a deep breath, as if his mind was passing into the last stages of   35
dissolution. "Well, I'm doggoned," he whispered to himself.

Scully wheeled suddenly and faced his son. "You've been troublin' this man!"

Johnnie's voice was loud with its burden of grievance. "Why, good Gawd, I ain't done nothin' to 'im."

The Swede broke in. "Gentlemen, do not disturb yourselves. I will leave this house. I will go away, because"—he accused them dramatically with his glance—"because I do not want to be killed."

Scully was furious with his son. "Will you tell me what is the matter, you young divil? What's the matter, anyhow? Speak out!"

"Blame it!" cried Johnnie in despair, "don't I tell you I don't know? He—he says   40
we want to kill him, and that's all I know. I can't tell what ails him."

The Swede continued to repeat: "Never mind, Mr. Scully; never mind. I will leave this house. I will go away, because I do not wish to be killed. Yes, of course, I am crazy—yes. But I know one thing! I will go away. I will leave this house. Never mind, Mr. Scully; never mind, I will go away."

"You will not go 'way," said Scully. "You will not go 'way until I hear the reason of this business. If anybody has troubled you I will take care of him. This is my house. You are under my roof, and I will not allow any peaceable man to be troubled here." He cast a terrible eye upon Johnnie, the cowboy, and the Easterner.

"Never mind, Mr. Scully; never mind. I will go away. I do not wish to be killed." The Swede moved toward the door which opened upon the stairs. It was evidently his intention to go at once for his baggage.

"No, no," shouted Scully peremptorily; but the white-faced man slid by him and disappeared. "Now," said Scully severely, "what does this mane?"°

Johnnie and the cowboy cried together: "Why, we didn't do nothin' to 'im!"   45

Scully's eyes were cold. "No," he said, "you didn't?"

Johnnie swore a deep oath. "Why, this is the wildest loon I ever see. We didn't do nothin' at all. We were just sittin' here playin cards, and he—"

The father suddenly spoke to the Easterner. "Mr. Blanc," he asked, "what has these boys been doin'?"

The Easterner reflected again. "I didn't see anything wrong at all," he said at last, slowly.

Scully began to howl, "But what does it mane?" He stared ferociously at his son. "I   50
have a mind to lather you for this, me boy."

Johnnie was frantic. "Well, what have I done?" he bawled at his father.

III

"I think you are tongue-tied," said Scully finally to his son, the cowboy, and the Easterner; and at the end of this scornful sentence he left the room.

Upstairs the Swede was swiftly fastening the straps of his great valise. Once his back happened to be half turned toward the door, and, hearing a noise there, he

---

mane: mean. Scully speaks with a slight Irish brogue (see, for example, paragraphs 58, 70, and 114).

wheeled and sprang up, uttering a loud cry. Scully's wrinkled visage showed grimly in the light of the small lamp he carried. This yellow effulgence, streaming upward, coloured only his prominent features, and left his eyes, for instance, in mysterious shadow. He resembled a murderer.

"Man! man!" he exclaimed, "have you gone daffy?"

"Oh, no! Oh, no!" rejoined the other. "There are people in this world who know   5 pretty nearly as much as you do—understand?"

For a moment they stood gazing at each other. Upon the Swede's deathly pale cheeks were two spots brightly crimson and sharply edged, as if they had been carefully painted. Scully placed the light on the table and sat himself on the edge of the bed. He spoke ruminatively. "By cracky, I never heard of such a thing in my life. It's a complete muddle. I can't, for the soul of me, think how you ever got this idea into your head." Presently he lifted his eyes and asked: "And did you sure think they were going to kill you?"

The Swede scanned the old man as if he wished to see into his mind. "I did," he said at last. He obviously suspected that this answer might precipitate an outbreak. As he pulled on a strap his whole arm shook, the elbow wavering like a bit of paper.

Scully banged his hand impressively on the footboard of the bed. "Why, man, we're goin' to have a line of ilictric street-cars in this town next spring."

"'A line of electric street-cars,'" repeated the Swede, stupidly.

"And," said Scully, "there's a new railroad goin' to be built down from Bro-   6 ken Arm to here. Not to mention the four churches and the smashin' big brick schoolhouse. Then there's the big factory, too. Why, in two years Romper'll be a met-tro-*pol*-is."

Having finished the preparation of his baggage, the Swede straightened himself. "Mr. Scully," he said, with sudden hardihood, "how much do I owe you?"

"You don't owe me anythin'," said the old man, angrily.

"Yes, I do," retorted the Swede. He took seventy-five cents from his pocket and tendered it to Scully; but the latter snapped his fingers in disdainful refusal. However, it happened that they both stood gazing in a strange fashion at three silver pieces on the Swede's open palm.

"I'll not take your money," said Scully at last. "Not after what's been goin' on here." Then a plan seemed to strike him. "Here," he cried, picking up his lamp and moving toward the door. "Here! Come with me a minute."

"No," said the Swede, in overwhelming alarm.   6

"Yes," urged the old man. "Come on! I want you to come and see a picter—just across the hall—in my room."

The Swede must have concluded that his hour was come. His jaw dropped and his teeth showed like a dead man's. He ultimately followed Scully across the corridor, but he had the step of one hung in chains.

Scully flashed the light high on the wall of his own chamber. There was revealed a ridiculous photograph of a little girl. She was leaning against a balustrade of gorgeous decoration, and the formidable bang to her hair was prominent. The figure was as graceful as an upright sled-stake, and, withal, it was of the hue of lead. "There," said Scully, tenderly, "that's the picter of my little girl that died. Her name was Carrie. She had the purtiest hair you even saw! I was that fond of her, she—"

Turning then, he saw that the Swede was not contemplating the picture at all, but, instead, was keeping keen watch on the gloom in the rear.

"Look, man!" cried Scully, heartily. "That's the picter of my little gal that died.   7 Her name was Carrie. And then here's the picter of my oldest boy, Michael. He's a lawyer in Lincoln, an' doin' well. I gave that boy a grand eddication, and I'm glad for it now. He's a fine boy. Look at 'im now. Ain't he bold as blazes, him there in Lincoln, an honoured an' respicted gintleman! An honoured and respicted gintleman," concluded Scully with a flourish. And, so saying, he smote the Swede jovially on the back.

The Swede faintly smiled.

"Now," said the old man, "there's only one more thing." He dropped suddenly to the floor and thrust his head beneath the bed. The Swede could hear his muffled voice. "I'd keep it under me piller if it wasn't for that boy Johnnie. Then there's the old woman—Where is it now? I never put it twice in the same place. Ah, now come out with you!"

Presently he backed clumsily from under the bed, dragging with him an old coat rolled into a bundle. "I've fetched him," he muttered. Kneeling on the floor, he unrolled the coat and extracted from its heart a large yellow-brown whiskey-bottle.

His first maneuver was to hold the bottle up to the light. Reassured, apparently, that nobody had been tampering with it, he thrust it with a generous movement toward the Swede.

The weak-kneed Swede was about to eagerly clutch this element of strength, but   75
he suddenly jerked his hand away and cast a look of horror upon Scully.

"Drink," said the old man affectionately. He had risen to his feet, and now stood facing the Swede.

There was a silence. Then again Scully said: "Drink!"

The Swede laughed wildly. He grabbed the bottle, put it to his mouth; and as his lips curled absurdly around the opening and his throat worked, he kept his glance, burning with hatred, upon the old man's face.

IV

After the departure of Scully the three men, with the card-board still upon their knees, preserved for a long time an astounded silence. Then Johnnie said: "That's the dod-dangedest Swede I ever see."

"He ain't no Swede," said the cowboy, scornfully.   80

"Well, what is he then?" cried Johnnie. "What is he then?"

"It's my opinion," replied the cowboy deliberately, "he's some kind of a Dutchman." It was a venerable custom of the country to entitle as Swedes all light-haired men who spoke with a heavy tongue. In consequence the idea of the cowboy was not without its daring. "Yes, sir," he repeated. "It's my opinion this feller is some kind of Dutchman."

"Well, he says he's a Swede, anyhow," muttered Johnnie, sulkily. He turned to the Easterner: "What do you think, Mr. Blanc?"

"Oh, I don't know," replied the Easterner.

"Well, what do you think makes him act that way?" asked the cowboy.   85

"Why, he's frightened." The Easterner knocked his pipe against the rim of the stove. "He's clear frightened out of his boots."

"What at?" cried Johnnie, and the cowboy together.

The Easterner reflected over his answer.

"What at?" cried the others again.

"Oh, I don't know, but it seems to me this man has been reading dime novels,   90
and he thinks he's right out in the middle of it—the shootin' and stabbin' and all."

"But," said the cowboy, deeply scandalized, "this ain't Wyoming, ner none of them places. This is Nebrasker."

"Yes," added Johnnie, "an' why don't he wait till he gits *out West?*"

The travelled Easterner laughed. "It isn't different there even—not in these days. But he thinks he's right in the middle of hell."

Johnnie and the cowboy mused long.

"It's awful funny," remarked Johnnie at last.   95

"Yes," said the cowboy. "This is a queer game. I hope we don't git snowed in, because then we'd have to stand this here man bein' around with us all the time. That wouldn't be no good."

"I wish pop would throw him out," said Johnnie.

Presently they heard a loud stamping on the stairs, accompanied by ringing jokes in the voice of old Scully, and laughter, evidently from the Swede. The men around the stove stared vacantly at each other. "Gosh!" said the cowboy. The door flew open, and old Scully, flushed and anecdotal, came into the room. He was jabbering at the Swede, who followed him, laughing bravely. It was the entry of two roisterers from a banquet hall.

"Come now," said Scully sharply to the three seated men, "move up and give us a chance at the stove." The cowboy and the Easterner obediently sidled their chairs to make room for the new-comers. Johnnie, however, simply arranged himself in a more indolent attitude, and then remained motionless.

"Come! Git over, there," said Scully.   100

"Plenty of room on the other side of the stove," said Johnnie.

"Do you think we want to sit in the draught?" roared the father.

But the Swede here interposed with a grandeur of confidence. "No, no. Let the boy sit where he likes," he cried in a bullying voice to the father.

"All right! All right!" said Scully, deferentially. The cowboy and the Easterner exchanged glances of wonder.

The five chairs were formed in a crescent about one side of the stove. The Swede   105
began to talk; he talked arrogantly, profanely, angrily. Johnnie, the cowboy, and the Easterner maintained a morose silence, while old Scully appeared to be receptive and eager, breaking in constantly with sympathetic ejaculations.

Finally the Swede announced that he was thirsty. He moved in his chair, and said that he would go for a drink of water.

"I'll git it for you," cried Scully at once.

"No," said the Swede contemptuously. "I'll get it for myself." He arose and stalked with the air of an owner off into the executive parts of the hotel.

As soon as the Swede was out of hearing Scully sprang to his feet and whispered intensely to the others: "Upstairs he thought I was tryin' to poison 'im."

"Say," said Johnnie, "this makes me sick. Why don't you throw 'im out in the   110
snow?"

"Why, he's all right now," declared Scully. "It was only that he was from the East, and he thought this was a tough place. That's all. He's all right now."

The cowboy looked with admiration upon the Easterner. "You were straight," he said. "You were on to that there Dutchman."

"Well," said Johnnie to his father, "he may be all right now, but I don't see it. Other time he was scared, but now he's too fresh."

Scully's speech was always a combination of Irish brogue and idiom, Western twang and idiom, and scraps of curiously formal diction taken from the storybooks and newspapers. He now hurled a strange mass of language at the head of his son. "What do I keep? What do I keep? What do I keep?" he demanded, in a voice of thunder. He slapped his knee impressively, to indicate that he himself was going to make reply, and that all should heed. "I keep a hotel," he shouted. "A hotel, do you mind? A guest under my roof has sacred privileges. He is to be intimidated by none. Not one word shall he hear that would prijudice him in favor of goin' away. I'll not have it. There's no place in this here town where they can say they iver took in a guest of mine because he was afraid to stay here." He wheeled suddenly upon the cowboy and the Easterner. "Am I right?"

"Yes, Mr. Scully," said the cowboy, "I think you're right."   115

"Yes, Mr. Scully," said the Easterner, "I think you're right."

V

At six-o'clock supper, the Swede fizzed like a fire-wheel. He sometimes seemed on the point of bursting into riotous song, and in all his madness he was encouraged by old Scully. The Easterner was encased in reserve; the cowboy sat in wide-mouthed amazement, forgetting to eat, while Johnnie wrathily demolished great plates of food. The daughters of the house, when they were obliged to replenish the biscuits, approached as warily as Indians, and, having succeeded in their purpose, fled with ill-concealed trepidation. The Swede domineered the whole feast, and he gave it the appearance of a cruel bacchanal. He seemed to have grown suddenly taller; he gazed, brutally disdainful, into every face. His voice rang through the room. Once when he jabbed out harpoon-fashion with his fork to pinion a biscuit, the weapon nearly impaled the hand of the Easterner, which had been stretched quietly out for the same biscuit.

After supper, as the men filed toward the other room, the Swede smote Scully ruthlessly on the shoulder. "Well, old boy, that was a good, square meal." Johnnie looked hopefully at his father; he knew that shoulder was tender from an old fall; and, indeed, it appeared for a moment as if Scully was going to flame out over the matter, but in the end he smiled a sickly smile and remained silent. The others understood from his manner that he was admitting his responsibility for the Swede's new viewpoint.

Johnnie, however, addressed his parent in an aside. "Why don't you license somebody to kick you downstairs?" Scully scowled darkly by way of reply.

When they were gathered about the stove, the Swede insisted on another game   120
of High-Five. Scully gently deprecated the plan at first, but the Swede turned a wolfish glare upon him. The old man subsided, and the Swede canvassed the others. In his tone there was always a great threat. The cowboy and the Easterner both remarked indifferently that they would play. Scully said that he would presently have to go to meet the 6:58 train, and so the Swede turned menacingly upon Johnnie. For a moment their glances crossed like blades, and then Johnnie smiled and said, "Yes, I'll play."

They formed a square, with the little board on their knees. The Easterner and the Swede were again partners. As the play went on, it was noticeable that the cowboy was not board-whacking as usual. Meanwhile, Scully, near the lamp, had put on his spectacles and, with an appearance curiously like an old priest, was reading a newspaper. In time he went out to meet the 6:58 train, and, despite his precautions, a gust of polar wind whirled into the room as he opened the door. Besides scattering the cards, it chilled the players to the marrow. The Swede cursed frightfully. When Scully returned, his entrance disturbed a cosy and friendly scene. The Swede again cursed. But presently they were once more intent, their heads bent forward and their hands moving swiftly. The Swede had adopted the fashion of board-whacking.

Scully took up his paper and for a long time remained immersed in matters which were extraordinarily remote from him. The lamp burned badly, and once he stopped to adjust the wick. The newspaper, as he turned from page to page, rustled with a slow and comfortable sound. Then suddenly he heard three terrible words: "You are cheatin'!"

Such scenes often prove that there can be little of dramatic import in environment. Any room can present a tragic front: any room can be comic. This little den was now hideous as a torture-chamber. The new faces of the men themselves had changed it upon the instant. The Swede held a huge fist in front of Johnnie's face, while the latter looked steadily over it into the blazing orbs of his accuser. The Easterner had grown pallid: the cowboy's jaw had dropped in that expression of bovine amazement which was one of his important mannerisms. After the three words, the first sound in the room was made by Scully's paper as it floated forgotten to his feet. His spectacles had also fallen from his nose, but by a clutch he had saved them in air. His hand, grasping the spectacles, now remained poised awkwardly and near his shoulder. He stared at the card-players.

Probably the silence was while a second elapsed. Then, if the floor had been suddenly twitched out from under the men they could not have moved quicker. The five had projected themselves headlong toward a common point. It happened that Johnnie, in rising to hurl himself upon the Swede, had stumbled slightly because of his curiously instinctive care for the cards and the board. The loss of the moment allowed time for the arrival of Scully, and also allowed the cowboy time to give the Swede a great push which sent him staggering back. The men found tongue together, and hoarse shouts of rage, appeal, or fear burst from every throat. The cowboy pushed and jostled feverishly at the Swede, and the Easterner and Scully clung wildly to Johnnie; but through the smoky air, above the swaying bodies of the peace-compellers, the eyes of the two warriors ever sought each other in glances of challenge that were at once hot and steely.

Of course the board had been overturned, and now the whole company of cards was scattered over the floor, where the boots of the men trampled the fat and painted kings and queens as they gazed with their silly eyes at the war that was waging above them.   125

Scully's voice was dominating the yells. "Stop now! Stop, I say! Stop, now—"

Johnnie, as he struggled to burst through the rank formed by Scully and the Easterner, was crying. "Well, he says I cheated! He says I cheated! I won't allow no man to say I cheated! If he says I cheated, he's a ——— ——!"

The cowboy was telling the Swede, "Quit, now! Quit, d'ye hear—"

The screams of the Swede never ceased: "He did cheat! I saw him! I saw him—"

As for the Easterner, he was importuning in a voice that was not heeded: "Wait a moment, can't you? Oh, wait a moment. What's the good of a fight over a game of cards? Wait a moment—"

In this tumult no complete sentences were clear. "Cheat"—"Quit"—"He says"— these fragments pierced the uproar and rang out sharply. It was remarkable that, whereas Scully undoubtedly made the most noise, he was the least heard of any of the riotous band.   130

Then suddenly there was a great cessation. It was as if each man had paused for breath; and although the room was still lighted with the anger of men, it could be seen that there was no danger of immediate conflict, and at once Johnnie, shouldering his way forward, almost succeeded in confronting the Swede. "What did you say I cheated for? What did you say I cheated for? I don't cheat, and I won't let no man say I do!"

The Swede said, "I saw you! I saw you!"

"Well," cried Johnnie, "I'll fight any man what says I cheat!"

"No, you won't," said the cowboy. "Not here."

"Ah, be still, can't you?" said Scully, coming between them.   135

The quiet was sufficient to allow the Easterner's voice to be heard. He was repeating, "Oh, wait a moment, can't you? What's the good of a fight over a game of cards? Wait a moment!"

Johnnie, his red face appearing above his father's shoulder, hailed the Swede again. "Did you say I cheated?"

The Swede showed his teeth. "Yes."

"Then," said Johnnie, "we must fight."

"Yes, fight," roared the Swede. He was like a demoniac. "Yes, fight! I'll show you   140 what kind of a man I am! I'll show you who you want to fight! Maybe you think I can't fight! Maybe you think I can't! I'll show you, you skin, you card-sharp! Yes, you cheated! You cheated! You cheated!"

"Well, let's go at it, then, mister," said Johnnie coolly.

The cowboy's brow was beaded with sweat from his efforts in intercepting all sorts of raids. He turned in despair to Scully. "What are you goin' to do now?"

A change had come over the Celtic visage of the old man. He now seemed all eagerness; his eyes glowed.

"We'll let them fight," he answered stalwartly. "I can't put up with it any longer. I've stood this damned Swede till I'm sick. We'll let them fight."

VI

The men prepared to go out of doors. The Easterner was so nervous that he had   145 great difficulty in getting his arms into the sleeves of his new leather coat. As the cowboy drew his fur cap down over his ears his hands trembled. In fact, Johnnie and old Scully were the only ones who displayed no agitation. These preliminaries were conducted without words.

Scully threw open the door. "Well, come on," he said. Instantly a terrific wind caused the flame of the lamp to struggle at its wick, while a puff of black smoke sprang from the chimney-top. The stove was in mid-current of the blast, and its voice swelled to equal the roar of the storm. Some of the scarred and bedabbled cards were caught up from the floor and dashed helplessly against the farther wall. The men lowered their heads and plunged into the tempest as into a sea.

No snow was falling, but great whirls and clouds of flakes, swept up from the ground by the frantic winds, were streaming southward with the speed of bullets. The covered land was blue with the sheen of an unearthly satin, and there was no other hue save where, at the low, black railway station—which seemed incredibly distant—one light gleamed like a tiny jewel. As the men floundered into a thigh-deep drift, it was known that the Swede was bawling out something. Scully went to him, put a hand on his shoulder, and projected an ear. "What's that you say?" he shouted.

"I say," bawled the Swede again. "I won't stand much show against this gang, I know you'll all pitch on me."

Scully smote him reproachfully on the arm. "Tut, man!" he yelled. The wind tore the words from Scully's lips and scattered them far alee.

"You are all a gang of—" boomed the Swede, but the storm also seized the remainder of this sentence.   150

Immediately turning their backs upon the wind, the men had swung around a corner to the sheltered side of the hotel. It was the function of the little house to preserve here, amid this great devastation of snow, an irregular V-shape of heavily encrusted grass, which crackled beneath the feet. One could imagine the great drifts piled against the windward side. When the party reached the comparative peace of this spot it was found that the Swede was still bellowing.

"Oh, I know what kind of a thing this is! I know you'll all pitch on me. I can't lick you all!"

Scully turned upon him panther-fashion. "You'll not have to whip all of us. You'll have to whip my son Johnnie. An' the man what troubles you durin' that time will have me to dale with."

The arrangements were swiftly made. The two men faced each other, obedient to the harsh commands of Scully, whose face, in the subtly luminous gloom, could be seen set in the austere impersonal lines that are pictured on the countenances of the Roman veterans. The Easterner's teeth were chattering, and he was hopping up and down like a mechanical toy. The cowboy stood rock-like.

The contestants had not stripped off any clothing. Each was in his ordinary attire. Their fists were up, and they eyed each other in a calm that had the elements of leonine cruelty in it.

During this pause, the Easterner's mind, like a film, took lasting impressions of three men—the iron-nerved master of the ceremony; the Swede, pale, motionless, terrible; and Johnnie, serene yet ferocious, brutish yet heroic. The entire prelude had in it a tragedy greater than the tragedy of action, and this aspect was accentuated by the long, mellow cry of the blizzard, as it sped the tumbling and wailing flakes into the black abyss of the south.

"Now!" said Scully.

The two combatants leaped forward and crashed together like bullocks. There was heard the cushioned sound of blows, and of a curse squeezing out from between the tight teeth of one.

As for the spectators, the Easterner's pent-up breath exploded from him with a pop of relief, absolute relief from the tension of the preliminaries. The cowboy bounded into the air with a yowl. Scully was immovable as from supreme amazement and fear at the fury of the fight which he himself had permitted and arranged.

For a time the encounter in the darkness was such a perplexity of flying arms that it presented no more detail than would a swiftly revolving wheel. Occasionally a face, as if illumined by a flash of light, would shine out, ghastly and marked with pink spots. A moment later, the men might have been known as shadows, if it were not for the involuntary utterance of oaths that came from them in whispers.

Suddenly a holocaust of warlike desire caught the cowboy, and he bolted forward with the speed of a broncho. "Go it, Johnnie! go it! Kill him! Kill him!"

Scully confronted him. "Kape back," he said; and by his glance the cowboy could tell that this man was Johnnie's father.

To the Easterner there was a monotony of unchangeable fighting that was an abomination. This confused mingling was eternal to his sense, which was concentrated in a longing for the end, the priceless end. Once the fighters lurched near him, and as he scrambled hastily backward he heard them breathe like men on the rack.

"Kill him, Johnnie! Kill him! Kill him! Kill him!" The cowboy's face was contorted like one of those agony masks in museums.

"Keep still," said Scully, icily.

Then there was a sudden loud grunt, incomplete, cut short, and Johnnie's body swung away from the Swede and fell with sickening heaviness to the grass. The cowboy was barely in time to prevent the mad Swede from flinging himself upon his prone adversary. "No, you don't," said the cowboy, interposing an arm. "Wait a second."

Scully was at his son's side. "Johnnie! Johnnie, me boy!" His voice had a quality of melancholy tenderness. "Johnnie! Can you go on with it?" He looked anxiously down into the bloody, pulpy face of his son.

There was a moment of silence, and then Johnnie answered in his ordinary voice, "Yes, I—it—yes."

Assisted by his father he struggled to his feet. "Wait a bit now till you git your wind," said the old man.

A few paces away the cowboy was lecturing the Swede. "No, you don't! Wait a second!" 170

The Easterner was plucking at Scully's sleeve. "Oh, this is enough," he pleaded. "This is enough! Let it go as it stands. This is enough!"

"Bill," said Scully, "git out of the road." The cowboy stepped aside. "Now." The combatants were actuated by a new caution as they advanced toward collision. They glared at each other, and then the Swede aimed a lightning blow that carried with it his entire weight. Johnnie was evidently half stupid from weakness, but he miraculously dodged, and his fist sent the over-balanced Swede sprawling.

The cowboy, Scully, and the Easterner burst into a cheer that was like a chorus of triumphant soldiery, but before its conclusion the Swede has scuffed agilely to his feet and come in berserk abandon at his foe. There was another perplexity of flying arms, and Johnnie's body again swung away and fell, even as a bundle might fall from a roof. The Swede instantly staggered to a little wind-waved tree and leaned upon it, breathing like an engine, while his savage and flamelit eyes roamed from face to face as the men bent over Johnnie. There was a splendour of isolation in his situation at this time which the Easterner felt once when, lifting his eyes from the man on the ground, he beheld that mysterious and lonely figure, waiting.

"Are you any good yet, Johnnie?" asked Scully in a broken voice.

The son gasped and opened his eyes languidly. After a moment he answered, 175 "No—I ain't—any good—any—more." Then, from shame, and bodily ill, he began to weep, the tears furrowing down through the blood-stains on his face. "He was too—too—too heavy for me."

Scully straightened and addressed the waiting figure.

"Stranger," he said, evenly, "it's all up with our side." Then his voice changed into that vibrant huskiness which is commonly the tone of the most simple and deadly announcements. "Johnnie is whipped."

Without replying, the victor moved off on the route to the front door of the hotel.

The cowboy was formulating new and unspellable blasphemies. The Easterner was startled to find that they were out in a wind that seemed to come direct from the shadowed arctic floes. He heard again the wail of the snow as it was flung to its grave in the south. He knew now that all this time the cold had been sinking into him deeper and deeper, and he wondered that he had not perished. He felt indifferent to the condition of the vanquished man.

"Johnnie, can you walk?" asked Scully. 180

"Did I hurt—hurt him any?" asked the son.

"Can you walk, boy? Can you walk?"

Johnnie's voice was suddenly strong. There was a robust impatience in it. "I asked you whether I hurt him any!"

"Yes, yes, Johnnie," answered the cowboy, consolingly; "he's hurt a good deal."

They raised him from the ground, and as soon as he was on his feet he went   18
tottering off, rebuffing all attempts at assistance. When the party rounded the corner
they were fairly blinded by the pelting of the snow. It burned their faces like fire. The
cowboy carried Johnnie through the drift to the door. As they entered, some cards again
rose from the floor and beat against the wall.

The Easterner rushed to the stove. He was so profoundly chilled that he almost
dared to embrace the glowing iron. The Swede was not in the room. Johnnie sank into a
chair and, folding his arms on his knees, buried his face in them. Scully, warming one
foot and then the other at a rim of the stove, muttered to himself with Celtic mournful-
ness. The cowboy had removed his fur cap, and with a dazed and rueful air he was running one hand through his tousled locks. From overhead they could hear the creaking
of boards, as the Swede tramped here and there in his room.

The sad quiet was broken by the sudden flinging open of a door that led toward
the kitchen. It was instantly followed by an inrush of women. They precipitated themselves upon Johnnie amid a chorus of lamentation. Before they carried their prey off to
the kitchen, there to be bathed and harangued with that mixture of sympathy and abuse
which is a feat of their sex, the mother straightened herself and fixed old Scully with an
eye of stern reproach, "Shame be upon you, Patrick Scully!" she cried. "Your own son,
too. Shame be upon you!"

"There, now! Be quiet, now!" said the old man, weakly.

"Shame be upon you, Patrick Scully!" The girls, rallying to this slogan, sniffed disdainfully in the direction of those trembling accomplices, the cowboy and the Easterner.
Presently they bore Johnnie away, and left the three men to dismal reflection.

VII

"I'd like to fight this here Dutchman myself," said the cowboy, breaking a long   19⦁
silence.

Scully wagged his head sadly. "No, that wouldn't do. It wouldn't be right. It
wouldn't be right."

"Well, why wouldn't it?" argued the cowboy. "I don't see no harm in it."

"No," answered Scully, with mournful heroism. "It wouldn't be right. It was
Johnnie's fight, and now we mustn't whip the man just because he whipped Johnnie."

"Yes, that's true enough," said the cowboy; "but—he better not get fresh with me,
because I couldn't stand no more of it."

"You'll not say a word to him," commanded Scully, and even then they heard the   19⦁
tread of the Swede on the stairs. His entrance was made theatric. He swept the door
back with a bang and swaggered to the middle of the room. No one looked at him.
"Well," he cried, insolently, at Scully, "I s'pose you'll tell me now how much I owe you?"

The old man remained stolid. "You don't owe me nothin'."

"Huh!" said the Swede, "huh! Don't owe 'im nothin'."

The cowboy addressed the Swede. "Stranger, I don't see how you come to be so
gay around here."

Old Scully was instantly alert. "Stop!" he shouted, holding his hand forth, fingers
upward. "Bill, you shut up!"

The cowboy spat carelessly into the sawdust-box. "I didn't say a word, did I?"   20⦁
he asked.

"Mr. Scully," called the Swede, "how much do I owe you?" It was seen that he was
attired for departure, and that he had his valise in his hand.

"You don't owe me nothin'," repeated Scully in the same imperturbable way.

"Huh!" said the Swede. "I guess you're right. I guess if it was any way at all, you'd owe me somethin'. That's what I guess." He turned to the cowboy. "'Kill him! Kill him! Kill him!'" he mimicked, and then guffawed victoriously. "'Kill him!'" He was convulsed with ironical humour.

But he might have been jeering the dead. The three men were immovable and silent, staring with glassy eyes at the stove.

The Swede opened the door and passed into the storm, giving one derisive glance   205
backward at the still group.

As soon as the door was closed, Scully and the cowboy leaped to their feet and began to curse. They trampled to and fro, waving their arms and smashing into the air with their fists. "Oh, but that was a hard minute!" wailed Scully. "That was a hard minute! Him there leerin' and scoffin'! One bang at his nose was worth forty dollars to me that minute! How did you stand it, Bill?"

"How did I stand it?" cried the cowboy in a quivering voice. "How did I stand it? Oh!"

The old man burst into sudden brogue. "I'd loike to take that Swade," he wailed, "and hould 'im down on a shtone flure and bate 'im to a jelly wid a shtick!"

The cowboy groaned in sympathy. "I'd like to git him by the neck and hammer him"—he brought his hand down on a chair with a noise like a pistol-shot— "hammer that there Dutchman until he couldn't tell himself from a dead coyote!"

"I'd bate 'im until he—"   210

"I'd show *him* some things—"

And then together they raised a yearning, fanatic cry—"Oh-o-oh! if we only could—"

"Yes!"

"Yes!"

"And then I'd—"   215

"O-o-oh!"

VIII

The Swede, tightly gripping his valise, tacked across the face of the storm as if he carried sails. He was following a line of little naked, gasping trees which, he knew, must mark the way of the road. His face, fresh from the pounding of Johnnie's fists, felt more pleasure than pain in the wind and the driving snow. A number of square shapes loomed upon him finally, and he knew them as the houses of the main body of the town. He found a street and made travel along it, leaning heavily upon the wind whenever, at a corner, a terrific blast caught him.

He might have been in a deserted village. We picture the world as thick with conquering and elate humanity, but here, with the bugles of the tempest pealing, it was hard to imagine a peopled earth. One viewed the existence of man then as marvel, and conceded a glamour of wonder to these lice which were caused to cling to a whirling, fire-smitten, ice-locked, disease-stricken, space-lost bulb. The conceit of man was explained by this storm to be the very engine of life. One was a coxcomb not to die in it. However, the Swede found a saloon.

In front of it an indomitable red light was burning, and the snowflakes were made blood-colour as they flew through the circumscribed territory of the lamp's shining. The Swede pushed open the door of the saloon and entered. A sanded expanse was before him, and at the end of it four men sat about a table drinking. Down one side of the room extended a radiant bar, and its guardian was leaning upon his elbows listening to the talk of the men at the table. The Swede dropped his valise upon the floor and, smiling fraternally upon the barkeeper, said, "Gimme some whisky, will you?" The man placed a bottle, a whisky-glass, and a glass of ice-thick water upon the bar. The Swede poured himself an abnormal portion of whisky and drank it in three gulps. "Pretty bad night," remarked the bartender, indifferently. He was making the pretension of blindness which is usually a distinction of his class; but it could have been seen that he was furtively studying the half-erased blood-stains on the face of the Swede. "Bad night," he said again.

"Oh, it's good enough for me," replied the Swede, hardily, as he poured himself   220
some more whisky. The barkeeper took his coin and manoeuvred it through its reception by the highly nickelled cash-machine. A bell rang; a card labelled "20 cts." had appeared.

"No," continued the Swede, "this isn't too bad weather. It's good enough for me."

"So?" murmured the barkeeper, languidly.

The copious drams made the Swede's eyes swim, and he breathed a trifle heavier. "Yes, I like this weather. I like it. It suits me." It was apparently his design to impart a deep significance to these words.

"So?" murmured the bartender again. He turned to gaze dreamily at the scroll-like birds and bird-like scrolls which had been drawn with soap upon the mirrors in back of the bar.

"Well, I guess I'll take another drink," said the Swede, presently. "Have   225
something?"

"No, thanks; I'm not drinkin'," answered the bartender. Afterward he asked, "How did you hurt your face?"

The Swede immediately began to boast loudly. "Why, in a fight. I thumped the soul out of a man down here at Scully's hotel."

The interest of the four men at the table was at last aroused.

"Who was it?" said one.

"Johnnie Scully," blustered the Swede. "Son of the man what runs it. He will be   230
pretty near dead for some weeks, I can tell you. I made a nice thing of him. I did. He couldn't get up. They carried him in the house. Have a drink?"

Instantly the men in some subtle way encased themselves in reserve. "No, thanks," said one. The group was of curious formation. Two were prominent local business men; one was the district attorney; and one was a professional gambler of the kind known as "square." But a scrutiny of the group would not have enabled an observer to pick the gambler from the men of more reputable pursuits. He was, in fact, a man so delicate in manner, when among people of fair class, and so judicious in his choice of victims, that in the strictly masculine part of the town's life he had come to be explicitly trusted and admired. People called him a thoroughbred. The fear and contempt with which his craft was regarded were undoubtedly the reason why his quiet dignity shone conspicuous above the quiet dignity of men who might be merely hatters, billiard-markers, or grocery clerks. Beyond an occasional unwary traveller who came by rail, this gambler was supposed to prey solely upon reckless and senile farmers, who, when flush with good crops, drove into town in all the pride and confidence of an absolutely invulnerable stupidity. Hearing at times in circuitous fashion of the despoilment of such a farmer, the important men of Romper invariably laughed in contempt of the victim, and if they thought of the wolf at all, it was with a kind of pride at the knowledge that he would never dare think of attacking their wisdom and courage. Besides, it was popular that this gambler had a real wife and two real children in a neat cottage in a suburb, where he led an exemplary home life; and when any one even suggested a discrepancy in his character, the crowd immediately vociferated descriptions of this virtuous family circle. Then men who led exemplary home lives, and men who did not lead exemplary home lives, all subsided in a bunch, remarking that there was nothing more to be said.

However, when a restriction was placed upon him—as, for instance, when a strong clique of members of the new Pollywog Club refused to permit him, even as a spectator, to appear in the rooms of the organization—the candour and gentleness with which he accepted the judgment disarmed many of his foes and made his friends more desperately partisan. He invariably distinguished between himself and a respectable Romper man so quickly and frankly that his manner actually appeared to be a continual broadcast compliment.

And one must not forget to declare the fundamental fact of his entire position in Romper. It is irrefutable that in all affairs outside his business, in all matters that occur eternally and commonly between man and man, this thieving cardplayer was so generous, so just, so moral, that, in a contest, he could have put to flight the consciences of nine tenths of the citizens of Romper.

And so it happened that he was seated in this saloon with the two prominent local merchants and the district attorney.

The Swede continued to drink raw whisky, meanwhile babbling at the barkeeper   235
and trying to induce him to indulge in potations. "Come on. Have a drink. Come on. What—no? Well, have a little one, then. By gawd, I've whipped a man tonight, and I want to celebrate. I whipped him good, too. Gentlemen," the Swede cried to the men at the table, "have a drink?"

"Ssh!" said the barkeeper.

The group at the table, although furtively attentive, had been pretending to be deep in talk, but now a man lifted his eyes toward the Swede and said, shortly, "Thanks. We don't want any more."

At this reply the Swede ruffled out his chest like a rooster. "Well," he exploded, "it seems I can't get anybody to drink with me in this town. Seems so, don't it? Well!"

"Ssh!" said the barkeeper.

"Say," snarled the Swede, "don't you try to shut me up. I won't have it. I'm a   240
gentleman, and I want people to drink with me. And I want 'em to drink with me now. *Now*—do you understand?" He rapped the bar with his knuckles.

Years of experience had calloused the bartender. He merely grew sulky. "I hear you," he answered.

"Well," cried the Swede, "listen hard then. See those men over there? Well, they're going to drink with me, and don't you forget it. Now you watch."

"Hi!" yelled the barkeeper, "this won't do!"

"Why won't it?" demanded the Swede. He stalked over to the table, and by chance laid his hand upon the shoulder of the gambler. "How about this?" he asked wrathfully. "I asked you to drink with me."

The gambler simply twisted his head and spoke over his shoulder. "My friend, I   245
don't know you."

"Oh, hell!" answered the Swede, "come and have a drink."

"Now, my boy," advised the gambler, kindly, "take your hand off my shoulder and go 'way and mind your own business." He was a little, slim man, and it seemed strange to hear him use this tone of heroic patronage to the burly Swede. The other men at the table said nothing.

"What! You won't drink with me, you little dude? I'll make you, then! I'll make you!" The Swede had grasped the gambler frenziedly at the throat, and was dragging him from his chair. The other men sprang up. The barkeeper dashed around the corner of his bar. There was a great tumult, and then was seen a long blade in the hand of the gambler. It shot forward, and a human body, this citadel of virtue, wisdom, power, was pierced as easily as if it had been a melon. The Swede fell with a cry of supreme astonishment.

The prominent merchants and the district attorney must have at once tumbled out of the place backward. The bartender found himself hanging limply to the arm of a chair and gazing into the eyes of a murderer.

"Henry," said the latter, as he wiped his knife on one of the towels that hung   25 beneath the bar rail, "you tell 'em where to find me. I'll be home, waiting for 'em." Then he vanished. A moment afterward the barkeeper was in the street dinning through the storm for help and, moreover, companionship.

The corpse of the Swede, alone in the saloon, had its eyes fixed upon a dreadful legend that dwelt atop the cash-machine: "This registers the amount of your purchase."

IX

Months later, the cowboy was frying pork over the stove of a little ranch near the Dakota line, when there was a quick thud of hoofs outside, and presently the Easterner entered with the letters and the papers.

"Well," said the Easterner at once, "the chap that killed the Swede has got three years. Wasn't much, was it?"

"He has? Three years?" The cowboy poised his pan of pork, while he ruminated upon the news. "Three years. That ain't much."

"No. It was a light sentence," replied the Easterner as he unbuckled his spurs.   25 "Seems there was a good deal of sympathy for him in Romper."

"If the bartender had been any good," observed the cowboy, thoughtfully, "he would have gone in and cracked that there Dutchman on the head with a bottle in the beginnin' of it and stopped all this here murderin'."

"Yes, a thousand things might have happened," said the Easterner, tartly.

The cowboy returned his pan of pork to the fire, but his philosophy continued. "It's funny, ain't it? If he hadn't said Johnnie was cheatin' he'd be alive this minute. He was an awful fool. Game played for fun, too. Not for money. I believe he was crazy."

"I feel sorry for that gambler," said the Easterner.

"Oh, so do I," said the cowboy. "He don't deserve none of it for killin' who he did."   26

"The Swede might not have been killed if everything had been square."

"Might not have been killed?" exclaimed the cowboy. "Everythin' square? Why, when he said that Johnnie was cheatin' and acted like such a jackass? And then in the saloon he fairly walked up to git hurt?" With these arguments the cowboy browbeat the Easterner and reduced him to rage.

"You're a fool!" cried the Easterner, viciously. "You're a bigger jackass than the Swede by a million majority. Now let me tell you one thing. Let me tell you something. Listen! Johnnie *was* cheating!"

"'Johnnie,'" said the cowboy, blankly. There was a minute of silence, and then he said, robustly, "Why, no. The game was only for fun."

"Fun or not," said the Easterner, "Johnnie was cheating. I saw him. I know it. I saw   26 him. And I refused to stand up and be a man. I let the Swede fight it out alone. And you—you were simply puffing around the place wanting to fight. And then old Scully himself! We are all in it! This poor gambler isn't even a noun. He is a kind of an adverb. Every sin is the result of collaboration. We, five of us, have collaborated in the murder of this Swede. Usually there are from a dozen to forty women really involved in every murder, but in this case it seems to be only five men—you, I, Johnnie, old Scully; and that fool of an unfortunate gambler came merely as a culmination, the apex of a human movement, and gets all the punishment."

The cowboy, injured and rebellious, cried out blindly into this fog of mysterious theory: "Well, I didn't do anythin', did I?"

QUESTIONS

1. Describe the conflict in the story. Why is the Swede the major antagonist? How could he be seen as protagonist, instead of antagonist? Why do the others stress his identity as a Swede, and why is he never named?

2. Consider the Easterner's analysis (paragraph 90) as a plausible explanation of the Swede's behavior before the fight. How fully does this analysis explain these actions? How could the analysis be used in an argument that "The Blue Hotel" is a critique of conventional, dime-store views of the wild west?

3. Analyze the structure of the story. What relationship do the parts of abstract formal structure (described on pp. 112–13) have to the part divisions marked by Crane himself? Why is most of the story about events at the Blue Hotel, and why do events at the saloon, where the murder occurs, occupy only a small section? Explain, in relation to the story's structure, why we do not learn until the very end that Johnny actually *was* cheating.

4. How adequately does the Easterner's "noun-adverb" analysis in the concluding paragraphs explain the events of the story? Could such events be stopped at a certain point, or are they inevitable regardless of the Easterner's theory about collaborative control and responsibility?

THOMAS HARDY   (1840–1928)

Hardy was born in Dorsetshire, in southwest England, which he called "Wessex" in his novels and poems. He began a career as an architect but gave it up to become a novelist. In 1898, after he had published his stories and more than a dozen novels, including Tess of the D'Urbervilles, The Return of the Native, *and* Jude the Obscure, *he gave up novels and devoted himself to poetry. Before his death in 1928, he had published eight volumes of verse, which were collected and published posthumously in 1931.*

The Three Strangers _____ 1888

Among the few features of agricultural England which retain an appearance but little modified by the lapse of centuries may be reckoned the high, grassy and furzy downs, coombs, or ewe-leases, as they are indifferently called, that fill a large area of certain counties in the south and southwest. If any mark of human occupation is met with hereon, it usually takes the form of the solitary cottage of some shepherd.

Fifty years ago such a lonely cottage stood on such a down, and may possibly be standing there now. In spite of its loneliness, however, the spot, by actual measurement, was not more than five miles from a county-town. Yet that affected it little. Five miles of irregular upland, during the long inimical seasons, with their sleets, snows, rains, and mists, afford withdrawing space enough to isolate a Timon or a Nebuchadnezzar;° much less, in fair weather, to please that less repellent tribe, the poets, philosophers, artists, and others who "conceive and meditate of pleasant things."

Some old earthen camp or barrow, some clump of trees, at least some starved fragment of ancient hedge is usually taken advantage of in the erection of these forlorn dwellings. But, in the present case, such a kind of shelter had been disregarded. Higher Crowstairs, as the house was called, stood quite detached and undefended. The only reason for its precise situation seemed to be the crossing of two footpaths at right angles hard by, which may have crossed there and thus for a good five hundred years. Hence the house was exposed to the elements on all sides. But, though the wind up here blew unmistakably when it did blow, and the rain hit hard whenever it fell, the various weathers of the winter season were not quite so formidable on the coomb as they were imagined to be by dwellers on low ground. The raw rimes° were not so pernicious as in the hollows, and the frosts were scarcely so severe. When the shepherd and his family who tenanted the house were pitied for their sufferings from the exposure, they said that upon the whole they were less inconvenienced by "wuzzes and flames" (hoarses and phlegms) than when they had lived by the stream of a snug neighboring valley.

The night of March 28, 182–, was precisely one of the nights that were wont to call forth these expressions of commiseration. The level rainstorm smote walls, slopes, and hedges like the clothyard shafts of Senlac and Crécy.° Such sheep and outdoor animals as had no shelter stood with their buttocks to the winds; while the tails of little birds trying to roost on some scraggy thorn were blown inside-out like umbrellas. The gable-end of the cottage was stained with wet, and the eavesdroppings flapped against the wall. Yet never was commiseration for the shepherd more misplaced. For that cheerful rustic was entertaining a large party in glorification of the christening of his second girl.

The guests had arrived before the rain began to fall, and they were all now assembled in the chief or living room of the dwelling. A glance into the apartment at eight o'clock on this eventful evening would have resulted in the opinion that it was as cozy and comfortable a nook as could be wished for in boisterous weather. The calling of its inhabitant was proclaimed by a number of highly polished sheep crooks without stems that were hung ornamentally over the fireplace, the curl of each shining crook varying from the antiquated type engraved in the patriarchal pictures of old family Bibles to the most approved fashion of the last local sheep-fair. The room was lighted by half a dozen candles having wicks only a trifle smaller than the grease which enveloped them, in candlesticks that were never used but at high-days, holy-days, and family feasts. The lights were scattered about the room, two of them standing on the chimney piece. This position of candles was in itself significant. Candles on the chimney piece always meant a party.

Timon or a Nebuchadnezzar: Both were proverbial for their solitude. The ancient Greek Timon was disappointed because he did not receive the advancement he expected, and he therefore withdrew from society totally. Nebuchadnezzar was the Babylonian king who, suffering from the delusion that he was an ox, was driven away from society to eat with beasts (Daniel 4).

raw rimes: coatings of frost.

clothyard shafts of Senlac and Crécy: Clothyard shafts were thirty-six inch arrows. Senlac and Crécy were battlefields in France where, in the Middle Ages, armies of English bowmen defeated numerically superior French forces.

On the hearth, in front of a back-brand° to give substance, blazed a fire of thorns, that crackled "like the laughter of the fool."°

Nineteen persons were gathered here. Of these, five women, wearing gowns of various bright hues, sat in chairs along the wall; girls shy and not shy filled the window-bench; four men, including Charley Jake the hedge-carpenter, Elijah New the parish-clerk, and John Pitcher, a neighboring dairyman, the shepherd's father-in-law, lolled in the settle; a young man and maid, who were blushing over tentative *pourparlers* on a life-companionship,° sat beneath the corner-cupboard; and an elderly engaged man of fifty or upward moved restlessly about from spots where his betrothed was not to the spot where she was. Enjoyment was pretty general, and so much the more prevailed in being unhampered by conventional restrictions. Absolute confidence in each other's good opinion begat perfect ease, while the finishing stroke of manner, amounting to a truly princely serenity, was lent to the majority by the absence of any expression or trait denoting that they wished to get on in the world, enlarge their minds, or do any eclipsing thing whatever—which nowadays so generally nips the bloom and *bonhomie* of all except the two extremes of the social scale.

Shepherd Fennel had married well, his wife being a dairyman's daughter from a vale at a distance, who brought fifty guineas in her pocket and kept them there, till they should be required for ministering to the needs of a coming family. This frugal woman had been somewhat exercised as to the character that should be given to the gathering. A sit-still party had its advantages; but an undisturbed position of ease in chairs and settles was apt to lead on the men to such an unconscionable deal of toping that they would sometimes fairly drink the house dry. A dancing-party was the alternative; but this, while avoiding the foregoing objection on the score of good drink, had a counterbalancing disadvantage in the matter of good victuals, the ravenous appetites engendered by the exercise causing immense havoc in the buttery. Shepherdess Fennel fell back upon the intermediate plan of mingling short dances with short periods of talk and singing, so as to hinder any ungovernable rage in either. But this scheme was entirely confined to her own gentle mind: the shepherd himself was in the mood to exhibit the most reckless phases of hospitality.

The fiddler was a boy of those parts, about twelve years of age, who had a wonderful dexterity in jigs and reels, though his fingers were so small and short as to necessitate a constant shifting for the high notes, from which he scrambled back to the first position with sounds not of unmixed purity of tone. At seven the shrill tweedle-dee of this youngster had begun, accompanied by a booming ground-bass from Elijah New, the parish-clerk, who had thoughtfully brought with him his favorite musical instrument, the serpent. Dancing was instantaneous, Mrs. Fennel privately enjoining the players on no account to let the dance exceed the length of a quarter of an hour.

But Elijah and the boy, in the excitement of their position, quite forgot the injunction. Moreover, Oliver Giles, a man of seventeen, one of the dancers, who was enamored of his partner, a fair girl of thirty-three rolling years, had recklessly handed a new crown-piece to the musicians, as a bribe to keep going as long as they had muscle and wind. Mrs. Fennel, seeing the steam begin to generate on the countenances of her guests, crossed over and touched the fiddler's elbow and put her hand on the serpent's mouth. But they took no notice, and fearing she might lose her character of genial

10

---

back-brand: a back-log, a big log or branch placed at the back of a fire.
"like the laughter of the fool": Ecclesiastes 7:6.
pourparlers on a life-companionship: conversations held prior to the negotiation of a marriage.

hostess if she were to interfere too markedly, she retired and sat down helpless. And so the dance whizzed on with cumulative fury, the performers moving in their planet-like courses, direct and retrograde, from apogee to perigee, till the hand of the well-kicked clock at the bottom of the room had traveled over the circumference of an hour.

While these cheerful events were in course of enactment within Fennel's pastoral dwelling, an incident having considerable bearing on the party had occurred in the gloomy night without. Mrs. Fennel's concern about the growing fierceness of the dance corresponded in point of time with the ascent of a human figure to the solitary hill of Higher Crowstairs from the direction of the distant town. This personage strode on through the rain without a pause, following the little-worn path which, further on in its course, skirted the shepherd's cottage.

It was nearly the time of full moon, and on this account, though the sky was lined with a uniform sheet of dripping cloud, ordinary objects out of doors were readily visible. The sad, wan light revealed the lonely pedestrian to be a man of supple frame; his gait suggested that he had somewhat passed the period of perfect and instinctive agility, though not so far as to be otherwise than rapid of motion when occasion required. At a rough guess, he might have been about forty years of age. He appeared tall, but a recruit-ing sergeant, or other person accustomed to the judging of men's heights by the eye, would have discerned that this was chiefly owing to his gauntness, and that he was not more than five-feet eight or nine.

Notwithstanding the regularity of his tread, there was caution in it, as in that of one who mentally feels his way; and despite the fact that it was not a black coat nor a dark garment of any sort that he wore, there was something about him which suggested that he naturally belonged to the black-coated tribes of men. His clothes were of fustian,° and his boots hobnailed, yet in his progress he showed not the mud-accustomed bearing of hobnailed and fustianed peasantry.

By the time that he had arrived abreast of the shepherd's premises the rain came down, or rather came along, with yet more determined violence. The outskirts of the little settlement partially broke the force of wind and rain, and this induced him to stand still. The most salient of the shepherd's domestic erections was an empty sty at the for-ward corner of his hedgeless garden, for in these latitudes the principle of masking the homelier features of your establishment by a conventional frontage was unknown. The traveler's eye was attracted to this small building by the pallid shine of the wet slates that covered it. He turned aside, and, finding it empty, stood under the pent-roof for shelter.

While he stood, the boom of the serpent within the adjacent house, and the lesser strains of the fiddler, reached the spot as an accompaniment to the surging hiss of the flying rain on the sod, its louder beating on the cabbage-leaves of the garden, on the eight or ten beehives just discernible by the path, and its dripping from the eaves into a row of buckets and pans that had been placed under the walls of the cottage. For at Higher Crowstairs, as at all such elevated domiciles, the grand difficulty of housekeeping was an insufficiency of water; and a casual rainfall was utilized by turning out, as catchers, every utensil that the house contained. Some queer stories might be told of the con-trivances for economy in suds and dishwaters that are absolutely necessitated in upland habitations during the droughts of summer. But at this season there were no such exi-gencies; a mere acceptance of what the skies bestowed was sufficient for an abundant store.

fustian: a thick, coarse cloth.

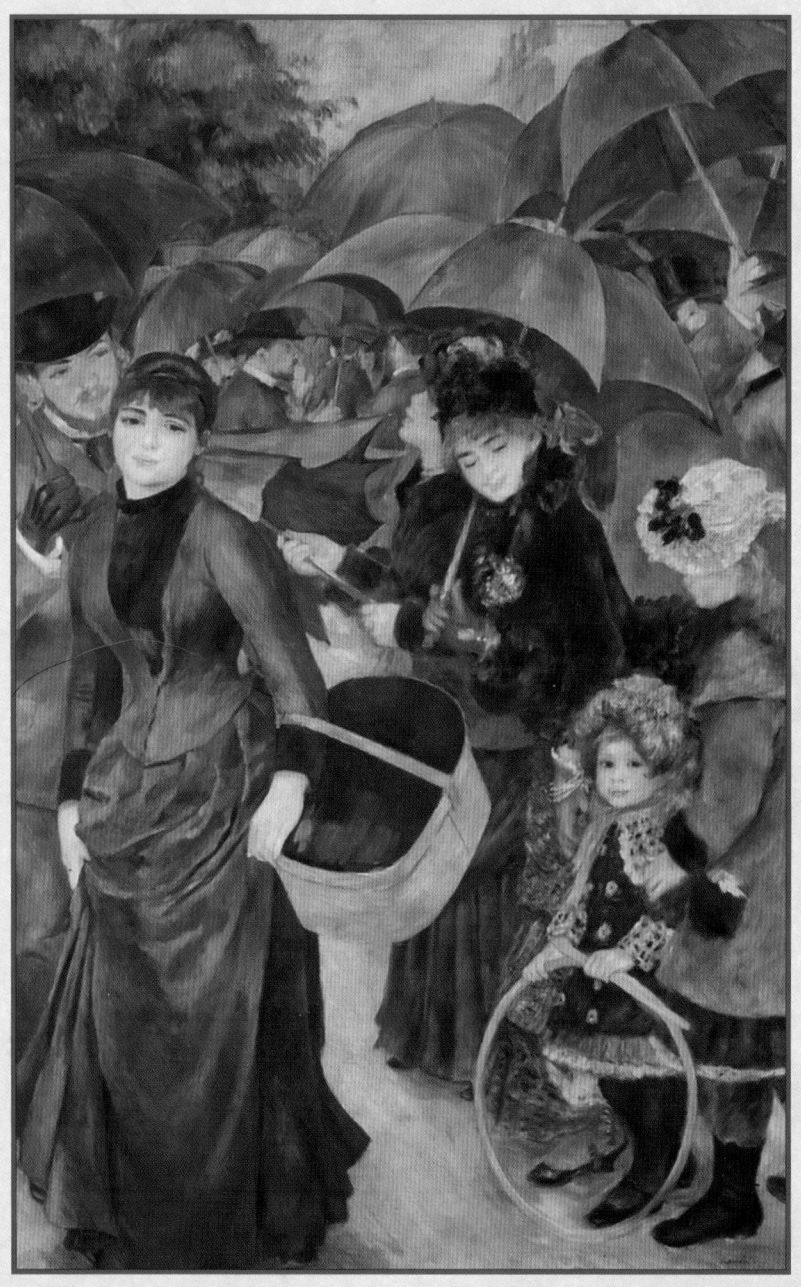

Auguste Renoir, *The Umbrellas (Les Parapluies)*, c. 1881-1886.
Oil on canvas, 180.3 x 114.9 cm. DN 93837. National Gallery,
London, England. Bridgeman/Art Resource, New York, NY.

Henri Matisse, *Harmony in Red (The Red Room)*, 1908–1909. Oil on canvas, 70 7/8 x 86 5/8 in. The Hermitage, St. Petersburg, Russia. George Roos/Art Resource, New York, NY.

At last the notes of the serpent ceased and the house was silent. This cessation of activity aroused the solitary pedestrian from the reverie into which he had elapsed, and, emerging from the shed, with an apparently new intention, he walked up the path to the house-door. Arrived here, his first act was to kneel down on a large stone beside the row of vessels, and to drink a copious draught from one of them. Having quenched his thirst, he rose and lifted his hand to knock, but paused with his eye upon the panel. Since the dark surface of the wood revealed absolutely nothing, it was evident that he must be mentally looking through the door, as if he wished to measure thereby all the possibilities that a house of this sort might include, and how they might bear upon the question of his entry.

In his indecision he turned and surveyed the scene around. Not a soul was anywhere visible. The garden path stretched downward from his feet, gleaming like the track of a snail; the roof of the little well (mostly dry), the well-cover, the top rail of the garden-gate, were varnished with the same dull liquid glaze; while, far away in the vale, a faint whiteness of more than usual extent showed that the rivers were high in the meads. Beyond all this winked a few bleared lamplights through the beating drops—lights that denoted the situation of the county-town from which he had appeared to come. The absence of all notes of life in that direction seemed to clinch his intentions, and he knocked at the door.

Within, a desultory chat had taken the place of movement and musical sound. The hedge-carpenter was suggesting a song to the company, which nobody just then was inclined to undertake, so that the knock afforded a not unwelcome diversion.

"Walk in!" said the shepherd, promptly.

The latch clicked upward, and out of the night our pedestrian appeared upon the door-mat. The shepherd arose, snuffed two of the nearest candles, and turned to look at him.

Their light disclosed that the stranger was dark in complexion and not unprepossessing as to feature. His hat, which for a moment he did not remove, hung low over his eyes, without concealing that they were large, open, and determined, moving with a flash rather than a glance round the room. He seemed pleased with his survey, and, baring his shaggy head, said, in a rich, deep voice: "The rain is so heavy friends, that I ask leave to come in and rest awhile."

"To be sure, Stranger," said the shepherd. "And faith, you've been lucky in choosing your time, for we are having a bit of a fling for a glad cause—though, to be sure, a man could hardly wish that glad cause to happen more than once a year."

"Nor less," spoke up a woman. "For 'tis best to get your family over and done with, as soon as you can, so as to be all the earlier out of the fag o't."

"And what may be this glad cause?" asked the stranger.

"A birth and christening," said the shepherd.

The stranger hoped his host might not be made unhappy either by too many or too few of such episodes and, being invited by a gesture to a pull at the mug, he readily acquiesced. His manner, which, before entering, had been so dubious, was now altogether that of a careless and candid man.

"Late to be traipsing athwart this coom—hey?" said the engaged man of fifty.

"Late it is, Master, as you say.—I'll take a seat in the chimney corner, if you have nothing to urge against it, Ma'am; for I am a little moist on the side that was next the rain."

Mrs. Shepherd Fennel assented, and made room for the self-invited comer, who, having got completely inside the chimney corner, stretched out his legs and arms with the expansiveness of a person quite at home.

20

25

"Yes, I am rather cracked in the vamp," he said freely, seeing that the eyes of the   30
shepherd's wife fell upon his boots, "and I am not well fitted either. I have had some
rough times lately, and have been forced to pick up what I can get in the way of wearing,
but I must find a suit better fit for working-days when I reach home."

"One of hereabouts?" she inquired.

"Not quite that—further up the country."

"I thought so. And so be I; and by your tongue you come from my neighborhood."

"But you would hardly have heard of me," he said quickly. "My time would be long
before yours, Ma'am, you see."

This testimony to the youthfulness of his hostess had the effect of stopping her   35
cross-examination.

"There is only one thing more wanted to make me happy," continued the newcomer, "and that is a little baccy, which I am sorry to say I am out of."

"I'll fill your pipe," said the shepherd.

"I must ask you to lend me a pipe likewise."

"A smoker, and no pipe about 'ee?"

"I have dropped it somewhere on the road."   40

The shepherd filled and handed him a new clay pipe, saying, as he did so, "Hand
me your baccy-box—I'll fill that too, now I am about it."

The man went through the movement of searching his pockets.

"Lost that too?" said his entertainer, with some surprise.

"I am afraid so," said the man with some confusion. "Give it to me in a screw of
paper." Lighting his pipe at the candle with a suction that drew the whole flame into
the bowl, he resettled himself in the corner and bent his looks upon the faint steam
from his damp legs, as if he wished to say no more.

Meanwhile the general body of guests had been taking little notice of this visitor   45
by reason of an absorbing discussion in which they were engaged with the band about a
tune for the next dance. The matter being settled, they were about to stand up when
an interruption came in the shape of another knock at the door.

At sound of the same the man in the chimney corner took up the poker and
began stirring the brands as if doing it thoroughly were the one aim of his existence;
and a second time the shepherd said, "Walk in!" In a moment another man stood upon
the straw-woven door-mat. He too was a stranger.

This individual was one of a type radically different from the first. There was more
of the commonplace in his manner, and a certain jovial cosmopolitanism sat upon his
features. He was several years older than the first arrival, his hair being slightly frosted, his
eyebrows bristly, and his whiskers cut back from his cheeks. His face was rather full and
flabby, and yet it was not altogether a face without power. A few grog-blossoms marked the
neighborhood of his nose. He flung back his long drab greatcoat, revealing that beneath
it he wore a suit of cinder-gray shade throughout, large heavy seals, of some metal or
other that would take a polish, dangling from his fob as his only personal ornament.
Shaking the water drops from his low-crowned glazed hat, he said, "I must ask for a few
minutes' shelter, comrades, or I shall be wetted to my skin before I get to Casterbridge."

"Make yourself at home, Master," said the shepherd, perhaps a trifle less heartily
than on the first occasion. Not that Fennel had the least tinge of niggardliness in his
composition; but the room was far from large, spare chairs were not numerous, and
damp companions were not altogether desirable at close quarters for the women and
girls in their bright-colored gowns.

However, the second comer, after taking off his greatcoat, and hanging his hat on
a nail in one of the ceiling-beams as if he had been specially invited to put it there,

advanced and sat down at the table. This had been pushed so closely into the chimney corner, to give all available room to the dancers, that its inner edge grazed the elbow of the man who had ensconced himself by the fire; and thus the two strangers were brought into close companionship. They nodded to each other by way of breaking the ice of unacquaintance, and the first stranger handed his neighbor the family mug—a huge vessel of brown ware, having its upper edge worn away like a threshold by the rub of whole generations of thirsty lips that had gone the way of all flesh, and bearing the following inscription burnt upon its rotund side in yellow letters:

THERE IS NO FUN
UNTIL i CUM

The other man, nothing loath, raised the mug to his lips, and drank on, and on, and on—till a curious blueness overspread the countenance of the shepherd's wife, who had regarded with no little surprise the first stranger's free offer to the second of what did not belong to him to dispense.

"I knew it!" said the toper to the shepherd with much satisfaction. "When I walked   50
up your garden before coming in, and saw the hives all of a row, I said to myself, 'Where there's bees there's honey, and where there's honey there's mead.' But mead of such a truly comfortable sort as this I really didn't expect to meet in my older days." He took yet another pull at the mug, till it assumed an ominous elevation.

"Glad you enjoy it!" said the shepherd, warmly.

"It is goodish mead," assented Mrs. Fennel, with an absence of enthusiasm which seemed to say that it was possible to buy praise for one's cellar at too heavy a price. "It is trouble enough to make—and really I hardly think we shall make any more. For honey sells well, and we ourselves can make shift with a drop o' small mead and metheglin° for common use from the comb-washings."

"Oh, but you'll never have the heart!" reproachfully cried the stranger in cinder-gray, after taking up the mug a third time and setting it down empty. "I love mead, when 'tis old like this, as I love to go to church o' Sundays, or to relieve the needy any day of the week."

"Ha, ha, ha!" said the man in the chimney corner, who, in spite of the taciturnity induced by the pipe of tobacco, could not or would not refrain from this slight testimony to his comrade's humor.

Now the old mead of those days, brewed of the purest first-year or maiden honey,   55
four pounds to the gallon—with its due complement of white of eggs, cinnamon, ginger, cloves, mace, rosemary, yeast, and processes of working, bottling, and cellaring—tasted remarkably strong; but it did not taste so strong as it actually was. Hence, presently, the stranger in cinder-gray at the table, moved by its creeping influence, unbuttoned his waistcoat, threw himself back in his chair, spread his legs, and made his presence felt in various ways.

"Well, well, as I say," he resumed, "I am going to Casterbridge, and to Casterbridge I must go. I should have been almost there by this time; but the rain drove me into your dwelling, and I'm not sorry for it."

"You don't live in Casterbridge?" said the shepherd.

"Not as yet; though I shortly mean to move there."

---

mead and metheglin: Mead is an alcoholic drink made from honey. Metheglin was a cheaper drink made with spices and water rinsed from the honeycomb after the better honey was extracted. See paragraph 55.

"Going to set up in trade, perhaps?"

"No, no," said the shepherd's wife. "It is easy to see that the gentleman is rich, 60
and don't want to work at anything."

The cinder-gray stranger paused, as if to consider whether he would accept that
definition of himself. He presently rejected it by answering, "Rich is not quite the word
for me, Dame. I do work, and I must work. And even if I only get to Casterbridge by
midnight I must begin work there at eight tomorrow morning. Yes, het or wet, blow or
snow, famine or sword, my day's work tomorrow must be done."

"Poor man! Then, in spite o' seeming, you be worse off than we," replied the shepherd's wife.

"'Tis the nature of my trade, men and maidens. 'Tis the nature of my trade more
than my poverty. . . . But really and truly I must up and off, or I shan't get a lodging in
the town." However, the speaker did not move, and directly added, "There's time for
one more draught of friendship before I go; and I'd perform it at once if the mug were
not dry."

"Here's a mug o' small," said Mrs. Fennel. "Small, we call it, though to be sure 'tis
only the first wash o' the combs."

No," said the stranger, disdainfully. "I won't spoil your first kindness by partaking 65
o' your second."

"Certainly not," broke in Fennel. "We don't increase and multiply every day, and
I'll fill the mug again." He went away to the dark place under the stairs where the barrel
stood. The shepherdess followed him.

"Why should you do this?" she said, reproachfully, as soon as they were alone.
"He's emptied it once, though it held enough for ten people; and now he's not contented wi' the small, but must needs call for more o' the strong! And a stranger unbe-
known to any of us. For my part, I don't like the look o' the man at all."

"But he's in the house, my honey; and 'tis a wet night, and a christening. Daze it,
what's a cup of mead more or less? There'll be plenty more next bee-burning."

"Very well—this time, then," she answered, looking wistfully at the barrel. "But what
is the man's calling, and where is he one of, that he should come in and join us like this?"

"I don't know. I'll ask him again."   70

The catastrophe of having the mug drained dry at one pull by the stranger in
cinder-gray was effectually guarded against this time by Mrs. Fennel. She poured out his
allowance in a small cup, keeping the large one at a discreet distance from him. When
he had tossed off his portion the shepherd renewed his inquiry about the stranger's
occupation.

The latter did not immediately reply, and the man in the chimney corner, with
sudden demonstrativeness, said, "Anybody may know my trade—I'm a wheelwright."

"A very good trade for these parts," said the shepherd.

"And anybody may know mine—if they've the sense the find it out," said the
stranger in cinder-gray.

"You may generally tell what a man is by his claws," observed the hedge-carpenter, 75
looking at his own hands. "My fingers be as full of thorns as an old pincushion is of pins."

The hands of the man in the chimney corner instinctively sought the shade, and
he gazed into the fire as he resumed his pipe. The man at the table took up the hedge-
carpenter's remark, and added smartly, "True; but the oddity of my trade is that, instead
of setting a mark upon me, it sets a mark upon my customers."

No observation being offered by anybody in elucidation of this enigma, the shepherd's wife once more called for a song. The same obstacles presented themselves as at

the former time—one had no voice, another had forgotten the first verse. The stranger at the table, whose soul had now risen to a good working temperature, relieved the difficulty by exclaiming that, to start the company, he would sing himself. Thrusting one thumb into the armhold of his waistcoat, he waved the other hand in the air, and, with an extemporizing gaze at the shining sheepcrooks above the mantelpiece, began:

> O my trade it is the rarest one,
>> Simple shepherds all—
> My trade is a sight to see;
> For my customers I tie, and take them up on high,
>> And waft 'em to a far countree!

The room was silent when he had finished the verse—with one exception, that of the man in the chimney corner, who at the singer's word, "Chorus!" joined him in a deep bass voice of musical relish:

> And waft 'em to a far countree!

Oliver Giles, John Pitcher the dairyman, the parish-clerk, the engaged man of fifty, the row of young women against the wall, seemed lost in thought not of the gayest kind. The shepherd looked meditatively on the ground, the shepherdess gazed keenly at the singer, and with some suspicion; she was doubting whether this stranger were merely singing an old song from recollection, or was composing one there and then for the occasion. All were as perplexed at the obscure revelation as the guests at Belshazzar's Feast,° except the man in the chimney corner, who quietly said, "Second verse, stranger," and smoked on.

The singer thoroughly moistened himself from his lips inward, and went on with the next stanza as requested:

> My tools are but common ones,
>> Simple shepherds all—
> My tools are no sight to see:
> A little hempen string, and a post whereon to swing,
>> Are implements enough for me!

Shepherd Fennel glanced round. There was no longer any doubt that the stranger was answering his question rhythmically. The guests one and all started back with suppressed exclamations. The young woman engaged to the man of fifty fainted halfway, and would have proceeded, but finding him wanting in alacrity for catching her she sat down trembling.

"Oh, he's the!" whispered the people in the background, mentioning the name of an ominous public officer. "He's come to do it! 'Tis to be at Casterbridge jail tomorrow—the man for sheep-stealing—the poor clockmaker we heard of, who used to live at Shottsford and had no work to do—Timothy Summers, whose family were astarving, and so he went out of Shottsford by the highroad, and took a sheep in open daylight, defying the farmer and the farmer's wife and the farmer's lad, and every man jack

80

Belshazzar's Feast: where the famous handwriting on the wall predicting the downfall of the ancient Babylonian kingdom happened (Daniel 5).

among 'em. He" (and they nodded toward the stranger of the deadly trade) "is come from up the country to do it because there's not enough to do in his own county-town, and he's got the place here now our own county-man's dead; he's going to live in the same cottage under the prison wall."

The stranger in cinder-gray took no notice of this whispered string of observations, but again wetted his lips. Seeing that his friend in the chimney corner was the only one who reciprocated his joviality in any way, he held out his cup toward that appreciative comrade, who also held out his own. They clinked together, the eyes of the rest of the room hanging upon the singer's actions. He parted his lips for the third verse; but at that moment another knock was audible upon the door. This time the knock was faint and hesitating.

The company seemed scared; the shepherd looked with consternation toward the entrance, and it was with some effort that he resisted his alarmed wife's deprecatory glance, and uttered for the third time the welcoming words, "Walk in!"

The door was gently opened, and another man stood upon the mat. He, like those who had preceded him, was a stranger. This time it was a short, small personage, of fair complexion, and dressed in a decent suit of dark clothes.

"Can you tell me the way to—?" he began: when, gazing round the room to observe the nature of the company among whom he had fallen, his eyes lighted on the stranger in cinder-gray. It was just at the instant when the latter, who had thrown his mind into his song with such a will that he scarcely heeded the interruption, silenced all whispers and inquiries by bursting into his third verse:

> Tomorrow is my working day,
> > Simple shepherds all—
> Tomorrow is a working day for me:
> For the farmer's sheep is slain, and the lad who did it ta'en,
> And on his soul may God ha' merc-y!

The stranger in the chimney corner, waving cups with the singer so heartily that his mead splashed over on the hearth, repeated in his bass voice as before:

> And on his soul may God ha' merc-y!

All this time the third stranger had been standing in the doorway. Finding now   85
that he did not come forward or go on speaking, the guests particularly regarded him. They noticed to their surprise that he stood before them the picture of abject terror—his knees trembling, his hand shaking so violently that the door-latch by which he supported himself rattled audibly: his white lips were parted, and his eyes fixed on the merry officer of justice in the middle of the room. A moment more and he had turned, closed the door, and fled.

"What a man can it be?" said the shepherd.

The rest, between the awfulness of their late discovery and the odd conduct of this third visitor, looked as if they knew not what to think, and said nothing. Instinctively they withdrew further and further from the grim gentleman in their midst, whom some of them seemed to take for the Prince of Darkness° himself, till they formed a remote circle, an empty space of floor being left between them and him—

Prince of Darkness: the devil.

. . . circulas, cujus centrum diabolus.°

The room was so silent—though there were more than twenty people in it—that nothing could be heard but the patter of the rain against the window-shutters, accompanied by the occasional hiss of a stray drop that fell down the chimney into the fire, and the steady puffing of the man in the corner, who had now resumed his pipe of long clay.

The stillness was unexpectedly broken. The distant sound of a gun reverberated through the air—apparently from the direction of the county-town.

"Be jiggered!" cried the stranger who had sung the song, jumping up.

"What does that mean?" asked several.

"A prisoner escaped from the jail—that's what it means."

All listened. The sound was repeated, and none of them spoke but the man in the chimney corner, who said quietly, "I've often been told that in this county they fire a gun at such times; but I never heard it till now."

"I wonder if it is *my* man?" murmured the personage in cinder-gray.

"Surely it is!" said the shepherd involuntarily. "And surely we've zeed him! That little man who looked in at the door by now, and quivered like a leaf when he zeed ye and heard your song!"

"His teeth chattered, and the breath went out of his body," said the dairyman.

"And his heart seemed to sink within him like a stone," said Oliver Giles.

"And he bolted as if he'd been shot at," said the hedge-carpenter.

"True—his teeth chattered, and his heart seemed to sink; and he bolted as if he'd been shot at," slowly summed up the man in the chimney corner.

"I didn't notice it," remarked the hangman.

"We were all awondering what made him run off in such a fright," faltered one of the women against the wall, "and now 'tis explained!"

The firing of the alarm-gun went on at intervals, low and sullenly, and their suspicions became a certainty. The sinister gentleman in cinder-gray roused himself. "Is there a constable here?" he asked, in thick tones. "If so, let him step forward."

The engaged man of fifty stepped quavering out from the wall, his betrothed beginning to sob on the back of the chair.

"You are a sworn constable?"

"I be, Sir."

"Then pursue the criminal at once, with assistance, and bring him back here. He can't have gone far."

"I will, Sir, I will—when I've got my staff. I'll go home and get it, and come sharp here, and start in a body."

"Staff!—never mind your staff; the man'll be gone!"

"But I can't do nothing without my staff—can I, William, and John, and Charles Jake? No; for there's the king's royal crown apainted on en in yaller and gold, and the lion and the unicorn, so as when I raise en up and hit my prisoner, 'tis made a lawful blow thereby. I wouldn't 'tempt to take up a man without my staff—no, not I. If I hadn't the law to gie me courage, why, instead o' my taking up him he might take up me!"

circulas, cujus centrum diabolus: circles, whose center [is] the devil.

"Now, I'm a king's man myself, and can give you authority enough for this," said the formidable officer in gray. "Now then, all of ye, be ready. Have ye any lanterns?"

"Yes—have ye any lanterns? I demand it!" said the constable.   110

"And the rest of you able-bodied—"

"Able-bodied men—yes—the rest of ye!" said the constable.

"Have you some good stout staves and pitchforks—"

"Staves and pitchforks—in the name o' the law! And take 'em in yer hands and go in quest, and do as we in authority tell ye!"

Thus aroused, the men prepared to give chase. The evidence was, indeed, though   115 circumstantial, so convincing, that but little argument was needed to show the shepherd's guests that after what they had seen it would look very much like connivance if they did not instantly pursue the unhappy third stranger, who could not as yet have gone more than a few hundred yards over such uneven country.

A shepherd is always well provided with lanterns; and, lighting these hastily, and with hurdle-staves in their hands, they poured out of the door, taking a direction along the crest of the hill, away from the town, the rain having fortunately a little abated.

Disturbed by the noise, or possibly by unpleasant dreams of her baptism, the child who had been christened began to cry heart-brokenly in the room overhead. These notes of grief came down through the chinks of the floor to the ears of the women below, who jumped up one by one, and seemed glad of the excuse to ascend and comfort the baby, for the incidents of the last half-hour greatly oppressed them. Thus in the space of two or three minutes the room on the ground-floor was deserted quite.

But it was not for long. Hardly had the sound of footsteps died away when a man returned round the corner of the house from the direction the pursuers had taken. Peeping in at the door, and seeing nobody there, he entered leisurely. It was the stranger of the chimney corner, who had gone out with the rest. The motive of his return was shown by his helping himself to a cut piece of skimmer cake that lay on a ledge beside where he had sat, and which he had apparently forgotten to take with him. He also poured out half a cup more mead from the quantity that remained, ravenously eating and drinking these as he stood. He had not finished when another figure came in just as quietly—his friend in cinder-gray.

"Oh—you here?" said the latter, smiling. "I thought you had gone to help in the capture." And this speaker also revealed the object of his return by looking solicitously round for the fascinating mug of old mead.

"And I thought you had gone," said the other, continuing his skimmer-cake with   120 some effort.

"Well, on second thoughts, I felt there were enough without me," said the first confidentially, "and such a night as it is, too. Besides, 'tis the business o' the Government to take care of its criminal—not mine."

"True; so it is. And I felt as you did, that there were enough without me."

"I don't want to break my limbs running over the humps and hollows of this wild country."

"Nor I neither, between you and me."

"These shepherd-people are used to it—simple-minded souls, you know, stirred   125 up to anything in a moment. They'll have him ready for me before the morning, and no trouble to me at all."

"They'll have him, and we shall have saved ourselves all labor in the matter."

"True, true. Well, my way is to Casterbridge; and 'tis as much as my legs will do to take me that far. Going the same way?"

"No, I am sorry to say! I have to get home over there" (he nodded indefinitely to the right), "and I feel as you do, that it is quite enough for my legs to do before bedtime."

The other had by this time finished the mead in the mug, after which, shaking hands heartily at the door, and wishing each other well, they went their several ways.

In the meantime the company of pursuers had reached the end of the hog's-back   130
elevation which dominated this part of the down. They had decided on no particular plan of action; and, finding that the man of the baleful trade was no longer in their company, they seemed quite unable to form any such plan now. They descended in all directions down the hill, and straightway several of the party fell into the snare set by Nature for all misguided midnight ramblers over this part of the cretaceous formation. The "lanchets," or flint slopes, which belted the escarpment at intervals of a dozen yards, took the less cautious ones unawares, and losing their footing on the rubbly steep they slid sharply downward, the lanterns rolling from their hands to the bottom, and there lying on their sides till the horn was scorched through.

When they had again gathered themselves together, the shepherd, as the man who knew the country best, took the lead, and guided them round these treacherous inclines. The lanterns, which seemed rather to dazzle their eyes and warn the fugitive than to assist them in the exploration, were extinguished, due silence was observed; and in this more rational order they plunged into the vale. It was a grassy, briery, moist defile, affording some shelter to any person who had sought it; but the party perambulated it in vain, and ascended on the other side. Here they wandered apart, and after an interval closed together again to report progress. At the second time of closing in they found themselves near a lonely ash, the single tree on this part of the coomb, probably sown there by a passing bird some fifty years before. And here, standing a little to one side of the trunk, as motionless as the trunk itself appeared the man they were in quest of, his outline being well defined against the sky beyond. The band noiselessly drew up and faced him.

"Your money or your life!" said the constable sternly to the still figure.

"No, no," whispered John Pitcher. "'Tisn't our side ought to say that. That's the doctrine of vagabonds like him, and we be on the side of the law."

"Well, well," replied the constable, impatiently; "I must say something, mustn't I? and if you had all the weight o' this undertaking upon your mind, perhaps you'd say the wrong thing, too!—Prisoner at the bar, surrender in the name of the Father—the Crown, I mane!"

The man under the tree seemed now to notice them for the first time, and, giving   135
them no opportunity whatever for exhibiting their courage, he strolled slowly toward them. He was, indeed, the little man, the third stranger; but his trepidation had in a great measure gone.

"Well, travelers," he said, "did I hear you speak to me?"

"You did; you've got to come and be our prisoner at once!" said the constable. "We arrest 'ee on the charge of not biding in Casterbridge jail in a decent proper manner to be hung tomorrow morning. Neighbors, do your duty, and seize the culprit!"

On hearing the charge, the man seemed enlightened, and, saying not another word, resigned himself with preternatural civility to the search-party, who, with their staves in their hands, surrounded him on all sides, and marched him back toward the shepherd's cottage.

It was eleven o'clock by the time they arrived. The light shining from the open door, a sound of men's voices within, proclaimed to them as they approached the house that some new events had arisen in their absence. On entering they discovered the shepherd's living-room to be invaded by two officers from Casterbridge jail, and a well-known magistrate who lived at the nearest county-seat, intelligence of the escape having become generally circulated.

"Gentlemen," said the constable, "I have brought back your man—not without   140
risk and danger; but everyone must do his duty! He is inside this circle of able-bodied persons, who have lent me useful aid, considering their ignorance of Crown work.— Men, bring forward your prisoner!" And the third stranger was led to the light.

"Who is this?" said one of the officials.

"The man," said the constable.

"Certainly not," said the turnkey; and the first corroborated his statement.

"But how can it be otherwise?" asked the constable. "Or why was he so terrified at sight o' the singing instrument of the law who sat there?" Here he related the strange behavior of the third stranger on entering the house during the hangman's song.

"Can't understand it," said the officer coolly. "All I know is that it is not the con-   145
demned man. He's quite a different character from this one; a gauntish fellow, with dark hair and eyes, rather good-looking, and with a musical bass voice that if you heard it once you'd never mistake as long as you lived."

"Why, souls—'twas the man in the chimney corner!"

"Hey—what?" said the magistrate, coming forward after inquiring particulars from the shepherd in the background. "Haven't you got the man after all?"

"Well, Sir," said the constable, "he's the man we were in search of, that's true; and yet he's not the man we were in search of. For the man we were in search of was not the man we wanted, Sir, if you understand my everyday way; for 'twas the man in the chimney corner!"

"A pretty kettle of fish altogether!" said the magistrate. "You had better start for the other man at once."

The prisoner now spoke for the first time. The mention of the man in the chim-   150
ney corner seemed to have moved him as nothing else could do. "Sir," he said, stepping forward to the magistrate, "take no more trouble about me. The time is come when I may as well speak. I have done nothing; my crime is that the condemned man is my brother. Early this afternoon I left home at Shottsford to tramp it all the way to Casterbridge jail to bid him farewell. I was benighted, and called here to rest and ask the way. When I opened the door I saw before me the very man, my brother, that I thought to see in the condemned cell at Casterbridge. He was in this chimney corner; and jammed close to him, so that he could not have got out if he had tried, was the executioner who'd come to take his life, singing a song about it and not knowing that it was his victim who was close by, joining in to save appearances. My brother looked a glance of agony at me, and I know he meant, 'Don't reveal what you see; my life depends on it.' I was so terror-struck that I could hardly stand, and, not knowing what I did, I turned and hurried away."

The narrator's manner and tone had the stamp of truth, and his story made a great impression on all around. "And do you know where your brother is at the present time?" asked the magistrate.

"I do not. I have never seen him since I closed this door."

"I can testify to that, for we've been between ye ever since," said the constable.

"Where does he think to fly to?—what is his occupation?"

"He's a watch-and-clock-maker, Sir."   15[5]

"'A said 'a was a wheelwright—a wicked rogue," said the constable.

"The wheels of clocks and watches he meant, no doubt," said Shepherd Fennel. "I thought his hands were palish for's trade."

"Well, it appears to me that nothing can be gained by retaining this poor man in custody," said the magistrate; "your business lies with the other, unquestionably."

And so the little man was released off-hand; but he looked nothing the less sad on that account, it being beyond the power of magistrate or constable to raze out the written troubles in his brain, for they concerned another whom he regarded with more solicitude than himself. When this was done, and the man had gone his way, the night was found to be so far advanced that it was deemed useless to renew the search before the next morning.

Next day, accordingly, the quest for the clever sheep-stealer became general and keen, to all appearance at least. But the intended punishment was cruelly disproportioned to the transgression, and the sympathy of a great many country-folk in that district was strongly on the side of the fugitive. Moreover, his marvelous coolness and daring in hob-and-nobbing with the hangman, under the unprecedented circumstances of the shepherd's party, won their admiration. So that it may be questioned if all those who ostensibly made themselves so busy in exploring woods and fields and lanes were quite so thorough when it came to the private examination of their own lofts and outhouses. Stories were afloat of a mysterious figure being occasionally seen in some old overgrown trackway or other, remote from turnpike roads, but when a search was instituted in any of these suspected quarters nobody was found. Thus the days and weeks passed without tidings.

160

In brief, the bass-voiced man of the chimney corner was never recaptured. Some said that he went across the sea, others that he did not, but buried himself in the depths of a populous city. At any rate, the gentleman in cinder-gray never did his morning's work at Casterbridge, nor met anywhere at all, for business purposes, the genial comrade with whom he had passed an hour of relaxation in the lonely house on the coomb.

The grass has long been green on the graves of Shepherd Fennel and his frugal wife; the guests who made up the christening parry have mainly followed their entertainers to the tomb; the baby in whose honor they all had met is a matron in the sere and yellow leaf. But the arrival of the three strangers at the shepherd's that night, and the details connected therewith, is a story as well-known as ever in the country about Higher Crowstairs.

QUESTIONS

1. Describe the appearances of conflicts in this story. Which conflicts are real?

2. Describe the reasons for which the narrator tells so much about the people of Higher Crowstairs. How are these descriptions related to the story's major conflict?

3. Why does the author withhold the identities of the various strangers? How does this delay condition your attitudes toward the first stranger?

4. What kind of story might "The Three Strangers" be, structurally, if the first stranger were named and identified when he first enters the cottage, before the entrance of the other strangers?

JAMAICA KINCAID   (b. 1949)

Jamaica Kincaid was born and educated in Antigua in the West Indies and now lives in Vermont. Her stories and novels are usually set in her native Antigua and often concern mother-daughter relationships, as in "Girl," one of her best-known (and very brief) stories. At the Bottom of the River *(1983), from which "What I Have Been Doing Lately" is taken, was her first collection of stories. Novels are* Annie John *(1985).* A Small Place *(1988),* Lucy *(1990), and more recently* The Autobiography of My Mother *(1996). Although some critics are concerned that Kincaid's fiction contains less action than situation, all agree that she superbly renders the speech rhythms and simple, primal concerns of her native islands.*

What I Have Been Doing Lately ———————————————— *1983*

What I have been doing lately: I was lying in bed and the doorbell rang. I ran downstairs. Quick. I opened the door. There was no one there. I stepped outside. Either it was drizzling or there was a lot of dust in the air and the dust was damp. I stuck out my tongue and the drizzle or the damp dust tasted like government school ink. I looked north. I looked south. I decided to start walking north. While walking north, I noticed that I was barefoot. While walking north, I looked up and saw the planet Venus. I said, "It must be almost morning." I saw a monkey in a tree. The tree had no leaves. I said, "Ah, a monkey. Just look at that. A monkey." I walked for I don't know how long before I came up to a big body of water. I wanted to get across it but I couldn't swim. I wanted to get across it but it would take me years to build a boat. I wanted to get across it but it would take me I didn't know how long to build a bridge. Years passed and then one day, feeling like it, I got into my boat and rowed across. When I got to the other side, it was noon and my shadow was small and fell beneath me. I set out on a path that stretched out straight ahead. I passed a house, and a dog was sitting on the verandah but it looked the other way when it saw me coming. I passed a boy tossing a ball in the air but the boy looked the other way when he saw me coming. I walked and I walked but I couldn't tell if I walked a long time because my feet didn't feel as if they would drop off. I turned around to see what I had left behind me but nothing was familiar. Instead of the straight path, I saw hills. Instead of the boy with his ball, I saw tall flowering trees. I looked up and the sky was without clouds and seemed near, as if it were the ceiling in my house and, if I stood on a chair, I could touch it with the tips of my fingers. I turned around and looked ahead of me again. A deep hole had opened up before me. I looked in. The hole was deep and dark and I couldn't see the bottom. I thought, What's down there?, so on purpose I fell in. I fell and I fell, over and over, as if I were an old suitcase. On the sides of the deep hole I could see things written, but perhaps it was in a foreign language because I couldn't read them. Still I fell, for I don't know how long. As I fell I began to see that I didn't like the way falling made me feel. Falling made me feel sick and I missed all the people I had loved. I said, I don't want to fall anymore, and I reversed myself. I was standing again on the edge of the deep hole. I looked at the deep hole and I said, You can close up now, and it did. I walked some more without knowing distance. I only knew that I passed through days and nights, I only knew that I passed through rain and shine, light and darkness. I was never thirsty and I felt no pain. Looking at the horizon, I made a joke for myself: I said, "The earth has thin lips," and I laughed.

Looking at the horizon again, I saw a lone figure coming toward me, but I wasn't frightened because I was sure it was my mother. As I got closer to the figure, I could see that it wasn't my mother, but still I wasn't frightened because I could see that it was a woman.

When this woman got closer to me, she looked at me hard and then she threw up her hands. She must have seen me somewhere before because she said, "It's you. Just look at that. It's you. And just what have you been doing lately?"

I could have said, "I have been praying not to grow any taller."

I could have said, "I have been listening carefully to my mother's words, so as to   5
make a good imitation of a dutiful daughter."

I could have said, "A pack of dogs, tired from chasing each other all over town, slept in the moonlight."

Instead, I said, What I have been doing lately: I was lying in bed on my back, my hands drawn up, my fingers interlaced lightly at the nape of my neck. Someone rang the doorbell. I went downstairs and opened the door but there was no one there. I stepped outside. Either it was drizzling or there was a lot of dust in the air and the dust was damp. I stuck out my tongue and the drizzle or the damp dust tasted like government school ink. I looked north and I looked south. I started walking north. While walking north, I wanted to move fast, so I removed the shoes from my feet. While walking north, I looked up and saw the planet Venus and I said, "If the sun went out, it would be eight minutes before I would know it." I saw a monkey sitting in a tree that had no leaves and I said, "A monkey. Just look at that. A monkey." I picked up a stone and I threw it at the monkey. The monkey, seeing the stone, quickly moved out of its way. Three times I threw a stone at the monkey and three times it moved away. The fourth time I threw the stone, the monkey caught it and threw it back at me. The stone struck me on my forehead over my right eye, making a deep gash. The gash healed immediately but now the skin on my forehead felt false to me. I walked for I don't know how long before I came to a big body of water. I wanted to get across, so when the boat came I paid my fare. When I got to the other side, I saw a lot of people sitting on the beach and they were having a picnic. They were the most beautiful people I had ever seen. Everything about them was black and shiny. Their skin was black and shiny. Their shoes were black and shiny. Their hair was black and shiny. The clothes they wore were black and shiny. I could hear them laughing and chatting and I said, I would like to be with these people, so I started to walk toward them, but when I got up close to them I saw that they weren't at a picnic and they weren't beautiful and they weren't chatting and laughing. All around me was black mud and the people all looked as if they had been made up out of the black mud. I looked up and saw that the sky seemed far away and nothing I could stand on would make me able to touch it with my fingertips. I thought, If only I could get out of this, so I started to walk. I must have walked for a long time because my feet hurt and felt as if they would drop off. I thought, If only just around the bend I would see my house and inside my house I would find my bed, freshly made at that, and in the kitchen I would find my mother or anyone else that I loved making me a custard. I thought, If only it was a Sunday and I was sitting in a church and I had just heard someone sing a psalm. I felt very sad so I sat down. I felt so sad that I rested my head on my own knees and smoothed my own head. I felt so sad I couldn't imagine feeling any other way again. I said, I don't like this. I don't want to do this anymore. And I went back to lying in bed, just before the doorbell rang.

QUESTIONS

1. Is the story told as if it were real or a dream? Why is the dreamlike quality introduced? How soon do you learn that the dreamlike narration has begun?

2. To what level of existence do the various descriptions and actions belong? In what ways do the actions and descriptions exceed everyday reality? Why does the author not introduce specific elements that might be considered appropriate in a world of dreams or in a future world?

3. Structurally, why does the story become repetitive at paragraph 7? What differences are there between the second narration and the first? Why does the story end with the third sound of the doorbell? What is the meaning of the repetitive actions?

4. Should this work be considered a story at all? What makes it a story? In what ways is it unlike a story?

EUDORA WELTY   (b. 1909)

One of the major southern writers, Welty was born in Jackson, Mississippi. She attended the Mississippi State College for Women and the University of Wisconsin, and she began her writing career during the Great Depression. By 1943 she had published two major story collections, Curtain of Green *(1941, including "A Worn Path") and* The Wide Net *(1943). She is the author of many stories and was awarded the Pulitzer Prize in 1973 for her short novel* The Optimist's Daughter *(1972). "A Worn Path" received an O. Henry Award in 1941.*

A Worn Path _____ *1941*

It was December—a bright frozen day in the early morning. Far out in the country there was an old Negro woman with her head tied in a red rag, coming along a path through the pinewoods. Her name was Phoenix Jackson. She was very old and small and she walked slowly in the dark pine shadows, moving a little from side to side in her steps, with the balanced heaviness and lightness of a pendulum in a grandfather clock. She carried a thin, small cane made from an umbrella, and with this she kept tapping the frozen earth in front of her. This made a grave and persistent noise in the still air, that seemed meditative like the chirping of a solitary little bird.

She wore a dark striped dress reaching down to her shoe tops, and an equally long apron of bleached sugar sacks, with a full pocket: all neat and tidy, but every time she took a step she might have fallen over her shoelaces, which dragged from her unlaced shoes. She looked straight ahead. Her eyes were blue with age. Her skin had a pattern all its own of numberless branching wrinkles and as though a whole little tree stood in the middle of her forehead, but a golden color ran underneath, and the two knobs of her cheeks were illuminated by a yellow burning under the dark. Under the rag her hair came down on her neck in the frailest of ringlets, still black, and with an odor like copper.

Now and then there was a quivering in the thicket. Old Phoenix said, "Out of my way, all you foxes, owls, beetles, jack rabbits, coons and wild animals! . . . Keep out from under these feet, little bob-whites. . . . Keep the big wild hogs out of my path. Don't let none of those come running my direction. I got a long way." Under her small black-freckled hand her cane, limber as a buggy whip, would switch at the brush as if to rouse up any hiding things.

On she went. The woods were deep and still. The sun made the pine needles almost too bright to look at, up where the wind rocked. The cones dropped as light as feathers. Down in the hollow was the mourning dove—it was not too late for him.

The path ran up a hill. "Seem like there is chains about my feet, time I get this far," she said, in the voice of argument old people keep to use with themselves. "Something always take a hold of me on this hill—pleads I should stay."   5

After she got to the top she turned and gave a full, severe look behind her where she had come. "Up through pines," she said at length. "Now down through oaks."

Her eyes opened their widest, and she started down gently. But before she got to the bottom of the hill a bush caught her dress.

Her fingers were busy and intent, but her skirts were full and long, so that before she could pull them free in one place they were caught in another. It was not possible to allow the dress to tear. "I in the thorny bush," she said. "Thorns, you doing your appointed work. Never want to let folks pass, no sir. Old eyes thought you was a pretty little *green* bush."

Finally, trembling all over, she stood free, and after a moment dared to stoop for her cane.

"Sun so high!" she cried, leaning back and looking, while the thick tears went over her eyes. "The time getting all gone here."   10

At the foot of this hill was a place where a log was laid across the creek.

"Now comes the trial," said Phoenix.

Putting her right foot out, she mounted the log and shut her eyes. Lifting her skirt, leveling her cane fiercely before her, like a festival figure in some parade, she began to march across. Then she opened her eyes and she was safe on the other side.

"I wasn't as old as I thought," she said.

But she sat down to rest. She spread her skirts on the bank around her and folded her hands over her knees. Up above her was a tree in a pearly cloud of mistletoe. She did not dare to close her eyes, and when a little boy brought her a plate with a slice of marble-cake on it she spoke to him. "That would be acceptable," she said. But when she went to take it there was just her own hand in the air.   15

So she left that tree, and had to go through a barbed-wire fence. There she had to creep and crawl, spreading her knees and stretching her fingers like a baby trying to climb the steps. But she talked loudly to herself: she could not let her dress be torn now, so late in the day, and she could not pay for having her arm or leg sawed off if she got caught fast where she was.

At last she was safe through the fence and risen up out in the clearing. Big dead trees, like black men with one arm, were standing in the purple stalks of the withered cotton field. There sat a buzzard.

"Who you watching?"

In the furrow she made her way along.

"Glad this is not the season for bulls," she said, looking sideways, "and the good   20
Lord made his snakes to curl up and sleep in the winter. A pleasure I don't see no two-
headed snake coming around that tree, where it come once. It took a while to get by
him, back in the summer."

She passed through the old cotton and went into a field of dead corn. It whispered and shook and was taller than her head. "Through the maze now," she said, for
there was no path.

Then there was something tall, black, and skinny there, moving before her.

At first she took it for a man. It could have been a man dancing in the field. But
she stood still and listened, and it did not make a sound. It was as silent as a ghost.

"Ghost," she said sharply, "who be you the ghost of? For I have heard of nary death
close by."

But there was no answer—only the ragged dancing in the wind.   25

She shut her eyes, reached out her hand, and touched a sleeve. She found a coat
and inside that an emptiness, cold as ice.

"You scarecrow," she said. Her face lighted. "I ought to be shut up for good," she
said with laughter. "My senses is gone. I too old, I the oldest people I ever know. Dance,
old scarecrow," she said, "while I dancing with you."

She kicked her foot over the furrow, and with mouth drawn down, shook her head
once or twice in a little strutting way. Some husks blew down and whirled in steamers
about her skirts.

Then she went on, parting her way from side to side with the cane, through the
whispering field. At last she came to the end, to a wagon track where the silver grass
blew between the red ruts. The quail were walking around like pullets, seeming all dainty
and unseen.

"Walk pretty," she said. "This is the easy place. This the easy going."   30

She followed the track, swaying through the quiet bare fields, through the little
strings of trees silver in their dead leaves, past cabins silver from weather, with the doors
and windows boarded shut, all like old women under a spell sitting there. "I walking in
their sleep," she said, nodding her head vigorously.

In a ravine she went where a spring was silently flowing through a hollow log. Old
Phoenix bent and drank. "Sweet-gum makes the water sweet," she said, and drank more.
"Nobody know who made this well, for it was here when I was born."

The track crossed a swampy part where the moss hung as white as lace from every
limb. "Sleep on, alligators, and blow your bubbles." Then the track went into the road.

Deep, deep the road went down between the high green-colored banks. Overhead
the live-oaks met, and it was as dark as a cave.

A black dog with a lolling tongue came up out of the weeds by the ditch. She was   35
meditating, and not ready, and when he came at her she only hit him a little with her
cane. Over she went in the ditch, like a little puff of milkweed.

Down there, her sense drifted away. A dream visited her, and she reached her
hand up, but nothing reached down and gave her a pull. So she lay there and presently
went to talking. "Old woman," she said to herself, "that black dog come up out of the
weeds to stall you off, and now there he sitting on his fine tail smiling at you."

A white man finally came along and found her—a hunter, a young man, with his
dog on a chain.

"Well, Granny!" he laughed. "What are you doing there?"

"Lying on my back like a June-bug waiting to be turned over, mister," she said,
reaching up her hand.

He lifted her up, gave her a swing in the air, and set her down. "Anything broken, Granny?"   40

"No sir, them old dead weeds is springy enough," said Phoenix, when she had got her breath. "I thank you for your trouble."

"Where do you live, Granny?" he asked, while the two dogs were growling at each other.

"Away back yonder, sir, behind the ridge. You can't even see it from here."

"On your way home?"

"No sir, I goin to town."   45

"Why, that's too far! That's as far as I walk when I come out myself, and I get something for my trouble." He patted the stuffed bag he carried, and there hung down a little closed claw. It was one of the bob-whites, with its beak hooked bitterly to show it was dead. "Now you go on home, Granny!"

"I bound to go to town, mister," said Phoenix. "The time come around."

He gave another laugh, filling the whole landscape. "I know you old colored people! Wouldn't miss going to town to see Santa Claus!"

But something held old Phoenix very still. The deep lines in her face went into a fierce and different radiation. Without warning, she had seen with her own eyes a flashing nickel fall out of the man's pocket onto the ground.

"How old are you, Granny?" he was saying.   50

"There is no telling, mister," she said, "no telling."

Then she gave a little cry and clapped her hands and said, "Git on away from here, dog! Look! Look at that dog!" She laughed as if in admiration. "He ain't scared of nobody. He a big black dog." She whispered, "Sic him!"

"Watch me get rid of that cur," said the man. "Sic him, Pete! Sic him!"

Phoenix heard the dogs fighting, and heard the man running and throwing sticks. She even heard a gunshot. But she was slowly bending forward by that time, further and further forward, the lids stretched down over her eyes, as if she were doing this in her sleep. Her chin was lowered almost to her knees. The yellow palm of her hand came out from the fold of her apron. Her fingers slid down and along the ground under the piece of money with the grace and care they would have in lifting an egg from under a setting hen. Then she slowly straightened up, she stood erect, and the nickel was in her apron pocket. A bird flew by. Her lips moved. "God watching me the whole time. I come to stealing."

The man came back, and his own dog panted about them. "Well, I scared him off   55
that time," he said, and then he laughed and lifted his gun and pointed it at Phoenix.

She stood straight and faced him.

"Doesn't the gun scare you?" he said, still pointing it.

"No, sir. I seen plenty go off closer by, in my day, and for less than what I done," she said, holding utterly still.

He smiled, and shouldered the gun. "Well, Granny," he said, "you must be a hundred years old, and scared of nothing. I'd give you a dime if I had any money with me. But you take my advice and stay home, and nothing will happen to you."

"I bound to go on my way, mister," said Phoenix. She inclined her head in the red   60
rag. Then they went in different directions, but she could hear the gun shooting again and again over the hill.

She walked on. The shadows hung from the oak trees to the road like curtains. Then she smelled wood-smoke, and smelled the river, and she saw a steeple and the cabins on their steep steps. Dozens of little black children whirled around her. There ahead was Natchez shining. Bells were ringing. She walked on.

In the paved city it was Christmas time. There were red and green electric lights strung and crisscrossed everywhere, and all turned on in the daytime. Old Phoenix would have been lost if she had not distrusted her eyesight and depended on her feet to know where to take her.

She paused quietly on the sidewalk where people were passing by. A lady came along in the crowd, carrying an armful of red-, green-, and silver-wrapped presents; she gave off perfume like the red roses in hot summer, and Phoenix stopped her.

"Please, missy, will you lace up my shoe?" She held up her foot.

"What do you want, Grandma?" 65

"See my shoe," said Phoenix. "Do all right for out in the country, but wouldn't look right to go in a big building."

"Stand still then, Grandma," said the lady. She put her packages down on the sidewalk beside her and laced and tied both shoes tightly.

"Can't lace 'em with a cane," said Phoenix. "Thank you, missy. I doesn't mind asking a nice lady to tie up my shoe, when I gets out on the street."

Moving slowly and from side to side, she went into the big building, and into a tower of steps, where she walked up and around and around until her feet knew to stop.

She entered a door, and there she saw nailed up on the wall the document that 70
had been stamped with the gold seal and framed in the gold frame, which matched the dream that was hung up in her head.

"Here I be," she said. There was a fixed and ceremonial stiffness over her body.

"A charity case, I suppose," said an attendant who sat at the desk before her.

But Phoenix only looked above her head. There was sweat on her face, the wrinkles in her skin shone like a bright net.

"Speak up, Grandma," the woman said, "What's your name? We must have your history, you know. Have you been here before? What seems to be the trouble with you?"

Old Phoenix only gave a twitch to her face as if a fly were bothering her. 75

"Are you deaf?" cried the attendant.

But then the nurse came in.

"Oh, that's just old Aunt Phoenix," she said. "She doesn't come for herself—she has a little grandson. She makes these trips just as regular as clockwork. She lives away back off the Old Natchez Trace." She bent down. "Well, Aunt Phoenix, why don't you just take a seat? We won't keep you standing after your long trip." She pointed.

The old woman sat down, bolt upright in the chair.

"Now, how is the boy?" asked the nurse. 80

Old Phoenix did not speak.

"I said, how is the boy?"

But Phoenix only waited and stared straight ahead, her face very solemn and withdrawn into rigidity.

"Is his throat any better?" asked the nurse. "Aunt Phoenix, don't you hear me? Is your grandson's throat any better since the last time you came for the medicine?"

With her hands on her knees, the old woman waited, silent, erect, and motionless, just as if she were in armor. 85

"You mustn't take up our time this way, Aunt Phoenix," the nurse said. "Tell us quickly about your grandson, and get it over. He isn't dead, is he?"

At last there came a flicker and then a flame of comprehension across her face, and she spoke.

"My grandson. It was my memory had left me. There I sat and forgot why I made my long trip."

"Forgot?" the nurse frowned. "After you came so far?"

Then Phoenix was like an old woman begging a dignified forgiveness for waking   90
up frightened in the night. "I never did go to school, I was too old at the Surrender," she
said in a soft voice. "I'm an old woman without an education. It was my memory fail me.
My little grandson, he is just the same, and I forgot it in the coming."

"Throat never heals, does it?" said the nurse, speaking in a loud, sure voice to old
Phoenix. By now she had a card with something written on it, a little list. "Yes. Swallowed
lye. When was it—January—two, three years ago—"

Phoenix spoke unasked now. "No missy, he not dead, he just the same. Every little
while his throat begin to close up again, and he not able to swallow. He not get his
breath. He not able to help himself. So the time come around, and I go on another trip
for the soothing medicine."

"All right. The doctor said as long as you came to get it, you could have it," said
the nurse. "But it's an obstinate case."

"My little grandson, he sit up there in the house all wrapped up, waiting by himself," Phoenix went on. "We is the only two left in the world. He suffer and it don't seem
to put him back at all. He got a sweet look. He going to last. He wear a little patch quilt
and peep out holding his mouth open like a little bird. I remembers so plain now. I not
going to forget him again, no, the whole enduring time. I could tell him from all the
others in creation."

"All right." The nurse was trying to hush her now. She brought her a bottle of   95
medicine. "Charity," she said, making a check mark in a book.

Old Phoenix held the bottle close to her eyes, and then carefully put it into her
pocket.

"I thank you," she said.

"It's Christmas time, Grandma," said the attendant. "Could I give you a few pennies out of my purse?"

"Five pennies is a nickel," said Phoenix stiffly.

"Here's a nickel," said the attendant.   100

Phoenix rose carefully and held out her hand. She received the nickel and then
fished the other nickel out of her pocket and laid it beside the new one. She stared at
her palm closely, with her head on one side.

Then she gave a tap with her cane on the floor.

"This is what come to me to do," she said, "I going to the store and buy my child a
little windmill they sells, made out of paper. He going to find it hard to believe there
such a thing in the world. I'll march myself back where he waiting, holding it straight up
in this hand."

She lifted her free hand, gave a little nod, turned around, and walked out of the
doctor's office. Then her slow step began on the stairs, going down.

QUESTIONS

1.   From the description of Phoenix, what do you conclude about her economic
     condition? How do you know that she has taken the path through the woods
     before? Is she accustomed to being alone? What do you make of her speaking
     to animals, and of her imagining a boy offering her a piece of cake? What does
     her speech show about her education and background?

2.   Describe the plot of the story. With Phoenix as the protagonist, what are the obstacles ranged against her? How might Phoenix be considered to be in the grip of large and indifferent social and political forces?

3.   Comment on the meaning of this dialogue between Phoenix and the hunter:

"Doesn't the gun scare you?" he said, still pointing it.

"No, sir. I seen plenty go off closer by, in my day, and for less than what I done," she said, holding utterly still.

4.   A number of responses might be made to this story, among them admiration for Phoenix, pity for her and her grandson and for the downtrodden generally, anger at her impoverished condition, and apprehension about her approaching senility. Do you share in any of these responses? Do you have any others?

TOM WHITECLOUD   (1914–1972)

Thomas St. Germain Whitecloud was born in New York City. However, he spent much of his youth on the Lac du Flambeau Indian Reservation near Woodruff, Wisconsin, the town mentioned in paragraph 20 of "Blue Winds Dancing." After attending colleges in New Mexico and California, he received his degree in medicine from Tulane University. He lived in Louisiana and Texas throughout his medical career, and at the time of his death he was a consultant for the Texas Commission on Alcoholism and Drug Abuse for Indians. "Blue Winds Dancing," which can be considered as either a story or a fictionalized autobiographical fragment, received a prize in 1938 from both Scribner's Magazine, *in which it was published, and the Phi Beta Kappa National Honor Society.*

Blue Winds Dancing ————————————————————————— *1938*

There is a moon out tonight. Moon and stars and clouds tipped with moonlight. And there is a fall wind blowing in my heart. Ever since this evening, when against a fading sky I saw geese wedge southward. They were going home. . . . Now I try to study, but against the pages I see them again, driving southward. Going home.

Across the valley there are heavy mountains holding up the night sky, and beyond the mountains there is home. Home, and peace, and the beat of drums, and blue winds dancing over snowfields. The Indian lodge will fill with my people, and our gods will come and sit among them. I should be there then. I should be at home.

But home is beyond the mountains, and I am here. Here where fall hides in the valleys, and winter never comes down from the mountains. Here where all the trees grow in rows; the palms stand stiffly by the roadsides, and in the groves the orange trees line in military rows, and endlessly bear fruit. Beautiful, yes; there is always beauty in order, in rows of growing things! But it is the beauty of captivity. A pine fighting for existence on a windy knoll is much more beautiful.

In my Wisconsin, the leaves change before the snows come. In the air there is the smell of wild rice and venison cooking; and when the winds come whispering through the forests, they carry the smell of rotting leaves. In the evenings, the loon calls, lonely; and birds sing their last songs before leaving. Bears dig roots and eat late fall berries, fattening for their long winter sleep. Later, when the first snows fall, one awakens in the morning to find the world white and beautiful and clean. Then one can look back over his trail and see the tracks following. In the woods there are tracks of deer and snow-shoe rabbits, and long streaks where partridges slide to alight. Chipmunks make tiny footprints on the limbs and one can hear squirrels busy in hollow trees, sorting acorns. Soft lake waves wash the shores, and sunsets burst each evening over the lakes, and make them look as if they were afire.

That land which is my home! Beautiful, calm—where there is no hurry to get any-   5
where, no driving to keep up in a race that knows no ending and no goal. No classes where men talk and talk and then stop now and then to hear their own words come back to them from the students. No constant peering into the maelstrom of one's mind; no worries about grades and honors; no hysterical preparing for life until that life is half over; no anxiety about one's place in the thing they call Society.

I hear again the ring of axes in deep woods, the crunch of snow beneath my feet. I feel again the smooth velvet of ghost-birch bark. I hear the rhythm of the drums. . . . I am tired. I am weary of trying to keep up this bluff of being civilized. Being civilized means trying to do everything you don't want to, never doing anything you want to. It means dancing to the strings of custom and tradition; it means living in houses and never knowing or caring who is next door. These civilized white men want us to be like them—always dissatisfied—getting a hill and wanting a mountain.

Then again, maybe I am not tired. Maybe I'm licked. Maybe I am just not smart enough to grasp these things that go to make up civilization. Maybe I am just too lazy to think hard enough to keep up.

Still, I know my people have many things that civilization has taken from the whites. They know how to give; how to tear one's piece of meat in two and share it with one's brother. They know how to sing—how to make each man his own songs and sing them; for their music they do not have to listen to other men singing over a radio. They know how to make things with their hands, how to shape beads into design and make a thing of beauty from a piece of birch bark.

But we are inferior. It is terrible to have to feel inferior; to have to read reports of intelligence tests, and learn that one's race is behind. It is terrible to sit in classes and hear men tell you that your people worship sticks of wood—that your gods are all false, that the Manitou forgot your people and did not write them a book.

I am tired. I want to walk again among the ghost-birches. I want to see the leaves   10
turn in autumn, the smoke rise from the lodgehouses, and to feel the blue winds. I want to hear the drums; I want to hear the drums and feel the blue whispering winds.

There is a train wailing into the night. The trains go across the mountains. It would be easy to catch a freight. They will say he has gone back to the blanket; I don't care. The dance at Christmas. . . .

A bunch of bums warming at a tiny fire talk politics and women and joke about the Relief and the WPA and smoke cigarettes. These men in caps and overcoats and dirty overalls living on the outskirts of civilization are free, but they pay the price of being free in civilization. They are outcasts. I remember a sociology professor lecturing on adjustment to society; hobos and prostitutes and criminals are individuals who never adjusted, he said. He could learn a lot if he came and listened to a bunch of bums talk. He would learn that work and a woman and a place to hang his hat are all the ordinary man wants. These are all he wants, but other men are not content to let him want only these. He must be taught to want radios and automobiles and a new suit every spring. Progress would stop if he did not want these things. I listen to hear if there is any talk of communism or socialism in the hobo jungles. There is none. At best there is a sort of disgusted philosophy about life. They seem to think there should be a better distribution of wealth, or more work, or something. But they are not rabid about it. The radicals live in the cities.

I find a fellow headed for Albuquerque, and talk road-talk with him. "It is hard to ride fruit cars. Bums break in. Better to wait for a cattle car going back to the Middle West, and ride that." We catch the next east-bound and walk the tops until we find a cattle car. Inside, we crouch near the forward wall, huddle, and try to sleep. I feel peaceful and content at last. I am going home. The cattle car rocks. I sleep.

Morning and the desert. Noon and the Salton Sea, lying more lifeless than a mirage under a somber sun in a pale sky. Skeleton mountains rearing on the skyline, thrusting out of the desert floor, all rock and shadow and edges. Desert. Good country for an Indian reservation. . . .

Yuma and the muddy Colorado. Night again, and I wait shivering for the dawn.   15

Phoenix. Pima country. Mountains that look like cardboard sets on a forgotten stage. Tucson, Papago country. Giant cacti that look like petrified hitchhikers along the highways. Apache country. At El Paso my road-buddy decides to go on to Houston. I leave him, and head north to the mesa country. Las Cruces and the terrible Organ Mountains, jagged peaks that instill fear and wondering. Albuquerque. Pueblos along the Rio Grande. On the boardwalk there are some Indian women in colored sashes selling bits of pottery. The stone age offering its art to the twentieth century. They hold up a piece and fix the tourist with black eyes until, embarrassed, he buys or turns away. I feel suddenly angry that my people should have to do such things for a living. . . .

Santa Fe trains are fast, and they keep them pretty clean of bums. I decide to hurry and ride passenger coaltenders. Hide in the dark, judge the speed of the train as it leaves, and then dash out, and catch it. I hug the cold steel wall of the tender and think of the roaring fire in the engine ahead, and of the passengers back in the dining car reading their papers over hot coffee. Beneath me there is a blur of rails. Death would come quick if my hands should freeze and I fall. Up over the Sangre De Cristo range, around cliffs and through canyons to Denver. Bitter cold here, and I must watch out for Denver Bob. He is a railroad bull who has thrown bums from fast freights. I miss him. It is too cold, I suppose. On north to the Sioux country.

Small towns lit for the coming Christmas. On the streets of one I see a beam-shouldered young farmer gazing into a window filled with shining silver toasters. He is tall and wears a blue shirt buttoned, with no tie. His young wife by his side looks at him hopefully. He wants decorations for his place to hang his hat to please his woman. . . .

Northward again. Minnesota, and great white fields of snow; frozen lakes, and dawn running into dusk without noon. Long forests wearing white. Bitter cold, and one night the northern lights. I am nearing home.

I reach Woodruff at midnight. Suddenly I am afraid, now that I am but twenty   20
miles from home. Afraid of what my father will say, afraid of being looked on as a stranger by my own people. I sit by a fire and think about myself and all other young Indians. We just don't seem to fit in anywhere—certainly not among the whites, and not among the older people. I think again about the learned sociology professor and his professing. So many things seem to be clear now that I am away from school and do not

have to worry about some man's opinion of my ideas. It is easy to think while looking at dancing flames.

Morning, I spend the day cleaning up, and buying some presents for my family with what is left of my money. Nothing much, but a gift is a gift, if a man buys it with his last quarter. I wait until evening, then start up the track toward home.

Christmas Eve comes in on a north wind. Snow clouds hang over the pines, and the night comes early. Walking along the railroad bed, I feel the calm peace of snow-bound forests on either side of me. I take my time; I am back in a world where time does not mean so much now. I am alone; alone but not nearly so lonely as I was back on the campus at school. Those are never lonely who love the snow and the pines; never lonely when the pines are wearing white shawls and snow crunches coldly underfoot. In the woods I know there are the tracks of deer and rabbit; I know that if I leave the rails and go into the woods I shall find them. I walk along feeling glad because my legs are light and my feet seem to know that they are home. A deer comes out of the woods ahead of me, and stands silhouetted on the rails. The North, I feel, has welcomed me home. I watch him and am glad that I do not wish for a gun. He goes into the woods quietly, leaving only the design of his tracks in the snow. I walk on. Now and then I pass a field, white under the night sky, with houses at the far end. Smoke comes from the chimneys of the houses, and I try to tell what sort of wood each is burning by the smoke; some burn pine, others aspen, others tamarack. There is one from which comes black coal smoke that rises lazily and drifts out over the tops of the trees. I like to watch houses and try to imagine what might be happening in them.

Just as a light snow begins to fall I cross the reservation boundary; somehow it seems as though I have stepped into another world. Deep woods in a white-and-black winter night. A faint trail leading to the village.

The railroad on which I stand comes from a city sprawled by a lake—a city with a million people who walk around without seeing one another; a city sucking the life from all the country around; a city with stores and police and intellectuals and criminals and movies and apartment houses; a city with its politics and libraries and zoos.

Laughing, I go into the woods. As I cross a frozen lake I begin to hear the drums. 25 Soft in the night the drums beat. It is like the pulse beat of the world. The white line of the lake ends at a black forest, and above the trees the blue winds are dancing.

I come to the outlying houses of the village. Simple box houses, etched black in the night. From one or two windows soft lamplight falls on the snow. Christmas here, too, but it does not mean much; not much in the way of parties and presents. Joe Sky will get drunk. Alex Bodidash will buy his children red mittens and a new sled. Alex is a Carlisle man, and tries to keep his home up to white standards. White standards. Funny that my people should be ever falling farther behind. The more they try to imitate whites the more tragic the result. Yet they want us to be imitation white men. About all we imitate well are their vices.

The village is not a sight to instill pride, yet I am not ashamed; one can never be ashamed of his own people when he knows they have dreams as beautiful as white snow on a tall pine.

Father and my brother and sister are seated around the table as I walk in. Father stares at me for a moment, then I am in his arms, crying on his shoulder. I give them the presents I have brought, and my throat tightens as I watch my sister save carefully bits of red string from the packages. I hide my feelings by wrestling with my brother when he strikes my shoulder in token of affection. Father looks at me, and I know he has many questions, but he seems to know why I have come. He tells me to go alone to the lodge, and he will follow.

I walk along the trail to the lodge, watching the northern lights forming in the heavens. White waving ribbons that seem to pulsate with the rhythm of the drums. Clean snow creaks beneath my feet, and a soft wind sighs through the trees, singing to me. Everything seems to say, "Be happy! You are home now—you are free. You are among friends—we are your friends; we, the trees, and the snow, and the lights." I follow the trail to the lodge. My feet are light, my heart seems to sing to the music, and I hold my head high. Across white snow fields blue winds are dancing.

Before the lodge door I stop, afraid, I wonder if my people will remember me. I   30
wonder—"Am I Indian, or am I white?" I stand before the door a long time. I hear the ice groan on the lake, and remember the story of the old woman under the ice, trying to get out, so she can punish some runaway lovers. I think to myself, "If I am white I will not believe that story; If I am Indian, I will know that there is an old woman under the ice." I listen for a while, and I know that there is an old woman under the ice. I look again at the lights, and go in.

Inside the lodge there are many Indians. Some sit on benches around the walls, others dance in the center of the floor around a drum. Nobody seems to notice me. It seems as though I were among a people I have never seen before. Heavy women with long hair. Women with children on their knees—small children that watch with intent black eyes the movements of the dancers, whose small faces are solemn and serene. The faces of the old people are serene, too, and their eyes are merry and bright. I look at the old men. Straight, dressed in dark trousers and beaded velvet vests, wearing soft moccasins. Dark, lined faces intent on the music. I wonder if I am at all like them. They dance on, lifting their feet to the rhythm of the drums swaying lightly, looking upward. I look at their eyes, and am startled at the rapt attention to the rhythm of the music.

The dance stops. The men walk back to the walls, and talk in low tones or with their hands. There is little conversation, yet everyone seems to be sharing some secret. A woman looks at a small boy wandering away, and he comes back to her.

Strange, I think and then remember. These people are not sharing words—they are sharing a mood. Everyone is happy. I am so used to white people that it seems strange so many people could be together without someone talking. These Indians are happy because they are together, and because the night is beautiful outside, and the music is beautiful. I try hard to forget school and white people, and be one of these—my people. I try to forget everything but the night, and it is a part of me that I am one with my people and we are all a part of something universal. I watch eyes, and see now that the old people are speaking to me. They nod slightly, imperceptibly, and their eyes laugh into mine. I look around the room. All the eyes are friendly; they all laugh. No one questions my being here. The drums begin to beat again, and I catch the invitation in the eyes of the old men. My feet begin to lift to the rhythm, and I look out beyond the walls into the night and see the lights. I am happy. It is beautiful. I am home.

QUESTIONS

1. Describe the first section of the story in terms of the structure. Could a case be made that this first section contains its own crisis and climax and that the rest of the story is really a resolution?

2. What do you learn in the first section about the conflict in the attitudes of the narrator? What is his attitude about "civilization"? What values make him think this way? If he is the protagonist, who or what is the antagonist?

3. What does the narrator mean by saying, "I am alone; alone but not nearly so lonely as I was back on the campus at school" (paragraph 22)?

4. What is meant by the dancing of the blue winds—what kind of wisdom? What is the place for such wisdom in a computerized, industrialized society?

WRITING ABOUT THE PLOT OF A STORY

An essay about plot is an analysis of the conflict and its developments. The organization of the essay should not be modeled on sequential sections and principal events, however, because these invite only a retelling of the story. Instead, the organization is to be developed from the important elements of conflict. Ask yourself the following questions as you look for ideas about plot.

Questions for Discovering Ideas

- Who are the protagonist and antagonist, and how do their characteristics put them in conflict? How would you describe the conflict?
- How does the action develop from the conflict?
- If the conflict stems from contrasting ideas or values, what are these, and how are they brought out?
- What problems does the major character (or do the major characters) face? How does the character (characters) deal with these problems?
- How do the major characters achieve (or not achieve) their major goal(s)? What obstacles do they overcome? What obstacles overcome them or alter them?
- At the end, are the characters successful or unsuccessful, happy or unhappy, satisfied or dissatisfied, changed or unchanged, enlightened or ignorant? How has the resolution of the major conflict produced these results?

Strategies for Organizing Ideas

To keep your essay brief, be selective. Rather than detailing everything a major character does, for example, stress the major elements in his or her conflict. Such an essay on Eudora Welty's "A Worn Path" might emphasize Phoenix as she encounters the various obstacles both in the woods and in town. When there is a conflict between two major characters, the obvious approach is to focus equally on both. For brevity, however, emphasis might be placed on just one. Thus, an essay on the plot of "The Blue Hotel" might stress the things we learn about the Swede that are important to his being a major participant in the conflict.

In addition, the plot may be analyzed more broadly in terms of impulses, goals, values, issues, and historical perspectives. Thus, you might emphasize the elements of chance working against Mathilde in Maupassant's "The Necklace" (Chapter 1) as a contrast to her dreams about wealth. A discussion of the plot of Poe's "The Masque of the Red Death" (Chapter 11) might stress the haughtiness of Prospero, the major character, because the plot could not develop without his egotism and pride.

The conclusion may contain a brief summary of the points you have made. It is also a fitting location for a brief consideration of the effect or *impact* produced by the conflict. Additional ideas might focus on whether the author has arranged actions and dialogue to direct your favor toward one side or the other or whether the plot is possible or impossible, serious or comic, fair or unfair, or powerful or weak.

DEMONSTRATIVE STUDENT ESSAY

Conflicting Values in Hardy's "The Three Strangers"°

[1] As one begins reading Thomas Hardy's "The Three Strangers," the nature of the plot is not immediately clear. There is no apparent protagonist, no single major character but rather a number of characters, and there is no apparent conflict. At first the major character seems to be Shepherd Fennel, but he stands out only as the cooperative host and opener of doors for the strangers entering his home during the stormy night. The first stranger might then seem to be the choice as major character, and this possibility is strengthened because of the jarring and obnoxious second stranger. Here the story establishes the beginning of a conflict, but a puzzling one because it seems no more than a contrast of personalities. The third stranger to enter the cottage does not stay long enough to make him seem a protagonist, for he leaves as quickly as he enters. However, it is clear, once all the characters have been involved in the story, that Hardy's plot stems not so much from the conflict of individual characters as from a conflict between aspects of legality and the law. On one side is justice and on the other injustice.* This opposition can be analyzed according to the characters on each side.†

[2] In the order in which Hardy interweaves the opposing parts of his plot, the unjust side--the side opposing the people at the Fennels' cottage--is represented by the second stranger, the Hangman. The cruelty of the hangman's duties is underlined by his own personal selfishness, egotism, and arrogance. He drinks all the mead in the large common cup, never caring about the wants of anyone else. He sings a merry song about his grisly job as hangman. He is obnoxiously demanding when ordering the guests to chase the third stranger. He shows his contempt for the people by calling them "simple-minded souls, you know, stirred

---

° See pages 133–47 for this story.
* Central idea.
† Thesis sentence.

up to anything in a moment" (paragraph 125). To make clear just how terrible the hangman is, Hardy compares him to the devil (paragraph 87). In short, the hangman, because of these qualities, is the story's cruel and thoughtless antagonist, and for this reason he stands as the negative part of Hardy's plot.

[3] By far the most powerful aspect of the plot is the positive and just side, represented by the Fennels, their guests, and the first and third strangers. They are ordinary, good folk, no more and no less, and their feelings about life are best shown by their celebration of the christening of the daughter of the Fennels. With regard to law, the story makes clear that such people favor fairness and compassion above strict punishment. Thus, when one of the guests explains that Timothy Summers (the first stranger) has been sentenced to be hanged because he had stolen a sheep when his "family were astarving" (paragraph 80), the other guests fall silent. Further, when the hangman starts pushing them to start a search, they are slow and unwilling, and when they go out looking, they produce the wrong man. As we learn, the first stranger is really the fugitive Summers, whose crime is justifiable in the eyes of the people, and the third stranger is the fugitive's brother, who flees not because he is guilty but because he wants to deflect suspicion from Summers. These are the characters toward whom Hardy directs our understanding, admiration, and sympathy. Any attempt to sentence anyone harshly, as the law has done with Summers, brings out their hesitation and resistance.

[4] An integral aspect of Hardy's plot is the countryside itself, which during the search becomes an almost active opponent of the legal capriciousness represented by the Hangman. The treacherous hill, containing the "flint slopes" of the hog's-back elevation near Higher Crowstairs, causes the searchers to stumble and tumble and make mistakes (paragraph 130). After the initial search for Summers proves fruitless, the people and the countryside unite to foil the thoughtlessly harsh law. The "woods and fields and lanes," together with the "lofts and outhouses" (paragraph 160), furnish hiding places for Summers, so that this man, the first stranger, is "never recaptured" (paragraph 161).

[5] This side of rightness represented by the people is shown by Hardy as not just occasional but rather eternal. He carefully sets the story in the framework of "the lapse of centuries" (paragraph 1), and he includes references to the ancient figures Timon and Nebuchadnezzar, as though the happenings at the Fennels' party are as ageless as human history (paragraph 2). Beyond this, Hardy compares the activities of the shepherd folk to the movements of the universe itself, for the energetic dancing moves "in planet-like courses, direct and retrograde, from apogee to perigee" (paragraph 10). When the third stranger is discovered, he steps out from behind an ash tree that was "probably sown there by a passing bird some fifty years before" (paragraph 131). Hardy's concluding paragraph places the entire story in the fabric of history and myth, thus stressing the continuum from the past to the present, a common humanity that is as old as time.

[6] This brief description of the major conflict making up the plot of "The Three Strangers" does not account for the story's power. Hardy skillfully paints a sympathetic picture of the shepherds and their way--a way of friendliness and good will in which the literal and harsh application of law has little place. His contrasting antagonist, the Hangman, personally violates the shepherd's home just as the law he represents violates the concept of justice felt by the people there. Admittedly, the complete intermeshing of the plot does not seem certain until the

circumstances are explained by the brother of Timothy Summers--an explanation that makes clear the opposition between the people's justice and the Hangman's injustice. Hardy's plot in "The Three Strangers" is strong because it is real and because the people themselves are presented as a collective force for fairness and justice over an application of law that is unfair and unjust.

Commentary on the Essay

Because the subject is plot, this essay emphasizes the conflicting elements in Hardy's "The Three Strangers"—the forces of understanding and humanity, on the one hand, and of harshness and cruelty, on the other. The first paragraph demonstrates how this conflict emerges in the story after a somewhat hesitant opening. Throughout the body of the essay, the conflict is stressed as the major element of Hardy's plot.

Note that the essay assumes that readers know the story already. Hence the essay is not a plot summary but is instead an analysis of the elements making up the plot. As much summary as is included here occurs in paragraph 6, in which the explanations by the third stranger are cited to show how Hardy does not make all aspects of his plot clear until near the story's end.

In the body of the essay, paragraph 2 deals with the characteristics of the antagonist, the hangman. Following this, the greater portion of the body considers the collective (not individual) protagonist arrayed against the hangman and the harsh law he represents. Thus the human protagonists are the people and the first and third strangers (paragraph 3), the geographical protagonist is the countryside around Higher Crowstairs (paragraph 4), and the historical protagonist is time itself (paragraph 5).

The last paragraph summarizes the conflicts of the plot and concludes with a final reference to the central idea, that the story exalts fairness and justice and deplores unfairness and injustice.

WRITING ABOUT STRUCTURE IN A STORY

Your essay should concern arrangement and shape. In form, the essay should not restate or summarize the part-by-part unfolding of the narrative or argument. Rather, it should explain why things are where they are: "Why is this here and not there?" is the fundamental question you need to answer. Thus it is possible to begin with a consideration of a work's crisis, and then to consider how the exposition and complication have built up to it. A vital piece of information, for example, might have been withheld in the earlier exposition (as in Ambrose Bierce's "An Occurrence at Owl Creek Bridge" [Chapter 5] and Hardy's "The Three Strangers") and introduced only at or near the conclusion; therefore, the crisis might be heightened because there would have been less suspense if the detail had been introduced earlier. Consider the following questions as you examine the story's structure.

Questions for Discovering Ideas

• If spaces or numbers divide the story into sections or parts, what structural importance do these parts have?

• If there are no marked divisions, what major sections can you discover? (You might make divisions according to places where actions occur, various times of day, changing weather, or increasingly important events.)

• If the story departs in major ways from the formal structure of exposition, complication, crisis, climax, and resolution, what purpose do these departures have?

• What variations in chronological order, if any, appear in the story (for example, gaps in the time sequence, flashbacks or selective recollection)? What effects are achieved by these variations?

• Does the story delay any crucial details of exposition? Why? What effect is achieved by the delay?

• Where does an important action or a major section (such as the climax) begin? End? How is it related to the other formal structural elements, such as the crisis? Is the climax an action, a realization, or a decision? To what degree does it relieve the work's tension? What is the effect of the climax on your understanding of the characters involved in it? How is this effect related to the arrangement of the climax?

Strategies for Organizing Ideas

Your essay should show why an entire story is arranged the way it is—to reveal the nature of a character's situation, to create surprise, or to bring out maximum humor. You might also, however, explain the structure of no more than a part of the story, such as the climax or the complication.

The essay is best developed in concert or agreement with what the work contains. The location of scenes is an obvious organizing element. Thus, essays on the structure of Hawthorne's "Young Goodman Brown" (Chapter 9) and Whitecloud's "Blue Winds Dancing" might be based on the fact that both take place outdoors (a dark forest for one and series of railway locations and a winter scene for the other). Similarly, an essay might explore the structure of Maupassant's "The Necklace" (Chapter 1) by contrasting the story's indoor and outdoor locations. In Glaspell's "A Jury of Her Peers" (Chapter 4), much is made of the various parts of a kitchen in an early-twentieth-century Iowa farmhouse, and an essay might trace the structural importance of these.

Other ways to consider structure may be derived from a work's notable aspects, such as the growing suspense and horrible conclusion of Poe's "The Cask of Amontillado" (Chapter 11) or the revelations about the "sinfulness" of Goodman Brown's father and neighbors in Hawthorne's "Young Goodman Brown."

The conclusion should highlight the main parts of your essay. You may also deal briefly with the relationship of structure to the plot. If the work you have analyzed departs from chronological order, you might stress the effects of this departure. Your aim should be to focus on the success of the work as it has been brought about by the author's choices in development.

DEMONSTRATIVE STUDENT ESSAY

Conflict and Suspense in Hardy's "The Three Strangers"°

[1]   Thomas Hardy's "The Three Strangers" is a finely woven story of conflict and suspense. The suspense is essential to the conflict, which is an opposition of right and wrong when applied to criminal justice. Hardy controls the structure to develop this opposition, which embodies the idea that the letter of the law is insignificant when compared with the spirit of the law.* The application of strict legality in Hardy's story is made wrong, while understanding and forgiveness, even if in a nominally illegal context, is made to seem right. As the basis of this idea, Hardy builds the story toward a major incident that presents a conflict for his Wessex shepherds between (1) duty toward law and (2) duty toward a human being who has been legally condemned but whose crime has been extenuated. Hardy develops his conflict and brings out his idea by showing the lives of his country people positively, by portraying his hangman negatively, and by creating suspense about his first stranger, who is the legally condemned "criminal."†

[2]   Although readers may not be aware of it during the early part of the story, Hardy arranges events to demonstrate a generous view of right and wrong. The first one-sixth of the story is an exposition of the way of life of the natives of Higher Crowstairs, who are shown to be warm and human. But in the service of his idea, Hardy is actually building up one side of the conflict by demonstrating that his natives are such nice, ordinary peasant folk that their judgments on matters of life and death are to be trusted. This is the positive side of Hardy's narratively presented argument.

[3]   When Hardy does engage both sides of the conflict--a complication occurring about midway through the story--by introducing the second stranger (the hangman), he has already established the grounds for his case, but he solidifies his argument by negatively presenting this ghoulish figure as brash, selfish, and obnoxious. When the natives learn of the second stranger's identity as the hangman, they are startled "with suppressed exclamations" (paragraph 79). The exclamations apparently take the form that if men like the hangman are associated with the letter of the law, the natives--along with the reader--will prefer the spirit even if the spirit may lead people to support apparently illegal actions. This reaction could not be sustained if the crime of the escaped criminal had been a violent one, but the "crime" was really the theft of a sheep to feed his starving family (paragraph 80). One may grant that Hardy is mitigating the crime here, but the conflict is not between right when it is right and wrong when it is wrong, but rather between legality when it is wrong and illegality when it is right. As Hardy structures the events in the story, it is not possible to disagree with the

---

° See pp. 133–47 for this story.
* Central idea.
† Thesis sentence.

judgment of the natives at the end that the intended hanging of the thief "was cruelly disproportioned to the transgression" (paragraph 160), for even if a reader wanted to disagree with Hardy's argument on legal grounds, the emotional thrust of the story leads toward extenuation.

[4]

Critical to this extenuation is Hardy's creation of suspense about the identity of the first stranger as Timothy Summers, the escaped prisoner. Because throughout the story readers have assented to the values and way of life of Shepherd Fennel and his guests, Hardy's crisis and climax forestall a purely legalistic reaction. Hardy puts Summers before the eyes of both country folk and readers as a brave and witty human being, not as a fugitive who has just escaped hanging. The revelation at the end therefore causes a second view of Summers. In retrospect, readers join the natives in admiring this first stranger's "marvelous coolness and daring in hob-and-nobbing with the hangman" (paragraph 160) and consequently would be indignant if such a person were actually to be hanged. As a result of Hardy's judicious withholding and disclosing of detail, he leads readers to deny the law when it is used unfairly.

[5]

Related to the major conflict are a number of lesser but still important conflicts that Hardy includes in the narrative. At crucial points, for example, he establishes that the natives living marginally "in the country about Higher Crowstairs" (paragraph 162) are uneasy and fearful of the law. When they realize that the second stranger is the hangman, they start "back," and one of them begins trembling (paragraph 79). Hardy invites readers to conclude that the natives view the conviction of Summers as a threat also to themselves. In a comic vein, Hardy contrasts the law with the ineptness of the shepherds who are called upon to enforce it (paragraphs 106–34). He makes the law so remote from their lives that when they actually make an arrest--of the third stranger-- they use words more appropriate to criminals or to priests (paragraphs 132–34). As an ironic dénouement of the story, Hardy tells us that the shepherds, resisting the legal but troubling hangman and magistrate, diligently search for Summers everywhere but where they know he can be found (paragraph 160).

[6]

In addition, Hardy includes other little but human contrasts in order to develop sympathy for the folk and therefore to strengthen his argument. Although the Fennels have twenty guests in their home, Mrs. Fennel is alarmed about giving them too much food and drink, and she is disturbed when the hangman selfishly depletes her store of mead. There is a small family disagreement on this score. Another minor and amusing conflict is set up by Hardy when Mrs. Fennel asks the musicians to stop playing, but they continue because they have been bribed by the amorous shepherd, Oliver Giles. There are also some noticeable contrasts in age among couples. Beyond these contrasts or opposites, which are vital to the story's structure, the technique of suspense is a conflict in itself, for it forces readers to consider and evaluate elements of the story a second time. These are all conflicts that Hardy employs in developing his major conflict between the right of the spirit and the wrong of the letter in "The Three Strangers."

Commentary on the Essay

As expressed in paragraph 1, this essay focuses on how Hardy structures character and action in "The Three Strangers" to achieve a contrast between right and wrong. The discussion of all events leading to the people's exoneration of the fugitive is seen not as narrative but as a contributing part of Hardy's argument. The essay thus argues that the parts of the story are placed where they are because they are aspects of Hardy's own argument. To emphasize this aim, words and phrases are introduced, such as "arranges events," "engage both sides of the conflict," "structures the events," "creation of suspense," "establishes," and "in order to develop sympathy." All these expressions are intended as reminders that the subject of the essay is the way in which Hardy structures the story.

In the body, paragraph 2 explains how Hardy introduces the shepherds and their guests at the Fennels' cottage to illustrate their qualities of warmth and humanity. Paragraph 3 stresses the negative reaction of the country folk when they learn that the second stranger is the hangman. Together, then, paragraphs 2 and 3 serve to explain the underlying causes of Hardy's arrangement of the narrative.

In paragraph 4 the essay explains Hardy's delay in identifying the fugitive: This delay allows Hardy to elaborate on his positive picture of the country folk and their values, and it also helps him in persuading readers of the story to concur in the decision for justice that the shepherds make. Paragraph 5 states that other conflicts in the story show that the shepherds are uneasy with the law and fearful of it—attitudes that reinforce their decision to favor the first stranger. The last paragraph argues that additional "but human" contrasts are placed so as to augment Hardy's favorable portraits of the Fennels and their guests.

SPECIAL TOPICS FOR WRITING AND ARGUMENT ABOUT PLOT AND STRUCTURE

1. What kind of story might "A Worn Path" be, structurally, if the detail about the invalid grandson were introduced at the start, before Phoenix begins her walk to town?

2. Compare the structuring of the interior scenes in "The Three Strangers," "A Worn Path," and "Blue Winds Dancing." How do these scenes bring out the various conflicts of the stories? How do characters in the interiors contribute to plot developments? What is the relationship of these characters to the major themes of the stories?

3. Consider the surprises in "An Occurrence at Owl Creek Bridge" (Chapter 5), "The Story of an Hour" (Chapter 8), and "The Three Strangers." How much preparation is made for the surprises? In retrospect, to what degree are the surprises not surprises at all but rather necessary outcomes of the preceding parts of the works?

4. Compare "Everyday Use" (Chapter 2) and "Blue Winds Dancing" as stories developing plots about clashing social and racial values. In what ways are the plots similar and different?

5. Analyze the repetitiveness in Kincaid's "What I Have Been Doing Lately." In what ways does the repetition seem to be a structural defect? In what ways does it seem to be an essential aspect of Kincaid's ideas as presented in the story?

6. Consider those aspects of "A Worn Path" that seem socially and politically significant. You might consider questions such as whether elderly women like Phoenix are living in such remote areas today, or whether her grandson should be left entirely in her care, or whether she should be near public transportation so that she would not need to walk great distances to attend to her needs. You might also consider her as a representative of a group suffering discrimination and treat her as an example of the need for legislation that would improve her condition.

7. Select a circumstance in your life that caused you doubt, difficulty, and conflict. Making yourself anonymous (give yourself a fictitious name and put yourself in a fictitious location), write a brief story about the occasion, stressing how your conflict began, how it affected you, and how you resolved it. You might choose to describe the details in chronological order, or you might begin the story in the present tense and introduce details in flashback.

8. Eudora Welty is considered one of the major contemporary southern writers. Using books and articles that you obtain from your library to substantiate your arguments, how valid is this assertion? What is particularly southern about her work? What is less regional and more general about what she is saying? (You may use "A Worn Path" as representative of her writing.)

4

Characters: The People in Fiction

Writers of fiction create narratives that enhance and deepen our understanding of human character and human life. In our own day, under the influences of pioneers like Freud, Jung, and Skinner, the science of psychology has influenced both the creation and the study of literature. It is well known that Freud buttressed some of his psychological conclusions by referring to literary works, especially plays by Shakespeare. Widely known films such as *Spellbound, The Snake Pit,* and *Final Analysis* have popularized the relationships between literary character and psychology. Without doubt, the presentation and understanding of character is a major aim of fiction (and literature generally).

In literature, a **character** can be defined as a verbal representation of a human being. Through action, speech, description, and commentary, authors portray characters who are worth caring about, cheering for, and even loving, although there are also characters you may laugh at, dislike, or even hate.

In a story or play emphasizing a major character, you may expect that each action or speech, no matter how small, is part of a total presentation of that complex combination of both the inner and the outer self that constitutes a human being. Whereas in life things may "just happen," in literature all actions, interactions, speeches, and observations are deliberate. Thus, you read about important actions like a long period of work and sacrifice (Maupassant's "The Necklace" [Chapter 1]), the taking of a regular journey of mercy (Welty's "A Worn Path" [Chapter 3]), an act of vengeance (Poe's "The Cask of Amontillado" [Chapter 11]), or a young man's poignant dream of freedom (Bierce's "An Occurrence at Owl Creek Bridge" [Chapter 5]). By making such actions interesting, authors help you understand and appreciate not only their major characters but also life itself.

CHARACTER TRAITS

In studying a literary character, try to determine the character's outstanding traits. A **trait** is a quality of mind or habitual mode of behavior, such as never repaying borrowed money, avoiding eye contact, or always thinking oneself the center of attention. If we study the facial expression of Andrea del Verrocchio's bust of Lorenzo de' Medici, for example (below), we can see that Verrocchio is presenting a negative view of his subject. Lorenzo's firm mouth, his fixed stare, his closely knit eyebrows suggest his pride and ruthlessness. Sometimes, of course, the traits we encounter are minor and therefore negligible, but often a trait may be a person's *primary* characteristic (not only in fiction but also in life). Thus, characters may be ambitious or lazy, serene or anxious, aggressive or fearful, thoughtful or inconsiderate, open or secretive, confident or self-doubting, kind or cruel, quiet or noisy, visionary or practical, careful or care-less, impartial or biased, straightforward or underhanded, "winners" or "losers," and so on.

With this sort of list, to which you may add at will, you can analyze and develop conclusions about character. For example, Mathilde in Maupassant's "The Necklace" (Chapter 1) indulges in dreams of unattainable wealth and comfort, and is so swept up in her visions that she scorns her comparatively good life with her reliable but dull husband. It is fair to say that this aversion to reality is her major trait. It is also a major weakness, because Maupassant shows how her dream life harms her real life. By contrast, the narrator of Anderson's "I'm a Fool" (Chapter 5) describes the lies he told about himself when courting a young woman. Although he regrets his foolishness, the self-awareness he shows also indicates his increasing character strength. By similarly analyzing the

Andrea del Verrochio, "Bust of Lorenzo de'Medici." National Gallery of Art, Washington, DC, Samuel H. Kress Collection.

actions, speeches, and thoughts of the literary characters you encounter, you can also draw conclusions about their qualities and strengths.

Distinguish between Circumstances and Character Traits

When you study a fictional person, distinguish between circumstances and character, for circumstances have value *only if they demonstrate important traits.* Thus, if our friend Sam wins a lottery, let us congratulate him on his luck; but the win does not say much about his *character*—not much, that is, unless we also learn that he has been spending hundreds of dollars each week for lottery tickets. In other words, making the effort to win a lottery *is* a character trait but winning (or losing) *is not.*

Or, let us suppose that an author stresses the neatness of one character and the sloppiness of another. If you accept the premise that people care for their appearance according to choice—and that choices develop from character—you can use these details to make conclusions about a person's self-esteem or the lack of it. In short, when reading about characters in literature, look beyond circumstances, actions, and appearances, and *determine what these things show about character.* Always try to get from the outside to the inside, for it is the *internal* quality that determines the *external* behavior.

HOW AUTHORS DISCLOSE CHARACTER IN LITERATURE

Authors use five methods of making their characters live. Remember that you must use your own knowledge and experience to make judgments about the qualities of the characters being revealed.

1. ACTIONS BY CHARACTERS REVEAL THEIR NATURES.   What characters *do* is our best clue to understanding what they *are.* For example, walking in the woods is recreation for most people, and it shows little about their characters except a fondness for the outdoors (perhaps a significant trait). But Phoenix's walk through the woods in Welty's "A Worn Path" (Chapter 3) is difficult and dangerous for her. Her walk, seen within the context of her age and her mission, can be taken as the expression of her loving, responsible character. Similar strength may be seen when a character faces psychological difficulties, as in Joy Williams's "Taking Care" (Chapter 2). For Jones, the central character who is also a minister, all aspects of life are going badly—with his wife, his daughter, and his own religious faith. Despite these incentives to despair, however, he preserves his caring and loving role, thus showing his quiet determination and devotion.

Like ordinary human beings, fictional characters do not necessarily understand how they may be changing or why they do the things they do. Nevertheless, their actions express their characters. Sarty of Faulkner's "Barn Burning" is such a character. He is developing a sense of rightness and responsibility, but he does not show the knowledge that is causing his growth. Actions may also signal qualities such as naiveté, weakness, deceit, a scheming personality, strong inner conflicts, a realization, or other growth or change. The actions of Abner Snopes in "Barn Burning" indicate a character of suspicion and resentment. Similarly, the strong inner conflict experienced by the two women in Glaspell's "A Jury of Her Peers" brings out their character strength. Theoretically, they have a strong obligation to the law, but they discover that they have an even stronger personal obligation to the accused killer, Minnie. Hence their silence about the incriminating evidence they uncover shows their adaptability and their willingness to change their views under new circumstances.

2. THE AUTHOR'S DESCRIPTIONS TELL US ABOUT CHARACTERS. Appearance and environment reveal much about a character's social and economic status, and they also tell us about character traits. Mathilde in Maupassant's "The Necklace" (Chapter 1) dreams about wealth and unlimited purchasing power. Although her unrealizable desires ultimately destroy her way of life, they also cause her character strength to emerge. The descriptions of country folkways in Hardy's "The Three Strangers" (Chapter 3) are independently interesting and unique, but they also make plain the personal loyalty of the peasants and their social stability and solidity.

3. WHAT CHARACTERS SAY REVEALS WHAT THEY ARE LIKE. Although the speeches of most characters are functional—essential to keeping the action moving along—they provide material from which you may draw conclusions. When the second traveler of Hawthorne's "Young Goodman Brown" (Chapter 9) speaks, for example, he reveals his devious and deceptive nature even though ostensibly he appears friendly. The lawmen in "A Jury of Her Peers" speak straightforwardly and directly, and these speeches suggest that their characters are similarly orderly. Their constant ridicule of the two women, however, indicates their limitations.

Often, characters use speech to hide their motives, though we as readers should see through such a ploy. The narrator Montresor in Poe's "The Cask of Amontillado" (Chapter 11), for example, is a vengeful schemer, and we conclude this much from his indirect and manipulative language to the equally unpleasant but gullible Fortunato. To Fortunato, Montresor seems friendly and sociable, but to us, he is lurid and demonic.

4. WHAT OTHERS SAY ABOUT A CHARACTER MAY REVEAL TRAITS ABOUT THAT CHARACTER. By studying what characters say about each other, you can enhance your understanding of the character being discussed. Thus the two medical attendants talking about Phoenix's condition in Welty's "A Worn Path" (Chapter 3) tell us much about her difficult life, and more importantly they provide a basis for conclusions about Phoenix's great strength.

Ironically, speeches often indicate something other than what the speakers intend, perhaps because of prejudice, stupidity, or foolishness. Lengel's disparagement of the girls in bathing suits in Updike's "A & P" (Chapter 7), for example, reveals to us not his wisdom but his rigidity and limited judgment.

Similarly, the sister in O'Connor's "First Confession" (Chapter 7) tells about her brother's violent outburst against her, but in effect she describes the boy's individuality just as she also discloses her own spitefulness.

5. THE AUTHOR, SPEAKING AS A STORYTELLER OR AN OBSERVER, MAY PRESENT JUDGMENTS ABOUT CHARACTERS.   What the author, speaking as a work's authorial voice, says about a character is usually accurate, and the authorial voice can be accepted factually. However, when the authorial voice interprets actions and characteristics, as in Hawthorne's "Young Goodman Brown" (Chapter 9) the author himself or herself assumes the role of a reader or critic, and any opinions may be questioned. For this reason, authors frequently avoid interpretations and devote their skill to arranging events and speeches so that readers can draw their own conclusions.

TYPES OF CHARACTERS: ROUND AND FLAT

No writer can present an entire life history of a protagonist, nor can each character in a story get "equal time" for development. Accordingly, some characters grow to be full and alive, while others remain shadowy. The British novelist and critic E. M. Forster, in his critical work *Aspects of the Novel,* calls the two major types "round" and "flat." [1]

1. ROUND CHARACTERS UNDERGO CHANGE.   The basic trait of **round characters** is that authors present enough detail about them to render them full, lifelike, and memorable. Their roundness is characterized by both individuality and unpredictability. A complementary quality about round characters is therefore that they are **dynamic.** That is, they *recognize, change with,* or *adjust to* circumstances. Such changes may be shown in (1) an action or actions, (2) the realization of new strength and therefore the affirmation of previous decisions, (3) the acceptance of a new condition and the need for making changes, or (4) the discovery of unrecognized truths. For example, Minnie Wright, in Glaspell's "A Jury of Her Peers," is dynamic. We learn that as a young woman she was happy and musical, though shy, but that she has been deprived and blighted by her twenty-year marriage. Finally, however, a particularly cruel action by her husband so enrages her that she breaks out of her subservient role and commits an act of violence. In short, her action shows her as a dynamic character capable of radical change.

Because a round character usually plays a major role in a story, he or she is often called the **hero** or **heroine.** Some round characters are not particularly heroic, however, so it is preferable to use the more neutral word **protagonist** (the "first actor"). The protagonist is central to the action, moves against an **antagonist** (the "opposing actor"), and exhibits the ability to adapt to new circumstances.

---

[1]See Forster's story "The Point of It" in Chapter 12.

2. FLAT CHARACTERS STAY THE SAME.   Unlike round characters, **flat characters** do not grow. They remain the same because they are stupid or insensitive or because they lack knowledge or insight. They end where they begin and thus are **static,** not dynamic. Flat characters are not worthless, however, for they highlight the development of the round characters, as with the lawmen in Glaspell's "A Jury of Her Peers." Usually, flat characters are minor (e.g., relatives, acquaintances, functionaries), but not all minor characters are necessarily flat.

Sometimes flat characters are prominent in certain types of literature, such as cowboy, police, and detective stories, where the focus is less on character than on performance. Such characters might be lively and engaging, even though they do not develop or change. They must be strong, tough, and clever enough to perform recurring tasks such as solving a crime, overcoming a villain, or finding a treasure. The term **stock character** refers to characters in these repeating situations. To the degree that stock characters have many common traits, they are **representative** of their class or group. Such characters, with variations in names, ages, and sexes, have been constant in literature since the ancient Greeks. Some regular stock characters are the insensitive father, the interfering mother, the sassy younger sister or brother, the greedy politician, the resourceful cowboy or detective, the overbearing or henpecked husband, the submissive or nagging wife, the angry police captain, the lovable drunk, and the town do-gooder.

Stock characters stay flat as long as they do no more than perform their roles and exhibit conventional and unindividual traits. When they possess no attitudes except those of their class, they are called **stereotype** characters, because they all seem to have been cast in the same mold.

When authors bring characters into focus, however, no matter what roles they perform, the characters emerge from flatness and move into roundness. For example, though most of us would expect grocery-store checkout clerks to be flat, the clerk Sammy in Updike's "A & P" (Chapter 7) is round, not flat, because he grows quickly under the special circumstances in the store where he works. Similarly, Sarty of Faulkner's "Barn Burning" is just a little boy, but he grows morally in opposition to his father's criminal acts. In sum, the ability to grow and develop and to be altered by circumstances makes characters round and dynamic. Absence of these traits makes characters flat and static.

REALITY AND PROBABILITY: VERISIMILITUDE

Characters in fiction should be true to life. Therefore their actions, statements, and thoughts must all be what human beings are *likely* to do, say, and think under the conditions presented in the literary work. This is the standard of **verisimilitude, probability,** or **plausibility.** One may readily admit that there are people *in life* who perform tasks or exhibit characteristics that are difficult or seemingly impossible (such as always leading the team to victory, always getting A+'s on every test, always being cheerful and helpful, or always understanding the needs of others). However, such characters *in fiction* would not be true to life because they do not fit within *normal* or *usual* behavior.

You should therefore distinguish between what characters may *possibly* do and what they *most frequently* or *most usually* do. Thus, in Maupassant's "The Necklace" (Chapter 1) it is possible that Mathilde could be truthful and tell her friend Jeanne Forrestier about the lost necklace. In light of her pride and sense of self-respect, however, it is more in character for her and her husband to hide the loss, borrow money for a replacement, and endure the consequences for ten years. Granted the possibilities of the story (either self-sacrifice or the admission of a fault or a possible crime), the decision she makes with her husband is the more *probable* one.

Nevertheless, probability does not rule out surprise or even exaggeration. It is unusual that young Sarty tries to inform on his father in Faulkner's "Barn Burning," but it is not improbable because he has been developing a sense of morality throughout the story. Likewise, in Katherine Anne Porter's "The Jilting of Granny Weatherall" (Chapter 12) the accomplishments of Granny—such as fencing a hundred acres of farmland all by herself—do not seem impossible even if they do seem unlikely. But we learn that when she was young she became compulsively determined to overcome the betrayal of her unfaithful lover. It is therefore probable that she would be capable of a monumental achievement like building the fence.

There are many ways of rendering probability in character. Works that attempt to mirror life—realistic, naturalistic, or "slice of life" stories like Hardy's "The Three Strangers"(Chapter 3)—set up a pattern of everyday probability. Less realistic conditions establish different frameworks of probability, in which characters are *expected* to be unusual. Such an example is Hawthorne's "Young Goodman Brown" (Chapter 9). Because a major way of explaining this story is that Brown is having a nightmarish psychotic trance, his bizarre and unnatural responses are probable. Equally probable is the way the doctors explain Louise Mallard's sudden death at the end of Kate Chopin's "The Story of an Hour" (Chapter 8) even though their smug analysis is totally (and comically) wrong.

You might also encounter works containing *supernatural* figures such as the second traveler in "Young Goodman Brown." You may wonder whether such characters are probable or improbable. Usually, gods and goddesses embody qualities of the best and most moral human beings, and devils like Hawthorne's guide take on attributes of the worst. However, you might remember that the devil is often given dashing and engaging qualities so that he can deceive gullible sinners and lead them into hell. The friendliness of Brown's guide is therefore not an improbable trait. In judging characters of this or any other type, your best criteria are probability, consistency, and believability.

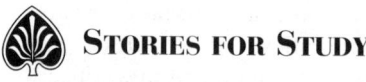 ## STORIES FOR STUDY

WILLA CATHER (1873–1947)

Willa Cather is acknowledged as one of America's foremost writers. Her life spanned the period from the decade after the Civil War to the conclusion of World War II. She was born in Virginia and as a girl was taken to Nebraska during mass migrations of homesteaders into the Midwest in the decades after the Civil War. She received a degree from the University of Nebraska in 1895 and spent time after that as a teacher in both Pittsburgh and New York. In 1911 she decided to become a writer, ultimately living in New York. During her career she published twelve novels and fifty-eight short stories. Her best-known novels are O Pioneers! *(1913),* My Antonía *(1918),* A Lost Lady *(1923), and* Death Comes for the Archbishop *(1927). She was the recipient of the Pulitzer Prize for 1923 for her novel* One of Ours. *"Paul's Case" was one of her earliest stories, appearing in her collection* The Troll Garden *(1905).*

Paul's Case ————————————————————— 1905

A Study in Temperament

It was Paul's afternoon to appear before the faculty of the Pittsburgh High School to account for his various misdemeanors. He had been suspended a week ago, and his father had called at the Principal's office and confessed his perplexity about his son. Paul entered the faculty room suave and smiling. His clothes were a trifle outgrown, and the tan velvet on the collar of his open overcoat was frayed and worn; but for all that there was something of the dandy about him, and he wore an opal pin in his neatly knotted black four-in-hand, and a red carnation in his buttonhole. This latter adornment the faculty somehow felt was not properly significant of the contrite spirit befitting a boy under the ban of suspension.

Paul was tall for his age and very thin, with high, cramped shoulders and a narrow chest. His eyes were remarkable for a certain hysterical brilliancy, and he continually used them in a conscious, theatrical sort of way, peculiarity offensive in a boy. The pupils were abnormally large, as though he were addicted to belladonna, but there was a glassy glitter about them which that drug does not produce.

When questioned by the Principal as to why he was there, Paul stated, politely enough, that he wanted to come back to school. This was a lie, but Paul was quite accustomed to lying; found it, indeed, indispensable for overcoming friction. His teachers were asked to state their respective charges against him, which they did with such a rancor and aggrievedness as evinced that this was not a usual case. Disorder and impertinence were among the offenses named, yet each of his instructors felt that it was scarcely possible to put into words the real cause of the trouble, which lay in a sort of hysterically defiant manner of the boy's; in the contempt which they all knew he felt for them, and which he seemingly made not the least effort to conceal. Once, when he had been making a synopsis of a paragraph at the blackboard, his English teacher had stepped to his side and attempted to guide his hand. Paul had started back with a shudder and thrust his hands violently behind him. The astonished woman could scarcely have been more hurt and embarrassed had he struck at her. The insult was so involuntary and definitely personal as to be unforgettable. In one way and another, he had made all his teachers, men and women alike, conscious of the same feeling of physical aversion. In one class he habitually sat with his hand shading his eyes; in another he always looked out of the window during the recitation; in another he made a running commentary on the lecture, with humorous intent.

His teachers felt this afternoon that his whole attitude was symbolized by his shrug and his flippantly red carnation flower, and they fell upon him without mercy, his English teacher leading the pack. He stood through it smiling, his pale lips parted over his white teeth. (His lips were continually twitching, and he had a habit of raising his eyebrows that was contemptuous and irritating to the last degree.) Older boys than Paul had broken down and shed tears under that ordeal, but his set smile did not once desert him, and his only sign of discomfort was the nervous trembling of the fingers that toyed with the buttons of his overcoat, and an occasional jerking of the other hand which held his hat. Paul was always smiling, always glancing about him, seeming to feel that people might be watching him and trying to detect something. This conscious expression, since it was as far as possible from boyish mirthfulness, was usually attributed to insolence or "smartness."

As the inquisition proceeded, one of his instructors repeated an impertinent   5
remark of the boy's, and the Principal asked him whether he thought that a courteous speech to make to a woman. Paul shrugged his shoulders slightly and his eyebrows twitched.

"I don't know," he replied, "I didn't mean to be polite or impolite, either. I guess it's a sort of way I have, of saying things regardless."

The Principal asked him whether he didn't think that a way it would be well to get rid of. Paul grinned and said he guessed so. When he was told that he could go, he bowed gracefully and went out. His bow was like a repetition of the scandalous red carnation.

His teachers were in despair, and his drawing master voiced the feeling of them all when he declared there was something about the boy which none of them understood. He added, "I don't really believe that smile of his comes altogether from insolence; there's something sort of haunted about it. The boy is not strong, for one thing. There is something wrong about the fellow."

The drawing master had come to realize that, in looking at Paul, one saw only his white teeth and the forced animation of his eyes. One warm afternoon the boy had gone to sleep at his drawing board, and his master had noted with amazement what a white, blue-veined face it was; drawn and wrinkled like an old man's about the eyes, the lips twitching even in his sleep.

His teachers left the building dissatisfied and unhappy; humiliated to have felt so   10
vindictive toward a mere boy, to have uttered this feeling in cutting terms, and to have set each other on, as it were, in the gruesome game of intemperate reproach. One of them remembered having seen a miserable street cat set at bay by a ring of tormentors.

As for Paul, he ran down the hill whistling the Soldiers' Chorus from *Faust,*° looking wildly behind him now and then to see whether some of his teachers were not there to witness his light-heartedness. As it was now late in the afternoon and Paul was on duty that evening as usher at Carnegie Hall,° he decided that he would not go home to supper. When he reached the concert hall the doors were not yet open. It was chilly outside, and he decided to go up into the picture gallery—always deserted at this hour—where there were some of Raffaëlli's° gay studies of Paris streets and an airy blue Venetian scene or two that always exhilarated him. He was delighted to find no one in the gallery but the old guard, who sat in the corner, a newspaper on his knee, a black patch over one eye and the other closed. Paul possessed himself of the place and walked confidently up and down, whistling under his breath. After a while he sat down before a blue Rico° and lost himself. When he bethought him to look at his watch, it was after seven o'clock, and he rose with a start and ran downstairs, making a face at Augustus Caesar,° peering out from the cast-room, and an evil gesture at the Venus of Milo° as he passed her on the stairway.

When Paul reached the ushers' dressing-room half a dozen boys were there already, and he began excitedly to tumble into his uniform. It was one of the few that at all approached fitting, and Paul thought it very becoming—though he knew the tight, straight coat accentuated his narrow chest, about which he was exceedingly sensitive. He was always excited while he dressed, twanging all over to the tuning of the strings and preliminary flourishes of the horns in the music-room; but tonight he seemed quite beside himself, and he teased and plagued the boys until, telling him that he was crazy, they put him down on the floor and sat on him.

Somewhat calmed by his suppression, Paul dashed out to the front of the house to seat the early comers. He was a model usher. Gracious and smiling he ran up and down the aisles. Nothing was too much trouble for him; he carried messages and brought programs as though it were his greatest pleasure in life, and all the people in his section thought him a charming boy, feeling that he remembered and admired them. As the house filled, he grew more and more vivacious and animated, and the color came to his cheeks and lips. It was very much as though this were a great reception and Paul were the host. Just as the musicians came out to take their places, his English teacher arrived with checks for the seat which a prominent manufacturer had taken for the season. She betrayed some embarrassment when she handed Paul the tickets, and a *hauteur* which subsequently made her feel very foolish. Paul was startled for a moment and had the feeling of wanting to put her out; what business had she here among all these fine people and gay colors? He looked her over and decided that she was not appropriately dressed and must be a fool to sit downstairs in such togs. The tickets had probably been sent her out of kindness, he reflected, as he put down a seat for her, and she had about as much right to sit there as he had.

When the symphony began Paul sank into one of the rear seats with a long sigh of relief, and lost himself as he had done before the Rico. It was not that symphonies, as

15

Faust: the most popular opera of Charles Gounod (1818–1893), first produced in 1859.

Carnegie Hall: in Pittsburgh, not the more famous one in New York.

Raffaëlli: Jean-François Rafaëlli (1850–1924), impressionist painter, sculptor, and engraver, known for his scenes of Parisian life.

Rico: Martin Rico (1833–1908). Spanish painter, known for his landscapes.

Caesar . . . Milo: copies of the famous statues of Augustus in the Vatican Museum and the Venus de Milo in the Louvre.

such, meant anything in particular to Paul, but the first sigh of the instruments seemed to free some hilarious spirit within him; something that struggled there like the Genius in the bottle found by the Arab fisherman.° He felt a sudden zest of life; the lights danced before his eyes and the concert hall blazed into unimaginable splendor. When the soprano soloist came on, Paul forgot even the nastiness of his teacher's being there, and gave himself up to the peculiar intoxication such personages always had for him. The soloist chanced to be a German woman, by no means in her first youth, and the mother of many children; but she wore a satin gown and a tiara, and she had that indefinable air of achievement, that world-shine upon her, which always blinded Paul to any possible defects.

After a concert was over, Paul was often irritable and wretched until he got to sleep—and tonight he was even more than usually restless. He had the feeling of not being able to let down; of its being impossible to give up this delicious excitement which was the only thing that could be called living at all. During the last number he withdrew and, after hastily changing his clothes in the dressing-room, slipped out to the side door where the singer's carriage stood. Here he began pacing rapidly up and down the walk, waiting to see her come out.

Over yonder the Schenley, in its vacant stretch, loomed big and square through the fine rain, the windows of its twelve stories glowing like those of a lighted cardboard house under a Christmas tree. All the actors and singers of any importance stayed there when they were in the city, and a number of the big manufacturers of the place lived there in the winter. Paul had often hung about the hotel, watching the people go in and out, longing to enter and leave schoolmasters and dull care° behind him forever.

As last the singer came out, accompanied by the conductor, who helped her into her carriage and closed the door with a cordial *auf Wiedersehen*°—which set Paul to wondering whether she were not an old sweetheart of his. Paul followed the carriage over to the hotel, walking so rapidly as not to be far from the entrance when the singer alighted and disappeared behind the swinging glass doors which were opened by a Negro in a tall hat and a long coat. In the moment that the door was ajar, it seemed to Paul that he, too, entered. He seemed to feel himself go after her up the steps, into the warm, lighted building, into an exotic, a tropical world of shiny, glistening surfaces and basking ease. He reflected upon the mysterious dishes that were brought into the dining-room, the green bottles in buckets of ice, as he had seen them in the supper party pictures of the Sunday supplement. A quick gust of wind brought the rain down with sudden vehemence, and Paul was startled to find that he was still outside in the slush of the gravel driveway; that his boots were letting in the water and his scanty overcoat was clinging wet about him; that the lights in front of the concert hall were out, and that the rain was driving in sheets between him and the orange glow of the windows above him. There it was, what he wanted—tangibly before him, like the fairy world of Christmas pantomime; as the rain beat in his face, Paul wondered whether he were destined always to shiver in the black night outside looking up at it.

He turned and walked reluctantly toward the car° tracks. The end had to come some time; his father in his night-clothes at the top of the stairs, explanations that did not explain, hastily improvised fictions that were forever tripping him up, his upstairs

---

    Arab fisherman: reference to the tale of "The Fisherman and the Jinni" from *The Arabian Nights.*
    dull care: phrase from the popular seventeenth-century song "Begone, Dull Care."
    auf Wiedersehen: German for "goodbye" (literally "until the seeing again").
    car: streetcar.

room and its horrible yellow wallpaper, the creaking bureau with the greasy plush collar-box, and over his painted wooden bed the pictures of George Washington and John Calvin,° and the framed motto, "Feed my Lambs,"° which had been worked in red worsted by his mother, whom Paul could not remember.

Half an hour later, Paul alighted from the Negley Avenue car and went slowly   20
down one of the side streets off the main thoroughfare. It was a highly respectable street, where all the houses were exactly alike, and where business men of moderate means begot and reared large families of children, all of whom went to Sabbath-school and learned the shorter catechism, and were interested in arithmetic; all of whom were as exactly alike as their homes, and of a piece with the monotony in which they lived. Paul never went up Cordelia Street without a shudder of loathing. His home was next to the house of the Cumberland° minister. He approached it tonight with the nerveless sense of defeat, the hopeless feeling of sinking back forever into ugliness and commonness that he had always had when he came home. The moment he turned into Cordelia Street he felt the waters close above his head. After each of these orgies of living, he experienced all the physical depression which follows a debauch; the loathing of respectable beds, of common food, of a house permeated by kitchen odors; a shudder-ing repulsion for the flavorless, colorless mass of everyday existence; a morbid desire for cool things and soft lights and fresh flowers.

The nearer he approached the house, the more absolutely unequal Paul felt to the sight of it all; his ugly sleeping chamber, the cold bathroom with the grimy zinc tub, the cracked mirror, the dripping spigots; his father, at the top of the stairs, his hairy legs sticking out from his nightshirt, his feet thrust into carpet slippers. He was so much later than usual that there would certainly be inquiries and reproaches. Paul stopped short before the door. He felt that he could not be accosted by his father tonight; that he could not toss again on that miserable bed. He would not go in. He would tell his father that he had no car fare, and it was raining so hard he had gone home with one of the boys and stayed all night.

Meanwhile, he was wet and cold. He went around to the back of the house and tried one of the basement windows, found it open, raised it cautiously, and scrambled down the cellar wall to the floor. There he stood, holding his breath, terrified by the noise he had made; but the floor above him was silent, and there was no creak on the stairs. He found a soap-box and carried it over to the soft ring of light that streamed from the furnace door, and sat down. He was horribly afraid of rats, so he did not try to sleep, but sat looking distrustfully at the dark, still terrified lest he might have awakened his father. In such reactions, after one of the experiences which made days and nights out of the dreary blanks of the calendar, when his senses were deadened, Paul's head was always singularly clear. Suppose his father had heard him getting in at the window and had come down and shot him for a burglar? Then, again, suppose his father had come down, pistol in hand, and he had cried out in time to save himself, and his father had been horrified to think how nearly he had killed him? Then, again, suppose a day should come when his father would remember that night, and wish there had been no warning cry to stay his hand? With this last supposition Paul entertained himself until daybreak.

John Calvin: John Calvin (1509–1564), a major theologian of the early Reformation in Switzerland.
   "Feed my Lambs:" See John 21:15–17.
   Cumberland: an independent, Evangelical branch of the Presbyterian Church, established in 1810.

The following Sunday was fine; the sodden November chill was broken by the last flash of autumnal summer. In the morning Paul had to go to church and Sabbath-school, as always. On seasonable Sunday afternoons the burghers of Cordelia Street usually sat out on their front "stoops," and talked to their neighbors on the next stoop, or called to those across the street in neighborly fashion. The men sat placidly on gay cushions placed upon the steps that led down to the sidewalk, while the women, in their Sunday "waists,"° sat in rockers on the cramped porches, pretending to be greatly at their ease. The children played in the streets; there were so many of them that the place resembled the recreation grounds of a kindergarten. The men on the steps—all in their shirt sleeves, their vests unbuttoned—sat with their legs well apart, their stomachs comfortably protruding, and talked of the prices of things, or told anecdotes of the sagacity of their various chiefs and overloads. They occasionally looked over the multitude of squabbling children, listened affectionately to their high-pitched, nasal voices, smiling to see their own proclivities reproduced in their offspring, and interspersed their legends of the iron kings with remarks about their son's progress at school, their grades in arithmetic, and the amounts they had saved in their toy banks. On this last Sunday of November, Paul sat all the afternoon on the lowest step of his "stoop," staring into the street, while his sisters, in their rockers, were talking to the minister's daughters next door about how many shirtwaists they had made in the last week, and how many waffles someone had eaten at the last church supper. When the weather was warm, and his father was in a particularly jovial frame of mind, the girls made lemonade, which was always brought out in a red-glass pitcher, ornamented with forget-me-nots in blue enamel. This the girls thought very fine, and the neighbors joked about the suspicious color of the pitcher.

Today Paul's father, on the top step, was talking to a young man who shifted a restless baby from knee to knee. He happened to be the young man who was daily held up to Paul as a model, and after whom it was his father's dearest hope that he would pattern. This young man was of a ruddy complexion, with a compressed, red mouth, and faded, nearsighted eyes, over which he wore thick spectacles, with gold bows that curved about his ears. He was clerk to one of the magnates of a great steel corporation, and was looked upon in Cordelia Street as a young man with a future. There was a story that, come five years ago—he was now barely twenty-six—he had been a trifle 'dissipated,' but in order to curb his appetites and save the loss of time and strength that a sowing of wild oats might have entailed, he had taken his chief's advice, oft reiterated to his employees, and at twenty-one had married the first woman whom he could persuade to share his fortunes. She happened to be an angular school mistress, much older than he, who also wore thick glasses, and who had now borne him four children, all nearsighted, like herself.

The young man was relating how his chief, now cruising in the Mediterranean, kept in touch with all the details of the business, arranging his office hours on his yacht just as though he were at home, and "knocking off work enough to keep two stenographers busy." His father told, in turn, the plan his corporation was considering, of putting in an electric railway plant at Cairo. Paul snapped his teeth; he had an awful apprehension that they might spoil it all before he got there. Yet he rather liked to hear these legends of the iron kings, that were told and retold on Sundays and holidays; these stories of palaces in Venice, yachts on the Mediterranean, and high play at Monte Carlo appealed to his fancy, and he was interested in the triumphs of cash boys° who had become famous, though he had no mind for the cash-boy stage. 25

---

waists: laced, close-fitting vests or jackets.

cash boys: The Cash Boy, a novel by Horatio Alger (1832–1899), tells about the progress of a young boy from a $156 a year "cash boy" position to the inheritance of a million dollars.

After supper was over, and he had helped to dry the dishes, Paul nervously asked his father whether he could go to George's to get some help in his geometry, and still more nervously asked for car fare. This latter request he had to repeat, as his father, on principle, did not like to hear requests for money, whether much or little. He asked Paul whether he could not go to some boy who lived nearer, and told him that he ought not to leave his school work until Sunday; but he gave him the dime. He was not a poor man, but he had a worthy ambition to come up in the world. His only reason for allowing Paul to usher was that he thought a boy ought to be earning a little.

Paul bounded upstairs, scrubbed the greasy odor of the dishwater from his hands with the ill-smelling soap he hated, and then shook over his fingers a few drops of violet water from the bottle he kept hidden in his drawer. He left the house with his geometry conspicuously under his arm, and the moment he got out of Cordelia Street and boarded a downtown car, he shook off the lethargy of two deadening days, and began to live again.

The leading juvenile of the permanent stock company which played at one of the downtown theaters was an acquaintance of Paul's, and the boy had been invited to drop in at the Sunday night rehearsals whenever he could. For more than a year Paul had spent every available moment loitering about Charley Edwards's dressing-room. He had won a place among Edwards's following not only because the young actor, who could not afford to employ a dresser, often found him useful, but because he recognized in Paul something akin to what churchmen term "vocation."

It was at the theater and at Carnegie Hall that Paul really lived; the rest was but a sleep and a forgetting.° This was Paul's fairy tale, and it had for him all the allurement of a secret love. The moment he inhaled the gassy, painty, dusty odor behind the scenes, he breathed like a prisoner set free, and felt within him the possibility of doing or saying splendid, brilliant things. The moment the cracked orchestra beat out the overture for *Martha,*° or jerked at the serenade from *Rigoletto,*° all stupid and ugly things slid from him, and his senses were deliciously, yet delicately fired.

Perhaps it was because, in Paul's world, the natural nearly always wore the guise of ugliness, that a certain element of artificiality seemed to him necessary in beauty. Perhaps it was because his experience of life elsewhere was so full of Sabbath-school picnics, petty economies, wholesome advice as to how to succeed in life, and the unescapable odors of cooking, that he found this existence so alluring, these smartly-clad men and women so attractive, that he was so moved by these starry apple orchards that bloomed perennially under the limelight. 30

It would be difficult to put it strongly enough how convincingly the stage entrance of that theater was for Paul the actual portal of Romance. Certainly none of the company ever suspected it, least of all Charley Edwards. It was very like the old stories that used to float about London of fabulously rich Jews, who had subterranean halls, with palms, and fountains, and soft lamps and richly apparelled women who never saw the disenchanting light of London day. So, in the midst of that smoke-palled city, enamored of figures and grimy toil, Paul had his secret temple, his wishing-carpet, his bit of blue-and-white Mediterranean shore bathed in perpetual sunshine.

Several of Paul's teachers had a theory that his imagination had been perverted by garish fiction; but the truth was, he scarcely ever read at all. The books at home were

---

a sleep and a forgetting: from "Intimations of Immortality," an ode by William Wordsworth (1770–1850), published in 1807. See Chapter 24.

Martha: opera by Friedrich von Flotow (1812–1883), first performed in 1847, the source of "The Last Rose of Summer."

Rigoletto: one of the best-known operas of Giuseppe Verdi (1813–1901), first performed in 1851.

not such as would either tempt or corrupt a youthful mind, and as for reading the novels that some of his friends urged upon him—well, he got what he wanted much more quickly from music; any sort of music, from an orchestra to a barrel organ. He needed only the spark, the indescribable thrill that made his imagination master of his senses, and he could make plots and pictures enough of his own. It was equally true that he was not stage-struck—not at any rate, in the usual acceptation of that expression. He had no desire to become an actor, any more than he had to become a musician. He felt no necessity to do any of these things; what he wanted was to see, to be in the atmosphere, float on the wave of it, to be carried out, blue league after blue league, away from everything.

After a night behind the scenes, Paul found the school-room more than ever repulsive; the bare floors and naked walls; the prosy men who never wore frock coats, or violets in their buttonholes; the women with their dull gowns, shrill voices, and pitiful seriousness about prepositions that govern the dative. He could not bear to have the other pupils think, for a moment, that he took these people seriously; he must convey to them that he considered it all trivial, and was there only by way of a joke, anyway. He had autograph pictures of all the members of the stock company which he showed to classmates, telling them the most incredible stories of his familiarity with these people, of his acquaintance with the soloists who came to Carnegie Hall, his suppers with them and the flowers he sent them. When these stories lost their effect, and his audience grew listless, he would bid all the boys good-by, announcing that he was going to travel for a while; going to Naples, to California, to Egypt. Then, next Monday, he would slip back, conscious and nervously smiling; his sister was ill, and he would have to defer his voyage until spring.

Matters went steadily worse with Paul at school. In the itch to let his instructors know how heartily he despised them, and how thoroughly he was appreciated elsewhere, he mentioned once or twice that he had no time to fool with theorems; adding—with a twitch of the eyebrows and a touch of that nervous bravado which so perplexed them—that he was helping the people down at the stock company; they were old friends of his.

The upshot of the matter was, that the Principal went to Paul's father, and Paul was taken out of school and put to work. The manager at Carnegie Hall was told to get another usher in his stead; the door-keeper at the theater was warned not to admit him to the house; and Charley Edwards remorsefully promised the boy's father not to see him again.   35

The members of the stock company were vastly amused when some of Paul's stories reached them—especially the women. They were hard-working women, most of them supporting indolent husbands or brothers, and they laughed rather bitterly at having stirred the boy to such fervid and florid inventions. They agreed with the faculty and with his father, that Paul's was a bad case.

The east-bound train was plowing through a January snowstorm; the dull dawn was beginning to show gray when the engine whistled a mile out of Newark.° Paul started up from the seat where he had lain curled in uneasy slumber, rubbed the breath-misted window glass with his hand, and peered out. The snow was whirling in curling eddies above the white bottom lands, and the drifts lay already deep in the fields and along the fences, while here and there the long dead grass and dried weed stalks protruded black

Newark: New Jersey city within twenty miles of New York.

above it. Lights shone from the scattered houses, and a gang of laborers who stood beside the track waved their lanterns.

Paul had slept very little, and he felt grimy and uncomfortable. He had made the all-night journey in a day coach because he was afraid if he took a Pullman he might be seen by some Pittsburgh business man who had noticed him in Denny & Carson's office. When the whistle woke him, he clutched quickly at his breast pocket, glancing about him with an uncertain smile. But the little, clay-bespattered Italians were still sleeping, the slatternly women across the aisle were in open-mouthed oblivion, and even the crumby, crying babies were for the nonce stilled. Paul settled back to struggle with his impatience as best he could.

When he arrived at the Jersey City° station, he hurried through his breakfast, manifestly ill at ease and keeping a sharp eye about him. After he reached the Twenty-third Street station° he consulted a cabman, and had himself driven to a men's furnishing establishment which was just opening for the day. He spent upward of two hours there, buying with endless reconsidering and great care. His new street suit he put on in the fitting-room; the frock coat and dress clothes he had bundled into the cab with his new shirts. Then he drove to a hatter's and a shoe house. His next errand was at Tiffany's, where he selected silver-mounted brushes° and a scarf-pin. He would not wait to have his silver marked, he said. Lastly, he stopped at a trunk shop on Broadway, and had his purchases packed into various traveling bags.

It was a little after one o'clock when he drove up to the Waldorf, and, after settling with the cabman, went into the office. He registered from Washington; said his mother and father had been abroad, and that he had come down to await the arrival of their steamer. He told his story plausibly and had no trouble, since he offered to pay for them in advance, in engaging his rooms; a sleeping-room, sitting room and bath. 40

Not once, but a hundred times Paul had planned this entry into New York. He had gone over every detail of it with Charley Edwards, and in his scrap book at home there were pages of description about New York hotels, cut from the Sunday papers.

When he was shown to his sitting room on the eighth floor, he saw at a glance that everything was as it should be; there was but one detail in his mental picture that the place did not realize, so he rang for the bell boy and sent him down for flowers. He moved about nervously until the boy returned, putting away his new linen and fingering it delightedly as he did so. When the flowers came, he put them hastily into water, and then tumbled into a hot bath. Presently he came out of his white bathroom, resplendent in his new silk underwear, and playing with the tassels of his red robe. The snow was whirling so fiercely outside his windows that he could scarcely see across the street; but within, the air was deliciously soft and fragrant. He put the violets and jonquils on the tabouret beside the couch, and threw himself down with a long sigh, covering himself with a Roman blanket. He was thoroughly tired; he had been in such haste, he had stood up to such a strain, covered so much ground in the last twenty-four hours, that he wanted to think how it had all come about. Lulled by the sound of the wind, the warm air, and the cool fragrance of the flowers, he sank into deep, drowsy retrospection.

It had been wonderfully simple; when they had shut him out of the theater and concert hall, when they had taken away his bone, the whole thing was virtually determined. The rest was a mere matter of opportunity. The only thing that at all surprised

Jersey City: New Jersey city on the Hudson River, directly across from the southern tip of Manhattan.

Twenty-third Street station: Paul's final destination in Manhattan.

brushes: hairbrushes.

him was his own courage—for he realized well enough that he had always been tormented by fear, a sort of apprehensive dread that, of late years, as the meshes of the lies he had told closed about him, had been pulling the muscles of his body tighter and tighter. Until now, he could not remember a time when he had not been dreading something. Even when he was a little boy, it was always there—behind him or before, or on either side. There had always been the shadowed corner, the dark place into which he dared not look, but from which something seemed always to be watching him—and Paul had done things that were not pretty to watch, he knew.

But now he had a curious sense of relief, as though he had at least thrown down the gauntlet to the thing in the corner.

Yet it was but a day since he had been sulking in the traces; but yesterday after-   45
noon that he had been sent to the bank with Denny & Carson's deposit, as usual—but this time he was instructed to leave the book to be balanced. There was above two thousand dollars in checks, and nearly a thousand in the bank notes which he had taken from the book and quietly transferred to his pocket. At the bank he had made out a new deposit slip. His nerves had been steady enough to permit of his returning to the office, where he had finished his work and asked for a full day's holiday tomorrow, Saturday, giving a perfectly reasonable pretext. The bank book, he knew, would not be returned before Monday or Tuesday, and his father would be out of town for the next week. From the time he slipped the bank notes into his pocket until he boarded the night train for New York, he had not known a moment's hesitation.

How astonishingly easy it had all been; here he was, the thing done; and this time there would be no awakening, no figure at the top of the stairs. He watched the snow-flakes whirling by his window until he fell asleep.

When he awoke, it was four o'clock in the afternoon. He bounded up with a start; one of his precious days gone already! He spent nearly an hour in dressing, watching every stage of his toilet carefully in the mirror. Everything was quite perfect; he was exactly the kind of boy he had always wanted to be.

When he went downstairs, Paul took a carriage and drive up Fifth Avenue toward the Park.° The snow had somewhat abated; carriages and tradesmen's wagons were hurrying soundlessly to and fro in the winter twilight; boys in woolen mufflers were shoveling off the doorsteps; the avenue stages° made fine spots of color against the white street. Here and there on the corners whole flower gardens blooming behind glass windows, against which the snow flakes stuck and melted; violets, roses, carnations, lilies of the valley—somehow vastly more lovely and alluring that they blossomed thus unnaturally in the snow. The Park itself was a wonderful stage winter-piece.

When he returned, the pause of the twilight had ceased, and the tune of the streets had changed. The snow was falling faster, lights streamed from the hotels that reared their many stories fearlessly up into the storm, defying the raging Atlantic winds. A long, black stream of carriages poured down the avenue, intersected here and there by other streams, tending horizontally. There were a score of cabs about the entrance of his hotel, and his driver had to wait. Boys in livery were running in and out of the awning stretched across the sidewalk, up and down the red velvet carpet laid from the door to the street. Above, about, within it all, was the rumble and roar, the hurry and toss of thousands of human beings as hot for pleasure as himself, and on every side of him towered the glaring affirmation of the omnipotence of wealth.

the Park: Central Park.
avenue stages: display windows.

The boy set his teeth and drew his shoulders together in a spasm of realization;   50
the plot of all dramas, the text of all romances, the nerve-stuff of all sensations was
whirling about him like the snowflakes. He burnt like a faggot in a tempest.

When Paul came down to dinner, the music of the orchestra floated up the elevator shaft to greet him. As he stepped into the thronged corridor, he sank back into one
of the chairs against the wall to get his breath. The lights, the chatter, the perfumes, the
bewildering medley of color—he had, for a moment, the feeling of not being able to
stand it. But only for a moment; these were his own people, he told himself. He went
slowly about the corridors, through the writing-rooms, smoking-rooms, reception-rooms,
as though he were exploring the chambers of an enchanted palace, built and peopled
for him alone.

When he reached the dining room he sat down at a table near a window. The
flowers, the white linen, the many-colored wine glasses, the gay toilettes of the women,
the low popping of corks, the undulating repetitions of the *Blue Danube*° from the
orchestra, all flooded Paul's dream with bewildering radiance. When the roseate tinge of
his champagne was added—that cold, precious, bubbling stuff that creamed and foamed
in his glass—Paul wondered that there were honest men in the world at all. This was
what all the world was fighting for, he reflected; this was what all the struggle was about.
He doubted the reality of his past. Had he ever known a place called Cordelia Street, a
place where fagged-looking business men boarded the early car? Mere rivets in a
machine they seemed to Paul—sickening men, with combings of children's hair always
hanging to their coats, and the smell of cooking in their clothes. Cordelia Street—Ah,
that belonged to another time and country! Had he not always been thus, had he not sat
here night after night, from as far back as he could remember, looking pensively over
just such shimmering textures, and slowly twirling the stem of a glass like this one
between his thumb and middle finger? He rather thought he had.

He was not in the least abashed or lonely. He had no special desire to meet or to
know any of these people; all he demanded was the right to look on and conjecture, to
watch the pageant. The mere stage properties were all he contended for. Nor was he
lonely later in the evening, in his loge at the Opera. He was entirely rid of his nervous
misgivings, of his forced aggressiveness, of the imperative desire to show himself different from his surroundings. He felt now that his surroundings explained him. Nobody
questioned the purple;° he had only to wear it passively. He had only to glance down at
his dress coat to reassure himself that here it would be impossible for anyone to humiliate him.

He found it hard to leave his beautiful sitting room to go to bed that night, and sat
long watching the raging storm from his turret window. When he went to sleep, it was
with the lights turned on in his bedroom; partly because of his old timidity, and partly so
that, if he should wake in the night, there would be no wretched moment of doubt, no
horrible suspicion of yellow wall-paper, or of Washington and Calvin above his bed.

On Sunday morning the city was practically snow-bound. Paul breakfasted late,   55
and in the afternoon he fell in with a wild San Francisco boy, a freshman at Yale, who
said he had run down for a "little flyer" over Sunday. The young man offered to show
Paul the night side of the town, and the two boys went off together after dinner, not
returning to the hotel until seven o'clock the next morning. They had started out in

---

Blue Danube: Composed in 1866, "The Blue Danube" is perhaps the best-known waltz of
Johann Strauss (1825–1899).
    purple: that is, clothing fit for royalty.

the confiding warmth of a champagne friendship, but their parting in the elevator was singularly cool. The freshman pulled himself together to make his train, and Paul went to bed. He woke at two o'clock in the afternoon, very thirsty and dizzy, and rang for ice water, coffee, and the Pittsburgh papers.

On the part of the hotel management, Paul excited no suspicion. There was this to be said for him, that he wore his spoils with dignity and in no way made himself conspicuous. His chief greediness lay in his ears and eyes, and his excesses were not offensive ones. His dearest pleasures were the gray winter twilights in his sitting room; his quiet enjoyment of his flowers, his clothes, his wide divan, his cigarette and his sense of power. He could not remember a time when he had felt so at peace with himself. The mere release from the necessity of petty lying, lying every day and every day, restored his self-respect. He had never lied for pleasure, even at school; but to make himself noticed and admired, to assert his difference from other Cordelia Street boys; and he felt a good deal more manly, more honest, even, now that he had no need for boastful pretensions, now that he could, as his actor friends used to say, "dress the part." It was characteristic that remorse did not occur to him. His golden days went by without a shadow, and he made each as perfect as he could.

On the eighth day after his arrival in New York, he found the whole affair exploited in the Pittsburgh papers, exploited with a wealth of detail which indicated that local news of a sensational nature was at a low ebb. The firm of Denny & Carson announced that the boy's father had refunded the full amount of his theft, and that they had no intention of prosecuting. The Cumberland minister had been interviewed, and expressed his hope of yet reclaiming the motherless lad, and Paul's Sabbath-school teacher declared that she would spare no effort to that end. The rumor had reached Pittsburgh that the boy had been seen in a New York hotel, and his father had gone East to find him and bring him home.

Paul had just come in to dress for dinner; he sank into a chair, weak in the knees, and clasped his head in his hands. It was to be worse than jail, even; the tepid waters of Cordelia Street were to close over him finally and forever. The gray monotony stretched before him in hopeless, unrelieved years; Sabbath-school, Young People's Meeting, the yellow-papered room, the damp dish-towels; it all rushed back upon him with sickening vividness. He had the old feeling that the orchestra had suddenly stopped, the sinking sensation that the play was over. The sweat broke out on his face, and he sprang to his feet, looked about him with his white, conscious smile, and winked at himself in the mirror. With something of the childish belief in miracles with which he had so often gone to class, all his lessons unlearned, Paul dressed and dashed whistling down the corridor to the elevator.

He had no sooner entered the dining room and caught the measure of the music, than his remembrance was lightened by his old elastic power of claiming the moment, mounting with it, and finding it all sufficient. The glare and glitter about him, the mere scenic accessories had again, and for the last time, their old potency. He would show himself that he was game, he would finish the thing splendidly. He doubted, more than ever, the existence of Cordelia Street, and for the first time he drank his wine recklessly. Was he not, after all, one of these fortunate beings? Was he not still himself, and in his own place? He drummed a nervous accompaniment to the music and looked about him, telling himself over and over that it had paid.

He reflected drowsily, to the swell of the violin and the chill sweetness of his wine, that he might have done it more wisely. He might have caught an outbound steamer and been well out of their clutches before now. But the other side of the world had seemed too far away and too uncertain then; he could not have waited for it; his need had been too sharp. If he had to choose over again, he would do the same thing tomorrow. He looked affectionately about the dining room, now gilded with a soft mist. Ah, it has paid indeed!

Paul was awakened the next morning by a painful throbbing in his head and feet. He had thrown himself across the bed without undressing, and had slept with his shoes on. His limbs and hands were lead heavy, and his tongue and throat were parched. There came upon him one of those fateful attacks of clear-headedness that never occurred except when he was physically exhausted and his nerves hung loose. He lay still and closed his eyes and let the tide of realities wash over him.

His father was in New York: "stopping at some joint or other," he told himself. The memory of successive summers on the front stoop fell upon him like a weight of black water. He had not a hundred dollars left, and he knew now, more than ever, that money was everything, the wall that stood between all he loathed and all he wanted. The thing was winding itself up; he had thought of that on his first glorious day in New York, and had even provided a way to snap the threat. It lay on his dressing-table now; he had got it out last night when he came blindly up from dinner—but the shiny metal hurt his eyes, and he disliked the look of it, anyway.

He rose and moved about with a painful effort, succumbing now and again to attacks of nausea. It was the old depression exaggerated; all the world had become Cordelia Street. Yet somehow he was not afraid of anything, was absolutely calm; perhaps because he had looked into the dark corner at last, and knew. It was bad enough, what he saw there, but somehow not so bad as his long fear of it had been. He saw everything clearly now. He had a feeling that he had made the best of it, that he had lived the sort of life he was meant to live, and for half an hour he sat staring at the revolver. But he told himself that was not the way, so he went downstairs and took a cab to the ferry.

When Paul arrived at Newark, he got off the train and took another cab, directing the driver to follow the Pennsylvania tracks out of town. The snow lay heavy on the roadways and had drifted deep in the open fields. Only here and there the dead grass or dried weed stalks projected, singularly black, above it. Once well into the country, Paul dismissed the carriage and walked, floundering along the tracks, his mind a medley of irrelevant things. He seemed to hold in his brain an actual picture of everything he had seen that morning. He remembered every feature of both his drivers, the toothless old woman from whom he had bought the red flowers in his coat, the agent from whom he had got his ticket, and all of his fellow-passengers on the ferry. His mind, unable to cope with vital matters near at hand, worked feverishly and deftly at sorting and grouping these images. They made for him a part of the ugliness of the world, of the ache in his head, and the bitter burning on his tongue. He stopped and put a handful of snow into his mouth as he walked, but that, too, seemed hot. When he reached a little hillside, where the tracks ran through a cut some twenty feet below him, he stopped and sat down.

The carnations in his coat were drooping with the cold, he noticed; all their red glory over. It occurred to him that all the flowers he had seen in the show windows that first night must have gone the same way, long before this. It was only one splendid breath they had, in spite of their brave mockery at the winter outside the glass. It was a losing game in the end, it seemed, this revolt against the homilies by which the world is run. Paul took one of the blossoms carefully from his coat and scooped a little hole in the snow, where he covered it up. Then he dozed a while, from his weak condition, seeming insensible to the cold.

65

The sound of an approaching train woke him, and he started to his feet, remembering only his resolution, and afraid lest he should be too late. He stood watching the approaching locomotive, his teeth chattering, his lips drawn away from them in a frightened smile; once or twice he glanced nervously sidewise, as though he were being watched. When the right moment came, he jumped. As he fell, the folly of his haste occurred to him with merciless clearness, the vastness of what he had left undone. There flashed through his brain, clearer than ever before, the blue of Adriatic water, the yellow of Algerian sands.

He felt something strike his chest—his body was being thrown swiftly through the air, on and on, immeasurably far and fast, while his limbs gently relaxed. Then, because the picture-making mechanism was crushed, the disturbing visions flashed into black, and Paul dropped back into the immense design of things.

QUESTIONS

1. Describe Paul as a character. How does he grow, or change? What are his strengths? Weaknesses? What do his preferences and annoyances show about him? What is shown by his meeting with the college boy in New York? Why is the story called "Paul's Case"?

2. Describe the speaker. How does the speaker describe Paul? The other characters? When does the speaker shift attention exclusively to Paul? Why?

3. What future does Paul see for himself? To what degree is his dislike of the life on Cordelia Street justified? Why does he think that forgiveness and correction would be worse for him than imprisonment? How can the story be seen as a criticism not of Paul but of early-twentieth-century society?

WILLIAM FAULKNER   (1897–1962)

Faulkner spent his childhood in Mississippi and became one of the foremost American novelists of the twentieth century. He twice received the Pulitzer Prize (in 1955 and 1963), and he also received the Nobel Prize in literature in 1949. Throughout his extensive fiction about the special world he called "Yoknapatawpha County," he treats life in the southern United States as a symbol of humankind generally, emphasizing the decline of civilization and culture in the wake of the Civil War. Often he deals with degraded, sullen, and degenerate characters, and in this respect Abner Snopes of "Barn Burning" is typical. The loyalty he tries to exact from his son Sarty is one that excludes any allegiance to morality. Faulkner also uses the Snopes family as subjects in The Hamlet *(1940),* The Town *(1957), and* The Mansion *(1960).*

Barn Burning _____ 1939

The store in which the Justice of the Peace's court was sitting smelled of cheese. The boy, crouched on his nail keg at the back of the crowded room, knew he smelled cheese, and more; from where he sat he could see the ranked shelves close-packed with the solid, squat, dynamic shapes of tin cans whose labels his stomach read, not from the lettering which meant nothing to his mind but from the scarlet devils and the silver curve of fish—this, the cheese which he knew he smelled and the hermetic meat° which his intestines believed he smelled coming in intermittent gusts momentary and brief between the other constant one, the smell and sense just a little of fear because mostly of despair and grief, the old fierce pull of blood. He could not see the table where the Justice sat and before which his father and his father's enemy (*our enemy* he thought in that despair; *ourn! mine and his both! He's my father!*) stood, but he could hear them, the two of them that is, because his father had said no word yet:

"But what proof have you, Mr. Harris?"

"I told you. The hog got into my corn. I caught it up and sent it back to him. He had no fence that would hold it. I told him so, warned him. The next time I put the hog in my pen. When he came to get it I gave him enough wire to patch up his pen. The next time I put the hog up and kept it. I rode down to his house and saw the wire I gave him still rolled on to the spool in his yard. I told him he could have the hog when he paid me a dollar pound fee. That evening a nigger came with the dollar and got the hog. He was a strange nigger. He said, 'He say to tell you wood and hay kin burn.' I said, 'What?' 'That what he say to tell you,' the nigger said. 'Wood and hay kin burn.' That night my barn burned. I got the stock out but I lost the barn."

"Where is the nigger? Have you got him?"

"He was a strange nigger, I tell you. I don't know what became of him."   5

"But that's not proof. Don't you see that's not proof?"

"Get that boy up here. He knows." For a moment the boy thought too that the man meant his older brother until Harris said. "Not him. The little one. The boy," and, crouching, small for his age, small and wiry like his father, in patched and faded jeans even too small for him, with straight, uncombed, brown hair and eyes gray and wild as storm scud, he saw the men between himself and the table part and become a lane of grim faces, at the end of which he saw the Justice, a shabby, collarless, graying man in spectacles, beckoning him. He felt no floor under his bare feet; he seemed to walk beneath the palpable weight of the grim turning faces. His father, stiff in his black Sunday coat donned not for the trial but for the moving, did not even look at him. *He aims for me to lie,* he thought, again with that frantic grief and despair. *And I will have to do hit.*

"What's your name, boy?" the Justice said.

"Colonel Sartoris Snopes," the boy whispered.

"Hey?" the Justice said. "Talk louder. Colonel Sartoris? I reckon anybody named   10 for Colonel Sartoris in this country can't help but tell the truth, can they?" The boy said nothing. *Enemy! Enemy!* he thought; for a moment he could not even see, could not see that the Justice's face was kindly nor discern that his voice was troubled when he spoke to the man named Harris: "Do you want me to question this boy?" But he could hear, and during those subsequent long seconds there was absolutely no sound in the crowded little room save that of quiet and intent breathing it was as if he had swung outward at the end of a grape vine, over a ravine, and at the top of the swing had been caught in a prolonged instant of mesmerized gravity, weightless in time.

"No!" Harris said violently, explosively. "Damnation! Send him out of here!" Now time, the fluid world, rushed beneath him again, the voices coming to him again through the smell of cheese and sealed meat, the fear and despair and the old grief of blood:

hermetic meat: canned meat.

"This case is closed. I can't find against you, Snopes, but I can give you advice. Leave this country and don't come back to it."

His father spoke for the first time, his voice cold and harsh, level, without emphasis: "I aim to. I don't figure to stay in a country among people who . . ." he said something unprintable and vile, addressed to no one.

"That'll do," the Justice said, "Take your wagon and get out of this country before dark. Case dismissed."

His father turned, and he followed the stiff black coat, the wiry figure walking a   15
little stiffly, from where a Confederate provost's man's musket ball had taken him in the heel on a stolen horse thirty years ago, followed the two backs now, since his older brother had appeared from somewhere in the crowd, no taller than the father but thicker, chewing tobacco steadily, between the two lines of grim-faced men and out of the store and across the worn gallery and down the sagging steps and among the dogs and half-grown boys in the mild May dust, where as he passed a voice hissed:

"Barn burner!"

Again he could not see, whirling; there was a face in a red haze, moonlike, bigger than the full moon, the owner of it half again his size, he leaping in the red haze toward the face, feeling no blow, feeling no shock when his head struck the earth, scrabbling up and leaping again, feeling no blow this time either and tasting no blood, scrabbling up to see the other boy in full flight and himself already leaping into pursuit as his father's hand jerked him back, the harsh, cold voice speaking above him: "Go get in the wagon."

It stood in a grove of locusts and mulberries across the road. His two hulking sisters in their Sunday dresses and his mother and her sister in calico and sunbonnets were already in it, sitting on and among the sorry residue of the dozen and more movings which even the boy could remember—the battered stove, the broken beds and chairs, the clock inlaid with mother-of-pearl, which would not run, stopped at some fourteen minutes past two o'clock of a dead and forgotten day and time, which had been his mother's dowry. She was crying, though when she saw him she drew her sleeve across her face and began to descend from the wagon. "Get back," the father said.

"He's hurt, I got to get some water and wash his . . ."

"Get back in the wagon." his father said. He got in too, over the tail-gate. His   20
father mounted to the seat where the older brother already sat and struck the gaunt mules two savage blows with the peeled willow, but without heat. It was not even sadistic; it was exactly that same quality which in later years would cause his descendants to over-run the engine before putting a motor car into motion, striking and reining back in the same movement. The wagon went on, the store with its quiet crowd of grimly watching men dropped behind; a curve in the road hid it. *Forever* he thought. *Maybe he's done satisfied now, now that he has . . .* stopping himself, not to say it aloud even to himself. His mother's hand touched his shoulder.

"Does hit hurt?" she said.

"Naw," he said. "Hit don't hurt. Lemme be."

"Can't you wipe some of the blood off before hit dries?"

"I'll wash tonight," he said. "Lemme be, I tell you."

The wagon went on. He did not know where they were going. None of them ever   2
did or ever asked, because it was always somewhere, always a house of sorts waiting for them a day or two days or even three days away. Likely his father had already arranged to make a crop on another farm before he. . . . Again he had to stop himself. He (the father) always did. There was something about his wolflike independence and even courage when the advantage was at least neutral which impressed strangers, as if they

got from his latent ravening ferocity not so much a sense of dependability as a feeling that his ferocious conviction in the rightness of his own actions would be of advantage to all whose interest lay with his.

That night they camped, in a grove of oaks and beeches where a spring ran. The nights were still cool and they had a fire against it, of a rail lifted from a nearby fence and cut into lengths—a small fire, neat, niggard almost, a shrewd fire; such fires were his father's habit and custom always, even in freezing weather. Older, the boy might have remarked this and wondered why not a big one; why should not a man who had not only seen the waste and extravagance of war, but who had in his blood an inherent prodigality with material not his own, have burned everything in sight? Then he might have gone a step farther and thought that that was the reason; that niggard blaze was the living fruits of nights passed during those four years in the woods hiding from all men, blue or grey, with his strings of horses (captured horses, he called them). And older still, he might have divined the true reason: that the element of fire spoke to some deep mainspring of his father's being, as the element of steel or of powder spoke to other men, as the one weapon for the preservation of integrity, else breath were not worth the breathing, and hence to be regarded with respect and used with discretion.

But he did not think this now and he had seen those same niggard blazes all his life. He merely ate his supper beside it and was already half asleep over his iron plate when his father called him, and once more he followed the stiff back, the stiff and ruthless limp, up the slope and on to the starlit road where, turning, he could see his father against the stars but without face or depth—a shape black, flat, and bloodless as though cut from tin in the iron folds of the frockcoat which had not been made for him, the voice harsh like tin and without heat like tin:

"You were fixing to tell them. You would have told him." He didn't answer. His father struck him with the flat of his hand on the side of the head, hard but without heat, exactly as he had struck the two mules at the store, exactly as he would strike either of them with any stick in order to kill a horse fly, his voice still without heat or anger: "You're getting to be a man. You got to learn. You got to learn to stick to your own blood or you ain't going to have any blood to stick to you. Do you think either of them, any man there this morning, would? Don't you know all they wanted was a chance to get at me because they knew I had them beat? Eh?" Later, twenty years later, he was to tell himself, "If I had said they wanted only truth, justice, he would have hit me again." But now he said nothing. He was not crying. He just stood there. "Answer me," his father said.

"Yes," he whispered. His father turned.

"Get on to bed. We'll be there tomorrow."   30

Tomorrow they were there. In the early afternoon the wagon stopped before a paintless two-room house identical almost with the dozen others it had stopped before even in the boy's ten years, and again, as on the other dozen occasions, his mother and aunt got down and began to unload the wagon, although his two sisters and his father and brother had not moved.

"Likely hit ain't fitten for hawgs," one of the sisters said.

"Nevertheless, fit it will and you'll hog it and like it," his father said. "Get out of them chairs and help your Ma unload."

The two sisters got down, big, bovine, in a flutter of cheap ribbons; one of them drew from the jumbled wagon bed a battered lantern, the other a worn broom. His father handed the reins to the older son and began to climb stiffly over the wheel. "When they get unloaded, take the team to the barn and feed them." Then he said, and at first the boy thought he was still speaking to his brother: "Come with me."

"Me?" he said.   35

"Yes," his father said. "You."

"Abner," his mother said. His father paused and looked back—the harsh level stare beneath the shaggy, graying, irascible brows.

"I reckon I'll have a word with the man that aims to begin tomorrow owning me body and soul for the next eight months."

They went back up the road. A week ago—or before last night, that is—he would have asked where they were going, but not now. His father had struck him before last night but never before had he paused afterward to explain why; it was as if the blow and the following calm, outrageous voice still rang, repercussed, divulging nothing to him save the terrible handicap of being young, the light weight of his few years, just heavy enough to prevent his soaring free of the world as it seemed to be ordered but not heavy enough to keep footed solid in it, to resist it and try to chance the course of its events.

Presently he could see the grove of oaks and cedars and the other flowering trees   40
and shrubs where the house would be, though not the house yet. They walked beside a fence massed with honeysuckle and Cherokee roses and came to a gate swinging open between two brick pillars, and now, beyond a sweep of drive, he saw the house for the first time and at that instant he forgot his father and the terror and despair both, and even when he remembered his father again (who had stopped) the terror and despair did not return. Because, for all the twelve movings, they had sojourned until now in a poor country, a land of small farms and fields and houses, and he had never seen a house like this before. *Hit's big as a courthouse* he thought quietly, with a surge of peace and joy whose reason he could not have thought into words, being too young for that: *They are safe from him. People whose lives are a part of this peace and dignity are beyond his touch, he no more to them than a buzzing wasp: capable of stinging for a little moment but that's all; the spell of this peace and dignity rendering even the barns and stable and cribs which belong to it impervious to the puny flames he might contrive . . .* this, the peace and joy, ebbing for an instant as he looked again at the stiff black back, the stiff and implacable limp of the figure which was not dwarfed by the house, for the reason that it had never looked big anywhere and which now, against the serene columned backdrop, had more than ever that impervious quality of something cut ruthlessly from tin, depthless, as though, side-wise to the sun, it would cast no shadow. Watching him, the boy remarked the absolutely undeviating course which his father held and saw the stiff foot come squarely down in a pile of fresh droppings where a horse had stood in the drive and which his father could have avoided by a simple change of stride. But it ebbed only for a moment, though he could not have thought this into words either, walking on in the spell of the house, which he could even want but without envy, without sorrow, certainly never with that ravening and jealous rage which unknown to him walked in the ironlike black coat before him: *Maybe he will feel it too. Maybe it will even change him now from what maybe he couldn't help but be.*

They crossed the portico. Now he could hear his father's stiff foot as it came down on the boards with clocklike finality, a sound out of all proportion to the dis-placement of the body it bore and which was not dwarfed either by the white door before it, as though it had attained to a sort of vicious and ravening minimum not to be dwarfed by anything—the flat, wide, black hat, the formal coat of broadcloth which had once been black but which had now that friction-glazed greenish cast of the bodies of old house flies, the lifted sleeve which was too large, the lifted hand like a curled claw. The door opened so promptly that the boy knew the Negro must have been watching them all the time, an old man with neat grizzled hair, in a linen jacket, who stood barring the door with his body, saying "Wipe yo foots, white man, fo you come in here. Major ain't home nohow."

"Get out of my way, nigger," his father said, without heat too, flinging the door back and the Negro also and entering, his hat still on his head. And now the boy saw the prints of the stiff foot on the doorsill and saw them appear on the pale rug behind the machinelike deliberation of the foot which seemed to bear (or transmit) twice the weight which the body compassed. The Negro was shouting "Miss Lula! Miss Lula!" somewhere behind them, then the boy, deluged as though by a warm wave by a suave turn of carpeted stair and a pendant glitter of chandeliers and a mute gleam of gold frames, heard the swift feet and saw her too, a lady—perhaps he had never seen her like before either—in a gray, smooth gown with lace at the throat and an apron tied at the waist and the sleeves turned back, wiping cake or biscuit dough from her hands with a towel as she came up the hall, looking not at his father at all but at the tracks on the blond rug with an expression of incredulous amazement.

"I tried," the Negro cried. "I tole him to . . ."

"Will you please go away?" she said in a shaking voice. "Major de Spain is not at home. Will you please go away?"

His father had not spoken again. He did not speak again. He did not even look at her. He just stood stiff in the center of the rug, in his hat, the shaggy iron-gray brows twitching slightly above the pebble-colored eyes as he appeared to examine the house with brief deliberation. Then with the same deliberation he turned; the boy watched him pivot on the good leg and saw the stiff foot drag round the arc of the turning, leaving a final long and fading smear. His father never looked at it, he never once looked down at the rug. The Negro held the door. It closed behind them, upon the hysteric and indistinguishable woman-wail. His father stopped at the top of the steps and scraped his boot clean on the edge of it. At the gate he stopped again. He stood for a moment, planted stiffly on the stiff foot, looking back at the house. "Pretty and white, ain't it?" he said. "That's sweat. Nigger sweat. Maybe it ain't white enough yet to suit him. Maybe he wants to mix some white sweat with it."

45

Two hours later the boy was chopping wood behind the house within which his mother and aunt and the two sisters (the mother and aunt, not the two girls, he knew that; even at this distance and muffled by walls the flat loud voices of the two girls emanated an incorrigible idle inertia) were setting up the stove to prepare a meal, when he heard the hooves and saw the linen-clad man on a fine sorrel mare, whom he recognized even before he saw the rolled rug in front of the Negro youth following on a fat bay carriage horse—a suffused, angry face vanishing, still at full gallop, beyond the corner of the house where his father and brother were sitting in the two tilted chairs; and a moment later, almost before he could have put the axe down, he heard the hooves again and watched the sorrel mare go back out of the yard, already galloping again. Then his father began to shout one of the sisters' names, who presently emerged backward from the kitchen door dragging the rolled rug along the ground by one end while the other sister walked behind it.

"If you ain't going to tote, go on and set up the wash pot," the first said.

"You, Sarty!" the second shouted. "Set up the wash pot!" His father appeared at the door, framed against that shabbiness, as he had been against that other bland perfection, impervious to either, the mother's anxious face at his shoulder.

"Go on," the father said. "Pick it up." The two sisters stooped, broad, lethargic; stooping, they presented an incredible expanse of pale cloth and a flutter of tawdry ribbons.

"If I thought enough of a rug to have to git hit all the way from France I   50
wouldn't keep hit where folks coming in would have to tromp on hit," the first said.
They raised the rug.

"Abner," the mother said. "Let me do it."

"You go back and git dinner," his father said. "I'll tend to this."

From the woodpile through the rest of the afternoon the boy watched them, the
rug spread flat in the dust beside the bubbling wash pot, the two sisters stooping over it
with that profound and lethargic reluctance, while the father stood over them in turn,
implacable and grim, driving them though never raising his voice again. He could smell
the harsh homemade lye they were using; he saw his mother come to the door once and
look toward them with an expression not anxious now but very like despair; he saw his
father turn, and he fell to with the axe and saw from the corner of his eye his father raise
from the ground a flattish fragment of field stone and examine it and return to the pot,
and this time his mother actually spoke: "Abner. Abner. Please don't. Please, Abner."

Then he was done too. It was dusk; the whippoorwills had already begun. He
could smell coffee from the room where they would presently eat the cold food remaining from the mid-afternoon meal, though when he entered the house he realized they
were having coffee again because there was a fire on the hearth, before which the rug
now lay spread over the backs of the two chairs. The tracks of his father's foot were gone.
Where they had been were now long, water-cloudy scoriations resembling the sporadic
course of a Lilliputian mowing machine.

It still hung there while they ate the cold food and then went to bed, scattered   55
without order or claim up and down the two rooms, his mother in one bed, where his
father would later lie, the older brother in the other, himself, the aunt, and the two sisters on pallets on the floor. But his father was not in bed yet. The last thing the boy
remembered was the depthless, harsh silhouette of the hat and coat bending over the
rug and it seemed to him that he had not even closed his eyes when the silhouette was
standing over him, the fire almost dead behind it, the stiff foot prodding him awake.
"Catch up the mule," his father said.

When he returned with the mule his father was standing in the black door, the
rolled rug over his shoulder. "Ain't you going to ride?" he said.

"No. Give me your foot."

He bent his knee into his father's hand, the wiry, surprising power flowed
smoothly, rising, he rising with it, on to the mule's bare back (they had owned a saddle
once; the boy could remember it though not when or where) and with the same effort-
lessness his father swung the rug up in front of him. Now in the starlight they retraced
the afternoon's path, up the dusty road rife with honeysuckle, through the gate and up
the black tunnel of the drive to the lightless house, where he sat on the mule and felt the
rough warp of the rug drag across his thighs and vanish.

"Don't you want me to help?" he whispered. His father did not answer and now he
heard again that stiff foot striking the hollow portico with that wooden and clocklike
deliberation, that outrageous overstatement of the weight it carried. The rug, hunched,
not flung (the boy could tell that even in the darkness) from his father's shoulder, struck
the angle of wall and floor with a sound unbelievably loud, thunderous, then the foot
again, unhurried and enormous; a light came on in the house and the boy sat, tense,
breathing steadily and quietly and just a little fast, though the foot itself did not increase
its beat at all, descending the steps now; now the boy could see him.

"Don't you want to ride now?" he whispered. "We kin both ride now," the light   6
within the house altering now, flaring up and sinking. *He's coming down the stairs now,* he

thought. He had already ridden the mule up beside the horse block; presently his father was up behind him and he doubled the reins over and slashed the mule across the neck, but before the animal could begin to trot the hard, thin arm came round him, the hard, knotted hand jerking the mule back to a walk.

In the first red rays of the sun they were in the lot, putting plow gear on the mules. This time the sorrel mare was in the lot before he heard it at all, the rider collarless and even bareheaded, trembling, speaking in a shaking voice as the woman in the house had done, his father merely looking up once before stooping again to the hame he was buckling, so that the man on the mare spoke to his stooping back:

"You must realize you have ruined that rug. Wasn't there anybody here, any of your women . . ." He ceased, shaking, the boy watching him, the older brother leaning now in the stable door, chewing, blinking slowly and steadily at nothing apparently. "It cost a hundred dollars. But you never had a hundred dollars. You never will. So I'm going to charge you twenty bushels of corn against your crop. I'll add it in your contract and when you come to the commissary you can sign it. That won't keep Mrs. de Spain quiet but maybe it will teach you to wipe your feet off before you enter her house again."

Then he was gone. The boy looked at his father, who still had not spoken or even looked up again, who was now adjusting the logger-head in the hame.

"Pap," he said. His father looked at him—the inscrutable face, the shaggy brows beneath which the gray eyes glinted coldly. Suddenly the boy went toward him, fast, stopping as suddenly. "You done the best you could!" he cried. "If he wanted hit done different why didn't he wait and tell you how? He won't git no twenty bushels! He won't git none! We'll get hit and hide hit! I kin watch . . ."

"Did you put the cutter back in that straight stock like I told you?"   65

"No, sir," he said.

"Then go do it."

That was Wednesday. During the rest of that week he worked steadily, at what was within his scope and some which was beyond it, with an industry that did not need to be driven nor even commanded twice; he had this from his mother, with the difference that some at least of what he did he liked to do, such as splitting wood with the half-size axe which his mother and aunt had earned, or saved money somehow, to present him with at Christmas. In company with the two older women (and on one afternoon even one of the sisters), he built pens for the shoat and the cow which were a part of his father's contract with the landlord, and one afternoon, his father being absent, gone somewhere on one of the mules, he went to the field.

They were running a middle buster now, his brother holding the plow straight while he handled the reins, and walking beside the straining mule, the rich black soil shearing cool and damp against his bare ankles, he thought *Maybe this is the end of it. Maybe even that twenty bushels that seems hard to have to pay for just a rug will be a cheap price for him to stop forever and always from being what he used to be;* thinking, dreaming now, so that his brother had to speak sharply to him to mind the mule: *Maybe he even won't collect the twenty bushels. Maybe it will all add up and balance and vanish—corn, rug, fire; the terror and grief, the being pulled two ways like between two teams of horses—gone, done with forever and ever.*

Then it was Saturday; he looked up from beneath the mule he was harnessing   70
and saw his father in the black coat and hat. "Not that," his father said. "The wagon gear." And then, two hours later, sitting in the wagon bed behind his father and brother on the seat, the wagon accomplished a final curve, and he saw the weathered paintless store with its tattered tobacco- and patent-medicine posters and the tethered wagons and saddle animals below the gallery. He mounted the gnawed steps behind

his father and brother, and there again was the lane of quiet, watching faces for the three of them to walk through. He saw the man in spectacles sitting at the plank table and he did not need to be told this was a Justice of the Peace; he sent one glare of fierce, exultant, partisan defiance at the man in collar and cravat now, whom he had seen but twice in his life, and that on a galloping horse, who now wore on his face an expression not of rage but of amazed unbelief which the boy could not have known was at the incredible circumstance of being sued by one of his own tenants, and came and stood against his father and cried at the Justice: "He ain't done it! He ain't burnt . . ."

"Go back to the wagon," his father said.

"Burnt?" the Justice said. "Do I understand this rug was burned too?"

"Does anybody here claim it was?" his father said. "Go back to the wagon." But he did not, he merely retreated to the rear of the room, crowded as that other had been, but not to sit down this time, instead, to stand pressing among the motionless bodies, listening to the voices:

"And you claim twenty bushels of corn is too high for the damage you did to the rug?"

"He brought the rug to me and said he wanted the tracks washed out of it. I   75
washed the tracks out and took the rug back to him."

"But you didn't carry the rug back to him in the same condition it was in before you made the tracks on it."

His father did not answer, and now for perhaps half a minute there was no sound at all save that of breathing, the faint, steady suspiration of complete and intent listening.

"You decline to answer that, Mr. Snopes?" Again his father did not answer. "I'm going to find against you, Mr. Snopes. I'm going to find that you were responsible for the injury to Major de Spain's rug and hold you liable for it. But twenty bushels of corn seems a little high for a man in your circumstances to have to pay. Major de Spain claims it cost a hundred dollars. October corn will be worth about fifty cents. I figure that if Major de Spain can stand a ninety-five-dollar loss on something he paid cash for, you can stand a five-dollar loss you haven't earned yet. I hold you in damages to Major de Spain to the amount of ten bushels of corn over and above your contract with him, to be paid to him out of your crop at gathering time. Court adjourned."

It had taken no time hardly, the morning was but half begun. He thought they would return home and perhaps back to the field, since they were late, far behind all other farmers. But instead his father passed on behind the wagon, merely indicating with his hand for the older brother to follow with it, and crossed the road toward the blacksmith shop opposite, pressing on after his father, overtaking him, speaking, whispering up at the harsh, calm face beneath the weathered hat: "He won't git no ten bushels neither. He won't git one. We'll . . ." until his father glanced for an instant down on him, the face absolutely calm, the grizzled eyebrows tangled above the cold eyes, the voice almost pleasant, almost gentle:

"You think so? Well, we'll wait till October anyway."   8•

The matter of the wagon—the setting of a spoke or two and the tightening of the tires—did not take long either, the business of the tires accomplished by driving the wagon into the spring branch behind the shop and letting it stand there, the mules nuzzling into the water from time to time, and the boy on the seat with the idle reins, looking up the slope and through the sooty tunnel of the shed where the slow hammer rang and where his father sat on an upended cypress bolt, easily, either talking or listening, still sitting there when the boy brought the dripping wagon up out of the branch and halted it before the door.

"Take them on to the shade and hitch," his father said. He did so and returned. His father and the smith and a third man squatting on his heels inside the door were talking, about crops and animals; the boy, squatting too in the ammoniac dust and hoof-parings and scales of rust, heard his father tell a long and unhurried story out of the time before the birth of the older brother even when he had been a professional horse-trader. And then his father came up beside him where he stood before a tattered last year's circus poster on the other side of the store, gazing rapt and quiet at the scarlet horses, the incredible poisings and convolutions of tulle and tights and the painted leers of comedians, and said, "It's time to eat."

But not at home. Squatting beside his brother against the front wall, he watched his father emerge from the store and produce from a paper sack a segment of cheese and divided it carefully and deliberately into three with his pocket knife and produce crackers from the same sack. They all three squatted on the gallery and ate slowly, without talking; then in the store again, they drank from a tin dipper tepid water smelling of the cedar bucket and of living beech trees. And still they did not go home. It was a horse lot this time, a tall rail fence upon and along which men stood and sat and out of which one by one horses were led, to be walked and trotted and then cantered back and forth along the road while the slow swapping and buying went on and the sun began to slant westward, they—the three of them—watching and listening, the older brother with his muddy eyes and his steady inevitable tobacco, the father commenting now and then on certain of the animals, to no one in particular.

It was after sundown when they reached home. They ate supper by lamplight, then, sitting on the doorstep, the boy watched the night fully accomplish, listening to the whippoorwills and the frogs, when he heard his mother's voice: "Abner! No! No! Oh, God, Oh, God, Abner!" and he rose, whirled, and saw the altered light through the door where a candle stub now burned in a bottle neck on the table and his father, still in the hat and coat, at once formal and burlesque as though dressed carefully for some shabby and ceremonial violence, emptying the reservoir of the lamp back into the five-gallon kerosene can from which it had been filled, while the mother tugged at his arm until he shifted the lamp to the other hand and flung her back, not savagely or viciously, just hard, into the wall, her hands flung out against the wall for balance, her mouth open and in her face the same quality of hopeless despair as had been in her voice. Then his father saw him standing in the door.

"Go to the barn and get that can of oil we were oiling the wagon with," he said. 85 The boy did not move. Then he could speak.

"What . . ." he cried. "What are you . . ."

"Go get that oil," his father said. "Go."

Then he was moving, running, outside the house, toward the stable: this the old habit, the old blood which he had not been permitted to choose for himself, which had been bequeathed him willy nilly and which had run for so long (and who knew where, battening on what of outrage and savagery and lust) before it came to him. *I could keep on,* he thought. *I could run on and on and never look back, never need to see his face again. Only I can't. I can't,* the rusted can in his hand now, the liquid sloshing in it as he ran back to the house and into it, into the sound of his mother's weeping in the next room, and handed the can to his father.

"Ain't you going to even send a nigger?" he cried. "At least you sent a nigger before!"

This time his father didn't strike him. The hand came even faster than the blow   90
had, the same hand which had set the can on the table with almost excruciating care
flashing from the can toward him too quick for him to follow it, gripping him by the
back of his shirt and on to tiptoe before he had seen it quit the can, the face stooping at
him in breathless and frozen ferocity, the cold, dead voice speaking over him to the
older brother who leaned against the table, chewing with that steady, curious, sidewise
motion of cows:

"Empty the can into the big one and go on. I'll catch up with you."

"Better tie him up to the bedpost," the brother said.

"Do like I told you," the father said. Then the boy was moving, his bunched shirt
and the hard, bony hand between his shoulder-blades, his toes just touching the floor,
across the room and into the other one, past the sisters sitting with spread heavy thighs
in the two chairs over the cold hearth, and to where his mother and aunt sat side by side
on the bed, the aunt's arms about the mother's shoulders.

"Hold him," the father said. The aunt made a startled movement. "Not you," the
father said. "Lennie. Take hold of him. I want to see you do it." His mother took him by
the wrist. "You'll hold him better than that. If he gets loose don't you know what he is
going to do? He will go up yonder." He jerked his head toward the road. "Maybe I'd
better tie him."

"I'll hold him," his mother whispered.   95

"See you do then." Then his father was gone, the stiff foot heavy and measured
upon the boards, ceasing at last.

Then he began to struggle. His mother caught him in both arms, he jerking and
wrenching at them. He would be stronger in the end, he knew that. But he had not time
to wait for it. "Lemme go!" he cried. "I don't want to have to hit you!"

"Let him go!" the aunt said. "If he don't go, before God, I am going up there
myself!"

"Don't you see I can't?" his mother cried. "Sarty! Sarty! No! No! Help me, Lizzie!"

Then he was free. His aunt grasped at him but it was too late. He whirled, run-   100
ning, his mother stumbled forward on to her knees behind him, crying to the nearer
sister: "Catch him, Net! Catch him!" But that was too late too, the sister (the sisters were
twins, born at the same time, yet either of them now gave the impression of being,
encompassing as much living meat and volume and weight as any other two of the
family) not yet having begun to rise from the chair, her head, face, alone merely turned,
presenting to him in the flying instant an astonishing expanse of young female features
untroubled by any surprise even, wearing only an expression of bovine interest. Then he
was out of the room, out of the house, in the mild dust of the starlit road and the heavy
rifeness of honeysuckle, the pale ribbon unspooling with terrific slowness under his running feet, reaching the gate at last and turning in, running, his heart and lungs drumming, on up the drive toward the lighted house, the lighted door. He did not knock, he
burst in, sobbing for breath, incapable for the moment of speech; he saw the astonished
face of the Negro in the linen jacket without knowing when the Negro had appeared.

"De Spain!" he cried, panted. "Where's . . ." then he saw the white man too emerging from a white door down the hall. "Barn!" he cried. "Barn!"

"What?" the white man said. "Barn?"

"Yes!" the boy cried. "Barn!"

"Catch him!" the white man shouted.

But it was too late this time too. The Negro grasped his shirt, but the entire sleeve,   10
rotten with washing, carried away, and he was out that door too and in the drive again,

and had actually never ceased to run even while he was screaming into the white man's face.

Behind him the white man was shouting. "My horse! Fetch my horse!" and he thought for an instant of cutting across the park and climbing the fence into the road, but he did not know the park nor how high the vine-massed fence might be and he dared not risk it. So he ran on down the drive, blood and breath roaring; presently he was in the road again though he could not see it. He could not hear either: the galloping mare was almost upon him before he heard her, and even then he held his course, as if the very urgency of his wild grief and need must in a moment more find him wings, waiting until the ultimate instant to hurl himself aside and into the weed-choked road-side ditch as the horse thundered past and on, for an instant in furious silhouette against the stars, the tranquil early summer night sky which, even before the shape of the horse and rider vanished, strained abruptly and violently upward: a long, swirling roar incredible and soundless, blotting the stars, and he springing up and into the road again, running again, knowing it was too late yet still running even after he heard the shot and, an instant later, two shots, pausing now without knowing he had ceased to run, crying "Pap! Pap!," running again before he knew he had begun to run, stumbling, tripping over something and scrabbling up again without ceasing to run, looking backward over his shoulder at the glare as he got up, running on among the invisible trees, panting, sobbing, "Father! Father!"

At midnight he was sitting on the crest of a hill. He did not know it was midnight and he did not know how far he had come. But there was no glare behind him now and he sat now, his back toward what he had called home for four days anyhow, his face toward the dark woods which he would enter when breath was strong again, small, shaking steadily in the chill darkness, hugging himself into the remainder of his thin, rotten shirt, the grief and despair now no longer terror and fear but just grief and despair. *Father. My father*, he thought. "He was brave!" he cried suddenly, aloud but not loud, no more than a whisper: "He was! He was in the war! He was in Colonel Sartoris' cav'ry!" not knowing that his father had gone to that war a private in the fine old European sense, wearing no uniform, admitting the authority of and giving fidelity to no man or army or flag, going to war as Malbrouck° himself did: for booty—it meant nothing and less than nothing to him if it were enemy booty or his own.

The slow constellations wheeled on. It would be dawn and then sun-up after a while and he would be hungry. But that would be tomorrow and now he was only cold, and walking would cure that. His breathing was easier now and he decided to get up and go on, and then he found that he had been asleep because he knew it was almost dawn, the night almost over. He could tell that from the whippoorwills. They were everywhere now among the dark trees below him, constant and inflectioned and ceaseless, so that, as the instant for giving over to the day birds drew nearer and nearer, there was no interval at all between them. He got up. He was a little stiff, but walking would cure that too as it would the cold, and soon there would be the sun. He went on down the hill, toward the dark woods within which the liquid silver voices of the birds called unceasing—the rapid and urgent beating of the urgent and quiring heart of the late spring night. He did not look back.

Malbrouck: hero of an old French ballad ("Malbrouck s'en va-t-en guerre"). The original Malbrouck, the English Duke of Marlborough (1650–1722) had been accused of profiteering during the War of the Spanish Succession (1702–1713).

QUESTIONS

1. Explain why Sarty's character is round rather than flat. In what ways does he change and grow? What conflicts does he face? What does he learn? How does he feel about the things his father does? Why does he leave and "not look back" at the end?

2. In the Bible, 2 Samuel, Chapters 2 and 3, Abner, the cousin of King Saul, is a powerful commander, warrior, and king maker. He is loyal to the son of King Saul and fights against the supporters of King David. Abner's death makes it possible for David to become uncontested ruler. Why do you think that Faulkner chose the name Abner for the father of the Snopes family? What actions of Abner Snopes make him seem heroic? Antiheroic? Why?

3. When and where is the story occurring? How does Faulkner convey this information to you?

4. Describe the characters of Sarty's mother and sisters. What do you learn about them? To what extent do any of them exhibit growth or development?

5. At the story's end, who is the rider of the horse? Who fires the three shots? Why does Faulkner not tell us the result of the shooting? (In Book I of *The Hamlet*, Faulkner explains that Abner and his other son, Flem, escape.)

SUSAN GLASPELL   (1882–1948)

For a brief biography, please see Chapter 26.

A Jury of Her Peers° _____ *1917*

When Martha Hale opened the storm-door and got a cut of the north wind, she ran back for her big woolen scarf. As she hurriedly wound that round her head her eye made a scandalized sweep of her kitchen. It was no ordinary thing that called her away— it was probably further from ordinary than anything that had ever happened in Dickson County. But what her eye took in was that her kitchen was in no shape for leaving: her bread all ready for mixing, half the flour sifted and half unsifted.

She hated to see things half done; but she had been at that when the team from town stopped to get Mr. Hale, and then the sheriff came running in to say his wife wished Mrs. Hale would come too—adding, with a grin, that he guessed she was getting scary and wanted another woman along. So she had dropped everything right where it was.

Glaspell's play *Trifles*, with which this story may be compared, appears in Chapter 26.

"Martha!" now came her husband's impatient voice. "Don't keep folks waiting out here in the cold."

She again opened the storm-door, and this time joined the three men and the one woman waiting for her in the big two-seated buggy.

After she had the robes tucked around her she took another look at the woman   5
who sat beside her on the back seat. She had met Mrs. Peters the year before at the county fair, and the thing she remembered about her was that she didn't seem like a sheriff's wife. She was small and thin and didn't have a strong voice. Mrs. Gorman, sheriff's wife before Gorman went out and Peters came in, had a voice that somehow seemed to be backing up the law with every word. But if Mrs. Peters didn't look like a sheriff's wife, Peters made it up in looking like a sheriff. He was to a dot the kind of man who could get himself elected sheriff—a heavy man with a big voice, who was particularly genial with the law-abiding, as if to make it plain that he knew the difference between criminals and non-criminals. And right there it came into Mrs. Hale's mind, with a stab, that this man who was so pleasant and lively with all of them was going to the Wrights' now as a sheriff.

"The country's not very pleasant this time of year," Mrs. Peters at last ventured, as if she felt they ought to be talking as well as the men.

Mrs. Hale scarcely finished her reply, for they had gone up a little hill and could see the Wright place now, and seeing it did not make her feel like talking. It looked very lonesome this cold March morning. It had always been a lonesome-looking place. It was down in a hollow, and the poplar trees around it were lonesome-looking trees. The men were looking at it and talking about what had happened. The county attorney was bending to one side of the buggy, and kept looking steadily at the place as they drew up to it.

"I'm glad you came with me," Mrs. Peters said nervously, as the two women were about to follow the men in through the kitchen door.

Even after she had her foot on the door-step, her hand on the knob, Martha Hale had a moment of feeling she could not cross that threshold. And the reason it seemed she couldn't cross it now was simply because she hadn't crossed it before. Time and time again it had been in her mind, "I ought to go over and see Minnie Foster"—she still thought of her as Minnie Foster, though for twenty years she had been Mrs. Wright. And then there was always something to do and Minnie Foster would go from her mind. But *now* she could come.

The men went over to the stove. The women stood close together by the door.   10
Young Henderson, the county attorney, turned around and said, "Come up to the fire, ladies."

Mrs. Peters took a step forward, then stopped. "I'm not—cold," she said.

And so the two women stood by the door, at first not even so much as looking around the kitchen.

The men talked for a minute about what a good thing it was the sheriff had sent his deputy out that morning to make a fire for them, and then Sheriff Peters stepped back from the stove, unbuttoned his outer coat, and leaned his hands on the kitchen table in a way that seemed to mark the beginning of official business. "Now, Mr. Hale," he said in a sort of semi-official voice, "before we move things about, you tell Mr. Henderson just what it was you saw when you came here yesterday morning."

The county attorney was looking around the kitchen.

"By the way," he said, "has anything been moved?" He turned to the sheriff. "Are   15
things just as you left them yesterday?"

Peters looked from cupboard to sink; from that to a small worn rocker a little to one side of the kitchen table.

"It's just the same."

"Somebody should have been left here yesterday," said the county attorney.

"Oh—yesterday," returned the sheriff, with a little gesture as of yesterday having been more than he could bear to think of. "When I had to send Frank to Morris Center for that man who went crazy—let me tell you. I had my hands full *yesterday*. I knew you could get back from Omaha by today, George, and as long as I went over everything here myself—"

"Well, Mr. Hale," said the county attorney, in a way of letting what was past and   20
gone go, "tell just what happened when you came here yesterday morning."

Mrs. Hale, still leaning against the door, had that sinking feeling of the mother whose child is about to speak a piece. Lewis often wandered along and got things mixed up in a story. She hoped he would tell this straight and plain, and not say unnecessary things that would just make things harder for Minnie Foster. He didn't begin at once, and she noticed that he looked queer—as if standing in that kitchen and having to tell what he had seen there yesterday morning made him almost sick.

"Yes, Mr. Hale?" the county attorney reminded.

"Harry and I had started to town with a load of potatoes," Mrs. Hale's husband began.

Harry was Mrs. Hale's oldest boy. He wasn't with them now, for the very good reason that those potatoes never got to town yesterday and he was taking them this morning, so he hadn't been home when the sheriff stopped to say he wanted Mr. Hale to come over to the Wright place and tell the county attorney his story there, where he could point it all out. With all Mrs. Hale's other emotions came the fear now that maybe Harry wasn't dressed warm enough—they hadn't any of them realized how that north wind did bite.

"We come along this road," Hale was going on, with a motion of his hand to the   25
road over which they had just come, "and as we got in sight of the house I says to Harry, 'I'm goin' to see if I can't get John Wright to take a telephone.' You see," he explained to Henderson, "unless I can get somebody to go in with me they won't come out this branch road except for a price *I* can't pay. I'd spoke to Wright about it once before; but he put me off, saying folks talked too much anyway, and all he asked was peace and quiet—guess you know about how much he talked himself. But I thought maybe if I went to the house and talked about it before his wife, and said all the women-folks liked the telephones, and that in this lonesome stretch of road it would be a good thing— well, I said to Harry that that was what I was going to say—though I said at the same time that I didn't know as what his wife wanted made much difference to John—"

Now there he was!—saying things he didn't need to say. Mrs. Hale tried to catch her husband's eye, but fortunately the county attorney interrupted with:

"Let's talk about that a little later, Mr. Hale. I do want to talk about that, but I'm anxious now to get along to just what happened when you got here."

When he began this time, it was very deliberately and carefully:

"I didn't see or hear anything. I knocked at the door. And still it was all quiet inside. I knew they must be up—it was past eight o'clock. So I knocked again, louder, and I thought I heard somebody say, 'Come in.' I wasn't sure—I'm not sure yet. But I opened the door—this door," jerking a hand toward the door by which the two women stood, "and there, in that rocker"—pointing to it—"sat Mrs. Wright."

Everyone in the kitchen looked at the rocker. It came into Mrs. Hale's mind that   30
that rocker didn't look in the least like Minnie Foster—the Minnie Foster of twenty years
before. It was a dingy red, with wooden rungs up the back, and the middle rung was
gone, and the chair sagged to one side.

"How did she—look?" the county attorney was inquiring.

"Well," said Hale, "she looked—queer."

"How do you mean—queer?"

As he asked it he took out a note-book and pencil. Mrs. Hale did not like the sight
of that pencil. She kept her eye fixed on her husband, as if to keep him from saying
unnecessary things that would go into that note-book and make trouble.

Hale did speak guardedly, as if the pencil had affected him too.   35

"Well, as if she didn't know what she was going to do next. And kind of—
done up."

"How did she seem to feel about your coming?"

"Why, I don't think she minded—one way or other. She didn't pay much attention. I said, 'Ho' do, Mrs. Wright? It's cold, ain't it?' And she said. 'Is it?'—and went on
pleatin' at her apron.

"Well, I was surprised. She didn't ask me to come up to the stove, or to sit down,
but just set there, not even lookin' at me. And so I said: 'I want to see John.'

"And then she—laughed. I guess you would call it a laugh.   40

"I thought of Harry and the team outside, so I said, a little sharp, 'Can I see John?'
'No,' says she—kind of dull like. 'Ain't he home?' says I. Then she looked at me. 'Yes,'
says she, 'he's home.' 'Then why can't I see him?' I asked her, out of patience with her
now. ''Cause he's dead' says she, just as quiet and dull—and fell to pleatin' her apron.
'Dead?' says I, like you do when you can't take in what you've heard.

"She just nodded her head, not getting a bit excited, but rockin' back and forth.

"'Why—where is he?' says I, not knowing *what* to say.

"She just pointed upstairs—like this"—pointing to the room above.

"I got up, with the idea of going up there myself. By this time I—didn't know what   45
to do. I walked from there to here; then I says: 'Why, what did he die of?'

"'He died of a rope around his neck,' says she; and just went on pleatin' at her
apron."

Hale stopped speaking, and stood staring at the rocker, as if he were still seeing
the woman who had sat there the morning before. Nobody spoke; it was as if every one
were seeing the woman who had sat there the morning before.

"And what did you do then?" the county attorney at last broke the silence.

"I went out and called Harry. I thought I might—need help. I got Harry in,
and we went upstairs." His voice fell almost to a whisper. "There he was—lying over
the—"

"I think I'd rather have you go into that upstairs," the county attorney interrupted, 50
"where you can point it all out. Just go on now with the rest of the story."

"Well, my first thought was to get that rope off. It looked—"

He stopped, his face twitching.

"But Harry, he went up to him, and he said. 'No, he's dead all right, and we'd
better not touch anything.' So we went downstairs.

"She was still sitting that same way. 'Has anybody been notified?' I asked. 'No,'
says she, unconcerned.

"'Who did this, Mrs. Wright?' said Harry. He said it businesslike, and she stopped   55
pleatin' at her apron. 'I don't know,' she says. 'You don't *know?*' says Harry. 'Weren't you
sleepin' in the bed with him?' 'Yes,' says she, 'but I was on the inside.' 'Somebody slipped
a rope round his neck and strangled him, and you didn't wake up?' says Harry. 'I didn't
wake up,' she said after him.

"We may have looked as if we didn't see how that could be, for after a minute she
said, 'I sleep sound.'

"Harry was going to ask her more questions, but I said maybe that weren't our
business; maybe we ought to let her tell her story first to the coroner or the sheriff.
So Harry went fast as he could over to High Road—the Rivers' place, where there's a
telephone."

"And what did she do when she knew you had gone for the coroner?" The attorney got his pencil in his hand all ready for writing.

"She moved from that chair to this one over here"—Hale pointed to a small chair
in the corner—"and just sat there with her hands held together and looking down. I
got a feeling that I ought to make some conversation, so I said I had come in to see if
John wanted to put in a telephone; and at that she started to laugh, and then she
stopped and looked at me—scared."

At the sound of a moving pencil the man who was telling the story looked up.   60

"I dunno—maybe it wasn't scared," he hastened: "I wouldn't like to say it was.
Soon Harry got back, and then Dr. Lloyd came, and you, Mr. Peters, and so I guess that's
all I know that you don't."

He said that last with relief, and moved a little, as if relaxing. Everyone moved a
little. The county attorney walked toward the stair door.

"I guess we'll go upstairs first—then out to the barn and around there."

He paused and looked around the kitchen.

"You're convinced there was nothing important here?" he asked the sheriff.   65
"Nothing that would—point to any motive?"

The sheriff too looked all around, as if to re-convince himself.

"Nothing here but kitchen things," he said, with a little laugh for the insignificance of kitchen things.

The county attorney was looking at the cupboard—a peculiar, ungainly structure,
half closet and half cupboard, the upper part of it being built in the wall, and the lower
part just the old-fashioned kitchen cupboard. As if its queerness attracted him, he got a
chair and opened the upper part and looked in. After a moment he drew his hand away
sticky.

"Here's a nice mess," he said resentfully.

The two women had drawn nearer, and now the sheriff's wife spoke.   7●

"Oh—her fruit," she said, looking to Mrs. Hale for sympathetic understanding.
She turned back to the county attorney and explained: "She worried about that when it
turned so cold last night. She said the fire would go out and her jars might burst."

Mrs. Peters' husband broke into a laugh.

"Well, can you beat the woman! Held for murder, and worrying about her
preserves!"

The young attorney set his lips.

"I guess before we're through with her she may have something more serious than   7●
preserves to worry about."

"Oh, well," said Mrs. Hale's husband, with good-natured superiority, "women are
used to worrying over trifles."

The two women moved a little closer together. Neither of them spoke. The county attorney seemed suddenly to remember his manners—and think of his future.

"And yet," said he, with the gallantry of a young politician. "for all their worries, what would we do without the ladies?"

The women did not speak, did not unbend. He went to the sink and began washing his hands. He turned to wipe them on the roller towel—whirled it for a cleaner place.

"Dirty towels! Not much of a housekeeper, would you say, ladies?"   80

He kicked his foot against some dirty pans under the sink.

"There's a great deal of work to be done on a farm," said Mrs. Hale stiffly.

"To be sure. And yet"—with a little bow to her—"I know there are some Dickson County farm-houses that do not have such roller towels." He gave it a pull to expose its full length again.

"Those towels get dirty awful quick. Men's hands aren't always as clean as they might be."

"Ah, loyal to your sex, I see," he laughed. He stopped and gave her a keen look.   85 "But you and Mrs. Wright were neighbors. I suppose you were friends, too."

Martha Hale shook her head.

"I've seen little enough of her of late years. I've not been in this house—it's more than a year."

"And why was that? You didn't like her?"

"I liked her well enough," she replied with spirit. "Farmers' wives have their hands full, Mr. Henderson. And then—" She looked around the kitchen.

"Yes?" he encouraged.   90

"It never seemed a very cheerful place," said she, more to herself than to him.

"No," he agreed; "I don't think anyone would call it cheerful. I shouldn't say she had the home-making instinct."

"Well, I don't know as Wright had, either," she muttered.

"You mean they didn't get on very well?" he was quick to ask.

"No; I don't mean anything," she answered, with decision. As she turned a little   95 away from him, she added: "But I don't think a place would be any the cheerfuller for John Wright's bein' in it."

"I'd like to talk to you about that a little later, Mrs. Hale," he said. "I'm anxious to get the lay of things upstairs now."

He moved toward the stair door, followed by the two men.

"I suppose anything Mrs. Peters does'll be all right?" the sheriff inquired. "She was to take in some clothes for her, you know—and a few little things. We left in such a hurry yesterday."

The county attorney looked at the two women whom they were leaving alone there among the kitchen things.

"Yes—Mrs. Peters," he said, his glance resting on the woman who was not Mrs.   100 Peters, the big farmer woman who stood behind the sheriff's wife. "Of course Mrs. Peters is one of us," he said, in a manner of entrusting responsibility. "And keep your eye out, Mrs. Peters, for anything that might be of use. No telling; you women might come upon a clue to the motive—and that's the thing we need."

Mr. Hale rubbed his face after the fashion of a showman getting ready for a pleasantry.

"But would the women know a clue if they did come upon it?" he said; and, having delivered himself of this, he followed the others through the stair door.

The women stood motionless and silent, listening to the footsteps, first upon the stairs, then in the room above them.

Then, as if releasing herself from something strange. Mrs. Hale began to arrange the dirty pans under the sink, which the county attorney's disdainful push of the foot had deranged.

"I'd hate to have men comin' into my kitchen," she said testily—"snoopin' round and criticizin'."   105

"Of course it's no more than their duty," said the sheriff's wife, in her manner of timid acquiescence.

"Duty's all right," replied Mrs. Hale bluffly; "but I guess that deputy sheriff that come out to make the fire might have got a little of this on." She gave the roller towel a pull. "Wish I'd thought of that sooner! Seems mean to talk about her for not having things slicked up, when she had to come away in such a hurry."

She looked around the kitchen. Certainly it was not "slicked up." Her eye was held by a bucket of sugar on a low shelf. The cover was off the wooden bucket, and beside it was a paper bag—half full.

Mrs. Hale moved toward it.

"She was putting this in there," she said to herself—slowly.   110

She thought of the flour in her kitchen at home—half sifted, half not sifted. She had been interrupted, and had left things half done. What had interrupted Minnie Foster? Why had that work been left half done? She made a move as if to finish it,—unfinished things always bothered her,—and then she glanced around and saw that Mrs. Peters was watching her—and she didn't want Mrs. Peters to get that feeling she had got of work begun and then—for some reason—not finished.

"It's a shame about her fruit," she said, and walked toward the cupboard that the county attorney had opened, and got on the chair, murmuring: "I wonder if it's all gone."

It was a sorry enough looking sight, but "Here's one that's all right," she said at last. She held it toward the light. "This is cherries, too." She looked again. "I declare I believe that's the only one."

With a sigh, she got down from the chair, went to the sink, and wiped off the bottle.

"She'll feel awful bad, after all her hard work in the hot weather. I remember the   115
afternoon I put up my cherries last summer."

She set the bottle on the table, and, with another sigh, started to sit down in the rocker. But she did not sit down. Something kept her from sitting down in that chair. She straightened—stepped back, and, half turned away, stood looking at it, seeing the woman who had sat there "pleatin' at her apron."

The thin voice of the sheriff's wife broke in upon her: "I must be getting those things from the front-room closet." She opened the door into the other room, started in, stepped back. "You coming with me, Mrs. Hale?" she asked nervously. "You—you could help me get them."

They were soon back—the stark coldness of that shut-up room was not a thing to linger in.

"My!" said Mrs. Peters, dropping the things on the table and hurrying to the stove.

Mrs. Hale stood examining the clothes the woman who was being detained in   12
town had said she wanted.

"Wright was close!"° she exclaimed, holding up a shabby black skirt that bore the marks of much making over. "I think maybe that's why she kept so much to herself. I s'pose she felt she couldn't do her part; and then, you don't enjoy things when you feel shabby. She used to wear pretty clothes and be lively—when she was Minnie Foster, one of the town girls, singing in the choir. But that—oh, that was twenty years ago."

With a carefulness in which there was something tender, she folded the shabby clothes and piled them at one corner of the table. She looked up at Mrs. Peters, and there was something in the other woman's look that irritated her.

"She don't care," she said to herself. "Much difference it makes to her whether Minnie Foster had pretty clothes when she was a girl."

Then she looked again, and she wasn't so sure; in fact, she hadn't at any time been perfectly sure about Mrs. Peters. She had that shrinking manner, and yet her eyes looked as if they could see a long way into things.

"This all you was to take in?" asked Mrs. Hale.   125

"No," said the sheriff's wife; "she said she wanted an apron. Funny thing to want," she ventured in her nervous little way, "for there's not much to get you dirty in jail, goodness knows. But I suppose just to make her feel more natural. If you're used to wearing an apron—. She said they were in the bottom drawer of this cupboard. Yes—here they are. And then her little shawl that always hung on the stair door."

She took the small gray shawl from behind the door leading upstairs, and stood a minute looking at it.

Suddenly Mrs. Hale took a quick step toward the other woman.

"Mrs. Peters!"

"Yes, Mrs. Hale?"

"Do you think she—did it?"   130

A frightened look blurred the other thing in Mrs. Peters' eyes.

"Oh, I don't know," she said, in a voice that seemed to shrink away from the subject.

"Well, I don't think she did," affirmed Mrs. Hale stoutly. "Asking for an apron, and her little shawl. Worryin' about her fruit."

"Mr. Peters says—." Footsteps were heard in the room above; she stopped, looked   135
up, then went on in a lowered voice: "Mr. Peters says—it looks bad for her. Mr. Henderson is awful sarcastic in a speech, and he's going to make fun of her saying she didn't—wake up."

For a moment Mrs. Hale had no answer. Then, "Well, I guess John Wright didn't wake up—when they was slippin' that rope under his neck," she muttered.

"No, it's *strange*," breathed Mrs. Peters. "They think it was such a—funny way to kill a man."

She began to laugh; at sound of the laugh, abruptly stopped.

"That's just what Mr. Hale said," said Mrs. Hale, in a resolutely natural voice. "There was a gun in the house. He says that's what he can't understand."

"Mr. Henderson said, coming out, that what was needed for the case was a motive.   140
Something to show anger—or sudden feeling."

"Well, I don't see any signs of anger around here," said Mrs. Hale, "I don't—" She stopped. It was as if her mind tripped on something. Her eye was caught by a dish-towel

close: that is, frugal, tightfisted.

in the middle of the kitchen table. Slowly she moved toward the table. One half of it was wiped clean, the other half messy. Her eyes made a slow, almost unwilling turn to the bucket of sugar and the half empty bag beside it. Things begun—and not finished.

After a moment she stepped back, and said, in that manner of releasing herself:

"Wonder how they're finding things upstairs? I hope she had it a little more red up° up there. You know,"—she paused, and feeling gathered,—"it seems kind of *sneaking:* locking her up in town and coming out here to get her own house to turn against her!"

"But, Mrs. Hale," said the sheriff's wife, "the law is the law."

"I s'pose 'tis," answered Mrs. Hale shortly.   145

She turned to the stove, saying something about that fire not being much to brag of. She worked with it a minute, and when she straightened up she said aggressively:

"The law is the law—and a bad stove is a bad stove. How'd you like to cook on this?"—pointing with the poker to the broken lining. She opened the oven door and started to express her opinion of the oven; but she was swept into her own thoughts, thinking of what it would mean, year after year, to have that stove to wrestle with. The thought of Minnie Foster trying to bake in that oven—and the thought of her never going over to see Minnie Foster—.

She was startled by hearing Mrs. Peters say: "A person gets discouraged—and loses heart."

The sheriff's wife had looked from the stove to the sink—to the pail of water which had been carried in from outside. The two women stood there silent, above them the footsteps of the men who were looking for evidence against the woman who had worked in that kitchen. That look of seeing into things, of seeing through a thing to something else, was in the eyes of the sheriff's wife now. When Mrs. Hale next spoke to her, it was gently:

"Better loosen up your things, Mrs. Peters. We'll not feel them when we go out."   150

Mrs. Peters went to the back of the room to hang up the fur tippet she was wearing. A moment later she exclaimed, "Why, she was piecing a quilt," and held up a large sewing basket piled high with quilt pieces.

Mrs. Hale spread some of the blocks on the table.

"It's a log-cabin pattern," she said, putting several of them together, "Pretty, isn't it?"

They were so engaged with the quilt that they did not hear the footsteps on the stairs. Just as the stair door opened Mrs. Hale was saying:

"Do you suppose she was going to quilt it or just knot it?"   155

The sheriff threw up his hands.

"They wonder whether she was going to quilt it or just knot it!"

There was a laugh for the ways of women, a warming of hands over the stove, and then the county attorney said briskly:

"Well, let's go right out to the barn and get that cleared up."

"I don't see as there's anything so strange," Mrs. Hale said resentfully, after the out-   160
side door had closed on the three men—"our taking up our time with little things while we're waiting for them to get the evidence. I don't see as it's anything to laugh about."

"Of course they've got awful important things on their minds," said the sheriff's wife apologetically.

red up: neat.

They returned to an inspection of the block for the quilt. Mrs. Hale was looking at the fine, even sewing, and preoccupied with thoughts of the woman who had done that sewing, when she heard the sheriff's wife say, in a queer tone:

"Why, look at this one."

She turned to take the block held out to her.

"The sewing," said Mrs. Peters, in a troubled way, "All the rest of them have been   165
so nice and even—but—this one. Why, it looks as if she didn't know what she was about!"

Their eyes met—something flashed to life, passed between them; then, as if with an effort, they seemed to pull away from each other. A moment Mrs. Hale sat there, her hands folded over that sewing which was so unlike all the rest of the sewing. Then she had pulled a knot and drawn the threads.

"Oh, what are you doing, Mrs. Hale?" asked the sheriff's wife, startled.

"Just pulling out a stitch or two that's not sewed very good," said Mrs. Hale mildly.

"I don't think we ought to touch things," Mrs. Peters said, a little helplessly.

"I'll just finish up this end," answered Mrs. Hale, still in that mild, matter-of-fact   170
fashion.

She threaded a needle and started to replace bad sewing with good. For a little while she sewed in silence. Then, in that thin, timid voice, she heard:

"Mrs. Hale!"

"Yes, Mrs. Peters?"

"What do you suppose she was so—nervous about?"

"Oh, *I* don't know," said Mrs. Hale, as if dismissing a thing not important enough   175
to spend much time on. "I don't know as she was—nervous. I sew awful queer sometimes when I'm just tired."

She cut a thread, and out of the corner of her eye looked up at Mrs. Peters. The small, lean face of the sheriff's wife seemed to have tightened up. Her eyes had that look of peering into something. But next moment she moved, and said in her thin, indecisive way:

"Well, I must get those clothes wrapped. They may be through sooner than we think. I wonder where I could find a piece of paper—and string."

"In that cupboard, maybe," suggested to Mrs. Hale, after a glance around.

One piece of the crazy sewing remained unripped. Mrs. Peter's back turned, Martha Hale now scrutinized that piece, compared it with the dainty, accurate sewing of the other blocks. The difference was startling. Holding this block made her feel queer, as if the distracted thoughts of the woman who had perhaps turned to it to try and quiet herself were communicating themselves to her.

Mrs. Peters' voice roused her.   180

"Here's a bird-cage," she said. "Did she have a bird, Mrs. Hale?"

"Why, I don't know whether she did or not." She turned to look at the cage Mrs. Peters was holding up. "I've not been here in so long." She sighed. "There was a man round last year selling canaries cheap—but I don't know as she took one. Maybe she did. She used to sing real pretty herself."

Mrs. Peters looked around the kitchen.

"Seems kind of funny to think of a bird here." She half laughed—an attempt to put up a barrier. "But she must have had one—or why would she have a cage? I wonder what happened to it."

"I suppose maybe the cat got it," suggested Mrs. Hale, resuming her sewing.   185

"No; she didn't have a cat. She's got that feeling some people have about cats—being afraid of them. When they brought her to our house yesterday, my cat got in the room, and she was real upset and asked me to take it out."

"My sister Bessie was like that," laughed Mrs. Hale.

The sheriff's wife did not reply. The silence made Mrs. Hale turn round. Mrs. Peters was examining the bird-cage.

"Look at this door," she said slowly. "It's broke. One hinge has been pulled apart." Mrs. Hale came nearer.

"Looks as if someone must have been—rough with it."   190

Again their eyes met—startled, questioning, apprehensive. For a moment neither spoke nor stirred. Then Mrs. Hale, turning away, said brusquely:

"If they're going to find any evidence, I wish they'd be about it. I don't like this place."

"But I'm awful glad you came with me, Mrs. Hale." Mrs. Peters put the bird-cage on the table and sat down. "It would be lonesome for me—sitting here alone."

"Yes, it would, wouldn't it?" agreed Mrs. Hale, a certain determined naturalness in   195
her voice. She had picked up the sewing, but now it dropped in her lap, and she murmured in a different voice: "But I tell you what I *do* wish, Mrs Peters. I wish I had come over sometimes when she was here. I wish—I had."

"But of course you were awful busy, Mrs. Hale. Your house—and your children."

"I could've come," retorted Mrs. Hale shortly. "I stayed away because it weren't cheerful—and that's why I ought to have come. I"—she looked around—"I've never liked this place. Maybe because it's down in a hollow and you don't see the road. I don't know what it is, but it's a lonesome place, and always was. I wish I had come over to see Minnie Foster sometimes. I can see now—" She did not put it into words.

"Well, you mustn't reproach yourself," counseled Mrs. Peters. "Somehow, we just don't see how it is with other folks till—something comes up."

"Not having children makes less work," mused Mrs. Hale, after a silence, "but it makes a quiet house—and Wright out to work all day—and no company when he did come in. Did you know John Wright, Mrs. Peters?"

"Not to know him. I've seen him in town. They say he was a good man."   200

"Yes—good," conceded John Wright's neighbor grimly. "He didn't drink, and kept his word as well as most, I guess, and paid his debts. But he was a hard man, Mrs. Peters. Just to pass the time of day with him—." She stopped, shivered a little. "Like a raw wind that gets to the bone." Her eye fell upon the cage on the table before her, and she added, almost bitterly: "I should think she would've wanted a bird!"

Suddenly she leaned forward, looking intently at the cage. "But what do you s'pose went wrong with it?"

"I don't know," returned Mrs. Peters; "unless it got sick and died."

But after she said it she reached over and swung the broken door. Both women watched it as if somehow held by it.

"You didn't know—her?" Mrs. Hale asked, a gentler note in her voice.   205

"Not till they brought her yesterday," said the sheriff's wife.

"She—come to think of it, she was kind of like a bird herself. Real sweet and pretty, but kind of timid and—fluttery. How—she—did—change."

That held her for a long time. Finally, as if struck with a happy thought and relieved to get back to everyday things, she exclaimed:

"Tell you what, Mrs. Peters, why don't you take the quilt in with you? It might take up her mind."

"Why, I think that's a real nice idea, Mrs. Hale," agreed the sheriff's wife, as if she   210
too were glad to come into the atmosphere of a simple kindness. "There couldn't possibly be any objection to that, could there? Now, just what will I take? I wonder if her
patches are in here—and her things?"

They turned to the sewing basket.

"Here's some red," said Mrs. Hale, bringing out a roll of cloth. Underneath that
was a box. "Here, maybe her scissors are in here—and her things." She held it up.
"What a pretty box! I'll warrant that was something she had a long time ago—when
she was a girl."

She held it in her hand a moment; then, with a little sigh, opened it.

Instantly her hand went to her nose.

"Why—!"   215

Mrs. Peters drew nearer—then turned away.

"There's something wrapped up in this piece of silk," faltered Mrs. Hale.

"This isn't her scissors," said Mrs. Peters, in a shrinking voice.

Her hand not steady, Mrs. Hale raised the piece of silk. "Oh, Mrs. Peters!" she
cried. "It's—"

Mrs. Peters bent closer.   220

"It's the bird," she whispered.

"But, Mrs. Peters!" cried Mrs. Hale. "*Look* at it! Its *neck*—look at its neck! It's all—
other side *to*."

She held the box away from her.

The sheriff's wife again bent closer.

"Somebody wrung its neck," said she, in a voice that was slow and deep.   225

And then again the eyes of the two women met—this time clung together in a
look of dawning comprehension, of growing horror. Mrs. Peters looked from the dead
bird to the broken door of the cage. Again their eyes met. And just then there was a
sound at the outside door.

Mrs. Hale slipped the box under the quilt pieces in the basket, and sank into the
chair before it. Mrs. Peters stood holding to the table. The county attorney and the sheriff came in from outside.

"Well, ladies," said the county attorney, as one turning from serious things to little
pleasantries, "have you decided whether she was going to quilt it or knot it?"

"We think," began the sheriff's wife in a flurried voice, "that she was going to—
knot it."

He was too preoccupied to notice the change that came in her voice on that last.   230

"Well, that's very interesting, I'm sure," he said tolerantly. He caught sight of the
bird-cage. "Has the bird flown?"

"We think the cat got it," said Mrs. Hale in a voice curiously even.

He was walking up and down, as if thinking something out.

"Is there a cat?" he asked absently.

Mrs. Hale shot a look up at the sheriff's wife.   235

"Well, not *now*," said Mrs. Peters. "They're superstitious, you know; they leave."

She sank into her chair.

The county attorney did not heed her. "No sign at all of anyone having come in
from the outside," he said to Peters, in the manner of continuing an interrupted conversation. "Their own rope. Now let's go upstairs again and go over it, piece by piece. It
would have to have been someone who knew just the—"

The stair door closed behind them and their voices were lost.

The two women sat motionless, not looking at each other, but as if peering into   240
something and at the same time holding back. When they spoke now it was as if they
were afraid of what they were saying, but as if they could not help saying it.

"She liked the bird," said Martha Hale, low and slowly. "She was going to bury it in
that pretty box."

"When I was a girl," said Mrs. Peters, under her breath, "my kitten—there was a
boy took a hatchet, and before my eyes—before I could get there—" She covered her
face an instant. "If they hadn't held me back I would have"—she caught herself, looked
upstairs where footsteps were heard, and finished weakly—"hurt him."

Then they sat without speaking or moving.

"I wonder how it would seem," Mrs. Hale at last began, as if feeling her way over
strange ground—"never to have had any children around?" Her eyes made a slow sweep
of the kitchen, as if seeing what that kitchen had meant through all the years. "No,
Wright wouldn't like the bird," she said after that—"a thing that sang. She used to sing.
He killed that too." Her voice tightened.

Mrs. Peters moved uneasily.   245

"Of course we don't know who killed the bird."

"I knew John Wright," was Mrs. Hale's answer.

"It was an awful thing was done in this house that night, Mrs. Hale," said the sheriff's wife. "Killing a man while he slept—slipping a thing round his neck that choked
the life out of him."

Mrs. Hale's hand went out to the bird cage.

"His neck. Choked the life out of him."   250

"We don't *know* who killed him," whispered Mrs. Peters wildly. "We don't *know*."

Mrs. Hale had not moved. "If there had been years and years of—nothing, then a
bird to sing to you, it would be awful—still—after the bird was still."

It was as if something within her not herself had spoken, and it found in Mrs.
Peters something she did not know as herself.

"I know what stillness is," she said, in a queer, monotonous voice. "When we
homesteaded in Dakota, and my first baby died—after he was two years old—and me
with no other then—"

Mrs. Hale stirred.   255

"How soon do you suppose they'll be through looking for the evidence?"

"I know what stillness is," repeated Mrs. Peters, in just that same way. Then she
too pulled back. "The law has got to punish crime, Mrs. Hale," she said in her tight
little way.

"I wish you'd seen Minnie Foster," was the answer, "when she wore a white dress
with blue ribbons, and stood up there in the choir and sang."

The picture of that girl, the fact that she had lived neighbor to that girl for twenty
years, and had let her die for lack of life, was suddenly more than she could bear.

"Oh, I *wish* I'd come over here once in a while!" she cried. "That was a crime!   260
Who's going to punish that?"

"We mustn't take on," said Mrs. Peters, with a frightened look toward the stairs.

"I might 'a' *known* she needed help! I tell you, it's *queer*, Mrs. Peters. We live close
together, and we live far apart. We all go through the same things—it's all just a different
kind of the same thing! If it weren't—why do you and I *understand?* Why do we *know*—
what we know this minute?"

She dashed her hand across her eyes. Then, seeing the jar of fruit on the table,
she reached for it and choked out:

"If I was you I wouldn't *tell* her her fruit was gone! Tell her it *ain't.* Tell her it's all right—all of it. Here—take this in to prove it to her! She—she may never know whether it was broke or not."

She turned away.   265

Mrs. Peters reached out for the bottle of fruit as if she were glad to take it—as if touching a familiar thing, having something to do, could keep her from something else. She got up, looked about for something to wrap the fruit in, took a petticoat from the pile of clothes she had brought from the front room, and nervously started winding that round the bottle.

"My!" she began, in a high, false voice, "it's a good thing the men couldn't hear us! Getting all stirred up over a little thing like a—dead canary." She hurried over that. "As if that could have anything to do with—with—My, wouldn't they *laugh?*"

Footsteps were heard on the stairs.

"Maybe they would," muttered Mrs. Hale—"maybe they wouldn't."

"No, Peters," said the county attorney incisively; "it's all perfectly clear, except the   270
reason for doing it. But you know juries when it comes to women. If there was some definite thing—something to show. Something to make a story about. A thing that would connect up with this clumsy way of doing it."

In a covert way Mrs. Hale looked at Mrs. Peters. Mrs. Peters was looking at her. Quickly they looked away from each other. The outer door opened and Mr. Hale came in.

"I've got the team° round now," he said. "Pretty cold out there."

"I'm going to stay here awhile by myself," the county attorney suddenly announced. "You can send Frank out for me, can't you?" he asked the sheriff. "I want to go over everything. I'm not satisfied we can't do better."

Again, for one brief moment, the two women's eyes found one another.

The sheriff came up to the table.   275

"Did you want to see what Mrs. Peters was going to take in?"

The county attorney picked up the apron. He laughed.

"Oh, I guess they're not very dangerous things the ladies have picked out."

Mrs. Hale's hand was on the sewing basket in which the box was concealed. She felt that she ought to take her hand off the basket. She did not seem able to. He picked up one of the quilt blocks which she had piled on to cover the box. Her eyes felt like fire. She had a feeling that if he took up the basket she would snatch it from him.

But he did not take it up. With another little laugh, he turned away, saying: 280

"No; Mrs. Peters doesn't need supervising. For that matter, a sheriff's wife is married to the law. Ever think of it that way, Mrs. Peters?"

Mrs. Peters was standing beside the table. Mrs. Hale shot a look up at her; but she could not see her face. Mrs. Peters had turned away. When she spoke, her voice was muffled.

"Not—just that way," she said.

"Married to the law!" chuckled Mrs. Peters' husband. He moved toward the door into the front room, and said to the county attorney:

"I just want you to come in here a minute, George. We ought to take a look at   285
these windows."

"Oh—windows," said the county attorney scoffingly.

"We'll be right out, Mr. Hale," said the sheriff to the farmer, who was still waiting by the door.

team: team of horses pulling the buggy in which the group had come.

Hale went to look after the horses. The sheriff followed the county attorney into the other room. Again—for one final moment—the two women were alone in that kitchen.

Martha Hale sprang up, her hands tight together, looking at that other woman, with whom it rested. At first she could not see her eyes, for the sheriff's wife had not turned back since she turned away at that suggestion of being married to the law. But now Mrs. Hale made her turn back. Her eyes made her turn back. Slowly, unwillingly, Mrs. Peters turned her head until her eyes met the eyes of the other woman. There was a moment when they held each other in a steady, burning look in which there was no evasion nor flinching. Then Martha Hale's eyes pointed the way to the basket in which was hidden the thing that would make certain the conviction of the other woman—that woman who was not there and yet who had been there with them all through that hour.

For a moment Mrs. Peters did not move. And then she did it. With a rush forward, she threw back the quilt pieces, got the box, tried to put it in her handbag. It was too big. Desperately she opened it, started to take the bird out. But there she broke—she could not touch the bird. She stood there helpless, foolish.

There was the sound of a knob turning in the inner door. Martha Hale snatched the box from the sheriff's wife, and got it in the pocket of her big coat just as the sheriff and the county attorney came back into the kitchen.

"Well, Henry," said the county attorney facetiously, "at least we found out that she was not going to quilt it. She was going to—what is it you call it, ladies?"

Mrs. Hale's hand was against the pocket of her coat.

"We call it—knot it, Mr. Henderson."

QUESTIONS

1. Who is the central character? That is, on whom does the story focus?
2. Describe the differences between Mrs. Hale and Mrs. Peters, in terms of their status, backgrounds, and comparative strengths of character.
3. Why do the two women not voice their conclusions about the murderer? How does Glaspell show that they both know the murderer's identity, the reasons, and the method? Why do they both "cover up" at the story's conclusion?

JOYCE CAROL OATES   (b. 1938)

An astoundingly productive author of more than twenty novels, many collections of stories, and books of poems, Oates received her education at Syracuse University and the University of Wisconsin. She began her teaching career at the University of Detroit and currently, in addition to guest positions, is Distinguished Professor in the Humanities at Princeton University. Some of her many novels are With Shuddering Fall *(1964),* Angel of Light *(1981),* Solstice *(1985), and* Foxfire *(1993). Among her awards are a Guggenheim Fellowship, the Continuing Achievement Award of the O. Henry Award Prize Stories series, a National Book Award, and the Lotos Club Award of Merit. "Shopping" is taken from* Heat and Other Stories *(1991).*

Shopping ————————————————— 1991

An old ritual, Saturday morning shopping. Mother and daughter. Mrs. Dietrich and Nola. Shops in the village, stores and boutiques at the splendid Livingstone Mall on

Route 12: Bloomingdale's, Saks, Lord & Taylor, Bonwit's, Neiman-Marcus, and the rest. Mrs. Dietrich would know her way around the stores blindfolded but there is always the surprise of lavish seasonal displays, extraordinary holiday sales, the openings of new stores at the mall like Laura Ashley, Paraphernalia. On one of their mall days Mrs. Dietrich and Nola would try to get there at midmorning, have lunch around 1 P.M. at one or another of their favorite restaurants, shop for perhaps an hour after lunch, then come home. Sometimes the shopping trips were more successful than at other times, but you have to have faith, Mrs. Dietrich tells herself. Her interior voice is calm, neutral, free of irony. Even since her divorce her interior voice has been free of irony. You have to have faith.

Tomorrow morning Nola returns to school in Maine; today will be spent at the mall. Mrs. Dietrich has planned it for days—there are numerous things Nola needs, mainly clothes, a pair of good shoes; Mrs. Dietrich must buy a birthday present for one of her aunts; mother and daughter need the time together. At the mall, in such crowds of shoppers, moments of intimacy are possible as they rarely are at home. (Seventeen-year-old Nola, home on spring break for a brief eight days, seems always to be *busy,* always out with her *friends,* the trip to the mall has been postponed twice.) But Saturday, 10:30 A.M., they are in the car at last headed south on Route 12, a bleak March morning following a night of freezing rain; there's a metallic cast to the air and no sun anywhere in the sky but the light hurts Mrs. Dietrich's eyes just the same. "Does it seem as if spring will ever come? It must be twenty degrees colder up in Maine," she says. Driving in heavy traffic always makes Mrs. Dietrich nervous and she is overly sensitive to her daughter's silence, which seems deliberate, perverse, when they have so little time remaining together—not even a full day.

Nola asks politely if Mrs. Dietrich would like her to drive and Mrs. Dietrich says no, of course not, she's fine, it's only a few more miles and maybe traffic will lighten. Nola seems about to say something more, then thinks better of it. So much between them is precarious, chancy—but they've been kind to each other these past seven days. Nola's secrets remain her own and Mrs. Dietrich isn't going to pry; she's beyond that. She loves Nola with a fierce unreasoned passion stronger than any she felt for the man who had been her husband for thirteen years, certainly far stronger than any she ever felt for her own mother. Sometimes in weak despondent moods, alone, lonely, self-pitying, when she has had too much to drink, Mrs. Dietrich thinks she is in love with her daughter, but this is a thought she can't contemplate for long. And how Nola would snort in amused contempt, incredulous, mocking—"Oh, *Mother!*"—if she were told.

("Why do you make so much of things? Of people who don't seem to care about you?" Mr. Dietrich once asked. He had been speaking of one or another of their Livingstone friends, a woman in Mrs. Dietrich's circle; he hadn't meant to be insulting but Mrs. Dietrich was stung as if he'd slapped her.)

Mrs. Dietrich tries to engage her daughter in conversation of a harmless sort but Nola answers in monosyllables; Nola is rather tired from so many nights of partying with her friends, some of whom attend the local high school, some of whom are home for spring break from prep schools—Exeter, Lawrenceville, Concord, Andover, Portland. Late nights, but Mrs. Dietrich doesn't consciously lie awake waiting for Nola to come home; they've been through all that before. Now Nola sits beside her mother looking wan, subdued, rather melancholy. Thinking her private thoughts. She is wearing a bulky quilted jacket Mrs. Dietrich has never liked, the usual blue jeans, black calfskin boots zippered tightly to mid-calf. Her delicate profile, thick-lashed eyes. Mrs. Dietrich must

5

resist the temptation to ask, Why are you so quiet, Nola? What are you thinking? They've been through all that before.

Route 12 has become a jumble of small industrial parks, high-rise office and apartment buildings, torn-up landscapes: mountains of raw earth, uprooted trees, ruts and ditches filled with muddy water. Everywhere are yellow bulldozers, earth-movers, construction workers operating cranes, ACREAGE FOR SALE signs. When Mr. and Mrs. Dietrich first moved out to Livingstone from the city sixteen years ago this strength along Route 12 was quite attractive, mainly farmland, woods, a scattering of small suburban houses; now it has nearly all been developed. There is no natural sequence to what you see—buildings, construction work, leveled woods, the lavish grounds owned by Squibb. Though she has driven this route countless times, Mrs. Dietrich is never quite certain where the mall is and must be prepared for a sudden exit. She remembers getting lost the first several times, remembers the excitement she and her friends felt about the grand opening of the mall, stores worthy of serious shopping at last. Today is much the same. No, today is worse. Like Christmas when she was a small child, Mrs. Dietrich thinks. She'd hoped so badly to be happy she'd felt actual pain, a constriction in her throat like crying.

"*Are* you all right, Nola? You've been so quiet all morning," Mrs. Dietrich asks, half scolding. Nola stirs from her reverie, says she's fine, a just perceptible edge to her reply, and for the remainder of the drive there's some stiffness between them. Mrs. Dietrich chooses to ignore it. In any case she is fully absorbed in driving—negotiating a tricky exit across two lanes of traffic, then the hairpin curve of the ramp, the numerous looping drives of the mall. Then the enormous parking lot, daunting to the inexperienced, but Mrs. Dietrich always heads for the area behind Lord & Taylor on the far side of the mall, Lot D; her luck holds and she finds a space close in. "Well, we made it," she says, smiling happily at Nola. Nola laughs in reply—what does a seventeen-year-old's laughter *mean?*—*but* she remembers, getting out, to lock both doors on her side of the car. Even here at the Livingstone Mall unattended cars are no longer safe. The smile Nola gives Mrs. Dietrich across the car's roof is careless and beautiful and takes Mrs. Dietrich's breath away.

The March morning tastes of grit with an undercurrent of something acrid, chemical; inside the mall, beneath the first of the elegant brass-buttressed glass domes, the air is fresh and tonic, circulating from invisible vents. The mall is crowded, rather noisy—it *is* Saturday morning—but a feast for the eyes after that long trip on Route 12. Tall slender trees grow out of the mosaic-tiled pavement; there are beds of Easter lilies, daffodils, jonquils, tulips of all colors. There are cobblestone walkways, fountains illuminated from within, wide promenades as in an Old World setting. Mrs. Dietrich smiles with relief. She senses that Nola too is relieved, cheered. It's like coming home.

The shopping excursions began when Nola was a small child but did not acquire their special significance until she was twelve or thirteen years old and capable of serious, sustained shopping with her mother. Sometimes Mrs. Dietrich and Nola would shop with friends, another mother and daughter perhaps, sometimes Mrs. Dietrich invited one or two of Nola's school friends to join them, but she preferred to be alone with Nola and she believed Nola preferred to be alone with her. This was about the time when Mr. Dietrich moved out of the house and back into their old apartment building in the city—a separation, he'd called it initially, to give them perspective, though Mrs. Dietrich had no illusions about what "perspective" would turn out to entail—so the shopping trips were all the more significant. Not that Mrs. Dietrich and Nola spent very much money; they really didn't, *really* they didn't, when compared to friends and neighbors. And Mr. Dietrich rarely objected: the financial arrangement he made with Mrs. Dietrich was surprisingly generous.

At seventeen Nola is shrewd and discerning as a shopper, not easy to please, knowledgeable as a mature woman about certain aspects of fashion, quality merchandise, good stores. She studies advertisements, she shops for bargains. Her closets, like Mrs. Dietrich's, are crammed, but she rarely buys anything that Mrs. Dietrich thinks shoddy or merely faddish. Up in Portland, at the academy, she hasn't as much time to shop, but when she is home in Livingstone it isn't unusual for her and her girlfriends to shop nearly every day. Sometimes she shops at the mall with a boyfriend—but she prefers girls. Like all her friends she has charge accounts at the better stores, her own credit cards, a reasonable allowance. At the time of their settlement Mr. Dietrich said guiltily that it was the least he could do for them: if Mrs. Dietrich wanted to work part-time, she could (she was trained, more or less, in public relations of a small-scale sort); if not, not. Mrs. Dietrich thought, It's the most you can do for us too.

Near Baumgarten's entrance mother and daughter see a disheveled woman sitting by herself on one of the benches. Without seeming to look at her, shoppers are making a discreet berth around her, a stream following a natural course. Nola, taken by surprise, stares. Mrs. Dietrich has seen the woman from time to time at the mall, always alone, smirking and talking to herself, frizzed gray hair in a tangle, puckered mouth. Always wearing the same black wool coat, a garment of fairly good quality but shapeless, rumpled, stained, as if she sleeps in it. She might be anywhere from forty to sixty years of age. Once Mrs. Dietrich saw her make menacing gestures at children who were teasing her, another time she'd seen the woman staring belligerently at *her.* A white paste had gathered in the corners of her mouth.

"My God, that poor woman," Nola says. "I didn't think there were people like her here—I mean, I didn't think they would allow it."

"She doesn't seem to cause any disturbance," Mrs. Dietrich says. "She just sits. Don't stare, Nola, she'll see you."

"You've seen her here before? Here?"

"A few times this winter."

"Is she always like that?"

"I'm sure she's harmless, Nola. She just *sits.*"

Nola is incensed, her pale blue eyes like washed glass. "I'm sure *she's* harmless, Mother. It's the harm the poor woman has to endure that is the tragedy."

Mrs. Dietrich is surprised and a little offended by her daughter's passionate tone but she knows enough not to argue. They enter Baumgarten's, taking their habitual route. So many shoppers! So much merchandise! Dazzling displays of tulips, chrome, neon, winking lights, enormous painted Easter eggs in wicker baskets. Nola speaks of the tragedy of women like that woman—the tragedy of the homeless, the mentally disturbed: bag ladies out on the street, outcasts of an affluent society—but she's soon distracted by the busyness on all sides, the attractive items for sale. They take the escalator up to the third floor, to the Clubhouse Juniors department, where Nola often buys things. From there they will move on to Young Collector, then to Act IV then to Petite Corner, then one or another boutique and designer—Liz Claiborne, Christian Dior, Calvin Klein, Carlos Falchi, and the rest. And after Baumgarten's the other stores await, to be visited each in turn. Mrs. Dietrich checks her watch and sees with satisfaction that there's just enough time before lunch but not *too* much time. She gets ravenously hungry, shopping at the mall.

Nola is efficient and matter-of-fact about shopping, though she acts solely upon instinct. Mrs. Dietrich likes to watch her at a short distance, holding items of clothing up to herself in the three-way mirrors, modeling things she thinks especially promising. A twill blazer, a dress with rounded shoulders and blouson jacket, a funky zippered jumpsuit in white sailcloth, a pair of straight-leg Evan Picone pants, a green leather vest: Mrs. Dietrich watches her covertly. At such times Nola is perfectly content, fully absorbed in the task at hand; Mrs. Dietrich knows she isn't thinking about anything that would distress her. (Like Mr. Dietrich's betrayal. Like Nola's difficulties with her friends. Like her difficulties at school—as much as Mrs. Dietrich knows of them.) When Nola glances in her mother's direction Mrs. Dietrich pretends to be examining clothes for her own purposes. As if she's hardly aware of Nola. Once, at the mall, perhaps in this very store in this very department, Nola saw Mrs. Dietrich watching her and walked away angrily, and when Mrs. Dietrich caught up with her she said, "I can't stand it, Mother." Her voice was choked and harsh, a vein prominent in her forehead. "Let me go. For Christ's sake will you let me go." Mrs. Dietrich didn't dare touch her though she could see Nola was trembling. For a long terrible moment mother and daughter stood side by side near a display of bright brash Catalina beachwear while Nola whispered, "Let me go. *Let me go.*" How the scene ended Mrs. Dietrich can't recall—it erupts in an explosion of light, like a bad dream—but she knows better than to risk it again.

Difficult to believe that girl standing so poised and self-assured in front of the three-way mirror was once a plain, rather chunky, unhappy child. She'd been unpopular at school. Overly serious. Anxious. Quick to tears. Aged eleven she hid herself away in her room for hours at a time, reading, drawing pictures, writing little stories she could sometimes be prevailed upon to read aloud to her mother, sometimes even to her father, though she dreaded his judgment. She went through a "scientific" phase a little later; Mrs. Dietrich remembers an ambitious bas-relief map of North America, meticulous illustrations for "photosynthesis," a pastel drawing of an eerie ball of fire labeled RED GIANT (a dying star?), which won a prize in a state competition for junior high students. Then for a season it was stray facts Nola confronted them with, often at the dinner table. Interrupting her parents' conversation to say brightly, "Did you know that Nero's favorite color was green? He carried a giant emerald and held it up to his eye to watch Christians being devoured by lions." And, "Did you ever hear of the raving ghosts of Siberia, with their mouths always open, starving for food, screaming?" And once at a large family gathering, "Did you all know that last week downtown a little baby's nose was chewed off by rats in his crib—a little *black* baby?" Nola meant only to call attention to herself, but you couldn't blame her listeners for being offended. They stared at her, not knowing what to say. What a strange child! What queer glassy-pale eyes! Mr. Dietrich told her curtly to leave the table; he'd had enough of the game she was playing and so had everyone else.

Nola stared at him, her eyes filling with tears. Game?

When they were alone Mr. Dietrich said angrily to Mrs. Dietrich, "Can't you control her in front of other people, at least?" Mrs. Dietrich was angry, too, and frightened. She said, "I *try*."

They sent her off aged fourteen to the Portland Academy up in Maine, and without their help she matured into a girl of considerable beauty. A heart-shaped face, delicate features, glossy red-brown hair scissor-cut to her shoulders. Five feet seven inches tall weighing less than one hundred pounds, the result of constant savage dieting. (Mrs. Dietrich, who has weight problems herself, doesn't dare inquire as to details. They've been through that already.) All the girls sport flat bellies, flat buttocks, jutting pelvic bones. Many, like Nola, are wound tight, high-strung as pedigreed dogs, whippets for instance, the breed that lives for running. Thirty days after they'd left her at the Portland Academy, Nola telephoned home at 11 P.M. one Sunday giggly and high, telling Mrs. Dietrich she adored the school she adored her suite-mates she adored most of her teachers particularly her riding instructor Tern, Tern the Terrier they called the woman because she was so fierce, such a character, eyes that bore right through your skull, wore belts with the most amazing silver buckles! Nola loved Tern but she wasn't *in* love—there's a difference!

Mrs. Dietrich broke down weeping, *that* time. 25

Now of course Nola has boyfriends. Mrs. Dietrich has long since given up trying to keep track of their names. And, in any case, the Paul of this spring isn't necessarily the Paul of last November, nor are all the boys necessarily students at the academy. There is even one "boy"—or young man—who seems to be married: who seems to be, in fact, one of the junior instructors at the school. (Mrs. Dietrich does not eavesdrop on her daughter's telephone conversations but there are things she cannot help overhearing.) Is your daughter on the pill? the women in Mrs. Dietrich's circle asked one another for awhile, guiltily, surreptitiously. Now they no longer ask.

But Nola has announced recently that she loathes boys—she's fed up.

She's never going to get married. She'll study languages in college, French, Italian, something exotic like Arabic, go to work for the American foreign service. Unless she drops out of school altogether to become a model.

"Do you think I'm too fat, Mother?" she asks frequently, worriedly, standing in front of the mirror, twisted at the waist to reveal her small round belly which, it seems, can't help being round: she bloats herself on diet Cokes all day long. "Do you think it *shows?*"

When Mrs. Dietrich was pregnant with Nola she'd been twenty-nine years old and 30 she and Mr. Dietrich had tried to have a baby for nearly five years. She'd lost hope, begun to despise herself; then suddenly it happened: like grace. Like happiness swelling so powerfully it can barely be contained. I can hear its heartbeat! her husband exclaimed. He'd been her lover then, young, vigorous, dreamy. Caressing the rock-hard belly, splendid white tight-stretched skin, that roundness like a warm pulsing melon. Never before so happy, and never since. Husband and wife. One flesh. Mr. Dietrich gave Mrs. Dietrich a reproduction on stiff glossy paper of Dante Gabriel Rossetti's *Beata Beatrix*, embarrassed, apologetic, knowing it was sentimental and perhaps a little silly but that was how he thought of her—so beautiful, rapturous, pregnant with their child. Her features were ordinarily pretty, her wavy brown hair cut short; Mrs. Dietrich looked nothing like the extraordinary woman in Rossetti's painting in her transport of ecstasy but she was immensely flattered and moved by her husband's gift, knowing herself adored, worthy of adoration. She told no one, but she knew the baby was to be a girl. It would be herself again, reborn and this time perfect.

Not until years later did she learn by chance that the woman in Rossetti's painting was in fact his dead wife Lizzy Siddal, who had killed herself with an overdose of laudanum after the stillbirth of their only child.

"Oh, Mother, isn't it *beautiful!*" Nola exclaims.

It is past noon. Past twelve-thirty. Mrs. Dietrich and Nola have made the rounds of a half dozen stores, traveled countless escalators, one clothing department has blended into the next and the chic smiling saleswomen have become indistinguishable, and Mrs. Dietrich is beginning to feel the urgent need for a glass of white wine. Just a glass. "Isn't it beautiful? It's *perfect*," Nola says. Her eyes glow with pleasure, her smooth skin is radiant. Modeling in the three-way mirror a queer little yellow-and-black striped sweater with a ribbed waist, punk style, mock cheap (though the sweater by Sergio Valente, even "drastically reduced," is certainly not cheap), Mrs. Dietrich feels the motherly obligation to register a mild protest, knowing Nola will not hear. She must have it and will have it. She'll wear it a few times, then retire it to the bottom of a drawer with so many other novelty sweaters, accumulated since sixth grade. (She's like her mother in that regard—can't bear to throw anything away. Clothes, shoes, cosmetics, records; once bought by Nola Dietrich they are hers forever, crammed in drawers and closets.)

"*Isn't* it beautiful?" Nola demands, studying her reflection in the mirror.

Mrs. Dietrich pays for the sweater on her charge account.   35

Next they buy Nola a good pair of shoes. And a handbag to go with them. In Paraphernalia where rock music blasts overhead and Mrs. Dietrich stands to one side, rather miserable, Nola chats companionably with two girls—tall, pretty, cutely made up—she'd gone to public school in Livingstone with. She says afterward with an upward rolling of her eyes, "God, I was afraid they'd latch onto us!" Mrs. Dietrich has seen women friends and acquaintances of her own in the mall this morning but has shrunk from being noticed, not wanting to share her daughter with anyone. She has a sense of time passing ever more swiftly, cruelly.

Nola wants to try on an outfit in Paraphernalia, just for fun, a boxy khaki-colored jacket with matching pants, fly front, zippers, oversized buttons, so aggressively ugly it must be chic, yes of course it *is* chic, "drastically reduced" from $245 to $219. An import by Julio Vicente and Mrs. Dietrich can't reasonably disapprove of Julio Vicente, can she. She watches Nola preening in the mirror, watches other shoppers watching her. My daughter. Mine. But of course there is no connection between them, they don't even resemble each other. A seventeen-year-old, a forty-seven-year-old. When Nola is away she seems to forget her mother entirely—doesn't telephone, certainly doesn't write. It's the way all their daughters are, Mrs. Dietrich's friends tell her. It doesn't *mean* anything. Mrs. Dietrich thinks how when she was carrying Nola, those nine long months, they'd been completely happy—not an instant's doubt or hesitation. The singular weight of the body. A state like trance you are tempted to mistake for happiness because the body is incapable of thinking, therefore incapable of anticipating change. Hot rhythmic blood, organs packed tight and moist, the baby upside down in her sac in her mother's belly, always present tense, always *now*. It was a shock when the end came so abruptly, but everyone told Mrs. Dietrich she was a natural mother, praised and pampered her. For a while. Then of course she'd had her baby, her Nola. Even now Mrs. Dietrich can't really comprehend the experience. *Giving birth. Had a baby. Was born.* Mere words, absurdly inadequate. She knows no more of how love ends than she knew as a child, she knows only of how love begins—in the belly, in the womb, where it is always present tense.

The morning's shopping has been quite successful, but lunch at La Crêperie doesn't go well. For some reason—surely there can be no reason?—lunch doesn't go well at all.

La Crêperie is Nola's favorite mall restaurant, always amiably crowded, bustling, a simulated sidewalk cafe with red-striped umbrellas, wrought-iron tables and chairs, menus in French, music piped in overhead. Mrs. Dietrich's nerves are chafed by the pretense of gaiety, the noise, the openness onto one of the mall's busy promenades where at any minute a familiar face might emerge, but she is grateful for her glass of chilled white wine—isn't it red wine that gives you headaches, hangovers?—white wine is safe. She orders a small tossed salad and a creamed chicken crepe and devours it hungrily—she *is* hungry—while Nola picks at her seafood crepe with a disdainful look. A familiar scene: mother watching while daughter pushes food around on her plate. Suddenly Nola is tense, moody, corners of her mouth downturned. Mrs. Dietrich wants to ask, What's wrong? She wants to ask, Why are you unhappy? She wants to smooth Nola's hair back from her forehead, check to see if her forehead is overly warm, wants to hug her close, hard. Why, why? What did I do wrong? Why do you hate me?

Calling the Portland Academy a few weeks ago Mrs. Dietrich suddenly lost control, began crying. She hadn't been drinking and she hadn't known she was upset. A girl unknown to her, one of Nola's suitemates, was saying, "Please, Mrs. Dietrich, it's all right, I'm sure Nola will call you back later tonight—or tomorrow, Mrs. Dietrich? I'll tell her you called, all right, Mrs. Dietrich?" as embarrassed as if Mrs. Dietrich had been her own mother.   40

How love begins. How love ends.

Mrs. Dietrich orders a third glass of wine. This is a celebration of sorts, isn't it? Their last shopping trip for a long time. But Nola resists, Nola isn't sentimental. In casual defiance of Mrs. Dietrich she lights up a cigarette—yes, Mother, Nola has said ironically, since you stopped smoking *everybody* is supposed to stop—and sits with her arms crossed, watching streams of shoppers pass. Mrs. Dietrich speaks lightly of practical matters, tomorrow morning's drive to the airport and will Nola telephone when she gets to Portland to let Mrs. Dietrich know she has arrived safely? La Crêperie opens onto an atrium three stories high, vast, airy, lit with artificial sunlight, tastefully decorated with trees, potted spring flowers, a fountain, a gigantic white Easter bunny, cleverly mechanized, atop a nest of brightly painted wooden eggs. The bunny has an animated tail, an animated nose; paws, ears, eyes that move. Children stand watching it, screaming with excitement, delight. Mrs. Dietrich notes that Nola's expression is one of faint contempt and says, "It is noisy here, isn't it?"

"Little kids have all the fun," Nola says.

Then with no warning—though of course she'd been planning this all along—Nola brings up the subject of a semester in France, in Paris and Rouen, the fall semester of her senior year it would be; she has put in her application, she says, and is waiting to hear if she's been accepted. She smokes her cigarette calmly, expelling smoke from her nostrils in a way Mrs. Dietrich thinks particularly coarse. Mrs. Dietrich, who believed that particular topic was finished, takes care to speak without emotion. "I just don't think it's a very practical idea right now, Nola," she says. "We've been through it, haven't we? I—"

"I'm going," Nola says.   45

"The extra expense, for one thing. Your father—"

"If I get accepted, I'm going."

"Your father—"

"The hell with him too."

Mrs. Dietrich would like to slap her daughter's face. Bring tears to those steely eyes. But she sits stiff, turning her wineglass between her fingers, patient, calm; she's heard all this before; she says, "Surely this isn't the best time to discuss it, Nola."   50

Mrs. Dietrich is afraid her daughter will leave the restaurant, simply walk away; that has happened before and if it happens today she doesn't know what she will do.

But Nola sits unmoving, her face closed, impassive. Mrs. Dietrich feels her quickened heartbeat. It's like seeing your own life whirling in a sink, in a drain, one of those terrible dreams in which you're paralyzed—the terror of losing her daughter. Once after one of their quarrels Mrs. Dietrich told a friend of hers, the mother too of a teenaged daughter, "I just don't know her any longer; how can you keep living with someone you don't know?" and the woman said, "Eventually you can't."

Nola says, not looking at Mrs. Dietrich, "Why don't we talk about it, Mother."

"Talk about what?" Mrs. Dietrich asks.

"You know."

"The semester in France? Again?"   55

"No."

"What then?"

"You *know*."

"I don't know, really. Really!" Mrs. Dietrich smiles, baffled. She feels the corners of her eyes pucker white with strain.

Nola says, sighing, "How exhausting it is."   60

"How *what?*"

"How exhausting it is."

"What is?"

"You and me."

"What?"   65

"Being together."

"Being together how?"

"The two of us, like this—"

"But we're hardly ever together, Nola," Mrs. Dietrich says.

Her expression is calm but her voice is shaking. Nola turns away, covering her face   70
with a hand; for a moment she looks years older than her age—in fact exhausted. Mrs. Dietrich sees with pity that her daughter's skin is fair and thin and dry—unlike her own, which tends to be oily—it will wear out before she's forty. Mrs. Dietrich reaches over to squeeze her hand. The fingers are limp, ungiving. "You're going back to school tomorrow, Nola," she says. "You won't come home again until June twelfth. And you probably will go to France—if your father consents."

Nola gets to her feet, drops her cigarette to the flagstone terrace, and grinds it out beneath her boot. A dirty thing to do, Mrs. Dietrich thinks, considering there's an ashtray right on the table, but she says nothing. She dislikes La Crêperie anyway.

Nola laughs, showing her lovely white teeth. "Oh, the hell with him," she says. "Fuck Daddy, right?"

They separate for an hour, Mrs. Dietrich to Neiman-Marcus to buy a birthday gift for her elderly aunt, Nola to the trendy new boutique Pour Vous. By the time Mrs. Dietrich rejoins her daughter she's quite angry, blood beating hot and hard and measured in resentment; she has had time to relive old quarrels between them, old exchanges, stray humiliating memories of her marriage as well; these last-hour disagreements are the cruelest and they are Nola's specialty. She locates Nola in the rear of the boutique amid blaring rock music, flashing neon lights, chrome-edged mirrors, her face still hard, closed, prim, pale. She stands beside another teenaged girl, looking in a desultory way through a rack of blouses, shoving the hangers roughly along, taking no care when a blouse falls to the floor. Mrs. Dietrich remembers seeing Nola slip a pair of panty hose into her purse in a village shop because, she said afterward, the saleswoman was so damned slow coming to wait on her; fortunately Mrs. Dietrich was there, took the panty hose right out, and replaced it on the counter. No big deal, Mother, Nola said, don't have a stroke or something. Seeing Nola now, Mrs. Dietrich is charged with hurt, rage; the injustice of it, she thinks, the cruelty of it, and why, and why? And as Nola glances up, startled, not prepared to see her mother in front of her, their eyes lock for an instant and Mrs. Dietrich stares at her with hatred. Cold calm clear unmistakable hatred. She is thinking, Who are *you?* What have I to do with *you?* I don't know *you,* I don't love *you,* why should I?

Has Nola seen, heard? She turns aside as if wincing, gives the blouses a final dismissive shove. Her eyes look tired, the corners of her mouth downturned. Anxious, immediately repentant, Mrs. Dietrich asks if she has found anything worth trying on. Nola says with a shrug, "Not a thing, Mother."

On their way out of the mall Mrs. Dietrich and Nola see the disheveled woman in the black coat again, this time sitting prominently on a concrete ledge in front of Lord & Taylor's busy main entrance, shopping bag at her feet, shabby purse on the ledge beside her. She is shaking her head in a series of annoyed twitches as if arguing with someone but her hands are loose, palms up, in her lap. Her posture is unfortunate—she sits with her knees parted, inner thighs revealed, fatty, dead white, the tops of cotton stockings rolled tight cutting into the flesh. Again, streams of shoppers are making a careful berth around her. Alone among them Nola hesitates, seems about to approach the woman— Please don't, Nola, please! Mrs. Dietrich thinks—then changes her mind and keeps on walking. Mrs. Dietrich murmurs, "Isn't it a pity, poor thing, don't you wonder where she lives, who her family is?" but Nola doesn't reply. Her pace through the first floor of Lord & Taylor is so rapid that Mrs. Dietrich can barely keep up.

But she's upset. Strangely upset. As soon as they are in the car, packages and bags in the back seat, she begins crying.

It's childish helpless crying, as though her heart is broken. But Mrs. Dietrich knows it isn't broken; she has heard these very sobs before. Many times before. Still she comforts her daughter, embraces her, hugs her hard, hard. A sudden fierce passion. Vehemence. "Nola honey, Nola dear, what's wrong, dear? Everything will be all right, dear," she says, close to weeping herself. She would embrace Nola even more tightly except for the girl's quilted jacket, that bulky L. L. Bean thing she has never liked, and Nola's stubborn lowered head. Nola has always been ashamed, crying, frantic to hide her face. Strangers are passing close by the car, curious, staring. Mrs. Dietrich wishes she had a cloak to draw over her daughter and herself, so that no one would see.

QUESTIONS

1. Describe the characters of Mrs. Dietrich and Nola. What is the basis of the opposition between the two? Why does Nola seem to resent her mother? Should Nola's resentment be construed as a mark of her growth? Why do the two argue about the semester abroad? How does Mrs. Dietrich's attitude toward Nola seem to change in paragraph 73? Does her anger indicate a cessation of love for Nola?

2. Is this story more about Mrs. Dietrich or Nola? In what ways are the two women different? The same? Why does the story end as it does, in the car?

3. Explain the meaning of the vagabond woman at the beginning and ending of the story (paragraphs 11, 75). How should this woman be considered a symbol of the shortcomings of the way of life represented by the shopping mall?

4.   Why is the story told in the present tense, with excursions into the past?

5.   Consider the proposition "Never before so happy, and never since" (paragraph 30) as a theme of the story.

AMY TAN   (b. 1952)

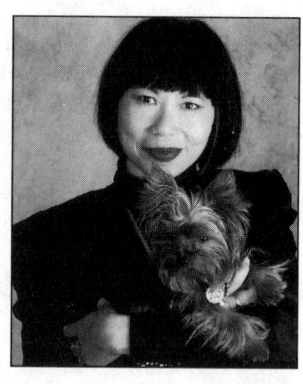

Tan was born almost three years after her parents left China during the Maoist revolution in that country. They settled in California and moved frequently within that state when Tan was a child. She attended schools in California and in Switzerland and received an M.A. at Berkeley. In addition to working as a freelance writer, she has been on many committees and boards serving the interests of minorities. As an imaginative writer she has drawn upon her own experiences as a Chinese-American growing up in the United States. Her most successful work to date is The Joy Luck Club *(1989), which was made into a movie (1993) and from which "Two Kinds" is excerpted. She has also published two other novels,* The Kitchen God's Wife *(1991) and* The Hundred Secret Senses *(1995), in addition to children's books. She edited* Best American Short Stories, 1999 *(1999).*

Two Kinds _____ 1989

My mother believed you could be anything you wanted to be in America. You could open a restaurant. You could work for the government and get good retirement. You could buy a house with almost no money down. You could become rich. You could become instantly famous.

"Of course you can be prodigy, too," my mother told me when I was nine. "You can be best anything. What does Auntie Lindo know? Her daughter, she is only best tricky."

America was where all my mother's hopes lay. She had come here in 1949 after losing everything in China: her mother and father, her family home, her first husband, and two daughters, twin baby girls. But she never looked back with regret. There were so many ways for things to get better.

We didn't immediately pick the right kind of prodigy. At first my mother thought I could be a Chinese Shirley Temple. We'd watch Shirley's old movies on TV as though they were training films. My mother would poke my arm and say, *"Ni kan"*—You watch. And I would see Shirley tapping her feet, or singing a sailor song, or pursing her lips into a very round O while saying, "Oh my goodness."

"Ni kan," said my mother as Shirley's eyes flooded with tears. "You already know how. Don't need talent for crying!"

Soon after my mother got this idea about Shirley Temple, she took me to a beauty training school in the Mission district and put me in the hands of a student who could barely hold the scissors without shaking. Instead of getting big fat curls, I emerged with an uneven mass of crinkly black fuzz. My mother dragged me off to the bathroom and tried to wet down my hair.

"You look like Negro Chinese," she lamented, as if I had done this on purpose.

The instructor of the beauty training school had to lop off these soggy clumps to make my hair even again. "Peter Pan is very popular these days," the instructor assured my mother. I now had hair the length of a boy's, with straight-across bangs that hung at a slant two inches above my eyebrows. I liked the haircut and it made me actually look forward to my future fame.

In fact, in the beginning, I was just as excited as my mother, maybe even more so. I pictured this prodigy part of me as many different images, trying each one on for size. I was a dainty ballerina girl standing by the curtains, waiting to hear the right music that would send me floating on my tiptoes. I was like the Christ child lifted out of the straw manger, crying with holy indignity. I was Cinderella stepping from her pumpkin carriage with sparkly cartoon music filling the air.

In all of my imaginings, I was filled with a sense that I would soon become *perfect*. 10 My mother and father would adore me. I would be beyond reproach. I would never feel the need to sulk for anything.

But sometimes the prodigy in me became impatient. "If you don't hurry up and get me out of here, I'm disappearing for good," it warned. "And then you'll always be nothing."

Every night after dinner, my mother and I would sit at the Formica kitchen table. She would present new tests, taking her examples from stories of amazing children she had read in *Ripley's Believe It or Not*, or *Good Housekeeping, Reader's Digest,* and a dozen other magazines she kept in a pile in our bathroom. My mother got these magazines from people whose houses she cleaned. And since she cleaned many houses each week, we had a great assortment. She would look through them all, searching for stories about remarkable children.

The first night she brought out a story about a three-year-old boy who knew the capitals of all the states and even most of the European countries. A teacher was quoted as saying the little boy could also pronounce the names of the foreign cities correctly.

"What's the capital of Finland?" my mother asked me, looking at the magazine story.

All I knew was the capital of California, because Sacramento was the name of the 15 street we lived on in Chinatown. "Nairobi!" I guessed, saying the most foreign word I could think of. She checked to see if that was possibly one way to pronounce "Helsinki" before showing me the answer.

The tests got harder—multiplying numbers in my head, finding the queen of hearts in a deck of cards, trying to stand on my head without using my hands, predicting the daily temperatures in Los Angeles, New York, and London.

One night I had to look at a page from the Bible for three minutes and then report everything I could remember. "Now Jehoshaphat had riches° and honor in abundance and . . . that's all I remember, Ma," I said.

And after seeing my mother's disappointed face once again, something inside of me began to die. I hated the tests, the raised hopes and failed expectations. Before going to bed that night, I looked in the mirror above the bathroom sink and when I saw only my face staring back—and that it would always be this ordinary face—I began to cry. Such a sad, ugly girl! I made high-pitched noises like a crazed animal, trying to scratch out the face in the mirror.

Now Jehoshaphat had riches: Jing-Mei had been told to report on the Hebrew monarch Jehoshaphat as narrated in the eighteenth chapter of II Chronicles.

And then I saw what seemed to be the prodigy side of me—because I had never seen that face before. I looked at my reflection, blinking so I could see more clearly. The girl staring back at me was angry, powerful. This girl and I were the same. I had new thoughts, willful thoughts, or rather thoughts filled with lots of won'ts. I won't let her change me, I promised myself. I won't be what I'm not.

So now on nights when my mother presented her tests, I performed listlessly, my   20
head propped on one arm. I pretended to be bored. And I was. I got so bored I started counting the bellows of the foghorns out on the bay while my mother drilled me in other areas. The sound was comforting and reminded me of the cow jumping over the moon. And the next day, I played a game with myself, seeing if my mother would give up on me before eight bellows. After a while I usually counted only one, maybe two bellows at most. At last she was beginning to give up hope.

Two or three months had gone by without any mention of my being a prodigy again. And then one day my mother was watching *The Ed Sullivan Show*° on TV. The TV was old and the sound kept shorting out. Every time my mother got halfway up from the sofa to adjust the set, the sound would go back on and Ed would be talking. As soon as she sat down, Ed would go silent again. She got up, the TV broke into loud piano music. She sat down. Silence. Up and down, back and forth, quiet and loud. It was like a stiff embraceless dance between her and the TV set. Finally she stood by the set with her hand on the sound dial.

She seemed entranced by the music, a little frenzied piano piece with this mesmerizing quality, sort of quick passages and then teasing lilting ones before it returned to the quick playful parts.

"*Ni kan,*" my mother said, calling me over with hurried hand gestures, "Look here."

I could see why my mother was fascinated by the music. It was being pounded out by a little Chinese girl, about nine years old, with a Peter Pan haircut. The girl had the sauciness of a Shirley Temple. She was proudly modest like a proper Chinese child. And she also did this fancy sweep of a curtsy, so that the fluffy skirt of her white dress cascaded slowly to the floor like the petals of a large carnation.

In spite of these warning signs, I wasn't worried. Our family had no piano and we   25
couldn't afford to buy one, let alone reams of sheet music and piano lessons. So I could be generous in my comments when my mother bad-mouthed the little girl on TV.

"Play note right, but doesn't sound good! No singing sound," complained my mother.

"What are you picking on her for?" I said carelessly. "She's pretty good. Maybe she's not the best, but she's trying hard." I knew almost immediately I would be sorry I said that.

"Just like you," she said. "Not the best. Because you not trying." She gave a little huff as she let go of the sound dial and sat down on the sofa.

The little Chinese girl sat down also to play an encore of "Anitra's Dance" by Grieg.° I remember the song, because later on I had to learn how to play it.

Three days after watching *The Ed Sullivan Show*, my mother told me what my   30
schedule would be for piano lessons and piano practice. She had talked to Mr. Chong,

---

Ed Sullivan Show: Ed Sullivan (1902–1974), originally a newspaper columnist, hosted this popular variety television show from 1948 to 1971.
    "Anitra's Dance" by Grieg: a portion of the suite composed for Ibsen's *Peer Gynt* by Norwegian composer Edvard Grieg (1843–1907).

who lived on the first floor of our apartment building. Mr. Chong was a retired piano teacher and my mother had traded housecleaning services for weekly lessons and a piano for me to practice on every day, two hours a day, from four until six.

When my mother told me this, I felt as though I had been sent to hell. I whined and then kicked my foot a little when I couldn't stand it anymore.

"Why don't you like me the way I am? I'm *not* a genius! I can't play the piano. And even if I could, I wouldn't go on TV if you paid me a million dollars!" I cried.

My mother slapped me. "Who ask you be genius?" she shouted. "Only ask you be your best. For you sake. You think I want you be genius? Hnnh! What for! Who ask you!"

"So ungrateful," I heard her mutter in Chinese. "If she had as much talent as she has temper, she would be famous now."

Mr. Chong, whom I secretly nicknamed Old Chong, was very strange, always tap- 35 ping his fingers to the silent music of an invisible orchestra. He looked ancient in my eyes. He had lost most of the hair on top of his head and he wore thick glasses and had eyes that always looked tired and sleepy. But he must have been younger than I thought, since he lived with his mother and was not yet married.

I met Old Lady Chong once and that was enough. She had this peculiar smell like a baby that had done something in its pants. And her fingers felt like a dead person's, like an old peach I once found in the back of the refrigerator; the skin just slid off the meat when I picked it up.

I soon found out why Old Chong had retired from teaching piano. He was deaf. "Like Beethoven!" he shouted to me. "We're both listening only in our head!" And he would start to conduct his frantic silent sonatas.

Our lessons went like this. He would open the book and point to different things, explaining their purpose: "Key! Treble! Bass! No sharps or flats! So this is C major! Listen now and play after me!"

And then he would play the C scale a few times, a simple chord, and then, as if inspired by an old, unreachable itch, he gradually added more notes and running trills and a pounding bass until the music was really something quite grand.

I would play after him, the simple scale, the simple chord, and then I just played 40 some nonsense that sounded like a cat running up and down on top of garbage cans. Old Chong smiled and applauded and then said, "Very good! But now you must learn to keep time!"

So that's how I discovered that Old Chong's eyes were too slow to keep up with the wrong notes I was playing. He went through the motions in half-time. To help me keep rhythm, he stood behind me, pushing down on my right shoulder for every beat. He balanced pennies on top of my wrists so I would keep them still as I slowly played scales and arpeggios. He had me curve my hand around an apple and keep that shape when playing chords. He marched stiffly to show me how to make each finger dance up and down, staccato like an obedient little soldier.

He taught me all these things, and that was how I also learned I could be lazy and get away with mistakes, lots of mistakes. If I hit the wrong notes because I hadn't prac- ticed enough, I never corrected myself. I just kept playing in rhythm. And Old Chong kept conducting his own private reverie.

So maybe I never really gave myself a fair chance. I did pick up the basics pretty quickly, and I might have become a good pianist at that young age. But I was so deter- mined not to try, not to be anybody different that I learned to play only the most ear- splitting preludes, the most discordant hymns.

Over the next year, I practiced like this, dutifully in my own way. And then one day I heard my mother and her friend Lindo Jong both talking in a loud bragging tone of voice so others could hear. It was after church, and I was leaning against the brick wall wearing a dress with stiff white petticoats. Auntie Lindo's daughter, Waverly, who was about my age, was standing farther down the wall about five feet away. We had grown up together and shared all the closeness of two sisters squabbling over crayons and dolls. In other words, for the most part, we hated each other. I thought she was snotty. Waverly Jong had gained a certain amount of fame as "Chinatown's Littlest Chinese Chess Champion."

"She bring home too many trophy," lamented Auntie Lindo that Sunday. "All day she play chess. All day I have no time do nothing but dust off her winnings." She threw a scolding look at Waverly, who pretended not to see her.   45

"You lucky you don't have this problem," said Auntie Lindo with a sigh to my mother.

And my mother squared her shoulders and bragged: "Our problem worser than yours. If we ask Jing-Mei wash dish, she hear nothing but music. It's like you can't stop this natural talent."

And right then, I was determined to put a stop to her foolish pride.

A few weeks later, Old Chong and my mother conspired to have me play in a talent show which would be held in the church hall. By then, my parents had saved up enough to buy me a secondhand piano, a black Wurlitzer spinet with a scarred bench. It was the showpiece of our living room.

For the talent show, I was to play a piece called "Pleading Child" from Schumann's   50
Scenes from Childhood.° It was a simple, moody piece that sounded more difficult than it was. I was supposed to memorize the whole thing, playing the repeat parts twice to make the piece sound longer. But I dawdled over it, playing a few bars and then cheating, looking up to see what notes followed. I never really listened to what I was playing. I day-dreamed about being somewhere else, about being someone else.

The part I liked to practice best was the fancy curtsy: right foot out, touch the rose on the carpet with a pointed foot, sweep to the side, left leg bends, look up and smile.

My parents invited all the couples from the Joy Luck Club to witness my debut. Auntie Lindo and Uncle Tin were there. Waverly and her two older brothers had also come. The first two rows were filled with children both younger and older than I was. The littlest ones got to go first. They recited simple nursery rhymes, squawked out tunes on miniature violins, twirled Hula Hoops, pranced in pink ballet tutus, and when they bowed or curtsied, the audience would sigh in unison, "Awww," and then clap enthusiastically.

When my turn came, I was very confident. I remember my childish excitement. It was as if I knew, without a doubt, that the prodigy side of me really did exist. I had no fear whatsoever, no nervousness. I remember thinking to myself, This is it! This is it! I looked out over the audience, at my mother's blank face, my father's yawn, Auntie Lindo's stiff-lipped smile, Waverly's sulky expression. I had on a white dress layered with sheets of lace, and a pink bow in my Peter Pan haircut. As I sat down I envisioned people jumping to their feet and Ed Sullivan rushing up to introduce me to everyone on TV.

And I started to play. It was so beautiful. I was so caught up in how lovely I looked that at first I didn't worry how I would sound. So it was a surprise to me when I hit the first wrong note and I realized something didn't sound quite right. And then I hit

---

Scenes from Childhood: Scenes from Childhood, or *Kinderszenen* (1836), is one of the best-known works for piano by Robert Schumann (1810–1856).

another and another followed that. A chill started at the top of my head and began to trickle down. Yet I couldn't stop playing, as though my hands were bewitched. I kept thinking my fingers would adjust themselves back, like a train switching to the right track. I played this strange jumble through two repeats, the sour notes staying with me all the way to the end.

When I stood up, I discovered my legs were shaking. Maybe I had just been nervous and the audience, like Old Chong, had seen me go through the right motions and had not heard anything wrong at all. I swept my right foot out, went down on my knee, looked up and smiled. The room was quiet, except for Old Chong, who was beaming and shouting, "Bravo! Bravo! Well done!" But then I saw my mother's face, her stricken face. The audience clapped weakly, and as I walked back to my chair, with my whole face quivering as I tried not to cry, I heard a little boy whisper loudly to his mother, "That was awful," and the mother whispered back, "Well, she certainly tried."

And now I realized how many people were in the audience, the whole world it seemed. I was aware of eyes burning into my back. I felt the shame of my mother and father as they sat stiffly throughout the rest of the show.

We could have escaped during intermission. Pride and some strange sense of honor must have anchored my parents to their chairs. And so we watched it all: the eighteen-year-old boy with a fake mustache who did a magic show and juggled flaming hoops while riding a unicycle. The breasted girl with white makeup who sang from *Madama Butterfly*° and got honorable mention. And the eleven-year-old boy who won first prize playing a tricky violin song that sounded like a busy bee.°

After the show, the Hsus, the Jongs, and the St. Clairs from the Joy Luck Club came up to my mother and father.

"Lots of talented kids," Auntie Lindo said vaguely, smiling broadly.

"That was somethin' else," said my father, and I wondered if he was referring to me in a humorous way, or whether he even remembered what I had done.

Waverly looked at me and shrugged her shoulders. "You aren't a genius like me," she said matter-of-factly. And if I hadn't felt so bad, I would have pulled her braids and punched her stomach.

But my mother's expression was what devastated me: a quiet, blank look that said she had lost everything. I felt the same way, and it seemed as if everybody were now coming up, like gawkers at the scene of an accident, to see what parts were actually missing. When we got on the bus to go home, my father was humming the busy-bee tune and my mother was silent. I kept thinking she wanted to wait until we got home before shouting at me. But when my father unlocked the door to our apartment, my mother walked in and then went to the back, into the bedroom. No accusations. No blame. And in a way, I felt disappointed. I had been waiting for her to start shouting, so I could shout back and cry and blame her for all my misery.

I assumed my talent-show fiasco meant I never had to play the piano again. But two days later, after school, my mother came out of the kitchen and saw me watching TV.

Madama Butterfly: The girl probably sang "Un Bel Di," the signature soprano aria from the opera *Madama Butterfly* by Giacomo Puccini (1858–1924).

   busy bee: probably the well-known "Flight of the Bumblebee" by Nikolay Rimsky-Korsakov (1844–1908).

"Four clock," she reminded me as if it were any other day. I was stunned, as though she were asking me to go through the talent-show torture again. I wedged myself more tightly in front of the TV.

"Turn off TV," she called from the kitchen five minutes later. 65

I didn't budge. And then I decided. I didn't have to do what my mother said anymore. I wasn't her slave. This wasn't China. I had listened to her before and look what happened. She was the stupid one.

She came out from the kitchen and stood in the arched entryway of the living room. "Four clock," she said once again, louder.

"I'm not going to play anymore," I said nonchalantly. "Why should I? I'm not a genius."

She walked over and stood in front of the TV. I saw her chest was heaving up and down in an angry way.

"No!" I said, and I now felt stronger, as if my true self had finally emerged. So this 70 was what had been inside me all along.

"No! I won't!" I screamed.

She yanked me by the arm, pulled me off the floor, snapped off the TV. She was frighteningly strong, half pulling, half carrying me toward the piano as I kicked the throw rugs under my feet. She lifted me up and onto the hard bench. I was sobbing by now, looking at her bitterly. Her chest was heaving even more and her mouth was open, smiling crazily as if she were pleased I was crying.

"You want me to be someone that I'm not!" I sobbed. "I'll never be the kind of daughter you want me to be!"

"Only two kinds of daughters," she shouted in Chinese. "Those who are obedient and those who follow their own mind! Only one kind of daughter can live in this house. Obedient daughter!"

"Then I wish I wasn't your daughter. I wish you weren't my mother," I shouted. 75 As I said these things I got scared. It felt like worms and toads and slimy things crawling out of my chest, but it also felt good, as if this awful side of me had surfaced, at last.

"Too late change this," said my mother shrilly.

And I could sense her anger rising to its breaking point. I wanted to see it spill over. And that's when I remembered the babies she had lost in China, the ones we never talked about. "Then I wish I'd never been born!" I shouted. "I wish I were dead! Like them."

It was as if I had said the magic words. Alakazam!—and her face went blank, her mouth closed, her arms went slack, and she backed out of the room, stunned, as if she were blowing away like a small brown leaf, thin, brittle, lifeless.

It was not the only disappointment my mother felt in me. In the years that followed, I failed her so many times, each time asserting my own will, my right to fall short of expectations. I didn't get straight As. I didn't become class president. I didn't get into Stanford. I dropped out of college.

For unlike my mother, I did not believe I could be anything I wanted to be. I could 80 only be me.

And for all those years, we never talked about the disaster at the recital or my terrible accusations afterward at the piano bench. All that remained unchecked, like a betrayal that was now unspeakable. So I never found a way to ask her why she had hoped for something so large that failure was inevitable.

And even worse, I never asked her what frightened me the most: Why had she given up hope?

For after our struggle at the piano, she never mentioned my playing again. The lessons stopped. The lid to the piano was closed, shutting out the dust, my misery, and her dreams.

So she surprised me. A few years ago, she offered to give me the piano, for my thirtieth birthday. I had not played in all those years. I saw the offer as a sign of forgiveness, a tremendous burden removed.

"Are you sure?" I asked shyly. "I mean, won't you and Dad miss it?"   85

"No, this your piano," she said firmly. "Always your piano. You only one can play."

"Well, I probably can't play anymore," I said. "It's been years."

"You pick up fast," said my mother, as if she knew this was certain. "You have natural talent. You could been genius if you want to."

"No I couldn't."

"You just not trying," said my mother. And she was neither angry nor sad. She   90
said it as if to announce a fact that could never be disproved. "Take it," she said.

But I didn't at first. It was enough that she had offered it to me. And after that, every time I saw it in my parents' living room, standing in front of the bay windows, it made me feel proud, as if it were a shiny trophy I had won back.

Last week I sent a tuner over to my parents' apartment and had the piano reconditioned, for purely sentimental reasons. My mother had died a few months before and I had been getting things in order for my father, a little bit at a time. I put the jewelry in special silk pouches. The sweaters she had knitted in yellow, pink, bright orange—all the colors I hated—I put those in moth-proof boxes. I found some old Chinese silk dresses, the kind with little slits up the sides. I rubbed the old silk against my skin, then wrapped them in tissue and decided to take them home with me.

After I had the piano tuned, I opened the lid and touched the keys. It sounded even richer than I remembered. Really, it was a very good piano. Inside the bench were the same exercise notes with handwritten scales, the same secondhand music books with their covers held together with yellow tape.

I opened up the Schumann book to the dark little piece I had played at the recital. It was on the left-hand side of the page, "Pleading Child." It looked more difficult than I remembered. I played a few bars, surprised at how easily the notes came back to me.

And for the first time, or so it seemed, I noticed the piece on the right-hand side.   95
It was called "Perfectly Contented." I tried to play this one as well. It had a lighter melody but the same flowing rhythm and turned out to be quite easy. "Pleading Child" was shorter but slower; "Perfectly Contented" was longer, but faster. And after I played them both a few times, I realized they were two halves of the same song.

QUESTIONS

1.   What major characteristics about the narrator, Jing-Mei, are brought out in the story?

2.   Describe the relationship between Jing-Mei and her mother. Why does Jing-Mei resist all efforts to develop her talents?

3.   Characterize the mother. To what degree is she sympathetic? Unsympathetic? At the story's end, how does Jing-Mei feel about her mother?

4.   What general details about the nature of first- and second-generation immigrants are presented in the story? For a broader comparison, you might relate "Two Kinds" to Zabytko's "Home Soil" (Chapter 10) and Cisneros's "The House on Mango Street" (Chapter 10).

WRITING ABOUT CHARACTERS

Usually your topic will be a major character in a story or drama, although you might also study one or more minor characters. After your customary overview, begin taking notes. List as many traits as you can, and also determine how the author presents details about the character through actions, appearance, speeches, comments by others, or authorial explanations. If you discover unusual traits, determine what they show. The following suggestions and questions will help you get started.

Questions for Discovering Ideas

• Who is the major character? What do you learn about this character from his or her own actions and speeches? From the speeches and actions of other characters? How else do you learn about the character?

• How important is the character to the work's principal action? Which characters oppose the major character? How do the major character and the opposing character(s) interact? What effects do these interactions create?

• What actions bring out important traits of the main character? To what degree is the character creating or just responding to events?

• Characterize the main character's actions: Are they good or bad, intelligent or stupid, deliberate or spontaneous? How do they help you understand the protagonist?

• Describe and explain the traits, both major and minor, of the character you plan to discuss. To what extent do the traits permit you to judge the character? What is your judgment?

• What descriptions (if any) of the character's appearance do you discover in the story? What does the appearance demonstrate about the character?

• In what ways is the character's major trait a strength—or a weakness? As the story progresses, to what degree does the trait become more (or less) prominent?

• Is the character round and dynamic? How does the character recognize, change with, or adjust to circumstances?

• If the character you are analyzing is flat or static, what function does he or she perform in the story (for example, by doing a task or by bringing out qualities of the major character)?

• If the character is a stereotype, to what type does he or she belong? To what degree does the character stay in the stereotypical role or rise above it? How?

- What do any of the other characters do, say, or think to give you insight into the character you are analyzing? What does the character say or think about himself or herself? What does the storyteller or narrator say? How valid are their comments and insights? How helpful in providing insights into the character?
- Is the character lifelike or unreal? Consistent or inconsistent? Believable or not believable?

Strategies for Organizing Ideas

Identify the character you are studying, and refer to noteworthy problems in determining this character's qualities. Use your central idea and thesis sentence to create the form for the body of your essay. Consider one of the following approaches to organize your ideas and form the basis for your essay.

1. *Plan to develop a central trait or major characteristic,* such as "a single-minded dedication to vengeance" (Montresor of Poe's "The Cask of Amontillado" [Chapter 11]) or "the habit of seeing the world only in one's own terms" (Abner Snopes of "Barn Burning"). This kind of structure shows how the work embodies the trait. For example, in one part of the story a trait may be brought out through speeches that characters make about the major character (as in Cather's "Paul's Case") and in another part through that character's own speeches and actions. Studying the trait thus enables you to focus on the differing ways in which the author presents the character, and it also enables you to focus on separate parts of the work.

2. *Plan to explain a character's growth or change.* This type of essay describes a character's traits at the work's beginning and then analyzes changes or developments. *It is important to stress the actual alterations as they emerge but at the same time to avoid retelling the major actions in the work.* Additionally, you should not only describe the changing traits but also analyze how they are brought out within the work (such as the dream of Young Goodman Brown [Chapter 9] or Minnie Wright's long ordeal).

3. *Plan to organize your essay around central actions, objects, or quotations that reveal primary characteristics.* Key incidents may stand out (such as walking on a fine rug with barnyard dirt on one's shoes), along with objects closely associated with the character being analyzed (such as a broken birdcage). There may be important quotations spoken by the character or by someone else in the work. Show how such elements serve as signposts or guides to understanding the character. (See the following demonstrative student essay for an illustration of this type of development.)

4. *Plan to develop qualities of a flat character or characters.* If the character is flat (such as the sisters in "Barn Burning" or the cowboy in Crane's "The Blue Hotel" [Chapter 3]), you might develop topics such as the function and relative significance of the character, the group the character represents, the relationship of the flat character to the round ones, the importance of this relationship, and any additional qualities or traits. For a flat character, you should

explain the circumstances or defects that keep the character from being round, as well as the importance of these shortcomings in the author's presentation of character.

In your conclusion, show how the character's traits are related to the work as a whole. If the person was good but came to a bad end, does this misfortune make him or her seem especially worthy? If the person suffers, does this fact suggest any attitudes about the class or type of which he or she is a part? Or does it illustrate the author's general view of human life? Or both? Do the characteristics explain why the person helps or hinders other characters? How does your essay help to clear up first-reading misunderstandings?

DEMONSTRATIVE STUDENT ESSAY

The Character of Minnie Wright in Glaspell's "A Jury of Her Peers"°

[1]
Minnie Wright is Susan Glaspell's major character in "A Jury of Her Peers." We learn about her, however, not from seeing and hearing her, for she is not a speaking or an acting character in the story, but rather from the secondhand evidence provided by the story's actual characters. Lewis Hale, a neighboring farmer, tells about Minnie's behavior after the body of her husband, John, was found strangled. Mrs. Hale, Hale's wife, tells about Minnie's young womanhood and about how she became alienated from her nearest neighbors because of John's stingy and unfriendly ways. Both Mrs. Hale and Mrs. Peters, the sheriff's wife, make observations about Minnie based on the condition of her kitchen. From this information we get a full portrait of Minnie, who has changed from passivity to destructive assertiveness.* Her change in character is indicated by her clothing, her dead canary, and her unfinished patchwork quilt.†

[2]
The clothes that Minnie has worn in the past and in the present indicate her character as a person of charm who has withered under neglect and contempt. Martha mentions Minnie's attractive and colorful dresses as a young woman, even recalling a "white dress with blue ribbons" (paragraph 258). Martha also recalls that Minnie, when young, was "sweet and pretty, but kind of timid and--fluttery" (paragraph 207). In light of these recollections, Martha observes that Minnie had changed, and changed for the worse, during her twenty years of marriage with John Wright, who is characterized as "a raw wind that gets to the bone" (paragraph 201). As more evidence for Minnie's acceptance of her drab life, Mrs. Peters says that Minnie asks for no more than an apron and a shawl when under arrest in the sheriff's home. This modest clothing, as contrasted with the colorful dresses of her youth, suggests her suppression of spirit.

[3]
The end of this suppression of spirit and also the emergence of Minnie's rage are shown by the discovery of her dead canary. We learn that Minnie, who when young had been in love with music, has endured her cheerless farm home

---
° See pp 202–216 for this story.
* Central idea.
† Thesis sentence.

for twenty years. During this time her husband's contempt has made her life solitary, cheerless, unmusical, and depressingly impoverished. But her buying the canary (paragraph 182) suggests the reemergence of her love of song, just as it also suggests her growth toward self-assertion. That her husband wrings the bird's neck may thus be seen as the cause not only of her immediate sorrow, shown by the dead bird in a "pretty box" (paragraphs 212–225), but also of the anger that marks her change from a stock, obedient wife to a person angry enough to kill.

[4]
Like her love of song, her unfinished quilt indicates her creativity. In twenty years on the farm, never having had children, she has nothing creative to do except for needlework like the quilt. Mrs. Hale comments on the beauty of Minnie's log-cabin design (paragraph 153) and observes the colorful patches of cloth in her sewing basket (paragraph 212). The inference is that even though Minnie's life has been bleak, she has been able to indulge her characteristic love of color and form--and also of warmth, granted the purpose of a quilt.

[5]
Ironically, the quilt also shows Minnie's creativity in the murder of her husband. Both Mrs. Hale and Mrs. Peters interpret the breakdown of her stitching on the quilt as signs of her distress about the dead canary and also of her nervousness in planning revenge. Further, even though nowhere in the play is it said that John is strangled with a quilting knot, no other conclusion is possible. Both Mrs. Hale and Mrs. Peters agree that Minnie probably intended to knot the quilt rather than sew it in a quilt stitch, and Glaspell pointedly causes the men to learn this detail even though they scoff at it and ignore it. In other words, we learn that Minnie's only outlet for creativity--needlework--has enabled her to perform the murder in the only way she can, by strangling John with a slip-proof quilting knot. Even though her plan for the murder is deliberate--Mrs. Peters reports that the arrangement of the rope was "*strange*" and a "funny way to kill" (paragraph 137)-Minnie is not cold or remorseless. Her passivity after the crime demonstrates that planning to evade guilt, beyond simple denial, is not in her character. She is not so diabolically creative that she plans or even understands the irony of strangling her husband (he killed the bird by wringing its neck). Glaspell, however, makes the irony plain.

[6]
It is important to emphasize again that we learn about Minnie from others. Nevertheless, Minnie is fully realized, round, and poignant. For the greater part of her adult life, she has patiently accepted her drab and colorless marriage even though it is so cruelly different from her youthful expectations. In the dreary surroundings of the Wright farm, she suppresses her grudges, just as she suppresses her prettiness, colorfulness, and creativity. In short, she had been nothing more than a flat character. The killing of the canary, however, causes her to change and to destroy her husband in an assertive rejection of her stock role as the suffering wife. She is a patient woman whose patience finally reaches the breaking point.

Commentary on the Essay

The strategy of the argument of this essay is to use details from the story to support the central idea that Minnie Wright is a round, developing character. Hence the essay illustrates one of the types in strategy 3 described on page 235. Other plans of organization could also have been chosen, such as the qualities of acquiescence, fortitude, and potential for anger (strategy 1); the change in Minnie from submission to vengefulness (strategy 2); or the reported actions of Minnie's singing, knotting quilts, and sitting in the kitchen on the morning after the murder (another way to use strategy 3).

Because Minnie does not appear in the play but is described only in the words of the major characters, the introductory paragraph of the sample essay deals with the way we learn about her. The essay thus highlights how Glaspell uses methods 2 and 4 (see pp. 172–74) as the ways of rendering the story's main character, while omitting methods 1, 3, and 5.

The essay's argument is developed through inferences made from details in the story, namely, Minnie's clothing (paragraph 2), her canary (paragraph 3), and her quilt (paragraphs 4 and 5). The last paragraph summarizes a number of these details, and it also considers how Minnie transcends the stock qualities of her role as a farm wife and gains roundness as a result of this outbreak.

As a study in composition, paragraph 3 demonstrates how discussion of a specific character trait, together with related details, can contribute to the essay's main argument. The trait is Minnie's love of music (shown by her canary). The connecting details, selected from study notes, are the loss of music in her life, her isolation, her lack of pretty clothing, the contemptibility of her husband, and her grief when putting the dead bird into the box. In short, the paragraph weaves together enough material to show the relationship between Minnie's trait of loving music and the crisis of her developing anger—a change that marks her as a round character.

SPECIAL TOPICS FOR WRITING AND ARGUMENT ABOUT CHARACTER

1. Compare the ways in which actions (or speeches, or the comments of others) are used to bring out the character traits of Sarty in "Barn Burning," Jing-Mei's mother in "Two Kinds," and Paul in "Paul's Case."

2. Write a brief essay comparing the changes or developments of two major or *round* characters in stories included in this chapter. You might deal with issues such as what the characters are like at the beginning; what conflicts they confront, deal with, or avoid; what qualities are brought out that signal the characters' changes or developments; and so on.

3. Compare the qualities and functions of two or more *flat* characters (e.g., Paul's father, Paul's teachers, one of the men in Glaspell's "A Jury of Her Peers," the twins in Faulkner's "Barn Burning"). How do they bring out qualities of the major characters? What do you discover about their own character traits?

4. Topics for argument or brief essays:

   a. Why does Abner Snopes burn barns? What qualities of character do these actions reveal? In light of your assessment of his character, how might Abner justify to himself his role as an arsonist?

   b. Develop this argument: To friends who haven't seen us for a time, we are round, but to ourselves and most other people, we are flat.

5. Using Sarty, Minnie Wright, and Jing-Mei as examples, describe the effects of circumstance on character. Under the rubric "circumstance" you may consider elements such as education, family, economic and social status, wartime conditions, and geographic isolation.

6. Write a brief story about an important decision you have made (e.g., choosing a school, beginning or leaving a job, declaring a major, starting or ending a friendship). Show how your qualities of character (to the extent that you understand them), together with your experiences, have gone into the decision. You may write more comfortably if you give yourself another name and describe your actions in the third person.

7. Using the card catalogue or computer catalogue in your library, find two critical studies of William Faulkner published by university presses. How fully do these studies describe and explain the characters living in Yoknapatawpha County, the imaginary place where Faulkner locates much of his fiction? Referring to these studies, write a short research-based essay on the characters and activities of the Snopes family.

5

Point of View:
The Position or Stance
of the Narrator
or Speaker

The term **point of view** refers to the **speaker, narrator, persona,** or **voice** created by authors to tell stories, present arguments, and express attitudes and judgments. Point of view involves not only the speaker's physical position as an observer and recorder but also the ways in which the speaker's social, political, and mental circumstances affect the narrative. For this reason, point of view is one of the most complex and subtle aspects of literary study.

Bear in mind that authors try not only to make their works vital and interesting but also to bring their *presentations* alive. The presentation is similar to a dramatic performance: In a play, the actors are always themselves, but in their roles they *impersonate* and temporarily *become* the characters whom they act. In fictional works, not only do authors impersonate or pretend to be characters who do the talking, but also they *create* these characters. One such character is Jackie, the narrator of Frank O'Connor's "First Confession" (Chapter 7) who is telling about events that occurred when he was a child. Because he is the subject as well as the narrator, he has firsthand knowledge of the actions, even though he also says things indicating that he, as an adult, has not fully assimilated his childhood experience. Another speaking character is Sammy of Updike's "A & P" (Chapter 7). Sammy is visualized as a real person describing an important event in his own life. We read Sammy's words, and we know that Sammy is a distinct though fictional character; but because Updike is the author we know that he is the one putting the words in Sammy's mouth. In Poe's "The Cask of Amontillado" (Chapter 11) we constantly hear the speaker's voice and are influenced not only by his narration but also by his attitudes. We are similarly affected by the unnamed narrator of Hardy's "The Three Strangers" (Chapter 3). This speaker obviously has strong opinions about the opposition between the country folk and the intrusive second stranger, and he arranges the narrative to make us sympathetic to his views.

Because of the ramifications of creating a narrative voice, point of view may also be considered as the centralizing or guiding intelligence in a work— the mind that filters the fictional experience and presents only the most important details to create the maximum impact. It may be compared to the perspectives utilized by painters. As we noted in Chapter 3, Claude Lorrain's painting *Seaport at Sunset* (p. 111) puts all the buildings, ships, landscape, and foreground figures into the perspective of the distant sun's mysterious glow. A contrasting painting is Henri Matisse's *Harmony in Red/The Red Room* (Insert I), which abandons the illusion of three dimensions while creating a perspective in which all the major details—chair, table, designs, still life, woman, and wall— are dominated not by dimensionality but rather by the color red. While Matisse concentrates on the connections of both life and color, Claude suggests that human artifacts and activities, however beautiful, are minor when compared with the vastness of the universe. In other words, the way reality is presented in each painting—the point of view or guiding intelligence presented by the painter—determines our perceptions and understanding of the painting. Similarly, the point of view or guiding intelligence created by the author determines how we read, understand, and respond.

AN EXERCISE IN POINT OF VIEW: REPORTING AN ACCIDENT

As an exercise to show that point of view is derived from lifelike situations, let us imagine that there has been an auto accident: Two cars, driven by Alice and Bill, have collided, and the scene is as we see it in the drawing on page 242. How might this accident be reported by a number of people? What would Alice say? What would Bill say?

Now assume that Frank, who is Bill's best friend, and Mary, who knows neither Bill nor Alice, were witnesses. What might Frank say about who was responsible? What might Mary say? Additionally, assume that you are a reporter for a local newspaper and are sent to report on the accident. You know none of the people involved. How will your report differ from the other reports? Finally, to what degree are all the statements designed to persuade listeners and readers of the correctness of the details and claims made in the respective reports?

The likely differences in the various reports may be explained by reference to point of view. Obviously, because both Alice and Bill are deeply involved—each of them is a major participant or what may be called a **major mover**—they will arrange their words to make themselves seem blameless. Frank, because he is Bill's best friend, will likely report things in Bill's favor. Mary will favor neither Alice nor Bill, but let us assume that she did not look up to see the colliding cars until she heard the crash. Thus, she did not see the accident happening but saw only the immediate aftereffects. Amid all this mixture of partial and impartial views of the action, to whom should we attribute the greatest reliability?

It seems clear that each person's report will have the "hidden agenda" of making herself or himself seem honest, objective, intelligent, impartial, and thorough. Thus, although both Alice and Bill may be truthful in their own eyes, it is unlikely that their reports will be reliable because they both have something to gain from avoiding responsibility for the accident. Also, Frank may be questionable as a witness because he is Bill's friend and may report things to Bill's advantage. Mary could be reliable, but she did not see everything; therefore she is unreliable not because of motivation but rather because of her location as a witness. Most likely, *your* account as an impartial reporter will be the most reliable and objective of all, because your major interest is to learn all the details and to report the truth accurately, with no concern about the personal interests of either Alice or Bill.

As you can see, the ramifications of describing actions are far-reaching, and the consideration of the various interests and situations is subtle. Indeed, of all the aspects of literature, point of view is the most complex because it is so much like life itself. On the one hand, point of view is intertwined with the many interests and wishes of humanity at large; on the other hand, it is linked to the enormous difficulty of uncovering and determining truth.

CONDITIONS THAT AFFECT POINT OF VIEW

As this exercise in observation and expression demonstrates, point of view depends on two major factors. The first factor is *the physical situation of the narrator, or speaker, as an observer.* How close to the action is the speaker? Is the speaker a major mover or major participant or no more than a witness, either close or distant? How much is he or she privileged to know? How accurate and complete are his or her reports? How do the speaker's characteristics emerge from the narration? What are his or her qualifications or limitations as an observer? The second factor is the speaker's intellectual and emotional position: How might the speaker gain or lose from what takes place in the story? Are the speaker's observations and words colored by these interests? Does he or she have any persuasive purpose beyond being a straightforward recorder or observer? What values does the speaker impose upon the action?

In a story, as in many poems using narrative, authors take into account all these subtleties. For example, Poe's narrator Montresor in "The Cask of Amontillado" (Chapter 11) is a man who describes the details of a murderous act of revenge that he carried out fifty years before the time of narration. O'Connor's speaker in "First Confession" (Chapter 7) tells about boyhood family problems and his first experience with the sacrament of confession, but he has not yet fully separated himself from some of his youthful antagonisms. Whitecloud's speaker in "Blue Winds Dancing" (Chapter 3) is filled with misgivings about the life he leaves and relief about the life to which he is returning. For these reasons, these narrators show their own involvement and concern about the events they describe. The speaker in Jackson's "The Lottery," however, does not seem personally involved in the action. This narrator listens, sees, and reports but does not express deep personal involvement in the events of the story's country village. As readers, we need to determine how such differing modes of presentation determine the effects of these and all other stories and narrative poems.

DISTINGUISH POINT OF VIEW FROM OPINION

Sometimes people mistakenly equate point of view with *opinions* or *beliefs*. It must be stressed that point of view is not synonymous with ideas. Rather, point of view refers to a work's mode of narration, comprising narrator, language, audience, and perceptions of events and characters. Opinions and beliefs are thoughts and ideas that may have nothing to do with a narration. A discussion of point of view should therefore emphasize how the dramatic situation of a work actually *shapes* and *creates* the work. If ideas seem to be particularly important in a story, your objective should not be to analyze and discuss the ideas *as ideas,* but rather to consider *if and how these ideas affect what the narrator concludes and says about the story's actions and situations.*

DETERMINING A WORK'S POINT OF VIEW

In your reading you will encounter a wide variety of points of view. To begin your analysis, first determine the work's grammatical voice (i.e., first, second, or third person). Then, study the ways in which the subject, characterization, dialogue, and form interact with the point of view.

In the First-Person Point of View, *the Narrator Tells about Events He or She Has Personally Witnessed*

If the voice of the work is an "I," the author is using the **first-person point of view**—the impersonation of a fictional narrator or speaker who may be named or unnamed. In our hypothetical accident reports, both Alice and Bill are first-person speakers who are named. In literature, the narrator of Poe's "The Cask of Amontillado" (Chapter 11) is clearly named and identified. By contrast, the narrator of Américo Parédes's "The Hammon and the Beans" (Chapter 8) is an unnamed first-person speaker. In Mark Twain's "Luck" (Chapter 7) there are two unnamed first-person speakers (the first "I" introduces the second "I").

First-person speakers might report events as though they have acquired their knowledge in a number of ways:

- What they themselves have done, said, heard, and thought (firsthand experience).
- What they have observed others doing and saying (firsthand witness).
- What others have said to them or otherwise communicated to them (secondhand testimony and hearsay).
- What they are able to infer or deduce from the information they have found (inferential information).
- What they are able to conjecture about how a character or characters might think and act, given their knowledge of a situation (conjectural, imaginative, or intuitive information).

Of all the points of view, that of the first person is the most independent of the author, because the first-person speaker may have a unique identity, with name, job, and economic and social position. Often, however, the author creates a more anonymous but still independent first-person speaker, as with the unnamed narrator of Poe's "The Masque of the Red Death" (Chapter 11). There are also situations in which an "I" narrative is pluralized by "we" when the first person includes other characters. Such a first-person plural point of view lends reliability to the narrative, as in Anderson's "I'm a Fool" and Zabytko's "Home Soil" (Chapter 10) because the characters included as "we" can be considered additional witnesses.

DETERMINE THE SPEAKER'S RELIABILITY OR LACK OF IT.   When you encounter a first-person narrative (whether a story or poem), determine the narrator's position and ability, prejudices or self-interest, and judgment of his or her readers or listeners. Most first-person speakers describing their own experiences are to be accepted as **reliable** and authoritative. But sometimes first-person speakers are **unreliable** because they may have interests or limitations that lead them to mislead, distort, or even lie. There is reason to question that the narrator Montresor of Poe's "The Cask of Amontillado" (Chapter 11) is telling the complete truth about his enmity against Fortunato, for example, because his act of revenge against Fortunato is motivated less by wounded honor than by a psychopathic and demonic personality. Whether first-person speakers are reliable or unreliable, however, they are one of the means by which authors confer an authentic, lifelike aura to their works.

In the Second-Person Point of View, the Narrator Is Speaking to Someone Else Who Is Called "You"

The **second-person point of view,** the least common of the points of view, offers the writer two major possibilities. In the first, a narrator (almost necessarily a first-person speaker) tells a present and involved listener what he or she has done and said at a past time. The actions might be a simple retelling of events, as when a parent tells an older child about something the child did during infancy, or when a doctor tells a patient with amnesia about events before the causative injury. The actions might also be subject to dispute and interpretation, as when a prosecuting attorney describes a crime for which a defendant is on trial or when a spouse lists grievances against an alienated spouse in a custody or divorce case. Still another situation of the second-person point of view might occur when an angry person accuses the listener of a betrayal or some other wrong. In such instances, it is worth bearing in mind that the point of view may possibly be considered first rather than second, for the speaker is likely to be speaking subjectively about his or her own perception about the listener's actions.

The second possibility is equally complex. Some narrators seem to be addressing a "you" but are instead referring mainly to themselves—and to listeners only tangentially—in preference to an "I." In addition, some narrators follow the usage—common in colloquial speech—of the indefinite "you," as in Anderson's "I'm a Fool." In this kind of narration, speakers use *you* to refer not to a specific listener but rather to anyone at all—in this way avoiding the more formal use of words like *one, a person,* or *people.* (Incidentally, the selection of *you* is non-gender-specific, because it eliminates the need for pronouns such as *he, she,* or *he or she.*). A clever variation of the "you" point of view is seen in Lorrie Moore's "How to Become a Writer," in which the narrator is apparently describing her own experiences under the guise of giving directions to a listener interested in developing a writing career.

In the Third-Person Point of View, *the Speaker Emphasizes the Actions and Speeches of Others*

If events in the work are described in the third person (*he, she, it, they*), the author is using the **third-person point of view.** It is not always easy to characterize the voice in this point of view. Sometimes the speaker may use an "I" (as in Poe's "The Masque of the Red Death" [Chapter 11]) and be seemingly identical with the author, but at other times the author may create a distinct **authorial voice,** as in Faulkner's "Barn Burning" (Chapter 4). There are three variants of the third-person point of view: *dramatic* or *objective, omniscient,* and *limited omniscient.*

THE DRAMATIC OR OBJECTIVE POINT OF VIEW IS THE MOST BASIC METHOD OF NARRATION.   The most direct presentation of action and dialogue is the **dramatic** or **objective point of view** (also called **third-person objective**). It is the basic method of rendering action and speech that all the points of view share. The narrator of the dramatic point of view is an unidentified speaker who reports things in a way that is analogous to a hovering or tracking motion-picture camera or to what some critics have called "a fly on the wall (or tree)." Somehow, the narrator is always on the spot—in rooms, forests, village squares, moving vehicles, or even in outer space—to tell us what is happening and what is being said.

The dramatic presentation is limited *only* to what is said and what happens. There is no attempt to draw conclusions or make interpretations, because the premise of the dramatic point of view is that readers, like a jury, can form their own interpretations if they are given the right evidence. Jackson's "The Lottery"—a powerful example of the dramatic point of view—is an objective story about a bizarre small-town lottery. We the readers draw many conclusions about this story (such as that people are tradition bound, insensitive, cruel, and so on), but because of the dramatic point of view Jackson does not *state* any of these conclusions for us.

THE NARRATOR IN THE OMNISCIENT POINT OF VIEW CAN SEE ALL AND DISCLOSE ALL. The third-person point of view is **omniscient** (all-knowing) when the speaker not only presents action and dialogue but also is able to report what goes on in the minds of the characters. In our everyday real world, we can never absolutely know what other people are thinking. However, we always make assumptions about the thoughts of others, and these assumptions are the basis of the omniscient point of view. Authors use it freely but judiciously to explain responses, thoughts, feelings, and plans—an additional dimension that aids in the development of character. For example, in Maupassant's "The Necklace" (Chapter 1) the speaker assumes omniscience to explain the responses and thoughts of the major character and also, though to a lesser degree, of her husband.

THE NARRATOR IN THE LIMITED, OR LIMITED-OMNISCIENT, POINT OF VIEW FOCUSES ON THOUGHTS AND DEEDS OF A MAJOR CHARACTER.   More common than the omniscient point of view is the *limited third-person* or **limited omniscient third-person point of view,** in which the author concentrates on or *limits* the narration to the actions and thoughts of a major character. In our accident case, Frank, being Bill's friend, would be sympathetic to Bill; thus his report of the collision would likely be third-person limited, with Bill as the center of interest. Depending on whether a narration focuses on action or motivation, the narrative may explore the mentalities of the characters either lightly or in depth. The name given to the central figure on whom the third-person omniscient point of view is focused is the **point-of-view character.** Thus, Barrett Clare in Gilchrist's "The Song of Songs," Peyton Farquhar in Bierce's "An Occurrence at Owl Creek Bridge," and Goodman Brown in Hawthorne's "Young Goodman Brown" (Chapter 9) are all point-of-view characters. Almost everything in these stories is there because the point-of-view characters see it, hear it, respond to it, think about it, imagine it entirely, do it or share in it, try to control it, or are controlled by it.

MINGLING POINTS OF VIEW

In some works, authors mingle points of view in order to imitate reality. For example, many first-person narrators use various types of the third-person point of view during much of their narration. Authors may also vary points of view to sustain interest, create suspense, or put the burden of response entirely upon readers. For example, Gilchrist in "The Song of Songs" preserves an almost exclusive focus on the major character, Barrett, until the final three paragraphs of the story, when there is a shift to a dramatic point of view as she meets her mother. As a result it appears that Barrett's emotional turmoil is at an end and that her life is taking a positive and more normal turn. A comparable but contrasting change in point of view occurs at the end of Hawthorne's "Young Goodman Brown" (Chapter 9) where the narrator shifts the story's major focus and objectively and almost brutally summarizes Brown's morose and loveless life after his nightmare about evil.

POINT OF VIEW AND VERB TENSE

Usually *point of view* refers to the ways narrators and speakers perceive and report actions and speeches, but in the broadest sense, point of view may be considered as a total way of rendering truth, and for this reason the *tense* chosen by the narrators is important. Most narratives rely on the past tense: The actions happened in the past, and they are now over. The introduction of dialogue, however, even in a past-tense narration, is a dramatic means of bringing the story into the present. The dialogue concluding Maupassant's "The Necklace," for example, emphasizes the immediacy of Mathilde's problems.

The narrator of a past-tense narrative may also introduce present-tense commentary during the narration—a strong means of signifying the importance of past events. Examples of such narrators are seen in Anderson's "I'm a Fool," where the narrator expresses regret over his own past mistakes, and in Mark Twain's "Luck," where the second narrator expresses amazement over the mistakes of the main character. In addition, as noted in Chapter 9, the narrators of *parables* and *fables* use past-tense narratives as vehicles for teaching current lessons in philosophy and religion.

A number of writers use the present tense as their principal time reference. With the present tense, the narrative story or poem is rendered as a virtual drama that is unfolded moment by moment. In "Blue Winds Dancing," for instance, Whitecloud employs the present tense to emphasize the immediate experience of the narrator's return home. Joy Williams uses the present tense in "Taking Care" as a means not only of emphasizing the immediacy of the main character's situation but also of demonstrating his future challenges.

Some writers intermingle tenses to show how time itself can be merged with the human consciousness and to show the fusion of past, present, and future within a character's mind. The intermingling of tenses may also demonstrate how characters perceive their social worlds, including the listeners and/or readers, as in Updike's "A & P," where Sammy's mixing of tenses shows the vividness of his memory of events in the store (past), and it also shows his friendliness and informality (present).

GUIDELINES FOR POINTS OF VIEW

The following guidelines summarize and further classify the types of points of view. Use them to distinguish differences and shades of variation in stories and poems.

1. **First person (*I, my, mine, me*, and sometimes *we, our,* and *us*).** First-person speakers are involved to at least some degree in the actions of the work. Such narrators may have (1) complete understanding, (2) partial or incorrect understanding, (3) no understanding at all, or (4) complete understanding with the motive to mislead or lie. Although the narrators described in 2 through 4 usually are *reliable* and tell the truth, they may also sometimes be *unreliable*.

   a. *Major participant*

      i. Who tells his or her own story and thoughts as a major mover.

  ii. Who tells a story about others and also about herself or himself as one of the major movers.

  iii. Who tells a story mainly about others, and about himself or herself only tangentially.

 b. *Minor participant,* who tells a story about events experienced and witnessed.

 c. *Nonparticipating but identifiable speaker,* who learns about events in other ways (e.g., listening to participants, examining documents, hearing news reports, imagining what might have occurred). The narrative of such a speaker is a combination of fact and conjectural reconstruction.

2. **Second person (*you*).** Occurs (1) when the speaker (e.g., parent, psychologist) knows more about a character's actions than the character himself or herself, or (2) when the speaker (e.g., lawyer, spouse, friend, sports umpire, angry person) is explaining to another person (the "you") that person's disputable actions and statements. The speaker may also use "you" to mean (3) himself or herself or (4) anyone at all.

3. **Third person (*she, he, it, they*).** The speaker is outside the action and is mainly a reporter of actions and speeches. Some speakers may have unique and distinguishing traits even though no separate identity is claimed for them ("the unnamed third-person narrator"). Other third-person speakers who are not separately identifiable may represent the words and views of the authors themselves ("the authorial voice").

 a. *Dramatic or third-person objective.* The narrator reports only what can be seen and heard. The thoughts of characters are included only if they are spoken or written (dialogue, reported or overheard conversation, letters, reports, etc.).

 b. *Omniscient.* The omniscient speaker knows all, sees all, reports all, and explains the inner workings of the minds of any or all characters (when necessary).

 c. *Limited, or limited omniscient.* The focus is on the actions, responses, thoughts, and feelings of a single major character. The narration may involve primarily what the character does, and it may also probe deeply within the consciousness of the character.

❀ STORIES FOR STUDY

SHERWOOD ANDERSON   (1876–1941)

Anderson was a native of Ohio. His early years showed no particular career objective: He worked at many odd jobs and served in the Spanish-American War. He married and worked briefly as manager of a paint factory. Soon, however, he deserted his family and moved to Chicago to pursue a career in writing. In 1916 he published his first book, a semiautobiographical novel entitled Windy McPherson's Son, *which established him as a master of naturalistic fiction (i.e., things never work out right). His major triumph was* Winesburg, Ohio, *published in 1919. In this collection of 23 stories, conflict develops from the characters' attempts (usually unsuccessful) to fit into society's norms and patterns. "I'm a Fool," which shares these conflicts, is taken from the collection* Horses and Men *(1924).*

I'm a Fool _____ *1924*

It was a hard jolt for me, one of the most bitterest I ever had to face. And it all came about through my own foolishness, too. Even yet sometimes, when I think of it, I want to cry or swear or kick myself. Perhaps, even now, after all this time, there will be a kind of satisfaction in making myself look cheap by telling of it.

It began at three o'clock one October afternoon as I sat in the grandstand at the fall trotting and pacing meet at Sandusky, Ohio.

To tell the truth, I felt a little foolish that I should be sitting in the grandstand at all. During the summer before I had left my home town with Harry Whitehead and, with a nigger named Burt, had taken a job as swipe° with one of the two horses Harry was campaigning through the fall race meets that year. Mother cried and my sister Mildred, who wanted to get a job as a schoolteacher in our town that fall, stormed and scolded about the house all during the week before I left. They both thought it something disgraceful that one of our family should take a place as a swipe with race horses. I've an idea Mildred thought my taking the place would stand in the way of her getting the job she'd been working so long for.

But after all I had to work, and there was no other work to be got. A big lumbering fellow of nineteen couldn't just hang around the house and I had got too big to mow people's lawns and sell newspapers. Little chaps who could get next to people's sympathies by their sizes were always getting jobs away from me. There was one fellow who kept saying to everyone who wanted a lawn mowed or a cistern cleaned that he was saving money to work his way through college, and I used to lay awake nights thinking up ways to injure him without being found out. I kept thinking of wagons running over him and bricks falling on his head as he walked along the street. But never mind him.

I got the place with Harry and I liked Burt fine. We got along splendid together. He was a big nigger with a lazy sprawling body and soft-, kind eyes, and when it came to a

---

swipe: a groom and general handyman; the narrator describes a swipe's duties in paragraph 7.

fight he could hit like Jack Johnson.° He had Bucephalus, a big black pacing stallion that could do 2.09 or 2.10 if he had to, and I had a little gelding named Doctor Fritz that never lost a race all fall when Harry wanted him to win.

We set out from home late in July, in a box car with the two horses and after that, until late November, we kept moving along to the race meets and the fairs. It was a peachy time for me, I'll say that. Sometimes now I think that boys who are raised regular in houses, and never have a fine nigger like Burt for best friend, and go to high schools and college, and never steal anything, or get drunk a little, or learn to swear from fellows who know how, or come walking up in front of a grandstand in their shirt sleeves and with dirty horsy pants on when the races are going on and the grandstand is full of people all dressed up—What's the use of talking about it? Such fellows don't know nothing at all. They've never had no opportunity.

But I did. Burt taught me how to rub down a horse and put the bandages on after a race and steam a horse out and a lot of valuable things for any man to know. He could wrap a bandage on a horse's leg so smooth that if it had been the same color you would think it was his skin, and I guess he'd have been a big driver, too, and got to the top like Murphy and Walter Cox and the others if he hadn't been black.

Gee whizz! it was fun. You got to a county-seat town, maybe say on a Saturday or Sunday, and the fair began the next Tuesday and lasted until Friday afternoon. Doctor Fritz would be, say, in the 2.25 trot on Tuesday afternoon and on Thursday afternoon Bucephalus would knock 'em cold in the "free-for-all" pace. It left you a lot of time to hang around and listen to horse talk, and see Burt knock some yap cold that got too gay,° and you'd find out about horses and men and pick up a lot of stuff you could use all the rest of your life, if you had some sense and salted down what you heard and felt and saw.

And then at the end of the week when the race meet was over, and Harry had run home to tend up to his livery-stable business, you and Burt hitched the two horses to carts and drove slow and steady across country, to the place for the next meeting, so as to not overheat the horses, etc., etc., you know.

Gee whizz! Gosh amighty! the nice hickory-nut and beechnut and oaks and other kinds of trees along the roads, all brown and red, and the good smells, and Burt singing a song called "Deep River,"° and the country girls at the windows of houses and everything. You can stick your colleges up your nose for all me. I guess I know where I got my education.

Why, one of those little burgs of towns you came to on the way, say now on a Saturday afternoon, and Burt says, "Let's lay up here." And you did.

And you took the horses to a livery stable and fed them, and you got your good clothes out of a box and put them on.

And the town was full of farmers gaping, because they could see you were race-horse people, and the kids maybe never see a nigger before and was afraid and run away when the two of us walked down their main street.

And that was before prohibition and all that foolishness, and so you went into a saloon, the two of you, and all the yaps come and stood around, and there was always some one pretended he was horsy and knew things and spoke up and began asking questions, and all you did was to lie and lie all you could about what horses you had, and I said I owned them, and then some fellow said, "Will you have a drink of whisky?" and

10

Jack Johnson: (1878–1946), the first black heavyweight champion, 1910–1915.
gay: high-spirited.
"Deep River": well-known spiritual.

Kid @who feels like he
has done the wrong
thing, told a lie to a
girl he wan'ts to
impress.

Burt knocked his eye out the way he could say, offhand like, "Oh, well, all right, I'm agreeable to a little nip. I'll split a quart with you." Gee whizz!

But that isn't what I want to tell my story about. We got home late in November   15
and I promised mother I'd quit the race horses for good. There's a lot of things you've got to promise a mother because she don't know any better.

And so, there not being any work in our town any more than when I left there to go to the races, I went off to Sandusky and got a pretty good place taking care of horses for a man who owned a teaming and delivery and storage and coal and real-estate business there. It was a pretty good place with good eats, and a day off each week, and sleeping on a cot in a big barn, and mostly just shoveling in hay and oats to a lot of big good-enough skates of horses that couldn't have trotted a race with a toad. I wasn't dissatisfied and I could send money home.

And then, as I started to tell you, the fall races come to Sandusky and I got the day off and I went. I left the job at noon and had on my good clothes and my new brown derby hat I'd bought the Saturday before, and a stand-up collar.

First of all I went downtown and walked about with the dudes. I've always thought to myself, "Put up a good front," and so I did it. I had forty dollars in my pockets and so I went into the West House, a big hotel, and walked up to the cigar stand. "Give me three twenty-five cent cigars," I said. There was a lot of horsemen and strangers and dressed-up people from other towns standing around in the lobby and in the bar, and I mingled amongst them. In the bar there was a fellow with a cane and a Windsor tie on, that it made me sick to look at him. I like a man to be a man and dressed up, but not to go put on that kind of airs. So I pushed him aside, kind of rough, and had me a drink of whisky. And then he looked at me, as though he thought maybe he'd get gay, but he changed his mind and didn't say anything. And then I had another drink of whisky, just to show him something, and went out and had a hack out to the races, all to myself, and when I got there I bought myself the best seat I could get up in the grandstand, but didn't go in for any of these boxes. That's putting on too many airs.

And so there I was, sitting up in the grandstand as gay as you please and looking down on the swipes coming out with their horses, and with their dirty horsy pants on and the horseblankets swung over their shoulders, same as I had been doing all the year before. I liked one thing about the same as the other, sitting up there and feeling grand and being down there and looking up at the yaps and feeling grander and more important, too.

One thing's about as good as another, if you take it just right. I've often said that.   20

Well, right in front of me, in the grandstand that day, there was a fellow with a couple of girls and they was about my age. The young fellow was a nice guy, all right. He was the kind maybe that goes to college and then comes to be a lawyer or maybe a newspaper editor or something like that, but he wasn't stuck on himself. There are some of that kind are all right and he was one of the ones.

He had his sister with him and another girl and the sister looked around over his shoulder, accidental at first, not intending to start anything—she wasn't that kind—and her eyes and mine happened to meet.

You know how it is. Gee, she was a peach! She had on a soft dress, kind of a blue stuff and it looked carelessly made, but was well sewed and made and everything. I knew that much. I blushed when she looked right at me and so did she. She was the nicest girl I've ever seen in my life. She wasn't stuck on herself and she could talk proper grammar without being like a schoolteacher or something like that. What I mean is, she was O.K. I think maybe her father was well-to-do, but not rich to make her chesty because she was his daughter, as some are. Maybe he owned a drug store or a dry-goods store in their home town, or something like that. She never told me and I never asked.

My own people are all O.K. too, when you come to that. My grandfather was Welsh and over in the old country, in Wales he was—but never mind that.

The first heat of the first race come off and the young fellow setting there with the two girls left them and went down to make a bet. I knew what he was up to, but he didn't talk big and noisy and let everyone around know he was a sport, as some do. He wasn't that kind. Well, he come back and I heard him tell the two girls what horse he'd bet on, and when the heat trotted they all half got to their feet and acted in the excited, sweaty way people do when they've got money down on a race, and the horse they bet on is up there pretty close at the end, and they think maybe he'll come on with a rush, but he never does because he hasn't got the old juice in him, come right down to it.

And then, pretty soon, the horses came out for the 2.18 pace and there was a horse in it I knew. He was a horse Bob French had in his string but Bob didn't own him. He was a horse owned by a Mr. Mathers down at Marietta, Ohio.

This Mr. Mathers had a lot of money and owned some coal mines or something and he had a swell place out in the country, and he was stuck on race horses, but was a Presbyterian or something, and I think more than likely his wife was one, too, maybe a stiffer one than himself. So he never raced his horses hisself, and the story round the Ohio race tracks was that when one of his horses got ready to go to the races he turned him over to Bob French and pretended to his wife he was sold.

So Bob had the horses and he did pretty much as he pleased and you can't blame Bob, at least, I never did. Sometimes he was out to win and sometimes he wasn't. I never cared much about that when I was swiping a horse. What I did want to know was that my horse had the speed and could go out in front, if you wanted him to.

And, as I'm telling you, there was Bob in this race with one of Mr. Mathers' horses, was named "About Ben Ahem"° or something like that, and was fast as a streak. He was a gelding and had a mark of 2.21, but could step in .08 or .09.

Because when Burt and I were out, as I've told you, the year before, there was a nigger Burt knew, worked for Mr. Mathers and we went out there one day when we didn't have no race on at the Marietta Fair and our boss Harry was gone home.

And so everyone was gone to the fair but just this one nigger and he took us all through Mr. Mathers' swell house and he and Burt tapped a bottle of wine Mr. Mathers had hid in his bedroom, back in a closet, without his wife knowing, and he showed us this Ahem horse. Burt was always stuck on being a driver but didn't have much chance to get to the top, being a nigger, and he and the other nigger gulped the whole bottle of wine and Burt got a little lit up.

So the nigger let Burt take this About Ben Ahem and step him a mile in a track Mr. Mathers had all to himself, right there on the farm. And Mr. Mathers had one child, a daughter, kinda sick and not very good looking, and she came home and we had to hustle to get About Ben Ahem stuck back in the barn.

I'm only telling you to get everything straight. At Sandusky, that afternoon I was at the fair, this young fellow with the two girls was fussed, being with the girls and losing his bet. You know how a fellow is that way. One of them was his girl and the other his sister. I had figured that out.

"Gee whizz," I say to myself, "I'm going to give him the dope."

"*About Ben Ahem*":· more likely "Abou Ben Adhem," from the poem "Abou Ben Adhem and the Angel" (1834) by Leigh Hunt (1784–1859).

He was mighty nice when I touched him on the shoulder. He and the girls were   35
nice to me right from the start and clear to the end. I'm not blaming them.

And so he leaned back and I give him the dope on About Ben Ahem. "Don't bet a
cent on this first heat because he'll go like an oxen hitched to a plow, but when the first
heat is over go right down and lay on your pile." That's what I told him.

Well, I never saw a fellow treat any one sweller. There was a fat man sitting beside
the little girl, that had looked at me twice by this time, and I at her, and both blushing,
and what did he do but have the nerve to turn and ask the fat man to get up and change
places with me so I could set with his crowd.

Gee whizz, craps amighty. There I was. What a chump I was to go and get gay up
there in the West House bar, and just because that dude was standing there with a cane
and that kind of a necktie on, to go and get all balled up and drink that whisky, just to
show off.

Of course she would know, me setting right beside her and letting her smell of
my breath. I could have kicked myself right down out of that grand stand and all around
that race track and made a faster record than most of the skates of horses they had there
that year.

Because that girl wasn't any mutt of a girl. What wouldn't I have give right then for   40
a stick of chewing gum to chew, or a lozenger, or some licorice, or most anything. I was
glad I had those twenty-five cent cigars in my pocket and right away I give that fellow
one and lit one myself. Then that fat man got up and we changed places and there I
was, plunked right down beside her.

They introduced themselves and the fellow's best girl, he had with him, was
named Miss Elinor Woodbury, and her father was a manufacturer of barrels from a place
called Tiffin, Ohio. And the fellow himself was named Wilbur Wessen and his sister was
Miss Lucy Wessen.

I suppose it was their having such swell names that got me off my trolley. A fellow,
just because he has been a swipe with a race horse, and works taking care of horses for a
man in the teaming, delivery, and storage business isn't any better or worse than any
one else. I've often thought that, and said it too.

But you know how a fellow is. There's something in that kind of nice clothes, and
the kind of nice eyes she had, and the way she had looked at me, awhile before, over
her brother's shoulder, and me looking back at her, and both of us blushing.

I couldn't show her up for a boob, could I?

I made a fool of myself, that's what I did. I said my name was Walter Mathers from   45
Marietta, Ohio, and then I told all three of them the smashingest lie you ever heard.
What I said was that my father owned the horse About Ben Ahem and that he had let
him out to this Bob French for racing purposes, because our family was proud and had
never gone into racing that way, in our own name, I mean, and Miss Lucy Wessen's eyes
were shining, and I went the whole hog.

I told about our place down at Marietta, and about the big stables and the grand
brick house we had on a hill, up above the Ohio River, but I knew enough not to do it in
no bragging way. What I did was to start things and then let them drag the rest out of
me. I acted just as reluctant to tell as I could. Our family hasn't got any barrel factory,
and since I've known us, we've always been pretty poor, but not asking anything of any
one at that, and my grandfather, over in Wales—but never mind that.

We set there talking like we had known each other for years and years, and I went
and told them that my father had been expecting maybe this Bob French wasn't on the
square, and had sent me up to Sandusky on the sly to find out what I could.

And I bluffed it through I had found out all about the 2.18 pace, in which About Ben Ahem was to start.

I said he would lose the first heat by pacing like a lame cow and then he would come back and skin 'em alive after that. And to back up what I said I took thirty dollars out of my pocket and handed it to Mr. Wilbur Wessen and asked him, would he mind, after the first heat, to go down and place it on About Ben Ahem for whatever odds he could get. What I said was that I didn't want Bob French to see me and none of the swipes.

Sure enough the first heat come off and About Ben Ahem went off his stride, up the back stretch, and looked like a wooden horse or a sick one, and come in to be last. Then this Wilbur Wessen went down to the betting place under the grandstand and there I was with the two girls, and when that Miss Woodbury was looking the other way once, Lucy Wessen kinda, with her shoulder you know, kinda touched me. Not just tucking down, I don't mean. You know how a woman can do. They get close, but not getting gay either. You know what they do. Gee whizz. 50

And then they give me a jolt. What they had done, when I didn't know, was to get together, and they had decided Wilbur Wessen would bet fifty dollars, and the two girls had gone and put in ten dollars each, of their own money, too. I was sick then, but I was sicker later.

About the gelding, About Ben Ahem, and their winning their money, I wasn't worried a lot about that. It came out O.K. Ahem stepped the next three heats like a bushel of spoiled eggs going to market before they could be found out, and Wilbur Wessen had got nine to two for the money. There was something else eating at me.

Because Wilbur come back, after he had bet the money, and after that he spent most of his time talking to that Miss Woodbury, and Lucy Wessen and I was left alone together like on a desert island. Gee, if I'd only been on the square or if there had been any way of getting myself on the square. There ain't any Walter Mathers, like I said to her and them, and there hasn't ever been one, but if there was, I bet I'd go to Marietta, Ohio, and shoot him tomorrow.

There I was, big boob that I am. Pretty soon the race was over, and Wilbur had gone down and collected our money, and we had a hack downtown, and he stood us a swell supper at the West House, and a bottle of champagne beside.

And I was with the girl and she wasn't saying much, and I wasn't saying much either. One thing I know. She wasn't stuck on me because of the lie about my father being rich and all that. There's a way you know . . . Craps amighty. There's a kind of girl you see just once in your life, and if you don't get busy and make hay, then you're gone for good and all, and might as well go jump off a bridge. They give you a look from inside of them somewhere, and it ain't no vamping, and what it means is—you want that girl to be your wife, and you want nice things around her like flowers and swell clothes, and you want her to have the kids you're going to have, and you want good music played and no ragtime. Gee whizz. 55

There's a place over near Sandusky, across a kind of bay, and it's called Cedar Point. And after we had supper we went over to it in a launch, all by ourselves. Wilbur and Miss Lucy and that Miss Woodbury had to catch a ten o'clock train back to Tiffin, Ohio, because, when you're out with girls like that you can't get careless and miss any trains and stay out all night, like you can with some kinds of Janes.

And Wilbur blowed himself to the launch and it cost him fifteen cold plunks, but I wouldn't never have knew if I hadn't listened. He wasn't no tin horn kind of a sport.

Over at the Cedar Point place, we didn't stay around where there was a gang of common kind of cattle at all.

There was big dance halls and dining places for yaps, and there was a beach you could walk along and get where it was dark, and we went there.

She didn't talk hardly at all and neither did I, and I was thinking how glad I was   60
my mother was all right, and always made us kids learn to eat with a fork at the table, and not swill soup, and not be noisy and rough like a gang you see around a race track that way.

Then Wilbur and his girl went away up the beach and Lucy and I sat down in a dark place, where there was some roots of old trees the water had washed up, and after that the time, till we had to go back in the launch and they had to catch their trains, wasn't nothing at all. It went like winking your eye.

Here's how it was. The place we were setting in was dark, like I said, and there was the roots from that old stump sticking up like arms, and there was a watery smell, and the night was like—as if you could put your hand out and feel it—so warm and soft and dark and sweet like an orange.

I most cried and I most swore and I most jumped up and danced, I was so mad and happy and sad.

When Wilbur come back from being alone with his girl, and she saw him coming, Lucy she says, "We got to go to the train now," and she was most crying too, but she never knew nothing I knew, and she couldn't be so all busted up. And then, before Wilbur and Miss Woodbury got up to where we was, she put her face up and kissed me quick, and put her head up against me and she was all quivering and—Gee whizz.

Sometimes I hope I have cancer and die. I guess you know what I mean. We went   65
in the launch across the bay to the train like that, and it was dark, too. She whispered and said it was like she and I could get out of the boat and walk on water, and it sounded foolish, but I knew what she meant.

And then quick we were right at the depot, and there was a big gang of yaps, the kind that goes to the fairs, and crowded and milling around like cattle, and how could I tell her? "It won't be long because you'll write and I'll write you." That's all she said.

I got a chance like a hay barn afire. A swell chance I got.

And maybe she would write me, down at Marietta that way, and the letter would come back, and stamped on the front of it by the U.S.A. "there ain't any such guy," or something like that, whatever they stamp on a letter that way.

And me trying to pass myself off for a big-bug and a swell—to her, as decent a little body as God ever made. Craps amighty—swell chance I got!

And then the train come in, and she got on it, and Wilbur Wessen, he come and   70
shook hands with me, and that Miss Woodbury was nice too and bowed to me, and I at her, and the train went and I busted out and cried like a kid.

Gee, I could have run after the train and made Dan Patch° look like a freight train after a wreck but, socks amighty, what was the use? Did you ever see such a fool?

I'll bet you what—if I had an arm broke right now or a train had run over my foot—I wouldn't go to no doctor at all. I'd go set down and let her hurt and hurt—that's what I'd do.

I'll bet you what—if I hadn't a drunk that booze I'd never been such a boob as to go tell such a lie—that couldn't never be made straight to a lady like her.

I wish I had that fellow right here that had on a Windsor tie and carried a cane. I'd smash him for fair. Gosh darn his eyes. He's a big fool—that's what he is.

Dan Patch: One of the fastest pace horses, Dan Patch still held records at the time of the story. Legendary for his speed, his records were not broken until well into the 1930s.

And if I'm not another you just go find me one and I'll quit working and be a bum and give him my job. I don't care nothing for working, and earning money, and saving it for no such boob as myself.

QUESTIONS

1. Describe the point of view of "I'm a Fool." How completely does the narrator describe himself? What is the level and effect of the narrator's diction? Why, in paragraphs 8 and 10–14, does he shift to the second-person point of view?

2. What changes does the narrator undergo during the events of the story?

3. Compare the characters of Lucy and the narrator. How successful might a match have been between the two if the narrator had not made things impossible by his false stories about himself?

4. Describe the importance of location and background. How does the narrator's familiarity with racing enable him to impress the Wessens?

AMBROSE BIERCE   (1842–1914?)

Bierce was a native of Ohio, the youngest of nine children in the highly religious family of a poor farmer. When the Civil War began he enlisted in the Union army as a drummer boy and rose to the rank of major by the war's end. After the war he went to San Francisco to begin a career in journalism. At various times he reported, edited, and wrote reviews for papers such as the San Francisco Examiner *and the* San Francisco News-Letter. *After he married he and his wife spent five years in England, but eventually she left him and their two children died—events that had an embittering effect on him. In 1913 he traveled to Mexico, and nothing further is known about him; he is presumed to have died in revolutionary fighting there in 1914. Bierce published his first story in 1871 and later published two volumes of stories:* In the Midst of Life *(1892, originally published in 1891 as* Tales of Soldiers and Civilians, *which included "An Occurrence at Owl Creek Bridge"), and* Can Such Things Be? *(1893). He is perhaps best known for his sometimes cynical* The Devil's Dictionary *(1911). He favored the short story as a form over the novel on much the same grounds as Poe, namely that the story could be designed to produce a single effect. He believed that fiction should be realistic and should build to concluding twists and surprises—goals that are seen in "An Occurrence at Owl Creek Bridge." His complete works, which he edited himself, appeared in twelve volumes from 1909 to 1912.*

American Civil War

An Occurrence at Owl Creek Bridge _____ *1891*

A man stood upon a railroad bridge in northern Alabama, looking down into the swift water twenty feet below. The man's hands were behind his back, the wrists bound with a cord. A rope closely encircled his neck. It was attached to a stout cross-timber above his head and the slack fell to the level of his knees. Some loose boards laid upon the sleepers supporting the metals of the railway supplied a footing for him and his executioners—two private soldiers of the Federal army, directed by a sergeant who in civil life may have been a deputy sheriff. At a short remove upon the same temporary platform was an officer in the uniform of his rank, armed. He was a captain. A sentinel at each end of the bridge stood with his rifle in the position known as "support," that is to say, vertical in front of the left shoulder, the hammer resting on the forearm thrown straight across the chest—a formal and unnatural position, enforcing an erect carriage of the body. It did not appear to be the duty of these two men to know what was occurring at the center of the bridge; they merely blockaded the two ends of the foot planking that traversed it.

Beyond one of the sentinels nobody was in sight; the railroad ran straight away into a forest for a hundred yards, then, curving, was lost to view. Doubtless there was an outpost farther along. The other bank of the stream was open ground—a gentle acclivity topped with a stockade of vertical tree trunks, loopholed for rifles, with a single embrasure through which protruded the muzzle of a brass cannon commanding the bridge. Midway of the slope between the bridge and fort were the spectators—a single company of infantry in line, at "parade rest," the butts of the rifles on the ground, the barrels inclining slightly backward against the right shoulder, the hands crossed upon the stock. A lieutenant stood at the right of the line, the point of his sword upon the ground, his left hand resting upon his right. Excepting the group of four at the center of the bridge, not a man moved. The company faced the bridge, staring stonily, motionless. The sentinels, facing the banks of the stream, might have been statues to adorn the bridge. The captain stood with folded arms, silent, observing the work of his subordinates, but making no sign. Death is a dignitary who when he comes announced is to be received with formal manifestations of respect, even by those most familiar with him. In the code of military etiquette silence and fixity are forms of deference.

The man who was engaged in being hanged was apparently about thirty-five years of age. He was a civilian, if one might judge from his habit, which was that of a planter. His features were good—a straight nose, firm mouth, broad forehead, from which his long, dark hair was combed straight back, falling behind his ears to the collar of his well-fitting frock coat. He wore a mustache and pointed beard, but no whiskers; his eyes were large and dark gray, and had a kindly expression which one would hardly have expected in one whose neck was in the hemp. Evidently this was no vulgar assassin. The liberal military code makes provision for hanging many kinds of persons, and gentlemen are not excluded.

The preparations being complete, the two private soldiers stepped aside and each drew away the plank upon which he had been standing. The sergeant turned to the captain, saluted and placed himself immediately behind that officer, who in turn moved apart one pace. These movements left the condemned man and the sergeant standing on the two ends of the same plank, which spanned three of the cross-ties of the bridge. The end upon which the civilian stood almost, but not quite, reached a fourth. This plank had been held in place by the weight of the captain; it was now held by that of the sergeant. At a signal from the former the latter would step aside, the plank would tilt and the condemned man go down between two ties. The arrangement commended itself to his judgment as simple and effective. His face had not been covered nor his eyes bandaged. He looked a moment at his "unsteadfast footing," then let his gaze wander to the swirling water of the stream racing madly beneath his feet. A piece of dancing driftwood caught his attention and his eyes followed it down the current. How slowly it appeared to move! What a sluggish stream!

He closed his eyes in order to fix his last thoughts upon his wife and children. The water, touched to gold by the early sun, the brooding mists under the banks at some distance down the stream, the fort, the soldiers, the piece of driftwood—all had distracted him. And now he became conscious of a new disturbance. Striking through the thought of his dear ones was a sound which he could neither ignore nor understand, a sharp, distinct, metallic percussion like the stroke of a blacksmith's hammer upon the anvil; it had the same ringing quality. He wondered what it was, and whether immeasurably distant or near by—it seemed both. Its recurrence was regular, but as slow as the tolling of a death knell. He awaited each stroke with impatience and—he knew not why—apprehension. The intervals of silence grew progressively longer; the delays became maddening. With their greater infrequency the sounds increased in strength and sharpness. They hurt his ear like the thrust of a knife; he feared he would shriek. What he heard was the ticking of his watch.

He unclosed his eyes and saw again the water below him. "If I could free my hands," he thought, "I might throw off the noose and spring into the stream. By diving I could evade the bullets and, swimming vigorously, reach the bank, take to the woods and get away home. My home, thank God, is as yet outside their lines; my wife and little ones are still beyond the invader's farthest advance."

As these thoughts, which have here to be set down in words, were flashed into the doomed man's brain rather than evolved from it the captain nodded to the sergeant. The sergeant stepped aside.

II

Peyton Farquhar was a well-to-do planter, of an old and highly respected Alabama family. Being a slave owner and like other slave owners a politician he was naturally an original secessionist and ardently devoted to the Southern cause. Circumstances of an imperious nature, which it is unnecessary to relate here, had prevented him from taking service with the gallant army that had fought the disastrous campaigns ending with the fall of Corinth,° and he chafed under the inglorious restraint, longing for the release of his energies, the larger life of the soldier, the opportunity for distinction. That opportunity, he felt, would come, as it comes to all in war time. Meanwhile he did what he could. No service was too humble for him to perform in aid of the South, no adventure too perilous for him to undertake if consistent with the character of a civilian who was at heart a soldier, and who in good faith and without too much qualification assented to at least a part of the frankly villainous dictum that all is fair in love and war.

One evening while Farquhar and his wife were sitting on a rustic bench near the entrance to his grounds, a gray-clad soldier rode up to the gate and asked for a drink of water. Mrs. Farquhar was only too happy to serve him with her own white hands. While she was fetching the water her husband approached the dusty horseman and inquired eagerly for news from the front.

"The Yanks are repairing the railroads," said the man, "and are getting ready for another advance. They have reached the Owl Creek bridge, put it in order and built a stockade on the north bank. The commandant has issued an order, which is posted everywhere, declaring that any civilian caught interfering with the railroad, its bridges, tunnels or trains will be summarily hanged. I saw the order."

"How far is it to the Owl Creek bridge?" Farquhar asked.

"About thirty miles."

"Is there no force on this side of the creek?"

10

Corinth: In the northeast corner of Mississippi, near the Alabama state line, Corinth was the site of a battle in 1862 won by the Union army.

"Only a picket post half a mile out, on the railroad, and a single sentinel at this end of the bridge."

"Suppose a man—a civilian and student of hanging—should elude the picket post   15
and perhaps get the better of the sentinel," said Farquhar, smiling, "what could he accomplish?"

The soldier reflected. "I was there a month ago," he replied. "I observed that the flood of last winter had lodged a great quantity of driftwood against the wooden pier at this end of the bridge. It is now dry and would burn like tow."

The lady had now brought the water, which the soldier drank. He thanked her ceremoniously, bowed to her husband and rode away. An hour later, after nightfall, he repassed the plantation, going northward in the direction from which he had come. He was a Federal scout.

III

As Peyton Farquhar fell straight downward through the bridge he lost consciousness and was as one already dead. From this state he was awakened—ages later, it seemed to him—by the pain of a sharp pressure upon his throat, followed by a sense of suffocation. Keen, poignant agonies seemed to shoot from his neck downward through every fiber of his body and limbs. These pains appeared to flash along well-defined lines of ramification and to beat with an inconceivably rapid periodicity. They seemed like streams of pulsating fire heating him to an intolerable temperature. As to his head, he was conscious of nothing but a feeling of fulness—of congestion. These sensations were unaccompanied by thought. The intellectual part of his nature was already effaced; he had power only to feel, and feeling was torment. He was conscious of motion. Encompassed in a luminous cloud, of which he was now merely the fiery heart, without material substance, he swung through unthinkable arcs of oscillation, like a vast pendulum. Then all at once, with terrible suddenness, the light about him shot upward with the noise of a loud plash; a frightful roaring was in his ears, and all was cold and dark. The power of thought was restored; he knew that the rope had broken and he had fallen into the stream. There was no additional strangulation; the noose about his neck was already suffocating him and kept the water from his lungs. To die of hanging at the bottom of a river!—the idea seemed to him ludicrous. He opened his eyes in the darkness and saw above him a gleam of light, but how distant, how inaccessible! He was still sinking, for the light became fainter and fainter until it was a mere glimmer. Then it began to grow and brighten, and he knew that he was rising toward the surface—knew it with reluctance, for he was now very comfortable. "To be hanged and drowned," he thought, "that is not so bad; but I do not wish to be shot. No; I will not be shot; that is not fair."

He was not conscious of an effort, but a sharp pain in his wrist apprised him that he was trying to free his hands. He gave the struggle his attention, as an idler might observe the feat of a juggler, without interest in the outcome. What splendid effort—what magnificent, what superhuman strength! Ah, that was a fine endeavor! Bravo! The cord fell away; his arms parted and floated upward; the hands dimly seen on each side in the growing light. He watched them with a new interest as first one and then the other pounced upon the noose at his neck. They tore it away and thrust it fiercely aside, its undulations resembling those of a water snake. "Put it back, put it back!" He thought he shouted these words to his hands, for the undoing of the noose had been succeeded by the direst pang that he had yet experienced. His neck ached horribly; his brain was on fire; his heart, which had been fluttering faintly, gave a great leap, trying to force itself out at his mouth. His whole body was racked and wrenched with an insupportable anguish! But his disobedient hands gave no heed to the command. They beat the water vigorously with quick, downward strokes, forcing him to the surface. He felt his head emerge; his eyes were blinded by the sunlight; his chest expanded convulsively, and with a supreme and crowning agony his lungs engulfed a great draught of air, which instantly he expelled in a shriek!

He was now in full possession of his physical senses. They were indeed, preternat- 20 urally keen and alert. Something in the awful disturbance of his organic system had so exalted and refined them that they made record of things never before perceived. He felt the ripples upon his face and heard their separate sounds as they struck. He looked at the forest on the bank of the stream, saw the individual trees, the leaves and the vein- ing of each leaf—saw the very insects upon them: the locusts, the brilliant-bodied flies, the gray spiders stretching their webs from twig to twig. He noted the prismatic colors in all the dewdrops upon a million blades of grass. The humming of the gnats that danced above the eddies of the stream, the beating of the dragon flies' wings, the strokes of the water-spiders' legs, like oars which had lifted their boat—all these made audible music. A fish slid along beneath his eyes and he heard the rush of its body parting the water.

He had come to the surface facing down the stream; in a moment the visible world seemed to wheel slowly round, himself the pivotal point, and he saw the bridge, the fort, the soldiers upon the bridge, the captain, the sergeant, the two privates, his executioners. They were in silhouette against the blue sky. They shouted and gesticu- lated, pointing at him. The captain had drawn his pistol, but did not fire; the others were unarmed. Their movements were grotesque and horrible, their forms gigantic.

Suddenly he heard a sharp report and something struck the water smartly within a few inches of his head, spattering his face with spray. He heard a second report, and saw one of the sentinels with his rifle at his shoulder, a light cloud of blue smoke rising from the muzzle. The man in the water saw the eye of the man on the bridge gazing into his own through the sights of the rifle. He observed that it was a gray eye and remembered having read that gray eyes were keenest, and that all famous marksmen had them. Nevertheless, this one had missed.

A counter-swirl had caught Farquhar and turned him half round; he was again looking into the forest on the bank opposite the fort. The sound of a clear, high voice in a monotonous singsong now rang out behind him and came across the water with a dis- tinctness that pierced and subdued all other sounds, even the beating of the ripples in his ears. Although no soldier, he had frequented camps enough to know the dread sig- nificance of that deliberate, drawling, aspirated chant; the lieutenant on shore was taking a part in the morning's work. How coldly and pitilessly—with what an even, calm intonation, presaging, and enforcing tranquility in the men—with what accurately mea- sured intervals fell those cruel words:

"Attention, company! . . . Shoulder arms! . . . Ready! . . . Aim! . . . Fire!"

Farquhar dived—dived as deeply as he could. The water roared in his ears like 25 the voice of Niagara, yet he heard the dulled thunder of the volley and, rising again toward the surface, met shining bits of metal, singularly flattened, oscillating slowly downward. Some of them touched him on the face and hands, then fell away, continu- ing their descent. One lodged between his collar and neck; it was uncomfortably warm and he snatched it out.

As he rose to the surface, gasping for breath, he saw that he had been a long time under water; he was perceptibly farther down stream—nearer to safety. The soldiers had almost finished reloading; the metal ramrods flashed all at once in the sunshine as they were drawn from the barrels, turned in the air, and thrust into their sockets. The two sentinels fired again, independently and ineffectually.

The hunted man saw all this over his shoulder; he was now swimming vigorously with the current. His brain was as energetic as his arms and legs; he thought with the rapidity of lightning.

"The officer," he reasoned, "will not make that martinet's error a second time. It is as easy to dodge a volley as a single shot. He has probably already given the command to fire at will. God help me, I cannot dodge them all!"

An appalling plash within two yards of him was followed by a loud, rushing sound, *diminuendo,* which seemed to travel back through the air to the fort and died in an explosion which stirred the very river to its deeps! A rising sheet of water curved over him, fell down upon him, blinded him, strangled him! The cannon had taken a hand in the game. As he shook his head free from the commotion of the smitten water he heard the deflected shot humming through the air ahead, and in an instant it was cracking and smashing the branches in the forest beyond.

"They will not do that again," he thought; "the next time they will use a charge of grape. I must keep my eye upon the gun; the smoke will apprise me—the report arrives too late; it lags behind the missile. That is a good gun." 30

Suddenly he felt himself whirled round and round—spinning like a top. The water, the banks, the forests, the now distant bridge, fort and men—all were commingled and blurred. Objects were represented by their colors only; circular horizontal streaks of color—that was all he saw. He had been caught in a vortex and was being whirled on with a velocity of advance and gyration that made him giddy and sick. In a few moments he was flung upon the gravel at the foot of the left bank of the stream— the southern bank—and behind a projecting point which concealed him from his enemies. The sudden arrest of his motion, the abrasion of one of his hands on the gravel, restored him, and he wept with delight. He dug his fingers into the sand, threw it over himself in handfuls and audibly blessed it. It looked like diamonds, rubies, emeralds; he could think of nothing beautiful which it did not resemble. The trees upon the bank were giant garden plants; he noted a definite order in their arrangement, inhaled the fragrance of their blooms. A strange, roseate light shone through the spaces among their trunks and the wind made in their branches the music of Æolian harps. He had no wish to perfect his escape—was content to remain in that enchanting spot until retaken.

A whiz and rattle of grapeshot among the branches high above his head roused him from his dream. The baffled cannoneer had fired him a random farewell. He sprang to his feet, rushed up the sloping bank, and plunged into the forest.

All that day he traveled, laying his course by the rounding sun. The forest seemed interminable; nowhere did he discover a break in it, not even a woodman's road. He had not known that he lived in so wild a region. There was something uncanny in the revelation.

By nightfall he was fatigued, footsore, famishing. The thought of his wife and children urged him on. At last he found a road which led him in what he knew to be the right direction. It was as wide and straight as a city street, yet it seem untraveled. No fields bordered it, no dwelling anywhere. Not so much as the barking of a dog suggested human habitation. The black bodies of the trees formed a straight wall on both sides, terminating on the horizon in a point, like a diagram in a lesson in perspective. Overhead, as he looked up through this rift in the wood, shone great golden stars looking unfamiliar and grouped in strange constellations. He was sure they were arranged in some order which had a secret and malign significance. The wood on either side was full of singular noises, among which—once, twice, and again—he distinctly heard whispers in an unknown tongue.

His neck was in pain and lifting his hand to it found it horribly swollen. He knew   35
that it had a circle of black where the rope had bruised it. His eyes felt congested; he could no longer close them. His tongue was swollen with thirst; he relieved its fever by thrusting it forward from between his teeth into the cold air. How softly the turf had carpeted the untraveled avenue—he could no longer feel the roadway beneath his feet!

Doubtless, despite his suffering, he had fallen asleep while walking, for now he sees another scene—perhaps he has merely recovered from a delirium. He stands at the gate of his own home. All is as he left it, and all bright and beautiful in the morning sunshine. He must have traveled the entire night. As he pushes open the gate and passes up the wide white walk, he sees a flutter of female garments; his wife, looking fresh and cool and sweet, steps down from the veranda to meet him. At the bottom of the steps she stands waiting, with a smile of ineffable joy, an attitude of matchless grace and dignity. Ah, how beautiful she is! He springs forward with extended arms. As he is about to clasp her he feels a stunning blow upon the back of the neck; a blinding white light blazes all about him with a sound like the shock of a cannon—then all is darkness and silence!

Peyton Farquhar was dead; his body, with a broken neck, swung gently from side to side beneath the timbers of the Owl Creek bridge.

QUESTIONS

1. What is the situation in the story? What did Farquhar do to deserve his execution?

2. Describe the various shifts in the story's point of view, particularly as indicated in paragraphs 5 and 37. How does Bierce make you aware of Farquhar's heightened consciousness?

3. According to Farquhar's perception of time, how long does it take him to get home after his escape (see paragraphs 33 and 36)?

4. What evidence can you find to indicate that Farquhar is experiencing great pain, despite his feelings that he is escaping?

5. What is the effect of the shift into the present tense in paragraph 36?

ELLEN GILCHRIST   (b. 1935)

A writer of novels, short stories, and poems, Gilchrist was born in Mississippi and received her higher education at Vanderbilt and Millsaps College. Among her novels are The Annunciation *(1984) and* I Cannot Get You Close Enough *(1990), which is a collection of three novellas. Story Collections are* In the Land of Dreamy Dreams *(1981),* Drunk with Love *(1986), and* Light Can Be Both Wave and Particle *(1989), from which "The Song of Songs" is taken.*

The Song of Songs _____ *1989*

It was Christmas morning. A bright clear day. Almost cool. The city of New Orleans lay in peace. Sleeeeep in heavenly peeeace. Sleep in heavenly peace.°

Strains of hymns from midnight mass echoed in the ears of the faithful. For unto us a child is born. Unto us a son is given.° The smell of lilies and candles. Morning.

Children were waking. Cats prowled the marble floors of the mansions of the Garden District and the lesser mansions of the Lower Garden District and the Victorian houses of the university section.

Barrett Clare had slept like a baby on two Valiums and a Seconal, safe in the high bedroom of the biggest whitest house on State Street. She had fought for that house. If it had been up to him, Charlie Clare would have settled for the old Phipps place, that tacky brick box.

She opened her eyes. The sun was slanting in the wooden shutters, casting bright demarcations over everything on the floor, her red wool dress, her De Liso Debs, her satin, hand-embroidered slip, her underpants, her bra. She had slept alone in the walnut bed. I have always been alone, she thought, and rose from the bed, shaking off the fuzzy feeling of the drugs, worrying that Charles was already awake, looking for her. Her baby, her one and only love, her boy. Damn, she thought, and shook her head again. The Seconal was too much. That was going too far. Still, it was better than not sleeping. It was better than dreams.

She picked up the slacks she had been wearing the day before and squeezed them in her hand. She had been wearing them when the tall blond boy came with his terrible message. That nightmare. Only it was true. He had come out of nowhere at eleven o'clock in the morning on Christmas Eve to tell her where her mother was. Her real mother, the one that had borne her into the world and given her away. She never touched me, Barrett had told Gustave over and over. No, I know she didn't. I would remember if she had. No one can remember that far back, he would say, and move around ever so gradually in his old brown chair. An enormous response from Gustave. She never touched me, Barrett would insist. I know. I would know. They got me from the home when I was five days old. I weighed eight pounds. I was a huge baby. I was alone when I was born and I have been alone ever since. She had me and then she never even looked at me. Gustave would move again in his chair. When she talked of *it* at least he listened. Well, he always listened. He was a wonderful doctor. A member of the Academy. He was the best. The very best. The best that money could buy.

Where was he now that she needed him? Where had he gone to? How dare he leave town at Christmas. Why couldn't they find him? They could find him if they really wanted to. She sat down on the bed and rang his answering service.

"You know you can find him. You must tell him it's an emergency. Tell him it's Barrett, Barrett Clare. You must reach him for me. All right, I'll be waiting. Yes, please try." She hung up. Who do they think they are? Those answering-service people.

Amanda McCamey is my mother. I'll call her on the phone. The thought was like an arrow. It flew across the room and disappeared. No, it's her place to call me. If she knows where I am. Your mother is named Amanda McCamey and she is up in Arkansas

---

Sleeeeep . . . peace: from the Christmas hymn "Silent Night."
For . . . given: chorus from *Messiah* (1741) by George Frideric Handel (1685–1759).

and she is going to have a baby any day now. That is what the blond boy said. I am going there now. I will tell her that I told you.

I'll go too, she had answered. I will go and talk to her. You can't go, he said. She is going to have a baby. She doesn't know you know. She doesn't know I'm here. 10

I want to tell someone, Barrett thought. I need to tell someone who my mother is. She is so beautiful. Didn't I touch her? That day at Loyola? When Brummette introduced us. I think I touched her. I think I shook her hand. She called me Shelley. She thought my name was Shelley. Why hasn't she called me if she knows who I am? Here is your mother, the blond boy said. And now I am taking her away.

A rush of fuzziness passed across her brain. She shook her head. She picked up Charlie's coat from the chair and started going through the pockets looking for a cigarette. He had come in from Vail at three or four. He had tried to get in bed with her. "It was a snowstorm, baby. They closed the airport. I couldn't help it."

"Get out of here, you bastard. Don't get near me."

"It's Christmas," he said.

"Go away, Charlie." 15

She went into the dressing room and washed her face and hands. She combed her hair. She looked deep into the mirror, searching her face for the face of her mother. It was there. Yes, anyone could see it. I could go on living, she thought. If it never would be Christmas. If I never had to hang that dead tree in the window. Well, Charles will be waking up. I must act normal. I must act like everything's okay. It's Christmas morning. She laughed at that. Suddenly her sadness and self-absorption seemed the silliest thing in all New Orleans.

She went downstairs and found Charles and Charlie in the breakfast room. Charlie still looked drunk. He was reading the paper. Charles had already started opening his presents. "Daddy slept with me," he said. "In my bed." He tore open a package containing a white shirt with his initials on the cuffs. He pulled it out of the package and took the pins out and tried it on. He was five years old, a sturdy wild little boy, excitable, hard to control.

The shirt was too big. The cuffs came down and hid his new Rolex watch. "It hides my watch," he said. "It doesn't fit. You have to take it back."

"You aren't supposed to be opening things yet," Charlie said. "I told you to wait for her. Is Lorraine coming, Barrett? Are we going to have breakfast?"

"She'll be here later. She has to cook for her family. I'll make breakfast. How was 20 Vail?" He didn't answer. She rolled up the sleeves of her robe and set the table with red placemats and a set of Christmas china Charlie's sister had given them the year before. In a while she put a breakfast of bacon and eggs on the plates.

"Let's sit together now," she said. "Let's hold hands and say grace. Charles, do you want to say the prayer?" They were holding hands around the table. She could feel the thick wiry hair on Charlie's hand, tough reddish blond hair. Wire, she thought. Like his mind. A piece of wire. I'll put that in a poem.

At least there's Patsy, he was thinking. God love her soft little buns. God love her laughter.

"Lord make us thankful for these and all our many other blessings, for Christ's sake, amen. Ahh, men. That's what old maids say, isn't it, Daddy?"

"You all go on and eat," Barrett said. "I'm going upstairs for a while." She reached over and hugged the little boy. "I love you, Sweetie Pie," she said. "Don't you ever forget that." Charlie sighed and put butter on a biscuit. He took a bite and put the other half on Charles's plate. They were beautiful plates, white porcelain decorated with holly. "I love you too, Charlie," she said. "No matter what you do." She gave him a very small kiss on the cheek.

"Don't you want to see your presents?"   25

"Not yet," she said. She unrolled the sleeves of her robe and walked out of the kitchen past the painted porch swing. She was the only woman in town with a porch swing in her kitchen. She walked into the hall and up the stairs past the stained-glass window depicting Saint George slaying the dragon. She walked into Charlie's room and took a pistol with handmade wooden handles out of a gun case and walked over to the window looking out on the avenue. *Now I will pull the trigger and blow my old blue and brown coiled-up brains all over the Pande Camaroon and some will spill on the Andrew Wyeth and, why not, some of them can move out onto the balcony and festoon the iron railings. You know, they will say, those old railings New Orleans is so famous for? Yes, it will make a good story around town. It will make everybody's day. They'll forget them-selves in the story of my willfulness.*

She put the gun in her mouth and sucked the barrel. It was a game she liked to play. It was the only power she knew she had. The phone was ringing, a lovely ring, soft, like bells. Barrett took it down from its hanger on the wall. "Is this Barrett Clare?" the voice said. The voice was tearing into her ears. "This is Amanda McCamey. I am your mother. If this is Mrs. Charles Clare. If you are an adopted child, I am your mother. Oh, forgive me, oh, my God, forgive me. I need you so terribly dreadfully much. Will you talk to me? Will you let me talk to you?"

"This is me," she said. "I knew you would call me up. I've been waiting all day."

"I've been waiting all my life," the voice said. "Forgive me for calling you instead of coming there. I should have come. But I can't come for several days, perhaps a week. Will you come to me? Will you come to where I am? Will you bring your little boy? Your father will be here. I will have him here. He's the one that found you. I'll send him for you. Oh, yes, that's what I'll do."

"No," Barrett said. "Don't do that. I'll come today. Tell me where to go. Tell me   30 how to get there." There was a sound on the other end, like sobbing, or something else, something she had never heard. "Don't cry," she said to her mother. "I am going to come to where you are as fast as I can get there. And I'm bringing Charles, my little boy. I will stay a long long time . . . I might come and stay forever. I might not ever leave. Can you hear me? I know you. Do you know that? I know who you are."

"How is that? How do you know?"

"I mean we met. At Loyola. Don Brummette introduced us. I used to read every-thing you wrote. I guess I had a crush on you that year."

"What do you look like? How could I not have known? I can't remember. So many things have happened today. A friend of mine was in a terrible wreck, someone I love. And everything else. Are you really coming here? You will come to me? You will come here?"

"I'm coming as soon as I can pack a bag and leave. I look like you. Yes, I think I look like you. We will look in a mirror. The two of us. We will look at one another. Tell me where you are. How to get there. How to go."

"Here's Katie," Amanda said. "She's my friend. She'll tell you what to do."

Then a woman named Katie got on the phone and told Barrett how to get to Fayetteville, Arkansas, from New Orleans, Louisiana. It was not that simple. "I'll be there this afternoon," Barrett said. "Tell my mother that I love her. Tell her I'll be there very soon." She put the phone back on the wall and picked the gun up off the dresser and walked across the room and put it back into the case and turned the key. Then she took the key and walked out on the balcony and threw it far out into the branches of a Japanese magnolia tree. Then she ran down the stairs to her husband and her child.

Charlie was sitting on the floor in a sea of wrapping paper drinking a brandy and playing with Charles. The great hanging tree for which the Clares were famous on State Street swayed softly above him. "Well," he said. "You're going to join us. How charming of you, Barrett."

"My mother just called me on the phone," she said. "My real mother. The one who had me. I'm going there today and taking Charles with me. Now get up please and help me. I want you to call and charter us a plane. She lives up in Arkansas. It's a long way and inaccessible. Do it right now, Charlie. This is not a joke. Something's happened to her. She needs me."

"Your mother?"

"Yes, my mother. Please get me a plane right now, Charlie. While I pack. Charles, you are going with me somewhere. We're going to see your grandmother. Your real grandmother. Someone you've never seen." The child did not move, but her husband, Charlie, got up. He came toward her, reaching out to her. "All right," he said. "That's wonderful. What else? What else can I do?"

"What will we wear?" Charles said. "What will we take to wear?"

"It doesn't matter what we wear," she said. "We're going to see my mother. My mother. I'm going to see my mother." She picked him up off the floor and hugged him fiercely and danced him around the room. I exist, she was singing inside her head. I am here. I am really here. Everything that happens from this day forward will be better. Whatever happens next will be better and better and better. My mother is waiting for me.

A woman named Katie met them at the airport and drove them to a house on top of a small mountain overlooking the university. "It was brave of you to come like this," Katie said. "What a brave thing to do."

"Where are we?" Charles said. "I don't know where we are."

Then they turned into a driveway and Barrett's mother was standing in the doorway of a small wooden house. A tall woman with hair that fell like a cascade almost to her waist. She walked out across the yard and took her daughter into her arms.

QUESTIONS

1. Describe the point of view of this story. Which character is the center of attention? Describe the narrator's attitude toward this character. What are the various ways in which this character is presented to us?

2. What is happening in Barrett's life? Why does she feel "alone ever since" she was born (paragraph 6)? What kind of relationship does she have with her husband, Charlie? Why does she go to her room and take out the gun? What does she do after she speaks with her mother?

3. Of what significance is it that the story takes place on Christmas day?

4. What view does the story present toward adoption and its effect on adopted children as adults?

SHIRLEY JACKSON   (1919–1965)

Jackson was a native of California. She graduated from Syracuse University in New York and lived much of her life in Vermont. Although her life was short, she was a successful writer of novels, short stories, biographies, and children's fiction. Her stories often depict unusual, unreal, or bizarre events in common settings, of which "The Lottery" is a major example. She wrote the story in only two hours and submitted it to the New Yorker *without major revisions. When it was published many readers raised questions about how to interpret the conclusion. Jackson steadfastly refused to explain, leaving readers to decide for themselves.*

The Lottery _____ *1948*

The morning of June 27th was clear and sunny, with the fresh warmth of a full summer day; the flowers were blossoming profusely and the grass was richly green. The people of the village began to gather in the square, between the post office and the bank, around ten o'clock; in some towns there were so many people that the lottery took two days and had to be started on June 26th, but in this village, where there were only about three hundred people, the whole lottery took less than two hours, so it could begin at ten o'clock in the morning and still be through in time to allow the villagers to get home for noon dinner.

The children assembled first, of course. School was recently over for the summer, and the feeling of liberty sat uneasily on most of them; they tended to gather together quietly for a while before they broke into boisterous play, and their talk was still of the classroom and the teacher, of books and reprimands. Bobby Martin had already stuffed his pockets full of stones, and the other boys soon followed his example, selecting the smoothest and roundest stones; Bobby and Harry Jones and Dickie Delacroix—the villagers pronounced this name "Dellacroy"—eventually made a great pile of stones in one corner of the square and guarded it against the raids of the other boys. The girls stood aside, talking among themselves, looking over their shoulders at the boys, and the very small children rolled in the dust or clung to the hands of their older brothers or sisters.

Soon the men began to gather, surveying their own children, speaking of planting and rain, tractors and taxes. They stood together, away from the pile of stones in the corner, and their jokes were quiet and they smiled rather than laughed. The women, wearing faded house dresses and sweaters, came shortly after their menfolk. They greeted one another and exchanged bits of gossip as they went to join their husbands. Soon the women, standing by their husbands, began to call to their children, and the children came reluctantly, having to be called four or five times. Bobby Martin ducked under his mother's grasping hand and ran, laughing, back to the pile of stones. His father spoke up sharply, and Bobby came quickly and took his place between his father and his oldest brother.

The lottery was conducted—as were the square dances, the teen-age club, the Halloween program—by Mr. Summers, who had time and energy to devote to civic activities. He was a round-faced, jovial man and he ran the coal business, and people were sorry for him, because he had no children and his wife was a scold. When he arrived in the square, carrying the black wooden box, there was a murmur of conversation among the villagers, and he waved and called, "Little late today, folks." The postmaster, Mr. Graves, followed him, carrying a three-legged stool, and the stool was put in the center of the square and Mr. Summers set the black box down on it. The villagers kept their distance, leaving a space between themselves and the stool, and when Mr. Summers said, "Some of you fellows want to give me a hand?" there was a hesitation before two men, Mr. Martin and his oldest son, Baxter, came forward to hold the box steady on the stool while Mr. Summers stirred up the papers inside it.

The original paraphernalia for the lottery had been lost long ago, and the black box now resting on the stool had been put into use even before Old Man Warner, the oldest man in town, was born. Mr. Summers spoke frequently to the villagers about making a new box, but no one liked to upset even as much tradition as was represented by the black box. There was a story that the present box had been made with some pieces of the box that had preceded it, the one that had been constructed when the first people settled down to make a village here. Every year, after the lottery, Mr. Summers began talking again about a new box, but every year the subject was allowed to fade off without anything's being done. The black box grew shabbier each year; by now it was no longer completely black but splintered badly along one side to show the original wood color, and in some places faded or stained.

Mr. Martin and his oldest son, Baxter, held the black box securely on the stool until Mr. Summers had stirred the papers thoroughly with his hand. Because so much of the ritual had been forgotten or discarded, Mr. Summers had been successful in having slips of paper substituted for the chips of wood that had been used for generations. Chips of wood, Mr. Summers had argued, had been all very well when the village was tiny, but now that the population was more than three hundred and likely to keep on growing, it was necessary to use something that would fit more easily into the black box. The night before the lottery, Mr. Summers and Mr. Graves made up the slips of paper and put them in the box, and it was then taken to the safe of Mr. Summers' coal company and locked up until Mr. Summers was ready to take it to the square next morning. The rest of the year, the box was put away, sometimes one place, sometimes another; it had spent one year in Mr. Graves's barn and another year underfoot in the post office, and sometimes it was set on a shelf in the Martin grocery and left there.

There was a great deal of fussing to be done before Mr. Summers declared the lottery open. There were the lists to make up—of heads of families, heads of households in each family, members of each household in each family. There was the proper swearing-in of Mr. Summers by the postmaster, as the official of the lottery; at one time, some people remembered, there had been a recital of some sort, performed by the official of the lottery, a perfunctory, tuneless chant that had been rattled off duly each year; some people believed that the official of the lottery used to stand just so when he said or sang it, others believed that he was supposed to walk among the people, but years and years ago this part of the ritual had been allowed to lapse. There had been, also, a ritual salute, which the official of the lottery had had to use in addressing each person who came up to draw from the box, but this also had changed with time, until now it was felt necessary only for the official to speak to each person approaching. Mr. Summers was very good at all this; in his clean white shirt and blue jeans, with one hand resting carelessly on the black box, he seemed very proper and important as he talked interminably to Mr. Graves and the Martins.

Just as Mr. Summers finally left off talking and turned to the assembled villagers, Mrs. Hutchinson came hurriedly along the path to the square, her sweater thrown over

5

her shoulders, and slid into place in the back of the crowd. "Clean forgot what day it was," she said to Mrs. Delacroix, who stood next to her, and they both laughed softly. "Thought my old man was out back stacking wood," Mrs. Hutchinson went on, "and then I looked out the window and the kids was gone, and then I remembered it was the twenty-seventh and came a-running." She dried her hands on her apron, and Mrs. Delacroix said, "You're in time, though. They're still talking away up there."

Mrs. Hutchinson craned her neck to see through the crowd and found her husband and children standing near the front. She tapped Mrs. Delacroix on the arm as a farewell and began to make her way through the crowd. The people separated good-humoredly to let her through; two or three people said, in voices just loud enough to be heard across the crowd, "Here comes your Missus, Hutchinson," and "Bill, she made it after all." Mrs. Hutchinson reached her husband, and Mr. Summers, who had been waiting, said cheerfully, "Thought we were going to have to get on without you, Tessie." Mrs. Hutchinson said, grinning, "Wouldn't have me leave m'dishes in the sink, now, would you, Joe?," and soft laughter ran through the crowd as the people stirred back into position after Mrs. Hutchinson's arrival.

"Well, now," Mr. Summers said soberly, "guess we better get started, get this over with, so's we can go back to work. Anybody ain't here?"   10

"Dunbar," several people said. "Dunbar, Dunbar."

Mr. Summers consulted his list. "Clyde Dunbar," he said. "That's right. He's broke his leg, hasn't he? Who's drawing for him?"

"Me, I guess," a woman said, and Mr. Summers turned to look at her. "Wife draws for her husband," Mr. Summers said. "Don't you have a grown boy to do it for you, Janey?" Although Mr. Summers and everyone else in the village knew the answer perfectly well, it was the business of the official of the lottery to ask such questions formally. Mr. Summers waited with an expression of polite interest while Mrs. Dunbar answered.

"Horace's not but sixteen yet," Mrs. Dunbar said regretfully. "Guess I gotta fill in for the old man this year."

"Right," Mr. Summers said. He made a note on the list he was holding. Then he asked, "Watson boy drawing this year?"   15

A tall boy in the crowd raised his hand. "Here," he said. "I'm drawing for m'mother and me." He blinked his eyes nervously and ducked his head as several voices in the crowd said things like "Good fellow, Jack," and "Glad to see your mother's got a man to do it."

"Well," Mr. Summers said, "guess that's everyone. Old Man Warner make it?"

"Here," a voice said, and Mr. Summers nodded.

A sudden hush fell on the crowd as Mr. Summers cleared his throat and looked at the list. "All ready?" he called. "Now, I'll read the names—heads of families first—and the men come up and take a paper out of the box. Keep the paper folded in your hand without looking at it until everyone has had a turn. Everything clear?"

The people had done it so many times that they only half listened to the directions; most of them were quiet, wetting their lips, not looking around. Then Mr. Summers raised one hand high and said, "Adams." A man disengaged himself from the crowd and came forward. "Hi, Steve," Mr. Summers said, and Mr. Adams said, "Hi, Joe." They grinned at one another humorlessly and nervously. Then Mr. Adams reached into the black box and took out a folded paper. He held it firmly by one corner as he turned and went hastily back to his place in the crowd, where he stood a little apart from his family, not looking down at his hand.

"Allen," Mr. Summers said. "Anderson. . . . Bentham."

"Seems like there's no time at all between lotteries any more," Mrs. Delacroix said to Mrs. Graves in the back row. "Seems like we got through with the last one only last week."

"Time sure goes fast," Mrs. Graves said.

"Clark. . . . Delacroix."

"There goes my old man," Mrs. Delacroix said. She held her breath while her husband went forward.   25

"Dunbar," Mr. Summers said, and Mrs. Dunbar went steadily to the box while one of the women said, "Go on, Janey," and another said, "There she goes."

"We're next," Mrs. Graves said. She watched while Mr. Graves came around from the side of the box, greeted Mr. Summers gravely, and selected a slip of paper from the box. By now, all through the crowd there were men holding the small folded papers in their large hands, turning them over and over nervously. Mrs. Dunbar and her two sons stood together, Mrs. Dunbar holding the slip of paper.

"Harburt. . . . Hutchinson."

"Get up there, Bill," Mrs. Hutchinson said, and the people near her laughed.

"Jones."   30

"They do say," Mr. Adams said to Old Man Warner, who stood next to him, "that over in the north village they're talking of giving up the lottery."

Old Man Warner snorted. "Pack of crazy fools," he said. "Listening to the young folks, nothing's good enough for *them*. Next thing you know, they'll be wanting to go back to living in caves, nobody work any more, live *that* way for a while. Used to be a saying about 'Lottery in June, corn be heavy soon.' First thing you know, we'd all be eating stewed chickweed and acorns. There's *always* been a lottery," he added petulantly. "Bad enough to see young Joe Summers up there joking with everybody."

"Some places have already quit lotteries," Mrs. Adams said.

"Nothing but trouble in *that*," Old Man Warner said stoutly. "Pack of young fools."

"Martin." And Bobby Martin watched his father go forward. "Overdyke. . . . Percy."   35

"I wish they'd hurry," Mrs. Dunbar said to her older son. "I wish they'd hurry."

"They're almost through," her son said.

"You get ready to run tell Dad," Mrs. Dunbar said.

Mr. Summers called his own name and then stepped forward precisely and selected a slip from the box. Then he called, "Warner."

"Seventy-seventh year I been in the lottery," Old Man Warner said as he went through the crowd. "Seventy-seventh time."   40

"Watson." The tall boy came awkwardly through the crowd. Someone said, "Don't be nervous, Jack," and Mr. Summers said, "Take your time, son."

"Zanini."

After that, there was a long pause, a breathless pause, until Mr. Summers, holding his slip of paper in the air, said, "All right, fellows." For a minute, no one moved, and then all the slips of paper were opened. Suddenly, all the women began to speak at once, saying, "Who is it?" "Who's got it?" "Is it the Dunbars?" "Is it the Watsons?" Then the voices began to say, "It's Hutchinson. It's Bill," "Bill Hutchinson's got it."

"Go tell your father," Mrs. Dunbar said to her older son.

People began to look around to see the Hutchinsons. Bill Hutchinson was standing quiet, staring down at the paper in his hand. Suddenly, Tessie Hutchinson shouted to Mr. Summers, "You didn't give him time enough to take any paper he wanted. I saw you. It wasn't fair!"   45

"Be a good sport, Tessie," Mrs. Delacroix called, and Mrs. Graves said, "All of us took the same chance."

"Shut up, Tessie," Bill Hutchinson said.

"Well, everyone," Mr. Summers said, "that was done pretty fast, and now we've got to be hurrying a little more to get done in time." He consulted his next list. "Bill," he said, "you draw for the Hutchinson family. You got any other households in the Hutchinsons?"

"There's Don and Eva," Mrs. Hutchinson yelled. "Make *them* take their chance!"

"Daughters draw with their husbands' families, Tessie," Mr. Summers said   50
gently. "You know that as well as anyone else."

"It wasn't *fair*," Tessie said.

"I guess not, Joe," Bill Hutchinson said regretfully. "My daughter draws with her husband's family, that's only fair. And I've got no other family except the kids."

"Then, as far as drawing for families is concerned, it's you," Mr. Summers said in explanation, "and as far as drawing for households is concerned, that's you, too. Right?"

"Right," Bill Hutchinson said.

"How many kids, Bill?" Mr. Summers asked formally.   55

"Three," Bill Hutchinson said. "There's Bill, Jr., and Nancy, and little Dave. And Tessie and me."

"All right, then," Mr. Summers said. "Harry, you got their tickets back?"

Mr. Graves nodded and held up the slips of paper. "Put them in the box, then," Mr. Summers directed. "Take Bill's and put it in."

"I think we ought to start over," Mrs. Hutchinson said, as quietly as she could. "I tell you it wasn't *fair*. You didn't give him time enough to choose. *Every*body saw that."

Mr. Graves had selected the five slips and put them in the box, and he dropped all   60
the papers but those onto the ground, where the breeze caught them and lifted them off.

"Listen, everybody," Mrs. Hutchinson was saying to the people around her.

"Ready, Bill?" Mr. Summers asked, and Bill Hutchinson, with one quick glance around at his wife and children, nodded.

"Remember," Mr. Summers said, "take the slips and keep them folded until each person has taken one. Harry, you help little Dave." Mr. Graves took the hand of the little boy, who came willingly with him up to the box. "Take a paper out of the box, Davy," Mr. Summers said. Davy put his hand into the box and laughed. "Take just *one* paper," Mr. Summers said. "Harry, you hold it for him." Mr. Graves took the child's hand and removed the folded paper from the tight fist and held it while little Dave stood next to him and looked up at him wonderingly.

"Nancy next," Mr. Summers said. Nancy was twelve, and her school friends breathed heavily as she went forward, switching her skirt, and took a slip daintily from the box. "Bill, Jr.," Mr. Summers said, and Billy, his face red and his feet over-large, nearly knocked the box over as he got a paper out. "Tessie," Mr. Summers said. She hesitated for a minute, looking around defiantly, and then set her lips and went up to the box. She snatched a paper out and held it behind her.

"Bill," Mr. Summers said, and Bill Hutchinson reached into the box and felt   6
around, bringing his hand out at last with the slip of paper in it.

The crowd was quiet. A girl whispered, "I hope it's not Nancy," and the sound of the whisper reached the edges of the crowd.

"It's not the way it used to be," Old Man Warner said clearly. "People ain't they way they used to be."

"All right," Mr. Summers said. "Open the papers. Harry, you open little Dave's."

Mr. Graves opened the slip of paper and there was a general sigh through the crowd as he held it up and everyone could see that it was blank. Nancy and Bill, Jr., opened theirs at the same time, and both beamed and laughed, turning around to the crowd and holding their slips of paper above their heads.

"Tessie," Mr. Summers said. There was a pause, and then Mr. Summers looked at Bill Hutchinson, and Bill unfolded his paper and showed it. It was blank.   70

"It's Tessie," Mr. Summers said, and his voice was hushed. "Show us her paper, Bill."

Bill Hutchinson went over to his wife and forced the slip of paper out of her hand. It had a black spot on it, the black spot Mr. Summers had made the night before with the heavy pencil in the coal-company office. Bill Hutchinson held it up, and there was a stir in the crowd.

"All right, folks," Mr. Summers said. "Let's finish quickly."

Although the villagers had forgotten the ritual and lost the original black box, they still remembered to use stones. The pile of stones the boys had made earlier was ready; there were stones on the ground with the blowing scraps of paper that had come out of the box. Mrs. Delacroix selected a stone so large she had to pick it up with both hands and turned to Mrs. Dunbar. "Come on," she said. "Hurry up."

Mrs. Dunbar had small stones in both hands, and she said, gasping for breath, "I   75
can't run at all. You'll have to go ahead and I'll catch up with you."

The children had stones already, and someone gave little Davy Hutchinson a few pebbles.

Tessie Hutchinson was in the center of a cleared space by now, and she held her hands out desperately as the villagers moved in on her. "It isn't fair," she said. A stone hit her on the side of the head.

Old Man Warner was saying, "Come on, come on, everyone." Steve Adams was in the front of the crowd of villagers with Mrs. Graves beside him.

"It isn't fair, it isn't right," Mrs. Hutchinson screamed, and then they were upon her.

QUESTIONS

1. Describe the point of view of the story. What seems to be the position from which the narrator sees and describes the events? How much extra information does the narrator provide?

2. What would the story be like if it were done with an omniscient point of view? With the first person? Could the story be as suspenseful as it is? In what other ways might the story be different with another point of view?

3. Does the conclusion of "The Lottery" seem to come as a surprise? In retrospect, what hints earlier in the story tell about what is to come?

4. A scapegoat, in the ritual of purification described in the Old Testament, was an actual goat that was released into the wilderness after having been ceremonially heaped with the "iniquities" of the people (Leviticus 16:22). What traces of such a ritual are suggested in "The Lottery"? Can you think of any other kinds of rituals that are retained today even though their purpose is now remote or even nonexistent?

5. Is "The Lottery" a horror story or a surprise story, or neither or both? Explain.

LORRIE MOORE   (b. 1957)

One of the youngest writers represented in this book, Lorrie Moore teaches at the University of Wisconsin. She was born in upstate New York and received a master of fine arts degree from Cornell. Following her first collection of stories, Self-Help (1985), from which "How to Become a Writer" is taken, she published her first novel, Anagrams, in 1986. A recent work is Like Life *(1991), a collection of eight stories taking its title from the last story, a grim portrait of life in a polluted, deteriorating future. She has received awards from the National Endowment for the Humanities and the Rockefeller Foundation, and her book* Birds of America *was nominated for the 1999 National Book Critics Circle fiction prize. Her fiction has been heralded for its combination of wry humor, deep feeling, and impending tragedy.*

How to Become a Writer _____ *1985*

First, try to be something, anything, else. A movie star/astronaut. A movie star/missionary. A movie star/kindergarten teacher. President of the World. Fail miserably. It is best if you fail at an early age—say, fourteen. Early, critical disillusionment is necessary so that at fifteen you can write long haiku sequences about thwarted desire. It is a pond, a cherry blossom, a wind brushing against sparrow wing leaving for mountain. Count the syllables. Show it to your mom. She is tough and practical. She has a son in Vietnam and a husband who may be having an affair. She believes in wearing brown because it hides spots. She'll look briefly at your writing, then back up at you with a face blank as a donut. She'll say: "How about emptying the dishwasher?" Look away. Shove the forks in the fork drawer. Accidentally break one of the freebie gas station glasses. This is the required pain and suffering. This is only for starters.

In your high school English class look only at Mr. Killian's face. Decide faces are important. Write a villanelle about pores. Struggle. Write a sonnet. Count the syllables: nine, ten, eleven, thirteen. Decide to experiment with fiction. Here you don't have to count syllables. Write a short story about an elderly man and woman who accidentally shoot each other in the head, the result of an inexplicable malfunction of a shotgun which appears mysteriously in their living room one night. Give it to Mr. Killian as your final project. When you get it back, he has written on it: "Some of your images are quite nice, but you have no sense of plot." When you are home, in the privacy of your own room, faintly scrawl in pencil beneath his black-inked comments: "Plots are for dead people, pore-face."

Take all the babysitting jobs you can get. You are great with kids. They love you. You tell them stories about old people who die idiot deaths. You sing them songs like "Blue Bells of Scotland," which is their favorite. And when they are in their pajamas and have finally stopped pinching each other, when they are fast asleep, you read every sex manual in the house, and wonder how on earth anyone could ever do those things with someone they truly loved. Fall asleep in a chair reading Mr. McMurphy's *Playboy*. When the McMurphys come home, they will tap you on the shoulder, look at the magazine in your lap, and grin. You will want to die. They will ask you if Tracey took her medicine all right. Explain, yes, she did, that you promised her a story if she would take it like a big girl and that seemed to work out just fine. "Oh, marvelous," they will exclaim.

Try to smile proudly.

Apply to college as a child psychology major. 5

As a child psychology major, you have some electives. You've always liked birds. Sign up for something called "The Ornithological Field Trip." It meets Tuesdays and Thursdays at two. When you arrive at Room 134 on the first day of class, everyone is sitting around a seminar table talking about metaphors. You've heard of these. After a short, excruciating while, raise your hand and say diffidently, "Excuse me, isn't this Bird-watching One-oh-one?" The class stops and turns to look at you. They seem to all have one face—giant and blank as a vandalized clock. Someone with a beard booms out, "No, this is Creative Writing." Say: "Oh—right," as if perhaps you knew all along. Look down at your schedule. Wonder how the hell you ended up here. The computer, apparently, has made an error. You start to get up to leave and then don't. The lines at the registrar this week are huge. Perhaps you should stick with this mistake. Perhaps your creative writing isn't all that bad. Perhaps it is fate. Perhaps this is what your dad meant when he said, "It's the age of computers, Francie, it's the age of computers."

Decide that you like college life. In your dorm you meet many nice people. Some are smarter than you. And some, you notice, are dumber than you. You will continue, unfortunately, to view the world in exactly these terms for the rest of your life.

The assignment this week in creative writing is to narrate a violent happening. Turn in a story about driving with your Uncle Gordon and another one about two old people who are accidentally electrocuted when they go to turn on a badly wired desk lamp. The teacher will hand them back to you with comments: "Much of your writing is smooth and energetic. You have, however, a ludicrous notion of plot." Write another story about a man and a woman who, in the very first paragraph, have their lower torsos accidentally blitzed away by dynamite. In the second paragraph, with the insurance money, they buy a frozen yogurt stand together. There are six more paragraphs. You read the whole thing out loud in class. No one likes it. They say your sense of plot is outrageous and incompetent. After class someone asks you if you are crazy.

Decide that perhaps you should stick to comedies. Start dating someone who is funny, someone who has what in high school you called a "really great sense of humor" and what now your creative writing class calls "self-contempt giving rise to comic form." Write down all of his jokes, but don't tell him you are doing this. Make up anagrams of his old girlfriend's name and name all of your socially handicapped characters with them. Tell him his old girlfriend is in all of your stories and then watch how funny he can be, see what a really great sense of humor he can have.

Your child psychology advisor tells you you are neglecting courses in your major. 10 What you spend the most time on should be what you're majoring in. Say yes, you understand.

In creative writing seminars over the next two years, everyone continues to smoke cigarettes and ask the same things: "But does it work?" "Why should we care about this character?" "Have you earned this cliché?" These seem like important questions.

On days when it is your turn, you look at the class hopefully as they scour your mimeographs for a plot. They look back up at you, drag deeply, and then smile in a sweet sort of way.

You spend too much time slouched and demoralized. Your boyfriend suggests bicycling. Your roommate suggests a new boyfriend. You are said to be self-mutilating and losing weight, but you continue writing. The only happiness you have is writing something new, in the middle of the night, armpits damp, heart pounding, something no one has yet seen. You have only those brief, fragile, untested moments of exhilaration when you know: you are a genius. Understand what you must do. Switch majors. The kids in your nursery project will be disappointed, but you have a calling, an urge, a delusion, an unfortunate habit. You have, as your mother would say, fallen in with a bad crowd.

Why write? Where does writing come from? These are questions to ask yourself. They are like: Where does dust come from? Or: Why is there war? Or: If there's a God, then why is my brother now a cripple?

These are questions that you keep in your wallet, like calling cards. These are   15
questions, your creative writing teacher says, that are good to address in your journals but rarely in your fiction.

The writing professor this fall is stressing the Power of the Imagination. Which means he doesn't want long descriptive stories about your camping trip last July. He wants you to start in a realistic context but then to alter it. Like recombinant DNA. He wants you to let your imagination sail, to let it grow big-bellied in the wind. This is a quote from Shakespeare.

Tell your roommate your great idea, your great exercise of imaginative power: a transformation of Melville to contemporary life. It will be about monomania and the fish-eat-fish world of life insurance in Rochester, New York. The first line will be "Call me Fishmeal," and it will feature a menopausal suburban husband named Richard, who because he is so depressed all the time is called "Mopey Dick" by his witty wife Elaine. Say to your roommate: "Mopey Dick, get it?" Your roommate looks at you, like a buddy, and puts an arm around your burdened shoulders. "Listen, Francie," she says, slow as speech therapy. "Let's go out and get a big beer."

The seminar doesn't like this one either. You suspect they are beginning to feel sorry for you. They say: "You have to think about what is happening. Where is the story here?"

The next semester the writing professor is obsessed with writing from personal experience. You must write from what you know, from what has happened to you. He wants deaths, he wants camping trips. Think about what has happened to you. In three years there have been three things: you lost your virginity; your parents got divorced; and your brother came home from a forest ten miles from the Cambodian border with only half a thigh, a permanent smirk nestled into one corner of his mouth.

About the first you write: "It created a new space, which hurt and cried in a voice   2
that wasn't mine, 'I'm not the same anymore, but I'll be okay.'"

About the second you write an elaborate story of an old married couple who stumble upon an unknown land mine in their kitchen and accidentally blow themselves up. You call it: "For Better or for Liverwurst."

About the last you write nothing. There are no words for this. Your typewriter hums. You can find no words.

At undergraduate cocktail parties, people say, "Oh, you write? What do you write about?" Your roommate, who has consumed too much wine, too little cheese, and no crackers at all, blurts: "Oh, my god, she always writes about her dumb boyfriend."

Later on in life you will learn that writers are merely open, helpless texts with no real understanding of what they have written and therefore must half-believe anything and everything that is said of them. You, however, have not yet reached this stage of literary criticism. You stiffen and say, "I do not," the same way you said it when someone in the fourth grade accused you of really liking oboe lessons and your parents really weren't just making you take them.

Insist you are not very interested in any one subject at all, that you are interested in the music of language, that you are interested in—in—syllables, because they are the atoms of poetry, the cells of the mind, the breath of the soul. Begin to feel woozy. Stare into your plastic wine cup.

25

"Syllables?" you will hear someone ask, voice trailing off, as they glide slowly toward the reassuring white of the dip.

Begin to wonder what you do write about. Or if you have anything to say. Or if there even is such a thing as a thing to say. Limit these thoughts to no more than ten minutes a day; like sit-ups, they can make you thin.

You will read somewhere that all writing has to do with one's genitals. Don't dwell on this. It will make you nervous.

Your mother will come visit you. She will look at the circles under your eyes and hand you a brown book with a brown briefcase on the cover. It is entitled: *How to Become a Business Executive.* She has also brought the *Names for Baby* encyclopedia you asked for; one of your characters, the aging clown–school teacher, needs a new name. You mother will shake her head and say: "Francie, Francie, remember when you were going to be a child psychology major?"

30

Say: "Mom, I like to write."

She'll say: "Sure you like to write. Of course. Sure you like to write."

Write a story about a confused music student and title it: "Schubert Was the One with the Glasses, Right?" It's not a big hit, although your roommate likes the part where the two violinists accidentally blow themselves up in a recital room. "I went out with a violinist once," she says, snapping her gum.

Thank god you are taking other courses. You can find sanctuary in nineteenth-century ontological snags and invertebrate courting rituals. Certain globular mollusks have what is called "Sex by the Arm." The male octopus, for instance, loses the end of one arm when placing it inside the female body during intercourse. Marine biologists call it "Seven Heaven." Be glad you know these things. Be glad you are not just a writer. Apply to law school.

From here on in, many things can happen. But the main one will be this: you decide not to go to law school after all, and, instead, you spend a good, big chunk of your adult life telling people how you decided not to go to law school after all. Somehow you end up writing again. Perhaps you go to graduate school. Perhaps you work odd jobs and take writing courses at night. Perhaps you are working on a novel and writing down all the clever remarks and intimate personal confessions you hear during the day. Perhaps you are losing your pals, your acquaintances, your balance.

You have broken up with your boyfriend. You now go out with men who, instead   35
of whispering "I love you," shout: "Do it to me, baby." This is good for your writing.

Sooner or later you have a finished manuscript more or less. People look at it in a vaguely troubled sort of way and say, "I'll bet becoming a writer was always a fantasy of yours, wasn't it?" Your lips dry to salt. Say that of all the fantasies possible in the world, you can't imagine being a writer even making the top twenty. Tell them you were going to be a child psychology major. "I bet," they always sigh, "you'd be great with kids." Scowl fiercely. Tell them you're a walking blade.

Quit classes. Quit jobs. Cash in old savings bonds. Now you have time like warts on your hands. Slowly copy all of your friends' addresses into a new address book.

Vacuum. Chew cough drops. Keep a folder full of fragments.

An eyelid darkening sideways.
World as conspiracy.
Possible plot? A woman gets on a bus.
Suppose you threw a love affair and nobody came.

At home drink a lot of coffee. At Howard Johnson's order the cole slaw. Consider how it looks like the soggy confetti of a map: where you've been, where you're going— "You Are Here," says the red star on the back of the menu.

Occasionally a date with a face blank as a sheet of paper asks you whether writers   40
often become discouraged. Say that sometimes they do and sometimes they do. Say it's a lot like having polio.

"Interesting," smiles your date, and then he looks down at his arm hairs and starts to smooth them, all, always, in the same direction.

QUESTIONS

1.   To whom does the "you" in the story refer? How strong a case may be made that the "you" refers really to "I," and that Francie is actually telling a story about herself?

2.   In light of the title, how adequate are Francie's "directions" for becoming a writer?

3.   Describe some of the comic elements of the story. What serious ideas about the development of a writer's profession undergird the story's humor?

WRITING ABOUT POINT OF VIEW

The purpose of this essay is to explain how point of view contributes to making the work exactly as it is. In prewriting, therefore, consider language, authority and opportunity for observation, the involvement or detachment of the speaker, the selection of detail, interpretive commentaries, and narrative development. The following questions will help you get started.

Questions for Discovering Ideas

- How is the narration made to seem real or probable? Are the actions and speeches reported authentically, as they might be seen and reported in life? Is the narrator identifiable? What are the narrator's qualifications as an observer? How much of the story seems to result from the imaginative or creative powers of the narrator?
- How does the narrator perceive the time of the actions? If the predominant tense is the past, what relationship, if any, does the speaker establish between the past and the present (e.g., providing explanations, making conclusions)? If the tense is present, what effect does this tense have on your understanding of the story?
- To what extent does the point of view make the work interesting and effective, or uninteresting and ineffective?

FIRST-PERSON POINT OF VIEW

- What situation prompts the speaker to tell the story or explain the situation? What is the speaker's background?
- Is the speaker talking to the reader, a listener, or herself? How does her audience affect what she is saying? Is the level of language appropriate to her and the situation? How much does she tell about herself?
- To what degree is the narrator involved in the action (i.e., as a major participant or major mover, minor participant, or nonparticipating observer)? Does he make himself the center of humor or admiration? How? Does he seem aware of changes he undergoes?
- Does the speaker criticize other characters? Why? Does she seem to report fairly and accurately what others have told her?
- How reliable is the speaker? Does the speaker seem to have anything to hide? Does it seem that he may be using the story for self-justification or exoneration? What effect does this complexity have on the story?

SECOND-PERSON POINT OF VIEW

- What situation prompts the use of the second person? How does the speaker acquire the authority to explain things to the listener? How directly involved is the listener? What is the relationship between the speaker and listener? If the listener is indefinite, why does the speaker choose to use "you" as the basis of the narration?

THIRD-PERSON POINT OF VIEW

- Does the author speak in an authorial voice, or has the author adopted a special but unnamed voice for the work?
- What is the speaker's level of language (i.e., formal and grammatical, informal or intimate and ungrammatical)? Are actions, speeches, and explanations made fully or sparsely?
- From what apparent vantage point does the speaker report action and speeches?

Does this vantage point make the characters seem distant or close? How much sympathy does the speaker express for the characters?

- To what degree is your interest centered on a particular character? Does the speaker give you thoughts and responses of this character (limited third person)?

- If the work is third-person omniscient, how extensive is this omniscience (e.g., all the characters or just a few)? Generally, what limitations or freedoms can be attributed to this point of view?

- What special kinds of knowledge does the narrator assume that the listeners or readers possess (e.g., art, religion, history, navigation, music)?

Strategies for Organizing Ideas

Throughout your essay, your object should be to develop your analysis of how the point of view determines such aspects as situation, form, general content, and language. The questions in the preceding section will help you decide how the point of view interacts with these other elements.

Begin by briefly stating the major influence of the point of view on the work. (*Examples:* "The omniscient point of view permits many insights into the major character," or "The first-person point of view permits the work to resemble an exposé of back-room political deals.") How does the point of view make the work interesting and effective? How will your analysis support your central idea or main argument?

An excellent way to build your argument is to explore how some other point of view might affect the work you are considering. Anderson's "I'm a Fool," for example, uses a first-person narrator—a young man telling about the greatest mistake in his life. You might consider whether this story could work with a third-person narration. A third-person limited narration would certainly state that the protagonist is self-critical and repentant. The first-person is superior, however, because we learn firsthand about the narrator's actual feelings. Indeed, the story seems totally dependent on the responses and thoughts of the first-person narrator. Conversely, Welty's "A Worn Path" (Chapter 3) largely employs the third-person limited point of view, from which we derive just enough information about the major character to understand and sympathize deeply with her plight. If Phoenix herself were the narrator, we would likely get not an objective but rather a sentimental view of her circumstances, and the story would not be as powerful as it is.

You can see that this approach requires creative imagination, for you must speculate about a point of view that is not present. Considering alternative points of view deeply, however, will greatly enhance your analytical and critical abilities.

In your conclusion, evaluate the success of the point of view: Is it consistent, effective, truthful? What does the writer gain or lose (if anything) by the selection of point of view?

DEMONSTRATIVE STUDENT ESSAY

Shirley Jackson's Dramatic Point of View in "The Lottery"°

[1] The dramatic point of view in Shirley Jackson's "The Lottery" is essential to her success in rendering horror in the midst of the ordinary.* The story, however, is not only one of horror: It may also be called a surprise story, an allegory, or a portrayal of human insensitivity and cruelty. But the validity of all other claims for "The Lottery" hinges on the author's control over point of view to make the events develop out of a seemingly everyday, matter-of-fact situation--a control that could not be easily maintained with another point of view. The success of Jackson's point of view is achieved through her characterization, selection of details, and diction.†

[2] Because of the dramatic point of view, Jackson succeeds in presenting the villagers as ordinary folks attending a normal, festive event--in contrast to the horror of their real purpose. The contrast depends on Jackson's speaker, who is emotionally uninvolved and who tells only enough about the three hundred townsfolk and their customs to permit the conclusion that they are normal, common people. The principal character is a local housewife, Tessie Hutchinson, but the speaker presents little about her except that she is just like everyone else--an important characteristic when she, like any person being singled out for punishment, objects not to the lottery itself but to the "unfairness" of the drawing. The same commonness applies also to the other characters, whose brief conversations are recorded but not analyzed. This detached, reportorial method of making the villagers seem common and one-dimensional is fundamental to Jackson's dramatic point of view, and the cruel twist of the ending depends on the method.

[3] While there could be much description, Jackson's speaker omits some of the important details to conceal the lottery's horrifying purpose. For example, the speaker presents enough information about the lottery to permit readers to understand its rules but does not disclose the grim prize for the "winner." The short saying "Lottery in June, corn be heavy soon" is mentioned as a remnant of a long-forgotten ritual, but the speaker does not explain anything more about this connection with scapegoatism and human sacrifice (paragraph 32). None of these references seems unusual as the narrator first presents them, and it is only the conclusion that reveals, in reconsideration, their shocking ghastliness.

[4] Without doubt, a point of view other than the dramatic would spoil Jackson's concluding horror because it would require more explanatory detail. A first-person speaker, for example, would not be credible without explaining the situation and revealing feelings that would give away the ending. Such an "I" speaker would need to say something like "The little boys gathered rocks but seemed not to be thinking about their forthcoming use in the stoning." But how would such detail affect the reader's response to the terrifying conclusion?

° See pp. 268–73 for this story.
* Central idea.
† Thesis sentence.

Similarly, an omniscient narrator would need to include details about people's reactions (how could he or she be omniscient otherwise?). A more suitable alternative might be a limited omniscient point of view confined to, say, a stranger in town or one of the local children. But any intelligent stranger would be asking "giveaway" questions, and any child but a tiny tot would know about the lottery's sinister outcome. Either hypothetical point-of-view character would therefore require revealing the information too soon. The only conclusion is that Jackson's point of view--the dramatic--is best for this story. Because it permits her naturally to hold back crucial details, it is essential for the suspenseful delay of horror.

Appropriate both to the suspenseful ending and also to the simple character of the villagers is the speaker's language. The words are accurate and descriptive but not elaborate. When Tessie Hutchinson appears, for example, she dries "her hands on her apron" (paragraph 8)--words that define her role as a housewife. Most of these simple, bare words may be seen as part of Jackson's technique of withholding detail to delay the reader's understanding. A prime example is the pile of stones, which is in truth a thoughtless and cruel preparation for the stoning, yet this conclusion cannot be drawn from the easy words describing it (paragraph 2):

[5]   Bobby Martin had already stuffed his pockets full of stones, and the other boys soon followed his example, selecting the smoothest and roundest stones; Bobby and Harry Jones and Dickie Delacroix--the villagers pronounced this name "Dellacroy"--eventually made a great pile of stones in one corner of the square and guarded it against the raids of the other boys.

Both the nicknames and the connotation of boyhood games divert attention and obscure the horrible purpose of the stones. Even at the end, the speaker uses the word "pebbles" to describe the stones given to Tessie's son Davy (paragraph 76). The implication is that Davy is playing a game, not participating in the ritual stoning of his own mother!

Such masterly control over point of view is a major cause of Jackson's success in "The Lottery." Her narrative method is to establish the appearance of everyday, uneventful reality, which she maintains up to the beginning of the last scene. She is so successful that a reader's first response to the stoning is, "Such an event could not take place among such common, earthy folks." Yet it is this

[6]   reality that validates Jackson's vision. Horror is not to be found on moors and in haunted castles but among everyday people like Jackson's three hundred villagers. Without her control of the dramatic point of view, there could be little of this power of suggestion, and it would not be possible to claim such success for the story.

Commentary on the Essay

The strategy of this essay is to argue for the importance of Jackson's dramatic point of view in building toward the shocking ending. Words of tribute throughout the essay are "success," "control," "essential," "appropriate," and "masterly." The introductory paragraph sets out three areas for exploration in the body: character, detail, and diction.

The body begins with paragraph 2, in which the aim is *not* to present a full character study (since the essay is not about character but point of view) but rather to discuss the ways in which the dramatic point of view *enables* the characters to be rendered. The argument of the paragraph is that the villagers are to be judged not as complete human beings but as "ordinary folks."

The second part of the body (paragraphs 3 and 4) emphasizes that the sparseness of detail permitted by the dramatic point of view aids Jackson in deferring conclusions about the horror of the drawing. Paragraph 4, which continues the topic of paragraph 3, shows how talking about alternative points of view may aid understanding of the story's actual point of view (see p. 280). The material for the paragraph is derived from notes speculating about whether Jackson's technique of withholding detail to build toward the concluding horror (the topic of paragraph 3) could be maintained with differing points of view. A combination of analysis and imagination is therefore at work in the paragraph.

The third section of the body (paragraph 5) emphasizes the idea that the flat, colorless diction defers awareness of what is happening; therefore the point of view is vital in the story's surprise and horror. The concluding paragraph emphasizes the way in which general response to the story is conditioned by the detached, dramatic point of view.

SPECIAL TOPICS FOR WRITING AND ARGUMENT ABOUT POINT OF VIEW

1. Write a short narrative from the point of view of one of these characters:
   a. Sheriff Peters in "A Jury of Her Peers" (Chapter 4): *Why are the women so concerned about that quilt?*
   b. Lucy Wessen in "I'm a Fool": *That young man seemed so nice. Why don't I see him any more?*
   c. Old Man Warner in "The Lottery": *People ain't the way they used to be.*
   d. Lengel in "A & P" (Chapter 7): *How could Sammy object to what I said to the girls?*
   e. Faith in "Young Goodman Brown" (Chapter 9): *I do not understand what has made my husband so sour and sullen all the time.*
   f. Charles in "Song of Songs": *Why is Barrett making such a fuss over going to see her mother?*

2. How would Hawthorne's story "Young Goodman Brown" (Chapter 9) be affected if told by a narrator with a different point of view (different knowledge, different interests, different purposes for telling the story), such as the narrators of Welty's "A Worn Path" (Chapter 3), Bierce's "An Occurrence at Owl Creek Bridge," and the second narrator of Mark Twain's "Luck" (Chapter 7)?

3. Recall a childhood occasion on which you were punished. Write an explanation of the punishment as though you were the adult who was in the position of punishing you. Be sure to consider your childhood self objectively, in the third person. Present things from the viewpoint of the adult, and try to determine how the adult would have learned about your action, judged it, and decided on your punishment.

4. Write an essay about the proposition that people often have something to gain when they speak and that therefore we need to be critical about what others tell us. Are they trying to change our judgments and opinions? Are they telling the truth? Are they leaving out any important details? Are they trying to sell us something? In your discussion you may strengthen your ideas by referring to stories that you have been reading.

5. In the reference section of your library, find two books on literary terms and concepts. How completely and clearly do these works explain the concept of point of view? With the aid of these books, together with the materials in this chapter, describe the interests and views of the narrators in Moore's "How to Become a Writer," Anderson's "I'm a Fool," or another story of your choice.

6
Setting:
The Background
of Place, Objects,
and Culture in Stories

Like all human beings, literary characters do not exist in isolation. Just as they become human by interacting with other characters, they gain identity because of their cultural and political allegiances, their possessions, their jobs, and where they live, and move, and have their being. Plays, stories, and narrative poems must therefore necessarily include descriptions of places, objects, and backgrounds—the **setting.**

WHAT IS SETTING?

Setting is the natural, manufactured, political, cultural, and temporal environment, including everything that characters know and own. Characters may be either helped or hurt by their surroundings, and they may fight about possessions and goals. Further, as characters speak with each other, they reveal the degree to which they share the customs and ideas of their times.

There Are Three Basic Types of Settings

NATURE AND THE OUTDOORS.   The natural world is an obvious location for the action of many narratives and plays. It is therefore important to note natural surroundings (hills, shorelines, valleys, mountains, meadows, fields, trees, lakes, streams), living creatures (birds, dogs, horses, snakes), and also the times, seasons, and conditions in which things happen (morning or night, summer or winter, sunlight or cloudiness, wind or calmness, rain or shine, sunlight or darkness, summer or winter, snowfall or blizzard, heat or cold)—any or all of which may influence character and action.

OBJECTS OF HUMAN MANUFACTURE AND CONSTRUCTION.   To reveal or highlight qualities of character, and also to make literature lifelike, authors include many

François Boucher, *Madame de Pompadour.* The Wallace Collection, London, England.

details about objects of human manufacture and construction. Houses, both interiors and exteriors, are common, as are possessions such as walking sticks, garden paths, park benches, toys, necklaces, or hair ribbons. In Maupassant's "The Necklace" (Chapter 1) the loss of a comfortable home brings out the best in a character by causing her to adjust to her economic reversal. The lugubrious vaults in Poe's "The Cask of Amontillado" (Chapter 11) reveal the similarly lugubrious and sinister nature of Poe's narrator.

Objects also enter directly into fictional action and character. The wearing of bathing suits within a supermarket is a cause of conflict in Updike's "A & P" (Chapter 7); a broken birdcage reveals the pathetic husband-wife relationship in Glaspell's "A Jury of Her Peers" (Chapter 4), and a bottle of medicine

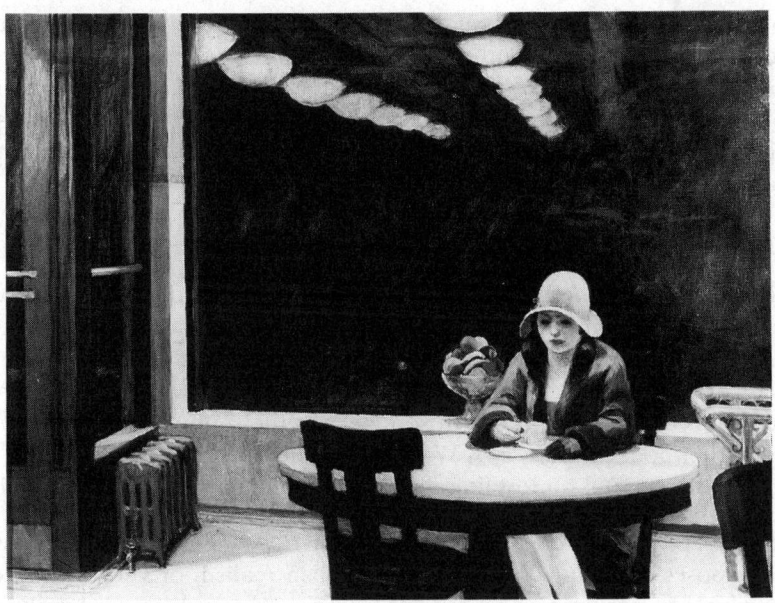

Edward Hopper, *Automat,* 1927. Des Moines Art Center, Permanent Collection, 1958.2.

represents the beauty of a character's love as well as the goal of her journey in Welty's "A Worn Path" (Chapter 3).

CULTURAL CONDITIONS AND ASSUMPTIONS.   Just as physical setting influences characters, so do historical and cultural conditions and assumptions. The broad cultural setting of Jackson's "The Lottery"(Chapter 5) is built on the persistence of a primitive belief in our modern and scientific age. The brutal oppressiveness and obscene prison-camp conditions in Ozick's "The Shawl" causes the major character to conceal a small child as the only way to keep that child alive. In Clark's "The Portable Phonograph" we see that an artistic and peaceful way of life breaks down when the culture on which it depends has been destroyed.

THE LITERARY USES OF SETTING

Authors use setting to create meaning, just as painters include backgrounds and objects to render ideas. The contrasting settings of François Boucher's portrait *Madame de Pompadour,* for example, and Edward Hopper's *Automat* demonstrate how the same subject—a single female figure—can show divergent views of human life, one elegant and pampered, the other ordinary and forlorn (pp. 286 and 287).

Writers manipulate literary locations in a comparable way. For example, in Welty's "A Worn Path" (Chapter 3) and Hawthorne's "Young Goodman Brown"

(Chapter 9) woodland paths that are difficult to trace and filled with obstacles are a major topographical feature. These are central to the time and circumstances of the stories, but they also convey the idea that life is difficult and uncertain. Similarly, in Glaspell's "A Jury of Her Peers" (Chapter 4) the fixtures and utensils in the kitchen of the Wright farm indicate that midwestern homesteads early in the twentieth century were bleak and oppressive.

The Setting of a Work Is Important in a Number of Ways

To study the setting in a narrative (or play), discover the important details and then try to explain their function. Depending on the author's purpose, the amount of detail may vary. Poe provides many graphic and also impressionistic details in "The Cask of Amontillado" so that we can follow, almost visually, the bizarre action at the story's end. In some works the setting is so intensely present, like the woods in Welty's "A Worn Path" and the Captain's cabin in "The Secret Sharer," that it is almost literally an additional participant in the action.

THE SETTING MAY HELP MAKE A WORK REALISTIC AND CREDIBLE.   One of the major purposes of literary setting is to establish **realism** or **verisimilitude.** As the description of location and objects becomes particular and detailed, the events of the work become more believable. Maupassant places "The Necklace" in real locations in late-nineteenth-century Paris, and for this reason the story has all the semblance of having actually happened. Even futuristic, symbolic, and fantastic stories, as well as ghost stories, seem more believable if they include places and objects from everyday experience. Hawthorne's "Young Goodman Brown" (Chapter 9) and Poe's "The Purloined Letter" (Chapter 11) are such stories. Although they make no pretenses at everyday realism, their credibility is enhanced because their settings are so realistic.

THE SETTING MAY BRING OUT QUALITIES OF CHARACTER.   Setting may intersect with character as a means by which authors underscore the influence of place, circumstance, and time on human growth and change. Glaspell's setting in "A Jury of Her Peers" (Chapter 4) is the kitchen of the lonely, dreary Wright farm. This kitchen is a place of such hard work, oppression, and unrelieved joylessness that it explains the extinguishing of Minnie's early brightness and promise and also helps us understand her angry act. (A blending of setting and character as seen in Maupassant's "The Necklace" is explored in the two drafts of the demonstrative student essay in Chapter 1).

The way characters respond and adjust to setting can reveal their strength or weakness. Peyton Farquhar's scheme to make an escape from his fate, even when it is almost literally hanging before him, suggests his character strength (Bierce's "An Occurrence at Owl Creek Bridge" [Chapter 5]). In contrast, Goodman Brown's Calvinistic religious conviction that human beings are totally depraved, which his nightmarish encounter confirms, indicates the weakness of his character because it alienates him from family and community (Hawthorne's "Young Goodman Brown" [Chapter 9]).

THE SETTING MAY BE AN ASPECT OF A STORY'S ORGANIZATION. Authors often use setting as one of the means of organizing their stories, as in Maupassant's "The Necklace," (Chapter 1), when Mathilde and her husband move from a respectable apartment to a cheap attic flat. The story's final scene is believable because Mathilde takes a nostalgic walk on the Champs-Elysées, the most fashionable street in Paris. Without this shift of setting, she could not have encountered Jeanne Forrestier again, for their usual ways of life would no longer bring them together.

Another organizational application of place, time, and object is the **framing** or **enclosing setting,** when an author opens with a particular description and then returns to the same setting at the end. An example is Welty's "A Worn Path," (Chapter 3), which begins with the major character walking toward Natchez and ends with her walking away from it. The framing use of passing time may be noted in Lessing's "The Old Chief Mshlanga" (Chapter 12), which opens and closes with references to "the years" and "about a year afterwards." In such ways, framing creates a formal completeness, just as it may underscore the author's ideas about the human condition.

SETTINGS MAY BE SYMBOLIC. If the scenes and materials of setting are highlighted or emphasized, they also may be taken as symbols through which the author expresses ideas. Such an emphasis is made in Ozick's "The Shawl," in which the shawl has the ordinary function of providing cover and warmth for the baby. Because it is so prominent, however, the shawl also suggests or symbolizes the attempt to preserve future generations, and because its loss also produces a human loss, it symbolizes the helplessness of the Nazi extermination camp victims during World War II. In Updike's "A & P" (Chapter 7), the reference to the local Congregational church symbolizes the decorum and restraint that the people of the town—including those shopping at the A & P—are expected to exercise.

THE SETTING MAY CREATE ATMOSPHERE AND MOOD. Most actions *require* no more than a functional description of setting. Thus, taking a walk in a forest needs just the statement that there are trees. However, if you find descriptions of shapes, light and shadows, animals, wind, and sounds, you may be sure that the author is creating an **atmosphere** or **mood** for the action (as in Hawthorne's "Young Goodman Brown" [Chapter 9]). There are many ways to develop moods. Descriptions of bright colors (red, orange, yellow) may contribute to a mood of happiness. Darkness and dark colors, like those in Poe's "The Cask of Amontillado" (Chapter 11) may invoke gloom or augment hysteria. References to smells and sounds further bring the setting to life by asking additional sensory responses from the reader. The setting of a story in a small town or large city, in green or snow-covered fields, or in middle- or lower-class residences may evoke responses to these places that contribute to the work's atmosphere.

THE SETTING MAY EMPHASIZE A STORY'S IRONY.   Just as setting may reinforce character and theme, so it may establish expectations that are the opposite of what occurs. At the beginning of "The Lottery" (Chapter 5), for example, Jackson describes the folksiness of the assembling townspeople—details that make the conclusion ironic, for it is just these real, everyday folks who participate in the final horror. A bizarre irony is created by Poe in "The Cask of Amontillado" (Chapter 11), when Montresor repeats Fortunato's appeal "For the love of God" as he puts in place the final bricks of Fortunato's living tomb. The ironic use of setting is by no means limited only to fiction, for it is often significant in both poems and plays. A particularly ironic situation, for example, is created by Thomas Hardy in the poem "Channel Firing" (Chapter 14) when the noise of large guns at sea wakens the skeletons buried in an English churchyard. The irony is that those engaged in the gunnery practice, if "red war" gets still redder, will soon join the skeletons.

STORIES FOR STUDY

SANDRA CISNEROS   (b. 1954)

Cisneros, a Mexican-American, was born in Illinois and now lives in Texas. She has been a "poet in the schools" in addition to teaching and also working as a college recruiter. She has held two NEA fellowships. Currently she serves a number of colleges as a visiting writer. The House on Mango Street, *which includes the story by the same name, was Cisneros's first book. Originally published in 1983, it was reissued in 1991, when her second book of stories,* Woman Hollering Creek *and Other* Stories, *was published. A recent book is a volume of poems,* Loose Woman: Poems, *which appeared in 1995.*

The House on Mango Street _____ *1983*

We didn't always live on Mango Street. Before that we lived on Loomis on the third floor, and before that we lived on Keeler. Before Keeler it was Paulina, and before that I can't remember. But what I remember most is moving a lot. Each time it seemed there'd be one more of us. By the time we got to Mango Street we were six—Mama, Papa, Carlos, Kiki, my sister Nenny and me.

The house on Mango Street is ours and we don't have to pay rent to anybody or share the yard with the people downstairs or be careful not to make too much noise and there isn't a landlord banging on the ceiling with a broom. But even so, it's not the house we'd thought we'd get.

We had to leave the flat on Loomis quick. The water pipes broke and the landlord wouldn't fix them because the house was too old. We had to leave fast. We were using the washroom next door and carrying water over in empty milk gallons. That's why Mama and Papa looked for a house, and that's why we moved into the house on Mango Street, far away, on the other side of town.

They always told us that one day we would move into a house, a real house that would be ours for always so we wouldn't have to move each year. And our house would have running water and pipes that worked. And inside it would have real stairs, not hallway stairs, but stairs inside like the houses on T.V. And we'd have a basement and at least three washrooms so when we took a bath we didn't have to tell everybody. Our house would be white with trees around it, a great big yard and grass growing without a fence. This was the house Papa talked about when he held a lottery ticket and this was the house Mama dreamed up in the stories she told us before we went to bed.

But the house on Mango Street is not the way they told it at all. It's small and 5
red with tight little steps in front and windows so small you'd think they were holding their breath. Bricks are crumbling in places, and the front door is so swollen you have to push hard to get in. There is no front yard, only four little elms the city planted by the curb. Out back is a small garage for the car we don't own yet and a small yard that looks smaller between the two buildings on either side. There are stairs in our house, but they're ordinary hallway stairs, and the house has only one washroom, very small. Everybody has to share a bedroom—Mama and Papa, Carlos and Kiki, me and Nenny.

Once when we were living on Loomis, a nun from my school passed by and saw me playing out front. The laundromat downstairs had been boarded up because it had been robbed two days before and the owner had painted on the wood YES WE'RE OPEN so as not to lose business.

Where do you live? she asked.

There, I said pointing up to the third floor.

You live *there*?

There. I had to look to where she pointed—the third floor, the paint peeling, 10
wooden bars Papa had nailed on the windows so we wouldn't fall out. You live *there*? The way she said it made me feel like nothing. *There*. I lived *there*. I nodded.

I knew then I had to have a house. A real house. One I could point to. But this isn't it. The house on Mango Street isn't it. For the time being, Mama says. Temporary, says Papa. But I know how those things go.

QUESTIONS

1. Why is the speaker concerned with the nature of the houses she has lived in? What feeling does she show about these houses?

2. Describe the house on Mango Street. How does the condition of this house and the other houses explain the economic circumstances of the speaker's family?

3. What is the speaker like as a character? How do you learn about her? How much do you learn?

WALTER VAN TILBURG CLARK   (1909–1971)

Clark was born in Maine, but he spent most of his life as a professor of English in the western United States. His best-known novel, The Ox-Bow Incident *(1940), which was popularized as a movie, deals with fairness and justice on the Nevada frontier. His other major novel was* The City of Trembling Leaves *(1945), a haunting story of initiation about a young man whose ambition it is to be a composer. "The Portable Phonograph" appeared in 1942, early in World War II, when American forces were being regularly defeated by the Japanese armies and navies in the South Pacific, and two years before the Allies invaded France. The atomic bomb was not known at this time, and hence the desolation envisioned in the story is the result of the "conventional" weaponry of bombs and tanks. Clark's stories were collected in* The Watchful Gods *(1950).*

In the middle of World War II.

The Portable Phonograph ———————————————————— 1942

The red sunset, with narrow, black cloud strips like threats across it, lay on the curved horizon of the prairie. The air was still and cold, and in it settled the mute darkness and greater cold of night. High in the air there was wind, for through the veil of the dusk the clouds could be seen gliding rapidly south and changing shapes. A sensation of torment, of two-sided, unpredictable nature, arose from the stillness of the earth air beneath the violence of the upper air. Out of the sunset, through the dead, matted grass and isolated weed stalks of the prairie, crept the narrow and deeply rutted remains of a road. In the road, in places, there were crusts of shallow, brittle ice. There were little islands of an old oiled pavement in the road too, but most of it was mud, now frozen rigid. The frozen mud still bore the toothed impress of great tanks, and a wanderer on the neighboring undulations might have stumbled, in this light, into large, partially filled-in and weed-grown cavities, their banks channeled and beginning to spread into badlands. These pits were such as might have been made by falling meteors, but they were not. They were the scars of gigantic bombs, their rawness already made a little natural by rain, seed and time. Along the road there were rakish remnants of fence. There was also, just visible, one portion of tangled and multiple barbed wire still erect, behind which was a shelving ditch with small caves, now very quiet and empty, at intervals in its back wall. Otherwise there was no structure or remnant of a structure visible over the dome of the darkling earth, but only, in sheltered hollows, the darker shadows of young trees trying again.

Under the wuthering arch of the high wind a V of wild geese fled south. The rush of their pinions sounded briefly, and the faint, plaintive notes of their expeditionary talk. Then they left a still greater vacancy. There was the smell and expectation of snow, as there is likely to be when the wild geese fly south. From the remote distance, toward the red sky, came faintly the protracted howl and quick yap-yap of a prairie wolf.

North of the road, perhaps a hundred yards, lay the parallel and deeply intrenched course of a small creek, lined with leafless alders and willows. The creek was already silent under ice. Into the bank above it was dug a sort of cell, with a single opening, like the mouth of a mine tunnel. Within the cell there was a little red of fire, which showed dully through the opening, like a reflection or a deception of the imagination. The light came from the chary burning of four blocks of poorly aged peat, which gave off a petty warmth and much acrid smoke. But the precious remnants of wood, old fence posts and timbers from the long-deserted dugouts, had to be saved for the real cold, for the time when a man's breath blew white, the moisture in his nostrils stiffened at once when he stepped out, and the expansive blizzards paraded for days over the vast open, swirling and settling and thickening, till the dawn of the cleared day when the sky was a thin blue-green and the terrible cold, in which a man could not live for three hours unwarmed, lay over the uniformly drifted swell of the plain.

Around the smoldering peat four men were seated cross-legged. Behind them, traversed by their shadows, was the earth bench, with two old and dirty army blankets, where the owner of the cell slept. In a niche in the opposite wall were a few tin utensils which caught the glint of the coals. The host was rewrapping in a piece of daubed burlap, four fine, leather-bound books. He worked slowly and very carefully, and at last tied the bundle securely with a piece of grass-woven cord. The other three looked intently upon the process, as if a great significance lay in it. As the host tied the cord, he spoke. He was an old man, his long, matted beard and hair gray to nearly white. The shadows made his brows and cheekbones appear gnarled, his eyes and cheeks deeply sunken. His big hands, rough with frost and swollen by rheumatism, were awkward but gentle at their task. He was like a prehistoric priest performing a fateful ceremonial rite. Also his voice had in it a suitable quality of deep, reverent despair, yet perhaps, at the moment, a sharpness of selfish satisfaction.

"When I perceived what was happening," he said, "I told myself, 'It is the end. I cannot take much; I will take these.'"   5

"Perhaps I was impractical," he continued. "But for myself, I do not regret, and what do we know of those who will come after us? We are the doddering remnant of a race of mechanical fools. I have saved what I love; the soul of what was good in us here; perhaps the new ones will make a strong enough beginning not to fall behind when they become clever."

He rose with slow pain and placed the wrapped volumes in the niche with his utensils. The others watched him with the same ritualistic gaze.

"Shakespeare, the Bible, *Moby Dick*,° *The Divine Comedy*,"° one of them said softly. "You might have done worse; much worse."

"You will have a little soul left until you die," said another harshly. "That is more than is true of us. My brain becomes thick, like my hands." He held the big, battered hands, with their black nails, in the glow to be seen.

"I want paper to write on," he said. "And there is none."   10

The fourth man said nothing. He sat in the shadow farthest from the fire, and sometimes his body jerked in its rags from the cold. Although he was still young, he was sick, and coughed often. Writing implied a greater future than he now felt able to consider.

The old man seated himself laboriously, and reached out, groaning at the movement, to put another block of peat on the fire. With bowed heads and averted eyes, his three guests acknowledged his magnanimity.

"We thank you, Doctor Jenkins, for the reading," said the man who had named the books.

They seemed then to be waiting for something. Doctor Jenkins understood, but was loath to comply. In an ordinary moment he would have said nothing. But the words of *The Tempest*,° which he had been reading, and the religious attention of the three, made this an unusual occasion.

Moby Dick: by Herman Melville (1819–1891), a classic American novel published in 1851.
The Divine Comedy: by Dante (1265–1321), regarded as the supreme poem of the Italian Renaissance, circulated about 1300.
The Tempest: Shakespeare's last play, first performed about 1611.

"You wish to hear the phonograph,"° he said grudgingly.   15

The two middle-aged men stared into the fire, unable to formulate and expose the enormity of their desire.

The young man, however, said anxiously, between suppressed coughs, "Oh, please," like an excited child.

The old man rose again in his difficult way, and went to the back of the cell. He returned and placed tenderly upon the packed floor, where the firelight might fall upon it, an old, portable phonograph in a black case. He smoothed the top with his hand, then opened it. The lovely green-felt-covered disk became visible.

"I have been using thorns as needles," he said. "But tonight, because we have a musician among us"—he bent his head to the young man, almost invisible in the shadow—"I will use a steel needle. There are only three left."

The two middle-aged men stared at him in speechless adoration. The one with   20
the big hands, who wanted to write, moved his lips, but the whisper was not audible.

"Oh, don't," cried the young man, as if he were hurt. "The thorns will do beautifully."

"No," the old man said. "I have become accustomed to the thorns—but they are not really good. For you, my young friend, we will have good music tonight.

"After all," he added generously, and beginning to wind the phonograph, which creaked, "they can't last forever."

"No, nor we," the man who needed to write said harshly. "The needle, by all means."

"Oh, thanks," said the young man. "Thanks," he said again, in a low, excited voice,   25
and then stifled his coughing with a bowed head.

"The records, though," said the old man when he had finished winding, "are a different matter. Already they are very worn. I do not play them more than once a week. One, once a week, that is what I allow myself.

"More than a week I cannot stand it; not to hear them," he apologized.

"No, how could you?" cried the young man. "And with them here like this."

"A man can stand anything," said the man who wanted to write, in his harsh, antagonistic voice.

"Please, the music," said the young man.   30

"Only the one," said the old man. "In the long run we will remember more that way."

He had a dozen records with luxuriant gold and red seals. Even in that light the others could see that the threads of the records were becoming worn. Slowly he read out the titles, and the tremendous, dead names of the composers and the artists and the orchestras. The three worked upon the names in their minds, carefully. It was difficult to select from such a wealth what they would at once most like to remember. Finally the man who wanted to write named Gershwin's "New York."°

---

phonograph: Early phonographs, in use before electrically driven record players, had to be wound up by hand. They played records at a speed of 78 revolutions per minute and used steel needles that had to be changed very often. The phonograph is especially valuable to the characters in this story because they have no electricity.

George Gershwin (1898–1937): American composer who wrote in jazz idiom, not in the classical manner.

"Oh, no," cried the sick young man, and then could say nothing more because he had to cough. The others understood him, and the harsh man withdrew his selection and waited for the musician to choose.

The musician begged Doctor Jenkins to read the titles again, very slowly, so that he could remember the sounds. While they were read, he lay back against the wall, his eyes closed, his thin, horny hand pulling at his light beard, and listened to the voices and the orchestras and the single instruments in his mind.

When the reading was done he spoke despairingly. "I have forgotten," he complained. "I cannot hear them clearly. 35

"There are things missing," he explained.

"I know," said Doctor Jenkins. "I thought that I knew all of Shelley° by heart. I should have brought Shelley."

"That's more soul than we can use," said the harsh man. "*Moby Dick* is better."

"By God, we can understand that," he emphasized.

The doctor nodded. 40

"Still," said the man who had admired the books, "we need the absolute if we are to keep a grasp on anything.

"Anything but these sticks and peat clods and rabbit snares," he said bitterly.

"Shelley desired an ultimate absolute," said the harsh man. "It's too much," he said. "It's no good; no earthly good."

The musician selected a Debussy° nocturne. The others considered and approved. They rose to their knees to watch the doctor prepare for the playing, so that they appeared to be actually in an attitude of worship. The peat glow showed the thinness of their bearded faces, and the deep lines in them, and revealed the condition of their garments. The other two continued to kneel as the old man carefully lowered the needle onto the spinning disk, but the musician suddenly drew back against the wall again, with his knees up, and buried his face in his hands.

At the first notes of the piano the listeners were startled. They stared at each other. 45 Even the musician lifted his head in amazement, but then quickly bowed it again, strainingly, as if he were suffering from a pain he might not be able to endure. They were all listening deeply, without movement. The wet, blue-green notes tinkled forth from the old machine, and were individual, delectable presences in the cell. The individual, delectable presences swept into a sudden tide of unbearably beautiful dissonance, and then continued fully the swelling and ebbing of that tide, the dissonant inpourings, and the resolutions, and the diminishments, and the little, quiet wavelets of interlude lapping between. Every sound was piercing and singularly sweet. In all the men except the musician, there occurred rapid sequences of tragically heightened recollection. He heard nothing but what was there. At the final, whispering disappearance, but moving quietly, so that the others would not hear him and look at him, he let his head fall back in agony, as if it were drawn there by the hair, and clenched the fingers of one hand over his teeth. He sat that way while the others were silent, and until they began to breathe again normally. His drawn-up legs were trembling violently.

Percy Bysshe Shelley (1792–1822): English poet who wrote poems about the soul, intellectual beauty, and mutability.

Claude Debussy (1862–1918): French composer. His *Nocturnes* for piano was first published in 1890.

Quickly Doctor Jenkins lifted the needle off, to save it, and not to spoil the recollection with scraping. When he had stopped the whirling of the sacred disk, he courteously left the phonograph open and by the fire, in sight.

The others, however, understood. The musician rose last, but then abruptly, and went quickly out at the door without saying anything. The others stopped at the door and gave their thanks in low voices. The doctor nodded magnificently.

"Come again," he invited, "in a week. We will have the 'New York.'"

When the two had gone together, out toward the rimmed road, he stood in the entrance, peering and listening. At first there was only the resonant boom of the wind overhead, and then, far over the dome of the dead, dark plain, the wolf cry lamenting. In the rifts of clouds the doctor saw four stars flying. It impressed the doctor that one of them had just been obscured by the beginning of a flying cloud at the very moment he heard what he had been listening for, a sound of suppressed coughing. It was not near by, however. He believed that down against the pale alders he could see the moving shadow.

With nervous hands he lowered the piece of canvas which served as his door, and   50
pegged it at the bottom. Then quickly and quietly, looking at the piece of canvas frequently, he slipped the records into the case, snapped the lid shut, and carried the phonograph to his couch. There, pausing often to stare at the canvas and listen, he dug earth from the wall and disclosed a piece of board. Behind this there was a deep hole in the wall, into which he put the phonograph. After a moment's consideration, he went over and reached down his bundle of books and inserted it also. Then, guardedly, he once more sealed up the hole with the board and the earth. He also changed his blankets, and the grass-stuffed sack which served as a pillow, so that he could lie facing the entrance. After carefully placing two more blocks of peat on the fire, he stood for a long time watching the stretched canvas, but it seemed to billow naturally with the first gusts of a lowering wind. At last he prayed, and got in under his blankets, and closed his smoke-smarting eyes. On the inside of the bed, next to the wall, he could feel with his hand, the comfortable piece of lead pipe.

QUESTIONS

1. What kind of environment is described in the first three paragraphs of this story? What has happened before the story opens? To what extent do these paragraphs establish the tone and atmosphere of the story?

2. The first three descriptive paragraphs are loaded with adjectives. In the first, for example, we find *narrow, black, still, cold, mute, dead, isolated, shallow, brittle, old, frozen, tangled, quiet,* and *empty*. What do most of these adjectives contribute to the establishment of setting and, in turn, mood?

3. How is "the host's" home described? What do the details tell us about the host, humanity, and existence in the world of the story?

4. What record do the men choose to hear? What do the phonograph and the music represent to these men?

5. What does Dr. Jenkins do with his things after the men leave? How does he readjust his bed? Why does he do these things?

JOSEPH CONRAD   (1857–1924)

Conrad (Jósef Teodor Konrad Korzeniowski), whose parents were Polish, was born in Ukraine. He did not start learning English until he shipped aboard English sailing vessels. He ultimately became an English ship's captain. He always spoke English with a Polish accent, but his command of written English, as readers of "The Secret Sharer" will quickly discover, was masterly. He always maintained that he might never have become a writer if he had not been able to write in English. In 1895 he left the sea to take up his entirely new career in his adopted language, having published his first novel, Almayer's Folly. *From this time until his death twenty-nine years later, he regularly produced novels as well as personal reminiscences and observations on "life and letters." His best-known novels are* Lord Jim *(1900) and* Nostromo *(1904). His best-known tale, or lengthy short story, is* Heart of Darkness *(1902). His work has come to great attention in recent years because of the movie* Apocalypse Now *(1979), directed by Francis Ford Coppola, which is an adaptation of* Heart of Darkness *as the details of the story may be applied to American participation in the war in Vietnam.*

The Secret Sharer _____ *1912*

1

On my right hand there were lines of fishing stakes resembling a mysterious system of half-submerged bamboo fences, incomprehensible in its division of the domain of tropical fishes, and crazy of aspect as if abandoned forever by some nomad tribe of fishermen now gone to the other end of the ocean; for there was no sign of human habitation as far as the eye could reach. To the left a group of barren islets, suggesting ruins of stone walls, towers, and block-houses, had its foundations set in a blue sea that itself looked solid, so still and stable did it lie below my feet; even the track of light from the westering sun shone smoothly, without that animated glitter which tells of an imperceptible ripple. And when I turned my head to take a parting glance at the tug which had just left us anchored outside the bar, I saw the straight line of the flat shore joined to the stable sea, edge to edge, with a perfect and unmarked closeness, in one leveled floor half brown, half blue under the enormous dome of the sky. Corresponding in their insignificance to the islets of the sea, two small clumps of trees, one on each side of the only fault in the impeccable joint, marked the mouth of the river Meinam° we had just left on the first preparatory stage of our homeward journey; and, far back on the inland level, a larger and loftier mass, the grove surrounding the great Paknam pagoda, was the only thing on which the eye could rest from the vain task of exploring the monotonous sweep of the horizon. Here and there gleams as of a few scattered pieces of silver marked the windings of the great river; and on the nearest of them, just within the bar, the tug steaming right into the land became lost to my

Meinam: The locations Conrad describes in the story are all real, although many have been renamed since his time. The river Meinam, or Mae Nam, is the Chao Phraya River, which empties into the Gulf of Siam (now the Gulf of Thailand), where the story's action begins. The "great Paknam" Pagoda is the Phra Samut Chedi Pagoda. The location of the ship at the story's end is near the island Kaôh Rüng (Koh-ring), near Cambodia (Cambodje), many miles to the southeast of where the story begins (see paragraphs 202, 248).

sight, hull and funnel and masts, as though the impassive earth had swallowed her up without an effort, without a tremor. My eye followed the light cloud of her smoke, now here, now there, above the plain, according to the devious curves of the stream, but always fainter and farther away, till I lost it at last behind the miter-shaped hill of the great pagoda. And then I was left alone with my ship, anchored at the head of the Gulf of Siam.

She floated at the starting point of a long journey, very still in an immense still-ness, the shadows of her spars flung far to the eastward by the setting sun. At that moment I was alone on her decks. There was not a sound in her—and around us noth-ing moved, nothing lived, not a canoe on the water, not a bird in the air, not a cloud in the sky. In this breathless pause at the threshold of a long passage we seemed to be mea-suring our fitness for a long and arduous enterprise, the appointed task of both our exis-tences to be carried out, far from all human eyes, with only sky and sea for spectators and for judges.

There must have been some glare in the air to interfere with one's sight, because it was only just before the sun left us that my roaming eyes made out beyond the highest ridge of the principal islet of the group something which did away with the solemnity of perfect solitude. The tide of darkness flowed on swiftly; and with tropical suddenness a swarm of stars came out above the shadowy earth, while I lingered yet, my hand resting lightly on my ship's rail as if on the shoulder of a trusted friend. But, with all that multi-tude of celestial bodies staring down at one, the comfort of quiet communion with her was gone for good. And there were also disturbing sounds by this time—voices, foot-steps forward; the steward flitted along the main deck, a busily ministering spirit; a hand bell tinkled urgently under the poop deck. . . .

I found my two officers waiting for me near the supper table, in the lighted cuddy.° We sat down at once, and as I helped the chief mate, I said:

"Are you aware that there is a ship anchored inside the islands? I saw her mast-   5
heads above the ridge as the sun went down."

He raised sharply his simple face, overcharged by a terrible growth of whisker, and emitted his usual ejaculations: "Bless my soul, sir! You don't say so!"

My second mate was a sound-cheeked, silent young man, grave beyond his years, I thought; but as our eyes happened to meet I detected a slight quiver on his lips. I looked down at once. It was not my part to encourage sneering on board my ship. It must be said, too, that I knew very little of my officers. In consequence of certain events of no particular significance, except to myself, I had been appointed to the command only a fortnight before. Neither did I know much of the hands forward. All these people had been together for eighteen months or so, and my position was that of the only stranger on board. I mention this because it has some bearing on what is to follow. But what I felt most was my being a stranger to the ship; and if truth must be told, I was somewhat of a stranger to myself. The youngest man on board (barring the second mate), and untried as yet by a position of the fullest responsibility, I was willing to take the adequacy of the others for granted. They had simply to be equal to their tasks: but I wondered how far I should turn out faithful to that ideal conception of one's own personality every man sets up for himself secretly.

Meantime the chief mate, with an almost visible effect of collaboration on the part of his round eyes and frightful whiskers, was trying to evolve a theory of the anchored

---

cuddy: a small mess hall next to the ship's kitchen.

ship. His dominant trait was to take all things into earnest consideration. He was of a painstaking turn of mind. As he used to say, he "liked to account to himself" for practically everything that came in his way, down to a miserable scorpion he had found in his cabin a week before. The why and the wherefore of that scorpion—how it got on board and came to select his room rather than the pantry (which was a dark place and more what a scorpion would be partial to), and how on earth it managed to drown itself in the inkwell of his writing desk—had exercised him infinitely. The ship within the islands was much more easily accounted for; and just as we were about to rise from the table he made his pronouncement. She was, he doubted not, a ship from home lately arrived. Probably she drew too much water to cross the bar except at the top of spring tides. Therefore she went into the natural harbor to wait for a few days in preference to remaining in an open roadstead.

"That's so," confirmed the second mate, suddenly, in his slightly hoarse voice. "She draws over twenty feet. She's the Liverpool ship *Sephora* with a cargo of coal. Hundred and twenty-three days from Cardiff."

We looked at him in surprise.   10

"The tugboat skipper told me when he came on board for your letters, sir," explained the young man. "He expects to take her up the river the day after tomorrow."

After thus overwhelming us with the extent of his information he slipped out of the cabin. The mate observed regretfully that he "could not account for that young fellow's whims." What prevented him telling us all about it at once, he wanted to know.

I detained him as he was making a move. For the last two days the crew had had plenty of hard work, and the night before they had very little sleep. I felt painfully that I—a stranger—was doing something unusual when I directed him to let all hands turn in without setting an anchor watch. I proposed to keep on deck myself till one o'clock or thereabouts. I would get the second mate to relieve me at that hour.

"He will turn out the cook and the steward at four," I concluded, "and then give you a call. Of course at the lightest sign of any sort of wind we'll have the hands up and make a start at once."

He concealed his astonishment. "Very well, sir." Outside the cuddy he put his head   15
in the second mate's door to inform him of my unheard-of caprice to take a five hours' anchor watch on myself. I heard the other raise his voice incredulously:

"What? The captain himself?" Then a few more murmurs, a door closed, then another. A few moments later I went on deck.

My strangeness, which had made me sleepless, had prompted that unconventional arrangement, as if I had expected in those solitary hours of the night to get on terms with the ship of which I knew nothing, manned by men of whom I knew very little more. Fast alongside a wharf, littered like any ship in port with a tangle of unrelated things, invaded by unrelated shore people, I had hardly seen her yet properly. Now, as she lay cleared for sea, the stretch of her main deck seemed to me very fine under the stars. Very fine, very roomy for her size, and very inviting. I descended the poop and paced the waist, my mind picturing to myself the coming passage through the Malay Archipelago, down the Indian Ocean, and up the Atlantic. All its phases were familiar enough to me, every characteristic, all the alternatives which were likely to face me on the high seas—everything! . . . except the novel responsibility of command. But I took heart from the reasonable thought that the ship was like other ships, the men like other men, and that the sea was not likely to keep any special surprises expressly for my discomfiture.

Arrived at that comforting conclusion, I bethought myself of a cigar and went below to get it. All was still down there. Everybody at the after end of the ship was sleeping profoundly. I came out again on the quarter-deck, agreeably at ease in my sleeping suit on that warm breathless night, barefooted, a glowing cigar in my teeth, and, going forward, I was met by the profound silence of the fore end of the ship. Only as I passed the door of the forecastle I heard a deep, quiet, trustful sigh of some sleeper inside. And suddenly I rejoiced in the great security of the sea as compared with the unrest of the land, in my choice of that untempted life presenting no disquieting problems, invested with an elementary moral beauty by the absolute straightforwardness of its appeal and by the singleness of its purpose.

The riding light in the fore-rigging burned with a clear, untroubled, as if symbolic, flame, confident and bright in the mysterious shades of the night. Passing on my way aft along the other side of the ship, I observed that the rope side ladder, put over, no doubt, for the master of the tug when he came to fetch away our letters, had not been hauled in as it should have been. I became annoyed at this, for exactitude in small matters is the very soul of discipline. Then I reflected that I had myself peremptorily dismissed my officers from duty, and by my own act had prevented the anchor watch being formally set and things properly attended to. I asked myself whether it was wise ever to interfere with the established routine of duties even from the kindest of motives. My action might have made me appear eccentric. Goodness only knew how that absurdly whiskered mate would "account" for my conduct, and what the whole ship thought of that informality of their new captain. I was vexed with myself.

Not from compunction certainly, but, as it were mechanically, I proceeded to get   20
the ladder in myself. Now a side ladder of that sort is a light affair and comes in easily, yet my vigorous tug, which should have brought it flying on board, merely recoiled upon my body in a totally unexpected jerk. What the devil! . . . I was so astounded by the immovableness of that ladder that I remained stock-still, trying to account for it to myself like that imbecile mate of mine. In the end, of course, I put my head over the rail.

The side of the ship made an opaque belt of shadow on the darkling glassy shimmer of the sea. But I saw at once something elongated and pale floating very close to the ladder. Before I could form a guess a faint flash of phosphorescent light, which seemed to issue suddenly from the naked body of a man, flickered in the sleeping water with the elusive, silent play of summer lightning in a night sky. With a gasp I saw revealed to my stare a pair of feet, the long legs, a broad livid back immersed right up to the neck in a greenish cadaverous glow. One hand, awash, clutched the bottom rung of the ladder. He was complete but for the head. A headless corpse! The cigar dropped out of my gaping mouth with a tiny plop and a short hiss quite audible in the absolute stillness of all things under heaven. At that I suppose he raised up his face, a dimly pale oval in the shadow of the ship's side. But even then I could only barely make out down there the shape of his black-haired head. However, it was enough for the horrid, frostbound sensation which had gripped me about the chest to pass off. The moment of vain exclamations was past, too. I only climbed on the spare spar and leaned over the rail as far as I could, to bring my eyes nearer to that mystery floating alongside.

As he hung by the ladder, like a resting swimmer, the sea lightning played about his limbs at every stir; and he appeared in it ghastly, silvery, fishlike. He remained as mute as a fish, too. He made no motion to get out of the water, either. It was inconceivable that he should not attempt to come on board, and strangely troubling to suspect that perhaps he did not want to. And my first words were prompted by just that troubled incertitude.

"What's the matter?" I asked in my ordinary tone, speaking down to the face upturned exactly under mine.

"Cramp," it answered, no louder. Then slightly anxious, "I say, no need to call anyone."

"I was not going to," I said.   25

"Are you alone on deck?"

"Yes."

I had somehow the impression that he was on the point of letting go the ladder to swim away beyond my ken—mysterious as he came. But, for the moment, this being appearing as if he had risen from the bottom of the sea (it was certainly the nearest land to the ship) wanted only to know the time. I told him. And he, down there, tentatively:

"I suppose your captain's turned in?"

"I am sure he isn't," I said.   30

He seemed to struggle with himself, for I heard something like the low, bitter murmur of doubt. "What's the good?" His next words came out with a hesitating effort.

"Look here, my man. Could you call him out quietly?"

I thought the time had come to declare myself.

"*I* am the captain."

I heard a "By Jove!" whispered at the level of the water. The phosphorescence   35
flashed in the swirl of the water all about his limbs, his other hand seized the ladder.

"My name's Leggatt."

The voice was calm and resolute. A good voice. The self-possession of that man had somehow induced a corresponding state in myself. It was very quietly that I remarked:

"You must be a good swimmer."

"Yes. I've been in the water practically since nine o'clock. The question for me now is whether I am to let go this ladder and go on swimming till I sink from exhaustion, or—to come on board here."

I felt this was no mere formula of desperate speech, but a real alternative in the   40
view of a strong soul. I should have gathered from this that he was young; indeed, it is only the young who are ever confronted by such clear issues. But at this time it was pure intuition on my part. A mysterious communication was established already between us two—in the face of that silent darkened tropical sea. I was young, too; young enough to make no comment. The man in the water began suddenly to climb up the ladder, and I hastened away from the rail to fetch some clothes.

Before entering the cabin I stood still, listening in the lobby at the foot of the stairs. A faint snore came through the closed door of the chief mate's room. The second mate's door was on the hook, but the darkness in there was absolutely soundless. He, too, was young and could sleep like a stone. Remained the steward, but he was not likely to wake up before he was called. I got a sleeping suit out of my room and, coming back on deck, saw the naked man from the sea sitting on the main hatch, glimmering white in the darkness, his elbows on his knees and his head in his hands. In a moment he had concealed his damp body in a sleeping suit of the same gray-stripe pattern as the one I was wearing and followed me like my double on the poop. Together we moved right aft, barefooted, silent.

"What is it?" I asked in a deadened voice, taking the lighted lamp out of the binnacle, and raising it to his face.

"An ugly business."

He had rather regular features; a good mouth; light eyes under somewhat heavy, dark eyebrows; a smooth, square forehead; no growth on his cheeks; a small, brown mustache, and a well-shaped, round chin. His expression was concentrated, meditative, under the inspecting light of the lamp I held up to his face; such as a man thinking hard in solitude might wear. My sleeping suit was just right for his size. A well-knit young fellow of twenty-five at most. He caught his lower lip with the edge of white, even teeth.

"Yes," I said, replacing the lamp in the binnacle. The warm, heavy tropical night   45
closed upon his head again.

"There's a ship over there," he murmured.

"Yes, I know. The *Sephora*. Did you know of us?"

"Hadn't the slightest idea. I am the mate of her—" He paused and corrected himself. "I should say I was."

"Aha! Something wrong?"

"Yes. Very wrong indeed. I've killed a man."   50

"What do you mean? Just now?"

"No, on the passage. Weeks ago. Thirty-nine south. When I say a man—"

"Fit of temper," I suggested, confidently.

The shadowy, dark head, like mine, seemed to nod imperceptibly above the ghostly gray of my sleeping suit. It was, in the night, as though I had been faced by my own reflection in the depths of a somber and immense mirror.

"A pretty thing to have to own up for a Conway boy,"° murmured my double,   55
distinctly.

"You're a Conway boy?"

"I am," he said, as if startled. Then, slowly . . . "Perhaps you too—"

It was so; but being a couple of years older I had left before he joined. After a quick interchange of dates a silence fell; and I thought suddenly of my absurd mate with his terrific whiskers and the "Bless my soul—you don't say so" type of intellect. My double gave me an inkling of his thoughts by saying:

"My father's a parson in Norfolk. Do you see me before a judge and jury on that charge? For myself I can't see the necessity. There are fellows that an angel from heaven—And I am not that. He was one of those creatures that are just simmering all the time with a silly sort of wickedness. Miserable devils that have no business to live at all. He wouldn't do his duty and wouldn't let anybody else do theirs. But what's the good of talking! You know well enough the sort of ill-conditioned snarling cur—"

He appealed to me as if our experiences had been as identical as our clothes. And   60
I knew well enough the pestiferous danger of such a character where there are no means of legal repression. And I knew well enough also that my double there was no homicidal ruffian. I did not think of asking him for details, and he told me the story roughly in brusque, disconnected sentences. I needed no more. I saw it all going on as though I were myself inside that other sleeping suit.

"It happened while we were setting a reefed foresail, at dusk. Reefed foresail! You understand the sort of weather. The only sail we had left to keep the ship running; so you may guess what it had been like for days. Anxious sort of job, that. He gave me some of his cursed insolence at the sheet. I tell you I was overdone with this terrific weather that seemed to have no end to it. Terrific, I tell you—and a deep ship. I believe the fellow himself was half crazed with funk. It was no time for gentlemanly reproof, so I turned round and felled him like an ox. He up and at me. We closed just as an awful sea

Conway boy: a graduate of the Conway Merchant Marine Academy at Conway, in north Wales.

made for the ship: All hands saw it coming and took to the rigging, but I had him by the throat, and went on shaking him like a rat, the men above us yelling, 'Look out! look out!' Then a crash as if the sky had fallen on my head. They say that for over ten minutes hardly anything was to be seen of the ship—just the three masts and a bit of the forecastle head and of the poop all awash driving along in a smother of foam. It was a miracle that they found us, jammed together behind the forebits. It's clear that I meant business, because I was holding him by the throat still when they picked us up. He was black in the face. It was too much for them. It seems they rushed us aft together, gripped as we were, screaming 'Murder!' like a lot of lunatics, and broke into the cuddy. And the ship running for her life, touch and go all the time, any minute her last in a sea fit to turn your hair gray only a-looking at it. I understand that the skipper, too, started raving like the rest of them. The man had been deprived of sleep for more than a week, and to have this sprung on him at the height of a furious gale nearly drove him out of his mind. I wonder they didn't fling me overboard after getting the carcass of their precious ship-mate out of my fingers. They had rather a job to separate us, I've been told. A suffi-ciently fierce story to make an old judge and a respectable jury sit up a bit. The first thing I heard when I came to myself was the maddening howling of that endless gale, and on that the voice of the old man. He was hanging on to my bunk, staring into my face out of his sou'wester.

"'Mr. Leggatt, you have killed a man. You can act no longer as chief mate of this ship.'"

His care to subdue his voice made it sound monotonous. He rested a hand on the end of the skylight to steady himself with, and all that time did not stir a limb, so far as I could see. "Nice little tale for a quiet tea party," he concluded in the same tone.

One of my hands, too, rested on the end of the skylight; neither did I stir a limb, so far as I knew. We stood less than a foot from each other. It occurred to me that if old "Bless my soul—you don't say so" were to put his head up the companion and catch sight of us, he would think he was seeing double, or imagine himself come upon a scene of weird witchcraft; the strange captain having a quiet confabulation by the wheel with his own gray ghost. I became very much concerned to prevent anything of the sort. I heard the other's soothing undertone.

"My father's a parson in Norfolk," it said. Evidently he had forgotten he had told   65
me this important fact before. Truly a nice little tale.

"You had better slip down into my stateroom now," I said, moving off stealthily. My double followed my movements; our bare feet made no sound; I let him in, closed the door with care, and, after giving a call to the second mate, returned on deck for my relief.

"Not much sign of any wind yet," I remarked when he approached.

"No, sir. Not much," he assented, sleepily, in his hoarse voice, with just enough deference, no more, and barely suppressing a yawn.

"Well, that's all you have to look out for. You have got your orders."

"Yes, sir."   70

I paced a turn or two on the poop and saw him take up his position face forward with his elbow in the rat-lines of the mizzen-rigging before I went below. The mate's faint snoring was still going on peacefully. The cuddy lamp was burning over the table on which stood a vase with flowers, a polite attention from the ships' provision merchant— the last flowers we should see for the next three months at the very least. Two bunches of bananas hung from the beam symmetrically, one on each side of the rudder casing. Everything was as before in the ship—except that two of her captain's sleeping suits were simultaneously in use, one motionless in the cuddy, the other keeping very still in the captain's stateroom.

It must be explained here that my cabin had the form of the capital letter L, the door being within the angle and opening into the short part of the letter. A couch was to the left, the bed-place to the right; my writing desk and the chronometers table faced the door. But anyone opening it, unless he stepped right inside, had no view of what I call the long (or vertical) part of the letter. It contained some lockers surmounted by a book-case; and a few clothes, a thick jacket or two, caps, oilskin coat, and such like, hung on hooks. There was at the bottom of that part a door opening into my bathroom, which could be entered also directly from the saloon. But that way was never used.

The mysterious arrival had discovered the advantage of this particular shape. Entering my room, lighted strongly by a big bulkhead lamp swung on gimbals above my writing desk, I did not see him anywhere till he stepped out quietly from behind the coats hung in the recessed part.

"I heard somebody moving about, and went in there at once," he whispered.

I, too, spoke under my breath.   75

"Nobody is likely to come in here without knocking and getting permission."

He nodded. His face was thin and the sunburn faded, as though he had been ill. And no wonder. He had been, I heard presently, kept under arrest in his cabin for nearly seven weeks. But there was nothing sickly in his eyes or in his expression. He was not a bit like me, really; yet, as we stood leaning over my bed-place, whispering side by side, with our dark heads together and our backs to the door, anybody bold enough to open it stealthily would have been treated to the uncanny sight of a double captain busy talk-ing in whispers with his other self.

"But all this doesn't tell me how you came to hang on to our side ladder," I inquired, in the hardly audible murmurs we used, after he had told me something more of the proceedings on board the *Sephora* once the bad weather was over.

"When we sighted Java Head I had had time to think all those matters out several times over. I had six weeks of doing nothing else, and with only an hour or so every evening for a tramp on the quarter-deck."

He whispered, his arms folded on the side of my bed-place, staring through the   80
open port. And I could imagine perfectly the manner of this thinking out—a stubborn if not a steadfast operation; something of which I should have been perfectly incapable.

"I reckoned it would be dark before we closed with the land," he continued, so low that I had to strain my hearing, near as we were to each other, shoulder touching shoulder almost. "So I asked to speak to the old man. He always seemed very sick when he came to see me—as if he could not look me in the face. You know, that foresail saved the ship. She was too deep to have run long under bare poles. And it was I that managed to set it for him. Anyway, he came. When I had him in my cabin—he stood by the door looking at me as if I had the halter around my neck already—I asked him right away to leave my cabin door unlocked at night while the ship was going through Sunda Straits. There would be the Java coast within two or three miles, off Angier Point. I wanted nothing more. I've had a prize for swimming my second year in the Conway."

"I can believe it," I breathed out.

"God only knows why they locked me in every night. To see some of their faces you'd have thought they were afraid I'd go about at night strangling people. Am I a murdering brute? Do I look it? By Jove! if I had been he wouldn't have trusted himself like that into my room. You'll say I might have chucked him aside and bolted out, there and then—it was dark already. Well, no. And for the same reason I wouldn't think of trying to smash the door. There would have been a rush to stop me at the noise, and I did not mean to get into a confounded scrimmage. Somebody else might have got killed—for I would not have broken out only to get chucked back, and I did not want any more of that work. He refused, looking more sick than ever. He was afraid of the men, and also of that old second mate of his who had been sailing with him for years—a gray-headed old humbug; and his steward, too, had been with him devil knows how long—seventeen years or more—a dogmatic sort of loafer who hated me like poison, just because I was the chief mate. No chief mate ever made more than one voyage in the *Sephora,* you know. Those two old chaps ran the ship. Devil only knows what the skipper wasn't afraid of (all his nerve went to pieces altogether in that hellish spell of bad weather we had)—of what the law would do to him—of his wife, perhaps. Oh, yes! she's on board. Though I don't think she would have meddled. She would have been only too glad to have me out of the ship in any way. The 'brand of Cain' business, don't you see. That's all right. I was ready enough to go off wandering on the face of the earth—and that was price enough to pay for an Abel of that sort. Anyhow, he wouldn't listen to me. 'This thing must take its course. I represent the law here.' He was shaking like a leaf. 'So you won't?' 'No!' 'Then I hope you will be able to sleep on that,' I said, and turned my back on him. 'I wonder that you can,' cries he, and locks the door.

"Well, after that, I couldn't. Not very well. That was three weeks ago. We have had a slow passage through the Java Sea; drifted about Carimata for ten days. When we anchored here they thought, I suppose, it was all right. The nearest land (and that's five miles) is the ship's destination; the consul would soon set about catching me; and there would have been no object in bolting to these islets there. I don't suppose there's a drop of water on them. I don't know how it was, but tonight that steward, after bringing me my supper, went out to let me eat it, and left the door unlocked. And I ate it—all there was, too. After I had finished I strolled out on the quarter-deck. I don't know that I meant to do anything. A breath of fresh air was all I wanted, I believe. Then a sudden temptation came over me. I kicked off my slippers and was in the water before I had made up my mind fairly. Somebody heard the splash and they raised an awful hullabaloo. 'He's gone! Lower the boats! He's committed suicide! No, he's swimming.' Certainly I was swimming. It's not so easy for a swimmer like me to commit suicide by drowning. I landed on the nearest islet before the boat left the ship's side. I heard them pulling about in the dark, hailing, and so on, but after a bit they gave up. Everything quieted down and the anchorage became as still as death. I sat down on a stone and began to think. I felt certain they would start searching for me at daylight. There was no place to hide on those stony things—and if there had been, what would have been the good? But now I was clear of that ship, I was not going back. So after a while I took off my clothes, tied them up in a bundle with a stone inside, and dropped them in the deep water on the outer side of the islet. That was suicide enough for me. Let them think what they liked, but I didn't mean to drown myself. I meant to swim till I sank—but that's not the same thing. I struck out for another of these little islands, and it was from that one that I first saw your riding light. Something to swim for. I went on easily, and on the way I came upon a flat rock a foot or two above water. In the daytime, I dare say, you might make it out with a glass from your poop. I scrambled up on it and rested myself for a bit. Then I made another start. That last spell must have been over a mile."

His whisper was getting fainter and fainter, and all the time he stared straight out through the porthole, in which there was not even a star to be seen. I had not interrupted him. There was something that made comment impossible in his narrative, or perhaps in himself; a sort of feeling, a quality, which I can't find a name for. And when he ceased, all I found was a futile whisper. "So you swam for our light?"

"Yes—straight for it. It was something to swim for. I couldn't see any stars low down because the coast was in the way, and I couldn't see the land, either. The water was like glass. One might have been swimming in a confounded thousand feet deep cistern with no place for scrambling out anywhere; but what I didn't like was the notion of swimming round and round like a crazed bullock before I gave out; and as I didn't mean to go back . . . No. Do you see me being hauled back, stark naked, off one of these little islands by the scruff of the neck and fighting like a wild beast? Somebody would have got killed for certain, and I did not want any of that. So I went on. Then your ladder—"

"Why didn't you hail the ship?" I asked, a little louder.

He touched my shoulder lightly. Lazy footsteps came right over our heads and stopped. The second mate had crossed from the other side of the poop and might have been hanging over the rail, for all we knew.

"He couldn't hear us talking—could he?" My double breathed into my very ear, anxiously.

His anxiety was an answer, a sufficient answer, to the question I had put to him. An answer containing all the difficulty of that situation. I closed the porthole quietly, to make sure. A louder word might have been overheard.   90

"Who's that?" he whispered then.

"My second mate. But I don't know much more of the fellow than you do."

And I told him a little about myself. I had been appointed to take charge while I least expected anything of the sort, not quite a fortnight ago. I didn't know either the ship or the people. Hadn't had the time in port to look about me or size anybody up. And as to the crew, all they knew was that I was appointed to take the ship home. For the rest, I was almost as much of a stranger on board as himself, I said. And at the moment I felt it most acutely. I felt that it would take very little to make me a suspect person in the eyes of the ship's company.

He had turned about meantime; and we, the two strangers in the ship, faced each other in identical attitudes.

"Your ladder—" he murmured, after a silence. "Who'd have thought of finding a   95
ladder hanging over at night in a ship anchored out here! I felt just then a very unpleasant faintness. After the life I've been leading for nine weeks, anybody would have got out of condition. I wasn't capable of swimming round as far as your rudder chains. And, lo and behold! there was a ladder to get hold of. After I gripped it I said to myself, 'What's the good?' When I saw a man's head looking over I thought I would swim away presently and leave him shouting—in whatever language it was. I didn't mind being looked at. I—I liked it. And then you speaking to me so quietly—as if you had expected me—made me hold on a little longer. It had been a confounded lonely time—I don't mean while swimming. I was glad to talk a little to somebody that didn't belong to the *Sephora*. As to asking for the captain, that was a mere impulse. It could have been no use, with all the ship knowing about me and the other people pretty certain to be round here in the morning. I don't know—I wanted to be seen, to talk with somebody, before I went on. I don't know what I would have said . . . 'Fine night, isn't it?' or something of the sort."

"Do you think they will be round here presently?" I asked with some incredulity.

"Quite likely," he said, faintly.

He looked extremely haggard all of a sudden. His head rolled on his shoulders.

"H'm. We shall see then. Meantime get into that bed," I whispered. "Want help? There."

It was a rather high bed-place with a set of drawers underneath. This amazing swimmer really needed the lift I gave him by seizing his leg. He tumbled in, rolled over on his back, and flung one arm across his eyes. And then, with his face nearly hidden, he must have looked exactly as I used to look in that bed. I gazed upon my other self for a while before drawing across carefully the two green serge curtains which ran on a brass rod. I thought for a moment of pinning them together for greater safety, but I sat down on the couch, and once there I felt unwilling to rise and hunt for a pin. I would do it in a moment. I was extremely tired, in a peculiarly intimate way, by the strain of stealthiness, by the effort of whispering and the general secrecy of this excitement. It was three o'clock by now and I had been on my feet since nine, but I was not sleepy; I could not have gone to sleep. I sat there, fagged out, looking at the curtains, trying to clear my mind of the confused sensation of being in two places at once, and greatly bothered by an exasperating knocking in my head. It was a relief to discover suddenly that it was not in my head at all, but on the outside of the door. Before I could collect myself the words "Come in" were out of my mouth, and the steward entered with a tray, bringing in my morning coffee. I had slept, after all, and I was so frightened that I shouted, "This way! I am here, steward," as though he had been miles away. He put down the tray on the table next the couch and only then said, very quietly, "I can see you are here, sir." I felt him give me a keen look, but I dared not meet his eyes just then. He must have wondered why I had drawn the curtains of my bed before going to sleep on the couch. He went out, hooking the door open as usual.

I heard the crew washing decks above me. I knew I would have been told at once if there had been any wind. Calm, I thought, and I was doubly vexed. Indeed, I felt dual more than ever. The steward reappeared suddenly in the doorway. I jumped up from the couch so quickly that he gave a start.

"What do you want here?"

"Close your port, sir—they are washing decks."

"It is closed," I said, reddening.

"Very well, sir." But he did not move from the doorway and returned my stare in an extraordinary, equivocal manner for a time. Then his eyes wavered, all his expression changed, and in a voice unusually gentle, almost coaxingly:

"May I come in to take the empty cup away, sir?"

"Of course!" I turned my back on him while he popped in and out. Then I unhooked and closed the door and even pushed the bolt. This sort of thing could not go on very long. The cabin was as hot as an oven, too. I took a peep at my double, and discovered that he had not moved, his arm was still over his eyes; but his chest heaved; his hair was wet; his chin glistened with perspiration. I reached over him and opened the port.

"I must show myself on deck," I reflected.

Of course, theoretically, I could do what I liked, with no one to say nay to me within the whole circle of the horizon; but to lock my cabin door and take the key away I did not dare. Directly I put my head out of the companion I saw the group of my two officers, the second mate barefooted, the chief mate in long india-rubber boots, near the break of the poop, and the steward halfway down the poop ladder talking to them eagerly. He happened to catch sight of me and dived, the second ran down on the main deck shouting some order or other, and the chief mate came to meet me, touching his cap.

There was a sort of curiosity in his eye that I did not like. I don't know whether the   110
steward had told them that I was "queer" only, or downright drunk, but I know the man
meant to have a good look at me. I watched him coming with a smile which, as he got
into point-blank range, took effect and froze his very whiskers. I did not give him time to
open his lips.

"Square the yards by lifts and braces before the hands go to breakfast."

It was the first particular order I had given on board that ship; and I stayed on
deck to see it executed, too. I had felt the need of asserting myself without loss of time.
That sneering young cub got taken down a peg or two on that occasion, and I also
seized the opportunity of having a good look at the face of every foremast man as they
filed past me to go to the after braces. At breakfast time, eating nothing myself, I
presided with such frigid dignity that the two mates were only too glad to escape from
the cabin as soon as decency permitted; and all the time the dual working of my mind
distracted me almost to the point of insanity. I was constantly watching myself, my secret
self, as dependent on my actions as my own personality, sleeping in that bed, behind
that door which faced me as I sat at the head of the table. It was very much like being
mad, only it was worse because one was aware of it.

I had to shake him for a solid minute, but when at last he opened his eyes it was in
the full possession of his senses, with an inquiring look.

"All's well so far," I whispered. "Now you must vanish into the bathroom."

He did so, as noiseless as a ghost, and I then rang for the steward, and facing him   115
boldly, directed him to tidy up my stateroom while I was having my bath—"and be quick
about it." As my tone admitted of no excuses, he said, "Yes, sir," and ran off to fetch his
dustpan and brushes. I took a bath and did most of my dressing, splashing, and whistling
softly for the steward's edification, while the secret sharer of my life stood drawn up bolt
upright in that little space, his face looking very sunken in daylight, his eyelids lowered
under the stern, dark line of his eyebrows drawn together by a slight frown.

When I left him there to go back to my room the steward was finished dusting. I
sent for the mate and engaged him in some insignificant conversation. It was, as it were,
trifling with the terrific character of whiskers; but my object was to give him an opportunity for a good look at my cabin. And then I could at last shut, with a clear conscience,
the door of my stateroom and get my double back into the recessed part. There was
nothing else for it. He had to sit still on a small folding stool, half smothered by the
heavy coats hanging there. We listened to the steward going into the bathroom out of
the saloon, filling the water bottles there, scrubbing the bath, setting things to rights,
whisk, bang, clatter—out again into the saloon—turn the key—click. Such was my
scheme for keeping my second self invisible. Nothing better could be contrived under
the circumstances. And there we sat; I at my writing desk ready to appear busy with some
papers, he behind me, out of sight of the door. It would not have been prudent to talk in
daytime; and I could not have stood the excitement of that queer sense of whispering to
myself. Now and then, glancing over my shoulder, I saw him far back there, sitting rigidly
on the low stool, his bare feet close together, his arms folded, his head hanging on his
breast—and perfectly still. Anybody would have taken him for me.

I was fascinated by it myself. Every moment I had to glance over my shoulder. I was
looking at him when a voice outside the door said:

"Beg pardon, sir."

"Well!" . . . I kept my eyes on him, and so, when the voice outside the door
announced, "There's a ship's boat coming our way, sir," I saw him give a start—the first
movement he had made for hours. But he did not raise his bowed head.

"All right. Get the ladder over."

I hesitated. Should I whisper something to him? But what? His immobility seemed to have been never disturbed. What could I tell him he did not know already? . . . Finally I went on deck.

2

The skipper of the *Sephora* had a thin red whisker all round his face, and the sort of complexion that goes with hair of that color; also the particular, rather smeary shade of blue in the eyes. He was not exactly a showy figure; his shoulders were high, his stature but middling—one leg slightly more bandy than the other. He shook hands, looking vaguely around. A spiritless tenacity was his main characteristic, I judged. I behaved with a politeness which seemed to disconcert him. Perhaps he was shy. He mumbled to me as if he were ashamed of what he was saying; gave his name (it was something like Archbold—but at this distance of years I hardly am sure), his ship's name, and a few other particulars of that sort, in the manner of a criminal making a reluctant and doleful confession. He had had terrible weather on the passage out—terrible—terrible—wife aboard, too.

By this time we were seated in the cabin and the steward brought in a tray with a bottle and glasses. "Thanks! No." Never took liquor. Would have some water, though. He drank two tumblerfuls. Terrible thirsty work. Ever since daylight had been exploring the islands round his ship.

"What was that for—fun?" I asked, with an appearance of polite interest.

"No!" He sighed. "Painful duty."

As he persisted in his mumbling and I wanted my double to hear every word, I hit upon the notion of informing him that I regretted to say I was hard of hearing.

"Such a young man, too!" he nodded, keeping his smeary blue, unintelligent eyes fastened upon me. What was the cause of it—some disease? he inquired, without the least sympathy and as if he thought that, if so, I'd got no more than I deserved.

"Yes; disease," I admitted in a cheerful tone which seemed to shock him. But my point was gained, because he had to raise his voice to give me his tale. It is not worth while to record that version. It was just over two months since all this had happened, and he had thought so much about it that he seemed completely muddled as to its bearings, but still immensely impressed.

"What would you think of such a thing happening on board your own ship? I've had the *Sephora* for these fifteen years. I am a well-known shipmaster."

He was densely distressed—and perhaps I should have sympathized with him if I had been able to detach my mental vision from the unsuspected sharer of my cabin as though he were my second self. There he was on the other side of the bulkhead, four or five feet from us, no more, as we sat in the saloon. I looked politely at Captain Archbold (if that was his name), but it was the other I saw, in a gray sleeping suit, seated on a low stool, his bare feet close together, his arms folded, and every word said between us falling into the ears of his dark head bowed on his chest.

"I have been at sea now, man and boy, for seven-and-thirty years, and I've never heard of such a thing happening in an English ship. And that it should be my ship. Wife on board, too."

I was hardly listening to him.

"Don't you think," I said, "that the heavy sea which, you told me, came aboard just then might have killed the man? I have seen the sheer weight of a sea kill a man very neatly, by simply breaking his neck."

"Good God!" he uttered, impressively, fixing his smeary blue eyes on me. "The sea! No man killed by the sea ever looked like that." He seemed positively scandalized at my suggestion. And as I gazed at him, certainly not prepared for anything original on his part, he advanced his head close to mine and thrust his tongue out at me so suddenly that I couldn't help starting back.

After scoring over my calmness in this graphic way he nodded wisely. If I had seen the sight, he assured me, I would never forget it as long as I lived. The weather was too bad to give the corpse a proper sea burial. So next day at dawn they took it up on the poop, covering its face with a bit of bunting; he read a short prayer, and then, just as it was, in its oilskins and long boots, they launched it amongst those mountainous seas that seemed ready every moment to swallow up the ship herself and the terrified lives on board of her.

"That reefed foresail saved you," I threw in.

"Under God—it did," he exclaimed fervently. "It was by a special mercy, I firmly believe, that it stood some of those hurricane squalls."

"It was the setting of that sail which—" I began.

"God's own hand in it," he interrupted me. "Nothing less could have done it. I don't mind telling you that I hardly dared give the order. It seemed impossible that we could touch anything without losing it, and then our last hope would have been gone."

The terror of that gale was on him yet. I let him go on for a bit, then said, casually—as if returning to a minor subject:

"You were very anxious to give up your mate to the shore people, I believe?"

He was. To the law. His obscure tenacity on that point had in it something incomprehensible and a little awful; something, as it were, mystical, quite apart from his anxiety that he should not be suspected of "countenancing any doings of that sort." Seven-and-thirty virtuous years at sea, of which over twenty of immaculate command, and the last fifteen in the *Sephora,* seemed to have laid him under some pitiless obligation.

"And you know," he went on, groping shamefacedly amongst his feelings, "I did not engage that young fellow. His people had some interest with my owners. I was in a way forced to take him on. He looked very smart, very gentlemanly, and all that. But do you know—I never liked him, somehow. I am a plain man. You see, he wasn't exactly the sort for the chief mate of a ship like the *Sephora.*"

I had become so connected in thoughts and impressions with the secret sharer of my cabin that I felt as if I, personally, were being given to understand that I, too, was not the sort that would have done for the chief mate of a ship like the *Sephora.* I had no doubt of it in my mind.

"Not at all the style of man. You understand," he insisted, superfluously, looking hard at me.

I smiled urbanely. He seemed at a loss for a while.

"I suppose I must report a suicide."

"Beg pardon?"

"Sui-cide! That's what I'll have to write to my owners directly I get in."

"Unless you manage to recover him before tomorrow," I assented, dispassionately. . . . "I mean, alive."

He mumbled something which I really did not catch, and I turned my ear to him in a puzzled manner. He fairly bawled:

"The land—I say, the mainland is at least seven miles off my anchorage."

135

140

145

150

"About that."

My lack of excitement, of curiosity, of surprise, of any sort of pronounced interest, began to arouse his distrust. But except for the felicitous pretense of deafness I had not tried to pretend anything. I had felt utterly incapable of playing the part of ignorance properly, and therefore was afraid to try. It is also certain that he had brought some ready-made suspicions with him, and that he viewed my politeness as a strange and unnatural phenomenon. And yet how else could I have received him? Not heartily! That was impossible for psychological reasons, which I need not state here. My only object was to keep off his inquiries. Surlily? Yes, but surliness might have provoked a point-blank question. From its novelty to him and from its nature, punctilious courtesy was the manner best calculated to restrain the man. But there was the danger of his breaking through my defense bluntly. I could not, I think, have met him by a direct lie, also for psychological (not moral) reasons. If he had only known how afraid I was of his putting my feeling of identity with the other to the test! But, strangely enough—(I thought of it only afterward)—I believe that he was not a little disconcerted by the reverse side of that weird situation, by something in me that reminded him of the man he was seeking—suggested a mysterious similitude to the young fellow he had distrusted and disliked from the first.

However that might have been, the silence was not very prolonged. He took 155
another oblique step.

"I reckon I had no more than a two-mile pull to your ship. Not a bit more."

"And quite enough, too, in this awful heat," I said.

Another pause full of mistrust followed. Necessity, they say, is mother of invention, but fear, too, is not barren of ingenious suggestions. And I was afraid he would ask me point-blank for news of my other self.

"Nice little saloon, isn't it?" I remarked, as if noticing for the first time the way his eyes roamed from one closed door to the other. "And very well fitted out, too. Here, for instance," I continued reaching over the back of my seat negligently and flinging the door open, "is my bathroom."

He made an eager movement, but hardly gave it a glance. I got up, shut the door 160
of the bathroom, and invited him to have a look round, as if I were very proud of my accommodation. He had to rise and be shown round, but he went through the business without any raptures whatever.

"And now we'll have a look at my stateroom," I declared, in a voice as loud as I dared to make it, crossing the cabin to the starboard side with purposely heavy steps.

He followed me in and gazed around. My intelligent double had vanished. I played my part.

"Very convenient—isn't it?"

"Very nice. Very comf . . ." He didn't finish, and went out brusquely as if to escape from some unrighteous wiles of mine. But it was not to be. I had been too frightened not to feel vengeful; I felt I had him on the run, and I meant to keep him on the run. My polite insistence must have had something menacing in it, because he gave in suddenly. And I did not let him off a single item; mate's room, pantry, storerooms, the very sail locker which was also under the poop—he had to look into them all. When at last I showed him out on the quarter-deck he drew a long, spiritless sigh, and mumbled dismally that he must really be going back to his ship now. I desired my mate, who had joined us, to see to the captain's boat.

The man of whiskers gave a blast on the whistle which he used to wear hanging 165
round his neck, and yelled, "*Sephora* away!" My double down there in my cabin must have heard, and certainly could not feel more relieved than I. Four fellows came

running out from somewhere forward and went over the side, while my own men, appearing on deck too, lined the rail. I escorted my visitor to the gangway ceremoniously, and nearly overdid it. He was a tenacious beast. On the very ladder he lingered, and in that unique, guiltily conscientious manner of sticking to the point:

"I say . . . you . . . you don't think that—"

I covered his voice loudly:

"Certainly not. . . . I am delighted. Good-by."

I had an idea of what he meant to say, and just saved myself by the privilege of defective hearing. He was too shaken generally to insist, but my mate, close witness of that parting, looked mystified and his face took on a thoughtful cast. As I did not want to appear as if I wished to avoid all communication with my officers, he had the opportunity to address me.

"Seems a very nice man. His boat's crew told our chaps a very extraordinary story,   170
if what I am told by the steward is true. I suppose you had it from the captain, sir?"

"Yes. I had a story from the captain."

"A very horrible affair—isn't it, sir?"

"It is."

"Beats all these tales we hear about murders in Yankee ships."

"I don't think it beats them. I don't think it resembles them in the least."   175

"Bless my soul—you don't say so! But of course I've no acquaintance whatever with American ships, not I, so I couldn't go against your knowledge. It's horrible enough for me. . . . But the queerest part is that these fellows seemed to have some idea the man was hidden aboard here. They had really. Did you ever hear of such a thing?"

"Preposterous—isn't it?"

We were walking to and fro athwart the quarter-deck. No one of the crew forward could be seen (the day was Sunday), and the mate pursued:

"There was some little dispute about it. Our chaps took offense. 'As if we would harbor a thing like that,' they said. 'Wouldn't you like to look for him in our coal hole?' Quite a tiff. But they made it up in the end. I suppose he did drown himself. Don't you, sir?"

"I don't suppose anything."   180

"You have no doubt in the matter, sir?"

"None whatever."

I left him suddenly. I felt I was producing a bad impression, but with my double down there it was most trying to be on deck. And it was almost as trying to be below. Altogether a nerve-trying situation. But on the whole I felt less torn in two when I was with him. There was no one in the whole ship whom I dared take into my confidence. Since the hands had got to know his story, it would have been impossible to pass him off for anyone else, and an accidental discovery was to be dreaded now more than ever. . . .

The steward being engaged in laying the table for dinner, we could talk only with our eyes when I first went down. Later in the afternoon we had a cautious try at whispering. The Sunday quietness of the ship was against us; the stillness of air and water around her was against us; the elements, the men were against us—everything was against us in our secret partnership; time itself—for this could not go on forever. The very trust in Providence was, I suppose, denied to his guilt. Shall I confess that this thought cast me down very much? And as to the chapter of accidents which counts for so much in the book of success, I could only hope that it was closed. For what favorable accident could be expected?

"Did you hear everything?" were my first words as soon as we took up our position side by side, leaning over my bed-place.   185

He had. And the proof of it was his earnest whisper, "The man told you he hardly dared to give the order."

I understood the reference to be to that saving foresail.

"Yes. He was afraid of it being lost in the setting."

"I assure you he never gave the order. He may think he did, but he never gave it. He stood there with me on the break of the poop after the maintopsail blew away, and whimpered about our last hope—positively whimpered about it and nothing else— and the night coming on! To hear one's skipper go on like that in such weather was enough to drive any fellow out of his mind. It worked me up into a sort of desperation. I just took it into my hands and went away from him, boiling, and—But what's the use telling you? *You* know! . . . Do you think that if I had not been pretty fierce with them I should have got the men to do anything? Not it! The bosun perhaps? Perhaps! It wasn't a heavy sea—it was a sea gone mad! I suppose the end of the world will be something like that; and a man may have the heart to see it coming once and be done with it—but to have to face it day after day—I don't blame anybody. I was precious little better than the rest. Only—I was an officer of that old coal-wagon, anyhow—"

"I quite understand," I conveyed that sincere assurance into his ear. He was out of   190
breath with whispering; I could hear him pant slightly. It was all very simple. The same strung-up force which had given twenty-four men a chance, at least, for their lives, had, in a sort of recoil, crushed an unworthy mutinous existence.

But I had no leisure to weigh the merits of the matter—footsteps in the saloon, a heavy knock. "There's enough wind to get under way with, sir." Here was the call of a new claim upon my thoughts and even upon my feelings.

"Turn the hands up," I cried through the door. "I'll be on deck directly."

I was going out to make the acquaintance of my ship. Before I left the cabin our eyes met—the eyes of the only two strangers on board. I pointed to the recessed part where the little campstool awaited him and laid my finger on my lips. He made a gesture—somewhat vague—a little mysterious, accompanied by a faint smile, as if of regret.

This is not the place to enlarge upon the sensations of a man who feels for the first time a ship move under his feet to his own independent word. In my case they were not unalloyed. I was not wholly alone with my command; for there was that stranger in my cabin. Or rather, I was not completely and wholly with her. Part of me was absent. That mental feeling of being in two places at once affected me physically as if the mood of secrecy had penetrated my very soul. Before an hour had elapsed since the ship had begun to move, having occasion to ask the mate (he stood by my side) to take a compass bearing of the Pagoda, I caught myself reaching up to his ear in whispers. I say I caught myself, but enough had escaped to startle the man. I can't describe it otherwise than by saying that he shied. A grave, preoccupied manner, as though he were in possession of some perplexing intelligence, did not leave him henceforth. A little later I moved away from the rail to look at the compass with such a stealthy gait that the helmsman noticed it—and I could not help noticing the unusual roundness of his eyes. These are trifling instances, though it's to no commander's advantage to be suspected of ludicrous eccentricities. But I was also more seriously affected. There are to a seaman certain words, gestures, that should in given conditions come as naturally, as instinctively as the winking of a menaced eye. A certain order should spring on to his lips without thinking; a certain sign should get itself made, so to speak, without reflection. But all unconscious alertness had abandoned me. I had to make an effort of will to recall myself back (from the cabin) to the conditions of the moment. I felt that I was appearing an irresolute commander to those people who were watching me more or less critically.

And, besides, there were the scares. On the second day out, for instance, coming off the deck in the afternoon (I had straw slippers on my bare feet) I stopped at the open pantry door and spoke to the steward. He was doing something there with his back to me. At the sound of my voice he nearly jumped out of his skin, as the saying is, and incidentally broke a cup.   195

"What on earth's the matter with you?" I asked, astonished.

He was extremely confused. "Beg your pardon, sir. I made sure you were in your cabin."

"You see I wasn't."

"No, sir. I could have sworn I had heard you moving in there not a moment ago. It's most extraordinary . . . , very sorry, sir."

I passed on with an inward shudder. I was so identified with my secret double that I did not even mention the fact in those scanty, fearful whispers we exchanged. I suppose he had made some slight noise of some kind or other. It would have been miraculous if he hadn't at one time or another. And yet, haggard as he appeared, he looked always perfectly self-controlled, more than calm—almost invulnerable. On my suggestion he remained almost entirely in the bathroom, which, upon the whole, was the safest place. There could be really no shadow of an excuse for anyone ever wanting to go in there, once the steward had done with it. It was a very tiny place. Sometimes he reclined on the floor, his legs bent, his head sustained on one elbow. At others I would find him on the campstool, sitting in his gray sleeping suit and with his cropped dark hair like a patient, unmoved convict. At night I would smuggle him into my bed-place, and we would whisper together, with the regular footfalls of the officer of the watch passing and repassing over our heads. It was an infinitely miserable time. It was lucky that some tins of fine preserves were stowed in a locker in my stateroom; hard bread I could always get hold of; and so he lived on stewed chicken, pate de foie gras, asparagus, cooked oysters, sardines—on all sorts of abominable sham delicacies out of tins. My early morning coffee he always drank; and it was all I dared do for him in that respect.   200

Every day there was the horrible maneuvering to go through so that my room and then the bathroom should be done in the usual way. I came to hate the sight of the steward, to abhor the voice of that harmless man. I felt that it was he who would bring on the disaster of discovery. It hung like a sword over our heads.

The fourth day out, I think (we were working down the east side of the Gulf of Siam, tack for tack, in light winds and smooth water)—the fourth day, I say, of this miserable juggling with the unavoidable, as we sat at our evening meal, that man, whose slightest movement I dreaded, after putting down the dishes ran up on deck busily. This could not be dangerous. Presently he came down again; and then it appeared that he had remembered a coat of mine which I had thrown over a rail to dry after having been wetted in a shower which had passed over the ship in the afternoon. Sitting stolidly at the head of the table I became terrified at the sight of the garment on his arm. Of course he made for my door. There was no time to lose.

"Steward," I thundered. My nerves were so shaken that I could not govern my voice and conceal my agitation. This was the sort of thing that made my terrifically whiskered mate tap his forehead with his forefinger. I had detected him using that gesture while talking on deck with a confidential air to the carpenter. It was too far to hear a word, but I had no doubt that this pantomime could only refer to the strange new captain.

"Yes, sir," the pale-faced steward turned resignedly to me. It was this maddening course of being shouted at, checked without rhyme or reason, arbitrarily chased out of my cabin, suddenly called into it, sent flying out of his pantry on incomprehensible errands, that accounted for the growing wretchedness of his expression.

"Where are you going with that coat?"   205

"To your room, sir."

"Is there another shower coming?"

"I'm sure I don't know, sir. Shall I go up again and see, sir?"

"No! never mind."

My object was attained, as of course my other self in there would have heard every-   210
thing that passed. During this interlude my two officers never raised their eyes off their respective plates; but the lip of that confounded cub, the second mate, quivered visibly.

I expected the steward to hook my coat on and come out at once. He was very slow about it; but I dominated my nervousness sufficiently not to shout after him. Suddenly I became aware (it could be heard plainly enough) that the fellow for some reason or other was opening the door of the bathroom. It was the end. The place was literally not big enough to swing a cat in. My voice died in my throat and I went stony all over. I expected to hear a yell of surprise and terror, and made a movement, but had not the strength to get on my legs. Everything remained still. Had my second self taken the poor wretch by the throat? I don't know what I would have done next moment if I had not seen the steward come out of my room, close the door, and then stand quietly by the sideboard.

Saved, I thought. But, no! Lost! Gone! He was gone!

I laid my knife and fork down and leaned back in my chair. My head swam. After a while, when sufficiently recovered to speak in a steady voice, I instructed my mate to put the ship round at eight o'clock himself.

"I won't come on deck," I went on. "I think I'll turn in, and unless the wind shifts I don't want to be disturbed before midnight. I feel a bit seedy."

"You did look middling bad a little while ago," the chief mate remarked without   215
showing any great concern.

They both went out, and I stared at the steward clearing the table. There was nothing to be read on that wretched man's face. But why did he avoid my eyes I asked myself. Then I thought I should like to hear the sound of his voice.

"Steward!"

"Sir!" Startled as usual.

"Where did you hang up that coat?"

"In the bathroom, sir." The usual anxious tone. "It's not quite dry yet, sir."   220

For some time longer I sat in the cuddy. Had my double vanished as he had come? But of his coming there was an explanation, whereas his disappearance would be inexplicable. . . . I went slowly into my dark room, shut the door, lighted the lamp, and for a time dared not turn round. When at last I did I saw him standing bolt upright in the narrow recessed part. It would not be true to say I had a shock, but an irresistible doubt of his bodily existence flitted through my mind. Can it be, I asked myself, that he is not visible to other eyes than mine? It was like being haunted. Motionless, with a grave face, he raised his hands slightly at me in a gesture which meant clearly, "Heavens! what a narrow escape!" Narrow indeed. I think I had come creeping quietly as near insanity as any man who has not actually gone over the border. That gesture restrained me, so to speak.

The mate with the terrific whiskers was now putting the ship on the other tack. In the moment of profound silence which follows upon the hands going to their stations I heard on the poop his raised voice: "Hard alee!" and the distant shout of the order repeated on the maindeck. The sails, in that light breeze, made but a faint fluttering noise. It ceased. The ship was coming round slowly; I held my breath in the renewed stillness of expectation; one wouldn't have thought that there was a single living soul on her decks. A sudden brisk shout, "Mainsail haul!" broke the spell, and in the noisy cries and rush overhead of the men running away with the main brace we two, down in my cabin, came together in our usual position by the bed-place.

He did not wait for my question. "I heard him fumbling here and just managed to squat myself down in the bath," he whispered to me. "The fellow only opened the door and put his arm in to hang the coat up. All the same—"

"I never thought of that," I whispered back, even more appalled than before at the closeness of the shave, and marveling at that something unyielding in his character which was carrying him through so finely. There was no agitation in his whisper. Whoever was being driven distracted, it was not he. He was sane. And the proof of his sanity was continued when he took up the whispering again.

"It would never do for me to come to life again."   225

It was something that a ghost might have said. But what he was alluding to was his old captain's reluctant admission of the theory of suicide. It would obviously serve his turn—if I had understood at all the view which seemed to govern the unalterable purpose of his action.

"You must maroon me as soon as ever you can get amongst these islands off the Cambodje shore," he went on.

"Maroon you! We are not living in a boy's adventure tale," I protested. His scornful whispering took me up.

"We aren't indeed! There's nothing of a boy's tale in this. But there's nothing else for it. I want no more. You don't suppose I am afraid of what can be done to me? Prison or gallows or whatever they may please. But you don't see me coming back to explain such things to an old fellow in a wig and twelve respectable tradesmen, do you? What can they know whether I am guilty or not—or of *what* I am guilty, either? That's my affair. What does the Bible say? 'Driven off the face of the earth.' Very well. I am off the face of the earth now. As I came at night so I shall go."

"Impossible!" I murmured. "You can't."   230

"Can't? . . . Not naked like a soul on the Day of Judgment. I shall freeze on to this sleeping suit. The Last Day is not yet—and . . . , you have understood thoroughly. Didn't you?"

I felt suddenly ashamed of myself. I may say truly that I understood—and my hesitation in letting that man swim away from my ship's side had been a mere sham sentiment, a sort of cowardice.

"It can't be done now till next night," I breathed out. "The ship is on the offshore tack and the wind may fail us."

"As long as I know that you understand," he whispered. "But of course you do. It's a great satisfaction to have got somebody to understand. You seem to have been there on purpose." And in the same whisper, as if we two whenever we talked had to say things to each other which were not fit for the world to hear, he added, "It's very wonderful."

We remained side by side talking in our secret way—but sometimes silent or just   235
exchanging a whispered word or two at long intervals. And as usual he stared through
the port. A breath of wind came now and again into our faces. The ship might have
been moored in dock, so gently and on an even keel she slipped through the water, that
did not murmur even at our passage, shadowy and silent like a phantom sea.

At midnight I went on deck, and to my mate's great surprise put the ship round
on the other tack. His terrible whiskers flitted round me in silent criticism. I certainly
should not have done it if it had been only a question of getting out of that sleepy gulf as
quickly as possible. I believe he told the second mate, who relieved him, that it was a
great want of judgment. The other only yawned. That intolerable cub shuffled about so
sleepily and lolled against the rails in such a slack, improper fashion that I came down
on him sharply.

"Aren't you properly awake yet?"

"Yes, sir! I am awake."

"Well, then, be good enough to hold yourself as if you were. And keep a lookout.
If there's any current we'll be closing with some islands before daylight."

The east side of the gulf is fringed with islands, some solitary, others in groups.   240
On the blue background of the high coast they seem to float on silvery patches of calm
water, arid and gray, or dark green and rounded like clumps of evergreen bushes, with
the larger ones, a mile or two long, showing the outlines of ridges, ribs of gray rock
under the dark mantle of matted leafage. Unknown to trade, to travel, almost to geography, the manner of life they harbor is an unsolved secret. There must be villages—
settlements of fishermen at least—on the largest of them, and some communication
with the world is probably kept up by native craft. But all forenoon, as we headed for
them, fanned along by the faintest of breezes, I saw no sign of man or canoe in the field
of the telescope I kept on pointing at the scattered group.

At noon I gave no orders for a change of course, and the mate's whiskers became
much concerned and seemed to be offering themselves unduly to my notice. At last I
said:

"I am going to stand right in. Quite in—as far as I can take her."

The stare of extreme surprise imparted an air of ferocity also to his eyes, and he
looked truly terrific for a moment.

"We're not doing well in the middle of the gulf," I continued, casually. "I am going
to look for the land breezes tonight."

"Bless my soul! Do you mean, sir, in the dark amongst the lot of all them islands   245
and reefs and shoals?"

"Well—if there are any regular land breezes at all on this coast one must get close
inshore to find them, mustn't one?"

"Bless my soul!" he exclaimed again under his breath. All that afternoon he wore
a dreamy, contemplative appearance which in him was a mark of perplexity. After dinner
I went into my stateroom as if I meant to take some rest. There we two bent our dark
heads over a half-unrolled chart lying on my bed.

"There," I said. "It's got to be Koh-ring. I've been looking at it ever since sunrise.
It has got two hills and a low point. It must be inhabited. And on the coast opposite
there is what looks like the mouth of a biggish river—with some town, no doubt, not far
up. It's the best chance for you that I can see."

"Anything. Koh-ring let it be."

He looked thoughtfully at the chart as if surveying chances and distances from a   250
lofty height—and following with his eyes his own figure wandering on the blank land

of Cochin China, and then passing off that piece of paper clean out of sight into
uncharted regions. And it was as if the ship had two captains to plan her course for her.
I had been so worried and restless running up and down that I had not had the patience
to dress that day. I had remained in my sleeping suit, with straw slippers and a soft floppy
hat. The closeness of the heat in the gulf had been most oppressive, and the crew were
used to see me wandering in that airy attire.

"She will clear the south point as she heads now," I whispered into his ear.
"Goodness only knows when, though, but certainly after dark. I'll edge her in to half a
mile, as far as I may be able to judge in the dark—"

"Be careful," he murmured, warningly—and I realized suddenly that all my future,
the only future for which I was fit, would perhaps go irretrievably to pieces in any mishap
to my first command.

I could not stop a moment longer in the room. I motioned him to get out of sight
and made my way on the poop. That unplayful cub had the watch. I walked up and
down for a while thinking things out, then beckoned him over.

"Send a couple of hands to open the two quarter-deck ports," I said, mildly.

He actually had the impudence, or else so forgot himself in his wonder at such   255
an incomprehensible order, as to repeat:

"Open the quarter-deck ports! What for, sir?"

"The only reason you need concern yourself about is because I tell you to do so.
Have them open wide and fastened properly."

He reddened and went off, but I believe made some jeering remark to the carpenter as to the sensible practice of ventilating a ship's quarter-deck. I know he popped
into the mate's cabin to impart the fact to him because the whiskers came on deck, as it
were by chance, and stole glances at me from below—for signs of lunacy or drunkenness, I suppose.

A little before supper, feeling more restless than ever, I rejoined, for a moment,
my second self. And to find him sitting so quietly was surprising, like something against
nature, inhuman.

I developed my plan in a hurried whisper.   260

"I shall stand in as close as I dare and then put her round. I shall presently find
means to smuggle you out of here into the sail locker, which communicates with the
lobby. But there is an opening, a sort of square for hauling the sails out, which gives
straight on the quarter-deck and which is never closed in fine weather, so as to give air
to the sails. When the ship's way is deadened in stays and all the hands are aft at the
main braces you shall have a clear road to slip out and get overboard through the open
quarter-deck port. I've had them both fastened up. Use a rope's end to lower yourself
into the water so as to avoid a splash—you know. It could be heard and cause some
beastly complication."

He kept silent for a while, then whispered, "I understand."

"I won't be there to see you go," I began with an effort. "The rest . . . I only hope
I have understood, too."

"You have. From first to last," and for the first time there seemed to be a faltering,
something strained in his whisper. He caught hold of my arm, but the ringing of the
supper bell made me start. He didn't, though; he only released his grip.

After supper I didn't come below again till well past eight o'clock. The faint,   26.
steady breeze was loaded with dew; and the wet, darkened sails held all there was of pro-
pelling power in it. The night, clear and starry, sparkled darkly, and the opaque, lightless

patches shifting slowly against the low stars were the drifting islets. On the port bow there was a big one more distant and shadowily imposing by the great space of sky it eclipsed.

On opening the door I had a back view of my very own self looking at a chart. He had come out of the recess and was standing near the table.

"Quite dark enough," I whispered.

He stepped back and leaned against my bed with a level, quiet glance. I sat on the couch. We had nothing to say to each other. Over our heads the officer of the watch moved here and there. Then I heard him move quickly. I knew what that meant. He was making for the companion; and presently his voice was outside my door.

"We are drawing in pretty fast, sir. Land looks rather close."

"Very well," I answered. "I am coming on deck directly."   270

I waited till he was gone out of the cuddy, then rose. My double moved too. The time had come to exchange our last whispers, for neither of us was ever to hear each other's natural voice.

"Look here!" I opened a drawer and took out three sovereigns.° "Take this, anyhow. I've got six and I'd give you the lot, only I must keep a little money to buy some fruit and vegetables for the crew from native boats as we go through Sunda Straits."

He shook his head.

"Take it," I urged him, whispering desperately. "No one can tell what—"

He smiled and slapped meaningly the only pocket of the sleeping jacket. It was   275
not safe, certainly. But I produced a large old silk handkerchief of mine, and tying the three pieces of gold in a corner, pressed it on him. He was touched, I suppose, because he took it at last and tied it quickly round his waist under the jacket, on his bare skin.

Our eyes met; several seconds elapsed, till, our glances still mingled, I extended my hand and turned the lamp out. Then I passed through the cuddy, leaving the door of my room wide open. "Steward!"

He was still lingering in the pantry in the greatness of his zeal, giving a rub-up to a plated cruet stand the last thing before going to bed. Being careful not to wake up the mate, whose room was opposite, I spoke in an undertone.

He looked round anxiously. "Sir!"

"Can you get me a little hot water from the galley?"

"I am afraid, sir, the galley fire's been out for some time now."   280

"Go and see."

He fled up the stairs.

"Now," I whispered, loudly, into the saloon—too loudly, perhaps, but I was afraid I couldn't make a sound. He was by my side in an instant—the double captain slipped past the stairs—through the tiny dark passage . . . a sliding door. We were in the sail locker, scrambling on our knees over the sails. A sudden thought struck me. I saw myself wandering barefooted, bareheaded, the sun beating on my dark poll. I snatched off my floppy hat and tried hurriedly in the dark to ram it on my other self. He dodged and fended off silently. I wonder what he thought had come to me before he understood and suddenly desisted. Our hands met gropingly, lingered united in a steady, motionless clasp for a second. . . . No word was breathed by either of us when they separated.

I was standing quietly by the pantry door when the steward returned.

"Sorry, sir. Kettle barely warm. Shall I light the spirit lamp?"   285

sovereigns: gold coins worth a pound each.

"Never mind."

I came out on deck slowly. It was not a matter of conscience to shave the land as close as possible—for now he must go overboard whenever the ship was put in stays. Must! There could be no going back for him. After a moment I walked over to leeward and my heart flew into my mouth at the nearness of the land on the bow. Under any other circumstances I would not have held on a minute longer. The second mate had followed me anxiously.

I looked on till I felt I could command my voice.

"She will weather," I said then in a quiet tone.

"Are you going to try that, sir?" he stammered out incredulously.   290

I took no notice of him and raised my tone just enough to be heard by the helmsman.

"Keep her good full."

"Good full, sir."

The wind fanned my cheek, the sails slept, the world was silent. The strain of watching the dark loom of the land grow bigger and denser was too much for me. I had shut my eyes—because the ship must go closer. She must! The stillness was intolerable. Were we standing still?

When I opened my eyes the second view started my heart with a thump. The black   295
southern hill of Koh-ring seemed to hang right over the ship like a towering fragment of the everlasting night. On that enormous mass of blackness there was not a gleam to be seen, not a sound to be heard. It was gliding irresistibly toward us and yet seemed already within reach of the hand. I saw the vague figures of the watch grouped in the waist, gazing in awed silence.

"Are you going on, sir?" inquired an unsteady voice at my elbow.

I ignored it. I had to go on.

"Keep her full. Don't check her way. That won't do now," I said warningly.

"I can't see the sails very well," the helmsman answered me, in strange, quavering tones.

Was she close enough? Already she was, I won't say in the shadow of the land, but   300
in the very blackness of it, already swallowed up as it were, gone too close to be recalled, gone from me altogether.

"Give the mate a call," I said to the young man who stood at my elbow still as death. "And turn all hands up."

My tone had a borrowed loudness reverberated from the height of the land. Several voir ^s cried out together. "We are all on deck, sir."

Then stillness again, with the great shadow gliding closer, towering higher, without a light, without a sound. Such a hush had fallen on the ship that she might have been a bark of the dead floating in slowly under the very gate of Erebus.

"My God! Where are we?"

It was the mate moaning at my elbow. He was thunderstruck, and as it were   305
deprived of the moral support of his whiskers. He clapped his hands and absolutely cried out, "Lost!"

"Be quiet," I said sternly.

He lowered his tone, but I saw the shadowy gesture of his despair. "What are we doing here?"

"Looking for the land wind."

He made as if to tear his hair, and addressed me recklessly.

"She will never get out. You have done it, sir. I knew it'd end in something like   310
this. She will never weather, and you are too close now to stay. She'll drift ashore before
she's round. O my God!"

I caught his arm as he was raising it to batter his poor devoted head, and shook it
violently.

"She's ashore already," he wailed, trying to tear himself away. "Is she? . . . Keep
good full there!"

"Good full, sir," cried the helmsman in a frightened, thin, childlike voice.

I hadn't let go the mate's arm and went on shaking it. "Ready about, do you hear?
You go forward"—shake—"and stop there"—shake—"and hold your noise"—shake—
"and see these head sheets properly overhauled"—shake, shake— shake.

And all the time I dared not look toward the land lest my heart should fail me. I   315
released my grip at last and he ran forward as if fleeing for dear life.

I wondered what my double there in the sail locker thought of this commotion.
He was able to hear everything—and perhaps he was able to understand why, on my
conscience, it had to be thus close—no less. My first order "Hard alee!" reechoed ominously under the towering shadow of Koh-ring as if I had shouted in a mountain gorge.
And then I watched the land intently. In that smooth water and light wind it was impossible to feel the ship coming-to. No! I could not feel her. And my second self was
making now ready to slip out and lower himself overboard. Perhaps he was gone
already . . . ?

The great black mass brooding over our very mastheads began to pivot away from
the ship's side silently. And now I forgot the secret stranger ready to depart, and remembered only that I was a total stranger to the ship. I did not know her. Would she do it?
How was she to be handled?

I swung the mainyard and waited helplessly. She was perhaps stopped, and her very
fate hung in the balance, with the black mass of Koh-ring like the gate of the everlasting
night towering over her taffrail. What would she do now? Had she way on her yet?
I stepped to the side swiftly, and on the shadowy water I could see nothing except a faint
phosphorescent flash revealing the glassy smoothness of the sleeping surface. It was
impossible to tell—and I had not learned yet the feel of my ship. Was she moving? What
I needed was something easily seen, a piece of paper, which I could throw overboard and
watch. I had nothing on me. To run down for it I didn't dare. There was no time. All at
once my strained, yearning stare distinguished a white object floating within a yard of
the ship's side. White on the black water. A phosphorescent flash passed under it. What
was that thing? . . . I recognized my own floppy hat. It must have fallen off his
head . . . and he didn't bother. Now I had what I wanted—the saving mark for my eyes.
But I hardly thought of my other self, now gone from the ship, to be hidden forever from
all friendly faces, to be a fugitive and a vagabond on the earth, with no brand of the curse
on his sane forehead to stay a slaying hand . . . too proud to explain.

And I watched the hat—the expression of my sudden pity for his mere flesh. It
had been meant to save his homeless head from the dangers of the sun. And now—
behold—it was saving the ship, by serving me for a mark to help out the ignorance of my
strangeness. Ha! It was drifting forward, warning me just in time that the ship had gathered sternway.

"Shift the helm," I said in a low voice to the seaman standing still like a statue.   320

The man's eyes glistened wildly in the binnacle light as he jumped round to the
other side and spun round the wheel.

I walked to the break of the poop. On the overshadowed deck all hands stood by the forebraces waiting for my order. The stars ahead seemed to be gliding from right to left. And all was so still in the world that I heard the quiet remark "She's round," passed in a tone of intense relief between two seamen.

"Let go and haul."

The foreyards ran round with a great noise, amidst cheery cries. And now the frightful whiskers made themselves heard giving various orders. Already the ship was drawing ahead. And I was alone with her. Nothing! no one in the world should stand now between us, throwing a shadow on the way of silent knowledge and mute affection, the perfect communion of a seaman with his first command.

Walking to the taffrail, I was in time to make out, on the very edge of a darkness   325
thrown by a towering black mass like the very gateway of Erebus—yes, I was in time to catch an evanescent glimpse of my white hat left behind to mark the spot where the secret sharer of my cabin and of my thoughts, as though he were my second self, had lowered himself into the water to take his punishment: a free man, a proud swimmer striking out for a new destiny.

QUESTIONS

1. Analyze the first three paragraphs of the story. What is the purpose of all the details of setting? How might a person claim that Conrad's great attention to detail is overdone?

2. Who is the narrator? What sort of person is he? Why does he determine to help Leggatt? What do the Captain and Leggatt have in common? Why does the Captain constantly think of Leggatt as his double?

3. How do the details of the Captain's cabin enable the Captain to conceal Leggatt successfully?

4. What details does the story provide about the techniques of sailing and handling ships in a storm? Why does Conrad provide these details?

5. What moral issue must the Captain deal with as he learns Leggatt's story and then decides to help Leggatt? Compare this issue with the issue confronted by Mrs. Hale and Mrs. Peters in "A Jury of Her Peers" (Chapter 4)?

JOANNE GREENBERG   (b. 1932)

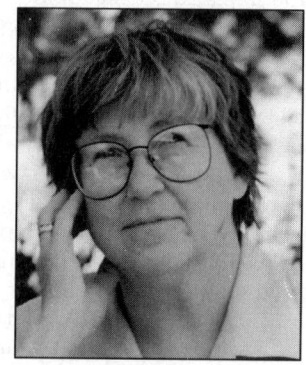

Greenberg, a resident of Colorado, graduated from American University in Washington and also attended the University of London. Under the pseudonym "Hannah Green," she achieved wide recognition in 1964 with the novel I Never Promised You a Rose Garden, *which describes the struggles of a teenage girl against schizophrenia. In 1977, the story was made into a successful film, featuring Kathleen Quinlan. Greenberg's fiction reflects her deep concern for "problems of the less fortunate." She is a member of the National Association for the Deaf and has taught sign language. As a writer she has been prolific, producing nearly a dozen novels. "And Sarah Laughed" is taken from her collection* Rites of Passage *(1972). Recent works are* With the Snow Queen *(1991) and* No Reck'ning Made *(1993).*

And Sarah Laughed°_____1972

She went to the window every fifteen minutes to see if they were coming. They would be taking the new highway cutoff; it would bring them past the south side of the farm; past the unused, dilapidated outbuildings instead of the orchards and fields that were now full and green. It would look like a poor place to the new bride. Her first impression of their farm would be of age and bleached-out, dried-out buildings on which the doors hung open like a row of gaping mouths that said nothing.

All day, Sarah had gone about her work clumsy with eagerness and hesitant with dread, picking up utensils to forget them in holding, finding them two minutes later a surprise in her hand. She had been planning and working ever since Abel wrote to them from Chicago that he was coming home with a wife. Everything should have been clean and orderly. She wanted the bride to know as soon as she walked inside what kind of woman Abel's mother was—to feel, without a word having to be said, the house's dignity, honesty, simplicity, and love. But the spring cleaning had been late, and Alma Yoder had gotten sick—Sarah had had to go over to the Yoders and help out.

Now she looked around and saw that it was no use trying to have everything ready in time. Abel and his bride would be coming any minute. If she didn't want to get caught shedding tears of frustration, she'd better get herself under control. She stepped over the pile of clothes still unsorted for the laundry and went out on the back porch.

The sky was blue and silent, but as she watched, a bird passed over the fields crying. The garden spread out before her, displaying its varying greens. Beyond it, along the creek, there was a row of poplars. It always calmed her to look at them. She looked today. She and Matthew had planted those trees. They stood thirty feet high now, stately as figures in a procession. Once—only once and many years ago—she had tried to describe in words the sounds that the wind made as it combed those trees on its way west. The little boy to whom she had spoken was a grown man now, and he was bringing home a wife. Married. . . .

Ever since he had written to tell them he was coming with his bride, Sarah had been going back in her mind to the days when she and Matthew were bride and groom and then mother and father. Until now, it hadn't seemed so long ago. Her life had flowed on past her, blurring the early days with Matthew when this farm was strange and new to her and when the silence of it was sharp and bitter like pain, not dulled and familiar like an echo of old age.

Matthew hadn't changed much. He was a tall, lean man, but he had had a boy's spareness then. She remembered how his smile came, wavered and went uncertainly, but how his eyes had never left her. He followed everything with his eyes. Matthew had always been a silent man; his face was expressionless and his body stiff with reticence, but his eyes had sought her out eagerly and held her and she had been warm in his look.

Sarah and Matthew had always known each other—their families had been neighbors. Sarah was a plain girl, a serious "decent" girl. Not many of the young men asked her out, and when Matthew did and did again, her parents had been pleased. Her father told her that Matthew was a good man, as steady as any woman could want. He came from honest, hardworking people and he would prosper any farm he had. Her mother spoke shyly of how his eyes woke when Sarah came into the room, and how they followed her. If she married him, her life would be full of the things she knew and loved, an

5

And Sarah Laughed: See Genesis 18:12.

easy, familiar world with her parents' farm not two miles down the road. But no one wanted to mention the one thing that worried Sarah: the fact that Matthew was deaf. It was what stopped her from saying yes right away; she loved him, but she was worried about his deafness. The things she feared about it were the practical things: a fall or a fire when he wouldn't hear her cry for help. Only long after she had put those fears aside and moved the scant two miles into his different world, did she realize that the things she had feared were the wrong things.

Now they had been married for twenty-five years. It was a good marriage—good enough. Matthew was generous, strong, and loving. The farm prospered. His silence made him seem more patient, and because she became more silent also, their neighbors saw in them the dignity and strength of two people who do not rail against misfortune, who were beyond trivial talk and gossip; whose lives needed no words. Over the years of help given and meetings attended, people noticed how little they needed to say. Only Sarah's friend Luita knew that in the beginning, when they were first married, they had written yearning notes to each other. But Luita didn't know that the notes also were mute. Sarah had never shown them to anyone, although she kept them all, and sometimes she would go up and get the box out of her closet and read them over. She had saved every scrap, from questions about the eggs to the tattered note he had left beside his plate on their first anniversary. He had written it when she was busy at the stove and then he'd gone out and she hadn't seen it until she cleared the table.

The note said: "I love you derest wife Sarah. I pray you have happy day all day your life."

When she wanted to tell him something, she spoke to him slowly, facing him, and he took the words as they formed on her lips. His speaking voice was thick and hard to understand and he perceived that it was unpleasant. He didn't like to use it. When he had to say something, he used his odd, grunting tone, and she came to understand what he said. If she ever hungered for laughter from him or the little meaningless talk that confirms existence and affection, she told herself angrily that Matthew talked through his work. Words die in the air; they can be turned one way or another, but Matthew's work prayed and laughed for him. He took good care of her and the boys, and they idolized him. Surely that counted more than all the words—words that meant and didn't mean—behind which people could hide. 10

Over the years she seldom noticed her own increasing silence, and there were times when his tenderness, which was always given without words, seemed to her to make his silence beautiful.

She thought of the morning she had come downstairs feeling heavy and off balance with her first pregnancy—with Abel. She had gone to the kitchen to begin the day, taking the coffeepot down and beginning to fill it when her eye caught something on the kitchen table. For a minute she looked around in confusion. They had already laid away what the baby would need: diapers, little shirts and bedding, all folded away in the drawer upstairs, but here on the table was a bounty of cloth, all planned and scrimped for and bought from careful, careful study of the catalogue—yards of patterned flannel and plissé, coat wool and bright red corduroy. Sixteen yards of yellow ribbon for bindings. Under the coat wool was cloth Matthew had chosen for her; blue with a little gray figure. It was silk, and there was a card on which was rolled precisely enough lace edging for her collar and sleeves. All the long studying and careful planning, all in silence.

She had run upstairs and thanked him and hugged him, but it was no use showing delight with words, making plans, matching cloth and figuring which pieces would be for the jacket and which for sleepers. Most wives used such fussing to tell their husbands how much they thought of their gifts. But Matthew's silence was her silence too.

When he had left to go to the orchard after breakfast that morning, she had gone to their room and stuffed her ears with cotton, trying to understand the world as it must be to him, with no sound. The cotton dulled the outside noises a little, but it only magnified all the noises in her head. Scratching her cheek caused a roar like a downpour of rain; her own voice was like thunder. She knew Matthew could not hear his own voice in his head. She could not be deaf as he was deaf. She could not know such silence ever.

So she found herself talking to the baby inside her, telling it the things she would have told Matthew, the idle daily things: Didn't Margaret Amson look peaked in town? Wasn't it a shame the drugstore had stopped stocking lump alum—her pickles wouldn't be the same.

Abel was a good baby. He had Matthew's great eyes and gentle ways. She chattered to him all day, looking forward to his growing up, when there would be confidences between them. She looked to the time when he would have his own picture of the world, and with that keen hunger and hope she had a kind of late blooming into a beauty that made people in town turn to look at her when she passed in the street holding the baby in the fine clothes she had made for him. She took Abel everywhere, and came to know a pride that was very new to her, a plain girl from a modest family who had married a neighbor boy. When they went to town, they always stopped over to see Matthew's parents and her mother.

Mama had moved to town after Pa died. Of course they had offered to have Mama come and live with them, but Sarah was glad she had gone to a little place in town, living where there were people she knew and things happening right outside her door. Sarah remembered them visiting on a certain spring day, all sitting in Mama's new front room. They sat uncomfortably in the genteel chairs, and Abel crawled around on the floor as the women talked, looking up every now and then for his father's nod of approval. After a while he went to catch the sunlight that was glancing off a crystal nut dish and scattering rainbow bands on the floor. Sarah smiled down at him. She too had a radiance, and, for the first time in her life, she knew it. She was wearing the dress she had made from Matthew's cloth—it became her and she knew that too, so she gave her joy freely as she traded news with Mama.

Suddenly they heard the fire bell ringing up on the hill. She caught Matthew's eye and mouthed, "Fire engines," pointing uphill to the firehouse. He nodded.

In the next minutes there was the strident, off-key blare as every single one of Arcadia's volunteer firemen—his car horn plugged with a matchstick and his duty before him—drove hellbent for the firehouse in an ecstasy of bell and siren. In a minute the ding-ding-ding-ding careened in deafening, happy privilege through every red light in town.

"Big bunch of boys!" Mama laughed. "You can count two Saturdays in good weather when they don't have a fire, and that's during the hunting season!"

They laughed. Then Sarah looked down at Abel, who was still trying to catch the wonderful colors. A madhouse of bells, horns, screaming sirens had gone right past them and he hadn't cried, he hadn't looked, he hadn't turned. Sarah twisted her head sharply away and screamed to the china cats on the whatnot shelf as loud as she could, but Abel's eyes only flickered to the movement and then went back to the sun and its colors.

Mama whispered, "Oh, my dear God!"

Sarah began to cry bitterly, uncontrollably, while her husband and son looked on, confused, embarrassed, unknowing.

The silence drew itself over the season and the seasons layered into years. Abel was a good boy; Matthew was a good man.

Later, Rutherford, Lindsay, and Franklin Delano came. They too were silent. Hereditary nerve deafness was rare, the doctors all said. The boys might marry and produce deaf children, but it was not likely. When they started to school, the administrators and teachers told her that the boys would be taught specially to read lips and to speak. They would not be "abnormal," she was told. Nothing would show their handicap, and with training no one need know that they were deaf. But the boys seldom used their lifeless voices to call to their friends; they seldom joined games unless they were forced to join. No one but their mother understood their speech. No teacher could stop all the jumping, turning, gum-chewing schoolboys, or remember herself to face front from the blackboard to the sound-closed boys. The lip-reading exercises never seemed to make plain differences—"man," "pan," "began."

But the boys had work and pride in the farm. The seasons varied their silence with colors—crows flocked in the snowy fields in winter, and tones of golden wheat darkened across acres of summer wind. If the boys couldn't hear the bedsheets flapping on the washline, they could see and feel the autumn day. There were chores and holidays and the wheel of birth and planting, hunting, fishing, and harvest. The boys were familiar in town; nobody ever laughed at them, and when Sarah met neighbors at the store, they praised her sons with exaggerated praise, well meant, saying that no one could tell, no one could really tell unless they knew, about the boys not hearing.

Sarah wanted to cry to these kindly women that the simple orders the boys obeyed by reading her lips were not a miracle. If she could ever hear in their long-practiced robot voices a question that had to do with feelings and not facts, and answer it in words that rose beyond the daily, tangible things done or not done, *that* would be a miracle.

Her neighbors didn't know that they themselves confided to one another from a universe of hopes, a world they wanted half lost in the world that was; how often they spoke pitting inflection against meaning to soften it, harden it, make a joke of it, curse by it, bless by it. They didn't realize how they wrapped the bare words of love in gentle humor or wild insults that the loved ones knew were ways of keeping the secret of love between the speaker and the hearer. Mothers lovingly called their children crow-bait, mouse-meat, devils. They predicted dark ends for them, and the children heard the secrets beneath the words, heard them and smiled and knew, and let the love said-unsaid caress their souls. With her own bitter knowledge Sarah could only thank them for well-meaning and return to silence.

Standing on the back porch now, Sarah heard the wind in the poplars and she sighed. It was getting on to noon. Warm air was beginning to ripple the fields. Matthew would be ready for lunch soon, but she wished she could stand out under the warm sky forever and listen to birds stitching sounds into the endless silence. She found herself thinking about Abel again, and the bride. She wondered what Janice would be like. Abel had gone all the way to Chicago to be trained in drafting. He had met her there, in the school. Sarah was afraid of a girl like that. They had been married quickly, without family or friends or toasts or gifts or questions. It hinted at some kind of secret shame. It frightened her. That kind of girl was independent and she might be scornful of a dowdy mother-in-law. And the house was still a mess.

From down the road, dust was rising. Matthew must have seen it too. He came   30
over the rise and toward the house walking faster than usual. He'd want to slick his hair
down and wash up to meet the stranger his son had become. She ran inside and bundled up the unsorted laundry, ran upstairs and pulled a comb through her hair, put on
a crooked dab of lipstick, banged her shin, took off her apron and saw a spot on her
dress, put the apron on again and shouted a curse to all the disorder she suddenly saw
around her.

Now the car was crunching up the thin gravel of the driveway. She heard Matthew
downstairs washing up, not realizing that the bride and groom were already at the house.
Protect your own, she thought, and ran down to tell him. Together they went to the
door and opened it, hoping that at least Abel's familiar face would comfort them.

They didn't recognize him at first, and he didn't see them. He and the tiny bride
might have been alone in the world. He was walking around to open the door for her,
helping her out, bringing her up the path to the house, and all the time their fingers
and hands moved and spun meanings at which they smiled and laughed; they were
talking somehow, painting thoughts in the air so fast with their fingers that Sarah
couldn't see where one began and the other ended. She stared. The school people had
always told her that such finger-talk set the deaf apart. It was abnormal; it made freaks of
them. . . . How soon Abel had accepted someone else's strangeness and bad ways. She
felt so dizzy she thought she was going to fall, and she was more bitterly jealous than
she had ever been before.

The little bride stopped before them appealingly and in her dead, deaf-rote voice,
said, "Ah-am pliizd to meet'ou." Sarah put out her hand dumbly and it was taken and the
girl's eyes shone. Matthew smiled, and this time the girl spoke and waved her hands in
time to her words, and then gave Matthew her hand. So Abel had told that girl about
Matthew's deafness. It had never been a secret, but Sarah felt somehow betrayed.

They had lunch, saw the farm, the other boys came home from their summer
school and met Janice. Sarah put out cake and tea and showed Abel and Janice up to
the room she had made ready for them, and all the time the two of them went on with
love-talk in their fingers; the jokes and secrets knitted silently between them, fears told
and calmed, hopes spoken and echoed in the silence of a kitchen where twenty-five
years of silence had imprisoned her. Always they would stop and pull themselves back to
their good manners, speaking or writing polite questions and answers for the family;
but in a moment or two, the talk would flag, the urgent hunger would overcome them
and they would fight it, resolutely turning their eyes to Sarah's mouth. Then the signs
would creep into their fingers, and the joy of talk into their faces, and they would fall
before the conquering need of their communion.

Sarah's friend Luita came the next day, in the afternoon. They sat over tea with   35
the kitchen window open for the cool breeze and Sarah was relieved and grateful to
hold to a familiar thing now that her life had suddenly become so strange to her. Luita
hadn't changed at all, thank God—not the hand that waved her tea cool or the high
giggle that broke into generous laughter.

"She's darling!" Luita said after Janice had been introduced, and, thankfully, had
left them. Sarah didn't want to talk about her, so she agreed without enthusiasm.

Luita only smiled back. "Sarah, you'll never pass for pleased with a face like that."

"It's just—just her ways," Sarah said. "She never even wrote to us before the wedding, and now she comes in and—and changes everything. I'll be honest, Luita, I
didn't want Abel to marry someone who was deaf. What did we train him for, all those

special classes? . . . *not* to marry another deaf person. And she hangs on him like a wood tick all day . . ." She didn't mention the signs. She couldn't.

Luita said, "It's just somebody new in the house, that's all. She's important to you, but a stranger. Addie Purkhard felt the same way and you know what a lovely girl Velma turned out to be. It just took time. . . . She's going to have a baby, did she tell you?"

"Baby? Who?" Sarah cried, feeling cold and terrified.   40

"Why, *Velma.* A baby due about a month after my Dolores'."

It had never occurred to Sarah that Janice and Abel could have a baby. She wanted to stop thinking about it and she looked back at Luita whose eyes were glowing with something joyful that had to be said. Luita hadn't been able to see beyond it to the anguish of her friend.

Luita said, "You know, Sarah, things haven't been so good between Sam and me. . . ." She cleared her throat. "You know how stubborn he is. The last few weeks, it's been like a whole new start for us. I came over to tell you about it because I'm so happy, and I had to share it with you."

She looked away shyly, and Sarah pulled herself together and leaned forward, putting her hand on her friend's arm. "I'm so happy for you. What happened?"

"It started about three weeks ago—a night that neither of us could get to sleep. We   45
hadn't been arguing; there was just that awful coldness, as if we'd both been frozen stiff. One of us started talking—just lying there in the dark. I don't even know who started, but pretty soon we were telling each other the most secret things—things we never could have said in the light. He finally told me that Dolores having a baby makes him feel old and scared. He's afraid of it, Sarah, and I never knew it, and it explains why he hates to go over and see them, and why he argues with Ken all the time. Right there beside me he told me so many things I'd forgotten or misunderstood. In the dark it's like thinking out loud—like being alone and yet together at the same time. I love him so and I came so close to forgetting it. . . ."

Sarah lay in bed and thought about Luita and Sam sharing their secrets in the dark. Maybe even now they were talking in their flower-papered upstairs room, moving against the engulfing seas of silence as if in little boats, finding each other and touching and then looking out in awe at the vastness all around them where they might have rowed alone and mute forever. She wondered if Janice and Abel fingered those signs in the dark on each other's body. She began to cry. There was that freedom, at least; other wives had to strangle their weeping.

When she was cried out, she lay in bed and counted all the good things she had: children, possessions, acres of land, respect of neighbors, the years of certainty and success. Then she conjured the little bride, and saw her standing in front of Abel's old car as she had at first—with nothing; all her virtues still unproven, all her fears still forming, and her bed in another woman's house. Against the new gold ring on the bride's finger, Sarah threw all the substance of her years to weigh for her. The balance went with the bride. It wasn't fair! The balance went with the bride because she had put that communion in the scales as well, and all the thoughts that must have been given and taken between them. It outweighed Sarah's twenty-five years of muteness; outweighed the house and barn and well-tended land, and the sleeping family keeping their silent thoughts.

The days went by. Sarah tortured herself with elaborate courtesy to Janice and politeness to the accomplice son, but she couldn't guard her own envy from herself and she found fault wherever she looked. Now the silence of her house was throbbing with her anger. Every morning Janice would come and ask to help, but Sarah was too restless to teach her, so Janice would sit for a while waiting and then get up and go outside to look for Abel. Then Sarah would decide to make coleslaw and sit with the chopping bowl in her lap, smashing the chopper against the wood with a vindictive joy that she alone could hear the sounds she was making, that she alone knew how savage they were and how satisfying.

At church she would see the younger boys all clean and handsome, Matthew greeting friends, Janice demure and fragile, and Abel proud and loving, and she would feel a terrible guilt for her unreasonable anger; but back from town afterwards, and after Sunday dinner, she noticed as never before how disheveled the boys looked, how ugly their hollow voices sounded. Had Matthew always been so patient and unruffled? He was like one of his own stock, an animal, a dumb animal.

Janice kept asking to help and Sarah kept saying there wasn't time to teach her.   50
She was amazed when Matthew, who was very fussy about his fruit, suggested to her that Janice might be able to take care of the grapes and, later, work in the orchard.

"I haven't time to teach her!"

"Ah owill teeech Ja-nuss," Abel said, and they left right after dinner in too much of a hurry.

Matthew stopped Sarah when she was clearing the table and asked why she didn't like Janice. Now it was Sarah's turn to be silent, and when Matthew insisted, Sarah finally turned on him. "You don't understand," she shouted. "You don't understand a thing!" And she saw on his face the same look of confusion she had seen that day in Mama's fussy front room when she had suddenly begun to cry and could not stop. She turned away with the plates, but suddenly his hand shot out and he struck them to the floor, and the voice he couldn't hear or control rose to an awful cry, "Ah ahm dehf! Ah ahm dehf!" Then he went out, slamming the door without the satisfaction of its sound.

If a leaf fell or a stalk sprouted in the grape arbor, Janice told it over like a set of prayers. One night at supper, Sarah saw the younger boys framing those dumb-signs of hers, and she took them outside and slapped their hands. "*We* don't do that!" she shouted at them, and to Janice later she said, "Those . . . signs you make—I know they must have taught you to do that, but out here . . . well, it isn't our way."

Janice looked back at her in a confusion for which there were no words.   55

It was no use raging at Janice. Before she had come there had never been anything for Sarah to be angry about. . . . What did they all expect of her? Wasn't it enough that she was left out of a world that heard and laughed without being humiliated by the love-madness they made with their hands? It was like watching them undressing.

The wind cannot be caught. Poplars may sift it, a rising bird can breast it, but it will pass by and no one can stop it. She saw the boys coming home at a dead run now, and they couldn't keep their hands from taking letters, words, and pictures from the fingers of the lovers. If they saw an eagle, caught a fish, or got scolded, they ran to their brother or his wife, and Sarah had to stand in the background and demand to be told.

One day Matthew came up to her and smiled and said, "Look." He put out his two index fingers and hooked the right down on the left, then the left down gently on the right. "Fwren," he said, "Ja-nuss say, fwren."

To Sarah there was something obscene about all those gestures, and she said, "I don't like people waving their hands around like monkeys in a zoo!" She said it very clearly so that he couldn't mistake it.

He shook his head violently and gestured as he spoke. "Mouth eat; mouth kiss,   60
mouth tawk! Fin-ger wohk; fin-ger tawk. E-ah" (and he grabbed his ear, violently),
"e-ah dehf. *Mihn*," (and he rapped his head, violently, as if turning a terrible impatience
against himself so as to spare her) "*mihn not* dehf!"

Later she went to the barn after something and she ran into Lindsay and Franklin
Delano standing guilty, and when she caught them in her eye as she turned, she saw
their hands framing signs. They didn't come into the house until it was nearly dark. Was
their hunger for those signs so great that only darkness could bring them home? They
weren't bad boys, the kind who would do a thing just because you told them not to. Did
their days have a hunger too, or was it only the spell of the lovers, honey-honeying to
shut out a world of moving mouths and silence?

At supper she looked around the table and was reassured. It could have been any
farm family sitting there, respectable and quiet. A glance from the father was all that
was needed to keep order or summon another helping. Their eyes were lowered, their
faces composed. The hands were quiet. She smiled and went to the kitchen to fix the
shortcake she had made as a surprise.

When she came back, they did not notice her immediately. They were all busy
talking. Janice was telling them something and they all had their mouths ridiculously
pursed with the word. Janice smiled in assent and each one showed her his sign and she
smiled at each one and nodded, and the signers turned to one another in their joy,
accepting and begging acceptance. Then they saw Sarah standing there; the hands came
down, the faces faded.

She took the dinner plates away and brought in the dessert things, and when she
went back to the kitchen for the cake, she began to cry. It was beyond envy now; it was
too late for measuring or weighing. She had lost. In the country of the blind, Mama
used to say, the one-eyed man is king. Having been a citizen of such a country, she knew
better. In the country of the deaf, the hearing man is lonely. Into that country a girl had
come who, with a wave of her hand, had given the deaf ears for one another, and
had made Sarah the deaf one.

Sarah stood, staring at her cake and feeling for that moment the profundity of   65
the silence which she had once tried to match by stuffing cotton in her ears. Everyone
she loved was in the other room, talking, sharing, standing before the awful, impersonal heaven and the unhearing earth with pictures of his thoughts, and she was the
deaf one now. It wasn't "any farm family," silent in its strength. It was a yearning family,
silent in its hunger, and a demure little bride had shown them all how deep the hunger
was. She had shown Sarah that her youth had been sold into silence. She was too old to
change now.

An anger rose in her as she stared at the cake. Why should they be free to move
and gesture and look different while she was kept in bondage to their silence? Then she
remembered Matthew's mute notes, his pride in Abel's training, his face when he had
cried, "I am deaf!" over and over. She had actually fought that terrible yearning, that
hunger they all must have had for their own words. If they could all speak somehow,
what would the boys tell her?

She knew what she wanted to tell them. That the wind sounds through the poplar
trees, and people have a hard time speaking to one another even if they aren't deaf.
Luita and Sam had to have a night to hide their faces while they spoke. It suddenly
occurred to her that if Matthew made one of those signs with his hands and she could
learn that sign, she could put her hands against his in the darkness, and read the meaning—that if she learned those signs she could hear him. . . .

She dried her eyes hurriedly and took in the cake. They saw her and the hands stopped, drooping lifelessly again; the faces waited mutely. Silence. It was a silence she could no longer bear. She looked from face to face. What was behind those eyes she loved? Didn't everyone's world go deeper than chores and bread and sleep?

"I want to talk to you," she said. "I want to talk, to know what you think." She put her hands out before her, offering them.

Six pairs of eyes watched her.   70

Janice said, "Mo-ther."

Eyes snapped away to Janice; thumb was under lip: the Sign.

Sarah followed them. "Wife," she said, showing her ring.

"Wife," Janice echoed, thumb under lip to the clasp of hands.

Sarah said, "I love. . . ."   75

Janice showed her and she followed hesitantly and then turned to Matthew to give and to be received in that sign.

QUESTIONS

1. Characterize Sarah. What do we learn about her character from the way she cares for her surroundings and tends to her tasks?

2. What kinds of detail about the appearance and circumstances of the farm appear in the story? Why are these details included?

3. Why does Greenberg not disclose right away that Matthew is deaf? Why does she withhold the same detail about Abel? How does Sarah respond when she learns that Abel is deaf?

4. What attitudes toward deafness and communication does Janice, with her mastery of sign language, bring out in Sarah? To what degree may her attitudes be considered a crisis? How does Sarah respond to the crisis? Why?

CYNTHIA OZICK   (b. 1928)

Ozick has published three novels, Trust *(1966),* The Cannibal Galaxy *(1983), and* The Messiah of Stockholm *(1987); three short-story collections,* The Pagan Rabbi *(1971),* Bloodshed *(1976), and* Levitation *(1982); and frequent essays and reviews, among which is the recent collection* Fame and Folly *(1996). Among her many recognitions and awards, she serves on the Board of Advisers of the* American Poetry Review. *Her 1990 novella "Puttermesser Paired" was the first story featured in* Prize Stories 1992: The O. Henry Awards, *edited by William Abrahams. "The Shawl," first published in the* New Yorker *in 1980, was republished in* The Shawl *in 1989, with a companion story describing the heroine's experiences in the United States after surviving the death camp.*

The Shawl _____ Magda is a baby. _____ *1980*

Stella, cold, cold the coldness of hell. How they walked on the roads together, Rosa with Magda curled up between sore breasts, Magda wound up in the shawl. Sometimes Stella carried Magda. But she was jealous of Magda. A thin girl of fourteen, too small, with thin breasts of her own, Stella wanted to be wrapped in a shawl, hidden away, asleep, rocked by the march, a baby, a round infant in arms. Magda took Rosa's nipple, and Rosa never stopped walking, a walking cradle. There was not enough milk; sometimes Magda sucked air; then she screamed. Stella was ravenous. Her knees were tumors on sticks, her elbows chicken bones.

Rosa did not feel hunger; she felt light, not like someone walking but like someone in a faint, in trance, arrested in a fit, someone who is already a floating angel, alert and seeing everything, but in the air, not there, not touching the road. As if teetering on the tips of her fingernails. She looked into Magda's face through a gap in the shawl: a squirrel in a nest, safe, no one could reach her inside the little house of the shawl's windings. The face, very round, a pocket mirror of a face: but it was not Rosa's bleak complexion, dark like cholera, it was another kind of face altogether, eyes blue as air, smooth feathers of hair nearly as yellow as the Star sewn into Rosa's coat. You could think she was one of *their* babies.

baby looked like this

Rosa, floating, dreamed of giving Magda away in one of the villages. She could leave the line for a minute and push Magda into the hands of any woman on the side of the road. But if she moved out of line they might shoot. And even if she fled the line for half a second and pushed the shawl-bundle at a stranger, would the woman take it? She might be surprised, or afraid; she might drop the shawl, and Magda would fall out and strike her head and die. The little round head. Such a good child, she gave up screaming, and sucked now only for the taste of the drying nipple itself. The neat grip of the tiny gums. One mite of a tooth tip sticking up in the bottom gum, how shining, an elfin tombstone of white marble gleaming there. Without complaining, Magda relinquished Rosa's teats, first the left, then the right; both were cracked, not a sniff of milk. The duct crevice extinct, a dead volcano, blind eye, chill hole, so Magda took the corner of the shawl and milked it instead. She sucked and sucked, flooding the threads with wetness. The shawl's good flavor, milk of linen.

It was a magic shawl, it could nourish an infant for three days and three nights. Magda did not die, she stayed alive, although very quiet. A peculiar smell, of cinnamon and almonds, lifted out of her mouth. She held her eyes open every moment, forgetting how to blink or nap, and Rosa and sometimes Stella studied their blueness. On the road they raised one burden of a leg after another and studied Magda's face. "Aryan," Stella said, in a voice grown as thin as a string; and Rosa thought how Stella gazed at Magda like a young cannibal. And the time that Stella said "Aryan," it sounded to Rosa as if Stella had really said "Let us devour her."

But Magda lived to walk. She lived that long, but she did not walk very well, partly because she was only fifteen months old, and partly because the spindles of her legs could not hold up her fat belly. It was fat with air, full and round. Rosa gave almost all her food to Magda, Stella gave nothing; Stella was ravenous, a growing child herself, but not growing much. Stella did not menstruate. Rosa did not menstruate. Rosa was ravenous, but also not; she learned from Magda how to drink the taste of a finger in one's mouth. They were in a place without pity, all pity was annihilated in Rosa, she looked at Stella's bones without pity. She was sure that Stella was waiting for Magda to die so she could put her teeth into the little thighs.

Rosa knew Magda was going to die very soon; she should have been dead already, but she had been buried away deep inside the magic shawl, mistaken there for the shivering mound of Rosa's breasts; Rosa clung to the shawl as if it covered only herself. No one took it away from her. Magda was mute. She never cried. Rosa hid her in the barracks, under the shawl, but she knew that one day someone would inform; or one day someone, not even Stella, would steal Magda to eat her. When Magda began to walk Rosa knew that Magda was going to die very soon, something would happen. She was afraid to fall asleep; she slept with the weight of her thigh on Magda's body; she was afraid she would smother Magda under her thigh. The weight of Rosa was becoming less and less; Rosa and Stella were slowly turning into air.

Magda was quiet, but her eyes were horribly alive, like blue tigers. She watched. Sometimes she laughed—it seemed a laugh, but how could it be? Magda had never seen anyone laugh. Still, Magda laughed at her shawl when the wind blew its corners, the bad wind with pieces of black in it, that made Stella's and Rosa's eyes tear. Magda's eyes were always clear and tearless. She watched like a tiger. She guarded her shawl. No one could touch it; only Rosa could touch it. Stella was not allowed. The shawl was Magda's own baby, her pet, her little sister. She tangled herself up in it and sucked on one of the corners when she wanted to be very still.

Then Stella took the shawl away and made Magda die.

Afterward Stella said: "I was cold."

And afterward she was always cold, always. The cold went into her heart: Rosa saw that Stella's heart was cold. Magda flopped onward with her little pencil legs scribbling this way and that, in search of the shawl; the pencils faltered at the barracks opening, where the light began. Rosa saw and pursued. But already Magda was in the square outside the barracks, in the jolly light. It was the roll-call arena. Every morning Rosa had to conceal Magda under the shawl against a wall of the barracks and go out and stand in the arena with Stella and hundreds of others, sometimes for hours, and Magda, deserted, was quiet under the shawl, sucking on her corner. Every day Magda was silent, and so she did not die. Rosa saw that today Magda was going to die, and at the same time a fearful joy ran into Rosa's two palms, her fingers were on fire, she was astonished, febrile: Magda, in the sunlight, swaying on her pencil legs, was howling. Ever since the drying up of Rosa's nipples, ever since Magda's last scream on the road, Magda had been devoid of any syllable; Magda was a mute. Rosa believed that something had gone wrong with her vocal cords, with her windpipe, with the cave of her larynx; Magda was defective, without a voice; perhaps she was deaf; there might be something amiss with her intelligence; Magda was dumb. Even the laugh that came when the ash-stippled wind made a clown out of Magda's shawl was only the air-blown showing of her teeth. Even when the lice, head lice and body lice, crazed her so that she became as wild as one of the big rats that plundered the barracks at daybreak looking for carrion, she rubbed and scratched and kicked and bit and rolled without a whimper. But now Magda's mouth was spilling a long viscous rope of clamor.

"Maaaa—"

It was the first noise Magda had ever sent out from her throat since the drying up of Rosa's nipples.

"Maaaa . . . aaa!"

Again! Magda was wavering in the perilous sunlight of the arena, scrabbling on such pitiful little bent shins. Rosa saw. She saw that Magda was grieving for the loss of her shawl, she saw that Magda was going to die. A tide of commands hammered in Rosa's nipples: Fetch, get, bring! But she did not know which to go after first, Magda or the

10

shawl. If she jumped out into the arena to snatch Magda up, the howling would not stop, because Magda would still not have the shawl; but if she ran back into the barracks to find the shawl, and if she found it, and if she came after Magda holding it and shaking it, then she would get Magda back, Magda would put the shawl in her mouth and turn dumb again.

Rosa entered the dark. It was easy to discover the shawl. Stella was heaped under   15
it, asleep in her thin bones. Rosa tore the shawl free and flew—she could fly, she was only air—into the arena. The sunheat murmured of another life, of butterflies in summer. The light was placid, mellow. On the other side of the steel fence, far away, there were green meadows speckled with dandelions and deep-colored violets; beyond them, even farther, innocent tiger lilies, tall, lifting their orange bonnets. In the barracks they spoke of "flowers," of "rain": excrement, thick turd-braids, and the slow stinking maroon waterfall that slunk down from the upper bunks, the stink mixed with a bitter fatty floating smoke that greased Rosa's skin. She stood for an instant at the margin of the arena. Sometimes the electricity inside the fence would seem to hum; even Stella said it was only an imagining, but Rosa heard real sounds in the wire: grainy sad voices. The farther she was from the fence, the more clearly the voices crowded at her. The lamenting voices strummed so convincingly, so passionately, it was impossible to suspect them of being phantoms. The voices told her to hold up the shawl, high; the voices told her to shake it, to whip with it, to unfurl it like a flag. Rosa lifted, shook, whipped, unfurled. Far off, very far, Magda leaned across her air-fed belly, reaching out with the rods of her arms. She was high up, elevated, riding someone's shoulder. But the shoulder that carried Magda was not coming toward Rosa and the shawl, it was drifting away, the speck of Magda was moving more and more into the smoky distance. Above the shoulder a helmet glinted. The light tapped the helmet and sparkled it into a goblet. Below the helmet a black body like a domino and a pair of black boots hurled themselves in the direction of the electrified fence. The electric voices began to chatter wildly. "Maa-maa, maaamaaa," they all hummed together. How far Magda was from Rosa now, across the whole square, past a dozen barracks, all the way on the other side! She was no bigger than a moth.

All at once Magda was swimming through the air. The whole of Magda traveled through loftiness. She looked like a butterfly touching a silver vine. And the moment Magda's feathered round head and her pencil legs and balloonish belly and zigzag arms splashed against the fence, the steel voices went mad in their growling, urging Rosa to run and run to the spot where Magda had fallen from her flight against the electrified fence; but of course Rosa did not obey them. She only stood, because if she ran they would shoot, and if she tried to pick up the sticks of Magda's body they would shoot, and if she let the wolf's screech ascending now through the ladder of her skeleton break out, they would shoot; so she took Magda's shawl and filled her own mouth with it, stuffed it in and stuffed it in, until she was swallowing up the wolf's screech and tasting the cinnamon and almond depth of Magda's saliva; and Rosa drank Magda's shawl until it dried.

QUESTIONS

1. Describe how Ozick presents the setting. Why do you not receive a clear picture of how things look? Why does Ozick present the details as she does?

2. In paragraph 15, what is on the other side of the fence? Explain Ozick's description here. Why does Ozick include these details so close to the story's end?

3. What character is the center of interest in "The Shawl"? Why is she being treated as she is? What are her impressions of the conditions and circumstances around her? What are her responses to her hunger and deprivation?

4. Explain the function of the more unpleasant and brutal details. What do you need to know about the circumstances of the story to respond to these details

WRITING ABOUT SETTING

In preparing to write about setting, determine the number and importance of locations, artifacts, and customs. Ask questions like the following:

- How extensive are the visual descriptions? Does the author provide such vivid and carefully arranged detail about surroundings that you could draw a map or plan? Or is the scenery vague and difficult to imagine?

- What connections, if any, are apparent between locations and characters? Do the locations bring characters together, separate them, facilitate their privacy, make intimacy and conversation difficult?

- How fully are objects described? How vital are they to the action? How important are they in the development of the plot or idea? How are they connected to the mental states of the characters?

- How important to plot and character are shapes, colors, times of day, clouds, storms, light and sun, seasons of the year, and conditions of vegetation?

- Are the characters poor, moderately well-off, or rich? How does their economic condition affect their actions and attitudes? How does their economic lot determine what happens to them?

- What cultural, religious, and political conditions are brought out in the story? How do the characters accept and adjust to these conditions? How do the conditions affect the characters' judgments and actions?

- What is the state of houses, furniture, and objects (e.g., new and polished, old and worn)? What connections can you find between this condition and the outlook and behavior of the characters?

- How important are sounds or silences? To what degree is music or other sound important in the development of character and action?

- Do characters respect or mistreat the environment? If there is an environmental connection, how central is it to the story?

- What conclusions do you think the author expects you to draw as a result of the neighborhood, culture, and larger world of the story?

Strategies for Organizing Ideas

Begin by making a brief description of the setting or scenes of the work, specifying the amount and importance of detail. Choosing one of the approaches in the following list, describe the approach you plan to develop. As you gather material for your essay, however, you may find it necessary to combine your major approach with one or more of the others. Whatever approach you use, be sure to consider setting not as an end in itself but rather as illustration and evidence for claims you are making about the particular story.

1. *Setting and action.* Explore the importance of setting in the work. How extensively is the setting described? Are locations essential or incidental to the actions? Does the setting serve as part of the action (e.g., places of flight or concealment; public places where people meet openly, or hidden places where they meet privately; natural or environmental conditions; seasonal conditions such as searing heat or numbing cold; customs and conventions)? Do any objects cause inspiration, difficulty, or conflict (for example, a bridge, a cellar, a walking stick, a necklace, a nickel, a hair ribbon, a toy windmill, a dead bird)? How directly do these objects influence the action?

2. *Setting and organization.* How is the setting connected to the various parts of the work? Does it undergo any changes as the action develops? Why are some parts of the setting more important than others? Is the setting used as a structural frame or enclosure for the story? How do objects, such as money or property, affect the motivation of the characters? How do descriptions made at the start become important in the action later on?

3. *Setting and character.* (For examples of this approach, see the two drafts of the demonstrative student essay in Chapter 1.) Analyze the degree to which setting influences and interacts with character. Are the characters happy or unhappy where they live? Do they get into discussions or arguments about their home environments? Do they want to stay or leave? Do the economic, philosophical, religious, or ethnic aspects of the setting make the characters undergo changes? What jobs do the characters perform because of their ways of life? What freedoms or restraints do these jobs cause? How does the setting influence their decisions, transportation, speech habits, eating habits, attitudes about love and honor, and general behavior?

4. *Setting and atmosphere.* To what extent does setting contribute to mood? Does the setting go beyond the minimum needed for action or character? How do descriptive words paint verbal pictures and evoke moods through references to colors, shapes, sounds, smells, or tastes? Does the setting establish a mood, say, of joy or hopelessness, plenty or scarcity? Do events happen in daylight or at night? Do the movements and locations of the characters suggest permanence or impermanence (like the return to a darkened room, the creation of a brick wall, the description of ocean currents, or the purchase of a fragile toy)? Are things warm and pleasant, or cold and harsh? What connection do you find between the atmosphere and the author's expressed or apparent thoughts about existence?

5. *Setting and other aspects.* Does setting reinforce the story's meaning? Does it establish irony about the circumstances and ideas in the story? If you choose this approach, consult the earlier sections of this chapter (the introductory paragraph on "The Literary Uses of Setting," the discussion of the importance of setting). If you want to write about the symbolic implications of a setting, consult Chapter 9.

To conclude, summarize your major points or write about related aspects of setting that you have not considered. Thus, if your essay treats the relationship of setting and action, your conclusion could mention connections of the setting with character or atmosphere. You might also point out whether your central idea about setting also applies to other major aspects of the story.

DEMONSTRATIVE STUDENT ESSAY

The Setting of Conrad's "The Secret Sharer"°

[1] In "The Secret Sharer" Joseph Conrad makes his setting an integral and inseparable part of his action and ideas.* The story is a sea story, which could not exist without the many details about ocean, ships, currents, cabins, and the men who sail. While some of Conrad's ideas about guilt, human sympathies, and the connection of divinity to human beings may be vague, the physical details about the setting are completely realized. The integration of setting and story can be followed in details about the Captain's cabin and the ocean itself and also in Conrad's suggestions that human affairs are linked to large, cosmic forces.†

[2] The Captain's cabin is essential to the story's main action because it enables the Captain successfully to conceal Leggatt, the stowaway. The tension resulting from the near-discoveries by the steward depends on Conrad's detailed descriptions of the cabin (see, for example, paragraphs 71-72, 200). It is described as having the shape of an L, with the door on "the short part of the letter" (paragraph 72). Because the "vertical" part is not visible to anyone entering, and because the coats, the curtained bunk, and the bathroom all furnish concealment, Leggatt can avoid the steward's searching eyes. Further, the noise made by sailors walking on the deck above the cabin permits the Captain and Leggatt to speak together without being overheard, and therefore the plans for the escape can be safely communicated between the two men.

[3] While it is obvious that a sea story takes the presence of the ocean for granted, the ocean is, for the story's purposes, equally important as the cabin. It was during a severe storm that Leggatt decided to "reef" the sail that saved his ship, the *Sephora.* It was the disobedient sailor's insults, probably brought about by fear of the storm, that enraged Leggatt and made him strangle this sailor. Thus the ocean itself produces both a good and a bad result, and it is the bad result that causes Leggatt to flee the *Sephora.* When he escapes he swims to the Captain's ship at night, thus connecting the two men, who otherwise would never have met. When Leggatt leaves the Captain's ship at the end of the story, he does so by going into the sea from a rope hung from the sail locker, and, because the Captain wishes to keep Leggatt as safe as possible, he steers too close to shore. Therefore the potential shallowness of the ocean becomes an immediate danger to the Captain, who risks his entire career (which could "go irretrievably to pieces") on the chance that he will not run aground (paragraph 252).

° See pp 297-322 for this story.
* Central idea.
† Thesis sentence.

While the setting of ocean and cabin helps create the story's adventure and tension, the descriptions also form part of Conrad's religious and philosophic setting. At the beginning, for example, we read the Captain's words:

> In this breathless pause at the threshold of a long passage we seemed to be measuring our fitness for a long and arduous enterprise, the appointed task . . . to be carried out, far from all human eyes, with only sky and sea for spectators and for judges. (paragraph 2)

[4] When the captain of the *Sephora* agrees that Leggatt's reefing of the sail saved his ship, he asserts that "God's own hand" was "in it. . . . Nothing less could have done it" (paragraph 139). In reflecting on Leggatt's both saving the *Sephora* and strangling the sailor, the Captain draws the following paradoxical conclusion:

> The same strung-up force which had given twenty-four men a chance, at least, for their lives, had, in a sort of recoil, crushed an unworthy mutinous existence. (paragraph 190)

At the end of the story, when the Captain's hat floating on the water enables the Captain to save his ship by turning around (paragraph 319), it is clear that the setting, through the currents of water, is intended to suggest cosmic approval of the Captain's decision to help Leggatt.

[5] An additional merging of setting and story should be mentioned in conclusion. This concerns the character of the Captain, the unnamed narrator. In his role as narrator, the Captain's observations about the sea, the sky, and the things the ship will encounter on the way back to England all show him as a clear-sighted man who understands the sea and the forces that control it. It is his knowledge of the danger of the sea during storms that makes possible his own personal "verdict" acquitting Leggatt for having strangled the mutinous sailor. Conrad's setting in this instance is so vital to the story that it becomes the very material of the Captain's morality, and it is this morality that causes the central decision around which all the events in the story turn. Because of this and all the other details, it is no exaggeration to say that Conrad's setting and his story are totally integrated and intertwined.

Commentary on the Essay

This essay focuses on the connection between Conrad's setting and the action and ideas of the story. In its emphasis on action and setting, the essay illustrates some aspects of strategy 1 described on page 336. In showing the connection between setting, character, and ideas, it illustrates strategies 2 and 3.

The introductory paragraph indicates the closeness of setting and story and lays out the areas to be developed in the essay. Paragraph 2 is developed with details showing the importance of the Captain's cabin. Paragraph 3 presents details about the relationship of the ocean to the story: in storm as a cause of Leggatt's good and bad actions, in calm and night as a link between the Captain and Leggatt, and in shallow water as a means of safety for Leggatt but as a threat to the Captain and the ship. Paragraph 4 presents details about the larger, cosmic aspects of the setting, for Conrad's story is not only about physical details but about the unseen forces that control human beings. The concluding paragraph illustrates the significance that knowledge of the ocean plays in the moral decision—and hence in the character—of the Captain.

SPECIAL TOPICS FOR WRITING AND ARGUMENT ABOUT SETTING

1. How do Dr. Jenkins and the young musician respond to the setting in "The Portable Phonograph"? How do they adjust to physical conditions? In light of this story, together with knowledge you have gained elsewhere from your reading and experience, what conclusions can you draw about the effects of warfare on character?

2. Compare and contrast how details of setting establish qualities and traits of the following female characters: Sarah of "And Sarah Laughed," Stella of "The Shawl," Mrs. Johnson of "Everyday Use" (Chapter 2), and the narrator of "The Yellow Wallpaper" (Chapter 12). To add to your comparison, you might discuss how the painters Boucher and Hopper portray background and dress to highlight the character of their female subjects (pp. 286 and 287).

3. In what ways might we say that both "The House on Mango Street" and "The Secret Sharer" are inseparable from their settings? To answer this question, consider the relationship of character to place and circumstance. How could the actions of the stories happen without the locations in which they occur?

4. Choose one story included in this chapter and rewrite a page or two, taking the characters out of their setting and placing them in an entirely new setting or in the setting of another story (you choose). Then write a brief analysis dealing with these questions: How were your characters affected by their new settings? Did you make them change slowly or rapidly? Why? As a result of your rewriting, what can you conclude about the uses of setting in fiction?

5. Write a short narrative as though it is part of a story (which you may also wish to write for the assignment) using option *a* and/or *b*.

   a. Relate a natural setting or type of day to a mood—for example, a nice day to happiness and satisfaction or a cold, cloudy, rainy day to sadness. Or create irony by relating the nice day to sadness or the rainy day to happiness.

   b. Indicate how an object or circumstance becomes the cause of conflict or reconciliation (such as the books and records in "The Portable Phonograph," the shawl in "The Shawl," or the sign language in "And Sarah Laughed").

6. In your library locate two books on the career of Joseph Conrad. On the basis of information you find in these sources, write a brief account of Conrad's uses of setting and place to evoke atmosphere and to bring out qualities of human character.

Style: The Words That Tell the Story

Style, derived from the Latin word *stilus* (a writing instrument), means the way writers assemble words to tell the story, develop the argument, dramatize the play, or compose the poem. Sometimes style is distinguished from content, but it is wiser not to make this separation, for style is best considered as the choice of words in the *service* of content. The written expression of a fictional action or scene, in other words, cannot be separated from the action or scene itself.

Style is also individual, because all authors put words together uniquely to fit the specific conditions in specific works. We may therefore speak of the style of Ernest Hemingway, for example, and of Mark Twain, even though both writers adapt words to situations. Thus an author may have a distinct style for narrative and descriptive passages but a very different style for dialogue. For a visual comparison of styles, look again at the paintings by François Boucher and Edward Hopper in Chapter 6 (pp. 286, 287). While the painters treat the same subject—a female figure—the *styles* are different: Boucher achieves a beautiful, flattering image of his aristocratic subject; by contrast, Hopper invests his more ordinary subject with an impression of emptiness and bleakness. These differing painting styles convey different outlooks on life. Similarly, writers vary their styles in the interest of content. In judging style the important criterion, therefore, is the author's *adaptability*. The more appropriately the words fit the situation, the better the style. Jonathan Swift defined style as the right words in the right places. We may add to this definition that style is also the right words at the right time and in the right circumstances.

DICTION: THE WRITER'S CHOICE AND CONTROL OF WORDS

Diction refers to the qualities of the writer's word choices. The selection should be accurate and explicit, so that all actions, scenes, and ideas are clear. If a passage is effective—if it conveys an idea well or gets at the essence of an action vividly and powerfully—we may confidently say that the words are right. For example, a passage describing action should employ many active verbs, whereas a description of a place should contain nouns and adjectives indicating locations, relationships, colors, and shapes. An explanatory or reflective passage should include words that convey thoughts, states of mind and emotion, and conditions of various human relationships.

Formal, Neutral, and Informal Diction Create Unique Effects

One aspect of word choice is the degree of formality. There are three levels of diction: **formal** or *high,* **neutral** or *middle,* and **informal** or *low. Formal* or *high* diction consists of standard and also "elegant" words (frequently polysyllabic), the retention of correct word order, and the absence of contractions. The sentence "It is I," for example, is formal. The following sentences from Poe's "The Masque of the Red Death" (Chapter 11) demonstrate formal language:

> They resolved to leave means neither of ingress nor egress to the sudden impulses of despair or frenzy from within. The abbey was amply provisioned. With such precautions the courtiers might bid defiance to contagion. (paragraph 2)

Note here the words *ingress, egress, amply provisioned, bid defiance,* and *contagion.* Though the sentences are brief and simple and all the words are accurate and apt, the italicized words are more "elegant" than those most of us normally use. These words may thus be considered formal or high diction.

Neutral or *middle* diction is ordinary, everyday standard vocabulary, shunning longer words but using contractions when necessary. The sentence "It's me" is an example of what many people naturally say in preference to the more formal "It is I." Words in the neutral style may be thought of as clear window glass, with words in the formal or high style being more decorative, like stained glass. An example of neutral, middle diction is the following passage from Munro's "The Found Boat":

> What surprised them in the second place was that when the boys did actually see what boat was meant, this old flood-smashed wreck held up in the branches, they did not understand that they had been fooled, that a joke had been played on them. They did not show a moment's disappointment, but seemed as pleased at the discovery as if the boat had been whole and new. They were already barefoot, because they had been wading in the water to get lumber, and they waded in here without a stop, surrounding the boat and appraising it and paying no attention even of an insulting kind to Eva and Carol who bobbed up and down on their log. Eva and Carol had to call to them. (paragraph 23)

The words of this passage are ordinary and easy. They are centered directly on the subject and do not draw attention to themselves. Even the longer words, like *surprised, disappointment, surrounding, appraising,* and *insulting,* would not be out of place in ordinary conversation, although *appraising* and *surrounding* would also be appropriate in a more formal passage.

Informal or *low* diction may range from *colloquial*—the language of relaxed, common activities—to the level of *substandard* or *slang* expressions. A person speaking to a close friend uses diction that would not be seemly in public and formal situations, and even in some social situations. Informal or low diction is thus correct for a good deal of narrative dialogue, depending, of course, on individual speakers. It is also a natural choice for stories told in the first-person point of view as though the speaker is talking directly to sympathetic and relaxed close friends. In Updike's "A & P," Sammy's first sentence illustrates informal, low diction:

> In walks these three girls in nothing but bathing suits.

Note the idiomatic and ungrammatical "In walks these three girls," a singular verb followed by a plural subject. Note also the colloquial use of "these" as a demonstrative adjective with no antecedent.

Specific-General and Concrete-Abstract Diction Guides Readers to Perceptions of Numbers and Qualities

Another aspect of language is its degree of explicitness. **Specific** refers to words that bring real and genuine situations to mind. "My dog Teddie is barking" is specific. **General** statements refer to broad classes, such as "All people like pets" and "Dogs make good pets." There is an ascending order of generality from (1) very specific to (2) less specific to (3) general, as though the words themselves climb a stairway. Thus *peach* is a specific fruit. *Fruit* is specific but more general because it also includes apples, oranges, and all other fruits. *Dessert* is a still more general word, which can encompass all sweets, including peaches and other fruits and also confections such as ice cream. *Food* is more general yet, for the word includes everything eaten by living creatures. If you report that you are having "food" for dinner, you are facetiously general, but if you say that the main course is a charcoal-broiled tenderloin steak with peaches for dessert, you are seriously specific.

While *specific–general* refers to categories, *concrete–abstract* refers to qualities or conditions. **Concrete words** describe qualities of immediate perception. If you say "Ice cream is cold," the word *cold* is concrete because it describes a condition that you can feel, just as you can *taste* ice cream's sweetness and *feel* its creamy texture in your mouth. **Abstract words** refer to broader, less palpable qualities; they may therefore apply to many separate things. If we describe ice cream as *good,* we are abstract because *good* is far removed from ice cream itself and conveys no descriptive information about it. A vast number of things may be *good,* just as they may be *bad, fine, "cool," excellent,* and so on.

Usually, writers of stories make most of their words specific and concrete to make us readily perceive actions, situations, objects, and scenes, for with more specificity and concreteness there is less ambiguity. Because exactness and vividness are goals of most fiction, specific and concrete words are the writer's basic tools, with general and abstract words being used sparingly.

The point, however, is not that abstract and general words have no place at all but rather that *words should be appropriate in the context.* Good writers control style to match their purposes. Observe, for example, Hemingway's diction in "Soldier's Home," a story about a young veteran who has just returned from World War I and is having difficulty adjusting to life back home. By combining specific and abstract language to convey this situation, Hemingway appropriately fits style to subject. In paragraph 6, for example, he uses abstract terms to describe the mental state of Krebs, the young veteran. We read that Krebs feels "nausea in regard to experience that is the result of untruth or exaggeration," that he goes into the "easy pose of the old soldier" when he meets another veteran, and that he "lost everything" during his time abroad. Because the words are mainly abstract and general, it is not possible to determine the precise details underlying Krebs's uneasinesss.

By contrast, Hemingway's description of Krebs's daily activities is specific: getting out of bed, walking to the library, eating lunch, reading on the front porch, and ambling down to the local pool hall. These details show that Krebs's activities are repetitive and meaningless. The two paragraphs therefore complement each other, with the specificity of paragraph 7 clarifying the abstraction of paragraph 6. In short, Hemingway skillfully combines abstract and specific words to build his portrait of a young man caught between two worlds—foreign warfare and peaceful life at home—and because of changing circumstances having no place in either.

Denotation *and* Connotation *Refer to Stages of Meaning and Suggestion*

Another way to understand style is to study the author's control of *denotation* and *connotation*. **Denotation** refers to what a word means, **connotation** to what the word suggests. For example, if a person in a social situation behaves in ways that are *friendly, warm, polite,* or *cordial,* these words all suggest slight differences in behavior because they have different connotations. Most of us prefer people who are friendly and warm rather than polite and cordial. Similarly, the words *dog* and *puppy* are close to each other denotatively, but *puppy* connotes more playfulness and cuteness than *dog.* Consider the connotations of words describing physical appearance. It is one thing to call a person *thin,* for example, but another to use the words *skinny, gaunt,* or *skeletal* and still something else to say *fit, trim, svelte, slim,* or *slender.*

Through the careful choice of words, not only for denotation but also for connotation, authors create unique effects even though they might be describing similar or even identical situations. Let us look briefly at Eudora Welty's description of Phoenix's walk through the woods in "A Worn Path" (Chapter 3):

> Her eyes were blue with age. Her skin had a pattern all its own of numberless branching wrinkles and as though a whole little tree stood in the middle of her forehead, but a golden color ran underneath, and the two knobs of her cheeks

were illumined by a yellow burning under the dark. Under the rag her hair came down on her neck in the frailest of ringlets, still black, and with an odor like copper. (paragraph 2)

The description conveys a compelling note of admiration. Specifically, the words *golden color* and *illumined* would be appropriate in the description of delicate and lovely medieval book paintings; *frailest of ringlets, still black* suggests girlishness and personal care, despite Phoenix's advancing age and weakness. Comparably, in "A & P," Sammy's words describing the "queen" (paragraphs 2–4) suggest his admiration of both her sexual beauty and her grace. Shirley Jackson's less full description of Tessie Hutchinson (paragraph 8) in "The Lottery" (Chapter 5) reduces Tessie to no more than an average woman of the village. The meager details are that she has a "sweater thrown over her shoulders" and that she dries her hands "on her apron." All these descriptive examples demonstrate the ways in which connotation may complement an author's descriptive intentions.

RHETORIC: THE WRITER'S CHOICES OF EFFECTIVE ARRANGEMENTS AND FORMS

Rhetoric refers to the art of effective and persuasive writing and, more broadly, to the art of writing generally. In studying style, you may consider the rhetorical qualities of a passage. Some relatively straightforward basic approaches are (1) counting various elements in a passage and (2) analyzing the types of sentences.

Counting Permits Conclusions about Brevity or Expansiveness

Counting various elements is a quick and easy way to begin the study of style. The number of words in a sentence; the number of verbs, adjectives, prepositions, and adverbs in a passage; or the number of syllables in relation to the total number of words—any of these can provide valuable clues about the style, especially if the count is related to other aspects of the passage. For illustration, let us say that Author A uses words mainly of one or two syllables, while Author B includes many words of three, four, and five syllables. Going further, let us say that A uses an average of twelve words per sentence and that B uses thirty-five. It would be fair to conclude that Author A is brief and Author B is more expansive. This is not to say that Author A's passage would be easier or superior, however, for a long string of short sentences with short words might seem choppy and tiresome. Remember that conclusions based on a count will provide tendencies of a particular author rather than absolutes.

Recognize Sentence Types as an Aspect of a Writer's Style

You can also study the rhetorical qualities of a passage by determining its various sentence types. Let us review the basic sentence types:

1. **Simple sentences** contain one subject and one verb, together with modifiers and complements. Usually simple sentences are short and are therefore appropriate for actions and declarations. Often they are idiomatic, particularly in dialogue.

    Example: Nora sat in front of me by the confession box. (Frank O'Connor's "First Confession")

2. **Compound sentences** contain two simple sentences joined by a conjunction (*and, but, for, or, nor,* or *yet*) and a comma or by a semicolon without a conjunction. Frequently, compound sentences are formed by three or four simple sentences joined by conjunctions. Like simple sentences, compound sentences are appropriate for actions and declarations.

    Example: Later he felt the need to talk but no one wanted to hear about it. (Hemingway's "Soldier's Home")

3. **Complex sentences** contain a main clause and a subordinate clause. Because of the subordinate clause, the complex sentence is suitable for describing cause-and-effect relationships in narrative and also for analysis and reflection.

    Example: It was the Wawanash River, which every spring overflowed its banks. (Munro's "The Found Boat")

4. **Compound-complex sentences** contain two main clauses and a subordinate clause. In practice many authors produce sentences that contain a number of main and subordinate clauses.

    Example: And yet, though the elder person was as simply clad as the younger, and as simple in manner too, he had an indescribable air of one who knew the world, and would not have felt abashed at the governor's dinner-table, or in King William's court, were it possible that his affairs should call him thither. (Hawthorne's "Young Goodman Brown" [Chapter 9]).

Parallelism Permits Balance, Order, and Economy of Diction

Parallelism is one of the most popular rhetorical devices. It refers to the repetition of the same grammatical form (nouns, verbs, phrases, clauses) to balance expressions, conserve words, and build climaxes. Here, for example, is a sentence by Poe from the story "The Black Cat" (Chapter 11):

I grew, day by day, more moody, more irritable, more regardless of the feelings of others.

Arrangements like this are called *parallel* because they can be laid out graphically, according to parts of speech, in parallel lines, as in the following (with the adverbial phrase "day to day" left out):

$$I \text{ grew} \begin{cases} \text{more moody} \\ \text{more irritable} \\ \text{more regardless of the feelings of others} \end{cases}$$

Poe's sentence increases in the severity of psychological depression, from personal to social. Such an ascending order marks a deliberate attempt at climax, unlike the parallelism in the following sentence from the concluding paragraph of Clark's "The Portable Phonograph" (Chapter 6):

1   2

Then quickly and quietly, looking at the piece of canvas frequently,

1   2

he slipped the records into the case, snapped the lid shut,

3

and carried the phonograph to his couch.

Here are two parallel adverbs at the beginning, both ending in *-ly,* and three past tense verbs ending in *-ed,* all of which have direct objects. The order here is time. Although the sentence is short, Clark uses parallelism to pack in a great deal of action.

You may also see parallel arrangements in individual sentences within a paragraph. In the following passage from Munro's "The Found Boat," for example, there are a number of identically formed sentences that sum up the exhilaration of young adolescents dashing naked to swim in a river. There are seven parallel clauses containing *they* followed by active verbs, which are underlined here:

> Nobody said a word this time, <u>they all bent and stripped themselves.</u> Eva, naked first, started running across the field, and then all the others ran, all five of them running bare through the knee-high hot grass, running towards the river. Not caring now about being caught but in fact leaping and yelling to call attention to themselves, if there was anybody to hear or see. <u>They felt</u> as if they were going to jump off a cliff and fly. <u>They felt</u> that something was happening to them different from anything that had happened before, and it had to do with the boat, the water, the sunlight, the dark ruined station, and each other. <u>They thought</u> of each other now hardly as names or people, but as echoing shrieks, reflections, all bold and white and loud and scandalous, and as fast as arrows. <u>They went running</u> without a break into the cold water and when it came almost to the tops of their legs <u>they fell on it and swam.</u> It stopped their noise. Silence, amazement, came over them in a rush. <u>They dipped and floated and separated,</u> sleek as mink. (paragraph 87)

You may not often encounter such readily detected parallel patterns, but you should always be alert to effective arrangements. You need not use technically correct names for the patterns you discover, as long as you focus on what you think is especially noteworthy.

STYLE IN GENERAL

If a story is good, you probably do not notice its style, for clear expressions and easy reading are marks of a writer's success. By studying style, however, you can discover and appreciate the author's achievement. The action described in a particular passage, the relationship of the passage to the entire work, the level of the diction, the vividness of the descriptions—all these should figure in your judgment.

In the paragraph from "The Found Boat," for example, Munro's masterly style can be perceived beyond the parallelism that we noted. The passage could be considered the climax of the story, which is, among other things, about emerging sexuality. In an almost ritualistic way, the paragraph describes the boys and girls running impetuously toward a river and diving in—a sexually symbolic action. Note that after the first two sentences of objective description, Munro's narrator presents us with four sentences of omniscient analysis describing the young people's feelings. If her intention had been to create searching psychological scrutiny, she might have selected words from the language of psychology (*libido, urge, sublimation,* and so on). Instead, she uses words that could have been in the vocabularies of the characters. Hence the young people feel "as if they were going to jump off a cliff and fly" and feel "that something was happening to them different from anything that had happened before." With these neutral words, the passage focuses on the excitement of the situation rather than on hidden psychological significance. In light of these considerations, Munro's style is exactly right—in fact, perfect.

Observations of this kind may not occur to you at first, but as long as you relate words to content, your analysis of style will be fruitful. The more you consider stories for style, the more you will discover your own analytical power.

❧ STORIES FOR STUDY

ERNEST HEMINGWAY   (1899–1961)

Hemingway was born in Illinois. During World War I he served in the Ambulance Corps in France, where he was wounded. In the 1920s he published The Sun Also Rises *(1926) and* A Farewell to Arms *(1929), and the resulting critical fame made him a major literary celebrity. He developed a sparse style in keeping with the elemental, stark lives of many of the characters he depicted. "Soldier's Home," from the collection* In Our Time *(1925), typifies that pared, annealed style. Notice the ambiguity and irony of the title. It may mean either "The soldier is home" or "The home of the soldier," but, ironically, the soldier's home no longer seems to be home.*

Soldier's Home _____ 1925

Krebs went to the war from a Methodist college in Kansas. There is a picture which shows him among his fraternity brothers, all of them wearing exactly the same height and style collar. He enlisted in the Marines in 1917 and did not return to the United States until the second division returned from the Rhine in the summer of 1919.

There is a picture which shows him on the Rhine with two German girls and another corporal. Krebs and the corporal look too big for their uniforms. The German girls are not beautiful. The Rhine does not show in the picture.

By the time Krebs returned to his home town in Oklahoma the greeting of heroes was over. He came back much too late. The men from the town who had been drafted had all been welcomed elaborately on their return. There had been a great deal of hysteria. Now the reaction had set in. People seemed to think it was rather ridiculous for Krebs to be getting back so late, years after the war was over.

At first Krebs, who had been at Belleau Wood, Soissons, the Champagne, St. Mihiel and in the Argonne did not want to talk about the war at all. Later he felt the need to talk but no one wanted to hear about it. His town had heard too many atrocity stories to be thrilled by actualities. Krebs found that to be listened to at all he had to lie, and after he had done this twice he, too, had a reaction against the war and against talking about it. A distaste for everything that had happened to him in the war set in because of the lies he had told. All of the times that had been able to make him feel cool and clean inside himself when he thought of them; the times so long back when he had done the one thing, the only thing for a man to do, easily and naturally, when he might have done something else, now lost their cool, valuable quality and then were lost themselves.

His lies were quite unimportant lies and consisted in attributing to himself things other men had seen, done or heard of, and stating as facts certain apocryphal incidents familiar to all soldiers. Even his lies were not sensational at the pool room. His acquaintances, who had heard detailed accounts of German women found chained to machine guns in the Argonne forest and who could not comprehend, or were barred by their patriotism from interest in, any German machine gunners who were not chained, were not thrilled by his stories.

Krebs acquired the nausea in regard to experience that is the result of untruth or exaggeration, and when he occasionally met another man who had really been a soldier and they talked a few minutes in the dressing room at a dance he fell into the easy pose of the old soldier among other soldiers: that he had been badly, sickeningly frightened all the time. In this way he lost everything.

During this time, it was late summer, he was sleeping late in bed, getting up to walk down town to the library to get a book, eating lunch at home, reading on the front porch until he became bored and then walking down through the town to spend the hottest hours of the day in the cool dark of the pool room. He loved to play pool.

In the evening he practised on his clarinet, strolled down town, read and went to bed. He was still a hero to his two young sisters. His mother would have given him break-fast in bed if he had wanted it. She often came in when he was in bed and asked him to tell her about the war, but her attention always wandered. His father was non-committal.

Before Krebs went away to the war he had never been allowed to drive the family motor car. His father was in the real estate business and always wanted the car to be at his command when he required it to take clients out into the country to show them a piece of farm property. The car always stood outside the First National Bank building where his father had an office on the second floor. Now, after the war, it was still the same car.

Nothing was changed in the town except that the young girls had grown up. But they lived in such a complicated world of already defined alliances and shifting feuds that Krebs did not feel the energy or the courage to break into it. He liked to look at them, though. There were so many good-looking young girls. Most of them had their hair cut short. When he went away only little girls wore their hair like that or girls that were fast. They all wore sweaters and shirt waists with round Dutch collars. It was a pattern. He liked to look at them from the front porch as they walked on the other side of the street. He liked to watch them walking under the shade of the trees. He liked the round Dutch collars above their sweaters. He liked their silk stockings and flat shoes. He liked their bobbed hair and the way they walked. 10

When he was in town their appeal to him was not very strong. He did not like them when he saw them in the Greek's ice cream parlor. He did not want them them-selves really. They were too complicated. There was something else. Vaguely he wanted a girl but he did not want to have to work to get her. He would have liked to have a girl but he did not want to have to spend a long time getting her. He did not want to get into the intrigue and the politics. He did not want to have to do any courting. He did not want to tell any more lies. It wasn't worth it.

He did not want any consequences. He did not want any consequences ever again. He wanted to live along without consequences. Besides he did not really need a girl. The army had taught him that. It was all right to pose as though you had to have a girl. Nearly everybody did that. But it wasn't true. You did not need a girl. That was the funny thing. First a fellow boasted how girls mean nothing to him, that he never thought of them, that they could not touch him. Then a fellow boasted that he could not get along without girls, that he had to have them all the time, that he could not go to sleep without them.

That was all a lie. It was all a lie both ways. You did not need a girl unless you thought about them. He learned that in the army. Then sooner or later you always got one. When you were really ripe for a girl you always got one. You did not have to think about it. Sooner or later it would come. He had learned that in the army.

Now he would have liked a girl if she had come to him and not wanted to talk. But here at home it was all too complicated. He knew he could never get through it all again. It was not worth the trouble. That was the thing about French girls and German girls. There was not all this talking. You couldn't talk much and you did not need to talk. It was simple and you were friends. He thought about France and then he began to think about Germany. On the whole he had liked Germany better. He did not want to leave Germany. He did not want to come home. Still, he had come home. He sat on the front porch.

He liked the girls that were walking along the other side of the street. He liked   15
the look of them much better than the French girls or the German girls. But the world they were in was not the world he was in. He would like to have one of them. But it was not worth it. They were such a nice pattern. He liked the pattern. It was exciting. But he would not go through all the talking. He did not want one badly enough. He liked to look at them all, though. It was not worth it. Not now when things were getting good again.

He sat there on the porch reading a book on the war. It was a history and he was reading about all the engagements he had been in. It was the most interesting reading he had ever done. He wished there were more maps. He looked forward with a good feeling to reading all the really good histories when they would come out with good detail maps. Now he was really learning about the war. He had been a good soldier. That made a difference.

One morning after he had been home about a month his mother came into his bedroom and sat on the bed. She smoothed her apron.

"I had a talk with your father last night, Harold," she said, "and he is willing for you to take the car out in the evenings."

"Yeah?" said Krebs, who was not fully awake. "Take the car out? Yeah?"

"Yes. Your father has felt for some time that you should be able to take the car out   20
in the evenings whenever you wished but we only talked it over last night."

"I'll bet you made him," Krebs said.

"No. It was your father's suggestion that we talk the matter over."

"Yeah. I'll bet you made him," Krebs sat up in bed.

"Will you come down to breakfast, Harold?" his mother said.

"As soon as I get my clothes on," Krebs said.   25

His mother went out of the room and he could hear her frying something downstairs while he washed, shaved and dressed to go down into the dining-room for breakfast. While he was eating breakfast his sister brought in the mail.

"Well, Hare," she said. "You old sleepy-head. What do you ever get up for?"

Krebs looked at her. He liked her. She was his best sister.

"Have you got the paper?" he asked.

She handed him *The Kansas City Star* and he shucked off its brown wrapper and   30
opened it to the sporting page. He folded *The Star* open and propped it against the water pitcher with his cereal dish to steady it, so he could read while he ate.

"Harold," his mother stood in the kitchen doorway, "Harold, please don't muss up the paper. You father can't read his *Star* if it's been mussed."

"I won't muss it," Krebs said.

His sister sat down at the table and watched him while he read.

"We're playing indoor° over at school this afternoon," she said. "I'm going to pitch."

"Good," said Krebs. "How's the old wing?"   s

"I can pitch better than lots of the boys. I tell them all you taught me. The other girls aren't much good."

"Yeah?" said Krebs.

indoor: that is, a softball game.

"I tell them all you're my beau. Aren't you my beau, Hare?"

"You bet."

"Couldn't your brother really be your beau just because he's your brother?"   40

"I don't know."

"Sure you know. Couldn't you be my beau, Hare, if I was old enough and if you wanted to?"

"Sure. You're my girl now."

"Am I really your girl?"

"Sure."

"Do you love me?"   45

"Uh, huh."

"Will you love me always?"

"Sure."

"Will you come over and watch me play indoor?"   50

"Maybe."

"Aw, Hare, you don't love me. If you loved me, you'd want to come over and watch me play indoor."

Krebs's mother came into the dining-room from the kitchen. She carried a plate with two fried eggs and some crisp bacon on it and a plate of buckwheat cakes.

"You run along, Helen," she said. "I want to talk to Harold."

She put eggs and bacon down in front of him and brought in a jug of maple syrup   55
for the buckwheat cakes. Then she sat down across the table from Krebs.

"I wish you'd put down the paper a minute, Harold," she said.

Krebs took down the paper and folded it.

"Have you decided what you are going to do yet, Harold?" his mother said, taking off her glasses.

"No," said Krebs.

"Don't you think it's about time?" His mother did not say this in a mean way. She   60
seemed worried.

"I hadn't thought about it," Krebs said.

"God has some work for every one to do," his mother said. "There can be no idle hands in His Kingdom."

"I'm not in His Kingdom," Krebs said.

"We are all of us in His Kingdom."

Krebs felt embarrassed and resentful as always.   65

"I've worried about you so much, Harold," his mother went on. "I know the temptations you must have been exposed to. I know how weak men are. I know what your own dear grandfather, my own father, told us about the Civil War and I have prayed for you. I pray for you all day long, Harold."

Krebs looked at the bacon fat hardening on his plate.

"Your father is worried, too," his mother went on. "He thinks you have lost your ambition, that you haven't got a definite aim in life. Charley Simmons, who is just your age, has a good job and is going to be married. The boys are all settling down; they're all determined to get somewhere; you can see that boys like Charley Simmons are on their way to being really a credit to the community."

Krebs said nothing.

"Don't look that way, Harold," his mother said. "You know we love you and I want   70
to tell you for your own good how matters stand. Your father does not want to hamper your freedom. He thinks you should be allowed to drive the car. If you want to take some

of the nice girls out riding with you, we are only too pleased. We want you to enjoy yourself. But you are going to have to settle down to work, Harold. Your father doesn't care what you start in at. All work is honorable as he says. But you've got to make a start at something. He asked me to speak to you this morning and then you can stop in and see him at his office."

"Is that all?" Krebs said.

"Yes. Don't you love your mother, dear boy?"

"No," Krebs said.

His mother looked at him across the table. Her eyes were shiny. She started crying.

"I don't love anybody," Krebs said.   75

It wasn't any good. He couldn't tell her, he couldn't make her see it. It was silly to have said it. He had only hurt her. He went over and took hold of her arm. She was crying with her head in her hands.

"I didn't mean it," he said. "I was just angry at something. I didn't mean I didn't love you."

His mother went on crying. Krebs put his arm on her shoulder.

"Can't you believe me, mother?"

His mother shook her head.   80

"Please, please, mother. Please believe me."

"All right," his mother said chokily. She looked up at him. "I believe you, Harold."

Krebs kissed her hair. She put her face up to him.

"I'm your mother," she said. "I held you next to my heart when you were a tiny baby."

Krebs felt sick and vaguely nauseated.

"I know, Mummy," he said. "I'll try and be a good boy for you."   85

"Would you kneel and pray with me, Harold?" his mother asked.

They knelt down beside the dining-room table and Krebs's mother prayed.

"Now, you pray, Harold," she said.

"I can't," Krebs said.   90

"Try, Harold."

"I can't."

"Do you want me to pray for you?"

"Yes."

So his mother prayed for him and then they stood up and Krebs kissed his mother   95
and went out of the house. He had tried so to keep his life from being complicated. Still, none of it had touched him. He had felt sorry for his mother and she had made him lie. He would go to Kansas City and get a job and she would feel all right about it. There would be one more scene maybe before he got away. He would not go down to his father's office. He would miss that one. He wanted his life to go smoothly. It had just gotten going that way. Well, that was all over now, anyway. He would go over to the schoolyard and watch Helen play indoor baseball.

QUESTIONS

1. Even though Hemingway is often praised for his specific writing, there are a number of vague passages in this story. Why does Hemingway include them? By what stylistic means does he control the vagueness?

, Hemingway's sentences. What relationship is there between the things ~scribes and the length and complexity of his sentences?

.1alyze Hemingway's descriptive style. What is the level of his diction? What /ords does he use for things and actions? How vivid are his descriptions?

:scribe Harold Krebs. How do we learn about him? What does his relation- p with his sister show about him? How does he change in the story?

ALICE MUNRO   (b. 1931)

Munro, who is a writer almost exclusively of short stories, grew up in Western Ontario, twenty miles east of Lake Huron—the locale of the town of Jubilee explored in the story collection Something I've Been Meaning to Tell You *(1974), from which "The Found Boat" is selected. She received her higher education at the University of Western Ontario, after which she married and moved to British Columbia, where she began her writing career. Her first col- lection was* Dance of the Happy Shades *(1968), fol- lowed three years later by the novelistic* Lives of Girls and Women. *Later volumes are* The Beggar Maid *(1978),* The Moons of Jupiter *(1982),* The Progress of Love *(1986),* Friend of My Youth *(1990),* Open Secrets *(1995), and* The Love of a Good Woman *(1998). Her stories are mainly regional and have a realistic basis in her own experiences. The stories are not autobiographical, however; her characters and their actions develop out of her powerful imagination and strong sympathy and compassion. Recipient of Canada's Governor-General's Award for her very first work, she has merited additional honors throughout her distinguished career, the most recent being the 1999 National Book Critics Circle fiction prize for* The Love of a Good Woman.

The Found Boat _____ *1974*

At the end of Bell Street, McKay Street, Mayo Street, there was the Flood. It was the Wawanash River, which every spring overflowed its banks. Some springs, say one in every five, it covered the roads on that side of town and washed over the fields, creating a shal- low choppy lake. Light reflected off the water made everything bright and cold, as it is in a lakeside town, and woke or revived in people certain vague hopes of disaster. Mostly during the late afternoon and early evening, there were people straggling out to look at it, and discuss whether it was still rising, and whether this time it might invade the town. In general, those under fifteen and over sixty-five were most certain that it would.

Eva and Carol rode out on their bicycles. They left the road—it was the end of Mayo Street, past any houses—and rode right into a field, over a wire fence entirely flat- tened by the weight of the winter's snow. They coasted a little way before the long grass stopped them, then left their bicycles lying down and went to the water.

"We have to find a log and ride on it," Eva said.

"Jesus, we'll freeze our legs off."

"Jesus, we'll freeze our legs off!" said one of the boys who were there too at the water's edge. He spoke in a sour whine, the way boys imitated girls although it was   5 nothing like the way girls talked. These boys—there were three of them—were all in the same class as Eva and Carol at school and were known to them by name (their names being Frank, Bud and Clayton), but Eva and Carol, who had seen and recognized them from the road, had not spoken to them or looked at them or, even yet, given any sign of knowing they were there. The boys seemed to be trying to make a raft, from lumber they had salvaged from the water.

Eva and Carol took off their shoes and socks and waded in. The water was so cold it sent pain up their legs, like blue electric sparks shooting through their veins, but they went on, pulling their skirts high, tight behind and bunched so they could hold them in front.

"Look at the fat-assed ducks in wading."

"Fat-assed fucks."

Eva and Carol, of course, gave no sign of hearing this. They laid hold of a log and climbed on, taking a couple of boards floating in the water for paddles. There were always things floating around in the Flood—branches, fence-rails, logs, road signs, old lumber; sometimes boilers, washtubs, pots and pans, or even a car seat or stuffed chair, as if somewhere the Flood had got into a dump.

They paddled away from shore, heading out into the cold lake. The water was per-   10
fectly clear, they could see the brown grass swimming along the bottom. Suppose it was the sea, thought Eva. She thought of drowned cities and countries. Atlantis. Suppose they were riding in a Viking boat—Viking boats on the Atlantic were more frail and narrow than this log on the Flood—and they had miles of clear sea beneath them, then a spired city, intact as a jewel irretrievable on the ocean floor.

"This is a Viking boat," she said. "I am the carving on the front." She stuck her chest out and stretched her neck, trying to make a curve, and she made a face, putting out her tongue. Then she turned and for the first time took notice of the boys.

"Hey, you sucks!" she yelled at them. "You'd be scared to come out here, this water is ten feet deep!"

"Liar," they answered without interest, and she was.

They steered the log around a row of trees, avoiding floating barbed wire, and got into a little bay created by a natural hollow of the land. Where the bay was now, there would be a pond full of frogs later in the spring, and by the middle of summer there would be no water visible at all, just a low tangle of reeds and bushes, green, to show that mud was still wet around their roots. Larger bushes, willows, grew around the steep bank of this pond and were still partly out of the water. Eva and Carol let the log ride in. They saw a place where something was caught.

It was a boat, or part of one. An old rowboat with most of one side ripped out,   1
the board that had been the seat just dangling. It was pushed up among the branches, lying on what would have been its side, if it had a side, the prow caught high.

Their idea came to them without consultation, at the same time:

"You guys! Hey, you guys!"

"We found you a boat!"

"Stop building your stupid raft and come and look at the boat!"

What surprised them in the first place was that the boys really did come, scram-
bling overland, half running, half sliding down the bank, wanting to see.

"Hey, where?"

"Where is it. I don't see no boat."

What surprised them in the second place was that when the boys did actually see what boat was meant, this old flood-smashed wreck held up in the branches, they did not understand that they had been fooled, that a joke had been played on them.

They did not show a moment's disappointment, but seemed as pleased at the discovery as if the boat had been whole and new. They were already barefoot, because they had been wading in the water to get lumber, and they waded in here without a stop, surrounding the boat and appraising it and paying no attention even of an insulting kind to Eva and Carol who bobbed up and down on their log. Eva and Carol had to call to them.

"How do you think you're going to get it off?"

"It won't float anyway."   25

"What makes you think it will float?"

"It'll sink. Glub-blub-blub, you'll all be drownded."

The boys did not answer, because they were too busy walking around the boat, pulling at it in a testing way to see how it could be got off with the least possible damage. Frank, who was the most literate, talkative and inept of the three, began referring to the boat as *she*, an affectation which Eva and Carol acknowledged with fishmouths of contempt.

"She's caught two places. You got to be careful not to tear a hole in her bottom. She's heavier than you'd think."

It was Clayton who climbed up and freed the boat, and Bud, a tall fat boy, who   30
got the weight of it on his back to turn it into the water so that they could half float, half carry it to shore. All this took some time. Eva and Carol abandoned their log and waded out of the water. They walked overland to get their shoes and socks and bicycles. They did not need to come back this way but they came. They stood at the top of the hill, leaning on their bicycles. They did not go on home, but they did not sit down and frankly watch, either. They stood more or less facing each other, but glancing down at the water and at the boys struggling with the boat, as if they had just halted for a moment out of curiosity, and staying longer than they intended, to see what came of this unpromising project.

About nine o'clock, or when it was nearly dark—dark to people inside the houses, but not quite dark outside—they all returned to town, going along Mayo Street in a sort of procession. Frank and Bud and Clayton came carrying the boat, upside-down, and Eva and Carol walked behind, wheeling their bicycles. The boys' heads were almost hidden in the darkness of the overturned boat, with its smell of soaked wood, cold swampy water. The girls could look ahead and see the street lights in their tin reflectors, a necklace of lights climbing Mayo Street, reaching all the way up to the standpipe. They turned onto Burns Street heading for Clayton's house, the nearest house belonging to any of them. This was not the way home for Eva or for Carol either, but they followed along. The boys were perhaps too busy carrying the boat to tell them to go away. Some younger children were still out playing, playing hopscotch on the sidewalk though they could hardly see. At this time of year the bare sidewalk was still such a novelty and delight. These children cleared out of the way and watched the boat go by with unwilling respect; they shouted questions after it, wanting to know where it came from and what was going to be done with it. No one answered them. Eva and Carol as well as the boys refused to answer or even look at them.

The five of them entered Clayton's yard. The boys shifted weight, as if they were going to put the boat down.

"You better take it round to the back where nobody can see it," Carol said. That was the first thing any of them had said since they came into town.

The boys said nothing but went on, following a mud path between Clayton's house and a leaning board fence. They let the boat down in the back yard.

"It's a stolen boat, you know," said Eva, mainly for the effect. "It must've belonged   35
to somebody. You stole it."

"You was the ones who stole it then," Bud said, short of breath. "It was you seen it
first."

"It was you took it."

"It was all of us then. If one of us gets in trouble then all of us does."

"Are you going to tell anybody on them?" said Carol as she and Eva rode home,
along the streets which were dark between the lights now and potholed from winter.

"It's up to you, I won't if you won't."   40

"I won't if you won't."

They rode in silence, relinquishing something, but not discontented.

The board fence in Clayton's back yard had every so often a post which supported
it, or tried to, and it was on these posts that Eva and Carol spent several evenings sitting,
jauntily but not very comfortably. Or else they just leaned against the fence while the
boys worked on the boat. During the first couple of evenings neighborhood children
attracted by the sound of hammering tried to get into the yard to see what was going
on, but Eva and Carol blocked their way.

"Who said you could come in here?"

"Just us can come in this yard."   45

These evenings were getting longer, the air milder. Skipping was starting on the
sidewalks. Further along the street there was a row of hard maples that had been tapped.
Children drank the sap as fast as it could drip into the buckets. The old man and woman
who owned the trees, and who hoped to make syrup, came running out of the house
making noises as if they were trying to scare away crows. Finally, every spring, the old
man would come out on his porch and fire his shotgun into the air, and then the thieving would stop.

None of those working on the boat bothered about stealing sap, though all had
done so last year.

The lumber to repair the boat was picked up here and there, along back lanes. At
this time of year things were lying around—old boards and branches, sodden mitts,
spoons flung out with the dishwater, lids of pudding pots that had been set in the snow to
cool, all the debris that can sift through and survive winter. The tools came from Clayton's
cellar—left over, presumably, from the time when his father was alive—and though they
had nobody to advise them the boys seemed to figure out more or less the manner in
which boats are built, or rebuilt. Frank was the one who showed up with diagrams from
books and *Popular Mechanics* magazines. Clayton looked at these diagrams and listened to
Frank read the instructions and then went ahead and decided in his own way what was
to be done. Bud was best at sawing. Eva and Carol watched everything from the fence
and offered criticism and thought up names. The names for the boat that they thought of
were: Water Lily, Sea Horse, Flood Queen, and Caro-Eve, after them because they had
found it. The boys did not say which, if any, of these names they found satisfactory.

The boat had to be tarred. Clayton heated up a pot of tar on the kitchen stove
and brought it out and painted slowly, his thorough way, sitting astride the overturned
boat. The other boys were sawing a board to make a new seat. As Clayton worked, the
tar cooled and thickened so that finally he could not move the brush any more. He
turned to Eva and held out the pot and said, "You can go in and heat this on the
stove."

Eva took the pot and went up the back steps. The kitchen seemed black after outside, but it must be light enough to see in, because there was Clayton's mother standing
at the ironing board, ironing. She did that for a living, took in wash and ironing.

"Please may I put the tar pot on the stove?" said Eva, who had been brought up to talk politely to parents, even wash-and-iron ladies, and who for some reason especially wanted to make a good impression on Clayton's mother.

"You'll have to poke up the fire then," said Clayton's mother, as if she doubted whether Eva would know how to do that. But Eva could see now, and she picked up the lid with the stove-lifter, and took the poker and poked up a flame. She stirred the tar as it softened. She felt privileged. Then and later. Before she went to sleep a picture of Clayton came to her mind; she saw him sitting astride the boat, tar-painting, with such concentration, delicacy, absorption. She thought of him speaking to her, out of his isolation, in such an ordinary peaceful taking-for-granted voice.

On the twenty-fourth of May, a school holiday in the middle of the week, the boat was carried out of town, a long way now, off the road over fields and fences that had been repaired, to where the river flowed between its normal banks. Eva and Carol, as well as the boys, took turns carrying it. It was launched in the water from a cow-trampled spot between willow bushes that were fresh out in leaf. The boys went first. They yelled with triumph when the boat did float, when it rode amazingly down the river current. The boat was painted black, and green inside, with yellow seats, and a strip of yellow all the way around the outside. There was no name on it, after all. The boys could not imagine that it needed any name to keep it separate from the other boats in the world.

Eva and Carol ran along the bank, carrying bags full of peanut butter-and-jam sandwiches, pickles, bananas, chocolate cake, potato chips, graham crackers stuck together with corn syrup and five bottles of pop to be cooled in the river water. The bottles bumped against their legs. They yelled for a turn.

"If they don't let us they're bastards," Carol said, and they yelled together. "We found it! We found it!"   55

The boys did not answer, but after a while they brought the boat in, and Carol and Eva came crashing, panting down the bank.

"Does it leak?"

"It don't leak yet."

"We forgot a bailing can," wailed Carol, but nevertheless she got in, with Eva, and Frank pushed them off, crying. "Here's to a Watery Grave!"

And the thing about being in a boat was that it was not solidly bobbing, like a log,   60
but was cupped in the water, so that riding in it was not like being on something in the water, but like being in the water itself. Soon they were all going out in the boat in mixed-up turns, two boys and a girl, two girls and a boy, a girl and a boy, until things were so confused it was impossible to tell whose turn came next, and nobody cared anyway. They went down the river—those who weren't riding, running along the bank to keep up. They passed under two bridges, one iron, one cement. Once they saw a big carp just resting, it seemed to smile at them, in the bridge-shaded water. They did not know how far they had gone on the river, but things had changed—the water had got shallower, and the land flatter. Across an open field they saw a building that looked like a house, abandoned. They dragged the boat up on the bank and tied it and set out across the field.

"That's the old station," Frank said. "That's Pedder Station." The others had heard this name but he was the one who knew, because his father was the station agent in town. He said that this was a station on a branch line that had been torn up, and that there had been a sawmill here, but a long time ago.

Inside the station it was dark, cool. All the windows were broken. Glass lay in shards and in fairly big pieces on the floor. They walked around finding the larger pieces of glass and tramping on them, smashing them, it was like cracking ice on puddles. Some partitions were still in place, you could see where the ticket window had been. There was a bench lying on its side. People had been here, it looked as if people came here all the time, though it was so far from anywhere. Beer bottles and pop bottles were lying around, also cigarette packages, gum and candy wrappers, the paper from a loaf of bread. The walls were covered with dim and fresh pencil and chalk writings and carved with knives.

> I LOVE RONNIE COLES
>
> I WANT TO FUCK
>
> KILROY WAS HERE
>
> RONNIE COLES IS AN ASS-HOLE
>
> WHAT ARE YOU DOING HERE?
>
> WAITING FOR A TRAIN
>
> DAWNA   MARY-LOU   BARBARA   JOANNE

It was exciting to be inside this large, dark, empty place, with the loud noise of breaking glass and their voices ringing back from the underside of the roof. They tipped the old beer bottles against their mouths. That reminded them that they were hungry and thirsty and they cleared a place in the middle of the floor and sat down and ate the lunch. They drank the pop just as it was, lukewarm. They ate everything there was and licked the smears of peanut butter and jam off the bread-paper in which the sandwiches had been wrapped.

They played Truth or Dare.

"I dare you to write on the wall, I am a Stupid Ass, and sign your name."

"Tell the truth—what is the worst lie you ever told?"

"Did you ever wet the bed?"

"Did you ever dream you were walking down the street without any clothes on?"

"I dare you to go outside and pee on the railway sign."

It was Frank who had to do that. They could not see him, even his back, but they knew he did it, they heard the hissing sound of his pee. They all sat still, amazed, unable to think of what the next dare would be.

"I dare everybody," said Frank from the doorway. "I dare—Everybody."

"What?"

"Take off all our clothes."

Eva and Carol screamed.

"Anybody who won't do it has to walk—has to *crawl*—around this floor on their hands and knees."

They were all quiet, till Eva said, almost complacently, "What first?"

"Shoes and socks."

"Then we have to go outside, there's too much glass here."

They pulled off their shoes and socks in the doorway, in the sudden blinding sun. The field before them was bright as water. They ran across where the tracks used to go.

"That's enough, that's enough," said Carol. "Watch out for thistles!"

"Tops! Everybody take off their tops!"

"I won't! We won't, will we, Eva?"

But Eva was whirling round and round in the sun where the track used to be. "I don't care, I don't care! Truth or Dare! Truth or Dare!"

She unbuttoned her blouse as she whirled, as if she didn't know what her hand was doing, she flung it off.

Carol took off hers. "I wouldn't have done it, if you hadn't!"

"Bottoms!"

Nobody said a word this time, they all bent and stripped themselves. Eva, naked first, started running across the field, and then all the others ran, all five of them running bare through the knee-high hot grass, running towards the river. Not caring now about being caught but in fact leaping and yelling to call attention to themselves, if there was anybody to hear or see. They felt as if they were going to jump off a cliff and fly. They felt that something was happening to them different from anything that had happened before, and it had to do with the boat, the water, the sunlight, the dark ruined station, and each other. They thought of each other now hardly as names or people, but as echoing shrieks, reflections, all bold and white and loud and scandalous, and as fast as arrows. They went running without a break into the cold water and when it came almost to the tops of their legs they fell on it and swam. It stopped their noise. Silence, amazement, came over them in a rush. They dipped and floated and separated, sleek as mink.

Eva stood up in the water her hair dripping, water running down her face. She was waist deep. She stood on smooth stones, her feet fairly wide apart, water flowing between her legs. About a yard away from her Clayton also stood up, and they were blinking the water out of their eyes, looking at each other. Eva did not turn or try to hide; she was quivering from the cold of the water, but also with pride, shame, boldness, and exhilaration.

Clayton shook his head violently, as if he wanted to bang something out of it, then bent over and took a mouthful of river water. He stood up with his cheeks full and made a tight hole of his mouth and shot the water at her as if it was coming out of a hose, hitting her exactly, first one breast and then the other. Water from his mouth ran down her body. He hooted to see it, a loud self-conscious sound that nobody would have expected, from him. The others looked up from wherever they were in the water and closed in to see.

Eva crouched down and slid into the water, letting her head go right under. She swam, and when she let her head out, downstream, Carol was coming after her and the boys were already on the bank, already running into the grass, showing their skinny backs, their white, flat buttocks. They were laughing and saying things to each other but she couldn't hear, for the water in her ears. 90

"What did he do?" said Carol.

"Nothing."

They crept in to shore. "Let's stay in the bushes till they go," said Eva. "I hate them anyway. I really do. Don't you hate them?"

"Sure," said Carol, and they waited, not very long, until they heard the boys still noisy and excited coming down to the place a bit upriver where they had left the boat. They heard them jump in and start rowing.

"They've got all the hard part, going back," said Eva, hugging herself and shivering violently. "Who cares? Anyway. It never was our boat." 95

"What if they tell?" said Carol.

"We'll say it's all a lie."

Eva hadn't thought of this solution until she said it, but as soon as she did she felt almost light-hearted again. The ease and scornfulness of it did make them both giggle, and slapping themselves and splashing out of the water they set about developing one of those fits of laughter in which, as soon as one showed signs of exhaustion, the other would snort and start up again, and they would make helpless—soon genuinely helpless—faces at each other and bend over and grab themselves as if they had the worst pain.

QUESTIONS

1. Consider the details used in passages of description in the story. What kinds of details are included?

2. What is the level of diction in the dialogue of the story? From the dialogue, what do you learn about the various speakers?

3. Study paragraph 10. What does the paragraph tell you about Eva as a limited-point-of-view center of interest? How?

4. Consider the last paragraph in the story as a paragraph of action. What verbs are used, and how well do they help you visualize and imagine the sounds of the scene? What is the effect of the verb "snort"?

5. From the lifestyle and artifacts mentioned, what do you learn about the time of the events and the economic level of the town? What is the effect of the facts that it is early springtime, that the water is still cold, but that in May the water is swimmable? What are the implications for summer?

FRANK O'CONNOR (1903–1966)

Frank O'Connor, the nom de plume *of Michael O'Donovan, was an only child of poor parents in County Cork, Ireland. He began writing when young, and for a time he was a director of Ireland's national theater. His output as a writer was considerable, with sixty-seven stories appearing in the posthumous* Collected Stories *of 1981. A meticulous writer, he was constantly revising his work. "First Confession," for example, went through a number of stages before the final version included here.*

First Confession _____ 1951

All the trouble began when my grandfather died and my grandmother—my father's mother—came to live with us. Relations in the one house are a strain at the best of times, but, to make matters worse, my grandmother was a real old countrywoman and quite unsuited to the life in town. She had a fat, wrinkled old face, and, to Mother's great indignation, went round the house in bare feet—the boots had her crippled, she said. For dinner she had a jug of porter° and a pot of potatoes with—sometimes—a bit of salt fish, and she poured out the potatoes on the table and ate them slowly, with great relish, using her fingers by way of a fork.

Now, girls are supposed to be fastidious, but I was the one who suffered most from this. Nora, my sister, just sucked up to the old woman for the penny she got every Friday out of the old-age pension, a thing I could not do. I was too honest, that was my trouble; and when I was playing with Bill Connell, the sergeant-major's son, and saw my grandmother steering up the path with the jug of porter sticking out from beneath her shawl I was mortified. I made excuses not to let him come into the house, because I could never be sure what she would be up to when we went in.

porter: a dark-brown beer.

When Mother was at work and my grandmother made the dinner I wouldn't touch it. Nora once tried to make me, but I hid under the table from her and took the bread-knife with me for protection. Nora let on to be very indignant (she wasn't, of course, but she knew Mother saw through her, so she sided with Gran) and came after me. I lashed out at her with the bread-knife, and after that she left me alone. I stayed there till Mother came in from work and made my dinner, but when Father came in later Nora said in a shocked voice: "Oh, Dadda, do you know what Jackie did at dinnertime?" Then, of course, it all came out; Father gave me a flaking; Mother interfered, and for days after that he didn't speak to me and Mother barely spoke to Nora. And all because of that old woman! God knows, I was heart-scalded.

Then, to crown my misfortune, I had to make my first confession and communion. It was an old woman called Ryan who prepared us for these. She was about the one age with Gran; she was well-to-do, lived in a big house on Montenotte, wore a black cloak and bonnet, and came every day to school at three o'clock when we should have been going home, and talked to us of hell. She may have mentioned the other place as well, but that could only have been by accident, for hell had the first place in her heart.

She lit a candle, took out a new half-crown, and offered it to the first boy who would hold one finger—only one finger!—in the flame for five minutes by the school clock. Being always very ambitious I was tempted to volunteer, but I thought it might look greedy. Then she asked were we afraid of holding one finger—only one finger!—in a little candle flame for five minutes and not afraid of burning all over in roasting hot furnaces for all eternity. "All eternity! Just think of that! A whole lifetime goes by and it's nothing, not even a drop in the ocean of your sufferings." The woman was really interesting about hell, but my attention was all fixed on the half-crown. At the end of the lesson she put it back in her purse. It was a great disappointment; a religious woman like that, you wouldn't think she'd bother about a thing like a half-crown.

Another day she said she knew a priest who woke one night to find a fellow he didn't recognize leaning over the end of his bed. The priest was a bit frightened— naturally enough—but he asked the fellow what he wanted, and the fellow said in a deep, husky voice that he wanted to go to confession. The priest said it was an awkward time and wouldn't it do in the morning, but the fellow said that last time he went to confession, there was one sin he kept back, being ashamed to mention it, and now it was always on his mind. Then the priest knew it was a bad case, because the fellow was after making a bad confession and committing a mortal sin. He got up to dress, and just then the cock crew in the yard outside, and—lo and behold!—when the priest looked round there was no sign of the fellow, only a smell of burning timber, and when the priest looked at his bed didn't he see the print of two hands burned in it? That was because the fellow had made a bad confession. This story made a shocking impression on me.

But the worst of all was when she showed us how to examine our conscience. Did we take the name of the Lord, our God, in vain? Did we honour our father and our mother? (I asked her did this include grandmothers and she said it did.) Did we love our neighbours as ourselves? Did we covet our neighbour's goods? (I thought of the way I felt about the penny that Nora got every Friday.) I decided that, between one thing and another, I must have broken the whole ten commandments, all on account of that old woman, and so far as I could see, so long as she remained in the house I had no hope of ever doing anything else.

I was scared to death of confession. The day the whole class went I let on to have a toothache, hoping my absence wouldn't be noticed; but at three o'clock, just as I was feeling safe, along comes a chap with a message from Mrs. Ryan that I was to go to

5

confession myself on Saturday and be at the chapel for communion with the rest. To make it worse, Mother couldn't come with me and sent Nora instead.

Now, that girl had ways of tormenting me that Mother never knew of. She held my hand as we went down the hill, smiling sadly and saying how sorry she was for me, as if she were bringing me to the hospital for an operation.

"Oh, God help us!" she moaned. "Isn't it a terrible pity you weren't a good boy? Oh, Jackie, my heart bleeds for you! How will you ever think of all your sins? Don't forget you have to tell him about the time you kicked Gran on the shin."   10

"Lemme go!" I said, trying to drag myself free of her. "I don't want to go to confession at all."

"But sure, you'll have to go to confession, Jackie," she replied in the same regretful tone. "Sure, if you didn't the parish priest would be up to the house, looking for you. 'Tisn't, God knows, that I'm not sorry for you. Do you remember the time you tried to kill me with the bread-knife under the table? And the language you used to me? I don't know what he'll do with you at all, Jackie. He might have to send you up to the bishop."

I remember thinking bitterly that she didn't know the half of what I had to tell— if I told it. I knew I couldn't tell it, and understood perfectly why the fellow in Mrs. Ryan's story made a bad confession; it seemed to me a great shame that people wouldn't stop criticizing him. I remember that steep hill down to the church, and the sunlit hill-sides beyond the valley of the river, which I saw in the gaps between the houses like Adam's last glimpse of Paradise.°

Then, when she had manœuvered me down the long flight of steps to the chapel yard, Nora suddenly changed her tone. She became the raging malicious devil she really was.

"There you are!" she said with a yelp of triumph, hurling me through the church   15
door. "And I hope he'll give you the penitential psalms, you dirty little caffler."

I knew then I was lost, given up to eternal justice. The door with the coloured-glass panels swung shut behind me, the sunlight went out and gave place to deep shadow, and the wind whistled outside so that the silence within seemed to crackle like ice under my feet. Nora sat in front of me by the confession box. There were a couple of old women ahead of her, and then a miserable-looking poor devil came and wedged me in at the other side, so that I couldn't escape even if I had the courage. He joined his hands and rolled his eyes in the direction of the roof, muttering aspirations in an anguished tone, and I wondered had he a grandmother too. Only a grandmother could account for a fellow behaving in that heartbroken way, but he was better off than I, for he at least could go and confess his sins; while I would make a bad confession and then die in the night and be continually coming back and burning people's furniture.

Nora's turn came, and I heard the sound of something slamming, and then her voice as if butter wouldn't melt in her mouth, and then another slam, and out she came. God, the hypocrisy of women! Her eyes were lowered, her head was bowed, and her hands were joined very low down on her stomach, and she walked up the aisle to the side altar looking like a saint. You never saw such an exhibition of devotion, and I remembered the devilish malice with which she had tormented me all the way from our door, and wondered were all religious people like that, really. It was my turn now. With the fear of damnation in my soul I went in, and the confessional door closed of itself behind me.

It was pitch-dark and I couldn't see priest or anything else. Then I really began to be frightened. In the darkness it was a matter between God and me, and He had all

Adam's last glimpse of Paradise: Genesis 3:23–24.

the odds. He knew what my intentions were before I even started; I had no chance. All I had ever been told about confession got mixed up in my mind, and I knelt to one wall and said: "Bless me, father, for I have sinned; this is my first confession." I waited for a few minutes, but nothing happened, so I tried it on the other wall. Nothing happened there either. He had me spotted all right.

It must have been then that I noticed the shelf at about one height with my head. It was really a place for grown-up people to rest their elbows, but in my distracted state I thought it was probably the place you were supposed to kneel. Of course, it was on the high side and not very deep, but I was always good at climbing and managed to get up all right. Staying up was the trouble. There was room only for my knees, and nothing you could get a grip on but a sort of wooden moulding a bit above it. I held on to the moulding and repeated the words a little louder, and this time something happened all right. A slide was slammed back; a little light entered the box, and a man's voice said: "Who's there?"

"'Tis me, father," I said for fear he mightn't see me and go away again. I   20 couldn't see him at all. The place the voice came from was under the moulding, about level with my knees, so I took a good grip of the moulding and swung myself down till I saw the astonished face of a young priest looking up at me. He had to put his head on one side to see me, and I had to put mine on one side to see him, so we were more or less talking to one another upside-down. It struck me as a queer way of hearing confessions, but I didn't feel it my place to criticize.

"Bless me, father, for I have sinned; this is my first confession," I rattled off all in one breath, and swung myself down the least shade more to make it easier for him.

"What are you doing up there?" he shouted in an angry voice, and the strain the politeness was putting on my hold of the moulding, and the shock of being addressed in such an uncivil tone, were too much for me. I lost my grip, tumbled, and hit the door an unmerciful wallop before I found myself flat on my back in the middle of the aisle. The people who had been waiting stood up with their mouths open. The priest opened the door of the middle box and came out, pushing his biretta back from his forehead; he looked something terrible. Then Nora came scampering down the aisle.

"Oh, you dirty little caffler!" she said. "I might have known you'd do it. I might have known you'd disgrace me. I can't leave you out of my sight for one minute."

Before I could even get to my feet to defend myself she bent down and gave me a clip across the ear. This reminded me that I was so stunned I had even forgotten to cry, so that people might think I wasn't hurt at all, when in fact I was probably maimed for life. I gave a roar out of me.

"What's all this about?" the priest hissed, getting angrier than ever and pushing   25 Nora off me. "How dare you hit the child like that, you little vixen?"

"But I can't do my penance with him, father," Nora cried, cocking an outraged eye up to him.

"Well, go and do it, or I'll give you some more to do," he said, giving me a hand up. "Was it coming to confession you were, my poor man?" he asked me.

"'Twas, father," said I with a sob.

"Oh," he said respectfully, "a big hefty fellow like you must have terrible sins. Is this your first?"

"'Tis, father," said I.   30

"Worse and worse," he said gloomily. "The crimes of a lifetime. I don't know will I get rid of you at all today. You'd better wait now till I'm finished with these old ones. You can see by the looks of them they haven't much to tell."

"I will, father," I said with something approaching joy.

The relief of it was really enormous. Nora stuck out her tongue at me from behind his back, but I couldn't even be bothered retorting. I knew from the very moment that man opened his mouth that he was intelligent above the ordinary. When I had time to think, I saw how right I was. It only stood to reason that a fellow confessing after seven years would have more to tell than people that went every week. The crimes of a lifetime, exactly as he said. It was only what he expected, and the rest was the cackle of old women and girls with their talk of hell, the bishop, and the penitential psalms. That was all they knew. I started to make my examination of conscience, and barring the one bad business of my grandmother it didn't seem so bad.

The next time, the priest steered me into the confession box himself and left the shutter back the way I could see him get in and sit down at the further side of the grille from me.

"Well, now," he said, "what do they call you?"   35

"Jackie, father," said I.

"And what's a-trouble to you, Jackie?"

"Father," I said, feeling I might as well get it over while I had him in good humour, "I had it all arranged to kill my grandmother."

He seemed a bit shaken by that, all right, because he said nothing for quite a while.

"My goodness," he said at last, "that'd be a shocking thing to do. What put that   40
into your head?"

"Father," I said, feeling very sorry for myself, "she's an awful woman."

"Is she?" he asked. "What way is she awful?"

"She takes porter, father," I said, knowing well from the way Mother talked of it that this was a mortal sin, and hoping it would make the priest take a more favourable view of my case.

"Oh, my!" he said, and I could see he was impressed.

"And snuff, father," said I.   4;

"That's a bad case, sure enough, Jackie," he said.

"And she goes round in her bare feet, father," I went on in a rush of self-pity, "and she knows I don't like her, and she gives pennies to Nora and none to me, and my da sides with her and flakes me, and one night I was so heartscalded I made up my mind I'd have to kill her."

"And what would you do with the body?" he asked with great interest.

"I was thinking I could chop that up and carry it away in a barrow I have," I said.

"Begor, Jackie," he said, "do you know you're a terrible child?"   5

"I know, father," I said, for I was just thinking the same thing myself. "I tried to kill Nora too with a bread-knife under the table, only I missed her."

"Is that the little girl that was beating you just now?" he asked.

"'Tis, father."

"Someone will go for her with a bread-knife one day, and he won't miss her," he said rather cryptically. "You must have great courage. Between ourselves, there's a lot of people I'd like to do the same to but I'd never have the nerve. Hanging is an awful death."

"Is it, father?" I asked with the deepest interest—I was always very keen on hanging. "Did you ever see a fellow hanged?"

"Dozens of them," he said solemnly. "And they all died roaring."

"Jay!" I said.

"Oh, a horrible death!" he said with great satisfaction. "Lots of fellows I saw killed their grandmothers too, but they all said 'twas never worth it."

He had me there for a full ten minutes talking, and then walked out the chapel yard with me. I was genuinely sorry to part with him, because he was the most entertaining character I'd ever met in the religious line. Outside, after the shadow of the church, the sunlight was like the roaring of waves on a beach; it dazzled me; and when the frozen silence melted and I heard the screech of trams on the road my heart soared. I knew now I wouldn't die in the night and come back, leaving marks on my mother's furniture. It would be a great worry to her, and the poor soul had enough.

Nora was sitting on the railing, waiting for me, and she put on a very sour puss when she saw the priest with me. She was made jealous because a priest had never come out of the church with her.

"Well," she asked coldly, after he left me, "what did he give you?"

"Three Hail Marys," I said.

"Three Hail Marys," she repeated incredulously. "You mustn't have told him anything."

"I told him everything," I said confidently.

"About Gran and all?"

"About Gran and all."

(All she wanted was to be able to go home and say I'd made a bad confession.)

"Did you tell him you went for me with the bread-knife?" she asked with a frown.

"I did to be sure."

"And he only gave you three Hail Marys?"

"That's all."

She slowly got down from the railing with a baffled air. Clearly, this was beyond her. As we mounted the steps back to the main road she looked at me suspiciously.

"What are you sucking?" she asked.

"Bullseyes."

"Was it the priest gave them to you?"

"'Twas."

"Lord God," she wailed bitterly, "some people have all the luck! 'Tis no advantage to anybody trying to be good. I might just as well be a sinner like you."

QUESTIONS

1. Describe Jackie as a narrator. What is the level of his language? To whom does he seem to be speaking or writing? What elements of language do you find in the story that seem characteristically Irish?

2. Describe Jackie's character. How old do you think he is at the time of the narration? Is there evidence that he has grown as a person since the time of the story's events? Do you think his attitutdes have changed about his grandmother? His parents? His sister? Mrs. Ryan? The priest?

3. Is Jackie's confession a "good" one? Whose religion seems more appealing, Mrs. Ryan's or the priest's?

4. To what degree are the relationships within Jackie's family either ordinary or unusual?

5. "First Confession" is a funny story. What contributions are made to the humor by the situations? The language?

MARK TWAIN   (1835–1910)

Mark Twain (born Samuel Clemens) is one of the literary giants of nineteenth- and early-twentieth-century America. Largely because of his use of colloquial and regional English in Huckleberry Finn, *he was acknowledged by Hemingway as a founder of American literature. He was born in Missouri and spent much of his youth as a Mississippi River pilot, Confederate soldier, journalist, and miner. In 1863 he adopted "Mark Twain" as his nom de plume. His most famous works are the novels* Tom Sawyer *(1876) and* Huckleberry Finn *(1884–1885).* Huckleberry Finn *is today the subject of controversy for characterizations some people consider racist, even though more than a century has passed since its publication.*

"Luck" is a brief story (Twain calls it a "sketch") illustrating Twain's art of comic debunking, a characteristic that he also shows in works such as The Innocents Abroad *and the short critical essay "Fenimore Cooper's Literary Offenses." The technique in "Luck" is to present an inside, private view of a person of high reputation and in effect to show that "the emperor has no clothes."*

Luck[1] _____ *1891*

It was at a banquet in London in honor of one of the two or three conspicuously illustrious English military names of this generation. For reasons which will presently appear, I will withhold his real name and titles and call him Lieutenant-General Lord Arthur Scoresby, Y.C., K.C.B., etc., etc. What a fascination there is in a renowned name! There sat the man, in actual flesh, whom I had heard of so many thousands of times since that day, thirty years before, when his name shot suddenly to the zenith from a Crimean battlefield,° to remain forever celebrated. It was food and drink to me to look, and look, and look at that demi-god; scanning, searching, noting: the quietness, the reserve, the noble gravity of his countenance; the simple honesty that expressed itself all over him; the sweet unconsciousness of his greatness—unconsciousness of the hundreds of admiring eyes fastened upon him, unconsciousness of the deep, loving, sincere worship welling out of the breasts of those people and flowing toward him.

The clergyman at my left was an old acquaintance of mine—clergyman now, but had spent the first half of his life in the camp and field and as an instructor in the military school at Woolwich. Just at the moment I have been talking about a veiled and singular light glimmered in his eyes and he leaned down and muttered confidentially to me—indicating the hero of the banquet with a gesture:

"Privately—he's an absolute fool."

This verdict was a great surprise to me. If its subject had been Napoleon, or Socrates, or Solomon, my astonishment could not have been greater. Two things I was well aware of: that the Reverend was a man of strict veracity and that his judgment

---

[1] This is not a fancy sketch. I got it from a clergyman who was an instructor at Woolwich forty years ago, and who vouched for its truth. [Twain's note.]

Crimean battlefield: In the Crimean War (1853–1856), England was one of the allies that fought against Russia.

of men was good. Therefore I knew, beyond doubt or question, that the world was mistaken about this hero: he *was* a fool. So I meant to find out, at a convenient moment, how the Reverend, all solitary and alone, had discovered the secret.

Some days later the opportunity came, and this is what the Reverend told me: 5

About forty years ago I was an instructor in the military academy at Woolwich. I was present in one of the sections when young Scoresby underwent his preliminary examination. I was touched to the quick with pity, for the rest of the class answered up brightly and handsomely, while he—why, dear me, he didn't know *anything*, so to speak. He was evidently good, and sweet, and lovable, and guileless; and so it was exceedingly painful to see him stand there, as serene as a graven image, and deliver himself of answers which were veritably miraculous for stupidity and ignorance. All the compassion in me was aroused in his behalf. I said to myself, when he comes to be examined again he will be flung over, of course; so it will be simply a harmless act of charity to ease his fall as much as I can. I took him aside and found that he knew a little of Caesar's history; and as he didn't know anything else, I went to work and drilled him like a galley-slave on a certain line of stock questions concerning Caesar which I knew would be used. If you'll believe me, he went through with flying colors on examination day! He went through on that purely superficial "cram," and got compliments too, while others, who knew a thousand times more than he, got plucked. By some strangely lucky accident—an accident not likely to happen twice in a century—he was asked no question outside of the narrow limits of his drill.

It was stupefying. Well, all through his course I stood by him, with something of the sentiment which a mother feels for a crippled child; and he always saved himself—just by miracle, apparently.

Now, of course, the thing that would expose him and kill him at last was mathematics. I resolved to make his death as easy as I could; so I drilled him and crammed him, and crammed him and drilled him, just on the line of questions which the examiners would be most likely to use, and then launched him on his fate. Well, sir, try to conceive of the result: to my consternation, he took the first prize! And with it he got a perfect ovation in the way of compliments.

Sleep? There was no more sleep for me for a week. My conscience tortured me day and night. What I had done I had done purely through charity, and only to ease the poor youth's fall. I never had dreamed of any such preposterous results as the thing that had happened. I felt as guilty and miserable as Frankenstein. Here was a wooden-head whom I had put in the way of glittering promotions and prodigious responsibilities, and but one thing could happen: he and his responsibilities would all go to ruin together at the first opportunity.

The Crimean War had just broken out. Of course there had to be a war, I said to   10
myself. We couldn't have peace and give this donkey a chance to die before he is found out. I waited for the earthquake. It came. And it made me reel when it did come. He was actually gazetted to a captaincy in a marching regiment! Better men grow old and gray in the service before they climb to a sublimity like that. And who could ever have foreseen that they would go and put such a load of responsibility on such green and inadequate shoulders? I could just barely have stood it if they had made him a cornet; but a captain—think of it! I thought my hair would turn white.

Consider what I did—I who so loved repose and inaction. I said to myself, I am responsible to the country for this, and I must go along with him and protect the country against him as far as I can. So I took my poor little capital that I had saved up through years of work and grinding economy, and went with a sigh and bought a cornetcy in his regiment, and away we went to the field.

And there—oh, dear, it was awful. Blunders?—why he never did anything *but* blunder. But, you see, nobody was in the fellow's secret. Everybody had him focused wrong, and necessarily misinterpreted his performance every time. Consequently they took his idiotic blunders for inspirations of genius. They did, honestly! His mildest blunders were enough to make a man in his right mind cry; and they did make me cry—and rage and rave, too, privately. And the thing that kept me always in a sweat of apprehension was the fact that every fresh blunder he made increased the luster of his reputation! I kept saying to myself, he'll get so high that when discovery does finally come it will be like the sun falling out of the sky.

He went right along, up from grade to grade, over the dead bodies of his superiors, until at last, in the hottest moment of the battle of——— down went our colonel, and my heart jumped into my mouth, for Scoresby was next in rank! Now for it, said I: we'll all land in Sheol in ten minutes, sure.

The battle was awfully hot; the allies were steadily giving way all over the field. Our regiment occupied a position that was vital; a blunder now must be destruction. At this crucial moment, what does this immortal fool do but detach the regiment from its place and order a charge over a neighboring hill where there wasn't a suggestion of an enemy! "There you go!" I said to myself; "this *is* the end at last."

And away we did go, and were over the shoulder of the hill before the insane movement could be discovered and stopped. And what did we find? An entire and unsuspected Russian army in reserve! And what happened? We were eaten up? That is necessarily what would have happened in ninety-nine cases out of a hundred. But no; those Russians argued that no single regiment would come browsing around there at such a time. It must be the entire English army, and that the sly Russian game was detected and blocked, so they turned tail, and away they went, pell-mell, over the hill and down into the field, in wild confusion, and we after them; they themselves broke the solid Russian center in the field, and tore through, and in no time there was the most tremendous rout you ever saw, and the defeat of the allies was turned into a sweeping and splendid victory! Marshall Canrobert looked on, dizzy with astonishment, admiration, and delight; and sent right off for Scoresby, and hugged him, and decorated him on the field in presence of all the armies!

And what was Scoresby's blunder that time? Merely the mistaking his right hand for his left—that was all. An order had come to him to fall back and support our right; and, instead, he fell *forward* and went over the hill to the left. But the name he won that day as a marvelous military genius filled the world with his glory, and that glory will never fade while history books last.

He is just as good and sweet and lovable and unpretending as a man can be, but he doesn't know enough to come in when it rains. Now that is absolutely true. He is the supremest ass in the universe; and until half an hour ago nobody knew it but himself and me. He has been pursued, day by day and year by year, by a most phenomenal astonishing luckiness. He has been a shining soldier in all our wars for a generation; he has littered his whole military life with blunders, and yet has never committed one that didn't make him a knight or a baronet or a lord or something. Look at his breast; why, he is just clothed in domestic and foreign decorations. Well, sir, every one of them is the record of some shouting stupidity or other; and, taken together, they are proof that the very best thing in all this world that can befall a man is to be born lucky. I say again, as I said at the banquet, Scoresby's an absolute fool.

15

QUESTIONS

1. Describe Twain's style as a writer of narrative prose. What kinds of detail does he present? Does he give you enough detail about the battle during the Crimean War, for example, to justify an assertion that he describes action vividly? Or does he confine his detail to illuminate the life of Scoresby?

2. What elements in the story are amusing? How does the development of humor depend on Twain's arrangement of words?

3. Study the first paragraph. What does Twain intend after the "look, and look, and look" phrase? Why do you think he begins the story with such a description, which might even be called heroic? Contrast this paragraph with paragraph 12, where the word *blunder* is repeated.

4. Who begins the story? Who finally tells it? How does the second narrator learn about Scoresby? How does he summarize Scoresby's career?

JOHN UPDIKE   (b. 1932)

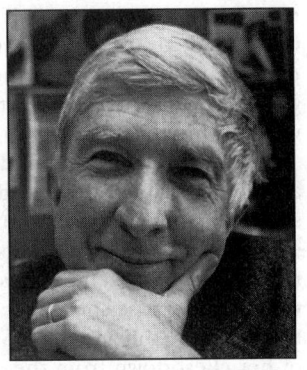

Updike was born and reared in Pennsylvania during the Great Depression. His parents were diligent about his education, and in 1950 he received a scholarship for study at Harvard, graduating in 1954. He worked for the New Yorker *for two years before deciding to devote himself exclusively to his own writing, but since then he has remained a frequent contributor of stories and poems to that magazine. In 1959, he published his first story collection,* The Same Door, *and his first novel,* The Poorhouse Fair. *In 1960, with* Rabbit, Run, *he began his extensive* Rabbit *chronicles. In 1981 he received the Pulitzer Prize for* Rabbit Is Rich. *His collected poems were published in 1993, and he is continually productive in writing new stories and poems. Today he is considered one of the best of America's major writers of fiction and poetry.*

A & P° _____ *1961*

In walks these three girls in nothing but bathing suits. I'm in the third checkout slot, with my back to the door, so I don't see them until they're over by the bread. The one that caught my eye first was the one in the plaid green two-piece. She was a chunky kid, with a good tan and a sweet broad soft-looking can with those two crescents of white just under it, where the sun never seems to hit, at the top of the backs of her legs. I stood there with my hand on a box of HiHo crackers trying to remember if I rang it up or not. I ring it up again and the customer starts giving me hell. She's one of these cash-register-watchers, a witch about fifty with rouge on her cheekbones and no eyebrows, and I know it made her day to trip me up. She'd been watching cash registers for fifty years and probably never seen a mistake before.

A & P: the Great Atlantic and Pacific Tea Company, a large grocery chain established in 1859 and still flourishing in 18 states, with more than 800 A & P stores in the United States and 200 in Canada.

By the time I got her feathers smoothed and her goodies into a bag—she gives me a little snort in passing, if she'd been born at the right time they would have burned her over in Salem—by the time I get her on her way the girls had circled around the bread and were coming back, without a pushcart, back my way along the counters, in the aisle between the checkouts and the Special bins. They didn't even have shoes on. There was this chunky one, with the two-piece—it was bright green and the seams on the bra were still sharp and her belly was still pretty pale so I guessed she just got it (the suit)—there was this one, with one of those chubby berry-faces, the lips all bunched together under her nose, this one, and a tall one, with black hair that hadn't quite frizzed right, and one of these sunburns right across under the eyes, and a chin that was too long—you know, the kind of girl other girls think is very "striking" and "attractive" but never quite makes it, as they very well know, which is why they like her so much—and then the third one, that wasn't quite so tall. She was the queen. She kind of led them, the other two peeking around and making their shoulders round. She didn't look around, not this queen, she just walked straight on slowly, on these long white prima-donna legs. She came down a little hard on her heels, as if she didn't walk in her bare feet that much, putting down her heels and then letting the weight move along to her toes as if she was testing the floor with every step, putting a little deliberate extra action into it. You never know for sure how girls' minds work (do you really think it's a mind in there or just a little buzz like a bee in a glass jar?) but you got the idea she had talked the other two into coming in here with her, and now she was showing them how to do it, walk slow and hold yourself straight.

She had on a kind of dirty-pink—beige, maybe, I don't know—bathing suit with a little nubble all over it and, what got me, the straps were down. They were off her shoulders looped loose around the cool tops of her arms, and I guess as a result the suit had slipped a little on her, so all around the top of the cloth there was this shining rim. If it hadn't been there you wouldn't have known there could have been anything whiter than those shoulders. With the straps pushed off, there was nothing between the top of the suit and the top of her head except just *her,* this clean bare plane of the top of her chest down from the shoulder bones like a dented sheet of metal tilted in the light. I mean, it was more than pretty.

She had sort of oaky hair that the sun and salt had bleached, done up in a bun that was unraveling, and a kind of prim face. Walking into the A & P with your straps down, I suppose it's the only kind of face you *can* have. She held her head so high her neck, coming up out of those white shoulders, looked kind of stretched, but I didn't mind. The longer her neck was, the more of her there was.

She must have felt in the corner of her eye me and over my shoulder Stokesie in the second slot watching, but she didn't tip. Not this queen. She kept her eyes moving across the racks, and stopped, and turned so slow it made my stomach rub the inside of my apron, and buzzed to the other two, who kind of huddled against her for relief, and then they all three of them went up the cat-and-dog-food-breakfast-cereal-macaroni-rice-raisins-seasonings-spreads-spaghetti-soft-drinks-crackers-and-cookies aisle. From the third slot I look straight up this aisle to the meat counter, and I watched them all the way. The fat one with the tan sort of fumbled with the cookies, but on second thought she put the package back. The sheep pushing their carts down the aisle—the girls were walking against the usual traffic (not that we have one-way signs or any-thing)—were pretty hilarious. You could see them, when Queenie's white shoulders dawned on them, kind of jerk, or hop, or hiccup, but their eyes snapped back to their own baskets and on they pushed. I bet you could set off dynamite in an A & P and the people would by and large keep reaching and checking oatmeal off their lists and muttering "Let me see, there was a third thing, began with A, asparagus, no ah, yes, applesauce!" or whatever it is they do mutter. But there was no doubt, this jiggled them. A few houseslaves in pin curlers even looked around after pushing their carts past to make sure what they had seen was correct.

You know, it's one thing to have a girl in a bathing suit down on the beach, where what with the glare nobody can look at each other much anyway, and another thing in the cool of the A & P, under the fluorescent lights, against all those stacked packages, with her feet paddling along naked over our checkerboard green-and-cream rubber-tile floor.

"Oh Daddy," Stokesie said beside me. "I feel so faint."

"Darling," I said. "Hold me tight." Stokesie's married, with two babies chalked up on his fuselage already, but as far as I can tell that's the only difference. He's twenty-two, and I was nineteen this April.

"Is it done?" he asks, the responsible married man finding his voice. I forgot to say he thinks he's going to be manager some sunny day, maybe in 1990 when it's called the Great Alexandrov and Petrooshki° Tea Company or something.

What he meant was, our town is five miles from the beach, with a big summer 10 colony out on the Point, but we're right in the middle of town, and the women generally put on a shirt or shorts or something before they get out of the car into the street. And anyway these are usually women with six children and varicose veins mapping their legs and nobody, including them, could care less. As I say, we're right in the middle of town, and if you stand at our front doors you can see two banks and the Congregational church and the newspaper store and three real-estate offices and about twenty-seven old freeloaders tearing up Central Street because the sewer broke again. It's not as if we're on the Cape,° we're north of Boston and there's people in this town haven't seen the ocean for twenty years.

The girls had reached the meat counter and were asking McMahon something. He pointed, they pointed, and they shuffled out of sight behind a pyramid of Diet Delight peaches. All that was left for us to see was old McMahon patting his mouth and looking after them sizing up their joints. Poor kids, I began to feel sorry for them, they couldn't help it.

Now here comes the sad part of the story, at least my family says it's sad, but I don't think it's so sad myself. The store's pretty empty, it being Thursday afternoon, so there was nothing much to do except lean on the register and wait for the girls to show up again. The whole store was like a pinball machine and I didn't know which tunnel they'd come out of. After a while they come around out of the far aisle, around the light bulbs, records at discount of the Caribbean Six or Tony Martin Sings or some such gunk you wonder they waste the wax on, sixpacks of candy bars, and plastic toys done up in cellophane that fall apart when a kid looks at them anyway. Around they come, Queenie still leading the way, and holding a little gray jar in her hand. Slots Three through Seven are unmanned and I could see her wondering between Stokes and me, but Stokesie with his usual luck draws an old party in baggy gray pants who stumbles up with four giant cans of pineapple juice (what do these bums *do* with all that pineapple juice? I've often

---

Great Alexandrov and Petrooshki: apparently a reference to the possibility that someday Russia might rule the United States.

the Cape: Cape Cod, the southeastern area of Massachusetts, a place of many resorts and beaches.

asked myself) so the girls come to me. Queenie puts down the jar and I take it into my fingers icy cold. Kingfish Fancy Herring Snacks in Pure Sour Cream: 49¢. Now her hands are empty, not a ring or a bracelet, bare as God made them, and I wonder where the money's coming from. Still with that prim look she lifts a folded dollar bill out of the hollow at the center of her nubbed pink top. The jar went heavy in my hand. Really, I thought that was so cute.

Then everybody's luck begins to run out. Lengel comes in from haggling with a truck full of cabbages on the lot and is about to scuttle into that door marked MANAGER behind which he hides all day when the girls touch his eye. Lengel's pretty dreary, teaches Sunday school and the rest, but he doesn't miss that much. He comes over and says, "Girls, this isn't the beach."

Queenie blushes, though maybe it's just a brush of sunburn I was noticing for the first time, now that she was so close. "My mother asked me to pick up a jar of herring snacks." Her voice kind of startled me, the way voices do when you see the people first, coming out so flat and dumb yet kind of tony, too, the way it ticked over "pick up" and "snacks." All of a sudden I slid right down her voice into her living room. Her father and the other men were standing around in ice-cream coats and bow ties and the women were in sandals picking up herring snacks on toothpicks off a big glass plate and they were all holding drinks the color of water with olives and sprigs of mint in them. When my parents have somebody over they get lemonade and if it's a real racy affair Schlitz in tall glasses with "They'll Do It Every Time"° cartoons stenciled on.

"That's all right," Lengel said. "But this isn't the beach." His repeating this struck   15
me as funny, as if it had just occurred to him, and he had been thinking all these years the A & P was a great big dune and he was the head lifeguard. He didn't like my smiling—as I say he doesn't miss much—but he concentrates on giving the girls that sad Sunday-school-superintendent stare.

Queenie's blush is no sunburn now, and the plump one in plaid, that I liked better from the back—a really sweet can—pipes up, "We weren't doing any shopping. We just came in for the one thing."

"That makes no difference," Lengel tells her, and I could see from the way his eyes went that he hadn't noticed she was wearing a two-piece before. "We want you decently dressed when you come in here."

"We *are* decent," Queenie says suddenly, her lower lip pushing, getting sore now that she remembers her place, a place from which the crowd that runs the A & P must look pretty crummy. Fancy Herring Snacks flashed in her very blue eyes.

"Girls, I don't want to argue with you. After this come in here with your shoulders covered. It's our policy." He turns his back. That's policy for you. Policy is what the king-pins want. What the others want is juvenile delinquency.

All this while, the customers had been showing up with their carts but, you know, sheep, seeing a scene, they had all bunched up on Stokesie, who shook open a paper bag as gently as peeling a peach, not wanting to miss a word. I could feel in the silence everybody getting nervous, most of all Lengel, who asks me, "Sammy, have you rung up their purchase?"

I thought and said "No" but it wasn't about that I was thinking. I go through the punches, 4, 9, GROC, TOT—it's more complicated than you think, and after you do it often enough, it begins to make a little song, that you hear words to, in my case "Hello (*bing*) there, you (*gung*) hap-py *pee*-pul (*splat*)!"—the *splat* being the drawer flying out.

"*They'll Do It Every Time*": syndicated daily and Sunday cartoon created by Jimmy Hatlo.

I uncrease the bill, tenderly as you may imagine, it just having come from between the two smoothest scoops of vanilla I had ever known were there, and pass a half and a penny into her narrow pink palm, and nestle the herrings in a bag and twist its neck and hand it over, all the time thinking.

The girls, and who'd blame them, are in a hurry to get out, so I say "I quit" to Lengel quick enough for them to hear, hoping they'll stop and watch me, their unsuspected hero. They keep right on going, into the electric eye; the door flies open and they flicker across the lot to their car, Queenie and Plaid and Big Tall Goony-Goony (not that as raw material she was so bad), leaving me with Lengel and a kink in his eyebrow.

"Did you say something, Sammy?"

"I said I quit."

"I thought you did."   25

"You didn't have to embarrass them."

"It was they who were embarrassing us."

I started to say something that came out "Fiddle-de-doo." It's a saying of my grandmother's, and I know she would have been pleased.

"I don't think you know what you're saying," Lengel said.

"I know you don't," I said. "But I do." I pull the bow at the back of my apron and   30
start shrugging it off my shoulders. A couple customers that had been heading for my slot begin to knock against each other, like scared pigs in a chute.

Lengel sighs and begins to look very patient and old and gray. He's been a friend of my parents for years. "Sammy, you don't want to do this to your Mom and Dad," he tells me. It's true, I don't. But it seems to me that once you begin a gesture it's fatal not to go through with it. I fold the apron, "Sammy" stitched in red on the pocket, and put it on the counter, and drop the bow tie on top of it. The bow tie is theirs, if you've ever wondered. "You'll feel this for the rest of your life," Lengel says, and I know that's true, too, but remembering how he made that pretty girl blush makes me so scrunchy inside I punch the No Sale tab and the machine whirs "pee-pul" and the drawer splats out. One advantage to this scene taking place in summer, I can follow this up with a clean exit, there's no fumbling around getting your coat and galoshes, I just saunter into the electric eye in my white shirt that my mother ironed the night before, and the door heaves itself open, and outside the sunshine is skating around on the asphalt.

I look around for my girls, but they're gone, of course. There wasn't anybody but some young married screaming with her children about some candy they didn't get by the door of a powder-blue Falcon° station wagon. Looking back in the big windows, over the bags of peat moss and aluminum lawn furniture stacked on the pavement, I could see Lengel in my place in the slot, checking the sheep through. His face was dark gray and his back stiff, as if he'd just had an injection of iron, and my stomach kind of fell as I felt how hard the world was going to be to me hereafter.   long sentences

QUESTIONS

1.   From Sammy's language, what do you learn about his view of himself? About his educational and class level? The first sentence, for example, is grammatically incorrect in standard English but not uncommon in colloquial English. Point out and explain similar passages.

Falcon: small car that had recently been introduced by the Ford Motor Company.

2. Consider the first eleven paragraphs as exposition, in which you learn about the location, the issues, and the participants in the story's conflict. Is there anything inessential in this section? Do you learn enough to understand the story? How might someone other than Sammy present the material?

3. How do you learn that Sammy is an experienced "girl watcher"? What does *he think* he thinks about most girls? To what degree is this estimate inconsistent with what he finally does after the girls leave?

4. Why does Sammy say "I quit" so abruptly? What does he mean when he says that the world is going to be hard to him after his experience at the A & P?

because he quite his job,
he was a fool,

WRITING ABOUT STYLE

In prewriting, consider the selected passage in the context of the entire story. If you can answer questions such as the following, you will readily assemble materials for your essay on the style of a passage from a story.

Questions for Discovering Ideas

• Use a dictionary to discover the meaning of any words you do not recognize. Are there any unusual words? Any especially difficult or uncommon words? Do any of the words distract you as you read?

• Are the words the most common ones that might be used? Can you think of more difficult ones? Easier ones? More accurate ones? How many words are particularly short (one or two syllables)? How many are long (three syllables and more)?

• How varied are the sentence lengths? Do you find mostly short sentences (five to twenty words) or mostly long ones (twenty-one and longer), or is there a mixture of long and short sentences? What relationships do you find between the nature of the material and the lengths of the sentences?

• Are the sentences simple, compound, or complex? What is the connection between sentence types and the topics? What variations do you discover within sentences at the beginning, middle, and end of the story?

• Can you easily visualize and imagine the situations described by the words? If you find it easy, or hard, to what degree does your success or difficulty stem from the level of diction?

• For passages describing *action*, how vivid are the words? How do they help you picture the action? How do they hold your attention?

• For passages describing *exterior or interior scenery*, how specific are the words? How much detail does the writer provide? Should there be more or fewer words? How spatial are the descriptions of scenery? How many words are devoted to colors, shapes and sizes?

• For passages of *dialogue*, what does the level of speech indicate about the characters doing the talking? How do a person's speeches help to establish her or his character? For what purposes does the author use formal or informal diction? How much slang do you find? Why is it there?

- What words belong only to particular occupations or ways of life (e.g., foreign words, specialized or technical words referring to things like horses, airplanes, flowers, medicine, psychology, and warfare)? What use do speakers make of contractions?

- What noteworthy rhetorical devices do you find? In how many sentences can you find parallelism (parallel words, phrases, clauses)? What effect is gained by the use of this device?

Strategies for Organizing Ideas

To describe and evaluate the style of the passage, first consider the style in relationship to the story. For example, suppose the speaker has just returned home after a long and painful journey, or has just finished a race with a close competitor, or is recalling an event of the long-distant past, or is anticipating future happiness or frustration. Keep such conditions in mind throughout your analysis.

To focus your essay, either single out one aspect of style or discuss everything, depending on the length of the assignment. Be sure to treat topics like *levels of diction,* categories like *specific-general* and *concrete-abstract,* the degree of *simplicity* or *complexity, length, numbers* of words, and *denotation-connotation.* In discussing rhetorical aspects, go as far as you can with the terminology at your command. For example, at a minimum, you should be able to consider simple-compound-complex for sentence types and parallelism for rhetorical devices. If you can draw attention to the elements in a parallel structure by using grammatical terms, do so. If you are able to detect the ways in which the sentences are kept simple or made complex, describe these ways. Be sure to use examples from the passage to illustrate your claims.

Your essay should reflect your awareness of style at your own stage of development as a reader. Later, when you have gained sharper perceptions and a wider descriptive vocabulary, you will be able to write more detailed and expert analyses.

In your conclusion, try to evaluate the author's style. To what extent has your analysis increased or reinforced your appreciation of the author's technique? Does the passage take on any added importance as a result of your study? Is there anything elsewhere in the work comparable to the content, words, or ideas that you have discussed in the passage?

Numbers for Easy Reference

Include a copy of your passage at the beginning of your essay, as in the sample that follows. For your readers' convenience, number the sentences in the passage, and use these numbers when you refer to them.

DEMONSTRATIVE STUDENT ESSAY

Mark Twain's Blending of Style and Purpose in Paragraphs 14 and 15 of "Luck"°

[¶14]

[1] The battle was awfully hot; the allies were steadily giving way all over the field. [2] Our regiment occupied a position that was vital; a blunder now must be destruction. [3] At this crucial moment, what does this immortal fool do but detach the regiment from its place and order a charge over a neighboring hill where there wasn't a suggestion of an enemy! [4] "There you go!" I said to myself; "this *is* the end at last."

[¶15]

[5] And away we did go, and were over the shoulder of the hill before the insane movement could be discovered and stopped. [6] And what did we find? [7] An entire and unsuspected Russian army in reserve! [8] And what happened? [9] We were eaten up? [10] That is necessarily what would have happened in ninety-nine cases out of a hundred. [11] But no; those Russians argued that no single regiment would come browsing around there at such a time. [12] It must be the entire English army, and that the sly Russian game was detected and blocked; so they turned tail, and away they went, pell-mell, over the hill and down into the field, in wild confusion, and we after them; they themselves broke the solid Russian center in the field, and tore through, and in no time there was the most tremendous rout you ever saw, and the defeat of the allies was turned into a sweeping and splendid victory! [13] Marshall Canrobert looked on, dizzy with astonishment, admiration, and delight; and sent right off for Scoresby, and hugged him, and decorated him on the field in presence of all the armies!

[1]

Appearing close to the end of "Luck," these two paragraphs are important in Twain's satiric design to puncture the bubble of Scoresby, the widely recognized and decorated general who has earned his recognition with luck and not skill. In the story, the paragraphs come as a climax. By presenting a brief account of a battle in the Crimean War, in which Scoresby's regiment is decisive, they bring out his stupidity and luck to the highest degree. Though the passages are narrative, the mark of Twain's style is to underscore how the hero's blundering foolishness is always saved by luck.* In every respect--description, word level, use of general and abstract diction, grammatical patterns, and the narrator's involvement--the passage embodies Twain's satiric and comic goal.†

[2]

The descriptions in the paragraphs are designed to expose Scoresby's idiocy. In fact, the descriptions are not about the battle at all. The military matter presented in the thirteen sentences is that the allies are giving way, that Scoresby orders a charge, and that the Russians turn tail and dash away. There is no report of clashing soldiers and dying men and horses—beyond the claim that the Russians themselves "tore through" their own ranks—and there are no

---

° See pp. 366-69 for this story.
* Central idea.
† Thesis sentence.

vivid words, beyond these, describing the circumstances of victory. Indeed, the descriptions are minimal, containing just enough to describe Scoresby's lucky blunder, but no more. The paragraphs would be unsuccessful as an account of a battle, but as part of this story they superbly serve Twain's satiric goal.

[3] In keeping with the exposé, Twain uses a middle, or neutral, level of diction. The words are not unusual or difficult. What could be more ordinary, for example, than words like "battle," "awfully," "steadily," "occupied," "discovered," "stopped," "argued," and "victory"? One may grant that "splendid," "astonishment," "pell-mell," "immortal," and "crucial" are not common in everyday speech, but in this context they are appropriate, for they fall within the vocabulary of responses to battle. Because of their aptness, they enable the reader to focus on the subject and on the narrator's expressions of humor, and in this respect they fit into the middle level of diction.

[4] Not only is the level neutral, but many words are general and abstract, in accord with the intention of debunking Scoresby. The "allies were steadily giving way," for example, and the "movement" of many individuals is described as "insane." These broad words are fitting for groups and mass actions but not for specific individuals. When the Russians conclude from Scoresby's senseless charge that their "game" is "detected," they turn "tail" and run "pell-mell," dashing in such "wild confusion" that there is "the most tremendous rout you ever saw," resulting in "sweeping and splendid victory"--all general and abstract words. Even the "hero," Scoresby, is not detailed anywhere as a specific leader and fighter; it is as though he is less significant than the gigantic forces of stupidity he unleashes. The last sentence of the paragraphs, the thirteenth, continues in this mode with the abstract but worshipful responses of the commander, Marshall Canrobert, who is "dizzy with astonishment, admiration, and delight." These abstract words reflect the public renown of Scoresby, which we, as the narrator's listeners, know to be untrue. Both general and abstract words thus jell perfectly with Twain's debunking humor.

[5] Grammatically, as well, there is great emphasis on the contrast between Scoresby's stupidity and his success. Twain's first two sentences are neatly balanced with contrasting ideas: Sentence 1 tells us that the battle is "hot" (part 1) and that the allies are losing (part 2). Sentence 2 tells us that the regiment is important (part 1) and that a mistake would be disastrous (part 2). But as the battle descends into the sweeping chaos caused by the charge of Scoresby's regiment, the grammar takes on the same chaotic pattern. Sentence 12, containing all the battle details, is eighty-one words long. It is broken up by semicolons and commas into a variety of separate statements and structures describing the panic of retreat and the splendidness of victory. In other words, the sentence has the same wildness, sweep, and madness of the events being described--a blending of grammar and subject.

[6] The major quality of Twain's style, however, is the narrator's amused and scornful language. His words frame the suspense and anticlimax of the battle, as is shown in the first paragraph (sentences 1-4). He tells us (sentence 3) that the "immortal fool" orders a mistaken charge. His lamenting prediction, "this *is* the end at last" (sentence 4), is designed for full dramatic and suspenseful effect. The narrator's involvement is also shown by his simply phrased questions just before he tells about the results of the charge: "And what did we find?" "And what happened?" "We were eaten up?" His attitude is most amusingly shown by the

word "browsing" (sentence 11), which suggests grazing animals, not charging armies. This word emphasizes the dimwittedness of Scoresby's command to attack. Throughout the paragraphs, the speaker thus lends his own wry insights to the language. The skill, naturally, belongs to Twain.

[7]   In all respects, the passage is a model of the right use of words in the right places for the author's intended purpose. If the writing were about an actual military combat, it would be poor. But because it is part of a comic exposé of a fortunate fool, it is hard to imagine better language of description. Twain's speaker gives us what we need to know: namely, that Scoresby has a Midas touch in everything he does, no matter how potentially disastrous his decisions might originally seem. The sentences are clear and direct, and they convey the facts about Scoresby that show his imbecility. Even the longest and most confused sentence, the twelfth, is appropriate to the confusion that Scoresby converts to triumph. For these reasons, the paragraphs are examples of Twain's accurate and purposeful narrative prose.

Commentary on the Essay

This essay shows how separate stylistic topics can be unified. Important in this objective are the transitions from paragraph to paragraph, such as "not only . . . but," "in keeping with the exposé," "as well," and "in all respects." These transitional phrases enable the reader to move easily from one topic to the next.

The beginning of the essay demonstrates the importance of relating the passage being studied to the work as a whole. Because the central idea is connected to Twain's debunking objective, the point is made that style and satiric intention are merged and integrated.

In the body, paragraph 2 treats the absence of specifically descriptive words, explaining this lack by reference to the satiric subject. Paragraph 3 treats the neutral diction, making the point that this language is appropriate because it permits a direct focus on the asinine blunders of the major character. Twain's use of general and abstract language is treated in paragraph 4, which makes the point that this language is appropriate because the story exposes Scoresby's empty-headedness. Paragraph 5, which addresses the grammar of the passage, indicates that the movement from balance to grammatical chaos complements the actual battlefield chaos. Paragraph 6, the last of the body, is the high point of the discussion; it asserts that the most important aspect of the writing is the narrative speaker, whose ideas and words permit Twain to keep the narrative brief while emphasizing his hero's stupidity. Paragraph 7, the conclusion, is a tribute to Twain's style, emphasizing again how his satiric objective governs word choices.

SPECIAL TOPICS FOR WRITING AND ARGUMENT ABOUT STYLE

1. In "Luck" there are two narrators. What purposes do these narrators serve? How do they differ in style (word choices, expressions of opinion, use of questions)?

2. Write an essay that answers the following questions: To what degree are the narrative and descriptive styles of "Soldier's Home" appropriate to the nature of the story? What would be the effect on the story if Hemingway had used the style of Faulkner in "Barn Burning" (Chapter 4), or Updike in "A & P," or Whitecloud in "Blue Winds Dancing" (Chapter 3)?

3. Stories like Munro's "The Found Boat" and Crane's "The Blue Hotel" (Chapter 2) are characterized by full descriptions, so that the reader needs to imagine few details. How appropriate would similarly full descriptions be in stories like Hemingway's "Soldier's Home" and Twain's "Luck"?

4. Write two brief character sketches, or a description of an action, to be included in a longer story. Make the first favorable and the second negative. Analyze your word choices in the contrasting accounts: What kinds of words do you select, and on what principles do you select them? What kinds of words might you select if you wanted to create a neutral account? On the basis of your answers, what can you conclude about the development of a fiction writer's style?

5. Munro's "The Found Boat," and Gilman's "The Yellow Wallpaper" (Chapter 12) feature the psychological makeup of their major characters (see also Chapters 4 and 33). Write an essay considering the nature and effectiveness of the psychological portraiture in these stories.

6. Using your library's card or computer catalogue, or else a university press book about Hemingway containing a substantial bibliography, list five works about Hemingway as a writer of fiction. Study at least one of the books, and write a brief summary of the author's discussion of Hemingway's style (i.e., Hemingway's descriptions, diction, brevity, dialogue).

8

Tone: The Expression
of Attitude in Fiction

Tone refers to the methods by which writers and speakers reveal attitudes or feelings. It is an aspect of all spoken and written statements, whether declarations of earnest love, requests to pass a dinner dish, letters asking parents for money, or official government notices threatening penalties if taxes and fines are not paid. Because tone is often equated with *attitude,* it is important to realize that tone refers not so much to attitude itself but instead *to those techniques and modes of presentation that reveal or create attitude.*

As a literary concept, *tone* is adapted from the phrase *tone of voice* in speech. Tone of voice reflects attitudes toward a particular object or situation, and also toward listeners. Let us suppose that Mary has a difficult assignment, on which she expects to work all day. Things go well, and she finishes quickly. She happily tells her friend Anne, "I'm so pleased. I needed only two hours for that." Then she decides to buy tickets for a popular play and must wait through a long and slow line. After getting her tickets, she tells the people at the end of the line, "I'm so pleased. I needed only two hours for that." The sentences are exactly the same, but by changing her emphasis and vocal inflection, Mary indicates her disgust and impatience with her long wait and also shows her sympathy with the people still in line. By controlling the *tone* of her statements, in other words, Mary conveys attitudes of satisfaction at one time and indignation and also sympathy at another.

Tone and the expression of attitude are vital components of all forms of communication. In Whistler's painting *The White Girl,* for example (p. 381), the young woman dressed in white seems at first to be loveliness personified. But certain features of the painting indicate ambiguity: The girl is standing on a rug of wolf's fur (the animal's expression makes it seem alive), some of her flowers have fallen and the ones she holds are wilted, and she appears detached, gazing vacantly into space. These details reveal that Whistler's attitude toward his beautiful subject is somewhat negative and ironic.

As the example about Mary indicates, an attitude itself may be summarized with a word or phrase (satisfaction or indignation, love or contempt, deference or command, and so on), but the study of tone examines those aspects of situation, language, action, and background that *bring out* the attitude. In

James McNeill Whistler, *The White Girl (Symphony in White, No. 1)*, 1862. National Gallery of Art, Washington, DC, Harris Whittlemore Collection.

Welty's "A Worn Path" (Chapter 3), for example, the attendant offers Phoenix "a few pennies," but Phoenix wants more. Being a recipient of charity but also being an independent sort, Phoenix makes the following response:

> "Five pennies is a nickel," said Phoenix stiffly. (paragraph 99)

This request is indirect, but it is nevertheless demanding. Although Phoenix is not a literary master, she is a master of tone in this conversational situation.

TONE AND ATTITUDES

In most literary works, attitudes point in a number of directions, so that tone becomes a highly complex matter. The following things to look for, however, should help you in understanding and describing literary tone.

Determine the Writer's Attitude Toward the Material

By reading a story carefully, we may deduce the author's attitude or attitudes toward the subject matter. In "The Story of an Hour" for example, Kate Chopin sympathetically portrays a young wife's secret wishes for freedom, just as she also humorously reveals the unwitting smugness that often pervades men's relationships with women. In "The Hammon and the Beans," Parédes shows revulsion against the effects of poverty, and also pity for the dead young girl who might have been saved with proper health care. Joy Williams in "Taking Care" (Chapter 2) reveals deep admiration for Jones, her major character. "Rape Fantasies" reveals Atwood's amused affection for Estelle, the narrator. All these stories exhibit various types of **irony,** which is one of the most significant aspects of authorial tone (see below, p. 384).

Discover the Writer's Attitude Toward Readers

Authors recognize that readers participate in the creative act and that all elements of a story—word choice, characterization, allusions, levels of reality—must take readers' responses into account (see the discussion of Reader-Response criticism in Chapter 33). When Hawthorne's woodland guide in "Young Goodman Brown" (Chapter 9) refers to "King Philip's War," for example, Hawthorne assumes that his readers know that this seventeenth-century war was inhumanly greedy and cruel. By not explaining this part of history, he indicates respect for the knowledge of his readers, and he also assumes their agreement with his interpretation. Updike in "A & P" (Chapter 7) assumes that readers understand his use of Sammy's diction to reveal Sammy as a perceptive and independent but insecure young man. Authors always make such considerations about readers by implicitly complimenting them on their knowledge and also by satisfying their curiosity and desire to be interested, stimulated, and pleased.

Determine Other Dominant Attitudes

Beyond general authorial tone, you will discover many internal and dramatically rendered expressions of attitude. For example, the speaker of Laurence's "The Loons" is a woman describing her memory of a childhood summer vacation when her family was accompanied by Piquette, an Indian girl, who had nowhere else to go. The narrator asks Piquette to "come and play," and Piquette responds scornfully, "I ain't a kid." The narrator's immediate reaction is to reject Piquette completely, but on mature reflection she decides to gain Piquette's trust. This change of attitude is the ultimate cause of the speaker's decision to tell Piquette's story, and therefore it is also the cause of the story's focus on the inevitability of change and loss.

In addition, as characters interact, their tone dramatically shows their judgments about other characters and situations. A complicated control of tone occurs at the end of Glaspell's "A Jury of Her Peers" (Chapter 4) where the two major characters, Mrs. Hale and Mrs. Peters, begin covering up incriminating evidence about Minnie Wright. When Mrs. Peters agrees to this obstruction of justice, however, she speaks not about illegality but rather about the possible embarrassment of the action:

> "My!" she began, in a high, false voice, "it's a good thing the men couldn't hear us! Getting all stirred up over a little thing like a—dead canary." She hurried over that. "As if that could have anything to do with—with—My, wouldn't they *laugh?*" (paragraph 267)

Notice that her words reveal her knowledge that men scoff at feminine concerns, like Minnie's quilting knots, and therefore she openly anticipates the men's amusement. The reader, however, knows that she is joining Mrs. Hale in hiding evidence.

TONE AND HUMOR

A major aspect of tone is humor. Everyone likes to laugh, and shared laughter is part of good human relationships; but not everyone can explain why things are funny. Laughter resists close analysis; it is unplanned, personal, idiosyncratic, and unpredictable. Nonetheless, there are a number of common elements:

1. *There must be something to laugh at.* Laughter is commonly *directed at* a person, thing, situation, custom, habit of speech or dialect, or arrangement of words. Because laughter requires an object or "butt," it is sometimes classified as *homicidal* (general laughter against something or someone), *fratricidal* (laughter against someone close), and *suicidal* (laughter against oneself).

2. *Laughter stems out of disproportion or incongruity.* We normally know what to expect under given conditions, and anything contrary to these expectations is *incongruous* and may therefore generate laughter. A traditional joke about the prototypical absent-minded professor has the professor lighting his pipe with a flaming ten-dollar bill. Such behavior is *inappropriate* or incongruous—and therefore funny—because it violates our expectations about ordinary and normal care of money. A student in a language class once wrote about a "*congregation* of verbs" and also about parts of speech as "nouns, verbs, and *proverbs.*" The student meant the *conjugation* of verbs, of course, and also (maybe) either *adverbs* or *pronouns,* but somehow his understanding slipped and he created a comic incongruity. Such inadvertent verbal errors are called **malapropisms,** after Mrs. Malaprop, a character in Richard Brinsley Sheridan's eighteenth-century play *The Rivals.* In the literary creation of malapropisms, the tone is directed against the speaker, for the amusement of both readers and author alike.

3. *Safety and/or good will prevents harm and ensures humor.* Seeing a person slip on a banana peel and hurtle through the air may cause laughter, but only if we ourselves are not that person, for laughter depends on insulation from danger and pain. In comic situations that involve physical abuse—falling down stairs or being hit in the face by cream pies—the abuse never harms the participants. The incongruity of such situations causes laughter, and the immunity from pain and injury prevents a response of horror. Good will enters into humor in romantic comedy or in any other work in which we are drawn into general sympathy with the major figures, such as Elizabeth and Nelson in Colwin's "An Old-Fashioned Story" (Chapter 2). As the author leads the characters toward recognizing that they love each other, our involvement produces happiness, smiles, and (perhaps) even sympathetic laughter.

4. *Unfamiliarity, newness, and uniqueness produce the spontaneity that prompts laughter.* Laughter depends on seeing something new or unique, on experiencing something familiar in a new light, and on flashes of insight. It is always spontaneous, even when readers already know what they are laughing at. Indeed, the task of the comic writer is to develop ordinary materials to that point at which spontaneity frees readers to laugh. Thus you can read and reread O'Connor's "First Confession" (Chapter 7) and laugh each time because, even though you know what will happen, the story shapes your acceptance of how reconciliation penetrates a wall of anger and guilt. Young Jackie's comic troubles with his sister and grandmother are always comic because his experiences are so spontaneous and incongruous.

TONE AND IRONY

The capacity to have more than one attitude toward someone or something is a uniquely human trait. We know that people are not perfect, but we love a number of them anyway. Therefore we speak to them not only with love and praise, but also with banter and criticism. On occasion, you may have given mildly insulting greeting cards to your loved ones, not to affront them but to amuse them. You share smiles and laughs, and at the same time you also remind them of your affection.

The word *irony* describes such contradictory statements or situations. Irony is natural to human beings who are aware of life's ambiguities and complexities. It develops from the realization that life does not always measure up to promise, that friends and loved ones are sometimes angry at each other, that the universe contains incomprehensible mysteries, that the social and political structure is often oppressive rather than liberating, that doubt exists even in the certainty of knowledge and faith, and that human character is built through chagrin, regret, and pain as much as through emulation and praise. In expressing an idea ironically, writers pay the greatest compliment to their audience, for they assume that readers have sufficient intelligence and skill to discover the real meaning of quizzical or ambiguous statements and situations.

The Four Major Kinds of Irony Are **Verbal,** **Situational, Cosmic,** *and* **Dramatic**

VERBAL IRONY DEPENDS ON THE INTERPLAY OF WORDS.   In **verbal irony,** one thing is said, but the opposite is meant. In the example opening this chapter, Mary's ironic expression of pleasure after her two-hour wait for tickets really means that she is disgusted. There are important types of verbal irony. In **understatement**, the expression does not fully describe the importance of a situation and therefore makes its point by implication. For example, in Bierce's "An Occurrence at Owl Creek Bridge" (Chapter 5) the condemned man, Farquhar, contemplates the apparatus designed by the soldiers to hang him. His response is described by the narrator: "The arrangement commended itself to his judgment as simple and effective" (paragraph 4). These words would be appropriate for the appraisal of ordinary machinery, but because the apparatus is going to kill Farquhar, his understated observation is ironic.

By contrast, in **overstatement** or **hyperbole,** the words are far in excess of the situation, and readers or listeners therefore understand that the true meaning is considerably less than what is said. An example is the priest's exaggerated dialogue with Jackie in "First Confession" (paragraphs 35–58). Though the priest makes incongruously hyperbolic comments on Jackie's plans for slaughtering his grandmother, readers know he means no such thing. The gulf between what is said and what is meant produces smiles and chuckles.

Often verbal irony is ambiguous, having double meaning or **double entendre.** Midway through "Young Goodman Brown," for example, the woodland guide leaves Brown alone while stating, "When you feel like moving again, there is my staff to help you along" (paragraph 40). The word "staff" is ambiguous, for it refers to the staff that resembles a serpent (paragraph 13). The word therefore suggests that the devilish guide is leaving Brown not only with a real staff but also with the spirit of evil, unlike the divine "staff" of Psalm 23 that gives comfort. Ambiguity, of course, may be used in relation to any topic. Quite often double entendre is used in statements about sexuality, usually for the amusement of listeners or readers.

SITUATIONAL IRONY FILLS THE GAP BETWEEN HOPE AND REALITY.   **Situational irony** or **irony of situation** refers to the chasm between what we hope for or expect and what actually happens. It is often pessimistic because it emphasizes that human beings usually have little or no control over their lives or anything else. The forces of opposition may be psychological, social, cultural, political, or environmental. In Atwood's "Rape Fantasies," for example, the narrator Estelle states her inability to understand why men cannot be satisfied by human relationships with women rather than rapacious ones. "Rape Fantasies" is not a sociological document, but Estelle's uneasiness underscores the irony of the political and social conditions that produce rape. Although situational irony often involves disaster, it need not always do so. For example, a happier occurrence of situational irony is in Chekhov's play *The Bear*

(Chapter 28), for the two characters shift from anger to love as they fall into the grips of emotions that are "bigger than both of them."

COSMIC IRONY STEMS FROM THE POWER OF CHANCE AND FATE.   A special kind of situational irony that emphasizes the pessimistic and fatalistic side of life is **cosmic irony** or **irony of fate.** By the standard of cosmic irony, the universe is indifferent to individuals, who are subject to blind chance, accident, uncontrollable emotions, perpetual misfortune, and misery. Even if things temporarily go well, people's lives end badly, and their best efforts do not rescue them or make them happy. A work illustrating cosmic irony is Glaspell's "A Jury of Her Peers," which develops out of the stultifying conditions of farm life experienced by Minnie Wright. She has no profession, no other hope, no other life except the lonely, dreary farm—nothing. After nineteen years of wretchedness, she buys a canary that warbles for her to make her life pleasant. Within a year, her boorish husband wrings the bird's neck, and she in turn wreaks vengeance against him. Her situation is cosmically ironic, for the implication of "A Jury of Her Peers" is that human beings are caught in a web of disastrous circumstances from which there is no escape.

DRAMATIC IRONY RESULTS FROM MISUNDERSTANDING AND LACK OF KNOWLEDGE. Like cosmic irony, **dramatic irony** is a special kind of situational irony. It happens when a character either has no information about a situation or else misjudges it, but readers (and often some of the other characters) see everything completely and correctly. As might be expected, dramatic irony is derived from drama, and the quintessentially ironic model is found in Sophocles' ancient Greek play *Oedipus the King* (Chapter 27). In this play, everyone—other characters and readers alike—knows the truth long before Oedipus knows it. It is also important to recognize that dramatic irony may also be found in fiction (and in poetry). It is seen in Chopin's "The Story of an Hour," where the doctors are ignorant of Louise's reaction to the reports of her husband's death. The story's readers, however, do indeed know and understand her feelings, and therefore they also know that the doctors reveal their own pompous vanity as they misdiagnose the cause of her sudden death.

❁ STORIES FOR STUDY

MARGARET ATWOOD (b. 1939)

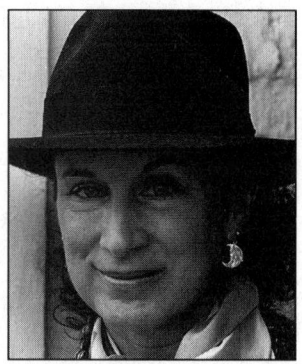

Atwood is one of Canada's premier writers, having published many books of poetry, a number of novels and stories, and much criticism. In addition, she is editor of The Oxford Book of Canadian Verse *(1982). One of her most widely recognized works is the anti-utopian novel.* The Handmaid's Tale *(1986), which describes a futuristic nightmare society of fear and repression for women. This story was adapted as a movie in 1990. The stories in a collection,* Wilderness Tips *(1992) reflect regret and diminished hopes, unlike the more comic topics of her story "Rape Fantasies" and her poem "Siren Song." The scope of her work may be inferred from recent publications:* The Robber Bride *(1993),* Good Bones and Simple Murders *(1994),* Poems *(1994),* Princess Prunella and the Purple Peanut *(1995), and* Morning in the Burned House *(1995).*

Rape Fantasies _____ Girl telling the story is Estelle _____ *1977*

The way they're going on about it in the magazines you'd think it was just invented, and not only that but it's something terrific, like a vaccine for cancer. They put it in capital letters on the front cover, and inside they have these questionnaires like the ones they used to have about whether you were a good enough wife or an endomorph or an ectomorph, remember that? with the scoring upside down on page 73, and then these numbered do-it-yourself dealies, you know? RAPE, TEN THINGS TO DO ABOUT IT, like it was ten new hairdos or something. I mean, what's so new about it?

So at work they all have to talk about it because no matter what magazine you open, there it is, staring you right between the eyes, and they're beginning to have it on the television, too. Personally I'd prefer a June Allyson° movie anytime but they don't make them any more and they don't even have them that much on the Late Show. For instance, day before yesterday, that would be Wednesday, thank god it's Friday as they say, we were sitting around in the women's lunch room—the *lunch* room, I mean you'd think you could get some peace and quiet in there—and Chrissy closes up the magazine she's been reading and says, "How about it, girls, do you have rape fantasies?"

The four of us were having our game of bridge the way we always do, and I had a bare twelve points counting the singleton with not that much of a bid in anything. So I said one club, hoping Sondra would remember about the one club convention, because the time before when I used that she thought I really meant clubs and she bid us up to three, and all I had was four little ones with nothing higher than a six, and we went down two and on top of that we were vulnerable. She is not the world's best bridge player. I mean, neither am I but there's a limit.

Darlene passed but the damage was done, Sondra's head went round like it was on ball bearings and she said, "*What* fantasies?"

June Allyson: actress (b. 1917) known for her bright smile and scratchy voice. She specialized in "sweet" movie and musical roles, 1943–1959, and for a long time she appeared in TV commercials.

make up all over

"Rape fantasies," Chrissy said. She's a receptionist and she looks like one; she's   5
pretty but cool as a cucumber, like she's been painted all over with nail polish, if you
know what I mean. Varnished. "It says here all women have rape fantasies."

"For Chrissake, I'm eating an egg sandwich," I said, "and I bid one club and
Darlene passed."

"You mean, like some guy jumping you in an alley or something," Sondra said.
She was eating her lunch, we all eat our lunches during the game, and she bit into a
piece of that celery she always brings and started to chew away on it with this thoughtful
expression in her eyes and I knew we might as well pack it in as far as the game was
concerned.

"Yeah, sort of like that," Chrissy said. She was blushing a little, you could see it
even under her makeup.

"I don't think you should go out alone at night," Darlene said, "you put yourself in
a position," and I may have been mistaken but she was looking at me. She's the oldest,
Darlene→ she's forty-one though you wouldn't know it and neither does she, but I looked it up in
the employees' file. I like to guess a person's age and then look it up to see if I'm right.
I let myself have an extra pack of cigarettes if I am, though I'm trying to cut down. I
figure it's harmless as long as you don't tell. I mean, not everyone has access to that file,
it's more or less confidential. But it's all right if I tell you, I don't expect you'll ever meet
her, though you never know, it's a small world. Anyway.

"For *heaven's* sake, it's only *Toronto*," Greta said. She worked in Detroit for three   10
years and she never lets you forget it, it's like she thinks she's a war hero or something,
we should all admire her just for the fact that she's still walking this earth, though she
was really living in Windsor° the whole time, she just worked in Detroit. Which for me
doesn't really count. It's where you sleep, right?

"Well, do you?" Chrissy said. She was obviously trying to tell us about hers but she
wasn't about to go first, she's cautious, that one.

"I certainly don't," Darlene said, and she wrinkled up her nose, like this, and I
had to laugh. "I think it's disgusting." She's divorced, I read that in the file too, she never
talks about it. It must've been years ago anyway. She got up and went over to the coffee
machine and turned her back on us as though she wasn't going to have anything more
to do with it.

"Well," Greta said. I could see it was going to be between her and Chrissy. They're
both blondes, I don't mean that in a bitchy way but they do try to outdress each other.
Greta would like to get out of Filing, she'd like to be a receptionist too so she could
meet more people. You don't meet much of anyone in Filing except other people in
Filing. Me, I don't mind it so much, I have outside interests.

"Well," Greta said, "I sometimes think about, you know my apartment? It's got
this little balcony, I like to sit out there in the summer and I have a few plants out
there. I never bother that much about locking the door to the balcony, it's one of
those sliding glass ones, I'm on the eighteenth floor for heaven's sake, I've got a good
view of the lake and the CN Tower and all. But I'm sitting around one night in my
housecoat, watching TV with my shoes off, you know how you do, and I see this guy's
feet, coming down past the window, and the next thing you know he's standing on
the balcony, he's let himself down by a rope with a hook on the end of it from the
floor above, that's the nineteenth, and before I can even get up off the chesterfield

---

Windsor: city south of Detroit, noted as the only place where any portion of Canada is south
of the United States.

he's inside the apartment. He's all dressed in black with black gloves on"—I knew right away what show she got the black gloves off because I saw the same one—"and then he, well, you know."

"You know what?" Chrissy said, but Greta said, "And afterwards he tells me that he goes all over the outside of the apartment building like that, from one floor to another, with his rope and his hook . . . and then he goes out to the balcony and tosses his rope, and he climbs up it and disappears."

"Just like Tarzan," I said, but nobody laughed.

"Is that all?" Chrissy said. "Don't you ever think about, well, I think about being in the bathtub, with no clothes on . . ."

"So who takes a bath in their clothes?" I said, you have to admit it's stupid when you come to think of it, but she just went on, ". . . with lots of bubbles, what I use is Vitabath, it's more expensive but it's so relaxing, and my hair pinned up, and the door opens and this fellow's standing there. . . ."

"How'd he get in?" Greta said.

"Oh, I don't know, through a window or something. Well, I can't very well get out of the bathtub, the bathroom's too small and besides he's blocking the doorway, so I just *lie* there, and he starts to very slowly take his own clothes off, and then he gets into the bathtub with me."

"Don't you scream or anything?" said Darlene. She'd come back with her cup of coffee, she was getting really interested. "I'd scream like bloody murder."

"Who'd hear me?" Chrissy said. "Besides, all the articles say it's better not to resist, that way you don't get hurt."

"Anyway you might get bubbles up your nose," I said, "from the deep breathing," and I swear all four of them looked at me like I was in bad taste, like I'd insulted the Virgin Mary or something. I mean, I don't see what's wrong with a little joke now and then. Life's too short, right?

"Listen," I said, "those aren't *rape* fantasies. I mean, you aren't getting *raped*, it's just some guy you haven't met formally who happens to be more attractive than Derek Cummins"—he's the Assistant Manager, he wears elevator shoes or at any rate they have these thick soles and he has this funny way of talking, we call him Derek Duck—"and you have a good time. Rape is when they've got a knife or something and you don't want to."

"So what about you, Estelle," Chrissy said, she was miffed because I laughed at her fantasy, she thought I was putting her down. Sondra was miffed too, by this time she'd finished her celery and she wanted to tell about hers, but she hadn't got in fast enough.

"All right, let me tell you one," I said. "I'm walking down this dark street at night and this fellow comes up and grabs my arm. Now it so happens that I have a plastic lemon in my purse, you know how it always says you should carry a plastic lemon in your purse? I don't really do it, I tried it once but the darn thing leaked all over my cheque-book, but in this fantasy I have one, and I say to him, "You're intending to rape me, right?" and he nods, so I open my purse to get the plastic lemon, and I can't find it! My purse is full of all this junk, Kleenex and cigarettes and my change purse and my lipstick and my driver's licence, you know the kind of stuff: so I ask him to hold out his hands, like this, and I pile all this junk into them and down at the bottom there's the plastic lemon, and I can't get the top off. So I hand it to him and he's very obliging, he twists the top off and hands it back to me, and I squirt him in the eye."

I hope you don't think that's too vicious. Come to think of it, it is a bit mean, especially when he was so polite and all.

"*That's* your rape fantasy?" Chrissy says, "I don't believe it."

"She's a card," Darlene says, she and I are the ones that've been here the longest and she never will forget the time I got drunk at the office party and insisted I was going to dance under the table instead of on top of it, I did a sort of Cossack number° but then I hit my head on the bottom of the table—actually it was a desk—when I went to get up, and I knocked myself out cold. She's decided that's the mark of an original mind and she tells everyone new about it and I'm not sure that's fair. Though I did do it.

"I'm being totally honest," I say. I always am and they know it. There's no point in being anything else, is the way I look at it, and sooner or later the truth will out so you might as well not waste the time, right? "You should hear the one about the Easy-Off Cleaner."   30

But that was the end of the lunch hour, with one bridge game shot to hell, and the next day we spent most of the time arguing over whether to start a new game or play out the hands we had left over from the day before, so Sondra never did get a chance to tell about her rape fantasy.

It started me thinking though, about my own rape fantasies. Maybe I'm abnormal or something, I mean I have fantasies about handsome strangers coming in through the window too, like Mr. Clean, I wish one would, please god somebody without flat feet and big sweat marks on his shirt, and over five feet five, believe me being tall is a handicap though it's getting better, tall guys are starting to like someone whose nose reaches higher than their belly button. But if you're being totally honest you can't count those as rape fantasies. In a real rape fantasy, what you should feel is this anxiety, like when you think about your apartment building catching on fire and whether you should use the elevator or the stairs or maybe just stick your head under a wet towel, and you try to remember everything you've read about what to do but you can't decide.

❋   For instance, I'm walking along this dark street at night and this short, ugly fellow comes up and grabs my arm, and not only is he ugly, you know, with a sort of puffy nothing face, like those fellows you have to talk to in the bank when your account's overdrawn—of course I don't mean they're all like that—but he's absolutely covered in pimples. So he gets me pinned against the wall, he's short but he's heavy, and he starts to undo himself and the zipper gets stuck. I mean, one of the most significant moments in a girl's life, it's almost like getting married or having a baby or something, and he sticks the zipper.

So I say, kind of disgusted, "Oh for Chrissake," and he starts to cry. He tells me he's never been able to get anything right in his entire life, and this is the last straw, he's going to go jump off a bridge.

"Look," I say, I feel so sorry for him, in my rape fantasies I always end up feeling   35 sorry for the guy, I mean there has to be something *wrong* with them, if it was Clint Eastwood° it'd be different but worse luck it never is. I was the kind of little girl who buried dead robins, know what I mean? It used to drive my mother nuts, she didn't like me touching them, because of the germs I guess. So I say, "Listen, I know how you feel. You really should do something about those pimples, if you got rid of them you'd be quite good looking, honest; then you wouldn't have to go around doing stuff like this. I had them myself once," I say, to comfort him, but in fact I did, and it ends up I give him the name of my old dermatologist, the one I had in high school, that was back in

Cossack number: a Ukrainian folk dance movement performed in a squatting position, with much hand clapping.

Clint Eastwood: born 1930, star of many tough-guy detective and western movies; most famous "Dirty Harry" (1971).

Leamington,° except I used to go to St. Catharine's for the dermatologist. I'm telling you, I was really lonely when I first came here; I thought it was going to be such a big adventure and all, but it's a lot harder to meet people in a city. But I guess it's different for a guy.

Or I'm lying in bed with this terrible cold, my face is all swollen up, my eyes are red and my nose is dripping like a leaky tap, and this fellow comes in through the window and *he* has a terrible cold too, it's a new kind of flu that's been going around. So he says, "I'b goig do rabe you"—I hope you don't mind me holding my nose like this but that's the way I imagine it—and he lets out this terrific sneeze, which slows him down a bit, also I'm no object of beauty myself, you'd have to be some kind of pervert to want to rape someone with a cold like mine, it'd be like raping a bottle of LePages mucilage the way my nose is running. He's looking wildly around the room, and I realize it's because he doesn't have a piece of Kleenex! "Id's ride here," I say, and I pass him the Kleenex, god knows why he even bothered to get out of bed, you'd think if you were going to go around climbing in windows you'd wait till you were healthier, right? I mean, that takes a certain amount of energy. So I ask him why doesn't he let me fix him a NeoCitran and scotch, that's what I always take, you still have the cold but you don't feel it, so I do and we end up watching the Late Show together. I mean, they aren't all sex maniacs, the rest of the time they must lead a normal life. I figure they enjoy watching the Late Show just like anybody else.

I do have a scarier one though . . . where the fellow says he's hearing angel voices that're telling him he's got to kill me, you know, you read about things like that all the time in the papers. In this one I'm not in the apartment where I live now, I'm back in my mother's house in Leamington and the fellow's been hiding in the cellar, he grabs my arm when I go downstairs to get a jar of jam and he's got hold of the axe too, out of the garage, that one is really scary. I mean, what do you say to a nut like that?

So I start to shake but after a minute I get control of myself and I say, is he sure the angel voices have got the right person, because I hear the same angel voices and they've been telling me for some time that I'm going to give birth to the reincarnation of St. Anne who in turn has the Virgin Mary and right after that comes Jesus Christ and the end of the world, and he wouldn't want to interfere with that, would he? So he gets confused and listens some more, and then he asks for a sign and I show him my vaccination mark, you can see it's sort of an odd-shaped one, it got infected because I scratched the top off, and that does it, he apologizes and climbs out the coal chute° again, which is how he got in in the first place, and I say to myself there's some advantage in having been brought up a Catholic even though I haven't been to church since they changed the service into English,° it just isn't the same, you might as well be a Protestant. I must write to Mother and tell her to nail up that coal chute, it always has bothered me. Funny, I couldn't tell you at all what this man looks like but I know exactly what kind of shoes he's wearing, because that's the last I see of him, his shoes going up the coal chute, and they're the old-fashioned kind that lace up the ankles, even though he's a young fellow. That's strange, isn't it?

Leamington: in Ontario on the north shore of Lake Erie, southeast of Windsor.

coal chute: trough for delivering coal from a truck into a basement coal bin. Estelle's remark indicates that the chute was not fastened over the opening to the bin, thus permitting an illegal entry.

into English: In accord with the Second Vatican Council (1962–1965), the Latin Mass was replaced by vernacular languages in the late 1960s.

Let me tell you though I really sweat until I see him safely out of there and I go upstairs right away and make myself a cup of tea. I don't think about that one much. My mother always said you shouldn't dwell on unpleasant things and I generally agree with that, I mean, dwelling on them doesn't make them go away. Though not dwelling on them doesn't make them go away either, when you come to think of it.

Sometimes I have these short ones where the fellow grabs my arm but I'm really a Kung-Fu° expert, can you believe it, in real life I'm sure it would just be a conk on the head and that's that, like getting your tonsils out, you'd wake up and it would be all over except for the sore places, and you'd be lucky if your neck wasn't broken or something, I could never even hit the volleyball in gym and a volleyball is fairly large, you know?—and I just go *zap* with my fingers into his eyes and that's it, he falls over, or I flip him against a wall or something. But I could never really stick my fingers in anyone's eyes, could you? It would feel like hot jello and I don't even like cold jello, just thinking about it gives me the creeps. I feel a bit guilty about that one, I mean how would you like walking around knowing someone's been blinded for life because of you?

But maybe it's different for a guy.

The most touching one I have is when the fellow grabs my arm and I say, sad and kind of dignified, "You'd be raping a corpse." That pulls him up short and I explain that I've just found out I have leukaemia and the doctors have only given me a few months to live. That's why I'm out pacing the streets alone at night, I need to think, you know, come to terms with myself. I don't really have leukaemia but in the fantasy I do, I guess I chose that particular disease because a girl in my grade four class died of it, the whole class sent her flowers when she was in the hospital. I didn't understand then that she was going to die and I wanted to have leukaemia too so I could get flowers. Kids are funny, aren't they? Well, it turns out that he has leukaemia himself, and *he* only has a few months to live, that's why he's going around raping people, he's very bitter because he's so young and his life is being taken from him before he's really lived it. So we walk along gently under the street lights, it's spring and sort of misty, and we end up going for coffee, we're happy we've found the only other person in the world who can understand what we're going through, it's almost like fate, and after a while we just sort of look at each other and our hands touch, and he comes back with me and moves into my apartment and we spend our last months together before we die, we just sort of don't wake up in the morning, though I've never decided which one of us gets to die first. If it's him I have to go on and fantasize about the funeral, if it's me I don't have to worry about that, so it just about depends on how tired I am at the time. You may not believe this but sometimes I even start crying. I cry at the end of movies, even the ones that aren't all that sad, so I guess it's the same thing. My mother's like that too.

❋ The funny thing about these fantasies is that the man is always someone I don't know, and the statistics in the magazines, well, most of them anyway, they say it's often someone you do know, at least a little bit, like your boss or something—I mean, it wouldn't be *my* boss, he's over sixty and I'm sure he couldn't rape his way out of a paper bag, poor old thing, but it might be someone like Derek Duck, in his elevator shoes, perish the thought—or someone you just met, who invites you up for a drink, it's getting so you can hardly be sociable any more, and how are you supposed to meet people if you can't trust them even that basic amount? You can't spend your whole life in the Filing Department or cooped up in your own apartment with all the doors and windows locked and the shades down. I'm not what you would call a drinker but I like to go out

---

Kung-Fu: elaborate self-defense system developed in China, similar to karate.

now and then for a drink or two in a nice place, even if I am by myself, I'm with Women's Lib on that even though I can't agree with a lot of the other things they say. Like here for instance, the waiters all know me and if anyone, you know, bothers me . . . I don't know why I'm telling you all this, except I think it helps you get to know a person, especially at first, hearing some of the things they think about. At work they call me the office worry wart, but it isn't so much like worrying, it's more like figuring out what you should do in an emergency, like I said before.

Anyway, another thing about it is that there's a lot of conversation, in fact I spend most of my time, in the fantasy that is, wondering what I'm going to say and what he's going to say, I think it would be better if you could get a conversation going. Like, how could a fellow do that to a person he's just had a long conversation with, once you let them know you're human, you have a life too, I don't see how they could go ahead with it, right? I mean, I know it happens but I just don't understand it, that's the part I really don't understand.

QUESTIONS

1.   What elements of the various rape fantasies are comic? How is the comedy brought out (e.g., through subject matter, circumstances of description, attitudes and understanding of the characters, <u>comments by the narrator</u>)?

2.   What do the various fantasies of Estelle have in common, and what do they show about her? How does Atwood control the tone so as to keep Estelle from considering rape as a problem in psychology or criminology? *She always end up helping the guys*

3.   Describe the story's tone. How does tone affect your perception of Estelle?

4.   Consider the tone of the very last paragraph. What is Atwood's apparent attitude toward the subject? How is it tempered by her attitude toward Estelle?

5.   Studies point out that rape is an act of violence. What do the women in the story do to deflect the seriousness of the potential violence involved?

KATE CHOPIN   (1851–1904)

Born in St. Louis, Chopin lived in Louisiana from the time of her marriage until 1882. After her husband's death she returned to St. Louis and began to write. She published two collections of stories based on the life she had known back in Louisiana: Bayou Folk *(1894) and* A Night in Acadie *(1897). However, she became best known for her major novel,* The Awakening *(1899), which aroused negative reactions because it mentioned taboo subjects like adultery and miscegenation. Indeed, the critical disapproval was so intense that Chopin published no further works, even though she was at the height of her literary power and lived five years after the controversy.*

The Story of an Hour _____ *1894*

Knowing that Mrs. Mallard was afflicted with a heart trouble, great care was taken to break to her as gently as possible the news of her husband's death.

It was her sister Josephine who told her, in broken sentences: veiled hints that revealed in half concealing. Her husband's friend Richards was there, too, near her. It was he who had been in the newspaper office when intelligence of the ~~railroad disaster~~ *died in a* was received, with ~~Brently Mallard's name~~ *her husband's name* leading the list of "killed." He had only taken the time to assure himself of its truth by a second telegram, and had hastened to forestall any less careful, less tender friend in bearing the sad message.

She did not hear the story as many women have heard the same, with a paralyzed inability to accept its significance. She wept at once, with sudden, wild abandonment, in her sister's arms. When the storm of grief had spent itself she went away to her room alone. She would have no one follow her.

There stood, facing the open window, a comfortable, roomy armchair. Into this she sank, pressed down by a physical exhaustion that haunted her body and seemed to reach into her soul.

She could see in the open square before her house the tops of trees that were all   5
aquiver with the new spring life. The delicious breath of rain was in the air. In the street below a peddler was crying his wares. The notes of a distant song which some one was singing reached her faintly, and countless sparrows were twittering in the eaves.

There were patches of blue sky showing here and there through the clouds that had met and piled one above the other in the west facing her window.

She sat with her head thrown back upon the cushion of the chair, quite motion-less, except when a sob came up into her throat and shook her, as a child who has cried itself to sleep continues to sob in its dreams.

She was young, with a fair, calm face, whose lines bespoke repression and even a certain strength. But now there was a dull stare in her eyes, whose gaze was fixed away off yonder on one of those patches of blue sky. It was not a glance of reflection, but rather indicated a suspension of intelligent thought.

There was something coming to her and she was waiting for it, fearfully. What was it? She did not know; it was too subtle and elusive to name. But she felt it, creeping out of the sky, reaching toward her through the sounds, the scents, the color that filled the air.

Now her bosom rose and fell tumultuously. She was beginning to recognize this   10
thing that was approaching to possess her, and she was striving to beat it back with her will—as powerless as her two white slender hands would have been.

When she abandoned herself a little whispered word escaped her slightly parted lips. She said it over and over under her breath: "free, free, free!" The vacant stare and the look of terror that had followed it went from her eyes. They stayed keen and bright. Her pulses beat fast, and the coursing blood warmed and relaxed every inch of her body.

She did not stop to ask if it were or were not a monstrous joy that held her. A clear and exalted perception enabled her to dismiss the suggestion as trivial.

She knew that she would weep again when she saw the kind, tender hands folded in death; the face that had never looked save with love upon her, fixed and gray and dead. But she saw beyond that bitter moment a long procession of years to come that would belong to her absolutely. And she opened and spread her arms out to them in welcome.

There would be no one to live for during those coming years; she would live for herself. There would be no powerful will bending hers in that blind persistence with which men and women believe they have a right to impose a private will upon a fellow-creature. A kind intention or a cruel intention made the act seem no less a crime as she looked upon it in that brief moment of illumination.

And yet she had loved him—sometimes. Often she had not. What did it matter! What could love, the unsolved mystery, count for in face of this possession of self-assertion which she suddenly recognized as the strongest impulse of her being!

"Free! Body and soul free!" she kept whispering.

Josephine was kneeling before the closed door with her lips to the keyhole, imploring for admission. "Louise, open the door! I beg; open the door—you will make yourself ill. What are you doing, Louise? For heaven's sake open the door."

"Go away. I am not making myself ill." No; she was drinking in a very elixir of life through that open window.

Her fancy was running riot along those days ahead of her. Spring days, and summer days, and all sorts of days that would be her own. She breathed a quick prayer that life might be long. It was only yesterday she had thought with a shudder that life might be long.

She arose at length and opened the door to her sister's importunities. There was a   20
feverish triumph in her eyes, and she carried herself unwittingly like a goddess of Victory. She clasped her sister's waist, and together they descended the stairs. Richards stood waiting for them at the bottom.

Some one was opening the front door with a latchkey. It was Brently Mallard who entered, a little travel-stained, composedly carrying his grip-sack and umbrella. He had been far from the scene of accident, and did not even know there had been one. He stood amazed at Josephine's piercing cry: at Richards' quick motion to screen him from the view of his wife.

But Richards was too late.

When the doctors came they said she had died of heart disease—of joy that kills.

QUESTIONS

1. What do we learn about Louise's husband? How has he justified her responses? How are your judgments about him controlled by the context of the story?

2 Analyze the tone of paragraph 5. How is the imagery here (and in the following paragraphs) appropriate for her developing mood?

3. What is the apparent attitude of the narrator toward the institution of marriage, and what elements of tone make this apparent?

4. What do Louise's sister and Richards have in common? How do their attitudes contribute to the irony of the story?

5. Consider the tone of the last paragraph. What judgment is being made about how men view their importance to women?

JACK HODGINS   (b. 1938)

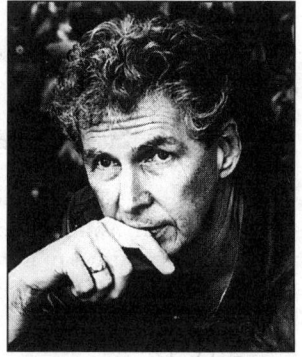

Both a novelist and short-story writer, Hodgins is a native of British Columbia. His works, some quite realistic and others tinged with the aura of "magic realism," are derived from his knowledge of the people and the countryside of this area. Among his novels are The Invention of the Word *(1977),* The Resurrection of Joseph Bourne *(1979),* The Honorary Patron *(1987), and* The Macken Charm *(1995). He has also written works for children and is the editor of three anthologies. His ideas about writing fiction are the substance of* A Passion for Narrative, *which was published in 1993. His story collections are* Spit Delaney's Island

(1977) and The Barclay Family Theater *(1981), in which Hodgins included "The Concert Stages of Europe."*

The Concert Stages of Europe _____ *1978*

Now I know Cornelia Horncastle would say I'm blaming the wrong person. I know that. I know too that she would say thirty years is a long time to hold a grudge, and that if I needed someone to blame for the fact that I made a fool of myself in front of the whole district and ruined my life in the process, then I ought to look around for the person who gave me my high-flown ideas in the first place. But she would be wrong; because there is no doubt I'd have led a different sort of life if it weren't for her, if it weren't for that piano keyboard her parents presented her with on her eleventh birthday. And everything—everything would have been different if that piano keyboard hadn't been the kind made out of stiff paper that you unfolded and laid out across the kitchen table in order to do your practising.

I don't suppose there would have been all that much harm in her having the silly thing, if only my mother hadn't got wind of it. What a fantastic idea, she said. You could learn to play without even making a sound! You could practise your scales without having to hear that awful racket when you hit a wrong note! A genius must have thought of it, she said. Certainly someone who'd read his Keats: *Heard melodies are sweet, but those unheard are sweeter.* "And don't laugh," she said, "because Cornelia Horncastle is learning to play the piano and her mother doesn't even have to miss an episode of *Ma Perkins* while she does it."

That girl, people had told her, would be giving concerts in Europe some day, command performances before royalty, and her parents hadn't even had to fork out the price of a piano. It was obvious proof, if you needed it, that a person didn't have to be rich to get somewhere in this world.

In fact, Cornelia's parents hadn't needed to put out even the small amount that paper keyboard would have cost. A piano teacher named Mrs. Humphries had moved onto the old Dendoff place and, discovering that almost no one in the district owned a piano, gave the keyboard to the Horncastles along with a year's free lessons. It was her idea, apparently, that when everyone heard how quickly Cornelia was learning they'd be lining up to send her their children for lessons. She wanted to make the point that having no piano needn't stop anyone from becoming a pianist. No doubt she had a vision of paper keyboards in every house in Waterville, of children everywhere thumping their scales out on the kitchen table without offending anyone's ears, of a whole generation turning silently into Paderewskis without ever having played a note.

They would, I suppose, have to play a real piano when they went to her house for lessons once a week, but I was never able to find out for myself, because all that talk of Cornelia's marvellous career on the concert stages of Europe did not prompt my parents to buy one of those fake keyboards or sign me up for lessons with Mrs. Humphries. My mother was born a Barclay, which meant she had a few ideas of her own, and Cornelia's glorious future prompted her to go one better. We would buy a *real* piano, she announced. And I would be sent to a teacher we could trust, not to that newcomer. If those concert stages of Europe were ever going to hear the talent of someone from the stump ranches of Waterville, it wouldn't be Cornelia Horncastle, it would be Barclay Desmond. Me.

Narrator

My father nearly choked on his coffee. "But Clay's a boy!"

"So what?" my mother said. *All* those famous players used to be boys. What did he think Chopin was? Or Tchaikovsky?

My father was so embarrassed that his throat began to turn a dark pink. Some things were too unnatural even to think about.

But eventually she won him over. "Think how terrible you'd feel," she said, "if he ended up in the bush, like you. If Mozart's father had worked for the Comox Logging Company and thought piano-playing was for sissies, where would the world be today?"

My father had no answer to that. He'd known since before his marriage that though my mother would put up with being married to a logger, expecting every day to be made a widow, she wouldn't tolerate for one minute the notion that a child of hers would follow him up into those hills. The children of Lenora Barclay would enter the professions.

She was right, he had to agree; working in the woods was the last thing in the world he wanted for his sons. He'd rather they take up ditch-digging or begging than have to work for that miserable logging company, or take their orders from a son-of-a-bitch like Tiny Beechman, or get their skulls cracked open like Stanley Kirck. It was a rotten way to make a living, and if he'd only had a decent education he could have made something of himself.

Of course, I knew he was saying all this just for my mother's benefit. He didn't really believe it for a minute. My father loved his work. I could tell by the way he was always talking about Ab Jennings and Shorty Cresswell, the men he worked with. I could tell by the excitement that mounted in him every year as the time grew near for the annual festival of loggers' sports where he usually won the bucking contest. It was obvious, I thought, that the man really wanted nothing more in this world than that one of his sons should follow in his footsteps. And much as I disliked the idea, I was sure that I was the one he'd set his hopes on. Kenny was good in school. Laurel was a girl. I was the obvious choice. I even decided that what he'd pegged me for was high-rigger. I was going to be one of those men who risked their necks climbing hundreds of feet up the bare lonely spar tree to hang the rigging from the top. Of course I would fall and kill myself the first time I tried it, I knew that, but there was no way I could convey my hesitation to my father since he would never openly admit that this was really his goal for me.

And playing the piano on the concert stages of Europe was every bit as unattractive. "Why not Kenny?" I said, when the piano had arrived, by barge, from Vancouver.

"He's too busy already with his school work," my mother said. Kenny was hoping for a scholarship, which meant he got out of just about everything unpleasant.

"What about Laurel?"

"With her short fat fingers?"

In the meantime, she said, though she was no piano-player herself (a great sigh here for what might have been), she had no trouble at all identifying which of those ivory keys was the all-important Middle C and would show it to me, to memorize, so that I wouldn't look like a total know-nothing when I showed up tomorrow for my first lesson. She'd had one piano lesson herself as a girl, she told me, and had learned all about Mister Middle C, but she'd never had a second lesson because her time was needed by her father, outside, helping with the chores. Seven daughters altogether, no sons, and she was the one who was the most often expected to fill the role of a boy. The rest of them had found the time to learn chords and chromatic scales and all those magic things she'd heard them practising while she was scrubbing out the dairy and cutting the runners off strawberry plants. They'd all become regular show-offs in one way or another, learning other instruments as well, putting on their own concerts and playing in dance bands and earning a reputation all over the district as entertaining livewires—The Barclay Sisters. And no one ever guessed that all the while she was dreaming about herself at that keyboard, tinkling away, playing beautiful music before huge audiences in elegant theatres.

"Then it isn't me that should be taking lessons," I said. "It's you."

"Don't be silly." But she walked to the new piano and pressed down one key, a black one, and looked as if I'd tempted her there for a minute. "It's too late now," she said. And then she sealed my fate: "But I just know that you're going to be a great pianist."

When my mother "just knew" something, that was as good as guaranteeing it   20
already completed. It was her way of controlling the future and, incidentally, the rest of us. By "just knowing" things, she went through life commanding the future to fit into certain patterns she desired while we scurried around making sure that it worked out that way so she'd never have to be disappointed. She'd had one great disappointment as a girl—we were never quite sure what it was, since it was only alluded to in whispers with far-off looks—and it was important that it never happen again. I was trapped.

People were always asking what you were going to be when you grew up. As if your wishes counted. In the first six years of my life the country had convinced me it wanted me to grow up and get killed fighting Germans and Japanese. I'd seen the coils of barbed wire along the beach and knew they were there just to slow down the enemy while I went looking for my gun. The teachers at school obviously wanted me to grow up and become a teacher just like them, because as far as I could see nothing they ever taught me could be of any use or interest to a single adult in the world except someone getting paid to teach it to someone else. My mother was counting on my becoming a pianist with a swallow-tail coat and standing ovations. And my father, despite all his noises to the contrary, badly wanted me to climb into the crummy every morning with him and ride out those gravelly roads into mountains and risk my life destroying forests.

I did not want to be a logger. I did not want to be a teacher. I did not want to be a soldier. And I certainly did not want to be a pianist. If anyone had ever asked me what I did want to be when I grew up, in a way that meant they expected the truth, I'd have said quite simply that what I wanted was to be a Finn.

Our new neighbours, the Korhonens, were Finns. And being a Finn, I'd been told, meant something very specific. A Finn would give you the shirt off his back, a Finn was as honest as the day is long, a Finn could drink anybody under the table and beat up half a dozen Germans and Irishmen without trying, a Finn was not afraid of work, a Finn kept a house so clean you could eat off the floors. I knew all these things before ever meeting our neighbours, but as soon as I had met them I was able to add a couple more generalizations of my own to the catalogue: Finnish girls were blonde and beautiful and flirtatious, and Finnish boys were strong, brave, and incredibly intelligent. These conclusions were reached immediately after meeting Lilja Korhonen, whose turned-up nose and blue eyes fascinated me from the beginning, and Larry Korhonen, who was already a teenager and told me for starters that he was actually Superman, having learned to fly after long hours of practice off their barn roof. Mr. and Mrs. Korhonen, of course, fitted exactly all the things my parents had told me about Finns in general. And so I decided my ambition in life was to be just like them.

I walked over to their house every Saturday afternoon and pretended to read their coloured funnies. I got in on the weekly steam-bath with Larry and his father in the sauna down by the barn. Mr. Korhonen, a patient man whose eyes sparkled at my eager attempts, taught me to count to ten—*yksi, kaksi, kolme, nelja, viisi, kuusi, seitseman, kahdeksan, yhdeksan, kymmenen.* I helped Mrs. Korhonen scrub her linoleum floors and put down newspapers so no one could walk on them, then I gorged myself on cinnamon cookies and *kala loota* and coffee sucked through a sugar cube. If there was something to be caught from just being around them, I wanted to catch it. And since being a Finn seemed to be a full-time occupation, I didn't have much patience with my parents, who behaved as if there were other things you had to prepare yourself for.

The first piano teacher they sent me to was Aunt Jessie, who lived in a narrow, cramped house up a gravel road that led to the mountains. She'd learned to play as a girl in Toronto, but she had no pretensions about being a real teacher, she was only doing this as a favour to my parents so they wouldn't have to send me to that Mrs. Humphries, an outsider. But one of the problems was that Aunt Jessie—who was no aunt of mine at all, simply one of those family friends who somehow get saddled with an honorary family title—was exceptionally beautiful. She was so attractive, in fact, that even at the age of ten I had difficulty keeping my eyes or my mind on the lessons. She exuded a dreamy sort of delicate femininity; her soft, intimate voice made the hair on the back of my neck stand on end. Besides that, her own playing was so much more pleasant to listen to than my own stumbling clangs and clunks that she would often begin to show me how to do something and become so carried away with the sound of her own music that she just kept right on playing through the rest of my half-hour. It was a simple matter to persuade her to dismiss me early every week so that I'd have a little time to play in the creek that ran past the back of her house, poling a homemade raft up and down the length of her property while her daughters paid me nickels and candies for a ride. At the end of a year my parents suspected I wasn't progressing as fast as I should. They found out why on the day I fell in the creek and nearly drowned, had to be revived by a distraught Aunt Jessie, and was driven home soaked and shivering in the back seat of her old Hudson.

Mr. Korhonen and my father were huddled over the taken-apart cream separator on the verandah when Aunt Jessie brought me up to the door. My father, when he saw me, had that peculiar look on his face that was halfway between amusement and concern, but Mr. Korhonen laughed openly. "That boy lookit like a drowny rat."

I felt like a drowned rat too, but I joined his laughter. I was sure this would be the end of my piano career, and could hardly wait to see my mother roll her eyes to the ceiling, throw out her arms, and say, "I give up."

She did nothing of the sort. She tightened her lips and told Aunt Jessie how disappointed she was. "No wonder the boy still stumbles around on that keyboard like a blindfolded rabbit; he's not going to learn the piano while he's out risking his life on the *river!*"

When I came downstairs in dry clothes Aunt Jessie had gone, no doubt wishing she'd left me to drown in the creek, and my parents and the Korhonens were all in the kitchen drinking coffee. The Korhonens sat at either side of the table, smoking hand-rolled cigarettes and squinting at me through the smoke. Mrs. Korhonen could blow beautiful white streams down her nostrils. They'd left their gumboots on the piece of newspaper just inside the door, of course, and wore the same kind of grey work-socks on their feet that my father always wore on his. My father was leaning against the wall with both arms folded across his chest inside his wide elastic braces, as he sometimes did, swishing his mug gently as if he were trying to bring something up from the bottom. My mother, however, was unable to alight anywhere. She slammed wood down into the firebox of the stove, she rattled dishes in the sink water, she slammed cupboard doors, she went around the room with the coffee pot, refilling mugs, and all the while she sang the song of her betrayal, cursing her own stupidity for sending me to a friend instead of

25

to a professional teacher, and suddenly in a flash of inspiration dumping all the blame on my father: "If you hadn't made me feel it was somehow pointless I wouldn't have felt guilty about spending more money!"

From behind the drifting shreds of smoke Mr. Korhonen grinned at me. Sucked 30 laughter between his teeth. "Yust *teenk*, boy, looks like-it you're saved!"

Mrs. Korhonen stabbed out her cigarette in an ashtray, picked a piece of tobacco off her tongue, and composed her face into the most serious and ladylike expression she could muster. "Yeh! Better he learn to drive the tractor." And swung me a conspirator's grin.

"Not on your life," my mother said. Driving a machine may have been a good enough ambition for some people, she believed, but the Barclays had been in this country for four generations and she knew there were a few things higher. "What we'll do is send him to a real teacher. Mrs. Greensborough."

Mrs. Greensborough was well known for putting on a public recital in town once a year, climaxing the program with her own rendition of Grieg's Piano Concerto—so beautiful that all went home, it was said, with tears in their eyes. The problem with Mrs. Greensborough had nothing to do with her teaching. She was, as far as I could see, an excellent piano teacher. And besides, there was something rather exciting about playing on her piano, which was surrounded and nearly buried by a thousand tropical plants and dozens of cages full of squawking birds. Every week's lesson was rather like putting on a concert in the midst of the Amazon jungle. There was even a monkey that swung through the branches and sat on the top of the piano with the metronome between its paws. And Mrs. Greensborough was at the same time warm and demanding, complimentary and hard to please—though given a little, like Aunt Jessie, to taking off on long passages of her own playing, as if she'd forgotten I was there.

It took a good hour's hard bicycling on uphill gravel roads before I could present myself for the lesson—past a dairy farm, a pig farm, a turkey farm, a dump, and a good long stretch of bush—then more washboard road through heavy timber where driveways disappeared into the trees and one dog after another lay in wait for its weekly battle with my right foot. Two spaniels, one Irish setter, and a bulldog. But it wasn't a spaniel or a setter or even a bulldog that met me on the driveway of the Greensborough's chicken farm, it was a huge German shepherd that came barking down the slope the second I had got the gate shut, and stuck its nose into my crotch. And kept it there, growling menacingly, the whole time it took me to back him up to the door of the house. There was no doubt in my mind that I would come home from piano lesson one Saturday minus a few parts. Once I had got to the house, I tried to get inside quickly and shut the door in his face, leaving him out there in the din of cackling hens; but he always got his nose between the door and the jamb, growled horribly and pushed himself inside so that he could lie on the floor at my feet and watch me hungrily the whole time I sat at the kitchen table waiting for Ginny Stamp to finish off her lesson and get out of there. By the time my turn came around my nerves were too frayed for me to get much benefit out of the lesson.

Still, somehow I learned. That Mrs. Greensborough was a marvellous teacher, my 3 mother said. The woman really knew her stuff. And I was such a fast-learning student that it took less than two years for my mother to begin thinking it was time the world heard from me.

"Richy Ryder," she said, "is coming to town."

"What?"

"Richy Ryder, CJMT. *The Talent Show.*"

I'd heard the program. Every Saturday night Richy Ryder was in a different town somewhere in the province, hosting his one-hour talent contest from the stage of a local theatre and giving away free trips to Hawaii.

Something rolled over in my stomach.   40

"And here's the application form right here," she said, whipping two sheets of paper out of her purse to slap down on the table.

"No thank you," I said. If she thought I was going in it, she was crazy.

"Don't be silly. What harm is there in trying?" My mother always answered objections with great cheerfulness, as if they were hardly worth considering.

"I'll make a fool of myself."

"You play beautifully," she said. "It's amazing how far you've come in only two   45
years. And besides, even if you don't win, the experience would be good for you."

"You have to go door-to-door ahead of time, begging for pledges, for money."

"Not begging," she said. She plunged her hands into the sink, peeling carrots so fast I couldn't see the blade of the vegetable peeler. "Just giving people a chance to vote for you. A dollar a vote." The carrot dropped, skinned naked, another one was picked up. She looked out the window now toward the barn and, still smiling, delivered the argument that never failed. "I just know you'd win it if you went in, I can feel it in my bones."

"Not this time!" I shouted, nearly turning myself inside out with the terror. "Not this time. I just can't do it."

Yet somehow I found myself riding my bicycle up and down all the roads around Waterville, knocking at people's doors, explaining the contest, and asking for their money and their votes. I don't know why I did it. Perhaps I was doing it for the same reason I was tripping over everything, knocking things off tables, slamming my shoulder into doorjambs; I just couldn't help it, everything had gone out of control. I'd wakened one morning that year and found myself six feet two inches tall and as narrow as a fence stake. My feet were so far away they seemed to have nothing to do with me. My hands flopped around on the ends of those lanky arms like fish, something alive. My legs had grown so fast the bones in my knees parted and I had to wear elastic bandages to keep from falling apart. When I turned a corner on my bicycle, one knee would bump the handlebar, throwing me into the ditch. I was the same person as before, apparently, saddled with this new body I didn't know what to do with. Everything had gone out of control. I seemed to have nothing to do with the direction of my own life. It was perfectly logical that I should end up playing the piano on the radio, selling myself to the countryside for a chance to fly off to Hawaii and lie on the sand under the whispering palms.

There were actually two prizes offered. The all-expense, ten-day trip to Hawaii   50
would go to the person who brought in the most votes for himself, a dollar a vote. But lest someone accuse the radio station of getting its values confused, there was also a prize for the person judged by a panel of experts to have the most talent. This prize, which was donated by Nelson's Hardware, was a leatherette footstool.

"It's not the prize that's important," people told me. "It's the chance to be heard by all those people."

I preferred not to think of all those people. It seemed to me that if I were cut out to be a concert pianist it would be my teacher and not my parents encouraging me in this thing. Mrs. Greensborough, once she'd forked over her two dollars for two votes, said nothing at all. No doubt she was hoping I'd keep her name out of it.

But it had taken no imagination on my part to figure out that if I were to win the only prize worth trying for, the important thing was not to spend long hours at the keyboard, practising, but to get out on the road hammering at doors, on the telephone calling relatives, down at the General Store approaching strangers who stopped for gas. Daily piano practice shrank to one or two quick run-throughs of "The Robin's Return," school homework shrank to nothing at all, and home chores just got ignored. My brother and sister filled in for me, once in a while, so the chickens wouldn't starve to death and the woodbox would never be entirely empty, but they did it gracelessly. It was amazing, they said, how much time a great pianist had to spend out on the road, meeting his public. Becoming famous, they said, was more work than it was worth.

And becoming famous, I discovered, was what people assumed I was after. "You'll go places," they told me. "You'll put this place on the old map." I was a perfect combination of my father's down-to-earth get-up-and-go and my mother's finer sensitivity, they said. How wonderful to see a young person with such high ambition!

"I always knew this old place wouldn't be good enough to hold you," my grand-   55
mother said as she fished out a five-dollar bill from her purse. But my mother's sisters, who appeared from all parts of the old farmhouse in order to contribute a single collective vote, had some reservations to express. Eleanor, the youngest, said she doubted I'd be able to carry it off, I'd probably freeze when I was faced with a microphone, I'd forget what a piano was for. Christina announced she was betting I'd faint, or have to run out to the bathroom right in the middle of my piece. And Mabel, red-headed Mabel who'd played accordion once in an amateur show, said she remembered a boy who made such a fool of himself in one of these things that he went home and blew off his head. "Don't be so morbid," my grandmother said. "The boy probably had no talent. Clay here is destined for higher things."

From behind her my grandfather winked. He seldom had a chance to contribute more than that to a conversation. He waited until we were alone to stuff a five-dollar bill in my pocket and squeeze my arm.

I preferred my grandmother's opinion of me to the aunts'. I began to feed people lies so they'd think that about me—that I was destined for dizzying heights. I wanted to be a great pianist, I said, and if I won that trip to Hawaii I'd trade it in for the money so that I could go off and study at the Toronto Conservatory. I'd heard of the Toronto Conservatory only because it was printed in big black letters on the front cover of all those yellow books of finger exercises I was expected to practise.

I don't know why people gave me their money. Pity, perhaps. Maybe it was impossible to say no to a six-foot-two-inch thirteen-year-old who trips over his own bike in front of your house, falls up your bottom step, blushes red with embarrassment when you open the door, and tells you he wants your money for a talent contest so he can become a Great Artist. At any rate, by the day of the contest I'd collected enough money to put me in the third spot. I would have to rely on pledges from the studio audience and phone-in pledges from the radio audience to rocket me up to first place. The person in second place when I walked into that theatre to take my seat down front with the rest of the contestants was Cornelia Horncastle.

I don't know how she managed it so secretly. I don't know where she found the people to give her money, living in the same community as I did, unless all those people who gave me their dollar bills when I knocked on their doors had just given her two the day before. Maybe she'd gone into town, canvassing street after street, something my parents wouldn't let me do on the grounds that town people already had enough strangers banging on their doors every day. Once I'd got outside the vague boundaries of Waterville I was to approach only friends or relatives or people who worked in the woods with my dad, or stores that had—as my mother put it—done a good business out of us over the years. Cornelia Horncastle, in order to get herself secretly into that second place, must have gone wild in town. Either that or discovered a rich relative.

She sat at the other end of the front row of contestants, frowning over the sheets   60
of music in her hands. A short nod and a quick smile were all she gave me. Like the other contestants, I was kept busy licking my dry lips, rubbing my sweaty palms together, wondering if I should whip out to the bathroom one last time, and rubbernecking to get a look at people as they filled up the theatre behind us. Mrs. Greensborough, wearing dark glasses and a big floppy hat, was jammed into the far corner at the rear, studying her program. Mr. and Mrs. Korhonen and Lilja came partway down the aisle and found seats near the middle. Mr. Korhonen winked at me. Larry, who was not quite the hero he had once been, despite the fact that he'd recently beat up one of the teachers and set fire to the bus shelter, came in with my brother Kenny—both of them looking uncomfortable—and slid into a back seat. My parents came all the way down front, so they could look back up the slope and pick out the seats they wanted. My mother smiled as she always did in public, as if she expected the most delightful surprise at any moment. They took seats near the front. Laurel was with them, reading a book.

My mother's sisters—with husbands, boyfriends, a few of my cousins—filled up the entire middle section of the back row. Eleanor, who was just a few years older than myself, crossed her eyes and stuck out her tongue when she saw that I'd turned to look. Mabel pulled in her chin and held up her hands, which she caused to tremble and shake. Time to be nervous, she was suggesting, in case I forgot. Bella, Christina, Gladdy, Frieda—all sat puffed up like members of a royal family, or the owners of this theatre, looking down over the crowd as if they believed every one of these people had come here expressly to watch their nephew and for no other reason. "Look, it's the Barclay girls," I heard someone behind me say. And someone else: "Oh, *them.*" The owner of the first voice giggled. "It's a wonder they aren't all entered in this thing, you know how they like to perform." A snort. "They *are* performing, just watch them." I could tell by the muffled "Shhh" and the rustling of clothing that one of them was nudging the other and pointing at me, at the back of my neck. "One of them's son." When I turned again, Eleanor stood up in the aisle by her seat, did a few steps of a tap dance, and quickly sat down. In case I was tempted to take myself seriously. *None of his family members except his father took him seriously.*

When my mother caught my eye, she mouthed a silent message: stop gawking at the audience, I was letting people see how unusual all this was to me, instead of taking it in my stride like a born performer. She indicated with her head that I should notice the stage.

As if I hadn't already absorbed every detail. It was exactly as she must have hoped. A great black concert grand with the lid lifted sat out near the front of the stage, against a painted backdrop of palm trees along a sandy beach, and—in great scrawled letters— the words "Richy Ryder's CJMT Talent Festival." A long blackboard leaned against one end of the proscenium arch, with all the contestants' names on it and the rank order of each. Someone named Brenda Roper was in first place. On the opposite side of the stage, a microphone seemed to have grown up out of a heap of pineapples. I felt sick.

Eventually Richy Ryder came out of whatever backstage room he'd been hiding in and passed down the row of contestants, identifying us and telling us to get up onto the stage when our turns came without breaking our necks on those steps. "You won't be nervous, when you get up there," he said. "I'll make you feel at ease." He was looking off somewhere else as he said it, and I could see his jaw muscles straining to hold back a yawn. And he wasn't fooling me with his "you won't be nervous" either, because I knew without a doubt that the minute I got up on that stage I would throw up all over the piano.

Under the spotlight, Richy Ryder acted like a different person. He did not look   65
the least bit like yawning while he told the audience the best way of holding their hands
to get the most out of applause, cautioned them against whistling or yelling obscenities,
painted a glorious picture of the life ahead for the talented winner of this contest, complimented the audience on the number of happy, shiny faces he could see out there in
the seats, and told them how lucky they were to have this opportunity of showing off the
fine young talent of the valley to all the rest of the province. I slid down in my seat, sure
that I would rather die than go through with this thing.

The first contestant was a fourteen-year-old girl dressed up like a gypsy, singing
something in a foreign language. According to the blackboard she was way down in
ninth place, so I didn't pay much attention until her voice cracked open in the middle
of a high note and she clutched at her throat with both hands, a look of incredulous
surprise on her face. She stopped right there, face a brilliant red, and after giving the
audience a quick curtsey hurried off the stage. A great beginning, I thought. If people
were going to fall to pieces like that through the whole show no one would even notice
my upchucking on the Heintzman. I had a vision of myself dry-heaving the whole way
through "The Robin's Return."

Number two stepped up to the microphone and answered all of Richy Ryder's
questions as if they were some kind of test he had to pass in order to be allowed to perform. Yes sir, his name was Roger Casey, he said with a face drawn long and narrow with
seriousness, and in case that wasn't enough he added that his father was born in Digby,
Nova Scotia, and his mother was born Esther Romaine in a little house just a couple of
blocks up the street from the theatre, close to the Native Sons' Hall, and had gone to
school with the mayor though she'd dropped out of Grade Eight to get a job at the
Safeway cutting meat. And yes sir, he was going to play the saxophone because he'd
taken lessons for four years from Mr. D. P. Rowbottom on Seventh Street though he'd
actually started out on the trumpet until he decided he didn't like it all that much. He
came right out to the edge of the stage, toes sticking over, leaned back like a rooster
about to crow, and blasted out "Softly As in a Morning Sunrise" so loud and hard that I
thought his bulging eyes would pop right out of his head and his straining lungs would
blast holes through that red-and-white shirt. Everyone moved forward, tense and straining, waiting for something terrible to happen—for him to fall off the stage or explode or
go sailing off into the air from the force of his own fantastic intensity—but he stopped
suddenly and everyone fell back exhausted and sweaty to clap for him.

The third contestant was less reassuring. A kid with talent. A smart-aleck ten-year-
old with red hair, who told the audience he was going into show business when he grew
up, started out playing "Swanee River" on his banjo, switched in the middle of a bar to
a mouth organ, tap-danced across the stage to play a few bars on the piano, and finished off on a trombone he'd had stashed away behind the palm tree. He bowed,
grinned, flung himself around the stage as if he'd spent his whole life on it, and looked
as if he'd do his whole act again quite happily if the audience wanted him to. By the
time the tremendous applause had died down my jaw was aching from the way I'd been
grinding my teeth the whole time he was up there. The audience would not have gone
quite so wild over him, I thought, if he hadn't been wearing a hearing aid and a leg
brace.

Then it was my turn. A strange calm fell over me when my name was called, the
kind of calm that I imagine comes over a person about to be executed when his mind
finally buckles under the horror it has been faced with, something too terrible to believe
in. I wondered for a moment if I had died. But no, my body at least hadn't died, for it

transported me unbidden across the front of the audience, up the staircase (with only a slight stumble on the second step, hardly noticeable), and across the great wide stage of the theatre to stand facing Richy Ryder's enormous expanse of white smiling teeth, beside the microphone.

"And you are Barclay Philip Desmond," he said.   70

"Yes," I said.

And again "yes," because I realized that not only had my voice come out as thin and high as the squeal of a dry buzz-saw, but the microphone was at least a foot too low. I had to bend my knees to speak into it.

"You don't live in town, do you?" he said. He had no intention of adjusting that microphone. "You come from a place called . . . Waterville. A logging and farming settlement?"

"Yes," I said.

And again "yes" because while he was speaking my legs had straightened up, I'd   75
returned to my full height and had to duck again for the microphone.

He was speaking to me but his eyes, I could see, were busy keeping all that audience gathered together, while his voice and his mind were obviously concentrated on the thousands of invisible people who were crouched inside that microphone, listening, the thousands of people who—I imagined now—were pulled up close to their sets all over the province, wondering if I was actually a pair of twins or if my high voice had some peculiar way of echoing itself, a few tones lower.

"Does living in the country like that mean you have to milk the cows every morning before you go to school?"

"Yes."

And again "yes."

I could see Mrs. Greensborough cowering in the back corner. I promise not to   80
mention you, I thought. And the Korhonens, grinning. I had clearly passed over into another world they couldn't believe in.

"If you've got a lot of farm chores to do, when do you find the time to practise the piano?"

He had me this time. A "yes" wouldn't be good enough. "Right after school," I said, and ducked to repeat. "Right after school. As soon as I get home. For an hour."

"And I just bet," he said, throwing the audience an enormous wink, "that like every other red-blooded country kid you hate every minute of it. You'd rather be outside playing baseball."

The audience laughed. I could see my mother straining forward; she still had the all-purpose waiting-for-the-surprise smile on her lips but her eyes were frowning at the master of ceremonies. She did not approve of the comment. And behind that face she was no doubt thinking to herself "I just know he's going to win" over and over so hard that she was getting pains in the back of her neck. Beside her, my father had a tight grin on his face. He was chuckling to himself, and sliding a look around the room to see how the others were taking this.

Up at the back, most of my aunts—and their husbands, their boyfriends—had   85
tilted their chins down to their chests, offering me only the tops of their heads. Eleanor, however, had both hands behind her neck. She was laughing harder than anyone else.

Apparently I was not expected to respond to the last comment, for he had another question as soon as the laughter had died. "How old are you, son?"

"Thirteen."

For once I remembered to duck the first time.

"Thirteen. Does your wife like the idea of your going on the radio like this?"

Again the audience laughed. My face burned. I felt tears in my eyes. I had no con-   90
trol over my face. I tried to laugh like everyone else but realized I probably looked like
an idiot. Instead, I frowned and looked embarrassed and kicked at one shoe with the
toe of the other.

"Just a joke," he said, "just a joke." The jerk knew he'd gone too far. "And now
seriously, one last question before I turn you loose on those ivories over there."

My heart had started to thump so noisily I could hardly hear him. My hands, I
realized, had gone numb. There was no feeling at all in my fingers. How was I ever going
to play the piano?

"What are you going to be when you grow up?"

The thumping stopped. My heart stopped. A strange, cold silence settled over the
world. I was going to die right in front of all those people. What I was going to be was a
corpse, dead of humiliation, killed in a trap I hadn't seen being set. What must have
been only a few seconds crawled by while something crashed around in my head, trying
to get out. I sensed the audience, hoping for some help from them. My mother had settled back in her seat and for the first time that surprise-me smile had gone. Rather, she
looked confident, sure of what I was about to say.

And suddenly, I was aware of familiar faces all over that theatre. Neighbours.   95
Friends of the family. My aunts. People who had heard me answer that question at their
doors, people who thought they knew what I wanted.

There was nothing left of Mrs. Greensborough but the top of her big hat. My
father, too, was looking down at the floor between his feet. I saw myself falling from that
spar tree, high in the mountains.

"Going to be?" I said, turning so fast that I bumped the microphone with my
hand, which turned out after all not to be numb.

I ducked.

"Nothing," I said. "I don't know. Maybe . . . maybe nothing at all."

I don't know who it was that snorted when I screwed up the stool, sat down, and   100
stood up to screw it down again. I don't know how well I played, I wasn't listening. I
don't know how loud the audience clapped, I was in a hurry to get back to my seat. I
don't know what the other contestants did, I wasn't paying any attention except when
Cornelia Horncastle got up on the stage, told the whole world she was going to be a
professional pianist, and sat down to rattle off Rachmaninoff's Rhapsody on a Theme of
Paganini as if she'd been playing for fifty years. As far as I know it may have been the first
time she'd ever heard herself play it. She had a faint look of surprise on her face the
whole time, as if she couldn't quite get over the way the keys went down when you
touched them.

As soon as Cornelia came down off the stage, smiling modestly, and got back into
her seat, Richy Ryder announced a fifteen-minute intermission while the talent judges
made their decision and the studio audience went out into the lobby to pledge their
money and their votes. Now that the talent had been displayed, people could spend
their money according to what they'd heard rather than according to who happened to
come knocking on their door. Most of the contestants got up to stretch their legs but I
figured I'd stood up once too often that night and stayed in my seat. The lower exit was
not far away; I contemplated using it; I could hitch-hike home and be in bed before any
of the others got out of there.

I was stopped, though, by my father, who sat down in the seat next to mine and
put a greasy carton of popcorn in my lap.

"Well," he said, "that's that."

His neck was flushed. This must have been a terrible evening for him. He had a carton of popcorn himself and tipped it up to gather a huge mouthful. I had never before in my life, I realized, seen my father eat popcorn. It must have been worse for him than I thought.

Not one of the aunts was anywhere in sight! I could see my mother standing in   105
the far aisle, talking to Mrs. Korhonen. Still smiling. She would never let herself fall apart in public, no matter what happened. My insides ached with the knowledge of what it must have been like right then to be her. I felt as if I had just betrayed her in front of the whole world. Betrayed everyone.

"Let's go home," I said.

"Not yet. Wait a while. Might as well see this thing to the end."

True, I thought. Wring every last drop of torture out of it.

He looked hard at me a moment, as if he were trying to guess what was going on in my head. And he did, he did, he always knew. "My old man wanted me to be a doctor," he said. "My mother wanted me to be a florist. She liked flowers. She thought if I was a florist I'd be able to send her a bouquet every week. But what does any of that matter now?"

Being part of a family was too complicated. And right then I decided I'd be a loner.   110
No family for me. Nobody whose hearts could be broken every time I opened my mouth. Nobody expecting anything of me. Nobody to get me all tangled up in knots trying to guess who means what and what is it that's really going on inside anyone else. No temptations to presume I knew what someone else was thinking or feeling or hoping for.

When the lights had flickered and dimmed, and people had gone back to their seats, a young man with a beard came out onto the stage and changed the numbers behind the contestants' names. I'd dropped to fifth place, and Cornelia Horncastle had moved up to first. She had also, Richy Ryder announced, been awarded the judges' footstool for talent. The winner of the holiday in sunny Hawaii would not be announced until the next week, he said, when the radio audience had enough time to mail in their votes.

"And that," my mother said when she came down the aisle with her coat on, "is the end of a long and tiring day." I could find no disappointment showing in her eyes, or in the set of her mouth. Just relief. The same kind of relief that I felt myself. "You did a good job," she said, "and thank goodness it's over."

As soon as we got in the house I shut myself in the bedroom and announced I was never coming out. Lying on my bed, I tried to read my comic books but my mind passed from face to face all through the community, imagining everyone having a good laugh at the way my puffed-up ambition had got its reward. My face burned. Relatives, the aunts, would be ashamed of me. Eleanor would never let me forget. Mabel would remind me of the boy who'd done the only honourable thing, blown off his head. Why wasn't I doing the same? I lay awake the whole night, torturing myself with these thoughts. But when morning came and the hunger pains tempted me out of the bedroom as far as the breakfast table, I decided the whole wretched experience had brought one benefit with it: freedom from ambition. I wouldn't worry any more about becoming a pianist for my mother. Nor would I worry any more about becoming a high-rigger for my father. I was free at last to concentrate on pursing the only goal that ever really mattered to me: becoming a Finn.

Of course I failed at that too. But then neither did Cornelia Horncastle become a great pianist on the concert stages of Europe. In fact, I understand that once she got back from her holiday on the beaches of Hawaii she announced to her parents that she was never going to touch a piano again as long as she lived, ivory, or cardboard, or any other kind. She had already, she said, accomplished all she'd ever wanted from it. And as far as I know, she's kept her word to this day.

QUESTIONS

1. Describe the attitude of Barclay Desmond toward his own experience as a young pianist and recitalist. Why does the story devote so much attention to Richy Ryder's introductory questions to Clay? Might Clay's experience have been different if he could have had a different kind of introduction?

2. How does Hodgins make the story comic? Describe the uses of farce, verbal humor, and fancifulness. Even though Clay makes himself the object of much humor, what is your attitude toward him at the story's end?

3. In what ways is the story serious? How seriously do you treat Clay's statements about his own ambitions (see paragraphs 22, 94–99, 113)?

4. Why do you think Clay begins and ends by referring to Cornelia Horncastle? In what ways do you think Clay is similar to Cornelia, and also different from her?

MARGARET LAURENCE   (1926–1987)

Laurence wss born in Neepawa, Manitoba, and was edu-cated in Winnipeg, the provincial capital. She spent her twenties in Somalia and Ghana, and one of her earliest writing efforts was to make translations from the Somali language. Eventually she lived in both England and Canada. Afer publication of her first novel, This Side Jordan *(1960), and her first collection of stories,* The Tomorrow-Tamer *(1964), she wrote prolifically, her most acclaimed work being her novels and stories dramatizing the lives of women in Manawaka, her fictionalized name for Neepawa. The best known of the Manawaka novels is* The Diviners *(1974). Laurence also wrote travel books, collec-tions of essays, and children's stories; her autobiographical memoir* Dance on the Earth *was published in 1989, two years after her death.* "The Loons" *is taken from* A Bird in the House *(1970), her collection of eight Manawaka stories.*

The Loons   ‪The narrator is Vanessa‬   *1970*

Just below Manawaka, where the Wachakwa River ran brown and noisy over the pebbles, the scrub oak and grey-green willow and chokecherry bushes grew in a dense thicket. In a clearing at the centre of the thicket stood the Tonnerre family's shack. The basis of this dwelling was a small square cabin made of poplar poles and chinked with mud, which had been built by Jules Tonnerre some fifty years before, when he came back from Batoche with a bullet in his thigh, the year that Riel was hung and the voices of the Metis entered their long silence. Jules had only intended to stay the winter in the Wachakwa Valley, but the family was still there in the thirties, when I was a child. As the Tonnerres had increased, their settlement had been added to, until the clearing at the foot of the town hill was a chaos of lean-tos, wooden packing cases, warped lumber, discarded car tyres, ramshackle chicken coops, tangled strands of barbed wire and rusty tin cans.

The Tonnerres were French halfbreeds, and among themselves they spoke a *patois* that was neither Cree nor French. Their English was broken and full of obscenities. They did not belong among the Cree of the Galloping Mountain reservation, further north, and they did not belong among the Scots-Irish and Ukrainians of Manawaka, either. They were, as my Grandmother MacLeod would have put it, neither flesh, fowl, nor good salt herring. When their men were not working at odd jobs or as section hands on the C.P.R., they lived on relief. In the summers, one of the Tonnerre youngsters, with a face that seemed totally unfamiliar with laughter, would knock at the doors of the town's brick houses and offer for sale a lard-pail full of bruised wild strawberries, and if he got as much as a quarter he would grab the coin and run before the customer had time to change her mind. Sometimes old Jules, or his son Lazarus, would get mixed up in a Saturday-night brawl, and would hit out at whoever was nearest, or howl drunkenly among the offended shoppers on Main Street, and then the Mountie would put them for the night in the barred cell underneath the Court House, and the next morning they would be quiet again.

Piquette Tonnerre, the daughter of Lazarus, was in my class at school. She was older than I, but she had failed several grades, perhaps because her attendance had always been sporadic and her interest in schoolwork negligible. Part of the reason she had missed a lot of school was that she had had tuberculosis of the bone, and had once spent many months in hospital. I knew this because my father was the doctor who had looked after her. Her sickness was almost the only thing I knew about her, however. Otherwise, she existed for me only as a vaguely embarrassing presence, with her hoarse voice and her clumsy limping walk and her grimy cotton dresses that were always miles too long. I was neither friendly nor unfriendly towards her. She dwelt and moved somewhere within my scope of vision, but I did not actually notice her very much until that peculiar summer when I was eleven.

"I don't know what to do about that kid," my father said at dinner one evening. "Piquette Tonnerre, I mean. The damn bone's flared up again. I've had her in hospital for quite a while now, and it's under control all right, but I hate like the dickens to send her home again."

"Couldn't you explain to her mother that she has to rest a lot?" my mother said. 5

"The mother's not there," my father replied. "She took off a few years back. Can't say I blame her. Piquette cooks for them, and she says Lazarus would never do anything for himself as long as she's there. Anyway, I don't think she'd take much care of herself, once she got back. She's only thirteen, after all. Beth, I was thinking—what about taking her up to Diamond Lake with us this summer? A couple of months rest would give that bone a much better chance."

My mother looked stunned.

"But Ewen—what about Roddie and Vanessa?"

"She's not contagious," my father said. "And it would be company for Vanessa."

"Oh dear," my mother said in distress, "I'll bet anything she has nits in her hair." 10

"For Pete's sake," my father said crossly, "do you think Matron would let her stay in the hospital for all this time like that? Don't be silly, Beth."

Grandmother MacLeod, her delicately featured face as rigid as a cameo, now brought her mauve-veined hands together as though she were about to begin a prayer.

"Ewen, if that half-breed youngster comes along to Diamond Lake, I'm not going," she announced. "I'll go to Morag's for the summer."

I had trouble in stifling my urge to laugh, for my mother brightened visibly and quickly tried to hide it. If it came to a choice between Grandmother MacLeod and Piquette, Piquette would win hands down, nits or not.

"It might be quite nice for you, at that," she mused. "You haven't seen Morag for over a year, and you might enjoy being in the city for a while. Well, Ewen dear, you do what you think best. If you think it would do Piquette some good, then we'll be glad to have her, as long as she behaves herself."

15

So it happened that several weeks later, when we all piled into my father's old Nash, surrounded by suitcases and boxes of provisions and toys for my ten-month-old brother, Piquette was with us and Grandmother MacLeod, miraculously, was not. My father would only be staying at the cottage for a couple of weeks, for he had to get back to his practice, but the rest of us would stay at Diamond Lake until the end of August.

Our cottage was not named, as many were, "Dew Drop Inn," or "Bide-a-Wee," or "Bonnie Doon." The sign on the roadway bore in austere letters only our name, MacLeod. It was not a large cottage, but it was on the lakefront. You could look out the windows and see, through the filigree of the spruce trees, the water glistening greatly as the sun caught it. All around the cottage were ferns, and sharp-branched raspberry bushes, and moss that had grown over fallen tree trunks. If you looked carefully among the weeds and grass, you could find wild strawberry plants which were in white flower now and in another month would bear fruit, the fragrant globes hanging like miniature scarlet lanterns on the thin hairy stems. The two gray squirrels were still there, gossiping at us from the tall spruce beside the cottage, and by the end of the summer they would again be tame enough to take pieces of crust from my hands. The broad moose antlers that hung above the back door were a little more bleached and fissured after the winter, but otherwise everything was the same. I raced joyfully around my kingdom, greeting all the places I had not seen for a year. My brother, Roderick, who had not been born when we were here last summer, sat on the car rug in the sunshine and examined a brown spruce cone, meticulously turning it round and round in his small and curious hands. My mother and father toted the luggage from car to cottage, exclaiming over how well the place had wintered, no broken windows, thank goodness, no apparent damage from storm-felled branches or snow.

Only after I had finished looking around did I notice Piquette. She was sitting on the swing, her lame leg held stiffly out, and her other foot scuffing the ground as she swung slowly back and forth. Her long hair hung black and straight around her shoulders, and her broad coarse-featured face bore no expression—it was blank, as though she no longer dwelt within her own skull, as though she had gone elsewhere. I approached her very hesitantly.

"Want to come and play?"

Piquette looked at me with a sudden flash of scorn.

"I ain't a kid," she said.

2

Wounded, I stamped angrily away, swearing I would not speak to her for the rest of the summer. In the days that followed, however, Piquette began to interest me, and I began to want to interest her. My reasons did not appear bizarre to me. Unlikely as it may seem, I had only just realised that the Tonnerre family, whom I had always heard called half-breeds, were actually Indians, or as near as made no difference. My acquaintance with Indians was not extensive. I did not remember ever having seen a real Indian, and my new awareness that Piquette sprang from the people of Big Bear and Poundmaker, of Tecumseh, of the Iroquois who had eaten Father Brebeuf's heart—all this gave her an instant attraction in my eyes. I was a devoted reader of Pauline Johnson at this age, and sometimes would orate aloud and in an exalted voice, *West Wind, blow from your prairie nest; Blow from the mountains, blow from the west*—and so on. It seemed to me that Piquette must be in some way a daughter of the forest, a kind of junior prophetess of the wilds, who might impart to me, if I took the right approach, some of the secrets which she undoubtedly knew—where the whippoorwill made her nest, how the coyote reared her young, or whatever it was that it said in Hiawatha.

I set about gaining Piquette's trust. She was not allowed to go swimming, with her bad leg, but I managed to lure her down to the beach—or rather, she came because there was nothing else to do. The water was always icy, for the lake was fed by springs, but I swam like a dog, thrashing my arms and legs around at such speed and with such an output of energy that I never grew cold. Finally, when I had had enough, I came out and sat beside Piquette on the sand. When she saw me approaching, her hand squashed flat the sand castle she had been building, and she looked at me sullenly, without speaking.

"Do you like this place?" I asked, after a while, intending to lead on from there into the question of forest lore.

Piquette shrugged. "It's okay. Good as anywhere."   25

"I love it," I said. "We come here every summer."

"So what?" Her voice was distant, and I glanced at her uncertainly, wondering what I could have said wrong.

"Do you want to come for a walk?" I asked her. "We wouldn't need to go far. If you walk just around the point there, you come to a bay where great big reeds grow in the water, and all kinds of fish hang around there. Want to? Come on."

She shook her head.

"Your dad said I ain't supposed to do no more walking than I got to."   30

I tried another line.

"I bet you know a lot about the woods and all that, eh ?" I began respectfully.

Piquette looked at me from her large dark unsmiling eyes.

"I don't know what in hell you're talkin' about," she replied. "You nuts or somethin'? If you mean where my old man, and me, and all them live, you better shut up, by Jesus, you hear?"

I was startled and my feelings were hurt, but I had a kind of dogged perseverance.   35
I ignored her rebuff.

"You know something, Piquette? There's loons here, on this lake. You can see their nests just up the shore there, behind those logs. At night, you can hear them even from the cottage, but it's better to listen from the beach. My dad says we should listen and try to remember how they sound, because in a few years when more cottages are built at Diamond Lake and more people come in, the loons will go away."

Piquette was picking up stones and snail shells and then dropping them again.

"Who gives a good goddamn?" she said.

It became increasingly obvious that, as an Indian, Piquette was a dead loss. That evening I went out by myself, scrambling through the bushes that overhung the steep path, my feet slipping on the fallen spruce needles that covered the ground. When I reached the shore, I walked along the firm damp sand to the small pier that my father had built, and sat down there. I heard someone else crashing through the undergrowth and the bracken, and for a moment I thought Piquette had changed her mind, but it turned out to be my father. He sat beside me on the pier and we waited, without speaking.

At night the lake was like black glass with a streak of amber which was the path of   40
the moon. All around, the spruce trees grew tall and close-set, branches blackly sharp
against the sky, which was lightened by a cold flickering of stars. Then the loons began
their calling. They rose like phantom birds from the nests on the shore, and flew out
onto the dark still surface of the water.

No one can ever describe that ululating sound, the crying of the loons, and no
one who has heard it can ever forget it. Plaintive, and yet with a quality of chilling mockery, those voices belonged to a world separated by aeons from our neat world of summer
cottages and the lighted lamps of home.

"They must have sounded just like that," my father remarked, "before any person
ever set foot here."

Then he laughed. "You could say the same, of course, about sparrows, or chipmunks, but somehow it only strikes you that way with the loons."

"I know," I said.

Neither of us suspected that this would be the last time we would ever sit here   45
together on the shore, listening. We stayed for perhaps half an hour, and then we went
back to the cottage. My mother was reading beside the fireplace. Piquette was looking at
the burning birch log, and not doing anything.

"You should have come along," I said, although in fact I was glad she had not.

"Not me," Piquette said. "You wouldn' catch me walkin' way down there jus' for a
bunch of squawkin' birds."

Piquette and I remained ill at ease with one another. I felt I had somehow failed
my father, but I did not know what was the matter, nor why she would not or could
not respond when I suggested exploring the woods or playing house. I thought it was
probably her slow and difficult walking that held her back. She stayed most of the time
in the cottage with my mother, helping her with the dishes or with Roddie, but hardly
ever talking. Then the Duncans arrived at their cottage, and I spent my days with
Mavis, who was my best friend. I could not reach Piquette at all, and I soon lost interest in trying. But all that summer she remained as both a reproach and a mystery to
me.

That winter my father died of pneumonia, after less than a week's illness. For
some time I saw nothing around me, being completely immersed in my own pain and
my mother's. When I looked outward once more, I scarcely noticed that Piquette
Tonnerre was no longer at school. I do not remember seeing her at all until four years
later, one Saturday night when Mavis and I were having Cokes in the Regal Café. The
jukebox was booming like tuneful thunder, and beside it, leaning lightly on its chrome
and its rainbow glass, was a girl.

Piquette must have been seventeen then, although she looked about twenty. I   5
stared at her, astounded that anyone could have changed so much. Her face, so stolid
and expressionless before, was animated now with a gaiety that was almost violent. She
laughed and talked very loudly with the boys around her. Her lipstick was bright
carmine, and her hair was cut short and frizzily permed. She had not been pretty as a
child, and she was not pretty now, for her features were still heavy and blunt. But her
dark and slightly slanted eyes were beautiful, and her skin-tight skirt and orange sweater
displayed to enviable advantage a soft and slender body.

She saw me, and walked over. She teetered a little, but it was not due to her once-
tubercular leg, for her limp was almost gone.

Narrator   "Hi, Vanessa." Her voice still had the same hoarseness. "Long time no see, eh?"

"Hi," I said. "Where've you been keeping yourself, Piquette?"

"Oh, I been around," she said. "I been away almost two years now. Been all over the place—Winnipeg, Regina, Saskatoon. Jesus, what I could tell you! I come back this summer, but I ain't stayin'. You kids goin' to the dance?"

"No," I said abruptly, for this was a sore point with me. I was fifteen, and thought I   55
was old enough to go to the Saturday-night dances at the Flamingo. My mother, however, thought otherwise.

"Y'oughta come," Piquette said. "I never miss one. It's just about the on'y thing in this jerkwater town that's any fun. Boy, you couldn' catch me stayin' here. I don' give a shit about this place. It stinks."

She sat down beside me, and I caught the harsh over-sweetness of her perfume.

"Listen, you wanna know something, Vanessa?" she confided, her voice only slightly blurred. "Your dad was the only person in Manawaka that ever done anything good to me."

I nodded speechlessly. I was certain she was speaking the truth. I knew a little more than I had that summer at Diamond Lake, but I could not reach her now any more than I had then. I was ashamed, ashamed of my own timidity, the frightened tendency to look the other way. Yet I felt no real warmth towards her—I only felt that I ought to, because of that distant summer and because my father had hoped she would be company for me, or perhaps that I would be for her, but it had not happened that way. At this moment, meeting her again, I had to admit that she repelled and embarrassed me, and I could not help despising the self-pity in her voice. I wished she would go away. I did not want to see her. I did not know what to say to her. It seemed that we had nothing to say to one another.

"I'll tell you something else," Piquette went on. "All the old bitches an' biddies in   60
this town will sure be surprised. I'm gettin' married this fall—my boyfriend, he's an English fella, works in the stockyards in the city there, a very tall guy, got blond wavy hair. Gee, is he ever handsome. Got this real classy name. Alvin Gerald Cummings— *Piquette's boyfriend's* some handle, eh? They call him Al." *name.*

For the merest instant, then, I saw her. I really did see her, for the first and only time in all the years we had both lived in the same town. Her defiant face, momentarily, became unguarded and unmasked, and in her eyes there was a terrifying hope.

"Gee, Piquette—" I burst out awkwardly, "that's swell. That's really wonderful. Congratulations—good luck—I hope you'll be happy—"

As I mouthed the conventional phrases, I could only guess how great her need must have been, that she had been forced to seek the very things she so bitterly rejected.

When I was eighteen, I left Manawaka and went away to college. At the end of my first year, I came back home for the summer. I spent the first few days in talking non-stop with my mother, as we exchanged all the news that somehow had not found its way into letters—what had happened in my life and what had happened here in Manawaka while I was away. My mother searched her memory for events that concerned people I knew.

"Did I ever write you about Piquette Tonnerre, Vanessa?" she asked one morning.   65

"No, I don't think so," I replied. "Last I heard of her, she was going to marry some guy in the city. Is she still there?"

My mother looked perturbed, and it was a moment before she spoke, as though she did not know how to express what she had to tell and wished she did not need to try.

"She's dead," she said at last. Then, as I stared at her, "Oh, Vanessa, when it happened, I couldn't help thinking of her as she was that summer—so sullen and gauche and badly dressed. I couldn't help wondering if we could have done something more at that time—but what could we do? She used to be around in the cottage there with me all day, and honestly, it was all I could do to get a word out of her. She didn't even talk to your father very much, although I think she liked him, in her way."

"What happened?" I asked.

"Either her husband left her, or she left him," my mother said. "I don't know which. Anyway, she came back here with two youngsters, both only babies—they must have been born very close together. She kept house, I guess, for Lazarus and her brothers, down in the valley there, in the old Tonnerre place. I used to see her on the street sometimes, but she never spoke to me. She'd put on an awful lot of weight, and she looked a mess, to tell you the truth, a real slattern, dressed any old how. She was up in court a couple of times—drunk and disorderly, of course. One Saturday night last winter, during the coldest weather, Piquette was alone in the shack with the children. The Tonnerres made home brew all the time, so I've heard, and Lazarus said later she'd been drinking most of the day when he and the boys went out that evening. They had an old woodstove there—you know the kind, with exposed pipes. The shack caught fire. Piquette didn't get out, and neither did the children."

I did not say anything. As so often with Piquette, there did not seem to be anything to say. There was a kind of silence around the image in my mind of the fire and the snow, and I wished I could put from my memory the look that I had seen once in Piquette's eyes.

I went up to Diamond Lake for a few days that summer, with Mavis and her family. The MacLeod cottage had been sold after my father's death, and I did not even go to look at it, not wanting to witness my long-ago kingdom possessed now by strangers. But one evening I went down to the shore by myself.

The small pier which my father had built was gone, and in its place there was a large and solid pier built by the government, for Galloping Mountain was now a national park, and Diamond Lake had been re-named Lake Wapakata, for it was felt that an Indian name would have a greater appeal to tourists. The one store had become several dozen, and the settlement had all the attributes of a flourishing resort—hotels, a dance-hall, cafés with neon signs, the penetrating odours of potato chips and hot dogs.

I sat on the government pier and looked out across the water. At night the lake at least was the same as it had always been, darkly shining and bearing within its black glass the streak of amber that was the path of the moon. There was no wind that evening, and everything was quiet all around me. It seemed too quiet, and then I realized that the loons were no longer here. I listened for some time, to make sure, but never once did I hear that long-drawn call, half mocking and half plaintive, spearing through the stillness across the lake.

I did not know what had happened to the birds. Perhaps they had gone away to some far place of belonging. Perhaps they had been unable to find such a place, and had simply died out, having ceased to care any longer whether they lived or not.

I remembered how Piquette had scorned to come along, when my father and I sat there and listened to the lake birds. It seemed to me now that in some unconscious and totally unrecognised way, Piquette might have been the only one, after all, who had heard the crying of the loons.

QUESTIONS

1. Describe the narrator. Granted the passage of time in the story, why is it essential for the narrator to be approximately the same age as Piquette?

2. How does the narrator's attitude toward Piquette change as the story develops (see especially paragraph 61)? As a result of this change, what happens to your attitude toward Piquette?

3. Describe what happens to the lake and the loons and how these conditions reflect the circumstances of Piquette's life (see paragraphs 1, 6, 16, 17, 36–45, 72–73). If one assumes that in a previous age Piquette would have inherited the traditions of the Cree Indians, what is Piquette's legacy in the changing modern world?

AMÉRICO PARÉDES   (1915–1999)

Parédes was a Mexican-American storyteller, folklorist, essayist, and poet, closely identified with Mexican-Americans living in Texas, his native state. He received his Ph.D. at the University of Texas in 1956 and also taught there for many years. His dissertation was published in 1958 as With His Pistol in His Hand, *a study of an early twentieth-century popular ballad about a fugitive, Gregorio Cortés. Deeply interested in the culture of the "lower border," he was one of the leaders of the Chicano movement in cultural-literary studies. He edited the* Journal of American Folklore *and also edited* Folklore and Culture on the Texas-Mexican Border *(1993). Among his honors was a Guggenheim Fellowship in 1962 and the Aztec Eagle medal from the Mexican government in 1991. "The Hammon and the Beans" was first published in the* Texas Observer *in 1963 and was republished in* The Hammon and the Beans and Other Stories *in 1994.*

The Hammon and the Beans _____ *1963*

> name of the City * Johesville - on-the-Grande

Once we lived in one of my grandfather's houses near Fort Jones.° It was just a block from the parade grounds, a big frame house painted a dirty yellow. My mother hated it, especially because of the pigeons that cooed all day about the eaves. They had fleas, she said. But it was a quiet neighborhood at least, too far from the center of town for automobiles and too near for musical, night-roaming drunks.

At this time Jonesville-on-the-Grande was not the thriving little city that it is today. We told off our days by the routine on the post. At six sharp the flag was raised on the parade grounds to the cackling of the bugles, and a field piece thundered out a salute. The sound of the shot bounced away through the morning mist until its echoes worked their way into every corner of town. Jonesville-on-the-Grande woke to the cannon's roar, as if to battle, and the day began.

At eight the whistle from the post laundry sent us children off to school. The whole town stopped for lunch with the noon whistle, and after lunch everybody went back to work when the post laundry said that it was one o'clock, except for those who could afford to be old-fashioned and took the siesta. The post was the town's clock, you might have said, or like some insistent elder person who was always there to tell you it was time.

Fort Jones: The setting of Fort Jones and Jonesville-on-the-Grande in Texas is fictional. The story takes place in the mid-1920s, one of the most turbulent periods of Mexican history and only a few years after the deaths of two of the greatest heroes of the Mexican revolution—Pancho Villa (1877–1923) and Emiliano Zapata (ca. 1879–1919).

At six the flag came down, and we went to watch through the high wire fence that divided the post from the town. Sometimes we joined in the ceremony, standing at salute until the sound of the cannon made us jump. That must have been when we had just studied about George Washington in school, or recited "The Song of Marion's Men"° about Marion the Fox and the British cavalry that chased him up and down the broad Santee. But at other times we stuck out our tongues and jeered at the soldiers. Perhaps the night before we had hung at the edges of a group of old men and listened to tales about Aniceto Pizaña and the "border troubles,"° as the local paper still called them when it referred to them gingerly in passing.

It was because of the border troubles, ten years or so before, that the soldiers had   5
come back to old Fort Jones. But we did not hate them for that; we admired them even, at least sometimes. But when we were thinking about the border troubles instead of Marion the Fox we hooted them and the flag they were lowering, which for the moment was theirs alone, just as we would have jeered an opposing ball team, in a friendly sort of way. On these occasions even Chonita would join in the mockery, though she usually ran home at the stroke of six. But whether we taunted or saluted, the distant men in khaki uniforms went about their motions without noticing us at all.

The last word from the post came in the night when a distant bugle blew. At nine it was all right because all the lights were on. But sometimes I heard it at eleven when everything was dark and still, and it made me feel that I was all alone in the world. I would even doubt that I was me, and that put me in such a fright that I felt like yelling out just to make sure I was really there. But next morning the sun shone and life began all over again. With its whistles and cannon shots and bugles blowing. And so we lived, we and the post, side by side with the wire fence in between.

The wandering soldiers whom the bugle called home at night did not wander in our neighborhood, and none of us ever went into Fort Jones. None except Chonita. Every evening when the flag came down she would leave off playing and go down towards what was known as the "lower" gate of the post, the one that opened not on Main Street but against the poorest part of town. She went into the grounds and to the mess halls and pressed her nose against the screens and watched the soldiers eat. They sat at long tables calling to each other through food-stuffed mouths.

"Hey bud, pass the coffee!"

"Give me the ham!"

"Yeah, give me the beans!"

After the soldiers were through the cooks came out and scolded Chonita, and then they gave her packages with things to eat.

Chonita's mother did our washing, in gratefulness—as my mother put it—for the use of a vacant lot of my grandfather's which was a couple of blocks down the street. On the lot was an old one-room shack which had been a shed long ago, and this Chonita's father had patched up with flattened-out pieces of tin. He was a laborer. Ever since the end of the border troubles there had been a development boom in the Valley, and Chonita's father was getting his share of the good times. Clearing brush

"Song of Marion's Men": a poem by William Cullen Bryant (1794–1878) about Colonel Francis Marion (ca. 1732–1795), who was a leader of irregular guerrilla forces in South Carolina during the Revolutionary War. Because of his hit-and-run tactics, involving his hiding in the swamps near the "broad Santee" river in South Carolina, Marion was nicknamed the "Swamp Fox."

border troubles: The most serious border incidents occurred in 1916, when Pancho Villa was responsible for deaths of Americans on both sides of the border. He made repeated raids into New Mexico and Texas.

and building irrigation ditches he sometimes pulled down as much as six dollars a week. He drank a good deal of it up, it was true. But corn was just a few cents a bushel in those days. He was the breadwinner, you might say, while Chonita furnished the luxuries. ᴺᵃʳʳᵃᵗᵒʳˢ ᶠʳⁱᵉⁿᵈ

Chonita was a poet too. I had just moved into the neighborhood when a boy came up to me and said, "Come on! Let's go hear Chonita make a speech."

She was already on top of the alley fence when we got there, a scrawny little girl of about nine, her bare dirty feet clinging to the fence almost like hands. A dozen other kids were there below her, waiting. Some were boys I knew at school; five or six were her younger brothers and sisters.

"Speech! Speech!" they all cried. "Let Chonita make a speech! Talk in English,   15 Chonita!"

They were grinning and nudging each other except for her brothers and sisters, who looked up at her with proud serious faces. She gazed out beyond us all with a grand, distant air and then she spoke.

"Give me the hammon and the beans!" she yelled. "Give me the hammon and the beans!"

She leaped off the fence and everybody cheered and told her how good it was and how she could talk English better than the teachers at the grammar school.

I thought it was a pretty poor joke. Every evening almost, they would make her get up on the fence and yell, "Give me the hammon and the beans!" And everybody would cheer and make her think she was talking English. As for me, I would wait there until she got it over with so we could play at something else. I wondered how long it would be before they got tired of it all. I never did find out because just about that time I got the chills and fever, and when I got up and around Chonita wasn't there anymore.

In later years I thought of her a lot, especially during the thirties when I was grow-   20 ing up. Those years would have been just made for her. Many's the time I have seen her in my mind's eyes, in the picket lines demanding not bread, not cake, but the hammon and the beans. But it didn't work out that way.

One night Doctor Zapata came into our kitchen through the back door. He set his bag on the table and said to my father, who had opened the door for him, "Well, she is dead."

My father flinched. "What was it?" he asked.

The doctor had gone to the window and he stood with his back to us, looking out toward the light of Fort Jones. "Pneumonia, flu, malnutrition, worms, the evil eye," he said without turning around. "What the hell difference does it make?"

"I wish I had known how sick she was," my father said in a very mild tone. "Not that it's really my affair, but I wish I had."

The doctor snorted and shook his head.   25

My mother came in and I asked her who was dead. She told me. It made me feel strange but I did not cry. My mother put her arm around my shoulders. "She is in Heaven now," she said. "She is happy."

I shrugged her arm away and sat down in one of the kitchen chairs.

"They're like animals," the doctor was saying. He turned round suddenly and his eyes glistened in the light. "Do you know what that brute of a father was doing when I left? He was laughing! Drinking and laughing with his friends."

"There's no telling what the poor man feels," my mother said.

My father made a deprecatory gesture. "It wasn't his daughter anyway."   30

"No?" the doctor said. He sounded interested.

"This is the woman's second husband," my father explained. "First one died before the girl was born, shot and hanged from a mesquite limb. He was working too close to the tracks the day the Olmito train was derailed."

"You know what?" the doctor said. "In classical times they did things better. Take Troy, for instance. After they stormed the city they grabbed the babies by the heels and dashed them against the wall. That was more humane."

My father smiled. "You sound very radical. You sound just like your relative down there in Morelos."°

"No relative of mine," the doctor said. "I'm a conservative, the son of a conservative, and you know that I wouldn't be here except for that little detail."   35

"Habit," my father said. "Pure habit, pure tradition. You're a radical at heart."

"It depends on how you define radicalism," the doctor answered. "People tend to use words too loosely. A dentist could be called a radical, I suppose. He pulls up things by the roots."

My father chuckled.

"Any bandit in Mexico nowadays can give himself a political label," the doctor went on, "and that makes him respectable. He's a leader of the people."

"Take Villa, now—" my father began.   40

"Villa was a different type of man," the doctor broke in.

"I don't see any difference."

The doctor came over to the table and sat down. "Now look at it this way," he began, his finger in front of my father's face. My father threw back his head and laughed.

"You'd better go to bed and rest," my mother told me. "You're not completely well, you know."

So I went to bed, but I didn't go to sleep, not right away. I lay there for a long time while behind my darkened eyelids Emiliano Zapata's cavalry charged down to the broad Santee, where there were grave men with hoary hairs.° I was still awake at eleven when the cold voice of the bugle went gliding in and out of the dark like something that couldn't find its way back to wherever it had been. I thought of Chonita in Heaven, and I saw her in her torn and dirty dress, with a pair of bright wings attached, flying round and round like a butterfly shouting, "Give me the hammon and the beans!"   45

Then I cried. And whether it was the bugle, or whether it was Chonita or what, to this day I do not know. But cry I did, and I felt much better after that.

QUESTIONS

1. How does Parédes establish the setting of the story? What is the significance of the fort? Of the "dirty yellow" paint? Of the vacant lot and the shack?

2. Is Chonita a round or flat character? To what extent does the author make her symbolic and representative?

3. What is the tone of the story (some possibilities: ironic, cynical, resigned, bitter, resentful)? What techniques does Parédes use to control the tone?

Morelos: the home state of Zapata.
grave men with hoary hairs: Cf. lines 49–52 of Bryant's "Song of Marion's Men":

> Grave men there are by broad Santee,
>   Grave men with hoary hairs;
> Their hearts are all with Marion,
>   For Marion are their prayers.

4. How does Doctor Zapata's attitude toward Chonita's death, and the words he uses to announce it, help to control the tone?

5. How does the tale of Chonita's brief life and her death fit into the political, social, and broadly human framework of the story?

6. Near the end of Bryant's "Song of Marion's Men" (lines 53–56) the following four lines appear:

> And lovely ladies greet our band [i.e., of soldiers]
> With kindliest welcoming,
> And smiles like those of summer,
> And tears like those of spring.

Contrast these lines with the narrator's vision of Chonita in heaven.

WRITING ABOUT TONE

Begin with a careful reading, noting those elements of the work that convey attitudes. Consider whether the work genuinely creates the attitudes it is designed to evoke. In Poe's "The Cask of Amontillado" for example, (Chapter 11), do the gloomy catacombs evoke emotions of fear, or do they seem exaggerated? In Laurence's "The Loons," does the narrator provide sufficient information about Piquette to permit genuine sympathy for her plight? In "The Hammon and the Beans," does the conclusion justify the narrator's recovery of "better" feelings? Developing responses to questions such as these will help you in creating ideas for your essay.

Questions for Discovering Ideas

- How strongly do you respond to the story? What attitudes can you identify and characterize? What elements in the story elicit your concern, indignation, fearfulness, anguish, amusement, or sense of affirmation?

- What causes you to sympathize or not to sympathize with the characters, situations, or ideas? What makes the circumstances in the work admirable or understandable (or deplorable)?

- What does the dialogue suggest about the author's attitudes toward the characters? How does it influence your attitudes? What qualities of diction permit and encourage your responses?

- To what degree, if any, does the story supersede any previous ideas you might have had about the same or similar subject matter? What do you think made changes in your attitude?

- What role does the narrator/speaker play in your attitudes toward the story material? Does the speaker seem intelligent or stupid, friendly or unfriendly, sane or insane, or idealistic or pragmatic?

- In an amusing or comic story, what elements of plot, character, and diction are particularly comic? How strongly do you respond to humor-producing situations? Why?

- What ironies do you find in the story (verbal, situational, cosmic, dramatic)? How is the irony connected to philosophies of marriage, family, society, politics, religion, or morality?

- To what extent are the characters controlled by fate, social or racial discrimination, limitations of intelligence, economic and political inequality, and limited opportunity?

- Do any words seem unusual or noteworthy, such as words in dialect, polysyllabic words, or foreign words or phrases that the author assumes you know? Are there any especially connotative or emotive words? What do these words suggest about the author's apparent assumptions about the readers?

Strategies for Organizing Ideas

Your goal is to show how the author establishes the dominant moods of the story—for example, the pathos of "The Loons" or the comedy of "Rape Fantasies." Some possibilities are the use or misuse of language, the exposé of a pretentious speaker, the use of exact and specific descriptions, the isolation of a major character, the failure of plans, and the continuance of naiveté in a disillusioned world. Some of the things to discuss are these:

1. *Audience, situation, and characters.* Is any person or group directly addressed by the speaker? What attitude is expressed (love, respect, condescension, confidentiality, confidence, etc.)? What is the basic situation in the story? Do you find irony? If so, what kind is it? What does the irony show (optimism or pessimism, for example)? How is the situation controlled to shape your responses? That is, can actions, situations, or characters be seen as expressions of attitude or as embodiments of certain favorable or unfavorable ideas or positions? What is the nature of the speaker or persona? Why does the persona speak exactly as he or she does? How is the persona's character manipulated to show apparent authorial attitude and to elicit reader response? Does the story promote respect, admiration, dislike, or other feelings about character or situation? How?

2. *Descriptions, diction.* Your concern here is not to analyze descriptions or diction for themselves alone but to relate these matters to attitude. *For descriptions:* To what degree do descriptions of natural scenery and conditions (snowstorms, cold, rain, ice, intense sunlight) convey an attitude that complements or opposes the circumstances of the characters? Are there any systematic references to colors, sounds, or noises that collectively reflect an attitude? *For diction:* Do connotative meanings of words (see Chapter 7) control response in any way? To what degree does the diction require readers to have a large or technical vocabulary? Do speech patterns or the use of dialect evoke attitudes about speakers or their condition of life? Is the level of diction normal, slang, standard, or substandard? What is the effect of such a level? Are there unusual or particularly noteworthy expressions? If so, what attitudes do these show? Does the author use verbal irony? To what effect?

3. *Humor.* Is the story funny? How funny, how intense? How is the humor achieved? Does the humor develop out of incongruous situations or language

or both? What is the underlying basis of attack in the humor? Are the objects of laughter still respected or even loved, though they cause amusement?

4. *Ideas.* Are any ideas advocated, defended mildly, or attacked? How does the author clarify his or her attitude toward these ideas—directly, by statement, or indirectly, through understatement, overstatement, or a character's speeches? In what ways does the story assume a common ground of assent between author and reader? That is, what common assumptions do you find about behavior, religion, politics, morality, and so on? Is it easy to give assent (temporary or permanent) to these ideas, or is any concession needed by the reader to approach the story? (For example, a major subject of O'Connor's "First Confession" [Chapter 7] is the preparation for a child going to first confession in the Catholic faith. Not everyone can relate to this situation, but even a skeptical reader can find common ground in the psychological situation of the story or in the desire to learn as much as possible about human beings.)

5. *Unique characteristics of the story.* Each story has unique properties that contribute to the tone. In Atwood's "Rape Fantasies" the center of interest is the narrator, Estelle, and the ideas about rape she expresses both in conversation and narration. The speaker of Hodgins's "The Concert Stages of Europe" demonstrates a willingness to describe embarrassing situations that someone else might omit or mitigate. In other stories you might discover a recurring word or phrase that seems special. For example, Mark Twain in "Luck" (Chapter 7) develops a passage centering on the word *blunder,* and thereby makes his attitude clear about the boob hero, Scoresby (paragraph 12).

In the conclusion, first summarize your main points and then go on to redefinitions, explanations, or afterthoughts, together with ideas reinforcing earlier points. You might also mention some other major aspect of the story's tone that you did not develop in the body.

DEMONSTRATIVE STUDENT ESSAY

Chopin's Use of Irony in "The Story of an Hour"°

[1]   "The Story of an Hour" is a brief story that exhibits Kate Chopin's complex control over tone. There are many ironies in the story, which grow out of error, misunderstanding, incorrect expectation, and a certain degree of pride.* In addition, the story raises an ironic question about the nature of marriage as an institution. All this is a great deal for so short a story, yet it is all there. The story contains a rich mixture of situational, cosmic, and dramatic irony.†

° See pp. 393-95 for this story.
* Central idea.
† Thesis sentence

[2] The center of the story's situational irony is Louise Mallard, the central character. Not much is disclosed about her character, her major circumstances being that she is a faithful and dedicated housewife and that she suffers from heart disease. Her situation reaches a crisis when she is told that her husband has died. As a loving wife, she weeps convulsively at the news and then retreats to her room to grieve in solitude. Once alone, she experiences a unique and unsuspected feeling that with her sorrow she has become "free." In other words, she realizes that her marriage has put her in bondage, even though at the same time she recognizes that her husband "had never looked save with love upon her" (paragraph 13). For the first time she recognizes the gap between her life and her hidden hopes and expectations--a virtual definition of situational irony.

[3] Both situational and cosmic ironies are focused on the people closest to Louise, namely her sister Josephine and Brently Mallard's friend Richards. They are kindly and have the best intentions toward her. Richards confirms the truth of the train wreck before coming to the Mallard household with the news. But first he tells Josephine, who in turn breaks the news gently to Louise in "veiled hints that revealed in half concealing" (paragraph 2) so as to forestall the shock that would bring on a fatal heart attack. Josephine is successful, and her concern causes her to beg Louise to come out of her room, for Josephine believes that Louise will make herself ill with grief (paragraph 17). With these best intentions, Josephine becomes the inadvertent cause of escorting Louise to the front door just as Brently Mallard enters it, and the shock of seeing him causes her heart to fail. Thus, through no fault of her own, Josephine brings about the blow of fate that she and Richards have tried to avoid.

[4] Another major cosmic irony in the story results from the inaccuracy and unreliability of information. At the time of the story (1894), the best and most modern method of sending information over distances was by telegraph. Richards is in the newspaper office "when intelligence of the railroad disaster was received, with Brently Mallard's name leading the list of 'killed'" (paragraph 2). Since the news could never have come so rapidly in the days before telegraphy, we may suppose that Louise would never have experienced the emotional crisis brought about by the prompt but inaccurate news. The error of information may be caused by human mistake, but the consequences are cosmic for Louise--and, one might add, for her unsuspecting husband, who enters the house only to witness his wife's sudden death.

[5] This irony-filled story also contains dramatic irony found in two details. None of the characters understands what Louise begins feeling as she sits upstairs. Their experience and their imagination make it impossible to comprehend her feelings. This failure of understanding is particularly sad with regard to Josephine and Richards, for these two are the closest ones to her. In effect, Louise dies alone even though she is surrounded by the people who love her most. In the case of the doctors who diagnose the cause of Louise's death, the lack of understanding is bitterly ironic:

> When the doctors came they said she had died of heart disease--of joy that kills. (paragraph 23)

These somewhat pompous doctors find it impossible to imagine the true reason for Louise's shock, for, they clearly think, what other reason than joy at seeing her restored husband could bring about such a powerful assault on her system? "The Story of an Hour" ends on this grim but also comic note.

The story's crowning situational irony is the discrepancy between normal and conventional ideas of marriage as an ideal and the reality of marriage as a fact. One senses the authorial voice insisting strongly on uncomfortable reality when Louise contemplates a future life free of the need for satisfying anyone else:

[6]
> There would be no powerful will bending hers in that blind persistence with which men and women believe they have a right to impose a private will upon a fellow-creature. (paragraph 14)

Louise's marriage has not been bad, but the story at this point goes to the heart of the conflict between personal freedom and marital obligation. Chopin's words "blind persistence" are particularly effective here in establishing an attitude of disapproval if not of protest.

[7]
Even though "The Story of an Hour" can thus be considered a tract against marriage, it is above all a superbly crafted story. In just twenty-three paragraphs it introduces a number of complex ironies revolving about the crisis created by the mistakes and misunderstandings of a single hour. It is the sudden fusion of all the ironies that crash in on Louise Mallard and destroy her. In her case, these ironies come into full play only when she believes that her husband has been killed and then quickly discovers that he is alive. In life, for most people, such crises may never come into play. As a general principle, the story's major irony is that even the best and most enviable circumstances of life contain imperfections, unarticulated frustration, and potential unhappiness.

Commentary on the Essay

The topic of this essay is Chopin's complex use of irony in "The Story of an Hour." Throughout the essay, a good deal of the story's action is used to exemplify the sorts of irony being discussed. Links and connections supporting the argument are brought out by the phrases "even though," "also," "the story's crowning situational irony," "another," and "both."

Paragraph 1, the introduction, contains the central idea that announces the causes producing irony. The thesis sentence indicates that the combination of situational, cosmic, and dramatic irony will be explored in the body. Paragraph 2 demonstrates how situational irony applies to the circumstances of the major character, Louise. Paragraph 3 shows how both situational and cosmic irony enter into the story through Louise's sister Josephine and Brently's friend Richards. An additional element of cosmic irony is introduced in paragraph 4. This irony is made to seem particularly unfortunate because the telegraphic errors are totally modern and could never have occurred in a pre-technological age.

Paragraph 5 brings out the story's dramatic irony. This irony results from the lack of understanding by those closest to Louise and from the intellectual blindness of the examining physicians. Paragraph 6 introduces Chopin's major idea criticizing marriage as an institution. Connected to the argumentative purpose of the essay, however, this idea is shown to be integrated with the story's major situational irony. The final paragraph pays tribute to the story as a story and speculates about how Chopin deals truthfully with difficult issues of life and marriage.

SPECIAL TOPICS FOR WRITING AND ARGUMENT ABOUT TONE

1. Write an essay comparing and contrasting attitudes toward two or more of the following female characters: Louise in "The Story of an Hour," Piquette in "The Loons," Mathilde in "The Necklace" (Chapter 1), and Phoenix in "A Worn Path" (Chapter 3). How does the author's presentation control your understanding of them? What details of tone are important in a feminist approach to these works (see Chapter 33)?

2. Consider a short story in which the narrator is the central character (for example, "The Concert Stages of Europe," "A & P" (Chapter 7), "First Confession" (Chapter 7), "Everyday Use" (Chapter 2), and "Blue Winds Dancing" (Chapter 3). Write an essay showing how the language of the narrator affects your attitudes toward him or her (that is, your sympathy for the narrator, your interest in the narrative, your feelings toward the other characters and what they do). Be sure to emphasize the relationship between the narrator's language and your responses.

3. Describe the attitude of Estelle, the narrator in "Rape Fantasies," toward sexual molestation. How does her character influence the tone of the story (e.g., treating the subject of rape in an amusing, uncomprehending, or serious manner)?

4. In "The Hammon and the Beans" how does Parédes express irony about the fact that Mexican-American children are taught United States history, but learn nothing about the Mexican political movements represented by Villa and Zapata?

5. Write a fragment of a story of your own about, for example, a student, a supervisor, or a politician. Treat your main character with dramatic irony; that is, your character thinks he or she knows all the details about a situation but really does not (e.g., a male student declares interest in a female student without realizing that she is already engaged; a supervisor expresses distrust in one of the best workers in the firm; a politician accuses an opponent of actions that were initiated not by the opponent but by a supporter). Through what actions, words, and situations do you make your irony clear?

6. In your school library, consult the most recent copy of the *MLA International Bibliography of Books and Articles on the Modern Languages and Literatures,* and make a short list of books and articles on Margaret Atwood or Kate Chopin. Consult at least three of the works you have listed, and using these, together with your own insights, write a short description of the writer's irony (comic or serious) and social criticism.

9

Symbolism and Allegory: Keys to Extended Meaning

Symbolism and **allegory,** like metaphors and similes (see Chapter 17), are modes that expand meaning. They are literary devices developed from the connections that real-life people make between their own existence and particular objects, places, or occurrences—either through experience or reading. A young man might remember making a vital realization about honesty and morality during a rowboat ride. A failed examination might cause a person to study harder than ever before and therefore to excel. A bereaved mother might associate personal grief with ordinary packing boxes. The significance of details like these can be meaningful not just at the time they occur but throughout an entire lifetime. Merely bringing them to mind or speaking about them unlocks their meanings, implications, and consequences. It is as though the reference alone can be the same as pages of explanation and analysis.

It is from this principle that both symbolism and allegory are derived. By highlighting details as *symbols,* and stories or parts of stories as *allegories,* writers expand their meaning while keeping their works within reasonable lengths.

SYMBOLISM

The words **symbol** and **symbolism** are derived from the Greek word meaning "to throw together" (*syn,* "together," and *ballein,* to "throw"). A symbol creates a direct meaningful equation between (1) a specific object, scene, character, or action and (2) ideas, values, persons, or ways of life. In effect, a symbol is a *substitute* for the elements being signified, much as the flag stands for the ideals of the nation.

In painting and sculpture, symbols are easily recognized, for to tell a story visually, the artist must make every object count. In the anonymous fresco *Hercules and the Infant Telephus* from ancient Herculaneum, for example, the painter has depicted a crucial event in the life of the mythical hero Hercules— the choice he had to make early in his life between pleasure or toil. By symbolically turning his head away from the seated figure representing Pleasure,

Hercules and the Infant Telephus. A Roman fresco from Herculaneum,
copy of a lost Greek original. National Archeological Museum, Naples, Italy.

Hercules is rejecting the life of ease that she symbolizes. Instead, his life will be
one of work, hardship, battle, victory, and glory, as symbolized by the lion, the
eagle, and the sheaf of arrows. The image of his child, Telephus, whom he later
abandons and who is being suckled by a donkey, symbolizes Hercules's insensitivity, verging on cruelty, which became a part of his single-minded existence
as a warrior and hero.

     When we first encounter a symbol in a story (or poem or play), it may
seem to carry no more weight than its surface or obvious meaning. It can be a
description of a character, an object, a place, an action, or a situation, and it
may function perfectly well in this capacity. What makes a symbol symbolic,
however, is its capacity to signify additional levels of meaning—major ideas,
simple or complex emotions, or philosophical or religious qualities or values.
There are two types of symbols—*cultural* and *contextual*.

Cultural Symbols Are Derived from Our Cultural and Historical Heritage

Many symbols are *generally* or *universally* recognized and are therefore **cultural** (also called **universal**). They embody ideas and emotions that writers and readers share as heirs of the same historical and cultural tradition. When using cultural symbols, a writer assumes that readers already know what the symbols represent. An example is the character Sisyphus of ancient Greek myth. As a punishment for trying to overcome death not just once but twice, Sisyphus is doomed by the underworld gods to roll a large boulder up a high hill forever. Just as he gets the boulder to the top, it rolls down, and then he is fated to roll it up again—and again—and again—because the boulder always rolls back. The plight of Sisyphus has been interpreted as a symbol of the human condition: In spite of constant struggle, a person rarely if ever completes anything. Work must always be done over and over from day to day and from generation to generation, and the same problems confront humanity throughout all time. Because of such fruitless effort, life seems to have little or no meaning. Nevertheless, there is hope: People who confront their tasks, as Sisyphus does, stay involved and active, and their work makes their lives meaningful. A writer referring to Sisyphus would expect us to understand that this ancient mythological figure symbolizes these conditions.

Similarly, ordinary water, because living creatures cannot live without it, is recognized as a symbol of life. It has this meaning in the ceremony of baptism, and it may convey this meaning and dimension in a variety of literary contexts. Thus, a spouting fountain may symbolize optimism (as upwelling, bubbling life), and a stagnant pool may symbolize the pollution and diminution of life. Water is also a universal symbol of sexuality, and its condition or state may symbolize various romantic relationships. For instance, stories in which lovers meet near a turbulent stream, a roaring waterfall, a beach with high breakers, a wide river, a stormy sea, a mud puddle, or a calm lake symbolically represent love relationships that range from uncertainty to serenity.

Contextual Symbols Are Symbolic Only in Individual Works

Objects and descriptions that are not universal symbols can be symbols *only if they are made so within individual works*. These are **contextual, private,** or **authorial symbols.** Unlike cultural symbols, contextual symbols derive their meaning from the context and circumstances of individual works. For example, the standing clock in Poe's "The Masque of the Red Death" (Chapter 11) is a large timepiece that in the story symbolizes not only the passage of time but also the sinister forces of death. Similarly, Elisa's chrysanthemums in Steinbeck's "The Chrysanthemums" seem at first nothing more than prized flowers. As the story progresses, however, they gain symbolic significance. The traveling tinsmith's apparent interest in them is the wedge he uses to get a small mending job from Elisa. Her description of the care needed in planting and tending them suggests that they signify her kindness, love, orderliness, femininity, and motherliness.

Like Poe's clock, Steinbeck's chrysanthemums are a major contextual symbol. But there is no carryover: In other stories, clocks and flowers are not symbolic unless the authors of these stories deliberately give them symbolic meaning. Further, if they are symbolic, they may be given different meanings than in the Poe and Steinbeck stories.

Determine What Is Symbolic (and Not Symbolic)

In determining whether a particular object, action, or character is a symbol, you need to judge the importance that the author gives to it. If the element is prominent and also maintains a constancy of meaning, you may justify interpreting it as a symbol. For example, the loons of Laurence's "The Loons" (Chapter 8) are water birds that ordinarily inhabit lakeshores, and their absence at the story's end is an expected result of the increased number of lakeside residences described in the story. Although the loons are ordinary, they are also symbolic, for the story is about loss and change (the death of the narrator's father and Piquette, the loss of the way of life of the Indians, the changes accompanying increased population). Here, the importance of the birds has invested them with symbolic meaning. Importance is therefore a key to the determination of symbolism, as at the end of Welty's "A Worn Path" (Chapter 3). Phoenix, Welty's major character, plans to spend all her money for a toy windmill for her sick grandson. Readers will note that the windmill is small and fragile, like her life and that of her grandson, but that Phoenix wants to give the boy a little pleasure despite their poverty and hopelessness. For these reasons the windmill is a contextual or authorial symbol of Phoenix's strong character, generous nature, and pathetic existence.

ALLEGORY

An **allegory** is like a symbol because it transfers and broadens meaning. The term is derived from the Greek word *allegorein,* which means "to speak so as to imply other than what is said." Allegory, however, is more sustained than symbolism. An allegory is to a symbol as a motion picture is to a still picture. In form, an allegory is a complete and self-sufficient narrative, but it also signifies another series of events or conditions. Although some stories are allegories from beginning to end, many stories that are not allegories may nevertheless contain brief sections or episodes that are *allegorical.*

Understand the Applications and Meaning of Allegory

Allegories and the allegorical method are more than literary exercises. Without question, readers and listeners learn and memorize stories and tales more easily than moral lessons, and therefore allegory is a favorite method of teaching morality. In addition, thought and expression have not always been free. The threat of censorship and the danger of reprisal have sometimes caused authors to express their views indirectly in the form of allegory rather than to write openly, name names, and risk political reprisal or accusations of libel. Hence, the double meaning of many allegories is based in both need and reality.

In studying allegory, determine whether all or part of a work may have an extended, allegorical meaning. The popularity of George Lucas's film *Star Wars* and its sequels (in videotape and newly refurbished rereleases and also its "prequel" *The Phantom Menace*), for example, is attributable at least partly to its being an allegory about the conflict between good and evil. Obi-Wan Kenobi (intelligence) assists Luke Skywalker (heroism, boldness) and instructs him in "the force" (moral or religious faith). Thus armed and guided, Skywalker opposes the powers of Darth Vader (evil) to rescue the Princess Leia (purity and goodness) with the aid of the latest spaceships and weaponry (technology). The story has produced a set of popular adventure films, accompanied by dramatic music and ingenious visual and sound effects. With the obvious allegorical overtones, however, it stands for any person's quest for self-fulfillment.

To apply a part of the allegory more specifically, consider that for a time the evil Vader imprisons Skywalker and that Skywalker must exert all his skill and strength to get free and overcome Vader. In the allegorical application of the episode, this imprisonment signifies those moments of doubt, discouragement, and depression that people experience while trying to better themselves through education, work, self-improvement, friendship, marriage, and so on.

Almost from the beginning of recorded literature, similar heroic deeds have been represented in allegorical forms. From ancient Greece, the allegorical hero Jason sails the *Argo* to distant lands to gain the Golden Fleece (those who take risks are rewarded). From Anglo-Saxon England, the hero Beowulf saves King Hrothgar's throne by killing Grendel and his monstrous mother (victory comes to those who rely on the forces of good). From seventeenth-century England, Bunyan's *The Pilgrim's Progress* tells how the hero Christian overcomes difficulties and temptations while traveling from this world to the next (belief, perseverance, and resistance to temptation save the faithful). As long as the parallel connections are close and consistent, such as those mentioned here, an allegorical interpretation is valid.

FABLE, PARABLE, AND MYTH

Closely related to symbolism and allegory in the ability to extend and expand meaning are three additional forms—*fable, parable,* and *myth.*

FABLE. The **fable** (from Latin *fabula,* a story or narration) is an old, brief, and popular form. Often but not always, fables are about animals who possess human traits (such fables are called **beast fables**). Past collectors and editors of fables have attached "morals" or explanations to the brief stories, as is the case with Aesop, the most enduringly popular of fable writers. Tradition has it that Aesop was a slave who composed fables in ancient Greece. His fable "The Fox and the Grapes" signifies the trait of belittling things we cannot have. More recent contributions to the fable tradition include Walt Disney's "Mickey Mouse," Walt Kelly's "Pogo," and Berke Breathed's "Bloom County." The adjective *fabulous* refers to the collective body of fables of all sorts, even though the word is often used as little more than a vague term of approval.

PARABLE.   A **parable** (from Greek *parabolé,* a "setting beside" or comparison) is a short, simple allegory with a moral or religious bent. Parables are most often associated with Jesus, who used them to embody unique religious insights and truths. His parables "The Good Samaritan" and "The Prodigal Son," for example, are interpreted to show God's love, concern, understanding, and forgiveness.

MYTH.   A **myth** (from Greek *muthos,* a story or plot) is a traditional story that embodies and codifies the religious, philosophical, and cultural values of the civilization in which it is composed. Usually the central figures of mythical stories are heroes, gods, and demigods, such as Zeus, Hera, Prometheus, Athena, Sisyphus, Oedipus, and Atalanta from ancient Greece. Most myths are of course fictional, but some have a basis in historical truth. They are by no means confined to the past, for the word *myth* may also refer to abstractions and ideas that people today hold collectively, such as the concept of never-ending economic growth or the idea that problems can be solved by science. Sometimes the words *myth* and *mythical* are used with the meaning "fanciful" or "untrue." Such disparagement is misleading because the truths of mythology are not to be found literally in the myths themselves but rather in their symbolic and allegorical interpretations.

ALLUSION IN SYMBOLISM AND ALLEGORY

Cultural or universal symbols and allegories often allude to other works from our cultural heritage, such as the Bible, ancient history and literature, and works of the British and American traditions. Sometimes understanding a story may require knowledge of politics and current events.

If the meaning of a symbol is not immediately clear to you, you will need a dictionary or other reference work. The scope of your college dictionary will surprise you. If you cannot find an entry there, however, try one of the major encyclopedias, or ask your reference librarian, who can direct you to shelves loaded with helpful books. A few excellent guides are *The Oxford Companion to Classical Literature* (ed. M. C. Howatson and Ian Chilvers), *The Oxford Companion to English Literature* (ed. Margaret Drabble), William Rose Benét's *The Reader's Encyclopedia,* Timothy Gantz's *Early Greek Myth: A Guide to Literary and Artistic*

Sources, and Richmond Y. Hathorn's *Greek Mythology.* Useful aids in finding biblical references are *Cruden's Complete Concordance,* which in various editions has been used since 1737, and *Strong's Exhaustive Concordance,* which has been revised and expanded regularly since it first appeared in the nineteenth century. These concordances list all the major words used in the Bible, so you can easily locate the chapter and verse of any and all biblical passages. If you still have trouble after using sources like these, see your instructor.

 ## STORIES FOR STUDY

AESOP   (ca. 6th c. B.C.E.)

> *Not much is known about the ancient fabulist Aesop. According to tradition, he was a freed slave who lived from about 620 to 560 B.C.E. Aristotle claimed that he had been a public defender, but there is no other evidence that he existed at all. In fact, versions of some of the fables were known a millennium before his time. Aesop might therefore be considered as much a collector as a creator of fables.*

Fable signifies the trait of belittling things we cannot have.

The Fox and the Grapes _____ *(ca. 6th c. B.C.E.)*

A hungry Fox came into a vineyard where there hung delicious clusters of ripe Grapes; his mouth watered to be at them; but they were nailed up to a trellis so high, that with all his springing and leaping he could not reach a single bunch. At last, growing tired and disappointed, "Let who will take them!" says he, "they are but green and sour; so I'll e'en let them alone."

QUESTIONS

1. How much do you learn about the characteristics of the fox? How are these characteristics related to the moral or message of the fable?
2. What is the conflict in the fable? What is the resolution?
3. In your own words, explain the meaning of the fable. Is the "sour grapes" explanation a satisfactory excuse, or is it a rationalization for failure?
4. From your reading of "The Fox and the Grapes," explain the characteristics of the fable as a type of literature.

THE MYTH OF ATALANTA

The story of Atalanta is an anonymous myth that was known throughout both the ancient Greek and Roman worlds. Because communication in ancient times was uncertain, there were variations in some of the details of the story, such as the names of Atalanta's father and her suitors. However, there was general agreement about the details of her story, which was told by many different writers, such as Apollodorus, Aelian, and Pacuvius. The best-known ancient text of the story appears in Ovid's Metamorphoses. *The story included here is slightly adapted from the brief but comprehensive version by Richmond Y. Hathorn* (Greek Mythology, *1977).*

Atalanta _____ *(5th–1st c. B.C.E.)*

There was once a man from Arcadia, in southern Greece, who hoped very much for a son, and when his wife gave birth to a daughter, he abandoned the child in the woods. A she-bear that lived there suckled the baby, until some hunters chanced on the child and reared it, calling it Atalanta [i.e., "the invincible one"]. Atalanta grew up to be a true daughter of the wilderness, an incomparable hunter, being instructed by the Goddess of the Hunt, Artemis, herself. Atalanta was a runner who could outrace any man, and a skillful wrestler, on one occasion defeating the hero Peleus at Pelias' funeral games. She tried also to go on the expedition with the Argonauts to recover the Golden Fleece, but she was turned away by Jason, who was afraid of the trouble a beautiful young woman might cause in a crew of young men.

Then Atalanta took part in the hunting of the Calydonian Boar, falling in love with the Calydonian Prince Meleager and being loved in return. But as this love brought about Meleager's death and as Atalanta was already inclined toward celibacy because of her allegiance to Artemis, she resolved on leading a solitary manless life henceforth, especially because the oracle at Delphi warned her that marriage would cause her whole nature to be changed. So when she gave birth to Meleager's child on her way back from Calydon to Arcadia, she kept it a secret and exposed the baby boy on Mount Parthenion. This child, called Parthenopaeus, was found by the same shepherds who had found and reared Telephus (the son of Hercules and the Princess Auge), and he grew up to be Telephus' companion in early adventures. Eventually Parthenopaeus met his death in the war of the Seven against Thebes.

Meanwhile Atalanta had returned to her old hunting haunts, fighting off attacks of satyrs and discouraging the proposals of mortal men by stipulating that each suitor should compete with her in a race, in which she would be armed with a spear. The condition was that if she overtook her opponent she might stab him to death. And in this way she had disposed of three suitors, cutting off their heads and displaying them beside the racecourse.

There was a young Arcadian named Milanion, who hated women as much as Atalanta hated men, and who was as fond of the chase as she was. He encountered Atalanta frequently during his hunts, and imperceptibly he fell in love with her. More and more he put himself in her way, until he was faithfully following her around, carrying her hunting-nets and enduring her endless disdain. Once when a centaur, Hylaeus, whom Atalanta had rejected, attacked her in anger, Milanion intervened, receiving the blows of the centaur's club and even being wounded by one of the centaur's arrows while protecting Atalanta with his body. Atalanta killed the man-beast, and then nursed the injured Milanion back to health, her feeling for him growing warmer all the while.

Still there was no way of winning Atalanta short of defeating her in the footrace; so in spite of all her discouragements Milanion challenged her. But before the day of the race he prayed to Aphrodite, the Goddess of Love, for aid, and the Goddess plucked three golden apples from the Garden of the Hesperides and instructed him in their use. When the race had begun and Atalanta was drawing near, Milanion dropped one golden apple and the young woman stopped to pick it up. Again she drew near, and again he dropped an apple, the Goddess causing them to weigh heavily in Atalanta's bosom. So when the third apple was dropped and picked up, Milanion was able to reach the goal unscathed and to claim Atalanta as his bride.

But in the flush of his victory and her willing defeat they both forgot to give thanks to Aphrodite. The Goddess punished them by inflicting a rage of lust on both of them, so that they lost all control of themselves. Passing by a sanctuary of Cybele, the Great Mother of Gods, they fell immediately to lovemaking in the holy grotto near the holy temple. They behaved with such abandon that the very statues averted their eyes. The Great Mother was incensed and thought of killing them at once, but instead she changed Milanion into a Lion and Atalanta into a lioness and made them the team that draws her chariot.

QUESTIONS

1. What abilities does Atalanta have? How does she try to preserve her independence?   *hunter, runner, wrestler*

2. Why does Atalanta vow to shun men? What causes her to change her mind? What finally happens to her?

3. Consider the symbolic significance of Atalanta's name, the golden apples, the chopping off of the heads of slow-running suitors, the father's abandonment of Atalanta, the exposure of the infant Parthenopaeus, the battle with the centaur, the way in which Atalanta loses the race, and the lovemaking in the holy grotto of the Great Mother of Gods.

ANITA SCOTT COLEMAN   (1890–1960)

Coleman, a writer of stories, poems, and essays, was born in Mexico and educated in New Mexico. Her mother had been a slave who had been bought out of slavery by her father. She published mainly in magazines. "Unfinished Masterpieces," for example, was published in Crisis: A Record of the Darker Races, *the magazine begun in 1910 that heralded the development of the Harlem Renaissance.*

Unfinished Masterpieces _____ *1927*

There are days which stand out clearly like limpid pools beside the dusty road; when your thoughts, crystal clear as water, are pinioned in loveliness like star-points. Solitary days, which come often, if you are given to browsing in fields of past adventure; or rarely, if you are seldom retrospective; and not at all, if you are too greatly concerned with rushing onward to a nebulous future. Days whereupon your experiences glimmer before you waveringly like motion-pictures and the people you have known stroll through the lanes of memory, arrayed in vari-colored splendor or in amusing disarray. Days like these are to be revered, for they have their humors and their whimsicalities. Hurry your thoughts and the gathering imageries take flight. Perplexity but makes the lens of introspection blur. And of annoyance beware, for it is an evil vapor that disseminates and drowns the visions in the sea of grim realities. Such days must be cultivated. Scenes for their reception must be set. Cushions perhaps, and warmth of fire. Above all, the warmth of sweet content. Ease and comfort, comfort and ease and moods of receptivity. Then hither, come hither the places and the people we have known, the associations that withstand time's effacements. Backward ho, through the mazes of the past.

STOP! "Why howdy, Dora Johns." Darling playmate of my child-years. With wooly hair a length too short for even pigtails. Mud-spatters upon your funny black face. Mud-spatters all over your dress and your little black hands mud-spattered too.

[handwritten: black girl]

Why? What? Come on and see. And lo! I am a child again.

Hand in hand, unmindful of her muddy ones, we skip around the old ramshackle house, back to the furthest corner of an unkempt yard, impervious to the tin cans, the ash-heap, the litter, the clutter that impedes our way, our eyes upon, our thoughts bent upon one small clean-swept corner, where there is mud. More mud and water in a battered tin can. And row after row of mud. No, not mud—not merely mud, but things made out of mud. Row on row, drying in the sun.

Carefully, I sit down, doubling up, to be as small as possible, for only this corner where mud things are drying is clean and corners are seldom, if ever, quite large enough. Besides, I must not touch the things made out of mud. If the dried ones fall, they break. If the moist ones are molested, be it with ever so gentle a finger, they lose their shape. Moreover I must not disturb Dora.

Her little hands are busied with the mud. Little moulder's fingers are deftly playing their skill. Her child's face is alight. What has splashed her grave child's face with such a light? I wondered. I wonder now. The glitter of brittle talent, a gleam of sterling genius or the glow from artistic fires burning within the soul of a little black child?

Little Dora shaping figures out of mud. Vases and urns, dolls and toys, flying birds and trotting horses, frisking dogs and playing kittens, marvelous things out of mud. Crying aloud as though dealt a blow if one of the dried mud-figures is broken. Working in mud for endless hours, while the neighbor children play. Their hilarious merriment dropping like bombs into the quiet of our clean-swept corner. Deadly missiles seeking to find a mark. The insistent halloes of futile mirth forever bubbling on the other side of a high-board fence. The dividing fence and upon one side the clean-swept corner and the row on row of mud things drying in the sun. And Dora seeming not to heed the seething bubbles upon the other side, shaping, shaping marvelous things out of mud.

Yet, Oh Dora, now that the day is ours, will you not say, "When did the bombs of futile mirth strike their target? When did the tin-cans and the rags and the old ash-heap crowd you out from your clean-swept corner? What rude hand caused the dried mud shapes to fall and break? Who set a ruthless foot in the midst of your damp mud things?" Or were you too plastic, as plastic as your mud? You dare not tell. Only this you can whisper into the mists of our today. You are one of the Master's unfinished shapes which He will some day gather to mould anew into the finished masterpiece.

[handwritten: Someone ruined the statues]

A lump of mud. Now, there is a sobriquet for you—you funny, funny man. Mr. William Williams. I saw you but once. We chanced to meet in the home of a mutual

Narrator *fifty one year old,*
friend is Dora Johns, Coleman *Unfinished Masterpieces* **435**
lives in the South

friend. I thought you so very funny then. Uncouth and very boorish, but ever, when these pageants of the past, these dumb shows of inarticulate folks arise before me upon retrospective days, you appear garbed in the tatters of pathos.

"I am fifty-one years old," you kept repeating. How pitiful those fifty-one years are. You wear a child's simplicity, the sort that is so sad to see upon a man. Fifty-one and penniless. Fifty-one and possessed of naught else but the clothing you wore. Fifty-one and no place on earth you might call home. You confessed to being a vagabond though "bum" was the term you used and you were very proud of your one accomplishment, an ability to avoid all labour.

"I've given no man a full day's honest work in all my fifty-one years," you boasted. "I gambles. I ain't no cotton-pickin' nigger." Your one and only boast after holding life, the fathomless fountain of eternal possibilities, in your possession for fifty-one priceless years.

Nevertheless you have lived and so intensely. You held us against our will. Clustered around you, listening to you talk. Relating clippings as it were from the scrapbook of your life.

Tales of the road, of the only places you knew. Roads leading away from plantations where the cotton waited to be picked by numberless "cotton-pickin' niggers." Roads leading to pool halls and gambling dens. Roads beginning and roads ending in "riding the roads," carrying backward and forward, here and yon through the weird goblin land of the South's black belt.

With a hardened casualness you told stories that revolted and at the same time cheered us with an all sufficing glow of thankfulness that life had spared us the sordidness of yours. Offhandily, you gave us humorous skits that tempered our laughter with wishes that we might know at least a bit of such a droll existence as had been yours. With magical words you painted pictures so sharply they cut scars upon our hearts. You drew others so filled with rollicking delight their gladsomeness was contagious. With the nonchalance of a player shuffling cards you flipped your characters before us, drawn directly from the cesspool of your contacts and spellbound we listened.

Someone remarked how wonderful you talked and you replied, "Once, I sorter wanted to write books. Once, I uster read a heaps. See times when I was broke and nobody would stake me for a game. I'd lay around and read. I've read the Bible through and through and every Police Gazette I could lay my hands on. Yes, suh, I've read a heap. And I've wished a lot'er times I'd sense enough to write a book."

Lump of mud. Containing the you, the splendid artist in you, the soul of you, the unfinished you in the ungainly lump of you, awaiting the gathering-up to be molded anew into the finished masterpiece.

What a day! Here is my friend at whose fire-side I have lingered beholding Mr. William Williams, great lump of mud. To be sure, she also is an unfinished production. Though it is apparent that the Master had all but done when she slipped from his hands and dropped to earth to lie groping like the rest of us thereon.

Let us sit here together, friend, and enjoy this day.

I shall try to discover what recent gift you have given to the poor the while you are quietly stitching upon the garments, linens and scarlet, with which to clothe your household. Sit here and smile with the welcoming light in your eyes, knowing that your door is open to such as William Williams and Dora Johns, the Dora who is become as the mud beneath one's feet. Kind mistress of the widely opened door where white and black, rich and poor, of whatever caste or creed may enter and find comfort and ease and food and drink.

QUESTIONS

1. What talents do Dora and William possess? Why have they not lived up to their talents? What has kept them down? Why are they "unfinished masterpieces"?

2. How may Dora and William be seen as symbols? What do they symbolize?

3. Characterize the narrator. What attitude does she exhibit toward the lack of fulfillment of the major characters (see particularly paragraph 19)? How might the story have been different if the narrator had shown hostility, for example, or extreme bitterness?

NATHANIEL HAWTHORNE   (1804–1864)

Hawthorne, a friend and associate of the fourteenth president of the United States, Franklin Pierce, is one of the great American writers of the nineteenth century. His most famous work is The Scarlet Letter *(1850), the sale of which gave him a degree of independence. During the administration of President Pierce (1853–1857), Hawthorne served as American consul in Liverpool, England, and this opportunity enabled him to travel extensively in Europe. Throughout his writing there runs a conflict between freedom and conventionality, with those choosing freedom sometimes suffering from the guilt that their choice brings. "Young Goodman Brown," which is one of the early stories that he included in* Twice-Told Tales *(1837, 1842), embodies this conflict.*

Young Goodman Brown _____ *1835*

Young Goodman Brown came forth at sunset, into the street of Salem village,° but put his head back, after crossing the threshold, to exchange a parting kiss with his young wife. And Faith, as the wife was aptly named, thrust her own pretty head into the street, letting the wind play with the pink ribbons of her cap, while she called to Goodman Brown.

"Dearest heart," whispered she, softly and rather sadly, when her lips were close to his ear, "prithee, put off your journey until sunrise, and sleep in your own bed tonight. A lone woman is troubled with such dreams and such thoughts, that she's afeared of herself, sometimes. Pray, tarry with me this night, dear husband, of all nights in the year!"

"My love and my Faith," replied young Goodman Brown, "of all nights in the year, this one night must I tarry away from thee. My journey, as thou callest it, forth and back again, must needs be done 'twixt now and sunrise. What, my sweet, pretty wife, dost thou doubt me already, and we but three months married!"

"Then God bless you!" said Faith with the pink ribbons, "and may you find all well, when you come back."

"Amen!" cried Goodman Brown. "Say thy prayers, dear Faith, and go to bed at dusk, and no harm will come to thee."

_____

Salem village: in Massachusetts, about fifteen miles north of Boston. The time of the story is the late seventeenth or early eighteenth century.

So they parted; and the young man pursued his way, until, being about to turn the corner by the meeting-house, he looked back and saw the head of Faith still peeping after him, with a melancholy air, in spite of her pink ribbons.

"Poor little Faith!" thought he, for his heart smote him. "What a wretch am I, to leave her on such an errand! She talks of dreams, too. Methought, as she spoke, there was trouble in her face, as if a dream had warned her what work is to be done tonight. But no, no! 't would kill her to think it. Well; she's a blessed angel on earth; and after this one night, I'll cling to her skirts and follow her to Heaven."

With this excellent resolve for the future, Goodman Brown felt himself justified in making more haste on his present evil purpose. He had taken a dreary road, darkened by all the gloomiest trees of the forest, which barely stood aside to let the narrow path creep through, and closed immediately behind. It was all as lonely as could be; and there is this peculiarity in such a solitude, that the traveller knows not who may be concealed by the innumerable trunks and the thick boughs overhead; so that, with lonely footsteps, he may yet be passing through an unseen multitude.

"There may be a devilish Indian behind every tree," said Goodman Brown to himself; and he glanced fearfully behind him, as he added, "What if the devil himself should be at my very elbow!"

His head being turned back, he passed a crook of the road, and looking forward again, beheld the figure of a man, in grave and decent attire, seated at the foot of an old tree. He arose at Goodman Brown's approach, and walked onward, side by side with him.   10

"You are late, Goodman Brown," said he. "The clock of the Old South° was striking, as I came through Boston; and that is full fifteen minutes agone."

"Faith kept me back awhile," replied the young man, with a tremor in his voice, caused by the sudden appearance of his companion, though not wholly unexpected.

It was now deep dusk in the forest, and deepest in that part of it where these two were journeying. As nearly as could be discerned, the second traveller was about fifty years old, apparently in the same rank of life as Goodman Brown, and bearing a considerable resemblance to him, though perhaps more in expression than features. Still, they might have been taken for father and son. And yet, though the elder person was as simply clad as the younger, and as simple in manner too, he had an indescribable air of one who knew the world, and would not have felt abashed at the governor's dinner-table, or in King William's° court, were it possible that his affairs should call him thither. But the only thing about him that could be fixed upon as remarkable, was his staff, which bore the likeness of a great black snake, so curiously wrought, that it might almost be seen to twist and wriggle itself like a living serpent. This, of course, must have been an ocular deception, assisted by the uncertain light.

"Come, Goodman Brown!" cried his fellow-traveller, "this is a dull pace for the beginning of a journey. Take my staff, if you are so soon weary."

"Friend," said the other, exchanging his slow pace for a full stop, "having kept   15 covenant by meeting thee here, it is my purpose now to return whence I came. I have scruples, touching the matter thou wot'st of."°

Old South: The Old South Church, in Boston, is still there.
King William: William III was king of England from 1688 to 1701 (the time of the story). William IV was king from 1830 to 1837 (the period when Hawthorne wrote the story).
thou wot'st: you know.

"Sayest thou so?" replied he of the serpent, smiling apart. "Let us walk on, nevertheless, reasoning as we go, and if I convince thee not, thou shalt turn back. We are but a little way in the forest, yet."

"Too far, too far!" exclaimed the goodman, unconsciously resuming his walk. "My father never went into the woods on such an errand, nor his father before him. We have been a race of honest men and good Christians, since the days of the martyrs.° And shall I be the first of the name of Brown that ever took this path and kept—"

"Such company, thou wouldst say," observed the elder person, interrupting his pause. "Well said, Goodman Brown! I have been as well acquainted with your family as ever a one among the Puritans; and that's no trifle to say. I helped your grandfather, the constable, when he lashed the Quaker woman so smartly through the streets of Salem. And it was I that brought your father a pitch-pine knot, kindled at my own hearth, to set fire to an Indian village, in King Philip's war.° They were my good friends, both; and many a pleasant walk have we had along this path, and returned merrily after midnight. I would fain be friends with you, for their sake."

"If it be as thou sayest," replied Goodman Brown, "I marvel they never spoke of these matters. Or, verily, I marvel not, seeing that the least rumor of the sort would have driven them from New England. We are a people of prayer, and good works to boot, and abide no such wickedness."

"Wickedness or not," said the traveller with twisted staff, "I have a very general acquaintance here in New England. The deacons of many a church have drunk the communion wine with me; the selectmen, of divers towns, make me their chairman; and a majority of the Great and General Court are firm supporters of my interest. The governor and I, too—but these are state secrets." ~~everyones evil,~~   20

"Can this be so!" cried Goodman Brown, with a stare of amazement at his undisturbed companion. "Howbeit, I have nothing to do with the governor and council; they have their own ways, and are no rule for a simple husbandman like me. But, were I to go on with thee, how should I meet the eye of that good old man, our minister, at Salem village? Oh, his voice would make me tremble, both Sabbath-day and lecture-day!"

Thus far, the elder traveller had listened with due gravity, but now burst into a fit of irrepressible mirth, shaking himself so violently, that his snakelike staff actually seemed to wriggle in sympathy.

"Ha! ha! ha!" shouted he, again and again; then composing himself, "Well, go on, Goodman Brown, go on; but, prithee, don't kill me with laughing!"

"Well, then, to end the matter at once," said Goodman Brown, considerably nettled, "there is my wife, Faith. It would break her dear little heart; and I'd rather break my own!"

"Nay, if that be the case," answered the other, "e'en go thy ways, Goodman Brown. I would not, for twenty old women like the one hobbling before us, that Faith should come to any harm."   2?

As he spoke, he pointed his staff at a female figure on the path, in whom Goodman Brown recognized a very pious and exemplary dame, who had taught him

---

days of the martyrs: the martyrdoms of Protestants in England during the reign of Queen Mary (1553–1558).

King Philip's war: This war (1675–1676), infamous for the atrocities committed by the New England settlers, resulted in the suppression of Indian tribal life and prepared the way for unlimited settlement of New England by European immigrants. "Philip" was the English name of Chief Metacomet of the Wampanoag tribe.

his catechism in youth, and was still his moral and spiritual adviser, jointly with the minister and Deacon Gookin.

"A marvel, truly, that Goody° Cloyse should be so far in the wilderness, at nightfall!" said he. "But, with your leave, friend, I shall take a cut through the woods, until we have left this Christian woman behind. Being a stranger to you, she might ask whom I was consorting with, and whither I was going."

"Be it so," said his fellow-traveller. "Betake you to the woods, and let me keep the path."

Accordingly, the young man turned aside, but took care to watch his companion, who advanced softly along the road, until he had come within a staff's length of the old dame. She, meanwhile, was making the best of her way, with singular speed for so aged a woman, and mumbling some indistinct words, a prayer, doubtless, as she went. The traveller put forth his staff, and touched her withered neck with what seemed the serpent's tail.

"The devil!" screamed the pious old lady. 30

"Then Goody Cloyse knows her old friend?" observed the traveller, confronting her, and leaning on his writhing stick.

"Ah, forsooth, and is it your worship, indeed?" cried the good dame. "Yea, truly is it, and in the very image of my old gossip,° Goodman Brown, the grandfather of the silly fellow that now is. But, would your worship believe it? My broomstick hath strangely disappeared, stolen, as I suspect, by that unhanged witch, Goody Cory,° and that, too, when I was all anointed with the juice of smallage and cinquefoil and wolf's-bane—"°

"Mingled with fine wheat and the fat of a new-born babe," said the shape of old Goodman Brown.

"Ah, your worship knows the recipe," cried the old lady, cackling aloud. "So, as I was saying, being all ready for the meeting, and no horse to ride on, I made up my mind to foot it; for they tell me there is a nice young man to be taken into communion tonight. But now your good worship will lend me your arm, and we shall be there in a twinkling."

"That can hardly be," answered her friend. "I will not spare you my arm, Goody 35 Cloyse, but here is my staff, if you will."

So saying, he threw it down at her feet, where, perhaps, it assumed life, being one of the rods which its owner had formerly lent to the Egyptian Magi.° Of this fact, however, Goodman Brown could not take cognizance. He had cast up his eyes in astonishment, and looking down again, beheld neither Goody Cloyse nor the serpentine staff, but his fellow-traveller alone, who waited for him as calmly as if nothing had happened.

"That old woman taught me my catechism!" said the young man; and there was a world of meaning in this simple comment.

They continued to walk onward, while the elder traveller exhorted his companion to make good speed and persevere in the path, discoursing so aptly, that his arguments seemed rather to spring up in the bosom of his auditor, than to be suggested by himself.

Goody: shortened form of "goodwife," a respectful name for a married woman of low rank. A "Goody Cloyse" was one of the women sentenced to execution by Hawthorne's great-grandfather, Judge John Hathorne.

gossip: from "good sib" or "good relative."

Goody Cory: name of a woman who was also sent to execution by Judge Hathorne.

smallage and cinquefoil and wolf's-bane: plants commonly used by witches in making ointments.

lent to the Egyptian Magi: See Exodus 7:10–12.

As they went he plucked a branch of maple, to serve for a walking-stick, and began to strip it of the twigs and little boughs, which were wet with evening dew. The moment his fingers touched them, they became strangely withered and dried up, as with a week's sunshine. Thus the pair proceeded, at a good free pace, until suddenly, in a gloomy hollow of the road, Goodman Brown sat himself down on the stump of a tree, and refused to go any farther.

"Friend," said he, stubbornly, "my mind is made up. Not another step will I budge on this errand. What if a wretched old woman do choose to go to the devil, when I thought she was going to Heaven! Is that any reason why I should quit my dear Faith, and go after her?"

"You will think better of this by and by," said his acquaintance, composedly. "Sit   40
here and rest yourself a while; and when you feel like moving again, there is my staff to help you along."

Without more words, he threw his companion the maple stick, and was as speedily out of sight as if he had vanished into the deepening gloom. The young man sat a few moments by the roadside, applauding himself greatly, and thinking with how clear a conscience he should meet the minister, in his morning walk, nor shrink from the eye of good old Deacon Gookin. And what calm sleep would be his, that very night, which was to have been spent so wickedly, but purely and sweetly now, in the arms of Faith! Amidst these pleasant and praiseworthy meditations, Goodman Brown heard the tramp of horses along the road, and deemed it advisable to conceal himself within the verge of the forest, conscious of the guilty purpose that had brought him thither, though now so happily turned from it.

On came the hoof-tramps and the voices of the riders, two grave old voices, conversing soberly as they drew near. These mingled sounds appeared to pass along the road, within a few yards of the young man's hiding-place; but owing, doubtless, to the depth of the gloom, at that particular spot, neither the travellers nor their steeds were visible. Though their figures brushed the small boughs by the wayside, it could not be seen that they intercepted, even for a moment, the faint gleam from the strip of bright sky, athwart which they must have passed. Goodman Brown alternately crouched and stood on tiptoe, pulling aside the branches, and thrusting forth his head as far as he durst, without discerning so much as a shadow. It vexed him the more, because he could have sworn, were such a thing possible, that he recognized the voices of the minister and Deacon Gookin, jogging° along quietly, as they were wont to do, when bound to some ordination or ecclesiastical council. While yet within hearing, one of the riders stopped to pluck a switch.

"Of the two, reverend Sir," said the voice like the deacon's, "I had rather miss an ordination dinner than to-night's meeting. They tell me that some of our community are to be here from Falmouth and beyond, and others from Connecticut and Rhode Island; besides several of the Indian powwows,° who, after their fashion, know almost as much deviltry as the best of us. Moreover, there is a goodly young woman to be taken into communion."

"Mighty well, Deacon Gookin!" replied the solemn old tones of the minister. "Spur up, or we shall be late. Nothing can be done, you know, until I get on the ground."

jogging: riding a horse at a slow trot.
powwow: a Narragansett Indian word describing a priest or cult leader who led ritual ceremonies of dance, incantation, and magic.

The hoofs clattered again, and the voices, talking so strangely in the empty air,   45
passed on through the forest, where no church had ever been gathered, nor solitary
Christian prayed. Whither, then, could these holy men be journeying, so deep into the
heathen wilderness? Young Goodman Brown caught hold of a tree, for support, being
ready to sink down on the ground, faint and over-burthened with the heavy sickness of
his heart. He looked up to the sky, doubting whether there really was a Heaven above
him. Yet, there was the blue arch, and the stars brightening in it.

"With Heaven above, and Faith below, I will yet stand firm against the devil!" cried
Goodman Brown.

While he still gazed upward, into the deep arch of the firmament, and had lifted
his hands to pray, a cloud, though no wind was stirring, hurried across the zenith, and
hid the brightening stars. The blue sky was still visible, except directly overhead, where
this black mass of cloud was sweeping swiftly northward. Aloft in the air, as if from the
depths of the cloud, came a confused and doubtful sound of voices. Once, the listener
fancied that he could distinguish the accents of town's people of his own, men and
women, both pious and ungodly, many of whom he had met at the communion-table,
and had seen others rioting at the tavern. The next moment, so indistinct were the
sounds, he doubted whether he had heard aught but the murmur of the old forest, whispering without a wind. Then came a stronger swell of those familiar tones, heard daily in
the sunshine, at Salem village, but never, until now, from a cloud at night. There was
one voice, of a young woman, uttering lamentations, yet with an uncertain sorrow, and
entreating for some favor, which, perhaps, it would grieve her to obtain. And all the
unseen multitude, both saints and sinners, seemed to encourage her onward.

"Faith!" shouted Goodman Brown, in a voice of agony and desperation; and the
echoes of the forest mocked him, crying—"Faith! Faith!" as if bewildered wretches were
seeking her, all through the wilderness.

The cry of grief, rage, and terror was yet piercing the night, when the unhappy
husband held his breath for a response. There was a scream, drowned immediately in a
louder murmur of voices fading into far-off laughter, as the dark cloud swept away, leaving the clear and silent sky above Goodman Brown. But something fluttered lightly down
through the air, and caught on the branch of a tree. The young man seized it and
beheld a pink ribbon.

"My Faith is gone!" cried he, after one stupefied moment. "There is no good on   50
earth, and sin is but a name. Come, devil! for to thee is this world given."

And maddened with despair, so that he laughed loud and long, did Goodman
Brown grasp his staff and set forth again, at such a rate, that he seemed to fly along the
forest path, rather than to walk or run. The road grew wilder and drearier, and more
faintly traced, and vanished at length, leaving him in the heart of the dark wilderness,
still rushing onward, with the instinct that guides mortal man to evil. The whole forest
was peopled with frightful sounds; the creaking of the trees, the howling of wild beasts,
and the yell of Indians; while, sometimes, the wind tolled like a distant church bell, and
sometimes gave a broad roar around the traveller, as if all Nature were laughing him to
scorn. But he was himself the chief horror of the scene, and shrank not from its other
horrors.

"Ha! ha! ha!" roared Goodman Brown, when the wind laughed at him. "Let us
hear which will laugh loudest! Think not to frighten me with your deviltry! Come witch,
come wizard, come Indian powwow, come devil himself! and here comes Goodman
Brown. You may as well fear him as he fear you!"

In truth, all through the haunted forest, there could be nothing more frightful than the figure of Goodman Brown. On he flew, among the black pines, brandishing his staff with frenzied gestures, now giving vent to an inspiration of horrid blasphemy, and now shouting forth such laughter, as set all the echoes of the forest laughing like demons around him. The fiend in his own shape is less hideous than when he rages in the breast of man. Thus sped the demoniac on his course, until, quivering among the trees, he saw a red light before him, as when the felled trunks and branches of a clearing have been set on fire, and throw up their lurid blaze against the sky, at the hour of midnight. He paused, in a lull of the tempest that had driven him onward, and heard the swell of what seemed a hymn, rolling solemnly from a distance, with the weight of many voices. He knew the tune. It was a familiar one in the choir of the village meeting-house. The verse died heavily away, and was lengthened by a chorus, not of human voices, but of all the sounds of the benighted wilderness, pealing in awful harmony together. Goodman Brown cried out; and his cry was lost to his own ear, by its unison with the cry of the desert.

In the interval of silence, he stole forward, until the light glared full upon his eyes. At one extremity of an open space, hemmed in by the dark wall of the forest, arose a rock, bearing some rude, natural resemblance either to an altar or a pulpit, and surrounded by four blazing pines, their tops aflame, their stems untouched, like candles at an evening meeting. The mass of foliage, that had overgrown the summit of the rock, was all on fire, blazing high into the night, and fitfully illuminating the whole field. Each pendent twig and leafy festoon was in a blaze. As the red light arose and fell, a numerous congregation alternately shone forth, then disappeared in shadow, and again grew, as it were, out of the darkness, peopling the heart of the solitary woods at once.

"A grave and dark-clad company!" quoth Goodman Brown.   55

In truth, they were such. Among them, quivering to-and-fro, between gloom and splendor, appeared faces that would be seen, next day, at the council-board of the province, and others which, Sabbath after Sabbath, looked devoutly heavenward, and benignantly over the crowded pews, from the holiest pulpits in the land. Some affirm that the lady of the governor was there. At least, there were high dames well known to her, and wives of honored husbands, and widows a great multitude, and ancient maidens, all of excellent repute, and fair young girls, who trembled lest their mothers should espy them. Either the sudden gleams of light, flashing over the obscure field, bedazzled Goodman Brown, or he recognized a score of the church members of Salem village, famous for their especial sanctity. Good old Deacon Gookin had arrived, and waited at the skirts of that venerable saint, his reverend pastor. But, irreverently consorting with these grave, reputable, and pious people, these elders of the church, these chaste dames and dewy virgins, there were men of dissolute lives and women of spotted fame, wretches given over to all mean and filthy vice, and suspected even of horrid crimes. It was strange to see, that the good shrank not from the wicked, nor were the sinners abashed by the saints. Scattered, also, among their pale-faced enemies, were the Indian priests, or pow-wows, who had often scared their native forest with more hideous incantations than any known to English witchcraft.

"But, where is Faith?" thought Goodman Brown; and, as hope came into his heart, he trembled.

Another verse of the hymn arose, a slow and mournful strain, such as the pious love, but joined to words which expressed all that our nature can conceive of sin, and darkly hinted at far more. Unfathomable to mere mortals is the lore of fiends. Verse after verse was sung, and still the chorus of the desert swelled between, like the deepest tone of a mighty organ. And, with the final peal of that dreadful anthem, there came a sound, as if the roaring wind, the rushing streams, the howling beasts, and every other voice of the unconverted wilderness were mingling and according with the voice of guilty man, in homage to the prince of all. The four blazing pines threw up a loftier flame, and obscurely discovered shapes and visages of horror on the smoke-wreaths, above the impious assembly. At the same moment, the fire on the rock shot redly forth, and formed a glowing arch above its base, where now appeared a figure. With reverence be it spoken, the apparition bore no slight similitude, both in garb and manner, to some grave divine of the New England churches.

"Bring forth the converts!" cried a voice, that echoed through the field and rolled into the forest.

At the word, Goodman Brown stepped forth from the shadow of the trees, and approached the congregation, with whom he felt a loathful brotherhood, by the sympathy of all that was wicked in his heart. He could have well-nigh sworn, that the shape of his own dead father beckoned him to advance, looking downward from a smoke-wreath, while a woman, with dim features of despair, threw out her hand to warn him back. Was it his mother? But he had no power to retreat one step, nor to resist, even in thought, when the minister and good old Deacon Gookin seized his arms, and led him to the blazing rock. Thither came also the slender form of a veiled female, led between Goody Cloyse, that pious teacher of the catechism, and Martha Carrier, who had received the devil's promise to be queen of hell. A rampant hag was she! And there stood the prose-lytes, beneath the canopy of fire.

"Welcome, my children," said the dark figure, "to the communion of your race! Ye have found, thus young, your nature and your destiny. My children, look behind you!"

They turned; and flashing forth, as it were, in a sheet of flame, the fiend-worshippers were seen; the smile of welcome gleamed darkly on every visage.

"There," resumed the sable form, "are all whom ye have reverenced from youth. Ye deemed them holier than yourselves, and shrank from your own sin, contrasting it with their lives of righteousness and prayerful aspirations heavenward. Yet, here are they all, in my worshipping assembly! This night it shall be granted you to know their secret deeds; how hoary-bearded elders of the church have whispered wanton words to the young maids of their households; how many a woman, eager for widow's weeds, has given her husband a drink at bedtime, and let him sleep his last sleep in her bosom; how beardless youths have made haste to inherit their father's wealth; and how fair damsels—blush not, sweet ones!—have dug little graves in the garden, and bidden me, the sole guest, to an infant's funeral. By the sympathy of your human hearts for sin, ye shall scent out all the places—whether in church, bed-chamber, street, field, or forest—where crime has been committed, and shall exult to behold the whole earth one stain of guilt, one mighty blood-spot. Far more than this! It shall be yours to penetrate, in every bosom, the deep mystery of sin, the fountain of all wicked arts, and which inexhaustibly supplies more evil impulses than human power—than my power, at its utmost!—can make manifest in deeds. And now, my children, look upon each other."

They did so; and, by the blaze of the hell-kindled torches, the wretched man beheld his Faith, and the wife her husband, trembling before that unhallowed altar.

"Lo! there ye stand, my children," said the figure, in a deep and solemn tone, almost sad, with its despairing awfulness, as if his once angelic nature° could yet mourn

---

once angelic nature: Lucifer ("light bearer"), another name for the Devil, led the traditional revolt of the angels and was thrown into hell as his punishment. See Isaiah 14:12–15.

for our miserable race. "Depending upon one another's hearts, ye had still hoped that virtue were not all a dream! Now are ye undeceived!—Evil is the nature of mankind. Evil must be your only happiness. Welcome, again, my children, to the communion of your race!"

"Welcome!" repeated the fiend-worshippers, in one cry of despair and triumph.

And there they stood, the only pair, as it seemed, who were yet hesitating on the verge of wickedness, in this dark world. A basin was hollowed, naturally, in the rock. Did it contain water, reddened by the lurid light? or was it blood? or, perchance, a liquid flame? Herein did the Shape of Evil dip his hand, and prepare to lay the mark of baptism upon their foreheads, that they might be partakers of the mystery of sin, more conscious of the secret guilt of others, both in deed and thought, than they could now be of their own. The husband cast one look at his pale wife, and Faith at him. What polluted wretches would the next glance show them to each other, shuddering alike at what they disclosed and what they saw!

"Faith! Faith!" cried the husband. "Look up to Heaven, and resist the Wicked One!"

Whether Faith obeyed, he knew not. Hardly had he spoken, when he found himself amid calm night and solitude, listening to a roar of the wind, which died heavily away through the forest. He staggered against the rock, and felt it chill and damp, while a hanging twig, that had been all on fire, besprinkled his cheek with the coldest dew.

The next morning, young Goodman Brown came slowly into the street of Salem village staring around him like a bewildered man. The good old minister was taking a walk along the grave-yard, to get an appetite for breakfast and meditate his sermon, and bestowed a blessing, as he passed, on Goodman Brown. He shrank from the venerable saint, as if to avoid an anathema. Old Deacon Gookin was at domestic worship, and the holy words of his prayer were heard through the open window. "What God doth the wizard pray to?" quoth Goodman Brown. Goody Cloyse, that excellent old Christian, stood in the early sunshine, at her own lattice, catechising a little girl, who had brought her a pint of morning's milk. Goodman Brown snatched away the child, as from the grasp of the fiend himself. Turning the corner by the meetinghouse, he spied the head of Faith, with the pink ribbons, gazing anxiously forth, and bursting into such joy at the sight of him that she skipt along the street, and almost kissed her husband before the whole village. But Goodman Brown looked sternly and sadly into her face, and passed on without a greeting.

Had Goodman Brown fallen asleep in the forest, and only dreamed a wild dream of a witch-meeting?

Be it so, if you will. But, alas! it was a dream of evil omen for young Goodman Brown. A stern, a sad, a darkly meditative, a distrustful, if not a desperate man did he become, from the night of that fearful dream. On the Sabbath day, when the congregation were singing a holy psalm, he could not listen, because an anthem of sin rushed loudly upon his ear, and drowned all the blessed strain. When the minister spoke from the pulpit, with power and fervid eloquence, and with his hand on the open Bible, of the sacred truths of our religion, and of saint-like lives and triumphant deaths, and of future bliss or misery unutterable, then did Goodman Brown turn pale, dreading lest the roof should thunder down upon the gray blasphemer and his hearers. Often, awaking suddenly at midnight, he shrank from the bosom of Faith, and at morning or eventide, when the family knelt down in prayer, he scowled, and muttered to himself, and gazed sternly at his wife, and turned away. And when he had lived long, and was borne to his grave, a hoary corpse, followed by Faith, an aged woman, and children and grandchildren,

70

[handwritten margin note: Goodman Brown ignores his wife]

a goodly procession, besides neighbors not a few, they carved no hopeful verse upon his tombstone; for his dying hour was gloom.

QUESTIONS

1. Near the end of the story the narrator asks the following: "Had Goodman Brown fallen asleep in the forest, and only dreamed a wild dream of a witch-meeting?" What is the answer? If Goodman Brown's visions come out of his own dreams (mind, subconscious), what do they tell us about him?

2. Is Goodman Brown round or flat? To what extent is he a symbolic "everyman" or representative of humankind?

3. Consider Hawthorne's use of symbolism, such as sunset and night, the walking stick, the witches' sabbath, the marriage to Faith, and the vague shadows amid the darkness, together with other symbols that you may find.

4. What details establish the two settings? What characterizes Salem? The woods? Why might we be justified in seeing the forest as a symbolic setting?

5. To what extent are the people, objects, and events in Goodman Brown's adventure invested with enough *consistent* symbolic resonance to justify calling his episode in the woods an allegory? Consider Brown's wife, Faith, as an allegorical figure. What do you make of Brown's statements that "I'll cling to her skirts and follow her to Heaven" (paragraph 7) and "Faith kept me back awhile" (paragraph 12)? In this same light, consider the other characters Brown meets in the forest, the sunset, the walk into the forest, and the staff "which bore the likeness of a great black snake" (paragraph 13).

ST. LUKE   (1st c. C.E.)

Although little is known about St. Luke, evidence in Colossians, Philemon, and 2 Timothy indicates that a man named Luke was the "beloved physician" and traveling companion of the apostle Paul, who journeyed in the Mediterranean area during the middle of the first century C.E. Scholars indicate that Luke built his gospel from the Gospel of St. Mark and also from written sources known as "Q," some of which were also used by St. Matthew. Luke also relied on other sources that were available only to him. In addition to his gospel, Luke is also accepted as the author of the Acts of the Apostles.

The Parable of the Prodigal Son (Luke 15:11–32) _____ *(ca. 90 C.E.)*

11 And he [Jesus] said, A certain man had two sons:

12 And the younger of them said to *his* father, Father, give me the portion of goods that falleth *to me.* And he divided unto them *his* living.°

13 And not many days after the younger son gathered all together, and took his journey into a far country,° and there wasted his substance with riotous living.

divided . . . his living: one-third of the father's estate; the son had to renounce all further claim.

far country: countries of the Jewish dispersal, or diaspora, in the areas bordering the Mediterranean Sea.

14 And when he had spent all, there arose a mighty famine in that land; and he began to be in want.

15 And he went and joined himself to a citizen of that country; and he sent him into his fields to feed swine.°

16 And he would fain have filled his belly with the husks° that the swine did eat: and no man gave unto him.

17 And when he came to himself, he said, How many hired servants of my father's have bread enough and to spare, and I perish with hunger!

18 I will arise and go to my father, and will say unto him, Father, I have sinned against heaven, and before thee.

19 And am no more worthy to be called thy son: make me as one of thy hired servants.

20 And he arose, and came to his father. But when he was yet a great way off, his father saw him, and had compassion, and ran, and fell on his neck, and kissed him.

21 And the son said unto him, Father, I have sinned against heaven, and in thy sight, and am no more worthy to be called thy son.

22 But the father said to his servants, Bring forth the best robe, and put *it* on him; and put a ring on his hand, and shoes on *his* feet:

23 And bring hither the fatted calf,° and kill *it;* and let us eat, and be merry:

24 For this my son was dead, and is alive again; he was lost, and is found. And they began to be merry.

25 Now his elder son was in the field: and as he came and drew nigh to the house, he heard music and dancing.

26 And he called one of the servants, and asked what these things meant.

27 And he said unto him, Thy brother is come; and thy father hath killed the fatted calf, because he hath received him safe and sound.

28 And he was angry, and would not go in: therefore came his father out, and intreated him.

29 And he answering said to *his* father, Lo, these many years do I serve thee, neither transgressed I at any time thy commandment: and yet thou never gavest me a kid, that I might make merry with my friends:

30 But as soon as this thy son was come, which hath devoured thy living with harlots, thou hast killed for him the fatted calf.

31 And he said unto him, Son, thou art ever with me, and all that I have is thine.

32 It was meet° that we should make merry, and be glad: for this thy brother was dead, and is alive again: and was lost, and is found.

QUESTIONS

1. Describe the character of the Prodigal Son. Is he flat or round, representative or individual? Why is it necessary that the character be considered representatively, even though he has individual characteristics?

2. What is the plot? What is the antagonism against which the Prodigal Son contends? Why is it necessary that the brother resent the brother's return?

feed swine: In Jewish custom, pigs were unclean.
husks: pods of the carob tree, the eating of which was thought to be penitential.
fatted calf: grain-fed calf.
meet: appropriate.

3. What is the resolution of the parable? Why is there no "they lived happily ever after" ending?

4. Using verse numbers, analyze the structure of the parable. What determines your division of the parts? Do these parts coincide with the development of the plot? Describe the relationship of plot to structure in the parable.

5. What is the point of view here? How does the emphasis shift with verse 22?

6. On the basis of the fact that there are many characteristics here of many stories you have read, write a description of the parable as a type of literature.

JOHN STEINBECK   (1902–1968)

Steinbeck was born in Salinas, California, and for a time attended Stanford University. In the 1920s, while working at jobs such as surveying, picking fruit, and hatching trout, he began his writing career. A number of stories and novels preceded his best-known novel, The Grapes of Wrath *(1939), for which he was awarded the Pulitzer Prize in 1940. He received the Nobel Prize in literature in 1962. His fiction, often set in rural areas, features a realistic and pessimistic view of life. A number of his novels have been made into films, the best known of which is* The Grapes of Wrath. *His home in Salinas is open to the visiting public.*

The Chrysanthemums _____ 1937

The high grey-flannel fog of winter closed off the Salinas Valley° from the sky and from all the rest of the world. On every side it sat like a lid on the mountains and made of the great valley a closed pot. On the broad, level land floor the gang plows bit deep and left the black earth shining like metal where the shares had cut. On the foothill ranches across the Salinas River, the yellow stubble fields seemed to be bathed in pale cold sunshine, but there was no sunshine in the valley now in December. The thick willow scrub along the river flamed with sharp and positive yellow leaves.

It was a time of quiet and of waiting. The air was cold and tender. A light wind blew up from the southwest so that the farmers were mildly hopeful of a good rain before long; but fog and rain do not go together.

Across the river, on Henry Allen's foothill ranch there was little work to be done, for the hay was cut and stored and the orchards were plowed up to receive the rain deeply when it should come. The cattle on the higher slopes were becoming shaggy and rough-coated.

Elisa Allen, working in her flower garden, looked down across the yard and saw Henry, her husband, talking to two men in business suits. The three of them stood by the tractor shed, each man with one foot on the side of the little Fordson.° They smoked cigarettes and studied the machines as they talked.

Salinas Valley: in Monterey County, California, about 50 miles south of San Jose.
Fordson: a tractor manufactured by the Ford Motor Company, with large steel-lugged rear wheels.

Elisa watched them for a moment and then went back to her work. She was thirty-five. Her face was lean and strong and her eyes were as clear as water. Her figure looked blocked and heavy in her gardening costume, a man's black hat pulled low down over her eyes, clodhopper shoes, a figured print dress almost completely covered by a big corduroy apron with four big pockets to hold the snips, the trowel and scratcher, the seeds and the knife she worked with. She wore heavy leather gloves to protect her hands while she worked.

She was cutting down the old year's chrysanthemum stalks with a pair of short and powerful scissors. She looked down toward the men by the tractor shed now and then. Her face was eager and mature and handsome; even her work with the scissors was over-eager, over-powerful. The chrysanthemum stems seemed too small and easy for her energy.

She brushed a cloud of hair out of her eyes with the back of her glove, and left a smudge of earth on the cheek in doing it. Behind her stood the neat white farm house with red geraniums close-banked around it as high as the windows. It was a hard-swept looking little house, with hard-polished windows, and a clean mud-mat on the front steps.

Elisa cast another glance toward the tractor shed. The strangers were getting into their Ford coupe. She took off a glove and put her strong fingers down into the forest of new green chrysanthemum sprouts that were growing around the old roots. She spread the leaves and looked down among the close-growing stems. No aphids were there, no sowbugs or snails or cutworms. Her terrier fingers destroyed such pests before they could get started.

Elisa started at the sound of her husband's voice. He had come near quietly, and he leaned over the wire fence that protected her flower garden from cattle and dogs and chickens.

"At it again," he said. "You've got a strong new crop coming."

Elisa straightened her back and pulled on the gardening glove again. "Yes. They'll be strong this coming year." In her tone and on her face there was a little smugness.

"You've got a gift with things," Henry observed. "Some of those yellow chrysanthemums you had this year were ten inches across. I wish you'd work out in the orchard and raise some apples that big."

Her eyes sharpened. "Maybe I could do it, too. I've a gift with things, all right. My mother had it. She could stick anything in the ground and make it grow. She said it was having planters' hands that knew how to do it."

"Well, it sure works with flowers," he said.

"Henry, who were those men you were talking to?"

"Why, sure, that's what I came to tell you. They were from the Western Meat Company. I sold those thirty head of three-year-old steers. Got nearly my own price, too."

"Good," she said. "Good for you."

"And I thought," he continued, "I thought how it's Saturday afternoon, and we might go to Salinas for dinner at a restaurant, and then to a picture show—to celebrate, you see."

"Good," she repeated. "Oh, yes. That will be good."

Henry put on his joking tone. "There's fights tonight. How'd you like to go to the fights?"

"Oh, no," she said breathlessly. "No, I wouldn't like fights."

"Just fooling, Elisa. We'll go to a movie. Let's see. It's two now. I'm going to take Scotty and bring down those steers from the hill. It'll take us maybe two hours. We'll go in town about five and have dinner at the Cominos Hotel. Like that?"

"Of course I'll like it. It's good to eat away from home."

"All right, then. I'll go get up a couple of horses."

She said, "I'll have plenty of time to transplant some of these sets, I guess."   25

She heard her husband calling Scotty down by the barn. And a little later she saw the two men ride up the pale yellow hillside in search of the steers.

There was a little square sandy bed kept for rooting the chrysanthemums. With her trowel she turned the soil over and over, and smoothed it and patted it firm. Then she dug ten parallel trenches to receive the sets. Back at the chrysanthemum bed she pulled out the little crisp shoots, trimmed off the leaves of each one with her scissors and laid it on a small orderly pile.

A squeak of wheels and plod of hoofs came from the road. Elisa looked up. The country road ran along the dense bank of willows and cottonwoods that bordered the river, and up this road came a curious vehicle, curiously drawn. It was an old spring-wagon, with a round canvas top on it like the cover of a prairie schooner. It was drawn by an old bay horse and a little grey-and-white burro. A big stubble-bearded man sat between the cover flaps and drove the crawling team. Underneath the wagon, between the hind wheels, a lean and rangy mongrel dog walked sedately. Words were painted on the canvas in clumsy, crooked letters. "Pots, pans, knives, sisors, lawn mores. Fixed." Two rows of articles and the triumphantly definitive "Fixed" below. The black paint had run down in little sharp points beneath each letter.

Elisa, squatting on the ground, watched to see the crazy, loose-jointed wagon pass by. But it didn't pass. It turned into the farm road in front of her house, crooked old wheels skirling and squeaking. The rangy dog darted from between the wheels and ran ahead. Instantly the two ranch shepherds flew out at him. Then all three stopped, and with stiff and quivering tails, with taut straight legs, with ambassadorial dignity, they slowly circled, sniffing daintily. The caravan pulled up to Elisa's wire fence and stopped. Now the newcomer dog, feeling outnumbered, lowered his tail and retired under the wagon with raised hackles and bared teeth.

The man on the wagon seat called out. "That's a bad dog in a fight when he gets   30
started."

Elisa laughed. "I see he is. How soon does he generally get started?"

The man caught up her laughter and echoed it heartily. "Sometimes not for weeks and weeks," he said. He climbed stiffly down, over the wheel. The horse and the donkey dropped like unwatered flowers.

Elisa saw that he was a very big man. Although his hair and beard were greying, he did not look old. His worn black suit was wrinkled and spotted with grease. The laughter had disappeared from his face and eyes the moment his laughing voice ceased. His eyes were dark and they were full of the brooding that gets in the eyes of teamsters and of sailors. The calloused hands he rested on the wire fence were cracked, and every crack was a black line. He took off his battered hat.

"I'm off my general road, ma'am," he said. "Does this dirt road cut over across the river to the Los Angeles highway?"

Elisa stood up and shoved the thick scissors in her apron pocket. "Well, yes, it   35
does, but it winds around and then fords the river. I don't think your team could pull through the sand."

He replied with some asperity, "It might surprise you what them beasts can pull through."

"When they get started?" she asked.

He smiled for a second. "Yes. When they get started."

"Well," said Elisa, "I think you'll save time if you go back to the Salinas road and pick up the highway there."

He drew a big finger down the chicken wire and made it sing. "I ain't in any hurry, ma'am. I go from Seattle to San Diego and back every year. Takes all my time. About six months each way. I aim to follow nice weather."   40

Elisa took off her gloves and stuffed them in the apron pocket with the scissors. She touched the under edge of her man's hat, searching for fugitive hairs. "That sounds like a nice kind of a way to live," she said.

He leaned confidentially over the fence. "Maybe you noticed the writing on my wagon. I mend pots and sharpen knives and scissors. You got any of them things to do?"

"Oh, no," she said quickly. "Nothing like that." Her eyes hardened with resistance.

"Scissors is the worst thing," he explained. "Most people just ruin scissors trying to sharpen 'em, but I know how. I got a special tool. It's a little bobbit kind of thing, and patented. But it sure does the trick."

"No. My scissors are all sharp."   45

"All right, then. Take a pot," he continued earnestly, "a bent pot, or a pot with a hole. I can make it like new so you don't have to buy no new ones. That's a saving for you."

"No," she said shortly. "I tell you I have nothing like that for you to do."

His face fell to an exaggerated sadness. His voice took on a whining undertone. "I ain't had a thing to do today. Maybe I won't have no supper tonight. You see I'm off my regular road. I know folks on the highway clear from Seattle to San Diego. They save their things for me to sharpen up because they know I do it so good and save them money."

"I'm sorry," Elisa said irritably. "I haven't anything for you to do."

His eyes left her face and fell to searching the ground. They roamed about until   50
they came to the chrysanthemum bed where she had been working. "What's them plants, ma'am?"

The irritation and resistance melted from Elisa's face. "Oh, those are chrysanthemums, giant whites and yellows. I raise them every year, bigger than anybody around here."

"Kind of a long-stemmed flower? Looks like a quick puff of colored smoke?" he asked.

"That's it. What a nice way to describe them."

"They smell kind of nasty till you get used to them," he said.

"It's a good bitter smell," she retorted, "not nasty at all."   5.

He changed his tone quickly. "I like the smell myself."

"I had ten-inch blooms this year," she said.

The man leaned farther over the fence. "Look. I know a lady down the road a piece, has got the nicest garden you ever seen. Got nearly every kind of flower but no chrysantheums. Last time I was mending a copper-bottom washtub for her (that's a hard job but I do it good), she said to me, 'If you ever run acrost some nice chrysantheums I wish you'd try to get me a few seeds.' That's what she told me."

Elisa's eyes grew alert and eager. "She couldn't have known much about chrysanthemums. You can raise them from seed, but it's much easier to root the little sprouts you see there."

"Oh," he said. "I s'pose I can't take none to her, then."

"Why yes you can," Elisa cried. "I can put some in damp sand, and you can carry them right along with you. They'll take root in the pot if you keep them damp. And then she can transplant them."

"She'd sure like to have some, ma'am. You say they're nice ones?"

"Beautiful," she said. "Oh, beautiful." Her eyes shone. She tore off the battered hat and shook out her dark pretty hair. "I'll put them in a flower pot, and you can take them right with you. Come into the yard."

While the man came through the picket gate Elisa ran excitedly along the geranium-bordered path to the back of the house. And she returned carrying a big red flower pot. The gloves were forgotten now. She kneeled on the ground by the starting bed and dug up the sandy soil with her fingers and scooped it into the bright new flower pot. Then she picked up the little pile of shoots she had prepared. With her strong fingers she pressed them into the sand and tamped around them with her knuckles. The man stood over her. "I'll tell you what to do," she said. "You remember so you can tell the lady."

"Yes, I'll try to remember."   65

"Well, look. These will take root in about a month. Then she must set them out, about a foot apart in good rich earth like this, see?" She lifted a handful of dark soil for him to look at. "They'll grow fast and tall. Now remember this. In July tell her to cut them down, about eight inches from the ground."

"Before they bloom?" he asked.

"Yes, before they bloom." Her face was tight with eagerness. "They'll grow right up again. About the last of September the buds will start."

She stopped and seemed perplexed. "It's the budding that takes the most care," she said hesitantly. "I don't know how to tell you." She looked deep into his eyes, searchingly. Her mouth opened a little, and she seemed to be listening. "I'll try to tell you," she said. "Did you ever hear of planting hands?"

"Can't say I have, ma'am."   70

"Well, I can only tell you what it feels like. It's when you're picking off the buds you don't want. Everything goes right down into your fingertips. You watch your fingers work. They do it themselves. You can feel how it is. They pick and pick the buds. They never make a mistake. They're with the plant. Do you see? Your fingers and the plant. You can feel that, right up your arm. They know. They never make a mistake. You can feel it. When you're like that you can't do anything wrong. Do you see that? Can you understand that?"

She was kneeling on the ground looking up at him. Her breast swelled passionately.

The man's eyes narrowed. He looked away self-consciously. "Maybe I know," he said. "Sometimes in the night in the wagon there—"

Elisa's voice grew husky. She broke in on him. "I've never lived as you do, but I know what you mean. When the night is dark—why, the stars are sharp-pointed, and there's quiet. Why, you rise up and up! Every pointed star gets driven into your body. It's like that. Hot and sharp and—lovely."

Kneeling there, her hand went out toward his legs in the greasy black trousers.   75
Her hesitant fingers almost touched the cloth. Then her hand dropped to the ground. She crouched low like a fawning dog.

He said, "It's nice, just like you say. Only when you don't have no dinner, it ain't."

She stood up then, very straight, and her face was ashamed. She held the flower pot out to him and placed it gently in his arms. "Here. Put it in your wagon, on the seat, where you can watch it. Maybe I can find something for you to do."

At the back of the house she dug in the can pile and found two old and battered aluminum saucepans. She carried them back and gave them to him. "Here, maybe you can fix these."

His manner changed. He became professional. "Good as new I can fix them." At the back of his wagon he set a little anvil, and out of an oily tool box dug a small machine hammer. Elisa came through the gate to watch him while he pounded out the dents in the kettles. His mouth grew sure and knowing. At a difficult part of the work he sucked his under-lip.

"You sleep right in the wagon?" Elisa asked.   80

"Right in the wagon, ma'am. Rain or shine. I'm dry as a cow in there."

"It must be nice," she said. "It must be very nice. I wish women could do such things."

"It ain't the right kind of a life for a woman."

Her upper lip raised a little, showing her teeth. "How do you know? How can you tell?" she said.

"I don't know ma'am," he protested. "Of course I don't know. Now here's your   85
kettles, done. You don't have to buy no new ones."

"How much?"

"Oh, fifty cents'll do. I keep my prices down and my work good. That's why I have all them satisfied customers up and down the highway."

Elisa brought him a fifty-cent piece from the house and dropped it in his hand. "You might be surprised to have a rival some time. I can sharpen scissors, too. And I can beat the dents out of little pots. I could show you what a woman might do."

He put his hammer back in the oily box and shoved the little anvil out of sight. "It would be a lonely life for a woman, ma'am, and a scarey life, too, with animals creeping under the wagon all night." He climbed over the single-tree, steadying himself with a hand on the burro's white rump. He settled himself in the seat, picked up the lines. "Thank you kindly, ma'am," he said. "I'll do like you told me; I'll go back and catch the Salinas road."

"Mind," she called, "if you're long in getting there, keep the sand damp."   90

"Sand, ma'am? . . . Sand? Oh, sure. You mean round the chrysantheums. Sure I will." He clucked his tongue. The beasts leaned luxuriously into their collars. The mongrel dog took his place between the back wheels. The wagon turned and crawled out the entrance road and back the way it had come, along the river.

Elisa stood in front of her wire fence watching the slow progress of the caravan. Her shoulders were straight, her head thrown back, her eyes half-closed, so that the scene came vaguely into them. Her lips moved silently, forming the words "Good-bye—good-bye." Then she whispered, "That's a bright direction. There's a glowing there." The sound of her whisper startled her. She shook herself free and looked about to see whether anyone had been listening. Only the dogs had heard. They lifted their heads toward her from their sleeping in the dust, and then stretched out their chins and settled asleep again. Elisa turned and ran hurriedly into the house.

In the kitchen she reached behind the stove and felt the water tank. It was full of hot water from the noonday cooking. In the bathroom she tore off her soiled clothes and flung them into the corner. And then she scrubbed herself with a little block of pumice, legs and thighs, loins and chest and arms, until her skin was scratched and red. When she had dried herself she stood in front of a mirror in her bedroom and looked at her body. She tightened her stomach and threw out her chest. She turned and looked over her shoulder at her back.

After a while she began to dress, slowly. She put on her newest under-clothing and her nicest stockings and the dress which was the symbol of her prettiness. She worked carefully on her hair, pencilled her eyebrows and rouged her lips.

Before she was finished she heard the little thunder of hoofs and the shouts of   95
Henry and his helper as they drove the red steers into the corral. She heard the gate
bang shut and set herself for Henry's arrival.

His step sounded on the porch. He entered the house calling "Elisa, where are
you?"

"In my room, dressing. I'm not ready. There's hot water for your bath. Hurry up.
It's getting late."

When she heard him splashing in the tub, Elisa laid his dark suit on the bed, and
shirt and socks and tie beside it. She stood his polished shoes on the floor beside the
bed. Then she went to the porch and sat primly and stiffly down. She looked toward the
river road where the willow-line was still yellow with frosted leaves so that under the high
grey fog they seemed a thin band of sunshine. This was the only color in the grey afternoon. She sat unmoving for a long time. Her eyes blinked rarely.

Henry came banging out of the door, shoving his tie inside his vest as he came.
Elisa stiffened and her face grew tight. Henry stopped short and looked at her. "Why—
why, Elisa. You look so nice!"

"Nice? You think I look nice? What do you mean by 'nice'?"   100

Henry blundered on. "I don't know. I mean you look different, strong and
happy."

"I am strong? Yes, strong. What do you mean 'strong'?"

He looked bewildered. "You're playing some kind of a game," he said helplessly.
"It's a kind of a play. You look strong enough to break a calf over your knee, happy
enough to eat it like watermelon."

For a second she lost her rigidity. "Henry! Don't talk like that. You didn't know
what you said." She grew complete again. "I'm strong," she boasted. "I never knew
before how strong."

Henry looked down toward the tractor shed, and when he brought his eyes back   105
to her, they were his own again. "I'll get out the car. You can put on your coat while I'm
starting."

Elisa went into the house. She heard him drive to the gate and idle down his
motor, and then she took a long time to put on her hat. She pulled it here and pressed
it there. When Henry turned the motor off she slipped into her coat and went out.

The little roadster bounced along on the dirt road by the river, raising the birds
and driving the rabbits into the brush. Two cranes flapped heavily over the willow-
line and dropped into the river-bed.

Far ahead on the road Elisa saw a dark speck. She knew.

She tried not to look as they passed it, but her eyes would not obey. She whispered
to herself sadly. "He might have thrown them off the road. That wouldn't have been
much trouble, not very much. But he kept the pot," she explained. "He had to keep the
pot. That's why he couldn't get them off the road."

The roadster turned a bend and she saw the caravan ahead. She swung full   110
around toward her husband so she could not see the little covered wagon and the mis-
matched team as the car passed them.

In a moment it was over. The thing was done. She did not look back. She said
loudly, to be heard above the motor, "It will be good, tonight, a good dinner."

"Now you're changed again," Henry complained. He took one hand from the
wheel and patted her knee. "I ought to take you in to dinner oftener. It would be good
for both of us. We get so heavy out on the ranch."

"Henry," she asked, "could we have wine at dinner?"

"Sure we could. Say! That will be fine."

She was silent for a little while; then she said, "Henry, at those prize fights, do the   115
men hurt each other very much?"

"Sometimes a little, not often. Why?"

"Well, I've read how they break noses, and blood runs down their chests. I've read
how the fighting gloves get heavy and soggy with blood."

He looked around at her. "What's the matter, Elisa? I didn't know you read things
like that." He brought the car to a stop, then turned to the right over the Salinas River
bridge.

"Do any women ever go to the fights?" she asked.

"Oh, sure, some. What's the matter, Elisa? Do you want to go? I don't think you'd   120
like it, but I'll take you if you really want to go."

She relaxed limply in the seat. "Oh, no. No. I don't want to go. I'm sure I don't."
Her face was turned away from him. "It will be enough if we can have wine. It will be
plenty." She turned up her coat collar so he could not see that she was crying weakly—
like an old woman.

QUESTIONS

1. What point of view is used in the story? What are the advantages of this point of view?

2. Consider the symbolism of the setting in this story with respect to the Salinas Valley, the time of year, and the description of the Allen house. What do these things tell us about Elisa Allen and her world?

3. To what extent is Steinbeck's description of Elisa in paragraphs 5 and 6 symbolic? What is she wearing? What do her clothes hide or suppress?

4. What do the chrysanthemums symbolize for Elisa? What do they symbolize *about* her? What role do these flowers play in her life?

5. How does Elisa's character or sense of self change during the episode in which she washes and dresses for dinner? To what extent is this washing-dressing episode symbolic? How would you explain the symbolism?

6. Consider the symbolic impact of Elisa's seeing the chrysanthemum sprouts at the roadside. What does her reaction tell us about her values?

MICHEL TREMBLAY   (b. 1942)

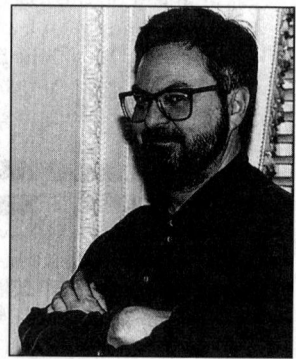

*Tremblay, a French-Canadian native of Montreal, is both a
dramatist and writer of fiction. He is known as an experimental and avant-garde writer. In one of his plays,
for example* (Albertine, en cinq temps *[1984]*), *five
actresses play one character at various times of life. His
innovativeness and boldness extend to his treating subjects
such as incest, transvestitism, and prostitution. His works
are strongly symbolic and, as with "The Thimble," allegorical. He has written a number of novels, including the autobiographical* The Fat Woman Next Door Is Pregnant
(1981). His collection of stories Contes pour buveurs
attardés *(1966; translated as* Stories for Late-Night
Drinkers, *1974) included "The Thimble."*

The Thimble ————————————————————————————— *1966*

Translated by Jay Bochner

If Bobby Stone had known what was to happen that day, he probably would never have got out of bed. And . . . well, the catastrophe might have been avoided.

Bobby Stone wasn't bad fellow. He worked in an office, drank in moderation, went to mass every Sunday, and had a weakness for plump women. He was neither old nor young, though he wore a hat to cover an expanding bald spot.   ~middleaged~

Bobby Stone had not the slightest inkling that he was going to be the cause of the catastrophe.

"Now, now, my dear lady, please stop this silly game. People are looking at us!" He was right. A throng of loafers had gathered around them and some were beginning to eye Bobby Stone reproachfully, because this woman was weeping and wailing. "Sir, I beg of you," she cried, "take it! Take it! I give it to you. It's yours!" But Bobby Stone didn't want it; he didn't want to have anything to do with it. "What do you expect me to do with it?" he said. "And besides, it's a . . . thing that belongs to women." More and more people gathered on the sidewalk and Bobby Stone began to sweat. He took out his hand-kerchief to wipe his forehead, but he didn't remove his hat. *She's crazy. That's it, she's crazy. And all those people looking at us. But I don't want to have her thimble!*

A man emerged from the crowd and grabbed Bobby Stone by the collar. "So," he said, breathing a rotten smell into his face, "we make women cry in the middle of the street?" Bobby Stone was trembling. "But Mister, I don't know this woman! She wants to give me her thimble, and I don't want her thimble, I don't. . . . " Really, Bobby Stone had had enough. In an abrupt surge of courage—or was it cowardice?—he slammed his fist into the face of the man who was threatening him and took off, knocking over two or three people who tried to stop him.

As you might have expected, he worked very poorly that day. The columns of figures swayed on the page, and when he closed his eyes Bobby Stone saw the strange woman offering him the thimble. "It is yours."

The five o'clock bell rang. Bobby Stone slumped in his desk chair, his tie undone and one hand on his chest. *I never would have believed such a stupid incident. . . . Oh, no that's too much, following me to my office!* But it was no vision this time; his eyes were wide open. She was sitting in the chair directly in front of him on the other side of his desk. "If you do not take it immediately," said the woman, "I will have to forbid you from taking it, and then you'll run after me to steal it from me. I'm telling you, you'll steal it from me." Bobby Stone, mad with fear, jumped up and ran towards the door. "Very well then," the woman cried out, "I forbid you to take my thimble!" Bobby Stone stopped short. Oh, what a fine thimble, such a fine beautiful thimble! Made out of plastic with tiny dimples in it. A fine thimble! He must have this thimble. Nothing else in the world existed outside of this pink and yellow thimble. He ran after the woman, who pretended to flee but was careful to lose ground all the while. . . .

Smack! And another! You bitch! So, you wanted to keep it all to yourself, did you? The thim-ble for you and nothing for me! This is for you. Some good kicks, you see, and the back of my hand, and a few with the knee. . . .

When he left the building his clothes were all mussed and there was some blood on his fingernails, but he had the thimble. It was his and no one—but no one, do you hear?—would ever be able to take it from him. He knew the secret of the thimble now.

5

Before she died the woman had whispered, "In the thimble . . . in the thimble . . . I have locked the universe."

When he awoke the next morning Bobby Stone remembered nothing. He found a pink and yellow thimble on his night-table. What an ugly thimble! He threw it in the garbage. But before he left for the office Bobby Stone tore a loose button from his overcoat. He found some thread and a needle and thought of the thimble at the bottom of the garbage pail. He went and got it. And so as not to prick himself while he sewed on his coat button, Bobby Stone pushed his little finger into the little thimble. He squashed the entire universe.   10

QUESTIONS

1.   Why does the story begin with a premonition of "catastrophe"? What is the catastrophe? To what degree is the narrative realistic or unrealistic?

2.   What does the woman say is the significance of the thimble? What does Bobby do with the thimble after he takes it from her? Might some other object have worked as well, for purposes of the story?

3.   Explain the story as an allegory of desire, denial, and the consequences of these emotions. What happens when Bobby puts his finger into the thimble? Is there a scientific basis for this happening, and if so, what is it? What is the allegorical meaning?

4.   What elements of "The Thimble" may be compared with Aesop's "The Fox and the Grapes"?

WRITING ABOUT SYMBOLISM OR ALLEGORY

To discover possible parallels that determine the presence of symbolism or allegory, consider the following questions.

Questions for Discovering Ideas

A. *SYMBOLISM*

- What cultural or universal symbols can you discover in names, objects, places, situations, or actions in a work (e.g., the character Faith, the woods, and the walking stick in "Yound Goodman Brown," the lumps of mud in "Unfinished Masterpieces," the bleakness of the weather in "The Chrysanthemums," or the straying young man in "The Parable of the Prodigal Son")?

- What contextual symbolism can be found in a work? What makes you think it is symbolic? What is being symbolized? How definite or direct is the symbolism? How systematically is it used? How necessary to the work is it? To what degree does it strengthen the work? How strongly does the work stand on its own without the reading for symbolism?

- Is it possible to make parallel lists to show how qualities of a particular symbol match the qualities of a character or an action? Here is such a list for the shepherd's home and the shepherds in Hardy's "The Three Strangers" (Chapter 3):

CIRCUMSTANCES OF THE SHEPHERD'S HOME	COMPARABLE QUALITIES IN THE SHEPHERDS AND THEIR LIVES
1. Remote	1. Unfamiliar with the outside world and the law
2. Solitary	2. Individualistic and resentful of outside interference
3. Weather-beaten	3. Adaptable and self-reliant
4. Humble	4. Poor
5. Providing an assembling place for guests	5. Hospitable

B. ALLEGORY

- How clearly does the author point you toward an allegorical reading (i.e., through names and allusions, consistency of narrative, literary context)?
- How consistent is the allegorical application? Does the entire work, or only a part, embody the allegory? On what basis do you draw these conclusions?
- How complete is the allegorical reading? How might the allegory yield to a diagram such as the following one on Hawthorne's "Young Goodman Brown," which shows how characters, actions, objects, and ideas correspond allegorically?

	Young Goodman Brown	Brown Himself	Citizens of the Village	The Forest Figure (Father), the Devil	Faith	The Forest Meeting	Retreat into suspicion and distrust
Allegorical Application to Morality and Faith	Potential for good	Culture and religious reinforcement	Forces of evil and deceit	Salvation and love; ideals to be rescued and preserved	Attack on ideals; incentive to disillusionment	Destruction of faith; doubt, spiritual negligence, loss of certainty, increase of gloom and suspicion
Allegorical Application to Personal and General Concerns	Individual in pursuit of goals	External support for personal strength and growth	Obstacles to overcome, or by which to be overcome	Personal involement, steadiness, happiness, religious conviction	Susceptibility to deceit, lack of conviction, misunderstanding, min-interpretation of others.	Failure, depression, discouragement, disappointment, bitterness.

C. OTHER FORMS

- What enables you to identify the story as a parable or fable? What lesson or moral is either clearly stated or implicit?

- What mythological identification is established in the work? What do you find in the story (names, situations, etc.) that enables you to determine its mythological significance? How is the myth to be understood? What symbolic value does the myth have? What current and timeless application does it have?

Strategies for Organizing Ideas

Relate the central idea of your essay to the meaning of the major symbols or allegorical thrust of the story. An idea about "Young Goodman Brown," for example, is that fanaticism darkens and limits the human soul. An early incident in the story provides symbolic support for this idea. Specifically, when Goodman Brown enters the woods, he resolves to "stand firm against the devil," and he then looks up toward "Heaven above him." As he looks, a "black mass of cloud" appears to hide the "brightening stars" (paragraph 45). Within the limits of our central idea, the cloud can be seen as a symbol, just like the widening path or the night walk itself. Look for ways to make solid connections like this when you designate something as a symbol or allegory.

Also, your essay will need to include justifications for your symbols or allegorical parallels. If you treat Montresor's vaults in Poe's "The Cask of Amontillado" (Chapter 11) as a symbol of deterioration and death, for example, it is important to draw attention to its skeletons and the increasingly stagnant air. These defects justify treating the vaults symbolically. In the same way, in describing the allegorical elements in "Young Goodman Brown," you need to establish a comprehensive statement such as the following: People lose ideals and forsake principles not because they are evil but because they misunderstand the people around them.

For the body of your essay, there are a number of strategies for discussing symbolism and allegory. You might use one exclusively or a combination.

SYMBOLISM.   If you want to write about symbolism, you might consider the following.

1. *The meaning of a major symbol.* Identify the symbol and what it stands for. Then answer questions such as these: Is the symbol cultural or contextual? How do you decide? How do you derive your interpretation of the symbolic meaning? What is the extent of the meaning? Does the symbol undergo modification or new applications if it reappears? How does the symbol affect your understanding of the story? Does the symbol bring out any ironies? How does the symbol add strength and depth to the story?

2. *The development and relationship of symbols.* For two or more symbols, consider issues such as these: How do the symbols connect with each other (like night and the cloud in "Young Goodman Brown" as symbols of a darkening mind)? What additional meanings do the symbols provide? (The windmill and the medicine in "A Worn Path" [Chapter 3], for example, are ironic because the windmill suggests cheer while the medicine suggests hopelessness.) Do the symbols control the form of the work? How? (For example, in Poe's "The Cask of Amontillado" the descent into the Montresor catacombs begins at dusk, and

the time lapse of the story suggests that the conclusion takes place in total darkness. At the beginning of Steinbeck's "The Chrysanthemums" the barren wintry countryside is compared to a "closed pot," and at the ending Elisa learns that the tinsmith has dumped the earth out of the pot which she had given to him as a gift. In a similar vein, Joyce's "Araby" [Chapter 10] begins with the "blind" or dead-end street and ends with the darkness of the closed bazaar.) Can these comparable objects and conditions be viewed symbolically in relationship to the development of the two stories? Other issues are whether the symbols fit naturally or artificially into the context of the story or whether and how the writer's symbols create unique quality or excellence.

ALLEGORY.   When writing about allegory, you might use one of the following approaches.

1. *The application and meaning of the allegory.* What is the subject of the story (allegory, fable, parable, myth)? How can it be more generally applied to ideas or to qualities of human character, not only of its own time but also of our own? What other versions of the story do you know, if any? Does it illustrate, either closely or loosely, particular philosophies or religious views? If so, what are these? How do you know?

2. *The consistency of the allegory.* Is the allegory used consistently throughout the story, or is it used intermittently? Explain and illustrate this use. Would it be correct to call your story *allegorical* rather than an *allegory*? Can you determine how parts of the story are introduced for their allegorical importance? Examples are the increasingly dark pathway home in Bierce's "An Occurrence at Owl Creek Bridge" (Chapter 5) and the frozen preserves in Glaspell's "A Jury of Her Peers" (Chapter 4), which are allegorical equivalents of life's destructive difficulties, and the Paris street in Maupassant's "The Necklace" (Chapter 1), which corresponds to the temptation to live beyond one's means.

In concluding, you might summarize main points, describe general impressions, explain the impact of the symbolic or allegorical methods, indicate personal responses, or suggest further lines of thought and application. You might also assess the quality and appropriateness of the symbolism or allegory (such as Hawthorne's "Young Goodman Brown" opening in darkness and closing in gloom).

DEMONSTRATIVE STUDENT ESSAY

Allegory and Symbolism in Hawthorne's "Young Goodman Brown"°

[1]   It is hard to read beyond the third paragraph of Nathaniel Hawthorne's "Young Goodman Brown" without recognizing the story's allegory and symbolism.

° See pp. 436-47 for this story.

The opening at first seems realistic. Goodman Brown, a young Puritan, leaves his home in colonial Salem to take an overnight trip. His wife's name, "Faith," however, suggests a symbolic reading, and as soon as Brown goes into the forest, his ordinary walk changes into an allegorical trip into evil. The idea that Hawthorne shows by this trip is that rigid belief destroys even the best human qualities.* He develops this thought in the allegory and in many symbols, particularly the sunset, the walking stick, and the path.†

[2] The allegory of the story concerns the ways in which people develop destructive ideas. Most of the story is dreamlike and unreal, and the ideas that Brown gains are also unreal. At the weird "witch meeting," he concludes that everyone he knows is sinful. He then permits mistrust and loathing to distort his previous love for his wife and neighbors, and he becomes harsh and gloomy forever after. The location of the story in colonial Salem indicates that Hawthorne's allegorical target is the zealous pursuit of religious principles that exclude love while dwelling on sinfulness. However, modern readers can also apply the allegory to the ways in which people blindly follow *any* ideal (most often political loyalties or racial or national prejudices) and thereby reject the integrity and rights of others. Through such blind obedience, they never try to understand those they condemn. In this way, Hawthorne's allegory applies to any narrow-minded acceptance of ideals or systems that exclude the importance of love, understanding, and tolerance.

[3] Hawthorne's attack on such dehumanizing belief is found not just in the allegory but also in his many symbols. For example, because of the nature of the story, the word "sunset," the seventh word, stands out as a symbol. In reality, sunset merely indicates the end of day, but at the story's beginning it suggests that Goodman Brown is about to start his long night of hatred, his spiritual death. For him the night will never end because his final days are shrouded in "gloom" (paragraph 72).

Equally symbolic is the guide's walking stick or staff, which points out the arbitrariness of the standard by which Brown judges his neighbors. Hawthorne's description of the staff invites us to consider it a symbol:

[4]
> . . . the only thing about him [the guide] that could be fixed upon as remarkable, was his staff, which bore the likeness of a great black snake, so curiously wrought, that it might almost be seen to twist and wriggle itself like a living serpent. This, of course, must have been an ocular deception, assisted by the uncertain light. (paragraph 13)

The serpent suggests Satan, who in Genesis (3:1-7) is the originator of all evil, but the phrase "ocular deception" creates an interesting and realistic ambiguity about the symbol. Since the perception of the snake may depend on nothing more than the "uncertain" light, the staff may be less symbolic of evil than of the tendency to find evil where it does not exist (and could the uncertain light symbolize the uncertainty of human understanding?).

---

* Central idea.
† Thesis sentence.

[5]

In the same vein, the path through the forest is a major symbol of the destructive mental confusion that overcomes Brown. As he follows the path it grows "wilder and drearier, and more faintly traced," and "at length" it vanishes (paragraph 51). This is like the biblical description of the "broad" way that leads "to Destruction" (Matthew 7:13). As a symbol, the path implies that most human acts are bad, and only a small number, like the "narrow" way to life (Matthew 7:14), are good. Goodman Brown's path at first seems clear, as though sin is a part of everyday life, indistinguishable from all the other choices that people make. Soon, however, the path is so indistinct that Brown can find only sin wherever he turns. The symbol suggests that when people follow evil, their moral vision becomes blurred and they soon fall prey to "the instinct that guides mortal man to evil" (paragraph 51).

[6]

Through Hawthorne's allegory and symbols, "Young Goodman Brown" presents the paradox of how noble beliefs can backfire. Goodman Brown dies in gloom because he believes that his wrong vision is true. This form of evil is the hardest to stop, because wrongdoers who are convinced of their own goodness are beyond reach. In view of such self-righteous evil, whether cloaked in the apparent virtues of Puritanism or of some other blindly rigorous doctrine (political as well as religious), Hawthorne writes that "the fiend in his own shape is less hideous than when he rages in the breast of man" (paragraph 53). Young Goodman Brown thus is the central symbol of the story. He is one of those who think they walk in light but who really create their own darkness.

Commentary on the Essay

The introduction presents the argument that a treatment of allegory and symbolism are justified because Hawthorne early in the story invites such a reading. The central idea relates Hawthorne's method to the idea that rigid belief destroys the best human qualities.

Paragraph 2 considers the allegory as a criticism of rigid Puritan morality. The major thread running through the paragraph is the hurtful effect of monomaniacal views like those of Brown. Paragraphs 3, 4, and 5 deal with three major symbols: sunset, the staff, and the path. The argument of this discussion is to show how the symbols apply to Hawthorne's attack on unquestioning belief. Throughout these three paragraphs, the central idea—the relationship of rigidity to destructiveness—is stressed. Hawthorne's allusions to both the Old and New Testaments are pointed out in paragraphs 4 and 5. The last paragraph builds to the conclusion that Brown symbolizes the idea that the primary cause of evil is the inability to separate reality from unreality.

If you write exclusively about allegory, you can use paragraph 2 of the demonstrative student essay as a guide for either a single paragraph or, when expanded, an entire essay. If the allegory of "Young Goodman Brown," for example, were to be expanded, additional topics might be Brown's gullibility, the meaning of faith and the requirements for maintaining it, and the causes for preferring to think evil rather than good of other people. Such points are sufficiently important to sustain an entire essay on the topic of allegory.

SPECIAL TOPICS FOR WRITING AND ARGUMENT ABOUT SYMBOLISM AND ALLEGORY

1. Compare and contrast the symbolism in Steinbeck's "The Chrysanthemums," Tremblay's "The Thimble," and Munro's "The Found Boat" (Chapter 7). To what degree do the stories rely on contextual symbols? On universal symbols? On the basis of your comparison, what is the case for asserting that realism and fantasy are directly related to the nature of the symbolism employed by the writer? (Consult Chapter 35 for a discussion of comparison and contrast essays.)

2. Why do writers who advocate moral, philosophical, or religious issues frequently use symbolism or allegory? In treating this question, you might introduce references from "The Parable of the Prodigal Son," Tremblay's "The Thimble," and Hawthorne's "Young Goodman Brown."

3. Write an essay on the allegorical method of one or more of the allegories included in the Gospel of St. Luke, such as "The Bridegroom" (5:34–35), "The Garments and the Wineskins" (5:36–39), "The Sower" (8:4–15), "The Good Samaritan" (10:25–37), "The Prodigal Son" (15:11–32), "The Ox in the Well" (14:5–6), "The Watering of Animals on the Sabbath" (13:15–17), "The Rich Fool" (12:16–21), "Lazarus" (16:19–31), "The Widow and the Judge" (18:1–8), and "The Pharisee and the Publican" (18:9–14).

4. Consider the story of Atalanta, first as a myth about male dominance in man-woman relationships and second as a myth about the obstacles to a woman's freedom and independence.

5. Write your own brief story using a widely recognized cultural symbol such as the flag (patriotism, love of country, a certain type of politics), water (life, sexuality, regeneration), or the population explosion (the end of life on earth). By arranging actions and dialogue, make clear the issues conveyed by your symbol, and also try to resolve conflicts the symbol might raise among your characters.

6. Write a brief story in which you develop your own contextual symbol. You might, for example, demonstrate how holding a job brings out character strengths that are not at first apparent or how neglecting to care for the inside or outside of a house indicates a character's decline. The principle is to take something that may at first seem normal and ordinary, then to make that thing symbolic as you develop your story.

7. Using the card or computer catalogue of your library, discover a recent critical-biographical book or books about Hawthorne. Explain what the book says about Hawthorne's uses of symbolism. To what extent does the book relate Hawthorne's symbolism to his religious and family heritage?

10

Idea or Theme:
The Meaning and the
Message in Fiction

The word **idea** refers to the result or results of general and abstract thinking. Synonymous words are *concept, thought, opinion,* and *principle.* In literary study the consideration of ideas relates to *meaning, interpretation, explanation,* and *significance.* Although ideas are usually extensive and complex, separate ideas may be named by single words, such as *right, good, love, piety, causation, wilderness,* and, not surprisingly, *idea* itself.

IDEAS AND ASSERTIONS

Although single words alone may name ideas, we must put these words into operation in *sentences* or *assertions* before they can advance our understanding. Good operational sentences about ideas are not the same as ordinary conversational statements such as "It's a nice day." An observation of this sort may be true (depending on the weather), but it gives us no ideas and does not stimulate our minds. Rather, a sentence asserting an idea should initiate a thought or argument about the day's quality, such as "A nice day requires light breezes, blue sky, a warm sun, and relaxation." Because this sentence makes an assertion about the word "nice," it allows us to consider and develop the idea of a nice day.

In studying literature, always express ideas as assertions. For example, you might state that an idea in Lawrence's "The Horse Dealer's Daughter" is "love," but it would be difficult to discuss anything more unless you make an assertion promising an argument such as "This story demonstrates the idea that love is irresistible and irrational." This assertion would lead you to explain the unlikely love that bursts out in the story. Similarly, for Welty's "A Worn Path" (Chapter 3) an assertion like the following would advance further argument: "Phoenix embodies the idea that caring for others gives no reward but the continuation of the duty itself."

Pablo Picasso, *Guernica*, 1937. Centro de Arte Reina Sofía, Madrid, Spain. Giraudon/Art Resource. © 1998 Estate of Pablo Picasso/Artists Rights Society (ARS), New York, NY.

Although we have noted only one idea in these two works, most stories contain many ideas. When one of the ideas seems to be the major one, it is called the **theme.** In practice, the words *theme* and *major idea* are the same.

IDEAS AND VALUES

Literature embodies **values** along with ideas. *Value,* of course, commonly refers to the price of something, but in the realm of ideas and principles, it is a standard of what is desired, sought, esteemed, and treasured. For example, *democracy* refers to our political system, but it is also a complex idea of representative government that we esteem most highly, and so also do we esteem concepts like honor, cooperation, generosity, and love. A vital idea/value is *justice,* which, put most simply, involves equality before the law and also the fair evaluation of conduct that is deemed unacceptable or illegal. Such an idea of justice is a major topic of Glaspell's "A Jury of Her Peers" (Chapter 4). Glaspell dramatizes the story of a farm wife who, for twenty years, endures her husband's intimidation and her abject circumstances of life, but finally rises up to strangle her husband in his sleep. By a rigid concept of justice as guilt-conviction-punishment, the wife, Minnie Wright, is guilty and should be convicted and punished. But justice as an idea also involves a full and fair consideration of the circumstances and motivation of wrongdoing, and it is such a consideration that the two women in the story make during their examination of Minnie's kitchen. Many of their speeches showing their sympathy to Minnie are equivalent to a jurylike deliberation. Their final decision is like a verdict, and their final covering up of Minnie's crime is evidence for their idea that justice, to be most highly valued, should be tempered with understanding—even if they do not use these exact words in their discussions of Minnie's situation. In short, the idea of justice underlying Glaspell's "A Jury of Her Peers" also involves a deeply felt value.

A graphic connection of ideas and values may be seen in Picasso's massive painting *Guernica* (p. 464). The painting superbly illustrates the agony of Guernica, the Spanish town bombed by Nazi planes in 1937. The agonized horse and the screaming man, the disembodied head and arms, the mother holding her dead infant—all convey the idea that war is an unspeakable crime against humanity. Picasso's condemnation of war and the man responsible for the slaughter at Guernica, Francisco Franco, is also clear. That Picasso wanted his values to be understood is confirmed by his instruction that the painting was not to be displayed in Spain until after Franco died.

THE PLACE OF IDEAS IN LITERATURE

Because writers of poems, plays, and stories are usually not systematic philosophers, it is not appropriate to go "message hunting" as though their works contained nothing but ideas. Indeed, there is great benefit and pleasure to be derived from just savoring a work—following the patterns of narrative and conflict, getting to like the characters, understanding the work's implications and suggestions, and listening to the sounds of the author's words—to name only a few of the reasons for which literature is treasured.

Nevertheless, ideas are vital to understanding and appreciating literature: Writers have ideas and want to communicate them. For example, in "The Horse Dealer's Daughter" Lawrence tells us about two unlikely characters who fall suddenly and unpredictably in love. This love is unusual, and the story is therefore effective, but the story is also provocative because it raises the idea that love pushes aside other decisions that people make. Gaines in "The Sky Is Gray" describes the extraordinary difficulty and pain experienced by a young child and his mother when trying to keep a dental appointment, but the story embodies *ideas* about the need for equality, the strength of human character, and the beauty of human kindness.

Distinguish between Ideas and Actions

As you analyze works for ideas, it is important to avoid the trap of confusing ideas and actions. Such a trap is contained in the following sentence about O'Connor's "First Confession" (Chapter 7): "The major character, Jackie, misbehaves at home and tries to stab his sister with a bread knife." This sentence successfully describes a major action in the story, but it does not express an *idea* that connects characters and events, and for this reason it obstructs understanding. Some possible connections might be achieved with sentences like these: "'First Confession' illustrates the idea that family life sometimes produces anger and potential violence" or "'First Confession' shows that compelling children to accept authority may produce effects that are the opposite of adult intentions." A study based on these connecting formulations could be focused on ideas and would not be sidetracked into doing no more than retelling O'Connor's story.

Distinguish between Ideas and Situations

You should also distinguish between ideas and situations. For example, in Joyce's "Araby," the narrator describes his frustration and embarrassment at the "Araby" bazaar in Dublin. This is a *situation,* but it is not the *idea* brought out by the situation. Joyce's idea here is rather that immature love causes unreal dreams and hopes that result in disappointment and self-reproach. If you are able to distinguish a story's various situations from the writer's major idea or ideas, as we have done here, you will be able to focus on ideas and therefore sharpen your own thinking.

HOW TO FIND IDEAS

Ideas are not as obvious as characters or setting. To determine an idea, you need to consider the meaning of what you read and then to develop explanatory and comprehensive assertions. Your assertions need not be the same as those that others might make. People notice different things, and individual formulations vary. In Chopin's "The Story of an Hour" (Chapter 8), for example, an initial expression of some of the story's ideas might take any of the following forms: (1) Partners in even a good marriage may have ambivalent feelings about their married life. (2) An accident may bring out negative but previously unrecognized thoughts in a woman. (3) Even those closest to a person may never realize that person's innermost feelings. Although any one of these choices could be a basic idea for studying "The Story of an Hour," they all have in common the main character's surprising feelings of release when she is told that her husband has been killed. In discovering ideas, you should follow a similar process—making a number of formulations for an idea and then selecting one for further development.

As you read, be alert to the different ways in which authors convey ideas. One author might prefer an indirect way through a character's speeches, whereas another may prefer direct statement. In practice, authors may employ any or all the following methods.

1. STUDY THE AUTHORIAL VOICE.   Although authors mainly render action, dialogue, and situation, they sometimes state ideas to guide us and deepen our understanding. In the second paragraph of Maupassant's "The Necklace" (Chapter 1), for example, the authorial voice presents the idea that women have only charm and beauty to get on in the world. Ironically, Maupassant uses the story to show that for the major character Mathilde, nothing is effective, for her charm cannot prevent disaster. Hawthorne, in "Young Goodman Brown" (Chapter 9), expresses this powerful idea: "The fiend in his own shape is less hideous than when he rages in the breast of man" (paragraph 53). This statement is made as authorial commentary just when the major character, Goodman Brown, is speeding through "the benighted wilderness" on his way to the satanic meeting. Although the idea is complex and will bear extensive discussion, its essential aspect is that the causes of evil originate within human beings themselves, with the implication that we alone are responsible for all our actions, whether good or evil.

2. STUDY THE FIRST-PERSON SPEAKER.   First-person narrators or speakers frequently express ideas along with their depiction of actions and situations, and they also make statements from which you can make inferences about ideas. (See also Chapter 5.) Because what they say is part of a dramatic presentation, they may be right or wrong, well considered or thoughtless, good or bad, or brilliant or half-baked, depending on the speaker. The narrator of Atwood's "Rape Fantasies" (Chapter 8), for example, is not noteworthy for her intelligence, yet she voices penetrating ideas about the relationships of men and women. In Zabytko's "Home Soil" the narrator considers the idea that war always causes regret and guilt, no matter when it is fought or who fights in it. A somewhat half-baked speaker, but yet an interesting one, is Sammy, the narrator of Updike's "A & P" (Chapter 7), who seems engulfed in intellectual commonplaces, particularly in his insinuation about the intelligence of women (paragraph 2). In his defense, however, Sammy *acts* on the worthy idea that people generally have the freedom and right to wear any clothes they please. If the speaker possesses a dubious character, such as the narrator Montresor of Poe's "The Cask of Amontillado" (Chapter 11), you may nevertheless still study and evaluate such a speaker's ideas. Montresor, for example, begins his narrative by describing his idea of personal revenge—an unpleasant idea, but an idea just the same.

3. STUDY THE STATEMENTS MADE BY CHARACTERS.   In many stories, characters express their own views, which may be right or wrong, admirable or contemptible. When you consider such dramatic speeches, you must do considerable interpreting and evaluating yourself. For example, Old Man Warner in "The Lottery" (Chapter 5) states that the lottery is valuable even though we learn from the narrator that the beliefs underlying it have long been forgotten. Because Warner is a zealous and noisy person, however, his words show that outdated ideas continue to do harm even when there is strong reason to throw them out and adopt new ones. The unnamed young man in the dentist's office in "The Sky Is Gray" speaks in contradictions, but when he amplifies them we learn a number of his ideas about the failure of America to live up to its professed principles of equality. The men in Glaspell's "A Jury of Her Peers" (Chapter 4) express conventional masculine ideas about the need for men to control women. The story itself, however, demonstrates the shortcomings and pomposity of their thought.

4. STUDY THE WORK'S FIGURATIVE LANGUAGE.   Figurative language is one of the major components of poetry, but it also abounds in prose fiction (see also Chapter 17). In Joyce's "Araby," for example, the narrator uses a beautiful figure of speech to describe his youthful admiration for his friend's sister. He says that his body "was like a harp and her words and gestures were like fingers running upon the wires." Another notable figure occurs in Glaspell's "A Jury of Her Peers" (Chapter 4), when a character compares John Wright, the murdered husband, with "a raw wind that gets to the bone" (paragraph 201). With this figurative language, Glaspell conveys the idea that bluntness, indifference, and cruelty create great personal damage.

5. STUDY HOW CHARACTERS MAY STAND FOR IDEAS.   Characters and their actions may often be equated with certain ideas and values. The power of Mathilde's story in Maupassant's "The Necklace," (Chapter 1), for example, enables us to explain that she represents the idea that unrealizable dreams may invade and damage the real world. Two diverse or opposed characters may embody contrasting ideas, as with Louise and Josephine of Chopin's "The Story of an Hour." (Chapter 8). Each woman may be taken to represent differing views about the role of women in marriage. In effect, characters who stand for ideas may assume symbolic status, as in Hawthorne's "Young Goodman Brown," (Chapter 9), where the protagonist symbolizes the alienation accompanying zealousness, or in Ozick's "The Shawl" (Chapter 6), where the small child Magda embodies the vulnerability and helplessness of human beings in the face of dehumanizing state brutality. Such characters may be equated directly with particular ideas, and to talk about them is a shorthand way of talking about the ideas.

6. STUDY THE WORK ITSELF AS AN EMBODIMENT OF IDEAS. One of the most important ways in which authors express ideas is to interlock them within all parts and aspects of the work. The art of painting is instructive here, for a painting can be taken in with a single view that comprehends all the aspects of color, form, action, and expression, which can also be considered separately. Thus, the broken and distorted figures in Picasso's Guernica (p. 464), which can be viewed together, all emphasize the idea that war creates unspeakable horror and suffering for both human beings and animals. In the same way, when a work is considered in its totality, the various parts collectively may embody major ideas, as in Gaines's "The Sky Is Gray," where Gaines dramatizes the urgency of ending racial barriers. He does not use these exact words, but the story powerfully embodies this idea. The third section of Bierce's "An Occurrence at Owl Creek Bridge" (Chapter 5) is based on the idea that under great stress, the human mind operates with lightning speed. Most works represent ideas in a similar way. Even "escape literature," which ostensibly enables readers to forget immediate problems, contains conflicts between good and evil, love and hate, good spies and bad, earthlings and aliens, and so on. Thereby, such works *do* embody ideas, even though their avowed intention is not to make readers think but rather to help them forget.

❧ STORIES FOR STUDY

TONI CADE BAMBARA   (1939–1995)

Bambara (an African tribal name that Toni Cade appropriated from an old manuscript) was brought up in Harlem and Bedford Stuyvesant in New York. She received a B.A. from Queens College and an M.A. in American Studies from the City College of New York. For a time she was a social worker, and later she taught at many schools, including Rutgers, Duke, and the Scribe Video Center in Philadelphia. She also collaborated in the writing of television documentaries, including a life of W. E. B. DuBois. In her fiction she treats the subjects of the black and also the female experience. She avoids using this material for political purposes, however, even though the subjects could easily fall within the political realm. Instead, she deals with her characters on the human level, trying to offer her readers "nourishment." Story Collections are Gorilla, My Love *(1972), from which "The Lesson" is taken, and* The Sea Birds Are Still Alive *(1977). Her novels are* The Salt Eaters *(1980) and* If Blessing Comes *(1987).*

The Lesson ———————————————————————————— *1972*

Back in the days when everyone was old and stupid or young and foolish and me and Sugar were the only ones just right, this lady moved on our block with nappy hair and proper speech and no makeup. And quite naturally we laughed at her, laughed the way we did at the junk man who went about his business like he was some big-time president and his sorry-ass horse his secretary. And we kinda hated her too, hated the way we did the winos who cluttered up our parks and pissed on our handball walls and stank up our hallways and stairs so you couldn't halfway play hide-and-seek without a goddamn gas mask. Miss Moore was her name. The only woman on the block with no first name. And she was black as hell, cept for her feet, which were fish-white and spooky. And she was always planning these boring-ass things for us to do, us being my cousin, mostly, who lived on the block cause we all moved North the same time and to the same apartment then spread out gradual to breathe. And our parents would yank our heads into some kinda shape and crisp up our clothes so we'd be presentable for travel with Miss Moore, who always looked like she was going to church, though she never did. Which is just one of the things the grownups talked about when they talked behind her back like a dog. But when she came calling with some sachet she'd sewed up or some gingerbread she'd made or some book, why then they'd all be too embarrassed to turn her down and we'd get handed over all spruced up. She'd been to college and said it was only right that she should take responsibility for the young ones education, and she not even related by marriage or blood. So they'd go for it. Specially Aunt Gretchen. She was the main gofer in the family. You got some ole dumb shit foolishness you want somebody to go for, you send for Aunt Gretchen. She been screwed into the go-along for so long, it's a blood-deep natural thing with her. Which is how she got saddled with me and Sugar and Junior in the first place while our mothers were in a la-de-da apartment up the block having a good ole time.

So this one day Miss Moore rounds us all up at the mailbox and it's purdee° hot and she's knockin herself out about arithmetic. And school suppose to let up in summer I heard, but she don't never let up. And the starch in my pinafore scratching the shit outta me and I'm really hating this nappy-head bitch and her goddamn college degree. I'd much rather go to the pool or to the show where it's cool. So me and Sugar leaning on the mailbox being surly, which is a Miss Moore word. And Flyboy checking out what

---

purdee: pretty.

everybody brought for lunch. And Fat Butt already wasting his peanut-butter-and-jelly sandwich like the pig he is. And Junebug punchin on Q.T.'s arm for potato chips. And Rosie Giraffe shifting from one hip to the other waiting for somebody to step on her foot or ask her if she from Georgia so she can kick ass, preferably Mercedes'. And Miss Moore asking us do we know what money is, like we a bunch of retards. I mean real money, she say, like it's only poker chips or Monopoly papers we lay on the grocer. So right away I'm tired of this and say so. And would much rather snatch Sugar and go to the Sunset and terrorize the West Indian kids and take their hair ribbons and their money too. And Miss Moore files that remark away for next week's lesson on brother-hood, I can tell. And finally I say we oughta get to the subway cause it's cooler and besides we might meet some cute boys. Sugar done swiped her mama's lipstick, so we ready.

So we heading down the street and she's boring us silly about what things cost and what our parents make and how much goes for rent and how money ain't divided up right in this country. And then she gets to the part about we all poor and live in the slums, which I don't feature. And I'm ready to speak on that, but she steps out in the street and hails two cabs just like that. Then she hustles half the crew in with her and hands me a five-dollar bill and tells me to calculate 10 percent tip for the driver. And we're off. Me and Sugar and Junebug and Flyboy hangin out the window and hollering to everybody, putting lipstick on each other cause Flyboy a faggot anyway, and making farts with our sweaty armpits. But I'm mostly trying to figure how to spend this money. But they all fascinated with the meter ticking and Junebug starts laying bets as to how much it'll read when Flyboy can't hold his breath no more. Then Sugar lays bets as to how much it'll be when we get there. So I'm stuck. Don't nobody want to go for my plan, which is to jump out at the next light and run off to the first bar-b-que we can find. Then the driver tells us to get the hell out cause we there already. And the meter reads eighty-five cents. And I'm stalling to figure out the tip and Sugar say give him a dime. And I decide he don't need it bad as I do, so later for him. But then he tries to take off with Junebug foot still in the door so we talk about his mama something ferocious. Then we check out that we on Fifth Avenue and everybody dressed up in stockings. One lady in a fur coat, hot as it is. White folks crazy.

"This is the place," Miss Moore say, presenting it to us in the voice she uses at the museum. "Let's look in the windows before we go in."

"Can we steal?" Sugar asks very serious like she's getting the ground rules squared 5
away before she plays. "I beg your pardon," say Miss Moore, and we fall out. So she leads us around the windows of the toy store and me and Sugar screamin, "This is mine, that's mine, I gotta have that, that was made for me, I was born for that," till Big Butt drowns us out.

"Hey, I'm going to buy that there."

"That there? You don't even know what it is, stupid."

"I do so," he say punchin on Rosie Giraffe. "It's a microscope."

"Whatcha gonna do with a microscope, fool?"

"Look at things." 10

"Like what, Ronald?" ask Miss Moore. And Big Butt ain't got the first notion. So here go Miss Moore gabbing about the thousands of bacteria in a drop of water and the somethinorother in a speck of blood and the million and one living things in the air around us is invisible to the naked eye. And what she say that for? Junebug go to town on that "naked" and we rolling. Then Miss Moore ask what it cost. So we all jam into the window smudgin it up and the price tag say $300. So then she ask how long'd take for

Big Butt and Junebug to save up their allowances. "Too long," I say. "Yeh," adds Sugar, "outgrown it by that time." And Miss Moore say no, you never outgrow learning instruments. "Why, even medical students and interns and," blah, blah, blah. And we ready to choke Big Butt for bringing it up in the first damn place.

"This here costs four hundred eighty dollars," say Rosie Giraffe. So we pile up all over her to see what she pointin out. My eyes tell me it's a chunk of glass cracked with something heavy, and different-color inks dripped into the splits, then the whole thing put into a oven or something. But for $480 it don't make sense.

"That's a paperweight made of semi-precious stones fused together under tremendous pressure," she explains slowly, with her hands doing the mining and all the factory work.

"So what's a paperweight?" asks Rosie Giraffe.

"To weigh paper with, dumbbell," say Flyboy, the wise man from the East.

"Not exactly," say Miss Moore, which is what she say when you warm or way off too. "It's to weigh paper down so it won't scatter and make your desk untidy." So right away me and Sugar curtsy to each other and then to Mercedes who is more the tidy type.

"We don't keep paper on top of the desk in my class," say Junebug, figuring Miss Moore crazy or lyin one.

"At home, then," she say. "Don't you have a calendar and a pencil case and a blotter and a letter-opener on your desk at home where you do your homework?" And she know damn well what our homes look like cause she nosys around in them every chance she gets.

"I don't even have a desk," say Junebug. "Do we?"

"No. And I don't get no homework neither," says Big Butt.

"And I don't even have a home," say Flyboy like he do at school to keep the white folks off his back and sorry for him. Send this poor kid to camp posters, is his specialty.

"I do," says Mercedes. "I have a box of stationery on my desk and a picture of my cat. My godmother bought the stationery and the desk. There's a big rose on each sheet and the envelopes smell like roses."

"Who wants to know about your smelly-ass stationery," say Rosie Giraffe fore I can get my two cents in.

"It's important to have a work area all your own so that. . . ."

"Will you look at this sailboat, please," say Flyboy, cuttin her off and pointin to the thing like it was his. So once again we tumble all over each other to gaze at this magnificent thing in the toy store which is just big enough to maybe sail two kittens across the pond if you strap them to the posts tight. We all start reciting the price tag like we in assembly. "Handcrafted sailboat of fiberglass at one thousand one hundred ninety-five dollars."

"Unbelievable," I hear myself say and am really stunned. I read it again for myself just in case the group recitation put me in a trance. Same thing. For some reason this pisses me off. We look at Miss Moore and she lookin at us, waiting for I dunno what.

"Who'd pay all that when you can buy a sailboat set for a quarter at Pop's, a tube of glue for a dime, and a ball of string for eight cents? It must have a motor and a whole lot else besides," I say. "My sailboat cost me about fifty cents."

"But will it take water?" say Mercedes with her smart ass.

"Took mine to Alley Pond Park once," say Flyboy. "String broke. Lost it. Pity."

"Sailed mine in Central Park and it keeled over and sank. Had to ask my father for   30
another dollar."

"And you got the strap," laugh Big Butt. "The jerk didn't even have a string on it.
My old man wailed on his behind."

Little Q.T. was staring hard at the sailboat and you could see he wanted it bad.
But he too little and somebodyd just take it from him. So what the hell. "This boat for
kids, Miss Moore?"

"Parents silly to buy something like that just to get all broke up," say Rosie Giraffe.

"That much money it should last forever," I figure.

"My father'd buy it for me if I wanted it."   35

"Your father, my ass," say Rosie Giraffe getting a chance to finally push Mercedes.

"Must be rich people shop here," say Q.T

"You are a very bright boy," say Flyboy. "What was your first clue?" And he rap him
on the head with the back of his knuckles, since Q.T. the only one he could get away
with. Though Q.T. liable to come up behind you years later and get his licks in when
you half expect it.

"What I want to know is," I says to Miss Moore though I never talk to her, I wouldn't
give the bitch that satisfaction, "is how much a real boat costs? I figure a thousand'd get
you a yacht any day."

"Why don't you check that out," she says, "and report back to the group?" Which   40
really pains my ass. If you gonna mess up a perfectly good swim day least you could do is
have some answers. "Let's go in," she say like she something up her sleeve. Only she
don't lead the way. So me and Sugar turn the corner to where the entrance is, but when
we get there I kinda hang back. Not that I'm scared, what's there to be afraid of, just a
toy store. But I feel funny, shame. But what I got to be shamed about? Got as much right
to go in as anybody. But somehow I can't seem to get hold of the door, so I step away
from Sugar to lead. But she hangs back too. And I look at her and she looks at me and
this is ridiculous. I mean, damn, I have never ever been shy about doing nothing or
going nowhere. But then Mercedes steps up and then Rosie Giraffe and Big Butt crowd
in behind and shove, and next thing we all stuffed into the doorway with only Mercedes
squeezing past us, smoothing out her jumper and walking right down the aisle. Then
the rest of us tumble in like a glued-together jigsaw done all wrong. And people lookin at
us. And it's like the time me and Sugar crashed into the Catholic church on a dare. But
once we got in there and everything so hushed and holy and the candles and the bowin
and the handkerchiefs on all the drooping heads, I just couldn't go through with the
plan. Which was for me to run up to the altar and do a tap dance while Sugar played the
nose flute and messed around in the holy water. And Sugar kept givin me the elbow.
Then later teased me so bad I tied her up in the shower and turned it on and locked her
in. And she'd be there till this day if Aunt Gretchen hadn't finally figured I was lyin
about the boarder takin a shower.

Same thing in the store. We all walkin on tiptoe and hardly touchin the games
and puzzles and things. And I watched Miss Moore who is steady watchin us like she
waitin for a sign. Like Mama Drewery watches the sky and sniffs the air and takes note of
just how much slant is in the bird formation. Then me and Sugar bump smack into each
other, so busy gazing at the toys, 'specially the sailboat. But we don't laugh and go into
our fat-lady bump-stomach routine. We just stare at that price tag. Then Sugar run a
finger over the whole boat. And I'm jealous and want to hit her. Maybe not her, but I
sure want to punch somebody in the mouth.

"Whatcha bring us here for, Miss Moore?"

"You sound angry, Sylvia. Are you mad about something?" Givin me one of them grins like she tellin a grown-up joke that never turns out to be funny. And she's lookin very closely at me like maybe she plannin to do my portrait from memory. I'm mad, but I won't give her that satisfaction. So I slouch around the store bein very bored and say, "Let's go."

Me and Sugar at the back of the train watchin the tracks whizzin by large then small then gettin gobbled up in the dark. I'm thinking about this tricky toy I saw in the store. A clown that somersaults on a bar then does chin-ups just cause you yank lightly at his leg. Cost $35. I could see me askin my mother for a $35 birthday clown. "You wanna who that costs what?" she'd say, cocking her head to the side to get a better view of the hole in my head. Thirty-five dollars could buy new bunk beds for Junior and Gretchen's boy. Thirty-five dollars and the whole household could go visit Granddaddy Nelson in the country. Thirty-five dollars would pay for the rent and the piano bill too. Who are these people that spend that much for performing clowns and $1000 for toy sailboats? What kinda work they do and how they live and how come we ain't in on it? Where we are is who we are. Miss Moore always pointin out. But it don't necessarily have to be that way, she always adds then waits for somebody to say that poor people have to wake up and demand their share of the pie and don't none of us know what kind of pie she talking about in the first damn place. But she ain't so smart cause I still got her four dollars from the taxi and she sure ain't gettin it. Messin up my day with this shit. Sugar nudges me in my pocket and winks.

Miss Moore lines us up in front of the mailbox where we started from, seem like   45
years ago, and I got a headache for thinkin so hard. And we lean all over each other so we can hold up under the draggy-ass lecture she always finishes us off with at the end before we thank her for borin us to tears. But she just looks at us like she readin tea leaves. Finally she say, "Well, what did you think of F. A. O. Schwarz?"

Rosie Giraffe mumbles, "White folks crazy."

"I'd like to go there again when I get my birthday money," says Mercedes, and we shove her out the pack so she has to lean on the mailbox by herself.

"I'd like a shower. Tiring day," say Flyboy.

Then Sugar surprises me by sayin, "You know, Miss Moore, I don't think all of us here put together eat in a year what that sailboat costs." And Miss Moore lights up like somebody goosed her. "And?" she say, urging Sugar on. Only I'm standin on her foot so she don't continue.

"Imagine for a minute what kind of society it is in which some people can spend   5
on a toy what it would cost to feed a family of six or seven. What do you think?"

"I think," say Sugar pushing me off her feet like she never done before, cause I whip her ass in a minute, "that this is not much of a democracy if you ask me. Equal chance to pursue happiness means an equal crack at the dough, don't it?" Miss Moore is besides herself and I am disgusted with Sugar's treachery. So I stand on her foot one more time to see if she'll shove me. She shuts up, and Miss Moore looks at me, sorrow-fully I'm thinkin. And somethin weird is goin on, I can feel it in my chest.

"Anybody else learn anything today?" lookin dead at me. I walk away and Sugar has to run to catch up and don't even seem to notice when I shrug her arm off my shoulder.

"Well, we got four dollars anyway," she says.

"Uh hunh."

"We could go to Hascombs and get half a chocolate layer and then go to the   55
Sunset and still have plenty money for potato chips and ice cream sodas."

"Uh hunh."

"Race you to Hascombs," she say.

We start down the block and she gets ahead which is O.K. by me cause I'm going
to the West End and then over to the Drive to think this day through. She can run if
she want to and even run faster. But ain't nobody gonna beat me at nuthin.

QUESTIONS

1. Who is Miss Moore? Why does she take an interest in the neighborhood chil-
    dren? Where does she take them? How does she attempt to teach them?

2. Describe Sylvia, the narrator, as a character. Why does she keep $4 of the five-
    dollar bill given her by Miss Moore? What does she mean by "ain't nobody
    gonna beat me at nuthin" in the story's final paragraph?

3. Describe the level of language of the narrator. Is she writing the story or speak-
    ing it? How do you know?

4. Consider paragraphs 44–50. What ideas about equality and inequality are
    brought out in the story? Do you think the children will remember the "lesson"
    or that they will forget it? Why?

ERNEST J. GAINES (b. 1933)

*A native of Louisiana, Gaines has spent much of his life in San Francisco. Since 1964,
when he published his first novel,* Catherine Carmier, *he has written a number of novels
chronicling the lives of southern blacks, the best known of which is* The Autobiography of
Miss Jane Pittman *(1971), which was translated into German in 1975. His most recent
novel is* A Lesson Before Dying *(1993). Two important recent publications featuring
interviews with him are* Porch Talk with Ernest Gaines, *edited by Marcia Gau (1990),
and* Conversations with Ernest Gaines, *edited by John Lowe (1995). "The Sky Is Gray"
is selected from his 1968 collection of stories,* Bloodlines.

The Sky Is Gray _____ *1968*

1

Go'n be coming in a few minutes. Coming round that bend down there full speed. And
I'm go'n get out my handkerchief and wave it down, and we go'n get on it and go.

I keep on looking for it, but Mama don't look that way no more. She's looking
down the road where we just come from. It's a long old road, and far 's you can see you
don't see nothing but gravel. You got dry weeds on both sides, and you got trees on both
sides, and fences on both sides, too. And you got cows in the pastures and they standing
close together. And when we was coming out here to catch the bus I seen the smoke
coming out of the cows's noses.

I look at my mama and I know what she's thinking. I been with Mama so much, just me and her, I know what she's thinking all the time. Right now it's home—Auntie and them. She's thinking if they got enough wood—if she left enough there to keep them warm till we get back. She's thinking if it go'n rain and if any of them go'n have to go out in the rain. She's thinking 'bout the hog—if he go'n get out, and if Ty and Val be able to get him back in. She always worry like that when she leaves the house. She don't worry too much if she leave me there with the smaller ones, 'cause she know I'm go'n look after them and look after Auntie and everything else. I'm the oldest and she say I'm the man.

I look at my mama and I love my mama. She's wearing that black coat and that black hat and she's looking sad. I love my mama and I want put my arm round her and tell her. But I'm not supposed to do that. She say that's weakness and that's crybaby stuff, and she don't want no crybaby round her. She don't want you to be scared, either. 'Cause Ty's scared of ghosts and she's always whipping him. I'm scared of the dark, too, but I make 'tend I ain't. I make 'tend I ain't 'cause I'm the oldest, and I got to set a good sample for the rest. I can't ever be scared and I can't ever cry. And that's why I never said nothing 'bout my teeth. It's been hurting me and hurting me close to a month now, but I never said it. I didn't say it 'cause I didn't want act like a crybaby, and 'cause I know we didn't have enough money to go have it pulled. But, Lord, it been hurting me. And look like it wouldn't start till at night when you was trying to get yourself little sleep. Then soon 's you shut your eyes—ummm-ummm, Lord, look like it go right down to your heartstring.

"Hurting, hanh?" Ty'd say.   5

I'd shake my head, but I wouldn't open my mouth for nothing. You open your mouth and let that wind in, and it almost kill you.

I'd just lay there and listen to them snore. Ty there, right 'side me, and Auntie and Val over by the fireplace. Val younger than me and Ty, and he sleeps with Auntie. Mama sleeps round the other side with Louis and Walker.

I'd just lay there and listen to them, and listen to that wind out there, and listen to that fire in the fireplace. Sometimes it'd stop long enough to let me get little rest. Sometimes it just hurt, hurt, hurt. Lord, have mercy.

2

Auntie knowed it was hurting me. I didn't tell nobody but Ty, 'cause we buddies and he ain't go'n tell nobody. But some kind of way Auntie found out. When she asked me, I told her no, nothing was wrong. But she knowed it all the time. She told me to mash up a piece of aspirin and wrap it in some cotton and jugg it down in that hole. I did it, but it didn't do no good. It stopped for a little while, and started right back again. Auntie wanted to tell Mama, but I told her, "Uh-uh." 'Cause I knowed we didn't have any money, and it just was go'n make her mad again. So Auntie told Monsieur Bayonne, and Monsieur Bayonne came over to the house and told me to kneel down 'side him on the fireplace. He put his finger in his mouth and made the Sign of the Cross on my jaw. The tip of Monsieur Bayonne's finger is some hard, 'cause he's always playing on that guitar. If we sit outside at night we can always hear Monsieur Bayonne playing on his guitar. Sometimes we leave him out there playing on the guitar.

Monsieur Bayonne made the Sign of the Cross over and over on my jaw, but that   10
didn't do no good. Even when he prayed and told me to pray some, too, that tooth still
hurt me.

"How you feeling?" he say.

"Same," I say.

He kept on praying and making the Sign of the Cross and I kept on praying, too.

"Still hurting?" he say.

"Yes, sir."   15

Monsieur Bayonne mashed harder and harder on my jaw. He mashed so hard he
almost pushed me over on Ty. But then he stopped.

"What kind of prayers you praying, boy?" he say.

"Baptist," I say.

"Well, I'll be—no wonder that tooth still killing him. I'm going one way and he
pulling the other. Boy, don't you know any Catholic prayers?"

"I know 'Hail Mary,'" I say.   20

"Then you better start saying it."

"Yes, sir."

He started mashing on my jaw again, and I could hear him praying at the same
time. And, sure enough, after while it stopped hurting me.

Me and Ty went outside where Monsieur Bayonne's two hounds was and we
started playing with them. "Let's go hunting," Ty say. "All right," I say; and we went
on back in the pasture. Soon the hounds got on a trail, and me and Ty followed
them all 'cross the pasture and then back in the woods, too. And then they cornered
this little old rabbit and killed him, and me and Ty made them get back, and we
picked up the rabbit and started on back home. But my tooth had started hurting
me again. It was hurting me plenty now, but I wouldn't tell Monsieur Bayonne. That
night I didn't sleep a bit, and first thing in the morning Auntie told me to go back
and let Monsieur Bayonne pray over me some more. Monsieur Bayonne was in his
kitchen making coffee when I got there. Soon 's he seen me he knowed what was
wrong.

"All right, kneel down there 'side that stove," he say. "And this time make sure you   25
pray Catholic. I don't know nothing 'bout that Baptist, and I don't want know nothing
'bout him."

3

Last night Mama say, "Tomorrow we going to town."

"It ain't hurting me no more," I say. "I can eat anything on it."

"Tomorrow we going to town," she say.

And after she finished eating, she got up and went to bed. She always go to bed
early now. 'Fore Daddy went in the Army,° she used to stay up late. All of us sitting out
on the gallery or round the fire. But now, look like soon 's she finish eating she go to
bed.

Daddy went in the Army: The time of the story is about 1942, early in World War II, when millions of men were being drafted into the armed services.

This morning when I woke up, her and Auntie was standing 'fore the fireplace.   30
She say: "Enough to get there and back. Dollar and a half to have it pulled. Twenty-five
for me to go, twenty-five for him. Twenty-five for me to come back, twenty-five for him.
Fifty cents left. Guess I get little piece of salt meat with that."

"Sure can use it," Auntie say. "White beans and no salt meat ain't white beans."

"I do the best I can," Mama say.

They was quiet after that, and I made 'tend I was still asleep.

"James, hit the floor," Auntie say.

I still made 'tend I was asleep. I didn't want them to know I was listening.   35

"All right," Auntie say, shaking me by the shoulder. "Come on. Today's the day."

I pushed the cover down to get out, and Ty grabbed it and pulled it back.

"You, too, Ty," Auntie say.

"I ain't getting no teef pulled," Ty say.

"Don't mean it ain't time to get up," Auntie say. "Hit it, Ty."   40

Ty got up grumbling.

"James, you hurry up and get in your clothes and eat your food," Auntie say.
"What time y'all coming back?" she say to Mama.

"That 'leven o'clock bus," Mama say. "Got to get back in that field this evening."

"Get a move on you, James," Auntie say.

I went in the kitchen and washed my face, then I ate my breakfast. I was having   45
bread and syrup. The bread was warm and hard and tasted good. And I tried to make it
last a long time.

Ty came back there grumbling and mad at me.

"Got to get up," he say. "I ain't having no teefes pulled. What I got to be getting
up for?"

Ty poured some syrup in his pan and got a piece of bread. He didn't wash his
hands, neither his face, and I could see that white stuff in his eyes.

"You the one getting your teef pulled," he say. "What I got to get up for. I bet if I
was getting a teef pulled, you wouldn't be getting up. Shucks; syrup again. I'm getting
tired of this old syrup. Syrup, syrup, syrup. I'm go'n take with the sugar diabetes. I want
me some bacon sometime."

"Go out in the field and work and you can have your bacon," Auntie say. She stood   50
in the middle door looking at Ty. "You better be glad you got syrup. Some people ain't
got that—hard's time is."

"Shucks," Ty say. "How can I be strong."

"I don't know too much 'bout your strength," Auntie say; "but I know where
you go'n be hot at, you keep that grumbling up. James, get a move on you; your mama
waiting."

I ate my last piece of bread and went in the front room. Mama was standing 'fore
the fireplace warming her hands. I put on my coat and my cap, and we left the house.

4

I look down there again, but it still ain't coming. I almost say, "It ain't coming
yet," but I keep my mouth shut. 'Cause that's something else she don't like. She don't
like for you to say something just for nothing. She can see it ain't coming. I can see it
ain't coming, so why say it ain't coming. I don't say it, I turn and look at the river that's
back of us. It's so cold the smoke's just raising up from the water. I see a bunch of

pool-doos not too far out—just on the other side of the lilies. I'm wondering if you can eat pool-doos.° I ain't too sure, 'cause I ain't never ate none. But I done ate owls and blackbirds, and I done ate redbirds,° too. I didn't want kill the redbirds, but she made me kill them. They had two of them back there. One in my trap, one in Ty's trap. Me and Ty was go'n play with them and let them go, but she made me kill them 'cause we needed the food.

"I can't," I say. "I can't."   55

"Here," she say. "Take it."

"I can't," I say. "I can't. I can't kill him, Mama, please."

"Here," she say. "Take this fork, James."

"Please, Mama, I can't kill him," I say.

I could tell she was go'n hit me. I jerked back, but I didn't jerk back soon enough.   60

"Take it," she say.

I took it and reached in for him, but he kept on hopping to the back.

"I can't, Mama," I say. The water just kept on running down my face. "I can't," I say.

"Get him out of there," she say.

I reached in for him and he kept on hopping to the back. Then I reached in far-   65
ther, and he pecked me on the hand.

"I can't, Mama," I say.

She slapped me again.

I reached in again, but he kept on hopping out my way. Then he hopped to one side and I reached there. The fork got him on the leg and I heard his leg pop. I pulled my hand out 'cause I had hurt him.

"Give it here," she say, and jerked the fork out my hand.

She reached in and got the little bird right in the neck. I heard the fork go in his   70
neck, and I heard it go in the ground. She brought him out and helt him right in front of me.

"That's one," she say. She shook him off and gived me the fork. "Get the other one."

"I can't, Mama," I say, "I'll do anything, but don't make me do that."

She went to the corner of the fence and broke the biggest switch over there she could find. I knelt 'side the trap, crying.

"Get him out of there," she say.

"I can't, Mama."   75

She started hitting me 'cross the back. I went down on the ground, crying.

"Get him," she say.

"Octavia?" Auntie say.

'Cause she had come out of the house and she was standing by the tree looking at us.

"Get him out of there," Mama say.   80

"Octavia," Auntie say, "explain to him. Explain to him. Just don't beat him. Explain to him."

But she hit me and hit me and hit me.

---

pool-doos: Pool-doo is a local Louisiana pronunciation of French *poule d'eau,* or "bird of water." It refers to a marsh hen, or bird of the rail family—most likely the American coot.
redbirds: cardinals.

I'm still young—I ain't no more than eight; but I know now; I know why I had to do it. (They was so little, though. They was so little. I 'member how I picked the feathers off them and cleaned them and helt them over the fire. Then we all ate them. Ain't had but a little bitty piece each, but we all had a little bitty piece, and everybody just looked at me 'cause they was so proud.) Suppose she had to go away? That's why I had to do it. Suppose she had to go away like Daddy went away? Then who was go'n look after us? They had to be somebody left to carry on. I didn't know it then, but I know it now. Auntie and Monsieur Bayonne talked to me and made me see.

5

Time I see it I get out my handkerchief and start waving. It's still 'way down there, but I keep waving anyhow. Then it come up and stop and me and Mama get on. Mama tell me go sit in the back while she pay. I do like she say, and the people look at me. When I pass the little sign that say "White" and "Colored," I start looking for a seat. I just see one of them back there, but I don't take it, 'cause I want my mama to sit down herself. She comes in the back and sit down, and I lean on the seat. They got seats in the front, but I know I can't sit there, 'cause I have to sit back of the sign. Anyhow, I don't want sit there if my mama go'n sit back here.

They got a lady sitting 'side my mama and she looks at me and smiles little bit. I smile back, but I don't open my mouth, 'cause the wind'll get in and make that tooth ache. The lady take out a pack of gum and reach me a slice, but I shake my head. The lady just can't understand why a little boy'll turn down gum, and she reach me a slice again. This time I point at my jaw. The lady understands and smiles little bit, and I smile little bit, but I don't open my mouth, though.

They got a girl sitting 'cross from me. She got on a red overcoat and her hair's plaited in one big plait. First, I make 'tend I don't see her over there, but then I start looking at her little bit. She make 'tend she don't see me, either, but I catch her looking that way. She got a cold, and every now and then she h'ist that little handkerchief to her nose. She ought to blow it, but she don't. Must think she's too much a lady or something.

Every time she h'ist that little handkerchief, the lady 'side her say something in her ear. She shakes her head and lays her hands in her lap again. Then I catch her kind of looking where I'm at. I smile at her little bit. But think she'll smile back? Uh-uh. She just turn up her little old nose and turn her head. Well, I show her both of us can turn us head. I turn mine too and look out at the river.

The river is gray. The sky is gray. They have pool-doos on the water. The water is wavy, and the pool-doos go up and down. The bus go round a turn, and you got plenty trees hiding the river. Then the bus go round another turn, and I can see the river again.

I look toward the front where all the white people sitting. Then I look at that little old gal again. I don't look right at her, 'cause I don't want all them people to know I love her. I just look at her little bit, like I'm looking out that window over there. But she knows I'm looking that way, and she kind of look at me, too. The lady sitting 'side her catch her this time, and she leans over and says something in her ear.

"I don't love him nothing," that little old gal says out loud.

Everybody back there hear her mouth, and all of them look at us and laugh.

"I don't love you, either," I say. "So you don't have to turn up your nose, Miss."

"You the one looking," she say.

"I wasn't looking at you," I say. "I was looking out that window, there."

85

"Out that window, my foot," she say. "I seen you. Everytime I turned round you   95
was looking at me."

"You must of been looking yourself if you seen me all them times," I say.

"Shucks," she say, "I got me all kind of boyfriends."

"I got girlfriends, too," I say.

"Well, I just don't want you getting your hopes up," she say.

I don't say no more to that little old gal 'cause I don't want have to bust her in   100
the mouth. I lean on the seat where Mama sitting, and I don't even look that way no
more. When we get to Bayonne, she jugg her little old tongue out at me. I make 'tend
I'm go'n hit her, and she duck down 'side her mama. And all the people laugh at us
again.

6

Me and Mama get off and start walking in town. Bayonne is a little bitty town.
Baton Rouge is a hundred times bigger than Bayonne. I went to Baton Rouge once—
me, Ty, Mama, and Daddy. But that was 'way back yonder, 'fore Daddy went in the Army.
I wonder when we go'n see him again. I wonder when. Look like he ain't ever coming
back home. . . . Even the pavement all cracked in Bayonne. Got grass shooting right out
the sidewalk. Got weeds in the ditch, too; just like they got at home.

It's some cold in Bayonne. Look like it's colder than it is home. The wind blows in
my face, and I feel that stuff running down my nose. I sniff. Mama says use that handkerchief. I blow my nose and put it back.

We pass a school and I see them white children playing in the yard. Big old red
school, and them children just running and playing. Then we pass a café, and I see a
bunch of people in there eating. I wish I was in there 'cause I'm cold. Mama tells me
keep my eyes in front where they belong.

We pass stores that's got dummies, and we pass another café, and then we pass a
shoe shop, and that bald-head man in there fixing on a shoe. I look at him and I butt
into that white lady, and Mama jerks me in front and tells me stay there.

We come up to the courthouse, and I see the flag waving there. This flag ain't like   105
the one we got at school. This one here ain't got but a handful of stars.° One at school
got a big pile of stars—one for every state. We pass it and we turn and there it is—the
dentist office. Me and Mama go in, and they got people sitting everywhere you look.
They even got a little boy in there younger than me.

Me and Mama sit on that bench, and a white lady come in there and ask me what
my name is. Mama tells her and the white lady goes on back. Then I hear somebody
hollering in there. Soon 's that little boy hear him hollering, he starts hollering, too. His
mama pats him and pats him, trying to make him hush up, but he ain't thinking 'bout
his mama.

The man that was hollering in there comes out holding his jaw. He is a big old
man and he's wearing overalls and a jumper.

"Got it, hanh?" another man asks him.

The man shakes his head—don't want open his mouth.

"Man, I thought they was killing you in there," the other man says. "Hollering like   110
a pig under a gate."

handful of stars: The Confederate flag contains thirteen stars. At the time of the story, the
American flag had forty-eight.

The man don't say nothing. He just heads for the door, and the other man follows him.

"John Lee," the white lady says. "John Lee Williams."

The little boy juggs his head down in his mama's lap and holler more now. His mama tells him go with the nurse, but he ain't thinking 'bout his mama. His mama tells him again, but he don't even hear her. His mama picks him up and takes him in there, and even when the white lady shuts the door I can still hear little old John Lee.

"I often wonder why the Lord let a child like that suffer," a lady says to my mama. The lady's sitting right in front of us on another bench. She's got on a white dress and a black sweater. She must be a nurse or something herself, I reckon.

"Not us to question," a man says.   115

"Sometimes I don't know if we shouldn't," the lady says.

"I know definitely we shouldn't," the man says. The man looks like a preacher. He's big and fat and he's got on a black suit. He's got a gold chain, too.

"Why?" the lady says.

"Why anything?" the preacher says.

"Yes," the lady says. "Why anything?"   120

"Not us to question," the preacher says.

The lady looks at the preacher a little while and looks at Mama again.

"And look like it's the poor who suffers the most," she says. "I don't understand it."

"Best not to even try," the preacher says. "He works in mysterious ways—wonders to perform."°

Right then little John Lee bust out hollering, and everybody turn they head to   125
listen.

"He's not a good dentist," the lady says. "Dr. Robillard is much better. But more expensive. That's why most of the colored people come here. The white people go to Dr. Robillard. Y'all from Bayonne?"

"Down the river," my mama says. And that's all she go'n say, 'cause she don't talk much. But the lady keeps on looking at her, and so she says, "Near Morgan."

"I see," the lady says.

7

"That's the trouble with the black people in this country today," somebody else says. This one here's sitting on the same side me and Mama's sitting, and he is kind of sitting in front of that preacher. He looks like a teacher or somebody that goes to college. He's got on a suit, and he's got a book that he's been reading. "We don't question is exactly our problem," he says. "We should question and question and question—question everything."

The preacher just looks at him a long time. He done put a toothpick or something in his mouth, and he just keeps on turning it and turning it. You can see he don't like that boy with that book.

"Maybe you can explain what you mean," he says.

He works . . . perform: an allusion to the well-known hymn "God moves in a mysterious way / His wonders to perform," by William Cowper (1731–1800).

"I said what I meant," the boy says. "Question everything. Every stripe, every star, every word spoken. Everything."

"It 'pears to me that this young lady and I was talking 'bout God, young man," the preacher says.

"Question Him, too," the boys says.

"Wait," the preacher says. "Wait now."   135

"You heard me right," the boy says. "His existence as well as everything else. Everything."

The preacher just looks across the room at the boy. You can see he's getting madder and madder. But mad or no mad, the boy ain't thinking 'bout him. He looks at that preacher just 's hard 's the preacher looks at him.

"Is this what they coming to?" the preacher says. "Is this what we educating them for?"

"You're not educating me," the boy says. "I wash dishes at night so that I can go to school in the day. So even the words you spoke need questioning."

The preacher just looks at him and shakes his head.   140

"When I come in this room and seen you there with your book, I said to myself, 'There's an intelligent man.' How wrong a person can be."

"Show me one reason to believe in the existence of a God," the boy says.

"My heart tells me," the preacher says.

"'My heart tells me,'" the boys says. "'My heart tells me.' Sure, 'My heart tells me.' And as long as you listen to what your heart tells you, you will have only what the white man gives you and nothing more. Me, I don't listen to my heart. The purpose of the heart is to pump blood throughout the body, and nothing else."

"Who's your paw, boy?" the preacher says.   145

"Why?"

"Who is he?"

"He's dead."

"And you mom?"

"She's in Charity Hospital with pneumonia. Half killed herself, working for   150
nothing."

"And 'cause he's dead and she's sick, you mad at the world?"

"I'm not mad at the world. I'm questioning the world. I'm questioning it with cold logic, sir. What do words like Freedom, Liberty, God, White, Colored mean? I want to know. That's why *you* are sending us to school, to read and to ask questions. And because we ask these questions, you call us mad. No sir, it is not us who are mad."

"You keep saying 'us'?"

"'Us.' Yes—us. I'm not alone."

The preacher just shakes his head. Then he looks at everybody in the room—   155
everybody. Some of the people look down at the floor, keep from looking at him. I kind of look 'way myself, but soon 's I know he done turn his head, I look that way again.

"I'm sorry for you," he says to the boy.

"Why?" the boy says. "Why not be sorry for yourself? Why are you so much better off than I am? Why aren't you sorry for these other people in here? Why not be sorry for the lady who had to drag her child into the dentist office? Why not be sorry for the lady sitting on that bench over there? Be sorry for them. Not for me. Some way or the other I'm going to make it."

"No, I'm sorry for you," the preacher says.

"Of course, of course," the boy says, nodding his head. "You're sorry for me because I rock that pillar you're leaning on."

"You can't ever rock the pillar I'm leaning on, young man. It's stronger than any-   160
thing man can ever do."

"You believe in God because a man told you to believe in God," the boy says. "A white man told you to believe in God. And why? To keep you ignorant so he can keep his feet on your neck."

"So now we the ignorant?" the preacher says.

"Yes," the boy says. "Yes." And he opens his book again.

The preacher just looks at him sitting there. The boy done forgot all about him. Everybody else make 'tend they done forgot the squabble, too.

Then I see that preacher getting up real slow. Preacher's a great big old man and   165
he got to brace himself to get up. He comes over where the boy is sitting.

He just stands there a little while looking down at him, but the boy don't raise his head.

"Get up, boy," preacher says.

The boy looks up at him, then he shuts his book real slow and stands up. Preacher just hauls back and hit him in the face. The boy falls back 'gainst the wall, but he straightens himself up and looks right back at that preacher.

"You forgot the other cheek," he says.°

The preacher hauls back and hit him again on the other side. But this time the   170
boy braces himself and don't fall.

"That hasn't changed a thing," he says.

The preacher just looks at the boy. The preacher's breathing real hard like he just run up a big hill. The boy sits down and opens his book again.

"I feel sorry for you," the preacher says. "I never felt so sorry for a man before."

The boy makes 'tend he don't even hear that preacher. He keeps on reading his book. The preacher goes back and gets his hat off the chair.

"Excuse me," he says to us. "I'll come back some other time. Y'all, please excuse   175
me."

And he looks at the boy and goes out the room. The boy h'ist his hand up to his mouth one time to wipe 'way some blood. All the rest of the time he keeps on reading. And nobody else in there say a word.

8

Little John Lee and his mama come out the dentist office, and the nurse calls somebody else in. Then little bit later they come out, and the nurse calls another name. But fast 's she calls somebody in there, somebody else comes in the place where we sitting, and the room stays full.

The people coming in now, all of them wearing big coats. One of them says something 'bout sleeting, another one says he hope not. Another one says he think it ain't nothing but rain. 'Cause, he says, rain can get awful cold this time of year.

All round the room they talking. Some of them talking to people right by them, some of them talking to people clear 'cross the room, some of them talking to any-body'll listen. It's a little bitty room, no bigger than us kitchen, and I can see everybody

---

other cheek: Matthew 5:39.

in there. The little old room's full of smoke, 'cause you got two old men smoking pipes over by that side door. I think I feel my tooth thumping me some, and I hold my breath and wait. I wait and wait, but it don't thump me no more. Thank God for that.

I feel like going to sleep, and I lean back 'gainst the wall. But I'm scared to go to sleep. Scared 'cause the nurse might call my name and I won't hear her. And Mama might go to sleep, too, and she'll be mad if neither one of us heard the nurse.

I look up at Mama. I love my mama. I love my mama. And when cotton come I'm go'n get her a new coat. And I ain't go'n get a black one, either. I think I'm go'n get her a red one.

"They got some books over there," I say. "Want read one of them?"

Mama looks at the books, but she don't answer me.

"You got yourself a little man there," the lady says.

Mama don't say nothing to the lady, but she must've smiled, 'cause I seen the lady smiling back. The lady looks at me a little while, like she's feeling sorry for me.

"You sure got that preacher out here in a hurry," she says to that boy.

The boy looks up at her and looks in his book again. When I grow up I want be just like him. I want clothes like that and I want keep a book with me, too.

"You really don't believe in God?" the lady says.

"No," he says.

"But why?" the lady says.

"Because the wind is pink," he says.

"What?" the lady says.

The boy don't answer her no more. He just reads in his book.

"Talking 'bout the wind is pink," that old lady says. She's sitting on the same bench with the boy and she's trying to look in his face. The boy makes 'tend the old lady ain't even there. He just keeps on reading. "Wind is pink," she says again. "Eh, Lord, what children go'n be saying next?"

The lady 'cross from us bust out laughing.

"That's a good one," she says. "The wind is pink. Yes sir, that's a good one."

"Don't you believe the wind is pink?" the boy says. He keeps his head down in the book.

"Course I believe it, honey," the lady says. "Course I do." She looks at us and winks her eye. "And what color is grass, honey?"

"Grass? Grass is black."

She bust out laughing again. The boy looks at her.

"Don't you believe grass is black?" he says.

The lady quits her laughing and looks at him. Everybody else looking at him, too. The place quiet, quiet.

"Grass is green, honey," the lady says. "It was green yesterday, it's green today, and it's go'n be green tomorrow."

"How do you know it's green?"

"I know because I know."

"You don't know it's green," the boy says. "You believe it's green because someone told you it was green. If someone had told you it was black you'd believe it was black."

"It's green," the lady says. "I know green when I see green."

"Prove it's green," the boy says.

"Sure, now," the lady says. "Don't tell me it's coming to that."

"It's coming to just that," the boy says. "Words mean nothing. One means no more than the other."

"That's what it all coming to?" that old lady says. That old lady got on a turban and she got on two sweaters. She got a green sweater under a black sweater. I can see the green sweater 'cause some of the buttons on the other sweater's missing.

"Yes, ma'am," the boy says. "Words mean nothing. Action is the only thing. Doing. That's the only thing."

"Other words, you want the Lord to come down here and show Hisself to you?" she says.

"Exactly, ma'am," he says.   215

"You don't mean that, I'm sure?" she says.

"I do, ma'am," he says.

"Done, Jesus," the old lady says, shaking her head.

"I didn't go 'long with that preacher at first," the other lady says; "but now—I don't know. When a person say the grass is black, he's either a lunatic or something's wrong."

"Prove to me that it's green," the boy says.   220

"It's green because the people say it's green."

"Those same people say we're citizens of these United States," the boy says.

"I think I'm a citizen," the lady says.

"Citizens have certain rights," the boy says. "Name me one right that you have. One right, granted by the Constitution, that you can exercise in Bayonne."

The lady don't answer him. She just looks at him like she don't know what he's talking 'bout. I know I don't.

"Things changing," she says.   225

"Things are changing because some black men have begun to think with their brains and not their hearts," the boy says.

"You trying to say these people don't believe in God?"

"I'm sure some of them do. Maybe most of them do. But they don't believe that God is going to touch these white people's hearts and change things tomorrow. Things change through action. By no other way."

Everybody sit quiet and look at the boy. Nobody says a thing. Then the lady 'cross the room from me and Mama just shakes her head.

"Let's hope that not all your generation feel the same way you do," she says.   23(

"Think what you please, it doesn't matter," the boy says. "But it will be men who listen to their heads and not their hearts who will see that your children have a better chance than you had."

"Let's hope they ain't all like you, though," the old lady says. "Done forgot the heart absolutely."

"Yes ma'am, I hope they aren't all like me," the boy says. "Unfortunately, I was born too late to believe in your God. Let's hope that the ones who come after will have your faith—if not in your God, then in something else, something definitely that they can lean on. I haven't anything. For me, the wind is pink, the grass is black."

9

The nurse comes in the room where we all sitting and waiting and says the doctor won't take no more patients till one o'clock this evening.° My mama jumps up off the bench and goes up to the white lady.

evening: local dialect for *afternoon.*

"Nurse, I have to go back in the field this evening," she says.   235

"The doctor is treating his last patient now," the nurse says. "One o'clock this evening."

"Can I at least speak to the doctor?" my mama asks.

"I'm his nurse," the lady says.

"My little boy's sick," my mama says. "Right now his tooth almost killing him."

The nurse looks at me. She's trying to make up her mind if to let me come in.   240
I look at her real pitiful. The tooth ain't hurting me at all, but Mama say it is, so I
make 'tend for her sake.

"This evening," the nurse says, and goes on back in the office.

"Don't feel 'jected, honey," the lady says to Mama. "I been round them a long
time—they take you when they want to. If you was white, that's something else; but we
the wrong color."

Mama don't say nothing to the lady, and me and her go outside and stand
'gainst the wall. It's cold out there. I can feel that wind going through my coat. Some
of the other people come out of the room and go up the street. Me and Mama stand
there a little while and we start walking. I don't know where we going. When we come
to the other street we just stand there.

"You don't have to make water, do you?" Mama says.

"No, ma'am," I say.   245

We go on up the street. Walking real slow. I can tell Mama don't know where
she's going. When we come to a store we stand there and look at the dummies. I look
at a little boy wearing a brown overcoat. He's got on brown shoes, too. I look at my
old shoes and look at his'n again. You wait till summer, I say.

Me and Mama walk away. We come up to another store and we stop and look at
them dummies, too. Then we go on again. We pass a café where the white people in
there eating. Mama tells me keep my eyes in front where they belong, but I can't help
from seeing them people eat. My stomach starts to growling 'cause I'm hungry. When
I see people eating, I get hungry; when I see a coat, I get cold.

A man whistles at my mama when we go by a filling station. She makes 'tend
she don't even see him. I look back and I feel like hitting him in the mouth. If I was
bigger, I say; if I was bigger, you'd see.

We keep on going. I'm getting colder and colder, but I don't say nothing. I feel
that stuff running down my nose and I sniff.

"That rag," Mama says.   250

I get it out and wipe my nose. I'm getting cold all over now—my face, my
hands, my feet, everything. We pass another little café, but this'n for white people,
too, and we can't go in there, either. So we just walk. I'm so cold now I'm 'bout ready
to say it. If I knowed where we was going I wouldn't be so cold, but I don't know
where we going. We go, we go, we go. We walk clean out of Bayonne. Then we cross
the street and we come back. Same thing I seen when I got off the bus this morning.
Same old trees, same old walk, same old weeds, same old cracked pave—same old
everything.

I sniff again.

"That rag," Mama says.

I wipe my nose real fast and jugg that handkerchief back in my pocket 'fore my
hand gets too cold. I raise my head and I can see David's hardware store. When we
come up to it, we go in. I don't know why, but I'm glad.

It's warm in there. It's so warm in there you don't ever want to leave. I look for the   255
heater, and I see it over by them barrels. Three white men standing round the heater
talking in Creole.° One of them comes over to see what my mama want.

"Got any axe handles?" she says.

Me, Mama and the white man start to the back, but Mama stops me when we
come up to the heater. She and the white man go on. I hold my hands over the heater
and look at them. They go all the way to the back, and I see the white man pointing to
the axe handles 'gainst the wall. Mama takes one of them and shakes it like she's trying
to figure how much it weighs. Then she rubs her hand over it from one end to the
other end. She turns it over and looks at the other side, then she shakes it again, and
shakes her head and puts it back. She gets another one and she does it just like she did
the first one, then she shakes her head. Then she gets a brown one and do it that, too.
But she don't like this one, either. Then she gets another one, but 'fore she shakes it or
anything, she looks at me. Look like she's trying to say something to me, but I don't
know what it is. All I know is I done got warm now and I'm feeling right smart better.
Mama shakes this axe handle just like she did the others, and shakes her head and says
something to the white man. The white man just looks at his pile of axe handles, and
when Mama pass him to come to the front, the white man just scratch his head and
follows her. She tells me come on and we go on out and start walking again.

We walk and walk, and no time at all I'm cold again. Look like I'm colder now
'cause I can still remember how good it was back there. My stomach growls and I suck it
in to keep Mama from hearing it. She's walking right 'side me, and it growls so loud you
can hear it a mile. But Mama don't say a word.

10

When we come up to the courthouse, I look at the clock. It's got quarter to twelve.
Mean we got another hour and a quarter to be out here in the cold. We go and stand
'side a building. Something hits my cap and I look up at the sky. Sleet's falling.

I look at Mama standing there. I want stand close 'side her, but she don't like that.   260
She say that's crybaby stuff. She say you got to stand for yourself, by yourself.

"Let's go back to that office," she says.

We cross the street. When we get to the dentist office I try to open the door, but
I can't. I twist and twist, but I can't. Mama pushes me to the side and she twist the knob,
but she can't open the door, either. She turns 'way from the door. I look at her, but
I don't move and I don't say nothing. I done seen her like this before and I'm scared
of her.

"You hungry?" she says. She says it like she's mad at me, like I'm the cause of
everything.

"No, ma'am," I say.

"You want eat and walk back, or you rather don't eat and ride?"   26

"I ain't hungry," I say.

I ain't just hungry, but I'm cold, too. I'm so hungry and cold I want to cry. And
look like I'm getting colder and colder. My feet done got numb. I try to work my toes,
but I don't even feel them. Look like I'm go'n die. Look like I'm go'n stand right here
and freeze to death. I think 'bout home. I think 'bout Val and Auntie and Ty and Louis
and Walker. It's 'bout twelve o'clock and I know they eating dinner now. I can hear Ty

Creole: the French Cajun dialect in Louisiana.

making jokes. He done forgot 'bout getting up early this morning and right now he's probably making jokes. Always trying to make somebody laugh. I wish I was right there listening to him. Give anything in the world if I was home round the fire.

"Come on," Mama says.

We start walking again. My feet so numb I can't hardly feel them. We turn the corner and go on back up the street. The clock on the courthouse starts hitting for twelve.

The sleet's coming down plenty now. They hit the pave and bounce like rice. Oh, Lord; oh, Lord, I pray. Don't let me die, don't let me die, don't let me die, Lord.   270

11

Now I know where we going. We going back of town where the colored people eat. I don't care if I don't eat. I been hungry before. I can stand it. But I can't stand the cold.

I can see we go'n have a long walk. It's 'bout a mile down there. But I don't mind. I know when I get there I'm go'n warm myself. I think I can hold out. My hands numb in my pockets and my feet numb, too, but if I keep moving I can hold out. Just don't stop no more, that's all.

The sky's gray. The sleet keeps on falling. Falling like rain now—plenty, plenty. You can hear it hitting the pave. You can see it bouncing. Sometimes it bounces two times 'fore it settles.

We keep on going. We don't say nothing. We just keep on going, keep on going.

I wonder what Mama's thinking. I hope she ain't mad at me. When summer come   275
I'm go'n pick plenty cotton and get her a coat. I'm go'n get her a red one.

I hope they'd make it summer all the time. I'd be glad if it was summer all the time—but it ain't. We got to have winter, too. Lord, I hate the winter. I guess everybody hate the winter.

I don't sniff this time. I get out my handkerchief and wipe my nose. My hand's so cold I can hardly hold the handkerchief.

I think we getting close, but we ain't there yet. I wonder where everybody is. Can't see a soul but us. Look like we the only two people moving round today. Must be too cold for the rest of the people to move round in.

I can hear my teeth. I hope they don't knock together too hard and make that bad one hurt. Lord, that's all I need, for that bad one to start off.

I hear a church bell somewhere. But today ain't Sunday. They must be ringing for   280
a funeral or something.

I wonder what they doing at home. They must be eating. Monsieur Bayonne might be there with his guitar. One day Ty played with Monsieur Bayonne's guitar and broke one of the strings. Monsieur Bayonne was some mad with Ty. He say Ty wasn't go'n ever 'mount to nothing. Ty can go just like Monsieur Bayonne when he ain't there. Ty can make everybody laugh when he starts to mocking Monsieur Bayonne.

I used to like to be with Mama and Daddy. We used to be happy. But they took him in the Army. Now, nobody happy no more . . . I be glad when Daddy comes home.

Monsieur Bayonne say it wasn't fair for them to take Daddy and give Mama nothing and give us nothing. Auntie say, "Shhh, Etienne. Don't let them hear you talk like that." Monsieur Bayonne say, "It's God truth. What they giving his children? They have to walk three and a half miles to school hot or cold. That's anything to give for a paw? She's got to work in the field rain or shine just to make ends meet. That's anything to give for a husband?" Auntie say, "Shhh, Etienne, shhh." "Yes, you right," Monsieur Bayonne say. "Best don't say it in front of them now. But one day they go'n find out. One day." "Yes, I suppose so," Auntie say. "Then what, Rose Mary?" Monsieur Bayonne say. "I don't know, Etienne," Auntie say. "All we can do is us job, and leave everything else in His hand . . ."

We getting closer, now. We getting closer. I can even see the railroad tracks.

We cross the tracks, and now I see the café. Just to get in there, I say. Just to get in   285
there. Already I'm starting to feel little better.

12

We go in. Ahh, it's good. I look for the heater; there 'gainst the wall. One of them little brown ones. I just stand there and hold my hands over it. I can't open my hands too wide 'cause they almost froze.

Mama's standing right 'side me. She done unbuttoned her coat. Smoke rises out of the coat, and the coat smells like a wet dog.

I move to the side so Mama can have more room. She opens out her hands and rubs them together. I rub mine together, too, 'cause this keeps them from hurting. If you let them warm too fast, they hurt you sure. But if you let them warm just little bit at a time, and you keep rubbing them, they be all right every time.

They got just two more people in the café. A lady back of the counter, and a man on this side the counter. They been watching us even since we come in.

Mama gets out the handkerchief and count up the money. Both of us know how   290
much money she's got there. Three dollars. No, she ain't got three dollars, 'cause she had to pay us way up here. She ain't got but two dollars and a half left. Dollar and a half to get my tooth pulled, and fifty cents for us to go back on, and fifty cents worth of salt meat.

She stirs the money round with her finger. Most of the money is change 'cause I can hear it rubbing together. She stirs it and stirs it. Then she looks at the door. It's still sleeting. I can hear it hitting 'gainst the wall like rice.

"I ain't hungry, Mama," I say.

"Got to pay them something for they heat," she says.

She takes a quarter out the handkerchief and ties the handkerchief up again. She looks over her shoulder at the people, but she still don't move. I hope she don't spend the money. I don't want her spending it on me. I'm hungry, I'm almost starving I'm so hungry, but I don't want her spending the money on me.

She flips the quarter over like she's thinking. She's must be thinking 'bout us walk-   295
ing back home. Lord, I sure don't want walk home. If I thought it'd do any good to say something, I'd say it. But Mama makes up her own mind 'bout things.

She turns 'way from the heater right fast, like she better hurry up and spend the quarter 'fore she change her mind. I watch her go toward the counter. The man and the lady look at her, too. She tells the lady something and the lady walks away. The man keeps on looking at her. Her back's turned to the man, and she don't even know he's standing there.

The lady puts some cakes and a glass of milk on the counter. Then she pours a cup of coffee and sets it 'side the other stuff. Mama pays her for the things and comes on back where I'm standing. She tells me sit down at the table 'gainst the wall.

The milk and the cake's for me; the coffee's for Mama. I eat slow and I look at her. She's looking outside at the sleet. She's looking real sad. I say to myself, I'm go'n make all this up one day. You see, one day, I'm go'n make all this up. I want say it now; I want tell her how I feel right now; but Mama don't like for us to talk like that.

"I can't eat all this," I say.

They ain't got but just three little old cakes there. I'm so hungry right now, the Lord knows I can eat a hundred times three, but I want my mama to have one.

Mama don't even look my way. She knows I'm hungry, she knows I want it. I let it stay there a little while, then I get it and eat it. I eat just on my front teeth, though, 'cause if cake touch that back tooth I know what'll happen. Thank God it ain't hurt me at all today.

After I finish eating I see the man go to the juke box. He drops a nickel in it, then he just stand there a little while looking at the record. Mama tells me keep my eyes in front where they belong. I turn my head like she say, but then I hear the man coming toward us.

"Dance, pretty?" he says.

Mama gets up to dance with him. But 'fore you know it, she done grabbed the little man in the collar and done heaved him 'side the wall. He hit the wall so hard he stop the juke box from playing.

"Some pimp," the lady back of the counter says. "Some pimp."

The little man jumps up off the floor and starts toward my mama. 'Fore you know it, Mama done sprung open her knife and she's waiting for him.

"Come on," she says. "Come on. I'll gut you from your neighbo° to your throat. Come on."

I go up to the little man to hit him, but Mama makes me come and stand 'side her. The little man looks at me and Mama and goes on back to the counter.

"Some pimp," the lady back of the counter says. "Some pimp." She starts laughing and pointing at the little man. "Yes sir, you a pimp, all right. Yes sirree."

13

"Fasten that coat, let's go," Mama says.

"You don't have to leave," the lady says.

Mama don't answer the lady, and we right out in the cold again. I'm warm right now—my hands, my ears, my feet—but I know this ain't go'n last too long. It done sleet so much now you got ice everywhere you look.

We cross the railroad tracks, and soon's we do, I get cold. That wind goes through this little old coat like it ain't even there. I got on a shirt and a sweater under the coat, but that wind don't pay them no mind. I look up and I can see we got a long way to go. I wonder if we go'n make it 'fore I get too cold.

We cross over to walk on the sidewalk. They got just one sidewalk back here, and it's over there.

After we go just a little piece, I smell bread cooking. I look, then I see a baker shop. When we get closer, I can smell it more better. I shut my eyes and make 'tend I'm eating. But I keep them shut too long and I butt up 'gainst a telephone post. Mama grabs me and see if I'm hurt. I ain't bleeding or nothing and she turns me loose.

I can feel I'm getting colder and colder, and I look up to see how far we still got to go. Uptown is 'way up yonder. A half mile more, I reckon. I try to think of something. They say think and you won't get cold. I think of that poem, "Annabel Lee."° I ain't been to school in so long—this bad weather—I reckon they done passed "Annabel Lee" by

neighbo: navel.
"Annabel Lee": poem (1849) by Edgar Allan Poe (1809–1849). See pp. 869-70.

now. But passed it or not, I'm sure Miss Walker go'n make me recite it when I get there. That woman don't never forget nothing. I ain't never seen nobody like that in my life.

I'm still getting cold. "Annabel Lee" or no "Annabel Lee," I'm still getting cold. But I can see we getting closer. We getting there gradually.

Soon 's we turn the corner, I see a little old white lady up in front of us. She's the only lady on the street. She's all in black and she's got a long black rag over her head.

"Stop," she says.

Me and Mama stop and look at her. She must be crazy to be out in all this bad   320
weather. Ain't got but a few other people out there, and all of them's men.

"Y'all done ate?" she says.

"Just finish," Mama says.

"Y'all must be cold then?" she says.

"We headed for the dentist," Mama says. "We'll warm up when we get there."

"What dentist?" the old lady says. "Mr. Bassett?"   325

"Yes, ma'am," Mama says.

"Come on in," the old lady says. "I'll telephone him and tell him y'all coming."

Me and Mama follow the old lady in the store. It's a little bitty store, and it don't have much in there. The old lady takes off her head rag and folds it up.

"Helena?" somebody calls from the back.   330

"Yes, Alnest?" the old lady says.

"Did you see them?"

"They're here. Standing beside me."

"Good. Now you can stay inside."

The old lady looks at Mama. Mama's waiting to hear what she brought us in here for. I'm waiting for that, too.

"I saw y'all each time you went by," she says. "I came out to catch you, but you   335
were gone."

"We went back of town," Mama says.

"Did you eat?"

"Yes, ma'am."

The old lady looks at Mama a long time, like she's thinking Mama might be just saying that. Mama looks right back at her. The old lady looks at me to see what I have to say. I don't say nothing. I sure ain't going 'gainst my mama.

"There's food in the kitchen," she says to Mama. "I've been keeping it warm."   340

Mama turns right around and starts for the door.

"Just a minute," the old lady says. Mama stops. "The boy'll have to work for it. It isn't free."

"We don't take no handout," Mama says.

"I'm not handing out anything," the old lady says. "I need my garbage moved to the front. Ernest has a bad cold and can't go out there."

"James'll move it for you," Mama says.   34

"Not unless you eat," the old lady says. "I'm old, but I have my pride, too, you know."

Mama can see that she ain't go'n beat this old lady down, so she just shakes her head.

"All right," the old lady says. "Come into the kitchen."

She leads the way with that rag in her hand. The kitchen is a little bitty little old thing, too. The table and the stove just 'bout fill it up. They got a little room to the side.

Somebody in there laying 'cross the bed—'cause I can see one of his feet. Must be the person she was talking to: Ernest or Alnest—something like that.

"Sit down," the old lady says to Mama. "Not you," she says to me. "You have to   350
move the cans."

"Helena?" the man says in the other room.

"Yes, Alnest?" the old lady says.

"Are you going out there again?"

"I must show the boy where the garbage is, Alnest," the old lady says.

"Keep that shawl over your head," the old man says.   355

"You don't have to remind me, Alnest. Come, boy," the old lady says.

We go out in the yard. Little old back yard ain't no bigger than the store or the kitchen. But it can sleet here just like it can sleet in any big back yard. And 'fore you know it, I'm trembling.

"There," the old lady says, pointing to the cans. I pick up one of the cans and set it right back down. The can's so light, I'm go'n see what's inside of it.

"Here," the old lady says. "Leave that can alone."

I look back at her standing there in the door. She's got that black rag wrapped   360
round her shoulders, and she's pointing one of her little old fingers at me.

"Pick it up and carry it to the front," she says. I go by her with the can, and she's looking at me all the time. I'm sure the can's empty. I'm sure she could've carried it herself—maybe both of them at the same time. "Set it on the sidewalk by the door and come back for the other one," she says.

I go and come back, and Mama looks at me when I pass her. I get the other can and take it to the front. It don't feel a bit heavier than that first one. I tell myself I ain't go'n be nobody's fool, and I'm go'n look inside this can to see just what I been hauling. First, I look up the street, then down the street. Nobody coming. Then I look over my shoulder toward the door. That little old lady done slipped up there quiet 's mouse, watching me again. Look like she knowed what I was go'n do.

"Ehh, Lord," she says. "Children, children. Come in here, boy, and go wash your hands."

I follow her in the kitchen. She points toward the bathroom, and I go in there and wash up. Little bitty old bathroom, but it's clean, clean. I don't use any of her towels; I wipe my hands on my pants legs.

When I come back in the kitchen, the old lady done dished up the food. Rice,   365
gravy, meat—and she even got some lettuce and tomato in a saucer. She even got a glass of milk and a piece of cake there, too. It looks so good, I almost start eating 'fore I say my blessing.

"Helena?" the old man says.

"Yes, Alnest?"

"Are they eating?"

"Yes," she says.

"Good," he says. "Now you'll stay inside."   370

The old lady goes in there where he is and I can hear them talking. I look at Mama. She's eating slow like she's thinking. I wonder what's the matter now. I reckon she's thinking 'bout home.

The old lady comes back in the kitchen.

"I talked to Dr. Bassett's nurse," she says. "Dr. Bassett will take you as soon as you get there."

"Thank you, ma'am," Mama says.   375

"Perfectly all right," the old lady says. "Which one is it?"

Mama nods toward me. The old lady looks at me real sad. I look sad, too.

"You're not afraid, are you?" she says.

"No, ma'am," I say.

"That's a good boy," the old lady says. "Nothing to be afraid of. Dr. Bassett will not hurt you."

When me and Mama get through eating, we thank the old lady again.   380

"Helena, are they leaving?" the old man says.

"Yes, Alnest."

"Tell them I say good-bye."

"They can hear you, Alnest."

"Good-bye both mother and son," the old man says. "And may God be with you." 385

Me and Mama tell the old man good-bye, and we follow the old lady in the front room. Mama opens the door to go out, but she stops and comes back in the store.

"You sell salt meat?" she says.

"Yes."

"Give me two bits worth."

"That isn't very much salt meat," the old lady says.   390

"That's all I have," Mama says.

The old lady goes back of the counter and cuts a big piece off the chunk. Then she wraps it up and puts it in a paper bag.

"Two bits," she says.

"That looks like awful lot of meat for a quarter," Mama says.

"Two bits," the old lady says. "I've been selling salt meat behind this counter   395
twenty-five years. I think I know what I'm doing."

"You got a scale there," Mama says.

"What?" the old lady says.

"Weigh it," Mama says.

"What?" the old lady says. "Are you telling me how to run my business?"

"Thanks very much for the food," Mama says.   400

"Just a minute," the old lady says.

"James," Mama says to me. I move toward the door.

"Just one minute, I said," the old lady says.

Me and Mama stop again and look at her. The old lady takes the meat out of the bag and unwraps it and cuts 'bout half of it off. Then she wraps it up again and juggs it back in the bag and gives the bag to Mama. Mama lays the quarter on the counter.

"Your kindness will never be forgotten," she says. "James," she says to me.   40

We go out, and the old lady comes to the door to look at us. After we go a little piece I look back, and she's still there watching us.

The sleet's coming down heavy, heavy now, and I turn up my coat collar to keep my neck warm. My mama tells me turn it right back down.

"You not a bum," she says. "You a man."

QUESTIONS

1. What does Gaines establish by using the eight-year-old boy, James, as the narrator who tells the story in the present tense and in his own dialect?

2. Why does James describe the family's need to kill and eat the small birds?

3. What is the major action in the story? What is the result of James and his mother Octavia taking the trip to the dentist? What is gained by the delays, which require the boy and his mother to wait in the office and then to walk out into the cold and sleet?

4. What is the significance of the discussions of suffering occasioned by the protesting child in the dentist's office? What ideas does the young man present (section 7)? When the minister hits him and reproaches him, what is demonstrated about the old and new ideas professed by African-Americans?

5. What values are represented by the elderly couple in the store? Why doesn't the woman phone Dr. Robillard, the "better" but "more expensive" dentist? Why doesn't Octavia accept the portion of salt meat the woman first offers her? What causes the woman to cut the salt meat in half?

JAMES JOYCE   (1882–1941)

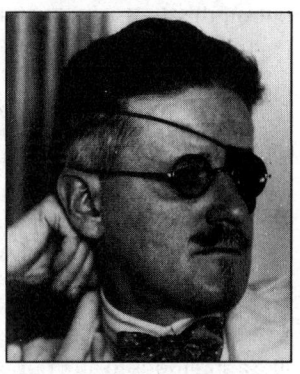

Joyce, one of the greatest twentieth-century writers, was born in Ireland and received a vigorous and thorough education there. He left Ireland in 1902 and spent most of the rest of his life in Switzerland and France. His best-known works are Dubliners *(1914),* A Portrait of the Artist as a Young Man *(1914–1915),* Ulysses *(1922), and* Finnegans Wake *(1939). Much of his work has been called "fictionalized autobiography," a quality shown in "Araby," which is selected from* Dubliners. *As a young child, Joyce had lived on North Richmond Street, just like the narrator of the story. The bazaar that the narrator visits actually did take place in Dublin, from May 14 to 19, 1894, when Joyce was the same age as the narrator. It was called "Araby in Dublin" and was advertised as a "Grand Oriental Fete."*

Araby _____ *1914*

North Richmond Street,° being blind,° was a quiet street except at the hour when the Christian Brothers' School set the boys free. An uninhabited house of two storeys stood at the blind end, detached from its neighbours in a square ground. The other houses of the street, conscious of decent lives within them, gazed at one another with brown imperturbable faces.

The former tenant of our house, a priest, had died in the back drawing room. Air, musty from having long been enclosed, hung in all the rooms, and the waste room behind the kitchen was littered with old useless papers. Among these I found a few paper-covered books, the pages of which were curled and damp: *The Abbott,* by Walter Scott, *The Devout Communicant*° and *The Memoirs of Vidocq.*° I liked the last best because its

North Richmond Street: name of a real street in Dublin on which Joyce lived as a boy.
blind: dead-end street.
The Devout Communicant: a book of meditations by Pacificus Baker, published 1873.
   The Memoirs of Vidocq: published 1829, the story of François Vidocq, a Parisian chief of detectives.

leaves were yellow. The wild garden behind the house contained a central apple-tree and a few straggling bushes under one of which I found the late tenant's rusty bicycle-pump. He had been a very charitable priest; in his will he had left all his money to institutions and the furniture of his house to his sister.

When the short days of winter came dusk fell before we had well eaten our dinners. When we met in the street the houses had grown sombre. The space of sky above us was the colour of ever-changing violet and towards it the lamps of the street lifted their feeble lanterns. The cold air stung us and we played till our bodies glowed. Our shouts echoed in the silent street. The career of our play brought us through the dark muddy lanes behind the houses where we ran the gauntlet of the rough tribes from the cottages, to the back doors of the dark dripping gardens where odours arose from the ashpits, to the dark odorous stables where a coachman smoothed and combed the horse or shook music from the buckled harness. When we returned to the street light from the kitchen windows had filled the areas. If my uncle was seen turning the corner we hid in the shadow until we had seen him safely housed. Or if Mangan's sister came out on the doorstep to call her brother in to his tea we watched her from our shadow peer up and down the street. We waited to see whether she would remain or go in and, if she remained, we left our shadow and walked up to Mangan's steps resignedly. She was waiting for us, her figure defined by the light from the half-opened door. Her brother always teased her before he obeyed and I stood by the railings looking at her. Her dress swung as she moved her body and the soft rope of her hair tossed from side to side.

Every morning I lay on the floor in the front parlor watching her door. The blind was pulled down within an inch of the sash so that I could not be seen. When she came out on the doorstep my heart leaped. I ran to the hall, seized my books and followed her. I kept her brown figure always in my eye and, when we came near the point at which our ways diverged, I quickened my pace and passed her. This happened morning after morning. I had never spoken to her, except for a few casual words, and yet her name was like a summons to all my foolish blood.

Her image accompanied me even in places the most hostile to romance. On Saturday evenings when my aunt went marketing I had to go to carry some of the parcels. We walked through the flaring street, jostled by drunken men and bargaining women, amid the curses of labourers, the shrill litanies of shop-boys who stood on guard by the barrels of pigs' cheeks, the nasal chanting of street singers, who sang a *come-all-you* about O'Donovan Rossa,° or a ballad about the troubles in our native land. These noises converged in a single sensation of life for me: I imagined that I bore my chalice safely through the throng of foes. Her name sprang to my lips at moments in strange prayers and praises which I myself did not understand. My eyes were often full of tears (I could not tell why) and at times a flood from my heart seemed to pour itself out into my bosom. I thought little of the future. I did not know whether I would ever speak to her or not or, if I spoke to her, how I could tell her of my confused adoration. But my body was like a harp and her words and gestures were like fingers running upon the wires.

One evening I went into the back drawing-room in which the priest had died. It was a dark rainy evening and there was no sound in the house. Through one of the broken panes I heard the rain impinge upon the earth, the fine incessant needles of

5

O'Donovan Rossa: popular ballad about Jeremiah O'Donovan (1831–1915), a leader in the movement to free Ireland from English control. He was called "Dynamite Rossa."

water playing in the sodden beds. Some distant lamp or lighted window gleamed below me. I was thankful that I could see so little. All my senses seemed to desire to veil themselves and, feeling that I was about to slip from them, I pressed the palms of my hands together until they trembled, murmuring: *O love! O love!* many times.

At last she spoke to me. When she addressed the first words to me I was so confused that I did not know what to answer. She asked me was I going to *Araby.*° I forget whether I answered yes or no. It would be a splendid bazaar, she said; she would love to go.

—And why can't you? I asked.

While she spoke she turned a silver bracelet round and round her wrist. She could not go, she said, because there would be a retreat° that week in her convent. Her brother and two other boys were fighting for their caps and I was alone at the railings. She held one of the spikes, bowing her head towards me. The light from the lamp opposite our door caught the white curve of her neck, lit up her hair that rested there and, falling, lit up the hand upon the railing. It fell over one side of her dress and caught the white border of a petticoat, just visible as she stood at ease.

—It's well for you, she said.   10

—If I go, I said, I will bring you something.

What innumerable follies laid waste my waking and sleeping thoughts after that evening! I wished to annihilate the tedious intervening days. I chafed against the work of school. At night in my bedroom and by day in the classroom her image came between me and the page I strove to read. The syllables of the word *Araby* were called to me through the silence in which my soul luxuriated and cast an Eastern enchantment over me. I asked for leave to go to the bazaar on Saturday night. My aunt was surprised and hoped it was not some Freemason° affair. I answered few questions in class. I watched my master's face pass from amiability to sternness; he hoped I was not beginning to idle. I could not call my wandering thoughts together. I had hardly any patience with the serious work of life which, now that it stood between me and my desire, seemed to me child's play, ugly monotonous child's play.

On Saturday morning I reminded my uncle that I wished to go to the bazaar in the evening. He was fussing at the hall-stand, looking for the hatbrush, and answered me curtly:

—Yes, boy, I know.

As he was in the hall I could not go into the front parlour and lie at the window. I   15
left the house in bad humour and walked slowly towards the school. The air was pitilessly raw and already my heart misgave me.

When I came home to dinner my uncle had not yet been home. Still, it was early. I sat staring at the clock for some time and, when its ticking began to irritate me, I left the room. I mounted the staircase and gained the upper part of the house. The high cold empty gloomy rooms liberated me and I went from room to room singing. From the front window I saw my companions playing below in the street. Their cries reached me weakened and indistinct and, leaning my forehead against the cool glass, I looked over at the dark house where she lived. I may have stood there for an hour, seeing nothing but the brown-clad figure cast by my imagination, touched discreetly by the

Araby: the bazaar held in Dublin from May 14–19, 1894.
retreat: a special time set aside for concentrated religious instruction, discussion, and prayer.
Freemason: and therefore Protestant.

lamplight at the curved neck, at the hand upon the railing and at the border below the dress.

When I came downstairs again I found Mrs. Mercer sitting at the fire. She was an old garrulous woman, a pawnbroker's widow, who collected used stamps for some pious purpose. I had to endure the gossip of the tea-table. The meal was prolonged beyond an hour and still my uncle did not come. Mrs. Mercer stood up to go: she was sorry she couldn't wait any longer, but it was after eight o'clock and she did not like to be out late, as the night air was bad for her. When she had gone I began to walk up and down the room, clenching my fists. My aunt said:

—I'm afraid you may put off your bazaar for this night of Our Lord.

At nine o'clock I heard my uncle's latchkey in the halldoor. I heard him talking to himself and heard the hall-stand rocking when it had received the weight of his overcoat. I could interpret these signs. When he was midway through his dinner I asked him to give me the money to go to the bazaar. He had forgotten.

—The people are in bed and after their first sleep now, he said.

I did not smile. My aunt said to him energetically:

—Can't you give him the money and let him go? You've kept him late enough as it is.

My uncle said he was very sorry he had forgotten. He said he believed in the old saying: *All work and no play makes Jack a dull boy.* He asked me where I was going and, when I had told him a second time he asked me did I know *The Arab's Farewell to his Steed.*° When I left the kitchen he was about to recite the opening lines of the piece to my aunt.

I held a florin° tightly in my hand as I strode down Buckingham Street towards the station. The sight of the streets thronged with buyers and glaring with gas recalled to me the purpose of my journey. I took my seat in a third-class carriage of a deserted train. After an intolerable delay the train moved out of the station slowly. It crept onward among ruinous houses and over the twinkling river. At Westland Row Station a crowd of people pressed to the carriage doors; but the porters moved them back, saying that it was a special train for the bazaar. I remained alone in the bare carriage. In a few minutes the train drew up beside an improvised wooden platform. I passed out on to the road and saw by the lighted dial of a clock that it was ten minutes to ten. In front of me was a large building which displayed the magical name.

I could not find any sixpenny entrance and, fearing that the bazaar would be closed, I passed in quickly through a turnstile, handing a shilling to a weary-looking man. I found myself in a big hall girdled at half its height by a gallery. Nearly all the stalls were closed and the greater part of the hall was in darkness. I recognized a silence like that which pervades a church after a service. I walked into the centre of the bazaar timidly. A few people were gathered about the stalls which were still open. Before a curtain, over which the words *Café Chantant* were written in coloured lamps, two men were counting money on a salver. I listened to the fall of the coins.

Remembering with difficulty why I had come I went over to one of the stalls and examined porcelain vases and flowered tea-sets. At the door of the stall a young lady was talking and laughing with two young gentlemen. I remarked their English accents and listened vaguely to their conversation.

—O, I never said such a thing!

The Arab's Farewell to his Steed: poem by Caroline Norton (1808–1877).
     florin: a two-shilling coin in the 1890s (when the story takes place), worth perhaps twenty dollars in today's money.

—O, but you did!
—O, but I didn't!
—Didn't she say that?   30
—Yes I heard her.
—O, there's a . . . fib!

Observing me the young lady came over and asked me did I wish to buy anything. The tone in her voice was not encouraging; she seemed to have spoken to me out of a sense of duty. I looked humbly at the great jars that stood like eastern guards at either side of the dark entrance to the stall and murmured:

—No, thank you.

The young lady changed the position of one of the vases and went back to the   35
two young men. They began to talk of the same subject. Once or twice the young lady glanced at me over her shoulder.

I lingered before her stall, though I knew my stay was useless, to make my interest in her wares seem the more real. Then I turned away slowly and walked down the middle of the bazaar. I allowed the two pennies to fall against the sixpence in my pocket. I heard a voice call from one end of the gallery that the light was out. The upper part of the hall was now completely dark.

Gazing up into the darkness I saw myself as a creature driven and derided by vanity; and my eyes burned with anguish and anger.

QUESTIONS

1. Describe what you consider to be the story's major idea.

2. How might the bazaar, "Araby," be considered symbolically in the story? To what extent does this symbol embody the story's central idea?

3. Consider the attitude of the speaker toward his home as indicated in the first paragraph. Why do you think the speaker uses the word *blind* to describe the dead-end street? What relationship exists between the speaker's pain at the end of the story to the ideas in the first paragraph?

4. Who is the narrator? About how old is he at the time of the story? About how old when he tells the story? What effect is produced by this difference in age between narrator-as-character and narrator-as-storyteller?

D. H. LAWRENCE   (1885–1930)

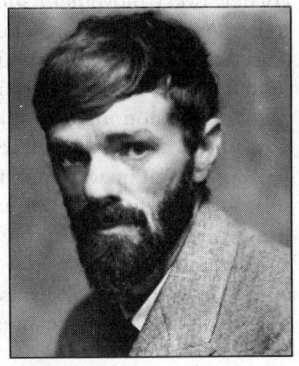

Lawrence was born in an English mining community, but he received a sufficient education to enable him to become a teacher and writer. He fictionalized the early years of his life in the novel Sons and Lovers *(1913). His most controversial work,* Lady Chatterley's Lover, *was printed privately in Italy in 1928 but was not published in an uncut version in the United States until the 1960s. He shocked his contemporaries with his emphasis on the importance of sexuality, an idea that is central to "The Horse Dealer's Daughter." He was afflicted with tuberculosis and lived in a number of warm, sunny places, including Italy, New Zealand, and New Mexico, in an*

attempt to restore his health. Nevertheless, his illness claimed him in 1930, when he was only forty-five years old.

The Horse Dealer's Daughter _____ 1922

"Well, Mabel, and what are you going to do with yourself?" asked Joe, with foolish flippancy. He felt quite safe himself. Without listening for an answer, he turned aside, worked a grain of tobacco to the tip of his tongue, and spat it out. He did not care about anything, since he felt safe himself.

The three brothers and the sister sat round the desolate breakfast table, attempting some sort of desultory consultation. The morning's post had given the final tap to the family fortunes, and all was over. The dreary dining-room itself, with its heavy mahogany furniture, looked as it were waiting to be done away with.

But the consultation amounted to nothing. There was a strange air of ineffectuality about the three men, as they sprawled at table, smoking and reflecting vaguely on their own condition. The girl was alone, a rather short, sullen-looking young woman of twenty-seven. She did not share the same life as her brothers. She would have been good-looking, save for the impassive fixity of her face, "bulldog," as her brothers called it.

There was a confused tramping of horses' feet outside. The three men all sprawled round in their chairs to watch. Beyond the dark holly-bushes that separated the strip of lawn from the high-road, they could see a cavalcade of shire horses swinging out of their own yard, being taken for exercise. This was the last time. These were the last horses that would go through their hands. The young men watched with critical, callous look. They were all frightened at the collapse of their lives, and the sense of disaster in which they were involved left them no inner freedom.

Yet they were three fine, well-set fellows enough. Joe, the eldest, was a man of thirty-three, broad and handsome in a hot, flushed way. His face was red, he twisted his black moustache over a thick finger, his eyes were shallow and restless. He had a sensual way of uncovering his teeth when he laughed, and his bearing was stupid. Now he watched the horses with a glazed look of helplessness in his eyes, a certain stupor of downfall.

The great draught-horses swung past. They were tied head to tail, four of them, and they heaved along to where a lane branched off from the highroad, planting their great hoofs floutingly in the fine black mud, swinging their great rounded haunches sumptuously, and trotting a few sudden steps as they were led into the lane, round the corner. Every movement showed a massive, slumbrous strength, and a stupidity which held them in subjection. The groom at the head looked back, jerking the leading rope. And the cavalcade moved out of sight up the lane, the tail of the last horse, bobbed up tight and stiff, held out taut from the swinging great haunches as they rocked behind the hedges in a motionlike sleep.

Joe watched with glazed hopeless eyes. The horses were almost like his own body to him. He felt he was done for now. Luckily, he was engaged to a woman as old as himself, and therefore her father, who was steward of a neighbouring estate, would provide him with a job. He would marry and go into harness. His life was over, he would be a subject animal now.

He turned uneasily aside, the retreating steps of the horses echoing in his ears. Then, with foolish restlessness, he reached for the scraps of bacon-rind from the plates, and making a faint whistling sound, flung them to the terrier that lay against the fender. He watched the dog swallow them, and waited till the creature looked into his eyes. Then a faint grin came on his face, and in a high, foolish voice he said:

"You won't get much more bacon, shall you, you little b———?"

The dog faintly and dismally wagged its tail, then lowered its haunches, circled   10
round, and lay down again.

There was another helpless silence at the table. Joe sprawled uneasily in his seat, not willing to go till the family conclave was dissolved. Fred Henry, the second brother, was erect, clean-limbed, alert. He had watched the passing of the horses with more *sang-froid*.° If he was an animal, like Joe, he was an animal which controls, not one which is controlled. He was master of any horse, and he carried himself with a well-tempered air of mastery. But he was not master of the situations of life. He pushed his coarse brown moustache upwards, off his lip, and glanced irritably at his sister, who sat impassive and inscrutable.

"You'll go and stop with Lucy for a bit, shan't you?" he asked. The girl did not answer.

"I don't see what else you can do," persisted Fred Henry.

"Go as a skivvy,"° Joe interpolated laconically.

The girl did not move a muscle.   15

"If I was her, I should go in for training for a nurse," said Malcolm, the youngest of them all. He was the baby of the family, a young man of twenty-two, with a fresh, jaunty *museau*.°

But Mabel did not take any notice of him. They had talked at her and round her for so many years, that she hardly heard them at all.

The marble clock on the mantel-piece softly chimed the half-hour, the dog rose uneasily from the hearthrug and looked at the party at the breakfast table. But still they sat on in ineffectual conclave.

"Oh, all right," said Joe suddenly, *à propos* of nothing. "I'll get a move on."

He pushed back his chair, straddled his knees with a downward jerk, to get them   20
free, in horsey fashion, and went to the fire. Still he did not go out of the room; he was curious to know what the others would do or say. He began to charge his pipe, looking down at the dog and saying, in a high, affected voice:

"Going wi' me? Going wi' me are ter? Tha'rt goin' further than tha counts on just now, dost hear?"

The dog faintly wagged its tail, the man stuck out his jaw and covered his pipe with his hands, and puffed intently, losing himself in the tobacco, looking down all the while at the dog, with an absent brown eye. The dog looked up at him in mournful distrust. Joe stood with his knees stuck out, in real horsey fashion.

"Have you had a letter from Lucy?" Fred Henry asked of his sister.

"Last week," came the neutral reply.

"And what does she say?"   25

There was no answer.

"Does she *ask* you to go and stop there?" persisted Fred Henry.

"She says I can if I like."

sang-froid: unconcern (literally, cold blood).
skivvy: British slang for housemaid.
museau: French for nose, snout.

"Well, then, you'd better. Tell her you'll come on Monday."

This was received in silence.   30

"That's what you'll do then, is it?" said Fred Henry, in some exasperation.

But she made no answer. There was a silence of futility and irritation in the room. Malcolm grinned fatuously.

"You'll have to make up your mind between now and next Wednesday," said Joe loudly, "or else find yourself lodgings on the kerbstone."

The face of the young woman darkened, but she sat on immutable.

"Here's Jack Fergusson!" exclaimed Malcolm, who was looking aimlessly out of   35
the window.

"Where?" exclaimed Joe, loudly.

"Just gone past."

"Coming in?"

Malcolm craned his neck to see the gate.

"Yes," he said.   40

There was a silence. Mabel sat on like one condemned, at the head of the table. Then a whistle was heard from the kitchen. The dog got up and barked sharply. Joe opened the door and shouted:

"Come on."

After a moment, a young man entered. He was muffled up in overcoat and a purple woolen scarf, and his tweed cap, which he did not remove, was pulled down on his head. He was of medium height, his face was rather long and pale, his eyes looked tired.

"Hello, Jack! Well, Jack!" exclaimed Malcolm and Joe. Fred Henry merely said "Jack!"

"What's doing?" asked the newcomer, evidently addressing Fred Henry.   45

"Same. We've got to be out by Wednesday—Got a cold?"

"I have—got it bad, too."

"Why don't you stop in?"

"*Me* stop in? When I can't stand on my legs, perhaps I shall have a chance." The young man spoke huskily. He had a slight Scotch accent.

"It's a knock-out, isn't it," said Joe boisterously, "if a doctor goes round croaking   50
with a cold. Looks bad for the patients, doesn't it?"

The young doctor looked at him slowly.

"Anything the matter with *you,* then?" he asked, sarcastically.

"Not as I know of. Damn your eyes, I hope not. Why?"

"I thought you were very concerned about the patients, wondered if you might be one yourself."

"Damn it, no, I've never been patient to no flaming doctor, and hope I never shall   55
be," returned Joe.

At this point Mabel rose from the table, and they all seemed to become aware of her existence. She began putting the dishes together. The young doctor looked at her, but did not address her. He had not greeted her. She went out of the room with the tray, her face impassive and unchanged.

"When are you off then, all of you?" asked the doctor.

"I'm catching the eleven-forty," replied Malcolm. "Are you goin' down wi' th' trap,° Joe?"

"Yes, I've told you I'm going down wi' th' trap, haven't I?"

trap: small wagon.

"We'd better be getting her in then.—So long, Jack, if I don't see you before I 60 go," said Malcolm, shaking hands.

He went out, followed by Joe, who seemed to have his tail between his legs.

"Well, this is the devil's own," exclaimed the doctor, when he was left alone with Fred Henry. "Going before Wednesday, are you?"

"That's the orders," replied the other.

"Where, to Northampton?"

"That's it." 65

"The devil!" exclaimed Fergusson, with quiet chagrin.

And there was silence between the two.

"All settled up, are you?" asked Fergusson.

"About."

There was another pause. 70

"Well, I shall miss yer, Freddy boy," said the young doctor.

"And I shall miss thee, Jack," returned the other.

"Miss you like hell," mused the doctor.

Fred Henry turned aside. There was nothing to say. Mabel came in again, to finish clearing the table.

"What are *you* going to do then, Miss Pervin?" asked Fergusson. "Going to your 75 sister's, are you?"

Mabel looked at him with her steady, dangerous eyes, that always made him uncomfortable, unsettling his superficial ease.

"No," she said.

"Well, what in the name of fortune *are* you going to do? Say what you *mean* to do," cried Fred Henry, with futile intensity.

But she only averted her head, and continued her work. She folded the white table-cloth, and put on the chenille cloth.

"The sulkiest bitch that ever trod!" muttered her brother. 80

But she finished her task with perfectly impassive face, the young doctor watching her interestedly all the while. Then she went out.

Fred Henry stared after her, clenching his lips, his blue eyes fixing in sharp antagonism, as he made a grimace of sour exasperation.

"You could bray her into bits, and that's all you'd get out of her," he said, in a small, narrowed tone.

The doctor smiled faintly.

"What's she *going* to do then?" he asked. 85

"Strike me if *I* know!" returned the other.

There was a pause. Then the doctor stirred.

"I'll be seeing you to-night, shall I?" he said to his friend.

"Ay—where's it to be? Are we going over to Jessdale?"

"I don't know. I've got such a cold on me. I'll come round to the Moon and Stars, 90 anyway."

"Let Lizzie and May miss their night for once, eh?"

"That's it—if I feel as I do now."

"All's one—"

The two young men went through the passage and down to the back door together. The house was large, but it was servantless now, and desolate. At the back was a small bricked house-yard, and beyond that a big square, gravelled fine and red, and having stables on two sides. Sloping, dank, winter-dark fields stretched away on the open sides.

But the stables were empty. Joseph Pervin, the father of the family, had been a   95
man of no education, who had become a fairly large horse dealer. The stables had been
full of horses, there was a great turmoil and come-and-go of horses and of dealers and
grooms. Then the kitchen was full of servants. But of late things had declined. The old
man had married a second time, to retrieve his fortunes. Now he was dead and everything was gone to the dogs, there was nothing but debt and threatening.

For months, Mabel had been servantless in the big house, keeping the home
together in penury for her ineffectual brothers. She had kept house for ten years. But
previously, it was with unstinted means. Then, however brutal and coarse everything was,
the sense of money had kept her proud, confident. The men might be foul-mouthed,
the women in the kitchen might have bad reputations, her brothers might have illegiti-
mate children. But so long as there was money, the girl felt herself established, and brutally proud, reserved.

No company came to the house, save dealers and coarse men. Mabel had no associates of her own sex, after her sister went away. But she did not mind. She went regularly
to church, she attended to her father. And she lived in the memory of her mother, who
had died when she was fourteen, and whom she had loved. She had loved her father,
too, in a different way, depending upon him, and feeling secure in him, until at the age
of fifty-four he married again. And then she had set hard against him. Now he had died
and left them all hopelessly in debt.

She had suffered badly during the period of poverty. Nothing, however, could
shake the curious sullen, animal pride that dominated each member of the family. Now,
for Mabel, the end had come. Still she would not cast about her. She would follow her
own way just the same. She would always hold the keys of her own situation. Mindless
and persistent, she endured from day to day. Why should she think? Why should she
answer anybody? It was enough that this was the end, and there was no way out.
She need not pass any more darkly along the main street of the small town, avoiding
every eye. She need not demean herself any more, going into the shops and buying the
cheapest food. This was at an end. She thought of nobody, not even of herself. Mindless
and persistent, she seemed in a sort of ecstasy to be coming nearer to her fulfilment,
her own glorification, approaching her dead mother, who was glorified.°

In the afternoon she took a little bag, with shears and sponge and a small scrubbing brush, and went out. It was a grey, wintry day, with saddened, dark-green fields and
an atmosphere blackened by the smoke of foundries not far off. She went quickly, darkly
along the causeway, heeding nobody, through the town to the churchyard.

There she always felt secure, as if no one could see her, although as a matter of   1
fact she was exposed to the stare of everyone who passed along under the churchyard
wall. Nevertheless, once under the shadow of the great looming church, among the
graves, she felt immune from the world, reserved within the thick churchyard wall as in
another country.

Carefully she clipped the grass from the grave, and arranged the pinky-white,
small chrysanthemums in the tin cross. When this was done, she took an empty jar from
a neighbouring grave, brought water, and carefully, most scrupulously sponged the
marble headstone and the coping-stone.

It gave her sincere satisfaction to do this. She felt in immediate contact with the
world of her mother. She took minute pains, went through the park in a state bordering

who was glorified: See Romans 8:17, 30.

on pure happiness, as if in performing this task she came into a subtle, intimate connection with her mother. For the life she followed here in the world was far less real than the world of death she inherited from her mother.

The doctor's house was just by the church. Fergusson, being a mere hired assistant, was slave to the countryside. As he hurried now to attend to the outpatients in the surgery, glancing across the graveyard with his quick eye, he saw the girl at her task at the grave. She seemed so intent and remote, it was like looking into another world. Some mystical element was touched in him. He slowed down as he walked, watching her as if spell-bound.

She lifted her eyes, feeling him looking. Their eyes met. And each looked again at once, each feeling, in some way, found out by the other. He lifted his cap and passed on down the road. There remained distinct in his consciousness, like a vision, the memory of her face, lifted from the tombstone in the churchyard, and looking at him with slow, large, portentous eyes. It *was* portentous, her face. It seemed to mesmerise him. There was a heavy power in her eyes which laid hold of his whole being, as if he had drunk some powerful drug. He had been feeling weak and done before. Now the life came back into him, he felt delivered from his own fretted, daily self.

He finished his duties at the surgery as quickly as might be, hastily filling up the bottles of the waiting people with cheap drugs. Then, in perpetual haste, he set off again to visit several cases in another part of his round, before teatime. At all times he preferred to walk, if he could, but particularly when he was not well. He fancied the motion restored him.

105

The afternoon was falling. It was grey, deadened, and wintry, with a slow, moist, heavy coldness sinking in and deadening all the faculties. But why should he think or notice? He hastily climbed the hill and turned across the dark-green fields, following the black cinder-track. In the distance, across a shallow dip in the country, the small town was clustered like smouldering ash, a tower, a spire, a heap of low, raw, extinct houses. And on the nearest fringe of the town, sloping into the dip, was Oldmeadow, the Pervins' house. He could see the stables and the outbuildings distinctly, as they lay towards him on the slope. Well, he would not go there many more times! Another resource would be lost to him, another place gone: the only company he cared for in the alien, ugly little town he was losing. Nothing but work, drudgery, constant hastening from dwelling to dwelling among the colliers and the iron-workers. It wore him out, but at the same time he had a craving for it. It was a stimulant to him to be in the homes of the working people, moving as it were through the innermost body of their life. His nerves were excited and gratified. He could come so near, into the very lives of the rough, inarticulate, powerfully emotional men and women. He grumbled, he said he hated the hellish hole. But as a matter of fact it excited him, the contact with the rough, strongly-feeling people was a stimulant applied direct to his nerves.

Below Oldmeadow, in the green, shallow, soddened hollow of fields, lay a square, deep pond. Roving across the landscape, the doctor's quick eye detected a figure in black passing through the gate of the field, down towards the pond. He looked again. It would be Mabel Pervin. His mind suddenly became alive and attentive.

Why was she going down there? He pulled up on the path on the slope above, and stood staring. He could just make sure of the small black figure moving in the hollow of the failing day. He seemed to see her in the midst of such obscurity, that he was like a clairvoyant, seeing rather with the mind's eye than with ordinary sight. Yet he could see her positively enough, whilst he kept his eye attentive. He felt, if he looked away from her, in the thick, ugly falling dusk, he would lose her altogether.

He followed her minutely as she moved, direct and intent, like something transmitted rather than stirring in voluntary activity, straight down the field towards the pond. There she stood on the bank for a moment. She never raised her head. Then she waded slowly into the water.

He stood motionless as the small black figure walked slowly and deliberately   110
towards the centre of the pond, very slowly, gradually moving deeper into the motionless water, and still moving forward as the water got up to her breast. Then he could see her no more in the dusk of the dead afternoon.

"There!" he exclaimed. "Would you believe it?"

And he hastened straight down, running over the wet, soddened fields, pushing through the hedges, down into the depression of callous wintry obscurity. It took him several minutes to come to the pond. He stood on the bank, breathing heavily. He could see nothing. His eyes seemed to penetrate the dead water. Yes, perhaps that was the dark shadow of her black clothing beneath the surface of the water.

He slowly ventured into the pond. The bottom was deep, soft clay, he sank in, and the water clasped dead cold round his legs. As he stirred he could smell the cold, rotten clay that fouled up into the water. It was objectionable in his lungs. Still, repelled and yet not heeding, he moved deeper into the pond. The cold water rose over his thighs, over his loins, upon his abdomen. The lower part of his body was all sunk in the hideous cold element. And the bottom was so deeply soft and uncertain, he was afraid of pitching with his mouth underneath. He could not swim, and was afraid.

He crouched a little, spreading his hands under the water and moving them round, trying to feel for her. The dead cold pond swayed upon his chest. He moved again, a little deeper, and again, with his hands underneath, he felt all around under the water. And he touched her clothing. But it evaded his fingers. He made a desperate effort to grasp it.

And so doing he lost his balance and went under, horribly, suffocating in the   11
foul earthy water, struggling madly for a few moments. At last, after what seemed an eternity, he got his footing, rose again into the air and looked around. He gasped, and knew he was in the world. Then he looked at the water. She had risen near him. He grasped her clothing, and drawing her nearer, turned to take his way to land again.

He went very slowly, carefully, absorbed in the slow progress. He rose higher, climbing out of the pond. The water was not only about his legs; he was thankful, full of relief to be out of the clutches of the pond. He lifted her and staggered on to the bank, out of the horror of wet, grey clay.

He laid her down on the bank. She was quite unconscious and running with water. He made the water come from her mouth, he worked to restore her. He did not have to work very long before he could feel the breathing begin again in her; she was breathing naturally. He worked a little longer. He could feel her live beneath his hands; she was coming back. He wiped her face, wrapped her in his overcoat, looked round into the dim, dark-grey world, then lifted her and staggered down the bank and across the fields.

It seemed an unthinkably long way, and his burden so heavy he felt he would never get to the house. But at last he was in the stable-yard, and then in the house-yard. He opened the door and went into the house. In the kitchen he laid her down on the hearthrug, and called. The house was empty. But the fire was burning in the grate.

Then again he kneeled to attend to her. She was breathing regularly, her eyes were wide open as if conscious, but there seemed something missing in her look. She was conscious in herself, but unconscious of her surroundings.

He ran upstairs, took blankets from a bed, and put them before the fire to warm. 120 Then he removed her saturated, earthy-smelling clothing, rubbed her dry with a towel, and wrapped her naked in the blankets. Then he went into the dining-room, to look for spirits. There was a little whiskey. He drank a gulp himself, and put some into her mouth.

The effect was instantaneous. She looked full into his face, as if she had been seeing him for some time, and yet had only just become conscious of him.

"Dr. Fergusson?" she said.

"What?" he answered.

He was divesting himself of his coat, intending to find some dry clothing upstairs. He could not bear the smell of the dead, clayey water, and he was mortally afraid for his own health. 125

"What did I do?" she asked.

"Walked into the pond," he replied. He had begun to shudder like one sick, and could hardly attend to her. Her eyes remained full on him, he seemed to be going dark in his mind, looking back at her helplessly. The shuddering became quieter in him, his life came back in him, dark and unknowing, but strong again.

"Was I out of my mind?" she asked, while her eyes were fixed on him all the time.

"Maybe, for the moment," he replied. He felt quiet, because his strength had come back. The strange fretful strain had left him.

"Am I out of my mind now?" she asked.

"Are you?" he reflected a moment. "No," he answered truthfully, "I don't see that 130 you are." He turned his face aside. He was afraid, now, because he felt dazed, and felt dimly that her power was stronger than his, in this issue. And she continued to look at him fixedly all the time. "Can you tell me where I shall find some dry things to put on?" he asked.

"Did you dive into the pond for me?" she asked.

"No," he answered. "I walked in. But I went in overhead as well."

There was silence for a moment. He hesitated. He very much wanted to go upstairs to get into dry clothing. But there was another desire in him. And she seemed to hold him. His will seemed to have gone to sleep, and left him, standing there slack before her. But he felt warm inside himself. He did not shudder at all, though his clothes were sodden on him.

"Why did you?" she asked.

"Because I didn't want you to do such a foolish thing," he said. 135

"It wasn't foolish," she said, still gazing at him as she lay on the floor, with a sofa cushion under her head. "It was the right thing to do. *I* knew best, then."

"I'll go and shift these wet things," he said. But still he had not the power to move out of her presence, until she sent him. It was as if she had the life of his body in her hands, and he could not extricate himself. Or perhaps he did not want to.

Suddenly she sat up. Then she became aware of her own immediate condition. She felt the blankets about her, she knew her own limbs. For a moment it seemed as if her reason were going. She looked round, with wild eye, as if seeking something. He stood still with fear. She saw her clothing lying scattered.

"Who undressed me?" she asked, her eyes resting full and inevitable on his face.

"I did," he replied, "to bring you round." 140

For some moments she sat and gazed at him awfully, her lips parted.

"Do you love me then?" she asked.

He only stood and stared at her, fascinated. His soul seemed to melt.

She shuffled forward on her knees, and put her arms round him, round his legs, as he stood there, pressing her breasts against his knees and thighs, clutching him with strange, convulsive certainty, pressing his thighs against her, drawing him to her face, her throat, as she looked up at him with flaring, humble eyes of transfiguration, triumphant in first possession.

"You love me," she murmured, in strange transport, yearning and triumphant and   145
confident. "You love me. I know you love me, I know."

And she was passionately kissing his knees, through the wet clothing, passionately and indiscriminately kissing his knees, his legs, as if unaware of everything.

He looked down at the tangled wet hair, the wild, bare, animal shoulders. He was amazed, bewildered, and afraid. He had never thought of loving her. He had never wanted to love her. When he rescued her and restored her, he was a doctor, and she was a patient. He had had no single personal thought of her. Nay, this introduction of the personal element was very distasteful to him, a violation of his professional honour. It was horrible to have her there embracing his knees. It was horrible. He revolted from it, violently. And yet—and yet—he had not the power to break away.

She looked at him again, with the same supplication of powerful love, and that same transcendent, frightening light of triumph. In view of the delicate flame which seemed to come from her face like a light, he was powerless. And yet he had never intended to love her. He had never intended. And something stubborn in him could not give way.

"You love me," she repeated, in a murmur of deep, rhapsodic assurance. "You love me."

Her hands were drawing him, drawing him down to her. He was afraid, even a   150
little horrified. For he had, really, no intention of loving her. Yet her hands were drawing him towards her. He put out his hand quickly to steady himself, and grasped her bare shoulder. A flame seemed to burn the hand that grasped her soft shoulder. He had no intention of loving her: his whole will was against his yielding. It was horrible—And yet wonderful was the touch of her shoulder, beautiful the shining of her face. Was she perhaps mad? He had a horror of yielding to her. Yet something in him ached also.

He had been staring away at the door, away from her. But his hand remained on her shoulder. She had gone suddenly very still. He looked down at her. Her eyes were now wide with fear, with doubt, the light was dying from her face, a shadow of terrible greyness was returning. He could not bear the touch of her eyes' question upon him, and the look of death behind the question.

With an inward groan he gave way, and let his heart yield towards her. A sudden gentle smile came on his face. And her eyes, which never left his face, slowly, slowly filled with tears. He watched the strange water rise in her eyes, like some slow fountain coming up. And his heart seemed to burn and melt away in his breast.

He could not bear to look at her any more. He dropped on his knees and caught her head with his arms and pressed her face against his throat. She was very still. His heart, which seemed to have broken, was burning with a kind of agony in his breast. And he felt her slow, hot tears wetting his throat. But he could not move.

He felt the hot tears wet his neck and the hollows of his neck, and he remained motionless, suspended through one of man's eternities. Only now it had become indispensable to him to have her face pressed close to him; he could never let her go again. He could never let her head go away from the close clutch of his arm. He wanted to remain like that for ever, with his heart hurting him in a pain that was also life to him. Without knowing, he was looking down on her damp, soft brown hair.

Then, as it were suddenly, he smelt the horrid stagnant smell of the water. And at the same moment she drew away from him and looked at him. Her eyes were wistful and unfathomable. He was afraid of them, and he fell to kissing her, not knowing what he was doing. He wanted her eyes not to have that terrible, wistful, unfathomable look. 155

When she turned her face to him again, a faint delicate flush was glowing, and there was again dawning that terrible shining of joy in her eyes, which really terrified him, and yet which he now wanted to see, because he feared the look of doubt still more.

"You love me?" she said, rather faltering.

"Yes." The word cost him a painful effort. Not because it wasn't true. But because it was too newly true, the *saying* seemed to tear open again his newly-torn heart. And he hardly wanted it to be true, even now.

She lifted her face to him, and he bent forward and kissed her on the mouth gently, with the one kiss that is an eternal pledge. And as he kissed her his heart strained again in his breast. He never intended to love her. But now it was over. He had crossed over the gulf to her, and all that he had left behind had shrivelled and become void.

After the kiss, her eyes again slowly filled with tears. She sat still, away from him, 160 with her face drooped aside, and her hands folded in her lap. The tears fell very slowly. There was complete silence. He too sat there motionless and silent on the hearthrug. The strange pain of his heart that was broken seemed to consume him. That he should love her? That this was love! That he should be ripped open in this way!—Him, a doctor!—How they would all jeer if they knew!—It was agony to him to think they might know.

In the curious naked pain of the thought he looked again to her. She was sitting there drooped into a muse. He saw a tear fall, and his heart flared hot. He saw for the first time that one of her shoulders was quite uncovered, one arm bare, he could see one of her small breasts; dimly, because it had become almost dark in the room.

"Why are you crying?" he asked, in an altered voice.

She looked up at him, and behind her tears the consciousness of her situation for the first time brought a dark look of shame to her eyes.

"I'm not crying, really," she said, watching him half frightened.

He reached his hand, and softly closed it on her bare arm. 165

"I love you! I love you!" he said in a soft, low vibrating voice, unlike himself.

She shrank, and dropped her head. The soft, penetrating grip of his hand on her arm distressed her. She looked up at him.

"I want to go," she said. "I want to go and get you some dry things."

"Why?" he said. "I'm all right."

"But I want to go," she said. "And I want you to change your things." 170

He released her arm, and she wrapped herself in the blanket, looking at him rather frightened. And still she did not rise.

"Kiss me," she said wistfully.

He kissed her, but briefly, half in anger.

Then, after a second, she rose nervously, all mixed up in the blanket. He watched her in her confusion, as she tried to extricate herself and wrap herself up so that she could walk. He watched her relentlessly, as she knew.

And as she went, the blanket trailing, and as he saw a glimpse of her feet and her   175
white leg, he tried to remember her as she was when he had wrapped her in the blanket. But then he didn't want to remember, because she had been nothing to him then,
and his nature revolted from remembering her as she was when she was nothing to
him.

A tumbling muffled noise from within the dark house startled him. Then he
heard her voice:—"There are clothes." He rose and went to the foot of the stairs, and
gathered up the garments she had thrown down. Then he came back to the fire, to
rub himself down and dress. He grinned at his own appearance, when he had finished.

The fire was sinking, so he put on coal. The house was now quite dark, save for the
light of a street-lamp that shone in faintly from beyond the holly trees. He lit the gas
with matches he found on the mantel-piece. Then he emptied the pockets of his own
clothes, and threw all his wet things in a heap into the scullery. After which
he gathered up her sodden clothes, gently, and put them in a separate heap on the
copper-top in the scullery.

It was six o'clock on the clock. His own watch had stopped. He ought to be back
to the surgery. He waited, and still she did not come down. So he went to the foot of
the stairs and called:

"I shall have to go."

Almost immediately he heard her coming down. She had on her best dress of   18(
black voile, and her hair was tidy, but still damp. She looked at him—and in spite of herself, smiled.

"I don't like you in those clothes," she said.

"Do I look a sight?" he answered.

They were shy of one another.

"I'll make you some tea," she said.

"No, I must go."   18

"Must you?" And she looked at him again with the wide, strained, doubtful eyes.
And again, from the pain of his breast, he knew how he loved her. He went and bent to
kiss her, gently, passionately, with his heart's painful kiss.

"And my hair smells so horrible," she murmured in distraction. "And I'm so awful,
I'm so awful! Oh, no, I'm too awful." And she broke into bitter, heartbroken sobbing.
"You can't want to love me, I'm horrible."

"Don't be silly, don't be silly," he said, trying to comfort her, kissing her, holding
her in his arms. "I want you, I want to marry you, we're going to be married, quickly,
quickly—to-morrow if I can."

But she only sobbed terribly, and cried.

"I feel awful. I feel awful. I feel I'm horrible to you."   1

"No, I want you, I want you," was all he answered blindly, with that terrible intonation which frightened her almost more than her horror lest he should *not* want
her.

QUESTIONS

1. What idea is Lawrence illustrating by the breakup of the Pervin household?

2. What does the comparison of Joe Pervin and the draft horses mean with regard
   specifically to Joe, and generally to people without love?

3.   What kind of person is Mabel? How do her brothers treat her? How does she feel about her brothers? What dilemma does she face as the story begins?

4.   What effect does Mabel have on Fergusson as he watches her in her home, in the churchyard, and at the pond? What does this effect contribute to Lawrence's ideas about love?

5.   What do Mabel and Fergusson realize as he revives and warms her? How do their responses signify their growth as characters?

6.   Why does the narrator tell us at the story's end that Fergusson "had no intention of loving" Mabel? What idea does this repeated assertion convey?

7.   In this story, there is an extensive exploration of the ambiguous feelings of both Fergusson and Mabel after they realize their love. Why does Lawrence explore these feelings so extensively?

IRENE ZABYTKO   (b. 1954)

Irene Zabytko was born in Chicago's Ukrainian neighborhood and took her undergraduate and graduate study at Vermont College. A proficient speaker of Ukrainian, she has lived in Ukraine and taught English language courses there. She is a past winner of the PEN Syndicated Fiction Project, and has held fellowships at the Helene Wurlitzer Foundation, the Hambidge Center, the Virginia Center for the Creative Arts and Sciences, and the Millay Colony for the Arts. She is the founder/publisher of OdessaPressa Productions of Lyndonvile, Vermont. She has been heard on "The Sound of Writing" program of National Public Radio. Her fiction has appeared in Catholic Girls *(1992) and* Earth Tones *(1994).* Don't Call Me Fluffy: Radical Feline Poetry, *is a collection of poems "written" by her cat. Her most recent work is* The Sky Unwashed *(2000), a novel based on the nuclear accident in Chernobyl, Russia.*

Home Soil _____ *1992*

I watch my son crack his knuckles, oblivious to the somber sounds of the Old Slavonic hymns the choir behind us is singing.

We are in the church where Bohdan, my son, was baptized nineteen years ago. It is Sunday. The pungent smell of frankincense permeates the darkened atmosphere of this cathedral. Soft sun rays illuminate the stained-glass windows. I sit near the one that shows Jesus on the cross looking down on some unidentifiable Apostles who are kneeling beneath His nailed feet. In the background, a tiny desperate Judas swings from a rope, the thirty pieces of silver thrown on the ground.

There is plenty of room in my pew, but my son chooses not to sit with me. I see him staring at the round carapace of a ceiling, stoic icons staring directly back at him. For the remainder of the Mass, he lightly drums his nervous fingers on top of the cover of *My Divine Friend,* the Americanized prayer book of the Ukrainian service. He took bongo lessons before he graduated high school, and learned the basic rolls from off a record, "Let's Swing with Bongos." I think it was supposed to make him popular with the girls at parties. I also think he joined the army because he wanted the virile image men in uniforms have that the bongos never delivered. When he returned from Nam, he mentioned after one of our many conversational silences that he lost the bongos, and the record is cracked, with the pieces buried somewhere deep inside the duffel bag he still hasn't unpacked.

Bohdan, my son, who calls himself Bob, has been back for three weeks. He looks so "American" in his green tailored uniform: his spit-shined vinyl dress shoes tap against the red-cushioned kneelers. It was his idea to go to church with me. He has not been anywhere since he came home. He won't even visit my garden.

Luba, my daughter, warned me he would be moody. She works for the Voice of   5
America and saw him when he landed from Nam in San Francisco. "Just don't worry, *tato*,"° she said to me on the telephone. "He's acting weird. Culture shock."

"Explain what you mean."

"Just, you know, strange." For a disc jockey, and a bilingual one at that, she is so inarticulate. She plays American jazz and tapes concerts for broadcasts for her anonymous compatriots in Ukraine. That's what she was doing when she was in San Francisco, taping some jazz concert. Pure American music for the huddled gold-toothed youths who risk their *komsomol* privileges and maybe their lives listening to these clandestine broadcasts and to my daughter's sweet voice. She will never be able to visit our relatives back there because American security won't allow it, and she would lose her job. But it doesn't matter. After my wife died, I have not bothered to keep up with anyone there, and I don't care if they have forgotten all about me. It's just as well.

I noticed how much my son resembled my wife when I first saw him again at the airport. He was alone, near the baggage claim ramp. He was taller than ever, and his golden hair was bleached white from the jungle sun. He inherited his mother's high cheekbones, but he lost his baby fat, causing his cheeks to jut out from his lean face as sharp as the arrowheads he used to scavenge for when he was a kid.

We hugged briefly. I felt his medals pinch through my thin shirt. "You look good, son," I lied. I avoided his eyes and concentrated on a pin shaped like an open parachute that he wore over his heart.

"Hi, *tato*," he murmured. We spoke briefly about his flight home from San   10
Francisco, how he'd seen Luba. We stood apart, unlike the other soldiers with their families who were hugging and crying on each other's shoulders in a euphoric delirium.

He grabbed his duffle bag from the revolving ramp and I walked behind him to see if he limped or showed any signs of pain. He showed nothing.

"Want to drive?" I asked, handing him the keys to my new Plymouth.

"Nah," he said. He looked around at the cars crowding the parking lot, and I thought he seemed afraid. "I don't remember how the streets go anymore."

An usher in his best borscht-red polyester suit waits for me to drop some money into the basket. It is old Pan° Medved, toothless except for the prominent gold ones he flashes at me as he pokes me with his basket.

---

tato: "Father" or "Dad."
Pan: a term of respect for adult males, the equivalent of *Mr.*

"*Nu*, give," he whispers hoarsely, but loud enough for a well-dressed woman with   15
lacquered hair who sits in front of me to turn around and stare in mute accusation.

I take out the gray and white snakeskin wallet Bohdan brought back for me, and
transfer out a ten dollar bill. I want the woman to see it before it disappears into the
basket. She smiles at me and nods.

Women always smile at me like that. Especially after they see my money and find
out that I own a restaurant in the neighborhood. None of the Ukies° go there; they
don't eat fries and burgers much. But the "jackees"—the Americans—do when they're
sick of eating in the cafeteria at the plastics factory. My English is pretty good for a D.P.,
and no one has threatened to bomb my business because they accuse me of being a no-
god bohunk commie. Not yet anyway.

But the women are always impressed. I usually end up with the emigrés—some of
them Ukrainians. The Polish women are the greediest for gawdy trinkets and for a man
to give them money so that they can return to their husbands and children in Warsaw. I
like them the best anyway because they laugh more than the other women I see, and
they know how to have a good time.

Bohdan knows nothing about my lecherous life. I told the women to stay clear
after my son arrived. He is so lost with women. I think he was a virgin when he joined the
army, but I'm sure he isn't now. I can't ask him.

After mass ends, I lose Bohdan in the tight clusters of people leaving their pews   20
and genuflecting toward the iconostasis. He waits for me by the holy water font. It looks
like a regular porcelain water fountain but without a spout. There is a sponge in the
basin that is moistened with the holy water blessed by the priests here. Bohdan stands
towering over the font, dabs his fingers into the sponge, but doesn't cross himself the
way he was taught to do as a boy.

"What's the matter?" I ask in English. I hope he will talk to me if I speak to him in
his language.

But Bohdan ignores me and watches an elderly woman gingerly entering the door
of the confessional. "What she got to say? Why is she going in there?"

"Everyone has sins."

"Yeah, but who forgives?"

"God forgives," I say. I regret it because it makes me feel like a hypocrite when-   25
ever I parrot words I still find difficult to believe.

We walk together in the neighborhood; graffiti visible in the alley-ways despite the
well-trimmed lawns with flowers and "bathtub" statues of the Blessed Mary smiling
benevolently at us as we pass by the small bungalows. I could afford to move out of here,
out of Chicago and into some nearby cushy suburb, Skokie or something. But what for?
Some smart Jewish lawyer or doctor would be my next door neighbor and find out that
I'm a Ukie and complain to me about how his grandmother was raped by Petliura.° I've
heard it before. Anyway, I like where I am. I bought a three-flat apartment building after
my wife died and I live in one of the apartments rent-free. I can walk to my business,
and see the past—old women in babushkas sweeping the sidewalks in front of their cherished gardens; men in Italian-made venetian-slat sandals and woolen socks rushing to a
chess match at the Soyuiez, a local meeting place where the D.P.s sit for hours rehashing
the war over beers and chess.

Ukies: Ukrainian Americans.
Petliura: Simeon Petliura (1879–1926), an anti-Bolshevik Ukrainian leader who was accused
of responsibility for Jewish pogroms during World War I. When his forces were defeated by the
Russians he went into exile in Paris, where he was ultimately assassinated by a Jewish nationalist.

Bohdan walks like a soldier. Not exactly a march, but a stiff gait that a good posture in a rigid uniform demands. He looks masculine, but tired and worn. Two pimples are sprouting above his lip where a faint moustache is starting.

"Want a cigarette?" I ask. Soldiers like to smoke. During the forties, I smoked that horrible cheap tobacco, *mahorka*. I watch my son puff heavily on the cigarette I've given him, with his eyes partially closed, delicately cupping his hands to protect it from the wind. In my life, I have seen so many soldiers in that exact pose; they all look the same. When their faces are contorted from sucking the cigarette, there is an unmistakable shadow of vulnerability and fear of living. That gesture and stance are more eloquent than the blood and guts war stories men spew over their beers.

Pan Medved, the battered gold-toothed relic in the church, has that look. Pan Holewski, one of my tenants, has it too. I would have known it even if he never openly displayed his old underground soldier's cap that sits on a bookshelf in the living room between small Ukrainian and American flags. I see it every time I collect the rent.

I wish Bohdan could tell me what happened to him in Vietnam. What did he do? 30 What was done to him? Maybe now isn't the time to tell me. He may never tell me. I never told anyone either.

I was exactly his age when I became a soldier. At nineteen, I was a student at the university in L'vov, which the Poles occupied. I was going to be a poet, to study poetry and write it, but the war broke out, and my family could not live on the romantic epics I tried to publish, so I was paid very well by the Nazis to write propaganda pamphlets. "Freedom for Ukrainians" I wrote—"Freedom for our people. Fight the Poles and Russians alongside our German brothers" and other such dreck. I even wrote light verse that glorified Hitler as the protector of the free Ukrainian nation that the Germans promised us. My writing was as naïve as my political ideas.

My new career began in a butcher shop, commandeered after the Polish owner was arrested and shot. I set my battered Underwood typewriter atop an oily wooden table where crescents of chicken feathers still clung between the cracks. Meat hooks that once held huge sides of pork hung naked in a back room, and creaked ominously like a deserted gallows whenever anyone slammed the front door. Every shred of meat had been stolen by looters after the Germans came into the city. Even the little bell that shopkeepers kept at the entrance was taken. But I was very comfortable in my surroundings. I thought only about how I was to play a part in a historical destiny that my valiant words would help bring about. That delusion lasted only about a week or so until three burly Nazis came in. *"Schnell!"* they said to me, pushing me out of my chair and pointing to the windows where I saw crowds chaotically swarming about. Before I could question the soldiers, one of them shoved a gun into my hands and pushed me out into the streets. I felt so bewildered until the moment I pointed my rifle at a man who was about—I thought—to hit me with a club of some sort. Suddenly, I felt such an intense charge of power, more so than I had ever felt writing some of my best poems. I was no longer dealing with abstract words and ideas for a mythological cause; I was responsible for life and death.

I enjoyed that power, until it seeped into my veins and poisoned my soul. It was only an instant, a brief interlude, a matter of hours until that transformation occurred. I still replay that scene in my mind almost forty years after it happened, no matter what I am doing, or who I am with.

I think she was a village girl. Probably a Jew, because on that particular day, the Jews were the ones chosen to be rounded up and sent away in cattle cars. Her hair was golden red, short and wavy as was the style, and her neck was awash in freckles. It was a crowded station in the center of the town, not far from the butcher shop. There were Germans shouting and women crying and church bells ringing. I stood with that German regulation rifle I hardly knew how to handle, frozen because I was too light-headed and excited. I too began to yell at people and held the rifle against my chest, and I was very much aware of how everyone responded to my authority.

Then, this girl appeared in my direct line of vision. Her back was straight, her shoulders tensed; she stopped in the middle of all the chaos. Simply stopped. I ran up and pushed her. I pushed her hard, she almost fell. I kept pushing her, feeling the thin material of her cheap wool jacket against my chapped eager hand; her thin muscles forced forward by my shoves. Once, twice, until she toppled into the open door of a train and fell toward a heap of other people moving deeper into the tiny confines of the stinking cattle car. She never turned around.   35

I should have shot her. I should have spared her from whatever she had to go through. I doubt she survived. I should have tried to find out what her name was, so I could track down her relatives and confess to them. At least in that way, they could have spat at me in justice and I would have finally received the absolution I will probably never find in this life.

* * *

I don't die. Instead, I go to the garden. It is Sunday evening. I am weeding the crop of beets and cabbages I planted in the patch in my backyard. The sun is lower, a breeze kicks up around me, but my forehead sweats. I breathe in the thick deep earth smells as the dirt crumbles and rotates against the blade of my hoe. I should destroy the honeysuckle vine that is slowly choking my plants, but the scent is so sweet, and its intoxicating perfume reminds me of a woman's gentleness.

I hoe for a while, but not for long, because out of the corner of my eye, I see Bohdan sitting on the grass tearing the firm green blades with his clenched hands. He is still wearing his uniform, all except the jacket, tie, and cap. He sits with his legs apart, his head down, ignoring the black flies that nip at his ears.

I wipe my face with a bright red bandana, which I brought with me to tie up the stalks of my drooping sunflowers. "Bohdan," I say to my son. "Why don't we go into the house and have a beer. I can finish this another time." I look at the orange sun. "It's humid and there's too many flies—means rain will be coming."

My son is quietly crying to himself.   40

"*Tato,* I didn't know anything," he cries out. "You know, I just wanted to jump out from planes with my parachute. I just wanted to fly . . ."

"I should have stopped you," I say more to myself than to him. Bohdan lets me stroke the thin spikes of his army regulation crew-cut which is soft and warm and I am afraid of how easily my hand can crush his skull.

I rock him in my arms the way I saw his mother embrace him when he was afraid to sleep alone.

There is not much more I can do right now except to hold him. I will hold him until he pulls away.

QUESTIONS

1. Where does the narrator live now, and what does he do? What do you learn about his past? What event remains fixed in his memory? Why?

2. What ideas about the exercise of power during warfare are brought out by the narrator's speaking of "the absolution I will probably never find in this life" (paragraph 36)?

3. Why is the narrator's son Bohdan in tears (paragraph 40)? How are Bohdan's experiences parallel with the narrator's? What ideas underlie this paralleling of experience?

4. What is the significance of the narrator's saying "I am afraid of how easily my hand can crush his skull" (paragraph 42)?

WRITING ABOUT A MAJOR IDEA IN FICTION

Most likely you will write about a major idea or theme, but you may also get interested in one of your story's other ideas. As you begin brainstorming and developing your first drafts, consider questions such as the following.

Questions for Discovering Ideas

GENERAL IDEAS

- What ideas do you discover in the work? How do you discover them (through action, character depiction, scenes, language)?

- To what do the ideas pertain? To the individuals themselves? To individuals and society? To religion? To social, political, or economic justice?

- How balanced are the ideas? If a particular idea is strongly presented, what conditions and qualifications are also presented (if any)? What contradictory ideas are presented?

- Are the ideas limited to members of any groups represented by the characters (age, race, nationality, personal status)? Or are the ideas applicable to general conditions of life? Explain.

- Which characters in their own right represent or embody ideas? How do their actions and speeches bring these ideas out?

- If characters state ideas directly, how persuasive is their expression, how intelligent and well considered? How germane are the ideas to the work? How germane to more general conditions?

- With children, young adults, or the old, how do the circumstances express or embody an idea?

A SPECIFIC IDEA

- What idea seems particularly important in the work? Why? Is it asserted directly, indirectly, dramatically, ironically? Does any one method predominate? Why?

- How pervasive in the work is the idea (throughout or intermittent)? To what degree is it associated with a major character or action? How does the structure of the work affect or shape your understanding of the idea?

- What value or values are embodied in the idea? Of what importance are the values to the work's meaning?
- How compelling is the idea? How could the work be appreciated without reference to any idea at all?

Strategies for Organizing Ideas

Narrative and dramatic elements have a strong bearing on ideas in well-written stories, poems, and plays. In this sense, an idea is like a key in music or like a continuous thread tying together actions, characters, statements, symbols, and dialogue. As readers, we can trace such threads throughout the entire fabric of the work.

As you write about ideas, you may find yourself relying most heavily on the direct statements of the authorial voice or on a combination of these and your interpretation of characters and action, or you might focus exclusively on a first-person speaker and use his or her ideas to develop your analysis. Always make clear the sources of your details and distinguish the sources from your own commentary.

In your essay, your general goal is to describe an idea and show its importance in the story. Each separate work will invite its own approach, but here are a number of strategies you might use to organize your essay:

1. *Analyze the idea as it applies to character. Example:* "Minnie Wright embodies the idea that living with cruelty and insensitivity leads to alienation, unhappiness, despair, and maybe to violence."

2. *Show how actions bring out the idea. Example:* "That Mabel and Dr. Fergusson fall in love rather than go their separate ways indicates Lawrence's idea that love literally rescues human lives."

3. *Show how dialogue and separate speeches bring out the idea. Example:* "The priest's responses to Jackie's confession embody the idea that kindness and understanding are the best means to encourage religious and philosophical commitment."

4. *Show how the story's structure is determined by the idea. Example:* "The idea that horror may exist in ordinary things leads to a structure in which Jackson (in 'The Lottery') introduces seemingly commonplace people, builds suspense about an impending misfortune, and develops a conclusion of mob destructiveness."

5. *Treat variations or differing manifestations of the idea. Example:* "The idea that zealousness leads to harm is shown in Brown's nightmarish distortion of reality, his rejection of others, and his dying gloom."

6. *Deal with a combination of these (together with any other significant aspect). Example:* "The idea in 'Araby' that devotion is complex and contradictory is shown in the narrator's romantic mission as a carrier of parcels, his outcries to love in the back room of his house, and his self-reproach and shame at the story's end." (Here the idea is traced through both speech and action.)

Your conclusion might begin with a summary, together with your evaluation of the validity or force of the idea. If you have been convinced by the author's ideas, you might say that the author has expressed the idea forcefully and convincingly, or else you might show the relevance of the idea to current conditions. If you are not persuaded by the idea, you should demonstrate the idea's shortcomings or limitations. If you wish to mention a related idea, whether in the story you have studied or in some other story, you might introduce that here, but be sure to stress the connections.

DEMONSTRATIVE STUDENT ESSAY

D. H. Lawrence's "The Horse Dealer's Daughter" as an Expression of the Idea That Commitment Is Essential in Life°

[1]   Lawrence's "The Horse Dealer's-Daughter" is an unusual love story. We learn that the lovers--Mabel Pervin (the "Horse Dealer's-Daughter") and Dr. Jack Fergusson--have known each other for many years but have never thought of themselves as lovers. It is not until after a potentially disastrous event that the two recognize that they love each other. Lawrence makes clear that this new love is about to bring new meaning and new direction to their lives. Most important about this love is that it fulfills Lawrence's idea that it is dedicated commitment that gives life meaning.* Lawrence brings out this idea first by showing characters with no sense of commitment and then by developing the two major characters whose lives are to be fulfilled by commitment.†

[2]   Negatively, Lawrence introduces his idea through the Pervin brothers, who have no sense of service or commitment and who therefore are leading obtuse, insensitive, somewhat cruel, and basically "ineffectual" lives (paragraph 96). It is true that Joe, the oldest brother, is planning to marry, and, one might assume, is also undertaking the promises and commitments that marriage brings. But Joe is seeking marriage only to receive a job from his future father-in-law. His only duty is to himself, in other words, and even though that is a commitment of sorts, it is only a limited one. In line with Lawrence's idea, Joe's life therefore has little if any meaning. Lawrence's speaker dismisses him with the cutting words that he is not much better than the large draught horses on the Pervin farm, whose "stupidity . . . [holds] them in subjection" (paragraph 6).

[3]   Lawrence's first use of his major characters, Mabel Pervin and Dr. Jack Fergusson, also embodies the negative aspect of his idea that lack of service and commitment to others leaves people weak and sick. When Jack first enters

---

° See pp. 500–10 for this story.
* Central idea.
† Thesis sentence.

the story his eyes look "tired" (paragraph 43), and he is suffering from a severe cold. His social life seems to be confined to spending time at a nearby pub and drinking with one of the Pervin brothers, Fred Henry, and two women named "Lizzie and May" (paragraphs 90-91). These outward signs of illness and aimlessness suggest an inner lack of conviction and commitment. But nevertheless, Jack is a good doctor. He may sometimes think of himself as a "slave" to his patients (paragraph 103), but he is dedicated to his work and finds excitement in it (paragraph 106). Therefore he declares that he cannot take a brief rest from serving his patients even to overcome his cold (paragraph 49). Clearly he is committed to his profession, but the commitment that comes from love is lacking in his life. When he goes into the pond to rescue Mabel, it is as a professional, not as a committed lover. His action, however, will change him and point him in the path of completeness.

[4] Mabel is in a similar position. Lawrence introduces her as "a rather short, sullen-looking young woman" with an "impassive fixity of her face" (paragraph 3). Her brothers all seem to dislike her. Like Jack, she is living only half a life, even though she has gained some little meaning through service, of a sort, to others. In the past she has been "keeping the home together" for her father and her brothers as the family fortunes declined. As long as the family had had money, her life was adequate, even if the household to which she was committed was "brutal and coarse" in many ways (paragraph 96). But with the family now "hopelessly in debt," requiring the breakup of the household, her duties are vanishing, and this loss also brings the loss of the meaning that her service has brought to her (paragraphs 97-98).

[5] In line with the idea, Lawrence makes plain that Mabel's developing despair will end her existence and that Jack's rootlessness, if unchanged, will keep him incomplete. Mabel's situation is, of course, the more critical. After completing her chores at home she sets about to care for the grave of her dead mother, to whom her commitment has been complete (paragraphs 98-101). Once she finishes this last loving task, she has nowhere to go, nothing more to do, and she therefore walks purposefully to the nearby pond and enters it in an attempt to drown herself (paragraph 109). One may read her attempted suicide as a symbol of Lawrence's idea that once a person's commitments end, meaning is gone and life is over.

[6] The paragraphs devoted by Lawrence to the interchanges of Mabel and Jack after he has rescued her from the pond demonstrate the interconnectedness of love and commitment. When he brings her to the shore he works "to restore her" (paragraph 117). After he carries her home--a long and difficult task--he disrobes her and wraps her in blankets to bring back warmth and life to her. At this point his commitment to her, however, is not to a loved one but to a victim. But when Mabel recovers, her first thought is to associate her nakedness with a newly discovered love for her. She asks him, "Do you love me then?" (paragraph 142). Once she has extracted a declaration of love, her first wishes are an enactment of Lawrence's idea of the power of commitment. She wants to get him "dry things" and then to make him some tea (paragraphs 170, 184). She has been awakened to a new life by a man who suddenly appears in a totally new light, and her response is immediately to begin the simple tasks that follow naturally from commitment. For his part, Jack demonstrates his newly found commitment

by stating that he wants the two of them "to be married" (paragraph 188). The idea is that love is for the moment, but commitment is for the long term.

The major and most truthful aspect of Lawrence's idea is that the transformation to commitment and responsibility is not easy but is both tentative and complex. Lawrence demonstrates this complexity by showing that both Mabel and Jack are uneasy and uncertain, for neither one can easily give up the past (even though Mabel was willing to give up everything by killing herself). When Jack expresses love for Mabel it is in a voice that is "unlike himself" (paragraph 166), and her response is to say "I feel I'm horrible to you" (paragraph 190). Difficult and fearful as the change to their new commitment is, however, it is leading them into the lives they have been designed for. Generally, people who evade such a change, like the Pervin brothers, may find life easy, but they are permanently incomplete because they lack the bravery of commitment shown by Mabel and Jack. Thus, Lawrence's idea in "The Horse Dealer's Daughter" emphasizes that a full life requires commitment, no matter how difficult, and that without such commitment lives can be lived only in the shadows.

[7]

Commentary on the Essay

This essay follows the strategy 6 (p. 517) by showing how separate components of the story exhibit the idea's pervasiveness. Throughout, citations of characters, actions, and speeches, together with observations about the story's organization, are used as evidence for the various conclusions. Transitions between paragraphs are effected by the words and phrases "introduces," "similar," "after he has rescued her," and "the major and most truthful aspect," all of which emphasize the continuity of the topic.

The first paragraph asserts that the story's major action—the development of love between the major characters—brings out the Lawrence's idea that commitment gives meaning to life. The idea is to be developed as it applies to characters without commitment and then to those who find it.

The argument of paragraphs 2 through 4 is to show how Lawrence brings out his idea negatively by demonstrating the shortcomings of characters, including the story's two major characters, who are living without commitment. The essay thus asserts that Joe is following a path of stupidity, Jack a life of rootlessness, and Mabel an action of suicide. These details are brought out in support of the essay's central idea or argument. Paragraphs 5 and 6 treat the positive aspects of the main idea, focusing on the renewing effect of commitment for both Jack and Mabel. The last paragraph pays tribute to Lawrence's idea by demonstrating that it is realistic and true to life because both Jack and Mabel discover that their new commitments are not made easily but require profound and disturbing changes in their lives.

SPECIAL TOPICS FOR WRITING AND ARGUMENT ABOUT IDEAS

1. Compare two stories containing similar themes. *Examples:* Colwin's "An Old-Fashioned Story" (Chapter 2) and Lawrence's "The Horse Dealer's Daughter,"

Zabytko's "Home Soil" and Hemingway's "Soldier's Home" (Chapter 7), Ozick's "The Shawl" (Chapter 6) and Clark's "The Portable Phonograph" (Chapter 6), Faulkner's "Barn Burning" (Chapter 4) and Munro's "The Found Boat" (Chapter 7), Chopin's "The Story of an Hour" (Chapter 8) and Gilman's "The Yellow Wallpaper" (Chapter 12). For help in developing your essay, consult Chapter 35 on the technique of comparison-contrast.

2. Consider "The Sky Is Gray" as an example of the idea of economic determinism (see also Chapter 33). That is, to what degree are the circumstances and traits of the characters, particularly James, controlled and limited by their economic status? According to the idea, how likely is it that the characters can ever rise above their circumstances?

3. Write an essay criticizing the ideas in a story in this anthology which you dislike or to which you are indifferent. With what statements in the story do you disagree? What actions? What characters? How do your own beliefs and values cause you to dislike the story's ideas? How might the story be changed to illustrate ideas with which you would agree?

4. Select an idea that particularly interests you, and write a story showing how characters may or may not live up to the idea. If you have difficulty getting started, try one of these possible ideas:

   a. Interest and enthusiasm are hard to maintain for long.

   b. People always want more than they have or need.

   c. The concerns of adults are different from those of children.

   d. It is awkward to confront another person about a grievance.

   e. Making a romantic or career decision is hard because it requires a change in life's directions.

5. Using books that you discover in the card or computer catalogue in your college or local library, search for discussions of only one of the following topics, and write a brief report on what you find.

   a. D. H. Lawrence or Thomas Hardy on the power of the working classes.

   b. James Joyce on the significance of religion.

   c. Cynthia Ozick on the effects of the Holocaust.

   d. Ernest Hemingway on individualism and self-realization.

   e. Stephen Crane on the power of chance in life.

   f. The ideas underlying Poe's concept of the short story as a form.

   g. Nathaniel Hawthorne on the significance of religion, both good and bad.

11

A Career in Fiction:
A Collection of Stories
by Edgar Allan Poe

POE'S LIFE AND CAREER

Edgar Poe was born in Boston in January 1809. His
parents, who were actors, separated before he was a
year old. Needing to make an independent living,
his mother, Elizabeth Poe, went on an acting tour,
taking Edgar, his infant sister, and his older brother
along with her. Shortly before Poe's third birthday,
Elizabeth died, and the three children were separated. Poe was rescued from a childhood of poverty
when he was taken into foster care by John and
Francis Allan of Richmond, Virginia, who were
childless. The Allans did not make a formal adoption, but when Poe was christened he was given *Allan* as his middle name. In 1815 John Allan, who was an
importer, took his family to England, where they spent five years and where Poe
received his elementary education. In 1820 the Allans returned to America and
Poe resumed his studies at a private school. He was successful both as a student
and as an athlete, one of his noteworthy achievements being a broad jump of
21 feet, 6 inches, a record at the time. In 1826, at the age of seventeen, he
matriculated at the University of Virginia, which had recently been founded by
Thomas Jefferson.

Although Poe was a natural student, personal problems, primarily an
increasingly strained relationship with Allan, upset his studies. Within a year
he left college and went to Boston, where he published his first volume of
poetry in 1827 *(Tamerlane and Other Poems)*. In the same year he joined the
army, and by the time he left service in 1829 he had gained the highest rank
of noncommissioned officers. In 1830, during a truce with Allan following
the death of Mrs. Allan, he was granted an appointment at the United States
Military Academy. Unfortunately, he got into debt, and Allan refused to help

him out despite having become wealthy as the result of an inheritance. In fact, Allan, who had quickly remarried and was beginning a new family, stopped supporting Poe and cut him out of his will entirely. In 1831, lacking the financial help that he needed to maintain his life as a cadet, Poe deliberately got himself expelled from West Point by refusing to obey orders. After this time he never again used *Allan* in his name even though he kept *A* as his middle initial. Now totally dependent on his own resources, he embarked on a career as a writer.

Despite his difficulties with Allan, Poe had been held in high esteem by his fellow West Point cadets, who took up a collection to subsidize the second edition of his poetry in 1832. In the following years, and throughout his career as a writer and editor, he struggled constantly against poverty. It was not that he did not work hard and prolifically. He was always writing reviews, criticism, lectures, poetry, and fiction, and he even tried his hand as a playwright. As with his college and West Point experiences, however, he was unable to stay anywhere for long. He also struggled against alcohol, and excessive drinking caused him to lose some of his positions, although at other times his jobs simply vanished through no fault of his own.

Early in his writing career he went to live in Baltimore with his aunt, Maria ("Muddy") Clemm, and her daughter Virginia ("Sissy"). In 1836, he and Sissy, who was then only thirteen, were married. Mrs. Clemm continued to live with the couple and also managed household affairs as Poe moved from city to city to take new editorial positions. The marriage lasted eleven years until Sissy died of tuberculosis in 1847, when the Poes were living in Fordham, New York (later incorporated into the Bronx). The house they lived in (the "Poe Cottage") still stands and is open to the public.

Although Sissy's death marked a low point in Poe's life, he continued his writing, reviewing, and lecturing. In September 1849, he went on an extended lecture tour, including Richmond, where he had been brought up, as one of his destinations. When there he proposed to Sarah Elmira Royster Shelton, a wealthy widow to whom he had been engaged when he was in his late teens. Elmira's father had objected to the first engagement, and now her three brothers and two children objected because they believed that Poe was an opportunistic drunkard who wanted to marry Elmira only for her money. Despite these objections, Elmira appears genuinely to have loved Poe (she wrote that he was "the *dearest object* on earth" to her), and she accepted his proposal. The couple set a date in mid-October 1849 for the wedding.

It seems clear that Poe was trying to build a new life. He had just taken an oath of sobriety, he was about to marry the sweetheart of his youth, his lectures were increasingly popular, and he was developing an idea for a new critical journal. He had also just received an offer of a short-term but lucrative editing job in Philadelphia. So on September 27, 1849, he left Richmond for the boat and train ride to Philadelphia, after which he was planning to go north to New York to bring Mrs. Clemm to Richmond for the wedding. However, he never reached his destination in Philadelphia, he never did the editing job, and five days after his departure from Richmond he was found in Baltimore in a drunken and incoherent state. He was no longer dressed in his traveling suit but instead was wearing cheap and worn clothing, and he no longer possessed any of the money he had been carrying (which may have been considerable). What had brought him to this condition is a mystery. Existing evidence is inconclusive and sometimes contradictory, but it seems that he may have been waylaid, robbed, beaten, and encouraged or forced to drink a huge amount of liquor. Although it does not seem that anyone made an attempt on his life, as some accounts would have it, it does appear that at some period during the unexplained lapse of time he was under the control of people who were hostile to him.

Whatever actually did happen, and for whatever reason, Poe was in grave condition on October 3, when he was found and taken to the Washington College Hospital (now Church Hospital) in Baltimore. Because he was delirious and sometimes comatose in the hospital, he was unable to tell anyone what had happened to him. He worsened, and on October 7 he died. The following day he was buried in Baltimore's Presbyterian Cemetery. The *Baltimore Clipper* reported that he had died of "congestion of the brain." Since then a number of possible diagnoses have been offered, including acute alcoholic poisoning, hypoglycemia, head trauma, diabetic shock, and even rabies. According to recent scholarship, however, there "simply is not enough medical evidence at hand" to determine the exact cause of death.[1] What we can safely conclude is that Poe died abruptly and under mysterious, suspicious, or even sinister circumstances just when his life and career seemed to be taking a new and positive turn.

POE'S WORK AS A JOURNALIST AND WRITER OF FICTION

During his seventeen-year career as a writer, Poe did editorial work for a number of magazines in Richmond, Philadelphia, and New York, with the most important of his associations being the *Southern Literary Messenger, Burton's Magazine, Graham's Magazine,* the *Broadway Journal,* and the *New York Mirror.* He sometimes had a regular income, although the largest salary he ever received was $800 from his editorship at *Graham's Magazine* in 1841–1842. In 1845 he seemed on the way to success when he began running the *Broadway Journal,* but this publication ran out of money early in 1846 and he was once again in financial trouble.

Along with his uncertain career in journalism and editing, Poe steadily wrote fiction. As a theoretical critic, he provided a foundation for short fiction

---

[1] See John Evangelist Walsh, *Midnight Dreary: The Mysterious Death of Edgar Allan Poe* (New Brunswick: Rutgers UP, 1998), p. 179.

and paved the way for subsequent writers of short stories. His critical review of Hawthorne's *Twice-Told Tales* (1842) is accepted as his theory of fiction.[2] In it he tells us that the special aim of the writer of a short prose tale is to create a concentrated emotional impact. Assuming that the writing is of high quality, the impact is directly related to the brevity of the narrative, which Poe states should take the reader no more than a single sitting of an hour or perhaps two. As a practical fact of reading, he indicates, longer stories and novels diffuse the desired effect because time itself produces inevitable distractions and the need for personal business. Therefore Poe's concept of the story stresses the primacy of effect. The implication of his theory is that, to achieve maximum impact, stories should be based on swiftly moving situations and descriptions, intricate plotting, and moods of fear and horror.

As a practitioner of fiction, Poe was both original and creative. It is to him that we owe the genres of detective story, murder story, horror story, suspense story, and psychological story (sometimes overlapping in the same work). Although he apparently considered himself a poet first and a fiction writer second, his complete stories, or tales, total more than seventy. He sought to capture his readers' attention by freely including material from his wide reading and by using his vivid and often sensational and macabre imagination. Some of his better-known tales are *The Narrative of A. Gordon Pym* (one of his longest stories, sometimes called a novel, 1837), "The Fall of the House of Usher" (1839), "The Murders in the Rue Morgue" (1841), "A Descent into the Maelström" (1841), "The Pit and the Pendulum" (1842), "The Masque of the Red Death" (1842), "The Tell-Tale Heart" (1843), "The Gold Bug" (1843), "The Black Cat" (1843), "The Purloined Letter" (1844), and "The Cask of Amontillado" (1846). He also assembled many of his tales into two major collections: *Tales of the Grotesque and Arabesque* (1840) and *Tales* (1845).

Because Poe as a practicing writer followed his own theory of fiction, he does not seek to create full-blown, "round" character development in his tales, but instead he focuses on situations, actions, and his characters' responses. His subject matter varies widely: He includes faraway, exotic, and often lugubrious locations such as Paris, the sea, American islands, dreary and collapsible mansions, Gothic interiors, cellars, subterranean vaults, and mythological ends of the earth. Few of his characters fall within the spectrum of what we think of as normal, and a number who start out as normal take a turn into the unusual or bizarre. Some characters are driven by pride and/or guilt; some commit deranged and grisly crimes; some are dead, either recently or for centuries; some of the dead are revivified long enough to claim possession over the living. The actions in Poe's stories are uncanny and often weird, consisting of intricate punishments, self-destructiveness, live burials, mysterious substitutions of personality, journeys into unknown regions, trips to the moon, total physical and psychological collapse, and strange and sometimes comic resurrections of the dead.

---

[2] See also Chapter 2, p. 53.

POE'S REPUTATION

In his lifetime Poe was not highly regarded in America. Perhaps his lack of recognition resulted from his own combativeness, for he constantly alienated people who might have supported him. From time to time he was involved in lawsuits, literary quarrels, and even a fistfight. He accused Henry Wadsworth Longfellow, one of the major poets of the time, of plagiarism—certainly not a way to make himself popular and respected within the nineteenth-century American literary community. He achieved success to the degree that he won a few prizes for stories, but his chief recognition was the praise heaped upon his poem "The Raven" in 1845 (for which he received little money). In 1846 he received a letter from Elizabeth Barrett Browning congratulating him on the warm reception of his works in England, and in the same year he was commended by Nathaniel Hawthorne even though he had written negative criticism of some of Hawthorne's fiction. The highest public recognition Poe received in his lifetime was his representation in *Prose Writers of America* (1847), edited by his sometime friend, Rufus Griswold, who also was his literary executor.

After Poe died, the decline of his reputation was hastened by Griswold, who published a short but poisonous biography, most of which was later included in various editions of Poe's collected works. (Griswold stated, in italics, that *"few will be grieved by"* Poe's death, and that Poe *"had few or no friends."*) Before long the public perception of Poe was that he had been an alcoholic and brooding loner who wrote about characters beyond the fringes of sanity. Poe's works did not contradict this image, for many unsophisticated readers readily believed that some of his disturbed fictional and poetic narrators (such as those of "The Black Cat," "The Cask of Amontillado," and "The Tell-Tale Heart") were the writer himself in his own person.

His work therefore fell into relative obscurity except in France, where he was considered a brilliant and creative though eccentric visionary. In the United States his reputation as a writer was obscured by the more objectionable and unexplainable aspects of his life, principally his marriage to his thirteen-year-old cousin together with reports of alcoholism and drug addiction and the mysterious circumstances of his death. As his writings have become more available, and as the early opinions about him have been modified, his literary reputation has risen. He is seen today as a romantic who asserted the need for artistic individuality and integrity and who in his works explored the exotic, the passionate, the puzzling, the intricate, the uncontrollable, the vengeful, and—in the face of human violence—the power of conscience. Because many of his works are unrealistic, grisly, and macabre, general readers often appreciate him for the shudder of sensational horror, while critics find ample materials for readings that are symbolic, allegorical, feminist, psychological, structuralist, and formalist. Today, of all nineteenth-century American writers of fiction, Poe is the most widely published and still the most widely read. His stature as a writer was fully acknowledged in 1986, when his name was placed in the Hall of Fame of American Authors.

BIBLIOGRAPHIC SOURCES

The number of books and essays about Poe is vast. The standard edition of the works is the three-volume *Collected Works of Edgar Allan Poe,* edited by Thomas Olive Mabbott (1969–1978). The Library of America edition of Poe's *Poetry and Tales* and *Essays and Reviews* appeared in 1984 in two volumes. A convenient popular edition has been regularly available for the last sixty years in the Modern Library edition of *The Complete Tales and Poems of Edgar Allan Poe,* with an introduction by Hervey Allen (1938). This volume includes seventy-three stories and fifty-three poems. Another readily available edition is G. R. Thompson, ed., *Great Short Works of Edgar Allan Poe* (1970). A thoroughgoing edition of the stories is *The Short Fiction of Edgar Allan Poe: An Annotated Edition* (1976, rpt. 1990), edited by Stuart and Susan Levine. This volume also contains a comprehensive introduction, a useful arrangement of the stories, copious notes, and an excellent working bibliography. An interesting popular edition is *18 Best Stories by Edgar Allan Poe* (1965), edited by Vincent Price and Chandler Brossard, with an introduction by Vincent Price, a film actor who specialized in movie villains and starred in film adaptations of Poe stories. Price's introduction, though brief, is therefore of independent interest.

Biographies of Poe are Kenneth Silverman, *Edgar A. Poe: Mournful and Never-ending Remembrance* (1991); Jeffrey Meyers, *Edgar Allan Poe: His Life and Legacy* (1992); and Scott Peeples, *Edgar Allan Poe Revisited* (1998). Other excellent biographies are Arthur H. Quinn, *Edgar Allan Poe: A Critical Biography* (1941); and Edward Wagenknecht, *Edgar Allan Poe: The Man Behind the Legend* (1963). George E. Woodberry's biography *Edgar Allan Poe,* originally published in 1885, was reprinted in 1980 with an introduction and evaluation by R. W. B. Lewis. To these biographies should be added John Evangelist Walsh, *Midnight Dreary: The Mysterious Death of Edgar Allan Poe* (1998), a study of the relevant evidence concerning Poe's death.

Significant criticism may be found in Kenneth Silverman, ed., *New Essays on Poe's Major Tales* (1993); William L. Howarth, ed., *Twentieth Century Interpretations of Poe's Tales* (1971); Charles E. May, *Edgar Allan Poe: A Study of the Short Fiction* (1991); Vincent Buranelli, *Edgar Allan Poe* (1961); A. Robert Lee, ed., *Edgar Allan Poe: The Design of Order* (1987); Eric W. Carlson, ed., *Critical Essays on Edgar Allan Poe* (1987); Shawn Rosenheim and Stephen Rachman, eds., *The American Face of Edgar Allan Poe* (1995); J. R. Hammond, *An Edgar Allan Poe Companion* (1981); and Bonnie Szumski and Carol Prime, eds., *Readings on Edgar Allan Poe* (1998). Eric W. Carlson in *The Recognition of Edgar Allan Poe* (1966) reprints essays and portions of essays selected to show the changes and growth of Poe's reputation from the time of his death through 1965, the year of publication. Louis Broussard, *The Measure of Poe* (1969), includes a fifty-nine-page bibliography, up to date through 1969, and May includes a ten-page bibliography, up to date through 1991. These works are complemented by the selected bibliography provided by Peeples (pp. 196–203), which reflects criticism through 1998. In 1993 a video recording was issued with the title *Homage to Edgar Allan Poe.*

Foreign interest in Poe was pioneered by the nineteenth-century French poet Charles Baudelaire, whose *Edgar Allan Poe: Sa Vie et ses Ouvrages* of 1852 was reprinted in 1994. A recent Italian work on Poe is by Giorgio Ghidetti, *Poe, L'Eresia de un Americano Maledetto* (1989).

Poe's works have been the subject of many musical settings. More than one composer has adapted *The Fall of the House of Usher* as a musical drama, and another of Poe's stories, *Ligeia,* has also been set to music. As one might expect, composers writing music for Poe's works have found the poetry to be of greater interest than the fiction. The most significant musical version of Poe is by Sergei Rachmaninoff (1873–1943), who composed "The Bells" (see Chapter 19) in 1913 for soloists, chorus, and orchestra to a Russian adaptation of the poem by Konstantin Balmont. Two more recent musical versions of Poe's poems are Norman Dello Joio's chorus *The Quest* (1991) and Paul Moravec's song cycle *Evensong* (1992).

SPECIAL TOPICS FOR WRITING AND ARGUMENT ABOUT POE

1. Poe's idea that fiction should create a single and clearly focused impression or impact on the reader.
2. Poe's explorations of the eerie and bizarre.
3. Poe's use of setting in one or more stories.
4. Poe's use of irony and humor.
5. Poe and psychology: the meaning of evil in the lives of his characters.
6. The inevitability of guilt and punishment following criminal and immoral behavior.
7. The social background of Poe's stories (the people and their ways of life, work habits, husband-wife relationships, involvement in the world at large).
8. Poe's use of symbolism and/or allegory.
9. Poe's use of dramatic dialogue and indirect discourse.
10. The nature of the "ratiocinative" or reasoning (or "detective") story.
11. Poe's use of the first-person narrator.

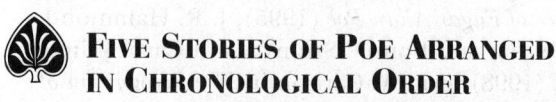

FIVE STORIES OF POE ARRANGED IN CHRONOLOGICAL ORDER

The Fall of the House of Usher (1839), 529
The Masque of the Red Death (1842), 541
The Black Cat (1843), 545
The Purloined Letter (1844), 551
The Cask of Amontillado (1846), 563

The Fall of the House of Usher ———————————————— *1839*

> *Son cœur est un luth suspendu;*
> *Sitôt qu'on le touche il resonne.*
> *—De Béranger.°*

During the whole of a dull, dark, and soundless day in the autumn of the year, when the clouds hung oppressively low in the heavens, I had been passing alone, on horse-back, through a singularly dreary tract of country; and at length found myself, as the shades of the evening drew on, within view of the melancholy House of Usher. I know not how it was—but, with the first glimpse of the building, a sense of insufferable gloom pervaded my spirit. I say insufferable; for the feeling was unrelieved by any of that half-pleasurable, because poetic, sentiment, with which the mind usually receives even the sternest natural images of the desolate or terrible. I looked upon the scene before me—upon the mere house, and the simple landscape features of the domain—upon the bleak walls—upon the vacant eye-like windows—upon a few rank sedges—and upon a few white trunks of decayed trees—with an utter depression of soul which I can com-pare to no earthly sensation more properly than to the afterdream of the reveller upon opium—the bitter lapse into everyday life—the hideous dropping off of the veil. There was an iciness, a sinking, a sickening of the heart—an unredeemed dreariness of thought which no goading of the imagination could torture into aught of the sublime. What was it—I paused to think—what was it that so unnerved me in the contempla-tion of the House of Usher? It was a mystery all insoluble; nor could I grapple with the shadowy fancies that crowded upon me as I pondered. I was forced to fall back upon the unsatisfactory conclusion, that while, beyond doubt, there *are* combinations of very simple natural objects which have the power of thus affecting us, still the analysis of this power lies among considerations beyond our depth. It was possible, I reflected, that a mere different arrangement of the particulars of the scene, of the details of the picture, would be sufficient to modify, or perhaps to annihilate its capacity for sorrowful impression; and, acting upon this idea, I reined my horse to the precipitous brink of a black and lurid tarn that lay in unruffled lustre by the dwelling, and gazed down—but with a shudder even more thrilling than before—upon the remodelled and inverted images of the gray sedge, and the ghastly tree-stems, and the vacant and eye-like win-dows.

Nevertheless, in this mansion of gloom I now proposed to myself a sojourn of some weeks. Its proprietor, Roderick Usher, had been one of my boon companions in boyhood; but many years had elapsed since our last meeting. A letter, however, had lately reached me in a distant part of the country—a letter from him—which, in its wildly importunate nature, had admitted of no other than a personal reply. The MS. gave evidence of ner-vous agitation. The writer spoke of acute bodily illness—of a mental disorder which oppressed him—and of an earnest desire to see me, as his best, and indeed his only per-sonal friend, with a view of attempting, by the cheerfulness of my society, some alleviation of his malady. It was the manner in which all this, and much more, was said—it was the apparent *heart* that went with his request—which allowed me no room for hesitation; and I accordingly obeyed forthwith what I still considered a very singular summons.

Son cœur . . . De Béranger: a passage of a poem by Pierre-Jean de Béranger (1780–1857): "His heart is a tightly strung lute; / It rings as soon as it is touched."

Although, as boys, we had been even intimate associates, yet I really knew little of my friend. His reserve had been always excessive and habitual. I was aware, however, that his very ancient family had been noted, time out of mind, for a peculiar sensibility of temperament, displaying itself, through long ages, in many works of exalted art, and manifested, of late, in repeated deeds of munificent yet unobtrusive charity, as well as in a passionate devotion to the intricacies, perhaps even more than to the orthodox and easily recognisable beauties, of musical science. I had learned, too, the very remarkable fact, that the stem of the Usher race, all time-honored as it was, had put forth, at no period, any enduring branch; in other words, that the entire family lay in the direct line of descent, and had always, with very trifling and very temporary variation, so lain. It was this deficiency, I considered, while running over in thought the perfect keeping of the character of the premises with the accredited character of the people, and while speculating upon the possible influence which the one, in the long lapse of centuries, might have exercised upon the other—it was this deficiency, perhaps, of collateral issue, and the consequent undeviating transmission, from sire to son, of the patrimony with the name, which had, at length, so identified the two as to merge the original title of the estate in the quaint and equivocal appellation of the "House of Usher"—an appellation which seemed to include, in the minds of the peasantry who used it, both the family and the family mansion.

I have said that the sole effect of my somewhat childish experiment—that of looking down within the tarn—had been to deepen the first singular impression. There can be no doubt that the consciousness of the rapid increase of my superstition—for why should I not so term it?—served mainly to accelerate the increase itself. Such, I have long known, is the paradoxical law of all sentiments having terror as a basis. And it might have been for this reason only, that, when I again uplifted my eyes to the house itself, from its image in the pool, there grew in my mind a strange fancy—a fancy so ridiculous, indeed, that I but mention it to show the vivid force of the sensations which oppressed me. I had so worked upon my imagination as really to believe that about the whole mansion and domain there hung an atmosphere peculiar to themselves and their immediate vicinity—an atmosphere which had no affinity with the air of heaven, but which had reeked up from the decayed trees, and the gray wall, and the silent tarn—pestilent and mystic vapor, dull, sluggish, faintly discernible, and leaden-hued.

Shaking off from my spirit what *must* have been a dream, I scanned more narrowly the real aspect of the building. Its principal feature seemed to be that of an excessive antiquity. The discoloration of ages had been great. Minute fungi overspread the whole exterior, hanging in a fine tangled web-work from the eaves. Yet all this was apart from any extraordinary dilapidation. No portion of the masonry had fallen; and there appeared to be a wild inconsistency between its still perfect adaptation of parts, and the crumbling condition of the individual stones. In this there was much that reminded me of the specious totality of old wood-work which has rotted for long years in some neglected vault, with no disturbance from the breath of the external air. Beyond this indication of extensive decay, however, the fabric gave little token of instability. Perhaps the eye of a scrutinizing observer might have discovered a barely perceptible fissure, which, extending from the roof of the building in front, made its way down the wall in a zigzag direction, until it became lost in the sullen waters of the tarn.

Noticing these things, I rode over a short causeway to the house. A servant in waiting took my horse, and I entered the Gothic archway of the hall. A valet, of stealthy step, thence conducted me, in silence, through many dark and intricate passages in my progress to the *studio* of his master. Much that I encountered on the way contributed, I know not how, to heighten the vague sentiments of which I have already spoken. While the objects around me—while the carvings of the ceilings, the sombre tapestries of the walls, the ebon blackness of the floors, and the phantasmagoric armorial trophies which rattled as I strode, were but matters to which, or to such as which, I had been accustomed from my infancy—while I hesitated not to acknowledge how familiar was all this—I still wondered to find how unfamiliar were the fancies which ordinary images were stirring up. On one of the staircases, I met the physician of the family. His countenance, I thought, wore a mingled expression of low cunning and perplexity. He accosted me with trepidation and passed on. The valet now threw open a door and ushered me into the presence of his master.

The room in which I found myself was very large and lofty. The windows were long, narrow, and pointed, and at so vast a distance from the black oaken floor as to be altogether inaccessible from within. Feeble gleams of encrimsoned light made their way through the trellissed panes, and served to render sufficiently distinct the more prominent objects around; the eye, however, struggled in vain to reach the remoter angles of the chamber, or the recesses of the vaulted and fretted ceiling. Dark draperies hung upon the walls. The general furniture was profuse, comfortless, antique, and tattered. Many books and musical instruments lay scattered about, but failed to give any vitality to the scene. I felt that I breathed an atmosphere of sorrow. An air of stern, deep, and irredeemable gloom hung over and pervaded all.

Upon my entrance, Usher arose from a sofa on which he had been lying at full length, and greeted me with a vivacious warmth which had much in it, I at first thought, of an overdone cordiality—of the constrained effort of the *ennuyé* man of the world. A glance, however, at his countenance, convinced me of his perfect sincerity. We sat down; and for some moments, while he spoke not, I gazed upon him with a feeling half of pity, half of awe. Surely, man had never before so terribly altered, in so brief a period, as had Roderick Usher! It was with difficulty that I could bring myself to admit the identity of the wan being before me with the companion of my early boyhood. Yet the character of his face had been at all times remarkable. A cadaverousness of complexion; an eye large, liquid, and luminous beyond comparison; lips somewhat thin and very pallid, but of a surpassingly beautiful curve; a nose of a delicate Hebrew model, but with a breadth of nostril unusual in similar formations; a finely moulded chin, speaking, in its want of prominence, of a want of moral energy; hair of a more than web-like softness and tenuity; these features, with an inordinate expansion above the regions of the temple, made up altogether a countenance not easily to be forgotten. And now in the mere exaggeration of the prevailing character of these features, and of the expression they were wont to convey, lay so much of change that I doubted to whom I spoke. The now ghastly pallor of the skin, and the now miraculous lustre of the eye, above all things startled and even awed me. The silken hair, too, had been suffered to grow all unheeded, and as, in its wild gossamer texture, it floated rather than fell about the face, I could not, even with effort, connect its Arabesque expression with any idea of simple humanity.

In the manner of my friend I was at once struck with an incoherence—an inconsistency; and I soon found this to arise from a series of feeble and futile struggles to overcome an habitual trepidancy—an excessive nervous agitation. For something of this nature I had indeed been prepared, no less by his letter, than by reminiscences of certain boyish traits, and by conclusions deduced from his peculiar physical conformation and temperament. His action was alternately vivacious and sullen. His voice varied rapidly from a tremulous indecision (when the animal spirits seemed utterly in abeyance) to that species of energetic concision—that abrupt, weighty, unhurried, and hollow-sounding enunciation—that leaden, self-balanced and perfectly modulated gut-tural utterance, which may be observed in the lost drunkard, or the irreclaimable eater of opium, during the periods of his most intense excitement.

It was thus that he spoke of the object of my visit, of his earnest desire to see me, and of the solace he expected me to afford him. He entered, at some length, into what he conceived to be the nature of his malady. It was, he said, a constitutional and a family evil, and one for which he despaired to find a remedy—a mere nervous affection, he immediately added, which would undoubtedly soon pass off. It displayed itself in a host of unnatural sensations. Some of these, as he detailed them, interested and bewildered me; although, perhaps, the terms, and the general manner of the narration had their weight. He suffered much from a morbid acuteness of the senses; the most insipid food was alone endurable; he could wear only garments of certain texture; the odors of all flowers were oppressive; his eyes were tortured by even a faint light; and there were but peculiar sounds, and these from stringed instruments, which did not inspire him with horror.

To an anomalous species of terror I found him a bounden slave. "I shall perish," said he, "I *must* perish in this deplorable folly. Thus, thus, and not otherwise, shall I be lost. I dread the events of the future, not in themselves, but in their results. I shudder at the thought of any, even the most trivial, incident, which may operate upon this intoler-able agitation of soul. I have, indeed, no abhorrence of danger, except in its absolute effect—in terror. In this unnerved—in this pitiable condition—I feel that the period will sooner or later arrive when I must abandon life and reason together, in some strug-gle with the grim phantasm, FEAR."

I learned, moreover, at intervals, and through broken and equivocal hints, another singular feature of his mental condition. He was enchained by certain superstitious impressions in regard to the dwelling which he tenanted, and whence, for many years, he had never ventured forth—in regard to an influence whose supposititious force was con-veyed in terms too shadowy here to be re-stated—an influence which some peculiarities in the mere form and substance of his family mansion, had, by dint of long sufferance, he said, obtained over his spirit—an effect which the *physique* of the gray walls and turrets, and of the dim tarn into which they all looked down, had, at length, brought about upon the *morale* of his existence.

He admitted, however, although with hesitation, that much of the peculiar gloom which thus afflicted him could be traced to a more natural and far more palpable origin—to the severe and long-continued illness—indeed to the evidently approach-ing dissolution—of a tenderly beloved sister—his sole companion for long years—his last and only relative on earth. "Her decease," he said, with a bitterness which I can never forget, "would leave him (him the hopeless and the frail) the last of the ancient race of the Ushers." While he spoke, the lady Madeline (for so was she called) passed slowly through a remote portion of the apartment, and, without having noticed my presence, disappeared. I regarded her with an utter astonishment not unmingled with dread—and yet I found it impossible to account for such feelings. A sensation of stupor oppressed me, as my eyes followed her retreating steps. When a door, at length, closed upon her, my glance sought instinctively and eagerly the countenance of the brother—but he had buried his face in his hands, and I could only perceive that a far more than ordinary wanness had overspread the emaciated fingers through which trickled many passionate tears.

The disease of the lady Madeline had long baffled the skill of her physicians. A settled apathy, a gradual wasting away of the person, and frequent although transient affections of a partially cataleptical character, were the unusual diagnosis. Hitherto she had steadily borne up against the pressure of her malady, and had not betaken herself finally to bed; but, on the closing in of the evening of my arrival at the house, she succumbed (as her brother told me at night with inexpressible agitation) to the prostrating power of the destroyer; and I learned that the glimpse I had obtained of her person would thus probably be the last I should obtain—that the lady, at least while living, would be seen by me no more.

For several days ensuing, her name was unmentioned by either Usher or myself: 15
and during this period I was busied in earnest endeavors to alleviate the melancholy of my friend. We painted and read together; or I listened, as if in a dream, to the wild improvisations of his speaking guitar. And thus, as a closer and still closer intimacy admitted me more unreservedly into the recesses of his spirit, the more bitterly did I perceive the futility of all attempt at cheering a mind from which darkness, as if an inherent positive quality, poured forth upon all objects of the moral and physical universe, in one unceasing radiation of gloom.

I shall ever bear about me a memory of the many solemn hours I thus spent alone with the master of the House of Usher. Yet I should fail in any attempt to convey an idea of the exact character of the studies, or of the occupations, in which he involved me, or led me the way. An excited and highly distempered ideality threw a sulphureous lustre over all. His long improvised dirges will ring forever in my ears. Among other things, I hold painfully in mind a certain singular perversion and amplification of the wild air of the last waltz of Von Weber.° From the paintings over which his elaborate fancy brooded, and which grew, touch by touch, into vaguenesses at which I shuddered the more thrillingly, because I shuddered knowing not why;—from these paintings (vivid as their images now are before me) I would in vain endeavor to educe more than a small portion which should lie within the compass of merely written words. By the utter simplicity, by the nakedness of his designs, he arrested and overawed attention. If ever mortal painted an idea, that mortal was Roderick Usher. For me at least—in the circumstances then surrounding me—there arose out of the pure abstractions which the hypochondriac contrived to throw upon his canvass, an intensity of intolerable awe, no shadow of which felt I ever yet in the contemplation of the certainly glowing yet too concrete reveries of Fuseli.°

One of the phantasmagoric conceptions of my friend, partaking not so rigidly of the spirit of abstraction, may be shadowed forth, although feebly, in words. A small picture presented the interior of an immensely long and rectangular vault or tunnel, with low walls, smooth, white, and without interruption or device. Certain accessory points of the design served well to convey the idea that this excavation lay at an exceeding depth below the surface of the earth. No outlet was observed in any portion of its vast extent, and no torch, or other artificial source of light was discernible; yet a flood of intense rays rolled throughout, and bathed the whole in a ghastly and inappropriate splendor.

I have just spoken of that morbid condition of the auditory nerve which rendered all music intolerable to the sufferer, with the exception of certain effects of stringed instruments. It was, perhaps, the narrow limits to which he thus confined himself upon the guitar, which gave birth, in great measure, to the fantastic character of his performances. But the fervid *facility* of his *impromptus* could not be so accounted for. They must have been, and were, in the notes, as well as in the words of his wild fantasias (for he not unfrequently accompanied himself with rhymed verbal improvisations), the result

Von Weber: Carl Maria Von Weber (1786–1826), German composer.
Fuseli: Henry Fuseli (1741–1825), Swiss-English painter whose best-known work is "The Nightmare" (1781).

of that intense mental collectedness and concentration to which I have previously alluded as observable only in particular moments of the highest artificial excitement. The words of one of these rhapsodies I have easily remembered. I was, perhaps, the more forcibly impressed with it, as he gave it, because, in the under or mystic current of its meaning, I fancied that I perceived, and for the first time, a full consciousness on the part of Usher, of the tottering of his lofty reason upon her throne. The verses, which were entitled "The Haunted Palace," ran very nearly, if not accurately, thus:

I

In the greenest of our valleys,
  By good angels tenanted,
Once a fair and stately palace—
  Radiant palace—reared its head.
In the monarch Thought's dominion—
  It stood there!
Never seraph spread a pinion
  Over fabric half so fair.

II

Banners yellow, glorious, golden,
  On its roof did float and flow;
(This—all this—was in the olden
  Time long ago)
And every gentle air that dallied,
  In that sweet day,
Along the ramparts plumed and pallid,
  A winged odor went away.

20

III

Wanderers in that happy valley
  Through two luminous windows saw
Spirits moving musically
  To a lute's well-tunéd law,
Round about a throne, where sitting
  (Porphyrogene!)°
In state his glory well befitting,
  The ruler of the realm was seen.

IV

And all with pearl and ruby glowing
  Was the fair palace door,
Through which came flowing, flowing, flowing,
  And sparkling evermore,
A troop of Echoes whose sweet duty
  Was but to sing,
In voices of surpassing beauty,
  The wit and wisdom of their king.

Porphyrogene: i.e., made of porphyry, a red stone that takes a high-gloss finish.

V

But evil things, in robes of sorrow,
  Assailed the monarch's high estate;
(Ah, let us mourn, for never morrow
  Shall dawn upon him, desolate!)
And, round about his home, the glory
  That blushed and bloomed
Is but a dim-remembered story
  Of the old time entombed.

VI

And travellers now within that valley,
  Through the red-litten windows, see
Vast forms that move fantastically
  To a discordant melody;
While, like a rapid ghastly river,
  Through the pale door,
A hideous throng rush out forever,
  And laugh—but smile no more.

I well remember that suggestions arising from this ballad, led us into a train of 25
thought wherein there became manifest an opinion of Usher's which I mention not so
much on account of its novelty, (for other men* have thought thus,) as on account of
the pertinacity with which he maintained it. This opinion, in its general form, was that
of the sentience of all vegetable things. But, in his disordered fancy, the idea had
assumed a more daring character, and trespassed, under certain conditions, upon the
kingdom of inorganization. I lack words to express the full extent, or the earnest *abandon* of his persuasion. The belief, however, was connected (as I have previously hinted)
with the gray stones of the home of his forefathers. The conditions of the sentience had
been here, he imagined, fulfilled in the method of collocation of these stones—in the
order of their arrangement, as well as in that of the many *fungi* which overspread them,
and of the decayed trees which stood around—above all, in the long undisturbed
endurance of this arrangement, and in its reduplication in the still waters of the tarn. Its
evidence—the evidence of the sentience—was to be seen, he said, (and I here started as
he spoke,) in the gradual yet certain condensation of an atmosphere of their own about
the waters and the walls. The result was discoverable, he added, in that silent, yet importunate and terrible influence which for centuries had moulded the destinies of his
family, and which made *him* what I now saw him—what he was. Such opinions need no
comment, and I will make none.

  Our books—the books which, for years, had formed no small portion of the
mental existence of the invalid—were, as might be supposed, in strict keeping with this
character of phantasm. We pored together over such works as the Ververt et Chartreuse
of Gresset; the Belphegor of Machiavelli; the Heaven and Hell of Swedenborg; the
Subterranean Voyage of Nicholas Klimm by Holberg; the Chiromancy of Robert Flud, of
Jean D'Indaginé, and of De la Chambre; the Journey into the Blue Distance of Tieck;
and the City of the Sun of Campanella. One favorite volume was a small octavo edition

  * Watson, Dr. Percival, Spallanzani, and especially the Bishop of Landaff.—See "Chemical
Essays," vol. v. [Poe's own note. He is citing these scientific and historical writers as support for his
assertions.]

of the *Directorium Inquisitorium,* by the Dominican Eymeric de Gironne; and there were passages in Pomponius Mela, about the old African Satyrs and Œgipans, over which Usher would sit dreaming for hours. His chief delight, however, was found in the perusal of an exceedingly rare and curious book in quarto Gothic—the manual of a forgotten church—the *Vigiliae Mortuorum secundum Chorum Ecclesiae Maguntinae.*°

I could not help thinking of the wild ritual of this work, and of its probable influence upon the hypochondriac, when, one evening, having informed me abruptly that the lady Madeline was no more, he stated his intention of preserving her corpse for a fortnight, (previously to its final internment,) in one of the numerous vaults within the main walls of the building. The worldly reason, however, assigned for this singular proceeding, was one which I did not feel at liberty to dispute. The brother had been led to his resolution (so he told me) by consideration of the unusual character of the malady of the deceased, of certain obtrusive and eager inquiries on the part of her medical men, and of the remote and exposed situation of the burial-ground of the family. I will not deny that when I called to mind the sinister countenance of the person whom I met upon the staircase, on the day of my arrival at the house, I had no desire to oppose what I regarded as at best but a harmless, and by no means an unnatural, precaution.

At the request of Usher, I personally aided him in the arrangements for the temporary entombment. The body having been encoffined, we two alone bore it to its rest. The vault in which we placed it (and which had been so long unopened that our torches, half smothered in its oppressive atmosphere, gave us little opportunity for investigation) was small, damp, and entirely without means of admission for light; lying, at great depth, immediately beneath that portion of the building in which was my own sleeping apartment. It had been used, apparently, in remote feudal times, for the worst purposes of a donjon-keep and, in later days, as a place of deposit for powder, or some other highly combustible substance, as a portion of its floor, and the whole interior of a long archway through which we reached it, were carefully sheathed with copper. The door, of massive iron, had been, also, similarly protected. Its immense weight caused an unusually sharp grating sound, as it moved upon its hinges.

Having deposited our mournful burden upon tressels within this region of horror, we partially turned aside the yet unscrewed lid of the coffin, and looked upon the face of the tenant. A striking similitude between the brother and sister now first arrested my attention; and Usher, divining, perhaps, my thoughts, murmured out some few words from which I learned that the deceased and himself had been twins, and that sympathies of a scarcely intelligible nature had always existed between them. Our glances, however, rested not long upon the dead—for we could not regard her unawed. The disease which had thus entombed the lady in the maturity of youth, had left, as usual in all maladies of a strictly cataleptical character, the mockery of a faint blush upon the bosom and the face, and that suspiciously lingering smile upon the lip which is so terrible in death. We replaced and screwed down the lid, and, having secured the door of iron, made our way, with toil, into the scarcely less gloomy apartments of the upper portion of the house.

And now, some days of bitter grief having elapsed, an observable change came over the features of the mental disorder of my friend. His ordinary manner had vanished. His ordinary occupations were neglected or forgotten. He roamed from chamber

Our books . . . Maguntinae (paragraph 27): Poe's speaker characterizes the works of the writers contained in the paragraph as being "in keeping with this character of phantasm." This judgment is right; the works are about mysticism, utopias, travels to fantastic underworld countries, palmistry, and forest deities such as Pan. The concluding reference is to a 1500 publication describing ceremonies and prayers for the dead.

to chamber with hurried, unequal, and objectless step. The pallor of his countenance had assumed, if possible, a more ghastly hue—but the luminousness of his eye had utterly gone out. The once occasional huskiness of his tone was heard no more; and a tremulous quaver, as if of extreme terror, habitually characterized his utterance. There were times, indeed, when I thought his unceasingly agitated mind was laboring with some oppressive secret, to divulge which he struggled for the necessary courage. At times, again, I was obliged to resolve all into the mere inexplicable vagaries of madness, for I beheld him gazing upon vacancy for long hours, in an attitude of the profoundest attention, as if listening to some imaginary sound. It was no wonder that condition terrified—that it infected me. I felt creeping upon me, by slow yet certain degrees, the wild influences of his own fantastic yet impressive superstitions.

It was, especially, upon retiring to bed late in the night of the seventh or eighth day after the placing of the lady Madeline within the donjon, that I experienced the full power of such feelings. Sleep came not near my couch—while the hours waned and waned away. I struggled to reason off the nervousness which had dominion over me. I endeavored to believe that much, if not all of what I felt, was due to the bewildering influence of the gloomy furniture of the room—of the dark and tattered draperies, which, tortured into motion by the breath of a rising tempest, swayed fitfully to and fro upon the walls, and rustled uneasily about the decorations of the bed. But my efforts were fruitless. An irrepressible tremor gradually pervaded my frame; and, at length, there sat upon my very heart an incubus of utterly causeless alarm. Shaking this off with a gasp and a struggle, I uplifted myself upon the pillows, and, peering earnestly within the intense darkness of the chamber, harkened—I know not why, except that an instinctive spirit prompted me—to certain low and indefinite sounds which came, through the pauses of the storm, at long intervals, I knew not whence. Overpowered by an intense sentiment of horror, unaccountable yet unendurable, I threw on my clothes with haste (for I felt that I should sleep no more during the night), and endeavored to arouse myself from the pitiable condition into which I had fallen, by pacing rapidly to and fro through the apartment.

I had taken but few turns in this manner, when a light step on an adjoining staircase arrested my attention. I presently recognised it as that of Usher. In an instant afterward he rapped, with a gentle touch, at my door, and entered, bearing a lamp. His countenance was, as usual, cadaverously wan—but, moreover, there was a species of mad hilarity in his eyes—an evidently restrained *hysteria* in his whole demeanor. His air appalled me—but anything was preferable to the solitude which I had so long endured, and I even welcomed his presence as a relief.

"And you have not seen it?" he said abruptly, after having stared about him for some moments in silence—"you have not then seen it?—but, stay! you shall." Thus speaking, and having carefully shaded his lamp, he hurried to one of the casements, and threw it freely open to the storm.

The impetuous fury of the entering gust nearly lifted us from our feet. It was, indeed, a tempestuous yet sternly beautiful night, and one wildly singular in its terror and its beauty. A whirlwind had apparently collected its force in our vicinity; for there were frequent and violent alterations in the direction of the wind; and the exceeding density of the clouds (which hung so low as to press upon the turrets of the house) did not prevent our perceiving the life-like velocity with which they flew careering from all points against each other, without passing away into the distance. I say that even their exceeding density did not prevent our perceiving this—yet we had no glimpse of the moon or stars—nor was there any flashing forth of the lightning. But the under surfaces of the huge masses of agitated vapor, as well as all terrestrial objects immediately around us, were glowing in the unnatural light of a faintly luminous and distinctly visible gaseous exhalation which hung about and enshrouded the mansion.

"You must not—you shall not behold this!" said I, shudderingly, to Usher, as I led him, with a gentle violence, from the window to a seat. "These appearances, which bewilder you, are merely electrical phenomena not uncommon—or it may be that they have their ghastly origin in the rank miasma of the tarn. Let us close this casement;—the air is chilling and dangerous to your frame. Here is one of your favorite romances. I will read, and you shall listen;—and so we will pass away this terrible night together."

35

The antique volume which I had taken up was the "Mad Trist" of Sir Launcelot Canning;° but I had called it a favorite of Usher's more in sad jest than in earnest; for, in truth, there is little in its uncouth and unimaginative prolixity which could have had interest for the lofty and spiritual ideality of my friend. It was, however, the only book immediately at hand; and I indulged a vague hope that the excitement which now agitated the hypochondriac, might find relief (for the history of mental disorder is full of similar anomalies) even in the extremeness of the folly which I should read. Could I have judged, indeed, by the wild overstrained air of vivacity with which he harkened, or apparently harkened, to the words of the tale, I might well have congratulated myself upon the success of my design.

I had arrived at that well-known portion of the story where Ethelred, the hero of the Trist, having sought in vain for peaceable admission into the dwelling of the hermit, proceeds to make good an entrance by force. Here, it will be remembered, the words of the narrative run thus:

"And Ethelred, who was by nature of a doughty heart, and who was now mighty withal, on account of the powerfulness of the wine which he had drunken, waited no longer to hold parley with the hermit, who, in sooth, was of an obstinate and maliceful turn, but, feeling the rain upon his shoulders, and fearing the rising of the tempest, uplifted his mace outright, and, with blows, made quickly room in the plankings of the door for his gauntleted hand; and now pulling therewith sturdily, he so cracked, and ripped, and tore all asunder, that the noise of the dry and hollow-sounding wood alarummed and reverberated throughout the forest."

At the termination of this sentence I started, and for a moment, paused; for it appeared to me (although I at once concluded that my excited fancy had deceived me)—it appeared to me that, from some very remote portion of the mansion, there came, indistinctly, to my ears, what might have been, in its exact similarity of character, the echo (but a stifled and dull one certainly) of the very cracking and ripping sound which Sir Launcelot had so particularly described. It was, beyond doubt, the coincidence alone which had arrested my attention; for, amid the rattling of the sashes of the casements, and the ordinary commingled noises of the still increasing storm, the sound, in itself, had nothing, surely, which should have interested or disturbed me. I continued the story:

"But the good champion Ethelred, now entering within the door, was sore enraged and amazed to perceive no signal of the maliceful hermit; but, in the stead thereof, a dragon of a scaly and prodigious demeanor, and of a fiery tongue, which sate in guard

---

the "Mad Trist" of Sir Launcelot Canning: There was no Sir Launcelot Canning, unlike the authors cited in paragraph 27. The "passages" from "Canning" read by the narrator to Usher were all written by Poe.

before a palace of gold, with a floor of silver; and upon the wall there hung a shield of shining brass with this legend enwritten—

Who entereth herein, a conqueror hath bin;
Who slayeth the dragon, the shield he shall win;

And Ethelred uplifted his mace, and struck upon the head of the dragon, which fell before him, and gave up his pesty breath, with a shriek so horrid and harsh, and withal so piercing, that Ethelred had fain to close his ears with his hands against the dreadful noise of it, the like whereof was never before heard."

Here again I paused abruptly and now with a feeling of wild amazement—for there could be no doubt whatever that, in this instance, I did actually hear (although from what direction it proceeded I found it impossible to say) a low and apparently distant, but harsh, protracted, and most unusual screaming or grating sound—the exact counterpart of what my fancy had already conjured up for the dragon's unnatural shriek as described by the romancer.

Oppressed, as I certainly was, upon the occurrence of this second and most extraordinary coincidence, by a thousand conflicting sensations, in which wonder and extreme terror were predominant, I still retained sufficient presence of mind to avoid exciting, by any observation, the sensitive nervousness of my companion. I was by no means certain that he had noticed the sounds in question; although, assuredly, a strange alteration had, during the last few minutes, taken place in his demeanor. From a position fronting my own, he had gradually brought round his chair, so as to sit with his face to the door of the chamber; and thus I could but partially perceive his features, although I saw that his lips trembled as if he were murmuring inaudibly. His head had dropped upon his breast—yet I knew that he was not asleep, from the wide and rigid opening of the eye as I caught a glance of it in profile. The motion of his body, too, was at variance with this idea—for he rocked from side to side with a gentle yet constant and uniform sway. Having rapidly taken notice of all this, I resumed the narrative of Sir Launcelot, which thus proceeded:

"And now, the champion, having escaped from the terrible fury of the dragon, bethinking himself of the brazen shield, and of the breaking up of the enchantment which was upon it, removed the carcass from out of the way before him, and approached valorously over the silver pavement of the castle to where the shield was upon the wall; which in sooth tarried not for his full coming, but fell down at his feet upon the silver floor, with a mighty great and terrible ringing sound."

No sooner had these syllables passed my lips, than—as if a shield of brass had indeed, at the moment, fallen heavily upon a floor of silver—I became aware of a distinct, hollow, metallic, and clangorous, yet apparently muffled reverberation. Completely unnerved, I leaped to my feet; but the measured rocking movement of Usher was undisturbed. I rushed to the chair in which he sat. His eyes were bent fixedly before him, and throughout his whole countenance there reigned a stony rigidity. But, as I placed my hand upon his shoulder, there came a strong shudder over his whole person; a sickly smile quivered about his lips; and I saw that he spoke in a low, hurried, and gibbering murmur, as if unconscious of my presence. Bending closely over him, I at length drank in the hideous import of his words.

"Not hear it?—yes, I hear it, and *have* heard it. Long—long—long—many minutes, many hours, many days, have I heard it—yet I dared not—oh, pity me, miserable

45

wretch that I am!—I dared not—*I dared* not speak! *We have put her living in the tomb!* Said I not that my senses were acute? I *now* tell you that I heard her first feeble movements in the hollow coffin I heard them—many, many days ago—yet I dared not—I *dared not speak!* And now—to-night—Ethelred—ha! ha!—the breaking of the hermit's door, and the death-cry of the dragon, and the clangor of the shield!—say, rather, the rending of her coffin, and the grating of the iron hinges of her prison, and her struggles within the coppered archway of the vault! Oh whither shall I fly? Will she not be here anon? Is she not hurrying to upbraid me for my haste? Have I not heard her footstep on the stair? Do I not distinguish that heavy and horrible beating of her heart? Madman!"— here he sprang furiously to his feet, and shrieked out his syllables, as if in the effort he were giving up his soul—*"Madman! I tell you that she now stands without the door!"*

As if in the superhuman energy of his utterance there had been found the potency of a spell—the huge antique pannels to which the speaker pointed, threw slowly back, upon the instant, their ponderous and ebony jaws. It was the work of the rushing gust—but then without those doors there *did* stand the lofty and enshrouded figure of the lady Madeline of Usher. There was blood upon her white robes, and the evidence of some bitter struggle upon every portion of her emaciated frame. For a moment she remained trembling and reeling to and fro upon the threshold—then, with a low moaning cry, fell heavily inward upon the person of her brother, and in her violent and now final death-agonies, bore him to the floor a corpse, and victim to the terrors he had anticipated.

From that chamber, and from that mansion, I fled aghast. The storm was still abroad in all its wrath as I found myself crossing the old causeway. Suddenly there shot along the path a wild light, and I turned to see whence a gleam so unusual could have issued; for the vast house and its shadows were alone behind me. The radiance was that of the full, setting, and blood-red moon, which now shone vividly through that once barely-discernible fissure, of which I have before spoken as extending from the roof of the building, in a zigzag direction, to the base. While I gazed, this fissure rapidly widened—there came a fierce breath of the whirlwind—the entire orb of the satellite burst at once upon my sight—my brain reeled as I saw the mighty walls rushing asunder—there was a long tumultuous shouting sound like the voice of a thousand waters— and the deep and dank tarn at my feet closed sullenly and silently over the fragments of the *"House of Usher."*

QUESTIONS

1. Consider Poe's use of setting in "The Fall of the House of Usher." What details (e.g., landscape, weather) seem realistic? What is the condition of the house, both outside and inside? What is the relationship between the house and the Usher family?

2. Should Poe's descriptions be taken literally or symbolically, or both? Explain.

3. What is the relationship between the narrator and Usher? Why is the narrator not named? Is he as involved in the events as, say, the unnamed narrator of "The Black Cat" or the named narrator of "The Cask of Amontillado"?

4. In what ways is Madeline a double of Usher himself? Why is Usher unwilling or unable to rescue her from the burial vault? What is the meaning of her falling on him and bringing about his death?

5. Why is Usher's poem included as part of the story? How does the poem explain the condition of the Usher household?

The Masque of the Red Death _____ *1842*

The "Red Death" had long devastated the country. No pestilence had ever been so fatal, or so hideous. Blood was its Avatar° and its seal—the redness and the horror of blood. There were sharp pains, and sudden dizziness, and then profuse bleeding at the pores, with dissolution. The scarlet stains upon the body and especially upon the face of the victim, were the pest ban which shut him out from the aid and from the sympathy of his fellow-men. And the whole seizure, progress, and termination of the disease, were the incidents of half an hour.

But the Prince Prospero° was happy and dauntless and sagacious. When his dominions were half depopulated, he summoned to his presence a thousand hale and light-hearted friends from among the knights and dames of his court, and with these retired to the deep seclusion of one of his castellated abbeys. This was an extensive and magnificent structure, the creation of the prince's own eccentric yet august taste. A strong and lofty wall girdled it in. This wall had gates of iron. The courtiers, having entered, brought furnaces and massy hammers and welded the bolts. They resolved to leave means neither of ingress nor egress to the sudden impulses of despair or of frenzy from within. The abbey was amply provisioned. With such precautions the courtiers might bid defiance to contagion. The external world could take care of itself. In the meantime it was folly to grieve, or to think. The prince had provided all the appliances of pleasure. There were buffoons, there were improvisatori, there were ballet-dancers, there were musicians, there was Beauty, there was wine. All these and security were within. Without was the "Red Death."

It was toward the close of the fifth or sixth month of his seclusion, and while the pestilence raged most furiously abroad, that the Prince Prospero entertained his thousand friends at a masked ball of the most unusual magnificence.

It was a voluptuous scene, that masquerade. But first let me tell of the rooms in which it was held. There were seven—an imperial suite. In many palaces, however, such suites form a long and straight vista, while the folding doors slide back nearly to the walls on either hand, so that the view of the whole extent is scarcely impeded. Here the case was very different; as might have been expected from the duke's love of the *bizarre*. The apartments were so irregularly disposed that the vision embraced but little more than one at a time. There was a sharp turn at every twenty or thirty yards, and at each turn a novel effect. To the right and left, in the middle of each wall, a tall and narrow Gothic window looked out upon a closed corridor which pursued the windings of the suite. These windows were of stained glass whose color varied in accordance with the prevailing hue of the decorations of the chamber into which it opened. That at the eastern extremity was hung, for example, in blue—and vividly blue were its windows. The second chamber was purple in its ornaments and tapestries, and here the panes were purple. The third was green throughout, and so were the casements. The fourth was furnished and lighted with orange—the fifth with white—the sixth with violet. The seventh apartment was closely shrouded in black velvet tapestries that hung all over the ceiling and down the walls, falling in heavy folds upon a carpet of the same material and hue. But in this chamber only, the color of the windows failed to correspond with the decorations. The panes here were scarlet—a deep blood color. Now in

---

Avatar: model, incarnation, manifestation.
Prospero: that is, "prosperous." In Shakespeare's play *The Tempest*, the principal character is Prospero.

no one of the seven apartments was there any lamp or candelabrum, amid the profusion of golden ornaments that lay scattered to and fro or depended from the roof. There was no light of any kind emanating from lamp or candle within the suite of chambers. But in the corridors that followed the suite, there stood, opposite to each window, a heavy tripod, bearing a brazier of fire, that projected its rays through the tinted glass and so glaringly illumined the room. And thus were produced a multitude of gaudy and fantastic appearances. But in the western or black chamber the effect of the fire-light that streamed upon the dark hangings through the blood-tinted panes was ghastly in the extreme, and produced so wild a look upon the countenances of those who entered, that there were few of the company bold enough to set foot within its precincts at all.

It was in this apartment, also, that there stood against the western wall, a gigantic clock of ebony. Its pendulum swung to and fro with a dull, heavy, monotonous clang; and when the minute-hand made the circuit of the face, and the hour was to be stricken, there came from the brazen lungs of the clock a sound which was clear and loud and deep and exceedingly musical, but of so peculiar a note and emphasis that, at each lapse of an hour, the musicians of the orchestra were constrained to pause, momentarily, in their performance, to hearken to the sound; and thus the waltzers perforce ceased their evolutions; and there was a brief disconcert of the whole gay company; and, while the chimes of the clock yet rang, it was observed that the giddiest grew pale, and the more aged and sedate passed their hands over their brows as if in confused revery or meditation. But when the echoes had fully ceased, a light laughter at once pervaded the assembly; the musicians looked at each other and smiled as if at their own nervousness and folly, and made whispering vows, each to the other, that the next chiming of the clock should produce in them no similar emotion; and then, after the lapse of sixty minutes (which embrace three thousand and six hundred seconds of the Time that flies), there came yet another chiming of the clock, and then were the same disconcert and tremulousness and meditation as before.

But, in spite of these things, it was a gay and magnificent revel. The tastes of the duke were peculiar. He had a fine eye for colors and effects. He disregarded the *decora*° of mere fashion. His plans were bold and fiery, and his conceptions glowed with barbaric lustre. There are some who would have thought him mad. His followers felt that he was not. It was necessary to hear and see and touch him to be *sure* that he was not.

He had directed, in great part, the movable embellishments of the seven chambers, upon occasion of this great fête,° and it was his own guiding taste which had given character to the masqueraders. Be sure they were grotesque. There were much glare and glitter and piquancy and phantasm—much of what has been since seen in "Hernani."° There were arabesque figures with unsuited limbs and appointments. There were delirious fancies such as the madman fashions. There were much of the beautiful, much of the wanton, much of the *bizarre*, something of the terrible, and not a little of that which might have excited disgust. To and fro in the seven chambers there stalked, in fact, a multitude of dreams. And these—the dreams—writhed in and about, taking hue from the rooms, and causing the wild music of the orchestra to seem as the echo

decora: schemes, patterns.
fête: party, revel.
Hernani: tragedy by Victor Hugo (1802–1885), featuring elaborate scenes and costumes.

of their steps. And, anon, there strikes the ebony clock which stands in the hall of the velvet. And then, for a moment, all is still, and all is silent save the voice of the clock. The dreams are stiff-frozen as they stand. But the echoes of the chime die away—they have endured but an instant—and a light, half-subdued laughter floats after them as they depart. And now again the music swells, and the dreams live, and writhe to and fro more merrily than ever, taking hue from the many-tinted windows through which stream the rays from the tripods. But to the chamber which lies most westwardly of the seven there are now none of the maskers who venture; for the night is waning away; and there flows a ruddier light through the blood-colored panes; and the blackness of the sable drapery appalls; and to him whose foot falls upon the sable carpet, there comes from the near clock of ebony a muffled peal more solemnly emphatic than any which reaches *their* ears who indulge in the more remote gaieties of the other apartments.

But these other apartments were densely crowded, and in them beat feverishly the heart of life. And the revel went whirlingly on, until at length there commenced the sounding of midnight upon the clock. And then the music ceased, as I have told; and the evolutions of the waltzers were quieted; and there was an uneasy cessation of all things as before. But now there were twelve strokes to be sounded by the bell of the clock; and thus it happened, perhaps that more of thought crept, with more of time, into the meditations of the thoughtful among those who revelled. And thus, too, it happened, perhaps, that before the last echoes of the last chime had utterly sunk into silence, there were many individuals in the crowd who had found leisure to become aware of the presence of a masked figure which had arrested the attention of no single individual before. And the rumor of this new presence having spread itself whisperingly around, there arose at length from the whole company a buzz, or murmur, expressive of disapprobation and surprise—then, finally, of terror, of horror, and of disgust.

In an assembly of phantasms such as I have painted, it may well be supposed that no ordinary appearance could have excited such sensation. In truth the masquerade license of the night was nearly unlimited; but the figure in question had out-Heroded Herod,° and gone beyond the bounds of even the prince's indefinite decorum. There are chords in the hearts of the most reckless which cannot be touched without emotion. Even with the utterly lost, to whom life and death are equally jests, there are matters of which no jest can be made. The whole company, indeed, seemed now deeply to feel that in the costume and bearing of the stranger neither wit nor propriety existed. The figure was tall and gaunt, and shrouded from head to foot in the habiliments of the grave. The mask which concealed the visage was made so nearly to resemble the countenance of a stiffened corpse that the closest scrutiny must have had difficulty in detecting the cheat. And yet all this might have been endured, if not approved, by the mad revellers around. But the mummer had gone so far as to assume the type of the Red Death. His vesture was dabbled in *blood*—and his broad brow, with all the features of the face, was besprinkled with the scarlet horror.

When the eyes of Prince Prospero fell upon this spectral image (which, with a slow and solemn movement, as if more fully to sustain its *rôle*, stalked to and fro among the waltzers) he was seen to be convulsed, in the first moment with a strong shudder either of terror or distaste; but, in the next, his brow reddened with rage.

10

---

out-Heroded Herod: quoted from Shakespeare's *Hamlet*, Act III, scene 2, line 13, in reference to extreme overacting.

"Who dares"—he demanded hoarsely of the courtiers who stood near him—"who dares insult us with this blasphemous mockery? Seize him and unmask him—that we may know whom we have to hang, at sunrise, from the battlements!"

It was in the eastern or blue chamber in which stood the Prince Prospero as he uttered these words. They rang throughout the seven rooms loudly and clearly, for the prince was a bold and robust man, and the music had become hushed at the waving of his hand.

It was in the blue room where stood the prince, with a group of pale courtiers by his side. At first, as he spoke, there was a slight rushing movement of this group in the direction of the intruder, who, at the moment was also near at hand, and now, with deliberate and stately step, made closer approach to the speaker. But from a certain nameless awe with which the mad assumptions of the mummer had inspired the whole party, there were found none who put forth hand to seize him; so that, unimpeded, he passed within a yard of the prince's person; and, while the vast assembly, as if with one impulse, shrank from the centres of the rooms to the walls, he made his way uninterruptedly, but with the same solemn and measured step which had distinguished him from the first, through the blue chamber to the purple—through the purple to the green—through the green to the orange—through this again to the white—and even thence to the violet, ere a decided movement had been made to arrest him. It was then, however, that the Prince Prospero, maddening with rage and the shame of his own momentary cowardice, rushed hurriedly through the six chambers, while none followed him on account of a deadly terror that had seized upon all. He bore aloft a drawn dagger, and had approached, in rapid impetuosity, to within three or four feet of the retreating figure, when the latter, having attained the extremity of the velvet apartment, turned suddenly and confronted his pursuer. There was a sharp cry—and the dagger dropped gleaming upon the sable carpet, upon which, instantly afterward, fell prostrate in death the Prince Prospero. Then, summoning the wild courage of despair, a throng of the revellers at once threw themselves into the black apartment, and, seizing the mummer, whose tall figure stood erect and motionless within the shadow of the ebony clock, gasped in unutterable horror at finding the grave cerements and corpse-like mask, which they handled with so violent a rudeness, untenanted by any tangible form.

And now was acknowledged the presence of the Red Death. He had come like a thief in the night.° And one by one dropped the revellers in the blood-bedewed halls of their revel, and died each in the despairing posture of his fall. And the life of the ebony clock went out with that of the last of the gay. And the flames of the tripods expired. And Darkness and Decay and the Red Death held illimitable dominion over all.

QUESTIONS

1. What is happening throughout the country in this story? What does the Prince's reaction to these events tell us about him?

2. How do the details of number, color, and lighting help create the atmosphere and mood of the story?

3. Why do the color and window of the last room disturb the revellers? To what extent does this last room reflect the plot and ideas of the story?

thief in the night: 2 Peter 3:10.

4. What single object is located in this last room? How is this object described?
    What effect does its sound have on the revellers? What do you think Poe is sug-
    gesting by this object and its effects?
5. How are the nobles dressed for the masquerade? Why is the "masked figure"
    remarkable? How does Prospero react to him?

The Black Cat _____ *1843*

For the most wild, yet most homely narrative which I am about to pen, I neither expect
nor solicit belief. Mad indeed would I be to expect it, in a case where my very senses
reject their own evidence. Yet, mad am I not—and very surely do I not dream. But
to-morrow I die, and to-day I would unburthen my soul. My immediate purpose is to place
before the world, plainly, succinctly, and without comment, a series of mere household
events. In their consequences, these events have terrified—have tortured—have
destroyed me. Yet I will not attempt to expound them. To me, they have presented little
but Horror—to many they will seem less terrible than *barroques*. Hereafter, perhaps,
some intellect may be found which will reduce my phantasm to the common-place—some
intellect more calm, more logical, and far less excitable than my own, which will perceive, in the circumstances I detail with awe, nothing more than an ordinary succession
of very natural causes and effects.

From my infancy I was noted for the docility and humanity of my disposition. My
tenderness of heart was even so conspicuous as to make me the jest of my companions.
I was especially fond of animals, and was indulged by my parents with a great variety of
pets. With these I spent most of my time, and never was so happy as when feeding and
caressing them. This peculiarity of character grew with my growth, and, in my manhood,
I derived from it one of my principal sources of pleasure. To those who have cherished
an affection for a faithful and sagacious dog, I need hardly be at the trouble of explaining the nature or the intensity of the gratification thus derivable. There is something in
the unselfish and self-sacrificing love of a brute, which goes directly to the heart of him
who has had frequent occasion to test the paltry friendship and gossamer fidelity of
mere *Man*.

I married early, and was happy to find in my wife a disposition not uncongenial
with my own. Observing my partiality for domestic pets, she lost no opportunity of
procuring those of the most agreeable kind. We had birds, gold-fish, a fine dog, rabbits,
a small monkey, and *a cat*.

This latter was a remarkably large and beautiful animal, entirely black, and sagacious to an astonishing degree. In speaking of his intelligence, my wife, who at heart
was not a little tinctured with superstition, made frequent allusion to the ancient popular notion, which regarded all black cats as witches in disguise. Not that she was ever
serious upon this point—and I mention the matter at all for no better reason than that it
happens, just now, to be remembered.

Pluto°—this was the cat's name—was my favorite pet and playmate. I alone fed   5
him, and he attended me wherever I went about the house. It was even with difficulty
that I could prevent him from following me through the streets.

Our friendship lasted, in this manner, for several years, during which my
general temperament and character—through the instrumentality of the Fiend

---

Pluto: the Roman name of Hades, the ancient god of the underworld.

Intemperance—had (I blush to confess it) experienced a radical alteration for the worse. I grew, day by day, more moody, more irritable, more regardless of the feelings of others. I suffered myself to use intemperate language to my wife. At length, I even offered her personal violence. My pets, of course, were made to feel the change in my disposition. I not only neglected, but ill-used them. For Pluto, however, I still retained sufficient regard to restrain me from maltreating him, as I made no scruple of maltreating the rabbits, the monkey, or even the dog, when by accident, or through affection, they came in my way. But my disease grew upon me—for what disease is like Alcohol!—and at length even Pluto, who was now becoming old, and consequently somewhat peevish—even Pluto began to experience the effects of my ill temper.

One night, returning home, much intoxicated, from one of my haunts about town, I fancied that the cat avoided my presence. I seized him; when, in his fright at my violence, he inflicted a slight wound upon my hand with his teeth. The fury of a demon instantly possessed me. I knew myself no longer. My original soul seemed, at once, to take its flight from my body; and a more than fiendish malevolence, gin-nurtured, thrilled every fibre of my frame. I took from my waistcoat-pocket a pen-knife, opened it, grasped the poor beast by the throat, and deliberately cut one of its eyes from the socket! I blush, I burn, I shudder, while I pen the damnable atrocity.

When reason returned with the morning—when I had slept off the fumes of the night's debauch—I experienced a sentiment half of horror, half of remorse, for the crime of which I had been guilty; but it was, at best, a feeble and equivocal feeling, and the soul remained untouched. I again plunged into excess, and soon drowned in wine all memory of the deed.

In the meantime the cat slowly recovered. The socket of the lost eye presented, it is true, a frightful appearance, but he no longer appeared to suffer any pain. He went about the house as usual, but, as might be expected, fled in extreme terror at my approach. I had so much of my old heart left, as to be at first grieved by this evident dislike on the part of a creature which had once so loved me. But this feeling soon gave place to irritation. And then came, as if to my final and irrevocable overthrow, the spirit of PERVERSENESS. Of this spirit philosophy takes no account. Yet I am not more sure that my soul lives, than I am that perverseness is one of the primitive impulses of the human heart—one of the indivisible primary faculties, or sentiments, which give direction to the character of Man. Who has not, a hundred times, found himself committing a vile or a silly action, for no other reason than because he knows he should *not*? Have we not a perpetual inclination, in the teeth of our best judgment, to violate that which is *Law*, merely because we understand it to be such? This spirit of perverseness, I say, came to my final overthrow. It was this unfathomable longing of the soul *to vex itself*—to offer violence to its own nature—to do wrong for the wrong's sake only—that urged me to continue and finally to consummate the injury I had inflicted upon the unoffending brute. One morning, in cool blood, I slipped a noose about its neck and hung it to the limb of a tree;—hung it with the tears streaming from my eyes, and with the bitterest remorse at my heart;—hung it *because* I knew that it had loved me, and *because* I felt it had given me no reason of offence;—hung it *because* I knew that in so doing I was committing a sin—a deadly sin that would so jeopardize my immortal soul as to place it—if such a thing were possible—even beyond the reach of the infinite mercy of the Most Merciful and Most Terrible God.

On the night of the day on which this cruel deed was done, I was aroused from sleep by the cry of fire. The curtains of my bed were in flames. The whole house was blazing. It was with great difficulty that my wife, a servant, and myself, made our escape from the conflagration. The destruction was complete. My entire worldly wealth was swallowed up, and I resigned myself thenceforward to despair.

I am above the weakness of seeking to establish a sequence of cause and effect, between the disaster and the atrocity. But I am detailing a chain of facts—and wish not to leave even a possible link imperfect. On the day succeeding the fire, I visited the ruins. The walls, with one exception, had fallen in. This exception was found in a compartment wall, not very thick, which stood about the middle of the house, and against which has rested the head of my bed. The plastering had here, in great measure, resisted the action of the fire—a fact which I attributed to its having been recently spread. About this wall a dense crowd were collected, and many persons seemed to be examining a particular portion of it with very minute and eager attention. The words "strange!" "singular!" and other similar expressions, excited my curiosity. I approached and saw, as if graven in *bas relief* upon the white surface, the figure of a gigantic *cat*. The impression was given with an accuracy truly marvellous. There was a rope about the animal's neck.

When I first beheld this apparition—for I could scarcely regard it as less—my wonder and my terror were extreme. But at length reflection came to my aid. The cat, I remembered, had been hung in a garden adjacent to the house. Upon the alarm of fire, this garden had been immediately filled by the crowds—by some one of whom the animal must have been cut from the tree and thrown, through an open window, into my chamber. This had probably been done with the view of arousing me from sleep. The falling of other walls had compressed the victim of my cruelty into the substance of the freshly-spread plaster; the lime of which, with the flames, and the *ammonia* from the carcass, had then accomplished the portraiture as I saw it.

Although I thus readily accounted to my reason, if not altogether to my conscience, for the startling fact just detailed, it did not the less fail to make a deep impression upon my fancy. For months I could not rid myself of the phantasm of the cat; and, during this period, there came back into my spirit a half-sentiment that seemed, but was not, remorse. I went so far as to regret the loss of the animal, and to look about me, among the vile haunts which I now habitually frequented, for another pet of the same species, and of somewhat similar appearance, with which to supply its place.

One night as I sat, half stupified, in a den of more than infamy, my attention was suddenly drawn to some black object, reposing upon the head of one of the immense hogsheads of Gin, or of Rum, which constituted the chief furniture of the apartment. I had been looking steadily at the top of this hogshead for some minutes, and what now caused me surprise was the fact that I had not sooner perceived the object thereupon. I approached it, and touched it with my hand. It was a black cat—a very large one—fully as large as Pluto, and closely resembling him in every respect but one. Pluto had not a white hair upon any portion of his body; but this cat had a large, although indefinite splotch of white, covering nearly the whole region of the breast.

Upon my touching him, he immediately arose, purred loudly, rubbed against my hand, and appeared delighted with my notice. This, then, was the very creature of which I was in search. I at once offered to purchase it of the landlord; but this person made no claim to it—knew nothing of it—had never seen it before.

I continued my caresses, and, when I prepared to go home, the animal evinced a disposition to accompany me. I permitted it to do so; occasionally stooping and patting it as I proceeded. When it reached the house it domesticated itself at once, and became immediately a great favorite with my wife.

15

For my own part, I soon found a dislike to it arising within me. This was just the reverse of what I had anticipated; but—I know not how or why it was—its evident fondness for myself rather disgusted and annoyed. By slow degrees, these feelings of disgust and annoyance rose into the bitterness of hatred. I avoided the creature; a certain sense of shame, and the remembrance of my former deed of cruelty, preventing me from physically abusing it. I did not, for some weeks, strike, or otherwise violently ill use it; but gradually—very gradually—I came to look upon it with unutterable loathing, and to flee silently from its odious presence, as from the breath of a pestilence.

What added, no doubt, to my hatred of the beast, was the discovery, on the morning after I brought it home, that, like Pluto, it also had been deprived of one of its eyes. This circumstance, however, only endeared it to my wife, who, as I have already said, possessed, in a high degree, that humanity of feeling which had once been my distinguishing trait, and the source of many of my simplest and purest pleasures.

With my aversion to this cat, however, its partiality for myself seemed to increase. It followed my footsteps with a pertinacity which it would be difficult to make the reader comprehend. Whenever I sat, it would crouch beneath my chair, or spring upon my knees, covering me with its loathsome caresses. If I arose to walk it would get between my feet and thus nearly throw me down, or, fastening its long and sharp claws in my dress, clamber, in this manner, to my breast. At such times, although I longed to destroy it with a blow, I was yet withheld from so doing, partly by a memory of my former crime, but chiefly—let me confess it at once—by absolute *dread* of the beast.

This dread was not exactly a dread of physical evil—and yet I should be at a loss how otherwise to define it. I am almost ashamed to own—yes, even in this felon's cell, I am almost ashamed to own—that the terror and horror with which the animal inspired me, had been heightened by one of the merest chimæras it would be possible to conceive. My wife had called my attention, more than once, to the character of the mark of white hair, of which I have spoken, and which constituted the sole visible difference between the strange beast and the one I had destroyed. The reader will remember that this mark, although large, had been originally very indefinite; but, by slow degrees—degrees nearly imperceptible, and which for a long time my Reason struggled to reject as fanciful—it had, at length, assumed a rigorous distinctness of outline. It was now the representation of an object that I shudder to name—and for this, above all, I loathed, and dreaded, and would have rid myself of the monster *had I dared*—it was now, I say, the image of a hideous—of a ghastly thing—of the Gallows!—oh, mournful and terrible engine of Horror and of Crime—of Agony and of Death!

And now was I indeed wretched beyond the wretchedness of mere Humanity. And *a brute beast*—whose fellow I had contemptuously destroyed—*a brute beast* to work out for *me*—for me a man, fashioned in the image of the High God—so much of insufferable woe! Alas! neither by day nor by night knew I the blessing of Rest any more! During the former, the creature left me no moment alone; and, in the latter, I started, hourly, from dreams of unutterable fear, to find the hot breath of *the thing* upon my face, and its vast weight—an incarnate Night-Mare that I had no power to shake off—incumbent eternally upon my *heart!*

Beneath the pressure of torments such as these, the feeble remnant of the good within me succumbed. Evil thoughts became my sole intimates—the darkest and most evil of thoughts. The moodiness of my usual temper increased to hatred of all things and of all mankind; while, from the sudden, frequent, and ungovernable outbursts of a fury to which I now blindly abandoned myself, my uncomplaining wife, alas! was the most usual and the most patient of sufferers.

20

One day she accompanied me, upon some household errand, into the cellar of the old building which our poverty compelled us to inhabit. The cat followed me down the steep stairs, and, nearly throwing me headlong, exasperated me to madness. Uplifting an axe, and forgetting, in my wrath, the childish dread which had hitherto stayed my hand, I aimed a blow at the animal which, of course, would have proved instantly fatal had it descended as I wished. But this blow was arrested by the hand of my wife. Goaded, by the interference, into a rage more than demoniacal, I withdrew my arm from her gasp and buried the axe in her brain. She fell dead upon the spot, without a groan.

This hideous murder accomplished, I set myself forthwith, and with entire deliberation, to the task of concealing the body. I knew that I could not remove it from the house, either by day or by night, without the risk of being observed by the neighbors. Many projects entered my mind. At one period I thought of cutting the corpse into minute fragments, and destroying them by fire. At another, I resolved to dig a grave for it in the floor of the cellar. Again, I deliberated about casting it in the well in the yard— about packing it in a box, as if merchandize, with the usual arrangements, and so getting a porter to take it from the house. Finally I hit upon what I considered a far better expedient than either of these. I determined to wall it up in the cellar—as the monks of the middle ages are recorded to have walled up their victims.

For a purpose such as this the cellar was well adapted. Its walls were loosely constructed, and had lately been plastered throughout with a rough plaster, which the dampness of the atmosphere had prevented from hardening. Moreover, in one of the walls was a projection, caused by a false chimney, or fireplace, that had been filled up, and made to resemble the rest of the cellar. I made no doubt that I could readily displace the bricks at this point, insert the corpse, and wall the whole up as before, so that no eye could detect any thing suspicious.

And in this calculation I was not deceived. By means of a crow-bar I easily dislodged the bricks, and, having carefully deposited the body against the inner wall, I propped it in that position, while, with little trouble, I re-laid the whole structure as it originally stood. Having procured mortar, sand, and hair, with every possible precaution, I prepared a plaster which could not be distinguished from the old, and with this I very carefully went over the new brick-work. When I had finished, I felt satisfied that all was right. The wall did not present the slightest appearance of having been disturbed. The rubbish on the floor was picked up with the minutest care. I looked around triumphantly, and said to myself—"Here at least, then, my labor has not been in vain."

My next step was to look for the beast which had been the cause of so much wretchedness; for I had, at length, firmly resolved to put it to death. Had I been able to meet with it, at the moment, there could have been no doubt of its fate; but it appeared that the crafty animal had been alarmed at the violence of my previous anger, and forebore to present itself in my present mood. It is impossible to describe, or to imagine, the deep, the blissful sense of relief which the absence of the detested creature occasioned in my bosom. It did not make its appearance during the night—and thus for one night at least, since its introduction into the house, I soundly and tranquilly slept; aye, *slept* even with the burden of murder upon my soul!

The second and third day passed, and still my tormentor came not. Once again I breathed as a free man. The monster, in terror, had fled the premises forever! I should behold it no more! My happiness was supreme! The guilt of my dark deed disturbed me but little. Some few inquiries had been made, but these had been readily answered. Even a search had been instituted—but of course nothing was to be discovered. I looked upon my future felicity as secured.

25

Upon the fourth day of the assassination, a party of the police came, very unexpectedly, into the house, and proceeded again to make rigorous investigation of the premises. Secure, however, in the inscrutability of my place of concealment, I felt no embarrassment whatever. The officer bade me accompany them in their search. They left no nook or corner unexplored. At length, for the third or fourth time, they descended into the cellar. I quivered not in a muscle. My heart beat calmly as that of one who slumbers in innocence. I walked the cellar from end to end. I folded my arms upon my bosom, and roamed easily to and fro. The police were thoroughly satisfied and prepared to depart. The glee at my heart was too strong to be restrained. I burned to say if but one word, by way of triumph, and to render doubly sure their assurance of my guiltlessness.

"Gentlemen," I said at last, as the party ascended the steps, "I delight to have 30
allayed your suspicions. I wish you all health, and a little more courtesy. By the bye, gentlemen, this—this is a very well constructed house." [In the rabid desire to say something easily, I scarcely knew what I uttered at all.]—"I may say an *excellently* well constructed house. These walls—are you going, gentlemen?—these walls are solidly put together," and here, through the mere phrenzy of bravado, I rapped heavily, with a cane which I held in my hand, upon that very portion of the brick-work behind which stood the corpse of the wife of my bosom.

But may God shield and deliver me from the fangs of the Arch-Fiend! No sooner had the reverberation of my blows sunk into silence, than I was answered by a voice from within the tomb!—by a cry, at first muffled and broken, like the sobbing of a child, and then quickly swelling into one long, loud, and continuous scream, utterly anomalous and inhuman—a howl—a wailing shriek, half of horror and half of triumph, such as might have arisen only out of hell, conjointly from the throats of the damned in their agony and of the demons that exult in the damnation.

Of my own thoughts it is folly to speak. Swooning, I staggered to the opposite wall. For one instant the party upon the stairs remained motionless, through extremity of terror and of awe. In the next, a dozen stout arms were toiling at the wall. It fell bodily. The corpse, already greatly decayed and clotted with gore, stood erect before the eyes of the spectators. Upon its head, with red extended mouth and solitary eye of fire, sat the hideous beast whose craft had seduced me into murder, and whose informing voice had consigned me to the hangman. I had walled the monster up within the tomb!

QUESTIONS

1. Does the first paragraph establish clarity or ambiguity about the narrator and the events he is about to describe? Explain.

2. What changes occur in the narrator's character? Are the narrator's explanations of the changes plausible and convincing?

3. What does the narrator, in considering what he does to Pluto, mean by "perverseness" (paragraph 9)? Why does Poe introduce the details about perverseness? In what ways should the house fire and the resulting consequences be considered as punishment for the narrator's actions?

4. How does the second cat resemble the first? What does the gallows mark represent when it takes shape on the new cat (paragraph 20)?

5. When the narrator knocks on the wall (paragraph 30), should his doing so be considered a mark of arrogance or a recognition of guilt? Explain.

The Purloined Letter ———————————————————— *1844*

> *Nil sapientiae odiosius acumine nimio.*
> —*Seneca*°

At Paris, just after dark one gusty evening in the autumn of 18—, I was enjoying the twofold luxury of meditation and a meerschaum, in company with my friend C. Auguste Dupin, in his little back library, or book-closet, *au troisiême*, No. 33, *Rue Dunôt, Faubourg St. Germain*. For one hour at least we had maintained a profound silence; while each, to any casual observer, might have seemed intently and exclusively occupied with the curling eddies of smoke that oppressed the atmosphere of the chamber. For myself, however, I was mentally discussing certain topics which had formed matter for conversation between us at an earlier period of the evening; I mean the affair of the Rue Morgue, and the mystery attending the murder of Marie Rogêt.° I looked upon it, therefore, as something of a coincidence, when the door of our apartment was thrown open and admitted our old acquaintance, Monsieur G——, the Prefect of the Parisian police.

We gave him a hearty welcome; for there was nearly half as much of the entertaining as of the contemptible about the man, and we had not seen him for several years. We had been sitting in the dark, and Dupin now arose for the purpose of lighting a lamp, but sat down again, without doing so, upon G.'s saying that he had called to consult us, or rather to ask the opinion of my friend, about some official business which had occasioned a great deal of trouble.

"If it is any point requiring reflection," observed Dupin, as he forebore to enkindle the wick, "we shall examine it to better purpose in the dark."

"That is another of your odd notions," said the Prefect, who had a fashion of calling every thing "odd" that was beyond his comprehension, and thus lived amid an absolute legion of "oddities."

"Very true," said Dupin, as he supplied his visiter with a pipe, and rolled towards   5
him a comfortable chair.

"And what is the difficulty now?" I asked. "Nothing more in the assassination way, I hope?"

"Oh no; nothing of that nature. The fact is, the business is *very* simple indeed, and I make no doubt that we can manage it sufficiently well ourselves; but then I thought Dupin would like to hear the details of it, because it is so excessively *odd*."

"Simple and odd," said Dupin.

"Why, yes; and not exactly that, either. The fact is, we have all been a good deal puzzled because the affair *is* so simple, and yet baffles us altogether."

"Perhaps it is the very simplicity of the thing which puts you at fault," said my   10
friend.

"What nonsense you *do* talk!" replied the Prefect, laughing heartily.

"Perhaps the mystery is a little *too* plain," said Dupin.

"Oh, good heavens! who ever heard of such an idea?"

Nil sapientiae . . . Seneca: "Nothing is more odious to wisdom than guilefulness." Poe attributes this quotation to the ancient Latin author Seneca (ca. 4 B.C.E.–65 C.E.), but he may have discovered it elsewhere, or else created it from his reading of Sir Francis Bacon (1561–1626) or Samuel Johnson (1709–1784).

Rue Morgue . . . Marie Rogêt: references to Poe's stories "The Murders in the Rue Morgue" (1841) and "The Mystery of Marie Rogêt" (1842). Note that Poe is establishing a sense of reality and continuity by introducing these references to his own earlier work.

"A little *too* self-evident."

"Ha! ha! ha!—ha! ha! ha!—ho! ho! ho!" roared our visiter, profoundly amused, 15 "oh, Dupin, you will be the death of me yet!"

"And what, after all, is the matter on hand?" I asked.

"Why, I will tell you," replied the Prefect, as he gave a long, steady, and contemplative puff, and settled himself in his chair. "I will tell you in a few words; but, before I begin, let me caution you that this is an affair demanding the greatest secrecy, and that I should most probably lose the position I now hold, were it known that I confided it to any one."

"Proceed," said I.

"Or not," said Dupin.

"Well, then; I have received personal information, from a very high quarter, that a 20 certain document of the last importance, has been purloined from the royal apartments. The individual who purloined it is known; this beyond a doubt; he was seen to take it. It is know, also, that it still remains in his possession."

"How is this known?" asked Dupin.

"It is clearly inferred," replied the Prefect, "from the nature of the document, and from the non-appearance of certain results which would at once arise from its passing *out* of the robber's possession;—that is to say, from his employing it as he must design in the end to employ it."

"Be a little more explicit," I said.

"Well, I may venture so far as to say that the paper gives its holder a certain power in a certain quarter where such power is immensely valuable." The Prefect was fond of the cant of diplomacy.

"Still I do not quite understand," said Dupin. 2[

"No? Well; the disclosure of the document to a third person, who shall be nameless, would bring in question the honor of a personage of most exalted station; and this fact gives the holder of the document an ascendancy over the illustrious personage whose honor and peace are so jeopardized."

"But this ascendancy," I interposed, "would depend upon the robber's knowledge of the loser's knowledge of the robber. Who would dare—"

"The thief," said G., "is the Minister D——, who dares all things, those unbecoming as well as those becoming a man. The method of the theft was not less ingenious than bold. The document in question—a letter, to be frank—had been received by the personage robbed while alone in the royal *boudoir*. During its perusal she was suddenly interrupted by the entrance of the other exalted personage from whom especially it was her wish to conceal it. After a hurried and vain endeavor to thrust it in a drawer, she was forced to place it, open as it was, upon a table. The address, however, was uppermost, and, the contents thus unexposed, the letter escaped notice. At this juncture enters the Minister D——. His lynx eye immediately perceives the paper, recognizes the handwriting of the address, observes the confusion of the personage addressed, and fathoms her secret. After some business transactions, hurried through in his ordinary manner, he produces a letter somewhat similar to the one in question, opens it, pretends to read it, and then places it in close juxtaposition to the other. Again he converses, for some fifteen minutes, upon the public affairs. At length, in taking leave, he takes also from the table the letter to which he had no claim. Its rightful owner saw, but, of course, dared not call attention to the act, in the presence of the third personage who stood at her elbow. The minister decamped; leaving his own letter—one of no importance—upon the table."

"Here, then," said Dupin to me, "you have precisely what you demand to make the ascendancy complete—the robber's knowledge of the loser's knowledge of the robber."

"Yes," replied the Prefect; "and the power thus attained has, for some months past, been wielded, for political purposes, to a very dangerous extent. The personage robbed is more thoroughly convinced, every day, of the necessity of reclaiming her letter. But this, of course, cannot be done openly. In fine, driven to despair, she has committed the matter to me."

"Than whom," said Dupin, amid a perfect whirlwind of smoke, "no more sagacious agent could, I suppose, be desired, or even imagined."

"You flatter me," replied the Prefect; "but it is possible that some such opinion may have been entertained."

"It is clear," said I, "as you observe, that the letter is still in possession of the minister; since it is this possession, and not any employment of the letter, which bestows the power. With the employment the power departs."

"True," said G., "and upon this conviction I proceeded. My first care was to make thorough search of the minister's hotel; and here my chief embarrassment lay in the necessity of searching without his knowledge. Beyond all things, I have been warned of the danger which would result from giving him reason to suspect our design."

"But," said I, "you are quite *au fait*° in these investigations. The Parisian police have done this thing often before."

"O yes; and for this reason I did not despair. The habits of the minister gave me, too, a great advantage. He is frequently absent from home all night. His servants are by no means numerous. They sleep at a distance from their master's apartment, and, being chiefly Neapolitans, are readily made drunk. I have keys, as you know, with which I can open any chamber or cabinet in Paris. For three months a night has not passed, during the greater part of which I have not been engaged, personally, in ransacking the D—— Hotel. My honor is interested, and, to mention a great secret, the reward is enormous. So I did not abandon the search until I had become fully satisfied that the thief is a more astute man than myself. I fancy that I have investigated every nook and corner of the premises in which it is possible that the paper can be concealed."

"But is it not possible," I suggested, "that although the letter may be in possession of the minister, as it unquestionably is, he may have concealed it elsewhere than upon his own premises?"

"This is barely possible," said Dupin. "The present peculiar condition of affairs at court, and especially of those intrigues in which D—— is known to be involved, would render the instant availability of the document—its susceptibility of being produced at a moment's notice—a point of nearly equal importance with its possession."

"Its susceptibility of being produced?" said I.

"That is to say, of being *destroyed*," said Dupin.

"True," I observed; "the paper is clearly then upon the premises. As for its being upon the person of the minister, we may consider that as out of the question."

"Entirely," said the Prefect. "He has been twice waylaid, as if by footpads, and his person rigorously searched under my own inspection."

"You might have spared yourself this trouble," said Dupin. "D——, I presume, is not altogether a fool, and, if not, must have anticipated these waylayings, as a matter of course."

au fait: according to precedent (literally, "to the fact").

"Not *altogether* a fool," said G., "but then he's a poet, which I take to be only one remove from a fool."

"True," said Dupin, after a long and thoughtful whiff from his meerschaum, "although I have been guilty of certain doggerel myself."   45

"Suppose you detail," said I, "the particulars of your search."

"Why the fact is, we took our time, and we searched *every where*. I have had long experience in these affairs. I took the entire building, room by room; devoting the nights of a whole week to each. We examined, first, the furniture of each apartment. We opened every possible drawer; and I presume you know that, to a properly trained police agent, such a thing as a *secret* drawer is impossible. Any man is a dolt who permits a 'secret' drawer to escape him in a search of this kind. The thing is *so* plain. There is a certain amount of bulk—of space—to be accounted for in every cabinet. Then we have accurate rules. The fiftieth part of a line could not escape us. After the cabinets we took the chairs. The cushions we probed with the fine long needles you have seen me employ. From the tables we removed the tops."

"Why so?"

"Sometimes the top of a table, or other similarly arranged piece of furniture, is removed by the person wishing to conceal an article; then the leg is excavated, the article deposited within the cavity, and the top replaced. The bottoms and tops of bedposts are employed in the same way."

"But could not the cavity be detected by sounding?" I asked.   50

"By no means, if, when the article is deposited, a sufficient wadding of cotton be placed around it. Besides, in our case, we were obliged to proceed without noise."

"But you could not have removed—you could not have taken to pieces *all* articles of furniture in which it would have been possible to make a deposit in the manner you mention. A letter may be compressed into a thin spiral roll, not differing much in shape or bulk from a large knitting-needle, and in this form it might be inserted into the rung of a chair, for example. You did not take to pieces all the chairs?"

"Certainly not; but we did better—we examined the rungs of every chair in the hotel, and, indeed, the jointings of every description of furniture, by the aid of a most powerful microscope. Had there been any traces of recent disturbance we should not have failed to detect it instantly. A single grain of gimlet-dust,° for example, would have been as obvious as an apple. Any disorder in the glueing—any unusual gaping in the joints—would have sufficed to insure detection."

"I presume you looked to the mirrors, between the boards and the plates, and you probed the beds and the bed-clothes, as well as the curtains and carpets."

"That of course; and when we had absolutely completed every particle of the furniture in this way, then we examined the house itself. We divided its entire surface into compartments, which we numbered, so that none might be missed; then we scrutinized each individual square inch throughout the premises, including the two houses immediately adjoining, with the microscope, as before."

"The two houses adjoining!" I exclaimed; "you must have had a great deal of trouble."

"We had; but the reward offered is prodigious."

"You include the *grounds* about the houses?"

"All the grounds are paved with brick. They gave us comparatively little trouble. We examined the moss between the bricks, and found it undisturbed."

gimlet-dust: waste wood left by a hand drill.

"You looked among D——'s papers, of course, and into the books of the library?"   60

"Certainly; we opened every package and parcel; we not only opened every book, but we turned over every leaf in each volume, not contenting ourselves with a mere shake, according to the fashion of some of our police officers. We also measured the thickness of every book-*cover,* with the most accurate admeasurement, and applied to each the most jealous scrutiny of the microscope. Had any of the bindings been recently meddled with, it would have been utterly impossible that the fact should have escaped observation. Some five or six volumes, just from the hands of the binder, we carefully probed, longitudinally, with the needles."

"You explored the floors beneath the carpets?"

"Beyond doubt. We removed every carpet, and examined the boards with the microscope."

"And the paper on the walls?"

"Yes."   65

"You looked into the cellars?"

"We did."

"Then," I said, "you have been making a miscalculation, and the letter is *not* upon the premises, as you suppose."

"I fear you are right there," said the Prefect. "And now, Dupin, what would you advise me to do?"

"To make a thorough re-search of the premises."   70

"That is absolutely needless," replied G——. "I am not more sure that I breathe than I am that the letter is not at the Hotel."

"I have no better advice to give you," said Dupin. "You have, of course, an accurate description of the letter?"

"Oh yes!"—And here the Prefect, producing a memorandum-book, proceeded to read aloud a minute account of the internal, and especially of the external appearance of the missing document. Soon after finishing the perusal of this description, he took his departure, more entirely depressed in spirits than I had ever known the good gentleman before.

In about a month afterwards he paid us another visit, and found us occupied very nearly as before. He took a pipe and a chair and entered into some ordinary conversation. At length I said,—

"Well, but G——, what of the purloined letter? I presume you have at last made   75
up your mind that there is no such thing as overreaching the Minister?"

"Confound him, say I—yes; I made the re-examination, however, as Dupin suggested—but it was all labor lost, as I knew it would be."

"How much was the reward offered, did you say?" asked Dupin.

"Why, a very great deal—a *very* liberal reward—I don't like to say how much, precisely; but one thing I *will* say, that I wouldn't mind giving my individual check for fifty thousand francs to any one who could obtain me that letter. The fact is, it is becoming of more and more importance every day; and the reward has been lately doubled. If it were trebled, however, I could do no more than I have done."

"Why, yes," said Dupin, drawlingly, between the whiffs of his meerschaum, "I really—think, G——, you have not exerted yourself—to the utmost in this matter. You might—do a little more, I think, eh?"

"How?—in what way?"   80

"Why—puff, puff—you might—puff, puff—employ counsel in the matter, eh?—puff, puff, puff. Do you remember the story they tell of Abernethy?"

"No; hang Abernethy!"

"To be sure! hang him and welcome. But, once upon a time, a certain rich miser conceived the design of sponging upon this Abernethy for a medical opinion. Getting up, for this purpose, an ordinary conversation in a private company, he insinuated his case to the physician, as that of an imaginary individual.

" 'We will suppose,' said the miser, 'that his symptoms are such and such; now, doctor, what would *you* have directed him to take?'

" 'Take!' said Abernethy, 'why, take *advice,* to be sure.' "

"But," said the Prefect, a little discomposed, "*I* am *perfectly* willing to take advice, and to pay for it. I would *really* give fifty thousand francs to any one who would aid me in the matter."

85

"In that case," replied Dupin, opening a drawer, and producing a check-book, "you may as well fill me up a check for the amount mentioned. When you have signed it, I will hand you the letter."

I was astounded. The Prefect appeared absolutely thunderstricken. For some minutes he remained speechless and motionless, looking incredulously at my friend with open mouth, and eyes that seemed starting from their sockets; then, apparently recovering himself in some measure, he seized a pen, and after several pauses and vacant stares, finally filled up and signed a check for fifty thousand francs, and handed it across the table to Dupin. The latter examined it carefully and deposited it in his pocket-book; then, unlocking an *escritoire,* took thence a letter and gave it to the Prefect. This functionary grasped it in a perfect agony of joy, opened it with a trembling hand, cast a rapid glance at its contents, and then, scrambling and struggling to the door, rushed at length unceremoniously from the room and from the house, without having uttered a syllable since Dupin had requested him to fill up the check.

When he had gone, my friend entered into some explanations.

"The Parisian police," he said, "are exceedingly able in their way. They are persevering, ingenious, cunning, and thoroughly versed in the knowledge which their duties seem chiefly to demand. Thus, when G—— detailed to us his mode of searching the premises at the Hotel D——, I felt entire confidence in his having made a satisfactory investigation—so far as his labors extended."

90

"So far as his labors extended?" said I.

"Yes," said Dupin. "The measures adopted were not only the best of their kind, but carried out to absolute perfection. Had the letter been deposited within the range of their search, these fellows would, beyond a question, have found it."

I merely laughed—but he seemed quite serious in all that he said.

"The measures, then," he continued, "were good in their kind, and well executed; their defect lay in their being inapplicable to the case, and to the man. A certain set of highly ingenious resources are, with the Prefect, a sort of Procrustean bed, to which he forcibly adapts his designs. But he perpetually errs by being too deep or too shallow, for the matter in hand; and many a schoolboy is a better reasoner than he. I knew one about eight years of age, whose success at guessing in the game of 'even and odd' attracted universal admiration. This game is simple, and is played with marbles. One player holds in his hand a number of these toys, and demands of another whether that number is even or odd. If the guess is right, the guesser wins one; if wrong, he loses one. The boy to whom I allude won all the marbles of the school. Of course he had some principle of guessing; and this lay in mere observation and admeasurement of the astuteness of his opponents. For example, an arrant simpleton is his opponent, and, holding up his closed hand, asks, 'are they even or odd?' Our schoolboy replies, 'odd,' and loses; but upon the second trial he wins, for he then says to himself, 'the simpleton had them even upon the first trial, and his amount of cunning is just sufficient to make him have them odd upon the second; I will therefore guess odd;'—he guesses odd, and wins. Now, with a simpleton a degree above the first, he would have reasoned thus: 'This fellow finds that in the first instance I guessed odd, and, in the second, he will propose to himself, upon the first impulse, a simple variation from even to odd, as did the first simpleton; but then a second thought will suggest that this is too simple a variation, and finally he will decide upon putting it even as before. I will therefore guess even;'—he guesses even, and wins. Now this mode of reasoning in the schoolboy, whom his fellows termed 'lucky,'—what, in its last analysis, is it?"

"It is merely," I said, "an identification of the reasoner's intellect with that of his opponent."   95

"It is," said Dupin; "and, upon inquiring of the boy by what means he effected the *thorough* identification in which his success consisted, I received answer as follows: 'When I wish to find out how wise, or how stupid, or how good, or how wicked is any one, or what are his thoughts at the moment, I fashion the expression of my face, as accurately as possible, in accordance with the expression of his, and then wait to see what thoughts or sentiments arise in my mind or heart, as if to match or correspond with the expression.' This reponse of the schoolboy lies at the bottom of all the spurious profundity which has been attributed to Rochefoucault, to La Bougive, to Machiavelli, and to Campanella."°

"And the identification," I said, "of the reasoner's intellect with that of his opponent, depends, if I understand you aright, upon the accuracy with which the opponent's intellect is admeasured."

"For its practical value it depends upon this," replied Dupin; "and the Prefect and his cohort fail so frequently, first, by default of this identification, and, secondly, by ill-admeasurement, or rather through non-admeasurement, of the intellect with which they are engaged. They consider only their *own* ideas of ingenuity; and, in searching for anything hidden, advert only to the modes in which *they* would have hidden it. They are right in this much—that their own ingenuity is a faithful representative of that of *the mass;* but when the cunning of the individual felon is diverse in character from their own, the felon foils them, of course. This always happens when it is above their own, and very usually when it is below. They have no variation of principle in their investigations; at best, when urged by some unusual emergency—by some extraordinary reward—they extend or exaggerate their old modes of *practice*, without touching their principles. What, for example, in this case of D——, has been done to vary the principle of action? What is all this boring, and probing, and sounding, and scrutinizing with the microscope, and dividing the surface of the building into registered square inches—what is it all but an exaggeration *of the application* of the one principle or set of principles of search, which are based upon the one set of notions regarding human ingenuity, to which the Prefect, in the long routine of his duty, has been accustomed? Do you not see he has taken it for granted that *all* men proceed to conceal a letter,—not exactly in a gimlet-hole bored in a chair-leg—but, at least, in *some* out-of-the-way hole or corner suggested by the same tenor of thought which would urge a man to secrete a letter in a gimlet-hole bored in a chair-leg? And do you not see also, that such *recherchés*° nooks for concealment are adapted only for ordinary occasions, and would be adopted only by ordinary intellects; for, in all cases of concealment, a disposal of the article concealed— a disposal of it in this *recherché* manner,—is, in the very first instance, presumable and

---

Rochefoucault . . . Campanella: These writers are cited because they are commonly associated with the idea that human beings are motivated by self-interest. "La Bougive" may be a name invented by Poe.

recherchés: hidden, hard to find.

presumed; and thus its discovery depends, not at all upon the acumen, but altogether upon the mere care, patience, and determination of the seekers; and where the case is of importance—or, what amounts to the same thing in the policial eyes, when the reward is of magnitude,—the qualities in question have *never* been known to fail. You will now understand what I meant in suggesting that, had the purloined letter been hidden any where within the limits of the Prefect's examination—in other words, had the principle of its concealment been comprehended within the principles of the Prefect—its discovery would have been a matter altogether beyond question. This functionary, however, has been thoroughly mystified; and the remote source of his defeat lies in the supposition that the Minister is a fool, because he has acquired renown as a poet. All fools are poets; this the Prefect *feels;* and he is merely guilty of a non *distributio medii*° in thence inferring that all poets are fools."

"But is this really the poet?" I asked. "There are two brothers, I know; and both have attained reputation in letters. The Minister I believe has written learnedly on the Differential Calculus. He is a mathematician, and no poet."

"You are mistaken; I know him well; he is both. As poet *and* mathematician, he   100
would reason well; as mere mathematician, he could not have reasoned at all, and thus would have been at the mercy of the Prefect."

"You surprise me," I said, "by these opinions, which have been contradicted by the voice of the world. You do not mean to set at naught the well-digested idea of centuries. The mathematical reason has long been regarded as *the* reason *par excellence.*"

"'*Il y à parièr,'*" replied Dupin, quoting from Chamfort, "'*que toute idée publique, toute convention reçue, est une sottise, car elle a convenue au plus grand nombre.*'° The mathematicians, I grant you, have done their best to promulgate the popular error to which you allude, and which is none the less an error for its promulgation as truth. With an art worthy a better cause, for example, they have insinuated the term 'analysis' into application to algebra. The French are the originators of this particular deception; but if a term is of any importance—if words derive any value from applicability—then 'analysis' conveys 'algebra' about as much as, in Latin, '*ambitus*' implies 'ambition,' '*religio*' 'religion,' or '*homines honesti,*'° a set of *honorable* men."

"You have a quarrel on hand, I see," said I, "with some of the algebraists of Paris; but proceed."

"I dispute the availability, and thus the value, of that reason which is cultivated in any especial form other than the abstractly logical. I dispute, in particular, the reason educed by mathematical study. The mathematics are the science for form and quantity; mathematical reasoning is merely logic applied to observation upon form and quantity. The great error lies in supposing that even the truths of what is called *pure* algebra, are abstract or general truth. And this error is so egregious that I am

---

non distributio medii: In logic, an "undistributed middle term." The faulty syllogism criticized by Dupin is this: All fools are poets. The Minister is a poet. Therefore the Minister is a fool. The minor premise "The Minister is a poet" is a bad proposition because the Minister is not assigned or distributed to the class of fools, but only of poets. Therefore, the conclusion "the Minister is a fool" does not follow logically.

Il y à . . . nombre: From Nicholas Chamfort (1741–1794), translated freely as "It appears that all popular ideas, all accepted conventions, are blunders because they have been shaped to suit the greatest number [of people]."

ambitus . . . religio . . . honesti: Dupin's point here is that the original Latin meanings of these words do not correspond with the meanings of their English derivatives. *Ambitus* or *ambitio* meant going about to solicit votes. *Religio* referred to fastening or connecting. *Honesti* (*honestus*) signified decency and respectability.

confounded at the universality with which it has been received. Mathematical axioms are *not* axioms of general truth. What is true of *relation*—of form and quantity—is often grossly false in regard to morals, for example. In this latter science it is very usually *un*true that the aggregated parts are equal to the whole. In chemistry also the axiom fails. In the consideration of motive it fails; for two motives, each of a given value, have not, necessarily, a value when united, equal to the sum of their values apart. There are numerous other mathematical truths which are only truths within the limits of *relation*. But the mathematician argues, from his *finite truths*, through habit, as if they were of an absolutely general applicability—as the world indeed imagines them to be. Bryant,° in his very learned 'Mythology,' mentions an analogous source of error, when he says that 'although the Pagan fables are not believed, yet we forget ourselves continually, and make inferences from them as existing realities.' With the algebraists, however, who are Pagans themselves, the 'Pagan fables' *are* believed, and the inferences are made, not so much through lapse of memory, as through an unaccountable addling of the brains. In short, I never yet encountered the mere mathematician who could be trusted out of equal roots, or one who did not clandestinely hold it as a point of his faith that $x^2 + px$ was absolutely and unconditionally equal to q. Say to one of these gentlemen, by way of experiment, if you please, that you believe occasions may occur where $x^2 + px$ is *not* altogether equal to q, and, having made him understand what you mean, get out of his reach as speedily as convenient, for, beyond doubt, he will endeavor to knock you down.

"I mean to say," continued Dupin, while I merely laughed at his last observations, "that if the Minister had been no more than a mathematician, the Prefect would have been under no necessity of giving me this check. I knew him, however, as both mathematician and poet, and my measures were adapted to his capacity, with reference to the circumstances by which he was surrounded. I knew him as a courtier, too, and as a bold *intriguant*.° Such a man, I considered, could not fail to be aware, of the ordinary policial modes of action. He could not have failed to ancitipate—and events have proved that he did not fail to anticipate—the waylayings to which he was subjected. He must have foreseen, I reflected, the secret investigations of his premises. His frequent absences from home at night, which were hailed by the Prefect as certain aids to his success, I regarded only as *ruses*, to afford opportunity for thorough search to the police, and thus the sooner to impress them with the conviction to which G——, in fact, did finally arrive—the conviction that the letter was not upon the premises. I felt, also, that the whole train of thought, which I was at some pains in detailing to you just now, concerning the invariable principle of policial action in searches for articles concealed—I felt that this whole train of thought would necessarily pass through the mind of the Minister. It would imperatively lead him to despise all the ordinary *nooks* of concealment. *He* could not, I reflected, be so weak as not to see that the most intricate and remote recess of his hotel would be as open as his commonest closets to the eyes, to the probes, to the gimlets, and to the microscopes of the Prefect. I saw, in fine, that he would be driven, as a matter of course, to *simplicity*, if not deliberately induced to it as a matter of choice. You will remember, perhaps, how desperately the Prefect laughed when I suggested, upon our first interview, that it was just possible this mystery troubled him so much on account of its being so *very* self-evident."

"Yes," said I, "I remember his merriment well. I really thought he would have fallen into convulsions."

Bryant: Jacob Bryant (1715–1804), English historian and antiquarian.
intriguant: one who engages in schemes.

"The material world," continued Dupin, "abounds with very strict analogies to the immaterial; and thus some color of truth has been given to the rhetorical dogma, that metaphor, or simile, may be made to strengthen an argument, as well as to embellish a description. The principle of the *vis inertiæ*, for example, seems to be identical in physics and metaphysics. It is not more true in the former, that a large body is with more difficulty set in motion than a smaller one, and that its subsequent *momentum* is commensurate with this difficulty, than it is, in the latter, that intellects of the vaster capacity, while more forcible, more constant, and more eventful in their movements than those of inferior grade, are yet the less readily moved, and more embarrassed and full of hesitation in the first few steps of their progress. Again: have you ever noticed which of the street signs, over the shop-doors, are the most attractive of attention?"

"I have never given the matter a thought," I said.

"There is a game of puzzles," he resumed, "which is played upon a map. One party playing requires another to find a given word—the name of town, river, state or empire—any word, in short, upon the motley and perplexed surface of the chart. A novice in the game generally seeks to embarrass his opponents by giving them the most minutely lettered names; but the adept selects such words as stretch, in large characters, from one end of the chart to the other. These, like the over-largely lettered signs and placards of the street, escape observation by dint of being excessively obvious; and here the physical oversight is precisely analogous with the moral inapprehension by which the intellect suffers to pass unnoticed those considerations which are too obtrusively and too palpably self-evident. But this is a point, it appears, somewhat above or beneath the understanding of the Prefect. He never once thought it probable, or possible, that the Minister had deposited the letter immediately beneath the nose of the whole world, by way of best preventing any portion of that world from perceiving it.

"But the more I reflected upon the daring, dashing, and discriminating ingenuity of D——; upon the fact that the document must always have been *at hand,* if he intended to use it to good purpose; and upon the decisive evidence, obtained by the Prefect, that it was not hidden within the limits of that dignitary's ordinary search— the more satisfied I became that, to conceal this letter, the Minister had resorted to the comprehensive and sagacious expedient of not attempting to conceal it at all.

"Full of these ideas, I prepared myself with a pair of green spectacles, and called one fine morning, quite by accident, at the Ministerial hotel. I found D—— at home, yawning, lounging, and dawdling, as usual, and pretending to be in the last extremity of *ennui*. He is, perhaps, the most really energetic human being now alive—but that is only when nobody sees him.

"To be even with him, I complained of my weak eyes, and lamented the necessity of the spectacles, under cover of which I cautiously and thoroughly surveyed the apartment, while seemingly intent only upon the conversation of my host.

"I paid especial attention to a large writing-table near which he sat, and upon which lay confusedly, some miscellaneous letters and other papers, with one or two musical instruments and a few books. Here, however, after a long and very deliberate scrutiny, I saw nothing to excite particular suspicion.

"At length my eyes, in going the circuit of the room, fell upon a trumpery fillagree card-rack of pasteboard, that hung dangling by a dirty blue ribbon, from a little brass knob just beneath the middle of the mantel-piece. In this rack, which had three or four compartments, were five or six visiting cards and a solitary letter. This last was much soiled and crumpled. It was torn nearly in two, across the middle—as if a design, in the first instance, to tear it entirely up as worthless, had been altered, or stayed, in the second. It had a large black seal, bearing the D—— cipher *very* conspicuously, and was addressed, in a diminutive female hand, to D——, the minister, himself. It was thrust carelessly, and even, as it seemed, contemptuously, into one of the upper divisions of the rack.

"No sooner had I glanced at this letter, than I concluded it to be that of which I   115
was in search. To be sure, it was, to all appearance, radically different from the one of which the Prefect had read us so minute a description. Here the seal was large and black, with the D—— cipher; there it was small and red, with the ducal arms of the S—— family. Here, the address, to the Minister, was diminutive and feminine; there the superscription, to a certain royal personage, was markedly bold and decided; the size alone formed a point of correspondence. But, then, the *radicalness* of these differences, which was excessive; the dirt; the soiled and torn condition of the paper, so inconsistent with the *true* methodical habits of D——, and so suggestive of a design to delude the beholder into an idea of the worthlessness of the document; these things, together with the hyperobtrusive situation of this document, full in the view of every visiter, and thus exactly in accordance with the conclusions to which I had previously arrived; these things, I say, were strongly corroborative of suspicion, in one who came with the intention to suspect.

"I protracted my visit as long as possible, and, while I maintained a most animated discussion with the Minister, on a topic which I knew well had never failed to interest and excite him, I kept my attention really riveted upon the letter. In this examination, I committed to memory its external appearance and arrangement in the rack; and also fell, at length, upon a discovery which set at rest whatever trivial doubt I might have entertained. In scrutinizing the edges of the paper, I observed them to be more *chafed* than seemed necessary. They presented the *broken* appearance which is manifested when a stiff paper, having been once folded and pressed with a folder, is refolded in a reversed direction, in the same creases or edges which had formed the original fold. This discovery was sufficient. It was clear to me that the letter had been turned, as a glove, inside out, re-directed, and re-sealed. I bade the Minister good morning, and took my departure at once, leaving a gold snuff-box upon the table.

"The next morning I called for the snuff-box, when we resumed, quite eagerly, the conversation of the preceding day. While thus engaged, however, a loud report, as if of a pistol, was heard immediately beneath the windows of the hotel, and was succeeded by a series of fearful screams, and the shoutings of a mob. D—— rushed to a casement, threw it open, and looked out. In the meantime, I stepped to the card-rack, took the letter, put it in my pocket, and replaced it by a *fac-simile,* (so far as regards externals,) which I had carefully prepared at my lodgings; imitating the D—— cipher, very readily, by means of a seal formed of bread.

"The disturbance in the street had been occasioned by the frantic behavior of a man with a musket. He had fired it among a crowd of women and children. It proved, however, to have been without ball, and the fellow was suffered to go his way as a lunatic or a drunkard. When he had gone, D—— came from the window, whither I had followed him immediately upon securing the object in view. Soon afterwards I bade him farewell. The pretended lunatic was a man in my own pay."

"But what purpose had you," I asked, "in replacing the letter by a *fac-simile?* Would it not have been better, at the first visit, to have seized it openly, and departed?"

"D——," replied Dupin, "is a desperate man, and a man of nerve. His hotel, too, is   120
not without attendants devoted to his interests. Had I made the wild attempt you suggest, I might never have left the Ministerial presence alive. The good people of Paris might have heard of me no more. But I had an object apart from these considerations. You know my political prepossessions. In this matter, I act as a partisan of the lady concerned. For eighteen months the Minister has had her in his power. She has now him in hers;

since, being unaware that the letter is not in his possession, he will proceed with his exactions as if it was. Thus will he inevitably commit himself, at once, to his political destruction. His downfall, too, will not be more precipitate than awkward. It is all very well to talk about the *facilis descensus Averni;*° but in all kinds of climbing, as Catalani° said of singing, it is far more easy to get up than to come down. In the present instance I have no sympathy—at least no pity—for him who descends. He is that *monstrum horrendum,*° an unprincipled man of genius. I confess, however, that I should like very well to know the precise character of his thoughts, when, being defied by her whom the Prefect terms 'a certain personage,' he is reduced to opening the letter which I left for him in the card-rack."

"How? did you put any thing particular in it?"

"Why—it did not seem altogether right to leave the interior blank—that would have been insulting. D——, at Vienna once, did me an evil turn, which I told him, quite good-humoredly, that I should remember. So, as I knew he would feel some curiosity in regard to the identity of the person who had outwitted him, I thought it a pity not to give him a clue. He is well acquainted with my MS., and I just copied into the middle of the blank sheet the words—

—Un dessein si funeste,
S'il n'est digne d'Atrée, est digne de Thyeste.

They are to be found in Crébillon's 'Atrée.'"°

QUESTIONS

1. What problem is posed for Dupin to solve? In what way does Dupin affront Monsieur G——?

2. Who is the speaker of the story? What is his relationship to Dupin? Is he named? What is gained by having this speaker as the narrator rather than Dupin?

3. What startling disclosure does Dupin make in the story? Why does Monsieur G—— have nothing to say after the event?

4. Aside from the obvious motive of the reward, what is Dupin's interest in recovering the letter?

5. Explain Dupin's elaborate processes of reasoning that enable him to deduce the letter's location. How correct is this reasoning?

6. This story is often considered one of the very first "detective" stories, a genre created by Poe. What elements does it contain that you associate with other detective stories you have read? What elements have later writers added to the form?

facilis descensus Averni [Averno]: from Virgil's *Aeneid,* VI.126, "It is easy to go down into Avernus [hell]."

Catalani: Angelica Catalani (1780–1849), one of the best-known singers of her day. She was also a theater manager.

monstrum horrendum: "a horrible monster," the description of the Cyclops Polyphemus in Virgil's *Aeneid,* III.658.

Crébillon's "Atrée": Prosper de Crébillon (1674–1762), author of the play *Atreus and Thyestes* (1707). "If so lethal a plot is not worthy of Atreus, it is worthy of Thyestes."

The Cask of Amontillado _____ *1846*

The thousand injuries of Fortunato I had borne as I best could; but when he ventured upon insult, I vowed revenge. You, who so well know the nature of my soul, will not suppose, however, that I gave utterance to a threat. *At length* I would be avenged: this was a point definitively settled—but the very definitiveness with which it was resolved, precluded the idea of risk. I must not only punish, but punish with impunity. A wrong is unredressed when retribution overtakes its redresser. It is equally unredressed when the avenger fails to make himself felt as such to him who has done the wrong.

It must be understood, that neither by word nor deed had I given Fortunato cause to doubt my good-will. I continued, as was my wont, to smile in his face, and he did not perceive that my smile *now* was at the thought of his immolation.

He had a weak point—this Fortunato—although in other regards he was a man to be respected and even feared. He prided himself on his connoisseurship in wine. Few Italians have the true virtuoso spirit. For the most part their enthusiasm is adopted to suit the time and opportunity—to practice imposture upon the British and Austrian millionaires. In painting and gemmary Fortunato, like his countrymen, was a quack—but in the matter of old wines he was sincere. In this respect I did not differ from him materially: I was skilful in the Italian vintages myself, and bought largely whenever I could.

It was about dusk, one evening during the supreme madness of the carnival season, that I encountered my friend. He accosted me with excessive warmth, for he had been drinking much. The man wore motley. He had on a tight-fitting parti-striped dress, and his head was surmounted by the conical cap and bells. I was so pleased to see him, that I thought I should never have done wringing his hand.

I said to him: "My dear Fortunato, you are luckily met. How remarkably well you are looking today! But I have received a pipe of what passes for Amontillado, and I have my doubts."   5

"How?" said he. "Amontillado? A pipe? Impossible! And in the middle of the carnival!"

"I have my doubts," I replied; "and I was silly enough to pay the full Amontillado price without consulting you in the matter. You were not to be found, and I was fearful of losing a bargain."

"Amontillado!"

"I have my doubts."

"Amontillado!"

"And I must satisfy them."   10

"Amontillado!"

"As you are engaged, I am on my way to Luchesi. If anyone has a critical turn, it is he: He will tell me—"

"Luchesi cannot tell Amontillado from Sherry."

"And yet some fools will have it that his taste is a match for your own."   15

"Come, let us go."

"Whither?"

"To your vaults."

"My friend, no; I will not impose upon your good nature. I perceive you have an engagement. Luchesi—"

"I have no engagement;—come."   20

"My friend, no. It is not the engagement, but the severe cold with which I perceive you are afflicted. The vaults are insufferably damp. They are encrusted with nitre."

"Let us go, nevertheless. The cold is merely nothing. Amontillado! You have been imposed upon. And as for Luchesi, he cannot distinguish Sherry from Amontillado."

Thus speaking, Fortunato possessed himself of my arm. Putting on a mask of black silk, and drawing a *roquelaure*° about my person, I suffered him to hurry me to my palazzo.

There were no attendants at home; they had absconded to make merry in honor of the time. I had told them that I should not return until the morning, and had given them explicit orders not to stir from the house. These orders were sufficient, I well knew, to insure their immediate disappearance, one and all, as soon as my back was turned.

I took from their sconces two flambeaux, and giving one to Fortunato, bowed him through several suites of rooms to the archway that led into the vaults. I passed down a long and winding staircase, requesting him be cautious as he followed. We came at length to the foot of the descent, and stood together on the damp ground of the catacombs of the Montresors.   25

The gait of my friend was unsteady, and the bells upon his cap jingled as he strode.

"The pipe?" said he.

"It is farther on," said I; "but observe the white webwork which gleams from these cavern walls."

He turned toward me, and looked into my eyes with two filmy orbs that distilled the rheum of intoxication.

"Nitre?" he asked, at length.

"Nitre," I replied. "How long have you had that cough?"   30

"Ugh! ugh! ugh!—ugh! ugh! ugh!—ugh! ugh! ugh!—ugh! ugh! ugh!—ugh! ugh! ugh!"

My poor friend found it impossible to reply for many minutes.

"It is nothing," he said at last.

"Come," I said, with decision, "we will go back; your health is precious. You are rich, respected, admired, beloved; you are happy, as once I was. You are a man to be missed. For me it is no matter. We will go back; you will be ill, and I cannot be responsible. Besides, there is Luchesi—"   35

"Enough," he said; "the cough is a mere nothing; it will not kill me. I shall not die of a cough."

"True—true," I replied; "and, indeed, I had no intention of alarming you unnecessarily; but you should use all proper caution. A draught of this Medoc will defend us from the damps."

Here I knocked off the neck of a bottle which I drew from a long row of its fellows that lay upon the mould.

"Drink," I said, presenting him the wine.

He raised it to his lips with a leer. He paused and nodded to me familiarly, while his bells jingled.   4

"I drink," he said, "to the buried that repose around us."

"And I to your long life."

He again took my arm, and we proceeded.

"These vaults," he said, "are extensive."

"The Montresors," I replied, "were a great and numerous family."

"I forget your arms."

---

roquelaure: a type of cloak.

"A huge human foot *d'or*, in a field azure; the foot crushes a serpent rampant whose fangs are imbedded in the heel."

"And the motto?"

"Nemo me impune lacessit."°

"Good!" he said.   50

The wine sparkled in his eyes and the bells jingled. My own fancy grew warm with the Medoc. We had passed through walls of piled bones, with casks and puncheons intermingling, into the inmost recesses of the catacombs. I paused again, and this time I made bold to seize Fortunato by an arm above the elbow.

"The nitre!" I said; "see, it increases. It hangs like moss upon the vaults. We are below the river's bed. The drops of moisture trickle among the bones. Come, we will go back ere it is too late. Your cough—"

"It is nothing," he said; "let us go on. But first, another draught of the Medoc."

I broke and reached him a flagon of De Grâve. He emptied it at a breath. His eyes flashed with a fierce light. He laughed and threw the bottle upward with a gesticulation I did not understand.

I looked at him in surprise. He repeated the movement—a grotesque one.   55

"You do not comprehend?" he said.

"Not I," I replied.

"Then you are not of the brotherhood."

"How?"

"You are not of the Masons."   60

"Yes, yes," I said; "yes, yes."

"You? Impossible! A Mason?"

"A Mason," I replied.

"A sign," he said.

"It is this," I answered, producing a trowel from beneath the folds of my   65
roquelaure.

"You jest," he exclaimed, recoiling a few paces. "But let us proceed to the Amontillado."

"Be it so," I said, replacing the tool beneath the cloak, and again offering him my arm. He leaned upon it heavily. We continued our route in search of the Amontillado. We passed through a range of low arches, descended, passed on, and descending again, arrived at a deep crypt, in which the foulness of the air caused our flambeaux rather to glow than flame.

At the most remote end of the crypt there appeared another less spacious. Its walls had been lined with human remains, piled to the vault overhead, in the fashion of the great catacombs of Paris. Three sides of this interior crypt were still ornamented in this manner. From the fourth the bones had been thrown down, and lay promiscuously upon the earth, forming at one point a mound of some size. Within the wall thus exposed by the displacing of the bones, we perceived a still interior recess, in depth about four feet, in width three, in height six or seven. It seemed to have been constructed for no especial use within itself, but formed merely the interval between two of the colossal supports of the roof of the catacombs, and was backed by one of their circumscribing walls of solid granite.

It was in vain that Fortunato, uplifting his dull torch, endeavored to pry into the depth of the recess. Its termination the feeble light did not enable us to see.

Nemo me impune lacessit: No one attacks me with impunity.

"Proceed," I said; "herein is the Amontillado. As for Luchesi—"   70

"He is an ignoramus," interrupted my friend, as he stepped unsteadily forward, while I followed immediately at his heels. In an instant he had reached the extremity of the niche, and finding his progress arrested by the rock, stood stupidly bewildered. A moment more and I had fettered him to the granite. In its surface were two iron staples, distant from each other about two feet, horizontally. From one of these depended a short chain, from the other a padlock. Throwing the links about his waist, it was but the work of a few seconds to secure it. He was too much astounded to resist. Withdrawing the key I stepped back from the recess.

"Pass your hand," I said, "over the wall; you cannot help feeling the nitre. Indeed it is *very* damp. Once more let me *implore* you to return. No? Then I must positively leave you. But I must first render you all the little attentions in my power."

"The Amontillado!" ejaculated my friend, not yet recovered from his astonishment.

"True," I replied; "the Amontillado."

As I said these words I busied myself among the pile of bones of which I have   75
before spoken. Throwing them aside, I soon uncovered a quantity of building stone and mortar. With these materials and with the aid of my trowel, I began vigorously to wall up the entrance of the niche.

I had scarcely laid the first tier of the masonry when I discovered that the intoxication of Fortunato had in a great measure worn off. The earliest indication I had of this was a low moaning cry from the depth of the recess. It was *not* the cry of a drunken man. There was then a long and obstinate silence. I laid the second tier, and the third, and the fourth; and then I heard the furious vibrations of the chain. The noise lasted for several minutes, during which, that I might hearken to it with the more satisfaction, I ceased my labors and sat down upon the bones. When at last the clanking subsided, I resumed the trowel, and finished without interruption the fifth, the sixth, and the seventh tier. The wall was now nearly upon a level with my breast. I again paused, and holding the flambeaux over the mason-work, threw a few feeble rays upon the figure within.

A succession of loud and shrill screams, bursting suddenly from the throat of the chained form, seemed to thrust me violently back. For a brief moment I hesitated— I trembled. Unsheathing my rapier, I began to grope with it about the recess; but the thought of an instant reassured me. I placed my hand upon the solid fabric of the catacombs, and felt satisfied. I reapproached the wall. I replied to the yells of him who clamored. I reechoed—I aided—I surpassed them in volume and in strength. I did this, and the clamorer grew still.

It was now midnight, and my task was drawing to a close. I had completed the eighth, the ninth, and the tenth tier. I had finished a portion of the last and the eleventh; there remained but a single stone to be fitted and plastered in. I struggled with its weight; I placed it partially in its destined position. But now there came from out the niche a low laugh that erected the hairs upon my head. It was succeeded by a sad voice, which I had difficulty in recognizing as that of the noble Fortunato. The voice said—

"Ha! ha! ha!—he! he!—a very good joke indeed—an excellent jest. We will have many a rich laugh about it at the palazzo—he! he! he!—over our wine—he! he! he!"

"The Amontillado!" I said.

"He! he! he!—he! he! he!—yes, the Amontillado. But is it not getting late? Will not they be awaiting us at the palazzo, the Lady Fortunato and the rest? Let us be gone."

"Yes," I said, "let us be gone."

"For the love of God, Montresor!"

"Yes," I said, "for the love of God!"

But to these words I hearkened in vain for a reply. I grew impatient. I called aloud: 85
"Fortunato!"

No answer. I called again:

"Fortunato!"

No answer still. I thrust a torch through the remaining aperture and let it fall within. There came forth in return only a jingling of the bells. My heart grew sick—on account of the dampness of the catacombs. I hastened to make an end of my labor. I forced the last stone into its position. I plastered it up. Against the new masonry I reerected the old rampart of bones. For the half of a century no mortal has disturbed them. *In pace requiescat!*°

QUESTIONS

1. What is the nature of the narration? Who is speaking? To whom is he speaking? What is the purpose of the narrator's "May he rest in peace" at the end? Why is the nature of Fortunato's insult against Montresor not explained?

2. What do you learn about revenge from Montresor? What do you learn about Montresor from his analysis of revenge and from his family's coat of arms?

3. How does Montresor manipulate Fortunato so that Fortunato seems to be the originator of the trip to examine the Amontillado? Who is Luchesi? What does Fortunato think of Luchesi?

4. Describe Poe's use of setting in "The Cask of Amontillado" (e.g., the cap and bells, Montresor's clothing, the interior recess in which Fortunato is pinioned, etc.).

EDITED SELECTIONS
FROM CRITICISM OF POE'S STORIES

The following selections are intended to supply details and ideas for essays on Poe's stories. For a selective bibliography, consult the *Bibliographical Sources* section above (p. 527), which may be augmented with your college library catalogue and the most recent volumes of the *MLA International Bibliography* available in your library's reference room. The bracketed page numbers refer to the original pagination of the sources included here. Footnotes in the sources have been deleted.

1. Poe's Irony*

Poe's "serious" tales, clearly, are only apparently serious in the manner that they pur-   [36]
port to be. The whole of Poe's Gothic fiction can be read not only as an ambivalent

---

In pace requiescat: May he rest in peace.
    * Selections 1–6 are from G. R. Thompson, ed., *Great Short Works of Edgar Allen Poe* (New York: Harper, 1970).

parody of the world of Gothic horror tales, but also as an extended grotesquerie of the human condition. Nothing quite works out for his heroes, even though they sometimes make superhuman efforts, and even though they are occasionally rescued from their predicaments. They undergo extended series of ironic reverses in fictional structures so ironically twisted that the form itself, even the very plot, approaches an absurd hoax perpetrated on the characters. The universe created in Poe's fiction is one in which the human mind tries vainly to perceive order and meaning. The universe is deceptive; its basic mode seems almost to be a constant shifting of appearances; reality is a flux vari-   [37] ously interpreted, or even created, by the individual human mind. In its deceptiveness, the universe of Poe's Gothic fiction seems not so much malevolent as mocking or "perverse." The universe is much like a gigantic hoax that God has played on man, an idea which is the major undercurrent of Poe's essay on the universe, *Eureka.* Thus, the hoax-like irony of Poe's technique has its parallel in the dramatic world in which his characters move.

The ultimate irony of this universe, however, is the "perversity" of man's own mind. The mind, and the mind only, seems to sustain Poe's heroes in their most desperate predicaments; yet in an instant the mind is capable of slipping into confusion, hysteria, madness—even while it seems most rational. From a more "Gothicist" point of view, Edward H. Davidson, without using the term *irony,* and without reading Poe's Gothic tales ironically or satirically, comes to much the same conclusion regarding Poe's universe. "Poe's nightmare universe," Davidson writes, "is one in which . . . people . . . are condemned to live as if they are in some long aftertime of belief and morality." The evil-doer is driven by "some maggot in the brain" that leaves him a kind of "moral freak" in a universe that also has some fantastic defect in it. In Poe's universe, Davidson suggests, evil and suffering are "the capacity and measure of man to feel and to know"; pain is the basis of life, and death is the only release from his "grotesque condition of 'perversity.'"

This view of Poe's "perverse" universe is, I think, essentially correct. Poe's fiction developed from a basically satiric mode into an ironic mode in which a tragic reponse to the perversities of fortune and to the treacheries of one's own mind is contrasted by a near-comic perception of the absurdity of man's condition in the universe. Such a double perception, according to the German Ironists, leads, through art, to a momentary   [38 transcendence of the dark chaos of the universe. If the artist (and through him the reader) can mock man's absurd condition at the same time that he feels it deeply, he transcends earthly or finite limits in an artistic paralleling of God's infinite perception. In Poe, however, such transcendence is always at the expense of the less perceptive mind. Poe plays a constant intellectual game with his readers; he tries to draw the reader into the "Gothic" world of the mind, but he is ready at any moment to mock the simplistic Gothic vision (under the trappings of which Poe saw man's real estrangement and isolation) that contemporary readers insisted on in the popular magazines.

2. The Narrators of "The Cask of Amontillado" and "The Fall of the House of Usher"

When we come to the tales, the comic and ironic side of Poe is clearer and more   [1 emphatic. And it is here, rather than among the poems, I believe, that we find the *great* works of Poe. (All of Poe's works, except his one novel, *Arthur Gordon Pym,* are "short.") His criticism, though historically interesting in its specificity and topicality, and the best of his time (barring only Coleridge's criticism), is valuable today mainly for its precise enunciation of principles of rational control over even the wildest materials—for its enunciation of a principle, not merely of "unity," but of "*totality* of effect." "If [the] very first sentence," Poe wrote in his 1847 review of Hawthorne's *Twice-Told Tales,* "tend not to [19] the outbringing of this effect, then in his very first step has [the artist] committed a blunder. In the whole composition there should be no word written of which the tendency, direct *or indirect,* is not to the pre-established design" (my italics). This principle he observed in each and every one of his tales—and not only in the well-known Gothic tales and detective stories, but also in the underrated comic and satiric tales, even though in these he was "slapping" (as he said in a letter to Joseph Snodgrass in 1841) "left & right at things in general."

In Poe's characteristically intricate, even involuted patterns of dramatic irony, the apparent narrative "voice" which pervades the surface atmosphere of the work is also seen within a qualifying frame. Several of the tales (for example "The Black Cat," "The Tell-Tale Heart," "Ligeia," "The Imp of the Perverse," "The Cask of Amontillado") involve a confessional element, wherein a first-person narrator, like Montresor, seems calmly or gleefully to recount horrible deeds, but which generally implies a listener to whom the agonized soul is revealing his torment. Especially revealing of the ironic structure thus achieved is Montresor in "The Cask of Amontillado." In the surface story, Montresor seems to be chuckling over his flawlessly executed revenge upon unfortunate "Fortunato" fifty years before. But a moment's reflection suggests that the indistinct "you" whom Montresor addresses in the first paragraph is probably his death-bed confessor—for if Montresor has murdered Fortunato fifty years before, he must now be some seventy to eighty years of age. None of this is explicitly stated; it is presented dramatically, and we get the double effect of feeling the coldly calculated murder at the same time that we see the larger point that Montresor, rather than having successfully taken his revenge "with impunity," as he says, has instead suffered a fifty-year's ravage [20] of conscience. Likewise, many of Poe's Gothic tales seem to involve supernatural happenings; but insinuated into them, like clues in a detective story, are details which begin to construct dramatic frames around the narrative "voice" of the work. These dramatic frames suggest the elusiveness of the experience as the first-person narrator renders it. As in Henry James and Joseph Conrad, there is often in Poe a tale within a tale within a tale; and the meaning of the whole lies in the relationship of the various implied stories and their frames rather than in the explicit meaning given to the surface story by the dramatically involved narrator.

Only within the last ten to fifteen years have critics begun to examine Poe's narrators as characters in the total design of his tales and poems, and to suspect that even his most famous Gothic works—like "Usher" and "Ligeia"—have ironic double and triple perspectives playing upon them: supernatural from one point of view, psychological from another point of view, and often burlesque from yet a third. Not only is nearly half of Poe's fiction satiric and comic in an obvious way, but the Gothic tales contain within them satiric and comic elements thematically related to the macabre elements. Poe seems very carefully to have aimed at the ironic effect of touching his readers simultaneously on an archetypal emotional level of fear and on an (almost subliminal) level of intellectual and philosophical perception of the Absurd. The result in the Gothic tales, as in many of the poems, is a kind of ambivalent mockery. We can respond to Poe's scenes of horror or despair at the same time that we are aware of their caricatural quality.

3. "The Fall of the House of Usher"

Between 1838 and 1840, the middle years of his career, Poe published three of his most   [34]
famous Gothic stories: "Ligeia," "The Fall of the House of Usher," and "William Wilson."
Like "Ligeia," the other two tales involve "doubles" and dramatize a weird universe as
perceived by a subjective mind. "Usher," despite the supernatural atmosphere, can be
read as the tale of the frenzied fantasies of *both* the narrator and Usher, fantasies engendered by a vague fear that something ominous *may* happen and by the disconnected,
alien environment. The overriding theme is the mechanism of fear itself, which has per-
versely operated on Roderick Usher before the narrator arrives, and which operates on
the narrator *through* Usher afterwards. When the narrator rides his horse up to the
House of Usher and gazes at its leaden-eyed aspect and at the tarn, with its sickly white
stems of dead plants sticking up through the stagnant water, he is immediately seized by
a vague apprehension. Later in the tale, he remarks that the "mental disorder" and "hysteria" of his friend Roderick Usher "terrified" and "infected" him: "I felt creeping upon   [35]
me, by slow yet certain degrees, the wild influences of his own fantastic yet impressive
superstitions." The narrator's confrontation with (and submission to) a mind gone mad
is imaged in the facelike appearance of the House itself, with its leaden-hued eyelike windows and its zigzag crack down the middle, and in the wild "arabesque" face of Roderick
Usher. The poem "The Haunted Palace," which Usher has composed, is also a symbolic,
indeed allegorical, portrait of a facelike structure. The "face" of the palace changes when
the "Monarch Thought" topples from his throne within, and the palace comes to resemble the face of Usher and his House as the narrator has described them. Moreover, when
the narrator first looks down into the tarn, what he should see of course is his own face
since he is on its very brink, but instead he sees the inverted image of the "face" of the
House of Usher. His next action is to go inside and meet Usher face to face. Immediately,
his attention is arrested by certain details of Usher's face; though he does not articulate
the resemblances, as such, the narrator so describes the weblike hair of Usher that we are
compelled to remember the webwork of fungi about the eaves of the House.

By the time the narrator "sees" the "return" of Madeline Usher from her grave,
the themes of narcissism and inversion are so clear that the relevance of the absurdist
interlude, "The Mad Trist of Sir Lancelot Canning" to the story as a whole (that is, to the
dramatic situation of the narrator rather than merely to Roderick's "trist" with his twin
sister) is obvious. The tale is the story of the "mad trist" of the twin, hysterical personalities of the narrator and Usher. Finally, we do not know for sure *what* has happened for,
as our narrator flees "aghast" from the scene, the face of the House splits apart and sinks
into that tarn which first merged the images of the faces of both the House and the
narrator. The tale has long been hailed as a masterpiece of Gothic horror; it is also a   [ⁱ
masterpiece of dramatic irony and structural symbolism.

4. "The Black Cat" and "The Tell-Tale Heart"*

"The Tell-Tale Heart" (1843), a study in obsessive paranoia, is yet another story of the
mind watching itself disintegrate under the stresses of delusion in an alienated world. It   [
is the perverse fortune of the narrator to become fearful of the grotesque eye of a kindly

---

* "The Tell-Tale Heart" is not included in this book.

old man, whom he says he loves. With a double perversity, he gives himself away to the police at the moment of success. Yet the narrator is caught in a weird world in which he [41] loves the old man yet displays no real emotion toward him, in which he cannot let the "beloved" old man live and yet cannot kill him without remorse, in which he cannot expose his crime and yet must do so. Perhaps the final irony is that the apparent beating of his own heart which he mistakes as, first, the beating of the still-living heart of the old man, and which, second, seems to be an emblem of his own guilt (and which, finally, compels him to confess), may very well be initially the peculiar thumping sound of the wood-beetles gnawing at the walls. "The Black Cat" (1843) carries the same themes further and details more clearly the irrational desire, almost the ultimate irony, to act against oneself, with an ambiguous conclusion suggesting the agency of malevolent fortune at the same time that it suggests subconscious self-punishment. The major absurdist irony, perhaps, is that the murder which the narrator commits is the result of subconscious remorse over the *cat* he has previously mistreated.

5. Dupin of "The Purloined Letter"

Poe's six ratiocinative tales of the 1840s represent the few successes of the acute mind in [43] overcoming the bewildering deceptiveness of the perverse world. Five of the tales are ostensibly serious ("Murders in the Rue Morgue," "Marie Roget," "The Purloined Letter," "Goldbug," "Descent into the Maelström") and one is comic and suggests self-parody (" 'Thou Art the Man' "). The Dupin kind of mentality assumes a godlike omniscience, the "I" and the reader, the role of dull-witted dupes. The major ironies of these tales are consistent with Poe's more clearly Gothic tales: their basis is the discrepancy between appearance and actuality; and the ease of Dupin's solutions contrasts with our mystification.

6. "The Masque of the Red Death"

"The Masque of The Red Death" (1842), a tale of the supernatural visitation of Death [39] himself, can also be read as a tone poem about hysteria, engendered by mood and setting, with a sarcastic concluding echo from Pope's *Dunciad*. Prince Prospero's sinister stronghold, of course, contrasts directly with the enchanted island of his namesake, Prospero, the magician in Shakespeare's *The Tempest*. The ironic theme of Poe's tale focuses on the grimly perverse joke of Prospero's having walled *in* death in a frenetic attempt to wall it out.

7. "The Purloined Letter"*

Dupin as Transcendental Hero

While the matter of Poe's real beliefs is perhaps still debatable, the importance for his [162] fiction of the world-view which we have been discussing is fairly easy to define: Poe was a [163] transcendentalist in that he wrote tales about the act of artistic perception, and his

* From Stuart Levine, *Edgar Poe: Seer and Craftsman* (Deland, FL: Everett/Edwards, 1972).

understanding of the nature of that act is substantially that to which the Transcendentalists subscribed. The number of different types of stories which are "about" perception is surprising, especially if one has read the more mechanical passages of Poe's criticism. One might, for example, expect the detective tales to be far removed from the pattern of complex-vision and perception because they seem like logic-games. I think we feel this way partially because of certain preconceptions we have regarding detective tales. We know what the modern whodunnit is like; we see similar features in the Dupin stories, and we conclude that the significant thing about Dupin is that he is a precursor of Sherlock Holmes and Perry Mason. Well, that is true enough, but it is not the whole truth.

When Émile Gaboriau became acquainted with Dupin through Baudelaire's translation, he was inspired to write the first novel-length detective story, and the extent to which the mystery-writing craft is indebted to Poe is indicated by Conan Doyle's words, "If every man who receives a cheque for a story which owes its springs to Poe were to pay tithe to a monument for the Master, he would have a pyramid as big as that of Cheops." Moreover, there are devices in Poe's tales which have proved remarkably durable. The outbursts of amazement from Watson and other "righthand men" are lineal descendents of those of Poe's narrator; they constitute "one of the hardiest devices that Poe gave to the form." There are still other elements which can be traced to Poe: the idea of the detective as a "thinking machine" (one famous fictional detective was so called; several deserve the appellation); the frequent use, in the hero's "logic," of the paradox. The Dupin tales have all these elements which by now are traditional, but they have something else, which becomes apparent when one examines the language with which Poe describes Dupin's method.

Poe's detective succeeds not because of a superior mechanical ability to piece together facts, but because he is an artist, and one who has more than a little in common with the artist described by Emerson in "The Poet." Speaking of the Prefect—prototype of all the literal-minded and unimaginative police chiefs and sergeants of our current detective stories—Dupin observes, ". . . our friend . . . is somewhat too cunning to be pro- [164 found. In his wisdom is no *stamen*. It is all head and no body. . . ." Dupin's complaint is essentially the message of *Eureka,* or of the "Sonnet—to Science." Science, Poe laments, has become too concerned with minute facts; it loses sight of the beauty of the greater scheme of which the facts are only small details. "SCIENCE! true daughter of the Old Time thou art!/Who alterest all things with thy peering eyes./Why preyest thou thus upon the poet's heart,/Vulture, whose wings are dull realities?" Emerson preached the same message in almost every paragraph of his work; Poe, similarly, embodied his conception of inspiration in numerous different pieces. Dupin has a great deal in common with Ellison, the creator of the Landscape Garden, and even something in common with the unnamed narrators of the tales of terror. The common element is to be found in the ways in which these very different people perceive the complex patterns which Poe admired. The Prefect of Police or a scientist following the unimaginative *credo* unfavorably described in Poe's sonnet are analogous to the uninspired scholar against whom Emerson warned in *The American Scholar.*

Poe was not intrinsically hostile to science, but he was hostile to mechanical fact-hunting. He was again surprisingly close to the ideas of the Transcendentalism he professed to scorn. "All head and no body" was the usual Transcendental plea for the instincts. Emerson said "books are for the scholar's idle times"; Poe thumbed his nose at facts-for-facts'-sake. As was very plain in "The Poetic Principle," Poe believed in something very like the Oversoul, which, if not specifically divine, was clearly the source of an artist's inspiration. As one moves chronologically through Poe's work, this "something" becomes more clearly divine and Poe comes to look more and more like an occultist. Hence his attempt, in *Eureka,* to write a prose poem which would, through "inspiration," present a large scientific thesis in an artistic way: if the end of knowledge is merger with "the universal oneness," then art and science are the same.

Dupin is different from Perry Mason because he understands this. He does not merely piece together clues; he creates a beautiful pattern. He uses more than logic. In "The Purloined Letter," Poe has him say of the Minister from whom he recovers the letter, "I know him . . . as both mathematician and poet, and my measures were adapted [165] to his capacity." He can imaginatively project himself into the complex personality of another, become one with him.

At the opening of "The Murders in the Rue Morgue," Poe's narrator explains the nature of Dupin's genius as an analyst: ". . . the analyst throws himself into the spirit of his opponent, identifies himself therewith. . . ." Analysis, then, involves the imagination, and is an artistic process.

> Between ingenuity and the analytic ability there exists a difference far greater, indeed, than that between the fancy and the imagination, but of a character very strictly analogous. It will be found, in fact, that the ingenious are always fanciful, and the *truly* imaginative never otherwise than analytic.

I have elsewhere mentioned the article in which Robert Daniel points out that Dupin can, with justice, be called "Poe's Detective God." We have also seen that several critics have noticed the similarity between Poe's conception of the role of the artist and that of certain of his contemporaries. One can say, without distorting the literary history of the early nineteenth century, that there is a certain common area shared by the critical theories of men as different as Shelley, Emerson, Coleridge and Edgar Poe, or, indeed, any writer who believed that it was the artist's duty to act as humanity's listening post to the music of the spheres. The artist's gift is defined as an ability to attune his mind to the correct frequencies. Shelley's Prometheus and Emerson's Poet have, in this sense, a common mission; they are heroic examples of man perceiving.

There are curious and paradoxical matters involved here. We have been discussing the philosophical consistency of Poe's fiction. Indeed, we have been demonstrating that the fiction is a dramatization of an esoteric philosophy, one in which the artist is understood to be a "seer," in direct communion with some source of supernal inspiration. And yet, in reviewing the various ways in which these stories illustrate perception and inspiration, we have come to something of a formula, a rather mechanical formula, at that: the easier the perception, the less tension. We may want to state it even more strongly: the easier the perception, the less plot. If the perceiving character in the story is naturally gifted with the artistic ability it takes to see the "vision," the story will be almost without plot. "The Domain of Arnheim" is hardly more than an extended sketch [166] because the garden is the creation of Ellison; the apocalyptic tales are plotless celestial conversations because the voices belonged to enlightened spirits; the detective stories contain practically no action because Dupin, like Ellison, is one of Poe's ideal artists. Plenty happens, of course, in the detective stories, but it is almost always in the past. Dupin and the narrator discuss it as history, and Dupin intuits its key. There is very little action in the present: Dupin places an advertisement and sits at home to await results, or tells us (again, in the past) how he found the Purloined Letter. We might even borrow a page from Poe, who invited readers to send in cryptograms for him to solve, by claiming to be able to "solve" the plot-structure of one of his stories which we have not read if the reader will send in only a description of the manner in which the perceiving character perceives. The trouble is that in the present case the author has read all of Poe's stories already, and the chances are that most of his readers have, too.

It should really not seem too strange to us that stories which embody an esoteric philosophy should lend themselves this readily to mechanical analysis. The apparent paradox is one for which Poe adequately prepared us in his criticism. . . . Poe's criticism acknowledges the importance of both inspiration and craftsmanship. A good craftsman has his favorite procedures, and the fact that we as readers have caught on to them in no sense makes him a formula writer. We may want to claim that we have found a "key" to Poe, but there is no point in claiming that we have unmasked him.

Our main point at present is that the detective stories should not be considered as an isolated handful of experiments in a totally different genre. Rather, they fit in perfectly well with the pattern which we have seen operating in so many of Poe's stories. If we were to arrange Poe's fiction along sort of a scale, running from those in which the narrator has a relatively difficult time in perceiving to those in which he has no trouble at all, the Dupin stories would come near the end of our list. At the other end of the scale would go tales such as "Ligeia," "Berenice," "The Fall of the House of Usher," "The Pit and the Pendulum" and "A Descent into the Maelstrom." What they have in common is that to "get through" to whatever "vision" he is to experience, the [167] perceiver in each of them has to go through a process far more arduous than do Ellison or Dupin. The patterns of crime which Dupin perceives will "take" the usual adjectives. They are ornate, complex, bizarre, but Dupin himself does not have to undergo a harrowing experience in order to see them. (He does, on the other hand, need more help than does Ellison. Dupin takes drugs.)

I do not think that it is overstating the case to claim that Dupin can be understood not merely as the prototype for a large number of whodunnit heroes, but also as an example of the transcendental hero, the character whom the author uses to show the transcendental way, or to demonstrate its hazards. The sense in which Henry Thoreau's work represents a testing of the Emersonian advice is sufficiently obvious; indeed, *Walden* may properly be understood as the "utopian novel" of the movement, and its persona, the modest transcendentalist hero. Similarly, Whitman's bardic pose clearly grows from Emersonian instructions. The mighty "I" of his poems is another example of the type, a God-like super-poet tuned to the broad frequencies of humanity *en mass*, the gain turned up to maximum. Much less optimistic are the versions of the character which appear in the fiction of Hawthorne and Melville. From *Mardi* on, for example, Melville's major fiction deals to a great extent with the attempts of "seekers" to obey the commands within, to step to the personal drumming which, according to the Concord gospel, echoed the eternal rhythms. The result is always disaster. Ahab's *Pequod* sinks into the serene Pacific; Pierre blows out his brains in a jail, and Taji seems doomed to an endless quest; Serenia will not satisfy him once "eternity is in his eye." It seems odd, perhaps, ever to group Poe with "bright" authors, but clearly his Dupin has more in common with Whitman's "I" and with the persona of *Walden* than he does with Ahab, Taji, or Pierre. Poe probably would resent our saying that his character was demonstrating the validity of Emersonian assumptions. He could point out, truthfully, that Emerson did not invent them. But that hardly matters, for the Transcendentalists share them with other writers of their age, and their truth seems sufficiently obvious to Poe for him to assert, in Agathos' words, that they are "simply true." Dupin makes use of them, and they work.

Poe's philosophical position would be clear had he left the world nothing but *Eureka,* the colloquies, and "The Rationale of Verse," but it would be equally clear, if less [168] obvious, had he written nothing but the major tales. I have been using Dupin as an example of his use of the transcendental hero because Dupin appears in several stories, and is well known, but what I have said about the detective stories really applies to most of Poe's best fiction. Taken collectively, his stories form a great drama in which the hero, as in *Walden,* "The Poet," or "Song of Myself," is the artist in the act of perceiving.

8. Sources and Analogues of "The Cask of Amontillado"*

"The Cask of Amontillado" is a prime example of Poe's ability to sculpt materials from [93] popular literature and culture into a masterwork of terror. At once derivative and freshly individualistic, the tale enacts Poe's belief that "the truest and surest test of *originality* is the manner of handling a hackneyed subject."

It has long been surmised that this story of murderous revenge reflects Poe's vindictive hatred of two prominent New York literary figures, the author Thomas Dunn English and the newspaper editor Hiram Fuller. If "The Cask" is on some level, a retaliatory document, surely Poe could not have envisioned a more ghoulish type of retaliation. Seen against the background of the war of the literati, the narrator Montresor (Poe) gets back at his enemy Fortunato (English) for a recent insult, using their mutual friend Luchesi (Fuller) as a foil in his scheme. Although we know from the start that Montresor is bent on revenge, and we have ominous feelings as he takes his foe into the depths of his skeleton-filled wine vaults, the tale's atmosphere is deceptively convivial; the two connoisseurs banter and drink as they go in search of the cask of Amontillado (a fine Spanish sherry) Montresor says he has received. Only when Montresor lures Fortunato into a small niche, quickly chains up his stupefied victim, and proceeds to wall up the niche with bricks and mortar are we overwhelmed by the horrifying fact of live burial.

Poe's animus against the literati may have motivated the revenge theme, but it fails to account for specific details of plot, character, and imagery. For those we must look to the tale's popular cultural context. Poe was a great borrower, and he had an eye on the popular market. On one level, his terror tales were clearly designed to cater to a [94] public increasingly enamored of horror and sensationalism. Writing in the era of the crime-filled penny papers and mass-produced pamphlet novels, he was well aware of the demands of the sensation-loving public. His letters are peppered with excited boasts about some work of his that has made a "sensation" or a "hit." In his tale "The Psyche Zenobia," he had the editor of a popular magazine declare: "Sensations are the great thing after all. Should you ever be drowned or hung, be sure and make a note of your sensations—they will be worth to you ten guineas a sheet." Following the lead of the sensation mongers, Poe made use of some of the wildest situations imaginable.

One such situation was live burial. In "The Premature Burial" Poe wrote that *"no* event is so terribly well adapted to inspire the supremeness of bodily and of mental distress, as is burial before death," a topic that creates "a degree of appalling and

* From David S. Reynolds, "Poe's Art of Transformation: 'The Cask of Amontillado in Its Cultural Context,'" in Kenneth Silverman, ed., *New Essays on Poe's Major Tales* (New York: Cambridge, 1993), pp. 93–112.

intolerable horror from which the most daring imagination must recoil." The specific work which established the premise of "The Cask of Amontillado" was Joel Tyler Headley's "A Man Built in a Wall," first published in the *Columbian Magazine* in 1844 and collected in Headley's *Letters from Italy* (1845). Headley reports having visited an Italian church containing a niche in which was discovered the skeleton of a man who had been buried alive by a workman under the direction of the man's smirking archenemy. After a detailed description of the grotesque posture of the skeleton, suggesting an excruciatingly painful death, Headley recreates the murder:

> The workman began at the feet, and with his mortar and trowel built up with the same carelessness he would exhibit in filling any broken wall. The successful enemy stood leaning on his sword—a smile of scorn and revenge on his features—and watched the face of the man he hated, but no longer feared. . . . It was slow work fitting the pieces nicely, so as to close up the aperture with precision. . . . With care and precision the last stone was fitted in the narrow space—the trowel passed smoothly over it—a stifled groan as if from the centre of a rock, broke the stillness—one strong shiver and all was over. The agony had passed—revenge was satisfied, and a secret locked up for the great revelation day.

Several details in Headley's piece—the premise of live burial in a hidden niche, the careful placement of the bricks, the revenge motive, the victim's agonized groaning and numbed stillness—anticipate "The Cask of Amontillado."   [95

Also analogous to Poe's story is Honoré de Balzac's "La Grande Bretêche," an adaptation of which appeared in the *Democratic Review* in November 1843. Balzac describes a jealous husband who, on discovering that his wife's lover is hiding in her closet, has the closet walled up as the lady watches. Poe most likely also knew the story "Apropos of Bores" (*New-York Mirror,* December 2, 1837), in which a man at a party tells of going with a porter into the vast wine vaults of Lincoln's Inn to view several pipes of Madeira that were stored there. They found the pipes in good condition but had a terrifying accident: When their candle was extinguished, they groped to the cellar door only to have the key break off in the lock. They impulsively decided to forget their sorrows by staving in a wine pipe and getting drunk in order to forget "the horrible death that awaits us." Giving up this impulse, they soberly faced the fact that their remains would not be discovered until all traces of identity were destroyed. We never learn the outcome of the tale, for the narrator and his listeners are called to tea before he is finished.

Another predecessor of Poe's tale, hitherto unacknowledged, was the sensational best-seller *The Quaker City; or The Monks of Monk Hall* (1845) by George Lippard, Poe's friend from his Philadelphia days. Monk Hall, a huge mansion where Philadelphia's prominent citizens gather in secret revels and debauchery, has below it a so-called "dead-vault," a vast cellar with labyrinthine passages and hidden recesses. The cellar is anticipatory of the vast vault beneath Montresor's mansion in several ways: It is lined with countless skeletons, its walls are clammy with moisture, and it is the scene of live burial. One critic has called "absurd" Poe's notion in "Cask" of "an ossuary . . . gruesomely combined with the appurtenances of a wine cellar," but many of Poe's contemporary readers had been prepared for such an odd coupling by the description of Monk Hall, where not only are the wine cellar and dead-vault side-by-side but the dead-vault is littered with liquor bottles strewn amid the skeletons. In a scene that presages Montresor's long descent with his victim into the catacombs, Devil-Bug, the sadistic keeper of Monk

Hall, slowly takes a victim, Luke Harvey, down an extensive staircase into the depths of the dead-vault. Hardly as subtle as Montresor, Devil-Bug mutters to his victim, "I am a-goin' to bury you alive! D'ye hear that? I'm a-goin' to bury you alive!" Just as Montresor howls and laughs at the enchained Fortunato, so Devil-Bug takes noisy pleasure in the sufferings of his victim. "He shrieked forth a horrible peal of laughter, more like the howl of a hyena, than the sound of a human laugh." Unlike Montresor, Devil-Bug does not succeed in his murderous scheme; his intended victim escapes. Devil-Bug, however, is haunted by the vision of a previous murder victim, just as (according to one reading) Montresor is tortured by the recollection of his crime. [96]

A larger cultural phenomenon that influenced Poe was the temperance movement, which produced a body of literature and lectures filled with the kinds of horrifying images that fascinated him. Poe's bouts with the bottle, leading eventually to his death, are well known. Less familiar is Poe's ambiguous relationship with the American temperance movement. In the 1830s Poe had befriended the Baltimore writer John Lofland, who delivered temperance lectures even though, like several other backsliding reformers of the period, he drank and took drugs in private. Another of Poe's acquaintances, Timothy Shay Arthur, wrote some of the most popular (and darkest) temperance tales of the day, including *Six Nights with the Washingtonians* (1842) and *Ten Nights in a Bar-room* (1854). In the early 1840s, the rise of the Washingtonians—reformed drunkards who told grisly tales of alcoholism in an effort to frighten listeners into signing a pledge of abstinence—brought to temperance rhetoric a new sensationalism. Walt Whitman's novel *Franklin Evans* (1842), for example, written on commission for the Washingtonians, luridly depicts the ill results of alcohol, including shattered homes, infanticide, crushing poverty that leads to crime, and delirium tremens with its nightmare visions. Poe had direct association with the Washingtonians. In 1843, after a period of heavy drinking, he promised a temperance friend from whom he hoped to gain a political appointment that he would join the Washingtonians. Whether or not he did so at that time, he did join a related group, the Sons of Temperance, in the last year of his life. When on August 31,1849, the *Banner of Temperance* announced Poe's initiation into the order, it said: "We trust his pen will sometimes be employed in its behalf. A vast amount of good might be accomplished by so pungent and forcible a writer." [97]

What the *Banner of Temperance* neglected to say was that Poe had already written temperance fiction, or more precisely, his own version of what I would call dark temperance, a popular mode that left didacticism behind and emphasized the perverse results of alcoholism. Following the lead of many dark temperance writers who portrayed once-happy families ripped asunder by a husband's inebriety, Poe in "The Black Cat" (1843) dramatized alcohol's ravages on an initially peaceful couple. The narrator tells us that he had once been known for his docility and gentleness but that his character—"through the instrumentality of the Fiend Intemperance—had (I blush to confess it) experienced a radical alteration for the worse. I grew, day by day, more moody, more irritable, more regardless of the feelings of others." As in popular temperance literature, the first sip is followed by escalating pathological behavior. The narrator declares that "my disease grew upon me—for what disease is like Alcohol!" One night a "fiendish malevolence, gin-nurtured" impels him to cut out the eye of his cat with a pen-knife, a deed he tries unsuccessfully to drown in wine. Before long he has been driven by alcohol to paranoia and crime, even to the extent of murdering his wife.

"The Cask of Amontillado" also studies the diseased psyche associated with alcohol. Everything in the story revolves around alcohol obsession. The object of the descent

into the vault is a pipe of wine. Both of the main characters are wine connoisseurs, as is their mentioned friend Luchesi. The narrator, Montresor, boasts, "I was skilful in the Italian vintages myself, and bought largely whenever I could." As for Fortunato, he is so vain about his knowledge of wine and so fixated on the supposed Amontillado that he goes willingly to his own destruction. When we meet him, we learn "he had been drinking much" in the carnival revelry, and as he walks unsteadily into the vault his eyes look like "two filmy orbs that distilled the rheum of intoxication." He gets drunker after sharing the bottle of Médoc that Montresor breaks open in the cellar, and even more so when he subsequently gulps down the flacon of De Grave (one of several puns that point to his fate). Fortunato's name has a double meaning: from his perspective he is "fortu-[98]
nate" to have an opportunity to show off his expertise in wines; from the reader's viewpoint, it is his bad "fortune" to be sucked to doom by his overriding interest in liquor. Poe's contemporary readers, accustomed to dark temperance rhetoric, would have found special significance in the interweaving of alcohol and death images in passages like this:

> The wine sparkled in his eyes and the bells jingled.
> My own fancy grew warm with Medoc. We had passed through walls of piled bones, with casks and puncheons intermingling, into the inmost depths of the catacombs.

The jingling of the bells reminds us of the fool Fortunato has become because of his destructive obsession. The wine-instilled agitation of Montresor's fancy reflects his role in this devilish communion, while the intermingled casks and bones, besides recalling Lippard's Monk Hall, enhance the eerie dark temperance atmosphere. After Montresor chains Fortunato to the wall, their dialogue takes on a dreary circularity that shows once again the importance of alcohol obsession to the story. "The Amontillado!" exclaims the victim; "True, the Amontillado," replies the murderer. Even after he has been walled in, the hapless Fortunato, in a desperate attempt to pass off the situation as a joke, returns to the subject of drinking:

> "We will have many a rich laugh about it at the palazzo—he! he! he!—over our wine—he! he! he!"
> "The Amontillado!" I said.
> "He! he! he!—he! he! he!—yes, the Amontillado!"

The dark temperance mode gives the tale a grim inevitability and another cultural phenomenon—anti-Masonry—contributes to its black humor and mysterious aura. At the center of the story is a dialogue that shows Poe tapping into his contemporaries' concerns about the Masons, a private all-male order widely thought to be involved in heinous crime. After drinking the bottle of De Grave, Fortunato throws it upward with a grotesque gesture Montresor does not understand.

> "You do not comprehend?" he said.
> "Not I," I replied.
> "Then you are not of the brotherhood."
> "How?"
> "You are not of the masons."
> "Yes, yes," I said, "yes, yes."
> "You? Impossible! A mason?"

"A mason," I replied.

"A sign," he said.

"It is this," I answered, producing a trowel from beneath the fold of my *roquelaire.*

"You jest," he exclaimed, recoiling a few paces. "But let us proceed to the Amontillado."

This marvelous moment of black humor has a range of historical associations rooted in the anti-Masonry mania that had swept America during Poe's apprentice period. The pun on "mason" (referring both to the fraternal order and to a worker in brick and stone) seems to have a specific historical referent. At the center of the Masonry controversy was one William Morgan, a brick-and-stone mason of Batavia, New York, who in 1826, after thirty years of membership in the Masons, was determined to publish a harsh exposé of the order but was silenced before he could, most likely by vindictive members of the order. Morgan's disappearance was wreathed in mystery. One night in September 1826 he was seized, gagged, and spirited away in a carriage to the Niagara frontier, where all trace of him was lost. The story spread that a group of Masons, viewing Morgan as a traitor, had drowned him in the Niagara River. (It is perhaps meaningful, in this context, that Montresor leads his victim "below the river bed.") Anti-Masonry sentiment snowballed and became a substantial political movement, peaking in the mid–1830s and then feeding into the ascendant Whig party. The Masonic order was viewed as undemocratic and as a tangible threat to American institutions. In particular, its oath, whereby members swore to uphold rational secular values (without reference to God or Christianity), was seen as sacrilegious. When Poe has Fortunato make a "grotesque" movement signaling membership in the order, he is introducing a sign that many of his readers would have regarded as demonic. When Montresor gives the sign of the trowel, he is not only foretelling the story's climax but is also summoning [100] up the associations of brick-and-stone masonry, murderous revenge, and mysterious disappearance surrounding American Masonry.

So central is the Masonic image that the tale has been interpreted as an enactment of the historical conflict between Catholics and Masons. In this reading, Fortunato's real crime is that he is a Mason, whereas Montresor, a Roman Catholic, assumes a perverted priestly function in his ritualistic murder of his Masonic foe. It should be pointed out, however, that in the predominantly evangelical Protestant America of Poe's day *both* Masons and Catholics were held suspect. If anti-Masonic feeling feeds into the portrait of Fortunato, anti-Catholic sentiment lies behind several of the grim images in the tale. In the 1830s and 1840s, American Protestant authors, fearful of the rapid growth of the Catholic church with the sudden flood of immigrants arriving from abroad, produced a large body of lurid literature aimed at exposing alleged depravity and criminality among Catholics. In 1838 one alarmed commentator wrote of the "tales of lust, and blood, and murder . . . with which the ultra protestant is teeming." Of special interest in connection with Poe's tale is Maria Monk's best-selling *Awful Disclosures of . . . the Hotel Dieu Nunnery at Montreal* (1836), which featured a huge cellar that served as both a torture chamber and a tomb, where priests had killed some 375 people and cast their remains into a lime pit. Whether or not Poe had Maria Monk and her ilk in mind when he concocted his tale of torture behind cellar walls, it is notable that he made use of Catholic images: The story is set during the *Carnivale,* a Catholic season just before Lent; Montresor's family motto about the heel crushing the serpent refers to Genesis 3:14 (the curse upon the serpent) and historically symbolizes the Church militant triumphing over the forces of evil; the early history of the Church is recalled when the underground passages are called "catacombs"; and the final words, *"In pace requiescat!"* are the last words of a requiem mass. The Catholic connection is further strengthened if we accept the idea that Poe derived the name Montresor from an old French Catholic family. Although not explicitly anti-Catholic, the tale combines religious criminal imagery in a way reminiscent of the anti-Catholic best-sellers of the day.   [101]

Though grounded in nineteenth-century American culture, "The Cask of Amontillado" transcends its time-specific referents because it is crafted in such a way that it remains accessible to generations of readers unfamiliar with such sources as anti-Catholicism, temperance, and live-burial literature. The special power of the tale can be understood if we take into account Poe's theories about fiction writing, developed largely in response to emerging forms of popular literature that aroused both his interest and his concern. On the one hand, as a literary professional writing for popular periodicals ("Cask" appeared in the most popular of all, *Godey's Lady's Book*) Poe had to keep in mind the demands of an American public increasingly hungry for sensation. On the other hand, as a scrupulous craftsman he was profoundly dissatisfied with the way in which other writers handled sensational topics. John Neal's volcanic, intentionally disruptive fiction seemed energetic but formless to Poe, who saw in it "no precision, no finish . . . —always an excessive *force* but little of refined art." Similarly, he wrote of the blackly humorous stories in Washington Irving's *Tales of a Traveller* that "the interest is subdivided and frittered away, and their conclusions are insufficiently *climacic* [sic]." George Lippard's *The Ladye Annabel,* a dizzying novel involving medieval torture and necrophilic visions, struck him as indicative of genius yet chaotic. A serial novel by Edward Bulwer-Lytton wearied him with its "continual and vexatious shifting of scene," while N. P. Willis's sensational play *Tortesa* exhibited "the great error" of "*inconsequence.* Underplot is piled on underplot," as Willis gives us "vast designs that terminate in nothing."

In his own fiction Poe tried to correct the mistakes he saw in other writers. The good plot, he argued, was that from which nothing can be taken without detriment to the whole. If, as he rightly pointed out, much sensational fiction of the day was digressive and directionless, his best tales were tightly unified. Of them all, "The Cask of Amontillado" perhaps most clearly exemplifies the unity he aimed for.

The tale's compactness becomes instantly apparent when we compare it with the popular live-burial works mentioned earlier. Headley's journalistic "A Man Built in a   [102 Wall" begins with a long passage about a lonely Italian inn and ends with an account of the countryside around Florence; the interpolated story about the entombed man dwells as much on the gruesome skeleton as on the vindictive crime. Balzac's "La Grande Brêteche" is a slowly developing tale in which the narrator gets mixed accounts about an old abandoned mansion near the Loire; only in the second half of the story does he learn from his landlady that the mansion had been the scene of a live burial involving a husband's jealous revenge. The entombment in "Apropos of Bores" is purely accidental (two unlucky men find themselves trapped in a wine vault) and is reduced to frivolous chatter when the narrator breaks off at the climactic moment and his listeners crack jokes and disperse to tea. Closest in spirit to Poe, perhaps, is the "dead-vault" scene in Lippard's *The Quaker City:* There is the same ritualistic descent into an immense cellar by a sadistic murderer intent on burying his victim alive. Lippard, however, constantly interrupts the scene with extraneous descriptions (he's especially fascinated by the skeletons and caskets strewn around the cellar). In addition, this is just one of countless bloodcurdling scenes in a meandering novel light-years distant, structurally, from Poe's carefully honed tale.

So tightly woven is "The Cask" that it may be seen as an effort at literary one-upsmanship on Poe's part, designed pointedly as a contrast to other, more casually constructed live-burial pieces. In his essays on popular literature, Poe expressed particular impatience with irrelevancies of plot or character. For instance, commenting on J. H. Ingraham's perfervid best-seller *Lafitte, the Pirate of the Gulf,* he wrote: "We are surfeited with unnecessary details. . . . Of outlines there are none. Not a dog yelps, unsung."

There is absolutely no excess in "The Cask of Amontillado." Every sentence points inexorably to the horrifying climax. In the interest of achieving unity, Poe purposely leaves several questions unanswered. The tale is remarkable for what it leaves out. What are the "thousand injuries" Montresor has suffered at the hands of Fortunato? In particular, what was the "insult" that has driven Montresor to the grisly extreme of murder by live burial? What personal misfortune is he referring to when he tells his foe, "you are happy, as once I was"? Like a painter who leaves a lot of suggestive white canvas, [103] Poe sketches character and setting lightly, excluding excess material. Even so simple a detail as the location of the action is unknown. Most assume the setting is Italy, but one commentator makes a good case for France. What do we know about the main characters? As discussed, both are bibulous and proud of their connoisseurship in wines. Fortunato, besides being a Mason, is "rich, respected, admired, beloved," and there is a Lady Fortunato who will miss him. Montresor is descended from "a great and numerous family" and is wealthy enough to sustain a palazzo, servants, and extensive wine vaults.

Other than that, Poe tells very little about the two. Both exist solely to fulfill the imperatives of the plot Poe has designed. Everything Montresor does and says furthers his strategy of luring his enemy to his death. Everything Fortunato does and says reveals the fatuous extremes his vanity about wines will lead him to. Though limited, these characters are not what E. M. Forster would call flat. They swiftly come alive before our eyes because Poe describes them with acute psychological realism. Montresor is a complex Machiavellian criminal, exhibiting a full range of traits from clever ingratiation to stark sadism. Fortunato, the dupe whose pride leads to his own downfall, nevertheless exhibits enough admirable qualities that one critic has seen him as a wronged man of courtesy and good will. The drama of the story lies in the carefully orchestrated interaction between the two. Poe directs our attention away from the merely sensational and toward the psychological.

Herein lies another key difference between the tale and its precursors. In none of the popular live-burial works is the *psychology* of revenge a factor. In Headley and Lippard, the victim is unconscious and thus incognizant of the murderer's designs; similarly, in Balzac there is no communication at all between the murderer and the entombed. In Poe, the relationship between the two is, to a large degree, the story. Montresor says at the start, murder is most successful if the victim is made painfully aware of what is happening: "A wrong is unredressed . . . when the avenger fails to make himself felt as such to him who has done the wrong." By focusing on the process of [104] vanity falling prey to sly revenge, Poe shifts attention to psychological subtleties ignored by the other live-burial writers.

9. Poe's Idea of Unity and "The Fall of the House of Usher"*

One of Poe's most characteristic ideas is *unity*. This is the key to the philosophy of *Eureka* [15] and the visionary dialogues; this is the essence of his contribution to the theory and practice of the short story. In his review of Hawthorne's *Twice-Told Tales* he speaks of the

*From Thomas Woodson, ed., *Twentieth-Century Interpretations of "The Fall of the House of Usher"* (Englewood Cliffs: Prentice Hall, 1969).

need for totality, for "a certain unique single *effect* to be wrought out": every word of a piece of fiction should contribute to the realization of this aim. Many critics have noticed the intensity of the concentration on unity in "Usher"—how the opening description of the House and the narrator's reactions lead swiftly and inevitably to the final catastrophe. It is perhaps instructive to see the story's structure as three sections of about equal length: paragraphs 1–14 introduce the House, the circumstances of the narrator's visit, and Roderick and Madeline Usher; the movement is of entrance, of the opening of doors (there is perhaps a pun on the family name when the valet "threw open a door and ushered me into the presence of his master"). The middle section, paragraphs 15 to 29, develops the narrator's initial impressions through the analysis of Roderick's aesthetic ideas, and the application of his most abstract and intellectual madness to his relationship with his sister. The final part, paragraphs 30 to 47 logically completes these themes by building rapidly to Madeline's reappearance and the simultaneous collapse of both Ushers and their house. Here there is a final door-opening, as Madeline reels on the threshold; then the tarn finally "closes" over the fragments of the fallen house. As often in Poe's fiction, the protagonist (here the narrator and both Ushers combined) ends teetering on the verge of a supreme revelation that is also his destruction, an opening that mockingly also closes everything.

Poe attains an effect of structural symmetry by placing certain actions and images [16] only in the first and third parts: the sullen tarn; the appearances of Madeline in the apartment; and the speeches of Roderick (there is little dialogue; Roderick speaks only twice at length, once early in the story to confirm his "intolerable agitation of soul," and then at the end to announce, *"We have put her living in the tomb!"*).

This unity of structure is reinforced by the style. From the magnificent opening sentences to the end, Poe's language is highly charged with emotion, but at the same time, quite abstract: for instance, the narrator remarks at the beginning, "a sense of insufferable gloom pervaded my spirit." Instead of simple, direct description, we experience the narrator's *sense* of things. *Pervaded* is also a key word, evoking the notorious "atmosphere" of the House, the "condensation" of "vapours" from the tarn. As Poe's note about "sentience" suggests, he seeks credibility for his psychological claims by using the vocabulary of nineteenth century chemistry. *Pervaded* is also important in introducing the theme of *oppression,* which recurs throughout: something sinister presses down on the mind, anticipating the collapse of the House. Later the narrator says: "An irrepressible terror pervaded my frame; and, at length, there sat upon my very heart an incubus of utterly causeless alarm." *Frame* hints at the identity of the human body with the building, as does the similarity of appearance between Roderick's head and the House, and the imagery of his poem, "The Haunted Palace." In fact, a close study of the story's style reveals a very high degree of recurrence of a rather small and special vocabulary. The effect of this stylistic narrowness is to bring together, almost to the verge of solipsism, the sensations of both Roderick and the narrator, and the "sentience" of Madeline and the House, Madeline being less a character than an object to be perceived.

Another peculiarity of Poe's diction is his emphasis on the negative. In the first paragraph alone we find, in addition to *insufferable,* these adjectives and verbs: *unrelieved, unredeemed, unnerved, insoluble,* and *unsatisfactory.* The story is full of words beginning with *un-* or *in-,* or ending in *-less,* and expressions containing *no, not, mere,* or *scarcely.* Poe uses these words to maintain an excited, exaggerated tone, but also to evoke the results of oppression on the mind: the nightmare of a vacant, featureless world—imaged by sinking beneath the surface of the tarn—a world where meaning and value have dissolved into nothingness.

Through these devices Poe has made style his weapon to redeem, as William   [17]
Hedges has put it, the sensational material of popular fiction for the analysis of the soul.
In the speeches of Roderick Usher this style is speeded up, intensified, almost to the
point of hysterical incoherence. This style is then counterpointed to the burlesque
extravagance of the "Mad Trist" of Sir Launcelot Canning, which the narrator describes
as a style of "uncouth and unimaginative prolixity," portentously empty of meaning (perhaps Poe's attempt to imitate the effect of the porter's knocking on the door in
Macbeth).

10. The Narrators of "The Cask of Amontillado" and "The Black Cat"*

It goes without saying that Poe, like other creative men, is sometimes at the mercy of his   [309]
own worst qualities. Yet the contention that he is fundamentally a bad or tawdry stylist
appears to me to be rather facile and sophistical. It is based, ultimately, on the untenable
and often unanalyzed assumption that Poe and his narrators are identical literary twins
and that he must be held responsible for all their wild or perfervid utterances; their
shrieks and groans are too often conceived as originating from Poe himself. I believe, on
the contrary, that Poe's narrators possess a character and consciousness distinct from
those of their creator. These protagonists, I am convinced, speak their own thoughts
and are the dupes of their own passions. In short, Poe understands them far better than
they can possibly understand themselves. Indeed, he often so designs his tales as to show
his narrators' limited comprehension of their own problems and states of mind; the
structure of many of Poe's stories clearly reveals an ironical and comprehensive intelligence critically and artistically ordering events so as to establish a vision of life and character which the narrator's very inadequacies help to "prove."

The structure of Poe's stories compels realization that they are more than the effu-   [310]
sions of their narrators' often disordered mentalities. Through the irony of his characters' self-betrayal and through the development and arrangement of his dramatic
actions, Poe suggests to his readers ideas never entertained by the narrators. Poe intends
his readers to keep their powers of analysis and judgment ever alert; he does not require
or desire complete surrender to the experience of the sensations being felt by his characters. The point of Poe's technique, then, is not to enable us to lose ourselves in strange
or outrageous emotions, but to see these emotions and those obsessed by them from a
rich and thoughtful perspective. I do not mean to advocate that, while reading Poe, we
should cease to feel; but feeling should be "simultaneous" with an analysis carried on
with the composure and logic of Poe's great detective, Dupin. For Poe is not merely a
Romanticist; he is also a chronicler of the consequences of the Romantic excesses which
lead to psychic disorder, pain, and disintegration.

Evidence of Poe's "seriousness" seems to me indisputable in "The Cask of   [313]
Amontillado. . . ." Far from being his author's mouthpiece, the narrator, Montresor, is
one of the supreme examples in fiction of a deluded rationalist who cannot glimpse the
moral implications of his planned folly. Poe's fine ironic sense makes clear that
Montresor, the stalker of Fortunato, is both a compulsive and pursued man; for in committing a flawless crime against another human being, he really (like Wilson and the
protagonist in "The Tell-Tale Heart") commits the worst of crimes against himself. His

*From James W. Gargano, "The Question of Poe's Narrators," in *The Recognition of Edgar
Allan Poe*, ed. Eric W. Carlson (Ann Arbor: U of Michigan P, 1966), pp. 308–316.

reasoned, "cool" intelligence weaves an intricate plot which, while ostensibly satisfying his revenge, despoils him of humanity. His impeccably contrived murder, his weird mask of goodness in an enterprise of evil, and his abandonment of all his life-energies in one pet project of hate convict him of a madness which he mistakes for the inspiration of genius. The brilliant masquerade setting of Poe's tale intensifies the theme of Montresor's apparently successful duplicity; Montresor's ironic appreciation of his own deviousness seems further to justify his arrogance of intellect. But the greatest irony of all, to which Montresor is never sensitive, is that the "injuries" supposedly perpetrated by Fortunato are illusory and that the vengeance meant for the victim recoils upon Montresor himself. In immolating Fortunato, the narrator unconsciously calls him the "noble" Fortunato and confesses that his own "heart grew sick." Though Montresor attributes this sickness to "the dampness of the catacombs," it is clear that his crime has begun to "possess" him. We see that, after fifty years, it remains the obsession of his life; [314] the meaning of his existence resides in the tomb in which he has, symbolically, buried himself. In other words, Poe leaves little doubt that the narrator has violated his own mind and humanity, that the external act has had its destructive inner consequences.

The same artistic integrity and seriousness of purpose evident in "The Cask of Amontillado" can be discovered in "The Black Cat." No matter what covert meanings one may find in this much-discussed story, it can hardly be denied that the nameless narrator does not speak for Poe. Whereas the narrator, at the beginning of his "confession," admits that he cannot explain the events which overwhelmed him, Poe's organization of his episodes provides an unmistakable clue to his protagonist's psychic deterioration. The tale has two distinct, almost parallel parts: in the first, the narrator's inner moral collapse is presented in largely symbolic narrative; in the second part, the consequences of his self-violation precipitate an act of murder, punishable by society. Each section of the story deals with an ominous cat, an atrocity, and an exposé of a "crime." In the first section, the narrator's house is consumed by fire after he has mutilated and subsequently hanged Pluto, his pet cat. Blindly, he refuses to grant any connection between his violence and the fire; yet the image of a hanged cat on the one remaining wall indicates that he will be haunted and hag-ridden by his deed. The sinister figure of Pluto, seen by a crowd of neighbors, is symbolically both an accusation and a portent, an enigma to the spectators but an infallible sign to the reader.

In the second section of "The Black Cat," the reincarnated cat goads the narrator into the murder of his wife. As in "William Wilson," "The Tell-Tale Heart," and "The Cask of Amontillado," the narrator cannot understand that his assault upon another person derives from his own moral sickness and unbalance. Like his confreres, too, he seeks psychic release and freedom in a crime which completes his torture. To the end of his life he is incapable of locating the origin of his evil and damnation within himself.

The theme of "The Black Cat" is complicated for many critics by the narrator's dogged assertion that he was pushed into evil and self-betrayal by the "imp of the perverse." This imp is explained, by a man who, it must be remembered, eschews [31?] explanation, as a radical, motiveless, and irresistible impulse within the human soul. Consequently, if his self-analysis is accepted, his responsibility for his evil life vanishes. Yet, it must be asked if it is necessary to give credence to the words of the narrator. William Wilson, too, regarded himself as a "victim" of a force outside himself and Montresor speaks as if he has been coërced into his crime by Fortunato. The narrator in "The Black Cat" differs from Wilson in bringing to his defense a well-reasoned theory with perhaps a strong appeal to many readers. Still, the narrator's pat explanation is contradicted by the development of the tale, for instead of being pushed into crime, he pursues a life which makes crime inevitable. He cherishes the intemperate self-indulgence which blunts his powers of self-analysis; he is guided by his delusions to the climax of damnation. Clearly, Poe does not espouse his protagonist's theory any more than he approves of the specious rationalizations of his other narrators. Just as the narrator's well constructed house has a fatal flaw, so the theory of perverseness is flawed because it really explains nothing. Moreover, even the most cursory reader must be struck by the fact that the narrator is most "possessed and maddened" when he most proudly boasts of self-control. If the narrator obviously cannot be believed at the end of the tale, what argument is there for assuming that he must be telling the truth when he earlier tries to evade responsibility for his "sin" by slippery rationalizations?

A close analysis of "The Black Cat" must certainly exonerate Poe of the charge of merely sensational writing. The final frenzy of the narrator, with its accumulation of superlatives, cannot be ridiculed as an example of Poe's style. The breakdown of the shrieking criminal does not reflect similar breakdown in the author. Poe, I maintain, is a serious artist who explores the neuroses of his characters with probing intelligence. He permits his narrator to revel and flounder in torment, but he sees beyond the torment to its causes.

In conclusion, then, the five tales I have commented on display Poe's deliberate craftsmanship and penetrating sense of irony. If my thesis is correct, Poe's narrators should not be construed as his mouthpieces; instead they should be regarded as express-ing, in "charged" language indicative of their internal disturbances, their own peculiarly [316] nightmarish visions. Poe, I contend, is conscious of the abnormalities of his narrators and does not condone the intellectual ruses through which they strive, only too earnestly, to justify themselves. In short, though his narrators are often febrile or demented. Poe is conspicuously "sane." They may be "decidedly primitive" or "wildly incoherent," but Poe, in his stories at least, is mature and lucid.

11. Poe, Women, and "The Fall of the House of Usher"*

Like the Egyptians, Poe would preserve bodies so as to prolong their historical effects. [340] Corpses, particularly female ones, are regularly revived in Poe's tales: Ligeia, Morella, Berenice, and Eleanora all revisit the scenes of their lives. Many readers of Poe have noted the prevalence of female deaths in his work. His dictum that "the death . . . of a beautiful woman is, unquestionably, the most poetical topic in the world" has long sug-gested both a personal obsession with lost women—stemming from the early loss of his mother, a loss then recapitulated in the death of his young wife—and an aesthetic misogy-ny working to delimit and destroy women. Yet however much Poe's stories and poems seem to propel and be propelled by the deaths of women, the morbidity of his treat-ment of women is regularly accompanied by the imagination of their regeneration. The horror, and sometimes solace, for the husbands, brothers, and lovers of these women [341] is that they cannot be extinguished: they return as indestructible forces to haunt their partners. At the same time, these resurrected women testify to the stories their partners tell; they verify the narratives about themselves. Their regenerate corpses thus embody a principle of preservation, safeguarding the consciousnesses in which they figure as mem-ories and thus poetic subjects.

*From Gillian Brown, "The Poetics of Extinction," in Shawn Rosenheim and Stephen Rachman, eds., *The American Face of Edgar Allan Poe* (Baltimore: Johns Hopkins UP, 1995.), pp. 310–344.

The misogyny in Poe's representations of women consists less in his death plots than in his revivification of women in service to the history of consciousness. Poe's necrophilic interest in women quite distinctively eschews their given generative power and their role in the perpetuation of the species. He fantasizes a self that is always and only self-transmitting. . . . In the tales, he assuages the fear of termination with the notion of succession through regeneration, a regeneration of women's bodies to prolong not themselves but men's minds. The ghoulishness of Poe's portrayal of women lies in this single-minded prohibition of female generativity in order to produce evidence of a particular existence.

The anthropological and andocentric function of such figures as Ligeia, Morella, Berenice, and Eleanora is also to supply a legibility, albeit a problematic one, to death. Their returns, like Madeline's, suggest an uncertainty, both hopeful and horrific, about death. On the one hand, bodies somehow survive death, but on the other hand, bodies seem subject to many forms of death, or to conditions that seem indistinguishable from death. Madeline suffers from catalepsy. The loss of consciousness and rigidification of the muscles caused by this disease make its sufferers likely candidates for premature burial. As Poe explains in "The Premature Burial," even "the most rigorous medical tests fail to establish any material distinction between the state of the sufferer and what we conceive of absolute death." Thus bodies in such states can be misread, and effectively murdered by misreading. Such fatal misreadings anticipate the eventuality of death, making it the result of human (mis)calculations. The horror of premature burial in "The Fall of the House of Usher" and other Poe tales ("Berenice," "The Cask of Amontillado," and "Loss of Breath") lies in the body's helplessness to govern interpretations of itself. Individual intention always exists amidst other intentionalities, other agents. The con- [342] sciousness that resurrected bodies signify is not just their own. Corpses in Poe, then, are always potential evidence of murder.

Murder narratives nicely serve Poe's anthropological purposes because they highlight the presence of some form of agency. When Madeline emerges from her premature interment, she reveals her brother's murderous mistake, literally scaring him to death. In her "now final death-agonies," she bears "him to the floor a corpse, and a victim to the terrors he had anticipated." He dies in a "struggle with the grim phantasm, FEAR," just as he had foreseen. Since Roderick's anticipation produces both deaths, the story of the extinction of his family reads as the record of his sensibility. Anticipation thus operates as an engine of transmission, disseminating the traces of human agency in death.

Not just any human agency: what survives is evidence of Roderick's consciousness, imprinted on his friend the narrator, who has shared his presentiments and aided Roderick in entombing Madeline. . . .

12. The Deceptive Narrator of "The Black Cat"*

Like "The Tell-Tale Heart," "The Black Cat" is not so much a confession as it is a murderer's attempt to rationalize his crime. "What disease is like Alcohol!" the narrator cries, elsewhere referring to the "Fiend Intemperance" and the "demon" that "possessed me" in order to shift responsibility from himself to his illness. Temperance crusaders

*From Scott Peeples, *Edgar Allan Poe Revisited,* Twayne's United States Authors Series No. 705. (New York: Twayne, 1998), pp. 96–98.

sought to change public opinion on alcoholism, to treat it as a disease rather than as a moral failing or vice of the alcoholic. But . . . the story undercuts the narrator's insistence that the demon alcohol made him do it; readers see that his entire story is built on implausibilities and lame excuses, and his crime is motivated by impulses more sinister than a weakness for drink. As with "The Tell-Tale Heart," we must read against the narrator of "The Black Cat," establish which parts of his testimony should be believed and which should not, and try to discover the deeper motivations for the crime.

Once again, the concept of doubling provides a means for making sense of the narrator's strange logic. The black cat that replaces Pluto is certainly a kind of doppelgänger: uncannily, he too is missing an eye, he too is loved by the wife, and he too torments the narrator. . . . I see both cats as doubles for the wife, in the narrator's mind, at least: . . . Whenever the narrator mentions his wife, a black cat is close by. He physically   [97] abuses both wife and cat, he tells us, even before hanging Pluto, and when he does hang it, its image mysteriously appears, of all places, on the wall above the unhappy couple's bed. Immediately after the second cat became "a great favorite with my wife," he explains, "For my own part, I soon found a dislike to it arising within me": as soon he associates cat with wife, he begins to loathe the cat. It is his wife who calls his attention to the gallows shape of the white spot on the cat's breast—appropriately so, for the gallows not only reflects Pluto's fate but forecasts the narrator's punishment for killing his wife. Finally, he unknowingly walls up the living cat with the wife, so that the cat's crying leads the police to the wife and leads the narrator to the story's final image of the cat perched on the dead wife's head. Although the context makes clear that the narrator's literal reference is to the cat in the last sentence, one can imagine cat and wife converging in the narrator's mind when he says "I had walled the monster up within the tomb!"

But why would the narrator want to kill his wife? For the very reason he gives for killing Pluto: "[I] hung it *because* I knew that it had loved me." He describes his wife as tender, possessing "that humanity of feeling which had once been my distinguishing trait," so it is reasonable to assume she would be affectionate and loving toward him. When the cat "spring[s] upon my knees, covering me with its loathsome caresses," or follows him closely, the narrator "long[s] to destroy it with a blow"; this exaggerated reaction to the cat's behavior leads one to suspect that the cat's expressions of love remind him of his wife's. When he does destroy his wife with a blow, his nonchalance is chilling, in contrast with his reaction to the murder of Pluto, which he calls "a deadly sin that would so jeopardize my immortal soul as to place it—if such a thing were possible—even beyond the reach of the infinite mercy of the Most Merciful and Most Terrible God." Either this guilt actually stems from his decision at that moment to kill his wife, having already killed her surrogate, or . . . he actually does kill his wife at the point when he *says* he killed Pluto, and in his confession fabricates the incident on the cellar stairs and the existence of a second cat. In either case, he responds to killing the cat as he ought to respond to killing his a wife, a sin that *is* deadly and unforgivable because of his wife's innocence, because she died for loving him.

Such a paradox—death as the penalty for love—seems consistent with the contradictions that make up the narrator's initial description of his story. It is "wild, yet most   [98] homely." The incidents have presented "little but Horror," yet he also refers to it as "a series of mere household events" and believes it could be perceived as "an ordinary succession of very natural causes and effects." And although he does not expect to be believed, he tries hard to explain his behavior as the result of all-too-human perverse impulses and the disease of alcoholism. One can attribute these contradictions, like the crime itself, to the narrator's madness, but again the story's network of uncanny images and plot twists warrants some consideration of how these bizarre occurrences might also be "mere household events." What the narrator does is horrible, shocking, and yet perhaps his motivations *are* common to marriages and other intimate relationships. . . . The narrator's hidden hatred of his wife, his unwillingness to acknowledge that hatred, his displacement of it onto the family pet, and certainly his turning to alcohol could be categorized as common "household events." His ultimate response, of course, is "wild" and "horrible"—but equally frightening is the implication that his predicament is not so uncommon, that, like the perverse impulse to do wrong for wrong's sake, the fear of intimacy is "one of the primitive impulses of the human heart—one of the indivisible primary faculties, or sentiments, which give direction to the character of Man."

12

Stories for Additional Study

ROBERT OLEN BUTLER (b. 1945)

*Butler was born in Granite City, Illinois, and was edu-
cated at Northwestern and Iowa (M.A., 1969). He served
in Army Intelligence in Vietnam from 1969–1972 and
became proficient in the Vietnamese language. After his
discharge he worked in a steel mill, drove a cab, and
taught high school. At the present time he lives in
Louisiana, where he teaches at McNeese State University.
He has been prolific as a novelist and story writer ever
since the first of his nine novels,* The Alleys of Eden,
*was published in 1981 after it had been rejected by twenty-
one publishers. He has had many honors, including a
Guggenheim Fellowship in fiction and a grant from the
National Endowment for the Arts. For* A Good Scent
from a Strange Mountain *(1993), a collection of stories about Vietnam and its aftermath, he received the Pulitzer Prize in fiction for 1993. He has written for movies and television. His most recent collection of stories is* Tabloid Dreams *(1996) and his most recent
novel is* Mr. Spaceman *(1999). The story "Snow" is taken from* A Good Scent from a
Strange Mountain.

Snow _____ *1992*

I wonder how long he watched me sleeping. I still wonder that. He sat and he did not wake me to ask about his carry-out order. Did he watch my eyes move as I dreamed? When I finally knew he was there and I turned to look at him, I could not make out his whole face at once His head was turned a little to the side. His beard was neatly trimmed, but the jaw it covered was long and its curve was like a sampan sail and it held my eyes the way a sail always did when I saw one on the sea. Then I raised my eyes and looked at his nose. I am Vietnamese, you know, and we have a different sense of these proportions. Our noses are small and his was long and it also curved, gently, a reminder of his jaw, which I looked at again. His beard was dark gray, like he'd crawled out of a charcoal kiln. I make these comparisons to things from my country and village, but it is only to clearly say what this face was like. It is not that he reminded me of home. That was the farthest thing from my mind when I first saw Mr. Cohen. And I must have stared at him in those first moments with a strange look because when his face turned full to me and I could finally lift my gaze to his eyes, his eyebrows made a little jump like he was asking me, What is it? What's wrong?

I was at this same table before the big window at the front of the restaurant. The Plantation Hunan does not look like a restaurant, though. No one would give it a name like that unless it really was an old plantation house. It's very large and full of antiques. It's quiet right now. Not even five, and I can hear the big clock—I had never seen one till I came here. No one in Vietnam has a clock as tall as a man. Time isn't as important as that in Vietnam. But the clock here is very tall and they call it Grandfather, which I like, and Grandfather is ticking very slowly right now, and he wants me to fall asleep again. But I won't.

This plantation house must feel like a refugee. It is full of foreign smells, ginger and Chinese pepper and fried shells for wonton, and there's a motel on one side and a gas station on the other, not like the life the house once knew, though there are very large oak trees surrounding it, trees that must have been here when this was still a plantation. The house sits on a busy street and the Chinese family who owns it changed it from Plantation Seafood into a place that could hire a Vietnamese woman like me to be a waitress. They are very kind, this family, though we know we are different from each other. They are Chinese and I am Vietnamese and they are very kind, but we are both here in Louisiana and they go somewhere with the other Chinese in town—there are four restaurants and two laundries and some people, I think, who work as engineers at the oil refinery. They go off to themselves and they don't seem to even notice where they are.

I was sleeping that day he came in here. It was late afternoon of the day before Christmas. Almost Christmas Eve. I am not a Christian. My mother and I are Buddhist. I live with my mother and she is very sad for me because I am thirty-four years old and I am not married. There are other Vietnamese here in Lake Charles, Louisiana, but we are not a community. We are all too sad, perhaps, or too tired. But maybe not. Maybe that's just me saying that. Maybe the others are real Americans already. My mother has two Vietnamese friends, old women like her, and her two friends look at me with the same sadness in their faces because of what they see as my life. They know that once I might have been married, but the fiancé I had in my town in Vietnam went away in the Army and though he is still alive in Vietnam, the last I heard, he is driving a cab in Hô Chí Minh City and he is married to someone else. I never really knew him, and I don't feel any loss. It's just that he's the only boy my mother ever speaks of when she gets frightened for me.

I get frightened for me, too, sometimes, but it's not because I have no husband. That Christmas Eve afternoon I woke slowly. The front tables are for cocktails and for waiting for carry-out, so the chairs are large and stuffed so that they are soft. My head was very comfortable against one of the high wings of the chair and I opened my eyes without moving. The rest of me was still sleeping, but my eyes opened and the sky was still blue, though the shreds of cloud were turning pink. It looked like a warm sky. And it was. I felt sweat on my throat and I let my eyes move just a little and the live oak in front of the restaurant was quivering—all its leaves were shaking and you might think that it would look cold doing that, but it was a warm wind, I knew. The air was thick and wet, and cutting through the ginger and pepper smell was the fuzzy smell of mildew.

Perhaps it was from my dream but I remembered my first Christmas Eve in America. I slept and woke just like this, in a Chinese restaurant. I was working there. But it was in a distant place, in St. Louis. And I woke to snow. The first snow I had ever seen. It scared me. Many Vietnamese love to see their first snow, but it frightened me in some very deep way that I could not explain, and even remembering that moment—especially as I woke from sleep at the front of another restaurant—frightened me. So I turned my face sharply from the window in the Plantation Hunan and that's when I saw Mr. Cohen.

I stared at those parts of his face, like I said, and maybe this was a way for me to hide from the snow, maybe the strangeness that he saw in my face had to do with the snow. But when his eyebrows jumped and I did not say anything to explain what was going on inside me, I could see him wondering what to do. I could feel him thinking: Should I ask her what is wrong or should I just ask her for my carry-out? I am not an especially shy person, but I hoped he would choose to ask for the carry-out. I came to myself with a little jolt and I stood up and faced him—he was sitting in one of the stuffed chairs at the next table. "I'm sorry," I said, trying to turn us both from my dreaming. "Do you have an order?"

He hesitated, his eyes holding fast on my face. These were very dark eyes, as dark as the eyes of any Vietnamese, but turned up to me like this, his face seemed so large that I had trouble taking it in. Then he said, "Yes. For Cohen." His voice was deep, like a movie actor who is playing a grandfather, the kind of voice that if he asked what it was that I had been dreaming, I would tell him at once.

But he did not ask anything more. I went off to the kitchen and the order was not ready. I wanted to complain to them. There was no one else in the restaurant, and everyone in the kitchen seemed like they were just hanging around. But I don't make any trouble for anybody. So I just went back out to Mr. Cohen. He rose when he saw me, even though he surely also saw that I had no carry-out with me.

"It's not ready yet," I said. "I'm sorry."

"That's okay," he said, and he smiled at me, his gray beard opening and showing teeth that were very white.

"I wanted to scold them," I said. "You should not have to wait for a long time on Christmas Eve."

"It's okay," he said. "This is not my holiday."

I tilted my head, not understanding. He tilted his own head just like mine, like he wanted to keep looking straight into my eyes. Then he said, "I am Jewish."

I straightened my head again, and I felt a little pleasure at knowing that his straightening his own head was caused by me. I still didn't understand, exactly, and he clearly read that in my face. He said, "A Jew doesn't celebrate Christmas."

"I thought all Americans celebrated Christmas," I said.

5

10

15

"Not all. Not exactly." He did a little shrug with his shoulders, and his eyebrows rose like the shrug, as he tilted his head to the side once more, for just a second. It all seemed to say, What is there to do, it's the way the world is and I know it and it all makes me just a little bit weary. He said, "We all stay home, but we don't all celebrate."

He said no more, but he looked at me and I was surprised to find that I had no words either on my tongue or in my head. It felt a little strange to see this very American man who was not celebrating the holiday. In Vietnam we never miss a holiday and it did not make a difference if we were Buddhist or Cao Đài or Catholic. I thought of this Mr. Cohen sitting in his room tonight alone while all the other Americans celebrated Christmas Eve. But I had nothing to say and he didn't either and he kept looking at me and I glanced down at my hands twisting at my order book and I didn't even remember taking the book out. So I said, "I'll check on your order again," and I turned and went off to the kitchen and I waited there till the order was done, though I stood over next to the door away from the chatter of the cook and the head waiter and the mother of the owner.

Carrying the white paper bag out to the front, I could not help but look inside to see how much food there was. There was enough for two people. So I did not look into Mr. Cohen's eyes as I gave him the food and rang up the order and took his money. I was counting his change into his palm—his hand, too, was very large—and he said, "You're not Chinese, are you?"

I said, "No. I am Vietnamese," but I did not raise my face to him, and he went away.   20

Two days later, it was even earlier in the day when Mr. Cohen came in. About four-thirty. The grandfather had just chimed the half hour like a man who is really crazy about one subject and talks of it at any chance he gets. I was sitting in my chair at the front once again and my first thought when I saw Mr. Cohen coming through the door was that he would think I am a lazy girl. I started to jump up, but he saw me and he motioned with his hand for me to stay where I was, a single heavy pat in the air, like he'd just laid this large hand of his on the shoulder of an invisible child before him. He said, "I'm early again."

"I am not a lazy girl," I said.

"I know you're not," he said and he sat down in the chair across from me.

"How do you know I'm not?" This question just jumped out of me. I can be a cheeky girl sometimes. My mother says that this was one reason I am not married, that this is why she always talks about the boy I was once going to marry in Vietnam, because he was a shy boy, a weak boy, who would take whatever his wife said and not complain. I myself think this is why he is driving a taxi in Hô Chí Minh City. But as soon as this cheeky thing came out of my mouth to Mr. Cohen, I found that I was afraid. I did not want Mr. Cohen to hate me.

But he was smiling. I could even see his white teeth in this smile. He said, "You're right. I have no proof."

"I am always sitting here when you come in," I said, even as I asked myself, Why are you rubbing on this subject?

I saw still more teeth in his smile, then he said, "And the last time you were even sleeping."

I think at this I must have looked upset, because his smile went away fast. He did not have to help me seem a fool before him. "It's all right," he said. "This is a slow time of day. I have trouble staying awake myself. Even in court."

I looked at him more closely, leaving his face. He seemed very prosperous. He was wearing a suit as gray as his beard and it had thin blue stripes, almost invisible, running through it. "You are a judge?"

"A lawyer," he said.

"You will defend me when the owner fires me for sleeping."

This made Mr. Cohen laugh, but when he stopped, his face was very solemn. He seemed to lean nearer to me, though I was sure he did not move. "You had a bad dream the last time," he said.

How did I know he would finally come to ask about my dream? I had known it from the first time I'd heard his voice. "Yes," I said. "I think I was dreaming about the first Christmas Eve I spent in America. I fell asleep before a window in a restaurant in St. Louis, Missouri. When I woke, there was snow on the ground. It was the first snow I'd ever seen. I went to sleep and there was still only a gray afternoon, a thin little rain, like a mist. I had no idea things could change like that. I woke and everything was covered and I was terrified."

I suddenly sounded to myself like a crazy person. Mr. Cohen would think I was lazy and crazy both. I stopped speaking and I looked out the window. A jogger went by in the street, a man in shorts and a T-shirt, and his body glistened with sweat. I felt beads of sweat on my own forehead like little insects crouching there and I kept my eyes outside, wishing now that Mr. Cohen would go away.

"Why did it terrify you?" he said.

"I don't know," I said, though this wasn't really true. I'd thought about it now and then, and though I'd never spoken them, I could imagine reasons.

Mr. Cohen said, "Snow frightened me, too, when I was a child. I'd seen it all my life, but it still frightened me."

I turned to him and now he was looking out the window.

"Why did it frighten you?" I asked, expecting no answer.

But he turned from the window and looked at me and smiled just a little bit, like he was saying that since he had asked this question of me, I could ask him, too. He answered, "It's rather a long story. Are you sure you want to hear it?"

"Yes," I said. Of course I did.

"It was far away from here," he said. "My first home and my second one. Poland and then England. My father was a professor in Warsaw. It was early in 1939. I was eight years old and my father knew something was going wrong. All the talk about the corridor to the sea was just the beginning. He had ears. He knew. So he sent me and my mother to England. He had good friends there. I left that February and there was snow everywhere and I had my own instincts, even at eight. I cried in the courtyard of our apartment building. I threw myself into the snow there and I would not move. I cried like he was sending us away from him forever. He and my mother said it was only for some months, but I didn't believe it. And I was right. They had to lift me bodily and carry me to the taxi. But the snow was in my clothes and as we pulled away and I scrambled up to look out the back window at my father, the snow was melting against my skin and I began to shake. It was as much from my fear as from the cold. The snow was telling me he would die. And he did. He waved at me in the street and he grew smaller and we turned a corner and that was the last I saw of him."

Maybe it was foolish of me, but I thought not so much of Mr. Cohen losing his father. I had lost a father, too, and I knew that it was something that a child lives through. In Vietnam we believe that our ancestors are always close to us, and I could tell that about Mr. Cohen, that his father was still close to him. But what I thought about

30

35

40

was Mr. Cohen going to another place, another country, and living with his mother. I live with my mother, just like that. Even still.

He said, "So the snow was something I was afraid of. Every time it snowed in England I knew that my father was dead. It took a few years for us to learn this from others, but I knew it whenever it snowed."

"You lived with your mother?" I said.

45

"Yes. In England until after the war and then we came to America. The others from Poland and Hungary and Russia that we traveled with all came in through New York City and stayed there. My mother loved trains and she'd read a book once about New Orleans, and so we stayed on the train and we came to the South. I was glad to be in a place where it almost never snowed."

I was thinking how he was a foreigner, too. Not an American, really. But all the talk about the snow made this little chill behind my thoughts. Maybe I was ready to talk about that. Mr. Cohen had spoken many words to me about his childhood and I didn't want him to think I was a girl who takes things without giving something back. He was looking out the window again, and his lips pinched together so that his mouth disappeared in his beard. He seemed sad to me. So I said, "You know why the snow scared me in St. Louis?"

He turned at once with a little humph sound and a crease on his forehead between his eyes and then a very strong voice saying, "Tell me," and it felt like he was scolding himself inside for not paying attention to me. I am not a vain girl, always thinking that men pay such serious attention to me that they get mad at themselves for ignoring me even for a few moments. This is what it really felt like and it surprised me. If I was a vain girl, it wouldn't have surprised me. He said it again: "Tell me why it scared you."

I said, "I think it's because the snow came so quietly and everything was underneath it, like this white surface was the real earth and everything had died—all the trees and the grass and the streets and the houses—everything had died and was buried. It was all lost. I knew there was snow above me, on the roof, and I was dead, too."

"Your own country was very different," Mr. Cohen said.

It pleased me that he thought just the way I once did. You could tell that he wished there was an easy way to make me feel better, make the dream go away. But I said to him, "This is what I also thought. If I could just go to a warm climate, more like home. So I came down to New Orleans, with my mother, just like you, and then we came over to Lake Charles. And it is something like Vietnam here. The rice fields and the heat and the way the storms come in. But it makes no difference. There's no snow to scare me here, but I still sit alone in this chair in the middle of the afternoon and I sleep and I listen to the grandfather over there ticking."

I stopped talking and I felt like I was making no sense at all, so I said, "I should check on your order."

Mr. Cohen's hand came out over the table. "May I ask your name?"

"I'm Miss Giàu," I said.

"Miss Giàu?" he asked, and when he did that, he made a different word, since Vietnamese words change with the way your voice sings them.

I laughed. "My name is Giàu, with the voice falling. It means 'wealthy' in Vietnamese. When you say the word like a question, you say something very different. You say I am Miss Pout."

Mr. Cohen laughed and there was something in the laugh that made me shiver just a little, like a nice little thing, like maybe stepping into the shower when you are covered with dust and feeling the water expose you. But in the back of my mind was his carry-out and there was a bad little feeling there, something I wasn't thinking about, but it made me go off now with heavy feet to the kitchen. I got the bag and it was feeling different as I carried it back to the front of the restaurant. I went behind the counter and I put it down and I wished I'd done this a few moments before, but even with his eyes on me, I looked into the bag. There was one main dish and one portion of soup.

Then Mr. Cohen said, "Is this a giau I see on your face?" And he pronounced the word exactly right, with the curling tone that made it "pout."

I looked up at him and I wanted to smile at how good he said the word, but even wanting to do that made the pout worse. I said, "I was just thinking that your wife must be sick. She is not eating tonight."

He could have laughed at this. But he did not. He laid his hand for a moment on his beard, he smoothed it down. He said, "The second dinner on Christmas Eve was for my son passing through town. My wife died some years ago and I am not remarried."   60

I am not a hard-hearted girl because I knew that a child gets over the loss of a father and because I also knew that a man gets over the loss of a wife. I am a good girl, but I did not feel sad for Mr. Cohen. I felt very happy. Because he laid his hand on mine and he asked if he could call me. I said yes, and as it turns out, New Year's Eve seems to be a Jewish holiday. Vietnamese New Year comes at a different time, but people in Vietnam know to celebrate whatever holiday comes along. So tonight Mr. Cohen and I will go to some restaurant that is not Chinese, and all I have to do now is sit here and listen very carefully to Grandfather as he talks to me about time.

STEPHEN DIXON   (b. 1936)

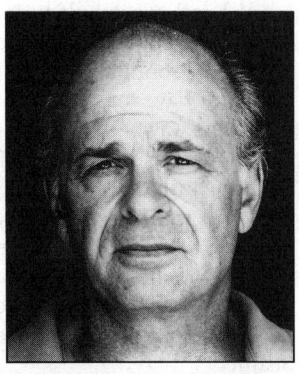

A New York native, Dixon received his B.A. from the City College of New York in 1958. His first collections of stories were No Relief *(1976) and* Quite Contrary *(1979). Early in 1992, his novel* Frog *was under consideration for the PEN/Faulkner Award for Fiction. His selected short stories appeared in 1994, followed in the next year by his novel* Interstate. *Among many distinctions are the O. Henry Award and the Pushcart Prize. "All Gone" (1990) is somewhat like Dixon's novel* Too Late *(1978), in which the protagonist, Art, goes in search of his lost woman friend, Donna. His search reveals the city as a bizarre and dangerous place, reminiscent of Eliot's experience on the subway platform in "All Gone."*

All Gone _____ *1990*

He says goodbye, we kiss at the door, he rings for the elevator, I say "I'll call you when I find out about the tickets," he says "Anytime, as I'll be in all day working on that book jacket I'm behind on," waves to me as the elevator door opens and I shut the door.

I find out about the tickets and call him and he doesn't answer. Maybe he hasn't gotten home yet, though he usually does in half an hour. But it's Saturday and the subway's always much slower on weekends, and I call him half an hour later and he doesn't answer.

He could have got home and I missed him because he right away might have gone out to buy some necessary art supply or something, and I call him an hour later and he doesn't answer. I do warm-ups, go out and run my three miles along the river, come back and shower and call him and he doesn't answer. I dial him every half hour after that for the next three hours and then call Operator and she checks and says his phone's in working order.

I call his landlord and say "This is Maria Pierce, Eliot Schulter's good friend for about the last half-year—you know me. Anyway, could you do me a real big favor and knock on his door? I know it's an inconvenience but he's only one flight up and you see, he should be home and doesn't answer and I've been phoning and phoning him and am getting worried. I'll call you back in fifteen minutes. If he's in and for his own reasons didn't want to answer the phone or it actually is out of order, could you have him call me at home?"

I call the landlord back in fifteen minutes and he says "I did what you said and he   5
didn't answer. That would've been enough for me. But you got me worried also, so I went downstairs for his duplicate keys and opened his door just a ways and yelled in for him and then walked in and he wasn't there, though his place looked okay."

"Excuse me, I just thought of something. Was his night light on?"

"You mean the little small-watt-bulb lamp on his fireplace mantel?"

"That's the one. He always keeps it on at night to keep away burglars who like to jump in from his terrace."

"What burglars jumping in from where? He was never robbed that I know."

"The tenant before him said she was. Was it on?"   1▪

"That's different. Yes. I thought he'd forgotten about the light, so I shut if off. I was thinking about his electricity cost, but you think I did wrong?"

"No. It only means he never got home. Thanks."

I call every half hour after that till around six, when he usually comes to my apartment. But he never comes here without our first talking on the phone during the afternoon about all sorts of things: how our work's going, what the mail brought, what we might have for dinner that evening and do later and if there's anything he can pick up on the way here and so on. The concert's at eight and I still have to pick up the tickets from my friend who's giving them to me and can't go herself because her baby's sick and her husband won't go without her. I call her and say "I don't see how we can make the concert. Eliot's not here, hasn't called, doesn't answer his phone and from what his landlord said, I doubt he ever got home after he left me this morning."

"Does he have any relatives or close friends in the city for you to call?"

"No, he would have gone to his apartment directly—I know him. He had important work to finish, and the only close person other than myself to him is his mother in Seattle."

"Maybe he did get home but got a very sudden call to drop everything and fly out to her, so he didn't have the time to phone you, or when he did, your line was busy."

"No, we're close enough that he'd know it would worry me. He'd have called from the airport, someplace."

"Your line still could have been busy all the times you were trying to get him. But I'm sure everything's okay, and don't worry about the tickets. Expensive as they are, I'll put them down as a total loss. Though if you are still so worried about him, phone the police in his neighborhood or even his mother in Seattle."

"Not his mother. There's no reason and I'd just worry her and Eliot would get angry at me. But the police is a good idea."

I call the police station in his precinct. The officer who answers says "We've noth-   20
ing on a Mr. Schulter. But being that you say he left your apartment this morning, phone
your precinct station," and she gives me the number. I call it and the officer on duty
says "Something did come in today about someone of his name—let me think."

"Oh no."

"Hey, take it easy. It could be nothing. I'm only remembering that I saw an earlier
bulletin, but what it was went right past me. What's your relationship to him before I
start searching for it?"

"His closest friend. We're really very very close and his nearest relative is three
thousand miles from here."

"Well, I don't see it in front of me. I'll locate it, though don't get excited when I'm
away. It could be nothing. I might even be wrong. It was probably more like a Mr. Fullter
or Schulton I read about, but not him. Want me to phone you back?"

"I'll wait, thanks."   25

"Let me take your number anyway, just in case I get lost."

He goes, comes back in a minute. "Now take it easy. It's very serious. He had no
I.D. on him other than this artist society card with only his signature on it, which we
were checking into, so we're grateful you called."

"Please, what is it?"

"According to this elderly witness, he was supposedly thrown on the subway tracks
this morning and killed."

I scream, break down, hang up, pound the telephone table with my fists, the offi-   30
cer calls back and says "If you could please revive yourself, Miss, we'd like you to come to
the police station here and then, if you could by the end of the night sometime, to the
morgue to identify your friend."

I say no, I could never go to the morgue, but then go with my best friend. She
stays outside the body room when I go in, look and say "That's him." Later I call Eliot's
mother and the next day her brother comes to the city and takes care of the arrangements to have Eliot flown to Seattle and his apartment closed down and most of his
belongings sold or given away or put on the street. The uncle asks if I'd like to attend the
funeral, but doesn't mention anything about providing air fare or where I would stay.
Since I don't have much money saved and also think I'll be out of place there and maybe
even looked down upon by his family I've never seen, I stay here and arrange on that
same funeral day a small ceremony in the basement of a local church, where I and several of our friends and his employers speak about Eliot and read aloud excerpts of his
letters to a couple of us and listen to parts of my opera records he most liked to play
and for a minute bow our heads, hold hands and pray.

According to that elderly witness, Eliot was waiting for a train on the downtown
platform of my stop when he saw a young man speaking abusively to a girl of about fifteen. When the girl continued to ignore him, he made several obscene gestures and
said he was going to throw her to the platform and force her to do all sorts of sordid
things to him and if he couldn't get her to do them there because people were watching,
then in the men's room upstairs. The girl was frightened and started to walk away. The
young man grabbed her wrist, started to twist it, stopped and said he would rip her arm
off if she gave him a hard time, but didn't let go. There were a few people on the platform. Nobody said anything or tried to help her and in fact all of them except Eliot and
this elderly man eventually moved to the other end of the platform or at least away from
what was going on. Then Eliot went over to the young man, who was still holding the girl
by her wrist, and very politely asked him to let her alone. Something like "Excuse me, I

don't like to interfere in anyone's problems. But if this young lady doesn't want to be bothered by you, then I would really think you'd let her go."

"Listen, I know her, so mind your business," the young man said and she said to Eliot "No he don't." Then out of nowhere a friend of the young man ran down the subway stairs and said to him "What's this chump doing, horning in on your act?" The elderly man got up from a bench and started for the upstairs to get help. "You stay right here, grandpa," the first young man said, "or you'll get thrown on your back too." The elderly man stopped. Eliot said to the young men "Please, nobody should be getting thrown on their backs. And I hate to get myself any more involved in this but for your own good you fellows ought to go now or just leave everybody here alone."

"And for your own good," one of the young men said, "you'd be wiser moving your ass out of here."

"I can only move it once I know this girl's out of danger with you two." 35

"She'll be plenty out of danger when you move your ass out of here, now move."

"Believe me, I'd like to, but how can I? Either you leave her completely alone now or I'll have to get the police."

That's when they jumped him, beat him to the ground and, when he continued to fight back with his feet, fists and butting his head, picked him up and threw him on the tracks. He landed on his head and cracked his skull and something like a blood clot suddenly shot through to the brain, a doctor later said. The girl had already run away. The young men ran the opposite way. The elderly man shouted at Eliot to get up, then at people to jump down to the tracks to help Eliot up, then ran in the direction the young men went to the token booth upstairs and told the attendant inside that an unconscious man was lying on the tracks and for her to do something quick to prevent a train from running over him. She phoned from the booth. He ran back to the platform and all the way to the other end of it yelling to the people around him "Stop the train. Man on the tracks, stop the local train." When the downtown local entered the station a minute later, he and most of the people along the platform screamed and waved the motorman to stop the train because someone was on the tracks. The train came to a complete stop ten feet from Eliot. A lot of the passengers were thrown to the floor and the next few days a number of them sued the city for the dizzy spells and sprained fingers and ripped clothes they said they got from the sudden train stop and also for the days and weeks they'd have to miss from their jobs because of their injuries. Anyway, according to that same doctor who examined Eliot at the hospital, he was dead a second or two after his head hit the train rail.

For a week after the funeral I go into my own special kind of mourning: seeing nobody, never leaving the apartment or answering phone calls, eating little and drinking too much, but mostly just sleeping or watching television while crying and lying in bed. Then I turn the television off, answer every phone call, run along the river for twice as many miles than I usually do, go out for a big restaurant dinner with a friend and return to my job.

The Saturday morning after the next Saturday after that I sit on the bench near the place on the subway platform where Eliot was thrown off. I stay there from eight to around one, on the lookout for the two young men. I figure they live in the neighborhood and maybe every Saturday have a job or something to go to downtown and after a few weeks they'll think everything's forgotten about them and their crime and they can go safely back to their old routines, like riding the subway to work at the station nearest their homes. The descriptions I have of them are the ones the elderly witness gave. He said he was a portrait painter or used to be and so he was absolutely exact about their height, age, looks, mannerisms and hair color and style and clothes. He also made detailed drawings of the men for the police, which I have copies of from the newspaper, and which so far haven't done the police any good in finding them.

What I'm really looking out for besides those descriptions are two young men who will try and pick up or seriously annoy or molest a teen-age girl on the platform or do that to any reasonably young woman, including me. If I see them and I'm sure it's them I'll summon a transit policeman to arrest them and if there's none around then I'll follow the young men, though discreetly, till I see a policeman. And if they try and molest or terrorize me on the bench and no policeman's around, I'll scream at the top of my lungs till someone comes and steps in, and hopefully a policeman. But I just want those two young men caught, that's all, and am willing to risk myself a little for it, and though there's probably not much chance of it happening, I still want to give it a good try.

I do this every Saturday morning for months. I see occasional violence on the platform, like a man slapping his woman friend in the face or a mother hitting her infant real hard, but nothing like two or even one man of any description close to those young men terrorizing or molesting a woman or girl or even trying to pick one up. I do see men, both old and young, and a few who look no more than nine years old or ten, leer at women plenty as if they'd like to pick them up or molest them. Some men, after staring at a woman from a distance, then walk near to her when the train comes just to follow her through the same door into the car. But that's as far as it goes on the platform. Maybe when they both get in the car and especially when it's crowded, something worse happens. I know that a few times a year when I ride the subway, a pull or poke from a man has happened to me.

A few times a man has come over to the bench and once even a woman who looked manly and tried to talk to me, but I brushed them off with silence or a remark. Then one morning a man walks over when I'm alone on the bench and nobody else is around. I'm not worried, since he has a nice face and is decently dressed and I've seen him before here waiting for the train and all it seems he wants now is to sit down. He's a big man, so I move over a few inches to the far end of the bench to give him more room.

"No," he says, "I don't want to sit—I'm just curious. I've seen you in this exact place almost every Saturday for the last couple of months and never once saw you get on the train. Would it be too rude—"

"Yes."   45

"All right. I won't ask it. I'm sorry."

"No, go on, ask it. What is it you want to know? Why I sit here? Well I've been here every Saturday for more than three months straight, if you're so curious to know, and why you don't see me get on the car is none of your business, okay?"

"Sure," he says, not really offended or embarrassed. "I asked for and got it and should be satisfied. Excuse me," and he walks away and stands near the edge of the platform, never turning around to me. When the local comes, he gets on it.

Maybe I shouldn't have been that sharp with him, but I don't like to be spoken to by men I don't know, especially in subways.

Next Saturday around the same time he comes downstairs again and stops by my   50
bench.

"Hello," he says.

I don't say anything and look the other way.

"Still none of my business why you sit here every Saturday like this?"

I continue to look the other way.

"I should take a hint, right?"   55

"Do you think that's funny?"

"No."

"Then what do you want me to do, call a policeman?"

"Of course not. I'm sorry and I am being stupid."

"Look, I wouldn't call a policeman. You seem okay. You want to be friendly or so it   60
seems. You're curious besides, which is good. But to me it is solely my business and not
yours why I am here and don't want to talk to you and so forth and I don't know why
you'd want to persist in it."

"I understand," and he walks away, stays with his back to me and gets on the train
when it comes.

Next Saturday he walks down the stairs and stays near the platform edge about
ten feet away reading a book. Then he turns to me and seems just about to say something and I don't know what I'm going to say in return, if anything, because he does
seem polite and nice and intelligent and I actually looked forward a little to seeing and
speaking civilly to him, when the train comes. He waves to me and gets on it. I lift my
hand to wave back but quickly put it down. Why start?

Next Saturday he runs down the stairs to catch the train that's pulling in. He
doesn't even look at me this time, so in a rush is he to get on the car. He gets past the
doors just before they close and has his back to me when the train leaves. He must
be late for someplace.

The next Saturday he comes down the stairs and walks over to me with two containers of coffee or tea while the train's pulling in. He keeps walking to me while the
train doors open, close, and the train goes. I look at the advertisement clock. He's about
fifteen minutes earlier than usual.

"How do you like your coffee if I can ask, black or regular? Or maybe you don't   6
want any from me, if you do drink coffee, which would of course be all right too."

"Regular, but I don't want any, thanks."

"Come on, take it, it's not toxic and I can drink my coffee any old way. And it'll
perk you up, not that you need perking up and certainly not from me," and he gives
me a container. "Sugar?" and I say "Really, this is—" and he says "Come on: sugar?" and
I nod and he pulls out of his jacket pocket a couple of sugar packets and a stirring stick.
"I just took these on the way out of the shop without waiting for a bag, don't ask me
why. The stick's probably a bit dirty, do you mind?" and I shake my head and wipe the
stick though there's nothing on it. "Mind if I sit and have my coffee also?" and I say "Go
ahead. It's not my bench and all that and I'd be afraid to think what you'd pull out of
your pocket if I said no—probably your own bench and cocktail table," and he says
"Don't be silly," and sits.

He starts talking about the bench, how the same oak one has been here for at
least thirty years because that's how long he's lived in the neighborhood, then about the
coffee, that it's good though always from the shop upstairs a little bitter, then why he
happens to see me every Saturday: that he's recently divorced and has a child by that
marriage who he goes to in Brooklyn once a week to spend the whole day with. He
seems even nicer and more intelligent than I thought and comfortable to be with and
for the first time I think he's maybe even goodlooking when before I thought his ears
stuck out too far and he had too thin a mouth and small a nose. He dresses well anyway
and has a nice profile and his hair's stylish and neat and his face shaven clean which I

like and no excessive jewelry or neck chain which I don't and in his other jacket pocket are a paperback and small ribbon-wrapped package, the last I guess a present for his little girl.

His train comes and when the doors open I say "Shouldn't you get on it?" and he says "I'll take the next one if you don't mind," and I say "I don't think it's up to me to decide," and he hunches his shoulders and gives me that expression "Well I don't know what to say," and the train goes and when it's quiet again he continues the conversation, now about what I think of something that happened in Africa yesterday which he read in the paper today. I tell him I didn't read it and that maybe when I do read my paper it won't be the same as his and so might not have that news story and he says "What paper you read?" and I tell him and he says "Same one—front page, left-hand column," and I say "Anyway, on Saturdays I don't, and for my own reasons, have time for the newspaper till I get home later and really also don't have the time to just sit here and talk," and he says "Of course, of course," but seriously, as if he believes me, and we're silent for a while, drinking our coffees and looking at the tracks.

We hear another train coming and I say "I think you better get on this one," and 70
he says "Okay. It's been great and I hope I haven't been too much of a nuisance," and I say "You really haven't at all," and he says "Mind if I ask your name?" and I say "Your train," and he yells to the people going into the subway car "Hold the door," and gets up and says to me "Mine's Vaughn," and shakes my hand and says "Next week," and runs to the train with his container and he's not past the door a second when the man who kept it open for him lets it close.

I picture him on his way to Brooklyn, reading his book, later in Prospect Park with his daughter as he said they would do if the good weather holds up and in an indoor ice-skating rink if it doesn't, and then go back to my lookout. People spit and throw trash on the tracks, a drunk or crazy man urinates on the platform, a boy defaces the tile wall with a marker pen and tells me to go shoot myself when I very politely suggest he stop, there's almost a fight between a man trying to get off the train and the one blocking his way who's trying to get on, which I doubt would have happened if both sides of the double door had opened, but again no sign of my two young men.

Vaughn's not there the next Saturday and the Saturday after that and the third Saturday he's not there I begin thinking that I'm thinking more about him than I do of anybody or thing and spending more time looking at the staircase and around the platform for him than I do for those young men. I've gradually lost interest in finding them and over the last four months my chances have gotten worse and worse that I'll even recognize them if they ever do come down here and as far as their repeating that harassing-the-girl incident at this particular station, well forget it, and I leave the station at noon instead of around my usual two and decide that was my last Saturday there.

A month later I meet Vaughn coming out of a supermarket when I'm going in. He's pulling a shopping cart filled with clean laundry at the bottom and two big grocery bags on top. It's Saturday, we're both dressed in T-shirts and shorts for the warm weather now, and I stop him by saying "Vaughn, how are you?" He looks at me as if he doesn't remember me. "Maybe because you can't place me anywhere else but on a subway bench. Maria Pierce. From the subway station over there."

"That's right. Suddenly your face was familiar, but you never gave me your name. What's been happening?" and I say "Nothing much I guess," and he says "You don't wait in subway stations anymore for whatever you were waiting for those days?" and I say "How would you know? You stopped coming yourself there and to tell you the truth I was sort of looking forward to a continuation of that nice chat we last had."

"Oh, let me tell you what went wrong. My ex-wife, giving me a day's notice, changed jobs and locations and took my daughter to Boston with her. I could have fought it, but don't like arguments. I only get to see her when I get up there, which hasn't happened yet, and maybe for August if I want."

"That's too bad. I remember how devoted you were."

"I don't know it's so bad. I'm beginning to enjoy my freedom every Saturday, as much as I miss my kid. But I got to go. Ice cream in the bag will soon be melting," and he says goodbye and goes.

If I knew his last name I might look him up in the phone book and call him and say something like "Since we live in the same neighborhood, would you care to have a cup of coffee one of these days? I owe you one and I'll even, if you're still curious, let you in on my big secret why I every Saturday for months waited at our favorite subway station." Then I think no, even if I did have his phone number. I gave him on the street a couple of openings to make overtures about seeing me again and he didn't take them because he didn't want to or whatever his reasons but certainly not because of his melting ice cream.

Several weeks later I read in the newspaper that those two young men got caught. They were in the Eighth Street subway station and tried to molest a policewoman dressed like an artist with even a sketchbook and drawing pen, and two plain-clothesmen were waiting nearby. The police connected them up with Eliot's death. The two men later admitted to being on my subway platform that day but said they only started a fight with him because he tried to stop one of them from making a date with a girl the young man once knew. They said they told Eliot to mind his business, he refused, so they wrestled him to the ground and then said he could get up if he didn't make any more trouble. Eliot said okay, got up and immediately swung at them, missed, lost his footing and before either of them could grab him away, fell to the tracks. They got scared and ran to the street. They don't know the girl's last name or where she lives except that it's somewhere in the Bronx.

I buy all the newspapers that day and the next. One of them has a photo of the young men sticking their middle fingers up to the news photographers. They don't look anything like the young men I was on the lookout for, so either the witness's description of them or the printing of the photograph was bad, because I don't see how they could have physically changed so much in just a few months.

I continue to read the papers for weeks after that, hoping to find something about the young men going to trial, but don't. Then a month later a co-worker of mine who knew about Eliot and me says she saw on the television last night that the young men were allowed to plead guilty to a lesser charge of negligent manslaughter or something and got off with a jail term of from one to three years. "It seems the elderly man, that main witness to Eliot's murder, died of a fatal disease a while ago and the young woman witness could never be found. As for molesting the policewoman, that charge was dropped, though the news reporter never said why."

ANDRE DUBUS   (1936–1999)

Dubus was born in Louisiana and received degrees from McNeese State College and the University of Iowa. He taught at Bradford College in Massachusetts before he was struck and disabled by a speeding automobile. He lived northwest of Boston near the Merrimack River, an area he often employed as the setting in his ficiton. The stories in his Selected Stories *(1988), from which "The Curse" is taken, touch the darker areas of human existence, but nevertheless have a compelling force. In "They Now Live in Texas," for example, a woman sees a horror ghost movie on her VCR and then awaits her own demons. In another story, "Townies," a drifting, purposeless young man kills his girlfriend and then achieves a curious serenity as he waits for the police. Dubus's last short story collection was* Dancing After Hours *(1996). He also worked in the longer form of the novella and published several novellas in* We Don't Live Here Anymore *(1984). He gained many honors, among them a Guggenheim Fellowship and a MacArthur Fellowship.*

The Curse _____ *1988*

Mitchell Hayes was forty-nine years old, but when the cops left him in the bar with Bob, the manager, he felt much older. He did not know what it was like to be very old, a shrunken and wrinkled man, but he assumed it was like this: fatigue beyond relieving by rest, by sleep. He also was not a small man: his weight moved up and down in the hundred and seventies and he was five feet, ten inches tall. But now his body seemed short and thin. Both stood at one end of the bar; he was a large blackhaired man, and there was nothing in front of him but an ash tray he was using. He looked at Mitchell at the cash register and said: "Forget it. You heard what Smitty said."

Mitchell looked away, at the front door. He had put the chairs upside down on the table. He looked from the door past Bob to the empty space of floor at the rear; sometimes people danced there, to the jukebox. Opposite Bob, on the wall behind the bar, was a telephone; Mitchell looked at it. He had told Smitty there were five guys and when he moved to the phone one of them stepped around the corner of the bar and shoved him: one hand against Mitchell's chest, and it pushed him backward; he nearly fell. That was when they were getting rough with her at the bar. When they took her to the floor Mitchell looked once at her sounds, then looked down at the duckboard he stood on, or at the belly or chest of a young man in front of him.

He knew they were not drunk. They had been drinking before they came to his place, a loud popping of motorcycles outside, then walking into the empty bar, young and sunburned and carrying helmets and wearing thick leather jackets in August. They stood in front of Mitchell and drank drafts. When he took their first order he thought they were on drugs and later, watching them, he was certain. They were not relaxed, in the way of most drinkers near closing time. Their eyes were quick, alert as wary animals, and they spoke loudly, with passion, but their passion was strange and disturbing, because they were only chatting, bantering. Mitchell knew nothing of the effects of drugs, so could not guess what was in their blood. He feared and hated drugs because of his work and because he was the stepfather of teenagers: a boy and a girl. He gave last call and served them and leaned against the counter behind him.

Then the door opened and the girl walked in from the night, a girl he had never seen, and she crossed the floor toward Mitchell. He stepped forward to tell her she had missed last call, but before he spoke she asked for change for the cigarette machine. She was young, he guessed nineteen to twenty-one, and deeply tanned and had dark hair. She was sober and wore jeans and a dark blue tee shirt. He gave her the quarters but she was standing between two of the men and she did not get to the machine.

When it was over and she lay crying on the cleared circle of floor, he left the bar and picked up the jeans and tee shirt beside her and crouched and handed them to her. She did not look at him. She lay the clothes across her breasts and what Mitchell thought of now as her wound. He left her and dialed 911, then Bob's number. He woke

5

up Bob. Then he picked up her sneakers from the floor and placed them beside her and squatted near her face, her crying. He wanted to speak to her and touch her, hold a hand or press her brow, but he could not.

The cruiser was there quickly, the siren coming east from town, then slowing and deepening as the car stopped outside. He was glad Smitty was one of them; he had gone to high school with Smitty. The other was Dave, and Mitchell knew him because it was a small town. When they saw the girl Dave went out to the cruiser to call for an ambulance, and when he came back he said two other cruisers had those scumbags and were taking them in. The girl was still crying and could not talk to Smitty and Dave. She was crying when a man and woman lifted her onto a stretcher and rolled her out the door and she vanished forever in a siren.

Bob came in while Smitty and Dave were sitting at the bar drinking coffee and Smitty was writing his report; Mitchell stood behind the bar. Bob sat next to Dave as Mitchell said: "I could have stopped them, Smitty."

"That's our job," Smitty said. "You want to be in the hospital now?"

Mitchell did not answer. When Smitty and Dave left, he got a glass of Coke from the cobra and had a cigarette with Bob. They did not talk. Then Mitchell washed his glass and Bob's cup and they left, turning off the lights. Outside Mitchell locked the front door, feeling the sudden night air after almost ten hours of air conditioning. When he had come to work the day had been very hot, and now he thought it would not have happened in winter. They had stopped for a beer on their way somewhere from the beach; he had heard them say that. But the beach was not the reason. He did not know the reason, but he knew it would not have happened in winter. The night was cool and now he could smell trees. He turned and looked at the road in front of the bar. Bob stood beside him on the small porch.

"If the regulars had been here," Bob said.

He turned and with his hand resting on the wooden rail he walked down the ramp to the ground. At his car he stopped and looked over its roof at Mitchell.

"You take it easy," he said.

Mitchell nodded. When Bob got in his car and left, he went down the ramp and drove home to his house on a street that he thought was neither good nor bad. The houses were small and there were old large houses used now as apartments for families. Most of the people had work, most of the mothers cared for their children, and most of the children were clean and looked like they lived in homes, not caves like some he saw in town. He worried about the older kids, one group of them anyway. They were idle. When he was a boy in a town farther up the Merrimack River, he and his friends committed every mischievous act he could recall on afternoons and nights when they were idle. His stepchildren were not part of that group. They had friends from the high school. The front porch light was on for him and one in the kitchen at the rear of the house. He went in the front door and switched off the porch light and walked through the living and dining rooms to the kitchen. He got a can of beer from the refrigerator, turned out the light, and sat at the table. When he could see, he took a cigarette from Susan's pack in front of him.

Down the hall he heard Susan move on the bed then get up and he hoped it wasn't for the bathroom but for him. He had met her eight years ago when he had given up on ever marrying and having kids, then one night she came into the bar with two of her girl friends from work. She made six dollars an hour going to homes of invalids, mostly what she called her little old ladies, and bathing them. She got the house from her marriage, and child support the guy paid for a few months till he left town and went

tetracycline
cups

south. She came barefoot down the hall and stood in the kitchen doorway and said:
"Are you all right?"

"No."   15

She sat across from him, and he told her. Very soon she held his hand. She was
good. He knew if he had fought all five of them and was lying in pieces in a hospital
bed she would tell him he had done the right thing, as she was telling him now. He liked
her strong hand on his. It was a professional hand and he wanted from her something
he had never wanted before: to lie in bed while she bathed him. When they went to bed
he did not think he would be able to sleep, but she kneeled beside him and massaged
his shoulders and rubbed his temples and pressed her hands on his forehead. He woke
to the voices of Marty and Joyce in the kitchen. They had summer jobs, and always when
they woke him he went back to sleep till noon, but now he got up and dressed and went
to the kitchen door. Susan was at the stove, her back to him, and Marty and Joyce were
talking and smoking. He said good morning, and stepped into the room.

"What are you doing up?" Joyce said.

She was a pretty girl with her mother's wide cheekbones and Marty was a tall good-
looking boy, and Mitchell felt as old as he had before he slept. Susan was watching him.
Then she poured him a cup of coffee and put it at his place and he sat. Marty said: "You
getting up for the day?"

"Something happened last night. At the bar." They tried to conceal their excitement, but he saw it in their eyes. "I should have stopped it. I think I *could* have stopped
it. That's the point. There were these five guys. They were on motorcycles but they
weren't bikers. Just punks. They came in late, when everybody else had gone home. It
was a slow night anyway. Everybody was at the beach."

"They rob you?" Marty said.   20

"No. A girl came in. Young. Nice looking. You know: just a girl, minding her
business."

They nodded, and their eyes were apprehensive.

"She wanted cigarette change, that's all. Those guys were on dope. Coke or something. You know: they were flying in place."

"Did they rape her?" Joyce said.   25

"Yes, honey."

"The *fuckers.*"

Susan opened her mouth then closed it and Joyce reached quickly for Susan's
pack of cigarettes. Mitchell held his lighter for her and said: "When they started getting
rough with her at the bar I went for the phone. One of them stopped me. He shoved
me, that's all. I should have hit him with a bottle."

Marty reached over the table with his big hand and held Mitchell's shoulder.

"No, Mitch. Five guys that mean. And coked up or whatever. No way. You
wouldn't be here this morning."

"I don't know. There was always a guy with me. But just one guy, taking turns."   30

"Great," Joyce said. Marty's hand was on Mitchell's left shoulder; she put hers on
his right hand.

"They took her to the hospital," he said. "The guys are in jail."

"They are?" Joyce said.

"I called the cops. When they left."

"You'll be a good witness," Joyce said.   35

He looked at her proud face.

"At the trial," she said.

The day was hot but that night most of the regulars came to the bar. Some of the younger ones came on motorcycles. They were a good crowd: they all worked, except the retired ones and no one ever bothered the women, not even the young ones with their summer tans. Everyone talked about it: some had read the newspaper story, some had heard the story in town, and they wanted to hear it from Mitchell. He told it as often as they asked but he did not finish it because he was working hard and could not stay with any group of customers long enough.

He watched their faces. Not one of them, even the women, looked at him as if he had not cared enough for the girl, or was a coward. Many of them even appeared sympathetic, making him feel for moments that he was a survivor of something horrible, and when that feeling left him he was ashamed. He felt tired and old, making drinks and change, moving and talking up and down the bar. At the stool at the far end Bob drank coffee and whenever Mitchell looked at him he smiled or nodded and once raised his right fist, with the thumb up.

Reggie was drinking too much. He did that two or three times a month and Mitchell had to shut him off and Reggie always took it humbly. He was a big gentle man with a long brown beard. But tonight shutting off Reggie demanded from Mitchell an act of will, and when the eleven o'clock news came on the television and Reggie ordered another shot and a draft, Mitchell pretended not to hear him. He served the customers at the other end of the bar, where Bob was. He could hear Reggie calling: Hey Mitch; shot and a draft, Mitch. Mitchell was close to Bob now. Bob said softly: "He's had enough."

Mitchell nodded and went to Reggie, leaned closer to him so he could speak quietly, and said: "Sorry, Reggie. Time for coffee. I don't want you dead out there."

Reggie blinked at him.

"Okay, Mitch." He pulled some bills from his pocket and put them on the bar. Mitchell glanced at them and saw at least a ten dollar tip. When he rang up Reggie's tab the change was sixteen dollars and fifty cents, and he dropped the coins and shoved the bills into the beer mug beside the cash register. The mug was full of bills, as it was on most nights, and he kept his hand in there, pressing Reggie's into the others, and saw the sunburned young men holding her down on the floor and one kneeling between her legs, spread and held, and he heard their cheering voices and her screaming and groaning and finally weeping and weeping and weeping, until she was the siren crying then fading into the night. From the floor behind him, far across the room, he felt her pain and terror and grief, then her curse upon him. The curse moved into his back and spread down and up his spine, into his stomach and legs and arms and shoulders until he quivered with it. He wished he were alone so he could kneel to receive it.

E. M. FORSTER (1879–1970)

A novelist, story writer, essayist, and travel-book writer, Edward Morgan Forster was a natural member of the British upper classes. He attended a public (i.e., private) school but disliked the atmosphere of social conformity he experienced there. He found life at Cambridge much more congenial to his disposition. Later he criticized the public school system and exalted personal values and relationships above all else. He spent time in Egypt and afterward wrote a guidebook to Alexandria (1922, 1938). He also spent time in India as a personal secretary to a Maharajah, and the result was perhaps his best-known novel, A Passage to India *(1924). In recent years his works have come to wide public attention because of various well-produced films, including* Howards End *(a 1992 version of his 1910 novel),* A Room with a View *(a 1985 version of his 1908 novel),* A Passage to India *(1984), and* Maurice *(a 1987 version of his posthumous 1971 novel).* "The Point of It" *is taken from his collection* The Celestial Omnibus *(1911).*

The Point of It _____ 1911

"I don't see the point of it," said Micky, through much imbecile laughter.

Harold went on rowing. They had spent too long on the sand-dunes, and now the tide was running out of the estuary strongly. The sun was setting, the fields on the opposite bank shone bright, and the farm-house where they were stopping glowed from its upper windows as though filled to the brim with fire.

"We're going to be carried out to sea," Micky continued. "You'll never win unless you bust yourself a bit, and you a poor invalid, too. I back the sea."

They were reaching the central channel, the backbone, as it were, of the retreating waters. Once past it, the force of the tide would slacken, and they would have easy going until they beached under the farm. It was a glorious evening. It had been a most glorious day. They had rowed out to the dunes at the slack, bathed, raced, eaten, slept, bathed and raced and eaten again. Micky was in roaring spirits. God had never thwarted him hitherto, and he could not suppose that they would really be made late for supper by an ebbing tide. When they came to the channel, and the boat, which had been slowly edging upstream, hung motionless among the moving waters, he lost all semblance of sanity, and shouted:

> It may be that the gulfs will wash us down,
> It may be we shall touch the Happy Isles,
> And see the great Achilles, whom we knew.°

Harold, who did not care for poetry, only shouted. His spirits also were roaring, and he neither looked nor felt a poor invalid. Science had talked to him seriously of late, shaking her head at his sunburnt body. What should Science know? She had sent him down to the sea to recruit,° and Micky to see that he did not tire himself. Micky had been a nuisance at first, but common sense had prevailed, as it always does among the young. A fortnight ago, he would not let the patient handle an oar. Now he bid him "bust" himself, and Harold took him at his word and did so. He made himself all will and muscle. He began not to know where he was. The thrill of the stretcher against his feet, and of the tide up his arms, merged with his friend's voice towards one nameless sensation; he was approaching the mystic state that is the athlete's true though unacknowledged goal: he was beginning to be.   5

Micky chanted, "One, two—one, two," and tried to help by twitching the rudder. But Micky had imagination. He looked at the flaming windows and fancied that the farm was a star and the boat its attendant satellite. Then the tide was the rushing ether stream of the universe, the interstellar surge that beats for ever. How jolly! He did not formulate his joys, after the weary fashion of older people. He was far too happy to be thankful.

It may be . . . : Tennyson, *Ulysses,* lines 62–64.
recruit: to convalesce, to recover after an illness.

"Remember now thy Creator in the days of thy youth,"° are the words of one who has left his youth behind, and all that Micky sang was "One, two."

Harold laughed without hearing. Sweat poured off his forehead. He put on a spurt, as did the tide.

"Wish the doctor could see you," cried Micky.

No answer. Setting his teeth, he went berserk. His ancestors called to him that it was better to die than to be beaten by the sea. He rowed with gasps and angry little cries, while the voice of the helmsman lashed him to fury.

"That's right—one, two—plug it in harder. . . . Oh, I say, this is a bit stiff, though.   10
Let's give it up, old man, perhaps."

The gulls were about them now. Some wheeled overhead, others bobbed past on the furrowed waters. The song of a lark came faintly from the land, and Micky saw the doctor's trap° driving along the road that led to the farm. He felt ashamed.

"Look here, Harold, you oughtn't to—I oughtn't to have let you. I—I don't see the point of it."

"Don't you?" said Harold with curious distinctness. "Well, you will some day," and so saying dropped both oars. The boat spun round at this, the farm, the trap, the song of the lark vanished, and he fell heavily against the rowlock. Micky caught at him. He had strained his heart. Half in the boat and half out of it, he died, a rotten business.

II

A rotten business. It happened when Michael was twenty-two, and he expected never to be happy again. The sound of his own voice shouting as he was carried out, the doctor's voice saying, "I consider you responsible," the coming of Harold's parents, the voice of the curate summarizing Harold's relations with the unseen—all these things affected him so deeply that he supposed they would affect him for ever. They did not, because he lived to be over seventy, and with the best will in the world, it is impossible to remember clearly for so long. The mind, however sensitive and affectionate, is coated with new experiences daily; it cannot clear itself of the steady accretion, and is forced either to forget the past or to distort it. So it was with Michael. In time only the more dramatic incidents survived. He remembered Harold's final gesture (one hand grasping his own, the other plunged deep into the sea), because there was a certain æsthetic quality about it, not because it was the last of his friend. He remembered the final words for the same reason. "Don't you see the point of it? Well, you will some day." The phrase struck his fancy, and passed into his own stock; after thirty or forty years he forgot its origin. He is not to blame; the business of life snowed him under.

There is also this to say: he and Harold had nothing in common except youth. No spiritual bond could survive. They had never discussed theology or social reform, or any of the problems that were thronging Michael's brain, and consequently, though they had been intimate enough, there was nothing to remember. Harold melted the more one thought of him. Robbed of his body, he was so shadowy. Nor could one imagine him as a departed spirit, for the world beyond death is surely august. Neither in heaven nor hell is there place for athletics and aimless good temper, and if these were taken from Harold, what was left? Even if the unseen life should prove an archetype of this,

---

"*Remember . . .*": Ecclesiastes 12:1.
trap: horse and buggy.

even if it should contain a sun and stars of its own, the sunburn of earth must fade off our faces as we look at it, the muscles of earth must wither before we can go rowing on its infinite sea. Michael sadly resigned his friend to God's mercy. He himself could do nothing, for men can only immortalize those who leave behind them some strong impression of poetry or wisdom.

For himself he expected another fate. With all humility, he knew that he was not as Harold. It was no merit of his own, but he had been born of a more intellectual stock, and had inherited powers that rendered him worthier of life, and of whatever may come after it. He cared for the universe, for the tiny tangle in it that we call civilization, for his fellow-men who had made the tangle and who transcended it. Love, the love of humanity, warmed him; and even when he was thinking of other matters, was looking at Orion perhaps in the cold winter evenings, a pang of joy, too sweet for description, would thrill him, and he would feel sure that our highest impulses have some eternal value, and will be completed hereafter. So full a nature could not brood over death.

To summarize his career.

Soon after the tragedy, when he in his turn was recruiting, he met the woman who was to become his helpmate through life. He had met her once before, and had not liked her; she had seemed uncharitable and hard. Now he saw that her hardness sprang from a morality that he himself lacked. If he believed in love, Janet believed in truth. She tested all men and all things. She had no patience with the sentimentalist who shelters from the world's rough and tumble. Engaged at that time to another man, she spoke more freely to Michael than she would otherwise have done, and told him that it is not enough to feel good and to feel that others are good; one's business is to make others better, and she urged him to adopt a profession. The beauty of honest work dawned upon the youth as she spoke. Mentally and physically, he came to full manhood, and, after due preparation, he entered the Home Civil Service—the British Museum.

Here began a career that was rather notable, and wholly beneficial to humanity. With his ideals of conduct and culture, Michael was not content with the official routine. He desired to help others, and, since he was gifted with tact, they consented to the operation. Before long he became a conciliatory force in his department. He could mollify his superiors, encourage his inferiors, soothe foreign scholars, and show that there is something to be said for all sides. Janet, who watched his rise, taxed him again with instability. But now she was wrong. The young man was not a mere opportunist. He always had a sincere opinion of his own, or he could not have retained the respect of his colleagues. It was really the inherent sweetness of his nature at work, turned by a woman's influence towards fruitful ends.

At the end of a ten years' acquaintance the two married. In the interval Janet had suffered much pain, for the man to whom she had been engaged had proved unworthy of her. Her character was set when she came to Michael, and, as he knew, strongly contrasted with his own; and perhaps they had already interchanged all the good they could. But the marriage proved durable and sufficiently happy. He, in particular, made endless allowances, for toleration and sympathy were becoming the cardinal points of his nature. If his wife was unfair to the official mind, or if his brother-in-law, an atheist, denounced religion, he would say to himself, "They cannot help it; they are made thus, and have the qualities of their defects. Let me rather think of my own, and strive for a wider outlook ceaselessly." He grew sweeter every day.

It was partly this desire for a wider outlook that turned him to literature. As he was crossing the forties it occurred to him to write a few essays, somewhat retrospective in tone, and thoughtful rather than profound in content. They had some success. Their

20

good taste, their lucid style, the tempered Christianity of their ethics, whetted the half-educated public, and made it think and feel. They were not, and were not intended to be, great literature, but they opened the doors to it, and were indubitably a power for good. The first volume was followed by "The Confessions of a Middle-aged Man." In it Michael paid melodious tribute to youth, but showed that ripeness is all.° Experience, he taught, is the only humanizer; sympathy, balance and many-sidedness cannot come to a man until he is elderly. It is always pleasant to be told that the best is yet to be, and the sale of the book was large. Perhaps he would have become a popular author, but his wife's influence restrained him from writing anything that he did not sincerely feel. She had borne him three children by now—Henry, Catherine, and Adam. On the whole they were a happy family. Henry never gave any trouble. Catherine took after her mother. Adam, who was wild and uncouth, caused his father some anxiety. He could not understand him, in spite of careful observation, and they never became real friends. Still, it was but a little cloud in a large horizon. At home, as in his work, Michael was more successful than most men.

Thus he slipped into the fifties. On the death of his father he inherited a house in the Surrey hills, and Janet, whose real interests were horticultural, settled down there. After all, she had not proved an intellectual woman. Her fierce manner had misled him and perhaps herself into believing it. She was efficient enough in London society, but it bored her, for she lacked her husband's pliancy, and aged more rapidly than he did. Nor did the country suit her. She grew querulous, disputing with other ladies about the names of flowers. And, of course, the years were not without their effect on him, too. By now he was somewhat of a valetudinarian.° He had given up all outdoor sports, and, though his health remained good, grew bald, and rather stout and timid. He was against late hours, violent exercise, night walks, swimming when hot, muddling about in open boats, and he often had to check himself from fidgeting the children. Henry, a charming sympathetic lad, would squeeze his hand and say, "All right, father." But Catherine and Adam sometimes frowned. He thought of the children more and more. Now that his wife was declining, they were the future, and he was determined to keep in touch with them, remembering how his own father had failed with him. He believed in gentleness, and often stood between them and their mother. When the boys grew up he let them choose their own friends. When Catherine, at the age of nineteen, asked if she might go away and earn some money as a lady gardener, he let her go. In this case he had his reward, for Catherine, having killed the flowers, returned. She was a restless, scowling young woman, a trial to her mother, who could not imagine what girls were coming to. Then she married and improved greatly; indeed, she proved his chief support in the coming years.

For, soon after her marriage, a great trouble fell on him. Janet became bedridden, and, after a protracted illness, passed into the unknown. Sir Michael—for he had been knighted—declared that he should not survive her. They were so accustomed to each other, so mutually necessary, that he fully expected to pass away after her. In this he was mistaken. She died when he was sixty, and he lived to be over seventy. His character had passed beyond the clutch of circumstance and he still retained his old interests and his unconquerable benignity.

A second trouble followed hard on the first. It transpired that Adam was devoted to his mother, and had only tolerated home life for her sake. After a brutal scene he

---

Ripeness is all: Shakespeare, *King Lear,* V.2.11.
valetudinarian: one who is chronically ill.

left. He wrote from the Argentine that he was sorry, but wanted to start for himself. "I don't see the point of it," quavered Sir Michael. "Have I ever stopped him or any of you from starting?" Henry and Catherine agreed with him. Yet he felt that they understood their brother better than he did. "I have given him freedom all his life," he continued. "I have given him freedom, what more does he want?" Henry, after hesitation, said, "There are some people who feel that freedom cannot be given. At least I have heard so. Perhaps Adam is like that. Unless he took freedom he might not feel free." Sir Michael disagreed. "I have now studied adolescence for many years," he replied, "and your conclusions, my dear boy, are ridiculous."

The two rallied to their father gallantly; and, after all, he spent a dignified old age. Having retired from the British Museum, he produced a little aftermath of literature. The great public had forgotten him, but the courtliness of his "Musings of a Pensioner" procured him some circulation among elderly and educated audiences. And he found a new spiritual consolation. *Anima naturaliter Anglicana,°* he had never been hostile to the Established Church; and, when he criticized her worldliness and occasional inhumanity, had spoken as one who was outside her rather than against her. After his wife's death and the flight of his son he lost any lingering taste for speculation. The experience of years disposed him to accept the experience of centuries, and to merge his feeble personal note in the great voice of tradition. Yes; a serene and dignified old age. Few grudged it to him. Of course, he had enemies, who professed to see through him, and said that Adam had seen through him too; but no impartial observer agreed. No ulterior motive had ever biased Sir Michael. The purity of his record was not due to luck, but to purity within, and his conciliatory manner sprang from a conciliated soul. He could look back on failures and mistakes, and he had not carried out the ideals of his youth. Who has? But he had succeeded better than most men in modifying those ideals to fit the world of facts, and if love had been modified into sympathy and sympathy into compromise, let one of his contemporaries cast the first stone.

One fact remained—the fact of death. Hitherto, Sir Michael had never died, and at times he was bestially afraid. But more often death appeared as a prolongation of his present career. He saw himself quietly and tactfully organizing some corner in infinity with his wife's assistance; Janet would be greatly improved. He saw himself passing from a sphere in which he had been efficient into a sphere which combined the familiar with the eternal, and in which he would be equally efficient—passing into it with dignity and without pain. This life is a preparation for the next. Those who live longest are consequently the best prepared. Experience is the great teacher; blessed are the experienced, for they need not further modify their ideals.

The manner of his death was as follows. He, too, met with an accident. He was walking from his town house to Catherine's by a short cut through a slum; some women were quarrelling about a fish, and as he passed they appealed to him. Always courteous, the old man stopped, said that he had not sufficient data to judge on, and advised them to lay the fish aside for twenty-four hours. This chanced to annoy them, and they grew more angry with him than with one another. They accused him of "doing them," of "getting round them," and one, who was the worse for drink, said, "See if he gets round that," and slapped him with the fish in the face. He fell. When he came to himself he was lying in bed with one of his headaches.

Anima naturaliter Anglicana: with a naturally Anglican soul.

He could hear Catherine's voice. She annoyed him. If he did not open his eyes, it was only because he did not choose.

"He has been like this for nearly two years," said Henry's voice.

It was, at the most, ten minutes since he had fallen in the slum. But he did not choose to argue.

"Yes, he's pretty well played out," said a third voice—actually the voice of Adam; how and when had Adam returned? "But, then, he's been that for the last thirty years."

"Gently, old boy," said Henry.

"Well, he has," said Adam. "I don't believe in cant. He never did anything since Mother died, and damned little before. They've forgotten his books because they aren't first-hand; they're rearranging the cases he arranged in the British Museum. That's a lot. What else has he done except tell people to dress warmly, but not too warm?"

"Adam, you really mustn't—"

"It's because nobody speaks up that men of the old man's type get famous. It's a sign of your sloppy civilization. You're all afraid—afraid of originality, afraid of work, afraid of hurting one another's feelings. You let any one come to the top who doesn't frighten you, and as soon as he dies you forget him and knight some other figurehead instead."

An unknown voice said, "Shocking, Mr. Adam, shocking. Such a dear old man, and quite celebrated, too."

"You'll soon get used to me, nurse."

The nurse laughed.

"Adam, it is a relief to have you," said Catherine after a pause. "I want you and your boy to help me with mine." Her voice sounded dimmer; she had turned from her father without a word of farewell. "One must profit by the mistakes of others . . . after all, more heroism. . . . I am determined to keep in touch with my boy—"

"Larrup° him," said Adam. "That's the secret." He followed his sister out of the room.

Then Henry's delightful laugh sounded for the last time. "You make us all feel twenty years younger," he said; "more like when—"

The door shut.

Sir Michael grew cold with rage. This was life, this was what the younger generation had been thinking. Adam he ignored, but at the recollection of Henry and Catherine he determined to die. If he chose, he could have risen from bed and driven the whole pack into the street. But he did not choose. He chose rather to leave this shoddy and ungrateful world. The immense and superhuman cynicism that is latent in all of us came at last to the top and transformed him. He saw the absurdity of love, and the vision so tickled him that he began to laugh. The nurse, who had called him a dear old man, bent over him, and at the same moment two boys came into the sick-room.

"How's grandpapa?" asked one of them—Catherine's boy.

"Not so well," the nurse answered.

There was a silence. Then the other boy said, "Come along, let's cut."

"But they told us not to."

"Why should we do what old people tell us! Dad's pretty well played out, and so's your mother."

"Shocking; be off with you both," said the nurse; and, with a little croon of admiration, Catherine's boy followed his cousin out of the room. Their grandfather's mirth

larrup: punish, beat.

increased. He rolled about in the bed; and, just as he was grasping the full irony of the situation, he died, and pursued it into the unknown.

III

Micky was still in bed. He was aware of so much through long melancholy dreams. But when he opened his mouth to laugh, it filled with dust. Choosing to open his eyes; he found that he had swollen enormously, and lay sunk in the sand of an illimitable plain. As he expected, he had no occasion greatly to modify his ideals; infinity had merely taken the place of his bedroom and of London. Nothing moved on its surface except a few sand-pillars, which would sometimes merge into each other as though confabulating, and then fall with a slight hiss. Save for these, there was no motion, no noise, nor could he feel any wind.

How long had he lain here? Perhaps for years, long before death perhaps, while his body seemed to be walking among men. Life is so short and trivial, that who knows whether we arrive for it entirely, whether more than a fraction of the soul is aroused to put on flesh? The bud and the blossom perish in a moment, the husk endures, and may not the soul be a husk? It seemed to Micky that he had lain in the dust for ever, suffering and sneering, and that the essence of all things, the primal power that lies behind the stars, is senility. Age, toothless, dropsical age; ungenerous to age and to youth; born before all ages, and outlasting them; the universe as old age.

The place degraded while it tortured. It was vast, yet ignoble. It sloped downward into darkness and upward into cloud, but into what darkness, what clouds! No tragic splendour glorified them. When he looked at them he understood why he was so unhappy, for they were looking at him, sneering at him while he sneered. Their dirtiness was more ancient than the hues of day and night, their irony more profound; he was part of their jest, even as youth was part of his, and slowly he realized that he was, and had for some years been, in Hell.

All around him lay other figures, huge and fungous. It was as if the plain had festered. Some of them could sit up, others scarcely protruded from the sand, and he knew that they had made the same mistake in life as himself, though he did not know yet what the mistake had been; probably some little slip, easily avoided had one but been told.

Speech was permissible. Presently a voice said, "Is not ours a heavenly sky? Is it not beautiful?"

"Most beautiful," answered Micky, and found each word a stab of pain. Then he knew that one of the sins here punished was appreciation; he was suffering for all the praise that he had given to the bad and mediocre upon earth; when he had praised out of idleness, or to please people, or to encourage people; for all the praise that had not been winged with passion. He repeated "Most beautiful," and the sky quivered, for he was entering into fuller torments now. One ray of happiness survived: his wife could not be in this place. She had not sinned with the people of the plain, and could not suffer their distortion. Her view of life had proved right after all; and, in his utter misery, this comforted him. Janet should again be his religion, and as eternity dragged forward and returned upon itself and dragged forward she would show him that old age, if rightly managed, can be beautiful; that experience, if rightly received, can lead the soul of man to bliss. Then he turned to his neighbour, who was continuing his hymn of praise.

"I could lie here for ever," he was saying. "When I think of my restlessness during life—that is to say, during what men miscall life, for it is death really—this is life—when

I think of my restlessness on earth, I am overcome by so much goodness and mercy, I could lie here for ever.

"And will you?" asked Micky.

"Ah, that is the crowning blessing—I shall, and so will you."

Here a pillar of sand passed between them. It was long before they could speak or see. Then Micky took up the song, chafed by the particles that were working into his soul.

"I, too, regret my wasted hours," he said, "especially the hours of my youth. I regret all the time I spent in the sun. In later years I did repent, and that is why I am admitted here where there is no sun; yes, and no wind and none of the stars that drove me almost mad at night once. It would be appalling, would it not, to see Orion again, the central star of whose sword is not a star but a nebula, the golden seed of worlds to be. How I dreaded the autumn on earth when Orion rises, for he recalled adventure and my youth. It was appalling. How thankful I am to see him no more." 60

"Ah, but it was worse," cried the other, "to look high leftward from Orion and see the Twins. Castor and Pollux were brothers, one human, the other divine; and Castor died. But Pollux went down to Hell that he might be with him."

"Yes; that is so. Pollux went into Hell."

"Then the gods had pity on both, and raised them aloft to be stars whom sailors worship, and all who love and are young. Zeus was their father, Helen their sister, who brought the Greeks against Troy. I dreaded them more than Orion."

They were silent, watching their own sky. It approved. They had been cultivated men on earth, and these are capable of the nicer torments hereafter. Their memories will strike exquisite images to enhance their pain. "I will speak no more," said Micky to himself. "I will be silent through eternity." But the darkness prised open his lips, and immediately he was speaking.

"Tell me more about this abode of bliss," he asked. "Are there grades in it? Are there ranks in our heaven?" 65

"There are two heavens," the other replied, "the heaven of the hard and of the soft. We here lie in the heaven of the soft. It is a sufficient arrangement, for all men grow either hard or soft as they grow old."

As he spoke the clouds lifted, and, looking up the slope of the plain, Micky saw that in the distance it was bounded by mountains of stone, and he knew, without being told, that among those mountains Janet lay, rigid, and that he should never see her. She had not been saved. The darkness would mock her, too, for ever. With him lay the sentimentalists, the conciliators, the peacemakers, the humanists, and all who have trusted the warmer vision; with his wife were the reformers and ascetics and all sword-like souls. By different paths they had come to Hell, and Micky now saw what the bustle of life conceals: that the years are bound either to liquefy a man or to stiffen him, and that Love and Truth, who seem to contend for our souls like angels, hold each the seeds of our decay.

"It is, indeed, a sufficient arrangement," he said; "both sufficient and simple. But answer one question more that my bliss may be perfected; in which of these two heavens are the young?"

His neighbour answered, "In neither; there are no young."

He spoke no more, and settled himself more deeply in the dust. Micky did the same. He had vague memories of men and women who had died before reaching maturity, of boys and unwedded maidens and youths lowered into the grave before their parents' eyes. Whither had they gone, that undeveloped minority? What was the point of their brief existence? Had they vanished utterly, or were they given another chance of accreting experiences until they became like Janet or himself? One thing was certain: there were no young, either in the mountains or the plain, and perhaps the very memory of such creatures was an illusion fostered by cloud.

The time was now ripe for a review of his life on earth. He traced his decomposition—his work had been soft, his books soft, he had softened his relations with other men. He had seen good in everything, and this is itself a sign of decay. Whatever occurred he had been appreciative, tolerant, pliant. Consequently he had been a success; Adam was right; it was the moment in civilization for his type. He had mistaken self-criticism for self-discipline, he had muffled in himself and others the keen, heroic edge. Yet the luxury of repentance was denied him. The fault was his, but the fate humanity's, for every one grows hard or soft as he grows old.

"This is my life," thought Micky; "my books forgotten, my work superseded. This is the whole of my life." And his agony increased, because all the same there had been in that life an elusive joy which, if only he could have distilled it, would have sweetened infinity. It was part of the jest that he should try, and should eternally oscillate between disgust and desire. For there is nothing ultimate in Hell; men will not lay aside all hope on entering it, or they would attain to the splendour of despair. To have made a poem about Hell is to mistake its very essence; it is the imagination of men, who will have beauty, that fashions it as ice or flame. Old, but capable of growing older, Micky lay in the sandy country, remembering that once he had remembered a country—a country that had not been sand. . . .

He was aroused by the mutterings of the spirits round him. An uneasiness such as he had not noted in them before had arisen. "A pillar of sand," said one. Another said, "It is not; it comes from the river."

He asked, "What river?"

"The spirits of the damned dwell over it; we never speak of that river."   75

"Is it a broad river?"

"Swift, and very broad."

"Do the damned ever cross it?"

"They are permitted, we know not why, to cross it now and again."

And in these answers he caught a new tone, as if his companions were frightened,   80
and were finding means to express their fear. When he said, "With permission, they can do us no harm," he was answered, "They harm us with light and a song." And again, "They harm us because they remember and try to remind."

"Of what would they remind us?"

"Of the hour when we were as they."

As he questioned a whisper arose from the low-lying verges. The spirits were crying to each other faintly. He heard, "It is coming; drive it back over the river, shatter it, compel it to be old." And then the darkness was cloven, and a star of pain broke in his soul. He understood now; a torment greater than any was at hand.

"I was before choice," came the song. "I was before hardness and softness were divided. I was in the days when truth was love. And I am."

All the plain was convulsed. But the invader could not be shattered. When it   85
pressed the air parted and the sand-pillars fell, and its path was filled with senile weeping.

"I have been all men, but all men have forgotten me. I transfigured the world for them until they preferred the world. They came to me as children, afraid; I taught them, and they despised me. Childhood is a dream about me, experience a slow forgetting: I govern the magic years between them, and am."

"Why trouble us?" moaned the shades. "We could bear our torment, just bear it, until there was light and a song. Go back again over the river. This is Heaven, we were saying, that darkness is God; we could praise them till you came. The book of our deeds is closed; why open it? We were damned from our birth; leave it there. Oh supreme jester, leave us. We have sinned, we know it, and this place is death and Hell."

"Death comes," the voice pealed, "and death is not a dream or a forgetting.° Death is real. But I, too, am real, and whom I will I save. I see the scheme of things, and in it no place for me, the brain and the body against me. Therefore I rend the scheme in two, and make a place, and under countless names have harrowed Hell. Come." Then, in tones of inexpressible sweetness, "Come to me all who remember. Come out of your eternity into mine. It is easy, for I am still at your eyes, waiting to look out of them; still in your hearts, waiting to beat. The years that I dwelt with you seemed short, but they were magical, and they outrun time."

The shades were silent. They could not remember.

"Who desires to remember? Desire is enough. There is no abiding home for strength and beauty among men.° The flower fades, the seas dry up in the sun, the sun and all the stars fade as a flower. But the desire for such things, that is eternal,° that can abide, and he who desires me is I."

Then Micky died a second death. This time he dissolved through terrible pain, scorched by the glare, pierced by the voice. But as he died he said, "I do desire," and immediately the invader vanished, and he was standing alone on the sandy plain. It had been merely a dream. But he was standing. How was that? Why had he not thought to stand before? He had been unhappy in Hell, and all that he had to do was to go elsewhere. He passed downwards, pained no longer by the mockery of its cloud. The pillars brushed against him and fell, the nether darkness went over his head. On he went till he came to the banks of the infernal stream, and there he stumbled—stumbled over a piece of wood, no vague substance, but a piece of wood that had once belonged to a tree. At his impact it moved, and water gurgled against it. He had embarked. Some one was rowing. He could see the blades of oars moving towards him through the foam, but the rower was invisible in cloud. As they neared mid-channel the boat went more slowly, for the tide was ebbing, and Micky knew that once carried out he would be lost eternally; there was no second hope of salvation. He could not speak, but his heart beat time to the oars—one, two. Hell made her last effort, and all that is evil in creation, all the distortions of love and truth by which we are vexed, came surging down the estuary, and the boat hung motionless. Micky heard the pant of breath through the roaring, the crack of angelic muscles; then he heard a voice say, "The point of it . . ." and a weight fell off his body and he crossed mid-stream.

It was a glorious evening. The boat had sped without prelude into sunshine. The sky was cloudless, the earth gold, and gulls were riding up and down on the furrowed waters. On the bank they had left were some sand-dunes rising to majestic hills; on the bank in front was a farm, full to the brim with fire.

90

. . . *forgetting:* Wordsworth, "Ode: Intimations of Immortality," stanza 5. See Chapter 25.
. . . *among men:* Hebrews 13:14.
. . . *eternal:* Isaiah 40:6–8.

CHARLOTTE PERKINS GILMAN (1860–1938)

Born in 1860, Gilman did not begin writing seriously until after the birth of her daughter in the 1880s, which was followed by her "nervous breakdown." Attempting to establish her own independence, she left her husband in 1890 and went to California, where she launched what was to become a distinguished career as an advocate for women's rights. For many decades she lectured and wrote extensively, her touchstone work being Women and Economics *(1898), in which she championed the need for women's financial independence. Among her many writings were* Concerning Children *(1900),* Human Work *(1904), and* His Religion and Hers *(1923). In the 1930s she became incurably ill, and with death facing her, she took her own life in 1938.*

The Yellow Wallpaper° _____ *1892*

It is very seldom that mere ordinary people like John and myself secure ancestral halls for the summer.

A colonial mansion, a hereditary estate, I would say a haunted house and reach the height of romantic felicity—but that would be asking too much of fate!

Still I will proudly declare that there is something queer about it.

Else, why should it be let so cheaply? And why have stood so long untenanted?

John laughs at me, of course, but one expects that.   5

John is practical in the extreme. He has no patience with faith, an intense horror of superstition, and he scoffs openly at any talk of things not to be felt and seen and put down in figures.

John is a physician, and *perhaps*—(I would not say it to a living soul, of course, but this is dead paper and a great relief to my mind)—*perhaps* that is one reason I do not get well faster.

You see, he does not believe I am sick! And what can one do?

If a physician of high standing, and one's own husband, assures friends and relatives that there is really nothing the matter with one but temporary nervous depression—a slight hysterical tendency—what is one to do?

My brother is also a physician, and also of high standing, and he says the same   10
thing.

So I take phosphates or phosphites—whichever it is—and tonics, and air and exercise, and journeys, and am absolutely forbidden to "work" until I am well again.

Personally, I disagree with their ideas.

Personally, I believe that congenial work, with excitement and change, would do me good.

The Yellow Wallpaper: The story is based on the "rest cure" developed after the Civil War by the famous Philadelphia physician S. Weir Mitchell (1829–1914); see paragraph 83. The Mitchell treatment required confining the patient to a hospital, hotel, or some other remote residence. Once isolated, the patient was to have complete bed rest, increased food intake, iron supplements, exercise, and sometimes massage and electric shock therapy. Gilman had experienced Mitchell's "cure," and sent a copy of this story to him as criticism. After receiving the story Mitchell modified his methods.

But what is one to do?

I did write for a while in spite of them; but it *does* exhaust me a good deal—having   15
to be so sly about it, or else meet with heavy opposition.

I sometimes fancy that in my condition, if I had less opposition and more society
and stimulus—but John says the very worst thing I can do is to think about my condition,
and I confess it always makes me feel bad.

So I will let it alone and talk about the house.

The most beautiful place! It is quite alone, standing well back from the road, quite
three miles from the village. It makes me think of English places that you read about, for
there are hedges and walls and gates that lock, and lots of separate little houses for the
gardeners and people.

There is a *delicious* garden! I never saw such a garden—large and shady, full of
box-bordered paths, and lined with long grape-covered arbors with seats under them.

There were greenhouses, but they are all broken now.   20

There was some legal trouble, I believe, something about the heirs and co-heirs;
anyhow, the place has been empty for years.

That spoils my ghostliness, I am afraid, but I don't care—there is something
strange about the house—I can feel it.

I even said so to John one moonlight evening, but he said what I felt was a
draught, and shut the window.

I get unreasonably angry with John sometimes. I'm sure I never used to be so sensitive. I think it is due to this nervous condition.

But John says if I feel so I shall neglect proper self-control; so I take pains to con-   25
trol myself—before him, at least, and that makes me very tired.

I don't like our room a bit. I wanted one downstairs that opened onto the
piazza and had roses all over the window, and such pretty old-fashioned chintz hangings! But John would not hear of it.

He said there was only one window and not room for two beds, and no near room
for him if he took another.

He is very careful and loving, and hardly lets me stir without special direction.

I have a schedule prescription for each hour in the day; he takes all care from me,
and so I feel basely ungrateful not to value it more.

He said he came here solely on my account, that I was to have perfect rest and all   3
the air I could get. "Your exercise depends on your strength, my dear," said he, "and
your food somewhat on your appetite; but air you can absorb all the time." So we took
the nursery at the top of the house.

It is a big, airy room, the whole floor nearly, with windows that look all ways, and
air and sunshine galore. It was nursery first, and then playroom and gymnasium, I
should judge, for the windows are barred for little children, and there are rings and
things in the walls.

The paint and paper look as if a boys' school had used it. It is stripped off—the
paper—in great patches all around the head of my bed, about as far as I can reach, and
in a great place on the other side of the room low down. I never saw a worse paper in my
life. One of those sprawling, flamboyant patterns committing every artistic sin.

It is dull enough to confuse the eye in following, pronounced enough constantly
to irritate and provoke study, and when you follow the lame uncertain curves for a little
distance they suddenly commit suicide—plunge off at outrageous angles, destroy themselves in unheard-of contradictions.

The color is repellent, almost revolting: a smouldering unclean yellow, strangely faded by the slow-turning sunlight. It is a dull yet lurid orange in some places, a sickly sulphur tint in others.

No wonder the children hated it! I should hate it myself if I had to live in this room long. 35

There comes John, and I must put this away—he hates to have me write a word.

We have been here two weeks, and I haven't felt like writing before, since that first day.

I am sitting by the window now, up in this atrocious nursery, and there is nothing to hinder my writing as much as I please, save lack of strength.

John is away all day, and even some nights when his cases are serious.

I am glad my case is not serious! 40

But these nervous troubles are dreadfully depressing.

John does not know how much I really suffer. He knows there is no reason to suffer, and that satisfies him.

Of course it is only nervousness. It does weigh on me so not to do my duty in any way!

I meant to be such a help to John, such a real rest and comfort, and here I am a comparative burden already!

Nobody would believe what an effort it is to do what little I am able—to dress and entertain, and order things. 45

It is fortunate Mary is so good with the baby. Such a dear baby!

And yet I *cannot* be with him, it makes me so nervous.

I suppose John never was nervous in his life. He laughs at me so about this wallpaper!

At first he meant to repaper the room, but afterward he said that I was letting it get the better of me, and that nothing was worse for a nervous patient than to give way to such fancies.

He said that after the wallpaper was changed it would be the heavy bedstead, and then the barred windows, and then that gate at the head of the stairs, and so on. 50

"You know the place is doing you good," he said, "and really, dear, I don't care to renovate the house just for a three months' rental."

"Then do let us go downstairs," I said. "There are such pretty rooms there."

Then he took me in his arms and called me a blessed little goose, and said he would go down cellar, if I wished, and have it whitewashed into the bargain.

But he is right enough about the beds and windows and things.

It is as airy and comfortable a room as anyone need wish, and, of course, I would not be so silly as to make him uncomfortable just for a whim. 55

I'm really getting quite fond of the big room, all but that horrid paper.

Out of one window I can see the garden—those mysterious deep-shaded arbors, the riotous old-fashioned flowers, and bushes and gnarly trees.

Out of another I get a lovely view of the bay and a little private wharf belonging to the estate. There is a beautiful shaded lane that runs down there from the house. I always fancy I see people walking in these numerous paths and arbors, but John has cautioned me not to give way to fancy in the least. He says that with my imaginative power and habit of story-making, a nervous weakness like mine is sure to lead to all manner of excited fancies, and that I ought to use my will and good sense to check the tendency. So I try.

I think sometimes that if I were only well enough to write a little it would relieve the press of ideas and rest me.

But I find I get pretty tired when I try.   60

It is so discouraging not to have any advice and companionship about my work. When I get really well, John says we will ask Cousin Henry and Julia down for a long visit; but he says he would as soon put fireworks in my pillow-case as to let me have those stimulating people about now.

I wish I could get well faster.

But I must not think about that. This paper looks to me as if it *knew* what a vicious influence it had!

There is a recurrent spot where the pattern lolls like a broken neck and two bulbous eyes stare at you upside down.

I get positively angry with the impertinence of it and the everlastingness. Up and   65
down and sideways they crawl, and those absurd unblinking eyes are everywhere. There is one place where two breadths didn't match, and the eyes go all up and down the line, one a little higher than the other.

I never saw so much expression in an inanimate thing before, and we all know how much expression they have! I used to lie awake as a child and get more entertainment and terror out of blank walls and plain furniture than most children could find in a toy-store.

I remember what a kindly wink the knobs of our big old bureau used to have, and there was one chair that always seemed like a strong friend.

I used to feel that if any of the other things looked too fierce I could always hop into that chair and be safe.

The furniture in this room is no worse than inharmonious, however, for we had to bring it all from downstairs. I suppose when this was used as a playroom they had to take the nursery things out, and no wonder! I never saw such ravages as the children have made here.

The wallpaper, as I said before, is torn off in spots, and it sticketh closer than a   7(
brother°—they must have had perseverance as well as hatred.

Then the floor is scratched and gouged and splintered, the plaster itself is dug out here and there, and this great heavy bed, which is all we found in the room, looks as if it had been through the wars.

But I don't mind it a bit—only the paper.

There comes John's sister. Such a dear girl as she is, and so careful of me! I must not let her find me writing.

She is a perfect and enthusiastic housekeeper, and hopes for no better profession. I verily believe she thinks it is the writing which made me sick!

But I can write when she is out, and see her a long way off from these windows.   7

There is one that commands the road, a lovely shaded winding road, and one that just looks off over the country. A lovely country, too, full of great elms and velvet meadows.

This wallpaper has a kind of sub-pattern in a different shade, a particularly irritating one, for you can only see it in certain lights, and not clearly then.

---

sticketh closer than a brother: Proverbs 18:24.

But in the places where it isn't faded and where the sun is just so—I can see a strange, provoking, formless sort of figure that seems to skulk about behind that silly and conspicuous front design.

There's sister on the stairs!

Well, the Fourth of July is over! The people are all gone, and I am tired out. John   80
thought it might do me good to see a little company, so we just had Mother and Nellie and the children down for a week.

Of course I didn't do a thing. Jennie sees to everything now.

But it tired me all the same.

John says if I don't pick up faster he shall send me to Weir Mitchell° in the fall.

But I don't want to go there at all. I had a friend who was in his hands once, and she says he is just like John and my brother, only more so!

Besides, it is such an undertaking to go so far.   85

I don't feel as if it was worthwhile to turn my hand over for anything, and I'm getting dreadfully fretful and querulous.

I cry at nothing, and cry most of the time.

Of course I don't when John is here, or anybody else, but when I am alone.

And I am alone a good deal just now. John is kept in town very often by serious cases, and Jennie is good and lets me alone when I want her to.

So I walk a little in the garden or down that lovely lane, sit on the porch under the   90
roses, and lie down up here a good deal.

I'm getting really fond of the room in spite of the wallpaper. Perhaps *because* of the wallpaper.

It dwells in my mind so!

I lie here on this great immovable bed—it is nailed down, I believe—and follow that pattern about by the hour. It is as good as gymnastics, I assure you. I start, we'll say, at the bottom, down in the corner over there where it has not been touched, and I determine for the thousandth time that I *will* follow that pointless pattern to some sort of a conclusion.

I know a little of the principle of design, and I know this thing was not arranged on any laws of radiation, or alternation, or repetition, or symmetry, or anything else that I ever heard of.

It is repeated, of course, by the breadths, but not otherwise.   95

Looked at in one way, each breadth stands alone; the bloated curves and flourishes—a kind of "debased Romanesque" with delirium tremens go waddling up and down in isolated columns of fatuity.

But, on the other hand, they connect diagonally, and the sprawling outlines run off in great slanting waves of optic horror, like a lot of wallowing sea-weeds in full chase.

The whole thing goes horizontally, too, at least it seems so, and I exhaust myself trying to distinguish the order of its going in that direction.

They have used a horizontal breadth for a frieze, and that adds wonderfully to the confusion.

There is one end of the room where it is almost intact, and there, when the   100
crosslights fade and the low sun shines directly upon it, I can almost fancy radiation after

Weir Mitchell: See note on page 617.

all—the interminable grotesque seems to form around a common center and rush off in headlong plunges of equal distraction.

It makes me tired to follow it. I will take a nap, I guess.

I don't know why I should write this.

I don't want to.

I don't feel able.

And I know John would think it absurd. But I *must* say what I feel and think in   105
some way—it is such a relief!

But the effort is getting to be greater than the relief.

Half the time now I am awfully lazy, and lie down ever so much. John says I mustn't lose my strength, and has me take cod liver oil and lots of tonics and things, to say nothing of ale and wine and rare meat.

Dear John! He loves me very dearly, and hates to have me sick. I tried to have a real earnest reasonable talk with him the other day, and tell him how I wish he would let me go and make a visit to Cousin Henry and Julia.

But he said I wasn't able to go, nor able to stand it after I got there; and I did not make out a very good case for myself, for I was crying before I had finished.

It is getting to be a great effort for me to think straight. Just this nervous weak-   110
ness, I suppose.

And dear John gathered me up in his arms, and just carried me upstairs and laid me on the bed, and sat by me and read to me till it tired my head.

He said I was his darling and his comfort and all he had, and that I must take care of myself for his sake, and keep well.

He says no one but myself can help me out of it, that I must use my will and self-control and not let any silly fancies run away with me.

There's one comfort—the baby is well and happy, and does not have to occupy this nursery with the horrid wallpaper.

If we had not used it, that blessed child would have! What a fortunate escape!   115
Why, I wouldn't have a child of mine, an impressionable little thing, live in such a room for worlds.

I never thought of it before, but it is lucky that John kept me here after all; I can stand it so much easier than a baby, you see.

Of course I never mention it to them any more—I am too wise—but I keep watch for it all the same.

There are things in that wallpaper that nobody knows about but me, or ever will.

Behind that outside pattern the dim shapes get clearer every day.

It is always the same shape, only very numerous.   120

And it is like a woman stooping down and creeping about behind that pattern. I don't like it a bit. I wonder—I begin to think—I wish John would take me away from here!

It is so hard to talk with John about my case, because he is so wise, and because he loves me so.

But I tried it last night.

It was moonlight. The moon shines in all around just as the sun does.

I hate to see it sometimes, it creeps so slowly, and always comes in by one window   125
or another.

John was asleep and I hated to waken him, so I kept still and watched the moonlight on that undulating wallpaper till I felt creepy.

The faint figure behind seemed to shake the pattern, just as if she wanted to get out.

I got up softly and went to feel and see if the paper *did* move, and when I came back John was awake.

"What is it, little girl?" he said. "Don't go walking about like that—you'll get cold."

I thought it was a good time to talk, so I told him that I really was not gaining 130
here, and that I wished he would take me away.

"Why, darling!" said he. "Our lease will be up in three weeks, and I can't see how to leave before.

"The repairs are not done at home, and I cannot possibly leave town just now. Of course, if you were in any danger, I could and would, but you really are better, dear, whether you can see it or not. I am a doctor, dear, and I know. You are gaining flesh and color, your appetite is better, I feel really much easier about you."

"I don't weigh a bit more," said I, "nor as much; and my appetite may be better in the evening when you are here but it is worse in the morning when you are away!"

"Bless her little heart!" said he with a big hug. "She shall be as sick as she pleases! But now let's improve the shining hours by going to sleep, and talk about it in the morning!"

"And you won't go away?" I asked gloomily. 135

"Why, how can I, dear? It is only three weeks more and then we will take a nice little trip of a few days while Jennie is getting the house ready. Really, dear, you are better!"

"Better in body perhaps—" I began, and stopped short, for he sat up straight and looked at me with such a stern, reproachful look that I could not say another word.

"My darling," said he, "I beg of you, for my sake and for our child's sake, as well as for your own, that you will never for one instant let that idea enter your mind! There is nothing so dangerous, so fascinating, to a temperament like yours. It is a false and foolish fancy. Can you not trust me as a physician when I tell you so?"

So of course I said no more on that score, and we went to sleep before long. He thought I was asleep first, but I wasn't, and lay there for hours trying to decide whether that front pattern and the back pattern really did move together or separately.

On a pattern like this, by daylight, there is a lack of sequence, a defiance of law, 140
that is a constant irritant to a normal mind.

The color is hideous enough, and unreliable enough, and infuriating enough, but the pattern is torturing.

You think you have mastered it, but just as you get well under way in following, it turns a back-somersault and there you are. It slaps you in the face, knocks you down, and tramples upon you. It is like a bad dream.

The outside pattern is a florid arabesque, reminding one of a fungus. If you can imagine a toadstool in joints, an interminable string of toadstools, budding and sprouting in endless convolutions—why, that is something like it.

That is, sometimes!

There is one marked peculiarity about this paper, a thing nobody seems to notice 145
but myself, and that is that it changes as the light changes.

When the sun shoots in through the east window—I always watch for that first long, straight ray—it changes so quickly than I never can quite believe it.

That is why I watch it always.

By moonlight—the moon shines in all night when there is a moon—I wouldn't know it was the same paper.

At night in any kind of light, in twilight, candlelight, lamplight, and worst of all by moonlight, it becomes bars! The outside pattern, I mean, and the woman behind it is as plain as can be.

I didn't realize for a long time what the thing was that showed behind, that dim   150
sub-pattern, but now I am quite sure it is a woman.

By daylight she is subdued, quiet. I fancy it is the pattern that keeps her so still. It is so puzzling. It keeps me quiet by the hour.

I lie down ever so much now. John says it is good for me, and to sleep all I can.

Indeed he started the habit by making me lie down for an hour after each meal.

It is a very bad habit, I am convinced, for you see, I don't sleep.

And that cultivates deceit, for I don't tell them I'm awake—oh, no!   155

The fact is I am getting a little afraid of John.

He seems very queer sometimes, and even Jennie has an inexplicable look.

It strikes me occasionally, just as a scientific hypothesis, that perhaps it is the paper!

I have watched John when he did not know I was looking, and come into the room suddenly on the most innocent excuses, and I've caught him several times *looking at the paper!* And Jennie too. I caught Jennie with her hand on it once.

She didn't know I was in the room, and when I asked her in a quiet, a very quiet   160
voice, with the most restrained manner possible, what she was doing with the paper, she turned around as if she had been caught stealing, and looked quite angry—asked me why I should frighten her so!

Then she said that the paper stained everything it touched, that she had found yellow smooches on all my clothes and John's and she wished we would be more careful!

Did not that sound innocent? But I know she was studying that pattern, and I am determined that nobody shall find it out but myself.

Life is very much more exciting now than it used to be. You see, I have something more to expect, to look forward to, to watch. I really do eat better, and am more quiet than I was.

John is so pleased to see me improve! He laughed a little the other day, and said I seemed to be flourishing in spite of my wallpaper.

I turned it off with a laugh. I had no intention of telling him it was *because* of the   16
wallpaper—he would make fun of me. He might even want to take me away.

I don't want to leave now until I have found it out. There is a week more, and I think that will be enough.

I'm feeling so much better!

I don't sleep much at night, for it is so interesting to watch developments; but sleep a good deal during the daytime.

In the daytime it is tiresome and perplexing.

There are always new shoots on the fungus, and new shades of yellow all over it. I   1
cannot keep count of them, though I have tried conscientiously.

It is the strangest yellow, that wallpaper! It makes me think of all the yellow things I ever saw—not beautiful ones like buttercups, but old, foul, bad yellow things.

But there is something else about that paper—the smell! I noticed it the moment we came into the room, but with so much air and sun it was not bad. Now we have had a week of fog and rain, and whether the windows are open or not, the smell is here.

It creeps all over the house.

I find it hovering in the dining-room, skulking in the parlor, hiding in the hall, lying in wait for me on the stairs.

It gets into my hair.   175

Even when I go to ride, if I turn my head suddenly and surprise it—there is that smell!

Such a peculiar odor, too! I have spent hours in trying to analyze it, to find what it smelled like.

It is not bad—at first—and very gentle, but quite the subtlest, most enduring odor I ever met.

In this damp weather it is awful. I wake up in the night and find it hanging over me.

It used to disturb me at first. I thought seriously of burning the house—to reach   180
the smell.

But now I am used to it. The only thing I can think of that it is like is the *color* of the paper! A yellow smell.

There is a very funny mark on this wall, low down, near the mopboard. A streak that runs round the room. It goes behind every piece of furniture, except the bed, a long, straight, even *smooch*, as if it had been rubbed over and over.

I wonder how it was done and who did it, and what they did it for. Round and round and round—round and round and round—it makes me dizzy!

I really have discovered something at last.

Through watching so much at night, when it changes so, I have finally found   185
out.

The front pattern *does* move—and no wonder! The woman behind shakes it!

Sometimes I think there are a great many women behind, and sometimes only one, and she crawls around fast, and her crawling shakes it all over.

Then in the very bright spots she keeps still, and in the very shady spots she just takes hold of the bars and shakes them hard.

And she is all the time trying to climb through. But nobody could climb through that pattern—it strangles so; I think that is why it has so many heads.

They get through and then the pattern strangles them off and turns them upside   190
down, and makes their eyes white!

If those heads were covered or taken off it would not be half so bad.

I think that woman gets out in the daytime!

And I'll tell you why—privately—I've seen her!

I can see her out of every one of my windows!

It is the same woman, I know, for she is always creeping, and most women do not   195
creep by daylight.

I see her in that long shaded lane, creeping up and down. I see her in those dark grape arbors, creeping all around the garden.

I see her on that long road under the trees, creeping along, and when a carriage comes she hides under the blackberry vines.

I don't blame her a bit. It must be very humiliating to be caught creeping by daylight!

I always lock the door when I creep by daylight. I can't do it at night, for I know John would suspect something at once.

And John is so queer now that I don't want to irritate him. I wish he would take   200
another room! Besides, I don't want anybody to get that woman out at night but myself.

I often wonder if I could see her out of all the windows at once.

But, turn as fast as I can, I can only see out of one at a time.

And though I always see her, she *may* be able to creep faster than I can turn! I have watched her sometimes away off in the open country, creeping as fast as a cloud shadow in a wind.

If only that top pattern could be gotten off from the under one! I mean to try it, little by little.

I have found out another funny thing, but I shan't tell it this time! It does not do   205
to trust people too much.

There are only two more days to get this paper off, and I believe John is beginning to notice. I don't like the look in his eyes.

And I heard him ask Jennie a lot of professional questions about me. She had a very good report to give.

She said I slept a good deal in the daytime.

John knows I don't sleep very well at night, for all I'm so quiet!

He asked me all sorts of questions, too, and pretended to be very loving and kind.   210
As if I couldn't see through him!

Still, I don't wonder he acts so, sleeping under this paper for three months.

It only interests me, but I feel sure John and Jennie are affected by it.

Hurrah! This is the last day, but it is enough. John is to stay in town over night, and won't be out until this evening.

Jennie wanted to sleep with me—the sly thing; but I told her I should undoubt-   215
edly rest better for a night all alone.

That was clever, for really I wasn't alone a bit! As soon as it was moonlight and that poor thing began to crawl and shake the pattern, I got up and ran to help her.

I pulled and she shook. I shook and she pulled, and before morning we had peeled off yards of that paper.

A strip about as high as my head and half around the room.

And then when the sun came and that awful pattern began to laugh at me, I declared I would finish it today!

We go away tomorrow, and they are moving all my furniture down again to leave   22●
things as they were before.

Jennie looked at the wall in amazement, but I told her merrily that I did it out of pure spite at the vicious thing.

She laughed and said she wouldn't mind doing it herself, but I must not get tired.

How she betrayed herself that time!

But I am here, and no person touches this paper but Me—not *alive!*

She tried to get me out of the room—it was too patent! But I said it was so quiet   22
and empty and clean now that I believed I would lie down again and sleep all I could, and not to wake me even for dinner—I would call when I woke.

So now she is gone, and the servants are gone, and the things are gone, and there is nothing left but that great bedstead nailed down, with the canvas mattress we found on it.

We shall sleep downstairs tonight, and take the boat home tomorrow.

I quite enjoy the room, now it is bare again.

How those children did tear about here!

This bedstead is fairly gnawed!

But I must get to work.

I have locked the door and thrown the key down into the front path.

I don't want to go out, and I don't want to have anybody come in, till John comes.

I want to astonish him.

I've got a rope up here that even Jennie did not find. If that woman does get out, and tries to get away, I can tie her!

235

But I forgot I could not reach far without anything to stand on!

This bed will *not* move!

I tried to lift and push it until I was lame, and then I got so angry I bit off a little piece at one corner—but it hurt my teeth.

Then I peeled off all the paper I could reach standing on the floor. It sticks horribly and the pattern just enjoys it! All those strangled heads and bulbous eyes and waddling fungus growths just shriek with derision!

I am getting angry enough to do something desperate. To jump out of the window would be admirable exercise, but the bars are too strong even to try.

240

Besides I wouldn't do it. Of course not. I know well enough that a step like that is improper and might be misconstrued.

I don't like to *look* out of the windows even—there are so many of those creeping women, and they creep so fast.

I wonder if they all came out of that wallpaper as I did?

But I am securely fastened now by my well-hidden rope—you don't get *me* out in the road there!

I suppose I shall have to get back behind the pattern when it comes night, and that is hard!

245

It is so pleasant to be out in this great room and creep around as I please!

I don't want to go outside. I won't, even if Jennie asks me to.

For outside you have to creep on the ground, and everything is green instead of yellow.

But here I can creep smoothly on the floor, and my shoulder just fits in that long smooch around the wall, so I cannot lose my way.

Why, there's John at the door!

250

It is no use, young man, you can't open it!

How he does call and pound!

Now he's crying to Jennie for an axe.

It would be a shame to break down that beautiful door!

"John, dear!" said I in the gentlest voice. "The key is down by the front steps, under a plantain leaf!"

255

That silenced him for a few moments.

Then he said, very quietly indeed, "Open the door, my darling!"

"I can't," said I. "The key is down by the front door under a plantain leaf!" And then I said it again, several times, very gently and slowly, and said it so often that he had to go and see, and he got it of course, and came in. He stopped short by the door.

"What is the matter?" he cried. "For God's sake, what are you doing!"

I kept on creeping just the same, but I looked at him over my shoulder.

260

"I've got out at last," said I, "in spite of you and Jane. And I've pulled off most of the paper, so you can't put me back!"

Now why should that man have fainted? But he did, and right across my path by the wall, so that I had to creep over him every time!

DORIS LESSING   (b. 1919)

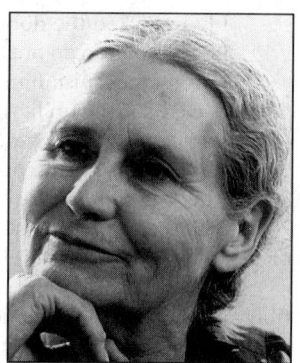

> Doris Lessing—née Taylor—was born in Persia, and at the age of five went with her family to Southern Rhodesia, where she grew up. She took a number of non-literary jobs after leaving school when she was fifteen, and in 1949 she went to England to take up the writer's craft. Her best-known novel is The Golden Notebook (1962), and she has written many stories and novels since then. "The Old Chief Mshlanga" is from That Was the Old Chief's Country (1951), a part of her African stories, and it reflects her early career as a writer.

The Old Chief Mshlanga ————————————————— 1951

They were good, the years of ranging the bush over her father's farm which, like every white farm, was largely unused, broken only occasionally by small patches of cultivation. In between, nothing but trees, the long sparse grass, thorn and cactus and gully, grass and outcrop and thorn. And a jutting piece of rock which had been thrust up from the warm soil of Africa unimaginable eras of time ago, washed into hollows and whorls by sun and wind that had travelled so many thousands of miles of space and bush, would hold the weight of a small girl whose eyes were sightless for anything but a pale willowed river, a pale gleaming castle—a small girl singing: "Out flew the web and floated wide, the mirror cracked from side to side . . ."

Pushing her way through the green aisles of the mealie° stalks, the leaves arching like cathedrals veined with sunlight far overhead, with the packed red earth underfoot, a fine lace of red starred witchweed would summon up a black bent figure croaking premonitions: the Northern witch, bred of cold Northern forests, would stand before her among the mealie fields, and it was the mealie fields that faded and fled, leaving her among the gnarled roots of an oak, snow falling thick and soft and white, the wood-cutter's fire glowing red welcome through crowding tree trunks.

A white child, opening its eyes curiously on a sun-suffused landscape, a gaunt and violent landscape, might be supposed to accept it as her own, to take the msasa trees and the thorn trees as familiars, to feel her blood running free and responsive to the swing of the seasons.

This child could not see a msasa tree, or the thorn, for what they were. Her books held tales of alien fairies, her rivers ran slow and peaceful, and she knew the shape of the leaves of an ash or an oak, the names of the little creatures that lived in English streams, when the words "the veld"° meant strangeness, though she could remember nothing else.

Because of this, for many years, it was the veld that seemed unreal; the sun was a foreign sun, and the wind spoke a strange language.

The black people on the farm were as remote as the trees and the rocks. They were an amorphous black mass, mingling and thinning and massing like tadpoles, face-less, who existed merely to serve, to say "Yes, Baas,"° take their money and go. They

mealie: a word for corn in Southern Africa.
veld: also *veldt,* a vast open grass-covered area used for grazing.
Baas: boss.

changed season by season, moving from one farm to the next, according to their out-landish needs, which one did not have to understand, coming from perhaps hundreds of miles North or East, passing on after a few months—where? Perhaps even as far away as the fabled gold mines of Johannesburg, where the pay was so much better than the few shillings a month and the double handful of mealie meal twice a day which they earned in that part of Africa.

The child was taught to take them for granted: the servants in the house would come running a hundred yards to pick up a book if she dropped it. She was called "Nkosikaas"—Chieftainess, even by the black children her own age.

Later, when the farm grew too small to hold her curiosity, she carried a gun in the crook of her arm and wandered miles a day, from vlei° to vlei, from *kopje* to *kopje*,° accompanied by two dogs: the dogs and the gun were an armour against fear. Because of them she never felt fear.

If a native came into sight along the kaffir° paths half a mile away, the dogs would flush him up a tree as if he were a bird. If he expostulated (in his uncouth language which was by itself ridiculous) that was cheek. If one was in a good mood, it could be a matter for laughter. Otherwise one passed on, hardly glancing at the angry man in the tree.

On the rare occasions when white children met together they could amuse them- 10
selves by hailing a passing native in order to make a buffoon of him; they could set the dogs on him and watch him run; they could tease a small black child as if he were a puppy—save that they would not throw stones and sticks at a dog without a sense of guilt.

Later still, certain questions presented themselves in the child's mind: and because the answers were not easy to accept, they were silenced by an even greater arrogance of manner.

It was even impossible to think of the black people who worked about the house as friends, for if she talked to one of them, her mother would come running anxiously: "Come away; you mustn't talk to natives."

It was this instilled consciousness of danger, of something unpleasant, that made it easy to laugh out loud, crudely, if a servant made a mistake in his English or if he failed to understand an order—there is a certain kind of laughter that is fear, afraid of itself.

One evening, when I was about fourteen, I was walking down the side of a mealie field that had been newly ploughed, so that the great red clods showed fresh and tumbling to the vlei beyond, like a choppy red sea; it was that hushed and listening hour, when the birds send long sad calls from tree to tree, and all the colours of earth and sky and leaf are deep and golden. I had my rifle in the curve of my arm, and the dogs were at my heels.

In front of me, perhaps a couple of hundred yards away, a group of three Africans 15
came into sight around the side of a big antheap. I whistled the dogs close in to my skirts and let the gun swing in my hand, and advanced, waiting for them to move aside, off the path, in respect for my passing. But they came on steadily, and the dogs looked up at me for the command to chase. I was angry. It was "cheek" for a native not to stand off a path, the moment he caught sight of you.

---

vlei: a slough or pond (valley).
kopje: a small hill covered with vegetation and rocks. Usually pronounced "copy."
kaffir: pejorative word for the various Bantu peoples and their languages.

In front walked an old man, stooping his weight on to a stick, his hair grizzled white, a dark red blanket slung over his shoulders like a cloak. Behind him came two young men, carrying bundles of pots, assegais, hatchets.

The group was not a usual one. They were not natives seeking work. These had an air of dignity, of quietly following their own purpose. It was the dignity that checked my tongue. I walked quietly on, talking softly to the growling dogs, till I was ten paces away. Then the old man stopped, drawing his blanket close.

"Morning, Nkosikaas," he said, using the customary greeting for any time of the day.

"Good morning," I said. "Where are you going?" My voice was a little truculent.

The old man spoke in his own language, then one of the young men stepped for- 20
ward politely and said in careful English: "My Chief travels to see his brothers beyond the river."

A Chief! I thought, understanding the pride that made the old man stand before me like an equal—more than an equal, for he showed courtesy, and I showed none.

The old man spoke again, wearing dignity like an inherited garment, still standing ten paces off, flanked by his entourage, not looking at me (that would have been rude) but directing his eyes somewhere over my head at the trees.

"You are the little Nkosikaas from the farm of Baas Jordan?"

"That's right," I said.

"Perhaps your father does not remember," said the interpreter for the old man, 25
"but there was an affair with some goats. I remember seeing you when you were . . ." The young man held his hand at knee level and smiled.

We all smiled.

"What is your name?" I asked.

"This is Chief Mshlanga," said the young man.

"I will tell my father that I met you," I said.

The old man said: "My greetings to your father, little Nkosikaas." 3

"Good morning," I said politely, finding the politeness difficult, from lack of use.

"Morning, little Nkosikaas," said the old man, and stood aside to let me pass.

I went by, my gun hanging awkwardly, the dogs sniffing and growling, cheated of their favorite game of chasing natives like animals.

Not long afterwards I read in an old explorer's book the phrase: "Chief Mshlanga's country." It went like this: "Our destination was Chief Mshlanga's country, to the north of the river; and it was our desire to ask his permission to prospect for gold in his territory."

The phrase "ask his permission" was so extraordinary to a white child, brought up ⋮
to consider all natives as things to use, that it revived those questions, which could not be suppressed: they fermented slowly in my mind.

On another occasion one of those old prospectors who still move over Africa look-ing for neglected reefs, with their hammers and tents, and pans for sifting gold from crushed rock, came to the farm and, in talking of the old days, used that phrase again: "This was the Old Chief's country," he said. "It stretched from those mountains over there way back to the river, hundreds of miles of country." That was his name for our dis-trict: "The Old Chief's Country"; he did not use our name for it—a new phrase which held no implication of usurped ownership.

As I read more books about the time when this part of Africa was opened up, not much more than fifty years before, I found Old Chief Mshlanga had been a famous man, known to all the explorers and prospectors. But then he had been young: or maybe it was his father or uncle they spoke of—I never found out.

During that year I met him several times in the part of the farm that was traversed by natives moving over the country. I learned that the path up the side of the big red field where the birds sang was the recognized highway for migrants. Perhaps I even haunted it in the hope of meeting him: being greeted by him, the exchange of courtesies, seemed to answer the questions that troubled me.

Soon I carried a gun in a different spirit; I used it for shooting food and not to give me confidence. And now the dogs learned better manners. When I saw a native approaching, we offered and took greetings; and slowly that other landscape in my mind faded, and my feet struck directly on the African soil, and I saw the shapes of tree and hill clearly, and the black people moved back, as it were, out of my life: it was as if I stood aside to watch a low intimate dance of landscape and men, a very old dance, whose steps I could not learn.

But I thought: this is my heritage, too; I was bred here; it is my country as well as the black man's country; and there is plenty of room for all of us, without elbowing each other off the pavements and roads.   40

It seemed it was only necessary to let free that respect I felt when I was talking with old Chief Mshlanga, to let both black and white people meet gently, with tolerance for each other's differences: it seemed quite easy.

Then, one day, something new happened. Working in our house as servants were always three natives: cook, houseboy, garden boy. They used to change as the farm natives changed: staying for a few months then moving on to a new job, or back home to their kraals.° They were thought of as "good" or "bad" natives; which meant: how did they behave as servants? Were they lazy, efficient, obedient, or disrespectful? If the family felt good-humoured, the phrase was: "What can you expect from raw black savages?" If we were angry, we said: "These damned niggers, we would be much better off without them."

One day, a white policeman was on his rounds of the district, and he said laughingly: "Did you know you have an important man in your kitchen?"

"What!" exclaimed my mother sharply. "What do you mean?"

"A Chief's son." The policeman seemed amused. "He'll boss the tribe when the   45
old man dies."

"He'd better not put on a Chief's son act with me," said my mother.

When the policeman left, we looked with different eyes at our cook: he was a good worker, but he drank too much at week-ends—that was how we knew him.

He was a tall youth, with very black skin, like black polished metal, his tightly-growing black hair parted white man's fashion at one side, with a metal comb from the store stuck into it; very polite, very distant, very quick to obey an order. Now that it had been pointed out, we said: "Of course, you can see. Blood always tells."

My mother became strict with him now she knew about his birth and prospects. Sometimes, when she lost her temper, she would say: "You aren't the Chief yet, you know." And he would answer her very quietly, his eyes on the ground: "Yes, Nkosikaas."

One afternoon he asked for a whole day off, instead of the customary half-day, to   50
go home next Sunday.

"How can you go home in one day?"

"It will take me half an hour on my bicycle," he explained.

I watched the direction he took; and the next day I went off to look for this kraal; I understood he must be Chief Mshlanga's successor: there was no other kraal near enough our farm.

kraals: fenced-in native villages.

Beyond our boundaries on that side the country was new to me. I followed unfamiliar paths past *kopjes* that till now had been part of the jagged horizon, hazed with distance. This was Government land, which had never been cultivated by white men; at first I could not understand why it was that it appeared, in merely crossing the boundary, I had entered a completely fresh type of landscape. It was a wide green valley, where a small river sparkled, and vivid water-birds darted over the rushes. The grass was thick and soft to my calves, the trees stood tall and shapely.

I was used to our farm, whose hundreds of acres of harsh eroded soil bore trees   55
that had been cut for the mine furnaces and had grown thin and twisted, where the cattle had dragged the grass flat, leaving innumerable criss-crossing trails that deepened each season into gullies, under the force of the rains.

This country had been left untouched, save for prospectors whose picks had struck a few sparks from the surface of the rocks as they wandered by; and for migrant natives whose passing had left, perhaps, a charred patch on the trunk of a tree where their evening fire had nestled.

It was very silent: a hot morning with pigeons cooing throatily, the midday shadows lying dense and thick with clear yellow spaces of sunlight between and in all that wide green park-like valley, not a human soul but myself.

I was listening to the quick regular tapping of a woodpecker when slowly a chill feeling seemed to grow up from the small of my back to my shoulders, in a constricting spasm like a shudder, and at the roots of my hair a tingling sensation began and ran down over the surface of my flesh, leaving me goosefleshed and cold, though I was damp with sweat. Fever? I thought; then uneasily, turned to look over my shoulder; and realized suddenly that this was fear. It was extraordinary, even humiliating. It was a new fear. For all the years I had walked by myself over this country I had never known a moment's uneasiness; in the beginning because I had been supported by a gun and the dogs, then because I had learnt an easy friendliness for the Africans I might encounter.

I had read of this feeling, how the bigness and silence of Africa, under the ancient sun, grows dense and takes shape in the mind, till even the birds seem to call menacingly, and a deadly spirit comes out of the trees and the rocks. You move warily, as if your very passing disturbs something old and evil, something dark and big and angry that might suddenly rear and strike from behind. You look at groves of entwined trees, and picture the animals that might be lurking there; you look at the river running slowly, dropping from level to level through the vlei, spreading into pools where at night the bucks come to drink, and the crocodiles rise and drag them by their soft noses into underwater caves. Fear possessed me. I found I was turning round and round, because of that shapeless menace behind me that might reach out and take me; I kept glancing at the files of *kopjes* which, seen from a different angle, seemed to change with every step so that even known landmarks, like a big mountain that had sentinelled my world since I first became conscious of it, showed an unfamiliar sunlit valley among its foothills. I did not know where I was. I was lost. Panic seized me. I found I was spinning round and round, staring anxiously at this tree and that, peering up at the sun which appeared to have moved into an eastern slant, shedding the sad yellow light of sunset. Hours must have passed! I looked at my watch and found that this state of meaningless terror had lasted perhaps ten minutes.

The point was that it was meaningless. I was not ten miles from home: I had only to take my way back along the valley to find myself at the fence; away among the foothills of the *kopjes* gleamed the roof of a neighbor's house, and a couple of hours' walking would reach it. This was the sort of fear that contracts the flesh of a dog at night and sets him howling at the full moon. It had nothing to do with what I thought or felt; and I was more disturbed by the fact that I could become its victim than of the physical sensation itself: I walked steadily on, quietened, in a divided mind, watching my own pricking nerves and apprehensive glances from side to side with a disgusted amusement. Deliberately I set myself to think of this village I was seeking, and what I should do when I entered it—if I could find it, which was doubtful, since I was walking aimlessly and it might be anywhere in the hundreds of thousands of acres of bush that stretched about me. With my mind on that village, I realized that a new sensation was added to the fear: loneliness. Now such a terror of isolation invaded me that I could hardly walk; and if it were not that I came over the crest of a small rise and saw a village below me, I should have turned and gone home. It was a cluster of thatched huts in a clearing among trees. There were neat patches of mealies and pumpkins and millet, and cattle grazed under some trees at a distance. Fowls scratched among the huts, dogs lay sleeping on the grass, and goats friezed a *kopje* that jutted up beyond a tributary of the river lying like an enclosing arm round the village.

As I came close I saw the huts were lovingly decorated with patterns of yellow and red and ochre mud on the walls; and the thatch was tied in place with plaits of straw.

This was not at all like our farm compound, a dirty and neglected place, a temporary home for migrants who had no roots in it.

And now I did not know what to do next. I called a small black boy, who was sitting on a lot playing a stringed gourd, quite naked except for the strings of blue beads round his neck, and said: "Tell the Chief I am here." The child stuck his thumb in his mouth and stared shyly back at me.

For minutes I shifted my feet on the edge of what seemed a deserted village, till at last the child scuttled off, and then some women came. They were draped in bright cloths, with brass glinting in their ears and on their arms. They also stared, silently; then turned to chatter among themselves.

I said again: "Can I see Chief Mshlanga?" I saw they caught the name: they did not understand what I wanted. I did not understand myself.

At last I walked through them and came past the huts and saw a clearing under a big shady tree, where a dozen old men sat cross-legged on the ground, talking. Chief Mshlanga was leaning back against the tree, holding a gourd in his hand, from which he had been drinking. When he saw me, not a muscle of his face moved, and I could see he was not pleased: perhaps he was afflicted with my own shyness, due to being unable to find the right forms of courtesy for the occasion. To meet me, on our own farm, was one thing; but I should not have come here. What had I expected? I could not join them socially: the thing was unheard of. Bad enough that I, a white girl, should be walking the veld alone as a white man might: and in this part of the bush where only Government officials had the right to move.

Again I stood, smiling foolishly, while behind me stood the groups of brightly clad, chattering women, their faces alert with curiosity and interest, and in front of me sat the old men, with old lined faces, their eyes guarded, aloof. It was a village of ancients and children and women. Even the two young men who kneeled beside the Chief were not those I had seen with him previously: the young men were all away working on the white men's farms and mines, and the Chief must depend on relatives who were temporarily on holiday for his attendants.

"The small white Nkosikaas is far from home," remarked the old man at last.

"Yes," I agreed, "it is far." I wanted to say: "I have come to pay you a friendly visit, Chief Mshlanga." I could not say it. I might now be feeling an urgent helpless desire to get to know these men and women as people, to be accepted by them as a friend, but the truth was I had set out in a spirit of curiosity: I had wanted to see the village that our

65

cook, the reserved and obedient young man who got drunk on Sundays, would one day rule over.

"The child of Nkosi Jordan is welcome," said Chief Mshlanga.   70

"Thank you," I said, and could think of nothing more to say. There was a silence, while the flies rose and began to buzz around my head: and the wind shook a little in the thick green tree that spread its branches over the old men.

"Good morning," I said at last. "I have to return now to my home."

"Morning, little Nkosikaas," said Chief Mshlanga.

I walked away from the indifferent village, over the rise past the staring amber-eyed goats, down through the tall stately trees into the great rich green valley where the river meandered and the pigeons cooed tales of plenty and the woodpecker tapped softly.

The fear was gone; the loneliness had set into stiff-necked stoicism; there was now   75
a queer hostility in the landscape, a cold, hard, sullen indomitability that walked with me, as strong as a wall, as intangible as smoke; it seemed to say to me: you walk here as a destroyer. I went slowly homewards, with an empty heart: I had learned that if one cannot call a country to heel like a dog, neither can one dismiss the past with a smile in an easy gush of feeling, saying: I could not help it, I am also a victim.

I only saw Chief Mshlanga once again.

One night my father's big red land was trampled down by small sharp hooves, and it was discovered that the culprits were goats from Chief Mshlanga's kraal. This had happened once before, years ago.

My father confiscated all the goats. Then he sent a message to the old Chief that if he wanted them he would have to pay for the damage.

He arrived at our house at the time of sunset one evening, looking very old and bent now, walking stiffly under his regally draped blanket, leaning on a big stick. My father sat himself down in his big chair below the steps of the house; the old man squatted carefully on the ground before him, flanked by his two young men.

The palaver was long and painful, because of the bad English of the young man   80
who interpreted, and because my father could not speak dialect, but only kitchen kaffir.

From my father's point of view, at least two hundred pounds' worth of damage had been done to the crop. He knew he could not get the money from the old man. He felt he was entitled to keep the goats. As for the old Chief, he kept repeating angrily: "Twenty goats! My people cannot lose twenty goats! We are not rich; like the Nkosi Jordan, to lose twenty goats at once."

My father did not think of himself as rich, but rather as very poor. He spoke quickly and angrily in return, saying that the damage done meant a great deal to him, and that he was entitled to the goats.

At last it grew so heated that the cook, the Chief's son, was called from the kitchen to be interpreter, and now my father spoke fluently in English, and our cook translated rapidly so that the old man could understand how very angry my father was. The young man spoke without emotion, in a mechanical way, his eyes lowered, but showing how he felt his position by a hostile uncomfortable set of the shoulders.

It was now in the late sunset, the sky a welter of colours, the birds singing their last songs, and the cattle, lowing peacefully, moving past us towards their sheds for the night. It was the hour when Africa is most beautiful; and here was this pathetic, ugly scene, doing no one any good.

At last my father stated finally: "I'm not going to argue about it. I am keeping the   8
goats."

The old Chief flashed back in his own language: "That means that my people will go hungry when the dry season comes."

"Go to the police, then," said my father, and looked triumphant.

There was, of course, no more to be said.

The old man sat silent, his head bent, his hands dangling helplessly over his withered knees. Then he rose, the young men helping him, and he stood facing my father. He spoke once again, very stiffly; and turned away and went home to his village.

"What did he say?" asked my father of the young man, who laughed uncomfortably and would not meet his eyes. 90

"What did he say?" insisted my father.

Our cook stood straight and silent, his brows knotted together. Then he spoke. "My father says: All this land, this land you call yours, is his land, and belongs to our people."

Having made this statement, he walked off into the bush after his father, and we did not see him again.

Our next cook was a migrant from Nyasaland, with no expectations of greatness.

Next time the policeman came on his rounds he was told this story. He remarked: 95 "That kraal has no right to be there; it should have been moved long ago. I don't know why no one has done anything about it. I'll have a chat with the Native Commissioner next week. I'm going over for tennis on Sunday, anyway."

Some time later we heard that Chief Mshlanga and his people had been moved two hundred miles east, to a proper Native Reserve; the Government land was going to be opened up for white settlement soon.

I went to see the village again, about a year afterwards. There was nothing there. Mounds of red mud, where the huts had been, had long swathes of rotting thatch over them, veined with the red galleries of the white ants. The pumpkin vines rioted everywhere, over the bushes, up the lower branches of trees so that the great golden balls rolled underfoot and dangled overhead: it was a festival of pumpkins. The bushes were crowding up, the new grass sprang vivid green.

The settler lucky enough to be allotted the lush warm valley (if he chose to cultivate this particular section) would find, suddenly, in the middle of a mealie field, the plants were growing fifteen feet tall, the weight of the cobs dragging at the stalks, and wonder what unsuspected vein of richness he had struck.

FLANNERY O'CONNOR   (1925–1964)

Mary Flannery O'Connor, a Georgia native, graduated from the Women's College of Georgia and received a master of fine arts degree from the University of Iowa in 1947. She contracted lupus, a disorder of the immune system, and was an invalid for the last ten years of her life. Despite her illness, she wrote extensively, publishing two novels and many short stories. Her first collection was A Good Man Is Hard to Find, *in 1955. A posthumous collection,* Everything That Rises Must Converge, *was published in 1965, and* Complete Stories *appeared in 1971. Her works combine flat realism with grotesque situations; violence occurs without apparent reason or preparation. Many of her characters*

are odd, eccentric, and bizarre. Others, such as the Misfit in "A Good Man Is Hard to Find," are gratuitously cruel. Ironically, however, their cold and depraved actions highlight the need for religious awakening because they enable some of the characters, such as the grandmother in the following story, to achieve spiritual elevation.

A Good Man Is Hard to Find _____ 1955

The grandmother didn't want to go to Florida. She wanted to visit some of her connections in east Tennessee and she was seizing at every chance to change Bailey's mind.
Bailey was the son she lived with, her only son. He was sitting on the edge of his chair at
the table, bent over the orange sports section of the *Journal.* "Now look here, Bailey,"
she said, "see here, read this," and she stood with one hand on her thin hip and the
other rattling the newspaper at his bald head. "Here this fellow that calls himself The
Misfit is aloose from the Federal Pen and headed toward Florida and you read here
what it says he did to these people. Just you read it. I wouldn't take my children in any
direction with a criminal like that aloose in it. I couldn't answer to my conscience if
I did."

Bailey didn't look up from his reading so she wheeled around then and faced
the children's mother, a young woman in slacks, whose face was as broad and innocent
as a cabbage and was tied round with a green head-kerchief that had two points on the
top like rabbit's ears. She was sitting on the sofa, feeding the baby his apricots out of a
jar. "The children have been to Florida before," the old lady said. "You all ought to
take them somewhere else for a change so they would see different parts of the world
and be broad. They never have been to east Tennessee."

The children's mother didn't seem to hear her but the eight-year-old boy, John
Wesley, a stocky child with glasses, said, "If you don't want to go to Florida, why dontcha
stay at home?" He and the little girl, June Star, were reading the funny papers on the
floor.

"She wouldn't stay at home to be queen for a day," June Star said without raising
her yellow head.

"Yes and what would you do if this fellow, The Misfit, caught you?" the grandmother asked.

"I'd smack his face," John Wesley said.

"She wouldn't stay at home for a million bucks," June Star said. "Afraid she'd
miss something. She has to go everywhere we go."

"All right, Miss," the grandmother said. "Just remember that the next time you
want me to curl your hair."

June Star said her hair was naturally curly.

The next morning the grandmother was the first one in the car, ready to go. She
had her big black valise that looked like the head of a hippopotamus in one corner,
and underneath it she was hiding a basket with Pitty Sing, the cat, in it. She
didn't intend for the cat to be left alone in the house for three days because he would
miss her too much and she was afraid he might brush against one of the gas burners
and accidentally asphyxiate himself. Her son, Bailey, didn't like to arrive at a motel with
a cat.

She sat in the middle of the back seat with John Wesley and June Star on either
side of her. Bailey and the children's mother and the baby sat in the front and they left
Atlanta at eight forty-five with the mileage on the car at 55890. The grandmother wrote

this down because she thought it would be interesting to say how many miles they had been when they got back. It took them twenty minutes to reach the outskirts of the city.

The old lady settled herself comfortably, removing her white cotton gloves and putting them up with her purse on the shelf in front of the back window. The children's mother still had on slacks and still had her head tied up in a green kerchief, but the grandmother had on a navy blue straw sailor hat with a bunch of white violets on the brim and a navy blue dress with a small white dot in the print. Her collar and cuffs were white organdy trimmed with lace and at her neckline she had pinned a purple spray of cloth violets containing a sachet. In case of an accident, anyone seeing her dead on the highway would know at once that she was a lady.

She said she thought it was going to be a good day for driving, neither too hot nor too cold, and she cautioned Bailey that the speed limit was fifty-five miles an hour and that the patrolmen hid themselves behind billboards and small clumps of trees and sped out after you before you had a chance to slow down. She pointed out interesting details of the scenery: Stone Mountain; the blue granite that in some places came up to both sides of the highway; the brilliant red clay banks slightly streaked with purple; and the various crops that made rows of green lacework on the ground. The trees were full of silver-white sunlight and the meanest of them sparkled. The children were reading comic magazines and their mother had gone back to sleep.

"Let's go through Georgia fast so we won't have to look at it much," John Wesley said.

"If I were a little boy," said the grandmother, "I wouldn't talk about my native state that way. Tennessee has the mountains and Georgia has the hills." 15

"Tennessee is just a hillbilly dumping ground," John Wesley said, "and Georgia is a lousy state too."

"You said it," June Star said.

"In my time," said the grandmother, folding her thin veined fingers, "children were more respectful of their native states and their parents and everything else. People did right then. Oh look at the cute little pickaninny!" she said and pointed to a Negro child standing in the door of a shack. "Wouldn't that make a picture, now?" she asked and they all turned and looked at the little Negro out of the back window. He waved.

"He didn't have any britches on," June said.

"He probably didn't have any," the grandmother explained. "Little niggers in the country don't have things like we do. If I could paint, I'd paint that picture," she said. 20

The children exchanged comic books.

The grandmother offered to hold the baby and the children's mother passed him over the front seat to her. She set him on her knee and bounced him and told him about the things they were passing. She rolled her eyes and screwed up her mouth and stuck her leathery thin face into his smooth bland one. Occasionally he gave her a far-away smile. They passed a large cotton field with five or six graves fenced in the middle of it, like a small island. "Look at the graveyard!" the grandmother said, pointing it out. "That was the old family burying ground. That belonged to the plantation."

"Where's the plantation?" John Wesley asked.

"Gone With the Wind," said the grandmother. "Ha. Ha."

When the children finished all the comic books they had brought, they opened the lunch and ate it. The grandmother ate a peanut butter sandwich and an olive and would not let the children throw the box and the paper napkins out the window. When there was nothing else to do they played a game by choosing a cloud and making the other two guess what shape it suggested. John Wesley took one the shape of a cow and 25

June Star guessed a cow and John Wesley said, no, an automobile, and June Star said he didn't play fair, and they began to slap each other over the grandmother.

The grandmother said she would tell them a story if they would keep quiet. When she told a story, she rolled her eyes and waved her head and was very dramatic. She said once when she was a maiden lady she had been courted by a Mr. Edgar Atkins Teagarden from Jasper, Georgia. She said he was a very good-looking man and a gentleman and that he brought her a watermelon every Saturday afternoon with his initials cut in it, E. A. T. Well, one Saturday, she said, Mr. Teagarden brought the watermelon and there was nobody at home and he left it on the front porch and returned in his buggy to Jasper, but she never got the watermelon, she said, because a nigger boy ate it when he saw the initials, E. A. T.! This story tickled John Wesley's funny bone and he giggled and giggled but June Star didn't think it was any good. She said she wouldn't marry a man that just brought her a watermelon on Saturday. The grandmother said she would have done well to marry Mr. Teagarden because he was a gentleman and had bought Coca-Cola stock when it first came out and that he had died only a few years ago, a very wealthy man.

They stopped at The Tower for barbecued sandwiches. The Tower was a part stucco and part wood filling station and dance hall set in a clearing outside of Timothy. A fat man named Red Sammy Butts ran it and there were signs stuck here and there on the building and for miles up and down the highway saying, TRY RED SAMMY'S FAMOUS BARBECUE. NONE LIKE FAMOUS RED SAMMY'S! RED SAM! THE FAT BOY WITH THE HAPPY LAUGH. A VETERAN! SAMMY'S YOUR MAN!

Red Sammy was lying on the bare ground outside The Tower with his head under a truck while a gray monkey about a foot high, chained to a small chinaberry tree, chattered nearby. The monkey sprang back into the tree and got on the highest limb as soon as he saw the children jump out of the car and run toward him.

Inside, The Tower was a long dark room with a counter at one end and tables at the other and dancing space in the middle. They all sat down at a broad table next to the nickelodeon and Red Sam's wife, a tall burnt-brown woman with hair and eyes lighter than her skin, came and took their order. The children's mother put a dime in the machine and played "The Tennessee Waltz," and the grandmother said the tune always made her want to dance. She asked Bailey if he would like to dance but he only glared at her. He didn't have a naturally sunny disposition like she did and trips made him nervous. The grandmother's brown eyes were very bright. She swayed her head from side to side and pretended she was dancing in her chair. June Star said play something she could tap to so the children's mother put in another dime and played a fast number and June Star stepped out onto the dance floor and did her tap routine.

"Ain't she cute?" Red Sam's wife said, leaning over the counter. "Would you like to come be my little girl?"

"No I certainly wouldn't," June Star said. "I wouldn't live in a broken-down place like this for a million bucks!" and she ran back to the table.

"Ain't she cute?" the woman repeated, stretching her mouth politely.

"Aren't you ashamed?" hissed her grandmother.

Red Sam came in and told his wife to quit lounging on the counter and hurry with these people's order. His khaki trousers reached just to his hip bones and his stomach hung over them like a sack of meal swaying under his shirt. He came over and sat down at a table nearby and let out a combination sigh and yodel. "You can't win," he said. "You can't win," and he wiped his sweating red face with a gray handkerchief. "These days you don't know who to trust," he said. "Ain't that the truth?"

"People are certainly not nice like they used to be," said the grandmother.   35

"Two fellers come in here last week," Red Sammy said, "driving a Chrysler. It was a old beat-up car but it was a good one and these boys looked all right to me. Said they worked at the mill and you know I let them fellers charge the gas they bought? Now why did I do that?"

"Because you're a good man!" the grandmother said at once.

"Yes'm, I suppose so," Red Sam said as if he were struck with the answer.

His wife brought the orders, carrying the five plates all at once without a tray, two in each hand and one balanced on her arm. "It isn't a soul in this green world of God's that you can trust," she said. "And I don't count anybody out of that, not nobody," she repeated, looking at Red Sammy.

"Did you read about that criminal, The Misfit, that's escaped?" asked the   40
grandmother.

"I wouldn't be a bit surprised if he didn't attack this place right here," said the woman. "If he hears about it being here, I wouldn't be none surprised to see him. If he hears it's two cent in the cash register, I wouldn't be a tall surprised if he . . ."

"That'll do," Red Sam said. "Go bring these people their Co'Colas," and the woman went off to get the rest of the order.

"A good man is hard to find," Red Sammy said. "Everything is getting terrible. I remember the day you could go off and leave your screen door unlatched. Not no more."

He and the grandmother discussed better times. The old lady said that in her opinion Europe was entirely to blame for the way things were now. She said the way Europe acted you would think we were made of money and Red Sam said it was no use talking about it, she was exactly right. The children ran outside into the white sunlight and looked at the monkey in the lacy chinaberry tree. He was busy catching fleas on himself and biting each one carefully between his teeth as if it were a delicacy.

They drove off again into the hot afternoon. The grandmother took cat naps and   45
woke up every few minutes with her own snoring. Outside of Toombsboro she woke up and recalled an old plantation that she had visited in this neighborhood once when she was a young lady. She said the house had six white columns across the front and that there was an avenue of oaks leading up to it and two little wooden trellis arbors on either side in front where you sat down with your suitor after a stroll in the garden. She recalled exactly which road to turn off to get to it. She knew that Bailey would not be willing to lose any time looking at an old house, but the more she talked about it, the more she wanted to see it once again and find out if the little twin arbors were still standing. "There was a secret panel in this house," she said craftily, not telling the truth but wishing that she were, "and the story went that all the family silver was hidden in it when Sherman° came through but it was never found . . ."

"Hey!" John Wesley said, "Let's go see it! We'll find it! We'll poke all the woodwork and find it! Who lives there? Where do you turn off at? Hey Pop, can't we turn off there?"

"We never have seen a house with a secret panel!" June Star shrieked. "Let's go to the house with the secret panel! Hey, Pop, can't we go see the house with the secret panel!"

"It's not far from here, I know," the grandmother said. "It wouldn't take over twenty minutes."

Bailey was looking straight ahead. His jaw was as rigid as a horseshoe. "No," he said.

Sherman: William Tecumseh Sherman (1820–1892), Union general during the Civil War.

The children began to yell and scream that they wanted to see the house with   50
the secret panel. John Wesley kicked the back of the front seat and June Star hung over
her mother's shoulder and whined desperately into her ear that they never had any
fun even on their vacation, and that they could never do what THEY wanted to do. The
baby began to scream and John Wesley kicked the back of the seat so hard that his
father could feel the blows in his kidney.

"All right!" he shouted, and drew the car to a stop at the side of the road. "Will
you all shut up? Will you all just shut up for one second? If you don't shut up, we won't
go anywhere."

"It would be very educational for them," the grandmother murmured.

"All right," Bailey said, "but get this: this is the only time we're going to stop for
anything like this. This is the one and only time."

"The dirt road that you have to turn down is about a mile back," the grandmother directed. "I marked it when we passed."

"A dirt road," Bailey groaned.   55

After they had turned around and were headed toward the dirt road, the grandmother recalled other points about the house, the beautiful glass over the front doorway and the candle-lamp in the hall. John Wesley said that the secret panel was probably
in the fireplace.

"You can't go inside this house," Bailey said. "You don't know who lives there."

"While you all talk to the people in front, I'll run around behind and get in a
window," John Wesley suggested.

"We'll all stay in the car," his mother said.

They turned onto the dirt road and the car raced roughly along in swirl of pink   60
dust. The grandmother recalled the times when there were no paved roads and thirty
miles was a day's journey. The dirt road was hilly and there were sudden washes in it
and sharp curves on dangerous embankments. All at once they would be on a hill, looking down over the blue tops of trees for miles around, then the next minute, they
would be in a red depression with the dust-coated trees looking down on them.

"This place had better turn up in a minute," Bailey said, "or I'm going to turn
around."

The road looked as if no one had traveled on it in months.

"It's not much farther," the grandmother said and just as she said it, a horrible
thought came to her. The thought was so embarrassing that she turned red in the
face and her eyes dilated and her feet jumped up, upsetting her valise in the corner.
The instant the valise moved, the newspaper top she had over the basket under it rose
with a snarl and Pitty Sing, the cat, sprang onto Bailey's shoulder.

The children were thrown to the floor and their mother, clutching the baby, was
thrown out the door onto the ground; the old lady was thrown into the front seat. The
car turned over once and landed right-side-up in a gulch on the side of the road. Bailey
remained in the driver's seat with the cat—gray-striped with a broad white face and an
orange nose—clinging to his neck like a caterpillar.

As soon as the children saw they could move their arms and legs, they scrambled
out of the car, shouting, "We've had an ACCIDENT!" The grandmother was curled up
under the dashboard, hoping she was injured so that Bailey's wrath would not come
down on her all at once. The horrible thought she had had before the accident was
that the house she had remembered so vividly was not in Georgia but in Tennessee.

Bailey removed the cat from his neck with both hands and flung it out the
window against the side of a pine tree. Then he got out of the car and started looking

for the children's mother. She was sitting against the side of the red gutted ditch, holding the screaming baby, but she only had a cut down her face and a broken shoulder. "We've had an ACCIDENT!" the children screamed in a frenzy of delight.

"But nobody's killed," June Star said with disappointment as the grandmother limped out of the car, her hat still pinned to her head but the broken front brim standing up at a jaunty angle and the violet spray hanging off the side. They all sat down in the ditch, except the children, to recover from the shock. They were all shaking.

"Maybe a car will come along," said the children's mother hoarsely.

"I believe I have injured an organ," said the grandmother, pressing her side, but no one answered her. Bailey's teeth were clattering. He had on a yellow sport shirt with bright blue parrots designed in it and his face was as yellow as the shirt. The grandmother decided that she would not mention that the house was in Tennessee.

The road was about ten feet above and they could see only the tops of the trees   70
on the other side of it. Behind the ditch they were sitting in there were more woods, tall and dark and deep. In a few minutes they saw a car some distance away on top of a hill, coming slowly as if the occupants were watching them. The grandmother stood up and waved both arms dramatically to attract their attention. The car continued to come on slowly, disappeared around a bend and appeared again, moving even slower, on top of the hill they had gone over. It was a big black battered hearse-like automobile. There were three men in it.

It came to a stop just over them and for some minutes, the driver looked down with a steady expressionless gaze to where they were sitting, and didn't speak. Then he turned his head and muttered something to the other two and they got out. One was a fat boy in black trousers and a red sweat shirt with a silver stallion embossed on the front of it. He moved around on the right side of them and stood staring, his mouth partly open in a kind of loose grin. The other had on khaki pants and a blue striped coat and a gray hat pulled down very low, hiding most of his face. He came around slowly on the left side. Neither spoke.

The driver got out of the car and stood by the side of it, looking down at them. He was an older man than the other two. His hair was just beginning to gray and he wore silver-rimmed spectacles that gave him a scholarly look. He had a long creased face and didn't have on any shirt or undershirt. He had on blue jeans that were too tight for him and was holding a black hat and a gun. The two boys also had guns.

"We've had an ACCIDENT!" the children screamed.

The grandmother had the peculiar feeling that the bespectacled man was someone she knew. His face was as familiar to her as if she had known him all her life but she could not recall who he was. He moved away from the car and began to come down the embankment, placing his feet carefully so that he wouldn't slip. He had on tan and white shoes and no socks, and his ankles were red and thin. "Good afternoon," he said. "I see you all had a little spill."

"We turned over twice!" said the grandmother.   75

"Oncet," he corrected. "We seen it happen. Try their car and see will it run, Hiram," he said quietly to the boy with the gray hat.

"What you got that gun for?" John Wesley asked, "Whatcha gonna do with that gun?"

"Lady," the man said to the children's mother, "would you mind calling them children to sit down by you? Children make me nervous. I want all you all to set down right together there where you're at."

"What are you telling us what to do for?" June Star asked.

Behind them the line of woods gaped like a dark open mouth. "Come here," said   80
their mother.

"Look here now," Bailey began suddenly, "we're in a predicament! We're in . . ."

The grandmother shrieked. She scrambled to her feet and stood staring. "You're The Misfit!" she said. "I recognized you at once."

"Yes'm" the man said, smiling slightly as if he were pleased in spite of himself to be known, "but it would have been better for all of you, lady, if you hadn't reckernized me."

Bailey turned his head sharply and said something to his mother that shocked even the children. The old lady began to cry and The Misfit reddened.

"Lady," he said, "don't you get upset: Sometimes a man says things he don't   85
mean. I don't reckon he meant to talk to you thataway."

"You wouldn't shoot a lady, would you?" the grandmother said and removed a clean handkerchief from her cuff and began to slap at her eyes with it.

The Misfit pointed the toe of his shoe into the ground and made a little hole and then covered it up again. "I would hate to have to," he said.

"Listen," the grandmother almost screamed, "I know you're a good man. You don't look a bit like you have common blood. I know you must come from nice people!"

"Yes mam," he said, "finest people in the world." When he smiled he showed a row of strong white teeth. "God never made a finer woman than my mother and my daddy's heart was pure gold," he said. The boy with the red sweat shirt had come around behind them and was standing with his gun at his hip. The Misfit squatted down on the ground. "Watch them children, Bobby Lee," he said. "You know they make me nervous." He looked at the six of them huddled together in front of him and he seemed to be embarrassed as if he couldn't think if anything to say. "Ain't a cloud in the sky," he remarked, looking up at it. "Don't see no sun but don't see no cloud neither."

"Yes, it's a beautiful day," said the grandmother. "Listen," she said, "you   9
shouldn't call yourself The Misfit because I know you're a good man at heart. I can just look at you and tell."

"Hush!" Bailey yelled. "Hush! Everybody shut up and let me handle this!" He was squatting in the position of a runner about to sprint forward but he didn't move.

"I pre-chate that, lady," The Misfit said and drew a little circle in the ground with the butt of his gun.

"It'll take a half a hour to fix this here car," Hiram called, looking over the raised hood of it.

"Well, first you and Bobby Lee get him and that little boy to step over yonder with you," The Misfit said, pointing to Bailey and John Wesley. "The boys want to ask you something," he said to Bailey. "Would you mind stepping back in them woods there with them?"

"Listen," Bailey began, "we're in a terrible predicament. Nobody realizes what this is," and his voice cracked. His eyes were as blue and intense as the parrots in his shirt and he remained perfectly still.

The grandmother reached up to adjust her hat brim as if she were going to the woods with him but it came off in her hand. She stood staring at it and after a second she let it fall to the ground. Hiram pulled Bailey up by the arm as if he were assisting an old man. John Wesley caught hold of his father's hand and Bobby Lee followed. They went off toward the woods and just as they reached the dark edge, Bailey turned and supporting himself against a gray naked pine trunk, he shouted, "I'll be back in a minute, Mamma, wait on me!"

"Come back this instant!" his mother shrilled but they all disappeared into the woods.

"Bailey Boy!" the grandmother called in a tragic voice but she found she was looking at The Misfit squatting on the ground in front of her. "I just know you're a good man," she said desperately. "You're not a bit common!"

"Nome, I ain't a good man," The Misfit said after a second as if he had considered her statement carefully, "but I ain't the worst in the world neither. My daddy said I was different breed of dog from my brothers and sisters. 'You know,' Daddy said, 'it's some that can live their whole life out without asking about it and it's others has to know why it is, and this boy is one of the latters. He's going to be into everything!'" He put on his black hat and looked up suddenly and then away deep into the woods as if he were embarrassed again. "I'm sorry I don't have on a shirt before you ladies," he said, hunching his shoulders slightly. "We buried our clothes that we had on when we escaped and we're just making do until we can get better. We borrowed these from some folks we met," he explained.

"That's perfectly all right," the grandmother said. "Maybe Bailey has an extra shirt in his suitcase." 100

"I'll look and see terrectly," the Misfit said.

"Where are they taking him?" the children's mother screamed.

"Daddy was a card himself," the Misfit said. "You couldn't put anything over on him. He never got in trouble with the Authorities though. Just had the knack of handling them."

"You could be honest too if you'd only try," said the grandmother. "Think how wonderful it would be to settle down and live a comfortable life and not have to think about somebody chasing you all the time."

The Misfit kept scratching in the ground with the butt of his gun as if he were thinking about it. "Yes'm, somebody is always after you," he murmured. 105

The grandmother noticed how thin his shoulder blades were just behind his hat because she was standing up looking down on him. "Do you ever pray?" she asked.

He shook his head. All she saw was the black hat wiggle between his shoulder blades. "Nome," he said.

There was a pistol shot from the woods, followed closely by another. Then silence. The old lady's head jerked around. She could hear the wind move through the tree tops like a long satisfied insuck of breath. "Bailey Boy!" she called.

"I was a gospel singer for a while," The Misfit said. "I been most everything. Been in the arm service, both land and sea, at home and abroad, been twict married, been an undertaker, been with the railroads, plowed Mother Earth, been in a tornado, seen a man burnt alive oncet," and he looked up at the children's mother and the little girl who were sitting close together, their faces white and their eyes glassy; "I even seen a woman flogged," he said.

"Pray, pray," the grandmother began, "pray, pray . . ." 110

"I never was a bad boy that I remember of," The Misfit said in an almost dreamy voice, "but somewheres along the line I done something wrong and got sent to the penitentiary. I was buried alive," and he looked up and held her attention to him by a steady stare.

"That's when you should have started to pray," she said. "What did you do to get sent to the penitentiary that first time?"

"Turn to the right, it was a wall," The Misfit said, looking up again at the cloudless sky. "Turn to the left, it was a wall. Look up it was a ceiling, look down it was a floor. I forgot what I done, lady. I set there and set there, trying to remember what it was I done and I ain't recalled it to this day. Oncet in a while, I would think it was coming to me, but it never come."

"Maybe they put you in by mistake," the old lady said vaguely.

"Nome," he said. "It wasn't no mistake. They had the papers on me." 115

"You must have stolen something," she said.

The Misfit sneered slightly. "Nobody had nothing I wanted," he said. "It was a head-doctor at the penitentiary said what I had done was kill my daddy but I know that for a lie. My daddy died in nineteen ought nineteen of the epidemic flu and I never had a thing to do with it. He was buried in the Mount Hopewell Baptist churchyard and you can go there and see for yourself."

"If you would pray," the old lady said, "Jesus would help you."

"That's right," The Misfit said.

"Well then, why don't you pray?" she asked trembling with delight suddenly. 120

"I don't want no hep," he said. "I'm doing all right by myself."

Bobby Lee and Hiram came ambling back from the woods. Bobby Lee was dragging a yellow shirt with bright blue parrots in it.

"Throw me that shirt, Bobby Lee," The Misfit said. The shirt came flying at him and landed on his shoulder and he put it on. The grandmother couldn't name what the shirt reminded her of. "No, lady," The Misfit said while he was buttoning it up. "I found out the crime don't matter. You can do one thing or you can do another, kill a man or take a tire off his car, because sooner or later you're going to forget what it was you done and just be punished for it."

The children's mother had begun to make heaving noises as if she couldn't get her breath. "Lady," he asked, "would you and that little girl like to step off yonder with Bobby Lee and Hiram and join your husband?"

"Yes, thank you," the mother said faintly. Her left arm dangled helplessly and she 12. was holding the baby, who had gone to sleep, in the other. "Hep that lady up, Hiram," The Misfit said as she struggled to climb out of the ditch, "and Bobby Lee, you hold onto that little girl's hand."

"I don't want to hold hands with him," June Star said. "He reminds me of a pig."

The fat boy blushed and laughed and caught her by the arm and pulled her off into the woods after Hiram and her mother.

Alone with The Misfit, the grandmother found that she had lost her voice. There was not a cloud in the sky nor any sun. There was nothing around her but woods. She wanted to tell him that he must pray. She opened and closed her mouth several times before anything came out. Finally she found herself saying, "Jesus, Jesus," meaning Jesus will help you, but the way she was saying it, it sounded as if she might be cursing.

"Yes'm," The Misfit said as if he agreed. "Jesus thown everything off balance. It was the same case with Him as with me except He hadn't committed any crime and they could prove I had committed one because they had the papers on me. Of course," he said, "they never shown me any papers. That's why I sign myself now. I said long ago, you get you a signature and sign everything you do and keep a copy of it. Then you'll know what you done and you can hold up the crime to the punishment and see do they match and in the end you'll have something to prove you ain't been treated right. I call myself The Misfit," he said, "because I can't make what all I done wrong fit what all I gone through in punishment."

There was a piercing scream from the woods, followed closely by a pistol report. 130 "Does it seem right to you, lady, that one is punished a heap and another ain't punished at all?"

"Jesus!" the old lady cried. "You've got good blood! I know you wouldn't shoot a lady! I know you come from nice people! Pray! Jesus, you ought not to shoot a lady: I'll give you all the money I've got!"

"Lady," The Misfit said, looking beyond her far into the woods, "there never was a body that give the undertaker a tip."

There were two more pistol reports and the grandmother raised her head like a parched old turkey hen crying for water and called, "Bailey Boy, Bailey Boy!" as if her heart would break.

"Jesus was the only One that ever raised the dead," The Misfit continued, "and He shouldn't have done it. He thown everything off balance. If He did what He said then it's nothing for you to do but thow away everything and follow Him, and if He didn't, then it's nothing for you to do but enjoy the few minutes you got left the best way you can—by killing somebody or burning down his house or doing some other meanness to him. No pleasure but meanness," he said and his voice had become almost a snarl.

"Maybe He didn't raise the dead," the old lady mumbled, not knowing what she 135 was saying and feeling so dizzy that she sank down in the ditch with her legs twisted under her.

"I wasn't there so I can't say He didn't." The Misfit said, "I wisht I had of been there," he said, hitting the ground with his fist. "It ain't right I wasn't there because if I had of been there I would of known. Listen lady," he said in a high voice, "if I had of been there I would of known and I wouldn't be like I am now." His voice seemed about to crack and the grandmother's head cleared for an instant. She saw the man's face twisted close to her own as if he were going to cry and she murmured, "Why you're one of my babies. You're one of my own children!" She reached out and touched him on the shoulder. The Misfit sprang back as if a snake had bitten him and shot her three times through the chest. Then he put his gun down on the ground and took off his glasses and began to clean them.

Hiram and Bobby Lee returned from the woods and stood over the ditch, looking down at the grandmother who half sat and half lay in a puddle of blood with her legs crossed under her like a child's and her face smiling up at the cloudless sky.

Without his glasses, The Misfit's eyes were red-rimmed and pale and defenseless-looking. "Take her off and thow her where you thown the others," he said, picking up the cat that was rubbing itself against his leg.

"She was a talker, wasn't she?" Bobby Lee said, sliding down the ditch with a yodel.

"She would of been a good woman," The Misfit said, "if it had been somebody 140 there to shoot her every minute of her life."

"Some fun!" Bobby Lee said.

"Shut up, Bobby Lee," The Misfit said. "It's no real pleasure in life."

TILLIE OLSEN   (b. ca. 1913)

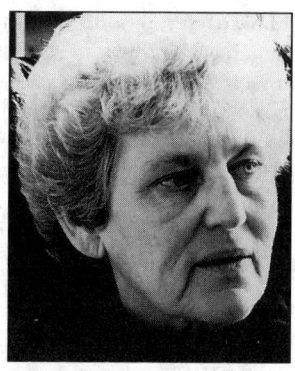

Tillie Olsen was born in 1912 or 1913 in Nebraska. Although she did not have an extensive formal education, she has been the recipient of five honorary degrees and a number of other honors, including a Guggenheim Fellowship. Her early efforts at writing were tentative, and after the mid 1930s she put her career on hold while she devoted herself to her four daughters, "everyday jobs," and marriage. In the 1950s she resumed writing, lecturing, and advocating feminist and minority issues, all of which have characterized her career since then. Her total output has not been great, for her work has been deliberate, careful, and slow. In 1974 she completed her long-developing novel, Yonnondio, From the Thirties, *which she had begun while in her teens (she had published a single chapter from the novel in 1943). The subject of the novel, which could be considered as a virtual life's work, is a working-class family during the depression years. "I Stand Here Ironing" is from her 1956 prize-winning collection* Tell Me a Riddle *(1961). If one judges the story as being related to Olsen's own experiences, it is visualized as happening in about 1951, when the narrator, the mother, is thirty-eight, and Emily, the daughter, is nineteen.*

I Stand Here Ironing _____ *1953–1954*

I stand here ironing, and what you asked me moves tormented back and forth with the iron.

"I wish you would manage the time to come in and talk with me about your daughter. I'm sure you can help me understand her. She's a youngster who needs help and whom I'm deeply interested in helping."

"Who needs help." . . . Even if I came, what good would it do? You think because I am her mother I have a key, or that in some way you could use me as a key? She has lived for nineteen years. There is all that life that has happened outside of me, beyond me.

And when is there time to remember, to sift, to weigh, to estimate, to total? I will start and there will be an interruption and I will have to gather it all together again. Or I will become engulfed with all I did or did not do, with what should have been and what cannot be helped.

She was a beautiful baby. The first and only one of our five that was beautiful at birth. You do not guess how new and uneasy her tenancy in her now-loveliness. You did not know her all those years she was thought homely, or see her poring over her baby pictures, making me tell her over and over how beautiful she had been—and would be, I would tell her—and was now, to the seeing eye. But the seeing eyes were few or nonexistent. Including mine.

I nursed her. They feel that's important nowadays. I nursed all the children, but with her, with all the fierce rigidity of first motherhood, I did like the books then said. Though her cries battered me to trembling and my breasts ached with swollenness, I waited till the clock decreed.

Why do I put that first? I do not even know if it matters, or if it explains anything.

She was a beautiful baby. She blew shining bubbles of sound. She loved motion, loved light, loved color and music and textures. She would lie on the floor in her blue overalls patting the surface so hard in ecstasy her hands and feet would blur. She was a miracle to me, but when she was eight months old I had to leave her daytimes with the woman downstairs to whom she was no miracle at all, for I worked or looked for work and for Emily's father, who "could no longer endure" (he wrote in his good-bye note) "sharing want with us."

I was nineteen. It was the pre-relief, pre-WPA world of the depression. I would start running as soon as I got off the streetcar, running up the stairs, the place smelling sour, and awake or asleep to startle awake, when she saw me she would break into a clogged weeping that could not be comforted, a weeping I can hear yet.

After a while I found a job hashing at night so I could be with her days, and it was   10
better. But it came to where I had to bring her to his family and leave her.

It took a long time to raise the money for her fare back. Then she got chicken pox and I had to wait longer. When she finally came, I hardly knew her, walking quick and nervous like her father, looking like her father, thin, and dressed in a shoddy red that yellowed her skin and glared at the pockmarks. All the baby loveliness gone.

She was two. Old enough for nursery school they said, and I did not know then what I know now—the fatigue of the long day, and the lacerations of group life in the kinds of nurseries that are only parking places for children.

Except that it would have made no difference if I had known. It was the only place there was. It was the only way we could be together, the only way I could hold a job.

And even without knowing, I knew. I knew the teacher that was evil because all these years it has curdled into my memory, the little boy hunched in the corner, her rasp, "why aren't you outside, because Alvin hits you? that's no reason, go out, scaredy." I knew Emily hated it even if she did not clutch and implore "don't go Mommy" like the other children, mornings.

She always had a reason why we should stay home. Momma, you look sick.   15
Momma, I feel sick. Momma, the teachers aren't there today, they're sick. Momma, we can't go, there was a fire there last night. Momma, it's a holiday today, no school, they told me.

But never a direct protest, never rebellion. I think of our others in their three-, four-year-oldness—the explosions, the tempers, the denunciations, the demands—and I feel suddenly ill. I put the iron down. What in me demanded that goodness in her? And what was the cost, the cost to her of such goodness?

The old man living in the back once said in his gentle way: "You should smile at Emily more when you look at her." What *was* in my face when I looked at her? I loved her. There were all the acts of love.

It was only with the others I remembered what he said, and it was the face of joy, and not of care or tightness or worry I turned to them—too late for Emily. She does not smile easily, let alone almost always as her brothers and sisters do. Her face is closed and sombre, but when she wants, how fluid. You must have seen it in her pantomimes, you spoke of her rare gift for comedy on the stage that rouses a laughter out of the audience so dear they applaud and applaud and do not want to let her go.

Where does it come from, that comedy? There was none of it in her when she came back to me that second time, after I had had to send her away again. She had a new daddy now to learn to love, and I think perhaps it was a better time.

Except when we left her alone nights, telling ourselves she was old enough.   20

"Can't you go some other time, Mommy, like tomorrow?" she would ask. "Will it be just a little while you'll be gone? Do you promise?"

The time we came back, the front door open, the clock on the floor in the hall. She rigid awake. "It wasn't just a little while. I didn't cry. Three times I called you, just three times, and then I ran downstairs to open the door so you could come faster. The clock talked loud. I threw it away, it scared me what it talked."

She said the clock talked loud again that night I went to the hospital to have Susan. She was delirious with the fever that comes before red measles, but she was fully conscious all the week I was gone and the week after we were home when she could not come near the new baby or me.

She did not get well. She stayed skeleton thin, not wanting to eat, and night after night she had nightmares. She would call for me, and I would rouse from exhaustion to sleepily call back: "You're all right, darling, go to sleep, it's just a dream," and if she still called, in a sterner voice, "now go to sleep, Emily, there's nothing to hurt you." Twice, only twice, when I had to get up for Susan anyhow, I went in to sit with her.

Now when it is too late (as if she would let me hold and comfort her like I do the others) I get up and go to her at once at her moan or restless stirring. "Are you awake, Emily? Can I get you something?" And the answer is always the same: "No, I'm all right, go back to sleep, Mother."

They persuaded me at the clinic to send her away to a convalescent home in the country where "she can have the kind of food and care you can't manage for her, and you'll be free to concentrate on the new baby." They still send children to that place. I see pictures on the society page of sleek young women planning affairs to raise money for it, or dancing at the affairs, or decorating Easter eggs or filling Christmas stockings for the children.

They never have a picture of the children so I do not know if the girls still wear those gigantic red bows and the ravaged looks on the every other Sunday when parents can come to visit "unless otherwise notified"—as we were notified the first six weeks.

Oh it is a handsome place, green lawns and tall trees and fluted flower beds. High up on the balconies of each cottage the children stand, the girls in their red bows and white dresses, the boys in white suits and giant red ties. The parents stand below shrieking up to be heard and the children shriek down to be heard, and between them the invisible wall "Not To Be Contaminated by Parental Germs or Physical Affection."

There was a tiny girl who always stood hand in hand with Emily. Her parents never came. One visit she was gone. "They moved her to Rose Cottage" Emily shouted in explanation. "They don't like you to love anybody here."

She wrote once a week, the labored writing of a seven-year-old. "I am fine. How is the baby. If I write my leter nicly I will have a star. Love." There never was a star. We wrote every other day, letters she could never hold or keep but only hear read—once. "We simply do not have room for children to keep any personal possessions," they patiently explained when we pieced one Sunday's shrieking together to plead how much it would mean to Emily, who loved so to keep things, to be allowed to keep her letters and cards.

Each visit she looked frailer. "She isn't eating," they told us.

(They had runny eggs for breakfast or mush with lumps, Emily said later, I'd hold it in my mouth and not swallow. Nothing ever tasted good, just when they had chicken.)

It took us eight months to get her released home, and only the fact that she gained back so little of her seven lost pounds convinced the social worker.

I used to try to hold and love her after she came back, but her body would stay stiff, and after a while she'd push away. She ate little. Food sickened her, and I think much of life too. Oh she had physical lightness and brightness, twinkling by on skates, bouncing like a ball up and down up and down over the jump rope, skimming over the hill; but these were momentary.

She fretted about her appearance, thin and dark and foreign-looking at a time   35
when every little girl was supposed to look or thought she should look a chubby blonde replica of Shirley Temple. The doorbell sometimes rang for her, but no one seemed to come and play in the house or be a best friend. Maybe because we moved so much.

There was a boy she loved painfully through two school semesters. Months later she told me how she had taken pennies from my purse to buy him candy. "Licorice was his favorite and I brought him some every day, but he still liked Jennifer better'n me. Why, Mommy?" The kind of question for which there is no answer.

School was a worry to her. She was not glib or quick in a world where glibness and quickness were easily confused with ability to learn. To her overworked and exasperated teachers she was an overconscientious "slow learner" who kept trying to catch up and was absent entirely too often.

I let her be absent, though sometimes the illness was imaginary. How different from my now-strictness about attendance with the others. I wasn't working. We had a new baby, I was home anyhow. Sometimes, after Susan grew old enough, I would keep her home from school, too, to have them all together.

Mostly Emily had asthma, and her breathing, harsh and labored, would fill the house with a curiously tranquil sound. I would bring the two old dresser mirrors and her boxes of collections to her bed. She would select beads and single earrings, bottle tops and shells, dried flowers and pebbles, old postcards and scraps, all sorts of odd-ments; then she and Susan would play Kingdom, setting up landscapes and furniture, peopling them with action.

Those were the only times of peaceful companionship between her and Susan. I   40
have edged away from it, that poisonous feeling between them, that terrible balancing of hurts and needs I had to do between the two, and did so badly, those earlier years.

Oh there are conflicts between the others too, each one human, needing, demanding, hurting, taking—but only between Emily and Susan, no, Emily toward Susan that corroding resentment. It seems so obvious on the surface, yet it is not obvi-ous. Susan, the second child, Susan, golden- and curly-haired and chubby, quick and articulate and assured, everything in appearance and manner Emily was not; Susan, not able to resist Emily's precious things, losing or sometimes clumsily breaking them; Susan telling jokes and riddles to company for applause while Emily sat silent (to say to me later; that was *my* riddle, Mother, I told it to Susan); Susan, who for all the five years' dif-ference in age was just a year behind Emily in developing physically.

I am glad for that slow physical development that widened the difference between her and her contemporaries, though she suffered over it. She was too vulnerable for that terrible world of youthful competition, of preening and parading, of constant mea-suring of yourself against every other, of envy, "If I had that copper hair," "If I had that skin. . . ." She tormented herself enough about not looking like the others, there was enough of the unsureness, the having to be conscious of words before you speak, the constant caring—what are they thinking of me? without having it all magnified by the merciless physical drives.

Ronnie is calling. He is wet and I change him. It is rare there is such a cry now. That time of motherhood is almost behind me when the ear is not one's own but must always be racked and listening for the child cry, the child call. We sit for a while and I hold him, looking out over the city spread in charcoal with its soft aisles of light, "*Shoogily*," he breathes and curls closer. I carry him back to bed, asleep. *Shoogily*. A funny word, a family word, inherited from Emily, invented by her to say: *comfort*.

In this and other ways she leaves her seal, I say aloud. And startle at my saying it. What do I mean? What did I start to gather together, to try and make coherent? I was at the terrible, growing years. War years. I do not remember them well. I was working, there were four smaller ones now, there was not time for her. She had to help be a mother, a housekeeper, and shopper. She had to set her seal. Mornings of crisis and near hysteria trying to get lunches packed, hair combed, coats and shoes found, everyone to school or Child Care on time, the baby ready for transportation. And always the paper scribbled on by a smaller one, the book looked at by Susan then mislaid, the homework not done. Running out to that huge school where she was one, she was lost, she was a drop; suffering over the unpreparedness, stammering and unsure in her classes.

There was so little time left at night after the kids were bedded down. She would struggle over books, always eating (it was in those years she developed her enormous appetite that is legendary in our family) and I would be ironing, or preparing food for the next day, or writing V-mail to Bill, or tending the baby. Sometimes, to make me laugh, or out of her despair, she would imitate happenings or types at school.

I think I said once: "Why don't you do something like this in the school amateur show?" One morning she phoned me at work, hardly understandable through the weeping: "Mother, I did it. I won, I won; they gave me first prize; they clapped and clapped and wouldn't let me go."

Now suddenly she was Somebody, and as imprisoned in her difference as she had been in anonymity.

She began to be asked to perform at other high schools, even in colleges, then at city and statewide affairs. The first one we went to, I only recognized her that first moment when thin, shy, she almost drowned herself into the curtains. Then: Was this Emily? The control, the command, the convulsing and deadly clowning, the spell, then the roaring, stamping audience, unwilling to let this rare and precious laughter out of their lives.

Afterwards: You ought to do something about her with a gift like that—but without money or knowing how, what does one do? We have left it all to her, and the gift has as often eddied inside, clogged and clotted, as been used and growing.

She is coming. She runs up the stairs two at a time with her light graceful step, and I know she is happy tonight. Whatever it was that occasioned your call did not happen today.

"Aren't you ever going to finish the ironing, Mother? Whistler painted his mother in a rocker. I'd have to paint mine standing over an ironing board." This is one of her communicative nights and she tells me everything and nothing as she fixes herself a plate of food out of the icebox.

She is so lovely. Why did you want me to come in at all? Why were you concerned? She will find her way.

She starts up the stairs to bed. "Don't get me up with the rest in the morning." "But I thought you were having midterms." "Oh, those," she comes back in, kisses me, and says quite lightly, "in a couple of years when we'll all be atom-dead they won't matter a bit."

She has said it before. She *believes* it. But because I have been dredging the past, and all that compounds a human being is so heavy and meaningful in me, I cannot endure it tonight.

I will never total it all. I will never come in to say: She was a child seldom smiled at. Her father left me before she was a year old. I had to work her first six years when there was work, or I sent her home and to his relatives. There were years she had care she hated. She was dark and thin and foreign-looking in a world where the prestige went to blondeness and curly hair and dimples, she was slow where glibness was prized. She was a child of anxious, not proud, love. We were poor and could not afford for her the soil of easy growth. I was a young mother, I was a distracted mother. There were the other children pushing up, demanding. Her younger sister seemed all that she was not. There were years she did not want me to touch her. She kept too much in herself, her life was such she had to keep too much in herself. My wisdom came too late. She has much to her and probably little will come of it. She is a child of her age, of depression, of war, of fear.

Let her be. So all that is in her will not bloom—but in how many does it? There is still enough left to live by. Only help her to know—help make it so there is cause for her to know—that she is more than this dress on the ironing board, helpless before the iron.

KATHERINE ANNE PORTER (1894–1980)

Porter was a native of Texas but made her home in many places during her life, spending considerable time in Mexico and Germany. She established her reputation with her early collections Flowering Judas *(1930) and* Pale Horse Pale Rider *(1939), for which she was praised for her analyses and insights into human character. A later collection of stories was* The Leaning Tower *(1944). Her major novel,* Ship of Fools, *appeared in 1962 and was made into a motion picture. She was awarded the Pulitzer Prize for fiction and also the National Book Award in 1966 for her* The Collected Stories. *"The Jilting of Granny Weatherall" first appeared in* Flowering Judas.

The Jilting of Granny Weatherall _____ *1930*

She flicked her wrist neatly out of Doctor Harry's pudgy careful fingers and pulled the sheet up to her chin. The brat ought to be in knee breeches. Doctoring around the country with spectacles on his nose! "Get along now, take your schoolbooks and go. There's nothing wrong with me."

Doctor Harry spread a warm paw like a cushion on her forehead where the forked green vein danced and made her eyelids twitch. "Now, now, be a good girl, and we'll have you up in no time."

"That's no way to speak to a woman nearly eighty years old just because she's down. I'd have you respect your elders, young man."

"Well, Missy, excuse me." Doctor Harry patted her cheek. "But I've got to warn you, haven't I? You're a marvel, but you must be careful or you're going to be good and sorry."

"Don't tell me what I'm going to be. I'm on my feet now, morally speaking. It's Cornelia. I had to go to bed to get rid of her." 5

Her bones felt loose, and floated around in her skin, and Doctor Harry floated like a balloon around the foot of the bed. He floated and pulled down his waistcoat and swung his glasses on a cord. "Well, stay where you are, it certainly can't hurt you."

"Get along and doctor your sick." said Granny Weatherall. "Leave a well woman alone. I'll call for you when I want you. . . . Where were you forty years ago when I pulled through milk-leg and double pneumonia? You weren't even born. Don't let Cornelia lead you on." she shouted, because Doctor Harry appeared to float up to the ceiling and out. "I pay my own bills, and I don't throw my money away on nonsense!"

She meant to wave good-by, but it was too much trouble. Her eyes closed of themselves, it was like a dark curtain drawn around the bed. The pillow rose and floated under her, pleasant as a hammock in a light wind. She listened to the leaves rustling outside the window. No, somebody was swishing newspapers: no, Cornelia and Doctor Harry were whispering together. She leaped broad awake, thinking they whispered in her ear.

"She was never like this, *never* like this!" "Well, what can we expect?" "Yes, eighty years old. . . . "

Well, and what if she was? She still had ears. It was like Cornelia to whisper around   10
doors. She always kept things secret in such a public way. She was always being tactful and kind. Cornelia was dutiful; that was the trouble with her. Dutiful and good: "So good and dutiful," said Granny, "that I'd like to spank her." She saw herself spanking Cornelia and making a fine job of it.

"What'd you say, Mother?"

Granny felt her face tying up in hard knots.

"Can't a body think, I'd like to know?"

"I thought you might want something."

"I do. I want a lot of things. First off, go away and don't whisper."   15

She lay and drowsed, hoping in her sleep that the children would keep out and let her rest a minute. It had been a long day. Not that she was tired. It was always pleasant to snatch a minute now and then. There was always so much to be done, let me see: tomorrow.

Tomorrow was far away and there was nothing to trouble about. Things were finished somehow when the time came; thank God there was always a little margin over for peace: then a person could spread out the plan of life and tuck in the edges orderly. It was good to have everything clean and folded away, with the hair brushes and tonic bottles sitting straight on the white embroidered linen: the day started without fuss and the pantry shelves laid out with rows of jelly glasses and brown jugs and white stone-china jars with blue whirligigs and words painted on them: coffee, tea, sugar, ginger, cinnamon, allspice: and the bronze clock with the lion on top nicely dusted off. The dust that lion could collect in twenty-four hours! The box in the attic with all those letters tied up, well she'd have to go through that tomorrow. All those letters—George's letters and John's letters and her letters to them both—lying around for the children to find afterwards made her uneasy. Yes, that would be tomorrow's business. No use to let them know how silly she had been once.

While she was rummaging around she found death in her mind and it felt clammy and unfamiliar. She had spent so much time preparing for death there was no need for bringing it up again. Let it take care of itself now. When she was sixty she had felt very old, finished, and went around making farewell trips to see her children and grandchildren, with a secret in her mind: This is the very last of your mother, children! Then she made her will and came down with a long fever. That was all just a notion like a lot of other things, but it was lucky too, for she had once for all got over the idea of dying for a long time. Now she couldn't be worried. She hoped she had better sense now. Her father had lived to be one hundred and two years old and had drunk a noggin of strong hot toddy on his last birthday. He told the reporters it was his daily habit, and he owed his long life to that. He had made quite a scandal and was very pleased about it. She believed she'd just plague Cornelia a little.

"Cornelia! Cornelia!" No footsteps, but a sudden hand on her cheek. "Bless you, where have you been?"

"Here, mother."   20

"Well, Cornelia, I want a noggin of hot toddy."

"Are you cold, darling?"

"I'm chilly, Cornelia. Lying in bed stops the circulation. I must have told you that a thousand times."

Well, she could just hear Cornelia telling her husband that Mother was getting childish and they'd have to humor her. The thing that most annoyed her was that Cornelia thought she was deaf, dumb, and blind. Little hasty glances and tiny gestures tossed around her and over her head saying. "Don't cross her, let her have her way, she's eighty years old," and she sitting there as if she lived in a thin glass cage. Sometimes Granny almost made up her mind to pack up and move back to her own house where nobody could remind her every minute that she was old. Wait, wait, Cornelia, till your own children whisper behind your back!

In her day she had kept a better house and had got more work done. She   25 wasn't too old yet for Lydia to be driving eighty miles for advice when one of the children jumped the track, and Jimmy still dropped in and talked things over: "Now, Mammy, you've a good business head, I want to know what you think of this? . . ." Old Cornelia couldn't change the furniture around without asking. Little things, little things! They had been so sweet when they were little. Granny wished the old days were back again with the children young and everything to be done over. It had been a hard pull, but not too much for her. When she thought of all the food she had cooked, and all the clothes she had cut and sewed, and all the gardens she had made—well, the children showed it. There they were, made out of her, and they couldn't get away from that. Sometimes she wanted to see John again and point to them and say, Well, I didn't do so badly, did I? But that would have to wait. That was for tomorrow. She used to think of him as a man, but now all the children were older than their father, and he would be a child beside her if she saw him now. It seemed strange and there was something wrong in the idea. Why, he couldn't possibly recognize her. She had fenced in a hundred acres once, digging the post holes herself and clamping the wires with just a negro boy to help. That changed a woman. John would be looking for a young woman with the peaked Spanish comb in her hair and the painted fan. Digging post holes changed a woman. Riding country roads in the winter when women had their babies was another thing: sitting up nights with sick horses and sick negroes and sick children and hardly ever losing one. John, I hardly ever lost one of them! John would see that in a minute, that would be something he could understand, she wouldn't have to explain anything!

It made her feel like rolling up her sleeves and putting the whole place to rights again. No matter if Cornelia was determined to be everywhere at once, there were a great many things left undone on this place. She would start tomorrow and do them. It was good to be strong enough for everything, even if all you made melted and changed and slipped under your hands, so that by the time you finished you almost forgot what you were working for. What was it I set out to do? she asked herself intently, but she could not remember. A fog rose over the valley, she saw it marching across the creek swallowing the trees and moving up the hill like an army of ghosts. Soon it would be at the near edge of the orchard, and then it was time to go in and light the lamps. Come in children, don't stay out in the night air.

Lighting the lamps had been beautiful. The children huddled up to her and breathed like little calves waiting at the bars in the twilight. Their eyes followed the match and watched the flame rise and settle in a blue curve, then they moved away from her. The lamp was lit, they didn't have to be scared and hang on to mother any more. Never, never, never more. God, for all my life I thank Thee. Without Thee, my God, I could never have done it. Hail, Mary, full of grace.

I want you to pick all the fruit this year and see that nothing is wasted. There's always someone who can use it. Don't let good things rot for want of using. You waste life when you waste good food. Don't let things get lost. It's bitter to lose things. Now, don't let me get to thinking, not when I am tired and taking a little nap before supper. . . .

The pillow rose about her shoulders and pressed against her heart and the memory was being squeezed out of it: oh, push down the pillow, somebody: it would smother her if she tried to hold it. Such a fresh breeze blowing and such a green day with no threats in it. But he had not come, just the same. What does a woman do when she has put on the white veil and set out the white cake for a man and he doesn't come? She tried to remember. No, I swear he never harmed me but in that. He never harmed me but in that . . . and what if he did? There was the day, the day, but a whirl of dark smoke rose and covered it, crept up and over into the bright field where everything was planted so carefully in orderly rows. That was hell, she knew hell when she saw it. For sixty years she had prayed against remembering him and against losing her soul in the deep pit of hell, and now the two things were mingled in one and the thought of him was a smoky cloud from hell that moved and crept in her head when she had just got rid of Doctor Harry and was trying to rest a minute. Wounded vanity, Ellen, said a sharp voice in the top of her mind. Don't let your wounded vanity get the upper hand of you. Plenty of girls get jilted. You were jilted, weren't you. Then stand up to it. Her eyelids wavered and let in streamers of blue-gray light like tissue paper over her eyes. She must get up and pull the shades down or she'd never sleep. She was in bed again and the shades were not down. How could that happen? Better turn over, hide from the light, sleeping in the light gave you nightmares. "Mother, how do you feel now?" and a stinging wetness on her forehead. But I don't like having my face washed in cold water!

Hapsy? George? Lydia? Jimmy? No, Cornelia, and her features were swollen and full of little puddles. "They're coming, darling, they'll all be here soon." Go wash your face, child, you look funny.

Instead of obeying, Cornelia knelt down and put her head on the pillow. She seemed to be talking but there was no sound. "Well, are you tongue-tied? Whose birthday is it? Are you going to give a party?"

Cornelia's mouth moved urgently in strange shapes. "Don't do that, you bother me, daughter."

"Oh, no, Mother, Oh, no . . ."

Nonsense. It was strange about children. They disputed your every word. "No what, Cornelia?"

"Here's Doctor Harry."

"I won't see that boy again. He just left five minutes ago."

"That was this morning, Mother. It's night now. Here's the nurse."

"This is Doctor Harry, Mrs. Weatherall. I never saw you look so young and happy!"

"Ah, I'll never be young again—but I'd be happy if they'd let me lie in peace and get rested."

She thought she spoke up loudly, but no one answered. A warm weight on her   40
forehead, a warm bracelet on her wrist, and a breeze went on whispering, trying to tell
her something. A shuffle of leaves in the everlasting hand of God. He blew on them and
they danced and rattled. "Mother, don't mind, we're going to give you a little hypoder-
mic." "Look here, daughter, how do ants get in this bed? I saw sugar ants yesterday." Did
you send for Hapsy too?

It was Hapsy she really wanted. She had to go a long way back through a great
many rooms to find Hapsy standing with a baby on her arm. She seemed to herself to be
Hapsy also, and the baby on Hapsy's arm was Hapsy and himself and herself, all at once,
and there was no surprise in the meeting. Then Hapsy melted from within and turned
flimsy as gray gauze and the baby was a gauzy shadow, and Hapsy came up close and
said, "I thought you'd never come," and looked at her very searchingly and said, "You
haven't changed a bit!" They leaned forward to kiss, when Cornelia began whispering
from a long way off, "Oh, is there anything you want to tell me? Is there anything I can
do for you?"

Yes, she had changed her mind after sixty years and she would like to see George.
I want you to find George. Find him and be sure to tell him I forgot him. I want him to
know I had my husband just the same and my children and my house like any other
woman. A good house too and a good husband that I loved and fine children out of
him. Better than I hoped for even. Tell him I was given back everything he took away
and more. Oh, no, oh, God, no, there was something else besides the house and the
man and the children. Oh, surely they were not all? What was it? Something not given
back. . . . Her breath crowded down under her ribs and grew into a monstrous frightening shape with cutting edges; it bored up into her head, and the agony was unbelievable: Yes, John, get the doctor now, no more talk, my time has come.

When this one was born it should be the last. The last. It should have been born
first, for it was the one she had truly wanted. Everything came in good time. Nothing left
out, left over. She was strong, in three days she would be as well as ever. Better. A woman
needed milk in her to have her full health.

"Mother, do you hear me?"

"I've been telling you—"   45

"Mother, Father Connolly's here."

"I went to Holy Communion only last week. Tell him I'm not so sinful as all that."

"Father just wants to speak to you."

He could speak as much as he pleased. It was like him to drop in and inquire
about her soul as if it were a teething baby, and then stay on for a cup of tea and a round
of cards and gossip. He always had a funny story of some sort, usually about an Irishman
who made his little mistakes and confessed them, and the point lay in some absurd thing
he would blurt out in the confessional showing his struggles between native piety and
original sin. Granny felt easy about her soul. Cornelia, where are your manners? Give
Father Connolly a chair. She had her secret comfortable understanding with a few
favorite saints who cleared a straight road to God for her. All as surely signed and sealed
as the papers for the new Forty Acres. Forever . . . heirs and assigns forever. Since the day
the wedding cake was not cut, but thrown out and wasted. The whole bottom dropped
out of the world, and there she was blind and sweating with nothing under her feet and
the walls falling away. His hand had caught her under the breast, she had not fallen,

there was the freshly polished floor with the green rug on it, just as before. He had cursed like a sailor's parrot and said. "I'll kill him for you." Don't lay a hand on him, for my sake leave something to God. "Now, Ellen, you must believe what I tell you. . . ."

So there was nothing, nothing to worry about any more, except sometimes in the night one of the children screamed in a nightmare, and they both hustled out shaking and hunting for the matches and calling, "There, wait a minute, here we are!" John, get the doctor now. Hapsy's time has come. But there was Hapsy standing by the bed in a white cap. "Cornelia, tell Hapsy to take off her cap. I can't see her plain."

Her eyes opened very wide and the room stood out like a picture she had seen somewhere. Dark colors with the shadow rising towards the ceiling in long angles. The tall black dresser gleamed with nothing on it but John's picture, enlarged from a little one, with John's eyes very black when they should have been blue. You never saw him, so how do you know how he looked? But the man insisted the copy was perfect, it was very rich and handsome. For a picture, yes, but it's not my husband. The table by the bed had a linen cover and a candle and a crucifix. The light was blue from Cornelia's silk lampshades. No sort of light at all, just frippery. You had to live forty years with kerosene lamps to appreciate honest electricity. She felt very strong and she saw Doctor Harry with a rosy nimbus around him.

"You look like a saint, Doctor Harry, and I vow that's as near as you'll ever come to it."

"She's saying something."

"I heard you, Cornelia. What's all this carrying-on?"

"Father Connolly's saying—"

Cornelia's voice staggered and bumped like a cart in a bad road. It rounded corners and turned back again and arrived nowhere. Granny stepped up in the cart very lightly and reached for the reins, but a man sat beside her and she knew him by his hands, driving the cart. She did not look in his face, for she knew without seeing, but looked instead down the road where the trees leaned over and bowed to each other and a thousand birds were singing a Mass. She felt like singing too, but she put her hand in the bosom of her dress and pulled out a rosary, and Father Connolly murmured Latin in a very solemn voice and tickled her feet. My God, will you stop that nonsense? I'm a married woman. What if he did run away and leave me to face the priest by myself? I found another a whole world better. I wouldn't have exchanged my husband for anybody except St. Michael himself, and you may tell him that for me with a thank you in the bargain.

Light flashed on her closed eyelids, and a deep roaring shook her. Cornelia, is that lightning? I hear thunder. There's going to be a storm. Close all the windows. Call the children in . . . "Mother, here we are, all of us." "Is that you, Hapsy?" "Oh, no, I'm Lydia. We drove as fast as we could." Their faces drifted above her, drifted away. The rosary fell out of her hands and Lydia put it back. Jimmy tried to help, their hands fumbled together, and Granny closed two fingers around Jimmy's thumb. Beads wouldn't do, it must be something alive. She was so amazed her thoughts ran round and round. So, my dear Lord, this is my death and I wasn't even thinking about it. My children have come to see me die. But I can't, it's not time. Oh, I always hated surprises. I wanted to give Cornelia the amethyst set—Cornelia, you're to have the amethyst set, but Hapsy's to wear it when she wants, and, Doctor Harry, do shut up. Nobody sent for you. Oh, my dear Lord, do wait a minute. I meant to do something about the Forty Acres, Jimmy doesn't need it and Lydia will later on with that worthless husband of hers. I meant to finish the altar cloth and send six bottles of wine to Sister Borgia for her dyspepsia.

I want to send six bottles of wine to Sister Borgia, Father Connolly, now don't let me forget.

Cornelia's voice made short turns and tilted over and crashed. "Oh, Mother, oh, Mother, oh, Mother. . . ."

"I'm not going, Cornelia. I'm taken by surprise. I can't go."

You'll see Hapsy again. What about her? "I thought you'd never come." Granny   60
made a long journey outward, looking for Hapsy. What if I don't find her? What then? Her heart sank down and down, there was no bottom to death, she couldn't come to the end of it. The blue light from Cornelia's lampshade drew into a tiny point in the center of her brain, it flickered and winked like an eye, quietly it fluttered and dwindled. Granny lay curled down within herself, amazed and watchful, staring at the point of light that was herself; her body was now only a deeper mass of shadow in an endless darkness and this darkness would curl around the light and swallow it up. God, give a sign!

For the second time there was no sign. Again no bridegroom and the priest in the house. She could not remember any other sorrow because this grief wiped them all away. Oh, no, there's nothing more cruel than this—I'll never forgive it. She stretched herself with a deep breath and blew out the light.

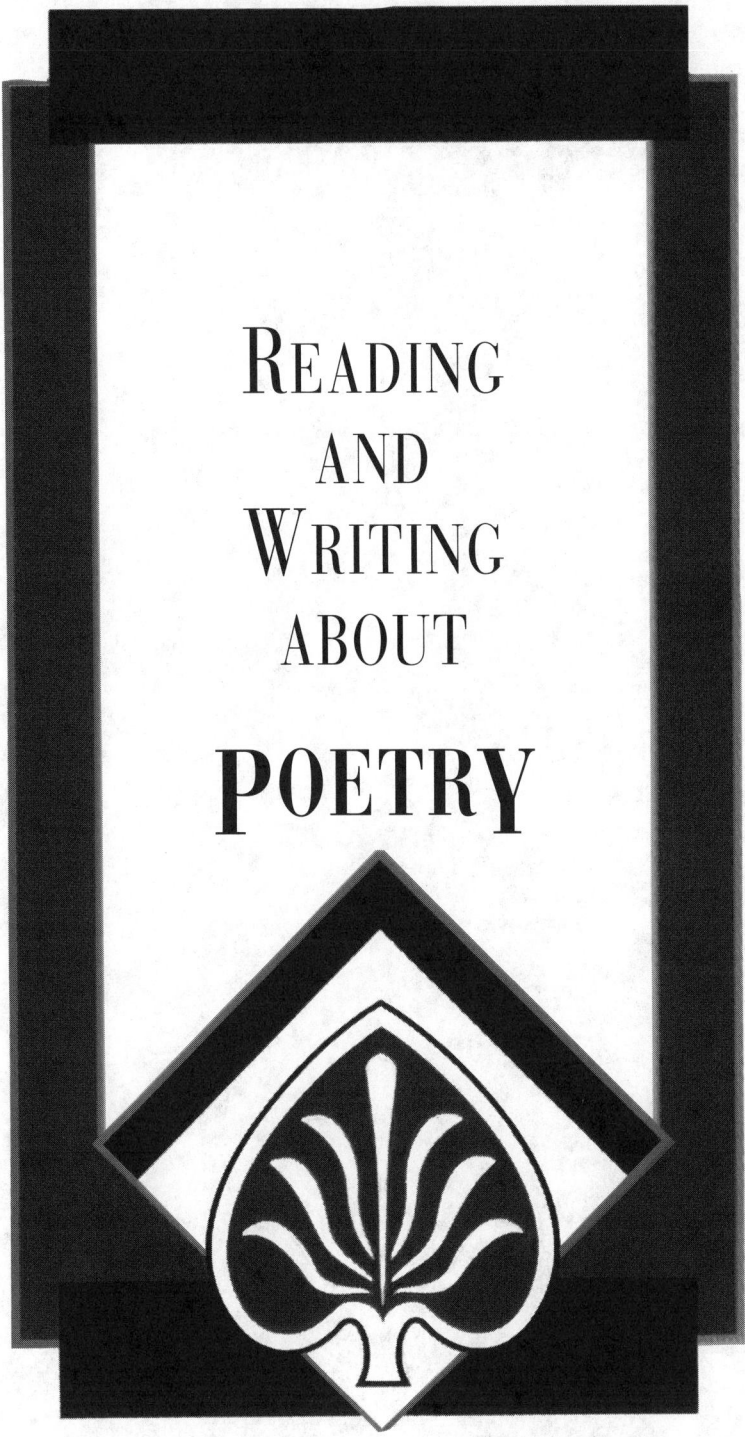

READING
AND
WRITING
ABOUT

POETRY

13

Meeting Poetry: An Overview

Poetry and **poem** describe a wide variety of spoken and written forms, styles, and patterns, and also a wide variety of subjects. Because of the variety, it is not possible to give a single, comprehensive definition. The origin of the words is the Greek word *poiema*, "something made or fashioned [in words]"—a meaning that applies both to poetry and to poems. Naturally, a **poet** was, and is, a person who writes or speaks poems. Rather than trying to create an understanding of poetry by defining it, we believe the best way to understand it is to read it, learn it, savor it, ponder it, and enjoy it. As your experience with poetry deepens, you will develop your own ideas and definitions.

THE NATURE OF POETRY

We begin with a poem based in the thoughts and experiences of just about everyone, young and old.

LISEL MUELLER (b. 1924)

Hope _____ *1976*

It hovers in dark corners   *hope preceeds the light*
before the lights are turned on,
   it shakes sleep from its eyes
   and drops from mushroom gills,
     it explodes in the starry heads   5
     of dandelions turned sages, *dandelions loves me,* *green is the color*
       it sticks to the wings of green angels *love me not,* *of hope,*
       that sail from the tops of maples. *leaves on top of a maple tree.*

It sprouts in each occluded eye
of the many-eyed potato,   10
   it lives in each earthworm segment
   surviving cruelty,

it is the motion that runs   *dog thinks you are going to*
from the eyes to the tail of a dog,   *give it something.*
    it is the mouth that inflates the lungs   15
    of the child that has just been born.

says It is the singular gift
other We cannot destroy in ourselves,   *saying we can not destroy*
people   *hope for ourselves,*
can't The argument that refutes death,   *hope is the argument that refutes*
destroy The genius that invents the future,   *death, hope survives*   20
it, All we know of God.   *death,*
we can   *if we have no hope*
Survive   *we will not know God,*
It is the serum which makes us swear
Not to betray one another;
It is in this poem, trying to speak.

QUESTIONS

1. How does the poem illustrate the meaning of hope? How true or adequate are the specific locations where hope may be found? How do these locations provide the grounds for a broadened understanding of hope?

2. What does the poet mean by saying that hope is a "singular gift / we cannot destroy in ourselves" and that hope is a "serum" that prevents people from betraying each other?

3. According to the illustrations in the poem, how strong is the connection between hope and life? Can anything or anyone be without hope?

4. Why does the poet write "trying to speak" rather than "speaking" in the final line?

"Hope" demonstrates that poetry is identifiable with life and the living. Mueller takes us on a journey we have not previously traveled, even though most of us take hope for granted as a regular part of our lives. We constantly hope for better weather, good luck, happier times, love, successful academic and athletic performance, more money, more and better friendships, and so on. But Mueller reminds us that hope exists in common things around us where we have never even thought about seeing it, such as the fluttering seeds ("angels") of maple trees, the expanding lungs of a newborn baby, the "genius that invents the future," and even the blind eyes of a potato. As we read the poem we find something new in it, a way of looking at things that we normally consider ordinary but which the poem makes extraordinary. Thus it is true that a common, everyday potato planted in the ground is an embodiment of hope because its potential growth is the same growth that we find in all forms of vegetable life. The poem even leaves us with a speculative and unusual conclusion, giving life to hope by stating that hope speaks simultaneously with poetry itself. These connections, which Mueller naturally and easily makes for us, cause us to say yes, to agree that hope is essential to life. Like all good poetry, "Hope" leads us into areas of thought which we have never before considered.

It is not necessary that poetry always be serious. Sometimes it can be clever and fanciful, and by this means it leads our thoughts, as in "Schoolsville" by Billy Collins.

BILLY COLLINS (b. 1941)

Schoolsville ————————————————— An English teacher's *1985*
Poem

Glancing over my shoulder at the past,
I realize the number of students I have taught   exaggeration,
is enough to populate a small town.   town called Schoolsville,

I can see it nestled in a paper landscape,
chalk dust flurrying down in winter,   5
nights dark as a blackboard.

The population ages but never graduates.
On hot afternoons they sweat the final in the park
and when it's cold they shiver around stoves
reading disorganized essays out loud.   10
A bell rings on the hour and everybody zigzags
in the streets with their books.

I forgot all their last names first and their
first names last in alphabetical order.
But the boy who always had his hand up   15
is an alderman and owns the haberdashery.
The girl who signed her papers in lipstick
leans against the drugstore, smoking,
brushing her hair like a machine.

Their grades are sewn into their clothes   20
like references to Hawthorne.°   *i.e., The Scarlet Letter*
The A's stroll along with other A's.
The D's honk whenever they pass another D.

All the creative writing students recline
on the courthouse lawn and play the lute.   25
Wherever they go, they form a big circle.

Needless to say, I am the mayor.
I live in the white colonial at Maple and Main.
I rarely leave the house. The car deflates
in the driveway. Vines twirl around the porchswing.   30

Once in a while a student knocks on the door
with a term paper fifteen years late
or a question about Yeats or double-spacing.
And sometimes one will appear in a window pane
to watch me lecturing the wall paper,   35
quizzing the chandelier, reprimanding the air.

QUESTIONS

1. What recognizable school experiences does the poem mention? Why is "Schoolsville" the title?
2. Describe the speaker. How does he indicate affection for students?
3. What details indicate that the poem is fantasy and not reality? To what degree is the poem humorous?
4. Compare the details of this poem with those in Roethke's "Dolor" (Chapter 15, p. 738). What similarities do you find in the choice and appropriateness of detail? What differences?
5. Each poem you read may help you understand, and therefore define, poetry. How might this poem help you begin making a definition?

"Schoolsville" reveals the variety and freedom of poetry. Unlike poems that are set out in strict line lengths, rhythms, and rhymes, "Schoolsville," though arranged in lines, does not follow measured rhythmical or rhyming patterns. The language is not difficult, the descriptions are straightforward, and the scenes seem both real and amusing. Many details—such as the "chalk dust flurrying down" like snow, "the girl who signed her name in lipstick," and the students forming a circle when they meet—are outrightly funny. But the poem moves from apparent reality to something beyond reality. Unifying the poem is the fanciful idea that school life is, like life generally, at once comical, serious, memorable, and poignant. It is therefore clear that this poem describing a school community is designed to shape our responses through its underlying insight and power.

We should always recognize that good poems, regardless of their topic, have similar power. To see this, let us look at another poem, by the seventeenth-century English poet Robert Herrick.

ROBERT HERRICK   (1591–1664)

Here a Pretty Baby Lies _____ *1648*

Here a pretty baby lies
Sung asleep with lullabies:
Pray be silent, and not stir
Th'easy earth that covers her.

QUESTIONS

1. What situation is described in this poem? To what degree is this situation either ordinary or unusual?
2. How does the final line change your perception of the first three lines? How does it change your response to the poem?

3. Consider the double meanings of the following words and phrases: "Here . . . lies"; "sung asleep"; "lullabies"; "stir."

The first three lines of this short poem seem ordinary. A scene is described that takes place over and over again everywhere in the world: A baby is sleeping quietly, and we are told to make no sounds that would awaken her. But the last line strikes us unexpectedly and powerfully, making us realize that nothing in the poem is what we understood at first. We immediately change our initial impressions and realize that the baby is not just sleeping but dead, lying not in a cradle but in a coffin; the lullabies are not only lullabies sung by a grieving mother but religious songs sung at a funeral ceremony; and the stirring is not just making noise but disturbing the still-loose earth that has just been shoveled onto the baby's grave. The effect of this poem has legitimately been called overwhelming.

The three poems have much in common; they are serious, engaging, original, and powerful. The first, however, is serious and thought-provoking; the second is amusing and slightly perplexing; the third is sad and deeply moving. There are no other poems like them. Once we understand them, we will never forget them. Even if we never read them again, they will echo in our minds as time passes, sometimes with great vividness and power, sometimes with less. In reading them again we may rediscover our original feelings, and often we may experience entirely new feelings about them. In short, like all good poetry, these poems live, and as long as we too live, they will be a permanent part of our thoughts.

Preliminary Statements about Poetry Can Help Our Understanding

As "Hope," "Schoolsville," and "Here a Pretty Baby Lies" demonstrate, all good poems are unique, and each poem we read will extend our understanding of the nature of poetry. Because this is so, we cannot formulate a single definition that can fit all poems. Nevertheless, we can offer a number of preliminary statements as a help to our understanding. To begin with, poems are imaginative works expressed in words that are used with the utmost compression, force, and economy. Unlike prose, which is expansive if not exhaustive, many poems are brief. But poetry is also comprehensive, offering us high points of thought, feeling, reflection, and resolution. Poems may be formed in just about any coherent and developed shape, from a line of a single word to lines of twenty, thirty, or more words; and these lines may be organized into any number of repeating or nonrepeating patterns. Some poems make us think, give us new and unexpected insights, and generally instruct us. Other poems arouse our emotions, surprise, amuse us, and inspire us. Ideally, reading and understanding poetry should prompt us to reexamine, reinforce, and reshape our ideas, our attitudes, our feelings, and our lives.

POETRY OF THE ENGLISH LANGUAGE

Today, most nations with their own languages have their own literatures, including poetry, with their own unique histories and characteristics. In this anthology, however, we are concerned primarily, but not exclusively, with poetry in our own language by American, British, and Canadian poets.

The earliest poems in English date back to the period of *Old English* (450–1100). Many of these early English poems reflect the influence of Christianity. Indeed, the most famous poem, the epic *Beowulf,* was probably interpreted as a Christian allegory even though it concerns the secular themes of adventure, courage, and war. Ever since the *Middle English* period (1100–1500), poets have written about many other subjects, although religious themes have remained important. Today, we find poetry on virtually all topics, including worship, music, love, society, sports, individuality, sexuality, warfare, strong drink, government, and politics; some poems treat special and unusual topics such as fishing, computers, exotic birds, and car crashes.

In short, poetry is alive and flourishing. Some people read it aloud in front of audiences, friends, and families; others read it silently in private. A poem set to music and sung aloud is especially powerful. Francis Scott Key's "The Star-Spangled Banner," for example, which he wrote about a battle in the War of 1812, has become our national anthem. More recently, musical groups like the Beatles, U2, and Smashing Pumpkins, along with singer Bruce Springsteen, have given poetic expression to ideas that huge masses of people have taken to heart. Ever since the 1960s, people devoted to civil rights have been unified and strengthened by the simple poetic lyrics of "We Shall Overcome," not only in the United States but throughout the world. The strength and vitality of poetry could be similarly documented time and time again.

HOW TO READ A POEM

With poetry, as with any other literary form, the more effort we put into understanding, the greater will be our reward. Poems are often about subjects that we have never experienced directly. We have never met the poet, never had his or her exact experiences, and never thought about things in exactly the same way. To recapture the experience of the poem, we need to understand the language, ideas, attitudes, and frames of reference that bring the poem to life.

We must therefore read all poems carefully, thoughtfully, and sympathetically—words that sum up the best approach to reading poetry. The economy and compression of poetry mean that every part of the poem must carry some of the impact and meaning, and thus every part repays careful attention. Try to interact with the poem. Do not expect the poem (or the poet) to do all the work. The poem contributes its language, imagery, rhythms, ideas, and all the other aspects that make it poetry, but you, the reader, will need to open your mind and your heart to the poem's impact.

There is no single technique for reading, absorbing, and appreciating poetry. In Chapter 1 we offer a number of guidelines for studying any work of literature (pp. 12–13). In addition to following the guidelines, read each poem more than once and keep in mind these objectives.

1. *Read straight through to get a general sense of the poem.* In this first reading, do not stop to puzzle out hard passages or obscure words; just read through from beginning to end.

2. *Try to understand the poem's meaning and organization.* As you read and reread the poem, study these elements:

- *important*
  The title. The title is almost always informative. The title of Collins's "Schoolsville" suggests that the poem will contain a somewhat flippant treatment of school life. The title of Frost's "Stopping by Woods on a Snowy Evening" suggests that the poem will present ideas derived from the natural world in cold and darkness.

- *The speaker.* Poems are dramatic, having points of view just like prose fiction. First-person speakers talk from the "inside" because they are directly involved in the action (like the speaker in Collins's "Schoolsville"). Other speakers are "outside" observers demonstrating the third-person limited and omniscient points of view, as in the anonymous "Sir Patrick Spens" (see also Chapter 5).

- *The meanings of all words, whether familiar or unfamiliar.* The words in many poems are immediately clear, as in Herrick's "Here a Pretty Baby Lies," but other poems may contain unfamiliar words and references that need looking up. You will need to consult dictionaries, encyclopedias, and other sources until you gain a grasp of the poem's content. If you have difficulty with meanings even after using your sources, speak to your instructor.

- *The poem's setting and situation.* Some poems establish their settings and circumstances vividly. Frost's "Stopping by Woods on a Snowy Evening," for example, describes an evening scene in which the speaker stops his sleigh by a woods so that he can watch snow falling amid the trees. Although not all poems are so clear, you should learn as much as you can about setting and situation in every poem you read.

- *The poem's basic form and development.* Some poems, like the anonymous "Sir Patrick Spens," are narratives; others, like Northrup's "Ogichidag," are personal statements; still others may be speeches to another person, like Herrick's "Here a Pretty Baby Lies." The poems may be laid out in a sonnet form or may develop in two-line sequences (couplets). They may contain stanzas, as in Mueller's "Hope," each unified by a particular action or thought. Try to determine the form and to trace the way in which the poem unfolds, part by part.

- *The poem's subject and theme.* The **subject** indicates the general or specific topic, while the **theme** refers to the idea or ideas that the poem explores. Jarrell's "The Death of the Ball Turret Gunner" announces its subject in the title. However, you must usually infer the theme. Jarrell's theme is the repulsive ugliness of war, the poignancy of untimely death, the callousness of the living toward the dead, and the suddenness with which war forces young people to face cruelty and horror.

3. *Read the poem aloud, sounding each word clearly.* Although this step may seem unnecessary, reading aloud will enable you to judge the effect of sound, rhythm, and rhyme. If you read Jarrell's "The Death of the Ball Turret Gunner" aloud, for example, you will notice the impact of rhyming *froze* with *hose* and the suggestion of the percussive sounds of cannon fire in the repeated and rhyming *l*, *a*, and *k* sounds of *black flak*. (For further discussion of sounds in poetry, see Chapter 19.)

   4. *Prepare a paraphrase of the poem, and make an explication of the ideas and themes.* A paraphrase (discussed later in this chapter) is a restatement of the poem in your own words which helps crystallize your understanding (see also Chapter 2, pp. 102–107). An explication, which is both explanation and interpretation, goes beyond paraphrase to consider significance—either of brief passages or of the entire poem.

STUDYING POETRY

Let us now look in detail at a poem, in this case one that tells a story. It was composed orally as a song sometime during the late Middle Ages or early Renaissance, when most people got information about the outside world from strolling balladeers who sang the news to them (there were no newspapers, and besides, few people could read). It tells a story that is probably true, or at least based on a real event.

ANONYMOUS

Sir Patrick Spens ——————————————————————— *Fifteenth century*

The king sits in Dumferline° town,
   Drinking the blood-red wine:
"O where will I get a good sailor
   To sail this ship of mine?"

Up and spoke an eldern° knight   *old, senior*
   Sat° at the king's right knee: *who sat*
"Sir Patrick Spens is the best sailor
   That sails upon the sea."

The king has written a braid° letter   *large, commanding*
   And signed it wi° his hand,   *with*
And sent it to Sir Patrick Spens,
   Was° walking on the sand.   *who was*

The first line that Sir Patrick read,
   A loud laugh laughèd he;
The next line that Sir Patrick read,
   A tear blinded his eye.

"O who is this has° done this deed,   *who has*
    This ill deed done to me,
To send me out this time o'° the year,   *of*
    To sail upon the sea?   20

"Make haste, make haste, my merry men all,
    Our good ship sails the morn."°   *in the morning*
"O say not so, my master dear,
    For I fear a deadly storm.

Late late yestere'en° I saw the new moon   *yesterday evening*   25
    With the old moon in her arm,
And I fear, I fear, my dear master,
    That we will come to harm."

O our Scots nobles were right loath
    To wet their cork-heeled shoon,°   *shoes*   30
But long ere a'° the play were played   *all*
    Their hats they swam aboon.°   *about (in the water)*

O long, long may their ladies sit
    Wi' their fans into their hand,
Or e'er they see Sir Patrick Spens
    Come sailing to the land.
                                                                                                 35

O long, long may the ladies stand,
    Wi' their gold combs in their hair,
Waiting for their own dear lords,
    For they'll see them no more.

Half o'er, half o'er to Aberdour°   40
    It's fifty fathom deep,
And there lies good Sir Patrick Spens,
    Wi' the Scots lords at his feet.

QUESTIONS

1. What action does the poem describe? Who are the principal individual figures? What groups of people are involved with and concerned about the action?

2. What do you learn about the principal figure, Sir Patrick Spens? Why does he follow the king's orders rather than his own judgment?

3. What conflicts do you find in the poem? Do they seem personal or political?

4. What emotions are conveyed in the last two stanzas? Since the poem does not explain why the king sends Sir Patrick and his men to sea, how might the emotions have been expressed more strongly?

SIR PATRICK SPENS.   1 *Dumferline:* a town on the Firth of Forth, in Scotland.   41 *Aberdour:* Aberdeen, on the east coast of Scotland on the North Sea, about eighty miles north of Dumberline.

5. Describe the poem's use of dialogue. How many people speak? How do the speeches assist in conveying the poem's action?

"Sir Patrick Spens" is a **narrative ballad.** A narrative tells a story, and the term *ballad* defines the poem's shape or form. The first two stanzas set up the situation: The king needs a sailor to undertake a vital mission, and an old knight—one of the king's close advisers—suggests choosing Sir Patrick Spens, who is obviously a competent and reliable sea captain. The rest of the poem focuses on the feelings and eventual death of Sir Patrick and his men. The third stanza provides a transition from the king to Sir Patrick. The king orders Sir Patrick to sea, and Sir Patrick reads the order. At first he laughs—probably sardonically, because Sir Patrick's response is that an order to go to sea at an obvious time of danger is nothing more than a grim joke. But when he realizes that the order is real, he foresees disaster. Our sense of impending calamity is increased when we learn that Sir Patrick's crew is also frightened (lines 23–28).

The shipwreck, described in the eighth stanza, is presented with ironic understatement. There is no description of the storm or of the crew's panic, nor does the speaker describe the masts splitting or the ship sinking under the waves. Although these horrors are omitted, the floating hats are grim evidence of destruction and death. The remainder of the poem continues in this vein of understatement. In the ninth and tenth stanzas the focus shifts back to the land, and to the ladies who will wait a "long, long" time (forever) for Sir Patrick and his men to return. The poem ends with a vision of Sir Patrick and the "Scots lords" lying "fifty fathom deep."

On first reflection, "Sir Patrick Spens" tells a sad tale without complications. The subject seems to describe no more than Sir Patrick's unfortunate drowning, along with his crew and the Scots noblemen. One might therefore claim that the poem does not have a clear theme. Even the understated irony of the floating hats and the waiting ladies is straightforward and unambiguous.

However, you might consider what the poem suggests about the contradictions and conflicts between authority and individuals. Sir Patrick knows the danger, yet he still obeys the king. In addition, there is a suggestion in lines 5, 17 to 20, and 32 of political infighting. The "eldern knight" is in effect responsible for dooming the ship. Moreover, the "play" being "played" suggests that a political game is taking place over and beyond the grim game of the men caught in the deadly storm (if Sir Patrick knows the danger, would not the knight also know it, and would not this knight also know the consequences of choosing Sir Patrick?). These political motives are not spelled out, but they are implied. Thus the poem is not only a sad tale but also a poignant dramatization of how power operates, of how a loyal person responds to a tragic dilemma, and of the pitiful consequences of that response.

In reading poetry, then, let the poem be your guide. Get all the words, try to understand dramatic situations, follow the emotional cues the poet gives you, and try to explain everything that is happening. If you find implications that you believe are important, as with the political overtones of "Sir Patrick Spens," use specific details from the poem to support your observations. Resist the temptation to "uncover" unusual or far-fetched elements in the poem (such as that hope is a tiny spirit who can inhabit human beings, trees, and vegetables in the blink of an eye, or that the "man he killed" was literally the speaker's brother). Draw only those conclusions that the poem itself will support.

 ## POEMS FOR STUDY

EMILY DICKINSON (1830–1886)

Because I Could Not Stop for Death _____ 1890 (ca. 1863)

Because I could not stop for Death–
He kindly stopped for me–
The Carriage held but just Ourselves–
And Immortality.

We slowly drove–He knew no haste   5
And I had put away
My labor and my leisure too,
For His Civility–

We passed the School, where Children strove
At Recess–in the Ring–   10
We passed the Fields of Gazing Grain–
We passed the Setting Sun–

Or rather–He passed Us–
The Dews drew quivering and chill–
For only Gossamer,° my Gown–   *thin fabric*   15
My Tippet°–only Tulle°–   *cape, scarf; thin silk*

We passed before a House that seemed
A Swelling of the Ground—
The Roof was scarcely visible—
The Cornice—in the Ground—   20

Since then—'tis Centuries—and yet
Feels shorter than the Day
I first surmised the Horses' Heads
Were toward Eternity—

QUESTIONS

1. Who is the speaker, and what is she like? Why couldn't she stop for Death? What
    perspective does her present position give the poem?
2. In what unusual ways does the poem characterize death?
3. What does the carriage represent? Where is it headed? Who are the riders?
    What is meant by the things the carriage passes?
4. What is represented by the house in line 17? Why does the poet use the word
    "House" in preference to some other word?

ROBERT FRANCIS   (1901–1987)

Catch _____ *1950*

Two boys uncoached are tossing a poem together,
Overhand, underhand, backhand, sleight of hand, every hand,
Teasing with attitudes, latitudes, interludes, altitudes,
High, make him fly off the ground for it, low, make him stoop,
Make him scoop it up, make him as-almost-as-possible miss it,
Fast, let him sting from it, now, fool him slowly,
Anything, everything tricky, risky, nonchalant,
Anything under the sun to outwit the prosy,
Over the tree and the long sweet cadence down,
Over his head, make him scramble to pick up the meaning,
And now, like a posy, a pretty one plump in his hands.

QUESTIONS

1. Describe the language of "Catch." How does the poet establish that there are
    two meanings to most of the words in the game of catch played by the "boys"?
2. How accurately does the poem describe a game of ordinary catch in which the
    participants are throwing a baseball? How interesting would a game of catch be
    if the participants stood still and merely threw the ball back and forth to each
    other ? How interesting would poetry be if the poet did not create variety just as
    the catch players vary their throws?

3. How well does the analogy of the game of catch explain why poetry sometimes requires extra efforts of understanding?

ROBERT FROST (1874–1963)

Stopping by Woods on a Snowy Evening _____ 1923

Whose woods these are I think I know.   *a — starts w/ w sound end with w sound.*
His house is in the village though;   *a — " w/ n " end*
He will not see me stopping here   *b* *w/ n "*
To watch his woods fill up with snow.   *a*

My little horse must think it queer   *a*   5
To stop without a farmhouse near   *a*
Between the woods and frozen lake   *b*
The darkest evening of the year.   *a*

He gives his harness bells a shake   *a*
To ask if there is some mistake.   *a*   10
The only other sound's the sweep   *b*
Of easy wind and downy flake.   *a*

The woods are lovely, dark and deep,   *a*   *realizes he has*
But I have promises to keep,   *a*   *responsibilities,*
And miles to go before I sleep,   *a*   *miles to* *people depend on them.*   15
And miles to go before I sleep.   *a*   *go before*
I die   *for someone*
                                         who just
                                         might commit
                                         suicide.

QUESTIONS

1. What do we learn about the speaker? Where is he? What is he doing?
2. What is the setting (place, weather, time) of this poem? *woods, winter, night*
3. Why does the speaker want to watch the "woods fill up with snow"?
4. What evidence suggests that the speaker is embarrassed or self-conscious about stopping? Consider the words "though" in line 2 and "must" in line 5.
5. The last stanza offers two alternative attitudes and courses of action. What are they? Which does the speaker choose? *commit Suicide, don't Commit Suicide*
6. To what extent do the sound and rhyme of this poem contribute to its impact? Note especially the *s* sounds in line 11 and the *w* sounds in line 12.

THOMAS HARDY (1840–1928)

The Man He Killed _____ 1902

"Had he and I but met
  By some old ancient inn,
We should have sat us down to wet
  Right many a nipperkin!°   *half-pint cup*

"But ranged as infantry,   5
   And staring face to face,
I shot at him as he at me,
   And killed him in his place.

"I shot him dead because—
   Because he was my foe.   10
Just so: my foe of course he was;
   That's clear enough; although

"He thought he'd 'list,° perhaps,   *enlist*
   Off-hand like—just as I—
Was out of work—had sold his traps°—   *possessions*   15
   No other reason why.

"Yes; quaint and curious war is!
   You shoot a fellow down
You'd treat if met where any bar is,
   Or help to half-a-crown."°   20

THE MAN HE KILLED.   20 *half a crown:* at the time, the equivalent of $20 or $30.

QUESTIONS

1. Who and what is the speaker? What do you learn about him from his language?
2. What situation and event is the speaker recalling and relating?
3. What is the effect produced by repeating the word "because" in lines 9 and 10 and using the word "although" in line 12?
4. What is the speaker's attitude toward his "foe" and toward what he has done?
5. What point, if any, does this poem make about war? How are this poem and Jarrell's "The Death of the Ball Turret Gunner" similar and different?

JOY HARJO   (b. 1951)

Eagle Poem _____ *1990*

To pray you open your whole self
To sky, to earth, to sun, to moon
To one whole voice that is you.
And know there is more
That you can't see, can't hear,
Can't know except in moments
Steadily growing, and in languages
That aren't always sound but other
Circles of motion.
Like eagle that Sunday morning
Over Salt River. Circled in blue sky
In wind, swept our hearts clean

With sacred wings.
We see you, see ourselves and know
That we must take the utmost care   15
And kindness in all things.
Breathe in, knowing we are made of
All this, and breathe, knowing
We are truly blessed because we
Were born, and die soon within a   20
True circle of motion,
Like eagle rounding out the morning
Inside us.
We pray that it will be done
In beauty.   25
In beauty.

QUESTIONS

1. What is meant by the requirement that "to pray you open your whole self / To sky, to earth, to sun, to moon"? What is the meaning of lines 4–9?
2. Why is the eagle significant to the speaker? Of what importance is the figure that the eagle makes?
3. Why does the poet repeat the phrase "In beauty" at the poem's end? (For comparison, see the Navajo Healing Prayer from the Beautyway Chant, Chapter 25.)

A. E. HOUSMAN   (1859–1936)

Loveliest of Trees, the Cherry Now _____ *1896*

Loveliest of trees, the cherry now
Is hung with bloom along the bough,
And stands about the woodland ride°   *path*
Wearing white for Eastertide.
                                                        5
Now, of my threescore years and ten,
Twenty will not come again,
And take from seventy springs a score,
It only leaves me fifty more.

And since to look at things in bloom   10
Fifty springs are little room,
About the woodland I will go
To see the cherry hung with snow.

QUESTIONS

1. How old is the speaker? How can you tell? Why does he assume he will live seventy years ("threescore years and ten")?

2. How would you describe the speaker's perception or sense of time? What is the effect of the words "only" (line 8) and "little" (line 10)?

3. What ideas about time, beauty, and life does this poem explore? What does it suggest about the way we should live?

RANDALL JARRELL   (1914–1965)

The Death of the Ball Turret Gunner° _____ *1945*

From my mother's sleep I fell into the State
And I hunched in its belly till my wet fur froze.°
Six miles from earth, loosed from its dream of life,
I woke to black flak° and the nightmare fighters.
When I died they washed me out of the turret with a hose.   5

THE DEATH OF THE BALL TURRET GUNNER.   *Ball Turret Gunner:* High-altitude bombers in World War II (1941–1945) contained a revolvable gun turret both at the top and at the bottom, from which a machine-gunner could shoot at attacking fighter planes. Gunners in these turrets were sometimes mutilated by the gunfire of attacking planes.   2 *froze:* The stratospheric below-zero temperatures caused the moisture in the gunner's breath to freeze as it contacted the collar of his flight jacket.   4 *flak:* the round, black explosions of antiaircraft shells fired at bombers from the ground, an acronym of the German word *Fliegerabwehrkanone.*

QUESTIONS

1. Who is the speaker? Where has he been, and what has he been doing? What has happened to him?

2. In the first line, what is the poet saying about the age of the speaker and the opportunities he had for living before he was killed? How may this line be read politically and polemically?

3. What is a turret? What is your response to the last line?

LOUIS MACNEICE   (1907–1963)

Snow _____ *1935*

The room was suddenly rich and the great bay-window was
Spawning snow and pink roses against it
Soundlessly collateral and incompatible:
World is suddener than we fancy it.

World is crazier and more of it than we think,
Incorrigibly plural. I peel and portion
A tangerine and spit the pips and feel
The drunkenness of things being various.

And the fire flames with a bubbling sound for world
Is more spiteful and gay than one supposes—   10
On the tongue on the eyes on the ears in the palms of one's hands—
There is more than glass between the snow and the huge roses.

QUESTIONS

1. Where is the speaker at the time of the poem? What is the contrast between the roses and the snow? Why is this contrast important?

2. What words describe snow in lines 1–3? What words in lines 4, 5, 6, 8, 10 describe the world generally? Why does the speaker choose these words rather than more descriptive ones?

3. What does the last line suggest?

4. What similarities and differences do you find between "Snow" and Frost's "Stopping by Woods on a Snowy Evening"?

JIM NORTHRUP   (b. 1943)

Ogichidag° _____ *1993*

I was born in war, WW Two.
Listened as the old men told stories
of getting gassed in the trenches, WW One.
Saw my uncles come back from
Guadalcanal, North Africa,   5
and the Battle of the Bulge.
Memorized the war stories
my cousins told of Korea.
Felt the fear in their voices.
Finally it was my turn,   10
my brothers too.
Joined the marines in time
for the Cuban Missile Crisis.
Heard the crack of rifles
in the rice paddies south of Da Nang.   15
Watched my friends die there
then tasted the bitterness of
the only war America ever lost.
My son is now a warrior.
Will I listen to his war stories   20
or cry into his open grave?

OGICHIDAG.   The title is the Ojibway word for "warriors."

QUESTIONS

1. What battles are mentioned in the poem, and over what period of time do these battles extend?
2. How does the speaker state that he learned about the battles? Why is this method of gaining knowledge important? What experience has the speaker had with war?
3. Why does the speaker finish the poem by referring to his son? In relationship to the poem's structure, why is the concluding question important?

NAOMI SHIHAB NYE   (b. 1952)

Where Children Live _____ *1982*

Homes where children live exude a pleasant rumpledness,
like a bed made by a child, or a yard littered with balloons.

To be a child again one would need to shed details
till the heart found itself dressed in the coat with a hood.
Now the heart has taken on gloves and mufflers,   5
the heart never goes outside to find someting to "do."
And the house takes on a new face, dignified.
No lost shoes blooming under bushes.
No chipped trucks in the drive.
Grown-ups like swings, leafy plants, slow-motion back and forth.   10
While the yard of a child is strewn with the corpses
of bottle-rockets and whistles,
anything whizzing and spectacular, brilliantly short-lived.

Trees in children's yards speak in clearer tongues.
Ants have more hope. Squirrels dance as well as hide.   15
The fence has a reason to be there, so children can go in and out.
Even when the children are at school, the yards glow
with the leftovers of their affection,
the roots of the tiniest grasses curl toward one another
like secret smiles.   20

QUESTIONS

1. How accurately does the poem present the "pleasant rumpledness" of children?
2. What is the speaker's view of the comparative dependence or independence of children? What does the speaker think of children?
3. Sometimes poems about children can be overly sentimental. How well does this poem present sentiment about children? Does it go too far, or is it about right?

WILLIAM SHAKESPEARE   (1564–1616)

Sonnet 55:
Not Marble, Nor the Gilded Monuments ———————————————— *1609*

Not marble, nor the gilded monuments
Of princes, shall outlive this powerful rhyme;
But you shall shine more bright in these contents
Than unswept stone, besmeared with sluttish time.
When wasteful war shall statues overturn,   5
And broils root out the work of masonry,
Nor° Mars his° sword nor war's quick fire shall burn   *Neither; Mars's*
The living record of your memory.
'Gainst death and all-oblivious enmity
Shall you pace forth; your praise shall still find room   10
Even in the eyes of all posterity
That wear this world out to the ending doom.°   *Judgment Day*
So, till the judgment that yourself arise,
You live in this, and dwell in lovers' eyes.

QUESTIONS

1. Who is the speaker of the poem, and who is being addressed?
2. What powers of destruction does the speaker mention? What, according to the speaker, will survive these powers?
3. What does "the living record of your memory" (line 8) mean?
4. What is the poem's subject? Theme?

WRITING A PARAPHRASE OF A POEM

Paraphrasing is especially useful in the study of poetry. It fixes both the general shape and the details of a poem in your mind, and it also reveals the poetic devices at work. A comparison of the original poem with the paraphrase highlights the techniques and the language that make the poem effective.

To paraphrase a poem, rewrite it in prose, in your own words. Decide what details to include—a number that you determine partly by the length of the poem and partly by the total length of your paraphrase. When you deal with lyrics, sonnets, and other short poems, you may include all the details, and thus your paraphrase may be as long as the work, or longer. Paraphrases of long poems, however, will be shorter than the originals because some details must be summarized briefly while others may be cut entirely.

It is vital to make your paraphrase accurate and also to use *only your own words*. To make sure that your words are all your own, read through the poem several times. Then, put the poem out of sight and write your paraphrase. Once you've finished, check yourself both for accuracy and vocabulary. If you find that you've borrowed too many of the poem's words, choose other words that mean the same thing, or else use quotation marks to set off the original words (but do not overuse quotations).

Above all, remain faithful to the poem, but *avoid drawing conclusions and giving unnecessary explanations.* It would be wrong in a paraphrase of Jarrell's "The Death of the Ball Turret Gunner," for example, to state, "This poem makes a forceful argument against the brutal and wasteful deaths caused by war." This assertion states the poem's *theme,* but it *does not* describe the poem's actual *content.*

Organizing Your Paraphrase

The organization of your paraphrase should reflect the poem's form or development. Include material in the order in which it occurs. With short poems, organize your paraphrase to reflect the poem's development line by line or stanza by stanza. In paraphrasing Shakespeare's "Not Marble, Nor the Gilded Monuments," for example, you should deal with each quatrain in sequence and then consider the final couplet. With longer poems, look for natural divisions such as groups of related stanzas, verse paragraphs, or other possible organizational units. In every situation, the poem's shape should determine the form of your paraphrase.

DEMONSTRATIVE STUDENT ESSAY

A Paraphrase of Thomas Hardy's "The Man He Killed"°

[1]   If the man I killed had met me in an inn, we would have sat down together and had many drinks. Because we belonged to armies of warring foot soldiers lined up on a battlefield, however, we shot at each other, and my shot killed him.

[2]   The reason I killed him, I think, was that he and I were enemies--just that. But as I think of it, I realize that he had enlisted in just the way I did. Perhaps he did it on a whim, or perhaps he had lost his job, and sold everything he owned. There was no other reason to enlist.

[3]   Being at war is unusual and strange. Instead of buying a man a drink or helping him out with a little money, you have to kill him.

Commentary on the Essay

Because Hardy's poem is short, the paraphrase attempts to include all its details. The organization closely follows the poem's development. Paragraph 1, for example, restates the contents of the first two stanzas. Paragraph 2 restates

° See p. 673 for this poem.

the third and fourth stanzas. Finally, the last paragraph separately paraphrases the last stanza, which contains the reflections made by the poem's "I" speaker. This paragraph concludes the paraphrase just as the last stanza concludes the poem.

Notice that the essay does not abstract details from the poem, such as "The dead man might have become a good friend in peacetime" for stanza 5; nor does it extend details, such as "We would have gotten acquainted, had drinks together, told many stories, and done quite a bit of laughing" for stanza 1 (even though both stanzas suggest these details). Although the paraphrase reflects the poem's strong antiwar sentiments, an interpretive sentence like "By his very directness, the narrator brings out the senselessness and brutality of warfare" would be out of place. What is needed is a short restatement of the poem to demonstrate the essay writer's understanding of the poem's content, and no more.

WRITING AN EXPLICATION OF A POEM

Explication goes beyond the assimilation required for a paraphrase and thus provides you with the opportunity to show your understanding. There is no need, however, to explain everything in the poem. A complete, or total, explication would theoretically require you to explain the meaning and implications of each word and every line—a technique that obviously would be exhaustive (and exhausting). It would also be self-defeating, for explicating everything would prohibit you from using your judgment and deciding what is important.

A more manageable and desirable technique is therefore the **general explication,** which devotes attention to the meaning of individual parts in relationship to the entire work, as in the discussion of "Sir Patrick Spens" (p. 670). You might think of a general explication as your explanation or "reading" of the poem. Because it does not require you to go into exhaustive detail, you will need to be selective and to consider only those details that are significant in themselves and vital to your own thematic development.

Questions for Discovering Ideas

- What does the title contribute to the reader's understanding?
- Who is speaking? Where is the speaker when the poem is happening?
- What is the situation? What has happened in the past, or what is happening in the present, that has brought about the speech?
- What difficult, special, or unusual words does the poem contain? What references need explaining? How does an explanation assist in the understanding of the poem?
- How does the poem develop? Is it a personal statement? Is it a story?
- What is the main idea of the poem? What details make possible the formulation of the main idea?

Strategies for Organizing Ideas

Your general explication demonstrates your ability to (1) follow the essential details of the poem (the same as in a paraphrase), (2) understand the issues and the meaning the poem reveals, (3) explain some of the relationships of content to technique, and (4) note and discuss especially important or unique aspects of the poem.

In your introduction, use your central idea to express a general view of the poem, which your essay will bear out. The discussion of the anonymous "Sir Patrick Spens" (p. 670) suggests some possible central ideas, namely that (1) the poem highlights a conflict between self-preservation and obedience to authority, and (2) innocent people may be caught in political infighting. In the following demonstrative student essay explicating Hardy's "The Man He Killed," the central idea is that war is senseless.

In the body of your essay, first explain the poem's content—not with a paraphrase but with a description of the poem's major organizing elements. Hence, if the speaker of the poem is "inside" the poem as a first-person involved "I," you do not need to reproduce this voice yourself in your description. Instead, *describe* the poem in your own words, with whatever brief introductory phrases you find necessary, as in the second paragraph of the following demonstrative student essay.

Next, explicate the poem in relation to your central idea. Choose *your own* order of discussion, depending on your topics. You should, however, keep stressing your central idea with each new topic. Thus, you might wish to follow your description by discussing the poem's meaning, or even by presenting two or more possible interpretations. You might also wish to refer to significant techniques. For example, in the anonymous "Sir Patrick Spens" a noteworthy technique is the unintroduced quotations (i.e., quotations appearing without any "he said" or "quoth he" phrases) as the ballad writer's means of dramatizing the commands and responses of Sir Patrick and his doomed crew.

You might also introduce special topics, such as the crewman who explains that there will be bad luck because the new moon has "the old moon in her arm" (line 26). Such a reference to superstition might include the explanation of the crewman's assumptions, the relationship of his uneasiness to the remainder of the poem, and also how the ballad writer keeps the narrative brief. In short, discuss those aspects of meaning and technique that bear upon your central idea.

In your conclusion, you may repeat your major idea to reinforce your essay's thematic structure. Because your essay is a general explication, there will be parts of the poem that you have not discussed. You might therefore mention what might be gained from an exhaustive discussion of various parts of the poem (do not, however, begin to exhaust any subject in the conclusion of your essay). The last stanza of Hardy's "The Man He Killed," for example, contains the words "quaint and curious" in reference to war. These words are unusual, particularly because the speaker might have chosen *hateful, senseless, destructive,* or other similarly descriptive words. Why did Hardy have his speaker make such a choice? With brief attention to such a problem, you may conclude your essay.

DEMONSTRATIVE STUDENT ESSAY

An Explication of Hardy's "The Man He Killed"°

[1] Thomas Hardy's "The Man He Killed" exposes the senselessness of war.* It does this through a silent contrast between the needs of ordinary people, as represented by a young man--the speaker--who has killed an enemy soldier in battle, and the antihuman and unnatural deaths of war. Of major note in this contrast are the speaker's circumstances, his language, his sense of identity with the dead man, and his concerns and wishes.†

[2] The speaker begins by contrasting the circumstances of warfare with those of peace. He does not identify himself, but his speech reveals that he is common and ordinary--a person, one of "the people"--who enjoys drinking in a bar and who prefers friendship and helpfulness to violence. If he and the man he killed had met in an inn, he says, they would have shared many drinks, but because they met on a battlefield they shot at each other, and he killed the other man. The speaker tries to justify the killing but can produce no stronger reason than that the dead man was his "foe." Once he states this reason, he again thinks of the similarities between himself and the dead man, and then he concludes that warfare is "quaint and curious" (line 17) because it forces a man to kill another man whom he would have befriended if they had met during peacetime.

[3] To make the irony of warfare clear, the poem uses easy, everyday language to bring out the speaker's ordinary qualities. His manner of speech is conversational, as in "We should have sat us down" (line 3), and "'list" (for "enlist," line 13), and his use of "you" in the last stanza. Also, his word choices, shown in words like "nipperkin," "traps," and "fellow" (lines 4, 15, and 18), are common and informal, at least in British usage. This language is important because it establishes that the speaker is an average man whom war has thrown into an unnatural role.

[4] As another means of stressing the stupidity of war, the poem makes clear that the two men--the live soldier who killed and the dead soldier who was killed--were so alike that they could have been brothers or even twins. They had similar ways of life, similar economic troubles, similar wishes to help other people, and similar motives in doing things like enlisting in the army. Symbolically, at least, the "man he killed" is the speaker himself, and hence the killing is a form of suicide. The poem thus raises the question of why two people who are almost identical should be shoved into opposing battle lines in order to kill each other. This question is rhetorical, for the obvious answer is that there is no good reason.

°See p. 673 for this poem.
*Central idea.
†Thesis sentence.

[5]

Because the speaker (and also, very likely, the dead man) is shown as a person embodying the virtues of friendliness and helpfulness, Hardy's poem is a strong disapproval of war. Clearly, political reasons for violence as policy are irrelevant to the characters and concerns of the men who fight. They, like the speaker, would prefer to follow their own needs rather than remote and meaningless ideals. The failure of complex but irrelevant political explanations is brought out most clearly in the third stanza, in which the speaker tries to give a reason for shooting the other man. Hardy's use of punctuation--the dashes--stresses the fact that the speaker has no commitment to the cause he served when killing. Thus the speaker stops at the word "because--" and gropes for a reason (line 9). Not being articulate, he can say only "Because he was my foe. / Just so: my foe of course he was; / That's clear enough" (lines 10-12). These short bursts of words indicate that he cannot explain things to himself or to anyone else except in the most obvious and trite terms, and in apparent embarrassment he inserts "of course" as a way of emphasizing hostility even though he felt none toward the man he killed.

[6]

A reading thus shows the power of the poem's dramatic argument. Hardy does not establish closely detailed reasons against war as a policy but rather dramatizes the idea that all political arguments are unimportant in view of the central and glaring brutality of war--killing. Hardy's speaker is not able to express deep feelings; rather he is confused because he is an average sort who wants only to live and let live and to enjoy a drink in a bar with friends. But this very commonness stresses the point that everyone is victimized by war--both those who die and those who kill. The poem is a powerful argument for peace and reconciliation.

Commentary on the Essay

This explication begins by stating a central idea about "The Man He Killed," then indicates the topics to follow that will develop the idea. Although nowhere does the speaker state that war is senseless, the essay takes the position that the poem embodies this idea. A more detailed examination of the poem's themes might develop the idea by discussing the ways in which individuals are caught up in social and political forces, or the contrast between individuality and the state. In this essay, however, the simple statement of the idea is enough.

Paragraph 2 describes the major details of the poem, with guiding phrases like "The speaker begins," "he says," and "he again thinks." Thus the paragraph goes over the poem, like a paraphrase, but explains how things occur, as is appropriate for an explication. Paragraph 3 is devoted to the speaker's words and idioms, with the idea that his conversational manner is part of the poem's contrasting method of argument. If these brief references to style were more detailed, this topic could be more fully developed as an aspect of Hardy's implied argument against war.

Paragraph 4 extends paragraph 3 inasmuch as it points out the similarities of the speaker and the man he killed. If the situation were reversed, the dead man might say exactly the same things about the present speaker. This affinity underscores the suicidal nature of war. Paragraph 5 treats the style of the poem's fourth stanza. In this context, the treatment is brief. The last paragraph reiterates the main idea and concludes with a tribute to the poem as an argument.

The entire essay therefore represents a reading and explanation of the poem's high points. It stresses a particular interpretation and briefly shows how various aspects of the poem bear it out.

SPECIAL TOPICS FOR WRITING AND ARGUMENT
ABOUT THE NATURE OF POETRY

1. Skim the titles of poems listed in the table of contents of this book. Judging by the subjects of these poems, describe and discuss the possible range of subject matter for poetry. What topics seem most suitable? Why? Do any topics seem to be ruled out? Why? What additional subject matter would you suggest as possible topics for poems?

2. How accurate is the proposition that poetry is a particularly compressed form of expression? To support your position, you might refer to poems such as Hardy's "The Man He Killed," MacNeice's "Snow," Francis's "Catch," and Frost's "Stopping by Woods on a Snowy Evening."

3. Consider the subject of war as brought out in Jarrell's "The Death of the Ball Turret Gunner," Hardy's "The Man He Killed," and Northrop's "Ogichidag." What ideas are common to the poems? What ideas are distinct and unique? On the basis of your comparison, consider the use of poetry as a vehicle for the expression of moral and political ideas.

4. Write two poems of your own about your future plans. In one, assume that the world is stable and will go on forever. In the other, assume that a large asteroid is out of orbit and is hurtling toward earth at great speed and that a collision six months from now will bring untold destruction and may even end life on earth. After composing your poems, write a brief explanation of how and why they differ in terms of language, references, and attitudes toward friends, family, country, religion, and so on.

5. Consult the brief section on reader-response criticism in Chapter 33. Then write an essay about your responses to one poem, or a number of poems, in this chapter. Assume that your own experiences are valuable guides for your judgment. In the poems that you have read, what has had a bearing on your experiences? What in your own experiences has given you insights into the poems? Try to avoid being anecdotal; instead, try to find a relationship between your experiences and the poetry.

6. In the reference section of your library, find two books (anthologies, encyclopedias, introductions, dictionaries of literary terms) about the general subject of poetry. On the basis of how these two sources define and explain poetry, write a brief essay telling a person younger than you what to expect from the reading of poems.

Character and Setting: Who, What, Where, and When in Poetry

Poets, like other writers, bring their works alive through the interactions of fictional characters who experience love and hatred, pleasure and pain, and most of the other conditions and situations of life. Just as in fiction, poetic characters are defined by what they say, what they do, and how they react, and also by what other characters say about them. Not all poetry is narrative, however. Hence we will study character in poems in relation to someone or something else—such as the interactions of speakers with listeners or with the reader, the inner conflicts of a speaker discussing the state of his or her spirit, and conditions such as love, hate, acceptance, disagreement, emulation, decision making, and action—brought out in personal, social, and political life.

In addition, we will examine the **setting** of a poem as one of the major means of measuring character (see also Chapter 6). Poetic protagonists, like those in stories, are necessarily influenced by their possessions, the places they inhabit, the conditions of their lives, and the times in which they live. The period that people have spent in a relationship, their relative wealth or poverty, their surroundings, their social and economic circumstances—all have a bearing on their characters. Poems therefore abound with references to events and situations and also to objects such as beaches, forests, battlefields, graveyards, teaspoons, melons, museums, and paintings.

CHARACTERS IN POETRY

The Speaker *or* Persona *Is the Voice of the Poem*

The most significant character in poetry is the **speaker,** also called the **persona** (plural *personae,* a term that comes from the Etruscan-Latin word meaning "mask"). In prose fiction, we also use *speaker* and *persona,* but we often prefer the word *narrator* because of the obvious role of storyteller. This distinction emphasizes the personal and psychological importance of poetic speakers. Sometimes the speaker is a distinct character, with individual traits and well-imagined circumstances, as in Browning's "My Last Duchess," Piercy's "Wellfleet Sabbath," and Marlowe's "The Passionate Shepherd to His Love." In Dickinson's "Because I Could Not Stop for Death" (Chapter 13), for example, the speaker is unique, for she states that she has been dead for hundreds of years and is now looking back from eternity to the occasion of her death.

Not all poetic speakers have separate identities, for some embody a position or stance that the poet selects to present detail or advance an argument. The poet is thus the undeniable speaker, but the voice we hear may be considered as a brief dramatization of the poet's personality or need. John Donne in "Batter My Heart" (Chapter 15) adopts such a stance—a supplicant or penitent praying for divine favor. In this sonnet Donne is not creating a separate dramatic character in deep religious anguish, but is expressing his own hope and fear.

Expectedly, poets use many sorts of speakers to voice their poems. In this anthology, for example, there are poems spoken by kings and dukes, husbands and wives, lovers and killers, shepherds and secretaries, believers and nonbelievers, adults and children, and almost every other kind of person you can imagine. In addition, you meet speakers who are mythological heroes and heroines, dead people, skeletons, ordinary people, machines, philosophers, lovers, former slaves, and ghosts. In fact, speakers do not have to be human; they can be animals, clouds, buildings, computers, or whatever the poet's imagination may create.

Inside Speakers Use the First Person Voice and Are Involved in the Poem's Actions. A poetic speaker may be *inside* or *outside* the poem, depending on the **point of view** used by the poet (see Chapter 5). If the point of view is first person, the speaker is *inside* the poem. Here is such a poem, written by an unknown late medieval poet.

ANONYMOUS

Western Wind, When Will Thou Blow _____ *Fifteenth century?*

Western wind, when will thou blow?
The small rain down can rain?
Christ, if my love were in my arms,
And I in my bed again.

In this poem the "my" and "I" pronouns indicate that the speaker is *inside* the poem speaking in the first person, wishing for warm spring rains and the renewal of life and love that is signaled by spring.

Outside Speakers Use the Third Person and Are Objective about the Poem's Actions. The speaker is *outside* the poem, however, if the third person is used.

In such poems, the speaker is not involved with the action; he or she describes what is happening to others, as in this anonymous Scots ballad.

ANONYMOUS

Bonny George Campbell _____ *Late sixteenth century*

High upon Highlands
   And low upon Tay,°
Bonny George Campbell
   Rode out on a day.

But toom° came his saddle,   *empty*   5
   All bloody to see,
Oh, home came his good horse,
   But never came he.

Down came his old mother,
   Greeting full sair°   *weeping full sore*   10
And down came his bonny wife,
   Wringing her hair.

Saddled, and bridled,
   And booted rode he;
And home came his good horse,   15
   But never came he.

"My meadow lies green,
   And my corn is unshorn,°   *grain is not harvested*
My barn is to build°   *yet to be built*
   And my babe is unborn."   2C

Saddled, and bridled,
   And booted rode he;
Toom home came the saddle,
   But never came he.

BONNY GEORGE CAMPBELL.   2 *Tay:* Loch Tay, a lake in Perth County, in central Scotland, about sixty miles north of Glasgow.

QUESTIONS

   1.   What can you deduce about the character, social status, way of life, and feelings of the three persons mentioned in the poem?

   2.   Why must you infer the exact nature of what happened to Bonny George Campbell?

   3.   Who is the speaker of the fifth stanza? What effect has Campbell's absence had on this speaker?

In this ballad the speaker limits his or her perspective to the people left behind, who loved Campbell. They do not know Campbell's fate beyond what they infer from the bloody saddle—nor do we, because the speaker does not tell us. However, the speaker does describe the effects upon Campbell's mother and wife, even quoting the wife's lamentation because Campbell's absence has deprived her of husband and breadwinner. By avoiding entering the poem as an "I," the speaker maintains objectivity and lets the details speak for themselves.

ADDITIONAL INFORMATION ABOUT SPEAKERS MAY BE GAINED FROM OTHER DETAILS IN POEMS. There is a great deal more to learn about poetic speakers. An obvious place to begin is the title. Take, for example, Marlowe's "The Passionate Shepherd to His Love," which reveals that the speaker is a young shepherd and that he is passionately in love.

We can also learn from the speaker's diction. In Housman's "Loveliest of Trees" (Chapter 13), the speaker reveals that he is twenty years old, that he doesn't think his remaining fifty years (assuming a lifetime of seventy years, the biblical life expectancy) will give him enough time to experience and observe life fully, that he enjoys the flowering of spring, that he knows enough about church rituals to claim that the whiteness of cherry blossoms coincides with the liturgical color of white for Easter, and that he is meditative and somber rather than extroverted and hilarious. All this is quite a bit of information from so short a poem.

If we look at all poems with the same care, we will discover many other details. Grammatical forms and word levels may define the speaker's social class or educational level. Similarly, the selection of topics may indicate the speaker's emotional state, self-esteem, knowledge, attitudes, habits, hobbies, and much more.

The Person with Whom or to Whom the Speaker Is Talking Is the Listener

The second type of character in poetry is the **listener**—a person, not the reader, whom the speaker addresses directly and who is therefore "inside" the poem. Occasionally we find poems in the form of a **dialogue** between two persons, so that the characters are *both* speakers and listeners, as in Randall's "Ballad of Birmingham" (Chapter 20). Whatever the form, the speaker-listener relationship creates drama and tension. In effect, we as readers are an audience, hearing either conversational exchanges or one-way conversations. The speakers of course identify themselves with the "I" pronoun and address their listeners with the pronouns "thou-thy-thee" and "you-your-yours."

In some poems the listener is passive, merely hearing the speaker's words without response, as in Marlowe's "The Passionate Shepherd to His Love" and Glück's "Snowdrops." In a variation of this situation, the listener may not be present but may instead be the speaker's intended recipient. In this case the speaker is like a letter writer and the listener is the "addressee." Such a listener is the "thou-thee-thine" of Ben Jonson's well-known "Drink to Me, Only, with Thine Eyes."

BEN JONSON   (1573–1637)

Drink to Me, Only, with Thine Eyes ————————————— *1616*

Drink to me, only, with thine eyes,
    And I will pledge° with mine;   *drink a toast*
Or leave a kiss but in the cup,
    And I'll not look for wine.
The thirst that from the soul doth rise   5
    Doth° ask a drink divine: *does*
But might I of Jove's nectar sup
    I would not change° for thine.   *exchange it [i.e., nectar]*

I sent thee, late,° a rosy wreath,   *lately, a short time ago*
    Not so much honoring thee,   10
As giving it a hope, that there
    It could not withered be.
But thou thereon did'st only breathe,
    And sent'st it back to me:
Since when° it grows, and smells, I swear,   *that time, then*   15
    Not of itself, but thee.

DRINK TO ME, ONLY, WITH THINE EYES.   7 *Jove's nectar:* Jove, or Jupiter, was the principal
Roman god. Nectar (a word meaning "overcoming death") was the drink of the gods; a human
being who drank it would become immortal.

QUESTIONS

   1. Who is the speaker? What do you learn about him, his knowledge, his wit, and
      his concern for the listener?
   2. What has the speaker sent to the listener? What did she do, and why is he still
      writing to her?
   3. How can the poem be seen as an attempt to "top" the listener's disdain? Explain
      why the speaker seems just as interested in showing his wittiness as in compli-
      menting the listener.

This poem demonstrates that the listener has not been passive; she has returned the speaker's gift and thus has spurned him. Therefore the poem may
be seen at least partly as the speaker's attempt, by demonstrating his wit, to
ingratiate himself with the listener. In similar poems involving a speaker and a
silent listener, we should consider both the dramatic situation and the listener's
stated and implied responses.

    A related but distinct type of situation involving a listener is the **dramatic
monologue,** in which the speaker talks directly to an on-the-spot listener whose
reactions may directly affect the course of the poem. Browning's "My Last
Duchess" is such a poem, in which the speaker, the duke, addresses an envoy of
a "count," a "you" listener, who has been given the task of arranging financial
terms about the dowry to be given by the count when the duke marries the
count's daughter.

Ultimately, we as readers are the listeners of all poems. In this capacity we are the poet's uninvolved, outside audience. Thus, in poems like Hardy's "The Workbox" (Chapter 18) and Browning's "My Last Duchess," we are a virtual hearing and viewing audience, and in a poem like Housman's "Loveliest of Trees," we are outside listeners, eavesdropping as the speaker meditates on time, death, and beauty. Sometimes, however, the poet may address us directly in our role as readers, as in this brief dedicatory poem that Ben Jonson uses to begin his book of epigrams published in 1616.

BEN JONSON   (1573–1637)

To the Reader _____ *1616*

Pray thee, take care, that tak'st my book in hand,
To read it well: that is, to understand.

In this couplet Jonson establishes intimacy with us as readers by using the second-person singular pronoun *thee*. Though we are clearly *outside* the poem, Jonson invites us *inside* by asking us to read well and understand all his forthcoming poems. As much as a poet can, he therefore closes the distance that exists between poem and reader.

Only rarely do poets address us directly, as Jonson does. For this reason it is important to determine what is meant when a poet uses the "you" pronoun (see also Chapter 5, p. 245). Sometimes the "you" suggests that we are on-the-spot listeners and even colleagues or chums of poetic speakers, but more often the "you" is a conversational way by which the speaker refers to himself or herself. Hardy's speaker in "The Man He Killed," for example (p. 673), uses an indirect "you" in this way, and thereby he establishes our assent to the idea that war is "quaint and curious." Even when we are invited to become inside listeners in this way, however, our responses do not enter the poem structurally, and therefore our role as spectators or witnesses does not change. We remain an audience of outside listeners.

Poems Are Sometimes Little Dramas with Major and Minor Participants

Because many poems are dramatic, they often involve a third type of character—major or minor participants. We learn about these characters from appearance, speech, action, and reaction. In the anonymous "Sir Patrick Spens" (p. 668), for example, we learn from Sir Patrick's outcry that he is distressed but from his action that he is obedient. In Hardy's "Channel Firing," we learn that the ages-old skeletons are sorry that they sacrificed personal enjoyment when they were alive because their strict living did nothing to improve humankind.

Most poetic speakers are reliable reporters about the actions and characters of the major and minor participants. For example, the speaker-narrator of the anonymous "Sir Patrick Spens" is honest and straightforward, and his assessment of Sir Patrick is reliable. But we should also be aware that poetic speakers, as in all fiction, can have interests beyond those of reportorial accuracy. A speaker who uses language for distortion and intimidation is the duke in Browning's "My Last Duchess." His words make clear that he is a liar and that we must look beyond his distortions to learn the character of the duchess and the nature of his life.

Not all participants, of course, are human. Poets frequently include descriptions of the animal kingdom, such as swimmers (sharks, large game fish, otters), flyers (orioles, nightingales, larks), and walkers and runners (bears, deer, lambs, woodchucks, and tigers). Although some of these animals are given character traits, as with the horse in Frost's "Stopping by Woods on a Snowy Evening" (Chapter 13) and the boobies in Tate's "The Blue Booby" (Chapter 25), they are mainly pictorial or symbolic.

SETTING AND CHARACTER IN POETRY

The people in poetry do not exist in a vacuum. When they speak and act, they reflect the time, place, thought, social conventions, and general circumstances of their lives. Love poetry, for example, is not about desire alone but rather about love within the possible ranges provided by culture and environment. Religion, economic circumstances, leisure, and the condition of the natural world may all enter into a lover's pronouncements. Thus, the speaker of Marlowe's "The Passionate Shepherd to His Love" daydreams about spending time in open nature with his love, sharing the songs of birds and the sights of "valleys, groves, hills, and fields." Here the setting of an Arcadian dream world—without work, want, or illness—reinforces his desire. In contrast, the speaker of Cowper's "The Poplar Field" speaks about Nature as the occasion to meditate on change and, ultimately, death. Cowper cites examples of how the woodsman's axe has caused the inhabitants of a once ideal world to flee, such as the winds and the blackbird that formerly sang in the leaves of the trees that have now been "felled." Thus, one poem deals directly with the reality of change while the other ignores it, although both poems yearn for an ideal natural world.

As in Cowper's "The Poplar Field," settings readily occasion personal, political, philosophical, and religious thought. Gray's "Elegy Written in a Country Churchyard" shows how important such thought can be when it is integrated into poetry. Here the approaching "darkness" causes the speaker to think of the "rude forefathers of the hamlet" in their churchyard graves. This thought leads him to speculate about how death cuts off those who are talented and potentially great. The interaction here is complex, interweaving character and history with natural and cultural situations and images. A poem similarly connecting character and setting is Wordsworth's "Lines Composed a Few Miles above Tintern Abbey" (Chapter 24). This poem, based on the relationship of the past, present, and future of the speaker to the natural scenes he describes, is a model of how poetic setting and character can be fused.

It is no exaggeration to say that setting interacts with character in endless numbers of ways. Thus in Browning's "My Last Duchess," the duke's display of valuable art creates a setting that exposes his greed and cruelty. In "London," Blake introduces bleak sights and anguished sounds that evoke a response of repulsion and rejection. As the representation of a philosophical judgment, the setting of Arnold's "Dover Beach" demonstrates changeability and impermanence. The speaker's solution is to establish personal fidelity as a fixture against change, dissolution, and brutality. To greater or lesser degrees, most poems offer similar connections of setting and character.

 ## POEMS FOR STUDY

MATTHEW ARNOLD   (1822–1888)

Dover Beach _____ *1867 (1849)*

The sea is calm tonight.
The tide is full, the moon lies fair
Upon the straits—on the French coast the light
Gleams and is gone; the cliffs of England stand,
Glimmering and vast, out in the tranquil bay.   5

Come to the window, sweet is the night air!
Only, from the long line of spray
Where the sea meets the moon-blanched land,
Listen! you hear the grating roar
Of pebbles which the waves draw back, and fling,   10
At their return, up the high strand,
Begin, and cease, and then again begin,
With tremulous cadence slow, and bring
The eternal note of sadness in.

                                                                                    15
Sophocles long ago
Heard it on the Aegean, and it brought
Into his mind the turbid ebb and flow
Of human misery; we
Find also in the sound a thought,
                                                                                    20
Hearing it by this distant northern sea.

The Sea of Faith
Was once, too, at the full, and round earth's shore
Lay like the folds of a bright girdle furled.
But now I only hear
Its melancholy, long, withdrawing roar,   25
Retreating, to the breath
Of the night wind, down the vast edges drear
And naked shingles° of the world.   *beaches*

Ah, love, let us be true
To one another! for the world, which seems   3(
To lie before us like a land of dreams,
So various, so beautiful, so new,
Hath really neither joy, nor love, nor light,
Nor certitude, nor peace, nor help for pain;
And we are here as on a darkling plain   3.
Swept with confused alarms of struggle and flight,
Where ignorant armies clash by night.

QUESTIONS

1. What words and details establish the setting?

2. Where are the speaker and listener? What can they see? Hear?

3. What sort of movement may be topographically traced in the first six lines of the poem, so that the scene finally focuses on the speaker and the listener?

4. What is meant by comparing the English Channel to the Aegean Sea, and relating the Aegean surf to the thought of Sophocles?

5. What faith remains after the loss of religious faith? Defend the claim that the faith is the speaker's commitment to personal fidelity rather than love.

WILLIAM BLAKE   (1757–1827)

London _____ *1794*

I wander thro' each charter'd° street,
Near where the charter'd Thames does flow,
And mark in every face I meet
Marks of weakness, marks of woe.

In every cry of every Man,   5
In every Infant's cry of fear,
In every voice, in every ban,°   *public pronouncement*
The mind-forg'd manacles I hear.

How the Chimney-sweeper's cry
Every blackning Church appalls;°   10
And the hapless Soldier's sigh
Runs in blood down Palace walls.

But most thro' midnight streets I hear
How the youthful Harlot's curse
Blasts the new-born Infant's tear,   15
And blights with plagues the Marriage hearse.

LONDON.   1 *charter'd:* privileged, licensed, authorized.   10 *appalls:* weakens, makes pale, shocks.

QUESTIONS

1. What does London represent to the speaker? How do the persons who live there contribute to the poem's ideas about the state of humanity?

2. What sounds does the speaker mention as a part of the London scene? Characterize these sounds in relation to the poem's main idea.

3. Because of the tension in the poem between civilized activity (as represented in the chartering of the street and the river) and free human impulses, explain how the poem might be considered revolutionary.

4. The poem appeared in *Songs of Experience,* published in 1794. Explain the appropriateness of Blake's including the poem in a collection so named.

ROBERT BROWNING   (1812–1889)

My Last Duchess° _____ *1842*

FERRARA
That's my last Duchess painted on the wall,
Looking as if she were alive. I call
That piece a wonder, now: Frà Pandolf's° hands

MY LAST DUCHESS.   The poem is based on incidents in the life of Alfonso II, duke of Ferrara, whose first wife died in 1561. Some claimed she was poisoned. The duke negotiated his second marriage to the daughter of the count of Tyrol through an agent.   3 *Frà Pandolf:* an imaginary painter who is also a monk.

Worked busily a day, and there she stands.
Will't please you sit and look at her? I said   5
"Frà Pandolf" by design, for never read
Strangers like you that pictured countenance,
The depth and passion of its earnest glance,
But to myself they turned (since none puts by
The curtain I have drawn for you, but I)   10
And seemed as they would ask me, if they durst,°   *dared*
How such a glance came there; so, not the first
Are you to turn and ask thus. Sir, 'twas not
Her husband's presence only, called that spot
Of joy into the Duchess' cheek: perhaps   15
Frà Pandolf chanced to say "Her mantle laps
Over my lady's wrist too much," or "Paint
Must never hope to reproduce the faint
Half-flush that dies along her throat": such stuff
Was courtesy, she thought, and cause enough   20
For calling up that spot of joy. She had
A heart—how shall I say?—too soon made glad,
Too easily impressed; she liked whate'er
She looked on, and her looks went everywhere.
Sir, 'twas all one! My favor at her breast,   25
The dropping of the daylight in the West,
The bough of cherries some officious fool
Broke in the orchard for her, the white mule
She rode with round the terrace—all and each
Would draw from her alike the approving speech,   30
Or blush, at least. She thanked men—good! but thanked
Somehow—I know not how—as if she ranked
My gift of a nine-hundred-years-old name
With anybody's gift. Who'd stoop to blame
This sort of trifling? Even had you skill   35
In speech—(which I have not)—to make your will
Quite clear to such a one, and say, "Just this
Or that in you disgusts me; here you miss,
Or there exceed the mark"—and if she let
Herself be lessoned so, nor plainly set   40
Her wits to yours, forsooth, and made excuse
—E'en then would be some stooping; and I choose
Never to stoop. Oh sir, she smiled, no doubt,
Whene'er I passed her; but who passed without
Much the same smile? This grew; I gave commands;   45
Then all smiles stopped together. There she stands
As if alive. Will't please you rise? We'll meet
The company below, then. I repeat,
The Count your master's known munificence
Is ample warrant that no just pretense   50
Of mine for dowry will be disallowed;
Though his fair daughter's self, as I avowed

At starting, is my object. Nay, we'll go
Together down, sir. Notice Neptune,° though,
Taming a sea horse, thought a rarity,   55
Which Claus of Innsbruck° cast in bronze for me!

54 *Neptune:* Roman god of the sea.   56 *Claus of Innsbruck:* an imaginary sculptor.

QUESTIONS

1. Who dominates the conversation in this poem? Who is the listener? Why does
   the main speaker avoid the obvious purpose of the conversation until near the
   poem's end?
2. What third character does the speaker describe? In what ways are his descriptions accurate or innacurate? What judgment do you think Browning wants you
   to make of the speaker? Why?
3. How does the poem illustrate the speaker's misuse of power?

WILLIAM COWPER   (1731–1800)

The Poplar Field _____ *1782*

The poplars are felled,° farewell to the shade   *cut down*
And the whispering sound of the cool colonnade.
The winds play no longer, and sing in the leaves,
Nor Ouse° on his bosom their image receives.

Twelve years have elapsed since I last took a view   5
Of my favourite field and the bank where they grew,
And now in the grass behold they are laid,
And the tree is my seat that once lent me a shade.

The blackbird has fled to another retreat
Where the hazels afford him a screen from the heat,   10
And the scene where his melody charmed me before,
Resounds with his sweet-flowing ditty no more.

My fugitive years are all hasting away,
And I must ere long lie as lowly as they,
With a turf on my breast, and a stone at my head,   15
Ere another such grove shall arise in its stead.

'Tis a sight to engage me, if any thing can,
To muse on the perishing pleasures of man;
Though his life be a dream, his enjoyments, I see,
Have a being less durable even than he.   20

THE POPLAR FIELD.   4 *Ouse:* river in northern England, near which Cowper lived.

QUESTIONS

1. What situation does the speaker describe? How has the scene changed from what he knew twelve years before? Why does the speaker refer to the passage of time? What kind of person is he?

2. How has the situation affected the blackbird? Why does the speaker care?

3. How does the scene affect the speaker? What idea does he express about what has occurred?

LOUISE GLÜCK (b. 1943)

Snowdrops _____ *1992*

Do you know what I was, how I lived? You know
what despair is; then
winter should have meaning for you.

I did not expect to survive,
earth suppressing me. I didn't expect   5
to waken again, to feel
in damp earth my body
able to respond again, remembering
after so long how to open again
in the cold light   10
of earliest spring—

afraid, yes, but among you again
crying yes risk joy

in the raw wind of the new world.

QUESTIONS

1. How much does the speaker say about her previous condition? What does she say about how she has changed? What has happened to make her change? To what degree, if any, has the speaker's change altered her general view of the world?

2. How much about her circumstances does the speaker leave vague? Why? Why is the poem titled "Snowdrops"? What is the meaning of the phrase "yes risk joy"?

3. Why does the poet not capitalize the first words in each line?

THOMAS GRAY (1716–1771)

Elegy Written in a Country Churchyard _____ *1751*

writing for the poor people

The curfew tolls the knell of parting day,
   The lowing herd wind slowly o'er the lea,
The ploughman homeward plods his weary way,
   And leaves the world to darkness and to me.

Now fades the glimm'ring landscape on the sight,   5
    And all the air a solemn stillness holds,
Save where the beetle wheels his droning flight,
    And drowsy tinklings lull the distant folds;

Save that from yonder ivy-mantled tower
    The moping owl does to the moon complain   10
Of such as wand'ring near her secret bower
    Molest her ancient solitary reign.

Beneath those rugged elms, that yew-tree's shade,
    Where heaves the turf in many a mold'ring heap,
Each in his narrow cell forever laid,   15
    The rude forefathers of the hamlet sleep.

The breezy call of incense-breathing morn,
    The swallow twitt'ring from the straw-built shed,
The cock's shrill clarion, or the echoing horn,°   *hunting horn*
    No more shall rouse them from their lowly bed.   20

For them no more the blazing hearth shall burn,
    Or busy housewife ply her evening care;
No children run to lisp their sire's return,
    Or climb his knees the envied kiss to share.

Oft did the harvest to their sickle yield,   25
    Their furrow oft the stubborn glebe° has broke;   *church land*
How jocund did they drive their team afield!
    How bowed the woods beneath their sturdy stroke!

Let not Ambition mock their useful toil
    Their homely joys, and destiny obscure;   30
Nor Grandeur hear with a disdainful smile
    The short and simple annals of the poor.

The boast of heraldry, the pomp of power,
    And all that beauty, all that wealth e'er gave,
Awaits alike th'inevitable hour.   35
    The paths of glory lead but to the grave.

Nor you, ye proud, impute to these the fault,
    If mem'ry o'er their tomb no trophies raise,
Where through the long-drawn aisle and fretted vault
    The pealing anthem swells the note of praise.   40

Can storied urn or animated bust
    Back to its mansion call the fleeting breath?
Can Honor's voice provoke the silent dust,
    Or Flatt'ry soothe the dull cold ear of death?

Perhaps in this neglected spot is laid   45
    Some heart once pregnant with celestial fire;
Hands that the rod of empire might have swayed,
    Or waked to ecstasy the living lyre.

But Knowledge to their eyes her ample page
   Rich with the spoils of time did ne'er unroll;   50
Chill Penury repressed their noble rage,
   And froze the genial current of the soul.

Full many a gem of purest ray serene,
   The dark unfathomed caves of ocean bear;
Full many a flower is born to blush unseen,   55
   And waste its sweetness on the desert air.

Some village Hampden,° that with dauntless breast
   The little tyrant of his fields withstood;
Some mute inglorious Milton here may rest,
   Some Cromwell guiltless of his country's blood.   60

Th'applause of list'ning senates to command,
   The threats of pain and ruin to despise,
To scatter plenty o'er a smiling land,
   And read their hist'ry in a nation's eyes.

Their lot forbade: nor circumscribed alone   65
   Their growing virtues, but their crimes confined;
Forbade to wade through slaughter to a throne,
   And shut the gates of mercy on mankind,

The struggling pangs of conscious truth to hide,
   To quench the blushes of ingenuous shame,   70
Or heap the shrine of luxury and pride
   With incense kindled at the Muse's flame.

Far from the madding° crowd's ignoble strife,   *raving*
   Their sober wishes never learned to stray;
Along the cool sequestered vale of life   75
   They kept the noiseless tenor of their way.

Yet ev'n these bones from insult to protect
   Some frail memorial still erected nigh,
With uncouth° rhymes and shapeless sculpture decked,   *uneducated, unsophisticated*
   Implores the passing tribute of a sigh.   80

Their names, their years, spelt by th'unlettered Muse,
   The place of fame and elegy supply;
And many a holy text around she strews,
   That teach the rustic moralist to die.

For who to dumb forgetfulness a prey,
   This pleasing anxious being e'er resigned,

ELEGY WRITTEN IN A COUNTRY CHURCHYARD. 57 *Hampden:* John Hampden (1594–1643), English statesman who defended the rights of the people against King Charles I and who died in the English Civil War of 1642–1646.

Left the warm precincts of the cheerful day,
  Nor cast one longing ling'ring look behind?

On some fond breast the parting soul relies,
  Some pious drops the closing eye requires;   90
Ev'n from the tomb the voice of Nature cries,
  Ev'n in our ashes live their wonted fires.

For thee, who mindful of th'unhonored dead
  Dost in these lines their artless tale relate;
If chance, by lonely contemplation led,   95
  Some kindred spirit shall inquire thy fate.

Haply some hoary-headed swain may say,
  "Oft have we seen him at the peep of dawn
Brushing with hasty steps the dews away
  To meet the sun upon the upland lawn.   100

"There, at the foot of yonder nodding beech
  That wreathes its old fantastic° roots so high,   *fancifully extravagant, grotesque*
His listless length at noontide would he stretch
  And pore upon the brook that babbles by.

"Hard by yon wood, now smiling as in scorn,   105
  Mutt'ring his wayward fancies he would rove,
Now drooping, woeful wan, like one forlorn,
  Or crazed with care, or crossed in hopeless love.

"One morn I missed him on the 'customed hill,
  Along the heath and near his fav'rite tree;   110
Another came; nor yet beside the rill,
  Nor up the lawn, nor at the wood was he;

"The next with dirges due in sad array
  Slow through the church-way path we saw him borne.
Approach and read (for thou canst read) the lay,   115
  Graved on the stone beneath yon aged thorn."

THE EPITAPH

Here rests his head upon the lap of earth
  A youth to fortune and to fame unknown;
Fair Science frowned not on his humble birth,
  And Melancholy marked him for her own.   120

Large was his bounty, and his soul sincere,
  Heav'n did a recompense as largely send:
He gave to mis'ry all he had, a tear:
  He gain'd from Heav'n ('twas all he wished) a friend.

No farther seek his merits to disclose,   125
  Or draw his frailties from their dread abode
(There they alike in trembling hope repose),
  The bosom of his Father and his God.

QUESTIONS

1. What is the time of day of the speaker's meditation? What is happening in nature as the poem opens? Whom is the speaker addressing?
2. Who are the people buried in the church graveyard? What point does Gray make about the contributions they might have made if they had not died?
3. How does Gray's use of sights and sounds complement the poem's mood?
4. Who is "thee" (line 93)? What happens to him? Why is he included in the poem?

THOMAS HARDY   (1840–1928)

The Ruined Maid _____ *1866*

"O 'melia,° my dear, this does everything crown!°   *i.e., Amelia*
Who could have supposed I should meet you in Town?
And whence such fair garments, such prosperi-ty"—
"O didn't you know I'd been ruined?" said she.

—"You left us in tatters, without shoes or socks,   5
Tired of digging potatoes, and spudding up docks;°   *digging up weeds*
And now you've gay bracelets and bright feathers three!"
"Yes: that's how we dress when we're ruined," said she.

—"At home in the barton° you said 'thee' and 'thou,'
And 'thik oon,' and 'theäs oon,' and 't'other';° but now   10
Your talking quite fits 'ee° for high compa-ny!"—   *thee*
"Some polish is gained with one's ruin," said she.

—"Your hands were like paws then, your face blue and bleak
But now I'm bewitched by your delicate cheek,
And your little gloves fit as on any la-dy!"—   15
"We never do work when we're ruined," said she.

—"You used to call home-life a hag-ridden dream,
And you'd sigh, and you'd sock°; but at present you seem   *moan, groan*
To know not of megrims° or melancho-ly!"—   *migraine headaches*
"True. One's pretty lively when ruined," said she.   20

—"I wish I had feathers, a fine sweeping gown,
And a delicate face, and could strut about Town!"—
"My dear—a raw country girl, such as you be,
Cannot quite expect that. You ain't ruined," said she.

THE RUINED MAID.   1 *does everything crown:* crowns everything; is a great surprise.   9 *At home in the barton:* when you lived at home on the farm.   9–10 *'thee'. . . . 't'other':* i.e., you spoke familiarly in the country dialect (using the second-person pronoun), saying "thik oon" for "that one" and "theäs oon" for "this one."

QUESTIONS

1. Who are the two speakers? How have they come together? What are their present economic circumstances? Who is 'melia (Amelia)? Does she seem to be bragging to the first speaker? Why has not the first speaker learned about 'melia earlier, before their encounter in town?

2. How aware of her situation is 'melia? Is she happy or unhappy about it? How completely has she shed her country habits of speech?

3. What double meaning does the word "ruined" have in this poem? To what extent does Hardy use the poem to challenge conventional moral judgments?

THOMAS HARDY (1840–1928)

Channel Firing _____ *1914*

That night your great guns, unawares,
Shook all our coffins° as we lay,
And broke the chancel window-squares,
We thought it was the Judgment Day

And sat upright. While drearisome   5
Arose the howl of wakened hounds:
The mouse let fall the altar-crumb,
The worms drew back into the mounds,

The glebe° cow drooled. Till God called, "No;
It's gunnery practice out at sea   10
Just as before you went below;
The world is as it used to be:

"All nations striving strong to make
Red war yet redder. Mad as hatters
They do no more for Christés sake   15
Than you who are helpless in such matters.

"That this is not the judgment hour
For some of them's a blessed thing,
For if it were they'd have to scour
Hell's floor for so much threatening. . . .   20

"Ha, ha. It will be warmer when
I blow the trumpet (if indeed
I ever do; for you are men,
And rest eternal sorely need)."

CHANNEL FIRING. 2 *coffins:* It has been common practice in England for hundreds of years to bury people in the floors or basements of churches. 9 *glebe:* a parcel of land adjoining and belonging to a church. Cows were grazed there to keep the grass short.

So down we lay again. "I wonder,   25
Will the world ever saner be,"
Said one, "than when He sent us under
In our indifferent century!"

And many a skeleton shook his head.
"Instead of preaching forty year,"   30
My neighbor Parson Thirdly said,
"I wish I had stuck to pipes and beer."

Again the guns disturbed the hour,
Roaring their readiness to avenge,
As far inland as Stourton Tower,°   35
And Camelot,° and starlit Stonehenge.°

35 *Stourton Tower:* tower commemorating King Alfred the Great's defeat of the Danes in
A.C.E. 879.   36 *Camelot:* legendary seat of King Arthur's court.   *Stonehenge:* group of standing stones on Salisbury Plain, probably built as a place of worship before 1000 B.C.E.

QUESTIONS

1. Who is the speaker in this poem? What is the setting? The situation?
2. To whom does the "your" in line 1 refer? The "our" in line 2?
3. What has awakened the speaker and his companions? What mistake have they made?
4. What three other voices are heard in the poem? How are their traits revealed?
5. What ideas about war and the nature of humanity does this poem explore?

C. DAY LEWIS   (1904–1972)

Song _____ *1935*

Come, live with me and be my love,
And we will all the pleasures prove
Of peace and plenty, bed and board,
That chance employment may afford.

I'll handle dainties on the docks
And thou shalt read of summer frocks:
At evening by the sour canals
We'll hope to hear some madrigals.

Care on thy maiden brow shall put
A wreath of wrinkles, and thy foot
Be shod with pain: not silken dress
But toil shall tire thy loveliness.

Hunger shall make thy modest zone
And cheat fond death of all but bone—
If these delights thy mind may move, 15
Then live with me and be my love.

QUESTIONS

1. What is the connection and contrast between this poem and Marlowe's "Passionate Shepherd to His Love"?
2. To what other poems in this chapter is this poem related? How?
3. Who is the speaker in this poem? The listener?
4. What is the effect of words like "chance employment" (line 4), "read" (line 6), and "hope" (line 8)?

CHRISTOPHER MARLOWE   (1564–1593)

The Passionate Shepherd to His Love _____ *1599*

Come live with me and be my love,
And we will all the pleasures prove°   test, try out
That valleys, groves, hills, and fields,
Woods, or steepy mountain yields.

And we will sit upon the rocks, 5
Seeing the shepherds feed their flocks,
By shallow rivers to whose falls
Melodious birds sing madrigals.

And I will make thee beds of roses
And a thousand fragrant posies, 10
A cap of flowers, and a kirtle°   long dress
Embroidered all with leaves of myrtle;

A gown made of the finest wool
Which from our pretty lambs we pull;
Fair lined slippers for the cold, 15
With buckles of the purest gold;

A belt of straw and ivy buds,
With coral clasps and amber studs;
And if these pleasures may thee move,
Come live with me, and be my love. 20

The shepherds' swains° shall dance and sing   lovers
For thy delight each May morning:
If these delights thy mind may move,
Then live with me and be my love.

QUESTIONS

1. Describe the speaker. What does he do? What is he like? What does he want?
2. Who is the listener? What is the relationship between speaker and listener?
3. What sort of life does the speaker offer the listener?
4. What is the speaker's understanding of reality?

MARGE PIERCY   (b. 1934)

Wellfleet° Sabbath _____ 1988

The hawk eye of the sun slowly shuts.
The breast of the bay is softly feathered
dove grey. The sky is barred like the sand
when the tide trickles out.

The great doors of the sabbath are swinging   5
open over the ocean, loosing the moon
floating up slow distorted vast, a copper
balloon just sailing free.

The wind slides over the waves, patting
them with its giant hand, and the sea   10
stretches its muscles in the deep,
purrs and rolls over.

The sweet beeswax candles flicker
and sigh, standing between the phlox
and the roast chicken. The wine shines   15
its red lantern of joy.

Here on this piney sandspit, the Shekinah°
comes on the short strong wings of the seaside
sparrow raising her song and bringing
down the fresh clean night.   20

WELLFLEET SABBATH.   *Wellfleet:* a seaside town close to the northern tip of Cape Cod,
Massachusetts.   17 *Shekinah:* in the Jewish faith, a visible sign or manifestation of divinity.

QUESTIONS

1. Who is the speaker? Where is she? What is the special occasion? Who, if anyone, is being addressed?
2. What attributes do the speaker's descriptions confer upon the exterior natural world? How do these attributes, together with the interior scene, contribute to the speaker's apparent mood?
3. Who, if anyone, is being addressed? What is the reader's relationship to the poem?

AL PURDY   (1918–2000)

Poem _____ *1971*

You are ill and so I lead you away
and put you to bed in the dark room
—you lie breathing softly and I hold your hand
feeling the fingertips relax as sleep comes

You will not sleep more than a few hours   5
and the illness is less serious than my anger or cruelty
and the dark bedroom is like a foretaste of other darknesses
to come later which all of us must endure alone
but here I am permitted to be with you

After a while in sleep your fingers clutch tightly   10
and I know that whatever may be happening
the fear coiled in dreams or the bright trespass of pain
there is nothing at all I can do except hold your hand
and not go away

QUESTIONS

1. What is the dramatic situation of this poem? Who is speaking to whom? What is their relationship?
2. What is the condition of the speaker? Of the listener? What traits of character does the speaker exhibit?

SIR WALTER RALEIGH   (1552–1618)

The Nymph's Reply to the Shepherd _____ *1600*

If all the world and love were young,
And truth in every shepherd's tongue,
These pretty pleasures might me move
To live with thee and be thy love.

Time drives the flocks from field to fold°   *fenced field*   5
When rivers rage and rocks grow cold,
And Philomel° becometh dumb;   *the nightingale*
The rest complains of cares to come.

The flowers do fade, and wanton fields
To wayward winter reckoning yields;   10
A honey tongue, a heart of gall,
Is fancy's spring, but sorrow's fall.

Thy gowns, thy shoes, thy beds of roses,
Thy cap, thy kirtle,° and thy posies°   *long dress; flowers and poems*
Soon break, soon wither, soon forgotten—   15
In folly ripe, in reason rotten.

Thy belt of straw and ivy buds,
Thy coral clasps and amber studs,
All these in me no means can move
To come to thee and be thy love.   20

But could youth last and love still° breed,   *always*
Had joys no date nor age no need,
Then these delights my mind might move
To live with thee and be thy love.

QUESTIONS

1. Who is the speaker? What do we learn about the speaker? Who is the listener?

2. How are the ideas of love and the world in this poem different from those in Marlowe's poem?

3. To what extent is this poem a parody (an imitation that makes fun) of Marlowe's poem? To what extent is it a refutation of Marlowe's poem?

4. Determine the steps of the speaker's logical argument in this poem.

CHRISTINA ROSSETTI   (1830–1894)

A Christmas Carol _____ *1872*

In the bleak mid-winter
  Frosty wind made moan,
Earth stood hard as iron,
  Water like a stone;
Snow had fallen, snow on snow,
  Snow on snow,
In the bleak mid-winter
  Long ago.

Our God, Heaven cannot hold Him
  Nor earth sustain;
Heaven and earth shall flee away
  When He comes to reign:
In the bleak mid-winter
  A stable-place sufficed°   *see Luke 2:7*
The Lord God Almighty
  Jesus Christ.

Enough for Him whom cherubim
  Worship night and day,
A breastful of milk
  And a mangerful of hay;   20
Enough for Him whom angels
  Fall down before,
The ox and ass and camel
  Which adore.

Angels and archangels   25
  May have gathered there,
Cherubim and seraphim
  Throng'd the air,
But only His mother
  In her maiden bliss   30
Worshipped the Beloved
  With a kiss.

What can I give Him,
  Poor as I am?
If I were a shepherd°   *see Luke 2:8–20*   35
  I would bring a lamb,
If I were a wise man°   *see Matthew 2:1–12*
  I would do my part,—
Yet what I can I give Him,
  Give my heart.   40

QUESTIONS

1. Why does Rossetti stress the bitterness and bleakness of the winter setting in this poem?

2. Why does the speaker stress the simplicity of the birthplace of "The Lord God Almighty"? What is the origin and tradition of this setting?

3. How does the fourth stanza prepare you for the speaker's description of her own condition in the fifth stanza?

4. How are the objects considered gifts by the speaker a part of the setting traditionally associated with the birth of Jesus? How does the speaker's gift reveal her character and condition?

JANE SHORE   (b. 1947)

A Letter Sent to Summer _____ *1977*

Oh summer if you would only come
with your big baskets of flowers,
dropping by like an old friend
just passing through the neighborhood!

If you came to my door disguised   5
as a thirsty biblical angel
I'd buy all your hairbrushes and magazines!
I'd be more hospitable
than any ancient king.

I'd personally carry your luggage in,   10
Your monsoons. Your squadrons of bugs,
Your plums and lovely melons.
Let the rose let out its long long sigh
And Desire return to the hapless rabbit.

This request is also in my own behalf.   15
Inside my head it is always snowing,
even when I sleep. When I wake up,
and still you have not arrived,
I curl back into my blizzard of linens.

Not like winter's buckets of whitewash.   20
Please wallpaper my bedroom
with leafy vegetables and farms.
If you knocked right now,
I would not interfere.
Start near the window.   25
Start right here.

QUESTIONS

1. Describe the speaker. What do you learn about her and how she is responding to the time of year?

2. Describe what summer means to the speaker. What attributes does she give to summer? What contrasts are brought out by references to "bugs" and "monsoons" in addition to "plums" and "the rose"?

3. What does the phrase "always snowing" contribute to your understanding of the speaker's yearning for summer?

MAURA STANTON   (b. 1946)

Childhood _____ *1984*

I used to lie on my back, imagining
A reverse house on the ceiling of my house
Where I could walk around in empty rooms
All by myself. There was no furniture
Up there, only a glass globe on the floor.
And knee-high barriers at every door.
The low silled windows opened on blue air.
Nothing hung in the closet; even the kitchen

Seemed immaculate, a place for thought.
I liked to walk across the swirling plaster   10
Into the parts of the house I couldn't see.
The hum from the other house, now my ceiling,
Reached me only faintly. I'd look up
To find my brothers watching old cartoons,
Or my mother vacuuming the ugly carpet.   15
I'd stare amazed at unmade beds, the clutter,
Shoes, half-dressed dolls, the telephone,
Then return dizzily to my perfect floorplan
Where I never spoke or listened to anyone.

I must have turned down the wrong hall,   20
Or opened a door that locked shut behind me,
For I live on the ceiling now, not the floor.
This is my house, room after empty room.
How do I ever get back to the real house
Where my sisters spill milk, my father calls,   25
And I am at the table, eating cereal?
I fill my white rooms with furniture,
Hang curtains over the piercing blue outside.
I lie on my back. I strive to look down,
This ceiling is higher than it used to be,   30
The floor so far away I can't determine
Which room I'm in, which year, which life.

QUESTIONS

1. How do the first four lines introduce the poem? To what degree is the situation
    normal? Unusual? Humorous?

2. How accurate is the imaginative explanation of details about the ceiling? About
    the rooms of the house?

3. How does line 20 constitute a shift in the poem? What purpose is served by
    these final thirteen lines?

4. Characterize the speaker. How does she explain what has happened to her? In
    relationship to her opening sentence, explain the last four lines.

JAMES WRIGHT   (1927–1980)

A Blessing ————————————————————————— *1963*

Just off the highway to Rochester, Minnesota,
Twilight bounds softly forth on the grass.
And the eyes of those two Indian ponies
Darken with kindness.
They have come gladly out of the willows   5
To welcome my friend and me.
We step over the barbed wire into the pasture

Where they have been grazing all day, alone.
They ripple tensely, they can hardly contain their happiness
That we have come.   10
They bow shyly as wet swans. They love each other.
There is no loneliness like theirs.
At home once more,
They begin munching the young tufts of spring in the darkness.
I would like to hold the slenderer one in my arms.   15
For she has walked over to me
And nuzzled my left hand.
She is black and white,
Her mane falls wild on her forehead,
And the light breeze moves me to caress her long ear   20
That is delicate as the skin over a girl's wrist.
Suddenly I realize
That if I stepped out of my body I would break
Into blossom.

QUESTIONS

1. What has happened just before the poem opens? Account for the poet's use of the present tense in his descriptions.
2. Is the setting specific or general? What happens as the poem progresses?
3. What realization overtakes the speaker? How does this realization constitute a "blessing," and what does it show about his character?
4. Why is it necessary for the poet to include all the detail of the first twenty-one lines before the realization of the last three?

WRITING ABOUT CHARACTER AND SETTING IN POETRY

Writing about character and setting involves many of the same considerations whether you deal with prose fiction or poetry. You might therefore review the material on character presented in Chapter 4. However, there are some important differences between the two writing tasks. One of these is the way you find out about characters. In prose fiction, you can usually judge a character by the details about his or her actions, words, thoughts, appearance, and opinions. In poetry, the speaker is less likely to provide full details. Consequently, many conclusions must be inferred from the speaker's suggestions and hints.

Another difference between fiction and poetry concerns the types of character. Fiction presents a broad range of writing options: You may write about the protagonist, the antagonist, the narrator, or any of the incidental characters. In poetry you are usually limited to the speaker or to one of the characters described by the speaker (although you may sometimes be able to discuss the

Fernand Léger (French, 1881-1955), *The City*, 1919. Oil on canvas, 90 3/4 x 117 1/4 in. Philadelphia Museum of Art: A.E. Gallatin Collection, Philadelphia, PA.

Francisco de Goya, *The Giant* or *The Colossus*, 1808-1810. Oil on canvas, 116 x 105 cm. Museo del Prado, Madrid, Spain. Scala/Art Resource, New York, NY.

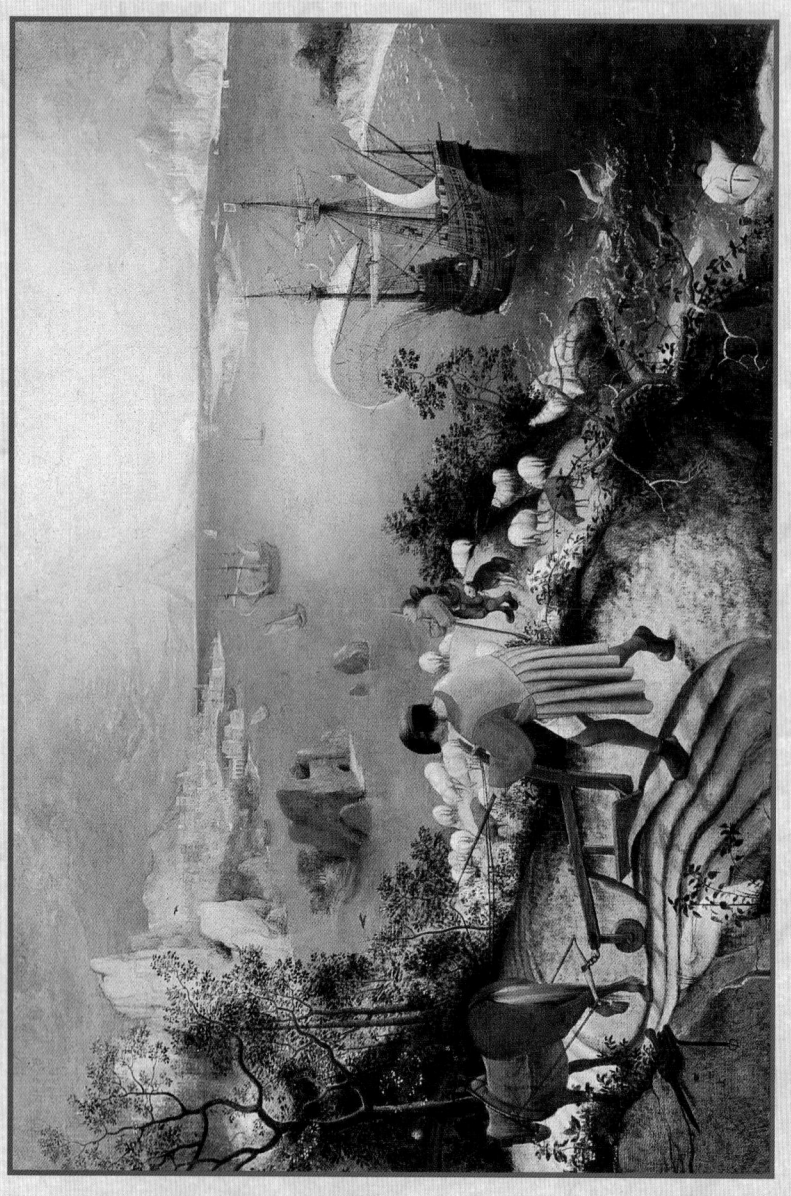

Pieter Brueghel the Elder, *Landscape with the Fall of Icarus*, c. 1554-1555.
Oil on panel (transferred to canvas), 29 x 44 1/8 in. Musées Royaux des
Beaux-Arts, Brussels, Belgium. Scala/Art Resource, New York, NY.

listener, too). In writing about Browning's "My Last Duchess," for example, you learn enough about both the duke and the duchess to write about either.

In planning and prewriting, you should find out as much as you can about the characters and their relationship to their situations, that is, to the action, emotion, ideas, setting, and other characters. Answering the following questions will help you to focus your ideas.

Questions for Discovering Ideas

ABOUT THE SPEAKER

- Who is the speaker? What is he or she doing? What does he or she say about himself or herself? About others?
- What conclusions can you draw about occurrences involving the speaker that took place before the poem begins? Why?
- How reliable is the speaker as an observer and reporter? What knowledge enables the speaker to make judgments and opinions?
- What do the speaker's word choices reveal about his or her education and social standing? How does the language reveal his or her assumptions?
- What tone of voice is suggested in the speaker's presentation?
- How deeply is the speaker involved with the action of the poem? What connection does she or he make with the other characters? With the poem's actions?

ABOUT OTHER CHARACTERS

- How vividly does the poem describe action, appearance, emotions, responses, and ideas? How strong a picture do you get of any other character (characters)?
- How does each significant character respond to the surroundings described and implied in the poem?
- What is the character trying to gain or learn?
- How is the character affected by others, and how do others respond to her or to him?
- What degree of control does the character exert, and what does his or her effort tell you?
- How does the character speak and behave, and what do you learn from these words and actions?

Strategies for Organizing Ideas

When you write about a single character, formulate a central idea that focuses on his or her personality or status. If you are writing about the duke in Browning's "My Last Duchess," for example, your idea might be that he is arrogant, cruel, greedy, and power-mad. In writing about Sir Patrick Spens (Chapter 13), your idea would likely be about his self-sacrificing fidelity to the king. If the topic is a set of characters, the central idea should express some relationship or commonality among them. Thus the grieving characters in the anonymous "Bonny George Campbell" show their love for Campbell, and the characters in Blake's "London" illustrate the withering effects of discriminatory law and religion.

Consider organizing your essay along the lines of one of the following approaches.

1. *Character as revealed by action.* Often the speaker describes himself or herself as a major character or major mover. What does the action reveal about this speaker? In Shore's "A Letter Sent to Summer," the speaker indicates that she would be willing to buy "hairbrushes and magazines" from Summer. What does this proposed action demonstrate? In Gray's "Elegy Written in a Country Churchyard," the speaker enters the churchyard at sunset, and his action causes him to think of life, glory, fame, fortune, and religious dedication. What do his speculations and conclusions reveal about his character?

In a parallel way, the speaker of Glück's "Snowdrops" may be an animated snowdrop (snowflake) that has undergone a transformation from winter to spring. Or is the speaker a person describing what appears to be an episode of depression that coincided with the fall of snow in winter? The springtime recovery is accompanied by the words "suppressing," "remembering," "earth," and "damp earth." What do these words, and the use of the word "risk" near the poem's end, suggest about the speaker's character and her relationship with the cyclical patterns of nature?

2. *Character as revealed by interaction.* Poems based in a dramatic situation yield best to this treatment. Browning's "My Last Duchess" is a fine example, as are Hardy's "Channel Firing," and Jonson's "Drink to Me, Only, with Thine Eyes." The situation in Purdy's "Poem" is that the speaker is talking directly to a listener who seems gravely ill. What does the speaker's attitude toward the listener reveal about his character? In this and other poems, what do you learn about relationships and how they have affected the poetic characters?

3. *Character as revealed by circumstance or setting.* The essay based on the interrelationship of character and setting assumes that time, place, artifact, money, family, culture, and history influence character and motivation, and also that individual and collective traits are developed as people try to control their surroundings. For instance, the speaker of Wright's "A Blessing" describes the thrill of looking at a roadside pasture, and at the end of the poem he feels as though he is about to "break / Into blossom." What enables him to reach this joyful conclusion? Why does he feel safe rather than frightened? Why does he believe in the benevolence of the two ponies, and, in turn, why do the ponies treat him with affection? What aspects of character enable him to step over the barbed wire without fear and to believe that the experience is really a "blessing"? Would such an experience have been possible at a more suspicious, less civilized time, when people stepping uninvited onto property might have been considered intruders and peppered with buckshot? In short, how has setting in the broadest sense entered into the speaker's character?

In dealing with the interrelationship of character and external situation, you might be able to organize the body of your essay by relying on certain aspects of the setting. Thus you might select the details about past, present, and future time in Gray's "Elegy Written in a Country Churchyard." Similarly, the details about the roaring surf and the dim lights in Arnold's "Dover Beach" can provide thematic links for a discussion of the speaker's sense of alienation, loss, and dedication. In such ways, you may use aspects of setting not only as topics to shed light on character but also to guide and shape your essay.

Whatever strategy you choose, remember that your organization will finally be determined by your poem. Each poem suggests its own avenues of exploration, directing your thought and organization.

In your conclusion you might summarize your major points about the character or characters, or you might tie your conclusions into an assessment of the poem as a whole. Thus, you might briefly discuss the connection between character and character, character and environment, character and death, character and greed, character and love, and so on, and deal with these topics generally as you write your final sentences.

DEMONSTRATIVE STUDENT ESSAY

The Character of the Duke in Browning's "My Last Duchess"°

[1]   In this dramatic monologue, Browning skillfully develops the character of his speaker, who holds the high position of Duke of Ferrara (in Italy) during the sixteenth century, a period of aristocratic absolutism. Because the duke is at the top of the aristocracy, he exerts absolute control, whether for good or for bad. Browning's duke is bad; not only is he bad, but he is totally evil.* He reveals this evil in his one-way conversation with the listener, who is an envoy of a less powerful aristocrat, the count, whose daughter the duke is claiming in marriage. The duke's evil character is brought out by his indulgence in power, his intimidation of others, his manipulation of his dead wife, and his general contempt for others.†

[2]   The duke's indulgence in power, the basis of his evil, is apparent in his use of indirect speech. On the surface, Browning makes him seem intelligent, civilized, and friendly. The duke begins speaking by pointing out to his listener the beauty of a painting of his "last Duchess," but his entire speech--comprising the entire poem--reveals the horror of his self-indulgence. His indirect but threatening description of how he treated the duchess shows that he delights in evil. When he says, "I gave commands; / Then all smiles stopped together" (lines 45-46), he is actually bragging about how he had the duchess killed. He is coldly horrible, the more so because he masks his evil with quiet words and a love of good art.

°See p. 695 for this poem.
*Central idea.
†Thesis sentence.

[3] Another horrible quality is the way the duke intimidates people. At first it seems that he is doing no more than telling about his dead wife, but the poem makes clear that he is intimidating both his listener and also the count, the listener's master. The last nine lines (48-56) indicate that his *monologue* should have been a *dialogue,* in which he should have negotiated the terms for the dowry he is to receive from the count. The fact that he has talked only about how he got rid of his "last Duchess" shows his arrogance. Thus, there is no mention of dowry until lines 48-53, when the duke states that he will make a "just pretense" for a dowry which of course the count will honor (for "just pretense," read a demand for all the count's money and land). In addition, the duke's commands, "Will't please you rise? We'll meet / The company below, then," indicate that the negotiation that never began is now over and that the envoy is totally in his power. This is intimidation of the most ruthless and inhuman sort.

The duke's evil nature is also brought out in his description of the duchess. If we study his words to determine what the duchess was really like, we conclude that she was even-tempered and pleasant to all--the soul of graciousness and courtesy. In fact, it would be hard to say that she was anything but perfect. But the duke, rather than indicating pleasure with her, states that she was ungrateful because she was not submissive. He complains that the smile she gave to others was the same as the smile she gave to him (it probably was not; we may conclude that her smile to him probably covered fear):

[4]
> O sir, she smiled, no doubt,
> Whene'er I passed her; but who passed without
> Much the same smile? (lines 43-45)

These lines show that the duke is a manipulator and that the poor duchess was in an impossible situation. Very likely he would have complained also if she had smiled only at him and not at others—thereby leaving herself open to the duke's perverted judgment that she did not show the graciousness toward others that he expected from his wife. No matter how good she was, there was no way for her to have pleased him. He would have manipulated her into an unfavorable position that would have justified his giving the "commands" to remove her.

[5] Perhaps the worst of this monster's traits is the contempt he shows for people by thinking of them not as human beings but rather as things. Most notable is the way he thinks of the duchess; he calls her painting a "piece" (line 3) to hang on a wall, looking "as if she were alive" (line 2). He does not even name her, or recognize her humanity by calling her "the *late* Duchess," and he speaks about the bronze statue of Neptune "taming a sea horse" (line 55) as being equal to her. This same contempt for people is shown in his claim that his interest in the count's daughter is the "fair daughter's self" (line 52), while the rest of the poem makes clear that he wants only wealth and power out of the new marriage. Oddly, also, he seems to think of himself less as a person than as a "nine-hundred-years-old name" (line 33), and it is this intangible distinction that he prizes above his own humanity. In other words, he views even himself with contempt.

[6] Browning's duke, then, is a person with absolute power but without the kindness and understanding to use it for anyone but himself. His complaints about the dead Duchess are meaningless, for they are no more than pretexts for cruel self-indulgence. He is at the top of the aristocratic power structure, and

therefore he is able to do what he wants without reprisal. People must defer to him and obey him, but only because he makes everyone afraid. His intimidation, his manipulation, his lust for power--all govern him and leave him unable to look at human beings as anything more than pawns in his game for control. <u>He is an example of the saying that absolute power corrupts absolutely, and his character is therefore a frightening portrait of evil.</u>

Commentary on the Essay

Because the subject of the discussion, the duke, is the speaker, the essay is based partially on details presented by him, but it is also partially based on interpretations. The principal subject matter is the interaction of the duke and the subject of the poem—the "last Duchess"—in addition to his interaction with the listener, who is a representative of an inferior aristocrat, and whom he therefore treats with contempt. Elements of setting are also introduced to illuminate the duke's character: his works of art, his absolute power, his pride in his name and title, and his wealth. The essay thus demonstrates how character can be analyzed with reference (1) to interactions between persons and persons and also (2) to the connections of persons with their surroundings.

The central idea is that the duke is evil. This point is made in paragraph 1, with sufficient accompanying detail to explain that the duke's position enables him to exercise absolute power. Paragraph 2 discloses that indulgence in power is one of the duke's primary evil traits, while paragraphs 3, 4, and 5 bring out traits of intimidation, manipulation, and contempt. The final paragraph summarizes but also asserts that the duke's justifications for killing his wife are irrelevant to his real motives of greed and lust for power.

As the essay develops, transitions are effected by words such as "another," "also," "worst," and "then." The assertions in the essay are supported by references to specific details from the poem, quotations from the poem (with line numbers noted), and interpretations of details.

SPECIAL TOPICS FOR WRITING AND ARGUMENT ABOUT CHARACTER AND SETTING IN POETRY

1. Write an essay comparing the speakers of the "passionate shepherd" poems (by Marlowe, Raleigh, and Lewis). How are the speakers alike, and how are they different? How do their words and references indicate their characters? How do the speakers influence your judgments of the poems in which they appear?

2. Write an essay discussing the relationships between location, thought, and character as asserted in the poems by Arnold, Blake, Cowper, Hardy, and Shore (or poems in other chapters). What importance do place and time have on the opportunity for life and the development of character? How do responses to time, historical period, and place influence ideas about how to live?

3. Write a short poem, biographical or autobiographical, showing how a certain time, place, or experience has shaped a present quality of character and/or a certain decision about life, friendships, and goals.

4. Consider Piercy's "Wellfleet Sabbath," Gray's "Elegy Written in a Country Churchyard," Rossetti's "A Christmas Carol," and Wright's "A Blessing" as poems embodying a type or types of religious experience. What common or similar circumstances occasion the religious reflections in the poems? What common ideas and conclusions do the poems express? What philosophical or sectarian differences do you find? On the basis of your study, explain typical patterns of religious experience. (For ideas about how to approach this topic, you may wish to consult Chapter 35 and also the section titled "Archetypal Criticism" in Chapter 32.)

5. Use your library to locate two university press books about Robert Browning. Analyze the extent to which they discuss Browning's use of dramatic monologue. With the aid of what you discover, write a brief essay on Browning's use of the dramatic monologue as a means of disclosing character.

15
Words:
The Building Blocks
of Poetry

Words are the spoken and written signifiers of thoughts, objects, and actions. They are also the building blocks of both poetry and prose, but poetry is unique because by its nature it uses words with the utmost economy. The words of poetry create rhythm, rhyme, meter, and form. They define the poem's speaker, the characters, the setting, and the situation, and they also carry its ideas and emotions. For this reason, each poet searches for perfect and indispensable words, words that convey all the compressed meanings, overtones, and emotions that each poem requires, and also the words that sound right and look right.

Life—and poetry—might be simpler (but less interesting) if there were an exact one-to-one correspondence between words and the objects or ideas they signify. Such close correspondences exist in artificial language systems such as chemical equations and computer languages. This identical correlation, however, is not characteristic of English or any other natural language. Instead, words have the independent and glorious habit of acquiring a vast array of different meanings.

Even if we have not thought much about language, most of us recognize that words are sometimes ambiguous, and much literature is built on ambiguity. For instance, in Shakespeare's *Romeo and Juliet,* when Mercutio says, "Seek for me tomorrow and you shall find me a grave man," the joke works because *grave* has two separate meanings, both of which come into play. In reading poetry, we recognize that poets rejoice in this shifting and elusive but also rich nature of language.

CHOICE OF DICTION: SPECIFIC AND CONCRETE, GENERAL AND ABSTRACT

Because poets always try to use only the exactly right words, they constantly make conscious and subconscious decisions about diction. One of the major categories of their choice is diction that is either specific and concrete or general and abstract.

Specific language refers to objects or conditions that can be perceived or imagined, and general language signifies broad classes of persons, objects, and phenomena. Concrete diction describes conditions or qualities that are exact and particular; abstract diction refers to qualities that are rarefied and theoretical. In practice, poems using specific and concrete words tend to be visual, familiar, and compelling. By contrast, poems using general and abstract words tend to be detached and cerebral, frequently dealing with universal questions or emotions.

These distinctions become clear when we compare Housman's "Loveliest of Trees" (Chapter 13) and Eberhart's "The Fury of Aerial Bombardment." Many of the terms and images that Housman uses, such "cherry . . . hung with bloom" and "three score years and ten," are specific and concrete; they evoke exact time and clear visualization. By contrast, Eberhart's terms, such as "infinite spaces" and "eternal truth," are general and abstract, and it is therefore hard to define them with clarity and exactness. This contrast, which by no means implies that Housman's poem is superior to Eberhart's, reflects differences in word choices for different objectives.

Most poets employ mixtures of words in these categories because in many poems they draw general observations and abstract conclusions from specific situations and concrete responses. They therefore interweave their words to fit their situations and ideas, as in Roethke's "Dolor," which uses specific and concrete words to define a series of abstract emotional states.

LEVELS OF DICTION

Like ordinary speakers and writers of prose, poets choose words from the category of the three levels of diction: high or formal, middle or neutral, and low or informal. Often, the high and middle levels are considered standard or "right" while low language is dismissed as substandard or "wrong." In poetry, however, none of the classes is more "correct" than any other, for what counts is that they all function according to the poet's wishes, from broadly formal and intellectual to ordinary and popular.

High or Formal Diction Is Elevated and Elaborate

High or formal diction exactly follows the rules of syntax and seeks accuracy of expression even if unusually elevated or complex words are brought into play. Beyond "correctness," formal language is characterized by complex words and a lofty tone. In general, formal diction freely introduces words of French, Latin, and Greek derivation, some of which are quite long, so that some persons might think that formal language is "difficult." Graves uses formal diction in "The Naked and the Nude" when the speaker asserts that the terms in the title are "By *lexicographers construed* / As synonyms that should *express* / The same *deficiency* of dress." The Latinate words, italicized here, stiffen and generalize the passage. We find *lexicographers* instead of *dictionary writers, construed* (from Latin) instead of *thought* (native English), *express* (from Latin) instead of *say* or *show* (native English), and *deficiency* (Latin) instead of *lack* (English). It is simply a fact that our language contains thousands of words that were originally French, Latin, or Greek and that many of these are long and abstract. But not all words of this sort are necessarily long, nor are they abstract and stiff. Many of our short words, for example, are French in origin, such as *class, face, fort, paint, bat, tend, gain, cap, trace, order,* and *very.* A good college-level dictionary contains brief descriptions of word origins, or etymologies; as an exercise, you might trace the origins of a number of words in a poem.

Middle or Neutral Diction Stresses Simplicity Rather than Complexity

Middle or **neutral diction** maintains the correct language and word order of formal diction but avoids elaborate words and elevated tone just as it also avoids idioms, colloquialisms, contractions, slang, jargon, and fads of speech. For example, Emily Dickinson's "Because I Could Not Stop for Death" (Chapter 13) is almost entirely in middle diction.

Low or Informal Diction Is the Language in Common, Everyday Use

Low or **informal diction** is relaxed and unself-conscious, the language of people buying groceries, gasoline, and pizza, and of people who may be "hanging out" while guzzling beer or soda pop. Poems using informal diction include common and simple words, idiomatic expressions, substandard expressions, foreign expressions, slang, "swearwords" or "cusswords," grammatical "errors," and contractions. Informal diction is seen in Hardy's "The Man He Killed" (Chapter 13), in which the speaker uses words and phrases like "many a nipperkin," "He thought he'd 'list," and "off-hand like."

SPECIAL TYPES OF DICTION

Depending on their subjects and purposes, poets (and writers of prose) may wish to introduce four special types of diction into their poems: idiom, dialect, slang, and jargon.

Idiom Refers to Forms of Diction and Word Order that Are Unique to a Language

The words **idiom** and **idioms,** originally meaning "making one's own," refer to words, phrases, and expressions that are common and acceptable in a particular language, even though they might, upon analysis, seem peculiar or even wrong. Standard English idioms are so ingrained into our thought that we hardly notice them. Poems automatically reflect these idioms. Thus, for example, a poet may "think *of*" an idea, speak of "living *in*" a house, talk of "going *out* to play," or describe a woman "lovely *as* chandeliers." Poets hardly have choices about such idioms as long as they are using standard English. Real choice occurs when poets select idioms that are unusual or even ungrammatical, as in phrases like "had he and I but met," "we was happy," and "except that You than He." Idioms like these enable poets to achieve levels of ordinary and colloquial diction, depending on their purposes.

Dialect Refers to Regional and Group Usage and Pronunciation

Although we recognize English as a common language, in practice the language is made up of many habits of speech or **dialects** that are characteristic of many groups, regions, and nations. In addition to "general American," we can recognize many common dialects such as Southern, Midwestern, New England, Brooklynese, American Black English, Yiddish English, and Texan, together with "upper" British, Cockney, and Scottish and Australian English. Dialect is concerned with whether we refer to a *pail* (general American) or a *bucket* (southern), or sit down on a *sofa* (eastern) or a *couch* (general American) or *davenport* (midwestern), or drink *soda* (eastern), *pop* (midwestern), *soda pop* (a confused midwesterner living in the east, or a confused easterner living in the midwest), or *tonic* (Bostonian). The anonymous "Bonny George Campbell" (Chapter 14) and Burns's "Green Grow the Rashes, O" illustrate the poetic use of dialect.

Slang Refers to Informal and Substandard Vocabulary and Idiom

Much of the language that people use every day is **slang.** Sometimes slang is impermanent, appearing among certain speakers and then vanishing. The use of the word *bad* to mean "good" illustrates how a new slang meaning can develop, and even stay for a time, and then diminish in use or even disappear entirely. This is not to say that slang is not persistent, for permanent slang forms a significant part of the language. There is a continuous word stock of substandard or "impolite" words, some of which are so-called four-letter words, that everyone knows but speaks only privately. There are also innumerable slang expressions. For example, we have many slang phrases describing dying, such as *kick the bucket, croak, be wasted, buy the farm, be disappeared,* and *be offed.* A nonnative speaker of English, unfamiliar with our slang, would have difficulty understanding that a person who "kicked the bucket," "bought the farm," or "was offed" had actually died.

Even though slang is a permanent part of our language, it usually confined to colloquial or conversational levels. Interestingly, people with perfect command of standard English regularly use slang in private among their friends and acquaintances. If slang is introduced into a standard context, therefore, it mars and jars, as in Larkin's "Next, Please" (Chapter 23), where the speaker describes the female statue at the bow of a ship as "the figurehead with golden tits." Because this poem is designed to expose the fatuousness of unreal hopes, the slang word creates a clashing, deflating effect that underscores this intention.

Jargon Is the Special Language and Terminology of Groups

Particular groups develop **jargon,** special words and expressions to fit needs and circumstances. Without an initiation of some kind (including intensive college and university study), people not in the group cannot understand the jargon. Usually such groups are members of specific professions or trades, such as astronauts, doctors, lawyers, computer experts, plumbers, and football players. Although jargon at its worst befuddles rather than informs, it is significant when it becomes part of mainstream English or is used in literature. Poets may introduce jargon for special effects. For example, Paul Zimmer, in "The Day Zimmer Lost Religion" (Chapter 25), wryly uses the phrase "ready for Him now," a boxing expression that describes a fighter in top condition. Linda Pastan uses "gives me an A" and "I'm dropping out," both phrases from school

---

DECORUM IS THE MATCHING OF SUBJECT AND WORD

A vital literary concept is **decorum;** that is, words and subjects should be exactly appropriate—formal words for serious subjects, and informal words for low subjects and comedy. In Shakespeare's *A Midsummer Night's Dream,* for example, the nobles usually speak poetry and the "mechanicals" speak prose. When the nobility are relaxed and in the forest, however, they speak prose. *Decorum* governs such choices of language.

In the eighteenth century, writers aimed to make the English language as dignified as ancient Latin, which was the international language of discourse. They therefore asserted that only formal diction was appropriate for poetry; common life and colloquial language were excluded except in drama and popular ballads. These rules of decorum required standard and elevated language rather than common words and phrases. The development of scientific terminology during the eighteenth century also influenced language. In the scientific mode, poets of the time used genus-species phrases like "lowing herd" for cattle (Gray) and "finny prey" for fish (Pope). In this vein, Thomas Gray observed the dependence of color on light in the line "cheerful fields resume their green attire" from the "Sonnet on the Death of Richard West."

Alexander Pope, one of the greatest eighteenth-century poets, maintained these rules of decorum—and also made fun of them—in his mock-epic poem *The Rape of the Lock,* and more fully in the mock-critical work *The Art of Sinking in Poetry.* In *The Rape of the Lock,* he refers to a scissors as a "glittering forfex." Similarly, in the following couplet he elevates the simple act of pouring coffee:

> From silver spouts the grateful liquors glide,
> While China's earth receives the smoking tide.

After William Wordsworth transformed poetic diction early in the nineteenth century, the topics and language of people of all classes, with a special stress on common folk, have become a feature of poetry (see Chapter 24). Poets have continued to follow rules of decorum, however, inasmuch as the use of colloquial diction and even slang is a necessary consequence of popular subject matter.

life, to create comic effects in "Marks" (Chapter 25). Poems in this chapter employing jargon are Reed's "Naming of Parts" and Eberhart's "The Fury of Aerial Bombardment." Both poems use technical terms about firearms to establish the authenticity of their references and therefore to reinforce their judgments about warfare.

SYNTAX

Syntax refers to word order and sentence structure. Normal English word order is firmly fixed in a *subject-verb-object* sequence. At the simplest level, we say, "A dog (*subject*) bites (*verb*) a man (*object*)." This order is so central to our communication that any change significantly affects meaning: "A dog bites a man" is not the same as "A man bites a dog."

Much of the time, poets follow normal word order. In "The Lamb," for example, Blake creates a simple, easy order in keeping with the poem's purpose of presenting a childlike praise of God. Many modern poets such as James Wright (Chapter 14) go out of their way to create ordinary, everyday syntax, on the theory that a poem's sentence structures should not get in the way of the reader's perceptions.

Yet, just as good poets always explore the limits of ideas, so also do they sometimes explore the many possibilities of syntax, as in line 7 of Donne's "Batter My Heart": "Reason, Your viceroy in me, me should defend." In prose, this sentence would read "Reason, who is Your viceroy in me, should defend me." But note that Donne drops the "who is," thus making an appositive instead of a relative clause. In the predicate, he places the direct object "me" before and not after the verb. The resulting emphasis on the pronoun *me* is appropriate to the personal-divine relationship that is the topic of the sonnet. The alteration also meets the demand of the poem's rhyme scheme. A set of particularly noteworthy syntactic variations occurs in Roethke's "Dolor." The poet uses an irregular and idiosyncratic combination of direct objects, prepositional phrases, and appositives to create ambiguity and uncertainty that reflects the poem's meaning—that school and office routines produce aimlessness and depression.

In addition to these techniques used by Blake, Wright, Donne, and Roethke, there are many other ways in which poets shape word order to create emphasis. **Rhetoric,** for example, has an important influence on sentence structures. A fundamental and easily recognized device is **parallelism,** the duplication of forms and word order (see also Chapter 7). The simplest form of parallelism is the **repetition** of the same words and phrases, seen in Blake's "The Lamb." Through the use of the same *forms* of *different* words, parallelism produces lines or portions of lines that impress our minds strongly, as in this passage from Robinson's "Richard Cory," in which there are four parallel past-tense verbs (italicized here):

> So on we *worked,* and *waited* for the light,
> And *went* without the meat, and *cursed* the bread;

The final two lines of this poem demonstrate how parallelism may embody **antithesis**—a contrasting situation or idea that brings out surprise and climax:

And Richard Cory, one calm summer night,
Went home and *put* a bullet through his head.

A major quality of parallelism is the packing of words (the *economy* and *compression* of poetry), for by using a parallel structure the poet makes a single word or phrase function a number of times, with no need for repetition. The opening verb phrase "have known" in Roethke's "Dolor," though used once, controls six parallel direct objects. At the end of Donne's "Batter My Heart," parallelism (along with antithesis) permits Donne to omit the italicized words added and bracketed in the last line here:

for I,
Except° You enthrall° me, never shall be free,   *unless; enslave*
Nor *[shall I]* ever *[be]* chaste, except you ravish me.

Note also that parallelism and antithesis make possible the unique *a b b a* ordering of these two lines , with the pattern "enthrall" (verb) "free" (adjective) "chaste" (adjective) "ravish" (verb). This pattern is called **antimetabole** or **chiasmus** and is a common means of creating emphasis.

DENOTATION AND CONNOTATION

To achieve the maximum impact, poets depend not just on the simplest, most essential meanings of words but also on the suggestions and associations that words bring to us. For this reason, control over denotation and connotation (see also Chapter 7) is so important that it has been called the very soul of the poet's art.

Denotation Refers to a Word's Standard, Most Commonly Recognized Meaning

Denotation refers to the ordinary dictionary meaning of a word. It indicates conventional correspondences between a word and an object or idea. We might expect denotation to be straightforward. However, most English words have multiple denotations. The noun *house,* for example, can refer to a *building,* a *family,* a *branch of congress,* a *theater,* a *theater audience,* a *sorority* or *fraternity,* an *astrological classification,* or a *brothel.* Although context usually makes the denotation of *house* more specific, the various meanings confer a built-in ambiguity in this simple word.

Denotation presents problems because with the passing of time new meanings emerge and old ones are shed. In poems written in the eighteenth century and earlier, there are many words that have changed so completely that a modern dictionary is not much help. In Marvell's "To His Coy Mistress," for example (Chapter 23), the speaker asserts that his "vegetable love should grow / Vaster than empires, and more slow." At first reading, "vegetable" may seem to refer to something like a giant, loving cabbage. When we turn to a current dictionary, we discover that *vegetable* is an adjective meaning "plant-like," but *plantlike love* does not get us much beyond *vegetable love*. A reference to the *Oxford English Dictionary* (OED), however, tells us that *vegetable* was used as an adjective in the seventeenth century to mean "living or growing like a plant." Thus we find out that "vegetable love" means love that grows slowly but steadily greater.

Connotation Refers to a Word's Emotional, Psychological, Social, and Historical Overtones

The life of language, and the most difficult to control, is a result of the **connotations** of various words. Almost no word is without connotation. For instance, according to the dictionary, the words *childish* and *childlike* denote the state of being like a child. Nevertheless, they connote or imply different sets of characteristics. *Childish* suggests a person who is bratty, stubborn, immature, silly, and petulant, whereas *childlike* suggests that a person may be innocent, charming, and unaffected. These different meanings are based entirely on connotations, for the denotations make little distinction.

Connotation affects us in almost everything we hear and read. We constantly encounter the manipulation of connotation in advertising, for example, which could not exist without the controlled management of meaning. Such manipulation may be as simple as calling a *used car* a *pre-owned car* to avoid the negative connotations of *used*. On the other hand, the manipulation may be as sophisticated as the current use of the words *lite* or *light* to describe foods and drinks. In all such products, *lite* denotes "dietetic," "low-calorie," or even "weak." The distinction—and the selling point—is found in connotation. Imagine how difficult it would be to sell a drink called "dietetic beer" or "weak beer." *Light* and *lite*, however, carry none of the negative connotations and, instead, suggest products that are pleasant, sparkling, bright, and healthy.

Poets always try to make individual words carry as many appropriate and effective denotations and connotations as possible. Put another way, poets use *packed* or *loaded* words that carry a broad range of meaning and association. With this in mind, read the following poem by Robert Graves.

ROBERT GRAVES   (1895–1985)

The Naked and the Nude ———————————————————— *1957*

For me, the naked and the nude
(By lexicographers° construed

As synonyms that should express
The same deficiency of dress
Or shelter) stand as wide apart   5
As love from lies, or truth from art.

Lovers without reproach will gaze
On bodies naked and ablaze;
The Hippocratic° eye will see
In nakedness, anatomy;   10
And naked shines the Goddess when
She mounts her lion among men.

The nude are bold, the nude are sly
To hold each treasonable eye.
While draping by a showman's trick   15
Their dishabille° in rhetoric,
They grin a mock-religious grin
Of scorn at those of naked skin.

The naked, therefore, who compete
Against the nude may know defeat;   20
Yet when they both together tread
The briary pastures of the dead,
By Gorgons° with long whips pursued,
How naked go the sometime nude!

THE NAKED AND THE NUDE.   2 *lexicographers:* writers of dictionaries.   9 *Hippocratic:* medical; the adjective derives from Hippocrates (ca. 460–377 B.C.E.), the ancient Greek who is considered the "father of medicine."   16 *dishabille:* being carelessly or partly dressed.   23 *Gorgons:* mythological female monsters with snakes for hair.

QUESTIONS

1. How does the speaker explain the denotations and connotations of "naked" and "nude" in the first stanza? What is indicated by the fact that the word *naked* is derived from Old English *nacod* while *nude* comes from Latin *nudus*?
2. What examples of "the naked" and "the nude" do the second and third stanzas provide? What do the examples have in common?
3. How do the connotations of words like "sly," "draping," "dishabille," "rhetoric," and "grin" contribute to the poem's ideas about "the nude"?
4. What does "briary pastures of the dead" mean in line 22?

This poem explores the connotative distinctions between the title words, *naked* and *nude,* which share a common denotation. The title also suggests that the poem is about human customs, for if the speaker were considering the words alone, he would say "naked" and "nude" instead of "*the* naked and *the* nude." The speaker's use of *the* signifies a double focus on both language and human perspectives. In the first five lines, the poem establishes that the two key words should be "synonyms that should express / The same deficiency of dress" (lines 3–4). By introducing elevated and complex words such as "lex-icographers" and "construed," however, Graves implies that the connection between "the naked" and "the nude" is sophisticated and artificial.

In the rest of the poem, Graves develops this distinction, linking the word *naked* to virtues of love, truth, innocence, and honesty, while connecting *nude* to artifice, hypocrisy, and deceit. At the end, he visualizes a classical underworld in which all pretentiousness will disappear, and the nude will lose their sophistication and become merged with the naked. The implication is that artifice will vanish in the face of eternal reality. A thorough study of the words in the poem bears out the consistency of Graves's idea, not only about the two title words, but also about the accumulated layers of history, usage, and philosophy that weigh upon human life and thought.

 ## POEMS FOR STUDY

WILLIAM BLAKE   (1757–1827)

The Lamb _____ 1789

Little Lamb, who made thee?
  Dost thou know who made thee?
Gave thee life & bid thee feed,
By the stream & o'er the mead;
Gave thee clothing of delight,
Softest clothing wooly bright;

Gave thee such a tender voice,
Making all the vales rejoice!
   Little Lamb who made thee?
   Dost thou know who made thee?   10

   Little Lamb I'll tell thee,
   Little Lamb I'll tell thee!
He is called by thy name,
For he calls himself a Lamb:
He is meek & he is mild,   15
He became a little child:
I a child & thou a lamb,
We are callèd by his name.
   Little Lamb God bless thee.
   Little Lamb God bless thee.   20

QUESTIONS

1. Who or what is the speaker in this poem? The listener? How are they related?
2. What is the effect of repetition in the poem?
3. How would you characterize the diction in this poem? High, middle, or low? Abstract or concrete? How is it consistent with the speaker?
4. What are the connotations of "softest," "bright," "tender," "meek," and "mild"? What do these words imply about the Creator?
5. Describe the characteristics of God imagined in this poem. Contrast the image here with the image of God in Donne's "Batter My Heart."

ROBERT BURNS   (1756–1796)

Green Grow the Rashes, O _____ *1787*

1

There's naught but care on ev'ry han',°   *hand*
   In every hour that passes, O;
What signifies the life o'° man   *of*
   An' 'twere na° for the lasses, O?   *if it were not*
Chorus:
Green grow the rashes,° O;   *rushes*   5
Green grow the rashes, O;
The sweetest hours that e'er I spend
   Are spent among the lasses, O!

2

The war'ly° race may riches chase,   *worldly*
   An' riches still may fly them, O;   10
An' tho' at last they catch them fast,
   Their hearts can ne'er enjoy them, O.
Chorus.

3

But gie me a cannie° hour at e'en,°   *give me a happy; evening*
   My arms about my dearie, O,
An' war'ly cares an' war'ly men   15
   May a' gae tapsalteerie,° O!   *all go topsy-turvy*
Chorus.

4

For you sae douce° ye sneer at this,   *so sober, so straitlaced*
   Ye're naught but senseless asses, O:
The wisest man the warl' e'er° saw,   *world ever*
   He dearly loved the lasses, O.   20
Chorus.

5

Auld Nature swears the lovely dears
   Her noblest work she classes, O;
Her prentice han'° she tried on man,   *apprentice hand*
   An' then she made the lasses, O.
Chorus.

QUESTIONS

1. Who is the speaker? What is he like? What is his highest value? How seriously do you take his pronouncements?

2. How does the speaker justify his feelings? How does he compare his interests with those of other people?

3. What is the speaker's explanation of the origins of men and women? How might this explanation have been received in 1787, the year of publication, when most people accepted the creation story as told in Genesis?

LEWIS CARROLL   (1832–1898)

Jabberwocky° _____ *1871*

'Twas brillig, and the slithy toves
   Did gyre and gimble in the wabe;
All mimsy were the borogoves,
   And the mome raths outgrabe.

"Beware the Jabberwock, my son!
   The jaws that bite, the claws that catch!
Beware the Jubjub bird, and shun
   The frumious Bandersnatch!"

JABBERWOCKY.   The poem, which appears in the first chapter of *Through the Looking Glass*, is full of nonsense words that Carroll made up with the sound (rather than the sense) in mind. Alice admits that the poem makes some sense even though she does not know the words: "It seems very pretty . . . but it's rather hard to understand! . . . Somehow it seems to fill my head with ideas—only I don't exactly know what they are!"

He took his vorpal sword in hand;
   Long time the manxome foe he sought—   10
So rested he by the Tumtum tree,
   And stood awhile in thought.

And, as in uffish thought he stood,
   The Jabberwock, with eyes of flame,
Came whiffling through the tulgey wood,   15
   And burbled as it came!

One, two! One, two! And through and through
   The vorpal blade went snicker-snack!
He left it dead, and with its head
   He went galumphing back.   20

"And hast thou slain the Jabberwock?
   Come to my arms, my beamish boy!
O frabjous day! Callooh! Callay!"
   He chortled in his joy.

'Twas brillig, and the slithy toves   25
   Did gyre and gimble in the wabe;
All mimsy were the borogoves,
   And the mome raths outgrabe.

QUESTIONS

1. Summarize in your own words the story that this poem tells.
2. Humpty Dumpty begins to explain or explicate this poem for Alice in Chapter 6 of *Through the Looking Glass*. He explains that "'brillig' means four o'clock in the afternoon—the time when you begin *broiling* things for dinner." He also explains that "'slithy' means 'lithe' and 'slimy.' 'Lithe' is the same as 'active.' You see it's like a portmanteau—there are two meanings packed into one word." Go through the poem and determine what combinations of words are packed into these portmanteau words. *Brillig,* for example, might be seen as a combination of *broiling, brilliant,* and *light.*

JOHN DONNE   (1572–1631)

Holy Sonnet 14: Batter My Heart, Three-Personed God _____ *1633*

Batter my heart, three-personed God; for You
As yet but knock, breathe, shine, and seek to mend;
That I may rise and stand, o'erthrow me, and bend
Your force to break, blow, burn and make me new.
I, like an usurped° town, to another due,   *conquered* 5
Labor to admit You, but Oh, to no end;
Reason, Your viceroy in me, me should defend,
But is captived, and proves weak or untrue.

Yet dearly I love You, and would be loved fain,°   *gladly*
But am betrothed unto Your enemy.
Divorce me, untie or break that knot again;
Take me to You, imprison me, for I,
Except You enthrall me, never shall be free,
Nor ever chaste, except you ravish me.

QUESTIONS

1. What kind of God is suggested by the words "batter," "knock," "overthrow," and "break"? What does "three-personed God" mean?
2. With which person of God might the verbs "knock" and "break" be associated? The verbs "breathe" and "blow"? The verbs "shine" and "burn"?
3. What is the effect of the altered word order at the ends of lines 7 and 9?
4. Explain the words "enthrall" (line 13) and "ravish" (line 14) to resolve the apparent paradox or contradiction in the last two lines.

RICHARD EBERHART   (b. 1904)

The Fury of Aerial Bombardment _____ *1947*

You would think the fury of aerial bombardment
Would rouse God to relent; the infinite spaces
Are still silent. He looks on shock-pried faces.
History, even, does not know what is meant.

You would feel that after so many centuries
God would give man to repent; yet he can kill
As Cain could, but with multitudinous will,
No farther advanced than in his ancient furies.

Was man made stupid to see his own stupidity?
Is God by definition indifferent, beyond us all?
Is the eternal truth man's fighting soul
Wherein the Beast ravens in its own avidity?

Of Van Wettering I speak, and Averill,
Names on a list, whose faces I do not recall
But they are gone to early death, who late in school
Distinguished the belt feed lever from the belt holding pawl.

QUESTIONS

1. Who or what is the speaker in this poem? What does the last stanza tell you about him? (Eberhart was a gunnery instructor during World War II.)
2. What type and level of diction predominates in lines 1–12? What observations about God are made in these lines? Compare the image of God presented here

with the one found in Donne's "Batter My Heart, Three-Personed God" and Blake's "The Lamb." What similarities or differences do you find?

3. How does the level and type of diction change in the last stanza? What is the effect of these changes? How is jargon used here?

4. Compare this poem with Thomas Hardy's "Channel Firing" (p. 703). How are the ideas in the poems similar?

THOMAS GRAY   (1716–1771)

Sonnet on the Death of Richard West _____ *(1742) 1775*

In vain to me the smiling mornings shine,
    And redd'ning Phoebus° lifts his golden fire;
The birds in vain their amorous descant° join,   *love songs*
    Or cheerful fields resume their green attire:°
These ears, alas! for other notes repine;   5
    A different object do these eyes require.
My lonely anguish melts no heart but mine,
    And in my breast the imperfect joys expire.
Yet morning smiles the busy race to cheer,
    And new-born pleasure brings to happier men;   10
The fields to all their wonted tribute bear;°
    To warm their little loves the birds complain:°
I fruitless mourn to him that cannot hear,
    And weep the more because I weep in vain.

SONNET ON THE DEATH OF RICHARD WEST.   2 *Phoebus:* Apollo, the Sun God   4 *resume their green attire:* During the darkness of night, the "cheerful fields" have no color, but in the light of the morning sun they become green again.   11 *The fields: . . . bear:* The fields contribute their customary harvest to benefit all creation.   12 *complain:* sing love songs.

QUESTIONS

1. What is the poem's subject, the speaker or the dead friend? How effective is the poem as a lament or dirge?

2. Describe the poem's level of diction. Why does the speaker use phrases like "smiling mornings" (line 1), "redd'ning Phoebus" (2), "golden fire" (2), "resume their green attire" (4), and "notes" (5)? How common are these phrases? What is their effect?

3. Consider the syntax in lines 5, 6, 9, 10, 11, and 12. What is unusual about the word order in these lines? What is the effect of this word order?

4. In the 1800 *Preface* to *Lyrical Ballads,* William Wordsworth printed this poem. He italicized lines 6–8 and 13 and 14, and wrote, "It will easily be perceived, that the only part of this Sonnet which is of any value is the lines printed in Italics; it is equally obvious, that . . . the language of these lines does in no respect differ from that of prose." What does Wordsworth's criticism mean? To what degree is it justified?

CAROLYN KIZER   (b. 1925)

Night Sounds _____ *1984*

imitated from the Chinese

The moonlight on my bed keeps me awake;
Living alone now, aware of the voices of evening,
A child weeping at nightmares, the faint love-cries of a woman,
Everything tinged by terror or nostalgia.

No heavy, impassive back to nudge with one foot   5
While coaxing, "Wake up and hold me,"
When the moon's creamy beauty is transformed
Into a map of impersonal desolation.

But, restless in this mock dawn of moonlight
That so chills the spirit, I alter our history;   10
You were never able to lie quite peacefully at my side,
Not the night through. Always withholding something.

Awake before morning, restless and uneasy,
Trying not to disturb me, you would leave my bed
While I lay there rigidly, feigning sleep.   15
Still—the night was nearly over, the light not as cold
As a full cup of moonlight.

And there were the lovely times when, to the skies' cold *No*
You cried to me, *Yes!* Impaled me with affirmation.
Now when I call out in fear, not in love, there is no answer.   20
Nothing speaks in the dark but the distant voices,
A child with the moon in his face, a dog's hollow cadence.

QUESTIONS

1. To what degee may this poem be considered confessional? What is being confessed?

2. Who is the "you" of the poem? What has happened between the speaker and the "you"? With what contrasts does the speaker conclude the poem? How are these contrasts related to the relationship between the speaker and the "you"?

3. What situation and impressions are brought about by these words in the first stanza: "moonlight," "weeping," "nightmares," "tinged," "terror," "nostalgia"?

4. What is the effect of the participles in stanzas 1–4 ("living," "coaxing," "withholding," "trying," "feigning")?

MAXINE KUMIN   (b. 1925)

Hello, Hello Henry —————————————————————— *1982*

My neighbor in the country, Henry Manley,
with a washpot warming on his woodstove,
with a heifer and two goats and yearly chickens,
has outlasted Stalin, Roosevelt and Churchill
but something's stirring in him in his dotage.   5

Last fall he dug a hole and moved his privy
and a year ago in April reamed his well out.
When the county sent a truck and poles and cable,
his daddy ran the linemen off with birdshot
and swore he'd die by oil lamp, and did.   10

Now you tell me that all yesterday in Boston
you set your city phone at mine, and had it ringing
inside a dead apartment for three hours
room after empty room, to keep yours busy.
I hear it in my head, that ranting summons.   15

That must have been about the time that Henry
walked up two miles, shy as a girl come calling,
to tell me he has a phone now, 264, ring two.
It rang one time last week—wrong number.
He'd be pleased if one day I would think to call him.   20

Hello, hello Henry? Is that you?

QUESTIONS

1. What is the poem's level of diction? What does this level contribute to your
   response to the poem?
2. What words in this poem are appropriate for a country location? What do
   the words show about Henry Manley, and about the conditions on his
   farm?
3. Who is the speaker? What does the selection of words indicate about the
   speaker's character and state of mind?
4. How does the listener enter into the poem's action in the third stanza? What is
   the meaning of the listener's action?

DENISE LEVERTOV   (1923–1997)

Of Being _____ *1997*

I know this happiness
Is provisional:

      the looming presences—
      great suffering, great fear—

      withdraw only   5
      into peripheral vision:

but ineluctable this shimmering
of wind in the blue leaves:

this flood of stillness
widening the lake of sky: 10

this need to dance,
this need to kneel:

      this mystery:

QUESTIONS

1. What is meant by "this happiness / Is provisional"?
2. What is it that withdraws (line 5)? How does the poet connect withdrawing with the poem's title?
3. What do the words "peripheral vision," "ineluctable," "blue leaves," "flood of stillness," and "lake of sky" contribute to your understanding of the "mystery" with which the poem closes? What is noteworthy about these words?
4. Why does the poet end the poem with a colon rather than a period?

HENRY REED   (1914–1986)

Naming of Parts _____ *1946*

To-day we have naming of parts. Yesterday,
We had daily cleaning. And to-morrow morning,
We shall have what to do after firing. But to-day,
To-day we have naming of parts. Japonica
Glistens like coral in all of the neighboring gardens,
   And to-day we have naming of parts.

This is the lower sling swivel. And this
Is the upper sling swivel, whose use you will see,
When you are given your slings. And this is the piling swivel,
Which in your case you have not got. The branches
Hold in the gardens their silent, eloquent gestures,
   Which in our case we have not got.

This is the safety-catch, which is always released
With an easy flick of the thumb. And please do not let me
See anyone using his finger. You can do it quite easy   15
If you have any strength in your thumb. The blossoms
Are fragile and motionless, never letting anyone see
   Any of them using their finger.

And this you can see is the bolt. The purpose of this
Is to open the breech, as you see. We can slide it   20
Rapidly backwards and forwards: we call this
Easing the spring. And rapidly backwards and forwards
The early bees are assaulting and fumbling the flowers:
   They call it easing the Spring.

They call it easing the Spring: it is perfectly easy   25
If you have any strength in your thumb: like the bolt,
And the breech, and the cocking-piece, and the point of balance,
Which in our case we have not got; and the almond-blossom
Silent in all of the gardens and the bees going backwards and forwards,
   For to-day we have naming of parts.   30

QUESTIONS

1. There may be two speakers in this poem, or one speaker repeating the words of another and adding his own thoughts. What two voices do you hear?

2. What is the setting? The situation? How do these affect the speaker?

3. How and why is jargon used in the poem? With what set of "parts" is the jargon initially associated? How does this change?

4. How are phrases like "easing the spring" (lines 22, 24, 25) and "point of balance" (27) used ambiguously? What is the effect of repetition?

EDWIN ARLINGTON ROBINSON (1869–1935)

Richard Cory _____ *1897*

Whenever Richard Cory went down town,
We people on the pavement looked at him:
He was a gentleman from sole to crown,
Clean favored, and imperially slim.

And he was always quietly arrayed,   5
And he was always human when he talked;
But still he fluttered pulses when he said,
'Good-morning,' and he glittered when he walked.

And he was rich—yes, richer than a king—
And admirably schooled in every grace: 10
In fine, we thought that he was everything
To make us wish that we were in his place.

So on we worked, and waited for the light,
And went without the meat, and cursed the bread;
And Richard Cory, one calm summer night,   15
Went home and put a bullet through his head.

QUESTIONS

1. What is the effect of using "down town," "pavement," "meat," and "bread" in connection with the people who admire Richard Cory?
2. What are the connotations and implications of the name "Richard Cory"? Of the word "gentleman"?
3. Why does the poet use "sole to crown" instead of "head to toe" and "imperially slim" instead of "very thin" to describe Cory?
4. What effect does repetition produce in this poem? Consider especially the six lines that begin with "And."
5. What positive characteristic does Richard Cory possess (at least from the perspective of the speaker) besides wealth?

THEODORE ROETHKE   (1907–1963)

Dolor _____ *1943*

I have known the inexorable sadness of pencils,
Neat in their boxes, dolor of pad and paper-weight,
All the misery of manila folders and mucilage,
Desolation in immaculate public places,
Lonely reception room, lavatory, switchboard,
The unalterable pathos of basin and pitcher,
Ritual of multigraph, paper-clip, comma,
Endless duplication of lives and objects.
And I have seen dust from the walls of institutions,
Finer than flour, alive, more dangerous than silica,
Sift, almost invisible, through long afternoons of tedium,
Dropping a fine film on nails and delicate eyebrows,
Glazing the pale hair, the duplicate grey standard faces.

QUESTIONS

1. What does "dolor" mean? What words objectify the concept?
2. Why does "Dolor" not contain the fourteen lines usual in a sonnet?
3. What institutions, conditions, and places does the speaker associate with "dolor"? What do these have in common?
4. Describe the relationships of sentence structures and lines in "Dolor."

STEPHEN SPENDER   (1909–1995)

I Think Continually of Those Who Were Truly Great ————————— *1934*

I think continually of those who were truly great.
Who, from the womb, remembered the soul's history
Through corridors of light where the hours are suns,
Endless and singing. Whose lovely ambition
Was that their lips, still touched with fire,   5
Should tell of the spirit clothed from head to foot in song.
And who hoarded from the spring branches
The desires falling across their bodies like blossoms.

What is precious is never to forget
The delight of the blood drawn from ageless springs   10
Breaking through rocks in worlds before our earth;
Never to deny its pleasure in the simple morning light,
Nor its grave evening demand for love;
Never to allow gradually the traffic to smother
With noise and fog the flowering of the spirit.   15

QUESTIONS

1. How does this poem cause you to reconsider what is usually understood by the word "great"? What are the principal characteristics of people "who were truly great"?

2. Why does Spender use the words "were great" rather than "are great"? What difference, if any, does this distinction make to Spender's definition of greatness?

3. What is the meaning of phrases like "delight of the blood," "in worlds before our earth," "hours are suns," "still touched with fire"? What other phrases need similar thought and explanation?

4. How practical is the advice of the poem in the light of its definitions of "great" and "precious"? Why should the practicality or impracticality of these definitions probably not be considered in your judgment of the poem?

WALLACE STEVENS   (1879–1955)

Disillusionment of Ten O'Clock ———————————————— *1923*

The houses are haunted
By white night-gowns.
None are green,
Or purple with green rings,
Or green with yellow rings,   5
Or yellow with blue rings.
None of them are strange,
With socks of lace
And beaded ceintures.°   *belts*

People are not going   10
To dream of baboons and periwinkles.
Only, here and there, an old sailor,
Drunk and asleep in his boots,
Catches tigers
In red weather.   15

QUESTIONS

1. Is the "Ten O'Clock" here morning or night? How can you tell?

2. What do "haunted" and "white night-gowns" suggest about the people who live in the houses? What do the negative images in lines 3–9 suggest?

3. To whom are these people contrasted in lines 12–15?

4. What are the connotations of "socks with lace" and "beaded ceintures"? With which character in the poem would you associate these things?

5. What is the effect of using words and images like "baboons," "periwinkles," "tigers," and "red weather" in lines 11–15? Who will dream of these things?

6. Explain the term "disillusionment" and explore its relation to the point that this poem makes about dreams, images, and imagination.

MARK STRAND   (b. 1934)

Eating Poetry _____ *1968*

Ink runs from the corners of my mouth.
There is no happiness like mine.
I have been eating poetry.

The librarian does not believe what she sees.
Her eyes are sad
and she walks with her hands in her dress.

The poems are gone.
The light is dim.
The dogs are on the basement stairs and coming up.

Their eyeballs roll,
their blond legs burn like brush.
The poor librarian begins to stamp her feet and weep.

She does not understand.
When I get on my knees and lick her hand,
She screams.

I am a new man.
I snarl at her and bark.
I romp with joy in the bookish dark.

QUESTIONS

1. In the first three lines, which words tell you that the poem is not to be taken literally?
2. What is the serious topic of the poem? What words indicate that the poem has a serious intent?
3. What is the comic topic? Which words tell you that the poem's action is comic?

WRITING ABOUT DICTION AND SYNTAX IN POETRY

Study your poem carefully, line by line, to gain a general sense of its meaning. Try to establish how diction and syntax may be connected to elements such as tone, character, and idea. As you develop your ideas, look for effective and consistent patterns of word choice, connotation, repetition, and syntactic patterns that help create and reinforce the conclusions you have already reached about the poem. Ask questions like the following.

Questions for Discovering Ideas

- Who is the speaker? What is the speaker's profession or way of life? How does the speaker's background affect his or her power of observation? How does the background affect his or her level of speech?
- Who is the listener? How does the listener affect what the speaker says?
- What other characters are in the poem? How are their actions described? How accurate and fair do you think these descriptions are?
- Is the level of diction in the poem elevated, neutral, or informal, and how does this level affect your perception of the speaker, subject, and main idea or ideas?
- What patterns of diction or syntax do you discover in the poem? (*Example:* Consider words related to situation, action, setting, or particular characters.) How ordinary or unusual are these words? Which, if any, are unusual enough to warrant further examination?
- Does the poem contain many "loaded" or connotative words in connection with any single element, such as setting, speaker, or theme?
- Does the poem contain a large number of general and abstract or specific and concrete words? What is the effect of these choices?
- Does the poem contain dialect? Colloquialisms? Jargon? If so, how does this special diction shape your response to the poem?
- What is the nature of the poem's syntax? Is there any unusual word order? What seems to be the purpose or effect of syntactic variations?
- Has the poet used any striking patterns of sentence structure such as parallelism or repetition? If so, what is the effect?

Strategies for Organizing Ideas

When you narrow your examination to one or two specific areas of diction or syntax, you should list important words, phrases, and sentences and investigate the full range of meaning and effect that the examples produce. Begin grouping examples that work in similar ways or produce similar effects. Eventually you may be able to develop the related examples as units or sections for your essay.

Your central idea should emerge from your investigation of the specific diction or syntax that you find most fruitful and interesting. Let the poem be your guide. Since diction and syntax contribute to the poem's impact and meaning, try to connect your thesis and examples to your other conclusions. If you are writing about Stevens's "Disillusionment of Ten O'Clock," for example, your central idea might assert that Stevens uses words describing colors (i.e., "white," "green," "purple," "yellow," "blue," "red") to contrast life's visual reality with the psychological "disillusionment" of the "houses," "People," and "old sailor." Such a formulation makes a clear connection between diction and meaning.

There are many different ways to organize your material. If you deal with only one aspect of diction, such as connotative words, you might treat these in the order in which they appear in the poem. When you deal with two or three different aspects of diction and syntax, however, you might devote a series of paragraphs to related examples of multiple denotation, then connotation, and finally jargon (assuming the presence of jargon in the poem). In such an instance, your organization would be controlled by the types of material under consideration rather than by the order in which the words occur.

Alternatively, you might deal with the impact of diction or syntax on a series of other elements, such as character, setting, or situation. Such an essay would focus on a single type of lexical or syntactic device as it relates to these different elements in sequence. Thus, you might discuss the link between connotation and character, then setting, and finally situation. Whatever organization you select, keep in mind that each poem will suggest its own avenues of exploration and strategies of organization.

In your conclusion, summarize your ideas about the impact of the poem's diction or syntax. You might also consider the larger implications of your ideas in connection with the thoughts and emotions evoked by your reading.

DEMONSTRATIVE STUDENT ESSAY

Extraordinary Definitions in Spender's "I Think Continually of Those Who Were Truly Great"°

[1]   In the two-stanza poem "I Think Continually of Those Who Were Truly Great," Sir Stephen Spender considers the meaning of true greatness. He begins the poem as though the speaker has been talking to an unnamed person who

---

° See p. 739 for this poem.

has spoken about greatness as the word is usually understood. The poem itself might then be considered a one-sided response by the speaker in which he presents his own definition of greatness, with particular emphasis on the *truly* in "truly great." The poem creates a different and new concept of greatness.*
Spender develops his argument in two parts, each of which is knitted together by particular attitudes and grammatical structures.†

[2]   Because the poem concentrates on new definitions, it is important to discuss what Spender does with the ideas that readers might have about greatness. Usually the type of person most readers think of as great is a leader of some sort--a king, a president, an emperor, a general, or a financial mogul. It is presumably this understanding that Spender is contradicting in the poem. Readers find that he says nothing about leadership, nor are there any references at all to specific great persons. Instead, Spender goes beyond usual definitions and asks readers to consider the meaning of greatness in a deeply individual and personal way. His first line is designed to catch the interest of readers, just as the rest of the poem is designed to surprise and lead them. Something unusual is being said--something new, something extraordinary.

[3]   The first stanza of the poem presents a set of positive qualities that define true greatness. Spender carries out his definitions within three relative clauses that modify and therefore define the word "great" ("who . . . remembered," "whose . . . ambition / Was," and "who hoarded"). Interestingly, the speaker's reference to "history" (line 2) immediately puts readers on guard because it does not refer to history as a record of human accomplishments. Rather the history of greatness is "the soul's history," having no written record but composed of "corridors of light . . . / Endless and singing." The unusual idea here is that song, not business, gives form to the world through persons who become great by connecting themselves with the very origins of life. Going on, Spender provides a new definition of "tell" (line 6). Usually people telling about greatness describe politics, economics, or world domination, but in this poem the telling is about the "spirit." Spender introduces readers to the concept of hoarding, but, as with telling, readers discover that the truly great do not hoard wealth but rather accept and hoard "desires" (lines 7-8).

[4]   The key words in Spender's first stanza, in short, go beyond their commonly used economic and political meanings and refer instead to feelings and spirituality. Readers thus consider the poem's references as being not to documented history but rather to a deeper remembrance of a preexisting condition of glory. Spender's redefined meaning of greatness means that those who are great can tune themselves into the basic song of the human spirit. The words redefining "great" therefore enable readers to expand their understanding of greatness into new and unexamined areas of thought.

[5]   The second stanza of the poem is unified by three negatives, which are cast within infinitive phrases ("never to forget," "never to deny," and "never to allow") that define the word "precious" in line 9. As in the first stanza, Spender uses a common definition as a starting point: What is precious--a necessary part of greatness--is not a large bank account but rather the connection with ageless springs of human delight. Of highest value is the quality of joy that has been in

*Central idea.
†Thesis sentence.

our human blood long since before our world was created, existing in unknown worlds going back to the moment of divine creation. Preciousness also consists in accepting the pleasure of morning light and the more sober ("grave") needs of evening love (line 13). Spender's third definition of what is precious (lines 14-15) is the insistence that people should allow their spirits to flower despite the smothering grind of daily business ("the traffic"). In all these thoughts about what is precious, readers are faced with new definitions and new ways of seeing.

[6]   It is clear that the poem presents readers with the possibility of greatness in accord with Spender's unique definitions. Such greatness asks readers to forge a new being for themselves. From the poem, readers may conclude that this new being is a free spirit who achieves greatness through song, who finds joy in the morning light of endless and rhythmical sunshine, and who willingly accepts pleasure in desires and love. Greatness, in short, is the ability to reconnect oneself with the very springs of existence.

[7]   "I Think Continually of Those Who Were Truly Great," then, is a defining and also a guiding poem. It presents readers with a set of ordinary words defined in a completely new way. Readers find no advice to abandon the needs of ordinary living but rather are told of a need to reanalyze and freshen their assumptions of what life is about. The poem suggests to readers that everyone can become great by resisting the grind of daily living ("the traffic") and reconnecting with the age-old sources of human strength. Even if people are never in positions of political or military leadership--the usual avenue of greatness--they can reestablish such connections. Thus Spender's poem reaffirms life by offering new ways for readers to think about becoming "truly great."

Commentary on the Essay

This essay considers how Spender redefines the two major words within the poem: "great" and "precious," as well as how he redefines other words (e.g., "history," "tell"). In addition, it deals with how Spender's syntax unifies the poem's two major parts (through adjective or relative clauses and through infinitive phrases). Finally, it attempts to treat the subject matter of the poem in the light of reader responses (see Chapter 33). Note that throughout the essay there are references to readers, their expectations, and their responses. A major element of the essay is that Spender leads readers to new understanding along the pathway of usual or commonly accepted understanding.

The opening paragraph makes assertions about the poem's dramatic situation and also about Spender's goal of redefining the key word "great." The body of the essay, in five paragraphs, deals with definition and redefinition. Because the poem is concerned with redefinition, paragraph 2 describes how the word "great" is usually understood. On this basis, paragraphs 3 and 4 move ahead to consider how the poem redefines this word.

The next two paragraphs (5 and 6) focus on the meaning of "precious," which Spender uses as an equivalent to greatness. The examples are examined here in the order in which they appear in the poem. Thus, paragraph 5 shows how Spender establishes three areas of life that are particularly precious, unlike the large bank account that is often understood to confer preciousness. Paragraph 6 extends this idea by considering the implications of a reevaluated existence in the light of Spender's redefinition.

The conclusion in paragraph 7 reasserts that Spender's definitions are designed to show readers the ways to personal, not public, greatness and that therefore everyone and not just a few may become great. In this way, the words examined in the essay are linked to the poem's reaffirmation of life.

SPECIAL TOPICS FOR WRITING AND ARGUMENT ABOUT THE WORDS OF POETRY

1. Using the poems of Reed and Eberhart in this chapter, together with poems by Jarrell (Chapter 13) and Owen (Chapters 16, 18), study the words that these poets use to indicate the weapons and actions of warfare. In an essay, consider these questions: What shared details make the poems similar? What separate details make them different? How do the poets use word choices to make their points about war as action, tragedy, and horror?

2. Write an essay considering the sound qualities of the invented words in "Jabberwocky." Some obvious choices are "brillig," "frumious," "vorpal," and "manxome," but you are free to choose any or all of them. What is the relationship between the sound and apparent meaning of these words? What effect do the surrounding normal words and normal word order have on the special words? How does Carroll succeed in creating a narrative "structure" even though the key words are, on the surface, nonsense?

3. Analyze Robinson's use of diction in "Richard Cory." Be sure to discuss the words he uses to describe the populace. How are these words different from his words for Cory? What is the nature of the diction describing Cory's final action?

4. Write a brief essay discussing the use of connotation in Kumin's "Hello, Hello Henry," Levertov's "Of Being," Roethke's "Dolor," and Strand's "Eating Poetry." What particularities of meaning do the poets introduce? How does their control of connotation contribute to the various ideas you discover in the poems?

5. Write a short poem describing a violent crime and commenting on it. Then, assume that you are the "perpetrator" of the crime, and write another poem on the same topic. Even though you describe the same situation, how do your words differ, and why have you made these different choices? Explain the other different word choices you have made. You might also discuss words that you considered using but rejected.

6. Find a book or books in your library about the works of Robinson, Carroll, or another poet in this chapter. How fully do these sources discuss the style of any of these poets? Write a brief report explaining how the writers of the book or books deal with poetic diction.

Imagery:
The Poem's Link
to the Senses

In literature, **imagery** refers to words that trigger your imagination to recall and recombine **images**—memories or mental pictures of sights, sounds, tastes, smells, sensations of touch, and motions. The process is active and even vigorous, for when words or descriptions produce images, you are using your personal experiences with life and language to help you understand the works you are reading. In effect, you are re-creating the work *in your own way* through the controlled stimulation produced by the writer's words. Imagery is therefore one of the strongest modes of literary expression because it provides a channel to your active imagination, and along this channel, writers bring their works directly to you and into your consciousness.

For example, reading the word *lake* may bring to your mind your literal memory of a particular lake. Your mental picture—or image—may be a distant view of calm waters reflecting a blue sky, a nearby view of gentle waves rippling in the wind, a close-up view of the sandy lake bottom from a boat, or an overhead view of a sun-drenched shoreline. Similarly, the words *rose, apple, hot dog, malted milk,* and *pizza* all cause you to recollect these objects and, in addition, may cause you to recall their smells and tastes. Active and graphic words like *run, row, swim, vault,* and *dive* stimulate you to picture moving images of someone performing these actions.

RESPONSES AND THE WRITER'S USE OF DETAIL

In studying imagery, we try to comprehend and explain our imaginative reconstruction of the pictures and impressions evoked by the work's images. We let the poet's words simmer and percolate in our minds. To get our imaginations stirring, we might follow Coleridge in this description from lines 37–41 of "Kubla Khan":

A damsel with a dulcimer
In a vision once I saw:

It was an Abyssinian maid,
And on her dulcimer she played
Singing of Mount Abora.

We do not read about the color of the young woman's clothing or learn anything else about her appearance except that she is playing a stringed instrument, a dulcimer, and that she is singing a song about a mountain in a foreign,
remote land. But Coleridge's image is enough. From it we can imagine a vivid,
exotic picture of a young woman from a distant land singing, together with
the loveliness of her song (even though we never hear it or understand it). The
image lives.

THE RELATIONSHIP OF IMAGERY
TO IDEAS AND ATTITUDES

Images do more than elicit impressions. By the *authenticating* effects of the vision
and perceptions underlying them, they give you new ways of seeing
the world and of strengthening your old ways of seeing it. Shakespeare, in "Let
Me Not to the Marriage of True Minds" (Chapter 20), for example, develops
the idea that love provides people with consistency of purpose in their lives.
Rather than stating the idea directly, he uses images of a landmark or lighthouse
and also of a fixed star—sights with which we as his readers are quite familiar:

> . . . it [love] is an ever fixèd mark
> That looks on tempests and is never shaken;
> It is the star to every wandering bark
> Whose worth's unknown, although his height be taken.

These images form a link with readers that is clear and also verifiable by observation. Such uses of imagery comprise one of the strongest means by which literature reinforces ideas.

In addition, as you form mental pictures from a poet's images, you
respond with appropriate attitudes and feelings. Thus the phrase "Beside the
lake, beneath the trees," from Wordsworth's poem "Daffodils" (Chapter 24),
prompts both the visualization of a wooded lakeshore and also the related pleas-
antness of outdoor relaxation and happiness. A contrasting visualization is to
be found in Herkomer's painting *Hard Times* (p. 748), where all the images—
the tired faces, the heavy load, the tools, the bleak road, the leafless trees—
point toward the harsh life of the worker and his family, causing a response of
sadness and sympathy. Imagery used in a negative way is also found in Swift's "A
Description of the Morning" (Chapter 18), which triggers unpleasant responses
by offering images of street hawkers, thieves, bill collectors, and hesitant schoolboys. By using such imagery, artists and poets not only create sensory vividness;
they also influence and control the attitudes of their readers.

Sir Hubert von Herkomer, *Hard Times.* Copyright Manchester City Art Gallery.

CLASSIFICATION OF IMAGERY

Visual Imagery Is the Language of Sight

Sight is the most significant of our senses, for it is the key to our remembrance of other impressions. Therefore, the most frequently occurring literary imagery is to things we can visualize either exactly or approximately—**visual images.** In "Cargoes" (the subject of the demonstrative student essay on p. 742), Masefield asks us to re-create mental pictures or images of oceangoing merchant vessels from three periods of human history.

JOHN MASEFIELD   (1878–1967)

Cargoes _____ *1902*

Quinquereme° of Nineveh° from distant Ophir,°
Rowing home to haven in sunny Palestine,
With a cargo of ivory,
And apes and peacocks,°
Sandalwood, cedarwood,° and sweet white wine.

Stately Spanish galleon coming from the Isthmus,°
Dipping through the Tropics by the palm-green shores,
With a cargo of diamonds,

Emeralds, amethysts,
Topazes, and cinnamon, and gold moidores.°   10

Dirty British coaster with a salt-caked smoke-stack,
Butting through the Channel in the mad March days,
With a cargo of Tyne coal,°
Road-rails, pig-lead,
Firewood, iron-ware, and cheap tin trays.   15

CARGOES. 1 *quinquereme:* the largest of the ancient ships. It was powered by three tiers of oars and was named "quinquereme" because five men operated each vertical oar station. The top two oars were each taken by two men, while one man alone took the bottom oar.   1 *Nineveh:* capital of ancient Assyria, an "exceeding great city" (Jonah 3:3).   1 *Ophir:* Ophir probably was in Africa and was known for its gold (1 Kings 10:22; 1 Chron. 29:4). Masefield echoes some of the biblical verses in his first stanza.   4 *apes and peacocks:* See 1 Kings 10:22, 2 Chron. 9:21. 5 *cedarwood:* See 1 Kings 9:11.   6 *Isthmus:* the Isthmus of Panama.   10 *moidores:* coins used in Portugal and Brazil at the time the New World was being explored.   13 *Tyne coal:* coal from Newcastle upon Tyne, in northern England, reknowned for its coal production.

QUESTIONS

   1. Consider the images of life during three periods of history: ancient Israel at the time of Solomon (ca. 950 B.C.E.), sixteenth-century Spain, and modern England. What do these images tell you about Masefield's interpretation of modern commercial life?

   2. To what senses do most of the images refer (e.g., sight, taste, etc.)?

   3. The poem contains no complete sentences. Why do you think Masefield included only verbals ("rowing," "dipping," "butting") to begin the second line of each stanza, rather than finite verbs?

   4. In historical reality, the quinquereme was likely rowed by slaves, and the Spanish galleon likely carried riches stolen from Central American natives. How might these unpleasant details affect the impressions otherwise achieved in the first two stanzas?

Masefield's images are vivid as they stand and need no further amplification. For us to reconstruct them imaginatively, we do not need ever to have seen the ancient biblical lands or waters, or ever to have seen or handled the cheap commodities on a modern merchant ship. We have seen enough in our lives both in reality and in pictures to *imagine* places and objects like these, and hence Masefield is successful in fixing his visual images in our minds.

Auditory Imagery Is the Language of Sound

   Auditory images trigger our experiences with sound. For such images, let us consider Wilfred Owen's "Anthem for Doomed Youth," which is about the death of soldiers in warfare and the sorrow of their loved ones.

WILFRED OWEN   (1893–1918)

Young officer in World War I,

Anthem for Doomed Youth _____ 1920

judged the best, the brightest, most physically fit
to die.

Not happy about war.

What passing-bells° for these who die as cattle? *like a cattle slaughterhouse,*
Only the monstrous anger of the guns. *machine guns*
Only the stuttering rifles' rapid rattle
Can patter out their hasty orisons.°   *prayers*
No mockeries for them from prayers or bells,   5
Nor any voice of mourning save the choirs—
The shrill, demented choirs of wailing shells;
And bugles calling for them from sad shires.°

What candles may be held to speed them all?
Not in the hands of boys, but in their eyes   10
Shall shine the holy glimmers of good-byes. *tears in their eyes*
The pallor of girls' brows shall be their pall; *girlfriends their faces*
Their flowers the tenderness of patient minds, *are pale w/ grieving*
the flowers may wilt a bit
And each slow dusk a drawing-down of blinds.
a slow dusk that won't go away.

ANTHEM FOR DOOMED YOUTH.   1 *passing-bells:* church bells that are tolled at the entry of a funeral cortege into a church cemetery.   8 *shires:* British counties.

QUESTIONS

1. What type of imagery predominates in the first eight lines? How does the imagery change in the last six lines?

2. Contrast the images of death at home and death on the battlefield. How does this contrast affect your experience and understanding of the poem?

3. Consider these images: "holy glimmers of good-byes," "pallor of girls' brows," "patient minds," "drawing-down of blinds." What relationship do the people imagined in these images have to the doomed youth?

The poem begins with the question of "what passing-bells" may be tolled for "these who die as cattle." Owen's speaker is referring to the traditional tolling of a parish church bell to announce the burial of a parishioner. Reference to the sounds of such a ceremony suggests a period of peace and order, when there is time to pay respect to the dead. But the poem then points out that the only sound for those who have fallen in battle is the "rapid rattle" of "stuttering" rifles—in other words, not the solemn, dignified sounds of peace but the horrifying noises of war. Owen's auditory images evoke corresponding sounds in our imaginations, and they help us to experience the poem and to hate the uncivilized depravity of war.

Olfactory, Gustatory, and Tactile Imagery Refers to Smell, Taste, and Touch

In addition to sight and sound, you will find images from the other senses: smell, taste, and touch. Shakespeare includes an **olfactory** image of sweet perfumes in Sonnet 130: "My Mistress' Eyes Are Nothing Like the Sun," and the odor of roses is cited in Jonson's "Drink to Me, Only, with Thine Eyes" (Chapter 14) and Burns's "A Red, Red Rose" (Chapter 17).

Gustatory images are also common, though less frequent than those referring to sight and sound. Lines 5 and 10 of Masefield's "Cargoes," for example, includes images of "sweet white wine" and "cinnamon." Although the poem refers to these commodities as cargoes, the words themselves also register in our minds as gustatory images because they evoke our sense of taste.

Images of touch and texture are not as common because touch is difficult to render except in terms of effects. The speaker of Lowell's "Patterns," for example (Chapter 25), uses **tactile imagery** when imagining a never-to-happen embrace with her fiancé, who we learn has been killed on a wartime battlefield. Her imagery in lines 51–52 records the effect of the embrace ("bruised"), whereas her internalized feelings are expressed in metaphors ("aching, melting"):

> And the buttons of his waistcoat bruised my body as he clasped me
> Aching, melting, unafraid.

Tactile images are not uncommon in love poetry, where references to touch and feeling are natural. Usually, however, love poetry deals with yearning and hope rather than sexual fulfillment (as in Keats's "Bright Star").

Kinetic and Kinesthetic Imagery Refer to Motion and Activity

References to movement are also images. Images of general motion are **kinetic** (remember that *motion pictures* are called "cinema"; note the closeness of *kine* and *cine*), whereas the term **kinesthetic** is applied to human or animal movement. Imagery of motion is closely related to visual images, for motion is most often seen. Masefield's "British coaster," for example, is a visual image, but when it goes "Butting through the channel," the motion makes it also kinetic. When Hardy's skeletons sit upright at the beginning of "Channel Firing," the image is kinesthetic, as is the action of Lowell's speaker in "Patterns," walking in the garden after hearing about her fiancé's death (Chapter 25). Both types are seen at the conclusion of the following poem, Elizabeth Bishop's "The Fish."

ELIZABETH BISHOP   (1911–1979)

The Fish ——————————————————————— *1946*

I caught a tremendous fish
and held him beside the boat
half out of water, with my hook
fast in a corner of his mouth.
He didn't fight.   5

He hadn't fought at all.
He hung a grunting weight,
battered and venerable
and homely. Here and there
his brown skin hung in strips   10
like ancient wallpaper,
and its pattern of darker brown
was like wallpaper:
shapes like full-blown roses
stained and lost through age.   15
He was speckled with barnacles,
fine rosettes of lime,
and infested
with tiny white sea-lice,
and underneath two or three   20
rags of green weed hung down.
While his gills were breathing in
the terrible oxygen
—the frightening gills,
fresh and crisp with blood,   25
that can cut so badly—
I thought of the coarse white flesh
packed in like feathers,
the big bones and the little bones,
the dramatic reds and blacks   30
of his shiny entrails,
and the pink swim-bladder
like a big peony.
I looked into his eyes
which were far larger than mine   35
but shallower, and yellowed,
the irises backed and packed
with tarnished tinfoil
seen through the lenses
of old scratched isinglass.°   *mica*
They shifted a little, but not
to return my stare.
—It was more like the tipping
of an object toward the light.
I admired his sullen face,
the mechanism of his jaw,
and then I saw
that from his lower lip
—if you could call it a lip—
grim, wet, and weaponlike,
hung five old pieces of fish-line,
or four and a wire leader
with the swivel still attached,

with all their five big hooks
grown firmly in his mouth.   55
A green line, frayed at the end
where he broke it, two heavier lines,
and a fine black thread
still crimped from the strain and snap
when it broke and he got away.   60
Like medals with their ribbons
frayed and wavering,
a five-haired beard of wisdom
trailing from his aching jaw.
I stared and stared   65
and victory filled up
the little rented boat,
from the pool of bilge
where oil had spread a rainbow
around the rusted engine   70
to the bailer rusted orange,
the sun-cracked thwarts,
the oarlocks on their strings,
the gunnels—until everything
was rainbow, rainbow, rainbow!   75
And I let the fish go.

QUESTIONS

1. Describe the poem's images of action. What is unusual about them?

2. What impression does the fish make upon the speaker? Is the fish beautiful?
   Ugly? Why is the fish described in such detail?

3. What do the "five old pieces of fish line" indicate?

4. How is the rainbow formed around the boat's engine? Why does the speaker
   refer to the "pool of bilge"? What does the rainbow mean to the speaker?

5. What right does the speaker have to keep the fish? Why does she choose to
   relinquish this right?

The kinetic images at the end of "The Fish" are those of victory filling the boat
(difficult to visualize) and the oil spreading to make a rainbow in the bilgewater
(easier to visualize). The kinesthetic images are readily imagined—the speaker's
staring, observing, and letting the fish go—and they are vivid and real. The
final gesture is the necessary outcome of the observed contrast between the
deteriorating artifacts of human beings and the natural world of the fish, and it
is a vivid expression of the right of the natural world to exist without human
intervention. In short, Bishop's kinetic and kinesthetic images are designed to
objectivize the need for freedom not only for human beings but for all the
earth and animated Nature.

   The areas from which kinetic and kinesthetic imagery can be derived are too varied and unpredictable to describe. Occupations, trades, professions, businesses, recreational activities—all these might furnish images. One poet introduces references from gardening, another from money and banking, another from modern real estate developments, another from the falling of leaves in autumn, another from life in the jungle. The freshness, newness, and surprise of much poetry result from the many and varied areas from which writers draw their images.

 ## POEMS FOR STUDY

WILLIAM BLAKE   (1757–1827)

The Tyger° _____ *1794*

Tyger! Tyger! burning bright
In the forests of the night,
What immortal hand or eye
Could frame thy fearful symmetry?

In what distant deeps or skies
Burnt the fire of thine eyes?
On what wings dare he aspire?
What the hand, dare seize the fire?

And what shoulder, & what art,
Could twist the sinews of thy heart?

THE TYGER.   The title refers not only to a tiger but to any large, wild, ferocious cat.

And when thy heart began to beat,
What dread hand? & what dread feet?

What the hammer? what the chain?
In what furnace was thy brain?
What the anvil? what dread grasp   15
Dare its deadly terrors clasp?

When the stars threw down their spears,
And water'd heaven with their tears,
Did he smile his work to see?
Did he who made the Lamb make thee?   20

Tyger! Tyger! burning bright
In the forests of the night,
What immortal hand or eye
Dare frame thy fearful symmetry?

QUESTIONS

1.   What do the associations of the image of "burning" suggest? Why is the burning done at night rather than day? What does night suggest?

2.   Describe the kinesthetic images of lines 5–20. What ideas is Blake's speaker representing by these images? What attributes does the speaker suggest may belong to the blacksmith-type initiator of these actions?

3.   Line 20 presents the kinesthetic image of a creator. What is implied about the mixture of good and evil in the world? What answer does the poem offer? Why does Blake phrase this line as a question rather than an assertion?

4.   The sixth stanza repeats the first stanza with only one change of imagery of action. Contrast these stanzas, stressing the difference between "could" (line 4) and "dare" (24).

ELIZABETH BARRETT BROWNING   (1806–1861)

Sonnets from the Portuguese: Number 14 _____ *1850*

If thou must love me, let it be for nought
Except for love's sake only. Do not say
"I love her for her smile—her look—her way
Of speaking gently,—for a trick of thought
That falls in well with mine, and certes° brought   *certainly*   5
A sense of pleasant ease on such a day"—
For these things in themselves, Belovèd, may
Be changed, or change for thee,—and love, so wrought,°   *created*
May be unwrought so. Neither love me for
Thine own dear pity's wiping my cheeks dry,—   10
A creature might forget to weep, who bore

Thy comfort long, and lose thy love thereby!
But love me for love's sake, that evermore
Thou mayst love on, through love's eternity.

QUESTIONS

1. Who is the speaker of this poem? Why might you conclude that the speaker is female?

2. What images does the speaker use to indicate possible causes for loving? What kinds of images are they? How does the speaker explain why they should be rejected?

3. How does the idea of lines 1, 13, and 14 build upon the ideas in the rest of the poem?

SAMUEL TAYLOR COLERIDGE   (1772–1834)

Kubla Khan _____ *1816*

In Xanadu did Kubla Khan
A stately pleasure dome decree:
Where Alph,° the sacred river, ran
Through caverns measureless to man
  Down to a sunless sea.
So twice five miles of fertile ground
With walls and towers were girdled round:
And there were gardens bright with sinuous rills,
Where blossomed many an incense-bearing tree;
And here were forest ancient as the hills,
Enfolding sunny spots of greenery.

But oh! that deep romantic chasm which slanted
Down the green hill athwart a cedarn cover!
A savage place! as holy and enchanted
As e'er beneath a waning moon was haunted
By woman wailing for her demon lover!
And from this chasm, with ceaseless turmoil seething,
As if this earth in fast thick pants were breathing,
A mighty fountain momently was forced:
Amid whose swift half-intermitted burst
Huge fragments vaulted like rebounding hail,
Or chaffy grain beneath the thresher's flail:
And 'mid these dancing rocks at once and ever
It flung up momently the sacred river.
Five miles meandering with a mazy motion
Through wood and dale the sacred river ran,
Then reached the caverns measureless to man,

KUBLA KHAN.   3 *Alph:* possibly a reference to the river Alpheus in Greece, as described by the ancient writers Virgil and Pausanias.

And sank in tumult to a lifeless ocean:
And 'mid this tumult Kubla heard from far
Ancestral voices prophesying war!   30
  The shadow of the dome of pleasure
  Floated midway on the waves;
  Where was heard the mingled measure
  From the fountain and the caves.
It was a miracle of rare device,   35
A sunny pleasure dome with caves of ice!

  A damsel with a dulcimer
  In a vision once I saw:
  It was an Abyssinian maid,
  And on her dulcimer she played   40
  Singing of Mount Abora.°
Could I revive within me
Her symphony and song,
To such a deep delight 'twould win me,
That with music loud and long,   45
I would build that dome in air,
That sunny dome! those caves of ice!
And all who heard should see them there,
And all should cry, Beware! Beware!
His flashing eyes, his floating hair!   50
Weave a circle round him thrice,
And close your eyes with holy dread,
For he on honeydew hath fed,
And drunk the milk of Paradise.

QUESTIONS

1. How many of the poem's images might be sketched or visualized? Which ones would be panoramic landscapes? Which might be close-ups?

2. What is the effect of auditory images such as "wailing," "fast thick pants," "tumult," "ancestral voices prophesying war," and "mingled measure"?

3. When Coleridge was writing this poem, he was recalling it from a dream. At line 54 he was interrupted, and when he resumed he could write no more. How might an argument be made that the poem is finished?

4. How do lines 35–36 establish the pleasure dome as a place of mysterious oddity? What is the effect of the words "miracle" and "rare"? The effect of combining the images "sunny" and "caves of ice"?

5. Why does the speaker yearn for the power of the singing Abyssinian maid? What kinesthetic images end the poem? How are these images important in the speaker's desire to reconstruct the vision of the pleasure dome?

41 *Mount Abora:* a mountain of Coleridge's imagination. But see John Milton's *Paradise Lost,* IV. 268–284.

RICHARD CRASHAW (1613–1649)

On Our Crucified Lord, Naked and Bloody ———————— *1646*

Th' have° left Thee naked,° Lord, O that they had;   *they have*
This garment too I would they had denied.
Thee with Thyself they have too richly clad,
Opening the purple° wardrobe of Thy side.°
   O never could be found garments too good   5
   For Thee to wear, but these, of Thine own blood.

ON OUR CRUCIFIED LORD, NAKED AND BLOODY.   1 *naked:* See Mark 15:24.   3–4
Thee . . . side: John 20:34.   4 *purple:* Mark 15:17.

QUESTIONS

1. Explain the contradiction and irony in the poem. Why does clothing made by human beings seem unworthy of being draped upon the crucified Lord?

2. What is meant by "this garment" in line 2? What is the relationship between this phrase and "Thee with Thyself" in line 3?

3. Does the emphasis on the blood of Christ in this poem seem appropriate or inappropriate for a devotional poem?

RAY DUREM (1915–1963)

I Know I'm Not Sufficiently Obscure ———————— *1962*

I know I'm not sufficiently obscure
to please the critics—nor devious enough.
Imagery escapes me.
I cannot find those mild and gracious words
To clothe the carnage.
Blood is blood and murder's murder.
What's a lavender word for lynch?
Come, you pale poets, wan, refined and dreamy:
Here is a black woman working out her guts
in a white man's kitchen
for little money and no glory.
How should I tell that story?
There is a black boy, blacker still from death,
face down in the cold Korean mud.
Come on with your effervescent jive
explain to him why he ain't alive.
Reword our specific discontent
into some plaintive melody,
a little whine, a little whimper,
not too much—and no rebellion!

God, no! Rebellion's much too corny.
You deal with finer feelings,
very subtle—an autumn leaf
hanging from a tree—I see a body!

QUESTIONS

1. Who is the "you" listener addressed by the speaker (lines 8, 15, 22)? Why does the speaker admit that he is "not sufficiently obscure"? What issue is he dealing with by this admission?

2. In line 3 the speaker says, "Imagery escapes me." How does the rest of the poem contradict this statement?

3. Consider the images in lines 7, 13, and 23–24. To what degree are these images timely? Dated?

T. S. ELIOT   (1888–1965)

Preludes _____ *1910*

I

The winter evening settles down
With smell of steaks in passageways.
Six o'clock.
The burnt-out ends of smoky days.
And now a gusty shower wraps   5
The grimy scraps
Of withered leaves about your feet
And newspapers from vacant lots;
The showers beat
On broken blinds and chimney-pots,   10
And at the corner of the street
A lonely cab-horse steams and stamps.
And then the lighting of the lamps.

II

The morning comes to consciousness
Of faint stale smells of beer   15
From the sawdust-trampled street
With all its muddy feet that press
To early coffee-stands.
With the other masquerades
That time resumes,   20
One thinks of all the hands
That are raising dingy shades
In a thousand furnished rooms.

III

You tossed a blanket from the bed,
You lay upon your back, and waited;   25
You dozed, and watched the night revealing
The thousand sordid images
Of which your soul was constituted;
They flickered against the ceiling.
And when all the world came back   30
And the light crept up between the shutters
And you heard the sparrows in the gutters,
You had such a vision of the street,
As the street hardly understands;
Sitting along the bed's edge, where   35
You curled the papers from your hair,
Or clasped the yellow soles of feet
In the palms of both soiled hands.

IV

His soul stretched tight across the skies
That fade behind a city block,   40
Or trampled by insistent feet
At four and five and six o'clock;
And short square fingers stuffing pipes,
And evening newspapers, and eyes
Assured of certain certainties,   4
The conscience of a blackened street
Impatient to assume the world.

I am moved by fancies that are curled
Around these images, and cling:
The notion of some infinitely gentle   5
Infinitely suffering thing.

Wipe your hand across your mouth, and laugh;
The worlds revolve like ancient women
Gathering fuel in vacant lots.

QUESTIONS

1. From what locations are the images in the first stanza derived? How do the images shift in the second stanza? What is the connection between the images in the second and third stanzas?

2. Who is the "you" in the third stanza? What images are associated with this listener?

3. Who is the "His" of the fourth stanza? How do the images develop in this stanza? What is meant particularly in the images of lines 46–47?

4. What is the nature of the bodily imagery in the poem? The urban imagery? What impressions do these images cause?

5. In lines 48–51, what does the speaker conclude? How do the last two unnumbered stanzas constitute a contrast of attitude?

GEORGE HERBERT (1593–1633)

The Pulley _____ *1633*

When God at first made man,
Having a glass of blessings standing by,
  "Let us," said he, "pour on him all we can.
Let the world's riches, which dispersed lie,
    Contract into a span."° 5

So strength first made a way;
Then beauty flowed, then wisdom, honor, pleasure.
  When almost all was out, God made a stay,
Perceiving that, alone of all his treasure,
    Rest° in the bottom lay. 10

"For if I should," said he,
"Bestow this jewel also on my creature,
  He would adore my gifts instead of me.
And rest in Nature, not the God of Nature;
    So both should losers be. 15

"Yet let him keep the rest,
But keep them with repining restlessness.
  Let him be rich and weary, that at least,
If goodness lead him not, yet weariness
    May toss him to my breast." 20

THE PULLEY.   4 *into a span:* that is, within the control of human beings.   10 *rest:* (1) repose, security; (2) all that remains.

QUESTIONS

1. Describe the dramatic scene of the poem. Who is doing what?
2. What are the particular "blessings" that God confers on humanity, according to the speaker? Why should these be considered blessings?
3. Consider the image of the pulley as the means, or device (through "repining restlessness"), by which God compels people to become worshipful.
4. Analyze and discuss the meaning of the kinetic images signified by the words "pour," "flowed," "rest," and "toss."

GERARD MANLEY HOPKINS (1844–1889)

Spring _____ *1877*

Nothing is so beautiful as Spring—
  When weeds, in wheels, shoot long and lovely and lush;
  Thrush's eggs look little low heavens, and thrush
Through the echoing timber does so rinse and wring
The ear, it strikes like lightnings to hear him sing; 5

The glassy peartree leaves and blooms, they brush
    The descending blue; that blue is all in a rush
With richness; the racing lambs too have fair their fling.

What is all this juice and all this joy?
    A strain of the earth's sweet being in the beginning   10
In Eden garden.—Have, get, before it cloy,
    Before it cloud, Christ, lord, and sour with sinning,
Innocent mind and Mayday in girl and boy,
    Most, O maid's child, thy choice and worthy the winning.

QUESTIONS

1. What images does the speaker mention as support for his first line, "Nothing is so beautiful as Spring"? Are these images those that you would normally expect? To what degree do they seem to be new or unusual?

2. What images of motion and activity do you find in the poem? Are these mainly static or dynamic? What do these suggest about the speaker's view of spring?

3. What is the relationship between "Eden garden" in line 11 and the scene described in lines 1–8? To what extent are spring and "Innocent mind and Mayday" a glimpse of the Garden of Eden?

4. Christ is mentioned in lines 12 and 14 (as "maid's child"). Do these references seal the poem off from readers who are not Christian? Why or why not?

DENISE LEVERTOV   (1923–1997)

A Time Past _____ *1975*

The old wooden steps to the front door
where I was sitting that fall morning
when you came downstairs, just awake,
and my joy at sight of you (emerging
into golden day—

                    the dew almost frost)
pulled me to my feet to tell you
how much I loved you:

those wooden steps
are gone now, decayed
replaced with granite,
hard, gray, and handsome.
The old steps live
only in me:
my feet and thighs
remember them, and my hands
still feel their splinters.

Everything else about and around that house
brings memories of others—of marriage,
of my son. And the steps do too: I recall
sitting there with my friend and her little son who died,   20
or was it the second one who lives and thrives?
And sitting there 'in my life,' often, alone or with my husband.
Yet that one instant,
your cheerful, unafraid, youthful, 'I love you too,'
the quiet broken by no bird, no cricket, gold leaves   25
spinning in silence down without
any breeze to blow them,
                            is what twines itself
in my head and body across those slabs of wood
that were warm, ancient, and now
wait somewhere to be burnt.   30

QUESTIONS

1.   Describe the visual imagery of the poem. What tactile imagery is associated with the steps? What other images are part of the speaker's memory?

2.   How is the image of the "old wooden steps" developed in the poem? What has happened to the wooden steps? What meaning may be derived from their having been replaced by the granite steps? How are these steps tied to the speaker's "time past"?

3.   Why do you think the speaker expressly denies the recollection of any sounds of bird or cricket?

THOMAS LUX   (b. 1946)

The Voice You Hear When You Read Silently _____ *1997*

THE VOICE YOU HEAR WHEN YOU READ SILENTLY

is not silent, it is a speaking-
out-loud voice in your head: it is *spoken,*
a voice is *saying* it
as you read. It's the writer's words,   5
of course, in a literary sense
his or her "voice" but the sound
of that voice is the sound of *your* voice.
Not the sound your friends know
or the sound of a tape played back   10
but your voice
caught in the dark cathedral
of your skull, your voice heard
by an internal ear informed by internal abstracts

and what you know by feeling,   15
having felt. It is your voice
saying, for example, the word "barn"
that the writer wrote
but the "barn" you say
is a barn you know or knew. The voice   20
in your head, speaking as you read,
never says anything neutrally—some people
hated the barn they knew,
some people love the barn they know
so you hear the word loaded   25
and a sensory constellation
is lit: horse-gnawed stalls,
hayloft, black heat tape wrapping
a water pipe, a slippery
spilled *chirrr* of oats from a split sack,   30
the bony, filthy haunches of cows . . .
And "barn" is only a noun—no verb
or subject has entered into the sentence yet!
The voice you hear when you read to yourself
is the clearest voice: you speak it   35
speaking to you.

QUESTIONS

1. What is meant by the "constellation" being lit when the reader reads a word, in this case "barn"? How does "constellation" explain the development of the barn image in lines 26–30?
2. Why is the "voice you hear when you read silently / . . . not silent"?
3. Describe the meaning and associations of the "dark cathedral / of your skull" in lines 11–12. What is particularly significant about the use of "cathedral" in these lines?

P. K. PAGE   (b. 1917)

Photos of a Salt Mine _____ 1954

How innocent their lives look,
how like a child's
dream of caves and winter, both combined;
the steep descent to whiteness
and the stope°
with its striated walls
their folds all leaning as if pointing to

PHOTOS OF A SALT MINE.   5 *stope:* a mining excavation taking the form of huge steps.

the greater whiteness still,
that great white bank
with its decisive front,   10
that seam upon a slope,
salt's lovely ice.

And wonderful underfoot the snow of salt
the fine   15
particles a broom could sweep,
one thinks
muckers might make angels in its drifts
as children do in snow,
lovers in sheets,   20
lie down and leave imprinted where they lay
a feathered creature holier than they.

And in the outworked stopes
with lamps and ropes
up miniature matterhorns   25
the miners climb
probe with their lights
the ancient folds of rock—
syncline and anticline°—
and scoop from darkness an Aladdin's cave: 30
rubies and opals glitter from its walls.

But hoses douse the brilliance of these jewels,
melt fire to brine.
Salt's bitter water trickles thin and forms,
slow fathoms down,   35
a lake within a cave,
lacquered with jet—
white's opposite.
There grey on black the boating miners float
to mend the stays and struts of that old stope   40
and deeply underground
their words resound,
are multiplied by echo, swell and grow
and make a climate of a miner's voice.

So all the photographs like children's wishes   45
are filled with caves or winter,
innocence
has acted as a filter,
selected only beauty from the mine.
Except in the last picture,   50
it is shot
from an acute high angle. In a pit
figures the size of pins are strangely lit

---

27 *syncline and anticline:* A syncline is a U-shaped formation of rock strata; an anticline is a formation bending down from a high point.

and might be dancing but you know they're not.
Like Dante's vision of the nether hell   55
men struggle with the bright cold fires of salt,
locked in the black inferno of the rock:
the filter here, not innocence but guilt.

QUESTIONS

1. What "filter" conditions the images in the first 47 lines? What characterizes the images in this section of the poem?
2. What beauties does the poet bring out through such images? What impressions does she convey with images like "miniature matterhorns," "brilliance of these jewels," "lacquered with jet," and "striated walls"?
3. What "filter" conditions the images in the last nine lines? What significance should be placed on the "figures the size of pins" (line 51)? How do the images of "pit," "nether hell," and "black inferno" suggest the poet's view of the lives imposed on the people working in such a mine?
4. What images of motion and activity do you find in the poem? What ideas do these images convey?

EZRA POUND   (1885–1972)

In a Station of the Metro° _____ *1916*

The apparition of these faces in the crowd;
Petals on a wet, black bough.

IN A STATION OF THE METRO.   *Metro:* the Paris subway.

QUESTIONS

1. Is the image of the wet, black bough happy or sad? If the petals were on a tree in the sunlight, what would be the effect?
2. What is the meaning of the image suggested by "apparition"? Does it suggest a positive or negative view of human life?
3. This poem contains only two lines. Is it proper to consider it as a poem nevertheless? If it is not a poem, what is it?

FRIEDRICH RÜCKERT   (1788–1866)

If You Love for the Sake of Beauty _____ *1823*

Anonymous Translator

If you love for the sake of beauty, O never love me!
Love the sun, which has bright golden hair.
If you love for the sake of youth, O never love me!

Love the spring, which is reborn each year.
If you love for the sake of wealth, O never love me!   5
Love the mermaid, whose pearls are rich and clear.
If you love for the sake of love alone, O yes then, love me!
Love me as I love you—forever!

QUESTIONS

1. What is the poem's situation? Who is speaking? Who is the listener?
2. How do the images in lines 2, 4, and 6 exemplify the abstract concepts in lines 1, 3, and 5? How does the speaker use these images to reinforce his or her negative requests?
3. How may the final two lines be considered a climax of the first six lines?

WILLIAM SHAKESPEARE   (1564–1616)

Sonnet 130: My Mistress' Eyes Are Nothing Like the Sun _____ *1609*

My mistress' eyes are nothing like the sun;
Coral is far more red than her lips' red;
If snow be white, why then her breasts are dun;
If hairs be wires, black wires grow on her head.
I have seen roses damasked,° red and white,   *set in an elaborate bouquet*   5
But no such roses see I in her cheeks;
And in some perfumes is there more delight
Than in the breath that from my mistress reeks.
I love to hear her speak, yet well I know
That music hath a far more pleasing sound;   10
I grant I never saw a goddess go;
My mistress, when she walks, treads on the ground.
And yet, by heaven, I think my love as rare
As any she belied with false compare.

QUESTIONS

1. To what does the speaker negatively compare his mistress's eyes? Lips? Breasts? Hair? Cheeks? Breath? Voice? Walk? What kinds of images are created in these negative comparisons?
2. What conventional images does this poem ridicule? What sort of poem is Shakespeare mocking by using the negative images in lines 1–12?
3. In the light of the last two lines, do you think the speaker intends the images as insults? If not as insults, how should they be taken?
4. Are most of the images auditory, olfactory, visual, or kinesthetic? Explain.
5. What point does this poem make about love poetry? About human relationships? How does the imagery contribute to the development of both points?

DAVID WOJAHN   (b. 1953)

"It's Only Rock and Roll but I Like It": The Fall of Saigon ——————————————— *1975*

The guttural stammer of the chopper blades
Raising arabesques of dust, tearing leaves
From the orange trees lining the Embassy compound:
One chopper left, and a CBS cameraman leans
From inside its door, exploiting the artful   5
Mayhem. Somewhere a radio blares the Stones,
"I like it, like it, yes indeed. . . ." Carts full
Of files blaze in the yard. Flak-jacketed marines
Gunpoint the crowd away. The overloaded chopper strains
And blunders from the roof. An ice-cream-suited   10
Saigonese drops his briefcase; both hands
Now cling to the airborne skis. The camera gets
It all: the marine leaning out the copter bay,
His fists beating time. Then the hands giving way.

QUESTIONS

1. What actions take place in this poem? Why does the Saigonese "cling to the airborne skis"? What happens to him?

2. Describe the poem's images of sound. How many such images does the poem contain? What is their effect? What images of sight do you find? What other types of images?

3. Contrast the poem's title with its content.

4. Cumulatively, what is the relationship of the poem's images to the phrase "artful / Mayhem" in lines 5 and 6 and also to the poem's judgment about the American presence in Vietnam?

WRITING ABOUT IMAGERY

Questions for Discovering Ideas

In preparing to write, you should develop a set of thoughtful notes dealing with issues such as the following:

- What type or types of images prevail in the work? Visual (shapes, colors)? Auditory (sounds)? Olfactory (smells)? Tactile (touch and texture)? Gustatory (taste)? Kinetic or kinesthetic (motion)? Or is the imagery a combination of these?

- To what degree do the images reflect either the poet's actual observation or the poet's reading and knowledge of fields such as science or history?

- How well do the images stand out? How vivid are they? How does the poet make the images vivid?

- Within a group of images, say visual or auditory, do the images pertain to one location or area rather than another (e.g., natural scenes rather than interiors, snowy scenes rather than grassy ones, loud and harsh sounds rather than quiet and civilized ones)?

- What explanation is needed for the images? (Images might be derived from the classics or the Bible, the Vietnam War or World War II, the behaviors of four-footed creatures or birds, and so on.)

- What effect do the circumstances described in the poem (e.g., conditions of brightness or darkness, warmth or cold, etc.) have upon your responses to the images? What purpose do you think the poet achieves by controlling these responses?

- How well are the images integrated within the poem's argument or development?

Answering questions like these should provide you with a sizable body of ready-made material that you can convert directly to your essay.

Strategies for Organizing Ideas

Connect a brief overview of the poem to your plan for the body of your essay, noting perhaps that the writer uses images to strengthen ideas about war, character, or love or that the writer relies predominantly on images of sight, sound, and action. You might deal exclusively with one of the following aspects, or, equally likely, you may combine your approaches, as you wish.

1. *Images suggesting ideas and/or moods.* Such an essay should emphasize the effects of the imagery. What ideas or moods are evoked by the images? (The auditory images beginning Owen's "Anthem for Doomed Youth," for example, all point toward a condemnation of war's brutal cruelty. The visual images of Eliot's "Preludes" all point toward a loss of principle and vitality in modern urban life.) Do the images promote approval or disapproval? Cheerfulness? Melancholy? Are the images drab, exciting, vivid? How? Why? Are they conducive to humor or surprise? How does the writer achieve these effects? Are the images consistent, or are they ambiguous? (For example, the images in Masefield's "Cargoes" indicate first approval and then disapproval, with no ambiguity. By contrast, Shakespeare's images in "My Mistress' Eyes" might be construed as insults, but in context, they are really compliments.)

2. *The types of images.* Here the emphasis is on the categories of images themselves. Is there a predominance of a particular type of image (e.g., visual or auditory images), or is there a blending? Is there a bunching of types at particular points in the poem or story? If so, why? Is there any shifting as the work develops (as, for example, in Owen's "Anthem for Doomed Youth" the auditory images first suggest loudness and harshness, but later images describe quietness and sorrow)? Are the images appropriate, granting the nature and apparent intent of the work? Do they assist in making the ideas seem convincing? If any images seem inappropriate, is the inappropriateness intentional or inadvertent? What is the effect of the inappropriate imagery?

3. *Systems of images.* Here the emphasis should be on the areas from which the images are drawn. This is another way of considering the appropriateness of the imagery. Is there a pattern of similar or consistent images, such as dark and dreary urban scenes (Eliot's "Preludes") or color and activity (Hopkins's "Spring")? Do all the images adhere consistently to a particular frame of reference, such as a sunlit garden (Lowell's "Patterns" [Chapter 25]), an extensive recreational forest and garden (Coleridge's "Kubla Khan"), a front stair (Levertov's "A Time Past"), or a forest at night (Blake's "The Tyger")? What is unusual or unique about the set of images? What unexpected or new responses do they produce?

Your conclusion, in addition to recapitulating your major points, is the place for additional insights. It would not be proper to go too far in new directions here, but you might briefly take up one or more of the ideas that you have not developed in the body. In short, what have you learned from your study of imagery in your poem?

DEMONSTRATIVE STUDENT ESSAY

The Images of Masefield's "Cargoes"°

[1]   In the three-stanza poem "Cargoes," John Masefield develops contrasting imagery to create a negative impression of modern commercial life.* He does not explicitly state that modern commercialism is ugly and drab and that it affects modern human beings negatively, but he creates his word pictures to make this point for him. His first two stanzas contain idealized images of ships from ancient and Renaissance times, and his contrasting third stanza includes realistic images of a gritty and grimy modern "coaster." Masefield's images are thus both positive and lush, on the one hand, and negative and stark, on the other.†

[2]   The most evocative and pleasant images in the poem are in the first stanza. The speaker asks that we imagine a "Quinquereme of Nineveh from distant Ophir" (line 1), an oceangoing, many-oared vessel loaded with treasure at the time of the biblical King Solomon. As Masefield identifies the cargo, the visual images are lush and romantic (lines 3–5):

> With a cargo of ivory,
> And apes and peacocks,
> Sandalwood, cedarwood, and sweet white wine.

Ivory suggests richness, which is augmented by the exotic "apes and peacocks" in all their exciting strangeness. The "sandalwood, cedarwood, and sweet white

---

° See p. 748 for this poem.
* Central idea.
† Thesis sentence.

wine" evoke pungent smells and tastes. The "sunny" light of ancient Palestine (line 2) not only illuminates the imaginative scene (visual) but invites readers to imagine the sun's warming touch (tactile). The references to animals and birds also suggest the sounds made by these creatures (auditory). Thus, in this rich first stanza, images derived from all the senses evoke impressions of an ideal, romantic past.

[3]   Almost equally lush are the images of the second stanza, which completes the poem's first part. Here the visual imagery evokes the regal splendor of a tall-masted, full-sailed galleon (line 6) at the height of Spain's commercial power in the sixteenth century. The galleon's cargo suggests wealth, with sparkling diamonds and amethysts, and Portuguese "gold moidores" gleaming in open chests (line 10). With cinnamon in the second stanza's bill of lading (line 10), Masefield includes the image of an exotic, pleasant-tasting spice.

[4]   The negative images of the third stanza contrast starkly with those in the first two stanzas. The poem asks us to imagine a modern "Dirty British coaster" (line 11), which draws attention to the griminess and suffocation of modern civilization. This spray-swept ship is loaded with materials that pollute the earth with noise and smoke. The smoke-stack of the coaster (line 11) and the firewood it is carrying suggest choking smog. The Tyne coal (line 13) and road rails (line 14) suggest the noise and smoke of puffing railroad engines. As if this were not enough, the "pig-lead" (line 14) to be used in various industrial processes indicates not just more unpleasantness but also something poisonous and deadly. In contrast to the lush and stately imagery of the first two stanzas, the images in the third stanza invite the conclusion that people now, when the "Dirty British coaster" butts through the English Channel, are surrounded and threatened by visual, olfactory, and auditory pollution.

[5]   The poem thus establishes a romantic past and ugly present through images of sight, smell, and sound. The images of motion also emphasize this view: In the first two stanzas the quinquereme is "rowing" and the galleon is "dipping." These kinetic images suggest dignity and lightness. The British coaster, however, is "butting," an image indicating bull-like hostility and stupid force. These, together with all the other images, focus the poem's negative views of modern life. The facts that existence for both ancient Palestinians and Renaissance Spaniards included slavery (of those men rowing the quinquereme) and piracy (by those Spanish "explorers" who robbed and killed the natives of the isthmus) should probably not be emphasized as a protest against Masefield's otherwise valid contrasts in images. His final commentary may hence be thought of as the banging of his "cheap tin trays" (line 15), which makes a percussive climax of the oppressive images filling too large a portion of modern lives.

Commentary on the Essay

This essay illustrates strategy 1 for writing about imagery (p. 769), using images to develop ideas and moods. All the examples—derived directly from the poem—emphasize the qualities of Masefield's images. This method permits the introduction of imagery drawn from all the senses in order to demonstrate Masefield's ideas about the past and the present. Other approaches might have concentrated exclusively on Masefield's visual images or on his images drawn from trade and commerce. Because Masefield uses auditory and gustatory images but does not develop them extensively, sound or taste might be appropriately treated in short, paragraph-length essays.

The introductory paragraph of the essay presents the central idea that Masefield uses his images contrastingly to lead to his negative view of modern commercialism. The thesis sentence indicates that the topics to be developed are those of (1) lushness and (2) starkness.

Paragraphs 2 and 3 form a unit stressing the lushness and exoticism of the first stanza and the wealth and colorfulness of the second stanza. In particular, paragraph 2 uses the words "lush," "evoke," "rich," "exotic," "pungent," "exciting," and "romantic" to characterize the pleasing mental pictures prompted by the images. Although the paragraph indicates enthusiastic responses to the images, it does not go beyond the limits of the images themselves.

Paragraph 4 stresses the contrast of Masefield's images in the third stanza with those of the first two stanzas. To this end the paragraph illustrates the imaginative reconstruction needed to develop an understanding of this contrast. The unpleasantness, annoyance, and even danger of the cargoes mentioned in the third stanza are therefore emphasized as the qualities evoked by the images.

The last paragraph demonstrates that the imagery of motion—not much stressed in the poem—is in agreement with the rest of Masefield's imagery. As a demonstration of the need for fair, impartial judgment, the conclusion introduces the possible objection that Masefield may be slanting his images by including not a full but rather a partial view of their respective historical periods. Thus the concluding paragraph adds balance to the analysis illustrated in paragraphs 2, 3, and 4.

SPECIAL TOPICS FOR WRITING
AND ARGUMENT ABOUT IMAGERY IN POETRY

1. Compare the images of home in Owen's "Anthem for Doomed Youth" and Seeger's "I Have a Rendezvous with Death" (Chapter 25). Describe the differing effects of the images. How are the images used? How effectively do these images aid in the development of the attitudes toward war expressed in each poem? How is your reading of the poems affected by the knowledge that both Owen and Seeger were killed in war?

2. Based on the poems in this chapter by Blake, Coleridge, Crashaw, and Hopkins, write an essay discussing the poetic use of images drawn from the natural world. What sorts of references do the poets make? What attitudes do they express about the details they select? What is the relationship between the images and religious views? What judgments about God and nature do the poets show by their images?

3. Considering the imagery of Eliot's "Preludes," write an essay explaining the power of imagery. As you develop your thoughts, be sure to consider the dramatic nature of Eliot's images and to account for the impressions and ideas that

they create. You may also wish to introduce references to images from other poems that are relevant to your points.

4. Write a comparison of the imagery in Rückert's "If You Love Me for the Sake of Beauty" and Browning's "If Thou Must Love Me." Even though the poems are on comparable subjects, how does the selection of images make each poem distinct?

5. Write a poem describing one of these:
   a. Athletes who have just completed an exhausting run.
   b. Children getting out of school for the day.
   c. Your recollection of having been lost as a child.
   d. A cat that always sits down on your schoolwork.
   e. A particularly good meal you had recently.
   f. The best concert you ever attended.
   g. Driving to work or school on a rainy or snowy day.

   Then write an analysis of the images you selected for your poem, and explain your choices. What details stand out in your mind? What do you recall best—sight, smell, sound, action? What is the relationship between your images and the ideas you express in your poem?

6. Study the reproduction of Herkomer's painting *Hard Times* (p. 748). Then write an essay comparing and contrasting the artistic techniques with Hopkins's poem "Spring" and Pound's "In a Station of the Metro," along with other poems that you may wish to include. What similarities and differences do you find in subject matter, treatment, arrangement, and general idea? On the basis of your comparison, what relationships do you perceive between poetic and painterly technique?

7. Use the retrieval system (computer or card catalogue) in your library to research the topic of imagery in Shakespeare (see *imagery* or *style and imagery*). How many titles do you find? Over how many years have these works been published? Take one of the books out, and write a brief report on one of the chapters. What topics are discussed? What types of imagery are introduced? What relationship does the author make between imagery and content?

17

Figures of Speech, or Metaphorical Language: A Source of Depth and Range in Poetry

Figures of speech, metaphorical language, figurative language, figurative devices, and **rhetorical figures** are terms describing organized patterns of comparison that deepen, broaden, extend, illuminate, and emphasize meaning. Although figurative language is sometimes called "ornate," as though it were unnecessarily decorative, it is not uncommon in conversational speech, and it is essential in literary thought and expression. Unlike the writing of the social and "hard" sciences, imaginative literature does not purport to be direct and absolute, offering a one-to-one relationship of words to things. Yes, literature often presents specific and accurate descriptions and explanations, but it also moves in areas of implication and suggestiveness through the use of figurative language, which enables writers to amplify their ideas while still employing a relatively small number of words. Such language is therefore a sine qua non in imaginative literature, particularly poetry, where it compresses thought, promotes understanding, and shapes response.

The two most important figures of speech, and the most easily recognized, are *metaphor* and *simile*. There are also many other metaphorical figures, some of which are *paradox, anaphora, apostrophe, personification, synecdoche* and *metonymy, pun* (or *paronomasia*), *synesthesia, overstatement,* and *understatement.* All these figures are modes of comparison, and they may be expressed in single words, phrases, clauses, or entire structures.

METAPHORS AND SIMILES: THE MAJOR FIGURES OF SPEECH

A Metaphor Establishes Identity: Something Unknown Is Shown to Be Identical to Something Known

A **metaphor** (a "carrying out a change") *equates* known objects or actions with something that is unknown or to be explained (e.g., "Your words are *music* to my ears," "You are the *sunshine* of my life," "My life is *a squirrel cage*"). The equation not only explains the thing, let us say Yeats's "An aged man" (in "Sailing to Byzantium"), but also offers distinctive and original ways of seeing it, explaining it, and thinking about it (Yeats's metaphor is "A tattered coat upon a stick"). Metaphors are virtually inseparable from language. In a heavy storm, for example, trees may be said to *bow* constantly as the wind blows against them. *Bow* is a metaphor because the word usually refers to performers' bending forward to acknowledge the applause of an audience and to indicate their gratitude for the audience's approval. The metaphor therefore asks us to equate our knowledge of theater life (something known) to a weather occurrence (something to be explained). A comparable reference to theater life creates one of the best-known metaphors to appear in Shakespeare's plays: "All the world's a stage, / And all the men and women merely players." Here, Shakespeare's character Jacques (JAY-queez) from Act II, scene 7 of *As You Like It*, equates human life directly with stage life. In other words, the things said and done by stage actors are also said and done by living people in real life. It is important to recognize that Shakespeare's metaphor does not state that the world is *like* a stage but that it literally *is* a stage.

A Simile Shows the Resemblance of the Unknown to the Known

A **simile** (a "showing of likeness or resemblance") illustrates the *similarity* or *comparability* of the known to something unknown or to be explained. Whereas a metaphor merges identities, a simile focuses on resemblances (e.g., "Your words are *like music* to me," "You are *like sunshine* in my life," "I feel *like a squirrel in a cage*"). Similes are distinguishable from metaphors because they are introduced by *like* with nouns and *as* (also *as if* and *as though*) with clauses. If Yeats had written "An aged man is . . . *like* / A tattered coat upon a stick," his metaphor would have been a simile. Let us consider one of the best-known similes in poetry, from "A Valediction: Forbidding Mourning" by the seventeenth-century poet John Donne. This is a dramatic poem spoken by a lover about to go on a trip; his loved one is sorrowful, and he attempts to console her by claiming that even when he is gone, he will remain with her in spirit. The following stanza contains the famous simile embodying this idea:

> Our two souls therefore, which are one,
>> Though I must go, endure not yet
> A breach, but an expansion
>> Like gold to airy thinness beat.

The simile compares the souls of the speaker and his loved one to gold, a metal both valuable and malleable. By the simile, the speaker asserts that the impending departure will not be a separation but rather a thinning out, so that the relationship of the lovers will remain constant and rich even as the distance between them increases. Because the comparison is introduced by "like," the emphasis of the figurative language is on the *similarity* of the lovers' love to gold (which is always gold even when it is thinned out by the goldsmith's hammer), not on the *identification* of the two. Similarly, the sentence "Come with . . . eyes as bright / As sunlight on a stream," from Rossetti's "Echo" (Chapter 19), compares the listener's eyes to a bright and gleaming natural scene.

CHARACTERISTICS OF METAPHORICAL LANGUAGE

In Chapter 16, we explored how imagery stimulates the imagination and recalls memories *(images)* of sights, sounds, tastes, smells, sensations of touch, and motions. Metaphors and similes go beyond literal imagery to introduce perceptions and comparisons that can be unusual, unpredictable, and surprising, as in Donne's simile comparing the lovers' relationship to gold. How many people have ever perceived such a metaphorical connection—between the thinning out of metal and the constancy of lovers when they are apart? The comparison emphasizes the bond between the two lovers; the reference to gold shows how valuable the bond is; the unusual and original comparison is one of the elements that make the poem striking and memorable.

In this way, metaphorical language extends knowledge and awareness by introducing perceptions that otherwise would not occur to us. Perceptions such as these connect the thing or things to be communicated—such as qualities of love, the fear of advancing age, the need for psychological assurance, or the excitement of unexpected discovery—with a new insight that is made objective through the comparison of a simile or the equation of a metaphor. First and foremost, the use of metaphors and similes is a major characteristic by which great literature provides us with fresh and original ways of thinking, feeling, and understanding.

To see metaphorical language in further operation, let us take a commonly described condition—happiness. In everyday speech, we might use the sentence "She was happy" to state that a particular character was experiencing joy and excitement. The sentence is of course accurate, but it is not interesting. A more vivid way of saying the same thing is to use an image of action, such as "She jumped for joy." This image gives us a literal picture of a person demonstrating happiness. But another and better way of communicating joy is the following simile: "She felt as if she had just won the lottery." Because readers easily understand the disbelief, excitement, exhilaration, and delight that such an event would bring, they also understand—and feel—the character's happiness. It is the *simile* that evokes this perception and enables each reader to personalize the experience, for no simple description could help a reader comprehend the same degree of emotion.

As a parallel poetic example, let us look at Keats's sonnet "On First Looking into Chapman's Homer," which Keats wrote soon after reading the translation of Homer's great epics *The Iliad* and *The Odyssey* by the Renaissance poet George Chapman. Keats, a great poet himself, describes his enthusiasm about Chapman's successful and exciting work.

JOHN KEATS   (1795–1821)

On First Looking into Chapman's Homer° _____ 1816

Much have I travell'd in the realms of gold,°	*the world of great art*
And many goodly states and kingdoms seen:	
Round many western islands° have I been	*ancient literature*
Which bards in fealty to Apollo° hold.	
Oft of one wide expanse° had I been told	*epic poetry* 5
That deep-brow'd Homer ruled as his demesne;°	*realm, estate*
Yet did I never breathe its pure serene°	
Till I heard Chapman speak out loud and bold:	
Then felt I like some watcher of the skies	
When a new planet swims into his ken;°	*range of vision* 10
Or like stout Cortez° when with eagle eyes	
He star'd at the Pacific—and all his men	
Look'd at each other with a wild surmise°—	*conjecture, supposition*
Silent, upon a peak in Darien.	

ON FIRST LOOKING INTO CHAPMAN'S HOMER.   George Chapman (c. 1560–1634) published his translations of Homer's *Iliad* in 1612 and *Odyssey* in 1614–15.   4 *bards . . . Apollo:* writers who are sworn subjects of Apollo, the Greek god of light, music, poetry, prophecy, and the sun.   7 *serene:* a clear expanse of air; also grandeur, clarity; rulers were also sometimes called "serene majesty."   11 *Cortez:* Hernando Cortés (1485–1547), a Spanish general and the conqueror of Mexico. Keats confuses him with Vasco de Balboa (c. 1475–1519), the first European to see the Pacific Ocean (in 1510) from Darien, an old name for the Isthmus of Panama.

As a first step in understanding the power of metaphorical language, we can briefly paraphrase the sonnet's content:

> I have enjoyed much art and read much poetry, and I have been told that Homer is the best writer of all. However, I did not appreciate his works until I first read them in Chapman's clear and forceful translation. This discovery was exciting and awe-inspiring.

If all Keats had written had been a paragraph like this one, we would pay no attention to it at all, for it carries no sense of excitement or stimulation. But the last six lines of the sonnet contain two memorable similes ("like some watcher of the skies" and "like stout Cortez") that stand out and demand a special effort of imagination. To appreciate these similes fully, we need to imagine what it would be like to be an astronomer as he or she discovers a previously unknown planet, and what it would have been like to be one of the first explorers to see the Pacific Ocean. As we imagine ourselves in these roles, we get a sense of the amazement, wonder, excitement, exhilaration, and joy that would accompany such discoveries. With that experience comes the realization that the world—the universe—is far bigger and more wonderful than we had ever dreamed.

Metaphorical language therefore makes strong demands on our creative imagination. It bears repeating that as we develop our own mental pictures under the stimulation of metaphors and similes, we also develop appropriately associated attitudes and feelings. Let us consider once more Keats's metaphor "realms of gold," which invites us both to imagine brilliant and shining kingdoms and also to join Keats in valuing and loving not just poetry but all literature. The metaphorical "realms of gold" act upon our minds, liberating our imaginations, directing our understanding, and evoking our feelings. In such a way, reading and responding to the works of writers like Keats produces both mental and emotional experiences that were previously hidden to us. They constantly give us something new, and they increase our power to think and know. They enlarge us.

TENOR AND VEHICLE

To describe the relationship between a writer's ideas and the metaphors and similes chosen to objectify them, two useful terms have been coined by I. A. Richards (in *The Philosophy of Rhetoric*). First is the **tenor,** which is the totality of ideas and attitudes not only of the literary speaker but also of the author. Second is the **vehicle,** or the specific words of the metaphor or simile. For example, the tenor of Donne's simile in "A Valediction: Forbidding Mourning" is the inseparable love and unbreakable connection of the two lovers; the vehicle is the beating of gold "to airy thinness." Similarly, the tenor of the similes in the sestet of Keats's sonnet is awe and wonder; the vehicle is the description of astronomical and geographical discovery.

OTHER FIGURES OF SPEECH

A Paradox Brings Out the Truth in Apparent Error and Contradiction

A **paradox** is "a thought beyond a thought," a figurative device through which something apparently wrong or contradictory is shown to be truthful and noncontradictory. The phrase "I, a child, very old" in Whitman's "Facing West from California's Shores" is a paradox. The obvious contradiction is that no one can be old and young at the same time, but this contradiction can be reconciled if we realize that even as people get older they still retain many of the qualities of children (such as enthusiasm and hope). Thus Whitman's contradiction is not contradictory (is this clause a paradox?) and the speaker may genuinely be "a child, very old." The second line of Wyatt's sonnet "I Find No Peace" embodies two paradoxes. One opposes fear with hope, the other fire with ice: "I fear and hope, I burn and freeze like ice." These paradoxes genuinely reflect the contradictory states of people in love—wanting love ("hope," "burn") but also being uncertain and unsure about the relationship ("fear," "freeze"). The paradoxes thus highlight the truth that love is a complex and sometimes unsettling emotion.

Anaphora Provides Weight Through Repetition

Anaphora ("to carry again or repeat") is the repetition of the same word or phrase throughout a work or a section of a work in order to lend weight and emphasis. In "The Bells," for example, Poe repeats the word *bells* many times, both for emphasis and also to suggest tolling bells (Chapter 19). In Blake's "The Tyger" (Chapter 16) the interrogative word *what* is used five times to emphasize the mystery of evil (italics added):

> *What* the hammer? *what* the chain?
> In *what* furnace was thy brain?
> *What* the anvil? *what* dread grasp
> Dare its deadly terrors clasp?

Anaphora is the most obvious feature of Rukeyser's "Looking at Each Other," where the word *yes* begins each of the poem's twenty-five lines.

Apostrophe Creates the Drama of a Speaker Addressing an Audience

In an **apostrophe** (a "turning away," or redirection of attention) a speaker addresses a real or imagined listener who is not present. It is like a public speech, with readers as audience, and it therefore lends an element of drama to a poem. An apostrophe enables the speaker to develop ideas that might arise naturally on a public occasion, as in Wordsworth's sonnet "London, 1802," which is addressed to the long-dead English poet Milton. In Keats's sonnet "Bright Star," the speaker addresses a distant and inanimate star, yet through apostrophe he proceeds as though the star has human understanding and divine power.

JOHN KEATS (1795–1822)

Bright Star _____ *1838 (1819)*

Bright star! would I were steadfast as thou art—
   Not in lone splendor hung aloft the night,
And watching, with eternal lids apart,
   Like Nature's patient, sleepless eremite,°   *hermit*
The moving waters at their priestlike task   5
   Of pure ablution round earth's human shores,
Or gazing on the new soft-fallen mask
   Of snow upon the mountains and the moors;
No—yet still steadfast, still unchangeable,
   Pillowed upon my fair love's ripening breast,   10

To feel forever its soft fall and swell,
   Awake forever in a sweet unrest,
      Still, still to hear her tender-taken breath,
      And so live ever—or else swoon to death.

QUESTIONS

1. With what topic is the speaker concerned in this sonnet? How does he compare himself with the distant star?

2. What qualities does the speaker attribute specifically to the star? What role does he seem to assign to it? In light of this role, and the qualities needed to serve in it, how might the star be compared to a divine and benign presence?

3. In light of the emphasis on the words "forever" and "ever" in lines 11–14, how appropriate is the choice of the star as the subject of the apostrophe in the poem?

In this sonnet the speaker addresses the star as though it is a person or god, an object of adoration, and the poem is therefore like a petitional prayer. The star is idealized with qualities that the speaker wishes to establish in himself, namely, steadfastness, eternal watchfulness, and fidelity. The point of the apostrophe is thus to dramatize the speaker's yearning and to stress the permanence of space and eternity as contrasted with earthly impermanence.

Personification Is the Attribution of Human Traits to Abstractions or to Nonhuman Objects

A close neighbor of apostrophe is **personification,** another dramatic figurative device through which poets explore relationships to environment, ideals, and inner lives. In "Bright Star," as we have just seen, Keats personifies the star addressed by the speaker. Shakespeare, in Sonnet 146, "Poor Soul, the Center of My Sinful Earth" (Chapter 25), personifies his own soul so that he can deal with earthly versus heavenly concerns. Other important uses of personification are seen in Shelley's "Ode to the West Wind" and also in Keats's "To Autumn" (Chapter 17) and "Ode on a Grecian Urn" (Chapter 23).

Synecdoche and Metonymy Transfer Meanings by Parts and Associations

These figures are close in purpose and effect. **Synecdoche** ("taking one thing out of another") is a device in which a part stands for the whole or a whole for a part, like the expression "all hands aboard," which describes the whole of a ship's crew by their hands, that part of them that performs work. **Metonymy** (a "transfer of name") substitutes one thing for another with which it is closely identified, as when "Hollywood" is used to mean the movie industry, or when "the White House" signifies the policies and activities of the United States president. The purpose of both figures of speech is the creation of new insights and ideas, just like metaphors and similes.

Synecdoche is seen in Keats's "To Autumn," where the gourd and hazel shells, which are single instances of ripe produce, stand for the entire autumnal harvest. In Wordsworth's "London, 1802," the phrase "thy heart" (line 13) is a synecdoche in which a part—the heart—refers to the complete person. Metonymy is seen again in Keats's "To Autumn," when the "granary floor" (line 14), the place where grain is stored, bears the transferred meaning of the entire autumnal harvest. In "Exit, Pursued by a Bear," Ogden Nash metonymically uses brand names, the names of artists, and the names of cities to mean objects, artworks, and places.

Pun or Paronomasia Depends on Words Having Similar Sounds But Different Meanings

A **pun** ("a point or a puncture") or **paronomasia** ("something beside a name") is wordplay stemming from the fact that words with different meanings have similar or even identical sounds and that some individual words have differing and even contradictory meanings. Line 5 of Donne's poem "A Hymn to God the Father," for example (Chapter 25), is built on the identical pronunciation but different meanings of "done" (finished) and "Donne" (the poet's name):

> When Thou hast done, Thou hast not done,

Because puns are sometimes considered outrageous and often require a little bit of thinking, people may groan when they hear them (even while they enjoy them). Also, because many puns seem to play only with sound, they have not always enjoyed critical acclaim. Good puns can always be relished, however, because they work with sounds to reveal ideas. John Gay, for example, creates clever puns in the following song, sung by the gang of thieves in *The Beggar's Opera* (1728), a play which, incidentally, marked the beginning of the modern musical comedy tradition.

JOHN GAY   (1685–1732)

Let Us Take the Road _____ *1728*

Let us take the road.
   Hark! I hear the sound of coaches!
   The hour of attack approaches,
To your arms, brave boys, and load.
     See the ball I hold! [*holding up a bullet*]   5
   Let the chemists° toil like asses,   *alchemists*
   Our fire their fire surpasses,°   *Our fire is better than their fire.*
     And turns all our lead to gold.

QUESTIONS

1. What traits are shown by the singers of this poem? Why do they not seem frightening, despite their admission that they are holdup men?
2. Describe the puns in the poem. What kind of knowledge is needed to explain them fully? How many puns are there? How are they connected? Why do the puns seem both witty and outrageous?

Here "fire," "lead," and "gold" are puns. *Lead* was the "base" or "low" metal that the medieval alchemists ("chemists") tried to transform into ingots of *gold,* using the heat from their *fires.* The puns develop because the gang of cutthroats singing the song is about to go out to rob travelers at gunpoint. Hence their bullets are their lead, which they will transform into the gold coins they steal. Their fire is not the fire of alchemists but rather the firing of pistols. Through these puns, Gay's villains charm us by their wit and delight in their villainy, even though in real life they would scare us to death.

Synesthesia Demonstrates the Oneness or Unity of Feelings

In **synesthesia** (the "bringing together of feelings") a poet describes a feeling or perception with words that usually refer to a different or even opposite feeling or perception, as in darkness that is visible (Milton), a thought that is green (Marvell), or a soul that claps its hands (Yeats). Keats uses synesthesia extensively, as, for example, in the "Ode to a Nightingale" (Chapter 20), where a plot of ground is "melodious," a draught of wine tastes of "Dance, and Provençal song, and sunburnt mirth," and beaded bubbles of wine are "winking at the brim" of a glass.

Overstatement and Understatement Are Means of Creating Emphasis

Two important devices creating emphasis are overstatement or hyperbole, and understatement. **Overstatement,** also called the **overreacher,** is exaggeration for effect. In "London, 1802," for example, Wordsworth declares that England "is a fen / Of stagnant waters." That is, the country and its people make up collectively a stinking, polluted marsh, a muddy dump. What Wordsworth establishes by this overstatement is his judgment that England in 1802 was so morally and politically rotten that it needed a writer like Milton to unite the people around noble ideas.

In contrast with overstatement, **understatement** is the deliberate underplaying or undervaluing of a thing. One of the most famous poetic understatements is in Marvell's "To His Coy Mistress" (Chapter 23):

The grave's a fine and private place,
But none, I think, do there embrace.

Here Marvell's understatement wittily and grimly emphasizes the eternity of death by contrasting the motionless privacy of the grave with the active privacy of a trysting place. Another ironic use of understatement is in lines 17–20 of Nash's "Exit, Pursued by a Bear," where the speaker states that the "lion and the lizard" cannot hear "heavenly harmonies." In this figure Nash emphasizes that the people have been killed who once lived in the rooms where such melodies were played, and therefore he emphasizes the destructive ignorance of nuclear war.

POEMS FOR STUDY

ROBERT BURNS   (1759–1796)

A Red, Red Rose ————————————————————————— *1796*

O my Luve's like a red, red rose,
    That's newly sprung in June:
O my Luve's like the melodie
    That's sweetly play'd in tune.

As fair art thou, my bonnie lass,   5
   So deep in luve am I;
And I will luve thee still, my Dear,
   Till a'° the seas gang° dry.   *all; go*

Till a' the seas gang dry, my Dear,
   And the rocks melt wi'° the sun: *with*   10
And I will luve thee still, my Dear,
   While the sands o'° life shall run.   *of*

And fare thee weel, my only Luve!
   And fare thee weel, awhile!
And I will come again, my Luve,   15
   Tho' it were ten thousand mile!

QUESTIONS

1. In light of the character and background of the speaker, do the two opening similes seem common or unusual? If they are just ordinary, does that fact diminish their value? How and why?

2. Describe the shift of listener envisioned after the first stanza. How are the last three stanzas related to the first?

3. Consider the metaphors concerning time and travel. How do the metaphors assist you in comprehending the speaker's character?

JOHN DONNE   (1572–1631)

A Valediction: Forbidding Mourning ———————————————— *1633*

As virtuous men pass mildly away,
  And whisper to their souls to go,
Whilst some of their sad friends do say
   The breath goes now, and some say, No;

So let us melt, and make no noise,
  No tear-floods, nor sigh-tempests move,
'Twere profanation of our joys
   To tell the laity° our love.

Moving of th'earth° brings harm and fears,   *earthquakes*
  Men reckon what it did and meant:
But trepidation° of the spheres,
   Though greater far, is innocent.

A VALEDICTION: FORBIDDING MOURNING.   7, 8 *profanation . . . laity:* as though the lovers are priests of love, whose love is a mystery.   11 *trepidation:* Before Sir Isaac Newton explained the precession of the equinoxes, it was assumed that the positions of heavenly bodies should be constant and perfectly circular. The clearly observable irregularities (caused by the slow wobbling of the earth's axis) were explained by the concept of *trepidation,* or a trembling or oscillation that occurred in the outermost of the spheres surrounding the earth.

Dull sublunary lovers' love
    (Whose soul is sense°) cannot admit
Absence, because it doth remove   15
    Those things which elemented it.

But we by a love so much refined
    That our selves know not what it is,
Inter-assured of the mind,
    Care less, eyes, lips, and hands to miss.   20

Our two souls therefore, which are one,
    Though I must go, endure not yet
A breach, but an expansion
    Like gold to airy thinness beat.°

If they be two, they are two so   25
    As stiff twin compasses° are two;
Thy soul, the fixt foot, makes no show
    To move, but doth, if th'other do.

And though it in the center sit,
    Yet when the other far doth roam,   30
It leans and harkens after it,
    And grows erect, as that comes home.

Such wilt thou be to me, who must
    Like th'other foot, obliquely run;
Thy firmness draws my circle just,°   35
    And makes me end where I begun.

14 *soul is sense:* lovers whose attraction is totally physical.   24 *gold to airy thinness beat:* a reference to the malleability of gold.   26 *compasses:* a compass used for drawing circles.   35 *just:* perfectly round.

QUESTIONS

1.   What is the situation envisioned as the occasion for the poem? Who is talking to whom? What is their relationship?

2.   What is the intention of the first two stanzas? What is the effect of the phrases "tear-floods" and "sigh-tempests"?

3.   Describe the effect of the opening simile about men on their deathbeds.

4.   What is the metaphor of the third stanza (lines 9–12)? In what sense might the "trepidation of the spheres" be less harmful than the parting of the lovers?

5.   In lines 13–20 there is a comparison making the love of the speaker and his sweetheart superior to the love of average lovers. What is the basis for the speaker's claim?

6.   What is the comparison begun by the word "refined" in line 17 and continued by the simile in line 24?

T. S. ELIOT   (1888–1965)

Eyes That Last I Saw in Tears _____ *1924*

Eyes that last I saw in tears
Through division
Here in death's dream kingdom
The golden vision reappears
I see the eyes but not the tears   5
This is my affliction

This is my affliction
Eyes I shall not see again
Eyes of decision
Eyes I shall not see unless   1(
At the door of death's other kingdom
Where, as in this,
The eyes outlast a little while
A little while outlast the tears
And hold us in derision.   1

QUESTIONS

1. What do "eyes" and "tears" signify as a synecdoche and as a metonymy?
2. What is the cause of the tears (line 2)? What is meant by the eyes outlasting the tears (lines 13, 14)? Why should the eyes "hold us in derision"? In line 9 the eyes are "of decision." What does this synecdoche mean?
3. Explain the paradox of the speaker's declaration in line 5 that he sees the eyes but not the tears. Why does he say that this is his "affliction"?
4. Why might the entire poem be considered a paradox? What happened in life? What does the speaker look forward to in death?
5. What is the distinction in the poem between "death's dream kingdom" and "death's other kingdom"?

ABBIE HUSTON EVANS   (1881–1983)

The Iceberg Seven-eighths Under _____ *1961*

Under the sky at night, stunned by our guesses,
We know incredibly much and incredibly little.
Wrapped in the envelope of gossamer air,
A clinging mote whirled round in a blizzard of stars,
A chaff-cloud of great suns that has not settled,
By the barn's black shoulder where the gibbous moon
Hangs low, no other light making a glimmer
In the dark country, hearing the breathing of cattle—
I do not need that anyone should tell me

Most real goes secret, sunken, nigh-submerged: 10
   Yet does it dazzle with its least part showing,
      Like the iceberg seven-eighths under.

QUESTIONS

1. How does the simile of the "iceberg seven-eighths under" explain the "Most real" that "goes secret"? In what way is this simile, together with line 11, an extension of the idea in line 2?
2. What metaphors does the poet use to describe the earth and the people ("We") on it?
3. Explain the contrast between the metaphors of night and darkness (lines 1, 6, 8) and the use of the word "dazzle" in line 11. How does the poem express awe about the visible universe?

LANGSTON HUGHES   (1902–1967)

Harlem _____ *1951*

What happens to a dream deferred?

  Does it dry up
  like a raisin in the sun?
  Or fester like a sore—
  And then run?   5
  Does it stink like rotten meat?
  Or crust and sugar over—
  like a syrupy sweet?

  Maybe it just sags
  like a heavy load.   10

  Or does it explode?

QUESTIONS

1. In the light of the black experience with the "American Dream," what do you think is meant by the phrase "dream deferred"?
2. Explain the structure of the poem in terms of the speaker's questions and answers. How is the structure here similar to the one in Blake's "The Tyger" (p. 754)?
3. Explain the similes in lines 3, 4, 6, 8, and 10. Why are these apt comparisons? What sorts of human actions are implied in these figures?
4. What is the meaning of the metaphor in line 11? Why do you think Hughes shifted from similes to a metaphor in this line?

JOHN KEATS   (1795–1821)

To Autumn _____ *1820*

Season of mists and mellow fruitfulness!
　Close bosom-friend of the maturing sun;
Conspiring with him how to load and bless
　With fruit the vines that round the thatch-eaves run;
To bend with apples the mossed cottage-trees,   5
　And fill all fruit with ripeness to the core;
　　To swell the gourd, and plump the hazel shells
With a sweet kernel; to set budding more,
　And still more, later flowers for the bees,
　Until they think warm days will never cease,   10
　　For Summer has o'erbrimmed their clammy cells.

Who hath not seen thee oft amid thy store?
　Sometimes whoever seeks abroad may find
Thee sitting careless on a granary floor,
　Thy hair soft-lifted by the winnowing wind,   15
Or on a half-reaped furrow sound asleep,
Drowsed with the fume of poppies, while thy hook
　　Spares the next swath and all its twinèd flowers;
And sometimes like a gleaner thou dost keep
　　Steady thy laden head across a brook;   2
　　Or by a cider-press, with patient look,
　　Thou watchest the last oozings hours by hours.

Where are the songs of Spring? Ay, where are they?
　Think not of them, thou hast thy music too,—
While barrèd clouds bloom the soft-dying day,
　And touch the stubble-plains with rosy hue;
Then in a wailful choir the small gnats mourn
　Among the river sallows, borne aloft
　　Or sinking as the light wind lives or dies;
And full-grown lambs loud bleat from hilly bourn;
　Hedge-crickets sing; and now with treble soft
The redbreast whistles from a garden-croft;
　　And gathering swallows twitter in the skies.

QUESTIONS

1.   How is personification used in the first stanza? How does it change in the
second? What is the effect of such personification?

2.   How does Keats structure the poem to accord with his apostrophe to autumn?
That is, in what ways can the stanzas be distinguished by the type of discourse
addressed to the season?

3. Analyze Keats's metonymy in the first stanza and synecdoche in the second. What effects does he achieve with these devices?

4. How, through the use of images, does Keats develop his idea that autumn is a season of "mellow fruitfulness"?

JANE KENYON   (1947–1995)

Portrait of a Figure Near Water _____ *1996*

Rebuked, she turned and ran
uphill to the barn. Anger, the inner
arsonist, held a match to her brain.
She observed her life: against her will
it survived the unwavering flame.   5

The barn was empty of animals.
Only a swallow tilted
near the beams, and bats
hung from the rafters
the roof sagged between.   10

Her breath became steady
where, years past, the farmer cooled
the big tin amphorae of milk.
The stone trough was still
filled with water: she watched it   15
and received its calm.

So it is when we retreat in anger
we think we burn alone
and there is no balm.
Then water enters, though it makes   20
no sound.

QUESTIONS

1. What do you think has happened before the poem opens? What sort of rebuke has the woman received? What does it lead her to do?

2. What is the effect of "tilted" (line 7), and why does the speaker draw attention to the roof sagging between the rafters (line 10)? Why does the writer call the large milk cans "amphorae" (line 13)? How do these word choices affect the poem's context?

3. What is the metaphorical sense of anger as "the inner / arsonist" (lines 2–3)? In what way is the water in the stone trough for animals metaphorical? What metaphorical meanings should be attributed to water?

HENRY KING   (1592–1669)

Sic Vita° _____ *1657*

Like to the falling of a star,
Or as the flights of eagles are,
Or like the fresh spring's gaudy hue,
Or silver drops of morning dew,
Or like a wind that chafes the flood,   5
Or bubbles which on water stood:
Even such is man, whose borrowed light
Is straight called in, and paid to night.
  The wind blows out, the bubble dies;
  The spring entombed in autumn lies: 10
  The dew dries up, the star is shot;
  The flight is past, and man forgot.

SIC VITA (Latin).   Such is life.

QUESTIONS

1. How many similes do you find in lines 1–6? Describe the range of references; that is, from what sources are the similes derived? What do all these similes (and references) have in common?

2. Explain the two metaphors in lines 7–8. (One is brought out by the words "borrowed," "called in," and "paid," the other by "light" and "night.")

3. Explain the continuation in lines 9–12 of the similes in 1–6. Do you think that these last four lines are essential, or might the poem have been successfully concluded with line 8? Explain.

4. What point does this poem make about humanity? In what ways do the similes in the poem help explore these ideas and bring them to life?

JUDITH MINTY   (b. 1937)

Conjoined _____ *1981*

a marriage poem

The onion in my cupboard, a monster, actually
two joined under one transparent skin:
each half-round, then flat and deformed
where it pressed and grew against the other.

An accident, like the two-headed calf rooted
in one body, fighting to suck at its mother's teats;
or like those other freaks, Chang and Eng,° twins

CONJOINED.   7 *Chang and Eng:* born in 1811, the original and most famous Siamese twins. Although they were never separated, they nevertheless fathered twenty-two children. They died in 1874.

joined at the chest by skin and muscle, doomed
to live, even make love, together for sixty years.

Do you feel the skin that binds us   10
together as we move, heavy in this house?
To sever the muscle could free one,
but might kill the other. Ah, but men
don't slice onions in the kitchen, seldom see
what is invisible. We cannot escape each other.   15

QUESTIONS

1. What are the two things—the "us" and "we" of lines 10 and 11—that are conjoined? Since this is "a marriage poem," might they be the man and the woman?
   Why might they also be considered as the body and soul of the speaker; or the
   desire to be married and subordinated, on the one hand, and to be free and in
   control of destiny, on the other?

2. Explore the metaphor of the onion and the similes of the two-headed calf
   and the Siamese twins. Why do you think the poet introduces the words "monster," "accident," and "freaks" into these figures in lines 1, 5, and 7? In what
   sense do you believe that these words are applicable to the nature and plight
   of women?

3. Is it true that *all* "men / don't slice onions in the kitchen, seldom see / what is
   invisible"? Explain.

OGDEN NASH   (1902–1970)

Exit, Pursued by a Bear _____ *1954*

Chipmunk chewing the Chippendale,°
Mice on the Meissen° shelf,
Pigeon stains on the Aubusson,°
Spider lace on the delf.°

Squirrel climbing the Sheraton,°   5
Skunk on the Duncan Phyfe,°
Silverfish in the Gobelins°
And the calfbound volumes of *Life*.

Pocks on the pink Picasso,
Dust on the four Cézannes,   10

EXIT, PURSUED BY A BEAR.   The title is a stage direction in Shakespeare's *The Winter's Tale* (III.3. 58).
The character is torn apart by the bear. When this poem was first published, the atomic bomb had
existed for nine years, the hydrogen bomb for two. In late 1953, Russia, which is sometimes symbolized
by a bear, announced that it possessed the hydrogen bomb.   1 *Chippendale:* ornate furniture made by
Thomas Chippendale (1718–1779).   2 *Meissen:* expensive chinaware made in Meissen, Germany.
Also called "Dresden China."   3 *Aubusson:* carpet imported from France.   4 *delf:* expensive pottery made in Delft, The Netherlands.   5 *Sheraton:* furniture made by Thomas Sheraton
(1751–1806).   6 *Duncan Phyfe:* furniture made by Duncan Phyfe (1768–1854), a Scotsman who came
to America in 1783.   7 *Gobelins:* rare and exquisitely crafted tapestries made by Gobelin of Paris.

Kit on the keys of the Steinway,
Cat on the Louis Quinze.°

Rings on the Adam° mantel
From a thousand bygone thirsts,
Mold on the Henry Millers°   15
And the Ronald Firbank° firsts.

The lion and the lizard°
No heavenly harmonies hear
From the high-fidelity speaker
Concealed behind the Vermeer.   20

Jamshid° squats in a cavern
Screened by a waterfall,
Catered by Heinz and Campbell,
And awaits the fireball.

12 *Louis Quinze:* furniture made in France during the reign of Louis XV (1710–1774).   13 *Adam:*
Robert Adam (1728–1792) was one of the most famous English architects.   15 *Henry Miller:*
American author (1891–1980).   16 *Ronald Firbank:* Arthur Ainsley Ronald Firbank (1886–1926),
British author.   17 *The lion and the lizard:* See Edward Fitzgerald's (1809–1883) version of *The
Rubáiyát of Omar Khayyám*, stanza 18, particularly in reference to Nash's last stanza.   21 *Jamshid:* a
reference to the legendary Persian hero Jamshid, who found a cup containing the elixir of life and
lived for 700 years. At one point in the story Jamshid remained hidden for a hundred years. Note also
the reference to Fitzgerald's *Rubáiyát*, stanza 18.

QUESTIONS

1. In relationship to the serious subject matter of the poem, what is the effect of
    the title? What is the possible pun on the word "bear"?
2. What location is the speaker describing? How is metonymy used to suggest the
    wealth of the collections of household items and art? What sort of lifestyle is
    suggested by the metonymy?
3. Why is it that animals rather than people are living with the expensive artifacts?
    Judging from line 14, how long has this situation existed?
4. How might the situation presented in the poem be considered a paradox?

MARGE PIERCY   (b. 1934)

A Work of Artifice _____ *1973*

The bonsai tree
in the attractive pot
could have grown eighty feet tall
on the side of a mountain
till split by lightning.
But a gardener
carefully pruned it.

It is nine inches high.
Every day as he
whittles back the branches   10
the gardener croons,
It is your nature
to be small and cozy,
domestic and weak;
how lucky, little tree,   15
to have a pot to grow in.
With living creatures
one must begin very early
to dwarf their growth:
the bound feet,   20
the crippled brain,
the hair in curlers,
the hands you
love to touch.

QUESTIONS

1. What is a bonsai tree? In what ways is it an apt metaphor for women? The tree "could have grown eighty feet tall." What would be the comparable growth and development of a woman?

2. What do you make of the gardener's song (lines 12–16)? If the bonsai tree were able to respond, would it accept the gardener's consolation? What conclusions about women's lives are implied by the metaphor of the tree?

3. How does the poem shift at line 17? To what extent do the next images (lines 20–24) embody women's lives? How are the images metaphorical?

SYLVIA PLATH   (1932–1963)

Metaphors _____ *1960*

I'm a riddle in nine syllables,
An elephant, a ponderous house,
A melon strolling on two tendrils.
O red fruit, ivory, fine timbers!
This loaf's big with its yeasty rising.   5
Money's new-minted in this fat purse.
I'm a means, a stage, a cow in calf.
I've eaten a bag of green apples,
Boarded the train there's no getting off.

QUESTIONS

1. What evidence can you find in the poem that the speaker is a woman?

2. The speaker calls herself a "riddle in nine syllables." What is the answer to the riddle? Why nine syllables (as opposed to eight or ten)? In what sense is the poem also a riddle? How are the answers to both riddles related?

3. Which of the metaphors do you find amusing, shocking, or demeaning? What do these suggest about the speaker's attitude toward herself?

4. What aspect of the speaker's condition is captured in the "bag of green apples" metaphor (line 8)? What two meanings are suggested by the "stage" metaphor (line 7)? Why is the "train" metaphor (line 9) appropriate to the speaker's condition and the results of that condition?

MURIEL RUKEYSER   (1913–1980)

Looking at Each Other ————————————————————— 1978

Yes, we were looking at each other
Yes, we knew each other very well
Yes, we had made love with each other many times
Yes, we had heard music together
Yes, we had gone to the sea together
Yes, we had cooked and eaten together
Yes, we had laughed often day and night
Yes, we fought violence and knew violence
Yes, we hated the inner and outer oppression
Yes, that day we were looking at each other
Yes, we saw the sunlight pouring down
Yes, the corner of the table was between us
Yes, bread and flowers were on the table
Yes, our eyes saw each other's eyes
Yes, our mouths saw each other's mouth
Yes, our breasts saw each other's breasts
Yes, our bodies entire saw each other
Yes, it was beginning in each
Yes, it threw waves across our lives
Yes, the pulses were becoming very strong
Yes, the beating became very delicate
Yes, the calling   the arousal
Yes, the arriving   the coming
Yes, there it was for both entire
Yes, we were looking at each other

QUESTIONS

1. What is the dramatic situation of the poem? What sort of listener is the speaker addressing?

2. Describe the rhetorical device at work here. How many different words are being repeated?

3. What is the effect of the repetitions? What is their relationship to the emotions and experiences that the speaker is describing?

WILLIAM SHAKESPEARE   (1564–1616)

Sonnet 18: Shall I Compare Thee to a Summer's Day? ——————— *1609*

Shall I compare thee to a summer's day?
Thou art more lovely and more temperate:
Rough winds do shake the darling° buds of May,   *dear, cherished*
And summer's lease hath all too short a date:
Sometime too hot the eye of heaven° shines   *the sun*   5
And often is his° gold complexion dimmed;   *its*
And every fair from fair sometime declines,
By chance, or nature's changing course, untrimmed;
But thy eternal summer shall not fade,
Nor lose possession of that fair thou owest;°   *own, possess*   10
Nor shall Death brag thou wander'st in his shade,
When in eternal lines to time thou growest:
   So long as men can breathe, or eyes can see,
   So long lives this, and this gives life to thee.

QUESTIONS

1. What is the dramatic situation of the poem? Who is speaking to whom?
2. What do the metaphors in lines 1–8 assert? Why does the speaker emphasize life's brevity?
3. Describe the shift in topic beginning in line 9. How do these lines both deny and echo the subject of lines 1–8?
4. What relationship do the last two lines have to the rest of the poem? What is the meaning of "this" (line 14)? What sort of immortality does Shakespeare exalt in the sonnet?

WILLIAM SHAKESPEARE   (1564–1616)

Sonnet 30: When to the Sessions of Sweet Silent Thought ——————— *1609*

When to the sessions° of sweet silent thought   *holding of court*
I summon° up remembrance of things past,
I sigh the lack of many a thing I sought,
And with old woes new wail my dear time's waste:°
Then can I drown an eye (un-used to flow)   5

SONNET 30.   2 *summon:* to issue a summons to appear at a legal hearing.   4 *old woes . . . waste:* revive old sorrows about lost opportunities and express sorrow for them again.

For precious friends hid in death's dateless° night,   *endless*
And weep afresh love's long since canceled° woe,   *paid in full*
And moan th'expense° of many a vanished sight.   *cost, loss*
Then can I grieve at grievances foregone,
And heavily° from woe to woe tell° o'er   *sadly; count*   10
The sad account of fore-bemoanèd moan,
Which I new pay, as if not paid before.
   But if the while I think on thee (dear friend)
   All losses are restored, and sorrows end.

QUESTIONS

1. Explain the metaphor of "sessions" and "summon" in lines 1–2. Where are the "sessions" being held? What is a "summons" for remembrance?

2. What is the metaphor brought out by the word "canceled" in line 7? In what sense might a "woe" of love be canceled? Explain the metaphor of "expense" in line 8.

3. What type of transaction does Shakespeare refer to in the metaphor of lines 9–12? What understanding does the metaphor provide about the sadness and regret that a person feels about past mistakes and sorrows?

4. What role does the speaker assign to the "dear friend" of line 13 in relation to the metaphors of the poem?

ELIZABETH TUDOR, QUEEN ELIZABETH I   (1533–1603)

On Monsieur's Departure _____ *ca. 1560 (1964)*

I grieve° and dare not show my discontent,   *I am unhappy*
I love and yet am forced to seem to hate,
I do, yet dare not say I ever meant,
I seem stark mute but inwardly do prate.°   *chatter endlessly*
   I am and not, I freeze and yet am burned,
   Since from myself another self I turned.

My care° is like my shadow in the sun,   *loved one*
Follows me flying, flies when I pursue it,
Stands and lies by me, doth what I have done.
His too familiar care° doth make me rue it.   *attentiveness, love*
   No means I find to rid him from my breast,
   Till by the end of things it be supprest.

Some gentler passion slide into my mind,
For I am soft and made of melting snow;
Or be more cruel, love, and so be kind.
Let me or float or sink, be high or low.
   Or let me live with some more sweet content.
   Or die and so forget what love ere meant.

QUESTIONS

1. What is the significance of "Monsieur's Departure"? How does this detail prompt the patterns of thought in the poem?
2. Explain the speaker's use of antithesis in the poem to explain her ambivalent situation. How seriously should we take the ideas in lines 12 and 18? Assuming that this is a deeply personal and private lyric, why, granted the speaker's royal status, does she express such contradictory feelings?
3. What is the meaning of the shadow simile in lines 7–10? How well does this comparison reveal her situation?
4. What is explained by the paradoxes in lines 5 and15?

MONA VAN DUYN   (b. 1921)

Earth Tremors Felt in Missouri _____ *1964*

The quake last night was nothing personal,
you told me this morning. I think one always wonders,
unless, of course, something is visible: tremors
that take us, private and willy-nilly, are usual.

But the earth said last night that what I feel,   5
you feel; what secretly moves you, moves me.
One small, sensuous catastrophe
makes inklings letters, spelled in a worldly tremble.

The earth, with others on it, turns in its course
as we turn toward each other, less than ourselves, gross,   10
mindless, more than we were. Pebbles, we swell
to planets, nearing the universal roll,
in our conceit even comprehending the sun,
whose bright ordeal leaves cool men woebegone.

QUESTIONS

1. In what ways is this poem intensely personal, a "confessional" poem? How does the poem develop materials that might be considered less personal and more public?
2. Why does the speaker equate herself and her listener with the earth? Granted that this metaphor is apt, what is then meant by "earth tremors," "quake last night," "Pebbles, we swell / to planets," and "comprehending the sun"?
3. What feelings are brought out in the last line through the words "ordeal" and "woebegone"?
4. Compare the use of the earth/person metaphor as it is used in this poem and in Donne's "The Good Morrow" (Chapter 25).

DIANE WAKOSKI   (b. 1937)

Inside Out _____ *1965*

I walk the purple carpet into your eye,
carrying the silver butter server,
but a truck rumbles by,
    leaving its black tire prints on my foot,
and old images—   5
       the sound of banging screen doors on hot afternoons
       and a fly buzzing over Kool-Aid spilled on the sink—
flicker, as reflections on the metal surface.

Come in, you said,
inside your paintings, inside the blood factory, inside the   10
old songs that line your hands, inside
eyes that change like a snowflake every second,

inside spinach leaves holding that one piece of gravel,

inside the whiskers of a cat,

inside your old hat, and most of all inside your mouth where you   1
grind the pigments with your teeth, painting
with a broken bottle on the floor, and painting
with an ostrich feather on the moon that rolls out of my mouth.

You cannot let me walk inside you too long
inside the veins where my small feet touch   2
bottom.

You must reach inside and pull me
like a silver bullet°
from your arm.

INSIDE OUT.   23 *silver bullet:* According to legend, silver bullets were used to kill vampires. The
Lone Ranger, of the radio and television series popular in the 1940s and 1950s, always used silver
bullets as a trademark of his pursuit of justice.

QUESTIONS

1. What "inside out" details of the listener's anatomy does the speaker mention?
   What do you think is meant by the poem's title?
2. Consider details of the eye and the veins as synecdoche, the paintings and the
   old hat as metonymy. In the determination of the poem's characterization of
   the "you" inside the poem, what do these details stand for?
3. Consider the truck's black tire prints on the speaker's foot (lines 3–4) as an
   instance of synesthesia, that is, the application of one set of sensuous references
   to another sense. What might this figure mean? Do the same for the mouth
   with the ground pigments (lines 15–16), the ostrich feather and the rolling
   moon (line 18), and the walk inside the veins (lines 19–20).

4. What is meant by lines 19–24? Why, after the establishment of so personal and intimate a relationship, might the speaker express the reservations that are contained here? How might these lines be interpreted as a reflection upon the paradoxical nature of the love relationship generally?

5. Describe the paradox of the purple carpet and the silver butter server.

WALT WHITMAN   (1819–1892)

Facing West from California's Shores _____ *1860*

Facing west from California's shores,
Inquiring, tireless, seeking what is yet unfound,
I, a child, very old, over waves, towards the house of maternity,°
    the land of migrations, look afar,
Look off the shores of my Western sea, the circle almost circled;
For starting westward from Hindustan,° from the vales of Kashmir,   5
From Asia, from the north, from the God, the sage, and the hero,
From the south, from the flowery peninsulas° and the spice islands,°
Long having wandered since, round the earth having wandered
Now I face home again, very pleased and joyous.
(But where is what I started for so long ago?   10
And why is it yet unfound?)

FACING WEST FROM CALIFORNIA'S SHORES.   3 *house of maternity:* Asia, then considered the cradle of human civilization.   5 *Hindustan:* India.   7 *flowery peninsulas:* south India, south Burma, and the Maylay peninsula.   7 *spice islands:* the Molucca Islands of Indonesia.

QUESTIONS

1. What major paradox, or apparently contradictory situation, is described in this poem? How does the poet bring out this paradox? What has the speaker been seeking? Where has he looked for it?

2. Describe the meaning of the phrase "a child, very old"; "where is what I started for"; "the circle almost circled." In what ways are these phrases paradoxical?

3. Why does the speaker twice use the word "unfound" (lines 2, 11)? How might the word be considered a theme of the poem?

WILLIAM WORDSWORTH   (1770–1850)

London, 1802 _____ *1807 (1802)*

Milton! thou should'st be living at this hour:
England hath need of thee: she is a fen°   *bog, marsh*
Of stagnant waters: altar, sword, and pen,
Fireside, the heroic wealth of hall and bower,

Have forfeited their ancient English dower°   *widow's inheritance*   5
Of inward happiness. We are selfish men;
Oh! raise us up, return to us again;
And give us manners,° virtue, freedom, power.
Thy soul was like a star, and dwelt apart:
Thou hadst a voice whose sound was like the sea: 10
Pure as the naked heavens, majestic, free,
So didst thou travel on life's common way,
In cheerful godliness; and yet thy heart
The lowliest duties on herself did lay.

LONDON, 1802.   8 *manners:* customs, moral codes of social and political conduct.

QUESTIONS

1. What is the effect of Wordworth's apostrophe to Milton? What elements of Milton's career as a writer does Wordsworth emphasize?

2. In lines 3 and 4, the device of metonymy is used. How does Wordsworth judge the respective institutions represented by the details?

3. Consider the use of overstatement, or hyperbole, from lines 2–6. What effect does Wordsworth achieve by using the device as extensively as he does here?

4. What effect does Wordsworth make through his use of overstatement in his praise of Milton in lines 9–14? What does he mean by the metonymic references to "soul" (line 9) and "heart" (line 13)?

SIR THOMAS WYATT   (1503–1542)

I Find No Peace _____ *1557*

I find no peace, and all my war is done,
  I fear and hope, I burn and freeze like ice;
  I fly above the wind yet can I not arise;
  And naught I have and all the world I season.
That looseth nor locketh holdeth me in prison,°
  And holdeth me not, yet I can scape° nowise;   *escape*
  Nor letteth me live nor die at my devise,°   *choice*
  And yet of death it giveth none occasion.
Without eyen° I see, and without tongue I plain;°   *eyes*
  I desire to perish, and yet I ask health;
  I love another, and thus I hate myself;
I feed me in sorrow, and laugh in all my pain.
  Likewise displeaseth me both death and life°
  And my delight is causer of this strife.

I FIND NO PEACE.   5 *that . . . prison:* that is, "that which neither lets me go nor contains me holds me in prison." At the time of Wyatt, *-eth* was used for the third person singular present tense.   9 *plain:* express desires about love.   13 *likewise . . . life:* literally, "it is displeasing to me, in the same way, both death and life." That is, "both death and life are equally distasteful to me."

QUESTIONS

1. What situation is the speaker reflecting upon? What metaphors and similes express his feelings? How successful are these figures?

2. How many paradoxes are in the poem? What is their cumulative effect? What is the topic of the paradoxes in lines 1–4? In lines 5–8? Why does the speaker declare that hating himself is a consequence of loving another? Why is it ironic that his "delight" is the "causer of this strife"?

3. To what extent do you think the paradoxes express the feelings of a person in love, particularly because in the sixteenth century, the free and unchaperoned meetings of lovers were not easily arranged?

WRITING ABOUT FIGURES OF SPEECH

Begin by determining the use, line by line, of metaphors, similes, or other rhetorical figures. Obviously, similes are the easiest figures to recognize because they introduce comparisons with the word *like* or *as*. Metaphors can be recognized because the topics are discussed not as themselves but as other topics. If the poems speak of falling leaves or law courts, for example, but the subjects are memory or increasing age, you are looking at metaphors. Similarly, if the poet is addressing an absent person or a natural object, or if you find clear double meanings in words, you may have apostrophe, personification, or puns.

Questions for Discovering Ideas

- What figures of speech does the work contain? Where do they occur? Under what circumstances? How extensive are they?

- How do you recognize them? Are they signaled by a single word or phrase, such as "desert places" in Frost's "Desert Places" (Chapter 20), or are they more extensively detailed, as in Shakespeare's Sonnet 30, "When to the Sessions of Sweet Silent Thought"?

- How vivid are the figures? How obvious? How unusual? What kind of effort is needed to understand them in context?

- Structurally, how are the figures developed? How do they rise out of the situation envisioned in the poem? To what degree are the figures integrated into the poem's development of ideas? How do they relate to other aspects of the poem?

- Is one type of figure used in a particular section while another type predominates in another section? Why?

- If you have discovered a number of figures, what relationships can you find among them (such as the judicial and financial connections in Shakespeare's "When to the Sessions")?

- How do the figures of speech broaden, deepen, or otherwise assist in making the ideas in the poem forceful?

- In general, how appropriate and meaningful are the figures of speech in the poem? What effect do the figures have on the poem's tone and on your understanding and appreciation of the poem?

Strategies for Organizing Ideas

For this essay, two types of compositions are possible. One is a full-scale essay. The other, because some rhetorical figures may occupy only a small part of the poem, is a single paragraph. Let us consider the single paragraph first.

1. A PARAGRAPH.   For a single paragraph you need only one topic, such as the opening paradox and metonymy that begin Eliot's "Eyes That Last I Saw in Tears." The goal is to deal with the single figure and its relationship to the poem's main idea. Thus the essay should describe the figure and discuss its meaning and implications. It is important to begin with a comprehensive topic sentence, such as one that explains the cleverness of the puns in Gay's "Let Us Take the Road" or the use of synesthesia in Keats's "Ode to a Nightingale" (Chapter 20).

2. A FULL-LENGTH ESSAY.   One type of essay might examine just one figure, if the figure is pervasive enough in the poem to justify a full treatment. Most often, the poet's use of metaphors and similes is suitable for extensive discussion. A second type of essay might explore the meaning and effect of two or more figures, with the various parts of the body of the essay being taken up with each figure. The unity of this second kind of essay is achieved by the linking of a series of two or three different rhetorical devices to a single idea or emotion.

In the introduction, relate the quality of the figures to the general nature of the work. Thus, metaphors and similes of suffering might be appropriate to a religious, redemptive work, while those of sunshine and cheer might be right for a romantic one. If there is any discrepancy between the metaphorical language and the topic, you could consider that contrast as a possible central idea, for it would clearly indicate the writer's ironic perspective. Suppose that the topic of the poem is love, but the figures put you in mind of darkness and cold: What would the writer be saying about the quality of love? You should also try to justify any claims that you make about the figures. For example, one of the similes in Coleridge's "Kubla Khan" (Chapter 16) compares the sounds of a "mighty fountain" to the breathing of the earth in "fast thick pants." How is this simile to be taken? As a reference to the animality of the earth? As a suggestion that the fountain, and the earth, are dangerous? Or simply as a comparison suggesting immense, forceful noise? How do you explain your answer or answers? Your introduction is the place to establish ideas and justifications of this sort.

The following approaches for discussing rhetorical figures are not mutually exclusive, and you may combine them as you wish. Most likely, your essay will bring in most of the following classifications.

1. *Interpret the meaning and effect of the figures.* Here you explain how the figures enable you to make an interpretation. In the second stanza of "A Valediction: Forbidding Mourning," for example, the following metaphor equates love with hierarchical nomenclature of the church:

'Twere profanation of our joys
To tell the laity our love.

Here Donne emphasizes the mystical relationship of two lovers, drawing the metaphor from the religious tradition whereby any explanation of religious mysteries is considered a desecration. This interpretive approach is a direct one, requiring that metaphors, similes, or other figures be expanded and interpreted, including the explanation of necessary references and allusions.

2. *Analyze the frames of reference and their appropriateness to the subject matter.* Here you classify and locate the sources and types of the references and determine the appropriateness of these to the poem's subject matter. Ask questions similar to those you might ask in a study of imagery: Does the writer refer extensively to nature, science, warfare, politics, business, reading (e.g., Shakespeare's metaphor equating personal reverie with courtroom proceedings)? Does the metaphor seem appropriate? How? Why?

3. *Focus on the interests and sensibilities of the poet.* In a way this approach is like strategy 2, but the emphasis here is on what the selectivity of the writer might show about his or her vision and interests. You might begin by listing the figures in the poem and then determining the sources, just as you would do in discussing the sources of images generally. But then you should raise questions like the following: Does the writer use figures derived from one sense rather than another (i.e., sight, hearing, taste, smell, touch)? Does he or she record color, brightness, shadow, shape, depth, height, number, size, slowness, speed, emptiness, fullness, richness, drabness? Has the writer relied on the associations of figures of sense? Do metaphors and similes referring to green plants and trees, to red roses, or to rich fabrics, for example, suggest that life is full and beautiful, or do references to touch suggest amorous warmth? This approach is designed to help you to draw conclusions about the author's taste or sensibility.

4. *Examine the effect of one figure on the other figures and ideas of the poem.* The assumption of this approach is that each literary work is unified and organically whole, so that each part is closely related and inseparable from everything else. Usually it is best to pick a figure that occurs at the beginning of the poem and then determine how this figure influences your perception of the rest of the poem. Your aim is to consider the relationship of part to parts and part to whole. The beginning of Donne's "A Valediction: Forbidding Mourning," for example, contains a simile comparing the parting of the speaker and his listener to the quiet dying of "virtuous men." What is the effect of this comparison upon the poem? To help you with questions like this, you might substitute a totally different detail, such as, here, the violent death of a condemned criminal, or the slaughter of a domestic animal, rather than the deaths of "virtuous men." Such suppositions, which would clearly be out of place, may help you to understand and then explain the poet's rhetorical figures.

In your conclusion, summarize your main points, describe your general impressions, try to describe the impact of the figures, indicate your personal responses, or show what might further be done along the lines you have been developing. If you know other works by the same writer, or other works by other writers who use comparable or contrasting figures, you might explain the relationship of the other work or works to your present analysis.

DEMONSTRATIVE STUDENT ESSAY

Wordsworth's Use of Overstatement in "London, 1802"°

Through overstatement in "London, 1802," William Wordsworth emphasizes his tribute to Milton as a master of idealistic thought. The speaker's claim that England is "is a fen / Of stagnant waters" (lines 2-3) is overstated, as is the implication that people ("we") in England have no "manners, virtue, freedom, [or] power" (line 8). With the overstatements, however, Wordsworth implies that the nation's well-being depends on the constant flow of creative thoughts by persons of great ideas. Because Milton was clearly the greatest of these, in the view of Wordsworth's speaker, the overstatements stress the need for leadership. Milton is the model, and the overstated criticism lays the foundation in the real political and moral world for the rebirth of another Milton. Thus, through overstatement, Wordsworth emphasizes Milton's importance and in this way pays tribute to him.

° See p. 799 for this poem.

Commentary on the Paragraph

This essay shows how a short paragraph can deal with a single rhetorical figure, in this case Wordsworth's overstatements in "London, 1802." Although most often the figure will be prominent, as this one is, prominence is not a requirement. In addition, there is no need to write an excessively long paragraph. The goal here is not to describe all the details of Wordsworth's overstatement but to show how the figure affects his tribute to Milton. For this reason, the paragraph shows the need for clear and direct support of the major point.

DEMONSTRATIVE STUDENT ESSAY

A Study of Shakespeare's Metaphors in Sonnet 30: "When to the Sessions of Sweet Silent Thought"°

[1]   In this sonnet Shakespeare's speaker stresses the sadness and regret of remembered experience, but he states that a person with these feelings may be cheered by the thought of a friend. His metaphors, cleverly used, create new and fresh ways of seeing personal life in this perspective.* He presents

° See p. 795 for this poem.
* Central idea.

metaphors drawn from the public and business world of law courts, money, and banking or money-handling.†

[2] The courtroom metaphor of the first four lines shows that memories of past experience are constantly present and influential. Like a judge commanding defendants to appear in court, the speaker "summon[s]" his memory of "things past" to appear on trial before him. This metaphor suggests that people are their own judges and that their ideals and morals are like laws by which they measure themselves. The speaker finds himself guilty of wasting his time in the past. Removing himself, however, from the strict punishment that a real judge might require, he does not condemn himself for his "dear time's waste" but instead laments it (line 4). The metaphor is thus used to indicate that a person's consciousness is made up just as much of self-doubt and reproach as of more positive qualities.

[3] With the closely related reference of money in the next group of four lines, Shakespeare shows that living is a lifelong investment and is valuable for this reason. According to the money metaphor, living requires the spending of emotions and commitment to others. When friends move away and loved ones die, it is as though this expenditure has been lost. Thus, the speaker's dead friends are "precious" because he invested time and love in them, and the "sights" that have "vanished" from his eyes make him "moan" because he went to great "expense" for them (line 8).

[4] Like the money metaphor, the metaphor of banking or money-handling in the next four lines emphasizes that memory is a bank in which life's experiences are deposited. The full emotions surrounding experience are recorded there, and they may be withdrawn in moments of "sweet silent thought" just as a depositor may withdraw money. Thus the speaker states that he counts out the sad parts of his experience—his woe—just as a merchant or banker counts money: "And heavily from woe to woe tell o'er" (line 10). Because strong emotions still accompany his memories of past mistakes, the metaphor extends to borrowing and the payment of interest. The speaker thus says that he pays again with "new" woe the accounts that he had already paid with old woe. The metaphor suggests that the past is so much a part of the present that a person never stops feeling pain and regret.

[5] The legal, financial, and money-handling metaphors combine in the last two lines to show how a healthy present life may overcome past regrets. The "dear friend" being addressed in these lines has the resources (financial) to settle all the emotional judgments that the speaker as a self-judge has made against himself (legal). It is as though the friend is a rich patron who rescues him from emotional bankruptcy (legal and financial) and the doom resulting from a sentence of emotional misery and depression (legal).

[6] In these metaphors, therefore, Shakespeare's references are drawn from everyday public and business actions, but his use of them is creative and unusual. In particular, the idea of line 8 ("And moan th'expense of many a vanished sight") stresses that people spend much emotional energy on others. Without such personal commitment, one cannot have precious friends and loved ones. In keeping with this metaphor of money and investment, one could measure life not in months or years, but in the spending of emotion and involve-

---

†Thesis sentence.

ment in personal relationships. Shakespeare, by inviting readers to explore the values brought out by his metaphors, gives new insights into the nature and value of life.

Commentary on the Essay

This essay treats the three classes of metaphors that Shakespeare introduces in Sonnet 30. It thus illustrates stragegy 2 described on p. 803. But the aim of the discussion is not to explore the extent and nature of the comparison between the metaphors and the personal situations described in the sonnet. Instead, the goal is to explain how the metaphors develop Shakespeare's meaning. This essay therefore also illustrates strategy 1 described on page 802.

In addition to providing a brief description of the sonnet, the introduction brings out the central idea and the thesis sentence. Paragraph 2 deals with the meaning of Shakespeare's courtroom metaphor. His money metaphor is explained in paragraph 3. Paragraph 4 considers the banking or money-handling figure. Paragraph 5 shows how Shakespeare's last two lines bring together the three strands of metaphor. The conclusion comments generally on the creativity of Shakespeare's metaphors, and it also amplifies the way in which the money metaphor leads toward an increased understanding of life.

Throughout the essay, transitions are brought about by the linking words in the topic sentences. In paragraph 3, for example, the words "closely related" and "next group" move the reader from paragraph 2 to the new content. In paragraph 4, the words effecting the transition are "like the money metaphor" and "the next four lines." The opening sentence of paragraph 5 refers collectively to the subjects of paragraphs 2, 3, and 4, thereby focusing them on the new topic of paragraph 5.

SPECIAL TOPICS FOR WRITING AND ARGUMENT
ABOUT FIGURES OF SPEECH IN POETRY

1. Study the simile of the "stiff twin compasses" in Donne's "A Valediction: Forbidding Mourning." Using such a compass or a drawing of one, write an essay that demonstrates the accuracy, or lack of it, of Donne's descriptions. What light does the simile shed on the relationship of two lovers? How does it emphasize any or all of these aspects of love: closeness, immediacy, extent, importance, duration, intensity?

2. Consider some of the metaphors and similes in the poems included in this chapter. Write an essay that answers the following questions. How effective are the figures you select? (*Examples:* the bonsai tree [Piercy], the Siamese twins [Minty], the explosive [Hughes], the summer's day [Shakespeare].) What insights do the figures provide within the contexts of their respective poems? How appropriate are they? Might they be expanded more fully, and if they were, what would be the effect?

3. Consider some of the other rhetorical figures in the poems of this chapter. Write an essay describing the importance of figures of speech in creating

emphasis and in extending and deepening the ideas of poetry. These are some possible topics:

- Paradox in Wyatt's "I Find No Peace" or Whitman's "Facing West from California's Shores."
- The simile of the compass in Donne's "Valediction."
- Metaphor in Minty's "Conjoined," Piercy's "A Work of Artifice," or Wakoski's "Inside Out."
- Anaphora in Rukeyser's "Yes, We Were Looking at Each Other."
- A comparison of contrasts and paradoxes in Elizabeth I's "On Monsieur's Departure" and Wyatt's "I Find No Peace."
- Similes in King's "Sic Vita" or Hughes's "Harlem."
- Personification in the poems of Wordsworth or Keats.
- Metonymy in Keats's "To Autumn" or Nash's "Exit, Pursued by a Bear."

4. Write a poem in which you create a governing metaphor or simile. An example might be "My girlfriend/boyfriend is like (a) an opening flower, (b) a difficult book, (c) an insoluble mathematical problem, (d) a bill that cannot be paid, (e) a slow-moving chess game." Another example: "Teaching a person how to do a particular job is like (a) shoveling heavy snow, (b) climbing a mountain during a landslide, (c) having someone force you underwater when you're gasping for breath." When you finish, describe the relationship between your comparison and the development and structure of your poem.

5. In your library's reference section, find the third edition of J. A. Cuddon's *A Dictionary of Literary Terms and Literary Theory* (1991) or some other dictionary of literary terms. Study the entries for "metaphysical" and "conceit," and write a brief report on these sections. You might attempt to answer questions like these: What is meant by the word *conceit?* What are some of the kinds of conceit the reference work discusses? What is a metaphysical conceit? Who are some of the writers considered metaphysical? In the "Metaphysical" entry, of what importance is John Donne?

18

Tone:
The Creation of Attitude in Poetry

Tone (see also Chapter 8), a term derived from the phrase *tone of voice*, describes the shaping of attitudes in poetry. Each poet's choice of words governs the reader's responses, as do the participants and situations in the poem. In addition, the poet shapes responses through denotation and connotation, seriousness or humor, irony, metaphors, similes, understatement, overstatement, and other figures of speech. Of major importance is the poem's speaker. How much self-awareness does the speaker show? What is his or her background? What relationship does the speaker establish with listeners and readers? What does the speaker assume about the readers and about their knowledge? How do these assumptions affect the ideas and the diction?

To compare poetic tone with artistic tone, see the reproduction of Fernand Léger's painting *The City* (Insert II, front top). A viewer's response to the painting depends on the relationships of the various shapes to Léger's arrangement and color. The signs, stairs, pole, and human figures in the painting are all common in modern cities. By cutting them up or leaving them partially hidden, Léger creates an atmosphere suggesting that contemporary urban life is truncated, sinister, and even threatening.

The same control is necessary in poetry. The sentences must be just long enough to achieve the poet's intended effect—no shorter and no longer. In a conversational style there should be no formal words, just as in a formal style there should be no slang, no rollicking rhythms, and no frivolous rhymes—that is, unless the poet deliberately intends that readers be startled or shocked. In all the features that contribute to a poem's tone, the poet's consistency of intention is primary. Any unintentional deviations will cause the poem to sink and the poet to fail.

TONE, CHOICE, AND RESPONSE

Remember that a major objective of poets is to inform, enrich, and inspire readers. Poets may begin their poems with a brief idea, a vague feeling, or a fleeting impression. Then, in the light of their developing design, they *choose* what to say—the form of their material and the words and phrases to express their ideas. The poem "Theme for English B" by Langston Hughes (p. 822) illustrates this process in almost outline form. Hughes's speaker lays out many interests that he shares with his intended reader, his English teacher. In this way Hughes enables all readers to accept his ideas of human equality.

In the long run, readers might not accept all the ideas in any poem, but the successful poem gains the reader's agreement—at least for a time—because the poet's control over tone is right. Each poem attempts to evoke total responses, which might be destroyed by any lapses in tone. Let us look at a poem in which the tone misses, and misses badly.

CORNELIUS WHUR   (1782–1853)

The First-Rate Wife _____ *1837*

This brief effusion I indite,
    And my vast wishes send,
That thou mayst be directed right,
And have ere long within thy sight
    A most *enchanting* friend!   5

The *maiden* should have *lovely face,*
    And be of *genteel mien;*
If not, within thy dwelling place,
There may be vestige of disgrace,
    Not much admired—when seen.   10

Nor will thy dearest be complete
    Without *domestic* care;
If otherwise, howe'er discreet,
Thine eyes will very often meet
    What none desire to share!   15

And further still—thy future *dear,*
    Should have some *mental* ray;
If not, thou mayest drop a tear,
Because no *real sense* is there
    To charm life's dreary day!   20

QUESTIONS

1. What kind of person is the poem's speaker? The listener? What is the situation? What requirements does the speaker create for the "first-rate wife"?

2. Describe the poem's tone. How does the speaker's character influence the tone? In light of the tone, to what degree can the poem be considered insulting?

3. How might lines 14 and 15 be interpreted as a possible threat if the woman as a wife does not keep the house clean and straight?

In this poem the speaker is talking to a friend or associate and is explaining his requirements for a "first-rate wife." From his tone, he clearly regards getting married as little more than hiring a pretty housekeeper. In the phrase "some *mental* ray," for example, the word *some* does not mean "a great deal" but is more like "*at least* some," as though nothing more could be expected of a woman. Even allowing for the fact that the poem was written early in the nineteenth century and represents a benighted view of women and marriage, "The First-Rate Wife" offends most readers. Do you wonder why you've never heard of Cornelius Whur before?

TONE AND THE NEED FOR CONTROL

"The First-Rate Wife" demonstrates the need for the poet to be in control over all facets of the poem. The speaker must be aware of his or her situation and should not, like Whur's speaker, demonstrate any smugness or insensitivity, unless the poet is deliberately revealing the shortcomings of the speaker by dramatizing them for the reader's amusement, as e. e. cummings does in the poem "next to of course god america i" (Chapter 23). In a poem with well-controlled tone, details and situations should be factually correct; observations should be both logical and fair, within the poem's structure, and also comprehensive and generally applicable. The following poem, based on battlefield conditions in World War I, illustrates a masterly control over tone.

WILFRED OWEN   (1893–1918)

Dulce et Decorum Est° _____ *1920*

Bent double, like old beggars under sacks,
Knock-kneed, coughing like hags, we cursed through sludge,
Till on the haunting flares we turned our backs
And towards our distant rest began to trudge.
Men marched asleep. Many had lost their boots
But limped on, blood-shod. All went lame; all blind;
Drunk with fatigue; deaf even to the hoots
Of tired, outstripped Five-Nines° that dropped behind.

Gas!° GAS! Quick, boys!—An ecstasy of fumbling,
Fitting the clumsy helmets° just in time;
But someone still was yelling out and stumbling
And flound'ring like a man in fire or lime . . .

DULCE ET DECORUM EST.   The Latin title comes from Horace's *Odes*, book 3, line 13: *Dulce et decorum est pro patria mori* ("It is sweet and honorable to die for the fatherland").   8 *Five-Nines:* artillery shells that made a hooting sound just before landing.   9 *Gas:* Chlorine gas was used as an antipersonnel weapon in 1915 by the Germans at Ypres, in Belgium.   10 *helmets:* Soldiers carried gas masks as normal battle equipment.

Dim, through the misty panes and thick green° light,
As under a green sea, I saw him drowning.

In all my dreams, before my helpless sight,   15
He plunges at me, guttering, choking, drowning.

If in some smothering dreams you too could pace
Behind the wagon that we flung him in.
And watch the white eyes writhing in his face,
His hanging face, like a devil's sick of sin;   20
If you could hear, at every jolt, the blood
Come gargling from the froth-corrupted lungs,
Obscene as cancer, bitter as the cud
Of vile, incurable sores on innocent tongues.—
My friend, you would not tell with such high zest   25
To children ardent for some desperate glory,
The old Lie: Dulce et decorum est
Pro patria mori.

13 *thick green:* The chlorine gas used in gas attacks has a greenish-yellow color.

QUESTIONS

1. What is the scene described in lines 1–8? What expressions does the speaker use to indicate his attitude toward the conditions?
2. What does the title of the poem mean? What attitude or conviction does it embody?
3. Does the speaker really mean "my friend" in line 25? In what tone of voice might this phrase be spoken?
4. What is the tonal relationship between the patriotic fervor of the Latin phrase and the images of the poem? How does the tonal contrast create the dominant tone of the poem?

The tone of "Dulce et Decorum Est" never lapses. The poet intends the description to evoke a response of horror, for he contrasts the strategic goals of warfare with the speaker's up-close experience of terror in battle. The speaker's language skillfully emphasizes first the dreariness and fatigue of warfare (with words like "sludge," "trudge," "lame," and "blind") and second the agony of violent death from chlorine gas (embodied in the participles "guttering," "choking," "drowning," "smothering," and "writhing"). With these details established, the concluding attack against the "glory" of war is difficult to refute, even if warfare is undertaken to defend or preserve one's country. Although the details about the agonized death may distress or discomfort a sensitive reader, they are not designed to do that alone but instead are integral to the poem's argument. Ultimately, it is the contrast between the high ideals of the Latin phrase and the ugliness of battlefield death that creates the dominant tone of the poem. The Latin phrase treats war and death in the abstract; the poem makes images of battle and death vividly real. The resultant tone is that of controlled bitterness and irony.

TONE AND COMMON GROUNDS OF ASSENT

Not all those reading Owen's poem will deny that war is ever necessary. The issues of politics and warfare are far too complex for that. But the poem does show another important aspect of tone—namely, the degree to which the poet judges and tries to control responses through the establishment of a *common ground of assent*. An appeal to a bond of commonly held interests, concerns, and assumptions is essential if a poet is to maintain an effective tone. Owen, for example, does not create arguments against the necessity of a just war. Instead, he bases the poem upon realistic details about the writhing, spastic death suffered by the speaker's comrade, and he appeals to emotions that everyone, pacifist and militarist alike, would commonly feel—horror at the contemplation of violent death. Even assuming a widely divergent audience, in other words, the *tone* of the poem is successful because it is based on commonly acknowledged facts and commonly felt emotions. Knowing a poem like this one, even advocates of a strong military would need to defend their ideas on the grounds of *preventing* just such needless, ugly deaths. Owen wisely and carefully considers the responses of his readers, and he regulates speaker, situation, detail, and argument in order to make the poem acceptable for the broadest possible spectrum of opinion.

TONE IN CONVERSATION AND POETRY

Many readers think that tone is a subtle and difficult subject, but it is nevertheless true that in ordinary situations we master tone easily and expertly (see Chapter 8, p. 380). We constantly use standard questions and statements that deal with tone, such as "What do you mean by that?" "What I'm saying is this . . . ," and "Did I hear you correctly?" together with other comments that extend to humor and, sometimes, to hostility. In poetry we do not have everyday speech situations; we have only the poems themselves and are guided by the materials they provide us. Some poems are straightforward and unambiguous, but in other poems feeling and mood are essential to our understanding. In Hardy's "The Workbox," for example, the husband's gift to his wife indicates not love but suspicion. Also, the husband's relentless linking of the dead man's coffin to the gift reveals his underlying anger. Pope, in the passage from the "Epilogue to the Satires" included in this chapter, satirically describes deplorable habits and customs of his English contemporaries in the 1730s. His concluding lines (of the passage and also of the poem) emphasize his scorn:

> Yet may this verse (if such a verse remain)
> Show there was one who held it in disdain.

The speaker of Ondaatje's "Late Movies with Skyler" describes how he and Skyler watch the late show. The activities described in the poem clearly establish a friendly and companionable bond between the two men. Poems of course may also reveal respect and wonder, as shown in the last six lines of Keats's "On First Looking into Chapman's Homer" (Chapter 17). By attending carefully to the details of such poems, you can draw conclusions about poetic tone that are as accurate as those you draw in normal speech situations.

TONE AND IRONY

Irony is a mode of indirection, a means of making a point by emphasizing a discrepancy or opposite (see also Chapter 8). Thus Owen uses the title "Dulce et Decorum Est" to emphasize that death in warfare is not sweet and honorable but rather demeaning and horrible. The title ironically reminds us of eloquent holiday speeches at the tombs of unknown soldiers, but as we have seen, it also reminds us of the reality of the agonized death of Owen's soldier. As an aspect of tone, therefore, irony is a powerful way of conveying attitudes, for it draws your attention to at least two ways of seeing a situation, enabling you not only to *understand* but also to *feel.* Poetry shares with fiction the various kinds of ironies that afflict human beings. These are verbal irony, situational irony, and dramatic irony.

Verbal Irony, Through Word Selection, Emphasizes Ambiguities and Discrepancies

At almost any point in a poem, a poet may introduce employ the ironic effects of language itself—**verbal irony.** The poem "she being Brand / -new," by e. e. cummings, is built on the double meanings derived from the procedures of breaking in a new car. Indeed, the entire poem is a virtuoso piece of double entendre. Another example of verbal irony is seen in Roethke's "My Papa's Waltz," in which the speaker uses the name of this orderly, stately dance to describe his childhood memories of his father's whirling him around the kitchen in wild, boisterous drunkenness.

Situational Irony Develops from Life's Anomalies and Uncertainties

Situational irony is derived from the discrepancies between the ideal and the actual. People would like to live their lives in terms of a standard of love, friendship, honor, success, and general excellence, but the irony is that the reality of their lives often falls far short of such standards. Whereas in fiction ironic situations emerge from extended narrative, in poetry such situations are usually at a high point or climax, and we must usually infer the narrative circumstances that have gone on before. Thomas Hardy, in "The Workbox," skillfully exploits an ironic situation between a husband and a wife.

THOMAS HARDY   (1840–1928)

The Workbox _____ *1914*

"See, here's the workbox, little wife,
    That I made of polished oak."
He was a joiner,° of village° life;   *cabinetmaker*
    She came of borough° folk.

He holds the present up to her   5
    As with a smile she nears
And answers to the profferer,
    "'Twill last all my sewing years!"

"I warrant it will. And longer too.
    'Tis a scantling° that I got   10
Off poor John Wayward's coffin, who
    Died of they knew not what.

"The shingled pattern that seems to cease
    Against your box's rim
Continues right on in the piece   1
    That's underground with him.

"And while I worked it made me think
    Of timber's varied doom:
One inch where people eat and drink,
    The next inch in a tomb.   2

"But why do you look so white, my dear,
    And turn aside your face?
You knew not that good lad, I fear,
    Though he came from your native place?"

"How could I know that good young man,
    Though he came from my native town,
When he must have left far earlier than
    I was a woman grown?"

"Ah, no. I should have understood!
    It shocked you that I gave
To you one end of a piece of wood
    Whose other is in a grave?"

"Don't, dear, despise my intellect.
    Mere accidental things
Of that sort never have effect
    On my imaginings."

THE WORKBOX.   4, 5 *village, borough:* A village was small and rustic; a borough was larger and
more sophisticated.   10 *scantling:* a small leftover piece of wood.

Yet still her lips were limp and wan,
   Her face still held aside,
As if she had known not only John,
   But known of what he died.   40

QUESTIONS

1. Who does most of the speaking here? What does the speaker's tone show about the characters of the husband and the wife? What does the tone indicate about the poet's attitude toward them?

2. What do lines 21–40 indicate about the wife's knowledge of John and about her earlier relationship with him? Why does she deny such knowledge? What does the last stanza show about her? Why is John's death kept a mystery?

3. In lines 17–20, what irony is suggested by the fact that the wood was used both for John's coffin and the workbox?

4. Why is the husband's irony more complex than he realizes? What do his words and actions show about his character?

5. The narrator, or poet, speaks only in lines 3–7 and 37–40. How much of his explanation is essential? How much shows his attitude? How might the poem have been more effectively concluded?

"The Workbox" is a domestic drama of deception, cruelty, and sadness. The complex details are evidence of situational irony, that is, an awareness that human beings do not control their lives but are rather controlled by powerful forces—in this case by both death and earlier feelings and commitments. Beyond this irony evolving out of the domestic scene, Hardy also emphasizes symbolically the direct connection that death has with the living. As a result of her husband's gift, made of the wood with which he has also made a coffin for the dead man, the wife will never escape being reminded of this man. Within the life imagined in the poem, she will have to live with regret and the constant need to deny her true emotions, and her situation is therefore endlessly ironic.

Dramatic Irony Is Built on the Ignorance of Characters and the Greater Knowledge of Readers

In addition to situational irony, the wife's deception reveals that the husband is in a situation of **dramatic irony.** He does not know all the circumstances of his wife's past, but readers have a more complete understanding. In addition, the husband does not actually *know*—though he suspects—that his wife is not being truthful about her earlier relationship with the dead man, but the poem sufficiently enables readers to make positive conclusions. By emphasizing the wood, the husband is apparently trying to make his wife uncomfortable, even to the point of extracting a confession from her, but because he does not actually know the true circumstances, he remains unsure of the truth and also of his wife's feelings about him. Because of these uncertainties and suspicions, Hardy has deftly used dramatic irony to create a poem of great complexity and pathos.

TONE AND SATIRE

Satire, an important genre in the study of tone, is designed to expose human follies and vices. In method, a satiric poem may be bitter and vituperative, but often it employs humor and irony, on the grounds that anger turns readers away while a comic tone more easily wins agreement. The speaker of a satiric poem either may attack folly and vice *directly,* or it may dramatically *embody* the folly or vice and thus serve as an illustration of the subject of satire. An example of the first type is the following short poem by Alexander Pope, in which the speaker directly attacks a listener who has claimed to be a poet but whom the speaker considers a fool. The speaker cleverly uses insult as the tone of attack.

ALEXANDER POPE   (1688–1744)

Epigram from the French —————————————————— *1732*

Sir, I admit your general rule
That every poet is a fool:
But you yourself may serve to show it,
That every fool is not a poet.

QUESTIONS

1. What has the listener said before the poem begins? How does the speaker build on the listener's previous comment?
2. Considering this poem as a brief satire, describe the nature of satiric attack and the corresponding tone of attack.
3. Look at the pattern "poet," "fool," "fool," "poet." This is a pattern (*a, b, b, a*) called *chiasmus* or *antimetabole.* What does the pattern contribute to the poem's effectiveness?

An example of the second type of satiric poem is another of Pope's epigrams, in which the speaker is an actual embodiment of the subject being attacked.

ALEXANDER POPE   (1688–1744)

Epigram, Engraved on the Collar of a Dog
which I Gave to His Royal Highness —————————————— *1738*

I am his Highness' dog at Kew:°   *the royal palace near London*
Pray tell me sir, whose dog are you?

QUESTIONS

1. Who or what is the subject of the satiric attack?
2. What attitude is expressed toward social pretentiousness?

Here the speaker is the king's dog, and the listener an unknown dog. Pope's satire is directed not against canines, however, but against human pretentiousness based on class. The first line ridicules those who claim social status that is derived, not earned. The second implies an unwillingness to recognize the listener until the question of rank is resolved. Pope, by using the dog as a speaker, reduces such snobbishness to an absurdity. A similar satiric poem attacking pretentiousness is "next to of course god america i" by e. e. cummings (Chapter 23), where the speaker voices a set of patriotic platitudes and in doing so illustrates cummings's satiric point that most speeches of this sort are empty-headed. Satiric tone may thus range widely, being sometimes objective, comic, and distant; sometimes deeply concerned and scornful; and sometimes dramatic, ingenuous, and revelatory. Always, however, the satiric mode aims toward confrontation and exposé.

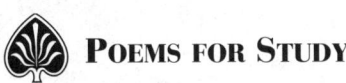

POEMS FOR STUDY

ANNE BRADSTREET   (1612–1672)

The Author to Her Book _____ *1678*

Thou ill-formed offspring of my feeble brain,
Who after birth did'st by my side remain,
Till snatched from thence by friends, less wise than true,
Who thee abroad exposed to public view;
Made thee in rags, halting, to the press to trudge,
Where errors were not lessened, all may judge.
At thy return my blushing was not small,
My rambling brat° (in print) should mother call;
I cast thee by as one unfit for light,
Thy visage was so irksome in my sight;
Yet being mine own, at length affection would
Thy blemishes amend, if so I could:
I washed thy face, but more defects I saw,
And rubbing off a spot, still made a flaw.
I stretched thy joints to make thee even feet,°   *regular poetic meter*
Yet still thou run'st more hobbling than is meet;
In better dress to trim thee was my mind,
But nought save homespun cloth, in the house I find.
In this array, 'mongst vulgars may'st thou roam;
In critics' hands beware thou dost not come;
And take thy way where yet thou art not known.
If for thy Father asked, say thou had'st none;
And for thy Mother, she alas is poor,
Which caused her thus to send thee out of door.

QUESTIONS

1.   What is the tone of the speaker's references to those friends who "exposed" her book to "public view" (that is, circulated it without her consent)? How does this tone indicate her ambiguous feelings about them?

2.   How does the speaker excuse the fact that she is issuing her book of poetry on her own initiative? How does the tone produce humor? How does the tone of the concluding metaphor encourage you to smile, or even to laugh?

3.   What attitude toward herself does the speaker express? How do you react to this attitude? How do you think you are expected by the poet to react?

4.   What is the tone of the extended metaphor of the child in lines 11–18?

THE AUTHOR TO HER BOOK.   8 *brat:* The word here emphasizes the insignificance rather than the unpleasant aspects of a child.

LUCILLE CLIFTON   (b. 1936)

homage to my hips _____ *1987*

these hips are big hips
they need space to
move around in.
they don't fit into little
petty places. these hips   5
are free hips.
they don't like to be held back.
these hips have never been enslaved.
they go where they want to go.
they do what they want to do.   10
these hips are mighty hips.
these hips are magic hips.
i have known them
to put a spell on a man and
spin him like a top!   15

QUESTIONS

1. What is unusual about the subject matter? Considering that some people are
    embarrassed to mention their hips, what attitudes does the speaker express
    here?

2. How do the words "enslaved," "want to go," "want to do," "mighty," and
    "spell" define the poem's ideas about the relationship between mentality and
    physicality?

3. To what degree is this a comic poem? What about the subject and the diction
    makes the poem funny?

e. e. cummings   (1894–1962)

she being Brand / -new _____ *1926*

she being Brand

-new;and you
know consequently a
little stiff i was
careful of her and(having   5
thoroughly oiled the universal
joint tested my gas felt of
her radiator made sure her springs were O.
K.)i went right to it flooded-the-carburetor cranked her

up,slipped the
clutch(and then somehow got into reverse she
kicked what
the hell)next
minute i was back in neutral tried and   10

again slo-wly;bare,ly nudg. ing(my   1!

lev-er Right-
oh and her gears being in

A 1 shape passed
from low through
second-in-to-high like   2
greasedlightning) just as we turned the corner of Divinity

avenue i touched the accelerator and give

her the juice,good

                        (it
was the first ride and believe i we was   :
happy to see how nice she acted right up to
the last minute coming back down by the Public
Gardens i slammed on
the

internalexpanding
&
externalcontracting
brakes Bothatonce and

brought allofher tremB
-ling
to a:dead.

stand-
;Still)

QUESTIONS

1. How extensive is the verbal irony, the double entendre, in this poem? This poem is considered comic. Do you agree? Why or why not? This poem might also be considered sexist. Do you agree? Why or why not?

2. How do the spacing and alignment affect your reading of the poem? How does the unexpected and sometimes absent punctuation—such as in line 15, "again slo-wly;bare,ly nudg. ing(my"—contribute to the humor?

3. Can this poem in any respect be called off-color or bawdy? How might you refute such charges in light of the tone the speaker uses to equate a first sexual experience with the breaking in of a new car?

MARI EVANS   (b. 1923)

I Am a Black Woman _____ *1970*

I am a black woman
the music of my song
some sweet arpeggio of tears
is written in a minor key
and I   5
can be heard humming in the night
Can be heard
    humming
in the night

I saw my mate leap screaming to the sea   10
and I/with these hands/cupped the lifebreath
from my issue in the canebreak
I lost Nat's swinging body° in a rain of tears

and heard my son scream all the way from Anzio°
for Peace he never knew. . . . I   15

learned Da Nang° and Pork Chop Hill°
in anguish
Now my nostrils know the gas
and these trigger tire/d fingers
seek the softness in my warrior's beard   20

I
am a black woman
tall as a cypress
strong
beyond all definition still   25
defying place
and time
and circumstance
    assailed
       impervious   30
          indestructible

Look
    on me and be
renewed

I AM A BLACK WOMAN.   13 *Nat's swinging body:* Nat Turner was hanged in 1831 for leading a
slave revolt in Southampton, Virginia.   14 *Anzio:* seacoast town in Italy, the scene of fierce fighting between the Allies and the Germans in 1943 during World War II.   16 *Da Nang:* major
American military base in South Vietnam, frequently attacked during the Vietnam War.   *Pork
Chop Hill:* site of a bloody battle between UN and Communist forces during the Korean War
(1950–1953).

QUESTIONS

1. What attitude is indicated by the phrase "sweet arpeggio of tears"? How does "in a minor key" complete both the idea and the comparison?

2. What phrases and descriptions does the speaker use to indicate her attitudes of anguish, despair, pain, and indignation?

3. In the last fourteen lines, what contrasting attitude is expressed? How does the speaker make this attitude clear? On balance, is the poem optimistic or pessimistic? Why?

LANGSTON HUGHES   (1902–1967)

Theme for English B _____ *1959*

The instructor said,

> Go home and write
> a page tonight.
> And let that page come out of you—
> Then, it will be true.

I wonder if it's that simple?

I am twenty-two, colored, born in Winston-Salem.
I went to school there, then Durham, then here
to this college on the hill above Harlem.°
I am the only colored student in my class.
The steps from the hill lead down to Harlem,
through a park, then I cross St. Nicholas,
Eighth Avenue, Seventh, and I come to the Y,
the Harlem Branch Y, where I take the elevator
up to my room, sit down, and write this page:

It's not easy to know what is true for you or me
at twenty-two, my age. But I guess I'm what
I feel and see and hear. Harlem, I hear you:
hear you, hear me—we two—you, me talk on this page.
(I hear New York, too.) Me—who?

Well, I like to eat, sleep, drink, and be in love.
I like to work, read, learn, and understand life.
I like a pipe for a Christmas present,
or records—Bessie,° bop,° or Bach.°

THEME FOR ENGLISH B.   9 *college . . . Harlem:* a reference to Columbia University in the Columbia Heights section of New York City. The other streets and buildings mentioned in lines 11–14 refer to specific places in the same vicinity.   24 *Bessie:* Bessie Smith (ca. 1898–1937), American jazz singer, famed as the "Empress of the Blues."   *bop:* a type of popular music that was in vogue in the 1940s through the 1960s.   *Bach:* Johann Sebastian Bach (1685–1750), German composer, considered the master of the baroque style of music.

I guess being colored doesn't make me not like 25
the same things other folks like who are other races.
So will my page be colored that I write?
Being me, it will not be white.
But it will be
a part of you, instructor. 30
You are white—
yet a part of me, as I am a part of you.
That's American.

Sometimes perhaps you don't want to be a part of me.
Nor do I often want to be a part of you. 35
But we are, that's true!
As I learn from you,
I guess you learn from me—
although you're older—and white—
and somewhat more free. 40

This is my page for English B.

QUESTIONS

1. What is the tone of the speaker's self-assessment? What does the tone indicate about his feelings toward the situation in the class and at the Y?
2. What tone is implicit in the fact that the speaker, in response to a theme assignment, has composed a poem rather than a prose essay?
3. What is the tone of lines 21–24, where the speaker indicates his likes? In what way may the characteristics brought out in these lines serve as an argument for social and political equality?
4. How does the tone in lines 27–40, particularly lines 34–36, prevent the statements of the speaker from becoming overly assertive or strident?

X. J. KENNEDY   (b. 1929)

John while swimming in the ocean _____ *1986*

John while swimming in the ocean
Rubbed sharks' backs with suntan lotion.
Now those sharks have skin of bronze
In their bellies—namely, John's.

QUESTIONS

1. What is the "action" of the poem? Why is it ludicrous?
2. What do the rhymes contribute to the poem's comic tone?
3. Describe the poem's attitude toward beach and ocean culture.

SHARON OLDS   (b. 1942)

The Planned Child ———————————————————————— *1996*

I hated the fact that they had planned me, she had taken
a cardboard out of his shirt from the laundry
as if sliding the backbone up out of his body,
and made a chart of the month and put
her temperature on it, rising and falling
to know the day to make me—I would have
liked to have been conceived in heat,
in haste, by mistake, in love, in sex,
not on cardboard, the little x on the
rising line that did not fall again.

But when a friend was pouring wine
and said that I seem to have been a child who had been wanted,
I took the wine against my lips
as if my mouth were moving along
that valved wall in my mother's body, she was
bearing down, and then breathing from the mask, and then
bearing down, pressing me out into
the world that was not enough for her without me in it,
not the moon, the sun, Orion
cartwheeling across the dark, not
the earth, the sea—none of it
was enough, for her, without me.

QUESTIONS

1. Who is the speaker? What is she like? What is she talking about? Why does she
   begin the poem talking about something she hated?
2. What change of attitudes is described by the poem? Why does the poem seem
   to require such a change?
3. What attitude is expressed in the concluding global, planetary, solar, and stellar
   refrences? Why does the speaker state that, to her mother, she has more value
   than this image?
4. What unique qualities of perception and expression does the speaker exhibit?
   Have you ever read a poem before in which details about conception and childbirth have been so prominent? Why are these details included in this poem?

MICHAEL ONDAATJE   (b. 1943)

Late Movies with Skyler ———————————————————————— *1979*

All week since he's been home
he has watched late movies alone

terrible one star films and then staggering
through the dark house to his bed
waking at noon to work on the broken car   5
he has come home to fix.

21 years old and restless
back from logging on Vancouver Island
with men who get rid of crabs with Raid
    2 minutes bending over in agony   10
    and then into the showers!

Last night I joined him for *The Prisoner of Zenda*
a film I saw three times in my youth
and which no doubt influenced me morally.
Hot coffee bananas and cheese   15
we are ready at 11.30 for adventure.

At each commercial Sky
breaks into midnight guitar practice
head down playing loud and intensely
till the movie comes on and the music suddenly stops.   20
Skyler's favourite hour's when he's usually alone
cooking huge meals of anything in the frying pan
thumbing through *Advanced Guitar* like a bible.
We talk during the film
and break into privacy during commercials   25
or get more coffee or push
the screen door open and urinate under the trees.

Laughing at the dilemmas of 1920 heroes
suggestive lines, cutaways to court officials
who raise their eyebrows at least 4 inches   30
when the lovers kiss . . .
only the anarchy of the evil Rupert of Hentzau°
is appreciated.
        And still somehow
by 1.30 we are moved
as Stewart Granger° girl-less and countryless   35
rides into the sunset with his morals and his horse.
The perfect world is over. Banana peels
orange peels ashtrays guitar books.
2 a.m. We stagger through
into the slow black rooms of the house.   40

I lie in bed fully awake. The darkness
breathes to the pace of a dog's snoring.
The film is replayed to sounds
of an intricate blues guitar.

LATE MOVIES WITH SKYLER.   32 *Rupert of Hentzau:* evil character in the *Prisoner of Zenda* (1952).
35 *Stewart Granger:* British actor (1913–1993) who appeared as the king in *The Prisoner of Zenda*.

Skyler is Rupert then the hero.   45
He will leave in a couple of days
for Montreal or the Maritimes.
In the movies of my childhood the heroes
after skilled swordplay and moral victories
leave with absolutely nothing   50
to do for the rest of their lives.

QUESTIONS

1. What value does the speaker place on old movies? What details does he intro-
    duce to contrast the world of movies with the world around him? What effect do
    the activities during the commercials have on the value of the film to Skyler
    and the speaker?

2. Who is Skyler? Where has he been? What has he been doing? What will he
    be doing in the future? What is the speaker's attitude toward Skyler and his
    activities?

3. What comic details can you discover in the poem? What makes them comic?
    How does this humor affect the speaker's sympathy for Skyler and for himself?

4. Describe the tone of the last four lines. In what way are the lines relevent to
    Skyler and to the speaker? To what degree are these lines integral to the poem?

ROBERT PINSKY   (b. 1940)

Dying _____ *1984*

Nothing to be said about it, and everything—
The change of changes, closer or further away:
The Golden Retriever next door, Gussie, is dead,

Like Sandy, the Cocker Spaniel from three doors down
Who died when I was small; and every day
Things that were in my memory fade and die.

Phrases die out: first, everyone forgets
What doornails are; then after certain decades
As a dead metaphor, *"dead as a doornail"* flickers

And fades away. But someone I know is dying—
And though one might say glibly, "everyone is,"
The different pace makes the difference absolute.

The tiny invisible spores in the air we breathe,
That settle harmlessly on our drinking water
And on our skin, happen to come together,

With certain conditions on the forest floor,
Or even a shady corner of the lawn—
And overnight the fleshy, pale stalks gather,

The colorless growth without a leaf or flower;
And around the stalks, the summer grass keeps growing   20
With steady pressure, like the insistent whiskers

That grow between shaves on a face, the nails
Growing and dying from the toes and fingers
At their own humble pace, oblivious

As the nerveless moths, that live their night or two—   25
Though like a moth a bright soul keeps on beating,
Bored and impatient in the monster's mouth.

QUESTIONS

1. What details about death does the poem introduce? How are they connected in the poem's development? What is the effect of these details on the tone of the poem?

2. What is meant by line 12, "The different pace makes the difference absolute"? How strongly does this statement counter the phrase "everyone is" in line 11?

3. Up until line 25 this poem can be considered negative or even despairing. What is the effect of lines 26 and 27 on this negative tone? What is the meaning of the phrase "monster's mouth" in these last two lines?

ALEXANDER POPE   (1685–1744)

From *Epilogue to the Satires, Dialogue I*
Lines 137–172 _____ *1738*

Virtue may choose the high or low degree,
'Tis just alike to Virtue, and to me;
Dwell in a monk, or light upon a king,
She's still the same, beloved, contented thing.   140
Vice is undone, if she forgets her birth,
And stoops from angels to the dregs of earth:
But 'tis the Fall degrades her to a whore;
Let Greatness own her, and she's mean no more:°
Her birth, her beauty, crowds and courts confess,°   145
Chaste matrons praise her, and grave bishops bless:
In golden chains the willing world she draws,
And hers the gospel is, and hers the laws:
Mounts the tribunal, lifts her scarlet head,

EPILOGUE TO THE SATIRES, DIALOGUE I.   144 *mean no more:* i.e., if the rich and powerful follow vice, vice is no longer low but fashionable.   145 *Her birth . . . confess:* i.e., under the dictates of fashion, both crowds and courts claim that Vice is both high-born and beautiful.

And sees pale Virtue carted° in her stead!   150
Lo! at the wheels of her triumphal car,°   *carriage*
Old England's genius, rough with many a scar,
Dragged in the dust! his arms hang idly round,
His flag inverted trails along the ground!°
Our youth, all liveried o'er with foreign gold,   155
Before her dance; behind her crawl the old!
See thronging millions to the pagod° run,
And offer country, parent, wife, or son!
Hear her black trumpet through the land proclaim,
That "not to be corrupted is the shame."   160
In soldier, churchman, patriot, man in power,
'Tis avarice all, ambition is no more!
See, all our nobles begging to be slaves!
See all our fools aspiring to be knaves!
The wit of cheats, the courage of a whore,   16
Are what ten thousand envy and adore.
All, all look up, with reverential awe,
On crimes that scape,° or triumph o'er the law: *escape*
While truth, worth, wisdom, daily they decry—
"Nothing is sacred now but villainy."   1
    Yet may this verse (if such a verse remain)
Show there was one who held it in disdain.

---

150 *carted:* It was an eighteenth-century punishment to display prostitutes in a cart; in addition, condemned criminals were carried in a cart from prison to Tyburn, in London, where they were hanged.   152–4 *Old England's genius . . . along the ground:* i.e., the spirit of England is humiliated by being tied to Vice's triumphal carriage and then dragged along the ground. The idea is that corrupt politicians have sacrificed England's defensive power for their own gain.   157 *pagod:* i.e., a pagoda, a symbol of how people have forsaken their own religion and adopted foreign religions.

QUESTIONS

1. The entire poem is in the form of a dialogue, in which these concluding lines are identified as being spoken by "P" (Pope). Should readers therefore take these lines as an expression of Pope's own ideas? In your answer, pay special attention to the final couplet.

2. Explain this poem as social satire. What is attacked? What evidence does the speaker advance to support his case that society has deserted virtue and religion?

3. Describe the poem's tone. What specific charges does the speaker make against the prevailing social-political structure?

4. How timely is the poem? To what degree might such charges be advanced in our society today?

SALVATORE QUASÍMODO   (1901–1968)

Auschwitz° ————————————————————————— *1983*

Translated by Jack Bevan

Far from the Vistula,° along the northern plain,
love, in a death-camp there at Auschwitz:
on the pole's rust and tangled fencing, rain
funeral cold.
No tree, no birds in the grey air   5
or above our thought, but limp
pain that memory leaves
to its silence without irony or anger.
You ask no elegies or idylls: only
the meaning of our destiny, you, here,   10
hurt by the mind's war,
uncertain at the clear
presence of life. For life is here
in every No that seems a certainty:
here we shall hear the angel weep, the monster, hear   15
our future time
beating the hereafter that is here, forever
in motion, not an image
of dreams, of possible pity.
Here are the myths, the metamorphoses.   20
Lacking the name of symbols or a god,
they are history, earth places,
they are Auschwitz, love. How suddenly
the dear forms of Alpheus and Arethusa°
changed into shadow-smoke!   25

Out of that hell hung with a white
inscription "work will make you free"°
there came the endless smoke
of many thousand women thrust at dawn
out of the kennels up to the firing-wall,   30
or, screaming for mercy to water, choked,
their skeleton mouths under the jets of gas.

AUSCHWITZ. *Auschwitz* is the German name for the town of Oswiecim in southern Poland, site
of the most notorious of the German concentration-extermination camps in World War II. There
were two major camps—Auschwitz itself, a former Polish army camp, and nearby Birkenau, which
contained many temporary barracks for worker-prisoners, together with gas chambers and cre-
matoria for the extermination of hundreds of thousands of victims.   1 *Vistula:* The Vistula
River rises in the northern Carpathian Mountains, south of Auschwitz.   24 *Alpheus and
Arethusa:* a river and fountain in Greece. In ancient mythology, Alpheus, who loved Arethusa, was
transformed into the river (bearing his name) to be united with Arethusa, who was transformed
into the fountain (bearing her name).   27 *work will make you free:* a translation of the large
metal sign *Arbeit macht frei*, which crested the main gate of Auschwitz and is still on display there. A
copy of the sign is displayed in the Holocaust Museum in Washington, D.C.

You, soldier, will find them in your annals
taking the forms of animals and rivers,
or are you too, now, ash of Auschwitz,   35
medal of silence?
Long tresses in glass urns can still be seen
bound up with charms, and an infinity
of ghostly little shoes and shawls of Jews:°
relics of a time of wisdom,   40
of man whose knowledge takes the shape of arms,
they are the myths, our metamorphoses.

Over the plains where love and sorrow
and pity rotted, there in the rain
a No inside us beat;   45
a No to death that died at Auschwitz
never from the pit of ashes
to show itself again.

37–39 *Long tresses . . . shawls of Jews:* Today the barracks at Auschwitz house permanent displays
that include the hair, shoes, eyeglasses, luggage, and clothing of thousands of the victims.

QUESTIONS

1. Compare the tone of the first ten lines with that of the last six. What differences
   do you notice? How does the idea of the last three lines answer the question
   posed in lines 9 and 10?

2. Even though the speaker is referring to the deadliest of all the camps, what
   does he mean by the lines "For life is here/in every No that seems a certainty"?

3. In line 20 the speaker mentions ancient myths about metamorphoses or transformations. What type of metamorphosis is linked to the death camps in lines
   26–42? What attitudes are brought out by this linkage?

ANNE RIDLER   (b. 1912)

Nothing Is Lost _____*1994*

Nothing is lost.
We are too sad to know that, or too blind;
Only in visited moments do we understand:
   It is not that the dead return—
      They are about us always, though unguessed.

      This penciled Latin verse
You dying wrote me, ten years past and more,
Brings you as much alive to me as the self you wrote it for,
   Dear father, as I read your words
      With no word but Alas.

Lines in a letter, lines in a face
Are faithful currents of life: the boy has written
His parents across his forehead, and as we burn
    Our bodies up each seven years,
        His own past self has left no plainer trace.   15

    Nothing dies.
The cells pass on their secrets, we betray them
Unknowingly: in a freckle, in the way
    We walk, recall some ancestor,
        And Adam in the color of our eyes.   20

    Yes, on the face of the new born,
Before the soul has taken full possession,
There pass, as over a screen, in succession
    The images of other beings:
        Face after face looks out, and then is gone.   25

    Nothing is lost, for all in love survive.
I lay my cheek against his sleeping limbs
To feel if he is warm, and touch in him
    Those children whom no shawl could warm,
        No arms, no grief, no longing could revive.   30

    Thus what we see, or know,
Is only a tiny portion, at the best,
Of the life in which we share; an iceberg's crest
    Our sunlit present, our partial sense,
        With deep supporting multitudes below.   35

QUESTIONS

1. What is unusual about the phrase "nothing dies" (line 16)? How successfully does the poet explain and exemplify the idea?
2. In what ways does the "face of the new born" reflect the "images of other beings" (lines 21–24)? How might the "color of our eyes" demonstrate that we are descended from Adam (line 20)? How true is it that "all in love survive" (line 26)?
3. In what ways might this poem offer comfort to readers who believe strongly in the concept of their own uniqueness and originality?

THEODORE ROETHKE   (1907–1963)

My Papa's Waltz ————————————————— *1942*

The whiskey on your breath
Could make a small boy dizzy;
But I hung on like death:
Such waltzing was not easy.

We romped until the pans   5
Slid from the kitchen shelf;
My mother's countenance
Could not unfrown itself.

The hand that held my wrist
Was battered on one knuckle;   10
At every step you missed
My right ear scraped a buckle.

You beat time on my head
With a palm caked hard by dirt,
Then waltzed me off to bed   15
Still clinging to your shirt.

QUESTIONS

1. What is the tone of the speaker's opening description of his father? What is the tone of the phrases "like death" and "such waltzing"?

2. What is the "waltz" the speaker describes? What is the tone of his words describing it in lines 5–15?

3. What does the reference to his "mother's countenance" contribute to the tone? What situation is suggested by the selection of the word "unfrown"?

4. What does the tone of the physical descriptions of the father contribute to your understanding of the speaker's attitude toward his childhood experiences as his father's dancing partner?

JONATHAN SWIFT   (1667–1745)

A Description of the Morning _____ *1709*

Now hardly here and there a hackney-coach
Appearing, showed the ruddy morn's approach.
Now Betty from her master's bed had flown,
And softly stole to discompose her own.
The slip-shod 'prentice from his master's door
Had pared the dirt, and sprinkled round the floor.
Now Moll had whirled her mop with dextrous airs,
Prepared to scrub the entry and the stairs.
The youth with broomy stumps began to trace
The kennel's edge,° where wheels had worn the place.
The small-coal man° was heard with cadence deep,   *charcoal seller*
Till drowned in shriller notes of chimney-sweep.
Duns° at his lordship's gate began to meet;   *bill collectors*
And brickdust Moll had screamed through half the street.

A DESCRIPTION OF THE MORNING.   10 *kennel's edge:* that is, the edge of the gutter. Swift annotated this line "To find old Nails."

The turnkey° now his flock returning sees,   15
Duly let out a-nights to steal for fees.
The watchful bailiffs take their silent stands,
And schoolboys lag° with satchels in their hands.

15 *turnkey:* an entrepreneur, operating a jail for profit, who allowed prisoners to go free at night so that they might bring him a night's booty to pay for the necessities provided them in jail. 18 *schoolboys lag:* cf. Shakespeare's *As You Like It,* II.7.145–147.

QUESTIONS

1. What images of life in early-eighteenth-century London are presented in this poem? Who is "Betty"? Why is she discomposing her bed? Are such images to be considered ordinary, heroic, or antiheroic? Why?

2. Why does Swift conclude with the reference to "schoolboys" lagging "with satchels in their hands"? Why would it not have been preferable to conclude with reference to adult behavior?

3. How do you know that Swift's poem is satiric? What is being satirized?

DAVID WAGONER   (b. 1926)

My Physics Teacher ——————————————————————— *1981*

He tried to convince us, but his billiard ball
Fell faster than his pingpong ball and thumped
To the floor first, in spite of Galileo.°
The rainbows from his prism skidded off-screen
Before we could tell an infra from an ultra.   5
His hand-cranked generator refused to spit
Sparks and settled for smoke. The dangling pith
Ignored the attractions of his amber wand,
No matter how much static he rubbed and dubbed
From the seat of his pants, and the housebrick   10
He lowered into a tub of water weighed
(Eureka!) more than the overflow.°

He believed in a World of Laws, where problems had answers,
Where tangible objects and intangible forces
Acting thereon could be lettered, numbered, and crammed   15

MY PHYSICS TEACHER.   3–12 *Galileo . . . overflow:* These lines describe classic classroom demonstrations in physics. Galileo first formulated the law of uniform falling bodies. Newton explained that a prism divides light into the colors of the rainbow. ("Infra" refers to infrared light; "ultra" to ultraviolet.) Sparks leaping across the space between two wires graphically demonstrate electrical generation and power. The motion of dried pith toward a charged piece of amber demonstrates the magnetic power of static electricity. Archimedes explained how the weight of a floating object is the same as the weight of water it displaces, and also how the volume of an immersed object (not the weight) is the same as the volume of displaced water. The physics teacher did not understand this distinction. (According to legend, Archimedes made this discovery when taking a bath, and then shouted "*Eureka!*" ["I have found it"].)

Through our tough skulls for lifetimes of homework.
But his only uncontestable demonstration
Came with our last class: he broke his chalk
On a formula, stooped to catch it, knocked his forehead
On the eraser-gutter, staggered slewfoot, and stuck   20
One foot forever into the wastebasket.

QUESTIONS

1. What idea underlies the physics teacher's use of classroom demonstrations?
   What is the speaker's apparent response to this idea?

2. What happens to these demonstrations? Why are these failures comic and farcical? What effect do the poem's farcical actions have upon the validity of the
   teacher's ideas?

C. K. WILLIAMS   (b. 1936)

Dimensions _____ *1969*

There is a world somewhere else that is unendurable.
Those who live in it are helpless in the hands of the elements,
they are like branches in the deep woods in wind
that whip their leaves off and slice the heart of the night
and sob. They are like boats bleating wearily in fog.

But here, no matter what, we know where we stand.
We know more or less what comes next. We hold out.
Sometimes a dream will shake us like little dogs, a fever
hang on so we're not ourselves or love wring us out,
but we prevail, we certify and make sure, we go on.

There is a world that uses its soldiers and widows
for flour, its orphans for building stone, its legs for pens.
In that place, eyes are softened and harmless like God's
and all blend in the traffic of their tragedy and pass by
like people. And sometimes one of us, losing the way,
will drift over the border and see them there, dying,
laughing, being revived. When we come home, we are half way.
Our screams heal the torn silence. We are like scars.

QUESTIONS

1. Why should this poem be called ironic? Should the irony be called situational?
   Cosmic? Why?

2. What is intended by the poem's title? What is the implication of the first line?
   What irony does the line bring out? Describe the irony of the second stanza
   (lines 6–10).

3. What is meant by "losing the way" and drifting " over the border" (lines 15–16)? What is the meaning and the irony of the last three lines? What does it mean to be "like scars" (line 18)?

WRITING ABOUT TONE IN POETRY

Be careful to note those elements of the work that touch particularly on attitudes or authorial consideration. Thus, for example, you may be studying Hughes's "Theme for English B," where it is necessary to consider the force of the poet's claim for equality. How serious is the claim? Does the speaker's apparent matter-of-factness make him seem less than enthusiastic? Or does this tone indicate that equality is so fundamental a right that its realization should be an everyday part of life? Devising and answering such questions can help you understand the degree to which authors show control of tone. Similar questions apply when you study internal qualities such as style and characterization.

Questions for Discovering Ideas

- What is the speaker like? Is he or she intelligent, observant, friendly, idealistic, realistic, trustworthy? How do you think you should respond to the speaker's characteristics?
- Do all the speeches seem right for the speaker and situation? Are all descriptions appropriate, all actions believable?
- If the work is comic, at what is the comedy directed? At situations? At characters? At the speaker himself or herself? What is the poet's apparent attitude toward the comic objects?
- Does the writer ask you to (1) sympathize with those in misfortune, (2) rejoice with those who have found happiness, (3) lament the human condition, (4) become angry against unfairness and inequality, (5) admire examples of noble human behavior, (6) have another appropriate emotional response?
- Do any words seem unusual or especially noteworthy, such as dialect, polysyllabic words, foreign words or phrases that the author assumes you know, or especially connotative words? What is the effect of such words on the poem's tone?

Strategies for Organizing Ideas

The goal of your essay is to examine all aspects bearing on the tone. Consider the following topics.

1. *The audience, situation, and characters.* Is any person or group directly addressed by the speaker? What attitude is expressed (love, respect, condescension, confidentiality, confidence, etc.)? What is the basic situation in the work? What is the nature of the speaker or persona? What is the relationship of the speaker to the material? What is the speaker's authority? Does the speaker give you the whole truth? Is he or she trying to withhold anything? Why? How is

the speaker's character manipulated to show apparent authorial attitude and to stimulate responses? Do you find any of the various sorts of irony? If so, what does the irony show (optimism or pessimism, for example)? How is the situation controlled to shape your responses? That is, can actions, situations, or characters be seen as expressions of attitude or as embodiments of certain favorable or unfavorable ideas or positions? How does the work promote respect, admiration, dislike, or other feelings about character or situation?

2. *Descriptions and diction.* Your concern here is to relate attitudes to the poet's use of language and description. Are there any systematic references, such as to colors, sounds, noises, natural scenes, and so on, that collectively reflect an attitude? Do connotative meanings of words control response in any way? Is any special knowledge of references or unusual words expected of readers? What is the extent of this knowledge? Do speech or dialect patterns indicate attitudes about speakers or their condition of life? Are speech patterns normal and standard or slang and substandard? What is the effect of these patterns? Are there unusual or particularly noteworthy expressions? If so, what attitudes do these show? Does the author use verbal irony? To what effect?

3. *Humor.* Is the work funny? How funny, how intense? How is the humor achieved? Does the humor develop out of incongruous situations or language, or both? Is there an underlying basis of attack in the humor, or are the objects of laughter still respected or even loved despite having humor directed against them?

4. *Ideas.* Ideas may be advocated, defended mildly, attacked, or ridiculed. Which attitude is present in the work you have been studying? How does the author make his or her attitude clear—directly, by statement, or indirectly, through understatement, overstatement, or the language of a character? In what ways does the work assume a common ground of assent between author and reader? That is, are there apparently common assumptions about religious views, political ideas, moral and behavioral standards, and so on? Are these common ideas readily acceptable, or is any concession needed by the reader to approach the work? (For example, a major subject of "Dover Beach" is that absolute belief in the truth of Christianity has been lost. This subject may not be important to everyone, but even an irreligious reader, or a follower of another faith, may find common ground in the poem's psychological situation or in the desire to learn as much as possible about so important an institution as religion.)

5. *Unique characteristics.* Each work has unique properties that contribute to the tone. Anne Bradstreet, for example, in "The Author to Her Book," introduces the metaphor that her work is like an unwanted child whom she is sending out into the world. Her apology hence introduces a tone of amused but sincere self-effacement that the reader must consider. Theodore Roethke's "My Papa's Waltz" is a brief narrative in which the speaker's recollected feelings about his father's boisterously drunken behavior must be inferred from understatement. Hardy's "Channel Firing" develops from the comic idea that the firing of guns at sea is so loud it could awaken the dead. Be alert for such

special circumstances in the poem you are considering, and as you plan and develop your essay, take them into account.

Your conclusion may summarize your main points and from there go on to any needed definitions, explanations, or afterthoughts, together with ideas reinforcing earlier points. If you have changed your mind or have made new realizations, briefly explain these. Finally, you might mention some other major aspect of the work's tone that you did not develop in the body.

DEMONSTRATIVE STUDENT ESSAY

The Shifting Attitudes of Sharon Olds's Speaker in "The Planned Child"°

[1]   "The Planned Child" is a striking and unusual poem because in it Sharon Olds deals frankly with her speaker's concern about the circumstances of her conception and birth. Few people ever learn about how they were conceived, and even fewer ever think about it enough to criticize it, and yet the poem's details concern this topic. As unusual as such details are, however, the poem's power results from the way the speaker traces the development of her attitudes toward her conception and birth--from hate, to uncertainty, to acceptance.* These attitudes are traceable in the development of the poem's two stanzas, Olds's ordinary diction, and her use of the first-person pronoun.†

[2]   Olds's first stanza contrasts the speaker's hatred for planning and organization with her preference for disorganization. The stanza is arresting because in it the speaker considers her feelings about how her mother calculated ovulation times to ensure conception. Rather than finding it humorous that she owes her existence to the chart her mother made on a laundry cardboard, the speaker says she hated this planned record keeping. To her way of thinking, such planning reduced her to little more than a cold and impersonal X on a rising graph line. From the description the speaker makes of conception in lines 7 and 8, it would seem that spontaneous and disorganized love by her parents would have made the act of her creation more warm and welcoming.

[3]   The second stanza is continuous with the first because it stems out of feelings occasioned by an unplanned but significant moment. A friend serves wine to the speaker and tells her that she seems to have been "a child who had been *wanted*" (line 12, italics added). This casual social event is symbolic (is it a kind of communion experience?) because it gives the speaker a life-giving insight into her existence. The conclusion of the poem is then devoted to the speaker's newly created feelings of involvement with her mother. She finds affection for her mother in the details of childbirth--bearing down, breathing, pressing, and the speaker's emergence into life. The poem's climax is the speaker's apparently amazed realization that her friend was right; she herself was actually *wanted*. The X on the graph therefore was a means of achieving a far greater

---

° See p. 824 for this poem.
* Central idea.
† Thesis sentence.

goal, for her mother valued her more than the world or the galaxy. This realization makes the speaker recognize the love that created her, and she then senses her own vital importance.

[4]

With such an unusual topic, one might expect a fair amount of abstract and medical diction, but such is not the case. Most of the words are flat and ordinary (e.g., "a friend was pouring wine"). Despite this simplicity, however, the diction confronts readers with direct physical details of planned conception and the labor of childbirth. The speaker refers matter-of-factly to a temperature chart, the birth canal, and breathing into a mask and bearing down during labor. Of major note is the intensity that Olds achieves through the selection of simple but strong verbs and verbals ("hated," "planned," "had taken," "sliding," "made," "pouring," "were moving," "bearing down," "breathing," "pressing," and "cartwheeling"). All these words fit the speaker's aim to connect herself with one of life's most basic facts--conception and delivery.

[5]

As the poem's details indicate, the central concern is the speaker and her attitudes. This centrality is emphasized by Olds's constant use of the first person pronoun. A form of the pronoun appears twelve times, and the poem begins with "I" and concludes with "me." This number may not seem high in a personal poem of twenty-two lines, but it is high enough to support the idea that the poem is about attitudes toward oneself. These attitudes emerge through the speaker's implied personal questions: Could she still love herself while knowing that she was planned and not spontaneous? Her answer is clearly no, not when these calculations seemed to result from nothing more than cold science. But could she love herself after learning that the calculations were preceded by love for her? Yes, and as a result the speaker makes inferences from this new information. She imagines that nothing in the world was more important to her mother than she. She therefore has more value than the earth and stars themselves, and this vision closes the poem on a strongly positive and affirmative note in lines 19-22:

> not the moon, the sun, Orion
> cartwheeling across the dark, not
> the earth, the sea--none of it
> was enough, for her, without me.

[6]

Thus, "The Planned Child" is a confession of changing attitudes in the light of a growing sense of personal origin. Olds develops these attitudes through the commonness and universality of details about birth. Yet the poem is not overly personal or egocentric because it is about the need of discovering who one is. Without this knowledge, the poem's speaker is uncertain and hostile. But once she sees that she is part of a pattern of love and creativity, she becomes positive and assertive. "The Planned Child" shows the growth of confidence resulting from increased knowledge and awareness.

Commentary on the Essay

Because this essay embodies a number of approaches by which tone may be studied in any work (situation, diction, special characteristics), it is typical of many essays that use a combined approach. The central idea, expressed in the first paragraph, is that the dominant attitudes in "The Planned Child" are the speaker's change from uncertainty and hostility to certainty and love.

Paragraph 2 considers the poem's first section, in which the speaker explains why a preference for spontaneity caused her initial hatred of how she came into being (see strategy 4, p. 836). Paragraph 3 shows how the explanation of a unique situation can be seen as a feature of tone (strategy 5). The paragraph pursues the speaker's thoughts that develop from an unexpected comment from a friend. In this sense, a casual moment explains how the speaker's confusion gives way to greater self-confidence and an acceptance of her mother's labors to bring her into the world.

Paragraph 4 concerns the poem's treatment of the unusual subject matter through comparatively simple diction (strategy 2). Words in the paragraph that indicate attitudes are "flat and ordinary," "confronts," "matter-of-factly," and "intensity." Paragraph 5 considers how the frequent appearance of the first-person pronoun fits into the poem's recognition of the speaker's importance (strategy 1). The paragraph asserts that the poem's positive conclusion is augmented by images on a planetary, solar, galactic, geographic, and marine scale (strategy 5).

The concluding paragraph points out that the speaker's concern with her origins is not a matter of egocentrism but rather results from her need to connect with an attitude that is more human and loving than calculated planning might indicate.

SPECIAL TOPICS FOR WRITING AND ARGUMENT ABOUT TONE IN POETRY

1. Consider "homage to my hips," "she being Brand / -new," "The Workbox," and "The First-Rate Wife" as poems about love. What similarities do you find? That is, do the poets state that love creates joy, satisfaction, distress, embarrassment, trouble? How does the tone of each of the poems enable you to draw your conclusions? What differences do you find in the ways the poets either control or do not control tone?

2. Consider these same poems from a feminist viewpoint (see Chapter 33). What importance and value do the poems give to women? How do they view women's actions? Generally, what praise or blame do the poems deserve because of their treatment of women?

3. a. Consider the tone of Roethke's "My Papa's Waltz." Some readers have concluded that the speaker is expressing fond memories of his childhood experiences with his father. Others believe that the speaker is ambiguous about the father and that he blocks out remembered pain as he describes the father's boisterousness in the kitchen. Basing your conclusion on the tone of the poem alone, how should the poem be interpreted?

   b. In your library, find two critical biographies about Theodore Roethke published by university presses. What do these books disclose about Roethke's childhood and his family, particularly his father? On the basis of what you learn, should your interpretation of the tone of "My Papa's Waltz" be changed or unchanged? Why?

4. Write a poem about a person or occasion that has made you either glad or angry. Try to create the same feelings in your reader, but create these feelings through your rendering of situation and your choices of the right words. (Possible topics: a social injustice, an unfair grade, a compliment you have received on a task well done, the landing of a good job, the winning of a game, a rise in the price of gasoline, a good book or movie, and so on.)

5. What judgments about modern city life do you think that Léger conveys in his painting *The City* (Insert II, front top)? If the tone of paintings can be considered similar to poetic tone, in what ways is *The City* comparable to the presentation of detail in Blake's "London" (Chapter 14), Eliot's "Preludes" (Chapter 16), Sandburg's "Chicago" (Chapter 25), and Swift's "A Description of the Morning"—together with any other poems you wish to include?

6. Quasímodo's "Auschwitz" concerns one of the twentieth century's central evils, about which people have expressed anger, horror, indignation, outrage, disgust, hatred, and vengefulness. To what degree do you find these attitudes in Quasímodo's poem? Do these attitudes, or others, govern the poem's tone?

Prosody: Sound, Rhythm, and Rhyme in Poetry

Prosody (the pronunciation of a song or poem) is the general word describing the study of poetic sounds and rhythms. Common alternative words are **metrics, versification, mechanics of verse,** and the **music of poetry.** Most readers, when reading poetry aloud, interpret the lines and develop an appropriate speed and expressiveness of delivery—a proper *rhythm*. Indeed, some people think of rhythm and sound as the *music* of poetry because they convey musical rhythms and tempos. Like music, poetry often requires a regular beat. The tempo and loudness of poetry may vary freely, however, and a reader may stop at any time to repeat the sounds and to think about the words and ideas.

In considering prosody, we should recognize that poets, being especially attuned to language, blend words and ideas together so that "the sound" becomes "an echo to the sense" (Pope, *An Essay on Criticism*). The consequence of this idea is that *prosodic technique cannot be separated from a poem's content.* For this reason, the study of prosody aims to determine how poets control their words so that the sound of a poem complements its expression of emotions and ideas.

IMPORTANT DEFINITIONS FOR STUDYING PROSODY

To understand and discuss prosody, you need to be able to explain the various sounds of both speech and poetry. Let us grant that the subject is technical, detailed, and also subtle, and as a result, the study of vocal production can take, and has taken, entire careers. An introductory knowledge of spoken sound, however, will enable you to analyze that aspect of the poet's craft that pertains to qualities of pronunciation and rhythm.

Vowel Sounds Create the Flow of Poetic Speech

The continuous stream of speech, whether conversation, oratory, or poetry, is provided mainly by **vowel sounds.** A vowel (from the Latin word *vox,* or "voice") results from vibrations resonating in the space between the tongue and the top of the mouth. As our tongues go up or down or forward or backward, or as they curl or flatten out, and as our lips move synchronously with our tongues, we form vowels. Some vowels are "long," such as ē (flee), ā (stay), ō (open), and ōō (food). Others are "short," such as ĭ (fit), ŭ (fun) and ĕ (set). Some vowels are called "front" (e.g., see, play) and some are called "back" (knowing, moon), depending on the position of the tongue in the production of the sound. Some are rounded (hōpe, hōōp) because their production requires pursed lips, but more are unrounded (green, swim).

Many of our English vowel sounds are pronounced as a **schwa,** or minimal vowel sound, despite their spellings (e.g., the *e* in "th*e* boy," the *a* in "*a*lone"). Thus, *a*bout," "stag*e*s," "rap*i*d," "nati*o*n," and "circ*u*s" contain the vowels *a, e, i, o,* and *u,* but all the italicized letters make the same schwa sound, which in pronunciation receives a light stress.

Of special importance is the **diphthong** (two voices, two sounds), that is, a meaningful sound that begins with one vowel sound and then is completed by the movement to another vowel sound. The three English diphthongs are *i* (try, appl*i*ance), *ou* (h*ou*se, sh*ou*t), and *oi* (f*oi*l, empl*oy*).

Consonant Sounds Are Meaningful Sounds Produced through the Creation of Vocal Obstructions in the Mouth

Consonant sounds "sounds made at the same time [as vowels]" result from the touching and near touching of various parts of the mouth (lips, tongue, teeth, palate), thus producing meaningful sounds obstructing the flow of vowel sound. Some consonants are continuous (e.g., *m, h, sh*), while others are momentary (*t, k*). In combination, consonants and vowels make for understandable speech. The consonants are classified into three major groups.

1. STOP SOUNDS, ALSO CALLED PLOSIVES, ARE PERCUSSIVE AND ABRUPT.   There are six stop sounds, which are made by the momentary stoppage and release of breath either when the lips touch each other (*p* and *b*) or when the tongue touches the palate (*k* and *g*) or the alveolar ridge above the teeth (*t* and *d*).

2. CONTINUANT SOUNDS ARE SMOOTH AND FLOWING.   They are produced by the steady release of the breath in conjunction with various positions of the tongue in relation to the lips, teeth, and palate, as in *n, ng, l, r, th* (as in *th*orn), *th* (as in *th*e), *f, v, s, z, sh* (as in *sh*arp), and *zh* (as in plea*s*ure); or with the touching of the lower lip and upper teeth for the sounds *f* and *v*; or with the touching of both lips for the sound *m*. Two special sounds called *affricates*

begin with the stops *t* and *d* and then become the continuants *sh* and *zh* (as in *ch*ew and ju*dg*e).

3. Semivowel Sounds Are More Like Consonants Than Vowels.

They are midway between vowels and consonants, and they have in common that they move from an originating sound and then move to another vowel sound. They are *w* (*w*agon, *w*in, *w*eather), *y* (*y*es, *y*oung, *u*nion), and *h* (*h*ope, *h*eap).

Consonants may be either voiced or voiceless. Voiced consonants are produced with the vibration of the vocal chords (e.g., *b, d, g, v, z, zh*), and voiceless consonants are produced by the breath alone, in this way being whispered sounds (e.g., *p, t, k, f, s, sh*). Among the semivowels, w and y are voiced, but *h* is voiceless.

Nasal consonants result from the release of sound through the nose. Three consonants require the stoppage of the breath in the mouth so that the sound can be released through the nose. The consonants, called *nasals,* are *n, m,* and *ng* (as in su*n*, su*m*, and su*ng*). In English, the *n* and *m* sounds may begin and end words or may appear in the middle of a word, whereas the *ng* sound may appear in the middle or end but may not begin a word. The nasals affect the pronunciation of adjoining consonants, as in words like *mountain* and *student,* in which the *t* and *d* sounds are released nasally by many speakers of English. Adjoining consonants also affect the pronunciation of the nasal, as in words like *sink* and *think,* in which the concluding *k* sound causes the preceding nasal to be an *ng* sound, as in *sing* and *thing,* even though the sound is spelled with an *n* alone.

SEGMENTS: INDIVIDUALLY MEANINGFUL SOUNDS

Individual sounds in combination make up syllables and words, and separate words in combination make up lines of poetry. Syllables and words are made up of **segments,** or individually meaningful sounds (which linguists call *segmental phonemes*). In the word *top,* there are three segments: *t, o,* and *p.* When you hear these three sounds in order, you recognize the word *top,* as distinguished from, say, *tape* and *type.* It takes three alphabetical letters—*t, o,* and *p*—to spell (or *graph*) *top,* because each letter is identical with a segment. Quite often, however, English uses more than one letter to spell a segment. For example, in the word *enough,* there are four segments (*e, n, ŭ, f*), although six letters are required for the correct spelling: *e, n, ou,* and *gh.* The last two segments (*ŭ* and *f*) require two letters each (two letters forming one segment are called a *digraph*). In the word *through* there are three segments but *seven* letters. To be spelled correctly in this word, the *ōō* segment must have four letters (*ough*). Note, however, that in the word *flute,* the *ōō* segment requires only one letter, *u.* When we study the effects of various segments in relationship to the poetic rhythm, we deal with **sound;** usually our concern is with prosodic devices such as **alliteration, assonance,** and **rhyme.**

When segments are meaningfully combined, they make up syllables and words. A **syllable,** in both prose and poetry, consists of a single meaningful strand of sound such as the article *a* in "*a* table," the stem *lin* in "*lin*en," and the entire word *screech.* The article *a,* which is both a syllable and a word, has only one segment; *lin,* the first syllable of a two-syllable word, contains three segments (*lin* does not occur alone but is used in combinations such as *lingerie* and *linoleum*); *screech* is a complete word of one syllable consisting of the five segments *s, k, r, ee,* and *tch.* The past tense of *screech* (*screeched*) adds one meaningful sound, *t,* and two letters, *ed,* but this additional sound does not create a new syllable. The understanding of what constitutes syllables is important because poetic rhythm is determined by the positions of heavily stressed and less heavily stressed syllables.

Distinguish between Spellings and the Actual Sounds of Words

It is important—vital—to understand the differences between spelling, or **graphics,** and pronunciation, or **phonetics.** Not all English sounds are spelled and pronounced in the same way, as with *top.* Thus the letter s has three very different sounds in the words *sweet, sugar,* and *flows: s, sh* ("sharp"), and *z.* On the other hand, the words *shape, ocean, nation, sure, fissure, Eschscholtzia,* and *machine* use different letters or combinations of letters to spell the *sh* sound.

Vowel sounds may also be spelled in different ways. The *ē* sound, for example, can be spelled *i* in *machine, ee* in *speed, ea* in *eat, e* in *even,* and *y* in *funny,* yet the vowel sounds in *eat, break,* and *bear* are not the same even though they are spelled the same. Remember this: With both consonants and vowel sounds, *do not confuse spellings with sounds.*

POETIC RHYTHM

Rhythm in speech is a combination of vocal speeds, rises and falls, starts and stops, vigor and slackness, and relaxation and tension. In ordinary speech and in prose, rhythm is not as important as the flow of ideas. In poetry, rhythm is significant because poetry is emotionally charged, compact, and intense. Poets invite us to change speeds while reading—to slow down and linger over some words and sounds and to pass rapidly over others. They also invite us to give more-than-ordinary vocal stress or emphasis to certain syllables and less stress to others. The more intense syllables are called **heavy stress** syllables, and it is the heavy stresses that determine the **accent** or **beat** of a poetic line. The less intense syllables receive **light stress.** In traditional verse, poets select patterns called **feet,** which consist of a regularized relationship of heavy stresses to light stresses.

Scansion Is the Systematic Study of Poetic Rhythm

To study the patterns of versification in any poem, you **scan** the poem. The act of scanning—**scansion**—enables you to discover how the poem establishes a prevailing metrical pattern, and also how and why there are variations in the pattern.

DETERMINE STRESSES OR BEATS.   In the scansion of a poem, it is important to use a commonly recognized notational system to record stresses or accents. A *heavy* or *primary* stress (also called an **accented syllable**) is commonly indicated by a prime mark or acute accent (´). A *light* stress (also called an **unaccented syllable**) is indicated by a bowl-like half circle called a **breve** (˘) or sometimes by a raised circle or degree sign (°). To separate one foot from another, a **virgule** or slash (/) is used. Thus, the following line, from Coleridge's "The Rime of the Ancient Mariner," is schematized formally in this way:

$$\text{Wa - ter, / wa - ter, / ev - ery where, /}$$

Here the virgules or slashes show that the line contains two two-syllable feet followed by a single three-syllable foot.

DETERMINE THE METER OR MEASURE.   Another important part of scansion is the determination of a poem's **meter,** or the number of feet in its lines. Lines containing five feet are **pentameter,** four are **tetrameter,** three are **trimeter,** two are **dimeter,** and one is **monometer.** (To these may be added the less common line lengths **hexameter,** a six-foot line; **heptameter** or the **septenary,** seven feet; and **octameter,** eight feet.) In terms of accent or beat, a trimeter line has three beats (heavy stresses), a pentameter line five beats, and so on.

THE MAJOR METRICAL FEET

You are now ready to scan poems and to determine the patterns of metrical feet, which measure the relationships of syllables and stresses. In English the names of the feet are derived from Greek poetry. We may classify them as feet of two syllables, three syllables, and one syllable (or imperfect).

The Two-Syllable Foot

1. IAMB (LIGHT/HEAVY).   The most important poetic foot in English is the **iamb** (a word of unknown origin), which contains a light stress followed by a heavy stress:

the winds   *Meaning first*
              Sound second

The iamb is the most important and most common foot because it most nearly duplicates natural speech while also elevating speech to poetry. It is the most versatile of English poetic feet, and it is capable of great variation. Even within the same line, iambic feet vary in intensity, so that they may support or undergird the shades of meaning designed by the poet. For example, in this line of iambic pentameter from Wordsworth's sonnet "The World Is Too Much with Us," each foot is unique:

The winds / that will / be howl- / ing at / all hours, /

Even though "will" and "at" receive the heavy stress in their individual iambic positions, they are not as strongly emphasized as "winds," "howl-," and "hours" (indeed, they are also less strong than "all," which is in the light-stress position in the concluding iamb). Such variability, approximating the stresses and rhythms of actual speech, makes the iamb suitable for both serious and light verse, and it therefore helps poets to focus attention on ideas and emotions. If they use it with skill, it never becomes monotonous, for it does not distract readers by drawing attention to its own rhythm.

2. TROCHEE (HEAVY/LIGHT). The **trochee** (*running*), sometimes called the **choree** (*dancing*), consists of a heavy accent followed by a light one:

flow - er

Rhythmically, most two-syllable English words are trochaic, as may be seen in words like *author, early, follow, major, morning, often, singing, snowfall, something, story, water, walking, willow,* and *window.* A major exception is seen in many two-syllable words beginning with prefixes, such as *sublime, because,* and *impel.* Another exception is found in two-syllable words that are borrowed from another language but are still pronounced as in the original language, as with *machine, technique, garage,* and *chemise,* all of which are recent importations from French, in which an iambic structure prevails. Illustrating the strength of trochaic rhythms in English, however, the final stresses in many French words borrowed six hundred or more years ago now accent the next-to-last syllable, as with *apartment, cherry, expression, language, lesson, nation,* and *very.*

Because trochaic rhythm has often been called *falling, dying, light,* or *anti-climactic,* and because iambic rhythm has been called *rising, elevating, serious,* and *climactic,* poets have preferred the iambic foot. They therefore have arranged various placements of single- and multiple-syllable words, and have also used a variety of other means, so that the heavy-stress syllable is at the end of the foot, as in Shakespeare's

With - in / his bend - / ing sick - /le's com - / pass come, /

in which three successive trochaic words (*bending, sickle's,* and *compass*) are arranged to match the iambic meter.

3. Spondee (Heavy/Heavy).   The **spondee** (originally two long notes played at the pouring of an offering)—also called a **hovering accent**—consists of two successive, equally heavy accents, as in "men's eyes" in Shakespeare's line

When, in / dis -grace / with For - / tune and / men's eyes, /

The spondee is mainly a substitute foot in English verse because successive spondees usually become iambs or trochees. An entire poem written in spondees would be unlikely within traditional metrical patterns and ordinary English syntax (but see Brooks's poem "We Real Cool"). As a substitute, however, the spondee creates emphasis. The usual way to indicate the spondaic foot is to link the two syllables together with chevronlike marks like this:

men's eyes

4. Pyrrhic (Light/Light).   The **pyrrhic** (a foot, a war dance) consists of two unstressed syllables, even though one of them may be in a normally stressed position, as in "on their" in this line from Pope's *Pastorals:*

Now sleep - / ing flocks / on their / soft flee - /ces lie. /

The pyrrhic is made up of weakly accented words such as prepositions (e.g., *on, to*) and articles (*the, a*). Like the spondee, it is a substitute foot for an iamb or a trochee. An entire poem could not be in pyrrhics because the pyrrhics, like spondees, would be resolved as trochees and iambs. As a substitute foot, however, the pyrrhic acts as a rhythmic catapult to move the reader swiftly to the next heavy-stress syllable, and therefore it undergirds the ideas conveyed by more important words.

The Three-Syllable Foot

1. Dactyl (Heavy/Light/Light).   The **dactyl** (after the shape of a finger, which has a long joint and two shorter joints) has a heavy stress followed by two lights:

green as our / hope in it, / white as our/ faith in it. /   (Swinburne)

2. Anapest (Light/Light/Heavy).   The **anapest** ("beaten back", or "turned around"; the reverse of a dactyl) consists of two light accents followed by a heavy accent:

by the dawn's / ear-ly light.   (Key)

The Imperfect Foot

A single stressed syllable (´) by itself or an unstressed syllable (˘) by itself creates an **imperfect foot.** This foot is a variant or substitute occurring in a poem in which one of the major feet forms the metrical pattern. The second line of Key's "The Star-Spangled Banner," for example, is anapestic, but it contains an imperfect foot at the end:

What so proud -/ly we hailed/at the twi-/light's last gleam-/ing. /

SPECIAL METERS

In many poems you will find meters other than those described above. Poets like Browning, Tennyson, Poe, and Swinburne introduce special or unusual meters. Other poets manipulate pauses or **caesurae** (discussed later) to create the effects of unusual meters. For these reasons, you should know about metrical feet such as the following:

1. **Amphibrach** (short at both ends). A light, heavy, and light:

    Ah feed me / and fill me / with pleas - sure. (Swinburne)

2. **Amphimacer** (long at both ends) or **Cretic** (a song from the island of Crete). A heavy, light, and heavy:

    Love is best. (Browning)

3. **Bacchius** or **Bacchic** (pertaining to Bacchus, the god of wine and conviviality). A light stress followed by two heavy stresses:

    Some late lark / [sing -ing]. (Henley)

4. **Dipodic Measure** (literally, "two feet" combining to make one), or **syzygy** (a yoking together). Dipodic measure develops in longer lines when a poet submerges two regular feet under a stronger beat, so that a "galloping" or "rollicking" rhythm results. The following line from Masefield's "Cargoes," for example, can be scanned as trochaic hexameter, with the concluding foot being an iamb:

    Quin-que- / reme of / Nin-e- / veh from / dis-tant / O-phir,

    In reading, however, a stronger beat is superimposed, which makes one foot out of two—dipodic measure or syzygy:

    Quin-quer-eme of / Nin-e veh / from dis-tant O-phir,

SUBSTITUTION

Most regular poems (i.e., poems written according to the "rules" of prosody) follow a formal pattern that may be analyzed according to the feet we have been describing here. Too much formal regularity, however, sometimes makes for monotony, and so for interest and emphasis (and also, especially, because of the natural rhythms of English speech), poets frequently alter and enlarge the regular patterns through the **substitution** of a dominant foot by a variant foot. Thus in an iambic line the poet may insert a spondee or an anapest and by this means may provide a wider and more conversational rhythmical range than the unvarying use of the poem's chosen pattern can achieve. As an example, the pattern of Swift's "A Description of the Morning" (Chapter 18) is iambic pentameter (i.e., five iambs per line). However, Swift introduces a formal substitution at the beginning of the following line:

Duns at/ his lord - / ship's gate / be - gan / to meet;

The first foot is a trochee, and the strong accent on *Duns* enables Swift to stress his comic assertion that even a member of the nobility, who supposedly has the money to pay his bills, does not do so and therefore is dunned by bill collectors. Note also that the light accent on *at* enables the voice to move rapidly through *at his lord*. Thus, although the first two feet are a trochee and an iamb, the rhythmical effect is that of an imperfect foot followed by an anapest. This simple substitution helps Swift to emphasize and satirize the unglamorous side of London life early in the eighteenth century.

When studying rhythm, your main concern in noting substitutions is to determine the formal metrical pattern and then to analyze the variations on this pattern and their principal techniques and effects. Always try to show how these variations have enabled the poet to get points across and to achieve emphasis.

ACCENTUAL, STRONG-STRESS, AND "SPRUNG" RHYTHMS

The foregoing descriptions of poetic feet will enable the analysis of most so-called traditional poetry. A number of poets, however stretch the bounds of traditional feet and use generally unmeasured rhythms derived from accentual or strong stresses. Such lines are historically linked to the poetry of Old English (see Chapter 13). At that time, each line was divided in two, with two major stresses, also alliterated, occurring in each half. In the nineteenth century, Gerard Manley Hopkins (1844–1889) developed what he called "sprung" rhythm, a rhythm in which the major stresses would be released or "sprung" from the line. The method is complex, but a primary characteristic is the placement together of one-syllable stressed words, as in this line from "Pied Beauty":

Wĭth swíft, slów; sweét, soúr; adázzlĕ, dím;

Here a number of elements combine to create six major stresses. Many of Hopkins's lines combine alliteration and strong stresses in this way to create the same heavy emphasis.

A parallel instance of strongly stressed lines is seen in "We Real Cool" by Brooks. In this poem the effect is achieved by the exclusive use of monosyllabic stressed words combined with internal rhyme, repetition, and alliteration.

THE CAESURA: THE PAUSE CREATING VARIETY AND NATURAL RHYTHMS IN POETRY

Whenever we speak, we run words together rapidly, without pause, but we do stop briefly and almost unnoticeably between significant units or phrases. Intelligible conversation could not take place without these pauses, which, both grammatically and rhythmically, create separate units of meaning called **cadence groups.** In poetry using a regular meter, the cadence groups operate just as they do in prose to make ideas clear. That is, while we follow the poetic measures, we also pause briefly at the ends of phrases, and we pause longer, for emphasis, at the ends of sentences. In scansion, the name of these pauses, which linguists call *junctures,* is **caesura** (a "cutting off"), pluralized as **caesurae.** When writing out our scansion of a line, we use two diagonal slashes or virgules (//) to indicate a caesura so that the caesura can be distinguished from the single virgule separating feet. Often the caesura coincides with the end of a foot, as at the end of the second iamb in this line by William Blake ("To Mrs. Anna Flaxman"):

Wĭth hánds / dĭ- víne // hĕ móv'd / thĕ gén - / tlĕ Sód. /

The caesura, however, may fall within a foot, and there may be more than one in a line, as within the second and third iambs in this line by Ben Jonson:

Thŏu árt / nŏt, // Péns - / húrst, // búilt / tŏ én - / vĭous shów. /

When a caesura ends a line, usually marked by a comma, semicolon, or period, that line is **end-stopped**, as in this famous line opening Keats's "Endymion" :

Ă thíng / ŏf beáu - / tў // ĭs / ă jóy / fŏr - év - ĕr. //

If a line has no punctuation at the end and the thought carries over to the next line, it is called **run-on.** A term also used to indicate run-on lines is

enjambement. The following passage, a continuation of the line from Keats, contains three run-on lines:

> Its loveliness increases; // it will never
> Pass into nothingness; // but still will keep
> A bower quiet for us, // and a sleep
> Full of sweet dreams, // . . .

It is important to recognize that the formal rhythms of poetry are superimposed on the rhythms of natural speech, creating a tension between the two. By manipulating the placement of caesurae, the pauses that fall randomly in speech, poets create many of the variant rhythms that are provided by formal substitution. If the poet ends a cadence group within a foot, the pause, or caesura, may cause us actually to *hear* trochees, amphibrachs, and other variant feet even though the line may scan correctly and regularly in the established meter. This type of *de facto* variation is **rhetorical substitution.** A noteworthy example in an iambic pentameter line is this one from the first Epistle of Pope's *Essay on Man:*

> His ac-/tions', // pas-/sions', // be-/ing's, // use/and end.

This is the second line in a "heroic" couplet, which theoretically requires that there should be only a single caesura following the fourth syllable. In this line, however, Pope provides us with great rhythmical variety. He uses not one but rather three caesurae, each of them producing an emphatic pause or juncture. Pope's line is regularly iambic, but the effect is different in actual reading or speaking. Because of the caesurae after the third, fifth, and seventh syllables, the rhythm produces an amphibrach, a trochee, another trochee, and an amphimacer. The effect is a skillful line containing two inner two-syllable feet framed by two three-syllable feet thus:

> His ac-tions', // pas-sions', // be-ing's, // use and end./
>
> AMPHIBRACH   TROCHEE   TROCHEE   AMPHIMACER

The spoken substitutions effected by the caesurae in this regular line produce the effect of substitution—rhetorical substitution—and therefore tension and interest. Never believe that Pope did not know what he was doing.

SEGMENTAL POETIC DEVICES

Once you have completed your analysis of rhythms, you should consider the segmental poetic devices in the poem. Usually these devices are used to create emphasis, but sometimes in context they may echo or imitate actions and objects. The segmental devices most common in poetry are *assonance, alliteration, onomatopoeia,* and *euphony and cacophony.*

assonants
Contarants
us rhynes,

Identical Vowel Sounds Create Assonance

Assonance is the repetition of identical *vowel* sounds in different words—for example, the short *ĭ* in "sw*i*ft Cam*i*lla sk*i*ms." It is a strong means of emphasis, as in the following line, where the *ŭ* sound connects the two words *lull* and *slumber,* and the short *ĭ* connects *him, in,* and *his:*

And more, to l*ŭ*ll h*ĭ*m *ĭ*n h*ĭ*s sl*ŭ*mber soft.   (Spenser)

Identical Consonant Sounds Create Alliteration

Like assonance, **alliteration** is a means of highlighting ideas by words containing the same consonant sound—for example, the repeated *m* in Spenser's "*M*ixed with a *m*ur*m*uring wind," or the *s* sound in Edmund Waller's praise of Oliver Cromwell, "Your never-failing *s*word made war to cea*s*e," which emphasizes the connection between the words "sword" and "cease."

There are two kinds of alliteration. Most commonly, alliteration is regarded as the repetition of identical consonant sounds that begin syllables in close patterns—for example, in Pope's lines "La*b*orious, heavy, *b*usy, *b*old, and *b*lind," "While *p*ensive *p*oets *p*ainful vigils keep," and "*br*azen *br*ainless *br*others." When used judiciously, alliteration gives strength to ideas by emphasizing key words, but too much *c*an *c*ause *c*omic and *c*atastrophic *c*onsequences.

The second form of alliteration occurs when a poet repeats identical or similar consonant sounds that do not begin syllables but nevertheless create a pattern—for example, the *z* segment in the line "In the*s*e places free*z*ing bree*z*es ea*s*ily cau*s*e snee*z*es," or the *m, b,* and *p* segments (all of which are made *bilabially,* that is, with both lips) in "The *m*isera*b*ly *m*u*m*bling and *m*o*m*entously *m*ur*m*uring *b*eggar *p*ro*p*els *p*egs and *p*e*bb*les in the *b*u*bb*ling *p*ool." Such clearly designed patterns are hard to overlook.

Verbal Imitation of Real Sounds Is Onomatopoeia, Sometimes Called Poetic Sound Effects

Onomatopoeia is a blend of consonant and vowel sounds designed to *imitate* or *suggest* a situation or an action. It is made possible in poetry because many English words are **echoic** in origin; that is, they are verbal echoes of the actions they describe, such as *buzz, bump, slap,* and so on. In "The Bells," Poe uses such words to create onomatopoeia. Through the combined use of assonance and alliteration, he imitates the kinds of bells that he celebrates. Thus, wedding bells sound softly with "m*o*lten g*o*lden n*o*tes" (*o*), while alarm bells "*cl*ang and *cl*ash and roar" (*kl*). David Wagoner includes imitative words like *tweedledy, thump,* and *wheeze* to suggest the sounds of the music produced by the protagonist of his "March for a One-Man Band."

Pleasing Sounds Create Euphony
and Harsh Sounds Create Cacophony

Words describing smooth or jarring sounds, particularly those resulting from consonants, are euphony and cacophony. **Euphony** ("good sound") refers to words containing consonants that permit an easy and smooth flow of spoken sound. Although there is no rule that some consonants are inherently more pleasant than others, students of poetry often cite sounds like *m, n, ng, l, v,* and *z,* together with *w* and *y,* as being especially easy on the ears. The opposite of euphony is **cacophony** ("bad sound"), in which percussive and choppy sounds make for vigorous and noisy pronunciation, as in tongue twisters like "black bug's blood" and "shuffling shellfish fashioned by a selfish sushi chef." Obviously, unintentional cacophony is a mark of imperfect control. When a poet deliberately creates it for effect, however, as in Tennyson's line "The bare black cliff clang'd round him," in Pope's "The hoarse, rough verse should like the torrent roar" (*An Essay on Criticism*), and in Coleridge's "Huge fragments vaulted like rebounding hail, / Or chaffy grain beneath the thresher's flail" ("Kubla Khan"), cacophony is a mark of poetic skill. Although poets generally aim at easily flowing, euphonious lines, cacophony does have a place, always depending on the poet's intention and subject matter.

RHYME: THE DUPLICATION
AND SIMILARITY OF SOUNDS

Rhyme refers to words containing identical final syllables. One type of rhyme involves words with identical concluding vowel sounds, or assonance, as in *day, weigh, hey, bouquet, fiancé,* and *matinee.* A second type of rhyme is created by assonance combined with identical consonant sounds, as in *ache, bake, break,* and *opaque* or *turn, yearn, fern, spurn,* and *adjourn* or *apple* and *dapple,* or *slippery* and *frippery.* Rhymes like these, because their rhyming sounds are identical, are called **exact rhymes.** It is important to note that rhymes result from *sound* rather than from spelling; words do not have to be spelled the same way or look alike to rhyme. All the words rhyming with *day,* for example, are spelled differently, but because they all contain the same *ā* sound, they rhyme.

Rhyme, above all, gives delight. It also strengthens a poem's psychological impact. Through its network of similar sounds that echo and resonate in our minds, it promotes memory by clinching feelings and ideas. It has been an important aspect of poetry for hundreds of years, and, although many poets have shunned it because they find it restrictive and artificial, it is closely connected with how well particular poems move us or leave us flat. There are few restrictions on the types of words that poets may choose in making rhymes. Nouns may be rhymed with verbs, adjectives, adverbs, and other nouns or with any other rhyming word, regardless of part of speech.

Most often, rhymes are placed at the ends of lines. Two successive lines may rhyme, for example, or rhymes may appear in alternating lines. It is also possible to introduce rhyming words at intervals of four, five, or more lines. If rhyming sounds are too far away from each other, however, it is difficult for readers to recall them and they therefore lose their effectiveness. Sometimes poets use rhyme within individual lines—**internal rhyme.** Poe uses internal rhyme effectively in the concluding stanzas of "Annabel Lee," where he rhymes the words *ever dissever; beams, dreams; rise, eyes;* and *tide* and *side.* Internal rhyme is not common, but you should be alert for it and make note of it when it occurs.

Poets who are skillful and original rhymers are able to create fresh, unusual, and surprising turns of thought. We can therefore judge poets on their use of rhyme. Often poets become quite creative rhymers, putting together words like *bent 'em* and *Tarentem* or *masterly* and *dastardly.* Some rhymers, whom an anonymous sixteenth-century critic called a "rakehelly route of ragged rhymers," are satisfied with easy rhymes, or **cliché rhymes,** like *trees* and *breeze* (a rhyme that Alexander Pope criticized in 1711 in *An Essay on Criticism*). But good rhymes and good poets go together, in creative cooperation. The seventeenth-century poet John Dryden, who wrote volumes of rhyming couplets, acknowledged that the need to find rhyming words inspired ideas he had not anticipated. In this sense, rhyme has been—and still is—a vital element of poetic creativity.

RHYME AND METER

The effects of rhyme are closely bound to rhythm and meter. There is general agreement that rhymes coinciding with a strong accent are conducive to serious subjects. Commensurately, rhymes coinciding with syllables of light stress are appropriate for light and comic subject matter. There is no hard-and-fast rule about such matters, for the effects of rhyme always result from the poet's skill, regardless of rhymes. There is enough truth in the observations, however, to warrant considering the relationship of rhyme and accent.

Rising Rhymes Form the Climaxing Syllables of Iambs and Anapests

The most significant type of **rising rhyme** is **iambic rhyme,** which utilizes one-syllable words in an iambic foot (like *the west* and *in rest, of God* and *his rod*) and two-syllable words in which the accent falls on the second syllable (like *away* and *today, demand* and *command*). Such rhymes are also called **heavy-stress rhyme** or **accented rhyme.** Iambic rhyme is illustrated in the opening lines of Robert Frost's "Stopping by Woods on a Snowy Evening" (Chapter 13, italics added):

Whose woods / these are / I think / I know.//

His house is in / the vil - / lage though;//

Here, the rhyming sounds are produced by one-syllable words—*know* and *though*—that occur in the final heavy-stress positions of the lines. The rhyme climaxing a final syllable can also involve spondees, as in lines 2 and 4 of Countée Cullen's "Yet Do I Marvel" (Chapter 25, italics added):

> I doubt not God is good, well-meaning, kind,
> And did He stoop to quibble could *tell why*
> The little buried mole continues blind,
> Why flesh that mirrors Him must some *day die.*

Byron, in the anapestic poem "The Destruction of Sennacherib" (Chapter 25), similarly uses rising rhymes:

> The Assyrian came down like the wolf *on the fold,*
> And his cohorts were gleaming in pur*ple and gold.*

Falling Rhymes Conclude with One or Two or More Lightly Stressed Syllables

Rhymes using words of two or more syllables in which the heavy stress is followed by light syllables are **trochaic rhyme** or **double rhyme** for two-syllable rhymes, **dactylic rhyme** or **triple rhyme** for three-syllable rhymes. Less technically, these types of rhymes are also called **falling rhymes** or **dying rhymes** because the intensity of pronunciation decreases on the light accent or accents following the heavy accent. Falling rhyme is seen in lines 2 and 4 of the first stanza of "Miniver Cheevy" by Edwin Arlington Robinson (italics added):

> Miniver Cheevy, child of scorn
>   Grew lean while he assailed the *seasons;*
> He wept that he was ever born,
>   And he had *reasons.*

Here the double rhyme undergirds the humor of the passage, thus helping to make Miniver Cheevy seem self-centered and pathetic.

Double rhymes can also be used to bring out irony or anticlimax, as in "a-dying" and "flying" in Browning's "Soliloquy of the Spanish Cloister" (Chapter 25, lines 53–56, italics added):

> If I trip him just *a-dying,*
>   Sure of heaven as sure can be,

> Spin him round and send him *flying*
> Off to hell, a Manichee?

Browning uses trochaic rhymes freely throughout this poem, including the rhyming of English ("rose-acacia") and Latin (*"Plena gratiâ"*). The effect of such rhymes is to complement Browning's exposé of the anger and hypocrisy of the speaker, a monk, who condemns no one but himself as he inveighs against a saintly fellow monk.

Dactylic or **triple rhyme,** even more than trochaic rhyme, is light or humorous because it tends to minimize the subject matter and maximize the rhythm, as in Eliot's "Macavity: The Mystery Cat," where Eliot rhymes *Macavity* with *gravity, depravity,* and *suavity.* These are comic rhymes, totally in keeping with the nature of the poem's feline hero. Ogden Nash makes great use of such rhymes in "Very Like a Whale." There, among other ingenious and amusing rhymes, we see *better for* rhymed with *metaphor,* and *experience* with *Assyrians.*

Variations in Rhyme Extend the Boundaries of Rhyming Poetry

Unlike poets writing in other languages (such as Italian, for example, which offers virtually endless rhyming possibilities because most Italian words end in vowel sounds), English poets are limited in selecting rhymes because our language is short in identical word terminations. To compensate for this shortfall of English rhymes, a tradition has grown that many English words may be rhymed even if their sounds do not duplicate each other exactly.

Rhymes may therefore be created out of words with similar but not identical sounds—**inexact rhyme.** In most inexact rhymes, either the vowel segments are different while the consonants are the same, or vice versa. In addition to *inexact rhyme,* this type of rhyme is variously called **slant rhyme, near rhyme, half rhyme, off rhyme, analyzed rhyme,** or **suspended rhyme.** In employing slant rhyme, a poet can pair *bleak* with *broke* or *could* with *solitude.* Emily Dickinson uses slant rhyme extensively in "To Hear an Oriole Sing"; in the second stanza of the poem she rhymes *Bird, unheard,* and *Crowd. Bird* and *unheard* form an exact rhyme, but the vowel and consonant shift in *Crowd* produces a slant rhyme.

Another common variation is **eye rhyme** or **sight rhyme.** In eye rhyme, the sounds to be eye-rhymed are *identical in spelling* but *different in pronunciation.* Entire words may be eye-rhymed, so that *wind* (verb) may be joined to *wind* (noun), and *cóntest* (noun) may be used with *contést* (verb). In most eye rhymes, however, it is only the relevant parts of words that must be spelled identically. Thus *stove* may pair with *prove* and *above,* and *bough* may match *cough, dough, enough,* and *through,* despite all the differing pronunciations The following lines contain eye rhyme:

> Although his claim was not to praise but *bury,*
> His speech for Caesar roused the crowd to *fury.*

The different pronunciations of "bury" and "fury" make clear the contrast between exact rhyme and eye rhyme. In exact rhyme identical sound is crucial; spelling is usually the same but may be different as long as the sounds remain identical. In eye rhyme, the eye-rhyming patterns must be spelled identically but the sounds must be different.

An additional variation is **identical rhyme** (noted earlier); that is, the same words are placed into rhyming positions, such as *veil* and *veil* or *stone* and *stone*. Perhaps the most extreme variation is **vowel rhyme,** in which poets put words ending in vowels into rhyming positions, as in *day* and *sky* or *key* and *play*.

RHYME SCHEMES

A **rhyme scheme** refers to a poem's pattern of rhyming sounds, which can be schematized by alphabetical letters. The first rhyming sounds, such as *love* and *dove*, are marked with an *a*; the next rhyming sounds, such as *swell* and *fell*, receive a *b*; the next sounds, such as *first* and *burst*, receive a *c*; and so on. Thus, a pattern of lines ending with the words *love, moon, thicket; dove, June, picket;* and *above, croon, wicket* can be schematized as *a b c, a b c, a b c*.

To formulate a rhyme scheme or pattern, you include the meter and the number of feet in each line as well as the letters indicating rhymes. Here is such a formulation:

Iambic pentameter: *a b a b, c d c d, e f e f*

This scheme shows that all the lines in the poem are iambic, with five feet in each line. Commas are used here to mark a stanzaic pattern of three 4-line units, or **quatrains,** with the rhymes falling on the first and third, and the second and fourth, lines of each quatrain.

Should the number of feet in the lines of a poem or **stanza** vary, you show this fact by using a number in front of each letter:

Iambic: *4a 3b 4a 3b 5a 5a 4b*

This formulation shows an intricate pattern of rhymes and line- lengths in a stanza of seven lines. The first, third, fifth, and sixth lines rhyme and vary from four to five feet. The second, fourth, and seventh lines also rhyme and vary from three to four feet.

The absence of a rhyme sound is indicated by an *x*. Thus, you formulate the rhyme scheme of **ballad measure** like this:

Iambic: *4x 3a 4x 3a*

The formulation shows that the quatrain alternates iambic tetrameter (four feet) with iambic trimeter (three feet). In this ballad quatrain, only lines 2 and 4 rhyme; there is no end rhyme in lines 1 and 3.

 POEMS FOR STUDY

GWENDOLYN BROOKS   (b. 1917)

We Real Cool ⎯⎯⎯⎯⎯⎯⎯⎯⎯⎯⎯⎯⎯⎯⎯⎯⎯⎯⎯⎯⎯ *1959*

       The Pool Players.
      Seven at the Golden Shovel.

We real cool. We
Left school. We

Lurk late. We
Strike straight. We

Sing sin. We
Thin gin. We

Jazz June. We
Die soon.

QUESTIONS

1. What is the major idea of the poem? Who is the speaker? How is the last sentence a climax? How is this sentence consistent with the declarations in lines 1–7? How is the poet's attitude made clear?

2. Describe the patterning of stresses in the poem. Explain the absence of light stresses. What method is employed to achieve the constant strong stresses?

EMILY DICKINSON   (1830–1886)

To Hear an Oriole Sing (F402, J526) _____ *1891 (ca. 1862)*

To hear an Oriole sing
May be a common thing –
Or only a divine.

It is not of the Bird   *1st & ryme*   *1 & longer*
Who sings the same, unheard,   *last doesn't*   *than last;*   5
As unto Crowd –

The Fashion of the Ear
Attireth that it hear
In Dun, or fair –

So whether it be Rune,   10
Or whether it be none
Is of within.

The "Tune is in the Tree –"
The Skeptic – showeth me –
"No Sir! In Thee!"   15

QUESTIONS

1. What can you deduce about the speaker? The listener? Who speaks in line 13? To whom is line 15 addressed?

2. Formulate the rhyme scheme of this poem. How does it help subdivide the poem into cohesive units of thought? To what extent does it unify the poem?

3. Locate all the slant rhymes in this poem. What effect do these have on your reading and perception? How is the rhyme here like the oriole's song?

*why he should think
that poem is good
anything from
Ch. on poets*

3 -5 pgs

4. To what degree does rhyme reinforce meaning? Note especially the rhyme words in the final stanza.

JOHN DONNE   (1572–1631)

The Sun Rising ————————————————————————— *1633*

>   Busy old fool, unruly Sun,
>   Why dost thou thus,
> Through windows, and through curtains call on us?
> Must to thy motions lovers' seasons run?
>   Saucy pedantic wretch, go chide
>   Late school boys and sour prentices,°   *apprentices*
>   Go tell Court-huntsmen, that the King will ride,
>   Call country ants to harvest offices;°   *duties*
> Love, all alike, no season knows, nor clime,°   *climate*
> Nor hours, days, months, which are the rags of time.
>
>   Thy beams, so reverend, and strong
>   Why shouldst thou think?°
> I could eclipse and cloud them with a wink,
> But that I would not lose her sight so long;
>   If her eyes have not blinded thine,
>   Look, and tomorrow late, tell me,
>   Whether both the Indias of spice and Mine°
>   Be where thou leftst them, or lie here with me.
> Ask for those kings whom thou saw'st yesterday,
> And thou shalt hear, All here in one bed lay.
>
>   She'is° all States, and all Princes, I,
>   Nothing else is.
> Princes do but play us; compared to this,
> All honor's mimic; all wealth alchemy.°
>   Thou, sun, art half as happy'as° we,
>   In that the world's contracted thus;
>   Thine age asks ease, and since thy duties be
>   To warm the world, that's done in warming us.
> Shine here to us, and thou art everywhere;
> This bed thy center° is, these walls, thy sphere.

THE SUN RISING.   8 *Call . . . offices:* i.e., Notify the country's ants to carry out the duty of eating the harvest of grain and produce.   11, 12 *Thy beams . . . think?:* i.e., why shouldst thou think that thy beams are so reverend and strong?   17 *Indias of spice and Mine:* The India of "spice" is the East Indies; the India of "Mine" (gold) is the West Indies.   21 *She'is:* For scansion, these two words are to be considered one syllable ("shé's").   24 *all wealth alchemy:* i.e., all wealth is false because it has been created by alchemists.   25 *happy'as:* to be scanned as a trochee ("hápp-yǎz").   30 *center:* the earth, around which the sun revolves (according the the Ptolemaic view of the solar system).

QUESTIONS

1. What is the speaker like? How deeply does he seem to be in love? How does he feel about love? What evidence do you find that the speaker has a good sense of humor?

2. To whom is the poem addressed? What is the speaker's attitude toward this listener?

3. What solar, seasonal, geographical, and political metaphors are developed in the poem?

4. What is the poem's rhyme scheme? What is the metrical norm of the lines? What variations on this norm do you find in the poem?

T. S. ELIOT   (1888–1965)

Macavity: The Mystery Cat _____ *1939*

Macavity's a Mystery Cat: he's called the Hidden Paw—
For he's the master criminal who can defy the Law.
He's the bafflement of Scotland Yard, the Flying Squad's despair:
For when they reach the scene of the crime—*Macavity's not there!*   5

  Macavity, Macavity, there's no one like Macavity,
He's broken every human law, he breaks the law of gravity.
His powers of levitation would make a fakir stare,
And when you reach the scene of crime—*Macavity's not there!*
You may seek him in the basement, you may look up in the air—   10
But I tell you once and once again, *Macavity's not there!*

  Macavity's a ginger cat, he's very tall and thin;
You would know him if you saw him, for his eyes are sunken in.
His brow is deeply lined with thought, his head is highly domed;
His coat is dusty from neglect, his whiskers are uncombed.   15
He sways his head from side to side, with movements like a snake;
And when you think he's half asleep, he's always wide awake.

  Macavity, Macavity, there's no one like Macavity,
For he's a fiend in feline shape, a monster of depravity.
You may meet him in a by-street, you may see him in the square—   20
But when a crime's discovered, then *Macavity's not there!*

  He's outwardly respectable. (They say he cheats at cards.)
And his footprints are not found in any file of Scotland Yard's.
And when the larder's looted, or the jewel-case is rifled,
Or when the milk is missing, or another Peke's been stifled,°
Or the greenhouse glass is broken, and the trellis past repair—   25
Ay, there's the wonder of the thing! *Macavity's not there!*

MACAVITY: THE MYSTERY CAT.   24 *Peke's been stifled:* A Pekinese dog (a small animal, with silky hair) has been found dead.

And when the Foreign Office find a Treaty's gone astray,
Or the Admiralty lose some plans and drawings by the way,
There may be a scrap of paper in the hall or on the stair—
But it's useless to investigate—*Macavity's not there!*   30
And when the loss has been disclosed, the Secret Service say:
"It *must* have been Macavity!"—but he's a mile away.
You'll be sure to find him resting, or a-licking of his thumbs,
Or engaging in doing complicated long division sums.

Macavity, Macavity, there's no one like Macavity,   35
There never was a Cat of such deceitfulness and suavity.
He always has an alibi, and one or two to spare:
At whatever time the deed took place—MACAVITY WASN'T THERE!
And they say that all the Cats whose wicked deeds are widely known
(I might mention Mungojerrie, I might mention Griddlebone)   40
Are nothing more than agents for the Cat who all the time
Just controls their operations: the Napoleon of Crime!

QUESTIONS

1. What are some of Macavity's major "crimes" as a master criminal and "mystery cat"? How, if the "crimes" had been attributed to a human being, would they be grievous wrongs? Since they are attributed to a cat, how do they add to the comic qualities of the poem?

2. What is the basic metrical foot of the poem? How many feet are contained in each of the lines? What is the norm?

3. Once you begin reading and getting into the lines, what new kind of pattern emerges? How many major stresses appear in each line? In light of the nature of the poem, how is the dipodic rhythm appropriate?

ISABELLA GARDNER   (1915–1981)

At a Summer Hotel _____ *1979*

I am here with my bountiful womanful child
to be soothed by the sea not roused by these roses roving wild.
My girl is gold in the sun and bold in the dazzling water,
She drowses on the blond sand and in the daisy fields my daughter
dreams. Uneasy in the drafty shade I rock on the veranda
reminded of Europa Persephone Miranda.°

AT A SUMMER HOTEL.   6 *Europa Persephone Miranda:* Europa was a princess in Greek mythology who attracted the attention of Zeus, the king of the gods. He took the form of a bull and carried her over the sea to Crete. She bore him three sons. Persephone, in Greek mythology, was the daughter of Zeus and Demeter, the goddess of fertility. She attracted the attention of Hades, the god of the underworld, who forcibly carried her off and married her. Miranda is an innocent young woman in Shakespeare's play *The Tempest* who was exiled on an island for twelve years with her father, Prospero. One of his servants, the beastlike Caliban, attempted to rape her.

QUESTIONS

1. Why is the speaker "uneasy" (line 5)? How do the references to Europa, Persephone, and Miranda help define this uneasiness?

2. To what extent do alliteration and repetition unify the lines and make the sound echo sense? Note especially the *ful* sounds in line 1, the *s* and *r* sounds in line 2, and the *d* and *dr* sounds in lines 4–5.

3. What is the effect of internal rhyme in this poem?

4. What kind of rhyme (rising or falling, exact or slant) is in lines 1–2? To what extent does this rhyme highlight the poem's central idea? What rhyme is in lines 3–6? How does this rhyme affect the poem's tone and impact?

ROBERT HERRICK   (1591–1674)

Upon Julia's Voice _____ *1648*

So smooth, so sweet, so silv'ry is thy voice,
As, could they hear, the damned would make no noise,
But listen to thee (walking in thy chamber)
Melting melodious words, to lutes of amber.

QUESTIONS

1. How do the words "silv'ry" and "amber" contribute to the praise of Julia's voice? How powerful does the speaker claim her voice is?

2. What is the "joke" of the poem? How can the praise of Julia's voice be interpreted as general praise for Julia herself?

3. How and where is alliteration used in the poem? Which of the alliterative sounds best complement the words praising the sweetness of Julia's voice?

GERARD MANLEY HOPKINS   (1844–1889)

God's Grandeur _____ *1877*

The world is charged with the grandeur of God.
  It will flame out, like shining from shook foil;
  It gathers to a greatness, like the ooze of oil
Crushed. Why do men then now not reck his rod?
Generations have trod, have trod, have trod;   5
  And all is seared with trade; bleared, smeared with toil;
  And wears man's smudge and shares man's smell: the soil
Is bare now, nor can foot feel, being shod.

Howdoyou like unp know, now that i'm on my way used to think im crazy standing here today..

GOD'S GRANDEUR.   4 *reck his rod:* God as king holds a scepter, making official laws through scriptures which people ("men") disobey.

And for all this, nature is never spent;
  There lives the dearest freshness deep down things;   10
And though the last lights off the black West went
  Oh, morning, at the brown brink eastward, springs—
Because the Holy Ghost over the bent
  World broods with warm breast and with ah! bright wings.

QUESTIONS

1. What is the contrast between the assertions in lines 1–4 and 5–8 (the octave)? How do lines 9–14 (the sestet) develop out of this contrast?

2. Analyze Hopkins's use of alliteration. What alliterative patterns occur? How do these affect meter and emphasis? On the basis of your analysis, describe "sprung rhythm" as used by Hopkins.

3. What instances of assonance, repetitions, and internal rhyme do you find?

LANGSTON HUGHES   (1902–1967)

Let America Be America Again _____ *1936*

Let America be America again.
Let it be the dream it used to be.
Let it be the pioneer on the plain
Seeking a home where he himself is free.

(America never was America to me.)

Let America be the dream the dreamers dreamed—
Let it be that great strong land of love
Where never kings connive nor tyrants scheme
That any man be crushed by one above.

(It never was America to me.)

O, let my land be a land where Liberty
Is crowned with no false patriotic wreath,
But opportunity is real, and life is free,
Equality is in the air we breathe.

(There's never been equality for me,
Nor freedom in this "homeland of the free.")

Say who are you that mumbles in the dark?
And who are you that draws your veil across the stars?
I am the poor white, fooled and pushed apart,
I am the Negro bearing slavery's scars.
I am the red man driven from the land,
I am the immigrant clutching the hope I seek—
And finding only the same old stupid plan
Of dog eat dog, of mighty crush the weak.

I am the young man, full of strength and hope,   25
Tangled in that ancient endless chain
Of profit, power, gain, of grab the land!
Of grab the gold! Of grab the ways of satisfying need!
Of work the men! Of take the pay!
Of owning everything for one's own greed!   30

I am the farmer, bondsman to the soil.
I am the worker sold to the machine.
I am the Negro, servant to you all.
I am the people, worried, hungry, mean—
Hungry yet today despite the dream.   35
Beaten yet today—O, Pioneers!
I am the man who never got ahead,
The poorest worker bartered through the years.

Yet I'm the one who dreamt our basic dream
In the Old World while still a serf of kings,   40
Who dreamt a dream so strong, so brave, so true,
That even yet its mighty daring sings
In every brick and stone, in every furrow turned
That's made America the land it has become.
O, I'm the man who sailed those early seas   45
In search of what I meant to be my home—
For I'm the one who left dark Ireland's shore,
And Poland's plain, and England's grassy lea,
And torn from Black Africa's strand I came
To build a "homeland of the free."   50
The free?

A dream—
Still beckoning to me!

O, let America be America again—
The land that never has been yet—   55
And yet must be—
The land where *every* man is free.
The land that's mine—
The poor man's, Indian's, Negro's, ME—
Who made America,   60
Whose sweat and blood, whose faith and pain,
Whose hand at the foundry, whose plow in the rain,
Must bring back our mighty dream again.
Sure, call me any ugly name you choose—
The steel of freedom does not stain.   65
From those who live like leeches on the people's lives,
We must take back our land again,
America!

O, yes,
I say it plain,
America never was America to me,   70
And yet I swear this oath—

America will be!
An ever-living seed,
Its dream
Lies deep in the heart of me.   75

We, the people, must redeem
Our land, the mines, the plants, the rivers,
The mountains and the endless plain—
All, all the stretch of these great green states—
And make America again!   80

QUESTIONS

1. In light of the poet's ideas, what is the effect of the changing stanzaic patterns?
    After the opening, fairly regular quatrains, why do the groupings become
    irregular?

2. What is the effect of the refrains in lines 5, 10, and 15–16? Why does the poet
    stop using the refrain after the third quatrain and not bring it out again until
    line 71?

3. Describe the use of alliteration. In phrases like "pushed apart" and "slavery's
    scars," together with other phrases, how does the alliteration emphasize the
    poet's ideas?

4. Describe the use of assonance, rhyme, and slant rhyme. What is gained by the
    slant rhymes?

PHILIP LEVINE   (b. 1928)

A Theory of Prosody _____ *1988*

When Nellie, my old pussy
cat, was still in her prime,
she would sit behind me
as I wrote, and when the line
got too long she'd reach
one sudden black foreleg down
and paw at the moving hand,
the offensive one. The first
time she drew blood I learned
it was poetic to end
a line anywhere to keep her
quiet. After all, many mornings she'd gotten to the chair
long before I was even up.
Those nights I couldn't sleep
she'd come and sit in my lap
to calm me. So I figured

I owed her the short cat line.
She's dead now almost nine years,
and before that there was one
during which she faked attention   20
and I faked obedience.
Isn't that what it's about—
pretending there's an alert cat
who leaves nothing to chance.

                                                                              25

QUESTIONS

1. Why is this poem comic? How effective a "theory of prosody" is contained in the poem? What is suggested by the syllable break in line 12? How seriously are we to take the final lines?

2. What is the relationship between the speaker and his cat, Nellie? How true is it that cats sitting at a table with their masters and mistresses sometimes take a swipe at what they are writing?

3. Compare this poem with Robert Frost's "A Considerable Speck" (Chapter 24). In what ways do the poets seem to be having a good time? Nevertheless, what truths about writing are they advancing in the poems?

HENRY WADSWORTH LONGFELLOW (1807-1882)

The Sound of the Sea _____ *1875*

The sea awoke at midnight from its sleep,
    And round the pebbly beaches far and wide
    I heard the first wave of the rising tide
Rush onward with uninterrupted sweep;
A voice out of the silence of the deep,   5
    A sound mysteriously multiplied
    As of a cataract from the mountain's side,
Or roar of winds upon a wooded steep.
    So comes to us at times, from the unknown
        And inaccessible solitudes of being,   10
            The rushing of the sea-tides of the soul;
And inspirations, that we deem our own,
        Are some divine foreshadowing and foreseeing
            Of things beyond our reason or control.

QUESTIONS

1. What is the analogy on which this poem is based? How does the form of the poem follow this analogy? Is the poem to be considered philosophical, mystical, or religious? Why does the poet conclude with the idea of "things beyond our reason or control"?

2. Describe the form of this poem, its rhyme scheme, and its use of rhyme.

3. What is the basic meter of the poem? Describe variations gained through substitution.

4. Describe the effects of alliteration and assonance in the poem. How do these prosodic devices complement the meanings of the affected words?

OGDEN NASH   (1902–1971)

Very Like a Whale° _____ *1934*

One thing that literature would be greatly the better for
Would be a more restricted employment by authors of simile and metaphor.
Authors of all races, be they Greeks, Romans, Teutons or Celts,
Can't seem just to say that anything is the thing it is but have to go out of their
    way to say that it is like something else.
What does it mean when we are told
That the Assyrian came down like a wolf on the fold?
In the first place, George Gordon Byron° had had enough experience
To know that it probably wasn't just one Assyrian, it was a lot of Assyrians.
However, as too many arguments are apt to induce apoplexy and thus hinder
    longevity,
We'll let it pass as one Assyrian for the sake of brevity.
Now then, this particular Assyrian; the one whose cohorts were gleaming in purple
    and gold,
Just what does the poet mean when he says he came down like a wolf on the
    fold?
In heaven and earth more than is dreamed of in our philosophy there are a great
    many things,
But I don't imagine that among them there is a wolf with purple and gold cohorts
    or purple and gold anythings.
No, no, Lord Byron, before I'll believe that this Assyrian was actually like a wolf
    I must have some kind of proof;
Did he run on all fours and did he have a hairy tail and a big red mouth and big
    white teeth and did he say Woof woof woof?
Frankly I think it very unlikely, and all you were entitled to say, at the very most,
Was that the Assyrian cohorts came down like a lot of Assyrian cohorts about to
    destroy the Hebrew host.
But that wasn't fancy enough for Lord Byron, oh dear me no, he had to invent a
    lot of figures of speech and then interpolate them.
With the result that whenever you mention Old Testament soldiers to people they
    say Oh yes, they're the ones that a lot of wolves dressed up in gold and purple
    ate them.

VERY LIKE A WHALE.   See *Hamlet,* III.2.358.   7 *George Gordon Byron:* See Byron, "The Destruction of Sennacherib," (Chapter 25), which Nash is satirizing in this poem.

That's the kind of thing that's being done all the time by poets, from Homer to
    Tennyson;
They're always comparing ladies to lilies° and veal to venison.
How about the man who wrote,
Her little feet stole in and out like mice beneath her petticoat?°
Wouldn't anybody but a poet think twice   25
Before stating that his girl's feet were mice?
Then they always say things like that after a winter storm
The snow is a white blanket. Oh it is, is it, all right then, you sleep under a six-
    inch blanket of snow and I'll sleep under a half-inch blanket of unpoetical
    blanket material and we'll see which one keeps warm.
And after that maybe you'll begin to comprehend dimly
What I meant by too much metaphor and simile.   30

22 *ladies:* See Campion, "Cherry Ripe," stanza 1, and also Burns, "A Red, Red Rose."   24 *little feet . . . petticoat:* In Sir John Suckling's "A Ballad upon a Wedding" (1641), the following lines appear: "Her feet beneath her petticoat / Like little mice stole in and out." Also in a poem by Robert Herrick complimenting the feet of Susanna Southwell (1648), he wrote: "Her pretty feet / Like snails did creep."

QUESTIONS

1. How serious is Nash when he states that literature would be improved if poets would remove simile and metaphor from their works? How just is his "criticism" of metaphor in line 4?

2. Explain how Nash achieves humor in this poem. How does the ending of the first line indicate that the subject matter is to be considered with a smile?

3. Describe Nash's rhymes in this poem. What types of rhymes do you find here? In what ways are some of the rhymes comic? How original are Nash's rhymes?

EDGAR ALLAN POE   (1809–1849)

Annabel Lee _____ *1849*

It was many and many a year ago,
    In a kingdom by the sea,
That a maiden there lived whom you may know
    By the name of Annabel Lee;
And this maiden she lived with no other thought   5
    Than to love and be loved by me.

She was a child and *I* was a child,
    In this kingdom by the sea,
But we loved with a love that was more than love—
    I and my Annabel Lee—   10
With a love that the wingèd seraphs of Heaven
    Coveted her and me.

And this was the reason that, long ago,
   In this kingdom by the sea,
A wind blew out of a cloud by night   15
   Chilling my Annabel Lee;
So that her high-born kinsmen came
   And bore her away from me,
To shut her up in a sepulchre
   In this kingdom by the sea.   20

The angels, not half so happy in Heaven,
   Went envying her and me:—
Yes! that was the reason (as all men know,
   In this kingdom by the sea)
That the wind came out of the cloud chilling   2.
   And killing my Annabel Lee.

But our love it was stronger by far than the love
   Of those who were older than we—
   Of many far wiser than we—
And neither the angels in Heaven above   ?
   Nor the demons down under the sea
Can ever dissever my soul from the soul
   Of the beautiful Annabel Lee:—

For the moon never beams without bringing me dreams
   Of the beautiful Annabel Lee;
And the stars never rise but I feel the bright eyes
   Of the beautiful Annabel Lee:
And so all the night-tide, I lie down by the side
Of my darling, my darling, my life and my bride
   In her sepulchre there by the sea—
   In her tomb by the side of the sea.

QUESTIONS

1.   How does the speaker explain the death of Annabel Lee? What is his attitude about the cause of her death? How does this judgment explain the actions he describes at the poem's end?

2.   What basic meter does the poet establish in the poem? What variations do you find on this pattern?

3.   Why do stanzas 3, 5, and 6 contain more lines than stanzas 1, 2, and 4? Why does stanza 5 contain seven lines, concluding with a dash?

4.   Describe the poem's internal rhymes, repetitions, assonances, and alliterations. What is their effect? Why did Poe include them?

EDGAR ALLAN POE   (1809–1849)

The Bells ———————————————————————————— *1849*

I

Hear the sledges with the bells—
   Silver bells!
What a world of merriment their melody foretells!
How they tinkle, tinkle, tinkle,
   In the icy air of night!   5
While the stars that oversprinkle
All the heavens, seem to twinkle
   With a crystalline delight;
     Keeping time, time, time,
     In a sort of Runic rhyme,   10
To the tintinnabulation that so musically wells
     From the bells, bells, bells, bells,
       Bells, bells, bells—
From the jingling and the tinkling of the bells.

II

Hear the mellow wedding bells—   15
   Golden bells!
What a world of happiness their harmony foretells!
   Through the balmy air of night
   How they ring out their delight!—
     From the molten-golden notes,   20
     And all in tune,
   What a liquid ditty floats
To the turtle-dove that listens, while she gloats
     On the moon!
     Oh, from out the sounding cells,   25
What a gush of euphony voluminously wells!
     How is swells!
     How it dwells
     On the Future!—how it tells
     Of the rapture that impels   30
   To the swinging and the ringing
     Of the bells, bells, bells—
Of the bells, bells, bells, bells,
     Bells, bells, bells—
To the rhyming and the chiming of the bells!   35

III

Hear the loud alarum bells—
   Brazen bells!
What a tale of terror, now, their turbulency tells!
   In the startled ear of night

How they scream out their affright!   40
   Too much horrified to speak,
   They can only shriek, shriek,
      Out of tune,
In a clamorous appealing to the mercy of the fire,
In a mad expostulation with the deaf and frantic fire,   45
     Leaping higher, higher, higher,
    With a desperate desire,
   And a resolute endeavor
   Now—now to sit, or never,
By the side of the pale-faced moon,   50
    Oh, the bells, bells, bells!
   What a tale their terror tells
     Of Despair!
   How they clang, and clash, and roar!
   What a horror they outpour   55
On the bosom of the palpitating air!
   Yet the ear, it fully knows,
    By the twanging
    And the clanging,
   How the danger ebbs and flows;   60
   Yet the ear distinctly tells,
    In the jangling
    And the wrangling,
How the danger sinks and swells,
By the sinking or the swelling in the anger of the bells—   65
    Of the bells,—
Of the bells, bells, bells, bells,
    Bells, bells, bells—
In the clamor and the clangor of the bells!

       IV
Hear the tolling of the bells—
    Iron bells!
What a world of solemn thought their monody compels!
   In the silence of the night,
   How we shiver with affright
At the melancholy menace of their tone!
   For every sound that floats
   From the rust within their throats
     Is a groan.
    And the people—ah, the people—
    They that dwell up in the steeple,
     All alone,
   And who tolling, tolling, tolling,
    In that muffled monotone,
   Feel a glory in so rolling
     On the human heart a stone—

They are neither man nor woman—
They are neither brute nor human—
    They are Ghouls:—
  And their king it is who tolls:—
  And he rolls, rolls, rolls,   90
    Rolls
    A paean from the bells!
And his merry bosom swells
    With the paean of the bells!
And he dances, and he yells;   95
Keeping time, time, time,
In a sort of Runic rhyme,
    To the paean of the bells—
    Of the bells:
Keeping time, time, time,   100
In a sort of Runic rhyme,
    To the throbbing of the bells—
  Of the bells, bells, bells—
    To the sobbing of the bells;
Keeping time, time, time,   105
  As he knells, knells, knells,
In a happy Runic rhyme,
    To the rolling of the bells—
  Of the bells, bells, bells:—
    To the tolling of the bells—   110
Of the bells, bells, bells, bells,
  Bells, bells, bells—
To the moaning and the groaning of the bells.

QUESTIONS

1. What kinds of bells does Poe extol in each of the stanzas? What metals and images does he associate with each type of bell? How appropriate are these? Why do you think the stanzas become progressively longer?

2. What segmental sounds does Poe utilize as imitative of the various bells? What differences in vowels are observable between the silver sledge bells, for example, and the brass ("brazen") alarum bells? Between the vowels describing the iron bells and the golden bells?

3. What is the effect of the repetition of the word "bells" throughout? What onomatopoeic effect is created by these repetitions?

4. Describe the pattern of rhymes in this poem.

ALEXANDER POPE (1685-1744)

From *An Essay on Man, Epistle I* (lines 17-90) _____ *1734*

    I. Say first, of God above, or man.° below,   *men; humanity*
What can we reason but from what we know?
Of man, what see we but his station here,
From which to reason, or to which refer?   20
Through worlds unnumbered though the God be known,
'Tis ours to trace him° only in our own.   *God*
He who through vast immensity can pierce,
See worlds on worlds compose one universe,
Observe how system into system runs,   25
What other planets circle other suns,
What varied being peoples every star,
May tell why Heaven has made us as we are.
But of this frame the bearings and the ties,
The strong connections, nice dependencies,   30
Gradations just, has thy pervading soul
Looked through? or can a part contain the whole?
    Is the great chain that draws all to agree,
And drawn supports, upheld by God, or thee?
    II. Presumptuous man! the reason wouldst thou find,   35
Why formed so weak, so little, and so blind?
First, if thou canst, the harder reason guess,
Why formed no weaker, blinder, and no less!
Ask of thy mother earth, why oaks are made
Taller or stronger than the weeds they shade!   40
Or ask of yonder argent fields above,
Why Jove's satellites are less than Jove!
    Of systems possible, if 'tis confessed
That wisdom infinite must form the best,
Where all must full or not coherent be,
And all that rises, rise in due degree;
Then, in the scale of reasoning life, 'tis plain,
There must be, somewhere, such a rank as man:
And all the question (wrangle e'er so long)
Is only this, if God has placed him wrong.
    Respecting man, whatever wrong we call,
May, must be right, as relative to all.
In human works, though labored on with pain,
A thousand movements scarce one purpose gain;
In God's, one single can its end produce;
Yet serves to second too some other use.
So man, who here seems principal alone,
Perhaps acts second to some sphere unknown,
Touches some wheel, or verges to some goal;
'Tis but a part we see, and not a whole.
    When the proud steed shall know why man restrains
His fiery course, or drives him o'er the plains:

When the dull ox, why now he breaks the clod,
Is now a victim, and now Egypt's god:
Then shall man's pride and dullness comprehend   65
His actions', passions', being's, use and end;
Why doing, suffering, checked, impelled; and why
This hour a slave, the next a deity.
    Then say not man's imperfect, Heaven in fault;
Say rather, man's as perfect as he ought: 70
His knowledge measured to his state and place;
His time a moment, and a point his space.
If to be perfect in a certain sphere,
What matter, soon or late, or here or there?
The blessed today is as completely so,   75
As who began a thousand years ago.
    III.   Heaven from all creatures hides the book of fate,
All but the page prescribed, their present state;
From brutes what men, from men what spirits know,
Or who could suffer being here below?   80
The lamb thy riot dooms to bleed today,
Had he thy reason, would he skip and play?
Pleased to the last, he crops the flowery food,
And licks the hand just raised to shed his blood.
Oh blindness to the future! kindly given,   85
That each may fill the circle marked by Heaven:
Who sees with equal eye, as God of all,
A hero perish, or a sparrow fall,
Atoms or systems into ruin hurled,
And now a bubble burst, and now a world.   90

QUESTIONS

1. What is the topic of the passage? How appropriate is it to present such material in the form of couplets? How does Pope use the couplet to develop his thought in the poem?

2. Analyze five or six of the couplets. On the basis of your study, what principles of the couplet does Pope follow? You might consider the average lengths of words and the use of iambs, caesurae, and end-stopped lines.

3. Describe Pope's use of rhyme. What types of words does he rhyme? How helpful are the rhymes in the emphasis of Pope's ideas?

EDWIN ARLINGTON ROBINSON   (1869–1935)

Miniver Cheevy ———————————————————— *1910*

Miniver Cheevy, child of scorn,
    Grew lean while he assailed the seasons;
He wept that he was ever born,
    And he had reasons.

Miniver loved the days of old   5
  When swords were bright and steeds were prancing;
The vision of a warrior bold
  Would set him dancing.

Miniver sighed for what was not,
  And dreamed, and rested from his labors;   10
He dreamed of Thebes° and Camelot,°
  And Priam's° neighbors.

Miniver mourned the ripe renown
  That made so many a name so fragrant;
He mourned Romance, now on the town,   15
  And Art, a vagrant.

Miniver loved the Medici,°
  Albeit he had never seen one;
He would have sinned incessantly
  Could he have been one.   20

Miniver cursed the commonplace
  And eyed a khaki suit with loathing;
He missed the medieval grace
  Of iron clothing.

Miniver scorned the gold he sought,   25
  But sore annoyed was he without it;
Miniver thought, and thought, and thought,
  And thought about it.

Miniver Cheevy, born too late,
  Scratched his head and kept on thinking;
Miniver coughed, and called it fate,
  And kept on drinking.

MINIVER CHEEVY.   11 *Thebes:* a city in Greece prominent in Greek legend and mythology in connection with Cadmus and Oedipus.   *Camelot:* legendary seat of the Round Table and capital of Britain during the reign of King Arthur.   12 *Priam's:* Priam was the king of Troy during the Trojan War.   17 *Medici:* wealthy Italian family that ruled Florence from the fifteenth to the eighteenth century. During the Renaissance, Lorenzo de'Medici was an important patron of the arts.

QUESTIONS

1. What is the speaker's attitude toward the central character? How does rhyme help define this attitude?

2. How does repetition reinforce the image of the central character and the speaker's attitude? Consider the beginning of each stanza and lines 27–28.

3. What rhyme predominates in lines 2 and 4 of each stanza? How does this rhyme help make sound echo sense?

WILLIAM SHAKESPEARE (1564–1616)

Sonnet 73: That Time of Year Thou May'st in Me Behold _____ *1609*

That time of year thou may'st in me behold
When yellow leaves, or none, or few, do hang
Upon those boughs which shake against the cold,
Bare ruined choirs,° where late the sweet birds sang.
In me thou see'st the twilight of such day   5
As after sunset fadeth in the west;
Which by and by black night doth take away,
Death's second self,° that seals up all in rest.
In me thou see'st the glowing of such fire,
That on the ashes of his° youth doth lie,   *its*   10
As the death-bed whereon it must expire,
Consumed with that which it was nourished by,°
This thou perceivest, which makes thy love more strong,
To love that well which thou must leave ere long.

SONNET 73.   4 *choirs:* the part of a church just in front of the altar.   8 *Death's . . . self:* That is, night is a mirror image of death inasmuch as it brings the sleep of rest just as death brings the sleep of actual death.   12 *Consumed . . . by:* That is, the ashes of the fuel burned at the fire's height now prevent the fire from continuing, and in fact extinguish it.

QUESTIONS

1. Describe the content of lines 1–4, 5–8, and 9–12. What connects these three sections? How does the concluding couplet relate to the first twelve lines?

2. Analyze the iambic pentameter of the poem. Consider the spondees in lines 2 ("do hang"), 4 ("bare ru-" and "birds sang"), 5 ("such day"), 7 ("black night"), 8 ("death's sec-"), 9 ("such fire"), 10 ("doth lie"), 11 ("death-bed"), 13 ("more strong"), and 14 ("ere long"). What is the effect of these substitutions on the poem's ideas?

3. How does the enjambement of lines 1–3 and 5–6 permit these lines to seem to conclude *as lines* even though grammatically they carry over to form sentences?

4. In lines 2, 5, 6, and 9, where does Shakespeare place the caesurae? What relationship is there between the rhythms produced by these caesurae and the content of lines 1–12? In lines 13 and 14, how do the rising stressed caesurae relate to the content?

PERCY BYSSHE SHELLEY (1792–1822)

Ode to the West Wind _____ *1820*

I

O wild West Wind, thou breath of Autumn's being,
Thou, from whose unseen presence the leaves dead
Are driven, like ghosts from an enchanter fleeing,

Yellow, and black, and pale, and hectic° red,
Pestilence-stricken multitudes: O Thou,   5
Who chariotest to their dark wintry bed

The winged seeds, where they lie cold and low,
Each like a corpse within its grave, until
Thine azure sister of the Spring° shall blow

Her clarion o'er the dreaming earth, and fill   10
(Driving sweet buds like flocks to feed in air)
With living hues and odours plain and hill:

Wild Spirit, which art moving everywhere;
Destroyer and Preserver; hear, O hear!

II

Thou on whose stream, 'mid the steep sky's commotion,   15
Loose clouds like Earth's decaying leaves are shed,
Shook from the tangled boughs of Heaven and Ocean,

Angels of rain and lightning: there are spread
On the blue surface of thine aery surge,
Like the bright hair uplifted from the head   20

Of some fierce Maenad,° even from the dim verge
Of the horizon to the zenith's height,
The locks of the approaching storm. Thou Dirge

Of the dying year, to which this closing night
Will be the dome of a vast sepulchre,   2
Vaulted with all thy congregated might

Of vapours,° from whose solid atmosphere   *clouds*
Black rain and fire and hail will burst: O hear!

III

Thou who didst waken from his summer dreams
The blue Mediterranean, where he lay,
Lulled by the coil of his crystalline streams,

Beside a pumice isle in Baiae's bay,°
And saw in sleep old palaces and towers
Quivering within the wave's intenser day,

ODE TO THE WEST WIND.   4 *hectic:* a tubercular fever that produced flushed cheeks.
9 *Spring:* the wind that will blow in the spring.   21 *Maenad:* a frenzied female worshipper of
Dionysus, the god of wine and fertility in Greek mythology.   32 *Baiae's bay:* a bay of the
Mediterranean Sea west of Naples, famous for the elaborate villas built on the shore by Roman
emperors.

All overgrown with azure moss and flowers   35
So sweet, the sense faints picturing them! Thou
For whose path the Atlantic's level powers

Cleave themselves into chasms, while far below
The sea-blooms and the oozy woods which wear
The sapless foliage of the ocean, know   40

Thy voice, and suddenly grow grey with fear,
And tremble and despoil themselves: O hear!

IV

If I were a dead leaf thou mightest bear;
If I were a swift cloud to fly with thee;
A wave to pant beneath thy power, and share   45

The impulse of thy strength, only less free
Than thou, O Uncontrollable! If even
I were as in my boyhood, and could be

The comrade of thy wanderings over Heaven,
As then, when to outstrip thy skiey speed   50
Scarce seemed a vision; I would ne'er have striven

As thus with thee in prayer in my sore need,
Oh! lift me as a wave, a leaf, a cloud!
I fall upon thorns of life! I bleed!

A heavy weight of hours has chained and bowed   55
One too like thee: tameless, and swift, and proud.

V

Make me thy lyre,° even as the forest is:
What if my leaves are falling like its own!
The tumult of thy mighty harmonies

Will take from both a deep, autumnal tone,   60
Sweet though in sadness. Be thou, Spirit fierce,
My spirit! Be thou me, impetuous one!

Drive my dead thoughts over the universe
Like withered leaves to quicken a new birth!
And, by the incantation of this verse,   65

Scatter, as from an unextinguished hearth
Ashes and sparks, my words among mankind!
Be through my lips to unawakened Earth

The trumpet of a prophecy! O Wind,
If Winter comes, can Spring be far behind?   70

57 *Lyre:* an Aeolian harp, a musical device that is sounded by the wind blowing across strings.

QUESTIONS

1. To what extent are the speaker's thoughts and feelings organized by the poem's five sections? What is the logical progression from section to section?

2. What aspect of the natural world does the wind affect in the first section of the poem? The second stanza? The third? What does the West Wind symbolize? Why does the speaker state, "Make me thy lyre"?

3. Formulate the structure (meter and rhyme scheme) of the stanzas. How many times (and where) is the *e* rhyme of the first stanza repeated as a rhyming sound? What is the effect of this repetition?

4. Describe Shelley's use of alliteration and assonance in the poem.

ALFRED, LORD TENNYSON   (1809–1892)

From *Idylls of the King: The Passing of Arthur*
(lines 344–393) _____ *1869 (1842)*

But, as he walked, King Arthur panted hard,
Like one that feels a nightmare on his bed   345
When all the house is mute. So sighed the King,
Muttering and murmuring at his ear, "Quick, quick!
I fear it is too late, and I shall die."
But the other swiftly strode from ridge to ridge,
Clothed with his breath, and looking, as he walked,   350
Larger than human on the frozen hills.
He heard the deep behind him, and a cry
Before. His own thought drove him like a goad.
Dry clashed his harness in the icy caves
And barren chasms, and all to left and right   355
The bare black cliff clanged round him, as he based
His feet on juts of slippery crag that rang
Sharp-smitten with the dint of armèd heels—
And on a sudden, lo! the level lake,
And the long glories of the winter moon.   360

Then saw they how there hove a dusky barge,
Dark as a funeral scarf from stem to stern,
Beneath them; and descending they were ware°   *aware*
That all the decks were dense with stately forms,
Black-stoled, black-hooded, like a dream—by these   365
Three Queens with crowns of gold: and from them rose
A cry that shivered to the tingling stars,
And, as it were one voice, an agony
Of lamentation, like a wind that shrills
All night in a waste land, where no one comes,   370
Or hath come, since the making of the world.

Then murmured Arthur, "Place me in the barge."
So to the barge they came. There those three Queens
Put forth their hands, and took the King, and wept.
But she, that rose the tallest of them all   375
And fairest, laid his head upon her lap,
And loosed the shattered casque,° and chafed his hands,   *helmet*
And called him by his name, complaining loud,
And dropping bitter tears against a brow
Striped with dark blood: for all his face was white   380
And colorless, and like the withered moon
Smote by the fresh beam of the springing east;
And all his greaves and cuisses° dashed with drops   *pieces of armor*
Of onset;° and the light and lustrous curls—   *blood*
That made his forehead like a rising sun   385
High from the dais-throne—were parched with dust:
Or, clotted into points and hanging loose,
Mixed with the knightly growth that fringed his lips.
So like a shattered column lay the King:
Not like that Arthur who, with lance in rest,   390
From spur to plume a star of tournament,
Shot through the lists at Camelot, and charged
Before the eyes of ladies and of kings.

QUESTIONS

1. How does Tennyson develop the mood of depression and loss associated with the dying of Arthur? What is the effect of the concluding simile?

2. Analyze the patterns of assonance and alliteration in the passage. What patterns are developed most extensively? What effects are thus achieved?

3. Describe Tennyson's use of onomatopoeia in lines 349–360, 369–371, and 380–383. What segments contribute to this effect?

DAVID WAGONER   (b. 1926)

March for a One-Man Band _____ *1983*

He's *a boom a blat* in the uniform
Of an army *tweedledy* band *a toot*
Complete with medals *a honk* cornet
Against *a thump* one side of his lips
And the other stuck with *a sloop a tweet*   5
A whistle *a crash* on top of *a crash*
A helmet *a crash* a cymbal a drum
At his *bumbledy* knee and a *rimshot* flag
A click he stands at attention *a wheeze*
And plays the Irrational Anthem *bang*.   10

QUESTIONS

1. What attitude does the speaker convey about the one-man band? Why is the Anthem "Irrational" rather than "National"?

2. Describe the onomatopoeic effect of the italicized percussive words. What is the purpose of the rhythms that these words cause?

3. What ambiguity is suggested by the *bang* of line 10? How does this ambiguity make the poem seem more than simply an entertaining display of sounds?

WRITING ABOUT PROSODY

Because studying prosody requires a good deal of specific detail and description, it is best to limit your study to a short poem or to a short passage from a long poem. A sonnet, a stanza of a lyric poem, or a fragment from a long poem will usually be sufficient. If you choose a fragment, it should be self-contained, such as an entire speech or a short episode or scene (as in the example from Tennyson chosen for the demonstrative student essay on pp. 885–91).

The analysis of even a short poem, however, can grow long because of the need to describe word positions and stresses and also to determine the various effects. For this reason you do not have to exhaust your topic. Try to make your discussion representative of the prosody of your poem or passage.

Your first reading in preparation for your essay should be for comprehension. On second and third readings, make notes of sounds, accents, and rhymes by reading the poem aloud. To perceive sounds, one student helped herself by reading aloud in an exaggerated way in front of a mirror. If you have privacy or are not self-conscious, you might do the same. Let yourself go a bit. As you dramatize your reading (maybe even in front of fellow students), you will find that heightened levels of reading also accompany the poet's expression of important ideas. Mark these spots for later analysis so that you will be able to make strong assertions about the relationship of sound to sense.

In planning, it is vital to prepare study sheets so that your observations will be correct, for if your factual analysis is wrong, your writing will also be wrong. Experience has shown that it is best to make four triple-spaced copies of the poem or passage (use a copier or a computer). These will be for the separate analyses of rhythm, assonance, alliteration, and rhyme. If you have been assigned just one of these topics, of course, only one copy will be necessary. Leave spaces between syllables and words for marking the various feet of the poem. Ultimately, this duplication of the passage, with your markings, should be included as a first page, as in the demonstrative student essays in this chapter.

Carry out your study of the passage in the following way.

- Number each line of the passage, regardless of length, beginning with 1, so that you can use these numbers as location references in your essay.

- Determine the formal pattern of feet, using the short acute accent or stress mark for heavily stressed syllables (´) and the breve for unaccented or lightly stressed syllables (˘). Use chevrons to mark spondees (⌃⌃).

- Indicate the separate feet by a diagonal slash or virgule (/). Indicate caesurae and end-of-line pauses by double virgules (//).

- Use colored pencils to underline and circle, make boxes, or otherwise mark the formal and rhetorical substitutions that you discover. Because such substitutions may occur throughout the poem, develop a numbering system for each type (e.g., 1 = anapest, 6 = trochee, etc., as in the sample work sheet on p. 886). Provide a key to your numbers at the bottom of the page.

- Do the same for alliteration, assonance, onomatopoeia, and rhyme. It has proved particularly effective to draw lines to connect the repeating sounds, for these effects will be close together in the poem, and your connections will dramatize this closeness. The use of a separate color for each separate effect is helpful, for different colors make prosodic distinctions stand out clearly.

- Use your work sheets as a reference for your reader's benefit. In writing your essay, however, make your examples specific by including brief illustrative quotations, as in the demonstrative student essays (i.e., words, phrases, and entire lines, with proper marks and accents). Do not rely on line numbers alone.

Once you have analyzed the various effects in your poem and have recorded these on your work sheets and in your notes, you will be ready to formulate a central idea and organization. The focus of your essay should reflect the most significant features of prosody in relationship to some other element of the poem, such as speaker, tone, or ideas.

Strategies for Organizing Ideas

Depending on your assignment, you might wish to discuss all aspects of rhythm or sound, or perhaps just one, such as the poet's use of regular meter, a particular substitution, alliteration, or assonance. It is possible, for example, to devote an entire essay to (1) regular meter; (2) one particular variation in meter, such as the anapest or spondee; (3) the caesura; (4) assonance; (5) alliteration; (6) onomatopoeia; or (7) rhyme. For brevity, rhythm and segmental effects are treated together in one demonstrative student essay, and rhyme is considered alone in a separate essay.

After a brief description of the poem (such as that it is a sonnet, a two-stanza lyric, a dipodic burlesque poem, and so on), establish the scope of your essay. Your central idea will outline the thought that you wish to carry out through your prosodic analysis, such as that regularity of meter is consistent with a happy, firm vision of love or life, or that frequent spondees emphasize the solidity of the speaker's wish to love, or that particular sounds echo some of the poem's actions.

The body of your essay may include all the following elements or just one, depending on your instructor's assignment.

1. *Rhythm.* Establish the formal metrical pattern. What is the dominant metrical foot and line length? Are some lines shorter than the pattern? What relationship do the variable lengths have with the subject matter? If the poem is a lyric or a sonnet, are important words and syllables successfully placed in stressed positions in order to achieve emphasis? Try to relate line lengths to exposition, development of ideas, and rising or falling emotions. It is also important to look for either repeating or varying metrical patterns as the subject matter reaches peaks or climaxes. Generally, deal with the relationship between the formal rhythmical pattern and the poet's ideas and attitudes.

When noting substitutions, analyze the formal variations and the principal effects of these. If you concentrate on only one substitution, describe any apparent pattern in its use, that is, its locations, recurrences, and effects on meaning.

For caesurae, treat the effectiveness of the poet's control. Can you see any pattern of use? Are the pauses regular or random? Describe noticeable principles of placement, such as (1) the creation of rhythmical similarities in various parts of the poem, (2) the development of particular rhetorical effects, or (3) the creation of interest through rhythmical variety. Do the caesurae lead to important ideas and attitudes? Are the lines all end-stopped, or do some of them run over from one line to the next (enjambement)? How do these rhythmical characteristics aid in poet's descriptions and in the expression of the poet's ideas?

2. *Segmental effects.* Here you might be discussing, collectively or separately, the use and effects of assonance, alliteration, onomatopoeia, and cacophony and euphony. Be sure to establish that the instances you choose really occur systematically enough in the poem to form a pattern. Illustrate sounds by including relevant words within parentheses. You might make separate paragraphs on alliteration, assonance, and any other seemingly important pattern. Also, because space is always at a premium, you might concentrate on only one noteworthy effect, like a certain pattern of assonance, rather than on everything. Throughout your discussion, always keep foremost the relationship between content and sound.

To make illustrations clear, emphasize the sounds to which you are calling attention. If you use an entire word to illustrate a sound, underline or italicize only the sound, not the entire word, and put the word within quotation marks (for example, "The poet uses a *t* [' *t*ip,' '*t*op,' and '*t*errific']").

3. *Rhyme.* An essay on rhyme should describe the major features of the poem's rhymes, specifically the scheme and variants, the lengths and rhythms of the rhyming words, and noteworthy segmental characteristics. In discussing the grammar of the rhymes, note the kinds of words (i.e., verbs, nouns, etc.) used for rhymes: Are they all the same? Does one form predominate? Is there variety? Can you determine the grammatical positions of the rhyming words? How may these characteristics be related to the idea or theme of the poem?

You might also discuss the qualities of the rhyming words. Are the words specific? Concrete? Abstract? Are there any striking rhymes? Any surprises? Any rhymes that are particularly clever and witty? Do any rhymes give unique comparisons or contrasts? How?

Generally, note any striking or unique rhyming effects. Without becoming overly subtle or far-fetched, you can make valid and interesting conclusions. Do any sounds in the rhyming words appear in patterns of assonance or alliteration elsewhere in the poem? Do the rhymes contribute to onomatopoeia in the poem? Broadly, what aspects of rhyme are uniquely effective because they blend fully with the poem's thought and mood?

In your conclusion, try to develop a short evaluation of the poet's prosodic performance. If we accept the premise that poetry is designed not only to stimulate emotions but also to provide information and transfer attitudes, to what degree do the prosodic techniques of your poem contribute to these goals? Without going into excessive detail (and writing another essay), what more can you say here? What has been the value of your study to your understanding and appreciating the poem? If you think your analysis has helped you to develop new awareness of the poet's craft, it would be appropriate to state what you have learned.

DEMONSTRATIVE STUDENT ESSAY

A Study of Tennyson's Rhythm and Segments in "The Passing of Arthur," Lines 349–360[1]

[1]For illustration, this essay analyzes a passage from Tennyson's "The Passing of Arthur," which is part of *Idylls of the King*. Containing 469 lines, "The Passing of Arthur" describes the last battle and the death of Arthur, legendary king of early Britain. After the fight, in which Arthur has been mortally wounded by the traitor Mordred, only Arthur and his follower Sir Bedivere remain alive. Arthur commands Bedivere to throw the royal sword Excalibur into the lake from which Arthur had originally received it. After great hesitation and some false claims, Bedivere does throw the sword into the lake, and a hand rises out of the water to catch it. Bedivere then carries Arthur to the lakeshore, where the dying king is taken aboard a mysterious funeral barge. In the passage selected for discussion (lines 349–360), Tennyson describes Bedivere's carrying Arthur down the hills and cliffs from the battlefield to the lake below. See also pp. 880–81.

1. *RHYTHMICAL ANALYSIS**

But the o - / ther swift - / ly strode / / from ridge / to ridge, / /   1

Clothed with / his breath, / / and look - / ing, / / as / he walk'd, / /   2

Lar - ger / than hu - / man / / on / the fro - / zen hills. / /   3

He heard / the deep / be - hind / him, / / and / a cry   4

Be - fore. / / His own / thought drove / him / / like / a goad. / /   5

Dry clash'd / his har - / ness / / in / the i / cy caves   6

And bar - ren / chasms, / / and all / to left / and right   7

The bare / black cliff / clang'd round / him, / / as / he based   8

His feet / on juts / of slip - / pe-ry crag / / that rang   9

Sharp - smit - / ten / / with / the / dint / of ar - / med heels— / /   10

And on / a sud - / den, / / lo! / / the lev - / el lake, / /   11

And the / long glor - / ies / / of / the win - / ter moon. / /   12

1 = Anapest, or effect of anapest.	4 = Effect of imperfect foot.
2 = Amphibrach, or the effect of amphibrach.	5 = Pyrrhic.
3 = Spondee.	6 = Trochee, or the effect of trochee.

* Pronunciation symbols as in *Webster's New World Dictionary,* 2nd ed.

2. ALLITERATION

But the other (s)wiftly (s)trode from ridge to ridge,   1

Clothed with his breath, and looking, as (h)e walked,   2

Larger than (h)uman on the frozen (h)ills.   3

(H)e (h)eard the deep be(h)ind (h)im, and a cry   4

Before. (H)is own thought drove him like a goad.   5

Dry (c)lash'd (h)is (h)arness in the icy (c)aves   6

And (b)arren (ch)asms, and all to left and right   7

The (b)are (b)(l)ack (c)(l)iff (c)(l)ang'd round him, as he (b)ased   8

His feet on juts of s(l)ippery (c)rag that rang   9

Sharp-smitten with the dint of armed heels—   10

And on a sudden, (l)o! the (l)evel, (l)ake,   11

And the (l)ong g(l)ories of the winter moon.   12

ᾮᾮᾮ = s   ─────── = b

------ = h   ᾮᾮᾮ = l as second consonant
                                         sound in words
········ = k   ─·─··─··─ = l

3. ASSONANCE

But the other sw(i)ftly str(o)de from r(i)dge to r(i)dge,   1

Cl(o)thed w(i)th h(i)s breath, and looking, as he walked,   2

Larger than human on the fr(o)zen hills.   3

He heard the deep beh(i)nd him, and a cr(y)   4

Before. His (ow)n thought dr(o)ve him l(i)ke a g(oa)d.   5

Dr(y) clash'd his harness in the (i)cy caves   6

And barren ch(a)sms, and all to left and r(i)ght   7

The bare bl(a)ck cliff cl(a)ng'd round him, as he based   8

H(i)s feet on juts of sl(i)ppery cr(a)g that r(a)ng   9

Sh(ar)p-sm(i)tten w(i)th the d(i)nt of (ar)med heels—   10

And on a sudden, lo! the level lake,   11

And the long glories of the winter moon.   12

—————— = ō   ·—·—·—· = ä

---------- = ī   ⌢⌢⌢⌢⌢ = ĭ

·········· = ă

[1] In these twelve lines, Tennyson describes the ordeal of Sir Bedivere as he carries King Arthur, who is dying, from the mountainous heights, where he was wounded, down to the lake, where he will be sent to his final rest. Tennyson emphasizes the bleakness and hostility of this ghostly and deserted landscape. The metrical pattern he uses is unrhymed iambic pentameter--blank verse--which is suitable for descriptions of actions and scenes. Appropriately, the verse augments the natural descriptions and echoes first Bedivere's tenseness and then his relaxation.* Tennyson's control enables a true blending of sound and sense, as seen in his use of rhythm and in his manipulation of segmental devices, including onomatopoeia.†

[2] Tennyson controls his meter to emphasize exertions and moods. In line 1 the meter is regular, except for an anapest in the first foot. This regularity may be interpreted as emphasizing the swiftness and surefootedness of Bedivere. But he is about to undergo a severe test, and the rhythm quickly becomes irregular, as though to strain the pentameter verse in illustration of Bedivere's exertions. Tennyson therefore uses variations to highlight key words. For example, he uses the effect of anapests in a number of lines. In line 2 he emphasizes the chill air and Bedivere's vitality in the following way:

Clothed with / his breath, //

The image is one of being surrounded by one's own breath that vaporizes on hitting the cold air, and the rhythmical variation—a trochaic substitution in the first foot—enables the voice to build up to the word "breath," a most effective internal climax.

[3] Tennyson uses the same kind of rhythmical effect in line 3. He emphasizes the "frozen hills" by creating a caesura in the middle of the third foot, and then by making the heavy stress of the third foot fall on the preposition "on", which with "the" creates the effect of an anapest consisting of two unstressed syllables leading up to the first, stressed, syllable of "frozen". The effect is that the voice builds up to the word and thus emphasizes the extreme conditions in which Bedivere is walking:

// on / the fro - / zen hills. //

Tennyson uses this rhythmical effect twelve times in the passage. It is one of his major means of rhetorical emphasis.

[4] Tennyson's most effective metrical variation is the spondee, which appears in lines 5, 6, 8, (twice), 10, and 12. These substitutions, occurring mainly in the section describing how Bedivere forces his way down the frozen hills, permits the descriptive lines to ring out, as in

The bare / black cliff / clanged round /

---

* Central idea.
† Thesis sentence.

and

Dry clash'd / his har - / ness //

These substitutions are so strong that they seem to mimic the actual sounds of Bedivere's exertions. In addition to this use of the spondee as a sound effect, a remarkable use of the spondee for psychological effect occurs in line 5. Here, the stresses internalize Bedivere's distress, reaching a climax on the word "drove":

His own / thought drove / him //

There is other substitution, too, both formal and rhetorical, and the tension these variations create keeps the responsive reader aware of Bedivere's tasks. One type of variation is the appearance of amphibrachic rhythm, which is produced in lines 2, 3, 4, 6, 7, and 11. The effect is achieved by a pattern that complements the rhetorical anapests. A caesura in the middle of a foot leaves the three preceding syllables as a light, heavy, and light, the rhythmical form of the

[5]   amphibrach. In line 2, for example, it appears thus:

// and look - / ing, //

In line 6 it takes this form:

/ his har - / ness //

Still another related variation is that of the apparently imperfect feet in lines 5, 8, 11, and 12. These imperfect feet are produced by a caesura, which isolates the syllable, as him is in line 8:

The bare / black cliff / clang'd round / him, //

[6]

In line 11 the syllable (on the word "lo!") is surrounded by two caesurae and is therefore thrust into a position of great stress:

And on / a sud - / den, // lo! // the lev - / el lake,

Other, less significant substitutions are the trochees in lines 3 and 7 and the pyrrhic in line 12. All the described variations suggest the energy that Bedivere expends during his heroic action.

Many of the variations are produced by Tennyson's sentence structure,
[7]   which results in a free placement of the caesurae and in a free use of end-stopping and enjambement. Four of the first five lines are end-stopped (two by commas,

two by periods). Bedivere is exerting himself during these lines, and he is taking short rests to gather strength. His dangerous descent is described during the next four lines, and none of these lines is end-stopped. Bedivere is disturbed (being goaded by "his own thought"), but he must keep going, and the free sentence structure and free metrical variation underscore his physical and mental difficulties. But in the last two lines, when he has reached the lake, the lines "relax" with falling caesurae exactly at the fifth syllable. In other words, the sentence structure of the last two lines is regular, an effect suggesting the return to order and beauty after the previous, rugged chaos.

[8] This rhythmical virtuosity is accompanied by a similarly brilliant control over segmental devices. Alliteration is the most obvious, permitting Tennyson to tie key words and their signifying actions together, as in the s's in "swiftly strode" in line 1 or the b's in "barren", "bare", "black", and "based" in lines 7 and 8. Other notable examples are the aspirated h's in lines 2 to 6 ("he", "human", "hills", "heard", "behind", "him", "his", "harness"); the k's in lines 6 to 9 ("clashed", "caves", "chasms", "cliff", "clanged", "crag"); and the l's in lines 11 and 12 ("lo", "level", "lake", "long", "glories"). One might compare these l's with the l's in the more anguished context of lines 8 and 9, where the sounds appear as the second segment in the heavy, ringing words there ("black", "cliff", "clanged", "slippery"). The sounds are the same, and the emphasis is similar, but the effects are different.

[9] Assonance is also present throughout the passage. In the first five lines, for example, the ō appears in six words. The first three ō's are in descriptive or metaphoric words ("strode", "clothed", "frozen"), while the last three are in words describing Bedivere's pain and anguish ("own", "drove", "goad"). The o therefore ties the physical to the psychological. Other patterns of assonance are the ă in lines 7, 8, and 9 (chasms, clang'd, black, crag, rang); the ä of line 10 (shärp, ärmed); the ī of lines 4 to 7 ("behind", "cry", "like", "dry", "icy", "right"); and the short ĭ of lines 1 and 2, and 9 and 10 ("swiftly", "ridge", "with", "his", "slippery", "smitten", "with", "dint"). One might remark also that in the last two lines, which describe the level lake and the moon, Tennyson introduces a number of relaxed o and oo and similar vowel sounds:

> And on a sudden, lo! the level lake,
> And the long glories of the winter moon.

[10] The last two lines are, in fact, onomatopoeic, since the liquid l sounds suggest the gentle lapping of waves on a lake shore. There are other examples of onomatopoeia, too. In line 2 Tennyson describes Bedivere in the cold air as being "Clothed with his breath," and in the following five lines Tennyson employs many words with the aspirate h (e.g., "his harness"). In the context, these sounds enable readers to see and hear sights and sounds just like those of Bedivere as he carries his royal burden. Similarly, the explosive stops b, k, d, and t in lines 6 to 10 imitate the sounds of Sir Bedivere's feet on the "juts of slippery crag."

[11] This short passage is filled with many examples of poetic excellence. Tennyson's sounds and rhythms actually speak along with the meaning. They emphasize the grandeur of Arthur and his faithful follower, and for one brief moment they bear out the magic that Tennyson associated with the fading past.

Commentary on the Essay

This essay presents a full treatment of the prosody of the passage from Tennyson. Paragraphs 2 through 7 deal with the relationship of the rhythm to the content. Note that prosody is not discussed in isolation, but as it augments Tennyson's descriptions of action and scenes. Thus, paragraph 4 refers to the use of the spondee as a substitute foot to reinforce ideas. Also in this paragraph, there is a short comparison of alternative ways of saying what Tennyson says so well. While such a speculative comparison should not be attempted often, it is effective here in bringing out the quality of Tennyson's use of the spondee as a means of emphasis.

Paragraphs 8 and 9 present a discussion of the alliteration and assonance of the passage, and paragraph 10 considers onomatopoeia.

Of greatest importance for the clarity of the essay, there are many supporting examples, spaced, centered, accurately marked, and numbered by line. In any essay about prosody, readers are likely to be unsure of the validity of the writer's observation unless such examples are provided and are located within the essay.

DEMONSTRATIVE STUDENT ESSAY

The Rhymes in Christina Rossetti's "Echo"

1	*n* Come to me in the silence of the night;	5a
2	*n* Come in the speaking silence of a dream;	5b
3	*adj* Come with soft rounded cheeks and eyes as bright	5a
4	*n* As sunlight on a stream;	3b
5	*n* Come back in tears,	2c
6	*n* O memory, hope, love of finished years.	5c
7	*adj* O dream how sweet, too sweet, too bitter sweet,	5d
8	*n* Whose wakening should have been in paradise,	5e
9	*v* Where souls brimful of love abide and meet;	5d

n
10   Where thirsty longing eyes   3e

n
11   Watch the slow door   2f

adv
12   That opening, letting in, lets out no more.   5f

v
13   Yet come to me in dreams, that I may live   5g

n
14   My very life again though cold in death;   5h

v
15   Come back to me in dreams, that I may give   5g

n
16   Pulse for pulse, breath for breath: 3h

adv
17   Speak low, lean low,   2i

adj
18   As long ago, my love, how long ago!   5i

Repeated words		n = noun
～～～	dream, dreams	v = verb
——	sweet	adj = adjective
- · - · - ·	breath	adv = adverb
······	low	
- - - - -	long ago	
～～～～	come	

[1]   In the three-stanza lyric poem "Echo," Christina Rossetti uses rhyme as a way of saying that one might regain in dreams a love that is lost in reality.* As the real love is to the dream of love, so is an original sound to an echo. This connection underlies the poem's title and also Rossetti's unique use of rhyme. Aspects of her rhyme are the lyric pattern, the forms and qualities of the rhyming words, and the special use of repetition.†

[2]   The rhyme pattern is simple, and, like rhyme generally, it may be thought of as a pattern of echoes. Each stanza contains four lines of alternating rhymes concluded by a couplet, as follows:

Iambic: *5a, 5b, 5a, 3b, 2c, 5c.*

* Central idea.
† Thesis sentence.

There are nine separate rhymes throughout the poem, three in each stanza. Only two words are used for each rhyme, and no rhyme is used twice. Of the eighteen rhyming words, sixteen are one syllable long—almost all the rhymes. The remaining two words consist of two and three syllables. With such a great number of single-syllable words, the rhymes are all rising ones, on the accented halves of iambic feet, and the end-of-line emphasis is on simple words.

The grammatical forms and positions of the rhyming words lend support to the introspective subject matter. Although there is variety, more than half the rhyming words are nouns. There are ten in all, and eight are placed as the objects of prepositions (e.g., "of a dream," "on a stream," "of finished years"). The nouns that are not the objects of prepositions are the subject and object of the same subordinate clause (lines 10 and 11). It seems clear that much of the poem's verbal energy occurs in the first parts of the lines, leaving the rhymes to occur in modifying elements, as in these lines (italics added):

[3]

Come to me *in the silence of the night* (1)

Yet come to me in dreams, *that I may live* (13)
My very life again *though cold in death;* (14)

Most of the other rhymes are also in such internalized positions. This careful arrangement is consistent with the speaker's emphasis on her yearning to relive her love within dreams.

The qualities of the words are also consistent with the poem's emphasis on the speaker's internal life. Most of the rhyming words are impressionistic. Even the specific words-- "stream", "tears", "eyes", "door", and "breath"--reflect the speaker's mental condition. In this regard, the rhyming words of lines 1 and 3 are

[4]   effective. These are "night" and "bright", which contrast the bleakness of the speaker's solitary condition with the vitality of her inner life. Another effective contrast is in lines 14 and 16, where "death" and "breath" are rhymed. This rhyme underscores the sad fact that even though the speaker's love has vanished, it lives in present memory just as an echo continues after the original sound is gone.

It is in emphasizing how memory echoes experience that Rossetti creates her special use of rhyming words. She creates an ingenious repetition of a number of words; these are the poem's echoes. The major echoing word is the verb "come," which appears as identical rhyme six times at the beginnings of lines in stanzas 1 and 3. Some of the other rhyming words are also repeated.

[5]   The most notable is "dream," the rhyming word in line 2. Rossetti repeats the word in line 7 and uses the plural, "dreams," in lines 13 and 15. In line 7 the rhyming word *sweet* is the third use of that word, a climax of "how *sweet*, too *sweet*, too bitter *sweet*." Concluding the poem, Rossetti repeats "breath" (16), "low" (17), and the phrase "long ago" (18). These repeating identical rhymes justify the title "Echo," and they also stress the major idea that it is only in memory that experience has reality, even if dreams are no more than echoes.

Thus rhyme is not just ornamental in "Echo," but integral. The ease of

[6]   Rossetti's rhymes, like the poem's diction generally, keeps the focus on regret and yearning rather than self-indulgence. As in all rhyming poems, Rossetti's rhymes emphasize the line endings. The rhymes go beyond this effect, however,

because they are used internally as identical rhymes of the terminal rhyming words. "Echo" is a poem in which rhyme is inseparable from meaning.

Commentary on the Essay

Throughout, illustrative words are highlighted, and numbers are used to indicate the lines from which the illustrations are drawn. The introductory paragraph asserts that rhyme is vital in Rossetti's poem. It also attempts to explain the title "Echo." The thesis statement indicates the four topics to be developed in the body.

Paragraph 2 deals with the mechanical, mathematical aspects of the poem's rhymes. The high number of monosyllabic rhyming words is used to explain Rossetti's use of rising rhymes.

Paragraph 3 treats the grammar of the rhymes. For example, an analysis and count reveal that there are ten rhyming nouns and three rhyming verbs. The verb of command *come* is mentioned to show that most of the rhyming words exist within groups modifying this word. The grammatical analysis is thus related to the internalized nature of the poem's subject.

Paragraph 4 emphasizes the impressionistic nature of the rhyming words and also points out two instances in which rhymes stress the contrast between real life and the speaker's introspective life. Paragraph 5 deals with how Rossetti repeats five of the poem's rhyming words. This repetition creates a pattern of echoes, in keeping with the poem's title.

The final paragraph concludes that Rossetti uses rhyme integrally within "Echo," not ornamentally. In addition, the point is emphasized that the internal rhymes or echoes are another facet of Rossetti's rhyming skill.

SPECIAL TOPICS FOR WRITING AND ARGUMENT ABOUT RHYTHM AND RHYME IN POETRY

1. For Shakespeare's Sonnet 73, "That Time of Year Thou May'st in Me Behold," analyze the ways in which Shakespeare creates iambics. What is the relationship of lightly accented syllables to the heavily accented ones? Where does Shakespeare use articles (*the*), pronouns (*this, his*), prepositions (*upon, against, of*), relative clause markers (*which, that*), and adverb clause markers (*as, when*) in relation to syllables of heavy stress? On the basis of this study, how would you characterize Shakespeare's control of the iambic foot?

2. Eliot's "Macavity: The Mystery Cat," Robinson's "Miniver Cheevy," Poe's "The Bells," Nash's "Very Like a Whale," and Gardner's "At a Summer Hotel" all include falling rhymes. What is the effect of this rhyming pattern in the poems? To what degree do the poems achieve seriousness despite the fact that falling rhyme is often used generally to complement humorous and light verse?

3. Compare the sounds used in Poe's "The Bells" with those of Wagoner's "March for a One-Man Band." What effects are achieved by each poet? What is the relationship in each poem between sound and content? Which poem do you prefer on the basis of sound? Why?

4.   Analyze the rhymes in two of the following poems: Shakespeare's Sonnet No. 73, Hopkins's "God's Grandeur," Poe's "Annabel Lee," Shelley's "Ode to the West Wind," or the passage from Pope's "Essay on Man." What is interesting or unique about the various rhyming words? What relationships can you discover between the rhymes and the topics of the poems?

5.   Compare one of the rhyming poems with one of the nonrhyming poems included in this chapter. What differences in reading and sound can you discover as a result of the use or nonuse of rhyme? What benefits does rhyme give to the poem? What benefits does nonrhyme give?

6.   Analyze Hardy's use of rhymes in "Channel Firing" (Chapter 14). What effects does Hardy create by using trochaic rhyme, like *hatters* and *matters,* and also by using dactyllic rhyme, like *saner be* and *century*? What is the relationship of such rhymes to the heavy-stress rhymes in the poem?

7.   Write a short poem of your own, using rhymes with trochaic words or dactylic words such as *computer, emetic, scholastic, remarkable, along with me, inedible, moron, anxiously, emotion, fishing,* and so on. If you have trouble with exact rhymes, see what you can do with slant rhymes and eye rhymes. The idea is to use your ingenuity.

8.   Using the topical index in your library, take out a book on prosody, such as Harvey Gross's *Sound and Form in Modern Poetry* (1968) or *The Structure of Verse* (1966), or Gay Wilson Allen's *American Prosody* (1935, reprinted 1966). Select a topic (e.g., formal or experimental prosody) or a poet (e.g., Frost, Arnold, Shakespeare, Blake) and write a summary of the ideas and observations that the writers make on your subject. What relationship do the writers make about prosody and the poet's ideas? How does prosody enter into the writer's thought? Into the ways in which the poets emphasize ideas and images?

20

Form: The Shape
of the Poem

Because poetry is tightly compressed and highly rhythmical, it always exists under self-imposed restrictions, or conventions, some of which are examined in Chapter 19. Traditionally, many poets have chosen a variety of clearly recognizable shapes or forms—closed form poetry. Since the middle of the nineteenth century, however, many poets have rejected the more regular patterns in favor of poems that appear more free and spontaneous—open form poetry. These terms refer to the structure and technique of the poems, not to content or ideas.

CLOSED-FORM POETRY

Closed-form poetry is written in specific and traditional patterns of lines produced through *line length, meter, rhyme, and line groupings.* In the closed form (and also in the open form), the **line** is, loosely, the poetic equivalent of the prose sentence. A prime characteristic of the closed-form line, as opposed to a sentence, is that its length should be designated or restricted. Various numbers of lines may be grouped together through rhyme and other means to form a **stanza,** which is the poetic analogue of the prose paragraph. Individual lines may coincide exactly with sentences, although quite often sentences stretch out over two or more lines. Stanzas consist of groups of lines that are both connected and also separated by developments of subject, idea, or expression of feeling.

Over the centuries, English and American poetry has appropriated and evolved many closed forms. The most important of these are *blank verse,* the *couplet,* the *tercet* or *triplet,* and the *quatrain,* in addition to special forms, most commonly the *sonnet,* the *ballad,* the *song* or *lyric, common measure* or the *hymnal stanza,* the *ode,* and less significant forms like the *haiku,* the *epigram,* the *epitaph,* the *limerick,* the *clerihew,* and the *double dactyl.*

BLANK VERSE.   One of the most common closed forms of English poetry is **blank verse,** or unrhymed iambic pentameter, which represents the adaptation and fusion of sentences to poetic form. The master of blank verse is Shakespeare, who uses it extensively in his plays. Another master is Milton, who uses it exclusively in his long epic *Paradise Lost.* An example of Shakespeare's blank verse is this speech from the first act of *Hamlet,* in which the prince tells his mother that his sorrow over his father's death is real and not superficial (I. 2.77–86):

> Seems, madam? nay it is, I know not "seems."
> 'Tis not alone my inky cloak good mother,
> Nor customary suits of solemn black,
> Nor windy suspiration of forced breath,
> No, nor the fruitful river in the eye,
> Nor the dejected havior of the visage,
> Together with all forms, moods, shapes of grief,
> That can denote me truly: these indeed seem,
> For they are actions that a man might play,
> But I have that within which passes show,
> These but the trappings and the suits of woe.

While these lines are linked together to make up the entire speech, each one creates an identifiable unit of thought and grammatical coherence. (The rhyming lines mark the conclusion of the scene, not a new stylistic form.) In the footsteps of Shakespeare, poets of English have used blank verse again and again, for without forsaking its poetic identity, it sounds like normal speech.

THE COUPLET.   The **couplet,** consisting of two lines, is the shortest distinct closed form. The two lines are usually identical in length, meter, and rhyme, although ancient biblical poetry contains couplets unified by parallel ideas, not by meter and rhyme. Some couplets are short; even monometric lines like "Some play / All day" comprise a couplet. However, couplets are most often in iambic tetrameter (four stresses) and iambic pentameter (five stresses), and they have been a regular feature of English poetry ever since Chaucer used them in the fourteenth century. In the seventeenth and eighteenth centuries, the iambic-pentameter couplet was considered appropriate for epic, or heroic, poetry. For this reason it is often called a **heroic couplet.** Because the period is considered the "neoclassic" age of literature, the form is also called the **neoclassic couplet.** It was used with consummate skill by John Dryden (1631–1700) and also by Alexander Pope (1685–1744).

Usually, the heroic couplet expresses a complete idea and is grammatically self-sufficient. It thrives on the rhetorical strategies of **parallelism** and **antithesis.** Look, for example, at these two couplets from "The Rape of the Lock," Pope's well-known mock-epic poem (1711):

Here Britain's statesmen oft the fall foredoom
Of foreign tyrants, and of nymphs at home;
Here thou, great Anna! whom three realms obey,
Dost sometimes counsel take—and sometimes tea.

These lines describe activities at Hampton Court, the royal palace and residence of Queen Anne (reigned 1701–1714). Notice that the first couplet allows Pope to link "Britain's statesmen" with two related but antithetical events: the fall of nations and the "fall" of young women. Similarly, the second heroic couplet allows for the parallel and comic linking of royal meetings of state ("counsel") and teatime (in the early eighteenth century, *tea* was pronounced "tay"). The example thus demonstrates how the heroic couplet may place contrasting actions and situations in amusing and ironic parallels.

THE TERCET OR TRIPLET. A three-line stanza is called a **tercet** or **triplet.** Tercets may be written in any uniform line length or meter and most commonly contain three rhymes (*a a a, b b b,* and so on), which are, in effect, short stanzas. The following poem is in iambic tetrameter triplets.

ALFRED, LORD TENNYSON   (1809–1892)

The Eagle _____ *1851*

He clasps the crag with crooked hands;
Close to the sun in lonely lands,
Ring'd with the azure world, he stands.

The wrinkled sea beneath him crawls;
He watches from his mountain walls,
And like a thunderbolt he falls.

5

In the first tercet, we view the eagle as though at a distance. In the second, the perspective shifts, and we see through the eagle's eyes and follow his actions. In this tercet the verbs are active: the sea "crawls" and the eagle "falls." While the two tercets and the shift in perspective divide the poem, alliteration pulls things back together. This is especially true of the *k* sound in "*c*lasps," "*c*rag," "*c*rooked," "*c*lose," and "*c*rawls" and the *w* sound in "*w*ith," "*w*orld," "*w*atches," and "*w*alls."

There are two important variations on the tercet pattern, each requiring a high degree of ingenuity and control. The first tercet variation is **terza rima,** in which stanzas are interlocked through a pattern that requires the center termination in one tercet to be rhymed twice in the next: *a b a, b c b, c d c, d e d,* and so on. You can see an example of terza rima in Shelley's "Ode to the West Wind" (p. 877).

The most complex variation of the tercet pattern is the **villanelle,** a nineteen-line form containing six tercets, rhymed *a b a,* and concluded by four lines.

The first and third lines of the first tercet are repeated alternately in subsequent tercets as a refrain and also are used in the concluding four lines. For examples see Bishop's "One Art," Roethke's "The Waking," and Thomas's "Do Not Go Gentle into That Good Night."

THE QUATRAIN.   The most common and adaptable stanzaic building block is the four-line **quatrain.** This stanza has been popular for hundreds of years and has lent itself to many variations. Like couplets and tercets, quatrains may be written in any line length and meter; even the line lengths *within* a quatrain may vary. The determining factor is the rhyme scheme, and even that is variable, depending on the form and the poet's aims. Quatrains may be rhymed *a a a a,* but they can also be rhymed *a b a b, a b b a, a a b a,* or even *a b c b.* All these variations are determined, at least in part, by the larger patterns or forms in which quatrains are used. Quatrains are basic components of many traditional closed forms, most notably ballads and sonnets.

THE SONNET.   The **sonnet,** consisting of fourteen lines, is one of the most popular and durable closed poetic forms. Initially it was an Italian form (*sonnetto* means "little song") created and popularized by the medieval Italian poet Petrarch (1304–1374), who wrote collections or *cycles* of sonnets. The sonnet form as practiced by Petrarch is called the **Italian sonnet** or **Petrarchan sonnet** in Petrarch's honor. The form and style of Petrarchan sonnets were adapted to English poetry in the early sixteenth century, and with variations they have been used ever since. As a form, the Petrarchan sonnet is in iambic pentameter, and it contains two quatrains (the **octave**) and two tercets (the **sestet**). In terms of structure and meaning, the octave presents a problem or situation that is resolved in the sestet, as in Milton's "When I Consider How My Light Is Spent." The rhyme scheme of the Petrarchan octave is fixed in an *a b b a, a b b a* pattern. The sestet offers a number of different rhyming possibilities, including *c d c, c d c* and *c d e, c d e.*

Shakespeare was the most original adapter of the sonnet tradition. Recognizing that there are fewer rhyming words in English than in Italian, he developed the **Shakespearean sonnet** or **English sonnet** on seven rhymes (in the pattern *a b a b, c d c d, e f e f, g g*) rather than the five rhymes of the Italian sonnet. As indicated by the rhyme scheme, the Shakespearean sonnet contains three quatrains and a concluding couplet. The pattern of thought therefore shifts from the octave-sestet organization of the Italian sonnet to a four-part argument on a single thought or emotion. Each Shakespearean quatrain contains a separate development of the sonnet's central idea or problem, and the couplet provides a climax and resolution.

THE BALLAD.   The **ballad,** which fuses narrative description with dramatic dialogue, originated in folk literature and is one of the oldest closed forms in English poetry. Ballads consist of many quatrains in which lines of iambic tetrameter alternate with iambic trimeter. Normally, only the second and fourth lines of each stanza rhyme, in the pattern *x a x a, x b x b, x c x c,* and so on. The ballad was designed for singing, like the anonymous "Sir Patrick Spens" (Chapter 13). Popular ballad tunes were used over and over again by later balladeers, often as many as forty and fifty times, and many of the tunes have survived to the present day and are still popular, as with "Bonny Barbara Allan" and "Waly, Waly" (Chapter 25).

THE SONG OR LYRIC.　　The **song** or **lyric** is a stanzaic form that was originally designed to be sung to a repeating melody, although not all lyrics are written specifically for music. Even so, the line lengths and rhyme schemes of the first stanza are duplicated in all subsequent stanzas, as though for repeated singing to the same tune. The stanzas of a lyric may be built from any combination of single lines, couplets, triplets, and quatrains. The line lengths may shift, and a great deal of metrical variation is common.

There is theoretically no limit to the number of stanzas in a lyric, although there are usually no more than five or six. A. E. Housman's "Loveliest of Trees" (Chapter 13), for example, is made up of three quatrains containing two couplets each. It is in iambic tetrameter and rhymes *a a b b.* The second and third stanzas repeat the same pattern. Christina Rossetti's "Echo" (Chapter 19) is also a lyric, but its structure is different from that of Housman's poem. Here, the structural formulation of each stanza is iambic: *5a 5b 5a 3b 2c 5c.* Lyrics can have very complex and ingenious stanzaic structures. John Donne's "The Canonization," for instance (Chapter 21), contains five stanzas that repeat the following iambic pattern: *5a 4b 5b 5a 4c 4c 4c 4a 3a.* This nine-line stanza contains three different rhymes and three different line lengths. Nevertheless, the same intricate pattern is repeated in each of the five stanzas.

COMMON MEASURE OR THE HYMNAL STANZA.　　**Common measure,** a quatrain form, is similar to the ballad stanza. It shares with the ballad the alternation of four-beat and three-beat iambic lines but adds a second rhyme to the first and third lines of each quatrain: *a b a b, c d c d,* and so on. Because the measure is often used in hymns, it is sometimes called the **hymnal stanza.** Many of Emily Dickinson's poems, including "Because I Could Not Stop for Death" (Chapter 13), are written in common measure.

THE ODE.　　The **ode** is a more variable stanzaic form than the lyric, with varying line lengths and intricate rhyme schemes. There is no set form. Some odes have repeating patterns, while others offer no duplication and introduce a new structure in each stanza. Poets have developed their own structures according to their needs. John Keats's great odes were particularly congenial to his ideas, as in "Ode to a Nightingale," which consists of ten stanzas in iambic pentameter with the repeating form *a b a b c d e 3c d e.* Although many odes have been set to music, such as John Dryden's "A Song for St. Cecelia's Day" (Chapter 23), most do not fit repeating melodies.

THE HAIKU.   The **haiku** originated in Japan, where it has been a favorite genre for hundreds of years. It traditionally imposes strict rules on the writer: (1) The topic should be derived from nature. (2) There should be three lines of *five, seven,* and *five* syllables per line, for a total of seventeen syllables. Today, English-language poets have adapted the haiku but have taken liberties with the subject matter and have often reduced the syllable count. Whether variations are taken, however, the haiku must be short, simple, objective, clear, and (often) symbolic. The following anonymous haiku illustrates some of these qualities.

Spun in High, Dark Clouds

Spun in high, dark clouds,
Snow forms vast webs of white flakes
And drifts lightly down

In the tradition of haiku, the subject is derived from nature, and the line pattern is 5-7-5. The central metaphor equates gathering snow with the webs of silkworms or spiders. To supply tension, the lines contrast "high" with "down" and "dark" with "white." Because of the enforced brevity, the diction is simple and, except for the word "forms," of English derivation (the word *form* was originally French). In addition, the words are mainly monosyllabic, and the poem therefore fills the seventeen-syllable form with sixteen words.

ADDITIONAL CLOSED-FORM TYPES.   Many other closed forms have enjoyed long popularity. One of these, the **epigram,** is a short and witty poem that usually makes a humorous or satiric point. Epigrams are two to four lines long and are often written in couplets. The form was developed by the Roman poet Martial (ca. 40–103 C.E.) and is still popular. Humorous **epitaphs,** lines composed to mark the death of someone, can also be epigrams.

Another popular type is the **limerick,** a five-line form popularized by the English artist and humorist Edward Lear (1812–1888). Like the epigram, limericks are comic and usually bawdy, their humor being reinforced by falling rhymes.

Comic closed forms continue to be devised by enterprising writers. The **clerihew,** a two-couplet form invented in the late nineteenth century by Edmund Clerihew Bentley (1875–1956), is related to the epigram. A final illustration of closed-form humor is the **double dactyl,** devised in the 1960s by Anthony Hecht and John Hollander. The form is related to the epigram, limerick, and clerihew, and it has rules that govern the meter, line length, and specific topic material.

Poets Use the Closed Form to Shape and Polish Meaning

Although many contemporary poets consider closed forms restrictive and even stultifying, the closed form has always provided both a framework and a challenge for poets to express new and fresh ideas, attitudes, and feelings. Let us look at the way Shakespeare uses the sonnet form to shape thoughts and emotions.

WILLIAM SHAKESPEARE   (1564–1616)

Sonnet 116: Let Me Not to the Marriage of True Minds _____ *1609*

Let me not to the marriage of true minds
Admit impediments.° Love is not love
Which alters when it alteration finds,
Or bends with the remover to remove:
Oh, no! it is an ever-fixéd mark,   5
That looks on tempests and is never shaken;
It is the star to every wandering bark,
Whose worth's unknown, although his height° be taken   *altitude*
Love's not Time's fool,° though rosy lips and cheeks   *slave*
Within his° bending sickle's compass come;   *Time's*   10
Love alters not with his brief hours and weeks,
But bears it out even to the edge of doom.°   *the Last Judgment*
  If this be error and upon me proved,
  I never writ, nor no man ever loved.

SONNET 116.   2 *impediments:* a reference to "The Order of Solemnization of Matrimony" in the Anglican Church's *Book of Common Prayer:* "I require that if either of you know of any impediment why ye may not be lawfully joined together in Matrimony, ye do now confess it."

QUESTIONS

1.   Describe the restrictions of this closed form. How is the poem's argument structured by the form?

2.   What is the poem's meter? Rhyme scheme? Structure?

3.   Describe the varying ideas about love explored in the three quatrains.

4.   What does the concluding couplet contribute to the poem's argument about love?

Even if we did not know that the poem is Shakespeare's, we would instantly recognize that it is a Shakespearean sonnet. It is in iambic pentameter and contains three quatrains and a concluding couplet, rhyming *a b a b, c d c d, e f e f, g g*. The sonnet form provides the organization for the poem's argument—that real love is a "marriage of true minds" existing independent of earthly time and change. Each quatrain advances a new perspective on this idea.

This is not to say that Shakespeare exhausts the subject or that he wants to. The ideas in the third quatrain, for example, about how love transcends time, could be greatly expanded. A philosophical analysis of the topic might deal extensively with Platonic ideas about reality—whether it exists in *particulars* or *universals.* Similarly, the poem's very last line, if it became the topic of a prose inquiry, might include the introduction of evidence about the poet's own writing, and also about many examples of human love. But the two lines are enough, granted the restrictions of the form, and more would be superfluous. One might add that most readers find Shakespeare's poem interesting and vital, while extensive philosophical discourses often drop into laps as readers fall asleep.

The closed poetic form therefore may be viewed as a complex consequence of poetic compression. No matter what form a poet chooses—couplet, sonnet, song, ballad, ode—that form imposes restrictions, and it therefore challenges and shapes the poet's thought. The poet of the closed form shares with all writers the need to make ideas seem logical and well supported, but the challenge of the form is to make all this happen *within the form itself.* The thought must be developed clearly and also fully, and there should be no lingering doubts once the poem is completed. The words must be the most fitting and exact ones that could be selected. When we look at good poems in the closed form, in short, we may be sure that they represent the ultimate degree of poetic thought, discipline, and skill.

OPEN-FORM POETRY

Among the closed forms, as we have seen, the ode is the form that gives poets great opportunity for variability and expansion. The ode is thus the closed form that is most closely related, in spirit, to **open-form poetry,** but the open form eliminates the restrictions of the closed form. Each open-form poem is thus unique and unpredictable because it avoids traditional patterns of organization to produce order. Poetry of this type was once termed **free verse** (from the French *vers libre*) to signify its liberation from regular metrics and its embrace of spoken rhythms. But open-form poetry is not therefore disorganized or chaotic. Open-form poets have instead sought new ways to arrange words and lines, new ways to express thoughts and feelings, and new ways to order poetic experience.

Poets writing in the open form attempt to fuse form and content by stressing speechlike rhythms, creating a natural and easy-flowing word order, altering and varying line lengths according to the importance of ideas, and creating emphasis through the control of shorter and longer pauses. They often isolate individual words, phrases, and clauses as single lines, freely emphasize their ideas through the manipulation of spaces separating words and sentences, and sometimes even break up individual words in separate lines to highlight their importance. Sometimes they create poems that look exactly like prose and that are printed in blocks and paragraphs instead of stanzas or lines, as with "Museum" by Robert Hass. Such **prose poems** rely on a progression of images and the cadences of language.

Open-Form Poetry Is Free and Variable in All Ways in the Presentation of Ideas and Emotions

An early example of open-form poetry is Walt Whitman's "Reconciliation". This poem was included in *Drum Taps,* a collection of fifty-three poems about the poet's reactions to Civil War battles in Virginia.

WALT WHITMAN   (1819–1892)

Reconciliation ————————————————————————— *1865, 1881*

Word over all, beautiful as the sky,
Beautiful that war and all its deeds of carnage must in time be utterly lost,
That the hands of the sisters Death and Night incessantly softly wash again, and ever
   again, this soiled world;
For my enemy is dead, a man divine as myself is dead,
I look where he lies white-faced and still in the coffin—I draw near,   5
Bend down and touch lightly with my lips the white face in the coffin.

QUESTIONS

1. How do individual lines, varying line lengths, punctuation, pauses, and cadences create rhythm and organize the images and ideas in this poem?
2. How do alliteration, assonance, and the repetition of words unify the poem and reinforce its content?
3. What is the "word" referred to in line 1? What does the speaker find "beautiful" about this "word" and the passage of time?
4. What instances of personification can you find? What do these personified figures do? What does the speaker do in lines 5–6? Why does he do this?

Whitman's "Reconciliation" shows the power of open-form poetry. There is no dominant meter, rhyme scheme, or stanza pattern. Instead, the poet uses individual lines and varying line lengths to organize and emphasize the images, ideas, and emotions. He also uses repetition, alliteration, and assonance to make internal line connections.

Without going into every aspect of the poem, one may note the unifying elements in the first few lines. The "word over all" (i.e., reconciliation, peace) is linked to the second line by the repetition of the words "beautiful" and "all," while "beautiful" is grammatically complemented by the clauses "that . . . lost" (line 2) and "That . . . world" (line 3). The reconciling word is thus connected to the image of the two personified figures, Death and Night, who "wash" war and carnage (bloodshed) out of "this soiled world."

In the third line, unity and emphasis are created through the repetition of "again" and the alliteration on the *ly* sound of incessant*ly* and "soft*ly*," the *s* sound in "*si*sters," "in*ce*ssantly," "*s*oftly," and "*s*oil'd," and the *d* sound in

"han*d*s," "*D*eath," "soil'*d*," and "Wor*ld*." One may also note the unifying assonance patterns of *ĭ* in "*i*ts," "*i*n," "s*i*sters," "*i*ncessantly," and "th*i*s," and *ī* in
"sk*y*," "t*i*me," and "N*i*ght." The pauses, or junctures, of the line create remarkable internal rhythms that coincide with the thought: "That the hands // of
the sisters // Death and Night // incessantly softly // wash again and ever
again // this soiled world."

This selective analysis demonstrates that open-form poetry creates its own
unity. While some of the unifying elements, such as alliteration and assonance,
are also a property of closed-form poetry, many are unique to poetry of the
open form, such as the repetitions, the reliance on grammatical structures, and
the careful control of rhythms. The concept of the open form is that the topic
itself shapes the number of lines, the line lengths, and the physical appearance
on the page. Unity is there—development is there—but the open form
demands that there be as many shapes and forms as there are topics.

VISUAL AND CONCRETE POETRY

In **visual poetry,** also called **shaped verse** and **picture poetry,** poets not only
emphasize the idea and emotion of their subject but also fashion the poem into
a recognizable shape on the page, as with the figure of a cone in Charles H.
Webb's "The Shape of History." Some visual poetry seeks to balance the pleasures of seeing with those of hearing. Other visual poetry, however, abandons
sound completely and invests all its impact in our perception of the visual
image or picture.

Visual poetry is not a recent development. The Chinese have been producing it for thousands of years, and there are surviving examples from ancient
Greece. In the seventeenth century, traditional English poets were manipulating the lines of their poems to represent wings, altars, squares, triangles, stars,
and the like. This type of poetry was often more ingenious than significant.
Exceptional poets, however, produced shaped verse in which the visual image
and the meaning strikingly echo each other.

After World War II, picture poems experienced a revival when visual
poetry reentered the literary landscape with the birth of a new movement
called **concrete poetry.** Poets in this tradition focus almost completely on the
medium in which the poem is created. With printed work, this means that the
poets pay far more attention to the visual arrangement of letters, words, lines,
and white space than they do to content. Concrete poetry represents a fusion of
writing with painting or graphic design, and the emphasis is on the visual.

Visual Poetry Connects the Ideas
of Language with Visual Forms

In reading visual and concrete poems, you should seek correspondences
between images and poetic ideas. Describe the shape of the poem and the

figures it resembles, the varying line lengths, the placement of individual words and phrases, and the use of space. A superb example of seventeenth-century visual poetry is George Herbert's "Easter Wings," a religious poem that offers two differing but related shapes.

GEORGE HERBERT (1593–1633)

Easter Wings _____ *1633*

Lord, who createdst man in wealth and store,° *abundance*
   Though foolishly he lost the same,
      Decaying more and more
         Till he became
           Most poor: 5
         With thee
        O let me rise
     As larks, harmoniously,
   And sing this day thy victories:
Then shall the fall° further the flight in me. 10

My tender age in sorrow did I begin:
   And still with sicknesses and shame
      Thou didst so punish sin,
         That I became
           Most thin. 15
         With thee
        Let me combine,
     And feel this day thy victory;°
   For, if I imp° my wing on thine,
Affliction shall advance the flight in me. 20

EASTER WINGS.   10 *fall:* the biblical account of how sin and death were introduced as a punishment for humankind after Adam and Eve disobeyed God. See also line 2.   18 *victory:* 1 Corinthians 15:54–57.   19 *imp:* to repair a falcon's wing or tail by grafting on feathers.

QUESTIONS

  1. What does the poem look like when viewed straight on? When viewed sideways, with the left side at the top? How do these two images echo and emphasize the poem's content?

  2. How does the typographical arrangement echo the sense? In lines 5 and 15, for example, how are typography, shape, and meaning fused?

  3. What do lines 1–5 tell you about humanity's spiritual history, according to Herbert? What do lines 11–15 tell you about the speaker's spiritual state? How are these parallel?

This poem is an admission of sin and a prayer for redemption. It compares humanity's loss of Eden ("wealth and store") to the speaker's spiritual state as a petitioner seeking salvation. When viewed straight on, each stanza resembles an altar. Sideways, the stanzas resemble the wings of two angels. The images are thus linked with the title of the poem, and they connote contrition, prayer, grace, and angelic reward.

The correspondence between shape and meaning goes even further. Herbert reinforces the ideas by the careful manipulation of line lengths. Thus, in discussing humanity's spiritual history, the original "wealth and store" of Eden are described in the poem's longest line (line 1). As the fall from grace is described, the lines get progressively shorter (and the picture becomes narrower) until humanity's fallen state is described in a very short line, "most poor" (line 5). This same pattern is repeated in lines 11–15 to portray the "sickness and shame" that have made the speaker spiritually "Most thin." In the second half of both stanzas, this pattern is reversed; the lines expand to complement the speaker's prayers for grace and salvation. The full lengths of lines 10 and 20 depict the speaker's hope of a victorious redemption—in effect the restoration of the divine favor described in line 1.

 ## Poems for Study

ELIZABETH BISHOP   (1911-1979)

One Art _____ *1976*

The art of losing isn't hard to master;
so many things seem filled with the intent
to be lost that their loss is no disaster.

Lose something every day. Accept the fluster
of lost door keys, the hour badly spent.
The art of losing isn't hard to master.

Then practice losing farther, losing faster:
places, and names, and where it was you meant
to travel. None of these will bring disaster.

I lost my mother's watch. And look! my last, or
next-to-last, of three loved houses went.
The art of losing isn't hard to master.

I lost two cities, lovely ones. And, vaster,
some realms I owned, two rivers, a continent.
I miss them, but it wasn't a disaster.

—Even losing you (the joking voice, a gesture
I love) I shan't have lied. It's evident
the art of losing's not too hard to master
though it may look like (*Write* it!) like disaster.

5

10

15

QUESTIONS

1. This poem is written in a traditional closed form called the villanelle (originally an Italian peasant song), which was developed in France during the
   Middle Ages. A villanelle is nineteen lines long. Fairly strict rules govern the
   length and structure of stanzas, the rhyme scheme, and the repetition of complete lines. Try to formulate these rules. For comparison, see Roethke's "The
   Waking" and Thomas's "Do Not Go Gentle into That Good Night".

2. On what idea is the poem based? What evidence does the speaker produce
   about losing? What feelings does she express about her losses?

3. How could the speaker have lost "two cities"? What other things has she lost
   which justify her claim that "the art of losing isn't hard to master"? What might
   she mean by having lost the "you" to whom the poem is addressed?

BILLY COLLINS   (b. 1941)

Sonnet ———————————————————————————— *1999*

All we need is fourteen lines, well, thirteen now,
and after this next one just a dozen
to launch a little ship on love's storm-tossed seas,
then only ten more left like rows of beans.
How easily it goes unless you get Elizabethan   5
and insist the iambic bongos must be played
and rhymes positioned at the ends of lines,
one for every station of the cross.
But hang on here while we make the turn
into the final six where all will be resolved,   10
where longing and heartache will find an end,
where Laura will tell Petrarch to put down his pen,
take off those crazy medieval tights,
blow out the lights, and come at last to bed.

QUESTIONS

1. Why is this poem amusing? What makes it amusing?
2. What is the effect of lines 6 and 7? Why does the speaker refer to "every station of the cross" in line 8?
3. What is the "little ship" that is to be launched on "love's storm-tossed seas"? To what tradition of the sonnet form is this a reference?
4. Why does the poet conclude the poem with a description of a scene between Petrarch and Laura?

e.e. cummings   (1874–1963)

Buffalo Bill's Defunct° ———————————————————— *1923*

Buffalo Bill's
defunct
          who used to
          ride a watersmooth-silver
                                   stallion
and break onetwothreefourfive pigeonsjustlikethat
                                        Jesus
he was a handsome man
                    and what i want to know is
how do you like your blueeyed boy
Mister Death

BUFFALO BILL'S DEFUNCT.   The poem has no title; it is usually referred to as "Portrait" or by its first two lines. Buffalo Bill (William F. Cody, 1846–1917) was an American plainsman, hunter, army scout, sharpshooter, and showman whose Wild West show began touring the world in 1883; he became a symbol of the Wild West.

QUESTIONS

1. What is the effect of devoting a whole line to "Buffalo Bill's" (line 1), "defunct" (line 2), "stallion" (line 5), "Jesus" (line 7), and "Mister Death" (line 11)? How does this technique reflect and emphasize the content of the poem?

2. How does the typographical arrangement of line 6 contribute to the fusion of sound and sense? What other examples of this technique do you find?

3. Explain the denotations and connotations of *defunct.* What would be lost (or gained) by using the term *dead* or *deceased* instead?

4. To what extent is this poem a "portrait" of Buffalo Bill? What do we learn about him? Is the portrait respectful, mocking, or something in between?

JOHN DRYDEN   (1631–1700)

To the Memory of Mr. Oldham° _____ *1684*

Farewell, too little and too lately known,
Whom I began to think and call my own:
For sure our souls were near allied, and thine
Cast in the same poetic mold with mine.
One common note on either lyre did strike,   5
And knaves and fools we both abhorred alike.
To the same goal did both our studies drive;
The last set out the soonest did arrive.
Thus Nisus° fell upon the slipp'ry place,
While his young friend performed and won the race.   10
O early ripe! to thy abundant store
What could advancing age have added more?
It might (what nature never gives the young)
Have taught the numbers of thy native tongue.
But satire needs not those, and wit will shine   15
Through the harsh cadence of a rugged line;
A noble error, and but seldom made,
When poets are by too much force betrayed.
Thy gen'rous fruits, though gathered ere their prime,
Still showed a quickness; and maturing time   20
But mellows what we write to the dull sweets of rhyme.
Once more, hail and farewell;° farewell, thou young.
But ah too short, Marcellus° of our tongue;
Thy brows with ivy and with laurels° bound;
But fate and gloomy night encompass thee around.   25

TO THE MEMORY OF MR. OLDHAM.   John Oldham (1653–1683) was a young poet whom Dryden admired.   9 *Nisus:* a character in Virgil's *Aeneid* who slipped in a pool of blood while running a race, thus allowing his best friend to win.   22 *hail and farewell:* an echo of the Latin phrase "ave atque vale" spoken by gladiators about to fight.   23 *Marcellus:* a Roman general who was adopted by the Emperor Augustus as his successor but died at the age of twenty. 24 *laurels:* a plant sacred to Apollo, the Greek god of poetry; the traditional prize given to poets is a wreath of laurel.

QUESTIONS

1. What is the meter of this poem? Rhyme scheme? Closed form? How does the form control the tempo? Why is this tempo appropriate?

2. What does the speaker reveal about himself in lines 1–10? About Oldham? About his relationship with Oldham? What did the two have in common?

3. What is the effect of Dryden's frequent classical allusions? What pairs of rhyming words most effectively clinch ideas?

ROBERT FROST   (1874–1963)

Desert Places _____ *1936*

Snow falling and night falling fast, oh, fast
In a field I looked into going past,
And the ground almost covered smooth in snow,
But a few weeds and stubble showing last.

The woods around it have it—it is theirs.
All animals are smothered in their lairs.
I am too absent-spirited to count;
The loneliness includes me unawares.

And lonely as it is that loneliness
Will be more lonely ere it will be less—
A blanker whiteness of benighted snow
With no expression, nothing to express.

They cannot scare me with their empty spaces
Between stars—on stars where no human race is.
I have it in me so much nearer home
To scare myself with my own desert places.

QUESTIONS

1. What is the meter? The rhyme scheme? The form?

2. What setting and situation are established in lines 1–4? What does the snow affect here? What does it affect in lines 5–8? In lines 9–12?

3. What different kinds of "desert places" is this poem about? Which kind is the most important? Most frightening?

4. How does the type of rhyme (rising or falling) change in the last stanza? How does this change affect the tone and impact of the poem?

5. How does the stanzaic pattern of this poem organize the progression of the speaker's thoughts, feelings, and conclusions?

ALLEN GINSBERG   (1926–1997)

A Supermarket in California ——————————————————— *1955*

What thoughts I have of you tonight, Walt Whitman,° for
I walked down the sidestreets under the trees with a headache
self-conscious looking at the full moon.
   In my hungry fatigue, and shopping for images, I went
into the neon fruit supermarket, dreaming of your enumerations!°   5
   What peaches and what penumbras! Whole families
shopping at night! Aisles full of husbands! Wives in the
avocados, babies in the tomatoes!—and you, Garcia Lorca,° what
were you doing down by the watermelons?

   I saw you, Walt Whitman, childless, lonely old grubber,   10
poking among the meats in the refrigerator and eyeing the
grocery boys.
   I heard you asking questions of each: Who killed the pork
chops? What price bananas? Are you my Angel?
   I wandered in and out of the brilliant stacks of cans   15
following you, and followed in my imagination by the store
detective.
   We strode down the open corridors together in our solitary
fancy tasting artichokes, possessing every frozen delicacy, and
never passing the cashier.   20

   Where are we going, Walt Whitman? The doors close in
an hour. Which way does your beard point tonight?
   (I touch your book and dream of our odyssey in the supermarket
and feel absurd.)
   Will we walk all night through solitary streets? The trees   25
add shade to shade, lights out in the houses, we'll both be
lonely.

   Will we stroll dreaming of the lost America of love past blue
automobiles in driveways, home to our silent cottage?
   Ah, dear father, graybeard, lonely old courage-teacher,   30
what America did you have when Charon° quit poling his ferry
and you got out on a smoking bank and stood watching the
boat disappear on the black waters of Lethe?°

A SUPERMARKET IN CALIFORNIA.   1 *Walt Whitman:* American poet (1819–1892) who experimented with open forms and significantly influenced the development of twentieth-century
poetry.   5 *enumerations:* Many of Whitman's poems contain long lists.   8 *Garcia Lorca:*
Spanish surrealist poet and playwright (1896–1936) whose later poetry became progressively more
like prose.   31 *Charon:* boatman in Greek mythology who ferried the souls of the dead across
the river Styx into Hades, the underworld.   33 *Lethe:* the river of forgetfulness in Hades. The
dead drank from this river and forgot their former lives.

QUESTIONS

1. Where is the speaker? What is he doing? What is his condition?
2. What effect is produced by placing Whitman and Lorca in the market?
3. To what extent do we find Whitman-like enumerations in this work? What is the effect of such enumerations?
4. Why is this a poem? What poetic devices are employed here? To what extent might it make more sense to consider this prose rather than poetry?

NIKKI GIOVANNI   (b. 1943)

Nikki-Rosa _____ *1968*

childhood remembrances are always a drag
if you're Black
you always remember things like living in Woodlawn°
with no inside toilet
and if you become famous or something
they never talk about how happy you were to have your mother
all to yourself and
how good the water felt when you got your bath from one of those
big tubs that folk in chicago barbecue in
and somehow when you talk about home
it never gets across how much you
understood their feelings
as the whole family attended meetings about Hollydale
and even though you remember
your biographers never understand
your father's pain as he sells his stock
and another dream goes
and though you're poor it isn't poverty that
concerns you
and though they fought a lot
it isn't your father's drinking that makes any difference
but only that everybody is together and you
and your sister have happy birthdays and very good christmasses
and I really hope no white person ever has cause to write about me
because they never understand Black love is Black wealth and they'll
probably talk about my hard childhood and never understand that
all the while I was quite happy

NIKKI-ROSA.   3 *Woodlawn:* a predominantly black suburb of Cincinnati, Ohio.

QUESTIONS

1. To what extent do individual lines, caesurae, and cadences create a rhythm and reinforce the sense of this poem?
2. What points does the speaker make about childhood in general, the childhoods of blacks, and her own childhood?
3. What ideas about the ways in which whites understand or misunderstand blacks does this poem explore?

ROBERT HASS   (b. 1941)

Museum _____ *1989*

On the morning of the Käthe Kollwitz° exhibit, a young man and woman come into the museum restaurant. She is carrying a baby; he carries the air-freight edition of the Sunday *New York Times*. She sits in a high-backed wicker chair, cradling the infant in her arms. He fills a tray with fresh fruit, rolls, and coffee in white cups and brings it to the table. His hair is tousled, her eyes are puffy. They look like they were thrown down into sleep and then yanked out of it like divers coming up for air. He holds the baby. She drinks coffee, scans the front page, butters a roll and eats it in their little corner in the sun. After a while, she holds the baby. He reads the *Book Review* and eats some fruit. Then he holds the baby while she finds the section of the paper she wants and eats fruit and smokes. They've hardly exchanged a look. Meanwhile, I have fallen in love with this equitable arrangement, and with the baby who cooperates by sleeping. All around them are faces Käthe Kollwitz carved in wood of people with no talent or capacity for suffering who are suffering the numbest kinds of pain: hunger, helpless terror. But this young couple is reading the Sunday paper in the sun, the baby is sleeping, the green has begun to emerge from the rind of the cantaloupe, and everything seems possible.

MUSEUM.   1 *Käthe Kollwitz:* Kollwitz (1867–1945) was a German artist well known for her sculptures and engravings portraying the misery of poverty and war.

QUESTIONS

1. Does this poem contain material that you ordinarily think of as poetic? What seems "poetic"? "Unpoetic"? Why?
2. Why does Hass not present the poem in lines? On what principle (topical, grammatical) might you set it up in line form? How might its being in lines change the way you read it as well as see it?
3. How does the poem contrast the young couple and their baby with the art of Käthe Kollwitz?
4. In the light of this poem, how seriously should we take the final statement ("and everything seems possible")?

GEORGE HERBERT   (1593–1633)

Virtue° _____ *1633*

Sweet day, so cool, so calm, so bright,
The bridal of the earth and sky:
The dew shall weep thy fall tonight;
    For thou must die.

Sweet rose, whose hue, angry° and brave,°   *red; splendid* 5
Bids the rash° gazer wipe his eye:
Thy root is ever in its grave,
    And thou must die.

Sweet spring, full of sweet days and roses,
A box where sweets° compacted lie: *perfumes* 1⦅
My music shows ye have your closes,°
    And all must die.

Only a sweet and virtuous soul,
Like seasoned timber, never gives;°
But though the whole world turn to coal,°   1
    Then chiefly lives.

VIRTUE.   The title can allude to (*a*) divine Power operating both outside and inside an individual; (*b*) a characteristic quality or property; (*c*) conformity to divine and moral laws.   6 *rash:* eager or sympathetic.   11 *closes:* A *close* is the conclusion of a musical composition.   14 *never gives:* i.e., never gives in, never deteriorates and collapses (like rotted timber). 15 *turn to coal:* the burned-out residue of the earth and universe after the universal fire on Judgment Day.

QUESTIONS

1. What is the rhyme scheme of this poem? The meter? The form?
2. What points does the speaker make about the day, the rose, spring, and the "sweet and virtuous soul"?

WILLIAM HEYEN   (b. 1940)

Mantle° _____ *1980*

        Mantle ran so hard, they said,
      he tore his legs to pieces.
        What is this but spirit?

   52 homers in '56, the triple crown.
I was a high school junior, batting   5
   fourth behind him in a dream.

   I prayed for him to quit, before
his lifetime dropped below .300.
   But he didn't, and it did.

He makes Brylcreem commercials now,   10
models with open mouths draped around him
   as they never were in Commerce, Oklahoma,

      where the sandy-haired, wide-shouldered boy
       stood up against his barn,
      lefty for an hour (Ruth, Gehrig),   15

         then righty (DiMaggio),
      as his father winged them in,
       and the future blew toward him,

            now a fastball, now a slow
          curve hanging   20
            like a model's smile.

MANTLE.   Mickey Mantle (1931–1995), a Yankee outfielder from 1951–1968. A switch hitter, he hit eighteen world series home runs (a record) and 536 career home runs. He was the American League's most valuable player in 1956, the year he won the triple crown (line 4).

QUESTIONS

   1.   Describe the shape of the poem, being careful to study the last stanza. Why is this shape appropriate for a famous baseball player?

   2.   How does the poet use Mantle as a symbol in this poem?

   3.   Who are Ruth, Gehrig, and DiMaggio? In what ways are they like Mantle?

JOHN HOLLANDER   (b. 1929)

Swan and Shadow _____ *1969*

```
                            Dusk
                        Above the
                    water hang the
                                loud
                                flies
                            Here
                        O so
                        gray
                        then
                    What                          A pale signal will appear
                    When                      Soon before its shadow fades
                    Where                    Here in this pool of opened eye
                    In us          No Upon us As at the very edges
                        of where we take shape in the dark air
                            this object bares its image awakening
                            ripples of recognition that will
                            brush darkness up into light
even after this bird this hour both drift by atop the perfect sad instant now
                            already passing out of sight
                            toward yet-untroubled reflection
                            this image bears its object darkening
                            into memorial shades Scattered bits of
                    light          No of water Or something across
                    water              Breaking up No Being regathered
                    soon                Yet by then a swan will have
                    gone                Yes out of mind into what
                        vast
                        pale
                        hush
                        of a
                            place
                                past
                    sudden dark as
                        if a swan
                        sang
```

QUESTIONS

1. How effectively and consistently does the shape image reinforce the meaning?
2. What specific words, phrases, and lines are emphasized by the typographical arrangement? To what extent does this effect give added impact to the poem?
3. How well does the structure echo the verbal images of the poem?

4. Do you find Hollander's experiment with shaped verse as successful as Herbert's in "Easter Wings" (p. 916)? If so, demonstrate how it succeeds. If not, explain why.

JOHN KEATS   (1795–1821)

Ode to a Nightingale ———————————————————————— *1819*

1

My heart aches, and a drowsy numbness pains
  My sense, as though of hemlock° I had drunk,   *a poisonous herb*
Or emptied some dull opiate to the drains
  One minute past, and Lethe-wards° had sunk:
'Tis not through envy of thy happy lot,   5
  But being too happy in thine happiness,—
    That thou, light-winged Dryad° of the trees,
      In some melodious plot
  Of beechen green, and shadows numberless,
    Singest of summer in full-throated ease.   10

2

O, for a draught of vintage! that hath been
  Cool'd a long age in the deep-delved earth,
Tasting of Flora° and the country green,
  Dance, and Provençal song, and sunburnt mirth!
O for a beaker full of the warm South,   15
  Full of the true, the blushful Hippocrene,°
    With beaded bubbles winking at the brim,
      And purple-stainèd mouth;
  That I might drink, and leave the world unseen,
    And with thee fade away into the forest dim: 20

3

Fade far away, dissolve, and quite forget
  What thou among the leaves hast never known,
The weariness, the fever, and the fret
  Here, where men sit and hear each other groan;
Where palsy shakes a few, sad, last gray hairs,   25
  Where youth grows pale, and spectre-thin, and dies;
    Where but to think is to be full of sorrow
      And leaden-eyed despairs,

ODE TO A NIGHTINGALE.   4 *Lethe-wards:* toward the river of forgetfulness in Hades, the underworld of Greek mythology.   7 *Dryad:* in Greek mythology, a semidivine tree spirit.   13 *Flora:* the Roman goddess of flowers.   16 *Hippocrene:* the fountain of the Muses on Mt. Helicon in Greek mythology; the phrase thus refers to both the waters of poetic inspiration and a cup of wine.

Where Beauty cannot keep her lustrous eyes,
   Or new Love pine at them beyond to-morrow.   30

4

Away! away! for I will fly to thee,
   Not charioted by Bacchus° and his pards,°   *leopards*
But on the viewless wings of Poesy,°   *poetry*
   Though the dull brain perplexes and retards:
Already with thee! tender is the night,   35
   And haply the Queen-Moon is on her throne,
     Cluster'd around by all her starry Fays;°   *fairies*
      But here there is no light,
Save what from heaven is with the breezes blown
   Through verdurous glooms and winding mossy ways.   4[0]

5

I cannot see what flowers are at my feet,
   Nor what soft incense hangs upon the boughs,
But, in embalmed° darkness, guess each sweet   *fragrant*
   Wherewith the seasonable month endows
The grass, the thicket, and the fruit-tree wild;
   White hawthorn, and the pastoral eglantine;°   *honeysuckle*
     Fast fading violets cover'd up in leaves;
      And mid-May's eldest child,
The coming musk-rose, full of dewy wine,
     The murmurous haunt of flies on summer eves.

6

Darkling° I listen; and, for many a time   *in the dark*
   I have been half in love with easeful Death,
Call'd him soft names in many a musèd rhyme,
   To take into the air my quiet breath;
Now more than ever seems it rich to die,
   To cease upon the midnight with no pain,
     While thou art pouring forth thy soul abroad
      In such an ecstasy!
Still wouldst thou sing, and I have ears in vain—
   To thy high requiem become a sod.

7

Thou wast not born for death, immortal Bird!
   No hungry generations tread thee down;
The voice I hear this passing night was heard
   In ancient days by emperor and clown:

32 *Bacchus:* the Greek god of wine. See Chapter 27.

Perhaps the self-same song that found a path   65
  Through the sad heart of Ruth,° when, sick for home,
    She stood in tears amid the alien corn;°   *wheat, grain*
      The same that oft-times hath
Charm'd magic casements, opening on the foam
  Of perilous seas, in faery lands forlorn.   70

                          8
Forlorn! the very word is like a bell
To toll me back from thee to my sole self!
Adieu! the fancy° cannot cheat so well   *imagination*
  As she is fam'd to do, deceiving elf.
Adieu! adieu! thy plaintive anthem fades   75
  Past the near meadows, over the still stream,
    Up the hill-side; and now 'tis buried deep
      In the next valley-glades:
Was it a vision, or a waking dream?
  Fled is that music:—Do I wake or sleep?   80

66 *Ruth:* the widow of Boaz in the biblical Book of Ruth.

QUESTIONS

1. Formulate the structure (meter of each line and rhyme scheme) of the stanzas. What traditional form is employed here?

2. What is the speaker's mental and emotional state in stanza 1? What similes are employed to describe this condition?

3. What does the speaker want in stanza 2? Whom does he want to join? Why? From what aspects of the world (stanza 3) does he want to escape?

4. How do the speaker's mood and perspective change in stanza 4? How does he achieve this transition? What characterizes the world that the speaker enters in stanza 5? What senses are employed to describe this world?

5. What does the speaker establish about the nightingale's song in stanza 7? What does the song come to symbolize?

CLAUDE McKAY   (1890–1948)

In Bondage —————————————————————————— *1922*

I would be wandering in distant fields
Where man, and bird, and beast, lives leisurely,
And the old earth is kind, and ever yields
Her goodly gifts to all her children free;
Where life is fairer, lighter, less demanding,   5
And boys and girls have time and space for play

Before they come to years of understanding—
Somewhere I would be singing, far away.
For life is greater than the thousand wars
Men wage for it in their insatiate lust,   10
And will remain like the eternal stars,
When all that shines to-day is drift and dust.

But I am bound with you in your mean graves,
O black men, simple slaves of ruthless slaves.

QUESTIONS

1. What is the meter of this poem? The rhyme scheme? The form? To what extent does the form organize the speaker's thoughts?

2. Lines 1–8 present a conditional (rather than actual) situation that the speaker desires. What word signals this nature? What is the speaker's wish?

3. What point does the speaker make about life in lines 9–12?

4. How does the couplet undermine the rest of the poem? What single word conveys this reversal? How effectively do the rhymes clinch the poem's meaning? What is the speaker telling us about the lives of African Americans?

JOHN MILTON   (1608–1674)

When I Consider How My Light Is Spent° _____ 1655

When I consider how my light is spent
  Ere half my days, in this dark world and wide,
  And that one talent° which is death to hide,
  Lodged with me useless, though my soul more bent
To serve therewith my Maker, and present
  My true account, lest he returning chide;
  "Doth God exact day-labor, light denied?"
  I fondly° ask; but Patience to prevent°   *foolishly; forestall*
That murmur, soon replies, "God doth not need
  Either man's work or his own gifts; who best
  Bear his mild yoke, they serve him best. His state
Is kingly. Thousands at his bidding speed
  And post o'er land and ocean without rest;
  They also serve who only stand and wait."

WHEN I CONSIDER HOW MY LIGHT IS SPENT.   Milton began to go blind in the late 1640s and was completely blind by 1651.   3 *talent:* both a skill and a reference to the talents discussed in the parable in Matthew 25:14–30.

QUESTIONS

1. What is the meter of this poem? The rhyme scheme? The closed form?
2. To what extent do the two major divisions of this form organize the poem's ideas?
3. What problem is raised in the octave? What are the speaker's complaints? Who is the speaker in the sestet? How are the earlier conflicts resolved?
4. Explore the word *talent* and relate its various meanings to the poem as a whole.

DUDLEY RANDALL   (b. 1914)

Ballad of Birmingham° _____ *1966*

(On the bombing of a church in Birmingham, Alabama, 1963)

"Mother dear, may I go downtown
Instead of out to play,
And march the streets of Birmingham
In a Freedom March today?"

"No, baby, no, you may not go,   5
For the dogs are fierce and wild,
And clubs and hoses, guns and jails
Aren't good for a little child."

"But, mother, I won't be alone.
Other children will go with me,   10
And march the streets of Birmingham
To make our country free."

"No, baby, no, you may not go,
For I fear those guns will fire.
But you may go to church instead   15
And sing in the children's choir."

She has combed and brushed her night-dark hair,
And bathed rose petal sweet,
And drawn white gloves on her small brown hands,
And white shoes on her feet.   20

The mother smiled to know her child
Was in the sacred place,
But that smile was the last smile
To come upon her face.

BALLAD OF BIRMINGHAM.   Four black children were killed when the 16th Street Baptist Church in Birmingham, Alabama, was bombed in 1963. A man was finally indicted for the murders in 1977 and convicted in 1982.

For when she heard the explosion,   25
Her eyes grew wet and wild.
She raced through the streets of Birmingham
Calling for her child.

She clawed through bits of glass and brick,
Then lifted out a shoe   30
"Oh, here's the shoe my baby wore,
But, baby, where are you?"

QUESTIONS

1. Formulate the structure (meter, rhyme scheme, stanza form) of this poem. What traditional closed form is employed here?

2. Who is the speaker in stanzas 1 and 3? In stanzas 2 and 4? How are quotation and repetition employed to create tension?

3. What ironies do you find in the mother's assumptions? In the poem as a whole? In the society pictured in the poem?

4. Compare the poem to "Sir Patrick Spens" (p. 668) and to "Barbara Allan" (Chapter 25). How are the structures of all three alike? To what extent do all three deal with the same type of subject matter?

THEODORE ROETHKE (1908-1963)

The Waking ———————————————————————————— *1953*

I wake to sleep, and take my waking slow.
I feel my fate in what I cannot fear.
I learn by going where I have to go.

We think by feeling. What is there to know?
I hear my being dance from ear to ear.
I wake to sleep, and take my waking slow.

Of those so close beside me, which are you?
God bless the Ground! I shall walk softly there,
And learn by going where I have to go.

Light takes the Tree; but who can tell us how?
The lowly worm climbs up a winding stair;
I wake to sleep, and take my waking slow.

Great Nature has another thing to do
To you and me; so take the lively air,
And, lovely, learn by going where to go.

This shaking keeps me steady. I should know.
What falls away is always. And is near.
I wake to sleep, and take my waking slow.
I learn by going where I have to go.

QUESTIONS

1. Compare the form of this poem with the poems by Bishop and Thomas in this chapter.
2. In what way or ways does the speaker "wake to sleep"? What other apparent contradictions does the speaker develop in this poem? Why might a reader conclude that the poem is positive rather than negative?
3. What does the speaker mean by saying that he learns "by going where I have to go"? In what way does "always" fall away (line 17)?

PERCY BYSSHE SHELLEY   (1792–1822)

Ozymandias _____ *1818*

I met a traveller from an antique land,
Who said—"Two vast and trunkless legs of stone
Stand in the desert. . . . Near them, on the sand,
Half sunk, a shattered visage lies, whose frown,
And wrinkled lip, and sneer of cold command,   5
Tell that its sculptor well those passions read
Which yet survive, stamped on these lifeless things,
The hand that mocked them, and the heart that fed;
And on the pedestal, these words appear;
'My name is Ozymandias, King of Kings,   10
Look on my Works, ye Mighty, and despair!'
Nothing beside remains. Round the decay
Of that colossal Wreck, boundless and bare
The lone and level sands stretch far away."

QUESTIONS

1. What is the meter of this poem? The rhyme scheme? What traditional closed form is modified here? How do the modifications affect the poem?
2. To what extent are content and meaning shaped by the closed form? What is described in the octave? In the sestet?
3. Characterize Ozymandias (thought to be Ramses II, pharaoh of Egypt, who died in 1225 B.C.E.) from the way he is portrayed in this poem.

MAY SWENSON   (1919–1989)

Women _____ *1968*

Women   Or they
  should be   should be
    pedestals   little horses
      moving   those wooden
        pedestals   sweet   5
          moving   oldfashioned
            to the   painted
              motions   rocking
                of men   horses

            the gladdest things in the toyroom   10

            The   feelingly
              pegs   and then
                of their   unfeelingly
                  ears   To be
                    so familiar   joyfully   15
                      and dear   ridden
                        to the trusting   rockingly
                          fists   ridden until
                    To be chafed   the restored

egos dismount and the legs stride away   20

Immobile   willing
  sweetlipped   to be set
    sturdy   into motion
      and smiling   Women
        women   should be
          should always   pedestals
            be waiting   to men

QUESTIONS

1. Is this poem an instance of closed-form, open-form, or visual poetry? In what different ways or sequences can it be read? How do the different sequences change the meaning?

2. How well does the image of the poem reinforce its meaning? Would the effect be different if the columns of words were straight instead of undulating?

3. To what extent do repetition and alliteration help to organize the poem and underscore its sense? Note especially *w, m, f, r,* and *s* sounds.

4. What does this poem *say* that women should be? Does it mean what it says? How are men characterized? In what way is this poem ironic?

DYLAN THOMAS   (1914–1953)

Do Not Go Gentle into That Good Night _____ *1951*

Do not go gentle into that good night,
Old age should burn and rave at close of day;
Rage, rage against the dying of the light.

Though wise men at their end know dark is right,
Because their words had forked no lightning they   5
Do not go gentle into that good night.

Good men, the last wave by, crying how bright
Their frail deeds might have danced in a green bay,
Rage, rage against the dying of the light.

Wild men who caught and sang the sun in flight,   10
And learn, too late, they grieved it on its way,
Do not go gentle into that good night.

Grave men, near death, who see with blinding sight
Blind eyes could blaze like meteors and be gay,
Rage, rage against the dying of the light.   15

And you, my father, there on the sad height,
Curse, bless, me now with your fierce tears, I pray.
Do not go gentle into that good night.
Rage, rage against the dying of the light.

QUESTIONS

1.   What conclusions do you make about the speaker, listener, and situation in this poem?

2.   What connotative words do you find here? Consider "dying," the "good" of "good night," "gentle," "Curse, bless, me now with your fierce tears, I pray," and "grave."

3.   What five different kinds of men does the speaker discuss in stanzas 2-5? What do they have in common? Of what value are they to the speaker's father (line 16)?

4.   Compare the form of this poem with the poems by Bishop and Roethke in this chapter.

JEAN TOOMER   (1894–1967)

Reapers _____ *1923*

Black reapers with the sound of steel on stones
Are sharpening scythes. I see them place the hones
In their hip-pockets as a thing that's done,
And start their silent swinging, one by one.

Black horses drive a mower through the weeds,   5
And there, a field rat, startled, squealing bleeds,
His belly close to ground. I see the blade,
Blood-stained, continue cutting weeds and shade.

QUESTIONS

1. What is the poem's meter? The rhyme scheme? The form? What is the difference between Toomer's use of the form and Dryden's?

2. How do the images of this poem relate to each other? How does the image of
   the bleeding field rat and the "blood-stained" blade heighten the impact?

3. How does alliteration unify this poem and make sound echo sense? Note especially the *s* and *b* sounds and the phrase "silent swinging."

CHARLES H. WEBB   (b. 1952)

The Shape of History ————————————————————— *1995*

Turning and turning in the widening gyre . . .°

Today's paper is crammed full of news: pages and pages on the Somalia
Famine, the Balkan Wars, Gays in the Military. On this date a year ago,
only 1/365 of "The Year's Top Stories" happened. *Time* magazine fits a
decade into one thin retrospective. Barely enough occurred a century
ago to fill one sub-chapter in a high school text. 500 years ago, one
or two things happened every 50 years. 5000 years ago, a city
was founded, a grain cultivated, a civilization toppled every
other century. Still farther back, the years march by in
groups like graduates at a big state university: 10,000 to
20,000 BC; 50,000 – 100,000 BC; 1 – 10 million BC.
Before that, things happened once an Era: Mam-
mals in the Cenozoic, Dinosaurs in the Meso-
zoic, Forests in the Paleozoic, Protozoans in
the Pre-Cambrian. Below that, at the
very base of time's twisting gyre, its
cornucopia, its ram's-horn trumpet, its tornado tracking across
eternity, came what Christians call Creation, astro-
physicists call the Big
Bang. Then, for tril-
lions of years,
nothing at
all.

THE SHAPE OF HISTORY.   *Turning . . . gyre:* See line 1 of Yeats's "The Second Coming," p. 961.

QUESTIONS

1. What shape does the poet give to history? How accurate is this shape?

2. How do the lengths of the first and final two lines graphically show how civilization has grown? What "top stories" are mentioned in the first few lines? How representative of modern news are these stories? How long will it take for such stories to be replaced by new, similar stories?

3. In the light of the epigraph by Yeats, what does the speaker apparently think will happen in the future?

4. Considering the content and the diminishing shape of the poem's twenty-four lines, what do you think is meant by "nothing at / all"?

PHYLLIS WEBB   (b. 1927)

Poetics Against the Angel of Death° _____ *1962*

I am sorry to speak of death again
(some say I'll have a long life)
but last night Wordsworth's 'Prelude'°
suddenly made sense—I mean the measure,
the elevated tone, the attitude   5
of private Man speaking to public men.
Last night I thought I would not wake again
but now with this June morning I run ragged to elude
the Great Iambic Pentameter
who is the Hound of Heaven° in our stress   10
because I want to die
writing Haiku
or, better,
long lines, clean and syllabic as knotted bamboo. Yes!

POETICS AGAINST THE ANGEL OF DEATH.   *Angel of Death:* See Byron's "The Destruction of Sennacherib," stanza 3 (Chapter 25).   3 *Wordsworth's 'Prelude':* See Chapter 24.   10 *Hound of Heaven (The):* a long poem (1893) by Francis Thompson (1859–1907) about attempting to evade God's love.

QUESTIONS

1. In the poem itself, what is meant by the "Angel of Death"?

2. What attitude does the speaker express about iambic pentameter? How does the speaker explain this attitude? How defensible is the attitude?

3. For what poetic forms does the speaker express a preference? Why? How does the form of this poem bear out the preference?

Pieter Brueghel the Elder, *The Peasant Dance.* Kunsthistorisches Museum, Vienna, Austria. Foto
Marburg/Art Resource, New York, NY.

WILLIAM CARLOS WILLIAMS   (1883–1963)

The Dance _____ *1944*

In Brueghel's° great picture, The Kermess,
the dancers go round, they go round and
around, the squeal and the blare and the
tweedle of bagpipes, a bugle and fiddles
tipping their bellies (round as the thick-
sided glasses whose wash they impound)
their hips and their bellies off balance
to turn them. Kicking and rolling about
the Fair Grounds, swinging their butts, those
shanks must be sound to bear up under such
rollicking measures, prance as the dance
in Breughel's great picture, The Kermess.

THE DANCE.   1 *Brueghel's:* Pieter Brueghel (ca. 1525–1569), a Flemish painter. *The Kermess* shows
peasants dancing in celebration of the anniversary of the founding of a church (*church mass*).

QUESTIONS

1. What effect is produced by repeating the first line as the last line?

2. How do repetition, alliteration, assonance, onomatopoeia, and internal rhyme affect the tempo, feeling, and meaning of the poem? How do the numerous participles (like "tipping," "kicking," "rolling") make sound echo sense?

3. What words are capitalized? What effect is produced by omitting the capital letters at the beginning of each line? How does this typographical choice reinforce the sound and the sense of the poem?

4. Most of the lines of this poem are run-on rather than end-stopped, and many of them end with fairly weak words such as *and, the, about,* and *such.* What effect is produced through these techniques?

5. How successful is Williams in making the words and sentence rhythms echo the visual rhythms in Breughel's painting? Why is this open form more appropriate to the images of the poem than any closed form could be?

WRITING ABOUT FORM IN POETRY

An essay about form in poetry should demonstrate a relationship between a poem's sense and its form. Do not discuss form or shape in isolation, for such an essay would be no more than a detailed description. The first thing to do in prewriting is to examine the poem's main ideas. Consider the various elements that contribute to the poem's impact and effectiveness: the speaker, listener, setting, situation, diction, imagery, and rhetorical devices. Once you understand these, it will be easier to establish a connection between form and content.

It will be helpful to prepare a work sheet much like the ones for writing about prosody (Chapter 19). In this case the work sheet will highlight structural elements. For closed forms, these will include the rhyme scheme, meter, line lengths, and stanzaic pattern. They may also include significant words and phrases that connect stanzas. The work sheet for an open-form poem should indicate variables such as rhythm and phrases, pauses and enjambements, significant words that are isolated or emphasized through typography, and patterns of repeated sounds, words, phrases, and images.

Questions for Discovering Ideas

CLOSED FORM

• What is the principal meter? Line length? Rhyme scheme? To what extent do these establish and/or reinforce the form?

- What is the form of each stanza or unit? How many stanzas or divisions does the poem contain? How does the poem establish a pattern? How is the pattern repeated?

- What is the form of the poem (e.g., couplet, tercet, ballad, villanelle, sonnet)? In what ways is the poem traditional, and what variations does it introduce? What is the effect of the variations?

- How effectively does the structure create or reinforce the poem's internal logic? What are the topical, logical, or thematic progressions that unite the various parts of the poem?

- To what extent does the form organize the images of the poem? Are key images developed within single units or stanzas? Do images recur in several units?

- To what extent does the form organize and bring out the ideas or emotions of the poem?

OPEN FORM

- What does the poem look like on the page? What is the relationship of its shape to its meaning?

- How does the poet use variable line lengths, spaces, punctuation, capitalization, and the like to shape the poem? How do these variables contribute to the poem's sense and impact?

- What rhythms are built into the poem through language or typography? How are these relevant to the poem's content?

- What is the poem's progression of ideas, images, and/or emotions? How is the logic created, and what does it contribute?

- How does form or typography isolate or group, and thus emphasize, various words and phrases? What is the effect of such emphasis?

- What patterns do you discover of words and sounds? To what degree do the patterns create order and structure? How are they related to the sense of the poem?

Strategies for Organizing Ideas

In developing your central idea, you should illustrate the connections between form and meaning. For example, in planning an essay on Randall's "Ballad of Birmingham" you might develop your ideas according to the speeches that are a normal feature of the ballad form. The poem's first part is a dialogue between mother and child about the hazard of the local streets and the safety of the local church. In the second part, after the explosion, the mother runs toward the church and calls for her child, who, ironically, will never again engage with her in further dialogue. Another plan is needed for an essay on Williams's "The Dance"; such a plan might link the lively, bustling movement of the dancers pictured in Breughel's painting (p. 930) to the rhythms, repetitions, and run-on lines of the poem. Still another plan would be needed for a discussion of Heyen's "Mantle," the form of which requires enough stanzas of approximately equal length to make up the pattern of a pitched ball (what is this pattern?).

Your introduction may contain general remarks about the poem, but it should focus on the connection between form and substance. Describe the ways in which structure and content interact together, with a brief listing of your specific topics.

Early in the body, describe the formal characteristics of your poem, using schemes and numbers (as in paragraph 2 of the demonstrative student essay). With closed forms, your description should detail such standard features as the traditional form, meter, rhyme scheme, stanzaic structure, and number of stanzas. With open-form poetry, you should focus on the most striking and significant features of the verse (as in the brief discussion of Whitman's "Reconciliation" on p. 905).

Be sure to integrate your discussion of both form and content. It may be that you have uncovered a good deal of information about technical features such as alliteration or rhyme, or you may wish to stress how words, phrases, and clauses develop a pattern of ideas. Remember that you are not making a paraphrase or a general explication but instead are showing how the poet uses form—either an open or a closed one—in the service of meaning. The order in which you deal with your topics is entirely your decision.

The conclusion of your essay might contain additional relevant observations about shape or structure. It might also summarize your argument. Here, as in all essays about literature, make sure to reach an actual conclusion rather than simply a stopping point.

DEMONSTRATIVE STUDENT ESSAY

Form and Meaning in Herbert's "Virtue"°

[1]
George Herbert's devotional four-stanza poem "Virtue" (1633) contrasts the mortality of worldly things with the immortality of the "virtuous soul." This is not an uncommon topic in religious poetry and hymns, and there is nothing unusual about this contrast. What is unusual, however, is the simplicity and directness of Herbert's expressions and the way in which he integrates his ideas within his stanzaic song pattern. Each part of the poem organizes the images logically and underscores the supremacy of life over death."* Through control over line and stanza groupings, rhyme scheme, and repeated sounds and words, Herbert's stanzas create a structural and visual distinction between the "sweet" soul and the rest of creation.†

[2]
Herbert's control over lines within the stanzas is particularly strong. Each stanza follows the same basic *a b a b* rhyme scheme. Since some rhyme sounds and words are repeated throughout the first three stanzas, however, the structure

° See p. 916 for this poem.
* Central idea.
† Thesis sentence.

of the poem can be formulated as *4a 4b 4a 2b; 4c 4b 4c 2b; 4d 4b 4d 2b; 4e 4f 4e 2f.* Each stanza thus contains three lines of iambic tetrameter with a final line of iambic dimeter--an unusual pattern that creates a unique emphasis. In the first three stanzas, the dimeter lines repeat the phrase "must die," while in the last stanza the contrast is made on the words "Then chiefly lives." These rhythms require a sensitive reading, and they powerfully underscore Herbert's idea that death is conquered by eternal life.

[3]   Like individual lines, Herbert's stanzaic structure provides the poem's pattern of organization and logic. The first stanza focuses on the image of the "Sweet day," comparing the day to "The bridal of the earth and sky" (line 2) and asserting that the day inevitably "must die." Similarly, the second stanza focuses on the image of a "Sweet rose" and asserts that it too "must die." The third stanza shifts to the image of "Sweet spring." Here the poet blends the images of the first two stanzas into the third by noting that the "Sweet spring" is "full of sweet days and roses" (line 9). The stanza concludes with the summarizing claim that "all must die." In this way, the third stanza is the climax of Herbert's imagery of beauty and mortality. The last stanza introduces a new image--"a sweet and virtuous soul"--and an assertion that is the opposite of the ideas expressed in the previous three stanzas. Although the day, the rose, and the spring "must die," the soul "never" deteriorates but "chiefly lives" even though "the whole world turn to coal" (line 15). With its key image of the "virtuous soul," this last stanza marks the logical conclusion of Herbert's argument. His pattern of organization allows this key image of permanence to be separated structurally from the images of impermanence.

[4]   This structural organization of images and ideas is repeated and reinforced by other techniques. Herbert's rhyme scheme, for example, links the first three stanzas while isolating the fourth. That the *b* rhyme is repeated at the ends of the second and fourth lines of each of the first three stanzas makes these stanzas into a complete unit. The fourth stanza, however is different in both content and rhyme. The stanza introduces the concept of immortality, and it also introduces entirely new rhymes, replacing the *b* rhyme with an *f* rhyme. Thus the rhyme scheme, by sound alone, parallels the poem's imagery and logic.

[5]   As a complement to the rhyming sounds, the poem also demonstrates organizing patterns of assonance. Most notable is the *oo* sound, which is repeated throughout the first three stanzas in the words "cool," "dew," "whose," "hue," "root," and "music". In Herbert's time, the sound might still have been prominent in the word "thou," so that in the first three stanzas the *oo*, which is not unlike a moan (certainly appropriate to things that die), is repeated eight times. In the last stanza there is a stress on the *oh* sound, in "only," "soul," "though", "whole," and "coal". While *oh* may also be a moan, in this context it is more like an exclamation, in keeping with the triumph contained in the final line.

[6]   Herbert's repetition of key words and phrases also distinguishes the first three stanzas from the last stanza. Each of the first three stanzas begins with "sweet" and ends with "must die". These repetitions stress both the beauty and the mortality of worldly things. In the last stanza, however, this repetition is abandoned, just as the stress on immortality transcends mortality. The "sweet" that begins each of the first three stanzas is replaced by "Only" (line 13). Similarly, "must die" is replaced with "chiefly lives". Both substitutions separate this final stanza from the three previous stanzas. More important, the shift in the verbal

pattern emphasizes the conceptual transition from death to the virtuous soul's immortality.

[7]   It is clear that the lyric form of Herbert's "Virtue" provides an organizational pattern for the poem's images and ideas. At the same time, the pattern of stanzas and the rhyme scheme allow the poet to draw a strong distinction between the corruptible world and the immortal soul. The closed form of this poem is not arbitrary or incidental; it is an integral way of asserting the importance of the key image, the "sweet and virtuous soul."

Commentary on the Essay

The introductory paragraph establishes the groundwork of the essay—the treatment of form in relationship to content. The main idea is that each part of the poem represents a complete blending of image, logic, and meaning.

Paragraph 2 , the first in the body, demonstrates how the poem's schematic formulation is integrated into Herbert's contrast of death and life. In this respect the paragraph demonstrates how a formal enumeration can be integrated within an essay's thematic development.

The focus of paragraph 3 is the organization of both images and ideas from stanza to stanza. Paragraph 4 begins with a transitional sentence that repeats part of the essay's central idea and, at the same time, connects it to paragraph 3. In the same way, paragraph 4 is closely tied to both paragraphs 1 and 3. The main topic here, the rhyme scheme of "Virtue," is introduced in the second sentence. This paragraph also asserts that rhythm reinforces the division between mortality and immortality. On much the same topic, paragraph 5 introduces Herbert's use of assonance, which can be seen as integral in the poem's blending of form and content.

Paragraph 6 takes up the last structural element described in the introduction—repeated key words and phrases. The idea is that these repetitions emphasize the distinction in the poem between mortality and immortality.

Paragraph 7, the conclusion, provides a brief overview and summation of the essay's argument. In addition, it concludes that form in "Virtue" is neither arbitrary nor incidental but rather an integral part of the poem's meaning.

SPECIAL TOPICS FOR WRITING AND ARGUMENT ABOUT POETIC FORM

1. Describe the use of the ode form as exemplified by Shelley's "Ode to the West Wind" (Chapter 19) and Keats's "Ode to a Nightingale." What patterns of regularity do you find? What differences do you find in the form and content of the poems? How do you account for these differences?

2. How do cummings, Thomas, Randall, and Dryden use different forms to consider the subject of death (in "Buffalo Bill's defunct," "Do Not Go Gentle into That Good Night," "Ballad of Birmingham," and "To the Memory of Mr. Oldham")? What differences in form and treatment do you find? What similarities do you find, despite these differences?

3. Consider the structural arrangement and shaping of the following works: Brueghel's painting *La Kermesse* (p. 930), Ginsberg's "A Supermarket in

California," Hass's "Museum," Heyen's "Mantle," Hollander's "Swan and Shadow," Wagoner's "March for a One-Man Band" (Chapter 19), Webb's "The Shape of History," and Williams's "The Dance." How do painter and poets utilize topic, arrangement, shape, and space to draw attention to their main ideas? How do the shaped and prose poems (Hass, Heyen, Hollander, and Webb) blend poetic and artistic techniques?

4. Compare and contrast the use of the villanelle by Bishop ("One Art"), Roethke ("The Waking"), and Thomas ("Do Not Go Gentle into That Good Night"). What topics do the poets develop? Why do the poets choose the villanelle as their poetic form? What lines do they repeat? What is the effect of this repetition?

5. Write a visual poem, and explain the principles on which you develop your lines. Here are some possible topics (just to get you started): a "boom box," a duck, a car, a football, a snow shovel, a giraffe. After finishing your poem, write a short essay that considers these questions: What are the strengths and limitations of the visual form, according to your experience? How does the form help make your poem serious or comic? How does it encourage creative language and original development of ideas?

6. Write a haiku. Be sure to fit your poem to the 5–7–5 pattern of syllables. What challenges and problems do you encounter in this form? Once you have completed your haiku (which, to be traditional, should be on a topic concerned with nature), try to cut the number of syllables to 4–5–4. Explain how you establish the first haiku pattern, and also explain how you go about cutting the number of syllables. Be sure to explain what kinds of words you use (length, choice of diction, etc.).

7. Using a computer reference system or regular card catalogue, look up one of the following topics: "ballads, England," "concrete poetry," or "blank verse." How many references are included under these listings? What sorts of topics are included under the basic topic?

Symbolism and Allusion: Windows to a Wide Expanse of Meaning

Symbolism refers to the use of symbols in works of art. As we note in Chapter 9, a **symbol** has meaning in and of itself, but it also is understood to represent something else, like the flag for the country or the school song for the school. Symbols occur in stories as well as in poems, but poetry relies more heavily on symbols because it is more concise and because it comprises more forms than fiction, which is confined to narratives alone.

Words are symbols, for they stand for various objects without actually being those objects. When we say *horse*, for example, or *tree*, or *run*, these words are not horses or trees or people running but are only symbols of horses and trees and people running. They direct our minds to real horses, real trees, and real actions in the real world that we have seen and can therefore easily imagine. In literature, however, symbolism implies a special relationship that expands our ordinary understanding of words, descriptions, and arguments.

SYMBOLISM AND MEANING IN POETRY

Symbolism goes beyond the close referral of word to thing; it is more like a window through which one can glimpse the extensive world outside. Because poetry is compact, its descriptions and portrayals of experience are brief. Symbolism is therefore one of its primary characteristics. It is a shorthand way of referring to extensive ideas or attitudes that otherwise would be impossible to state in the brief format of a poem. Thus William Butler Yeats, who believed that the city of Constantinople, or Byzantium, represented a pinnacle of human civilization, used the city as a symbol of human achievement in peace, politics, and particularly art and literature. His poem "Sailing to Byzantium" does not expand upon the full meaning and interpretation of this idea, for it would take a long history and a detailed analysis of Byzantine art and literature to do that. But the poem does consider Byzantium as a symbol of excellence and as a standard by which, to Yeats, the deteriorating state of modern civilization may be measured.

Symbolism Extends Meaning Beyond
the Normal Connotations of Words

The use of symbols is a way of moving outward, a means of extending and crystallizing information and ideas. For example, at the time of William Blake (1757–1827), the word *tiger* meant both a large, wild cat and also the specific animal we know today as a tiger. The word's connotation therefore links it with wildness and predation. As a symbol in "The Tyger," however, Blake uses the animal as a stand-in for what he considers cosmic negativism—the savage, wild forces that constantly emerge among human beings to undermine the progress of civilization. Thus the tiger as a symbol is more meaningful than either the denotation or the connotation of the word would indicate. A visual comparison can be made with Goya's painting "The Colossus" (Insert II, front bottom) in which the giant pugilistic figure above the tiny figures in the landscape represents the combination of anger, defiance, and ruthlessness that is unleashed and unchecked during times of war.

CULTURAL OR UNIVERSAL SYMBOLS ARE WIDELY KNOWN AND RECOGNIZED.   In poetry, some symbols possess a ready-made, clearly agreed upon meaning. These are **cultural** or **universal symbols** (also described in Chapter 9). Many such symbols, like the tiger, are drawn directly from nature. Other natural universal symbols are springtime and morning, which signify beginnings, growth, hope, optimism, and love. In love poetry, such symbols are normal and appropriate. If the symbols are introduced into a poem about the suddenness and irevocability of death, however, they would be ironic, for their presence would emphasize the contrast between death and life.

Cultural symbols are drawn from history and custom, such as the many Judeo-Christian religious symbols that appear in poetry. References to the lamb, Eden, Egyptian bondage, shepherds, exile, the Temple, blood, water, bread, the cross, and wine—all Jewish and/or Christian symbols—occur over and over again. Sometimes these symbols are prominent in a purely devotional context. In other contexts, however, they may be contrasted with symbols of warfare and corruption to show how extensively people neglect their moral and religious obligations.

CONTEXTUAL, PRIVATE, OR AUTHORIAL SYMBOLS GAIN MEANING MAINLY WITHIN INDIVIDUAL WORKS.   Symbols that are not widely or universally recognized are termed **contextual, private,** or **authorial symbols** (also discussed in Chapter 9). Some of these have a natural relationship with the objects and ideas being symbolized. Let us consider snow, which is cold and white and covers everything when it falls. A poet can exploit this quality and make snow a symbol. At the beginning of the long poem "The Waste Land," T. S. Eliot does exactly that; he refers to snow as a symbol of retreat from life, a withdrawal into an intellectual and moral hibernation. Another poem utilizing snow as a symbol linking the living and the dead both literally and figuratively is the following one.

VIRGINIA SCOTT (b. 1938)

Snow _____ *1977*

A doe stands at the roadside,
spirit of those who have lived here
and passed known through our memory.
The doe stands at the edge of the icy road,
then darts back into the woods.   5

Snow falling,
mother-spirit hovering,
white on the drops in the road and fields,
light from the windows
of the old house   10
brightening the snow.

Presences: mother,
grandmother,
here in their place
at the foot of *ben lomond*,   15
green trees black in the hemlock night.

The doe stands at the edge of the icy road,
then darts back into the woods.

Golden Grove, New Brunswick, Canada
January 5, 1977

QUESTIONS

1. How is snow described in the poem? How and where is it seen? As a symbol, what does it signify in relationship to the doe, the memory of persons, the mother-spirit, the old house, the light, the presences, the mountains, and the trees?

2. Explain the structural purpose for which the doe is mentioned three times in the poem, with lines 17 and 18 repeating 4 and 5. As a symbol, what do you think the doe signifies?

3. What are the relationships described in the poem between memory of the past and existence in the present? What does the symbolism contribute to your understanding of these relationships?

This poem describes a real circumstance at a real place at a real time; the poet has even provided an actual location and date, just as we do when writing a letter. We can therefore presume that the snow is real snow, falling at a time in the evening when lights go on in the nearby houses. This detail by itself would be sufficient as a realistic image, but as Scott develops the poem, the snow symbolizes the link between the speaker's memory of the past and perception of the present. The reality of the moment is suffused with the memory of the people—"mother, / grandmother"—who "lived here." The poet is meditating on the idea that individuals, though they may often be alone like the speaker, are never alone as long as they have a vivid memory of the past. Symbolically, the past and present are always connected, just as the snow covers the scene.

At the poem's conclusion, the doe darting into the woods suggests a linking of present and future (i.e., as long as there are woods, there will be does darting into them). Both the snow and the deer are private and contextual symbols, for they are established and developed within the poem, and they do not have the same symbolic value elsewhere. Through the symbolism, therefore, the poet has converted a private moment into an idea of general significance.

Similarly, references to other ordinary materials may be symbolic if the poet emphasizes them sufficiently, as in Keats's "La Belle Dame Sans Merci," which opens and closes with the image of withered sedge, or grass. What might seem like nothing more than a natural detail becomes additionally important because it can be understood to symbolize the loss and bewilderment felt by people when the people they love seem to be unreal, faithless, and destructive rather than genuine, loyal, and supportive.

Symbols Are Integrated into Poetry in a Variety of Ways

Poets do not simply jam symbols into a poem artificially and arbitrarily. Rather, symbols are structurally important and meaningful first and are secondarily (and essentially) symbolic. We therefore find symbols in single words, and also in actions, scenes and settings, characters and characterizations, and various situations.

MANY INDIVIDUAL WORDS ARE SYMBOLIC IN THEMSELVES.   With general and universal symbols, a single word is often sufficient, as with references to the lamb, shepherd, cross, blood, bread, and wine; or to summer and winter; or to drought and flood, morning and night, heat and shade, storm and calm, or feast and famine. One of the most famous of all birds, the nightingale, is an example of a single word being instantly symbolic. Because the bird is known for its beautiful song, it symbolizes natural, unspoiled beauty as contrasted with the contrived attempts by human beings to create beauty. Keats refers to the bird in this way in his "Ode to a Nightingale," and he compares his own mortality with the virtually eternal beauty of this singer.

Another word also referring to a bird as a symbol is *geese*. Because migratory geese fly south in the fall, they symbolize the loss of summer abundance, seasonal change, alteration, and loss, with accompanying feelings of regret and sorrow. Because they return north in the spring, however, they also symbolize regeneration, newness, anticipation, and hope. These contrasting symbolic values are important in Jorie Graham's "The Geese" and Mary Oliver's "Wild Geese." Graham emphasizes that the geese are "crossing" overhead but nevertheless that human affairs of "the everyday" continue despite the changes symbolized by the geese. In contrast, Oliver emphasizes geese as symbols of renewal, for the geese returning in spring suggest that "the world offers itself to your imagination."

A SIMPLE ACTION MAY BE SHOWN TO BE SYMBOLIC.   Not only words but also actions may be presented as symbols. In Scott's "Snow," as we have just observed, the doe darting into the darkening woods symbolizes renewal and the mystery of life. In Hardy's "In Time of 'The Breaking of Nations,'" the action of the man plowing a field symbolizes the continued life and vitality of the folk, the people, despite the political wrangling and military warfare that constantly rage in the world.

SCENES AND SETTINGS MAY BE VIEWED AS SYMBOLS.   While settings and scenes may be no more than just that—settings and scenes—the poet may also develop them as symbols. We may note a symbolic setting in Wilbur's "Year's End." Wilbur draws our attention to a little dog, curled up as if sleeping, and its (presumable) owners, all of whom were killed by falling lava when the eruption of Mount Vesuvius destroyed Pompeii, the ancient Roman town, in 79 C.E. In the poem's context, this scene symbolizes the incompleteness of human achievements, a condition not only of present life but also of ancient life. Keats, in "La Belle Dame Sans Merci," introduces the "elfin grot" (grotto) of the "lady in the meads." This grotto is an unreal magical womblike location symbolizing both the allure and the disappointment that sometimes characterize sexual attraction.

CHARACTERS MAY BE GIVEN SYMBOLIC VALUE.   Poets also devise characters or people as symbols representing ideas or values, like the balloonman in e. e. cummings's "in Just-." Although the balloonman is simply mentioned and not described or visualized, cummings includes enough detail about him to make him symbolic of the primitive vitality, joy, and sexuality that calls children out of childhood. The "fairy's child" of "La Belle Dame Sans Merci" is a symbol of the mystery of love. The figures in Hardy's "In Time of 'The Breaking of Nations'" symbolize the power of average, ordinary people to endure even "though Dynasties pass."

SITUATIONS MAY BE VIEWED SYMBOLICALLY.   The poem's situations, circumstances, and conditions may also be symbolic. The position of the young gunner in the World War II bomber, six miles above the earth (Jarrell's "The Death of the Ball Turret Gunner", Chapter 13), makes him vulnerable and helpless, and his death symbolizes the condition of humankind in the modern age of fear and anxiety, when life is threatened by global war and technologically expert destructiveness. In "she being Brand / -new" (Chapter 18), e. e. cummings cleverly uses the situation of the speaker's breaking in a new automobile as the symbol of another kind of encounter involving the speaker.

Symbols Offer a Complete Range of Qualities

The meanings of symbols may be placed on a continuum of qualities from good to bad, high to low, favorable to unfavorable. For example, cummings's old balloonman of "in just-" is on the positive end, symbolizing the irresistible and joyful call of growth and sexuality. Outright horror is suggested by the symbol of the rough beast slouching toward Bethlehem in Yeats's "The Second Coming." Although the beast shares the same birthplace with Jesus, the commonality is ironic because the beast represents the extremes of anger, hatred, and brutality that in Yeats's judgment are dominant in modern politics.

ALLUSIONS AND POETIC MEANING

Just as symbolism enriches meaning, so also do **allusions** (see Chapter 9), which take the form of (1) unacknowledged brief quotations from other works and (2) references to historical events and any aspect of human culture—art, music, literature, and so on. The use of allusions is a means of connecting new literary works with the broader cultural tradition of which the works are a part. In addition, allusions presuppose a common bond of knowledge between the poet and the reader. On the one hand, poets making allusions compliment the past, and on the other, they salute readers able to discover how the meanings of the allusions are both retained and transformed in the new context.

Allusions Add Their Own Life to Poems Containing Them

An allusion carries with it the entire context of the work from which it is drawn. Perhaps the richest storehouses of such ready-made references and stories are the King James Bible and the plays of Shakespeare. Keats introduces a biblical allusion in "Ode to a Nightingale" (Chapter 20), where he refers to the story of Ruth, who was "sick for home" while standing "in tears amid the alien corn." This allusion is particularly rich, because Ruth became the mother of Jesse. According to the Gospel of Matthew it was from the line of Jesse that King David was born, and it was from the house of David that Jesus was born. Thus Keats's nightingale is not only a symbol of natural beauty, but through the biblical allusion it symbolizes regeneration and redemption, much in keeping with Keats's assertion that the bird is "not born for death." In Yeats's "The Second Coming," we encounter an allusion to *Macbeth,* by Shakespeare. Yeats uses the phrase "blood-dimmed tide," which refers to Macbeth's soliloquy in the second act of *Macbeth.* In the play, after murdering Duncan, Macbeth asks if there is enough water in Neptune's ocean to wash the blood from his hands. His immediate, guilt-ridden response is that Duncan's blood will instead turn the green water to red. This image of crime being bloody enough to stain the ocean's water is thus the allusive context of Yeats's "blood-dimmed tide."

Once works become well known, as with the Bible and the plays of Shakespeare, they may in turn become a source of allusions for subsequent writers. Such a well-known work is Frost's "Stopping by Woods on a Snowy Evening" (Chapter 13), which contains an often quoted last line: "And miles to go before I sleep." This line is so universally recognized that it has become a symbol of completing tasks and fulfilling responsibilities. Isabella Gardner alludes to the Frost line in her "Collage of Echoes," for example, a poem which is deliberately built out of allusions.

Allusions may be discovered in no more than a single word or phrase in a poem, provided that the expression is unusual enough or associative enough to bear the weight of the reference. Virginia Scott's "Snow," for example, speaks of "green trees black in the hemlock night." Of course, the word *hemlock* refers to a type of evergreen tree observed by the speaker, but a distillation of hemlock was also the poison drunk by Socrates when the ancient Athenians executed him, as described in Plato's dialogue "Phaedo." Because of this association, any use of the word *hemlock* can be construed as an allusion to the death of Socrates and the end of human achievement. Another allusion to hemlock occurs in the beginning lines of "Ode to a Nightingale," in which Keats refers to hemlock. His speaker declares that a "drowsy numbness" has overtaken him "as though of hemlock . . . [he] had drunk." As the poem continues, we realize that Keats's allusion refers to the way in which death might open a new plane of existence for the speaker—a life of immortal beauty. Thus Keats builds the single-word allusion into new ideas about the possible nature of death.

Phrases and also descriptions and situations may also signal allusions, as in Jacobsen's "Tears," where the following sentence occurs: "Yet the globe is salt / with that savor." This is a clear allusion to the book of Matthew, 5:13: "Ye are the salt of the earth: but if the salt have lost his savour, wherewith shall it be salted?" This biblical passage refers to the need for believers to retain their faith, for without such faith they are "good for nothing, but to be cast out." However, Jacobsen is discussing something different, namely the endlessness of grief as a condition of life, with the continuing facts of sorrow remaining on the earth as a silent legacy. By making this allusion, Jacobsen adds to her idea the implication that, throughout human history, sorrow and tears have been a result of the loss of faith and love in human relationships.

Allusions are therefore an important means by which poets broaden the context and deepen meaning. The issues a poet raises in a new poem, in other words, are not important only there but are linked through allusion to issues raised earlier by other thinkers or brought out by previous events, places, or persons. With connections made through allusions, poets clarify their own ideas. Allusion is hence not literary "theft" but is rather a means of enrichment.

STUDYING FOR SYMBOLS AND ALLUSIONS

As you study poetry for its symbols and allusions, remember that these devices do not come marked with special notice and fanfare. A decision to call a feature of a poem *symbolic* is based on the circumstances brought out in the poem. Let us say that the poet introduces a major item of importance at a climactic part of the poem, or that the poet introduces a description that is unusual or note-worthy, such as the connection between "stony sleep" and the "rough beast" in Yeats's "The Second Coming." When such a connection occurs, the element may no longer be taken just literally but should be read as a symbol.

Even after you have found a connection such as this, however, you will have to discover and understand symbolic meaning. For instance, in the context of Yeats's "The Second Coming," the phrase "rough beast" might refer to the person or persons hinted at in traditional interpretations of the New Testament as the "Antichrist." In a secular frame of reference, the associations of blank-ness and pitilessness suggest brutality and suppression. Still further, however, if the last hundred years had not been a period in which millions of people were persecuted and exterminated in military and secret police operations, even these associations might make the "rough beast" quizzical but not necessarily symbolic. But because of the rightness of the application, together with the tra-ditional biblical associations, the figure clearly should be construed as a symbol of heartless persecution and brutality.

As you can see, the interpretation of a symbol requires that you consider, in some depth, the person, object, situation, or action being considered as sym-bolic. If the element can be seen as general and representative—characteristic of the condition of a large number of human beings—it assumes symbolic sig-nificance. As a rule, the more ideas that you can associate with the element, the more likely it is to be a symbol.

As for allusions, the identification of an allusion is usually simple. A word, situation, or phrase either is an allusion or it is not, and hence the matter is easily settled once a source is located. The problem comes in determining how the allusion affects the context of the poem you are reading. Thus we under-stand that in the poem "Snow," Virginia Scott alludes to Robert Frost's "Desert Places" by borrowing Frost's phrase "Snow falling." Once this allusion is estab-lished, its purpose must still be learned. Thus, on the one hand, the allusion might mean that the situation in "Snow" is the same as in Frost's poem, namely, that the authorial speaker is making observations about interior blankness—the "desert places" of the mind, or soul. On the other hand, the poet may be using the allusion in a new sense, and this indeed is the case. Whereas Frost uses the falling snow to suggest coldness of spirit, Scott uses it, more warmly, to connect the natural scene to the memory of family. In other words, once the presence of an allusion is established, the challenge of reading and under-standing still continues.

❀ POEMS FOR STUDY

e. e. cummings   (1894–1962)

in Just- _____ *1923*

in Just-
spring   when the world is mud-
luscious the little
lame balloonman

whistles   far   and wee   5

and eddieandbill come
running from marbles and
piracies and it's
spring

when the world is puddle-wonderful   10

the queer
old balloonman whistles
far   and   wee
and bettyandisbel come dancing

from hop-scotch and jump-rope and   15
it's
spring
and
      the
            goat-footed°   20

balloonMan   whistles
far
and
wee

IN JUST-.   20 *goat-footed:* The mythological Greek god Pan, a free-spirited and lascivious god who presides over fields, forests, and herds, was portrayed with the body of a man and the legs of a goat.

QUESTIONS

1. Explain the following as symbols: "spring," "mud-luscious," "marbles," "puddle-wonderful," "hop-scotch." What does the whistle of the balloonman symbolize?
2. In what way is the balloonman symbolic?
3. Besides the balloonman, there are four other characters in the poem. Who are they? Why does cummings run their names together? What impulses do these characters represent symbolically?
4. Read the poem aloud. Taking into account the spacing and alignment, how does the physical arrangement on the page influence your perception?

JOHN DONNE   (1572–1731)

The Canonization° _____ *1633*

For Godsake hold your tongue, and let me love,
   Or chide my palsy, or my gout,
My five gray hairs, or ruin'd fortune flout,
    With wealth your state, your mind with Arts improve,°
      Take you a course,° get you a place,°
      Observe His Honor,° or his grace,°
Or the King's real, or his stampèd face
    Contemplate,° what you will, approve,°
    So you will let me love.

Alas, alas, who's injured by my love?
    What merchant's ships have my sighs drown'd?
Who says my tears have overflow'd his ground?
    When did my colds a forward spring° remove?
      When did the heats which my veins fill°
      Add one more to the plaguy Bill?°
Soldiers find wars, and Lawyers find out still
    Litigious men, which quarrels move,
    Though she and I do love.

Call us what you will, we are made such by love;
    Call her one, me another fly,°
We're Tapers° too, and at our own cost die,°   *candles*

THE CANONIZATION. *The Canonization:* the making of saints.   4 *With wealth . . . improve:* i.e., Improve your state with wealth and your mind with arts.   5 *Take you a course:* take up a career.   *place:* a political appointment.   6 *His Honor:* any important courtier.   *his grace:* a person of greatest eminence, such as a bishop or the king.   7, 8 *Or . . . contemplate:* i.e., Or contemplate either the king's real face (at court) or stamped face (on coins).   8 *What . . . approve:* Try anything you like (i.e., "Mind your own business").   13 *a forward spring:* an early spring (season).   14 *the heats . . . fill:* i.e., "the heats (fevers) that fill my veins." Donne apparently wrote this line before the discovery of blood circulation was announced by William Harvey in 1616.   15 *plaguy Bill:* a regularly published list of deaths caused by the plague.   20 *fly:* a butterfly or moth (and apparently superficial and light-headed).   21 *at . . . die:* It was supposed that sexual climax shortened life.

And we in us find the'Eagle and the Dove.°
   The Phoenix riddle° hath more wit
   By us, we two, being one, are it.
So, to one neutral thing both sexes fit,   25
   We die and rise the same, and prove
   Mysterious° by this love.

We can die by it, if not live by love,
   And if unfit for tombs and hearse
Our legend be, it will be fit for verse;   30
   And if no piece of Chronicle we prove,
     We'll build in sonnets pretty rooms;
     As well a well wrought urn becomes
The greatest ashes, as half-acre tombs,
   And by these hymns, all shall approve   35
   Us *Canoniz'd* for love:°

And thus invoke° us; "You whom reverend love   *pray to saints*
   Made one another's hermitage;°
You, to whom love was peace, that now is rage;
   Who did the whole world's soul extract, and drove   40
     Into the glasses of your eyes
     So made such mirrors, and such spies,
That they did all to you epitomize,°
   Countries, towns, courts: Beg from above
   A pattern of your love!"   45

22 *the'Eagle and the Dove:* masculine and feminine symbols.   23 *Phoenix riddle:* In ancient times the phoenix, a mythical bird that lived for a thousand years, was supposed to die and rise five hundred years later from its own ashes; hence the phoenix symbolized immortality and the renewal of life and desire. See Chapter 22.   27 *Mysterious:* unknowable to anyone but God, and therefore quintessentially holy.   35, 36 *by these hymns . . . Canoniz'd for love:* The idea is that later generations will remember the lovers and elevate them to the sainthood of a religion of love. Because the lovers' love is recorded so powerfully in the speaker's poems ("sonnets" in line 33), these later generations will use the poems as hymns in their worship of love.   38 *Made . . . hermitage:* made a religious retreat for each other.   40–43 *Who did . . . epitomize:* An allusion to reputed alchemical processes, and therefore to be understood approximately like this: "Who extracted the whole world's soul and, through your eyes, assimilated this soul into yours, so that you, whose eyes saw and reflected each other, embodied the love and desire felt by all human beings."

QUESTIONS

1. What is the situation of the poem? Whom is the speaker addressing? Why does he begin as he does? How does he defend his love?

2. What symbols do you find in the poem? What are the symbols? What is being symbolized?

3. What mythic and religious mysteries are linked with sexual love in the third stanza? What does "canonization" mean? What canonizes and immortalizes the lovers? How does the "canonization" symbolize the poem's idea about the nature of love?

4. What will future lovers ask of these saints of love? Of what use will the speaker's poem be at that time? What do you think of the speaker's claim about love?

ISABELLA GARDNER   (1915–1981)

Collage of Echoes _____ 1979

I have no promises to keep
Nor miles to go before I sleep,°
For miles of years I have made promises
and (mostly) kept them.
      It's time I slept.
Now I lay me down to sleep°
With no promises to keep.
      My sleaves are ravelled°
      I have travelled.°

COLLAGE OF ECHOES.   2 *miles to go before I sleep:* See Robert Frost, "Stopping by Woods on a Snowy Evening" (p. 673), lines 13–16.   6 *Now I lay me down to sleep:* from the child's prayer: Now I lay me down to sleep; / I pray the Lord my soul to keep. / If I should die before I wake, / I pray the Lord my soul to take.   8 *My sleaves are ravelled:* See *Macbeth*, II.2.37: "Sleep that knits up the ravelled sleave of care."   9 *I have travelled:* See Keats, "On First Looking into Chapman's Homer" (p. 777).

QUESTIONS

1. Given the allusions in the poem, what do you conclude about the speaker's judgment of the reader's knowledge of literature?
2. How reliant is "Collage of Echoes" upon the contexts being echoed? How do the echoes assist in enabling enjoyment and appreciation of the poem?
3. In relation to the speaker's character as demonstrated in the poem, consider the phrases "(mostly) kept them," "With no promises to keep," and "My sleaves are ravelled." What do they show about the speaker's self-assessment? In what way might these phrases be considered comic?

JORIE GRAHAM   (b. 1954)

The Geese _____ 1980

Today as I hang out the wash I see them again, a code
as urgent as elegant,
tapering with goals.
For days they have been crossing. We live beneath these geese

as if beneath the passage of time, or a most perfect heading.
Sometime I fear their relevance.
Closest at hand,
between the lines,

the spiders imitate the paths the geese won't stray from,
imitate them endlessly to no avail: 10
things will not remain connected,
will not heal,

and the world thickens with texture instead of history,
texture instead of place.
Yet the small fear of the spiders   15
binds and binds

the pins to the lines, the lines to the eaves, to the pincushion bush,
as if, at any time, things could fall further apart
and nothing could help them
recover their meaning. And if these spiders had their way,   20

chainlink over the visible world,
would we be in or out? I turn to go back in.
There is a feeling the body gives the mind
of having missed something, a bedrock poverty, like falling

without the sense that you are passing through one world,   25
that you could reach another
anytime. Instead the real
is crossing you,

your body an arrival
you know is false but can't outrun. And somewhere in between   30
these geese forever entering and
these spiders turning back

this astonishing delay, the everyday, takes place.

QUESTIONS

1. What is the dominant tense of the poem? What effect does this tense have on the speaker's conclusions?

2. What action does the speaker perform in the course of the poem? What is the relationship between this action and the final lines?

3. What do the geese symbolize? What do the spiders symbolize? How are these symbols contrasted?

4. The first half of this poem, particularly lines 11 and 18, is reminiscent of Yeats's "The Second Coming" (p. 961). In your judgment, what use does Graham make of this allusion?

THOMAS HARDY   (1840–1928)

In Time of "The Breaking of Nations"° _____ *1916 (1915)*

Only a man harrowing clods
  In a slow silent walk,
With an old horse that stumbles and nods
  Half asleep as they stalk.

Only thin smoke without flame   5
  From the heaps of couch grass:°   *quack grass*
Yet this will go onward the same
  Though Dynasties pass.

Yonder a maid and her wight°   *fellow*
  Come whispering by;   10
War's annals will fade into night
  Ere their story die.

IN TIME OF "THE BREAKING OF NATIONS."   See Jeremiah 51:20, "with you I break nations in pieces."

QUESTIONS

1. What does Hardy symbolize by the man, horse, smoke, and couple? How realistic and vivid are these symbols? Are they universal or contextual?
2. How does Hardy show that the phrase "breaking of nations" is to be taken symbolically? What meaning is gained by the biblical allusion of this phrase?
3. Contrast the structure of stanza 1 with that of stanzas 2 and 3. How does the form of stanzas 2 and 3 enable Hardy to emphasize the main idea?
4. How does the speaker show his evaluation of the life of the common people? You might consider that at the time (1915), World War I was raging in Europe.

GEORGE HERBERT   (1593–1633)

The Collar° _____ *1633*

I struck the board, and cry'd, "No more;
    I will abroad!
What? shall I ever sigh and pine?
My lines and life are free; free as the road,
  Loose as the wind, as large as store,
    Shall I be still in suit?°
  Have I no harvest but a thorn°
  To let me blood, and not restore
What I have lost with cordial fruit?
    Sure there was wine

THE COLLAR.   *collar:* (a) the collar worn by a member of the clergy; (b) the collar of the harness of a draft animal such as a horse; (c) a restraint placed on prisoners; (d) a pun on *choler* (yellow bile), a bodily substance that was thought to cause quick rages.   6 *in suit:* waiting upon a person of power to gain favor or position.   7 *thorn:* See Mark 15:17.

Before my sighs did dry it: there was corn
    Before my tears did drown it.
Is the year only lost to me?
    Have I no bays° to crown it?
No flowers, no garlands gay? all blasted?   15
      All wasted?
Not so, my heart: but there is fruit,
    And thou hast hands.
Recover all thy sigh-blown age
On double pleasures: leave thy cold dispute   20
Of what is fit, and not; forsake thy cage;
    Thy rope of sands,
Which petty thoughts have made, and made to thee
    Good cable, to enforce and draw,
      And be thy law,   25
While thou didst wink and wouldst not see.
    Away; take heed:
    I will abroad.
Call in thy death's head there: tie up thy fears.
    He that forbears   30
To suit° and serve his need,   *follow*
    Deserves his load."
But as I rav'd and grew more fierce and wild
    At every word,
Me thought I heard one calling, "Child:"   35
    And I replied, *"My Lord."*

14 *bays:* laurel crowns to signify victory and honor.

QUESTIONS

1. What is the opening situation? Why is the speaker angry? Against what role in life is he complaining?

2. In light of the many possible meanings of *collar* (see note), explain the title as a symbol in the poem.

3. Explain the symbolism of the thorn (line 7), blood (line 8), wine (line 10), bays (line 14), flowers and garlands (line 15), cage (line 21), rope of sands (line 22), death's head (line 29), and the dialogue in lines 35 and 36.

JOSEPHINE JACOBSEN   (b. 1908)

Tears ———————————————————————— *1981*

Tears leave no mark on the soil
or pavement; certainly not in sand
or in any known rain forest;
never a mark on stone.

One would think that no one in Persepolis°   5
or Ur° ever wept.

You would assume that, like Alice,°
we would all be swimming, buffeted
in a tide of tears.
But they disappear. Their heat goes.   10
Yet the globe is salt
with that savor.°

The animals want no part in this.
The hare both screams and weeps
at her death, one poet says.   15
The stag, at death, rolls round drops
down his muzzle; but he is in
Shakespeare's forest.°

These cases are mythically rare.
No, it is the human being who persistently   20
weeps; in some countries, openly, in others, not.
Children who, even when frightened, weep most hopefully;
women, licensed weepers.°
Men, in secret, or childishly; or nobly.

Could tears not make a sea of their mass?   25
It could be salt and wild enough;
it could rouse storms and sink ships,
erode, erode its shores:
tears of rage, of love, of torture,
of loss. Of loss.   30

Must we see the future
in order to weep? Or the past?
Is that why the animals
refuse to shed tears?
But what of the present, the tears of the present?   35
The awful relief, like breath

after strangling? The generosity
of the verb "to shed"?

TEARS. 5, 6 *Persepolis . . . Ur:* Persepolis was the capital city of ancient Persia (now Iran). Ur, on the Persian Gulf, was the capital city of the ancient Sumerian Empire. Today, both cities survive only in ruins. The Hebrew patriarch Abraham traveled from "Ur of the Chaldees" to settle in the land of Canaan, the "promised land."   7 *Alice:* In Lewis Carroll's *Alice in Wonderland* (Ch. 2), Alice sheds tears, and then is reduced in size and almost drowns in her own teardrops. 11–12 *Yet . . . savor:* Matthew 5:13.   14–18 *The hare . . . forest:* In the poem *Autumn* by James Thomson (1700–1748), lines 401–457, a cruel hunt of the hare and the stag is described. It is the stag who sheds "big round tears" and "groans in anguish" when dying. Jacobsen's allusion to Shakespeare—to whom Thomson is also alluding—is *As You Like It,* II.1.29–43.   23 *licensed weepers:* In certain countries, such as Greece, professional "weepers" weep and cry aloud at funerals.

They are a classless possession
yet are not found in the museum   40
of even our greatest city.
Sometimes what was human, turns
into an animal, dry-eyed.

QUESTIONS

1. What does the poem's major symbol, tears, mean? What significance does the poem attribute to tears? Why are tears sometimes disregarded?

2. How does the poem apply the symbol to various cultures and conditions?

3. How do tears differentiate human beings from animals? What is the symbolic value of this difference? In light of the contrast, what is the meaning of the last two lines?

4. Explain the poem's use of allusions (i.e., Persepolis, Ur, the New Testament, *Alice in Wonderland*, professional mourners, Shakespeare).

ROBINSON JEFFERS   (1887–1962)

The Purse-Seine _____ *1937*

1

Our sardine fishermen work at night in the dark of the moon; daylight or
    moonlight
They could not tell where to spread the net, unable to see the phosphorescence
    of the shoals of fish.
They work northward from Monterey, coasting Santa Cruz; off New Year's Point
    or off Pigeon Point
The look-out man will see some lakes of milk-color light on the seas's night-purple;
    he points, and the helmsman
Turns the dark prow, the motorboat circles the gleaming shoal and drifts out   5
    her seine-net. They close the circle
And purse the bottom of the net, then with great labor haul it in.

2

                            I cannot tell you
How beautiful the scene is, and a little terrible, then, when the crowded fish
Know they are caught, and wildly beat from one wall to the other of their closing
    destiny the phosphorescent
Water to a pool of flame, each beautiful slender body sheeted with flame, like a   10
    live rocket
A comet's tail wake of clear yellow flame; while outside the narrowing
Floats and cordage of the net great sea-lions come up to watch, sighing in the
    dark; the vast walls of night
Stand erect to the stars.

3

                Lately I was looking from a night mountain-top
On a wide city, the colored splendor, galaxies of light: how could I help but recall   15
    the seine-net

Gathering the luminous fish? I cannot tell you how beautiful the city appeared,
    and a little terrible.
I thought, We have geared the machines and locked all together into
    interdependence; we have built the great cities; now
There is no escape. We have gathered vast populations incapable of free survival,
    insulated
From the strong earth, each person in himself helpless, on all dependent. The
    circle is closed, and the net
Is being hauled in. They hardly feel the cords drawing, yet they shine already.
    The inevitable mass-disasters
Will not come in our time nor in our children's, but we and our children
Must watch the net draw narrower, government take all powers—or revolution,
    and the new government
Take more than all, add to kept bodies kept souls—or anarchy, the mass-disasters.

4

These things are Progress;
Do you marvel our verse is troubled or frowning, while it keeps its reason? Or it
    lets go, lets the mood flow
In the manner of the recent young men into mere hysteria, splintered gleams,
    crackled laughter. But they are quite wrong.
There is no reason for amazement: surely one always knew that cultures decay,
    and life's end is death.

QUESTIONS

1. Describe how the purse-seine is used to haul in the sardines. What is the speaker's reaction to the scene as described in stanza 2?

2. How does the speaker explain that the purse-seine is a symbol? What does it symbolize? What do the sardines symbolize?

3. Compare the ideas of Jeffers with those of Yeats in "The Second Coming." Are the ideas of Jeffers more or less methodical?

4. Is the statement at the end to be taken as a fact or as a resigned acceptance of that fact? Does the poem offer any solution to the problem?

5. How can the sea-lions of line 12, and their sighs, be construed as a symbol?

JOHN KEATS   (1795–1821)

La Belle Dame Sans Merci: A Ballad° _____ 1820 (1819)

1

O what can ail thee, knight at arms,
    Alone and palely loitering?

LA BELLE DAME SANS MERCI.   French for "The beautiful lady without pity" (that is, "The heartless woman"). "La Belle Dame Sans Merci" is the title of a medieval poem by Alain Chartier; Keats's poem bears no other relationship to the medieval poem, which was thought at the time to have been by Chaucer.

The sedge has wither'd from the lake,
   And no birds sing.

2

O what can ail thee, knight at arms,   5
   So haggard and so woe-begone?
The squirrel's granary is full,
   And the harvest's done.

3

I see a lily on thy brow
   With anguish moist and fever dew,   10
And on thy cheeks a fading rose
   Fast withereth too.

4

I met a lady in the meads,°   *meadows*
   Full beautiful, a fairy's child;
Her hair was long, her foot was light,   15
   And her eyes were wild.

5

I made a garland for her head,
   And bracelets too, and fragrant zone;°   *belt*
She look'd at me as she did love,
   And made sweet moan.   20

6

I set her on my pacing steed,
   And nothing else saw all day long,
For sidelong would she bend, and sing
   A fairy's song.

7

She found me roots of relish° sweet,   *magical potion*   25
   And honey wild, and manna° dew,   *see Exodus 16:14–36*
And sure in language strange she said—
   I love thee true.

8

She took me to her elfin grot,°   *grotto*
   And there she wept, and sigh'd full sore,   30
And there I shut her wild wild eyes
   With kisses four.

9

And there she lullèd me asleep,
   And there I dream'd—Ah! woe betide!
The latest° dream I ever dream'd   *last*   35
   On the cold hill's side.

10

I saw pale kings, and princes too,
  Pale warriors, death pale were they all;
They cried—"La belle dame sans merci
  Hath thee in thrall!"°   *slavery*   40

11

I saw their starv'd lips in the gloam
  With horrid warning gapèd wide,
And I awoke and found me here
  On the cold hill's side.

12

And this is why I sojourn here,   4
  Alone and palely loitering,
Though the sedge is wither'd from the lake,
  And no birds sing.

QUESTIONS

1. Who is the speaker of stanzas 1–3? Who speaks after that?
2. In light of the dreamlike content of the poem, how can the knight's experience be viewed as symbolic? What is being symbolized?
3. Consider "relish" (line 25), "honey" (line 26), and "manna" (line 26) as symbols. Are they realistic or mythical? What does the allusion to manna signify? What is symbolized by the "pale kings, and princes too" and "Pale warriors" (lines 37–38)?
4. Consider the poem's setting as symbols of the knight's state of mind.

X. J. KENNEDY   (b. 1929)

Old Men Pitching Horseshoes _____ *1985*

Back in a yard where ringers groove a ditch,
These four in shirtsleeves congregate to pitch
Dirt-burnished iron. With appraising eye,
One sizes up a peg, hoists and lets fly—
A clang resounds as though a smith had struck
Fire from a forge. His first blow, out of luck,
Rattles in circles. Hitching up his face,
He swings, and weight once more inhabits space,
Tumbles as gently as a new-laid egg.
Extended iron arms surround their peg
Like one come home to greet a long-lost brother.
Shouts from one outpost. Mutters from the other.

Now changing sides, each withered pitcher moves
As his considered dignity behooves
Down the worn path of earth where August flies   15
And sheaves of air in warm distortions rise.
To stand ground, fling, kick dust with all the force
Of shoes still hammered to a living horse.

QUESTIONS

1. How does the poet indicate that the pitching of horseshoes is symbolic? As symbols, why are old men chosen rather than young men?

2. Discuss the effects of the words "congregate," "outpost," "withered," "sheaves," "kick dust," and "force." What do these words contribute to the poem's symbolism?

3. Compare the topic of this poem with the concluding lines of T. S. Eliot's "Preludes" (p. 759), especially the last two lines. How is the symbolism of these poems similar? Different?

MARY OLIVER   (b. 1935)

Wild Geese _____ *1986*

You do not have to be good.
You do not have to walk on your knees
for a hundred miles through the desert, repenting.
You only have to let the soft animal of your body
    love what it loves.
Tell me about despair, yours, and I will tell you mine.   5
Meanwhile the world goes on.
Meanwhile the sun and the clear pebbles of the rain
are moving across the landscapes,
over the prairies and the deep trees,
the mountains and the rivers.   10
Meanwhile the wild geese, high in the clean blue air,
are heading home again.
Whoever you are, no matter how lonely,
the world offers itself to your imagination,
calls to you like the wild geese, harsh and exciting—   15
over and over announcing your place
in the family of things.

QUESTIONS

1. What idea is contained in the first five lines? What ideas are expressed in lines 6–12? In what ways are lines 13–17 a climax of the poem? How does this last section build on the poem's earlier parts?

2. What is symbolized by the references to "the sun and the clear pebbles of the rain," and so on, in lines 7–10? Do these symbols suggest futility or hope?

3.   What do the wild geese symbolize (lines 11–12, 15)? How is the symbol of the geese a response to the poem's first six lines? How well would the words *acceptance, self-knowledge,* or *adjustment* describe the poem's ideas? What other words would be better or more suitable? Why?

WALT WHITMAN   (1819–1892)

A Noiseless Patient Spider _____ 1868

A noiseless patient spider,
I marked where on a little promontory it stood isolated,
Marked how to explore the vacant vast surrounding,
It launched forth filament, filament, filament out of itself,
Ever unreeling them, ever tirelessly speeding them.

And you O my soul where you stand,
Surrounded, detached, in measureless oceans of space,
Ceaselessly musing, venturing, throwing, seeking the spheres
    to connect them,
Till the bridge you will need be formed, till the ductile anchor hold,
Till the gossamer thread you fling catch somewhere, O my soul.

QUESTIONS

1.   The subject of the second stanza is seemingly unrelated to the subject of the first. How are these stanzas related?

2.   In what way does the spider's web symbolize the soul and the poet's view of the isolation of human beings? How does the web symbolize the soul's ceaseless "musing . . . seeking" and the attempt "to connect"?

3.   Explain why the second stanza is not a complete sentence. How might this grammatical feature be related to the spider's web? To the poet's idea that life requires striving but does not offer completeness?

RICHARD WILBUR   (b. 1921)

Year's End _____ 1950

Now winter downs the dying of the year,
And Night is all a settlement of snow;
From the soft street the rooms of houses show
A gathered light, a shapen atmosphere,
Like frozen-over lakes whose ice is thin
And still allows some stirring down within.

I've known the wind by water banks to shake
The late leaves down, which frozen where they fell
And held in ice as dancers in a spell
Fluttered all winter long into a lake;   10
Graved on the dark in gestures of descent,
They seemed their own most perfect monument.

There was perfection in the death of ferns
Which laid their fragile cheeks against the stone
A million years. Great mammoths overthrown   15
Composedly have made their long sojourns,
Like palaces of patience, in the gray
And changeless lands of ice. And at Pompeii°

The little dog lay curled and did not rise
But slept the deeper as the ashes rose   20
And found the people incomplete, and froze
The random hands, the loose unready eyes
Of men expecting yet another sun
To do the shapely thing they had not done.

These sudden ends of time must give us pause.   25
We fray into the future, rarely wrought
Save in the tapestries of afterthought.
More time, more time. Barrages of applause
Come muffled from a buried radio.
The New-year bells are wrangling with the snow.   30

YEAR'S END.   18 *Pompeii:* the southern Italian Roman city covered by lava during the eruption
of Mount Vesuvius in 79 C.E. Many people and animals died trying to escape the lava flow and
were covered over where they fell. Modern excavators created statues of these fallen figures by
using plaster to fill in cavities left by their bodies. One of these was the "little dog" mentioned in
line 19.

QUESTIONS

1. What natural and historical symbols does Wilbur introduce in the poem? What ideas do the symbols present about time and the use people make of time?
2. Describe Wilbur's use of two-word groups united by assonance and consonance in the poem (e.g., "*pe*ople incompl*e*te," "*d*owns the *d*ying," "*st*ill . . . *st*irring"). How effective are these groups in drawing your attention to Wilbur's meaning?
3. Describe the symbols in the final stanza ("fray into the future," "tapestries of afterthought," "muffled from a buried radio"). Why does the poem conclude with the symbols of "New-year bells" and "snow"?
4. Consider the meaning of line 25. How can this line be interpreted so that the poem may have either positive or negative views of human activity?

WILLIAM BUTLER YEATS   (1865–1939)

Sailing to Byzantium° _____ *1927*

1

That is no country for old men. The young
In one another's arms, birds in the trees
—Those dying generations—at their song,
The salmon-falls, the mackerel-crowded seas,
Fish, flesh, or fowl, commend all summer long
Whatever is begotten, born, and dies.
Caught in that sensual music all neglect
Monuments of unaging intellect.

2

An aged man is but a paltry thing.
A tattered coat upon a stick, unless
Soul clap its hands and sing, and louder sing
For every tatter in its mortal dress,
Nor is there singing school but studying
Monuments of its own magnificence;
And therefore I have sailed the seas and come
To the holy city of Byzantium.

3

O sages standing in God's holy fire
As in the gold mosaic of a wall,
Come from the holy fire, perne in a gyre,°
And be the singing-masters of my soul.
Consume my heart away; sick with desire
And fastened to a dying animal
It knows not what it is; and gather me
Into the artifice of eternity.

4

Once out of nature I shall never take
My bodily form from any natural thing,
But such a form as Grecian goldsmiths make
Of hammered gold and gold enameling
To keep a drowsy Emperor awake;
Or set upon a golden bough to sing
To lords and ladies of Byzantium
Of what is past, or passing, or to come.

SAILING TO BYZANTIUM.   In Yeat's private mythology, Byzantium (called Constantinople in Roman times and Istanbul today) symbolizes art, artifice, sophistication, and eternity as opposed to the natural world and physicality.   19 *perne in a gyre:* turning about in a spiral motion. See the diagram on p. 961.

QUESTIONS

1. Why does the speaker state that Byzantium "is no country for old men"? What details does he bring out in the first stanza that support this claim?

2. What thoughts and descriptions does the speaker bring out about himself? What symbols does he employ in exemplifying his self-examination?

3. In stanza 4, what does the speaker mean by stating that he will take "such a form as Grecian goldsmiths make"? To what degree may this reference be taken as a symbol of the permanence of art as opposed to the impermanence of life?

4. Why does the speaker describe "eternity" as an "artifice" (line 24)? In what way, actual or symbolic, could the speaker be gathered into this artifice? What is being said here?

WILLIAM BUTLER YEATS   (1865–1939)

The Second Coming° _____ *1920 (1919)*

Turning and turning in the widening gyre°
The falcon cannot hear the falconer;
Things fall apart; the center cannot hold;
Mere anarchy is loosed upon the world,
The blood-dimmed tide° is loosed, and everywhere   5
The ceremony of innocence is drowned;
The best lack all conviction, while the worst
Are full of passionate intensity.

THE SECOND COMING.   The phrase "second coming" has been traditionally used to refer to expectations of the return of Jesus for the salvation of believers, as described in the New Testament. The prophecies foretold that Christ's return would be preceded by famine, epidemics, wars between nations, and general civil disturbance. Yeats believed that human history could be measured in cycles of approximately 2,000 years (see line 19, "twenty centuries"). According to this system, the birth of Jesus ended the Greco-Roman cycle and in 1919, when Yeats wrote "The Second Coming," it appeared to him that the Christian period was ending and a new era was about to take its place. The New Testament expectation was that Jesus would reappear. Yeats, by contrast, holds that the disruptions of the twentieth century were preceding a takeover by the forces of evil.   1 *gyre:* a radiating spiral, cone, or vortex. Yeats used the intersecting of two of these shapes as a visual symbol of his cyclic theory. As one gyre spiraled and widened out, to become dissipated, one period of history would end; at the same time a new gyre, closer to the center, would begin and spiral in a reverse direction to the starting point of the old gyre. A drawing of this plan looks like this:

The falcon of line 2 is at the broadest, centrifugal point of one gyre, symbolically illustrating the end of a cycle. The "indignant desert birds" of line 17 "reel" in a tighter circle, symbolizing the beginning of the new age in the new gyre.   5 *blood-dimmed tide:* quotation from Shakespeare's *Macbeth*, II.2.60–63.

Surely some revelation is at hand;
Surely the Second Coming is at hand.   10
The Second Coming! Hardly are those words out
When a vast image out of *Spiritus Mundi*°
Troubles my sight; somewhere in sands of the desert
A shape with lion body and the head of a man,°
A gaze blank and pitiless as the sun,   15
Is moving its slow thighs, while all about it
Reel shadows of the indignant desert birds.
The darkness drops again; but now I know
That twenty centuries of stony sleep
Were vexed to nightmare by a rocking cradle,   20
And what rough beast, its hour come round at last,
Slouches towards Bethlehem to be born?

12 *Spiritus Mundi:* literally, the spirit of the world, a collective human consciousness that furnished writers and thinkers with a common fund of images and symbols. Yeats referred to this collective repository as "a great memory passing on from generation to generation."   14 *lion body and the head of a man:* that is, the Sphinx, which in ancient Egypt symbolized the pharaoh as a spirit of the sun. Because of this pre-Christian origin, the reincarnation of a sphinx could therefore represent qualities associated in New Testament books like Revelation (11, 13, 17), Mark (13:14–20), and 2 Thessalonians (2:1–12) with a monstrous, superhuman, satanic figure. For a picture of the Sphinx, see p. 994.

QUESTIONS

1. Consider the following as symbols: the "gyre," the "falcon," the "blood-dimmed tide," the "ceremony of innocence," the "worst" who are "full of passionate intensity." What ideas and values do these symbolize in the poem?

2. Why does Yeats capitalize the phrase "Second Coming"? To what does this phrase refer? Explain the irony of Yeats's use of the phrase in this poem.

3. Contrast the symbols of the falcon of line 2 and the desert birds of line 17. Considering that these are realistically presented, how does the realism contribute to their identity as symbols?

4. What is symbolized by the sphinx being revealed as a "rough beast"? What is the significance of the beast's going "towards Bethlehem to be born"?

WRITING ABOUT SYMBOLISM AND ALLUSION IN POETRY

As you read your poem, take notes and make all the observations you can about the presence of symbols or allusions or both. Explanatory notes will help you establish basic information, but you also need to explain meanings and create interpretations in your own words. Use a dictionary for understanding words or phrases that require further study. For allusions, you might check out original sources to determine original contexts. Try to determine the ways in which your poem is similar to, or different from, the original work or source, and then determine the purpose served by the allusion.

Questions for Discovering Ideas

CULTURAL OR UNIVERSAL SYMBOLS

• What symbols that you can characterize as cultural or universal can you discover in names, objects, places, situations, or actions in the poem (e.g., nightingales, hemlock, a thorn, two lovers, Bethlehem)?

• How are these symbols used? What do they mean, both specifically, in the poem, and universally, in a broader context? What would the poem be like without the symbolic meaning?

CONTEXTUAL SYMBOLS

• What contextual symbols can you locate in the poem (e.g., withered sedge, a flock of birds, a doe running into a woods)? How are these symbols used specifically in the poem? What would the poem be like if the contextual symbol were not taken to be symbolic?

• What causes you to conclude that the symbols are truly symbolic? What is being symbolized? What do the symbols mean? How definite or direct is the symbolism?

• Is the symbolism used systematically throughout the poem, or is it used only once? How does the symbolism affect the ideas or emotions expressed in the poem?

ALLUSIONS

• Granted your knowledge of literature, science, geography, television, the Bible, film, popular culture, and other fields, what kinds of allusion are you likely to recognize immediately?

• Do you find any references that fit into any of these or other categories? What do these allusions mean in their original context? What do they mean in the poem's context?

• Do you see any possible allusions that you are not sure about? What help do you find in the explanatory notes in the text you are using? Consult a dictionary or other reference work to discover the nature of these allusions. See Chapter 9, p. 431, and feel free to ask your reference librarian for help.

Strategies for Organizing Ideas

Begin with a brief description of the poem and of the symbolism or allusions in it. A symbol might be central to the poem, or an allusion might be introduced at a particularly important point. Your central idea might take you in a number of directions: you might conclude that the symbolism is based on objects like flowers and natural scenes, or that it stems out of an action or set of actions, or that it is developed from an initial situation such as a time of the day or year. The symbols may be universal or contextual; they may be applicable particularly to personal life or to political or social life. Allusions may emphasize the differences between your poem and the work or event being alluded to, or they may highlight the circumstances of your poem. Also, you might make a point that the symbols and/or allusions make the poem seem optimistic, or pessimistic, and so on.

Here are some possible approaches for your essay, which may be combined as need arises.

1. *The meaning of symbols or allusions.* This approach is the most natural one to take for an essay on symbolism or allusion. If you have discovered a symbol or symbols or allusions, explain the meaning as best you can. Thus you need to answer questions like these: What is the poem's major idea? How do you know that your interpretation is valid? How do the poem's symbols and allusions contribute to your interpretation? How pervasive, how applicable, are these devices? If you have discovered many symbols and allusions, which ones predominate? What do they mean? Why are some more important than others? What connects them with each other and with the poem's main idea? How are you able to make conclusions about all this?

2. *The effect of symbols or allusions on the poem's form.* Here the goal is to determine how symbolism or allusion is related to the poetic structure. Where does the symbol occur in the poem? If it is early, how do the following parts relate to the ideas of the symbol? What logical or chronological function does the symbol serve in the poem's development? Is the symbol repeated, and if so, to what effect? If the symbol is introduced later, has it been anticipated earlier? How do you know? Can the symbol be considered climactic? What might the structure of the poem have been like if the symbolism had not been used? (Answering this question can help you judge how the symbol influences the poem's structure.) Many of these same questions might also be applied to an allusion or allusions. In addition, for an allusion, it is important to compare the contexts of the work you are studying and of the original to determine how the poet uses the allusion as a part of the poem's form or structure.

3. *The relationship between the literal and the symbolic.* The object here is to describe the literal nature of the symbols, and then to determine their appropriateness to the poem's context. If the symbol is part of a narrative, what is its literal function? If the symbol is a person, object, or setting, what physical aspects are described? Are colors included? Shapes? Sizes? Sounds? In light of this description, how applicable is the symbol to the ideas it embodies? How appropriate is the literal condition to the symbolic condition? The answers to questions like these should lead not so much to a detailed account of the meaning of the symbols but rather to an account of their appropriateness to the topics and ideas of the poem.

4. *The implications and resonances of symbols and allusions.* This type of essay is more personal than the others, for it is devoted to the suggestions and associations—the "implications and resonances"—that the poem's symbols and allusions bring out. The object of the essay is to describe your own responses or chain of thinking that the poem sets in motion. You are therefore free to move in your own direction as long as you base your discussion on the symbols and allusions in the poem. If the poet is speaking in general terms about the end of

an era, for example, as with the symbol of the rough beast in Yeats's "The Second Coming" and the giant fishnets in Jeffers's "The Purse-Seine," then you could apply these symbols to your own thinking. It is not easy to summon the knowledge and authority to contradict the work of any poet, but if you can point out shortcomings in the thought of the symbols or allusions, you should do so.

Your conclusion might contain a summary of your main points. If your poem is rich in symbols or allusions, you might also consider some of the elements that you have not discussed in the body and try to tie these together with those you have already discussed. It would also be appropriate to introduce any responses or new ideas you have developed as a result of your study.

DEMONSTRATIVE STUDENT ESSAY

Symbolism and Allusion in Yeats's "The Second Coming"°

[1] William Butler Yeats's "The Second Coming" is a prophetic poem that lays out reasons for being scared about the future. The poem's symbolism and allusiveness combine traditional materials from ancient history and literature together with Yeats's own scheme for visualizing the rise and fall of civilizations. These devices are arranged to explain both the disruption of our present but old culture and also the installation of a fearsome new one.* To make his prophecies clear, Yeats describes major symbols and allusions separately and combines them as a reflection of horror.†

[2] Yeats's first symbol, the gyre, or rather two interconnecting gyres, pervades the poem, for it outlines the cyclical nature of political changes. Flying outward at the widest point of the gyre--symbolizing our present era--a falcon is used by Yeats to introduce the idea that "the center cannot hold." The "desert birds," hovering around the "lion body and the head of a man" (the sphinx-like figure), show a tighter circle in a second gyre, symbolizing a new stage of human existence. Thus the widening symbolic gyre in line 1 is interpenetrating with the narrowing gyre pointing at the "rough beast." This intersecting and blending show that new things both emerge and separate from old things. The spatial and geometrical symbolism thus illustrates that the past is breaking up while the future is about to take the shape of the past--but at its worst, not at its best.

[3] Embodying this horror-to-be, the second major symbol is the sphinx-like creature moving its "slow thighs" in the sands of the desert. The attributes of the monstrous creature are blankness and pitilessness. Yeats describes it as a "rough beast," with the "indignant desert birds" flying in circles above it like vultures. This description symbolizes the brutal nature of the new age. Yeats wrote the poem in 1919, right after the conclusion of World War I, which had seen

---

° See p. 961 for this poem.
* Central idea.
† Thesis sentence.

particularly mindless and vicious trench warfare. The disruption of life caused by this war was a disturbing indicator of the repressiveness and brutality to come.

It is this forthcoming brutality that makes ironic the poem's major allusion--the "second coming. " Yeats alludes to the second coming in the poem's title and also in lines 9 and 10:

> Surely some revelation is at hand;
> Surely the Second Coming is at hand.

[4] The allusion is to the usual understanding of New Testament prophecies about the return of Christ at the end of historical time, when the Kingdom of God will come on earth. In the Bible, war and rumors of war are claimed as being the signs indicating that the return, or "second coming," is near. Thus far, both the biblical signs and the observations of Yeats coincide. The twist, however, is that Yeats is suggesting in the allusion that after the breakup of the present age, the new age will be marked not by God's Kingdom but by the "rough beast." Because Yeats describes the beast as a sphinx, his model is the kind of despotism known in ancient Egypt, when power was held absolutely by the pharaoh, and when the mass of people were denied freedom and civil rights.

[5] A unique aspect of Yeats's symbolism and allusiveness is that he fuses the two together. The "ceremony of innocence," for example (line 6), refers to the ritual of communion and also to its symbolic value of regeneration. By indicating that it is being drowned, he doubles the impact of his assertion that tradition is being lost and brutalized. The *Spiritus Mundi* is an abstract allusion to a common human bond of images and characteristics, but because of the image of brutality it produces, as a symbol it demonstrates that horror is a normal condition of human life. In addition, the "blood-dimmed tide" is an allusion to Shakespeare's Macbeth, who symbolically has stained the ocean red with King Duncan's blood. The "blood-dimmed tide" therefore both allusively and symbolically indicates the global scope of the evil age being born.

[6] "The Second Coming" is rich in symbols that are both traditional and personal, but there are additional symbols and allusions. The most easily visualized of these is the falcon out of control, flying higher and higher and farther away from the falconer, to symbolize the anarchy that Yeats mentions in line 4 as being "loosed" in the world. An example of a symbol being used ironically is the reference to Bethlehem, where, according to Matthew and Luke, Jesus, the "Prince of Peace," was born. In "The Second Coming," Yeats asserts that the new birth will not lead to peace but instead will bring about a future age of repression and brutality. The poem thus offers a complex and disturbing fabric of symbol and allusion.

Commentary on the Essay

This essay combines the topics of symbolism and allusion and illustrates how each can be treated. The introduction briefly characterizes Yeats's poem and asserts that the arguments are made through the use of symbols and allusions. The central idea is about the replacement of the old by the new, and the thesis sentence states that Yeats combines major symbols and allusions to achieve an effect of horror. Paragraph 2 describes the shape of the symbol, thus illustrating strategy 2 as described on page 000, and also explains it, illustrating strategy 1 (p. 964). Paragraph 3 considers the "rough beast" as a symbol of emerging brutality. Paragraph 4 treats the title's allusion to New Testament prophetic tradition, showing that Yeats makes his point by reversing the outcome that tradition had predicted. Paragraph 5 demonstrates the complexity of Yeats's poem by stressing how he fuses symbolism and allusion as a common topic. The sixth and last paragraph contains a brief summary and then proceeds to illustrate the richness of "The Second Coming" with brief references to additional symbols and allusions.

SPECIAL TOPICS FOR WRITING AND ARGUMENT ABOUT SYMBOLISM AND ALLUSIONS IN POETRY

1. Analyze the ways in which Keats, Herbert, and Jeffers use symbols to convey the fact and idea of capture and thralldom ("La Belle Dame Sans Merci," "The Collar," and "The Purse-Seine"). What major symbols do the three poets use? How appropriate is each symbol in its respective poem? How do the poets use the symbols to focus on the problems they present in their poems?

2. Describe the differences in the ways in which e. e. cummings, Jorie Graham, and W. B. Yeats use allusions in "in Just-," "The Geese," and "The Second Coming." How completely can we understand these poems without an explanation of the allusions? How extensive should explanations be? To what extent does the allusiveness make the poems difficult? Challenging? Interesting? Enriching?

3. Compare the use of religious symbols in Donne's "The Canonization" and Herbert's "The Collar." What are the locations from which the poets draw their symbols? How do the symbols figure into the major ideas and arguments of the poems?

4. Describe the nature of the symbols in cummings's "in Just-," Hardy's "In Time of 'The Breaking of Nations,'" and Whitman's "A Noiseless Patient Spider." What parallels in general topic matter do you discover? How do the poets make the poems diverge despite the common qualities of the symbols?

5. Write a poem in which you develop a major symbol, as Jeffers does in "The Purse-Seine" and Kennedy does in "Old Men Pitching Horseshoes." Some symbols you might consider are these:

   > Atomic waste or nuclear weapons
   > Foreign-made cars
   > A superstar athlete
   > A computer
   > A dog looking out a window as children leave for school

   Write an essay describing the process of your creation. How do you begin? How much detail is necessary? How many conclusions do you need to bring out about your symbol? When do you think you have said enough? Too much? How do you know?

6. Write a poem in which you make your own allusions to your own experiences, such as school, an activity, a team, a book, a movie character, or a recent artistic

or political event. What assumptions do you make about your reader when you bring out your allusions? How do you make the allusion (i.e., by a quotation, a name, a title, an indirect reference)? How does your allusion deepen your meaning? How does your allusion increase your own power of expression?

7. From your library, take out a critical study of Yeats or Jeffers that is published by a university press. How much detail is devoted in the study to either poet's use of symbols? How pervasively is symbolism employed by the poet? How does the poet use symbolism to express ideas about science or nationalism? What other use or uses does the poet make of symbolism?

22
Myth: Systems of Symbolic Allusion in Poetry

Our word *myth* is derived from the Greek word *muthos* or *mythos,* meaning a story, narrative, or plot. A **myth** is a story that deals with the relationships of gods to humanity (the *myths* of Oedipus or Odysseus) or with battles among heroes (the *myths* of Hercules or Achilles). A myth may also be a set of beliefs or assumptions among societies. **Mythology** refers collectively to all the stories and beliefs, either of a group (Greek *mythology*) or of a number of groups (*mythology of the Ancient Near East*). A system of beliefs and religious or historical doctrine is a **mythos** (the *Islamic mythos* or the *Buddhist mythos*).

MYTHOLOGY AS AN EXPLANATION OF HOW THINGS ARE

Throughout the ages, people have developed myths because they want to know who they are, where they have been, where they are going, how the world got the way it is, and whether anyone up there cares. Mythical stories and characters answer these questions. They comprise narrative systems that explain the history, culture, religion, and collective psychology of individual societies and civilizations. They also satisfy the human need to understand and humanize conditions that are otherwise mysterious and frightening.

Although many myths originated in primitive times, they still provide a wealth of material and allusion in literature and art. The world around us seems more rich, awesome, and divine when we know that many events, places, creatures, trees, and flowers are important in the beautiful stories and legends that we have inherited from the past.

Myth Should Be Distinguished from Science

Myth and science overlap, since both attempt to provide explanations for the universe. At the beginning of civilization, almost all the vital questions were answered by myths, such as those about gods, the creation of the earth and humanity, lightning and thunder, earthquakes and volcanoes, sexuality, birth, good, evil, and death.

As Western civilization became progressively more educated and sophisticated, particularly after the time of Copernicus (1473–1543), scientific discoveries replaced myths as the means of explaining the "how's" of life and existence. Thus we understand today that lightning and thunder are produced by electrically charged clouds, not by the great and powerful gods Zeus and Thor hurling lightning bolts from the sky (but lightning is still not a thoroughly understood phenomenon). Wherever volcanoes erupt, we know that the cause is molten rock deep within the earth's crust being vented violently through fissures in the volcanoes.

Even though myths are not scientific, they should not be dismissed. It is true that we know an immense amount scientifically about *how* things happen, but we do not really know *why* they happen. For instance, although cosmogonists tell us a great deal about the early stages of the universe and the development of galaxies, stars, the solar system, and our earth, they do not even approach answering the imponderable religious and philosophical questions about causes that myths attempt to explain.

Symbolic Mythical Truths Have Great Power Over Our Thought

Myths are ingrained in our minds and in our speech. For example, we *know* with scientific certainty that we have daylight when we are turned into the sun's direct light and that we have night when we are turned away from the sun and are in the earth's shadow. Nevertheless, we continue to use the phrases "the sun rises" and "the sun sets" to explain day and night, as though we still believed the mythical story about a flat earth with the sun circling around it. Such mythically originated language is inseparable from our minds. Even the belief that science and technology can solve all earthly problems may be seen as a myth. Human beings, in short, are **mythopoeic**—that is, not only do we live with myths, but we habitually create them. We could not continue to exist if we did not do so.

We should therefore realize that myths express truth symbolically even if mythical heroes and stories themselves are scientifically or historically nothing much more than fabrications. The truths are not to be found in mythical lore itself but rather what they show about our earthly existence. Thus, when we read about the problems of the ancient Theban king Oedipus, we can safely assume that the specific details of his life (if he actually ever did live) did not happen just as Sophocles dramatizes them in *Oedipus the King*. But we find in the play a powerful rendering of how human beings make mistakes and how they must pay for them. In short, the truth of the Oedipus myth is psychological, not literal and historical.

Ansel Adams, "Forest Floor, Yosemite Valley." Photograph by Ansel Adams. Copyright © 1994 by the Trustees of The Ansel Adams Publishing Rights Trust. All rights reserved.

Myths Help Us Understand Our Position in the World

We can broaden our consideration by adding that myths also imply a special perspective about how people see their place and purpose in the world. This kind of myth may be constructive and generative. Thus, at one time most North Americans accepted the myth that Nature was limitless and wild and in need of being conquered. With this concept in mind, settlers moved into every available corner of the land—to build, farm, create industries, and establish new ways of life. Without such an inspiring myth, people would have stayed put, and the nation would never have achieved its current prominence.

This is not to say that all myths are positive; indeed, some myths are destructive. Thus, the once-positive myth of limitless and inexhaustible nature has led us into the massive problems we face today with environmental exploitation and degradation. There is need for a different myth—a myth declaring that the earth is no longer inimical and in need of taming, but rather that the earth is beautiful, tender, and fragile and is in need of preservation and conservation. The Ansel Adams photograph "Forest Floor, Yosemite Valley" (above) is a visual embodiment of this more accepting myth of nature.

Mythological Themes or Motifs Are Common to Many Cultures

Since myths address our human need to know, it is not surprising to find that many civilizations, separated by time and space, have parallel myths, such as the many stories accounting for the creation of the universe. The details of these myths are different, but the *patterns* are similar inasmuch as they all posit both an original time and act of creation and a creator god or gods who also take part in human history. The principal god is perceived as a shaper, a modeler, a divine artisan, who has fashioned the orderly systems we find in the world, such as life, daylight, ecological dependence, tides, warmth, fertility, harvests, morality, and social stability.

One of the most crucial of all myths involves sin, disobedience, and evil, which are usually blamed for winter, natural calamities, illness, and death. A corollary of the myth is that a god-hero or goddess-heroine must undergo a sacrifice to atone for sin and to ensure the renewed vitality of spring. In *The Golden Bough,* a massive collection and analysis of mythic stories, Sir James Frazer (1854–1941) compares a series of mythical death-renewal motifs. Among such sacrificed and reborn gods are Thammuz (Babylonia), Attis (Phrygia), Osiris (Egypt), and Adonis, Dionysus, and Persephone (Greece). Again, the specific myths take different forms, but they reflect the same mysteries, fears, and hopes.

Scholars and anthropologists like Frazer were among the first to observe the interrelationships among myths produced by diverse cultures. The Swiss psychoanalyst Carl Gustav Jung (1875–1961) offered an explanation for this duplication. He noticed that images, characters, and events similar to those in literature, mythology, and religion also occurred in the dreams of his patients. He termed these recurring images **archetypes** (from the Greek word meaning "model" or "first mold") and developed a theory that all human beings share a universal or collective unconsciousness. Even if Jung's theory is ignored, the fact remains that types of mythic creatures such as dragons and centaurs, archetypal mother-daughter and father-son stories, and narratives involving sacrifices, heroic quests, and trips to the underworld recur throughout various mythologies and pervade our literature.[1]

MYTHOLOGY AND LITERATURE

When writing was invented, the first written works recorded oral mythologies; that is, the mythologies had already existed for long periods of time before they were written down. The ancient Greek poet Homer, for example (perhaps a mythical figure himself), told about the mythical gods and heroes of the Trojan War. Homer did not actually write (tradition says he was blind), but other writers recorded and transmitted his epics. The Latin writer Ovid (43 B.C.E.–17 C.E.)

---

[1] See also Chapter 33 for a further discussion of archetypes.

knew a large body of mythology and wrote poetic stories based on it. The result of this assimilation of myth into poetry was a combination of literature and religion that served the double purpose of teaching and entertaining. In this way, poets throughout antiquity used mythology as a mine for ideas, images, and symbols.

Although almost two thousand years have passed since Ovid lived, writers and artists still rely on mythology. In every generation since the earliest Anglo-Saxon poems and legends, poets of English have retold and updated mythological stories. Indeed, many of the poems in this chapter are from the twentieth century. Modern poetry utilizing mythology, however, is no longer designed to reinforce the dominant religion. Instead, it uses mythology to link past and present, to dramatize important concerns, and to symbolize universal patterns of thought.

Most Western poets who use mythological material in their verse turn to long-standing bodies of myth, particularly those of Greco-Roman, Norse-Teutonic, and Judeo-Christian origin. These systems of mythology are **universal** or **public,** since they are part of a vast common heritage. Like *cultural symbols,* they make up a reservoir of material that all writers are free to employ.

Mythological References Are Common in Poetry

When poets make references to a myth, as in poems like Tennyson's "Ulysses" and Parker's "Penelope," both of which refer to the myth of Odysseus (Ulysses), they assume that readers already understand something about the stories and characters. With these poems, readers are expected to know enough of Homer's *Odyssey* to recall that this hero fought in the Trojan War for ten years and then was forced to spend an additional ten years trying to return home. In other words, during most of his reign as king of Ithaca he was a warrior and adventurer—an absentee ruler—but at the same time his queen, Penelope, stayed at home.

Although you might have enough background in mythology to understand a poet's mythological references, you may sometimes need to fill in or reinforce your knowledge. A good place to start is a dictionary or general encyclopedia, where you will find brief identifications of mythic figures and a key to further reading. Eventually you will want access to more detailed information. Excellent books that retell the stories of Greco-Roman mythology are Richmond Hathorn's *Greek Mythology,* M. C. Howatson's *The Oxford Companion to Classical Literature,* and Timothy Gantz's *Early Greek Myth: A Guide to Literary and Artistic Sources.* Bulfinch's *The Age of Fable* and Edith Hamilton's *Mythology* are respected traditional books. There are also many classical dictionaries, such as the *Oxford Classical Dictionary,* that are immensely useful. John Keats learned much of his mythology from John Lemprière's *Classical Dictionary.* Many libraries have this book on their reference shelves, and your use of it will both inform you and impress you with a sense of bibliographical history. Not all allusions are classical. Should you want to understand allusions to the myths of Paul

Bunyan and Johnny Appleseed, for example, you would want a collection of American folk tales. References to Odin, Thor, the Valkyries, or Asgard should lead you to a collection of Norse-Teutonic mythology.

Myths Are Often Vitally Significant in Poetry

We are now ready to look at a poem that is built upon a myth. The poem is by William Butler Yeats, and it draws on Greco-Roman mythology.

WILLIAM BUTLER YEATS   (1865–1939)

Leda and the Swan _____ *1924 (1923)*

A sudden blow: the great wings beating still
Above the staggering girl, her thighs caressed
By the dark webs, her nape caught in his bill,
He holds her helpless breast upon his breast.

How can those terrified vague fingers push
The feathered glory from her loosening thighs?
And how can body, laid in that white rush,
But feel the strange heart beating where it lies?

A shudder in the loins engenders there
The broken wall, the burning roof and tower
And Agamemnon dead.
                Being so caught up,
So mastered by the brute blood of the air,
Did she put on his knowledge with his power
Before the indifferent beak could let her drop?

QUESTIONS

1. What mythic event does the poem retell? Who was Leda? The swan? Who were Leda's children? What events are alluded to in lines 10 and 11?
2. How is Leda described? What words suggest her helplessness? What phrases suggest the swan's mystery and divinity?
3. What question is raised in the last two lines? To what extent does the poem provide an answer to this question?

Yeats's sonnet focuses on a specific event of ancient Greek mythology: Zeus, king of the gods, having taken the form of a swan, raped Leda, a Spartan queen. According to the myth, this violent event was a starting point not only of Greek civilization but also of the angers and troubles of humanity in general. One of the children born of the rape was Helen of Troy, whose abduction by Paris precipitated the Trojan War. Yeats's phrase "The broken wall, the burning roof and tower" refers to the destruction of Troy. Another child was Clytemnestra, married to Agamemnon, king of Mycenae and leader of the allied Greek forces. Because Agamemnon had sacrificed their daughter Iphigeneia as a part of the war effort, Clytemnestra vowed revenge and had him murdered when he returned home from the Trojan War.

After a graphic recounting of the swan's attack on Leda and a brief reference to the sack of Troy and Agamemnon's death, Yeats's concluding lines raise a central issue stemming from the myth. While Leda took on some of Zeus's divine power with the rape (through the process of childbearing), the poem asks whether she also "put on" some of his divine knowledge—whether she acquired Zeus's foreknowledge of the fall of Troy, the murder of Agamemnon, and, by extension, the subsequent events in history. Of course, the question is rhetorical and the answer is negative.

If all the poem did were to question the ancient myth in this way, it would be of limited interest for modern readers. But it does more than that; it directs our attention to concerns of today. Thus, we may conclude from Yeats's use of the myth that human beings, like Leda, do not have foreknowledge, but have only their own culture, experience, and intelligence as their guides. If divine beings exist, they have no interest in human affairs, but are rather uninvolved and "indifferent" (line 14). By extension the myth suggests that the burden of civilization is on human beings themselves and that if knowledge and power are ever to be combined for constructive goals, that blending must be a human achievement.

Yeats thus employs mythic material in this sonnet to raise a searching question about the nature of existence, knowledge, and power. The historical process is embodied in the rape, the children born out of it, and their troubles. As the central figure of the myth, Leda is the focal point of circumstances and concerns that have extended from the distant past to the present, and that will likely extend into the future.

Because most myths similarly embody recurring issues, they have great value for modern readers. Muriel Rukeyser's "Myth," for example, uses the ancient myth about Oedipus to shed light amusingly on misperceptions about male-female relationships. Edward Field's "Icarus" (one of a number of Icarus poems we include here) uses the ancient Icarus myth to decry the impact of modern society upon individuals. In these and in other poems based in mythology, you may look for such original ways in which poets receive something old and make it new. Myths do not belong only to the past but are alive and well in the present.

The poems in this chapter feature mythical material about Odysseus, Icarus, the Phoenix, and Oedipus. Although all the poems delve into ancient mythology for their subjects, they are remarkably different; each offers its own meaning, impact, and poetic experience. The poets shape their mythic material to illustrate and symbolize ideas about pride, daring, disillusionment, suffering, indignation, creativity, idealism, and indifference to the plights of others, and therefore the poems demonstrate how myths can be used for original effects in new poetic contexts. As you study the poems, consider the following general questions along with the questions following the poems:

1.   How completely does the poem deal with the myth? What is included? What is excluded? What does the poet expect that you should know about the myth? How does the poet create a variation on the myth beyond the original?

2.   Why do modern poets treat mythical subjects? Are they simply interpreting or reinterpreting ancient stories, or are they using the ancient stories to shed light on modern circumstances? Why? How?

EIGHT POEMS RELATED TO THE MYTH OF ODYSSEUS

Odysseus was the mythical king of the island realm of Ithaca and a Greek general in the Trojan War. He spent ten years in Troy and then another ten years on his journey home. He encountered so many obstacles and delays, however, and his return took so long, that traveling became a way of life with him. For seven years he was confined on the island of Aeaea by Circe, a sorceress. Circe turned his men into swine, but Odysseus escaped this transformation by taking a magical herb. When he sailed near the Sirens, who lured sailors to death with the beauty of their songs, Odysseus resisted their attraction by having himself lashed to the mast of his ship. During this long absence, his kingdom was entrusted to his wife, Penelope. Penelope was dutiful and faithful, but she was besieged by crowds of suitors, each of whom sought to take over the Ithacan kingdom by marrying her. She promised to accept one of the suitors when she finished making a shroud for her father-in-law. During the day she would weave the shroud, but then at night she would unravel her day's work. By the time the suitors discovered her ruse, Odysseus returned and, with help, killed all the suitors and restored himself as king.

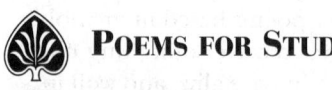

POEMS FOR STUDY

MARGARET ATWOOD   (b. 1939)

Siren Song _____ *1974*

This is the one song everyone
would like to learn: the song
that is irresistible:

the song that forces men
to leap overboard in squadrons   5
even though they see the beached skulls

the song nobody knows
because anyone who has heard it
is dead, and the others can't remember.

Shall I tell you the secret   10
and if I do, will you get me
out of this bird suit?

I don't enjoy it here
squatting on this island
looking picturesque and mythical   15

with these two feathery maniacs,
I don't enjoy singing
this trio, fatal and valuable.

I will tell the secret to you,
to you, only to you.   20
Come closer. This song

is a cry for help: Help me!
Only you, only you can,
you are unique

at last, Alas   25
it is a boring song
but it works every time.

QUESTIONS

1. Who were the Sirens in Greek mythology? What effect did their song have?
2. Who is the speaker in this poem? What is the effect of her colloquial diction?
    What does she tell you about her song?
3. Who is the "you" referred to in lines 10–24? What does the speaker say about
    her life? What "works every time"? To what extent is the conclusion amusing?

OLGA BROUMAS   (b. 1949)

Circe _____ 1977

The Charm

> The fire bites, the fire bites.   Bites
> to the little death.   Bites
>
> till she comes to nothing.   Bites
> on her own sweet tongue. She goes on.   Biting.

The Anticipation

> They tell me a woman waits, motionless
> till she's wooed.   I wait
>
> spiderlike, effortless as they weave
> even my web for me, tying the cord in knots
>
> with their courting hands. Such power
> over them.   And the spell
>
> their own.   Who could release them?   Who
> would untie the cord
>
> with a cloven hoof?

The Bite

> What I wear in the morning pleases
> me: green shirt, skirt of wine.   I am wrapped
>
> in myself as the smell of night
> wraps round my sleep when I sleep
>
> outside.   By the time
> I get to the corner
>
> bar, corner store, corner construction
> site, I become divine.   I turn
>
> men into swine.   Leave
> them behind me whistling, grunting, wild.

QUESTIONS

1. Who was Circe? What powers did she have?
2. Who or what is the speaker in this poem? What is the connection between the speaker and Circe? Why is the poem titled "Circe"?
3. What do Circe and the speaker symbolize in the poem? What is the source of Circe's power in the myth and the poem? What does this power symbolize?
4. What is the "fire" (lines 1–5)? Who are "they" (lines 7–15)? What is the effect of "spiderlike" (line 9) and "courting hands" (line 11)? What is "the spell" (line 12)? What is the significance of "a cloven hoof" (line 15)?

5. What is the speaker's attitude toward herself in lines 16–26? What happens to her in these lines? What happens to the men she encounters?

LOUISE GLÜCK (b. 1943)

Penelope's Song ——————————————————————— *1996*

Little soul, little perpetually undressed one,
do now as I bid you, climb
the shelf-like branches of the spruce tree;
wait at the top, attentive, like
a sentry or look-out. He will be home soon;   5
it behooves you to be
generous. You have not been completely
perfect either; with your troublesome body
you have done things you shouldn't
discuss in poems. Therefore   10
call out to him over the open water, over the bright water
with your dark song, with your grasping,
unnatural song—passionate,
like Maria Callas.° Who
wouldn't want you? Whose most demonic appetite   15
could you possibly fail to answer? Soon
he will return from wherever he goes in the meantime,
suntanned from his time away, wanting
his grilled chicken. Ah, you must greet him,
you must shake the boughs of the tree   20
to get his attention,
but carefully, carefully, lest
his beautiful face be marred
by too many falling needles.

PENELOPE'S SONG.   14 *Maria Callas:* Callas (1923–1977) was one of the best-known sopranos of the twentieth century, famous for her acting and her fiery interpretations of operatic heroines.

QUESTIONS

1. Who is the speaker of this poem? To whom is she speaking? What does she tell herself that she might not tell a companion or friend?
2. Describe your response to the poem if the speaker is Penelope, planning to welcome Odysseus after his twenty-year adventure in Troy and on the high seas.
3. Describe your response if the speaker is a modern woman planning to welcome her husband after he has spent Sunday afternoon seeing a professional football game. How does the poem seem to change under these circumstances?
4. If such were the circumstances, what use is Glück making of the Odysseus myth?

W. S. MERWIN   (b. 1927)

Odysseus _____ *1960*

Always the setting forth was the same,
Same sea, same dangers waiting for him
As though he had got nowhere but older.
Behind him on the receding shore
The identical reproaches, and somewhere   5
Out before him, the unravelling patience
He was wedded to. There were the islands
Each with its woman and twining welcome
To be navigated, and one to call "home."
The knowledge of all that he betrayed   10
Grew till it was the same whether he stayed
Or went. Therefore he went. And what wonder
If sometimes he could not remember
Which was the one who wished on his departure
Perils that he could never sail through,   1
And which, improbable, remote, and true,
Was the one he kept sailing home to?

QUESTIONS

1. What aspects of the Odysseus myth are evoked in this poem? What point does
    the poem make about Odysseus's experiences?
2. To what extent is Odysseus symbolic of a specific kind of life and attitude toward
    life? How does our knowledge of Odysseus contribute to the impact and mean-
    ing of the poem?
3. Compare this poem with Parker's "Penelope." How is the same mythic material
    used toward different ends in these poems?
4. Compare this poem with Tennyson's "Ulysses." Explain how and why the same
    mythic figure can be used to convey such different ideas.

DOROTHY PARKER   (1893–1967)

Penelope _____ *1936*

In the pathway of the sun,
   In the footsteps of the breeze,
Where the world and sky are one,
   He shall ride the silver seas,
      He shall cut the glittering wave.
I shall sit at home, and rock;
Rise, to heed a neighbor's knock;
Brew my tea, and snip my thread;
Bleach the linen for my bed.
      They will call him brave.

QUESTIONS

1. How does the speaker describe her life? How is her life different from that of the male figure described in lines 1–5?

2. To what extent is Penelope a symbol? What does she symbolize? How does our knowledge of the myth deepen our response to this symbolism?

LINDA PASTAN (b. 1932)

The Suitor _____ *1988*

There is always a story
that no one bothers to tell:
the younger son of a younger son,
hardly a suitor at all, sits
at the sharp edge of the table   5
among the boisterous men, not hungry
except for a glimpse of Penelope,
a woman wasted, he thinks—
those pale arms, that hair
a web she might have woven   10
around her own head.
Sometimes he tries to speak
to the son° who looks at him wonderingly,   *Telemachus*
but doesn't answer.
How could Odysseus have left?   15
he asks himself, but is grateful
for the chance to pretend
it could be him she'll choose.
He almost knows it must end badly,
though his will be a minor tributary   20
in that unplumbed sea
of wasted blood.

QUESTIONS

1. Why does Pastan choose a young man as the suitor of the poem? Who are the "boisterous men," and what is the suitor's relationship to them?

2. How does the suitor feel about Penelope? What does he have to gain by being a part of the suitors seeking her hand in marriage?

3. What will be the suitor's fate? Why does Pastan close on the note of "wasted blood"?

ALFRED, LORD TENNYSON   (1809–1892)

Ulysses _____ *1842 (1833)*

   It little profits that an idle king,
By this still hearth, among these barren crags,
Matched with an aged wife, I mete and dole
Unequal laws° unto a savage race,   *rewards and punishments*
That hoard, and sleep, and feed, and know not me.   5

   I cannot rest from travel; I will drink
Life to the lees.° All times I have enjoyed   *dregs*
Greatly, have suffered greatly, both with those
That loved me, and alone; on shore, and when
Through scudding drifts the rainy Hyades°   10
Vexed the dim sea. I am become a name;
For always roaming with a hungry heart
Much have I seen and known—cities of men
And manners, climates, councils, governments,
Myself not least, but honored of them all—   15
And drunk delight of battle with my peers,
Far on the ringing plains of windy Troy.
I am a part of all that I have met;
Yet all experience is an arch wherethrough
Gleams that untraveled world whose margin fades   20
Forever and forever when I move.
How dull it is to pause, to make an end,
To rust unburnished, not to shine in use!
As though to breathe were life! Life piled on life
Were all too little, and of one to me   25
Little remains; but every hour is saved
From that eternal silence, something more,
A bringer of new things; and vile it were
For some three suns to store and hoard myself,
And this gray spirit yearning in desire   30
To follow knowledge like a sinking star,
Beyond the utmost bound of human thought.

   This is my son, mine own Telemachus,
To whom I leave the scepter and the isle—°
Well-loved of me, discerning to fulfill
This labor, by slow prudence to make mild
A rugged people, and through soft degrees
Subdue them to the useful and the good.
Most blameless is he, centered in the sphere
Of common duties, decent not to fail

ULYSSES.   10 *Hyades:* nymphs who were placed among the stars by Zeus, the king of the gods. The name means "rain," and the rising of the stars was thought to precede a storm.   34 *isle:* Ithaca, the island realm ruled by Odysseus.

In offices of tenderness, and pay
Meet° adoration to my household gods,   *appropriate*
When I am gone. He works his work, I mine.

    There lies the port; the vessel puffs her sail;
There gloom the dark, broad seas. My mariners,   45
Souls that have toiled, and wrought, and thought with me—
That ever with a frolic welcome took
The thunder and the sunshine, and opposed
Free hearts, free foreheads—you and I are old;
Old age hath yet his honor and his toil.   50
Death closes all; but something ere the end,
Some work of noble note, may yet be done,
Not unbecoming men that strove with Gods.
The lights begin to twinkle from the rocks;
The long day wanes; the slow moon climbs; the deep   55
Moans round with many voices. Come, my friends,
'Tis not too late to seek a newer world.
Push off, and sitting well in order smite
The sounding furrows; for my purpose holds
To sail beyond the sunset, and the baths   60
Of all the western stars, until I die.
It may be that the gulfs will wash us down;
It may be we shall touch the Happy Isles,°
And see the great Achilles,° whom we knew.

Though much is taken, much abides; and though   65
We are not now that strength which in old days
Moved earth and heaven, that which we are, we are—
One equal temper of heroic hearts,
Made weak by time and fate, but strong in will
To strive, to seek, to find, and not to yield.   70

63 *Happy Isles:* the Elysian Fields, dwelling place of mortals who have been made immortal by the gods.   64 *Achilles:* Greek hero of the Trojan War who killed Hector and was, in turn, killed by Paris.

QUESTIONS

1. Who is the speaker of the poem? What is his attitude toward his life in Ithaca? What key phrases and adjectives in lines 1–5 establish this attitude?

2. Who is Telemachus? What is the speaker's attitude toward him? How are the speaker and Telemachus different?

3. What aspects of Ulysses are emphasized in this poem? To what extent does he become symbolic? What does he symbolize?

PETER ULISSE   (b. 1944)

Odyssey: 20 Years Later _____ *1995*

I battled Trojans with Odysseus.
Bludgeoning the eye of Polyphemus
I meandered past Scylla and Charybdis,
descended into Hades, outwitted Calypso.
I ate of the lotus, and forgot.
Twenty years I roamed—

Wandering Jew, Prodigal Son, opener
of doors in empty streets I
embraced strangers like a lover's quest,
searched for the beautiful which
alone
could make a life complete.
I released hands in bedrooms,
turned to St. Augustine

It is only now I feel the pull
of salmon swimming up current,
turtles drawn to Galapagos,
fowls finding a path through
a thousand mile sky,
only now I understand
Odyssey not as Cyclops, Sirens,
or unfavorable winds but

simply as
coming home.

QUESTIONS

1. Who is the "I" of line 1? How does this line reveal the identity of the "I"? How is this speaker different from the speaker of Tennyson's "Ulysses"? What do the final lines tell you about the speaker's and Odysseus's journeys?

2. Consider the speaker's description of having duplicated the actions performed by Odysseus and other ancient figures. What ideas does the speaker present about the repetitive or cyclical nature of human experience?

3. What autobiographical or confessional details are contained in lines 13–19? What educational experiences are alluded to in these lines?

SEVEN POEMS RELATED TO THE MYTH OF ICARUS

Icarus was the son of Daedalus, the greatest master of applied science in ancient Greek myth. The story begins with Minos, king of Crete, who ruled Athens and the rest of the Greek world. Each year (or, according to other versions of the story, every nine years) Minos compelled the Athenians to make a tribute of seven young people to be sacrificed to the Minotaur, an enormously powerful monster who was half man and half bull. Needing to control and confine the monster, Minos hired Daedalus to build an enclosure—a labyrinth—as a prison. Daedalus fulfilled his part of the bargain, but Minos did not. Instead, Minos wanted to have the technological skills of Daedalus readily at hand, and so Daedalus was not allowed to leave but was rather confined in the labyrinth with his son Icarus. Needless to say, Daedalus did not take kindly to this confinement, and, according to some accounts, he gained retribution by aiding the Athenian hero, Theseus, in killing the Minotaur, thereby freeing Athens from the burden of the living tribute. In order to leave his imprisonment, Daedalus exerted his great skills to carry out an aerial escape. He made two pairs of wings out of wax and feathers—one pair for himself and one for Icarus. Daedalus flew safely away and eventually made his home in Sicily. Icarus, however, flew too close to the sun: The wax melted and the wings fell apart; Icarus fell into the Icarian Sea (named after him), and he drowned.

POEMS FOR STUDY

BRIAN ALDISS   (b. 1925)

Flight 063 _____ *1994*

Why always speak of Icarus' fall?—
That legendary plunge
Amid a shower of tallow
And feathers and the poor lad's
Sweat? And that little splash   5
Which caught the eye of Brueghel°
While the sun remained
Aloof within its private zone?

    That fall remains
Suspended in the corporate mind.   10
Yet as our Boeing flies
High above the Arctic Circle

FLIGHT 063.   6 *Brueghel:* Pieter Brueghel or Breughel (ca. 1525–1569) was a Flemish painter whose subjects include the Nativity ("the miraculous birth"), the Crucifixion ("the dreadful martyrdom"), and the fall of Icarus. His *Landscape with the Fall of Icarus* is reproduced in color in Insert II.

Into the sun's eye, think—
Before the fall the flight was.
(So with Adam—just before   15
The Edenic Fall, he had
That first taste of Eve.)

Dinner is served aboard Flight 063.
We eat from plastic trays, oblivious
To the stratosphere.   20

But Icarus—his cliff-top jump,
The leap of heart, the blue air scaled—
His glorious sense of life
Imperiled. Time
Fell far below, the everyday   25
Was lost in his ascent.

Up, up, he sailed, unheeding
Such silly limitations as
The melting point of wax.

QUESTIONS

1. What attitude toward Icarus does the speaker present (see lines 21–26)? What emotions does he attribute to Icarus during the beginning of the flight? What is the significance of line 14 ("Before the fall the flight was")?

2. What do the words "dinner" and "oblivious" suggest about modern attitudes toward flight?

3. Why does the speaker emphasize the word "think" (line 13)? Why is the melting point of wax a "silly" limitation?

W. H. AUDEN   (1907–1973)

Musée des Beaux Arts° _____ *1940*

About suffering they were never wrong,
The Old Masters: how well they understood
Its human position; how it takes place
While someone else is eating or opening a window or just walking dully along;
How, when the aged are reverently, passionately waiting
For the miraculous birth, there always must be
Children who did not specially want it to happen, skating
On a pond at the edge of the wood:
They never forgot
That even the dreadful martyrdom must run its course
Anyhow in a corner, some untidy spot

MUSÉE DES BEAUX ARTS.   "Museum of Fine Arts."

Where the dogs go on with their doggy life and the torturer's horse
Scratches its innocent behind on a tree.
In Brueghel's *Icarus*, for instance: how everything turns away
Quite leisurely from the disaster; the ploughman may   15
Have heard the splash, the forsaken cry,
But for him it was not an important failure; the sun shone

As it had to on the white legs disappearing into the green
Water; and the expensive delicate ship that must have seen
Something amazing, a boy falling out of the sky,   20
Had somewhere to get to and sailed calmly on.

QUESTIONS

1. What does the speaker say about the perceptions of the "Old Masters" to suffering? What use does Auden make of the Brueghel painting?

2. What concern do those close to Icarus's fall show toward the fall and the drowning? In the light of this concern, what ideas does the poem express about the ultimate importance of heroism and great occurrences?

3. Compare this poem with Frost's "Out, Out—" (Chapter 24). What does each poet indicate about the attitudes of people toward the suffering of others? Would you characterize these poems as painfully truthful? Ironic? Disillusioned?

EDWARD FIELD   (b. 1924)

Icarus _____ *1963*

Only the feathers floating around the hat
Showed that anything more spectacular had occurred
Than the usual drowning. The police preferred to ignore
The confusing aspects of the case,
And the witnesses ran off to a gang war.   5
So the report filed and forgotten in the archives read simply
"Drowned," but it was wrong: Icarus
Had swum away, coming at last to the city
Where he rented a house and tended the garden.

"That nice Mr. Hicks" the neighbors called him,   10
Never dreaming that the gray, respectable suit
Concealed arms that had controlled huge wings
Nor that those sad, defeated eyes had once
Compelled the sun. And had he told them
They would have answered with a shocked, uncomprehending stare.   15
No, he could not disturb their neat front yards;
Yet all his books insisted that this was a horrible mistake:
What was he doing aging in a suburb?

Can the genius of the hero fall
To the middling stature of the merely talented? 20

And nightly Icarus probes his wound
And daily in his workshop, curtains carefully drawn,
Constructs small wings and tries to fly
To the lighting fixture on the ceiling:
Fails every time and hates himself for trying. 25

He had thought himself a hero, had acted heroically,
And dreamt of his fall, the tragic fall of the hero;
But now rides commuter trains,
Serves on various committees,
And wishes he had drowned. 30

QUESTIONS

1. What twist on the Icarus myth occurs in this poem?

2. How does Field undercut the heroic myth of Icarus? What happens to Icarus after he rents a house and tends his garden? What does Icarus, the daily suburban commuter with "sad, defeated eyes," wish at the poem's end?

3. What level of language does Field use in this poem? How does this language complement the poem's antiheroic view of Icarus?

MURIEL RUKEYSER (1913–1980)

Waiting for Icarus _____ *1973*

He said he would be back and we'd drink wine together
He said that everything would be better than before
He said we were on the edge of a new relation
He said he would never again cringe before his father
He said that he was going to invent full-time
He said he loved me that going into me
He said was going into the world and the sky
He said all the buckles were very firm
He said the wax was the best wax
He said Wait for me here on the beach
He said Just don't cry

I remember the gulls and the waves
I remember the islands going dark on the sea
I remember the girls laughing
I remember they said he only wanted to get away from me
I remember mother saying: Inventors are like poets,
                                a trashy lot
I remember she told me those who try out inventions are worse
I remember she added: Women who love such are the worst of all

I have been waiting all day, or perhaps longer.   20
I would have liked to try those wings myself.
It would have been been better than this.

QUESTIONS

1. Who is speaking? How long has she been waiting for Icarus? When is she speaking? Does she know what has happened to Icarus?

2. In what ways is the speaker's narration a complaint? What does she complain about? How do the things she says bring ancient and modern circumstances to a common level?

3. To what degree is this poem humorous? What effect does Rukeyser's use of anaphora (see p. 779) have on the development of the poem?

ANNE SEXTON (1928–1974)

To a Friend Whose Work Has Come to Triumph° _____ *1962*

Consider Icarus, pasting those sticky wings on,
testing that strange little tug at his shoulder blade,
and think of that first flawless moment over the lawn
of the labyrinth. Think of the difference it made!
There below are the trees, as awkward as camels;   5
and here are the shocked starlings pumping past
and think of innocent Icarus who is doing quite well:
larger than a sail, over the fog and the blast
of the plushy ocean, he goes. Admire his wings!
Feel the fire at his neck and see how casually   10
he glances up and is caught, wondrously tunneling
into that hot eye. Who cares that he fell back to the sea?
See him acclaiming the sun and come plunging down
while his sensible daddy goes straight into town.

TO A FRIEND WHOSE WORK HAS COME TO TRIUMPH.   The title alludes to and reverses the title of a poem by William Butler Yeats, "To a Friend Whose Work Has Come to Nothing" (1914).

QUESTIONS

1. Describe the contrast made in this poem between Icarus and Daedalus ("his sensible daddy"). What achievement does the speaker attribute to Icarus? Does the speaker seem to like or dislike Icarus?

2. In relation to line 12, what is the significance of the poem's title? In what sense has Icarus's life been a model for "Triumph"?

3. What tone is indicated by phrases like "sticky wings," "strange little tug," "awkward as camels," "plushy ocean," "hot eye," and "sensible daddy"?

STEPHEN SPENDER   (1909–1995)

Icarus ———————————————————— *1933*

He will watch the hawk with an indifferent eye
  Or pitifully;
Nor on those eagles that so feared him, now
  Will strain his brow;
Weapons men use, stone, sling and strong-thewed bow
  He will not know.

This aristocrat, superb of all instinct,
  With death close linked
Had paced the enormous cloud, almost had won
  War on the sun;
Till now, like Icarus mid-ocean-drowned,
  Hands, wings, are found.

QUESTIONS

1. Describe the structure of this poem. How many lines does Spender devote to the character of Icarus? Why does he consider Icarus an aristocrat?

2. Why does he say that Icarus had "almost" won a "War on the sun"? What modern lesson does Spender draw from the story of Icarus?

3. Why does the first stanza contain future tense verbs, and why in the second stanza do the verbs shift to past perfects ("had paced," "had won"), a present perfect ("are found"), and a past participle ("linked")?

WILLIAM CARLOS WILLIAMS   (1883–1963)

Landscape with the Fall of Icarus ———————————————— *1962*

According to Brueghel°
when Icarus fell
it was spring

a farmer was ploughing
his field
the whole pageantry

of the year was
awake tingling
near

LANDSCAPE WITH THE FALL OF ICARUS.   1 *Brueghel:* See the note for line 6 in Aldiss's "Flight 063," p. 985.

the edge of the sea   10
concerned
with itself

sweating in the sun
that melted
the wings' wax   15

unsignificantly
off the coast
there was

a splash quite unnoticed
this was   20
Icarus drowning

QUESTIONS

1. As the speaker presents the actual fall of Icarus as contained in Brueghel's painting, how significant is Icarus himself?

2. The poem is in tercets (three-line groups), and no line has more than four
   words. What is the effect of these sparse lines on the seriousness of Icarus's situation? Why does the poem not contain more detail?

3. Why does the speaker mention other things, specifically, the season, the farmer,
   the act of ploughing, the "tingling" pageant "of the year," and the shoreline—
   before he describes the splash in the last three lines?

4. Compare the view of Icarus in this poem with the views of Aldiss, Auden, Field,
   and Spender.

THREE POEMS RELATED
TO THE MYTH OF THE PHOENIX

In ancient myth, the phoenix was a gold and red Arabian bird resembling an
eagle. At the end of a long period—some accounts say five hundred years,
others say fifteen hundred—the phoenix would be mysteriously consumed by
fire. A new phoenix would then reconstitute itself from the ashes of the old,
and a new life cycle would begin. According to the myth, the process continued indefinitely. Because of this constant renewal, many religions have considered the phoenix story optimistically, as a symbol of life overcoming death.

 POEMS FOR STUDY

AMY CLAMPITT   (1920–1994)

Berceuse° _____ *1982*

Listen to Gieseking° playing a Berceuse
of Chopin°—the mothwing flutter
light as ash, perishable as burnt paper—

and sleep, now the furnaces of Auschwitz°
are all out, and tourists go there.
The purest art has slept with turpitude,

we all pay taxes. Sleep. The day of waking
waits, cloned from the phoenix—
a thousand replicas in upright silos,

nurseries of the ultimate enterprise.
Decay will undo what it can, the rotten
fabric of our repose connives with doomsday.

Sleep on, scathed felicity. Sleep, rare
and perishable relic. Imagining's no shutter
against the absolute, incorrigible sunrise.

BERCEUSE.   *Berceuse:* a lullaby or cradle song.   1 *Gieseking:* Walter Gieseking (1895–1956),
famous French pianist.   2 *Chopin:* Frédéric Chopin (1810–1849), Polish composer and pianist.
3 *Auschwitz:* World War II Nazi death camp near Kraków, Poland. See also Quasímodo's poem
"Auschwitz" (p. 829).

QUESTIONS

1. In what ways is this poem pessimistic? How does the speaker contrast the best and worst aspects of human life?
2. What is meant by line 6? What irony is contained in the image of the phoenix (stanza 3)? What objects are replicated in the "upright silos"?
3. What are the "felicity" and "relic" of lines 13 and 14? Why should these "sleep" (see also line 7)? What is meant by the "absolute, incorrigible sunrise" of line 15?

DENISE LEVERTOV (1923-1997)

Hunting the Phoenix _____ *1987*

Leaf through discolored manuscripts,
make sure no words
lie thirsting, bleeding,
waiting for rescue. No:
old loves half-
articulated, moments forced
out of the stream of perception
to play 'statue',
and never released—

they had no blood to shed.   10
You must seek
the ashy nest itself
if you hope to find
charred feathers, smouldering flightbones,
and a twist of singing flame   15
rekindling.

QUESTIONS

1. What use is Levertov making here of the phoenix myth? How does the poem's organization make the references to the phoenix clear?

2. What is the speaker referring to that might be recorded in "discolored manuscripts"? What might be the things that have "no blood to shed"?

3. Why, in the last six lines, does the speaker introduce a reference to "the ashy nest"? What is meant by the poem's advice to seek this nest? What is the promise if one does seek out the nest?

MAY SARTON   (1912–1995)

The Phoenix° Again _____ *1988*

On the ashes of this nest
Love wove with deathly fire
The phoenix takes its rest
Forgetting all desire.

After the flame, a pause,   5
After the pain, rebirth.
Obeying nature's laws
The phoenix goes to earth.

You cannot call it old
You cannot call it young.   10
No phoenix can be told,
This is the end of song.

It struggles now alone
Against death and self-doubt,
But underneath the bone   15
The wings are pushing out.

And one cold starry night
Whatever your belief
The phoenix will take flight
Over the seas of grief   20

THE PHOENIX AGAIN.   *Phoenix:* See the note to line 23 of John Donne's "The Canonization," (p. 946).

To hear her thrilling song
To stars and waves and sky
For neither old nor young
The phoenix does not die.

QUESTIONS

1. What is the phoenix? What does it signify?
2. What significance does the phoenix have for the speaker? What personal situation does the speaker seem to be describing? Why does the speaker invoke the details of the phoenix's return to life after death?
3. Compare Sarton's use of the phoenix with the uses by Donne in "The Canonization" (p. 946) and Clampitt in "Berceuse" (p. 992).

TWO POEMS RELATED TO THE MYTH OF OEDIPUS

For the story of Oedipus, see the introduction to *Oedipus the King* by Sophocles (Chapter 27).

The Great Sphinx, Gîza, Egypt. Foto Marburg/Art Resource, New York, NY.

 POEMS FOR STUDY

MURIEL RUKEYSER   (1913–1980)

Myth _____ *1978*

Long afterward, Oedipus, old and blinded, walked the
roads.   He smelled a familiar smell.   It was
the Sphinx.   Oedipus said, "I want to ask one question.
Why didn't I recognize my mother?"   "You gave the
wrong answer," said the Sphinx.   "But that was what   5
made everything possible," said Oedipus.   "No," she said.
"When I asked, What walks on four legs in the morning,
two at noon, and three in the evening, you answered,
Man.   You didn't say anything about woman."
"When you say Man," said Oedipus, "you include women   10
too. Everyone knows that."   She said, "That's what
you think."

QUESTIONS

1.   Who was Oedipus? The Sphinx? According to this poem, what was wrong with
      Oedipus's answer to the Riddle of the Sphinx?

2.   What elements and techniques in this work allow you to consider it a poem?

3.   What two myths and meanings of *myth* are embodied in the title?

4.   To what extent does the poem's colloquial language revitalize the mythic
      material?

JOHN UPDIKE   (b. 1932)

On the Way to Delphi _____ *1978*

Oedipus slew his father near this muddy field
the bus glides by as it glides by many another,
and Helicon° is real; the Muses hid and dwelled
on a hill, less than a mountain, that we could climb
if the bus would stop and give us the afternoon.   5

From these small sites, now overrun by roads and fame,
dim chieftains stalked into the world's fog and grew huge.
Where shepherds sang their mistaken kings, stray factories
mar with cement and smoke the lean geology
that wants to forget—*has* forgotten—the myths it bred.   10

We pass some slopes where houses, low, of stone, blend in
like utterings on the verge of sleep—accretions scarce

ON THE WAY TO DELPHI.   3 *Helicon:* a mountain in southwestern Greece. In ancient Greek
mythology, Helicon was the home of the Nine Muses.

distinguishable from scree,° on the uphill way rocks, rubble
to architecture and law. No men are visible.
All out: Parnassus.° The oracle's voice is wild.   1⁵

13 *Scree*: piles of loose rock at the base of a mountain or hill.   15 *Parnassus*: a mountain sacred
to Dionysus, Apollo, and the Muses. The geography of the poem indicates that the speaker's reflections take place on a tour bus ride from Athens north and west to Delphi, which is at the foot of
Mount Parnassus.

QUESTIONS

1. What is the situation of the speaker of this poem? Where is he? What is he
    doing? What prompts his observations about Oedipus and the sacred moun-
    tains of ancient Greece?

2. Why does the speaker observe that the field is "muddy" near where Oedipus
    killed his father?

3. In the second stanza, what prompts the contrast between the present and the
    mythical past? What does it mean to say that modern people have forgotten the
    ancient myths? What is symbolic about the low houses that are similar to
    "scree"?

WRITING ABOUT MYTH IN POETRY

An essay on myth in poetry will normally connect the mythic material in a
poem to some other element, such as speaker, character, action, tone, setting,
situation, imagery, form, or meaning. This suggests a two-part exploration of
the poem, one concerned with its general sense, and the other with the ways in
which myth shapes and controls that sense.

As you reexamine the poem, look for the ways in which myth enriches the
poem and focuses its meaning. The following questions should help.

Questions for Discovering Ideas

•   To what extent does the title identify the mythic content of the poem and thus
    provide a key for understanding?

•   How much of the poem's action, setting, and situation are borrowed from mythol-
    ogy? What is the significance of the action in the myth? What does this action
    symbolize? How does the poet reshape the action and its significance?

•   To what extent does our understanding of the myth explain the poem's speaker,
    characters, situations, and ideas? What characters, including the speaker, are
    drawn from mythology?

•   In what ways are these characters symbolic? What aspects of this symbolism are
    carried into the poem? How does the poem either maintain or change the
    symbolism?

•   How do the various formal elements of the poem, such as diction, rhyme, meter, and
    form, reshape the mythic material and affect the meaning and impact of the myth?

- How does the tone of the poem either reinforce or undercut the ideas and implications of the original myth? Cite specific words and phrases that lead you to your conclusions.

- Does the rhyme (if any) lead us to consider the mythic content as serious or comic?

- Generally, how does the mythic content help develop and clarify the poem?

Strategies for Organizing Ideas

A main challenge in writing about myths is to develop a focus or central idea. If, for example, you find that the poem retells a myth in order to make a point about history or society, you should fashion your central idea to reflect that connection. Similarly, if the poem employs a mythical speaker or character to convey ideas about war or heroism, your essay should focus on the links among myth, character, and those ideas.

When you formulate a central idea, draft it as a complete sentence that conveys the full scope of your ideas. It is not enough merely to assert that a given poem contains a great deal of mythic material. If you are writing about Yeats's "Leda and the Swan," for example, you might be tempted to form a central idea that argues that "William Butler Yeats's 'Leda and the Swan' retells the myth of Leda's rape by Zeus and the consequences of that event." That sentence does not tell the reader anything about the *way* the Leda myth works in the poem. Nor does it provide a basis for moving beyond summary and paraphrase. A more effective formulation would be the following: "In Yeats's 'Leda and the Swan,' the myth of Leda's rape by Zeus and the consequences of that rape illustrate the process of history and also question the connection between knowledge and power." This sentence points to a specific connection between mythological content and the poem's effect, and it gives a clear direction to the essay.

In your introductory paragraph or paragraphs, you should briefly summarize the significant parts of your poem's mythical elements, together with any noteworthy details about the poem's form or circumstances of composition. Your aim should be to focus on the poem (and the mythic material within the poem) rather than on the myth itself. Thus, you should link the mythical elements with other aspects of the poem and make assertions about the effects of this connection. You can employ various strategies to organize the body of your essay.

1. You might echo the organization of the poem, shaping the central paragraphs so as to reflect the poem's line-by-line or stanza-by-stanza logic.

2. You might choose an organization based on a series of different mythic elements or figures. For instance, if a poem alludes to Odysseus; his wife, Penelope; and his son, Telemachus, you might devote paragraphs to the way each figure shapes the poem's impact and meaning.

3. You might use the relevant elements of poetry as the focal points of organization. Thus, if you argue that diction, rhyme, and tone shape the mythological material to produce significant effects, you would deal with each element in turn.

To bring your essay to a convincing and assertive close, you might summarize your major points. At the same time, you might draw your reader's attention to the significance of your observations and to any further implications of the ways in which the myth is integrated into the poem you have considered.

DEMONSTATIVE STUDENT ESSAY

Myth and Meaning in Dorothy Parker's "Penelope"°

[1] Dorothy Parker's short lyric poem "Penelope" uses mythic allusion and symbolism to criticize conventional ideas about the roles of women and men. Her speaker is the mythic figure Penelope, the wife of King Odysseus of the ancient realm of Ithaca. Not only is Penelope the speaker, but she is also the poem's major figure. Parker uses her to assert that society has consistently misjudged and undervalued women's lives.* Her assertions are brought out through the poem's title, its mythic resonance, its diction, and its view of the representative lives of both Odysseus and Penelope.†

[2] The key to the poem's use of myth is the title, "Penelope." As the only place where the poem's mythological speaker is named, the title alludes to Homer's *Odyssey,* which tells that Penelope endures a twenty-year wait while her husband is at war and at sea. Her seemingly endless wait is filled with trouble. Her palace is occupied by boorish suitors who assume that Odysseus is dead and that his kingship is vacant. They therefore demand that Penelope choose a new husband. Only Penelope and Telemachus, her son, cling to the hope that Odysseus is still alive. She keeps the arrogant suitors at bay by promising to marry one of them after she finishes weaving a shroud for Odysseus's father. To delay this event, she works at the loom by day and unravels the work by night.

[3] Although the title refers directly to Penelope, the poem itself also deals with Odysseus. Lines 1-5 evoke the king's adventures in the phrases "He shall ride the silver seas" (line 4) and "He shall cut the glittering wave" (line 5). Because Odysseus is not identified by name, but only by the pronoun "he," readers might see this male figure as a symbol of all men who choose to lead their principal lives outside the home. The adjectives "silver" and "glittering" connote splendor and glory, while the verbs "ride" and "cut" suggest resoluteness and boldness. In addition, the phrases "pathway of the sun" (line 1) and "footsteps of the breeze" (line 2) add romance and mystery. In the same lines, however, one may perceive a subtle undercutting of the heroic figure. The phrase "ride the silver seas," for example, suggests that some of the Homeric lines are clichés. The implication is that an overglorified image of active heroes like Odysseus is both exaggerated and inaccurate.

[4] Just as this language has general implications for men, the language about Penelope is significant for women. In lines 6-9 she, as the speaker, contrasts her restricted life with the freedom of males. Here we find no adjectives at all;

° See p. 980 for this poem.
* Central idea.
† Thesis sentence.

the woman's existence is thus rendered factually, without adornment of any sort. In addition, the verbs represent passive and domestic activities: "sit", "rock", "rise", "brew", "snip", and "bleach". These last two verbs are especially effective. The phrase "snip my thread" (line 8) is the only allusion to Penelope's unhappy existence. It refers to her daring deception of the suitors through her nightly unraveling of the shroud. At the same time, "snip" is contrasted with the verb "cut" used earlier in the poem. While the words are synonyms, their connotations are different, for "cut" implies a degree of violence while "snip" suggests careful and delicate activity. "Bleach" is equally connotative; although it refers directly to "the linen for my bed," it is consistent with the view that Penelope's life is faded and colorless.

[5] The poem's final line ironically clarifies Penelope's attitude toward the different roles of men and women. Penelope asserts that "They will call him brave." "They" refers to society, to the world at large, and to generations of readers who have admired Odysseus in Homer's *Iliad* and *Odyssey*. The meter of the line--a concluding spondee--places a great emphasis on the word "him", thus demonstrating the speaker's realization, and the poet's assertion, that society ignores or dismisses the quiet bravery of women. In myth and in life, the woman's role demands just as much courage and conviction as the man's.

[6] "Penelope" thus employs mythic figures and events to criticize the historical perception of the roles of men and women. Odysseus, the mythical and typical male, is presented as a heroic figure, but he too is human, and his adventures are tinged with overdramatization. Parker's point is not to demean him, however, but rather to emphasize that women, too, have their own heroism. Biology and destiny may have traditionally confined women at home to keep house and weave tapestries while men are granted the freedom to find adventure in far-off lands. But waiting at home while meeting domestic challenges takes courage too. Penelope and Odysseus lived at a time of the old ways, but if Parker's poem is understood properly, it is time for new ways to begin. Penelope is right to express annoyance and irony when considering the judgment of history. Our knowledge of her courageous survival in Ithaca during the absence of Odysseus adds significantly to the truth and depth of her feelings.

Commentary on the Essay

This essay's major rhetorical purpose is to show how the poet uses the Penelope-Odysseus myth to shed new light on conventional attitudes about men and women. As a guide for your own writing aims, therefore, the essay illustrates how the mythological material can lead to ideas for development.

The body of the essay follows the organization of the poem itself. Thus, paragraph 2 focuses on the title, paragraph 3 on lines 1–5, paragraph 4 on lines 6–9, and paragraph 5 on the last line. Each of the paragraphs also advances a specific aspect of the essay's central idea. In paragraph 2, Penelope is identified and the relevant mythic material is reviewed. Logically, the information in this paragraph is essential for the remainder of the essay.

In paragraph 3, the title and its mythic importance introduce Odysseus and the symbol of the heroic male. Here, the point is that Parker's diction undercuts the active male image while seeming to glorify it. The first sentence of paragraph 4 provides a transition from Odysseus and heroic males to Penelope and the perceived passiveness of women. Again, the essay explores the way diction and mythic allusion in the poem demonstrate that there is more to the lives of women than usually is claimed. Paragraph 5 looks at the poem's final line in relation to the contrasted lives of "heroic" men and "passive" women. Here, the essay shows how tone and meter reveal the speaker's attitude toward these contrasting lives and society's misperception of them.

The conclusion goes quickly over the essay's basic points, and it emphasizes how the poem, with its ancient myth, brings new light to a traditional problem. The writer has ended with a brief personal essay that considers the poem's ideas and their current importance.

SPECIAL TOPICS FOR WRITING AND ARGUMENT ABOUT MYTH IN POETRY

1. In Atwood's "Siren Song," Broumas's "Circe," Glück's "Penelope's Song," Merwin's "Odysseus," Parker's "Penelope," Pastan's "The Suitor," Tennyson's "Ulysses," and Ulisse's "Odyssey: 20 Years Later," the poets evoke the same myth but for different purposes. What are these purposes? What views do you find about adventure, domesticity, and sexuality? What attitudes toward figures in the myth (Odysseus, Penelope, Calypso, the Siren, Circe) do the poets bring out? How do word choice, selection of detail, and point of view influence each poet's conclusions?

2. The myth of Icarus is used by Aldiss, Auden, Field, Rukeyser, Sexton, Spender, and Williams. Basing your conclusions on two or more of the poems in this group, what similarities and differences can you describe? How do the poets present the myth? How do they use the myth to create unusual or surprising endings, and to comment on contemporary but also permanent attitudes about life and the sufferings of others?

3. What point does Muriel Rukeyser's "Myth" make about both men and women and their attitudes toward each other? How does our knowledge of the Oedipus myth (See Sophocles' play *Oedipus the King*, Chapter 27) help clarify these aspects of the poem? In what respects is the poem contemporary?

4. Compare and contrast the use of the Phoenix myth by Clampitt, Levertov, and Sarton.

5. In your library, choose a book on myths, such as Kenneth McLeish, *Myth: Myths and Legends of the World Explored* (1996), or Richard Erdoes and Alfonso Ortiz, *American Indian Myths and Legends* (1984). Select a story from among the many myths described there (e.g., Oedipus, Jason, Prometheus, Antigone, Sisyphus, Beaver stealing fire from the Pines, Coyote placing the stars, A Tale of Elder Brother). To these you might add biblical stories (e.g., the fight between God and Satan, Noah, Leviathan, Joseph and his brothers, the Hebrew captivity in Egypt, the Exodus, the Babylonian captivity) and other legends and actual historical stories (Robin Hood, Paul Bunyan, Davy Crockett, the Amistad event,

the forty-niners, the Civil War, the Lone Ranger, the log cabin, the Rough Riders, etc.). Write a poem based on the story you choose. Try to present your own view about the importance, timeliness, intelligence, and truth of your story. What kinds of detail do you select? How do you give the figures mythic status? How do you make your own attitudes apparent by your arrangement of detail and your word choice?

23
Meaning:
Idea and Theme
in Poetry

When we talk about understanding poetry, we frequently use the words *idea, theme, motif,* and *meaning* (see also Chapter 10). Usually **idea** refers to a *concept, principle, scheme, method,* or *plan.* An idea may yield to extensive description and definition, such as the *idea of goodness,* the *idea of time,* and so on. When we use the word **theme** we refer to an idea, image, principle, or **motif** that, like a melody in music, is embodied, repeated, and developed within a literary work.

Going up the scale from idea, theme, and motif, we arrive at **meaning,** the word referring comprehensively to the ideas expressed within the poem—the poem's sense or message. For example, in the poem "Daffodils" (Chapter 24) Wordsworth begins with a description of how on a walk he saw large numbers ("a host") of daffodils blooming "beside a lake, beneath the trees." He goes on to describe his impressions upon seeing daffodils in bloom, and, at the poem's end, he points out how the remembered vision of this scene gives him spiritual joy and comfort (lines 19–24):

> For oft, when on my couch I lie
> In vacant or in pensive mood,
> They flash upon that inward eye
> Which is the bliss of solitude;
> And then my heart with pleasure fills,
> And dances with the daffodils.

By drawing general conclusions about his experience in this way, Wordsworth develops his theme and brings out the idea that intimate contact with natural scenes provides energy and creative renewal for the mind and spirit.

MEANING, POWER, AND POETIC THOUGHT

Poetry achieves much of its power through the expression of ideas. Such power is shown in Dryden's "A Song for St. Cecilia's Day," an ode, written in 1687, that exalts music, harmony, and the divine creation. Dryden's complex ideas are based on analogy and comparison, starting with the belief that in the very beginning of time (which was thought to be much more recent in his day than in ours), the divine principles of order and harmony created the universe out of a primeval chaos of "jarring atoms." Expanding this idea by analogy, Dryden asserts that the earthly counterpart of this creative heavenly harmony is music. In other words, just as harmony is the principle that began the "universal frame" of creation, so musical harmony is the principle that creates order and civilization on earth. In both the past and the present, then, harmony has been essential to human life and all life. It will be similarly essential in the future and even beyond, for musical harmony will continue triumphantly throughout eternity after our visible universe ends. These ideas combine biblical theology, late-seventeenth-century science, Dryden's understanding of music and musical instruments, and his reasoning based on analogy. For this reason the poem may not seem up to date by modern standards. However, we might consider that the discovery of universal principles of order has always been sought by scientists from Pythagoras to Newton to Einstein to Hubble, and that order and regularity are postulates of musical theory and composition. Dryden's idea about the vitality of harmony is therefore still current and contemporary, and his emphasis on this idea makes the poem both true and powerful. Modern readers can still learn from reading "A Song for St. Cecilia's Day" and can still be inspired by it.

This example also introduces the fact that poetry involves a unique form of thinking. Usually the direct presentation of ideas is concerned with organization, method, science, instruction, and reasoning and logic. Poetry is at once all and none of these things. It is both organized and methodical, but it usually advocates neither organization nor method; it is distant from science, but it often incorporates scientific details (see David Wagoner's "My Physics Teacher" in Chapter 18 and Donne's "A Valediction: Forbidding Mourning" in Chapter 17); it is always instructive even though pleasure, not instruction, is its primary aim; and it establishes patterns that follow reason and logic even though it is not primarily reasonable or logical. It is true that poetry benefits from the thinking processes necessary for discursive and ratiocinative prose (such as reports, articles, and persuasive speeches); its underlying thinking processes are additionally linked with association, suggestion, indirection, implication, analogy, metaphor, symbol, paradox, and ambiguity.

Expressing ideas is only one of a number of poetic aims, for poems may take the shape of narration, description, dialogue, observation, persuasive speech, self-analysis, confession, imaginary situations, and much else. In this respect, poetry as an instrument for ideas is like both music and painting. Music expresses ideas through complex melodic development, instrumentation, key, harmony or disharmony, and dynamics. Painting relies on ranges of color, light and shadow, action, expression, and arrangement. Both music and painting depend on nonlogical, nonverbal types of thought. Because poetry employs words, it is similar to more discursive presentations of ideas. But it is unique because it is an art form, and a poet controls words and ideas within the poem just as a painter controls paint on the canvas to make a meaningful picture, or a composer controls individual notes to create meaningful music.

PROBLEMS IN UNDERSTANDING THE MEANING OF POEMS

Our Understandings May Be Restricted by Time

A major problem in understanding poetic meaning lies in the nature of poetry itself: Poetry, like all literature and also like music, is a *time art*. Each poem's developing meaning depends on the poem itself, our interaction with it, and the passage of time. Naturally, our power of absorption sometimes lags. The early lines recede in our minds as we encounter the new words, images, ideas, symbols, sounds, and rhythms of later and concluding lines. The result is that we cannot express the poem's meaning comprehensively at a given single moment.

Personal Concerns May Divert Our Attention When Reading

Our own concerns and preoccupations also influence the impact that we allow poems to have on us. We may not always be ready to reach out to the poem we are reading. Almost without warning, parts that we think we understand escape our comprehension, and lines that we may have read inattentively yesterday burst upon us with great meaning and power today. As a public example of this fact, former president Dwight D. Eisenhower once introduced a new legislative proposal by quoting the following couplet from *An Essay on Criticism* by Alexander Pope:

> Be not the first by whom the new are tried,
> Nor yet the last to lay the old aside.

Everyone who studies Pope's poem reads these lines, which refer to the need for being cautious about immediately forsaking old approaches and accepting new ones. But the president—or more likely someone on his staff—thought the lines provided a meaningful justification for new legislation. Here we have a clear example of how meaning may emerge as time and circumstance change.

The Uniqueness and Autonomy of Poetry Limit Our Interpretive Power

When we interpret a poem for its meaning, it is important to recognize the limitations of our effort. What we say about a poem is no more than that. It demonstrates our own perception and understanding, but only the poem itself contains its *entire* meaning. Individual poems are made up of separate parts, each part with its own meaning, and the various parts together make up the whole, so that the poem is an artifact intricately connected to the poet's mind, the circumstances of composition, and the historical period of the poem's origin. As we continue to raise questions about individual poems—as one of the best ways to understand them—we recognize that our understanding often falls short of our efforts to comprehend and explain.

Yet even after we complete our analysis and determine what we consider to be a poem's meaning, the poem is still independent. Consider the conclusion of Keats's "Ode on a Grecian Urn," some of the most frequently quoted lines in poetry:

> When old age shall this generation waste,
> Thou shalt remain, in midst of other woe
> Than ours, a friend to man, to whom thou say'st,
> "Beauty is truth, truth beauty,"—that is all
> Ye know on earth, and all ye need to know.

The meaning of these lines has been analyzed and discussed ever since Keats wrote them. Their meaning will continue to be discussed as long as people read and talk about poetry, yet it still eludes us even as we feel that we know what it means. Perhaps no other passage so clearly shows that poems always possess their own identity and integrity. Poetic meaning is like the dancer who was once asked why she danced. Her response was that if she could explain her reasons in words, she would no longer feel the need to dance. In other words, no matter how well we follow a poem's intricate themes or motifs, or how comprehensively we determine its meaning, the poem is still out there—dancing.

MEANING AND POETIC TECHNIQUES

Even if we grant the unlikelihood of grasping a poem's entire meaning at a single instant, there is still much that we can do to increase our understanding. We can study each poem's ideas and relate these ideas to the intellectual and emotional impact of the poem. In effect, meaning involves us in a transfer of thought and experience from the poet's mind to our own, for reading poetry is a cooperative venture between poet and reader. It is no exaggeration to say that the structure and development of a poem are intended to produce a corresponding development of thoughts, reactions, considerations, and emotions in readers. To get at meaning is to get at all the ways in which poetry brings these effects about.

An initial understanding of meaning can be gained by a close, sentence-by-sentence reading. But for most poems the meaning emerges as a result of comprehending not only the direct statements but also the results of the poet's technique. In other chapters we have studied many of the elements of technique that the poet uses: those of speaker; character, setting, and action;

diction; imagery and figures of speech; tone; rhythm, meter, sound, and rhyme; structure and form; and symbol and allusion. A brief reminder of the techniques may be helpful here.

The Speaker Provides a Starting Point for Our Understanding of a Poem

It is important that we learn the identity and circumstances of the speaker (see Chapter 14). The speaker of Hardy's "Channel Firing" (Chapter 14), for example, is a skeleton who has been wakened in his grave by the noise of battleship guns being fired on the nearby sea. The speaker in Sharon Olds's "35/10" is a mother brushing her daughter's hair. The attitudes and ironies so essential to the meanings of these poems would not be clear if we did not know who these speakers are and what they are doing at the "time" the action of the poems is occurring. Similarly, we need to know whether a speaker is trustworthy or untrustworthy. The speaker of "next to of course god america i" by e. e. cummings, for example, demonstrates his unreliability because he voices nothing but political platitudes. Without knowing it, he is funny, because cummings makes the speaker's words parody the occasional speeches of politicians from the earliest times to our own. As these various examples show, each poem contains its own unique speaker, whose character has a vital bearing on poetic content and meaning.

Character, Setting, and Action Are Dramatic Elements of Meaning

Here are three important elements to observe and to study, for all of these can be considered as parts of the drama of poetry. A poem describing the painted scenes on an ancient Greek vase (Keats's "Ode on a Grecian Urn"), for example, conveys a different meaning from one giving details about a walk through the woodland in spring (Housman's "Loveliest of Trees," Chapter 13) or one that tells about an adult speaker searching the shadows of memory for a vision of dead childhood friends (Justice's "On the Death of Friends in Childhood"). All three of these poems introduce the subject of death, but their radically different contexts and actions produce a new perspective, a different emotional response, a new experience, and a different meaning.

The Selection of Words Shapes Our Perception of Ideas

The words of a poem—denotation, connotation, and syntax (see Chapter 15)—are basic to a poem's total meaning and impact. In Robert Herrick's "To the Virgins, to Make Much of Time," for example, the speaker advises virgins to gather "rosebuds," which could easily be interpreted as an invitation to promiscuous sexuality. However, the poem concludes on the advice to "go marry," and thereby it places the urgency of sex in the context of socially and religiously approved behavior. By contrast, in Ben Jonson's "To Celia," the speaker urges "sports of love" and "love's fruit" but provides no additional context. Thus the diction of "To Celia" primarily stresses seduction, while the diction of "To the Virgins" provides happy but mature advice about life, even though both poems belong to the *carpe diem* ("seize the day") tradition of love poetry.

Imagery and Figures of Speech Provide an Interpretative Basis of Ideas

Imagery, metaphor, simile, and other figures of speech (see Chapters 16 and 17) make abstract ideas and situations concrete and immediate. We have stressed how Keats creates the excitement of discovery through his simile of the "watcher of the skies" in "On First Looking into Chapman's Homer" (Chapter 17). Beyond such uses, a poet may introduce imagery and metaphorical language to reinforce or to negate what appears to be the speaker's major thrust. In Owen's "Dulce et Decorum Est," for example (Chapter 18), soldiers are described as "Bent double, like old beggars under sacks." The simile is consistent with the rest of the poem; it defines the speaker's abhorrence of the destructiveness of war, and it shapes the poem's sense that war is humiliating, dehumanizing, and vicious.

The Tone of a Poem Enables Us to Measure and Balance Ideas

A poem's tone (see Chapter 18) has a significant effect on the ways in which we perceive its ideas, as in "On the Death of Friends in Childhood" by Donald Justice, in which the sentences "We shall not ever meet them" and "let us seek them there in the shadows" show the speaker's unambiguous sorrow and regret over the loss of childhood friends and the potentially rewarding experience they might have offered him. Tone may sometimes create ambiguity, however, or it may even work against the stated purpose of the speaker, as in the duke's mentioning the marriage settlement in "My Last Duchess" (Chapter 14). The duke speaks of the count's "known munificence" as justification for his "just" claims, while we conclude that the duke will make confiscatory demands. Through irony, therefore, Browning shows the duke's smugness, cruelty, and inhumanity.

Prosody (Meter, Sound, and Rhyme) Distinguishes and Emphasizes Ideas

Prosodic devices are integral aspects of poetic meaning (see Chapter 19). Rhythm and meter are often controlled to emphasize important words and therefore to shape our perception of major ideas. In Dorothy Parker's "Penelope" (Chapter 22) the concluding line is "They will call him brave." The meter literally demands a strong accent on "him," thus underscoring the poem's powerful irony (i.e., "They will call *him* brave [but not me, even though I have been equally brave]"). Rhyme and other segmental effects may be employed to point up ideas, regulate the tone, and thus shape meaning. The strong, single-word rhymes in the final stanza of Larkin's "Next, Please," for example ("black," "back"; "wake," "break"), are integrated with heavy alliteration (the *b* and *br* sounds) and concluding palatal stops (the *k* sounds) to bring the poem to a powerful conclusion. The employment of such effects, in fact, is one of the best single poetic techniques for helping readers' memories, and therefore for both establishing and emphasizing ideas.

Structure and Form Permit Us to Follow the Development of Ideas

The form of a poem (see Chapter 20) orders and shapes its developing meaning. The units or stanzas usually reflect specific steps in a poetic argument or in the logical buildup from details to ideas. Such is the case in Dryden's "A Song for St. Cecilia's Day." In this closed-form ode, with stanzas of irregular length depending on the subject, the ideas begin with Dryden's opening paean to heavenly harmony and grow toward the concluding tribute to the universal and cosmological power of music. In Judith Viorst's open-form poem "True Love," the stanzas wryly complement the poem's movement from marital irritations and frustrations to the assertion of the meaning of "true love."

JUDITH VIORST   (b. 1931)

True Love _____ *1968*

It is true love because
I put on eyeliner and a concerto and make pungent observations about the great
   issues of the day
Even when there's no one here but him,
And because
I do not resent watching the Green Bay Packers
Even though I am philosophically opposed to football,
And because
When he is late for dinner and I know he must be either having an affair or lying dead
   in the middle of the street,
I always hope he's dead.

It's true love because
If he said quit drinking martinis but I kept drinking them and the next morning I
   couldn't get out of bed,
He wouldn't tell me he told me,
And because
He is willing to wear unironed undershorts
Out of respect for the fact that I am philosophically opposed to ironing,
And because
If his mother was drowning and I was drowning and he had to choose one of us to
   save,

TRUE LOVE.   See Shakespeare's *A Midsummer Night's Dream,* I.1.132: "The course of true love never did run smooth."

He says he'd save me.

It's true love because
When he went to San Francisco on business while I had to stay home with the painters
    and the exterminator and the baby who was getting the chicken pox,   20
He understood why I hated him,
And because
When I said that playing the stock market was juvenile and irresponsible and then the
    stock I wouldn't let him buy went up twenty-six points,
I understood why he hated me,
And because   25
Despite cigarette cough, tooth decay, acid indigestion, dandruff, and other features of
    married life that tend to dampen the fires of passion,
We still feel something
We can call
True love.

QUESTIONS

1. What does the poet mean by "true love"?
2. What situations described here are antiromantic? What importance do they have in the speaker's idea of the wife–husband relationship?
3. What comic situations and statements does the poem contain? How do these elements contribute to the poem's tone and meaning?
4. Explain why lines 2, 8, 11, 17, 20, 23, and 26 are the poem's longest lines. In what ways is the meaning of these lines contrasted with the meaning of the shorter lines?

Symbol, Allusion, and Myth Broaden the Scope of a Poem's Ideas

Poets employ symbol and allusion, and they use mythical materials (see Chapters 21 and 22) as a shorthand way of conveying complex ideas and a great deal of information as quickly and economically as possible. For instance, in Herrick's "To the Virgins, to Make Much of Time," two symbols—rosebuds and flowers—point beyond themselves to youth and the brevity of life as well as to sexuality, marriage, family, and full involvement in life. Allusion can be equally important, as in Marvell's "To His Coy Mistress," where we find that geographic and biblical allusions are integral to the poem's developing argument. The use of myth puts poems in a broad historical context. Poems devoted entirely to mythical subjects, such as Parker's "Penelope" and Field's "Icarus" (Chapter 22), may render unexpected insights into human problems. Even a brief reference to a myth, such as Dryden's lines about Orpheus in "A Song for St. Cecilia's Day," serve to introduce complex thoughts and enrich the total meaning of a poem.

Admittedly, these topics form a large number of variables to consider when you study each poem's central idea and meaning. However, with increasing experience as a disciplined reader, you will do much of this step-by-step analysis naturally and routinely. A point to remember about analyzing poetic meaning is that you can draw upon your available knowledge to develop your understanding.

 ## POEMS FOR STUDY

AMY CLAMPITT   (1920–1994)

Beach Glass _____ 1983

While you walk the water's edge,
turning over concepts
I can't envision, the honking buoy
serves notice that at any time
the wind may change,
the reef-bell clatters
its treble monotone, deaf as Cassandra°
to any note but warning. The ocean,
cumbered by no business more urgent
than keeping open old accounts
that never balanced,
goes on shuffling its millenniums
of quartz, granite, basalt.

          It behaves
toward the permutations of novelty—
driftwood and shipwreck, last night's
beer cans, spilt oil, the coughed-up

BEACH GLASS.   7 *Cassandra:* mythical Trojan prophetess who accurately foretold future disasters but whom no one believed.

residue of plastic—with random
impartiality, playing catch or tag
or touch-last like a terrier,   20
turning the same thing over and over,
over and over. For the ocean, nothing
is beneath consideration.

        The houses
of so many mussels and periwinkles   25
have been abandoned here, it's hopeless
to know which to salvage. Instead
I keep a lookout for beach glass—
amber of Budweiser, chrysoprase°
of Almadén and Gallo, lapis   30
by way of (no getting around it,
I'm afraid) Phillips'
Milk of Magnesia, with now and then a rare
translucent turquoise or blurred amethyst
of no known origin.   35

        The process
goes on forever: they came from sand,
they go back to gravel,
along with the treasuries
of Murano,° the buttressed   40
astonishments of Chartres,°
which even now are readying
for being turned over and over as gravely
and gradually as an intellect
engaged in the hazardous   45
redefinitions of structures
no one has yet looked at.

29 *chrysoprase:* a gold-green gemstone.   40 *Murano:* a Venetian island famous for its glass.
41 *Chartres:* the medieval cathedral of Chartres, France, which is unique because of the incredible
beauty of its stained glass windows.

QUESTIONS

1. What is the idea of the poet's description of the buoy near the shore? How does
   the reference to Cassandra support the poem's meaning?
2. What life forms, now jetsam, does the speaker observe on the shore? What
   human artifacts have been cast ashore? Why does she choose to collect some
   of these artifacts? Why does she use words like "chrysoprase," "lapis," and
   "amethyst" in reference to these objects?
3. What is the meaning of the last stanza? What is the purpose of the poem's contrast between the beach glass and the glass from Murano and Chartres? What
   do these objects symbolize?

e. e. cummings   (1894–1962)

next to of course god america i _____ *1926*

"next to of course god america i
love you land of the pilgrims' and so forth oh
say can you see by the dawn's early my
country 'tis of centuries come and go
and are no more what of it we should worry   5
in every language even deafanddumb
thy sons acclaim your glorious name by gorry
by jingo by gee by gosh by gum
why talk of beauty what could be more beaut-
iful than these heroic happy dead   10
who rushed like lions to the roaring slaughter
they did not stop to think they died instead
then shall the voice of liberty be mute?"

He spoke. And drank rapidly a glass of water.

QUESTIONS

1. What is the form of the poem? What is the rhyme scheme? What does cummings achieve by not using capitalization and punctuation?

2. Who is the speaker? What characteristics and capacities does he show? How do you respond to him?

3. What ideas does the poem bring out? In what ways does the speaker parody the speakers that one is likely to hear on the Fourth of July throughout the United States? What is cummings saying not only about the speakers but also about the crowds that listen to such speeches?

JOHN DRYDEN   (1631–1700)

A Song for St. Cecilia's Day° _____ *1687*

I

From harmony, from heavenly harmony
　　This universal frame began:
　　When Nature underneath a heap
　　　　Of jarring atoms lay,
　　And could not heave her head,
The tuneful voice was heard from high,
　　"Arise, ye more than dead."

SONG FOR ST. CECILIA'S DAY.   *St. Cecilia:* St. Cecilia, the patron saint of music, was traditionally considered the creator of the pipe organ. In London after 1683, she was celebrated annually
on November 22 by the performance of a poem set to orchestral and choral music. Dryden wrote
two poems for the occasion: this one in 1687, and the longer "Alexander's Feast" in 1697. The
best-known version of the "Song for St. Cecilia's Day" is by Georg Frideric Handel.

Then cold, and hot, and moist, and dry°
In order to their stations leap,
      And Music's pow'r obey.   10
From harmony, from heavenly harmony
     This universal frame began:
     From harmony to harmony
Through all the compass of the notes it ran,
The diapason° closing full in Man.°   15

II

What passion cannot Music raise and quell!
    When Jubal° struck the corded shell,
    His listening brethren stood around,
    And, wondering, on their faces fell
    To worship that celestial sound: 20
Less than a god they thought there could not dwell
    Within the hollow of that shell,
    That spoke so sweetly and so well.
What passion cannot Music raise and quell!

III

The trumpet's loud clangor   25
    Excites us to arms
With shrill notes of anger
    And mortal alarms.
The double double double beat
    Of the thundering drum   30
Cries, "Hark! the foes come;
Charge, charge, 'tis too late to retreat."

IV

The soft complaining flute
In dying notes discovers
    The woes of hopeless lovers,   35
Whose dirge is whispered by the warbling lute.

V

Sharp violins proclaim
Their jealous pangs, and desperation,
Fury, frantic indignation,
Depth of pains, and height of passion   40
    For the fair, disdainful dame.

8 *cold . . . dry:* Before the modern classification of elements, it was supposed that there were four "elements" having four primary qualities: earth = cold, fire = hot, water = moist, and air = dry. 15 *diapason:* the organ stop determining keys and chords; thus, metaphorically, the quality that created and shaped humankind.   15 *Man:* the human race.   17 *Jubal:* "the father of all such as handle the harp and organ" (Genesis 4:21).

VI

But O! what art can teach,
What human voice can reach
   The sacred organ's praise?
   Notes inspiring holy love,   45
Notes that wing their heavenly ways
     To mend the choirs above.

VII

Orpheus° could lead the savage race
And trees unrooted left their place,
   Sequacious of the lyre;   50
But bright Cecilia raised the wonder higher:
When to her organ vocal breath was given,
An angel heard, and straight appeared,
     Mistaking earth for heaven.

GRAND CHORUS

As from the power of sacred lays
   The spheres began to move,   5
And sung the great Creator's praise
   To all the blessed above;
So, when the last and dreadful hour
This crumbling pageant shall devour   6
The trumpet shall be heard on high,
The dead shall live, the living die,
And Music shall untune the sky.°

48 *Orpheus:* in Greek myth, the greatest of all musicians. His playing tamed wild animals, and trees uprooted themselves to go and hear him.   63 *And Music shall untune the sky:* The harmony of the sky (i.e., heavenly harmony) will be replaced eternally by musical harmony.

QUESTIONS

1. What is the central idea of "A Song for St. Cecilia's Day"? In light of this idea, what is the major attribute of the creator God (whom Dryden does not specifically mention)? Why does the angel mistake earth for heaven (stanza VII)? How is this example related to the poem's major idea?

2. Through what attribute is music related to the created universal order? How is music analogous to the ordering principles of creation? How long will music continue to exist? Why?

3. What powers are attributed to the various instruments? When is vocal music introduced? What is its effect?

4. Should Dryden's ideas in the poem be considered outdated? To what degree are the ideas still important and valid?

DONALD HALL   (b. 1928)

Whip-poor-will _____ *1981*

As the last light
of June withdraws
the whip-poor-will sings
his clear brief notes

by the darkening house, then   5
rises abruptly from sandy
ground, a brown bird
in the near-night, soaring
over shed and woodshed
to far dark fields. When   10
he returns at dawn,
in my sleep I hear
his three syllables make
a man's name, who slept
fifty years in this bed   15
and ploughed these fields:
Wes-ley-Wells °. . . *Wes-*
ley-Wells . . .
            It is good
to wake early in high   20
summer with work to do,
and look out the window
at a ghost bird lifting away
to drowse all morning
in his grassy hut.   25

WHIP-POOR-WILL.   17 *Wes-ley-Wells:* the name of the poet's grandfather.

QUESTIONS

1. What is a whippoorwill? How does its song figure into the poem's development?
    Why does the speaker stress that he hears the name *Wesley Wells* not when
    waking but when asleep?
2. Who was Wesley Wells? What connection is established between him and the
    home and life of the speaker?
3. Why is so much attention given to the flying and singing habits of the bird?
4. How comparable is this poem to Keats's "Ode to a Nightingale" (p. 919)? How
    do birds and their songs serve to bring out major ideas in both poems?

ROBERT HERRICK   (1591–1674)

To the Virgins, to Make Much of Time _____ *1648*

Gather ye rosebuds while ye may,
   Old time is still a-flying;
And this same flower that smiles today
   Tomorrow will be dying.

The glorious lamp of heaven, the sun,   5
   The higher he's a-getting,
The sooner will his race be run,
   And nearer he's to setting.

That age is best which is the first,
   When youth and blood are warmer;   10
But being spent, the worse, and worst
   Times still succeed the former.

Then be not coy, but use your time,
   And, while ye may, go marry;
For, having lost but once your prime,   15
   You may forever tarry.

QUESTIONS

1.   What does the title of this poem tell us? What can we deduce about the speaker? To whom is the poem addressed?

2.   What point does this poem make about time? Life? Love?

3.   How does symbolism help shape the message and meaning of the poem? Consider especially "rosebuds," "flower," and "the sun."

4.   How do rhyme and tone help create and focus the meaning of this poem?

5.   This type of poem is called *carpe diem* (Latin for "seize the day" or "enjoy the present"). Compare this poem with Jonson's "To Celia" and Marvell's "To His Coy Mistress," which are also *carpe diem* poems. How are the tone and message of this poem similar to and different from those in the poems by Jonson and Marvell?

LANGSTON HUGHES   (1902–1967)

The Negro Speaks of Rivers _____ *1926*

I've known rivers:
I've known rivers ancient as the world and older than the flow of human blood in
    human veins.

My soul has grown deep like the rivers.

I bathed in the Euphrates when dawns were young.
I built my hut near the Congo and it lulled me to sleep.

I looked upon the Nile and raised the pyramids above it.
I heard the singing of the Mississippi when Abe Lincoln went down to New Orleans,
    and I've seen its muddy bosom turn all golden in the sunset.

I've known rivers:
Ancient, dusky rivers.

My soul has grown deep like the rivers.   10

QUESTIONS

1. What does the speaker mean by stating that his soul has grown deep like the rivers? Does the speaker refer to himself individually, or to his race collectively, or to both?

2. What is meant by the citation of the Euphrates, the Congo, the Nile, and the Mississippi? To what civilizations does the speaker refer? What idea about the history of blacks is implied by these rivers?

3. How do the repeated and echoed lines (8–10 repeating and echoing 1–3) affect your understanding of the poem's ideas? Why does the poet conclude the poem in this way?

BEN JONSON   (1572–1632)

To Celia° _____ *1606*

Come my Celia, let us prove,°   *try*
While we may, the sports of love;
Time will not be ours forever;
He at length our good will sever.
Spend not then his gifts in vain.   5
Suns that set may rise again;
But if once we lose this light,
'Tis with us perpetual night.
Why should we defer our joys?
Fame° and rumor are but toys.   *reputation*   10
Cannot we delude the eyes
Of a few poor household spies,
Or his° easier ears beguile,   *Celia's husband*
So removed by our wile?
'Tis no sin love's fruit to steal;   15
But the sweet theft to reveal,
To be taken, to be seen,
These have crimes accounted been.

TO CELIA.   The poem is from Jonson's play *Volpone;* it is spoken by Volpone (the name means "the fox") to Celia, a married woman whom he is trying to seduce.

QUESTIONS

1. What is the speaker like? What is his attitude toward time? Love? Celia?
2. What is personified in lines 3–5? What power does this force have?
3. How is the idea of "seizing the day" relevant to the first eight lines of this poem?
4. How does the speaker's argument change in the last ten lines? What assertions does the poem make about time, love, reputation, and crime?
5. What is the tone of the poem? How does it affect the meaning?

DONALD JUSTICE   (b. 1925)

On the Death of Friends in Childhood _____ *1960*

We shall not ever meet them bearded in heaven,
Nor sunning themselves among the bald of hell;
If anywhere, in the deserted schoolyard at twilight,
Forming a ring, perhaps, or joining hands
In games whose very names we have forgotten,
Come, memory, let us seek them there in the shadows.

QUESTIONS

1. What is the subject of this poem: the living, or the dead? How accurate is the title as a guide to subject and theme?
2. What point (if any) does this poem make about death? Time? Memory? The living?
3. How do imagery, diction, rhetoric and tone contribute to the total meaning of this poem? Consider phrases like "bearded in heaven" and "sunning themselves among the bald of hell." What is personified in the last line?

JOHN KEATS   (1795–1821)

Ode on a Grecian Urn _____ *1820 (1819)*

1

Thou still unravish'd bride of quietness,
   Thou foster-child of silence and slow time,
Sylvan historian, who canst thus express
A flowery tale more sweetly than our rhyme:
What leaf-fring'd legend° haunts about thy shape   *border and tale*
   Of deities or mortals, or of both,

ODE ON A GRECIAN URN.   The imaginary Grecian urn to which the poem is addressed combines design motifs from many different existing urns. This imaginary one is decorated with a border of leaves and trees, men (or gods) chasing women, a young musician sitting under a tree, lovers, and a priest and congregation leading a heifer to sacrifice.

"The Krater of Thanagra," fourth century B.C.E., showing a wedding procession and musicians. National Museum, Athens, Greece. Alinari/Art Resource, New York, NY.

    In Tempe° or the dales of Arcady?°
  What men or gods are these? What maidens loth?
What mad pursuit? What struggle to escape?
    What pipes and timbrels? What wild ecstasy?   10

2

Heard melodies are sweet, but those unheard
  Are sweeter; therefore, ye soft pipes, play on;
Not to the sensual ear, but, more endear'd,
  Pipe to the spirit ditties of no tone:
Fair youth, beneath the trees, thou canst not leave   15
  Thy song, nor ever can those trees be bare;
    Bold lover, never, never canst thou kiss,
Though winning near the goal—yet, do not grieve;

7 *Tempe:* a beautiful rustic valley in Greece.   *Arcady:* refers to the valleys of Arcadia, a state in ancient Greece known for its beauty and peacefulness.

She cannot fade, though thou hast not thy bliss,
For ever wilt thou love, and she be fair!   20

3

Ah, happy, happy boughs! that cannot shed
  Your leaves, nor ever bid the spring adieu;
And, happy melodist, unwearied,
  For ever piping songs for ever new;
More happy love! more happy, happy love!   25
  For ever warm and still to be enjoy'd,
    For ever panting, and for ever young;
All breathing human passion far above,
  That leaves a heart high-sorrowful and cloy'd,
    A burning forehead, and a parching tongue.   30

4

Who are these coming to the sacrifice?
  To what green altar, O mysterious priest,
Lead'st thou that heifer lowing at the skies,
  And all her silken flanks with garlands drest?
What little town by river or sea shore,   3
  Or mountain-built° with peaceful citadel,   *built on a mountain*
    Is emptied of this folk, this pious morn?
And, little town, thy streets for evermore
  Will silent be; and not a soul to tell
    Why thou art desolate, can e'er return.   4

5

O Attic shape! Fair attitude! with brede°   *braid, pattern*
  Of marble men and maidens overwrought,°   *ornamented*
With forest branches and the trodden weed;
  Thou, silent form, dost tease us out of thought
As doth eternity: Cold Pastoral!
  When old age shall this generation waste,
    Thou shalt remain, in midst of other woe
Than ours, a friend to man, to whom thou say'st,
  "Beauty is truth, truth beauty,"—that is all
    Ye know on earth, and all ye need to know.

QUESTIONS

1. What is the dramatic situation? What does the speaker see and do?

2. What does the speaker call the urn in the first stanza? What is suggested in these lines about the urn's relationship to time and change? To poetry?

3. What are "unheard" melodies (line 11) and "ditties of no tone" (line 14)? Why are these "sweeter" than songs heard by "the sensual ear" (line 13)? What central contrast is created through this comparison?

4. What do the trees, the musician, and the lovers have in common? How are they all related to the real world of time and change?

PHILIP LARKIN   (1922–1985)

Next, Please _____ *1955*

Always too eager for the future, we
Pick up bad habits of expectancy.
Something is always approaching; every day
Till then we say,

Watching from a bluff the tiny, clear,   5
Sparkling armada of promises draw near.
How slow they are! And how much time they waste,
Refusing to make haste!

Yet still they leave us holding wretched stalks
Of disappointment, for, though nothing balks   10
Each big approach, leaning with brasswork prinked,°   *adorned*
Each rope distinct,

Flagged, and the figurehead with golden tits
Arching our way, it never anchors; it's
No sooner present than it turns to past.   15
Right to the last

We think each one will heave to and unload
All good into our lives, all we are owed
For waiting so devoutly and so long.
But we are wrong: 20

Only one ship is seeking us, a black-
Sailed unfamiliar, towing at her back
A huge and birdless silence. In her wake
No waters breed or break.

QUESTIONS

1. What is the subject of the poem? The theme? What point does it make about time, expectation, human nature, and the way we live our lives?

2. What cliché does the extended metaphor that begins in the second stanza ironically revitalize and reverse? How does this metaphor make the total meaning of the poem clearer and more palpable?

3. How do meter, rhyme, and diction help create meaning? Consider, for example, the metrical variation in the fourth line of each stanza, rhyming pairs such as "waste-haste" and "wake-break," or words such as "bluff" and "armada."

4. Compare this poem to the three *carpe diem* poems in this chapter, including Marvell's "To His Coy Mistress." To what extent is "Next, Please" a *carpe diem* poem?

ARCHIBALD MACLEISH   (1892–1982)

Ars Poetica _____ *1926*

A poem should be palpable and mute
As a globed fruit,

Dumb
As old medallions to the thumb,

Silent as the sleeve-worn stone   5
Of casement ledges where the moss has grown—

A poem should be wordless
As the flight of birds

                    *   *   *

A poem should be motionless in time
As the moon climbs.   1

Leaving, as the moon releases
Twig by twig the night-entangled trees,

Leaving, as the moon behind the winter leaves,
Memory by memory the mind—

A poem should be motionless in time   1
As the moon climbs.

                    *   *   *

A poem should be equal to:
Not true.

For all the history of grief
An empty doorway and a maple leaf

For love
The leaning grasses and two lights above the sea—

A poem should not mean
But be.

QUESTIONS

1. What do lines 1–8 assert about a poem? How do the similes make this assertion clear and concrete?

2. How do you resolve the paradoxes that a poem may be both "mute" and "dumb," and also "silent" and "wordless"?

3. How do symbolism and simile clarify the claims about poetry in lines 9–16? How can something be "motionless" and also "climb"?

4. What does the third section (lines 17–24) state about a poem? Why are the symbols of grief and love included here?

5. To what extent does "Ars Poetica" illustrate its own definition of poetry?

ANDREW MARVELL   (1621–1678)

To His Coy Mistress _____ *1681*

Had we but world enough, and time,
This coyness, lady, were no crime.
We would sit down, and think which way
To walk, and pass our long love's day.

Thou by the Indian Ganges° side   5
Shouldst rubies find; I by the tide
Of Humber° would complain. I would
Love you ten years before the flood,°   *Noah's flood*
And you should, if you please, refuse
Till the conversion of the Jews.°   10
My vegetable love should grow
Vaster than empires and more slow;
An hundred years should go to praise
Thine eyes, and on thy forehead gaze;
Two hundred to adore each breast,   15
But thirty thousand to the rest;
An age at least to every part,
And the last age should show your heart.
For, lady, you deserve this state,
Nor would I love at lower rate.   20
But at my back I always hear
Time's wingéd chariot hurrying near;
And yonder all before us lie
Deserts of vast eternity.
Thy beauty shall no more be found,   25
Nor, in thy marble vault, shall sound
My echoing song; then worms shall try
That long-preserved virginity,
And your quaint honor turn to dust,
And into ashes all my lust: 30
The grave's a fine and private place,
But none, I think, do there embrace.
Now therefore, while the youthful hue
Sits on thy skin like morning dew,
And while thy willing soul transpires   35
At every pore with instant fires,
Now let us sport us while we may,
And now, like amorous birds of prey,
Rather at once our time devour
Than languish in his slow-chapped° power.   *slow-jawed*   40

TO HIS COY MISTRESS.   5 *Ganges:* a large river that runs across most of India.   7 *Humber:* a small river that runs through the north of England to the North Sea.   10 *Jews:* Traditionally, this conversion is supposed to occur just before the Last Judgment.

Let us roll all our strength and all
Our sweetness up into one ball,
And tear our pleasures with rough strife
Thorough° the iron gates of life: *through*
Thus, though we cannot make our sun 45
Stand still, yet we will make him run.

QUESTIONS

1. In lines 1–20 the speaker sets up a hypothetical situation and the first part of a pseudological proof: If *A* then *B*. What specific words indicate the logic of this section? What hypothetical situation is established?

2. How do geographic and biblical allusions affect our sense of time and place?

3. In lines 21–32 the speaker refutes the hypothetical condition set up in the first twenty lines. What word indicates that this is a refutation? How does imagery help create and reinforce meaning here?

4. The last part of the poem (lines 33–46) presents the speaker's "logical" conclusion. What words indicate that this is a conclusion? What is the conclusion?

SHARON OLDS (b. 1942)

35/10 _____ *1984*

Brushing out my daughter's dark
silken hair before the mirror
I see the grey gleaming on my head,
the silver-haired servant behind her. Why is it
just as we begin to go
they begin to arrive, the fold in my neck
clarifying as the fine bones of her
hips sharpen? As my skin shows
its dry pitting, she opens like a small
pale flower on the tip of a cactus;
as my last chances to bear a child
are falling through my body, the duds among them,
her full purse of eggs, round and
firm as hard-boiled yolks, is about
to snap its clasp. I brush her tangled
fragrant hair at bedtime. It's an old
story—the oldest we have on our planet—
the story of replacement.

QUESTIONS

1. Who is the speaker in this poem? What is she doing? What is the setting?

2. How does the speaker contrast her own state of being to her daughter's stage of life? How are images, metaphors, and similes used to clarify this contrast? How does this contrast help convey the poem's meaning?

3. What point does this poem make about life and nature? To what extent does the last sentence clarify (or overclarify) the poem's theme?

LINDA PASTAN (b. 1932)

Ethics _____ *1980*

In ethics class so many years ago
our teacher asked this question every fall:
if there were a fire in a museum
which would you save, a Rembrandt painting
or an old woman who hadn't many   5
years left anyhow? Restless on hard chairs
caring little for pictures or old age
we'd opt one year for life, the next for art
and always half-heartedly. Sometimes
the woman borrowed my grandmother's face   10
leaving her usual kitchen to wander
some drafty, half-imagined museum.
One year, feeling clever, I replied
why not let the woman decide herself?
Linda, the teacher would report, eschews   15
the burdens of responsibility.
This fall in a real museum I stand
before a real Rembrandt, old woman,
or nearly so, myself. The colors
within this frame are darker than autumn,   20
darker even than winter—the browns of earth,
though earth's most radiant elements burn
through the canvas. I know now that woman
and painting and season are almost one
and all beyond saving by children.   25

QUESTIONS

1. What can we surmise about the speaker in this poem? How does this knowledge contribute to our understanding of theme?

2. What are the two settings, situations, and actions presented here? How are they related? How much time has passed between them? How does the contrast between them help create meaning?

3. How has the passage of time changed the speaker's attitudes? What does she now realize about "woman / and painting and season" (lines 23–24)? About children?

4. What is the subject of this poem? The theme? What point does it make about art, life, time, and values?

WRITING ABOUT THEME AND MEANING IN POETRY

The prewriting process for this essay includes reading and rereading, developing your initial ideas about the poem, testing those ideas against the poem itself, formulating a tentative central idea for your essay, and organizing your observations into coherent units. Always keep foremost that your essay should connect the poem's theme and meaning to other poetic elements, such as speaker, imagery, metaphor, symbol, and tone.

Questions for Discovering Ideas

- What does the title of the poem tell you about subject and meaning?
- What do you learn about the speaker? How does the speaker shape and communicate ideas?
- How do the other characters (if any) affect the poem's meaning?
- What impact do setting, situation, and action have on theme?
- How do diction, imagery, metaphor, simile, and other figures of speech affect the ideas? How are multiple denotations and connotations employed? To what extent are special types of diction or word order used?
- Describe the tone of the poem. What effect does the tone have on the ideas?
- What role do rhythm, meter, sound, and rhyme play in shaping and emphasizing important words and ideas?
- How does the poem's form shape its ideas? What effect does the form have on your response?
- How do symbol, allusion, or myth contribute to the poem's ideas?

You will find poems for which all these questions are relevant, for some poets employ every element and device in the poetic repertory to develop their meaning. Other poems touch on only a few of these areas. Look for major elements that have the strongest impact on the poem's ideas and on your consideration of the poem as an emotional and intellectual experience.

Strategies for Organizing Ideas

Be careful to distinguish between *subject* and *theme.* For example, in planning to discuss Larkin's "Next, Please," you might write the following: "Larkin's 'Next, Please' makes a clear assertion about human habits of expectation." This sentence describes the poem's *subject,* and it might even be a good beginning sentence for your essay. It is not, however, a good central idea because it tells the reader nothing about the poem's theme or meaning. A better central idea is "Larkin's 'Next, Please' exposes the futility of ignoring the present while anticipating the future." This sentence summarizes the theme of the poem and makes a strong statement on which to build an effective essay.

Next, focus on the relationship between your idea and the ways in which the poem creates meaning. Use the information you gain from answering the questions for discovering ideas (in the preceding section). Thus, if you find that a poem's theme is established through symbol and allusion, you should make this connection by relating meaning to these elements. Such a plan might be (1) theme, (2) theme and symbol, and (3) theme and allusion. Or it might be that the poet's meaning is made plain through a dominant image or metaphor. You might then plan to develop the idea part by part, showing how the metaphor develops it, or you might want to stress the metaphor itself as it grows and develops as support for the poem's idea, as in the demonstrative student essay that follows.

In your introductory paragraph, before stating your central idea, bring out any points that are relevant to the poem and your essay. If your poem is about life at the front in World War I, for example, or if the speaker is a woman walking along a sandy beach, it is important to make these basic facts clear right at the beginning.

As you organize and develop your paragraphs, keep in mind the following structural patterns. They will be useful for almost all the poems you encounter.

1. The poem may convey meaning through direct statement. In such a case you might organize your essay to reflect the line-by-line or sentence-by-sentence structure of the poem itself.

2. You might find that the speaker's reasoning or argument most effectively creates meaning. To follow such a pattern of logic, for example, would be useful in an essay about the meaning of Andrew Marvell's "To His Coy Mistress."

3. The poet's use of a *single element* (such as a metaphor, simile, or myth) or a set of consistent references (such as discussions of explorers, bankers, darkness, or rain) might bring out the poem's meaning. Your organization might reflect how the element is used in the poem.

4. Finally, it might be that a number of *different poetic elements* (e.g., rhythm, rhyme, metaphor, level of diction, imagery, and so on) work together to shape theme and impact. The structure of an essay dealing with such elements can be based on a sequential discussion of each element as it contributes to meaning.

Please note that these four structural patterns can be modified and combined. To accommodate the specific poem you are considering, you should always be ready to adjust whatever plan you choose.

In your conclusion, you might pull all the strands of the essay together and reaffirm the connection between the poem's method and meaning. This is most conveniently done through a summary of your major points. The conclusion is also the place where you can consider additional aspects of the poem's ideas. Your reactions and thoughts upon reading the poem often suggest additional ideas for inclusion in your essay. Similarly, you might want to consider the extent to which your own circumstances (such as age, interests, political views, religion) help determine your understanding of the poem.

DEMONSTRATIVE STUDENT ESSAY

Metaphor and Meaning in Larkin's "Next, Please"°

[1]   Philip Larkin's "Next, Please" exposes the futility of ignoring the present while anticipating the future.* The idea is borne out in the poem's contrast between the slowness of hope and fulfillment and the certainty of disappointment and death. The theme is conveyed through the extended metaphor that begins in the second stanza; within this metaphor, diction and meter reinforce the meaning of the poem and the human experience that it defines.†

[2]   "Next, Please" announces its subject and begins to develop its theme through the title and the direct statements of the first stanza. The title refers to the desire to hope and look ahead. It suggests that we are never satisfied with what we have but always expect happiness "just around the corner." These implications are brought into focus in the first stanza, where the speaker notes that we are "Always too eager for the future" and that "we / Pick up bad habits of expectancy" (lines 1-2). Our habitual hope for the future is captured in the speaker's observation that "every day / *Till then* we say" (lines 3-4). By using the pronouns "we" and "us" here and throughout, the speaker generalizes: It is not just he or she alone, but all human beings who habitually indulge in wishful thinking.

[3]   In the second stanza, the poem asserts that these "bad habits of expectancy" leave us disappointed. This point is made through an extended metaphor based on a hidden cliché, which may be expressed either as "Someday my ship will come in" or "Someday I'll win out over everything." This cliché, which Larkin expresses originally as a "Sparkling armada of promises," embodies the vain dream that we will eventually get everything we want or deserve . Larkin's metaphor suggests that these hopes are mostly doomed.

[4]   Larkin begins developing the metaphor's meaning by making it dramatic. We as readers are "Watching from a bluff" at not just one hope, but at a whole fleet of hopeful promises. Right at the beginning, however, Larkin's diction directs our attention to the vanity of hope. A "bluff" of course is a hill, but it is also an attempt to mislead or deceive. "Armada" is similarly loaded because it evokes the memory of the Spanish Armada that sailed against England in 1588 and was destroyed by bad planning, storms, and failure in battle. The clear prediction of wreckage is thus built into the metaphor.

[5]   The metaphor makes the poem's meaning vivid and immediate through a wealth of detail. We notice that the "armada of promises" moves very slowly: "How slow they are! And how much time they waste, / Refusing to make haste" (lines 7-8). The metaphor is extended, with more and more details, such as the shining "brasswork," "Each rope distinct," the flag, and "the figurehead with

° See p. 1021 for this poem.
* Central idea.
† Thesis sentence.

golden tits / Arching our way" (lines 11-14). The metaphor suggests through these details that our dreams enable us to visualize the shapes that success can take. Even as our promises draw closer, their elusiveness is also established: "Yet still they leave us holding wretched stalks / Of disappointment" (lines 9-10). This image of standing on the "bluff" and holding wilted flowers represents unrealized hopes.

This disappointment is brought into explicit focus as the "armada" metaphor continues in the fourth stanza. We see that the fleet "never anchors" because it is "No sooner present than it turns to past" (line 14-15). Most of these words carry double meanings. "It", for example, refers to both the ships and time. "Turns to" indicates both a change of course and the inevitable transformation of the present into the past. Similarly, "present" and "past" signify both the physical status of the ships and the movement of time. The metaphor thus conveys the experience of disappointment both in terms of the "armada of promises" and the time we waste waiting for a reward that never comes.

[6]

Larkin's last two stanzas conclude the armada metaphor and expand on the theme of disappointment. The speaker observes that we always expect one of our ships to "heave to" and deliver "All good into our lives" (line 18). The stanza's last line, however, completely undercuts all hope. Here, we sense the impact of a metrical technique that Larkin has employed throughout. The poem is mostly in iambic pentameter, but the fourth line of each stanza is cut short to two or three feet. This metrical falling-off parallels the loss of hope. Like the "armada" and the future, each stanza fails to deliver what we expect. The force of this device strikes us at the close of the fifth stanza, where the final two-beat line bleakly tells us, "But we are wrong" (line 20).

[7]

In the sixth stanza, Larkin makes absolutely clear his ironic contrast between hope and disappointment. Although we seek the ships of expectation, which never come, there is "one ship" that "is seeking us" (line 21). It is not a ship full of good things; instead, it is a "black- / Sailed unfamiliar" ship "towing at her back / A huge and birdless silence" (lines 22-23). This is the only ship that is sure to come—the ship of death.

[8]

"Next, Please" thus tells us that passive hope is vain. The poem lets us experience this meaning through an extended metaphor, in which an "armada of promises" seems to be coming close, but then leaves without unloading anything and without winning any battles for us. The meaning of the poem becomes our movement through the metaphor, and our experience of the metaphor is disappointment and a vision of death. At the same time, however, the poem is not totally bleak and hopeless. It implies that we should live in and for the present, making the most of what we have. To this extent, "Next, Please" is a *carpe diem* poem, suggesting that we should "seize" today, which is real, rather than waste our time in unreal expectation.

[9]

Commentary on the Essay

The essay illustrates the need to combine and adjust strategies of organization in dealing with a specific poem. It combines a focus on a specific poetic element (metaphor) with secondary interest in two other elements (diction and meter). The essay thus represents a modification and combination of organization strategies 3 and 4 on page 1027.

Paragraph 2 deals with the subject of the poem; it grows out of the first two sentences of the introduction. This discussion provides the foundation for the essay's subsequent treatment of theme and meaning.

Paragraphs 3 through 8 grow out of the last two sentences of the introduction; they treat the connection between metaphor and meaning, and they take up the additional subjects of diction and meter. Paragraph 3 provides transition from subject to theme, introduces the dominant metaphor, and explains the hidden cliché (or clichés) on which the metaphor is based. Paragraph 4 examines the way that the "armada" metaphor creates a palpable experience and how the poem's diction lessens the promise of the experience.

Paragraph 5 sustains the focus on the link between metaphor and meaning through attention to the details that the speaker mentions in the poem's second, third, and fourth stanzas. Again, the first sentence connects this paragraph to both the introduction and the previous paragraph. Similarly, the concluding sentence leads into paragraph 6, which takes up the next stage of the extended metaphor and the articulation of disappointment. This focus on the end of the metaphor and on the experience of disappointment is continued in paragraph 7, which explores the impact of the poem's meter. The poem's last stanza is discussed in paragraph 8, which, like the stanza, emphasizes the contrast between the uncertainty of hope and the certainty brought by the black-sailed ship.

The concluding paragraph briefly considers the implications of the poem's meaning, offers a second and implied theme for the poem, and connects "Next, Please" to the long-standing *carpe diem* poetic tradition. The value of this paragraph is that it is more than a summary, leaving the reader with new thoughts.

SPECIAL TOPICS FOR WRITING AND ARGUMENT
ABOUT MEANING IN POETRY

1. Compare two or all of the following as *carpe diem* poems: Jonson's "To Celia," Herrick's "To the Virgins," Marvell's "To His Coy Mistress," and Larkin's "Next, Please." How well does each poem express the central idea of the *carpe diem* tradition? What are the similarities and differences of the tone and ideas? If the poems involve invitations to seduction, how do they transcend their topic to deal with ideas and values?

2. On the basis of ideas about age, change, and the loss of time and life, compare Pastan's "Ethics," Olds's "35/10," Marvell's "To His Coy Mistress," and Justice's "On the Death of Friends in Childhood." How do the ideas of the poems merge, even though they are about different subjects? Which of the poems do you prefer? Why?

3. Basing your discussion on the poems of Viorst, cummings, and Pastan, explain how comic humor can be employed as a vehicle for serious ideas. How do the poets introduce comic humor into their poems? What relationship does the

humor have to ideas? How might the expression of ideas be better (or worse) if the poems were serious and not comic?

4. Write your own poem in which you stress a particular idea. You might write about a friend or acquaintance who has endured an illness, performed an important service, admitted a mistake or failure, or succeeded in a task. Other possible topics are a social, religious, or political issue or some aspect of education, work, or community life. When you finish, explain how you go about making the situation clear to your reader, and explain how you use the situation to bring out your ideas. Do not neglect the title as one of the means of expressing ideas.

5. In the reference section of your library, select a guide to ideas, such as Philip P. Wiener, ed., *Dictionary of the History of Ideas: Studies of Selected Pivotal Ideas* (1973). Read about one or more of the following: *allegory, beauty, holy, idea, love, realism, sublime*. Explain the depth and application of the idea. What writers are associated with the idea? How does the author of the article demonstrate the idea's development? Describe how the author of the article emphasizes and exemplifies the idea.

24

Three Poetic Careers: William Wordsworth, Emily Dickinson, and Robert Frost

In Chapters 13 to 23 we have considered poetry in terms of its elements and effects. In this chapter we examine collections of poems by three major poets: William Wordsworth (1770–1850), Emily Dickinson (1830–1886), and Robert Frost (1874–1963). Wordsworth, whose first poems were published late in the eighteenth century, was one of the first Romantic poets in England. He stands at the crossroad between classicism and modernity. Dickinson and Frost are both American poets and New Englanders. Dickinson is one of the most prominent poetic voices of the nineteenth century, and Frost is recognized as a poetic giant of the twentieth century. Although the poems included here comprise only a fraction of the work of each of these major poets, it has been our goal to select enough poems to illustrate the central concerns and major characteristics that are to be found in the study of their poetic careers.

WILLIAM WORDSWORTH (1770–1850)

Life and Work

William Wordsworth was born in 1770 in the Lake District of northern England. He had three brothers and one sister. His father, John Wordsworth, was an attorney who urged him to memorize many poems of the great English poets. His mother died when he was eight years old, and the children were separated. Wordsworth went to a school at Hawkshead, near Lake Windermere, where he was an undistinguished pupil but enjoyed a good deal of personal freedom. Having little money but boundless energy, he became a tireless walker, to which he attributed the "indomitable vigour" of his adult life. He walked everywhere. During his lifetime he walked more than 100,000 miles—and not

William Wordsworth

slowly, either. As he walked various English and European countrysides, often covering as much as forty miles a day, he met and conversed with many local people, an experience that is reflected in his poetry.

Wordsworth's thirteenth year was marked by the death of his father, who, unwisely, had loaned his life savings to his employer, Sir James Lowther, who later became the first Lord Lonsdale. Representatives of the children appealed to Lord Lonsdale to restore the money, but this honorable gentleman rebuffed every claim. Not until Lonsdale died, when Wordsworth was in his early thirties, was restitution finally made. Once Wordsworth received his share of the inheritance, life became somewhat easier for him.

In 1787, four years after his father's death and fifteen years before his belated inheritance, his uncles enabled him to enter Cambridge University. He found classes uninteresting, but he read voraciously, and between terms he went walking. In 1790 he took a walking tour of France and the Alps with a friend, Robert Jones, and in 1791, the year he graduated, he walked with Jones throughout Wales.

For a time after his graduation Wordsworth lived in France, then at the height of its revolution, and he shared the idealistic possibilities of the new age based on trust "in the People." Later he described his youthful optimism: "Bliss was it in that dawn to be alive, / But to be young was very Heaven!" (*The Prelude*, XI.108–09). Eventually, however, he was disillusioned by the excesses of the Reign of Terror and the militarism of Napoleon.

While in France Wordsworth began an affair with Annette Vallon, a woman who held royalist sympathies. In 1793 the couple had a daughter, Caroline. Wordsworth wanted to marry Annette, but his money ran out and he had to return home the same year. Also in 1793, England and France went to war, and Wordsworth was unable to return to France. After the war, in 1802, he and Annette agreed that they had grown too separate from each other to undertake a successful marriage. They parted as friends, and Wordsworth, who had just come into his inheritance, provided for the care of their daughter.

In Wordsworth's post-Cambridge years he spent much time deciding what to do with his life, his options being poetry (his preference), the clergy, the law, or the military. Fortune intruded on his behalf, because for a time in 1795 he had cared for a good friend, Raisley Calvert, who was dying. Calvert believed in Wordsworth's future as a poet and expressed his gratitude by leaving Wordsworth a bequest of £900. This substantial sum enabled Wordsworth to take a home in the south of England, where he was joined by his sister Dorothy, who remained his housekeeper, friend, and lifelong confidante. Here he met Samuel Taylor Coleridge, a young man with similar interests and enthusiasms. The two men walked and talked together for many months, developing plans for a magazine and then for a book of poems.

Their collaboration resulted in one of the most significant books in English literature despite its inauspicious title: *Lyrical Ballads, with a Few Other Poems*, published in 1798. The collection contained twenty-three poems, four by Coleridge (including "The Rime of the Ancient Mariner") and nineteen by Wordsworth. Although *Lyrical Ballads* did not create a great general stir, many poetry readers bought it, and Wordsworth and Coleridge soon issued new, expanded editions. For the 1800 edition, Wordsworth included his landmark "Preface," in which he lays out his poetic credo.

After Wordsworth and Annette separated amicably in 1802, he married a woman he had known since childhood, Mary Hutchinson. The couple moved into Dove Cottage, Wordsworth's home in Grasmere, in the Lake District. Eventually they had five children, and in 1813 they took up permanent residence at nearby Rydal Mount. Along with growing recognition as a poet, Wordsworth attained financial security when he was appointed revenue collector in the Lake District. Years later he received an annual government pension of £300. In 1843 he was named poet laureate, an honor he held until his death in 1850.

Wordsworth published his poetry regularly throughout his lifetime, the most notable publications, after *Lyrical Ballads,* being *Poems in Two Volumes* in 1807, *The Excursion* in 1814, and his collected poems in 1815. His long autobiographical poem *The Prelude,* which he wrote and revised for more than five decades, was not published until after his death in 1850. In later years, Dove Cottage, Wordsworth's first residence in Grasmere, has become a shrine. Rebuilt and greatly enlarged, the home is now operated as a national historic trust. Rydal Mount is similarly open to visitors.

Wordsworth and Romanticism

Wordsworth, along with Coleridge, is acknowledged as an originator of English Romantic poetry. It must be said that the writers living in the so-called Romantic period (1798–1832) did not describe themselves as romantics; the term was conferred by later critics. There are many ways to explain Romanticism—and little agreement about any of them—but the essence of Romanticism is a belief in the power and validity of human emotions as a means of knowing and as a guide to life. The result is a strong emphasis on the individual and also on common people, regardless of station, since all people are capable of learning through emotional experiences. Whereas previous periods considered a ruling class the proper center of power and human interest, the Romantic believed that this center exists among all people. Romanticism undoubtedly reflected many ideas of the period—the Protestant Reformation, with its emphasis on the sanctity of individual conscience and its skepticism toward hierarchy; the influences of the American and French Revolutions, with their emphasis on the "common man" and representative government; the cultivation of sensibility in aesthetics, with its focus on individual feelings; and the growth of scientific research and experimentation as opposed to the acceptance of authoritarian dicta.

ROMANTICISM AND NATURE.   Wordsworth has always been considered a poet of nature. In his own lifetime he spent much time outdoors in all seasons, and he records innumerable experiences in the natural world. He can therefore be considered a topographic or landscape poet. But his object is not to record details but rather to emphasize the meaning of nature. His descriptions of natural scenes are therefore impressionistic and interpretive. For example, when he considers a remembered vision of daffodils, a vision that filled him with joy, he describes them as "fluttering and dancing in the breeze" and outdoing "the sparkling waves in glee." He clearly states his belief that nature provides evidence for universal power, a power that he seeks to assimilate within himself through feeling and imagination. The concluding lines from "The Tables Turned" (1798) illustrate this idea:

Come forth, and bring with you a heart
That watches and receives.

Because Wordsworth is one of those with a heart that receives, he frequently writes of his excitement upon seeing the beauty of nature. He describes such a feeling in the following brief poem:

My Heart Leaps Up ———————————————————— *1802*

My heart leaps up when I behold
   A rainbow in the sky.
So was it when my life began;

So is it now I am a man;
So be it when I shall grow old,   5
     Or let me die!
The Child is father of the Man;
And I could wish my days to be
Bound each to each by natural piety.

His great paean to nature, the distillation of this kind of experience, occurs in
lines 93 to 102 of "Lines Composed a Few Miles above Tintern Abbey" (1798):

And I have felt
A presence that disturbs me with the joy
Of elevated thoughts; a sense sublime
Of something far more deeply interfused,
Whose dwelling is the light of setting suns,
And the round ocean, and the living air,
And the blue sky, and in the mind of man;
A motion and a spirit, that impels
All thinking things, all objects of all thought,
And rolls through all things. . . .

ROMANTICISM, THE SELF, AND THE MORAL SENSE.   In some writers, the
consequence of romanticism is extreme Egotism. One certainly finds self-
centeredness in Wordsworth, whose own experiences, responses, and emotions
are his major subject. There is, however, a tempering sense that individual emotions are not self-indulgent but rather that they lead to self-realization and to a
genial moral philosophy that he describes in "Tintern Abbey" as a "cheerful
faith, that all which we behold / Is full of blessings."

His poetry embodies this particular type of romanticism. Believing that
all lives are worthy of study and understanding, Wordsworth wrote many poems
that treat topics of ordinary life, over which is cast an imaginative and moral
perspective. Examples from *Lyrical Ballads* are an old huntsman, a little girl who
cannot understand death, a betrayed woman who forever laments her abandonment, and a man who can never get warm because he once denied a few
sticks of firewood to an aged woman. These subjects illustrate Wordsworth's
broad concern with the meaning of the common events of everyday life.

But his most characteristic poems are those in which he concentrates on
individual experience as illustrated by his own life and thought. Wordsworth
looks at his life as a revelation—even a divine revelation—and therefore as holy.
For him, poetry of personal testimony and self-concern is justifiable and even
necessary. His longest poem, which is about himself, is the posthumously published *The Prelude* (1850), his exhaustive autobiographical self-analysis focused
on the growth of his own poetic imagination. This long work is unique in
English literature. In the ode "Intimations of Immortality" (1807), Wordsworth
is equally concerned with his own change and development. In this poem he
traces the emergence of "the philosophic mind." Perhaps Wordsworth's most
serene description of himself is "Lines Composed a Few Miles above Tintern

Abbey." In this poem the speaker, whom we may take to be Wordsworth himself, describes how his moral sense has been evoked and shaped by his lifelong experiences with nature.

ROMANTICISM AND WORDSWORTH'S THEORY OF COMPOSITION.

Wordsworth's Romanticism, then, is based on the idea that human emotions are good and moral and that they are authoritative and trustworthy. In particular, poets—that is, persons of powerful intuition and imagination—are specially inspired recipients of universal wisdom, and their poetry is the record of their inspiration, set down for others to appreciate and recognize as paralleling their own experience. His brief preface to "Tintern Abbey" best tells the story:

> No poem of mine was composed under circumstances more pleasant for me to remember than this. I began it upon leaving Tintern, after crossing the Wye, and concluded it just as I was entering Bristol in the evening, after a ramble of four or five days, with my Sister. Not a line of it was altered and not any part of it written down till I reached Bristol.

Of major significance is Wordsworth's claim that he altered "not a line," for his belief is that the entire poem was inspired, and that he received it through his own intuition and imagination. He clarifies these ideas in the "Preface" to the second edition of *Lyrical Ballads,* in which he states that poetic composition is produced by "emotion recollected in tranquillity." That is, the poet, living life as all of us do, finds that the memory of past experiences comes to mind involuntarily, through random associations, and that in times of relaxation and meditation this recollection causes the poet to reexperience the accompanying emotions. Such reflection is the basis of poetry, for the renewal of once-felt emotions inspires the poet to begin writing. Although the outline of this process is clear, the specifics of recollection are unknown, unknowable, and unpredictable—mysterious—and therefore, for a romantic, the act of poetic creation is evidence for a transcendent source of wisdom.

This view of poetic composition is similar to the idea of "negative capability" of John Keats (1795–1821). According to Keats, writing in 1817, negative capability is a capacity to accept and preserve ideas without critical interference because poetic thoughts come to the poet through a "penetralium of mystery."[1] This is a quintessentially Romantic idea of composition, and it explains why at least some of the Romantics believed that poetry should be preserved without change or revision. Because the poetic process exceeds normal human understanding, it should be hallowed and left unaltered. We should not conclude that Wordsworth never scratched out words and lines or added others. He rewrote poems all the time. But he believed that his original

---

[1] Hyder Rollins, ed., *The Letters of John Keats, 1814–1821* (Cambridge: Harvard, 1972), 1.193–194. Keats explains negative capability as a state "when a man is capable of being in uncertainties, Mysteries, doubts, without any irritable reaching after fact & reason." *Penetralium* (more correctly, *penetralia*) refers to an innermost and holy area, usually said of a religious sanctuary, but Keats clearly uses the word to mean an unseen, remote, mysterious, and divine center of inspiration.

thoughts and ideas should be retained because they came to him from a mysterious and transcendent power. His revisions were therefore intended to bring his poems into line with his original inspiration.

Wordsworth's Poetic Diction

Wordsworth's poetry marks a unique turn that reflects not only developing democratic ideals but also the emphasis on direct and everyday language that had been a major goal of the scientific revolution begun more than a century earlier with the founding of the English Royal Society (1661). His ideas about poetic diction are found in his "Preface." He seeks to use words as denotatively as possible, and his aim is that the words should be "the real language of men in a state of vivid sensation." (He repeats the phrase "real language" a number of times.) His aim is to "look steadily" at his subject and to use the vocabulary of prose as his poetic medium, for, as he says, "there neither is, nor can be, any *essential* difference between the language of prose and metrical composition."

Wordsworth's theory about poetic language is consistent with his ideas about the nature of poetry: The poet's obligation is to render experiences accurately and to express them without resorting to traditional poetic conventions, which tend to divert the poem from its goal of re-creating the experiences. The object of poets, in short, is to connect their own imaginations with the imaginations of readers and to enable readers to duplicate or share the poet's heightened awareness. Such a theory of poetic language constitutes a marked change in poetic practice and theory, one we see continuing in much modern poetry.

BIBLIOGRAPHIC SOURCES

The standard edition of Wordsworth is Ernest De Selincourt and Helen Darbishire, eds., *The Poetical Works of William Wordsworth* in five volumes (Oxford: Clarendon, 1940–49; Volumes I–III were revised from 1952–54). Cornell University Press has been publishing *The Cornell Wordsworth* in separate volumes since 1975. These volumes are based on manuscript as well as published versions of the poems, and they are considered definitive. Standard one-volume editions are Andrew J. George, ed., *The Complete Poetical Works of Wordsworth* (Boston: Houghton Mifflin, 1932; frequently reprinted); Stephen Gill, ed., *William Wordsworth: A Life* (Oxford: Oxford UP, 1989); and John O. Hayden, ed., *William Wordsworth: The Poems*, 2 vols. (London: Penguin, 1977, rpt. 1989). The works first published in *Lyrical Ballads* are available in R. L. Brett and A. R. Jones, eds., *Lyrical Ballads: Wordsworth and Coleridge; The Text of the 1798 Edition with the Additional 1800 Poems and Prefaces* (New York: Barnes and Noble, 1963). Readily available selections of the poetry are the Penguin Classics edition by John O. Hayden, ed., *William Wordsworth: Selected Poems* (New York: Penguin, 1994), and Nicholas Roe, ed., *William Wordsworth: Selected Poetry* (London: Penguin, 1992). Another excellent selection is Jack Stillinger, ed.,

William Wordsworth: Selected Poems and Prefaces, Riverside Editions (Boston: Houghton Mifflin, 1965).

A brief critical biography is by Russell Noyes, *William Wordsworth,* 1971, revised by John O. Hayden (New York: Twayne, 1991). A fully illustrated brief biography (photographs, drawings, paintings) is F. E. Halliday, *Wordsworth and His World* (New York: Viking, 1970). A recent biography is Kenneth R. Johnston, *The Hidden Wordsworth: Poet, Lover, Rebel, Spy* (New York: Norton, 1999). Lane Cooper's *A Concordance to the Poems of Wordsworth* (London, 1911) is essential for studying Wordsworth's words and therefore his ideas.

Significant criticism is found in F. W. Bateson, *Wordsworth: A Re-Interpretation,* 2nd ed. (London: Longmans, 1956); Helen Darbishire, *The Poet Wordsworth* (Oxford: Clarendon, 1950, rpt. 1980); Alan Grob, *The Philosophic Mind: A Study of Wordsworth's Poetry and Thought,* 1797–1805 (Columbus: Ohio State UP, 1973); Richard E. Brantley, *Wordsworth's "Natural Methodism"* (New Haven: Yale UP, 1975); John Purkis, *A Preface to Wordsworth* (New York: Scribner, 1970; Thomas McFarland, *William Wordsworth: Intensity and Achievement* (Oxford: Clarendon, 1992); and John O. Hayden, *William Wordsworth and the Mind of Man: The Poet as Thinker* (Bibliophile Press, 1993). Useful collections of selected criticism are Meyer H. Abrams, ed., *Wordsworth: A Collection of Critical Essays* (Englewood Cliffs: Prentice Hall, 1972); Jack M. Davis, ed., *Discussions of William Wordsworth* (Boston: Heath, 1964); and Harold Bloom, ed., *William Wordsworth* (New York: Chelsea House, 1985). Lionel Trilling's *The Liberal Imagination: Essays on Literature and Society* (New York: Doubleday, 1953, rpt. 1976) contains a superb essay, "The Immortality Ode."

SPECIAL TOPICS FOR WRITING AND ARGUMENT ABOUT THE POETRY OF WORDSWORTH

1. The speakers of Wordsworth's poems: characteristics, observations, insights, philosophy.
2. Political ideas in Wordsworth's sonnets: attitudes toward freedom, human dignity. Implications for a democratic form of government.
3. The ideas and structure of "Ode: Intimations of Immortality from Recollections of Early Childhood."
4. Wordsworth's use of symbols: childhood, natural scenes, city vistas.
5. Wordsworth's poetic diction: description, action, introspection.
6. Wordsworth's (a) blank verse, (b) stanzaic poetry, (c) sonnets. His use of rhythm and rhyme.
7. Wordsworth's "cheerful faith": the moral effect of experience, the thoughts that lie too deep for tears.
8. Wordsworth's introduction of events of common life into his poetry.
9. Wordsworth's theory of poetic composition: the nature of the poet, the relationship of the poet to his audience, memory, emotion recollected in tranquillity.

10. Wordsworth as a topographic and landscape poet: description, response, meaning.

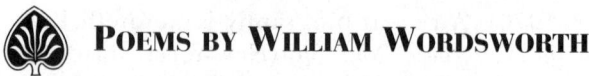

POEMS BY WILLIAM WORDSWORTH

BLANK VERSE POEMS

STANZAIC POEMS

SONNETS*

BLANK VERSE POETRY

From *The Prelude*, Book I,
Lines 301–474_____ *1850*

    Fair seed-time had my soul, and I grew up
Fostered alike by beauty and by fear:
Much favoured in my birth-place, and no less

In that beloved Vale to which erelong
We were transplanted—there were we let loose   305
For sports of wider range. Ere I had told
Ten birth-days, when among the mountain slopes
Frost, and the breath of frosty wind, had snapped
The last autumnal crocus, 'twas my joy
With store of springes o'er my shoulder hung   310
To range the open heights where woodcocks run
Along the smooth green turf. Through half the night,
Scudding away from snare to snare, I plied
That anxious visitation;—moon and stars
Were shining o'er my head. I was alone,   315
And seemed to be a trouble to the peace
That dwelt among them. Sometimes it befel
In these night wanderings, that a strong desire
O'erpowered my better reason, and the bird
Which was the captive of another's toil   320
Became my prey; and when the deed was done
I heard among the solitary hills
Low breathings coming after me, and sounds
Of undistinguishable motion, steps
Almost as silent as the turf they trod.   325

    Nor less when spring had warmed the cultured Vale,
Roved we as plunderers where the mother-bird
Had in high places built her lodge; though mean
Our object and inglorious, yet the end
Was not ignoble. Oh! when I have hung   330
Above the raven's nest, by knots of grass
And half-inch fissures in the slippery rock
But ill sustained, and almost (so it seemed)
Suspended by the blast that blew amain,
Shouldering the naked crag, oh, at that time   335
While on the perilous ridge I hung alone,
With what strange utterance did the loud dry wind
Blow through my ear! the sky seemed not a sky
Of earth—and with what motion moved the clouds!

    Dust as we are, the immortal spirit grows   340
Like harmony in music; there is a dark
Inscrutable workmanship that reconciles
Discordant elements, makes them cling together
In one society. How strange that all
The terror, pains, and early miseries,   345
Regrets, vexations, lassitudes interfused
Within my mind, should e'er have borne a part,
And that a needful part, in making up
The calm existence that is mine when I
Am worthy of myself! Praise to the end!   350

Thanks to the means which Nature deigned to employ;
Whether her fearless visitings, or those
That came with soft alarm, like hurtless light
Opening the peaceful clouds; or she may use
Severer interventions, ministry   355
More palpable, as best might suit her aim.

    One summer evening (led by her) I found
A little boat tied to a willow tree
Within a rocky cave, its usual home.
Straight I unloosed her chain, and stepping in   360
Pushed from the shore. It was an act of stealth
And troubled pleasure, nor without the voice
Of mountain-echoes did my boat move on;
Leaving behind her still, on either side,
Small circles glittering idly in the moon,   365
Until they melted all into one track
Of sparkling light. But now, like one who rows,
Proud of his skill, to reach a chosen point
With an unswerving line, I fixed my view
Upon the summit of a craggy ridge,   370
The horizon's utmost boundary; for above
Was nothing but the stars and the grey sky.
She was an elfin pinnace; lustily
I dipped my oars into the silent lake,
And, as I rose upon the stroke, my boat   375
Went heaving through the water like a swan;
When, from behind that craggy steep till then
The horizon's bound, a huge peak, black and huge,
As if with voluntary power instinct
Upreared its head. I struck and struck again,   380
And growing still in stature the grim shape
Towered up between me and the stars, and still,
For so it seemed, with purpose of its own
And measured motion like a living thing,
Strode after me. With trembling oars I turned,   385
And through the silent water stole my way
Back to the covert of the willow tree;
There in her mooring-place I left my bark,—
And through the meadows homeward went, in grave
And serious mood; but after I had seen   390
That spectacle, for many days, my brain
Worked with a dim and undetermined sense
Of unknown modes of being; o'er my thoughts
There hung a darkness, call it solitude
Or blank desertion. No familiar shapes   395
Remained, no pleasant images of trees,
Of sea or sky, no colours of green fields;
But huge and mighty forms, that do not live

Like living men, moved slowly through the mind
By day, and were a trouble to my dreams.   400

    Wisdom and Spirit of the universe!
Thou Soul that art the eternity of thought,
That givest to forms and images a breath
And everlasting motion, not in vain
By day or star-light thus from my first dawn   405
Of childhood didst thou intertwine for me
The passions that build up our human soul;
Not with the mean and vulgar works of man,
But with high objects, with enduring things—
With life and nature, purifying thus   410
The elements of feeling and of thought,
And sanctifying, by such discipline,
Both pain and fear, until we recognise
A grandeur in the beatings of the heart.
Nor was this fellowship vouchsafed to me   415
With stinted kindness. In November days,
When vapours rolling down the valley made
A lonely scene more lonesome, among woods,
At noon and 'mid the calm of summer nights,
When, by the margin of the trembling lake,   420
Beneath the gloomy hills homeward I went
In solitude, such intercourse was mine;
Mine was it in the fields both day and night,
And by the waters, all the summer long.

    And in the frosty season, when the sun   425
Was set, and visible for many a mile
The cottage windows blazed through twilight gloom,
I heeded not their summons: happy time
It was indeed for all of us—for me
It was a time of rapture! Clear and loud   430
The village clock tolled six,—I wheeled about,
Proud and exulting like an untired horse
That cares not for his home. All shod with steel,
We hissed along the polished ice in games
Confederate, imitative of the chase   435
And woodland pleasures,—the resounding horn,
The pack loud chiming, and the hunted hare.
So through the darkness and the cold we flew,
And not a voice was idle; with the din
Smitten, the precipices rang aloud;   440
The leafless trees and every icy crag
Tinkled like iron; while far distant hills
Into the tumult sent an alien sound
Of melancholy not unnoticed, while the stars
Eastward were sparkling clear, and in the west   445
The orange sky of evening died away.

Not seldom from the uproar I retired
Into a silent bay, or sportively
Glanced sideway, leaving the tumultuous throng,
To cut across the reflex of a star   450
That fled, and, flying still before me, gleamed
Upon the glassy plain; and oftentimes,
When we had given our bodies to the wind,
And all the shadowy banks on either side
Came sweeping through the darkness, spinning still   455
The rapid line of motion, then at once
Have I, reclining back upon my heels,
Stopped short; yet still the solitary cliffs
Wheeled by me—even as if the earth had rolled
With visible motion her diurnal round!   46(
Behind me did they stretch in solemn train,
Feebler and feebler, and I stood and watched
Till all was tranquil as a dreamless sleep.

    Ye Presences of Nature in the sky
And on the earth! Ye Visions of the hills!   46.
And Souls of lonely places! can I think
A vulgar hope was yours when ye employed
Such ministry, when ye through many a year
Haunting me thus among my boyish sports,
On caves and trees, upon the woods and hills,   47
Impressed upon all forms the characters
Of danger or desire; and thus did make
The surface of the universal earth
With triumph and delight, with hope and fear,
Work like a sea?   4'

Lines Composed a Few Miles above Tintern Abbey on Revisiting the Banks of the Wye During a Tour, June 13, 1798° _____ *1798*

Five years have past; five summers, with the length
Of five long winters! and again I hear
These waters, rolling from their mountain-springs
With a soft inland murmur.—Once again
Do I behold these steep and lofty cliffs,
That on a wild secluded scene impress
Thoughts of more deep seclusion, and connect
The landscape with the quiet of the sky.
The day is come when I again repose

LINES COMPOSED ABOVE TINTERN ABBEY.   Wordsworth first visited the valley of the Wye
in southwest England in August 1793 at age twenty-three. On this second visit he was accompanied by his sister Dorothy (the "friend" in line 115).

Here, under this dark sycamore, and view   10
These plots of cottage-ground, these orchard-tufts,
Which at this season, with their unripe fruits,
Are clad in one green hue, and lose themselves
'Mid groves and copses. Once again I see
These hedge-rows, hardly hedge-rows, little lines   15
Of sportive wood run wild; these pastoral farms,
Green to the very door; and wreaths of smoke
Sent up, in silence, from among the trees!
With some uncertain notice, as might seem
Of vagrant dwellers in the houseless woods,   20
Or of some Hermit's cave, where by his fire
The Hermit sits alone.
                              These beauteous forms,
Through a long absence, have not been to me
As is a landscape to a blind man's eye:
But oft, in lonely rooms, and 'mid the din   25
Of towns and cities, I have owed to them
In hours of weariness, sensations sweet,
Felt in the blood, and felt along the heart;
And passing even into my purer mind,
With tranquil restoration:—feelings too   30
Of unremembered pleasure: such, perhaps,
As have no slight or trivial influence
On that best portion of a good man's life,
His little, nameless, unremembered acts
Of kindness and of love. Nor less, I trust,   35
To them I may have owed another gift,
Of aspect more sublime; that blessed mood,
In which the burden of the mystery,
In which the heavy and the weary weight
Of all this unintelligible world,   40
Is lightened:—that serene and blessed mood,
In which the affections gently lead us on,—
Until, the breath of this corporeal frame
And even the motion of our human blood
Almost suspended, we are laid asleep   45
In body, and become a living soul:
While with an eye made quiet by the power
Of harmony, and the deep power of joy,
We see into the life of things.
                              If this
Be but a vain belief, yet, oh!—how oft—   50
In darkness and amid the many shapes
Of joyless daylight; when the fretful stir
Unprofitable, and the fever of the world,
Have hung upon the beatings of my heart—
How oft, in spirit, have I turned to thee,   55
O sylvan Wye! thou wanderer thro' the woods,

How often has my spirit turned to thee!
  And now, with gleams of half extinguished thought,
With many recognitions dim and faint,
And somewhat of a sad perplexity,   60
The picture of the mind revives again:
While here I stand, not only with the sense
Of present pleasure, but with pleasing thoughts
That in this moment there is life and food
For future years. And so I dare to hope,   65
Though changed, no doubt, from what I was when first
I came among these hills; when like a roe
I bounded o'er the mountains, by the sides
Of the deep rivers, and the lonely streams,
Wherever nature led: more like a man   70
Flying from something that he dreads, than one
Who sought the thing he loved. For nature then
(The coarser pleasures of my boyish days,
And their glad animal movements all gone by)
To me was all in all.—I cannot paint   75
What then I was. The sounding cataract
Haunted me like a passion: the tall rock,
The mountain, and the deep and gloomy wood,
Their colours, and their forms, were then to me
An appetite; a feeling and a love,   80
That had no need of a remoter charm,
By thought supplied, nor any interest
Unborrowed from the eye.—That time is past,
And all its aching joys are now no more,
And all its dizzy raptures. Not for this   85
Faint I, nor mourn nor murmur; other gifts
Have followed; for such loss, I would believe,
Abundant recompense. For I have learned
To look on nature, not as in the hour
Of thoughtless youth; but hearing oftentimes
The still, sad music of humanity,
Nor harsh nor grating, though of ample power
To chasten and subdue. And I have felt
A presence that disturbs me with the joy
Of elevated thoughts; a sense sublime
Of something far more deeply interfused,
Whose dwelling is the light of setting suns,
And the round ocean, and the living air,
And the blue sky, and in the mind of man;
A motion and a spirit, that impels
All thinking things, all objects of all thought,
And rolls through all things. Therefore am I still
A lover of the meadows and the woods,
And mountains; and of all that we behold
From this green earth; of all the mighty world

Of eye, and ear,—both what they half create,
And what perceive; well pleased to recognize
In nature and the language of the sense,
The anchor of my purest thoughts, the nurse,
The guide, the guardian of my heart, and soul   110
Of all my moral being.
                              Nor perchance,
If I were not thus taught, should I the more
Suffer my genial spirits to decay:
For thou art with me here upon the banks
Of this fair river; thou my dearest Friend,   115
My dear, dear Friend; and in thy voice I catch
The language of my former heart, and read
My former pleasures in the shooting lights
Of thy wild eyes. Oh! yet a little while
May I behold in thee what I was once,   120
My dear, dear Sister! and this prayer I make,
Knowing that Nature never did betray
The heart that loved her; 'tis her privilege,
Through all the years of this our life, to lead
From joy to joy: for she can so inform   125
The mind that is within us, so impress
With quietness and beauty, and so feed
With lofty thoughts, that neither evil tongues,
Rash judgments, nor the sneers of selfish men,
Nor greetings where no kindness is, nor all   130
The dreary intercourse of daily life,
Shall e'er prevail against us, or disturb
Our cheerful faith that all which we behold
Is full of blessings. Therefore let the moon
Shine on thee in thy solitary walk;   135
And let the misty mountain-winds be free
To blow against thee: and, in after years,
When these wild ecstasies shall be matured
Into a sober pleasure; when thy mind
Shall be a mansion for all lovely forms,   140
Thy memory be as a dwelling-place
For all sweet sounds and harmonies; oh! then,
If solitude, or fear, or pain, or grief,
Should be thy portion, with what healing thoughts
Of tender joy wilt thou remember me,   145
And these my exhortations! Nor, perchance—
If I should be where I no more can hear
Thy voice, nor catch from thy wild eyes these gleams
Of past existence—wilt thou then forget
That on the banks of this delightful stream   150
We stood together; and that I, so long
A worshipper of Nature, hither came
Unwearied in that service: rather say

With warmer love—oh! with far deeper zeal
Of holier love. Nor wilt thou then forget,   155
That after many wanderings, many years
Of absence, these steep woods and lofty cliffs,
And this green pastoral landscape, were to me
More dear, both for themselves and for thy sake!   160

STANZAIC POEMS

Daffodils (I Wandered Lonely as a Cloud) _____ *1807 (1804)*

I wandered lonely as a cloud
That floats on high o'er vales and hills,
When all at once I saw a crowd,
A host, of golden daffodils;
Beside the lake, beneath the trees,
Fluttering and dancing in the breeze.

Continuous as the stars that shine
And twinkle on the milky way,
They stretched in never-ending line
Along the margin of a bay: 1
Ten thousand saw I at a glance,
Tossing their heads in sprightly dance.

The waves beside them danced; but they
Out-did the sparkling waves in glee:
A poet could not but be gay,
In such a jocund° company: *cheerful, merry*
I gazed—and gazed—but little thought
What wealth the show to me had brought:

For oft, when on my couch I lie
In vacant or in pensive mood,
They flash upon that inward eye
Which is the bliss of solitude;
And then my heart with pleasure fills,
And dances with the daffodils.

Wordsworth's note: "Written at Town-end, Grasmere. Daffodils grew and still grow on the margin of Ullswater, and probably may be seen to this day as beautiful in the month of March, nodding their golden heads beside the dancing and foaming waves." Wordsworth also pointed out that lines 21 and 22, the "best lines," were by his wife, Mary.

Lines Written in Early Spring _____ *1798*

I heard a thousand blended notes,
While in a grove I sate° reclined,   *sat*
In that sweet mood when pleasant thoughts
Bring sad thoughts to the mind.

To her fair works did Nature link   5
The human soul that through me ran;
And much it grieved my heart to think
What man has made of man.

Through primrose tufts, in that green bower,
The periwinkle° trailed its wreaths;   10
And 'tis my faith that every flower
Enjoys the air it breathes.

The birds around me hopped and played,
Their thoughts I cannot measure—
But the least motion which they made,   15
It seemed a thrill of pleasure.

The budding twigs spread out their fan,
To catch the breezy air;
And I must think, do all I can,
That there was pleasure there.   20

If this belief from heaven be sent,
If such be Nature's holy plan,
Have I not reason to lament
What man has made of man?

LINES WRITTEN IN EARLY SPRING.   10 *periwinkle:* a trailing evergreen plant with blue or white flowers.

Ode: Intimations of Immortality from Recollections of Early Childhood ———————————————————————— *1807*

> *The Child is Father of the Man;*
> *And I could wish my days to be*
> *Bound each to each by natural piety.*

I

There was a time when meadow, grove, and stream,
The earth, and every common sight,
        To me did seem
        Apparelled in celestial light,
The glory and the freshness of a dream.   5
It is not now as it hath been of yore;—
        Turn wheresoe'er I may,
        By night or day,
The things which I have seen I now can see no more.

II

        The Rainbow comes and goes,   10
        And lovely is the Rose;

> The Moon doth with delight
> Look round her when the heavens are bare;
> Waters on a starry night
> Are beautiful and fair;
> The sunshine is a glorious birth;
> But yet I know, where'er I go,
> That there hath past away a glory from the earth.

III

> Now, while the birds thus sing a joyous song,
> And while the young lambs bound
> As to the tabor's sound,
> To me alone there came a thought of grief:
> A timely utterance gave that thought relief,
> And I again am strong:
> The cataracts blow their trumpets from the steep;
> No more shall grief of mine the season wrong;
> I hear the Echoes through the mountains throng,
> The Winds come to me from the fields of sleep,
> And all the earth is gay;
> Land and sea
> Give themselves up to jollity,
> And with the heart of May
> Doth every Beast keep holiday;—
> Thou Child of Joy,
> Shout round me, let me hear thy shouts, thou happy
> Shepherd-boy!

IV

> Ye blessèd Creatures, I have heard the call
> Ye to each other make; I see
> The heavens laugh with you in your jubilee;
> My heart is at your festival,
> My head hath its coronal,
> The fulness of your bliss, I feel—I feel it all.
> Oh evil day! if I were sullen
> While Earth herself is adorning,
> This sweet May-morning,
> And the Children are culling
> On every side,
> In a thousand valleys far and wide,
> Fresh flowers; while the sun shines warm,
> And the Babe leaps up on his Mother's arm:—
> I hear, I hear, with joy I hear!
> —But there's a Tree, of many, one,
> A single Field which I have looked upon,
> Both of them speak of something that is gone:
> The Pansy at my feet

15

20

25

30

35

Doth the same tale repeat:
Whither is fled the visionary gleam?
Where is it now, the glory and the dream?

V

Our birth is but a sleep and a forgetting:
The Soul that rises with us, our life's Star,   60
    Hath had elsewhere its setting,
        And cometh from afar:
    Not in entire forgetfulness,
    And not in utter nakedness,
But trailing clouds of glory do we come   65
    From God, who is our home:
Heaven lies about us in our infancy!
Shades of the prison-house begin to close
    Upon the growing Boy,
        But He   70
Beholds the light, and whence it flows,
    He sees it in his joy;
The Youth, who daily farther from the east
    Must travel, still is Nature's Priest,
    And by the vision splendid   75
    Is on his way attended;
At length the Man perceives it die away,
And fade into the light of common day.

VI

Earth fills her lap with pleasures of her own;
Yearnings she hath in her own natural kind,   80
And, even with something of a Mother's mind,
    And no unworthy aim,
    The homely Nurse doth all she can
To make her Foster-child, her Inmate Man,
    Forget the glories he hath known,   85
And that imperial palace whence he came.

VII

Behold the Child among his new-born blisses,
A six years' Darling of a pigmy size!
See, where 'mid work of his own hand he lies,
Fretted by sallies of his mother's kisses,
With light upon him from his father's eyes!   90
See, at his feet, some little plan or chart,
Some fragment from his dream of human life,
Shaped by himself with newly-learnèd art;
    A wedding or a festival,   95
    A mourning or a funeral;
    And this hath now his heart,

And unto this he frames his song:
　　Then will he fit his tongue   100
To dialogues of business, love, or strife;
　　But it will not be long
　　Ere this be thrown aside,
　　And with new joy and pride
The little Actor cons another part;   105
Filling from time to time his 'humorous stage'
With all the Persons, down to palsied Age,
That Life brings with her in her equipage;
　　As if his whole vocation
　　Were endless imitation.

VIII

Thou, whose exterior semblance doth belie   11(
　　Thy Soul's immensity;
Thou best Philosopher, who yet dost keep
Thy heritage, thou Eye among the blind,
That, deaf and silent, read'st the eternal deep,
Haunted for ever by the eternal mind,—   11
　　Mighty Prophet! Seer blest!
　　On whom those truths do rest,
Which we are toiling all our lives to find,
In darkness lost, the darkness of the grave;
Thou, over whom thy Immortality   12
Broods like the Day, a Master o'er a Slave,
A Presence which is not to be put by;
Thou little Child, yet glorious in the might
Of heaven-born freedom on thy being's height,
Why with such earnest pains dost thou provoke   1!
The years to bring the inevitable yoke,
Thus blindly with thy blessedness at strife?
Full soon thy Soul shall have her earthly freight,
And custom lie upon thee with a weight,
Heavy as frost, and deep almost as life!   1

IX

　　O joy! that in our embers
　　Is something that doth live,
　　That nature yet remembers
　　What was so fugitive!
The thought of our past years in me doth breed
Perpetual benediction: not indeed
For that which is most worthy to be blest;
Delight and liberty, the simple creed
Of Childhood, whether busy or at rest,
With new-fledged hope still fluttering in his breast:—
　　Not for these I raise

The song of thanks and praise;
But for those obstinate questionings
Of sense and outward things,
Fallings from us, vanishings;   145
    Blank misgivings of a Creature
Moving about in worlds not realized,
High instincts before which our mortal Nature
Did tremble like a guilty Thing surprised:
        But for those first affections,   150
        Those shadowy recollections,
    Which, be they what they may,
Are yet the fountain light of all our day,
Are yet a master light of all our seeing;
        Uphold us, cherish, and have power to make   155
Our noisy years seem moments in the being
Of the eternal Silence: truths that wake,
        To perish never;
    Which neither listlessness, nor mad endeavour,
        Nor Man nor Boy,   160
Nor all that is at enmity with joy,
Can utterly abolish or destroy!
        Hence in a season of calm weather
        Though inland far we be,
Our Souls have sight of that immortal sea   165
        Which brought us hither,
    Can in a moment travel thither,
And see the Children sport upon the shore,
And hear the mighty waters rolling evermore.

                        X
Then sing, ye Birds, sing, sing a joyous song!   170
        And let the young Lambs bound
        As to the tabor's sound!
We in thought will join your throng,
        Ye that pipe and ye that play,
        Ye that through your hearts today   175
        Feel the gladness of the May!
What though the radiance which was once so bright
Be now for ever taken from my sight,
        Though nothing can bring back the hour
Of splendour in the grass, of glory in the flower;   180
        We will grieve not, rather find
        Strength in what remains behind;
        In the primal sympathy
        Which having been must ever be;
        In the soothing thoughts that spring   185
        Out of human suffering;
        In the faith that looks through death,
In years that bring the philosophic mind.

XI

And O, ye Fountains, Meadows, Hills, and Groves,
Forebode not any severing of our loves!   190
Yet in my heart of hearts I feel your might;
I only have relinquished one delight
To live beneath your more habitual sway.
I love the Brooks which down their channels fret,
Even more than when I tripped lightly as they;   195
The innocent brightness of a new-born Day
      Is lovely yet;
The Clouds that gather round the setting sun
Do take a sober colouring from an eye
That hath kept watch o'er man's mortality;   200
Another race hath been, and other palms are won.
Thanks to the human heart by which we live,
Thanks to its tenderness, its joys, and fears,
To me the meanest flower that blows can give
Thoughts that do often lie too deep for tears.   20⅝

Expostulation and Reply ———————————————————————— *1798*

"Why, William, on that old grey stone,
Thus for the length of half a day,
Why, William, sit you thus alone,
And dream your time away?

"Where are your books?—that light bequeathed
To Beings else forlorn and blind!
Up! up! and drink the spirit breathed
From dead men to their kind.

"You look round on your Mother Earth,
As if she for no purpose bore you;
As if you were her first-born birth,
And none had lived before you!"

One morning thus, by Esthwaite lake,
When life was sweet, I knew not why,
To me my good friend Matthew spake,
And thus I made reply.

"The eye—it cannot choose but see;
We cannot bid the ear be still;
Our bodies feel, where'er they be,
Against or with our will.

"Nor less I deem that there are Powers
Which of themselves our minds impress;
That we can feed this mind of ours
In a wise passiveness.

"Think you, 'mid all this mighty sum   25
Of things for ever speaking,
That nothing of itself will come,
But we must still be seeking?

"—Then ask not wherefore, here, alone,
Conversing as I may,   30
I sit upon this old grey stone,
And dream my time away."

The Tables Turned _____ *1798*

An Evening Scene on the Same Subject

Up! up! my Friend, and quit your books;
Or surely you'll grow double:
Up! up! my Friend, and clear your looks;
Why all this toil and trouble?

The sun, above the mountain's head,   5
A freshening lustre mellow
Through all the long green fields has spread,
His first sweet evening yellow.

Books! 'tis a dull and endless strife:
Come, hear the woodland linnet,   10
How sweet his music! on my life,
There's more of wisdom in it.

And hark! how blithe the throstle sings!
He, too, is no mean preacher:
Come forth into the light of things,   15
Let Nature be your Teacher.

She has a world of ready wealth,
Our minds and hearts to bless—
Spontaneous wisdom breathed by health,
Truth breathed by cheerfulness.   20

One impulse from a vernal wood
May teach you more of man,
Of moral evil and of good,
Than all the sages can.

Sweet is the lore which Nature brings;   25
Our meddling intellect
Mis-shapes the beauteous forms of things:—
We murder to dissect.

Enough of Science and of Art;
Close up those barren leaves;   30

Come forth, and bring with you a heart
That watches and receives.

Stepping Westward _____ *1807*

"What, you are stepping westward?"—"Yea."
—'Twould be a *wildish* destiny,
If we, who thus together roam
In a strange Land, and far from home,
Were in this place the guests of Chance: 5
Yet who would stop, or fear to advance,
Though home or shelter he had none,
With such a sky to lead him on?

The dewy ground was dark and cold;
Behind, all gloomy to behold;   1
And stepping westward seemed to be
A kind of *heavenly* destiny:
I liked the greeting; 'twas a sound
Of something without place or bound;
And seemed to give me spiritual right   1
To travel through that region bright.

The voice was soft, and she who spake
Was walking by her native lake:
The salutation had to me
The very sound of courtesy: 2
Its power was felt; and while my eye
Was fixed upon the glowing Sky,
The echo of the voice enwrought
A human sweetness with the thought
Of travelling through the world that lay
Before me in my endless way.

Wordsworth's note: While my Fellow-traveller and I were walking by the side of Loch Ketterine, one fine evening after sunset, in our road to a Hut where, in the course of our Tour, we had been hospitably entertained some weeks before, we met, in one of the loneliest parts of that solitary region, two well-dressed Women, one of whom said to us, by way of greeting, "What, you are stepping westward?"

The Solitary Reaper _____ *1807*

Behold her, single in the field,
Yon solitary Highland Lass!
Reaping and singing by herself;
Stop here, or gently pass!

Alone she cuts and binds the grain,
And sings a melancholy strain;

O listen! for the Vale profound
Is overflowing with the sound.

No Nightingale did ever chaunt
More welcome notes to weary bands   10
Of travelers in some shady haunt,
Among Arabian sands;
A voice so thrilling ne'er was heard
In springtime from the Cuckoo bird,
Breaking the silence of the seas   15
Among the farthest Hebrides.°

Will no one tell me what she sings?°
Perhaps the plaintive numbers flow
For old, unhappy, far-off things,
And battles long ago;   20
Or is it some more humble lay,
Familiar matter of today?
Some natural sorrow, loss, or pain,
That has been, and may be again?

Whate'er the theme, the Maiden sang   25
As if her song could have no ending;
I saw her singing at her work,
And o'er the sickle bending—

I listened, motionless and still;
And, as I mounted up the hill,   30
The music in my heart I bore,
Long after it was heard no more.

THE SOLITARY REAPER.   16 *Hebrides*: a group of islands off the west coast of Scotland.
17 *Will . . . sings:* The speaker does not understand Scots Gaelic, the language in which the woman
sings.

SONNETS*

Composed upon Westminster Bridge, September 3, 1802 _____ *1807*

Earth has not any thing to show more fair:
Dull would he be of soul who could pass by
A sight so touching in its majesty:
This City now doth, like a garment, wear
The beauty of the morning; silent, bare,   5
Ships, towers, domes, theatres, and temples lie
Open unto the fields, and to the sky;
All bright and glittering in the smokeless air.
Never did sun more beautifully steep

* See also "London, 1802," p. 799.

In his first splendour, valley, rock, or hill;   10
Ne'er saw I, never felt, a calm so deep!
The river glideth at his own sweet will:
Dear God! the very houses seem asleep;
And all that mighty heart is lying still!

I Grieved for Buonaparté, with a Vain _____ *1807*

I grieved for Buonaparté, with a vain
And an unthinking grief! The tenderest mood
Of that Man's mind—what can it be? what food
Fed his first hopes? what knowledge could *he* gain?
'Tis not in battles that from youth we train   5
The Governor who must be wise and good,
And temper with the sternness of the brain
Thoughts motherly, and meek as womanhood.
Wisdom doth live with children round her knees:
Books, leisure, perfect freedom, and the talk   10
Man holds with week-day man in the hourly walk
Of the mind's business: these are the degrees
By which true Sway doth mount; this is the stalk
True Power doth grow on; and her rights are these.

It Is a Beauteous Evening, Calm and Free _____ *1807*

It is a beauteous evening calm and free,
The holy time is quiet as a Nun
Breathless with adoration; the broad sun
Is sinking down in its tranquillity;
The gentleness of heaven broods o'er the Sea:
Listen! the mighty Being is awake,
And doth with his eternal motion make
A sound like thunder—everlastingly.
Dear Child! dear Girl! that walkest with me here,
If thou appear untouched by solemn thought,
Thy nature is not therefore less divine:
Thou liest in Abraham's bosom all the year;
And worshipp'st at the Temple's inner shrine,
God being with thee when we know it not.

On the Extinction of the Venetian Republic _____ *1807*

Once did She hold the gorgeous east in fee;
And was the safeguard of the west: the worth
Of Venice did not fall below her birth,
Venice, the eldest Child of Liberty.
She was a maiden City, bright and free;

No guile seduced, no force could violate;
And, when she took unto herself a Mate,
She must espouse the everlasting Sea.
And what if she had seen those glories fade,   10
Those titles vanish, and that strength decay;
Yet shall some tribute of regret be paid
When her long life hath reached its final day:
Men are we, and must grieve when even the Shade
Of that which once was great, is passed away.   15

Scorn Not the Sonnet ———————————————————— *1827*

Scorn not the Sonnet; Critic, you have frowned,
Mindless of its just honours, with this key
Shakespeare unlocked his heart; the melody
Of this small lute gave ease to Petrarch's wound;
A thousand times this pipe did Tasso sound;   5
With it Camoëns soothed an exile s grief;
The Sonnet glittered a gay myrtle leaf
Amid the cypress with which Dante crowned
His visionary brow: a glow-worm lamp,
It cheered mild Spenser, called from Faery-land   10
To struggle through dark ways; and, when a damp
Fell round the path of Milton, in his hand
The Thing became a trumpet; whence he blew
Soul-animating strains—alas, too few!

To Toussaint L'Ouverture ——————————————— *1807*

Toussaint,° the most unhappy man of men!
Whether the whistling Rustic tend his plough
Within thy hearing, or thy head be now
Pillowed in some deep dungeon's earless den;—
O miserable Chieftain! where and when   5
Wilt thou find patience? Yet die not; do thou
Wear rather in thy bonds a cheerful brow:
Though fallen thyself, never to rise again,
Live, and take comfort. Thou hast left behind
Powers that will work for thee, air, earth, and skies;   10
There's not a breathing of the common wind
That will forget thee; thou hast great allies;
Thy friends are exultations, agonies,
And love, and man's unconquerable mind.

TO TOUSSAINT L'OUVERTURE.   1 *Toussaint:* Haitian revolutionary leader imprisoned by
Napoleon.

EMILY DICKINSON   (1830–1886)

Life and Work

Emily Elizabeth Dickinson, who is acknowledged as one of America's greatest poets, was born on December 10, 1830. She was raised in Amherst, Massachusetts, which in the nineteenth century was a small and tradition-bound town. Dominating the Dickinson family was Emily's father Edward, a lawyer, a legislator, and also a rigorous Calvinist, whose concept of life was stern religious observance and obedience to God's laws. Emily was taken to Sunday School, but late in her teens she declined to pronounce herself a believing Christian. She spent a number of years at primary school and eventually studied classics at Amherst Academy. She also enrolled at the South Hadley Seminary for Women (now Mount Holyoke College), but her parents withdrew her after a year because of ill health. At about this time she sat for a photograph, a daguerreotype showing her as a slender young woman. It is the only reliable likeness.[*]

During these years of childood and youth, she led a normally active life. She saw many people, liked school and her teachers, wrote essays, acquired a number of good friends, gossiped, sang at the piano to her own accompaniment, treasured spring flowers, amused her friends with impromptu stories, studied theology, read Pope's *Essay on Man,* and planned to become the "Belle of Amherst" at the age of seventeen. She also began writing poetry, which consisted mainly of occasional verses and valentines.

After leaving school she returned home. She was to spend the rest of her life there, sharing in family and household duties. In 1856 she won a second prize at the local fair for her recipe for rye and Indian bread. She took occasional trips, including long stays in Boston in 1864 and 1865 to be treated for an undisclosed eye ailment. Eventually, however, she stopped traveling altogether.

She included a number of men among her friends and correspondents. One was Benjamin Newton, a law student whom she met in 1848 and who undertook to guide her reading. This guidance was cut short, however, because Newton married, moved away, and died of tuberculosis in 1853. The second man was Reverend Charles Wadsworth, a Philadelphia minister whom she met in 1854. She regarded him as an intellectual adviser and her "dearest earthly friend." Her poetic activity increased considerably during the time she knew and corresponded with him, particularly after he left for San Francisco in 1862 to accept a ministerial call. The two saw each other only once more, in 1880, when he returned for a visit.

---

[*]Richard B. Sewall, includes a photograph of a young woman as the frontispiece of the second volume of his *The Life of Emily Dickinson* (1974). On the back of the original is written "Emily Dickenson 1860" in an unknown hand, and the features of the portrayed woman are consistent with those in the daguerrotype of Dickinson at seventeen. Although it is tempting to consider this photograph genuine, the attribution has been discredited. Still another photograph has come to light that may show Dickinson at the age of about 30–35. As yet the photo, an albumen print with Dickinson's name on the back, has not been authenticated, but it is fair to say that its resemblance to the one authentic photo is uncanny. See *The New Yorker* of May 22, 2000, pp. 30–31.

Emily Dickinson

After Wadsworth's departure, Dickinson began corresponding with Thomas Higginson, a literary critic and Civil War hero who had written an article encouraging young writers. She sent him some of her poetry and asked if her verses "breathed" enough to warrant publication. She may have viewed Higginson as another mentor, but she soon discovered that his literary judgments were stultifying. Indeed, some critics conclude that his inability to understand her poetic methods was a major reason she did not publish collections of her poems during her lifetime. He visited her in August 1870 and noted her nervousness and her girlish energy (she was 39 at the time). He listened more than he spoke, believing that to interrupt her would cause her to withdraw from conversation. Later he wrote that she exhibited a unique capacity to drain his "nerve power" and that he was therefore glad he did not live near her. Ironically, Higginson became one of the first editors of her work after her death in 1886.

Still another man of importance to her, to whom she wrote often, was Otis Lord, a judge who had been her father's closest friend (her father died in 1874). Lord was a regular guest in the Dickinson household. He and Dickinson seem to have loved each other, for he proposed marriage to her in 1878. She did not love him sufficiently to accept his offer, but afterwards the two continued to remain on good terms.

Although Dickinson had written poems since her school days, she did not devote herself to poetry until her late twenties—in about 1858. After this time her poetic output expanded, almost miraculously. Many of her poems are quite short, consisting of no more than a single stanza, but some are much longer. No more than ten of them were published during her lifetime, mostly against her wishes. Instead, her "publication" consisted of making fair copies of the poems in longhand (her writing is difficult to read). In the privacy of her own room she put numbers of poems together in what were later called "fascicles," which consisted of folded sheets of stationery bound with thread. These handwritten copies were for her eyes only, although she frequently sent copies in letters and also sent batches of poems to friends. The poems she didn't prepare carefully for her fascicles were kept in little packets. She locked away all these private literary treasures, which were discovered only after her death.

In all, 1,775 to 1,789 of her poems have been recovered. The figure 1,775 is the number of poems included by Thomas H. Johnson in his *The Complete Poems of Emily Dickinson* (1955), the first major complete edition of Dickinson's poetry. The figure 1,789 is the number included by Ralph W. Franklin in *The Poems of Emily Dickinson: Variorum Edition* (1998). Both editions are based on exhaustive studies of all the documentary evidence available at the times when the editors were doing their research. Beyond these major scholarly editions, a number of brief poems have been recently mined from Dickinson's letters and published, in 1993, as 498 new poems, on the theory that parts of the letters reach a succinctness and rhythm more characteristic of poetry than prose. These poems are short, some being no more than two lines long. If one accepts them as additional Dickinson poems, they bring the total count above 2,280.

At the same time Dickinson was creating this overwhelmingly large body of poetry, she also became reclusive. She removed herself from much of life's business, and she took to wearing only white dresses. Naturally, such behavior created interest and speculation. One of the stories about her was that her reclusiveness was so extreme that even when she gave gingerbread to local children she stayed at an upper window and lowered the sweets in a basket so that she might not be seen. Another was that she concealed herself behind doors when speaking to visitors (see "I Cannot Live with You," line 47). At first, at least, she was not housebound, for she shared both outside and inside household work, and she visited nearby friends. But by the time she was forty she refused invitations, staying almost exclusively in the family house. One of her major tasks was caring for her parents until they died. When she became an invalid herself during the last year of her life, she was cared for by her younger sister Lavinia. She died in May 1886.

POETIC CHARACTERISTICS

Dickinson's most productive years were between 1862 and 1865, when she wrote at least 760 poems. This amazingly high number is hard to account for on biographical grounds. As much as one can say is that, by her thirties, she had matured as an observer, thinker, and poet and that she compulsively turned to verse as the expression of her thought and meditation. What Dickinson sought in poetry—both what she read and what she wrote—was intensity more than form. When Thomas Higginson visited her in 1870, she declared her views positively. She said that if she was reading a book and found that

> it makes my whole body so cold no fire ever can warm me I know *that* is poetry. If I feel physically as if the top of my head were taken off, I know *that* is poetry. These are the only way I know it. Is there any other way.

In her poetry she successfully achieves such intensity. Her poems are energetic, imaginative, astoundingly creative, and also economical. Within a small number of lines she covers vast distances. Who but Dickinson, for example, could conceive the first line of "I Heard a Fly Buzz – When I Died," and even more, who could progress from this opening to the concluding sentence, "I could not see to see"? Because she covers so much territory, her style is sometimes elliptical and obscure, producing a rapid interplay of thoughts and images. Her diction is neutral, with a number of formal words that may be taken as evidence of her reading and general knowledge. In her desire for accuracy she regularly referred to Webster's *Dictionary*, one of the books she kept at her side. This fact has caused critics to observe that reading her poetry often requires the aid of a dictionary.

Her sentences are regularly broken by interjections and sentence fragments. She uses these grammatical irregularities deliberately, just as she employs capital letters to emphasize words. In addition, she indulges in eccentricities of punctuation. Because her poems are mostly private monologues, she usually ignores periods and commas, instead adopting dashes and exclamation points to mark rhythm and vocal modulations. To suggest varying degrees of expressiveness, she uses dashes of differing lengths, although printed texts obscure this subtlety.

Dickinson's earliest experiences with the poetry of others was with the quatrain form (see Chapter 20, p. 900), which abounds in the Protestant hymnals of the time. It is thus no surprise that in her own poems she most often uses common measure and the ballad stanza. She is no metronomic follower, however, for many of her stanzaic forms are irregular. She achieves flexibility and originality by shortening many lines, varying many of the meters, and freely inserting midline caesurae. She is a skilled rhymer, preferring exact rhymes but also using slant rhymes, eye rhymes, vowel rhymes, and repeated-word rhymes (*identical rhyme*). These irregularities, which confounded Dickinson's first editors, have since been recognized as important and effective elements of her poetic craft.

POETIC SUBJECTS

Although, as we have seen, a surprising amount of biographical information is available about Dickinson, the key details are missing—the connections between events in her life and her poems. For example, it seems obvious

that a real and powerful sadness underlies the poignant conclusion of "Safe in   0
Their Alabaster Chambers," just as a sense of personal inadequacy or reproach
may have caused her to write "I Felt a Funeral in My Brain." We can only guess,
however, about the specific situations that led her to write such poems.

Nevertheless, the general occasions inspiring some of her poems are
clear. The world she lived in was small, and she found subjects in her surroundings: house, garden, yard, and village. A lowly snake is the topic of one
of her poems—one of the few published when she was alive—as are butterflies, a singing oriole, and a vibrating hummingbird. She even wrote a poem
about the railroad locomotives servicing Amherst. Sometimes no more than a
recollection, a single word, a concept, or a paradox that arose from her own
interior monologue enabled her to originate poems. Such inspirations
account for topics such as a haunted mind, a memory, a state of solitude, the
nature of truth and beauty, the condition of self-reliance, the angle of winter
light. For one of the poems, "My Triumph Lasted Till the Drums," one may
postulate a connection with her thoughts about the Civil War. She was at the
height of her poetic power during this time, and she expresses feelings about
the horrors of the war in these ironic lines: "A Bayonet's contrition / Is nothing to the Dead."

Dickinson's poems on death and dying probably had occasional sources
also, even though these sources may be far removed from the time and circumstance of the poems. One of Dickinson's dearest childhood friends was
Sophia Holland, who died in 1844. Perhaps the loss of Sophia was one of her
memories when she wrote "I Never Lost as Much But Twice" and "This World Is
Not Conclusion," together with her other poems on death. (See pp. 1093-94.)

Much of her other poetry may have a similar if remote occasional origin.
She wrote poems about love and the psychology of personal relationships, even
though she never married or had a love affair that we know about. We may
therefore wonder about the internal necessity that caused her to write poems
like "Wild Nights – Wild Nights!" and "I Cannot Live with You," which portray
states of sexual ecstasy and final renunciation. And what sorts of personal experience and introspection underlay such poems as "After Great Pain, a Formal
Feeling Comes," "The Soul Selects Her Own Society," and "One Need Not Be a
Chamber — To Be Haunted"?

In the absence of specific details linking her life to her poetry, therefore,
the occasions of her poems must remain no more than peripherally relevant—
themselves unseen, though in the effects they remain. We are left to conclude
that her inspiration rose from within herself. She is a personal, contemplative,
confessional poet, whether she herself is the omnipresent "I" of her poems or
whether the "I" is an objective speaker to whom she assigns all the strength of
her imagination and her dreams. This speaker possesses bright wit, clever and
engaging playfulness, acute powers of observation, deep sensitivity, intense
introspection, and tender responsiveness. She is alive, quick, and inventive. She
enjoys riddles. She leads readers into new and unexplored regions of thought
and feeling.

All these characteristics are to be discovered everywhere in her poetry. Her speaker expresses a vital joy and delirious energy in the quizzical poem "I Taste a Liquor Never Brewed," an insouciant bluffness in "I'm Nobody! Who Are You?," inner terror in "One Need Not Be a Chamber – To Be Haunted," and overwhelming tenderness and regret at the end of "The Bustle in a House." In the last stanza of "I Cannot Live with You" she captures the deep anguish of a relationship that is ending:

> So We must meet apart –
> You there – I – here –
> With just the Door ajar
> That Oceans are – and Prayer –
> And that White Sustenance –
> Despair –

She is also reverent, and a number of poems introduce the topics of God, immortality, scripture, and the final judgment. But she can also be saucy and flippant about religion. Going to church on Sunday, for example, was expected of the dutiful Christian, but she explains why she prefers staying home with "a Bobolink for a Chorister":

> So instead of getting to Heaven, at last –
> I'm going, all along.

Undeniably, Dickinson's external daily life was uneventful. Her inner life was anything but uneventful, however, for she was always reflecting and thinking. What we know about her is that her inquiring and restless mind was the source of her compulsive poetic strength, and that her poetry expresses the vital personal feelings and psychological insights that emerged from her thoughts about life, love, death, Nature, and God. It is not possible to read her poems without revering her as a person and as a poet.

BIBLIOGRAPHIC SOURCES

After Dickinson died, her sister, Lavinia, was astonished to find the many fascicles and packets of poems that she had left. Lavinia recognized the significance of this work and eventually turned much of it over to Thomas Higginson and Mabel L. Todd for editing and publication. They published three separate volumes of Dickinson's verse (in 1890, 1891, and 1896), each containing about a hundred poems. In these volumes, the editors eliminated slant rhymes, smoothed out the meter, revised those metaphors that struck them as outrageous, and regularized the punctuation.

These well-intentioned editorial "adjustments" remained intact until 1955, when the Harvard University Press published Thomas H. Johnson's three-volume complete edition, which has already been mentioned. Johnson also published a single-volume edition of the poems in 1961 and, in addition, a paperback selection titled *Final Harvest: Emily Dickinson's Poems* (1961). Johnson's pioneering edition has been followed by the ambitious and comprehensive *The Poems of Emily Dickinson: Variorum Edition* in three volumes (Cambridge: Harvard UP, 1998), edited by Ralph W. Franklin, who also edited the facsimile edition of the handwritten poems, *The Manuscript Books of Emily Dickinson* (Cambridge: Harvard UP, 1981). The poems that have been extracted from Dickinson's letters, which we have already mentioned, were edited by William Shurr, with Anna Dunlap and Emily Shurr, as *New Poems of Emily Dickinson* (Chapel Hill: U of North Carolina P, 1993).

Definitive biographies of Dickinson are Richard B. Sewall, *The Life of Emily Dickinson* (New York: Farrar, 1974, rpt. 1980) and Cynthia Griffin Wolff, *Emily Dickinson* (New York: Knopf, 1986). A useful book containing biographical, critical, and many other details is Jane Donahue Eberwein, ed., *An Emily Dickinson Encyclopedia* (Westport: Greenwood, 1998). The numbers of important critical studies are legion. Some of these are Albert J. Gelpi, *Emily Dickinson: The Mind of the Poet* (Cambridge: Harvard UP, 1966); Joanne F. Diehl, *Dickinson and the Romantic Imagination* (Princeton: Princeton UP, 1981); David Porter, *Dickinson, the Modern Idiom* (Cambridge: Harvard UP, 1981); Susan Juhasz, *The Undiscovered Continent: Emily Dickinson and the Space of the Mind* (Bloomington: U of Indiana P, 1983); E. Miller Budick, *Emily Dickinson and the Life of Language: A Study in Symbolic Poetics* (Baton Rouge: Louisiana State UP, 1985); Donna Dickenson, *Emily Dickinson* (Leamington Spa: Berg, 1985); Sharon Leder and Andrea Abbott, *The Language of Exclusion: The Poetry of Emily Dickinson and Christina Rossetti* (New York: Greenwood, 1987); Cristanne Miller, *Emily Dickinson: A Poet's Grammar* (Cambridge: Harvard UP, 1987); Elizabeth Phillips, *Emily Dickinson: Personae and Performance* (University Park: Pennsylvania State UP, 1988); Joanne Dobson, *Dickinson and the Strategies of Reticence* (Bloomington: U of Indiana P, 1989); Paula Bennett, *Emily Dickinson: Woman Poet* (Iowa City: U of Iowa P, 1990); Gary Lee Stonum, *The Dickinson Sublime* (Madison: U of Wisconsin P, 1990); Joan Kirkby, *Emily Dickinson* (New York: St. Martin's, 1991); Judith Farr, *The Passion of Emily Dickinson* (Cambridge: Harvard UP, 1992); Claudia Ottlinger, *The Death-Motif in the Poetry of Emily Dickinson and Christina Rossetti* (Frankfurt: Lang, 1996); and Paul Crumbley, *Inflections of the Pen: Dash and Voice in Emily Dickinson* (Lexington: U of Kentucky P, 1996).

Collections of essays on Dickinson are Paul J. Ferlazzo, ed., *Critical Essays on Emily Dickinson* (Boston: Hall, 1958, a historical collection); Richard B. Sewall, ed., *Emily Dickinson: A Collection of Critical Essays* (Englewood Cliffs: Prentice Hall, 1963); Judith Farr, ed., *Emily Dickinson: A Collection of Critical Essays* (Upper Saddle River: Prentice Hall, 1996), and Gudrun Grabher et al., eds., *The Emily Dickinson Handbook* (Amherst: U of Massachusetts P, 1998). One of the hour-long programs in the PBS *Voices and Visions* series (1987) features Dickinson's work.

SPECIAL TOPICS FOR WRITING AND ARGUMENT
ABOUT THE POETRY OF DICKINSON

1. Dickinson's characteristic brevity in the explanation of situations and the expression of ideas.

2. Dickinson's use of personal but not totally disclosed subject matter.

3. Dickinson's use of imagery and symbolism: sources, types, meanings. Her humor and irony.

4. Dickinson's ideas about love, separation, personal pain, war, death, faith, religion, science, the soul.

5. Dickinson's power as a poet.

6. Dickinson's poems as they appear on the page: the relationship of meaning to lines, stanzas, capitalization, punctuation, the use of the dash.

7. The structuring of a number of Dickinson's poems: subject, development, conclusions.

8. The character of the speaker in a number of Dickinson's poems: personality, things noticed, accuracy of conclusions. If there appears to be a listener in the poems, what effect does this listener have on the speaker?

9. Dickinson's verse forms and use of rhymes.

10. Themes of exhilaration, sorrow, pity, triumph, and regret in Dickinson.

 ## POEMS BY EMILY DICKINSON*

After Great Pain, a Formal Feeling Comes, 1068
The Bustle in a House, 1068
"Faith" Is a Fine Invention, 1069
The Heart Is the Capital of the Mind, 1069
I Cannot Live with You, 1069
I Died for Beauty – but Was Scarce, 1070
I Felt a Funeral in My Brain, 1071
I Heard a Fly Buzz – When I Died, 1071

*For ease in locating the selections included here, the poems are arranged alphabetically by the first significant words in first lines. There are two numbers following the title of each poem. The first number (e.g., J501) refers to the poem numbers in Thomas H. Johnson's *The Complete Poems of Emily Dickinson*. Critics since Johnson's edition have unanimously employed these numbers. The second number (e.g., F373) refers to the new numbering in Ralph W. Franklin's *The Poems of Emily Dickinson: Variorum Edition*. It would appear that future Dickinson criticism will need to include both numbers if the poem under discussion is to be properly identified, as with the following title: *After Great Pain, a Formal Feeling Comes* (J341, F372).

Typographically, we have treated the dash as it is used in Franklin's edition, as in the following line, *After great pain, a formal feeling comes – .* Many past editions have utilized a longer and more obtrusive dash, as in *After great pain, a formal feeling comes—.*

See also two additional Dickinson poems in this anthology: "Because I Could Not Stop for Death" (J712, F479), p. 671, and "To Hear an Oriole Sing" (J52, F402), p. 859.

After Great Pain, a Formal Feeling Comes (J341, F372) _____ 1929 (ca. 1862)

After great pain, a formal feeling comes –
The Nerves sit ceremonious, like Tombs –
The Stiff Heart questions 'was it He, that bore,'
And 'Yesterday, or Centuries before'?

The Feet, mechanical, go round –
A Wooden way
Of Ground, or Air, or Ought° –   *anything, nothing*
Regardless grown,
A Quartz contentment, like a stone –

This is the Hour of Lead –
Remembered, if outlived,
As Freezing persons, recollect the Snow –
First – Chill – then Stupor – then the letting go –

The Bustle in a House (J1078, F1108) _____ 1890 (ca. 1865)

The Bustle in a House
The Morning after Death
Is solemnest of industries
Enacted upon Earth –

The Sweeping up the Heart   5
And putting Love away
We shall not want to use again
Until Eternity –

"Faith" Is a Fine Invention (J185, F202) ————————— 1891 (ca. 1861)

"Faith" is a fine invention
When Gentlemen can *see –* °
But Microscopes are prudent
In an Emergency.

FAITH IS A FINE INVENTION.   2 alternative wording: For Gentlemen who *see-*.

The Heart Is the Capital of the Mind (J1354, F1381) ——— 1929 (ca. 1875)

The Heart is the Capital of the Mind –
The Mind is a single State –
The Heart and the Mind together make
A single Continent.

One – is the Population –   5
Numerous enough –
This ecstatic Nation
Seek – it is Yourself –

I Cannot Live with You (J640, F706) ————————————— 1890 (ca. 1863)

I cannot live with You –
It would be Life –
And Life is over there –
Behind the Shelf

The Sexton keeps the Key to –   5
Putting up
Our Life – His Porcelain –
Like a Cup –

Discarded of the Housewife –
Quaint – or Broke –   10
A newer Sevres° pleases –   *a fine French porcelain*
Old Ones crack –

I could not die – with You –
For One must wait
To shut the Other's Gaze down –   15
You – could not –

And I – Could I stand by
And see You – freeze –
Without my Right of Frost –
Death's privilege? 20

Nor could I rise – with You –
Because Your Face
Would put out Jesus' –
That New Grace

Glow plain – and foreign 25
On my homesick eye –
Except that You than He
Shone closer by –

They'd judge Us – How –
For You – served Heaven – You know, 30
Or sought to –
I could not –

Because You saturated sight –
And I had no more eyes
For sordid excellence 35
As Paradise

And were You lost, I would be –
Though my name
Rang loudest
On the Heavenly fame – 40

And were You – saved –
And I – condemned to be
Where You were not
That self – were Hell to Me –

So We must meet apart –
You there – I – here –
With just the Door ajar
That Oceans are – and Prayer –
And that White Sustenance –
Despair –

I Died for Beauty – but Was Scarce (J449, F448) _____ *1890 (ca. 1862)*

I died for Beauty – but was scarce
Adjusted in the Tomb
When One who died for Truth, was lain
In an adjoining Room –

He questioned softly "Why I failed"?   5
"For Beauty", I replied –
"And I – for Truth – Themselves are One –
We Brethren, are", He said –

And so, as Kinsmen, met a Night –
We talked between the Rooms –   10
Until the Moss had reached our lips –
And covered up – Our names –

I Felt a Funeral in My Brain (J280, F340) _____ *1896 (ca. 1862)*

I felt a Funeral, in my Brain,
And Mourners to and fro
Kept treading – treading – till it seemed
That Sense was breaking through –

And when they all were seated,   5
A Service, like a Drum –
Kept beating – beating – till I thought
My mind was going numb –

And then I heard them lift a Box
And creak across my Soul   10
With those same Boots of Lead, again,
Then Space – began to toll,

As all the Heavens were a Bell,
And Being, but an Ear,
And I, and Silence, some strange Race   15
Wrecked, solitary, here –

And then a Plank in Reason, broke,
And I dropped down, and down –
And hit a World, at every plunge,
And Finished knowing – then –   20

I Heard a Fly Buzz – When I Died (J465, F591) _____ *1896 (ca. 1863)*

I heard a Fly buzz – when I died –
The Stillness in the Room
Was like the Stillness in the Air –
Between the Heaves of Storm –

The Eyes around – had wrung them dry –   5
And Breaths were gathering firm

For that last Onset – when the King
Be witnessed – in the Room –

I willed my Keepsakes – Signed away
What portion of me be   10
Assignable – and then it was
There interposed a Fly –

With Blue – uncertain – stumbling Buzz –
Between the light – and me –
And then the Windows failed – and then   15
I could not see to see –

I Like to See It Lap the Miles (J585, F383) _____ *1891 (ca. 1862)*

I like to see it lap the Miles –
And lick the Valleys up –
And stop to feed itself at Tanks –
And then – prodigious step

Around a Pile of Mountains –
And supercilious peer
In Shanties – by the sides of Roads –
And then a Quarry pare

To fit it's sides
And crawl between   1
Complaining all the while
In horrid – hooting stanza –
Then chase itself down Hill –

And neigh like Boanerges° –
Then – prompter than a Star
Stop – docile and omnipotent
At it's own stable door –

I LIKE TO SEE IT LAP THE MILES.   14 *Boanerges:* a surname meaning "the sons of thunder"
that appears in Mark 3:17.

I'm Nobody! Who Are You? (J288, F260) _____ *1891 (ca. 1861)*

I'm Nobody! Who are you?
Are you – Nobody – too?
Then there's a pair of us!
Don't tell! they'd banish us – you know!

How dreary – to be – Somebody!   5
How public – like a Frog –
To tell your name – the livelong June –
To an admiring Bog!

I Never Felt at Home – Below – (J413, F437) _____ *1929 (ca. 1862)*

I never felt at Home – Below –
And in the Handsome skies
I shall not feel at Home – I know –
I dont like Paradise –

Because it's Sunday – all the time –   5
And Recess – never comes –
And Eden'll be so lonesome
Bright Wednesday Afternoons –

If God could make a visit –
Or ever took a Nap –   10
So not to see us – but they say
Himself – a Telescope

Perennial beholds us –
Myself would run away
From Him – and Holy Ghost – and All –   15
But there's the "Judgment Day"!

I Never Lost as Much But Twice (J49, F39) _____ *1890 (ca. 1858)*

I never lost as much but twice –
And that was in the sod.
Twice have I stood a beggar
Before the door of God!

Angels – twice descending   5
Reimbursed my store –
Burglar! Banker – Father!
I am poor once more!

I Taste a Liquor Never Brewed (J214, F207) _____ *1861, 1890 (ca. 1860)*

I taste a liquor never brewed –
From Tankards scooped in Pearl –
Not all the Frankfort Berries°   *grapes*
Yield such an Alcohol!

Inebriate of Air – am I –   5
And Debauchee of Dew –
Reeling – thro endless summer days –
From inns of Molten Blue –

When "Landlords" turn the drunken Bee
Out of the Foxglove's door –   10
When Butterflies – renounce their "drams" –
I shall but drink the more!

Till Seraphs swing their Snowy Hats –
And Saints – to windows run –
To see the little Tippler   1
From Manzanilla° come!

I TASTE A LIQUOR NEVER BREWED.   16 *Manzanilla:* a pale sherry from Spain. Dickinson may also have been thinking of Manzanillo, a Cuban city known for rum.

Much Madness Is Divinest Sense (J435, F620) _____ *1890 (ca. 1863)*

Much Madness is divinest Sense –
To a discerning Eye –
Much Sense – the starkest Madness –
'Tis the Majority
In this, as all, prevail –
Assent – and you are sane –
Demur – you're straightway dangerous –
And handled with a Chain –

My Life Closed Twice Before Its Close (J1732, F1773) _____ *1896*

My life closed twice before it's close;
It yet remains to see
If Immortality unveil
A third event to me,

So huge, so hopeless to conceive
As these that twice befell.
Parting is all we know of heaven,
And all we need of hell.

My Triumph Lasted Till the Drums (J1227, F1212) _____ *1935 (ca. 1871)*

My Triumph lasted till the Drums
Had left the Dead alone
And then I dropped my Victory
And chastened stole along

To where the finished Faces   5
Conclusion turned on me
And then I hated Glory
And wished myself were They.

What is to be is best descried
When it has also been –   10
Could Prospect taste of Retrospect
The Tyrannies of Men
Were Tenderer, diviner
The Transitive toward –
A Bayonet's contrition   15
Is nothing to the Dead.

One Need Not Be a Chamber –
To Be Haunted (J670, F407) ———————————— *1891 (ca. 1862, 1864)*

One need not be a chamber – to be Haunted –
One need not be a House –
The Brain has Corridors – surpassing
Material Place –

Far safer, of a midnight meeting   5
External Ghost
Than it's interior confronting –
That cooler Host –

Far safer, through an Abbey gallop,
The Stones a'chase –   10
Than unarmed, one's a'self encounter –
In lonesome Place –

Ourself behind ourself, concealed –
Should startle most –
Assassin hid in our Apartment   15
Be Horror's least –

The Body – borrows a Revolver –
He bolts the Door –
O'erlooking a superior spectre –
Or More –   20

Safe in Their Alabaster Chambers (J216, F124) ——————— *1862 (ca. 1859)*

Safe in their Alabaster Chambers –
Untouched by Morning –
And untouched by Noon –

Lie the meek members of the Resurrection –
Rafter of Satin – and Roof of Stone! 5

Grand go the Years – in the Crescent – above them –
Worlds scoop their Arcs –
And Firmaments – row –
Diadems – drop – and Doges° – surrender –
Soundless as dots – on a Disc of snow – 1

SAFE IN THEIR ALABASTER CHAMBERS. 9 *Doges:* rulers of Venice and Genoa, Italian city-
states during the Renaissance.

Some Keep the Sabbath Going to Church (*J324, F236*) _____ *1864 (ca. 1861)*

Some keep the Sabbath going to Church –
I keep it, staying at Home –
With a Bobolink for a Chorister –
And an Orchard, for a Dome –

Some keep the Sabbath in Surplice –
I, just wear my Wings –
And instead of tolling the Bell, for Church,
Our little Sexton – sings.

God preaches, a noted Clergyman –
And the sermon is never long.
So instead of getting to Heaven, at last –
I'm going, all along.

The Soul Selects Her Own Society (*J303, F409*) _____ *1890 (ca. 1862)*

The Soul selects her own Society –
Then – shuts the Door –
To her divine Majority –
Present no more –

Unmoved – she notes the Chariots – pausing –
At her low Gate –
Unmoved – an Emperor be kneeling
Opon° her Mat –   *upon*

I've known her – from an ample nation –
Choose One –
Then – close the Valves of her attention –
Like Stone –

Success Is Counted Sweetest (J67, F112) _____ *1864 (ca. 1859)*

Success is counted sweetest
By those who ne'er succeed.
To comprehend a nectar
Requires sorest need.

Not one of all the purple Host   5
Who took the Flag today
Can tell the definition
So clear of Victory

As he defeated – dying –
On whose forbidden ear   10
The distant strains of triumph
Burst agonized and clear!

Tell All the Truth but Tell It Slant (J1129, F1263) _____ *1945 (ca. 1872)*

Tell all the truth but tell it slant –
Success in Circuit lies
Too bright for our infirm Delight
The Truth's superb surprise
As Lightning to the Children eased   5
With explanation kind
The Truth must dazzle gradually
Or every man be blind –

There's a Certain Slant of Light (J258, F320) _____ *1890 (ca. 1862)*

There's a certain Slant of light,
Winter Afternoons –
That oppresses, like the Heft
Of Cathedral Tunes –

Heavenly Hurt, it gives us –   5
We can find no scar,
But internal difference –
Where the Meanings, are –

None may teach it – Any –
'Tis the Seal Despair –   10
An imperial affliction
Sent us of the Air –

When it comes, the Landscape listens –
Shadows – hold their breath –
When it goes, 'tis like the Distance   15
On the look of Death –

This World Is Not Conclusion (J501, F373) —————— *1896, 1945 (ca. 1862)*

This World is not Conclusion.
A Species stands beyond –
Invisible, as Music –
But positive, as Sound –
It beckons, and it baffles –
Philosophy, dont know –
And through a Riddle, at the last –
Sagacity, must go –
To guess it, puzzles scholars –
To gain it, Men have borne
Contempt of Generations
And Crucifixion, shown –
Faith slips – and laughs, and rallies –
Blushes, if any see –
Plucks at a twig of Evidence –
And asks a Vane, the way –
Much Gesture, from the Pulpit –
Strong Hallelujahs roll –
Narcotics cannot still the Tooth
That nibbles at the soul –

Wild Nights – Wild Nights! (J249, F269) ——————— *1891 (ca. 1861)*

Wild Nights – Wild Nights!
Were I with thee
Wild Nights should be
Our luxury!

Futile – the winds –
To a Heart in port –
Done with the Compass –
Done with the Chart!

Rowing in Eden -
Ah - the Sea!
Might I but moor - tonight -
In thee!

EDITED SELECTIONS FROM CRITICISM
OF DICKINSON'S POEMS, WITH AN EMPHASIS
ON POEMS INCLUDED IN THIS CHAPTER

The following selections are intended to supply details and ideas for essays on Dickinson's poems. For a selective bibliography, consult the "Bibliographic Sources" section above (p. 1065), which may be augmented with your college library catalogue and the most recent volumes of the *MLA International Bibliography* available in the reference room of your college library. The bracketed page numbers refer to the original pagination of the sources included here. Footnotes in the sources have been deleted.

From "The Flower, the Bee, and the Spider"*

"Tell all the Truth," Emily instructed herself, "but tell it slant—/Success in Circuit lies." [144] When she said that "every suggestion is Dimension," she was really referring to what she called on another occasion "the circumference of Expression," and was thereby assigning to form and style all the connotations of the word "circumference": self contained fullness and totality; precision of outline and bounds; circuitous definition of center and dimension. In her mind the Bible, unlike poetry, spoke "with the Centre, not with the Circumference" of expression, because the Bible made emphatic, direct statements about God (the omnipresent Center) in God's own words, whereas poetry could only speak roundabout in her own words. So clearly did she realize that the particular style and form which a poet used was a projection of himself and his experience that she rejected—politely and gratefully but adamantly—every piece of practical literary advice that "Preceptor" Higginson offered.

What, then, was the basic element in the peculiar and distinctive style which Emily Dickinson made? Emerson had said that organic form depended on making every nuance of relation into a new word; the poet named things "sometimes after their appearance, sometimes after their essence," and gave "to every one its own name and not another's, thereby rejoicing the intellect, which delights in detachment or boundary." We might often want more conciseness and particularity in Emerson's style, but [145] Emily's friend Dr. Holland expressed a popular contemporary view when he observed of Emerson's writing: "There is no more spare language on his ideas, than there is flesh on his bones corporeal. A word less on the one, or an atom less on the other, and there would be a fatal catastrophe." In his journal Thoreau had formulated this same first commandment for the stylist: "By your few words show how insufficient would be many words . . . In breadth we may be patterns of conciseness, but in depth we may well be prolix." Emily Dickinson refined this tendency toward exactness and condensation even further. If Emerson and Thoreau wrote at their best in well-wrought and precisely tooled sentences, then Emily Dickinson compressed language into finely honed and deliberately placed words. Her mind did not move in abstract or even sequential logic, and so her language—whether in verse or prose—does not depend on its sweep or smoothness or exuberance or delicately woven texture or even on its syntactical coherence. Indeed, the very confusion of the syntax—a fairly common occurrence, actually—forces the

* From Albert J. Gelpi, *Emily Dickinson: The Mind of the Poet* (Cambridge: Harvard UP, 1966).

reader to concentrate on the basic verbal units and derive the strength and meaning largely from the circumference of words.

Therefore, while as the poet-seer she could bewail the inadequacy of words for the vision, as poet-craftsman she reveled time and again in the breadth and depth enclosed in one mighty word:

Could mortal lip divine
The undeveloped Freight
Of a delivered syllable
'Twould crumble with the weight.   [J1409, F1456]

Moreover, her concern was not just with the density or weight of the words but with the "life and palpitation" which Thoreau called for:

A word is dead
When it is said,
Some say.
I say it just
Begins to live
That day.   [J1212, F278]

The vigorous word lived primarily in itself—in its sensual concreteness or its conceptual precision or its connotative resonance or its metaphorical implications—but secondarily it lived in its effect on the verse pattern—that is, in its contribution to rhyme, rhythm, alliteration, and so on. "How lovely," Emily exclaimed to Mrs. Holland, "are the wiles of Words!" . . .

A good indication of her formalism is her insatiable and unabating interest in the [14
wiles of words. Emily told Higginson that for some years her lexicon had been her only companion, and throughout her life she pored over the dictionary as zealously as she read her Bible. From the native strength of words and from her experiments in expanding their scope she fashioned a unique language (Higginson thought it "spasmodic" and "uncontrolled.") She chose words with stinging freshness; she flavored speech with earthy New England colloquialisms; she often dropped the "s" of the third-person singular of the present tense to suggest the enduring quality of the action; she emphasized nouns by the striking addition or omission of the preceding article; she sometimes used singular nouns where plurals were expected and vice versa; she made parts of speech perform unorthodox functions, used words in startling contexts, coined words when none seemed available or apt. Like Ezra Pound, William Carlos Williams, Marianne Moore, and E. E. Cummings, Emily Dickinson sought to speak the uniqueness of her experience in a personal tongue by reconstituting and revitalizing—at the risk of eccentricity—the basic verbal unit.

For the framework in which to set her words, Emily Dickinson came naturally to depend on the standard hymn stanzas. She was familiar with them from church and was otherwise quite unsophisticated in the technicalities of metrics. The quatrains of short lines (mostly three and four beats) imposed the necessity for conciseness and control, and the association with the meetinghouse suggested (whether she realized it or not) [1
the religious basis of her poetic calling. Without relaxing the rigid formality of the quatrains she gave them variety and adaptability through the flexibility of the rhythms

(marked by those dots and dashes that serve as breathing points) and through the atonality of slant rimes and the internal harmonics of the vowels and consonants. She had worked out a stanza which was prescribed without monotony and which could be skillfully worked within strict limits.

Take for example this carefully constructed quatrain:

> The Clock strikes one that just struck two—
> Some schism in the Sum—
> A Vagabond from Genesis
> Has wrecked the Pendulum—   [J1569, F1598]

All the words are monosyllables accept for three trisyllabic words (Vagabond, Genesis, Pendulum), and these are reiterated in the trisyllabic rime "in the Sum" and in the three words beginning with "s" in the second line. The tone of the bell "strikes one" in the monosyllables and especially in the words "Clock," "strikes," "struck," and "wrecked." The "two" mentioned at the end of the first line is repeated in the "Some" and "Sum" of the second, which are in turn split by "schism." In the poem which begins "When Bells stop ringing—Church—begins—" (P 633 [J633, F601]) . . . the slow, solemn pace suggests the motionlessness which is the subject of the poem. Another quatrain is built on the tonal possibilities of the letter "o," on which every change is rung:

> The blonde Assassin passes on—
> The Sun proceeds unmoved
> To measure off another Day
> For an Approving God.   [J1624, F1668]

A more complex sound pattern becomes a chamber of echoes, in which "b," "l," and "e" tumble in rapid succession and the short "i"'s of the first line are picked up in the last:

> Admonished by her buckled lips
> Let every babbler be
> The only secret people keep
> Is Immortality.   [J1748, F1776]

This sort of analysis might best be left to the explorations of the individual reader of the poetry, especially since the point is by now plain. Like a good American craftsman, Emily Dickinson whittled her materials, within the limits of a rather strict form, into something of beauty and use. Moreover, the qualities of her style attest to the qualities of her consciousness; at its best the writing is terse, compact, concrete—and yet oblique, cryptic, surrendering its secret only in lightning-flashes of word and metaphor.

From "Orthodox Modernisms"*

Dickinson's power derives partly from a cluster of techniques, from certain themes, and [222] from tonal qualities that we consider modern and admire for their apparent newness.

---

* From David Porter, *Dickinson, the Modern Idiom* (Cambridge: Harvard UP, 1981).

Her work is a catalogue of these modernisms, conventional to us now in their familiarity and so commonly known in her repertoire that a summary here will suffice. She possessed an intuitive knack for exploiting the capacity of language under certain distortions or tensions to arrest, illuminate, pierce, astonish. Her wonderfully engaging first lines range from the controlled audacity of flatness and understatement ("Before I got my eye put out") to marvelous lines of great syntactic pressure involving mystery, lure, expectation, and which play sophisticatedly with line-end novelty and grammatical deception.

The animated lexical selection that is the heart of her craft comprises violations sometimes of great daring. She surprised with her language and, when it was not so deliberately concocted as to be coy or patent, it brings off its risks and shocks in a modern way. A corpse in poem 287 [J287, F259] is "This Pendulum of snow" and death's finality is in "Decades of Arrogance." Elsewhere her lexical surprises manage a careful deflation and austerity that dehumanize, objectify, as in these sciential lines about a corpse:

> The busy eyes—congealed—
> It straightened—that was all . . .
> It multiplied indifference

Dry and hard, spare in a Poundian sense, this cold language forms into an analytical instrument of great accuracy. There is also word parading of the sort we now admire as well in Marianne Moore. In Dickinson's little known poem about a June bug, the poly- [22?
syllables thump against the single-syllable vernacular:

> From Eminence remote
> Drives ponderous perpendicular
> . . . .
> Depositing his Thunder
> He hoists abroad again—
> A Bomb upon the Ceiling
> Is an improving thing
> It keeps conjecture flourishing—   [J1128, F1150]

Dickinson interrupted nineteenth-century poetic discourse with a vernacular so direct it seemed crude to her first public. She disarmingly called it in poem 373 [J373, F575] "my simple speech" and "plain word." It was in fact flattened speech, a *talking* that was depoetizing; and an escape from pomposity. Into her poems and particularly into those outrageous first lines came a natural breath and diction that created the illusion and the impact of real speech acts. . . .

Most modern, perhaps, among Dickinson's techniques is her use of language [2 realms as constitutive elements in analytical structure. She makes the language medium itself objective and able to cut like a tool, managing this in at least three ways: vernacular diction inserted in formal language for its cross-cut effect; deploying Anglo-Saxon abruptness against the formalities of Latinate diction (this has been much noticed); and cleverly treating a subject with an alien lexical set. An instance of this last, as I have noted elsewhere, is characterizing God in the language of law or commerce. Dickinson, intuitively audacious in this, makes one language subset cut against and criticize another level of lexical selection, making a drama of language itself as if lexicons were themselves characters. Here is God silently measured by cold legalisms.

> I read my sentence—steadily—
> Reviewed it with my eyes,
> To see that I made no mistake
> In it's extremest clause——
> The Date, and manner, of the shame—
> And then the Pious Form
> That "God have mercy" on the Soul
> The Jury voted Him—   [J412, F432]

Besides such strategies of diction choice at which she was so adept, Dickinson employed other techniques that we call modern. As noted, she elided syntax (for various reasons), omitted transitions, and dropped structural and even syntactical copulas. This habit of withholding connective material produces curiously vexatious ways we now choose to see as modern: discontinuity of structure and story, and remystification of phenomena that seem simple and clear, and those extinguishings of meaning by which we experience complexity and feel the intractable quality of existence again. Beyond this, Dickinson's habitual brevity seems modern in its glimpses and incompleteness. These are notes raised to literature, notation as authentic response. Wayward in punctuation, the poems disregard nicety and neglect finish. They have an aura of spontaneity and the status of randomness which, as when we look at impressionist or action painting, [226] we find congenial and not a counterfeiting of sensation and reality. Like Hardy, but apparently less knowingly, her poetry was revolutionary because it avoided the jeweled line. It was more a making of the irregular line through a rough simplicity and by drastic reduction. Indeed, sometimes the print version of her manuscripts unavoidably makes a modern line disposition.

> And Life was not so
> Ample I
> Could finish–Enmity—   [J478, F763]

Her partial rhymes and the structural instability and shifts in poems contribute to this impatient art.

Dickinson's rift vision, the ability to make language cut into the disparities between concept and reality, between the expectation and the actuality—this creation in language of cruel parallax—effects a disruption and penetration that we also call modern. It appeals to our suspicion of wholeness and seamless compatible meaning. This effect is behind Harold Bloom's accurate observation that Dickinson, as much as any modern, made the visible world a little hard to see.

The several techniques emphasized here as modern are well known and often displayed as the true source of Dickinson's modernity. Yet we shall see that her modernity operated at a more fundamental level than this. For now it is clear that these several conventional modernisms, what have now become part of the technical orthodoxy of modernist verse in English, contribute to the powerful effect that is indubitably of our time: the estrangement from outer reality and the resistance of common words to definitive meaning. The estrangement is accomplished by the compact, unsustained, raw power of language at the surface of her clipped-off poems.

In her themes, as well, Dickinson is with the moderns. Her language, animated by her selective cleverness, together with the snapshot brevity of her hymn form, courted instability and change and spotted the vulnerability of settled states. This is why sunsets evoked some of her best imagistic effort. The spectacle of day's end was intensely, exaggeratedly visual, it was naturally associated with death, and it was recurrent novelty, change taking place before the eyes. The sunset was thus a visual allegory for what most [227] centrally engaged this poet.

Her preoccupation with change led to more desperate visions of mutability where the price of each moment of transport qualified every ecstasy, showing by her allegorical terms the furrow that threatens every glow. Unlike Emerson and Whitman, Dickinson brought into view with her strange and critical metaphors the opaque being of man, the "mysterious peninsula" as she called it, the unmanageable, excruciatingly sensitive, and needful portion that was her preoccupation.

She possessed a modernist knowledge of the mind's hidden places, what she called "That awful stranger Consciousness," terrifying to face. Equipped with her estranging language, she raised to the reader's awareness the intricate workings out of sight, careful not to "Mistake the Outside for the in" as she said. It is this interior life, in (for this recluse) the inevitable metaphor of the house, that is "haunted" and is the crucial spot where we enact our ignorance of ourselves and the world. Here is the "interior Confronting," where "Unarmed, one's a'self encounter." Now become an orthodox element of modern themes—what Irving Howe has called a modern fondness for the signs of psychic division—the interior life and the language to see it were the particular loci of Dickinson's attention. Encountering the self both dictated the strategies of her language and was the act in which her language had its circumstantial reflection.

"I felt a Funeral in my Brain" [J280, F340] is the first coolly targeted modern interior in American poetry, and it is handled adroitly with modernist attention not to moral judgment but to judgment-free description. There is no emotional slither, to use Pound's term, or didactic assertion as in other poems such as "Bound—a trouble/And lives can bear it!" or "A Weight with Needles on the pounds," but rather psychological interiority seen minutely. The funeral-in-the-brain poem, representative of a substantial cluster of Dickinson's works on psychic distress, manifested two generations in advance the doctrine of imagism that Pound defined as the transfer of a complex of emotions in an instant of time.

It was Dickinson diving into the wreck and her devastated speaker indeed "wrecked" in the poem. Assurance of diction and line is firm. The poem has structure and lexical cohesion of a high order for Dickinson, and it is this firmness that operates so effectively against the subject matter of instability and disintegration. [22 It is a superb performance, thoroughly modernist in its dark vision clinically portrayed.

Such language . . . made visible a new category of psychic suffering. Minutely observant, its figure of the interior funeral sustained, the poem moves with impressive directness into its surrealist transformation at the line "Then Space—began to toll." The familiar terms make new equations: Heaven is a Bell, Being an ear, and Silence a strange Race, and the wreck itself an annihilating silence. The surreal landscape, haunted with Dickinson's sense of exclusion and ignorance, unfolds, at least to the somewhat redundant last stanza, with a sure finality of language and wholeness of vision. In its cold-blooded, unflinching way as well as in the interior location of its action, the poem is supremely modernist. From the broader view of the Dickinson canon, we see how her concern with the interior reflects an equally modern concern with intense self-consciousness extending even to self-torture and the poetry of breakdown. . . .

The protomodernist image of the durable face of technological violence, of assault [229] masked by dehumanized visages, is related in terror to another theme of Dickinson's that is hardly depictable by such momentary frissons. That is her vision of the *absence of an end.* I find this the most frightful of all Dickinson's modernist themes because it involves the pathological extremity of her familiar images such as this, of death in life, that ends an eight-line poem of utter inertness.

> I take my living place
> As one commuted led—
> A Candidate for Morning Chance
> But dated with the Dead.   [J1194, F1209]

The smell of nihilism rises from more than a few poems, sometimes in a complete flatness of tune where her theme is the loss that drains every gain: note the eight lines that tick off loss beginning "Finding is the first Act/The second, loss" [J870, F910]. Associated with this theme of lost purpose and the absence of an end is a fearful corollary: the prevention of ripeness, of completion and thereby of knowledge and identity. It is the vision we saw in "What ripeness after that": that is, a life of incompletion, of ignorance, of need without assuaging. It can stand for the quintessential modernist condition—until with Dickinson we find ourselves going deeper. . . .

Particular tones in Dickinson's poetry are also part of her commonly recognized [230] modernism. Currents of doubt and the snowman moments give certain poems a psychological desperation that was unfamiliar to much nineteenth-century poetry. The sharply discrepant tone in poems, their directness of statement, and the audacity of their attack on conventional belief and easy-going piety are elements that would have given offense in her own time and so did not appear in the first editions of her poetry in the 1890s. Her colloquial and irreverently casual heresy at times ("It's easy to invent a Life"), her deliberate inelegance in a primitive offbeat diction ("It is simple to ache in the Bone or the Rind"), and the seemingly sophisticated skepticism in offhand phrases ("Our Savior, by a Hair") combine to give a considerable portion of the poetry a discordant tone that undercuts the poetry of unquestioned assent with which her contemporaries filled the verse books of the day.

Satire and irreverence along a gamut from mild asides to bitter attack are also modernist elements that form part of our critical orthodoxy and the surfaces by which Dickinson can be labeled a modern. In the poem beginning "There's been a Death, in [231] the opposite house" [J389, F547] she creates a gentle satire on the impersonal organization that swings into action at a death, with its ritual movements and the professional mourners who take charge. In such verse of casual irreverence, the understatement and vernacular ease effectively counterpoint the regular common meter that arranges them. Deft lexical selection provides the edge that cuts in in the modern way. Her lines on the aurora borealis, where the common expectation would be for "paint" and "tint," Dickinson slips all askew by substituting "infection" and "taint":

> The North—Tonight . . .
> Infects my simple spirit
> With Taints of Majesty   [J290, F319]

She deflated a generically solemn occasion by unobtrusive negation and the one unexpected word "soldered":

I've seen a Dying Eye
Run round and round a Room . . .
And then—be soldered down
Without disclosing what it be
'Twere blessed to have seen   [J547, F648]

Her language pierced theological pomposities with strokes of marvelous wit, as here
with out-of-place words from the public hall set off against Resurrection:

No crowd that has occurred
Exhibit—I suppose
That General Attendance
That Resurrection–does   [J515, F653]

Dickinson's modernist tones include the confessional one. She excelled in creat- [23°
ing a sense of private immediacy because, by the strategy of seemingly autobiographical speech acts, she reproduced in writing the speaking voice. Archibald MacLeish has
written most knowingly on the unique voice by which we identify her. It is language signifying emotional experience close at hand that impresses us. The voice, quotation
marks invisible, contradicts a reader's conscious awareness of the deliberately written
text. This way in which Dickinson *did* speak out to strangers produces what we take to be
an immediate proximity to the mind. The flattened conversational tone depoetizes experience and gives it a confessional authenticity of the sort we are familiar with in our own
time.

To Ache is human—not polite—
The Film upon the eye
Mortality's Old Custom—
Just locking up—to Die   [J479, F458]

Toughness of attitude and candor couched in unstudied inelegance are further tonal
qualities by which twentieth-century readers have assigned Dickinson to the origins of
modernism along with Whitman. The blunt tones sound frequently along her lines, as
here in this bald assertion that seems to have no poetic pretentions: "Men die—externally—/It is a truth—of Blood" [J531, F584].

Boldly secular content and skeptical tone quite disjunct from the orderly arrangement of the hymn form make an ironic combination. The poems produce that most
modern of all attitudes, the ironicalization of experience. Beyond that, the disjunction
and tonal qualities together effect a modernist estrangement, dissonance, and thus a
critical perspective. Her bruskness deromanticizes, as in the moon poem that begins "I
watched the Moon around the House." Dickinson's daring comes out most clearly if her
moon is put alongside the famous protoimagist poem on the moon by T. E. Hulme.
Dickinson's lines have in their more compact shape a greater bravado. It is part of what
she shares with poets who followed her.

like a Head—a Guillotine
Slide carelessly away —
like a Stemless Flower—
Upheld in rolling Air—   [J629, F593]

The best summing up of these tonal qualities we now see as a modern set is in [233] that phrase *the ironicalization of experience.* The tonal undercutting, the evasion of stock sincerity, the protective irreverence and throwaway understatement, thus making the hymn form play a different tune: all these effects, even if there were behind them no perspective of mind much more fundamental, would withal make Dickinson a modern. Neither sophisticated nor sustained, hers was a poetic cunning working by stealth of language and subversion of form to create surprise by strangeness. Out of these strategies came a disordering of experience, a new confession of our precarious status.

From "The Landscape of the Spirit"*

Dickinson's poems frequently assert her sense of the mind's actuality with images of cav- [14] erns and corridors [J777, F877; J670, F407], windows and doors [J303, F409; J657, F466], [15] even cellars [J1182, F1234]. Because she took the mind to be her dwelling place, it is appropriate that she use these domestic figurative correspondences to describe it. Yet her poems using such architectural analogues go beyond pointing out how a mind might be like a house. They set out to show, as well, what happens in a mind that is as a house, so that the solidity which door and window frame provide grants substance both to the setting and to the events occurring within. The architectural vocabulary usually portrays the mind as an enclosed space, its confinement responsible for power, safety, yet fearful confrontation.

Poem 303 is a strong statement about the power of the self alone. The soul is shown living within a space defined by door, gate, and mat. The external world, with its nations and their rulers, is kept outside.

> The soul selects her own Society—
> Then—shuts the Door—
> To her divine Majority—
> Present no more—
>
> Unmoved—she notes the Chariots—pausing—
> At her low Gate—
> Unmoved—an Emperor be kneeling
> Upon her Mat—
>
> I've known her—from an ample nation—
> Choose One—
> Then—close the Valves of her attention—
> Like Stone—

Traditional ideas about power are reversed here. Not control over vast populations but the ability to construct a world for oneself comprises the greatest power, a godlike achievement, announces the opening stanza. Not only is the soul alone "divine," but it is also identified as "Society" and "Majority": the poem also challenges our ideas about what constitutes a social group. Consequently, the enclosed space of the soul's house is more than adequate for a queenly life, and ambassadors of the external world's glories,

* From Suzanne Juhasz, *"The Undiscovered Continent:" Emily Dickinson and The Space of the Mind* (Bloomington: Indiana UP, 1983).

even emperors, can easily be scorned. Yet while the speaker claims her equality with those most powerful in the outer world—they may be emperors, but she is "divine Majority," at the same time she asserts her difference from them; for her domestic vocabulary of door, low gate and mat establishes her dwelling as not a grand palace but rather a simple house.

While associating power with the enclosed space of the mind, the poem also [16 implies how isolation is confinement, too. When the soul turns in upon her own concerns, she closes "the Valves of her attention—/Like Stone—."

Valves permit the flow of whatever they regulate in one direction only: here from outside to inside. Either of the halves of a double door or any of the leaves of a folding door are valves. Valves seen as doors reinforce the poem's house imagery, while their association with stone makes the walls separating soul from world so solid as to be, perhaps, prison-like.

Prison-like because they allow no escape from the kinds of conflict, the kinds of terror, even, that must occur within. Poem 670 [J670, F407] exaggerating the architectural vocabulary, compares the chambers of the mind to the haunted castle of gothic fiction, a stereotypical setting for horror.

> One need not be a Chamber—to be Haunted—
> One need not be a House—
> The Brain has Corridors—surpassing
> Material Place—
>
> Far safer, of a Midnight Meeting
> External Ghost
> Than its interior Confronting—
> That Cooler Host.
>
> Far safer, through an Abbey gallop,
> The stones a'chase—
> Than Unarmed, one's a'self encounter—
> In lonesome Place—
>
> Ourself behind ourself, concealed—
> Should startle most—
> Assassin hid in our Apartment
> Be Horror's least.
>
> The Body—borrows a Revolver—
> He bolts the Door—
> O'erlooking a superior spectre—
> Or More—

The poem assumes that the mind is substantial, possessing corridors and chambers, because it is the dwelling place of "oneself." The extended comparison that is developed, between two kinds of dwellings, two binds of hauntings, is for the purpose of dramatizing how there can be something more frightening than the most frightening situation usually imaginable.

Both the second and third stanzas begin with the same phrase: "Far safer." Safer are the supernatural events of gothic castles, meeting ghosts at midnight; we are warned about "interior confronting," the everyday moments of the mind, another lonesome place, when "one's a'self encounter." One clue to the degree of difference in horror is the word, "Unarmed." We come prepared to find ghosts in spooky old castles, but not in what Dickinson calls in another poem "That polar privacy/A soul admitted to itself" [J1695, F1696].

There is, in fact, no way one can be armed against this particular kind of ghost. The murderer seeking to kill the body can be vanquished—one can borrow a revolver, bolt the door. But this assassin is hidden within oneself—is oneself. There is no escape. As Dickinson comments in poem 894 [J894, F1076], "Of Consciousness, her awful Mate/The Soul cannot be rid."

In the final stanza [of poem J670, F407] the quintessence of this horror is revealed. The rhetoric of the poem has been dramatic as well as concrete. Two dramas, in fact, have been enacted and contrasted. The external self has been venturing into lonesome abbeys, discovering hidden assassins in her chamber, even as the internal self has become aware of the existence of the "Cooler Host." Now the two plots turn into one. The self, who is, after all, body and mind at once, bolts the door, only to discover that she has locked herself in with herself. Adventuring in the external world, one need not confront one's own consciousness. But when one turns from "Horror's least" to live in the mind, that "superior spectre" can never be avoided again.

Because consciousness is self-confrontation, it establishes a "society" within, of "ourself" with "ourself." To represent the conflict and struggle engendered here, poem 642 uses an architectural vocabulary that provides a setting, fortress, for a drama of siege and defense. Yet even as "One need not be a Chamber—to be Haunted—" constructs a comparison between external and internal ghost stories only to conflate them, so the following poem's distinctions between inner and outer, protagonist and antagonist, turn out to be fictions.

> Me from Myself—to banish—
> Had I Art—
> Impregnable my Fortress
> Unto All Heart—
>
> But since Myself—assault Me—
> How have I peace
> Except by subjugating
> Consciousness?
>
> And since We're mutual Monarch
> How this be
> Except by Abdication—
> Me—of Me—?   [J642, F709]

The speaker of the poem "Myself" wishes for the ability to banish from her castle an enemy, called "Me." In the second stanza she admits to the complexity of the problem; more than skill is required to maintain the defense, because there is a profound connection between the combatants. Reversing their titles—"Me" is now the speaker, "Myself" the opponent—the poem acknowledges their interchangeability while at the same time continuing to deal with them as separate entities. The enemy is also identified as "Heart" in the first stanza, "Consciousness" in the second. That these are as much aspects of "Me" as they are of "Myself" the poem will not yet admit.

Although we know that the poem is discussing one person and not two, its dramatic fiction of attacker and attacked creates a situation that is surely war, albeit civil. When the dichotomy itself is collapsed in the final stanza, the effect is to intensify the situation, the pain, the impossibility of victory. "Mutual Monarch," the antagonists are revealed to be in actuality both within. There is nobody without. Without doesn't matter. Victory is impossible, is not a mere matter of "art," because enemy and friend are one. "Consciousness" is the self's awareness of itself and could be vanquished only through the annihilation of self, which would leave no victor, since no self is left. The very naming of the characters in this drama articulates and also anticipates this conclusion. If in stanza one the defender was Myself, the attacker, Me; and in stanza two the attacker was Myself, the defender, Me; in the final stanza they, as mutual Monarch, are "Me" and "Me."

The poem's structure dramatizes an experienced conflict. If the fictional dichotomy of within and without is necessary so that we might understand the problem, so is the final denial of the fiction, that we might better understand the conclusion: that self-consciousness means precisely the encounter of the self with itself, and that this is a perpetual struggle.

From "The American Plain Style"*

In a still broader sense of influence, the American idiom itself, in both its literary [14:
and daily forms, may have contributed to Dickinson's use of a style that is biblical in origin. By the mid-nineteenth century Puritan "plain style" had become the language of self-expression, the trusted idiom in America, although—or perhaps because—it had [14
lost its bolstering doctrinal and political contexts. According to Perry Miller's "An American Language," the plain style's demand that one speak from personal knowledge and as comprehensibly as possible made it the natural mode of discourse for a people living "in the wilderness:" and, by the late eighteenth century, attempting to form a democracy. All American writers, he claims, have had to deal with the consequences of this wholesale adoption of the principles and techniques of plain style. Because of its pervasiveness, Dickinson would inevitably have used language to some extent within its dictates. For epistemological reasons also, Dickinson may have felt some affinity for this style. Miller describes the plain style as inherently "defiant"—a style that both proclaims authority for the word and places the word's authority in individuals' articulate examinations of the truth; the style encourages practical discourse on theoretical or spiritual truths. Hence, it can as easily be turned against the idea of an authoritative God as it can be used to support that idea. Authority of language lies with the "plainest" (that is, apparently most artless yet still most commanding) speaker. The Puritans kept the style's implicit defiance in check by subordinating their word to God's Word; the latter was the law which theirs attempted to interpret and reflect. Emerson, Miller claims, partially maintained this check on defiance through his romantic belief in Nature as the origin of language, while Thoreau released the defiance of this style in his prose, "glory[ing] in his participation in the community of sin."

More covertly than Thoreau, Dickinson does the same. Her very disguise of defiance, however, may also stem in part from inherent characteristics of the plain style, which demands the simplicity reflected in its name but paradoxically also a kind of reticence that may prevent its complete message from being articulated. Ideally,

* From Christanne Miller, *Emily Dickinson: A Poet's Grammar* (Cambridge: Harvard UP, 1987).

the plain speaker "convey[s] the emphasis, the hesitancies, the searchings of language as it is spoken"; plainness lies in the apparent artlessness of the speaker's or writer's use of the word. Partly as a consequence, writers in the plain style leave much unsaid, and they claim that their discourse says even less than it does. Using words sparingly leaves much to implication, and making modest claims for a text may disguise the authority its author in fact feels. Thus the plain style frequently underplays its own importance and seriousness; even when it most anarchically expresses the perception of the individual, it maintains the guise of saying little, and that only matter-of-factly. Hence, while speaking "plain" truth, an individual may confound every doctrine that [145] the Puritans held true and believed the plain style must express. As Miller puts it: "The forthright method [plain style] proved to be . . . the most subversive power that the wicked could invoke against those generalities it had, long ago, been designed to protect." Through reticence, indirection, and disguised claims for the authority of her word, Dickinson manipulates characteristics of the plain use of language in poetry that contradict Puritan convictions about the individual's relation to God and His Word. The style that affirms God's truth for the Puritans, and denies that God's power is the only good (while still celebrating it) for Thoreau, becomes ironic with Dickinson: while appearing to affirm or naively question, she denies the trustworthiness of any superhuman power. . . .

It is in her attitude toward language and toward communication itself as much as in her characteristic manipulations of the word that Dickinson differs from her con- [146] temporaries and predecessors who wrote in plain style. Like them, she emphasizes the bare force of the word, eschewing elaborate syntax, modifiers, and extended conceits. Like them, she tends to stress the word's direct mediation between the individual and the world (for them, God). Like them, but to an unusual extreme, she makes small claims for her writing: her poems are "a letter to the World"; she is often a girl, or (like) a daisy, bird, spider, or gnat. Even when she has volcanic power, she generally appears harmless and unimportant: "A meditative spot—/An acre for a Bird to choose / Would be the General thought—" [J1677, F1743]. Dickinson, however, senses a different need for both plainness and reticence from those who believe in a natural or divine law of language. The word has two faces for her. Its effect may be epiphanic and it may come to her as a "gift," revealing "That portion of the Vision" she could not find without the help of "Cherubim" [J1126, F1243]. This is the language of poetry, of pure communication, "Like signal esoteric sips / Of the communion Wine" [J1452, F1476], or a "word of Gold" [J430, F388]. At other times the word is all but meaningless—an "Opinion" [J797, F849], an empty term. In a letter to Bowles she writes: "The old words are *numb*—and there *a'nt* any *new* ones—Brooks— are useless—in *Freshettime*—" (L 252). Her trick as poet is to make the old words new. To do this, she trusts "Philology," not God or Nature, and when she succeeds in doing this she feels that she has been lucky.

To Dickinson's mind, success in speaking plainly, in creating a word "that breathes" [J1651, F1715] does not prove spiritual salvation or make her a candidate for fame, partly because her sense of moral superiority depends on overthrowing the notion that God or the world can save her. The economical use of the words of ordinary life gives language its power. Speaking indirectly or subversively disguises the poet's usurpation of moral judgment from divine or human law, and thus saves her to speak again. As Perry Miller suggests, in Dickinson's poetry the pull between plainness and reticence subverts the whole idea of plainness. Because her meanings are not plain, they cannot be expressed plainly despite her use of simple words; her plainest speech *is* that of indirection.

As this conception of language implies, for Dickinson there is no stable relation between spiritual truth, the facts of existence, and the terms of language. Names are not adequate to things, and the function of language is not primarily to name. Things are perceived and understood through their relations to the rest of the world and by the process of cumulative, even contradictory, definition rather than by categorization or labeling. Dickinson has greater affinity with the lexicographer, the scientist of language seeking to clarify each word's various meanings, than she does with the Romantic *Ur*- [148 poet Adam. Her language stresses the relation between object and its effects or relations in an active world; meaning, for her, is not fixed by rules or even by her own previous perception of the world. The principles of Dickinson's world do not have to do with immutable properties and distinctions.

Dickinson manifests her belief in the flux or instability of relationship in the narratives of her poems more obviously than in her use of language. For example, the figures of her poems often change positions relative to each other, or prove to be undifferentiable rather than separate identities. In "The Moon is distant from the Sea," first "She" is the moon and "He" the water, then she becomes "the distant Sea—" and his are the ordering "Amber Hands—" of light [J429, F387]; the "single Hound" attending the Soul proves to be "It's own identity." [J822, F817]; in an early poem, she and her playmate Tim turn out to be "I—'Tim'—and—Me!" [J196, F231]. In a late poem, desired object, self, and "Messenger" are indistinguishable in both their presence and their absence; in a mockery of simplicity, all have the same name:

> We send the Wave to find the Wave—
> An Errand so divine,
> The Messenger enamored too,
> Forgetting to return,
> We make the wise distinction still,
> Soever made in vain,
> The sagest time to dam the sea is when the sea is gone—   [J1604, F1643]

Although this poem may be read as an elaboration of a truism—that one must give to receive, or that some losses cannot be prevented—it also ironically suggests that distinguishing present and absent sea (loved "Wave" from our own) is "vain." The "wise distinction" persists in failing to recognize the absurdity of damming what is not there and cannot be kept anyway. We attempt to conserve only what we have already lost.

Similarly, in "The Sea said 'Come' to the Brook" [J1210, F1275], the grown Brook takes the same form and title as the Sea that wanted to keep it small, as if to prove that the existence of one sea does not prevent the growth of innumerable physically indistinguishable others. In the last stanza it is not immediately clear which "Sea" is which:

> The Sea said "Go" to the Sea—
> The Sea said "I am he
> You cherished"—"Learned Waters—
> Wisdom is stale—to Me"

In countless other poems, unspecified and multiply referential "it" or "this" is as meaningful a subject for speculation as any clearly delineated event or object. Metaphor serves as the primary tool of definition and explanation because it allows for the greatest flexibility in its reference to fact.

From "The Histrionic Imagination"*

Dickinson recognized, early in her career, the value of the dramatic monologue and learned to use it with skill. A well-known poem, dated about 1858 or 1859 when the apprenticeship was nearing its end, serves both as an example in which she has not quite mastered the form but is alert to its efficacy and as a work in which she draws on her own experience but changes it in the act of speaking about it.

> I never lost as much but twice,
> And that was in the sod.
> Twice have I stood a beggar
> Before the door of God!
>
> Angels—twice descending
> Reimbursed my store—
> Burglar! Banker—Father!
> I am poor once more!   [J49, F39]

The story line of the verse is addressed to an imagined interlocutor on the subject of the power of God; when the poet allows the speaker to address God directly, however, the break in point of view discloses that Dickinson has not yet learned to integrate narration and drama. The austerely restricted language of the narrative is right for the recollection of painful loss in contrast to the defiant and improvident moment when the persona forgets the unidentified listener and turns in line seven to revile God directly, but an experienced poet does not lose awareness of the audience assumed in a mono- [83] logue even when the character being depicted rages on.

Despite the violation of point of view, or perhaps because of it, the supplicant's outburst continues to reverberate in our ears as we listen to the falling strain of a voice quickly regaining control and we believe we have overheard Emily Dickinson herself quarreling with God. When we find in a second poem, "Going to Heaven!" (#79, [J79, F128] c. 1859), that the persona, a young girl who both hopes to go and is glad she isn't going to heaven, says, "If you sh'd get there first / Save just a little place for me/ Close to the two I lost—," we look elsewhere for the experiences about which *she* is talking in the angry indictment of God. Who, among the people she loved, we ask, died during Dickinson's childhood and youth? And what other personal loss is of the enormity of death? Because neither poem gives any clues, we search the biography for them.

There was more anguish in the life of young Emily Dickinson than "I never lost as much but twice" enumerates. She recalled, in a letter of March 28, 1846, to Abiah Root, whose schoolmate had just died, an experience of early sorrow. The opening words of the recollection prefigure the idiomatic cadence in which the poem begins. She wrote: "I have never lost but one friend near my age & with whom my thoughts & her own were the same. It was before you came to Amherst. My friend was Sophia Holland. She was too lovely for earth & she was transplanted from earth to heaven. . . . Then it seemed to me I should die too." Emily, who was fourteen at the time of the death of her friend in the spring of 1844, gave way to "a fixed melancholy," told no one the cause of her grief, and was not well. Her parents sent her to Boston, where she stayed with relatives for a

---

*From Elizabeth Phillips, *Emily Dickinson: Personae and Performance* (University Park: Pennsylvania State UP, 1988).

month and her health improved so that her "spirits were better." In May 1846, her maternal grandfather, Joel Norcross, died; there is no record of how she felt about him, but she went again in August to Boston for her health. In May 1848, during her seventeenth year, Jacob Holt, a friend about whom she anxiously asked more than once in letters from Holyoke, died at the age of twenty-six; he wrote some rather commonplace poems, one of which she copied in her Bible. There were, also, other persons who are usually suggested as "the two" she lost in death. Since the emotions of loss became more complex as she matured, they well may be fused beyond one's ability to extricate them in the poem.

Leonard Humphrey, who was principal of the Amherst Academy in 1846–47, Emily's last year there, died at the age of twenty-six in November 1850; reporting the death of her "master" to Abiah, Emily mourned but did not give way to melancholy: "my [8⁴ rebellious thoughts," she asserted, "are many." Thereafter, Ben Newton, who introduced her to Emerson's poetry in 1850, left Amherst for Worcester, married in 1851, and died at the age of thirty-two on March 24, 1853. He taught her to read, she said, and was, "the first of my own friends." Had she forgotten Sophia Holland, who has not counted in explanations of the poet's loss?

Additional comments in the letters seem to lend support to readers who identify "the two she lost as Humphrey and Newton (Or are they "three": Holt, Humphrey, and Newton?) Writing on April 25, 1862, to Higginson, the poet said: "When a little Girl, I had a friend who taught me Immortality—but venturing too near, himself—he never returned—Soon after, my Tutor, died—and for several years, my Lexicon was my only companion." As if she were explaining "I never lost as much but twice," which Higginson had not seen, she added: "Then I found one more—but he was not contented I be his scholar—so he left the Land." This remark causes further speculation about whether the final loss in the poem is a kind different from that "in the sod." Casual readers then want to hear a name such as Charles Wadsworth or Samuel Bowles, neither of whom had "left the land" before or during the year in which Dickinson made a final copy of the verse ending with the dramatic cry: "Burglar! Banker—Father! / I am poor once more!"

There is not only too much evidence but too much uncertainty about what to choose from it for ascertaining the specific provocations of the poem's dramatic script. Nevertheless, if the letters to Abiah Root began the account of the incremental sorrow that is Dickinson's subject, one can say the soliloquy depends on events that are autobiographical but is not a literal recording of any one among them. The poet was rather finding words to make emotions *sound* true.

The recurrent experience of separations and loss may well be the source of another poem, which is more lyrical than dramatic. The emphasis is again on emotions related to a life "closed twice," but beyond the term "parting" there is no evidence that permits one to identity the events to which the persona refers. If the experiences are personal, they have been transmuted into flawless lines:

> My life closed twice before its close—
> It yet remains to see
> If Immortality unveil
> A third event to me
>
> So huge, so hopeless to conceive
> As these that twice befell.
> Parting is all we know of heaven,
> And all we need of hell.   [J1732, F1773, n.d.]

Although there is no autograph copy or date of composition for this justly famous poem, it points up Dickinson's practice of trying out different aspects of a theme in order to realize the perfection of form inherent in it. The poet ceased, moreover, to be an amateur in exploiting the possibilities of the dramatic monologue, which became the genre for a number of equally memorable Dickinson texts.

From "The Gothic Mode: 'Tis so appalling—it exhilarates—'"*

Emily Dickinson's gothic poems are perhaps her most startling challenge to the symbolic order. They are transgressive poems of great energy which explore taboo states usually excluded from consideration. In these poems the speakers spare the reader no excess in their relish of the macabre, as a selection of first lines suggests: 'As by the dead we love to sit' [J88, F78]; 'Do People moulder equally, / They bury, in the Grave?' [J432, F390] or 'If I may have it, when it's dead.' [J577, F431]. In many poems, the dead simply refuse to lie down; witty, garrulous corpses relentlessly address the reader from deathbed or grave: ''Twas just this time, last year, I died' [J445, F344]; 'I heard a Fly buzz—when I died—' [J465, F591}, 'I died for Beauty—' [J449, F448]. In others the speaker confronts an unknown self and experiences 'A doubt if it be Us' [J859, F903]. [87]

The Gothic poems fall into three main categories: those in which the speaker encounters unknown forces within the self; those in which the walking dead are women and continue Dickinson's explorations of gender; and those in which death is welcomed as a liberation from the confinements of the symbolic order. These poems challenge the ideals and propriety of the social order; they are disturbing because they question the certainty and rightness of its interpretations of the world. Madness suggests that there are forces within that are beyond its jurisdiction; human identity is not ultimately fixed, coherent, controlled, knowable. The dissolution of death is a permanent reminder of the fragility and artificiality of the social order and its rigid conventions. [88]

The nineteenth century saw the articulation of the idea of the unconscious and Dickinson's poems participate in that impulse. Dickinson was acutely aware of what Edward Young had referred to as 'the stranger within thee'. In his book *Night Thoughts* (1742–5), which was used as one of the textbooks at Amherst Academy, Young writes that reason is but 'a baffled counsellor': man looks within and finds 'an awful stranger'. Dickinson was similarly aware of an alien aspect to consciousness, writing in Poem 894: 'Of Consciousness, her awful Mate / The Soul cannot be rid—' [J894, F1076]. Sometimes consciousness was an oppressive companion:

> I do not know the man so bold
> He dare in lonely Place
> That awful stranger Consciousness
> Deliberately face—   [Poem J1323, F1325]

Several poems explore the encounter of the self with a stranger within. In Poem 670 [J670, F407], the internal ghost is an awesome force to be reckoned with:

> One need not be a Chamber—to be Haunted—
> One need not be a House—
> The Brain has Corridors—surpassing
> Material Place—

* From Joan Kirkby, *Emily Dickinson* (New York: St. Martin's, 1991).

Far safer, of a Midnight Meeting
External Ghost
Than its interior Confronting—   [89]
That Cooler Host.

Far safer, through an Abbey gallop,
The Stones a'chase—
Than Unarmed, one's a' self encounter—
In lonesome Place—

Ourself behind ourself, concealed—
Should startle most—
Assassin hid in our Apartment
Be Horror's least.

The Body—borrows a Revolver—
He bolts the Door—
O'erlooking a superior spectre—
Or More—

In this poem the mind itself is seen as more terrifying and dangerous than a haunted house; it has dark, unknown corridors surpassing 'Material place'. The encounter with one's concealed self is more dangerous than ghost, or graveyard, or assassin; they are 'Horror's least.' These could be fled on horseback, locked out or vanquished with revolver, but there is no escape from the self. Indeed the self hidden within the self is 'a superior spectre/—Or More', suggesting some terror greater than any hitherto conceived. The mind has within itself the potential for insurrection and dissolution. . . .

Dickinson's most famous Poem 712 [J712, F479] 'Because I could not stop for   [9 Death—' deals with a similar moment in which a woman is severed from her chosen tasks and carried off by an anonymous gentleman called 'Death'. Once again the fair theme of love is associated with 'a thought so mean'. However, this poem makes explicit the fact that the advent of the gentleman caller is nothing short of death for the woman. While this poem is usually read as a poem about death, revealing Dickinson's playfully macabre vision of death as a gentleman caller, it is a poem that identifies the gentleman caller as death; for him woman is expected to put away both her labour and her leisure. Like the woman in Poem 732 [J732, F857] she is expected to rise 'to His Requirement' and drop 'The Playthings of Her Life/To take the honorable Work/Of Woman, and of Wife—'.

Because I could not stop for Death—
He kindly stopped for me
The Carriage held but just Ourselves—
And Immortality.

We slowly drove—He knew no haste
And I had put away
My labor and my leisure too,
For His Civility—

We passed the School, where Children strove
At Recess—in the Ring—
We passed the Fields of Gazing Grain—   [99]
We passed the Setting Sun—

Or rather—He passed Us—
The Dews drew quivering and chill—
For only Gossamer, my Gown—
My Tippet—only Tulle—

We paused before a House that seemed
A Swelling of the Ground—
The Roof was scarcely visible—
The Cornice—in the Ground—

Since then—'tis Centuries—and yet
Feels shorter than the Day
I first surmised the Horses' Heads
Were toward Eternity—

The first stanza suggests that the female speaker is so deeply engaged in her own life that she does not wish to stop, but it also suggests the passivity of female desire. Courting is a male prerogative; she must wait to be called upon, but once chosen a surrender that is both quick and total is expected. She must give up her work and her leisure 'For His Civility'. He has all the privileges of authority; he nominates the time of execution but is regarded as 'kindly' and civil. That the death coach contains the new couple—'And Immortality'—suggests something of the enormous duration of the marriage journey. However, it also suggests that male authority extends into eternity; both earthly life and after life are in his hands; indeed that hypothesis underpins his authority here.

The second stanza highlights the slowness and solemnity of this journey to a bridal house that strongly resembles a grave. Like the anonymous 'He' in Poem 315 [J315, F477] 'He fumbles at your Soul', 'He knew no haste'. She is assumed to have no interest or activity separate from his. Rather like the woman in Poem 273 [J273, F330] 'He put [100] the Belt around my life—', she begins to sense her 'Lifetime folding up—'. As the journey progresses the speaker becomes increasingly aware that she has lost all agency and volition. Like the woman in Poem 443 [J443, F522] her 'ticking' has stopped. The fields of grain are 'gazing' at her; the setting sun 'passed Us'. In her bridal finery she experiences a mortal chill: 'For only Gossamer, my Gown— / My Tippet—only Tulle—'. Indeed the fine silk veil around her neck is a kind of noose; like the bride in Poem 1072 [J1072, F194] she is 'Born—Bridalled— Shrouded— / In a day—'. The wedding house turns out to be her grave; it is lowly and scarcely undifferentiated from the ground. Since this deathly bridal day, it seems like 'Centuries' and 'Eternity'. Dickinson's poem suggests the eternity of death-in-life endured after marriage, what the woman in Poem 443 [J443, F522] refers to as 'Miles on Miles of Nought—'.

In this poem woman is interrupted from her independent activities and brought to a house that seems 'A Swelling of the Ground', inevitably suggesting the house of biological destiny, the womb as tomb. There is the suggestion in the poem that female autonomy would threaten the existing order; a woman with her own work and her own leisure may be too busy 'to stop' for connubial death. In Poem 1445 [J1445, F1470]'Death is the supple Suitor', images of death and courtship are interwined in similar fashion; it is 'a stealthy Wooing'; a coach carries the woman away to 'Troth unknown' and 'Kindred as responsive/As Porcelain'.

Dickinson's most striking gothic poems are those in which the dead address the speaker from deathbed or grave. These poems bear out Gillian Beer's view that 'Ghost stories are to do with the insurrection, not the resurrection of the dead. It is the element of 'the insurrectionary' and 'the uncontrollable' that confounds. It goes without saying that these poems are disconcerting. Death is the ultimate taboo and the corpse [10] 'the ultimate impurity', 'the most sickening waste'. Yet Dickinson's speakers provocatively play on graves, sit by the dead, wonder if corpses moulder equally. In drawing near the corpse, the object that marks the limit between life and death, Dickinson invokes a place that is outside the rule of the symbolic order. In these poems, death marks the dissolution of the social order and becomes an emblem of liberation from its oppressive and artificial conventions. The corpse highlights the frailty of the symbolic order. As Julia Kristeva writes, a 'decaying body, lifeless, completely turned into dejection, blurred between the inanimate and the inorganic . . . the corpse represents fundamental pollution.' It is 'above all the opposite of the spiritual, of the symbolic, and of divine law.'

In Poem 465 [J465, F591] Dickinson presents a speaker beyond the limit of the symbolic order; she has 'Signed away/What portion of me be/Assignable—' and is henceforth to nature, a decomposing body subject only to the fly. The poem highlights the radical distance between the dying, who awaits the dissolution of the human into the undifferentiated matter of the corpse, and the living, who remain entirely bound up in the trappings of the social order, property, keepsakes, and the law of the father— 'the King' who is to be 'witnessed—in the Room—'.

> I heard a Fly buzz—when I died—
> The Stillness in the Room
> Was like the Stillness in the Air—
> Between the Heaves of Storm—
>
> The Eyes around—had wrung them dry—
> And Breaths were gathering firm
> For that last Onset—when the King
> Be witnessed—in the Room—
>
> I willed my Keepsakes—Signed away   [1]
> What portion of me be
> Assignable—and then it was
> There interposed a Fly—
>
> With Blue—uncertain stumbling Buzz—
> Between the light—and me—
> And then the Windows failed—and then
> I could not see to see—   [J465, F591]

At the moment of death, the speaker's attention is deflected by the buzz of a fly, lowly earthly representative of physical decay. For the dying person that simple presence erases all other concerns, social and religious alike. However, the living reaffirm their allegiance to the symbolic order. They turn their attention away from the dying person and what is represented by death to an affirmation of their faith; they prepare themselves to witness God's presence in the room, his taking of the dying person.

While the living await the 'King' and the re-inscription of the social order, the dying person awaits the fly and a decomposition of the self into corporeal waste. She has willed her keepsakes and signed away the portion of her with meaning in the social order, that is property, gender, social identity. The use of sign and assignable is significant in this context. In death the subject relinquishes the power to sign, to signify, to mark with characters, and to assign, to transfer or designate by writing. The corpse is outside the sign, outside the system of differences inscribed by the social order. The dead body is disconcertingly free of its rules, systems, distinctions and limits. In death there is also a dissolution of the gender-marked body. The corpse is an 'it', as the speaker notes in Poem 389 [J389, F547] 'There's been a Death, in the Opposite House':

> Somebody flings a Mattress out—
> The Children hurry by—
> They wonder if *it* died—on that   [103]
> I used to—when a Boy—

The buzzing fly blocks out the light of distinction and differentiation. The buzz of the fly is the antithesis of human language with its discrete units of modulated sounds. That the blue of the sky is transposed to the buzz of the fly suggests a further scrambling of the senses. Indeed the windows fail, which suggests a total breakdown of the social framing of experience. Windows are artificial barriers between inside and outside, nature and culture; windows frame and limit vision. However, in death the social framing of experience ends. There is darkness and a dissolution of all the restricting categories and hierarchies on which the social order is based.

A similar dynamics informs Poem 449 [J449, F448] which is Dickinson's witty retort to the closing lines of Keats' 'Ode on a Grecian Urn': 'Beauty is Truth, Truth Beauty,—that is all/ Ye know on earth and all ye need to know.' In Dickinson's poem death deposes pomp.

> I died for Beauty—but was scarce
> Adjusted in the Tomb
> When One who died for Truth, was lain
> In an adjoining Room—
>
> He questioned softly "Why I failed"?
> "For Beauty", I replied—
> "And I—for Truth—Themself are One—
> We Brethren, are", He said—
>
> And so, as Kinsmen, met a Night—
> We talked between the Rooms—
> Until the Moss had reached our lips—
> And covered up—our names—

The concepts and abstractions of the symbolic order avail for little here. The fact of   [104]
physical decomposition overtakes the speaker practically in mid sentence. The moss

covers up the speakers' names and makes the differences for which they died irrelevant. Each corpse has died as she thought in significance, for a large life ordering abstraction whose significance would continue after death. However, death marks the dissolution of the whole system of differences on which the social order is based. The moss like the fly signals the dissolution of the symbolic order as well as the decay of the body; the moss seals the lips, the locus of speech, and covers up 'our names—'.

ROBERT FROST   (1874–1963)

Life and Work

Robert Lee Frost (1874–1963) published his first book of poems, *A Boy's Will,* when he was living in England in 1913. At this time he was unrecognized and virtually unknown in the United States. Ezra Pound wrote that "it is a sinister thing that so American . . . a talent . . . should have to be exported before it can find due encouragement and recognition." Time, of course, made Frost the most visible and admired American poet of his day. He eventually received twenty-five honorary degrees and four Pulitzer Prizes. Although there was no officially recognized national poet until the 1980s (when the annual poet laureateships were established) he came as close as possible to being America's official poet when he read "The Gift Outright" at the inauguration of President John F. Kennedy in 1961. Writing in 1999, Joyce Carol Oates declared that "Frost's influence is so pervasive in American poetry, like Whitman's, as to be beyond assessment."[*] His collected poetic works continue to earn him this recognition.

Although in his person, and in his poetry, Frost presented himself as the quintessential New Englander, he was born on March 26, 1874, in California, where he spent his first ten years of life. His father, William Frost, had gone to San Francisco to take a job with the *San Francisco Bulletin,* and he and his wife Belle had their two children there. When William died in 1885, Frost's mother returned east to Lawrence, Massachusetts where Frost attended high school, studied classics, and began writing poetry. He graduated in 1892 as co-valedictorian with Elinor White, whom he married in 1895. After high school he attended Dartmouth College for seven weeks and then turned to newspaper work and teaching school. Two years after his marriage, he enrolled at Harvard (1897–1899), aiming at a specialty in classical literature. He had hoped to take classes with William James, but he was disappointed because James was on leave during the years of Frost's attendance. However, Frost was able to take a class taught by the famous philosopher George Santayana. Personal reasons, including an unwillingness to submit rigorously to academic discipline, led him to end his student days at Harvard without taking a degree.

The image that one gains of him at this time is that he had enormous capability, powerful energy, much anxiety and self-doubt, and uncertain focus. In later years he stated that his early interests inclined him toward a career in

[*] *American Poetry Review,* Vol. 28, No. 6 (Nov/Dec 1999): 9.

Robert Frost in 1915

archaeology, astronomy, farming, or teaching Latin. It does not seem that he had any vision of himself as the poet and man of letters he was to become. Even at the height of his fame he minimized his poetic achievement by telling an audience at Amherst College that all he ever wanted from his poetic career was to write "a few little poems it'd be hard to get rid of. That's all I ask."*

Much of Frost's early uncertainty resulted from his need to support his growing family. He gravitated toward farming as a way of life that would take up his physical energies and also give him the chance to think and to write. Fortunately, he had a supportive grandfather, William Frost, Sr., who backed up affection with financial support. In 1900 William Senior gave Robert a farm in Derry, New Hampshire, and for the next twelve years he lived in Derry, raised chickens and apples, wrote poetry, and taught English at Pinkerton Academy. His life was hard but satisfying, but, as he later said, he was "not much of a farmer." He preferred sitting up late at night to study, and then to sleep until noon. He did not see it as his obligation to get up with the sun and then go about the endless tasks needed for successful farming. He was also an unusual farmer because he had been acquiring an immense amount of erudition, including the study of Latin and Greek poets and large numbers of Shakespeare's sonnets. It was during this time in Derry, in the first decade of

---

* *Amherst Alumni News* (April 1954), quoted in Jay Parini, *Robert Frost: A Life* (New York: Henry Holt, 1999), p. 391.

the twentieth century, that he wrote many of his most famous poems, either in completed form or in draft form. He sent many of these poems to magazines, but was unsuccessful in getting them published.

By 1912 he was aching to devote himself to writing but was extremely discouraged with the way things were going. According to the terms of Grandfather Frost's gift, however, he was permitted to sell the farm and use the money for his own purposes. Because he believed that he might make a better start abroad, he planned a move to England, one of the many moves he was to make in his life. He also said that he might be poor abroad without embarrassing his relatives and friends. Once he landed in England, his poetic career was energized. He found a publisher who liked his poems and put him under contract. Almost overnight he emerged from obscurity through the publication of his first two poetic volumes, *A Boy's Will* (1913) and *North of Boston* (1914), which were favorably reviewed and which started to earn him acclaim in the United States. He also met a number of emerging and established poets, including Ezra Pound, T. S. Eliot, and William Butler Yeats.

Just as in 1913 he had been anxious to move abroad, early in 1915 he was anxious to return home. World War I had been declared, and he believed life would be better and safer in the United states. Once he got back he took up residence on a farm near Franconia, New Hampshire. His life after this time was one of increasing professional success together with a heavy burden of personal anxiety and grief. He and his wife had already lost two of their children in infancy. In addition, their daughter Marjorie died in 1934, and their son Carol, who suffered severe bouts of depression, committed suicide in 1940. Elinor herself had died in 1938. In addition, Frost was constantly stretching his finances to help his remaining adult children as they attempted to create their own lives. There is no question that the man who was becoming the most successful poet of his generation was also a person who suffered intensely in private.

But it must be emphasized that Frost's career as a poet flourished beyond his early hopes. In 1916 he published *Mountain Interval,* a book containing "The Road Not Taken," "Birches," and "Out, Out—." He soon was in constant demand as a teacher and speaker. Amherst College created the position of poet-in-residence for him, an honor that would continue for much of his life. He also regularly lectured at Michigan, Harvard, Yale, and Dartmouth. Stories abound about his brilliance in front of audiences, both large and small. Seminars that he began teaching in the afternoon would stretch late into the evening as he captivated his students with his insights and his immense knowledge. He was not popular only with students. With the development of television after 1950, Frost took to the new medium with great enthusiasm. With his memorable appearance and voice, he was interviewed on many early television shows, and as a result he became perhaps the most widely recognizable poet in the history of literature.

As he gained all these successes as a teacher and lecturer, his poetic output remained constant and regular. In 1923 he published *Selected Poems* and *New Hampshire*. The latter collection, for which he won a Pulitzer Prize, contains some of his best-known work: "Stopping by Woods on a Snowy Evening," "Fire and Ice," and "Nothing Gold Can Stay." Throughout his career there were many additional collections. *West Running Brook* appeared in 1928, *Collected Poems* in 1930. Additional collections were *A Further Range* (1936), *A Witness Tree* (1942), *Steeple Bush* (1947), *Complete Poems* (1949), *Aforesaid* (1954), and *In the Clearing* (1962).

Poetic Characteristics

Early in his career and throughout his long public experience as a speaker and lecturer, Frost cultivated his persona as a philosophical, wry, and wise country poet. This is the friendly, almost avuncular voice we most regularly hear, the one that expresses knowledge and concern for the land, history, and human nature. Even with this genial persona, however, there are complicated undertones of wit and irony. There is also what Randall Jarrell called "The Other Frost," the often agonized and troubled spirit whose voice is heard in poems like "Acquainted with the Night" and "Fire and Ice."

Regardless of the voice we hear, Frost preferred traditional poetic forms and rhythms, and he disapproved of free verse so strongly that he once asserted that writing it was like playing tennis without a net. He possessed complete knowledge of traditional forms (he knew much Latin poetry by heart). We therefore find that he uses conventional rhyme schemes and clear meters (with traditional metrical substitutions) in much of his poetry, together with closed forms such as couplets, sonnets (with interesting varying rhyme patterns), terza rima, quatrains, stanzas, and blank verse (see Chapter 20). Tension in the poems is created through the contrast of traditional form and Frost's characteristic conversational style. His diction is informal, plain, and colloquial, and his phrases are simple and direct. He uses and refines the natural speech patterns and rhythms of New England, polishing the language of everyday life and blending speech and formal patterns into a compact and unique poetic texture.

Structurally, Frost's poems typically move in a smooth, uninterrupted flow from an event or an object, through a metaphor, to an idea. Within this pattern, he usually describes a complete event rather than a single vision. The heart of the process is the image or metaphor. Frost's metaphors are sparse and careful; they are brought sharply into focus and skillfully interwoven within each poem. Frost himself saw metaphors as the beginning of the process. In *Education by Poetry* (1931) he states that "poetry begins in trivial metaphors, pretty metaphors, 'grace' metaphors, and goes on to the profoundest thinking that we have. Poetry provides the one permissible way of saying one thing and meaning another." In "The Figure a Poem Makes," a brief essay that he wrote as the Preface to his *The Complete Poems of Robert Frost* of 1949, he goes on further to describe what to him was the poetic process: "The figure a poem makes. It begins in delight and ends in wisdom. The figure is the same as for love. No one can really hold that the ecstasy should be static and stand still in one place. It begins in delight, it inclines to the impulse, it assumes direction with the first line laid down, it runs a course of lucky events, and ends in a clarification of life—not necessarily a great clarification, such as sects and cults are founded on, but in a momentary stay against confusion."

Poetic Subjects

Frost's poems are usually based in everyday life and rural settings. Poems are occasioned by flowers, stone fences, chopping wood, picking apples, sleigh riding, falling leaves, rain, snow, birch trees, insects, birds, hired men, and children, to name just a few of the topics. However, the Frostian poetic structure always moves from such subjects toward philosophical generalizations about life and death, survival and responsibility, and nature and humanity. As he said in "The Figure a Poem Makes," the "delight" of poetry "is in the surprise of remembering something I didn't know I knew."

One of Frost's major appeals is that his poems are easily accessible. They are by no means simplistic, however, but run deep, as seen, for example, in poems like "The Road Not Taken" and "Misgiving." They also may be complex and ambiguous, as in "Mending Wall," in which the philosophies of the speaker and his fence-repairing neighbor are well presented and contrasted. Readers often conclude that the speaker's wish to remove barriers is the poem's major idea, but the neighbor's argument for maintaining them is equally strong. Further, in "Desert Places" (Chapter 20) we are presented with a chilling view of the infinite desert within the human mind. In "Acquainted with the Night," Frost's sophisticated urban speaker tells us of the night of the city and also presents hints about the dark night of the soul.

BIBLIOGRAPHIC SOURCES

The standard edition of Frost's work is by Richard Poirier and Mark Richardson, eds., *Robert Frost: Collected Poems, Prose, & Plays* (New York: Library of America, 1995). Twelve of his lectures have been preserved in Reginald Cook, *Robert Frost, A Living Voice* (Amherst: U of Massachusetts P, 1974). The standard biography, although often hostile, is by Lawrance Thompson, in three volumes: *Robert Frost: The Early Years; The Years of Triumph;* and *The Later Years* (New York: Holt Rinehart, 1966–1977). The last volume was completed after Thompson's death by Roy H. Winnick. A supurb recent biography is Jay Parini, *Robert Frost: A Life* (New York: Henry Holt, 1999).

Useful criticism includes George Nitchie, *Human Values in the Poetry of Robert Frost* (Durham: Duke UP, 1960); Reuben Brower, *The Poetry of Robert Frost: Constellations of Intention* (New York: Oxford UP, 1963); Philip L. Gerber, *Robert Frost* (Boston: Twayne, 1966, rpt. 1982); Richard Poirier, *Robert Frost: The Work of Knowing* (Palo Alto: Stanford UP, 1990); John Kemp; *Robert Frost and New England: The Poet as Regionalist* (Princeton: Princeton UP, 1979); Richard Wakefield, *Robert Frost and the Opposing Lights of the Hour* (New York: Lang, 1985); James Potter, *A Robert Frost Handbook* (University Park: Pennsylvania State UP,

1980); Harold Bloom, ed., *Robert Frost* (New York: Chelsea House, 1986; a collection of critical essays); George Monteiro, *Robert Frost and the New England Renaissance* (Lexington: U of Kentucky P, 1988); Judith Oster, *Toward Robert Frost: The Reader and the Poet* (Athens: U of Georgia P, 1991); George F. Bagby, *Frost and the Book of Nature* (Knoxville: U of Tennessee P, 1993); and Katherine Kearns, *Robert Frost and a Poetics of Appetite* (New York: Cambridge UP, 1994). One of the hour-long programs in the PBS *Voices and Visions* series (1987) features his work.

SPECIAL TOPICS FOR WRITING AND ARGUMENT
ABOUT THE POETRY OF FROST

1. The nature of Frost's topics (situations, scenes, actions) and his use of them for observation, narration, and metaphor.
2. Frost's assessment of the human situation: work, love, death, choices, diminution of life, Stoicism, keeping or not keeping boundaries.
3. Frost's speaker: character, experiences, recollections, and reflections. In developing his subjects, to what degree does the speaker take a possible listener into account?
4. Frost as a poet of ideas. His vision of the way things are or should be.
5. Frost as a "confessional" poet: misgivings, the admission of personal error and personal fears.
6. Frost's use of narration and description in his poetry.
7. The structuring of Frost's poems: situation, observation, and generalization.
8. Frost's poetic diction: level and relationship to topic; conversational style.
9. Poetic forms in Frost: rhythm, meter, rhyme, and line and stanza patterns.
10. Frost's wry humor.

 POEMS BY ROBERT FROST*

*See also two additional poems by Frost in this anthology: "Desert Places," p. 912; and "Stopping by Woods on a Snowy Evening," (1923), p. 673.

A Line-Storm Song _____ 1913

The line-storm clouds fly tattered and swift.
   The road is forlorn all day,
Where a myriad snowy quartz stones lift,
   And the hoof-prints vanish away.
The roadside flowers, too wet for the bee,
   Expend their bloom in vain.
Come over the hills and far with me,
    And be my love in the rain.

The birds have less to say for themselves
   In the wood-world's torn despair
Than now these numberless years the elves,
   Although they are no less there:
All song of the woods is crushed like some
   Wild, easily shattered rose.
Come, be my love in the wet woods, come,
    Where the boughs rain when it blows.

There is the gale to urge behind
   And bruit our singing down,
And the shallow waters aflutter with wind
   From which to gather your gown.
What matter if we go clear to the west,
   And come not through dry-shod?
For wilding brooch shall wet your breast
    The rain-fresh goldenrod.

Oh, never this whelming east wind swells
   But it seems like the sea's return
To the ancient lands where it left the shells
   Before the age of the fern;
And it seems like the time when after doubt
   Our love came back amain.
Oh, come forth into the storm and rout
    And be my love in the rain.

Mending Wall _____ 1914

Something there is that doesn't love a wall,
That sends the frozen-ground-swell under it,

And spills the upper boulders in the sun;
And makes gaps even two can pass abreast.
The work of hunters is another thing: 5
I have come after them and made repair
Where they have left not one stone on a stone,
But they would have the rabbit out of hiding,
To please the yelping dogs. The gaps I mean,
No one has seen them made or heard them made,   10
But at spring mending-time we find them there.
I let my neighbor know beyond the hill;
And on a day we meet to walk the line
And set the wall between us once again.
We keep the wall between us as we go.   15
To each the boulders that have fallen to each.
And some are loaves and some so nearly balls
We have to use a spell to make them balance:
'Stay where you are until our backs are turned!'
We wear our fingers rough with handling them.   20
Oh, just another kind of outdoor game,
One on a side. It comes to little more:
There where it is we do not need the wall:
He is all pine and I am apple orchard.
My apple trees will never get across   25
And eat the cones under his pines, I tell him.
He only says, 'Good fences make good neighbors.'
Spring is the mischief in me, and I wonder
If I could put a notion in his head:
'*Why* do they make good neighbors? Isn't it   30
Where there are cows? But here there are no cows.
Before I built a wall I'd ask to know
What I was walling in or walling out,
And to whom I was like to give offense.
Something there is that doesn't love a wall,   35
That wants it down.' I could say 'Elves' to him,
But it's not elves exactly, and I'd rather
He said it for himself. I see him there
Bringing a stone grasped firmly by the top
In each hand, like an old-stone savage armed.   40
He moves in darkness as it seems to me,
Not of woods only and the shade of trees.
He will not go behind his father's saying,
And he likes having thought of it so well
He says again, 'Good fences make good neighbors.'   45

Birches ————————————————————————— *1915*

When I see birches bend to left and right
Across the lines of straighter darker trees,
I like to think some boy's been swinging them.

But swinging doesn't bend them down to stay
As ice-storms do. Often you must have seen them   5
Loaded with ice a sunny winter morning
After a rain. They click upon themselves
As the breeze rises, and turn many-colored
As the stir cracks and crazes their enamel.
Soon the sun's warmth makes them shed crystal shells   10
Shattering and avalanching on the snow-crust—
Such heaps of broken glass to sweep away
You'd think the inner dome of heaven had fallen.
They are dragged to the withered bracken by the load,
And they seem not to break; though once they are bowed   15
So low for long, they never right themselves:
You may see their trunks arching in the woods
Years afterwards, trailing their leaves on the ground
Like girls on hands and knees that throw their hair
Before them over their heads to dry in the sun.   20
But I was going to say when Truth broke in
With all her matter-of-fact about the ice-storm
I should prefer to have some boy bend them
As he went out and in to fetch the cows—
Some boy too far from town to learn baseball,   2
Whose only play was what he found himself,
Summer or winter, and could play alone.
One by one he subdued his father's trees
By riding them down over and over again
Until he took the stiffness out of them,   3
And not one but hung limp, not one was left
For him to conquer. He learned all there was
To learn about not launching out too soon
And so not carrying the tree away
Clear to the ground. He always kept his poise   3
To the top branches, climbing carefully
With the same pains you use to fill a cup
Up to the brim, and even above the brim.
Then he flung outward, feet first, with a swish,
Kicking his way down through the air to the ground.
So was I once myself a swinger of birches.
And so I dream of going back to be.
It's when I'm weary of considerations,
And life is too much like a pathless wood
Where your face burns and tickles with the cobwebs
Broken across it, and one eye is weeping
From a twig's having lashed across it open.
I'd like to get away from earth awhile
And then come back to it and begin over.
May no fate willfully misunderstand me
And half grant what I wish and snatch me away
Not to return. Earth's the right place for love:
I don't know where it's likely to go better.

I'd like to go by climbing a birch tree,
And climb black branches up a snow-white trunk   55
Toward Heaven, till the tree could bear no more,
But dipped its top and set me down again.
That would be good both going and coming back.
One could do worse than be a swinger of birches.

The Road Not Taken _____ *1915*

Two roads diverged in a yellow wood,
And sorry I could not travel both
And be one traveler, long I stood
And looked down one as far as I could
To where it bent in the undergrowth;   5

Then took the other, as just as fair,
And having perhaps the better claim,
Because it was grassy and wanted wear;
Though as for that the passing there
Had worn them really about the same,   10

And both that morning equally lay
In leaves no step had trodden black.
Oh, I kept the first for another day!
Yet knowing how way leads on to way,
I doubted if I should ever come back.   15

I shall be telling this with a sigh
Somewhere ages and ages hence:
Two roads diverged in a wood, and I—
I took the one less traveled by,
And that has made all the difference.   20

'Out, Out—' _____ *1916*

The buzz saw snarled and rattled in the yard
And made dust and dropped stove-length sticks of wood,
Sweet-scented stuff when the breeze drew across it.
And from there those that lifted eyes could count
Five mountain ranges one behind the other   5
Under the sunset far into Vermont.
And the saw snarled and rattled, snarled and rattled,
As it ran light, or had to bear a load.
And nothing happened: day was all but done.
Call it a day, I wish they might have said   10
To please the boy by giving him the half hour
That a boy counts so much when saved from work.
His sister stood beside them in her apron
To tell them 'Supper.' At the word, the saw,
As if to prove saws knew what supper meant,   15
Leaped out at the boy's hand, or seemed to leap—

He must have given the hand. However it was,
Neither refused the meeting. But the hand!
The boy's first outcry was rueful laugh,
As he swung toward them holding up the hand   2●
Half in appeal, but half as if to keep
The life from spilling. Then the boy saw all—
Since he was old enough to know, big boy
Doing a man's work, though a child at heart—
He saw all spoiled. 'Don't let him cut my hand off—   2.
The doctor, when he comes. Don't let him, sister!'
So. But the hand was gone already.
The doctor put him in the dark of ether.
He lay and puffed his lips out with his breath.
And then—the watcher at his pulse took fright.   3
No one believed. They listened at his heart.
Little–less–nothing!–and that ended it.
No more to build on there. And they, since they
Were not the one dead, turned to their affairs.

The Oven Bird _____ 1916

There is a singer everyone has heard,
Loud, a mid-summer and a mid-wood bird,
Who makes the solid tree trunks sound again.
He says that leaves are old and that for flowers
Mid-summer is to spring as one to ten.
He says the early petal-fall is past
When pear and cherry bloom went down in showers
On sunny days a moment overcast;
And comes that other fall we name the fall.
He says the highway dust is over all.
The bird would cease and be as other birds
But that he knows in singing not to sing.
The question that he frames in all but words
Is what to make of a diminished thing.

Fire and Ice _____ 1920

Some say the world will end in fire,
Some say in ice.
From what I've tasted of desire
I hold with those who favor fire.
But if it had to perish twice,
I think I know enough of hate
To say that for destruction ice
Is also great
And would suffice.

Misgiving ————————————————————— *1923*

All crying, 'We will go with you, O Wind!'
The foliage follow him, leaf and stem;
But a sleep oppresses them as they go,
And they end by bidding him stay with them.

Since ever they flung abroad in spring   5
The leaves had promised themselves this flight,
Who now would fain seek sheltering wall,
Or thicket, or hollow place for the night.

And now they answer his summoning blast
With an ever vaguer and vaguer stir,   10
Or at utmost a little reluctant whirl
That drops them no further than where they were.

I only hope that when I am free
As they are free to go in quest
Of the knowledge beyond the bounds of life   15
It may not seem better to me to rest.

Nothing Gold Can Stay ————————————————— *1923*

Nature's first green is gold,
Her hardest hue to hold.
Her early leaf's a flower;
But only so an hour.
Then leaf subsides to leaf.   5
So Eden sank to grief,
So dawn goes down to day.
Nothing gold can stay.

Acquainted with the Night ————————————— *1928*

I have been one acquainted with the night.
I have walked out in rain—and back in rain.
I have outwalked the furthest city light.

I have looked down the saddest city lane.
I have passed by the watchman on his beat   5
And dropped my eyes, unwilling to explain.

I have stood still and stopped the sound of feet
When far away an interrupted cry
Came over houses from another street,

But not to call me back or say good-by;   10
And further still at an unearthly height,
One luminary clock against the sky

Proclaimed the time was neither wrong nor right.
I have been one acquainted with the night.

Design ———————————————————————— *1936*

I found a dimpled spider, fat and white,
On a white heal-all,° holding up a moth
Like a white piece of rigid satin cloth—
Assorted characters of death and blight
Mixed ready to begin the morning right,
Like the ingredients of a witches' broth—
A snow-drop spider, a flower like a froth,
And dead wings carried like a paper kite.

What had that flower to do with being white,
The wayside blue and innocent heal-all?
What brought the kindred spider to that height,
Then steered the white moth thither in the night?
What but design of darkness to appall?—
If design govern in a thing so small.

DESIGN.   2 *heal-all:* a flower, usually blue, thought to have healing powers.

The Silken Tent ———————————————————— *1936*

She is as in a field a silken tent
At midday when a sunny summer breeze
Has dried the dew and all its ropes relent,
So that in guys it gently sways at ease,
And its supporting central cedar pole,
That is its pinnacle to heavenward
And signifies the sureness of the soul,
Seems to owe naught to any single cord,
But strictly held by none, is loosely bound
By countless silken ties of love and thought
To everything on earth the compass round,
And only by one's going slightly taut
In the capriciousness of summer air
Is of the slightest bondage made aware.

The Strong Are Saying Nothing ———————————— *1937*

The soil now gets a rumpling soft and damp,
And small regard to the future of any weed.
The final flat of the hoe's approval stamp
Is reserved for the bed of a few selected seed.

There is seldom more than a man to a harrowed piece.   5
Men work alone, their lots plowed far apart,
One stringing a chain of seed in an open crease,
And another stumbling after a halting cart.

To the fresh and black of the squares of early mold
The leafless bloom of a plum is fresh and white;   10
Though there's more than a doubt if the weather is not too cold
For the bees to come and serve its beauty aright.

Wind goes from farm to farm in wave on wave,
But carries no cry of what is hoped to be.
There may be little or much beyond the grave,   15
But the strong are saying nothing until they see.

A Considerable Speck ———————————————— *1942*

(Microscopic)

A speck that would have been beneath my sight
On any but a paper sheet so white
Set off across what I had written there.
And I had idly poised my pen in air
To stop it with a period of ink   5
When something strange about it made me think.
This was no dust speck by my breathing blown,
But unmistakably a living mite
With inclinations it could call its own.
It paused as with suspicion of my pen,   10
And then came racing wildly on again
To where my manuscript was not yet dry;
Then paused again and either drank or smelt—
With loathing, for again it turned to fly.
Plainly with an intelligence I dealt.   15
It seemed too tiny to have room for feet,
Yet must have had a set of them complete
To express how much it didn't want to die.
It ran with terror and with cunning crept.
It faltered: I could see it hesitate;   20
Then in the middle of the open sheet

Cower down in desperation to accept
Whatever I accorded it of fate.
I have none of the tenderer-than-thou
Collectivistic regimenting love   25
With which the modern world is being swept
But this poor microscopic item now!
Since it was nothing I knew evil of
I let it lie there till I hope it slept.
I have a mind myself and recognize   30
Mind when I meet with it in any guise.
No one can know how glad I am to find
On any sheet the least display of mind.

Choose Something like a Star ———————————————————————*1943*

O Star (the fairest one in sight),
We grant your loftiness the right
To some obscurity of cloud—
It will not do to say of night,
Since dark is what brings out your light.
Some mystery becomes the proud.
But to be wholly taciturn
In your reserve is not allowed.
Say something to us we can learn
By heart and when alone repeat.   1
Say something! And it says, 'I burn,'
But say with what degree of heat.
Talk Fahrenheit, talk Centigrade.
Use language we can comprehend.
Tell us what elements you blend.
It gives us strangely little aid,
But does tell something in the end.
And steadfast as Keats' Eremite,
Not even stooping from its sphere,
It asks a little of us here.
It asks of us a certain height,
So when at times the mob is swayed
To carry praise or blame too far,
We may choose something like a star
To stay our minds on and be staid.

25

Poems for Additional Study

POEMS FOR STUDY

A. R. AMMONS   (b. 1926)

80-Proof _____ 1975

A fifth of me's me:
the rest's chaser:
35 lbs.'s
my true self: but
chuck 10 lbs. or so for bones,
what's left's
steaks & chops &
chicken fat,
two-over-easy & cream-on-the-side:
strip off a sheath of hide,
strip out nerves & veins
& permeable membranes,
what's left's a greasy spot:

the question's
whether   15
to retain
the shallow stain
or go 100% spiritual
and fifth by fifth
achieve a whole,   20
highly transcendental.

MAYA ANGELOU   (b. 1928)

My Arkansas _____ *1978*

There is a deep brooding
in Arkansas.
Old crimes like moss pend
from poplar trees.
The sullen earth   5
is much too
red for comfort.

Sunrise seems to hesitate
and in that second
lose its   10
incandescent aim, and
dusk no more shadows
than the noon.
The past is brighter yet.

Old hates and   15
ante-bellum° lace, are rent
but not discarded.
Today is yet to come
in Arkansas.
It writhes. It writhes in awful   20
waves of brooding.

MY ARKANSAS.   16 *ante-bellum:* before the U.S. Civil War (1861–1865).

ANONYMOUS

Barbara Allan _____ *Sixteenth century*

It was in and about the Martinmas° time,   *November 11*
   When the green leaves were a-fallin',
That Sir John Graeme in the West Country
   Fell in love with Barbara Allan.

He sent his man down through the town   5
   To the place where she was dwellin':
"O haste and come to my master dear,
   Gin° ye be Barbara Allan."   *if*

O slowly, slowly rose she up,
   To the place where he was lyin',   10
And when she drew the curtain by:
   "Young man, I think you're dyin'."

"O it's I'm sick, and very, very sick,
   And 'tis all for Barbara Allan."
"O the better for me ye shall never be,   15
   Though your heart's blood were a-spillin'."

"O dinna ye mind,° young man," said she,   *don't you recall*
   "When ye the cups were fillin',
That ye made the healths° go round and round,   *toasts*
   And slighted Barbara Allan?"   20

He turned his face unto the wall,
   And death with him was dealin':
"Adieu, adieu,° my dear friends all,   *farewell*
   And be kind to Barbara Allan."

And slowly, slowly, rose she up,   25
   And slowly, slowly left him;
And sighing said she could not stay,
   Since death of life had reft him.°   *since death had bereft him of life*

She had not gone a mile but twa,°   *two*
   When she heard the dead-bell knellin',
And every jow° that the dead-bell ga'ed°   *stroke; made*
   It cried, "Woe to Barbara Allan!"

"O mother, mother, make my bed,
   O make it soft and narrow:
Since my love died for me today,
   I'll die for him tomorrow."

ANONYMOUS (NAVAJO)

Healing Prayer from the Beautyway Chant ———————————— *Traditional*

Out of the East, Beauty has come home,
Out of the South, Beauty has come home,
Out of the West, Beauty has come home,
Out of the North, Beauty has come home,
Out of the highest heavens and the lowest lands,
   Beauty has come home.
      Everywhere around us, Beauty has come home.

As we live each day, everything evil will leave us.
    We will be entirely healed,
    Our bodies will exult in the fresh winds,   10
    Our steps will be firm.
As we live each day,
    Everything before us will be Beautiful;
    Everything behind us will be Beautiful;
    Everything above us will be Beautiful;   15
    Everything below us will be Beautiful;
    Everything around us will be Beautiful;
    All our thoughts will be Beautiful;
    All our words will be Beautiful;
    All our dreams will be Beautiful.   20
We will be forever restored, forever whole.
All things will be Beautiful forever.

ANONYMOUS

Lord Randal ————————————————————— *Sixteenth century*

"Oh, where have you been, Lord Randal, my son?
Oh, where have you been, my handsome young man?"
"Oh, I've been to the wildwood; mother, make my bed soon,
I'm weary of hunting and I fain° would lie down."   *gladly*

"And whom did you meet there, Lord Randal, my son?   5
And whom did you meet there, my handsome young man?"
"Oh, I met with my true love; mother, make my bed soon,
I'm weary of hunting and I fain would lie down."

"What got you for supper, Lord Randal, my son?
What got you for supper, my handsome young man?"   10
"I got eels boiled in broth; mother, make my bed soon,
I'm weary of hunting and I fain would lie down."

"And who got your leavings, Lord Randal, my son?
And who got your leavings, my handsome young man?"
"I gave them to my dogs; mother, make my bed soon,   15
I'm weary of hunting and I fain would lie down."

"And what did your dogs do, Lord Randal, my son?
And what did your dogs do, my handsome young man?"
"Oh, they stretched out and died; mother, make my bed soon,
I'm weary of hunting and I fain would lie down."   20

"Oh, I fear you are poisoned, Lord Randal, my son,
Oh, I fear you are poisoned, my handsome young man."
"Oh, yes, I am poisoned; mother, make my bed soon,
For I'm sick at my heart and I fain would lie down."

"What will you leave your mother, Lord Randal, my son?
What will you leave your mother, my handsome young man?"
"My house and my lands; mother, make my bed soon,
For I'm sick at my heart and I fain would lie down." 25

"What will you leave your sister, Lord Randal, my son?
What will you leave your sister, my handsome young man?"
"My gold and my silver; mother, make my bed soon,
For I'm sick at my heart and I fain would lie down." 3

"What will you leave your brother, Lord Randal, my son?
What will you leave your brother, my handsome young man?"
"My horse and my saddle; mother, make my bed soon,
For I'm sick at my heart and I fain would lie down." 3

"What will you leave your true-love, Lord Randal, my son?
What will you leave your true-love, my handsome young man?"
"A halter to hang her; mother, make my bed soon,
For I'm sick at my heart and I want to lie down." 4

ANONYMOUS

The Three Ravens ———————————————————— *Sixteenth century*

There were three ravens sat on a tree,
  Down a down, hay down, hay down,
There were three ravens sat on a tree,
  With a down,
There were three ravens sat on a tree,
They were as black as they might be,
  With a down, derry, derry, derry, down, down.°

The one of them said to his mate,
"Where shall we our breakfast take?

"Down in yonder green field
There lies a knight slain under his shield.

"His hounds they lie down at his feet,
So well they can their master keep.

"His hawks they fly so eagerly,°   *fiercely*
There's no fowl° dare him come nigh."   *bird*

Down there comes a fallow° doe,   *light brown*
As great with young as she might go,°   *walk*

She lifted up his bloody head,
And kissed his wounds that were so red.

THE THREE RAVENS. 7 *down:* In singing this ballad, the first line of each stanza is repeated
three times and the refrain is repeated as in stanza 1.

She got him up upon her back,   20
And carried him to earthen lake.°   *pit*

She buried him before the prime,°   *morning prayer service*
She was dead herself ere evensong time.°
God send every gentleman
Such hawks, such hounds, and such a lemman.°   *mistress*

23 *evensong time:* the time for the evening prayer service.

ANONYMOUS

Waly, Waly ————————————————————— *Eighteenth century*

O waly, waly, up the bank,
    And waly, waly, down the brae,
And waly, waly, yon burn side,
    Where I and my love were wont to gae.

I leant my back upon an oak,   5
    I thought it was a trusty tree;
But first it bent, and then it broke,
    Just as my love proved false to me.

O waly, waly, love is bonny,
    A little while when it is new;   10
But when it's old, it waxes cold,
    And fades away like morning dew.

O wherefore should I busk my head?
    O wherefore should I comb my hair?
For my true love has me forsook,   15
    And says he'll never love me more.

Now Arthur's Seat shall be my bed,
    The sheets shall ne'er be filled by me:
Saint Anthony's well shall be my drink,
    Since my true love has forsaken me.   20

Martinmas wind, when wilt thou blow,
    And shake the green leaves off the tree?
O gentle death, when wilt thou come?
    For of my life I am weary.

'Tis not the frost, that freezes fell,   25
    Nor blowing snow's inclemency;
'Tis not such cold that makes me cry,
    But my love's heart grown cold to me.

When we came in by Glasgow town,
    We were a comely sight to see,   30

My love was clad in black velvet,
  And I myself in cramasie.°   crimson

But had I wist, before I kissed,
  That love had been so ill to win,
I'd locked my heart in a case of gold,   35
  And pinned it with a silver pin.

And oh! if my young babe were born,
  And set upon the nurse's knee,
And I my self were dead and gone:
  For a maid again I'll never be. ·   4(

MARGARET ATWOOD   (b. 1939)

Variation on the Word Sleep _____ *1981*

I would like to watch you sleeping,
which may not happen.
I would like to watch you,
sleeping. I would like to sleep
with you, to enter
your sleep as its smooth dark wave
slides over my head

and walk with you through that lucent
wavering forest of bluegreen leaves
with its watery sun & three moons
towards the cave where you must descend,
towards your worst fear

I would like to give you the silver
branch, the small white flower, the one
word that will protect you
from the grief at the center
of your dream, from the grief
at the center. I would like to follow
you up the long stairway
again & become
the boat that would row you back
carefully, a flame
in two cupped hands
to where your body lies
beside me, and you enter
it as easily as breathing in

I would like to be the air
that inhabits you for a moment
only. I would like to be that unnoticed
& that necessary.

W. H. AUDEN   (1907–1973)

The Unknown Citizen _____ *1940*

(To JS/07/M/378
This Marble Monument
Is Erected by the State)

He was found by the Bureau of Statistics to be
One against whom there was no official complaint,
And all the reports on his conduct agree
That, in the modern sense of an old-fashioned word, he was a saint,
For in everything he did he served the Greater Community.   5

Except for the War till the day he retired
He worked in a factory and never got fired,
But satisfied his employers, Fudge Motors Inc.
Yet he wasn't a scab° or odd in his views.   *strikebreaker*
For his Union reports that he paid his dues,   10
(Our report on his Union shows it was sound)
And our Social Psychology workers found
That he was popular with his mates° and liked a drink.   *co-workers*
The Press are convinced that he bought a paper every day
And that his reactions to advertisements were normal in every way.   15
Policies taken out in his name prove that he was fully insured,
And his Health-card shows he was once in hospital but left it cured.
Both Producers Research and High-Grade Living declare
He was fully sensible to the advantages of the Installment Plan
And had everything necessary to the Modern Man,   20
A phonograph, a radio, a car and a frigidaire.
Our reseachers into Public Opinion are content
That he held the proper opinions for the time of year;
When there was peace, he was for peace; when there was war, he went.
He was married and added five children to the population,   25
Which our Eugenist says was the right number for a parent of his generation,
And our teachers report that he never interfered with their education.
Was he free? Was he happy? The question is absurd:
Had anything been wrong, we should certainly have heard.

IMAMU AMIRI BARAKA (LEROI JONES)   (b. 1934)

Ka 'Ba _____ *1969*

A closed window looks down
on a dirty courtyard, and black people
call across or scream across or walk across
defying physics in the stream of their will

Our world is full of sound   5
Our world is more lovely than anyone's
tho we suffer, and kill each other
and sometimes fail to walk the air

We are beautiful people
with african imaginations   10
full of masks and dances and swelling chants
with african eyes, and noses, and arms,
though we sprawl in grey chains in a place
full of winters, when what we want is sun.

We have been captured,   15
brothers. And we labor
to make our getaway, into
the ancient image, into a new

correspondence with ourselves
and our black family. We need magic   20
now we need the spells, to raise up
return, destroy, and create. What will be

the sacred words?

WENDELL BERRY   (b. 1934)

Through the Weeks of Deep Snow _____ *1985*

Through the weeks of deep snow
we walked above the ground
on fallen sky, as though we did
not come of root and leaf, as though
we had only air and weather
for our difficult home.
                            But now
as March warms, and the rivulets
run like birdsong on the slopes,
and the branches of light sing in the hills,
slowly we return to earth.

EARLE BIRNEY   (1904–1995)

Can. Lit.° _____ *1962*

(or them able leave her ever)

since we'd always sky about
when we had eagles they flew out

CAN LIT.   The title is an abbreviation for "Canadian Literature."

leaving no shadow bigger than wren's
to trouble even our broodiest hens
too busy bridging loneliness   5
to be alone
we hacked in railway ties
what Emily° etched in bone

we French & English never lost
our civil war   10
endure it still
a bloody civil bore

the wounded sirened off
no Whitman° wanted
it's only by our lack of ghosts   15
we're haunted

---

8 *Emily:* Emily Dickinson (1830–1886), American poet (see pp. 1060–1100).   14 *Whitman:* Walt
Whitman (1819–1892), American poet.

LOUISE BOGAN   (1879–1970)

Women _____ *1923*

Women have no wilderness in them,
They are provident instead,
Content in the tight hot cell of their hearts
To eat dusty bread.

They do not see cattle cropping red winter grass,   5
They do not hear
Snow water going down under culverts
Shallow and clear.

They wait, when they should turn to journeys,
They stiffen, when they should bend.   10
They use against themselves that benevolence
To which no man is friend.

They cannot think of so many crops to a field
Or of clean wood cleft by an axe.
Their love is an eager meaninglessness   15
Too tense, or too lax.

They hear in every whisper that speaks to them
A shout and a cry.
As like as not, when they take life over their door-sills
They should let it go by.   20

ARNA BONTEMPS   (1902–1973)

A Black Man Talks of Reaping ———————————————————————— *1940*

I have sown beside all waters in my day.
I planted deep, within my heart the fear
that wind or fowl would take the grain away.
I planted safe against this stark, lean year.

I scattered seed enough to plant the land
in rows from Canada to Mexico
but for my reaping only what the hand
can hold at once is all that I can show.

Yet what I sowed and what the orchard yields
my brother's sons are gathering stalk and root;
small wonder then my children glean in fields
they have not sown, and feed on bitter fruit.

ANNE BRADSTREET   (1612–1672)

To My Dear and Loving Husband ———————————————————————— *1678*

If ever two were one, then surely we.
If ever man were loved by wife, then thee;
If ever wife was happy in a man,
Compare with me ye women if you can.
I prize thy love more than whole mines of gold,
Or all the riches that the East doth hold.
My love is such that rivers cannot quench,
Nor ought but love from thee give recompense.
Thy love is such I can no way repay;
The heavens reward thee manifold, I pray.
Then while we live, in love let's so persever,
That when we live no more we may live ever.

GWENDOLYN BROOKS   (b. 1917)

Primer for Blacks ———————————————————————— *1980*

Blackness
is a title,
is a preoccupation,
is a commitment Blacks
are to comprehend—
and in which you are
to perceive your Glory.

The conscious shout
of all that is white is
"It's Great to be white." 10
The conscious shout
of the slack in Black is
"It's Great to be white."
Thus all that is white
has white strength and yours. 15

The word Black
has geographic power,
pulls everybody in:
Blacks here—
Blacks there— 20
Blacks wherever they may be.
And remember, you Blacks, what they told you—
remember your Education:
"one Drop—one Drop
maketh a brand new Black." 25
    Oh mighty Drop.
——And because they have given us kindly
so many more of our people

Blackness
stretches over the land. 30
Blackness—
the Black of it,
the rust-red of it,
the milk and cream of it,
the tan and yellow-tan of it, 35
the deep-brown middle-brown high-brown of it,
the "olive" and ochre of it—
Blackness
marches on.

The huge, the pungent object of our prime out-ride 40
is to Comprehend,
to salute and to Love the fact that we are Black,
which *is* our "ultimate Reality,"
which is the lone ground
from which our meaningful metamorphosis, 45
from which our prosperous staccato,
group of individual, can rise.

Self-shriveled Blacks.
Begin with gaunt and marvelous concession:
YOU are our costume and our fundamental bone. 50

    All of you—
    You COLORED ones,
    you NEGRO ones,
those of you who proudly cry

"I'm half INDian"—   55
those of you who proudly screech
"I'VE got the blood of George WASHington in
    MY veins"—

ALL of you—
    you proper Blacks,   60
you half-Blacks,
you wish-I-weren't Blacks,
Niggeroes and Niggerenes.

You.

ELIZABETH BARRETT BROWNING   (1806–1861)

Sonnets from the Portuguese: Number 43 _____ *1850*

How do I love thee? Let me count the ways.
I love thee to the depth and breadth and height
My soul can reach, when feeling out of sight
For the ends of Being and ideal Grace.
I love thee to the level of every day's
Most quiet need, by sun and candlelight.
I love thee freely, as men strive for Right;
I love thee purely, as they turn from Praise.
I love thee with the passion put to use
In my old griefs, and with my childhood's faith.
I love thee with a love I seemed to lose
With my lost saints,—I love thee with the breath,
Smiles, tears, of all my life!—and, if God choose,
I shall but love thee better after death.

ROBERT BROWNING   (1812–1889)

Soliloquy of the Spanish Cloister _____ *1842*

1

Gr-r-r—there go, my heart's abhorrence!
    Water your damned flowerpots, do!
If hate killed men, Brother Lawrence,
    God's blood, would not mine kill you!
What? your myrtle bush wants trimming?
    Oh, that rose has prior claims—
Needs its leaden vase filled brimming?
    Hell dry you up with its flames!

2

At the meal we sit together:
    Salve tibi!° I must hear   *Hail to thee!*
Wise talk of the kind of weather,

Sort of season, time of year:
Not a plenteous cork-crop: scarcely
    Dare we hope oak-galls, I doubt:
What's the Latin name for "parsley"?   15
    What's the Greek name for Swine's Snout?

                          3
Whew! We'll have our platter burnished,
    Laid with care on our own shelf!
With a fire-new spoon we're furnished,
    And a goblet for ourself,   20
Rinsed like something sacrificial
    Ere 'tis fit to touch our chaps°   jaws
Marked with L. for our initial!
    (He-he! There his lily snaps!)

                          4
Saint, forsooth! While brown Dolores   25
    Squats outside the Convent bank
With Sanchicha, telling stories,
    Steeping tresses in the tank,
Blue-black, lustrous, thick like horsehairs,
    —Can't I see his dead eye glow,   30
Bright as 'twere a Barbary corsair's?°   pirate's
    (That is, if he'd let it show!)

                          5
When he finishes refection,°   dinner
    Knife and fork he never lays
Cross-wise, to my recollection,   35
    As do I, in Jesu's praise.
I the Trinity illustrate,
    Drinking watered orange-pulp—
In three sips the Arian° frustrate;   Anti-Trinitarian (a heretic)
    While he drains his at one gulp.   40

                          6
Oh, those melons? If he's able
    We're to have a feast! so nice!
One goes to the Abbot's table,
    All of us get each a slice.
How go on your flowers? None double?   45
    Not one fruit-sort can you spy?
Strange!—And I, too, at such trouble,
    Keep them close-nipped on the sly!

                          7
There's a great text in Galatians,°   perhaps 3:10 or 5:19–21
    Once you trip on it, entails   50
Twenty-nine distinct damnations,

One sure, if another fails:
    If I trip him just a-dying,
        Sure of heaven as sure can be,
Spin him round and send him flying   55
        Off to hell, a Manichee?°   *heretic*

8

Or, my scrofulous° French novel   *pornographic*
    On gray paper with blunt type!
Simply glance at it, you grovel
    Hand and foot in Belial's° gripe: *the Devil* 60
If I double down its pages
    At the woeful sixteenth print,
When he gathers his greengages,
    Ope a sieve and slip it in't?

9

Or, there's Satan!—one might venture   65
    Pledge one's soul to him, yet leave
Such a flaw in the indenture°   *contract*
    As he'd miss till, past retrieve,
Blasted lay that rose-acacia
    We're so proud of! *Hy, Zy, Hine* . . .   70
'St, there's Vespers! *Plena gratiâ*°   *full of grace*
    Ave, Virgo!° Gr-r-r—you swine!   *Hail, Virgin!*

GEORGE GORDON, LORD BYRON   (1788–1824)

The Destruction of Sennacherib° _____ *1815*

The Assyrian came down like the wolf on the fold,
And his cohorts were gleaming in purple and gold;
And the sheen of their spears was like stars on the sea,
When the blue wave rolls nightly on deep Galilee.

Like the leaves of the forest when summer is green,
That host with their banners at sunset were seen:
Like the leaves of the forest when autumn hath blown,
That host on the morrow lay withered and strown.

THE DESTRUCTION OF SENNACHERIB. Sennacherib was king of the ancient Near Eastern empire of Assyria from 705 to 681 B.C.E. He laid seige to Jerusalem in about 702 B.C.E., even though King Hezekiah had already rendered tribute to Assyria. According to 2 Kings 19:35–36, a miracle occurred to save the besieged Hebrews: "the angel of the Lord went out and smote . . . [185,000 Assyrian soldiers]; and when they [the Hebrews] arose early in the morning, behold, they [the Assyrians] were all dead corpses." See p. 791.

For the Angel of Death spread his wings on the blast,
And breathed in the face of the foe as he passed;   10
And the eyes of the sleepers waxed deadly and chill,
And their hearts but once heaved—and for ever grew still!

And there lay the steed with his nostril all wide,
But through it there rolled not the breath of his pride;
And the foam of his gasping lay white on the turf,   15
And cold as the spray of the rock-beating surf.

And there lay the rider distorted and pale,
With the dew on his brow, and the rust on his mail;
And the tents were all silent, the banners alone,
The lances unlifted, the trumpet unblown.   20

And the widows of Ashur° are loud in their wail,
And the idols are broke in the temple of Baal;°
And the might of the Gentile, unsmote by the sword,
Hath melted like snow in the glance of the Lord!

21 *Ashur:* the land of the Assyrians.   22 *Baal:* a god who supposedly controlled weather and
storms.

THOMAS CAMPION   (1567–1620)

Cherry Ripe _____ *1617*

There is a garden in her face,
Where roses and white lilies grow;
A heavenly paradise is that place,
Wherein all pleasant fruits do flow.
There cherries grow, which none may buy   5
Till "Cherry ripe" themselves do cry.

Those cherries fairly do enclose
Of orient pearl a double row;
Which when her lovely laughter shows,
They look like rosebuds filled with snow.   10
Yet them nor peer nor prince can buy
Till "Cherry ripe" themselves do cry.

Her eyes like angels watch them still;
Her brows like bended bows do stand,
Threatening with piercing frowns to kill   15
All that attempt, with eye or hand,
Those sacred cherries to come nigh
Till "Cherry ripe" themselves do cry.

LUCILLE CLIFTON   (b. 1936)

this morning
(for the girls of eastern high school) ————————————————— *1987*

this morning
this morning
           i met myself

coming in

a bright
jungle girl
shining
quick as a snake
a tall
tree girl a
me girl

           i met myself
this morning
coming in

and all day
i have been
a black bell
ringing
i survive

           survive

survive

LUCILLE CLIFTON   (b. 1936)

the poet ————————————————————————— *1987*

i beg my bones to be good but
they keep clicking music and
i spin in the center of myself
a foolish frightful woman
moving my skin against the wind and
tap dancing for my life.

LEONARD COHEN   (b. 1934)

'The killers that run . . .' ——————————————————— *1972*

The killers that run
           the other countries

are trying to get us
to overthrow the killers
       that run our own 5
I for one
prefer the rule
       of our native killers
I am convinced
       the foreign killer 10
will kill more of us
than the old familiar killer does
       Frankly I don't believe
anyone out there
really wants us to solve 15
our social problems
       I base this all on how I feel
about the man next door
I just hope he doesn't
       get any uglier 20
Therefore I am a patriot
I don't like to see
       a burning flag
because it excites
the killers on either side 25
to unfortunate excess
which goes on gaily
       quite unchecked
until everyone is dead

BILLY COLLINS (b. 1941)

Days ———————————————————— *1995*

Each one *is* a gift, no doubt.
mysteriously placed in your waking hand
or set upon your forehead
moments before you open your eyes.

Today begins cold and bright, 5
the ground heavy with snow
and the thick masonry of ice.
the sun glinting off the turrets of clouds.

Through the calm eye of the window
everything is in its place 10
but so precariously
this day might be resting somehow

on the one before it,
all the days of the past stacked high
like the impossible tower of dishes   15
entertainers used to build on stage.

No wonder you find yourself
perched on the top of a tall ladder
hoping to add one more.
Just another Wednesday   2C

you whisper,
then holding your breath,
place this cup on yesterday's saucer
without the slightest clink.

FRANCES CORNFORD   (1886–1960)

From a Letter to America on a Visit to Sussex: Spring 1942 _____ 1942

How simply violent things
Happen, is strange.
How strange it was to see
In the soft Cambridge sky our Squadron's wings,
And hear the huge hum in the familiar grey.
And it was odd today
On Ashdown Forest that will never change,
To find a gunner in the gorse, flung down,
Well-camouflaged, and bored and lion-brown.
A little further by those twisted trees
(As if it rose on humped preposterous seas
Out of a Book of Hours) up a bank
Like a large dragon, purposeful though drunk,
Heavily lolloped, swayed and sunk,
A tank.
All this because manoeuvres had begun.
But now, but soon,
At home on any usual afternoon,
High overhead
May come the Erinyes° winging   *the furies in Greek mythology*
Or here the boy may lie beside his gun,
His mud-brown tunic gently staining red,
While larks get on with their old job of singing.

STEPHEN CRANE   (1871–1900)

Do Not Weep, Maiden, for War Is Kind _____ *1896, 1899 (1895)*

Do not weep, maiden, for war is kind.
Because your lover threw wild hands toward the sky
And the affrighted steed ran on alone,
Do not weep.
War is kind.   5

    Hoarse, booming drums of the regiment
    Little souls who thirst for fight,
    These men were born to drill and die
    The unexplained glory flies above them
    Great is the battle-god, great, and his kingdom—   10
    A field where a thousand corpses lie.

Do not weep, babe, for war is kind.
Because your father tumbled in the yellow trenches,
Raged at his breast, gulped and died,
Do not weep.   15
War is kind.

    Swift, blazing flag of the regiment
    Eagle with crest of red and gold,
    These men were born to drill and die
    Point for them the virtue of slaughter   20
    Make plain to them the excellence of killing
    And a field where a thousand corpses lie.

Mother whose head hung humble as a button
On the bright splendid shroud of your son,
Do not weep.   25
War is kind.

COUNTÉE CULLEN   (1903–1946)

Yet Do I Marvel _____ *1925*

I doubt not God is good, well-meaning, kind,
And did He stoop to quibble could tell why
The little buried mole continues blind,
Why flesh that mirrors Him must some day die.
Make plain the reason tortured Tantalus°   5
Is baited by the fickle fruit, declare

YET I DO MARVEL.   5 *Tantalus:* a figure in Greek mythology condemned to eternal hunger and thirst. He stood in Hades chin deep in water with a fruit-laden branch just above his head, but he could never eat or drink.

If merely brute caprice dooms Sisyphus°
To struggle up a never-ending stair.
Inscrutable His ways are, and immune
To catechism by a mind too strewn   10
With petty cares to slightly understand
What awful brain compels His awful hand.
Yet do I marvel at this curious thing:
To make a poet black, and bid him sing!

7 *Sisyphus:* a figure in Greek mythology condemned to eternally useless labor. He was fated to roll a huge boulder up a hill in the underworld, but each time he neared the top, the stone slipped and he had to begin anew. See also p. 427.

e. e. cummings   (1894–1962)

if there are any heavens _____ *1931*

if there are any heavens my mother will(all by herself)have
one.   It will not be a pansy heaven nor
a fragile heaven of lilies-of-the-valley but
it will be a heaven of blackred roses

my father will be(deep like a rose
tall like a rose)

standing near my

swaying over her
(silent)
with eyes which are really petals and see

nothing with the face of a poet really which
is a flower and not a face with
hands
which whisper
This is my beloved my

                    (suddenly in sunlight

he will bow,

& the whole garden will bow)

JAMES DICKEY   (1923–1997)

Kudzu _____ *1964*

Japan invades. Far Eastern vines
Run from the clay banks they are

Supposed to keep from eroding,
Up telephone poles,
Which rear, half out of leafage,   5
As though they would shriek,
Like things smothered by their own
Green, mindless, unkillable ghosts.
In Georgia, the legend says
That you must close your windows   10

At night to keep it out of the house.
The glass is tinged with green, even so,

As the tendrils crawl over the fields.
The night the kudzu has
Your pasture, you sleep like the dead.   15
Silence has grown Oriental
And you cannot step upon ground:
Your leg plunges somewhere
It should not, it never should be,
Disappears, and waits to be struck   20

Anywhere between sole and kneecap:
For when the kudzu comes,

The snakes do, and weave themselves
Among its lengthening vines,
Their spade heads resting on leaves,   25
Growing also, in earthly power
And the huge circumstance of concealment.
One by one the cows stumble in,
Drooling a hot green froth,
And die, seeing the wood of their stalls   30

Strain to break into leaf.
In your closed house, with the vine

Tapping your window like lightning,
You remember what tactics to use.
In the wrong yellow fog-light of dawn   35
You herd them in, the hogs,
Head down in their hairy fat,
The meaty troops, to the pasture.
The leaves of the kudzu quake
With the serpents' fear, inside   40

The meadow ringed with men
Holding sticks, on the country roads.

The hogs disappear in the leaves.
The sound is intense, subhuman,
Nearly human with purposive rage.   45
There is no terror

Sound from the snakes.
No one can see the desperate, futile
Striking under the leaf heads.
Now and then, the flash of a long   5

Living vine, a cold belly,
Leaps up, torn apart, then falls

Under the tussling surface.
You have won, and wait for frost,
When, at the merest touch   5
Of cold, the kudzu turns
Black, withers inward and dies,
Leaving a mass of brown strings
Like the wires of a gigantic switchboard.
You open your windows,

With the lightning restored to the sky
And no leaves rising to bury
You alive inside your frail house,
And you think, in the opened cold,
Of the surface of things and its terrors,
And of the mistaken, mortal
Arrogance of the snakes

JAMES DICKEY   (1923–1997)

The Lifeguard _____ *1962*

In a stable of boats I lie still,
From all sleeping children hidden.
The leap of a fish from its shadow
Makes the whole lake instantly tremble.
With my foot on the water, I feel
The moon outside

Take on the utmost of its power.
I rise and go out through the boats.
I set my broad sole upon silver,
On the skin of the sky, on the moonlight,
Stepping outward from earth onto water
In quest of the miracle

This village of children believed
That I could perform as I dived
For one who had sunk from my sight.
I saw his cropped haircut go under.

I leapt, and my steep body flashed
Once, in the sun.

Dark drew all the light from my eyes.
Like a man who explores his death 20
By the pull of his slow-moving shoulders,
I hung head down in the cold,
Wide-eyed, contained, and alone
Among the weeds,

And my fingertips turned into stone 25
From clutching immovable blackness.
Time after time I leapt upward
Exploding in breath, and fell back
From the change in the children's faces
At my defeat. 30

Beneath them I swam to the boathouse
With only my life in my arms
To wait for the lake to shine back
At the risen moon with such power
That my steps on the light of the ripples 35
Might be sustained.

Beneath me is nothing but brightness
Like the ghost of a snowfield in summer.
As I moved toward the center of the lake,
Which is also the center of the moon, 40
I am thinking of how I may be
The saviour of one

Who has already died in my care.
The dark trees fade from around me.
The moon's dust hovers together. 45
I call softly out, and the child's
Voice answers through blinding water.
Patiently, slowly,

He rises, dilating to break
The surface of stone with his forehead. 50
He is one I do not remember
Having ever seen in his life.
The ground I stand on is trembling
Upon his smile.

I wash the black mud from my hands. 55
On a light given off by the grave
I kneel in the quick of the moon
At the heart of a distant forest
And hold in my arms a child
Of water, water, water. 60

JAMES DICKEY (1923–1997)

The Performance _____ *1967*

The last time I saw Donald Armstrong
He was staggering oddly off into the sun,
Going down, off the Philippine Islands.
I let my shovel fall, and put that hand
Above my eyes, and moved some way to one side
That his body might pass through the sun,

And I saw how well he was not
Standing there on his hands,
On his spindle-shanked forearms balanced,
Unbalanced, with his big feet looming and waving
In the great, untrustworthy air
He flew in each night, when it darkened.

Dust fanned in scraped puffs from the earth
Between his arms, and blood turned his face inside out,
To demonstrate its suppleness
Of veins, as he perfected his role.
Next day, he toppled his head off
On an island beach to the south,

And the enemy's two-handed sword
Did not fall from anyone's hands
At that miraculous sight,
As the head rolled over upon
Its wide-eyed face, and fell
Into the inadequate grave

He had dug for himself, under pressure.
Yet I put my flat hand to my eyebrows
Months later, to see him again
In the sun, when I learned how he died,
And imagined him, there,
Come, judged, before his small captors,

Doing all his lean tricks to amaze them—
The back somersault, the kip-up—
And at last, the stand on his hands,
Perfect, with his feet together,
His head down, evenly breathing,
As the sun poured up from the sea

And the headsmen broke down
In a blaze of tears, in that light
Of the thin, long human frame
Upside down in its own strange joy,
And, if some other one had not told him,
Would have cut off the feet

Instead of the head,
And if Armstrong had not presently risen
In kingly, round-shouldered attendance,   45
And then knelt down in himself
Beside his hacked, glittering grave, having done
All things in this life that he could.

JOHN DONNE   (1572–1631)

The Good Morrow _____ *1633*

I wonder, by my troth, what thou and I
Did, till we loved! Were we not weaned till then,
But sucked on country pleasures, childishly?
Or snorted we in the seven sleepers' den?°
T'was so; But this, all pleasures fancies be.   5
If ever any beauty I did see,
Which I desired, and got, t'was but a dream of thee.

And now good morrow to our waking souls,
Which watch not one another out of fear;
For love all love of other sights controls,°   10
And makes one little room an everywhere.
Let sea-discoverers to new worlds have gone,
Let maps to other, worlds on worlds have shown,°
Let us possess one world; each hath one, and is one.

My face in thine eye, thine in mine appears,°   15
And true plain hearts do in the faces rest;
Where can we find two better hemispheres
Without sharp North, without declining West?
Whatever dies was not mixed equally;
If our two loves be one, or thou and I   20
Love so alike, that none do slacken, none can die.°

THE GOOD MORROW.   4 *seven sleepers' den:* a reference to the miraculous legend of the Seven
Sleepers of Ephesus, in Asia Minor. Seven young nobles fled Ephesus to avoid religious persecution by the Emperor Decius (ca. 250 C.E.). They took refuge in a cave and were sealed inside. They
then slept for either 230 or 309 years, and they emerged praising God. After they died, their
remains were taken to St. Victor's Church in Marseilles, France, where they were encrypted.
10 *For love . . . controls:* i.e., Love is so powerful that it eliminates fear and makes everything in the
world worthy of love.   13, 14 *let sea-discoverers . . . shown:* i.e., let sea-explorers discover new
worlds, and let maps show other new worlds to other discoverers.   15 *My face . . . appears:* Each
face is reflected in the pupils of the other lover's eyes.   19–21 *Whatever . . . can die:* Scholastic
philosophy argued that elements which are united in perfect balance will never change or decay;
hence, such a mixture cannot die. Donne's analogy suggests—humorously—that the love of the
lovers is too pure to die, and that they may therefore go on making love forever.

JOHN DONNE   (1572–1631)

Holy Sonnet 6: This Is My Play's Last Scene _____ *1633*

This is my play's last scene; here heavens appoint
My pilgrimage's last mile; and my race
Idly, yet quickly run, hath this last pace,
My span's last inch, my minute's last point,
And gluttonous Death will instantly unjoint   5
My body, and soul, and I shall sleep a space,
But my ever-waking part° shall see that face,   *the soul*
Whose fear already shakes my every joint.
Then, as my soul, t'heaven her first seat, takes flight,
And earth-borne body, in the earth shall dwell,   10
So, fall my sins, that all may have their right,
To where they are bred, and would press me, to hell.
Impute me righteous, thus purged of evil,
For thus I leave the world, the flesh, and devil.

JOHN DONNE   (1572–1631)

Holy Sonnet 7: At the Round Earth's Imagined Corners _____ *1633*

At the round earth's imagined corners, blow
Your trumpets, angels,° and arise, arise
From death, you numberless infinities
Of souls, and to your scattered bodies go,
All whom the flood did, and fire shall o'erthrow,
All whom war, dearth, age, agues, tyrannies,
Despair, law, chance, hath slain, and you whose eyes
Shall behold God, and never taste death's woe.°
But let them sleep, Lord, and me mourn a space,
For, if above all these, my sins abound,
'Tis late to ask abundance of Thy grace,
When we are there. Here on this lowly ground,
Teach me how to repent; for that's as good
As if Thou hadst sealed my pardon with Thy blood.

AT THE ROUND EARTH'S IMAGINED CORNERS.   1–2 *At . . . angels:* The lines combine the
image of the angels or winds drawn at the four corners of old maps with an allusion to the four
angels mentioned in Revelations 7:1.   7–8 *you whose eyes . . . woe:* a reference to those people
who are still living on the day at the Last Judgment and thus move directly from life to judgment
without experiencing death.

JOHN DONNE   (1572–1631)

Holy Sonnet 10: Death Be Not Proud ──────────── *1633*

Death, be not proud, though some have callèd thee
Mighty and dreadful, for thou art not so;
For those whom thou think'st thou dost overthrow
Die not, poor Death, nor yet canst thou kill me.
From rest and sleep, which but thy pictures° be,   *imitations*   5
Much pleasure; then from thee much more must flow,
And soonest our best men with thee do go,
Rest of their bones, and soul's delivery.
Thou art slave to fate, chance, kings, and desperate men,
And dost with poison, war, and sickness dwell,   10
And poppy° or charms can make us sleep as well   *opium*
And better than thy stroke; why swell'st° thou then?   *puff up with pride*
One short sleep past, we wake eternally°   *on Judgment Day*
And death shall be no more; Death, thou shalt die.

JOHN DONNE   (1572–1631)

A Hymn to God the Father ──────────── *1633 (1623?)*

Wilt Thou forgive that sin where I begun,
    Which is my sin, though it were done before?
Wilt Thou forgive those sins through which I run,
    And do them still, though still I do deplore?
        When Thou hast done, Thou hast not done,   5
            For I have more.

Wilt Thou forgive that sin by which I won
    Others to sin and made my sin their door?
Wilt Thou forgive that sin which I did shun
    A year or two, but wallowed in a score?   10
        When Thou hast done, Thou hast not done,
            For I have more.

I have a sin of fear, that when I have spun
    My last thread, I shall perish on the shore;
Swear by Thy Self, that at my death Thy sun   15
    Shall shine as it shines now and heretofore;
        And, having done that, Thou hast done,
            I have no more.

JOHN DONNE   (1572–1631)

Song (Go, and Catch a Falling Star) _____ *1633*

Go, and catch a falling star,
  Get with child a mandrake root,°
Tell me where all past years are,
  Or who cleft the Devil's foot,
Teach me to hear mermaids singing,
Or to keep off envy's stinging,
    And find
    What wind
Serves to advance an honest mind.

If thou beest born to strange sights,
  Things invisible to see,
Ride ten thousand days and nights
  Till age snow white hairs on thee,
Thou, when thou return'st, wilt tell me
All strange wonders that befell thee
    And swear
    Nowhere
Lives a woman true, and fair.

If thou findst one, let me know,
  Such a Pilgrimage were sweet;
Yet do not, I would not go,
  Though at next door we might meet;
Though she were true when you met her,
And last till you write your letter,
    Yet she
    Will be
False, ere I come, to two, or three.

SONG.   2 *mandrake root:* The mandrake, or mandragora, is a European narcotic herb once considered an aphrodisiac because the two-pronged root was thought to resemble a women's torso and legs.

MICHAEL DRAYTON   (1563–1631)

Since There's No Help _____ *1619*

Since there's no help, come let us kiss and part;
Nay, I have done, you get no more of me,
And I am glad, yea glad with all my heart
That thus so cleanly I myself can free;
Shake hands forever, cancel all our vows,
And when we meet at any time again,
Be it not seen in either of our brows
That we one jot of former love retain.
Now at the last gasp of love's latest breath,

When, his pulse failing, passion speechless lies,   10
When faith is kneeling by his bed of death,
And innocence is closing up his eyes;
Now if thou wouldst, when all have given him over,
From death to life thou mightst him yet recover.

PAUL LAURENCE DUNBAR (1872–1906)

Sympathy ————————————————————————— *1895*

I know what the caged bird feels, alas!
When the sun is bright on the upland slopes;
When the wind stirs soft through the springing grass
And the river flows like a stream of glass;
When the first bird sings and the first bud opes,   5
And the faint perfume from its chalice steals—
I know what the caged bird feels!

I know why the caged bird beats his wing
Till its blood is red on the cruel bars;
For he must fly back to his perch and cling   10
When he fain would be on the bough a-swing;
And a pain still throbs in the old, old scars
And they pulse again with a keener sting—
I know why he beats his wing!

I know why the caged bird sings, ah me,   15
When his wing is bruised and his bosom sore,
When he beats his bars and would be free;
It is not a carol of joy or glee,
But a prayer that he sends from his heart's deep core,
But a plea, that upward to Heaven he flings—   20
I know why the caged bird sings!

T. S. ELIOT (1888–1965)

The Love Song of J. Alfred Prufrock° ——————————— *1915 (1910–1911)*

> *S'io credesse che mia risposta fosse°*
> *A persona che mai tornasse al mondo,*
> *Questa fiamma staria senza piu scosse.*
> *Ma perciocche giammai di questo fondo*

THE LOVE SONG OF J. ALFRED PRUFROCK. The poem is a monologue spoken by Prufrock; the name is invented but suggests a businessman.   EPIGRAPH: The Italian epigraph is quoted from Dante's *Inferno* (Canto 27, lines 61–66) and is spoken by a man who relates his evil deeds to Dante because he assumes that Dante will never return to the world: "If I believed that my response were made to a person who would ever revisit the world, this flame would stand motionless. But since none has ever returned from this depth alive, if I hear the truth, I answer you without fear of infamy."

Non torno vivo alcun, s'i'odo il vero,
Senza tema d'infamia ti rispondo.

Let us go then, you and I
When the evening is spread out against the sky
Like a patient etherized upon a table;
Let us go, through certain half-deserted streets,
The muttering retreats
Of restless nights in one-night cheap hotels
And sawdust restaurants with oyster shells;
Streets that follow like a tedious argument
Of insidious intent
To lead you to an overwhelming question . . .
Oh, do not ask, "What is it?"
Let us go and make our visit.

In the room the women come and go
Talking of Michelangelo.°

The yellow fog that rubs its back upon the windowpanes,
The yellow smoke that rubs its muzzle on the windowpanes
Licked its tongue into the corners of the evening,
Lingered upon the pools that stand in drains,
Let fall upon its back the soot that falls from chimneys,
Slipped by the terrace, made a sudden leap,
And seeing that it was a soft October night,
Curled once about the house, and fell asleep.

And indeed there will be time
For the yellow smoke that slides along the street,
Rubbing its back upon the windowpanes;
There will be time, there will be time°
To prepare a face to meet the faces that you meet;
There will be time to murder and create,
And time for all the works and days° of hands
That lift and drop a question on your plate;
Time for you and time for me,
And time yet for a hundred indecisions,
And for a hundred visions and revisions,
Before the taking of a toast and tea.

In the room the women come and go
Talking of Michelangelo.

And indeed there will be time
To wonder, "Do I dare?" and, "Do I dare?"

14 *Michelangelo:* one of the greatest Italian Renaissance painters and sculptors (1475–1564). The name suggests that the women are cultured, or at least pretending to be so.   26 *time:* a possible allusion to Andrew Marvell's "To His Coy Mistress" (p. 1023).   29 *works and days:* the title of a poem about farming by the Greek poet Hesiod. Here the phrase ironically refers to social gestures.

Time to turn back and descend the stair,
With a bald spot in the middle of my hair—   40
(They will say: "How his hair is growing thin!")
My morning coat, my collar mounting firmly to the chin,
My necktie rich and modest, but asserted by a simple pin—
(They will say: "But how his arms and legs are thin!")
Do I dare   45
Disturb the universe?
In a minute there is time
For decisions and revisions which a minute will reverse.

For I have known them all already, known them all—
Have known the evenings, mornings, afternoons,   50
I have measured out my life with coffee spoons;
I know the voices dying with a dying fall°
Beneath the music from a farther room.
    So how should I presume?

And I have known the eyes already, known them all—   55
The eyes that fix you in a formulated phrase,
And when I am formulated, sprawling on a pin,
When I am pinned and wriggling on the wall,
Then how should I begin
To spit out all the butt-ends of my days and ways?   60
And how should I presume?

And I have known the arms already, known them all—
Arms that are braceleted and white and bare
(But in the lamplight, downed with light brown hair!)
Is it perfume from a dress   65
That makes me so digress?
Arms that lie along a table, or wrap about a shawl.
    And should I then presume?
    And how should I begin?

Shall I say, I have gone at dusk through narrow streets   70
And watched the smoke that rises from the pipes
Of lonely men in shirt-sleeves, leaning out of windows? . . .

I should have been a pair of ragged claws
Scuttling across the floors of silent seas.

And the afternoon, the evening, sleeps so peacefully!   75
Smoothed by long fingers,
Asleep . . . tired . . . or it malingers,°
Stretched on the floor, here beside you and me.
Should I, after tea and cakes and ices,
Have the strength to force the moment to its crisis?   80
But though I have wept and fasted, wept and prayed,

---

52 *dying fall:* an allusion to a speech by Orsino in Shakespeare's *Twelfth Night* (I.1.4).
77 *malingers:* pretends to be ill.

Though I have seen my head (grown slightly bald) brought in upon a platter,°
I am no prophet—and here's no great matter;
I have seen the moment of my greatness flicker,
And I have seen the eternal Footman hold my coat, and snicker,   85
And in short, I was afraid.

And would it have been worth it, after all,
After the cups, the marmalade, the tea,
Among the porcelain, among some talk of you and me,
Would it have been worth while,   90
To have bitten off the matter with a smile,
To have squeezed the universe into a ball°
To roll it toward some overwhelming question,
To say: "I am Lazarus,° come from the dead,
Come back to tell you all, I shall tell you all"—   95
If one, setting a pillow by her head,
    Should say: "That is not what I meant at all.
    That is not it, at all."

And would it have been worth it, after all,
Would it have been worth while,   100
After the sunsets and the dooryards and the sprinkled streets,
After the novels, after the teacups, after the skirts that trail along the floor—
And this, and so much more?—
It is impossible to say just what I mean!
But as if a magic lantern threw the nerves in patterns on a screen: 105
Would it have been worth while
If one, setting a pillow or throwing off a shawl,
And turning toward the window, should say:
    "That is not it at all,
    That is not what I meant, at all."   110

No! I am not Prince Hamlet,° nor was meant to be;
Am an attendant lord, one that will do
To swell a progress,° start a scene or two,
Advise the prince; no doubt, an easy tool,
Deferential, glad to be of use,   115
Politic, cautious, and meticulous;
Full of high sentence,° but a bit obtuse;
At times, indeed, almost ridiculous—
Almost, at times, the Fool.

I grow old . . . I grow old . . .   120
I shall wear the bottoms of my trousers rolled.°

---

82 *platter:* as was the head of John the Baptist; see Mark 6:17–28 and Matthew 14:3–11.
92 *ball:* another allusion to Marvell's "Coy Mistress."   94 *Lazarus:* See John 11:1–44.
111 *Prince Hamlet:* the hero of Shakespeare's play *Hamlet.*   113 *swell a progress:* enlarge a royal
procession.   117 *sentence:* ideals, opinions, sentiment.   121 *rolled:* a possible reference to
cuffs, which were becoming fashionable in 1910.

Shall I part my hair behind? Do I dare to eat a peach?
I shall wear white flannel trousers, and walk upon the beach.
I have heard the mermaids singing, each to each.

I do not think that they will sing to me.   125

I have seen them riding seaward on the waves
Combing the white hair of the waves blown back
When the wind blows the water white and black.

We have lingered in the chambers of the sea
By sea-girls wreathed with seaweed red and brown   130
Till human voices wake us, and we drown.

JAMES EMANUEL   (b. 1921)

The Negro ————————————————————————————— *1968*

Never saw him.
Never can.
Hypothetical,
Haunting man:

Eyes a-saucer,   5
Yessir bossir,
Dice a-clicking,
Razor flicking.

The-ness froze him
In a dance.   10
A-ness never
Had a chance.

LYNN EMANUEL   (b. 1949)

Like God ————————————————————————————— *1998*

you hover above the page staring
down on a small town. By its roads
some scenery loafs in a hammock of
sleepy prose and here is a mongrel
loping and here is a train pulling into   5
a station in three long sentences and
here are the people in galoshes waiting.
But you know this story and it is not
about those travelers and their galoshes,

but about your life, so, like a diver   10
climbing over the side of a boat and
down into the ocean, you climb, sentence
by sentence, into this story on this page.

You have been expecting yourself
as the woman who purrs by in a dress   1!
by Patou, and a porter manacled to
the luggage, and a matron bulky as
the *Britannia,* and there, haunting
her ankles like a piece of ectoplasm
that barks is, once again, that small   2
white dog from chapter twenty.
These are your fellow travelers and
you become part of their logjam of
images of hats and umbrellas and
Vuitton luggage, you are a face   2
behind or inside these faces, a
heartbeat in the volley of these
heartbeats, as you choose, out of all
the passengers, the journey of a man
with a mustache scented faintly with   ￼
Prince Albert. "He must be a secret
sensualist," you think and your awareness
drifts to his trench coat, worn, softened,
and flabby, a coat with a lobotomy, just
as the train arrives at a destination.

No, you would prefer another stop
in a later chapter where the climate is
affable and sleek. But most of
the passengers are disembarking, and
you did not choose to be in the story
of the white dress. You did not choose
the story of the matron whose bosom
is like the prow of a ship and who is
launched toward lunch at The Hotel Pierre,
or even the story of the dog-on-a-leash,
even though this is now your story:
the story of the man-who-had-to-
take-the-train and walk the dark road
described hurriedly by someone sitting
at the café so you could discover it,
although you knew all along it would
be there, you, who have been hovering
above this page, holding the book in
your hands, like God, reading.

JOHN ENGELS   (b. 1931)

Naming the Animals ————————————————————————— *1981*

Since spring I've seen two deer,
one lashed to a fender. The other fed
in a clearing on the back slope
of Bean Hill, his big rack° still   *antlers*
in velvet. The shot buck bled,   5

its tongue frozen
to the rusty hood.
But the other, in its simpler stance,
felt merely the delicate itch
of antler skin.   10

And three does, mildly alert,
cocked ears toward where I watched from
in the hemlocks. I saw, of course,
five deer; but I
count only what by plain necessity of death   15

or feeding is oblivious to me,
does not watch back.

CAROLYN FORCHÉ   (b. 1950)

Because One Is Always Forgotten ———————————————— *1981*

IN MEMORIAM, JOSÉ RUDOLFO VIERA
1939–1981: EL SALVADOR

When Viera was buried we knew it had come to an end,
his coffin rocking into the ground like a boat or a cradle.

I could take my heart, he said, and give it to a *campesino*°   *peasant*
and he would cut it up and give it back:

you can't eat heart in those four dark   5
chambers where a man can be kept years.

A boy soldier in the bone-hot sun works his knife
to peel the face from a dead man

and hang it from the branch of a tree
flowering with such faces.   10

The heart is the toughest part of the body.
Tenderness is in the hands.

DAN GEORGAKAS   (b. 1938)

Hiroshima Crewman _____ *1969*

Somewhere in California
his body humbled by a hair shirt,
a vow of silence on his lips,
a Hiroshima crewman tries to find a life.
If he should ever choose to break his peace,
he might speak of death by fire
no Nazi ordered; he might tell how
war produces many brands of
Auschwitz soap and Dachau lampshade.

CHIEF DAN GEORGE   (1899-1981)

The Beauty of the Trees _____ *1974*

The beauty of the trees,
the softness of the air,
the fragrance of the grass,
    speaks to me.

The summit of the mountain,
the thunder of the sky,
the rhythm of the sea,
    speaks to me.

The faintness of the stars,
the freshness of the morning,
the dewdrop on the flower,
    speaks to me.

The strength of fire,
the taste of salmon,
the trail of the sun,
and the life that never goes away,
    they speak to me.

And my heart soars.

NIKKI GIOVANNI   (b. 1943)

Woman _____ *1978*

she wanted to be a blade
of grass amid the fields

but he wouldn't agree
to be the dandelion

she wanted to be a robin singing   5
through the leaves
but he refused to be
her tree

she spun herself into a web
    and looking for a place to rest   10
turned to him
but he stood straight
declining to be her corner

she tried to be a book
but he wouldn't read   15
she turned herself into a bulb
but he wouldn't let her grow

she decided to become
a woman
and though he still refused   20
to be a man
she decided it was all
right

MARILYN HACKER   (b. 1942)

Sonnet Ending with a Film Subtitle ———————————— *1979*

For Judith Landry

Life has its nauseating ironies:
The good die young, as often has been shown;
Chaste spouses catch Venereal Disease;
And feminists sit by the telephone.
Last night was rather bleak, tonight is starker.   5
I may stare at the wall till half-past-one.
My friends are all convinced Dorothy Parker
Lives, but is not well, in Marylebone.°   *a district in London*
I wish that I could imitate my betters
And fortify my rhetoric with guns.   10
Some day we women all will break our fetters
And raise our daughters to be Lesbians.
(I wonder if the bastard kept my letters?)
Here follow untranslatable French puns.

JOHN HAINES   (b. 1936)

Little Cosmic Dust Poem ———————————————————— *1985*

Out of the debris of dying stars,
this rain of particles
that waters the waste with brightness;
the sea-wave of atoms hurrying home,
collapse of the giant,
unstable guest who cannot stay;

the sun's heart reddens and expands,
his mighty aspiration is lasting,
as the shell of his substance
one day will be white with frost.

In the radiant field of Orion°
great hordes of stars are forming,
just as we see every night,
fiery and faithful to the end.

Out of the cold and fleeing dust
that is never and always,
the silence and waste to come—
this arm, this hand,
my voice, your face, this love.

LITTLE COSMIC DUST POEM.   11 *Orion:* a prominent winter constellation. Recent observations have led scientists to conclude that stars are being formed in the nebulous area in the "sword" of the constellation.

DONALD HALL   (b. 1928)

Scenic View ——————————————————————————— *1981*

Every year the mountains
get paler and more distant—
trees less green, rock piles
disappearing—as emulsion
from a billion Kodaks
sucks color out.
In fifteen years
Monadnock and Kearsarge,
the Green Mountains
and the White, will turn
invisible, all
tint removed
atom by atom to albums
in Medford and Greenwich,
while over the valleys

the still intractable granite
rears with unseeable peaks
fatal to airplanes.

DANIEL HALPERN (b. 1945)

Snapshot of Hué _____ *1982*

For Robert Stone

They are riding bicycles on the other side
of the Perfume River.

A few months ago the bridges were down
and there was no one on the streets.

There were the telling piles on corners,   5
debris that contained a little of everything.

There was nothing not under cover—
even the sky remained impenetrable

day after day. And if you were seen
on the riverbank you were knocked down.   10

It is clear today. The litter in the streets
has been swept away. It couldn't have been

that bad, one of us said, the river barely moving,
the bicycles barely moving, the sun posted above.

DANIEL HALPERN (b. 1945)

Summer in the Middle Class _____ *1991*

All over America
it's suddenly
mid-July
We're chasing
our sons around   5
the yard
with balls and sticks
We are lumbering
because we are overweight
and a little older   10
being survivors
of the baby boom
making good the legacy
At sundown

a million barbecues ignite   15
as if from a single match
Webers
Crestlines
international hibachis
and the sad slabs of meat   20
begin to emerge
from their various marinades
the tables get set
and the mosquitoes awaken
for the evening meal   25

When they have finished
what is rightfully theirs
the children are removed
from the tables
and the adults open   30
another bottle or can of beer
The evenings are special
this time of year
the heat finally bearable
the coals a coolish grey   35
dying into themselves
It's what happens in unison
that makes America America
the lights going off
the fluorescent show
of t.v. coming on
and then
the total darkness

H. S. (SAM) HAMOD   (b. 1936)

Leaves _____ *1973*

(for Sally)

Tonight, Sally and I are making stuffed
grapeleaves, we get out a package, it's
drying out, I've been saving it in the freezer, it's
one of the last things my father ever picked in this
life—they're over five years old
and up to now
we just kept finding packages of them in the
freezer, as if he were still picking them
somewhere packing them
carefully to send to us
making sure they didn't break into pieces.

***

"To my Dar Garnchildn
Davd and Lura
from Thr Jido"
twisted on tablet paper   15
between the lines
in this English lettering
hard for him even to print,
I keep this small torn record,
this piece of paper stays in the upstairs storage,   20
one of the few pieces of American
my father ever wrote. We find his Arabic letters
all over the place, even in the files we find
letters to him in English, one I found from Charles Atlas
telling him, in 1932,   25
"Of course, Mr. Hamod, you too can build
your muscles like mine . . ."

***

Last week my mother told me, when I was
asking why I became a poet, "But don't you remember,
your father made up poems, don't you remember him   30
singing in the car as we drove—those were poems."
Even now, at night, I sometimes
get out the Arabic grammar book
though it seems so late.

FRANCES E. W. HARPER   (1825–1911)

She's Free! _____ *1854*

How say that by law we may torture and chase
A woman whose crime is the hue of her face?—
With her step on the ice, and her arm on her child,
The danger was fearful, the pathway was wild. . . .
But she's free! yes, free from the land where the slave,   5
From the hand of oppression, must rest in the grave;
Where bondage and blood, where scourges and chains,
Have placed on our banner indelible stains. . . .

The bloodhounds have miss'd the scent of her way,
The hunter is rifled and foiled of his prey,   10
The cursing of men and clanking of chains
Make sounds of strange discord on Liberty's plains. . . .
Oh! poverty, danger and death she can brave,
For the child of her love is no longer a slave.

MICHAEL S. HARPER   (b. 1938)

Called _____ *1975*

Digging the grave
through black dirt,
gravel and rocks
that will hold her down,
we speak of her heat
which has driven her out
over the highway
in her first year.

A fly glides from her mouth
as we take her four legs,
and the great white neck
muddled at the lakeside
bends gracefully into the arc
of her tongue, colorless, now,
and we set her in the bed
of earth and rock
which will hold her as the sun
sets over her shoulders.

You had spoken of her brother,
100 lbs or more,
and her slight frame
from the diet of chain
she had broken;
on her back
as the spade cools her brow
with black dirt, rocks,
sand, white tongue,
what pups does she hold
that are seeds unspayed
in her broken body;
what does her brother say
to the seed gone out over
the prairie, on the hunt
of the unreturned:
and what do we say
to the master of the dog dead,
heat, highway, this bed
on the shoulder
of the road west
where her brother called, calls

ROBERT HASS   (b. 1941)

Spring Rain _____ *1989*

Now the rain is falling, freshly, in the intervals between sunlight,

a Pacific squall started no one knows where, drawn east as the drifts of
warm air make a channel;

it moves its own way, like water or the mind,

and spills this rain passing over. The Sierras will catch it as last snow   5
flurries before summer, observed only by the wakened marmots at ten
thousand feet,

and we will come across it again as larkspur and penstemon sprouting
along a creek above Sonora Pass next August,

where the snowmelt will have trickled into Dead Man's Creek and the   10
creek spilled into the Stanislaus and the Stanislaus into the San Joaquin
and the San Joaquin into the slow salt marshes of the bay.

That's not the end of it: the gray jays of the mountains eat larkspur seeds,
which cannot propagate otherwise.

To simulate the process, you have to soak gathered seeds all night in the   15
acids of coffee

and then score them gently with a very sharp knife before you plant them
in the garden.

ROBERT HAYDEN   (1913–1980)

Those Winter Sundays _____ *1962*

Sundays too my father got up early
and put his clothes on in the blueblack cold,
then with cracked hands that ached
from labor in the weekday weather made
banked fires blaze. No one ever thanked him.   5
I'd wake and hear the cold splintering, breaking,
When the rooms were warm, he'd call,
and slowly I would rise and dress,
fearing the chronic angers of that house,

Speaking indifferently to him,   10
who had driven out the cold
and polished my good shoes as well.
What did I know, what did I know
of love's austere and lonely offices?

SEAMUS HEANEY   (b. 1939)

The Otter _____ *1979*

When you plunged
The light of Tuscany wavered
And swung through the pool
From top to bottom.

I loved your wet head and smashing crawl,   5
Your fine swimmer's back and shoulders
Surfacing and surfacing again
This year and every year since.

I sat dry-throated on the warm stones.
You were beyond me.   10
The mellowed clarities, the grape-deep air
Thinned and disappointed.

Thank God for the slow loadening,
When I hold you now
We are closed and deep   15
As the atmosphere on water.

My two hands are plumbed water.
You are my palpable, lithe
Otter of memory
In the pool of the moment,   20

Turning to swim on your back,
Each silent, thigh-shaking kick
Re-tilting the light,
Heaving the cool at your neck.

And suddenly you're out,
Back again, intent as ever,
Heavy and frisky in your freshened pelt,
Printing the stones.

GEORGE HERBERT   (1593–1633)

Love (III)° _____ *1633*

Love bade me welcome: yet my soul drew back,
    Guilty of dust and sin.
But quick-eyed Love, observing me grow slack
    From my first entrance in,
Drew nearer to me, sweetly questioning
    If I lacked° anything.

LOVE (III).   cf. I John 4:8: "He that loveth not knoweth not God; for God is love."   6 *lacked:*
wanted; the phrase is a standard question asked by innkeepers.

"A guest," I answered, "worthy to be here":
    Love said, "You shall be he."
"I, the unkind, ungrateful? Ah, my dear,
    I cannot look on thee."   10
Love took my hand, and smiling did reply,
    "Who made the eyes but I?"

"Truth, Lord; but I have marred them; let my shame
    Go where it doth deserve."
"And know you not," says Love, "who bore the blame?"   15
    "My dear, then I will serve."
"You must sit down," says Love, "and taste my meat."°
    So I did sit and eat.

17 *and taste my meat:* Job 12:11: "Doth not the ear try words? and the mouth taste his meat?" Here, *meat* refers simply to food in general.   17–18 *You must sit down . . . eat:* Luke 13:37: "Blessed are those servants, whom the Lord when he cometh shall find watching: verily I say unto you, that he shall gird himself, and make them to sit down to meat, and will come forth and serve them."

WILLIAM HEYEN   (b. 1940)

The Hair: Jacob Korman's Story ————————————— *1980*

Ten kilometers from Warsaw,
I arrived in Rembertow where
hundreds of Jews had lived
until the wheel turned: *Judenrein.*°   *cleansed; rid of Jews*

You think they let themselves be taken?   5
They would not fill the trucks.
Men were shot trying to pull guns
from the guards' hands.

and hands of dead women
clutched hair, hair of SS guards   10
blood-patched hair everywhere,
a *velt mit hor,* a field of hair.

A. D. HOPE   (b. 1907)

Advice to Young Ladies ———————————————— *1970*

A.U.C.° 334: about this date
For a sexual misdemeanor, which she denied,
The vestal virgin Postumia was tried.
Livy records it among affairs of state.

A.U.C.   *A.U.C.* stands for *ab urbe condita,* "from the founding of the city." A.U.C. 334 therefore means 334 years after the founding of ancient Rome.

They let her off: it seems she was perfectly pure;   5
The charge arose because some thought her talk
Too witty for a young girl, her ways, her walk
Too lively, her clothes too smart to be demure.

The Pontifex Maximus, summing up the case,
Warned her in future to abstain from jokes,   10
To wear less modish and more pious frocks.
She left the court reprieved, but in disgrace.

What then? With her the annalist is less
Concerned than what the men achieved that year;
Plots, quarrels, crimes, with oratory to spare!   15
I see Postumia with her dowdy dress,

Stiff mouth and listless step; I see her strive
To give dull answers. She had to knuckle down.
A vestal virgin who scandalized that town
Had fair trial, then they buried her alive.   20

Alive, bricked up in suffocating dark,
A ration of bread, a pitcher if she was dry
Preserved the body they did not wish to die
Until her mind was quenched to the last spark.

How many the black maw has swallowed in its time!   25
Spirited girls who would not know their place.
Talented girls who found that the disgrace
Of being a woman made genius a crime;

How many others, who would not kiss the rod
Domestic bullying broke, or public shame?   ?
Pagan or Christian, it was much the same:
Husbands, Saint Paul declared, rank next to God.

Livy and Paul, it may be, never knew
That Rome was doomed; each spoke of her with pride.
Tacitus, writing after both had died,
Showed that whole fabric rotten through and through.

Historians spend their lives and lavish ink
Explaining how great commonwealths collapse
From great defects of policy—perhaps
The cause is sometimes simpler than they think.

It may not seem so grave an act to break
Postumia's spirit as Galileo's, to gag
Hypatia as crush Socrates, or drag
Joan as Giordano Bruno to the stake.

Can we be sure: Have more states perished, then,
For having shackled the enquiring mind,
Than those who, in their folly not less blind,
Trusted the servile womb to breed free men?

GERARD MANLEY HOPKINS   (1844–1889)

Pied Beauty ———————————————————————— *(1918) 1877*

Glory be to God for dappled things—
   For skies of couple-colour as a brinded cow;°
     For rose-moles all in stipple upon trout that swim;
Fresh-firecoal chestnut-falls;° finches' wings;
   Landscape plotted and pieced°—fold,° fallow,° and plough;   5
     And áll trádes, their gear and tackle and trim.

All things counter,° original, spare,° strange;
   Whatever is fickle, freckled (who knows how?)
     With swift, slow; sweet, sour; adazzle, dim;
He fathers-forth whose beauty is past change: 10
Praise him.

PIED BEAUTY.   2 *Brinded:* brindled, that is, grey with dark spots.   4 *chestnut-falls:* the meat
of a roasted chestnut.   5 *pieced:* divided into fields of different colors, depending on the crops
or use.   *fold:* an enclosed field for animals.   *fallow:* a plowed but unplanted field.
7 *counter:* opposed, as in contrasting patterns.   *spare:* rare.

GERARD MANLEY HOPKINS   (1844–1889)

The Windhover° ———————————————————————— *1918 (1877)*

To Christ Our Lord

I caught this morning morning's minion,° king-   *darling*
   dom of daylight's dauphin,° dapple-dawn-drawn Falcon, in his riding
     Of the rolling level underneath him steady air, and striding
High there, how he rung upon the rein of a wimpling wing   5
In his ecstasy! then off, off forth on swing,
   As a skate's heel sweeps smooth on a bow-bend: the hurl and gliding
     Rebuffed the big wind. My heart in hiding
Stirred for a bird,—the achieve of, the mastery of the thing!

Brute beauty and valour and act, oh, air, pride, plume, here   10
   Buckle!° AND the fire that breaks from thee then, a billion   *join*
Times told lovelier, more dangerous. O my chevalier!°   *knight*
   No wonder of it: shéer plód makes plough down sillion°
Shine, and blue-beak embers, ah my dear,
   Fall, gall themselves, and gash gold-vermilion.

THE WINDHOVER.   The poem's title refers to a kestrel—or falcon—that glides or hovers in the
wind.   2 *dauphin:* prince, heir to the throne of France.   12 *sillion:* the ridge of earth
between two plowed furrows in a field.

JULIA WARD HOWE   (1819–1910)

Battle Hymn of the Republic ———————————————————— *1862*

Mine eyes have seen the glory of the coming of the Lord;
He is trampling out the vintage where the grapes of wrath are stored:
He hath loosed the fateful lightning of His terrible swift sword;
  His truth is marching on!
    Glory! glory! hallelujah!   5
    Glory! glory! hallelujah!
    Glory! glory! hallelujah!
      Our God is marching on!

I have seen Him in the watch-fire of a hundred circling camps,
They have builded Him an altar in the evening dews and damps;   10
I can read His righteous sentence by the dim and flaring lamps;
  His day is marching on!
    Glory! etc.

I have read a fiery gospel writ in burnished rows of steel:
"As ye deal with my contemners so with you my grace shall deal!"   1
Let the Hero born of woman crush the serpent with his heel,
  Since God is marching on!
    Glory! etc.

He has sounded forth the trumpet that shall never call retreat;
He is sifting out the hearts of men before His judgment seat;   2
Oh! be swift, my soul, to answer Him, be jubilant, my feet!
  Our God is marching on!
    Glory! etc.

In the beauty of the lilies Christ was born across the sea,
With a glory in his bosom that transfigures you and me;
As he died to make men holy, let us die to make men free.
  While God is marching on!
    Glory! etc.

LANGSTON HUGHES   (1902–1967)

Negro ———————————————————————————————————— *1958*

I am a Negro:
  Black as the night is black,
  Black like the depths of my Africa.

I've been a slave:
  Caesar told me to keep his door-steps clean.
  I brushed the boots of Washington.

I've been a worker:
  Under my hand the pyramids arose.
  I made mortar for the Woolworth Building.

I've been a singer: 10
  All the way from Africa to Georgia
  I carried my sorrow songs.
  I made ragtime.

I've been a victim:
  The Belgians cut off my hands in the Congo.   15
  They lynch me still in Mississippi.

I am a Negro:
  Black as the night is black,
  Black like the depths of my Africa.

ROBINSON JEFFERS   (1887–1962)

The Answer ———————————————————————————— *1937*

Then what is the answer?—Not to be deluded by dreams.
To know that great civilizations have broken down into violence, and their tyrants
  come, many times before.
When open violence appears, to avoid it with honor or choose the least ugly faction;
  these evils are essential.
To keep one's own integrity, be merciful and uncorrupted and not wish for evil;
  and not be duped
By dreams of universal justice or happiness. These dreams will not be fulfilled.   5
To know this, and know that however ugly the parts appear the whole remains
  beautiful. A severed hand
Is an ugly thing, and man disseemed from the earth and stars and his history . . . for
  contemplation or in fact . . .

Often appears atrociously ugly. Integrity is wholeness, the greatest beauty is
Organic wholeness, the wholeness of life and things, the divine beauty of the universe.
  Love that, not man
Apart from that, or else you will share man's pitiful confusions, or drown in despair
  when his days darken.   10

ETHERIDGE KNIGHT   (1931–1991)

Haiku° ———————————————————————————————— *1968*

     1
Eastern guard tower
glints in sunset; convicts rest
like lizards on rocks.

HAIKU.   The haiku is a Japanese lyric verse form consisting of three lines that total seventeen syllables, divided 5-7-5. See the discussion on p. 902.

2
The piano man
is sitting at 3 am   5
his songs drop like plum.

3
Morning sun slants cell.
Drunks stagger like cripple flies
On the Jailhouse floor.

4
To write a blues song
is to regiment riots   10
and pluck gems from graves.

5
A bare pecan tree
slips a pencil shadow down
a moonlit snow slope.   1[5]

6
The falling snow flakes
Can not blunt the hard aches nor
Match the steel stillness.

7
Under moon shadows
A tall boy flashes knife and   2[0]
Slices star bright ice.

8
In the August grass
Struck by the last rays of sun
The cracked teacup screams.

9
Making jazz swing in
Seventeen syllables AIN'T
No square poet's job.

MAXINE KUMIN   (b. 1925)

Woodchucks _____ *1972*

Gassing the woodchucks didn't turn out right.
The knockout bomb from the Feed and Grain Exchange
was featured as merciful, quick at the bone
and the case we had against them was airtight,
both exits shoehorned shut with puddingstone,
but they had a sub-sub-basement out of range.

Next morning they turned up again, no worse
for the cyanide than we for our cigarettes
and state-store Scotch, all of us up to scratch.
They brought down the marigolds as a matter of course   10
and then took over the vegetable patch
nipping the broccoli shoots, beheading the carrots.

The food from our mouths, I said, righteously thrilling
to the feel of the .22, the bullet's neat noses.
I, a lapsed pacifist fallen from grace   15
puffed with Darwinian pieties° for killing,
now drew a bead on the littlest woodchuck's face.
He died down in the everbearing roses.

Ten minutes later I dropped the mother. She
flipflopped in the air and fell, her needle teeth   20
still hooked in a leaf of early Swiss chard.
Another baby next. O one-two-three
the murderer inside me rose up hard,
the hawkeye killer came on stage forthwith.

There's one chuck left. Old wily fellow, he keeps   25
me cocked and ready day after day after day.
All night I hunt his humped-up form. I dream
I sight along the barrel in my sleep.
If only they'd all consented to die unseen
gassed underground the quiet Nazi way.°   30

WOODCHUCKS.   16 *Darwinian pieties:* Charles Darwin (1809–1892) was a British naturalist who
formulated the theory of evolution; the piety is "survival of the fittest."   30 *gassed . . . way:* a reference to the extermination of millions of people in gas chambers by the Nazis during World War II.

IRVING LAYTON   (b. 1912)

Rhine Boat Trip° _____ 1977

The castles on the Rhine
are all haunted
by the ghosts of Jewish mothers
looking for their ghostly children

And the clusters of grapes   5
in the sloping vineyards
are myriads of blinded eyes
staring at the blind sun

The tireless Lorelei°
can never comb from their hair   10

RHINE BOAT TRIP: The title refers to the Rhine River, which flows through Germany.
9 *Lorelei:* legendary seductive nymphs who lived in the cliffs overlooking the Rhine, and whose
singing lured sailors to shipwreck.

the crimson beards
of murdered rabbis

However sweetly they sing
one hears only
the low wailing of cattle-cars°   15
moving invisibly across the land

15 *cattle-cars:* railroad cars designed to transport cattle but used by the Nazis to transport Jews
from the cities of Europe to extermination camps.

LI-YOUNG LEE   (b. 1957)

A Final Thing ———————————————————————— *1990*

I am that last, that
final thing, the body
in a white sheet listening,

the whole of me trained,
curled like one great ear on
a sound, a noise I know, a

woman talking
in another room,
the woman I love; and

though I can't hear
her words, by their voicing
I can guess

she is telling a story,

using a voice which speaks to another,
weighted with that other's attention,
and avowing it
by deepening in intention.

Rich with the fullness of what's declared,
this voice points
away from itself
to some place

in the hearer,
sends the hearer back
to himself
to find what he knows.

A saying full of hearing,
a murmuring full of telling
and compassion for the listener
and for what's told,

now interrupted by a second voice,   30

thinner, higher, uncertain.
Querying, it seems
an invitation to be met,
stirring anticipation, embodying
incompletion of time and the day.   35

My son, my first-born, and his mother
are involved in a story no longer only theirs,
for I am implicated,
all three of us now
clinging to expectancy, riding sound and air.   40

Will my first morning of heaven be this?
No. And this is not
my last morning on earth.
I am simply last
in my house   45

to waken, and the first
sound I hear
is the voice of one I love
speaking to one we love.
I hear it through the bedroom wall;   50

something, someday, I'll close my eyes to recall.

ALAN P. LIGHTMAN   (b. 1948)

In Computers ——————————————————————— *1982 (1981)*

In the magnets of computers will
   be stored

Blend of sunset over wheat
   fields.
Low thunder of gazelle.   5
Light, sweet wind on high
   ground.
Vacuum stillness spreading from
   a thick snowfall.

Men will sit in rooms   10
upon the smooth, scrubbed earth
or stand in tunnels on the moon
and instruct themselves in how it
   was.
Nothing will be lost.   15
Nothing will be lost.

LIZ LOCHHEAD   (b. 1947)

The Choosing —————————————————————— *1984*

We were first equal Mary and I
with same coloured ribbons in mouse-coloured hair
and with equal shyness,
we curtseyed to the lady councillor
for copies of Collins' Children's Classics.   5
First equal, equally proud.

Best friends too Mary and I
a common bond in being cleverest (equal)
in our small school's small class.
I remember   10
the competition for top desk
or to read aloud the lesson
at school service.
And my terrible fear
of her superiority at sums.   1
I remember the housing scheme
where we both stayed.
The same houses, different homes,
where the choices were made.

I don't know exactly why they moved,   2
but anyway they went.
Something about a three-apartment
and a cheaper rent.
But from the top deck of the high-school bus
I'd glimpse among the others on the corner
Mary's father, mufflered, contrasting strangely
with the elegant greyhounds by his side.
He didn't believe in high school education,
especially for girls,
or in forking out for uniforms.

Ten years later on a Saturday —
I am coming from the library —
sitting near me on the bus,
Mary
with a husband who is tall,
curly haired, has eyes
for no one else but Mary.
Her arms are round the full-shaped vase
that is her body.
Oh, you can see where the attraction lies
in Mary's life —
not that I envy her, really.

And I am coming from the library
with my arms full of books.
I think of those prizes that were ours for the taking   45
and wonder when the choices got made
we don't remember making.

AUDRE LORDE   (1934–1992)

Every Traveler Has One Vermont Poem _____ *(1986)*

Spikes of lavender aster under Route 91
hide a longing or confession
"I remember when air was invisible"
from Chamberlin Hill down to Lord's Creek
tree mosses point the way home.   5

Two nights of frost
and already the hills are turning
curved green against the astonished morning
sneeze-weed and ox-eye daisies
nor caring   I am a stranger   10
making a living choice.

Tanned boys I do not know
on their first proud harvest
wave from their father's tractor
one smiles as we drive past   15
the other hollers
nigger
into cropped and fragrant air.

RICHARD LOVELACE   (1618–1657)

To Lucasta, Going to the Wars _____ *1649*

Tell me not, Sweet, I am unkind
That from the nunnery
Of thy chaste breast and quiet mind,
To war and arms I fly.

True, a new mistress now I chase,   5
The first foe in the field;
And with a stronger faith embrace
A sword, a horse, a shield.

Yet this inconstancy is such
As you too shall adore;   10
I could not love thee, Dear, so much,
Loved I not honor more.

AMY LOWELL   (1874–1925)

Patterns _____ *1916*

I walk down the garden paths,
And all the daffodils
Are blowing, and the bright blue squills.
I walk down the patterned garden-paths
In my stiff, brocaded gown.   5
With my powdered hair and jewelled fan,
I too am a rare
Pattern. As I wander down
The garden paths.
My dress is richly figured,   10
And the train
Makes a pink and silver stain
On the gravel, and the thrift
Of the borders.
Just a plate of current fashion   15
Tripping by in high-heeled, ribboned shoes.
Not a softness anywhere about me,
Only whalebone° and brocade.
And I sink on a seat in the shade
Of a lime tree. For my passion   20
Wars against the stiff brocade.
The daffodils and squills
Flutter in the breeze
As they please.
And I weep;   25
For the lime-tree is in blossom
And one small flower has dropped upon my bosom.

And the plashing of waterdrops
In the marble fountain
Comes down the garden-paths.
The dripping never stops.

Underneath my stiffened gown
Is the softness of a woman bathing in a marble basin,
A basin in the midst of hedges grown
So thick, she cannot see her lover hiding,
But she guesses he is near,
And the sliding of the water
Seems the stroking of a dear
Hand upon her.
What is Summer in a fine brocaded gown!
I should like to see it lying in a heap upon the ground.
All the pink and silver crumpled up on the ground.

PATTERNS.   18 *whalebone:* Baleen from whales was used to make corsets for women because it
was strong and flexible, like an early plastic.

I would be the pink and silver as I ran along the paths,
And he would stumble after,
Bewildered by my laughter. 45
I should see the sun flashing from his sword-hilt and buckles on his shoes.
I would choose
To lead him in a maze along the patterned paths,
A bright and laughing maze for my heavy-booted lover.
Till he caught me in the shade, 50
And the buttons of his waistcoat bruised my body as he clasped me,
Aching, melting, unafraid.
With the shadows of the leaves and the sundrops,
And the plopping of the waterdrops,
All about us in the open afternoon— 55
I am very like to swoon
With the weight of this brocade,
For the sun sifts through the shade.

Underneath the fallen blossom
In my bosom, 60
Is a letter I have hid.
It was brought to me this morning by a rider from the Duke.
Madam, we regret to inform you that Lord Hartwell
Died in action Thursday se'nnight.°
As I read it in the white, morning sunlight, 65
The letters squirmed like snakes.
"Any answer, Madam," said my footman.
"No," I told him.
"See that the messenger takes some refreshment.

No, no answer." 70
And I walked into the garden,
Up and down the patterned paths,
In my stiff, correct brocade.
The blue and yellow flowers stood up proudly in the sun,
Each one. 75
I stood upright too,
Held rigid to the pattern
By the stiffness of my gown.
Up and down I walked.
Up and down. 80

In a month he would have been my husband.
In a month, here, underneath this lime,
We would have broken the pattern;
He for me, and I for him,
He as Colonel, I as Lady, 85
On this shady seat.
He had a whim
That sunlight carried blessing.

64 *se'nnight:* seven nights, hence a week ago.

And I answered, "It shall be as you have said."
Now he is dead.   90

In Summer and In Winter I shall walk
Up and down
The patterned garden-paths
In my stiff, brocaded gown.
The squills and daffodils   95
Will give peace to pillared roses, and to asters, and to snow.
I shall go
Up and down,
In my gown.
Gorgeously arrayed,   100
Boned and stayed.
And the softness of my body will be guarded from embrace
By each button, hook, and lace.
For the man who should loose me is dead,
Fighting with the Duke in Flanders,°   10
In a pattern called a war.
Christ! What are patterns for?

105 *Flanders:* a place of frequent warfare in Belgium. The speaker's clothing (lines 5, 6) suggests the time of the duke of Marlborough's Flanders campaigns of 1702–1710. The Battle of Waterloo (1815) was also fought nearby under the duke of Wellington. During World War I, fierce fighting against the Germans occurred in Flanders in 1914 and 1915, with great loss of life.

GWENDOLYN McEWEN   (b. 1941)

Dark Pines under Water _____ *1969*

This land like a mirror turns you inward
And you become a forest in a furtive lake;
The dark pines of your mind reach downward,
You dream in the green of your time,
Your memory is a row of sinking pines.

Explorer, you tell yourself this is not what you came for
Although it is good here, and green;
You had meant to move with a kind of largeness,
You had planned a heavy grace, an anguished dream.

But the dark pines of your mind dip deeper
And you are sinking, sinking, sleeper
In an elementary world;
There is something down there and you want it told.

HEATHER McHUGH   (b. 1948)

Lines _____ *1981*

Some are waiting, some can't wait.
The stores are full of necessities.

The sun dies down, the graveyard
grows, the subway is a wind
instrument with so many stops, but   5
even the underground comes
to an end, and all those flights
of fancy birds settle for one
telephone wire, the one on which
just now, the man in utterly   10
unheard-of love has caught
the word goodbye. He puts
the receiver back in the cradle
and stands. Outside his window
an old man with a hearing-aid walks   15
without aim, happy just to be alive.

CLAUDE McKAY   (1890–1948)

The White City _____ *1922*

I will not toy with it nor bend an inch.
Deep in the secret chambers of my heart
I muse my life-long hate, and without flinch
I bear it nobly as I live my part.
My being would be a skeleton, a shell,   5
If this dark Passion that fills my every mood,
And makes my heaven in the white world's hell,
Did not forever feed me vital blood.
I see the mighty city through a mist—
The strident trains that speed the goaded mass,   10
The poles and spires and towers vapor-kissed,
The fortressed port through which the great ships pass,
The tides, the wharves, the dens I contemplate,
Are sweet like wanton loves because I hate.

W. S. MERWIN   (b. 1927)

Listen _____ *1988*

Listen
with the night falling we are saying thank you

we are stopping on the bridges to bow from the railings
we are running out of the glass rooms
with our mouths full of food to look at the sky   5
and say thank you
we are standing by the water looking out
in different directions

back from a series of hospitals back from a mugging
after funerals we are saying thank you   10
after the news of the dead
whether or not we knew them we are saying thank you
looking up from tables we are saying thank you
in a culture up to its chin in shame
living in the stench it has chosen we are saying thank you   15

over telephones we are saying thank you
in doorways and in the backs of cars and in elevators
remembering wars and the police at the back door
and the beatings on stairs we are saying thank you
in the banks that use us we are saying thank you   20

with the animals dying around us
our lost feelings we are saying thank you
with the forests falling faster than the minutes
of our lives we are saying thank you
with the words going out like cells of a brain   25
with the cities growing over us like the earth
we are saying thank you faster and faster
with nobody listening we are saying thank you
we are saying thank you and waving
dark though it is

EDNA ST. VINCENT MILLAY   (1892–1950)

What Lips My Lips Have Kissed, and Where, and Why _____ *1923*

What lips my lips have kissed, and where, and why,
I have forgotten, and what arms have lain
Under my head till morning; but the rain
Is full of ghosts tonight, that tap and sigh
Upon the glass and listen for reply,
And in my heart there stirs a quiet pain
For unremembered lads that not again
Will turn to me at midnight with a cry.
Thus in the winter stands the lonely tree,
Nor knows what birds have vanished one by one,
Yet knows it boughs more silent than before:

I cannot say what loves have come and gone,
I only know that summer sang in me
A little while, that in me sings no more.

N. SCOTT MOMADAY   (b. 1934)

The Bear ————————————————————————— *1992*

What ruse of vision,
escarping the wall of leaves,
    rending incision
into countless surfaces,

    would cull and color   5
his somnolence, whose old age
    has outworn valor,
all but the fact of courage?

    Seen, he does not come,
move, but seems forever there,   10
    dimensionless, dumb
in the windless noon's hot glare.

    More scarred than others
these years since the trap maimed him,
    pain slants his withers,   15
drawing up the crooked limb.

    Then he is gone, whole,
without urgency, from sight,
    as buzzards control,
imperceptibly, their flight.   20

HOWARD NEMEROV   (1920–1991)

Life Cycle of Common Man ——————————————— *1960*

Roughly figured, this man of moderate habits,
This average consumer of the middle class,
Consumed in the course of his average life span
Just under half a million cigarettes,
Four thousand fifths of gin and about   5
A quarter as much vermouth; he drank
Maybe a hundred thousand cups of coffee,
And counting his parents' share it cost
Something like half a million dollars

To put him through life. How many beasts   10
Died to provide him with meat, belt and shoes
Cannot be certainly said.

                    But anyhow,
It is in this way that a man travels through time,
Leaving behind him a lengthening trail   15
Of empty bottles and bones, of broken shoes,
Frayed collars and worn out or outgrown
Diapers and dinnerjackets, silk ties and slickers.

Given the energy and security thus achieved,
He did . . . ? What? The usual things, of course,   20
The eating, dreaming, drinking and begetting,
And he worked for the money which was to pay
For the eating, et cetera, which were necessary
If he were to go on working for the money, et cetera,
But chiefly he talked. As the bottles and bones   2
Accumulated behind him, the words proceeded
Steadily from the front of his face as he
Advanced into the silence and made it verbal.
Who can tally the tale of his words? A lifetime
Would barely suffice for their repetition;
If you merely printed all his commas the result
Would be a very large volume, and the number of times
He said "thank you" or "very little sugar, please,"
Would stagger the imagination. There were also
Witticisms, platitudes, and statements beginning
"It seems to me" or "As I always say."
Consider the courage in all that, and behold the man
Walking into deep silence, with the ectoplastic
Cartoon's balloon of speech proceeding
Steadily out of the front of his face, the words
Borne along on the breath which is his spirit
Telling the numberless tale of his untold Word
Which makes the world his apple, and forces him to eat.

JIM NORTHRUP   (b. 1943)

wahbegan° _____ *1993*

Didja ever hear a sound
smell something
taste something
that brought you back

WAHBEGAN.   The title is an Ojibway name.

to Vietnam, instantly?   5
Didja ever wonder
when it would end?
It ended for my brother.
He died in the war
but didn't fall down   10
for fifteen tortured years.
His flashbacks are over,
another casualty whose name
will never be on the Wall.
Some can find peace   15
only in death.
The sound of his
family crying hurt.
The smell of the flowers
didn't comfort us.   20
The bitter taste
in my mouth
still sours me.
How about a memorial
for those who made it   25
through the war
but still died
before their time?

FRANK O'HARA (1926–1966)

Poem _____ *1952*

The eager note on my door said "Call me,
call when you get in!" so I quickly threw
a few tangerines into my overnight bag,
straightened my eyelids and shoulders, and
headed straight for the door. It was autumn   5
by the time I got around the corner, oh all
unwilling to be either pertinent or bemused, but
the leaves were brighter than grass on the sidewalk!

Funny, I thought, that the lights are on this late
and the hall door open; still up at this hour, a   10
champion jai-alai player like himself? Oh fie!
for shame! What a host, so zealous! And he was

there in the hall, flat on a sheet of blood that
ran down the stairs. I did appreciate it. There are few
hosts who so thoroughly prepare to greet a guest   15
only casually invited, and that several months ago.

MARY OLIVER   (b. 1935)

Ghosts _____ *1983*

1
Have you noticed?

2
Where so many millions of powerful bawling beasts
lay down on the earth and died
it's hard to tell now
what's bone, and what merely
was once.

The golden eagle, for instance,
has a bit of heaviness in him;
moreover the huge barns
seem ready, sometimes, to ramble off
toward deeper grass.

3
1805
near the Bitterroot Mountains:
a man named Lewis kneels down
on the prairie watching
a sparrow's nest cleverly concealed in the wild hyssop
and lined with buffalo hair. The chicks,
not more than a day hatched, lean
quietly into the thick wool as if
content, after all,
to have left the perfect world and fallen,
helpless and blind
into the flowered fields and the perils
of this one.

4
In the book of the earth it is written:
nothing can die.

In the book of the Sioux it is written:
they have gone away into the earth to hide.
Nothing will coax them out again
but the people dancing.

5
Said the old-timers:
the tongue
is the sweetest meat.

Passengers shooting from train windows
could hardly miss, they were   35
that many.

Afterward the carcasses
stank unbelievably, and sang with flies, ribboned
with slopes of white fat,
black ropes of blood—hellhunks   40
in the prairie heat.

        6
Have you noticed? how the rain
falls soft as the fall
of moccasins. *Have you noticed?*
how the immense circles still,   45
stubbornly, after a hundred years,
mark the grass where the rich droppings
from the roaring bulls
fell to the earth as the herd stood
day after day, moon after moon   50
in their tribal circle, outwaiting
the packs of yellow-eyed wolves that are also
have you noticed? gone now.

        7
Once only, and then in a dream,
I watched while, secretly   55
and with the tenderness of any caring woman,
a cow gave birth
to a red calf, tongued him dry and nursed him
in a warm corner
of the clear night   60
in the fragrant grass
in the wild domains
of the prairie spring, and I asked them,
in my dream I knelt down and asked them
to make room for me.   65

SIMON ORTIZ   (b. 1941)

A Story of How a Wall Stands _____ *1976*

> *At Aacqu there is a wall almost 400 years old which*
> *supports hundreds of tons of dirt and bones—it's a*
> *graveyard built on a steep incline—and it looks like*
> *it's about to fall down the incline but will not for a long time.*

My father, who works with stone,
says, "That's just the part you see,
the stones which seem to be
just packed in on the outside,"
and with his hands put the stone and mud
in place. "Underneath
what looks like loose stone,
there is stone woven together."
He ties one hand over the other,
fitting like the bones of his hands
and fingers. "That's what is
holding it together."

"It is built that carefully,"
he says, "the mud mixed
to a certain texture," patiently
"with the fingers," worked
in the palm of his hand. "So that
placed between the stones, they hold
together for a long, long time."

He tells me those things,
the story of them worked
with his fingers, in the palm
of his hands, working the stone
and the mud until they become
the wall that stands a long, long time.

DOROTHY PARKER   (1893–1967)

Résumé _____ 1936

Razors pain you;
Rivers are damp;
Acids stain you;
And drugs cause cramp.
Guns aren't lawful;
Nooses give;
Gas smells awful;
You might as well live.

LINDA PASTAN   (b. 1932)

Marks _____ 1978

My husband gives me an A
for last night's supper,
an incomplete for my ironing,

a B plus in bed.
My son says I am average,   5
an average mother, but if
I put my mind to it
I could improve.
My daughter believes
in Pass/Fail and tells me   10
I pass. Wait 'til they learn
I'm dropping out.

MARGE PIERCY   (b. 1936)

The Secretary Chant ————————————————— *1973*

My hips are a desk.
From my ears hang
chains of paper clips.
Rubber bands form my hair.
My breasts are wells of mimeograph ink.   5
My feet bear casters.
Buzz. Click.
My head is a badly organized file.
My head is a switchboard
where crossed lines crackle.   10
Press my fingers
and in my eyes appear
credit and debit.
Zing. Tinkle.
My navel is a reject button.   15
From my mouth issue canceled reams.
Swollen, heavy, rectangular
I am about to be delivered
of a baby
Xerox machine.   20
File me under W
because I wonce
was
a woman.

MARGE PIERCY   (b. 1936)

Will We Work Together? ———————————————— *1980*

You wake in the early grey
morning in bed alone and curse
me, that I am only
sometimes there. But when

I am with you, I light   5
up the corners, I am bright
as a fireplace roaring
with love, every bone in my back
and my fingers is singing
like a tea kettle on the boil.   10
My heart wags me, a big dog
with a bigger tail. I am
a new coin printed with
your face. My body wears
sore before I can express   15
on yours the smallest part
of what moves me. Words
shred and splinter.
I want to make with you
some bold new thing   20
to stand in the marketplace,
the statue of a goddess
laughing, armed and wearing
flowers and feathers. Like sheep
of whose hair is made   25
blankets and coats, I want
to force from this fierce sturdy
rampant love some useful thing.

SYLVIA PLATH   (1932–1963)

Last Words _____ *1971 (1961)*

I do not want a plain box, I want a sarcophagus
With tigery stripes, and a face on it
Round as the moon, to stare up.
I want to be looking at them when they° come
Picking among the dumb minerals, the roots,
I see them already—the pale, star-distance faces.
Now they are nothing, they are not even babies.
I imagine them without fathers or mothers, like the first gods.
They will wonder if I was important.
I should sugar and preserve my days like fruit!
My mirror is clouding over—
A few more breaths, and it will reflect nothing at all.
The flowers and the faces whiten to a sheet.

I do not trust the spirit. It escapes like steam
In dreams, through mouth-hole or eye-hole. I can't stop it.
One day it won't come back. Things aren't like that.

LAST WORDS.   4 *they:* possibly archeologists exploring the speaker's tomb or stone coffin
("sarcophagus").

They stay, their little particular lusters
Warmed by much handling. They almost purr.
When the soles of my feet grow cold,
The blue eye of my turquoise will comfort me.   20
Let me have my copper cooking pots, let my rouge pots
Bloom about me like night flowers, with a good smell.
They will roll me up in bandages, they will store my heart
Under my feet in a neat parcel.°
I shall hardly know myself. It will be dark,   25
And the shine of these small things sweeter than the face of Ishtar.°

19–24 *When . . . parcel:* The objects and procedures here refer to the household goods normally
entombed with a body in ancient Egypt and to the preparation of a mummy.   27 *Ishtar:* ancient
Babylonian goddess of fertility, love, and war.

SYLVIA PLATH   (1932–1963)

Mirror _____ *1965 (1961)*

I am silver and exact. I have no preconceptions.
Whatever I see I swallow immediately
Just as it is, unmisted by love or dislike.
I am not cruel, only truthful—
The eye of a little god, four-cornered.   5
Most of the time I meditate on the opposite wall.
It is pink, with speckles. I have looked at it so long
I think it is a part of my heart. But it flickers.
Faces and darkness separate us over and over.

Now I am a lake. A woman bends over me,   10
Searching my reaches for what she really is.
Then she turns to those liars, the candles or the moon.
I see her back, and reflect it faithfully.
She rewards me with tears and an agitation of hands.
I am important to her. She comes and goes.   15
Each morning it is her face that replaces the darkness.
In me she has drowned a young girl, and in me an old woman
Rises toward her day after day, like a terrible fish.

KATHA POLLITT   (b. 1949)

Archaeology _____ *1981*

> *"Our real poems are already in us
> and all we can do is dig."*
> —*Jonathan Galassi*

You knew the odds on failure from the start,
that morning you first saw, or thought you saw,

beneath the heartstruck plains of a second-rate country
the outline of buried cities. A thousand to one
you'd turn up nothing more than the rubbish heap   5
of a poor Near Eastern backwater:
a few chipped beads,
splinters of glass and pottery, broken tablets
whose secret lore, laboriously deciphered,
would prove to be only a collection of ancient grocery lists.   10
Still, the train moved away from the station without you.

How many lives ago
was that? How many choices?
Now that you've got your bushelful of shards
do you say, *give me back my years*   1.
or wrap yourself in the distant
glitter of desert stars,
telling yourself it was foolish after all
to have dreamed of uncovering
some fluent vessel, the bronze head of a god?   2
Pack up your fragments. Let the simoom°   *a desert sandstorm*
flatten the digging site. Now come
the passionate midnights in the museum basement
when out of that random rubble you'll invent
the dusty market smelling of sheep and spices,   2
streets, palmy gardens, courtyards set with wells
to which, in the blue of evening, one by one
come strong veiled women, bearing their perfect jars.

EZRA POUND   (1885–1972)

The River-Merchant's Wife: A Letter° ———————————— 1926 (1915)

While my hair was still cut straight across my forehead
I played about the front gate, pulling flowers.
You came by on bamboo stilts, playing horse,
You walked about my seat, playing with blue plums.
And we went on living in the village of Chokan:°
Two small people, without dislike or suspicion.

At fourteen I married My Lord you.
I never laughed, being bashful.
Lowering my head, I looked at the wall.
Called to, a thousand times, I never looked back.

At fifteen I stopped scowling,
I desired my dust to be mingled with yours

THE RIVER-MERCHANTS WIFE: A LETTER.   Freely translated from the Chinese of Li Po
(701–762).   5 *Chokan:* a suburb of Nanking, China.

Forever and forever and forever.
Why should I climb the look out?

At sixteen you departed,   15
You went into far Ku-tō-en,° by the river of swirling eddies,
And you have been gone five months.
The monkeys make sorrowful noise overhead.

You dragged your feet when you went out.
By the gate now, the moss is grown, the different mosses,   20
Too deep to clear them away!
The leaves fall early this autumn, in wind.
The paired butterflies are already yellow with August

Over the grass in the West garden;
They hurt me, I grow older.   25
If you are coming down through the narrows of the river Kiang,
Please let me know beforehand,
And I will come out to meet you
As far as Chō-fū-sa.°

16 *Ku-tō-en:* an island several hundred miles up the Kiang River from Nanking.   29 *Chō-fū-sa:*
a beach near Ku-tō-en.

JOHN CROWE RANSOM   (1888–1974)

Bells for John Whiteside's Daughter ⸻⸻⸻⸻⸻⸻ *1924*

There was such speed in her little body,
And such lightness in her footfall,
It is no wonder her brown study
Astonishes us all.

Her wars were bruited in our high window.   5
We looked among orchard trees and beyond
Where she took arms against her shadow,
Or harried unto the pond.

The lazy geese, like a snow cloud
Dripping their snow on the green grass,   10
Tricking and stopping, sleepy and proud,
Who cried in goose, Alas,

For the tireless heart within the little
Lady with rod that made them rise
From their noon apple-dreams and scuttle   15
Goose-fashion under the skies!

But now go the bells, and we are ready,
In one house we are sternly stopped
To say we are vexed at her brown study,
Lying so primly propped.   20

JOHN RAVEN (b. 1936)

Assailant _____ *1969*

He jumped me while I was asleep.
He was big and fat.
I been in many fights before,
but never one like that.
The only way I could survive,
was to get my hat . . .
His *name?*
Officers, I ain't talkin' 'bout no man;
I'm talkin' 'bout a rat!

ADRIENNE RICH (b. 1929)

Diving into the Wreck _____ *1973*

First having read the book of myths,
and loaded the camera,
and checked the edge of the knife-blade,
I put on
the body armor of black rubber
the absurd flippers
the grave and awkward mask.
I am having to do this
not like Cousteau with his
assiduous team
aboard the sun-flooded schooner
but here alone.

There is a ladder.
The ladder is always there
hanging innocently
close to the side of the schooner.
We know what it is for,
we who have used it.
otherwise
it is a piece of maritime floss
some sundry equipment.

I go down.
Rung after rung and still
the oxygen immerses me
the blue light
the clear atoms
of our human air.
I go down.

My flippers cripple me,
I crawl like an insect down the ladder   30
and there is no one
to tell me when the ocean
will begin.

First the air is blue and then
it is bluer and then green and then   35
black I am blacking out and yet
my mask is powerful
it pumps my blood with power
the sea is another story
the sea is not a question of power   40
I have to learn alone
to turn my body without force
in the deep element.

And now: it is easy to forget
what I came for   45
among so many who have always
lived here
swaying their crenellated fans
between the reefs
and besides   50
you breathe differently down here.

I came to explore the wreck.
The words are purposes.
The words are maps.
I came to see the damage that was done   55
and the treasures that prevail.
I stroke the beam of my lamp
slowly along the flank
of something more permanent
than fish or weed   60

the thing I came for:
the wreck and not the story of the wreck
the thing itself and not the myth
the drowned face always staring
toward the sun   65
the evidence of damage
worn by salt and sway into this threadbare beauty
the ribs of the disaster
curving their assertion
among the tentative haunters.   70

This is the place.
And I am here, the mermaid whose dark hair
streams black, the merman in his armored body.
We circle silently
about the wreck   75

we dive into the hold.
I am she: I am he

whose drowned face sleeps with open eyes
whose breasts still bear the stress
whose silver, copper, vermeil cargo lies   80
obscurely inside barrels
half-wedged and left to rot
we are the half-destroyed instruments
that once held to a course
the water-eaten log   85
the fouled compass

We are, I am, you are
by cowardice or courage
the one who find our way
back to this scene   90
carrying a knife, a camera
a book of myths
in which
our names do not appear.

THEODORE ROETHKE   (1908–1963)

The Light Comes Brighter _____ *1941*

The light comes brighter from the east; the caw
Of restive crows is sharper on the ear.
A walker at the river's edge may hear
A cannon crack announce an early thaw.

The sun cuts deep into the heavy drift,
Though still the guarded snow is winter-sealed,
At bridgeheads buckled ice begins to shift,
The river overflows the level field.

Once more the trees assume familiar shapes,
As branches loose last vestiges of snow.
The water stored in narrow pools escapes
In rivulets; the cold roots stir below.

Soon field and wood will wear an April look,
The frost be gone, for green is breaking now;
The ovenbird will match the vocal brook,
The young fruit swell upon the pear-tree bough.

And soon a branch, part of a hidden scene,
The leafy mind, that long was tightly furled,
Will turn its private substance into green,
And young shoots spread upon our inner world.

LUIS OMAR SALINAS   (b. 1937)

In a Farmhouse —————————————————————————— *1973*

Fifteen miles
out of Robstown
with the Texas sun
fading in the distance
I sit in the bedroom   5
profoundly,
animated by the day's work
in the cottonfields.

I made two dollars and
thirty cents today   10
I am eight years old
and I wonder
how the rest of the Mestizos°
do not go hungry
and if one were to die   15
of hunger
what an odd way
to leave for heaven.

IN A FARMHOUSE.   13 *Mestizos:* persons of mixed Spanish and Amerindian ancestry.

SONIA SANCHEZ   (b. 1934)

right on: white america —————————————————————— *1970*

this country might have
been a pio
   neer land
once.
   but.   there ain't   5
no mo
     indians   blowing
custer's° mind
     with a different
image of america.   10
         this country
might have
     needed shoot/
outs/ daily/
    once.   15
       but. there ain't

RIGHT ON: WHITE AMERICA.   8 *custer's:* General George Armstrong Custer (1839–1876) was
killed in his "last stand" at the Little Bighorn in Montana during a battle with Sioux Indians.

no mo real/ white/   allamerican
                        bad/guys.
just
        u & me.
                blk/ and un/armed.
this country might have
been a pion
                eer land.   once.
                                and it still is.
check out
        the falling
gun/shells   on our blk/tomorrows.

CARL SANDBURG   (1878–1967)

Chicago ———————————————————————— *1916*

Hog Butcher for the World,
Tool Maker, Stacker of Wheat,
Player with Railroads and the Nation's Freight Handler;
Stormy, husky, brawling,
City of the Big Shoulders:

They tell me you are wicked and I believe them, for I have seen your painted
women under the gas lamps luring the farm boys.
And they tell me you are crooked and I answer: Yes, it is true I have seen the
gunman kill and go free to kill again.
And they tell me you are brutal and my reply is: On the faces of women and
children I have seen the marks of wanton hunger.
And having answered so I turn once more to those who sneer at this my city,
and I give them back the sneer and say to them:
Come and show me another city with lifted head singing so proud to be alive
and coarse and strong and cunning.
Flinging magnetic curses amid the toil of piling job on job, here is a tall bold
slugger set vivid against the little soft cities;
Fierce as a dog with tongue lapping for action, cunning as a savage pitted against
the wilderness,
        Bareheaded,
        Shoveling,
        Wrecking,
        Planning,
        Building, breaking, rebuilding,
Under the smoke, dust all over his mouth, laughing with white teeth,
Under the terrible burden of destiny laughing as a young man laughs,
Laughing even as an ignorant fighter laughs who has never lost a battle,
Bragging and laughing that under his wrist is the pulse, and under his ribs the
heart of the people,
        Laughing!

Laughing the stormy, husky, brawling laughter of Youth, half-naked, sweating,
   proud to be Hog Butcher, Tool Maker, Stacker of Wheat, Player with Railroads
   and Freight Handler to the Nation.

SIEGFRIED SASSOON   (1886–1967)

Dreamers ————————————————————————— *1918*

Soldiers are citizens of death's grey land,
   Drawing no dividend from time's to-morrows.
In the great hour of destiny they stand,
   Each with his feuds, and jealousies, and sorrows.

Soldiers are sworn to action; they must win   5
   Some flaming, fatal climax with their lives.
Soldiers are dreamers; when the guns begin
   They think of firelit homes, clean beds, and wives.

I see them in foul dug-outs, gnawed by rats,
   And in the ruined trenches, lashed with rain,   10
Dreaming of things they did with balls and bats,
   And mocked by hopeless longing to regain
Bank-holidays,° and picture shows, and spats,
   And going to the office in the train.

DREAMERS.   13 *Bank-holidays:* legal holidays in Great Britain.

GJERTRUD SCHNACKENBERG   (b. 1953)

The Paperweight————————————————————— *1982*

The scene within the paperweight is calm,
A small white house, a laughing man and wife,
Deep snow. I turn it over in my palm
And watch it snowing in another life,

Another world, and from this scene learn what   5
It is to stand apart: she serves him tea
Once and forever, dressed from head to foot
As she is always dressed. In this toy, history

Sifts down through the glass like snow, and we
Wonder if her single deed tells much   10
Or little of the way she loves, and whether he
Sees shadows in the sky. Beyond our touch,

Beyond our lives, they laugh, and drink their tea.
We look at them just as the winter night
With its vast empty spaces bends to see   15
Our isolated little world of light,

Covered with snow, and snow in clouds above it,
And drifts and swirls too deep to understand.
Still I must try to think a little of it,
With so much winter in my head and hand.   20

ALAN SEEGER   (1886–1916)

I Have a Rendezvous with Death _____ *1916*

I have a rendezvous with Death
At some disputed barricade,
When Spring comes back with rustling shade
And apple blossoms fill the air—
I have a rendezvous with Death
When Spring brings back blue days and fair.

It may be he shall take my hand
And lead me into his dark land
And close my eyes and quench my breath—
It may be I shall pass him still.

I have a rendezvous with Death
On some scarred slope of battered hill,
When Spring comes round again this year
And the first meadow flowers appear.

God knows 'twere better to be deep
Pillowed in silk and scented down,
Where Love throbs out in blissful sleep,
Pulse nigh to pulse and breath to breath,
Where hushed awakenings are dear. . . .
But I've a rendezvous with Death
At midnight in some flaming town,
When Spring trips north again this year,
And I to my pledged word am true,
I shall not fail that rendezvous.

BRENDA SEROTTE   (b. 1946)

My Mother's Face _____ *1991*

Dressing for work
I glanced in the mirror

startled to see my mother's face
white, with the mouth turned down
her red frizzled hair   5
wild in all directions.
She turned sideways
to study my dress
standing tiptoe like I do
craning her long neck   10
in a futile attempt to see my feet.
Then without warning, the tears
rolling from the outer corners down
past slightly pitted cheeks
past that inverted smile   15
into the cave of her bosom
which heaved a sigh so forlorn
so weighted with loss
that had I not been standing silent
I would have surely thought it was me.   20

WILLIAM SHAKESPEARE   (1564–1616)

Fear No More the Heat o' the Sun° ———————————— *1623 (ca. 1609)*

Fear no more the heat o' the sun,
   Nor the furious winter's rages;
Thou thy worldly task hast done,
   Home art gone, and ta'en° thy wages: *taken*
Golden lads and girls all must,   5
As° chimney-sweepers, come to dust.   *like*

Fear no more the frown o' the great;
   Thou art past the tyrant's stroke;
Care no more to clothe and eat;
   To thee the reed is as the oak;   10
The scepter, learning, physic, must
All follow this, and come to dust.

Fear no more the lightning flash,
   Nor the all-dreaded thunder stone;°
Fear not slander, censure rash;   15
   Thou hast finished joy and moan:°   *sadness*
All lovers young, all lovers must
Consign to thee, and come to dust.

FEAR NO MORE THE HEAT O' THE SUN.   A dirge or lament sung over the supposedly dead body of Imogen in Act IV of Shakespeare's *Cymbeline.*   14 *thunder stone:* The sound of thunder was believed to be caused by stones falling from the sky.

No exorciser harm thee!
Nor no witchcraft charm thee!   20
Ghost unlaid forbear thee!
Nothing ill come near thee!
Quiet consummation have;
And renownéd be thy grave!

WILLIAM SHAKESPEARE   (1564–1616)

Sonnet 29: When in Disgrace with Fortune and Men's Eyes _____ *1609*

When, in disgrace with Fortune and men's eyes,
I all alone beweep my outcast state,
And trouble deaf heaven with my bootless° cries,   *futile, useless*
And look upon myself and curse my fate,
Wishing me like to one more rich in hope,
Featured like him, like him with friends possessed,
Desiring this man's art and that man's scope,
With what I most enjoy contented least;
Yet in these thoughts myself almost despising,
Haply I think on thee, and then my state,
(Like to the lark at break of day arising)
From sullen earth sings hymns at heaven's gate,
For thy sweet love remembered such wealth brings
That then I scorn to change my state with kings.

WILLIAM SHAKESPEARE   (1564–1616)

Sonnet 146: Poor Soul, The Center of My Sinful Earth _____ *1609*

Poor soul, the center of my sinful earth,
Thrall° to these rebel powers that thee array,°   *captive*
Why dost thou pine within and suffer dearth
Painting thy outward walls so costly gay?
Why so large cost having so short a lease,
Dost thou upon thy fading mansion spend?
Shall worms, inheritors of this excess,
Eat up thy charge? Is this thy body's end?
Then, soul, live thou upon thy servant's loss,°
And let that pine to aggravate thy store;°
Buy terms° divine in selling hours of dross°   *periods; refuse*

POOR SOUL.   2 *array:* surround or dress out, as in a military formation.   9 *thy servant's loss:*
the loss of the body.   10 *let . . . store:* let the body ("that") dwindle ("pine") to increase ("aggravate") the riches ("store") of the soul.

Within be fed, without be rich no more:
So shalt thou feed on Death, that feeds on men,
And Death once dead, there's no more dying then.

KARL SHAPIRO   (1913–2000)

Auto Wreck ———————————————————————— *1941*

Its quick soft silver bell beating, beating,
And down the dark one ruby flare
Pulsing out red light like an artery,
The ambulance at top speed floating down
Past beacons and illuminated clocks   5
Wings in a heavy curve, dips down,
And brakes speed, entering the crowd.
The doors leap open, emptying light;
Stretchers are laid out, the mangled lifted
And stowed into the little hospital.   10
Then the bell, breaking the hush, tolls once,
And the ambulance with its terrible cargo
Rocking, slightly rocking, moves away,
As the doors, an afterthought, are closed.

We are deranged, walking among the cops   15
Who sweep glass and are large and composed.
One is still making notes under the light.
One with a bucket douches ponds of blood
Into the street and gutter.
One hangs lanterns on the wrecks that cling,   20
Empty husks of locusts, to iron poles.
Our throats were tight as tourniquets,
Our feet were bound with splints, but now,
Like convalescents intimate and gauche,
We speak through sickly smiles and warn   25
With the stubborn saw of common sense,
The grim joke and the banal resolution.
The traffic moves around with care,
But we remain, touching a wound
That opens to our richest horror.   30
Already old, the question Who shall die?
Becomes unspoken Who is innocent?
For death in war is done by hands;
Suicide has cause and stillbirth, logic;
And cancer, simple as a flower, blooms.   35
But this invites the occult mind,
Cancels our physics with a sneer,
And spatters all we knew of dénouement
Across the expedient and wicked stones.

LESLIE MARMON SILKO   (b. 1948)

Where Mountain Lion Lay Down with Deer _____ *1974*

I climb the black rock mountain
  stepping from day to day
      silently.
I smell the wind for my ancestors
  pale blue leaves
  crushed wild mountain smell.
Returning
  up the gray stone cliff
  where I descended
      a thousand years ago.

Returning to faded black stone
  where mountain lion lay down with deer.
It is better to stay up here
      watching wind's reflection
      in tall yellow flowers.
The old ones who remember me are gone
    the old songs are all forgotten
and the story of my birth.
How I danced in snow-frost moonlight
    distant stars to the end of the Earth,
How I swam away
      in freezing mountain water
      narrow mossy canyon tumbling down
        out of the mountain
          out of the deep canyon stone
    down
      the memory
        spilling out
        into the world.

DAVE SMITH   (b. 1942)

Bluejays _____ *1981*

She tries to call them down,
quicknesses of air.
They bitch and scorn,
they roost away from her.

It isn't that she's brutal.
She's just a girl. Worse,
her touch is total.
Her play is dangerous.

Darkly they spit each at each,
from tops of pine and spruce.   10
Her words are shy and sweet,
but it's no use.

Ragged, blue, shrill,
they dart around like boys.
They fear the beautiful   15
but do not fly away.

STEVIE SMITH (1902–1971)

Not Waving But Drowning _____ *1957*

Nobody heard him, the dead man,
But still he lay moaning:
I was much further out than you thought
And not waving but drowning.

Poor chap, he always loved larking   5
And now he's dead
It must have been too cold for him his heart gave way,
They said.

Oh, no no no, it was too cold always
(Still the dead one lay moaning)   10
I was much too far out all my life
And not waving but drowning.

W. D. SNODGRASS (b. 1926)

These Trees Stand . . . _____ *1960*

These trees stand very tall under the heavens.
While *they* stand, if I walk, all stars traverse
This steep celestial gulf their branches chart.
Though lovers stand at sixes and at sevens
While civilizations come down with the curse,   5
Snodgrass is walking through the universe.

I can't make any world go around *your* house.
But note this moon. Recall how the night nurse
Goes ward-rounds, by the mild, reflective art
Of focusing her flashlight on her blouse.   10
Your name's safe conduct into love or verse;
Snodgrass is walking through the universe.

Your name's absurd, miraculous as sperm
And as decisive. If you can't coerce

One thing outside yourself, why you're the poet!
What irrefrangible atoms whirl, affirm
Their destiny and form Lucinda's skirts!
She can't make up your mind. Soon as you know it,
Your firmament grows touchable and firm.
If all this world runs battlefield or worse,
Come, let us wipe our glasses on our shirts:
Snodgrass is walking through the universe.

CATHY SONG   (b. 1955)

Lost Sister ————————————————————————————— *1983*

1

In China,
even the peasants
named their first daughters
Jade—°
the stone that in the far fields
could moisten the dry season,
could make men move mountains
for the healing green of the inner hills
glistening like slices of winter melon.
And the daughters were grateful:
they never left home.
To move freely was a luxury
stolen from them at birth.
Instead, they gathered patience,
learning to walk in shoes
the size of teacups,°
without breaking—
the arc of their movements
as dormant as the rooted willow,
as redundant as the farmyard hens.
But they traveled far
in surviving,
learning to stretch the family rice,
to quiet the demons,
the noisy stomachs.

2

There is a sister
across the ocean,
who relinquished her name,

LOST SISTER.   4. *Jade:* Both the mineral and the name are considered signs of good fortune and health in China.   16 *teacups:* Traditionally, girls' feet were bound at the age of seven in China because minuscule feet were considered beautiful and aristocratic. The binding inhibited the natural growth of the feet and made it painful and difficult to walk.

diluting jade green
with the blue of the Pacific.   30
Rising with a tide of locusts,
she swarmed with others
to inundate another shore.
In America,
there are many roads   35
and women can stride along with men.

But in another wilderness,
the possibilities,
the loneliness,
can strangulate like jungle vines.   40
The meager provisions and sentiments
of once belonging—
fermented roots, Mah-Jongg° tiles and firecrackers—
set but a flimsy household
in a forest of nightless cities.   45
A giant snake rattles above,
spewing black clouds into your kitchen.

Dough-faced landlords
slip in and out of your keyholes,
making claims you don't understand,   50
tapping into your communication systems
of laundry lines and restaurant chains.

You find you need China:
your one fragile identification,
a jade link   55
handcuffed to your wrist.
You remember your mother
who walked for centuries,
footless—
and like her,   60
you have left no footprints,
but only because
there is an ocean in between,
the unremitting space of your rebellion.

43. *Mah-Jongg:* a Chinese game played with 144 domino-like tiles marked in suits, counters, and dice.

GARY SOTO   (b. 1952)

Oranges _____ *1984*

The first time I walked
With a girl, I was twelve,
Cold, and weighted down

With two oranges in my jacket.
December. Frost cracking
Beneath my steps, my breath
Before me, then gone,
As I walked toward
Her house, the one whose
Porch light burned yellow
Night and day, in any weather.
A dog barked at me, until
She came out pulling
At her gloves, face bright
With rouge. I smiled,
Touched her shoulder, and led
Her down the street, across
A used car lot and a line
Of newly planted trees,
Until we were breathing
Before a drugstore. We
Entered, the tiny bell
Bringing a saleslady
Down a narrow aisle of goods.
I turned to the candies
Tiered like bleachers,
And asked what she wanted—
Light in her eyes, a smile
Starting at the corners
Of her mouth. I fingered
A nickel in my pocket,
And when she lifted a chocolate
That cost a dime,
I didn't say anything.
I took the nickel from
My pocket, then an orange,
And set them quietly on
The counter. When I looked up,
The lady's eyes met mine,
And held them, knowing
Very well what it was all
About.
      Outside,
A few cars hissing past,
Fog hanging like old
Coats between the trees.
I took my girl's hand
In mine for two blocks,
Then released it to let
Her unwrap the chocolate.
I peeled my orange
That was so bright against

The gray of December
That, from some distance,
Someone might have thought   55
I was making a fire in my hands.

GARY SOTO   (b. 1952)

Kearney Park ———————————————————————— *1985*

True Mexicans or not, let's open our shirts
And dance, a spark of heels
Chipping at the dusty cement. The people
Are shiny like the sea, turning
To the clockwork of rancheras,   5
The accordion wheezing, the drum-tap
Of work rising and falling.
Let's dance with our hats in hand.
The sun is behind the trees,
Behind my stutter of awkward steps   10
With a woman who is a brilliant arc of smiles,
An armful of falling water. Her skirt
Opens and closes. My arms
Know no better but to flop
On their own, and we spin, dip   15
And laugh into each other's faces—
Faces that could be famous
On the coffee table of my abuelita.°   *little grandmother*
But grandma is here, at the park, with a beer
At her feet, clapping   20
And shouting, "Dance, hijo,° dance!"   *son, child*
Laughing, I bend, slide, and throw up
A great cloud of dust,
Until the girl and I are no more.

WILLIAM STAFFORD   (1914–1993)

Traveling Through the Dark ———————————————— *1960*

Traveling through the dark I found a deer
dead on the edge of the Wilson River road.
It is usually best to roll them into the canyon:
that road is narrow; to swerve might make more dead.

By glow of the tail-light I stumbled back of the car   5
and stood by the heap, a doe, a recent killing;
she had stiffened already, almost cold.
I dragged her off; she was large in the belly.

My fingers touching her side brought me the reason—
her side was warm; her fawn lay there waiting,   10
alive, still, never to be born.
Beside that mountain road I hesitated.

The car aimed ahead its lowered parking lights;
under the hood purred the steady engine.
I stood in the glare of the warm exhaust turning red;   15
around our group I could hear the wilderness listen.
I thought hard for us all—my only swerving—,
then pushed her over the edge into the river.

GERALD STERN   (b. 1925)

Burying an Animal on the Way to New York _____ *1977*

Don't flinch when you come across a dead animal lying on the road;
you are being shown the secret of life.
Drive slowly over the brown flesh;
you are helping to bury it.
If you are the last mourner there will be no caress
at all from the crushed limbs
and you will have to slide over the dark spot imagining
the first suffering all by yourself
Shreds of spirit and little ghost fragments will be spread out
for two miles above the white highway.
Slow down with your radio off and your window open
to hear the twittering as you go by.

WALLACE STEVENS   (1879–1955)

The Emperor of Ice-Cream _____ *1923*

Call the roller of big cigars,
The muscular one, and bid him whip
In kitchen cups concupiscent curds.
Let the wenches dawdle in such dress
As they are used to wear, and let the boys
Bring flowers in last month's newspapers.
Let be be finale° of seem.
The only emperor is the emperor of ice-cream.
Take from the dresser of deal,°
Lacking the three glass knobs, that sheet
On which she embroidered fantails° once

THE EMPEROR OF ICE-CREAM.   7 *finale:* the grand conclusion.   9 *deal:* unfinished pine
or fir used to make cheap furniture.   11 *fantails:* fantail pigeons.

And spread it so as to cover her face.
If her horny feet protrude, they come
To show how cold she is, and dumb.
Let the lamp affix its beam.   15
The only emperor is the emperor of ice-cream.

MAY SWENSON   (1919–1989)

Question ———————————————————————— *1978*

Body my house
my horse my hound
what will I do
when you are fallen

Where will I sleep   5
How will I ride
What will I hunt

Where can I go
without my mount
all eager and quick   10
How will I know
in thicket ahead
is danger or treasure
when Body my good
bright dog is dead   15

How will it be
to lie in the sky
without roof or door
and wind for an eye

With cloud for shift   20
how will I hide?

JONATHAN SWIFT   (1667–1745)

A Riddle (The Vowels) ————————————————— *1746*

We are little airy Creatures,
All of different Voice and Features;
One of us in Glass is set,
One of us you'll find in Jet.
T'other you may see in Tin,   5
And the fourth a Box within.
If the fifth you shou'd pursue,
It can never fly from you.

JAMES TATE   (b. 1943)

The Blue Booby _____ *1969*

The blue booby lives
on the bare rocks
of Galápagos°
and fears nothing.
It is a simple life:
they live on fish,
and there are few predators.
Also, the males do not
make fools of themselves
chasing after the young
ladies. Rather,
they gather the blue
objects of the world
and construct from them
a nest—an occasional
Gaulois° package,
a string of beads,
a piece of cloth from
a sailor's suit. This
replaces the need for
dazzling plumage;
in fact, in the past
fifty million years
the male has grown
considerably duller,
nor can he sing well.
The female, though,

asks little of him—
the blue satisfies her
completely, has
a magical effect
on her. When she returns
from her day of
gossip and shopping,
she sees he has found her
a new shred of blue foil:
for this she rewards him
with her dark body,
the stars turn slowly
in the blue foil beside them
like the eyes of a mild savior.

THE BLUE BOOBY.   3 *Galápagos:* islands in the Pacific Ocean on the equator about six hundred miles west of Ecuador where many unique species of animals live.   16 *Gaulois:* a brand of French cigarettes with a blue package.

DYLAN THOMAS   (1914–1953)

A Refusal to Mourn the Death, by Fire, of a Child in London —————— *1946*

Never until the mankind making
Bird beast and flower
Fathering and all humbling darkness
Tells with silence the last light breaking
And the still hour   5
Is come of the sea tumbling in harness

And I must enter again the round
Zion of the water bead
And the synagogue of the ear of corn
Shall I let pray the shadow of a sound   10
Or sow my salt seed
In the least valley of sackcloth to mourn

The majesty and burning of the child's death.
I shall not murder
The mankind of her going with a grave truth   15
Nor blaspheme down the stations of the breath
With any further
Elegy of innocence and youth.

Deep with the first dead lies London's daughter,
Robed in the long friends,   20
The grains beyond age, the dark veins of her mother,
Secret by the unmourning water
Of the riding Thames.°
After the first death, there is no other.

A REFUSAL TO MOURN.   23 *Thames:* the River Thames, which flows through London.

CHASE TWICHELL   (b. 1950)

Blurry Cow ——————————————————————— *1983*

Two cows stand transfixed
by a trough of floating leaves,
facing as if into the camera,
black and white. One stamps
at the hot sting of a deerfly.   5

Seen from the window of a train,
the hoof lifts forever
over hay crosshatched by speed,
and the scales of the haunches
balance. The rest is lost: 10

the head a sudden slur of light,
the dog loping along the tracks
toward a farm yard
where a woman wavers
in her mirage of laundry.   15
A blurry cow, of all things,
strays into the mind's eye,
the afterimage
of this day on earth.

JOHN UPDIKE   (b. 1932)

Perfection Wasted _____ *1990*

And another regrettable thing about death
is the ceasing of your own brand of magic,
which took a whole life to develop and market—
the quips, the witticisms, the slant
adjusted to a few, those loved ones nearest
the lip of the stage, their soft faces blanched
in the footlight glow, their laughter close to tears,
their tears confused with their diamond earrings,
their warm pooled breath in and out with your heartbeat,
their response and your performance twinned.
The jokes over the phone. The memories packed
in the rapid-access file. The whole act.
Who will do it again? That's it: no one;
imitators and descendants aren't the same.

TINO VILLANUEVA   (b. 1941)

Day-Long Day _____ *1972*

> Again the drag of pisca,° pisca . . . pisca . . .
> Daydreams border on sun-fed hallucinations,
> eyes and hands automatically discriminate
> whiteness of cotton from field of vision.
> Pisca, pisca.
> > "Un Hijo del Sol,"°
> > Genaro Gonzales°

DAY-LONG DAY.   EPIGRAPH: *pisca:* picking cotton.   *Un Hijo del Sol:* a Son of the Sun.
Genaro Gonzales: Hispanic author, born 1949.

Third-generation timetable.
Sweat day-long dripping into open space;
sun blocks out the sky, suffocates the only breeze.
From el amo desgraciado,° a sentence:

"I wanna bale a day, and the boy here   5
don't hafta go to school."

*   *   *

In time-binding motion—
a family of sinews and backs,
row-trapped,
zigzagging through summer-long rows
of cotton: Lubbock by way of Wharton.°   10

"Está como si escupieran fuego,"° a mother moans
in sweat-patched jeans,
stooping
with unbending dreams.
"Estudia para que no seas burro como nosotros,"°   15
our elders warn, their gloves and cuffs
leaf-stained by seasons.
*   *   *
Bronzed and blurry-eyed by
the blast of degrees,
we blend into earth's rotation.   20
And sweltering toward Saturday, the
day-long day is sunstruck by 6:00 P.M.
One last chug-a-lug from a water jug
old as granddad.
Day-long sweat dripping into open space: 25
Wharton by way of Lubbock.

4 *el amo desgraciado:* the despicable boss.   11 *Lubbock* . . . *Wharton:* cities on opposite sides of
Texas.   12 *Está . . . fuego:* "It's as if they are spewing fire."   16 *Estudia . . . nosotros:* "Study so
that you will not be a burro like us."

SHELLY WAGNER   (b. ca. 1950)

The Boxes ————————————————————————————————— *1991*

When I told the police I couldn't find you,
they began a search that included everything—
even the boxes in the house:
the footlockers of clothes in the attic,
the hamper in the bathroom,
and the Chinese lacquered trunk by the sofa.   5
They made me raise every lid.

I told them you would never stay in a box,
not with all the commotion.
You would have jumped out,   10
found your flashlight
and joined the search.

Poor Thomas, taking these men
who don't know us   1*
through our neighbors' garages
where you never played,
hoping they were right
and we were wrong
and he would find you and   2
snatch you home by the hand

so the police cars could
get out of our driveway
and the divers would
get out of our river   2
because it was certainly
past our bedtime.
We would double-bolt our doors
like always,
say longer prayers than usual   ?
and go to bed. But during the night
I would have sat till morning
beside my sleeping boys.

But that's not what happened.
Thomas is still here, now older.
I still go to his room
when he is sleeping
just to look at him.
I still visit the cemetery,
not as often,
but the urge is the same:
to lie down on the grass,
put my arm around the hump of ground
and tell you, "Get out of this box!
Put a stop to this commotion. Come home.
You should be in bed."

ALICE WALKER   (b. 1944)

Revolutionary Petunias ————————————————— *1972*

Sammy Lou of Rue
sent to his reward
the exact creature who

murdered her husband,
using a cultivator's hoe   5
with verve and skill;
and laughed fit to kill
in disbelief
at the angry, militant
pictures of herself   10
the Sonneteers quickly drew:
not any of them people that
she knew.
A backwoods woman
her house was papered with   15
funeral home calendars and
faces appropriate for a Mississippi
Sunday School. She raised a George,
a Martha, a Jackie and a Kennedy. Also
a John Wesley Junior.°   20
"Always respect the word of God,"
she said on her way to she didn't
know where, except it would be by
electric chair, and she continued
"Don't yall forgit to *water*   25
my purple petunias."

REVOLUTIONARY PETUNIAS.   18–20 *George . . . Junior:* The children are named after George
and Martha Washington, Jackie and John Fitzgerald Kennedy (1917–1963, thirty-fifth U.S. president), and John Wesley (1703–1791), English evangelical preacher who founded Methodism.

EDMUND WALLER   (1606–1687)

Go, Lovely Rose ⸻ *1645*

   Go, lovely rose!
Tell her that wastes her time and me
   That now she knows,
When I resemble° her to thee,   *compare*
How sweet and fair she seems to be.   5

   Tell her that's young,
And shuns to have her graces spied,
   That hadst thou sprung
In deserts, where no men abide,
Thou must have uncommended died.   10

   Small is the worth
Of beauty from the light retired;

Bid her come forth,
Suffer herself to be desired,
And not blush so to be admired.

Then die! that she
The common fate of all things rare
    May read in thee;
How small a part of time they share
That are so wondrous sweet and fair.

ROBERT PENN WARREN   (1905–1989)

Heart of Autumn _____ *1978*

Wind finds the northwest gap, fall comes.
Today, under gray cloud-scud and over gray
Wind-flicker of forest, in perfect formation, wild geese
Head for a land of warm water, the *boom*, the lead pellet.

Some crumple in air, fall. Some stagger, recover control,
Then take the last glide for a far glint of water. None
Knows what has happened. Now, today, watching
How tirelessly *V* upon *V* arrows the season's logic,

Do I know my own story? At least, they know
When the hour comes for the great wing-beat. Sky-strider,
Star-strider—they rise, and the imperial utterance,
Which cries out for distance, quivers in the wheeling sky.

That much they know, and in their nature know
The path of pathlessness, with all the joy
Of destiny fulfilling its own name.
I have known time and distance, but not why I am here.

Path of logic, path of folly, all
The same—and I stand, my face lifted now skyward,
Hearing the high beat, my arms outstretched in the tingling
Process of transformation, and soon tough legs,

With folded feet, trail in the sounding vacuum of passage,
And my heart is impacted with a fierce impulse
To unwordable utterance—
Toward sunset, at a great height.

BRUCE WEIGL   (b. 1949)

Song of Napalm ——————————————————————— *1985*

For My Wife

After the storm, after the rain stopped pounding,
We stood in the doorway watching horses
Walk off lazily across the pasture's hill.
We stared through the black screen,
Our vision altered by the distance   5
So I thought I saw a mist
Kicked up around their hooves when they faded
Like cut-out horses
Away from us.
The grass was never more blue in that light, more   10
Scarlet; beyond the pasture
Trees scraped their voices in the wind, branches
Criss-crossed the sky like barbed-wire
But you said they were only branches.

Okay. The storm stopped pounding.   15
I am trying to say this straight: for once
I was sane enough to pause and breathe
Outside my wild plans and after the hard rain
I turned my back on the old curses, I believed
They swung finally away from me . . .   20

But still the branches are wire
And thunder is the pounding mortar,
Still I close my eyes and see the girl
Running from her village, napalm
Stuck to her dress like jelly,   25
Her hands reaching for the no one
Who waits in waves of heat before her.

So I can keep on living,
So I can stay here beside you,
I try to imagine she runs down the road and wings   30
Beat inside her until she rises
Above the stinking jungle and her pain
Eases, and your pain, and mine.
But the lie swings back again.
The lie works only as long as it takes to speak   35
And the girl runs only so far
As the napalm allows
Until her burning tendons and crackling
Muscles draw her up

Into that final position
Burning bodies so perfectly assume. Nothing
Can change that; she is burned behind my eyes
And not your good love and not the rain-swept air
And not the jungle green
Pasture unfolding before us can deny it.

PHILLIS WHEATLEY   (1754–1784)

On Being Brought from Africa to America _____ *1773*

'Twas mercy brought me from my *Pagan* land,
Taught my benighted soul to understand
That there's a God, that there's a *Saviour* too:
Once I redemption neither sought nor knew.
Some view our sable race with scornful eye,
"Their colour is a diabolic die."
Remember, *Christians*, *Negroes*, black as *Cain*,
May be refin'd, and join th' angelic train.

WALT WHITMAN   (1819–1892)

Full of Life Now _____ *1857*

Full of life now, compact, visible,
I, forty years old the eighty-third year of the States,
To one a century hence or any number of centuries hence,
To you yet unborn these, seeking you.

When you read these I that was visible am become invisible,
Now it is you, compact, visible, realizing my poems, seeking me,
Fancying how happy you were if I could be with you and become your comrade;
Be it as if I were with you. (Be not too certain but I am now with you.)

WALT WHITMAN   (1819–1892)

Beat! Beat! Drums! _____ *1861*

Beat! beat! drums!—blow! bugles! blow!
Through the windows—through doors—burst like a ruthless force,
Into the solemn church, and scatter the congregation,
Into the school where the scholar is studying;
Leave not the bridegroom quiet—no happiness must he have now with his bride,
Nor the peaceful farmer any peace, plowing his field or gathering his grain,
So fierce you whir and pound you drums—so shrill you bugles blow.

Beat! beat! drums!—blow! bugles! blow!
Over the traffic of cities—over the rumble of wheels in the streets;
Are beds prepared for sleepers at night in the houses? no sleepers must sleep in
    those beds,   10
No bargainers' bargains by day—no brokers or speculators—would they continue?
Would the talkers be talking? would the singer attempt to sing?
Would the lawyer rise in the court to state his case before the judge?
Beat! beat! drums—blow! bugles! blow!
Then rattle quicker, heavier drums—you bugles wilder blow.   15
Make no parley—stop for no expostulation,
Mind not the timid—mind not the weeper or prayer,
Mind not the old man beseeching the young man,
Let not the child's voice be heard, nor the mother's entreaties,
Make even the trestles to shake the dead where they lie awaiting the hearses,   20
So strong you thump O terrible drums—so loud you bugles blow.

WALT WHITMAN   (1819–1892)

Dirge for Two Veterans ———————————————————— *1865*

    The last sunbeam
Lightly falls from the finished Sabbath,
On the pavement here, and there beyond it is looking,
    Down a new-made double grave.

    Lo, the moon ascending,   5
Up from the east the silvery round moon,
Beautiful over the house-tops, ghastly, phantom moon,
    Immense and silent moon.

    I see a sad procession,
And I hear the sound of coming full-keyed bugles,   10
All the channels of the city streets they're flooding,
    As with voices and with tears.

    I hear the great drums pounding
And the small drums steady whirring,
And every blow of the great convulsive drums,   15
    Strikes me through and through.

    For the son is brought with the father,
(In the foremost ranks of the fierce assault they fell,
Two veterans son and father dropped together,
    And the double grave awaits them.)   20

    Now nearer blow the bugles,
And the drums strike more convulsive,
And the daylight o'er the pavement quite has faded,
    And the strong dead-march enwraps me.

In the eastern sky up-buoying,
The sorrowful vast phantom moves illumined,
('Tis some mother's large transparent face,
    In heaven brighter growing.)

O strong dead-march you please me!
O moon immense with your silvery face you soothe me!
O my soldiers twain! O my veterans passing to burial!
    What I have I also give you.

The moon gives you light,
And the bugles and the drums give you music,
And my heart, O my soldiers, my veterans,
    My heart gives you love.

RICHARD WILBUR   (b. 1921)

April 5, 1974 _____ *1976*

The air was soft, the ground still cold.
In the dull pasture where I strolled
Was something I could not believe.
Dead grass appeared to slide and heave,
Though still too frozen-flat to stir,
And rocks to twitch, and all to blur.
What was this rippling of the land?
Was matter getting out of hand
And making free with natural law?
I stopped and blinked, and then I saw
A fact as eerie as a dream.
There was a subtle flood of steam
Moving upon the face of things.
It came from standing pools and springs
And what of snow was still around;
It came of winter's giving ground
So that the freeze was coming out,
As when a set mind, blessed by doubt,
Relaxes into mother-wit.
Flowers, I said, will come of it.

WILLIAM CARLOS WILLIAMS   (1883–1963)

The Red Wheelbarrow _____ *1923*

            so much depends
            upon

a red wheel
barrow

glazed with rain   5
water

beside the white
chickens.

WILLIAM BUTLER YEATS   (1865–1939)

The Wild Swans at Coole ————————————————————————— *1919*

The trees are in their autumn beauty,
The woodland paths are dry,
Under the October twilight the water
Mirrors a still sky;
Upon the brimming water among the stones   5
Are nine-and-fifty swans.

The nineteenth autumn has come upon me
Since I first made my count;
I saw, before I had well finished,
All suddenly mount   10
And scatter wheeling in great broken rings
Upon their clamorous wings.

I have looked upon those brilliant creatures,
And now my heart is sore.
All's changed since I, hearing at twilight,   15
The first time on this shore,
The bell beat of their wings above my head,
Trod with a lighter tread.

Unwearied still, lover by lover,
They paddle in the cold   20
Companionable streams or climb the air;
Their hearts have not grown old;
Passion or conquest, wander where they will,
Attend upon them still.

But now they drift on the still water,   25
Mysterious, beautiful;
Among what rushes will they build,
By what lake's edge or pool
Delight men's eyes when I awake some day
To find they have flown away?   30

PAUL ZIMMER   (b. 1934)

The Day Zimmer Lost Religion _____ *1973*

The first Sunday I missed Mass on purpose
I waited all day for Christ to climb down
Like a wiry flyweight° from the cross and
Club me on my irreverent teeth, to wade into
My blasphemous gut and drop me like a
Red hot thurible,° the devil roaring in
Reserved seats until he got the hiccups.

It was a long cold way from the old days
When cassocked and surpliced° I mumbled Latin
At the old priest and rang his obscure bell.
A long way from the dirty wind that blew
The soot like venial sins° across the schoolyard
Where God reigned as a threatening,
One-eyed triangle high in the fleecy sky.

The first Sunday I missed Mass on purpose
I waited all day for Christ to climb down
Like the playground bully, the cuts and mice
Upon his face agleam, and pound me
Till my irreligious tongue hung out.
But of course He never came, knowing that
I was grown up and ready for Him now.

THE DAY ZIMMER LOST RELIGION.   3 *flyweight:* a boxer weighing less than 112 pounds.
6 *thurible:* a censer, a container in which incense is burned.   9 *cassocked and surpliced:* wearing
the traditional garb of an altar boy during Mass.   12 *venial sins:* minor inadvertent sins.

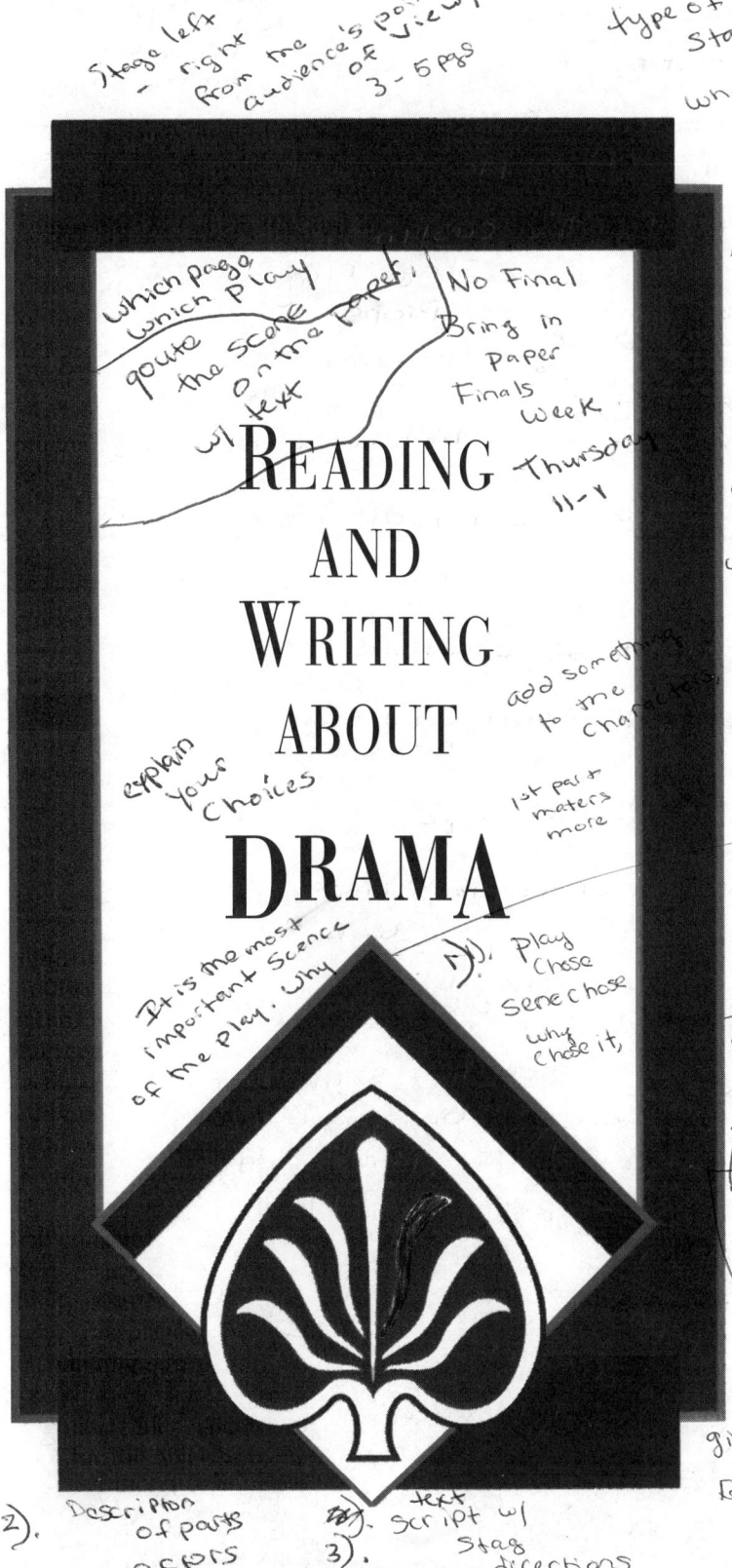

READING AND WRITING ABOUT DRAMA

Stage left - right from the one's point Audience's point of view 3 - 5 pgs

type of stage,

who moves when first

Which page which play qoute the scene on the paper w/ text

No Final Bring in Paper Finals Week Thursday 11-1

enter left Downstage

right upstage

when start to cross

when stop where stop

add something to the characters

explain your choices

1st part maters more

It is the most important Scene of the play. Why

1). Play Chose Sene chose why chose it

chose period or Contempory

What actors why Chose them

generly funny, good

describe Costumes

give a rational for what your doing

2). Description of parts actors

2). text script w/ stag directions

3).

Who's doing what at what point

Drama
    Theater

indicate the
actions of
the actors
on the stage

block a scene from a
    chosen play

Specify the customs
    Stage furn.
      Props.

explain who to cast
and what
- actual people names
- black, white, young

movement
    on stage

      between speeches

    we are the director,

like Ch 26 directions,

Pick about
30 lines
50 lines

Can cast hollywood stars
    in our paper,

us be in charge

One of the plays in the
      book

no chapter
30

Ch 31
Chose a scene

one of these
plays only
A Dollhouse
An enemy of the
people
Mulatto
The Glass menagerie

Paper

Pick the scene that
brings out the
Point in the
Play

1). Which scene
   why you chose that scene of
   the play

2). Script w/ fancy stage directions
   why you think it
   brings out the point
   what stage looks like
   where actors move
   what actors wearing
   what actors look
      like,

26
The Dramatic Vision: An Overview

Drama has much in common with the other genres of literature: Both drama and fiction, for example, focus on one or a few major characters who enjoy success or endure failure in facing challenges and in dealing with other characters. Many plays are written in prose, as is fiction, on the principle that the language of drama should resemble the language of life as much as possible.

Drama is also like poetry because both genres develop situations through speech and action. Indeed, a great number of plays, particularly those of past ages, exist as poetry. For example, the plays of ancient Athens were composed in intricate poetic forms. Many European plays from the Renaissance through the nineteenth century were written in blank verse or rhymed couplets, a tradition of poetic drama preserved by twentieth-century dramatists such as T. S. Eliot and Christopher Fry.

As separate genres, however, there are necessarily major differences among drama, fiction, and poetry. Fiction is distinguished from drama because the essence of fiction is narration—the relating or recounting of a sequence of events or actions, the actual telling of a story. Poetry is unlike both drama and fiction because it exists in many formal and informal shapes, and it is usually the shortest of the genres. Although we frequently read poetry silently and alone, it can be profitably read aloud by a single person to a group. Unlike both fiction and poetry, drama is literature designed for impersonation by people—actors—for the benefit and delight of other people—an audience.

DRAMA AS LITERATURE
AND DRAMA AS PERFORMANCE

Drama Is Both a Regular and Unique Form of Literature

Drama is unique because it can be presented and discussed both as *literature*—drama itself—and as *performance*—the production of plays in the theater. The major literary aspects of drama are the *text, language, characters, plot, structure, point of view, tone, symbolism,* and *theme* or *meaning*. All these elements have remained constant throughout the history of drama. In addition, drama written in poetic forms, such as Shakespeare's *Hamlet* and *A Midsummer Night's Dream*, includes elements such as *meter* and *rhyme*.

THE TEXT IS THE PRINTED (OR HANDWRITTEN) PLAY. The text of a play is in effect a plan for bringing the play into action on the stage. The most notable features of the text are dialogue, monologue, and stage directions. **Dialogue** is the conversation of two or more characters. A **monologue** is spoken by a single character who is usually alone onstage. **Stage directions** are the playwright's instructions about facial and vocal expression, movement and action, gesture and "body language," stage appearance, lighting, and similar matters. In addition, some dramatists, like Tennessee Williams, provide introductions and explanations for their plays. Such material can be considered as additional directions for interpretation and staging.

LANGUAGE, IMAGERY, AND STYLE ARE THE SPOKEN MEANS THROUGH WHICH WE UNDERSTAND THE PLAY. What we learn about characters, relationships, and conflicts is conveyed in dramatic language. Through dialogue, and sometimes through soliloquy and aside, characters use language to reveal intimate details about their lives and their deepest thoughts—their loves, hatreds, plans, and hopes.

To bring such revelations before the audience, dramatists employ words that have wide-ranging connotations and that acquire many layers of meaning. Such is the case with the words *trifle* and *knot* in Glaspell's *Trifles*. Similarly, playwrights can have their characters speak in similes or metaphors that contribute significantly to the play's meaning and impact. Again in *Trifles*, the major (but offstage) character is compared to a bird, and this simile becomes one of the play's central symbols.

Dramatists also make sure that the words of their characters fit the circumstances, the time, and the place of the play. Thus, in *Death of a Salesman* (Chapter 27) Miller's Willy Loman speaks the language of modern America, and Shakespeare's Hamlet speaks Elizabethan blank verse, almost academic prose, and "one-liner" remarks. In addition, dramatists employ accents, dialects, idiom, jargon, and clichés to indicate character traits. The gravediggers in *Hamlet* speak in a Renaissance English lower-class dialect that distinguishes them from the aristocratic characters in the play. Some of the characters in Williams's *The Glass Menagerie* (Chapter 29) speak in dialect, complete with slang expressions, that fits their southern locale.

CHARACTERS COME ALIVE THROUGH SPEECH AND ACTION. Drama necessarily focuses on its **characters**, who are persons the playwright creates to embody the play's actions, ideas, and attitudes. Of course characters are characters, no matter where we find them, and many of the character types that populate drama are also found in fiction. The major quality of characters in drama, however, is that they come alive through speech and action. To understand them we block scene

must listen to their words and watch and interpret how they react both to their circumstances and to the characters around them. They are also sometimes described and discussed by other characters, but primarily they are rendered dramatically.

Drama is not designed to present the full life stories of its characters. Rather, the plots of drama bring out intense and highly focused oppositions or conflicts in which the characters are engaged. In accord with such conflicts, most major dramatic characters are considered as protagonists and antagonists. The **protagonist** (the first or leading struggler or actor), usually the central character, is opposed by the **antagonist** (the one who struggles against). A classic conflict is seen in Shakespeare's *Hamlet*, in which Prince Hamlet, the protagonist, tries first to confirm and then to punish the crime committed by his uncle, King Claudius, the antagonist.

Just as in fiction, drama presents us with both round and flat characters. A **round, dynamic, developing,** and **growing character**, like Shakespeare's Hamlet and Ibsen's Nora, possesses great **motivation.** The round character profits from experience and undergoes a development in awareness, insight, understanding, moral capacity, and the ability to make decisions. A **flat, static, fixed,** and **unchanging character,** like the men in Glaspell's *Trifles*, does not undergo any change or growth. There is no rule, however, that flat characters must be dull. They can be charming, vibrant, entertaining, and funny, but even if they are memorable in these ways, they remain fixed and static.

Dramatic characters can also be considered as realistic, nonrealistic, stereotyped (or stock), ancillary, and symbolic. **Realistic characters** are designed to seem like individualized women and men; they are given thoughts, desires, motives, personalities, and lives of their own. **Nonrealistic characters** are often undeveloped and symbolic. An interesting example is Torvald Helmer of Ibsen's *A Dollhouse* (Chapter 31). In terms of his assumptions and expectations, he is nonrealistic for most of the play, but he becomes sadly realistic when he recognizes the disastrous effects of his previous outlook on life and marriage. He is unique because he does not so much grow as undergo an almost instant change.

Throughout the ages, drama and other types of literature have relied on **stereotype** or **stock characters**, that is, unindividualized characters whose actions and speeches make them seem to have been taken from a mold. The general types developed in the comedy of ancient Athens and Rome, and in the drama of the Renaissance, are the *stubborn father,* the *romantic hero* and *heroine,* the *clever male servant,* the *saucy maidservant,* the *braggart soldier,* the *bumpkin,* the *trickster,* the *victim,* the *insensitive husband,* the *shrewish wife,* and the *lusty youth.* Modern drama continues these stereotypes, and it has also invented many of its own, such as the *private eye,* the *stupid bureaucrat,* the *corrupt politician,* the *independent pioneer,* the *sensitive prostitute,* the *loner cowboy,* and the *town sheriff who never loses the draw in a showdown.*

There are also **ancillary characters** who set off or highlight the protagonist and who provide insight into the action. The first type, the **foil,** has been a feature of drama since its beginnings in ancient Athens. The foil is a character who is to be compared and contrasted with the protagonist. Laertes and Fortinbras are foils in *Hamlet*. Because of the play's circumstances, Laertes is swept into destruction along with Hamlet, whereas Fortinbras picks up the pieces and gets life moving again after the final death scene. The second type is the **choric figure**, who is loosely connected to the choruses of ancient drama. Usually the choric figure is a single character, often a confidant of the protagonist, such as Hamlet's friend Horatio. When the choric figure expresses ideas about the play's major issues and actions, he or she is called a **raisonneur** (the French word meaning "reasoner") or **commentator**.

Any of the foregoing types of characters can also be **symbolic** in the context of individual plays. They can symbolize ideas, moral values, religious concepts, ways of life, or some other abstraction. For instance, Linda in *Death of a Salesman* symbolizes helplessness before destructive forces, while Fred Higgins in Hughes's *Mulatto* (Chapter 29) symbolizes the cynicism, indifference, cruelty, and misuse of responsibility that accompany the concept of racial supremacy.

ACTION, CONFLICT, AND PLOT MAKE UP A PLAY'S DEVELOPMENT.   Plays are made up of a series of sequential and related **actions** or **incidents**. The actions are connected by **chronology**—the logic of time—and the term given to the principles underlying this ordered chain of actions and reactions is **plot**, which is a connected plan or pattern of causation. The impulse controlling the connections is **conflict,** which refers to people or circumstances—the antagonist—that the protagonist tries to overcome. Most dramatic conflicts are vividly apparent because the clashes of wills and characters take place onstage, right in front of our eyes. Conflicts can also exist between groups, although conflicts between individuals are more identifiable and therefore more suitable for plays.

Although dramatic plots can be simplified and schematized, most of them are as complicated as life itself. Special complications result from a **double** or **multiple plot**—two or more different but related lines of action. Usually one of these plots is the **main plot**, but the **subplot** can be independently important and sometimes even more interesting. Such a situation occurs in *A Midsummer Night's Dream*, where the exploits of Bottom and the "mechanicals," which form just one of the four strands of plot, are so funny that they usually steal the show.

STRUCTURE IS THE PLAY'S PATTERN OF ORGANIZATION.   The way a play is arranged or laid out is its **structure**. With variations, many traditional plays contain elements that constitute a structure of *five stages:* (1) *exposition* or *introduction,* (2) *complication* and *development,* (3) *crisis* or *climax,* (4) *falling action,* and (5) *dénouement, resolution,* or *catastrophe.* In the nineteenth century, the German novelist and critic Gustav Freytag (1816–1895) visualized this pattern as a pyramid (though he used six elements rather than five). In the so-called Freytag pyramid, the exposition and complication lead up to a high point of tension—the crisis or climax—followed by the falling action and the catastrophe.

The Freytag Pyramid

1. Exposition or Introduction
2. Complication and Development
3. Crisis or Climax
4. Falling Action
5. Dénouement, Resolution, or Catastrophe

This pyramidal pattern of organization can be observed to greater or lesser degrees throughout many plays. Some plays follow the pattern closely, but often there is uncertainty about when one phase of the structure ends and the next one begins. In addition, words defining some of the stages are variable. Even though students of drama agree about the meaning of the first two stages, the terms for the final three are not used with precision. With these reservations, the Freytag pyramid is valuable in the analysis of dramatic plot structure.

1. *The exposition or introduction brings out everything we need to know to understand and follow what is to happen in the play.* In the first part of a drama, the dramatist introduces the play's background, characters, situations, and conflicts. Although **exposition** is occasionally presented through direct statements to the audience, the better method is to render it dramatically. Both major and minor characters thus perform the task of exposition through dramatic dialogue—describing situations, actions, and plans, and also explaining the traits and motives of other characters. In such a way, in *Oedipus the King,* Sophocles provides expository material in the prologue featuring Oedipus, the Priest, and Creon; in *Trifles* Glaspell presents exposition in the early conversations of the two farm women. In *Hamlet,* Horatio's explanations to Barnardo and Marcellus provide vital information about circumstances in the Danish court.

2. *The complication and development mark the onset of the play's major conflicts.* In this second stage, also called the **rising action,** we see the beginning of difficulties that seem overwhelming and insoluble, as in both *Hamlet* and *Trifles,* where we learn in the exposition that a death has occurred before the play opens. **Complication** develops as the characters try to learn answers to some of the following perplexing questions: Was the death a murder? If so, who did it? How was it done? How can the murderer be identified? Is the murderer truly guilty? What should be done about the murder? What punishment should there be? In *A Midsummer Night's Dream,* less serious complications result from the **development** of issues like these: Can young lovers overcome parental opposition? Can a bumbling group of amateur actors successfully perform a play

before the highest social group in the nation? Can a squabble among supernatural beings be brought to a peaceful conclusion?

3. *The crisis or climax is the culmination of the play's conflicts and complications—the intense moments of decision.* The uncertainty and anxiety of the complication lead to the third stage, the **crisis** ("turning point") or **climax** ("high point"). In this third stage, all the converging circumstances compel the hero or heroine to recognize what needs to be done to resolve the play's major conflict. Another way of considering the crisis or climax is to define it as that point in the play when uncertainty ends and inevitability begins, as when Hamlet vows vengeance after drawing conclusions about the king's reaction to the player scene.

4. *The falling action is a time of avoidance and delay.* The downward slope of the pyramid is the **falling action**, which contains complicating elements deferring the play's conclusion. In *Hamlet*, for example, a number of scenes make up the falling action: Hamlet's decision not to kill Claudius at prayer, Hamlet's departure for England, the gravediggers scene and the conflicts at Ophelia's grave, and the murderous conspiracy of Claudius and Laertes. In *Oedipus the King*, Oedipus continues to seek confirming evidence about the death of his father, although by the end of Episode 3—the climax—he has all the information he needs to determine that he himself is the murderer.

5. *The dénouement is the end, the logical outcome of what has gone before.* In the **dénouement** ("unraveling") or **resolution** ("untying"), also called the **catastrophe** ("overturning"), all tragic protagonists undergo suffering or death, all mysteries are explained, all conflicts are resolved, all mistakes are corrected, all dastardly schemes are defeated, all long-lost children are identified, all obstacles to love are overcome, all deserving characters are rewarded, and the play ends. In short, the function of the dénouement is to end complications and conflicts, not to create new ones. It is important to observe that the word *catastrophe* for the final dramatic stage should not necessarily be construed in the sense of a calamity, even though most tragic catastrophes are calamitous. It is probably best, however, to use the words *dénouement* and *resolution* as general descriptions of a play's final stage and to reserve *catastrophe* for tragedies.

Of great significance is that the various points of the pyramid define an abstract model that is applicable to most plays—tragedy, comedy, and tragicomedy alike. Since the time of Shakespeare, however, most dramatists writing in English have been concerned less with dramatic *form* than with dramatic *effect*. As a result, many plays in English do not perfectly follow the pattern charted in the Freytag pyramid. You should therefore be prepared for plays that conceal or delay essential parts of the exposition; create a number of separate crises and climaxes; crowd the climax, falling action, and dénouement into a short space at the play's end; or modify the formal pattern in other significant ways.

POINT OF VIEW FOCUSES ATTENTION ON A PLAY'S MAJOR CHARACTER (OR CHARACTERS) AND IDEAS.   In fiction, the exceedingly complex concept of **point of view** refers to the narrative *voice* of the story, the speaker or guiding intelligence through which the characters and actions are presented. In drama, the term refers generally to a play's **perspective** or focus. Basically, dramatic point of view comprises the ways in which dramatists direct attention to the play's characters and their concerns. In the theater, dramatists govern our responses visually by putting certain major characters onstage and keeping them there. That these characters are always speaking and moving in front of us causes us to devote our attention to them, to become involved with them, and to see things pretty much through their eyes. For example, once the opening speeches of *Hamlet* are over, the play focuses directly on Hamlet and never wavers, even after he lies dead on the stage in the last act. In O'Neill's *Before Breakfast*, the entire play is a monologue spoken by Mrs. Rowland, and we therefore see things from her perspective even though we also become conscious of her shortcomings.

The dramatist can also keep characters and issues in our minds by causing other characters to speak about them. Thus all the speeches in Glaspell's *Trifles* are designed to shape our understanding of what Minnie Wright did to her husband on the lonely Wright farm, and why she did it. Because everyone is always talking about Minnie and her boorish but recently murdered husband, the play makes this perspective inescapable.

TONE OR ATMOSPHERE SIGNIFIES THE WAY MOODS AND ATTITUDES ARE CREATED AND PRESENTED. Authors of plays have unique ways of conveying tone beyond those used by poets and fiction writers. Some of these are vocal ranges and stage gestures (such as rolling one's eyes, throwing up one's hands, holding one's forehead in despair, jumping for joy, making side remarks, and staggering in grief). Even silence, intense stares, and shifting glances can be effective means for creating moods and controlling attitudes.

Whereas voice and movement establish mood onstage, we do not have these guides in reading. Nevertheless, there are guides to dramatic tone: Sometimes a playwright uses stage directions as an indication of tone, as Ibsen does in *A Dollhouse*, directing the inflections of a speaker's voice with the stage direction that she is shaking her head when speaking. Similarly, Hughes suggests the mood of one of his characters in *Mulatto* with the direction that he "runs" to his mother and hugs her "teasingly."

When such directions are absent—and usually they are—we need to take the diction, tempo, imagery, and context as clues to the tone of specific speeches and whole plays. In the opening scene of *Hamlet*, for example, Shakespeare uses short and rapidly delivered sentences to create a mood of fearfulness, anxiety, and apprehensiveness. This opening passage anticipates the Ghost's forthcoming charge of murder against Claudius, and it also prepares us for the ominous events of the rest of the play.

One of the most common methods playwrights employ to control the tone of the play is **dramatic irony**. This type of **situational** (as opposed to **verbal**) irony refers to circumstances in which characters have only a partial, incorrect, or misguided understanding of what is happening, while both readers and other characters understand the situation completely. Readers hence become concerned about the characters and hope that they will develop understanding quickly enough to avoid the problems bedeviling them and the threats endangering them. The classic example of dramatic irony occurs in Sophocles' *Oedipus the King:* As Oedipus condemns the murderer of his father, he also unwittingly condemns himself. Another example of dramatic irony occurs in Glaspell's *Trifles,* when the male characters mockingly dismiss the women's concerns by noting that "women are used to worrying about such trifles." The line acquires vast dramatic irony as we watch Mrs. Hale and Mrs. Peters achieve understanding through careful attention to the "trifles" that the men ignore.

SYMBOLISM AND ALLEGORY ARE NORMAL LITERARY DEVICES ALSO USED BY DRAMATISTS.[1]   In drama, as in fiction and poetry, the meaning of a **symbol** extends beyond its surface meaning. Dramatic symbols, which can be characters, settings, objects, actions, situations, or statements, can be both cultural or contextual. **Cultural** or **universal symbols**—such as crosses, flags, snakes, and flowers—are generally understood by the audience or reader regardless of the context in which they appear. In Act V of *Hamlet,* for example, we readily accept Yorick's skull as a symbol of death. **Contextual** or **private symbols** develop their impact only within the context of a specific play or even a particular scene. We often don't realize at first that such objects or actions are symbolic; they acquire symbolic meaning only through context and continued action. In the living-room setting of Hughes's *Mulatto,* for instance, there is a vestibule "leading to the porch." Initially, this location is not unusual, but as the play develops we realize that it symbolizes how the rights and privileges of whites on the plantation are denied to the African-Americans who work there.

When a play offers consistent and sustained symbols that refer to general human experiences, that play can be construed as an **allegory,** or at least as being **allegorical.** For example, Ibsen's *A Dollhouse* can be considered allegorically as an expression of the shortcomings of any way of life in which a grown person is infantilized and therefore is prevented from realizing the mature and independent life that she is entitled to seek as an adult.

SUBJECT AND THEME ARE THE COMPLEX OF IDEAS PRESENTED BY THE DRAMATIST. Most playwrights do not aim to propagandize their audience, but nevertheless they do embody ideas in their plays. The aspects of humanity a playwright explores constitute the play's **subject.** Plays can be *about* love, religion, hatred, war, ambition, death, envy, or anything else that is part of the human condition.

The ideas that the play dramatizes make up the play's **theme** or meaning. A play might explore the idea that love will always find a way or that marriage can be destructive, that pride always leads to disaster, or that grief can be conquered through strength and a commitment to life. Full, evening-long plays can contain many thematic strands. Ibsen creates such complexity in *A Dollhouse,*

---

[1] See also Chapters 9 and 21.

where he deals with themes of selfless devotion, egotism, pompousness, hypocrisy, betrayal, and women's self-determination. Even short plays can have complex themes, as in O'Neill's *Before Breakfast*, which explores the themes that anger can be stronger than love, that deceit is a consequence of alienation, and that despair and fear can conquer the normal wish to live.

The Unique Aspect of Drama Is Performance

As we read and talk about drama, we should always remind ourselves that plays are meant to be acted. It is **performance** that makes a play immediate, exciting, and powerful. The elements of performance are the *actors*, the *director* and the *producer*, the *stage, sets* or *scenery, lighting, costumes* and *makeup*, and the *audience*.

ACTORS BRING A PLAY TO LIFE.   Good actors are trained and experienced to exert their intelligence, emotions, imaginations, voices, and bodies to make their roles come alive. Actors speak as they imagine the characters might speak—earnestly, eagerly, calmly, excitedly, prayerfully, exultantly, sorrowfully, or angrily. When they respond, they respond as they imagine the characters might respond—with surprise, expectation, approval, happiness, irony, acceptance, rejection, resignation, or resolution. When they move about the stage according to patterns called **blocking**, they move as they imagine the characters might move—slowly, swiftly, smoothly, hesitatingly, furtively, stealthily, or clumsily, and gesturing broadly or subtly. Actors also frequently engage in **stage business**—gestures or movements that make the play dynamic, spontaneous, and often funny.

THE DIRECTOR AND THE PRODUCER SUPPORT AND CONTROL A PLAY'S PRODUCTION. In the theater, all aspects of performance are shaped and supervised by the **director** and the **producer**. The producer, the one with the money, is responsible for financing and arranging the production. Working closely with the producer is the director, who is probably the most significant member of the entire dramatic production. The director cooperates closely with the actors and guides them in speaking, responding, standing, and moving in ways that are consistent with his or her vision of the play. When a play calls for special effects (for example, the Ghost in *Hamlet*) both the producer and the director work with specialists such as musicians, choreographers, and sound and lighting technicians to enhance and enliven the performance.

THE STAGE IS THE LOCATION OF BOTH SPEECH AND ACTION.   Most modern theaters feature an interior **proscenium stage**—a picture-frame stage that is like a room with one wall missing so that the audience can look in on the action. In most proscenium stages, a large curtain representing that missing wall is usually opened and closed to indicate the beginning and ending of acts. Members of the audience seated directly before the stage are close to the action, but people seated at the sides, to the rear, behind a tall person, or in the balcony are to greater or lesser degrees removed from the vital and up-close involvement that is desirable in good theater. There is no question that such remoteness is a built-in disadvantage of many proscenium stages.

Modern theater designers have therefore experimented with stage designs inspired by theaters of the past. One notable success has been to revive the shape of the ancient Greek amphitheater (with seats rising from the stage in an expanding half-circle), a structure employed in theaters like the Tyrone Guthrie in Minneapolis and at the Shakespeare Festival in Ashland, Oregon. Because seats for the audience ascend in semicircular tiers around three sides of the stage, most of the audience is closer to the action—and better able to see—than in a theater with a proscenium stage. The audience is also, therefore, more closely involved in the dramatic action.

Like many other modern theaters, these theaters feature a **thrust stage** or **apron stage** (like the **platform stage** used in the time of Shakespeare), which enlarges the proscenium stage with an acting area projecting into the audience by twenty or more feet. It is on this apron that a good deal of the acting occurs. Closely related to the apron stage is **theater-in-the-round**, a stage open on all sides like a boxing ring, surrounded by the audience. Productions for both types of stages are especially lively because the actors usually enter and leave through the same doorways and aisles used by the audience.

SETS OR SCENERY CREATES THE LOCATION OF THE PLAY.   Most productions use **sets** (derived from the phrase "set scenes," i.e., fixed scenes) or **scenery** to establish the action in place and time, to underscore the ideas of the director, and to determine the level of reality of the production. Sets are constructed and decorated to indicate a specific place (a living room, a kitchen, a throne room, a forest, a graveyard) or a detached and indeterminate place with a specific atmosphere (an open plain, a heavenly or hellish location, a nightmarish future). When we first see the stage at the beginning of a performance, it is the scenery that we see, bringing the play to life through walls, windows, stairways, furniture, furnishings, and painted locations.

In most proscenium stages, the sets establish a permanent location or **scene** resembling a framed picture. All characters enter this setting, and they leave once they have achieved their immediate purpose. Such a fixed scene is established in *Oedipus the King*, which is set entirely in front of the royal palace of ancient Thebes, and in *Before Breakfast*, set in an apartment kitchen. Generally, one-act plays rely on a single setting and a short imagined time of action. Many full-length plays also confine the action to a single setting despite the longer imagined time during which the action takes place.

Because sets are often elaborate and costly, many producers use single fixed-scene sets that are flexible and easily changed. Some productions employ a single, neutral set throughout the play and then mark scene changes with the physical introduction of movable **properties** (or **props**)—chairs, tables, beds, flower vases, hospital curtain enclosures, trees, shovels, skulls, and so on. The use of props to mark separate scenes is a necessity in modern productions of plays that require constant scene changes, like *Hamlet.* Interestingly, many productions make scene changes an integral part of the drama by having costumed stagehands, or even the actors themselves, carry props on and off the stage. In a 1995 New York production of *Hamlet,* for example, Hamlet himself (actor Ralph Fiennes) carried in the chairs needed for the spectators of the player scene.

The constant changing of scenery is sometimes avoided by the use of a **unit set**—a series of platforms, rooms, stairs, and exits that form the locations for all the play's actions, as in Miller's *Death of a Salesman.* The movement of the characters from place to place within the unit set marks the shifting of scenes and the changing of topics.

Like characters, the setting can be realistic or nonrealistic. A **realistic setting**, sometimes called a **naturalistic setting**, requires extensive construction and properties, for the object is to create as lifelike a stage as possible. In Glaspell's *Trifles,* for example, the setting is a realistic copy of an early-twentieth-century midwestern farm kitchen. A **nonrealistic setting** is nonrepresentational and often symbolic, as in Wilder's *The Happy Journey to Trenton and Camden* (Chapter 29). Sometimes a realistic play can be made suggestive and expressive through the use of a nonrealistic setting.

LIGHTING CREATES CLARITY , EMPHASIS, AND MOOD.   In ancient and medieval times, plays were performed in daylight, and hence no artificial **lighting** was required. With the advent of indoor theaters and evening performances, lighting became a necessity. At first, artificial illumination was provided by lanterns, candelabras, sconces, and torches (yes, some theaters burned down), and indirect lighting was achieved by reflectors and valances—all of which were used with great ingenuity and effect. Later, gaslight and limelight lamps replaced the earlier open flames.

The evolution of theater lighting reached its climax with the development of electric lights in the nineteenth century. Today, dramatic performances are enhanced by virtually all the technical features of our electronic age, including specialized lamps, color filters, spotlights, dimmers, and simulated fires. This dazzling technology, which employs hundreds or even thousands of lights of varying intensity in unlimited combination, is used to highlight individual characters, to isolate and emphasize various parts of the stage, to establish times, and generally to shape the moods of individual scenes. Lighting can also divide the stage or a unit set into different acting areas simply through the illumination of one section and the darkening of the rest, as in productions of plays like Williams's *The Glass Menagerie* and Miller's *Death of a Salesman.* The result is that lighting has become an integral element of set design, especially when the dramatist uses a **scrim** (a curtain that becomes transparent when illuminated from behind), which permits great variety in the portrayal of scenes and great rapidity in scene changes. In our day it is a rare stage indeed that does not contain an elaborate, computerized, and complicated (and expensive) lighting system.

COSTUMES AND MAKEUP ESTABLISH THE NATURE AND APPEARANCE OF THE ACTORS. Actors make plays vivid by wearing **costumes** and using **makeup**, which help the audience understand a play's time period together with the occupations, mental outlooks, and socioeconomic conditions of the characters. Costumes, which include not only dress but items such as jewelry, good-luck charms, swords, firearms, and canes, can be used realistically (farm women in plain clothes, a salesman in a business suit, a king in rich robes) or symbolically (a depressed character wearing black). Makeup usually enhances an actor's facial features, just as it can fix the illusion of youth or age or emphasize a character's joy or sorrow.

THE AUDIENCE RESPONDS TO THE PERFORMANCE AND HELPS TO SHAPE IT. To be complete, plays require an interaction of actors and **audience**. Drama enacts fictional or historical events as if they were happening in the present, and members of the audience—whether spectators or readers—are direct witnesses to the dramatic action from start to finish. The audience most definitely has a creative impact on theatrical performances. Although audiences are made up of people who otherwise do not know each other, they have a common bond of interest in the play. Therefore, even though they are isolated by the darkness of the theater in which they sit, they create communal responses. Their reactions to the onstage action (e.g., laughter, gasps, applause) provide instant feedback to the actors and thus continually influence the delivery and pace of the performance. For this reason, drama *in the theater* is the most immediate and accessible of the literary arts. There is no intermediary between the audience and the stage action—no narrator, as in prose fiction, and no speaker, as in poetry.

DRAMA FROM ANCIENT TIMES TO OUR OWN: TRAGEDY, COMEDY, AND ADDITIONAL FORMS

Today, people interested in drama have more options than at any other time in human history. There is professional live theater in many major cities, and touring theatrical troupes reach areas with smaller populations. Many cities and towns have amateur community theaters that put on plays regularly. Movie theaters and multiplexes are flourishing. Television has brought film versions of plays to the home screen, together with innumerable situation comedies ("sitcoms"), continuous narrative dramas (including soap operas), made-for-TV films, documentary dramas ("docudramas"), short skits on comedy shows, and many other types. All these different genres ultimately spring from the drama that was developed twenty-six hundred years ago in Athens, the leading ancient Greek city-state. Although subsequent centuries have produced many variations, the types the Athenians created are still as important today as they were then. They are tragedy and comedy.[2]

Tragedy and Comedy Originated in Ancient Greece

During the sixth century B.C.E., drama first arose from choral presentations the Athenians held during religious festivals celebrating Dionysus, the god of wine, conviviality, sexual vitality, ecstasy, and freedom. The choruses comprised young men who sang or chanted lengthy songs that the Athenians called **dithyrambs;** the choruses also performed interpretive dance movements during the presentations. The dithyrambs were not dramatizations but rather recitations, which became dramatic when a member of the chorus was designated to step forward and impersonate—*act*—one of the heroes. Soon, additional men from the choruses took acting roles, and the focus of the performances shifted from the choral group to individual actors. Greek **tragedy** as we know it had come into being. It was this pattern of drama that during the fifth century B.C.E. produced a golden age of tragedy. Most of the tragedies have been lost, and only a small number of plays by the three great Athenian dramatists— Aeschylus, Sophocles, and Euripides—have survived.

Not long after the emergence of tragedy, **comedy** became an additional feature of the festivals. Because the ancient Athenians encouraged free speech, at least for males, the comedy writers created a boisterous, lewd, and freely critical type of burlesque comedy that later critics called **Old Comedy**. The eleven surviving plays of Aristophanes represent this tradition. In the fourth century B.C.E., after Athenian power and freedom had declined because of the debilitating Peloponnesian Wars at the end of the fifth century, this type of comedy was replaced by **Middle Comedy**, a more social, discreet, and international drama, and then by **New Comedy**, a type of play featuring the development of situation, plot, and character. The best-known writer of New Comedy was Menander, whose plays were long thought to be totally lost. In the last hundred years, however, a number of fragments of his work have been discovered, including one play in its entirety.

Both of these Greek dramatic types have proved long-lasting. The introduction of subject matter about loss in the earliest tragedies has led to today's common understanding that tragedy dramatizes an individual's fall from a secure and elevated position to social or personal defeat. Likewise, what we usually consider typical comedies are directly linked to the pattern of ancient New

---

[2] Fuller discussions of tragedy and comedy are presented in Chapters 27 and 28.

Comedy: plays that dramatize the regeneration of individuals who begin in insecurity and end with their troubles over and happiness before them.

Tragedy and Comedy Were of Less Significance in Ancient Rome

The two Athenian dramatic forms were adopted by the Romans during the periods of the Republic (before 29 B.C.E.) and the Empire (after 29 B.C.E.). Although Republican Rome produced writers of note who created comedies (Plautus, ca. 254-184 B.C.E., and Terence, ca. 195 or 185-159 B.C.E.), the only significant playwright of imperial times was the tragedian Seneca (4 B.C.E.–65 C.E.), who wrote "closet dramas"—that is, plays designed to be read but not performed.

Ancient Drama Faded along with the Breakup of the Western Roman Empire

As the Roman Empire in western Europe disintegrated in the fifth century C.E., many of its institutions, including the theater, disintegrated with it. In the next five centuries, often called the Dark Ages, Europe fell into feudalism, characterized by political decentralization and social fragmentation. The intellectuals of the period—most of them clergy—were creating Christian theology and establishing the growing church while abandoning the memories and records of the past, of which drama was a major element. As far as we know, there were no public theaters, no patrons able to support public performances, no popular audiences with the money to pay for admission, no official permission by secular and religious authorities to perform plays, and no practicing dramatists —in short, there was no organized theater. It is hard to believe, however, that the human need for stories and fantasies did not remain. Tales and songs were unquestionably passed on from parents to children and community to community throughout these dark centuries.

Medieval Drama Developed within Church Services

When drama emerged hundreds of years after the fall of Rome, it had little to do with the Greek and Roman dramatic tradition because it was a creation of the Christian church. It was at some time in the tenth century—approximately when the medieval period or Middle Ages were emerging from the Dark Ages—that the clergy started to realize the potentiality of dramatic presentations within the Mass. It was then that dramatic **tropes** (short interludes performed in conjunction with the mass, either with or without musical accompaniment) developed in the churches. These tropes were not considered as separate dramas, however, but instead were integrated within regular services.

The earliest tropes were written for Easter rituals. The prototype of the Easter trope, which is included here, represented the discovery of the empty tomb as evidence of Christ's resurrection. This is the *Visitatio Sepulchri*, or *The Visit to the Sepulchre*, often known as the *Quem Quaeritis* ("Whom are you seeking") trope. This is considered the first European drama, from which all subsequent dramas have developed. Authored by persons who are unknown and forever unknowable, the trope was in Latin and was chanted not for the people but for cloistered monks and priests. It was enacted many times both on the continent and the British Isles, and in later centuries it became a regular feature of Easter worship. It has survived in a variety of forms in medieval manuscripts. Some versions contain detailed directions about performance, and some are cast in a question-and-answer format.

Although the *Quem Quaeritis* trope was a part of ritual, it clearly involved impersonation—and therefore drama—to the degree that priests and monks represented the persons and scenes contained in the gospel accounts of the resurrection. The heart of the trope is that the Angel at the tomb announces the resurrection to the three Marys, who then leave to proclaim the news.

ANONYMOUS

The Visit to the Sepulchre (Visitatio Sepulchri) ————————— *Tenth century*

[CAST OF CHARACTERS]

[The Angel at the Tomb]
[Mary the Mother of Jesus]
[Mary Magdalen]
[Mary of Bethany, the Sister of Martha and Lazarus*]

*[*SCENE: *The Sepulchre in which Christ was entombed after the Crucifixion.* THE ANGEL, *dressed in white and holding a palm leaf, enters and sits beside a location curtained off to represent the tomb. Behind the curtain is a table or other surface representing a burial slab on which there is a linen sheet (i.e., the burial shroud supplied by Joseph of Aramathea). The three* MARYS *enter, carrying vessels [thuribles] as though they are intending to anoint Christ's body with aromatic oils and spices. At first they do not see the tomb, and they wander about until they do. Then they stop in front of the* ANGEL.*]*

ANGEL. Whom are you seeking in this sepulchre, O followers of Christ?
THE THREE HOLY WOMEN. [*Speaking together.*] Jesus of Nazareth, who was crucified, O heavenly one.

---

*Although gospel accounts are in general accord about the identity of the first two Marys, there is no agreement about the third woman, and none of the gospels indicates that Mary of Bethany was the third Mary. Nevertheless, medieval tradition fixed a tradition that there was a third Mary, and that it was Mary of Bethany, probably on the authority of John 12:7, where Jesus implies that this Mary will be one of those to anoint his dead body.

ANGEL. [*Pulling back the curtain to show the empty tomb.*] He is not here. He has been resurrected, as was predicted. Go forth, tell everyone that he is risen. Spread the news!

THE THREE HOLY WOMEN. [*Kneeling and singing.*] Alleluia! Today Christ the Lord, the Son of God, the Mighty Lion, has been resurrected! Thanks be to God! Tell it to all the world!

ANGEL. Come and see the place where the Lord was laid.

[*The Three Holy Women examine the empty tomb and, with the Angel, display the burial shroud.*]

ANGEL. Alleluia! Alleluia! Hurry, tell the disciples that the Lord has risen! Alleluia! Alleluia! [*He exits, singing alleluias.*]

THE THREE HOLY WOMEN. [*Rejoicing, and singing in unison.*] The Lord, who hung on the tree for us, has risen from the grave! Alleluia!

[*They exit, repeating these lines.*]

QUESTIONS

1. What dramatic characteristics, as opposed to the obvious theology, do you find in this brief play?

2. Describe the play's dramatic actions. What sorts of movement would have been carried out? How extensive might have been the use of properties?

3. How do you suppose this play would have affected people attending the service in which it was performed?

Comparable Dramatic Ceremonies Followed the Visitatio Sepulchri

During the eleventh and twelfth centuries, the *Visit to the Sepulchre* ceremony became more elaborate, with additional characters and actions, such as the race by Peter and John to the tomb and Mary Magdalen's recognition of the risen Christ after having first confused him for a gardener. Some of the ceremonies, which were eventually performed before congregations, became extensive enough to require a lengthy performance. Historians of drama observe that this Easter ceremony was *dramatic liturgy* rather than *liturgical drama*, but any congregations present would likely have ignored this distinction. Instead they would have welcomed the ceremony as something totally new, vital, exciting, and dramatic.

In addition to the Easter pageantry, the church also developed special Christmas ceremonies such as those for the Three Wise Men, the Shepherds, the scene at the stable, the ranting Herod, and the Slaughter of the Innocents (Innocents Day was December 28). These ceremonies were observed as regular parts of Easter and Christmas rituals for hundreds of years after their beginnings in the tenth century.

A New Kind of Drama, the Corpus Christi Play, Grew Independently of the Church

Growing out of the religious dramatic tradition, a full-blown religious and civic drama developed in the fourteenth century. This was the Corpus Christi (i.e., "Body of Christ") play, which evolved just as the drama of ancient Athens had developed out of religious festivals for the god Dionysus in the sixth century B.C.E.* The major expression of the new religious drama came during the celebration of Corpus Christi Day, a celebration of the doctrine of transubstantiation (i.e., during mass, Eucharistic bread and wine were said to become transformed miraculously into the real body and blood of Christ).

Corpus Christi Day regularly featured local processions devoted to the worship of the Eucharist, and in this way it brought religious celebration into the streets and before the public. Because the feast occurred at the end of the liturgical year, it coincided with the beginning of good weather. The winter and spring rains abated, daylight hours lengthened, short trips from country villages to nearby towns became possible, and people could spend an entire day outside and still be comfortable.

The goal of the new Corpus Christi, or mystery plays, was to create a complete sequence or **cycle** of plays dramatizing the biblical accounts of world history from the Creation to Judgment Day. The plays were produced by the local craft guilds, the members of whom were master tradesmen. Hence the plays were also known as *mysteries*, or *mystery plays*. Naturally, the guild masters wanted to boost the prestige of their towns and their own wealth and power. They therefore welcomed this annual religious celebration that attracted customers and patrons. Although there were as yet no professional acting companies like the one that Shakespeare joined in the late sixteenth century, the annual staging of the Corpus Christi plays required large numbers of participants. The planning by the local guilds was therefore complex and challenging; and the result was a vital, durable, instructive, and exciting drama.

As the Corpus Christi feasts grew in importance, the plays became a highlight of town life in the early summer. By the fifteenth century, as many as forty towns had their own cycles. Some were large and elaborate; some—probably those performed in the smaller towns—were modest. Often the performances took place not only on Corpus Christi Thursday but also on Friday and Saturday, thus creating an extensive religious and secular celebration. Although the texts of most of these plays have been lost, cycles from four towns have been preserved. These cycles, named after the towns that presented them, contain more than 150 plays.

English Replaced Latin as the Language of the Corpus Christi Plays

A major influence on the Corpus Christi drama—with profound implications for later drama—was the increasing importance of the English language

* See p. 1235.

at this time. During the two centuries following the Norman conquest in 1066, the ruling and intellectual languages of England had been French and Latin. By the fourteenth century, however, things were changing: English had been enriched with huge numbers of French words and was reasserting its role as the major language of England. More and more, the governing classes were committed to England—having a centuries-long tradition there—and used English as the language of intellectual and political discourse. Native writers began looking with increased favor on English as a literary language. A new literature in English—including drama—was ripe for development.

Other Religious Dramas Originated after the Corpus Christi Plays

In the course of time, additional types of religious dramas were developed. One of these was the **miracle play**, a devotional dramatization of the lives of saints. In addition, the **morality play** was developed as a genre instructing the faithful in the proper way to lead a devotional life. The most famous of these, in about 1500, was *Everyman*, which even today retains a good deal of interest and power.

Ancient and Medieval Traditions Fused in the Renaissance to Create a New Secular Drama

In the sixteenth century, drama became liberated from these religious foundations and began rendering the twists and turns of more secular human conflicts. It was also at this time that the drama of ancient Greece and Rome was rediscovered. Therefore, the performing tradition growing out of the medieval church was combined with the surviving ancient tragedies and comedies to create an entirely new drama that quickly reached its highest point in the plays of Shakespeare. In this way, tragedy and comedy, the forms originated by the Athenians, had a revival during the Renaissance in Europe.[3]

New Types of Drama Have Developed Since the Renaissance

Renaissance drama was by no means a copy of ancient forms, however, even though a number of sixteenth- and seventeenth-century playwrights, including Shakespeare, reworked many of the ancient plays. The plays of

---

[3] The Renaissance revival of drama also transformed the theater into a business. Earlier drama had been a product of the church and religious life, but during the Renaissance, actors and theater people found that they could make a living in the theater. Although at first there was little money in acting and in writing plays, the theater managers were often able to do quite well. Shakespeare, for example, was a theater manager as well as a dramatist and minor actor. He earned enough from his shares in the Globe Theatre to retire in 1611 and leave London to spend his remaining days in his native Stratford-upon-Avon.

Renaissance England, and later the plays of the United States, offer mixtures of tragedy and comedy. For example, some of Shakespeare's comedies treat disturbing and potentially destructive topics, just as many of his tragedies include scenes that are farcical, witty, and ironic. When the patterns and emotions are truly mixed, the play is called a **tragicomedy**, a term first used by the Roman playwright Plautus. In many ways tragicomedy is the dominant form of twentieth-century drama.

Additional types of drama that evolved from tragedy and comedy include farce, melodrama, and social drama. The major purpose of **farce**, which was also a strong element in the Athenian Old Comedy, is to make audiences laugh. Typically, it is crammed full of extravagant dialogue, stage business, and slapstick, with exaggerated emotions and rapid extremes of action. The "mechanicals" in Shakespeare's *A Midsummer Night's Dream* offer us a good example of farce, and the characters appearing at the end of Kauffmann's *The More the Merrier* are introduced in a farcical manner.

Resembling tragedy but stepping back from tragic outcomes is **melodrama**, a form in which most situations and characters are so exaggerated that they seem ridiculous. In its pure form, melodrama brings characters to the brink of ruin but saves them through the superhuman resources of a hero who always arrives just in time to pay the mortgage, save the business, and rescue the heroine while the grumbling villain flees the stage, muttering, "Curses, foiled again!"

The nineteenth century saw the creation of a form of topical drama known as **social drama** (sometimes called **problem drama**), a type that still exists as serious drama today. This type of play explores social problems and the individual's place in society. The plays can be tragic, comic, or mixed. Examples of social drama are Ibsen's *A Dollhouse*, Glaspell's *Trifles*, and Miller's *Death of a Salesman*.

Despite all these terms and types, keep in mind that classification is not the goal of reading or seeing plays. It is less important to identify the melodramatic elements in O'Neill's *Before Breakfast* or the farcical elements in Kauffmann's *The More the Merrier* than it is to understand and share the experiences and ideas that each play offers.

READING PLAYS

As we have noted, drama relies heavily on actors and directors to bring it to life. You might therefore ask why we bother to read plays without seeing them performed. The most obvious answer is that we may never get the chance actually to *see* a professional or amateur performance of a particular play. But we also read plays to familiarize ourselves with important literature. Plays are not simply maps to theatrical production; they are a significant and valuable part of our literary heritage. Dramas like Sophocles' *Oedipus the King*, Shakespeare's *Hamlet*,

Miller's *Death of a Salesman,* and Williams's *The Glass Menagerie* have become cultural touchstones. Finally, we read plays in order to have the time to study and understand them. Only through reading do we have the opportunity to look at the parts that make up the whole and to determine how they fit together to create a moving and meaningful experience.

Reading a play, as opposed to watching a performance, carries both advantages and disadvantages. The major disadvantage is that we lack the immediacy of live theater. We do not see a majestic palace or a rundown living room, the rich robes of a king or the pathetic rags of a beggar, a vital and smiling young person or a tired and tearful old person. We do not hear the lovers flirting, the servants complaining, the soldiers boasting, the opponents threatening, the conspirators plotting; nor do we hear fanfares of trumpets or the sounds of a wedding procession or a funeral march.

The major advantage of reading is that we can consider each element in the play at length, and we can "stage" the play in our imagination. In the theater, the action proceeds at the director's pace. There is no opportunity to turn back to an interesting scene or to reconsider an important speech. In addition, a performance always represents someone else's interpretation. The director and the actors have already made choices that emphasize certain avenues of exploration and cut off others. Reading a play lets us avoid these drawbacks—provided that we read attentively and with understanding. We can read at our own tempo, turn back and reread a particular speech or scene, or explore those implications or ideas that strike us as interesting.

Try to use the advantages of reading and study to compensate for the disadvantages. You have time and freedom to read carefully, reflect deeply, and follow your thoughts. Rely on your experiences in watching theatrical productions, movies, and television to enhance your reading. Use your imagination. Stage the play as fully as you can in the theater of your mind. Become the director, producer, set designer, lighting technician, costume designer, and all the actors. Build whatever mental sets you like, dress your actors as you see fit, and move the characters across the stage of your mind. Enjoy.

✿ PLAYS FOR STUDY

SUSAN GLASPELL, *TRIFLES*

Susan Glaspell, a writer of both plays and fiction, was a native of Iowa. She was educated at Drake University andthe University of Chicago. In her thirties she moved to the northeast and became interested in theater. Along with her husband, George Cook, she was a founder and director of the Provincetown Players of Cape Cod in 1914. The organization encouraged lesser-known young dramatists and was often experimental, but nevertheless it became successful enough to justify the opening of a second theater in New York. The first offerings of the theater were many one-act plays, featuring the earlier works of Glaspell herself, Eugene O'Neill, Edna Ferber, Edmund Wilson, and Edna St. Vincent Millay.

Glaspell wrote or coauthored over ten plays for the Provincetown Players, including *Suppressed Desires* (1914), *Close the Book* (1917), *Women's Honor* (1918), *Tickless Time* (1918), *Bernice* (1919, her first full-length play), *The Inheritors* (1921), and *The Verge* (1921). After 1922, however, she gave up the theater and turned almost exclusively to fiction. The exception was *Alison's House* (1930), a play loosely based on the life and family of Emily Dickinson, for which she won a Pulitzer Prize.

Glaspell deals with diverse topics in her drama, including misunderstood parentage, the effects of psychoanalysis, rejection of the machine age, the function and importance of honor, the tensions between political conservatives and liberals, and the onset of psychosis. Running through much of her work are strongly feminist ideas, based on a critique of the power—personal, social, and political—that men possess and that women are denied. Usually, Glaspell focuses on the negative and destructive effects that male-female relationships have on women, but she also stresses the ways in which women cope with their circumstances. To maintain character integrity and to preserve their domestic strength, they are forced into roles that are characterized not by direct but by indirect action.

Trifles, Glaspell's best-known drama, displays these characteristics. She wrote it in ten days for the Provincetown Players, who produced the play in 1916. Its inspiration was a murder trial she had covered while working as a reporter for a Des Moines newspaper before moving to the northeast. In 1917 she refashioned the material for the short story "A Jury of Her Peers," with which *Trifles* can be compared (see p. 202). Although Glaspell preserves a considerable amount of dramatic dialogue in the story, the additions and changes she makes are indicative of the differences between drama and fiction.

Trifles concerns a murder investigation, but the play is not a mystery. Soon after the characters enter and go about their business, the two women characters begin to uncover the circumstances that reveal the killer and the nature of the crime. Once the facts are established, however, the action focuses on the significant details of motive. Indeed, the heart of the play consists of the contrasting ways in which the men and the women attempt to uncover and understand the motive. The men—the county attorney and the sheriff—look for signs of violent rage, and they move onstage and offstage throughout the house in their search. The women—Mrs. Hale and Mrs. Peters—stay onstage and draw their conclusions from the ordinary, everyday details of a farm woman's kitchen. It is finally the women, not the men, who realize the true power that comes from understanding. Their realization—as well as their strength—leads them to their final decisions about how to judge the killer and treat the evidence.

The language that Glaspell gives to her characters is in keeping with the plain and simple lives the characters lead: simple, specific, and unadorned. Of the two groups, the women are more direct in the expression of their ideas. Once they realize the gravity of the situation they are exploring, however, they become indirect, but only because they fear to speak the words that describe the truths they have discovered. By contrast, the men usually talk convivially and smugly about the crime and their own roles in life, patronizingly among themselves about the women, and almost scornfully to the women about womanly concerns.

SUSAN GLASPELL   (1882–1948)

Trifles _____ *1916*

CAST OF CHARACTERS

George Henderson, *county attorney*
Henry Peters, *sheriff*
Lewis Hale, *a neighboring farmer*
Mrs. Peters
Mrs. Hale

SCENE. *The kitchen in the now abandoned farmhouse of* JOHN WRIGHT, *a gloomy kitchen, and left without having been put in order—unwashed pans under the sink, a loaf of bread outside the bread-box, a dish-towel on the table—other signs of incompleted work. At the rear the outer door opens and the* SHERIFF *comes in followed by the* COUNTY ATTORNEY *and* HALE. *The* SHERIFF *and* HALE *are men in middle life, the* COUNTY ATTORNEY *is a young man; all are much bundled up and go at once to the stove. They are followed by the two women—the* SHERIFF'S *wife first; she is a slight wiry woman, a thin nervous face.* MRS. HALE *is larger and would ordinarily be called more comfortable looking, but she is disturbed now and looks fearfully about as she enters. The women have come in slowly, and stand close together near the door.*

COUNTY ATTORNEY. [*Rubbing his hands.*] This feels good. Come up to the fire, ladies.

MRS. PETERS. [*After taking a step forward.*] I'm not—cold.

SHERIFF. [*Unbuttoning his overcoat and stepping away from the stove as if to mark the beginning of official business.*] Now, Mr. Hale, before we move things about, you explain to Mr. Henderson just what you saw when you came here yesterday morning.

COUNTY ATTORNEY. By the way, has anything been moved? Are things just as you left them yesterday?

SHERIFF. [*Looking about.*] It's just the same. When it dropped below zero last night 5
I thought I'd better send Frank out this morning to make a fire for us—no use getting pneumonia with a big case on, but I told him not to touch anything except the stove—and you know Frank.

COUNTY ATTORNEY. Somebody should have been left here yesterday.

SHERIFF. Oh—yesterday. When I had to send Frank to Morris Center for that man who went crazy—I want you to know I had my hands full yesterday. I knew you could get back from Omaha by today and as long as I went over everything here myself—

COUNTY ATTORNEY. Well, Mr. Hale, tell just what happened when you came here yesterday morning.

HALE. Harry and I had started to town with a load of potatoes. We came along the road from my place and as I got here I said, "I'm going to see if I can't get John Wright to go in with me on a party telephone." I spoke to Wright about it once before and he put me off, saying folks talked too much anyway, and all he asked was peace and quiet—I guess you know about how much he talked himself; but I thought maybe if I went to the house and talked about it before his wife, though I said to Harry that I didn't know as what his wife wanted made much difference to John—

COUNTY ATTORNEY. Let's talk about that later, Mr. Hale. I do want to talk about 10
that, but tell now just what happened when you got to the house.

HALE. I didn't hear or see anything; I knocked at the door, and still it was all quiet inside. I knew they must be up, it was past eight o'clock. So I knocked again, and I thought I heard somebody say, "Come in." I wasn't sure, I'm not sure yet, but I opened the door—this door [*Indicating the door by which the two women are still standing.*] and there in that rocker—[*Pointing to it.*] sat Mrs. Wright.

[*They all look at the rocker.*]

COUNTY ATTORNEY. What—was she doing?

HALE. She was rockin' back and forth. She had her apron in her hand and was kind of—pleating it.

COUNTY ATTORNEY. And how did she—look?

HALE. Well, she looked queer. 15

COUNTY ATTORNEY. How do you mean—queer?

HALE. Well, as if she didn't know what she was going to do next. And kind of done up.

COUNTY ATTORNEY. How did she seem to feel about your coming?

HALE. Why, I don't think she minded—one way or other. She didn't pay much attention. I said, "How do, Mrs. Wright, it's cold, ain't it?" And she said, "Is it?"—and went on kind of pleating at her apron. Well, I was surprised; she didn't ask me to come up to the stove, or to set down, but just sat there, not even looking at me, so I said, "I want to see John." And then she—laughed. I guess you would call it a laugh. I thought of

Harry and the team outside, so I said a little sharp: "Can't I see John?" "No," she says, kind o' dull like. "Ain't he home?" says I. "Yes," says she, "he's home." "Then why can't I see him?" I asked her, out of patience. "'Cause he's dead," says she. "*Dead?*" says I. She just nodded her head, not getting a bit excited, but rockin' back and forth. "Why— where is he?" says I, not knowing what to say. She just pointed upstairs—like that. [*Himself pointing to the room above.*] I got up, with the idea of going up there. I walked from there to here—then I says, "Why, what did he die of?" "He died of a rope round his neck," says she, and just went on pleatin' at her apron. Well, I went out and called Harry. I thought I might—need help. We went upstairs and there he was lyin'—

COUNTY ATTORNEY.   I think I'd rather have you go into that upstairs, where you can point it all out. Just go on now with the rest of the story.

HALE.   Well, my first thought was to get that rope off. It looked . . . [*Stops, his face twitches.*] . . . but Harry, he went up to him, and he said, "No, he's dead all right, and we'd better not touch anything." So we went back downstairs. She was still sitting that same way. "Has anybody been notified?" I asked. "No," says she, unconcerned. "Who did this, Mrs. Wright?" said Harry. He said it businesslike—and she stopped pleatin' of her apron. "I don't know," she says. "You don't *know?*" says Harry. "No," says she. "Weren't you sleepin' in the bed with him?" says Harry. "Yes," says she, "but I was on the inside." "Somebody slipped a rope round his neck and strangled him and you didn't wake up?" says Harry. "I didn't wake up," she said after him. We must 'a looked as if we didn't see how that could be, for after a minute she said, "I sleep sound." Harry was going to ask her more questions but I said maybe we ought to let her tell her story first to the coroner, or the sheriff, so Harry went fast as he could to Rivers' place, where there's a telephone.

COUNTY ATTORNEY.   And what did Mrs. Wright do when she knew that you had gone for the coroner?

HALE.   She moved from that chair to this one over here [*Pointing to a small chair in the corner.*] and just sat there with her hands held together and looking down. I got a feeling that I ought to make some conversation, so I said I had come in to see if John wanted to put in a telephone, and at that she started to laugh, and then she stopped and looked at me—scared. [*The COUNTY ATTORNEY, who has had his notebook out, makes a note.*] I dunno, maybe it wasn't scared. I wouldn't like to say it was. Soon Harry got back, and then Dr. Lloyd came, and you, Mr. Peters, and so I guess that's all I know that you don't.

COUNTY ATTORNEY.   [*Looking around.*] I guess we'll go upstairs first—and then out to the barn and around there. [*To the SHERIFF.*] You're convinced that there was nothing important here—nothing that would point to any motive.

SHERIFF.   Nothing here but kitchen things.

[*The COUNTY ATTORNEY, after again looking around the kitchen, opens the door of a cupboard closet. He gets up on a chair and looks on a shelf. Pulls his hand away, sticky.*]

COUNTY ATTORNEY.   Here's a nice mess.

[*The women draw nearer.*]

MRS. PETERS.   [*To the other woman.*] Oh, her fruit; it did freeze. [*To the LAWYER.*] She worried about that when it turned so cold. She said the fire'd go out and her jars would break.

SHERIFF.   Well, can you beat the women! Held for murder and worryin' about her preserves.

COUNTY ATTORNEY.   I guess before we're through she may have something more serious than preserves to worry about.

HALE.   Well, women are used to worrying over trifles.   30

[*The two women move a little closer together.*]

COUNTY ATTORNEY.   [*With the gallantry of a young politician.*] And yet, for all their worries, what would we do without the ladies? [*The women do not unbend. He goes to the sink, takes a dipperful of water from the pail and pouring it into a basin, washes his hands. Starts to wipe them on the roller-towel, turns it for a cleaner place.*] Dirty towels! [*Kicks his foot against the pans under the sink.*] Not much of a housekeeper, would you say, ladies?
MRS. HALE.   [*Stiffly.*] There's a great deal of work to be done on a farm.
COUNTY ATTORNEY.   To be sure. And yet [*With a little bow to her.*] I know there are some Dickson county farmhouses which do not have such roller towels.

[*He gives it a pull to expose its full length again.*]

MRS. HALE.   Those towels get dirty awful quick. Men's hands aren't always as clean as they might be.
COUNTY ATTORNEY.   Ah, loyal to your sex, I see. But you and Mrs. Wright were   35
neighbors. I suppose you were friends, too.
MRS. HALE.   [*Shaking her head.*] I've not seen much of her of late years. I've not been in this house—it's more than a year.
COUNTY ATTORNEY.   And why was that? You didn't like her?
MRS. HALE.   I liked her all well enough. Farmers' wives have their hands full, Mr. Henderson. And then—
COUNTY ATTORNEY.   Yes—?
MRS. HALE.   [*Looking about.*] It never seemed a very cheerful place.   40
COUNTY ATTORNEY.   No—it's not cheerful. I shouldn't say she had the homemaking instinct.
MRS. HALE.   Well, I don't know as Wright had, either.
COUNTY ATTORNEY.   You mean that they didn't get on very well?
MRS. HALE.   No, I don't mean anything. But I don't think a place'd be any cheerfuller for John Wright's being in it.
COUNTY ATTORNEY.   I'd like to talk more of that a little later. I want to get the lay   45
of things upstairs now.

[*He goes to the left, where three steps lead to a stair door.*]

SHERIFF.   I suppose anything Mrs. Peters does'll be all right. She was to take in some clothes for her, you know, and a few little things. We left in such a hurry yesterday.
COUNTY ATTORNEY.   Yes, but I would like to see what you take, Mrs. Peters, and keep an eye out for anything that might be of use to us.
MRS. PETERS.   Yes, Mr. Henderson.

[*The women listen to the men's steps on the stairs, then look about the kitchen.*]

MRS. HALE.   I'd hate to have men coming into my kitchen, snooping around and criticising.

[*She arranges the pans under the sink which the LAWYER had shoved out of place.*]

MRS. PETERS.   Of course it's no more than their duty.   50
MRS. HALE.   Duty's all right, but I guess that deputy sheriff that came out to make the fire might have got a little of this on. [*Gives the roller towel a pull.*] Wish I'd thought of

that sooner. Seems mean to talk about her for not having things slicked up when she had to come away in such a hurry.

MRS. PETERS.   [*Who had gone to a small table in the left rear corner of the room, and lifted one end of a towel that covers a pan.*] She had bread set.

[*Stands still.*]

MRS. HALE.   [*Eyes fixed on a loaf of bread beside the breadbox, which is on a low shelf at the other side of the room. Moves slowly toward it.*] She was going to put this in there. [*Picks up loaf, then abruptly drops it. In a manner of returning to familiar things.*] It's a shame about her fruit. I wonder if it's all gone. [*Gets up on the chair and looks.*] I think there's some here that's all right, Mrs. Peters. Yes—here; [*Holding it toward the window.*] this is cherries, too. [*Looking again.*] I declare I believe that's the only one. [*Gets down, bottle in her hand. Goes to the sink and wipes it off on the outside.*] She'll feel awful bad after all her hard work in the hot weather. I remember the afternoon I put up my cherries last summer.

[*She puts the bottle on the big kitchen table, center of the room. With a sigh, is about to sit down in the rocking-chair. Before she is seated realizes what chair it is; with a slow look at it, steps back. The chair which she has touched rocks back and forth.*]

MRS. PETERS.   Well, I must get those things from the front room closet. [*She goes to the door at the right, but after looking into the other room, steps back.*] You coming with me, Mrs. Hale? You could help me carry them.

[*They go in the other room; reappear, MRS. PETERS carrying a dress and skirt, MRS. HALE following with a pair of shoes.*]

MRS. PETERS.   My, it's cold in there.

[*She puts the clothes on the big table and hurries to the stove.*]

MRS. HALE.   [*Examining the skirt.*] Wright was close. I think maybe that's why she kept so much to herself. She didn't even belong to the Ladies Aid. I suppose she felt she couldn't do her part, and then you don't enjoy things when you feel shabby. She used to wear pretty clothes and be lively, when she was Minnie Foster, one of the town girls singing in the choir. But that—oh, that was thirty years ago. This all you was to take in?

MRS. PETERS.   She said she wanted an apron. Funny thing to want, for there isn't much to get you dirty in jail, goodness knows. But I suppose just to make her feel more natural. She said they was in the top drawer in this cupboard. Yes, here. And then her little shawl that always hung behind the door. [*Opens stair door and looks.*] Yes, here it is.

[*Quickly shuts door leading upstairs.*]

MRS. HALE.   [*Abruptly moving toward her.*] Mrs. Peters?
MRS. PETERS.   Yes, Mrs. Hale?
MRS. HALE.   Do you think she did it?
MRS. PETERS.   [*In a frightened voice.*] Oh, I don't know.
MRS. HALE.   Well, I don't think she did. Asking for an apron and her little shawl. Worrying about her fruit.
MRS. PETERS.   [*Starts to speak, glances up, where footsteps are heard in the room above. In a low voice.*] Mr. Peters says it looks bad for her. Mr. Henderson is awful sarcastic in a speech and he'll make fun of her sayin' she didn't wake up.

MRS. HALE.   Well, I guess John Wright didn't wake when they was slipping that rope under his neck.

MRS. PETERS.   No, it's strange. It must have been done awful crafty and still. They   65
say it was such a—funny way to kill a man, rigging it all up like that.

MRS. HALE.   That's just what Mr. Hale said. There was a gun in the house. He says that's what he can't understand.

MRS. PETERS.   Mr. Henderson said coming out that what was needed for the case was a motive; something to show anger, or—sudden feeling.

MRS. HALE.   [*Who is standing by the table.*] Well, I don't see any signs of anger around here. [*She puts her hand on the dish towel which lies on the table, stands looking down at table, one half of which is clean, the other half messy.*] It's wiped to here. [*Makes a move as if to finish work, then turns and looks at loaf of bread outside the breadbox. Drops towel. In that voice of coming back to familiar things.*] Wonder how they are finding things upstairs. I hope she had it a little more red-up° up there. You know, it seems kind of *sneaking*. Locking her up in town and then coming out here and trying to get her own house to turn against her!

MRS. PETERS.   But Mrs. Hale, the law is the law.

MRS. HALE.   I s'pose 'tis. [*Unbuttoning her coat.*] Better loosen up your things, Mrs.   70
Peters. You won't feel them when you go out.

[*MRS. PETERS takes off her fur tippet,° goes to hang it on hook at back of room, stands looking at the under part of the small corner table.*]

MRS. PETERS.   She was piecing a quilt.

[*She brings the large sewing basket and they look at the bright pieces.*]

MRS. HALE.   It's log cabin pattern. Pretty, isn't it? I wonder if she was goin' to quilt it or just knot it?

[*Footsteps have been heard coming down the stairs. The SHERIFF enters followed by HALE and the COUNTY ATTORNEY.*]

SHERIFF.   They wonder if she was going to quilt it or just knot it!

[*The men laugh; the women look abashed.*]

COUNTY ATTORNEY.   [*Rubbing his hands over the stove.*] Frank's fire didn't do much up there, did it? Well, let's go out to the barn and get that cleared up.

[*The men go outside.*]

MRS. HALE.   [*Resentfully.*] I don't know as there's anything so strange, our takin'   75
up our time with little things while we're waiting for them to get the evidence. [*She sits down at the big table smoothing out a block with decision.*] I don't see as it's anything to laugh about.

MRS. PETERS.   [*Apologetically.*] Of course they've got awful important things on their minds.

[*Pulls up a chair and joins MRS. HALE at the table.*]

---

68 *red-up:* neat, arranged in order.   70 S.D. *tippet:* scarf-like garment of fur or wool for the
neck and shoulders. See p. 671.

MRS. HALE. [*Examining another block.*] Mrs. Peters, look at this one. Here, this is the one she was working on, and look at the sewing! All the rest of it has been so nice and even. And look at this! It's all over the place! Why, it looks as if she didn't know what she was about!

[*After she has said this they look at each other, then start to glance back at the door. After an instant MRS. HALE has pulled at a knot and ripped the sewing.*]

MRS. PETERS. Oh, what are you doing, Mrs. Hale?

MRS. HALE. [*Mildly.*] Just pulling out a stitch or two that's not sewed very good. [*Threading a needle.*] Bad sewing always made me fidgety.

MRS. PETERS. [*Nervously.*] I don't think we ought to touch things.   80

MRS. HALE. I'll just finish up this end. [*Suddenly stopping and leaning forward.*] Mrs. Peters?

MRS. PETERS. Yes, Mrs. Hale?

MRS. HALE. What do you suppose she was so nervous about?

MRS. PETERS. Oh—I don't know. I don't know as she was nervous. I sometimes sew awful queer when I'm just tired. [*MRS. HALE starts to say something, looks at MRS. PETERS, then goes on sewing.*] Well I must get these things wrapped up. They may be through sooner than we think. [*Putting apron and other things together.*] I wonder where I can find a piece of paper, and string.

MRS. HALE. In that cupboard, maybe.

MRS. PETERS. [*Looking in cupboard.*] Why, here's a bird-cage. [*Holds it up.*] Did she have a bird, Mrs. Hale?

MRS. HALE. Why, I don't know whether she did or not—I've not been here for so long. There was a man around last year selling canaries cheap, but I don't know as she took one; maybe she did. She used to sing real pretty herself.

MRS. PETERS. [*Glancing around.*] Seems funny to think of a bird here. But she must have had one, or why would she have a cage? I wonder what happened to it?

MRS. HALE. I s'pose maybe the cat got it.

MRS. PETERS. No, she didn't have a cat. She's got that feeling some people have about cats—being afraid of them. My cat got in her room and she was real upset and asked me to take it out.

MRS. HALE. My sister Bessie was like that. Queer, ain't it?

MRS. PETERS. [*Examining the cage.*] Why, look at this door. It's broke. One hinge is pulled apart.

MRS. HALE. [*Looking too.*] Looks as if someone must have been rough with it.

MRS. PETERS. Why, yes.

[*She brings the cage forward and puts it on the table.*]

MRS. HALE. I wish if they're going to find any evidence they'd be about it. I don't like this place.

MRS. PETERS. But I'm awful glad you came with me, Mrs. Hale. It would be lonesome for me sitting here alone.

MRS. HALE. It would, wouldn't it? [*Dropping her sewing.*] But I tell you what I do wish, Mrs. Peters. I wish I had come over sometimes when *she* was here. I—[*Looking around the room.*]—wish I had.

MRS. PETERS. But of course you were awful busy, Mrs. Hale—your house and your children.

MRS. HALE.   I could've come. I stayed away because it weren't cheerful—and that's why I ought to have come. I—I've never liked this place. Maybe because it's down in a hollow and you don't see the road. I dunno what it is, but it's a lonesome place and always was. I wish I had come over to see Minnie Foster sometimes. I can see now—

[*Shakes her head.*]

MRS. PETERS.   Well, you mustn't reproach yourself, Mrs. Hale. Somehow we just   100
don't see how it is with other folks until—something comes up.

MRS. HALE.   Not having children makes less work—but it makes a quiet house, and Wright out to work all day, and no company when he did come in. Did you know John Wright, Mrs. Peters?

MRS. PETERS.   Not to know him; I've seen him in town. They say he was a good man.

MRS. HALE.   Yes—good; he didn't drink, and kept his word as well as most, I guess, and paid his debts. But he was a hard man, Mrs. Peters. Just to pass the time of day with him—[*Shivers.*] Like a raw wind that gets to the bone. [*Pauses, her eye falling on the cage.*] I should think she would 'a wanted a bird. But what do you suppose went with it?

MRS. PETERS.   I don't know, unless it got sick and died.

[*She reaches over and swings the broken door, swings it again, both women watch it.*]

MRS. HALE.   You weren't raised round here, were you? [*MRS. PETERS shakes her   105
head.*] You didn't know—her?

MRS. PETERS.   Not till they brought her yesterday.

MRS. HALE.   She—come to think of it, she was kind of like a bird herself—real sweet and pretty, but kind of timid and—fluttery. How—she—did—change. [*Silence; then as if struck by a happy thought and relieved to get back to everyday things.*] Tell you what, Mrs. Peters, why don't you take the quilt in with you? It might take up her mind.

MRS. PETERS.   Why, I think that's a real nice idea, Mrs. Hale. There couldn't possibly be any objection to it, could there? Now, just what would I take? I wonder if her patches are in here—and her things.

[*They look in the sewing basket.*]

MRS. HALE.   Here's some red. I expect this has got sewing things in it. [*Brings out a fancy box.*] What a pretty box. Looks like something somebody would give you. Maybe her scissors are in here. [*Opens box. Suddenly puts her hand to her nose.*] Why— [*MRS. PETERS bends nearer, then turns her face away.*] There's something wrapped up in this piece of silk.

MRS. PETERS.   Why, this isn't her scissors.   110

MRS. HALE.   [*Lifting the silk.*] Oh, Mrs. Peters—it's—

[*MRS. PETERS bends closer.*]

MRS. PETERS.   It's the bird.

MRS. HALE.   [*Jumping up.*] But, Mrs. Peters—look at it! Its neck! Look at its neck! It's all—other side *to.*

MRS. PETERS.   Somebody—wrung—its—neck.

[*Their eyes meet. A look of growing comprehension, of horror. Steps are heard outside. MRS. HALE slips box under quilt pieces, and sinks into her chair. Enter SHERIFF and COUNTY ATTORNEY. MRS. PETERS rises.*]

COUNTY ATTORNEY.   [*As one turning from serious things to little pleasantries.*] Well,   1
ladies, have you decided whether she was going to quilt it or knot it?

MRS. PETERS.   We think she was going to—knot it.

COUNTY ATTORNEY.   Well, that's interesting, I'm sure. [*Seeing the bird-cage.*] Has the
bird flown?

MRS. HALE.   [*Putting more quilt pieces over the box.*] We think the—cat got it.

COUNTY ATTORNEY.   [*Preoccupied.*] Is there a cat?

[*MRS. HALE glances in a quick covert way at MRS. PETERS.*]

MRS. PETERS.   Well, not *now*. They're superstitious, you know. They leave.   1

COUNTY ATTORNEY.   [*To SHERIFF PETERS, continuing an interrupted conversation.*] No
sign at all of anyone having come from the outside. Their own rope. Now let's go up
again and go over it piece by piece. [*They start upstairs.*] It would have to have been someone who knew just the—

[*MRS. PETERS sits down. The two women sit there not looking at one another, but as if peering
into something and at the same time holding back. When they talk now it is in the manner of feeling their way over strange ground, as if afraid of what they are saying, but as if they cannot
help saying it.*]

MRS. HALE.   She liked the bird. She was going to bury it in that pretty box.

MRS. PETERS.   [*In a whisper.*] When I was a girl—my kitten—there was a boy took
a hatchet, and before my eyes—and before I could get there—[*Covers her face an instant.*]
If they hadn't held me back I would have—[*Catches herself, looks upstairs where steps are
heard, falters weakly.*]—hurt him.

MRS. HALE.   [*With a slow look around her.*] I wonder how it would seem never to
have had any children around. [*Pause.*] No, Wright wouldn't like the bird—a thing that
sang. She used to sing. He killed that, too.

MRS. PETERS.   [*Moving uneasily.*] We don't know who killed the bird.   1

MRS. HALE.   I knew John Wright.

MRS. PETERS.   It was an awful thing was done in this house that night, Mrs. Hale.
Killing a man while he slept, slipping a rope around his neck that choked the life out
of him.

MRS. HALE.   His neck. Choked the life out of him.

[*Her hand goes out and rests on the bird-cage.*]

MRS. PETERS.   [*With rising voice.*] We don't know who killed him. We don't know.

MRS. HALE.   [*Her own feeling not interrupted.*] If there'd been years and   1
years of nothing, then a bird to sing to you, it would be awful—still, after the bird was
still.

MRS. PETERS.   [*Something within her speaking.*] I know what stillness is. When we
homesteaded in Dakota, and my first baby died—after he was two years old, and me with
no other then—

MRS. HALE.   [*Moving.*] How soon do you suppose they'll be through, looking for
the evidence?

MRS. PETERS.   I know what stillness is. [*Pulling herself back.*] The law has got to
punish crime, Mrs. Hale.

MRS. HALE.   [*Not as if answering that.*] I wish you'd seen Minnie Foster when she
wore a white dress with blue ribbons and stood up there in the choir and sang. [*A look*

around the room.] Oh, I *wish* I'd come over here once in a while! That was a crime! That was a crime! Who's going to punish that?

MRS. PETERS. [*Looking upstairs.*] We mustn't—take on.

MRS. HALE. I might have known she needed help! I know how things can be— for women. I tell you, it's queer, Mrs. Peters. We live close together and we live far apart. We all go through the same things—it's all just a different kind of the same thing. [*Brushes her eyes, noticing the bottle of fruit, reaches out for it.*] If I was you I wouldn't tell her her fruit was gone. Tell her it *ain't.* Tell her it's all right. Take this in to prove it to her. She—she may never know whether it was broke or not.

MRS. PETERS. [*Takes the bottle, looks about for something to wrap it in; takes petticoat from the clothes brought from the other room, very nervously begins winding this around the bottle. In a false voice.*] My, it's a good thing the men couldn't hear us. Wouldn't they just laugh! Getting all stirred up over a little thing like a—dead canary. As if that could have anything to do with—with—wouldn't they *laugh!*

[*The men are heard coming down stairs.*]

MRS. HALE. [*Under her breath.*] Maybe they would—maybe they wouldn't.

COUNTY ATTORNEY. No, Peters, it's all perfectly clear except a reason for doing it. But you know juries when it comes to women. If there was some definite thing. Something to show—something to make a story about—a thing that would connect up with this strange way of doing it—

[*The women's eyes meet for an instant. Enter HALE from outer door.*]

HALE. Well, I've got the team° around. Pretty cold out there. 140

COUNTY ATTORNEY. I'm going to stay here a while by myself. [*To the SHERIFF.*] You can send Frank out for me, can't you? I want to go over everything. I'm not satisfied that we can't do better.

SHERIFF. Do you want to see what Mrs. Peters is going to take in?

[*The COUNTY ATTORNEY goes to the table, picks up the apron, laughs.*]

COUNTY ATTORNEY. Oh, I guess they're not very dangerous things the ladies have picked out. [*Moves a few things about, disturbing the quilt pieces which cover the box. Steps back.*] No, Mrs. Peters doesn't need supervising. For that matter, a sheriff's wife is married to the law. Ever think of it that way, Mrs. Peters?

MRS. PETERS. Not—just that way.

SHERIFF. [*Chuckling.*] Married to the law. [*Moves toward the other room.*] I just want 145 you to come in here a minute, George. We ought to take a look at these windows.

COUNTY ATTORNEY. [*Scoffingly.*] Oh, windows!

SHERIFF. We'll be right out, Mr. Hale.

[*HALE goes outside. The SHERIFF follows the COUNTY ATTORNEY into the other room. Then MRS. HALE rises, hands tight together, looking intensely at MRS. PETERS, whose eyes make a slow turn, finally meeting MRS. HALE'S. A moment MRS. HALE holds her, then her own eyes point the way to where the box is concealed. Suddenly MRS. PETERS throws back quilt pieces and tries to put the box in the bag she is wearing. It is too big. She opens box, starts to take bird out, cannot touch it, goes to pieces, stands there helpless. Sound of a knob turning in the other room. MRS.*

140 *team:* team of horses drawing a wagon.

HALE *snatches the box and puts it in the pocket of her big coat. Enter* COUNTY ATTORNEY *and* SHERIFF.]

COUNTY ATTORNEY.   [*Facetiously.*] Well, Henry, at least we found out that she was not going to quilt it. She was going to—what is it you call it, ladies?

MRS. HALE.   [*Her hand against her pocket.*] We call it—knot it, Mr. Henderson.

CURTAIN

QUESTIONS

1. How does the first entrance of the characters establish a distinction between the men and women in the play? What is suggested by the different reactions of the men and women to the frozen preserves?

2. What does Mr. Hale report to the County Attorney in his extended narrative? How observant is he? How accurate?

3. What is needed for a strong legal case against Minnie? What does the Sheriff conclude about the kitchen? What do his conclusions tell you about the men?

4. What are the women's conclusions about the bad sewing? What does Mrs. Hale do about it? At this point, what might she be thinking about the murder?

5. Of what importance are Mrs. Hale's descriptions (a) of Minnie as a young woman and (b) of the Wrights' marriage?

6. What do the women deduce from the broken birdcage and the dead bird? How are these symbolic, and what do they symbolize?

7. How did Minnie Wright murder her husband? What hints lead you to this solution? What information permits the women to make the right inferences about the crime and the method of strangulation?

8. What does Mrs. Hale do with the "trifles" of evidence? Why? How is her reaction to the evidence different from that of Mrs. Peters? What conflict develops between these women? How is it resolved?

9. Why does Mrs. Hale feel guilty about her relationship with Minnie Wright? To what degree does her guilt shape her decisions and actions?

GENERAL QUESTIONS

1. To what does the title of this play refer? How does this irony of the word *trifles* help shape the play's meaning?

2. What are the men like? Are they round characters or flat? How observant are they? What is their attitude toward their jobs? Toward their own importance? Toward the women and "kitchen things"?

3. What is Mrs. Hale like? How observant is she? What is her attitude toward the men and their work, and toward herself?

4. Some critics argue that Minnie is the play's most important character, even though she never appears onstage. Do you agree? Why do you think Glaspell did not make Minnie a speaking character?

5. How is symbolism employed to establish and underscore the play's meaning? Consider especially the birdcage, the dead bird, and the repeated assertion that Mrs. Wright was going to "knot" (tie) rather than "quilt" (sew) the quilt.

STANLEY KAUFFMANN, *THE MORE THE MERRIER*

Stanley Kauffmann is a native New Yorker who received his higher education at New York University, graduating in 1935. In addition to the creation of a large number of plays, his professional activities have included acting, stage managing, editing, directing, writing stories and novels, writing screenplays, running a weekly television program about the art of film, and teaching. He is perhaps best known today as one of America's foremost theater and movie critics. For a time he wrote reviews for *The New York Times,* and for decades he has been a regular reviewer for *The New Republic,* also doing reviews for *The Saturday Review* and *The Atlantic Monthly.* He was a recipient of the George Jean Nathan Award for drama criticism in 1973, and he has taught at Yale, the Graduate Center of The City University of New York, and Hunter College. His early years in the theater gave him both a theoretical and practical knowledge of drama. Over a twelve-year period beginning in 1933, he wrote more than twenty comedies. Some of these were full-length productions, such as *How She Managed Her Marriage* (1935) and *The True Adventure* (1935); a greater number consisted of one act, such as *The Singer in Search of a King* (1935). In addition to writing under his own name, he used the pseudonym Spranger Barry for a small number of plays.

The More the Merrier is a brief and entertaining piece in the tradition of romantic farce. The play begins conventionally, with the two main characters agreeing to marry. In their action and dialogue, they demonstrate that they are smitten both with each other and with the idea of a perfect marriage that promises the new beginning of a separate and better life. When Simon enters, however, the subject matter begins to verge on social drama. The dialogue between Emily and Simon shifts the play away from the previous borderline frivolousness, for as they speak they introduce a more serious treatment of motivation and the causes and occasions of human relationships. Despite the fact that these characters are part of the upper-crust, social-club level of society, the dimensions of their lives include great concern and uncertainty about genuinely human problems. The farcical mixup closing the play, together with the dialogue between the offstage characters at the final curtain, underscores the fact that while human beings may aspire to separateness and individuality, they can grow, mature, and live their lives only as integral members of society.

STANLEY KAUFFMANN (b. 1916)

The More the Merrier _____ *1940*

CAST OF CHARACTERS

Emily Stringer
Raphael Thumb
Simon Latchflake
Vesta Frimpole
A Woman's Voice
A Man's Voice

PLACE. *A room with people in it.*

TIME. *An evening of their lives.*

SCENE. *A room, furnished enough to suggest the real, bare enough to be fantastic. Immediately on the rising of the curtain we should get a definite hint that the place is as improbable as the play. There is a door back center, a door right, and a door left.*

RAPHAEL *is kneeling for the seated* EMILY, *anxiously awaiting an answer to the question he has just asked.*

EMILY. Yes.
RAPHAEL. You—you will?
EMILY. Yes.
RAPHAEL. Darling! [*He embraces her. They kiss.*] Darling!
EMILY. Sweetheart! [*They kiss again.*] Dear, you'd better get up. It's hard to kiss you, leaning over like this.
RAPHAEL. Sorry, honeybunch. [*He gets to his feet, leans over her, and kisses her again.*] How wonderful. How delicious. How unbelievable.
EMILY. [*Her hands on his cheek.*] Dear, silly Raphael. Didn't you know?
RAPHAEL. I could only hope, Emily!
EMILY. [*Leaning forward.*] Raphael. [*They kiss.*]
RAPHAEL. When shall it be?
EMILY. As soon as possible.
RAPHAEL. Tomorrow—tonight—
EMILY. [*Laughs.*] Oh, my rash, impetuous boy! No, not tomorrow; not for at least a month. I'll have to shop for a trousseau, and it will take three weeks to cry the banns°—
RAPHAEL. The banns?
EMILY. The banns are so cute—and then we'll have our wedding, a beautiful wedding.
RAPHAEL. A symbol of the beginning of a beautiful new life.
EMILY. Yes.
RAPHAEL. [*Thinking.*] Emily.
EMILY. [*Leaning forward with pouted lips, thinking he wants to kiss her.*] Raphael. [*He does nothing. She stares at him.*] Well.

13 *banns:* declarations made in church, usually Anglican, of an intent to marry. According to convention, the banns must be declared on three successive Sundays before a marriage is permitted.

RAPHAEL.   Oh—excuse me— [*He is jarred out of his thoughtfulness and kisses her.*] I   20
was about to say: it will really be a new life, won't it?

EMILY.   A wonderful new life.

RAPHAEL.   Cut off from everyone else.

EMILY.   Just us two.

RAPHAEL.   Just us two. [*Thinking, again.*] Emily.

EMILY.   [*Leaning forward.*] Raphael.   25

RAPHAEL.   Oh—er—yes, dear. [*He kisses her.*] I was about to say: it will really be cut
off from everyone else, won't it? I mean, to me that's always been the marvelous thing
about marriage. It—it separates you from the rest of the world; gives you a life apart.

EMILY.   It will be as if we were born again.

RAPHAEL.   No old ties?

EMILY.   No old ties, no old bonds. You and I together, apart from the world.

RAPHAEL.   Oh— [*Clasping her hands.*] —oh, if you only knew how wonderful that   30
sounds. I have often thought to myself, "Raphael Thumb, you must make a fresh
start. You are slipping. You must cut loose from the past. You must take a fresh grip."
Our marriage will be that fresh grip, dear.

EMILY.   A very fresh grip, sweetest. Raphael.

RAPHAEL.   [*Leaning forward.*] Emily.

EMILY.   Sit back, dear. I only want to ask you a question.

RAPHAEL.   Oh. Of Course. [*He relaxes.*]

EMILY.   Raphael, what is it you want to cut loose from?   35

RAPHAEL.   My past.

EMILY.   You have a past?

RAPHAEL.   Haven't you?

EMILY.   It all depends. Do you mean past with a small "p" or a capital "P"?

RAPHAEL.   A small "p," I hope.   40

EMILY.   Well, yes, I have.

RAPHAEL.   So have I. But even more than forgetting the past, I want to lose all
the things and people that disappoint me. You know, dear, when we're very young, we—
we form ideals of friendship and living, and we're never quite able to adhere to them.
Consequently, we're usually looking for a chance to wipe the slate clean and begin over
again. That's what marriage is for. That's why I'm so happy.

EMILY.   [*Leaning forward.*] Raphael.

RAPHAEL.   [*Puzzled.*] Er—is it a question, dear—or—

EMILY.   Not a question. [*They kiss.*] Our marriage will be just like pulling two   45
straight, untangled threads out of a jumbled skein.

RAPHAEL.   There are so many things I despise. Cigars, for instance. I'll never
smoke cigars again.

EMILY.   Lipstick, for another instance. I'll never use it again.

RAPHAEL.   And the people I never want to see again! Susan Tellow . . . and Arnold
Brunt.

EMILY.   Lucy Fishpocket . . . and Seymour Prazey.

RAPHAEL.   How about Bertie Moxpitch?   50

EMILY.   And Adelaide Jarbus.

RAPHAEL.   And Prissie Yemling.

EMILY.   And Lester Warbeak.

RAPHAEL.   Dorothy Hosepull!

EMILY.   Chesterton Keith!   55
RAPHAEL.   I hate them all.
EMILY.   We'll never see them again. We'll be too busy being married.
RAPHAEL.   Ah, my life feels purged already. Emily.
EMILY.   [*Leaning forward.*] Raphael. [*They kiss.*]
RAPHAEL.   We two. Alone.   60
EMILY.   Sweetiekins.
RAPHAEL.   Honey lamb.

[*Yes, they kiss again.*]

EMILY.   Raphael, when did you discover that you loved me? Or was it gradual?
RAPHAEL.   Oh, it was sudden. Very sudden. I remember the day exactly. It was just
seven months ago at Sarah Bullhorn's birthday party. I glimpsed you coming through
the doorway with a lemon sherbet in your hand, and—
EMILY.   It couldn't have been lemon. I hate lemon.   65
RAPHAEL.   Well, perhaps it was orange. But anyway, that was the moment.
EMILY.   [*Hugging him.*] Sweetist Babykins!
RAPHAEL.   My own! And when did you learn you loved me?
EMILY.   The first time I danced with you. You're the only man I've ever known
whose hands aren't hot and sweaty by eleven p.m.
RAPHAEL.   Angelest!   70
EMILY.   Ducky diddle!

[*Right. Another kiss.*]

RAPHAEL.   And now we're each other's. Alone. Isn't love wonderful?
EMILY.   Wonderful. It's like a cold shower or a swift swim. It simply kills every-
thing mean and dirty in you and gives you a new outlook on life.
RAPHAEL.   Us—
EMILY.   Emily and Raphael.   75
RAPHAEL.   Alone forever. [*A knock at the door back center.*] Who can that be?
EMILY.   I haven't the faintest.
RAPHAEL.   Shall I answer?
EMILY.   [*After a moment's pouting deliberation.*] No, let him go away.
RAPHAEL.   [*Sighing happily.*] Ah! Now, where were we?   80
EMILY.   I think you were about to kiss me again.
RAPHAEL.   That must have been it. Well— [*He leans forward. Another knock.*] He
hasn't gone.
EMILY.   Persistent wretch.
RAPHAEL.   Hadn't I better answer?
EMILY.   Not until you've kissed me again.   85
RAPHAEL.   My ownest. My own, own darling.
EMILY.   My heart's treasure.

[*They kiss. Simultaneously, the doorbell rings. It has a really hideous sound.*]

RAPHAEL.   Drat that man!
EMILY.   [*Reclining languidly, her back to the door.*] I suppose you'd better answer,
dear.
RAPHAEL.   Yes, lamikins. [*As he goes to the door, the bell rings again.*] All right, all
right. Wait a moment, can't you? [*Muttering.*] People who don't know when other people

want to be alone— [*He opens the door. SIMON LATCHFLAKE stands there, his overcoat up around his ears, his hat down over his brows. You'd never have recognized him if we hadn't told you.*] Who is it?

SIMON.   [*In a voice slightly muffled by his coat.*] Me. It's me.

RAPHAEL.   [*Recognizing him.*] Oh, it's you, old man! Well, for goodness' sake, come in! However on earth did you know I was here? How did you find me? Come in.

[*SIMON enters. The door is shut behind him.*]

SIMON.   Oh, I managed to find you.

RAPHAEL.   I'm glad you did. Old man, congratulate me. This is the happiest day of my life. I want you to meet the girl who's just promised to be mine alone. Emily, darling.

EMILY.   [*Going to them.*] Yes, dear.   95

RAPHAEL.   Emily, I want you to meet my old friend—

EMILY.   Simon Latchflake.

SIMON.   Yes.

RAPHAEL.   What?

SIMON.   [*Nods.*] Simon Latchflake.   100

EMILY.   Oh.

RAPHAEL.   Well!

EMILY.   [*Whispering.*] Is it you?

RAPHAEL.   Yes, it's he; but how did you know?

EMILY.   Oh, dear. Tonight of all nights.   105

SIMON.   Rather disappointing, isn't it, Emily?

RAPHAEL.   Emily! I say, would someone mind very much explaining just what— what—

SIMON.   Shall I explain, Emily?

EMILY.   Yes, you'd better explain—now.

RAPHAEL.   Well, the first thing is—   110

SIMON.   —to take off my coat. [*Which he does.*]

RAPHAEL.   [*With a tinge of the sardonic.*] Oh, make yourself at home.

SIMON.   Thank you.

RAPHAEL.   Will you be seated?

SIMON.   Not yet.   115

RAPHAEL.   I shall sit. Emily?

EMILY.   No, no. Hurry, Simon. Explain.

SIMON.   Well, Raphael, I called at your home tonight to take you along to the club for a game of billiards. Your butler told me you'd gone to visit a lady, a lady you'd been visiting frequently, a Miss Emily Stringer. That was a jolt, I can tell you. Then when he told me how you'd been prancing and dancing around the house before you left, I knew you'd come here to propose. I followed at once and tried to arrive before it was too late. There's the whole thing in a nutshell.

RAPHAEL.   That's only the nutshell. What I want to know is, what was the jolt. How did Emily come to know you and you her?

SIMON.   Raphael, old man, this is going to be a shock. Here goes. Not many   120 months ago, I stood in your shoes.

RAPHAEL.   What! You mean—

SIMON.   Yes. Miss Stringer was engaged to me.

RAPHAEL.   Wha—Em—Emily, is this true?

EMILY.   Yes, Raphael, too true.

RAPHAEL.   But I—I don't understand.   125

EMILY.   Raphael, dear, it was before I knew you.

RAPHAEL.   Oh, of course. But—phew! And we were going to shut out the rest of the world. The first man who calls is my friend and your former fiancé. [*Sternly, to* SIMON.] Even so, how dare you presume to follow me and try to stop me?

SIMON.   Ah, Raphael, you don't know this woman as I know her.

RAPHAEL.   Stop! I won't hear a word against Emily.

EMILY.   Thank you, dear.   130

RAPHAEL.   Even though she was once engaged to you, I hold the highest opinion of her.

EMILY.   *Thank* you dear.

RAPHAEL.   But what's the matter with her?

SIMON.   Well, take tonight for instance. Haven't you noticed something wrong already?

RAPHAEL.   [*Troubled.*] Why—er—   13!

SIMON.   Fool! Utter fool!

RAPHAEL.   [*Worried by the fact that he may have missed something.*] I—I can't think of anything—

SIMON.   I'm here. That's what's wrong. I'm here.

RAPHAEL.   That's very wrong. But it's not her fault.

SIMON.   Oh, yes, it is. And it's only a sample of what your future life will be. I   14 know what you were talking about before I came . . . how you were going to seclude yourself from the world, how you were going to live alone. But, with this woman, that's impossible. Her life is knotted up with thousands of other people. She has hundreds of close friends. I'm only one of them. We keep coming. I came tonight.

RAPHAEL.   But you came—

SIMON.   Nevertheless, it's a sample.

RAPHAEL.   You mean, I'd never have—

SIMON.   With this woman, you'll never have what you want most from marriage; you'll never have the chance to break loose from the old . . . you'll never begin anew.

EMILY.   What's the matter with having friends?   1ₐ

SIMON.   Nothing, if you like it. But for a man like Raphael, who has ideals, who's dissatisfied with his past life and wants to begin a better one beginning with marriage, you're the wrong woman.

RAPHAEL.   Really, you know, you—er—have no right—

SIMON.   Raphael, old man. I have the great right—the desire for your welfare.

EMILY.   Raphael, are you going to listen to him?

RAPHAEL.   Well, dear, you can't deny that he speaks from experience. I—I don't   1 exactly know.

EMILY.   You don't love me.

RAPHAEL.   Oh, I do, I do. But I—I really ought to think it over. You see, one of my principal reasons for marrying—well, I must be sure.

SIMON.   That's all I want to hear. Raphael, old man, you're saved. Now you go right home and—

EMILY.   No, no!

RAPHAEL.   No, no!

SIMON.   Well, then, go inside and have a nice long talk with yourself.

RAPHAEL.   All right. [*Turning back tentatively.*] I wish I had something to smoke.

SIMON.   Have you promised to give up cigars? [*RAPHAEL nods.*] The usual thing. Here. [*He gives RAPHAEL a terribly long cigar.*] Take this, and don't come back till you've finished it.

RAPHAEL.   All right. [*He starts right, turns and looks back dubiously.*] All right. [*He exits.*]

EMILY.   [*Angrily.*] Well, he can think it over, if he wants to. I'm not to be bandied   160 about this way. After he's finished that cigar, perhaps I won't be so anxious to take him.

SIMON.   Good.

EMILY.   And you—what a beast you are! Not satisfied to wound my pride a year ago, you come here tonight to interfere with my happiness.

SIMON.   [*Taking a mirror from his pocket.*] Here, you look terrible. It's the kissing that's done it, I suppose. Fix yourself up.

EMILY.   You mind your own— [*Glancing in the mirror.*] I wish I had a lipstick.

SIMON.   [*Taking one from his pocket.*] Here.   165

EMILY.   [*Coldly.*] Thank you. [*She makes the necessary adjustments and turns away. He replaces the instruments of war in his pocket.*]

SIMON.   Do you know why I came here tonight and told those things to Raphael?

EMILY.   You said it was because—

SIMON.   That's not the reason. That was only to discourage him. I came because—well—I've reconsidered the matter. I want to marry you.

EMILY.   Indeed! Isn't that just too flattering!   170

SIMON.   Emily, I love you.

EMILY.   Liar.

SIMON.   Well, at least I want to marry you.

EMILY.   Why?

SIMON.   Oh, I'm sick of the old life: new girl every week, parties, dances, bright   175 conversations. I want to settle down.

EMILY.   [*Mockingly.*] Oh, but you forget. I'm a girl who has thousands of ties with the past. There'd be no escape with me.

SIMON.   I could take you away.

EMILY.   From my habits?

SIMON.   From people. We'll make new habits.

EMILY.   No, thank you. I'll marry the man I love, the man who loves me. That's   180 Raphael.

SIMON.   [*Cajolingly.*] You were engaged to me once.

EMILY.   Once was enough. Simon, you're a fool.

SIMON.   Am I?

EMILY.   For two reasons. First, for thinking you could discourage Raphael. Two minutes alone with him and I'll have him back again. Second, about this new life, turning over a new leaf.

SIMON.   Raphael believes it, too.   185

EMILY.   Yes, and I encourage him in it because it makes him happy to think about it; but I don't really believe it. Our lives are too closely caught up with other people and other things ever to extract them completely. When I was a child, someone put chewing gum in my hair. Have you ever tried to take chewing gum out of your hair?

SIMON.   No!

EMILY.   Well, it can't be done. You have to cut off the hair.

SIMON.   Who cares. I say that a new life—

EMILY. No. The chains of our old lives are linked and cross-linked. Pull one,   190
pull all.

SIMON. But, Emily—

EMILY. The proof? See how entangled our lives are: mine and yours; yours and
Raphael's; and Raphael's back again with mine.

SIMON. Coincidence, mere coincidence. I happened to know you and Raphael
happened to know you; and he and I happened to be friends. It—it just happened.

EMILY. Everything just happens. Don't you see? And there's probably someone
else whose life is tied up with all three of ours, although we don't know it. Nobody lives
alone.

[*A knock at the door.*]

SIMON. Don't answer.   195

EMILY. Why not?

SIMON. I have a horrible feeling that it's the person you just described, someone
who knows all three of us.

EMILY. [*Going to the door.*] We'll se.

SIMON. Wait! Things are complicated enough! Don't make them worse! Wait!

[*But* EMILY *has opened the door.* VESTA FRIMPOLE *is there.*]

EMILY. Vesta!   20

VESTA. Emily!

SIMON. Vesta!

VESTA. Simon!

EMILY. Another thread.

SIMON. I told you. [*To* VESTA.] How—how did you—   20

VESTA. I phoned your home. They told me you were at this address. I didn't
know that Emily lived here. How are you, Emily, dear? I haven't seen you in ages.

EMILY. I'm fine, dear. How are you?

VESTA. Oh, I can't complain. Has Simon been proposing to you?

EMILY. Yes.

VESTA. Have you accepted him?   2

EMILY. No.

VESTA. Good. [*Kneeling to* SIMON.] Simon, will you marry me?

SIMON. For Heaven's sake, get up.

VESTA. Will you?

SIMON. Oh, get up!   2

VESTA. [*Rising.*] All right, dear, don't be angry. I only did it to prove that I'm sincere.

EMILY. Shall I leave?

SIMON. No! [*To* VESTA.] Why on earth do you want to marry me?

VESTA. Oh, I don't know. I'm sort of tired of the old life; I want to turn over a
new leaf—

EMILY. [*Bored.*] Mother, mother, pin a rose on me.   2

SIMON. For I'm to be Queen of the May.°

VESTA. What?

SIMON. We've been through all that.

EMILY. It won't work.

221 *Queen of the May:* See Tennyson's "The May Queen" (1833).

VESTA.   But why—   225
SIMON.   Too many people!
EMILY.   Too many ties!
SIMON.   No clean starts!
EMILY.   Better make the best of it.
SIMON.   Chewing gum in the hair.   230
VESTA.   But I don't understand. Why couldn't we—
SIMON.   Everyone knows everyone else, and everyone's past is brought up into
his future every day of his life. That's why.
VESTA.   No, I still don't understand—

[*RAPHAEL comes in right.*]

RAPHAEL.   This cigar is pretty bad. Do I have to—
VESTA.   Raphael Thumb!   235
RAPHAEL.   Vesta Frimpole!
EMILY.   What!
SIMON.   I'm not surprised.
RAPHAEL.   Emily, I might as well tell you the truth immediately. Vesta and I were
engaged once.
VESTA.   Indeed we were.   240
SIMON.   [*To VESTA.*] Now do you understand?
VESTA.   But—but—
RAPHAEL.   [*To VESTA.*] What a pleasant surprise to see you here.
VESTA.   Oh—thanks.
SIMON.   Cease the amenities. Raphael, have you made up your mind?   245
RAPHAEL.   Yes. The unexpected sight of Vesta has made it up for me.
EMILY.   [*Fearfully.*] Raphael—you mean—
RAPHAEL.   I mean I realize now that there is no escape from the past, and I shall
marry you anyway.
EMILY.   Beloved!
RAPHAEL.   Adored one!   250

[*They embrace.*]

VESTA.   [*Coyly.*] Simon!
SIMON.   No!
VESTA.   Simon—
SIMON.   No!
VESTA.   [*Wheedlingly.*] Simon—   255
SIMON.   Oh—

[*They embrace, too. Suddenly there is a knock on the door center.*]

RAPHAEL.   Don't open. [*He goes to the switch next to the door and plunges the room
into comparative darkness, leaving just enough light for us to see their faces. Then he looks through
the keyhole.*] Oh, it's no one you know. A friend of mine. Name of Bussbones.
ALL THE OTHERS.   Arthur Bussbones? [*They look at each other.*]
RAPHAEL.   [*Wearily.*] Oh, dear. [*Another glance through the keyhole.*] Look! A cab's
stopping at the corner! Someone's getting out. It looks like that Vetborough girl.
THE OTHERS.   Virginia Vetborough? [*They look at each other again. More knocking at
the door.*]

EMILY.   There's only one chance for us! Don't open the door! [*She goes to the door,*   2'
quietly turns the key in the lock and hands it to RAPHAEL.] Swallow the key!

RAPHAEL.   What?

EMILY.   Please?

SIMON.   For all of us. Please.

VESTA.   To lock out the past. It's our only chance.

RAPHAEL.   Oh—very well. [*He swallows the key.*] Hm. Not as bad as I expected.   2'
Now what?

SIMON.   We must escape. We have a locked door across our lives, separating us
from the past. It's a headstart, small but nevertheless real. We must capitalize it. You take
Emily that way; Vesta and I will go this way; and may we never meet again.

RAPHAEL.   Amen.

SIMON.   Come, Vesta dear.

VESTA.   [*Cooingly.*] All right, darling.

RAPHAEL.   [*In the shadows.*] Wait a minute, I'm Raphael. Hey Simon, you've got   2'
Emily.

SIMON.   Excuse me, Emily.

EMILY.   Quite all right.

SIMON.   [*Tentatively.*] Vesta?

VESTA.   Yes, dear.

SIMON.   Come, Vesta.   2'

RAPHAEL.   Emily?

EMILY.   Yes, dear.

RAPHAEL.   Come, Emily.

[*One pair tiptoes to the right, the other to the left. More knocking at the door.*]

ONE PAIR.   [*Fingers to lips.*] Ssh!

THE OTHER PAIR.   [*Likewise.*] Ssh!   2'

[*All exit. A woman's footsteps approach the front door. More knocking. Voices are heard outside.*]

A WOMAN.   Isn't anyone home?

A MAN.   I don't think so. I've been knocking several minutes. No one answers. By
the way, madam, don't I know you? Aren't you Virginia Vetborough?

A WOMAN.   Why, Arthur Bussbones! Of all people!

A MAN.   Well, well!

[*They laugh.*]

A WOMAN.   And how have you been since we broke off our engagement?

[*They continue to chatter; but you have the idea.*]

CURTAIN

QUESTIONS

1.   Who are the two main characters in the play? What are they doing as the play
opens? What beliefs do they reveal about love and marriage?

2.   Who is Simon? When does he enter? What is his interest in interrupting the
conversation between Raphael and Emily?

3. What do Emily and Simon discuss after Raphael has left the stage? Why does Kauffmann have Emily discuss these matters with Simon when Raphael is not present?
4. In what way is the attitude toward marriage expressed by Vesta similar to the attitude of Simon? How are they "made for each other"?
5   Describe the language spoken by the characters in the play. What particular types of phrases do they use to indicate their affection? To what degree does this language seem out of date?
6   What changes or developments do the characters undergo in the course of the play, particularly with regard to attitudes about the possibilities of marriage?
7. What attitudes toward the material of the play and toward the audience are revealed in the stage directions? How seriously does the dramatist take the characters and their attitudes?
8. Why does the play end with the conversation of Virginia Vetborough and Arthur Bussbones after the major characters have left the stage?

GENERAL QUESTIONS

1. How generally true is Simon's claim, made about Emily, that our lives are "knotted up with thousands of other people" (speech 140), and Emily's point that "Our lives are too closely caught up with other people and other things ever to extract them completely" (speech 186)? How do these ideas relate to the intention of Raphael and Emily that their married life will give them a life "apart" from the lives of everyone else?
2. Describe the idea that "mere coincidence" and simple happenstance rather than decisiveness governs some of the most significant aspects of personal life (speeches 193, 194). What are the implications of this idea for relationships of love and marriage? Are love and marriage no more than accidental, the result of chance happenings? What is the role of deliberation in such circumstances of life?
3. How does this play illustrate the ways in which dramatists express ideas even through the substance of apparently light and "improbable" romantic farce?

BETTY KELLER, *TEA PARTY*

Betty Keller, a Canadian, has brought a wide variety of experience to her work for the theater, including such unlikely jobs as insurance adjuster, farmer, photographer's assistant, and prison matron. She served as a teacher for many theatrical workshops in Vancouver, including four years with Playhouse Holiday. She taught drama and theater at the Windsor Secondary School in North Vancouver until 1974, the year she published *Improvisations in*

Creative Drama, the collection of short plays and sketches from which *Tea Party* is selected. She also taught at Simon Fraser University and the University of British Columbia. She was the founder/producer of the western Canadian writers festival and workshop program *The Festival of the Written Arts* from 1983 to 1994. In addition to her work in drama, she has written biographical and historical works, including *Pauline: A Biography of E. Pauline Johnson* (1982); *Black Wolf: A Life of Ernest Thompson Seton* (1984); *On the Shady Side: Vancouver 1886–1914* (1986); *Sea Silver: Salmon Farming on the West Coast* (1996); and *Bright Seas and Pioneer Spirits* (1996).

Brief as *Tea Party* is, it illustrates the power of drama to depict character and situation and to convey emotion. The main characters are two lonely elderly sisters who have outlived their friends and relatives and have no one except the people who occasionally come to their house to perform various services, such as delivering the paper and reading the meters. The sketch presents their plight deftly and succinctly, touching with great tenderness on the pathos of their loneliness.

Tea Party is too short to present difficult choices for the characters, and hence they hardly get the opportunity to go through the responses and changes that are found in full-length plays. Both Alma and Hester are individualized, however, as they carry on a minor controversy about names and dates from their long-vanished past. Beyond this, in Alma's last speech, which ends the dramatic sketch, one might find a hint of the awareness and recognition that we expect of round, developed characters. Even though the paperboy is not a speaking part, his unkindness to the sisters is shown clearly, and in this way Keller dramatizes the poignant situation of persons whom life has passed by. It is difficult to find a play that conveys so much of life and feeling in so short a span of time and action.

BETTY KELLER   (b. 1930)

Tea Party ————————————————————————————— *1974*

CHARACTERS

Alma Evans: *seventy-five years old, small and spare framed. Her clothing is simple but not outdated, her grey hair cut short and neat. She walks with the aid of a cane, although she would not be classed as a cripple.*

Hester Evans: *seventy-nine years old. There is little to distinguish her physically from her sister, except perhaps a face a little more pinched and pain-worn. She sits in a wheelchair; but although her legs may be crippled, her mind certainly is not.*

The Boy: *in his early teens, seen only fleetingly.*

SCENE. *The sitting room of the Evans sisters' home. The door to the street is on the rear wall Upstage Left,° a large window faces the street Upstage Center. On the right wall is the door to the kitchen; on the left, a door to the remainder of the house. Downstage Left is an easy chair, Upstage Right a sofa, Downstage Right a tea trolley. The room is crowded with the knickknacks gathered by its inhabitants in three-quarters of a century of living.*

[*At rise,* ALMA *is positioning* HESTER'S *wheelchair Upstage Left.* ALMA'S *cane is on* HESTER'S *lap.*]

> HESTER.   That's it.

[ALMA *takes her cane from* HESTER. *They both survey the room.*]

> ALMA.   I think I'll sit on the sofa . . . at the far end.
> HESTER.   Yes. That will be cosy. Then he can sit on this end between us.

[ALMA *sits on the Downstage Right end of the sofa. They both study the effect.*]

> ALMA.   But then he's too close to the door, Hester!

[HESTER *nods, absorbed in the problem.*]

> ALMA.   [*Moving to the Upstage Left end of sofa.*] Then I'd better sit here.   5
> HESTER.   But now he's too far away from me, Alma.

[ALMA *stands; both of them study the room again.*]

> ALMA.   But if I push the tea trolley in front of you, he'll have to come to you, won't he?
> HESTER.   Oh, all right, Alma. You're sure it's today?
> ALMA.   [*Pushing the tea trolley laden with cups and napkins, etc. to* HESTER.] The first Thursday of the month.
> HESTER.   You haven't forgotten the chocolate biscuits?°   10
> ALMA.   No dear, they're on the plate. I'll bring them in with the tea. [*Goes to the window, peering up the street to the Right.*]
> HESTER.   And cocoa?
> ALMA.   I remembered.
> HESTER.   You didn't remember for Charlie's visit.
> ALMA.   Charlie drinks tea, Hester. I didn't make cocoa for him because he drinks   15
> tea.
> HESTER.   Oh. He didn't stay last time anyway.
> ALMA.   It was a busy day. . . .
> HESTER.   Rushing in and out like that. I was going to tell him about father and the *Bainbridge* . . . and he didn't stay.
> ALMA.   What about the *Bainbridge?*

Upstage Left: To visualize stage locations, assume that the stage directions are described from the viewpoint of an actor facing the audience. Thus "Right" is actually to the left of the audience, and "Left" is right. "Downstage" refers to the front of the stage, while "Upstage" is the back. The terms *down* and *up* were established at a time when stages were tilted toward the audience, so that spectators at floor level could have as complete a view as possible of the entire stage.   10 *chocolate biscuits:* chocolate cookies.

HESTER.   Her maiden voyage out of Liverpool . . . when father was gone three   2(
months and we thought he'd gone down with her.

ALMA.   That wasn't the *Bainbridge.*

HESTER.   Yes, it was. It was the *Bainbridge.* I remember standing on the dock in
the snow when she finally came in. That was the year I'd begun first form, and I could
spell out the letters on her side.

ALMA.   It was her sister ship, the *Heddingham.*

HESTER.   The *Bainbridge.* You were too young to remember. Let's see, the year
was . . .

ALMA.   Mother often told the story. It was the *Heddingham* and her engine broke   2
down off Cape Wrath beyond the Hebrides.

HESTER.   It was 1902 and you were just four years old.

ALMA.   The *Heddingham,* and she limped into port on January the fifth.

HESTER.   January the fourth just after nine in the morning, and we stood in the
snow and watched the *Bainbridge* nudge the pier, and I cried and the tears froze on my
cheeks.

ALMA.   The *Heddingham.*

HESTER.   Alma, mother didn't cry, you know. I don't think she ever cried. My   ‌
memory of names and places is sharp so that I don't confuse them as some others I
could mention, but sometimes I can't remember things like how people reacted. But I
remember that day. There were tears frozen on my cheeks but mother didn't cry.

ALMA.   [*Nodding.*] She said he didn't offer a word of explanation. Just marched
home beside her.

HESTER.   [*Smiling.*] He never did say much. . . . Is he coming yet?

ALMA.   No, can't be much longer though. Almost half past four.

HESTER.   Perhaps you'd better bring in the tea. Then it will seem natural.

ALMA.   Yes dear, I know. [*Exits out door Upstage Right.*] Everything's ready.

HESTER.   What will you talk about?

ALMA.   [*Re-entering with the teapot*] I thought perhaps . . . [*Carefully putting down
the teapot.*] . . . perhaps brother George!

HESTER.   And the torpedo? No, Alma, he's not old enough for that story!

ALMA.   He's old enough to know about courage. I thought I'd show him the
medal, too. [*She goes to the window, peers both ways worriedly, then carries on towards the
kitchen.*]

HESTER.   Not yet? He's late to-night. You're sure it's today?

ALMA.   He'll come. It's the first Thursday. [*Exit.*]

HESTER.   You have his money?

ALMA.   [*Returning with the plate of biscuits.*] I've got a twenty dollar bill, Hester.

HESTER.   Alma!

ALMA.   Well, we haven't used that one on him. It was Dennis, the last one, who
always had change. We could get two visits this way, Hester.

HESTER.   Maybe Dennis warned him to carry change for a twenty.

ALMA.   It seemed worth a try. [*Goes to the window again.*] Are you going to tell him
about the *Heddingham?*

HESTER.   The *Bainbridge.* Maybe . . . or maybe I'll tell him about the day the
Great War ended. Remember, Alma, all the noise, the paper streamers . . .

ALMA.   And father sitting silent in his chair.

HESTER.   It wasn't the same for him with George gone. Is he coming yet?

ALMA.   No dear, maybe he's stopped to talk somewhere. [*Looking to the right.*] . . . No . . . no, there he is, on the Davis' porch now!

HESTER.   I'll pour then. You get the cocoa, Alma.

ALMA.   [*Going out.*] It's all ready, I just have to add hot water.

HESTER.   Don't forget the marshmallows!

ALMA.   [*Reappearing*] Oh, Hester, what if he comes in and just sits down closest to   55
the door? He'll never stay!

HESTER.   You'll have to prod him along. For goodness sakes, Alma, get his cocoa!

[*ALMA disappears.*]

HESTER.   He must be nearly here. He doesn't go to the Leschynskis, and the Blackburns don't get home till after six.

ALMA.   [*Returning with the cocoa.*] Here we are! Just in . . .

[*The BOY passes the window. There is a slapping sound as the newspaper lands on the porch.*]

[*ALMA and HESTER look at the door and wait, hoping to hear a knock, but they both know the truth. Finally, ALMA goes to the door, opens it and looks down at the newspaper.*]

ALMA.   He's gone on by.

HESTER.   You must have had the day wrong.   60

ALMA.   No, he collected at the Davis'.

HESTER.   [*After a long pause.*] He couldn't have forgotten us.

ALMA.   [*Still holding the cocoa, she turns from the door.*] He's collecting at the Kerighan's now. [*She closes the door and stands forlornly.*]

HESTER.   Well, don't stand there with that cocoa! You look silly. [*ALMA brings the cocoa to the tea trolley.*] Here's your tea. [*ALMA takes the cup, sits on the Upstage Left end of the sofa. There is a long silence.*]

HESTER.   I think I'll save that story for the meter man.   65

ALMA.   The *Heddingham?*

HESTER.   The *Bainbridge.*

ALMA.   [*After a pause.*] They don't read the meters for two more weeks.

SLOW BLACKOUT

QUESTIONS

1.   What is the play's major conflict? The minor conflict?

2.   Why do the two sisters discuss their seating arrangements for the paperboy? How do we learn that they have made these arrangements before?

3.   What does Alma's plan for the twenty-dollar bill show about her? What does the discussion about both the money and the paperboys indicate about their own self-awareness?

4.   How does controversy about the names *Bainbridge* and *Heddingham* help you understand the two sisters?

GENERAL QUESTIONS

1. How does Keller's description of the sets aid you in understanding the action? The normal tasks of the women? From the setting of this play, what are your conclusions about the relationship of objects and spatial arrangements to the action and development of drama?

2. Consider the women, particularly with regard to their age. In the light of their health and their isolation, how does *Tea Party* present the circumstances of the aged? How can the play be construed as a sociological/political argument, with the elderly as the focus?

EUGENE O'NEILL, *BEFORE BREAKFAST*

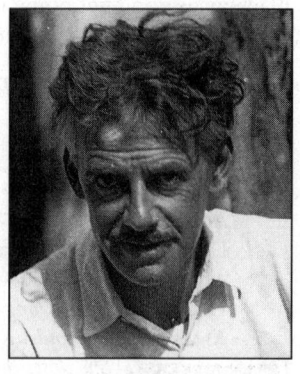

Eugene O'Neill is one of America's great playwrights. He wrote more than forty plays and won three Pulitzer Prizes. He is still the only American dramatist to have received the Nobel Prize for literature (1936).

O'Neill was born in New York, the son of a well-known actor, and was educated sporadically as his parents traveled from city to city on theatrical tours. Eventually he studied at Princeton, but he left to go to work, first in a mail-order house and then in Honduras, where he engaged in prospecting. He then began a brief career as a seaman, traveling on both sides of the Atlantic. He contracted tuberculosis in about 1912, and while in a sanitarium he began to write plays. Upon release he studied playwriting at Harvard, but by 1916 he had left to try his luck as a playwright with the Provincetown Players, the same company that Susan Glaspell had helped found and where she began her writing career. It was in 1916, the same year that Glaspell wrote *Trifles,* that the Provincetown Players produced O'Neill's first drama, *Bound East for Cardiff.*

O'Neill maintained a close connection with the Provincetown Players for several years, providing them with ten one-act plays between 1916 and 1920. Among these were *Thirst* (1916), *Before Breakfast* (1916), *Fog* ((1917), *The Long Voyage Home* (1917), *Ile* (1917), and *The Rope* (1917). His later (and longer) works include *The Emperor Jones* (1920), *Anna Christie* (1921), *Desire Under the Elms* (1924), *Strange Interlude* (1928), *Mourning Becomes Electra* (1931), and *The Iceman Cometh* (1946). O'Neill also wrote an autobiographical play, *Long Day's Journey into Night* (1936), that at his request was withheld until after his death. Staged on Broadway in 1956, it received the Pulitzer Prize in drama (O'Neill's third Pulitzer); it was later made into a film starring Katherine Hepburn.

Before Breakfast, though one of O'Neill's earliest plays, shows his characteristic control of point of view, conflict, character, and setting. The play was first staged in December 1916 by the Provincetown Players in New York City's

Greenwich Village (where Christopher Street, the address of the Rowlands' apartment, is located). The play contains little action, and yet it is charged with conflict. The plot is simple and straightforward—a wife onstage berates her off-stage husband for twenty minutes. The conflict between them is long-standing and bitter, and it is resolved in the play's horrifying conclusion.

Above all, *Before Breakfast* illustrates O'Neill's skillful control over the dramatic point of view. By giving Mrs. Rowland every word spoken on the stage, O'Neill causes the audience to understand everything as it is filtered through her mind. Indeed, the play is a bravura piece for a gifted actress. Because Mrs. Rowland dominates the stage so completely, it is tempting to see her character as one of constantly nagging spitefulness. It is to O'Neill's credit, however, that she is not without basic strength, and that her bitterness is not without cause. Alfred, the unseen and unheard offstage husband, has contributed to their estranged relationship.

Of particular note in indicating the impasse that the characters have reached are O'Neill's extensive stage directions describing the setting. We learn that the Rowlands' flat is in Greenwich Village, the traditional New York home of artists, poets, and actors. On the one hand, therefore, the flat suggests Alfred's artistic aspirations, but on the other, the poverty of the surroundings indicates the sad truth that such dreams cannot be sustained unless someone pays the rent.

The language of Mrs. Rowland, the only speaking character in the play, indicates both her lack of education and her intense dissatisfaction. Phrases such as "I got," "like I was," "liable" for "likely," and "sewing my fingers off" suggest that her knowledge of language has not been derived from education and study. Her speech also suggests the social gulf that originally separated her from Alfred, a gulf that they tried to bridge in their marriage but which now has opened up irretrievably. A number of other phrases embody the taunts that Mrs. Rowland directs at Alfred ("pawn, pawn, pawn," "like a man," " a fine life," "in trouble," etc.).

EUGENE O'NEILL   (1888–1953)

Before Breakfast ———————————————————— *1916*

CHARACTERS

> Mrs. Rowland, *the wife*
> Mr. Alfred Rowland, *the husband*

SCENE. *A small room serving both as kitchen and dining room in a flat on Christopher Street, New York City. In the rear, to the right, a door leading to the outer hallway. On the left of the doorway, a sink, and a two-burner gas stove. Over the stove, and extending to the left wall, a wooden closet for dishes, etc. On the left, two windows looking out on a fire escape where several potted plants are dying of neglect. Before the windows, a table covered with oilcloth. Two cane-bottomed chairs are placed by the table. Another stands against the wall to the right of door in rear. In the right wall, rear, a doorway leading into a bedroom. Farther forward, different articles of a man's and a woman's clothing are hung on pegs. A clothes line is strung from the left corner, rear, to the right wall, forward.*

It is about eight-thirty in the morning of a fine, sunshiny day in the early fall.

MRS. ROWLAND *enters from the bedroom, yawning, her hands still busy putting the finishing touches on a slovenly toilet by sticking hairpins into her hair which is bunched up in a drab-colored mass on top of her round head. She is of medium height and inclined to a shapeless stoutness, accentuated by her formless blue dress, shabby and worn. Her face is characterless, with small regular features and eyes of a nondescript blue. There is a pinched expression about her eyes and nose and her weak, spiteful mouth. She is in her early twenties but looks much older.*

She comes to the middle of the room and yawns, stretching her arms to their full length. Her drowsy eyes stare about the room with the irritated look of one to whom a long sleep has not been a long rest. She goes wearily to the clothes hanging on the right and takes an apron from a hook. She ties it about her waist, giving vent to an exasperated "damn" when the knot fails to obey her clumsy fingers. Finally gets it tied and goes slowly to the gas stove and lights one burner. She fills the coffee pot at the sink and sets it over the flame. Then slumps down into a chair by the table and puts a hand over her forehead as if she were suffering from headache. Suddenly her face brightens as though she had remembered something, and she casts a quick glance at the dish closet; then looks sharply at the bedroom door and listens intently for a moment or so.

MRS. ROWLAND.   [*In a low voice.*] Alfred! Alfred! [*There is no answer from the next room and she continues suspiciously in a louder tone.*] You needn't pretend you're asleep. [*There is no reply to this from the bedroom, and, reassured, she gets up from her chair and tiptoes cautiously to the dish closet. She slowly opens one door, taking great care to make no noise, and slides out, from their hiding place behind the dishes, a bottle of Gordon gin and a glass. In doing so she disturbs the top dish, which rattles a little. At this sound she starts guiltily and looks with sulky defiance at the doorway to the next room.*]

[*Her voice trembling.*] Alfred!

[*After a pause, during which she listens for any sound, she takes the glass and pours out a large drink and gulps it down; then hastily returns the bottle and glass to their hiding place. She closes the closet door with the same care as she had opened it, and, heaving a great sigh of relief, sinks down into her chair again. The large dose of alcohol she has taken has an almost immediate effect. Her features become more animated, she seems to gather energy, and she looks at the bedroom door with a hard, vindictive smile on her lips. Her eyes glance quickly about the room and are fixed on a man's coat and vest which hang from a hook at right. She moves stealthily over to the open doorway and stands there, out of sight of anyone inside, listening for any movement.*]

[*Calling in a half-whisper.*] Alfred!

[*Again there is no reply. With a swift movement she takes the coat and vest from the hook and returns with them to her chair. She sits down and takes the various articles out of each pocket but quickly puts them back again. At last, in the inside pocket of the vest, she finds a letter.*]

[*Looking at the handwriting—slowly to herself.*] Hmm! I knew it.

[*She opens the letter and reads it. At first her expression is one of hatred and rage, but as she goes on to the end it changes to one of triumphant malignity. She remains in deep thought for a moment, staring before her, the letter in her hands, a cruel smile on her lips. Then she puts the letter back in the pocket of the vest, and still careful not to awaken the sleeper, hangs the clothes up again on the same hook, and goes to the bedroom door and looks in.*]

[*In a loud, shrill voice.*] Alfred! [*Still louder.*] Alfred! [*There is a muffled, yawning groan from the next room.*] Don't you think it's about time you got up? Do you want to stay in bed all day? [*Turning around and coming back to her chair.*] Not that I've got any doubts about your being lazy enough to stay in bed forever. [*She sits down and looks out of the window, irritably.*] Goodness knows what time it is. We haven't even got any way of telling the time since you pawned your watch like a fool. The last valuable thing we had, and you knew it. It's been nothing but pawn, pawn, pawn, with you—anything to put off getting a job, anything to get out of going to work like a man. [*She taps the floor with her foot nervously, biting her lips.*]

[*After a short pause.*] Alfred! Get up, do you hear me? I want to make that bed before I go out. I'm sick of having this place in a continual muss on your account. [*With a certain vindictive satisfaction.*] Not that we'll be here long unless you manage to get some money some place. Heaven knows I do my part—and more—going out to sew every day while you play the gentleman and loaf around bar rooms with that good-for-nothing lot of artists from the Square.°

[*A short pause during which she plays nervously with a cup and saucer on the table.*]

And where are you going to get money, I'd like to know? The rent's due this week and you know what the landlord is. He won't let us stay a minute over our time. You say you *can't* get a job. That's a lie and you know it. You never even look for one. All you do is moon around all day writing silly poetry and stories that no one will buy—and no wonder they won't. I notice I can always get a position, such as it is; and it's only that which keeps us from starving to death.

[*Gets up and goes over to the stove—looks into the coffee pot to see if the water is boiling; then comes back and sits down again.*]

You'll have to get money to-day some place. I can't do it all, and I won't do it all. You've got to come to your senses. You've got to beg, borrow, or steal it somewheres. [*With a contemptuous laugh.*] But where, I'd like to know? You're too proud to beg, and you've borrowed the limit, and you haven't the nerve to steal.

[*After a pause—getting up angrily.*] Aren't you up yet, for heaven's sake? It's just like you to go to sleep again, or pretend to. [*She goes to the bedroom door and looks in.*] Oh, you are up. Well, it's about time. You needn't look at me like that. Your airs don't fool me a bit any more. I know you too well—better than you think I do—you and your goings-on. [*Turning away from the door—meaningly.*] I know a lot of things, my dear. Never mind what I know, now. I'll tell you before I go, you needn't worry. [*She comes to the middle of the room and stands there, frowning.*]

[*Irritably.*] Hmm! I suppose I might as well get breakfast ready—not that there's anything much to get. [*Questioningly.*] Unless you have some money? [*She pauses for an answer from the next room which does not come.*] Foolish question! [*She gives a short, hard laugh.*] I ought to know you better than that by this time. When you left here in such a huff last night I knew what would happen. You can't be trusted for a second. A nice condition you came home in! The fight we had was only an excuse for you to make a beast of yourself. What was the use pawning your watch if all you wanted with the money was to waste it in buying drink?

[*Goes over to the dish closet and takes out plates, cups, etc., while she is talking.*]

6 *Square:* Washington Square, at the center of Greenwich Village.

Hurry up! It don't take long to get breakfast these days, thanks to you. All we got this morning is bread and butter and coffee; and you wouldn't even have that if it wasn't for me sewing my fingers off. [*She slams the loaf of bread on the table with a bang.*]

The bread's stale. I hope you'll like it. *You* don't deserve any better, but I don't see why *I* should suffer.

[*Going over to the stove.*] The coffee'll be ready in a minute, and you needn't expect me to wait for you.

[*Suddenly with great anger.*] What on earth are you doing all this time? [*She goes over to the door and looks in.*] Well, you're *almost* dressed at any rate. I expected to find you back in bed. That'd be just like you. How awful you look this morning! For heaven's sake, shave! You're disgusting! You look like a tramp. No wonder no one will give you a job. I don't blame them—when you don't even look halfway decent. [*She goes to the stove.*] There's plenty of hot water right here. You've got no excuse. [*Gets a bowl and pours some of the water from the coffee pot into it.*] Here.

[*He reaches his hand into the room for it. It is a sensitive hand with slender fingers. It trembles and some of the water spills on the floor.*]

[*Tauntingly.*] Look at your hand tremble! You'd better give up drinking. You can't stand it. It's just your kind that get the D.T.'s. *That would be* the last straw! [*Looking down at the floor.*] Look at the mess you've made of this floor—cigarette butts and ashes all over the place. Why can't you put them on a plate? No, you wouldn't be considerate enough to do that. You never think of me. You don't have to sweep the room and that's all you care about.

[*Takes the broom and commences to sweep viciously, raising a cloud of dust. From the inner room comes the sound of a razor being stropped.*]°

[*Sweeping.*] Hurry up! It must be nearly time for me to go. If I'm late I'm liable to lose my position, and then I couldn't support you any longer. [*As an afterthought she adds sarcastically.*] And then you'd have to go to work or something dreadful like that. [*Sweeping under the table.*] What I want to know is whether you're going to look for a job to-day or not. You know your family won't help us any more. They've had enough of you, too. [*After a moment's silent sweeping.*] I'm about sick of all this life. I've a good notion to go home, if I wasn't too proud to let them know what a failure you've been—you, the millionaire Rowland's only son, the Harvard graduate, the poet, the catch of the town— Huh! [*With bitterness.*] There wouldn't be many of them now envy my catch if they knew the truth. What has our marriage been, I'd like to know? Even before your *millionaire* father died owing every one in the world money, you certainly never wasted any of your time on your wife. I suppose you thought I'd ought to be glad you were *honorable* enough to marry me—after getting me into trouble. You were ashamed of me with your fine friends because my father's only a grocer, that's what you were. At least he's honest, which is more than any one could say about yours. [*She is sweeping steadily toward the door. Leans on her broom for a moment.*]

You hoped every one'd think you'd been forced to marry me, and pity you, didn't you? You didn't hesitate much about telling me you loved me, and making me believe your lies, before it happened, did you? You made me think you didn't want your father to buy me off as he tried to do. I know better now. I haven't lived with you all this time

---

15 S.D. *stropped:* Alfred is using a leather strap to sharpen a straight razor, the kind barbers still use, with a very sharp steel blade that is hinged to a handle.

for nothing. [*Somberly.*] It's lucky the poor thing was born dead, after all. What a father you'd have been!

[*Is silent, brooding moodily for a moment—then she continues with a sort of savage joy.*]

But I'm not the only one who's got you to thank for being unhappy. There's one other, at least, and she can't hope to marry you now. [*She puts her head into the next room.*] How about Helen? [*She starts back from the doorway, half frightened.*]

Don't look at me that way! Yes, I read her letter. What about it? I got a right to. I'm your wife. And I know all there is to know, so don't lie. You needn't stare at me so. You can't bully me with your superior airs any longer. Only for me you'd be going without breakfast this very morning. [*She sets the broom back in the corner—whiningly.*] You never did have any gratitude for what I've done. [*She comes to the stove and puts the coffee into the pot.*] The coffee's ready. I'm not going to wait for you. [*She sits down in her chair again.*]

[*After a pause—puts her hand to her head—fretfully.*] My head aches so this morning. It's a shame I've got to go to work in a stuffy room all day in my condition. And I wouldn't if you were half a man. By rights I ought to be lying on my back instead of you. You know how sick I've been this last year; and yet you object when I take a little something to keep up my spirits. You even didn't want me to take that tonic I got at the drug store. [*With a hard laugh.*] I know you'd be glad to have me dead and out of your way; then you'd be free to run after all these silly girls that think you're such a wonderful, misunderstood person—this Helen and the others. [*There is a sharp exclamation of pain from the next room.*]

[*With satisfaction.*] There! I knew you'd cut yourself. It'll be a lesson to you. You know you oughtn't to be running around nights drinking with your nerves in such an awful shape. [*She goes to the door and looks in.*]

What makes you so pale? What are you staring at yourself in the mirror that way for? For goodness sake, wipe that blood off your face! [*With a shudder.*] It's horrible. [*In relieved tones.*] There, that's better. I never could stand the sight of blood. [*She shrinks back from the door a little.*] You better give up trying and go to a barber shop. Your hand shakes dreadfully. Why do you stare at me like that? [*She turns away from the door.*] Are you still mad at me about that letter? [*Defiantly.*] Well, I had a right to read it. I'm your wife. [*She comes to the chair and sits down again. After a pause.*]

I knew all the time you were running around with someone. Your lame excuses about spending the time at the library didn't fool me. Who is this Helen, anyway? One of those artists? Or does she write poetry, too? Her letter sounds that way. I'll bet she told you your things were the best ever, and you believed her, like a fool. Is she young and pretty? I was young and pretty, too, when you fooled me with your fine, poetic talk; but life with you would soon wear anyone down. What I've been through! [*Goes over and takes the coffee off the stove.*] Breakfast is ready. [*With a contemptuous glance.*] Breakfast! [*Pours out a cup of coffee for herself and puts the pot on the table.*] Your coffee'll be cold. What are you doing—still shaving, for heaven's sake? You'd better give it up. One of these mornings you'll give yourself a serious cut. [*She cuts off bread and butters it. During the following speeches she eats and sips her coffee.*]

I'll have to run as soon as I've finished eating. One of us has got to work. [*Angrily.*] Are you going to look for a job to-day or aren't you? I should think some of your fine friends would help you, if they really think you're so much. But I guess they just like to hear you talk. [*Sits in silence for a moment.*]

I'm sorry for this Helen, whoever she is. Haven't you got any feelings for other people? What will her family say? I see she mentions them in her letter. What is she going to do—have the child—or go to one of those doctors? That's a nice thing, I must say. Where can she get the money? Is she rich? [*She waits for some answer to this volley of questions.*]

Hmm! You won't tell me anything about her, will you? Much I care. Come to think of it, I'm not so sorry for her after all. She knew what she was doing. She isn't any school-girl, like I was, from the looks of her letter. Does she know you're married? Of course, she must. All your friends know about your unhappy marriage. I know they pity you, but they don't know my side of it. They'd talk different if they did.

[*Too busy eating to go on for a second or so.*]

This Helen must be a fine one, if she knew you were married. What does she expect, then? That I'll divorce you and let her marry you? Does she think I'm crazy enough for that—after all you've made me go through? I guess not! And you can't get a divorce from me and you know it. No one can say *I've* ever done anything wrong. [*Drinks the last of her cup of coffee.*]

She deserves to suffer, that's all I can say. I'll tell you what I think; I think your Helen is no better than a common street-walker, that's what I think. [*There is a stifled groan of pain from the next room.*]

Did you cut yourself again? Serves you right. [*Gets up and takes off her apron.*] Well, I've got to run along. [*Peevishly.*] This is a fine life for me to be leading! I won't stand for your loafing any longer. [*Something catches her ear and she pauses and listens intently.*] There! You've overturned the water all over everything. Don't say you haven't. I can hear it dripping on the floor. [*A vague expression of fear comes over her face.*] Alfred! Why don't you answer me?

[*She moves slowly toward the room. There is the noise of a chair being overturned and something crashes heavily to the floor. She stands, trembling with fright.*]

Alfred! Alfred! Answer me! What is it you knocked over? Are you still drunk? [*Unable to stand the tension a second longer she rushes to the door of the bedroom.*] Alfred!

[*She stands in the doorway looking down at the floor of the inner room, transfixed with horror. Then she shrieks wildly and runs to the other door, unlocks it and frenziedly pulls it open, and runs shrieking madly into the outer hallway.*]

[*The curtain falls.*]

QUESTIONS

1. What does the setting tell you about the Rowlands?
2. How is Mrs. Rowland described in the opening stage directions? How does O'Neill use adjectives to shape your initial response to her? How does the rest of the play sustain or alter this image?
3. How does Mrs. Rowland speak to Alfred? What does she complain about? What does she accuse Alfred of being and doing?
4. What happened during Mrs. Rowland's premarital affair with Alfred? Why didn't she let Alfred's father "buy her off"?

5. Where is the play's crisis? Which character comes to a crisis? What leads you to conclude that the character and play have reached a crisis?

6. Mrs. Rowland precipitates the climax by discussing Alfred's affair. What do we learn about Helen? What pushes Alfred over the edge?

GENERAL QUESTIONS

1. How does the setting define the characters, their relationship, and their life? What details of setting are most significant?

2. Is Mrs. Rowland flat or round? Static or dynamic? Individualized or stereotyped? Why does she have no first name?

3. Why is Alfred Rowland kept off stage (except for his hand) and given no dialogue? How does this affect the play?

4. Alfred is presented from his wife's point of view. How accurate is this portrait? To what degree does Alfred justify his wife's accusations?

5. Why does O'Neill present the history of Alfred's family and his relationship with Mrs. Rowland out of chronological order? What is the effect of this method of presentation?

WRITING ABOUT THE ELEMENTS OF DRAMA

Although some aspects of drama, such as lighting and stage movement, are purely theatrical, drama shares a number of elements with fiction and poetry. The planning and the writing processes for essays about drama are therefore similar to those used for essays on the other genres. As you plan, select a play and an appropriate element or series of elements. It would be inappropriate, for example, to attempt an essay about character development in *Tea Party* (pp. 1266–69) because this play is too short to probe the two characters deeply.

Once you select the play, choose a focus, which will be your central idea. For example, you might argue that a character is flat, static, nonrealistic, or symbolic of good or evil. Or, to assert relationships among elements, you might claim that a play's meaning is shaped and emphasized through setting or through conflict.

Topics for Discovering Ideas

PLOT, ACTION, CONFLICT.   (See also Chapter 3.) In planning an essay on plot or structure, demonstrate how actions and conflicts unfold. In addition, link this concern to other dramatic elements, such as tone or theme. In general, this topic breaks down into three areas—conflict, plot, and structure. For conflict, determine what the conflicts are, which one is central, and how it is resolved. What kind of conflict is it? Does it suggest any general behavioral patterns? For plot, determine the separate stages of development. What is the climax? The dénouement? How are they anticipated or foreshadowed? In examining plot structures and patterns, determine whether the play has a sub-plot or second plot. If so, how is it related to the main plot? Is a significant pattern of action repeated? If so, what is the effect? To what extent do these parallel or repetitive patterns influence theme and meaning? How do they control your responses?

CHARACTERS. (See also Chapter 4.) Focus on a significant figure and formulate a central idea about his or her personality, function, or meaning. Is the character round or flat? Static or dynamic? Individualized or stereotyped? Realistic or nonrealistic? Symbolic? How is the character described in the stage directions? By other characters? By himself or herself? What does he or she do, think, say? What is the character's attitude toward the environment? The action? Other characters? Himself or herself? To what extent does he or she articulate and/or embody key ideas in the play?

POINT OF VIEW AND PERSPECTIVE. (See also Chapter 5.) In many plays, such as *Hamlet* (Chapter 27), *Before Breakfast,* and *The Glass Menagerie* (Chapter 29), the playwright presents the action from the perspective of an individual character. The audience therefore sees things as this character sees the same things, influences them, and is influenced by them. When you deal with such a technique, consider how the perspective affects the play's structure and meaning. Why is this point of view useful or striking? What does it suggest about character? Theme? To what extent does your reaction to the play correspond with or diverge from this perspective?

Another feature of perspective is that characters may speak directly to the audience, in a *soliloquy,* or indirectly, in *a monologue.* In dealing with these perspectives, consider whether you sympathize with the character doing the speaking. What information does the character convey? What is he or she trying to prove? What is the tone of the speech? What do these devices contribute to your response? Generally, what does the perspective contribute to your understanding of the play?

SETTING, SETS, AND PROPS. (See also Chapter 6.) Normally, you will not write about setting and properties in isolation; such an essay would simply produce a detailed description of the setting(s) and objects. Instead, a discussion of setting in drama should be linked to another element, such as character, mood, or meaning. Such an essay can demonstrate the ways in which setting(s) and objects help establish the time, place, characters, lifestyle, values, or ideas.

When dealing with a single setting, pay close attention to the opening stage directions and any other directions or dialogue that describe the environment or objects. In plays with multiple settings, you will normally select one or two for examination. Ask yourself whether the setting is realistic or nonrealistic and to what extent it may be symbolic. What details and objects are specified? What do these tell you about the time, the place, and the characters and their way of life and values? To what extent does the setting contribute to the play's tone, atmosphere, impact, and meaning?

DICTION, IMAGERY, AND STYLE. (See also Chapters 7 and 15.) As with setting, try to connect the devices of language to some other element such as tone, character, or meaning. Investigate the play's levels of diction and types of dialect, jargon, slang, or clichés. To what extent do these techniques define the characters and support or undercut their ideas? What connotative words or phrases are repeated? Which are spoken at particularly significant moments? What striking or consistent threads of imagery, metaphor, tone, or meaning do you find? How do all these aspects of language shape your reaction?

TONE AND ATMOSPHERE. (See also Chapters 8 and 18.) Try to deal with *how* the tone is established and *what* impact it has on the play's meaning. Seek those devices the playwright employs to control your attitudes toward individual characters, situations, and outcomes. Look for clues in stage directions, diction, imagery, rhetorical devices, tempo, and context. Is tone articulated directly? Or indirectly, through irony? Also try to establish the presence of dramatic irony: To what extent do you (as a reader or spectator) know more than many of the onstage characters?

SYMBOLISM AND ALLEGORY. (See also Chapters 9 and 21.) Try to determine the characters, objects, settings, situations, actions, words or phrases, and/or costumes that seem to be symbolic. What do they symbolize, and how do you know that they are symbolic? Are they universal or contextual? Is the symbolism extensive and consistent enough to form an allegorical system? If so, what are the two levels of meaning addressed by the allegory? To what extent does the symbolism or allegory shape the play's meaning and your responses to it?

THEME. (See also Chapters 10 and 23.) The questions and areas of concern listed above should help you in discussing theme. Try to connect theme with various other aspects of the play such as character, conflict, action, setting, language, or symbolism. What key ideas does the play explore, and what aspects of the play convey these ideas most emphatically? In dealing with each topic and question, isolate the elements and devices that have the strongest impact on meaning.

REFERRING TO PLAYS AND PARTS OF PLAYS

<u>Underline</u> (or *italicize*) the titles of plays as you would a book title. In referring to speeches, assume that your reader may have a text different from yours. Therefore provide the information necessary for finding the exact location, regardless of text.

In the body of the essay, for a play with act, scene, and line or speech numbers, refer to *Act* (roman numeral), *scene* (Arabic numeral), and *line* or *speech* number (Arabic numeral). For clarity, spell out these words: *Hamlet accuses his mother of offenses against his father in Act III, scene 4, line 9* or *Claudius defends his own status as king in Act IV, scene 5, lines 120–23.*

In direct quotations, however, including block quotations (set apart from your own writing), write the numbers in parentheses following the quotation: (*III.1.33*) or (*III.1, speech 4*). When no word precedes the last number, it is understood to refer to a line; for clarity, it is best to spell out that you are referring to a speech number.

When a play is divided into acts but not scenes, or if the play contains only one act, spell out the details completely. Thus, in a play like *Death of a Salesman,* which contains two acts and an epilogue, you may refer to *Act I, speech 348* or *Epilogue, speech 5,* both in your text and in block quotations. If the play contains only numbered scenes, like *The Glass Menagerie,* spell things out similarly: *scene I, speech 29.* When referring to a one-act play like *The More the Merrier,* use the speech or line number: *speech 265.*

For stage directions, use the line or speech number immediately preceding the direction, and abbreviate *stage direction* as *S.D.: scene 1, speech 16 S.D.* Your reader will then know that you are referring to the stage direction following speech 16 in scene 1. If there are stage directions at the opening of the play before the speeches begin (as in *The Glass Menagerie* and *Before Breakfast*), use a zero and then a decimal point followed by an Arabic numeral to refer to the paragraph of directions. Thus *0.3 S.D.* refers to the third paragraph of directions at the play's beginning.

For prefaces, scene directions, and casts of characters, such as the "Production Notes" of *The Glass Menagerie,* use the title and then the paragraph number: *In the "Production Notes," Williams describes* The Glass Menagerie *as a "memory play" (paragraph 1).*

For scene directions at the beginning of acts or scenes, the most specific style spells out the circumstances: *The scene directions for Act III of Ibsen's* An Enemy of the People *describe the shabby editorial offices of the* People's Messenger.

For the cast of characters, the same principle applies. Spell out what you mean, such as *the cast of characters, the Characters list,* or *the Dramatis Personae.* The important thing about referring to parts of plays is that you be clear and exact. The guidance offered here will cover most situations, but complications and exceptions will occur. When they do, always ask your instructor for help.

Strategies for Organizing Ideas

For an essay on drama, you might choose from a number of strategies. If you are writing about loneliness and frustration in Keller's *Tea Party,* for example, you might select a number of objects or occurrences as the launching point for your discussion. Some of these might be the tea trolley and the sofa, the bringing in of the cocoa, or the paperboy's rapid movement past the window. In discussing the crimes of Claudius in Shakespeare's Hamlet, you might choose (1) the testimony of the Ghost to *Hamlet,* (2) Claudius's reaction to the players' scene, (3) his speech as he is praying, and (4) his poisoning of the cup, showing how these actions convincingly establish his villainy. For such essays, you might devote separate paragraphs to each element, or you might use two or more paragraphs for each element as you develop your ideas further.

Similar strategies can be found for every possible type of essay on drama. In dealing with character in Glaspell's *Trifles,* for example, you might claim that a number of symbolic props help to establish and reinforce the character of Minnie Wright or the ideas about marriage conveyed in the play. You might then use separate paragraphs to discuss these related symbols, such as Minnie's clothes, her dead canary, and her unfinished quilt. Similarly, in writing about language in plays like Chekhov's *The Bear,* (Chapter 28), you would establish how the particular play connects qualities of speech to revelations about topics such as character and idea. Thus, Smirnov's constant use of exclamations, shouts, and profanity, at least until shortly before the play's end, establish his irascibility.

DEMONSTRATIVE STUDENT ESSAY

The Symbolism of the Quilting Knot in Susan Glaspell's *Trifles*°

[1]

In Glaspell's *Trifles,* the quilting knot that women use in making quilts is an important symbol. We learn that the central (but unseen) character Minnie Wright was apparently intending to knot her quilt, and it is fair to conclude that she tied and tightened such a knot in the rope she put around the neck of her husband, John, in order to strangle him in his sleep. This use of knots is stressed so much, and the many speeches about knots are so significant (there are at least twelve references to knots, and the last words in the play are about knots), that the quilting knot is not to be considered just a trifle but rather must have special meaning. In fact, the knot may be taken as Glaspell's major contextual symbol of women's lives.* This symbol governs the play's vision of feminine skill, the work roles of women, female bonding, and male trivialization of women and women's work.†

° See p. 1244 for this play.
* Central idea.
† Thesis sentence.

[2]

The first symbolic meaning of the knot is female skill. As a practical matter, making a slip-proof quilting knot requires skill and force, because it is the way of keeping quilts from being lumpy. Such skill is typical in a number of other symbolic female services mentioned in *Trifles,* such as keeping a towel clean (speech 31), putting up home-canned preserves (speech 27), making bread (speech 52), and storing pots and pans (speech 31). All these concerns, common and trifling as they are, are essential to life, for without someone to do them, other work would stop. In addition, it is true that the knot in the rope strangling John Wright requires the same skill and strength that Minnie ordinarily has devoted to domestic work. For either positive or negative actions, then, the knot symbolizes female ability and power.

[3]

Some of the qualities of traditional female labor are also symbolized by the quilting knot. As the means by which women put quilts together, and therefore a means of creating warmth and rest, the knot symbolizes the nurturing and comforting nature of women's work. While such work is vital to home life, however, it is all done mostly in interiors, by women alone. This detail about the symbol suggests that women--at least farm women like Minnie--are doomed to isolation by their work. Specifically, Minnie is cut off from all outside sources of support and strength, and she has no way to correct the wrongs she has endured from her uncaring and cruel husband. The symbolism thus suggests that the traditional female role, ironically, also makes women vulnerable.

[4]

The most important value for the knot as a contextual symbol is that it is forms a bond between the women onstage and Minnie Wright offstage. Henderson, the county attorney, correctly notes that Mrs. Hale and Mrs. Peters are "loyal to . . . [their] sex" (speech 35). Mrs. Hale, seeing the circumstances of Minnie's life, sympathetically claims "I know how things can be--for women" (speech 136), and, by the end of the play, Mrs. Peters agrees with her. In both a visual and symbolic way, therefore, the knot connects two strands of the same loop--suggesting that women (in general) are together, united within a protective circle. This symbolic unity goes so far that Mrs. Hale and Mrs. Peters conceal Minnie's crime because they sympathize so deeply with her. The symbolic bond represented by the knot may go beyond the play itself to suggest the common lot of all women.

[5]

Just as the knot symbolizes female bonding, it symbolizes for men the trivial nature of women's lives. When Peters and Henderson learn about the women's concern for the knotting of Minnie's quilt, they laugh because they consider it trifling, and they continue to laugh even at the end of the play (speeches 73, 115, 148). By thus flaunting their ignorance, they show their low regard of women. Their responses reveal their smug belief that women exist only to cater to men (speech 31).

[6]

The knot as a major contextual symbol thus has important implications. The first is that it emphasizes the irony of male-female relationships. Believing themselves supreme, the men of the play are not equipped to learn Minnie Wright's motive for murder. They fail because they cannot understand the "trifles" so important to women. Thus the knot as a symbol suggests the limitations of the men, just as it points out the skill and sensitivity of the women. The second major implication of the knot as a symbol is Glaspell's point that there is a more important law than the law itself, particularly as long as the legal profession is run by males. Even if Mrs. Peters is "married to the law" (speeches 143-145), and even if she recognizes that "the law is the law" (speech 69), the knot as a symbol suggests that the law is wrong when it aims to punish a woman for rejecting a life of repression.

[7]   Just as Minnie Wright says no, both violently and cleverly, by using one of her major skills to wipe out the husband who had misused her, the two onstage women become accomplices after the fact because they understand Minnie's feelings so completely. Certainly their lot in life is not as severe as Minnie's. But through the symbolism of the kitchen artifacts, especially the knot so much mocked by the men, they recognize that with just a bit of ill luck, Minnie's condition might easily have been theirs. Symbolically, then, the major importance of the knot is that it leads to the conclusions that more status and recognition are needed by women and that more understanding is needed by men.

Commentary on the Essay

This essay is based entirely on conclusions drawn from the speeches and actions of the play. Because the play is dramatic, the central idea—that the apparently trifling quilting knot is a major contextual symbol—might be open to the counter-claim that nowhere in the play is the knot so described. To avoid this claim, the writer of the essay about the knot's symbolism is obligated to support conclusions by stressing the evidence that the play itself presents.

Paragraph 1 thus establishes that the stress on the use of knots in the play, together with the many speeches about knots, justifies treating the knot as a symbol. The logic is this: the knot is so important, and is emphasized so much, that it is virtually impossible to ignore its symbolic meaning. In this way the central idea, which is the basis of this feminist critique of *Trifles*, is made reasonable as the basis for the essay. This reasonableness is underscored by the thesis sentence, which indicates the major aspects of the symbolism to be explored in the body.

In the body, paragraphs 2 and 3 consider the meaning of the symbol as it pertains to female strength and the quality of "female labor." Paragraph 2, by connecting the quilting knot to the knot used in the murder of the farm husband, shows the extent to which female strength is symbolized. Paragraph 3 highlights the irony brought out by the symbol, for the nurturing role of women like Minnie also makes them subject to victimization. Paragraph 4 is a climax in this line of thought, for it suggests that the female understanding of Minnie's life and circumstances leads to the symbolic bonding felt by the two women onstage, and therefore also to their covering up of Minnie's crime.

Paragraph 5 moves in a related direction, emphasizing how the knot symbolically exposes the inability of the men to understand the lives of women. This idea leads to the two concluding paragraphs, 6 and 7. Paragraph 6 stresses the gaps between men and women, underscoring the irony of the relationship.

In keeping with the idea of paragraph 6, paragraph 7 concludes on the note that the symbolism can be interpreted constructively to point out need for improvement.

SPECIAL TOPICS FOR WRITING AND ARGUMENT ABOUT THE ELEMENTS OF DRAMA

1. *Tea Party* might be considered sentimental, on the grounds that the two elderly characters are presented to evoke sympathy and anguish, not to resemble the life of real persons. Write an essay defending the play against this judgment, being sure to make references to Keller's characterizations and her development of character.

2. Compare Kauffmann's *The More the Merrier* and Colwin's "An Old Fashioned Story" (Chapter 2). To what common social level do the characters belong? How do they apparently function within this level? What common concerns about personal life do you discover in the two sets of characters? What common patterns do the play and the story reveal about the previous lives and concerns of the characters? (For a method of treating comparison and contrast, see Chapter 35.)

3. *Before Breakfast* is set in an apartment in Greenwich Village in lower Manhattan around 1916. It was performed in Greenwich Village in December 1916. Write an essay that deals with the following questions:

   a. What do you make of this convergence of settings—artistic and realistic?

   b. What did O'Neill assume about his original audience's reaction to the setting?

4. Write an essay that considers the following questions. Is Glaspell's *Trifles* about crime? Rural life? Marriage? The roles of rural and frontier women? The way men regard women? The way in which anger that is bottled up must eventually explode? Write an essay detailing your response, using specific details from the play to support your argument. To what degree is the situation in the play realistic? If it were to be presented as a play about a similar murder in the 1980s and 1990s (there have been a number of them), what freedom would the women have to explore the kitchen?

5. Read the story "A Jury of Her Peers" (Chapter 4). Glaspell wrote this story a year after *Trifles*. Write an essay comparing and contrasting (see Chapter 35) the story and the play. You might wish to concentrate, for example, on the openings of the two works, the descriptions of the women's reactions, and the quantity of detail used in the play and in the story. On the basis of your essay, contrast the characteristics of drama and of fiction.

6. Write an essay on one of the following topics. Before you begin writing, consult Chapter 33 for a description of how to proceed.

   a. The viewpoint of the men in *Trifles*.

   b. A feminist analysis of Mrs. Rowland in *Before Breakfast*.

c. A close formal (new critical) analysis of the dialogue (speeches 160–194) between Emily and Simon in *The More the Merrier.*

d. The two sisters as archetypal old people in *Tea Party.*

7. On the basis of the plays included in this chapter, write an essay dealing with the characteristics of the dramatic form. Consider topics such as dialogue, monologue, soliloquy, action, vocal ranges, staging, comparative lengths of plays, pauses in speech, stage directions, laughter, seriousness, and the means by which the dramatists engage the audience in characters and situations.

8. Using the catalogue in your library, look up the category "Drama—Criticism" or "Drama—History and Criticism," whichever title your library uses. You will find there a number of categories, such as the relationship of drama to (a) elements, (b) history, (c) origin, (d) philosophy, (e) production, (f) religion, (g) stagecraft, and (h) themes. Develop a short bibliography on one of these topics and take out two or three of the relevant books. Describe them briefly, and explain—and criticize if possible—the principal ideas in one of the chapters.

27

The Tragic Vision:
Affirmation Through Loss

Tragedy is drama in which a major character undergoes a loss but also achieves illumination or a new perspective. It is considered the most elevated literary form because it concentrates affirmatively on the religious and cosmic implications of its major character's misfortunes. In ancient Greece, it originated as a key element in Athenian religious festivals during the decades before Athens became a major military, economic, and cultural power during the fifth century B.C.E.

Tragedy, however, was not religious in a sectarian sense. It did not dramatize religious doctrines and did not present a consistent religious view. To the Athenians, religion connected the past with the present and with the gods, and through this connection it served to enrich individuals, society, and the state.

Originally, tragedy in Athens was associated with the worship of a specific god—Dionysus, one of the twelve principal Athenian deities who, it was thought, transformed human personality and freed people from care and grief. To elevate this god in the eyes of his fellow Athenians, the Athenian tyrant Peisistratus (ruled 560–527 B.C.E.) added the worship of Dionysus to the regular religious festivals that the Athenians held for their gods.[1]

[1] Ancient religion is difficult for us to understand because of our completely different religious traditions and the passage of 2,500 years of history. In its origins, Greek religion was local in nature—a by-product of the comparative isolation of the various Greek city-states. Collective public worship of a centralized god within centrally located religious buildings—like the churches, temples, and mosques we know today—did not then exist. Instead, the Greeks believed in many gods with varying powers and interests who could travel invisibly and at will from place to place within their dominions. Consequently the Greeks erected many separate local shrines and sanctuaries, which were considered holy to particular gods and where people might place offerings and say prayers. Large temples built in important city-states like Athens and Corinth were dedicated to gods, such as Zeus, Athena, and Apollo, that important citizens especially revered. Even then, the temples were not designed for mass worship, but rather were considered resident sanctuaries for the gods themselves. Therefore, the major space in the temples was a holy-of-holies reserved only for the god. To make public this essentially private worship, the Greek city-states held religious festivals such as the Athenian celebrations of Dionysus and Athena. In short, the gods who became prominent and who were widely worshiped in ancient Greece achieved their status because of the political power of their principal worshipers.

THE ORIGIN OF TRAGEDY

Tragedy Is the Earliest of Our Dramatic Forms

From the standpoint of drama, the most significant of these Dionysiac festivals were the Lenaia and the Great or City Dionysia. The **Lenaia** was a short celebration held in January (the Greek month *Gamelion*), and the **City Dionysia** was a week-long event in March-April (*Elaphebolion*, the month of stags). In the sixth century B.C.E., ceremonies held during the festival of the City Dionysia began to include tragedy, although not in the form that has been transmitted to us. The philosopher and critic Aristotle (384–322 B.C.E.), writing almost two hundred years after the form appeared, claimed that the first tragedies developed from a choral ode called a **dithyramb**—an ode or song that was sung or chanted and also danced by large choruses at the festivals.[2] According to Aristotle, the first tragedies were choral improvisations originating with "the authors of the Dithyramb" (*Poetics* IV.12, p. 19).

The Subject Matter of Tragedy Was Drawn from Tales of Prehistoric Times

From Aristotle's claim, we can conclude that tragedy soon took on the characteristics and conventions that elevated it. For subject matter, writers turned to well-known myths about the heroes and demigods of the prehistoric period between the vanished age of bronze and the living age of iron. These myths described individual adventures and achievements, including epic explorations and battles that had taken place principally during the time of the Trojan War. Like the stories in the Bible, the Greek myths illustrated divine-human relationships and also served as examples or models of heroic behavior. With very few exceptions, these myths became the fixed tragic subject matter. Indeed, Aristotle called them the "received legends" that by his time had become the "usual subjects of tragedy" (*Poetics* IX.8, p. 37).

The mythical heroes—many of whom were objects of cult worship—were kings, queens, princes, and princesses. They engaged in conflicts; they suffered; and, often, they died. Though great, they were nevertheless human, and a common critical judgment is that they were dominated by **hubris** or **hybris** (arrogant pride, insolence, contemptuous violence), which was manifested in

---

[2] S. H. Butcher, *Aristotle's Theory of Poetry and Fine Art*, 4th ed. (New York: Dover, 1951), p. 19 (VI.12). All parenthetical references to Aristotle are from this edition. The origin of the word *dithyramb* is obscure. Some ancient etymologists claimed that the word was derived from the legendary "double birth" of Dionysus. This derivation is based on the idea that dithyramb is a compound (*dis*, "two," and *thyra*, "door") referring to the myth that Zeus removed Dionysus from the womb of his mother, Semele, and then placed the fetus within his thigh. When Zeus removed Dionysus, the god had "come through the door" of birth twice. This derivation, however, has been disputed. For a description of the origin of comedy during the festivals for Dionysus, see Chapter 28.

destructive actions such as deceit, subterfuge, lying, betrayal, revenge, murder, suicide, patricide, infanticide, and self-mutilation. By truthfully demonstrating the faults of these heroes along with their greatness, the writers of tragedy also invoked philosophical and religious issues that provide meaning and value in the face of misfortune and suffering.

The Word Tragedy Underwent an Elevation in Meaning

One of the puzzles of tragedy is the word itself, which combines the Greek words *tragos* ("goat") and *oide* ("ode" or "song")—a "goat ode" or "goat song." This meaning raises the question of how so unlikely a word is linked to the tragic form. One oft-repeated answer is that the word was first applied to choral ceremonials performed at the ritual sacrifice of a goat. Another is that the word described a choral competition in which a goat was the prize.

A more persuasive recent answer is that the word *tragedy* stemmed from the word *tragoidoi*, or "billy goat singers," which was applied pejoratively to the young men (*ephebes*) in the choruses.[3] The ephebes were military trainees between the ages of eighteen and twenty. Those trainees who were best at close-order drill were selected as choral members because the dramatic choruses required precision movements. Because they were young, however, they were still likened to goats.[4] Indeed, at first tragedy was apparently not called *tragodia* (tragedy) at all, but rather *tragoidoi*, as though the chorus members were more important than the words they spoke. This explanation is consistent with the improvisatory origins of tragedy that Aristotle describes. In the decades following its beginnings, the genre grew in importance, quality, and stature, and its name underwent the accompanying elevation that it still possesses.

Tragedy Evolved from a Choral Form to a Dramatic Form

Because the surviving Athenian plays are dominated by acting parts, modern readers sometimes conclude that the chorus parts annoyingly interrupt the main action. It may be surprising to recognize that in the beginning there were no individual actors at all, only choruses. The introduction of actors—and their eventual domination—was one of the improvisations that

[3] For this argument, see John J. Winkler, "The Ephebes' Song: *Tragodia* and *Polis*," in John J. Winkler and Froma I. Zeitlin, eds., *Nothing to Do with Dionysos? Athenian Drama in Its Social Context* (Princeton: Princeton UP, 1990), pp. 20–62. For a discussion of the military nature of the ancient Greek city-state, see Paul Rahe, "The Martial Republics of Classical Greece," *The Wilson Quarterly*, vol. 17, no. 1 (Winter 1993): 58–70.

[4] There is nothing unusual about this comparison. In modern English, for example, a common slang word for a child is *kid*, which is the standard word for a young goat and also other young animals.

Aristotle associates with the evolution of tragedy. We can surmise that during a festival performance of an unknown choral ode, the chorus leader stepped forward to deliver lines introducing and linking the choral speeches. Because of this special function, the new speaker—called a *hypocrites* (hip-POCK-rih-tayss), which became the word for actor—was soon separated and distinguished from the chorus.

The next essential step was *impersonation,* or the assuming of a role. The *hypocrites* would represent a hero, and the chorus would represent groups such as townspeople, worshipers, youths, or elders. With the commencement of such role-playing, genuine drama had begun. According to tradition, the first *hypocrites* or actor—and therefore the acknowledged founder of the acting profession—was the writer and choral leader Thespis, in about 536–533 B.C.E., during the time of Peisistratus.

THE ORIGIN OF TRAGEDY IN BRIEF

In Athens during the sixth century B.C.E., tragedy originated during the City Dionysia, one of the major Athenian religious festivals held to celebrate Dionysus, a liberating god and one of the twelve major gods. As a genre, tragedy first featured improvisations upon a type of choral ode called a *dithyramb.* It then evolved, as Aristotle says, "by slow degrees" (*Poetics,* IV.12, p. 19), developing new elements as they seemed appropriate and necessary.

One of the vital new elements was an emphasis on the death or misfortune of a major character.* This emphasis resulted *not* from a preconceived theoretical design, however, but rather from the reality of suffering in the lives of the heroic subjects. As writers of tragedy developed the cosmic and religious implications of such adversity, performances in effect offered philosophic, religious, moral, and civic benefits, and therefore the simple attendance at a tragedy came to be regarded as a religious experience.

Because tragedy was originally linked to the choral dithyrambs, it is important to stress that *tragedy, and therefore drama, began as a form for choruses, not for actors.* Even after actors became dominant in the plays, the chorus was important enough for Aristotle to state that "the chorus should be regarded as one of the actors" (XVIII.7, p. 69).

---

* Although the tragic protagonist often dies at the play's end, the extant Athenian tragedies do not follow this pattern rigidly. It is true that the major figures suffer, and sometimes they die, but often they escape punishment entirely, and they may even receive divine pardon.

THE ANCIENT COMPETITIONS IN TRAGEDY

Once Thespis set the pattern of action involving actor and chorus, the writing of tragedies as a competition within the Dionysiac festivals became institutionalized.

The Tragic Dramatists Competed for the Honor of Having Their Plays Performed

Early each summer, a number of dramatists vied for the honor of having their plays performed at the next City Dionysia, to be held the following spring. They prepared three tragedies (a **trilogy**)[5] together with a **satyr** play (a boisterous burlesque) and submitted the four works to the Eponymous Archon, one of the city's two principal magistrates and the man for whom the year was named. The three best submissions were approved, or "given a chorus," for performance at the festival. On the last day of the festival, after the performances were over, the archon awarded a prize to the tragic playwright voted best for that year; there was also a prize for the best writer of a comedy. The winner's prize was not money, but rather a crown of ivy and the glory of triumph.

The Three Greatest Athenian Tragic Playwrights Were Aeschylus, Sophocles, and Euripides

To gain the honor of victory during the centuries of the competitions, many playwrights wrote many hundreds, probably thousands, of plays. Most of these have long since vanished because the writers were insignificant and also because there were no more than a few copies of each play, all handwritten on perishable papyrus scrolls.

A small number of works by three tragic playwrights, however, have survived. These dramatists are **Aeschylus** (525–456 B.C.E.), who added a second actor; **Sophocles** (ca. 496–406/5 B.C.E.), who added a third actor, created scene design, and enlarged the chorus from twelve to fifteen; and **Euripides** (ca. 484–406 B.C.E.). Although these three playwrights did not win prizes every time they entered the competitions, a consensus grew that they were the best, and by the middle of the fourth century B.C.E., their works were recognized as classics. Although tragedies had originally been intended for only one performance—at the festival for which they competed—an exception was made for these three dramatists, whose tragedies were then performed repeatedly both in Athens and elsewhere in the Greek-speaking world.

The combined output of the three classic playwrights was slightly more than three hundred plays, of which three-fourths were tragedies and one-fourth were satyr plays. As many as eight hundred years after the end of the fifth century B.C.E., these plays, together with many other Greek tragedies, satyr plays, and comedies, were available to readers who could afford to buy copies

---

[5] In the earliest dramas, the trilogies shared a common subject, as may be seen in the *Oresteia* of Aeschylus, which is a cycle of three plays on the subject of the royal house of Agamemnon. But by the time of Sophocles and Euripides, connected trilogies were no longer required. Sophocles' *Oedipus the King* and *Oedipus at Colonus*, for example, were submitted at widely different times.

or commission scribes to copy them.[6] However, with the increasing dominance of Christianity, the plays fell into neglect because they were considered pagan and also because vellum or parchment, which made up the pages of the books (*codices*) that replaced papyrus scrolls, was enormously expensive and was reserved for Christian works. Most of the unique and priceless copies of Athenian plays were subsequently destroyed or thrown away.

Thirty-Three Tragedies by the Three Great Athenian Tragedians Have Survived to the Present Day

The Greek dramatic tradition might have vanished entirely had it not been for the efforts of Byzantine scholars during the ninth century, when Constantinople became the center of a revival of interest in classical Greek language and literature. A primary characteristic of this revival was the copying and preservation of important texts—including those of the major Greek writers. We may conclude that the scholars copied as many of the plays as they could locate, and that they tried to shelter their copies in the security of monastery libraries.

However, security was impossible to maintain during those years. Fire, neglect, time, political destabilization, and pillage (such as the sack of Constantinople by Crusaders in 1204) took an enormous toll on the Byzantine manuscript collections. Even so, seven tragedies by Aeschylus, seven by Sophocles, and ten by Euripides somehow were saved from destruction.[7] Additionally, in the fourteenth century, a scholar named Demetrius Triclinius made a lucky find of scrolls containing nine more plays by Euripides (part of what was once a complete set), bringing the total of Euripidean plays to nineteen. Therefore, of all the hundreds and thousands of plays written by all the Greek tragic playwrights, thirty-three still survive intact. These plays make up the complete Greek tragedies as we know them.[8]

---

[6] In the third century B.C.E., a complete and definitive hand-copied set of Greek plays was apparently deposited in the Egyptian Royal Library that formed a part of the Ptolemaic museum and palace of Alexandria, but at some point all the holdings were lost, thrown away, or destroyed, just as the palace and museum were destroyed. In modern Alexandria, not even the location of the ancient library is exactly known. See Luciano Canfora, *The Vanished Library: A Wonder of the Ancient World* (Berkeley: U of California P, 1990).

[7] Many standard reference works contain the assertion that these twenty-four plays were selected by an unnamed Byzantine schoolmaster for use in the Byzantine schools and that this anthology was widely adopted and exclusively used thereafter. This claim would explain why the anthologized plays were preserved while unanthologized plays were lost. L. D. Reynolds and N. G. Wilson, in their authoritative *Scribes and Scholars: A Guide to the Transmission of Greek and Latin Literature*, 3rd ed. (Oxford UP, 1991), question this hypothesis. They point out that there is no historical record that such an anthology was ever made, that modern scholars are in truth ignorant "of the origin of the selection," and that therefore "it is perhaps best to abandon the idea that a conscious act of selection by an individual was a primary factor in determining the survival of texts" (p. 54).

[8] The survival of Greek drama was under constant threat until the first printed editions were published at the beginning of the sixteenth century.

There is, however, just a little more: Many ancient writers often quoted brief passages from plays that were not otherwise preserved, and these portions therefore still exist. Moreover, collectors living in ancient Egypt owned many copies of the plays, and not everything from these collections was lost. In recent centuries, papyrus and vellum fragments—some quite extensive—have been recovered by archaeologists from such unlikely locations as ancient Egyptian rubbish heaps, tombs, and the linings of coffins.

ARISTOTLE AND THE NATURE OF TRAGEDY

Because Aristotle's *Poetics* (*Peri Poietikes*), the first section of his major critical work, survives intact from antiquity, he is in effect the Western world's first critic and aesthetician. From him, later critics derived the various "rules" of tragic composition. He also wrote a second part of the *Poetics* concerning comedy. This second work is lost, but enough fragments and summaries survive to permit a partial hypothetical reconstruction.[9] Aristotle also considered aspects of literature in parts of other philosophical works, principally the *Ethics* and the *Politics*. In addition he, along with his students, assembled a complete catalogue of Greek tragedy from its beginnings to his own time (the *Didaskaliae*). He was therefore able to base his criticism on virtually the entire body of Greek tragedy, including written copies of many plays that he had probably never seen performed. No one before or since has had more firsthand knowledge of Greek tragedy. His criticism is therefore especially valuable because it rests not only on his acute powers of observation, but also on his unique and encyclopedic knowledge.

As we have seen, Aristotle states that tragedy grew out of improvisations related to dithyrambic choral odes. He adds that once tragedy reached its "natural" or ideal form it stopped evolving (*Poetics* IV.12, p. 1). His criticism is designed to explain the ideal characteristics: Throughout the *Poetics* he stresses concepts of exactitude, proportion, appropriateness, and control. His famous definition of tragedy is in accord with these concepts. In the sixth chapter of the *Poetics*, he states that tragedy is "an imitation of an action that is serious, complete, and of a certain magnitude; in language embellished with each kind of artistic ornament, the several kinds being found in separate parts of the play; in the form of action, not of narrative; through pity and fear effecting the proper purgation of these emotions" (VI.2, p. 23).

---

[9] See Richard Janko, trans., *Aristotle, Poetics I with the Tractatus Coislinianus, A Hypothetical Reconstruction of Poetics II, the Fragments of the On Poets* (Indianapolis: Hackett, 1987), pp. 47–55.

To Aristotle, the Key to Tragedy Is the Concept of Catharsis

The last part of this definition—that purgation or **catharsis** is the end or goal of tragedy—crystallizes the earlier parts. In Aristotle's view, tragedy arouses the disturbing emotions of pity and fear (*eleos* and *phobos*), and, through the experience of the drama, brings about a "proper purgation" or purification of these emotions. Originally, the word *catharsis* was a medical term, and therefore many interpreters argue that tragedy produces a therapeutic effect through an actual purging or "vomiting" of emotions—a sympathetic release of feelings that produces emotional relief and encourages psychological health. In other words, tragedy heals.

A complementary view is that tragic catharsis has a larger public and moral purpose. In this sense, Aristotle's description of tragedy is an implicit argument defending literature itself against the strong disapproval of his teacher, Plato.[10] Both master and pupil accepted the premise that human beings behave thoughtlessly and stupidly as a result of uncontrolled emotion. While in the grip of deep feelings, people cannot be virtuous and can do no good for others because they make bad decisions that produce bad personal, social, political, military, and moral results. Consequently, if individual temperance and public justice are to prevail, there is a universal need to moderate and regulate the emotions. Because Plato states that the emotionalism of literature is untrue, undignified, and also unreasonable, he denies that literature can address this need.

But in the *Poetics* and in relevant parts of other works, Aristotle shows that tragedy indeed addresses this need and does so through the effect of catharsis. By arousing the powerful feelings of pity and fear, tragedy trains or shapes the emotions so that people become *habituated* to measuring, shaping, and channeling their feelings—controlling them, and not being controlled by them. Through catharsis, people are led to the development of an emotional *mean*, a condition of poise and balance among emotional forces, and they achieve this balanced state harmlessly because in the artistic context of tragedy they are immune to the damage such emotions may do in actual life. Tragedy therefore assists in the development of moral virtue, for people who have experienced the emotional catharsis or regulation of tragedy will be led to love and hate correctly, to direct their loyalties correctly, and also to make correct decisions and take correct actions, both for themselves and, more significantly, for the public.

It is important to stress that Aristotle states that catharsis is also brought about by other literary genres, especially comedy and epic, as well as by music. In other words, artistic works have in common that they cleanse or purify the emotions. It is through the continuous and renewed shaping and regulating of feelings—catharsis—that tragedy, like literature broadly, encourages moral virtue, and therefore on both philosophical and religious grounds it is defensible and necessary.

---

[10] See Janko, especially pp. xvi–xx, and Butcher's discussion on pp. 245–51 of *Aristotle's Theory of Poetry and Fine Art*.

The Tragic Plot Is Structured to Arouse and Shape Emotions

In the light of the concept of catharsis, Aristotle's description of the formal aspects and characteristics of tragedy can be seen as an outline of the ways in which these characteristics first arouse the emotions and then regulate and shape them.

THE TRAGIC PLOT REQUIRES THE REPRESENTATION OF A SINGLE MAJOR ACTION. Aristotle concedes that tragedy is not true in the sense that actual history is true. He therefore stresses that a tragic plot, or *muthos*, is not an exact imitation or duplication of life, but rather a **representation** or *mimesis*. The concept of representation acknowledges both the moral role of the writer and the artistic freedom needed to create works conducive to the proper responses. A tragic plot therefore consists of a self-contained and concentrated single action. Anything outside this action, such as unrelated incidents in the life of the major character, is not to be contained in the play. The action of *Oedipus the King,* for example, is focused on Oedipus's determination as king of Thebes to free his city from the pestilence that is destroying it. Although other aspects of his life are introduced in the play's dialogue because they are relevant to the action, they are reported rather than dramatized. Only those incidents integral to the action are included in the play.

TRAGIC RESPONSES ARE BROUGHT TO A HEAD THROUGH REVERSAL, RECOGNITION, AND SUFFERING. Aristotle's discussion of the three major elements of tragic plot is particularly significant. The elements all appear near the conclusion of a tragic play because they are the probable and inevitable results of the early elements of exposition and complication. First is the "**reversal** of the situation" (*peripeteia*) from apparent good to bad, or a "change [usually also a surprise] by which the action veers round to its opposite," as in *Oedipus the King,* where the outcome is the reverse of what Oedipus intends and expects (XI.1, p. 41). Even if the outcome is unhappy—especially if it is unhappy—it is "the right ending" (XIII.6, p. 47) because it is the most tragic; that is, it evokes the greatest degree of pity and fear.

Second is "a change from ignorance to knowledge, producing love or hate between the persons destined by the poet for good or bad fortune." Aristotle calls this change *anagnorisis* or **recognition** (XI.2, p. 41). In the best and most powerful tragedies, according to him, the reversal and the recognition occur together and create surprise. Aristotle considers recognition to be the discovery of the true identity and involvement of persons, the establishment of guilt or innocence, and the revelation of previously unknown details, for "it is upon such situations that the issues of good or bad fortune will depend" (XI.4, p. 41). One might add that recognition is of major importance because ideally, upon discovering the truth, the protagonist acknowledges errors and accepts responsibility. In *Oedipus the King,* for example, Oedipus finally recognizes the truth of his own guilt even though during most of the play he has been trying to evade it. He then becomes the agent of his own punishment. Because such recognition illustrates that human beings have the strength to preserve their integrity even in the depths of adversity, it is one of the elements making tragedy the highest of all literary forms.

Aristotle describes the third part of plot as a "scene of suffering" (*pathos*), which he defines as "a destructive or painful action, such as death on the stage, bodily agony, wounds, and the like" (XI.6, p. 43). He stresses that the destructive or painful action (not necessarily death) should be caused by "those who are near or dear to one another" (XIV.4, pp. 49–50). That is, violence should occur within a royal household or family rather than against a hostile foe. Because the trust, love, and protectiveness that one hopes for in a family is replaced by treachery, hate, and mayhem, the suffering of the tragic protagonist is one of the major ways in which tragedy arouses fear and pity.

To Aristotle, Additional Tragic Requirements Are Seriousness, Completeness, and Artistic Balance

The first part of Aristotle's definition, asserting that a tragedy is "serious, complete, and of a certain magnitude," can be seen as a vital aspect of his analysis of how tragedy shapes responses. The term **serious**, or noble or elevated, concerns the play's tone and level of life, in contrast with the boisterousness and ribaldry of Athenian comedies. While comedy represents human character as less serious than it is, tragedy shows it as more serious (II.4, p. 13). Seriousness is also a consequence of the political and cosmological dimensions of the issues in which the heroic characters are engaged. By **complete**, we understand that a tragedy must be shaped and perfected into a logical and finished whole. The beginning, the middle, and the ending must be so perfectly placed that changing or removing any part would spoil the work's integrity (VII.2–3, p. 31). By stating that a tragedy should be of a "certain" or proportional **magnitude**, Aristotle refers to a balance of length and subject matter. The play should be short enough to "be easily embraced by the memory " and long enough to "admit of a change . . . from good fortune to bad" (VII.5–7, p. 33). In other words, everything is artistically balanced; nothing superfluous is included, and nothing essential is omitted.

For Aristotle, Appropriate Diction and Song Are Necessary in Tragedy

For modern readers, Aristotle's description of tragic structure is more easily understood than his discussion of tragic language. His statement about tragic poetry—that it is the "mere metrical arrangement of the words" (VI.4, p. 25)—is clear as far as it goes, for the plays themselves show that the tragic playwrights used poetic forms deliberately and exactly. These characteristics, however, do not survive translation into modern English. As for **song** (*melos*),

Aristotle's claim that it is "a term whose sense everyone understands" (VI.4, p. 25) is not illuminating. What is therefore significant about his discussion of verse and song is his statement that the "several kinds of artistic ornament are to be found in separate parts of the play" (VI.2, p. 23). That is, where verse is appropriate, the tragic playwrights include poetry as a means of elevating the drama; where music and song are appropriate, they include these to increase beauty and intensify the drama. As with the other aspects of tragedy, therefore, placement, balance, and appropriateness are the most fitting standards of judgment.

The Tragedy's Hero Is the Focus of Sympathetic Tragic Emotions

Aristotle's description of the tragic protagonist or hero, though not included in his definition of tragedy, is integral to the concept of catharsis and therefore to his description of tragedy. As with the other parts of his analysis, he demonstrates the exact effects and limits of the topic—the perfected balance of form necessary to bring about proper tragic responses. To this end, he states that we, as normally imperfect human beings, are able to sympathize with a "highly renowned and prosperous" protagonist because that protagonist is also imperfect—a person who exists between extremes, just "like ourselves" (XIII.2, p. 45). The misfortunes of this noble protagonist are caused not by "vice" or "depravity" but rather by "some great error or frailty" (XIII.4, p. 47). Aristotle's word for such shortcomings is *hamartia*, which is often translated as **tragic flaw**, and it is this flaw that makes the protagonist human—neither a saint nor a villain. If the protagonist were a saint (one who is "eminently good and just"), his or her suffering would be undeserved and unfair, and our pity would be overwhelmed by indignation and anger—not a proper tragic reaction. Nor could we pity a villain experiencing adversity and pain, for we would judge the suffering to be deserved, and our primary response would then be satisfaction—also not a proper reaction. Therefore, an ideal tragedy is fine-tuned to control our emotions exactly, producing horror and fear because the suffering protagonist is a person like ourselves, and pity because the suffering far exceeds what the protagonist deserves.

ARISTOTLE'S VIEW OF TRAGEDY IN BRIEF

Aristotle's definition of tragedy hinges on his idea that tragedy, as a dramatic form, is designed to evoke powerful emotions and thereby, through catharsis, to serve both a salutary and ethical purpose. The tragic incidents and plot must be artistically constructed to produce the "essential tragic effect" (VI.12, p. 27). Therefore Aristotle stresses that plot and incidents, arranged for this effect, form the end or goal—the "chief thing of all"—of tragedy (VI.10, p. 27).

IRONY IN TRAGEDY

Implicit in the excessiveness of tragic suffering is the idea that the universe is mysterious and often unfair and that unseen but powerful forces—fate, fortune, circumstances, and the gods—directly intervene in human life. Ancient Athenian belief was that the gods give rewards or punishments to suit their own purposes, which mortals cannot understand, bring about, or prevent. For example, in *Prometheus Bound* (attributed to Aeschylus), the god Hephaestus binds Prometheus to a rock in the Scythian Mountains as punishment for having given fire and technology to humankind. (A good deed produces suffering.) Conversely, in *Medea*, Euripides shows that the god Apollo permits Medea to escape after killing her own children. (An evil deed produces reward.)

Situational and Cosmic Irony Are Essential in Tragedy

These examples illustrate the pervasiveness of situational and cosmic irony in tragedy. Characters are thrust into situations that are caused by others or that they themselves unwittingly cause. When they try to act responsibly and nobly to relieve their situations, their actions do not produce the expected results—this is consistent with Aristotle's idea of reversal—and usually things come out badly. For example, Oedipus brings suffering on himself just when he succeeds—and *because* he succeeds—in rescuing his city. Whether on the personal or cosmic level, therefore, there is no escape—no way to evade responsibility, and no way to change the universal laws that thrust human beings into such situations.

Situational and cosmic irony is not confined to ancient tragedies. Shakespeare's tragic hero Hamlet speaks about the "divinity that shapes our ends," thus expressing the unpredictability of hopes, plans, and achievements, and also the wisdom of resignation. In *Death of a Salesman*, Miller's hero, Willy Loman, is gripped not so much by divine power as by time—the agent of destruction being the inexorable force of economic circumstances.

The Tragic Dilemma Confronts the Problem of Free Will vs. Fate

These ironies are related to what is called the **tragic dilemma**—a situation that forces the tragic protagonist to make a difficult choice. The tragic dilemma has also been called a "lose-lose" situation. Thus, Oedipus cannot shirk his duty as king of Thebes because that would be ruinous. He therefore tries to eliminate his city's affliction, but that course also is ruinous. In other words, the choices posed in a tragic dilemma seemingly permit freedom of will, but the consequences of any choice demonstrate the inescapable fact that powerful forces, perhaps fate or inevitability, baffle even the most reasonable and noble intentions. As Hamlet states, "O cursèd spite, / That ever I was born to set it right" (I.5, 188–89).

Dramatic Irony Focuses Attention on the Tragic Limitations of Human Vision and Knowledge

It is from a perspective of something like divinity that we as readers or spectators perceive the action of tragedies. We are like the gods because we always know more than the characters. Such dramatic irony permits us, for example, to know what Oedipus does not know: In defensive rage, he killed his real father, and he himself is therefore his city's bane. Similar dramatic irony can be found in Shakespeare's *Hamlet*, for we realize that Claudius murdered Hamlet's father while Hamlet himself has only unconfirmable suspicions of this truth. The underlying basis of dramatic irony in real life is of course that none of us can know our own futures exactly, and few if any can anticipate accident, illness, and all the social, economic, and political adversity that may distress or destroy our way of life.

THE ANCIENT ATHENIAN AUDIENCE AND THEATER

Athenian audiences of the fifth century B.C.E., predominantly men but also a small number of women and slaves, took their theater seriously. Indeed, as young men many citizens had taken active parts in the parades and choruses. Admission was charged for those able to pay, but subsidies allowed poorer people to attend as well. Rich Athenians, as a duty (*liturgeia*) to the state, underwrote the costs of the productions—except for the three professional actors who were paid by the government. Each wealthy man, for his contribution, was known as a *choragos,* or choral sponsor. To gain public recognition, the choragos sometimes performed as the leader of the chorus.

Ancient Athenian Theater Originated in the Marketplace, or **Agora**

In the beginning, tragic performances were given specially designated space in the Athenian *agora,* or marketplace. In the center of the performing area was an altar dedicated to Dionysus, around which the choruses danced and chanted. Wooden risers were set up for the spectators.

Ancient Greek Plays Were Performed in the Athenian Theater of Dionysus

By the early fifth century B.C.E., a half-circular outdoor theater (*theatron,* or "place for seeing") was created out of the hill at the southern base of the Acropolis in the area sacred to Dionysus (see the photograph on the front of Insert III.). All later performances of tragedies were held at this **Theater of Dionysus**, which held as many as fourteen thousand people (the comic dramatist Aristophanes indicated that thirteen thousand were in attendance at one

Ancient theater at Epidauros, Greece. Gian Berto Vanni/Art Resource, New York, NY.

of his plays). In the earliest days of the theater, most spectators sat on the sloping ground, but eventually wooden and then stone benches were constructed in the rising semicircle, with more elegant seating for dignitaries in front. Although the Theater was outdoors, the acoustics were sufficiently good to permit audiences to hear both the chorus and the actors, provided that the spectators remained reasonably quiet during performances.

THE *ORCHESTRA* WAS THE FOCAL POINT OF BOTH SIGHT AND SOUND. Centered at the base of the hill—the focus of attention—was a round area modeled on the one that had been used in the agora. This was the ***orchestra*** (or-KESS-tra) or "dancing place," which was about sixty-five feet in diameter. Here, each chorus sang its odes and performed its dance movements to the rhythm of a double-piped flute (*aulos*), an instrument that was also used to mark the step in military drill. In the center was a permanent altar.

THE *SKENE* WAS A VERSATILE BUILDING USED FOR BOTH ACTION AND ENTRANCES. Behind the *orchestra* was a building for actors, costumes, and props called the ***skene*** ("tent"), from which is derived our modern word *scene*. Originally a tent or hut, the *skene* was later made of wood and decorated to provide backdrops for the various plays. Some theater historians argue that the stage itself was a wooden platform (*proskenion* or proscenium) in front of the *skene* to elevate the actors and set them off from the chorus. At the center of

View of modern production of Sophocles' *Oedipus at Colonus* at the Theater of Epidauros (see also p. 1299). Note the size of the *orchestra,* the formation and gestures of the chorus (fifteen members, in masks, together with the choral leader), the central altar, the reconstructed *skene,* and the single actor on the proscenium. D.A. Harissiadis/Benaki Museum, Athens, Greece, Photographic Archive.

the *skene* a double door for entrances and exits opened out to the stage and the *orchestra.* Through this door a large platform (*ekkyklyma*) could be rolled out to show interior scenes. There was no curtain.

The roof of the *skene* was sometimes used as a place of action (as in Aeschylus's *Agamemnon*). A *mechane* (may-KAH-nay), or crane, was also located there so that actors playing gods could be swung up, down, and around as a mark of divine power. It was this crane that gave rise to the Latin phrase *deus ex machina* ("a god out of the machine"), a term that refers to an artificial and/or illogical action or device introduced at a play's end to bring otherwise impossible conflicts to a satisfactory solution.

THE ACTORS PERFOMED IN ALL STAGE AND ORCHESTRA AREAS, AND THE CHORUS PERFORMED IN THE ORCHESTRA.   The performing space for the actors was mainly in front of the *skene.* The space for the chorus was the entire *orchestra.* The chorus entered the *orchestra*—and left it at the end of the play—along the aisles between the retaining wall of the hillside seats and the front of the *skene.* Each of these lateral walkways was known as a *parados* ("way in"), the name also given to the chorus's entry scene. The actors often used the *skene* for entrances and exits, but they were also free to use either of the walkways.

THE THEATER WAS REPAIRED AND RESTORED A NUMBER OF TIMES IN ANTIQUITY. In the centuries after it was built, the Theater of Dionysus was remodeled and restored a number of times. Aeschylus' trilogy the *Oresteia* was performed in 458 B.C.E., for example, not long after a renovation. The ruins existing on the south slope of the Acropolis today are not those of the theater known by Sophocles, but rather those of a Roman restoration. A better sense of how the theater looked during the time of Sophocles can be gained from the Theater of Epidaurus, which has been preserved in excellent condition (see the photographs, pp. 1299 and 1300) and which even in antiquity was considered one of the best Greek theaters.

ANCIENT GREEK TRAGIC ACTORS AND THEIR COSTUMES

The task of the three competing playwrights who had been "given a chorus" by the archon to stage their works during the City Dionysia (and later during the Lenaia) was to plan, choreograph, and direct the productions, usually with the aid of professionals. By performance time, the dramatists would already have spent many months preparing the three assigned actors and fifteen choristers. They also would have directed rehearsals for a small number of auxiliary chorus members and other silent extras in roles such as servants and soldiers.

Costumes Distinguished the Actors from the Chorus

All these participants needed costumes. The chorus members were lightly clad, for ease of movement, and were apparently barefoot. The main actors wore the identifying costumes of tragedy, namely, sleeved robes, boots, and masks. Their robes were heavily decorated and embroidered. Their calf-high leather boots, called *kothornoi* or, in English, **buskins**, were like the elegant boots worn by the patron god Dionysus in painting and statuary. During the following centuries, the buskins became elevator shoes that made the tragic actors taller, in keeping with their heroic stature.

Masks Worn by Chorus and Actors Helped the Audience Recognize and Distinguish the Characters

A vital aspect of ancient tragic costuming was the use of conventionalized plaster and linen masks, which were designed to identify and delineate characters. These were of particular help for those in the audience who sat at increasing distances away and up from the orchestra and stage, and who therefore would have had trouble seeing facial expressions. As many as twenty-eight different kinds of masks were in use for the tragic productions. Each mask portrayed a distinct facial type and expression (e.g., king, queen, young woman, old man). The choristers wore identical masks for their group roles. Apparently the masks covered the entire head, except for openings for seeing, breathing, and speaking. They included a high headdress and, when necessary, a beard.

The masks, along with costume changes, gave the actors great versatility. Each actor could assume a number of different roles simply by entering the *skene*, changing mask and costume, and reentering as a new character. Thus, in *Oedipus the King* a single actor could represent the seer Tiresias and later reappear as the Messenger. The masks even made it possible for two actors, or even all three, to perform as the same character in separate parts of the play if the need arose.

PERFORMANCE AND THE FORMAL ORGANIZATION OF GREEK TRAGEDY

On performance days, the competing playwrights staged their plays from morning to afternoon, first the tragedies, then the satyr plays (and after these, comedies by other writers). Because plays were performed with a minimum of scenery and props, dramatists used dialogue to establish times and locations. Each tragedy was performed in the order of the formally designated sections that modern editors have marked in the printed texts. It is therefore possible to describe the production of a play in terms of these structural divisions.

The First Part Was the Prologue, *the Play's Exposition*

There was considerable variety in the performance of the **prologue**. Sometimes it was given by a single actor, speaking as either a mortal or a god. In *Oedipus the King*, Sophocles used all three actors for the prologue (Oedipus, the Priest, and Creon), speaking to themselves and also to the extras acting as the Theban populace.

The Second Part Was the Parados, *the Entry of the Chorus into the Orchestra*

Once the chorus members entered the orchestra, they remained there until the play's end. Because they were required to project their voices to spectators in the top seats, they both sang and chanted their lines. They also moved rhythmically in a number of stanzaic *strophes* (turns), *antistrophes* (counterturns), and *epodes* (units following the songs). These dance movements, regulated by the rhythm of the *aulos* or flute as in military drill, were done in straight-line formations of five or three, but we do not know whether the chorus stopped or continued moving when delivering their lines. After the *parados*, the choristers would necessarily have knelt or sat at attention, in this way focusing on the activities of the actors and, when necessary, responding as a group.

The Play's Principal Action Consisted of Four Episodes *and* Stasimons

With the chorus as a model audience, the drama itself was developed in four full sections or acting units. The major part of each section was the **episode**. Each episode featured the actors, who presented both action and speech, including swift one-line interchanges known as **stichomythy**.

When the episode ended, the actors withdrew.[11] The following second part of the acting section was called a *stasimon* (plural *stasima*), performed by the chorus in the *orchestra*. Like the *parados*, the *stasima* required dance movements, along with the chanting and singing of strophes, antistrophes, and epodes. The topics concerned the play's developing action, although over time the *stasima* became more general and therefore less integral to the play.

The Play Concluded with the Exodos

When the last of the four episode-*stasimon* sections had been completed, the *exodos* (literally, "a way out"), or the final section, commenced. It contained the resolution of the drama, the exit of the actors, and the last pronouncements, dance movements, and exit of the chorus.

The Role of the Chorus Became Less Important as Greek Tragedy Evolved

We know little about tragic structure at the very beginning of the form, but Athenian tragedies of the fifth century B.C.E. followed the pattern just described. Aeschylus, the earliest of the Athenian writers of tragedy, lengthened the episodes, thus emphasizing the actors and minimizing the chorus (*Poetics* IV.13, p. 19). Sophocles made the chorus even less important. Euripides, Sophocles's younger contemporary, concentrated on the episodes, making the chorus almost incidental. In later centuries, dramatists dropped the choral sections completely, establishing a precedent for the five-act structure adopted by Roman dramatists and later by Renaissance dramatists.

🌼 PLAYS FOR STUDY

---

[11] For example, at the end of the first episode of *Oedipus the King,* Oedipus goes into the *skene*—the palace—while a servant leads Tiresias off along the *parados,* thus indicating that he is leaving Thebes entirely.

SOPHOCLES, *OEDIPUS THE KING*

Sophocles was born between 500 and 494 B.C.E. into an affluent Athenian family. He began acting and singing early, and he served as a choral leader in the celebrations for the defeat of the Persians at Marathon in 480 B.C.E. In 468 he won highest festival honors for the first play he submitted for competition, *Triptolemos*. He wrote at least 120 plays, approximately 90 of them tragedies, and he won the prize a record 24 times. He was also an active citizen. He was twice elected general of his tribe, and he served as a priest in the cult of Asclepius, the god of healing. Because of his dramatic and public 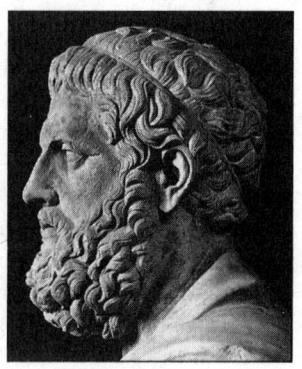 achievements, he was venerated during his lifetime, and after his death in 406–405 B.C.E., a cult was established in his honor.

When *Oedipus the King* was first performed between 430 and 425 B.C.E., most of the audience would have known the general outlines of the story inasmuch as it was one of the "received legends" of tragedy: the antagonism of the gods Hephaestus and Hera toward Cadmus of Thebes (of whom Oedipus was a descendant); the prophecy that the Theban king Laius would be killed by his own son; the exposure of the newly born Oedipus on a mountainside; his rescue by a well-meaning shepherd; his youth spent as the adopted son of King Polybus and Queen Merope of Corinth; his trip to Delphi to learn his origins; his impetuous murder of Laius (a stranger to him); his solution of the Sphinx's riddle; his ascension as king of Thebes and his marriage to Queen Jocasta, his mother; his reign as king; the plague that afflicted Thebes; his attempts at restoration; and Jocasta's suicide when the truth of Oedipus' past is revealed.

Although these details were commonly known, there was disagreement about the outcome of Oedipus' life. One version told that he remarried, had four children with his new wife, reigned long and successfully, died in battle, and was finally worshiped as a hero. Sophocles, however, dramatizes a version—either borrowed or of his own creation—that tells of Oedipus' self-imposed punishment.

As we have said, Aristotle prized *Oedipus the King* so highly that he used it to illustrate many of his principles of tragedy. Of particular interest is that the play embodies the so-called three **unities**, which are implicit in the *Poetics* although Aristotle does not stress them. Sophocles creates *unity of place* by using the front of the royal palace of Thebes as the location for the entire action. He creates *unity of action* by dramatizing only those activities leading to Oedipus' recognition of the true scourge of the city. Finally, he creates *unity of time* because the stage or action time coincides with real-life time. In fact, the play's time is considerably shorter than the "single revolution of the sun" (*sic*) that Aristotle recommends as the proper period for a complete tragic action (V.4, p. 23). Above all, *Oedipus the King* meets Aristotle's requirements for one of the very best plays because of the skill with which Sophocles makes Oedipus' recognition of his guilt coincide exactly with the disastrous reversal of his fortunes (XI.2, p. 41).

SOPHOCLES   (ca. 496–406 B.C.E.)

Oedipus the King ————————————————————————— *430–425* B.C.E.

Translated by Thomas Gould

CHARACTERS

> Oedipus,° *The King of Thebes*
> Priest of Zeus, *Leader of the Suppliants*
> Creon, *Oedipus's Brother-in-law*
> Chorus, *a Group of Theban Elders*
> Choragos, *Spokesman of the Chorus*
> Tiresias, *a blind Seer or Prophet*
> Jocasta, *The Queen of Thebes*
> Messenger, *from Corinth, once a Shepherd*
> Herdsman, *once a Servant of Laius*
> Second Messenger, *a Servant of Oedipus*

MUTES

> Suppliants, *Thebans seeking Oedipus's help*
> Attendants, *for the Royal Family*
> Servants, *to lead Tiresias and Oedipus*
> Antigone, *Daughter of Oedipus and Jocasta*
> Ismene, *Daughter of Oedipus and Jocasta*

[*The action takes place during the day in front of the royal palace in Thebes. There are two altars (left and right) on the Proscenium and several steps leading down to the Orchestra. As the play opens, Thebans of various ages who have come to beg Oedipus for help are sitting on these steps and in part of the Orchestra. These suppliants are holding branches of laurel or olive which have strips of wool° wrapped around them. Oedipus enters from the palace (the central door of the Skene).*]

PROLOGUE

OEDIPUS.   My children, ancient Cadmus'° newest care,
why have you hurried to those seats, your boughs
wound with the emblems of the suppliant?
The city is weighed down with fragrant smoke,
with hymns to the Healer° and the cries of mourners.
I thought it wrong, my sons, to hear your words
through emissaries, and have come out myself,
I, Oedipus, a name that all men know.   5

Oedipus: The name means "swollen foot." It refers to the mutilation of Oedipus's feet by his father, Laius, before the infant was sent to Mount Cithaeron to be put to death by exposure. 0.1 S.D *wool:* Branches wrapped with wool are traditional symbols of prayer or supplication. *Cadmus:* Oedipus's great-great-grandfather (although he does not know this) and the founder of Thebes.   5 *Healer:* Apollo, god of prophecy, light, healing, justice, purification, and destruction.

[*OEDIPUS addresses the PRIEST.*]

Old man—for it is fitting that you speak
for all—what is your mood as you entreat me,   10
fear or trust? You may be confident
that I'll do anything. How hard of heart
if an appeal like this did not rouse my pity!
PRIEST.   You, Oedipus, who hold the power here,
you see our several ages, we who sit   15
before your altars—some not strong enough
to take long flight, some heavy in old age,
the priests, as I of Zeus,° and from our youths
a chosen band. The rest sit with their windings
in the markets, at the twin shrines of Pallas,°   20
and the prophetic embers of Ismēnos.°
Our city, as you see yourself, is tossed
too much, and can no longer lift its head
above the troughs of billows red with death.
It dies in the fruitful flowers of the soil,   25
it dies in its pastured herds, and in its women's
barren pangs. And the fire-bearing god°
has swooped upon the city, hateful plague,
and he has left the house of Cadmus empty.
Black Hades° is made rich with moans and weeping.   30
Not judging you an equal of the gods,
do I and the children sit here at your hearth,
but as the first of men, in troubled times
and in encounters with divinities.
You came to Cadmus' city and unbound   35
the tax we had to pay to the harsh singer,°
did it without a helpful word from us,
with no instruction; with a god's assistance
you raised up our life, so we believe.

18 *Zeus:* father and king of the gods.   20 *Pallas:* Athena, goddess of wisdom, arts, crafts, and war.   21 *Ismēnos:* a reference to the temple of Apollo near the river Ismenos in Thebes. Prophecies were made here by "reading" the ashes of the altar fires.   27 *fire-bearing god:* contagious fever viewed as a god.   30 *Black Hades:* refers to both the underworld, where the spirits of the dead go, and the god of the underworld.   36 *harsh singer:* the Sphinx, a monster with a woman's head, a lion's body, and wings. The "tax" that Oedipus freed Thebes from was the destruction of all the young men who failed to solve the Sphinx's riddle and were subsequently devoured. The Sphinx always asked the same riddle: "What goes on four legs in the morning, two legs at noon, and three legs in the evening, and yet is weakest when supported by the largest number of feet?" Oedipus discovered the correct answer—man, who crawls in infancy, walks in his prime, and uses a stick in old age—and thus ended the Sphinx's reign of terror. The Sphinx destroyed herself when Oedipus answered the riddle. Oedipus's reward for freeing Thebes of the Sphinx was the throne and the hand of the recently widowed Jocasta. (A photograph of a Sphinx built in ancient Egypt appears on p. 994.)

Again now Oedipus, our greatest power,   40
we plead with you, as suppliants, all of us,
to find us strength, whether from a god's response,
or learned in some way from another man.
I know that the experienced among men
give counsels that will prosper best of all.   45
Noblest of men, lift up our land again!
Think also of yourself; since now the land
calls you its Savior for your zeal of old,
oh let us never look back at your rule
as men helped up only to fall again!   50
Do not stumble! Put our land on firm feet!
The bird of omen was auspicious then,
when you brought that luck; be that same man again!
The power is yours; if you will rule our country,
rule over men, not in an empty land.   55
A towered city or a ship is nothing
if desolate and no man lives within.
OEDIPUS.   Pitiable children, oh I know, I know
the yearnings that have brought you. Yes, I know
that you are sick. And yet, though you are sick,   60
there is not one of you so sick as I.
For your affliction comes to each alone,
for him and no one else, but my soul mourns
for me and for you, too, and for the city.
You do not waken me as from a sleep,   65
for I have wept, bitterly and long,
tried many paths in the wanderings of thought,
and the single cure I found by careful search
I've acted on: I sent Menoeceus' son,
Creon, brother of my wife, to the Pythian   70
halls of Phoebus,° so that I might learn
what I must do or say to save this city.
Already, when I think what day this is,
I wonder anxiously what he is doing.
Too long, more than is right, he's been away.   75
But when he comes, then I shall be a traitor
if I do not do all that the god reveals.
PRIEST.   Welcome words! But look, those men have signaled
that it is Creon who is now approaching!
OEDIPUS.   Lord Apollo! May he bring Savior Luck,   80
a Luck as brilliant as his eyes are now!
PRIEST.   His news is happy, it appears. He comes,
forehead crowned with thickly berried laurel.°
OEDIPUS.   We'll know, for he is near enough to hear us.

[*Enter* CREON *along one of the Parados.*]

70–71 *Pythian . . . Phoebus:* the temple of Phoebus Apollo's oracle or prophet at Delphi.
83 *laurel:* Creon is wearing a garland of laurel leaves, sacred to Apollo.

Lord, brother in marriage, son of Menoeceus!   85
What is the god's pronouncement that you bring?
CREON.   It's good. For even troubles, if they chance
to turn out well, I always count as lucky.
OEDIPUS.   But what was the response? You seem to say
I'm not to fear—but not to take heart either.   90
CREON.   If you will hear me with these men present,
I'm ready to report—or go inside.

[*CREON moves up the steps toward the palace.*]

OEDIPUS.   Speak out to all! The grief that burdens me
concerns these men more than it does my life.
CREON.   Then I shall tell you what I heard from the god.   95
The task Lord Phoebus sets for us is clear:
drive out pollution sheltered in our land,
and do not shelter what is incurable.
OEDIPUS.   What is our trouble? How shall we cleanse ourselves?
CREON.   We must banish or murder to free ourselves   100
from a murder that blows storms through the city.
OEDIPUS.   What man's bad luck does he accuse in this?
CREON.   My Lord, a king named Laius ruled our land
before you came to steer the city straight.
OEDIPUS.   I know. So I was told—I never saw him.   10
CREON.   Since he was murdered, you must raise your hand
against the men who killed him with their hands.
OEDIPUS.   Where are they now? And how can we ever find
the track of ancient guilt now hard to read?
CREON.   In our own land, he said. What we pursue,   11
that can be caught; but not what we neglect.
OEDIPUS.   Was Laius home, or in the countryside—
or was he murdered in some foreign land?
CREON.   He left to see a sacred rite, he said;
He left, but never came home from his journey.   11
OEDIPUS.   Did none of his party see it and report—
someone we might profitably question?
CREON.   They were all killed but one, who fled in fear,
and he could tell us only one clear fact.
OEDIPUS.   What fact? One thing could lead us on to more   1
if we could get a small start on our hope.
CREON.   He said that bandits chanced on them and killed him—
with the force of many hands, not one alone.
OEDIPUS.   How could a bandit dare so great an act—
unless this was a plot paid off from here!   1
CREON.   We thought of that, but when Laius was killed,
we had no one to help us in our troubles.
OEDIPUS.   It was your very kingship that was killed!
What kind of trouble blocked you from a search?
CREON.   The subtle-singing Sphinx asked us to turn   1
from the obscure to what lay at our feet.

OEDIPUS.   Then I shall begin again and make it plain.
It was quite worthy of Phoebus, and worthy of you,
to turn our thoughts back to the murdered man,
and right that you should see me join the battle   135
for justice to our land and to the god.
Not on behalf of any distant kinships,
it's for myself I will dispel this stain.
Whoever murdered him may also wish
to punish me—and with the selfsame hand.   140
In helping him I also serve myself.
Now quickly, children: up from the altar steps,
and raise the branches of the suppliant!
Let someone go and summon Cadmus' people:
say I'll do anything.

                    [*Exit an* ATTENDANT *along one of the Parados.*]

            Our luck will prosper   145
if the god is with us, or we have already fallen.
PRIEST.   Rise, my children; that for which we came,
he has himself proclaimed he will accomplish.
May Phoebus, who announced this, also come
as Savior and reliever from the plague.   150

[*Exit* OEDIPUS *and* CREON *into the Palace. The* PRIEST *and the* SUPPLIANTS *exit left and right
    along the Parados. After a brief pause, the* CHORUS *(including the* CHORAGOS*)
    enters the Orchestra from the Parados.*]

PARADOS

Strophe 1°

CHORUS.   Voice from Zeus,° sweetly spoken, what are you
that have arrived from golden
Pytho° to our shining
Thebes? I am on the rack, terror
        shakes my soul.   155
Delian Healer,° summoned by "iē!"
I await in holy dread what obligation, something new
or something back once more with the revolving years,
        you'll bring about for me.
Oh tell me, child of golden Hope,   160
        deathless Response!

---

151 *Strophe, Strophe and antistrophe (line 162) are* stanzaic units referring to movements, counter-
movements, and gestures that the Chorus performed while singing or chanting in the orchestra.
See p. 1300.   151 *Voice from Zeus:* a reference to Apollo's prophecy. Zeus taught Apollo how to
prophesy.   153 *Pytho:* Delphi.   156 *Delian Healer:* Apollo.

Antistrophe 1

I appeal to you first, daughter of Zeus,
    deathless Athena,
    and to your sister who protects this land,
    Artemis,° whose famous throne is the whole circle
    of the marketplace,
and Phoebus, who shoots from afar: iō!
Three-fold defenders against death, appear!
If ever in the past, to stop blind ruin
    sent against the city,
you banished utterly the fires of suffering,
    come now again!

Strophe 2

Ah! Ah! Unnumbered are the miseries
I bear. The plague claims all
our comrades. Nor has thought found yet a spear
by which a man shall be protected. What our glorious
earth gives birth to does not grow. Without a birth
from cries of labor
    do the women rise.
One person after another
    you may see, like flying birds,
faster than indomitable fire, sped
to the shore of the god that is the sunset.°

Antistrophe 2

And with their deaths unnumbered dies the city.
Her children lie unpitied on the ground,
spreading death, unmourned.
Meanwhile young wives, and gray-haired mothers with them,
on the shores of the altars, from this side and that,
suppliants from mournful trouble,
    cry out their grief.
A hymn to the Healer shines,
    the flute a mourner's voice.
Against which, golden goddess, daughter of Zeus,
    send lovely Strength.

Strophe 3

Cause raging Ares°—who,
    armed now with no shield of bronze,
    burns me, coming on amid loud cries—

---

165 *Artemis:* goddess of virginity, childbirth, and hunting.   183 *god . . . sunset:* Hades, god of
the underworld.   195 *Ares:* god of war and destruction.

to turn his back and run from my land,
with a fair wind behind, to the great
    hall of Amphitritē,° 200
or to the anchorage that welcomes no one,
Thrace's troubled sea!
If night lets something get away at last,
    it comes by day.
Fire-bearing god 205
    you who dispense the might of lightning,
Zeus! Father! Destroy him with your thunderbolt!

[*Enter* OEDIPUS *from the palace.*]

Antistrophe 3

Lycēan Lord!° From your looped
    bowstring, twisted gold,
I wish indomitable missiles might be scattered 210
and stand forward, our protectors; also fire-bearing
radiance of Artemis, with which
    she darts across the Lycian mountains.
I call the god whose head is bound in gold,
with whom this country shares its name, 215
Bacchus,° wine-flushed, summoned by "euoi!,"
    Maenads' comrade,
to approach ablaze
    with gleaming . . . . . .
pine, opposed to that god-hated god. 220

EPISODE 1

OEDIPUS.   I hear your prayer. Submit to what I say
and to the labors that the plague demands
and you'll get help and a relief from evils.
I'll make the proclamation, though a stranger
to the report and to the deed. Alone, 225
had I no key, I would soon lose the track.
Since it was only later that I joined you,
to all the sons of Cadmus I say this:
whoever has clear knowledge of the man
who murdered Laius, son of Labdacus, 230
I command him to reveal it all to me—
nor fear if, to remove the charge, he must
accuse himself: his fate will not be cruel—
he will depart unstumbling into exile.
But if you know another, or a stranger, 235
to be the one whose hand is guilty, speak:

200 *Amphitritē:* the Atlantic Ocean.   208 *Lycēan Lord:* Apollo.   216 *Bacchus:* Dionysus, god
of fertility and wine.

I shall reward you and remember you.
But if you keep your peace because of fear,
and shield yourself or kin from my command,
hear you what I shall do in that event:
I charge all in this land where I have throne
and power, shut out that man—no matter who—
both from your shelter and all spoken words,
nor in your prayers or sacrifices make
him partner, nor allot him lustral° water.
All men shall drive him from their homes: for he
is the pollution that the god-sent Pythian
response has only now revealed to me.
In this way I ally myself in war
with the divinity and the deceased.°
And this curse, too, against the one who did it,
whether alone in secrecy, or with others:
may he wear out his life unblest and evil!
I pray this, too: if he is at my hearth
and in my home, and I have knowledge of him,
may the curse pronounced on others come to me.
All this I lay to you to execute,
for my sake, for the god's, and for this land
now ruined, barren, abandoned by the gods.
Even if no god had driven you to it,
you ought not to have left this stain uncleansed,
the murdered man a nobleman, a king!
You should have looked! But now, since, as it happens,
It's I who have the power that he had once,
and have his bed, and a wife who shares our seed,
and common bond had we had common children
(had not his hope of offspring had back luck—
but as it happened, luck lunged at his head);
because of this, as if for my own father,
I'll fight for him, I'll leave no means untried,
to catch the one who did it with his hand,
for the son of Labdacus, of Polydorus,
of Cadmus before him, and of Agēnor.°
This prayer against all those who disobey:
the gods send out no harvest from their soil,
nor children from their wives. Oh, let them die
victims of this plague, or of something worse.
Yet for the rest of us, people of Cadmus,
we the obedient, may Justice, our ally,
and all the gods, be always on our side!
CHORAGOS.   I speak because I feel the grip of your curse:
the killer is not I. Nor can I point

245 *lustral:* purifying.   250 *the deceased:* Laius.   272–73 *son . . . Agēnor:* refers to Laius by
citing his genealogy.

to him. The one who set us to this search,
Phoebus, should also name the guilty man.
OEDIPUS. Quite right, but to compel unwilling gods—   285
no man has ever had that kind of power.
CHORAGOS. May I suggest to you a second way?
OEDIPUS. A second or a third—pass over nothing!
CHORAGOS. I know of no one who sees more of what
Lord Phoebus sees than Lord Tiresias.   290
My Lord, one might learn brilliantly from him.
OEDIPUS. Nor is this something I have been slow to do.
At Creon's word I sent an escort—twice now!
I am astonished that he has not come.
CHORAGOS. The old account is useless. It told us nothing.   295
OEDIPUS. But tell it to me. I'll scrutinize all stories.
CHORAGOS. He is said to have been killed by travelers.
OEDIPUS. I have heard, but the one who did it no one sees.
CHORAGOS. If there is any fear in him at all,
he won't stay here once he has heard that curse.   300
OEDIPUS. He won't fear words: he had no fear when he did it.

[*Enter TIRESIAS from the right, led by a SERVANT and two of Oedipus's ATTENDANTS.*]

CHORAGOS. Look there! There is the man who will convict him!
It's the god's prophet they are leading here,
one gifted with the truth as no one else.
OEDIPUS. Tiresias, master of all omens—   305
public and secret, in the sky and on the earth—
your mind, if not your eyes, sees how the city
lives with a plague, against which Thebes can find
no Saviour or protector, Lord, but you.
For Phoebus, as the attendants surely told you,   310
returned this answer to us: liberation
from the disease would never come unless
we learned without a doubt who murdered Laius—
put them to death, or sent them into exile.
Do not begrudge us what you may learn from birds   315
or any other prophet's path you know!
Care for yourself, the city, care for me,
care for the whole pollution of the dead!
We're in your hands. To do all that he can
to help another is man's noblest labor.   320
TIRESIAS. How terrible to understand and get
no profit from the knowledge! I knew this,
but I forgot, or I had never come.
OEDIPUS. What's this? You've come with very little zeal.
TIRESIAS. Let me go home! If you will listen to me,   325
You will endure your troubles better—and I mine.
OEDIPUS. A strange request, not very kind to the land
that cared for you—to hold back this oracle!

TIRESIAS.   I see your understanding comes to you
    inopportunely. So that won't happen to me . . .   330

OEDIPUS.   Oh, by the gods, if you understand about this,
    don't turn away! We're on our knees to you.

TIRESIAS.   None of you understands! I'll never bring
    my grief to light—I will not speak of yours.

OEDIPUS.   You know and won't declare it! Is your purpose   33£
    to betray us and to destroy this land?

TIRESIAS.   I will grieve neither of us. Stop this futile
    cross-examination. I'll tell you nothing!

OEDIPUS.   Nothing? You vile traitor! You could provoke
    a stone to anger! You still refuse to tell?   34●
    Can nothing soften you, nothing convince you?

TIRESIAS.   You blamed anger in me—you haven't seen.
    Can nothing soften you, nothing convince you?

OEDIPUS.   Who wouldn't fill with anger, listening
    to words like yours which now disgrace this city?   34

TIRESIAS.   It will come, even if my silence hides it.

OEDIPUS.   If it will come, then why won't you declare it?

TIRESIAS.   I'd rather say no more. Now if you wish,
    respond to that with all your fiercest anger!

OEDIPUS.   Now I am angry enough to come right out   3£
    with this conjecture: you, I think, helped plot
    the deed; you did it—even if your hand
    cannot have struck the blow. If you could see,
    I should have said the deed was yours alone.

TIRESIAS.   Is that right! Then I charge you to abide   3.
    by the decree you have announced: from this day
    say no word to either these or me,
    for you are the vile polluter of this land!

OEDIPUS.   Aren't you appalled to let a charge like that
    come bounding forth? How will you get away?   3

TIRESIAS.   You cannot catch me. I have the strength of truth.

OEDIPUS.   Who taught you this? Not your prophetic craft!

TIRESIAS.   You did. You made me say it. I didn't want to.

OEDIPUS.   Say what? Repeat it so I'll understand.

TIRESIAS.   I made no sense? Or are you trying me?   ?

OEDIPUS.   No sense I understood. Say it again!

TIRESIAS.   I say you are the murderer you seek.

OEDIPUS.   Again that horror! You'll wish you hadn't said that.

TIRESIAS.   Shall I say more, and raise your anger higher?

OEDIPUS.   Anything you like! Your words are powerless.   :

TIRESIAS.   You live, unknowing, with those nearest to you
    in the greatest shame. You do not see the evil.

OEDIPUS.   You won't go on like that and never pay!

TIRESIAS.   I can if there is any strength in truth.

OEDIPUS.   In truth, but not in you! You have no strength,
    blind in your ears, your reason, and your eyes.

TIRESIAS.   Unhappy man! Those jeers you hurl at me
　　before long all these men will hurl at you.
OEDIPUS.   You are the child of endless night; it's not
　　for me or anyone who sees to hurt you.　　　　　　　　　　　　　　380
TIRESIAS.   It's not my fate to be struck down by you.
　　Apollo is enough. That's his concern.
OEDIPUS.   Are these inventions Creon's or your own?
TIRESIAS.   No, your affliction is yourself, not Creon.
OEDIPUS.   Oh success!—in wealth, kingship, artistry,　　　　　　　385
　　in any life that wins much admiration—
　　the envious ill will stored up for you!
　　to get at my command, a gift I did not
　　seek, which the city put into my hands,
　　my loyal Creon, colleague from the start,　　　　　　　　　　　390
　　longs to sneak up in secret and dethrone me.
　　So he's suborned this fortuneteller—schemer!
　　deceitful beggar-priest!—who has good eyes
　　for gains alone, though in his craft he's blind.
　　Where were your prophet's powers ever proved?　　　　　　395
　　Why, when the dog who chanted verse° was here,
　　did you not speak and liberate this city?
　　Her riddle wasn't for a man chancing by
　　to interpret; prophetic art was needed,
　　but you had none, it seems—learned from birds　　　　　　400
　　or from a god. I came along, yes I,
　　Oedipus the ignorant, and stopped her—
　　by using thought, not augury from birds.
　　And it is I whom you may wish to banish,
　　so you'll be close to the Creontian throne.　　　　　　　　　405
　　You—and the plot's concocter—will drive out
　　pollution to your grief: you look quite old
　　or you would be the victim of that plot!
CHORAGOS.　　It seems to us that this man's words were said
　　in anger, Oedipus, and yours as well.　　　　　　　　　　　　410
　　Insight, not angry words, is what we need,
　　the best solution to the god's response.
TIRESIAS.   You are the king, and yet I am your equal
　　in my right to speak. In that I too am Lord,
　　for I belong to Loxias,° not you.　　　　　　　　　　　　　　415
　　I am not Creon's man. He's nothing to me.
　　Hear this, since you have thrown my blindness at me:
　　Your eyes can't see the evil to which you've come,
　　nor where you live, nor who is in your house.
　　Do you know your parents? Now knowing, you are　　　　420
　　their enemy, in the underworld and here.
　　A mother's and a father's double-lashing

396 *dog . . . verse:* the Sphinx.　　415 *Loxias:* Apollo.

terrible-footed curse will soon drive you out.
Now you can see, then you will stare into darkness.
What place will not be harbor to your cry,
or what Cithaeron° not reverberate
when you have heard the bride-song in your palace
to which you sailed? Fair wind to evil harbor!
Nor do you see how many other woes
will level you to yourself and to your children.
So, at my message, and at Creon, too,
splatter muck! There will never be a man
ground into wretchedness as you will be.
OEDIPUS.   Am I to listen to such things from him!
May you be damned! Get out of here at once!
Go! Leave my palace! Turn around and go!

[*TIRESIAS begins to move away from OEDIPUS.*]

TIRESIAS.   I wouldn't have come had you not sent for me.
OEDIPUS.   I did not know you'd talk stupidity,
or I wouldn't have rushed to bring you to my house.
TIRESIAS.   Stupid I seem to you, yet to your parents
who gave you natural birth I seemed quite shrewd.
OEDIPUS.   Who? Wait! Who is the one who gave me birth?
TIRESIAS.   This day will give you birth,° and ruin too.
OEDIPUS.   What murky, riddling things you always say!
TIRESIAS.   Don't you surpass us all at finding out?
OEDIPUS.   You sneer at what you'll find has brought me greatness.
TIRESIAS.   And that's the very luck that ruined you.
OEDIPUS.   I wouldn't care, just so I saved the city.
TIRESIAS.   In that case I shall go. Boy, lead the way!
OEDIPUS.   Yes, let him lead you off. Here, underfoot,
you irk me. Gone, you'll cause no further pain.
TIRESIAS.   I'll go when I have said what I was sent for.
Your face won't scare me. You can't ruin me.
I say to you, the man whom you have looked for
as you pronounced your curses, your decrees
on the bloody death of Laius—he is here!
A seeming stranger, he shall be shown to be
a Theban born, though he'll take no delight
in that solution. Blind, who once could see,
a beggar who was rich, through foreign lands
he'll go and point before him with a stick.
To his beloved children, he'll be shown
a father who is also brother; to the one
who bore him, son and husband; to his father,
his seed-fellow and killer. Go in
and think this out; and if you find I've lied,
say then I have no prophet's understanding!

426 *Cithaeron:* reference to the mountain on which Oedipus was to be exposed as an infant.
443 *give you birth:* that is, identify your parents.

[Exit TIRESIAS, *led by a* SERVANT. OEDIPUS *exits into the palace with his* ATTENDANTS.*]*

STASIMON 1

Strophe 1

CHORUS.   Who is the man of whom the inspired
    rock of Delphi° said
he has committed the unspeakable   470
    with blood-stained hands?
Time for him to ply a foot
mightier than those of the horses
    of the storm in his escape;
upon him mounts and plunges the weaponed   475
son of Zeus,° with fire and thunderbolts,
and in his train the dreaded goddesses
of Death, who never miss.

Antistrophe 1

The message has just blazed,
    gleaming from the snows   480
of Mount Parnassus: we must track
    everywhere the unseen man.
He wanders, hidden by wild
forests, up through caves
    and rocks, like a bull,   485
anxious, with an anxious foot, forlorn.
He puts away from him the mantic° words come from earth's
navel,° at its center, yet these live
forever and still hover round him.

Strophe 2

Terribly he troubles me,   490
    the skilled interpreter of birds!°
I can't assent, nor speak against him.
    Both paths are closed to me.
I hover on the wings of doubt,
    not seeing what is here nor what's to come.   495
What quarrel started in the house of Labdacus°
or in the house of Polybus,°
    either ever in the past
    or now, I never
heard, so that . . . with this fact for my touchstone   500

---

469 *rock of Delphi:* Apollo's oracle at Delphi.   476 *son of Zeus:* Apollo.   487 *mantic:* prophetic.
487–88 *earth's navel:* Delphi.   491 *interpreter of birds:* Tiresias. The Chorus is troubled by his accusations.   496 *house of Labdacus:* the line of Laius.   497 *Polybus:* Oedipus's foster father.

I could attack the public
    fame of Oedipus, by the side of the Labdaceans
an ally, against the dark assassination.

Antistrophe 2

No, Zeus and Apollo
    understand and know things
mortal; but that another man
    can do more as a prophet than I can—
for that there is no certain test,
    though, skill to skill,
one man might overtake another.
No, never, not until
    I see the charges proved,
when someone blames him shall I nod assent.
For once, as we all saw, the winged maiden° came
against him: he was seen then to be skilled,
    proved, by that touchstone, dear to the people. So,
never will my mind convict him of the evil.

EPISODE 2

[*Enter* CREON *from the right door of the skene and speaks to the* CHORUS.]

CREON.   Citizens, I hear that a fearful charge
    is made against me by King Oedipus!
    I had to come. If, in this crisis,
    he thinks that he has suffered injury
    from anything that I have said or done,
    I have no appetite for a long life—
    bearing a blame like that! It's no slight blow
    the punishment I'd take from what he said:
    it's the ultimate hurt to be called traitor
    by the city, by you, by my own people!
CHORAGOS.   The thing that forced that accusation out
    could have been anger, not the power of thought.
CREON.   But who persuaded him that thoughts of mine
    had led the prophet into telling lies?
CHORAGOS.   I do not know the thought behind his words.
CREON.   But did he look straight at you? Was his mind right
    when he said that I was guilty of this charge?
CHORAGOS.   I have no eyes to see what rulers do.
    But here he comes himself out of the house.

[*Enter* OEDIPUS *from the palace.*]

OEDIPUS.   What? You here? And can you really have
    the face and daring to approach my house

514 *winged maiden:* the Sphinx.

when you're exposed as its master's murderer
and caught, too, as the robber of my kingship?   540
Did you see cowardice in me, by the gods,
or foolishness, when you began this plot?
Did you suppose that I would not detect
your stealthy moves, or that I'd not fight back?
It's your attempt that's folly, isn't it—   545
tracking without followers or connections,
kingship which is caught with wealth and numbers?
CREON.   Now wait! Give me as long to answer back!
Judge me for yourself when you have heard me!
OEDIPUS.   You're eloquent, but I'd be slow to learn   550
from you, now that I've seen your malice toward me.
CREON.   That I deny. Hear what I have to say.
OEDIPUS.   Don't you deny it! You are the traitor here!
CREON.   If you consider mindless willfulness
a prized possession, you are not thinking sense.   555
OEDIPUS.   If you think you can wrong a relative
and get off free, you are not thinking sense.
CREON.   Perfectly just, I won't say no. And yet
what is this injury you say I did you?
OEDIPUS.   Did you persuade me, yes or no, to send   560
someone to bring that solemn prophet here?
CREON.   And I still hold to the advice I gave.
OEDIPUS.   How many years ago did your King Laius . . .
CREON.   Laius! Do what? Now I don't understand.
OEDIPUS.   Vanish—victim of a murderous violence?   565
CREON.   That is a long count back into the past.
OEDIPUS.   Well, was this seer then practicing his art?
CREON.   Yes, skilled and honored just as he is today.
OEDIPUS.   Did he, back then, ever refer to me?
CREON.   He did not do so in my presence ever.   570
OEDIPUS.   You did inquire into the murder then.
CREON.   We had to, surely, though we discovered nothing.
OEDIPUS.   But the "skilled" one did not say this then? Why not?
CREON.   I never talk when I am ignorant.
OEDIPUS.   But you're not ignorant of your own part.   575
CREON.   What do you mean? I'll tell you if I know.
OEDIPUS.   Just this: if he had not conferred with you
he'd not have told about my murdering Laius.
CREON.   If he said that, you are the one who knows.
But now it's fair that you should answer me.   580
OEDIPUS.   Ask on! You won't convict me as the killer.
CREON.   Well then, answer. My sister is your wife?
OEDIPUS.   Now there's a statement that I can't deny.
CREON.   You two have equal power in this country?
OEDIPUS.   She gets from me whatever she desires.   585
CREON.   And I'm a third? The three of us are equals?
OEDIPUS.   That's where you're treacherous to your kinship!

CREON.   But think about this rationally, as I do.
   First look at this: do you think anyone
   prefers the anxieties of being king
   to untroubled sleep—if he has equal power?
   I'm not the kind of man who falls in love
   with kingship. I am content with a king's power.
   And so would any man who's wise and prudent.
   I get all things from you, with no distress;
   as king I would have onerous duties, too.
   How could the kingship bring me more delight
   than this untroubled power and influence?
   I'm not misguided yet to such a point
   that profitable honors aren't enough.
   As it is, all wish me well and all salute;
   those begging you for something have me summoned,
   for their success depends on that alone.
   Why should I lose all this to become king?
   A prudent mind is never traitorous.
   Treason's a thought I'm not enamored of;
   nor could I join a man who acted so.
   In proof of this, first go yourself to Pytho°
   and ask if I brought back the true response.
   Then, if you find I plotted with that portent
   reader,° don't have me put to death by your vote
   only—I'll vote myself for my conviction.
   Don't let an unsupported thought convict me!
   It's not right mindlessly to take the bad
   for good or to suppose the good are traitors.
   Rejecting a relation who is loyal
   is like rejecting life, our greatest love.
   In time you'll know securely without stumbling,
   for time alone can prove a just man just,
   though you can know a bad man in a day
CHORAGOS.   Well said, to one who's anxious not to fall.
   Swift thinkers, Lord, are never safe from stumbling.
OEDIPUS.   But when a swift and secret plotter moves
   against me, I must make swift counterplot.
   If I lie quiet and await his move,
   he'll have achieved his aims and I'll have missed.
CREON.   You surely cannot mean you want me exiled!
OEDIPUS.   Not exiled, no. Your death is what I want!
CREON.   If you would first define what envy is . . .
OEDIPUS.   Are you still stubborn! Still disobedient?
CREON.   I see you cannot think!
OEDIPUS.   For me I can.
CREON.   You should for me as well!

608 *Pytho:* Delphi.   610–11 *portent reader:* Apollo's oracle or prophet.

OEDIPUS.   But you're a traitor!
CREON.   What if you're wrong?
OEDIPUS.   Authority must be maintained.
CREON.   Not if the ruler's evil.
OEDIPUS.   Hear that, Thebes!
CREON.   It is my city too, not yours alone!   635
CHORAGOS.   Please don't, my Lords! Ah, just in time, I see
    Jocasta there, coming from the palace.
    With her help you must settle your quarrel.

[*Enter JOCASTA from the Palace.*]

JOCASTA.   Wretched men! What has provoked this ill-
    advised dispute? Have you no sense of shame,   640
    with Thebes so sick, to stir up private troubles?
    Now go inside! And Creon, you go home!
    Don't make a general anguish out of nothing!
CREON.   My sister, Oedipus your husband here
    sees fit to do one of two hideous things: 645
    to have me banished from the land—or killed!
OEDIPUS.   That's right: I caught him, Lady, plotting harm
    against my person—with a malignant science.
CREON.   May my life fail, may I die cursed, if I
    did any of the things you said I did!   650
JOCASTA.   Believe his words, for the god's sake, Oedipus,
    in deference above all to his oath
    to the gods. Also for me, and for these men!

KOMMOS°

Strophe 1

CHORUS.   Consent, with will and mind,
    my king, I beg of you!   655
OEDIPUS.   What do you wish me to surrender?
CHORUS.   Show deference to him who was not feeble in time past
    and is now great in the power of his oath!
OEDIPUS.   Do you know what you're asking?
CHORUS.   Yes.
OEDIPUS.   Tell me then.
CHORUS.   Never to cast into dishonored guilt, with an unproved   660
    assumption, a kinsman who has bound himself by curse.
OEDIPUS.   Now you must understand, when you ask this,
    you ask my death or banishment from the land.

Strophe 2

CHORUS.   No, by the god who is the foremost of all gods,
    the Sun! No! Godless,   665

653 *Kommos:* a dirge or lament sung by the Chorus and one or more of the chief characters.

friendless, whatever death is worst of all,
let that be my destruction, if this
  thought ever moved me!
But my ill-fated soul
  this dying land
wears out—the more if to these older troubles
she adds new troubles from the two of you!
OEDIPUS.   Then let him go, though it must mean my death,
or else disgrace and exile from the land.
My pity is moved by your words, not by his—
he'll only have my hate, wherever he goes.
CREON.   You're sullen as you yield; you'll be depressed
when you've passed through this anger. Natures like yours
are hardest on themselves. That's as it should be.
OEDIPUS.   Then won't you go and let me be?
CREON.   I'll go.
Though you're unreasonable, they know I'm righteous.

                                        [*Exit* CREON.]

Antistrophe 1

CHORUS.   Why are you waiting, Lady?
Conduct him back into the palace!
JOCASTA.   I will, when I have heard what chanced.
CHORUS.   Conjectures—words alone, and nothing based on thought.
But even an injustice can devour a man.
JOCASTA.   Did the words come from both sides?
CHORUS.   Yes.
JOCASTA. What was said?
CHORUS.   To me it seems enough! enough! the land already troubled,
that this should rest where it has stopped.
OEDIPUS.   See what you've come to in your honest thought,
in seeking to relax and blunt my heart?

Antistrophe 2

CHORUS.   I have not said this only once, my Lord.
That I had lost my sanity,
  without a path in thinking—
be sure this would be clear
  if I put you away
who, when my cherished land
  wandered crazed
with suffering, brought her back on course.
Now, too, be a lucky helmsman!
JOCASTA.   Please, for the god's sake, Lord, explain to me
the reason why you have conceived this wrath?
OEDIPUS.   I honor you, not them,° and I'll explain
to you how Creon has conspired against me.

705 *them:* the Chorus.

JOCASTA.   All right, if that will explain how the quarrel started.
OEDIPUS.   He says I am the murderer of Laius!
JOCASTA.   Did he claim knowledge or that someone told him?
OEDIPUS.   Here's what he did: he sent that vicious seer   710
    so he could keep his own mouth innocent.
JOCASTA.   Ah then, absolve yourself of what he charges!
    Listen to this and you'll agree, no mortal
    is ever given skill in prophecy.
    I'll prove this quickly with one incident.   715
    It was foretold to Laius—I shall not say
    by Phoebus himself, but by his ministers—
    that when his fate arrived he would be killed
    by a son who would be born to him and me.
    And yet, so it is told, foreign robbers   720
    murdered him, at a place where three roads meet.
    As for the child I bore him, not three days passed
    before he yoked the ball-joints of its feet,°
    then cast it, by others' hands, on a trackless mountain.
    That time Apollo did not make our child   725
    a patricide, or bring about what Laius
    feared, that he be killed by his own son.
    That's how prophetic words determined things!
    Forget them. The things a god must track
    he will himself painlessly reveal.   730
OEDIPUS.   Just now, as I was listening to you, Lady,
    what a profound distraction seized my mind!
JOCASTA.   What made you turn around so anxiously?
OEDIPUS.   I thought you said that Laius was attacked
    and butchered at a place where three roads meet.   735
JOCASTA.   That is the story, and it is told so still.
OEDIPUS.   Where is the place where this was done to him?
JOCASTA.   The land's called Phocis, where a two-forked road
    comes in from Delphi and from Daulia.
OEDIPUS.   And how much time has passed since these events?   740
JOCASTA.   Just prior to your presentation here
    as king this news was published to the city.
OEDIPUS.   Oh, Zeus, what have you willed to do to me?
JOCASTA.   Oedipus, what makes your heart so heavy?
OEDIPUS.   No, tell me first of Laius' appearance,   745
    what peak of youthful vigor he had reached.
JOCASTA.   A tall man, showing his first growth of white.
    He had a figure not unlike your own.
OEDIPUS.   Alas! It seems that in my ignorance
    I laid those fearful curses on myself.   750
JOCASTA.   What is it, Lord? I flinch to see your face.
OEDIPUS.   I'm dreadfully afraid the prophet sees.
    But I'll know better with one more detail.

723 *ball-joints of its feet:* the ankles.

JOCASTA.   I'm frightened too. But ask: I'll answer you.
OEDIPUS.   Was his retinue small, or did he travel
　　with a great troop, as would befit a prince?
JOCASTA.   There were just five in all, one a herald.
　　There was a carriage, too, bearing Laius.
OEDIPUS.   Alas! Now I see it! But who was it,
　　Lady, who told you what you know about this?
JOCASTA.   A servant who alone was saved unharmed.
OEDIPUS.   By chance, could he be now in the palace?
JOCASTA.   No, he is not. When he returned and saw
　　you had the power of the murdered Laius,
　　he touched my hand and begged me formally
　　to send him to the fields and to the pastures,
　　so he'd be out of sight, far from the city.
　　I did. Although a slave, he well deserved
　　to win this favor, and indeed far more.
OEDIPUS.   Let's have him called back in immediately.
JOCASTA.   That can be done, but why do you desire it?
OEDIPUS.   I fear, Lady, I have already said
　　too much. That's why I wish to see him now.
JOCASTA.   Then he shall come; but it is right somehow
　　that I, too, Lord, should know what troubles you.
OEDIPUS.   I've gone so deep into the things I feared
　　I'll tell you everything. Who has a right
　　greater than yours, while I cross through this chance?
　　Polybus of Corinth was my father,
　　my mother was the Dorian Meropē.
　　I was first citizen, until this chance
　　attacked me—striking enough, to be sure,
　　but not worth all the gravity I gave it.
　　This: at a feast a man who'd drunk too much
　　denied, at the wine, I was my father's son.
　　I was depressed and all that day I barely
　　held it in. Next day I put the question
　　to my mother and father. They were enraged
　　at the man who'd let this fiction fly at me.
　　I was much cheered by them. And yet it kept
　　grinding into me. His words kept coming back.
　　Without my mother's or my father's knowledge
　　I went to Pytho. But Phoebus sent me away
　　dishonoring my demand. Instead, other
　　wretched horrors he flashed forth in speech.
　　He said that I would be my mother's lover,
　　show offspring to mankind they could not look at,
　　and be his murderer whose seed I am.°
　　When I heard this, and ever since, I gauged
　　the way to Corinth by the stars alone,

798 *be . . . am:* that is, murder my father.

running to a place where I would never see
the disgrace in the oracle's words come true.
But I soon came to the exact location
where, as you tell of it, the king was killed.
Lady, here is the truth. As I went on, 805
when I was just approaching those three roads,
a herald and a man like him you spoke of
came on, riding a carriage drawn by colts.
Both the man out front and the old man himself°
tried violently to force me off the road. 810
The driver, when he tried to push me off,
I struck in anger. The old man saw this, watched
me approach, then leaned out and lunged down
with twin prongs° at the middle of my head!
He got more than he gave. Abruptly—struck 815
once by the staff in this my hand—he tumbled
out, head first, from the middle of the carriage.
And then I killed them all. But if there is
a kinship between Laius and this stranger,
who is more wretched than the man you see? 820
Who was there born more hated by the gods?
For neither citizen nor foreigner
may take me in his home or speak to me.
No, they must drive me off. And it is I
who have pronounced these curses on myself! 825
I stain the dead man's bed with these my hands,
by which he died. Is not my nature vile?
Unclean?—if I am banished and even
in exile I may not see my own parents,
or set foot in my homeland, or else be yoked 830
in marriage to my mother, and kill my father,
Polybus, who raised me and gave me birth?
If someone judged a cruel divinity
did this to me, would he not speak the truth?
You pure and awful gods, may I not ever 835
see that day, may I be swept away
from men before I see so great and so
calamitous a stain fixed on my person!

CHORAGOS.   These things seem fearful to us, Lord, and yet,
until you hear it from the witness, keep hope! 840
OEDIPUS.   That is the single hope that's left to me,
to wait for him, that herdsman—until he comes.
JOCASTA.   When he appears, what are you eager for?
OEDIPUS.   Just this: if his account agrees with yours
then I shall have escaped this misery. 845
JOCASTA.   But what was it that struck you in my story?

---

809 *old man himself:* Laius.   813–14 *lunged . . . prongs:* Laius strikes Oedipus with a two-pronged
horse goad or whip.

OEDIPUS.   You said he spoke of robbers as the ones
    who killed him. Now: if he continues still
    to speak of many, then I could not have killed him.
    One man and many men just do not jibe.
    But if he says one belted man, the doubt
    is gone. The balance tips toward me. I did it.
JOCASTA.   No! He told it as I told you. Be certain.
    He can't reject that and reverse himself.
    The city heard these things, not I alone.
    But even if he swerves from what he said,
    he'll never show that Laius' murder, Lord,
    occurred just as predicted. For Loxias
    expressly said my son was doomed to kill him.
    The boy—poor boy—he never had a chance
    to cut him down, for he was cut down first.
    Never again, just for some oracle
    will I shoot frightened glances right and left.
OEDIPUS.   That's full of sense. Nonetheless, send a man
    to bring that farm hand here. Will you do it?
JOCASTA.   I'll send one right away. But let's go in.
    Would I do anything against your wishes?

        [*Exit OEDIPUS and JOCASTA through the central door into the palace.*]

STASIMON 2

Strophe 1

CHORUS.   May there accompany me
    the fate to keep a reverential purity in what I say,
    in all I do, for which the laws have been set forth
    and walk on high, born to traverse the brightest,
    highest upper air; Olympus° only
    is their father, nor was it
    mortal nature
    that fathered them, and never will
    oblivion lull them into sleep;
    the god in them is great and never ages.

Antistrophe 1

    The will to violate, seed of the tyrant,
    if it has drunk mindlessly of wealth and power,
    without a sense of time or true advantage,
    mounts to a peak, then
    plunges to an abrupt . . . destiny,
    where the useful foot

872 *Olympus:* Mount Olympus, home of the gods, treated as a god.

is of no use. But the kind
of struggling that is good for the city   885
I ask the god never to abolish.
The god is my protector: never will I give that up.

Strophe 2

But if a man proceeds disdainfully
　　in deeds of hand or word
and has no fear of Justice   890
　　or reverence for shrines of the divinities
(may a bad fate catch him
　　for his luckless wantonness!),
if he'll not gain what he gains with justice
and deny himself what is unholy,   895
or if he clings, in foolishness, to the untouchable
(what man, finally, in such an action, will have strength
enough to fend off passion's arrows from his soul?),
if, I say, this kind of
　　deed is held in honor—   900
why should I join the sacred dance?

Antistrophe 2

No longer shall I visit and revere
　　Earth's navel,° the untouchable,
nor visit Abae's° temple,
　　or Olympia,°   905
if the prophecies are not matched by events
　　for all the world to point to.
No, you who hold the power, if you are rightly called
Zeus the king of all, let this matter not escape you
and your ever-deathless rule,   910
for the prophecies to Laius fade . . .
and men already disregard them;
nor is Apollo anywhere
　　glorified with honors.
Religion slips away.   915

EPISODE 3

[*Enter JOCASTA from the palace carrying a branch wound with wool and a jar of incense. She is attended by two women.*]

JOCASTA.   Lords of the realm, the thought has come to me
　　to visit shrines of the divinities
　　with suppliant's branch in hand and fragrant smoke.

---

903 *Earth's navel:* Delphi.   904 *Abae:* a town in Phocis where there was another oracle of
Apollo.   905 *Olympia:* site of the oracle of Zeus.

For Oedipus excites his soul too much
with alarms of all kinds. He will not judge
the present by the past, like a man of sense.
He's at the mercy of all terror-mongers.

[*JOCASTA approaches the altar on the right and kneels.*]

Since I can do no good by counseling,
Apollo the Lycēan!—you are the closest—
I come a suppliant, with these my vows,
for a cleansing that will not pollute him.
For when we see him shaken we are all
afraid, like people looking at their helmsman.

[*Enter a MESSENGER along one of the Parados. He sees JOCASTA at the altar and then addresses the CHORUS.*]

MESSENGER.   I would be pleased if you would help me, stranger.
Where is the palace of King Oedipus?
Or tell me where he is himself, if you know.
CHORUS.   This is his house, stranger. He is within.
This is his wife and mother of his children.
MESSENGER.   May she and her family find prosperity,
if, as you say, her marriage is fulfilled.
JOCASTA.   You also, stranger, for you deserve as much
for your gracious words. But tell me why you've come.
What do you wish? Or what have you to tell us?
MESSENGER.   Good news, my Lady, both for your house and
           husband.
JOCASTA.   What is your news? And who has sent you to us?
MESSENGER.   I come from Corinth. When you have heard my
           news
you will rejoice, I'm sure—and grieve perhaps.
JOCASTA.   What is it? How can it have this double power?
MESSENGER.   They will establish him their king, so say
the people of the land of Isthmia.°
JOCASTA.   But is old Polybus not still in power?
MESSENGER.   He's not, for death has clasped him in the tomb.
JOCASTA.   What's this? Has Oedipus' father died?
MESSENGER.   If I have lied then I deserve to die.
JOCASTA.   Attendant! Go quickly to your master,
and tell him this.
                    [*Exit an ATTENDANT into the palace.*]
                    Oracles of the gods!
Where are you now? The man whom Oedipus
fled long ago, for fear that he should kill him—
he's been destroyed by chance and not by him!

945 *land of Isthmia:* Corinth, which is on an isthmus.

[*Enter OEDIPUS from the palace.*]

OEDIPUS.   Darling Jocasta, my beloved wife,   955
   Why have you called me from the palace?
JOCASTA.   First hear what this man has to say. Then see
   what the god's grave oracle has come to now!
OEDIPUS.   Where is he from? What is this news he brings me?
JOCASTA.   From Corinth. He brings news about your father: 960
   that Polybus is no more! that he is dead!
OEDIPUS.   What's this, old man? I want to hear you say it.
MESSENGER.   If this is what must first be clarified,
   please be assured that he is dead and gone.
OEDIPUS.   By treachery or by the touch of sickness?   965
MESSENGER.   Light pressures tip agéd frames into their sleep.
OEDIPUS.   You mean the poor man died of some disease.
MESSENGER.   And of the length of years that he had tallied.
OEDIPUS.   Aha! Then why should we look to Pytho's vapors,°
   or to the birds that scream above our heads?°   970
   If we could really take those things for guides,
   I would have killed my father. But he's dead!
   He is beneath the earth, and here am I,
   who never touched a spear. Unless he died
   of longing for me and I "killed" him that way!   975
   No, in this case, Polybus, by dying, took
   the worthless oracle to Hades with him.
JOCASTA.   And wasn't I telling you that just now?
OEDIPUS.   You were indeed. I was misled by fear.
JOCASTA.   You should not care about this anymore.   980
OEDIPUS.   I must care. I must stay clear of my mother's bed.
JOCASTA.   What's there for man to fear? The realm of chance
   prevails. True foresight isn't possible.
   His life is best who lives without a plan.
   This marriage with your mother—don't fear it.   985
   How many times have men in dreams, too, slept
   with their own mothers! Those who believe such things
   mean nothing endure their lives most easily.
OEDIPUS.   A fine, bold speech, and you are right, perhaps,
   except that my mother is still living,   990
   so I must fear her, however well you argue.
JOCASTA.   And yet your father's tomb is a great eye.
OEDIPUS.   Illuminating, yes. But I still fear the living.
MESSENGER.   Who is the woman who inspires this fear?
OEDIPUS.   Meropē, Polybus' wife, old man.   995
MESSENGER.   And what is there about her that alarms you?
OEDIPUS.   An oracle, god-sent and fearful, stranger.
MESSENGER.   Is it permitted that another know?

---

969 *Pytho's vapors:* the prophecies of the oracle at Delphi.   970 *birds . . . heads:* the prophecies
derived from interpreting the flights of birds.

OEDIPUS.   It is. Loxias once said to me
  I must have intercourse with my own mother   1'
  and take my father's blood with these my hands.
  So I have long lived far away from Corinth.
  This has indeed brought much good luck, and yet,
  to see one's parents' eyes is happiest.
MESSENGER.   Was it for this that you have lived in exile?   1
OEDIPUS.   So I'd not be my father's killer, sir.
MESSENGER.   Had I not better free you from this fear,
  my Lord? That's why I came—to do you service.
OEDIPUS.   Indeed, what a reward you'd get for that!
MESSENGER.   Indeed, this is the main point of my trip,   1
  to be rewarded when you get back home.
OEDIPUS.   I'll never rejoin the givers of my seed!°
MESSENGER.   My son, clearly you don't know what you're doing.
OEDIPUS.   But how is that, old man? For the gods' sake, tell me!
MESSENGER.   If it's because of them you won't go home.   1'
OEDIPUS.   I fear that Phoebus will have told the truth.
MESSENGER.   Pollution from the ones who gave you seed?
OEDIPUS.   That is the thing, old man, I always fear.
MESSENGER.   Your fear is groundless. Understand that.
OEDIPUS.   Groundless? Not if I was born their son.   1'
MESSENGER.   But Polybus is not related to you.
OEDIPUS.   Do you mean Polybus was not my father?
MESSENGER.   No more than I. We're both the same to you.
OEDIPUS.   Same? One who begot me and one who didn't?
MESSENGER.   He didn't beget you any more than I did.   1'
OEDIPUS.   But then, why did he say I was his son?
MESSENGER.   He got you as a gift from my own hands.
OEDIPUS.   He loved me so, though from another's hands?
MESSENGER.   His former childlessness persuaded him.
OEDIPUS.   But had you bought me, or begotten me?   1'
MESSENGER.   Found you. In the forest hallows of Cithaeron.
OEDIPUS.   What were you doing traveling in that region?
MESSENGER.   I was in charge of flocks which grazed those mountains.
OEDIPUS.   A wanderer who worked the flocks for hire?
MESSENGER.   Ah, but that day I was your savior, son.   1'
OEDIPUS.   From what? What was my trouble when you took me?
MESSENGER.   The ball-joints of your feet might testify.
OEDIPUS.   What's that? What makes you name that ancient trouble?
MESSENGER.   Your feet were pierced and I am your rescuer.
OEDIPUS.   A fearful rebuke those tokens left for me!   1'
MESSENGER.   That was the chance that names you who you are.
OEDIPUS.   By the gods, did my mother or my father do this?
MESSENGER.   That I don't know. He might who gave you to me.
OEDIPUS.   From someone else? You didn't chance on me?
MESSENGER.   Another shepherd handed you to me.   1'

1012 *givers of my seed:* that is, my parents. Oedipus still thinks Meropē and Polybus are his parents.

OEDIPUS.   Who was he? Do you know? Will you explain!
MESSENGER.   They called him one of the men of—was it Laius?
OEDIPUS.   The one who once was king here long ago?
MESSENGER.   That is the one! The man was shepherd to him.
OEDIPUS.   And is he still alive so I can see him?   1050
MESSENGER.   But you who live here ought to know that best.
OEDIPUS.   Does any one of you now present know
 about the shepherd whom this man has named?
 Have you seen him in town or in the fields? Speak out!
 The time has come for the discovery!   1055
CHORAGOS.   The man he speaks of, I believe, is the same
 as the field hand you have already asked to see.
 But it's Jocasta who would know this best.
OEDIPUS.   Lady, do you remember the man we just
 now sent for—is that the man he speaks of?   1060
JOCASTA.   What? The man he spoke of? Pay no attention!
 His words are not worth thinking about. It's nothing.
OEDIPUS.   With clues like this within my grasp, give up?
 Fail to solve the mystery of my birth?
JOCASTA.   For the love of the gods, and if you love your life,   1065
 give up this search! My sickness is enough.
OEDIPUS.   Come! Though my mothers for three generations
 were in slavery, you'd not be lowborn!
JOCASTA.   No, listen to me! Please! Don't do this thing!
OEDIPUS.   I will not listen; I will search out the truth.   1070
JOCASTA.   My thinking is for you—it would be best.
OEDIPUS.   This "best" of yours is starting to annoy me.
JOCASTA.   Doomed man! Never find out who you are!
OEDIPUS.   Will someone go and bring that shepherd here?
 Leave her to glory in her wealthy birth!   1075
JOCASTA.   Man of misery! No other name
 shall I address you by, ever again.

[Exit JOCASTA into the palace after a long pause.]

CHORAGOS.   Why has your lady left, Oedipus,
 hurled by a savage grief? I am afraid
 disaster will come bursting from this silence.   1080
OEDIPUS.   Let it burst forth! However low this seed
 of mine may be, yet I desire to see it.
 She, perhaps—she has a woman's pride—
 is mortified by my base origins.
 But I who count myself the child of Chance,   1085
 the giver of good, shall never know dishonor.
 She is my mother,° and the months my brothers
 who first marked out my lowness, then my greatness.
 I shall not prove untrue to such a nature
 by giving up the search for my own birth.   1090

1087 *She . . . mother:* Chance is my mother.

STASIMON 3

Strophe

CHORUS.   If I have mantic power
and excellence in thought,
by Olympus,
        you shall not, Cithaeron, at tomorrow's
full moon,   109
fail to hear us celebrate you as the countryman
of Oedipus, his nurse and mother,
or fail to be the subject of our dance,
        since you have given pleasure
to our king.   110
Phoebus, whom we summon by "iē!,"
may this be pleasing to you!

Antistrophe

Who was your mother, son?
which of the long-lived nymphs
after lying with Pan,°   110
        the mountain roaming . . . Or was it a bride
of Loxias?°
For dear to him are all the upland pastures.
Or was it Mount Cyllēnē's lord,°
or the Bacchic god,°   11
        dweller of the mountain peaks,
who received you as a joyous find
from one of the nymphs of Helicon,
the favorite sharers of his sport?

EPISODE 4

OEDIPUS.   If someone like myself, who never met him,   1▪
may calculate—elders, I think I see
the very herdsman we've been waiting for.
His many years would fit that man's age,
and those who bring him on, if I am right,
are my own men. And yet, in real knowledge,   1▪
you can outstrip me, surely: you've seen him.

[*Enter the old* HERDSMAN *escorted by two of Oedipus's* ATTENDANTS. *At first, the* HERDSM▪
will not look at OEDIPUS.]

CHORAGOS.   I know him, yes, a man of the house of Laius,
a trusty herdsman if he ever had one.

1105 *Pan:* god of shepherds and woodlands, half man and half goat.   1107 *Loxias:* Apollo.
1109 *Mount Cyllēnē's lord:* Hermes, messenger of the gods.   1110 *Bacchic god:* Dionysus.

OEDIPUS.   I ask you first, the stranger come from Corinth:
  is this the man you spoke of?
MESSENGER.   That's he you see.   1125
OEDIPUS.   Then you, old man. First look at me! Now answer:
  did you belong to Laius' household once?
HERDSMAN.   I did. Not a purchased slave but raised in the palace.
OEDIPUS.   How have you spent your life? What is your work?
HERDSMAN.   Most of my life now I have tended sheep.   1130
OEDIPUS.   Where is the usual place you stay with them?
HERDSMAN.   On Mount Cithaeron. Or in that district.
OEDIPUS.   Do you recall observing this man there?
HERDSMAN.   Doing what? Which is the man you mean?
OEDIPUS.   This man right here. Have you had dealings with him?   1135
HERDSMAN.   I can't say right away. I don't remember.
MESSENGER.   No wonder, master. I'll bring clear memory
  to his ignorance. I'm absolutely sure
  he can recall it, the district was Cithaeron,
  he with a double flock, and I, with one,   1140
  lived close to him, for three entire seasons,
  six months long, from spring right to Arcturus.°
  Then for the winter I'd drive mine to my fold,
  and he'd drive his to Laius' pen again.
  Did any of the things I say take place?   1145
HERDSMAN.   You speak the truth, though it's from long ago.
MESSENGER.   Do you remember giving me, back then,
  a boy I was to care for as my own?
HERDSMAN.   What are you saying? Why do you ask me that?
MESSENGER.   There, sir, is the man who was that boy!   1150
HERDSMAN.   Damn you! Shut your mouth! Keep your silence!
OEDIPUS.   Stop! Don't you rebuke his words.
  Your words ask for rebuke far more than his.
HERDSMAN.   But what have I done wrong, most royal master?
OEDIPUS.   Not telling of the boy of whom he asked.   1155
HERDSMAN.   He's ignorant and blundering toward ruin.
OEDIPUS.   Tell it willingly—or under torture.
HERDSMAN.   Oh god! Don't—I am old—don't torture me!
OEDIPUS.   Here! Someone put his hands behind his back!
HERDSMAN.   But why? What else would you find out, poor man?   1160
OEDIPUS.   Did you give him the child he asks about?
HERDSMAN.   I did. I wish that I had died that day!
OEDIPUS.   You'll come to that if you don't speak the truth.
HERDSMAN.   It's if I speak that I shall be destroyed.
OEDIPUS.   I think this fellow struggles for delay.   1165
HERDSMAN.   No, no! I said already that I gave him.
OEDIPUS.   From your own home, or got from someone else?

1142 *from spring right to Arcturus:* that is, from spring to early fall, when the summer star Arcturus
(in the constellation Boötes) is no longer visible in the early evening sky. It does not rise at night
again until the following spring.

HERDSMAN.　Not from my own. I got him from another.
OEDIPUS.　Which of these citizens? What sort of house?
HERDSMAN.　Don't—by the gods!—don't, master, ask me more!
OEDIPUS.　It means your death if I must ask again.
HERDSMAN.　One of the children of the house of Laius.
OEDIPUS.　A slave—or born into the family?
HERDSMAN.　I have come to the dreaded thing, and I shall say it.
OEDIPUS.　And I to hearing it, but hear I must.
HERDSMAN.　He was reported to have been—his son.
　　Your lady in the house could tell you best.
OEDIPUS.　Because she gave him to you?
HERDSMAN.　　　　　　　　　　　　Yes, my lord.
OEDIPUS.　What was her purpose?
HERDSMAN.　　　　　　　　　　I was to kill the boy.
OEDIPUS.　The child she bore?
HERDSMAN.　　　　　　　　　She dreaded prophecies.
OEDIPUS.　What were they?
HERDSMAN.　　　　　　　　The word was that he'd kill his parents.
OEDIPUS.　Then why did you give him up to this old man?
HERDSMAN.　In pity, master—so he would take him home,
　　to another land. But what he did was save him
　　for this supreme disaster. If you are the one
　　he speaks of—know your evil birth and fate!
OEDIPUS.　Ah! All of it was destined to be true!
　　Oh light, now may I look my last upon you,
　　shown monstrous in my birth, in marriage monstrous,
　　a murderer monstrous in those I killed.

[*Exit* OEDIPUS, *running into the palace.*]

STASIMON 4

Strophe 1

CHORUS.　Oh generations of mortal men,
　　while you are living, I will
　　　　appraise your lives at zero!
　　What man
　　comes closer to seizing lasting blessedness
　　than merely to seize its semblance,
　　and after living in this semblance, to plunge?
　　With your example before us,
　　with your destiny, yours,
　　　　suffering Oedipus, no mortal
　　can I judge fortunate.

Antistrophe 1

　　For he,° outranging everybody,
　　shot his arrow° and became the lord

1202 *he:* Oedipus.　　1203 *shot his arrow:* took his chances; made a guess at the Sphinx's riddle.

of wide prosperity and blessedness,
oh Zeus, after destroying   1205
the virgin with the crooked talons,°
singer of oracles; and against death,
in my land, he arose a tower of defense.
From which time you were called my king
and granted privileges supreme—in mighty   1210
Thebes the ruling lord.

Strophe 2

But now—whose story is more sorrowful than yours?
Who is more intimate with fierce calamities,
with labors, now that your life is altered?
Alas, my Oedipus, whom all men know: 1215
one great harbor°—
one alone sufficed for you,
as son and father,
when you tumbled,° plowman° of the woman's chamber.
How, how could your paternal   1220
    furrows, wretched man,
endure you silently so long.

Antistrophe 2

Time, all-seeing, surprised you living an unwilled life
and sits from of old in judgment on the marriage, not a marriage,
where the begetter is the begot as well.   1225
Ah, son of Laius . . . ,
would that—oh, would that
I had never seen you!
I wail, my scream climbing beyond itself
from my whole power of voice. To say it straight: 1230
    from you I got new breath—
but I also lulled my eye to sleep.°

EXODOS

[Enter the SECOND MESSENGER from the palace.]

SECOND MESSENGER.   You who are first among the citizens,
    what deeds you are about to hear and see!
    What grief you'll carry, if, true to your birth,   1235
    you still respect the house of Labdacus!
    Neither the Ister nor the Phasis river

1206 *virgin . . . talons:* the Sphinx.   1216 *one great harbor:* metaphorical allusion to Jocasta's body.   1219 *tumbled:* were born and had sex.   *plowman:* Plowing is used here as a sexual metaphor.   1232 *I . . . sleep:* I failed to see the corruption you brought.

could purify this house, such suffering
does it conceal, or soon must bring to light—
willed this time, not unwilled. Griefs hurt worst
which we perceive to be self-chosen ones.
CHORAGOS.   They were sufficient, the things we knew before,
to make us grieve. What can you add to those?
SECOND MESSENGER.   The thing that's quickest said and quickest heard:
our own, our royal one, Jocasta's dead.
CHORAGOS.   Unhappy queen! What was responsible?
SECOND MESSENGER.   Herself. The bitterest of these events
is not for you, you were not there to see,
but yet, exactly as I can recall it,
you'll hear what happened to that wretched lady.
She came in anger through the outer hall,
and then she ran straight to her marriage bed,
tearing her hair with the fingers of both hands.
Then, slamming shut the doors when she was in,
she called to Laius, dead so many years,
remembering the ancient seed which caused
his death, leaving the mother to the son
to breed again an ill-born progeny.
She mourned the bed where she, alas, bred double—
husband by husband, children by her child.
From this point on I don't know how she died,
for Oedipus then burst in with a cry,
and did not let us watch her final evil.
Our eyes were fixed on him. Wildly he ran
to each of us, asking for his spear
and for his wife—no wife: where he might find
the double mother-field, his and his children's.
He raved, and some divinity then showed him—
for none of us did so who stood close by.
With a dreadful shout—as if some guide were leading—
he lunged through the double doors; he bent the hollow
bolts from the sockets, burst into the room,
and there we saw her, hanging from above,
entangled in some twisted hanging strands.
He saw, was stricken, and with a wild roar
ripped down the dangling noose. When she, poor woman,
lay on the ground, there came a fearful sight:
he snatched the pins of worked gold from her dress,
with which her clothes were fastened: these he raised
and struck into the ball-joints of his eyes.°
He shouted that they would no longer see
the evils he had suffered or had done,
see in the dark those he should not have seen,
and know no more those he once sought to know.

1280 *ball-joints of his eyes:* his eyeballs. Oedipus blinds himself in both eyes at the same time.

Theatre of Dionysus, fourth century B.C.E., Athens, Greece.
Michael Holford Photographs.

Stage of the Globe Theatre, seventeenth century, London, England. Dr. Franklin J. Hildy, photographer.

While chanting this, not once but many times   1285
he raised his hand and struck into his eyes.
Blood from his wounded eyes poured down his chin,
not freed in moistening drops, but all at once
a stormy rain of black blood burst like hail.
These evils, coupling them, making them one,   1290
have broken loose upon both man and wife.
The old prosperity that they had once
was true prosperity, and yet today,
mourning, ruin, death, disgrace, and every
evil you could name—not one is absent.   1295
CHORAGOS.   Has he allowed himself some peace from all this grief?
SECOND MESSENGER.   He shouts that someone slide the bolts and show
to all the Cadmeians the patricide,
his mother's—I can't say it, it's unholy—
so he can cast himself out of the land,   1300
not stay and curse his house by his own curse.
He lacks the strength, though, and he needs a guide,
for his is a sickness that's too great to bear.
Now you yourself will see: the bolts of the doors
are opening. You are about to see   1305
a vision even one who hates must pity.

[*Enter the blinded* OEDIPUS *from the palace, led in by a household* SERVANT.]

CHORAGOS.   This suffering sends terror through men's eyes,
terrible beyond any suffering
my eyes have touched. Oh man of pain,
what madness reached you? Which god from far off,   1310
surpassing in range his longest spring,
struck hard against your god-abandoned fate?
Oh man of pain,
I cannot look upon you—though there's so much
I would ask you, so much to hear,   1315
so much that holds my eyes—
so awesome the convulsions you send through me.
OEDIPUS.   Ah! Ah! I am a man of misery.
Where am I carried? Pity me! Where
is my voice scattered abroad on wings?   1320
Divinity, where has your lunge transported me?
CHORAGOS.   To something horrible, not to be heard or seen.

KOMMOS

Strophe 1

OEDIPUS.   Oh, my cloud
of darkness, abominable, unspeakable as it attacks me,
not to be turned away, brought by an evil wind!   1325

> Alas!
> Again alas! Both enter me at once:
> the sting of the prongs,° the memory of evils!
> CHORUS.   I do not marvel that in these afflictions
> you carry double griefs and double evils.

Antistrophe 1

> OEDIPUS.   Ah, friend,
> so you at least are there, resolute servant!
> Still with a heart to care for me, the blind man.
> Oh! Oh!
> I know that you are there. I recognize
> even inside my darkness, that voice of yours.
> CHORUS.   Doer of horror, how did you bear to quench
> your vision? What divinity raised your hand?

Strophe 2

> OEDIPUS.   It was Apollo there, Apollo, friends,
> who brought my sorrows, vile sorrows to their perfection,
> these evils that were done to me.
> But the one who struck them with his hand,
> that one was none but I, in wretchedness.
> For why was I to see
> when nothing I could see would bring me joy?
> CHORUS.   Yes, that is how it was.
> OEDIPUS.   What could I see, indeed,
> or what enjoy—what greeting
> is there I could hear with pleasure, friends?
> Conduct me out of the land
> as quickly as you can!
> Conduct me out, my friends,
> the man utterly ruined,
> supremely cursed,
> the man who is by gods
> the most detested of all men!
> CHORUS.   Wretched in disaster and in knowledge:
> oh, I could wish you'd never come to know!

Antistrophe 2

> OEDIPUS.   May he be destroyed, whoever freed the savage shackles
> from my feet when I'd been sent to the wild pasture,
> whoever rescued me from murder
> and became my savior—
> a bitter gift:

1328 *prongs:* refers to both the whip that Laius used and the two gold pins Oedipus used to blind himself.

if I had died then,
   I'd not have been such grief to self and kin.   1365
CHORUS.   I also would have had it so.
OEDIPUS.   I'd not have returned to be my father's
   murderer; I'd not be called by men
   my mother's bridegroom.
   Now I'm without a god,   1370
      child of a polluted parent,
   fellow progenitor with him
      who gave me birth in misery.
   If there's an evil that
      surpasses evils, that   1375
   has fallen to the lot of Oedipus.
CHORAGOS.   How can I say that you have counseled well?
   Better not to be than live a blind man.
OEDIPUS.   That this was not the best thing I could do—
   don't tell me that, or advise me any more!   1380
   Should I descend to Hades and endure
   to see my father with these eyes? Or see
   my poor unhappy mother? For I have done,
   to both of these, things too great for hanging.
   Or is the sight of children to be yearned for,   1385
   to see new shoots that sprouted as these did?
   Never, never with these eyes of mine!
   Nor city, nor tower, nor holy images
   of the divinities! For I, all-wretched,
   most nobly raised—as no one else in Thebes—   1390
   deprived myself of these when I ordained
   that all expel the impious one—god-shown
   to be polluted, and the dead king's son!°
   Once I exposed this great stain upon me,
   could I have looked on these with steady eyes?   1395
   No! No! And if there were a way to block
   the source of hearing in my ears, I'd gladly
   have locked up my pitiable body,
   so I'd be blind and deaf. Evils shut out—
   that way my mind could live in sweetness.   1400
   Alas, Cithaeron,° why did you receive me?
   Or when you had me, not killed me instantly?
   I'd not have had to show my birth to mankind.
   Polybus, Corinth, halls—ancestral,
   they told me—how beautiful was your ward,   1405
   a scar that held back festering disease!
   Evil my nature, evil my origin.
   You, three roads, and you, secret ravine,

1391–1393 *I . . . son:* Oedipus refers to his own curse against the murderer as well as his sins of patricide and incest.   1401 *Cithaeron:* the mountain on which the infant Oedipus was exposed.

you oak grove, narrow place of those three paths
that drank my blood° from these my hands, from him   1‹
who fathered me, do you remember still
the things I did to you? When I'd come here,
what I then did once more? Oh marriages! Marriages!
You gave us life and when you'd planted us
you sent the same seed up, and then revealed   1
fathers, brothers, sons, and kinsman's blood,
and brides, and wives, and mothers, all the most
atrocious things that happen to mankind!
One should not name what never should have been.
Somewhere out there, then, quickly, by the gods,   1
cover me up, or murder me, or throw me
to the ocean where you will never see me more!

[*OEDIPUS moves toward the CHORUS and they back away from him.*]

Come! Don't shrink to touch this wretched man!
Believe me, do not be frightened! I alone
of all mankind can carry these afflictions.   1

[*Enter CREON from the palace with ATTENDANTS.*]

CHORAGOS.   Tell Creon what you wish for. Just when we need him
he's here. He can act, he can advise you.
He's now the land's sole guardian in your place.
OEDIPUS.   Ah! Are there words that I can speak to him?
What ground for trust can I present? It's proved   1
that I was false to him in everything.
CREON.   I have not come to mock you, Oedipus,
nor to reproach you for your former falseness.
You men, if you have no respect for sons
of mortals, let your awe for the all-feeding   1
flames of lordly Hēlius° prevent
your showing unconcealed so great a stain,
abhorred by earth and sacred rain and light.
Escort him quickly back into the house!
If blood kin only see and hear their own   1
afflictions, we'll have no impious defilement.
OEDIPUS.   By the gods, you've freed me from one terrible fear,
so nobly meeting my unworthiness:
grant me something—not for me; for you!
CREON.   What do you want that you should beg me so?   1‹
OEDIPUS.   To drive me from the land at once, to a place
where there will be no man to speak to me!
CREON.   I would have done just that—had I not wished
to ask first of the god what I should do.
OEDIPUS.   His answer was revealed in full—that I,   1‹
the patricide, unholy, be destroyed.

1410 *my blood:* that is, the blood of my father, Laius.   1436 *Hēlius:* the sun.

CREON.   He said that, but our need is so extreme,
  it's best to have sure knowledge what must be done.
OEDIPUS.   You'll ask about a wretched man like me?
CREON.   Is it not time you put your trust in the god?   1455
OEDIPUS.   But I bid you as well, and shall entreat you.
  Give her who is within what burial
  you will—you'll give your own her proper rites;
  but me—do not condemn my fathers' land
  to have me dwelling here while I'm alive,   1460
  but let me live on mountains—on Cithaeron
  famed as mine, for my mother and my father,
  while they yet lived, made it my destined tomb,
  and I'll be killed by those who wished my ruin!
  And yet I know: no sickness will destroy me,   1465
  nothing will: I'd never have been saved
  when left to die unless for some dread evil.
  Then let my fate continue where it will!
  As for my children, Creon, take no pains
  for my sons—they're men and they will never lack   1470
  the means to live, wherever they may be—
  but my two wretched, pitiable girls,
  who never ate but at my table, never
  were without me—everything that I
  would touch, they'd always have a share of it—   1475
  please care for them! Above all, let me touch
  them with my hands and weep aloud my woes!
  Please, my Lord!
  Please, noble heart! Touching with my hands,
  I'd think I held them as when I could see.   1480

[*Enter* ANTIGONE *and* ISMENE *from the palace with* ATTENDANTS.]

  What's this?
  Oh gods! Do I hear, somewhere, my two dear ones
  sobbing? Has Creon really pitied me
  and sent to me my dearest ones, my children?
  Is that it?   1485

CREON.   Yes, I prepared this for you, for I knew
  you'd feel this joy, as you have always done.
OEDIPUS.   Good fortune, then, and, for your care, be guarded
  far better by divinity than I was!
  Where are you, children? Come to me! Come here   1490
  to these my hands, hands of your brother, hands
  of him who gave you seed, hands that made
  these once bright eyes to see now in this fashion.

[*OEDIPUS embraces his daughters.*]

  He, children, seeing nothing, knowing nothing,
  he fathered you where his own seed was plowed.   1495
  I weep for you as well, though I can't see you,

imagining your bitter life to come,
the life you will be forced by men to live.
What gatherings of townsmen will you join,
what festivals, without returning home   1
in tears instead of watching holy rites?
And when you've reached the time for marrying,
where, children, is the man who'll run the risk
of taking on himself the infamy
that will wound you as it did my parents?   1
What evil is not here? Your father killed
his father, plowed the one who gave him birth,
and from the place where he was sown, from there
he got you, from the place he too was born.
These are the wounds: then who will marry you?   1.
No man, my children. No, it's clear that you
must wither in dry barrenness, unmarried.

[*OEDIPUS addresses CREON.*]

Son of Menoeceus! You are the only father
left to them—we two who gave them seed
are both destroyed: watch that they don't become   1!
poor, wanderers, unmarried—they are your kin.
Let not my ruin be their ruin, too!
No, pity them! You see how young they are,
bereft of everyone, except for you.
Consent, kind heart, and touch me with your hand!   1▪

[*CREON grasps OEDIPUS's right hand.*]

You, children, if you had reached an age of sense,
I would have counseled much. Now, pray you may live
always where it's allowed, finding a life
better than his was, who gave you seed.
CREON.   Stop this now. Quiet your weeping. Move away, into the house.   1▪
OEDIPUS.   Bitter words, but I obey them.
CREON.   There's an end to all things.
OEDIPUS.   I have first this request.
CREON.   I will hear it.
OEDIPUS.   Banish me from my homeland.
CREON.   You must ask that of the god.
OEDIPUS.   But I am the gods' most hated man!
CREON.   Then you will soon get what you want.
OEDIPUS.   Do you consent?
CREON.   I never promise when, as now, I'm ignorant.   1!
OEDIPUS.   Then lead me in.
CREON.   Come. But let your hold fall from your children.
OEDIPUS.   Do not take them from me, ever!
CREON.   Do not wish to keep all of the
power. You had power, but that power did not follow you through life.

[*OEDIPUS's daughters are taken from him and led into the palace by ATTENDANTS. OEDIPUS is led into the palace by a SERVANT. CREON and the other ATTENDANTS follow. Only the CHORUS remains.*]

CHORUS.   People of Thebes, my country, see: here is that Oedipus—
he who "knew" the famous riddle, and attained the highest power,   1535
whom all citizens admired, even envying his luck!
See the billows of wild troubles which he has entered now!
Here is the truth of each man's life: we must wait, and see his end,
scrutinize his dying day, and refuse to call him happy
till he has crossed the border of his life without pain.   1540

[*Exit the CHORUS along each of the Parados.*]

QUESTIONS

Prologue and Parados

1. What is the situation in Thebes as the play begins? Why does Oedipus want to find Laius's murderer?

Episode 1 and Stasimon 1

2. How does Oedipus react to Tiresias's refusal to speak? How is this reaction characteristic of Oedipus? What other instances of this sort of behavior can you find in Oedipus's story?
3. When Tiresias does speak, he answers the central question of the play and tells the truth. Why doesn't Oedipus recognize this as the truth?

Episode 2 and Stasimon 2

4. What does Oedipus accuse Creon of doing? How does Creon defend himself? Do you find Creon's defense convincing? Why?
5. What is Jocasta's attitude toward oracles and prophecy? Why does she have this attitude? How does it contrast with the attitude of the chorus?
6. At what point in the play does Oedipus begin to suspect that he killed Laius? What details make him begin to suspect himself?

Episode 3 and Stasimon 3

7. What news does the messenger from Corinth bring? Why does this news seem to be good at first? How is this situation reversed?

Episode 4 and Stasimon 4

8. What do you make of the coincidence that the same herdsman (1) saved the infant Oedipus from death, (2) was with Laius at the place where three roads meet and was the lone survivor of the attack, and (3) will now be the agent to destroy Oedipus?
9. What moral does the chorus see in Oedipus's life?

Exodos

10. Why does Oedipus blind himself? What is the significance of the instruments that he uses to blind himself?

11. Who or what does Oedipus blame for his tragic life and destruction?

GENERAL QUESTIONS

1. In *Oedipus*, the peripeteia, anagnorisis, and catastrophe all occur at the same moment. When is this moment? Who is most severely affected by it?

2. Sophocles tells the events of Oedipus's life out of chronological order. Put all the events of his life in chronological order and consider how you might dramatize them. Why does Sophocles's ordering of these events produce an effective play?

3. Each episode of the play introduces new conflicts: Oedipus against the plague, against Tiresias, against Creon. What is the central conflict of the play? Why is it central?

4. All the violent acts of this play—the suicide of Jocasta and the blinding of Oedipus—occur offstage and are reported rather than shown. What are the advantages and disadvantages of dealing with violence this way?

5. Discuss the use of coincidences in the play. How do you react to them? Do they seem convincing or forced, given the plot of the play?

6. Explore the ways in which Sophocles employs dramatic irony, with reference to three specific examples.

7. Consider that *Oedipus* is a tragedy of both the individual and the state. What do you think will happen to Thebes after Oedipus is exiled?

8. Discuss the functions of the chorus and the Choragos. What do the choral odes contribute to the play?

9. Early in the play Oedipus begins a search for a murderer. How does the object of his search change as the play progresses? Why does it change?

RENAISSANCE DRAMA AND SHAKESPEARE'S THEATER

In the early years of the English Renaissance, there was a flourishing native tradition of theater that had developed first within the church and then with the cooperation of the church.[12] The bridge from religious drama to the drama of the Renaissance was created in a number of ways. Of great importance was the growth of traveling dramatic professional companies, who performed their plays in local innyards—square or quadrangular spaces surrounded by the rooms of the inn. In addition, plays were performed at court, in the great rooms of aristocratic houses, in the law courts, and at universities.

---

[12] For an account of the medieval tradition, see Chapter 26, pp. 1236–40.

Aside from the performing tradition, the immediate influence on the creation of a new drama was the development of a taste for dramatic topics drawn from nonreligious sources. The earliest of such plays in the sixteenth century was the so-called **Tudor interlude,** named after the monarchs of the Tudor family who ruled England from 1485 to 1603. *Interlude* is a misnomer, for the plays were often quite long, one of them lasting an entire day. The interludes, supported by the nobility, were tragedies, comedies, or historical plays that were performed by both professional actors and students. They sometimes featured abstract and allegorical characters and provided opportunities for both music and farcical action.

After the middle of the sixteenth century, the revival of ancient drama and culture came increasingly to the fore. The dominating influence was the Roman dramatist Seneca (4 B.C.E.–65 C.E.), eight of whose tragedies, derived from Greek tragedy, had survived from antiquity. A vital quality of the Senecan tragedies was that they were violent and bloody, and thus they gave a classical precedent for the revenge and murder that were to be featured in the Elizabethan drama. Seneca became important not so much because he had written great works but rather because he had written in Latin. He could therefore be readily understood by a generation of new dramatists who had been schooled in Roman history, culture, and literature.

Shakespeare Became a Theater Entrepreneur as Well as a Writer

The first group of these Elizabethan playwrights included Christopher Marlowe, Thomas Kyd, Robert Greene, George Peele, Thomas Lodge, and John Lyly. These were the men whose plays William Shakespeare watched and acted in when he first arrived in London from Stratford-upon-Avon early in the 1590s. By 1594 Shakespeare had joined the Lord Chamberlain's Men, the most popular of the London acting companies. He rose swiftly as both an actor and a dramatist, and by 1599 he had become an active partner with the Lord Chamberlain's Men in a venture to construct a new theater, the Globe, within a stone's throw of the earlier theater, the Rose. It was at the Globe that Shakespeare's greatest plays (including *Hamlet*) were first produced.

Shakespeare Wrote His Major Plays for the Globe Theater (1599–1612)

Compared with the massive Greek outdoor amphitheaters, the Globe was small. Some theater historians have calculated that it could have held as many as 2,000 to 3,000 people, although this estimate seems excessive, for half of that number would have made an extremely large audience.

The front exterior of the newly reconstructed *Shakespeare's Globe Theater* in Southwark, London (with some scaffolding still in place). This theater duplicates the original Globe known by Shakespeare and his audiences. Plans for reconstruction were based on contemporary drawings and archaeological discoveries at the original site. Rebuilding was carried out in accord with authentic Elizabethan materials and methods; note the thatched roof, the half-timbering, the windows, and the building's many sides. Regular performances began here on August 21, 1996.

THE GLOBE WAS A "RING" TYPE THEATER OPEN TO THE SKY.   Recent archaeological excavations of the site of the Globe, together with a complete reconstruction based on the knowledge newly gained, show that it was a twenty-sided building. For practical purposes it was round—as it is shown in a contemporary drawing—and its outer diameter was approximately a hundred feet. From above, it would have resembled a ring, or, as Shakespeare called the type in *Henry V,* a "wooden O." Its central yard was open to the elements, a detail that it had appropriated from the confined areas of the inns. The thrust stage, covered by a roof, was built thirty feet into the yard at the building's south side.

THE GLOBE PROVIDED A NUMBER OF ACTING AREAS.   This thrust stage was close to five feet high—probably lower in front (*downstage*) and higher in back (*upstage*). Actors could move anywhere on this stage to deliver their lines. On the second level above the stage was a gallery for spectators, musicians, and actors (as in the balcony scene in Shakespeare's *Romeo and Juliet*). Actors might enter this gallery to deliver lines, and then they might also descend from there to the main stage. The area below the stage was called the *hell*. At center stage there was a trapdoor to the hell that was used for the entrances and exits of devils, monsters, and ghosts such as the Ghost of Hamlet's father. Downstage, holding up the protective roof, there were two columns. The ceiling of this roof, called the *heavens*, was decorated with colorful paintings. A hut on the roof itself contained machinery for lowering and raising actors who took the roles of fairies, witches, and gods. Behind the upstage area, which could be curtained off for interior scenes, there was a *tiring house* and storage area where actors changed their costumes and waited for their cues. Two or three doors opened out from the tiring house to the stage.

THERE WERE THREE LOCATIONS FOR THE AUDIENCE. The admission price permitted spectators into the ground area. Those who remained there stood during the entire performance and crowded as close as they could to the stage. These people were patronizingly called the *groundlings*. For additional charges, spectators could sit in one of the three seating levels within the roofed galleries (part of the "O"). Those who could afford it paid still another charge for seats directly on the stage—a custom that continued in English theaters until the time of David Garrick in the eighteenth century.

THE GLOBE, LIKE OTHER ELIZABETHAN THEATERS, MANDATED ITS OWN PRODUCTION AND STAGE CONVENTIONS. Just as in the Athenian theater, there was no artificial lighting, and performances therefore took place in the afternoon. The plays were performed rapidly, without intermissions or indications of act and scene changes except for occasional rhymed couplets. With no curtain and no scenery, shifts in scene were indicated by the exits and entrances of the actors. This type of scene division produced swift changes in time and place and made for great fluidity and fast pacing.

The conditions of performance and the physical shape of the theater produced a number of theatrical conventions. The two columns supporting the stage roof, for example, were versatile. Sometimes they represented trees or the sides of buildings, and conventionally they were used as places of concealment and for eavesdropping. Time, place, and circumstances of weather were established through dialogue, as in the opening scene of *Hamlet* when Horatio speaks of "the morn, in russet mantle clad" (line 166), or in *As You Like It*, when Rosalind says, "This is the forest of Arden" (II.4.15).

The Globe's relatively small size and its thrust stage made for intimate performances. There was little separation of the audience and the actors, unlike the case with the *orchestra* in Greek theaters that widened the distance between actors and spectators or the proscenium and curtain found in many modern theaters. Consequently, there was much interaction between actors and spectators. The closeness of spectators to the stage led to two unique stage conventions. One of these, the **aside**, permits a character to make brief remarks directly to the audience or to another character without the rest of the characters' hearing the words. In the other, the **soliloquy**, a character alone onstage speaks his or her thoughts or plans directly to the audience. For example, in Hamlet's second soliloquy, he criticizes his emotional detachment from his father's murder and explains how he plans to test Claudius's guilt (II.2.524–580). We should realize that actors using these conventions spoke directly to members of the audience who were sitting next to the action. These spectators almost literally became additional members of the cast.

THE ACTORS FOLLOWED ESTABLISHED CONVENTIONS IN GESTURE AND COSTUME. The actors in Shakespeare's day were legally bound to the company of which they were members. Without the protection of the company, they were considered "rogues and vagabonds." In England the actors were always male, with adolescent boys performing the women's roles because women were excluded from the stage. The actors used no masks. Instead, they developed expressions and gestures that would seem to us, today, excessively stylized. The acting mannerisms sometimes seemed excessive to Shakespeare, too, as is indicated by Hamlet's instructions to the traveling actors. He tells them not to "saw the air too much with your hand" and not to "tear a passion to tatters, to very rags" (III.2.4–9).

The actors wore elaborate costumes to demonstrate the nature and status of the characters. Thus kings always wore robes and crowns, and they carried orbs and scepters. A fool (a type of comic and ironic commentator) wore a multicolored or *motley* costume, and clowns and "mechanicals" wore the common clothing of the humble classes. Ragged clothing indicated a reduction in circumstances, as in *King Lear*, and Ophelia's description of Hamlet's disordered clothing in the second act of *Hamlet* indicates the prince's disturbed mental condition (1.74–82). Whenever characters took on a disguise, as in *As You Like It*, this disguise was impenetrable to the other characters.

THE NEW GLOBE THEATER HAS BEEN RECONSTRUCTED NEAR THE SITE OF SHAKESPEARE'S GLOBE.   Shakespeare's Globe burned in 1612, and the theater that replaced it was torn down by the Puritans under Oliver Cromwell in 1644. From then on the site was variously occupied by tenements, breweries, other buildings, and a road. In the late 1980s, however, archaeological excavations took place at the sites of both the Globe and the nearby Rose theater, and the subsequent discoveries have provided exciting new information about theaters and theatergoing in Shakespeare's day. A reconstruction of the Globe was undertaken and is now complete—not at the original location but close by; the original site could not be used because it is preempted by a protected building and a vital street leading to Southwark Bridge. Theatergoers in London are now able to attend performances of Shakespeare's plays in this new theater under conditions almost identical to those that Shakespeare's audiences and acting company knew (see the photograph of the reconstruction of the Globe stage, Insert III).[13]

WILLIAM SHAKESPEARE, *HAMLET*

Shakespeare was born in 1564 in Stratford-upon-Avon, in western England. He attended the Stratford grammar school, married in 1582, and had three children. He left his family and moved to London sometime between 1585 and 1592. During this period he became a professional actor, and he also began writing plays and poems. Because the London theaters were closed during the plague years 1592–1594, he apparently worked at other jobs, about which we know nothing. By 1595, however, he was recognized as a major writer of comedies and tragedies. He soon became a member of the Lord Chamberlain's Men, the leading theatrical company, and, as we have seen, he became a shareholder in the new Globe Theatre in 1599. Because he realized good returns from the business venture and also from his plays, he became moderately wealthy. He stopped writing for the stage in 1611, having written a total of thirty-seven plays, of which eleven were tragedies. He spent his retirement years in Stratford. He died in 1616 and is buried next to the altar of Stratford's Trinity Church, beneath a bust and an inscribed gravestone.

When the Lord Chamberlain's Men first staged *Hamlet* in 1602 at the Globe, it was not the first time the story had been dramatized on the London stage. There is evidence that a play based on the Hamlet story, now lost, had been performed before 1589. Therefore, at least some of the theatergoers might have known the story.

Even if none of them knew it, however, they would have known the tradition of **revenge tragedy.** The Elizabethans had been introduced to the drama of vengeance through the English translations of Seneca's tragedies during the 1570s and early 1580s. Another important precedent was Thomas Kyd's *Spanish Tragedy* (ca. 1587), the first English play in the revenge tradition, which featured a hero who commits suicide. The major conventions of the genre were a ghost who calls for vengeance and a revenger who pretends to be insane at least part of the time. Above all, the tradition required that the revenger would also die, no matter how good a person he was or how just his cause might have been.

---

[13] See J. R. Mulryne and Margaret Shewring, eds. *Shakespeare's Globe Rebuilt* (Cambridge: Cambridge UP, 1997). A current e-mail address for further information about the Globe Theatre is globe@uga.cc.uga.edu.

Although Elizabethan audiences were prepared for *Hamlet* by the revenge formula, they could have anticipated neither a protagonist of Hamlet's likeableness and complexity nor a play of such profundity. The earlier revengers were flat characters with a single fixation on getting even through personal vengeance. Hamlet, however, is acutely aware of the political and moral corruption of the Danish court, and he reflects on the fallen state of humanity. Experiencing despair and guilt, he even contemplates suicide. He learns from his experiences and meditations, discovering that he must look beyond reason and philosophy for ways of coping with the world. He also develops patience and learns to trust in Providence, the "divinity that shapes our ends" (V.2.10).

The play itself demonstrates the far-reaching effects of evil, which branches inexorably outward from Claudius's initial act of murder. The evil ensnares innocent and guilty alike. Hamlet, the avenger, becomes the direct and indirect cause of deaths, and as a result, he in turn also becomes an object of revenge. By the play's end, all the major and two of the minor characters are dead: Polonius, Ophelia, Rosencrantz, Guildenstern, Gertrude, Claudius, Laertes, and, finally, Hamlet himself. The play's crowning irony is that Hamlet does not complete his vengeance because of the murder of his father, King Hamlet. Rather, he kills Claudius immediately upon learning that the king has murdered Gertrude, his mother.

In the centuries since Shakespeare wrote *Hamlet*, the play has remained among the most popular, most moving, and most effective plays in the world. It has been translated into scores of languages. Major actors from Shakespeare's day to ours—including Richard Burbage as the first Hamlet and Derek Jacoby, Kevin Kline, Mel Gibson, Ralph Fiennes, and Kenneth Branagh as the most recent—have starred in the role. Beyond the play's stage popularity, *Hamlet* has become one of the central documents of Western civilization. Somehow, we all know about Hamlet, and we know passages like "to be, or not to be," "the play's the thing," and "The undiscovered country, from whose bourn/No traveller returns" even if we have never read the play or seen a live or filmed performance.

WILLIAM SHAKESPEARE   (1564–1616)

The Tragedy of Hamlet, Prince of Denmark _____ *ca. 1600*

Edited by Alice Griffin°

Professor Griffin's text for *Hamlet* was the Second Quarto (edition) published in 1604, with modifications based on the First Folio, published in 1623. Stage directions in those editions are printed here without brackets; added stage directions are printed within brackets. We have edited Griffin's notes for this text.

CHARACTERS

Claudius, *King of Denmark*
Hamlet, *Son to the former, and nephew to the present King*
Polonius, *Lord Chamberlain*
Horatio, *Friend to Hamlet*
Laertes, *Son to Polonius*
Valtemand ⎫
Cornelius ⎪
Rosencrantz ⎬ *Courtiers*
Guildenstern ⎪
Osric ⎭
A Gentleman
A Priest
Marcellus ⎫ *Officers*
Barnardo ⎬
Francisco, *a Soldier*
Reynaldo, *Servant to Polonius*
Players
Two Clowns, *gravediggers*
Fortinbras, *Prince of Norway*
A Norwegian Captain
English Ambassadors
Gertrude, *Queen of Denmark, mother to Hamlet*
Ophelia, *Daughter to Polonius*
Ghost of Hamlet's Father
Lords, Ladies, Officers, Soldiers, Sailors, Messengers, Attendants

[*Scene: Elsinore*]

ACT 1

Scene 1. *[A platform on the battlements of the castle]*

Enter BARNARDO *and* FRANCISCO, *two Sentinels.*

BARNARDO.	Who's there?
FRANCISCO.	Nay, answer me. Stand and unfold° yourself.
BARNARDO.	Long live the king.
FRANCISCO.	Barnardo?
BARNARDO.	He.
FRANCISCO.	You come most carefully upon your hour.
BARNARDO.	'Tis now struck twelve, get thee to bed Francisco.
FRANCISCO.	For this relief much thanks, 'tis bitter cold,
	And I am sick at heart.
BARNARDO.	Have you had quiet guard?
FRANCISCO.	Not a mouse stirring.

5

10

2 *unfold:* reveal.

BARNARDO.   Well, good night:
    If you do meet Horatio and Marcellus,
    The rivals° of my watch, bid them make haste.

Enter HORATIO and MARCELLUS.

FRANCISCO.   I think I hear them. Stand ho, who is there?
HORATIO.   Friends to this ground.
MARCELLUS.   And liegemen° to the Dane.°   15
FRANCISCO.   Give you good night.
MARCELLUS.   O, farewell honest soldier,
    Who hath relieved you?
FRANCISCO.   Barnardo hath my place;
    Give you good night.   *Exit FRANCISCO.*
MARCELLUS.   Holla, Barnardo!
BARNARDO.   Say,
    What, is Horatio there?
HORATIO.   A piece of him.
BARNARDO.   Welcome Horatio, welcome good Marcellus.   2(
HORATIO.   What, has this thing appeared again tonight?
BARNARDO.   I have seen nothing.
MARCELLUS.   Horatio says 'tis but our fantasy,°
    And will not let belief take hold of him,
    Touching this dreaded sight twice seen of us,   2:
    Therefore I have entreated him along
    With us to watch the minutes of this night,
    That if again this apparition come,
    He may approve° our eyes and speak to it.
HORATIO.   Tush, tush, 'twill not appear.
BARNARDO.   Sit down awhile,   3
    And let us once again assail your ears,
    That are so fortified against our story,
    What we have two nights seen.
HORATIO.   Well, sit we down,
    And let us hear Barnardo speak of this.   3
BARNARDO.   Last night of all,
    When yon same star that's westward from the pole°
    Had made his course t'illume that part of heaven
    Where now it burns, Marcellus and myself,
    The bell then beating one—

Enter GHOST.

MARCELLUS.   Peace, break thee off, look where it comes again.
BARNARDO.   In the same figure like the king that's dead.
MARCELLUS.   Thou art a scholar, speak to it Horatio.
BARNARDO.   Looks a' not like the king? mark it Horatio.
HORATIO.   Most like, it harrows me with fear and wonder.
BARNARDO.   It would be spoke to.

---

13 *rivals:* partners.   15 *liegemen:* subjects.   *Dane:* King of Denmark.   23 *fantasy:* imagination.   29 *approve:* prove reliable.   36 *pole:* North Star.

MARCELLUS.   Question it Horatio.   45
HORATIO.   What art thou that usurp'st° this time of night,
  Together with that fair and warlike form,
  In which the majesty of buried Denmark°
  Did sometimes° march? by heaven I charge thee speak.
MARCELLUS.   It is offended.
BARNARDO.   See, it stalks away.   50
HORATIO.   Stay, speak, speak, I charge thee speak.   *Exit GHOST.*
MARCELLUS.   'Tis gone and will not answer.
BARNARDO.   How now Horatio, you tremble and look pale,
  Is not this something more than fantasy?
  What think you on't?   55
HORATIO.   Before my God I might not this believe,
  Without the sensible and true avouch°
  Of mine own eyes.
MARCELLUS.   Is it not like the king?
HORATIO.   As thou art to thyself.
  Such was the very armour he had on,   60
  When he the ambitious Norway° combated:
  So frowned he once, when in an angry parle°
  He smote the sledded Polacks° on the ice.
  'Tis strange.
MARCELLUS.   Thus twice before, and jump° at this dead hour,   65
  With martial stalk hath he gone by our watch.
HORATIO.   In what particular thought to work, I know not,
  But in the gross and scope° of mine opinion,
  This bodes some strange eruption to our state.
MARCELLUS.   Good now sit down, and tell me he that knows,   70
  Why this same strict and most observant watch
  So nightly toils the subject° of the land,
  And why such daily cast of brazen cannon
  And foreign mart,° for implements of war,
  Why such impress° of shipwrights, whose sore° task   75
  Does not divide the Sunday from the week,
  What might be toward° that this sweaty haste
  Doth make the night joint-labourer with the day,
  Who is't that can inform me?
HORATIO.   That can I.
  At least the whisper goes so; our last king,   80
  Whose image even but now appeared to us,
  Was as you know by Fortinbras of Norway,
  Thereto pricked on by a most emulate° pride,
  Dared to the combat; in which our valiant Hamlet

46 *usurp'st:* wrongfully occupy (both the time and the shape of the dead king).   48 *buried*
Denmark: the buried King of Denmark.   49 *sometimes:* formerly.   57 *Sensible . . . avouch:*
assurance of the truth of the senses.   61 *Norway:* King of Norway.   62 *parle:* parley, verbal
battle.   63 *sledded Polacks:* Poles on sleds.   65 *jump:* just.   68 *gross and scope:* general view.
72 *toils the subject:* makes the subjects toil.   74 *mart:* trade.   75 *impress:* conscription.
sore: difficult.   77 *toward:* forthcoming.   83 *emulate:* rivaling

(For so this side of our known world esteemed him)
Did slay this Fortinbras, who by a sealed compact,°
Well ratified by law and heraldy,°
Did forfeit (with his life) all those his lands
Which he stood seized° of, to the conqueror:
Against the which a moiety competent°
Was gagèd° by our King, which had returned
To the inheritance of Fortinbras,
Had he been vanquisher; as by the same co-mart,°
And carriage of the article designed,°
His fell to Hamlet; now sir, young Fortinbras,
Of unimprovèd mettle° hot and full,
Hath in the skirts° of Norway here and there
Sharked up° a list of lawless resolutes°
For food and diet to some enterprise
That hath a stomach° in't, which is no other,
As it doth well appear unto our state,
But to recover of us by strong hand
And terms compulsatory, those foresaid lands
So by his father lost; and this I take it,
Is the main motive of our preparations,
The source of this our watch, and the chief head°
Of this post-haste and romage° in the land.
BARNARDO.   I think it be no other, but e'en so;
Well may it sort° that this portentous figure
Comes armèd through our watch so like the king
That was and is the question of these wars.
HORATIO.   A mote it is to trouble the mind's eye:
In the most high and palmy° state of Rome,
A little ere the mightest Julius fell,
The graves stood tenantless, and the sheeted dead
Did squeak and gibber in the Roman streets,
As stars with trains of fire,° and dews of blood,
Disasters° in the sun; and the moist star,°
Upon whose influence Neptune's empire stands,
Was sick almost to doomsday with eclipse.
And even the like precurse° of feared events,
As harbingers preceding still° the fates
And prologue to the omen° coming on,
Have heaven and earth together demonstrated
Unto our climatures° and countrymen.

86 *compact:* treaty.   87 *law and heraldy:* heraldic law regulating combats.   89 *seized:* possessed.
90 *moiety competent:* equal amount.   91 *gagèd:* pledged.   93 *co-mart:* joint bargain.   94 *carriage . . . designed:* intent of the treaty drawn up.   96 *unimprovèd mettle:* untested (1) metal (2)
spirit.   97 *skirts:* outskirts.   98 *Sharked up:* gathered up indiscriminately (as a shark preys).
lawless resolutes: determined outlaws.   100 *stomach:* show of courage.   106 *head:* fountainhead.
107 *romage:* bustle (rummage).   109 *sort:* turn out.   113 *palmy:* triumphant.   117*stars . . .
fire:* meteors.   118 *Disasters:* unfavorable portents.   *moist star:* moon.   121 *precurse:* portent.   122 *still:* always.   123 *omen:* disaster.   125 *climatures:* regions.

Enter GHOST.

But soft, behold, lo where it comes again.
I'll cross° it though it blast me: *Spreads his arms.*
                          stay illusion,
If thou hast any sound or use of voice,
Speak to me.
If there be any good thing to be done   130
That may to thee do ease, and grace° to me,
Speak to me.
If thou art privy° to thy country's fate
Which happily° foreknowing may avoid,
O speak: 135
Or if thou hast uphoarded in thy life
Extorted treasure in the womb of earth,
For which they say you spirits oft walk in death,

                                                    The cock crows.

Speak of it, stay and speak. Stop it Marcellus.
MARCELLUS.   Shall I strike at it with my partisan?°   140
HORATIO.   Do, if it will not stand
BARNARDO.   'Tis here.
HORATIO.   'Tis here.
MARCELLUS.   'Tis gone.   *Exit* GHOST.
We do it wrong being so majestical,
To offer it the show of violence,
For it is as the air, invulnerable,   145
And our vain blows malicious mockery.°
BARNARDO.   It was about to speak when the cock crew.°
HORATIO.   And then it started like a guilty thing,
Upon a fearful summons; I have heard,
The cock that is the trumpet to the morn,   150
Doth with his lofty and shrill-sounding throat
Awake the god of day, and at his warning
Whether in sea or fire, in earth or air,°
Th'extravagant and erring° spirit hies°
To his confine, and of the truth herein   155
This present object made probation.°
MARCELLUS.   It faded on the crowing of the cock.
Some say that ever 'gainst° that season comes
Wherein our Saviour's birth is celebrated
This bird of dawning singeth all night long,   160
And then they say no spirit dare stir abroad,

---

127 *cross:* (1) cross its path (2) spread my arms to make a cross of my body (to ward against evil).   131 *grace:* (1) honor (2) blessedness.   133 *art privy:* know secretly of.   134 *happily:* perhaps.   140 *partisan:* spear.   146 *malicious mockery:* mockery because they only imitate harm.   147 *cock crew:* (traditional signal for ghosts to return to their confines).   153 *sea . . . air:* the four elements (inhabited by spirits, each indigenous to a particular element).   154 *extravagant and erring:* going beyond its bounds (vagrant) and wandering.   *hies:* hastens.   156 *made probation:* gave proof.   158 *'gainst:* just before.

The nights are wholesome,° then no planets strike,°
No fairy takes,° nor witch hath power to charm,
So hallowed, and so gracious is that time.
HORATIO.   So have I heard and do in part believe it.
But look, the morn in russet° mantle clad
Walks o'er the dew of yon high eastward hill:
Break we our watch up and by my advice
Let us impart what we have seen tonight
Unto young Hamlet, for upon my life
This spirit dumb to us, will speak to him:
Do you consent we shall acquaint him with it,
As needful in our loves,° fitting our duty?
MARCELLUS.   Let's do't I pray, and I this morning know
Where we shall find him most convenient.   *Exeunt.*°

Scene 2. *[A room of state in the castle]*

Flourish.° Enter CLAUDIUS *King of Denmark,* GERTRUDE *the Queen,* [*members of the*] *Council: as* POLONIUS; *and his son* LAERTES, HAMLET, [VALTEMAND *and* CORNELIUS] *cum aliis.*°

KING.   Though yet of Hamlet our dear brother's death
The memory be green, and that it us befitted
To bear our hearts in grief, and our whole kingdom
To be contracted in one brow of woe,
Yet so far hath discretion fought with nature,°
That we° with wisest sorrow think on him
Together with remembrance of ourselves:°
Therefore our sometime° sister,° now our queen,
Th'imperial jointress° to this warlike state,
Have we as 'twere with a defeated joy,
With an auspicious, and a dropping eye,°
With mirth in funeral, and with dirge in marriage,
In equal scale weighing delight and dole,
Taken to wife: nor have we herein barred
Your better wisdoms,° which have freely gone
With this affair along—for all, our thanks.
Now follows that you know, young Fortinbras,
Holding a weak supposal of our worth,°
Or thinking by our late dear brother's death
Our state to be disjoint and out of frame,°
Colleaguèd° with this dream of his advantage,°

162 *wholesome:* healthy (night air was considered unhealthy).   *strike:* exert evil influence   163 *takes:* bewitches.   166 *russet:* reddish.   173 *needful . . . loves:* urged by our friendship.   175 S.D.: *Exeunt:* all exit.   0.1 S.D.: *Flourish:* fanfare of trumpets.   *cum aliis:* with others.   5 *nature:* natural impulse (of grief).   6 *we:* royal plural. The King speaks not only for himself, but for his entire government.   7 *remembrance of ourselves:* reminder of our duties.   8 *sometime:* former.   *sister:* sister-in-law.   9 *jointress:* widow who inherits the estate.   11 *auspicious . . . eye:* one eye happy, the other tearful.   14–15 *barred . . . wisdoms:* failed to seek and abide by your good advice.   18 *weak . . . worth:* low opinion of my ability in office.   20 *out of frame:* tottering.   21 *Colleaguèd:* supported.   *advantage:* superiority.

He hath not failed to pester us with message
Importing the surrender of those lands
Lost by his father, with all bands° of law,
To our most valiant brother—so much for him: 25
Now for ourself, and for this time of meeting,
Thus much the business is. We have here writ
To Norway, uncle of young Fortinbras—
Who impotent and bed-rid scarcely hears
Of this his nephew's purpose—to suppress   30
His further gait° herein, in that the levies,
The lists, and full proportions are all made
Out of his subject:° and we here dispatch
You good Cornelius, and you Valtemand,
For bearers of this greeting to old Norway,   35
Giving to you no further personal power
To business with the king, more than the scope
Of these delated° articles allow:
Farewell, and let your haste commend your duty.°
CORNELIUS, VALTEMAND.   In that, and all things, will we show our duty.   40
KING.   We doubt it nothing, heartily farewell.

                                        Exeunt VALTEMAND and CORNELIUS.

And now Laertes what's the news with you?
You told us of some suit, what is't Laertes?
You cannot speak of reason to the Dane
And lose your voice;° what wouldst thou beg Laertes,   45
That shall not be my offer, not thy asking?°
The head is not more native° to the heart,
The hand more instrumental to the mouth,
Than is the throne of Denmark to thy father.
What wouldst thou have Laertes?
LAERTES.   My dread lord,   50
Your leave and favour° to return to France,
From whence, though willingly I came to Denmark,
To show my duty in your coronation,
Yet now I must confess, that duty done,
My thoughts and wishes bend again toward France,   55
And bow them to your gracious leave and pardon.°
KING.   Have you your father's leave? What says Polonius?
POLONIUS.   He hath my lord wrung from me my slow leave
By laboursome petition, and at last
Upon his will I sealed my hard consent.°   60
I do beseech you give him leave to go.

---

24 *bands:* bonds.   31 *gait:* progress.   31–33 *levies . . . subject:* Taxes, conscriptions, and
supplies are all obtained from his subjects.   38 *delated:* accusing.   39 *haste . . . duty:* prompt
departure signify your respect.   45 *lose your voice:* speak in vain.   46 *offer . . . asking:* grant even
before requested.   47 *native:* related.   51 *leave and favour:* kind permission.   56 *pardon:*
allowance.   60 *Upon . . . consent:* (1) At his request, I gave my grudging consent. (2) On the soft
sealing wax of his (legal) will, I stamped my approval.

KING.   Take thy fair hour Laertes, time be thine,
And thy best graces spend it at thy will.
But now my cousin° Hamlet, and my son—
HAMLET.   [*Aside.*] A little more than kin,° and less than kind.°
KING.   How is it that the clouds still hang on you?
HAMLET.   Not so my lord, I am too much in the sun.°
QUEEN.   Good Hamlet cast they nighted colour° off
And let thine eye look like a friend on Denmark,°
Do not for ever with they vailèd° lids
Seek for thy noble father in the dust,
Thou know'st 'tis common, all that lives must die,
Passing through nature to eternity.
HAMLET.   Ay madam, it is common.°
QUEEN.   If it be,
Why seems it so particular with thee?
HAMLET.   Seems, madam? nay it is, I know not "seems."
'Tis not alone my inky cloak good mother,
Nor customary suits of solemn black,
Nor windy suspiration of forced breath,
No, nor the fruitful river in the eye,°
Nor the dejected haviour° of the visage,
Together with all forms, moods, shapes of grief,
That can denote me truly: these indeed seem,
For they are actions that a man might play,°
But I have that within which passes show,
These but the trappings and the suits of woe.°
KING.   'Tis sweet and commendable in your nature Hamlet,
To give these mourning duties to your father:
But you must know your father lost a father,
That father lost, lost his, and the survivor bound
In filial obligation for some term
To do obsequious sorrow:° but to persever
In obstinate condolement,° is a course
Of impious stubbornness, 'tis unmanly grief,
It shows a will most incorrect to heaven,
A heart unfortified, a mind impatient,
An understanding simple and unschooled:
For what we know must be, and is as common
As any the most vulgar thing to sense,°

64 *cousin:* kinsman (used for relatives outside the immediate family).   65 *more than kin:* too much of a kinsman, being both uncle and stepfather.   *less than kind:* (1) unkind because of being a kin (proverbial) and taking the throne from the former king's son (2) unnatural (as it was considered incest to marry the wife of one's dead brother).   67 *in the sun:* (1) in presence of the king (often associated metaphorically with the sun) (2) proverbial: "out of heaven's blessing into the warm sun" (3) of a "son."   68 *nighted colour:* black.   69 *Denmark:* the King of Denmark.   70 *vailèd:* downcast.   74 *common:* (1) general (2) vulgar.   79–80 *windy . . . eye:* (hyperbole used to describe exaggerated sighs and tears).   81 *haviour:* behavior.   84 *play:* act.   86 *trappings . . . woe:* outward, superficial costumes of mourning.   92 *do obsequious sorrow:* express sorrow befitting obsequies or funerals.   93 *condolement:* grief.   99 *As any . . . sense:* as the most ordinary thing the senses can perceive.

Why should we in our peevish opposition   100
Take it to heart? Fie, 'tis a fault to heaven,
A fault against the dead, a fault to nature,
To reason most absurd, whose common theme
Is death of fathers, and who still° hath cried
From the first corse,° till he that died today,   105
"This must be so." We pray you throw to earth
This unprevailing° woe, and think of us
As of a father, for let the world take note
You are the most immediate° to our throne,
And with no less nobility of love   110
Than that which dearest father bears his son,
Do I impart toward you. For your intent
In going back to school in Wittenberg,
It is most retrograde° to our desire,
And we beseech you, bend you° to remain   115
Here in the cheer and comfort of our eye,
Our chiefest courtier, cousin, and our son.
QUEEN.   Let not thy mother lose her prayers Hamlet,
    I pray thee stay with us, go not to Wittenberg.
HAMLET.   I shall in all my best obey you madam.   120
KING.   Why 'tis a loving and a fair reply,
    Be as ourself in Denmark. Madam come,
    This gentle and unforced accord of Hamlet
    Sits smiling to my heart, in grace whereof,
    No jocund health that Denmark drinks today,   125
    But the great cannon to the clouds shall tell,
    And the king's rouse° the heaven shall bruit° again,
    Re-speaking earthly thunder; come away.

Flourish, Exeunt all but HAMLET.

HAMLET.   O that this too too sullied° flesh would melt,
    Thaw and resolve itself into a dew,   130
    Or that the Everlasting had not fixed
    His canon° 'gainst self-slaughter. O God, God,
    How weary, stale, flat, and unprofitable
    Seems to me all the uses of this world!
    Fie on't, ah fie, 'tis an unweeded garden   135
    That grows to seed, things rank° and gross in nature
    Possess it merely.° That it should come to this,
    But two months dead, nay not so much, not two,
    So excellent a king, that was to this

---

104 *still:* always.   105 *corse:* corpse (of Abel, also, ironically, the first fratricide).   107 *unprevailing:* useless.   109 *most immediate:* next in succession (though Danish kings were elected by the council, an Elizabethan audience might feel that Hamlet, not Claudius, should be king).   114 *retrograde:* movement (of planets) in a reverse direction.   115 *beseech . . . you:* hope you will be inclined.   127 *rouse:* toast that empties the wine cup. *bruit:* sound.   129 *sullied:* tainted.   132 *canon:* divine edict.   136 *rank:* (1) luxuriant, excessive (2) bad-smelling.   137 *merely:* entirely.

Hyperion° to a satyr,° so loving to my mother,
That he might not beteem° the winds of heaven
Visit her face too roughly—heaven and earth,
Must I remember? why, she would hang on him
As if increase of appetite had grown
By what it fed on,° and yet within a month—
Let me not think on't: Frailty, thy name is woman—
A little month or ere those shoes were old
With which she followed my poor father's body
Like Niobe° all tears, why she, even she—
O God, a beast that wants° discourse of reason
Would have mourned longer—married with my uncle,
My father's brother, but no more like my father
Than I to Hercules: within a month,
Ere yet the salt of most unrighteous° tears
Had left the flushing° in her gallèd° eyes,
She married. O most wicked speed, to post°
With such dexterity to incestuous° sheets:
It is not, nor it cannot come to good,
But break my heart, for I must hold my tongue.

Enter HORATIO, MARCELLUS and BARNARDO.

HORATIO.   Hail to your lordship.
HAMLET.   I am glad to see you well;
    Horatio, or I do forget my self.
HORATIO.   The same my lord, and your poor servant ever.
HAMLET.   Sir my good friend, I'll change° that name with you:
    And what make you from Wittenberg, Horatio?
    Marcellus.
MARCELLUS.   My good lord.
HAMLET.   I am very glad to see you: good even, sir.
    But what in faith make you from Wittenberg?
HORATIO.   A truant disposition, good my lord.
HAMLET.   I would not hear your enemy say so,
    Nor shall you do mine ear that violence
    To make it truster of your own report
    Against yourself. I know you are no truant,
    But what is your affair in Elsinore?
    We'll teach you to drink deep ere you depart.
HORATIO.   My Lord, I came to see your father's funeral.
HAMLET.   I prithee do not mock me, fellow student,
    I think it was to see my mother's wedding.

140 *Hyperion:* god of the sun.   *satyr:* part-goat, part-man woodland deity (noted for lust).   141 *beteem:* allow.   144–145 *As if . . . on:* as if the more she fed, the more her appetite increased.   149 *Niobe:* (who boasted of her children before Leto and was punished by their destruction; Zeus changed the weeping mother to a stone dropping continual tears).   150 *wants:* lacks.   154 *unrighteous:* (because untrue).   155 *flushing:* redness.   *gallèd:* rubbed sore.   156 *post:* rush.   157 *incestuous:* (the church forbade marriage to one's brother's widow).   163 *change:* exchange (and be called your friend).

HORATIO.   Indeed my lord it followed hard upon.
HAMLET.   Thrift, thrift, Horatio, the funeral baked meats°   180
  Did coldly° furnish forth the marriage tables.
  Would I had met my dearest° foe in heaven
  Or ever I had seen that day Horatio.
  My father, methinks I see my father.
HORATIO.   Where my lord?
HAMLET.   In my mind's eye Horatio.   185
HORATIO.   I saw him once, a' was a goodly° king.
HAMLET.   A' was a man, take him for all in all,
  I shall not look upon his like again.
HORATIO.   My lord, I think I saw him yesternight.
HAMLET.   Saw? Who?   190
HORATIO.   My lord, the king your father.
HAMLET.   The king my father?
HORATIO.   Season your admiration° for a while
  With an attent ear till I may deliver
  Upon the witness of these gentlemen
  This marvel to you.
HAMLET.   For God's love let me hear!   195
HORATIO.   Two nights together had these gentlemen,
  Marcellus and Barnardo, on their watch
  In the dead waste and middle of the night,
  Been thus encountered. A figure like your father
  Armed at point exactly, cap-a-pe,°   200
  Appears before them, and with solemn march,
  Goes slow and stately by them; thrice he walked
  By their oppressed° and fear-surprisèd eyes
  Within his truncheon's° length, whilst they distilled°
  Almost to jelly with the act of fear,   205
  Stand dumb and speak not to him; this to me
  In dreadful secrecy° impart they did,
  And I with them the third night kept the watch,
  Where as they had delivered, both in time,
  Form of the thing, each word made true and good,   210
  The apparition comes: I knew your father,
  These hands are not more like.
HAMLET.   But where was this?
MARCELLUS.   My lord upon the platform where we watch.
HAMLET.   Did you not speak to it?
HORATIO.   My lord I did,
  But answer made it none, yet once methought   215
  It lifted up it° head, and did address
  Itself to motion° like as it would speak:

180 *funeral baked meats:* food prepared for the funeral.   181 *coldly:* when cold.   182 *dearest:*
direst.   186 *goodly:* handsome.   192 *Season your admiration:* control your wonder.   200
at point . . . cap-a-pe: in every detail, head to foot.   203 *oppressed:* overcome by horror.   204
truncheon: staff (of office).   *distilled:* dissolved.   207 *in dreadful secrecy:* as a dread
secret.   216 *it:* its.   216–217 *address . . . motion:* start to move.

But even then the morning cock crew loud,
And at the sound it shrunk in haste away
And vanished from our sight.
HAMLET.   'Tis very strange.
HORATIO.   As I do live my honoured lord 'tis true,
And we did think it writ down in our duty
To let you know of it.
HAMLET.   Indeed indeed sirs, but this troubles me.
Hold you the watch tonight?
ALL.   We do my lord.
HAMLET.   Armed say you?
ALL.   Armed my lord.
HAMLET.   From top to toe?
ALL.   My lord from head to foot.
HAMLET.   Then saw you not his face.
HORATIO.   O yes my lord, he wore his beaver° up.
HAMLET.   What, looked he frowningly?
HORATIO.   A countenance more in sorrow than in anger.
HAMLET.   Pale, or red?
HORATIO.   Nay, very pale.
HAMLET.   And fixed his eyes upon you?
HORATIO.   Most constantly.
HAMLET.   I would I had been there.
HORATIO.   It would have much amazed you.
HAMLET.   Very like, very like, stayed it long?
HORATIO.   While one with moderate haste might tell° a hundred.
MARCELLUS, BARNARDO.   Longer, longer.
HORATIO.   Not when I saw't.
HAMLET.   His beard was grizzled,° no?
HORATIO.   It was as I have seen it in his life,
A sable silvered.°
HAMLET.   I will watch tonight;
Perchance 'twill walk again.
HORATIO.   I warr'nt it will.
HAMLET.   If it assume my noble father's person,
I'll speak to it though hell itself should gape
And bid me hold my peace;° I pray you all
If you have hitherto concealed this sight
Let it be tenable° in your silence still,
And whatsoever else shall hap tonight,
Give it an understanding but no tongue.
I will requite your loves, so fare you well:
Upon the platform 'twixt eleven and twelve
I'll visit you.
ALL.   Our duty to your honour.

---

230 *beaver:* visor.   238 *tell:* count.   240 *grizzled:* grey.   242 *A sable silvered:* black flecked
with gray.   245–246 *though hell . . . peace:* despite the risk of hell (for speaking to a demon)
warning me to be silent.   248 *tenable:* held, kept.

HAMLET.   Your loves, as mine to you:° farewell.   *Exeunt.*
My father's spirit (in arms) all is not well,   255
I doubt° some foul play, would the night were come;
Till then sit still my soul, foul deeds will rise,
Though all the earth o'erwhelm them, to men's eyes.   *Exit.*

Scene 3. *[Polonius's chambers]*

Enter LAERTES *and* OPHELIA *his sister.*

LAERTES.   My necessaries are embarked, farewell,
And sister, as the winds give benefit
And convoy° is assistant, do not sleep
But let me hear from you.
OPHELIA.   Do you doubt that?
LAERTES.   For Hamlet, and the trifling of his favour,   5
Hold it a fashion, and a toy in blood,°
A violet in the youth of primy nature,°
Forward,° not permanent, sweet, not lasting,
The perfume and suppliance of° a minute,
No more.
OPHELIA.   No more but so?
LAERTES.   Think it no more.   10
For nature crescent° does not grow alone
In thews and bulk,° but as this temple waxes°
The inward service of the mind and soul
Grows wide withal.° Perhaps he loves you now,
And now no soil nor cautel° doth besmirch   15
The virtue of his will:° but you must fear,
His greatness weighed,° his will is not his own,
For he himself is subject to his birth:
He may not as unvalued persons° do,
Carve° for himself, for on his choice depends   20
The sanctity and health of this whole state,
And therefore must his choice be circumscribed
Unto the voice and yielding° of that body
Whereof he is the head. Then if he says he loves you,
It fits your wisdom so far to believe it   25
As he in his particular act and place
May give his saying deed,° which is no further
Than the main voice of Denmark goes withal.
Then weigh what loss your honour may sustain

---

254 *Your loves . . . you:* offer your friendship (rather than duty) in exchange for mine.   256 *doubt:*
fear.   3 *convoy:* conveyance.   6 *toy in blood:* whim of the passions.   7 *youth of primy nature:*
early spring.   8 *Forward:* premature.   9 *suppliance of:* supplying diversion for.   11 *nature
crescent:* man as he grows.   12 *thews and bulk:* sinews and body.   *temple waxes:* body grows
(1 Cor. 6:19).   14 *withal:* at the same time.   15 *cautel:* deceit.   16 *will:* desire.   17
weighed: considered.   19 *unvalued persons:* common people.   20 *Carve:* choose (as does the
one who carves the food).   23 *voice and yielding:* approving vote.   26–27 *in his . . . deed:* limited by personal responsibilities and rank, may perform what he promises.

If with too credent° ear you list° his songs,
Or lose your heart, or your chaste treasure open
To his unmast'red importunity.°
Fear it Ophelia, fear it my dear sister,
And keep you in the rear of your affection,
Out of the shot and danger of desire.
The chariest° maid is prodigal enough
If she unmask her beauty to the moon.
Virtue itself 'scapes not calumnious strokes.
The canker galls the infants° of the spring
Too oft before their buttons° be disclosed,
And in the morn and liquid dew of youth
Contagious blastments° are most imminent.
Be wary then, best safety lies in fear,
Youth to itself rebels,° though none else near.
OPHELIA.   I shall the effect° of this good lesson keep
As watchman to my heart: but good my brother,
Do not as some ungracious° pastors do,
Show me the steep and thorny way to heaven,
Whiles like a puffed and reckless libertine
Himself the primrose path of dalliance treads,
And recks not his own rede.°

Enter POLONIUS.

LAERTES.   O fear me not,°
I stay too long, but here my father comes:
A double blessing is a double grace,
Occasion smiles upon a second leave.°
POLONIUS.   Yet here Laertes? aboard, aboard for shame,
The wind sits in the shoulder of your sail,
And you are stayed for: there, my blessing with thee,
And these few precepts in thy memory
Look thou character.° Give thy thoughts no tongue,
Nor any unproportioned thought his act:
Be thou familiar, but by no means vulgar:°
Those friends thou hast, and their adoption tried,°
Grapple them unto thy soul with hoops of steel,
But do not dull° thy palm with entertainment
Of each new-hatched unfledged° comrade. Beware
Of entrance to a quarrel, but being in,
Bear't that th'opposèd may beware of thee.
Give every man thy ear, but few thy voice:

30 *credent:* credulous.   *list:* listen to.   31–32 *your chaste . . . importunity:* lose your virginity to his uncontrolled persistence.   36 *chariest:* most cautious.   39 *canker . . . infants:* cankerworm or caterpillar harms the young plants.   40 *buttons:* buds.   42 *blastments:* blights.   44 *to itself rebels:* lusts by nature.   45 *effect:* moral.   47 *ungracious:* lacking God's grace.   51 *recks . . . rede:* does not follow his own advice.   *fear me not:* Don't worry about me.   54 *Occasion . . . leave:* opportunity favors a second leave-taking.   59 *character:* write, impress, imprint.   61 *vulgar:* indiscriminately friendly.   62 *adoption tried:* loyalty proved.   64 *dull:* get callouses on.   65 *new-hatched unfledged:* new and untested.

Take each man's censure,° but reserve thy judgment.
Costly thy habit° as thy purse can buy,   70
But not expressed in fancy;° rich, not gaudy,
For the apparel oft proclaims the man,
And they in France of the best rank and station,
Are of a most select and generous chief° in that:
Neither a borrower nor a lender be,   75
For loan oft loses both itself and friend,
And borrowing dulls the edge of husbandry;°
This above all, to thine own self be true
And it must follow as the night the day,
Thou canst not then be false to any man.   80
Farewell, my blessing season° this in thee.

LAERTES.   Most humbly do I take my leave my lord.

POLONIUS.   The time invites you, go, your servants tend.°

LAERTES.   Farewell Ophelia, and remember well
What I have said to you.

OPHELIA.   'Tis in my memory locked,   85
And you yourself shall keep the key of it.

LAERTES.   Farewell.   *Exit LAERTES.*

POLONIUS.   What is't Ophelia he hath said to you?

OPHELIA.   So please you, something touching the Lord Hamlet.

POLONIUS.   Marry,° well bethought: 90
'Tis told me he hath very oft of late
Given private time to you, and you yourself
Have of your audience been most free and bounteous.
If it be so, as so 'tis put on me,
And that in way of caution, I must tell you,   95
You do not understand yourself so clearly
As it behooves my daughter, and your honour.
What is between you? give me up the truth.

OPHELIA.   He hath my lord of late made many tenders°
Of his affection to me.   100

POLONIUS.   Affection, puh, you speak like a green girl
Unsifted° in such perilous circumstance.
Do you believe his tenders as you call them?

OPHELIA.   I do not know my lord what I should think.

POLONIUS.   Marry, I will teach you; think yourself a baby   105
That you have ta'en these tenders° for true pay
Which are not sterling.° Tender yourself more dearly,°
Or (not to crack the wind of the poor phrase,
Running it thus°) you'll tender me a fool.°

---

69 *censure:* opinion.   70 *habit:* clothing.   71 *expressed in fancy:* so fantastic as to be
ridiculous.   74 *select . . . chief:* judicious and noble eminence.   77 *husbandry:* thrift.   81
season: bring to maturity.   83 *tend:* attend, wait.   90 *Marry:* (a mild oath, from "By the Virgin
Mary").   99 *tenders:* offers (see lines 106–109).   102 *Unsifted:* untested.   106 *tenders:* offers
(of money).   107 *sterling:* genuine (currency).   *Tender . . . dearly:* hold yourself at a higher
value.   108–109 *crack . . . thus:* make the phrase lose its breath.   109 *tender . . . fool:* (1) make
me look foolish (2) present me with a baby.

OPHELIA.   My lord he hath importuned me with love   11
    In honourable fashion.
POLONIUS.   Ay, fashion you may call it, go to, go to.
OPHELIA.   And hath given countenance° to his speech, my lord,
    With almost all the holy vows of heaven.
POLONIUS.   Ay, springes° to catch woodcocks.° I do know   11
    When the blood burns, how prodigal the soul
    Lends the tongue vows: these blazes daughter,
    Giving more light than heat, extinct in both,
    Even in their promise, as it is a-making,°
    You must not take for fire. From this time   1£
    Be something scanter of your maiden presence,
    Set your entreatments at a higher rate
    Than a command to parle;° for Lord Hamlet,
    Believe so much in him that he is young,
    And with a larger tether may he walk   1ʔ
    Than may be given you: in few° Ophelia,
    Do not believe his vows, for they are brokers°
    Not of that dye which their investments° show,
    But mere implorators° of unholy suits,
    Breathing° like sanctified and pious bonds,°
    The better to beguile. This is for all,
    I would not in plain terms from this time forth
    Have you so slander any moment leisure
    As to give words or talk with the Lord Hamlet.
    Look to't I charge you, come your ways.°   1
OPHELIA.   I shall obey, my lord.   [*Exeunt.*]

Scene 4. [*The platform on the battlements*]

Enter HAMLET, HORATIO and MARCELLUS.

HAMLET.   The air bites shrewdly,° it is very cold.
HORATIO.   It is a nipping and an eager° air.
HAMLET.   What hour now?
HORATIO.   I think it lacks of twelve.
MARCELLUS.   No, it is struck.
HORATIO.   Indeed? I heard it not: it then draws near the season,°
    Wherein the spirit held his wont to walk.

A flourish of trumpets, and two pieces [of ordnance] go off.

    What does this mean my lord?

---

113 *countenance:* confirmation.   115 *springes:* snares.   *woodcocks:* snipelike birds (believed to be stupid and therefore easily trapped).   118–119 *extinct . . . a-making:* losing both appearance, because of brevity, and substance, because of broken promises.   122–123 *Set . . . parle:* Don't rush to negotiate a surrender as soon as the besieger asks for a discussion of terms.   126 *few:* short.   127 *brokers:* (1) business agents (2) procurers.   128 *investments:* (1) business ventures (2) clothing.   129 *implorators:* solicitors.   130 *Breathing:* speaking softly.   *bonds:* pledges.   135 *come your ways:* come along.   1 *shrewdly:* piercingly.   2 *eager:* sharp.   5 *season:* time, period.

HAMLET.   The king doth wake° tonight and takes his rouse,°
Keeps wassail° and the swagg'ring up-spring° reels:
And as he drains his draughts of Rhenish° down,   10
The kettle-drum and trumpet thus bray out
The triumph of his pledge.°
HORATIO.   Is it a custom?
HAMLET.   Ay marry is't,
But to my mind, though I am native here
And to the manner born,° it is a custom   15
More honoured in the breach than the observance.°
This heavy-headed revel east and west
Makes us traduced and taxed of° other nations:
They clepe° us drunkards, and with swinish phrase
Soil our addition,° and indeed it takes   20
From our achievements, though performed at height,°
The pith and marrow of our attribute.°
So oft it chances in particular men,
That for some vicious mole of nature° in them,
As in their birth, wherein they are not guilty   25
(Since nature cannot choose his origin),
By the o'ergrowth of some complexion,°
Oft breaking down the pales° and forts of reason,
Or by some habit, that too much o'er-leavens°
The form of plausive° manners—that these men,   30
Carrying I say the stamp of one defect,
Being nature's livery,° or fortune's star,°
His virtues else be they as pure as grace,
As infinite as man may undergo,
Shall in the general censure° take corruption   35
From that particular fault: the dram of evil
Doth all the noble substance of a doubt,
To his own scandal.°

Enter GHOST.

HORATIO.   Look my lord, it comes.
HAMLET.   Angels and ministers of grace defend us:
Be thou a spirit of health, or goblin damned,°   40

---

8 *wake:* stay awake.   *rouse:* drinks that empty the cup.   9 *Keeps wassail:* holds drinking
bouts.   *up-spring:* a vigorous German dance.   10 *Rhenish:* Rhine wine.   12 *triumph* . . .
pledge: victory of emptying the cup with one draught.   15 *to* . . . *born:* accustomed to the practice since birth.   16 *More* . . . *observance:* better to break than to observe.   18 *traduced and*
taxed of: defamed and taken to task by.   19 *clepe:* call.   19–20 *with swinish* . . . *addition:* blemish our reputation by comparing us to swine.   21 *at height:* to the maximum.   22 *attribute:*
reputation.   24 *mole of nature:* natural blemish.   27 *o'er growth* . . . *complexion:* overbal-
ance of one of the body's four humors or fluids believed to determine temperament.   28 *pales:*
defensive enclosures.   29 *too much o'er-leavens:* excessively modifies (like too much leaven in
bread).   30 *plausive:* pleasing.   32 *nature's livery:* marked by nature.   *fortune's star:* destined by chance.   35 *general censure:* public opinion.   36–38 *the dram* . . . *scandal:* the minute
quantity of evil casts doubt upon his noble nature, to his shame.   40 *spirit* . . . *damned:* true
ghost or demon from hell.

Bring with thee airs from heaven, or blasts from hell,
Be thy intents wicked, or charitable,
Thou com'st in such a questionable° shape,
That I will speak to thee. I'll call thee Hamlet,
King, father, royal Dane. O answer me,
Let me not burst in ignorance, but tell
Why thy canonized° bones hearsèd° in death
Have burst their cerements°? why the sepulchre,
Wherein we saw thee quietly interred
Hath oped his ponderous and marble jaws,
To cast thee up again? What may this mean
That thou, dead corse, again in complete steel
Revisits thus the glimpses of the moon,
Making night hideous, and we fools of nature°
So horridly to shake our disposition
With thoughts beyond the reaches of our souls,
Say why is this? wherefore? what should we do?   GHOST *beckons HAM*
HORATIO.   It beckons you to go away with it,
   As if it some impartment did desire°
   To you alone.
MARCELLUS.   Look with what courteous action
   It waves you to a more removèd ground,
   But do not go with it.
HORATIO.   No, by no means.
HAMLET.   It will not speak, then I will follow it.
HORATIO.   Do not my lord.
HAMLET.   Why what should be the fear?
   I do not set my life at a pin's fee,°
   And for my soul, what can it do to that
   Being a thing immortal as itself;
   It waves me forth again, I'll follow it.
HORATIO.   What if it tempt you toward the flood my lord,
   Or to the dreadful summit of the cliff
   That beetles o'er° his base into the sea,
   And there assume some other horrible form
   Which might deprive your sovereignty of reason,°
   And draw you into madness? think of it,
   The very place puts toys of desperation,°
   Without more motive, into every brain
   That looks so many fathoms to the sea
   And hears it roar beneath.
HAMLET.   It waves me still:
   Go on, I'll follow thee.

---

43 *questionable:* question-raising.   47 *canonized:* buried in accordance with church edict.   *hearsèd:* entombed.   48 *cerements:* waxed cloth wrappings.   54 *fools of nature:* mocked by our natural limitations when faced with the supernatural.   59 *some . . . desire:* desired to impart something.   65 *fee:* value.   71 *beetles o'er:* overhangs.   73 *deprive . . . reason:* dethrone your reason from its sovereignty.   75 *toys of desperation:* desperate whims.

MARCELLUS.   You shall not go my lord.
HAMLET.   Hold off your hands.   80
HORATIO.   Be ruled, you shall not go.
HAMLET.   My fate cries out,
And makes each petty artire° in this body
As hardy as the Nemean lion's° nerve;°
Still am I called, unhand me gentlemen,
By heaven I'll make a ghost of him that lets° me: 85
I say away; go on, I'll follow thee.   *Exeunt GHOST and HAMLET.*
HORATIO.   He waxes desperate° with imagination.
MARCELLUS.   Let's follow, 'tis not fit thus to obey him.
HORATIO.   Have after—to what issue will this come?
MARCELLUS.   Something is rotten in the state of Denmark.   90
HORATIO.   Heaven will direct it.
MARCELLUS.   Nay, let's follow him.   *Exeunt.*

Scene 5. *[Another part of the platform]*

Enter GHOST and HAMLET.

HAMLET.   Whither wilt thou lead me? Speak, I'll go no further.
GHOST.   Mark me.
HAMLET.   I will.
GHOST.   My hour is almost come
When I to sulphurous and tormenting flames
Must render up myself.
HAMLET.   Alas poor ghost.
GHOST.   Pity me not, but lend thy serious hearing   5
To what I shall unfold.
HAMLET.   Speak, I am bound° to hear.
GHOST.   So art thou to revenge, when thou shalt hear.
HAMLET.   What?
GHOST.   I am thy father's spirit,
Doomed for a certain term to walk the night,   10
And for the day confined to fast in fires,
Till the foul crimes done in my days of nature°
Are burnt and purged away: but that I am forbid
To tell the secrets of my prison-house,
I could a tale unfold whose lightest word   15
Would harrow up thy soul, freeze thy young blood,
Make thy two eyes like stars start from their spheres,°
Thy knotted and combinèd locks to part,
And each particular hair to stand an° end,
Like quills upon the fretful porpentine:°   20

---

82 *artire:* ligament.   83 *Nemean lion:* (killed by Hercules as one of his twelve labors).   *nerve:*
sinew.   85 *lets:* prevents.   87 *waxes desperate:* grows frantic.   6 *bound:* obliged by
duty.   12 *crimes . . . nature:* sins committed during my life on earth.   17 *spheres:* (1) orbits
(according to Ptolemy, each planet was confined to a sphere revolving around the earth)
(2) sockets.   19 *an:* on.   20 *fretful porpentine:* angry porcupine.

But this eternal blazon° must not be
To ears of flesh and blood; list, list, O list:
If though didst ever thy dear father love—
HAMLET. O God!
GHOST. Revenge his foul and most unnatural murder.
HAMLET. Murder?
GHOST. Murder most foul, as in the best it is,
But this most foul, strange and unnatural.
HAMLET. Haste me to know't, that I with wings as swift
As meditation or the thoughts of love,
May sweep to my revenge.
GHOST.   I find thee apt,°
And duller shouldst thou be than the fat° weed
That rots itself in ease on Lethe wharf,°
Wouldst thou not stir in this; now Hamlet hear,
'Tis given out, that sleeping in my orchard,°
A serpent stung me, so the whole ear of Denmark
Is by a forgèd process° of my death
Rankly abused:° but know thou noble youth,
The serpent that did sting thy father's life
Now wears his crown.
HAMLET.   O my prophetic soul!
My uncle?
GHOST. Ay, that incestuous, that adulterate° beast,
With witchcraft of his wit, with traitorous gifts,
O wicked wit and gifts, that have the power
So to seduce; won to his shameful lust
The will of my most seeming-virtuous queen;
O Hamlet, what a falling-off was there,
From me whose love was of that dignity
That it went hand in hand, even with the vow
I made to her in marriage, and to decline
Upon° a wretch whose natural gifts were poor
To° those of mine;
But virtue, as it never will be moved,
Though lewdness court it in a shape of heaven,°
So lust, though to a radiant angle linked,
Will sate itself in a celestial bed
And prey on garbage.
But soft, methinks I scent the morning air,
Brief let me be; sleeping within my orchard,
My custom always of the afternoon,
Upon my secure° hour thy uncle stole

---

21 *eternal blazon:* revelation about eternity.   31 *apt:* ready.   32 *fat:* slimy.   33 *Lethe wharf:*
the banks of Lethe (river in Hades from which spirits drank to forget their past lives).   35
orchard: garden.   37 *process:* account.   38 *abused:* deceived.   42 *adulterate:*
adulterous.   50–51 *decline Upon:* descend to.   52 *To:* compared to.   54 *shape of heaven:*
angelic appearance.   61 *secure:* unsuspecting.

With juice of cursèd hebona° in a vial,
And in the porches of my ears did pour
The leperous° distilment, whose effect
Holds such an enmity with blood of man,   65
That swift as quicksilver it courses through
The natural gates and alleys of the body,
And with a sudden vigour it doth posset°
And curd, like eager° droppings into milk,
The thin and wholesome° blood; so did it mine,   70
And a most instant tetter° barked about°
Most lazar°-like with vile and loathsome crust
All my smooth body.
Thus was I sleeping by a brother's hand,
Of life, of crown, of queen at once dispatched,   75
Cut off even in the blossoms of my sin,
Unhouseled, disappointed, unaneled,°
No reck'ning° made, but sent to my account°
With all my imperfections on my head;
O horrible, O horrible, most horrible!   80
If thou hast nature in thee bear it not,
Let not the royal bed of Denmark be
A couch for luxury° and damnèd incest.
But howsoever thou pursues this act,
Taint not thy mind, nor let thy soul contrive   85
Against thy mother aught;° leave her to heaven,
And to those thorns that in her bosom lodge
To prick and sting her. Fare thee well at once,
The glow-worm shows the matin° to be near
And 'gins to pale this uneffectual fire:°   90
Adieu, adieu, adieu, remember me.   *Exit.*
HAMLET.   O all you host of heaven! O earth! what else?
And shall I couple° hell? O fie! Hold, hold my heart,
And you my sinews, grow not instant old,
But bear me stiffly up; remember thee?   95
Ay thou poor ghost, whiles memory holds a seat
In this distracted globe.° Remember thee?
Yea, from the table° of my memory
I'll wipe away all trivial fond° records,
All saws of books,° all forms, all pressures° past   100

62 *hebona:* poisonous sap of the ebony or henbane.   64 *leperous:* leprosy-causing.   68 *posset:*
curdle.   69 *eager:* sour.   70 *wholesome:* healthy.   71 *tetter:* skin eruption.   *barked about:*
covered (like bark on a tree).   72 *lazar:* leper.   77 *Unhouseled . . . unaneled:* without final
sacrament, unprepared (without confession) and lacking extreme unction (anointing).   78
reck'ning: (1) accounting (2) payment of my bill (3) confession and absolution.   *account:* judgment.   83 *luxury:* lust.   86 *aught:* anything.   89 *matin:* dawn.   90 *'gins . . . fire:* his
light becomes ineffective, made pale by day.   93 *couple:* engage in a contest against.   97 *distracted globe:* (his head).   98 *table:* tablet, "table-book."   99 *fond:* foolish.   100 *saws of
books:* maxims (sayings) copied from books.   *forms, pressures:* ideas, impressions.

That youth and observation copied there,
And thy commandment all alone shall live
Within the book and volume of my brain,
Unmixed with baser matter, yes by heaven:
O most pernicious woman!   1●
O villain, villain, smiling damnèd villain!
My tables,° meet° it is I set it down
That one may smile, and smile, and be a villain,
At least I am sure it may be so in Denmark.
So uncle, there you are: now to my word,°   1
It is 'Adieu, adieu, remember me.'
I have sworn't.

Enter HORATIO and MARCELLUS.

HORATIO.   My lord, my lord!
MARCELLUS.   Lord Hamlet!
HORATIO.   Heaven secure° him.
HAMLET.   So be it.
MARCELLUS.   Illo, ho, ho, my lord!   1
HAMLET.   Hillo, ho, ho, boy, come° bird, come.
MARCELLUS.   How is't my noble lord?
HORATIO.   What news my lord?
HAMLET.   O, wonderful!
HORATIO.   Good my lord, tell it.
HAMLET.   No, you will reveal it.
HORATIO.   Not I my lord, by heaven.
MARCELLUS.   Nor I my lord.   ∣
HAMLET.   How say you then, would heart of man once think it?
    But you'll be secret?
BOTH.   Ay, by heaven, my lord.
HAMLET.   There's ne'er a villain dwelling in all Denmark
    But he's an arrant° knave.
HORATIO.   There needs no ghost my lord, come from the grave
    To tell us this.
HAMLET.   Why right, you are in the right,
    And so without more circumstance° at all
    I hold it fit that we shake hands and part,
    You, as your business and desire shall point you,
    For every man hath business and desire
    Such as it is, and for my own poor part,
    Look you, I will go pray.
HORATIO.   These are but wild and whirling words my lord.
HAMLET.   I am sorry they offend you, heartily,
    Yes faith, heartily.
HORATIO.   There's no offence my lord.

---

107 *tables:* See note for line 98.   *meet:* fitting.   110 *word:* motto (to guide my actions).   113
secure: protect.   116 *Hillo . . . come:* falconer's cry with which Hamlet replies to their calls.   124
arrant: thoroughgoing.   127 *circumstance:* ceremony.

HAMLET.   Yes by Saint Patrick, but there is Horatio,
　　And much offence too: touching this vision here,
　　It is an honest° ghost, that let me tell you:
　　For your desire to know what is between us,
　　O'ermaster't as you may. And now good friends,   140
　　As you are friends, scholars, and soldiers,
　　Give me one poor request.
HORATIO.   What is't, my lord? we will.
HAMLET.   Never make known what you have seen tonight.
BOTH.   My lord we will not.
HAMLET.   Nay, but swear't.
HORATIO.   In faith   145
　　My lord, not I.
MARCELLUS.   Nor I my lord, in faith.
HAMLET.   Upon my sword.
MARCELLUS.   We have sworn my lord already.
HAMLET.   Indeed, upon my sword,° indeed.
GHOST.   Swear.   *Ghost cries under the stage.*
HAMLET.   Ha, ha, boy, say'st thou so, art thou there, truepenny°?   150
　　Come on, you hear this fellow in the cellarage,
　　Consent to swear.
HORATIO.   Propose the oath my lord.
HAMLET.   Never to speak of this that you have seen.
　　Swear by my sword.
GHOST.   [*Beneath.*] Swear.   155
HAMLET.   Hic et ubique?° then we'll shift our ground:
　　Come hither gentlemen,
　　And lay your hands again upon my sword,
　　Swear by my sword
　　Never to speak of this that you have heard.   160
GHOST.   [*Beneath.*] Swear by his sword.
HAMLET.   Well said old mole, canst work i'th' earth so fast?
　　A worthy pioner°—once more remove,° good friends.
HORATIO.   O day and night, but this is wondrous strange.
HAMLET.   And therefore as a stranger give it welcome.   165
　　There are more things in heaven and earth Horatio,
　　Than are dreamt of in your philosophy.
　　But come,
　　Here as before, never so help you mercy,
　　How strange or odd some'er I bear myself,   170
　　(As I perchance hereafter shall think meet
　　To put an antic disposition on°)
　　That you at such times seeing me, never shall
　　With arms encumbered° thus, or this head-shake,
　　Or by pronouncing of some doubtful phrase,   175

---

138 *honest:* true (not a devil in disguise).   148 *sword:* (the cross-shaped hilt).   150 *truepenny:*
old pal.   156 *Hic et ubique:* here and everywhere.   163 *pioner:* digger (army
trencher).   *remove:* move elsewhere.   172 *put . . . on:* assume a mad or grotesque behavior.   174 *encumbered:* folded.

As "Well, well, we know," or "We could and if we would,"
Or "If we list° to speak," or "There be and if they might,"
Or such ambiguous giving out, to note
That you know aught of me; this do swear,
So grace and mercy at your need help you.
GHOST.   [*Beneath.*] Swear.   [*They swear.*]
HAMLET.   Rest, rest, perturbed spirit: so gentlemen,
With all my love I do commend me to you,°
And what so poor a man as Hamlet is,
May do t'express his love and friending to you
God willing shall not lack: let us go in together,
And still° your fingers on your lips I pray.
The time is out of joint: O cursèd spite,
That ever I was born to set it right.
Nay come, let's go together.   *Exeunt.*

ACT 2

Scene 1. *[Polonius's chambers]*

Enter old POLONIUS *with his man* REYNALDO.

POLONIUS.   Give him this money, and these notes Reynaldo.
REYNALDO.   I will my lord.
POLONIUS.   You shall do marvellous° wisely, good Reynaldo,
Before you visit him, to make inquire
Of his behaviour.
REYNALDO.   My lord, I did intend it.
POLONIUS.   Marry, well said, very well said; look you sir,
Inquire me first what Danskers° are in Paris,
And how, and who, what means, and where they keep,°
What company, at what expense, and finding
By this encompassment° and drift of question
That they do know my son, come you more nearer
Than your particular demands° will touch it,
Take you as 'twere some distant knowledge of him,
As thus, "I know his father, and his friends,
And in part him"—do you mark this, Reynaldo?
REYNALDO.   Ay, very well my lord.
POLONIUS.   'And in part him, but,' you may say, 'not well,
But if't be he I mean, he's very wild,
Addicted so and so;' and there put on him
What forgeries° you please, marry none so rank°
As may dishonour him, take heed of that,

177 *list:* please.   183 *commend . . . you:* put myself in your hands.   187 *still:* always.   3
marvellous: wonderfully.   7 *danskers:* Danes.   8 *keep:* lodge.   10 *encompassment:* roundabout way.   12 *particular demands:* specific questions.   20 *forgeries:* inventions.   *rank:*
excessive.

But sir, such wanton, wild, and usual slips,
As are companions noted and most known
To youth and liberty.
REYNALDO.   As gaming my lord.
POLONIUS.   Ay, or drinking, fencing, swearing,   25
    Quarrelling, drabbing°—you may go so far.
REYNALDO.   My lord, that would dishonour him.
POLONIUS.   Faith no, as you may season it in the charge.°
    You must not put another scandal on him,
    That he is open to incontinency,°   30
    That's not my meaning, but breathe his faults so quaintly°
    That they may seem the taints of° liberty,
    The flash and outbreak of a fiery mind,
    A savageness in unreclaimèd blood,°
    Of general assault.°
REYNALDO.   But my good lord—   35
POLONIUS.   Wherefore° should you do this?
REYNALDO.   Ay my lord,
    I would know that.
POLONIUS.   Marry sir, here's my drift,
    And I believe it is a fetch of warrant:°
    You laying these slight sullies on my son,
    As 'twere a thing a little soiled i'th' working,°   40
    Mark you, your party in converse, him you would sound,
    Having ever seen° in the prenominate crimes°
    The youth you breathe of guilty, be assured
    He closes with you in this consequence,°
    "Good sir," or so, or "friend," or "gentleman,"   45
    According to the phrase, or the addition°
    Of man and country.
REYNALDO.   Very good my lord.
POLONIUS.   And then sir, does a'° this, a' does, what was I
        about to say?
    By the mass I was about to say something,
    Where did I leave?
REYNALDO.   At "closes in the consequence,"   50
    At "friend, or so, and gentleman."
POLONIUS.   At "closes in the consequence," ay marry,
    He closes thus, "I know the gentleman,
    I saw him yesterday, or th'other day,
    Or then, or then, with such or such, and as you say,   55
    There was a' gaming, there o'ertook in's rouse,°

---

26 *drabbing:* whoring.   28 *season . . . charge:* temper the charge as you make it.   30 *inconti-*
nency: uncontrolled lechery.   31 *quaintly:* delicately.   32 *taints of:* blemishes due to.   34
unreclaimèd blood: unbridled passion.   35 *general assault:* attacking all (young men).   36 *Where-*
fore: why.   38 *fetch of warrant:* trick guaranteed to succeed.   40 *working:* handling.   42
Having ever seen: if he has ever seen.   *prenominate crimes:* aforenamed sins.   44 *closes . . .*
consequence: comes to terms with you as follows.   46 *addition:* title, form of address.
48 *'a:* he.   56 *o'ertook in's rouse:* overcome by drunkenness.

There falling out at tennis," or perchance
"I saw him enter such a house of sale,"
Videlicet,° a brothel, or so forth. See you now,
Your bait of falsehood takes this carp of truth,
And thus do we of wisdom, and of reach,°
With windlasses,° and with assays of bias,°
By indirections find directions out:
So by my former lecture and advice
Shall you my son; you have me, have you not?

REYNALDO.   My lord I have.
POLONIUS.   God bye ye, fare ye well.
REYNALDO.   Good my lord.
POLONIUS.   Observe his inclination in yourself.°
REYNALDO.   I shall my lord.
POLONIUS.   And let him ply° his music.
REYNALDO.   Well my lord.
POLONIUS.   Farewell.

                                                        Exit REYNALDO.

Enter OPHELIA.

                            How now Ophelia, what's the matter?
OPHELIA.   O my lord, my lord, I have been so affrighted.
POLONIUS.   With what, i'th'name of God?
OPHELIA.   My lord, as I was sewing in my closet,°
    Lord Hamlet with his doublet all unbraced,°
    No hat upon his head, his stockings fouled,
    Ungart'red, and down-gyvèd° to his ankle,
    Pale as his shirt, his knees knocking each other,
    And with a look so piteous in purport°
    As if he had been loosèd out of hell
    To speak of horrors, he comes before me.
POLONIUS.   Mad for thy love?
OPHELIA.   My lord I do not know,
    But truly I do fear it.
POLONIUS.   What said he?
OPHELIA.   He took me by the wrist, and held me hard,
    Then goes he to the length of all his arm,°
    And with his other hand thus o'er his brow,
    He falls to such perusal of my face
    As° a' would draw it; long stayed he so,
    At last, a little shaking of mine arm,
    And thrice his head thus waving up and down,
    He raised a sigh so piteous and profound
    As it did seem to shatter all his bulk,°

59 *Videlicet:* namely.   61 *reach:* far-reaching knowledge.   62 *windlasses:* roundabout
approaches.   *assays of bias:* indirect attempts.   68 *in yourself:* personally.   70 *ply:* practice.   74 *closet:* private room.   75 *doublet all unbraced:* jacket all unfastened.   77 *down-*
gyvèd: down around his ankles (like prisoners' fetters or gyves).   79 *purport:* expression.   85
goes . . . arm: holds me at arm's length.   88 *As:* as if.   92 *bulk:* body.

And end his being; that done, he lets me go,
And with his head over his shoulder turned
He seemed to find his way without his eyes,   95
For out adoors he went without their helps,
And to the last bended their light on me.
POLONIUS. Come, go with me, I will go seek the king,
This is the very ecstasy° of love,
Whose violent property fordoes itself,°   100
And leads the will to desperate undertakings
As oft as any passion under heaven
That does afflict our natures: I am sorry.
What, have you given him any hard words of late?
OPHELIA. No my good lord, but as you did command   105
I did repel his letters, and denied
His access to me.
POLONIUS.   That hath made him mad.
I am sorry that with better heed and judgment
I had not quoted° him. I feared he did but trifle
And meant to wrack° thee, but beshrew my jealousy:°   110
By heaven it is as proper to our age
To cast beyond ourselves in our opinions,°
As it is common for the younger sort
To lack discretion; come, go we to the king,
This must be known, which being kept close, might move   115
More grief to hide, than hate to utter love.°   [*Exeunt.*]

Scene 2. [*A room in the Castle*]

Flourish. Enter KING *and* QUEEN, ROSENCRANTZ *and* GUILDENSTERN, *cum aliis.*

KING. Welcome dear Rosencrantz and Guildenstern.
Moreover° that we much did long to see you,
The need we have to use you did provoke
Our hasty sending. Something have you heard
Of Hamlet's transformation—so call it.   5
Sith° nor th'exterior nor the inward man
Resembles that it was. What it should be,
More than his father's death, that thus hath put him
So much from th'understanding of himself,
I cannot dream of: I entreat you both,   10
That being of so young days° brought up with him,
And sith so neighboured to his youth and haviour,
That you vouchsafe your rest° here in our court
Some little time, so by your companies

99 *ecstasy:* madness.   100 *Whose . . . itself:* that, by its violent nature, destroys the lover.   109
quoted: observed.   110 *wrack:* ruin.   *beshrew my jealousy:* curse my suspicion.   111–112
proper . . . opinions: natural for old people to read more into something than is actually
there.   115–116 *being kept . . . love:* if kept secret, might cause more grief than if we risked the
king's displeasure.   2 *Moreover:* in addition to the fact.   6 *Sith:* since.   11 *of . . . days:*
from your early days.   13 *vouchsafe your rest:* agree to stay.

To draw him on to pleasures, and to gather
So much as from occasion you may glean,
Whether aught to us unknown afflicts him thus,
That opened° lies within our remedy.

QUEEN. Good gentlemen, he hath much talked of you,
And sure I am, two men there are not living
To whom he more adheres. If it will please you
To show us so much gentry° and good will,
As to expend your time with us awhile,
For the supply and profit of our hope,
Your visitation shall receive such thanks
As fits a king's remembrance.

ROSENCRANTZ.   Both your majesties
Might by the sovereign power you have of us,
Put your dread pleasures more into command
Than to entreaty.

GUILDENSTERN.   But we both obey,
And here give up ourselves in the full bent,°
To lay our service freely at your feet
To be commanded.

KING. Thanks Rosencrantz, and gentle Guildenstern.

QUEEN. Thanks Guildenstern, and gentle Rosencrantz.
And I beseech you instantly to visit
My too much changèd son. Go some of you
And bring these gentlemen where Hamlet is.

GUILDENSTERN. Heavens make our presence and our practices°
Pleasant and helpful to him.

QUEEN.   Ay, amen.

Exeunt ROSENCRANTZ *and* GUILDENSTERN.

Enter POLONIUS.

POLONIUS. Th'ambassadors from Norway my good lord,
Are joyfully returned.

KING. Thou still° hast been the father of good news.

POLONIUS. Have I, my lord? Assure you, my good liege,
I hold my duty as I hold my soul,
Both to my God and to my gracious king;
And I do think, or else this brain of mine
Hunts not the trail of policy° so sure
As it hath used to do, that I have found
The very cause of Hamlet's lunacy.

KING. O speak of that, that do I long to hear.

POLONIUS. Give first admittance to th' ambassadors,
My news shall be the fruit° to that great feast.

18 *Opened:* discovered.   22 *gentry:* courtesy.   30 *in the full bent:* to the utmost (in archery, bending the bow).   38 *practices:* (1) actions (2) plots.   42 *still:* always.   47 *policy:* (1) politics (2) plots.   52 *fruit:* dessert.

KING.   Thyself do grace to them, and bring them in.   [*Exit POLONIUS.*]
    He tells me my dear Gertrude, he hath found
    The head and source of all your son's distemper.   55
QUEEN.   I doubt° it is no other but the main,
    His father's death and our o'erhasty marriage.
KING.   Well, we shall sift him.

Enter POLONIUS, VALTEMAND, and CORNELIUS.

                        Welcome, my good friends.
    Say Valtemand, what from our brother Norway?
VALTEMAND.   Most fair return of greetings and desires;   60
    Upon our first,° he sent out to suppress
    His nephew's levies, which to him appeared
    To be a preparation 'gainst the Polack,
    But better looked into, he truly found
    It was against your highness, whereat grieved   65
    That so his sickness, age, and impotence
    Was falsely borne in hand,° sends out arrests
    On Fortinbras, which he in brief obeys,
    Receives rebuke from Norway, and in fine,°
    Makes vow before his uncle never more   70
    To give th'assay° of arms against your majesty:
    Whereon old Norway, overcome with joy,
    Gives him threescore thousand crowns in annual fee,
    And his commission to employ those soldiers
    So levied (as before) against the Polack,   75
    With an entreaty herein further shown,
    That it might please you to give quiet pass°
    Through your dominions for this enterprise,
    On such regards of safety and allowance
    As therein are set down.   [*Giving a paper.*]
KING.   It likes° us well,   80
    And at our more considered time,° we'll read,
    Answer, and think upon this business:
    Meantime, we thank you for your well-took labour,
    Go to your rest, at night we'll feast together.
    Most welcome home.   *Exeunt AMBASSADORS.*
POLONIUS.   This business is well ended.   85
    My liege and madam, to expostulate°
    What majesty should be, what duty is,
    Why day is day, night night, and time is time.
    Were nothing but to waste night, day, and time.
    Therefore since brevity is the soul of wit,°   90
    And tediousness the limbs and outward flourishes,°

---

56 *doubt:* suspect.   61 *first:* first presentation.   67 *borne in hand:* deceived.   69 *fine:* finishing.   71 *assay:* test.   77 *pass:* passage.   80 *likes:* pleases.   81 *at . . . time:* when time is available for consideration.   86 *expostulate:* discuss.   90 *wit:* understanding.   91 *tediousness . . . flourishes:* embellishments and flourishes cause tedium.

I will be brief. Your noble son is mad:
Mad call I it, for to define true madness,
What is't but to be nothing else but mad?
But let that go.
QUEEN.   More matter, with less art.
POLONIUS.   Madam, I swear I use no art at all:
That he is mad 'tis true: 'tis true, 'tis pity,
And pity 'tis 'tis true: a foolish figure,°
But farewell it, for I will use no art.
Mad let us grant him then, and now remains
That we find out the cause of this effect,
Or rather say, the cause of this defect,
For this effect defective comes by cause:
Thus it remains, and the remainder thus.
Perpend.°
I have a daughter, have while she is mine,
Who in her duty and obedience, mark,
Hath given me this, now gather and surmise.
[*Reads.*] "To the celestial, and my soul's idol, the most
beautified° Ophelia,"—
That's an ill phrase, a vile phrase, "beautified" is a vile
phrase, but you shall hear. Thus: [*Reads.*]
      "In her excellent white bosom, these," &c.—
QUEEN.   Came this from Hamlet to her?
POLONIUS.   Good madam stay awhile, I will be faithful.   [*Reads.*]
    "Doubt thou the stars are fire,
      Doubt that the sun doth move,°
    Doubt° truth to be a liar,
      But never doubt I love.
O dear Ophelia, I am ill at these numbers, I have not
art to reckon° my groans, but that I love thee best, O
most best, believe it. Adieu.
    Thine evermore, most dear lady, whilst
      this machine° is to° him, Hamlet."
This in obedience hath my daughter shown me,
And more above hath his solicitings,
As they fell out by time, by means, and place,
All given to mine ear.
KING.   But how hath she
Received his love?
POLONIUS.   What do you think of me?
KING.   As of a man faithful and honourable.
POLONIUS.   I would fain prove so. But what might you think
When I had seen this hot love on the wing,
As I perceived it (I must tell you that)

---

98 *figure:* rhetorical figure.   105 *Perpend:* consider.   110 *beautified:* beautiful.   117 *move:*
(as it was believed to do, around the earth).   118 *Doubt:* suspect.   121 *reckon:* express in
meter.   124 *machine:* body.   *to:* attached to.

Before my daughter told me, what might you,
Or my dear majesty your queen here think,   135
If I had played the desk or table-book,°
Or given my heart a winking° mute and dumb,
Or looked upon this love with idle° sight,
What might you think? No, I went round to work,
And my young mistress this I did bespeak,   140
"Lord Hamlet is a prince out of thy star,°
This must not be:" and then I prescripts° gave her
That she should lock herself from his resort,°
Admit no messengers, receive no tokens:
Which done, she took the fruits of my advice,   145
And he repellèd, a short tale to make,
Fell into a sadness, then into a fast,
Thence to a watch,° thence into a weakness,
Thence to a lightness,° and by this declension,
Into the madness wherein now he raves,   150
And all we mourn for.
KING.   Do you think 'tis this?
QUEEN.   It may be very like.
POLONIUS.   Hath there been such a time, I would fain know that,
     That I have positively said "'Tis so,"
     When it proved otherwise?
KING.   Not that I know.   155
POLONIUS.   Take this, from this, if this be otherwise;

[*Points to his head and shoulder.*]

     If circumstances lead me, I will find
     Where truth is hid, though it were hid indeed
     Within the center.
KING.   How may we try° it further?
POLONIUS.   You know sometimes he walks four hours together   160
     Here in the lobby.
QUEEN.   So he does indeed.
POLONIUS.   At such a time, I'll loose° my daughter to him.
     Be you and I behind an arras° then,
     Mark the encounter: if he love her not,
     And be not from his reason fall'n thereon,   165
     Let me be no assistant for a state,°
     But keep a farm and carters.
KING.   We will try it.

Enter HAMLET reading on a book.

QUEEN.   But look where sadly the poor wretch comes reading.

136 *played . . . book:* kept it concealed as in a desk or personal notebook.   137 *given . . . winking:*
had my heart shut its eyes to the matter.   138 *idle:* unseeing.   141 *out . . . star:* out of your
sphere (above you in station).   142 *prescripts:* orders.   143 *resort:* company.   148 *watch:*
sleeplessness.   149 *lightness:* lightheadedness.   159 *try:* test.   162 *loose:* (1) release (2)
turn loose.   163 *arras:* hanging tapestry.   166 *assistant . . . state:* state official.

POLONIUS.   Away, I do beseech you both away,
I'll board him presently,° O give me leave.   *Exeunt KING and QUEEN.*   17
How does my good Lord Hamlet?

HAMLET.   Well, God-a-mercy.

POLONIUS.   Do you know me, my lord?

HAMLET.   Excellent well, you are a fishmonger.°

POLONIUS.   Not I my lord.   1'

HAMLET.   Then I would you were so honest a man.

POLONIUS.   Honest, my lord?

HAMLET.   Ay sir, to be honest as this world goes, is to be one
man picked out of ten thousand.

POLONIUS.   That's very true, my lord.   1.

HAMLET.   For if the sun breed maggots° in a dead dog, being a good
kissing carrion°—have you a daughter?

POLONIUS.   I have my lord.

HAMLET.   Let her not walk i'th'sun:° conception° is a blessing, but as
your daughter may conceive, friend look to'it.   1

POLONIUS.   [*Aside.*] How say you by that? Still harping on my daughter,
yet he knew me not at first, a' said I was a fishmonger.
A' is far gone, far gone, and truly in my youth, I suffered
much extremity for love, very near this. I'll speak to him
again. What do you read my lord?

HAMLET.   Words, words, words.

POLONIUS.   What is the matter my lord?

HAMLET.   Between who?

POLONIUS.   I mean the matter° that you read, my lord.

HAMLET.   Slanders sir; for the satirical rogue says here, that old men
have grey beards, that their faces are wrinkled, their eyes
purging thick amber and plum-tree gum,° and that they
have a plentiful lack of wit, together with most weak
hams. All which sir, though I most powerfully and
potently believe, yet I hold it not honesty° to have it thus set
down, for yourself sir shall grow old as I am: if like a crab
you could go backward.

POLONIUS.   [*Aside.*] Though this be madness, yet there is method
in't.
Will you walk out of the air° my lord?

HAMLET.   Into my grave.

POLONIUS.   [*Aside.*] Indeed that's out of the air; how pregnant°
sometimes his replies are, a happiness° that often

---

170 *board him presently:* approach him immediately.   174 *fishmonger:* (1) fish dealer (2)
pimp.   181 *breed maggots:* (in the belief that the rays of the sun caused maggots to breed in
dead flesh).   182 *kissing carrion:* piece of flesh for kissing.   184 *Let . . . sun:* (1) (proverbial: "out of God's blessing, into the warm sun") (2) because the sun is a breeder (3) don't let her
go near me (with a pun on "sun" and "son").   *conception:* (1) understanding (2) pregnancy.
194 *matter:* (1) content (Polonius's meaning) (2) cause of a quarrel (Hamlet's
interpretation).   197–198 *purging . . . gum:* exuding a viscous yellowish discharge.   200 *honesty:* decency.   205 *out . . . air:* (in the belief that fresh air was bad for the sick).   207 *pregnant:* full of meaning.   208 *happiness:* aptness.

madness hits on, which reason and sanity could not so
prosperously° be delivered of. I will leave him, and   210
suddenly contrive the means of meeting between him
and my daughter. My honourable lord, I will most
humbly take leave of you.

HAMLET.   You cannot sir take from me anything that I will more
willingly part withal: except my life, except my life,   215
except my life.

POLONIUS.   Fare you well my lord.

HAMLET.   These tedious old fools.

Enter ROSENCRANTZ and GUILDENSTERN.

POLONIUS.   You go to seek the Lord Hamlet, there he is.

ROSENCRANTZ.   [*To POLONIUS.*] God save you sir.   [*Exit POLONIUS.*]   220

GUILDENSTERN.   My honoured lord.

ROSENCRANTZ.   My most dear lord.

HAMLET.   My excellent good friends, how dost thou Guildenstern?
Ah Rosencrantz, good lads, how do you both?

ROSENCRANTZ.   As the indifferent° children of the earth.   225

GUILDENSTERN.   Happy, in that we are not over-happy:
On Fortune's cap we are not the very button.°

HAMLET.   Nor the soles of her shoe?

ROSENCRANTZ.   Neither my lord.

HAMLET.   Then you live about her waist, or in the middle of her   230
favours?

GUILDENSTERN.   Faith, her privates° we.

HAMLET.   In the secret parts of Fortune? O most true, she is a
strumpet.° What news?

ROSENCRANTZ.   None my lord, but that the world's grown honest.   235

HAMLET.   Then is doomsday near: but your news is not true. Let me
question more in particular: what have you my good
friends, deserved at the hands of Fortune, that she sends
you to prison hither?

GUILDENSTERN.   Prison, my lord?   240

HAMLET.   Denmark's a prison.

ROSENCRANTZ.   Then is the world one.

HAMLET.   A goodly one, in which there are many confines, wards,°
and dungeons; Denmark being one o'th'worst.

ROSENCRANTZ.   We think not so my lord.   245

HAMLET.   Why then 'tis none to you; for there is nothing either good
or bad, but thinking makes it so: to me it is a prison.

ROSENCRANTZ.   Why then your ambition makes it one: 'tis too narrow for
your mind.

HAMLET.   O God, I could be bounded in a nutshell, and count   250
myself a king of infinite space; were it not that I have bad
dreams.

---

210 *prosperously:* successfully.   225 *indifferent:* ordinary.   227 *on Fortune's . . . button:* we are not
at the height of our fortunes.   232 *privates:* (1) intimate friends (2) private parts.   234 *strumpet:* inconstant woman, giving favor to many.   243 *wards:* cells.

GUILDENSTERN.   Which dreams indeed are ambition: for the very substance
  of the ambitious, is merely the shadow of a dream.
HAMLET.   A dream itself is but a shadow.   25
ROSENCRANTZ.   Truly, and I hold ambition of so airy and light a quality,
  that it is but a shadow's shadow.
HAMLET.   Then are our beggars bodies, and our monarchs and
  outstretched heroes the beggars' shadows:° shall we to th'
  court? for by my fay,° I cannot reason.   26
BOTH.   We'll wait upon° you.
HAMLET.   No such matter. I will not sort° you with the rest of my
  servants: for to speak to you like an honest man, I am most
  dreadfully attended. But in the beaten way of friendship,
  what make you at Elsinore?   2
ROSENCRANTZ.   To visit you my lord, no other occasion.
HAMLET.   Beggar that I am, I am even poor in thanks, but I thank
  you, and sure dear friends, my thanks are too dear a
  halfpenny:° were you not sent for? is it your own inclining?
  is it a free° visitation? come, come, deal justly with me,   2
  come, come, nay speak.
GUILDENSTERN.   What should we say my lord?
HAMLET.   Anything but to th'purpose: you were sent for, and there
  is a kind of confession in your looks, which your modesties
  have not craft enough to colour: I know the good king and   2
  queen have sent for you.
ROSENCRANTZ.   To what end my lord?
HAMLET.   That you must teach me: but let me conjure° you, by the
  rights of our fellowship, by the consonancy of our youth,°
  by the obligation of our ever-preserved love, and by what   2
  more dear a better proposer can charge you withal,° be
  even and direct with me whether you were sent for or no.
ROSENCRANTZ.   [*Aside to Guildenstern.*] What say you?
HAMLET.   Nay then, I have an eye of° you: If you love me,
  hold not off.   2
GUILDENSTERN.   My lord, we were sent for.
HAMLET.   I will tell you why, so shall my anticipation prevent° your
  discovery,° and your secrecy to the king and queen moult
  no feather.° I have of late, but wherefore I know not, lost all
  my mirth, forgone all custom of exercises: and indeed it
  goes so heavily with my disposition, that this goodly
  frame the earth, seems to me a sterile promontory, this
  most excellent canopy the air, look you, this brave°
  o'erhanging firmament, this majestical roof fretted° with

258–259 *Then are . . . shadows:* then beggars are the true substance and ambitious kings and heroes
the elongated shadows of beggars' bodies (for only a real substance can cast a shadow).
260 *fay:* faith.   261 *wait upon:* attend.   262 *sort:* class.   268–269 *too dear a halfpenny:*
worth not even a halfpenny (as I have no influence).   270 *free:* voluntary.   278 *conjure:*
appeal to.   279 *consonancy . . . youth:* agreement in our ages.   281 *withal:* with.   284 *of:*
on.   287 *prevent:* forestall.   288 *discovery:* disclosure.   288–289 *moult no feather:* change in
no way.   293 *brave:* splendid.   294 *fretted:* ornamented with fretwork.

golden fire,° why it appeareth nothing to me but a foul and   295
pestilent congregation of vapours.° What a piece of work is
a man! How noble in reason, how infinite in faculties,° in
form and moving, how express° and admirable in action,
how like an angel in apprehension, how like a god: the
beauty of the world; the paragon of animals; and yet to   300
me, what is this quintessence of dust? Man delights not
me, no, nor woman neither, though by your smiling, you
seem to say so.
ROSENCRANTZ.   My lord, there was no such stuff in my thoughts.
HAMLET.   Why did ye laugh then, when I said 'man delights not me'?   305
ROSENCRANTZ.   To think, my lord, if you delight not in man, what lenten
entertainment° the players shall receive from you: we coted°
them on the way, and hither are they coming to offer you
service.
HAMLET.   He that plays the king shall be welcome, his majesty shall   310
have tribute of me, the adventurous knight° shall use his
foil and target,° the lover shall not sigh gratis,° the humorous
man° shall end his part in peace,° the clown shall make
those laugh whose lungs are tickle o'th'sere,° and the lady
shall say her mind freely: or the blank verse shall halt° for't.   315
What players are they?
ROSENCRANTZ.   Even those you were wont to take such delight in, the
tragedians of the city.
HAMLET.   How chances it they travel? Their residence° both in
reputation and profit was better both ways.   320
ROSENCRANTZ.   I think their inhibition comes by the means of the late
innovation.°
HAMLET.   Do they hold the same estimation they did when I was in
the city; are they so followed?
ROSENCRANTZ.   No indeed are they not.   325
HAMLET.   How comes it? Do they grow rusty?
ROSENCRANTZ.   Nay, their endeavour keeps in the wonted pace; but there
is sir an aery° of children, like eyases,° that cry out on the
top of question,° and are most tyrannically° clapped for't:
these are now the fashion, and so berattle° the common   330

---

295 *golden fire:* stars.   296 *pestilent . . . vapours:* (clouds were believed to carry contagion).
297 *faculties:* physical powers.   298 *express:* well framed.   306–307 *lenten entertainment:* meager
treatment.   307 *coted:* passed.   311 *adventurous knight:* knight errant (a popular stage character).   312 *foil and target:* sword blunted for stage fighting, and small shield.   312 *gratis:*
(without applause).   312–313 *humorous man:* eccentric character with a dominant trait, caused by
an excess of one of the four humors, or bodily fluids.   313 *in peace:* without interruption.
314 *tickle o'th'sere:* attuned to respond to laughter, as the finely adjusted gunlock responds to the
touch of the trigger (fr. hunting).   315 *halt:* limp (if she adds her own opinions and spoils the
meter).   319 *residence:* i.e., in a city theatre.   321–322 *inhibition . . . innovation:* i.e., they were
forced out of town by a more popular theatrical fashion. The following speeches allude to the "War
of the Theatres" (1601–1602) between the child and adult acting companies.   328 *aery:*
nest.   *eyases:* young hawks.   328–329 *that cry . . . question:* whose shrill voices can be heard
above all others.   329 *tyrannically:* strongly.   330 *berattle:* berate.   330–331 *common stages:*
public playhouses (the children's companies performed in private theatres).

stages° (so they call them) that many wearing rapiers° are
afraid of goose-quills,° and dare scarce come thither.
HAMLET.   What, are they children? Who maintains 'em? How are
they escoted°? Will they pursue the quality no longer than
they can sing°? Will they not say afterwards if they should
grow themselves to common players (as it is most like, if
their means are not better) their writers do them wrong, to
make them exclaim against their own succession°?
ROSENCRANTZ.   Faith, there has been much to-do on both sides: and the
nation holds it no sin to tarre° them to controversy. There
was for a while, no money bid for argument,° unless the
poet and the player went to cuffs in the question.°
HAMLET.   Is't possible?
GUILDENSTERN.   O there has been much throwing about of brains.
HAMLET.   Do the boys carry it away°?
ROSENCRANTZ.   Ay, that they do my lord, Hercules and his load too.°
HAMLET.   It is not very strange, for my uncle is king of Denmark,
and those that would make mows° at him while my father
lived, give twenty, forty, fifty, a hundred ducats apiece
for his picture in little.° 'Sblood,° there is something in this
more than natural, if philosophy° could find it out.

A flourish for the Players.

GUILDENSTERN.   There are the players.
HAMLET.   Gentlemen, you are welcome to Elsinore: your hands,
come then, th'appurtenance° of welcome is fashion and
ceremony; let me comply with you in this garb,° lest my
extent° to the players, which I tell you must show fairly
outwards, should more appear like entertainment than
yours.° You are welcome: but my uncle-father, and aunt-
mother, are deceived.
GUILDENSTERN.   In what my dear lord?
HAMLET.   I am but mad north-north-west; when the wind is southerly,
I know a hawk from a handsaw.°

Enter POLONIUS.

POLONIUS.   Well be with you, gentlemen.

---

331 *wearing rapiers:* (worn by gentlemen).   332 *goose-quills:* pens (of satirical dramatists who wrote
for the children).   334 *escoted:* supported.   334–335 *pursue . . . sing:* continue acting only until
their voices change.   338 *succession:* inheritance.   340 *tarre:* provoke.   341 *bid for
argument:* paid for the plot of a proposed play.   342 *went . . . question:* came to blows on the subject.   345 *carry it away:* carry off the prize.   346 *Hercules . . . too:* (Shakespeare's own company at the Globe Theatre, whose sign was Hercules carrying the globe of the world).
348 *mows:* mouths, grimaces.   350 *little:* a miniature.   *'Sblood:* by God's blood.   351 *philosophy:* science.   354 *appurtenance:* accessory.   355 *comply . . . garb:* observe the formalities
with you in this style.   356 *extent:* i.e., of welcome.   357–358 *should . . . yours:* should appear
more hospitable than yours.   362 *I know . . . handsaw:* I can tell the difference between two
things that are unlike ("hawk" = [1] bird of prey [2] mattock, pickaxe; "handsaw" = [1] hernshaw
or heron bird [2] small saw).

HAMLET. Hark you Guildenstern, and you too, at each ear a hearer: 365
    that great baby you see there is not yet out of his swaddling
    clouts.°
ROSENCRANTZ. Happily° he is the second time come to them, for they say
    an old man is twice a child.
HAMLET. I will prophesy, he comes to tell me of the players, mark
    it.—You say right sir, a Monday morning, 'twas then 370
    indeed.
POLONIUS. My lord, I have news to tell you.
HAMLET. My lord, I have news to tell you. When Roscius° was an
    actor in Rome—
POLONIUS. The actors are come hither, my lord. 375
HAMLET. Buz, buz.°
POLONIUS. Upon my honour.
HAMLET. Then came each actor on his ass—
POLONIUS. The best actors in the world, either for tragedy, comedy,
    history, pastoral, pastoral-comical, historical-pastoral, 380
    tragical-historical, tragical-comical-historical-pastoral,
    scene individable,° or poem unlimited.° Seneca cannot be
    too heavy, nor Plautus° too light for the law of writ, and the
    liberty:° these are the only men.
HAMLET. O Jephthah,° judge of Israel, what a treasure hadst thou. 385
POLONIUS. What a treasure had he, my lord?
HAMLET. Why
    'One fair daughter and no more,
      The which he lovèd passing° well.'
POLONIUS. [*Aside.*] Still on my daughter. 390
HAMLET. Am I not i'th' right, old Jephthah?
POLONIUS. If you call me Jephthah my lord, I have a daughter that I
    love passing well.
HAMLET. Nay, that follows not.
POLONIUS. What follows then, my lord? 395
HAMLET. Why
    "As by lot, God wot,"
    and then you know
    "It came to pass, as most like° it was:"
    the first row° of the pious chanson will show you more, for 400
    look where my abridgement° comes.

Enter four or five PLAYERS.

    You are welcome masters, welcome all. I am glad to see
    thee well: welcome, good friends. O my old friend, why

365–366 *swaddling clouts:* strips of cloth binding a newborn baby. 367 *Happily:* perhaps. 373
Roscius: famous Roman actor. 376 *Buz, buz:* (contemptuous). 382 *scene individable:* play
observing the unities (time, place, action). *poem unlimited:* play ignoring the unities. 382–383 *Seneca, Plautus:* Roman writers of tragedy and comedy, respectively. 383–384
law . . . liberty: "rules" regarding the unities and those exercising freedom from the unities. 385
Jephthah: (who was forced to sacrifice his only daughter because of a rash promise: Judges
11:29–39). 389 *passing:* surpassingly. 399 *like:* likely. 400 *row:* stanza. 401 *abridge-
ment:* (the players who will cut short my song).

thy face is valanced° since I saw thee last, com'st thou to
beard me in Denmark? What, my young lady° and   40!
mistress? by'r lady, your ladyship is nearer to heaven than
when I saw you last, by the altitude of a chopine.° Pray
God your voice, like a piece of uncurrent° gold, be not
cracked within the ring.° Masters, you are all welcome:
we'll e'en to't like French falconers, fly at any thing we see:°   41▪
we'll have a speech straight. Come give us a taste of your
quality: come, a passionate speech.

1. PLAYER.   What speech, my good lord?

HAMLET.   I heard thee speak me a speech once, but it was never
acted, or if it was, not above once, for the play I remember   41
pleased not the million, 'twas caviary to the general,° but it
was (as I received it, and others, whose judgments in such
matters cried in the top of mine°) an excellent play, well
digested in the scenes, set down with as much modesty as
cunning.° I remember one said there were no sallets° in the   4!
lines, to make the matter savoury, nor no matter in the
phrase that might indict the author of° affection, but called
it an honest method, as wholesome as sweet, and by very
much more handsome than fine:° one speech in't I chiefly
loved, 'twas Aeneas' tale to Dido, and thereabout of it   4!
especially where he speaks of Priam's slaughter.° If it live in
your memory begin at this line, let me see, let me see:
        "The rugged Pyrrhus,° like th'Hyrcanian beast"°—
'tis not so: it begins with Pyrrhus—
        "The rugged Pyrrhus, he whose sable° arms,   4
Black as his purpose, did the night resemble
When he lay couched in th'ominous horse,°
Hath now this dread and black complexion smeared
With heraldy more dismal: head to foot
Now is he total gules,° horridly tricked°   4
With blood of fathers, mothers, daughters, sons,
Baked and impasted° with the parching° streets,
That lend a tyrannous and damnèd light
To their lord's murder. Roasted in wrath and fire,
And thus o'er-sizèd° with coagulate gore,   4
With eyes like carbuncles,° the hellish Pyrrhus

---

404 *valanced:* fringed with a beard.   405 *lady:* boy playing women's role.   407 *chopine:* thick-
soled shoe.   408 *uncurrent:* not legal tender.   409 *ring:* (1) ring enclosing the design on a
gold coin (to crack it within the ring [to steal the gold] made it "uncurrent") (2) sound.
410 *fly . . . see:* undertake any difficulty.   416 *caviary . . . general:* like caviar, too rich for the
general public.   418 *cried . . . mine:* spoke with more authority than mine.   419–420 *modesty
as cunning:* moderation as skill.   420 *sallets:* spicy bits.   422 *indict . . . of:* charge . . .
with.   424 *handsome than fine:* dignified than finely wrought.   426 *Priam's slaughter:* the
murder of the King of Troy (as told in the Aeneid).   428 *Pyrrhus:* son of
Achilles.   *Hyrcanian beast:* tiger noted for fierceness.   430 *sable:* black.   432 *horse:* the
hollow wooden horse used by the Greeks to enter Troy.   435 *gules:* red.   *horridly tricked:*
horribly decorated.   437 *impasted:* coagulated.   *parching:* (because the city was on
fire).   440 *o'er-sizèd:* covered over.   441 *carbuncles:* red gems.

Old grandsire Priam seeks;"
So proceed you.
POLONIUS.   'Fore God, my lord, well spoken, with good accent and
   good discretion.°   445
1. PLAYER.   "Anon he finds him,
   Striking too short at Greeks, his antique° sword,
   Rebellious to his arm, lies where it falls,
   Repugnant to command;° unequal matched,
   Pyrrhus at Priam drives, in rage strikes wide,   450
   But with the whiff and wind of his fell° sword,
   Th'unnerved father falls: then senseless Ilium,°
   Seeming to feel this blow, with flaming top
   Stoops to his base; and with a hideous crash
   Takes prisoner Pyrrhus' ear. For lo, his sword   455
   Which was declining on the milky head
   Of reverend Priam, seemed i'th'air to stick;
   So as a painted° tyrant Pyrrhus stood,
   And like a neutral to his will and matter,°
   Did nothing: 460
   But as we often see, against° some storm,
   A silence in the heavens, the rack° stand still,
   The bold winds speechless, and the orb° below
   As hush as death, anon the dreadful thunder
   Doth rend the region, so after Pyrrhus' pause,   465
   A rousèd vengeance sets him new awork,
   And never did the Cyclops'° hammers fall
   On Mars's armour, forged for proof eterne,°
   With less remorse than Pyrrhus' bleeding sword
   Now falls on Priam.   470
   Out, out, thou strumpet Fortune: all you gods,
   In general synod° take away her power,
   Break all the spokes and fellies from her wheel,°
   And bowl the round nave° down the hill of heaven
   As low as to the fiends."°   475
POLONIUS.   This is too long.
HAMLET.   It shall to the barber's with your beard; prithee say on: he's
   for a jig, or a tale of bawdry, or he sleeps. Say on, come to
   Hecuba.
1. PLAYER.   "But who, ah woe, had seen the mobled° queen—"   480
HAMLET.   "The mobled queen"?
POLONIUS.   That's good, "mobled queen" is good.

---

445 *discretion:* interpretation.   447 *antique:* ancient.   449 *Repugnant to command:* refusing
to obey its commander.   451 *fell:* savage.   452 *senseless Ilium:* unfeeling Troy.   458
painted: pictured.   459 *like . . . matter:* unmoved by either his purpose or its achievement.
461 *against:* before.   462 *rack:* clouds.   463 *orb:* earth.   467 *Cyclops:* workmen of Vulcan,
armorer of the gods.   468 *for proof eterne:* to be eternally invincible.   472 *synod:*
assembly.   473 *fellies . . . wheel:* curved pieces of the rim of the wheel that fortune turns, representing a man's fortunes.   474 *nave:* hub.   475 *fiends:* i.e., of hell.   480 *mobled:* muffled
in a scarf.

1. PLAYER.   "Run barefoot up and down, threat'ning the flames
    With bissom rheum,° a clout° upon that head
    Where late the diadem stood, and for a robe,   485
    About her lank and all o'er-teemèd° loins,
    A blanket in the alarm of fear caught up—
    Who this had seen, with tongue in venom steeped,
    'Gainst Fortune's state° would treason have pronounced;
    But if the gods themselves did see her then,   490
    When she saw Pyrrhus make malicious sport
    In mincing with his sword her husband's limbs,
    The instant burst of clamour that she made,
    Unless things mortal move them not at all,
    Would have made milch° the burning eyes of heaven,   495
    And passion in the gods."
POLONIUS.   Look whe'r° he has not turned° his colour, and has tears in's
    eyes, prithee no more.
HAMLET.   'Tis well, I'll have thee speak out the rest of this soon.
    Good my lord, will you see the players well bestowed;° do   500
    you hear, let them be well used, for they are the abstract°
    and brief chronicles° of the time; after your death you were
    better have a bad epitaph than their ill report while you
    live.
POLONIUS.   My lord, I will use them according to their desert.°   505
HAMLET.   God's bodkin° man, much better. Use every man after° his
    desert, and who shall 'scape whipping? Use them after
    you own honour and dignity: the less they deserve, the
    more merit is in your bounty. Take them in.
POLONIUS.   Come sirs.   *Exeunt POLONIUS and PLAYERS.*   5
HAMLET.   Follow him friends, we'll hear a play tomorrow; [*Stops the
    First Player.*] dost thou hear me, old friend, can you play
    The Murder of Gonzago?
1. PLAYER.   Ay my lord.
HAMLET.   We'll ha't tomorrow night. You could for a need° study a   5
    speech of some dozen or sixteen lines, which I would set
    down and insert in't, could you not?
1. PLAYER.   Ay my lord.
HAMLET.   Very well, follow that lord, and look you mock him not.

                                 [*Exit FIRST PLAYER.*]

    [*To Rosencrantz and Guildenstern.*] My good friends, I'll   5
    leave you till night, you are welcome to Elsinore.
ROSENCRANTZ.   Good my lord.   [*Exeunt ROSENCRANTZ and GUILDENSTERN.*]
HAMLET.   Ay so, God bye to you, now I am alone.
    O what a rogue and peasant slave am I.

---

484 *bissom rheum:* binding tears.   *clout:* cloth.   486 *o'erteemed:* worn out by excessive childbearing.   489 *state:* reign.   495 *milch:* milky, moist.   497 *whe'r:* whether.   *turned:*
changed.   500 *bestowed:* lodged.   501 *abstract:* summary (noun).   502 *brief chronicles:* history in brief.   505 *desert:* merit.   506 *God's bodkin:* God's little body, the communion wafer
(an oath).   *after:* according to.   515 *for a need:* if necessary.

Is it not monstrous that this player here,   525
But in a fiction, in a dream of passion,°
Could force his soul so to his own conceit°
That from her working all his visage wanned,°
Tears in his eyes, distraction in his aspect,
A broken voice, and his whole function° suiting   530
With forms° to his conceit; and all for nothing,
For Hecuba!
What's Hecuba to him, or he to Hecuba,
That he should weep for her? what would he do,
Had he the motive and the cue for passion   535
That I have? he would drown the stage with tears,
And cleave the general ear° with horrid speech,
Make mad the guilty and appal the free,°
Confound° the ignorant, and amaze indeed
The very faculties of eyes and ears; yet I,   540
A dull and muddy-mettled° rascal, peak°
Like John-a-dreams,° unpregnant of° my cause,
And can say nothing; no, not for a king,
Upon whose property and most dear life,
A damned defeat was made: am I a coward?   545
Who calls me villain, breaks my pate° across,
Plucks off my beard° and blows it in my face,
Tweaks me by the nose, gives me the lie i'th'throat
As deep as to the lungs,° who does me this?
Ha, 'swounds,° I should take it; for it cannot be   550
But I am pigeon-livered,° and lack gall
To make oppression bitter, or ere this
I should ha' fatted all the region kites°
With this slave's offal: bloody, bawdy villain,
Remorseless, treacherous, lecherous, kindless° villain!   555
O vengeance!
Why what an ass am I, this is most brave,°
That I, the son of a dear father murdered,
Prompted to my revenge by heaven and hell,
Must like a whore unpack my heart with words,   560
And fall a-cursing like a very drab,°
A scullion,° fie upon't, foh.
About, my brains; hum, I have heard,
That guilty creatures sitting at a play,

---

526 *dream of passion:* portrayal of emotion.   527 *conceit:* imagination.   528 *wanned:* grew
pale.   530 *function:* bearing.   531 *With forms:* in appearance.   537 *general ear:* ears of all
in the audience.   538 *free:* innocent.   539 *Confound:* confuse.   541 *muddy-mettled:* dull-
spirited.   *peak:* pine, mope.   542 *John-a-dreams:* a daydreaming fellow.   *unpregnant of:*
unstirred by.   546 *pate:* head.   547 *Plucks . . . beard:* (a way of giving insult).   548–549
gives . . . lungs: insults me by calling me a liar of the worst kind (the lungs being deeper than the
throat).   550 *'swounds:* God's wounds.   551 *pigeon-livered:* meek and uncourageous.
553 *region kites:* vultures of the upper air.   555 *kindless:* unnatural.   557 *brave:* fine.
561 *drab:* whore.   562 *scullion:* kitchen wench.

Have by the very cunning of the scene
Been struck so to the soul, that presently°
They have proclaimed their malefactions:
For murder, though it have no tongue, will speak
With most miraculous organ: I'll have these players
Play something like the murder of my father
Before mine uncle, I'll observe his looks,
I'll tent° him to the quick, if a' do blench°
I know my course. The spirit that I have seen
May be a devil, and the devil hath power
T'assume a pleasing shape, yea, and perhaps
Out of my weakness, and my melancholy,
As he is very potent with such spirits,
Abuses me to damn me; I'll have grounds
More relative than this: the play's the thing
Wherein I'll catch the conscience of the king.

ACT 3

Scene 1. *[A room in the castle]*

Enter KING, QUEEN, POLONIUS, OPHELIA, ROSENCRANTZ, GUILDENSTERN, *and* LORDS.

KING.   And can you by no drift of conference°
　　Get from him why he puts on this confusion,°
　　Grating so harshly all his days of quiet
　　With turbulent and dangerous lunacy?
ROSENCRANTZ.   He does confess he feels himself distracted,
　　But from what cause, a' will by no means speak.
GUILDENSTERN.   Nor do we find him forward to be sounded,°
　　But with a crafty madness keeps aloof
　　When we would bring him on to some confession
　　Of his true state.
QUEEN.　　　　　　　　Did he receive you well?
ROSENCRANTZ.   Most like a gentleman.
GUILDENSTERN.   But with much forcing of his disposition.°
ROSENCRANTZ.   Niggard of question,° but of our demands
　　Most free in his reply.
QUEEN.　　　　　　　　Did you assay° him
　　To any pastime?
ROSENCRANTZ.   Madam, it so fell out that certain players
　　We o'er-raught° on the way: of these we told him,
　　And there did seem in him a kind of joy

---

566 *presently:* immediately.　　572 *tent:* probe.　　*blench:* flinch.　　1 *drift of conference:* turn of conversation.　　2 *puts . . . confusion:* seems so distracted ("puts on" indicates the king's private suspicion that Hamlet is playing mad).　　7 *forward . . . sounded:* disposed to be sounded out.　　12 *forcing . . . disposition:* forcing himself to be so.　　13 *Niggard of question:* unwilling to talk.　　14 *assay:* tempt.　　17 *o'er-raught:* overtook.

To hear of it: they are here about the court,
And as I think, they have already order   20
This night to play before him.

POLONIUS.   'Tis most true,
And he beseeched me to entreat your majesties
To hear and see the matter.°

KING.   With all my heart, and it doth much content me
To hear him so inclined.   25
Good gentlemen, give him a further edge,°
And drive his purpose into these delights.

ROSENCRANTZ.   We shall my lord.   *Exeunt ROSENCRANTZ and GUILDENSTERN.*

KING.   Sweet Gertrude, leave us too,
For we have closely° sent for Hamlet hither,
That he, as 'twere by accident, may here   30
Affront° Ophelia;
Her father and myself, lawful espials,°
Will so bestow° ourselves, that seeing unseen,
We may of their encounter frankly° judge,
And gather by him as he is behaved,   35
If't be th'affliction of his love or no
That thus he suffers for.

QUEEN.   I shall obey you.
And for your part Ophelia, I do wish
That your good beauties be the happy cause
Of Hamlet's wildness, so shall I hope your virtues   40
Will bring him to his wonted° way again,
To both your honours.

OPHELIA.   Madam, I wish it may.   *[Exit QUEEN.]*

POLONIUS.   Ophelia, walk you here—Gracious,° so please you,
We will bestow ourselves—read on this book,°
That show of such an exercise° may colour°   45
Your loneliness; we are oft to blame in this,
'Tis too much proved,° that with devotion's visage
And pious action, we do sugar o'er
The devil himself.

KING.   *[Aside.]* O 'tis too true,°
How smart a lash that speech doth give my conscience.   50
The harlot's cheek, beautied with plast'ring art,
Is not more ugly to° the thing that helps it,
Than is my deed to my most painted word:°
O heavy burden!

---

23 *matter:* i.e., of the play.   26 *give . . . edge:* encourage his keen interest.   29 *closely:*
secretly.   31 *Affront:* meet face to face with.   32 *espials:* spies.   33, 44 *bestow:*
place.   34 *frankly:* freely.   41 *wonted:* customary.   43 *Gracious:* i.e., Your Grace.   44
book: (of prayer).   45 *exercise:* religious exercise.   *colour:* make plausible.   47 *'Tis . . .
proved:* it is all too apparent.   49 *'tis too true:* (the king's first indication that he is guilty).   52
to: compared to.   51–53 *harlot's cheek . . . word:* just as the harlot's cheek is even uglier by contrast to the makeup that tries to beautify it, so my deed is uglier by contrast to the hypocritical
words under which I hide it.

POLONIUS.   I hear him coming, let's withdraw my lord.   *Exeunt.*

Enter HAMLET.

HAMLET.   To be, or not to be, that is the question,
        Whether 'tis nobler in the mind° to suffer
        The slings and arrows of outrageous fortune,
        Or to take arms against a sea of troubles,
        And by opposing, end them: to die, to sleep,
        No more; and by a sleep, to say we end
        The heart-ache, and the thousand natural shocks
        That flesh is heir to; 'tis a consummation
        Devoutly to be wished. To die, to sleep,
        To sleep, perchance to dream, ay there's the rub,°
        For in that sleep of death what dreams may come
        When we have shuffled off this mortal coil°
        Must give us pause—there's the respect°
        That makes calamity of so long life:°
        For who would bear the whips and scorns of time,
        Th'oppressor's wrong, the proud man's contumely,°
        The pangs of disprized love, the law's delay,°
        The insolence of office,° and the spurns
        That patient merit of th'unworthy takes,
        When he himself might his quietus° make
        With a bare bodkin;° who would fardels° bear,
        To grunt and sweat under a weary life,
        But that the dread of something after death,
        The undiscovered° country, from whose bourn°
        No traveller returns, puzzles the will,
        And makes us rather bear those ills we have,
        Than fly to others that we know not of.
        Thus conscience does make cowards of us all,
        And thus the native hue° of resolution
        Is sicklied o'er with the pale cast of thought,
        And enterprises of great pitch° and moment,°
        With this regard° their currents turn awry,°
        And lose the name of action. Soft you now,
        The fair Ophelia—Nymph, in thy orisons°
        Be all my sins remembered.
OPHELIA.   Good my lord,
        How does your honour for this many a day°?

---

57 *nobler in the mind:* best, according to "sovereign" reason.   65 *rub:* obstacle.   67 *mortal coil:* (1)turmoil of mortal life (2) coil of flesh encircling the body.   68 *respect:* consideration.   69 *makes calamity of so long life:* makes living long a calamity.   71 *contumely:* contempt.   72 *law's delay:* longevity of lawsuits.   73 *office:* officials.   75 *quietus:* settlement of his debt.   76 *bare bodkin:* mere dagger.   *fardels:* burdens.   79 *undiscovered:* unknown, unexplored.   *bourn:* boundary.   84 *native hue:* natural complexion.   86 *pitch:* height, excellence.   *moment:* importance.   87 *regard:* consideration.   *their currents turn awry:* change their course.   89 *orisons:* prayers (referring to her prayer book).   91 *this . . . day:* all these days.

HAMLET. I humbly thank you: well, well, well.

OPHELIA. My lord, I have remembrances of yours
That I have longèd long to re-deliver,
I pray you now receive them.

HAMLET.   No, not I,   95
I never gave you aught.

OPHELIA. My honoured lord, you know right well you did,
And with them words of so sweet breath° composed
As made the things more rich: their perfume lost,
Take these again, for to the noble mind   100
Rich gifts wax° poor when givers prove unkind.
There my lord.

HAMLET. Ha, ha, are you honest°?

OPHELIA. My lord.

HAMLET. Are you fair°?   105

OPHELIA. What means your lordship?

HAMLET. That if you be honest and fair, your honesty should admit
no discourse to your beauty.°

OPHELIA. Could beauty my lord, have better commerce than with
honesty?   110

HAMLET. Ay truly, for the power of beauty will sooner transform
honesty° from what it is to a bawd,° than the force of
honesty can translate beauty into his likeness. This was
sometime° a paradox, but now the time gives it proof. I did
love you once.   115

OPHELIA. Indeed my lord, you made me believe so.

HAMLET. You should not have believed me, for virtue cannot so
inoculate our old stock, but we shall relish of it.° I loved
you not.

OPHELIA. I was the more deceived.   120

HAMLET. Get thee to a nunnery,° why wouldst thou be a breeder of
sinners? I am myself indifferent honest,° but yet I could
accuse me of such things, that it were better my mother
had not borne me: I am very proud, revengeful, ambitious,
with more offences at my beck,° than I have thoughts   125
to put them in, imagination to give them shape, or time to
act them in: what should such fellows as I do, crawling
between earth and heaven? we are arrant° knaves all,
believe none of us, go thy ways to a nunnery. Where's
your father?   130

OPHELIA. At home my lord.

---

98 *breath:* speech.   101 *wax:* grow.   103 *honest:* (1) chaste (2) truthful.   105 *fair:* (1)
beautiful (2) honorable.   107–108 *admit . . . beauty:* (1) not allow communication with your
beauty (2) not allow your beauty to be used as a trap (Hamlet may have overheard the
Polonius–Claudius plot or spotted their movement behind the arras).   112 *honesty:*
chastity.   *bawd:* procurer, pimp.   114 *sometime:* once.   118 *inoculate . . . it:* change our
sinful nature (as a tree is grafted to improve it) but we will keep our old taste (as will the fruit of
the grafted tree).   121 *nunnery:* (1) cloister (2) slang for "brothel" (cf. "bawd" above).   122
indifferent honest: reasonably virtuous.   125 *beck:* beckoning.   128 *arrant:* absolute.

HAMLET.   Let the doors be shut upon him, that he may play the fool
   no where but in's own house. Farewell.
OPHELIA.   O help him, you sweet heavens.
HAMLET.   If thou dost marry, I'll give thee this plague° for thy dowry:
   be thou as chaste as ice, as pure as snow, thou shalt not
   escape calumny; get thee to a nunnery, go, farewell. Or if
   thou wilt needs marry, marry a fool, for wise men know
   well enough what monsters° you make of them: to a nunnery
   go, and quickly too, farewell.
OPHELIA.   O heavenly powers, restore him.
HAMLET.   I have heard of your paintings too, well enough. God hath
   given you one face, and you make yourselves another: you
   jig,° you amble, and you lisp,° you nick-name God's
   creatures, and make your wantonness your ignorance;° go to,
   I'll no more on't, it hath made me mad. I say we will have
   no moe° marriage. Those that are married already, all but
   one shall live, the rest shall keep as they are: to a nunnery,
   go.   *Exit* HAMLET.
OPHELIA.   O what a noble mind is here o'erthrown!
   The courtier's, soldier's, scholar's, eye, tongue, sword,
   Th'expectancy and rose° of the fair state,
   The glass° of fashion, and the mould of form,°
   Th'observed of all observers, quite quite down,
   And I of ladies most deject and wretched,
   That sucked the honey of his music vows,
   Now see that noble and most sovereign° reason
   Like sweet bells jangled, out of tune and harsh,
   That unmatched form and feature° of blown° youth
   Blasted with ecstasy.° O woe is me,
   T'have seen what I have seen, see what I see.

Enter KING *and* POLONIUS.

KING.   Love? his affections° do not that way tend,
   Nor what he spake, though it lacked form a little,
   Was not like madness. There's something in his soul
   O'er which his melancholy sits on brood,
   And I do doubt,° the hatch and the disclose°
   Will be some danger; which for to prevent,
   I have in quick determination
   Thus set it down: he shall with speed to England,
   For the demand of our neglected° tribute:

135 *plague:* curse.   139 *monsters:* horned cuckolds (men whose wives were unfaithful).   144
jig: walk in a mincing way.   *lisp:* put on affected speech.   145 *make your . . . ignorance:*
excuse your caprices as being due to ignorance.   147 *moe:* more.   152 *expectancy and rose:*
fair hope.   153 *glass:* mirror.   *mould of form:* model of manners.   157 *sovereign:* (because
it should rule).   159 *feature:* external appearance.   159 *blown:* flowering.   160 *Blasted
with ecstasy:* blighted by madness.   162 *affections:* emotions, afflictions.   166 *doubt:*
fear.   165–166 *on brood . . . hatch . . . disclose:* (metaphor of a hen sitting on eggs).   170
neglected: (being unpaid).

Haply° the seas, and countries different,
With variable° objects, shall expel
This something°-settled matter in his heart,
Whereon his brains still beating puts him thus
From fashion of himself.° What think you on't?   175
POLONIUS.   It shall do well. But yet do I believe
The origin and commencement of his grief
Sprung from neglected° love. How now Ophelia?
You need not tell us what Lord Hamlet said,
We heard it all. My lord, do as you please,   180
But if you hold it fit, after the play,
Let his queen-mother all alone entreat him
To show his grief, let her be round° with him,
And I'll be placed (so please you) in the ear
Of° all their conference. If she find° him not,   185
To England send him: or confine him where
Your wisdom best shall think.
KING.   It shall be so,
Madness in great ones must not unwatched go.   *Exeunt.*

Scene 2. *[A hall in the castle]*

Enter HAMLET *and three of the* PLAYERS.

HAMLET.   Speak the speech° I pray you as I pronounced it to you,
trippingly on the tongue, but if you mouth it° as many of
your players do, I had as lief the town-crier spoke my
lines. Nor do not saw the air too much with your hand
thus, but use all gently, for in the very torrent, tempest,   5
and as I may say, whirlwind of your passion, you must
acquire and beget° a temperance that may give it smoothness.
O it offends me to the soul, to hear a robustious°
periwig-pated° fellow tear a passion to tatters, to very rags,
to split the ears of the groundlings,° who for the most part   10
are capable of° nothing but inexplicable dumb shows° and
noise: I would have such a fellow whipped for o'erdoing
Termagant:° it out-herods Herod,° pray you avoid it.
1. PLAYER.   I warrant you honour.
HAMLET.   Be not too tame neither, but let your own discretion be   15
your tutor, suit the action to the word, the word to the

---

171 *Haply:* perhaps.   172 *variable:* varied.   173 *something-:* somewhat-.   175 *fashion of himself:* his usual self.   178 *neglected:* unrequited.   183 *round:* direct.   184–185 *in the ear Of:* so as to overhear.   185 *find:* find out.   1 *the speech:* i.e., that Hamlet has inserted.   2 *mouth it:* deliver it slowly and overdramatically.   7 *acquire and beget:* achieve for yourself and instill in other actors.   8 *robustious:* boisterous.   9 *periwig-pated:* wig-wearing.   10 *groundlings:* audience who paid least and stood on the ground floor.   11 *capable of:* able to understand.   *dumb shows:* pantomimed synopses of the action to follow (as below).   13 *Termagant:* violent, ranting character in the guild or mystery plays.   *out-herods Herod:* outdoes even Herod, King of Judea, who commanded the slaughter of the innocents and who was a ranting tyrant in the Corpus Christi plays. See pp. 1239–40.

action, with this special observance, that you o'erstep not
the modesty° of nature: for any thing so o'erdone, is from°
the purpose of playing, whose end both at the first, and
now, was and is, to hold as 'twere the mirror up to nature,   2●
to show virtue her own feature, scorn° her own image, and
the very age and body of the time his form and pressure.°
Now this overdone, or come tardy off,° though it make the
unskilful° laugh, cannot but make the judicious grieve, the
censure of the which one,° must in your allowance°   2.
o'erweigh a whole theatre of others. O there be players
that I have seen play, and heard others praise, and that
highly (not to speak it profanely) that neither having
th'accent of Christians, nor the gait of Christian, pagan,
nor man, have so strutted and bellowed, that I have   3
thought some of nature's journeymen° had made men, and
not made them well, they imitated humanity so
abominably.
1. PLAYER.   I hope we have reformed that indifferently° with us, sir.
HAMLET.   O reform it altogether, and let those that play your clowns   ●
speak no more than is set down for them,° for there be of
them that will themselves laugh, to set on some quantity
of barren° spectators to laugh too, though in the meantime,
some necessary question° of the play be then to be considered:
that's villainous, and shows a most pitiful ambition
in the fool that uses it. Go make you ready.   *Exeunt PLAYERS.*

Enter POLONIUS, ROSENCRANTZ, and GUILDENSTERN.

How now my lord, will the king hear this piece of work?
POLONIUS.   And the queen too, and that presently.
HAMLET.   Bid the players make haste.   *Exit POLONIUS.*
Will you two help to hasten them?
ROSENCRANTZ.   Ay my lord.   *Exeunt they two.*
HAMLET.   What ho, Horatio!

Enter HORATIO.

HORATIO.   Here sweet lord, at your service.
HAMLET.   Horatio, thou art e'en as just° a man
As e'er my conversation coped withal.°
HORATIO.   O my dear lord.
HAMLET.   Nay, do not think I flatter,
For what advancement may I hope from thee,

---

18 *modesty:* moderation.   *from:* away from.   21 *scorn:* that which should be scorned.
22 *age . . . pressure:* shape of the times in its accurate impression.   23 *come tardy off:* understated,
underdone.   24 *unskilful:* unsophisticated.   25 *one:* the judicious.   *allowance:* estimation.   31 *journeymen:* artisans working for others and not yet masters of their trades.
34 *indifferently:* reasonably well.   36 *speak no more . . . them:* stick to their lines.   38 *barren:*
witless.   39 *question:* dialogue.   49 *just:* well balanced.   50 *coped withal:* had to do with.

That no revenue hast but thy good spirits
To feed and clothe thee? Why should the poor be flattered?
No, let the candied° tongue lick° absurd pomp,   55
And crook the pregnant° hinges of the knee
Where thrift may follow fawning.° Dost thou hear,
Since my dear soul was mistress of her choice,
And could of men distinguish her election,°
Sh'hath sealed° thee for herself, for thou hast been   60
As one in suff'ring all that suffers nothing,
A man that Fortune's buffets° and rewards
Hast ta'en with equal thanks; and blest are those
Whose blood° and judgment are so well co-mingled,
That they are not a pipe for Fortune's finger   65
To sound what stop° she please:° give me that man
That is not passion's slave, and I will wear him
In my heart's core, ay in my heart of heart,
As I do thee. Something too much of this.
There is a play tonight before the king,   70
One scene of it comes near the circumstance
Which I have told thee of my father's death.
I prithee when thou seest that act afoot,
Even with the very comment° of thy soul
Observe my uncle: if his occulted° guilt   75
Do not itself unkennel° in one speech,
It is a damnèd ghost° that we have seen,
And my imaginations are as foul
As Vulcan's stithy;° give him heedful note,
For I mine eyes will rivet to his face,   80
And after we will both our judgments join
In censure of his seeming.°
HORATIO.   Well my lord,
If a' steal aught the whilst this play is playing,
And 'scape detecting, I will pay° the theft.   *Sound a flourish.*
HAMLET.   They are coming to the play. I must be idle,°   85
Get you a place.

Enter Trumpets and Kettledrums, KING, QUEEN, POLONIUS, OPHELIA, ROSENCRANTZ, GUILD-
ENSTERN, *and other* LORDS *attendant, with his* GUARD *carrying torches. Danish March.*

KING.   How fares° our cousin Hamlet?

55–57 *candied . . . fawning:* (metaphor of a dog licking and fawning for candy).   55 *candied:* flattering.   *lick:* pay court to.   56–57 *crook . . . fawning:* obsequiously kneel when personal profit
may ensue.   56 *pregnant:* quick in motion.   59 *election:* choice.   60 *sealed:*
confirmed.   62 *buffets:* blows.   64 *blood:* passions.   66 *sound . . . please:* play whatever tune
she likes.   *stop:* finger hole in wind instrument for varying the sound.   74 *very comment:*
acutest observation.   75 *occulted:* hidden.   76 *unkennel:* force from hiding.   77 *damnèd
ghost:* devil (not the ghost of my father).   79 *Vulcan's stithy:* the forge of the blacksmith of the
gods.   82 *censure . . . seeming:* (1) judgment of his appearance (2) disapproval of his pretending.   84 *pay:* i.e., for.   85 *be idle:* act mad.   87 *fares:* does, but Hamlet takes it to mean
"eats" or "dines."

HAMLET.   Excellent i'faith, of the chameleon's dish: I eat the air,°
promise-crammed, you cannot feed capons so.°

KING.   I have nothing with° this answer Hamlet, these words are
not mine.°

HAMLET.   No, nor mine now. [*To Polonius.*] My lord, you played
once i'th'university you say?

POLONIUS.   That did I my lord, and was accounted a good actor.

HAMLET.   What did you enact?

POLONIUS.   I did enact Julius Caesar, I was killed i'th'Capitol, Brutus
killed me.

HAMLET.   It was a brute part of him to kill so capital a calf there. Be
the players ready?

ROSENCRANTZ.   Ay my lord, they stay upon your patience.°

QUEEN.   Come hither my dear Hamlet, sit by me.

HAMLET.   No, good mother, here's metal more attractive.°

POLONIUS.   [*To the King.*] O ho, do you mark that?

HAMLET.   Lady, shall I lie in your lap?

OPHELIA.   No my lord.

HAMLET.   I mean, my head upon your lap?

OPHELIA.   Ay my lord.

HAMLET.   Do you think I meant country° matters?

OPHELIA.   I think nothing my lord.

HAMLET.   That's a fair thought to lie between maids' legs.

OPHELIA.   What is, my lord?

HAMLET.   Nothing.

OPHELIA.   You are merry my lord.

HAMLET.   Who, I?

OPHELIA.   Ay my lord.

HAMLET.   O God, your only jig-maker: what should a man do but be
merry, for look you how cheerfully my mother looks, and
my father died within's two hours.

OPHELIA.   Nay, 'tis twice two months my lord.

HAMLET.   So long? Nay then let the devil wear black, for I'll have a
suit of sables;° O heavens, die two months ago, and not
forgotten yet? Then there's hope a great man's memory
may outlive his life half a year, but by'r lady° a' must build
churches then, or else shall a' suffer not thinking on,° with
the hobby-horse,° whose epitaph is "For O, for O, the
hobby-horse is forgot."

88 *eat the air:* the chamelion supposedly ate air, but Hamlet also puns on "heir."   89 *you cannot . . .*
so: (1) even a capon cannot feed on air and your promises (2) like a capon stuffed with food before
being killed, I am stuffed (fed up) with your promises.   90 *nothing with:* nothing to do
with.   91 *not mine:* not in answer to my question.   100 *stay . . . patience:* await your permission.   102 *metal more attractive:* (1) iron more magnetic (2) stuff ("mettle") more
beautiful.   108 *country:* rustic, sexual (with a pun on a slang word for the female sexual
organ).   121 *sables:* (1) rich fur (2) black mourning garb.   123 *by'r lady:* by Our Lady (the
Virgin Mary).   124 *not thinking on:* being forgotten.   125 *hobby-horse:* (1) character in the
May games (2) slang for "prostitute."

The trumpets sound. The Dumb Show° follows. Enter a King and a Queen, very lovingly, the Queen embracing him, and he her. She kneels and makes show of protestation unto him. He takes her up, and declines his head upon her neck. He lies him down upon a bank of flowers; she seeing him asleep leaves him: anon comes in another man, takes off his crown, kisses it, pours poison in the sleeper's ears, and leaves him: the Queen returns, finds the King dead, and makes passionate action. The poisoner with some three or four mutes° comes in again, seeming to condole with her. The dead body is carried away. The poisoner wooes the Queen with gifts: she seems harsh and unwilling awhile, but in the end accepts his love. Exeunt.

OPHELIA.   What means this, my lord?

HAMLET.   Marry, this is miching mallecho,° it means mischief.

OPHELIA.   Belike this show imports the argument° of the play.

Enter PROLOGUE.

HAMLET.   We shall know by this fellow: the players cannot keep   130
  counsel,° they'll tell all.

OPHELIA.   Will a' tell us what this show meant?

HAMLET.   Ay, or any show that you will show him. Be not you
  ashamed to show, he'll not shame to tell you what it
  means.   135

OPHELIA.   You are naught,° you are naught, I'll mark the play.

PROLOGUE.   For us and for our tragedy,
  Here stooping to your clemency,
  We beg your hearing patiently.   [*Exit.*]

HAMLET.   Is this a prologue, or the posy° of a ring?   140

OPHELIA.   'Tis brief, my lord.

HAMLET.   As woman's love.

Enter Player KING and QUEEN.

PLAYER KING.   Full thirty times hath Phoebus' cart° gone round
  Neptune's salt wash,° and Tellus' orbèd ground,°
  And thirty dozen moons with borrowed sheen   145
  About the world have times twelve thirties been,
  Since love our hearts, and Hymen° did our hands
  Unite commutual,° in most sacred bands.

PLAYER QUEEN.   So many journeys may the sun and moon
  Make us again count o'er ere love be done,   150
  But woe is me, you are so sick of late,
  So far from cheer, and from your former state,
  That I distrust you:° yet though I distrust,
  Discomfort you, my lord, it nothing must.
  For women fear too much, even as they love,   155

126 S.D.: *Dumb Show:* pantomimed synopsis of the action to follow.   126 S.D.: *mutes:* actors without speaking parts.   128 *miching mallecho:* skulking mischief.   129 *imports the argument:* signifies the plot.   131 *counsel:* a secret.   136 *naught:* naughty, lewd.   140 *posy:* motto (engraved in a ring).   143 *Phoebus' cart:* chariot of the sun.   144 *wash:* sea.   *Tellus'. . . ground:* the earth (Tellus was a Roman earth goddess).   147 *Hymen:* Roman god of marriage.   148 *commutual:* mutually.   153 *distrust you:* am worried about you.

And women's fear and love hold quantity,°
In neither aught, or in extremity:°
Now what my love is, proof° hath made you know,
And as my love is sized, my fear is so.
Where love is great, the littlest doubts are fear,   160
Where little fears grow great, great love grows there.
PLAYER KING.   Faith, I must leave thee love, and shortly too,
My operant° powers their functions leave° to do,
And thou shalt live in this fair world behind,
Honoured, beloved, and haply° one as kind   165
For husband shalt thou—
PLAYER QUEEN.   O confound the rest:
Such love must needs be treason in my breast.
In second husband let me be accurst,
None wed the second, but who killed the first.
HAMLET.   [*Aside.*] That's wormwood,° wormwood.   17[]
PLAYER QUEEN.   The instances° that second marriage move°
Are base respects of thrift,° but none of love.
A second time I kill my husband dead,
When second husband kisses me in bed.
PLAYER KING.   I do believe you think what now you speak,   17[]
But what we do determine, oft we break:
Purpose is but the slave to memory,
Of violent birth but poor validity:°
Which now like fruit unripe sticks on the tree,
But fall unshaken when they mellow be.   18[]
Most necessary 'tis that we forget
To pay ourselves what to ourselves is debt:°
What to ourselves in passion we propose,
The passion ending, doth the purpose lose.
The violence of either grief or joy   18[]
Their own enactures° with themselves destroy:
Where joy most revels, grief doth most lament;
Grief joys, joy grieves, on slender accident.
This world is not for aye,° nor 'tis not strange
That even our loves should with our fortunes change: 19[]
For 'tis a question left us yet to prove,
Whether love lead fortune, or else fortune love.°
The great man down, you mark his favourite flies,
The poor advanced, makes friends of enemies:
And hitherto doth love on fortune tend,   1[]
For who not needs, shall never lack a friend,
And who in want a hollow friend doth try,

156 *quantity:* proportion.   157 *In neither . . . extremity:* their love and fear are either absent or
excessive.   158 *proof:* experience.   163 *operant:* vital.   *leave:* cease.   165 *haply:* perhaps.   170 *wormwood:* bitter (like the herb).   171 *instances:* causes.   *move:* moti-
vate.   172 *respects of thrift:* consideration of profit.   178 *validity:* strength.   181–182
Most . . . debt: we are easy creditors to ourselves and forget our former promises (debts).   186
enactures: fulfillments.   189 *aye:* ever.   192 *fortune love:* fortune lead love.

Directly seasons him° his enemy.
But orderly to end where I begun,
Our wills and fates do so contrary run,   200
That our devices still° are overthrown,
Our thoughts are ours, their ends none of our own.
So think thou wilt no second husband wed,
But die thy thoughts when thy first lord is dead.

PLAYER QUEEN.   Nor earth to me give food, nor heaven light,   205
Sport and repose lock from me day and night,
To desperation turn my trust and hope,
An anchor's° cheer in prison be my scope,
Each opposite that blanks° the face of joy,
Meet what I would have well, and it destroy,   210
Both here and hence° pursue me lasting strife,
If once a widow, ever I be wife.

HAMLET.   If she should break it now.

PLAYER KING.   'Tis deeply sworn: sweet, leave me here awhile,
My spirits grow dull, and fain° I would beguile   215
The tedious day with sleep.   *Sleeps.*

PLAYER QUEEN.   Sleep rock thy brain.
And never come mischance between us twain.   *Exit.*

HAMLET.   Madam, how like you this play?

QUEEN.   The lady doth protest too much methinks.

HAMLET.   O but she'll keep her word.   220

KING.   Have you heard the argument°? Is there no offence in't?

HAMLET.   No, no, they do but jest, poison in jest, no offence
i'th'world.

KING.   What do you call the play?

HAMLET.   The Mouse-trap. Marry, how? Tropically:° this play is the   225
image of a murder done in Vienna: Gonzago is the duke's
name, his wife Baptista, you shall see anon, 'tis a knavish
piece of work, but what of that? Your majesty, and we
that have free° souls, it touches us not: let the galled jade
winch,° our withers are unwrung.°   230

Enter LUCIANUS.

This is one Lucianus, nephew to the king.

OPHELIA.   You are as good as a chorus,° my lord.

HAMLET.   I could interpret between you and your love, if I could see
the puppets dallying.

OPHELIA.   You are keen my lord, you are keen.°   235

HAMLET.   It would cost you a groaning to take off mine edge.

---

198 *seasons him:* causes him to become.   201 *devices still:* plans always.   208 *anchor's:*
hermit's.   209 *opposite that blanks:* contrary event that pales.   211 *here and hence:* in this
world and the next.   215 *fain:* gladly.   221 *argument:* plot.   225 *Tropically:*
figuratively.   229 *free:* innocent.   229–230 *galled jade winch:* chafed old horse wince (from its
sores).   230 *withers are unwrung:* (1) shoulders are unchafed (2) consciences are clear.
232 *chorus:* actor who introduced the action.   235 *keen:* (1) sharp (Ophelia's meaning)
(2) sexually excited (Hamlet's interpretation).

OPHELIA.   Still better and worse.°

HAMLET.   So you mistake° your husbands. Begin, murderer. Pox,°
  leave thy damnable faces° and begin. Come, the croaking
  raven doth bellow for revenge.   240

LUCIANUS.   Thoughts black, hands apt, drugs fit, and time agreeing,
  Confederate season, else no creature seeing,°
  Thou mixture rank, of midnight weeds collected,
  With Hecate's° ban° thrice blasted, thrice infected,
  Thy natural magic, and dire property,   24!
  On wholesome° life usurps immediately.   *Pours the poison in his ears.*

HAMLET.   A' poisons him i'th'garden for's estate, his name's Gonzago,
  the story is extant, and written in very choice
  Italian, you shall see anon how the murderer gets the love
  of Gonzago's wife.   25•

OPHELIA.   The king rises.

HAMLET.   What, frighted with false fire°?

QUEEN.   How fares my lord?

POLONIUS.   Give o'er the play.

KING.   Give me some light. Away!   25

ALL.   Lights, lights, lights!   *Exeunt all but HAMLET and HORATIO.*

HAMLET.   Why, let the stricken deer go weep,
      The hart ungallèd° play,°
  For some must watch while some must sleep,
      Thus runs the world away.   2€
  Would not this° sir, and a forest of feathers,° if the rest of my
  fortunes turn Turk with° me, with two Provincial roses° on
  my razed° shoes, get me a fellowship° in a cry° of players?

HORATIO.   Half a share.°

HAMLET.   A whole one, I.   2•
  For thou dost know, O Damon° dear,
      This realm dismantled was
  Of Jove° himself, and now reigns here
      A very very—pajock.°

HORATIO.   You might have rhymed.°   2

HAMLET.   O good Horatio, I'll take the ghost's word for a thousand
  pound. Didst perceive?

HORATIO.   Very well my lord.

---

237 *better and worse:* better wit but a worse meaning, with a pun on "better" and "bitter."   238 *mistake:* mis-take.   *Pox:* a plague on it.   239 *faces:* exaggerated facial expressions.
242 *Confederate . . . seeing:* no one seeing me except time, my confederate.   244 *Hecate:* goddess of witchcraft.   *ban:* evil spell.   246 *wholesome:* healthy.   252 *false fire:* discharge of blanks (not gunpowder).   257–258 *deer . . . play:* (the belief that a wounded deer wept, abandoned by the others).   258 *ungallèd:* unhurt.   261 *this:* i.e., sample (of my theatrical talent).   *feathers:* plumes (worn by actors).   262 *turn Turk with:* cruelly turn against.   *Provincial roses:* rosettes named for Provins, France.   263 *razed:* slashed, decorated with cutouts.   *fellowship:* partnership.   *cry:* pack, troupe.   264 *share:* divisions of profits among members of a theatrical production company.   266 *Damon:* legendary ideal friend to Pythias.   268 *Jove:* (Hamlet's father).   269 *pajock:* peacock (associated with lechery).   270 *rhymed:* (used "ass" instead of "pajock").

HAMLET.   Upon the talk of the poisoning?
HORATIO.   I did very well note him.   275

Enter ROSENCRANTZ and GUILDENSTERN.

HAMLET.   Ah ha, come, some music. Come, the recorders.°
    For if the king like not the comedy,
    Why then belike he likes it not, perdy.°
    Come, some music.
GUILDENSTERN.   Good my lord, vouchsafe me a word with you.   280
HAMLET.   Sir, a whole history.
GUILDENSTERN.   The king, sir—
HAMLET.   Ay sir, what of him?
GUILDENSTERN.   Is in his retirement, marvellous distempered.
HAMLET.   With drink sir?   285
GUILDENSTERN.   No my lord, with choler.°
HAMLET.   Your wisdom should show itself more richer to signify
    this to the doctor: for, for me to put him to his purgation,°
    would perhaps plunge him into more choler.
GUILDENSTERN.   Good my lord, put your discourse into some frame,° and   290
    start not so wildly from my affair.
HAMLET.   I am tame sir, pronounce.
GUILDENSTERN.   The queen your mother, in most great affliction of spirit,
    hath sent me to you.
HAMLET.   You are welcome.   295
GUILDENSTERN.   Nay good my lord, this courtesy is not of the right breed.°
    If it shall please you to make me a wholesome° answer, I
    will do your mother's commandment: if not, your pardon°
    and my return shall be the end of my business.
HAMLET.   Sir I cannot.   300
ROSENCRANTZ.   What, my lord?
HAMLET.   Make you a wholesome answer: my wit's diseased. But
    sir, such answer as I can make, you shall command, or
    rather as you say, my mother: therefore no more, but to
    the matter. My mother you say.   305
ROSENCRANTZ.   Then thus she says, your behaviour hath struck her into
    amazement and admiration.°
HAMLET.   O wonderful son that can so 'stonish a mother. But is there
    no sequel at the heels of this mother's admiration? Impart.
ROSENCRANTZ.   She desires to speak with you in her closet°   310
    ere you go to bed.
HAMLET.   We shall obey, were she ten times our mother. Have you
    any further trade with us?
ROSENCRANTZ.   My lord, you once did love me.

276 *recorders:* soft-toned woodwind instruments, similar to flutes.   278 *perdy:* by God (*par dieu*).   286 *choler:* anger.   288 *purgation:* (1) purging of excessive bile (2) judicial investigations (3) purgatory.   290 *frame:* order.   296 *breed:* (1) species (2) manners.   297 *wholesome:* reasonable.   298 *pardon:* permission to depart.   307 *admiration:* wonder.   310 *closet:* private room, bedroom.

HAMLET.   And do still, by these pickers and stealers.°   315

ROSENCRANTZ.   Good my lord, what is your cause of distemper? You do
surely bar the door upon your own liberty, if you deny
your griefs to your friend.°

HAMLET.   Sir, I lack advancement.

ROSENCRANTZ.   How can that be, when you have the voice° of the king   320
himself for your succession in Denmark?

HAMLET.   Ay sir, but 'while the grass grows'°—the proverb is
something musty.°

Enter the PLAYERS with recorders.

O the recorders, let me see one. To withdraw° with you,
why do you go about to recover the wind of me,° as if you   32?
would drive me into a toil°?

GUILDENSTERN.   O my lord, if my duty be too bold, my love is too
unmannerly.°

HAMLET.   I do not well understand that. Will you play
upon this pipe°?   33

GUILDENSTERN.   My lord I cannot.

HAMLET.   I pray you.

GUILDENSTERN.   Believe me. I cannot.

HAMLET.   I do beseech you.

GUILDENSTERN.   I know no touch of it° my lord.   33

HAMLET.   It is as easy as lying; govern these ventages° with your
fingers and thumb, give it breath with your mouth, and it
will discourse most eloquent music. Look you, these are
the stops.

GUILDENSTERN.   But these cannot I command to any utt'rance of harmony,   34
I have not the skill.

HAMLET.   Why look you now how unworthy a thing you make of
me: you would play upon me, you would seem to know
my stops, you would pluck out the heart of my mystery,
you would sound me from my lowest note to the top of my   3
compass:° and there is much music, excellent voice in this
little organ,° yet cannot you make it speak. 'Sblood, do you
think I am easier to be played on than a pipe? Call me what
instrument you will, though you can fret° me, you cannot
play upon me.   3

Enter POLONIUS.

God bless you sir.

315 *pickers and stealers:* hands (from the prayer, "Keep my hands from picking and stealing").
317–318 *deny . . . friend:* refuse to let your friend know the cause of your suffering.   320 *voice:*
vote.   322 *while . . . grows:* (the proverb ends: "the horse starves").   323 *something musty:*
somewhat too old and trite (to finish).   324 *withdraw:* speak privately.   325 *recover . . . me:*
drive me toward the wind, as with a prey, to avoid its scenting the hunter.   326 *toil:* snare.
327–328 *is too unmannerly:* makes me forget my good manners.   330 *pipe:* recorder.
335 *know . . . it:* have no skill at fingering it.   336 *ventages:* holes, stops.   346 *compass:*
range.   347 *organ:* musical instrument.   349 *fret:* (1) irritate (2) play an instrument that
has "frets" or bars to guide the fingering.

POLONIUS.   My lord, the queen would speak with you, and presently.
HAMLET.   Do you see yonder cloud that's almost in shape of a camel?
POLONIUS.   By th'mass and 'tis, like a camel indeed.
HAMLET.   Methinks it is like a weasel.   355
POLONIUS.   It is backed like a weasel.
HAMLET.   Or like a whale?
POLONIUS.   Very like a whale.
HAMLET.   Then I will come to my mother by and by.°
    [*Aside.*] They fool me to the top of my bent.°   360
    I will come by and by.
POLONIUS.   I will say so.   *Exit.*
HAMLET.   "By and by" is easily said.
    Leave me, friends.   [*Exeunt all but* HAMLET.]
    'Tis now the very witching time of night.   365
    When churchyards yawn,° and hell itself breathes out
    Contagion° to this world: now could I drink hot blood,
    And do such bitter business as the day
    Would quake to look on: soft, now to my mother—
    O heart, lose not thy nature,° let not ever   370
    The soul of Nero° enter this firm bosom,
    Let me be cruel, not unnatural.
    I will speak daggers to her, but use none:
    My tongue and soul in this be hypocrites,°
    How in my words somever she be shent,°   375
    To give them seals,° never my soul consent.   *Exit.*

Scene 3. *[A room in the castle]*

Enter KING, ROSENCRANTZ, *and* GUILDENSTERN.

KING.   I like him not, nor stands it safe with us
    To let his madness range. Therefore prepare you,
    I your commission will forthwith dispatch,°
    And he to England shall along with you:
    The terms of our estate° may not endure   5
    Hazard so near's° as doth hourly grow
    Out of his brows.°
GUILDENSTERN.   We will ourselves provide:°
    Most holy and religious fear it is
    To keep those many many bodies safe
    That live and feed upon your majesty.   10
ROSENCRANTZ.   The single and peculiar° life is bound
    With all the strength and armour of the mind

359 *by and by:* very soon.   360 *fool me . . . bent:* force me to play the fool to my utmost.
366 *churchyards yawn:* graves open.   367 *Contagion:* (1) evil (2) diseases.   370 *nature:* natural affection.   371 *Nero:* (who killed his mother).   374 *My tongue . . . hypocrites:* I will speak
cruelly but intend no harm.   375 *shent:* chastised.   376 *give them seals:* confirm them with
action (as a legal "deed" is confirmed with a "seal").   3 *forthwith dispatch:* immediately have
prepared.   5 *terms . . . estate:* circumstances of my royal office.   6 *near's:* near us.   7 *brows:*
effronteries.   *provide:* prepare.   11 *peculiar:* individual.

To keep itself from noyance,° but much more
That spirit, upon whose weal° depends and rests
The lives of many; the cess° of majesty
Dies not alone, but like a gulf° doth draw
What's near it, with it. O 'tis a massy wheel
Fixed on the summit of the highest mount,
To whose huge spokes, ten thousand lesser things
Are mortised° and adjoined, which when it falls,
Each small annexment, petty consequence,
Attends° the boist'rous ruin. Never alone
Did the king sigh, but with a general groan.
KING.   Arm° you I pray you, to this speedy voyage,
For we will fetters put about this fear,
Which now goes too free-footed.
ROSENCRANTZ.   We will haste us.

                              Exeunt [*ROSENCRANTZ and GUILDENSTERN.*]

Enter POLONIUS.

POLONIUS.   My lord, he's going to his mother's closet:
Behind the arras I'll convey myself
To hear the process.° I'll warrant she'll tax him home,
And as you said, and wisely was it said,
'Tis meet° that some more audience than a mother,
Since nature makes them partial, should o'erhear
The speech of vantage;° fare you well my liege,°
I'll call upon you ere you go to bed,
And tell you what I know.
KING.   Thanks, dear my lord.   *Exit* [*POLONIUS.*]
O my offence is rank, it smells to heaven,
It hath the primal eldest curse° upon't,
A brother's murder. Pray can I not,
Though inclination be as sharp as will:°
My stronger guilt defeats my strong intent,
And like a man to double business bound,
I stand in pause where I shall first begin,
And both neglect; what if this cursèd hand
Were thicker than itself with brother's blood,
Is there not rain enough in the sweet heavens
To wash it white as snow? Whereto serves mercy
But to confront the visage of offence°?
And what's in prayer but this two-fold force,
To be forestallèd° ere we come to fall,
Or pardoned being down? Then I'll look up,

---

13 *noyance:* harm.   14 *weal:* well-being.   15 *cess:* cessation, death.   16 *gulf:* whirl-
pool.   20 *mortised:* securely fitted.   22 *Attends:* accompanies.   24 *Arm:* prepare.   29
the process: what proceeds.   31 *meet:* fitting.   33 *of vantage:* from an advantageous
position.   *liege:* lord.   37 *primal . . . curse:* curse of Cain.   39 *inclination . . . will:* my desire
to pray is as strong as my determination to do so.   47 *confront . . . offence:* plead in man's behalf
against sin (at the Last Judgment).   49 *forestallèd:* prevented.

My fault is past. But O what form of prayer
Can serve my turn? "Forgive me my foul murder":
That cannot be, since I am still possessed
Of those effects° for which I did the murder:
My crown, mine own ambition, and my queen.   55
May one be pardoned and retain th'offence?
In the corrupted currents of this world,
Offence's gilded hand may shove by justice,
And oft 'tis seen the wicked prize itself
Buys out the law;° but 'tis not so above,   60
There is no shuffling,° there the action lies
In his true nature,° and we ourselves compelled
Even to the teeth and forehead of our faults°
To give in evidence. What then? What rests°?
Try what repentance can. What can it not?   65
Yet what can it, when one can not repent?
O wretched state? O bosom black as death!
O limèd soul, that struggling to be free,
Art more engaged;° help, angels, make assay:°
Bow stubborn knees, and heart with strings of steel,   70
Be soft as sinews of the new-born babe,
All may be well.   [*He kneels.*]

Enter HAMLET.

HAMLET. Now might I do it pat,° now a' is a-praying,
    And now I'll do't, [*Draws his sword.*] and so a' goes to heaven,
    And so am I revenged: that would be scanned:°   75
    A villain kills my father, and for that,
    I his sole son, do this same villain send
    To heaven.
    Why, this is hire and salary, not revenge.
    A' took my father grossly,° full of bread,°   80
    With all his crimes° broad blown,° as flush° as May,
    And how his audit° stands who knows save heaven,
    But in our circumstance and course of thought,
    'Tis heavy° with him: and am I then revenged
    To take him in the purging of his soul,   85
    when he is fit and seasoned° for his passage?
    No.   [*Sheathes his sword.*]
    Up sword, and know thou a more horrid hent,°

54 *effects:* results.   59–60 *wicked . . . law:* fruits of the crime bribe the judge.   61 *shuffling:* evasion.   61–62 *action . . . nature.* (1) deed is seen in its true nature (2) legal action is sustained according to the truth.   63 *to the teeth . . . faults:* meeting our sins face to face.   64 *rests:* remains.   68–69 *limèd . . . engaged:* like a bird caught in lime (a sticky substance spread on twigs as a snare), the soul in its struggle to clear itself only becomes more entangled.   69 *make assay:* I'll make an attempt.   73 *pat:* opportunely.   75 *would be scanned:* needs closer examination.   80 *grossly:* unpurified (by final rites).   *bread:* self-indulgence.   81 *crimes:* sins.   *broad blown:* in full flower.   *flush:* lusty.   82 *audit:* account.   84 *heavy:* grievous.   86 *seasoned:* ready (prepared).   88 *horrid hent:* horrible opportunity ("hint") for seizure ("hent") by me.

When he is drunk asleep, or in his rage,
Or in th'incestuous pleasure of his bed,   9●
At game, a-swearing, or about some act
That has no relish° of salvation in't,
Then trip him that his heels may kick at heaven,
And that his soul may be as damned and black
As hell whereto it goes; my mother stays,   9
This physic° but prolongs thy sickly days.   *Exit.*

KING.   [*Rises.*] My words fly up, my thoughts remain below,
Words without thoughts never to heaven go.   *Exit.*

Scene 4. *[The queen's closet]*

Enter QUEEN and POLONIUS.

POLONIUS.   A' will come straight, look you lay home° to him,
Tell him his pranks have been too broad° to bear with,
And that your grace hath screened and stood between
Much heat° and him. I'll silence me° even here:
Pray you be round with him.

HAMLET.   [*Within.*] Mother, mother, mother.

QUEEN.   I'll war'nt you,
Fear me not. Withdraw, I hear him coming. [*POLONIUS hides behind the arras.*]

Enter HAMLET.

HAMLET.   Now mother, what's the matter?

QUEEN.   Hamlet, thou hast thy father much offended.

HAMLET.   Mother, you have my father much offended.

QUEEN.   Come, come, you answer with an idle° tongue.

HAMLET.   Go, go, you question with a wicked tongue.

QUEEN.   Why, how now Hamlet?

HAMLET.   What's the matter now?

QUEEN.   Have you forgot me?

HAMLET.   No by the rood,° not so,
You are the queen, your husband's brother's wife,
And would it were not so, you are my mother.

QUEEN.   Nay, then I'll set those to you that can speak.°

HAMLET.   Come, come, and sit you down, you shall not budge,
You go not till I set you up a glass°
Where you may see the inmost part of you.

QUEEN.   What wilt thou do? Thou wilt not murder me?
Help, help, ho!

POLONIUS.   [*Behind the arras.*] What ho! help, help, help!

HAMLET.   How now, a rat? dead for a ducat,° dead.

Kills POLONIUS [through the arras.]

92 *relish:* taste.   96 *physic:* (1) medicine (2) purgation of your soul by prayer.   1 *lay home:*
thrust home; speak sharply.   2 *broad:* unrestrained.   4 *heat:* anger.   *silence me:* hide in
silence.   11 *idle:* foolish.   14 *rood:* cross.   17 *speak:* i.e., to you as you should be spoken
to.   19 *glass:* looking glass.   23 *for a ducat:* I wager a ducat (an Italian gold coin).

POLONIUS. O I am slain!

QUEEN. O me, what hast thou done?

HAMLET.   Nay I know not,   25
   Is it the king?

QUEEN. O what a rash and bloody deed is this!

HAMLET. A bloody deed, almost as bad, good mother,
   As kill a king, and marry with his brother.

QUEEN. As kill a king?

HAMLET.   Ay lady, it was my word.   30
   [*To Polonius.*] Thou wretched, rash, intruding fool, farewell,
   I took thee for thy better,° take thy fortune,
   Thou find'st to be too busy is some danger.
   [*To the Queen.*] Leave wringing of your hands, peace, sit you down,
   And let me wring your heart, for so I shall   35
   If it be made of penetrable stuff,
   If damnèd custom° have not brazed° it so,
   That it be proof° and bulwark against sense.°

QUEEN. What have I done, that thou dar'st wag thy tongue
   In noise so rude against me?

HAMLET.   Such an act   40
   That blurs the grace and blush of modesty,
   Calls virtue hypocrite, takes off the rose°
   From the fair forehead of an innocent love
   And sets a blister there,° makes marriage vows
   As false as dicers' oaths, O such a deed,   45
   As from the body of contraction° plucks
   The very soul, and sweet religion makes
   A rhapsody° of words; heaven's face does glow,°
   Yea this solidity and compound mass°
   With heated visage, as against the doom,°   50
   Is thought-sick at the act.

QUEEN.   Ay me, what act,
   That roars so loud, and thunders in the index°?

HAMLET. Look here upon this picture, and on this,
   The counterfeit presentment° of two brothers:
   See what a grace was seated on this brow,   55
   Hyperion's° curls, the front° of Jove himself,
   An eye like Mars, to threaten and command,
   A station° like the herald Mercury,
   New-lighted on a heaven-kissing hill,
   A combination and a form indeed,   60
   Where every god did seem to set his seal

---

32 *thy better:* the king.   37 *custom:* habit.   *brazed:* brass-plated (brazened).   38 *proof:* armor.   *sense:* sensibility.   42 *rose:* (symbol of perfection and innocence).   44 *blister there:* (whores were punished by being branded on the forehead).   46 *body of contraction:* marriage contract.   48 *rhapsody:* (meaningless) mixture.   *glow:* blush.   49 *solidity . . . mass:* solid earth, compounded of the four elements.   50 *against the doom:* expecting Judgment Day.   52 *index:* (1) table of contents (2) prologue.   54 *counterfeit presentment:* painted likeness.   56 *Hyperion:* Greek sun god.   *front:* forehead.   58 *station:* bearing.

To give the world assurance of a man.
This was your husband. Look you now what follows.
Here is your husband, like a mildewed ear,°
Blasting° his wholesome brother. Have you eyes?   65
Could you on this fair mountain leave to feed,°
And batten° on this moor? Ha! Have you eyes?
You cannot call it love, for at your age
The hey-day in the blood° is tame, it's humble,
And waits upon the judgment, and what judgment   70
Would step from this to this? Sense° sure you have
Else could you not have motion,° but sure that sense
Is apoplexed,° for madness would not err,
Nor sense to ecstasy was ne'er so thralled°
But it reserved some quantity of choice   7
To serve in such a difference.° What devil was't
That thus hath cozened you at hoodman-blind°?
Eyes without feeling, feeling without sight,
Ears without hands or eyes, smelling sans all,°
Or but a sickly part of one true sense
Could not so mope:° O shame, where is thy blush?   8
Rebellious hell,
If thou canst mutine in a matron's bones,
To flaming youth let virtue be as wax
And melt in her own fire. Proclaim no shame
When the compulsive° ardour gives the charge,°
Since frost itself as actively doth burn,
And reason panders will.°
QUEEN.   O Hamlet, speak no more,
Thou turn'st my eyes into my very soul,
And there I see such black and grainèd° spots
As will not leave their tinct.°
HAMLET.   Nay, but to live
In the rank sweat of an enseamèd° bed,
Stewed in corruption, honeying, and making love
Over the nasty sty.
QUEEN.   O speak to me no more,
These words like daggers enter in mine ears,
No more, sweet Hamlet.
HAMLET.   A murderer and a villain,
A slave that is not twentieth part the tithe°

---

64 *ear:* i.e., of grain.   65 *Blasting:* blighting.   66 *leave to feed:* leave off feeding.   67 *batten:* gorge yourself.   69 *hey-day in the blood:* youthful passion.   71 *Sense:* perception by the senses.   72 *motion:* impulse.   73 *apoplexed:* paralyzed.   74 *sense . . . thralled:* sensibility was never so enslaved by madness.   76 *in . . . difference:* where the difference was so great.   77 *cozened . . . blind:* cheated you at blindman's bluff.   79 *sans all:* without the other senses.   81 *so mope:* be so dull.   86 *compulsive:* compelling.   *gives the charge:* attacks.   88 *panders will:* pimps for lust.   90 *grainèd:* dyed in grain, unfading.   91 *leave their tinct:* lose their color.   92 *enseamèd:* greasy.   97 *tithe:* one-tenth part.

Of your precedent lord, a vice° of kings,
A cutpurse° of the empire and the rule,
That from a shelf the precious diadem stole   100
And put it in his pocket.
QUEEN.   No more.
HAMLET.   A king of shreds and patches—

Enter the GHOST in his night-gown.°

Save me and hover o'er me with your wings,
You heavenly guards. What would your gracious figure?
QUEEN.   Alas, he's mad.   105
HAMLET.   Do you not come your tardy son to chide,
That lapsed in time and passion° lets go by
Th'important acting of your dread command?
O say!
GHOST.   Do not forget: this visitation   110
Is but to whet thy almost blunted purpose.
But look, amazement on thy mother sits,
O step between her and her fighting soul,
Conceit° in weakest bodies strongest works,
Speak to her Hamlet.
HAMLET.   How is it with you lady?   115
QUEEN.   Alas, how is't with you,
That you do bend your eye on vacancy,°
And with th'incorporal° air do hold discourse?
Forth at your eyes your spirits° wildly peep,
And as the sleeping soldiers in th'alarm,   120
Your bedded° hairs, like life in excrements,°
Start up and stand an° end. O gentle son,
Upon the heat and flame of thy distemper
sprinkle cool patience. Whereon do you look?
HAMLET.   On him, on him, look you how pale he glares,   125
His form and cause conjoined, preaching to stones,
Would make them capable.° Do not look upon me,
Lest with this piteous action you convert
My stern effects,° then what I have to do
Will want° true colour,° tears perchance for blood.   130
QUEEN.   To whom do you speak this?
HAMLET.   Do you see nothing there?
QUEEN.   Nothing at all, yet all that is I see.
HAMLET.   Nor did you nothing hear?

98 *vice:* buffoon (like the character of Vice in the morality plays).   99 *cutpurse:* pick-
pocket.   102.1 S.D.: *night-gown:* dressing gown.   107 *lapsed . . . passion:* having let time
elapse and passion cool.   114 *Conceit:* imagination.   117 *vacancy:* (she cannot see the
ghost).   118 *incorporal:* bodiless.   119 *spirits:* vital forces.   121 *bedded:* lying flat.   *excrements:* outgrowths (of the body).   122 *an:* on.   127 *capable:* i.e., of feeling pity.   128–129
convert . . . effects: transform my outward signs of sternness.   130 *want:* lack.   *colour:* (1)
complexion (2) motivation.

QUEEN.   No, nothing but ourselves.
HAMLET.   Why look you there, look how it steals away,
   My father in his habit as he lived,°   135
   Look where he goes, even now out at the portal.   *Exit* [*GHOST.*]
QUEEN.   This is the very coinage of your brain,
   This bodiless creation ecstasy
   Is very cunning in.°
HAMLET.   Ecstasy?
   My pulse as yours doth temperately keep time,   140
   And makes as healthful music. It is not madness
   That I have uttered; bring me to the test
   And I the matter will re-word, which madness
   Would gambol° from. Mother, for love of grace,
   Lay not that flattering unction° to your soul,   145
   That not your trespass but my madness speaks,
   It will but skin and film the ulcerous place,
   Whiles rank corruption mining° all within,
   Infects unseen. Confess yourself to heaven,
   Repent what's past, avoid what is to come,   150
   And do not spread the compost° on the weeds
   To make them ranker. Forgive me this my virtue,°
   For in the fatness° of these pursy° times
   Virtue itself of vice must pardon beg,
   Yea curb and woo° for leave to do him° good.   155
QUEEN.   O Hamlet, thou hast cleft my heart in twain.
HAMLET.   O throw away the worser part of it,
   And live the purer with the other half.
   Good night, but go not to my uncle's bed,
   Assume° a virtue if you have it not.   160
   That monster custom, who all sense doth eat
   Of habits evil,° is angel yet in this,
   That to the use° of actions fair and good,
   He likewise gives a frock or livery
   That aptly° is put on. Refrain tonight,   165
   And that shall lend a kind of easiness
   To the next abstinence, the next more easy:
   For use° almost can change the stamp° of nature,
   And either . . . the° devil, or throw him out
   With wondrous potency: once more good night,   170
   And when you are desirous to be blessed,
   I'll blessing beg of you. For this same lord,°   172

---

135 *habit . . . lived:* clothing he wore when alive.   138–139 *bodiless . . . cunning in:* madness (ecstasy) is very skillful in causing an affected person to hallucinate.   144 *gambol:* leap. 145 *unction:* salve.   148 *mining:* undermining.   151 *compost:* manure.   152 *virtue:* sermon on virtue.   153 *fatness:* grossness.   *pursy:* flabby.   155 *curb and woo:* bow and plead.   *him:* vice.   160 *Assume:* put on the guise of.   161–162 *all sense . . . evil:* confuses the sense of right and wrong in a habitué.   163 *use:* habit.   165 *aptly:* readily.   168 *use:* habit.   *stamp:* form.   169 *either . . . the:* (word omitted, for which "tame," "curls," and "quell" have been suggested).   172 *lord:* Polonius.

I do repent; but heaven hath pleased it so
To punish me with this, and this with me,
That I must be their scourge and minister.° 175
I will bestow° him and will answer well°
The death I gave him; so again good night.
I must be cruel only to be kind;
This bad begins, and worse remains behind.°
One word more, good lady.
QUEEN. What shall I do? 180
HAMLET. Not this by no means that I bid you do:
Let the bloat° king tempt you again to bed,
Pinch wanton on your cheek, call you his mouse,
And let him for a pair of reechy° kisses,
Or paddling in your neck with his damned fingers, 185
Make you to ravel° all this matter out
That I essentially am not in madness,
But mad in craft. 'Twere good you let him know,
For who that's but a queen, fair, sober, wise,
Would from a paddock, from a bat, a gib,° 190
Such dear concernings hide? who would do so?
No, in despite of sense and secrecy,
Unpeg the basket on the house's top,
Let the birds fly, and like the famous ape,
To try conclusions° in the basket creep, 195
And break your own neck down.°
QUEEN. Be thou assured, if words be made of breath,
And breath of life, I have no life to breathe
What thou hast said to me.
HAMLET. I must to England, you know that.
QUEEN. Alack, 200
I had forgot: 'tis so concluded on.
HAMLET. There's letters sealed, and my two school-fellows,
Whom I will trust as I will adders fanged,
They bear the mandate, they must sweep my way
And marshal me to knavery:° let it work, 205
For 'tis the sport to have the enginer°
Hoist with his own petar,° and't shall go hard
But I will delve one yard below their mines,
And blow them at the moon: O 'tis most sweet

---

175 *their . . . minister:* heaven's punishment and agent of retribution.   176 *bestow:* stow
away.   *answer well:* assume full responsibility for.   179 *bad . . . behind:* is a bad beginning to a
worse end to come.   182 *bloat:* bloated with dissipation.   184 *reechy:* filthy.   186 *ravel:*
unravel.   190 *paddock, bat, gib:* toad, bat, tomcat ("familiars" or demons in animal shape that
attend on witches).   193–196 *Unpeg . . . down:* (the story refers to an ape that climbs to the
top of a house and opens a basket of birds; when the birds fly away, the ape crawls into the basket,
tries to fly, and breaks his neck. The point is that if she gives away Hamlet's secret, she harms herself).   195 *try conclusions:* experiment.   204–205 *sweep . . . knavery:* (like the marshal who
went before a royal procession, clearing the way, so Rosencrantz and Guildenstern clear Hamlet's
path to some unknown evil).   206 *enginer:* maker of war engines.   207 *Hoist . . . petar:* blown
up by his own bomb.

When in one line two crafts directly meet.°   21●
This man shall set me packing,°
I'll lug the guts into the neighbour room;
Mother good night indeed. This counsellor
Is now most still, most secret, and most grave,
Who was in life a foolish prating knave.   21
Come sir, to draw toward an end with you.
Good night mother.   *Exit* HAMLET *tugging in* POLONIUS.

ACT 4

Scene 1. *[A room in the castle]*

Enter KING *and* QUEEN *with* ROSENCRANTZ *and* GUILDENSTERN.

KING.   There's matter in these sighs, these profound heaves,
       You must translate, 'tis fit we understand them.
       Where is your son?
QUEEN.   Bestow this place on us° a little while.

                    Exeunt ROSENCRANTZ *and* GUILDENSTERN.

       Ah mine own lord, what have I seen tonight!
KING.   What, Gertrude? How does Hamlet?
QUEEN.   Mad as the sea and wind when both contend
       Which is the mightier, in his lawless fit,
       Behind the arras hearing something stir,
       Whips out his rapier, cries "A rat, a rat,"
       And in this brainish apprehension° kills
       The unseen good old man.
KING.   O heavy deed!
       It had been so with us° had we been there:
       His liberty is full of threats to all,
       To you yourself, to us, to every one.
       Alas, how shall this bloody deed be answered?
       It will be laid to us,° whose providence°
       Should have kept short,° restrained, and out of haunt°
       This mad young man; but so much was our love,
       We would not understand what was most fit,
       But like the owner of a foul disease,
       To keep it from divulging,° let it feed
       Even on the pith of life: where is he gone?

---

210 *in one . . . meet:* the digger of the mine and the digger of the countermine meet halfway in
their tunnels.   211 *packing:* (1) i.e., my bags (2) rushing away (3) plotting.   4 *Bestow . . .*
us: leave us.   11 *brainish apprehension:* insane delusion.   13 *us:* me (royal plural).
17 *laid to us:* blamed on me.   *providence:* foresight.   18 *short:* tethered by a short
leash.   *out of haunt:* away from others.   22 *divulging:* being divulged.

QUEEN.   To draw apart the body he hath killed,
    O'er whom his very madness, like some ore   25
    Among a mineral of metals base,°
    Shows itself pure: a' weeps for what is done.
KING.   O Gertrude, come away:
    The sun no sooner shall the mountains touch,
    But we will ship him hence and this vile deed   30
    We must with all our majesty and skill
    Both countenance° and excuse. Ho Guildenstern!

Enter ROSENCRANTZ and GUILDENSTERN.

    Friends both, go join you with some further aid;
    Hamlet in madness hath Polonius slain,
    And from his mother's closet hath he dragged him.   35
    Go seek him out, speak fair, and bring the body
    Into the chapel; I pray you haste in this.   *[Exeunt Gentlemen.]*
    Come Gertrude, we'll call up our wisest friends,
    And let them know both what we mean to do
    And what's untimely done: [so haply slander,]   40
    Whose whisper o'er the world's diameter,
    As level° as the cannon to his blank°
    Transports his° poisoned shot, may miss our name,
    And hit the woundless° air. O come away,
    My soul is full of discord and dismay.   *Exeunt.*   45

Scene 2. *[Another room in the castle]*

Enter HAMLET.

HAMLET.   Safely stowed.
    Gentlemen within: Hamlet, Lord Hamlet!
    But soft, what noise, who calls on Hamlet?
    O here they come.

Enter ROSENCRANTZ and GUILDENSTERN.

ROSENCRANTZ.   What have you done my lord with the dead body?
HAMLET.   Compounded it with dust whereto 'tis kin.   5
ROSENCRANTZ.   Tell us where 'tis that we may take it thence,
    And bear it to the chapel.
HAMLET.   Do not believe it.
ROSENCRANTZ.   Believe what?
HAMLET.   That I can keep your counsel° and not mine own.° Besides,   10
    to be demanded of° a sponge, what replication° should be
    made by the son of a king?

25–26 *ore . . . base:* pure ore (such as gold) in a mine of base metal.   32 *countenance:*
defend.   42 *As level:* with a straight aim.   *blank:* while bull's-eye at the target's center.   43
his: slander's.   44 *woundless:* invulnerable.   10 *counsel:* (1) advice (2) secret.   *keep . . .*
own: follow your advice and not keep my own secret.   11 *demanded of:* questioned by.   *repli-*
cation: reply to a charge.

ROSENCRANTZ.   Take you me for a sponge, my lord?

HAMLET.   Ay sir, that soaks up the king's countenance,° his rewards,
  his authorities. But such officers do the king best service in   15
  the end; he keeps them like an apple in the corner of his
  jaw, first mouthed to be last swallowed: when he needs
  what you have gleaned, it is but squeezing you, and
  sponge, you shall be dry again.

ROSENCRANTZ.   I understand you not my lord.   20

HAMLET.   I am glad of it: a knavish speech sleeps in° a foolish ear.

ROSENCRANTZ.   My lord, you must tell us where the body is, and go with
  us to the king.

HAMLET.   The body is with the king, but the king° is not with the
  body. The king is a thing—   2

GUILDENSTERN.   A thing my lord?

HAMLET.   Of nothing, bring me to him. Hide fox, and all after.°   *Exeunt.*

Scene 3. *[Another room in the castle.]*

Enter KING *and two or three.*

KING.   I have sent to seek him, and to find the body:
  How dangerous is it that this man goes loose,
  Yet must not we put the strong law on him,
  He's loved of the distracted multitude,°
  Who like not in° their judgment, but their eyes,
  And where 'tis so, th'offender's scourge° is weighed
  But never the offence: to bear all° smooth and even,
  This sudden sending him away must seem
  Deliberate pause:° diseases desperate grown,
  By desperate appliance° are relieved,
  Or not at all.

Enter ROSENCRANTZ *and all the rest.*

                How now, what hath befallen?

ROSENCRANTZ.   Where the dead body is bestowed my lord,
  We cannot get from him.

KING.   But where is he?

ROSENCRANTZ.   Without, my lord, guarded,° to know your pleasure.

KING.   Bring him before us.

ROSENCRANTZ.   Ho, bring in the lord.

Enter HAMLET *(guarded) and* GUILDENSTERN.

KING.   Now Hamlet, where's Polonius?

HAMLET.   At supper.

KING.   At supper? where?

---

14 *countenance:* favor.   21 *sleeps in:* means nothing to.   24 *king . . . king:* Hamlet's father . . .
Claudius.   27 *Hide fox . . . after:* (cry in a children's game, like hide-and-seek).   4 *distracted
multitude:* confused mob.   5 *in:* according to.   6 *scourge:* punishment.   7 *bear all:* carry
out everything.   9 *Deliberate pause:* considered delay.   10 *appliance:* remedy.   14 *guarded:*
(Hamlet is under guard until he boards the ship).

HAMLET.   Not where he eats, but where a' is eaten: a certain
    convocation of politic° worms are e'en° at him. Your worm is your   20
    only emperor for diet, we fat all creatures else to fat us,
    and we fat ourselves for maggots. Your fat king and your
    lean beggar is but variable service,° two dishes but to one
    table, that's the end.
KING.   Alas, alas.   25
HAMLET.   A man may fish with the worm that hath eat of a king, and
    eat of the fish that hath fed of that worm.
KING.   What dost thou mean by this?
HAMLET.   Nothing but to show you how a king may go a progress°
    through the guts of a beggar.   30
KING.   Where is Polonius?
HAMLET.   In heaven, send thither to see. If your messenger find him
    not there, seek him i'th'other place yourself: but if indeed
    you find him not within this month, you shall nose him as
    you go up the stairs into the lobby.   35
KING.   [*To Attendants.*] Go seek him there.
HAMLET.   A' will stay till you come.   [*Exeunt.*]
KING.   Hamlet, this deed, for thine especial safety—
    Which we do tender,° as we dearly grieve
    For that which thou hast done—must send thee hence   40
    With fiery quickness. Therefore prepare thyself,
    The bark is ready, and the wind at help,°
    Th'associates tend,° and every thing is bent
    For England.
HAMLET.   For England.
KING.   Ay Hamlet.
HAMLET.   Good.
KING.   So is it if thou knew'st our purposes.   45
HAMLET.   I see a cherub° that sees them: but come, for England.
    Farewell dear mother.
KING.   Thy loving father, Hamlet.
HAMLET.   My mother: father and mother is man and wife, man and
    wife is one flesh, and so my mother: come, for England.   *Exit.* 50
KING.   [*To ROSENCRANTZ and GUILDENSTERN.*]
    Follow him at foot,° tempt him with speed aboard,
    Delay it not, I'll have him hence tonight.
    Away, for every thing is sealed and done
    That else leans on° th'affair, pray you make haste.   [*Exeunt.*]
    And England,° if my love thou hold'st at aught°—   55
    As my great power thereof may give thee sense,
    Since yet thy cicatrice° looks raw and red

---

20 *politic:* (1) statesmanlike (2) crafty.   *e'en:* even now.   23 *variable service:* different types
of food.   29 *go a progress:* make a splendid royal journey from one part of the country
to another.   39 *tender:* cherish.   42 *at help:* helpful.   43 *tend:* wait.   46 *cherub:* (considered the watchmen of heaven).   51 *at foot:* at his heels.   54 *leans on:* relates to.
55 *England:* King of England.   *my love . . . aught:* you place any value on my favor.   57 *cica-
trice:* scar.

After the Danish sword, and thy free awe
Pays homage° to us—thou mayst not coldly set°
Our sovereign process,° which imports at full   60
By letters congruing° to that effect,
The present° death of Hamlet. Do it England,
For like the hectic° in my blood he rages,
And thou must cure me; till I know 'tis done,
Howe'er my haps,° my joys were ne'er begun.   *Exit.*   6!

Scene 4. [*A plain in Denmark*]

Enter FORTINBRAS with his army over the stage.

FORTINBRAS.   Go captain, from me greet the Danish king,
    Tell him that by his license, Fortinbras
    Craves the conveyance° of a promised march
    Over his kingdom. You know the rendezvous:
    If that his majesty would aught with us,
    We shall express our duty in his eye,°
    And let him know so.
CAPTAIN.   I will do't, my lord.
FORTINBRAS.   Go softly° on.   *Exit.*

Enter HAMLET, ROSENCRANTZ, [GUILDENSTERN,] etc.

HAMLET.   Good sir whose powers° are these?
CAPTAIN.   They are of Norway sir.
HAMLET.   How purposed sir I pray you?
CAPTAIN.   Against some part of Poland.
HAMLET.   Who commands them sir?
CAPTAIN.   The nephew to old Norway, Fortinbras.
HAMLET.   Goes it against the main° of Poland sir,
    Or for some frontier?
CAPTAIN.   Truly to speak, and with no addition,
    We go to gain a little patch of ground
    That hath in it no profit but the name.°
    To pay five ducats, five, I would not farm it;
    Nor will it yield to Norway or the Pole
    A ranker° rate, should it be sold in fee.°
HAMLET.   Why then the Polack never will defend it.
CAPTAIN.   Yes, it is already garrisoned.
HAMLET.   Two thousand souls, and twenty thousand ducats
    Will not debate the question of° this straw:°
    This is th'imposthume of much wealth and peace,°

58–59 *free . . . homage:* awe which you, though free, still show by paying homage.   59 *coldly set:*
lightly estimate.   60 *process:* command.   61 *congruing:* agreeing.   62 *present:* immediate.   63 *hectic:* fever.   65 *haps:* fortunes.   3 *conveyance of:* escort for.   6 *in his eye:* face
to face.   8 *softly:* slowly.   9 *powers:* troops.   15 *main:* body.   19 *name:* glory.   22
ranker: higher (as annual interest on the total).   *in fee:* outright.   26 *debate . . . of:* settle the
dispute over.   *straw:* triviality.   27 *imposthume . . . peace:* swelling discontent (inner abscess)
resulting from too much wealth and peace.

That inward breaks, and shows no cause without
Why the man dies. I humbly thank you sir.
CAPTAIN. God bye you sir.   [*Exit.*]
ROSENCRANTZ.   Will't please you go my lord?   30
HAMLET.   I'll be with you straight, go a little before.

[*Exeunt all but HAMLET.*]

How all occasions do inform against me,
And spur my dull revenge. What is a man
If his chief good and market° of his time
Be but to sleep and feed? a beast, no more: 35
Sure he that made us with such large discourse,°
Looking before and after,° gave us not
That capability and god-like reason
To fust° in us unused. Now whether it be
Bestial oblivion,° or some craven° scruple   40
Of thinking too precisely on th'event°—
A thought which quartered hath but one part wisdom,
And ever three parts coward—I do not know
Why yet I live to say "This thing's to do,"
Sith I have cause, and will, and strength, and means   45
To do't; examples gross° as earth exhort me:
Witness this army of such mass and charge,°
Led by a delicate and tender° prince,
Whose spirit with divine ambition puffed,
Makes mouths° at the invisible event,°   50
Exposing what is mortal, and unsure,
To all that fortune, death, and danger dare,
Even for an egg-shell. Rightly to be great,
Is not to stir without great argument,
But greatly to find quarrel in a straw   55
When honour's at the stake.° How stand I then
That have a father killed, a mother stained,
Excitements° of my reason, and my blood,
And let all sleep, while to my shame I see
The imminent death of twenty thousand men,   60
That for a fantasy and trick° of fame
Go to their graves like beds, fight for a plot
Whereon the numbers cannot try the cause,°
Which is not tomb enough and continent°
To hide the slain. O from this time forth,   65
My thoughts be bloody, or be nothing worth.   *Exit.*

34 *market:* profit.   36 *discourse:* power of reasoning.   37 *Looking . . . after:* seeing causes and
effects.   39 *fust:* grow moldy.   40 *Bestial oblivion:* forgetfulness, as a beast forgets its
parents.   *craven:* cowardly.   41 *event:* outcome.   46 *gross:* obvious.   47 *charge:*
expense.   48 *delicate and tender:* gentle and young.   50 *mouths:* faces.   *event:*
outcome.   53–56 *Rightly . . . stake:* the truly great do not fight without just cause ("argument"),
but it is nobly ("greatly") done to fight even for a trifle if honor is at stake.   58 *Excitements:* incentives.   61 *fantasy and trick:* illusion and trifle.   63 *Whereon . . . cause:* too small to accommodate all the troops fighting for it.   64 *continent:* container.

Scene 5. *[A room in the castle]*

Enter QUEEN, HORATIO and a GENTLEMAN.

QUEEN.   I will not speak with her.
GENTLEMAN.   She is importunate, indeed distract,°
    Her mood will needs be° pitied.
QUEEN.   What would she have?
GENTLEMAN.   She speaks much of her father, says she hears
    There's tricks i'th'world, and hems,° and beats her heart,
    Spurns enviously at straws,° speaks things in doubt°
    That carry but half sense: her speech is nothing,
    Yet the unshapèd use of it doth move
    The hearers to collection;° they aim° at it,
    And botch° the words up fit to their own thoughts,
    Which as her winks, and nods, and gestures yield them,
    Indeed would make one think there might be thought,
    Though nothing sure, yet much unhappily.
HORATIO.   'Twere good she were spoken with, for she may strew
    Dangerous conjectures in ill-breeding minds.
QUEEN.   Let her come in.   *Exit GENTLEMAN.*
    [*Aside.*] To my sick soul, as sin's true nature is,°
    Each toy° seems prologue to some great amiss,°
    So full of artless jealousy° is guilt,
    It spills itself, in fearing to be spilt.

Enter OPHELIA, distracted.°

OPHELIA.   Where is the beauteous majesty of Denmark?
QUEEN.   How now Ophelia?
OPHELIA.   [*Sings.*] How should I your true love know
                    From another one?
                By his cockle hat and staff,°
                And his sandal shoon.°
QUEEN.   Alas sweet lady, what imports this song?
OPHELIA.   Say you? nay, pray you mark.
    [*Sings.*] He is dead and gone, lady,
                He is dead and gone,
            At his head a grass-green turf,
                At his heels a stone.
            O ho.
QUEEN.   Nay but Ophelia—
OPHELIA   Pray you mark.
    [*Sings.*] White his shroud as the mountain snow—

Enter KING.

2 *distract:* insane.   3 *will needs be:* needs to be.   5 *hems:* coughs.   6 *Spurns . . . straws:* reacts maliciously to trifles.   *in doubt:* ambiguous.   9 *collection:* inference.   *aim:* guess.   10 *botch:* patch.   17 *as sin's . . . is:* as is natural for the guilty.   18 *toy:* trifle.   *amiss:* disaster.   19 *artless jealousy:* uncontrollable suspicion.   20 S.D.: *distracted:* insane.   25 *cockle hat and staff.* (marks of the pilgrim, the cockle shell symbolizing his journey to the shrine of St. James; the pilgrim was a common metaphor for the lover).   26 *shoon:* shoes.

QUEEN.   Alas, look here my lord.   35
OPHELIA.   [*Sings.*] Larded° all with sweet flowers,
      Which bewept to the ground did not go,
        With true-love showers.
KING.   How do you, pretty lady?
OPHELIA.   Well, God 'ild° you. They say the owl was a baker's   40
   daughter.° Lord, we know what we are, but know not what
   we may be. God be at your table.°
KING.   Conceit° upon her father.
OPHELIA.   Pray you let's have no words of this, but when they ask
   you what it means, say you this: 45

    [*Sings.*] Tomorrow is Saint Valentine's day,
       All in the morning betime,°
       And I a maid at your window
         To be your Valentine.
       Then up he rose, and donned his clo'es,   50
        And dupped° the chamber door,
       Let in the maid, that out a maid,
        Never departed more.
KING.   Pretty Ophelia.
OPHELIA.   Indeed, la, without an oath I'll make an end on't.   55

    [*Sings.*] By Gis° and by Saint Charity,
       Alack and fie for shame,
       Young men will do't, if they come to't,
        By Cock° they are to blame.
       Quoth she, Before you tumbled me,   60
        You promised me to wed.

   (He answers)
       So would I ha' done, by yonder sun,
        An° thou hadst not come to my bed.
KING.   How long hath she been thus?   65
OPHELIA.   I hope all will be well. We must be patient, but I cannot
   choose but weep to think they would lay him i'th'cold
   ground. My brother shall know of it, and so I thank you
   for your good counsel. Come, my coach: good night
   ladies, good night. Sweet ladies, good night, good night.   [*Exit* OPHELIA.]   70
KING.   Follow her close, give her good watch I pray you.   [*Exit* HORATIO.]
   O this is the poison of deep grief, it springs
   All from her father's death, and now behold:
   O Gertrude, Gertrude,
   When sorrows come, they come not single spies,   75
   But in battalions: first her father slain,

---

36 *Larded:* trimmed.   40 *God 'ild:* God yield (reward).   40–41 *owl . . . daughter:* (in a medieval legend, a baker's daughter was turned into an owl because she gave Jesus short weight on a loaf of bread).   42 *God . . . table:* (a blessing at dinner).   43 *Conceit:* thinking.   47 *betime:* early (because the first woman a man saw on Valentine's Day would be his true love).   51 *dupped:* opened.   56 *Gis:* contraction of "Jesus."   59 *Cock:* (vulgarization of "God" in oaths).   64 *An:* if.

Next, your son gone, and he most violent author
Of his own just remove, the people muddied,°
Thick and unwholesome in their thoughts and whispers
For good Polonius' death: and we have done but greenly°   8(
In hugger-mugger° to inter him: poor Ophelia
Divided from herself and her fair judgment,
Without the which we are pictures or mere beasts,
Last, and as much containing° as all these,
Her brother is in secret come from France,   8!
Feeds on his wonder,° keeps himself in clouds,°
And wants not buzzers° to infect his ear
With pestilent speeches of his father's death,
Wherein necessity, of matter beggared,
Will nothing stick our person to arraign°   9
In ear and ear:° O my dear Gertrude, this
Like to a murdering-piece° in many places
Gives me superfluous death.   *A noise within.*

QUEEN.   Alack, what noise is this?
KING.   Attend!   *Enter a MESSENGER.*
Where are my Switzers°? Let them guard the door.   9
What is the matter?
MESSENGER.   Save yourself, my lord.
The ocean, overpeering of his list,°
Eats not the flats° with more impiteous haste
Than young Laertes in a riotous head°
O'erbears your officers: the rabble call him lord,   1(
And as the world were now but to begin,
Antiquity forgot, custom not known,
The ratifiers and props of every word,
They cry "Choose we, Laertes shall be king!"
Caps, hands, and tongues applaud it to the clouds,   1(
"Laertes shall be king, Laertes king!"   *A noise within.*
QUEEN.   How cheerfully on the false trail they cry.
O this is counter,° you false Danish dogs.
KING.   The doors are broke.

Enter LAERTES with others.

LAERTES.   Where is this king? Sirs, stand you all without.°
DANES.   No, let's come in.
LAERTES.   I pray you give me leave.°
DANES.   We will, we will.   [*They retire.*]

78 *muddied:* stirred up.   80 *done but greenly:* acted like amateurs.   81 *hugger-mugger:* secret
haste.   84 *containing:* i.e., cause for sorrow.   86 *Feeds . . . wonder:* sustains himself by wondering about his father's death.   *clouds:* gloom, obscurity.   87 *wants not buzzers:* lacks not
whispering gossips.   89–90 *Wherein . . . arraign:* in which the tellers, lacking facts, will not hesitate to accuse me.   91 *In ear and ear:* whispering from one ear to another.   92 *murdering-
piece:* small cannon shooting shrapnel, to inflict numerous wounds.   95 *Switzers:* Swiss
guards.   97 *overpeering . . . list:* rising above its usual limits.   98 *flats:* lowlands.   99 *head:*
armed force.   108 *counter:* following the scent backward.   110 *without:* outside.   111
leave: i.e., to enter alone.

LAERTES.   I thank you, keep the door. O thou vile king,
　　Give me my father.
QUEEN.　　　　　　　　Calmly, good Laertes.
LAERTES.   That drop of blood that's calm proclaims me bastard,　　　　　115
　　Cries cuckold° to my father, brands° the harlot
　　Even here between the chaste unsmirchèd brows
　　Of my true mother.
KING.　　　　　　　　What is the cause Laertes,
　　That thy rebellion looks so giant-like?
　　Let him go Gertrude, do not fear° our person,　　　　　120
　　There's such divinity° doth hedge a king,
　　That treason can but peep to° what it would,
　　Acts little of his° will. Tell me Laertes,
　　Why thou art this incensed. Let him go Gertrude.
　　Speak man.　　　　　　　　125
LAERTES.   Where is my father?
KING.　　　　　　　　Dead.
QUEEN.　　　　　　　　　　But not by him.
KING.   Let him demand his fill.
LAERTES.   How came he dead? I'll not be juggled with.
　　To hell allegiance, vows to the blackest devil,
　　Conscience and grace, to the profoundest pit.　　　　　130
　　I dare damnation: to this point I stand,
　　That both the worlds I give to negligence,°
　　Let come what comes, only I'll be revenged
　　Most throughly for my father.
KING.　　　　　　　　Who shall stay you?
LAERTES.   My will, not all the world's:°　　　　　135
　　And for my means, I'll husband° them so well,
　　They shall go far with little.
KING.　　　　　　　　Good Laertes,
　　If you desire to know the certainty
　　Of your dear father, is't writ in your revenge
　　That swoopstake,° you will draw both friend and foe,　　　　　140
　　Winner and loser?
LAERTES.   None but his enemies.
KING.　　　　　　　　Will you know them then?
LAERTES.   To his good friends thus wide I'll ope my arms,
　　And like the kind life-rend'ring pelican,°
　　Repast them with my blood.
KING.　　　　　　　　Why now you speak　　　　　145
　　Like a good child, and a true gentleman.
　　That I am guiltless of your father's death,

---

116 *cuckold:* betrayed husband.　　　*brands:* (so harlots were punished).　　　120 *fear:* i.e.,
for.　　　121 *divinity:* divine protection.　　　122 *peep to:* strain to see.　　　123 *his:* treason's.
132 *both . . . negligence:* I care nothing for this world or the next.　　　135 *world's:* i.e., will.
136 *husband:* economize.　　　140 *swoopstake:* sweeping in all the stakes in a game, both of winner
and loser.　　　144 *pelican:* (the mother pelican was believed to nourish her young with blood
pecked from her own breast).

And am most sensibly° in grief for it,
It shall as level° to your judgment 'pear
As day does to your eye.   150

[*A noise within.*]

[*Crowd shouts.*] Let her come in.
LAERTES.   How now, what noise is that?

Enter OPHELIA.

O heat, dry up my brains, tears seven time salt,
Burn out the sense and virtue° of mine eye!
By heaven, thy madness shall be paid with weight,°
Till our scale turn the beam,° O rose of May,   15
Dear maid, kind sister, sweet Ophelia:
O heavens, is't possible a young maid's wits
Should be as mortal as an old man's life?
Nature is fine in love, and where 'tis fine,
It sends some previous instance of itself   16
after the thing it loves.°
OPHELIA.   [*Sings.*] They bore him barefaced on the bier,
               Hey non nonny, nonny, hey nonny:
               And in his grave rained many a tear—
          Fare you well my dove.   16
LAERTES.   Hadst thou thy wits, and didst persuade revenge,
It could not move thus.
OPHELIA.   You must sing "adown adown," and you call him adown-a.
O how the wheel becomes it.° It is the false steward that
stole his master's daughter.   1
LAERTES.   This nothing's more than matter.°
OPHELIA.   There's rosemary,° that's for remembrance, pray you love
remember: and there is pansies, that's for thoughts.
LAERTES.   A document° in madness, thoughts and remembrance
fitted.°   1
OPHELIA.   There's fennel for you, and columbines.° There's rue° for
you, and here's some for me, we may call it herb of grace°
o'Sundays: O, you must wear your rue with a difference.°
There's a daisy,° I would give you some violets,° but they
withered all when my father died: they say a' made a good   1
end;
          [*Sings.*] For bonny sweet Robin is all my joy.

---

148 *sensibly:* feelingly.   149 *level:* plain.   153 *sense and virtue:* feeling and power.   154 *with weight:* with equal weight.   155 *turn the beam:* outweigh the other side.   159–161 *Nature . . . loves:* filial love that is so refined and pure sends some precious token (her wits) after the beloved dead.   169 *wheel becomes it:* refrain ("adown") suits the subject (Polonius's fall).   171 *more than matter:* more eloquent than sane speech.   172 *There's rosemary:* (given to Laertes; she may be distributing imaginary or real flowers).   174 *document:* lesson.   *thoughts . . . fitted:* thoughts of revenge matched with remembrance of Polonius.   176 *fennel, columbines:* (given to the king, symbolizing flattery and ingratitude).   *rue:* (given to the queen, symbolizing sorrow or repentance).   177 *herb of grace:* (because it symbolizes repentance).   178 *with a difference:* for a different reason (Ophelia's is for sorrow and the queen's for repentance).   179 *daisy:* (symbolizing dissembling).   *violets:* (symbolizing faithfulness).

LAERTES.   Thought and affliction, passion, hell itself,
  She turns to favour and to prettiness.
OPHELIA.   [*Sings.*] And will a' not come again,   185
      And will a' not come again?
        No, no, he is dead,
        Go to thy death-bed,
        He never will come again.
      His beard was as white as snow,   190
      All flaxen was his poll,°
        He is gone, he is gone,
        And we cast away moan,
        God ha' mercy on his soul.
  And of all Christian souls, I pray God. God bye you.   195

                                                           Exit OPHELIA.

LAERTES.   Do you see this, O God?
KING.   Laertes, I must commune with your grief,
  Or you deny me right: go but apart,
  Make choice of whom your wisest friends you will,
  And they shall hear and judge 'twixt you and me;   200
  If by direct or by collateral° hand
  They find us touched,° we will our kingdom give,
  Our crown, our life, and all that we call ours
  To you in satisfaction; but if not,
  Be you content to lend your patience to us,   205
  And we shall jointly labour with your soul
  To give it due content.
LAERTES.   Let this be so.
  His means of death, his obscure funeral,
  No trophy,° sword, nor hatchment° o'er his bones,
  No noble rite, nor formal ostentation,°   210
  Cry° to be heard as 'twere from heaven to earth,
  That I must call't in question.
KING.   So you shall,
  And where th'offence is, let the great axe fall.
  I pray you go with me.   [*Exeunt.*]

Scene 6. *[Another room in the castle]*

Enter HORATIO *and others.*

HORATIO.   What are they that would speak with me?
GENTLEMAN.   Seafaring men sir, they say they have letters for you.
HORATIO.   Let them come in.   [*Exit* ATTENDANT.]
  I do not know from what part of the world
  I should be greeted, if not from Lord Hamlet.   5

---

191 *flaxen . . . poll:* white was his head.   201 *collateral:* indirect.   202 *touched:* tainted with
guilt.   209 *trophy:* memorial.   *hatchment:* tablet displaying coat of arms.   210 *ostentation:*
ceremony.   211 *Cry:* cry out.

Enter SAILORS.

SAILOR.   God bless you sir.

HORATIO.   Let him bless thee too.

SAILOR.   A' shall sir, an't please him. There's a letter for you sir, it
came from th'ambassador that was bound for England, if
your name be Horatio, as I am let to know it is.

HORATIO.   [*Reads the letter.*] "Horatio, when thou shalt have
overlooked° this, give these fellows some means to the king,
they have letters for him. Ere we were two days old at sea,
a pirate of very warlike appointment° gave us chase.
Finding ourselves too slow of sail, we put on a compelled
valour, and in the grapple° I boarded them. On the instant
they got clear of our ship, so I alone became their prisoner.
They have dealt with me like thieves of mercy,° but they
knew what they did. I am to do a good turn for them. Let
the king have the letters I have sent, and repair° thou to me
with as much speed as thou wouldst fly death. I have
words to speak in thine ear will make thee dumb, yet are
they much too light for the bore° of the matter. These good
fellows will bring thee where I am. Rosencrantz and
Guildenstern hold their course for England. Of them I
have much to tell thee. Farewell.

He that thou knowest thine, Hamlet."

Come, I will give you way° for these your letters,
And do't the speedier that you may direct me
To him from whom you brought them.   *Exeunt.*

Scene 7. [*Another room in the castle*]

Enter KING *and* LAERTES.

KING.   Now must your conscience my acquittance seal,°
And you must put me in your heart for friend,
Sith you have heard and with a knowing ear,
That he which hath your noble father slain
Pursued my life.

LAERTES.   It well appears: but tell me
Why you proceeded not against these feats
So crimeful and so capital in nature,
As by your safety, greatness, wisdom, all things else,
You mainly were stirred up.°

KING.   O for two special reasons,
Which may to you perhaps seem much unsinewed,°
But yet to me they're strong. The queen his mother
Lives almost by his looks, and for myself,

12 *overlooked:* read over.   14 *appointment:* equipment.   16 *in the grapple:* when the pirate
ship hooked onto ours.   18 *of mercy:* merciful.   20 *repair:* come.   23 *bore:* size,
caliber.   28 *way:* access (to the king).   1 *my acquittance seal:* confirm my acquittal.
9 *mainly . . . up:* were strongly urged.   10 *much unsinewed:* very weak.

My virtue or my plague, be it either which,
She's so conjunctive° to my life and soul,
That as the star moves not but in his sphere,°   15
I could not but by her. The other motive,
Why to a public count° I might not go,
Is the great love the general gender° bear him,
Who dipping all his faults in their affection,
Would like the spring that turneth wood to stone,°   20
Convert his gyves to graces,° so that my arrows,
Too slightly timbered° for so loud a wind,
Would have reverted to my bow again,
And not where I had aimed them.

LAERTES.   And so have I a noble father lost,   25
A sister driven into desperate terms,°
Whose worth, if praises may go back° again,
Stood challenger on mount of all the age
For her perfections.° But my revenge will come.

KING.   Break not your sleeps for that, you must not think   30
That we are made of stuff so flat and dull,
That we can let our beard be shook with danger,
And think it pastime. You shortly shall hear more,
I loved your father, and we love ourself,
And that I hope will teach you to imagine—   35

Enter a MESSENGER with letters.

How now. What news?
MESSENGER.   Letters my lord, from Hamlet.
These to your majesty, this to the queen.
KING.   From Hamlet? Who brought them?
MESSENGER.   Sailors my lord they say, I saw them not:
They were given me by Claudio, he received them   40
Of him that brought them.
KING.   Laertes you shall hear them:
Leave us.   *Exit [MESSENGER]*
[*Reads*] "High and mighty, you shall know I am set naked° on
your kingdom. Tomorrow shall I beg leave to see your kingly
eyes, when I shall, first asking your pardon° thereunto,   45
recount the occasion of my sudden and more strange return.
                                             Hamlet."
What should this mean? Are all the rest come back?
Or is it some abuse,° and no such thing?

14 *conjunctive:* closely allied.   15 *in his sphere:* (referring to the Ptolemaic belief that each planet, fixed in its own sphere, revolved around the earth).   17 *count:* accounting.   18 *general gender:* common people.   20 *the spring . . . stone:* (the baths of King's Newnham in Warwickshire were described as being able to turn wood into stone because of their high concentrations of lime).   21 *Convert . . . graces:* regard his fetters (had he been imprisoned) as honors. 22 *slightly timbered:* light-shafted.   26 *desperate terms:* madness.   27 *go back:* i.e., before her madness.   28–29 *challenger . . . perfections:* like a challenger on horseback, ready to defend against the world her claim to perfection.   43 *naked:* without resources.   45 *pardon:* permission. 49 *abuse:* deception.

LAERTES.   Know you the hand?
KING.   'Tis Hamlet's character.° "Naked,"   5○
   And in a postscript here he says "alone."
   Can you devise° me?
LAERTES.   I am lost in it my lord, but let him come,
   It warms the very sickness in my heart
   That I shall live and tell him to his teeth,   5○
   "Thus didest thou."
KING.   If it be so Laertes—
   As how should it be so? how otherwise?—
   Will you be ruled by me?
LAERTES.   Ay my lord,
   So you will not o'errule me to a peace.
KING.   To thine own peace: if he be now returned,
   As checking at° his voyage, and that he means   6○
   No more to undertake it, I will work him
   To an exploit, now ripe in my device,°
   Under the which he shall not choose but fall:
   And for his death no wind of blame shall breathe,
   But even his mother shall uncharge the practice,°   ○
   And call it accident.
LAERTES.   My lord, I will be ruled,
   The rather if you could devise it so
   That I might be the organ.°
KING.   It falls right.
   You have been talked of since your travel much,
   And that in Hamlet's hearing, for a quality
   Wherein they say you shine: your sum of parts°
   Did not together pluck such envy from him
   As did that one, and that in my regard
   Of the unworthiest siege.°
LAERTES.   What part is that my lord?
KING.   A very riband° in the cap of youth,
   Yet needful too, for youth no less becomes°
   The light and careless livery° that it wears,
   Than settled age his sables° and his weeds°
   Importing health and graveness; two months since,°
   Here was a gentleman of Normandy—
   I have seen myself, and served against the French,
   And they can° well on horseback—but this gallant
   Had witchcraft in't, he grew unto his seat,
   And to such wondrous doing brought his horse,

---

50 *character:* handwriting.   52 *devise me:* explain it.   61 *checking at:* altering the course of (when the falcon forsakes one quarry for another).   63 *ripe in my device:* already planned by me.   66 *uncharge the practice:* acquit the plot (of treachery).   69 *organ:* instrument.   72 *your sum of parts:* all your accomplishments.   75 *siege:* rank.   76 *riband:* decoration.   77 *becomes:* befits.   78 *livery:* clothing (denoting rank or occupation).   79 *sables:* fur-trimmed gowns.   *weeds:* garments.   80 *since:* ago.   83 *can:* can do.

As had he been incorpsed and demi-natured°
With the brave beast. So far he topped my thought,
That I in forgery of° shapes and tricks
Come short of what he did.
LAERTES.   A Norman was't?
KING.   A Norman.   90
LAERTES.   Upon my life, Lamord.
KING.   The very same.
LAERTES.   I know him well, he is the brooch° indeed
And gem of all the nation.
KING.   He made confession° of you,
And gave you such a masterly report   95
For art and exercise in your defence,
And for your rapier most especial,
That he cried out 'twould be a sight indeed
If one could match you; the scrimers° of their nation
He swore had neither motion, guard, nor eye,   100
If you opposed them; sir this report of his
Did Hamlet so envenom° with his envy,
That he could nothing do but wish and beg
Your sudden coming o'er to play with him.
Now out of this—
LAERTES.   What out of this, my lord?   105
KING.   Laertes, was your father dear to you?
Or are you like the painting of a sorrow,
A face without a heart?
LAERTES.   Why ask you this?
KING.   Not that I think you did not love your father,
But that I know love is begun by time,   110
And that I see in passages of proof,°
Time qualifies° the spark and fire of it:
There lives within the very flame of love
A kind of wick or snuff that will abate it,°
And nothing is at a like goodness still,°   115
For goodness growing to a plurisy,°
Dies in his own too-much. That we would do
We should do when we would: for this "would"° changes,
And hath abatements and delays as many
As there are tongues, are hands, are accidents,   120
And then this "should"° is like a spendthrift sigh,
That hurts by easing;° but to the quick° of th'ulcer:

---

86 *incorpsed . . . natured:* made into one body, sharing half its nature.   88 *in forgery of:* imagining.   92 *brooch:* ornament.   94 *confession:* report.   99 *scrimers:* fencers.   102 *envenom:* poison.   111 *passages of proof:* examples drawn from experience.   112 *qualifies:* weakens.   114 *snuff . . . it:* charred end of the wick that will diminish the flame.   115 *still:* always.   116 *plurisy:* excess.   118 *"would":* will to act.   121*"should":* reminder of one's duty.   121–122 *spendthrift . . . easing:* A sigh which, though giving temporary relief, wastes life, as each sigh draws a drop of blood away from the heart (a common Elizabethan belief).   122 *quick:* most sensitive spot.

Hamlet comes back, what would you undertake
To show yourself in deed your father's son
More than in words?

LAERTES.   To cut his throat i'th'church.

KING.   No place indeed should murder sanctuarize,°
Revenge should have no bounds: but good Laertes,
Will you do this, keep close within your chamber:
Hamlet returned shall know you are come home,
We'll put on° those shall praise your excellence,
And set a double varnish on the fame
The Frenchman gave you, bring you in fine° together,
And wager on your heads; he being remiss,°
Most generous, and free from all contriving,
Will not peruse the foils, so that with ease,
Or with a little shuffling, you may choose
A sword unbated,° and in a pass of practice°
Requite him for your father.

LAERTES.   I will do't,
And for the purpose, I'll anoint my sword.
I bought an unction° of a mountebank°
So mortal,° that but dip a knife in it,
Where it draws blood, no cataplasm° so rare,
Collected from all simples° that have virtue°
Under the moon,° can save the thing from death
That is but scratched withal: I'll touch my point
With this contagion, that if I gall° him slightly,
It may be death.

KING.   Let's further think of this,
Weigh what convenience both of time and means
May fit us to our shape;° if this should fail,
And that our drift° look through° our bad performance,
'Twere better not assayed; therefore this project
Should have a back or second that might hold
If this did blast in proof;° soft, let me see,
We'll make a solemn wager on your cunnings°—
I ha't:
When in your motion you are hot and dry,
As make your bouts more violent to that end,
And that he calls for drink, I'll have prepared him
A chalice for the nonce,° whereon but sipping,
If he by chance escape your venomed stuck,°

---

126 *murder sanctuarize:* give sanctuary to murder.   130 *put on:* incite.   132 *in fine:* finally.   133 *remiss:* easy-going.   137 *unbated:* not blunted (the edges and points were blunted for fencing).   *pass of practice:* (1) match for exercise (2) treacherous thrust. 140 *unction:* ointment.   *mountebank:* quack doctor, medicine man.   141 *mortal:* deadly.   142 *cataplasm:* poultice.   143 *simples:* herbs.   *virtue:* power (of healing). 144 *Under the moon:* (when herbs were supposed to be collected to be most effective).   146 *gall:* scratch.   149 *shape:* plan.   150 *drift:* aim.   *look through:* be exposed by.   153 *blast in proof:* fail when tested (as a bursting cannon).   154 *cunnings:* skills.   159 *nonce:* occasion.   160 *stuck:* thrust.

Our purpose may hold there; but stay, what noise?

Enter QUEEN.

How, sweet queen?
QUEEN.   One woe doth tread upon another's heel,
　　So fast they follow; your sister's drowned, Laertes.
LAERTES.   Drowned! O where?   165
QUEEN.   There is a willow grows aslant a brook,
　　That shows his hoar° leaves in the glassy stream,
　　There with fantastic garlands did she make
　　Of crow-flowers,° nettles, daisies, and long purples,°
　　That liberal° shepherds give a grosser name,   170
　　But our cold° maids do dead men's fingers call them.
　　There on the pendent boughs her coronet weeds°
　　Clamb'ring to hang, an envious sliver° broke,
　　When down her weedy trophies and herself
　　Fell in the weeping brook: her clothes spread wide,   175
　　And mermaid-like awhile they bore her up,
　　Which time she chanted snatches of old tunes,
　　As one incapable of° her own distress,
　　Or like a creature native and indued
　　Unto° that element: but long it could not be   180
　　Till that her garments, heavy with their drink,
　　Pulled the poor wretch from her melodious lay
　　To muddy death.
LAERTES.　　　　　　　　　Alas, then she is drowned?
QUEEN.   Drowned, drowned.
LAERTES.   Too much of water hast thou, poor Ophelia,   185
　　And therefore I forbid my tears; but yet
　　It is our trick, nature her custom holds,
　　Let shame say what it will; when these° are gone,
　　The woman will be out.° Adieu my lord,
　　I have a speech o' fire that fain would blaze,   190
　　But that this folly douts it.°　　　　　　　　　　　　　　*Exit.*
KING.　　　　　　　　　Let's follow, Gertrude,
　　How much I had to do to calm his rage;
　　Now fear I this will give it start again,
　　Therefore let's follow.　　　　　　　　　　　　　　　　*Exeunt.*

ACT 5

Scene 1. [A churchyard]

Enter two CLOWNS.°

167 *hoar:* grey (on the underside).   169 *crow-flowers:* buttercups.   *long purples:* spike-
like early orchid.   170 *liberal:* libertine.   171 *cold:* chaste.   172 *coronet weeds:* garland
of weeds.   173 *envious sliver:* malicious branch   178 *incapable of:* unable to
understand.   179–180 *indued Unto:* endowed by nature to exist in.   188 *these:* i.e.,
tears.   189 *woman . . . out:* womanly habits will be out of me.   191 *folly douts it:* tears put it
out.   0.2 S.D.: *clowns:* rustics.

1. CLOWN.   Is she to be buried in Christian burial,° when she wilfully
seeks her own salvation?°
2. CLOWN.   I tell thee she is, therefore make her grave straight.° The
crowner hath sat on her,° and finds it Christian burial.
1. CLOWN.   How can that be, unless she drowned herself in her own
defence?°
2. CLOWN.   Why, 'tis found so.
1. CLOWN.   It must be "se offendendo,"° it cannot be else: for here lies
the point: if I drown myself wittingly, it argues an act,
and an act hath three branches, it is to act, to do, and to
perform; argal,° she drowned herself wittingly.
2. CLOWN.   Nay, but hear you, goodman delver.
1. CLOWN.   Give me leave: here lies the water, good. Here stands the
man, good. If the man go to this water and drown himself,
it is, will he nill he,° he goes, mark you that. But if the
water come to him, and drown him, he drowns not
himself. Argal, he that is not guilty of his own death, shortens not his own
life.
2. CLOWN.   But is this law?
1. CLOWN.   Ay marry is't, crowner's quest° law.
2. CLOWN.   Will you ha' the truth on't? If this had not been a
gentlewoman, she would have been buried out o'Christian
burial.
1. CLOWN.   Why there thou say'st, and the more pity that great folk
should have countenance° in this world to drown or hang
themselves more than their even-Christen.° Come, my
spade; there is no ancient gentlemen but gardeners,
ditchers and grave-makers; they hold up Adam's profession.
2. CLOWN.   Was he a gentleman?
1. CLOWN.   A' was the first that ever bore arms.°
2. CLOWN.   Why, he had none.
1. CLOWN.   What, art a heathen? How dost thou understand the
Scripture? The Scripture says Adam digged; could he dig
without arms? I'll put another question to thee; if thou
answerest me not to the purpose, confess thyself—
2. CLOWN.   Go to.
1. CLOWN.   What is he that builds stronger than either the mason, the
shipwright, or the carpenter?
2. CLOWN.   The gallows-maker, for that frame outlives a thousand
tenants.

---

1 *Christian burial:* consecrated ground within a churchyard (where suicides were not allowed burial).   2 *salvation:* i.e., "damnation." The gravediggers make a number of such "mistakes," later termed "malapropisms." See p. 383.   3 *straight:* straightaway, at once.   4 *crowner . . . her:* coroner has ruled on her case.   5–6 *her own defence:* (as self-defense justifies homicide, so may it justify suicide).   8 *"se offendendo":* (he means *"se defendendo,"* in self-defense).   11 *argal:* (corruption of "ergo" = therefore).   15 *will he nill he:* will he or will he not (willy nilly).   20 *quest:* inquest.   25 *countenance:* privilege.   26 *even-Christen:* fellow Christian.   30 *arms:* (with a pun on "coat of arms").

1. CLOWN.   I like thy wit well in good faith, the gallows does well, but
how does it well? It does well to those that do ill. Now
thou dost ill to say the gallows is built stronger than the
church. Argal, the gallows may do well to thee.° To't
again, come.   45
2. CLOWN.   'Who builds stronger than a mason, a shipwright, or a
carpenter?'
1. CLOWN.   Ay, tell me that, and unyoke.°
2. CLOWN.   Marry, now I can tell.
1. CLOWN.   To't.   50
2. CLOWN.   Mass,° I cannot tell.
1. CLOWN.   Cudgel thy brains no more about it, for your dull ass will
not mend his pace with beating, and when you are asked
this question next, say "a grave-maker:" the houses he
makes last till doomsday. Go get thee to Yaughan,° and   55
fetch me a stoup° of liquor.   [*Exit 2. CLOWN.*]

Enter HAMLET and HORATIO afar off.

1. CLOWN.   (*Sings.*) In youth when I did love, did love,
                      Methought it was very sweet,
                      To contract oh the time for a° my behove,°
                      O methought there a was nothing a meet.°   60
HAMLET.   Has this fellow no feeling of his business, that a'sings in
grave-making?
HORATIO.   Custom hath made it in him a property of easiness.°
HAMLET.   'Tis e'en so, the hand of little employment hath the
daintier sense.°   65
1. CLOWN.   (*Sings.*) But age with his stealing steps
                      Hath clawed me in his clutch,
                      And hath shipped me intil° the land,
                      As if I had never been such.   [*Throws up a skull.*]
HAMLET.   That skull had a tongue in it, and could sing once: how the   70
knave jowls° it to the ground, as if'twere Cain's jaw-bone,°
that did the first murder. This might be the pate of a
politician, which this ass now o'erreaches;° one that
would circumvent° God, might it not?
HORATIO.   It might my lord.   75
HAMLET.   Or of a courtier, which could say "Good morrow sweet
lord, how dost thou good lord?" This might be my lord
such-a-one, that praised my lord such-a-one's horse, when
a'meant to beg it, might it not?

---

44 *to thee:* i.e., by hanging you.   48 *unyoke:* unharness (your wits, after this exertion).   51 *Mass:*
by the mass.   55 *Yaughan:* probably a local innkeeper.   56 *stoup:* stein, drinking mug.   59
oh, a: (he grunts as he works).   *behove:* benefit.   60 *meet:* suitable.   63 *Custom . . . easiness:*
being accustomed to it has made him indifferent.   65 *daintier sense:* finer sensibility (being uncal-
loused).   68 *intil:* into.   71 *jowls:* casts (with obvious pun).   *Cain's jaw-bone:* the jawbone of
an ass with which Cain murdered Abel.   73 *o'erreaches:* (1) reaches over (2) gets the better
of.   74 *would circumvent:* tried to outwit.

HORATIO. It might my lord.

HAMLET. Why e'en so, and now my Lady Worm's, chopless,° and
knocked about the mazzard° with a sexton's spade; here's
fine revolution an° we had the trick° to see't. Did these
bones cost no more the breeding, but to play at loggets°
with them? Mine ache to think on't.

1. CLOWN. (*Sings.*) A pick-axe and a spade, a spade,
        For and a shrouding sheet,
     O a pit of clay for to be made
      For such a guest is meet.°   [*Throws up another skull.*]

HAMLET. There's another: why may not that be the skull of a
lawyer? Where be his quiddities° now, his quillets,° his
cases, his tenures,° and his tricks? Why does he suffer this
rude knave now to knock him about the sconce° with a
dirty shovel, and will not tell him of his action of battery?
Hum, this fellow might be in's time a great buyer of land,
with his statutes,° his recognizances,° his fines,° his double
vouchers,° his recoveries:° is this the fine° of his fines, and
the recovery° of his recoveries, to have his fine pate full of
fine dirt? Will his vouchers vouch him no more of his
purchases, and double ones too, than the length and
breadth of a pair of indentures?° The very conveyances° of
his lands will scarcely lie in this box,° and must th'inheritor°
himself have no more, ha?

HORATIO. Not a jot more my lord.

HAMLET. Is not parchment made of sheep-skins?

HORATIO. Ay my lord, and of calves'-skins too.

HAMLET. They are sheep and calves which seek out assurance° in
that. I will speak to this fellow. Whose grave's this, sirrah?

1. CLOWN. Mine sir:
     [*Sings.*] O a pit of clay for to be made
      For such a guest is meet.

HAMLET. I think it be thine indeed, for thou liest in't.

1. CLOWN. You lie out on't° sir, and therefore 'tis not yours; for my
part I do not lie in't, and yet it is mine.

HAMLET. Thous dost lie in't, to be in't and say it is thine: 'tis for the
dead, not for the quick,° therefore thou liest.

1. CLOWN. 'Tis a quick lie sir, 'twill away again from me to you.

HAMLET. What man dost thou dig it for?

---

81 *chopless:* lacking the lower jaw.   82 *mazzard:* head.   83 *an:* if.   *trick:* knack.   84
loggets: game in which small pieces of wood were thrown at fixed stakes.   89 *meet:* fitting.   91
quiddities: subtle definition.   *quillets:* minute distinctions.   92 *tenures:* property holdings.   93 *sconce:* head.   96 *statutes:* mortgages.   *recognizances:* promissory bonds.   96–97
fines, recoveries: legal processes for transferring real estate.   97 *vouchers:* persons who vouched for
a title to real estate.   *fine:* end.   98 *recovery:* attainment.   100–101 *length . . . indentures:*
contracts in duplicate, which spread out, would just cover his grave.   101 *conveyances:*
deeds.   102 *box:* the grave.   *inheritor:* owner.   107 *assurance:* (1) security (2) transfer of
land.   113 *on:* of.   116 *quick:* living.

1. CLOWN.   For no man sir.
HAMLET.   What woman then?
1. CLOWN.   For none neither.   120
HAMLET.   Who is to be buried in't?
1. CLOWN.   One that *was* a woman sir, but rest her soul she's dead.
HAMLET.   How absolute° the knave is, we must speak by the card,° or
  equivocation° will undo us. By the lord, Horatio, this   125
  three years I have took note of it, the age is grown so
  picked,° that the toe of the peasant comes so near the heel of
  the courtier, he galls his kibe.° How long hast thou been
  grave-maker?
1. CLOWN.   Of all the days i'th'year I came to't that day that our last   130
  king Hamlet overcame Fortinbras.
HAMLET.   How long is that since?
1. CLOWN.   Cannot you tell that? Every fool can tell that. It was the very
  day that young Hamlet was born: he that is mad and
  sent into England.   135
HAMLET.   Ay marry, why was he sent into England?
1. CLOWN.   Why because a' was mad: a' shall recover his wits there, or
  if a' do not, 'tis no great matter there.
HAMLET.   Why?
1. CLOWN.   'Twill not be seen in him there, there the men are as mad   140
  as he.
HAMLET.   How came he mad?
1. CLOWN.   Very strangely they say.
HAMLET.   How strangely?
1. CLOWN.   Faith, e'en with losing his wits.   145
HAMLET.   Upon what ground?
1. CLOWN.   Why here in Denmark: I have been sexton here man and
  boy thirty years.
HAMLET.   How long will a man lie i'th'earth ere he rot?
1. CLOWN.   Faith, if a' be not rotten before a' die, as we have many   150
  pocky° corses nowadays that will scarce hold the laying in,
  a' will last you some eight year, or nine year. A tanner will
  last you nine year.
HAMLET.   Why he more than another?
1. CLOWN.   Why sir, his hide is so tanned with his trade, that a' will   155
  keep out water a great while; and your water is a sore°
  decayer of your whoreson dead body. Here's a skull now:
  this skull hath lain you i'th'earth three-and-twenty years.
HAMLET.   Whose was it?
1. CLOWN.   A whoreson mad fellow's it was, whose do you think it   160
  was?
HAMLET.   Nay, I know not.

124 *absolute:* precise.   *by the card:* exactly to the point (card on which compass points are
marked).   125 *equivocation:* ambiguity.   127 *picked:* fastidious ("picky").   128 *galls his kibe:*
chafes the sore on the courtier's heel.   151 *pocky:* rotten (with venereal disease).   156 *sore:*
grievous.

1. CLOWN.   A pestilence on him for a mad rogue, a' poured a flagon of
Rhenish° on my head once; this same skull sir, was sir,
Yorick's skull, the king's jester.   16

HAMLET.   This?

1. CLOWN.   E'en that.

HAMLET.   Let me see. [*Takes the skull.*] Alas poor Yorick, I knew him
Horatio, a fellow of infinite jest, of most excellent fancy,°
he hath borne me on his back a thousand times: and now   17
how abhorred in my imagination it is: my gorge rises at it.
Here hung those lips that I have kissed I know not how
oft. Where be your gibes now? your gambols, your songs,
your flashes of merriment, that were wont to set the table
on a roar?° not one now to mock your own grinning? quite   17
chop-fallen?° Now get you to my lady's chamber, and tell
her, let her paint an inch thick, to this favour° she must
come. Make her laugh at that. Prithee Horatio, tell me one
thing.

HORATIO.   What's that, my lord?   18

HAMLET.   Dost thou think Alexander looked o' this fashion
i'th'earth?

HORATIO.   E'en so.

HAMLET.   And smelt so? pah.   [*Puts down the skull.*]

HORATIO.   E'en so my lord.   1

HAMLET.   To what base uses we may return, Horatio. Why may not
imagination trace the noble dust of Alexander, til a'find it
stopping a bung-hole?°

HORATIO.   'Twere to consider too curiously,° to consider so.

HAMLET.   No faith, not a jot, but to follow him thither with modesty°   1
enough, and likelihood to lead it; as thus: Alexander died,
Alexander was buried, Alexander returneth to dust, the
dust is earth, of earth we make loam,° and why of that loam
whereto he was converted, might they not stop a
beer-barrel?
    Imperious Caesar, dead and turned to clay,
    Might stop a hole to keep the wind away.
    O that that earth which kept the world in awe,
    Should patch a wall t'expel the winter's flaw.°
But soft, but soft awhile, here comes the king,
The queen, the courtiers.

Enter KING, QUEEN, LAERTES, *[Doctor of Divinity], and a coffin, with Lords attendant.*

Who is this they follow?
And with such maimèd° rites? This doth betoken
The corse they follow did with desp'rate hand

---

164 *Rhenish:* Rhine wine.   169 *fancy:* imagination.   175 *on a roar:* roaring with
laughter.   176 *chop-fallen:* (a) lacking a lower jaw (2) dejected, "down in the mouth."   177
favour: appearance.   188 *bung-hole:* hole in a cask.   189 *curiously:* minutely.   190 *modesty:* moderation.   193 *loam:* a clay mixture used as plaster.   199 *flaw:* windy gusts.   202
maimèd: abbreviated.

Fordo it° own life; 'twas of some estate.°
Couch° we awhile, and mark.   [*They retire.*] 205
HAMLET.   That is Laertes,
A very noble youth: mark.
LAERTES.   What ceremony else?
DOCTOR.   Her obsequies have been as far enlarged
As we have warranty: her death was doubtful,°   210
And but that great command o'ersways the order,
She should in ground unsanctified have lodged
Til the last trumpet: for charitable prayers,
Shards,° flints and pebbles should be thrown on her:
Yet here she is allowed her virgin crants,°   215
Her maiden strewments,° and the bringing home
Of° bell and burial.
LAERTES.   Must there no more be done?
DOCTOR.   No more be done:
We should profane the service of the dead,
To sing sage requiem° and such rest to her   220
As to peace-parted souls.
LAERTES.   Lay her i'th'earth,
And from her fair and unpolluted flesh
May violets spring: I tell thee churlish priest,
A minist'ring angel shall my sister be,
When thou liest howling.
HAMLET.   What, the fair Ophelia?   225
QUEEN.   [*Scattering flowers.*] Sweets to the sweet, farewell.
I hoped thou shouldst have been my Hamlet's wife:
I thought thy bride-bed to have decked, sweet maid,
And not have strewed thy grave.
LAERTES.   O treble woe
Fall ten times treble on that cursèd head   230
Whose wicked deed thy most ingenious sense°
Deprived thee of. Hold off the earth awhile,
Till I have caught her once more in mine arms;   *Leaps in the grave.*
Now pile your dust upon the quick° and dead,
Till of this flat a mountain you have made   235
T'o'ertop old Pelion,° or the skyish head
Of blue Olympus.
HAMLET.   [*Comes forward.*] What is he whose grief
Bears such an emphasis? whose phrase of sorrow
Conjures the wand'ring stars,° and makes them stand
Like wonder-wounded hearers? This is I,
Hamlet the Dane.   240
                                                           HAMLET leaps in after LAERTES.

204 *Fordo it:* destroy its.   *estate:* social rank.   205 *Couch:* hide.   210 *doubtful:* suspicious.   214 *Shards:* bits of broken pottery.   215 *crants:* garland.   216 *strewments:* flowers
strewn on the grave.   216–217 *bringing home Of:* laying to rest with.   220 *sage requiem:* solemn
dirge.   231 *sense:* mind.   234 *quick:* live.   236 *Pelion:* mountain (on which the Titans
placed Mt. Ossa, to scale Mt. Olympus and reach the gods).   239 *Conjures . . . stars:* casts a spell
over the planets.

LAERTES.   [*Grapples with him.*] The devil take thy soul.

HAMLET.   Thou pray'st not well,
I prithee take thy fingers from my throat,
For though I am not splenitive° and rash,
Yet have I in me something dangerous,
Which let thy wiseness fear; hold off thy hand.

KING.   Pluck them asunder.

QUEEN.   Hamlet, Hamlet!

ALL.   Gentlemen!

HORATIO.   Good my lord, be quiet.

[*Attendants part them, and they come out of the grave.*]

HAMLET.   Why, I will fight with him upon this theme
Until my eyelids will no longer wag.

QUEEN.   O my son, what theme?

HAMLET.   I loved Ophelia, forty thousand brothers
Could not with all their quantity of love
Make up my sum. What wilt thou do for her?

KING.   O he is mad, Laertes.

QUEEN.   For love of God, forbear° him.

HAMLET.   'Swounds,° show me what thou't do:
Woo't° weep? woo't fight? woo't fast? woo't tear thyself?
Woo't drink up eisel?° eat a crocodile?°
I'll do't. Dost thou come here to whine?
To outface me with leaping in her grave?
Be buried quick with her, and so will I.
And if thou prate of mountains, let them throw
Millions of acres on us, till our ground,
Singeing his pate against the burning zone,°
Make Ossa° like a wart. Nay, an thou'lt mouth,
I'll rant as well as thou.

QUEEN.   This is mere° madness,
And thus awhile the fit will work on him:
Anon as patient as the female dove
When that her golden couplets° are disclosed,
His silence will sit drooping.

HAMLET.   Hear you sir,
What is the reason that you use me thus?
I loved you ever; but it is no matter.
Let Hercules himself do what he may,
The cat will mew, and dog will have his day.

                                        Exit HAMLET.

KING.   I pray thee good Horatio, wait upon him.   [HORATIO *follows.*]

        [*Aside to Laertes.*] Strengthen your patience in our last night's speech,

244 *spenitive:* quick-tempered (anger was thought to originate in the spleen).   256 *forbear:*
be patient with.   257 *'Swounds:* corruption of "God's wounds."   258 *Woo't:* wilt
thou.   259 *eisel:* vinegar (thought to reduce anger and encourage melancholy).   *crocodile:*
(associated with hypocritical tears).   265 *burning zone:* sun's sphere.   266 *Ossa:* (see above,
line 236 n.).   267 *mere:* absolute.   270 *golden couplets:* fuzzy yellow twin fledglings.

We'll put the matter to the present push°—
Good Gertrude, set some watch over your son—
This grave shall have a living monument:°
An hour of quiet shortly shall we see,   280
Till then, in patience our proceeding be.   *Exeunt.*

Scene 2. *[A hall in the castle]*

Enter HAMLET *and* HORATIO.

HAMLET.   So much for this sir, now shall you see the other;
    You do remember all the circumstance.
HORATIO.   Remember it my lord!
HAMLET.   Sir, in my heart there was a kind of fighting
    That would not let me sleep; methought I lay
    Worse than the mutines in the bilboes.° Rashly—   5
    And praised be rashness for it: let us know,
    Our indiscretion sometimes serves us well
    When our deep plots do pall,° and that should learn us
    There's a divinity that shapes our ends,
    Rough-hew them how we will—   10
HORATIO.   That is most certain.
HAMLET.   Up from my cabin,
    My sea-gown° scarfed about me, in the dark
    Groped I to find out them, had my desire,
    Fingered° their packet, and in fine° withdrew
    To mine own room again, making so bold,   15
    My fears forgetting manners, to unseal
    Their grand commission; where I found, Horatio—
    Ah royal knavery—an exact command,
    Larded° with many several sorts of reasons,
    Importing Denmark's health, and England's too,   20
    With ho, such bugs and goblins in my life,°
    That on the supervise,° no leisure bated,°
    No, not to stay° the grinding of the axe,
    My head should be struck off.
HORATIO.   Is't possible?
HAMLET.   Here's the commission, read it at more leisure.   25
    But wilt thou hear now how I did proceed?
HORATIO.   I beseech you.
HAMLET.   Being thus be-netted round with villainies,
    Ere I could make a prologue to my brains,
    They had begun the play.° I sat me down,   30

---

278 *present push:* immediate test.   280 *living monument:* (1) lasting tombstone (2) living sacrifice (Hamlet) to memorialize it.   6 *mutines . . . bilboes:* mutineers in shackles.   9 *pall:* fail.   13 *sea-gown:* short-sleeved knee-length gown worn by seamen.   15 *Fingered:* got my fingers on.   *in fine:* to finish.   20 *Larded:* embellished.   22 *bugs . . . life:* imaginary evils attributed to me, like imaginary goblins ("bugs") meant to frighten children.   23 *supervise:* looking over (the commission).   *leisure bated:* delay excepted.   24 *stay:* await.   30–31 *Ere . . . play:* Before I could outline the action in my mind, my brains started to play their part.

Devised a new commission, wrote it fair°—
I once did hold it, as our statists° do,
A baseness° to write fair, and laboured much
How to forget that learning, but sir now
It did me yeoman's° service: wilt thou know
Th'effect of what I wrote?
HORATIO.   Ay, good my lord.
HAMLET.   An earnest conjuration° from the king,
As England was his faithful tributary,
As love between them like the palm might flourish,
As peace should still her wheaten garland wear
And stand a comma° 'tween their amities,
And many such like "as'es"° of great charge,°
That on the view and know of these contents,
Without debatement further, more or less,
He should those bearers put to sudden death,
Not shriving° time allowed.
HORATIO.   How was this sealed?
HAMLET.   Why even in that was heaven ordinant,°
I had my father's signet° in my purse,
Which was the model° of that Danish seal:
Folded the writ up in the form of th'other,
Subscribed° it, gave't th'impression,° placed it safely,
The changeling° never known: now the next day
Was our sea-fight, and what to this was sequent
Thou knowest already.
HORATIO.   So Guildenstern and Rosencrantz go to't.
HAMLET.   Why man, they did make love to this employment,°
They are not near my conscience, their defeat
Does by their own insinuation° grow:
'Tis dangerous when the baser nature comes
Between the pass° and fell° incensed points
Of mighty opposites.
HORATIO.   Why, what a king is this!
HAMLET.   Does it not, think thee, stand me now upon°—
He that hath killed my king, and whored my mother,
Popped in between th'election° and my hopes,
Thrown out his angle° for my proper° life,
And with such cozenage°—is't not perfect conscience

32 *wrote it fair:* wrote a finished (neat) copy, a "fair copy."   33 *statists:* statesmen.   34 *baseness:*
mark of humble status.   36 *yeoman's:* (in the sense of "faithful").   38 *conjuration:* entreaty (he
parodies the rhetoric of such documents).   42 *comma:* connection.   43 *as'es:* (1) the "as"
clauses in the commission (2) asses.   *charge:* (1) weight (in the clauses) (2) burdens (on the
asses).   47 *shriving:* confession and absolution.   48 *was heaven ordinant:* it was divinely
ordained.   49 *signet:* seal.   50 *model:* replica.   52 *Subscribed:* signed.   *impression:* i.e., of
the seal.   53 *changeling:* substitute (baby imp left when an infant was spirited away).   57 *did* . . .
employment: asked for it.   59 *insinuation:* intrusion.   61 *pass:* thrust.   *fell:* fierce.   63
stand . . . *upon:* become incumbent upon me now.   65 *election:* (the Danish king was so
chosen).   66 *angle:* fishing hook.   *proper:* very own.   67 *cozenage:* deception.

To quit° him with this arm? And is't not to be damned,
To let this canker of our nature° come
In further evil?

HORATIO.   It must be shortly known to him from England   70
What is the issue of the business there.

HAMLET.   It will be short, the interim is mine,
And a man's life's no more than to say "One."°
But I am very sorry good Horatio,   75
That to Laertes I forgot myself;
For by the image of my cause, I see
The portraiture of his;° I'll court his favours:
But sure the bravery° of his grief did put me
Into a towering passion.

HORATIO.   Peace, who comes here?
                                                                        80

Enter young OSRIC.

OSRIC.   Your lordship is right welcome back to Denmark.

HAMLET.   I humbly thank you sir. [*Aside to Horatio.*] Dost know this
water-fly?

HORATIO.   No my good lord.

HAMLET.   Thy state is the more gracious,° for 'tis a vice to know him: 85
he hath much land, and fertile: let a beast be lord of beasts,
and his crib shall stand at the king's mess;° 'tis a chough,°
but as I say, spacious in the possession of dirt.

OSRIC.   Sweet lord, if your lordship were at leisure, I should
impart a thing to you from his majesty.   90

HAMLET.   I will receive it sir, with all diligence of spirit; put your
bonnet° to his right use, 'tis for the head.

OSRIC.   I thank your lordship, it is very hot.

HAMLET.   No, believe me, 'tis very cold, the wind is northerly.

OSRIC.   It is indifferent° cold my lord indeed.   95

HAMLET.   But yet methinks it is very sultry and hot for my
complexion.°

OSRIC.   Exceedingly, my lord, it is very sultry, as 'twere, I cannot
tell how: but my lord, his majesty bade me signify to you
that a' has laid a great wager on your head. Sir, this is the   100
matter—

HAMLET.   [*Moves him to put on his hat.*] I beseech you remember—

OSRIC.   Nay good my lord, for mine ease,° in good faith. Sir, here
is newly come to court Laertes, believe me, an absolute
gentleman, full of most excellent differences,° of very soft   105
society, and great showing: indeed to speak feelingly of

---

68 *quit:* repay, requite.   69 *canker of our nature:* cancer of humanity.   74 *to say "One":* to
score one hit in fencing.   77–78 *by the image . . . his:* in the depiction of my situation, I see the
reflection of his.   79 *bravery:* ostentation.   85 *gracious:* favorable.   86–87 *let a beast . . .
mess:* An ass who owns enough property can eat with the king.   87 *chough:* chattering bird,
jackdaw.   92 *bonnet:* hat.   95 *indifferent:* reasonably.   97 *complexion:* temperament.   103 *for mine ease:* for my own comfort.   105 *differences:* accomplishments.

him, he is the card° or calendar of gentry: for you shall find
in him the continent of what part a gentleman would see.°

HAMLET. Sir, his definement° suffers no perdition° in you, though I   11•
know to divide him inventorially would dozy°
th'arithmetic of memory, and yet but yaw neither, in
respect of his quick sail,° but in the verity of extolment,° I
take him to be a soul of great article,° and his infusion° of
such dearth and rareness, as to make true diction of him,
his semblable° is his mirror, and who else would trace° him,   11
his umbrage,° nothing more.°

OSRIC. Your lordship speaks most infallibly of him.

HAMLET. The concernancy° sir? why do we wrap the gentleman in
our more rawer breath?°

OSRIC. Sir?   12

HORATIO. Is't not possible to understand in another tongue?° You
will do't sir, really.

HAMLET. What imports the nomination° of this gentleman?

OSRIC. Of Laertes?

HORATIO. His purse is empty already, all's golden words are spent.   1;

HAMLET. Of him, sir.

OSRIC. I know you are not ignorant—

HAMLET. I would you did sir, yet in faith if you did, it would not
much approve me.° Well, sir.

OSRIC. You are not ignorant of what excellence Laertes is—   1;

HAMLET. I dare not confess that, lest I should compare with him in
excellence, but to know a man well were to know himself.°

OSRIC. I mean sir for his weapon, but in the imputation° laid on
him by them in his meed,° he's unfellowed.°

HAMLET. What's his weapon?

OSRIC. Rapier and dagger.

HAMLET. That's two of his weapons—but well.

OSRIC. The king sir, hath wagered with him six Barbary horses,
against which he has impawned,° as I take it, six French
rapiers and poniards,° with their assigns,° as girdle, hangers,°   1
and so. Three of the carriages° in faith are very dear to

---

107 *card:* shipman's compass card.   108 *continent . . . see:* (continuing the marine metaphor)
(1) geographical continent (2) all the qualities a gentleman would look for.   109–116 *Sir . . .
more:* (Hamlet outdoes Osric in affected speech).   109 *definement:* description.   *perdition:*
loss.   110 *dozy:* dizzy.   111–112 *yaw . . . sail:* (1) moving in an unsteady course (as another
boat would do, trying to catch up with Laertes' "quick sail") (2) staggering to one trying to list his
accomplishments.   112 *in . . . extolment:* to praise him truthfully.   113 *article:* scope.   *infu-
sion:* essence.   114–116 *as to make . . . more:* to describe him truly I would have to employ his
mirror to depict his only equal—himself, and who would follow him is only a shadow.   115 *sem-
blable:* equal.   *trace:* (1) describe (2) follow.   116 *umbrage:* shadow.   118 *concernancy:* relevance.   119 *rawer breath:* crude speech.   121 *Is't not . . . tongue:* Cannot Osric understand
his own way of speaking when used by another?   123 *nomination:* naming.   128–129 *if you
did . . . me:* If you found me to be "not ignorant," it would prove little (as you are no judge of ignorance).   132 *to know . . . himself:* to know a man well, one must first know oneself.   133 *impu-
tation:* repute.   134 *meed:* worth.   *unfellowed:* unequaled.   139 *impawned:* staked.
140 *poniards:* daggers.   *assigns:* accessories.   *girdle, hangers:* belt, straps attached thereto,
from which swords were hung.   141 *carriages:* hangers.

fancy,° very responsive to the hilts, most delicate carriages,
and of very liberal conceit.°

HAMLET.   What call you the carriages?

HORATIO.   I knew you must be edified by the margent° ere you had
done.   145

OSRIC.   The carriages sir, are the hangers.

HAMLET.   The phrase would be more germane to the matter, if we
could carry a cannon by our sides: I would it might be
hangers till then, but on: six Barbary horses against six   150
French swords, their assigns, and three liberal-conceited
carriages—that's the French bet against the Danish. Why
is this all "impawned" as you call it?

OSRIC.   The king sir, hath laid sir, that in a dozen passes between
yourself and him, he shall not exceed you three hits°; he   155
hath laid on twelve for nine, and it would come to
immediate trial, if your lordship would vouchsafe the
answer.°

HAMLET.   How if I answer no?

OSRIC.   I mean my lord, the opposition of your person in trial.

HAMLET.   Sir, I will walk here in the hall; if it please his majesty, it is   160
the breathing time° of day with me; let the foils be brought,
the gentleman willing, and the king hold his purpose, I
will win for him an I can, if not, I will gain nothing but my
shame and the odd hits.

OSRIC.   Shall I re-deliver you° e'en so?   165

HAMLET.   To this effect sir, after what flourish your nature will.°

OSRIC.   I commend° my duty to your lordship.

HAMLET.   Yours, yours.
                                                                                          [*Exit OSRIC.*]
He does well to commend it himself, there are no tongues   170
else for's turn.°

HORATIO.   This lapwing° runs away with the shell on his head.

HAMLET.   A' did comply° sir, with his dug° before a' sucked it: thus
has he—and many more of the same bevy that I know the
drossy° age dotes on—only got the tune of the time, and   175
out of an habit of encounter,° a kind of yeasty collection,°
which carries them through and through the most fond
and winnowed° opinions; and do but blow them to their
trial, and bubbles are out.°

141–142 *dear to fancy:* rare in design.   143 *liberal conceit:* elaborate conception.   145 *margent:* marginal note.   154–155 *laid . . . three hits:* wagered that in twelve bouts Laertes must win
three more than Hamlet.   158 *answer:* acceptance of the challenge (Hamlet interprets as
"reply").   163 *breathing time:* exercise period.   166 *re-deliver you:* take back your answer.
167 *after . . . will:* embellished as you wish.   168 *commend:* offer (Hamlet interprets as
"praise").   170–171 *no tongues . . . turn:* no others who would.   172 *lapwing:* (reported to be
so precocious that it ran as soon as hatched).   173 *comply:* observe the formalities of courtesy.   *dug:* mother's breast.   175 *drossy:* frivolous.   176 *habit of encounter:* habitual association (with others as frivolous).   *yeasty collection:* frothy assortment of phrases.   177–178
fond and winnowed: trivial and considered.   178–179 *blow . . . out:* blow on them to test them
and they are gone.

Enter a LORD.

LORD.   My lord, his majesty commended him to you by young   18
Osric, who brings back to him that you attend him in
the hall. He sends to know if your pleasure hold to play
with Laertes, or that you will take longer time.

HAMLET.   I am constant to my purposes, they follow the king's
pleasure, if his fitness speaks,° mine is ready: now or   18
whensoever, provided I be so able as now.

LORD.   The king, and queen, and all are coming down.

HAMLET.   In happy time.

LORD.   The queen desires you to use some gentle entertainment°
to Laertes, before you fall to play.   19
                                                                            [*Exit* LORD.]

HAMLET.   She well instructs me.

HORATIO.   You will lose this wager, my lord.

HAMLET.   I do not think so, since we went into France, I have been in
continual practice, I shall win at the odds; but thou
wouldst not think how ill all's here about my heart: but it   1
is no matter.

HORATIO.   Nay good my lord—

HAMLET.   It is but a foolery, but it is such a kind of gaingiving° as
would perhaps trouble a woman.

HORATIO.   If your mind dislike any thing, obey it. I will forestall their   2
repair° hither, and say you are not fit.

HAMLET.   Not a whit, we defy augury;° there is a special providence
in the fall of a sparrow.° If it be now, 'tis not to come:
if it be not to come, it will be now; if it be not now,
yet it will come—the readiness is all. Since no man has   2
aught of what he leaves, what is't to leave betimes?° let
be.

A table prepared. Trumpets, Drums, and officers with cushions. Enter KING, QUEEN, *and all the*
state, [OSRIC], *foils daggers, and* LAERTES.

KING.   Come Hamlet, come and take this hand from me.
   [*Puts Laertes' hand into Hamlet's.*]

HAMLET.   Give me your pardon sir, I have done you wrong,
But pardon't as you are a gentleman.
This presence knows, and you must needs have heard,
How I am punished with a sore distraction.°
What I have done
That might your nature, honour, and exception°
Roughly awake, I here proclaim was madness:
Was't Hamlet wronged Laertes? never Hamlet.
If Hamlet from himself be ta'en away,

---

185 *his fitness speaks:* it agrees with his convenience.   189 *gentle entertainment:* friendly treatment.   198 *gaingiving:* misgiving.   201 *repair:* coming.   202 *augury:* omens.   202–203
special . . . sparrow: ("Are not two sparrows sold for a farthing? and one of them shall not fall on
the ground without your Father": Matthew 10:29).   206 *betimes:* early (before one's
time).   212 *sore distraction:* grievous madness.   214 *exception:* disapproval.

And when he's not himself, does wrong Laertes,
Then Hamlet does it not, Hamlet denies it:
Who does it then? his madness. If't be so,   220
Hamlet is of the faction that is wronged,
His madness is poor Hamlet's enemy.
Sir, in this audience,
Let my disclaiming from a purposed evil,
Free me so far in your most generous thoughts,   225
That I have shot my arrow o'er the house
And hurt my brother.°
LAERTES.   I am satisfied in nature,
Whose motive in this case should stir me most
To my revenge, but in my terms of honour
I stand aloof, and will no reconcilement,   230
Till by some elder masters of known honour
I have a voice and precedent° of peace
To keep my name ungored:° but till that time,
I do receive your offered love, like love,
And will not wrong it.
HAMLET.   I embrace it freely,   235
And will this brother's wager frankly° play.
Give us the foils: come on.
LAERTES.   Come, one for me.
HAMLET.   I'll be your foil° Laertes, in mine ignorance
Your skill shall like a star i'th' darkest night
Stick fiery off° indeed.   240
LAERTES.   You mock me sir.
HAMLET. No, by this hand.
KING.   Give them the foils young Osric. Cousin° Hamlet,
You know the wager.
HAMLET.   Very well my lord.
Your grace has laid the odds o'th'weaker side.
KING.   I do not fear it, I have seen you both,   245
But since he is bettered,° we have therefore odds.
LAERTES.   This is too heavy: let me see another.°
HAMLET.   This likes° me well, these foils have all a° length?
OSRIC.   Ay my good lord.   *Prepare to play.*
KING.   Set me the stoups° of wine upon that table: 250
If Hamlet give the first or second hit,
Or quit in answer of° the third exchange,
Let all the battlements their ordnance fire.

226–227 *That I have . . . brother:* (that it was accidental).   232 *voice and precedent:* opinion based
on precedent.   233 *name ungored:* reputation uninjured. Laertes says that he cannot accept
Hamlet's apology formally until he is assured that his acceptance will not harm his honor or
damage his reputation.   236 *frankly:* freely.   238 *foil:* (1) the blunted sword with which they
fence (2) leaf of metal set under a jewel to make it shine more brilliantly.   240 *Stick fiery off:*
show in shining contrast.   242 *Cousin:* kinsman.   246 *bettered:* either (a) judged to be better,
or (b) better trained.   247 *another:* (the unbated and poisoned sword).   248 *likes:*
pleases.   *all a:* all the same.   250 *stoups:* goblets.   252 *quit in answer of:* score a draw in.

The king shall drink to Hamlet's better breath,
And in the cup an union° shall he throw,
Richer than that which four successive kings
In Denmark's crown have worn: give me the cups,
And let the kettle° to the trumpet speak,
The trumpet to the cannoneer without,
The cannons to the heavens, the heaven to earth,
"Now the king drinks to Hamlet." Come begin.
And you the judges bear a wary eye.   *Trumpets the while.*
HAMLET.   Come on sir.
LAERTES.   Come my lord.   *They play.*
HAMLET.   One.
LAERTES.   No.
HAMLET.   Judgment.
OSRIC.   A hit, a very palpable hit.

Flourish. Drum, trumpets and shot. A piece° goes off.

LAERTES.   Well, again.
KING.   Stay, give me drink. Hamlet, this pearl is thine.
Here's to thy health: give him the cup.
HAMLET.   I'll play this bout first, set it by a while.
Come.   [*They play.*]
Another hit. What say you?
LAERTES.   A touch, a touch, I do confess't.
KING.   Our son shall win.
QUEEN.   He's fat° and scant of breath.
Here Hamlet, take my napkin,° rub thy brows.   [*She takes HAMLET'S cup.*]
The queen carouses° to thy fortune, Hamlet.
HAMLET.   Good madam.
KING.   Gertrude, do not drink.
QUEEN.   I will my lord, I pray you pardon me.
KING.   [*Aside.*] It is the poisoned cup, it is too late.
HAMLET.   I dare not drink yet madam: by and by.
QUEEN.   Come, let me wipe thy face.
LAERTES.   [*To the King.*] My lord, I'll hit him now.
KING.   I do not think't.
LAERTES.   [*Aside.*] And yet 'tis almost 'gainst my conscience.
HAMLET.   Come for the third Laertes, you do but dally,
I pray you pass° with your best violence,
I am afeard you make a wanton of me.°
LAERTES.   Say you so? Come on.   *Play.*
OSRIC.   Nothing neither way   [*They break off.*]
LAERTES.   Have at you now.°   [*Wounds Hamlet.*]

---

255 *union:* large pearl.   258 *kettle:* kettledrum.   264.1 S.D.: *piece:* i.e., a cannon.   270 *fat:* sweating (sweat was thought to be melted body fat).   271 *napkin:* handkerchief.   272 *carouses:* drinks.   281 *pass:* thrust.   282 *make a wanton of me:* are indulging me like a spoiled child.   285 *Have . . . now:* (the bout is over when Laertes attacks Hamlet and catches him off guard).

In scuffling they change rapiers.

KING.   Part them, they are incensed.   285
HAMLET.   Nay, come again.
                                                            [*The* QUEEN *falls.*]
OSRIC.   Look to the queen there, ho!

                                            [HAMLET *wounds* LAERTES.]

HORATIO.   They bleed on both side. How is it, my lord?
OSRIC.   How is't, Laertes?
LAERTES.   Why as a woodcock° to my own springe,° Osric,
   I am justly killed with mine own treachery.
HAMLET.   How does the queen?   290
KING.   She sounds° to see them bleed.
QUEEN.   No, no, the drink, the drink, O my dear Hamlet,
   The drink, the drink, I am poisoned:
HAMLET.   O villainy! ho! let the door be locked,   [*Dies.*]
   Treachery, seek it out!
LAERTES.   It is here Hamlet. Hamlet, thou art slain,   295
   No medicine in the world can do thee good,
   In thee there is not half an hour of life,
   The treacherous instrument is in thy hand,
   Unbated° and envenomed. The foul practice°   300
   Hath turned itself on me, lo, here I lie
   Never to rise again: thy mother's poisoned:
   I can no more: the king, the king's to blame.
HAMLET.   The point envenomed too:
   Then venom, to thy work.   *Hurts the* KING.   305
ALL.   Treason! treason!
KING.   O yet defend me friends, I am but hurt.°
HAMLET.   Here, thou incestuous, murderous, damnèd Dane,
   Drink off this potion: is thy union here?
   Follow my mother.   *King dies.*   310
LAERTES.   He is justly served,
   It is a poison tempered° by himself:
   Exchange forgiveness with me, noble Hamlet,
   Mine and my father's death come not upon thee,°
   Nor thine on me.   *Dies.*
HAMLET.   Heaven make thee free° of it, I follow thee.   315
   I am dead, Horatio; wretched queen, adieu.
   You that look pale, and tremble at this chance,
   That are but mutes,° or audience to this act,
   Had I but time, as this fell sergeant° Death
   Is strict in his arrest, O I could tell you—   320
   But let it be; Horatio, I am dead,

289 *woodcock:* snipe-like bird (believed to be foolish and therefore easily trapped).   *springe:* trap.   291 *sounds:* swoons.   300 *Unbated:* not blunted.   *practice:* plot.   307 *but hurt:* only wounded.   311 *tempered:* mixed.   313 *come . . . thee:* are not to be blamed on you.   315 *free:* guiltless.   318 *mutes:* actors without speaking parts.   319 *fell sergeant:* cruel sheriff's officer.

Thou livest, report me and my cause aright
      To the unsatisfied.°
HORATIO.   Never believe it;
      I am more an antique Roman° than a Dane:
      Here's yet some liquor left.
HAMLET.   As thou'rt a man,   32!
      Give me the cup, let go, by heaven I'll ha't.
      O God, Horatio, what a wounded name,
      Things standing thus unknown, shall live behind me.
      If thou didst ever hold me in thy heart,
      Absènt thee from felicity awhile,   33
      And in this harsh world draw thy breath in pain
      To tell my story.   *A march afar off, and shot within.*
                         What warlike noise is this?
OSRIC.   Young Fortinbras with conquest come from Poland,
      To th'ambassadors of England gives
      This warlike volley.
HAMLET.   O I die Horatio,   3℥
      The potent poison quite o'er-crows° my spirit,
      I cannot live to hear the news from England,
      But I do prophesy th'election° lights
      On Fortinbras, he has my dying voice,°   3·
      So tell him, with th'occurrents more and less°
      Which have solicited°—the rest is silence.   *Dies.*
HORATIO.   Now cracks a noble heart: good night sweet prince,
      And flights of angels sing thee to thy rest.
      Why does the drum come hither?

Enter FORTINBRAS *and English Ambassadors, with drum, colours, and attendants.*

FORTINBRAS.   Where is this sight?
HORATIO.   What is it you would see?   ℥
      If aught of woe, or wonder, cease your search.
FORTINBRAS.   This quarry cries on havoc.° O proud death,
      What feast is toward° in thine eternal cell,
      That thou so many princes at a shot
      So bloodily hast struck?
AMBASSADOR.   The sight is dismal,
      And our affairs from England come too late;
      The ears° are senseless that should give us hearing,
      To tell him his commandment is fulfilled,
      That Rosencrantz and Guildenstern are dead:
      Where should we have our thanks?
HORATIO.   Not from his mouth,
      Had it th'ability of life to thank you;

323 *unsatisfied:* uninformed.   324 *antique Roman:* ancient Roman (who considered suicide
honorable).   336 *o'er-crows:* overpowers, conquers.   338 *election:* (for king of Denmark).   339 *voice:* vote.   340 *occurrents more and less:* events great and small.   341 *solicited:*
incited me.   347 *quarry . . . havoc:* heap of dead bodies proclaims slaughter done here.
348 *toward:* in preparation.   352 *ears:* (of Claudius).

He never gave commandment for their death;
But since so jump° upon this bloody question,
You from the Polack wars, and you from England
Are here arrived, give order that these bodies
High on a stage be placèd to the view,   360
And let me speak to th'yet unknowing world
How these things came about; so shall you hear
Of carnal, bloody and unnatural acts,
Of accidental judgments, casual° slaughters,
Of deaths put on° by cunning and forced cause,°   365
And in this upshot, purposes mistook,
Fall'n on th'inventors' heads:° all this can I
Truly deliver.
FORTINBRAS.   Let us haste to hear it,
And call the noblest to the audience.
For me, with sorrow I embrace my fortune;   370
I have some rights of memory° in this kingdom,
Which now to claim my vantage° doth invite me.
HORATIO.   Of that I shall have also cause to speak,
And from his mouth whose voice will draw on more:°
But let this same° be presently performed,   375
Even while men's minds are wild,° lest more mischance
On° plots and errors happen.
FORTINBRAS.   Let four captains
Bear Hamlet like a soldier to the stage,
For he was likely, had he been put on,°
To have proved most royal; and for his passage,°   380
The soldiers' music and the rite of war
Speak loudly for him:
Take up the bodies, such a sight as this,
Becomes the field, but here shows much amiss.
Go bid the soldiers shoot.   385

Exeunt marching: after the which a peal of ordnance are shot off.

QUESTIONS

Act I

1. Discuss the various ways in which the first scene of *Hamlet* shows you that something is wrong in Denmark.

2. What impression does Claudius make in scene 2? Is he a rational man? A good administrator? A competent ruler? A loving husband and uncle?

3. What does Hamlet reveal about his own mental state in his first soliloquy?

358 *jump:* opportunely.   365 *casual:* unpremeditated.   366 *put on:* prompted by.   *forced cause:* being forced to act in self-defense.   367–368 *purposes . . . heads:* plots gone wrong and destroying their inventors.   372 *of memory:* remembered.   373 *vantage:* advantageous position.   375 *draw on more:* influence more (votes).   376 *this same:* this telling of the story.   377 *wild:* upset.   378 *On:* on top of.   380 *put on:* i.e., put on the throne.   381 *passage:* i.e., to the next world.

4. What attitude toward Ophelia's relationship with Hamlet do Laertes and Polonius share? What do they want Ophelia to do? Why?

5. What does the ghost tell Hamlet? What does the ghost want Hamlet to do and not to do? Why does Hamlet need proof that the ghost's words are true?

Act II

6. What does Polonius think is the cause of Hamlet's madness? What do Polonius's diagnosis and his handling of the situation show us about him?

7. What does Hamlet accuse himself of in the soliloquy that begins "O what a rogue and peasant slave am I" (II.2.524–580)? To what extent is his self-accusation justified?

Act III

8. How do you react to Hamlet's treatment of Ophelia in the first scene of Act III? What evidence might indicate that Hamlet knows that Claudius and Polonius are watching and listening to everything that occurs?

9. Hamlet sets up the performance of "The Murder of Gonzago"—the play-within-a-play—to test Claudius's guilt. What is the relationship between the events of this play-within-a-play and the events of *Hamlet*?

10. How does Claudius react to "The Murder of Gonzago"? What does this reaction tell Hamlet? Why do you suppose Claudius does not react to the dumb show presented at the beginning of the play-within-a-play?

11. What is Hamlet's reason for not killing Claudius at prayer?

12. How does Hamlet treat his mother during their confrontation in her closet? Is Hamlet's behavior overly nasty or justified? Why does the ghost reappear during this confrontation?

13. What crimes or sins does Hamlet accuse Gertrude of committing?

Act IV

14. Do you think Laertes's desire to avenge his father's murder is any more or less justified than Hamlet's desire?

15. How does Claudius plan to use Laertes's desire for revenge to manipulate him? To what extent does Laertes unwittingly allow himself to be used by Claudius?

Act V

16. The conversation between the two clowns (gravediggers) and between Hamlet and the first clown is seen as comic relief—a humorous episode designed to ease tension. Why is comic relief appropriate at this point?

17. How does this scene of comic relief reflect and broaden the play's themes?

18. Why does Hamlet describe Osric as a "water-fly"? How does Shakespeare use Osric's language and behavior to characterize him?

19. Discuss the lessons that Hamlet tells Horatio he has learned about life. How does this understanding change Hamlet? Why is it ironic?

20. How is Gertrude killed? Hamlet? Laertes? Claudius? Why does Hamlet insist that Horatio not commit suicide?

GENERAL QUESTIONS

1. Describe the character of Claudius. Do you consider him purely evil or merely a flawed human? Why? To what degree can you justify calling this play "The Tragedy of Claudius, King of Denmark"?

2. Characterize Horatio. Why does Hamlet admire and trust him? How is he different from Polonius or Rosencrantz and Guildenstern?

3. Describe Rosencrantz and Guildenstern. Are they round or flat? How does Claudius use them? Why do they cooperate with Claudius? How does Hamlet arrange their deaths? To what extent can this action be justified?

4. Evaluate Polonius's character. Is he a wise counselor? A fool? Sincere? Self-serving? Hypocritical? What are his motives? How is he like Rosencrantz and Guildenstern? How is his death like their deaths?

5. *Hamlet* is full of conflicts that oppose people to other people, to society, and to themselves. List all the conflicts you can find in the play. Decide which of these is the central conflict, and explain your choice.

6. What is the crisis of *Hamlet?* When does it occur? Whom does it affect? What is the catastrophe? The resolution?

7. In Act IV, Claudius notes that "sorrows come . . . in battalions." By the end of the play these sorrows include the deaths of Polonius, Rosencrantz, Guildenstern, Ophelia, Laertes, Gertrude, Claudius, and Hamlet. To what degree can Claudius be held responsible for all the sorrows of the play? Which sorrows are primarily Hamlet's responsibility?

8. Is *Hamlet* a tragedy of the state as well as a tragedy of the individual? In what condition is Denmark at the beginning of the play? Is the condition of Denmark better or worse at the end?

TRAGEDY FROM SHAKESPEARE TO ARTHUR MILLER

Shakespeare's tragedies feature people of elevated station, such as kings, princes, dukes, and generals. When Shakespeare uses characters of a lower status, he often treats them as comic, as we see in the gravediggers in *Hamlet* and the "mechanicals" in *A Midsummer Night's Dream.* This distinction, traditional in literature, was based on the realistic acceptance of the fact that the political and social order rested on the lives and trials of the powerful and the elite. Their intellectual, political, and emotional journeys held more dramatic interest than the lives and concerns of people in lower social orders. The magnitude of their deeds—and errors—was a primary element giving tragedy its larger dimensions. Yet it was to people of the lesser orders that the future belonged. They were to become the heirs of developing democratic beliefs in the dignity not just of the few, but of the many.

As long as monarchy and despotism remained the principal political systems in Europe, however, most writers of tragedy continued to draw their subject matter from the lives of the nobility. But one can see anticipations of things to come. In the eighteenth century, an interesting experiment in tragedy—and also therefore a play looking toward the future—was *The London Merchant*

(1731) by George Lillo (1693-1739), which forsook heroic characters altogether and instead dramatized the "history" of a young boy, apprentice George Barnwell, who makes an error in judgment that leads him to theft, murder, and finally the gallows. Lillo's aim was primarily moral and exemplary—the play was just as much a sermon as a drama. The impact of *The London Merchant* was not that the human spirit is elevated through adversity or that human beings should stand in awe before the tragic potential of their acts; rather it was that audiences should avoid mistakes such as those made by Lillo's gullible and misguided protagonist. It was clear that writers of tragedy would ultimately need to face the problem of reconciling the treatment of ordinary people with the tragic ideal of human dignity and nobility.

The late eighteenth century began a number of political revolutions that continued into and throughout much of the twentieth. Most of these depended on the belief that human beings are perfectible, but the political beliefs of modern democracy did not add to the tradition of tragedy until the mid-twentieth century with the emergence of the talent of Arthur Miller. Miller's tragedy is drawn from the modern world as we know it. His characters are common people—those who live in modern cities and walk, drive, or take the bus to work; those who go to modern schools, succeed or fail there, and then go on to make a living either in business for themselves or by working for others for their livelihoods. These are the people we know and see every day, and Miller bases their stories on the language and experiences that we all see, hear, or otherwise learn about. It is such people who in his eyes are worthy subjects for tragedy.

ARTHUR MILLER, *DEATH OF A SALESMAN*

Because of his large number of important dramas, Miller can justly be considered a dominant modern American playwright. He was born in New York in 1915 and educated at the University of Michigan, where he won a prize for a play he had written as an undergraduate. After graduation he wrote with the Federal Theater Project (part of President Roosevelt's New Deal). When that project lost funding, he began writing radio plays, a novel, and, during World War II, an account of military training. He then wrote a play, *The Man Who Had All the Luck*, which met little success on Broadway in 1944.

After the war he quickly catapulted into fame as a dramatist with *All My Sons* (1947), *Death of a Salesman* (1949), *An Enemy of the People* (1951, an adaptation of Ibsen's play), *The Crucible* (1953), and *A View from the Bridge* (1955). Many of these combine his interests in family relationships and sociopolitical issues. For instance, *All My Sons* explores the relationship between Joe Keller, an industrialist and war profiteer who had allowed faulty engines to be installed in U.S. military aircraft, and his son Chris, an army pilot returning home from World War II. The play investigates Joe Keller's guilt and his emerging realization that the airmen who died because of his defective engines were "all" his sons. Another of Miller's most important plays, *The Crucible*, reflects the suspicions and unfounded accusations rampant in the McCarthy era early in the 1950s.

Miller's later work includes the screenplay *The Misfits* (1961), the last film in which Marilyn Monroe, who was then his wife, starred, and the plays *After the Fall* (1964), *Incident at Vichy* (1964), *The Price* (1968), *Fame* (1970), *The Reason Why* (1972), *The Creation of the World and Other Business* (1972), *The Archbishop's Ceiling* (1976), *The American Clock* (1980), *Playing for Time* (1985), *I Can't Remember Anything* (1987), *Clara* (1987), a filmscript titled *Everybody Wins* (1990), and *Broken Glass* (1994). In 1996 *The Crucible* was revised and presented as a successful film with Daniel Day-Lewis and Winona Ryder. In 2000 his newest play, *The Ride Down Mount Morgan*, was performed to acclaim on Broadway.

Death of a Salesman, which opened on Broadway on February 10, 1949, is similar to both *Oedipus the King* and the traditional *well-made play* (see p. 1790). Miller's play dramatizes the end of a longer story. The stage action in the present (in Acts I and II) covers about twenty-four hours, from Monday evening to Tuesday evening. The story, however, covers much of Willy Loman's life, and his memories of past events constantly impose themselves on the present. One of the play's central conflicts stems from a secret known only to Willy and his son Biff, a secret that is concealed until near the end. Such secrets, having a profound significance in the action, are a feature of the traditional well-made play.

In writing a tragedy about the struggle and failure of Willy Loman, Miller effectively redefines the nature of tragedy in our modern period of democracy and belief in the significance of common people. In a *New York Times* essay published shortly after the Broadway opening, Miller argues that "the common man is as apt a subject for tragedy in its highest sense as kings were."[14] He asserts that tragedy springs from the individual's quest for a proper place in the world and from his or her readiness "to lay down . . . life, if need be, to secure . . . [a] sense of personal dignity." Willy is flawed: He is self-deluded, deceitful, unfaithful, and weak; he denies the truth when he is confronted with it. But Miller links Willy's defects with the quest for dignity: "the flaw or crack in the character is really . . . his inherent unwillingness to remain passive in the face of what he conceives to be a challenge to his dignity, his image of his rightful status." It is with great justice that Linda asserts to her sons that attention must be paid to such a person. In this sense, Miller meets the challenge of creating a modern character worthy of tragic elevation.

Accordingly, *Death of a Salesman* is developed around the character of Willy Loman. At first, Miller wanted to call the play "The Inside of His Head," and his initial vision was of "an enormous face the height of the proscenium arch that would appear and open up, and we would see the inside of a man's

---

[14] "Tragedy and the Common Man," *New York Times*, February 27, 1949, sec. 2, p. 1.

head."[15] The play contains two types of time and action: real and remembered. Present events are enacted and described realistically, but such action often triggers Willy's memory of the past, which is always with him, shaping the way he reacts to the present. Sometimes past events can even occur simultaneously with present action, as in Act I when Willy speaks with his dead brother, whom he is remembering, at the same time as he is playing cards with Charley. At other times, past events take over the play completely, although Willy continues to exist in the present.

Like the acting of past events, the setting of *Death of a Salesman* is symbolic and nonrealistic (see p. 1657). The play demonstrates the degree to which Miller relies on developments in the physical theater that took place between Shakespeare's day and our own. Miller adapts both the concepts of the picture-frame proscenium stage and the apron stage. Thus the Loman house—set on the proscenium stage—is a framework with three rooms (or acting areas) on three levels: the kitchen, the sons' bedroom, and Willy's bedroom. The forestage and apron are used for all scenes away from the house and for "memory" scenes. The house is hemmed in by apartment houses and lit with an "angry glow of orange," thus suggesting that Willy's present existence is urbanized and claustrophobic. When memory takes over, however, the apartment houses disappear (a technique of lighting), and the orange glow gives way to pastoral colors and the shadows of leaves—the setting for dreams about past times and hopes.

Death of a Salesman is very much about dreams, illusions, and self-deception. Dreams pervade Willy's thoughts, conversation, family, and house, and the staging allows fluid transitions between current action and memory. Willy's central illusion is the American dream of success and wealth through the merchandizing of the self. This dream is embodied in a series of smaller dreams (illusions, lies) that Willy has created out of hope and then tried to bequeath to his sons. But reality destroys these dreams. Willy's expectation of a New York City job and a salary, for example, founders on the reality of his disastrous encounter with his preoccupied and unsympathetic boss. Only Linda escapes the tyranny of dreams. While she serves and supports Willy completely, she remains firmly planted in the reality of house payments, insurance premiums, and Willy's need for dignity and attention as his world falls apart.

At the end of the play, we are left with a number of questions about the degree to which Willy recognizes and understands the illusory nature of his dreams and his self-image. He does understand that he has run out of lies and has nothing left to sell. He also understands—according to Miller—his alienation from true values:

> Had Willy been unaware of his separation from values that endure he would have died contentedly while polishing his car. . . . But he was agonized by his awareness of being in a false position, so constantly haunted by the

---

[15] Arthur Miller, "Introduction to the Collected Plays," *Arthur Miller's Collected Plays* (New York: Viking, 1957), p. 23.

Stage set for *Death of a Salesman*. Billy Rose Theater Collection, The New York Public Library at Lincoln Center, Astor, Lenox and Tilden Foundation.

hollowness of all he had placed his faith in, so aware, in short, that he must somehow be filled with his spirit or fly apart, that he staked his life on the ultimate assertion.[16]

Yet at the end of the play, Willy is still in the grip of delusion. He imagines that his insurance money will make Biff "magnificent," and he dreams that his funeral will be massive. Both visions are delusions, for Biff has already abandoned the business world, and the funeral is attended by only five people. In the Requiem scene, Biff states that Willy's dreams were illusory: "He had all the wrong dreams. All, all wrong" (speech 16). Only the character ironically named Happy retains his own unreconstructed version of Willy's dream: "He had a good dream. It's the only dream you can have—to come out number-one man" (speech 25). Miller leaves it to the audience to evaluate the truth and validity of each character's assertions.

ARTHUR MILLER   (b. 1915)

Death of a Salesman —————————————————— *1949*

pick the scene
— place takes place
apartment, condo,
house,
florida,
nj.

CHARACTERS

 Willy Loman
 Linda, *his wife*

when stop in the
etc. play

[16] *Ibid.*, pp. 34–35.

Biff ⎫
Happy ⎬ *his sons*
Uncle Ben
Charley
Bernard
The Woman
Howard Wagner
Jenny
Stanley
Miss Forsythe
Letta

The action takes place in WILLY LOMAN'*s house and yard and in various places he visits in the New York and Boston of today.*

ACT 1

A melody is heard, played upon a flute. It is small and fine, telling of grass and trees and the horizon. The curtain rises.

Before us is the Salesman's house. We are aware of towering, angular shapes behind it, surrounding it on all sides. Only the blue light of the sky falls upon the house and forestage; the surrounding area shows an angry glow of orange. As more light appears, we see a solid vault of apartment houses around the small, fragile-seeming home. An air of the dream clings to the place, a dream rising out of reality. The kitchen at center seems actual enough, for there is a kitchen table with three chairs, and a refrigerator. But no other fixtures are seen. At the back of the kitchen there is a draped entrance, which leads to the living-room. To the right of the kitchen, on a level raised two feet, is a bedroom furnished only with a brass bedstead and a straight chair. On a shelf over the bed a silver athletic trophy stands. A window opens onto the apartment house at the side.

Behind the kitchen, on a level raised six and a half feet, is the boys' bedroom, at present barely visible. Two beds are dimly seen, and at the back of the room a dormer window. (This bedroom is above the unseen living-room.) At the left a stairway curves up to it from the kitchen.

The entire setting is wholly or, in some places, partially transparent. The roof-line of the house is one-dimensional; under and over it we see the apartment buildings. Before the house lies an apron, curving beyond the forestage into the orchestra. This forward area serves as the back yard as well as the locale of all WILLY'*s imaginings and of his city scenes. Whenever the action is in the present the actors observe the imaginary wall-lines, entering the house only through its door at the left. But in the scenes of the past these boundaries are broken, and characters enter or leave a room by stepping "through" a wall onto the forestage.*

[*From the right,* WILLY LOMAN, *The Salesman, enters, carrying two large sample cases. The flute plays on. He hears but is not aware of it. He is past sixty years of age, dressed quietly. Even as he crosses the stage to the doorway of the house, his exhaustion is apparent. He unlocks the door, comes into the kitchen, and thankfully lets his burden down, feeling the soreness of his palms. A word-sigh escapes his lips—it might be "Oh, boy, oh, boy." He closes the door, then carries his cases out into the living-room, through the draped kitchen doorway.*]

[LINDA, *his wife, has stirred in her bed at the right. She gets out and puts on a robe, listening. Most often jovial, she has developed an iron repression of her exceptions to* WILLY'*s behavior—she more than loves him, she admires him, as though his mercurial nature, his temper, his massive dreams and little cruelties, served her only as sharp reminders of the turbulent longings within him, longings which she shares but lacks the temperament to utter and follow to their end.*]

LINDA. [*hearing* WILLY *outside the bedroom, calls with some trepidation*] Willy!

WILLY. It's all right. I came back.

LINDA. Why? What happened? [*slight pause*] Did something happen, Willy?

WILLY. No, nothing happened.

LINDA. You didn't smash the car, did you?   5

WILLY. [*with casual irritation*] I said nothing happened. Didn't you hear me?

LINDA. Don't you feel well?

WILLY. I'm tired to the death. [*The flute has faded away. He sits on the bed beside her, a little numb.*] I couldn't make it. I just couldn't make it, Linda.

LINDA. [*very carefully, delicately*] Where were you all day? You look terrible.

WILLY. I got as far as a little above Yonkers.° I stopped for a cup of coffee. Maybe   10
it was the coffee.

LINDA. What?

WILLY. [*after a pause*] I suddenly couldn't drive any more. The car kept going off onto the shoulder, y'know?

LINDA. [*helpfully*] Oh. Maybe it was the steering again. I don't think Angelo knows the Studebaker.

WILLY. No, it's me, it's me. Suddenly I realize I'm goin' sixty miles an hour and I don't remember the last five minutes. I'm—I can't seem to—keep my mind to it.

LINDA. Maybe it's your glasses. You never went for your new glasses.   15

WILLY. No, I see everything. I came back ten miles an hour. It took me nearly four hours from Yonkers.

LINDA. [*resigned*] Well, you'll just have to take a rest, Willy, you can't continue this way.

WILLY. I just got back from Florida.

LINDA. But you didn't rest your mind. Your mind is overactive, and the mind is what counts, dear.

WILLY. I'll start out in the morning. Maybe I'll feel better in the morning. [*She is*   20
taking off his shoes.] These goddam arch supports are killing me.

LINDA. Take an aspirin. Should I get you an aspirin? It'll soothe you.

WILLY. [*with wonder*] I was driving along, you understand? And I was fine. I was even observing the scenery. You can imagine, me looking at scenery, on the road every week of my life. But it's so beautiful up there, Linda, the trees are so thick, and the sun is warm. I opened the windshield and just let the warm air bathe over me. And then all of a sudden I'm goin' off the road! I'm tellin' ya, I absolutely forgot I was driving. If I'd've gone the other way over the white line I might've killed somebody. So I went on again—and five minutes later I'm dreamin' again, and I nearly— [*He presses two fingers against his eyes.*] I have such thoughts, I have such strange thoughts.

LINDA. Willy, dear. Talk to them again. There's no reason why you can't work in New York.

WILLY. They don't need me in New York. I'm the New England man. I'm vital in New England.

LINDA. But you're sixty years old. They can't expect you to keep traveling every   25
week.

---

10 *Yonkers:* Yonkers is immediately north of New York City, touching the city limits of the Bronx. Because Willy lives in Brooklyn, to the south, he got no more than thirty or thirty-five miles from home.

WILLY.   I'll have to send a wire to Portland. I'm supposed to see Brown and
Morrison tomorrow morning at ten o'clock to show the line. Goddammit, I could sell
them! [*He starts putting on his jacket.*]

LINDA.   [*taking the jacket from him*] Why don't you go down to the place tomorrow
and tell Howard you've simply got to work in New York? You're too accommodating, dear.

WILLY.   If old man Wagner was alive I'd a been in charge of New York now! That
man was a prince, he was a masterful man. But that boy of his, that Howard, he don't
appreciate. When I went north the first time, the Wagner Company didn't know where
New England was!

LINDA.   Why don't you tell those things to Howard, dear?

WILLY.   [*encouraged*] I will, I definitely will. Is there any cheese?   30

LINDA.   I'll make you a sandwich.

WILLY.   No, go to sleep. I'll take some milk. I'll be up right away. The boys in?

LINDA.   They're sleeping. Happy took Biff on a date tonight.

WILLY.   [*interested*] That so?

LINDA.   It was so nice to see them shaving together, one behind the other,   35
in the bathroom. And going out together. You notice? The whole house smells of shaving lotion.

WILLY.   Figure it out. Work a lifetime to pay off a house. You finally own it, and
there's nobody to live in it.

LINDA.   Well, dear, life is a casting off. It's always that way.

WILLY.   No, no, some people—some people accomplish something. Did Biff say
anything after I went this morning?

LINDA.   You shouldn't have criticized him, Willy, especially after he just got off
the train. You mustn't lose your temper with him.

WILLY.   When the hell did I lose my temper? I simply asked him if he was   40
making any money. Is that a criticism?

LINDA.   But, dear, how could he make any money?

WILLY.   [*worried and angered*] There's such an undercurrent in him. He became a
moody man. Did he apologize when I left this morning?

LINDA.   He was crestfallen, Willy. You know how he admires you. I think if he
finds himself, then you'll both be happier and not fight any more.

WILLY.   How can he find himself on a farm? Is that a life? A farmhand? In the
beginning, when he was young, I thought, well, a young man, it's good for him to tramp
around, take a lot of different jobs. But it's more than ten years now and he has yet to
make thirty-five dollars a week!

LINDA.   He's finding himself, Willy.

WILLY.   Not finding yourself at the age of thirty-four is a disgrace!

LINDA.   Shh!

WILLY.   The trouble is he's lazy, goddammit!

LINDA.   Willy, please!

WILLY.   Biff is a lazy bum!

LINDA.   They're sleeping. Get something to eat. Go on down.

WILLY.   Why did he come home? I would like to know what brought him home.

LINDA.   I don't know. I think he's still lost, Willy. I think he's very lost.

WILLY.   Biff Loman is lost. In the greatest country in the world a young man with
such—personal attractiveness, gets lost. And such a hard worker. There's one thing
about Biff—he's not lazy.

LINDA.   Never.

WILLY.   [*with pity and resolve*] I'll see him in the morning; I'll have a nice talk with him. I'll get him a job selling. He could be big in no time. My God! Remember how they used to follow him around in high school? When he smiled at one of them their faces lit up. When he walked down the street . . . [*He loses himself in reminiscences.*]

LINDA.   [*trying to bring him out of it*] Willy, dear, I got a new kind of American-type cheese today. It's whipped.

WILLY.   Why do you get American when I like Swiss?

LINDA.   I just thought you'd like a change—

WILLY.   I don't want a change! I want Swiss cheese. Why am I always being   60
contradicted?

LINDA.   [*with a covering laugh*] I thought it would be a surprise.

WILLY.   Why don't you open a window in here, for God's sake?

LINDA.   [*with infinite patience*] They're all open dear.

WILLY.   The way they boxed us in here. Bricks and windows, windows and bricks.

LINDA.   We should've bought the land next door.   65

WILLY.   The street is lined with cars. There's not a breath of fresh air in the neighborhood. The grass don't grow any more, you can't raise a carrot in the back yard. They should've had a law against apartment houses. Remember those two beautiful elm trees out there? When I and Biff hung the swing between them?

LINDA.   Yeah, like being a million miles from the city.

WILLY.   They should've arrested the builder for cutting those down. They massacred the neighborhood. [*lost*] More and more I think of those days, Linda. This time of year it was lilac and wisteria. And then the peonies would come out, and the daffodils. What fragrance in this room!

LINDA.   Well, after all, people had to move somewhere.

WILLY.   No, there's more people now.   70

LINDA.   I don't think there's more people. I think—

WILLY.   There's more people! That's what's ruining this country! Population is getting out of control. The competition is maddening! Smell the stink from that apartment house! And another one on the other side . . . How can they whip cheese?

[*On* WILLY's *last line,* BIFF *and* HAPPY *raise themselves up in their beds, listening.*]

LINDA.   Go down, try it. And be quiet.

WILLY.   [*turning to* LINDA, *guiltily*] You're not worried about me, are you, sweetheart?

BIFF.   What's the matter?   75

HAPPY.   Listen!

LINDA.   You've got too much on the ball to worry about.

WILLY.   You're my foundation and my support, Linda.

LINDA.   Just try to relax, dear. You make mountains out of molehills.

WILLY.   I won't fight with him any more. If he wants to go back to Texas, let   80
him go.

LINDA.   He'll find his way.

WILLY.   Sure. Certain men just don't get started till later in life. Like Thomas Edison, I think. Or B. F. Goodrich.° One of them was deaf. [*He starts for the bedroom doorway.*] I'll put my money on Biff.

---

82 *Thomas Edison, B. F. Goodrich:* Thomas A. Edison (1847–1931) was an American inventor who developed the electric light and the phonograph. Benjamin Franklin Goodrich (1841–1888) founded the B. F. Goodrich Rubber and Tire Company. It was Edison who suffered from deafness.

LINDA.   And Willy—if it's warm Sunday we'll drive in the country. And we'll open the windshield, and take lunch.

WILLY.   No, the windshields don't open on the new cars.

LINDA.   But you opened it today.

WILLY.   Me? I didn't. [*He stops.*] Now isn't that peculiar! Isn't that a remarkable— [*He breaks off in amazement and fright as the flute is heard distantly.*]

LINDA.   What, darling?

WILLY.   That is the most remarkable thing.

LINDA.   What, dear?

WILLY.   I was thinking of the Chevvy. [*slight pause*] Nineteen twenty-eight . . . when I had that red Chevvy— [*Breaks off.*] That funny? I coulda sworn I was driving that Chevvy today.

LINDA.   Well, that's nothing. Something must've reminded you.

WILLY.   Remarkable. Ts. Remember those days? The way Biff used to simonize that car? The dealer refused to believe there was eighty thousand miles on it. [*He shakes his head.*] Heh! [*to Linda*] Close your eyes, I'll be right up. [*He walks out of the bedroom.*]

HAPPY.   [*to BIFF*] Jesus, maybe he smashed up the car again!

LINDA.   [*calling after WILLY*] Be careful on the stairs, dear! The cheese is on the middle shelf! [*She turns, goes over to the bed, takes his jacket, and goes out of the bedroom.*]

[*Light has risen on the boys' room. Unseen, WILLY is heard talking to himself, "Eighty thousand miles," and a little laugh. BIFF gets out of bed, comes downstage a bit, and stands attentively. BIFF is two years older than his brother HAPPY, well built, but in these days bears a worn air and seems less self-assured. He has succeeded less, and his dreams are stronger and less acceptable than HAPPY's. HAPPY is tall, powerfully made. Sexuality is like a visible color on him, or a scent that many women have discovered. He, like his brother, is lost, but in a different way, for he has never allowed himself to turn his face toward defeat and is thus more confused and hard-skinned, although seemingly more content.*]

HAPPY.   [*getting out of bed*] He's going to get his license taken away if he keeps that up. I'm getting nervous about him, y'know, Biff?

BIFF.   His eyes are going.

HAPPY.   No, I've driven with him. He sees all right. He just doesn't keep his mind on it. I drove into the city with him last week. He stops at a green light and then it turns red and he goes. [*He laughs.*]

BIFF.   Maybe he's color-blind.

HAPPY.   Pop? Why he's got the finest eye for color in the business. You know that.

BIFF.   [*sitting down on his bed*] I'm going to sleep.

HAPPY.   You're not still sour on Dad, are you, Biff?

BIFF.   He's all right, I guess.

WILLY.   [*underneath them, in the living-room*] Yes, sir, eighty thousand miles—eighty-two thousand!

BIFF.   You smoking?

HAPPY.   [*holding out a pack of cigarettes*] Want one?

BIFF.   [*taking a cigarette*] I can never sleep when I smell it.

WILLY.   What a simonizing job, heh!

HAPPY.   [*with deep sentiment*] Funny, Biff y'know? Us sleeping in here again? The old beds. [*He pats his bed affectionately.*] All the talk that went across those two beds, huh? Our whole lives.

BIFF.   Yeah. Lotta dreams and plans.

HAPPY. [*with a deep and masculine laugh*] About five hundred women would like to 110
know what was said in this room.

[*They share a soft laugh.*]

BIFF. Remember that big Betsy something—what the hell was her name—over
on Bushwick Avenue?

HAPPY. [*combing his hair*] With the collie dog!

BIFF. That's the one. I got you in there, remember?

HAPPY. Yeah, that was my first time—I think. Boy, there was a pig! [*They laugh,
almost crudely.*] You taught me everything I know about women. Don't forget that.

BIFF. I bet you forgot how bashful you used to be. Especially with girls. 115

HAPPY. Oh, I still am, Biff.

BIFF. Oh, go on.

HAPPY. I just control it, that's all. I think I got less bashful and you got more so.
What happened, Biff? Where's the old humor, the old confidence? [*He shakes
BIFF's knee. BIFF gets up and moves restlessly about the room.*] What's the matter?

BIFF. Why does Dad mock me all the time?

HAPPY. He's not mocking you, he— 120

BIFF. Everything I say there's a twist of mockery on his face. I can't get near him.

HAPPY. He just wants you to make good, that's all. I wanted to talk to you about
Dad for a long time, Biff. Something's—happening to him. He—talks to himself.

BIFF. I noticed that this morning. But he always mumbled.

HAPPY. But not so noticeable. It got so embarrassing I sent him to Florida. And
you know something? Most of the time he's talking to you.

BIFF. What's he say about me? 125

HAPPY. I can't make it out.

BIFF. What's he say about me?

HAPPY. I think the fact that you're not settled, that you're still kind of up in the
air . . .

BIFF. There's one or two other things depressing him, Happy.

HAPPY. What do you mean?

BIFF. Never mind. Just don't lay it all to me. 130

HAPPY. But I think if you just got started—I mean—is there any future for you
out there?

BIFF. I tell ya, Hap, I don't know what the future is. I don't know—what I'm supposed to want.

HAPPY. What do you mean?

BIFF. Well, I spent six or seven years after high school trying to work myself up. 135
Shipping clerk, salesman, business of one kind or another. And it's a measly manner of
existence. To get on that subway on the hot mornings in summer. To devote your whole
life to keeping stock, or making phone calls, or selling or buying. To suffer fifty weeks of
the year for the sake of a two-week vacation, when all you really desire is to be outdoors,
with your shirt off. And always to have to get ahead of the next fella. And still—that's
how you build a future.

HAPPY. Well, you really enjoy it on a farm? Are you content out there?

BIFF. [*with rising agitation*] Hap, I've had twenty or thirty different kinds of jobs
since I left home before the war, and it always turns out the same. I just realized it lately.
In Nebraska when I herded cattle, and the Dakotas, and Arizona, and now in Texas. It's
why I came home now, I guess, because I realized it. This farm I work on, it's spring

there now, see? And they've got about fifteen new colts. There's nothing more inspiring or—beautiful than the sight of a mare and a new colt. And it's cool there now, see? Texas is cool now, and it's spring. And whenever spring comes to where I am, I suddenly get the feeling, my God, I'm not gettin' anywhere! What the hell am I doing, playing around with horses, twenty-eight dollars a week! I'm thirty-four years old, I oughta be makin' my future. That's when I come running home. And now, I get here, and I don't know what to do with myself. [*after a pause*] I've always made a point of not wasting my life, and everytime I come back here I know that all I've done is to waste my life.

HAPPY.   You're a poet, you know that, Biff? You're a—you're an idealist!

BIFF.   No, I'm mixed up very bad. Maybe I oughta get married. Maybe I oughta get stuck into something. Maybe that's my trouble. I'm like a boy. I'm not married, I'm not in business, I just—I'm like a boy. Are you content, Hap? You're a success, aren't you? Are you content?

HAPPY.   Hell, no!

BIFF.   Why? You're making money, aren't you?

HAPPY.   [*moving about with energy, expressiveness*] All I can do now is wait for the merchandise manager to die. And suppose I get to be merchandise manager? He's a good friend of mine, and he just built a terrific estate on Long Island. And he lived there about two months and sold it, and now he's building another one. He can't enjoy it once it's finished. And I know that's just what I would do. I don't know what the hell I'm workin' for. Sometimes I sit in my apartment—all alone. And I think of the rent I'm paying. And it's crazy. But then, it's what I always wanted. My own apartment, a car, and plenty of women. And still, goddammit, I'm lonely.

BIFF.   [*with enthusiasm*] Listen, why don't you come out West with me?

HAPPY.   You and I, heh?

BIFF.   Sure, maybe we could buy a ranch. Raise cattle, use our muscles. Men built like we are should be working out in the open.

HAPPY.   [*avidly*] The Loman Brothers, heh?

BIFF.   [*with vast affection*] Sure, we'd be known all over the counties!

HAPPY.   [*enthralled*] That's what I dream about, Biff. Sometimes I want to just rip my clothes off in the middle of the store and outbox that goddam merchandise manager. I mean I can outbox, outrun, and outlift anybody in that store, and I have to take orders from those common, petty sons-of-bitches till I can't stand it any more.

BIFF.   I'm tellin' you, kid, if you were with me I'd be happy out there.

HAPPY.   [*enthused*] See, Biff, everybody around me is so false that I'm constantly lowering my ideals . . .

BIFF.   Baby, together we'd stand up for one another, we'd have someone to trust.

HAPPY.   If I were around you—

BIFF.   Hap, the trouble is we weren't brought up to grub for money. I don't know how to do it.

HAPPY.   Neither can I!

BIFF.   Then let's go!

HAPPY.   The only thing is—what can you make out there?

BIFF.   But look at your friend. Builds an estate and then hasn't the peace of mind to live in it.

HAPPY.   Yeah, but when he walks into the store the waves part in front of him. That's fifty-two thousand dollars a year coming through the revolving door, and I got more in my pinky finger than he's got in his head.

BIFF.   Yeah, but you just said—

HAPPY.   I gotta show some of those pompous, self-important executives over   160
there that Hap Loman can make the grade. I want to walk into the store the way he
walks in. Then I'll go with you, Biff. We'll be together yet, I swear. But take those two we
had tonight. Now weren't they gorgeous creatures?
BIFF.   Yeah, yeah, most gorgeous I've had in years.
HAPPY.   I get that any time I want, Biff. Whenever I feel disgusted. The only trou-
ble is, it gets like bowling or something. I just keep knockin' them over and it doesn't
mean anything. You still run around a lot?
BIFF.   Naa. I'd like to find a girl—steady, somebody with substance.
HAPPY.   That's what I long for.
BIFF.   Go on! You'd never come home.   165
HAPPY.   I would! Somebody with character, with resistance! Like Mom, y'know?
You're gonna call me a bastard when I tell you this. That girl Charlotte I was with tonight
is engaged to be married in five weeks. [*He tries on his new hat.*]
BIFF.   No kiddin'!
HAPPY.   Sure, the guy's in line for the vice-presidency of the store. I don't know
what gets into me, maybe I just have an overdeveloped sense of competition or some-
thing, but I went and ruined her, and furthermore I can't get rid of her. And he's the
third executive I've done that to. Isn't that a crummy characteristic? And to top it all, I
go to their weddings! [*Indignantly, but laughing*] Like I'm not supposed to take bribes.
Manufacturers offer me a hundred-dollar bill now and then to throw an order their way.
You know how honest I am, but it's like this girl, see. I hate myself for it. Because I don't
want the girl, and, still, I take it and—I love it!
BIFF.   Let's go to sleep.
HAPPY.   I guess we didn't settle anything, heh?   170
BIFF.   I just got one idea that I think I'm going to try.
HAPPY.   What's that?
BIFF.   Remember Bill Oliver?
HAPPY.   Sure, Oliver is very big now. You want to work for him again?
BIFF.   No, but when I quit he said something to me. He put his arm on my   175
shoulder and he said, "Biff, if you ever need anything, come to me."
HAPPY.   I remember that. That sounds good.
BIFF.   I think I'll go to see him. If I could get ten thousand or even seven or eight
thousand dollars I could buy a beautiful ranch.
HAPPY.   I bet he'd back you. 'Cause he thought highly of you, Biff. I mean, they
all do. You're well liked, Biff. That's why I say to come back here, and we both have the
apartment. And I'm tellin' you, Biff, any babe you want . . .
BIFF.   No, with a ranch I could do the work I like and still be something. I just
wonder though. I wonder if Oliver still thinks I stole that carton of basketballs.
HAPPY.   Oh, he probably forgot that long ago. It's almost ten years. You're too   180
sensitive. Anyway, he didn't really fire you.
BIFF.   Well, I think he was going to. I think that's why I quit. I was never sure
whether he knew or not. I know he thought the world of me, though. I was the only one
he'd let lock up the place.
WILLY.   [*below*] You gonna wash the engine, Biff?
HAPPY.   Shh!

[*BIFF looks at HAPPY, who is gazing down, listening. WILLY is mumbling in the parlor.*]

HAPPY.   You hear that?

[*They listen. WILLY laughs warmly.*]

BIFF.   [*growing angry*] Doesn't he know Mom can hear that?
WILLY.   Don't get your sweater dirty, Biff!

[*A look of pain crosses BIFF's face.*]

HAPPY.   Isn't that terrible! Don't leave again, will you? You'll find a job here. You gotta stick around. I don't know what to do about him, it's getting embarrassing.
WILLY.   What a simonizing job!
BIFF.   Mom's hearing that!
WILLY.   No kiddin', Biff, you got a date? Wonderful!
HAPPY.   Go on to sleep. But talk to him in the morning, will you?
BIFF.   [*reluctantly getting into bed*] With her in the house. Brother!
HAPPY.   [*getting into bed*] I wish you'd have a good talk with him.

[*The light on their room begins to fade.*]

BIFF.   [*to himself in bed*] That selfish, stupid . . .
HAPPY.   Sh . . . Sleep, Biff.

[*Their light is out. Well before they have finished speaking, WILLY's form is dimly seen below in the darkened kitchen. He opens the refrigerator, searches in there, and takes out a bottle of milk. The apartment houses are fading out, and the entire house and surroundings become covered with leaves. Music insinuates itself as the leaves appear.*]

WILLY.   Just wanna be careful with those girls, Biff, that's all. Don't make any promises. No promises of any kind. Because a girl, y'know, they always believe what you tell 'em, and you're very young, Biff, you're too young to be talking seriously to girls.

[*Light rises on the kitchen. WILLY, talking, shuts the refrigerator door and comes downstage to the kitchen table. He pours milk into a glass. He is totally immersed in himself, smiling faintly.*]

WILLY.   Too young entirely, Biff. You want to watch your schooling first. Then when you're all set, there'll be plenty of girls for a boy like you. [*He smiles broadly at a kitchen chair.*] That so? The girls pay for you? [*He laughs.*] Boy, you must really be makin' a hit.

[*WILLY is gradually addressing—physically—a point offstage, speaking through the wall of the kitchen, and his voice has been rising in volume to that of a normal conversation.*]

WILLY.   I been wondering why you polish the car so careful. Ha! Don't leave the hubcaps, boys. Get the chamois to the hubcaps. Happy, use newspaper on the windows, it's the easiest thing. Show him how to do it, Biff! You see, Happy? Pad it up, use it like a pad. That's it, that's it, good work. You're doin' all right, Hap. [*He pauses, then nods in approbation for a few seconds, then looks upward.*] Biff, first thing we gotta do when we get time is clip that big branch over the house. Afraid it's gonna fall in a storm and hit the roof. Tell you what. We get a rope and sling her around, and then we climb up there with a couple of saws and take her down. Soon as you finish the car, boys, I wanna see ya. I got a surprise for you, boys.
BIFF.   [*offstage*] Whatta ya got, Dad?
WILLY.   No, you finish first. Never leave a job till you're finished—remember that. [*looking toward the "big trees"*] Biff, up in Albany I saw a beautiful hammock. I think I'll buy it next trip, and we'll hang it right between those two elms. Wouldn't that be something? Just swingin' there under those branches. Boy, that would be . . .

[*YOUNG BIFF and YOUNG HAPPY appear from the direction WILLY was addressing. HAPPY carries rags and a pail of water. BIFF, wearing a sweater with a block "S," carries a football.*]

BIFF. [*pointing in the direction of the car offstage*] How's that, Pop, professional?
WILLY. Terrific. Terrific job, boys. Good work, Biff.
HAPPY. Where's the surprise, Pop?
WILLY. In the back seat of the car.
HAPPY. Boy! [*He runs off.*]
BIFF. What is it, Dad? Tell me, what'd you buy?   205
WILLY. [*laughing, cuffs him*] Never mind, something I want you to have.
BIFF. [*turns and starts off*] What is it, Hap?
HAPPY. [*offstage*] It's a punching bag!
BIFF. Oh, Pop!
WILLY. It's got Gene Tunney's° signature on it!   210

[*HAPPY runs onstage with a punching bag.*]

BIFF. Gee, how'd you know we wanted a punching bag?
WILLY. Well, it's the finest thing for the timing.
HAPPY. [*lies down on his back and pedals with his feet*] I'm losing weight, you notice, Pop?
WILLY. [*to HAPPY*] Jumping rope is good too.   215
BIFF. Did you see the new football I got?
WILLY. [*examining the ball*] Where'd you get a new ball?
BIFF. The coach told me to practice my passing.
WILLY. That so? And he gave you the ball, heh?
BIFF. Well, I borrowed it from the locker room. [*He laughs confidentially.*]   220
WILLY. [*laughing with him at the theft*] I want you to return that.
HAPPY. I told you he wouldn't like it!
BIFF. [*angrily*] Well, I'm bringing it back!
WILLY. [*stopping the incipient argument, to HAPPY*] Sure, he's gotta practice with a regulation ball, doesn't he? [*to BIFF*] Coach'll probably congratulate you on your initiative!
BIFF. Oh, he keeps congratulating my initiative all the time, Pop.   225
WILLY. That's because he likes you. If somebody else took that ball there'd be an uproar. So what's the report, boys, what's the report?
BIFF. Where'd you go this time, Dad? Gee we were lonesome for you.
WILLY. [*pleased, puts an arm around each boy and they come down to the apron*] Lonesome, heh?
BIFF. Missed you every minute.
WILLY. Don't say? Tell you a secret, boys. Don't breathe it to a soul. Someday I'll   230
have my own business, and I'll never have to leave home any more.
HAPPY. Like Uncle Charley, heh?
WILLY. Bigger than Uncle Charley! Because Charley is not—liked. He's liked, but he's not—well liked.
BIFF. Where'd you go this time, Dad?
WILLY. Well, I got on the road, and I went north to Providence. Met the Mayor.
BIFF. The Mayor of Providence!   235
WILLY. He was sitting in the hotel lobby.

---

211 *Gene Tunney:* James Joseph Tunney, a boxer who won the heavyweight championship from Jack Dempsey in 1926 and retired undefeated in 1928.

BIFF. What'd he say?

WILLY. He said, "Morning!" And I said, "You got a fine city here, Mayor." And then he had coffee with me. And then I went to Waterbury. Waterbury is a fine city. Big clock city, the famous Waterbury clock. Sold a nice bill there. And then Boston—Boston is the cradle of the Revolution. A fine city. And a couple of other towns in Mass., and on to Portland and Bangor and straight home!

BIFF. Gee, I'd love to go with you sometime, Dad.

WILLY. Soon as summer comes.   240

HAPPY. Promise?

WILLY. You and Hap and I, and I'll show you all the towns. America is full of beautiful towns and fine, upstanding people. And they know me, boys, they know me up and down New England. The finest people. And when I bring you fellas up, there'll be open sesame for all of us, 'cause one thing, boys: I have friends. I can park my car in any street in New England, and the cops protect it like their own. This summer, heh?

BIFF and HAPPY. [*together*] Yeah! You bet!

WILLY. We'll take our bathing suits.

HAPPY. We'll carry your bags, Pop!   245

WILLY. Oh, won't that be something! Me comin' into the Boston stores with you boys carryin' my bags. What a sensation!

[*BIFF is prancing around, practicing passing the ball.*]

WILLY. You nervous, Biff, about the game?

BIFF. Not if you're gonna be there.

WILLY. What do they say about you in school, now that they made you captain?

HAPPY. There's a crowd of girls behind him everytime the classes change.   250

BIFF. [*taking WILLY's hand*] This Saturday, Pop, this Saturday—just for you, I'm going to break through for a touchdown.

HAPPY. You're supposed to pass.

BIFF. I'm takin' one play for Pop. You watch me, Pop, and when I take off my helmet, that means I'm breakin' out. Then you watch me crash through that line!

WILLY. [*kisses BIFF*] Oh, wait'll I tell this in Boston!

[*BERNARD enters in knickers. He is younger than BIFF, earnest and loyal, a worried boy.*]   255

BERNARD. Biff, where are you? You're supposed to study with me today.

WILLY. Hey, looka Bernard. What're you lookin' so anemic about, Bernard?

BERNARD. He's gotta study, Uncle Willy. He's got Regents° next week.

HAPPY. [*tauntingly, spinning BERNARD around*] Let's box, Bernard!

BERNARD. Biff! [*He gets away from HAPPY.*] Listen, Biff, I heard Mr. Birnbaum say that if you don't start studyin' math he's gonna flunk you, and you won't graduate. I heard him!

WILLY. You better study with him, Biff. Go ahead now.   260

BERNARD. I heard him!

BIFF. Oh, Pop, you didn't see my sneakers! [*He holds up a foot for WILLY to look at.*]

WILLY. Hey, that's a beautiful job of printing!

BERNARD. [*wiping his glasses*] Just because he printed University of Virginia on his sneakers doesn't mean they've got to graduate him, Uncle Willy!

257 *Regents:* a statewide high school proficiency examination administered in New York State.

WILLY. [*angrily*] What're you talking about? With scholarships to three uni- 265
versities they're gonna flunk him?

BERNARD. But I heard Mr. Birnbaum say—

WILLY. Don't be a pest, Bernard! [*to his boys*] What an anemic!

BERNARD. Okay, I'm waiting for you in my house, Biff.

[*BERNARD goes off. The LOMANS laugh.*]

WILLY. Bernard is not well liked, is he?

BIFF. He's liked, but he's not well liked. 270

HAPPY. That's right, Pop.

WILLY. That's just what I mean. Bernard can get the best marks in school, y'understand, but when he gets out in the business world, y'understand, you are going to be
five times ahead of him. That's why I thank Almighty God you're both built like
Adonises. Because the man who makes an appearance in the business world, the man
who creates personal interest, is the man who gets ahead. Be liked and you will never
want. You take me, for instance. I never have to wait in line to see a buyer. "Willy Loman
is here!" That's all they have to know, and I go right through.

BIFF. Did you knock them dead, Pop?

WILLY. Knocked 'em cold in Providence, slaughtered 'em in Boston.

HAPPY. [*on his back, pedaling again*] I'm losing weight, you notice, Pop? 275

[*LINDA enters, as of old, a ribbon in her hair, carrying a basket of washing.*]

LINDA. [*with youthful energy*] Hello, dear!

WILLY. Sweetheart!

LINDA. How'd the Chevvy run?

WILLY. Chevrolet, Linda, is the greatest car ever built. [*to the boys*] Since when do
you let your mother carry wash up the stairs?

BIFF. Grab hold there, boy!

HAPPY. Where to, Mom? 280

LINDA. Hang them up on the line. And you better go down to your friends, Biff.
The cellar is full of boys. They don't know what to do with themselves.

BIFF. Ah, when Pop comes home they can wait!

WILLY. [*laughs appreciatively*] You better go down and tell them what to do, Biff.

BIFF. I think I'll have them sweep out the furnace room. 285

WILLY. Good work, Biff.

BIFF. [*goes through wall-line of kitchen to doorway at back and calls down*] Fellas!
Everybody sweep out the furnace room! I'll be right down!

VOICES. All right! Okay, Biff.

BIFF. George and Sam and Frank, come out back! We're hangin' up the wash!
Come on, Hap, on the double! [*He and HAPPY carry out the basket.*]

LINDA. The way they obey him! 290

WILLY. Well, that's training, the training. I'm tellin' you, I was sellin' thousands
and thousands, but I had to come home.

LINDA. Oh, the whole block'll be at that game. Did you sell anything?

WILLY. I did five hundred gross in Providence and seven hundred gross in Boston.

LINDA. No! Wait a minute, I've got a pencil. [*She pulls pencil and paper out of her
apron pocket.*] That makes your commission . . . Two hundred—my God! Two hundred
and twelve dollars!

WILLY. Well, I didn't figure it yet, but . . . 295

LINDA.   How much did you do?

WILLY.   Well, I—I did—about a hundred and eighty gross in Providence. Well, no—it came to—roughly two hundred gross on the whole trip.

LINDA.   [*without hesitation*] Two hundred gross. That's . . . [*She figures.*]

WILLY.   The trouble was that three of the stores were half closed for inventory in Boston. Otherwise I woulda broke records.

LINDA.   Well, it makes seventy dollars and some pennies. That's very good.   300

WILLY.   What do we owe?

LINDA.   Well, on the first there's sixteen dollars on the refrigerator—

WILLY.   Why sixteen?

LINDA.   Well, the fan belt broke, so it was a dollar eighty.

WILLY.   But it's brand new.   305

LINDA.   Well, the man said that's the way it is. Till they work themselves in, y'know.

[*They move through the wall-line into the kitchen.*]

WILLY.   I hope we didn't get stuck on that machine.

LINDA.   They got the biggest ads of any of them!

WILLY.   I know, it's a fine machine. What else?

LINDA.   Well, there's nine-sixty for the washing machine. And for the vacuum   31
cleaner there's three and a half due on the fifteenth. Then the roof, you got twenty-one dollars remaining.

WILLY.   It don't leak, does it?

LINDA.   No, they did a wonderful job. Then you owe Frank for the carburetor.

WILLY.   I'm not going to pay that man! That goddam Chevrolet, they ought to prohibit the manufacture of that car!

LINDA.   Well, you owe him three and a half. And odds and ends, comes to around a hundred and twenty dollars by the fifteenth.

WILLY.   A hundred and twenty dollars! My God, if business don't pick up   3
I don't know what I'm gonna do!

LINDA.   Well, next week you'll do better.

WILLY.   Oh, I'll knock 'em dead next week. I'll go to Hartford. I'm very well liked in Hartford. You know, the trouble is, Linda, people don't seem to take to me.

[*They move onto the forestage.*]

LINDA.   Oh, don't be foolish.

WILLY.   I know it when I walk in. They seem to laugh at me.

LINDA.   Why? Why would they laugh at you? Don't talk that way, Willy.   3

[*WILLY moves to the edge of the stage. LINDA goes into the kitchen and starts to darn stockings.*]

WILLY.   I don't know the reason for it, but they just pass me by. I'm not noticed.

LINDA.   But you're doing wonderful, dear. You're making seventy to a hundred dollars a week.

WILLY.   But I gotta be at it ten, twelve hours a day. Other men—I don't know— they do it easier. I don't know why—I can't stop myself—I talk too much. A man oughta come in with a few words. One thing about Charley. He's a man of few words, and they respect him.

LINDA.   You don't talk too much, you're just lively.

WILLY.   [*smiling*] Well, I figure, what the hell, life is short, a couple of jokes.   3
[*to himself*] I joke too much! [*The smile goes.*]

LINDA.   Why? You're—

WILLY.   I'm fat. I'm very—foolish to look at, Linda. I didn't tell you, but Christmas time I happened to be calling on F. H. Stewarts, and a salesman I know, as I was going in to see the buyer I heard him say something about—walrus. And I—I cracked him right across the face. I won't take that. I simply will not take that. But they do laugh at me. I know that.

LINDA.   Darling . . .

WILLY.   I gotta overcome it. I know I gotta overcome it. I'm not dressing to advantage, maybe.

LINDA.   Willy, darling, you're the handsomest man in the world—   330

WILLY.   Oh, no, Linda.

LINDA.   To me you are. [*slight pause*] The handsomest.

[*From the darkness is heard the laughter of a woman. WILLY doesn't turn to it, but it continues through LINDA's lines.*]

LINDA.   And the boys, Willy. Few men are idolized by their children the way you are.

[*Music is heard as behind a scrim, to the left of the house, THE WOMAN, dimly seen, is dressing.*]

WILLY.   [*with great feeling*] You're the best there is, Linda, you're a pal, you know that? On the road—on the road I want to grab you sometimes and just kiss the life outa you.

[*The laughter is loud now, and he moves into a brightening area at the left, where THE WOMAN has come from behind the scrim and is standing, putting on her hat, looking into a "mirror" and laughing.*]

WILLY.   Cause I get so lonely—especially when business is bad and there's   335
nobody to talk to. I get the feeling that I'll never sell anything again, that I won't make a living for you, or a business, a business for the boys. [*He talks through THE WOMAN's subsiding laughter; THE WOMAN primps at the "mirror."*] There's so much I want to make for—

THE WOMAN.   Me? You didn't make me, Willy. I picked you.

WILLY.   [*pleased*] You picked me?

THE WOMAN.   [*who is quite proper-looking, WILLY's age*] I did. I've been sitting at that desk watching all the salesmen go by, day in, day out. But you've got such a sense of humor, and we do have such a good time together, don't we?

WILLY.   Sure, sure. [*He takes her in his arms.*] Why do you have to go now?

THE WOMAN.   It's two o'clock . . .   340

WILLY.   No, come on in! [*He pulls her.*]

THE WOMAN.   . . . my sisters'll be scandalized. When'll you be back?

WILLY.   Oh, two weeks about. Will you come up again?

THE WOMAN.   Sure thing. You do make me laugh. It's good for me. [*She squeezes his arm, kisses him.*] And I think you're a wonderful man.

WILLY.   You picked me, heh?   345

THE WOMAN.   Sure. Because you're so sweet. And such a kidder.

WILLY.   Well, I'll see you next time I'm in Boston.

THE WOMAN.   I'll put you right through to the buyers.

WILLY.   [*slapping her bottom*] Right. Well, bottoms up!

THE WOMAN.   [*slaps him gently and laughs*] You just kill me, Willy. [*He suddenly   350
grabs her and kisses her roughly.*] You kill me. And thanks for the stockings. I love a lot of stockings. Well, good night.

WILLY.   Good night. And keep your pores open!
THE WOMAN.   Oh, Willy!

[*THE WOMAN bursts out laughing, and LINDA's laughter blends in. THE WOMAN disappears into the dark. Now the area at the kitchen table brightens. LINDA is sitting where she was at the kitchen table, but now is mending a pair of her silk stockings.*]

LINDA.   You are, Willy. The handsomest man. You've got no reason to feel that—
WILLY.   [*coming out of THE WOMAN's dimming area and going over to LINDA*] I'll make it all up to you, Linda, I'll—
LINDA.   There's nothing to make up, dear. You're doing fine, better than—
WILLY.   [*noticing her mending*] What's that?
LINDA.   Just mending my stockings. They're so expensive—
WILLY.   [*angrily, taking them from her*] I won't have you mending stockings in this house! Now throw them out!

[*LINDA puts the stockings in her pocket.*]

BERNARD.   [*entering on the run*] Where is he? If he doesn't study!
WILLY.   [*moving to the forestage, with great agitation*] You'll give him the answers!
BERNARD   I do, but I can't on a Regents! That's a state exam! They're liable to arrest me!
WILLY.   Where is he? I'll whip him, I'll whip him!
LINDA.   And he'd better give back that football, Willy, it's not nice.
WILLY.   Biff! Where is he? Why is he taking everything?
LINDA.   He's too rough with the girls, Willy. All the mothers are afraid of him!
WILLY.   I'll whip him!
BERNARD.   He's driving the car without a license!

[*THE WOMAN's laugh is heard.*]

WILLY.   Shut up!
LINDA.   All the mothers—
WILLY.   Shut up!
BERNARD.   [*backing quietly away and out*] Mr. Birnbaum says he's stuck up.
WILLY.   Get outa here!
BERNARD.   If he doesn't buckle down he'll flunk math! [*He goes off.*]
LINDA.   He's right, Willy, you've gotta—
WILLY.   [*exploding at her*] There's nothing the matter with him! You want him to be a worm like Bernard? He's got spirit, personality . . .

[*As he speaks, LINDA, almost in tears, exits into the living-room. WILLY is alone in the kitchen, wilting and staring. The leaves are gone. It is night again, and the apartment houses look down from behind.*]

WILLY.   Loaded with it. Loaded! What is he stealing? He's giving it back, isn't he? Why is he stealing? What did I tell him? I never in my life told him anything but decent things.

[*HAPPY in pajamas has come down the stairs; WILLY suddenly becomes aware of HAPPY's presence.*]

HAPPY.   Let's go now, come on.

WILLY. [*sitting down at the kitchen table*] Huh! Why did she have to wax the floors herself? Everytime she waxes the floors she keels over. She knows that!

HAPPY. Shh! Take it easy. What brought you back tonight?

WILLY. I got an awful scare. Nearly hit a kid in Yonkers. God! Why didn't 380 I go to Alaska with my brother Ben that time! Ben! That man was a genius, that man was success incarnate! What a mistake! He begged me to go.

HAPPY. Well, there's no use in—

WILLY. You guys! There was a man started with the clothes on his back and ended up with diamond mines!

HAPPY. Boy, someday I'd like to know how he did it.

WILLY. What's the mystery? The man knew what he wanted and went out and got it! Walked into a jungle, and comes out, the age of twenty-one, and he's rich! The world is an oyster, but you don't crack it open on a mattress!

HAPPY. Pop, I told you I'm gonna retire you for life. 385

WILLY. You'll retire me for life on seventy goddam dollars a week? And your women and your car and your apartment, and you'll retire me for life! Christ's sake, I couldn't get past Yonkers today! Where are you guys, where are you? The woods are burning! I can't drive a car!

[*CHARLEY has appeared in the doorway. He is a large man, slow of speech, laconic, immovable. In all he says, despite what he says, there is pity, and now, trepidation. He has a robe over pajamas, slippers on his feet. He enters the kitchen.*]

CHARLEY. Everything all right?

HAPPY. Yeah, Charley, everything's . . .

WILLY. What's the matter?

CHARLEY. I heard some noise. I thought something happened. Can't we do 390 something about the walls? You sneeze in here, and in my house hats blow off.

HAPPY. Let's go to bed, Dad. Come on.

[*CHARLEY signals to HAPPY to go.*]

WILLY. You go ahead, I'm not tired at the moment.

HAPPY. [*to WILLY*] Take it easy, huh? [*He exits.*]

WILLY. What're you doin' up?

CHARLEY. [*sitting down at the kitchen table opposite WILLY*] Couldn't sleep good. 395 I had a heartburn.

WILLY. Well, you don't know how to eat.

CHARLEY. I eat with my mouth.

WILLY. No, you're ignorant. You gotta know about vitamins and things like that.

CHARLEY. Come on, let's shoot. Tire you out a little.

WILLY. [*hesitantly*] All right. You got cards? 400

CHARLEY. [*taking a deck from his pocket*] Yeah, I got them. Someplace. What is it with those vitamins?

WILLY. [*dealing*] They build up your bones. Chemistry.

CHARLEY. Yeah, but there's no bones in a heartburn.

WILLY. What are you talkin' about? Do you know the first thing about it?

CHARLEY. Don't get insulted. 405

WILLY. Don't talk about something you don't know anything about.

[*They are playing. Pause.*]

CHARLEY.   What're you doin' home?
WILLY.   A little trouble with the car.
CHARLEY.   Oh. [*Pause*] I'd like to take a trip to California.
WILLY.   Don't say.
CHARLEY.   You want a job?
WILLY.   I got a job, I told you that. [*after a slight pause*] What the hell are you offering me a job for?
CHARLEY.   Don't get insulted.
WILLY.   Don't insult me.
CHARLEY.   I don't see no sense in it. You don't have to go on this way.
WILLY.   I got a good job. [*slight pause*] What do you keep comin' in for?
CHARLEY.   You want me to go?
WILLY.   [*after a pause, withering*] I can't understand it. He's going back to Texas again. What the hell is that?
CHARLEY.   Let him go.
WILLY.   I got nothin' to give him, Charley, I'm clean, I'm clean.
CHARLEY.   He won't starve. None a them starve. Forget about him.
WILLY.   Then what have I got to remember?
CHARLEY.   You take it too hard. To hell with it. When a deposit bottle is broken you don't get your nickel back.
WILLY.   That's easy enough for you to say.
CHARLEY.   That ain't easy for me to say.
WILLY.   Did you see the ceiling I put up in the living-room?
CHARLEY.   Yeah, that's a piece of work. To put up a ceiling is a mystery to me. How do you do it?
WILLY.   What's the difference?
CHARLEY.   Well, talk about it.
WILLY.   You gonna put up a ceiling?
CHARLEY.   How could I put up a ceiling?
WILLY.   Then what the hell are you bothering me for?
CHARLEY.   You're insulted again.
WILLY.   A man who can't handle tools is not a man. You're disgusting.
CHARLEY.   Don't call me disgusting, Willy.

[UNCLE BEN, *carrying a valise and an umbrella, enters the forestage from around the right corner of the house. He is a stolid man, in his sixties, with a mustache and an authoritative air. He is utterly certain of his destiny, and there is an aura of far places about him. He enters exactly as* WILLY *speaks.*]

WILLY.   I'm getting awfully tired, Ben.

[BEN'*s music is heard.* BEN *looks around at everything.*]

CHARLEY.   Good, keep playing; you'll sleep better. Did you call me Ben?

[BEN *looks at his watch.*]

WILLY.   That's funny. For a second there you reminded me of my brother Ben.
BEN.   I only have a few minutes. [*He strolls, inspecting the place.* WILLY *and* CHARLEY *continue playing.*]
CHARLEY.   You never heard from him again, heh? Since that time?

WILLY.   Didn't Linda tell you? Couple of weeks ago we got a letter from his wife in Africa. He died.

CHARLEY.   That so.

BEN.   [*chuckling*] So this is Brooklyn, eh?

CHARLEY.   Maybe you're in for some of his money.

WILLY.   Naa, he had seven sons. There's just one opportunity I had with   445
that man . . .

BEN.   I must make a train, William. There are several properties I'm looking at in Alaska.

WILLY.   Sure, sure! If I'd gone with him to Alaska that time, everything would've been totally different.

CHARLEY.   Go on, you'd froze to death up there.

WILLY.   What're you talking about?

BEN.   Opportunity is tremendous in Alaska, William. Surprised you're not   450
up there.

WILLY.   Sure, tremendous.

CHARLEY.   Heh?

WILLY.   There was the only man I ever met who knew the answers.

CHARLEY.   Who?

BEN.   How are you all?   455

WILLY.   [*taking a pot, smiling*] Fine, fine.

CHARLEY.   Pretty sharp tonight.

BEN.   Is Mother living with you?

WILLY.   No, she died a long time ago.

CHARLEY.   Who?   460

BEN.   That's too bad. Fine specimen of a lady, Mother.

WILLY.   [*to CHARLEY*] Heh?

BEN.   I'd hoped to see the old girl.

CHARLEY.   Who died?

BEN.   Heard anything from Father, have you?   465

WILLY.   [*unnerved*] What do you mean, who died?

CHARLEY.   [*taking a pot*] What're you talkin' about?

BEN.   [*looking at his watch*] William, it's half-past eight!

WILLY.   [*As though to dispel his confusion he angrily stops CHARLEY's hand.*] That's my build!

CHARLEY.   I put the ace—   470

WILLY.   If you don't know how to play the game I'm not gonna throw my money away on you!

CHARLEY.   [*rising*] It was my ace, for God's sake!

WILLY.   I'm through, I'm through!

BEN.   When did Mother die?

WILLY.   Long ago. Since the beginning you never knew how to play cards.   475

CHARLEY.   [*picks up the cards and goes to the door*] All right! Next time I'll bring a deck with five aces.

WILLY.   I don't play that kind of game!

CHARLEY.   [*turning to him*] You ought to be ashamed of yourself!

WILLY.   Yeah?

CHARLEY.   Yeah! [*He goes out.*]   480

WILLY.   [*slamming the door after him*] Ignoramus!

BEN. [*as WILLY comes toward him through the wall-line of the kitchen*] So you're William.

WILLY. [*shaking BEN's hand*] Ben! I've been waiting for you so long! What's the answer? How did you do it?

BEN. Oh, there's a story in that.

[*LINDA enters the forestage, as of old, carrying the wash basket.*]

LINDA. Is this Ben? 485

BEN. [*gallantly*] How do you do, my dear.

LINDA. Where've you been all these years? Willy's always wondered why you—

WILLY. [*pulling BEN away from her impatiently*] Where is Dad? Didn't you follow him? How did you get started?

BEN. Well, I don't know how much you remember.

WILLY. Well, I was just a baby, of course, only three or four years old— 49(

BEN. Three years and eleven months.

WILLY. What a memory, Ben!

BEN. I have many enterprises, William, and I have never kept books.

WILLY. I remember I was sitting under the wagon in—was it Nebraska?

BEN. It was South Dakota, and I gave you a bunch of wild flowers. 49.

WILLY. I remember you walking away down some open road.

BEN. [*laughing*] I was going to find Father in Alaska.

WILLY. Where is he?

BEN. At that age I had a very faulty view of geography, William. I discovered after a few days that I was heading due south, so instead of Alaska, I ended up in Africa. 50

LINDA. Africa!

WILLY. The Gold Coast!

BEN. Principally diamond mines.

LINDA. Diamond mines!

BEN. Yes, my dear. But I've only a few minutes—

WILLY. No! Boys! Boys! [*YOUNG BIFF and HAPPY appear.*] Listen to this. This 5(
is your Uncle Ben, a great man! Tell my boys, Ben!

BEN. Why, boys, when I was seventeen I walked into the jungle, and when I was twenty-one I walked out. [*He laughs.*] And by God I was rich.

WILLY. [*to the boys*] You see what I been talking about? The greatest things can happen!

BEN. [*glancing at his watch*] I have an appointment in Ketchikan Tuesday week.

WILLY. No, Ben. Please tell about Dad. I want my boys to hear. I want them to know the kind of stock they spring from. All I remember is a man with a big beard, and I was in Mamma's lap, sitting around a fire, and some kind of high music.

BEN. His flute. He played the flute. 5

WILLY. Sure, the flute, that's right!

[*New music is heard, a high, rollicking tune.*]

BEN. Father was a very great and a very wild-hearted man. We would start in Boston, and he'd toss the whole family into the wagon, and then he'd drive the team right across the country; through Ohio, and Indiana, Michigan, Illinois, and all the Western states. And we'd stop in the towns and sell the flutes that he'd made on the way. Great inventor, Father. With one gadget he made more in a week than a man like you could make in a lifetime.

WILLY. That's just the way I'm bringing them up, Ben—rugged, well liked, all-around.

BEN. Yeah? [*to BIFF*] Hit that, boy—hard as you can. [*He pounds his stomach.*]

BIFF. Oh, no, sir! 515

BEN. [*taking boxing stance*] Come on, get to me! [*He laughs.*]

BIFF. Okay! [*He cocks his fists and starts in.*]

WILLY. Go to it, Biff! Go ahead, show him!

LINDA. [*to WILLY*] Why must he fight, dear?

BEN. [*sparring with BIFF*] Good boy! Good boy! 520

WILLY. How's that, Ben, heh?

HAPPY. Give him the left, Biff!

LINDA. Why are you fighting?

BEN. Good boy! [*suddenly comes in, trips BIFF, and stands over him, the point of his umbrella poised over BIFF's eye.*]

LINDA. Look out, Biff! 525

BIFF. Gee!

BEN. [*patting BIFF's knee*] Never fight fair with a stranger, boy. You'll never get out of the jungle that way. [*taking LINDA's hand and bowing*] It was an honor and a pleasure to meet you, Linda.

LINDA. [*withdrawing her hand coldly, frightened*] Have a nice—trip.

BEN. [*to WILLY*] And good luck with your—what do you do?

WILLY. Selling. 530

BEN. Yes. Well . . . [*He raises his hand in farewell to all.*]

WILLY. No, Ben, I don't want you to think . . . [*He takes BEN's arm to show him.*] It's Brooklyn, I know, but we hunt too.

BEN. Really, now.

WILLY. Oh, sure, there's snakes and rabbits and—that's why I moved out here. Why, Biff can fell any one of these trees in no time! Boys! Go right over to where they're building the apartment house and get some sand. We're gonna rebuild the entire front stoop right now! Watch this, Ben!

BIFF. Yes, sir! On the double, Hap! 535

HAPPY. [*as he and BIFF run off*] I lost weight, Pop, you notice?

[*CHARLEY enters in knickers, even before the boys are gone.*]

CHARLEY. Listen, if they steal any more from that building the watchman'll put the cops on them!

LINDA. [*to WILLY*] Don't let Biff . . .

[*BEN laughs lustily.*]

WILLY. You shoulda seen the lumber they brought home last week. At least a dozen six-by-tens worth all kinds a money.

CHARLEY. Listen, if that watchman— 540

WILLY. I gave them hell, understand. But I got a couple of fearless characters there.

CHARLEY. Willy, the jails are full of fearless characters.

BEN. [*clapping WILLY on the back, with a laugh at CHARLEY*] And the stock exchange, friend!

WILLY. [*joining in BEN's laughter*] Where are the rest of your pants?

CHARLEY. My wife bought them. 545

WILLY.   Now all you need is a golf club and you can go upstairs and go to sleep.
[*to BEN*] Great athlete! Between him and his son Bernard they can't hammer a nail!
BERNARD.   [*rushing in*] The watchman's chasing Biff!
WILLY.   [*angrily*] Shut up! He's not stealing anything!
LINDA.   [*alarmed, hurrying off left*] Where is he? Biff, dear! [*She exits.*]
WILLY.   [*moving toward the left, away from BEN*] There's nothing wrong. What's   5
the matter with you?
BEN.   Nervy boy. Good!
WILLY.   [*laughing*] Oh, nerves of iron, that Biff!
CHARLEY.   Don't know what it is. My New England man comes back and he's
bleedin', they murdered him up there.
WILLY.   It's contacts, Charley, I got important contacts!
CHARLEY.   [*sarcastically*] Glad to hear it, Willy. Come in later, we'll shoot a   5
little casino. I'll take some of your Portland money. [*He laughs at WILLY and exits.*]
WILLY.   [*turning to BEN*] Business is bad, it's murderous. But not for me, of course.
BEN.   I'll stop by on my way back to Africa.
WILLY.   [*longingly.*] Can't you stay a few days? You're just what I need, Ben,
because I—I have a fine position here, but I—well, Dad left when I was such a baby and
I never had a chance to talk to him and I still feel—kind of temporary about myself.
BEN.   I'll be late for my train.

[*They are at opposite ends of the stage.*]

WILLY.   Ben, my boys—can't we talk? They'd go into the jaws of hell for me, see,   5
but I—
BEN.   William, you're being first-rate with your boys. Outstanding, manly chaps!
WILLY.   [*hanging on to his words*] Oh, Ben, that's good to hear! Because sometimes I'm afraid that I'm not teaching them the right kind of—Ben, how should I teach
them?
BEN.   [*giving great weight to each word, and with a certain vicious audacity*] William,
when I walked into the jungle, I was seventeen. When I walked out I was twenty-one.
And, by God, I was rich! [*He goes off into darkness around the right corner of the house.*]
WILLY.   . . . was rich! That's just the spirit I want to imbue them with! To walk into
a jungle! I was right! I was right! I was right!

[*BEN is gone, but WILLY is still speaking to him as LINDA, in her nightgown and robe, enters the
kitchen, glances around for WILLY, then goes to the door of the house, looks out and sees him.
Comes down to his left. He looks at her.*]

LINDA.   Willy, dear? Willy?   5
WILLY.   I was right!
LINDA.   Did you have some cheese? [*He can't answer.*] It's very late, darling. Come
to bed, heh?
WILLY.   [*looking straight up*] Gotta break your neck to see a star in this yard.
LINDA.   You coming in?
WILLY.   Whatever happened to that diamond watch fob? Remember? When Ben   5
came from Africa that time? Didn't he give me a watch fob with a diamond in it?
LINDA.   You pawned it, dear. Twelve, thirteen years ago. For Biff's radio corre-
spondence course.
WILLY.   Gee, that was a beautiful thing. I'll take a walk.
LINDA.   But you're in your slippers.

WILLY.   [*starting to go around the house at the left*] I was right! I was! [*Half to* LINDA, *as*   575
he goes, shaking his head] What a man! There was a man worth talking to. I was right!

LINDA.   [*calling after* WILLY] But in your slippers, Willy!

[WILLY *is almost gone when* BIFF, *in his pajamas, comes down the stairs and enters the kitchen.*]

BIFF.   What is he doing out there?

LINDA.   Sh!

BIFF.   God Almighty, Mom, how long has he been doing this?

LINDA.   Don't, he'll hear you.   580

BIFF.   What the hell is the matter with him?

LINDA.   It'll pass by morning.

BIFF.   Shouldn't we do anything?

LINDA.   Oh, my dear, you should do a lot of things, but there's nothing to do, so
go to sleep.

[HAPPY *comes down the stairs and sits on the steps.*]

HAPPY.   I never heard him so loud, Mom.   585

LINDA.   Well, come around more often; you'll hear him. [*She sits down at the
table and mends the lining of* WILLY'S *jacket.*]

BIFF.   Why didn't you ever write me about this, Mom?

LINDA.   How would I write to you? For over three months you had no address.

BIFF.   I was on the move. But you know I thought of you all the time. You know
that, don't you, pal?

LINDA.   I know, dear, I know. But he likes to have a letter. Just to know that there's
still a possibility for better things.

BIFF.   He's not like this all the time, is he?   590

LINDA.   It's when you come home he's always the worst.

BIFF.   When I come home?

LINDA.   When you write you're coming, he's all smiles, and talks about the future,
and—he's just wonderful. And then the closer you seem to come, the more shaky he
gets, and then, by the time you get here, he's arguing, and he seems angry at you. I think
it's just that maybe he can't bring himself to—to open up to you. Why are you so hateful
to each other? Why is that?

BIFF.   [*evasively*] I'm not hateful, Mom.

LINDA.   But you no sooner come in the door than you're fighting!   595

BIFF.   I don't know why. I mean to change. I'm tryin', Mom, you understand?

LINDA.   Are you home to stay now?

BIFF.   I don't know. I want to look around, see what's doin'.

LINDA.   Biff, you can't look around all your life, can you?

BIFF.   I just can't take hold, Mom. I can't take hold of some kind of a life.   600

LINDA.   Biff, a man is not a bird, to come and go with the springtime.

BIFF.   Your hair . . . [*He touches her hair.*] Your hair got so gray.

LINDA.   Oh, it's been gray since you were in high school. I just stopped dyeing it,
that's all.

BIFF.   Dye it again, will ya? I don't want my pal looking old. [*He smiles.*]

LINDA.   You're such a boy! You think you can go away for a year and . . .
You've got to get it into your head now that one day you'll knock on this door and   605
there'll be strange people here—

BIFF.   What are you talking about? You're not even sixty, Mom.

LINDA.   But what about your father?

BIFF.   [*lamely*] Well, I meant him, too.

HAPPY.   He admires Pop.

LINDA.   Biff, dear, if you don't have any feeling for him, then you can't have any   6
feeling for me.

BIFF.   Sure I can, Mom.

LINDA.   No. You can't just come to see me, because I love him. [*with a threat, but
only a threat, of tears*] He's the dearest man in the world to me, and I won't have anyone
making him feel unwanted and low and blue. You've got to make up your mind now,
darling, there's no leeway any more. Either he's your father and you pay him that
respect, or else you're not to come here. I know he's not easy to get along with—nobody
knows that better than me—but . . .

WILLY.   [*from the left, with a laugh*] Hey, hey, Biffo!

BIFF.   [*starting to go out after WILLY*] What the hell is the matter with him? [*HAPPY
stops him.*]

LINDA.   Don't—don't go near him!   6

BIFF.   Stop making excuses for him! He always, always wiped the floor with you.
Never had an ounce of respect for you.

HAPPY.   He's always had respect for—

BIFF.   What the hell do you know about it?

HAPPY.   [*surlily*] Just don't call him crazy!

BIFF.   He's got no character—Charley wouldn't do this. Not in his own   6
house—spewing out that vomit from his mind.

HAPPY.   Charley never had to cope with what he's got to.

BIFF.   People are worse off than Willy Loman. Believe me, I've seen them!

LINDA.   Then make Charley your father, Biff. You can't do that, can you? I don't
say he's a great man. Willy Loman never made a lot of money. His name was never in the
paper. He's not the finest character that ever lived. But he's a human being, and a terrible thing is happening to him. So attention must be paid. He's not to be allowed to fall
into his grave like an old dog. Attention, attention must be finally paid to such a person.
You called him crazy—

BIFF.   I didn't mean—

LINDA.   No, a lot of people think he's lost his—balance. But you don't have   6
to be very smart to know what his trouble is. The man is exhausted.

HAPPY.   Sure!

LINDA.   A small man can be just as exhausted as a great man. He works for a company thirty-six years this March, opens up unheard-of territories to their trademark, and
now in his old age they take his salary away.

HAPPY.   [*indignantly*] I didn't know that, Mom.

LINDA.   You never asked, my dear! Now that you get your spending money someplace else you don't trouble your mind with him.

HAPPY.   But I gave you money last—   6

LINDA.   Christmas time, fifty dollars! To fix the hot water it cost ninety-seven fifty!
For five weeks he's been on straight commission,° like a beginner, an unknown!

BIFF.   Those ungrateful bastards!

---

631 *straight commission:* refers to the fact that Willy is receiving no salary, only a commission (per-
centage) on the sales he makes.

LINDA.   Are they any worse than his sons? When he brought them business, when he was young, they were glad to see him. But now his old friends, the old buyers that loved him so and always found some order to hand him in a pinch—they're all dead, retired. He used to be able to make six, seven calls a day in Boston. Now he takes his valises out of the car and puts them back and takes them out again and he's exhausted. Instead of walking he talks now. He drives seven hundred miles, and when he gets there no one knows him any more, no one welcomes him. And what goes through a man's mind, driving seven hundred miles home without having earned a cent? Why shouldn't he talk to himself? Why? When he has to go to Charley and borrow fifty dollars a week and pretend to me that it's his pay? How long can that go on? How long? You see what I'm sitting here and waiting for? And you tell me he has no character? The man who never worked a day but for your benefit? When does he get the medal for that? Is this his reward—to turn around at the age of sixty-three and find his sons, who he loved better than his life, one a philandering bum—

HAPPY.   Mom!

LINDA.   That's all you are, my baby! [*To* BIFF] And you! What happened to   635
the love you had for him? You were such pals! How you used to talk to him on the phone every night! How lonely he was till he could come home to you!

BIFF.   All right, Mom. I'll live here in my room, and I'll get a job. I'll keep away from him, that's all.

LINDA.   No, Biff. You can't stay here and fight all the time.

BIFF.   He threw me out of this house, remember that.

LINDA.   Why did he do that? I never knew why.

BIFF.   Because I know he's a fake and he doesn't like anybody around who knows!   640

LINDA.   Why a fake? In what way? What do you mean?

BIFF.   Just don't lay it all at my feet. It's between me and him—that's all I have to say. I'll chip in from now on. He'll settle for half my pay check. He'll be all right. I'm going to bed. [*He starts for the stairs.*]

LINDA.   He won't be all right.

BIFF.   [*turning on the stairs, furiously*] I hate this city and I'll stay here. Now what do you want?

LINDA.   He's dying, Biff.   645

[*HAPPY turns quickly to her, shocked.*]

BIFF.   [*after a pause*] Why is he dying?

LINDA.   He's been trying to kill himself.

BIFF.   [*with great horror*] How?

LINDA.   I live from day to day.

BIFF.   What're you talking about?   650

LINDA.   Remember I wrote you that he smashed up the car again? In February?

BIFF.   Well?

LINDA.   The insurance inspector came. He said that they have evidence. That all these accidents in the last year—weren't—weren't—accidents.

HAPPY.   How can they tell that? That's a lie.

LINDA.   It seems there's a woman . . . [*She takes a breath as*]   655

} BIFF.   [*sharply but contained*] What woman?

   LINDA.   [*simultaneously*] . . . and this woman . . .

   LINDA.   What?

BIFF.   Nothing. Go ahead.

LINDA.   What did you say?

BIFF.   Nothing. I just said what woman?

HAPPY.   What about her?

LINDA.   Well, it seems she was walking down the road and saw his car. She says that he wasn't driving fast at all, and that he didn't skid. She says he came to that little bridge, and then deliberately smashed into the railing, and it was only the shallowness of the water that saved him.

BIFF.   Oh, no, he probably just fell asleep again.

LINDA.   I don't think he fell asleep.

BIFF.   Why not?

LINDA.   Last month . . . [*with great difficulty*] Oh, boys, it's so hard to say a thing like this! He's just a big stupid man to you, but I tell you there's more good in him than in many other people. [*She chokes, wipes her eyes.*] I was looking for a fuse. The lights blew out, and I went down the cellar. And behind the fuse box—it happened to fall out—was a length of rubber pipe—just short.

HAPPY.   No kidding?

LINDA.   There's a little attachment on the end of it. I knew right away. And sure enough, on the bottom of the water heater there's a new little nipple on the gas pipe.

HAPPY.   [*angrily*] That—jerk.

BIFF.   Did you have it taken off?

LINDA.   I'm—I'm ashamed to. How can I mention it to him? Every day I go down and take away that little rubber pipe. But, when he comes home, I put it back where it was. How can I insult him that way? I don't know what to do. I live from day to day, boys. I tell you, I know every thought in his mind. It sounds so old-fashioned and silly, but I tell you he put his whole life into you and you've turned your backs on him. [*She is bent over in the chair, weeping, her face in her hands.*] Biff, I swear to God! Biff, his life is in your hands!

HAPPY.   [*to BIFF*] How do you like that damned fool!

BIFF.   [*kissing her*] All right, pal, all right. It's all settled now. I've been remiss. I know that, Mom. But now I'll stay, and I swear to you, I'll apply myself. [*kneeling in front of her, in a fever of self-reproach*] It's just—you see, Mom, I don't fit in business. Not that I won't try. I'll try, and I'll make good.

HAPPY.   Sure you will. The trouble with you in business was you never tried to please people.

BIFF.   I know, I—

HAPPY.   Like when you worked for Harrison's. Bob Harrison said you were tops, and then you go and do some damn fool thing like whistling whole songs in the elevator like a comedian.

BIFF.   [*against HAPPY*] So what? I like to whistle sometimes.

HAPPY.   You don't raise a guy to a responsible job who whistles in the elevator!

LINDA.   Well, don't argue about it now.

HAPPY.   Like when you'd go off and swim in the middle of the day instead of taking the line around.

BIFF.   [*his resentment rising*] Well, don't you run off? You take off sometimes, don't you? On a nice summer day?

HAPPY.   Yeah, but I cover myself!

LINDA.   Boys!

HAPPY.   If I'm going to take a fade the boss can call any number where I'm sup-   685
posed to be and they'll swear to him that I just left. I'll tell you something that I hate to
say, Biff, but in the business world some of them think you're crazy.
BIFF.   [*angered*] Screw the business world!
HAPPY.   All right, screw it! Great, but cover yourself!
LINDA.   Hap, Hap!
BIFF.   I don't care what they think! They've laughed at Dad for years, and you
know why? Because we don't belong in this nuthouse of a city! We should be mixing
cement on some open plain, or—or carpenters. A carpenter is allowed to whistle!

[*WILLY walks in from the entrance of the house, at left.*]

WILLY.   Even your grandfather was better than a carpenter. [*pause. They watch*   690
him.] You never grew up. Bernard does not whistle in the elevator, I assure you.
BIFF.   [*as though to laugh WILLY out of it*] Yeah, but you do, Pop.
WILLY.   I never in my life whistled in an elevator! And who in the business world
thinks I'm crazy?
BIFF.   I didn't mean it like that, Pop. Now don't make a whole thing out of it,
will ya?
WILLY.   Go back to the West! Be a carpenter, a cowboy, enjoy yourself!
LINDA.   Willy, he was just saying—   695
WILLY.   I heard what he said!
HAPPY.   [*trying to quiet WILLY*] Hey, Pop, come on now . . .
WILLY.   [*continuing over HAPPY's line*] They laugh at me, heh? Go to Filene's, go
to the Hub, go to Slattery's,° Boston. Call out the name Willy Loman and see what hap-
pens! Big shot!
BIFF.   All right, Pop.
WILLY.   Big!   700
BIFF.   All right!
WILLY.   Why do you always insult me?
BIFF.   I didn't say a word. [*to LINDA*] Did I say a word?
LINDA.   He didn't say anything, Willy.
WILLY.   [*going to the doorway of the living room*] All right, good night, good   705
night.
LINDA.   Willy, dear, he just decided . . .
WILLY.   [*to BIFF*] If you get tired hanging around tomorrow, paint the ceiling I
put up in the living-room.
BIFF.   I'm leaving early tomorrow.
HAPPY.   He's going to see Bill Oliver, Pop.
WILLY.   [*interestedly*] Oliver? For what?   710
BIFF.   [*with reserve, but trying, trying*] He always said he'd stake me. I'd like to go
into business, so maybe I can take him up on it.
LINDA.   Isn't that wonderful?
WILLY.   Don't interrupt. What's wonderful about it? There's fifty men in the City
of New York who'd stake him. [*to BIFF*] Sporting goods?
BIFF.   I guess so. I know something about it and—

698 *Filene's, the Hub, Slattery's:* department stores in New England.

WILLY. He knows something about it! You know sporting goods better than Spalding, for God's sake! How much is he giving you?

BIFF. I don't know. I didn't even see him yet, but—

WILLY. Then what're you talkin' about?

BIFF. [*getting angry*] Well, all I said was I'm gonna see him, that's all!

WILLY. [*turning away*] Ah, you're counting your chickens again.

BIFF. [*starting left for the stairs*] Oh, Jesus, I'm going to sleep!

WILLY. [*calling after him*] Don't curse in this house!

BIFF. [*turning*] Since when did you get so clean?

HAPPY. [*trying to stop them*] Wait a . . .

WILLY. Don't use that language to me! I won't have it!

HAPPY. [*grabbing Biff, shouts*] Wait a minute! I got an idea. I got a feasible idea. Come here, Biff, let's talk this over now, let's talk some sense here. When I was down in Florida last time, I thought of a great idea to sell sporting goods. It just came back to me. You and I, Biff—we have a line, the Loman Line. We train a couple of weeks, and put on a couple of exhibitions, see?

WILLY. That's an idea!

HAPPY. Wait! We form two basketball teams, see? Two waterpolo teams. We play each other. It's a million dollars' worth of publicity. Two brothers, see? The Loman Brothers. Displays in the Royal Palms—all the hotels. And banners over the ring and the basketball court: "Loman Brothers." Baby, we could sell sporting goods!

WILLY. That is a one-million-dollar idea!

LINDA. Marvelous!

BIFF. I'm in great shape as far as that's concerned.

HAPPY. And the beauty of it is, Biff, it wouldn't be like a business. We'd be out playin' ball again . . .

BIFF. [*enthused*] Yeah, that's . . .

WILLY. Million-dollar . . .

HAPPY. And you wouldn't get fed up with it, Biff. It'd be the family again. There'd be the old honor, and comradeship, and if you wanted to go off for a swim or somethin'—well, you'd do it! Without some smart cooky gettin' up ahead of you!

WILLY. Lick the world! You guys together could absolutely lick the civilized world.

BIFF. I'll see Oliver tomorrow. Hap, if we could work that out . . .

LINDA. Maybe things are beginning to—

WILLY. [*wildly enthused, to Linda*] Stop interrupting! [*to Biff*] But don't wear sport jacket and slacks when you see Oliver.

BIFF. No, I'll—

WILLY. A business suit, and talk as little as possible, and don't crack any jokes.

BIFF. He did like me. Always liked me.

LINDA. He loved you!

WILLY. [*to Linda*] Will you stop! [*to Biff*] Walk in very serious. You are not applying for a boy's job. Money is to pass. Be quiet, fine, and serious. Everybody likes a kidder, but nobody lends him money.

HAPPY. I'll try to get some myself, Biff. I'm sure I can.

WILLY. I see great things for you kids. I think your troubles are over. But remember, start big and you'll end big. Ask for fifteen. How much you gonna ask for?

BIFF. Gee, I don't know—

WILLY. And don't say "Gee." "Gee" is a boy's word. A man walking in for fifteen thousand dollars does not say "Gee!"

BIFF.   Ten, I think, would be top though.

WILLY.   Don't be so modest. You always started too low. Walk in with a big laugh. Don't look worried. Start off with a couple of your good stories to lighten things up. It's not what you say, it's how you say it—because personality always wins the day.

LINDA.   Oliver always thought the highest of him—   750

WILLY.   Will you let me talk?

BIFF.   Don't yell at her, Pop, will ya?

WILLY.   [*angrily*] I was talking, wasn't I?

BIFF.   I don't like you yelling at her all the time, and I'm tellin' you, that's all.

WILLY.   What're you, takin' over this house?   755

LINDA.   Willy—

WILLY.   [*turning on her*] Don't take his side all the time, godammit!

BIFF.   [*furiously*] Stop yelling at her!

WILLY.   [*suddenly pulling on his cheek, beaten down, guilt ridden*] Give my best to Bill Oliver—he may remember me.

[*He exits through the living-room doorway.*]

LINDA.   [*her voice subdued*] What'd you have to start that for? [*BIFF turns away.*]   760 You see how sweet he was as soon as you talked hopefully? [*She goes over to BIFF.*] Come up and say good night to him. Don't let him go to bed that way.

HAPPY.   Come on, Biff, let's buck him up.

LINDA.   Please, dear. Just say good night. It takes so little to make him happy. Come. [*She goes through the living-room doorway, calling upstairs from within the living-room.*] Your pajamas are hanging in the bathroom, Willy!

HAPPY.   [*looking toward where LINDA went out*] What a woman! They broke the mold when they made her. You know that, Biff?

BIFF.   He's off salary. My God, working on commission!   765

HAPPY.   Well, let's face it: he's no hot-shot selling man. Except that sometimes, you have to admit, he's a sweet personality.

BIFF.   [*deciding*] Lend me ten bucks, will ya? I want to buy some new ties.

HAPPY.   I'll take you to a place I know. Beautiful stuff. Wear one of my striped shirts tomorrow.

BIFF.   She got gray. Mom got awful old. Gee, I'm gonna go in to Oliver tomorrow and knock him for a—

HAPPY.   Come on up. Tell that to Dad. Let's give him a whirl. Come on.   770

BIFF.   [*steamed up*] You know, with ten thousand bucks, boy!

HAPPY.   [*as they go into the living-room*] That's the talk, Biff, that's the first time I've heard the old confidence out of you! [*from within the living-room, fading off*] You're gonna live with me, kid, and any babe you want just say the word . . . [*The last lines are hardly heard. They are mounting the stairs to their parents' bedroom.*]

LINDA.   [*entering her bedroom and addressing WILLY, who is in the bathroom. She is straightening the bed for him.*] Can you do anything about the shower? It drips.

WILLY.   [*from the bathroom*] All of a sudden everything falls to pieces! Goddam plumbing, oughta be sued, those people. I hardly finished putting it in and the thing . . . [*His words rumble off.*]

LINDA.   I'm just wondering if Oliver will remember him. You think he might?

WILLY.   [*coming out of the bathroom in his pajamas*] Remember him? What's   775 the matter with you, you crazy? If he'd've stayed with Oliver he'd be on top by now! Wait'll Oliver gets a look at him. You don't know the average caliber any more. The average young man today—[*He is getting into bed*]—is got a caliber of zero. Greatest thing in the world for him was to bum around.

[*BIFF and HAPPY enter the bedroom. Slight pause.*]

> WILLY.   [*stops short, looking at BIFF*] Glad to hear it, boy.
> HAPPY.   He wanted to say good night to you, sport.
> WILLY.   [*to BIFF*] Yeah. Knock him dead, boy. What'd you want to tell me?
> BIFF.   Just take it easy, Pop. Good night. [*He turns to go.*]
> WILLY.   [*unable to resist*] And if anything falls off the desk while you're talking to   78
> him—like a package or something—don't you pick it up. They have office boys for that.
> LINDA.   I'll make a big breakfast—
> WILLY.   Will you let me finish? [*to BIFF*] Tell him you were in the business in the West. Not farm work.
> BIFF.   All right, Dad.
> LINDA.   I think everything—
> WILLY.   [*going right through her speech*] And don't undersell yourself. No less   7
> than fifteen thousand dollars.
> BIFF.   [*unable to bear him*] Okay. Good night, Mom. [*He starts moving.*]
> WILLY.   Because you got a greatness in you, Biff, remember that. You got all kinds
> a greatness . . . [*He lies back, exhausted.*]

[*BIFF walks out.*]

> LINDA.   [*calling after BIFF*] Sleep well, darling!
> HAPPY.   I'm gonna get married, Mom. I wanted to tell you.
> LINDA.   Go to sleep, dear.   7
> HAPPY.   [*going*] I just wanted to tell you.
> WILLY.   Keep up the good work. [*HAPPY exits.*] God . . . remember that Ebbets
> Field° game? The championship of the city?
> LINDA.   Just rest. Should I sing to you?
> WILLY.   Yeah. Sing to me. [*LINDA hums a soft lullaby.*] When that team came out—
> he was the tallest, remember?
> LINDA.   Oh, yes. And in gold.

[*BIFF enters the darkened kitchen, takes a cigarette, and leaves the house. He comes downstage into a golden pool of light. He smokes, staring at the night.*]

> WILLY.   Like a young god. Hercules—something like that. And the sun, the sun
> all around him. Remember how he waved to me? Right up from the field, with the rep-
> resentatives of three colleges standing by? And the buyers I brought, and the cheers
> when he came out—Loman, Loman, Loman! God Almighty, he'll be great yet. A star
> like that, magnificent, can never really fade away!

[*The light on WILLY is fading. The gas heater begins to glow through the kitchen wall, near the stairs, a blue flame beneath red coils.*]

> LINDA.   [*timidly*] Willy dear, what has he got against you?
> WILLY.   I'm so tired. Don't talk any more.

---

792 *Ebbets Field:* the baseball stadium of the Brooklyn Dodgers before they moved to Los Angeles in 1958. Biff had played there in a city championship football game. See II.210 (p. 1495).

[BIFF *slowly returns to the kitchen. He stops, stares toward the heater.*]

LINDA. Will you ask Howard to let you work in New York?

WILLY. First thing in the morning. Everything'll be all right. 800

[BIFF *reaches behind the heater and draws out a length of rubber tubing. He is horrified and turns his head toward* WILLY'S *room, still dimly lit, from which the strains of* LINDA'S *desperate but monotonous humming rise.*]

WILLY. [*staring through the window into the moonlight*] Gee, look at the moon moving between the buildings!

[BIFF *wraps the tubing around his hand and quickly goes up the stairs.*]

ACT 2

[*Music is heard, gay and bright. The curtain rises as the music fades away.* WILLY, *in shirt sleeves, is sitting at the kitchen table, sipping coffee, his hat in his lap.* LINDA *is filling his cup when she can.*]

WILLY. Wonderful coffee. Meal in itself.

LINDA. Can I make you some eggs?

WILLY. No. Take a breath.

LINDA. You look so rested, dear.

WILLY. I slept like a dead one. First time in months. Imagine, sleeping till ten on 5
a Tuesday morning. Boys left nice and early, heh?

LINDA. They were out of here by eight o'clock.

WILLY. Good work!

LINDA. It was so thrilling to see them leaving together. I can't get over the shaving lotion in this house!

WILLY. [*smiling*] Mmm—

LINDA. Biff was very changed this morning. His whole attitude seemed to 10
be hopeful. He couldn't wait to get downtown to see Oliver.

WILLY. He's heading for a change. There's no question, there simply are certain men that take longer to get—solidified. How did he dress?

LINDA. His blue suit. He's so handsome in that suit. He could be a—anything in that suit!

[WILLY *gets up from the table.* LINDA *holds his jacket for him.*]

WILLY. There's no question, no question at all. Gee, on the way home tonight I'd like to buy some seeds.

LINDA. [*laughing*] That'd be wonderful. But not enough sun gets back there. Nothing'll grow any more.

WILLY. You wait, kid, before it's all over we're gonna get a little place out 15
in the country, and I'll raise some vegetables, a couple of chickens . . .

LINDA. You'll do it yet, dear.

[WILLY *walks out of his jacket,* LINDA *follows him.*]

WILLY. And they'll get married, and come for a weekend. I'd build a little guest house. 'Cause I got so many fine tools, all I'd need would be a little lumber and some peace of mind.

LINDA. [*joyfully*] I sewed the lining . . .

WILLY.   I could build two guest houses, so they'd both come. Did he decide how much he's going to ask Oliver for?

LINDA.   [*getting him into the jacket*] He didn't mention it, but I imagine ten or fifteen thousand. You going to talk to Howard today?

WILLY.   Yeah. I'll put it to him straight and simple. He'll just have to take me off the road.

LINDA.   And Willy, don't forget to ask for a little advance, because we've got the insurance premium. It's the grace period now.

WILLY.   That's a hundred . . . ?

LINDA.   A hundred and eight, sixty-eight. Because we're a little short again.

WILLY.   Why are we short?

LINDA.   Well, you had the motor job on the car . . .

WILLY.   That goddam Studebaker!

LINDA.   And you got one more payment on the refrigerator . . .

WILLY.   But it just broke again!

LINDA.   Well, it's old, dear.

WILLY.   I told you we should've bought a well-advertised machine. Charley bought a General Electric and it's twenty years old and it's still good, that son-of-a-bitch.

LINDA.   But, Willy—

WILLY.   Whoever heard of a Hastings refrigerator? Once in my life I would like to own something outright before it's broken! I'm always in a race with the junkyard! I just finished paying for the car and it's on its last legs. The refrigerator consumes belts like a goddam maniac. They time those things. They time them so when you finally paid for them, they're used up.

LINDA.   [*buttoning up his jacket as he unbuttons it*] All told, about two hundred dollars would carry us, dear. But that includes the last payment on the mortgage. After this payment, Willy, the house belongs to us.

WILLY.   It's twenty-five years!

LINDA.   Biff was nine years old when we bought it.

WILLY.   Well, that's a great thing. To weather a twenty-five year mortgage is—

LINDA.   It's an accomplishment.

WILLY.   All the cement, the lumber, the reconstruction I put in this house! There ain't a crack to be found in it any more.

LINDA.   Well, it served its purpose.

WILLY.   What purpose? Some stranger'll come along, move in, and that's that. If only Biff would take this house, and raise a family . . . [*He starts to go.*] Good-by, I'm late.

LINDA.   [*suddenly remembering*] Oh, I forgot! You're supposed to meet them for dinner.

WILLY.   Me?

LINDA.   At Frank's Chop House on Forty-eighth near Sixth Avenue.

WILLY.   Is that so! How about you?

LINDA.   No, just the three of you. They're gonna blow you to a big meal!

WILLY.   Don't say! Who thought of that?

LINDA.   Biff came to me this morning, Willy, and he said, "Tell Dad, we want to blow him to a big meal." Be there six o'clock. You and your two boys are going to have dinner.

WILLY.   Gee whiz! That's really somethin'. I'm gonna knock Howard for a loop, kid. I'll get an advance, and I'll come home with a New York job. Goddammit, now I'm gonna do it!

LINDA.   Oh, that's the spirit, Willy!   50
WILLY.   I will never get behind a wheel the rest of my life!
LINDA.   It's changing, Willy, I can feel it changing!
WILLY.   Beyond a question. G'by, I'm late. [*He starts to go again.*]
LINDA.   [*calling after him as she runs to the kitchen table for a handkerchief*] You got
your glasses?
WILLY.   [*feels for them, then comes back in*] Yeah, yeah, got my glasses.   55
LINDA.   [*giving him the handkerchief*] And a handkerchief.
WILLY.   Yeah, handkerchief.
LINDA.   And your saccharine?
WILLY.   Yeah, my saccharine.
LINDA.   Be careful on the subway stairs.   60

[*She kisses him, and a silk stocking is seen hanging from her hand. WILLY notices it.*]

WILLY.   Will you stop mending stockings? At least while I'm in the house. It gets
me nervous. I can't tell you. Please.

[*LINDA hides the stocking in her hand as she follows WILLY across the forestage in front of the house.*]

LINDA.   Remember, Frank's Chop House.
WILLY.   [*passing the apron*] Maybe beets would grow out there.
LINDA.   [*laughing*] But you tried so many times.
WILLY.   Yeah. Well, don't work hard today. [*He disappears around the right corner of*   65
the house.]
LINDA.   Be careful!

[*As WILLY vanishes, LINDA waves to him. Suddenly the phone rings. She runs across the stage
and into the kitchen and lifts it.*]

LINDA.   Hello? Oh, Biff! I'm so glad you called, I just . . . Yes, sure, I just told him.
Yes, he'll be there for dinner at six o'clock, I didn't forget. Listen, I was just dying to tell
you. You know that little rubber pipe I told you about? That he connected to the gas
heater? I finally decided to go down the cellar this morning and take it away and destroy
it. But it's gone! Imagine? He took it away himself, it isn't there! [*She listens.*] When? Oh,
then you took it. Oh—nothing, it's just that I'd hoped he'd taken it away himself. Oh,
I'm not worried, darling, because this morning he left in such high spirits, it was like
the old days! I'm not afraid any more. Did Mr. Oliver see you? . . . Well, you wait there
then. And make a nice impression on him, darling. Just don't perspire too much before
you see him. And have a nice time with Dad. He may have big news too! . . . That's right,
a New York job. And be sweet to him tonight, dear. Be loving to him. Because he's only a
little boat looking for a harbor. [*She is trembling with sorrow and joy.*] Oh, that's wonderful,
Biff, you'll save his life. Thanks, darling. Just put your arm around him when he comes
into the restaurant. Give him a smile. That's the boy . . . Good-by, dear . . . You got your
comb? . . . That's fine. Good-by, Biff dear.

[*In the middle of her speech, HOWARD WAGNER, thirty-six, wheels in a small typewriter table on
which is a wire-recording machine and proceeds to plug it in. This is on the left forestage. Light
slowly fades on LINDA as it rises on HOWARD. HOWARD is intent on threading the machine and
only glances over his shoulder as WILLY appears.*]

WILLY.   Pst! Pst!
HOWARD.   Hello, Willy, come in.
WILLY.   Like to have a little talk with you, Howard.   70

HOWARD.   Sorry to keep you waiting. I'll be with you in a minute.

WILLY.   What's that, Howard?

HOWARD.   Didn't you ever see one of these? Wire recorder.

WILLY.   Oh. Can we talk a minute?

HOWARD.   Records things. Just got delivery yesterday. Been driving me crazy, the most terrific machine I ever saw in my life. I was up all night with it.

WILLY.   What do you do with it?

HOWARD.   I bought it for dictation, but you can do anything with it. Listen to this. I had it home last night. Listen to what I picked up. The first one is my daughter. Get this. [*He flicks the switch and "Roll out the Barrel" is heard being whistled.*] Listen to that kid whistle.

WILLY.   That is lifelike, isn't it?

HOWARD.   Seven years old. Get that tone.

WILLY.   Ts, ts. Like to ask a little favor if you . . .

[*The whistling breaks off, and the voice of HOWARD'S DAUGHTER is heard.*]

HIS DAUGHTER.   "Now you, Daddy."

HOWARD.   She's crazy for me! [*Again the same song is whistled.*] That's me! Ha! [*He winks.*]

WILLY.   You're very good!

[*The whistling breaks off again. The machine runs silent for a moment.*]

HOWARD.   Sh! Get this now, this is my son.

HIS SON.   "The capital of Alabama is Montgomery; the capital of Arizona is Phoenix; the capital of Arkansas is Little Rock; the capital of California is Sacramento . . ." [*and on, and on*]

HOWARD.   [*holding up five fingers*] Five years old, Willy!

WILLY.   He'll make an announcer some day!

HIS SON.   [*continuing*] "The capital . . ."

HOWARD.   Get that—alphabetical order! [*The machine breaks off suddenly.*] Wait a minute. The maid kicked the plug out.

WILLY.   It certainly is a—

HOWARD.   Sh, for God's sake!

HIS SON.   "It's nine o'clock, Bulova watch time. So I have to go to sleep."

WILLY.   That really is—

HOWARD.   Wait a minute! The next is my wife.

[*They wait.*]

HOWARD'S VOICE.   "Go on, say something." [*pause*] "Well, you gonna talk?"

HIS WIFE.   "I can't think of anything."

HOWARD'S VOICE.   "Well, talk—it's turning."

HIS WIFE.   [*shyly, beaten*] "Hello." [*Silence*] "Oh, Howard, I can't talk into this . . ."

HOWARD.   [*snapping the machine off*] That was my wife.

WILLY.   That is a wonderful machine. Can we—

HOWARD.   I tell you, Willy, I'm gonna take my camera, and my bandsaw, and all my hobbies, and out they go. This is the most fascinating relaxation I ever found.

WILLY.   I think I'll get one myself.

HOWARD.   Sure, they're only a hundred and a half. You can't do without it. Supposing you wanna hear Jack Benny,° see? But you can't be at home at that hour. So

---

103 *Jack Benny:* (1894–1974), vaudeville, radio, television, and movie comedian.

you tell the maid to turn the radio on when Jack Benny comes on, and this automatically
goes on with the radio . . .

WILLY.   And when you come home you . . .

HOWARD.   You can come home twelve o'clock, one o'clock, any time you like,   105
and you get yourself a Coke and sit yourself down, throw the switch, and there's Jack
Benny's program in the middle of the night!

WILLY.   I'm definitely going to get one. Because lots of time I'm on the road, and
I think to myself, what I must be missing on the radio!

HOWARD.   Don't you have a radio in the car?

WILLY.   Well, yeah, but who ever thinks of turning it on?

HOWARD.   Say, aren't you supposed to be in Boston?

WILLY.   That's what I want to talk to you about, Howard. You got a minute?   110

[*He draws a chair in from the wing.*]

HOWARD.   What happened? What're you doing here?

WILLY.   Well . . .

HOWARD.   You didn't crack up again, did you?

WILLY.   Oh, no. No . . .

HOWARD.   Geez, you had me worried there for a minute. What's the trouble?   115

WILLY.   Well, tell you the truth, Howard, I've come to the decision that I'd rather
not travel any more.

HOWARD.   Not travel! Well, what'll you do?

WILLY.   Remember, Christmas time, when you had the party here? You said you'd
try to think of some spot for me here in town.

HOWARD.   With us?

WILLY.   Well, sure.

HOWARD.   Oh, yeah, yeah. I remember. Well, I couldn't think of anything for you,   120
Willy.

WILLY.   I tell ya, Howard. The kids are all grown up, y'know. I don't need much
any more. If I could take home—well, sixty-five dollars a week, I could swing it.

HOWARD.   Yeah, but Willy, see I—

WILLY.   I tell ya why, Howard. Speaking frankly and between the two of us,
y'know—I'm just a little tired.

HOWARD.   Oh, I could understand that, Willy. But you're a road man, Willy,   125
and we do a road business. We've only got a half-dozen salesmen on the floor here.

WILLY.   God knows, Howard, I never asked a favor of any man. But I was with the
firm when your father used to carry you up here in his arms.

HOWARD.   I know that, Willy, but—

WILLY.   Your father came to me the day you were born and asked me what I
thought of the name of Howard, may he rest in peace.

HOWARD.   I appreciate that, Willy, but there just is no spot here for you. If I had a
spot I'd slam you right in, but I just don't have a single solitary spot.

[*He looks for his lighter.* WILLY *has picked it up and gives it to him. Pause.*]

WILLY.   [*with increasing anger*] Howard, all I need to set my table is fifty dollars   130
a week.

HOWARD.   But where am I going to put you, kid?

WILLY.   Look, it isn't a question of whether I can sell merchandise, is it?

HOWARD.   No, but it's a business, kid, and everybody's gotta pull his own weight.

WILLY.   [*desperately*] Just let me tell you a story, Howard—

HOWARD.   'Cause you gotta admit, business is business.

WILLY.   [*angrily*] Business in definitely business, but just listen for a minute. You don't understand this. When I was a boy—eighteen, nineteen—I was already on the road. And there was a question in my mind as to whether selling had a future for me. Because in those days I had a yearning to go to Alaska. See, there were three gold strikes in one month in Alaska, and I felt like going out. Just for the ride, you might say.

HOWARD.   [*barely interested*] Don't say.

WILLY.   Oh, yeah, my father lived many years in Alaska. He was an adventurous man. We've got quite a little streak of self-reliance in our family. I thought I'd go out with my older brother and try to locate him, and maybe settle in the North with the old man. And I was almost decided to go, when I met a salesman in the Parker House.° His name was Dave Singleman. And he was eighty-four years old, and he'd drummed merchandise in thirty-one states. And old Dave, he'd go up to his room, y'understand, put on his green velvet slippers—I'll never forget—and pick up his phone and call the buyers, and without ever leaving his room, at the age of eighty-four, he made his living. And when I saw that, I realized that selling was the greatest career a man could want. 'Cause what could be more satisfying than to be able to go, at the age of eighty-four, into twenty or thirty different cities, and pick up a phone, and be remembered and loved and helped by so many different people? Do you know? when he died—and by the way he died the death of a salesman, in his green velvet slippers in the smoker of the New York, New Haven and Hartford, going into Boston—when he died, hundreds of salesmen and buyers were at his funeral. Things were sad on a lotta trains for months after that. [*He stands up.* HOWARD *has not looked at him.*] In those days there was personality in it, Howard. There was respect, and comradeship, and gratitude in it. Today, it's all cut and dried, and there's no chance for bringing friendship to bear—or personality. You see what I mean? They don't know me any more.

HOWARD.   [*moving away, to the right*] That's just the thing, Willy.

WILLY.   If I had forty dollars a week—that's all I'd need. Forty dollars, Howard.

HOWARD.   Kid, I can't take blood from a stone, I—

WILLY.   [*desperation is on him now*] Howard, the year Al Smith° was nominated, your father came to me and—

HOWARD.   [*starting to go off*] I've got to see some people, kid.

WILLY.   [*stopping him*] I'm talking about your father! There were promises made across this desk! You mustn't tell me you've got people to see—I put thirty-four years into this firm, Howard, and now I can't pay my insurance! You can't eat the orange and throw the peel away—a man is not a piece of fruit! [*after a pause*] Now pay attention. Your father—in 1928 I had a big year. I averaged a hundred and seventy dollars a week in commissions.

HOWARD.   [*impatiently*] Now, Willy, you never averaged—

WILLY.   [*banging his hand on the desk*] I averaged a hundred and seventy dollars a week in the year of 1928! And your father came to me—or rather, I was in the office here—it was right over this desk—and he put his hand on my shoulder—

HOWARD.   [*getting up*] You'll have to excuse me, Willy, I gotta see some people. Pull yourself together. [*going out*] I'll be back in a little while.

138 *Parker House:* a hotel in Boston.   142 *Al Smith:* Alfred E. Smith was governor of New York State (1919–1921, 1923–1929) and the Democratic presidential candidate defeated by Herbert Hoover in 1928.

[*On HOWARD's exit, the light on his chair grows very bright and strange.*]

WILLY. Pull myself together! What the hell did I say to him? My God, I was yelling at him! How could I! [*WILLY breaks off, staring at the light, which occupies the chair, animating it. He approaches this chair, standing across the desk from it.*] Frank, Frank, don't you remember what you told me that time? How you put your hand on my shoulder, and Frank . . . [*He leans on the desk and as he speaks the dead man's name he accidentally switches on the recorder, and instantly*]

HOWARD'S SON. ". . . of New York is Albany. The capital of Ohio is Cincinnati, the capital of Rhode Island is . . ." [*The recitation continues.*]

WILLY. [*leaping away with fright, shouting*] Ha! Howard! Howard! Howard!   150

HOWARD. [*rushing in*] What happened?

WILLY. [*pointing at the machine, which continues nasally, childishly, with the capital cities*] Shut it off! Shut it off!

HOWARD. [*pulling the plug out*] Look, Willy . . .

WILLY. [*pressing his hands to his eyes*] I gotta get myself some coffee. I'll get some coffee . . .

[*WILLY starts to walk out. HOWARD stops him.*]

HOWARD. [*rolling up the cord*] Willy, look . . .   155

WILLY. I'll go to Boston.

HOWARD. Willy, you can't go to Boston for us.

WILLY. Why can't I go?

HOWARD. I don't want you to represent us. I've been meaning to tell you for a long time now.

WILLY. Howard, are you firing me?

HOWARD. I think you need a good long rest, Willy.   160

WILLY. Howard—

HOWARD. And when you feel better, come back, and we'll see if we can work something out.

WILLY. But I gotta earn money, Howard. I'm in no position to—

HOWARD. Where are your sons? Why don't your sons give you a hand?   165

WILLY. They're working on a very big deal.

HOWARD. This is no time for false pride, Willy. You go to your sons and you tell them that you're tired. You've got two great boys, haven't you?

WILLY. Oh, no question, no question, but in the meantime . . .

HOWARD. Then that's that, heh?

WILLY. All right, I'll go to Boston tomorrow.   170

HOWARD. No, no.

WILLY. I can't throw myself on my sons. I'm not a cripple!

HOWARD. Look, kid, I'm busy this morning.

WILLY. [*grasping HOWARD's arm*] Howard, you've got to let me go to Boston!

HOWARD. [*hard, keeping himself under control*] I've got a line of people to see   175 this morning. Sit down, take five minutes, and pull yourself together, and then go home, will ya? I need the office, Willy. [*He starts to go, turns, remembering the recorder, starts to push off the table holding the recorder.*] Oh, yeah. Whenever you can this week, stop by and drop off the samples. You'll feel better, Willy, and then come back and we'll talk. Pull yourself together, kid, there's people outside.

[*Howard exits, pushing the table off left. Willy stares into space, exhausted. Now the music is heard—Ben's music—first distantly, then closer. As Willy speaks, Ben enters from the right. He carries valise and umbrella.*]

WILLY. Oh, Ben, how did you do it? What is the answer? Did you wind up the Alaska deal already?

BEN. Doesn't take much time if you know what you're doing. Just a short business trip. Boarding ship in an hour. Wanted to say good-by.

WILLY. Ben, I've got to talk to you.

BEN. [*glancing at his watch*] Haven't much time, William.

WILLY. [*crossing the apron to Ben*] Ben, nothing's working out. I don't know what to do.

BEN. Now, look here, William. I've bought timberland in Alaska and I need a man to look after things for me.

WILLY. God, timberland! Me and my boys in those grand outdoors!

BEN. You've a new continent at your doorstep, William. Get out of these cities, they're full of talk and time payments and courts of law. Screw on your fists and you can fight for a fortune up there.

WILLY. Yes, yes! Linda, Linda!

[*Linda enters as of old, with the wash.*]

LINDA. Oh, you're back?

BEN. I haven't much time.

WILLY. No, wait! Linda, he's got a proposition for me in Alaska.

LINDA. But you've got—[*to Ben*] He's got a beautiful job here.

WILLY. But in Alaska, kid, I could—

LINDA. You're doing well enough, Willy!

BEN. [*to Linda*] Enough for what, my dear?

LINDA. [*frightened of Ben and angry at him*] Don't say those things to him! Enough to be happy right here, right now. [*to Willy, while Ben laughs*] Why must everybody conquer the world? You're well liked, and the boys love you, and someday—[*to Ben*]—why old man Wagner told him just the other day that if he keeps it up he'll be a member of the firm, didn't he, Willy?

WILLY. Sure, sure. I am building something with this firm, Ben, and if a man is building something he must be on the right track, mustn't he?

BEN. What are you building? Lay your hand on it. Where is it?

WILLY. [*hesitantly*] That's true, Linda, there's nothing.

LINDA. Why? [*to Ben*] There's a man eighty-four years old—

WILLY. That's right, Ben, that's right. When I look at that man I say, what is there to worry about?

BEN. Bah!

WILLY. It's true, Ben. All he has to do is go into any city, pick up the phone, and he's making his living and you know why?

BEN. [*picking up his valise*] I've got to go.

WILLY. [*holding Ben back*] Look at this boy!

[*Biff, in his high school sweater, enters carrying suitcase. Happy carries Biff's shoulder guards, gold helmet, and football pants.*]

WILLY. Without a penny to his name, three great universities are begging for him, and from there the sky's the limit, because it's not what you do, Ben. It's who you know and the smile on your face! It's contacts, Ben, contacts! The whole wealth of Alaska passes over the lunch table at the Commodore Hotel,° and that's the wonder, the wonder of this country, that a man can end with diamonds here on the basis of being liked! [*He turns to BIFF*] And that's why when you get out on that field today it's impor-tant. Because thousands of people will be rooting for you and loving you. [*to BEN, who has again begun to leave*] And Ben! when he walks into a business office his name will sound out like a bell and all the doors will open to him! I've seen it, Ben, I've seen it a thousand times! You can't feel it with your hand like timber, but it's there!

BEN.   Good-by, William.

WILLY.   Ben, am I right? Don't you think I'm right? I value your advice.

BEN.   There's a new continent at your doorstep, William. You could walk out rich.   205
Rich! [*He is gone.*]

WILLY.   We'll do it here, Ben! You hear me? We're gonna do it here!

[*YOUNG BERNARD rushes in. The gay music of the Boys is heard.*]

BERNARD.   Oh, gee, I was afraid you left already!

WILLY.   Why? What time is it?

BERNARD.   It's half-past one!

WILLY.   Well, come on, everybody! Ebbets Field next stop! Where's the pennants?   210
[*He rushes through the wall-line of the kitchen and out into the dining-room.*]

LINDA.   [*to BIFF*] Did you pack fresh underwear?

BIFF.   [*who has been limbering up*] I want to go!

BERNARD.   Biff, I'm carrying your helmet, ain't I?

HAPPY.   No, I'm carrying the helmet.

BERNARD.   Oh, Biff, you promised me.   215

HAPPY.   I'm carrying the helmet.

BERNARD.   How am I going to get in the locker room?

LINDA.   Let him carry the shoulder guards. [*She puts her coat and hat on in the kitchen.*]

BERNARD.   Can I, Biff? 'Cause I told everybody I'm going to be in the locker room.

HAPPY.   In Ebbets Field it's the clubhouse.   220

BERNARD.   I meant the clubhouse. Biff!

HAPPY.   Biff!

BIFF.   [*grandly, after a slight pause.*] Let him carry the shoulder guards.

HAPPY.   [*as he gives BERNARD the shoulder guards*] Stay close to us now.

[*WILLY rushes in with the pennants.*]

WILLY.   [*handing them out*] Everybody wave when Biff comes out on the field.   225
[*HAPPY and BERNARD run off.*] You set now, boy?

[*The music has died away.*]

BIFF.   Ready to go, Pop. Every muscle is ready.

WILLY.   [*at the edge of the apron*] You realize what this means?

BIFF.   That's right, Pop.

WILLY.   [*feeling BIFF's muscles*] You're comin' home this afternoon captain of the All-Scholastic Championship Team of the City of New York.

202 *Commodore Hotel:* a large hotel in New York City.

BIFF.   I got it, Pop. And remember, pal, when I take off my helmet, that touch-   23⁴
down is for you.

WILLY.   Let's go! [*He is starting out, with his arm around BIFF, when CHARLEY enters, as
of old, in knickers.*] I got no room for you, Charley.

CHARLEY.   Room? For what?

WILLY.   In the car.

CHARLEY.   You goin' for a ride? I wanted to shoot some casino.

WILLY.   [*furiously*] Casino! [*incredulously*] Don't you realize what today is?   23

LINDA.   Oh, he knows, Willy. He's just kidding you.

WILLY.   That's nothing to kid about!

CHARLEY.   No, Linda, what's goin' on?

LINDA.   He's playing in Ebbets Field.

CHARLEY.   Baseball in this weather?   24

WILLY.   Don't talk to him. Come on, come on! [*He is pushing them out.*]

CHARLEY.   Wait a minute, didn't you hear the news?

WILLY.   What?

CHARLEY.   Don't you listen to the radio? Ebbets Field just blew up.

WILLY.   You go to hell! [*CHARLEY laughs. Pushing them out.*] Come on, come   2⁴
on! We're late.

CHARLEY.   [*as they go*] Knock a homer, Biff, knock a homer!

WILLY.   [*the last to leave, turning to CHARLEY*] I don't think that was funny, Charley.
This is the greatest day of his life.

CHARLEY.   Willy, when are you going to grow up?

WILLY.   Yeah, heh? When this game is over, Charley, you'll be laughing out the
other side of your face. They'll be calling him another Red Grange.° Twenty-five thousand a year.

CHARLEY.   [*kidding*] Is that so?   2

WILLY.   Yeah, that's so.

CHARLEY.   Well, then, I'm sorry, Willy. But tell me something.

WILLY.   What?

CHARLEY.   Who is Red Grange?

WILLY.   Put up your hands. Goddam you, put up your hands!   ⁵

[*CHARLEY, chuckling, shakes his head and walks away, around the left corner of the stage. WILLY
follows him. The music rises to a mocking frenzy.*]

WILLY.   Who the hell do you think you are, better than everybody else? You don't
know everything, you big, ignorant, stupid. . . . Put up your hands!

[*Light rises, on the right side of the forestage, on a small table in the reception room of CHARLEY'S
office. Traffic sounds are heard. BERNARD, now mature, sits whistling to himself. A pair of tennis
rackets and an overnight bag are on the floor beside him.*]

WILLY.   [*offstage*] What are you walking away for? Don't walk away! If you're going
to say something say it to my face! I know you laugh at me behind my back. You'll laugh
out of the other side of your goddam face after this game. Touchdown! Touchdown!
Eighty thousand people! Touchdown. Right between the goal posts.

---

249 *Red Grange:* Harold Edward Grange (1903–1991), all-America halfback (1923–1925) at the
University of Illinois.

[*BERNARD is a quiet, earnest, but self-assured young man. WILLY'S voice is coming from right upstage now. BERNARD lowers his feet off the table and listens. JENNY, his father's secretary, enters.*]

JENNY. [*distressed*] Say, Bernard, will you go out in the hall?

BERNARD. What is that noise? Who is it?

JENNY. Mr. Loman. He just got off the elevator. 260

BERNARD. [*getting up*] Who's he arguing with?

JENNY. Nobody. There's nobody with him. I can't deal with him any more, and your father gets all upset everytime he comes. I've got a lot of typing to do, and your father's waiting to sign it. Will you see him?

WILLY. [*entering*] Touchdown! Touch—[*He sees JENNY.*] Jenny, Jenny, good to see you. How're ya? Workin'? Or still honest?

JENNY. Fine. How've you been feeling?

WILLY. Not much any more, Jenny. Ha, ha! [*He is surprised to see the rackets.*] 265

BERNARD. Hello, Uncle Willy.

WILLY. [*almost shocked*] Bernard! Well, look who's here! [*He comes quickly, guiltily, to BERNARD and warmly shakes his hand.*]

BERNARD. How are you? Good to see you.

WILLY. What are you doing here?

BERNARD. Oh, just stopped off to see Pop. Get off my feet till my train leaves. I'm 270 going to Washington in a few minutes.

WILLY. Is he in?

BERNARD. Yes, he's in his office with the accountants. Sit down.

WILLY. [*sitting down*] What're you going to do in Washington?

BERNARD. Oh, just a case I've got there, Willy.

WILLY. That so? [*Indicating the rackets*] You going to play tennis there? 275

BERNARD. I'm staying with a friend who's got a court.

WILLY. Don't say. His own tennis court. Must be fine people, I bet.

BERNARD. They are, very nice. Dad tells me Biff's in town.

WILLY. [*with a big smile*] Yeah, Biff's in. Working on a very big deal, Bernard.

BERNARD. What's Biff doing? 280

WILLY. Well, he's been doing very big things in the West. But he decided to establish himself here. Very big. We're having dinner. Did I hear your wife had a boy?

BERNARD. That's right. Our second.

WILLY. Two boys! What do you know!

BERNARD. What kind of a deal has Biff got?

WILLY. Well, Bill Oliver—very big sporting-goods man—he wants Biff very 285 badly. Called him in from the West. Long distance, carte blanche, special deliveries. Your friends have their own private tennis court?

BERNARD. You still with the old firm, Willy?

WILLY. [*after a pause*] I'm—I'm overjoyed to see how you made the grade, Bernard, overjoyed. It's an encouraging thing to see a young man really—really—Looks very good for Biff—very—[*He breaks off, then*] Bernard—[*He is so full of emotion, he breaks off again.*]

BERNARD. What is it, Willy?

WILLY. [*small and alone*] What—what's the secret?

BERNARD. What secret? 290

WILLY. How—how did you? Why didn't he ever catch on?

BERNARD. I wouldn't know that, Willy.

WILLY. [*confidentially, desperately*] You were his friend, his boyhood friend. There's something I don't understand about it. His life ended after that Ebbets Field game. From the age of seventeen nothing good ever happened to him.

BERNARD. He never trained himself for anything.

WILLY. But he did, he did. After high school he took so many correspondence courses. Radio mechanics; television; God knows what, and never made the slightest mark.

BERNARD. [*taking off his glasses*] Willy, do you want to talk candidly?

WILLY. [*rising, faces BERNARD*] I regard you as a very brilliant man, Bernard. I value your advice.

BERNARD. Oh, the hell with the advice, Willy. I couldn't advise you. There's just one thing I've always wanted to ask you. When he was supposed to graduate, and the math teacher flunked him—

WILLY. Oh, that son-of-a-bitch ruined his life.

BERNARD. Yeah, but, Willy, all he had to do was go to summer school and make up that subject.

WILLY. That's right, that's right.

BERNARD. Did you tell him not to go to summer school?

WILLY. Me? I begged him to go. I ordered him to go!

BERNARD. Then why wouldn't he go?

WILLY. Why? Why! Bernard, that question has been trailing me like a ghost for the last fifteen years. He flunked the subject, and laid down and died like a hammer hit him!

BERNARD. Take it easy, kid.

WILLY. Let me talk to you—I got nobody to talk to. Bernard, Bernard, was it my fault? Y'see? It keeps going around in my mind, maybe I did something to him. I got nothing to give him.

BERNARD. Don't take it so hard.

WILLY. Why did he lay down? What is the story there? You were his friend!

BERNARD. Willy, I remember, it was June, and our grades came out. And he'd flunked math.

WILLY. That son-of-a-bitch!

BERNARD. No, it wasn't right then. Biff just got very angry, I remember, and he was ready to enroll in summer school.

WILLY. [*surprised*] He was?

BERNARD. He wasn't beaten by it at all. But then, Willy, he disappeared from the block for almost a month. And I got the idea that he'd gone up to New England to see you. Did he have a talk with you then?

[*WILLY stares in silence.*]

BERNARD. Willy?

WILLY. [*with a strong edge of resentment in his voice*] Yeah, he came to Boston. What about it?

BERNARD. Well, just that when he came back—I'll never forget this, it always mystifies me. Because I'd thought so well of Biff, even though he'd always taken advantage of me. I loved him, Willy, y'know? And he came back after that month and took his sneakers—remember the sneakers with "University of Virginia" printed on them? He was so proud of those, wore them every day. And he took them down in the cellar, and burned them up in the furnace. We had a fist fight. It lasted at least half an hour. Just the two of us, punching each other down the cellar, and crying right through it. I've often thought of how strange it was that I knew he'd given up his life. What happened in Boston, Willy?

[*WILLY looks at him as at an intruder.*]

> BERNARD. I just bring it up because you asked me.
> WILLY. [*angrily*] Nothing. What do you mean, "What happened?" What's that got to do with anything?
> BERNARD. Well, don't get sore.   320
> WILLY. What are you trying to do, blame it on me? If a boy lays down is that my fault?
> BERNARD. Now, Willy, don't get—
> WILLY. Well, don't—don't talk to me that way! What does that mean, "What happened?"

[*CHARLEY enters. He is in his vest, and he carries a bottle of bourbon.*]

> CHARLEY. Hey, you're going to miss that train. [*He waves the bottle.*]
> BERNARD. Yeah, I'm going. [*He takes the bottle.*] Thanks, Pop. [*He picks up*   325
> *his rackets and bag.*] Good-by, Willy, and don't worry about it. You know, "If at first you don't succeed . . ."
> WILLY. Yes, I believe in that.
> BERNARD. But sometimes, Willy, it's better for a man just to walk away.
> WILLY. Walk away?
> BERNARD. That's right.
> WILLY. But if you can't walk away?   330
> BERNARD. [*after a slight pause*] I guess that's when it's tough. [*extending his hand*] Good-by, Willy.
> WILLY. [*shaking BERNARD's hand*] Good-by, boy.
> CHARLEY. [*an arm on BERNARD's shoulder*] How do you like this kid? Gonna argue a case in front of the Supreme Court.
> BERNARD. [*protesting*] Pop!
> WILLY. [*genuinely shocked, pained, and happy*] No! The Supreme Court!   335
> BERNARD. I gotta run. 'By, Dad!
> CHARLEY. Knock 'em dead, Bernard!

[*BERNARD goes off.*]

> WILLY. [*as CHARLEY takes out his wallet*] The Supreme Court! And he didn't even mention it!
> CHARLEY. [*counting out money on the desk*] He don't have to—he's gonna do it.
> WILLY. And you never told him what to do, did you? You never took any   340
> interest in him.
> CHARLEY. My salvation is that I never took any interest in anything. There's some money—fifty dollars. I got an accountant inside.
> WILLY. Charley, look . . . [*with difficulty*] I got my insurance to pay. If you can manage it—I need a hundred and ten dollars.

[*CHARLEY doesn't reply for a moment; merely stops moving.*]

> WILLY. I'd draw it from my bank but Linda would know, and I . . .
> CHARLEY. Sit down, Willy.

WILLY. [*moving toward the chair*] I'm keeping an account of everything,   34₅
remember. I'll pay every penny back. [*He sits.*]

CHARLEY. Now listen to me, Willy . . .

WILLY. I want you to know I appreciate . . .

CHARLEY. [*sitting down on the table*] Willy, what're you doin'? What the hell is goin'
on in your head?

WILLY. Why? I'm simply . . .

CHARLEY. I offered you a job. You can make fifty dollars a week. And I won't send   35₀
you on the road.

WILLY. I've got a job.

CHARLEY. Without pay? What kind of job is a job without pay? [*He rises.*] Now,
look, kid, enough is enough. I'm no genius but I know when I'm being insulted.

WILLY. Insulted!

CHARLEY. Why don't you want to work for me?

WILLY. What's the matter with you? I've got a job.   35₅

CHARLEY. Then what're you walkin' in here every week for?

WILLY. [*getting up*] Well, if you don't want me to walk in here—

CHARLEY. I am offering you a job.

WILLY. I don't want your goddam job!

CHARLEY. When the hell are you going to grow up?   36₀

WILLY. [*furiously*] You big ignoramus, if you say that to me again I'll rap you one!
I don't care how big you are! [*He's ready to fight.*]

[*Pause.*]

CHARLEY. [*kindly, going to him*] How much do you need, Willy?

WILLY. Charley, I'm strapped. I'm strapped. I don't know what to do. I was just
fired.

CHARLEY. Howard fired you?

WILLY. That snotnose. Imagine that? I named him. I named him Howard.   3₆₅

CHARLEY. Willy, when're you gonna realize that them things don't mean anything? You named him Howard, but you can't sell that. The only thing you got in this
world is what you can sell. And the funny thing is that you're a salesman, and you don't
know that.

WILLY. I've tried to think otherwise, I guess. I always felt that if a man was impressive, and well liked, that nothing—

CHARLEY. Why must everybody like you? Who liked J. P. Morgan?° Was he impressive? In a Turkish bath he'd look like a butcher. But with his pockets on he was very well
liked. Now listen, Willy, I know you don't like me, and nobody can say I'm in love with
you, but I'll give you a job because—just for the hell of it, put it that way. Now what do
you say?

WILLY. I—I just can't work for you, Charley.

CHARLEY. What're you, jealous of me?   3₇₀

WILLY. I can't work for you, that's all, don't ask me why.

CHARLEY. [*angered, takes out more bills*] You been jealous of me all your life, you
damned fool! Here, pay your insurance. [*He puts the money in WILLY'S hand.*]

368 *J. P. Morgan:* John Pierpont Morgan (1837–1913) was the founder of U.S. Steel and the head
of a gigantic family fortune that was enlarged by his son, John Pierpont Morgan (1867–1943).
Charley is probably referring to the son.

WILLY.   I'm keeping strict accounts.

CHARLEY.   I've got some work to do. Take care of yourself. And pay your insurance.

WILLY.   [*moving to the right*] Funny, y'know? After all the highways, and the   375
trains, and the appointments, and the years, you end up worth more dead than alive.

CHARLEY.   Willy, nobody's worth nothin' dead. [*after a slight pause*] Did you hear
what I said?

[*WILLY stands still, dreaming.*]

CHARLEY.   Willy!

WILLY.   Apologize to Bernard for me when you see him. I didn't mean to argue
with him. He's a fine boy. They're all fine boys, and they'll end up big—all of them.
Someday they'll all play tennis together. Wish me luck, Charley. He saw Bill Oliver today.

CHARLEY.   Good luck.

WILLY.   [*on the verge of tears*] Charley, you're the only friend I got. Isn't that a   380
remarkable thing? [*He goes out.*]

CHARLEY.   Jesus!

[*CHARLEY stares after him a moment and follows. All light blacks out. Suddenly raucous music is
heard, and a red glow rises behind the screen at right. STANLEY, a young waiter, appears, carrying a table, followed by HAPPY, who is carrying two chairs.*]

STANLEY.   [*putting the table down*] That's all right, Mr. Loman. I can handle it
myself. [*He turns and takes the chairs from HAPPY and places them at the table.*]

HAPPY.   [*glancing around.*] Oh, this is better.

STANLEY.   Sure, in the front there you're in the middle of all kinds a noise.
Whenever you got a party, Mr. Loman, you just tell me and I'll put you back here.
Y' know, there's a lotta people they don't like it private, because when they go out they
like to see a lotta action around them because they're sick and tired to stay in the house
by theirself. But I know you, you ain't from Hackensack.° You know what I mean?

HAPPY.   [*sitting down*] So how's it coming, Stanley?   385

STANLEY.   Ah, it's a dog's life. I only wish during the war they'd a took me in the
Army. I coulda been dead by now.

HAPPY.   My brother's back, Stanley.

STANLEY.   Oh, he come back, heh? From the Far West.

HAPPY.   Yeah, big cattle man, my brother, so treat him right. And my father's
coming too.

STANLEY.   Oh, your father too!   390

HAPPY.   You got a couple of nice lobsters?

STANLEY.   Hundred per cent, big.

HAPPY.   I want them with claws.

STANLEY.   Don't worry. I don't give you no mice. [*HAPPY laughs.*] How about some
wine? It'll put a head on the meal.

HAPPY.   No. You remember, Stanley, that recipe I brought you from overseas?   395
With the champagne in it?

STANLEY.   Oh, yeah, sure. I still got it tacked up yet in the kitchen. But that'll have
to cost a buck apiece anyways.

HAPPY.   That's all right.

384 *Hackensack:* a city in northeastern New Jersey; Stanley uses the name as a reference to unsophisticated visitors to New York City.

STANLEY.   What'd you, hit a number or somethin'?

HAPPY.   No, it's a little celebration. My brother is—I think he pulled off a big deal today. I think we're going into business together.

STANLEY.   Great! That's the best for you. Because a family business, you know what I mean?—that's the best.

HAPPY.   That's what I think.

STANLEY.   'Cause what's the difference? Somebody steals? It's in the family. Know what I mean? [*sotto voce°*] Like this bartender here. The boss is goin' crazy what kinda leak he's got in the cash register. You put it in but it don't come out.

HAPPY.   [*raising his head*] Sh!

STANLEY.   What?

HAPPY.   You notice I wasn't lookin' right or left, was I?

STANLEY.   No.

HAPPY.   And my eyes are closed.

STANLEY.   So what's the—?

HAPPY.   Strudel's comin'.

STANLEY.   [*catching on, looks around*] Ah, no, there's no—

[*He breaks off as a furred, lavishly dressed GIRL enters and sits at the next table. Both follow her with their eyes.*]

STANLEY.   Geez, how'd ya know?

HAPPY.   I got radar or something. [*staring directly at her profile*] Oooooooo . . . Stanley.

STANLEY.   I think that's for you, Mr. Loman.

HAPPY.   Look at that mouth. Oh God. And the binoculars.

STANLEY.   Geez, you got a life, Mr. Loman.

HAPPY.   Wait on her.

STANLEY.   [*going to the GIRL's table*] Would you like a menu, ma'am?

GIRL.   I'm expecting someone, but I'd like a—

HAPPY.   Why don't you bring her—excuse me, miss, do you mind? I sell champagne, and I'd like you to try my brand. Bring her a champagne, Stanley.

GIRL.   That's awfully nice of you.

HAPPY.   Don't mention it. It's all company money. [*He laughs.*]

GIRL.   That's a charming product to be selling, isn't it?

HAPPY.   Oh, gets to be like everything else. Selling is selling, y'know.

GIRL.   I suppose.

HAPPY.   You don't happen to sell, do you?

GIRL.   No, I don't sell.

HAPPY.   Would you object to a compliment from a stranger? You ought to be on a magazine cover.

GIRL.   [*looking at him a little archly*] I have been.

[*STANLEY comes in with a glass of champagne.*]

HAPPY.   What'd I say before, Stanley? You see? She's a cover girl.

STANLEY.   Oh, I could see, I could see.

HAPPY.   [*to the GIRL*] What magazine?

GIRL.   Oh, a lot of them. [*She takes the drink.*] Thank you.

402 *sotto voce:* spoken in an undertone or "stage" whisper.

HAPPY.   You know what they say in France, don't you? "Champagne is the drink of the complexion"—Hya, Biff!

[*BIFF has entered and sits with HAPPY.*]

BIFF.   Hello, kid. Sorry I'm late.

HAPPY.   I just got here. Uh, Miss—?   435

GIRL.   Forsythe.

HAPPY.   Miss Forsythe, this is my brother.

BIFF.   Is Dad here?

HAPPY.   His name if Biff. You might've heard of him. Great football player.

GIRL.   Really? What team?   440

HAPPY.   Are you familiar with football?

GIRL.   No. I'm afraid I'm not.

HAPPY.   Biff is quarterback with the New York Giants.

GIRL.   Well, that is nice, isn't it? [*She drinks.*]

HAPPY.   Good health.   445

GIRL.   I'm happy to meet you.

HAPPY.   That's my name. Hap. It's really Harold, but at West Point they called me Happy.

GIRL.   [*now really impressed*] Oh, I see. How do you do? [*She turns her profile.*]

BIFF.   Isn't Dad coming?

HAPPY.   You want her?   450

BIFF.   Oh, I could never make that.

HAPPY.   I remember the time that idea would never come into your head. Where's the old confidence, Biff?

BIFF.   I just saw Oliver—

HAPPY.   Wait a minute. I've got to see that old confidence again. Do you want her? She's on call.

BIFF.   Oh, no. [*He turns to look at the GIRL.*]   455

HAPPY.   I'm telling you. Watch this. [*turning to the GIRL*] Honey? [*She turns to him.*] Are you busy?

GIRL.   Well, I am . . . but I could make a phone call.

HAPPY.   Do that, will you, honey? And see if you can get a friend. We'll be here for a while. Biff is one of the greatest football players in the country.

GIRL.   [*standing up*] Well, I'm certainly happy to meet you.

HAPPY.   Come back soon.   460

GIRL.   I'll try.

HAPPY.   Don't try, honey, try hard.

[*The GIRL exits. STANLEY follows, shaking his head in bewildered admiration.*]

HAPPY.   Isn't that a shame now? A beautiful girl like that? That's why I can't get married. There's not a good woman in a thousand. New York is loaded with them, kid!

BIFF.   Hap, look—

HAPPY.   I told you she was on call!   465

BIFF.   [*strangely unnerved*] Cut it out, will ya? I want to say something to you.

HAPPY.   Did you see Oliver?

BIFF.   I saw him all right. Now look, I want to tell Dad a couple of things and I want you to help me.

HAPPY.   What? Is he going to back you?

BIFF.   Are you crazy? You're out of your goddam head, you know that?   47◐

HAPPY.   Why? What happened?

BIFF.   [*breathlessly*] I did a terrible thing today, Hap. It's been the strangest day I ever went through. I'm all numb, I swear.

HAPPY.   You mean he wouldn't see you?

BIFF.   Well, I waited six hours for him, see? All day. Kept sending my name in. Even tried to date his secretary so she'd get me to him, but no soap.

HAPPY.   Because you're not showin' the old confidence, Biff. He remembered   47
you, didn't he?

BIFF.   [*stopping HAPPY with a gesture*] Finally, about five o'clock, he comes out. Didn't remember who I was or anything. I felt like such an idiot, Hap.

HAPPY.   Did you tell him my Florida idea?

BIFF.   He walked away. I saw him for one minute. I got so mad I could've torn the walls down! How the hell did I ever get the idea I was a salesman there? I even believed myself that I'd been a salesman for him! And then he gave me one look and— I realized what a ridiculous lie my whole life has been! We've been talking in a dream for fifteen years. I was a shipping clerk.

HAPPY.   What'd you do?

BIFF.   [*with great tension and wonder*] Well, he left, see. And the secretary   4⁸
went out. I was all alone in the waiting-room. I don't know what came over me, Hap. The next thing I know I'm in his office—paneled walls, everything. I can't explain it. I—Hap, I took his fountain pen.

HAPPY.   Geez, did he catch you?

BIFF.   I ran out. I ran down all eleven flights. I ran and ran and ran.

HAPPY.   That was an awful dumb—what'd you do that for?

BIFF.   [*agonized*] I don't know, I just—wanted to take something. I don't know. You gotta help me, Hap, I'm gonna tell Pop.

HAPPY.   You crazy? What for?

BIFF.   Hap, he's got to understand that I'm not the man somebody lends that   4
kind of money to. He thinks I've been spiting him all these years and it's eating him up.

HAPPY.   That's just it. You tell him something nice.

BIFF.   I can't.

HAPPY.   Say you got a lunch date with Oliver tomorrow.

BIFF.   So what do I do tomorrow?   ⁴

HAPPY.   You leave the house tomorrow and come back at night and say Oliver is thinking it over. And he thinks it over for a couple of weeks, and gradually it fades away and nobody's the worse.

BIFF.   But it'll go on forever!

HAPPY.   Dad is never so happy as when he's looking forward to something!

[*WILLY enters.*]

HAPPY.   Hello, scout!

WILLY.   Gee, I haven't been here in years!

[*STANLEY has followed WILLY in and sets a chair for him. STANLEY starts off but HAPPY stops him.*]

HAPPY.   Stanley!

[*STANLEY stands by, waiting for an order.*]

BIFF. [*going to WILLY with guilt, as to an invalid*] Sit down, Pop. You want a drink?

WILLY. Sure, I don't mind.

BIFF. Let's get a load on.

WILLY. You look worried.   500

BIFF. N-no. [*to STANLEY*] Scotch all around. Make it doubles.

STANLEY. Doubles, right. [*He goes.*]

WILLY. You had a couple already, didn't you?

BIFF. Just a couple, yeah.

WILLY. Well, what happened, boy? [*nodding affirmatively, with a smile*] Every-   505
thing go all right?

BIFF. [*takes a breath, then reaches out and grasps WILLY'S hand*] Pal . . . [*He is smiling bravely, and WILLY is smiling too.*] I had an experience today.

HAPPY. Terrific, Pop.

WILLY. That so? What happened?

BIFF. [*high, slightly alcoholic, above the earth*] I'm going to tell you everything from first to last. It's been a strange day. [*Silence. He looks around, composes himself as best he can, but his breath keeps breaking the rhythm of his voice.*] I had to wait quite a while for him, and—

WILLY. Oliver?   510

BIFF. Yeah, Oliver. All day, as a matter of cold fact. And a lot of—instances—facts, Pop, facts about my life came back to me. Who was it, Pop? Who ever said I was a sales-man with Oliver?

WILLY. Well, you were.

BIFF. No, Dad, I was a shipping clerk.

WILLY. But you were practically—

BIFF. [*with determination*] Dad, I don't know who said it first, but I was never   515
a salesman for Bill Oliver.

WILLY. What're you talking about?

BIFF. Let's hold on to the facts tonight, Pop. We're not going to get anywhere bullin' around. I was a shipping clerk.

WILLY. [*angrily*] All right, now listen to me—

BIFF. Why don't you let me finish?

WILLY. I'm not interested in stories about the past or any crap of that kind   520
because the woods are burning, boys, you understand? There's a big blaze going on all around. I was fired today.

BIFF. [*shocked*] How could you be?

WILLY. I was fired, and I'm looking for a little good news to tell your mother, because the woman has waited and the woman has suffered. The gist of it is that I haven't got a story left in my head, Biff. So don't give me a lecture about facts and aspects. I am not interested. Now what've you got to say to me?

[*STANLEY enters with three drinks. They wait until he leaves.*]

WILLY. Did you see Oliver?

BIFF. Jesus, Dad!

WILLY. You mean you didn't go up there?   525

HAPPY. Sure he went up there.

BIFF. I did. I—saw him. How could they fire you?

WILLY. [*on the edge of his chair*] What kind of a welcome did he give you?

BIFF. He won't even let you work on commission?

WILLY. I'm out! [*driving*] So tell me, he gave you a warm welcome?   530

HAPPY.   Sure, Pop, sure!

BIFF.   [*driven*] Well, it was kind of—

WILLY.   I was wondering if he'd remember you. [*to HAPPY*] Imagine, man doesn't see him for ten, twelve years and gives him that kind of a welcome!

HAPPY.   Damn right!

BIFF.   [*trying to return to the offensive*] Pop, look—

WILLY.   You know why he remembered you, don't you? Because you impressed him in those days.

BIFF.   Let's talk quietly and get this down to the facts, huh?

WILLY.   [*as though BIFF had been interrupting*] Well, what happened? It's great news, Biff. Did he take you into his office or'd you talk in the waiting-room?

BIFF.   Well, he came in, see, and—

WILLY.   [*with a big smile*] What'd he say? Betcha he threw his arm around you.

BIFF.   Well, he kinda—

WILLY.   He's a fine man. [*to HAPPY*] Very hard man to see, y'know.

HAPPY.   [*agreeing*] Oh, I know.

WILLY.   [*to BIFF*] Is that where you had the drinks?

BIFF.   Yeah, he gave me a couple of—no, no!

HAPPY.   [*cutting in*] He told him my Florida idea.

WILLY.   Don't interrupt. [*to BIFF*] How'd he react to the Florida idea?

BIFF.   Dad, will you give me a minute to explain?

WILLY.   I've been waiting for you to explain since I sat down here! What happened? He took you into his office and what?

BIFF.   Well—I talked. And—and he listened, see.

WILLY.   Famous for the way he listens, y'know. What was his answer?

BIFF.   His answer was—[*He breaks off, suddenly angry.*] Dad, you're not letting me tell you what I want to tell you!

WILLY.   [*accusing, angered*] You didn't see him, did you?

BIFF.   I did see him!

WILLY.   What'd you insult him or something? You insulted him, didn't you?

BIFF.   Listen, will you let me out of it, will you just let me out of it!

HAPPY.   What the hell!

WILLY.   Tell me what happened!

BIFF.   [*to HAPPY*] I can't talk to him!

[*A single trumpet note jars the ear. The light of green leaves stains the house, which holds the air of night and a dream. YOUNG BERNARD enters and knocks on the door of the house.*]

YOUNG BERNARD.   [*frantically*] Mrs. Loman, Mrs. Loman!

HAPPY.   Tell him what happened!

BIFF.   [*to HAPPY*] Shut up and leave me alone!

WILLY.   No, no! You had to go and flunk math!

BIFF.   What math? What're you talking about?

YOUNG BERNARD.   Mrs. Loman, Mrs. Loman!

[*LINDA appears in the house, as of old.*]

WILLY.   [*wildly*] Math, math, math!

BIFF.   Take it easy, Pop!

YOUNG BERNARD.   Mrs. Loman!

WILLY.   [*furiously*] If you hadn't flunked you'd've been set by now!

BIFF.   Now, look, I'm gonna tell you what happened, and you're going to   570
listen to me.

YOUNG BERNARD.   Mrs. Loman!

BIFF.   I waited six hours—

HAPPY.   What the hell are you saying?

BIFF.   I kept sending in my name but he wouldn't see me. So finally he . . .

[*He continues unheard as light fades low on the restaurant.*]

YOUNG BERNARD.   Biff flunked math!   575

LINDA.   No!

YOUNG BERNARD.   Birnbaum flunked him! They won't graduate him!

LINDA.   But they have to. He's gotta go to the university. Where is he? Biff! Biff!

YOUNG BERNARD.   No, he left. He went to Grand Central.

LINDA.   Grand—You mean he went to Boston!   580

YOUNG BERNARD.   Is Uncle Willy in Boston?

LINDA.   Oh, maybe Willy can talk to the teacher. Oh, the poor, poor boy!

[*Light on house area snaps out.*]

BIFF.   [*at the table, now audible, holding up a gold fountain pen*] . . . so I'm washed
up with Oliver, you understand? Are you listening to me?

WILLY.   [*at a loss*] Yeah, sure. If you hadn't flunked—

BIFF.   Flunked what? What're you talking about?   585

WILLY.   Don't blame everything on me! I didn't flunk math—you did! What pen?

HAPPY.   That was awful dumb, Biff, a pen like that is worth—

WILLY.   [*seeing the pen for the first time*] You took Oliver's pen?

BIFF.   [*weakening*] Dad, I just explained it to you.

WILLY.   You stole Bill Oliver's fountain pen!   590

BIFF.   I didn't exactly steal it! That's just what I've been explaining to you!

HAPPY.   He had it in his hand and just then Oliver walked in, so he got nervous
and stuck it in his pocket!

WILLY.   My God, Biff!

BIFF.   I never intended to do it, Dad!

OPERATOR'S VOICE.   Standish Arms, good evening!   595

WILLY.   [*shouting*] I'm not in my room!

BIFF.   [*frightened*] Dad, what's the matter? [*He and HAPPY stand up.*]

OPERATOR.   Ringing Mr. Loman for you!

WILLY.   I'm not there, stop it!

BIFF.   [*horrified, gets down on one knee before WILLY*] Dad, I'll make good, I'll   600
make good. [*WILLY tries to get to his feet. BIFF holds him down.*] Sit down now.

WILLY.   No, you're no good, you're no good for anything.

BIFF.   I am, Dad, I'll find something else, you understand? Now don't worry about
anything. [*He holds up WILLY's face.*] Talk to me, Dad.

OPERATOR.   Mr. Loman does not answer. Shall I page him?

WILLY.   [*attempting to stand, as though to rush and silence the OPERATOR*] No, no, no!

HAPPY.   He'll strike something, Pop.   605

WILLY.   No, no . . .

BIFF.   [*desperately, standing over WILLY*] Pop, listen! Listen to me! I'm telling you
something good. Oliver talked to his partner about the Florida idea. you listening? He—

he talked to his partner, and he came to me . . . I'm going to be all right, you hear? Dad, listen to me, he said it was just a question of the amount!

WILLY. Then you . . . got it?

HAPPY. He's gonna be terrific, Pop!

WILLY. [*trying to stand*] Then you got it, haven't you? You got it! You got it!

BIFF. [*agonized, holds WILLY down*] No, no. Look, Pop. I'm supposed to have lunch with them tomorrow. I'm just telling you this so you'll know that I can still make an impression, Pop. And I'll make good somewhere, but I can't go tomorrow, see?

WILLY. Why not? You simply—

BIFF. But the pen, Pop!

WILLY. You give it to him and tell him it was an oversight!

HAPPY. Sure, have lunch tomorrow!

BIFF. I can't say that—

WILLY. You were doing a crossword puzzle and accidentally used his pen!

BIFF. Listen, kid, I took those balls years ago, now I walk in with his fountain pen? That clinches it, don't you see? I can't face him like that! I'll try elsewhere.

PAGE'S VOICE. Paging Mr. Loman!

WILLY. Don't you want to be anything?

BIFF. Pop, how can I go back?

WILLY. You don't want to be anything, is that what's behind it?

BIFF. [*now angry at WILLY for not crediting his sympathy*] Don't take it that way! You think it was easy walking into that office after what I'd done to him? A team of horses couldn't have dragged me back to Bill Oliver!

WILLY. Then why'd you go?

BIFF. Why did I go? Why did I go? Look at you! Look at what's become of you!

[*Off left, THE WOMAN laughs.*]

WILLY. Biff, you're going to go to that lunch tomorrow, or—

BIFF. I can't go. I've got no appointment!

HAPPY. Biff, for . . . !

WILLY. Are you spiting me?

BIFF. Don't take it that way! Goddammit!

WILLY. [*strikes BIFF and falters away from the table*] You rotten little louse! Are you spiting me?

THE WOMAN. Someone's at the door, Willy!

BIFF. I'm no good, can't you see what I am?

HAPPY. [*separating them*] Hey, you're in a restaurant! Now cut it out, both of you! [*The girls enter.*] Hello, girls, sit down.

[*THE WOMAN laughs, off left.*]

MISS FORSYTHE. I guess we might as well. This is Letta.

THE WOMAN. Willy, are you going to wake up?

BIFF. [*ignoring WILLY*] How're ya, miss, sit down. What do you drink?

MISS FORSYTHE. Letta might not be able to stay long.

LETTA. I gotta get up very early tomorrow. I got jury duty. I'm so excited! Were you fellows ever on a jury?

BIFF. No, but I been in front of them! [*The girls laugh.*] This is my father.

LETTA. Isn't he cute? Sit down with us, Pop.

HAPPY.   Sit him down, Biff!

BIFF.   [*going to him*] Come on, slugger, drink us under the table. To hell with it! Come on, sit down, pal.

[*On BIFF's last insistence, WILLY is about to sit.*]

THE WOMAN.   [*now urgently*] Willy, are you going to answer the door!

[*THE WOMAN's call pulls WILLY back. He starts right, befuddled.*]

BIFF.   Hey, where are you going?   645
WILLY.   Open the door.
BIFF.   The door?
WILLY.   The washroom . . . the door . . . where's the door?
BIFF.   [*leading WILLY to the left*] Just go straight down.

[*WILLY moves left.*]

THE WOMAN.   Willy, Willy, are you going to get up, get up, get up, get up?   650

[*WILLY exits left.*]

LETTA.   I think it's sweet you bring your daddy along.
MISS FORSYTHE.   Oh, he isn't really your father!
BIFF.   [*at left, turning to her resentfully*] Miss Forsythe, you've just seen a prince walk by. A fine, troubled prince. A hard-working, unappreciated prince. A pal, you understand? A good companion. Always for his boys.
LETTA.   That's so sweet.
HAPPY.   Well, girls, what's the program? We're wasting time. Come on, Biff.   655
Gather round. Where would you like to go?
BIFF.   Why don't you do something for him?
HAPPY.   Me!
BIFF.   Don't you give a damn for him, Hap?
HAPPY.   What're you talking about? I'm the one who—
BIFF.   I sense it, you don't give a good goddam about him. [*He takes the rolled-up*   660
hose from his pocket and puts it on the table in front of HAPPY.] Look what I found in the cellar, for Christ's sake. How can you bear to let it go on?
HAPPY.   Me? Who goes away? Who runs off and—
BIFF.   Yeah, but he doesn't mean anything to you. You could help him—I can't! Don't you understand what I'm talking about? He's going to kill himself, don't you know that?
HAPPY.   Don't I know it! Me!
BIFF.   Hap, help him! Jesus . . . help him . . . Help me, help me, I can't bear to look at his face! [*Ready to weep, he hurries out, up right.*]
HAPPY.   [*staring after him*] Where are you going?   665
MISS FORSYTHE.   What's he so mad about?
HAPPY.   Come on, girls, we'll catch up with him.
MISS FORSYTHE.   [*as HAPPY pushes her out*] Say, I don't like that temper of his!
HAPPY.   He's just a little overstrung, he'll be all right!
WILLY.   [*off left, as THE WOMAN laughs*] Don't answer! Don't answer!   670
LETTA.   Don't you want to tell your father—
HAPPY.   No, that's not my father. He's just a guy. Come on, we'll catch Biff, and, honey, we're going to paint this town! Stanley, where's the check! Hey, Stanley!

[*They exit.* STANLEY *looks toward left.*]

STANLEY. [*calling to* HAPPY *indignantly*] Mr. Loman! Mr. Loman!

[STANLEY *picks up a chair and follows them off. Knocking is heard off left.* THE WOMAN *enters, laughing.* WILLY *follows her. She is in a black slip; he is buttoning his shirt. Raw, sensuous music accompanies their speech.*]

WILLY. Will you stop laughing? Will you stop?

THE WOMAN. Aren't you going to answer the door? He'll wake the whole hotel.

WILLY. I'm not expecting anybody.

THE WOMAN. Whyn't you have another drink, honey, and stop being so damn self-centered?

WILLY. I'm so lonely.

THE WOMAN. You know you ruined me, Willy? From now on, whenever you come to the office, I'll see that you go right through to the buyers. No waiting at my desk any more, Willy. You ruined me.

WILLY. That's nice of you to say that.

THE WOMAN. Gee, you are self-centered! Why so sad? You are the saddest, self-centeredest soul I ever did see-saw. [*She laughs. He kisses her.*] Come on inside, drummer boy. It's silly to be dressing in the middle of the night. [*As knocking is heard*] Aren't you going to answer the door?

WILLY. They're knocking on the wrong door.

THE WOMAN. But I felt the knocking! And he heard us talking in here. Maybe the hotel's on fire!

WILLY. [*his terror rising*] It's a mistake.

THE WOMAN. Then tell him to go away!

WILLY. There's nobody there.

THE WOMAN. It's getting on my nerves, Willy. There's somebody standing out there and it's getting on my nerves!

WILLY. [*pushing her away from him*] All right, stay in the bathroom here, and don't come out. I think there's a law in Massachusetts about it, so don't come out. It may be that new room clerk. He looked very mean. So don't come out. It's a mistake, there's no fire.

[*The knocking is heard again. He takes a few steps away from her, and she vanishes into the wing. The light follows him, and now he is facing* YOUNG BIFF, *who carries a suitcase.* BIFF *steps toward him. The music is gone.*]

BIFF. Why didn't you answer?

WILLY. Biff! What are you doing in Boston?

BIFF. Why didn't you answer? I've been knocking for five minutes, I called you on the phone—

WILLY. I just heard you. I was in the bathroom and had the door shut. Did anything happen home?

BIFF. Dad—I let you down.

WILLY. What do you mean?

BIFF. Dad . . .

WILLY. Biffo, what's this about? [*putting his arm around* BIFF] Come on, let's go downstairs and get you a malted.

BIFF. Dad, I flunked math.

WILLY. Not for the term?

BIFF. The term. I haven't got enough credits to graduate.

WILLY. You mean to say Bernard wouldn't give you the answers? 700

BIFF. He did, he tried, but I only got a sixty-one.

WILLY. And they wouldn't give you four points?

BIFF. Birnbaum refused absolutely. I begged him, Pop, but he won't give me those points. You gotta talk to him before they close the school. Because if he saw the kind of man you are, and you just talked to him in your way, I'm sure he'd come through for me. The class came right before practice, see, and I didn't go enough. Would you talk to him? He'd like you, Pop. You know the way you could talk.

WILLY. You're on. We'll drive right back.

BIFF. Oh, Dad, good work! I'm sure he'll change it for you! 705

WILLY. Go downstairs and tell the clerk I'm checkin' out. Go right down.

BIFF. Yes, sir! See, the reason he hates me, Pop—one day he was late for class so I got up at the blackboard and imitated him. I crossed my eyes and talked with a lithp.

WILLY. [*laughing*] You did? The kids like it?

BIFF. They nearly died laughing!

WILLY. Yeah? What'd you do? 710

BIFF. The thquare root of thixthy twee is . . . [*WILLY bursts out laughing; BIFF joins him.*] And in the middle of it he walked in!

[*WILLY laughs and THE WOMAN joins in offstage.*]

WILLY. [*without hesitation*] Hurry downstairs and—

BIFF. Somebody in there?

WILLY. No, that was next door.

[*THE WOMAN laughs offstage.*]

BIFF. Somebody got in your bathroom! 715

WILLY. No, it's the next room, there's a party—

THE WOMAN. [*enters, laughing. She lisps this.*] Can I come in? There's something in the bathtub, Willy, and it's moving!

[*WILLY looks at BIFF, who is staring open-mouthed and horrified at THE WOMAN.*]

WILLY. Ah—you better go back to your room. They must be finished painting by now. They're painting her room so I let her take a shower here. Go back, go back . . . [*He pushes her.*]

THE WOMAN. [*resisting*] But I've got to get dressed, Willy, I can't—

WILLY. Get out of here! Go back, go back . . . [*suddenly striving for the ordinary*] 720 This is Miss Francis, Biff, she's a buyer. They're painting her room. Go back, Miss Francis, go back . . .

THE WOMAN. But my clothes, I can't go out naked in the hall!

WILLY. [*pushing her offstage*] Get outa here! Go back, go back!

[*BIFF slowly sits down on his suitcase as the argument continues offstage.*]

THE WOMAN. Where's my stockings? You promised me stockings, Willy!

WILLY. I have no stockings here!

THE WOMAN. You had two boxes of size nine sheers for me, and I want them! 725

WILLY. Here, for God's sake, will you get outa here!

THE WOMAN.   [*enters holding a box of stockings*] I just hope there's nobody in the hall. That's all I hope. [*To* BIFF] Are you football or baseball?

BIFF.   Football.

THE WOMAN.   [*angry, humiliated*] That's me too. G'night. [*she snatches her clothes from* WILLY, *and walks out.*]

WILLY.   [*after a pause*] Well, better get going. I want to get to the school first thing   730▪
in the morning. Get my suits out of the closet. I'll get my valise. [BIFF *doesn't move.*]
What's the matter? [BIFF *remains motionless, tears falling*] She's a buyer. Buys for J. H.
Simmons. She lives down the hall—they're painting. You don't imagine—[*He breaks off.
After a pause*] Now listen, pal, she's just a buyer. She sees merchandise in her room and
they have to keep it looking just so . . . [*Pause. Assuming command*] All right, get my suits.
[BIFF *doesn't move.*] Now stop crying and do as I say. I gave you an order. Biff, I gave you
an order! Is that what you do when I give you an order? How dare you cry! [*putting his
arm around* BIFF] Now look, Biff, when you grow up you'll understand about these things.
You mustn't—you mustn't overemphasize a thing like this. I'll see Birnbaum first thing
in the morning.

BIFF.   Never mind.

WILLY.   [*getting down beside* BIFF] Never mind! He's going to give you those points.
I'll see to it.

BIFF.   He wouldn't listen to you.

WILLY.   He certainly will listen to me. You need those points for the U. of
Virginia.

BIFF.   I'm not going there.   73▪

WILLY.   Heh? If I can't get him to change that mark you'll make it up in summer
school. You've got all summer to—

BIFF.   [*his weeping breaking from him*] Dad . . .

WILLY.   [*infected by it*] Oh, my boy . . .

BIFF.   Dad . . .

WILLY.   She's nothing to me, Biff. I was lonely, I was terribly lonely.   74▪

BIFF.   You—you gave her Mama's stockings! [*His tears break through and he rises
to go.*]

WILLY.   [*grabbing for* BIFF] I gave you an order!

BIFF.   Don't touch me, you—liar!

WILLY.   Apologize for that!

BIFF.   You fake! You phony little fake! [*Overcome, he turns quickly and weeping   74▪
fully goes out with his suitcase.* WILLY *is left on the floor on his knees.*]

WILLY.   I gave you an order! Biff, come back here or I'll beat you! Come back
here! I'll whip you!

[STANLEY *comes quickly in from the right and stands in front of* WILLY.]

WILLY.   [*shouts at* STANLEY] I gave you an order . . .

STANLEY.   Hey, let's pick it up, pick it up, Mr. Loman. [*He helps* WILLY *to his feet.*]
Your boys left with the chippies. They said they'll see you home.

[*A* SECOND WAITER *watches some distance away.*]

WILLY.   But we were supposed to have dinner together.

[*Music is heard,* WILLY'S *theme.*]

STANLEY.   Can you make it?   7▪

WILLY.   I'll—sure, I can make it. [*suddenly concerned about his clothes*] Do I—I look all right?

STANLEY.   Sure, you look all right. [*He flicks a speck off WILLY's lapel.*]

WILLY.   Here—here's a dollar.

STANLEY.   Oh, your son paid me. It's all right.

WILLY.   [*putting it in STANLEY's hand*] No, take it. You're a good boy.   755

STANLEY.   Oh, no, you don't have to . . .

WILLY.   Here—here's some more, I don't need it any more. [*after a slight pause*] Tell me—is there a seed store in the neighborhood?

STANLEY.   Seeds? You mean like to plant?

[*As WILLY turns, STANLEY slips the money back into his jacket pocket.*]

WILLY.   Yes. Carrots, peas . . .

STANLEY.   Well, there's hardware stores on Sixth Avenue, but it may be too   760
late now.

WILLY.   [*anxiously*] Oh, I'd better hurry. I've got to get some seeds. [*He starts off to the right.*] I've got to get some seeds, right away. Nothing's planted. I don't have a thing in the ground.

[*WILLY hurries out as the light goes down. STANLEY moves over to the right after him, watches him off. The other waiter has been staring at WILLY.*]

STANLEY.   [*to the WAITER*] Well, whatta you looking at?

[*The WAITER picks up the chairs and moves off right. STANLEY takes the table and follows him. The light fades on this area. There is a long pause, the sound of the flute coming over. The light gradually rises on the kitchen, which is empty. HAPPY appears at the door of the house, followed by BIFF. HAPPY is carrying a large bunch of long-stemmed roses. He enters the kitchen, looks around for LINDA. Not seeing her, he turns to BIFF, who is just outside the house door, and makes a gesture with his hands, indicating "Not here, I guess." He looks into the living-room and freezes. Inside, LINDA, unseen, is seated, WILLY's coat on her lap. She rises ominously and quietly and moves toward HAPPY, who backs up into the kitchen, afraid.*]

HAPPY.   Hey, what're you doing up? [*LINDA says nothing but moves toward him implacably.*] Where's Pop? [*He keeps backing to the right, and now LINDA is in full view in the doorway to the living-room.*] Is he sleeping?

LINDA.   Where were you?

HAPPY.   [*trying to laugh it off*] We met two girls, Mom, very fine types. Here,   765
we brought you some flowers. [*offering them to her*] Put them in your room, Ma.

[*She knocks them to the floor at BIFF's feet. He has now come inside and closed the door behind him. She stares at BIFF, silent.*]

HAPPY.   Now what'd you do that for? Mom, I want you to have some flowers—

LINDA.   [*cutting HAPPY off, violently to BIFF*] Don't you care whether he lives or dies?

HAPPY.   [*going to the stairs*] Come upstairs, Biff.

BIFF.   [*with a flare of disgust, to HAPPY*] Go away from me! [*to LINDA*] What do you mean, lives or dies? Nobody's dying around here, pal.

LINDA.   Get out of my sight! Get out of here!   770

BIFF.   I wanna see the boss.

LINDA.   You're not going near him!

BIFF.   Where is he? [*He moves into the living-room and LINDA follows.*]

LINDA. [*shouting after BIFF*] You invite him for dinner. He looks forward to it all day—[*BIFF appears in his parents' bedroom, looks around, and exits.*]—and then you desert him there. There's no stranger you'd do that to!

HAPPY. Why? He had a swell time with us. Listen, when I—[*LINDA comes back into the kitchen.*]—desert him I hope I don't outlive the day!

LINDA. Get out of here!

HAPPY. Now look, Mom . . .

LINDA. Did you have to go to women tonight? You and your lousy rotten whores!

[*BIFF re-enters the kitchen.*]

HAPPY. Mom, all we did was follow Biff around trying to cheer him up! [*to BIFF*] Boy, what a night you gave me!

LINDA. Get out of here, both of you, and don't come back! I don't want you tormenting him any more. Go on now, get your things together! [*to BIFF*] You can sleep in his apartment. [*She starts to pick up the flowers and stops herself.*] Pick up this stuff, I'm not your maid any more. Pick it up, you bum, you!

[*HAPPY turns his back to her in refusal. BIFF slowly moves over and gets down on his knees, picking up the flowers.*]

LINDA. You're a pair of animals! Not one, not another living soul would have had the cruelty to walk out on that man in a restaurant!

BIFF. [*not looking at her*] Is that what he said?

LINDA. He didn't have to say anything. He was so humiliated he nearly limped when he came in.

HAPPY. But, Mom, he had a great time with us—

BIFF. [*cutting him off violently*] Shut up!

[*Without another word, HAPPY goes upstairs.*]

LINDA. You! You didn't even go in to see if he was all right!

BIFF. [*still on the floor in front of LINDA, the flowers in his hand; with self-loathing*] No. Didn't. Didn't do a damned thing. How do you like that, heh? Left him babbling in a toilet.

LINDA. You louse. You . . .

BIFF. Now you hit it on the nose! [*He gets up, throws the flowers in the wastebasket.*] The scum of the earth, and you're looking at him!

LINDA. Get out of here!

BIFF. I gotta talk to the boss, Mom. Where is he?

LINDA. You're not going near him. Get out of this house!

BIFF. [*with absolute assurance, determination*] No. We're gonna have an abrupt conversation, him and me.

LINDA. You're not talking to him!

[*Hammering is heard from outside the house, off right. BIFF turns toward the noise.*]

LINDA. [*suddenly pleading*] Will you please leave him alone?

BIFF. What's he doing out there?

LINDA. He's planting the garden!

BIFF. [*quietly*] Now? Oh, my God!

[*BIFF moves outside, LINDA following. The light dies down on them and comes up on the center of the apron as WILLY walks into it. He is carrying a flashlight, a hoe, and a handful of seed packets. He raps the top of the hoe sharply to fix it firmly, and then moves to the left, measuring off the distance with his foot. He holds the flashlight to look at the seed packets, reading off the instructions. He is in the blue of night.*]

WILLY.   Carrots . . . quarter-inch apart. Rows . . . one-foot rows. [*He measures it off.*] One foot. [*He puts down a package and measures off.*] Beets. [*He puts down another package and measures again.*] Lettuce. [*He reads the package, puts it down.*] One foot—[*He breaks off as* BEN *appears at the right and moves slowly down to him.*] What a proposition, ts, ts. Terrific, terrific. 'Cause she's suffered, Ben, the woman has suffered. You understand me? A man can't go out the way he came in, Ben, a man has got to add up to something. You can't, you can't—[BEN *moves toward him as though to interrupt.*] You gotta consider, now. Don't answer so quick. Remember, it's a guaranteed twenty-thousand-dollar proposition. Now look, Ben, I want you to go through the ins and outs of this thing with me. I've got nobody to talk to, Ben, and the woman has suffered, you hear me?

BEN.   [*standing still, considering*] What's the proposition?   800

WILLY.   It's twenty thousand dollars on the barrelhead. Guaranteed, gilt-edged, you understand?

BEN.   You don't want to make a fool of yourself. They might not honor the policy.

WILLY.   How can they dare refuse? Didn't I work like a coolie to meet every premium on the nose? And now they don't pay off? Impossible!

BEN.   It's called a cowardly thing, William.

WILLY.   Why? Does it take more guts to stand here the rest of my life ringing up   805
a zero?

BEN.   [*yielding*] That's a point, William. [*He moves, thinking, turns.*] And twenty thousand—that *is* something one can feel with the hand, it is there.

WILLY.   [*now assured, with rising power*] Oh, Ben, that's the whole beauty of it! I see it like a diamond, shining in the dark, hard and rough, that I can pick up and touch in my hand. Not like—like an appointment! This would not be another damned-fool appointment, Ben, and it changes all the aspects. Because he thinks I'm nothing, see, and so he spites me. But the funeral—[*straightening up*] Ben, that funeral will be massive! They'll come from Maine, Massachusetts, Vermont, New Hampshire! All the old-timers with the strange license plates—that boy will be thunder-struck, Ben, because he never realized—I am known! Rhode Island, New York, New Jersey—I am known, Ben, and he'll see it with his eyes once and for all. He'll see what I am, Ben! He's in for a shock, that boy!

BEN.   [*coming down to the edge of the garden*] He'll call you a coward.

WILLY.   [*suddenly fearful*] No, that would be terrible.

BEN.   Yes. And a damned fool.   810

WILLY.   No, no, he mustn't, I won't have that! [*He is broken and desperate.*]

BEN.   He'll hate you, William.

[*The gay music of the Boys is heard.*]

WILLY.   Oh, Ben, how do we get back to all the great times? Used to be so full of light, and comradeship, the sleigh-riding in winter, and the ruddiness on his cheeks. And always some kind of good news coming up, always something nice coming up ahead. And never even let me carry the valises in the house, and simonizing, simonizing that little red car! Why, why can't I give him something and not have him hate me?

BEN.   Let me think about it. [*He glances at his watch.*] I still have a little time. Remarkable proposition, but you've got to be sure you're not making a fool of yourself.

[*BEN drifts upstage and goes out of sight. BIFF comes down from the left.*]

WILLY.   [*suddenly conscious of BIFF, turns and looks up at him, then begins picking up the packages of seeds in confusion*] Where the hell is that seed? [*Indignantly*] You can't see nothing out here! They boxed in the whole goddam neighborhood!

BIFF.   There are people all around here. Don't you realize that?

WILLY.   I'm busy. Don't bother me.

BIFF.   [*taking the hoe from WILLY*] I'm saying good-by to you, Pop. [*WILLY looks at him, silent, unable to move.*] I'm not coming back any more.

WILLY.   You're not going to see Oliver tomorrow?

BIFF.   I've got no appointment, Dad.

WILLY.   He put his arm around you, and you've got no appointment?

BIFF.   Pop, get this now, will you? Everytime I've left it's been a fight that sent me out of here. Today I realized something about myself and I tried to explain it to you and I—I think I'm just not smart enough to make any sense out of it for you. To hell with whose fault it is or anything like that. [*He takes WILLY's arm.*] Let's just wrap it up, heh? Come on in, we'll tell Mom. [*He gently tries to pull WILLY to left.*]

WILLY.   [*frozen, immobile, with guilt in his voice*] No, I don't want to see her.

BIFF.   Come on! [*He pulls again, and WILLY tries to pull away.*]

WILLY.   [*highly nervous*] No, no, I don't want to see her.

BIFF.   [*tries to look into WILLY's face, as if to find the answer there*] Why don't you want to see her?

WILLY.   [*more harshly now*] Don't bother me, will you?

BIFF.   What do you mean, you don't want to see her? You don't want them calling you yellow, do you? This isn't your fault; it's me, I'm a bum. Now come inside! [*WILLY strains to get away.*] Did you hear what I said to you?

[*WILLY pulls away and quickly goes by himself into the house. BIFF follows.*]

LINDA.   [*to WILLY*] Did you plant, dear?

BIFF.   [*at the door, to LINDA*] All right, we had it out. I'm going and I'm not writing any more.

LINDA.   [*going to WILLY in the kitchen*] I think that's the best way, dear. 'Cause there's no use drawing it out, you'll just never get along.

[*WILLY doesn't respond.*]

BIFF.   People ask where I am and what I'm doing, you don't know, and you don't care. That way it'll be off your mind and you can start brightening up again. All right? That clears it, doesn't it? [*WILLY is silent, and BIFF goes to him.*] You gonna wish me luck, scout? [*He extends his hand.*] What do you say?

LINDA.   Shake his hand, Willy.

WILLY.   [*turning to her, seething with hurt*] There's no necessity to mention the pen at all, y'know.

BIFF.   [*gently*] I've got no appointment, Dad.

WILLY.   [*erupting fiercely*] He put his arm around . . . ?

BIFF.   Dad, you're never going to see what I am, so what's the use of arguing? If I strike oil I'll send you a check. Meantime forget I'm alive.

WILLY.   [*to LINDA*] Spite, see?

BIFF.   Shake hands, Dad.

WILLY.   Not my hand.

BIFF.   I was hoping not to go this way.

WILLY.   Well, this is the way you're going. Good-by.

[*BIFF looks at him a moment, then turns sharply and goes to the stairs.*]

WILLY.   [*stops him with*] May you rot in hell if you leave this house!

BIFF.   [*turning*] Exactly what is it that you want from me?

WILLY.   I want you to know, on the train, in the mountains, in the valleys,   845
wherever you go, that you cut down your life for spite!

BIFF.   No, no.

WILLY.   Spite, spite, is the word of your undoing! And when you're down and out,
remember what did it. When you're rotting somewhere beside the railroad tracks,
remember, and don't you dare blame it on me!

BIFF.   I'm not blaming it on you!

WILLY.   I won't take the rap for this, you hear?

[*HAPPY comes down the stairs and stands on the bottom step, watching.*]

BIFF.   That's just what I'm telling you!   850

WILLY.   [*sinking into a chair at the table, with full accusation*] You're trying to put a
knife in me—don't think I don't know what you're doing!

BIFF.   All right, phony! Then let's lay it on the line. [*He whips the rubber tube out of
his pocket and puts it on the table.*]

HAPPY.   You crazy—

LINDA.   Biff! [*She moves to grab the hose, but BIFF holds it down with his hand.*]

BIFF.   Leave it here! Don't move it!   855

WILLY.   [*not looking at it*] What is that?

BIFF.   You know goddam well what that is.

WILLY.   [*caged, wanting to escape*] I never saw that.

BIFF.   You saw it. The mice didn't bring it into the cellar! What is this supposed to
do, make a hero out of you? This supposed to make me sorry for you?

WILLY.   Never heard of it.   860

BIFF.   There'll be no pity for you, you hear it? No pity!

WILLY.   [*to LINDA*] You hear the spite!

BIFF.   No, you're going to hear the truth—what you are and what I am!

LINDA.   Stop it!

WILLY.   Spite!   865

HAPPY.   [*coming down toward BIFF*] You cut it now!

BIFF.   [*to HAPPY*] The man don't know who we are! The man is gonna know! [*to
WILLY*] We never told the truth for ten minutes in this house!

HAPPY.   We always told the truth!

BIFF.   [*turning on him*] You big blow, are you the assistant buyer? You're one of
the two assistants to the assistant, aren't you?

HAPPY.   Well, I'm practically—   870

BIFF.   You're practically full of it! We all are! And I'm through with it. [*to WILLY*]
Now hear this, Willy, this is me.

WILLY.   I know you!

BIFF.   You know why I had no address for three months? I stole a suit in Kansas
City and I was in jail. [*to LINDA, who is sobbing*] Stop crying. I'm through with it.

[*LINDA turns from them, her hands covering her face.*]

WILLY.   I suppose that's my fault!

BIFF.   I stole myself out of every good job since high school!

WILLY.   And whose fault is that?

BIFF.   And I never got anywhere because you blew me so full of hot air I could never stand taking orders from anybody! That's whose fault it is!

WILLY.   I hear that!

LINDA.   Don't, Biff!

BIFF.   It's goddam time you heard that! I had to be boss big shot in two weeks, and I'm through with it!

WILLY.   Then hang yourself! For spite, hang yourself!

BIFF.   No! Nobody's hanging himself, Willy! I ran down eleven flights with a pen in my hand today. And suddenly I stopped, you hear me? And in the middle of that office building, do you hear this? I stopped in the middle of that building and I saw—the sky. I saw the things that I love in this world. The work and the food and time to sit and smoke. And I looked at the pen and said to myself, what the hell am I grabbing this for? Why am I trying to become what I don't want to be? What am I doing in an office, making a contemptuous, begging fool of myself, when all I want is out there, waiting for me the minute I say I know who I am! Why can't I say that, Willy?

[*He tries to make* WILLY *face him, but* WILLY *pulls away and moves to the left.*]

WILLY.   [*with hatred, threateningly.*] The door of your life is wide open!

BIFF.   Pop! I'm a dime a dozen, and so are you!

WILLY.   [*turning on him now in an uncontrolled outburst*] I am not a dime a dozen! I am Willy Loman, and you are Biff Loman!

[*BIFF starts for* WILLY, *but is blocked by* HAPPY. *In his fury,* BIFF *seems on the verge of attacking his father.*]

BIFF.   I am not a leader of men, Willy, and neither are you. You were never anything but a hard-working drummer who landed in the ash can like all the rest of them! I'm one dollar an hour, Willy! I tried seven states and couldn't raise it. A buck an hour! Do you gather my meaning? I'm not bringing home any prizes any more, and you're going to stop waiting for me to bring them home!

WILLY.   [*directly to* BIFF] You vengeful, spiteful mutt!

[*BIFF breaks from* HAPPY. WILLY, *in fright, starts up the stairs.* BIFF *grabs him.*]

BIFF.   [*at the peak of his fury*] Pop I'm nothing! I'm nothing, Pop. Can't you understand that? There's no spite in it any more. I'm just what I am, that's all.

[*BIFF's fury has spent itself, and he breaks down, sobbing, holding on to* WILLY, *who dumbly fumbles for* BIFF's *face.*]

WILLY.   [*astonished*] What're you doing? What're you doing? [*to* LINDA] Why is he crying?

BIFF.   [*crying, broken*] Will you let me go, for Christ's sake? Will you take that phony dream and burn it before something happens? [*Struggling to contain himself, he pulls away and moves to the stairs.*] I'll go in the morning. Put him—put him to bed. [*Exhausted,* BIFF *moves up the stairs to his room.*]

WILLY.   [*after a long pause, astonished, elevated*] Isn't that—isn't that remarkable? Biff—he likes me!

LINDA.   He loves you, Willy!

HAPPY.   [*deeply moved*] Always did, Pop.

WILLY.   Oh, Biff! [*staring wildly*] He cried! Cried to me. [*He is choking with his love, and now cries out his promise.*] That boy—that boy is going to be magnificent!

[*BEN appears in the light just outside the kitchen.*]

BEN.   Yes, outstanding, with twenty thousand behind him.   895

LINDA.   [*sensing the racing of his mind, fearfully, carefully*] Now come to bed, Willy. It's all settled now.

WILLY.   [*finding it difficult not to rush out of the house*] Yes, we'll sleep. Come on. Go to sleep, Hap.

BEN.   And it does take a great kind of a man to crack the jungle.

[*In accents of dread, BEN's idyllic music starts up.*]

HAPPY.   [*his arm around LINDA*] I'm getting married, Pop, don't forget it. I'm changing everything. I'm gonna run that department before the year is up. You'll see, Mom. [*He kisses her.*]

BEN.   The jungle is dark but full of diamonds, Willy.   900

[*WILLY turns, moves, listening to BEN.*]

LINDA.   Be good. You're both good boys, just act that way, that's all.

HAPPY.   'Night, Pop. [*He goes upstairs.*]

LINDA.   [*to WILLY*] Come, dear.

BEN.   [*with greater force*] One must go in to fetch a diamond out.

WILLY.   [*to LINDA, as he moves slowly along the edge of the kitchen, toward the   905
door*] I just want to get settled down, Linda. Let me sit alone for a little.

LINDA.   [*almost uttering her fear*] I want you upstairs.

WILLY.   [*taking her in his arms*] In a few minutes, Linda. I couldn't sleep right now. Go on, you look awful tired. [*He kisses her.*]

BEN.   Not like an appointment at all. A diamond is rough and hard to the touch.

WILLY.   Go on now. I'll be right up.

LINDA.   I think this is the only way, Willy.   910

WILLY.   Sure, it's the best thing.

BEN.   Best thing!

WILLY.   The only way. Everything is gonna be—go on, kid, get to bed. You look so tired.

LINDA.   Come right up.

WILLY.   Two minutes.   915

[*LINDA goes into the living-room, then reappears in her bedroom. WILLY moves just outside the kitchen door.*]

WILLY.   Loves me. [*wonderingly*] Always loved me. Isn't that a remarkable thing? Ben, he'll worship me for it!

BEN.   [*with promise*] It's dark there, but full of diamonds.

WILLY.   Can you imagine that magnificence with twenty thousand dollars in his pocket?

LINDA.   [*calling from her room*] Willy! Come up!

WILLY.   [*calling into the kitchen*] Yes! Yes. Coming! It's very smart, you realize that,   920
don't you, sweetheart? Even Ben sees it. I gotta go, baby. 'By! 'By! [*going over to BEN, almost dancing*] Imagine? When the mail comes he'll be ahead of Bernard again!

BEN.   A perfect proposition all around.

WILLY.   Did you see how he cried to me? Oh, if I could kiss him, Ben!

BEN.   Time, William, time!

WILLY.   Oh, Ben, I always knew one way or another we were gonna make it, Biff and I!

BEN.   [*looking at his watch*] The boat. We'll be late. [*He moves slowly off into the*   925
darkness.]

WILLY.   [*elegiacally, turning to the house*] Now when you kick off, boy, I want a seventy-yard boot, and get right down the field under the ball, and when you hit, hit low and hit hard, because it's important, boy. [*He swings around and faces the audience.*] There's all kinds of important people in the stands, and the first thing you know . . . [*suddenly realizing he is alone*] Ben! Ben, where do I . . . ? [*He makes a sudden movement of search.*] Ben, how do I . . . ?

LINDA.   [*calling*] Willy, you coming up?

WILLY.   [*uttering a gasp of fear, whirling about as if to quiet her*] Sh! [*He turns around as if to find his way; sounds, faces, voices, seem to be swarming in upon him and he flicks at them, crying*] Sh! Sh! [*Suddenly music, faint and high, stops him. It rises in intensity, almost to an unbearable scream. He goes up and down on his toes, and rushes off around the house.*] Shhh!

LINDA.   Willy?

[*There is no answer. LINDA waits. BIFF gets up off his bed. He is still in his clothes. HAPPY sits up. BIFF stands listening.*]

LINDA.   [*with real fear*] Willy, answer me! Willy!   93[

[*There is the sound of a car starting and moving away at full speed.*]

LINDA.   No!

BIFF.   [*rushing down the stairs*] Pop!

[*As the car speeds off, the music crashes down in a frenzy of sound, which becomes the soft pulsation of a single cello string. BIFF slowly returns to his bedroom. He and HAPPY gravely don their jackets. LINDA slowly walks out of her room. The music has developed into a dead march. The leaves of day are appearing over everything. CHARLEY and BERNARD somberly dressed, appear and knock on the kitchen door. BIFF and HAPPY slowly descend the stairs to the kitchen as CHARLEY and BERNARD enter. All stop a moment when LINDA, in clothes of mourning, bearing a little bunch of roses, comes through the draped doorway into the kitchen. She goes to CHARLEY and takes his arm. Now all move toward the audience, through the wall-line of the kitchen. At the limit of the apron, LINDA lays down the flowers, kneels, and sits back on her heels. All stare down at the grave.*]

REQUIEM

CHARLEY.   It's getting dark, Linda.

[*LINDA doesn't react. She stares at the grave.*]

BIFF.   How about it, Mom? Better get some rest, heh? They'll be closing the gate soon.

[*LINDA makes no move. Pause.*]

HAPPY.   [*deeply angered*] He had no right to do that. There was no necessity for it. We would've helped him.

CHARLEY.   [*grunting*] Hmmm.
BIFF.   Come along, Mom.   5
LINDA.   Why didn't anybody come?
CHARLEY.   It was a very nice funeral.
LINDA.   But where are all the people he knew? Maybe they blame him.
CHARLEY.   Naa. It's a rough world, Linda. They wouldn't blame him.
LINDA.   I can't understand it. At this time especially. First time in thirty-five years   10
we were just about free and clear. He only needed a little salary. He was even finished
with the dentist.
CHARLEY.   No man only needs a little salary.
LINDA.   I can't understand it.
BIFF.   There were a lot of nice days. When he'd come home from a trip; or on
Sundays, making the stoop; finishing the cellar; putting on the new porch; when he built
the extra bathroom; and put up the garage. You know something, Charley, there's more
of him in that front stoop than in all the sales he ever made.
CHARLEY.   Yeah. He was a happy man with a batch of cement.
LINDA.   He was so wonderful with his hands.   15
BIFF.   He had all the wrong dreams. All, all, wrong.
HAPPY.   [*almost ready to fight BIFF*] Don't say that!
BIFF.   He never knew who he was.
CHARLEY.   [*stopping HAPPY's movement and reply. To BIFF*] Nobody dast blame this
man. You don't understand. Willy was a salesman. And for a salesman, there is no rock
bottom to the life. He don't put a bolt to a nut, he don't tell you the law or give you
medicine. He's a man way out there in the blue, riding on a smile and a shoeshine. And
when they start not smiling back—that's an earthquake. And then you get yourself a
couple of spots on your hat, and you're finished. Nobody dast blame this man. A salesman is got to dream, boy. It comes with the territory.
BIFF.   Charley, the man didn't know who he was.   20
HAPPY.   [*infuriated*] Don't say that!
BIFF.   Why don't you come with me, Happy?
HAPPY.   I'm not licked that easily. I'm staying right in this city, and I'm gonna
beat this racket! [*He looks at BIFF, his chin set.*] The Loman Brothers!
BIFF.   I know who I am, kid.
HAPPY.   All right, boy. I'm gonna show you and everybody else that Willy Loman   25
did not die in vain. He had a good dream. It's the only dream you can have—to come
out number-one man. He fought it out here, and this is where I'm gonna win it for him.
BIFF.   [*with a hopeless glance at HAPPY, bends toward his mother*] Let's go, Mom.
LINDA.   I'll be with you in a minute. Go on, Charley. [*He hesitates.*] I want to, just
for a minute. I never had a chance to say good-by.

[*CHARLEY moves away, followed by HAPPY. BIFF remains a slight distance up and left of LINDA.
She sits there, summoning herself. The flute begins, not far away, playing behind her speech.*]

LINDA.   Forgive me, dear. I can't cry. I don't know what it is, but I can't cry. I
don't understand it. Why did you ever do that? Help me, Willy, I can't cry. It seems to me
that you're just on another trip. I keep expecting you. Willy, dear, I can't cry. Why did
you do it? I search and search and I search, and I can't understand it, Willy. I made the
last payment on the house today. Today, dear. And there'll be nobody home. [*A sob rises
in her throat.*] We're free and clear. [*sobbing more fully, released*] We're free. [*BIFF comes
slowly toward her.*] We're free . . . We're free . . .

[*BIFF lifts her to her feet and moves out up right with her in his arms. LINDA sobs quietly. BERNARD and CHARLEY come together and follow them, followed by HAPPY. Only the music of the flute is left on the darkening stage as over the house the hard towers of the apartment buildings rise into sharp focus, and*

The curtain falls.*]

QUESTIONS

Act I

1. What do you learn about Willy from the first stage direction?
2. What instances of stealing are in the play? Why do Biff and Happy steal? Where did they learn about stealing? How is stealing related to salesmanship?
3. In Act I Willy claims that "I never in my life told him [Biff] anything but decent things." Is this assertion true? What does it show you about Willy?

Act II and Requiem

4. What does Willy's difficulty with machines—especially his car, the refrigerator, and Howard's tape recorder—suggest about him? To what extent are these machines symbolic?
5. When Willy sees Bernard in Charley's office, he asks, "What—what's the secret?" What secret is he asking about? Does such a secret exist?
6. In Act II Willy buys seeds and tries to plant a garden at night. Why is Willy so disturbed that "nothing's planted" and "I don't have a thing in the ground"? What do this garden and having "things in the ground" mean to Willy?
7. In Act II, speech 867, Biff claims that "we never told the truth for ten minutes in this house!" What does he mean? To what extent is he right?
8. Linda's last line in the play—"We're free . . . we're free"—seems to refer to the house mortgage. In what other ways, however, might you take it?

GENERAL QUESTIONS

1. How does Miller use lighting, the set, blocking, and music to differentiate between action in the present and "memory" action?
2. The stage directions are full of information that cannot be played. In describing Happy, for example, Miller notes that "sexuality is like a color on him." What is the function of such stage directions?
3. How is Willy's suicide foreshadowed throughout the play? To what extent does this foreshadowing create tension?
4. Which characters are "real" and which are "hallucinations" that spring from Willy's memory? What are the major differences between these two groups?
5. Which characters are symbolic and what do they symbolize?

6. Describe the character of Willy Loman. What are his good qualities? In what ways does he have heroic stature? What are his bad qualities? To what extent is his "fall" the result of his flaws, and to what extent is it caused by circumstances beyond his control?

7. How is the relationship between Charley and Bernard different from the one between Willy and his sons? Why is this difference important?

8. Discuss Linda's character and role. In what ways is she supportive of Willy? In what ways does she encourage his deceptions and self-delusions?

9. What sort of person is Happy? What has he inherited from Willy? How is he a debasement of Willy? To what degree is he successful or happy?

10. Willy claims that success in business is based not on "what you do" but on "who you know and the smile on your face! It's contacts . . . a man can end up with diamonds on the basis of being well liked." How does the play support or reject this assertion?

11. Most of Willy's memories—Ben's visit, Boston, the football game—are from 1928. Why does Willy's memory return to 1928? Why is the contrast between 1928 and the present significant for Willy and for the play as a whole?

WRITING ABOUT TRAGEDY

As you plan and write an essay about tragedy, keep in mind all the elements of drama. A full discussion of traditional approaches to these elements—plot, character, point of view, setting, language, tone, symbol, and theme—is found in Chapter 26. Review this material before you begin your essay.

Although the basic elements remain consistent in tragedy, the form requires a few special considerations. In planning to write about plot and conflict, you might explore the crisis or climax—that point at which the downfall becomes inevitable. Similarly, you might consider the degree to which the conflicts shape or accelerate the tragic action. With character, pay special attention to the tragic protagonist and the major antagonists: What is the connection between the protagonist's strengths and weaknesses? To what extent does the protagonist bring on or cooperate with his or her own destruction? What key characteristics and behavior patterns ensure both the protagonist's heroic stature and fall? In dealing with tone, consider the degree to which the play is ironic. Do you know more about what is going on than the protagonist? Than most of the characters? If so, how does your knowledge affect your understanding of the play?

Along with these considerations, all the traditional elements of drama can provide fruitful essays about tragic drama. Here, however, we introduce two new ways of writing about literature: an examination of a problem and a close reading of a passage. Both approaches have universal application. They can be employed to write about prose fiction, poetry, or any type of dramatic literature. Our discussion will naturally focus on tragedy—specifically *Hamlet*—and the plays in which problem solving and close reading can generate effective essays about tragic drama.

AN ESSAY ABOUT A PROBLEM

A **problem** is any question that you cannot answer easily and correctly about a body of material that you know. The question "Who is the major character in *Hamlet?*" is not a problem, because the obvious answer is Hamlet. Let us, however, ask another question: "Why is it *correct* to say that Hamlet is the major character?" This question is not as easy as the first, and for this reason it creates a problem. It requires that we think about our answer, even though we do not need to search very far. Hamlet is the title character. He is involved in most of the actions of the play. He is so much the center of our liking and concern that his death causes sadness and regret. To "solve" this problem has required a set of responses, all of which provide answers to the question *Why?*

More complex, however, and more typical of most problems, are questions like these: Why does Hamlet talk of suicide in his first soliloquy? Why does he treat Ophelia so coarsely in the "nunnery" scene? Why does he delay in avenging his father's death? Essays on a problem are normally concerned with such questions, because they require a good deal of thought, together with a number of interpretations knitted together into a whole essay. More broadly, dealing with problems is one of the major tasks of the intellectual, scientific, social, and political disciplines. Being able to advance and then explain solutions is therefore one of the most important techniques that you can acquire.

Strategies for Organizing Ideas

Your first purpose is to convince your reader that your solution is a good one. This you do by making sound conclusions from supporting evidence. In nonscientific subjects like literature, you rarely find absolute proofs, so your conclusions will not be *proved* in the way you prove triangles congruent in geometry. But your organization, your use of facts from the text, your interpretations, and your application of general or specific knowledge should all make your conclusions convincing. Thus your basic strategy is *persuasion*.

1. DEMONSTRATE THAT CONDITIONS FOR A SOLUTION ARE FULFILLED.   This type of development is the most basic in writing—namely, illustration. You first explain that certain conditions need to exist for your solution to be plausible. Your central idea—really a brief answer to the question—is that the conditions do indeed exist. Your development is to show how the conditions can be found in the work.

Suppose that you are writing on the problem of why Hamlet delays revenge against Claudius. Suppose also that you make the point that Hamlet delays because he is never sure that Claudius is guilty. This is your "solution" to the problem. In your essay you support your answer by by challenging the credibility of the information Hamlet receives about the crime (i.e., the two visits from the Ghost and Claudius's distress at the play within the play). Once you have "attacked" these sources of data on the grounds that they are unreliable, you have succeeded because your solution is consistent with the details of the play.

2. ANALYZE WORDS IN THE PHRASING OF THE PROBLEM.   Your object in this approach is to clarify important words in the statement of the problem, then to decide how applicable they are. This kind of attention to words, in fact, might give you enough material for all or part of your essay. Thus, an essay on the problem of Hamlet's delay might focus in part on a treatment of the word *delay:* What, really, does *delay* mean? For Hamlet, is there a difference between delay that is reasonable and delay that is unreasonable? Does Hamlet delay unreasonably? Is his delay the result of a psychological fault? Would speedy revenge be more or less reasonable than the delay? By the time you have answered such pointed questions, you will also have sufficient material for your full essay.

3. REFER TO LITERARY CONVENTIONS OR EXPECTATIONS   With this strategy, the argument is to establish that the problem can be solved by reference to the literary mode or conventions of a work, or to the limitations of the work itself. In other words, what appears to be a problem is really no more than a normal characteristic. A problem about the artificiality of the choruses in *Oedipus the King,* for example, might be resolved by reference to the fact that choruses were a normal feature of Greek drama. In a similar manner, the knowledge that delay is a convention of all revenge tragedy might provide a key to the problem of Hamlet's apparent procrastination. Similarly, a question about the differing functions of Tom in *The Glass Menagerie* (pp. 1704–54) can be explained by the free use that Tennessee Williams makes of nonrealistic stage conventions.

4. ARGUE AGAINST POSSIBLE OBJECTIONS.   With this strategy, you raise your own objections and then argue against them. Called **procatalepsis** or **anticipation,** this approach helps you sharpen your arguments, because *anticipating* and dealing with objections forces you to make analyses and use facts that you might otherwise overlook. Although procatalepsis can be used point by point throughout your essay, you may find it most useful at the end.

The situation to imagine is that someone is raising objections to your solution to the problem. It is then your task to show that the objections (1) are not accurate or valid, (2) are not strong or convincing, or (3) are based on unusual rather than usual conditions (on an exception and not the rule). Here are some examples of these approaches.

1. *The objection is not accurate or valid.* You reject this objection by showing that either the interpretation or the conclusions are wrong and also by emphasizing that the evidence supports your solution.

Although Hamlet's delay is reasonable, the claim might be made that his duty is to kill Claudius in revenge immediately after the Ghost's accusations. This claim is not persuasive because it assumes that Hamlet knows everything the audience knows. The audience accepts the Ghost's word that Claudius is guilty, but Hamlet has no certain reasons to believe the Ghost. Would it not seem insane for Hamlet to kill Claudius, who reigns legally, and then to claim he did it because of the Ghost's words? The argument for speedy revenge is not good because it is based on an incorrect view of Hamlet's situation.

2. *The objection is not strong or convincing.* You *concede* that the objection has some truth or validity, but you then try to show that it is weak and that your own solution is stronger.

One might claim that Claudius's distress at the play within the play is evidence for his guilt and that therefore Hamlet should carry out his revenge right away. This argument has merit, and Hamlet's speech after Claudius has fled the scene ("I'll take the Ghost's word for a thousand pound") shows that the "conscience of the king" has been caught. But the king's guilty behavior is not a strong cause for killing him. Hamlet could justifiably ask for an investigation of his father's death on these grounds, but he could not justify a revenge killing. Claudius could not be convicted in any court on the testimony that he was disturbed at seeing *The Murder of Gonzago.* Even after the play within the play, the reasons for delay are stronger than for action.

3. *The objection depends on unusual rather than usual conditions.* You reject the objection on the grounds that it could be valid only if normal conditions were suspended. The objection depends on an exception, not a rule.

The case for quick action is simple: Hamlet should kill Claudius right after seeing the Ghost (I.3) or else after seeing the king's reaction to the stage murder of Gonzago (III.2) or else after seeing the Ghost again (III.4). Redress under these circumstances, goes the argument, must be both personal and extralegal. This argument wrongly assumes that due process does not exist in the Denmark of Hamlet and Claudius. Nothing in the play indicates that the Danes, even though they carouse a bit, do not value legality and the rules of evidence. Thus Hamlet cannot rush out to kill Claudius, because he knows that the king has not had anything close to due process. The argument for quick action is poor because it rests on an exception being made from civilized law.

Remember that writing an essay on a problem requires you to argue a position: Either there is a solution or there is not. To develop your position requires that you show the steps to your conclusion. Your general thematic form is thus (1) to describe the conditions that need to be met for the solution you propose and then (2) to demonstrate that these conditions exist. If you assert that there is no solution, then your form would be the same for the first part, but your second part—the development—would show that these conditions have *not* been met.

In developing your response, use one or more of the strategies described in this chapter. These are, again, (1) to demonstrate that conditions for a solution are fulfilled, (2) to analyze the words in the phrasing of the problem, (3) to refer to literary conventions or expectations, and (4) to argue against possible objections. You might combine these. Thus, if we assume that your argument is that Hamlet's delay is reasonable, you might first consider the word *delay* (strategy 2). Then you might use strategy 1 to explain the reasons for Hamlet's delay. Finally, to answer objections to your argument, you might show that he acts promptly when he believes he is justified (strategy 4). Whatever your topic, the important thing is to use the method or methods that best help you make a good argument for your solution.

In your conclusion, try to affirm the validity of your solution in view of the supporting evidence. You might do this by reemphasizing your strongest points, or you might simply present a brief summary. Or you might think of your argument as still continuing and thus use the strategy of procatalepsis to raise and answer possible objections to your solution, as in the last paragraph of the demonstrative student essay that follows.

DEMONSTRATIVE STUDENT ESSAY

The Problem of Hamlet's Apparent Delay°

[1] For hundreds of years, readers and spectators of Shakespeare's *Hamlet* have been puzzled by the prince's apparent failure to kill Claudius quickly. Early in the play, the Ghost calls on his son to "Revenge his foul and most unnatural murder" (I.5.25). Hamlet, however, delays his vengeance until the end of the play. Why does he not act sooner? The answer is that there is no unjustified delay and that in fact Hamlet acts as quickly as possible.* This becomes evident when we examine the conventions of revenge tragedy, the actual "call to revenge," and the steps that Hamlet takes to achieve vengeance.†

[2] Revenge tragedy conventionally requires that vengeance be delayed until the closing moments of the play. Given this limitation, Shakespeare must justify the wide gap of time between the call to revenge in Act I and the killing of Claudius in Act V. We find such justification in the unreliability of the ghost's initial accusation, Hamlet's need for additional evidence, and the events that occur after this evidence is obtained.

[3] The Ghost's accusations and demands are straightforward: He accuses his brother of murdering him, and he calls on his son for vengeance. Shakespeare is careful, however, to establish that this testimony may be doubtful. Horatio questions the Ghost's truthfulness and motives, and he warns Hamlet that the spirit might "assume some other horrible form / Which might deprive your sovereignty of reason, / And draw you into madness" (I.4.72-74). Hamlet himself expresses doubt about the ghost: (II.2.573-579):

° See pp. 1350–1451 for this play.
* Central idea.
† Thesis sentence.

> The spirit that I have seen
> May be a devil, and the devil hath power
> T'assume a pleasing shape, yea, and perhaps
> Out of my weakness, and my melancholy,
> As he is very potent with such spirits,
> Abuses me to damn me; I'll have grounds
> More relative than this.

The prince thus cannot act on the unsupported word of the ghost; he needs more evidence.

[4] There is no delay at this point in the play, because Hamlet quickly begins developing a plan of action. Immediately after speaking with the Ghost, he decides to cover himself under an "antic disposition" while he gathers information. He swears his companions to silence and warns them not to react knowingly if he should seem to behave strangely or insanely (I.5.169-179). His idea is that this pose will make him less suspect and make others less careful.

Once Hamlet has begun his plan, he takes advantage of every opportunity to carry out his vengeance. When the players come to Elsinore, he adroitly plans to test Claudius by making him publicly view a play, *The Mousetrap*, which shows a murder just like Claudius's murder of Hamlet's father. Hamlet states that Claudius's appearance will give him the clue he needs to confirm the Ghost's information (II.2.571-573):

> I'll observe his looks,
> I'll tent him to the quick, if a' do blench
[5] > I know my course.

Once the king breaks up the performance in great agitation, which Hamlet correctly interprets as an admission of guilt, Hamlet declares confidence in the Ghost ("I'll take the ghost's word for a thousand pound" [III.2.271-272]). Moreover, he is psychologically ready to act against the king, for he asserts that he could "drink hot blood, / And do such bitter business as the day / Would quake to look on" (III.2.367–369). Without doubt, Hamlet is only a prayer away from stabbing Claudius, for when he sees the king kneeling, his opportunity has merged with his desire and also with his promise to the Ghost. He tells the audience, "Now might I do it pat, now a' is a-praying, / And now I'll do't" (III.3.73-74).

But he does not "do't," and for this reason he is open to the claim that he cannot act. Again, however, Shakespeare carefully justifies this hesitation. The prince does not want to send Claudius's soul to heaven by killing him at prayer. Rather, he wants the revenge to match Claudius's treacherous murder of old King Hamlet, who died without the chance to pray and repent (III.3.88-95):

[6]
> Up sword, and know thou a more horrid hent,
> When he is drunk asleep, or in his rage,
> Or in th'incestuous pleasure of his bed,
> At game, a-swearing, or about some act
> That has no relish of salvation in't
> Then trip him that his heels may kick at heaven,
> And that his soul may be as damned and black
> As hell whereto it goes.

This deferral is in keeping with the code of personal blood vengeance, whereby the revenge must match or exceed the original crime. There is no question of Hamlet's incapacity to act, because his putting up his sword is totally reasonable and justifiable.

[7]

From this point on, Hamlet acts or reacts to every situation as the opportunity presents itself. After he kills Polonius, Claudius initiates a counter-plot to send Hamlet off to England and execution. Clearly, Hamlet's chances to kill the king are thus reduced to zero. It is not until Act V that Hamlet gets back to Denmark, after having decisively thwarted Claudius's murderous instructions by turning them against Rosencrantz and Guildenstern. He makes it clear to Horatio, however, that he will take the earliest opportunity, and that "the readiness is all" (V.2.205). Once the rigged fencing match is under way, the opportunity finally comes. Claudius, Hamlet learns, has not only killed his father but has poisoned his mother, and he himself is about to die from Laertes's poisoned sword. Upon such certain information, Hamlet immediately kills Claudius. When the revenge is complete, the Ghost, who began the cry for vengeance, is nowhere to be heard or seen, and four bodies lie on the stage.

[8]

Thus, we see that the problem of Hamlet's delay--and the vengeance does take four acts to carry out--is really not a problem. The prince acts in accordance with the code of revenge as quickly as circumstances permit. Although the text of the play supports this solution, critics might still argue that procrastination is an issue because Hamlet twice accuses himself of delay. This objection does not take into consideration that Hamlet's perception of time and action is distorted by his eagerness for vengeance. From Hamlet's subjective point of view, any break in activity is delay. From our objective viewpoint, however, delay is not a true issue.

Commentary on the Essay

The structure of the essay illustrates strategy 1 (p. 1524). Paragraph 2, however, makes brief use of strategy 3 in its reference to the conventions of revenge tragedy. In both paragraphs 6 and 8, the argument is carried on by use of procatalepsis, or strategy 4, whereby a counterargument is presented and then answered.

The introductory paragraph raises the problem of Hamlet's apparent delay and offers a brief statement of the solution (the central idea). This plan is developed in paragraphs 2–7 in exactly the same order in which the issues are raised in the introduction. Paragraph 2 deals with the conventions of revenge tragedy, and paragraph 3 takes up the issue of the Ghost's reliability. Paragraphs 4 and 5 deal with Hamlet's attempts to corroborate the ghost's accusations, and paragraphs 6 and 7 consider the subsequent action. Note that each paragraph in the argument grows naturally out of the one that precedes it, just as all the paragraphs are linked to the introductory paragraph.

The concluding paragraph asserts that the original problem is solved; the paragraph then summarizes the steps of the solution. It also continues the argument by raising and then dealing with a possible objection.

AN ESSAY ON A CLOSE READING
OF A PASSAGE

An essay on a close reading is a detailed study of a passage of prose or verse that is either part of a longer work—in this chapter, a play—or an entire short poem. The close-reading essay is both specific, in that it focuses on the selected passage, and general, in that you consider not a single topic (such as character, setting, or theme) but rather *all* the elements to be found in the passage. If the passage describes a person, for example, you must discuss character, but your emphasis should be on what the passage itself brings out about the character. *The passage dictates the content of your essay.*

Focus on the general meaning and impact of the passage. Who speaks it? What is it about? What does it tell you about the speaker or the world of the play? Once these questions are answered, write notes that you can use later in paragraphs. Try to reach specific and focused conclusions: Does the passage (1) describe a scene, (2) develop a character, (3) present an action, (4) reveal a character's thoughts, (5) advance an argument, or (6) introduce an idea? What is the thematic content? How does the passage relate to earlier and later parts of the whole text? (To deal with this question, you can assume that your reader is familiar with the entire work.)

Strategies for Organizing Ideas

FOR AN EARLY PASSAGE, DETERMINE THE CONNECTIONS WITH WHAT COMES AFTER. If the passage is early in the play, you can conclude that the author is setting things in motion (exposition, complication). Thus, you should determine how themes, characterizations, and arguments in the passage are related to later developments. Always assume that everything is there for a purpose, and then find that purpose.

FOR A LATER, MIDPOINT PASSAGE, DETERMINE THE CONNECTIONS WITH WHAT COMES BOTH BEFORE AND AFTER.   In a passage at the play's midpoint, a character's fortunes can take either an expected or an unexpected turn. If the change is unexpected, you should explain how the passage focuses the various themes or ideas and then propels them toward the forthcoming crisis or climax (the turning point or high point). It may be that the work features surprises, and the passage thus acquires a different meaning on second reading. Or it may be that the speaker has one set of assumptions while the readers have others, and that the passage marks the speaker's increasing self-awareness. Any part of any work is part of a whole, and it is therefore your task to determine the extent to which the passage (1) builds on what has happened previously and (2) prepares the way for the outcome.

FOR A CONCLUDING PASSAGE, DETERMINE THE CONNECTIONS WITH WHAT HAS GONE ON EARLIER.   A passage at or near the play's end is designed to solve problems or to be a focal point or climax for all the cumulative situations and ideas. You will thus need to show how the passage brings together all details, ideas, and themes. What is happening? Is any action described in the passage a major action, or a step leading to the major action? Has everything in the passage been prepared for earlier, or are there any surprises?

When you prepare your essay, begin by quoting the entire passage just as it appears in the text. It is also helpful to number the lines for easy reference. Because the close-reading essay is concerned with details, you might have a problem developing a thematic structure. You can overcome this difficulty if you begin to work with either a generalization about the passage or a thesis based on the relationship of the passage to the work. Suppose, for example, that the passage is factually descriptive or that it introduces a major character or raises a major idea. Any one of these observations can serve as a thesis.

Develop the body of the essay according to what you find in the passage. For a passage of character description, analyze what is disclosed about the character, and also analyze what bearing this information has on the play as a whole. For a passage presenting an idea or ideas, analyze the idea and demonstrate how it is important for the rest of the work. In short, your aim in this kind of essay is double: first, discuss the passage itself, and second, show how the passage functions within the entire play.

To conclude, stress the important details of your analysis. In addition, you may want to deal with secondary issues that arise in the passage but do not merit full consideration. The passage may contain specific phrases or underlying assumptions that you have not considered in the body of your essay. The conclusion is the place to mention these matters, without developing them fully.

DEMONSTRATIVE STUDENT ESSAY

Appearance and Reality: A Close Reading of *Hamlet,* Act I, scene 2, lines 76–86°

76	Seems, madam? nay it is. I know not "seems."
77	'Tis not alone my inky cloak good mother,
78	Nor customary suits of solemn black,
79	Nor windy suspiration of forced breath,
80	No, nor the fruitful river of the eye,
81	Nor the dejected havior of the visage,
82	Together with all forms, moods, shapes of grief,
83	That can denote me truly: these indeed seem,
84	For they are actions that a man might play,
85	But I have that within which passes show,
86	These but the trappings and the suits of woe.

° See pp. 1350–1451 for this play.

Hamlet speaks these lines during his first appearance in Act I. Gertrude--his mother--has just tried to convince him that death is "common" to all humanity and that he "seems" to spinning out his grief over his father's death. Hamlet's [1] speech grows out of Gertrude's word "seems." In this way, Shakespeare introduces one of the play's central ideas: that there is a difference between appearance and reality.* This concept is stated directly, is then amplified, and shows up repeatedly throughout the play in both character and action.†

[2] The discrepancy between appearance and reality is introduced in Hamlet's first line: "Seems, madam? nay it is." In this disarmingly simple statement, Hamlet opposes things that seem to be and those that actually exist. This opposition of illusion or appearance ("seems") and reality ("is") becomes the cornerstone of his words.

Hamlet expands on the contrast in lines 77–86 with reference to the outward trappings of mourning. In an almost scholarly way (he has just come home from school), he lists five of the traditional signs of grief: an "inky cloak" (77); "suits of solemn black" (78); sighs, or the "windy suspiration of forced breath" (79); tears, or "the fruitful river of the eye" (80); and sad looks, or "the dejected [be]havior of the visage" (81). Having listed these items, Hamlet identifies them in three separate lines as the outward displays of mourning. First, he [3] calls them the "forms, moods, shapes of grief" (82). In line 84 he also notes that "they are actions that a man might play." And in line 86 he labels this list as "the trappings [costumes] and the suits of woe." These three lines thus show that the five signs of grief are all outward shows. His contrast is especially emphasized in the words "forms," "shapes," "play," and "trappings." His speech is capped off logically by his contrast of all the appearances of grief with his own real and internal feelings: "I have that within which [sur]passes show" (line 85). Again, we have the direct contrast between appearance ("show") and reality ("that within").

This contrast is a vital idea in the entire play, for it shows up repeatedly in both character and situation. Claudius, for example, appears to be a loving uncle, a good king, and a reasonable man, but we know that he is actually a murderer and a usurper. Rosencrantz and Guildenstern are Hamlet's school chums, but they easily succumb to Claudius's wiles, and they then become spies. Such discrepancies are also apparent in actions. For example, in Act III, Claudius appears [4] to be praying. In his brief soliloquy, however, he admits that he cannot be contrite, but rather he is "still possessed / Of those effects for which I did the murder" (III.3.53-54). Similarly, the duel between Hamlet and Laertes seems to be a straightforward fencing match, but is actually a complicated trap by which Claudius plans to kill Hamlet by either sword or poison.

Hamlet's speech therefore shows his wit in responding to his mother, and it also shows his scholarly nature in his assertions contrasting superficial grief with his own deep grief. The contrast obviously governs his own view of reality, and it also puts forward one of the play's most important issues. It is, after all, the [5] difference between appearance and reality that permits Claudius to reign even though he is a murderer, and it is the difficulty of distinguishing between appearance and reality that Hamlet encounters when trying to carry out the Ghost's cry

---

* Central idea.
† Thesis sentence.

for revenge. Generally, also, the difference is a cause of the confusion, and also the evil, that exists in the personal, social, and political world. Because characters and events in *Hamlet* are rarely what they appear to be, the passage thus provides a key to Shakespeare's profound tragedy.

Commentary on the Essay

This essay deals with one of Shakespeare's major themes in *Hamlet*: the difference between appearance and reality and the effects of these differences. The body takes up the specific details in Hamlet's speech and then shows how these details are developed throughout the play. Paragraph 2 deals with Hamlet's first statement of the idea, and paragraph 3 discusses how he applies the concept to the expression of grief. Paragraph 4 demonstrates the relationship of the idea to character and situation elsewhere in the text. The conclusion brings the arguments of the essay together, stressing that the contrast is important to our understanding of Hamlet's character, the play's major ideas, Hamlet's task of revenge, and, generally, the world at large.

SPECIAL TOPICS FOR WRITING AND ARGUMENT ABOUT TRAGEDY

1. Much has been made of the contrast in *Oedipus the King* between seeing and blindness. Write an essay that considers this contrast as it is related to the character of Oedipus. How are blindness and seeing reversed, with regard to his understanding about the curse on the city, his attempts to ferret out the guilty ones, his awakening perceptions of his own responsibility and guilt, and his self-blinding? How can Tiresias be compared and contrasted with Oedipus?

2. Develop an argument for one of these assertions:

    a. Oedipus's fall is the result of fate, predestination, and the gods, and it would happen despite his character.

    b. Oedipus's fall is the result only of his character and has nothing to do with fate or the gods.

3. Write an essay considering the degree to which Gertrude and Ophelia in *Hamlet* justify Hamlet's assertion "Frailty, thy name is woman" (I. 2. 146). Questions you might take into account concern the status of these women, their power to exert their own individuality and to make their own decisions, Gertrude as a royal queen and Ophelia as an aristocratic daughter, their capacity to undergo the pain of bereavement, Hamlet's own feelings about the death of his father, and so on. To what degree should issues concerning these women be subjected to a feminist critical analysis? (See Chapter 33, p. 1960.)

4. Hamlet, Laertes, and Fortinbras are all young men whose fathers have been killed and who set out to avenge these deaths. Their courses of action, however, are different. In an essay, consider these three as typical or archetypal sons. What characteristics do they share? What, in turn, makes them individual and distinct? Compare and contrast how each character deals with his father's death. Which approach seems most reasonable to you? Most emotional? Most effective? For additional directions, consult Chapter 35 (p. 1979).

5. *Death of a Salesman* was successfully produced in the People's Republic of China in 1983 and was revived on Broadway in 1984 with Dustin Hoffman and in 1999 with Brian Dennehy, and there were also successful television productions—by Lee J. Cobb in the 1950s and Dustin Hoffman in the 1980s. How do you account for the continuing interest in the play from the time it was first produced until the present moment, in other cultures as well as in contemporary America?

6. Write an essay discussing the ways in which *Death of a Salesman* comments on American life and values. What specific shortcomings of American life—social, economic, political, and personal—does Miller expose and attack? In what ways does Willy Loman represent these shortcomings? Conversely, how can he be seen as an innocent victim? To what degree might Willy's death be seen as redemptive and therefore as a defense of American life?

7. Considering *Oedipus the King*, *Hamlet*, and *Death of a Salesman*, write an essay defining and explaining tragedy. Include references to the nature of the tragic protagonists, the situations they face, their solutions to their problems, their responses to the consequences of their actions, and their worthiness of character. Be sure to compare and contrast the actions and speeches of the characters in the plays as evidence.

8. Use your library or the Internet to locate books on tragedy. Some general topics might be *ancient and modern tragedy, definitions, emotions, heroes, passions, problems*, and *questions*. You might also wish to locate specific books on Aristotle and tragedy or on *Oedipus the King*, *Hamlet*, and *Death of a Salesman*. Write a brief report on one of the books, being careful to consider topics such as the author's definitions of tragedy and the author's application of the topic to various specific plays. Try also to consider the completeness of the author's presentation of material and the persuasiveness of the author's arguments.

28

The Comic Vision: Restoring the Balance

Comedy as we know it arose in ancient Greece, just as tragedy did.[1] Comedy is therefore the fraternal twin of tragedy. Many comedies are filled with tragic potential, and many tragedies contain potentially comic plots. Indeed, tragedy can be seen as an abortive or incomplete comedy in which affairs go wrong, and comedy can be considered a tragedy in which the truth is discovered (or covered up), the hero saves the day, the villain is overcome, and equilibrium and balance are restored. The major differences are that tragedy moves toward despair or death, while comedy moves toward success, happiness, and marriage. Tragic diction is elevated and heroic. Comic diction can be elevated too, but often it is common or colloquial, and although it is frequently witty, it is also often witless and bawdy. The primary difference is that the mask of tragedy grieves and weeps, but the mask of comedy smiles and laughs.

THE ORIGINS OF COMEDY

In the *Poetics*, Aristotle states that he knows less about the origin of Athenian comedy than of tragedy because at first comedy was not taken as seriously as tragedy (V.2, p. 21). He does say, however, that comedy, like tragedy, developed as an improvisatory form (IV.12, p. 19). Most comic improvisations were an outgrowth of "phallic songs," which were bacchanalian processions that took place during the **Lenaia,** the religious festival held in January-February each year in *Gamelion*, the month of weddings, just following the winter solstice.

The word *comedy* is consistent with this explanation, for as "a *komos* song" its Greek meaning is "a song of revels" or "a song sung by merrymakers." The revels, like the tragedies, were religious in ways that the Greeks considered meaningful, although they seem secular to us today. During parades or processions at the Lenaia, the merrymakers expressed their joy boisterously, traded bawdy and obscene remarks with spectators, lampooned public persons, wore

---

[1] For a more detailed discussion of how drama developed within the anient Athenian religious festivals, see Chapter 27, pp. 1286–89.

ceremonial phalluses, and dressed in paunchy costumes suggesting feasting, fatness, fertility, and fun. We may conclude that these *komos* processions were encouraged officially in the belief and hope that human ceremonies would encourage divine favor and bring about prosperity and happiness. As the form developing out of such processions, comedy began with many of these characteristics and has retained them to the present day. If one briefly may generalize about subsequent comedies—even those that are cold sober rather than boisterous—it is clear that love, marriage, and ritualized celebrations of a happy future are usually major concerns.

The Athenians Held Competitions for Comedy, Just as for Tragedy

Tragedy originated in Athens, but the same does not appear to be true of comedy. Rather, comedy coexisted in the areas surrounding Greece called *Magna Graecia* ("Greater Greece"). Aristotle himself admitted that it was "late" when comic performances were separated from the phallic songs (V.2, p. 21); that is, comedy followed tragedy by many years. The earliest certain date for the existence of Athenian comedy is 486 B.C.E., when a state-sponsored comedy competition was won by a writer named Chionides. Although these earliest comedies apparently consisted of little more than loosely connected lampoons, they were highly enough regarded to justify regular competitions. Comedies were scheduled on each day of the festivals, following the tragedies and satyr plays.

According to Aristotle, the first writer to transform comedy by creating a thematic plot development was Crates, who won the first of his three prizes in about the mid-fifth century B.C.E. (V.3, p. 21). It was at this time that comedies became popular enough to justify an additional state comedy competition, which was instituted in about 440 B.C.E. For the remainder of the century, writers of comedy as well as tragedy tried to win prizes for their new plays at both the Lenaia and the City Dionysia.

THE EARLIEST GREEK COMEDY IS CALLED OLD COMEDY. The comedies of the fifth century B.C.E., called **Old Comedy** or **Old Attic Comedy** by later historians, followed intricate structural patterns and displayed complex poetic conventions. Nevertheless, they bore the marks of their origins in the bacchanalian *komos* processions. The actors (three or four men) and the members of the chorus (twenty-four), each dressed in a distortingly padded costume, wore a character-defining mask and displayed a ceremonial phallus. The role of the chorus usually dictated the comedy's title (e.g., *The Frogs, The Wasps*). Customarily, the plot was fantastic and impossible, and the dialogue was farcical and bawdy. In the tradition of satires and tirades associated with the phallic songs and with early comedy, the comic dramatists freely lashed public persons (usually but not always without legal reprisal).

Although the most successful comedy writer of the fifth century B.C.E. was Magnes (flourished 475–450 B.C.E.), who won eleven times, the only writer whose works survive is Aristophanes (ca. 450–385 B.C.E.), who won four times.

His work constitutes our principal firsthand knowledge of Greek Old Comedy. He wrote at least thirty-two comedies. Fortunately, eleven have survived, along with fragments of some of his other plays. His plots and actions are outrageous, his characters are funny, and his language is satirical, bawdy, and biting.

MIDDLE COMEDY CAME AFTER ARISTOPHANES. Aristophanes lived into the next period of Greek comedy, called **Middle Comedy**. His plays *Ecclesiazusae* (ca. 391 B.C.E.) and *Plutus* (388 B.C.E.), presaged Middle Comedy; all the Middle Comedy plays by other authors are lost, although there are many extant fragments. Middle Comedy eliminated some of the complex patterns of Old Comedy and treated more broadly international and less narrowly Athenian topics. Political criticism was abandoned, and character types such as the braggart soldier were introduced. The role of the chorus was diminished or eliminated (as with tragedy), and the exaggerated costumes were eliminated.

NEW COMEDY, A TYPE OF ROMANTIC COMEDY, FLOURISHED AFTER MIDDLE COMEDY. By the end of the fourth century B.C.E., Middle Comedy was replaced by **New Comedy**. The most important of the New Comedy dramatists was Menander (342–292 B.C.E.), who was heralded in ancient times as the greatest comic writer of them all. Everyone knows quotations from Menander, such as "calling a spade a spade" and "the gods first make mad those they intend to destroy." St. Paul quotes him in 1 Corinthians 15: 33 ("Bad company ruins good morals"), but after the fifth century C.E., copies of Menander's plays were no longer available and were presumed totally lost. In the last hundred years, however, many Menandrian manuscripts have been discovered, mostly in the sands of Egypt. We now have Menander's *Dyscolus* (*The Grouch*) in its entirety and near-complete versions of some of his other comedies, together with numerous fragments and passages. In total, the titles of close to one hundred of his plays are known. His comedies, which are romantic rather than satirical, employ such stock characters as young lovers, stubborn fathers, clever slaves, and long-separated relatives.

Roman Comedy Was Composed Largely in the Third and Second Centuries B.C.E.

After the time of Menander, Greek power in the Mediterranean waned and was replaced by the might of Rome. In the third century B.C.E. Roman comedy began and flourished, largely through the translation and adaptation of Greek New Comedies. The significant Roman writers were Plautus (ca. 254–184 B.C.E.), with twenty surviving comedies, and Terence (ca. 186–159 B.C.E.), whose six comedies all exist. Briefly, the comedies of Plautus are brisk, while those of Terence are more restrained. The central issue in most of the Roman comedies is the overcoming of a **blocking agent**, or obstruction to true love, that could be almost anyone or anything—a rival lover, an angry father, a family feud, an old law, a previously arranged marriage, or differences in social class. The pattern of action, traditionally called the **plot of intrigue**, stems from the subterfuges that young lovers undertake to overcome the blocking agent, so that the outcome frequently heralds the victory of youth over age and the passing of control from one generation to the next.

COMEDY FROM ROMAN TIMES TO THE RENAISSANCE

By the time the Roman Empire was established in 29 B.C.E., the writing of comedy had virtually disappeared because Roman dramatic creativity had been preempted by pantomime entertainments and public spectacles such as gladiatorial combat. Comedy thus accompanied tragedy into fifteen hundred years of obscurity—a period when the empire rose and fell, the Dark Ages descended, and the medieval period flourished. Although many comic and farcical scenes were included in the mystery cycles of late medieval times,[2] comedy as a form was not reestablished until the Renaissance.

Once reintroduced, comedy grew rapidly. By 1500 the six plays of Terence had been rediscovered and were achieving wide recognition, followed by the twenty surviving plays of Plautus. When English dramatists began writing comedies, they followed Roman conventions. The English plays of the mid-sixteenth century contained five acts and observed the unities of time, place, and action, thus following the rules and justifying the claim that they were "regular." Character types from the Roman comedies, such as the intriguing couple, the fussing father, and the bragging soldier, initially predominated. Soon, more specifically English types appeared, anticipating the roisterers in Shakespeare's *Henry IV* plays and the "mechanicals" in *A Midsummer Night's Dream*. By the end of the sixteenth century, when Shakespeare had completed many of his comedies, English comedy was in full bloom. It has commonly been observed that the comedy was Latin in structure but English in character.

When the seventeenth century began, the chief obstacle to a wide public assimilation of drama had been the absence of institutionalized theaters. London authorities, maintaining that playgoing was a sinful public nuisance, banned theaters within the city itself. Builders therefore had to construct theaters outside the London city limits. For example, the Rose and the Globe theaters, where Shakespeare saw his plays produced from the mid-1590s to 1611, were built in Southwark across the Thames. We should realize that most people in Shakespeare's audiences got to the theater by walking over London Bridge or by being ferried across the river and that they returned home the same way.

COMIC PATTERNS, CHARACTERS, AND LANGUAGE

Dictionaries sometimes give *funny* as a synonym for *comic*, but the two terms are not the same. Words like *funny, amusing,* or *humorous* define our emotional conditioning to incidents, and our reactions always depend on context. We usually

[2] For a description of the medieval mystery or Corpus Christi plays, see Chapter 26, pp. 1239-40.

think it is funny to see an actor in a slapstick routine being struck with a paddle, whereas if we leave the theater and see a person being beaten with a similar object, such as a baseball bat, we are repelled and horrified. The *context* makes the difference.

The Word Comic Suggests a Pattern of Humorous Action

Comic, the adjective derived from *comedy*, describes the pattern or context that conditions our responses. *Comic* means that a literary work or set of situations conforms to the patterns and characteristics of comedy. Within these patterns, we are conditioned to perceive most dialogue and action—even serious problems and dangerous situations—as being amusing. At heart, therefore, comedy and the term *comic* suggest a pattern of action, including funny situations and language, that we perceive as solvable and correctable. The pattern grows out of character or situation, and it leads to a resolution that satisfies us.

COMIC PROBLEMS FLOURISH IN DIFFICULTIES AND MISUNDERSTANDINGS THAT STOP SHORT OF DANGER. The problems with which comedies begin can be personal or social. Representative problems are thwarted love, eccentric behavior, corruption in high places, misinformation, disinformation, misguided suspicion, or a combination of other difficulties. As the comedies move from exposition to complication, the problems appear increasingly worse as they are fueled by confusion, misunderstanding, mistakes in identity, errors in judgment, excessive or unreasonable behavior, misinformed speech, and coincidences that stretch our credulity.

THE COMIC CLIMAX IS THE PEAK OF CONFUSION. In a comic climax, misunderstanding is dominant, pressure is at a high point, and choices must be made even though solutions seem impossible. The catastrophe—the changing or turning point—frequently introduces a sudden revelation in which a key fact, identity, or event is explained to characters and audience at the same time.

THE COMIC DÉNOUEMENT RESTORES SANITY AND CALM. In most comedies, the events of the dénouement resolve the initial problems and allow for the comic resolution, which involves setting things right at every level of action. Errors are therefore explained, personal lives are straightened out, people at odds with each other are reconciled, promises are made for the future, new families are formed through marriage, and a stable social order is reestablished.

COMEDY IS BASED ON EDUCATION AND CHANGE. In many comedies, at least some of the characters learn something about themselves, their society, or the way to love and live. They see past errors and are willing to amend them, and they also are human and humble enough to ask forgiveness, which is promptly awarded. Their education makes it possible for them to improve, and, by implication, for the world also to improve. In other comedies, however, particularly those that touch on major social and political problems, the *audience* is educated, and the playwright hopes that change will occur in the world as well as on the stage. Comedy therefore depends on the process of education, which culminates in the moment or moments of change.

Comic Characters Are More Limited than in Tragedy

Comic characters are relatively limited because they are almost necessarily common and representative rather than individual and heroic. Characters with the depth or individuality of Hamlet or Oedipus are therefore not characteristic of comedy. Instead, comedy gives us stock characters who represent classes, types, and generations. In Shakespeare's *A Midsummer Night's Dream*, for instance, most of the characters are representative and stock figures. Egeus is a conventional indignant father. Similarly, Hermia and Lysander (along with Helena and Demetrius) are typical young lovers. In Kauffmann's *The More the Merrier* (Chapter 26) the two lovers, Emily and Raphael, are drawn from a social elite that deals with mutual acquaintances and exclusive club life. Although the main characters do confront serious personal problems, it is difficult to imagine that they ever could reach the depth and height of a majestic character like Hamlet.

Comic Language Is a Vital Vehicle of Humor

As in other types of literature, comic dramatists use language to delineate character, to establish tone and mood, and to express ideas and feelings. In comedy, however, language is also one of the most important vehicles for humor. Some comedies are characterized by elegant and witty language, others by puns and bawdy jokes.

Characters in comedy tend either to be masters of language or to be mastered by it. Those who are skillful with language, such as Lisette in *Love Is the Doctor*, can use a witty phrase like a knife to satirize their foes and friends alike. Those who are unskilled with language, like Bottom in *A Midsummer Night's Dream*, bungle through a speech with their misuse of words and inadvertent puns. Both types of characters are amusing; we smile a knowing smile with the wits and laugh out loud at the bunglers.

TYPES OF COMEDY

Differences in comic style, content, and intent that have evolved over the centuries make it possible to divide comedy into various types. The broadest of these divisions, based on both style and content, separates all comic literature into *high comedy* and *low comedy*.

High Comedy Develops Mainly from Problems of Character

Ideally, **high comedy** (a term coined by George Meredith in 1877 in *The Idea of Comedy*) is witty, graceful, and sophisticated. The problems and complications are more closely related to character than to situation, even though, admittedly, they develop out of situations. The appeal of high comedy is therefore to the intellect, for the comic resolution must come about because the characters learn enough to accept adjustments and changes in their lives. A simple change of situation alone will not do for high comedy.

1. ROMANTIC COMEDY FOCUSES ON PROBLEMS OF YOUTHFUL LOVE. One of the major kinds of high comedy is **romantic comedy**, which views action and character from the standpoint of earnest young lovers like Hermia and Lysander in *A Midsummer Night's Dream*. Ultimately derived from Roman comedy, this kind of play is built on a plot of intrigue featuring lovers who try to overcome opposition (like Egeus) to achieve a successful union. The aim of such plays is amusement and entertainment rather than ridicule and reform. Although vice and folly may be exposed in romantic comedy, especially in the antagonists blocking the young lovers, the dominant impulse is toleration and amused indulgence.

2. COMEDY OF MANNERS TESTS THE STRENGTH OF SOCIAL CUSTOMS AND ASSUMPTIONS. Related to romantic comedy is the **comedy of manners**, an important type from the seventeenth century to our own times. The comedy of manners examines and satirizes attitudes and customs in the light of high intellectual and moral standards. The dialogue is witty and sophisticated, and characters are often measured according to their linguistic and intellectual powers. The love plots are serious and real, even though they share with romantic comedy the need to create intrigues to overcome blocking forces. The realism and seriousness in some of the manners comedies written in Restoration England (1660–1700) in fact are so great that one might consider them not only as plays of manners but also of social and personal problems.

3. SATIRIC COMEDY, LIKE ALL SATIRE, RIDICULES VICES AND FOLLIES. Midway between high and low comedy is **satiric comedy**, which is based in a comic attack on foolishness and/or viciousness. The playwright of satiric comedy assumes the perspective of a rational and moderate observer measuring human life against a moderate norm that is represented by high and serious characters. The spectators are invited to share this viewpoint as they, along with the dramatist, heap scorn upon the vicious and laugh loudly at the eccentric and the foolish.

Low Comedy Dwells amid the Silly and Bumbling

In **low comedy** emphasis is on funny remarks and outrageous circumstances; complications develop from situation and plot rather than from character. Plays of this type are by definition full of physical humor and stage business—a character rounds his forefinger and thumb to imitate a wall, through which other characters speak; an irascible man constantly breaks furniture; a character disguised as a doctor takes a father's pulse to determine his daughter's condition; characters who have just declared their love are visited by people to whom they formerly swore love.

The quintessential type of low comedy is **farce** (a word derived from the Latin word *farsus,* meaning "stuffed"), which is designed, in the words of Henry Fielding, to make us laugh. A farce is an outlandish physical comedy overflowing with silly characters, improbable happenings, wild clowning, pratfalls, extravagant language, and bawdy jokes.

Another type of farce was the ***commedia dell'arte,*** a prototypical, broadly comic drama, which developed among traveling companies in Italy and France in the sixteenth and seventeenth centuries. The broadly humorous characters of *commedia dell'arte* recurred from play to play with consistent names and characteristics. The action usually involved a plot of intrigue. The lovers were *Inamorato* and *Inamorata* (like Clitander and Lucinda in *Love Is the Doctor*), who were aided by Inamorata's clever servant, the *soubrette* (like Lisette), to overcome *Pantaloon,* the old man (like Sganarelle). The servant characters were *Harlequin* (who was invisible) and *Columbine* (his sweetheart, also invisible), who were joined in highjinks by *Pierrot* (a clown lover) and *Scaramouche* (the soldier). Other stock characters, most of whom were derived from Greek New Comedy by way of Roman comedy, have in turn become constant features of much subsequent comedy.

With characters of low comedy, of course, there is much tomfoolery and improvisation—the major qualities of the extreme form of farce, **slapstick**, which is named after the double paddles ("slap sticks") that made loud cracking noises when actors in the *commedia dell'arte* used them to whack each other. Slapstick depends heavily on exaggerated actions, poses, and facial expressions. In slapstick there is constant onstage business with objects like paddles, pies, pails, paint, paste, or toilet paper, along with wild and improbable actions such as squirming, hiding, tripping, stumbling, tumbling, falling, and flopping.

Other Kinds of Comedy Emphasize Complexity and Absurdity

Other types of modern and contemporary comedy include **ironic comedy, realistic comedy,** and **comedy of the absurd.** All of these usually shun the happy endings of traditional comedy. Often, the blocking agents are successful, the protagonists are defeated, and the initial problem—either a realistic or an absurdist dilemma—remains unresolved. Such comedies, which began to appear in the late nineteenth century, illustrate the complexities and absurdities of modern life and the funny but futile efforts that people make when coming to grips with existence.

Many of the types of comedy just discussed still flourish. Romantic comedies, comedies of manners, and farces can be found on innumerable stages and movie screens. They revolve about a central situation that might be quite ordinary (Will Hank get along with a visiting lodge member? Will Sue be accepted by schoolmates at her new school? Will Jim get a date for the prom?). Such situations find their ways into the many *sitcoms* (*situation comedies*) that occupy prime-time television programs.

In view of the variety of comedy, it is most important to recognize that comedy is rarely a pure and discrete form. High comedies might include crude physical humor, especially with characters to be disapproved. Low comedies can sometimes contain wit and elegance. Satiric comedies might deal with successful young lovers. Romantic comedies can mock the vices and follies of weird and eccentric characters. Farce and slapstick can contain satire on social values and conventions.

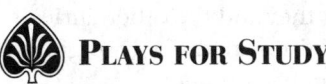 **PLAYS FOR STUDY**

WILLIAM SHAKESPEARE, *A MIDSUMMER NIGHT'S DREAM*

A Midsummer Night's Dream was written early in Shakespeare's career, in 1594 or 1595.[3] It is a romantic comedy dramatizing the idea that "the course of true love never did run smooth." This central line of action, which owes much to Roman comedy, involves blocked love, a journey of circumvention and education that takes the lovers from the world of laws and problems into an imaginary world of chaos and transformations, and an ultimate victory back in the world of daylight and order.

The subject of *A Midsummer Night's Dream* is love. Shakespeare skillfully interweaves this topic in the play's four separate plots, four groups of characters, and four styles of language. Each plot explores the nature of love, the madness of irrational love, and the harmony needed for regenerative love.

In the *overplot*—the action that establishes the time for the play—the relationship is between the rulers, Theseus and Hippolyta, who have undergone a change from irrational war to rational peace. As such, they represent the dynastic continuity of the state, the order of the daylight world of Athens,

---

[3] See Chapter 27, pp. 1345–50, for a description of Shakespeare's theater and career as a dramatist.

and the rigor of law. These characters are the rulers, and they speak predominantly in blank verse (unrhymed iambic pentameter; see Chapter. 19). The two connected *middle plots* concern the adventures of the four lovers and the actions of Oberon and Titania. The four lovers, embodying the most passionate and insistent phase of love, are from the middle class, and they speak mainly in rhymed couplets. During their long night of illusion in the woods, conjured by Oberon and his servant Puck, their adventures drive them toward rationality, and they recognize and accept the need for faithfulness and constancy.

The parallel middle love plot involves the conflict between Oberon and Titania, the king and queen of the fairies, because of their mutually exclusive wishes to control a "changeling" child. Oberon is "jealous" and wants the child as an attendant, but Titania wants to keep him in her service because his mother had been Titania's attendant, friend, and confidante. With great power over Titania, Oberon humbles her, and she then reacknowledges his superiority—the proper attitude of a wife, according to Elizabethan males. Oberon and Titania, of course, are supernatural forces. Although they and the other fairies speak in both blank verse and rhymed couplets, the fairies are the only singing characters and also the only characters to speak in iambic tetrameter.

The examination of love in the *subplot* occurs partly in Titania's relationship with Bottom—the most hilarious instance of love madness in the play—and partly in the play-within-a-play about Pyramus and Thisby. This ridiculous tragedy echoes the central plot of *A Midsummer Night's Dream* and demonstrates, again, the pitfalls and unpredictability of love. It also emphasizes the happy and harmonious marriages and rapprochements that occur in both the overplot and the middle plots.

While *A Midsummer Night's Dream* is chiefly about love, it is equally concerned with the complicated relationship of perception, imagination, passion, art, and illusion. In Act V Theseus asserts that "The lunatic, the lover, and the poet" are alike because they all try to make reality conform with their own imaginations and desires (1.7–22). It would seem that chaos would therefore be the normal state, but, as Hippolyta concludes in response to Theseus, order and certainty somehow prevail, "howsoever" extraordinary and almost miraculous this result may seem (lines 23–27). The movement of the play is governed by these ideas that, along with the brilliant language and comic actions, are directly attributable to the genius of Shakespeare.

WILLIAM SHAKESPEARE   (1564–1616)

A Midsummer Night's Dream _____ *1600 (ca. 1594)*

Edited by Alice Griffin°

THE NAMES OF THE ACTORS

Theseus, *Duke of Athens*
Egeus, *father of Hermia*

Lysander, *beloved of Hermia*
Demetrius, *in love with Hermia, favoured by Egeus*
Philostrate, *Master of the Revels to Theseus*
Peter Quince, *a carpenter (Prologue)**
Nick Bottom, *a weaver (Pyramus)**
Francis Flute, *a bellows-mender (Thisby)**
Tom Snout, *a tinker (Wall)**
Snug, *a joiner (Lion)**
Robin Starveling, *a tailor (Moonshine)**
Hippolyta, *Queen of the Amazons, betrothed to Theseus*
Hermia, *daughter of Egeus, in love with Lysander*
Helena, *in love with Demetrius*
Oberon, *King of the Fairies*
Titania, *Queen of the Fairies*
Puck, *or* Robin Goodfellow
Peaseblossom ⎫
Cobweb   ⎬ *Fairies*
Moth   ⎪
Mustardseed ⎭

Other Fairies attending Oberon and Titania. Attendants on Theseus and Hippolyta.

Scene: *Athens, and a wood nearby*

ACT 1

[*Scene 1. Athens. The palace of Theseus*]

Enter THESEUS, HIPPOLYTA,° [PHILOSTRATE,] *with others.*

THESEUS. Now fair Hippolyta, our nuptial hour
　　Draws on apace: four happy days bring in
　　Another moon: but O, methinks how slow
　　This old moon wanes! she lingers° my desires,
　　Like to a stepdame or a dowager,°　　　　　　　　　　　5
　　Long withering out° a young man's revenue.
HIPPOLYTA. Four days will quickly steep themselves in night:
　　Four nights will quickly dream away the time:
　　And then the moon, like to a silver bow
　　New-bent in heaven, shall behold the night　　　　　　　10
　　Of our solemnities.

Professor Griffin's text for *A Midsummer Night's Dream* is the First Quarto (edition) published in 1600, with modifications based on the Quarto edition of 1619 and the First Folio, published in 1623. Stage directions in those editions are printed here without brackets; added stage directions are printed within brackets. We have edited Griffin's notes for this text.　　*Characters who play in the interlude.　　0.3 S.D.: *Theseus, Hippolyta:* In Greek legend, Theseus captured the Amazon Queen Hippolyta and brought her to Athens where they were married.　　4 *lingers:* delays the fulfillment of.　　5 *dowager:* a widow supported by her dead husband's heirs.　　6 *withering out:* (1) depleting (2) growing withered.

THESEUS.   Go Philostrate,
  Stir up the Athenian youth to merriments,
  Awake the pert° and nimble spirit of mirth,
  Turn melancholy forth to funerals:
  The pale companion° is not for our pomp.   [*Exit PHILOSTRATE.*]
  Hippolyta, I wooed thee with my sword,
  And won thy love doing thee injuries;
  But I will wed thee in another key,
  With pomp, with triumph,° and with revelling.

Enter EGEUS and his daughter HERMIA, LYSANDER and DEMETRIUS.

EGEUS.   Happy be Theseus, our renownèd duke.
THESEUS.   Thanks good Egeus:° what's the news with thee?
EGEUS.   Full of vexation come I, with complaint
  Against my child, my daughter Hermia.
  Stand forth Demetrius. My noble lord,
  This man hath my consent to marry her.
  Stand forth Lysander. And my gracious duke,
  This man hath bewitched the bosom of my child.
  Thou, thou Lysander, thou hast given her rhymes,
  And interchanged love tokens with my child:
  Thou hast by moonlight at her window sung,
  With feigning voice, verses of feigning° love,
  And stol'n the impression of her fantasy°
  With bracelets of thy hair, rings, gauds,° conceits,°
  Knacks,° trifles, nosegays, sweetmeats—messengers
  Of strong prevailment in unhardened youth.
  With cunning hast thou filched my daughter's heart,
  Turned her obedience, which is due to me,
  To stubborn harshness. And my gracious duke,
  Be it so° she will not here before your grace
  Consent to marry with Demetrius,
  I beg the ancient privilege of Athens:
  As she is mine, I may dispose of her:
    Which shall be, either to this gentleman,
    Or to her death, according to our law
    Immediately° provided in that case.
THESEUS.   What say you, Hermia? Be advised, fair maid.
  To you your father should be as a god:
  One that composed your beauties: yea and one
  To whom you are but as a form in wax
  By him imprinted, and within his power
  To leave the figure, or disfigure it:
  Demetrius is a worthy gentleman.

13 *pert:* lively.   15 *companion:* fellow (contemptuous).   19 *triumph:* public festival.   21 *Egeus:* (trisyllabic).   31 *feigning:* (1) deceptive (2) desirous ("faining").   32 *stol'n . . . fantasy:* stealthily imprinted your image upon her fancy.   33 *gauds:* trinkets.   *conceits:* either (a) love poetry, or (b) love tokens.   34 *Knacks:* knick-knacks.   39 *Be it so:* if it be that.   45 *Immediately:* precisely.

HERMIA.   So is Lysander.
THESEUS   In himself he is:
But in this kind, wanting your father's voice,°
The other must be held the worthier.   55
HERMIA.   I would my father looked but with my eyes.
THESEUS.   Rather your eyes must with his judgment look.
HERMIA.   I do entreat your grace to pardon me.
I know not by what power I am made bold,
Nor how it may concern my modesty,   60
In such a presence, here to plead my thoughts:
But I beseech your grace that I may know
The worst that may befall me in this case,
If I refuse to wed Demetrius.
THESEUS.   Either to die the death, or to abjure   65
For ever the society of men.
Therefore fair Hermia, question your desires,
Know of your youth,° examine well your blood,°
Whether, if you yield not to your father's choice,
You can endure the livery° of a nun,   70
For aye° to be in shady cloister mewed,°
To live a barren sister all your life,
Chanting faint hymns to the cold fruitless moon.°
Thrice blessèd they that master so their blood,
To undergo such maiden pilgrimage: 75
But earthlier happy° is the rose distilled,°
Than that which, withering on the virgin thorn,
Grows, lives, and dies, in single blessedness.
HERMIA.   So will I grow, so live, so die my lord,
Ere I will yield my virgin patent° up   80
Unto his lordship, whose unwishèd yoke
My soul consents not to give sovereignty.
THESEUS.   Take time to pause, and by the next moon,
The sealing day betwixt my love and me,
For everlasting bond of fellowship,   85
Upon that day either prepare to die
For disobedience to your father's will,
Or else to wed Demetrius, as he would,
Or on Diana's altar to protest°
For aye, austerity and single life.   90
DEMETRIUS.   Relent, sweet Hermia, and Lysander, yield
Thy crazèd° title to my certain right.
LYSANDER.   You have her father's love, Demetrius:
Let me have Hermia's: do you marry him.

---

54 *in . . . voice:* in this respect, lacking your father's approval.   68 *Know . . . youth:* ask yourself as
a young person.   68 *blood:* passions.   70 *livery:* habit.   71 *aye:* ever.   *mewed:* shut
up.   73 *moon:* (the moon goddess Diana represented unmarried chastity).   76 *earthlier happy:*
more happy on earth.   *distilled:* i.e., into perfume (thus its essence is passed on, as to a
child).   80 *patent:* privilege.   89 *protest:* vow.

EGEUS.   Scornful Lysander, true, he hath my love:
　　And what is mine, my love shall render him.
　　And she is mine, and all my right of her
　　I do estate° unto Demetrius.
LYSANDER.   I am, my lord, as well derived° as he,
　　As well possessed:° my love is more than his:
　　My fortunes every way as fairly ranked
　　(If not with vantage) as° Demetrius':
　　And, which is more than all these boasts can be,
　　I am beloved of beauteous Hermia.
　　Why should not I then prosecute my right?
　　Demetrius, I'll avouch it to his head,°
　　Made love to Nedar's daughter, Helena,
　　And won her soul: and she, sweet lady, dotes,
　　Devoutly dotes, dotes in idolatry,
　　Upon this spotted° and inconstant man.
THESEUS.   I must confess that I have heard so much,
　　And with Demetrius thought to have spoke thereof:
　　But being over-full of self-affairs,
　　My mind did lose it. But Demetrius come,
　　And come Egeus, you shall go with me:
　　I have some private schooling for you both.
　　For you fair Hermia, look you arm yourself,
　　To fit your fancies to your father's will;
　　Or else the law of Athens yields you up
　　(Which by no means we may extenuate)
　　To death or to a vow of single life.
　　Come my Hippolyta, what cheer my love?
　　Demetrius and Egeus, go along:
　　I must employ you in some business
　　Against° our nuptial, and confer with you
　　Of something nearly° that concerns yourselves.
EGEUS.   With duty and desire we follow you.

Exeunt.° Manent° LYSANDER *and* HERMIA.

LYSANDER.   How now my love? Why is your cheek so pale?
　　How chance the roses there do fade so fast?
HERMIA.   Belike° for want of rain, which I could well
　　Beteem° them from the tempest of my eyes,
LYSANDER.   Ay me, for aught that I could ever read,
　　Could ever hear by tale or history,
　　The course of true love never did run smooth;
　　But either it was different in blood—
HERMIA.   O cross! too high° to be enthralled to low.°

92 *crazèd:* flawed.   98 *estate:* transfer.   99 *well derived:* well born.   100 *well possessed:* wealthy.   102 *with vantage, as:* better, than.   106 *avouch . . . head:* prove it to his face.   110 *spotted:* stained   125 *Against:* in preparation for.   126 *nearly:* closely.   127 S.D.: *Exeunt:* they exit.   *Manent:* they remain.   130 *Belike:* likely.   131 *Beteem:* (1) pour out on (2) allow.   136 *high:* highborn.   *enthralled to low:* made a slave to one of low birth.

LYSANDER.   Or else misgraffèd° in respect of years—
HERMIA.   O spite! too old to be engaged to young.
LYSANDER.   Or else it stood upon the choice of friends—
HERMIA.   O hell! to choose love by another's eyes.   140
LYSANDER.   Or if there were a sympathy in choice,
　　War, death, or sickness did lay siege to it;
　　Making it momentany° as a sound,
　　Swift as a shadow, short as any dream,
　　Brief as the lightning in the collied° night,   145
　　That, in a spleen,° unfolds both heaven and earth;
　　And ere a man hath power to say "Behold,"
　　The jaws of darkness do devour it up:
　　So quick bright things come to confusion.
HERMIA.   If then true lovers have been ever crossed,°   150
　　It stands as an edict in destiny:
　　Then let us teach our trial patience,°
　　Because it is a customary cross,
　　As due to love as thoughts and dreams and sighs,
　　Wishes and tears; poor Fancy's° followers.   155
LYSANDER.   A good persuasion: therefore hear me, Hermia:
　　I have a widow aunt, a dowager,
　　Of great revenue, and she hath no child:
　　From Athens is her house remote seven leagues,
　　And she respects° me as her only son: 160
　　There gentle Hermia, may I marry thee,
　　And to that place the sharp Athenian law
　　Cannot pursue us. If thou lov'st me then,
　　Steal forth thy father's house tomorrow night:
　　And in the wood, a league without the town,   165
　　Where I did meet thee once with Helena
　　To do observance to a morn of May,°
　　There will I stay° for thee.
HERMIA.　　　　　　　　　　　　My good Lysander,
　　I swear to thee, by Cupid's strongest bow,
　　By his best arrow, with the golden head,°   170
　　By the simplicity of Venus' doves,
　　By that which knitteth souls and prospers loves,
　　And by that fire which burned the Carthage queen,
　　When the false Troyan° under sail was seen,
　　By all the vows that ever men have broke,   175
　　(In number more than ever women spoke)
　　In that same place thou has appointed me,
　　Tomorrow truly will I meet with thee.

---

137 *misgraffèd:* badly joined.   143 *momentany:* momentary.   145 *collied:* black as coal.   146
in a spleen: impulsively, in a sudden outburst.   150 *ever crossed:* evermore thwarted.   152 *teach*
. . . *patience:* teach ourselves to be patient.   155 *Fancy:* love (sometimes infatuation).   160
respects: regards.   167 *do . . . May:* celebrate May Day.   168 *stay:* wait.   170 *golden head:*
(The arrow with the gold head causes love).   173–174 *Carthage Queen . . . false Troyan:* Dido,
who burned herself to death on a funeral pyre when Trojan Aeneas deserted her.

LYSANDER.   Keep promise love: look, here comes Helena.

Enter HELENA.

HERMIA.   God speed fair Helena: whither away?
HELENA.   Call you me fair? That fair again unsay.
Demetrius loves your fair:° O happy fair!
Your eyes are lodestars,° and your tongue's sweet air°
More tuneable than lark to shepherd's ear,
When wheat is green, when hawthorn buds appear.
Sickness is catching: O were favour° so,
Yours would I catch, fair Hermia, ere I go,
My ear should catch your voice,° my eye your eye,°
My tongue should catch your tongue's sweet melody.
Were the world mine, Demetrius being bated,°
The rest I'ld give to be to you translated.°
O teach me how you look, and with what art
You sway the motion of Demetrius' heart.
HERMIA.   I frown upon him; yet he loves me still.
HELENA.   O that your frowns would teach my smiles such skill.
HERMIA.   I give him curses; yet he gives me love.
HELENA.   O that my prayers could such affection move.
HERMIA.   The more I hate, the more he follows me.
HELENA.   The more I love, the more he hateth me.
HERMIA.   His folly, Helena, is no fault of mine.
HELENA.   None but your beauty; would that fault were mine.
HERMIA.   Take comfort: he no more shall see my face:
Lysander and myself will fly this place.
Before the time I did Lysander see,
Seemed Athens as a paradise to me:
O then, what graces in my love do dwell,
That he hath turned a heaven unto a hell!
LYSANDER.   Helen, to you our minds we will unfold:
Tomorrow night, when Phoebe° doth behold
Her silver visage in the wat'ry glass,°
Decking with liquid pearl the bladed grass
(A time that lovers' flights doth still° conceal)
Through Athens gates have we devised to steal.
HERMIA.   And in the wood, where often you and I
Upon faint primrose beds were wont to lie,
Emptying our bosoms of their counsel° sweet,
There my Lysander and myself shall meet,
And thence from Athens turn away our eyes,
To see new friends and stranger companies.°
Farewell, sweet playfellow: pray thou for us:

182 *your fair:* i.e., beauty.   183 *lodestars:* guiding stars.   *air:* music.   186 *favour:* appearance.   188 *My ear . . . voice:* my ear should catch the tone of your voice.   *my eye your eye:* my
eye should catch the way you glance.   190 *bated:* subtracted, excepted.   191 *translated:* transformed.   209 *Phoebe:* Diana, the moon.   210 *wat'ry glass:* mirror of the water.   212 *still:*
always.   216 *counsel:* secrets.   219 *stranger companies:* the companionship of strangers.

And good luck grant thee thy Demetrius.
Keep word Lysander: we must starve our sight
From lovers' food,° till morrow deep midnight.

LYSANDER.   I will my Hermia.   *Exit HERMIA.*
                       Helena adieu:
As you on him, Demetrius dote on you.°   *Exit LYSANDER.*   225

HELENA.   How happy some, o'er other some, can be!
Through Athens I am thought as fair as she.
But what of that? Demetrius thinks not so:
He will not know what all but he do know.
And as he errs, doting on Hermia's eyes,   230
So I, admiring of his qualities.
Things base and vile, holding no quantity.°
Love can transpose to form and dignity.
Love looks not with the eyes, but with the mind:
And therefore is winged Cupid painted blind.   235
Nor hath Love's mind of any judgment taste:
Wings, and no eyes, figure° unheedy haste.
And therefore is Love said to be a child:
Because in choice he is so oft beguiled.
As waggish boys in game themselves forswear: 240
So the boy Love is perjured everywhere.
For ere Demetrius looked on Hermia's eyne,°
He hailed down oaths that he was only mine.
And when this hail some heat from Hermia felt,
So he dissolved, and show'rs of oaths did melt.   245
I will go tell him of fair Hermia's flight:
Then to the wood will he tomorrow night
Pursue her: and for this intelligence,°
If I have thanks, it is a dear expense:°
But herein mean I to enrich my pain,   250
To have his sight° thither and back again.   *Exit.*

[*Scene 2. Quince's house*]

Enter QUINCE the Carpenter; and SNUG the Joiner; and BOTTOM the Weaver; and FLUTE the Bellows-mender; and SNOUT the Tinker; and STARVELING the Tailor.°

QUINCE.   Is all our company here?
BOTTOM.   You were the best to call them generally,° man by man,
   according to the scrip.

---

223 *lovers' food:* the sight of the loved one.   225 *As . . . you:* As you dote on Demetrius, so may
Demetrius also dote on you.   232 *holding no quantity:* out of proportion.   237 *figure:* symbolize.   242 *eyne:* eyes.   248 *intelligence:* information.   249 *dear expense:* costly outlay (on
Demetrius' part).   250–251 *But . . . sight:* but I will be rewarded just by the sight of him.   0.2
S.D.: the low characters' names describe their work: *Quince:* quoins, wooden wedges used in
building.   *Snug:* fitting snugly, suiting a joiner of furniture.   *Bottom:* bobbin or core on
which yarn is wound.   *Flute:* mender of fluted church organs and bellows.   *Snout:* spout
(of the kettles he mends).   *Starveling:* (tailors being traditionally thin).   2 *generally:* Bottom
often uses the wrong word; here he means the opposite: "severally, one-by-one."

QUINCE. Here is the scroll of every man's name which is thought
   fit, through all Athens, to play in our interlude° before
   the duke and the duchess, on his wedding-day at night.
BOTTOM. First good Peter Quince, say what the play treats on,
   then read the names of the actors: and so grow to a point.
QUINCE. Marry,° our play is "The most lamentable comedy, and
   most cruel death of Pyramus and Thisby."
BOTTOM. A very good piece of work I assure you, and a merry. Now
   good Peter Quince, call forth your actors by the scroll.
   Masters, spread yourselves.
QUINCE. Answer as I call you. Nick Bottom the weaver?
BOTTOM. Ready: name what part I am for, and proceed.
QUINCE. You, Nick Bottom, are set down for Pyramus.
BOTTOM. What is Pyramus? A lover, or a tyrant?
QUINCE. A lover that kills himself, most gallant, for love.
BOTTOM. That will ask some tears in the true performing of it. If I
   do it, let the audience look to their eyes: I will move
   storms: I will condole° in some measure. To the rest—
   yet my chief humour° is for a tyrant. I could play Ercles°
   rarely, or a part to tear a cat in, to make all split.°
       The raging rocks
       And shivering shocks,
       Shall break the locks
          Of prison gates,
       And Phibbus' car°
       Shall shine from far,
       And make and mar
          The foolish Fates.
   This was lofty. Now name the rest of the players. This is
   Ercles' vein, a tyrant's vein: a lover is more condoling.
QUINCE. Francis Flute, the bellows-mender?
FLUTE. Here Peter Quince.
QUINCE. Flute, you must take Thisby on you.
FLUTE. What is Thisby? A wand'ring knight?
QUINCE. It is the lady that Pyramus must love.
FLUTE. Nay faith, let not me play a woman: I have a beard
   coming.
QUINCE. That's all one:° you shall play it in a mask, and you may
   speak as small° as you will.
BOTTOM. And° I may hide my face, let me play Thisby too: I'll speak
   in a monstrous little voice; "Thisne, Thisne," "Ah
   Pyramus, my lover dear, thy Thisby dear, and lady
   dear."
QUINCE. No, no, you must play Pyramus: and Flute, you Thisby.

---

5 *interlude:* short play.   9 *Marry:* indeed (mild oath, corruption of "by the Virgin
Mary").   21 *condole:* lament.   22 *humour:* inclination.   *Ercles:* Hercules (typified by
ranting).   23 *tear . . . split:* (terms for ranting and raging on the stage).   28 *Phibbus' car:*
Phoebus Apollo's chariot.   41 *That's all one:* never mind.   42 *small:* softly.   43 *And:* if.

BOTTOM.   Well, proceed.

QUINCE.   Robin Starveling, the tailor?

STARVELING.   Here Peter Quince.   50

QUINCE.   Robin Starveling, you must play Thisby's mother. Tom
Snout, the tinker?

SNOUT.   Here Peter Quince.

QUINCE.   You, Pyramus' father; myself, Thisby's father; Snug the
joiner, you the lion's part: and I hope here is a play   55
fitted.°

SNUG.   Have you the lion's part written? Pray you, if it be, give
it me: for I am slow of study.

QUINCE.   You may do it extempore: for it is nothing but roaring.

BOTTOM.   Let me play the lion too. I will roar, that° I will do any   60
man's heart good to hear me. I will roar, that I will make
the duke say "Let him roar again: let him roar again."

QUINCE.   And you should do it too terribly, you would fright the
duchess and the ladies, that they would shriek: and
that were enough to hang us all.   65

ALL.   That would hang us, every mother's son.

BOTTOM.   I grant you, friends, if you should fright the ladies out of
their wits, they would have no more discretion but to
hang us: but I will aggravate° my voice so, that I will roar
you as gently as any sucking dove: I will roar you and   70
'twere° any nightingale.

QUINCE.   You can play no part but Pyramus: for Pyramus is a
sweet-faced man; a proper° man as one shall see in a
summer's day; a most lovely gentleman-like man: therefore
you must needs play Pyramus.   75

BOTTOM.   Well: I will undertake it. What beard were I best to play
it in?

QUINCE.   Why, what you will.

BOTTOM.   I will discharge it in either your straw-colour beard, your
orange-tawny beard, your purple-in-grain° beard, or your   80
French-crown-colour° beard, your perfit yellow.

QUINCE.   Some of your French crowns° have no hair at all; and
then you will play barefaced. But masters here are your
parts, and I am to entreat you, request you, and desire
you, to con° them by tomorrow night: and meet me in the   85
palace wood, a mile without the town, by moonlight;
there will we rehearse: for if we meet in the city, we
shall be dogged with company, and our devices° known.
In the meantime, I will draw a bill of properties,° such
as our play wants. I pray you fail me not.   90

---

56 *fitted:* cast.   60 *that:* so that.   69 *aggravate:* (he means "moderate").   70–71 *and 'twere:*
as if it were.   73 *proper:* handsome.   80 *purple-in-grain:* dyed permanently purple.   81
French-crown-colour: golden, like French crowns (gold coins).   82 *French crowns:* bald heads
believed to be caused by syphilis, the "French" disease.   85 *con:* learn by heart.   88 *devices:*
plans.   89 *bill of properties:* list of stage props.

BOTTOM.   We will meet, and there we may rehearse most obscenely°
and courageously. Take pain, be perfit: adieu.
QUINCE.   At the duke's oak we meet.
BOTTOM.   Enough: hold, or cut bow-strings.°   *Exeunt.*

ACT 2

[*Scene 1. A wood near Athens*]

Enter a FAIRY *at one door, and* ROBIN GOODFELLOW [*Puck*] *at another.*

PUCK.   How now spirit, whither wander you?
FAIRY.   Over hill, over dale,
    Thorough bush, thorough brier,
Over park, over pale,°
    Thorough flood, thorough fire:
I do wander everywhere,
Swifter than the moon's sphere:
And I serve the Fairy Queen,
To dew ° her orbs° upon the green.
The cowslips° tall her pensioners° be,
In their gold coats, spots you see:
Those be rubies, fairy favours:°
In those freckles live their savours.°
I must go seek some dewdrops here,
And hang a pearl in every cowslip's ear.
Farewell thou lob° of spirits: I'll be gone,
Our queen and all her elves come here anon.
PUCK.   The king doth keep his revels here tonight.
Take heed the queen come not within his sight.
For Oberon is passing fell° and wrath,
Because that she, as her attendant, hath
A lovely boy, stol'n from an Indian king:
She never had so sweet a changeling.°
And jealous Oberon would have the child
Knight of his train, to trace° the forests wild.
But she, perforce,° withholds the lovèd boy,
Crowns him with flowers, and makes him all her joy.
And now, they never meet in grove or green,
By fountain clear, or spangled starlight sheen,
But they do square,° that all their elves for fear
Creep into acorn cups, and hide them there.

91 *obscenely:* (he may mean "fittingly" or "obscurely").   94 *hold, or cut bow-strings:* (meaning uncertain, but equivalent to "fish, or cut bait").   4 *pale:* enclosure.   9 *dew:* bedew.   *orbs:* fairy rings (circles of high grass).   10 *cowslips:* primroses.   *pensioners:* royal bodyguards.   12 *favours:* gifts.   13 *savours:* perfumes.   16 *lob:* lout, lubber.   20 *passing fell:* surpassingly fierce.   23 *changeling:* creature exchanged by fairies for a stolen baby (among the fairies, the stolen child).   25 *trace:* traverse.   26 *perforce:* by force.   30 *square:* quarrel.

FAIRY. Either I mistake your shape and making quite,
Or else you are that shrewd and knavish sprite
Called Robin Goodfellow. Are not you he
That frights the maidens of the villagery,   35
Skim milk,° and sometimes labour in the quern,°
And bootless° make the breathless housewife churn,
And sometime make the drink to bear no barm,°
Mislead night-wanderers, laughing at their harm?
Those that Hobgoblin call you, and sweet Puck,   40
You do their work, and they shall have good luck.
Are not you he?
PUCK.   Thou speakest aright;
I am that merry wanderer of the night.
I jest to Oberon, and make him smile,
When I a fat and bean-fed horse beguile,   45
Neighing in likeness of a filly foal;
And sometime lurk I in a gossip's° bowl,
In very likeness of a roasted crab,°
And when she drinks, against her lips I bob,
And on her withered dewlap° pour the ale.   50
The wisest aunt, telling the saddest tale,
Sometime for three-foot stool mistaketh me:
Then slip I from her bum, down topples she,
And "tailor"° cries, and falls into a cough;
And then the whole quire° hold their hips and laugh,   55
And waxen° in their mirth, and neeze,° and swear
A merrier hour was never wasted° there.
But room° fairy: here comes Oberon.
FAIRY. And here, my mistress. Would that he were gone.

*Enter [OBERON] the King Of Fairies, at one door with his TRAIN, and the QUEEN [TITANIA], at
another, with hers.*

OBERON. Ill met by moonlight, proud Titania.   60
QUEEN. What, jealous Oberon? Fairy, skip hence.
I have forsworn his bed and company.
OBERON. Tarry, rash wanton.° Am not I thy lord?
QUEEN. Then I must be thy lady: but I know
When thou hast stol'n away from fairyland,   65
And in the shape of Corin° sat all day,
Playing on pipes of corn,° and versing love
To amorous Phillida.° Why art thou here

36 *Skim milk:* steals the cream off the milk.   *quern:* handmill for grinding grain.   37 *bootless:* without result.   38 *barm:* foamy head (therefore the drink was flat).   47 *gossip's:* old
woman's.   48 *crab:* crabapple (often put into ale).   50 *dewlap:* loose skin hanging about
the throat.   54 *"tailor":* (variously explained: perhaps the squatting position of the tailor, or
"tailard"—one with a tail).   55 *quire:* choir, group.   56 *waxen:* increase.   *neeze:*
sneeze.   57 *wasted:* spent.   58 *room:* make room.   63 *Tarry, rash wanton:* wait, headstrong
one.   66–68 *Corin, Phillida:* (traditional names in pastoral literature for a shepherd and his
loved one, respectively).   67 *corn:* wheat straws.

Come from the farthest steep of India?
But that, forsooth, the bouncing Amazon,°
Your buskined° mistress and your warrior love,
To Theseus must be wedded; and you come,
To give their bed joy and prosperity.
OBERON. How canst thou thus, for shame, Titania,
Glance at my credit with° Hippolyta,
Knowing I know thy love to Theseus?
Didst thou not lead him through the glimmering night,
From Perigenia, whom he ravishèd?
And make him with fair Aegles break his faith,
With Ariadne, and Antiopa°?
QUEEN. These are the forgeries of jealousy:
And never, since the middle summer's spring,°
Met we on hill, in dale, forest, or mead,
By pavèd° fountain, or by rushy brook,
Or in the beachèd margent° of the sea,
To dance our ringlets to the whistling wind,
But with thy brawls thou hast disturbed our sport.
Therefore the winds, piping to us in vain,
As in revenge, have sucked up from the sea
Contagious° fogs: which falling in the land,
Hath every pelting° river made so proud,
That they have overborne their continents.°
The ox hath therefore stretched his yoke in vain,
The ploughman lost his sweat, and the green corn°
Hath rotted, ere his youth attained a beard:°
The fold° stands empty in the drownèd field,
And crows are fatted with the murrion° flock.
The nine men's morris° is filled up with mud:
And the quaint mazes° in the wanton green,°
For lack of tread, are undistinguishable.
The human mortals want° their winter here,
No night is now with hymn or carol blest;
Therefore the moon, the governess of floods,
Pale in her anger, washes all the air,
That rheumatic diseases do abound.
And thorough this distemperature,° we see
The seasons alter: hoary-headed frosts

---

70 *Amazon:* Hippolyta.   71 *buskined:* wearing boots.   75 *Glance . . . credit with:* hint at my favors from.   78–80 *Perigenia . . . Antiopa:* women that Theseus supposedly loved and deserted.   82 *middle . . . spring:* beginning of midsummer.   84 *pavèd:* with a pebbly bottom.   85 *margent:* margin, shore.   88–117 *Therefore . . . original:* (the disturbance in nature reflects the discord between Oberon and Titania).   90 *Contagious:* spreading pestilence.   91 *pelting:* paltry.   92 *overborne their continents:* overflown the banks which contain them.   94 *corn:* grain.   95 *beard:* the tassels on ripened grain.   96 *fold:* enclosure for livestock.   97 *murrion:* dead from murrain, a cattle disease.   98 *nine men's morris:* game played on squares cut in the grass on which stones or disks are moved.   99 *quaint mazes:* intricate paths.   *wanton green:* luxuriant grass.   101 *want:* lack.   106 *distemperature:* upset in nature.

Fall in the fresh lap of the crimson rose,
And on old Hiems'° thin and icy crown,
An odorous chaplet° of sweet summer buds   110
Is, as in mockery, set. The spring, the summer,
The childing° autumn, angry winter change
Their wonted liveries:° and the mazèd° world,
By their increase, now knows not which is which:
And this same progeny of evils comes   115
From our debate, from our dissension:
We are their parents and original.
OBERON.   Do you amend it then: it lies in you.
Why should Titania cross her Oberon?
I do but beg a little changeling boy,   120
To be my henchman.°
QUEEN.   Set your heart at rest.
The fairy land buys not the child of me.
His mother was a vot'ress° of my order:
And in the spicèd Indian air, by night,
Full often hath she gossiped by my side.   125
And sat with me on Neptune's yellow sands,
Marking th' embarkèd traders° on the flood:
When we have laughed to see the sails conceive,
And grow big-bellied with the wanton° wind:
Which she, with pretty and with swimming gait,   130
Following (her womb then rich with my young squire)
Would imitate, and sail upon the land,
To fetch me trifles, and return again,
As from a voyage, rich with merchandise.
But she, being mortal, of that boy did die,   135
And for her sake, do I rear up her boy:
And for her sake, I will not part with him.
OBERON.   How long within this wood intend you stay?
QUEEN.   Perchance till after Theseus' wedding day.
If you will patiently dance in our round,°   140
And see our moonlight revels, go with us:
If not, shun me, and I will spare° your haunts.
OBERON.   Give me that boy, and I will go with thee.
QUEEN.   Not for thy fairy kingdom. Fairies away
We shall chide downright, if I longer stay.   145

                        Exeunt [*TITANIA and her* TRAIN.]

OBERON.   Well, go thy way. Thou shalt not from this grove,
Till I torment thee for this injury.
My gentle Puck come hither: thou rememb'rest,

---

109 *Hiems:* god of winter.   110 *odorous chaplet:* sweet-smelling wreath.   112 *childing:* fruitful.   113 *wonted liveries:* accustomed dress.   *mazèd:* amazed.   121 *henchman:*
attendant.   123 *vot'ress:* vowed and devoted follower.   127 *traders:* merchant ships.   129
wanton: sportive.   140 *round:* rounddance.   142 *spare:* shun.

Since° once I sat upon a promontory,
And heard a mermaid, on a dolphin's back,
Uttering such dulcet and harmonious breath,
That the rude° sea grew civil° at her song,
And certain stars shot madly from their spheres,
To hear the sea-maid's music.
PUCK.   I remember.
OBERON.   That very time, I saw (but thou couldst not)
Flying between the cold moon and the earth,
Cupid, all armed: a certain aim he took
At a fair Vestal,° thronèd by the west,
And loosed his love-shaft smartly from his bow,
As it should pierce a hundred thousand hearts:
But I might see young Cupid's fiery shaft
Quenched in the chaste beams of the wat'ry moon:
And the imperial vot'ress° passèd on,
In maiden meditation, fancy-free.°
Yet marked I where the bolt° of Cupid fell.
It fell upon a little western flower;
Before, milk-white; now purple with love's wound,
And maidens call it love-in-idleness.°
Fetch me that flow'r: the herb I showed thee once.
The juice of it, on sleeping eyelids laid,
Will make or man or woman madly dote
Upon the next live creature that it sees.
Fetch me this herb, and be thou here again
Ere the leviathan° can swim a league.
PUCK.   I'll put a girdle round about the earth,
In forty minutes.   [*Exit.*]
OBERON.   Having once this juice,
I'll watch Titania when she is asleep,
And drop the liquor of it in her eyes:
The next thing then she waking looks upon,
(Be it on lion, bear, or wolf, or bull,
On meddling monkey, or on busy° ape)
She shall pursue it, with the soul of love.
And ere I take this charm from off her sight
(As I can take it with another herb)
I'll make her render up her page to me.
But who comes here? I am invisible,
And I will overhear their conference.

Enter DEMETRIUS, HELENA *following him.*

149 *Since:* when.   152 *rude:* rough.   *civil:* calm.   158 *Vestal:* virgin, probable reference to
Queen Elizabeth.   163 *imperial vot'ress:* royal devotee (Queen Elizabeth) of Diana.   164
fancy-free: free from love.   165 *bolt:* arrow.   168 *love-in-idleness:* pansy.   174 *leviathan:*
whale.   181 *busy:* mischievous.

DEMETRIUS. I love thee not: therefore pursue me not.
 Where is Lysander and fair Hermia?
 The one I'll slay: the other slayeth me.   190
 Thou told'st me they were stol'n unto this wood:
 And here am I, and wood° within this wood:
 Because I cannot meet my Hermia.
 Hence, get thee gone, and follow me no more.
HELENA. You draw me, you hard-hearted adamant:°   195
 But yet you draw not iron, for my heart
 Is true as steel. Leave you your power to draw,
 And I shall have no power to follow you.
DEMETRIUS. Do I entice you? Do I speak you fair°?
 Or rather do I not in plainest truth   200
 Tell you I do not, nor I cannot love you?
HELENA. And even for that, do I love you the more:
 I am your spaniel: and Demetrius,
 The more you beat me, I will fawn on you.
 Use me but as your spaniel: spurn me, strike me, 205
 Neglect me, lose me: only give me leave,
 Unworthy as I am, to follow you.
 What worser place can I beg in your love
 (And yet a place of high respect with me)
 Than to be usèd as you use your dog.   210
DEMETRIUS. Tempt not too much the hatred of my spirit,
 For I am sick, when I do look on thee.
HELENA. And I am sick, when I look not on you.
DEMETRIUS. You do impeach° your modesty too much,
 To leave the city and commit yourself   215
 Into the hands of one that loves you not,
 To trust the opportunity of night,
 And the ill counsel of a desert° place,
 With the rich worth of your virginity.
HELENA. Your virtue is my privilege:° for that°   220
 It is not night, when I do see your face,
 Therefore I think I am not in the night.
 Nor doth this wood lack worlds of company,
 For you, in my respect,° are all the world.
 Then how can it be said I am alone,   225
 When all the world is here to look on me?
DEMETRIUS. I'll run from thee and hide me in the brakes,°
 And leave thee to the mercy of wild beasts.
HELENA. The wildest hath not such a heart as you.
 Run when you will: the story shall be changed; 230

---

192 *wood:* crazy. 195 *adamant:* (1) magnet (2) impenetrably hard lodestone. 199 *you fair:*
to you in a kindly way. 214 *impeach:* discredit. 218 *desert:* deserted. 220 *Your . . . privi-*
lege: your attraction is my excuse (for coming). *for that:* because. 224 *respect:*
regard. 227 *brakes:* thickets.

Apollo flies, and Daphne° holds the chase:
The dove pursues the griffin:° the mild hind°
Makes speed to catch the tiger. Bootless° speed,
When cowardice pursues, and valour flies.

DEMETRIUS.   I will not stay° thy questions. Let me go: 23£
Or if thou follow me, do not believe
But I shall do thee mischief in the wood.   [*Exit DEMETRIUS.*]

HELENA.   Ay, in the temple, in the town, the field,
You do me mischief. Fie Demetrius,
Your wrongs do set a scandal on my sex: 24€
We cannot fight for love, as men may do:
We should be wooed, and were not made to woo.
I'll follow thee and make a heaven of hell,
To die upon the hand I love so well.   *Exit.*

OBERON.   Fare thee well nymph. Ere he do leave this grove,   24.
Thou shalt fly him, and he shall seek thy love.

Enter PUCK.

Hast thou the flower there? Welcome wanderer.
PUCK.   Ay, there it is.
OBERON.   I pray thee give it me.
I know a bank where the wild thyme blows,
Where oxlips and the nodding violet grows,   25
Quite over-canopied with luscious woodbine,
With sweet musk-roses, and with eglantine:
There sleeps Titania, sometime of the night,
Lulled in these flowers, with dances and delight:
And there the snake throws° her enamelled skin,   25
Weed° wide enough to wrap a fairy in.
And with the juice of this, I'll streak her eyes,
And make her full of hateful fantasies.
Take thou some of it, and seek through this grove:
A sweet Athenian lady is in love   2(
With a disdainful youth: anoint his eyes.
But do it when the next thing he espies
May be the lady. Thou shalt know the man
By the Athenian garments he hath on.
Effect it with some care, that he may prove   2(
More fond° on her, than she upon her love:
And look thou meet me ere the first cock crow.
PUCK.   Fear not my lord: your servant shall do so.

                                                              Exeunt.

---

231 *Apollo . . . Daphne:* (in Ovid, Apollo pursues Daphne, who turns into a laurel tree).   232
griffin: legendary beast with the head of an eagle and the body of a lion.   *hind:* doe.   233
Bootless: useless.   235 *stay:* wait for.   255 *throws:* casts off.   256 *weed:* garment.   266
fond: doting, madly in love.

[*Scene 2. Another part of the wood*]

Enter TITANIA Queen of Fairies with her train.

QUEEN.   Come, now a roundel° and a fairy song:
Then, for the third part of a minute, hence—
Some to kill cankers in the musk-rose buds,
Some war with reremice° for their leathren wings,
To make my small elves coats, and some keep back   5
The clamorous owl, that nightly hoots and wonders
At our quaint° spirits. Sing me now asleep:
Then to your offices,° and let me rest.

Fairies sing.

You spotted snakes with double° tongue,
Thorny hedgehogs be not seen,   10
Newts and blind-worms° do no wrong,
Come not near our Fairy Queen.
Philomele,° with melody,
Sing in our sweet lullaby,
Lulla, lulla, lullaby, lulla, lulla, lullaby.   15
Never harm,
Nor spell, nor charm,
Come our lovely lady nigh.
So good night, with lullaby.
1. FAIRY.   Weaving spiders come not here: 20
Hence you long-legged spinners, hence:
Beetles black approach not near:
Worm nor snail do no offence.
Philomele, with melody, &c.   *She sleeps.*
2. FAIRY.   Hence away: now all is well: 25
One aloof stand sentinel.   [*Exeunt fairies.*]

Enter OBERON [and applies the flower juice to TITANIA's eyelids.]

OBERON.   What thou seest, when thou dost wake,
Do it for thy true love take:
Love and languish for his sake.
Be it ounce,° or cat, or bear,   30
Pard,° or boar with bristled hair,
In thy eye that shall appear,
When thou wak'st, it is thy dear:
Wake when some vile thing is near.   [*Exit.*]

Enter LYSANDER and HERMIA.

---

1 *roundel:* dance in a ring.   4 *reremice:* bats.   7 *quaint:* dainty.   8 *offices:* duties.   9
double: forked.   11 *blind-worms:* legless lizards.   13 *Philomele:* the nightingale.   30 *ounce:*
lynx.   31 *Pard:* leopard.

LYSANDER.   Fair love, you faint with wand'ring in the wood:
And to speak troth° I have forgot our way.
We'll rest us Hermia, if you think it good,
And tarry for the comfort of the day.
HERMIA.   Be't so Lysander: find you out a bed:
For I upon this bank will rest my head.
LYSANDER.   One turf shall serve as pillow for us both,
One heart, one bed, two bosoms, and one troth.°
HERMIA.   Nay good Lysander: for my sake, my dear,
Lie further off yet; do not lie so near.
LYSANDER.   O take the sense, sweet, of my innocence:°
Love takes the meaning in love's conference.°
I mean that my heart unto yours is knit,
So that but one heart we can make of it:
Two bosoms interchainèd with an oath,
So then two bosoms and a single troth.
Then by your side no bed-room me deny:
For lying so, Hermia, I do not lie.
HERMIA.   Lysander riddles very prettily.
Now much beshrew° my manners and my pride,
If Hermia meant to say Lysander lied.
But gentle friend, for love and courtesy,
Lie further off, in human modesty:
Such separation as may well be said
Becomes a virtuous bachelor and a maid,
So far be distant, and good night sweet friend:
Thy love ne'er alter till thy sweet life end.
LYSANDER.   Amen, amen, to that fair prayer say I,
And then end life, when I end loyalty.
Here is my bed: sleep give thee all his rest.
HERMIA.   With half that wish, the wisher's eyes be pressed.°

They sleep.

Enter PUCK.

PUCK.   Through the forest have I gone,
But Athenian found I none,
On whose eyes I might approve°
This flower's force in stirring love.
Night and silence. Who is here?
Weeds° of Athens he doth wear:
This is he (my master said)
Despisèd the Athenian maid:
And here the maiden, sleeping sound,

---

36 *troth:* truth.   42 *troth:* true love.   45 *take . . . innocence:* understand the innocence of my remark.   46 *Love . . . conference:* Love enables lovers to understand each other when they converse.   54 *beshrew:* curse.   65 *pressed:* i.e., by sleep.   68 *approve:* test   71 *Weeds:* garments.

On the dank and dirty ground.   75
Pretty soul, she durst not lie
Near this lack-love, this kill-courtesy.
Churl, upon thy eyes I throw
All the power this charm doth owe:°
When thou wak'st, let love forbid   80
Sleep his seat on thy eyelid.°
So awake when I am gone:
For I must now to Oberon.   *Exit.*

Enter DEMETRIUS and HELENA running.

HELENA.   Stay, thou kill me, sweet Demetrius.
DEMETRIUS.   I charge thee hence, and do not haunt me thus.
HELENA.   O, wilt thou darkling° leave me? Do not so.   85
DEMETRIUS.   Stay on thy peril: I alone will go.   *Exit DEMETRIUS.*
HELENA.   O, I am out of breath in this fond° chase:
The more my prayer, the lesser is my grace.°
Happy is Hermia, wheresoe'er she lies:
For she hath blessèd and attractive eyes.   90
How came her eyes so bright? Not with salt tears:
If so, my eyes are oft'ner washed than hers.
No, no: I am as ugly as a bear:
For beasts that meet me run away for fear.   95
Therefore no marvel, though Demetrius
Do as a monster, fly my presence thus.
What wicked and dissembling glass° of mine,
Made me compare with Hermia's sphery eyne°!
But who is here? Lysander, on the ground?   100
Dead, or asleep? I see no blood, no wound.
Lysander, if you live, good sir awake.
LYSANDER.   [*Wakes.*] And run through fire, I will for thy sweet sake.
Transparent° Helena, nature shows art,
That through thy bosom, makes me see thy heart.   105
Where is Demetrius? O how fit a word
Is that vile name to perish on my sword!
HELENA.   Do not say so, Lysander, say not so.
What though he love your Hermia? Lord, what though?
Yet Hermia still loves you: then be content.   110
LYSANDER.   Content with Hermia? No: I do repent
The tedious minutes I with her have spent.
Not Hermia, but Helena I love.
Who will not change a raven for a dove?
The will of man is by his reason swayed:°   115
And reason says you are the worthier maid.

---

79 *owe:* own.   80–81 *forbid . . . eyelid:* make you sleepless (with love).   86 *darkling:* in the
dark.   88 *fond:* foolishly doting.   89 *my grace:* favor shown to me.   98 *glass:* looking
glass.   99 *sphery eyne:* starry eyes.   104 *Transparent:* radiant.   115 *swayed:* ruled.   118
ripe: mature.

Things growing are not ripe until their season:
So I, being young, till now ripe° not to reason.
And touching now the point° of human skill,°
Reason becomes the marshal to my will,
And leads me to your eyes; where I o'erlook
Love's stories, written in love's richest book.

HELENA.   Wherefore° was I to this keen mockery born?
When at your hands did I deserve this scorn?
Is't not enough, is't not enough, young man,
That I did never, no, nor never can,
Deserve a sweet look from Demetrius' eye,
But you must flout° my insufficiency?
Good troth you do me wrong, good sooth you do,
In such disdainful manner me to woo.
But fare you well: perforce I must confess,
I thought you lord of more true gentleness.°
O, that a lady, of one man refused,
Should of another, therefore be abused!   *Exit.*

LYSANDER.   She sees not Hermia. Hermia, sleep thou there,
And never mayst thou come Lysander near.
For, as a surfeit of the sweetest things
The deepest loathing to the stomach brings:
Or as the heresies that men do leave,
Are hated most of those they did deceive:
So thou, my surfeit and my heresy,
Of all be hated; but the most, of me:
And all my powers, address your love and might,
To honour Helen, and to be her knight.

                                                                     Exit.

HERMIA.   [*Wakes.*] Help me Lysander, help me: do thy best
To pluck this crawling serpent from my breast.
Ay me, for pity. What a dream was here?
Lysander, look how I do quake with fear.
Methought a serpent eat my heart away,
And you sat smiling at his cruel prey.°
Lysander: what, removed? Lysander, lord!
What, out of hearing, gone? No sound, no word?
Alack, where are you? Speak, and if you hear:
Speak, of° all loves. I swoon almost with fear.
No? Then I well perceive you are not nigh:
Either death, or you, I'll find immediately.   *Exit.*

---

119 *point:* peak.   *skill:* knowledge.   123 *Wherefore:* why.   128 *flout:* mock.   132 *lord . . .*
gentleness: more of a gentleman.   150 *prey:* preying.   154 *of:* for the sake of.

ACT 3

[*Scene 1. The wood*]

Enter the CLOWNS [*QUINCE, SNUG, BOTTOM, FLUTE, SNOUT, and STARVELING.*]

BOTTOM.   Are we all met?
QUINCE.   Pat, pat: and here's a marvellous convenient place for
　　our rehearsal. This green plot shall be our stage, this
　　hawthorn brake° our tiring-house,° and we will do it in
　　action, as we will do it before the duke.   5
BOTTOM.   Peter Quince?
QUINCE.   What sayest thou, bully° Bottom?
BOTTOM.   There are things in this Comedy of Pyramus and Thisby
　　that will never please. First, Pyramus must draw a sword
　　to kill himself; which the ladies cannot abide. How   10
　　answer you that?
SNOUT.   By'r lakin,° a parlous° fear.
STARVELING.   I believe we must leave the killing out, when all is done.
BOTTOM.   Not a whit: I have a device to make all well. Write me
　　a prologue, and let the prologue seem to say, we will   15
　　do no harm with our swords, and that Pyramus is not
　　killed indeed: and for the more better assurance, tell
　　them that I Pyramus am not Pyramus, but Bottom the
　　weaver: this will put them out of fear.
QUINCE.   Well, we will have such a prologue, and it shall be   20
　　written in eight and six.°
BOTTOM.   No, make it two more: let it be written in eight and
　　eight.
SNOUT.   Will not the ladies be afeared of the lion?
STARVELING.   I fear it, I promise you.   25
BOTTOM.   Masters, you ought to consider with yourselves, to bring
　　in (God shield us) a lion among ladies, is a most dreadful
　　thing. For there is not a more fearful wild-fowl than
　　your lion living: and we ought to look to't.
SNOUT.   Therefore another prologue must tell he is not a lion.   30
BOTTOM.   Nay, you must name his name, and half his face must be
　　seen through the lion's neck, and he himself must speak
　　through, saying thus, or to the same defect:° "Ladies,"
　　or "Fair ladies—I would wish you," or "I would request
　　you," or "I would entreat you, not to fear,   35
　　not to tremble: my life for yours. If you think I come
　　hither as a lion, it were pity of my life. No, I am no
　　such thing: I am a man as other men are." And there

---

4 *brake:* thicket.　　*tiring-house:* dressing room.　　7 *bully:* "old pal."　　12 *By'r lakin:* mild oath,
"by Our Lady."　　*parlous:* awful, perilous.　　21 *eight and six:* alternate lines of eight and six
syllables (the ballad meter).　　33 *defect:* (he means "effect").

indeed let him name his name, and tell them plainly he
is Snug the joiner.   40

QUINCE.   Well, it shall be so, but there is two hard things: that is,
to bring the moonlight into a chamber: for you know,
Pyramus and Thisby meet by moonlight.

SNOUT.   Doth the moon shine that night we play our play?

BOTTOM.   A calendar, a calendar: look in the almanac: find out   45
moonshine, find out moonshine.

QUINCE.   Yes, it doth shine that night.

BOTTOM.   Why then may you leave a casement of the great
chamber window, where we play, open; and the moon may
shine in at the casement.   50

QUINCE.   Ay, or else one must come in with a bush of thorns° and
a lantern, and say he comes to disfigure,° or to present,
the person of Moonshine. Then, there is another thing;
we must have a wall in the great chamber: for Pyramus
and Thisby, says the story, did talk through the chink   55
of a wall.

SNOUT.   You can never bring in a wall. What say you, Bottom?

BOTTOM.   Some man or other must present wall: and let him have
some plaster, or some loam, or some rough-cast° about
him, to signify wall; and let him hold his fingers thus: 60
and through that cranny, shall Pyramus and Thisby whisper.

QUINCE.   If that may be, then all is well. Come, sit down every
mother's son, and rehearse your parts. Pyramus, you
begin: when you have spoken your speech, enter into that
brake, and so every one according to his cue.   65

Enter PUCK.

PUCK.   What hempen homespuns° have we swagg'ring here,
So near the cradle of the Fairy Queen?
What, a play toward°? I'll be an auditor,
An actor too perhaps, if I see cause.

QUINCE.   Speak Pyramus. Thisby stand forth.

PYRAMUS.   Thisby, the flowers of odious savours sweet—   70

QUINCE.   "Odorous, odorous."

PYRAMUS.   —odours savours sweet,
So hath thy breath, my dearest Thisby dear.
But hark, a voice: stay thou but here awhile,
And by and by I will to thee appear.   *Exit* PYRAMUS.   75
                                                                   [*Exit.*]

PUCK.   A stranger Pyramus than e'er played here.

THISBY.   Must I speak now?

QUINCE.   Ay marry must you. For you must understand he goes
but to see a noise that he heard, and is to come again.

---

51 *bush of thorns:* bundle of firewood (the man in the moon was supposed to have been placed
there as a punishment for gathering wood on Sundays).   52 *disfigure:* (he means "figure," symbolize).   59 *rough-cast:* coarse plaster of lime and gravel.   66 *hempen homespuns:* wearers of
clothing spun at home from hemp.   68 *toward:* in preparation.

THISBY.   Most radiant Pyramus, most lily-white of hue,
 Of colour like the red rose, on triumphant brier,
 Most brisky juvenal,° and eke most lovely Jew,°
 As true as truest horse, that yet would never tire,
 I'll meet thee Pyramus, at Ninny's tomb.   85
QUINCE.   "Ninus' tomb,"° man: why, you must not speak that yet.
 That you answer to Pyramus. You speak all your part
 at once, cues and all. Pyramus, enter; your cue is past:
 it is "never tire."
THISBY.   O—As true as truest horse, that yet would never tire. 90

Enter PYRAMUS with the ass-head [followed by PUCK].

PYRAMUS.   If I were fair, Thisby, I were only thine.
QUINCE.   O monstrous! O strange! We are haunted. Pray masters,
 fly masters. Help!   *The clowns all exeunt.*
PUCK.   I'll follow you: I'll lead you about a round,°
 Through bog, through bush, through brake, through brier. 95
 Sometime a horse I'll be, sometime a hound,
  A hog, a headless bear, sometime a fire,
 And neigh, and bark, and grunt, and roar, and burn,
 Like horse, hound, hog, bear, fire, at every turn.   *Exit.*
BOTTOM.   Why do they run away? This is a knavery of them to 100
 make me afeared.

Enter SNOUT.

SNOUT.   O Bottom, thou art changed. What do I see on thee?
BOTTOM.   What do you see? You see an ass-head of your own, do
 you?   *[Exit SNOUT.]*

Enter QUINCE.

QUINCE.   Bless thee Bottom, bless thee. Thou art translated.° *Exit.* 105
BOTTOM.   I see their knavery. This is to make an ass of me, to
 fright me if they could: but I will not stir from this
 place, do what they can. I will walk up and down here,
 and will sing that they shall hear I am not afraid.
  [*Sings.*] The woosel° cock, so black of hue,   110
   With orange tawny bill,
   The throstle,° with his note so true,
   The wren, with little quill.°
TITANIA.   What angel wakes me from my flow'ry bed?
BOTTOM.   [*Sings.*] The finch, the sparrow, and the lark, 115
   The plain-song° cuckoo gray:
   Whose note full many a man doth mark,
   And dares not answer, nay.

---

83 *brisky juvenal:* lively youth. *Jew:* diminutive of either "juvenal" or "jewel." 86 *Ninus'*
tomb: (tomb of the founder of Nineveh, and meeting place of the lovers in Ovid's version of the
Pyramus story). 94 *about a round:* in circles, like a round dance (round about). 105 *trans-*
lated: transformed. 110 *woosel:* ousel, blackbird. 112 *throstle:* thrush. 113 *quill:* piping
note. 116 *plain-song:* sounding a simple unvaried note.

For indeed, who would set his wit to° so foolish a bird?
Who would give a bird the lie,° though he cry "cuckoo"°
never so°?

TITANIA.   I pray thee, gentle mortal, sing again.
Mine ear is much enamoured of thy note:
So is mine eye enthrallèd to thy shape,
And thy fair virtue's force (perforce°) doth move me,
On the first view to say, to swear, I love thee.

BOTTOM.   Methinks mistress, you should have little reason for
that. And yet, to say the truth, reason and love keep
little company together now-a-days. The more the pity,
That some honest neighbours will not make them friends.
Nay, I can gleek° upon occasion.

TITANIA.   Thou art as wise as thou art beautiful.

BOTTOM.   Not so neither: but if I had wit enough to get out of
this wood, I have enough to serve mine own turn.

TITANIA.   Out of this wood do not desire to go:
Thou shalt remain here, whether thou wilt or no.
I am a spirit of no common rate:°
The summer still doth tend upon my state,°
And I do love thee: therefore go with me.
I'll give thee fairies to attend on thee:
And they shall fetch thee jewels from the deep,
And sing, while thou on pressèd flowers dost sleep:
And I will purge thy mortal grossness so,
That thou shalt like an airy spirit go.
Peaseblossom, Cobweb, Moth,° and Mustardseed!

Enter four FAIRIES.

PEASEBLOSSOM.   Ready.

COBWEB.   And I.

MOTH.   And I.

MUSTARDSEED.   And I.

ALL.   Where shall we go?

TITANIA.   Be kind and courteous to this gentleman,
Hop in his walks and gambol° in his eyes,
Feed him with apricocks° and dewberries,°
With purple grapes, green figs, and mulberries.
The honey-bags steal from the humblebees,°
And for night-tapers, crop° their waxen thighs,
And light them at the fiery glow-worm's eyes,

---

119 *set . . . to:* match his wit against.   120 *Who . . . lie:* who could call a bird a liar. *"cuckoo":*
(which sounded like "cuckold" = a deceived husband).   121 *never so:* i.e., often.   125 *per-*
force: by force.   131 *gleek:* joke satirically.   137 *rate:* rank, value   138 *still . . . state:* always
serves as an attendant in my royal train.   145 *Moth:* mote (so pronounced), tiny speck.   149
gambol in: caper before.   150 *apricocks:* apricots.   *dewberries:* blackberries.   152 *humble-*
bees: bumblebees.   153 *crop:* clip.

To have my love to bed and to arise: 155
And pluck the wings from painted butterflies,
To fan the moonbeams from his sleeping eyes.
Nod to him elves, and do him courtesies.
PEASEBLOSSOM. Hail, mortal.
COBWEB. Hail. 160
MOTH. Hail.
MUSTARDSEED. Hail.
BOTTOM. I cry your worships mercy,° heartily: I beseech your
  worship's name.
COBWEB. Cobweb. 165
BOTTOM. I shall desire you of more acquaintance, good Master
  Cobweb: if I cut my finger,° I shall make bold with you.
  Your name, honest gentleman?
PEASEBLOSSOM. Peaseblossom.
BOTTOM. I pray you commend me° to Mistress Squash,° your mother, 170
  and to Master Peascod,° your father. Good Master Peaseblossom,
  I shall desire you of more acquaintance, too.
  Your name I beseech you sir?
MUSTARDSEED. Mustardseed.
BOTTOM. Good Master Mustardseed, I know your patience well. 175
  That same cowardly giant-like ox beef hath devoured
  many a gentleman of your house. I promise you, your
  kindred hath made my eyes water ere now. I desire you
  of more acquaintance, good Master Mustardseed.
TITANIA. Come wait upon him: lead him to my bower. 180
    The moon methinks looks with a wat'ry eye:
    And when she weeps, weeps every little flower,
    Lamenting some enforcèd° chastity.
    Tie up my lover's tongue, bring him silently. *Exeunt.*

[Scene 2. Another part of the wood]

Enter [OBERON,] *King of Fairies, solus.*°

OBERON. I wonder if Titania be awaked;
    Then what it was that next came in her eye,
    Which she must dote on in extremity.

Enter PUCK.

    Here comes my messenger. How now, mad spirit?
    What night-rule° now about this haunted grove? 5
PUCK. My mistress with a monster is in love.
    Near to her close and consecrated bower,
    While she was in her dull° and sleeping hour,

---

163 *I . . . mercy:* I respectfully beg your pardons. 167 *cut my finger:* (cobwebs were used to stop
bleeding). 170 *commend me:* offer my respects. *Squash:* unripe peapod. 171 *Peascod:*
ripe peapod. 183 *enforcèd:* violated. S.D.: *solus:* alone. 5 *night-rule:* diversion ("mis-
rule") in the night. 8 *dull:* drowsy.

A crew of patches,° rude mechanicals,°
That work for bread upon Athenian stalls,°
Were met together to rehearse a play,
Intended for great Theseus' nuptial day:
The shallowest thickskin of that barren sort,°
Who Pyramus presented in their sport,
Forsook his scene and entered in a brake:
When I did him at this advantage take,
An ass's nole° I fixèd on his head.
Anon° his Thisby must be answerèd,
And forth my mimic° comes. When they him spy,
As wild geese, that the creeping fowler° eye,
Or russet-pated choughs,° many in sort,°
Rising and cawing at the gun's report,
Sever themselves and madly sweep the sky,
So at his sight away his fellows fly:
And at our stamp, here o'er and o'er one falls:
He murder cries, and help from Athens calls.
Their sense thus weak, lost with their fears thus strong,
Made senseless things begin to do them wrong.
For briers and thorns at their apparel snatch:
Some° sleeves, some hats; from yielders, all things catch.°
I led them on in this distracted° fear,
And left sweet Pyramus translated there:
When in that moment (so it came to pass)
Titania waked, and straightway loved an ass.
OBERON.   This falls out better than I could devise.
But has thou yet latched° the Athenian's eyes
With the love-juice, as I did bid thee do?
PUCK.   I took him sleeping (that is finished too)
And the Athenian woman by his side;
That when he waked, of force° she must be eyed.

Enter DEMETRIUS and HERMIA.

OBERON.   Stand close:° this is the same Athenian.
PUCK.   This is the woman: but not this the man.
DEMETRIUS.   O why rebuke you him that loves you so?
Lay breath so bitter on your bitter foe.
HERMIA.   Now I but chide: but I should use thee worse,
For thou, I fear, hast given me cause to curse.
If thou hast slain Lysander in his sleep,
Being o'er shoes in blood, plunge in the deep,
And kill me too.
The sun was not so true unto the day,

9 *patches:* fools.   *mechanicals:* workers.   10 *stalls:* shops.   13 *barren sort:* stupid
crew.   17 *nole:* head, noodle.   18 *Anon:* presently.   19 *mimic:* actor.   20 *fowler:* hunter
of fowl.   21 *russet-pated choughs:* grey-headed jackdaws.   *sort:* a flock.   30 *Some:* ie.,
snatch.   *from yielders . . . catch:* (everything joins in to harm the weak).   31 *distracted:* maddened.   36 *latched:* moistened.   40 *of force:* by necessity.   41 *close:* hidden.

As he to me. Would he have stolen away
From sleeping Hermia? I'll believe as soon
This whole° earth may be bored,° and that the moon
May through the center creep, and so displease
Her brother's noontide with th' Antipodes.°   55
It cannot be but thou hast murdered him.
So should a murderer look; so dead,° so grim.
DEMETRIUS.   So should the murdered look, and so should I,
Pierced through the heart with your stern cruelty.
Yet you, the murderer, look as bright, as clear,   60
As yonder Venus in her glimmering sphere.°
HERMIA.   What's this to my Lysander? Where is he?
Ah good Demetrius, wilt thou give him me?
DEMETRIUS.   I had rather give his carcass to my hounds.
HERMIA.   Out dog, out cur! Thou driv'st me past the bounds   65
Of maiden's patience. Hast thou slain him then?
Henceforth be never numbered among men.
O, once tell true: tell true, even for my sake:
Durst thou have looked upon him, being awake?
And hast thou killed him sleeping? O brave touch°!   70
Could not a worm,° an adder, do so much?
An adder did it: for with doubler tongue°
Than thine, thou serpent, never adder stung.
DEMETRIUS.   You spend your passion on a misprised mood:°
I am not guilty of Lysander's blood: 75
Nor is he dead, for aught that I can tell.
HERMIA.   I pray thee, tell me then that he is well.
DEMETRIUS.   And if I could, what should I get therefore?
HERMIA.   A privilege never to see me more:
And from thy hated presence part I so: 80
See me no more, whether he be dead or no.   *Exit.*
DEMETRIUS.   There is no following her in this fierce vein.
Here therefore for a while I will remain.
So sorrow's heaviness doth heavier grow
For debt that bankrout sleep doth sorrow owe:°   85
Which now in some slight measure it will pay,
If for his tender° here I make some stay.°   *Lies down.*
OBERON.   What hast thou done? Thou hast mistaken quite,
And laid the love-juice on some true-love's sight.
Of thy misprision° must perforce° ensue   90
Some true love turned, and not a false turned true.

---

53 *whole:* solid.   *be bored:* have a hole bored through it.   55 *Her brother's . . . Antipodes:* the
noon of her brother sun, by appearing among the Antipodes (the people on the other side of the
earth).   57 *dead:* deadly.   61 *sphere:* (in the Ptolemaic system, each planet moved in its own
sphere around the earth).   70 *brave touch:* splendid stroke (ironic).   71 *worm:* snake.   72
doubler tongue: (1) tongue more forked (2) more deceitful speech.   74 *on . . . mood:* in mistaken anger.   85 *For debt . . . owe:* because sleep cannot pay the debt of repose he owes the man
who is kept awake by sorrow.   87 *tender:* offer.   *stay:* pause.   90 *misprision:* mistake.   *perforce:* of necessity.

PUCK.   Then fate o'errules, that one man holding troth,
    A million fail, confounding° oath on oath.°
OBERON.   About the wood, go swifter than the wind,
    And Helena of Athens look thou find.
    All fancy-sick° she is, and pale of cheer,°
    With sighs of love, that costs the fresh blood dear.
    By some illusion see thou bring her here:
    I'll charm his eyes against she do appear.°
PUCK.   I go, I go, look how I go.
    Swifter than arrow from the Tartar's bow.°   *Exit.*
OBERON.   Flower of this purple dye,
    Hit with Cupid's archery,
    Sink in apple of his eye:
    When his love he doth espy,
    Let her shine as gloriously
    As the Venus of the sky.
    When thou wak'st, if she be by,
    Beg of her for remedy.

Enter PUCK.

PUCK.   Captain of our fairy band,
        Helena is here at hand,
        And the youth, mistook by me,
        Pleading for a lover's fee.°
        Shall we their fond pageant° see?
        Lord, what fools these mortals be!
OBERON.   Stand aside. The noise they make
        Will cause Demetrius to awake.
PUCK.   Then will two at once woo one:
        That must needs be sport alone.°
        And those things do best please me
        That befall prepost'rously.

Enter LYSANDER and HELENA.

LYSANDER.   Why should you think that I should woo in scorn?
        Scorn and derision never come in tears.
        Look when I vow, I weep: and vows so born,
          In their nativity all truth appears.°
        How can these things in me seem scorn to you,
          Bearing the badge° of faith to prove them true?
HELENA.   You do advance your cunning more and more.
        When truth kills truth,° O devilish-holy fray!
        These vows are Hermia's. Will you give her o'er?

---

93 *confounding:* destroying.   *oath on oath:* one oath after another.   96 *fancy-sick:*
lovesick.   *cheer:* face.   99 *against . . . appear:* in preparation for her appearance.   101
Tartar's bow: (the Tartars, who used powerful Oriental bows, were famed as archers).   113 *fee:*
reward.   114 *fond pageant:* foolish spectacle.   119 *alone:* unique.   124–125 *vows . . .*
appears: vows born in weeping must be true ones.   127 *badge:* (1) outward signs (2) family crest.
129 *truth kills truth:* Former true love is killed by vows of present true love.

Weigh oath with oath, and you will nothing weigh.
Your vows to her and me, put in two scales,
Will even weigh: and both as light as tales.
LYSANDER.   I had no judgment, when to her I swore.
HELENA.   Nor none, in my mind, now you give her o'er.   135
LYSANDER.   Demetrius loves her: and he loves not you.
DEMETRIUS.   (*Awakes.*) O Helen, goddess, nymph, perfect, divine,
   To what, my love, shall I compare thine eyne!
   Crystal is muddy. O, how ripe in show,
   Thy lips, those kissing cherries, tempting grow!   140
   That pure congealèd white, high Taurus'° snow,
   Fanned with the eastern wind, turns to a crow,
   When thou hold'st up thy hand. O let me kiss
   This princess of pure white,° this seal of bliss.
HELENA.   O spite! O hell! I see you all are bent   145
   To set against me, for your merriment.
   If you were civil,° and knew courtesy,
   You would not do me thus much injury.
   Can you not hate me, as I know you do,
   But you must join in souls° to mock me too?   150
   If you were men, as men you are in show,
   You would not use a gentle lady so;
   To vow, and swear, and superpraise my parts,°
   When I am sure you hate me with your hearts.
   You both are rivals, and love Hermia: 155
   And now both rivals, to mock Helena.
   A trim° exploit, a manly enterprise,
   To conjure tears up in a poor maid's eyes
   With your derision. None of noble sort
   Would so offend a virgin, and extort°   160
   A poor soul's patience, all to make you sport.
LYSANDER.   You are unkind, Demetrius: be not so.
   For you love Hermia: this you know I know.
   And here, with all good will, with all my heart,
   In Hermia's love I yield you up my part: 165
   And yours of Helena to be bequeath,
   Whom I do love, and will do to my death.
HELENA.   Never did mockers waste more idle breath.
DEMETRIUS.   Lysander, keep thy Hermia: I will none.°
   If e'er I loved her, all that love is gone.   170
   My heart to her but as guest-wise sojourned:°
   And now to Helen is it home returned,
   There to remain.
LYSANDER.   Helen, it is not so.

---

141 *Taurus:* mountain range in Asia Minor.   144 *princess . . . white:* sovereign example of whiteness (her hand).   147 *civil:* well behaved.   150 *join in souls:* agree in spirit.   153 *parts:*
qualities.   157 *trim:* fine (ironic).   160 *extort:* wring.   169 *none:* have none of
her.   171 *to her . . . sojourned:* visited her only as a guest.

DEMETRIUS.   Disparage not the faith thou dost not know,
Lest to thy peril thou aby it dear.°
Look where thy love comes: yonder is thy dear.

Enter HERMIA.

HERMIA.   Dark night, that from the eye his function takes,
The ear more quick of apprehension makes.
Wherein it doth impair the seeing sense,
It pays the hearing double recompense.
Thou art not by mine eye, Lysander, found:
Mine ear, I thank it, brought me to thy sound.
But why unkindly didst thou leave me so?
LYSANDER.   Why should he stay, whom love doth press to go?
HERMIA.   What love could press Lysander from my side?
LYSANDER.   Lysander's love, that would not let him bide—
Fair Helena: who more engilds the night
Than all your fiery oes and eyes of light.°
Why seek'st thou me? Could not this make thee know,
The hate I bare thee made me leave thee so?
HERMIA.   You speak not as you think: it cannot be.
HELENA.   Lo: She is one of this confederacy.
Now I perceive they have conjoined all three,
To fashion this false sport in spite of° me.
Injurious° Hermia, most ungrateful maid,
Have you conspired, have you with these contrived
To bait° me with this foul derision?
Is all the counsel° that we two have shared,
The sisters' vows, the hours that we have spent,
When we have chid the hasty-footed time
For parting us; O, is all forgot?
All schooldays' friendship, childhood innocence?
We Hermia, like two artificial° gods,
Have with our needles created both one flower,
Both on one sampler,° sitting on one cushion,
Both warbling of one song, both in one key;
As if our hands, our sides, voices, and minds
Had been incorporate.° So we grew together,
Like to a double cherry, seeming parted,
But yet an union in partition,
Two lovely berries moulded on one stem:
So with two seeming bodies, but one heart,
Two of the first, like coats in heraldry,
Due but to one, and crownèd with one crest.°
And will you rent° our ancient love asunder,

---

175 *aby it dear:* buy it at a high price.   188 *oes . . . light:* stars.   194 *in spite of:* to spite.   195
Injurious: insulting.   197 *bait:* attack.   198 *counsel:* secrets.   203 *artificial:* skilled in
art.   205 *sampler:* work of embroidery.   208 *incorporate:* in one body.   213–214 *Two . . .
crest:* (the two bodies being) like double coats of arms joined under one crest (with one
heart).   215 *rent:* rend, tear.

To join with men in scorning your poor friend?
It is not friendly, 'tis not maidenly.
Our sex, as well as I, may chide you for it;
Though I alone do feel the injury.

HERMIA.   I am amazèd at your passionate words: 220
I scorn you not. It seems that you scorn me.

HELENA.   Have you not set Lysander, as in scorn,
To follow me, and praise my eyes and face?
And made your other love, Demetrius
(Who even but now did spurn° me with his foot)   225
To call me goddess, nymph, divine, and rare,
Precious, celestial? Wherefore speaks he this
To her he hates? And wherefore doth Lysander
Deny your love, so rich within his soul,
And tender° me (forsooth) affection,   230
But by your setting on, by your consent?
What though I be not so in grace° as you,
So hung upon with love, so fortunate,
But miserable most, to love unloved?
This you should pity, rather than despise.   235

HERMIA.   I understand not what you mean by this.

HELENA.   Ay, do. Persèver, counterfeit sad° looks:
Make mouths upon° me when I turn my back:
Wink each at other, hold the sweet jest up.
This sport well carried, shall be chronicled.°   240
If you have any pity, grace, or manners,
You would not make me such an argument.°
But fare ye well: 'tis partly my own fault:
Which death or absence soon shall remedy.

LYSANDER.   Stay, gentle Helena: hear my excuse,   245
My love, my life, my soul, fair Helena.

HELENA.   O excellent!

HERMIA.   Sweet, do not scorn her so.

DEMETRIUS.   If she cannot entreat,° I can compel.

LYSANDER.   Thou canst compel no more than she entreat.
Thy threats have no more strength than her weak prayers.   250
Helen, I love thee, by my life I do:
I swear by that which I will lose for thee,
To prove° him false that says I love thee not.

DEMETRIUS.   I say I love thee more than he can do.

LYSANDER.   If thou say so, withdraw, and prove° it too.   255

DEMETRIUS.   Quick, Come.

HERMIA.   Lysander, whereto tends all this?

LYSANDER.   Away, you Ethiope.°

---

225 *spurn:* kick.   230 *tender:* offer.   232 *in grace:* favored.   237 *sad:* serious.   238 *mouths upon:* faces at.   240 *chronicled:* written down in the history books.   242 *argument:* subject (of your mockery).   248 *entreat:* sway you by entreaty.   253, 255 *prove:* i.e., by a duel.   257 *Ethiope:* (because she is a brunette).

DEMETRIUS.   No, no, sir,
  Seem to break loose: take on as you would follow;
  But yet come not.° You are a tame man, go.
LYSANDER.   Hang off,° thou cat, thou burr: vile thing, let loose;
  Or I will shake thee from me like a serpent.
HERMIA.   Why are you grown so rude? What change is this,
  Sweet love?
LYSANDER.   Thy love? Out, tawny Tartar, out:
  Out, loathèd med'cine: O hated potion, hence!
HERMIA.   Do you not jest?
HELENA.   Yes sooth: and so do you.
LYSANDER.   Demetrius, I will keep my word° with thee.
DEMETRIUS.   I would I had your bond.° For I perceive
  A weak bond holds you. I'll not trust your word.
LYSANDER.   What? Should I hurt her, strike her, kill her dead?
  Although I hate her, I'll not harm her so.
HERMIA.   What? Can you do me greater harm than hate?
  Hate me, wherefore°? O me, what news,° my love?
  Am not I Hermia? Are not you Lysander?
  I am as fair now, as I was erewhile.°
  Since night, you loved me; yet since night, you left me.
  Why then, you left me—O, the gods forbid—
  In earnest, shall I say?
LYSANDER   Ay, by my life:
  And never did desire to see thee more.
  Therefore be out of hope, of question, of doubt:
  Be certain: nothing truer: 'tis no jest
  That I do hate thee, and love Helena.
HERMIA.   O me, you juggler,° you canker blossom,°
  You thief of love: what, have you come by night,
  And stol'n my love's heart from him?
HELENA.   Fine, i' faith.
  Have you no modesty, no maiden shame,
  No touch of bashfulness? What, will you tear
  Impatient answers from my gentle tongue?
  Fie, fie, you counterfeit, you puppet,° you.
HERMIA.   Puppet? Why so—ay, that way goes the game.
  Now I perceive that she hath made compare
  Between our statures, she hath urged her height,
  And with her personage, her tall personage,
  Her height (forsooth) she hath prevailed with him.
  And are you grown so high in his esteem,
  Because I am so dwarfish and so low?
  How low am I, thou painted maypole? Speak:

258–259 *Seem . . . not:* You only seem to break loose from Hermia and pretend to follow me to a
duel, but you actually hold back.   260 *Hang off:* let go.   266 *keep my word:* i.e., to duel.   267
bond: written agreement.   272 *wherefore:* why.   *what news:* what's the matter.   274 *erewhile:*
a short while ago.   282 *juggler:* deceiver.   *canker blossom:* worm that causes canker in blossoms.   288 *puppet:* (Hermia is short and Helena tall).

How low am I? I am not yet so low,
But that my nails can reach unto thine eyes.
HELENA. I pray you, though you mock me, gentlemen,
Let her not hurt me. I was never curst:° 300
I have no gift at all in shrewishness:
I am a right maid for my cowardice:°
Let her not strike me. You perhaps may think,
Because she is something lower than myself,
That I can match her.
HERMIA.   Lower? Hark again. 305
HELENA. Good Hermia, do not be so bitter with me,
I evermore did love you Hermia.
Did ever keep your counsels, never wronged you;
Save that in love unto Demetrius,
I told him of your stealth unto this wood. 310
He followed you: for love I followed him.
But he hath chid me hence, and threatened me
To strike me, spurn me, nay to kill me too;
And now, so° you will let me quiet go,
To Athens will I bear my folly back, 315
And follow you no further. Let me go.
You see how simple and how fond° I am.
HERMIA. Why, get you gone. Who is't that hinders you?
HELENA. A foolish heart, that I leave here behind.
HERMIA. What, with Lysander?
HELENA.   With Demetrius. 320
LYSANDER. Be not afraid: she shall not harm thee Helena.
DEMETRIUS. No sir: she shall not, though you take her part.
HELENA. O when she's angry, she is keen and shrewd.°
She was a vixen when she went to school:
And though she be but little, she is fierce. 325
HERMIA. "Little" again? Nothing but "low" and "little"?
Why will you suffer her to flout° me thus?
Let me come to her.
LYSANDER.   Get you gone, you dwarf;
You minimus,° of hind'ring knot-grass° made;
You bead, you acorn.
DEMETRIUS.   You are too officious 330
In her behalf that scorns your services.
Let her alone: speak not of Helena,
Take not her part. For if thou dost intend°
Never so little show of love to her,
Thou shalt aby it.°

---

300 *curst:* bad-tempered.   302 *right . . . cowardice:* true woman in being cowardly.   314 *so:* if.   317 *fond:* foolish.   323 *keen and shrewd:* sharp and malicious.   327 *flout:* mock.   329 *minimus:* smallest of creatures.   *knot-grass:* weed believed to stunt the growth if eaten.   333 *intend:* extend.   335 *aby it:* buy it dearly.

LYSANDER.   Now she holds me not:
Now follow, if thou dar'st, to try whose right,
Of thine or mine, is most in Helena.°
DEMETRIUS.   Follow? Nay, I'll go with thee, cheek by jowl.

Exeunt LYSANDER and DEMETRIUS.

HERMIA.   You, mistress, all this coil is long of° you.
Nay, go not back.
HELENA.   I will not trust you, I,
Nor longer stay in your curst company
Your hands than mine are quicker for a fray:
My legs are longer though, to run away.   [*Exit.*]
HERMIA.   I am amazed,° and know not what to say.   *Exit.*
OBERON.   This is thy negligence: still thou mistak'st,
Or else commit'st thy knaveries wilfully.
PUCK.   Believe me, king of shadows, I mistook.
Did not you tell me I should know the man
By the Athenian garments he had on?
And so far blameless proves my enterprise,
That I have 'nointed an Athenian's eyes:
And so far am I glad it so did sort,°
As this their jangling I esteem a sport.
OBERON.   Thou seest these lovers seek a place to fight;
Hie therefore Robin, overcast the night,
The starry welkin° cover thou anon
With drooping fog as black as Acheron,°
And lead these testy° rivals so astray,
As° one come not within another's way.
Like to Lysander sometime frame thy tongue:
Then stir Demetrius up with bitter wrong:°
And sometime rail thou like Demetrius:
And from each other look thou lead them thus;
Till o'er their brows death-counterfeiting sleep
With leaden legs and batty wings doth creep:
Then crush this herb into Lysander's eye;
Whose liquor hath this virtuous° property,
To take from thence all error with his might,
And make his eyeballs roll with wonted° sight.
When they next wake, all this derision°
Shall seem a dream, and fruitless vision,
And back to Athens shall the lovers wend,
With league whose date° till death shall never end.
Whiles I in this affair do thee employ,
I'll to my queen and beg her Indian boy:

336–337 *try . . . Helena:* prove by fighting which of us has most right to Helena.   339 *coil is long
of:* turmoil is because of.   344 *amazed:* confused.   352 *sort:* turn out.   356 *welkin:*
sky.   357 *Acheron:* one of the four rivers in the underworld.   358 *testy:* irritable.   359 *As:*
so that.   361 *wrong:* insult.   367 *virtuous:* potent.   369 *wonted:* (previously) accustomed.   370 *derision:* laughable interlude.   373 *date:* term.

And then I will her charmèd eye release
From monster's view, and all things shall be peace.
PUCK. My fairy lord, this must be done with haste,
　For night's swift dragons cut the clouds full fast:
　And yonder shines Aurora's harbinger,°　　　　　　　　　　　　　380
　At whose approach, ghosts wand'ring here and there,
　Troop home to churchyards: damnèd spirits all,
　That in crossways° and floods° have burial,
　Already to their wormy beds are gone:
　For fear lest day should look their shames upon,　　　　　　　385
　They wilfully themselves exile from light,
　And must for aye consort° with black-browed night.
OBERON. But we are spirits of another sort.
　I with the morning's love have oft made sport,°
　And like a forester, the groves may tread　　　　　　　　　　390
　Even till the eastern gate all fiery red,
　Opening on Neptune, with fair blessèd beams,
　Turns into yellow gold his salt green streams.
　But notwithstanding, haste, make no delay:
　We may effect this business yet ere day.　　　　　*[Exit.]*　395
PUCK. Up and down, up and down,
　　I will lead them up and down.
　　I am feared in field and town.
　　Goblin, lead them up and down.
　　Here comes one.　　　　　　　　　　　　　　　　　　400

Enter LYSANDER.

LYSANDER. Where art thou, proud Demetrius? Speak thou now.
PUCK. Here villain, drawn° and ready. Where art thou?
LYSANDER. I will be with thee straight.
PUCK.　　　　　　　　　　　　Follow me then
　To plainer° ground.　　　　　　　　　　*[Exit* LYSANDER.*]*

Enter DEMETRIUS.

DEMETRIUS.　　　　　　　　Lysander, speak again.
　Thou runaway, thou coward, art thou fled?　　　　　　　　405
　Speak: in some bush? Where dost thou hide thy head?
PUCK. Thou coward, art thou bragging to the stars,
　Telling the bushes that thou look'st for wars,
　And wilt not come? Come recreant,° come thou child,
　I'll whip thee with a rod. He is defiled　　　　　　　　　410
　That draws a sword on thee.
DEMETRIUS.　　　　　　　　Yea, art thou there?

380 *Aurora's harbinger:* the morning star heralding Aurora, the dawn.　　383 *crossways:* crossroads, where suicides were buried.　　*floods:* those who drowned.　　387 *aye consort:* ever associate.　　389 *morning's . . . sport:* hunted with Cephalus (beloved of Aurora and himself devoted
to his wife Procris, whom he killed by accident; "sport" also = "amorous dalliance," and "love" =
Aurora's love for Oberon).　　402 *drawn:* with sword drawn.　　404 *plainer:* more level.　　409
recreant: oath-breaker, coward.

PUCK.   Follow my voice: we'll try no manhood° here.   *Exeunt.*

[*Enter* LYSANDER.]

LYSANDER.   He goes before me and still dares me on:
  When I come where he calls, then he is gone
  The villain is much lighter-heeled than I;   41
  I followed fast: but faster he did fly,
  That fallen am I in dark uneven way,
  And here will rest me. (*Lie down.*) Come thou gentle day,
  For if but once thou show me thy grey light.
  I'll find Demetrius and revenge this spite.   [*Sleeps.*]   4ᶻ

Enter PUCK *and* DEMETRIUS.

PUCK.   Ho, ho, ho! Coward, why com'st thou not?
DEMETRIUS.   Abide° me, if thou dar'st, for well I wot°
  Thou run'st before me, shifting every place,
  And dar'st not stand, nor look me in the face.
  Where art thou now?
PUCK.   Come hither: I am here.   4
DEMETRIUS.   Nay then thou mock'st me. Thou shalt buy this dear,°
  If ever I thy face by daylight see.
  Now go thy way. Faintness constraineth me
  To measure out my length on this cold bed.
  By day's approach look to be visited.   [*Lies down and sleeps.*]   4

Enter HELENA.

HELENA.   O weary night, O long and tedious night,
  Abate° thy hours; shine comforts° from the east,
  That I may back to Athens by daylight,
  From these that my poor company detest:
  And sleep, that sometimes shuts up sorrow's eye.   4
  Steal me awhile from mine own company.   *Sleeps.*
PUCK.   Yet but three? Come one more,
  Two of both kinds makes up four.
  Here she comes, curst° and sad.
  Cupid is a knavish lad,
  Thus to make poor females mad.   ·· ·

Enter HERMIA.

HERMIA.   Never so weary, never so in woe,
      Bedabbled with the dew, and torn with briers:
    I can no further crawl, no further go:
      My legs can keep no pace with my desires.
    Here will I rest me till the break of day.
    Heavens shield Lysander, if they mean a fray.   [*Lies down and sleeps.*]

412 *try no manhood:* test no valor.   422 *Abide:* wait for.   *wot:* know.   426 *buy this dear:* pay
dearly for this.   432 *Abate:* shorten.   *shine comforts:* may comforts shine.   439 *curst:*
cross.

PUCK.   On the ground,
  Sleep sound:
  I'll apply
  To your eye,   450
Gentle lover, remedy.   [*Squeezes the love-juice on* LYSANDER'S *eyelids.*]
  When thou wak'st,
  Thou tak'st
  True delight
  In the sight   455
Of thy former lady's eye:
And the country proverb known,
That every man should take his own,
In your waking shall be shown.   460
  Jack shall have Jill:
  Naught shall go ill:
The man shall have his mare again, and all shall be well.

         [*Exit* PUCK. *The lovers remain asleep on stage.*]

ACT 4

[*Scene 1. The wood*]

Enter [TITANIA] QUEEN OF FAIRIES, *and* [BOTTOM] THE CLOWN, *and* FAIRIES, *and the* KING
[OBERON] *behind them* [*unseen*].

TITANIA. Come sit thee down upon this flow'ry bed,
   While I thy amiable° cheeks do coy,°
    And stick musk-roses in thy sleek smooth head,
    And kiss thy fair large ears, my gentle joy.
BOTTOM. Where's Peaseblossom?   5
PEASEBLOSSOM. Ready.
BOTTOM. Scratch my head, Peaseblossom. Where's Mounsieur
  Cobweb?
COBWEB. Ready.
BOTTOM. Mounsieur Cobweb, good mounsieur, get you your weapons 10
  in your hand, and kill me a red-hipped humblebee on
  the top of a thistle: and good mounsieur, bring me the
  honey-bag. Do not fret yourself too much in the action,
  mounsieur: and good mounsieur have a care the honey-
  bag break not, I would be loath to have you overflowen 15
  with a honey bag, signior. Where's Mounsieur
  Mustardseed?
MUSTARDSEED. Ready.
BOTTOM. Give me your neaf,° Mounsieur Mustardseed. Pray you
  leave your curtsy,° good mounsieur.   20

---

2 *amiable:* lovely. *coy:* caress. 19 *neaf:* fist. 20 *leave your curtsy:* either (a) stop bowing,
or (b) replace your hat.

MUSTARDSEED.   What's your will?

BOTTOM.   Nothing, good mounsieur, but to help Cavalery° Cobweb
to scratch. I must to the barber's mounsieur, for
methinks I am marvellous hairy about the face. And I am
such a tender ass, if my hair do but tickle me, I must
scratch.

TITANIA.   What, will thou hear some music, my sweet love?

BOTTOM.   I have a reasonable good ear in music. Let's have the tongs°
and the bones.°

TITANIA.   Or say, sweet love, what thou desirest to eat.

BOTTOM.   Truly, a peck of provender. I could munch your good
dry oats. Methinks I have a great desire to a bottle° of hay.
Good hay, sweet hay, hath no fellow.

TITANIA.   I have a venturous fairy that shall seek
The squirrel's hoard, and fetch thee new nuts.

BOTTOM.   I had rather have a handful or two of dried pease. But
I pray you, let none of your people stir me: I have an
exposition of° sleep come upon me.

TITANIA.   Sleep thou, and I will wind thee in my arms.
Fairies, be gone, and be all ways° away.   [*Exeunt FAIRIES.*]
So doth the woodbine the sweet honeysuckle
Gently entwist: the female ivy so
Enrings the barky fingers of the elm.
O how I love thee! how I dote on thee!   [*They sleep.*]

Enter ROBIN GOODFELLOW [*PUCK.*]

OBERON.   [*Advances.*] Welcome good Robin. Seest thou this sweet sight?
Her dotage now I do begin to pity.
For meeting her of late behind the wood,
Seeking sweet favours° for this hateful fool,
I did upbraid her and fall out with her.
For she his hairy temples then had rounded
With coronet of fresh and fragrant flowers
And that same dew which sometime° on the buds
Was wont to° swell like round and orient° pearls,
Stood now within the pretty flowerets' eyes,
Like tears that did their own disgrace bewail.
When I had at my pleasure taunted her,
And she in mild terms begged my patience,
I then did ask of her her changeling child:
Which straight she gave me, and her fairy sent
To bear him to my bower in fairy land.

---

22 *Cavalery:* (he means "cavalier").   29 *tongs:* crude music made by striking tongs with a piece
of metal.   *bones:* pieces of bone held between the fingers and clapped together
rhythmically.   32 *bottle:* bundle.   38 *exposition of:* (he means "disposition to").   40 *all
ways:* in every direction.   48 *favours:* bouquets as love tokens.   52 *sometime:* formerly.   53
Was wont to: used to.   *orient:* (where the most beautiful pearls came from).

And now I have the boy, I will undo
This hateful imperfection of her eyes.
And gentle Puck, take this transformèd scalp
From off the head of this Athenian swain;
That he awaking when the other do,   65
May all to Athens back again repair,°
And think no more of this night's accidents,°
But as the fierce vexation of a dream.
But first I will release the Fairy Queen.
    Be as thou wast wont to be: 70
    See, as thou wast wont to see.
    Dian's bud o'er Cupid's flower°
    Hath such force and blessèd power.
Now my Titania, wake you, my sweet queen.
TITANIA.   My Oberon, what visions have I seen!   75
Methought I was enamoured of an ass.
OBERON.   There lies your love.
TITANIA.   How came these things to pass?
O, how mine eyes do loathe his visage now!
OBERON.   Silence awhile Robin, take off this head:
Titania, music call, and strike more dead   80
Than common sleep of all these five the sense.°
TITANIA.   Music, ho music! such as charmeth sleep.
PUCK.   Now, when thou wak'st, with thine own fools' eyes peep.
OBERON.   Sound music: *Music still.*°
    come my queen, take hands with me,
And rock the ground whereon these sleepers be.   [*Dance.*]   85
Now thou and I are new in amity,
And will tomorrow midnight solemnly
Dance in Duke Theseus' house triumphantly,°
And bless it to all fair prosperity.
There shall the pairs of faithful lovers be   90
Wedded, with Theseus, all in jollity.
PUCK.   Fairy King, attend and mark:
    I do hear the morning lark.
OBERON.   Then my queen, in silence sad,°
    Trip we after the night's shade: 95
    We the globe can compass soon,
    Swifter than the wand'ring moon.
TITANIA.   Come my lord, and in our flight,
    Tell me how it came this night,
    That I sleeping here was found,   100
    With these mortals on the ground.   *Exeunt.*

---

66 *repair:* return.   67 *accidents:* incidents.   72 *Dian's bud . . . flower:* (Diana's bud counteracts
the effects of love-in-idleness, the pansy).   80–81 *strike . . . sense:* Make these five (the lovers
and Bottom) sleep more soundly.   84.1 S.D.: *still:* continuously.   88 *triumphantly:* in celebration.   94 *sad:* serious.

Wind° horns. Enter THESEUS, HIPPOLYTA, EGEUS and all his train.

THESEUS.   Go one of you, find out the forester:
For now our observation° is performed.
And since we have the vaward° of the day,
My love shall hear the music of my hounds.
Uncouple° in the western valley, let them go:
Dispatch I say, and find the forester.   [*Exit an ATTENDANT.*]
We will, fair queen, up to the mountain's top,
And mark the musical confusion
Of hounds and echo in conjunction.
HIPPOLYTA.   I was with Hercules and Cadmus° once,
When in a wood of Crete they bayed the bear,°
With hounds of Sparta:° never did I hear
Such gallant chiding. For besides the groves,
The skies, the fountains, every region near
Seemed all one mutual cry. I never heard
So musical a discord, such sweet thunder.
THESEUS.   My hounds are bred out of the Spartan kind:
So flewed, so sanded:° and their heads are hung
With ears that sweep away the morning dew,
Crook-kneed, and dewlapped° like Thessalian bulls:
Slow in pursuit; but matched in mouth like bells,
Each under each.° A cry° more tuneable
Was never holloa'd to, nor cheered with horn,
In Crete, in Sparta, nor in Thessaly.
Judge when you hear. But soft.° What nymphs are these?
EGEUS.   My lord, this is my daughter here asleep,
And this Lysander, this Demetrius is,
This Helena, old Nedar's Helena.
I wonder of their being here together.
THESEUS.   No doubt they rose up early to observe
The rite of May: and hearing our intent,
Came here in grace° of our solemnity.
But speak Egeus, is not this the day
That Hermia should give answer of her choice?
EGEUS.   It is, my lord.
THESEUS.   Go bid the huntsmen wake them with their horns.

Shout within: wind horns. They all start up.

101.1 S.D.: *wind:* blow, sound.   103 *observation:* observance of the May Day rites.   104
vaward: vanguard, earliest part.   106 *Uncouple:* unleash (the dogs).   111 *Cadmus:* mythical
builder of Thebes.   112 *bayed the bear:* brought the bear to bay, to its last stand.   113 *hounds
of Sparta:* (a breed famous for their swiftness and quick scent).   119 *flewed, so sanded:* with
hanging cheeks, so sand-colored.   121 *dewlapped:* with skin hanging from the chin.   122–23
matched . . . each: with each voice matched for harmony with the next in pitch, like bells in a
chime.   123 *cry:* pack of dogs.   126 *soft:* wait.   133 *grace:* honor.

Good morrow, friends. Saint Valentine is past.
Begin these wood-birds but to couple now?°
LYSANDER.   Pardon, my lord.   [*They kneel.*]
THESEUS.   I pray you all, stand up.   140
I know you two are rival enemies.
How comes this gentle concord in the world,
That hatred is so far from jealousy,°
To sleep by hate° and fear no enmity?
LYSANDER.   My lord, I shall reply amazedly,   145
Half sleep, half waking. But as yet, I swear,
I cannot truly say how I came here.
But as I think—for truly would I speak,
And now I do bethink me, so it is—
I came with Hermia hither. Our intent   150
Was to be gone from Athens, where we might,
Without° the peril of the Athenian law—
EGEUS.   Enough, enough, my lord: you have enough.
I beg the law, the law upon his head:
They would have stol'n away, they would, Demetrius,   155
Thereby to have defeated you and me:
You of your wife, and me of my consent:
Of my consent that she should be your wife.
DEMETRIUS.   My lord, fair Helen told me of their stealth,
Of this their purpose hither, to this wood,   160
And I in fury hither followed them;
Fair Helena in fancy° following me.
But my good lord, I wot not by what power
(But by some power it is) my love to Hermia,
Melted as the snow, seems to me now   165
As the remembrance of an idle gaud,°
Which in my childhood I did dote upon:
And all the faith, the virtue of my heart,
The object and the pleasure of mine eye,
Is only Helena. To her, my lord,   170
Was I betrothed ere I saw Hermia:
But like a sickness,° did I loathe this food.
But as in health, come° to my natural taste,
Now I do wish it, love it, long for it.
And will for evermore be true to it.   175
THESEUS.   Fair lovers, you are fortunately met.
Of this discourse we more will hear anon.
Egeus, I will overbear your will:
For in the temple, by and by,° with us,

138–139 *Saint . . . now:* (birds traditionally chose their mates on St. Valentine's Day).   143 *jealousy:* suspicion.   144 *hate:* one it hates.   152 *Without:* beyond.   162 *in fancy:* out of doting love.   166 *idle gaud:* trifling toy.   172 *sickness:* sick person.   173 *come:* i.e., back.   179 *by and by:* immediately.

These couples shall eternally be knit.
And for the morning now is something worn,°
Our purposed hunting shall be set aside.
Away with us to Athens. Three and three,
We'll hold a feast in great solemnity.
Come Hippolyta.

Exeunt DUKE [HIPPOLYTA, EGEUS] and LORDS.

DEMETRIUS.   These things seem small and undistinguishable,
Like far-off mountains turnèd into clouds.
HERMIA.   Methinks I see these things with parted° eye,
When everything seems double.
HELENA.   So methinks:
And I have found Demetrius, like a jewel,
Mine own, and not mine own.°
DEMETRIUS.   Are you sure
That we are awake? It seems to me,
That yet we sleep, we dream. Do not you think
The duke was here, and bid us follow him?
HERMIA.   Yea, and my father.
HELENA.   And Hippolyta.
LYSANDER.   And he did bid us follow to the temple.
DEMETRIUS.   Why then, we are awake: let's follow him,
And by the way let us recount our dreams.   *Exeunt Lovers.*
BOTTOM.   (*Wakes.*) When my cue comes, call me, and I will answer.
My next is "Most fair Pyramus." Hey ho. Peter Quince?
Flute the bellows-mender? Snout the tinker? Starveling?
God's my life! Stol'n hence, and left me asleep? I have
had a most rare vision. I have had a dream, past the wit
of man to say what dream it was. Man is but an ass, if he
go about° to expound this dream. Methought I was—
there is no man can tell what. Methought I was, and
methought I had—but man is but a patched fool,° if he
will offer to say what methought I had. The eye of man
hath not heard, the ear of man hath not seen, man's hand is
not able to taste, his tongue to conceive, nor his
heart to report, what my dream was. I will get Peter
Quince to write a ballad of this dream: it shall be called
Bottom's Dream; because it hath no bottom: and I
will sing it in the latter end of our play, before the duke.
Peradventure, to make it the more gracious, I shall sing
it at her° death.   *Exit.*

---

181 *something worn:* somewhat worn on.   188 *parted:* divided (each eye seeing a separate image).   190–191 *like . . . own:* like a person who finds a jewel: the finder is the owner, but insecurely so.   205 *go about:* attempt.   207 *patched fool:* fool dressed in motley.   216 *her:* Thisby's.

[*Scene 2. Athens, Quince's house*]

Enter QUINCE, FLUTE, SNOUT, and STARVELING.

QUINCE.   Have you sent to Bottom's house? Is he come home yet?
STARVELING.   He cannot be heard of. Out of doubt he is transported.°
FLUTE.   If he come not, then the play is marred. It goes not forward,
     doth it?
QUINCE.   It is not possible. You have not a man in all Athens able   5
     to discharge° Pyramus but he.
FLUTE.   No, he hath simply the best wit of any handicraft man in Athens.
QUINCE.   Yea, and the best person too, and he is a very paramour
     for a sweet voice.
FLUTE.   You must say "paragon." A paramour is (God bless us)   10
     a thing of naught.°

Enter SNUG THE JOINER.

SNUG.   Masters, the duke is coming from the temple, and there
     is two or three lords and ladies more married. If our
     sport had gone forward, we had all been made men.°
FLUTE.   O sweet bully Bottom. Thus hath he lost sixpence a day°   15
     during his life: he could not have 'scaped sixpence a day.
     And the duke had not given him sixpence a day for playing
     Pyramus, I'll be hanged. He would have deserved it.
     Sixpence a day in Pyramus, or nothing.

Enter BOTTOM.

BOTTOM.   Where are these lads? Where are these hearts?   20
QUINCE.   Bottom! O most courageous° day! O most happy hour!
BOTTOM.   Masters, I am to discourse wonders: but ask me not what.
     For if I tell you, I am not true Athenian. I will tell you
     everything, right as it fell out.
QUINCE.   Let us hear, sweet Bottom.   25
BOTTOM.   Not a word of me. All that I will tell you is, that the
     duke hath dined. Get your apparel together, good
     strings to your beards, new ribbands to your pumps, meet
     presently° at the palace, every man look o'er his part: for
     the short and the long is, our play is preferred.° In any   30
     case, let Thisby have clean linen: and let not him that
     plays the lion pare his nails, for they shall hang out for
     the lion's claws. And most dear actors, eat no onions nor
     garlic, for we are to utter sweet breath: and I do not
     doubt but to hear them say it is a sweet comedy. No more   35
     words: away, go away.   *Exeunt.*

2 *transported:* carried away (by spirits).   6 *discharge:* portray.   11 *of naught:* wicked,
naughty.   14 *made men:* men made rich.   15 *sixpence a day:* i.e., as a pension   21 *coura-*
geous: (he may mean "auspicious").   29 *presently:* immediately.   30 *preferred:* recommended
(for presentation).

ACT 5

[*Scene 1. The palace of Theseus*]

Enter THESEUS, HIPPOLYTA, *and* PHILOSTRATE, *and his* LORDS.

HIPPOLYTA.   'Tis strange, my Theseus, that these lovers speak of.
THESEUS.   More strange than true. I never may believe
  These antick° fables, nor these fairy toys.°
  Lovers and madmen have such seething brains,
  Such shaping fantasies,° that apprehend
  More than cool reason ever comprehends.
  The lunatic, the lover, and the poet,
  Are of imagination all compact.°
  One sees more devils than vast hell can hold:
  That is the madman. The lover, all as frantic,
  Sees Helen's beauty in a brow of Egypt.°
  The poet's eye, in a fine frenzy rolling,
  Doth glance from heaven to earth, from earth to heaven.
  And as imagination bodies forth
  The forms of things unknown, the poet's pen
  Turns them to shapes, and gives to airy nothing,
  A local habitation and a name.
  Such tricks hath strong imagination,
  That if it would but apprehend some joy,
  It comprehends° some bringer of that joy.
  Or in the night, imagining some fear,
  How easy is a bush supposed a bear.
HIPPOLYTA.   But all the story of the night told over,
  And all their minds transfigured so together,
  More witnesseth than fancy's images,°
  And grows to something of great constancy:°
  But howsoever, strange and admirable.°

Enter LOVERS: LYSANDER, DEMETRIUS, HERMIA, *and* HELENA.

THESEUS.   Here come the lovers, full of joy and mirth.
  Joy, gentle friends, joy and fresh days of love
  Accompany your hearts.
LYSANDER.   More° than to us
  Wait in your royal walks, your board, your bed.
THESEUS.   Come now, what masques,° what dances shall we have,
  To wear away this long age of three hours
  Between our after-supper° and bed-time?

---

3 *antick:* fantastic.   *fairy toys:* trivial fairy stories.   5 *fantasies:* imaginations.   8 *of . . . compact:* totally composed of imagination.   11 *a brow of Egypt:* the swarthy face of a gypsy (believed to come from Egypt).   20 *comprehends:* includes.   25 *More . . . images:* testifies that it is more than just imagination.   26 *constancy:* certainty.   27 *admirable:* to be wondered at.   30 *More:* even more (joy and love).   32, 40 *masques:* lavish courtly entertainments combining song and dance.   34 *after-supper:* late supper.

Where is our usual manager of mirth?   35
What revels are in hand? Is there no play,
To ease the anguish of a torturing hour?
Call Philostrate.
PHILOSTRATE.   Here, mighty Theseus.
THESEUS.   Say, what abridgment° have you for this evening?
What masque,° what music? How shall we beguile   40
The lazy time, if not with some delight?
PHILOSTRATE.   There is a brief° how many sports are ripe:°
Make choice of which your highness will see first.

[*Gives a paper.*]

THESEUS.   "The battle with the Centaurs, to be sung
By an Athenian eunuch to the harp."   45
We'll none of that. That have I told my love
In glory of my kinsman Hercules.
"The riot of the tipsy Bacchanals,
Tearing the Thracian singer in their rage."°
That is an old device: and it was played   50
When I from Thebes came last a conqueror.
"The thrice three Muses mourning for the death
Of Learning, late deceased in beggary."
That is some satire keen and critical,
Not sorting with° a nuptial ceremony.   55
"A tedious brief scene of young Pyramus
And his love Thisby; very tragical mirth."
Merry and tragical? Tedious and brief?
That is hot ice and wondrous strange snow.
How shall we find the concord of this discord?   60
PHILOSTRATE.   A play there is, my lord, some ten words long,
Which is as brief as I have known a play:
But by ten words, my lord, it is too long,
Which makes it tedious: for in all the play
There is not one word apt, one player fitted.°   65
And tragical, my noble lord, it is:
For Pyramus therein doth kill himself.
Which when I saw rehearsed, I must confess,
Made mine eyes water; but more merry tears
The passion of loud laughter never shed.   70
THESEUS.   What are they that do play it?
PHILOSTRATE.   Hard-handed men, that work in Athens here,
Which never laboured in their minds till now:
And now have toiled their unbreathed° memories
With this same play, against° your nuptial.   75

39 *abridgment:* either (a) diversion to make the hours seem shorter or (b) short entertainment.   42 *brief:* list.   *ripe:* ready.   48–49 *riot . . . rage:* (The singer Orpheus of Thrace
was torn limb from limb by the Maenads, frenzied female priests of Bacchus).   55 *sorting with:*
befitting.   65 *fitted:* (well) cast.   74 *unbreathed:* unpracticed, unexercised.
75 *against:* in preparation for.

THESEUS.   And we will hear it.
PHILOSTRATE.   No, my noble lord,
    It is not for you. I have heard it over,
    And it is nothing, nothing in the world;
    Unless you can find sport in their intents,
    Extremely stretched and conned° with cruel pain.
    To do your service.
THESEUS.   I will hear that play.
    For never anything can be amiss,
    When simpleness and duty tender° it.
    Go bring them in, and take your places, ladies.   [*Exit PHILOSTRATE.*]
HIPPOLYTA.   I love not to see wretchedness o'ercharged,°
    And duty in his service perishing.
THESEUS.   Why, gentle sweet, you shall see no such thing.
HIPPOLYTA.   He says they can do nothing in this kind.°
THESEUS.   The kinder we, to give them thanks for nothing.
    Our sport shall be to take what they mistake.
    And what poor duty cannot do, noble respect
    Takes it in might, not merit.°
    Where I have come, great clerks° have purposèd
    To greet me with premeditated welcomes;
    Where I have seen them shiver and look pale,
    Make periods in the midst of sentences,
    Throttle° their practised accent in their fears,
    And in conclusion dumbly have broke off,
    Not paying me a welcome. Trust me, sweet,
    Out of this silence yet I picked a welcome:
    And in the modesty of fearful duty°
    I read as much as from the rattling tongue
    Of saucy and audacious eloquence.
    Love, therefore, and tongue-tied simplicity,
    In° least, speak most, to my capacity.°

[*Enter PHILOSTRATE.*]

PHILOSTRATE.   So please your grace, the Prologue is addressed.°
THESEUS.   Let him approach.

Flourish trumpets. Enter the PROLOGUE [QUINCE].

PROLOGUE.   If we offend, it is with our good will.
        That you should think, we come not to offend,
        But with good will. To show our simple skill,
        That is the true beginning of our end.

---

80 *stretched and conned:* strained and memorized.   83 *tender:* offer.   85 *wretchedness o'er-charged:* poor fellows taxing themselves too much.   88 *in this kind:* of this sort.   91–92 *noble . . . merit:* a noble nature considers the sincerity of effort rather than the skill of execution.   93 *clerks:* scholars.   97 *Throttle:* choke on.   101 *fearful duty:* subjects whose devotions gave them stage fright.   105 *In:* i.e., saying.   *capacity:* way of thinking.   106 *addressed:* ready.   108–117 *If . . . know:* (Quince's blunders in punctuation exactly reverse the meaning).

Consider then, we come but in despite.°
We do not come, as minding to content you,
Our true intent is. All for your delight,
We are not here. That you should here repent you,   115
The actors are at hand: and by their show,
You shall know all, that you are like to know.°

THESEUS. This fellow doth not stand upon points.°
LYSANDER. He hath rid his prologue like a rough colt: he knows
not the stop.° A good moral my lord: it is not enough   120
to speak; but to speak true.
HIPPOLYTA. Indeed he hath played on his prologue like a child on a
recorder:° a sound, but not in government.°
THESUS. His speech was like a tangled chain: nothing impaired, but
all disordered. Who is next?   125

Enter PYRAMUS and THISBY, WALL, MOONSHINE, and LION.

PROLOGUE. Gentles, perchance you wonder at this show,
But wonder on, till truth make all things plain.
This man is Pyramus, if you would know:
This beauteous lady, Thisby is certain.
This man, with lime and rough-cast,° doth present   130
Wall, that vile wall which did these lovers sunder:
And through Wall's chink, poor souls, they are content
To whisper. At the which, let no man wonder.
This man, with lantern, dog, and bush of thorn,
Presenteth Moonshine. For if you will know,   135
By moonshine did these lovers think no scorn
To meet at Ninus' tomb, there, there to woo:
This grisly beast (which Lion hight° by name)
The trusty Thisby, coming first by night,
Did scare away, or rather did affright: 140
And as she fled, her mantle she did fall:°
Which Lion vile with bloody mouth did stain.
Anon comes Pyramus, sweet youth and tall,°
And finds his trusty Thisby's mantle slain:
Whereat, with blade, with bloody blameful blade,   145
He bravely broached° his boiling bloody breast.
And Thisby, tarrying in mulberry shade,
His dagger drew, and died. For all the rest,
Let Lion, Moonshine, Wall, and lovers twain.
At large° discourse, while here they do remain.   150
THESEUS. I wonder if the lion be to speak.

---

112 *despite:* malice.   118 *stand upon points:* (1) pay attention to punctuation (2) bother about
the niceties (of expression).   120 *stop:* (1) halt (2) period.   123 *recorder:* flutelike wind
instrument.   *in government:* well managed.   130 *rough-cast:* rough plaster made of lime and
gravel.   138 *hight:* is called.   141 *fall:* let fall.   143 *tall:* brave.   146 *broached:* opened
(Shakespeare parodies the overuse of alliteration in the earlier bombastic Elizabethan
plays).   150 *At large:* in full.

DEMETRIUS.   No wonder, my lord: one lion may, when many asses do.

Exeunt [PROLOGUE, PYRAMUS,] LION, THISBY, MOONSHINE.

WALL.   In this same interlude° it doth befall
   That I, one Snout by name, present a wall:
   And such a wall, as I would have you think,   15
   That had in it a crannied hole or chink:
   Through which the lovers, Pyramus and Thisby,
   Did whisper often, very secretly.
   This loam, this rough-cast, and this stone doth show
   That I am that same wall: the truth is so.   16
   And this the cranny is, right and sinister,°
   Through which the fearful lovers are to whisper.
THESEUS.   Would you desire lime and hair to speak better?
DEMETRIUS.   It is the wittiest° partition° that ever I heard discourse,
   my lord.   1

Enter PYRAMUS.

THESEUS.   Pyramus draws near the wall: silence.
PYRAMUS.   O grim-looked night, O night with hue so black,
     O night, which ever art when day is not:
   O night, O night, alack, alack, alack,
     I fear my Thisby's promise is forgot.   1
   And thou O wall, O sweet, O lovely wall,
     That stand'st between her father's ground and mine,
   Thou wall, O wall, O sweet and lovely wall,
     Show me thy chink, to blink through with mine eyne.°

[*WALL holds up his fingers.*]

   Thanks, courteous wall. Jove shield thee well for this.   1
     But what see I? No Thisby do I see.
   O wicked wall, through whom I see no bliss,
     Cursed by thy stones for thus deceiving me.
THESEUS.   The wall methinks being sensible,° should curse again.°
PYRAMUS.   No in truth sir, he should not. "Deceiving me" is
   Thisby's cue: she is to enter now, and I am to spy her
   through the wall. You shall see it will fall pat° as I told you:
   yonder she comes.

Enter THISBY.

THISBY.   O wall, full often hast thou heard my moans,
   For parting my fair Pyramus and me.
   My cherry lips have often kissed thy stones;
     Thy stones with lime and hair knit up in thee.

---

153 *interlude:* short play.   161 *right and sinister:* from right to left (he probably uses the fingers of his right and left hands to form the cranny).   164 *wittiest:* most intelligent.   *partition:* (1) wall (2) section of a learned book or speech.   174 *eyne:* eyes.   179 *sensible:* capable of feelings and perception.   *again:* back.   182 *pat:* exactly.

PYRAMUS. I see a voice: now will I to the chink,
　　　　To spy and I can hear my Thisby's face.
　　　　Thisby?　　　　　　　　　　　　　　　　　190
THISBY. My love thou art, my love I think.
PYRAMUS. Think what thou wilt, I am thy lover's grace:
　　　　And, like Limander,° am I trusty still.
THISBY. And I like Helen,° till the Fates me kill.
PYRAMUS. Not Shafalus to Procrus,° was so true.　　　　195
THISBY. As Shafalus to Procrus, I to you.
PYRAMUS. O kiss me through the hole of this vile wall.
THISBY. I kiss the wall's hole, not your lips at all.
PYRAMUS. Wilt thou at Ninny's° tomb meet me straightway?
THISBY. Tide° life, tide death, I come without delay.　　　　200

　　　　　　　　　　　　[*Exeunt* PYRAMUS *and* THISBY.]

WALL. Thus have I, Wall, my part dischargèd so;
　　　　And being done, thus Wall away doth go.　　　　　*Exit.*
THESEUS. Now is the mural° down between the two neighbours.
DEMETRIUS. No remedy my lord, when walls are so wilful to hear
　　　　without warning.°　　　　　　　　　　　　　　205
HIPPOLYTA. This is the silliest stuff that ever I heard.
THESEUS. The best in this kind are but shadows:° and the worst are
　　　　no worse, if imagination amend them.
HIPPOLYTA. It must be your imagination then, and not theirs.
THESEUS. If we imagine no worse of them than they of themselves,　　210
　　　　they may pass for excellent men. Here come two noble
　　　　beasts in, a man and a lion.

Enter LION *and* MOONSHINE.

LION. You ladies, you, whose gentle hearts do fear
　　　　The smallest monstrous mouse that creeps on floor,
　　　　May now perchance both quake and tremble here.　　　215
　　　　When lion rough in wildest rage doth roar.
　　　　Then know that I, as Snug the joiner am
　　　　A lion fell,° nor else no lion's dam:°
　　　　For if I should as lion come in strife
　　　　Into this place, 'twere pity on my life.　　　　　　220
THESEUS. A very gentle beast, and of a good conscience.
DEMETRIUS. The very best at a beast,° my lord, that e'er I saw.
LYSANDER. This lion is a very fox for his valour.
THESEUS. True: and a goose for his discretion.
DEMETRIUS. Not so my lord: for his valour cannot carry his discretion,　　225
　　　　and the fox carries the goose.

193 *Limander:* (he means "Leander").　　194 *Helen:* (he means "Hero").　　195 *Shafalus to
Procrus:* (he means "Cephalus" and "Procris" [see III.2.389 n., p. 1579]).　　199 *Ninny:* fool (he
means "Ninus").　　200 *Tide:* come, betide.　　203 *mural:* wall.　　205 *without warning:* either
(a) without warning the parents or (b) unexpectedly.　　207 *in . . . shadows:* of this sort are only
plays (or only actors).　　218 *fell:* fierce.　　*nor . . . dam:* and not a lioness.　　222 *best, beast:*
(pronounced similarly).

THESEUS.   His discretion, I am sure, cannot carry his valour: for the
goose carries not the fox. It is well: leave it to his discretion,
and let us listen to the moon.

MOONSHINE.   This lanthorn° doth the hornèd moon present—

DEMETRIUS.   He should have worn the horns on his head.°

THESEUS.   He is no crescent, and his horns are invisible within the
circumference.

MOONSHINE.   This lanthorn doth the hornèd moon present,
Myself, the man i' th' moon do seem to be.

THESEUS.   This is the greatest error of all the rest; the man should
be put into the lanthorn. How is it else the man i' th'
moon?

DEMETRIUS.   He dares not come there for the candle; for you see, it
is already in snuff.°

HIPPOLYTA.   I am aweary of this moon. Would he would change.

THESEUS.   It appears, by his small light of discretion, that he is in
the wane: but yet in courtesy, in all reason, we must stay°
the time.

LYSANDER.   Proceed, Moon.

MOONSHINE.   All that I have to say, is to tell you that the lanthorn is
the moon, I the man i' th' moon, this thornbush my
thornbush, and this dog my dog.

DEMETRIUS.   Why, all these should be in the lanthorn: for all these are
in the moon. But silence: here comes Thisby.

Enter THISBY.

THISBY.   This is old Ninny's tomb. Where is my love?

LION.   Oh!   *The LION roars. THISBY runs off.*

DEMETRIUS.   Well roared, Lion.

THESEUS.   Well run, Thisby.

HIPPOLYTA.   Well shone, Moon. Truly, the moon shines with a good
grace.

[*The LION shakes THISBY's mantle.*]

THESEUS.   Well moused,° Lion.

DEMETRIUS.   And then came Pyramus.

Enter PYRAMUS. [Exit LION.]

LYSANDER.   And so the lion vanished.

PYRAMUS.   Sweet moon, I thank thee for thy sunny beams,
I thank thee, moon, for shining now so bright.
For by thy gracious, golden, glittering gleams,
I trust to take of truest Thisby sight.

---

230 *lanthorn:* lantern (once made of horn).   230–231 *hornèd . . . head:* (referring to the cuckold or deceived husband, who supposedly grew horns).   240 *in snuff:* (1) in need of snuffing
(having a long, burnt-out wick or snuff) (2) in a temper.   243 *stay:* await.   257 *moused:*
shaken, as a cat shakes a mouse.

But stay: O spite!
But mark, poor knight,   265
What dreadful dole° is here?
Eyes, do you see!
How can it be!
O dainty duck, O dear!
Thy mantle good,   270
What, stained with blood?
Approach, ye Furies° fell:
O Fates!° come, come:
Cut thread and thrum.°
Quail,° crush, conclude, and quell.°   275

THESEUS.   This passion, and the death of a dear friend, would go
near to make a man look sad.

HIPPOLYTA.   Beshrew° my heart, but I pity the man.

PYRAMUS.   O wherefore Nature, didst thou lions frame?
Since lion vile hath here deflowered my dear.   280
Which is—no, no—which was the fairest dame
That lived, that loved, that liked, that looked with cheer.
Come tears, confound:
Out sword, and wound
The pap° of Pyramus: 285
Ay, that left pap,
Where heart doth hop.   [*Stabs himself.*]
Thus die, I, thus, thus, thus.
Now am I dead,
Now am I fled,   290
My soul is in the sky.
Tongue lose thy light,
Moon° take thy flight,   [*Exit MOONSHINE.*]
Now die, die, die, die, die.   [*Dies.*]

DEMETRIUS.   No die,° but an ace° for him. For he is but one.   295

LYSANDER.   Less than an ace, man. For he is dead, he is nothing.

THESEUS.   With the help of a surgeon, he might yet recover, and
prove an ass.

HIPPOLYTA.   How chance Moonshine is gone before Thisby comes
back and finds her lover?   300

Enter THISBY.

THESEUS.   She will find him by starlight. Here she comes, and her
passion ends the play.

HIPPOLYTA.   Methinks she should not use a long one for such a
Pyramus: I hope she will be brief.

266 *dole:* grief.   272 *Furies:* classical spirits of the underworld who avenged murder.   273
Fates: three sisters who spun the thread of human destiny, which at will was cut with a
shears.   274 *thrum:* fringelike end of the warp in weaving.   275 *Quail:* subdue.   *quell:*
kill.   278 *Beshrew:* curse (meant lightly).   285 *pap:* breast.   292–293 *Tongue . . . Moon:*
(he reverses the two subjects).   295 *die:* (singular of "dice").   *ace:* a throw of one at dice.

DEMETRIUS.   A mote will turn the balance, which Pyramus, which
  Thisby, is the better: he for a man. God warr'nt° us;
  she for a woman, God bless us.
LYSANDER.   She hath spied him already with those sweet eyes.
DEMETRIUS.   And thus she means,° videlicet°—
THISBY.   Asleep my love?
    What, dead, my dove?
  O Pyramus, arise,
   Speak, speak. Quite dumb?
  Dead, dead? A tomb
  Must cover thy sweet eyes.
   These lily lips,
   This cherry nose,
  These yellow cowslip° cheeks,
   Are gone, are gone:
   Lovers, make moan:
  His eyes were green as leeks.
   O Sisters Three,°
   Come, come to me,
  With hands as pale as milk,
   Lay them in gore,
   Since you have shore
  With shears his thread of silk.
   Tongue, not a word:
   Come trusty sword,
  Come blade, my breast imbrue°   [*Stabs herself.*]
   And farewell friends:
   Thus Thisby ends:
  Adieu, adieu, adieu.   [*Dies.*]
THESEUS.   Moonshine and Lion are left to bury the dead.
DEMETRIUS.   Ay, and Wall too.
BOTTOM.   [*Starts up*] No, I assure you, the wall is down that parted
  their fathers. Will it please you to see the Epilogue, or
  to hear a Bergomask° dance between two of our company?
THESEUS.   No epilogue, I pray you; for your play needs no excuse.
  Never excuse: for when the players are all dead, there
  need none to be blamed. Marry, if he that writ it had
  played Pyramus and hanged himself in Thisby's garter,
  it would have been a fine tragedy: and so it is truly, and
  very notably discharged. But come, your Bergomask:
  let your Epilogue alone.   [*A dance.*]
  The iron tongue° of midnight hath told° twelve.
  Lovers, to bed, 'tis almost fairy time.°
  I fear we shall outsleep the coming morn,

---

306 *warr'nt:* warrant, protect. 309 *means:* laments. *videlicet:* namely. 318 *cowslip:*
yellow primrose. 322 *Sisters Three:* the Fates. 330 *imbrue:* stain with gore. 338
Bergomask: exaggerated country dance. 346 *iron tongue:* i.e., of the bell. *told:* counted,
tolled. 347 *fairy time:* (from midnight to daybreak).

As much as we this night have overwatched.
This palpable gross° play hath well beguiled   350
The heavy gait of night. Sweet friends, to bed.
A fortnight hold we this solemnity,
In nightly revels, and new jollity.   *Exeunt.*

Enter PUCK *[with a broom].*

PUCK.   Now the hungry lion roars,
             And the wolf behowls the moon;   355
       Whilst the heavy° ploughman snores,
             All with weary task fordone.°
       Now the wasted brands° do glow,
       Whilst the screech-owl, screeching loud,
             Puts the wretch that lies in woe°   360
       In remembrance of a shroud.
             Now it is the time of night,
       That the graves, all gaping wide,
             Every one lets forth his sprite,°
       In the church-way paths to glide.   365
             And we fairies, that do run
       By the triple Hecate's° team,°
             From the presence of the sun,
   Following darkness like a dream,
       Now are frolic:° not a mouse   370
   Shall disturb this hallowed house.
   I am sent with broom before,
   To sweep the dust° behind° the door.

Enter KING *and* QUEEN OF FAIRIES, *with all their train.*

OBERON.   Through the house give glimmering light,
             By the dead and drowsy fire,   375
       Every elf and fairy sprite,
             Hop as light as bird from brier,
       And this ditty after me,
       Sing, and dance it trippingly.
TITANIA.   First rehearse your song by rote,   380
   To each word a warbling note.
   Hand in hand, with fairy grace,
   Will we sing and bless this place.   *[Song and dance.]*
OBERON.   Now, until the break of day,
       Through this house each fairy stray.   385
       To the best bride-bed will we,
       Which by us shall blessèd be:

---

350 *palpable gross:* obvious and crude.   356 *heavy:* sleepy.   357 *fordone:* worn out, "done
in."   358 *wasted brands:* burnt logs.   360 *wretch . . . woe:* sick person.   364 *sprite:* spirit,
ghost.   367 *triple Hecate:* the moon goddess, identified as Cynthia in heaven, Diana on earth,
and Hecate in hell.   *team:* dragons that pull the chariot of the night moon.   370 *frolic:*
frolicsome.   373 *To sweep the dust:* (Puck often helped with household chores).   *behind:*
from behind.

And the issue° there create,°
Ever shall be fortunate:
So shall all the couples three   39
Ever true in loving be:
And the blots of Nature's hand°
Shall not in their issue° stand.
Never mole, harelip, nor scar,
Nor mark prodigious,° such as are   39
Despisèd in nativity,
Shall upon their children be.
With this field-dew consecrate.
Every fairy take his gait,°
And each several° chamber bless,   4
Through this palace, with sweet peace;
And the owner of its blest,
Ever shall in safety rest.
Trip away: make no stay: *Exeunt [all but PUCK].*   4
Meet me all by break of day.

PUCK.   If we shadows have offended,
Think but this, and all is mended,
That you have but slumbered here,
While these visions did appear.
And this weak and idle° theme,
No more yielding but° a dream,
Gentles, do not reprehend.
If you pardon, we will mend.°
And as I am an honest Puck,
If we have unearnèd luck,
Now to scape the serpent's tongue,°
We will make amends, ere long:
Else the Puck a liar call.
So, good night unto you all.
Give me your hands,° if we be friends;
And Robin shall restore amends.°   *[Exit.]*

QUESTIONS

Act I

1. Describe the relationship between Theseus and Hippolyta. What does each of them represent? How does Shakespeare show us that they have different attitudes toward their marriage?

2. Characterize Hermia and Lysander. What blocks their relationship? How do they plan to circumvent these obstructions?

388, 393 *issue:* children.   388 *create:* created.   392 *blots . . . hand:* birth defects.   395 *mark prodigious:* unnatural birthmark.   399 *take his gait:* proceed.   400 *several:* separate.   410 *idle:* foolish.   411 *No . . . but:* yielding nothing more than.   413 *mend:* improve.   416 *serpent's tongue:* hissing of the audience.   420 *hands:* applause.   421 *restore amends:* do better in the future.

3. What are Helena's feelings about herself? About Hermia? About Demetrius? How might you account for her self-image?

4. Why have the mechanicals gathered at Quince's house? How does Shakespeare show us that Bottom is eager, ill-educated, energetic, and funny?

Act II

5. What is Puck's job? What do you find out about his personality, habits, and pastimes in his first conversation?

6. Why are Titania and Oberon fighting with each other, and what are the specific consequences of their conflict?

7. What does Oberon plan to do to Titania? Why? What is "love-in-idleness"? What power does it have? What does it symbolize?

8. Why are Demetrius and Helena in the woods? What does Oberon decide to do to them? What error occurs? What happens to Lysander when Helena awakens him?

Act III

9. How and why does Puck change Bottom? How is this transformation appropriate? What happens when Bottom awakens Titania? Why?

10. What does Oberon decide to do when he realizes that Puck has made a mistake? What is Puck's attitude toward the confusion he has created?

11. What happens when Helena awakens Demetrius? How does this situation reverse the one that began the play? Explain Helena's reaction to the behavior of Demetrius and Lysander.

12. What real dangers (tragic potential) do the lovers face in Act III? How do Oberon and Puck deal with these dangers? What is their plan? How successful is it?

Act IV

13. Why does Oberon cure Titania of her infatuation with Bottom? How does the relationship between Oberon and Titania change? How is this change symbolized? Why is it significant?

14. How are the relationships among the four lovers straightened out? How does each explain his or her feelings? What does Theseus decide about the couples? Why is this significant?

15. What momentous event occurs offstage and is briefly reported in Act IV, scene 2?

Act V

16. Describe Pyramus and Thisby. What blocks their relationship? How do they plan to circumvent these obstructions? What happens to them?

17. What is the significance of the fairy masque (a combination of poetry, music, dance, and drama) that ends the play?

18. What does Puck's epilogue suggest about you as a reader or spectator? How does it reinforce the connections among dreaming, imagination, illusion, and drama?

GENERAL QUESTIONS

1. To what extent are the characters in this play conventional and representative types? What is the effect of Shakespeare's style of characterization?

2. Are any of the characters symbolic? If so, what do they symbolize? How does such symbolism reinforce the themes of the play?

3. How does Shakespeare employ language, imagery, and poetic form to define the characters in this play and differentiate among the various groups of characters?

4. To what extent do the two settings—city and woods—structure the play? Where does exposition occur? Complication and catastrophe? The comic resolution? How complete is the resolution? Why is the round-trip journey from one setting to the other necessary for the lovers? The rulers? The "hempen homespuns"?

5. What are the similarities or parallels in plot and theme between A Midsummer Night's Dream and "Pyramus and Thisby"? To what degree are they versions of the same play with different endings? Why do you think Shakespeare included the play-within-the-play in A Midsummer Night's Dream?

6. In the first soliloquy of the play, Helena discusses love. What kind of love is she talking about? What are its qualities and characteristics? How far do the relationships in the play bear out her ideas about love?

7. How well do the mechanicals understand the nature of dramatic illusion? What sorts of production problems concern them? How do they solve these?

8. What ideas about drama and the ways in which audiences respond to it does A Midsummer Night's Dream explore?

9. Compare the play-within-a-play in A Midsummer Night's Dream to the one in Act III of Hamlet. How are the internal plays and situations similar? Different? What parallels do you see in the connections between each play-within-a-play and the larger play in which each occurs?

THE THEATER OF MOLIÈRE

The seventeenth century was the golden age of French neoclassical theater (called *neo* or "new" because it marked the reintroduction of Greek and Latin models). The dominant political figure of the age was the "Sun King," Louis XIV, the absolute monarch of France. He and his court—a set of nobles, wits, would-be wits, and ladies- and gentlemen-in-waiting—dictated fashion to the world at large and made Paris the cultural center of Europe.

The members of this ruling class profoundly influenced the drama of the age because they were the theater's patrons and protectors. Writers of tragedy, the two most important of whom were Pierre Corneille (1606–1684) and Jean Racine (1639–1699), complimented the understanding and sympathy of the nobility by creating serious poetic dramas for them. More daring and risky was the role of the writers of comedy, who populated the stage with characters derived not so much from the nobility as from the middle classes, often mocking their appearance, customs, and tastes.

The most important of the comic writers, the acknowledged master of comedy, was Molière, the pen name of Jean Baptiste Poquelin. Born in 1622, he received a Jesuit education and took up the study of law at Orléans. His favorite reading, however, was not law, but rather the six surviving comedies of the Roman dramatist Terence.[4] In 1643 he shocked his family by abandoning both the law and his father's prosperous upholstering business and going into the theater, a career that was considered scandalous and sinful. He joined a company of actors called the Illustrious Theater, who established themselves in a playhouse, produced a tragedy, and then went bankrupt.

The acting company spent the next thirteen years touring the provinces of France, performing *commedia dell'arte* farces and short comic plays, many of them by Molière. These years gave him his real education in the theater. He soon developed into a superb actor, director, and—more important—writer.

Although the years in the provinces were not easy, the company was achieving recognition. The group returned to Paris in 1658 at the invitation of King Louis XIV. The king was pleased with Molière's comedies and publicly provided support and protection. He also gave the company the authorization to use the *Théâtre de Petit Bourbon* at Versailles. In 1659, when the *Théâtre* was torn down, Louis provided a royal patent to use the *Palais Royale* in Paris. With the king's support, Molière spent the rest of his career at this theater as an actor, director, manager, and playwright.

Molière's personal life was a great deal more troubled than his professional life. At the age of forty he began an unhappy marriage with Armande Béjart, the twenty-year-old daughter (or sister) of his former mistress Madeleine Béjart (his enemies whispered that Armande was also *his* daughter). He endured constant ill health, but he was a fighter. He performed even on the day he died, collapsing onstage in 1673 while acting the lead role in his *The Imaginary Invalid* and dying several hours later. Because of the suddenness of his death he was not given last rites, and he was denied burial in consecrated ground.

Despite the adversities of his life, his creative output was great. He wrote twenty-nine plays, ranging from broad farce to satirical comedies of manners. He observed the theatrical conventions of his age, and he drew his plots from Roman comedy, Italian *commedia dell'arte*, and French farce, all of which schooled him in comic character, tempo, and situation. His inspirations were the manners, morals, and customs of the French gentry and middle class.

Molière was also innovative as a dramatist. He elevated comedy to the seriousness of tragedy, as in his satiric comedies *The Ridiculous Dilettantes* (*Les Précieuses Ridicules*, 1659), *The Misanthrope* (1666), *The Miser* (1668), and *Tartuffe*

---

[4] See pp. 1236 and 1537 for a brief discussion of the Roman dramatists.

Molière in the character of Sganarelle

(1669). What is new in these serious comedies is Molière's thoughtful and detached perspective on vices and follies. His mainspring is character, and his norm is moderation in all forms of behavior. From this point of balance, his plots mock and expose religious posturing, personal greed, social snobbery, and professional hypocrisy. In short, whatever is excessive is the subject of his satiric thrusts.

The *Théâtre Royale*, the Paris theater in which most of Molière's plays were produced, was patterned on Italian theater design of the early seventeenth century—a design that by and large has dominated theater architecture up to the present. The building was rectangular, with a proscenium stage at one end and seating in the approximate shape of a horseshoe—orchestra and balcony—for as many as six hundred spectators at the other end and both sides. Also at the sides were galleries or private boxes. There may have been space in front of the stage for special dances and ballets. A major innovation in design was the use of footlights and large chandeliers, which were essential for indoor performances. Either candles or oil lamps provided the light, and there was a constant need for attentive stagehands and candle snuffers to forestall accidental fires.

The stage scenery could be lavish, but for economy much of it was probably used in the productions of many separate plays. Molière apparently favored sparse sets and only minimal stage properties. The actors and actresses (women were never excluded from the French stage) wore contemporary costumes. This convention made Molière's satires all the more effective. Since his performers were costumed like the social types being pictured and mocked, the comedies became images of the social scenes inhabited by his audiences.

MOLIÈRE, *LOVE IS THE DOCTOR (L'AMOUR MÉDECIN)*

Love Is the Doctor (*L'Amour Médecin*) was first performed in 1665 at the palace of Louis XIV at Versailles, where the king himself sometimes joined Molière's casts to indulge his own acting fantasies and to win applause from his courtiers. The play is typical of Molière's comic farces, relying heavily on pantomime, dance, and music in the *commedia dell'arte* tradition. The incidental music by Jean Baptiste Lully (1632–1687), who provided music for many other Molière plays, has survived and is available in a modern recording.

The central character in *Love Is the Doctor*, Sganarelle, appears with the same name in other Molière comedies, also in the tradition of the *commedia dell'arte*. Usually Sganarelle tries to beat others, but as often as not he is beaten himself, and therefore he is both the cause and the butt of laughter. His function in *Love Is the Doctor* is typical: He is a wealthy businessman and a traditional paterfamilias, with the final word in family matters (like Egeus in *A Midsummer Night's Dream* and Polonius in *Hamlet*). He closely guards his daughter, Lucinda, from suitors to avoid having to pay a massive dowry to a son-in-law who, as he complains, might be a perfect stranger.

The plan by Lucinda and her suitor Clitander to marry despite Sganarelle's opposition is an example of the traditional intrigue plot, in which the father (or guardian), acting as blocking agent, chooses another man for the young woman, or, as in *Love Is the Doctor*, tries to prevent marriage entirely.[5] The *soubrette* in the play, who aids and abets the intrigue, is Lisette. Although in some intrigue plots the blocker is reconciled by the fact that the young man is independently rich, that does not happen in this play, for at the end Sganarelle is frustrated and outraged despite the surrounding merriment.

---

[5] The origin and nature of intrigue plots are more fully described on pp. 1537 and 1541.

Molière's notable addition to the intrigue plot in *Love Is the Doctor* is his satiric treatment of doctors. Medical practice in the seventeenth century was based on the widely held theory that a healthy body contained a harmonious balance of the four bodily fluids or "humors"—blood, yellow bile, black bile, and phlegm. When one of the humors became excessive or "putrid," the imbalance made the patient sick. Illness, including mental illness, could also be caused by the *adust*, or burning, of a particular humor during a high fever. (The understanding of bacterial and viral causes of disease did not develop until two centuries after Molière.) When doctors made a diagnosis based on this system, their treatment was to purge the offending humor and its noxious pressures (as the doctors recommend for Lucinda many times in *Love Is the Doctor*). Depending on the humor, they employed one of four methods of purgation: (1) a lancing or "bleeding" to draw off blood, or "sanguine" (the most common purgation, but the patient, weakened by blood loss, would often die more speedily from the original disease); (2) an emetic to eliminate yellow bile, or "choler," through vomiting; (3) a laxative to purge black bile, or "melancholy"; and (4) various irritating (and sometimes poisonous) powders to eliminate "phlegm" through violent sneezing.

With such principles and treatments, doctors were open targets for satire, and *Love Is the Doctor* holds nothing back. Once Lisette reports Lucinda's illness, the play is invaded by Molière's cadre of funny physicians, who, like their real-life counterparts, were bearded men who dressed in black robes and hats. Molière satirizes his doctors on the grounds of cronyism, indifference to the condition of patients, pomposity, exploitation of gullibility, ignorance and indecision, resistance to innovation, and simple greed.

Despite the severity of his satire, however, Molière also presents the doctors in a comic-farcical light. Both when they are summoned and when they are paid, for example, they perform dances and pantomimes. Even the blatant self-exposure of Dr. Fillpocket (Filerin) can be construed as the excess one expects of farce, and therefore honest medical practitioners in Molière's day could have claimed that the doctors in *Love Is the Doctor* represented the exception, not the rule.

Although the following version of *L'Amour Médecin* follows Molière's text faithfully, I have taken latitude in a few instances to emphasize his sharp comic intentions. For example, his introduction of the quack elixir "Orviétan" in Act II, scene 6, requires explanation, which I have included as part of the dramatic text in preference to creating an extensive footnote. Because the names of the doctors are not particularly meaningful, I have given them "tag names" that I hope will be readily appreciated by today's readers. Thus Drs. Tomès, De Fonandrès, Macroton, Bahays, and Filerin are, respectively, Slicer, De Pits, Gouger, Golfer, and Fillpocket. Generally, the medical recommendations of these doctors cannot be translated into modern terms. Readers will therefore need to rely on the brief description given here about medical practice in Molière's day. Alert readers may notice some anachronisms and inconsistencies, such as the use of the words *pathological* and *psychosomatic;* these are not inadvertent, but are made in the hope that they are consistent with the comic spirit of Molière.

MOLIÈRE (JEAN BAPTISTE POQUELIN) (1622–1673)

Love Is the Doctor (L'Amour Médecin) _____ *1665*

Translated by Edgar V. Roberts

CHARACTERS

> Sganarelle, *a wealthy Parisian merchant, father of* Lucinda
> Aminta, *his neighbor*
> Lucretia, *his niece*
> Mr. Williams, *his friend, a seller of tapestries*
> Mr. Josse, *another friend, a jeweller*
> Lucinda, *daughter of* Sganarelle, *in love with* Clitander
> Lisette, *maid to* Lucinda, *a soubrette*
> Champagne, *an assistant to* Sganarelle, *a dancer*
> Dr. Slicer [Tomès]
> Dr. De Pits [De Fonandrès]
> Dr. Gouger [Macroton] } *doctors*
> Dr. Golfer [Bahays]
> Dr. Fillpocket [Filerin]
> Clitander, *in love with Lucinda*
> A Justice
> A Mountebank, *a quack, seller of the cure-all "Orviétan"*
> Buffoons and Scaramouches, *assistants to the Mountebank*
> The Spirit of Comedy
> Musicians
> Singers
> Dancers
> Servants, etc.

5

The action takes place in Paris, in the house and drawing room of SGANARELLE [*and also on a street in Paris*].

ACT I

Scene 1

Enter SGANARELLE, AMINTA, LUCRETIA, MR. WILLIAMS, *and* MR. JOSSE.

SGANARELLE.   Life is strange. I agree with that great classical philosopher who said that those who have wealth also have woe,° and that misery breeds more misery. I've been married only once, and my wife is now dead.

---

1 *woe:* Ecclesiastes 2:9–11.

MR. WILLIAMS.   How many wives would you have liked?

SGANARELLE.   Don't mock, Mr. Williams; my loss is great, and I'm still sad when I think about her. I never liked her lifestyle, and we argued a great deal, but Death, as they say, settles everything. She's dead and I'm sorry, but if she were alive we would still be fighting. Of all the children that Heaven blessed us with, only my daughter has survived, but she is my greatest sorrow because she is sad beyond belief—in a deep depression I can't get her out of. Beyond that, she won't tell me what's wrong. I'm almost beside myself, and I need your good advice. You [*to* LUCRETIA] are my niece. You [*to* AMINTA] are my neighbor. You [*to* MR. WILLIAMS *and* MR. JOSSE] are my friends and equals. What should I do?

MR. JOSSE.   I believe that jewelry is what young women like best, and if I were you I would buy her some nice necklaces, brooches, or rings set with expensive diamonds, rubies, and emeralds.

MR. WILLIAMS.   If I were in your position, I'd get her an elegant tapestry showing a landscape or historical scene. The sight of something like that in her room would pick up both her vision and her spirits.

AMINTA.   If you ask me, I wouldn't do anything of the sort. Rather, I'd get her married off as soon as possible—maybe to the man who, they say, asked you for her hand some time ago.

LUCRETIA.   I don't agree. She's not ready for marriage, and she's not strong enough to bear children. For her, having babies would be a quick way to go six feet under. She's too good for this world, and I think you should send her off to a convent, where she'll be able to do things to suit her special personality.

SGANARELLE.   I appreciate your thoughts, but they seem more to your interests than mine. You are a jeweler, Mr. Josse, and your advice would probably make you a handsome profit. You, Mr. Williams, have a tapestry shop, and I think you're trying to get rid of a little excess inventory. I've heard that your boyfriend, neighbor Aminta, is carrying a torch for my daughter, and you'd therefore like to have her married off and out of circulation. And as for you, my dear niece, you know that I have no plans to consent to a marriage for my daughter—I've got my reasons—but your advice to send her to religious orders suggests that you wouldn't mind becoming the only heir to all my money. So, ladies and gentlemen, your advice is perhaps the best in the world, but, if you please, I want none of it. Please go.

[*They leave, grumbling to themselves.* SGANARELLE *then speaks sarcastically to the audience.*]

There you have modern, up-to-date friends, who give their impersonal advice with no hope of gain whatever.

Act I, Scene 2

He remains. Enter LUCINDA.

SGANARELLE.   [*Aside.*] That's my daughter taking a walk for exercise. She doesn't see me; she's sighing. Now she's raising her eyes to Heaven. [*To* LUCINDA.] Bless you, Lucinda. What's the matter? Why so sad and sorrowful? Why don't you tell me what's wrong? You can trust your dear old dad, so tell me what's on your mind. Don't worry. Give me a kiss, like a good little girl. [*Aside.*] I can't stand seeing her like this. [*To*

LUCINDA.] Do you want me to die with unhappiness because of you? Won't you tell me what's troubling you? Tell me what's wrong and I'll do anything for you, I promise. Just tell me what's making you sad, because I swear on a stack of Bibles that there's nothing I won't do to make you happy. Tell me what you want. Are you jealous of any friends because they seem better dressed? I'll get you clothes that will make theirs seem like rags.—No? Does your room seem bare? I'll let you pick out the best furniture to be found anywhere.—No again? Well, maybe you want to learn music; I'll get you the best piano teacher there is.—Not that either? Maybe you're in love, and would like to be married. [*LUCINDA nods her head in agreement.*]

Act I, Scene 3

They remain. Enter LISETTE.

LISETTE.   Sir, you've just been chatting with your daughter. Did she tell you what's wrong?

SGANARELLE.   No, she's being bitchy and it's making me mad.

LISETTE.   Let me try; I'll sound her out a little.

SGANARELLE.   It won't work. Since she's so stubborn, let her alone.

LISETTE.   Just let me try. She may be more open with me than you. [*To LUCINDA.*   5
During LISETTE's speech, which SGANARELLE also overhears, he gets increasingly irritated with his daughter.] Now, Madam, let us know what's wrong; don't keep on like this and upset everybody. It seems to me that something really mysterious is bothering you, and if you won't tell your father, maybe you'll tell me. Do you want anything from him? You know that he'll spare no expense for you. Do you want him to give you more freedom? More promenades in the park? More presents to tempt your fancy?—No? Maybe you're angry with someone, then.—No? Well then, maybe you have a secret wish to get married, and you'd like your father's consent. [*LUCINDA nods enthusiastically.*]—Ah, that's it; why all the secrecy? Sir, the mystery is solved, and—

SGANARELLE.   [*Interrupting her.*] Get away, you ingrate; I won't talk to you any more. Be as stubborn as you like.

LUCINDA.   Father, since you want me to tell you—

SGANARELLE.   No, I'm finished with you.

LISETTE.   Sir, her sadness—

SGANARELLE.   She's a hussy, and enjoys hurting me.   10

LUCINDA.   Father, I want—

SGANARELLE.   Is this the gratitude I get for bringing you up so well?

LISETTE.   But, sir—

SGANARELLE.   No, I'm so mad I may have a stroke.

LUCINDA.   But, Father—   15

SGANARELLE.   I no longer have a speck of kindness for you.

LISETTE.   But—

SGANARELLE.   She's a cheap wench.

LISETTE.   But—

SGANARELLE.   An ungrateful slut.   20

LISETTE.   But—

SGANARELLE.   A trollop, who won't tell me what's wrong with her.

LISETTE.   It's a husband that she wants!

SGANARELLE.   [*Hearing but deliberately ignoring this piece of information.*] I'll turn her out of my house.

LISETTE.   A husband!

SGANARELLE.   I detest her.

LISETTE.   [*Shouting increasingly more loudly.*] A husband!

SGANARELLE.   And I disown her as my daughter.

LISETTE.   A husband!

SGANARELLE.   No, don't talk to me about it.

LISETTE.   A husband!

SGANARELLE.   Don't talk to me about it.

LISETTE.   A husband!

SGANARELLE.   Don't talk to me about it.

LISETTE.   A husband, a husband, a husband!

[*SGANARELLE stalks off.*]

Act I, Scene 4

LISETTE and LUCINDA remain.

LISETTE.   It's really true that none are so deaf as those who refuse to hear.

LUCINDA.   [*Ironically.*] Well, Lisette, you see how wrong I was to hide my feelings, and how all I had to do was to tell my father about everything I wanted.

LISETTE.   My God, he's a hard man. I swear, I'd enjoy playing some kind of trick on him to show him up. But why, Madam, did you hide your wishes from me?

LUCINDA.   Alas, what would I have gained? I might just as well have kept the secret for the rest of my life. Do you think I didn't foresee what he would do? I know his temper, and I'm in despair about the refusal he gave to the envoy sent to him to propose marriage to me. I've lost hope.

LISETTE.   [*As though recalling a forgotten incident.*] What's this? It's that stranger who arranged for the proposal, the one for whom you—

LUCINDA.   Perhaps it's not right for me to speak so freely, but I confess, if I had the liberty to choose, he's the one I'd want. We've never spoken together; he's never been able to tell me he loves me. But, in all the places where he's seen me, his looks and gestures have indicated such tenderness, and his formal request for my hand has given me such a sense of his honor, that I can't help believing he loves me. No matter; you see how my father's reaction has hardened all this tenderness.

LISETTE.   Well, I have to say, I think you shouldn't have kept things secret from me, but I'll still help you. You need to be certain of your determination—

LUCINDA.   But what should I do against my father's authority?—And if he won't listen to my hopes—

LISETTE.   Come on now, you can't let yourself be led around like a sheep. As long as you don't offend his honor, you can free yourself at least a little from him. What does he want with you? You're of age, and you're not made of stone. I say again I'll help you in this affair. Your interests are mine, and, you'll see, I know a thing or two—But I see your father; let's go in. Leave everything to me.

[*They hurry off.*]

Act I, Scene 5

Enter SGANARELLE.

SGANARELLE.   [*Laughing to himself.*] It's sometimes good to seem not to hear things you hear only too well. I was smart to sidestep that declaration of her hopes that I do not mean to satisfy. Is there anything more tyrannical than that custom by which marriage arrangements make paupers out of fathers?—Anything more futile and ridiculous than to spend your life grubbing and grabbing to get rich, and raising a daughter with care and love, only to be robbed of both of them at the hands of a total stranger, a nobody? No, no, I don't give a damn for that custom, and I'll keep my wealth and my daughter to myself.

Act I, Scene 6

He remains. Enter LISETTE.

LISETTE.   [*Pretending not to see SGANARELLE.*]—Oh unhappiness! Oh disgrace! Oh, poor Mr. Sganarelle! Where can I find him?
SGANARELLE.   [*Aside.*] What's all this?
LISETTE.   Oh unhappy father, what will you do when you learn about this?
SGANARELLE.   [*Aside.*] What's going on?
LISETTE.   My poor mistress!   5
SGANARELLE.   [*Aside.*] I'm lost!
LISETTE.   —Oh!
SGANARELLE.   [*Running after LISETTE.*] Lisette!
LISETTE.   [*Pretending not to hear him, but making sure he hears her.*] What a misfortune!
SGANARELLE.   —Lisette!   10
LISETTE.   [*Still pretending.*] What bad luck!
SGANARELLE.   —Lisette!
LISETTE.   [*Pretending yet.*] How ghastly awful!
SGANARELLE.   —Lisette!
LISETTE.   [*Pretending just now to have noticed him.*] Ah, Sir.   15
SGANARELLE.   What's going on? What's wrong?
LISETTE.   Sir, your daughter—
SGANARELLE.   Oh, no!
LISETTE.   Sir, sir, don't cry like that. [*Aside.*] You'll make me laugh if you keep on.
SGANARELLE.   Tell me quickly.   20
LISETTE.   You daughter was hurt by your words and scared by your anger. [*Dramatizing and exaggerating her following descriptions to the utmost.*] She went to her room and, in despair, she opened the window facing the river—
SGANARELLE.   Oh, my God, no!
LISETTE.   Then, raising her head heavenward, she said, "No, it's impossible for me to live with the anger of my father, and since he is disowning me, I want to die!"
SGANARELLE.   She threw herself out?

LISETTE.   No sir. She sorrowfully closed the window, and threw herself on her bed, where she wept bitterly. Suddenly, her face got pale, her eyes rolled in her head, her heart seemed to stop, and she fell into my arms!

SGANARELLE.   Oh, my poor daughter!

LISETTE.   By slapping her face and using smelling salts, I revived her. But she's getting worse, and I don't believe she can last the day.

SGANARELLE.   [*Calling to the offstage servant* CHAMPAGNE.] Champagne! Champagne! Champagne! [*Enter* CHAMPAGNE.] Quickly, go get the doctors, and as many as you can find! There can't be too many for this! Oh, my daughter, my poor daughter!

[*They leave quickly.*]

FIRST ENTR'ACTE

[CHAMPAGNE, *while dancing, knocks on the doors of four doctors, who begin dancing and then ceremoniously enter the house of the patient's father.*]

ACT II

Scene 1

Enter SGANARELLE *and* LISETTE.

LISETTE.   Why do you need four doctors, Sir? Just one alone is enough to kill you.

SGANARELLE.   Be quiet. Four opinions are better than one.

LISETTE.   Can't your daughter die by herself, without the help of these gentlemen?

SGANARELLE.   Do you mean to say that it's the doctor who causes death, and not the disease?

LISETTE.   Absolutely. I know a man who proved beyond doubt that we should never say, "This person died of a raging fever or a galloping consumption," but rather "That person was killed by the incompetence of two druggists and four doctors."

SGANARELLE.   Stop. You'll offend these gentlemen.

LISETTE.   Lord, Sir, our cat needed no drugs or treatment to recover from that jump she made from the rooftop to the street, and she didn't eat or move a muscle for three days. It's lucky for her there are no cat doctors, or they'd have wiped her out with their mindless purging and bleeding.

SGANARELLE.   Will you please keep your impertinent remarks to yourself? Here they are.

LISETTE.   Watch out. They'll tell you what you already know—that your daughter's sick. Only they'll bamboozle you by saying it in Latin!

Act II, Scene 2

Enter DR. SLICER, DR. GOUGER, DR. DE PITS, *and* DR. GOLFER.

SGANARELLE.   Welcome, gentlemen!

DR. SLICER.   [*Pompously.*] We have made our diagnosis of your daughter, and she unquestionably has many impurities in her.

SGANARELLE.   My daughter is impure?

DR. SLICER.   You must understand that it is her body that is full of impurities— many corrupt and putrid humors.°

SGANARELLE.   Oh, thank you, I understand.   5

DR. SLICER.   But, we plan to consult about her.

SGANARELLE.   [*To attending servants.*] Come, bring chairs for the doctors.

LISETTE.   [*To DR. SLICER.*] Doctor, is that you?

SGANARELLE.   How do you know Dr. Slicer?

LISETTE.   From having seen him the other day at the home of a good friend of   10
your niece.

DR. SLICER.   How is her coachman?

LISETTE.   Fabulous; he's dead.

DR. SLICER.   Dead?

LISETTE.   Yes, dead.

DR. SLICER.   That cannot be!   15

LISETTE.   I don't know if it couldn't happen, but I do know that it did.

DR. SLICER.   And I tell you he can't be dead.

LISETTE.   And I tell you he's dead and buried.

DR. SLICER.   You've made a mistake.

LISETTE.   I saw it with my own eyes.   20

DR. SLICER.   It's impossible. Hippocrates° says that patients don't die of this disease until the end of the second or third week, and he was sick for only six days.

LISETTE.   Let Hippocrates talk all he wants; the coachman is dead.

SGANARELLE.   [*To LISETTE.*] Be quiet, chatterbox; we should leave. [*To the doctors.*] Gentlemen, we will leave you in peace for your consultation. I know it's not customary to pay in advance, but I'll pay you now, before I forget.

[*He pays them, and each one, upon receiving the fee, makes a different show of thanks. SGANA-RELLE and LISETTE then leave.*]

Act II, Scene 3

DR. SLICER, DR. GOUGER, DR. DE PITS, and DR. GOLFER remain.

DR. DE PITS.   Paris is an incredibly large city, and a good medical practice requires long trips.

DR. SLICER.   I have an excellent mule for that; you won't believe the distances I make him go each day.

DR. DE PITS.   I have a marvelous horse; he never gets tired.

DR. SLICER.   Do you know the ground my mule has covered today? I was near the Arsenal first. Then I went to the suburb of St. Germain, from there to Le Marais, and then to St. Honoré Gate; after that to St. Jacques, to the Richelieu Gate, and finally here. When I leave, I'll go to the Place Royale.

---

4 *corrupt and putrid humors:* internal illness of body fluids.   21 *Hippocrates:* ancient Greek physician, known as the father of medicine.

DR. DE PITS.   My horse has gone to all those places today, and in addition I rode him all the way to Ruel so I could see a patient.

DR. SLICER.   By the way, what position do you gentlemen take in the controversy between Doctors Theophrastus and Artemius? This is a matter that's dividing the whole profession.

DR. DE PITS.   I think Artemius is right.

DR. SLICER.   I do too. It's true that his treatment killed the patient, and that the recommendation of Theophrastus was infinitely better, but in the circumstances, Theophrastus was wrong. He should not have ignored the recommendation of Artemius, who was, we must recognize, the senior physician in the case. What do you say about it?

DR. DE PITS.   Proper procedure should always be respected. I think we would be lost without our strict order of authority.

DR. SLICER.   I agree; I'm as severe about this as the devil—unless it's among friends. The other day three of us were consulting with an outside physician about a patient. I stopped the whole business until we proceeded in absolute order. Meanwhile, the people of the house did their best as the illness reached a crisis, but I continued to insist on proper consultative procedure. Before we could end our conference, the patient died—may he rest in peace.

DR. DE PITS.   Insisting on our rights like that is the best way to keep lay people in their place, and show them that we're in control.

DR. SLICER.   A dead person is a dead person, and of no importance; but any neglect of standard operating procedures puts our whole profession in a bad light.

Act II, Scene 4

They remain. Enter SGANARELLE.

SGANARELLE.   Gentlemen, my daughter's condition is becoming serious. Please tell me at once what you have decided.

DR. SLICER.   [*To DR. DE PITS.*] Sir, you speak.

DR. DE PITS.   No, Sir, you speak first.

DR. SLICER.   Please, Sir, don't be modest.

DR. DE PITS.   No, Sir, please, after you.

DR. SLICER.   Sir!

DR. DE PITS.   Sir!

SGANARELLE.   With all respect, gentlemen, forget your ceremony and remember our present urgency.

[*All four doctors now speak together.*]

DR. SLICER.   The illness of your daughter—

DR. DE PITS.   The judgment of all these gentlemen together—

DR. GOUGER.   After our most exhaustive consultation—

DR. GOLFER.   To consider the case step by step, we—

SGANARELLE.   Gentlemen, please, speak one at a time.

DR. SLICER.   Sir, we have reached a diagnosis of your daughter's illness. My opinion is that it stems from a sanguinary superabundance—too much blood, to you. So my recommendation is blood letting; as soon as possible you should let as much blood from her as you can.

DR. DE PITS. My best judgment is that her illness results from a putrefaction of   15
humors, caused by too much repletion. So my advice—listen carefully—is that she be
given an emetic.

DR. SLICER. I submit that an emetic will kill her.

DR. DE PITS. And I believe that a bleeding is contra-indicated; it will bring about
instant expiration—in other words, death.

DR. SLICER. [*Huffily, to DR. DE PITS.*] You of course are a great authority.

DR. DE PITS. [*Defensively, to DR. SLICER.*] Yes, I am; I'll outshine you in any branch
of medical knowledge.

DR. SLICER. Do you recall that your wrongheaded treatment killed a man the   20
other day?

DR. DE PITS. Do you recall that your bungling put a woman in her grave just
three days ago?

DR. SLICER. [*To SGANARELLE.*] I've given you my opinion.

DR. DE PITS. [*To SGANARELLE.*] And I've informed you of my professional
judgment.

DR. SLICER. If you don't bleed your daughter immediately, she'll be a goner. [*He
leaves.*]

DR. DE PITS. And if you do bleed her, she'll die in a quarter of an hour.   25

[*He leaves.*]

Act II, Scene 5

SGANARELLE, DR. GOUGER, and DR. GOLFER remain.

SGANARELLE. Which of the two should I believe, and what should I do with such
contrary advice? Gentlemen, I ask you to understand my predicament and tell me objectively what you believe would cure my daughter.

DR. GOUGER. [*He speaks agonizingly slowly, drawing out his syllables and even stressing
ordinarily silent letters.*] Sir, in these matters, we must proceed with circumspection, and, as
they say, do nothing rashly, because the mistakes that we may make, according to our
master, Hippocrates, may have dangerous consequences.

DR. GOLFER. [*This one speaks at breakneck speed.*] He's right; we must be careful in
what we do. This is not a child's game, and when we fail, it's not easy to repair the
damage and restore the dead to life: *Experimentum periculosum:* in other words, medicine
is a perilous experiment that we learn from as we go along. That's why we must reason
carefully, weigh the alternatives, consider individual cases, examine all the possible
causes of the illness, and see what remedies we may bring to the patient.

SGANARELLE. [*Aside.*] One is as slow as a turtle, the other as fast as a jackrabbit.

DR. GOUGER. [*He is the turtle.*] Therefore, Sir, to get down to the matter, I find   5
that your daughter is sick. She has a chronic sickness which will get worse unless it gets
better, for her symptoms indicate a pathological and mordant—that is to say, bad—vapor
which penetrates the membranes of the brain. Now this vapor, which is called *atmos* in
Greek, is caused by putrid, tenacious, and glutinous humors which are contained in the
lower bowel.

DR. GOLFER. [*He is the jackrabbit.*] And, inasmuch as these humors were engendered there during an extended period, they have turned adust—that is, they have been
overcooked, so to speak—and have produced the present pathology of the brain.

DR. GOUGER.   [*Still speaking slowly.*] Therefore, in order that we may draw out, detach, withdraw, expel, and evacuate these said humors, we must recommend an aggressive treatment of purgation. But first, I find, it would not be improper to prescribe anodynes of emollients° and cleansing solutions, together with refreshing medicinal juleps and syrups to be mixed with her herbal tea and her tonic.

DR. GOLFER.   After this, should come purging and bleeding, to be repeated as necessary.

DR. GOUGER.   This does not mean that your daughter won't die after all this, but at least you will have done your best, and may be consoled by the realization that she died in accordance with proper procedures.

DR. GOLFER.   It's much better to die by the rules than to recover in spite of them.

DR. GOUGER.   We are giving you our best professional advice.

DR. GOLFER.   And we have spoken to you as though you were our brother.

SGANARELLE.   [*To DR. GOUGER, drawing out his words.*] I thank you most humbly, Sir. [*To DR. GOLFER, as rapidly as possible.*] To you, Sir, I am infinitely obliged for the care that you have taken.

[*The doctors exit.*]

Act II, Scene 6

SGANARELLE, alone.

SGANARELLE.   Now I'm more uncertain than ever. What can I do? [*He ponders this question for a few moments.*] I've got an idea: I've heard about a medicine that can cure everything, which they make down in Orvieto, Italy. It's a marvelous new elixir called "Orviétan." The advertising says it's cured millions of people. I'll buy some for her. It's got to work.

[*He leaves.*]

Act II, Scene 7

A Street. Enter SGANARELLE and MOUNTEBANK, accompanied by his BUFFOONS and SCARAMOUCHES.

SGANARELLE.   Hello, Sir. Please give me a bottle of your amazing new drug, Orviétan. How much does it cost?

MOUNTEBANK.   [*Singing.*]

> *Would the gold in the richest of mines*
> *Be enough for this all-curing pill?*
> *By its magic it separates the ill*
> *From more ailments than forests have pines.*
> > *Agues and itches,*
> > *Fevers and twitches,*
> > *Plagues and neuroses,*
> > *Funks and psychoses,*
> > *Measles, congestions,*

7 *anodynes of emollients:* soothing lotions.

Strokes and depressions,
Organs that fail you,
All things that ail you—
All can be cured by my Orviétan, my Orviétan,
All can be cured by my Orviétan.

SGANARELLE.   Sir, I believe that all the gold in the world is not enough to pay you
for your medicine. However, here's five hundred for you.
MOUNTEBANK.   [*Singing.*]

Sing my praise, for these pills, I surmise—
Such a bargain for such a small cost—
Give new strength to those lives that are tossed
By diseases the heavens devise.
   Agues and itches,
   Fevers and twitches,
   Plagues and neuroses,
   Funks and psychoses,
   Measles, congestions,
   Strokes and depressions,
   Organs that fail you,
   All things that ail you—
All can be cured by my Orviétan, my Orviétan,
All can be cured by my Orviétan.

[*Exit SGANARELLE.*]

SECOND ENTR'ACTE
A dance by the MOUNTEBANK'S BUFFOONS and SCARAMOUCHES.

ACT III

Scene 1

Enter DR. FILLPOCKET, DR. SLICER, and DR. DE PITS.

DR. FILLPOCKET.   Gentlemen, as men of your experience you should be ashamed
to have been so imprudent as to quarrel like young blockheads. Don't you see that such
open arguments hurt us in the public eye? Isn't it enough that expert critics know all
about the controversy and dissension among our authorities and ancient masters, without disclosing our humbug to the world by wrangling in front of spectators? I'm concerned that some members of our profession mismanage their public relations so badly,
because lately we've been hurt, and if we're not careful we may ruin ourselves. I have
nothing to lose in this, because I've already made my pile. Let it blow, rain, and hail,
the dead are dead, and I'm rich enough not to fear the living. But in the long run, our
squabbles and disputes don't advance the medical profession. Since Heaven has smiled
on us and enabled us to hoodwink the public for centuries, let's not disabuse people by
our excesses, but let us go on taking advantage of the gullible—and thereby go on
making our bundles. You know we're not the only profession to prey on human vulnerability; it's the major study of half the world's population. Everyone wants to catch

people in moments of weakness in order to cash in. Flatterers, for example, benefit from the human need for praise, and so they lay it on with a trowel; some people have made huge fortunes in this way. Alchemists benefit from people's greed by promising mountains of gold to fools stupid enough to invest in their phony technology about making gold out of lead. And people even pour money into those consummate fakers, the psychics, who manipulate the vanity and ambition of their victims by making rosy predictions about the future. But the greatest weakness of humanity is the love of life—yes, our instinct for self-preservation—and we, as doctors, all profit from it, even with our pompous nonsense. We reap gigantic rewards because of the worship and adoration that our profession gains from our patients' fear of death. Let us then preserve the high esteem that human fallibility has given us, and let us, in the eyes of that world of believers out there, agree to take the credit for our cures while we deceive people by convincing them to blame Nature for our blunders. Let's not go about, I say, stupidly destroying the happy continuation of this public misperception which puts bread on our tables; and from the dead, whom we put into the ground, let us raise up our boundless wealth.

DR. SLICER.   [*Spellbound.*] You are so right—so very right. But our dispute arose simply from hot blood, which we cannot always control.

DR. FILLPOCKET.   All right, then, gentlemen, put rancor aside, and make your apologies now.

DR. DE PITS.   I agree, if my emetic can be given to our present patient then Dr. Slicer can do as he pleases with the next patient.

DR. FILLPOCKET.   I couldn't say it better myself, and I'm glad to see good sense prevail.

DR. DE PITS.   It's done.

DR. FILLPOCKET.   Shake hands, then. [*DR. DE PITS and DR. SLICER shake hands.*] Goodbye. And next time, be more careful.

[*Exit DR. FILLPOCKET.*]

Act III, Scene 2

DR. DE PITS and DR. SLICER remain. Enter LISETTE.

LISETTE.   Gentlemen, how can you stand there without seeking a way of getting even for the attack that has just been made against the practice of medicine?

DR. SLICER.   What do you mean?

LISETTE.   A brazen fellow has just had the nerve to practice your profession without a licence; he has just wiped out another fellow with a sword clean through the body.

DR. SLICER.   Listen, you can make fun of us now, but some day you'll be sick, and then we'll get you in our clutches.

LISETTE.   When I'm ready, then I'll give you permission to do me in.

[*Exit the doctors.*]

Act III, Scene 3

LISETTE remains. Enter CLITANDER, dressed as a doctor.

CLITANDER.   Well, Lisette, what do you think of my outfit? Do you think I can fool our gentleman with it? Do I look the part of a doctor?

LISETTE.   You look fine, but you're late. It's good that Heaven has made me so good-natured. I can't see two lovers sighing for each other without feeling soft myself, and wishing to satisfy their longing. Hang the consequences, I've sworn to free Lucinda from her tyranny and give her to you. I liked you from the first. I'm an authority when it comes to men, and she couldn't have made a better choice than you. True love requires great risks, and we have devised a scheme that we hope will succeed. Our plans are already moving ahead. The man we're dealing with is not one of your brightest in the world, and if we fail now, we can find a thousand other ways to reach our goal. Wait for me alone over there; I'll be right back to get you.

[*CLITANDER leaves.*]

Act III, Scene 4

LISETTE remains. Enter SGANARELLE.

LISETTE.   Sir, joy, joy!
SGANARELLE.   What's this?
LISETTE.   Rejoice.
SGANARELLE.   What for?
LISETTE.   And again, I say, rejoice!   5
SGANARELLE.   Tell me what's going on, and then I'll rejoice—maybe.
LISETTE.   No, I want you to rejoice in advance; I want you to sing and dance!
SGANARELLE.   Upon what?
LISETTE.   Upon my word.
SGANARELLE.   Okay, then. [*He sings and dances.*] La lera la la, la lera la. What the   10
devil!
LISETTE.   Sir, your daughter is cured!
SGANARELLE.   My daughter is cured?
LISETTE.   Yes. I am bringing you a doctor, but not just any doctor. He is the most important doctor on earth, who makes miraculous cures and puts all other doctors to shame.
SGANARELLE.   Where is he?
LISETTE.   I'll have him come in. [*She leaves.*]   15
SGANARELLE.   [*Alone.*] Let's see if this one will do better than the others.

Act III, Scene 5

SGANARELLE remains. Enter LISETTE and CLITANDER in his doctor's robes.

LISETTE.   [*Leading CLITANDER.*] Here he is.
SGANARELLE.   This doctor has only a small growth of beard.
LISETTE.   Science is not measured by a beard, and he did not get his degrees because of his chin.
SGANARELLE.   Sir, I'm told that you have effective medications for regular bowel movements.
CLITANDER.   Sir, my remedies are entirely unique. Other doctors use emetics,   5
bleeding, medicines, and enemas, but I cure by words, sounds, letters, signs, and mystical rings.

LISETTE.   What did I tell you?

SGANARELLE.   Here is a great man!

LISETTE.   Sir, since your daughter is up and around, I'll get her over here.

SGANARELLE.   Please do. [*LISETTE leaves.*]

CLITANDER.   [*Taking SGANARELLE's pulse.*] Your daughter is indeed sick.

SGANARELLE.   You know that from taking *my* pulse?

CLITANDER.   Yes, because of the sympathetic vibrations passing between father and daughter.

Act III, Scene 6

SGANARELLE and CLITANDER remain. Enter LUCINDA and LISETTE.

LISETTE.   [*To CLITANDER.*] Here, Sir, take this chair. [*To SGANARELLE.*] Let's go and leave them together.

SGANARELLE.   Why? I want to stay here.

LISETTE.   Are you kidding? We should go; a doctor has a hundred questions that it's not right for us to hear.

[*SGANARELLE and LISETTE move to a side of the stage.*]

CLITANDER.   [*Speaking to LUCINDA alone.*] Ah, Madam, I'm so overwhelmed with joy I hardly know how to begin speaking to you! When I could speak only with my eyes, I thought I had hundreds of things to say; but now that I have freedom to say what I want, I feel tongue-tied, and my happiness stifles my words.

LUCINDA.   I feel the same thing, and like you I sense movements of joy that catch in my throat and prevent my speaking.

CLITANDER.   Ah, Madam, I would be so happy if you felt everything I feel, and if I could judge your heart by mine! But, Madam, may I believe that you were the one who thought of this happy stratagem that gives me such joy in your presence?

LUCINDA.   If you don't owe me the idea, at least you should know that I approved it eagerly.

SGANARELLE.   [*To LISETTE.*] He seems very close to her.

LISETTE.   [*To SGANARELLE.*] He's a doctor, and he's studying her facial features.

CLITANDER.   [*To LUCINDA.*] Will you be faithful, Madam, in the promises you make to me?

LUCINDA.   And you, will you be firm in your present resolutions?

CLITANDER.   Ah, Madam, until death, and I'll demonstrate my love by what I'm now about to do.

SGANARELLE.   [*To CLITANDER.*] Well, our patient seems to be perking up.

CLITANDER.   That's because I've already tried one of the remedies of my great art on her. The mind has power over the body, and sickness often begins in the mind. My method is therefore to cure the spirit first before treating the body. Accordingly, I have studied her looks, her facial features, and the lines of her two hands; and by the science bestowed on me by Heaven, I have determined that her sickness is psychosomatic—she is sick in spirit. This disease comes entirely from her disordered imagination, which prompts her depraved wish to be married. My view is that there is nothing more extravagant or ridiculous than this wish for marriage.

SGANARELLE.   [*Aside.*] This is indeed a man of skill!

CLITANDER.   And all my life I have had, and will continue to have, an aversion for it.

SGANARELLE.   [*Aside.*] A great physician!

CLITANDER.   But, since it's necessary to flatter the imagination of patients, and because I see schizophrenic tendencies in her, and also because it would be perilous not to treat her quickly, I have taken advantage of her weakness and told her that I came here to ask you for her hand in marriage. When she heard that, her appearance changed for the better, her complexion brightened, and her eyes sparkled. I believe that if you keep her in this error for several days, you will see her recover completely.

SGANARELLE.   There's nothing I want more.

CLITANDER.   Afterwards we'll apply other remedies to cure her of this fantasy entirely.   20

SGANARELLE.   That will be marvellous! [*To* LUCINDA.] Well, daughter, here is a gentleman who wishes to marry you, and I have told him he has my blessing!

LUCINDA.   Dear me, is this possible?

SGANARELLE.   Yes.

LUCINDA.   I'm not dreaming?

SGANARELLE.   No, you're not dreaming.   25

LUCINDA.   [*To* CLITANDER.] You really want to be my husband?

CLITANDER.   Yes, Madam.

LUCINDA.   And my father consents?

SGANARELLE.   Yes, daughter.

LUCINDA.   If this is true, I couldn't be happier!   30

CLITANDER.   Don't doubt it, Madam. It is not just today that I began loving you and longing to marry you. I came here only to ask for your hand, and, if you want to know the whole truth exactly as it is, this doctor's costume is nothing more than a false front. I pretended to be a doctor only to come close to you, the more easily to realize my goal of marrying you.

LUCINDA.   This all shows me the proofs of your tender love. I am deeply moved by them.

SGANARELLE.   [*Aside.*] Oh, the fool! the fool! the fool!

LUCINDA.   You approve of this gentleman as my husband, father, and do so willingly?

SGANARELLE.   Yes. Give me your hand, and you, Sir, give me yours, too, by way of witness.   35

CLITANDER.   But, Sir—

SGANARELLE.   [*Stifling laughter.*] No, no, it's to—it's to ease her mind. Now, join hands. There, it's done.

CLITANDER.   Accept as a token of my faith this ring that I give you. [*Speaking low, to* SGANARELLE.] It's a special ring to cure her distracted mind.

LUCINDA.   Let us draw up the contract, so that everything will be complete.

CLITANDER.   Certainly; I would like that, Madam. [*To* SGANARELLE.] I'll show   40
her the man who writes my prescriptions, and make her believe he's a genuine Justice.

SGANARELLE.   Excellent!

CLITANDER.   [*Calling offstage.*] You there, send in the Justice I brought with me!

LUCINDA.   What, you brought along a Justice?

CLITANDER.   Yes, Madam.

LUCINDA.   I'm delighted!   45
SGANARELLE.   [*Chuckling.*] Oh, the fool! the fool!

Act III, Scene 7

They all remain. Enter the JUSTICE, *appropriately robed.* CLITANDER *whispers to the* JUSTICE.

SGANARELLE.   [*To the* JUSTICE.] Welcome, Sir. I commission you to draft a contract for these two young people. Please begin writing. [*While the* JUSTICE *is writing,* SGANARELLE *speaks to* LUCINDA.] This will be a contract to end all contracts. [*To the* JUSTICE.] I give her twenty million upon her marriage. Write that down!

LUCINDA.   I'm so overwhelmingly grateful to you, father.

JUSTICE.   [*Giving the contract to* SGANARELLE.] There, it's done; you need only to come and sign.

SGANARELLE.   How's that for a contract speedily finished?

CLITANDER.   [*To* SGANARELLE.] At least, Sir—

SGANARELLE.   No, no words of gratitude; say nothing, I beg you. [*Aside to* CLITANDER.] Don't we both know what we're doing? [*To the* JUSTICE.] Come, give him the pen. [*After* CLITANDER *signs,* SGANARELLE *gives the pen to* LUCINDA.] Come, come, sign it. Go ahead; I'll sign too. [*He signs.*]

LUCINDA.   No, no. I want to hold the contract myself.

SGANARELLE.   All right, take it. [*After she has signed.*] Now, are you happy?

LUCINDA.   More than you can imagine!

SGANARELLE.   I'm please. I'm very pleased.

CLITANDER.   As for the rest, I not only took the trouble to bring a Justice along, but to celebrate the occasion I brought singers and musicians too. Send them in! These are the people I take with me every day on my rounds; I direct them, with their harmony, to pacify the troubled minds of my patients.

Final Scene

All remain. Enter the SPIRIT OF COMEDY, DANCERS, *and* MUSICIANS.

ALL THREE [*COMEDY, DANCERS, and MUSICIANS*].
If you didn't have music and singing and dancing,
You'd spend your life with your mind in chains;
For it's we, with our wonderful songs and our prancing,
Who win the fight against aches and pains.

COMEDY

Do you want to break free,
In the happiest way,
From the mis'ry and grief
Of each long day?
Then sing your song
The whole day long;
Throw away your medicine,
Along with the jar it's in,

And join our throng
As we sing along.

ALL THREE

If you didn't have music and singing and dancing,
You'd spend your life with your mind in chains;
For it's we, with our wonderful songs and our prancing,
Who win the fight against aches and pains.

[*While they are singing and dancing, and amidst all the Games, Smiles, and Pleasures,*
CLITANDER *leads* LUCINDA *away.*]

SGANARELLE.   This is a marvelous way to cure someone! But where is my daughter,
and where is the doctor?
LISETTE.   They left—to complete the rest of the marriage ritual.
SGANARELLE.   What are you saying? What—what marriage?
LISETTE.   In truth, Sir, the game has been bagged, and what you thought was a
joke turns out to be the absolute truth!
SGANARELLE.   [*The* DANCERS *catch hold of him and bring him into the dance by force.*]
What's this? The devil! Let me go! Let me go, I tell you! Still more? A plague on
everything!

[*Finis.*]

QUESTIONS

Act I

1. What does the opening scene indicate about Sganarelle's responses to other
   people? Describe his traits. What do you learn about his economic status? Why
   is this status important in the plot?

2. Describe the father-daughter relationship that is brought out in scenes 2 and
   3. Why is the relationship made to seem comic and not serious?

3. Why is it important that we learn about a suitor whom Lucinda likes, and that
   there has been an "envoy" from him seeking to negotiate a marriage?

4. Describe Lisette. Is she flat or round, representative or individualized? Why is
   she important? What is her relationship with Lucinda?

5. Why does Sganarelle not want his daughter married? What do his reasons disclose about him? What effect does Sganarelle's behavior toward his daughter
   have on your attitude toward him at the play's conclusion?

Act II

6. Why is Sganarelle dramatized as a person with great faith in doctors? Why is
   Lisette skeptical about them?

7. Study the dialogue between Lisette and Dr. Slicer (scene 2, paragraphs 8–22).
   Describe how character and speech here produce laughter.

8. At the end of scene 2 a stage direction describes Sganarelle's payment to the doctors. Explain how pantomime and dance might be used here to augment Molière's satiric presentation of doctors. Be specific.

9. Though scene 3 is supposedly a medical "consultation" about the condition of Lucinda, the conversation has nothing to do with her. What does Molière achieve by introducing the topics the doctors actually discuss?

10. What treatments do the doctors prescribe for Lucinda? Though the doctors are contradictory, in what respects are some of them truthful? Why is their telling the truth comic?

11. Explain Sganarelle's role in the scenes with the doctors. What is the effect of these scenes on his seeking out the Mountebank, and also on his reception of Clitander in the next act when Clitander appears disguised as a doctor?

Act III

12. Why does Dr. Fillpocket make such a long speech? How honest is he? Would he give this speech to anyone but fellow doctors? Is Molière's treatment of the speech comic? Serious? True? Partly true? Untrue?

13. What is the stratagem devised by Lisette and Clitander? How is it related to Sganarelle's already proven faith in doctors and medication?

14. Explain the irony of Clitander's confession to Lucinda and also of Sganarelle's responses beginning in scene 6, and extending to the revelation in the last scene. How does Molière keep the final scene light and comic?

15. How does Sganarelle react to the news that the marriage of Lucinda and Clitander is real? How is his reaction kept from seeming serious? If you were a director, what might you tell the actor playing Sganarelle to do during the concluding dance? Why?

GENERAL QUESTIONS

1. Who is the protagonist of *Love Is the Doctor*? What conflicts develop? Who and what are the antagonists? Which "side" is triumphant at the end?

2. A traditional topic for laughter is that the "biter gets bitten" and the "tables are turned." To what degree does Molière use this topic in the play? How successful is it as a means of developing humor?

3. The critic Harold C. Knutson has observed that in *Love Is the Doctor* we have "a particularly biting commentary on doctors and doctoring," and that one of the modes of satire is that the doctors "drop the mask and betray their callousness" and "contentiousness," and that their "concern" is not with their patients but rather with rules and formalities (*Molière: An Archetypal Approach* [Toronto: U of Toronto Press, 1976], pp. 52–53). Do you agree or disagree with Professor Knutson's observations? Explain in detail.

4. Aside from the medical satire, describe the various doctors as characters. Which of the doctors is the most fully developed? Which are most amusing? Why?

COMEDY FROM MOLIÈRE TO THE PRESENT

The subject of comedy in the centuries from Molière to the present is vast. In all the major European countries, and eventually in the United States, there were many comic dramatists. Some of them were successful in their time but are neglected today, such as Eugène Scribe in France, and some are known for works other than their comedies. In England in the seventeenth century, dramatists such as William Wycherley (1640–1716) and William Congreve (1670–1729) created a sophisticated type of drama, in the comedy of manners tradition, that is termed **Restoration comedy** because it developed after King Charles II was restored to the English throne in 1660. The Restoration comedies combined and contrasted elegant and boisterous manners, and they often dealt with serious social and sexual problems. In the first part of the eighteenth century, dramatists created "sentimental" drama. Sentimental comedies showed individuals who verge on behavioral excesses but who eventually conform to morality because they are good at heart—hence the term *sentimental.*

The first half of the eighteenth century saw the popularity of other forms, such as the musical play and the burlesque play. The musical play was first known as **ballad opera**, and later it was called **comic opera** and **musical comedy**. The characteristic of the musical play was the combination of spoken dialogue and brief songs. The first such play was *The Beggar's Opera* (1728) by John Gay (1685–1732).[6] *The Beggar's Opera* was also a burlesque that satirized the Italian operas so popular in the early eighteenth century. Henry Fielding (1707–1754), known for his later novels, wrote perhaps the best of the burlesques, *Tom Thumb, or The Tragedy of Tragedies* (1730, 1731), and, in addition, he wrote ballad operas in the manner of *The Beggar's Opera.* Also unique in Fielding's comic writing were a number of five-act plays dealing with serious social situations. The comic opera reached its high point in the nineteenth century with the Savoy Operas of William Gilbert (1836–1911) and Arthur Sullivan (1842–1900). The Gilbert and Sullivan operas, such as *H.M.S. Pinafore* (1878) and *The Mikado* (1885), are regularly performed today by both professionals and amateurs. In the United States during the twentieth century, the musical comedy form became a major force, as with the plays of Richard Rodgers (1902–1979) and Oscar Hammerstein II (1895–1960) and of Alan Jay Lerner (1918–1986) and Frederick Loewe (1901–1987).

In the later nineteenth century, the major comic dramatists who were more or less in the pure comic tradition were Oscar Wilde (1854–1900) and George Bernard Shaw (1856–1950), whose plays are still regularly revived and well attended. The twentieth century marked the appearance of important comic dramatists, including many, like Eugene O'Neill and Tennessee Williams, who are better known for more serious plays (see pp. 1271 and 1704). A number of writers divided their time between theater and film, as with George Kaufman (1889–1961), whose *The Man Who Came to Dinner* (1939) was success-

---

[6] See p. 781 for a song from *The Beggar's Opera.*

ful both onstage and on the screen. For a time, Kaufman also wrote scripts for some of the early film comedies of the Marx Brothers. Many other comic playwrights experimented with comedy. Such a writer is Arthur Kopit (b. 1937), whose *Oh Dad, Poor Dad, Mamma's Hung You in the Closet and I'm Feelin' so Sad* (1961) created a great stir when it was first performed. Of particular note is the development of the Theater of the Absurd. Some significant plays in this tradition are *Waiting for Godot* (1953) by Samuel Becket (1906–1989), *Rhinocéros* (1960) by Jean Genet (1910–1986), *The Sandbox* (1959) by Edward Albee (b. 1928), and *The Homecoming* (1960) by Harold Pinter (b. 1930).

It is fair to say that comedy today is characterized by great variety. All the types described earlier are being written (see pp. 1540-43). Serious plays may contain comic and farcical elements. Comic and farcical plays may introduce serious sequences and also may contain strong elements of satire. Satirical plays may contain songs to complement the onstage action and also to divert and entertain. It is clear that writers at the end of the twentieth century were combining the various comic forms that were brought into prominence by writers since the time of Molière.

ANTON CHEKHOV, *THE BEAR*

Anton Chekhov was born in Taganrog in southern Russia in 1860, the son of a merchant and grandson of a serf. He entered medical school in Moscow in 1879, graduating in 1884. While a student he was also obligated to help support his family, and he turned to writing stories, jokes, and potboilers for pay under a variety of pen names, one of which was "The Doctor without Patients." *The Bear* belongs to the end of this early period, ten years before Chekhov's association with the Moscow Art Theater at the end of the century (see also p. 1659).

Chekhov minimized *The Bear*, referring to it as a "joke" and a "vaudeville"—both words suggesting a farcical work with little form or substance. Nevertheless, the play was greatly acclaimed and financially successful, to the author's amazement and delight. Three months after its first performance in 1888, he likened *The Bear* to a "milk cow" ("cash cow") because, to his happiness, it earned him a steady income.

The Bear is a farce, a dramatic form designed preeminently to evoke laughter, and it therefore contains extravagant language and boisterous and sudden action. But there is also an underlying seriousness that sustains the humor. In their way, both Smirnov and Mrs. Popov have been failures; they could conceivably sink into lives of depression and futility, and both are walking a very fine wire as the play begins. Chekhov makes clear that Mrs. Popov is filled with resentment at her unfaithful and now dead husband, and also that she is chafing under her self-imposed resolution to lead a life of mourning and self-denial in his memory. Smirnov is having difficulty with creditors, and he admits that his relationships with the many women he has known have ended unhappily. He is therefore both cynical and angry.

The climax of the play is the improbable and preposterous challenge that Smirnov offers Mrs. Popov, resolved by the equally sudden and preposterous outcome. Despite the improbabilities of the play, however, the actions are not impossible because they manifest the true internal needs of the main characters. Chekhov's friend Leo Tolstoy, who criticized some of Chekhov's late plays, laughed heartily at *The Bear*, and countless audiences and readers since then have joined him in laughter.

ANTON CHEKHOV (1860–1904)

The Bear, A Joke in One Act ——————————————— *1900*

CAST OF CHARACTERS

Mrs. Popov. *A widow of seven months, Mrs. Popov is small and pretty, with dimples. She is a landowner. At the start of the play, she is pining away in memory of her dead husband.*
Grigory Stepanovich Smirnov. *Easily angered and loud, Smirnov is older. He is a landowner, too, and a man of substance.*
Luka. *Luka is Mrs. Popov's footman (a servant whose main tasks were to wait table and attend the carriages, in addition to general duties). He is old enough to feel secure in telling Mrs. Popov what he thinks.*
Gardener, Coachman, Workmen, *who enter at the end.*

SCENE. *The drawing room of MRS. POPOV's country home.*

[*MRS. POPOV, in deep mourning, does not remove her eyes from a photograph.*]

LUKA. It isn't right, madam . . . you're only destroying yourself. . . . The chambermaid and the cook have gone off berry picking; every living being is rejoicing; even the cat knows how to be content, walking around the yard catching birds, and you sit in your room all day as if it were a convent, and you don't take pleasure in anything. Yes, really! Almost a year has passed since you've gone out of the house!

MRS. POPOV. And I shall never go out. . . . What for? My life is already ended. *He* lies in his grave; I have buried myself in these four walls . . . we are both dead.

LUKA. There you go again! Your husband is dead, that's as it was meant to be, it's the will of God, may he rest in peace. . . . You've done your mourning and that will do. You can't go on weeping and mourning forever. My wife died when her time came, too. . . . Well? I grieved, I wept for a month, and that was enough for her; the old lady wasn't worth a second more. [*Sighs.*] You've forgotten all your neighbors. You don't go anywhere or accept any calls. We live, so to speak, like spiders. We never see the light. The mice have eaten my uniform. It isn't as if there weren't any nice neighbors—the district is full of them . . . there's a regiment stationed at Riblov, such officers—they're like candy—you'll never get your fill of them! And in the barracks, never a Friday goes by without a dance; and, if you please, the military band plays music every day. . . . Yes, madam, my dear lady: you're young, beautiful, in the full bloom of youth—if only you took a little pleasure in life . . . beauty doesn't last forever, you know! In ten years' time, you'll be wanting to wave your fanny in front of the officers—and it will be too late.

MRS. POPOV.   [*Determined.*] I must ask you never to talk to me like that! You know that when Mr. Popov died, life lost all its salt for me. It may seem to you that I am alive, but that's only conjecture! I vowed to wear mourning to my grave and not to see the light of day. . . . Do you hear me? May his departed spirit see how much I love him. . . . Yes, I know, it's no mystery to you that he was often mean to me, cruel . . . and even unfaithful, but I shall remain true to the grave and show him I know how to love. There, beyond the grave, he will see me as I was before his death. . . .

LUKA.   Instead of talking like that, you should be taking a walk in the garden or have Toby or Giant harnessed and go visit some of the neighbors. . . .

MRS. POPOV.   Ai! [*She weeps.*]

LUKA.   Madam! Dear lady! What's the matter with you! Christ be with you!

MRS. POPOV.   Oh, how he loved Toby! He always used to ride on him to visit the Korchagins or the Vlasovs. How wonderfully he rode! How graceful he was when he pulled at the reins with all his strength! Do you remember? Toby, Toby! Tell them to give him an extra bag of oats today.

LUKA.   Yes, madam.

[*Sound of loud ringing.*]

MRS. POPOV.   [*Shudders.*] Who's that? Tell them I'm not at home!

LUKA.   Of course, madam. [*He exits.*]

MRS. POPOV.   [*Alone. Looks at the photograph.*] You will see, Nicholai, how much I can love and forgive . . . my love will die only when I do, when my poor heart stops beating. [*Laughing through her tears.*] Have you no shame? I'm a good girl, a virtuous little wife. I've locked myself in and I'll be true to you to the grave, and you . . . aren't you ashamed, you chubby cheeks? You deceived me, you made scenes, for weeks on end you left me alone . . .

LUKA.   [*Enters, alarmed.*] Madam, somebody is asking for you. He wants to see you. . . .

MRS. POPOV.   But didn't you tell them that since the death of my husband, I don't see anybody?

LUKA.   I did, but he didn't want to listen; he spoke about some very important business.

MRS. POPOV.   I am *not at home!*

LUKA.   That's what I told him . . . but . . . the devil . . . he cursed and pushed past me right into the room . . . he's in the dining room right now.

MRS. POPOV.   [*Losing her temper.*] Very well, let him come in . . . such manners! [*LUKA goes out.*] How difficult these people are! What does he want from me? Why should he disturb my peace? [*Sighs.*] But it's obvious I'll have to go live in a convent. . . . [*Thoughtfully.*] Yes, a convent. . . .

SMIRNOV.   [*Enters while speaking to LUKA.*] You idiot, you talk too much. . . . Ass! [*Sees MRS. POPOV and changes to dignified speech.*] Madam, may I introduce myself: retired lieutenant of the artillery and landowner, Grigory Stepanovich Smirnov! I feel the necessity of troubling you about a highly important matter. . . .

MRS. POPOV.   [*Refusing her hand.*] What do you want?

SMIRNOV.   Your late husband, whom I had the pleasure of knowing, has remained in my debt for two twelve-hundred-ruble notes. Since I must pay the interest at the agricultural bank tomorrow, I have come to ask you, madam, to pay me the money today.

MRS. POPOV.   One thousand two hundred. . . . And why was my husband in debt to you?

SMIRNOV.   He used to buy oats from me.

MRS. POPOV.   [*Sighing, to* LUKA.] So, Luka, don't you forget to tell them to give Toby an extra bag of oats.

[*LUKA goes out.*]

[*To* SMIRNOV.] If Nikolai, my husband, was in debt to you, then it goes without saying that I'll pay; but please excuse me today. I haven't any spare cash. The day after tomorrow, my steward will be back from town and I will give him instructions to pay you what is owed; until then I cannot comply with your wishes. . . . Besides, today is the anniversary—exactly seven months ago my husband died, and I'm in such a mood that I'm not quite disposed to occupy myself with money matters.

SMIRNOV.   And I'm in such a mood that if I don't pay the interest tomorrow, I'll   25
be owing so much that my troubles will drown me. They'll take away my estate!

MRS. POPOV.   You'll receive your money the day after tomorrow.

SMIRNOV.   I don't want the money the day after tomorrow. I want it today.

MRS. POPOV.   You must excuse me. I can't pay you today.

SMIRNOV.   And I can't wait until after tomorrow.

MRS. POPOV.   What can I do, if I don't have it now?   30

SMIRNOV.   You mean to say you can't pay?

MRS. POPOV.   I can't pay. . . .

SMIRNOV.   Hm! Is that your last word?

MRS. POPOV.   That is my last word.

SMIRNOV.   Positively the last?   35

MRS. POPOV.   Positively.

SMIRNOV.   Thank you very much. We'll make a note of that. [*Shrugs his shoulders.*] And people want me to be calm and collected! Just now, on the way here, I met a tax officer and he asked me: why are you always so angry, Grigory Stepanovich? Goodness' sake, how can I be anything but angry? I need money desperately . . . I rode out yesterday early in the morning, at daybreak, and went to see all my debtors; and if only one of them had paid his debt . . . I was dog-tired, spent the night God knows where—a Jewish tavern beside a barrel of vodka. . . . Finally I got here, fifty miles from home, hoping to be paid, and you treat me to a "mood." How can I help being angry?

MRS. POPOV.   It seems to me that I clearly said: My steward will return from the country and then you will be paid.

SMIRNOV.   I didn't come to your steward, but to you! What the hell, if you'll pardon the expression, would I do with your steward?

MRS. POPOV.   Excuse me, my dear sir, I am not accustomed to such profane   40
expressions nor to such a tone. I'm not listening to you any more. [*Goes out quickly.*]

SMIRNOV.   [*Alone.*] Well, how do you like that? "A mood." . . . "Husband died seven months ago"! Must I pay the interest or mustn't I? I ask you: Must I pay, or must I not? So, your husband's dead, and you're in a mood and all that finicky stuff . . . and your steward's away somewhere; may he drop dead. What do you want me to do? Do you think I can fly away from my creditors in a balloon or something? Or should I run and bash my head against the wall? I go to Gruzdev—and he's not at home; Yaroshevich is hiding, with Kuritsin it's a quarrel to the death and I almost throw him out the window; Mazutov has diarrhea, and this one is in a "mood." Not one of these swine wants to pay me! And all because I'm too nice to them. I'm a sniveling idiot, I'm spineless, I'm an old lady! I'm too delicate with them! So, just you wait! You'll find out what I'm like! I won't let you play around with me, you devils! I'll stay and stick it out until she pays. Rrr! . . . How furious I am today, how furious! I'm shaking inside from rage and I can hardly catch my breath. . . . Damn it! My God, I even feel sick! [*He shouts.*] Hey, you!

LUKA.   [*Enters.*] What do you want?

SMIRNOV.   Give me some beer or some water! [*LUKA exits.*] What logic is there in this! A man needs money desperately, it's like a noose around his neck—and she won't pay because, you see, she's not disposed to occupy herself with money matters! . . . That's the logic of a woman! That's why I never did like and do not like to talk to women. I'd rather sit on a keg of gunpowder than talk to a woman. Brr! . . . I even have goose pimples, this broad has put me in such a rage! All I have to do is see one of those spoiled bitches from a distance, and I get so angry it gives me a cramp in the leg. I just want to shout for help.

LUKA.   [*Entering with water.*] Madam is sick and won't see anyone.

SMIRNOV.   Get out! [*LUKA goes.*] Sick and won't see anyone! No need to see me . . . I'll stay and sit here until you give me the money. You can stay sick for a week, and I'll stay for a week . . . if you're sick for a year, I'll stay a year. . . . I'll get my own back, dear lady! You can't impress me with your widow's weeds and your dimpled cheeks . . . we know all about those dimples! [*Shouts through the window.*] Semyon, unharness the horses! We're not going away quite yet! I'm staying here! Tell them in the stable to give the horses some oats! You brute, you let the horse on the left side get all tangled up in the reins again! [*Teasing.*] "Never mind" . . . I'll give you a never mind! [*Goes away from the window.*] Shit! The heat is unbearable and nobody pays up. I slept badly last night and on top of everything else this broad in mourning is "in a mood" . . . my head aches . . . [*Drinks, and grimaces.*] Shit! This is water! What I need is a drink! [*Shouts.*] Hey, you!

LUKA.   [*Enters.*] What is it?

SMIRNOV.   Give me a glass of vodka. [*LUKA goes out.*] Oaf! [*Sits down and examines himself.*] Nobody would say I was looking well! Dusty all over, boots dirty, unwashed, unkept, straw on my waistcoat. . . . The dear lady probably took me for a robber. [*Yawns.*] It's not very polite to present myself in a drawing room looking like this; oh well, who cares? . . . I'm not here as a visitor but as a creditor, and there's no official costume for creditors. . . .

LUKA.   [*Enters with vodka.*] You're taking liberties, my good man. . . .

SMIRNOV.   [*Angrily.*] What?

LUKA.   I . . . nothing . . . I only . . .

SMIRNOV.   Who are you talking to? Shut up!

LUKA.   [*Aside.*] The devil sent this leech. An ill wind brought him. . . . [*LUKA goes out.*]

SMIRNOV.   Oh how furious I am! I'm so mad I could crush the whole world into a powder! I even feel faint! [*Shouts.*] Hey, you!

MRS. POPOV.   [*Enters, eyes downcast.*] My dear sir, in my solitude, I have long ago grown unaccustomed to the masculine voice and I cannot bear shouting. I must request you not to disturb my peace and quiet!

SMIRNOV.   Pay me my money and I'll go.

MRS. POPOV.   I told you in plain language: I haven't any spare cash now; wait until the day after tomorrow.

SMIRNOV.   And I also told you respectfully, in plain language: I don't need the money the day after tomorrow, but today. If you don't pay me today, then tomorrow I'll have to hang myself.

MRS. POPOV.   But what can I do if I don't have the money? You're so strange!

SMIRNOV.   Then you won't pay me now? No?

MRS. POPOV.   I can't. . . .

SMIRNOV.   In that case, I can stay here and wait until you pay. . . . [*Sits down.*] You'll pay the day after tomorrow? Excellent! In that case I'll stay here until the day after tomorrow. I'll sit here all that time . . . [*Jumps up.*] I ask you: Have I got to pay the interest tomorrow, or not? Or do you think I'm joking?

MRS. POPOV.   My dear sir, I ask you not to shout! This isn't a stable!

SMIRNOV.   I wasn't asking you about a stable but about this: Do I have to pay the interest tomorrow or not?

MRS. POPOV.   You don't know how to behave in the company of a lady!

SMIRNOV.   No, I don't know how to behave in the company of a lady!

MRS. POPOV.   No, you don't! You are an ill-bred, rude man! Respectable people don't talk to a woman like that!

SMIRNOV.   Ach, it's astonishing! How would you like me to talk to you? In French, perhaps? [*Lisps in anger.*] *Madame, je vous prie*° . . . how happy I am that you're not paying me the money. . . . Ah, pardon, I've made you uneasy! Such lovely weather we're having today! And you look so becoming in your mourning dress. [*Bows and scrapes.*]

MRS. POPOV.   That's rude and not very clever!

SMIRNOV.   [*Teasing.*] Rude and not very clever! I don't know how to behave in the company of ladies. Madam, in my time I've seen far more women than you've seen sparrows. Three times I've fought duels over women; I've jilted twelve women, nine have jilted me! Yes! There was a time when I played the fool; I became sentimental over women, used honeyed words, fawned on them, bowed and scraped. . . . I loved, suffered, sighed at the moon; I became limp, melted, shivered . . . I loved passionately, madly, every which way, devil take me, I chattered away like a magpie about the emancipation of women, ran through half my fortune as a result of my tender feelings; but now, if you will excuse me, I'm on to your ways! I've had enough! Dark eyes, passionate eyes, ruby lips, dimpled cheeks; the moon, whispers, bated breath—for all that I wouldn't give a good goddamn. Present company excepted, of course, but all women, young and old alike, are affected clowns, gossips, hateful, consummate liars to the marrow of their bones, vain, trivial, ruthless, outrageously illogical, and as far as this is concerned [*taps on his forehead.*], well, excuse my frankness, any sparrow could give pointers to a philosopher in petticoats! Look at one of those romantic creatures: muslin, ethereal demigoddess, a thousand raptures, and you look into her soul—a common crocodile! [*Grips the back of a chair; the chair cracks and breaks.*] But the most revolting part of it all is that this crocodile imagines that she has, above everything, her own privilege, a monopoly on tender feelings. The hell with it—you can hang me upside down by that nail if a woman is capable of loving anything besides a lapdog. All she can do when she's in love is slobber! While the man suffers and sacrifices, all her love is expressed in playing with her skirt and trying to lead him around firmly by the nose. You have the misfortune of being a

60

65

---

67 *Madame, je vous prie:* I beg you, Madam.

woman, you know yourself what the nature of a woman is like. Tell me honestly: Have you ever in your life seen a woman who is sincere, faithful, and constant? You never have! Only old and ugly ladies are faithful and constant! You're more liable to meet a horned cat or a white woodcock than a faithful woman!

MRS. POPOV.   Pardon me, but in your opinion, who is faithful and constant in love? The man?

SMIRNOV.   Yes, the man!

MRS. POPOV.   The man! [*Malicious laugh.*] Men are faithful and constant in love! That's news! [*Heatedly.*] What right have you to say that? Men are faithful and constant! For that matter, as far as I know, of all the men I have known and now know, my late husband was the best. . . . I loved him passionately, with all my being, as only a young intellectual woman can love; I gave him my youth, my happiness, my life, my fortune; he was my life's breath; I worshipped him as if I were a heathen, and . . . and, what good did it do—this best of men himself deceived me shamelessly at every step of the way. After his death, I found his desk full of love letters; and when he was alive—it's terrible to remember—he used to leave me alone for weeks at a time, and before my eyes he flirted with other women and deceived me. He squandered my money, made a mockery of my feelings . . . and, in spite of all that, I loved him and was true to him . . . and besides, now that he is dead, I am still faithful and constant. I have shut myself up in these four walls forever and I won't remove these widow's weeds until my dying day. . . .

SMIRNOV.   [*Laughs contemptuously.*] Widow's weeds! . . . I don't know what you take me for! As if I didn't know why you wear that black outfit and bury yourself in these four walls! Well, well! It's no secret, so romantic! When some fool of a poet passes by this country house, he'll look up at your window and think: "Here lives the mysterious Tamara, who, for the love of her husband, buried herself in these four walls." We know these tricks!

MRS. POPOV.   [*Flaring.*] What? How dare you say that to me?

SMIRNOV.   You may have buried yourself alive, but you haven't forgotten to powder yourself!

MRS. POPOV.   How dare you use such expressions with me?

SMIRNOV.   Please don't shout. I'm not your steward! You must allow me to call a spade a spade. I'm not a woman and I'm used to saying what's on my mind! Don't you shout at me!

MRS. POPOV.   I'm not shouting, you are! Please leave me in peace!

SMIRNOV.   Pay me my money and I'll go.

MRS. POPOV.   I won't give you any money!

SMIRNOV.   Yes, you will.

MRS. POPOV.   To spite you, I won't pay you anything. You can leave me in peace!

SMIRNOV.   I don't have the pleasure of being either your husband or your fiancé, so please don't make scenes! [*Sits down.*] I don't like it.

MRS. POPOV.   [*Choking with rage.*] You're sitting down?

SMIRNOV.   Yes, I am.

MRS. POPOV.   I ask you to get out!

SMIRNOV.   Give me my money . . . [*Aside.*] Oh, I'm so furious! Furious!

MRS. POPOV.   I don't want to talk to impudent people! Get out of here! [*Pause.*] You're not going? No?

SMIRNOV.   No.

MRS. POPOV.   No?

SMIRNOV.   No!

MRS. POPOV.   We'll see about that. [*Rings.*]

[*LUKA enters.*]

Luka, show the gentleman out!

LUKA.   [*Goes up to SMIRNOV.*] Sir, will you please leave, as you have been asked. You mustn't . . .

SMIRNOV.   [*Jumping up.*] Shut up! Who do you think you're talking to? I'll make mincemeat out of you!

LUKA.   [*His hand to his heart.*] Oh my God! Saints above! [*Falls into chair.*] Oh, I feel ill! I can't catch my breath!   95

MRS. POPOV.   Where's Dasha? Dasha! [*She shouts.*] Dasha! Pelagea! Dasha! [*She rings.*]

LUKA.   Oh! They've all gone berry picking . . . there's nobody at home . . . I'm ill! Water!

MRS. POPOV.   Will you please get out!

SMIRNOV.   Will you please be more polite?

MRS. POPOV.   [*Clenches her fist and stamps her feet.*] You're nothing but a crude bear! A brute! A monster!   100

SMIRNOV.   What? What did you say?

MRS. POPOV.   I said that you were a bear, a monster!

SMIRNOV.   [*Advancing toward her.*] Excuse me, but what right do you have to insult me?

MRS. POPOV.   Yes, I am insulting you . . . so what? Do you think I'm afraid of you?

SMIRNOV.   And do you think just because you're one of those romantic creations,   105
that you have the right to insult me with impunity? Yes? I challenge you!

LUKA.   Lord in Heaven! Saints above! . . . Water!

SMIRNOV.   Pistols!

MRS. POPOV.   Do you think just because you have big fists and you can bellow like a bull, that I'm afraid of you? You're such a bully!

SMIRNOV.   I challenge you! I'm not going to let anybody insult me, and I don't care if you are a woman, a delicate creature!

MRS. POPOV.   [*Trying to get a word in edgewise.*] Bear! Bear! Bear!   110

SMIRNOV.   It's about time we got rid of the prejudice that only men must pay for their insults! Devil take it, if women want to be equal, they should behave as equals! Let's fight!

MRS. POPOV.   You want to fight! By all means!

SMIRNOV.   This minute!

MRS. POPOV.   This minute! My husband had some pistols . . . I'll go and get them right away. [*Goes out hurriedly and then returns.*] What pleasure I'll have putting a bullet through that thick head of yours! The hell with you! [*She goes out.*]

SMIRNOV.   I'll shoot her down like a chicken! I'm not a little boy or a sentimental   115
puppy. I don't care if she is delicate and fragile.

LUKA.   Kind sir! Holy father! [*kneels.*] Have pity on a poor old man and go away from here! You've frightened her to death and now you're going to shoot her?

SMIRNOV.   [*Not listening to him.*] If she fights, then it means she believes in equality of rights and emancipation of women. Here the sexes are equal! I'll shoot her like a chicken! But what a woman! [*Imitates her.*] "The hell with you! . . . I'll put a bullet through that thick head of yours! . . . " What a woman! How she blushed, her eyes shone . . . she accepted my challenge! To tell the truth, it was the first time in my life I've seen a woman like that. . . .

LUKA. Dear sir, please go away! I'll pray to God on your behalf as long as I live!

SMIRNOV. That's a woman for you! A woman like that I can understand! A real woman! Not a sour-faced nincompoop but fiery, gunpowder! Fireworks! I'm even sorry to have to kill her!

LUKA. [*Weeps.*] Dear sir . . . go away! 12(

SMIRNOV. I positively like her! Positively! Even though she has dimpled cheeks, I like her! I'm almost ready to forget about the debt. . . . My fury has diminished. Wonderful woman!

MRS. POPOV. [*Enters with pistols.*] Here they are, the pistols. Before we fight, you must show me how to fire. . . . I've never had a pistol in my hands before . . .

LUKA. Oh dear Lord, for pity's sake. . . . I'll go and find the gardener and the coachman. . . . What did we do to deserve such trouble? [*Exit.*]

SMIRNOV. [*Examining the pistols.*] You see, there are several sorts of pistols . . . there are special dueling pistols, the Mortimer with primers. Then there are Smith and Wesson revolvers, triple action with extractors . . . excellent pistols! . . . they cost a minimum of ninety rubles a pair. . . . You must hold the revolver like this . . . [*Aside.*] What eyes, what eyes! A woman to set you on fire!

MRS. POPOV. Like this? 12

SMIRNOV. Yes, like this . . . then you cock the pistol . . . take aim . . . put your head back a little . . . stretch your arm out all the way . . . that's right . . . then with this finger press on this little piece of goods . . . and that's all there is to do . . . but the most important thing is not to get excited and aim without hurrying . . . try to keep your arm from shaking.

MRS. POPOV. Good . . . it's not comfortable to shoot indoors. Let's go into the garden.

SMIRNOV. Let's go. But I'm giving you advance notice that I'm going to fire into the air.

MRS. POPOV. That's the last straw! Why? 1!

SMIRNOV. Why? . . . Why . . . because it's my business, that's why.

MRS. POPOV. Are you afraid? Yes? Aahhh! No, sir. You're not going to get out of it that easily! Be so good as to follow me! I will not rest until I've put a hole through your forehead . . . that forehead I hate so much! Are you afraid?

SMIRNOV. Yes, I'm afraid.

MRS. POPOV. You're lying! Why don't you want to fight?

SMIRNOV. Because . . . because you . . . because I like you.

MRS. POPOV. [*Laughs angrily.*] He likes me! He dares say that he likes me! [*Points* 1. *to the door.*] Out!

SMIRNOV. [*Loads the revolver in silence, takes cap and goes; at the door, stops for half a minute while they look at each other in silence; then he approaches MRS. POPOV hesitantly.*] Listen. . . . Are you still angry? I'm extremely irritated, but, do you understand me, how can I express it . . . the fact is, that, you see, strictly speaking . . . [*He shouts.*] Is it my fault, really, for liking you? [*Grabs the back of a chair, which cracks and breaks.*] Why the hell do you have such fragile furniture! I like you! Do you understand? I . . . I'm almost in love with you!

MRS. POPOV. Get away from me—I hate you!

SMIRNOV. God, what a woman! I've never in my life seen anything like her! I'm lost! I'm done for! I'm caught like a mouse in a trap!

MRS. POPOV. Stand back or I'll shoot!

SMIRNOV. Shoot! You could never understand what happiness it would be to die under the gaze of those wonderful eyes, to be shot by a revolver which was held by those

little velvet hands. . . . I've gone out of my mind! Think about it and decide right away,   140
because if I leave here, then we'll never see each other again! Decide . . . I'm a nobleman,
a respectable gentleman, of good family. I have an income of ten thousand a year. . . . I can
put a bullet through a coin tossed in the air . . . I have some fine horses. . . . Will you be
my wife?

    MRS. POPOV.   [*Indignantly brandishes her revolver.*] Let's fight! I challenge you!

    SMIRNOV.   I'm out of my mind . . . I don't understand anything . . . [*Shouts.*] Hey,
you, water!

    MRS. POPOV.   [*Shouts.*] Let's fight!

    SMIRNOV.   I've gone out of my mind. I'm in love like a boy, like an idiot! [*He grabs
her hand, she screams with pain.*] I love you! [*Kneels.*] I love you as I've never loved before!
I've jilted twelve women, nine women have jilted me, but I've never loved one of them as
I love you. . . . I'm weak, I'm a limp rag. . . . I'm on my knees like a fool, offering you my
hand. . . . Shame, shame! I haven't been in love for five years, I vowed I wouldn't; and
suddenly I'm in love, like a fish out of water. I'm offering my hand in marriage. Yes or
no? You don't want to? You don't need to! [*Gets up and quickly goes to the door.*]

    MRS. POPOV.   Wait!

    SMIRNOV.   [*Stops.*] Well?

    MRS. POPOV.   Nothing . . . you can go . . . go away . . . wait. . . . No, get out, get   145
out! I hate you! But—don't go! Oh, if you only knew how furious I am, how angry!
[*Throws revolver on table.*] My fingers are swollen from that nasty thing. . . . [*Tears her handkerchief furiously.*] What are you waiting for? Get out!

    SMIRNOV.   Farewell!

    MRS. POPOV.   Yes, yes, go away! [*Shouts.*] Where are you going? Stop. . . . Oh, go
away! Oh, how furious I am! Don't come near me! Don't come near me!

    SMIRNOV.   [*Approaching her.*] How angry I am with myself! I'm in love like a stu-
dent. I've been on my knees. . . . It gives me the shivers. [*Rudely.*] I love you! A lot of
good it will do me to fall in love with you! Tomorrow I've got to pay the interest, begin   150
the mowing of the hay. [*Puts his arm around her waist.*] I'll never forgive myself for this. . . .

    MRS. POPOV.   Get away from me! Get your hands away! I . . . hate you! I . . . chal-
lenge you!

[*Prolonged kiss,* LUKA *enters with an ax, the* GARDENER *with a rake, the* COACHMAN *with a pitchfork, and* WORKMEN *with cudgels.*]

    LUKA.   [*Catches sight of the pair kissing.*] Lord in heaven! [*Pause.*]

    MRS. POPOV.   [*Lowering her eyes.*] Luka, tell them in the stable not to give Toby any
oats today.

CURTAIN

QUESTIONS

1.   What was Mrs. Popov's life like with her late husband? What did she learn about
him after his death? How has this knowledge affected her?

2.   Who is Smirnov? What is he like, and how do you know? Why does he say what
he does about women?

3.   Why is Luka important? How do his responses highlight the emotions developing between Smirnov and Mrs. Popov?

4. What causes Mrs. Popov to call Smirnov a bear, a brute, a monster? What is his immediate response?
5. Why is Toby significant? How does he symbolize Mrs. Popov's shifting emotions?

GENERAL QUESTIONS

1. Where did you laugh in the play? Analyze those moments and try to determine the causes of your laughter.
2. From this play, what conclusions can you draw about farce as a dramatic form? Consider the breaking chairs, the shouting, the challenge, the attitude of Smirnov about being shot, the shifting of feelings, etc.
3. How does Chekhov's presentation of Smirnov and Mrs. Popov make their reversal of feelings seem normal and logical, although sudden, unexpected, and surprising?
4. What are the major ideas or themes in *The Bear*? Consider vows made by the living to the dead, the difficulty of keeping resolutions, the nature of powerful emotions, the need to maintain conventions and expectations, etc.

BETH HENLEY, *AM I BLUE*

Brought up in Mississippi, Beth Henley attended Southern Methodist University, where in her sophomore year she wrote *Am I Blue*, which was first produced in December 1981. She attended acting school in Illinois and went to Hollywood to take up a career as a movie actress. However, at the same time she continued to work on new plays, and it is as a writer that she has been successful. Her most notable achievement is her "southern Gothic" play *Crimes of the Heart* (first titled *Crimes of Passion*), for which she won the Great American Play contest in 1978 and the Pulitzer Prize for Drama in 1981. She also wrote *The Wake of Jamey Foster* (1983), *The Lucky Spot* (1987), *The Debutante Ball* (1991), and *Abundance* (1991). The year 1992 saw the publication of four collected plays (*Beth Henley: Four Plays*), including *The Miss Firecracker Contest*, a two-act play written in 1979 and first performed in 1984. A recent play *Impossible Marriage* was produced off-Broadway in 1998 at the Laura Pels Theatre in New York. During the spring of 2000, her new play *Family Week* was produced in New York at the Century Center theater. In addition, she has seen some of her shorter scripts produced as television plays. *Crimes of the Heart* was made into a successful film in 1986, starring Diane Keaton, Jessica Lange, Sam Shepard, and Sissy Spacek.

In many of her plays, Henley's comedic manner develops out of the eccentricity or "kookiness" of her main female characters. The comic *donnée* is that an unusual or even disturbed action is accepted as a normal event that begins a course of dramatic action. A character in one of Henley's television plays, for example, inadvertently sets a house on fire, but the outcome turns out to be fortunate because of a rewarding home insurance policy. In *Crimes of the Heart,* one of the characters, after a failed suicide attempt, explains herself by saying that she has been having "a bad day." Even in the serious play *Abundance,* the two main female characters begin their twenty-five-year-long friendship after they have come west in the 1860s to become mail-order brides of men they have never seen. Ashbe of *Am I Blue* is an early original in the pattern, with her liking for hot Kool-Aid and colored marshmallows, her habit of stealing ashtrays and then donating them to a fellow tenant, and her dabbling in voodoo.

Although *Am I Blue* is an amusing play, it deals with the difficulties of adjustment to adulthood, misconceptions about social roles, unfulfilled dreams, general aimlessness and indecisiveness, and the attempt to develop individuality. The larger political and historical context of the year of the supposed events of the play, 1968, is mentioned by neither Ashbe nor John Polk, but one might connect their difficulties with some of the disturbances of that year, particularly the assassinations of Robert Kennedy and Martin Luther King, Jr., the frustrating and seemingly endless war in Vietnam, and the many antiwar demonstrations and riots, especially during the Democratic National Convention in Chicago in the summer. Henley is very specific in dating the action of *Am I Blue* on the night of November 11, 1968—in other words, after all these disturbing and destabilizing events had taken place, and also less than a week after the election that made Richard Nixon president. One might also note the irony that November 11 had before 1954 been called Armistice Day (now Veterans Day)—a holiday dedicated to peace and stability.

Am I Blue thus reflects the disturbances and disruptions of the late 1960s, even though it focuses on the individual concerns and problems of John Polk and Ashbe. Ashbe's father is an alcoholic who is absent when she needs him, and her mother has deserted the home entirely. John Polk is facing a difficult choice about his future career, and he is also trying to stay afloat in the swim of fraternity life. Unable to succeed in either situation, he seeks strength in rum instead of calling on his own inner resources. Nothing earthshaking is claimed for either John Polk or Ashbe at the play's end, but they both succeed in developing a degree of recognition—rejecting conventional behaviors and discovering their own capacities for friendship and dignity.

BETH HENLEY (b. 1952)

Am I Blue° _____ *(1973) 1982*

CHARACTERS

John Polk Richards, *seventeen*
Ashbe Williams, *sixteen*
Hilda, *a waitress, thirty-five*
Street People: Barker, Whore, Bum, Clareece

First produced in New York City by the Circle Repertory Company.

[*SCENE:* A bar, the street, the living room of a run-down apartment.]

[*TIME: Fall 1968.*]

The scene opens on a street in the New Orleans French Quarter on a rainy, blue bourbon night. Various people—a WHORE, BUM, STREET BARKER, CLAREECE—*appear and disappear along the street. The scene then focuses on a bar where a piano is heard from the back room playing softly and indistinctly "Am I Blue?" The lights go up on* JOHN POLK, *who sits alone at a table. He is seventeen, a bit overweight and awkward. He wears nice clothes, perhaps a navy sweater with large white monograms. His navy raincoat is slung over an empty chair. While drinking John Polk concentrates on the red and black card that he holds in his hand. As soon as the scene is established,* ASHBE *enters from the street. She is sixteen, wears a flowered plastic raincoat, a white plastic rain cap, red galoshes, a butterfly barrette, and jeweled cat-eye glasses. She is carrying a bag full of stolen goods. Her hair is very curly. Ashbe makes her way cautiously to John Polk's table. As he sees her coming, he puts the card into his pocket. She sits in the empty chair and pulls his raincoat over her head.*

ASHBE.   Excuse me . . . do you mind if I sit here please?

JOHN POLK.   [*Looks up at her—then down into his glass.*] What are you doing hiding under my raincoat? You're getting it all wet.

ASHBE.   Well, I'm very sorry, but after all it is a raincoat. [*He tries to pull off coat.*] It was rude of me I know, but look I just don't want them to recognize me.

JOHN POLK.   [*Looking about.*] Who to recognize you?

ASHBE.   Well, I stole these two ashtrays from the Screw Inn, ya know right down the street. [*She pulls out two glass commercial ashtrays from her white plastic bag.*] Anyway, I'm scared the manager saw me. They'll be after me I'm afraid.

JOHN POLK.   Well, they should be. Look, do you mind giving me back my raincoat? I don't want to be found protecting any thief.

ASHBE.   [*Coming out from under coat.*] Thief—would you call Robin Hood a thief?

JOHN POLK.   Christ.

ASHBE.   [*Back under coat.*] No, you wouldn't. He was valiant—all the time stealing from the rich and giving to the poor.

JOHN POLK.   But your case isn't exactly the same, is it? You're stealing from some crummy little bar and keeping the ashtrays for yourself. Now give me back my coat.

ASHBE.   [*Throws coat at him.*] Sure, take your old coat. I suppose I should have explained—about Miss Marcey. [*Silence.*] Miss Marcey, this cute old lady with a little hump in her back. I always see her in her sun hat and blue print dress. Miss Marcey lives in the apartment building next to ours. I leave all the stolen goods, as gifts on her front steps.

JOHN POLK.   Are you one of those kleptomaniacs? [*He starts checking his wallet.*]

ASHBE.   You mean when people all the time steal and they can't help it?

JOHN POLK.   Yeah.

ASHBE.   Oh, no. I'm not a bit careless. Take my job tonight, my very first night job, if you want to know. Anyway, I've been planning it for two months, trying to decipher which bar most deserved to be stolen from. I finally decided on the Screw Inn. Mainly because of the way they're so mean to Mr. Groves. He works at the magazine rack at Diver's Drugstore and is really very sweet, but he has a drinking problem. I don't think that's fair to be mean to people simply because they have a drinking problem—and, well, anyway, you see I'm not just stealing for personal gain. I mean, I don't even smoke.

JOHN POLK.   Yeah, well, most infants don't, but then again, most infants don't hang around bars.

ASHBE.   I don't see why not, Toulouse Lautrec did.

JOHN POLK.   They'd throw me out.

ASHBE.   Oh, they throw me out too, but I don't accept defeat. [*Slowly moves into him.*] Why it's the very same with my pickpocketing.

[*JOHN POLK sneers, turns away.*]

ASHBE.   It's a very hard act to master. Why every time I've done it, I've been   20
caught.

JOHN POLK.   That's all I need, is to have some slum kid tell me how good it is to steal. Everyone knows it's not.

ASHBE.   [*About his drink.*] That looks good. What is it?

JOHN POLK.   Hey, would you mind leaving me alone—I just wanted to be alone.

ASHBE.   Okay. I'm sorry. How about if I'm quiet?

[*JOHN POLK shrugs. He sips drink, looks around, catches her eye, she smiles and sighs.*]

ASHBE.   I was just looking at your pin. What fraternity are you in?

JOHN POLK.   S.A.E.   25

ASHBE.   Is it a good fraternity?

JOHN POLK.   Sure, it's the greatest.

ASHBE.   I bet you have lots of friends.

JOHN POLK.   Tons.

ASHBE.   Are you being serious?   30

JOHN POLK.   Yes.

ASHBE.   Hmm. Do they have parties and all that?

JOHN POLK.   Yeah, lots of parties, booze, honking horns, it's exactly what you would expect.

ASHBE.   I wouldn't expect anything. Why did you join?   35

JOHN POLK.   I don't know. Well, my brother . . . I guess it was my brother . . . he told me how great it was, how the fraternity was supposed to get you dates, make you study, solve all your problems.

ASHBE.   Gee, does it?

JOHN POLK.   Doesn't help you study.

ASHBE.   How about dates? Do they get you a lot of dates?

JOHN POLK.   Some.   40

ASHBE.   What were the girls like?

JOHN POLK.   I don't know—they were like girls.

ASHBE.   Did you have a good time?

JOHN POLK.   I had a pretty good time.

ASHBE.   Did you make love to any of them?   45

JOHN POLK.   [*To self.*] Oh, Christ . . .

ASHBE.   I'm sorry . . . I just figured that's why you had the appointment with the whore . . . cause you didn't have anyone else . . . to make love to.

JOHN POLK.   How did you know I had the, ah, the appointment?

ASHBE.   I saw you put the red card in your pocket when I came up. Those red cards are pretty familiar around here. The house is only about a block or so away. It's one of the best though, really very plush. Only two murders and a knifing in its whole history. Do you go there often?

JOHN POLK.   Yeah, I like to give myself a treat.   50

ASHBE.   Who do you have?

JOHN POLK.   What do you mean?

ASHBE.   I mean which girl. [*JOHN POLK gazes into his drink.*] Look, I just thought I might know her is all.

JOHN POLK.   Know her, ah, how would you know her?

ASHBE.   Well, some of the girls from my high school go there to work when they get out.

JOHN POLK.   G.G., her name is G.G.

ASHBE.   G.G. . . . Hmm, well, how does she look?

JOHN POLK.   I don't know.

ASHBE.   Oh, you've never been with her before?

JOHN POLK.   No.

ASHBE.   [*Confidentially.*] Are you one of those kinds that likes a lot of variety?

JOHN POLK.   Variety? Sure, I guess I like variety.

ASHBE.   Oh, yes, now I remember.

JOHN POLK.   What?

ASHBE.   G.G., that's just her working name. Her real name is Myrtle Reims, she's Kay Reims' older sister. Kay is in my grade at school.

JOHN POLK.   Myrtle? Her name is Myrtle?

ASHBE.   I never liked the name either.

JOHN POLK.   Myrtle, oh, Christ. Is she pretty?

ASHBE.   [*Matter of fact.*] Pretty, no she's not real pretty.

JOHN POLK.   What does she look like?

ASHBE.   Let's see . . . she's, ah, well, Myrtle had acne and there are a few scars left. It's not bad. I think they sort of give her character. Her hair's red, only I don't think it's really red. It sort of fizzles out all over her head. She's got a pretty good figure . . . big top . . . but the rest of her is kind of skinny.

JOHN POLK.   I wonder if she has a good personality.

ASHBE.   Well, she was a senior when I was a freshman; so I never really knew her. I remember she used to paint her fingernails lots of different colors . . . pink, orange, purple. I don't know, but she kind of scares me. About the only time I ever saw her true personality was around a year ago. I was over at Kay's making a health poster for school. Anyway, Myrtle comes busting in, screaming about how she can't find her spangled bra anywhere. Kay and I just sat on the floor cutting pictures of food out of magazines while she was storming about slamming drawers and swearing. Finally, she found it. It was pretty garish—red with black and gold sequined G's on each cup. That's how I remember the name—G.G.

[*As Ashbe illustrates the placement of the G's she spots Hilda, the waitress, approaching. Ashbe pulls the raincoat over her head and hides on the floor. Hilda enters through the beaded curtains spilling her tray. Hilda is a woman of few words.*]

HILDA.   Shit, damn curtain. Nuther drink?

JOHN POLK.   Mam?

HILDA.   [*Points to drink.*] Vodka coke?

JOHN POLK.   No, thank you. I'm not quite finished yet.

HILDA.   Napkins clean.

[*ASHBE pulls her bag off the table. HILDA looks at ASHBE then to JOHN POLK. She walks around the table, as ASHBE is crawling along the floor to escape. ASHBE runs into HILDA's toes.*]

ASHBE.   Are those real gold?

HILDA.   You again. Out.   80
ASHBE.   She wants me to leave. Why should a paying customer leave? [*Back to HILDA.*] Now I'll have a mint julip and easy on the mint.
HILDA.   This pre-teen with you?
JOHN POLK.   Well, I . . . No . . . I . . .
HILDA.   I.D.'s.
ASHBE.   Certainly, I always try to cooperate with the management.   85
HILDA.   [*Looking at JOHN POLK'S I.D.*] I.D., 11-12-50. Date: 11-11-68.
JOHN POLK.   Yes, but . . . well, 11-12 is less than two hours away.
HILDA.   Back in two hours.
ASHBE.   I seem to have left my identification in my gold lamé bag.
HILDA.   Well, boo-hoo. [*Motions for ASHBE to leave with a minimum of effort. She goes*   90
back to table.] No tip.
ASHBE.   You didn't tip her?
JOHN POLK.   I figured the drinks were so expensive . . . I just didn't . . .
HILDA.   No tip!
JOHN POLK.   Look, Miss, I'm sorry. [*Going through his pockets.*] Here would you like a . . . a nickel . . . wait, wait, here's a quarter.
HILDA.   Just move ass, sonny. You too, Barbie.   95
ASHBE.   Ugh, I hate public rudeness. I'm sure I'll refrain from ever coming here again.
HILDA.   Think I'll go in the back room and cry.

[*Ashbe and John Polk exit. Hilda picks up tray and exits through the curtain, tripping again.*]

HILDA.   Shit. Damn curtain.

[*ASHBE and JOHN POLK are now standing outside under the awning of the bar.*]

ASHBE.   Gee, I didn't know it was your birthday tomorrow. Happy birthday! Don't be mad. I thought you were at least twenty or twenty-one, really.
JOHN POLK.   It's o.k. Forget it.   100

[*As they begin walking, various blues are heard coming from the nearby bars.*]

ASHBE.   It's raining.
JOHN POLK.   I know.
ASHBE.   Are you going over to the house now?
JOHN POLK.   No, not till twelve.
ASHBE.   Yeah, the red and black cards—they mean all night. Midnight till   105
morning.

[*At this point a street BARKER beckons the couple into his establishment. Perhaps he is accompa-nied by a WHORE.*]

BARKER.   Hey mister, bring your baby on in, buy her a few drinks, maybe tonight ya get lucky.
ASHBE.   Keep walking.
JOHN POLK.   What's wrong with the place?
ASHBE.   The drinks are watery rot gut, and the show girls are boys . . .
BARKER.   Up yours, punk!   110

JOHN POLK.   [*Who has now sat down on a street bench.*] Look, just tell me where a cheap bar is. I've got to stay drunk, but I don't have much money left.

ASHBE.   Yikes, there aren't too many cheap bars around here, and a lot of them check I.D.'s.

JOHN POLK.   Well, do you know of any that don't?

ASHBE.   No, not for sure.

JOHN POLK.   Oh, God, I need to get drunk.

ASHBE.   Aren't you?

JOHN POLK.   Some, but I'm losing ground fast.

[*By this time a* BUM *who has been traveling drunkenly down the street falls near the couple and begins throwing up.*]

ASHBE.   Oh, I know! You can come to my apartment. It's just down the block. We keep one bottle of rum around. I'll serve you a grand drink, three or four if you like.

JOHN POLK.   [*Fretfully.*] No, thanks.

ASHBE.   But look, we're getting all wet.

JOHN POLK.   Sober too, wet and sober.

ASHBE.   Oh, come on! Rain's blurring my glasses.

JOHN POLK.   Well, how about your parents? What would they say?

ASHBE.   Daddy's out of town and Mama lives in Atlanta; so I'm sure they won't mind. I think we have some cute little marshmallows. [*Pulling on him.*] Won't you really come?

JOHN POLK.   You've probably got some gang of muggers waiting to kill me. Oh, all right . . . what the hell, let's go.

ASHBE.   Hurrah! Come on. It's this way. [*She starts across the stage, stops, and picks up an old hat.*] Hey, look at this hat. Isn't it something! Here, wear it to keep off the rain.

JOHN POLK.   [*Throwing hat back onto street.*] No, thanks, you don't know who's worn it before.

ASHBE.   [*Picking hat back up.*] That makes it all the more exciting. Maybe it was a butcher's who slaughtered his wife or a silver pirate with a black bird on his throat. Who do you guess?

JOHN POLK.   I don't know. Anyway what's the good of guessing? I mean you'll never really know.

ASHBE.   [*Trying the hat on.*] Yeah, probably not.

[*At this point* ASHBE *and* JOHN POLK *reach the front door.*]

ASHBE.   Here we are.

[ASHBE *begins fumbling for her key.* CLAREECE, *a teeny-bopper, walks up to* JOHN POLK.]

CLAREECE.   Hey, man, got any spare change?

JOHN POLK.   [*Looking through his pockets.*] Let me see . . . I . . .

ASHBE.   [*Coming up between them, giving* CLAREECE *a shove.*] Beat it, Clareece. He's my company.

CLAREECE.   [*Walks away and sneers.*] Oh, shove it, Frizzels.

ASHBE.   A lot of jerks live around here. Come on in. [*She opens the door. Lights go up on the living room of a run-down apartment in a run-down apartment house. Besides being merely run-down the room is a malicious pig sty with colors, paper hats, paper dolls, masks, torn up stuffed animals, dead flowers and leaves, dress-up clothes, etc., thrown all about.*] My bones are cold. Do you want a towel to dry off?

JOHN POLK.   Yes, thank you.

ASHBE.   [*She picks up a towel off the floor and tosses it to him.*] Here. [*He begins drying off, as she takes off her rain things; then she begins raking things off the sofa.*] Please do sit down. [*He sits.*] I'm sorry the place is disheveled, but my father's been out of town. I always try to pick up and all before he gets in. Of course, he's pretty used to messes. My mother never was too good at keeping things clean.

JOHN POLK.   When's he coming back?

ASHBE.   Sunday, I believe. Oh, I've been meaning to say . . .   140

JOHN POLK.   What?

ASHBE.   My name's Ashbe Williams.

JOHN POLK.   Ashbe?

ASHBE.   Yeah, Ashbe.

JOHN POLK.   My name's John Polk Richards.   145

ASHBE.   John Polk? They call you John Polk?

JOHN POLK.   It's family.

ASHBE.   [*Putting on socks.*] These are my favorite socks, the red furry ones. Well, here's some books and magazines to look at while I fix you something to drink. What do you want in your rum?

JOHN POLK.   Coke's fine.

ASHBE.   I'll see if we have any. I think I'll take some hot Kool-Aid myself.   150

[*She exits to the kitchen.*]

JOHN POLK.   Hot Kool-Aid?

ASHBE.   It's just Kool-Aid that's been heated, like hot chocolate or hot tea.

JOHN POLK.   Sounds great.

ASHBE.   Well, I'm used to it. You get so much for your dime, it makes it worth your while. I don't buy presweetened, of course, it's better to sugar your own.

JOHN POLK.   I remember once I threw up a lot of grape Kool-Aid when I was a   155
kid. I've hated it ever since. Hey, would you check on the time?

ASHBE.   [*She enters carrying a tray with several bottles of food coloring, a bottle of rum, and a huge glass.*] I'm sorry we don't have Coke. I wonder if rum and Kool-Aid is good? Oh, we don't have a clock either.

[*She pours a large amount of rum into the large glass.*]

JOHN POLK.   I'll just have it with water then.

ASHBE.   [*She finds an almost empty glass of water somewhere in the room and dumps it in with the rum.*] Would you like food coloring in the water? It makes a drink all the more aesthetic. Of course, some people don't care for aesthetics.

JOHN POLK.   No, thank you, just plain water.

ASHBE.   Are you sure? The taste is entirely the same. I put it in all my water.   160

JOHN POLK.   Well . . .

ASHBE.   What color do you want?

JOHN POLK.   I don't know.

ASHBE.   What's your favorite color?

JOHN POLK.   Blue, I guess.   165

[*She puts a few blue drops into the glass. As she has nothing to stir with, she blows into the glass turning the water blue.*]

JOHN POLK.   Thanks.

ASHBE.   [*Exits. She screams from kitchen.*] Come on, say come on, cat, eat your fresh, good milk.

JOHN POLK.   You have a cat?

ASHBE.   [*off.*] No.

JOHN POLK.   Oh.

ASHBE.   [*She enters carrying a tray with a cup of hot Kool-Aid and Cheerios and colored marshmallows.*] Here are some Cheerios and some cute, little, colored marshmallows to eat with your drink.

JOHN POLK.   Thanks.

ASHBE.   I one time smashed all the big white marshmallows in the plastic bag at the grocery store.

JOHN POLK.   Why did you do that?

ASHBE.   I was angry. Do you like ceramics?

JOHN POLK.   Yes.

ASHBE.   My mother makes them. It's sort of her hobby. She is very talented.

JOHN POLK.   My mother never does anything. Well, I guess she can shuffle the bridge deck okay.

ASHBE.   Actually, my mother is a dancer. She teaches at a school in Atlanta. She's really very talented.

JOHN POLK.   [*Indicates ceramics.*] She must be to do all these.

ASHBE.   Well, Madeline, my older sister, did the blue one. Madeline gets to live with Mama.

JOHN POLK.   And you live with your father.

ASHBE.   Yeah, but I get to go visit them sometimes.

JOHN POLK.   You do ceramics too?

ASHBE.   No, I never learned . . . but I have this great potholder set. [*Gets up to show him.*] See, I make lots of multicolored potholders and send them to Mama and Madeline. I also make paper hats. [*Gets material to show him.*] I guess they're more creative, but making potholders is more relaxing. Here, would you like to make a hat?

JOHN POLK.   I don't know, I'm a little drunk.

ASHBE.   It's not hard a bit. [*Hands him material.*] Just draw a real pretty design on the paper. It really doesn't have to be pretty, just whatever you want.

JOHN POLK.   It's kind of you to give my creative drives such freedom.

ASHBE.   Ha, ha, ha, I'll work on my potholder set a bit.

JOHN POLK.   What time is it? I've really got to check on the time.

ASHBE.   I know. I'll call the time operator.

[*She goes to the phone.*]

JOHN POLK.   How do you get along without a clock?

ASHBE.   Well, I've been late for school a lot. Daddy has a watch. It's 11:03.

JOHN POLK.   I've got a while yet. [*Ashbe twirls back to her chair, drops, and sighs.*] Are you a dancer, too?

ASHBE.   [*Delighted.*] I can't dance a bit, really. I practice a lot is all, at home in the afternoon. I imagine you go to a lot of dances.

JOHN POLK.   Not really, I'm a terrible dancer. I usually get bored or drunk.

ASHBE.   You probably drink too much.

JOHN POLK.   No, it's just since I've come to college. All you do there is drink more beer and write more papers.

ASHBE.   What are you studying for to be?

JOHN POLK.   I don't know.   200

ASHBE.   Why don't you become a rancher?

JOHN POLK.   Dad wants me to help run his soybean farm.

ASHBE.   Soybean farm. Yikes, that's really something. Where is it?

JOHN POLK.   Well, I live in the Delta, Hollybluff, Mississippi. Anyway, Dad feels I should go to business school first; you know, so I'll become, well, management-minded. Pass the blue.

ASHBE.   Is that what you really want to do?   205

JOHN POLK.   I don't know. It would probably be as good as anything else I could do. Dad makes good money. He can take vacations whenever he wants. Sure it'll be a ball.

ASHBE.   I'd hate to have to be management-minded. [*John Polk shrugs.*] I don't mean to hurt your feelings, but I would really hate to be a management mind. [*She starts walking on her knees, twisting her fists in front of her eyes, and making clicking sounds as a management mind would make.*]

JOHN POLK.   Cut it out. Just forget it. The farm could burn down, and I wouldn't even have to think about it.

ASHBE.   [*After a pause.*] Well, what do you want to talk about?

JOHN POLK.   I don't know.   210

ASHBE.   When was the last dance you went to?

JOHN POLK.   Dances. That's a great subject. Let's see, oh, I don't really remember—it was probably some blind date. God, I hate dates.

ASHBE.   Why?

JOHN POLK.   Well, they always say that they don't want popcorn, and they wind up eating all of yours.

ASHBE.   You mean, you hate dates just because they eat your popcorn? Don't you   215 think that's kind of stingy?

JOHN POLK.   It's the principle of the thing. Why can't they just say, yes, I'd like some popcorn when you ask them. But, no, they're always so damn coy.

ASHBE.   I'd tell my date if I wanted popcorn. I'm not that immature.

JOHN POLK.   Anyway, it's not only the popcorn. It's a lot of little things. I've finished coloring. What do I do now?

ASHBE.   Now you have to fold it. Here . . . like this. [*She explains the process with relish.*] Say, that's really something.

JOHN POLK.   It's kind of funny looking. [*Putting the hat on.*] Yeah, I like it, but you   220 could never wear it anywhere.

ASHBE.   Well, like what anyway?

JOHN POLK.   Huh?

ASHBE.   The things dates do to you that you don't like, the little things.

JOHN POLK.   Oh, well, just the way they wear those false eyelashes and put their hand on your knee when you're trying to parallel park, and keep on giggling and going off to the bathroom with their girl friends. It's obvious they don't want to go out with me. They just want to go out so that they can wear their new clothes and won't have to sit on their ass in the dormitory. They never want to go out with me. I can never even talk to them.

ASHBE.   Well, you can talk to me, and I'm a girl.   225

JOHN POLK.   Well, I'm really kind of drunk, and you're a stranger . . . well, I probably wouldn't be able to talk to you tomorrow. That makes a difference.

ASHBE.   Maybe it does. [*A bit of a pause and then extremely pleased by the idea she says.*] You know we're alike because I don't like dances either.

JOHN POLK.   I thought you said you practiced . . . in the afternoons.

ASHBE.   Well, I like dancing. I just don't like dances. At least not like . . . well, not like the one our school was having tonight . . . they're so corny.

JOHN POLK.   Yeah, most dances are.

ASHBE.   All they serve is potato chips and fruit punch, and then this stupid baby band plays and everybody dances around thinking they're so hot. I frankly wouldn't dance there. I would prefer to wait till I am invited to an exclusive ball. It doesn't really matter which ball, just one where they have huge, golden chandeliers and silver fountains, and serve delicacies of all sorts and bubble blue champagne. I'll arrive in a pink silk cape. [*Laughing.*] I want to dance in pink!

JOHN POLK.   You're mixed up. You're probably one of those people that live in a fantasy world.

ASHBE.   I do not. I accept reality as well as anyone. Anyway, you can talk to me, remember. I know what you mean by the kind of girls it's hard to talk to. There are girls a lot that way in the small clique at my school. Really tacky and mean. They expect everyone to be as stylish as they are, and they won't even speak to you in the hall. I don't mind if they don't speak to me, but I really love the orphans, and it hurts my feelings when they are so mean to them.

JOHN POLK.   What do you mean—they're mean to the "orpheens"? [*Giggles to himself at the wordplay.*]

ASHBE.   Oh, well, they sometimes snicker at the orphans' dresses. The orphans usually have hand-me-down, drab, ugly dresses. Once Shelly Maxwell wouldn't let Glinda borrow her pencil, even though she had two. It hurt her feelings.

JOHN POLK.   Are you best friends with these orphans?

ASHBE.   I hardly know them at all. They're really shy. I just like them a lot. They're the reason I put spells on the girls in the clique.

JOHN POLK.   Spells, what do you mean, witch spells?

ASHBE.   Witch spells? Not really, mostly just voodoo.

JOHN POLK.   Are you kidding? Do you really do voodoo?

ASHBE.   Sure, here I'll show you my doll. [*Goes to get doll, comes back with straw voodoo doll. Her air as she returns is one of frightening mystery.*] I know a lot about the subject. Cora, she used to wash dishes in the Moonlight Cafe, told me all about voodoo. She's a real expert on the subject, went to all the meetings and everything. Once she caused a man's throat to rot away and turn almost totally black. She's moved to Chicago now.

JOHN POLK.   It doesn't really work. Does it?

ASHBE.   Well, not always. The thing about voodoo is that both parties have to believe in it for it to work.

JOHN POLK.   Do the girls in school believe in it?

ASHBE.   Not really, I don't think. That's where my main problem comes in. I have to make the clique believe in it, yet I have to be very subtle. Mainly, I give reports in English class or Speech.

JOHN POLK.   Reports?

ASHBE.   On voodoo.

JOHN POLK.   That's really kind of sick, you know.

ASHBE.   Not really. I don't cast spells that'll do any real harm. Mainly, just the kind of thing to make them think . . . to keep them on their toes. [*Blue-drink intoxication begins to take over and JOHN POLK begins laughing.*] What's so funny?

JOHN POLK.   Nothing. I was just thinking what a mean little person you are.

ASHBE.   Mean! I'm not mean a bit.

JOHN POLK.   Yes, you are mean . . . [*Picking up color.*] . . . and green too.

ASHBE.   Green?

JOHN POLK.   Yes, green with envy of those other girls; so you play all those mean little tricks.

ASHBE.   Envious of those other girls, that stupid, close-minded little clique!   255

JOHN POLK.   Green as this marshmallow. [*Eats marshmallow.*]

ASHBE.   You think I want to be in some group . . . a sheep like you? A little sheep like you that does everything when he's supposed to do it!

JOHN POLK.   Me a sheep . . . I do what I want!

ASHBE.   Ha! I've known you for an hour and already I see you for the sheep you are!

JOHN POLK.   Don't take your green meanness out on me.   260

ASHBE.   Not only are you a sheep, you are a NORMAL sheep. Give me back my colors! [*Begins snatching colors away.*]

JOHN POLK.   [*Pushing colors at her.*] Green and mean! Green and mean! Green and mean!

ASHBE.   [*Throwing marshmallows at him.*] That's the reason you're in a fraternity and the reason you're going to manage your mind. And dates . . . you go out on dates merely because it's expected of you even though you have a terrible time. That's the reason you go to the whorehouse to prove you're a normal man. Well, you're much too normal for me.

JOHN POLK.   Infant bitch. You think you're really cute.

ASHBE.   That really wasn't food coloring in your drink, it was poison! [*She laughs,*   265
he picks up his coat to go, and she stops throwing marshmallows at him.] Are you going? I was only kidding. For Christ sake, it wasn't really poison. Come on, don't go. Can't you take a little friendly criticism?

JOHN POLK.   Look, did you have to bother me tonight? I had enough problems without . . .

[*Phone rings. Both look at phone, it rings for the third time. He stands undecided.*]

ASHBE.   Look, wait, we'll make it up. [*She goes to answer phone.*] Hello . . . Daddy. How are you? . . . I'm fine . . . Dad, you sound funny . . . What? . . . Come on, Daddy, you know she's not here. [*Pause.*] Look, I told you I wouldn't call anymore. You've got her number in Atlanta. [*Pause, as she sinks to the floor.*] Why have you started again? . . . Don't say that. I can tell it. I can. Hey, I have to go to bed now, I don't want to talk anymore, okay? [*Hangs up phone, then softly to self.*] Goddamnit.

JOHN POLK.   [*He has heard the conversation and is taking off his coat.*] Hey, Ashbe . . . [*She looks at him blankly, her mind far away.*] You want to talk?

ASHBE.   No. [*Slight pause.*] Why don't you look at my shell collection? I have this special shell collection. [*She shows him collection.*]

JOHN POLK.   They're beautiful, I've never seen colors like this. [ASHBE *is silent, he*   270
continues to himself.] I used to go to Biloxi° a lot when I was a kid . . . One time my brother and I, we camped out on the beach. The sky was purple. I remember it was really purple. We ate pork and beans out of a can. I'd always kinda wanted to do that. Every night for about a week after I got home, I dreamt about these waves foaming over my head and face. It was funny. Did you find these shells or buy them?

270 *Biloxi:* city in southern Mississippi, on the Gulf of Mexico.

ASHBE.   Some I found, some I bought. I've been trying to decipher their meaning. Here, listen, do you hear that?

JOHN POLK.   Yes.

ASHBE.   That's the soul of the sea. [*She listens.*] I'm pretty sure it's the soul of the sea. Just imagine when I decipher the language. I'll know all the secrets of the world.

JOHN POLK.   Yeah, probably you will. [*Looking into the shell.*] You know, you were right.

ASHBE.   What do you mean?

JOHN POLK.   About me, you were right. I am a sheep, a normal one. I've been trying to get out of it, but now I'm as big a sheep as ever.

ASHBE.   Oh, it doesn't matter. You're company. It was rude of me to say.

JOHN POLK.   No, because it was true. I really didn't want to go into a fraternity, I didn't even want to go to college, and I sure as hell don't want to go back to Hollybluff and work the soybean farm till I'm eighty.

ASHBE.   I still say you could work on a ranch.

JOHN POLK.   I don't know. I wanted to be a minister or something good, but I don't even know if I believe in God.

ASHBE.   Yeah.

JOHN POLK.   I never used to worry about being a failure. Now I think about it all the time. It's just I need to do something that's . . . fulfilling.

ASHBE.   Fulfilling, yes, I see what you mean. Well, how about college? Isn't it fulfilling? I mean, you take all those wonderful classes, and you have all your very good friends.

JOHN POLK.   Friends, yeah, I have some friends.

ASHBE.   What do you mean?

JOHN POLK.   Nothing . . . well, I do mean something. What the hell, let me try to explain. You see it was my "friends," the fraternity guys that set me up with G.G., excuse me, Myrtle, as a gift for my eighteenth birthday.

ASHBE.   You mean, you didn't want the appointment?

JOHN POLK.   No, I didn't want it. Hey, ah, where did my blue drink go?

ASHBE.   [*As she hands him the drink.*] They probably thought you really wanted to go.

JOHN POLK.   Yeah, I'm sure they gave a damn what I wanted. They never even asked me. Hell, I would have told them a handkerchief, a pair of argyle socks, but, no, they have to get me a whore just because it's a cool-ass thing to do. They make me sick. I couldn't even stay at the party they gave. All the sweaty T-shirts, and moron sex stories . . . I just couldn't take it.

ASHBE.   Is that why you were at the Blue Angel so early?

JOHN POLK.   Yeah, I needed to get drunk, but not with them. They're such creeps.

ASHBE.   Gosh, so you really don't want to go to Myrtle's?

JOHN POLK.   No, I guess not.

ASHBE.   Then are you going?

JOHN POLK.   [*Pause.*] Yes.

ASHBE.   That's wrong. You shouldn't go just to please them.

JOHN POLK.   Oh, that's not the point anymore, maybe at first it was, but it's not anymore. Now I have go for myself . . . to prove to myself that I'm not afraid.

ASHBE.   Afraid? [*Slowly, as she begins to grasp his meaning.*] You mean, you've never slept with a girl before?

JOHN POLK.   Well, I've never been in love.

ASHBE. [*In amazement.*] You're a virgin?

JOHN POLK. Oh, God.

ASHBE. No, don't feel bad, I am too.

JOHN POLK. I thought I should be in love . . .

ASHBE. Well, you're certainly not in love with Myrtle. I mean, you haven't even 305
met her.

JOHN POLK. I know, but, God, I thought maybe I'd never fall in love. What then?
You should experience everything . . . shouldn't you? Oh, what's it matter, everything's
so screwed.

ASHBE. Screwed? Yeah, I guess it is. I mean, I always thought it would be fun to
have a lot of friends who gave parties and go to dances all dressed up. Like the dance
tonight . . . it might have been fun.

JOHN POLK. Well, why didn't you go?

ASHBE. I don't know. I'm not sure it would have been fun. Anyway, you can't
go . . . alone.

JOHN POLK. Oh, you need a date? 310

ASHBE. Yeah, or something.

JOHN POLK. Say, Ashbe, ya wanna dance here?

ASHBE. No, I think we'd better discuss your dilemma.

JOHN POLK. What dilemma?

ASHBE. Myrtle. It doesn't seem right you should . . . 315

JOHN POLK. Let's forget Myrtle for now. I've got a while yet. Here have some
more of this blue-moon drink.

ASHBE. You're only trying to escape through artificial means.

JOHN POLK. Yeah, you got it. Now come on. Would you like to dance? Hey, you
said you liked to dance.

ASHBE. You're being ridiculous.

JOHN POLK. [*Winking at her.*] Dance? 320

ASHBE. John Polk, I just thought . . .

JOHN POLK. Hmm?

ASHBE. How to solve your problem . . .

JOHN POLK. Well . . .

ASHBE. Make love to me! 325

JOHN POLK. What?!

ASHBE. It all seems logical to me. It would prove you weren't scared, and you
wouldn't be doing it just to impress others.

JOHN POLK. Look, I . . . I mean, I hardly know you . . .

ASHBE. But we've talked. It's better this way, really. I won't be so apt to point out
your mistakes.

JOHN POLK. I'd feel great, stripping a twelve-year-old of her virginity. 330

ASHBE. I'm sixteen! Anyway, I'd be stripping you of yours just as well. I'll go put
on some Tiger Claw perfume. [*She runs out.*]

JOHN POLK. Hey, come back! Tiger Claw perfume, Christ.

ASHBE. [*Entering.*] I think one should have different scents for different moods.

JOHN POLK. Hey, stop spraying that! You know I'm not going to . . . well, you'd
get neurotic, or pregnant, or some damn thing. Stop spraying, will you!

ASHBE. Pregnant? You really think I could get pregnant? 335

JOHN POLK. Sure, it'd be a delightful possibility.

ASHBE.   It really wouldn't be bad. Maybe I would get to go to Tokyo for an abortion. I've never been to the Orient.

JOHN POLK.   Sure getting cut on is always a real treat.

ASHBE.   Anyway, I might just want to have my dear baby. I could move to Atlanta with Mama and Madeline. It'd be wonderful fun. Why I could take him to the supermarket, put him in one of those little baby seats to stroll him about. I'd buy peach baby food and feed it to him with a tiny golden spoon. Why I could take colored pictures of him and send them to you through the mail. Come on . . . [*Starts putting pillows onto the couch.*] Well, I guess you should kiss me for a start. It's only etiquette, everyone begins with it.

JOHN POLK.   I don't think I could even kiss you with a clear conscience. I mean,   340
you're so small with those little cat-eye glasses and curly hair . . . I couldn't even kiss you.

ASHBE.   You couldn't even kiss me? I can't help it if I have to wear glasses. I got the prettiest ones I could find.

JOHN POLK.   Your glasses are fine. Let's forget it, okay?

ASHBE.   I know, my lips are too purple, but if I eat carrots, the dye'll come off and they'll be orange.

JOHN POLK.   I didn't say anything about your lips being too purple.

ASHBE.   Well, what is it? You're just plain chicken, I suppose . . .   34!

JOHN POLK.   Sure, right, I'm chicken, totally chicken. Let's forget it. I don't know how, but, somehow, this is probably all my fault.

ASHBE.   You're darn right it's all your fault! I want to have my dear baby or at least get to Japan. I'm so sick of school I could smash every marshmallow in sight! [*She starts smashing.*] Go on to your skinny pimple whore. I hope the skinny whore laughs in your face, which she probably will because you have an easy face to laugh in.

JOHN POLK.   You're absolutely right, she'll probably hoot and howl her damn fizzle red head off. Maybe you can wait outside the door and hear her, give you lots of pleasure, you sadistic little thief.

ASHBE.   Thief! Was Robin Hood . . . Oh, what's wrong with this world? I just wasn't made for it, is all. I've probably been put in the wrong world, I can see that now.

JOHN POLK.   You're fine in this world.   35

ASHBE.   Sure, everyone just views me as an undesirable lump.

JOHN POLK.   Who?

ASHBE.   You, for one.

JOHN POLK.   [*Pause.*] You mean because I wouldn't make love to you?

ASHBE.   It seems clear to me.   35

JOHN POLK.   But you're wrong, you know.

ASHBE.   [*To self, softly.*] Don't pity me.

JOHN POLK.   The reason I wouldn't wasn't that . . . it's just that . . . well, I like you too much to.

ASHBE.   You like me?

JOHN POLK.   Undesirable lump, Jesus. Your cheeks they're . . . they're . . .   3•

ASHBE.   My cheeks? They're what?

JOHN POLK.   They're rosy.

ASHBE.   My cheeks are rosy?

JOHN POLK.   Yeah, your cheeks, they're really rosy.

ASHBE.   Well, they're natural, you know. Say, would you like to dance?   3•

JOHN POLK.   Yes.

ASHBE. I'll turn on the radio. [*She turns on radio. Ethel Waters is heard singing "Honey in the Honeycomb." ASHBE begins snapping her fingers.*] Yikes, let's jazz it out.

[*They dance.*]

JOHN POLK. Hey, I'm not good or anything . . .

ASHBE. John Polk.

JOHN POLK. Yeah? 370

ASHBE. Baby, I think you dance fine!

[*They dance on, laughing, saying what they want till end of song. Then a radio announcer comes on and says the 12:00 news will be in five minutes. Billie Holiday, or Terry Pierce, begins singing, "Am I Blue?"*]

JOHN POLK. Dance?

ASHBE. News in five minutes.

JOHN POLK. Yeah.

ASHBE. That means five minutes till midnight. 375

JOHN POLK. Yeah, I know.

ASHBE. Then you're not . . .

JOHN POLK. Ashbe, I've never danced all night. Wouldn't it be something to . . . to dance all night and watch the rats come out of the gutter?

ASHBE. Rats?

JOHN POLK. Don't they come out at night? I hear New Orleans has lots of rats. 380

ASHBE. Yeah, yeah, it's got lots of rats.

JOHN POLK. Then let's dance all night and wait for them to come out.

ASHBE. All right . . . but, but how about our feet?

JOHN POLK. Feet?

ASHBE. They'll hurt. 385

JOHN POLK. Yeah.

ASHBE. [*Smiling.*] Okay, then let's dance.

[*He takes her hand, and they dance as lights black out and the music soars and continues to play.*]

End.

QUESTIONS

1. What do Ashbe's actions at the start tell you about her (such as hiding under the coat, stealing and giving the stolen things away, crawling away from the waitress)? What is disclosed by her speeches?

2. Describe the circumstances of Ashbe and her family. To what degree can her character and behavior be explained by these circumstances?

3. What is Ashbe's intention in her description of G.G., or Myrtle? What does her description tell you about her? What do you learn about her from her description of the only sort of dance she would like to go to (speech 231)?

4. What personal, occupational, and social difficulties is John Polk experiencing? Why is he trying to stay drunk before going to G.G.? What are his reactions to fraternity life and to the family business?

5. Explain the effects of the arguments between Ashbe and John Polk. How does their occasionally taunting each other influence their developing relationship?

6. Why does John Polk not take up Ashbe's invitation to make love? How does this refusal suggest the development of his character? Of Ashbe's character? What may be inferred by their concluding decision to dance the night away?

GENERAL QUESTIONS

1. What is the plot of *Am I Blue?* Who is the protagonist (or protagonists)? Who or what is the antagonist? How is the plot resolved?

2. Describe and analyze the verbal comedy of the play, such as the "two murders and a knifing" (speech 49), Ashbe's description of Myrtle (speeches 71–73), and the inquiry about what to mix with rum (speech 148).

3. What is appealing (or not appealing) about Ashbe and John Polk? To what extent are you to consider them as realistic persons? How might they be seen as symbols, and what might they symbolize?

4. What are the major themes or ideas of the play? To what extent does the comic mode obscure these ideas? To what extent does it bring them out?

5. What is the effect of the setting in the New Orleans French Quarter and the characters to be found there? What is shown about Ashbe and John Polk by their brief interactions with the characters in the bar, especially Hilda, and on the street?

WRITING ABOUT COMEDY

For an essay about comedy, you can choose most of the conventional topics, such as *plot, conflict, character, point of view, setting, style, tone, symbolism,* or *theme.* You might choose one of these, or two or more; for example, how language and action define character, how character and symbol convey meaning, or how setting may influence comic structure.

Planning and prewriting strategies for each of these conventional elements are discussed at some length in Chapter 26 (pp. 1277–79) and in other chapters on prose fiction and poetry. As you develop your essay, you will find it helpful to look at these suggestions.

For the most part, planning and writing about specific features of comedy are much like addressing the same topics in other forms of drama, short stories, and poetry. However, a few areas of consideration—such as plot, character, and language—are especially significant in comic drama and can be handled in a distinctive fashion.

Questions for Discovering Ideas

PLOT, CONFLICT, STRUCTURE.   What problems, adversities, or abnormal situations are in place at the comedy's opening? How is this initial situation complicated? Do the complications spring mainly from character or from situation? If from character, what aspects of behavior or personality create the problems? If from situation, what dilemmas or troubles plague the characters? What kinds of complications dominate—misunderstandings, disagreements, mistakes in identity, situational problems, or emotional entanglements? How important is coincidence?

What problems and complications occur early? Who is the comic protagonist (or protagonists) and what is the protagonist's goal (money, success, marriage, land, freedom)? How is the protagonist blocked (fathers, rivals, laws, customs, his or her own personality)? How threatening is the obstruction? What plans are hatched to overcome the blocking agents? Are the plans sensible or silly? Who initiates and executes the plans? To what extent do plans succeed (or fail)—because of chance and good luck or because of skillful planning and manipulation?

Describe the conflicts. Which conflict is central, and whom do the conflicts involve? Do they result from personality clashes or from situations? To what degree are they related to blocking activities? How does the action reach the crisis, and which characters are involved? What choices, decisions, plans, or conclusions become necessary? What events or revelations (of character, emotion, background) produce the catastrophe, and how do these affect characters, circumstances, and relationships?

In the comic resolution, to what extent are loose ends tied up and lives straightened out? Is reasonable order restored and regeneration assured or implied? Is the resolution satisfying? Disturbing? Does it leave you happy or thoughtful, or both? Are you amused by farce, pleased by romance, or disturbed by satire? If there is to be a marriage, whom will it bring together? What will the marriage settle, or whom will it divide? Most important, how can you account for your responses to the resolution and the play as a whole? How do they reflect the general aims of comedy?

CHARACTER.   Which characters are realistic, conventional, round, flat, changing, standing still? Who is the protagonist or lover, the antagonist or blocking agent? Which characters seem excessive, eccentric, or irrational? What is the nature of their excesses? To what extent do the excesses define the characters? How do you respond to the excessive or exaggerated characters? Does the comedy provide a "cure" for the excesses? In other words, do the characters learn and change? If so, why and how? If not, why not?

From what classes are the characters derived? What class characteristics do you find? Who are the stock or stereotyped characters, and what is their significance to the protagonist? How does the playwright invigorate the characters? Who is the choric figure or *raisonneur,* if there is one? Who is the confidant? Which character can be considered a foil (or foils)?

LANGUAGE.   Does the language consist of witty turns of phrase, confusions, puns, misunderstandings, or a mixture? Which characters are masters of language and which are mastered by it? Do characters use the same type of language and level of diction consistently? To what extent does language expose a character's self-interest or hypocrisy? If the language is witty and sparkling, what devices make it work effectively? If it is garbled and filled with misunderstandings, what types of errors does the playwright put into the characters' mouths? How does the language shape your response to characters, to ideas, and to the play as a whole?

Strategies for Organizing Ideas

To develop a central idea, isolate the feature you wish to explore and consider how it affects the shape and impact of the play. For *A Midsummer Night's Dream,* for example, you might focus on Puck's character and function. You might also develop a link between Puck's conventional role as a tricky servant with his love of mischief and the chaos he creates. Remember that it is difficult to develop essays from sentences like "Puck is a comic character" or "*Love Is the Doctor* contains dramatic satire." A more focused assertion that also reveals your thematic development is necessary, such as "Puck, modeled on the tricky servant of Roman comedy, causes most of the play's confusion" or "*Love Is the Doctor* satirizes the medical profession on the grounds of ignorance and greed."

Organize your essay by grouping related types of details together (such as observations about characters, actions, direct statements, and specific words), and choose your own order of presentation. In writing about Puck as a tricky servant and creator of chaos, for example, you might present only one kind of detail—such as direct statements—and introduce these not in their order in the play but rather as they contribute to your analysis of Puck's character.

More often than not, your supporting details will represent a variety of types of evidence—dramatic dialogue and action, individual soliloquies, special properties (such as a love potion or a disguise), or the failure or development of various plans. For example, you might support an assertion about Puck by referring to his reputation, actions, and attitudes as though each of these is equally important. Other possible strategies are to demonstrate how the topics are related according to cause and effect, to build the topics from the least to the most significant, and to trace how a common idea or image provides unity. Whatever your method of development, be sure to validate your arguments with supporting details.

A summary of key points will make your conclusion useful and effective. In addition, you can show how your conclusions in the body of the essay bear upon larger aspects of the play's meaning.

DEMONSTRATIVE STUDENT ESSAY

**Setting as Symbol and Comic Structure
in *A Midsummer Night's Dream*°**

[1] Shakespeare's *A Midsummer Night's Dream* might superficially be considered light and inconsequential. The changes of mind undergone by the two sets of lovers, the placing of an ass's head on one of the characters, the presence of unrealistic fairies, the acting of a silly sketch--all seem far-fetched. But the play is real. It dramatizes the accidental and arbitrary origins of love, even though it considers this serious subject in the good-natured medium of comedy.* To bring out both message and merriment, Shakespeare uses two settings--the city of Athens and the nearby forest. The play's comic structure is governed by the movements between the order and the chaos that these two locations represent.†

[2] At the play's beginning, Athens is presented as a world of daylight, order, and law. In this setting, Duke Theseus has absolute authority, fathers are always right, and the law permits Egeus to "dispose" of Hermia "either to this gentleman [Demetrius], / Or to her death" (I.1.43–44). The city is also the place for the exposition and the beginning of complications. Here, we meet the various groups of characters (except the fairies), and we learn about the initial problem--namely, that the relationship between Hermia and Lysander is blocked by a raging father, a rival suitor, and an old law. To flee and then to overcome these obstructions, Lysander asks Hermia to meet him in the woods. Her agreement begins a journey from Athens to the forest that ultimately includes everyone in the play--the four lovers, Egeus, the city rulers, and the "mechanicals."

[3] The play's second setting, the woods outside Athens, is the kingdom of Oberon and Titania, the king and queen of the fairies. It is a world of darkness, moonlight, chaos, madness, and dreams, a world that symbolizes the power of imagination and passion. The disorder in this world has many sources, including Oberon's jealousy, Titania's infatuation, and Puck's delight in mischief. When the lovers and the mechanicals enter this setting, they also become disordered and chaotic.

[4] The woods are the setting for complication, crisis, and catastrophe. Confusion dominates the action here. Puck disrupts the mechanicals' rehearsal and transforms Bottom into an ass-headed monster. More important, the passions of the lovers are rearranged several times by Oberon and Puck through the magic of "love-in-idleness," a flower that symbolizes love's irrational but overwhelming power. Although the first two adjustments of the lovers' feelings are done to help, each has the effect of raising the levels of complication and disorder. Puck gleefully observes that his actions are the cause of the play's confusions (III.2.120–121):

° See pp. 1544–98 for this play.
* Central idea.
† Thesis sentence.

those things do best please me
That befall prepost'rously.

Puck is right; his first application of love-in-idleness causes Lysander to fall wildly in love with Helena, and his second does the same to Demetrius.

[5]   The crisis and dénouement of the main plot also occur in the woods. A crisis occurs when the two lovers challenge each other and the women attack each other. At this point, complication is at a peak, and the fairies must develop a plan to resolve the threats. Puck therefore misleads the lovers to end their potential duel, and he adjusts their emotions one more time. The dénouement--the revelation of the newly restored emotions--occurs the next morning at the edge of the woods, in the presence of Egeus, Theseus, and Hippolyta. Thus, it ends the confusing relationships occurring in the forest and begins the regularity of relationships in the orderly world of city and society.

[6]   Resolution--the marriages and the mechanicals' production of *Pyramus and Thisby*--occurs in the first setting, the city, which represents law and order. But the journey to the second setting has had a significant effect on the urban world both for Theseus and for the lovers. The law has been softened, Egeus overruled, the young lovers allowed to marry as they like, and lives set right. In the end, this second setting has also become the dream world of night and the supernatural, and the fairy dance and blessings closing the play only emphasize the harmony and the regenerative implications of the comic resolutions.

[7]   Setting, symbolism, and comic pattern thus combine in *A Midsummer Night's Dream* to produce an intricately plotted structure. Each element reinforces the others, bringing the play toward completion though time after time there seems to be no way out. The marvel of the play is that the two settings represent, realistically, two opposed states of being, and, dramatically, two distinct stages of comic structure. The journey *out of* Athens, *into* the woods, and then *back* to the city is also a journey *from* exposition and adversity, *through* complication, crisis, and catastrophe, *to* comic resolution.

Commentary on the Essay

This essay deals with three elements of *A Midsummer Night's Dream:* setting, symbol, and comic structure. It demonstrates the way a number of different topics can be combined in a single essay. Consequently, the essay is organized to reflect the journey from the city to the woods and then back to the city.

The body of the essay takes up the settings, their symbolic meaning, and the relationship between setting and structure. Paragraph 2 deals with Athens both as a world of law and order and as the setting for exposition and the beginnings of complication. The supporting details include circumstance, actions, and dialogue.

Paragraphs 3–5 deal with the middle of the journey and of the play. Paragraph 3 discusses the symbolic implications of the forest setting, and paragraphs 4 and 5 take up the connection between the setting and comic structure, specifically complication, crisis, and catastrophe. Again, the supporting details in these paragraphs are a mixture of actions, circumstances, and direct quotations.

Paragraph 6 deals briefly with the return to the city, linking this setting with the play's comic resolution. The concluding paragraph returns to the idea about how *A Midsummer Night's Dream* connects setting, symbol, and comic pattern.

SPECIAL TOPICS FOR WRITING AND ARGUMENT ABOUT COMEDY

1. Write an essay describing Shakespeare's comic technique in *A Midsummer Night's Dream*. Consider these questions: Is the basic situation serious? How does Shakespeare keep it comic? How does the boisterousness of the low characters influence your perceptions of the lovers and the courtly characters? Would the play be as interesting without Bottom and his crowd or without the fairies and their involvement? How does the comic outcome depend on the boisterousness and colorfulness provided by the players and the fairies? For research on Shakespeare as a comic dramatist, you might wish to consult Henry B. Charlton's classic study *Shakespeare's Comedies* (rpt. 1972) and/or a more recent book by Michael Mangan, *A Preface to Shakespeare's Comedies* (1996).

2. Although *Love Is the Doctor* is a farce, it deals with serious topic material, namely, a father trying to control his daughter's life, the exploitation of gullibility, and an illegal deception. How does Molière treat these topics and yet preserve the play's comic tone?

3. Write an essay that analyzes the relationship of situation to comedy in *Am I Blue*. How do the eccentricity of the characters and the improbability of their circumstances produce amusement? When you finish the play, do you believe that you have been seriously engaged? Simply entertained? Explain. For comparison with other Henley plays, you might wish to take out *Beth Henley: Four Plays* (1992) from your college library.

4. *The Bear* is one of Chekhov's most popular comedies. Read another Chekhov play (for example, *The Cherry Orchard, The Seagull, Three Sisters, Uncle Vanya*) and compare it to *The Bear* (characters with characters, dialogue with dialogue, situations with situations, and so on). As you make your comparison, attempt to explain the continued popularity of *The Bear*.

5. Write an essay about the nature of comedy, using *A Midsummer Night's Dream, Am I Blue, The Bear,* and *Love Is the Doctor* as material. Deal with issues like the following: How can comic material be defined? Does the happy outcome of a serious action qualify a play as a comedy, or should no action be serious? When is a comedy no longer comic but tragic? Are jokes necessary? Is farcical action necessary? Where are the edges between comedy and farce, on the one hand, and comedy and tragedy on the other? For a research component for this topic, you might wish to introduce materials from books by Wylie Sypher (1956, rpt. 1982, an edition of two classic essays on the comic), G. S. Amur (1963), Robert Corrigan (1965), Robert B. Heilman (1978), T. G. A. Nelson (1990), Athene Seyler (1990), Frances Teague (1994), and Janet Suzman (1995).

6. Treat the lovers in *A Midsummer Night's Dream* and *Love Is the Doctor* as types or archetypes (see Chapter 33). What is their situation? What problems block the fulfillment of their love? How serious are these problems? What actions and ruses do they plan to make things right? How are the pairs of lovers in the two plays similar? Different?

7. Write a comic scene of your own between two people, perhaps a boy and a girl, as in *Am I Blue;* or a father and daughter, as in *Love Is the Doctor;* or two people who are at first angry with each other, as in *The Bear;* or a person under a spell and a person in normal touch with reality, as in *A Midsummer Night's Dream.* After you finish your scene, write a short essay explaining the principles on which you've written your scene, such as the reasons for your choice of material, your use of jokes (if any), straightforward dialogue, anger, outrage, amused responses, and so on.

1658 ▪ 29 ▪ Visions of
break through
play is a play
nected to li

Visions of Dra...
and Nonreality: Varying th...
of Drama as Imitation

A major dimension of drama is the relationship to reality that dramatists seek to create. From Aristotle's description of the origin of tragedy, we may conclude that drama was originally considered to be an "imitation of an action"; that is, each play represents a significant and discrete series of actions that make up a complete story in the lives of the major characters. The drama focuses on only those actions and speeches that are integral to the story, and the outcome of the action is the logically necessary consequence of the conflicts and issues raised in the play. To achieve such concentration, dramatists introduce restrictions and nonrealistic conventions that aid the presentation of the story. Thus there can be no absolutely realistic drama in the sense of the straightforward duplication of life. Rather, the issue is how far drama goes either toward or away from reality.

REALISM AND NONREALISM IN DRAMA

The most important difference between realistic and nonrealistic drama concerns the play's relationships to the audience, the theater, and the world at large. In **realistic drama**, the playwright seeks to create an *illusion* of reality—*verisimilitude*. The situations, problems, characters, dialogue, and other elements are all those that might genuinely exist in the real world. The play presents a self-contained action in a world that professes to imitate reality. Ideally, the illusion of reality is never compromised; the actors never drop out of character, the audience is never addressed, and the play never acknowledges that it is a play.

In **nonrealistic drama**, even the pretense to achieve realism is abandoned, and the goal instead is to present essential features of character and society through techniques that *do not* try to mirror life. Nonrealistic drama employs whatever conventions the playwright finds useful. It can be full of devices that

the illusion on the stage (or the page) and scream out that the
—a work of art, a stylized imitation of something remotely con-
e.

Nonrealistic Drama Has Prevailed
During Most of Dramatic History

From ancient Greek tragedy through Victorian melodrama, plays were
artificial and conventionalized. The conventions of drama changed from age
to age—choruses and masks in Greek tragedy, soliloquies and blank verse in
Elizabethan plays, rhymed couplets in French and much English neoclassical
drama. Although these conventions were nonrealistic, audiences and readers
accepted them as normal features of dramatic presentation. The enduring eloquence and power of the nonrealistic tradition can be found in plays like
Sophocles' *Oedipus the King*, Shakespeare's *Hamlet*, and Miller's *Death of a
Salesman*.

By the nineteenth century, artificial and romantic drama dominated the
stage. These plays featured lavish sets, gorgeous costumes, flamboyant acting,
conventionalized plots, and happy endings. The characters were exaggerated
and idealized—heroes saving the day, heroines swooning at every opportunity,
and villains twirling their mustaches and leering at the audience as they plotted
to steal the hero's sweetheart and swindle him out of his money.

Realistic Drama Developed
in Opposition to Unrealistic Drama

In reaction to the unrealistic tradition, and as a likely development coincidental with democratic theories of society and government, a number of nineteenth-century dramatists created plays that presented realistic characters in
realistic situations and that explored the real problems of contemporary society.
The rebellion began slowly, and most of these writers were Europeans, among
them Émile Zola (French), Henrik Ibsen (Norwegian), Maxim Gorki
(Russian), and George Bernard Shaw (Irish-English). American realists, who
came to this tradition somewhat later than the Europeans, included Eugene
O'Neill, Langston Hughes, and Susan Glaspell (pp. 1270, 1663, and 1243).

**DRAMATIC REALISM ATTEMPTS TO EXPLORE THE LIVES OF PEOPLE AS THEY LIVE THEIR
LIVES.** In keeping with the goal of verisimilitude, realistic plays eliminate traditional but artificial dramatic conventions that do not occur in daily life, such
as disguises, overheard conversations, asides, soliloquies, and verse. At its best,
realistic drama is a close examination of character in conflict. The plots are
straightforward and progress chronologically. The characters look, speak, and
act as much as possible like real people. The settings are middle-class living
rooms, the country houses of the wealthy, the squalid slums of the poor. Usually

the plays explore ideas about the nature of humanity in conflict with social customs and prejudices.

REALISTIC THEATRICAL PRODUCTIONS EMPHASIZE LIFELIKE SETTINGS. The new realism called for equally new and realistic methods of production and action. Most theaters of the nineteenth century featured a darkened auditorium, a proscenium arch separating the audience from the players, and a picture-frame stage. The spectators watched the play as though the fourth wall of a room had been removed. The illusion was that the audience was eavesdropping on private conversations and events.

The settings and stage directions for realistic drama became as detailed and lifelike as possible. When the curtain went up, the audience saw a completely furnished room or office, much like the ones in which they themselves lived or worked. Ibsen's lengthy description of the setting for Acts I and II of *An Enemy of the People* (1882), for example, calls for the elaborate duplication of Norwegian middle-class living and dining rooms of the late nineteenth century (1882), complete with a sofa, a coffee table, a lighted lamp, a ceramic tile heating stove, a dining table at the end of a meal with all the china and utensils still on it, and a platter of roast beef. Lighting and costumes were equally realistic. Lighting was designed to duplicate the natural light at a particular time of day or the lamps burning in a room at night. Similarly, the lavish and beautiful costumes of nineteenth-century melodrama gave way to detailed realism in dress and makeup on the stage.

REALISTIC DRAMA REQUIRES ACTORS TO DUPLICATE THE SPEECH AND MANNERISMS OF LIVING PEOPLE. The most radical and permanent change caused by the new realism was in acting styles. In the Victorian theater, actors stood in one place, assumed a conventional stance, and declaimed their lines. In realistic drama the acting became more natural and intimate. Actors began to combine movement with dialogue and to play "within the scene" to each other rather than to the spectators.

These changes were due, in large measure, to Konstantin Stanislavsky (1863–1938), one of the founders of the Moscow Art Theater (1898) and the inventor of what we now term *method acting*. Stanislavski argued that actors had to build characterizations on a lifelong study of inner truths and motivation. He taught actors to search inwardly, within the depths of their own imaginations, for the feelings, motivations, and behavior of the characters they portray.

A New Nonrealistic Drama Was Created in Opposition to Realism

No sooner had realism taken over the stage than a new nonrealistic drama began to emerge as a reaction against realism. Many playwrights in Europe and the United States decided that realism had gone too far and that the quest for minutely realistic details had sacrificed the essence of drama—character and universal truth. Playwrights began to explore every avenue of antirealistic drama.

A CONSEQUENCE OF NONREALISTIC DRAMA WAS EXPERIMENTAL STAGING.   At the same time, new types of stages and theaters began to appear. The **thrust stage,** from Elizabethan theaters, was reintroduced. It projected into the audience, thus helping to destroy the fourth-wall principle of realistic drama. The **arena stage,** or **theater-in-the-round,** was developed, which also called for new concepts in drama and production.[1]

Playwrights like Luigi Pirandello (Italian, 1867–1936) and Bertolt Brecht (German, 1898–1956) wrote plays that required only minimal sets or no sets at all. Using this same tradition, Thornton Wilder wrote plays (such as *Our Town*) in which the action occurs on a bare stage, with the backstage area in full view showing brick walls, heating pipes, ropes, pulleys, and other stage appurtenances. To a degree, both Miller's *Death of a Salesman* and Williams's *The Glass Menagerie* share in this tradition. Miller presents us with three rooms for his characters, together with a thrust stage in which dream sequences take place, while Williams utilizes projected images and claims that his scenes are "not realistic." Such characteristics remind us constantly that we are reading or watching a play—an illusion and an imitation—rather than real life.

ELEMENTS OF REALISTIC
AND NONREALISTIC DRAMA

THE TWO KINDS OF DRAMA IMPLY GREAT DIFFERENCES IN THEIR PRESENTATION OF NARRATIVE.   Because realistic plays, like life, unfold chronologically, the *story* (as opposed to the *play*) is usually nearing conclusion when the stage action begins. In Glaspell's *Trifles*, for example, the story comprises incidents from Mrs. Wright's youth, her marital difficulties, and her reaction against her husband. All this, however, is presented in conversation; it all occurred *before* the play begins. Such events from the past have a profound impact on the present action in realistic drama, but the play itself presents only the last part of the story.

In nonrealistic drama, the structure of the plot is more fluid. Action shifts easily from the present to the past with little or no transition. Flashbacks are mixed with present action, and the entire play dramatizes the past through a present perspective. In Williams's *The Glass Menagerie*, recollected past action is revealed through the present memories of the narrator. Similarly, the action in

---

[1] For an additional discussion of stages, see pp. 1231–34.

Miller's *Death of a Salesman* constantly shifts between the present and memories of the past.

DRAMATIC CHARACTERS ARE SHAPED ACCORDING TO WHETHER THEY ARE CONCEIVED REALISTICALLY OR NONREALISTICALLY. The characters in realistic drama are as much as possible like living people. They can be representative, symbolic, or even stock characters, but they must sound and act like normal human beings, with backgrounds, emotions, motivations, and last names as well as first names. There must be reasons for their actions, words, conflicts, and relationships. Most important, they must be consistent. Their responses, decisions, and characteristics must be the same as in real life. Such fidelity to life is apparent in realistic plays like Glaspell's *Trifles* and Hughes's *Mulatto*.

In modern nonrealistic drama, the characters can be nameless figures who have no background or motivation and who drop in and out of character, or who assume a number of different functions at different times, according to the dramatist's need. Tom is such a character in Williams's *The Glass Menagerie*. At various times he is a character in the action, a narrator who provides background and commentary, and a stage manager. As a character, he interacts with Laura and Amanda; as a narrator, he speaks directly to the audience; as a stage manager, he occasionally cues the technicians offstage about music and lighting.

These distinctions do not mean that realistic characters are always round and nonrealistic ones always flat. The way in which a playwright develops characters, realistically or nonrealistically, does not control the degree to which they are developed. Thus, true-to-life characters like Mr. Hale in *Trifles* or Jim O'Connor in *The Glass Menagerie* are flat. By the same token, nonrealistic characters, like Tom in *The Glass Menagerie* or Willy Loman in *Death of a Salesman*, have enough depth and scope to be considered fully round.

LANGUAGE IS A SIGN OF THE DEGREES OF REALITY OR NONREALITY. In a realistic play, the language accurately represents the diction appropriate to the class or group of people portrayed. There is no poetry, no radical shift in style, and no direct address to the reader or speaker. In *Mulatto*, for instance, Cora and her uneducated children consistently use the vernacular speech patterns of African-Americans living in the south during the 1930s. Similarly, the characters in Glaspell's *Trifles* sound like midwestern farmers and small-town residents.

Such verisimilitude is not required in nonrealistic drama. Playwrights employ any linguistic devices that suit their needs. Some characters therefore speak in verse, clichés, or even nonsense sounds. Others have two or three separate speeds of presentation, as Tom does in *The Glass Menagerie*. Dramatists are free to introduce snippets of poetry or song into the play, as in Wilder's *The Happy Journey to Trenton and Camden*, and some characters speak directly to the audience. Often the characters talk as though they are in a dream, or are living through their memories, or are so preoccupied with their concerns that the other characters are incidental to them.

THE STAGE ITSELF IS A GRAPHIC GUIDE TO THE LEVEL OF REALITY.   Such differences in plot, characterization, and language are matched by differences in production techniques. Whereas the staging of a realistic drama must be as true to life as possible, as in *A Dollhouse*, nonrealistic drama is usually staged with few or no realistic effects. While the sets are based in reality, they are primarily symbolic and expressive of mood, employing lighting and a semitransparent painted cloth (called a **scrim**) to create the simultaneous effect of multiple places or times. Carefully controlled lighting indicates flashbacks, changes in mood, and shifts of location, and spotlights illuminate and emphasize objects and characters in ways that never happen in reality. In addition, the dramatist of a nonrealistic play is free to introduce music, special sound effects, words or images projected onto a wall or screen, action that flows off the stage into the auditorium, and speeches made directly to the spectators or the reader. All these and other devices break the illusion of reality and demand that we consider the play as an artistic construction. Such nonrealistic dramatic effects are described in the stage directions for both *Death of a Salesman* and *The Glass Menagerie*.

In this way, nonrealistic drama has moved progressively farther away from realism throughout the latter half of the twentieth century. With the development of flexible theaters, in which the seats in certain locations are removed, with acting areas being set up throughout the house, the action of plays has moved offstage and into the space once occupied by the audience.

Paradoxically, as such drama becomes more nonrealistic, the theater itself, as a place for acting and performing, becomes the dominant reality. In the 1960s and 1970s, acting companies like the Living Theater in New York experimented with plays that began onstage, moved into the audience, and ended on the streets outside. Such productions represent the edge of drama. In the mid-1980s, the Old Vic Company in England produced *The Creation*—a series of medieval mystery plays—in which the actors mingled among the spectators, separating only when their parts were called for. Whenever new scenes were introduced, the standing spectators were (literally) swept aside to provide space, so that acting areas were being shaped by the shifting audience. A production that has remained popular into the year 2000 is *Tony n' Tina's Wedding*, which is the staging of a wedding and reception (in two different locations, one a church and the other a restaurant).[2] Because performers and audience interact, particularly at the reception, many members of the audience take on impromptu acting and speaking roles. Every performance

---

[2] *Tony n' Tina's Wedding* is so firmly fixed that it has created its own Web site at <www.tonylovestina.com> and also <www.theatermania.com>, a practice now common with many long-running plays

is therefore spontaneous and unique. An argument might be made that such one-time performances represent superrealism, but in fact they blur the distinction between drama and the real world to the point where art almost ceases to be art, and all action everywhere—both real life and stage life—seems nothing but performance.

Most Plays Offer a Blend of Realism and Nonrealism

To this point we have been speaking as though realistic and nonrealistic drama were always at opposite extremes, but most plays are not purely realistic or nonrealistic. Rather, the terms represent the opposite ends of a continuum, and most plays fall somewhere between the extremes. Hughes's *Mulatto*, Glaspell's *Trifles*, and Ibsen's *A Dollhouse*, for example, are highly realistic, yet each modifies its realism through symbolism and selective emphasis. Conversely, the staging of *The Happy Journey to Trenton and Camden* is nonrealistic, yet the play's action is sufficiently realistic to justify the claim that it belongs at a midpoint between the two extremes. Both Miller's *Death of a Salesman* and Williams's *The Glass Menagerie* also fall near the middle of the continuum; they combine realistic language and characterization with nonrealistic settings, lighting, and structure.

PLAYS FOR STUDY

LANGSTON HUGHES, *MULATTO*

James Mercer Langston Hughes was born in Missouri in 1902 and reared in Kansas and Ohio. After living for a year in Mexico he attended Columbia University, but he left after one year. He received a B.A. from Lincoln University in Pennsylvania in 1929, and when he came to New York he soon became one of the leading figures in the Harlem Renaissance, an energetic burst of African-American literary creativity that also included Countée Cullen and Claude McKay (see Chapter 25). Over the next forty-five years, Hughes was to write in every major literary genre, including translations, regular columns for a weekly newspaper, and reports on the Spanish Civil War. His earliest works were poems that he published in the *Crisis*, the official journal of the National Association for the Advancement of Colored People. Eventually he published fourteen books of poems and two novels, together with a number of short-story collections and many plays and texts for musical plays.

The Great Depression, which began with the New York stock market crash in 1929, destroyed the economic underpinnings of the Harlem Renaissance. It was during the Depression that Hughes became radicalized. After visiting Haiti and Cuba he attacked what he considered U.S. imperialist interventions in those countries. He then spent a year in Soviet Russia, assisting in the preparation of a film on U.S. race relations. When he returned he published his first collection of stories, *The Ways of White Folks* (1934), in which he fictionalized his disaffection with the condition of both southern and northern African-Americans. One of the stories included in this collection was "Father and Son," a version of the material that he turned into the two-act play *Mulatto*, which was produced at the Vanderbilt Theater in New York in October 1935. The play had a run of 373 performances, the record at that time for a Broadway play by an African-American dramatist.

At that time, the growing African-American theater was dominated by two major themes, the first being the customs and problems of southern blacks. The most pressing problem was the cruelty and injustice of lynching. Angelina Weld Grimké's *Rachael* (1920) and James Miller's *Never No More* (1932) openly condemned the practice. Dennis Donaghue's *Legal Murder* (1934) was an attack on the false conviction for rape of nine young black men from Scottsboro, Alabama, a topic that Hughes also treated in his early drama *Scottsboro Limited: Four Poems and a Play in Verse* (1932). The second major theme concerned the adjustments that blacks needed to make after they left the south and migrated to cities in the north. Frank Wilson's *Meek Mose* was perhaps the most optimistic of these plays, in which dispossessed blacks discover oil on their new property. More typical were Garland Anderson's *Appearances* (1925), about how a black bellhop overcomes false charges of rape, and Wallace Thurman's *Harlem* (1929), about the difficulties of a black family living in Chicago. This theme also dominates Lorraine Hansberry's *A Raisin in the Sun* (1959), the classic drama that marked the coming of age of post–World War II African-American playwrights.

Although Langston Hughes is not thought of principally as a dramatist, he wrote plays throughout his career. In addition to the plays already mentioned, he wrote *Little Ham* (1936) and *Soul Gone Home* (1937), a short fantasy play. As the first production for the radical Suitcase Theater, which he founded after returning as a correspondent from the Spanish Civil War, he wrote *Don't You Want to Be Free* (1938). He collaborated with Arna Bontemps in *When the Jack Hollers* (1936) and with Zora Neale Hurston in *Mule Bone* (reissued in 1991). In 1948 he wrote the lyrics for the Kurt Weill and Elmer Rice musical

Street Scene, perhaps the best known of the plays in which he was involved. In 1951 he produced a libretto, *Just Around the Corner,* and in 1957 he wrote *Simply Heavenly,* a blues-musical play featuring the character Jesse Semple, whom he had created as a character in his weekly columns for the *Chicago Defender.* Although *Simply Heavenly* (which is a musical version of an earlier play, *Simple Takes a Wife*) concludes optimistically, one can find within it the serious theme of frustration resulting from the difficulties that African-Americans experience in seeking identity and recognition. Semple says, at one point:

> I'm broke, busted, and disgusted. And just spent mighty near my last nickel for a paper—and there ain't no news in it about colored folks. Unless we commit murder, robbery or rape, or are being chased by a mob, do we get on the front page, or hardly on the back. (I.5)

Hughes's interests in the last decades of his life were in the musical theater, particularly the introduction of gospel-related music and jazz. Three of his major efforts were *Black Nativity* (1961), *The Gospel Glory* (1962), and *Jericho-Jim Crow* (1964). His output as a dramatist was indeed great, even if it is overshadowed by his preeminence as a poet and fiction writer.

Hughes's *Mulatto* is one of his plays dealing with life in the south during the 1930s, a time when the system of white control over blacks was absolute and uncompromisingly harsh. Hughes's first conception of the play, as one dealing with father and son, is a perennial one. Colonel Tom Norwood and Robert Lewis, his mulatto son, recognize their relationship but also hate and reject each other. In *Mulatto* the realistic cause of conflict is the "color line"—the symbolic line that people of different races must cross in order to accept each other as human beings. Acceptance is an ideal goal, just as the color line is an insurmountable obstacle in the society that the play depicts. The lack of ability or will to cross the line governs the pattern of action and also the violent outcome. Colonel Norwood has lived in the same house with Cora Lewis for many years, and they do well together as long as he is not confronted with the issues of his paternity and his control over the plantation. There is no way he can recognize the four "yard blacks" on his plantation as his legitimate children, however, unless he is willing to forsake his identity as a white.

There are many other marks of dramatic realism, particularly the exploitation of black women (described in Act I, speech 61), the front entrance of the Norwood house, Robert's complaints about Miss Gray, and his speeding with the Ford. All of Robert's so-called "uppity" actions would not be unacceptable to white society if he were white, but because he is black they indicate a state of revolt. In addition, Robert's identity as half white, half black—he is called "yellow" by Colonel Tom—leaves him in an anomalous position, for he is not "white" enough to be equal or "black" enough to be subservient. The reality of his situation leads him to hate both whites and blacks alike, and the sudden eruption of his seething anger leads to his uncontrolled violence.

It is important to note that *Mulatto* reflects the reality of language in the south of the 1930s. Hughes's blacks, except for Robert and Sallie, use southern black vernacular (called "darky talk" by Hughes). The introduction of such speech in literature was controversial at the time. Many black intellectuals who had also been a part of the Harlem Renaissance believed that dialect should be shunned, on the principle that it reinforced negative African-American stereotypes. However, Hughes believed that using the vernacular was above all truthful and realistic, enabling writers to demonstrate that blacks are not stereotypes, that they face human problems just like everyone else, and that they succeed and fail just like everyone else. Moreover, there were precedents for the realistic use of dialect that had been set by Mark Twain in *Tom Sawyer* and *Huckleberry Finn*, both of which are acknowledged classics of American literature.

Mulatto is one of Hughes's most important plays. In 1950 he refashioned it as a libretto, titled *The Barrier*, that was set to music by the composer Jan Meyerowitz. In addition, the play was translated into Spanish and published in South America in 1954.

LANGSTON HUGHES   (1902–1967)

Mulatto _____ *1935*

CHARACTERS

Colonel Thomas Norwood. *Plantation owner, a still vigorous man of about sixty, nervous, refined, quick-tempered, and commanding; a widower who is the father of four living mulatto children by his Negro housekeeper.*

Cora Lewis. *A brown woman in her forties who has kept the house and been the mistress of Colonel Norwood for some thirty years.*

William Lewis. *The oldest son of Cora Lewis and the Colonel; a fat, easy-going, soft looking mulatto of twenty-eight; married.*

Sallie Lewis. *The seventeen-year-old daughter, very light with sandy hair and freckles, who could pass for white.*

Robert Lewis [Bert]. *Eighteen, the youngest boy; strong and well-built; a light mulatto with ivory-yellow skin and proud thin features like his father's; as tall as the Colonel, with the same gray-blue eyes, but with curly black hair instead of brown; of a fiery, impetuous temper—immature and willful—resenting his blood and the circumstances of his birth.*

Fred Higgins. *A close friend of Colonel Norwood; a county politician; fat and elderly, conventionally Southern.*

Sam. *An old Negro retainer, a personal servant of the Colonel.*

Billy. *The small son of William Lewis; a chubby brown kid about five.*

Talbot. *The overseer.*

Mose. *An elderly Negro, chauffeur for Mr. Higgins.*
A Storekeeper.
An Undertaker.
Undertaker's Helper. *Voice offstage only.*
The Mob.

ACT I

TIME.   An afternoon in early fall.
THE SETTING.   The living room of the Big House on a plantation in Georgia. Rear center of the room, a vestibule with double doors leading to the porch; at each side of the doors, a large window with lace curtains and green shades; at left a broad flight of stairs leading to the second floor; near the stairs, downstage, a doorway leading to the dining room and kitchen; opposite at right of stage, a door to the library. The room is furnished in the long outdated horsehair and walnut style of the nineties; a crystal chandelier, a large old-fashioned rug, a marble-topped table, upholstered chairs. At the right there is a small cabinet. It is a very clean, but somewhat shabby and rather depressing room, dominated by a large oil painting of NORWOOD's wife of his youth on the center wall. The windows are raised. The afternoon sunlight streams in.

ACTION.   As the curtain rises, the stage is empty. The door at the right opens and COLONEL NORWOOD enters, crossing the stage toward the stairs, his watch in his hand. Looking up, he shouts:

NORWOOD.   Cora! Oh Cora!
CORA.   [*Heard above*] Yes, sir, Colonel Tom.
NORWOOD.   I want to know if that child of yours means to leave here this afternoon?
CORA.   [*At head of steps now*] Yes, sir, she's goin' directly. I's gettin' her ready now, packin' up an' all. 'Course, she wants to tell you goodbye 'fore she leaves.
NORWOOD.   Well, send her down here. Who's going to drive her to the railroad?   5
The train leaves at three—and it's after two now. You ought to know you can't drive ten miles in no time.
CORA.   [*Above*] Her brother's gonna drive her. Bert. He ought to be back here most any time now with the Ford.
NORWOOD.   [*Stopping on his way back to the library*] Ought to be *back* here? Where's he gone?
CORA.   [*Coming downstairs nervously*] Why, he driv in town 'fore noon, Colonel Tom. Said he were lookin' for some tubes or somethin' 'nother by de mornin' mail for de radio he's been riggin' up out in de shed.
NORWOOD.   Who gave him permission to be driving off in the middle of the morning? I bought that Ford to be used when I gave orders for it to be used, not . . .
CORA. Yes, sir, Colonel Tom, but . . .   10
NORWOOD.   But what? [*Pausing. Then deliberately*] Cora, if you want that hardheaded yellow son of yours to get along around here, he'd better listen to me. He's no more than any other black buck on this plantation—due to work like the rest of 'em. I don't take such a performance from nobody under me—driving off in the middle of the day to town, after I've told him to bend his back in that cotton. How's Talbot going to keep the rest of those darkies working right if that boy's allowed to set that kind of an

example? Just because Bert's your son, and I've been damn fool enough to send him off to school for five or six years, he thinks he has a right to privileges, acting as if he owned this place since he's been back here this summer.

CORA.   But, Colonel Tom . . .

NORWOOD.   Yes, I know what you're going to say. I don't give a damn about him! There's no nigger-child of mine, yours, ours—no darkie—going to disobey me. I put him in that field to work, and he'll stay on this plantation till I get ready to let him go. I'll tell Talbot to use the whip on him, too, if he needs it. If it hadn't been that he's yours, he'd-a had a taste of it the other day. Talbot's a damn good overseer, and no saucy, lazy Nigras stay on this plantation and get away with it. [*To* CORA] Go on back upstairs and see about getting Sallie out of here. Another word from you and I won't send your [*Sarcastically*] pretty little half-white daughter anywhere, either. Schools for darkies! Huh! If you take that boy of yours for an example, they do 'em more harm than good. He's learned nothing in college but impudence, and he'll stay here on this place and work for me awhile before he gets back to any more schools. [*He starts across the room.*]

CORA.   Yes, sir, Colonel Tom. [*Hesitating*] But he's just young, sir. And he was mighty broke up when you said last week he couldn't go back to de campus. [*COLONEL NORWOOD turns and looks at CORA commandingly. Understanding, she murmurs*] Yes, sir. [*She starts upstairs, but turns back.*] Can't I run and fix you a cool drink, Colonel Tom?

NORWOOD.   No, damn you! Sam'll do it.

CORA.   [*Sweetly*] Go set down in de cool, then, Colonel. 'Taint good for you to be going' on this way in de heat. I'll talk to Robert maself soon's he comes in. He don't mean nothing—just smart and young and kinder careless, Colonel Tom, like ma mother said you used to be when you was eighteen.

NORWOOD.   Get on upstairs, Cora. Do I have to speak again? Get on! [*He pulls the cord of the servants' bell.*]

CORA.   [*On the steps*] Does you still be in the mind to tell Sallie good-bye?

NORWOOD.   Send her down here as I told you. [*Impatiently*] Where's Sam? Send him here first. [*Fuming*] Looks like he takes his time to answer that bell. You colored folks are running the house to suit yourself nowadays.

CORA.   [*Coming downstairs again and going toward door under the steps*] I'll get Sam for you.

[*CORA exits left. NORWOOD paces nervously across the floor. Goes to the window and looks out down the road. Takes a cigar from his pocket, sits in a chair with it unlighted, scowling. Rises, goes toward servants' bell and rings it again violently as SAM enters, out of breath.*]

NORWOOD.   What the hell kind of a tortoise race is this? I suppose you were out in the sun somewhere sleeping?

SAM.   No, sah, Colonel Norwood. Just tryin' to get Miss Sallie's valises down to de yard so's we can put 'em in de Ford, sah.

NORWOOD.   [*Out of patience*] Huh! Darkies waiting on darkies! I can't get service in my own house. Very well. [*Loudly*] Bring me some whiskey and soda, and ice in a glass. Is that damn Frigidaire working right? Or is Livonia still too thickheaded to know how to run it? Any ice cubes in the thing?

SAM.   Yes, sah, Colonel, yes, sah. [*Backing toward door left*] 'Scuse me, please sah, but [*as* NORWOOD *turns toward library*] Cora say for me to ask you is it all right to bring that big old trunk what you give Sallie down by de front steps. We ain't been able to tote it down them narrer little back steps, sah. Cora, say, can we bring it down de front way through here?

NORWOOD.   No other way? [*SAM shakes his head*] Then pack it on through the   25 back, quick. Don't let me catch you carrying any of Sallie's baggage out of that front door here. You-all'll be wanting to go in and out the front way next. [*Turning away, complaining to himself*] Darkies have been getting mighty fresh in this part of the country since the war. The damn Germans should've . . . [*To SAM*] Don't take that trunk out that front door.

SAM.   [*Evilly, in a cunning voice*] I's seen Robert usin' de front door—when you ain't here, and he comes up from de cabin to see his mammy. [*SALLIE, the daughter, appears at the top of the stairs, but hesitates about coming down.*]

NORWOOD.   Oh, you have, have you? Let me catch him and I'll break his young neck for him. [*Yelling at SAM*] Didn't I tell you some whiskey and soda an hour ago?

[*SAM exits left. SALLIE comes shyly down the stairs and approaches her father. She is dressed in a little country-style coat-suit ready for traveling. Her features are Negroid, although her skin is very fair. COLONEL NORWOOD gazes down at her without saying a word as she comes meekly toward him, half-frightened.*]

SALLIE.   I just wanted to tell you goodbye, Colonel Norwood, and thank you for letting me go back to school another year, and for letting me work here in the house all summer where mama is. [*NORWOOD says nothing. The girl continues in a strained voice as if making a speech*] You mighty nice to us colored folks certainly, and mama says you the best white man in Georgia. [*Still NORWOOD says nothing. The girl continues.*] You been mighty nice to your—I mean to us colored children, letting my sister and me go off to school. The principal says I'm doing pretty well and next year I can go to Normal and learn to be a teacher. [*Raising her eyes*] You reckon I can, Colonel Tom?

NORWOOD.   Stand up straight and let me see how you look. [*Backing away*] Humm-m! Getting kinder grown, ain't you? Do they teach you in that school to have good manners, and not be afraid of work, *and to respect white folks*?

SALLIE.   Yes, sir, I been taking up cooking and sewing, too.   30

NORWOOD.   Well, that's good. As I recall it, that school turned your sister out a right smart cook. Cora tells me she's got a good job in some big hotel in Chicago. I'm thinking about you going on up North there with her in a year or two. You're getting too old to be around here, and too womanish. [*He puts his hands on her arms as if feeling her flesh*]

SALLIE.   [*Drawing back slightly*] But I want to live down here with mama. I want to teach school in that there empty school house by the Cross Roads what hasn't had a teacher for five years.

[*SAM has been standing with the door cracked, overhearing the conversation. He enters with the drink and places it on the table, right. NORWOOD sits down, leaving the girl standing, as SAM pours out a drink.*]

NORWOOD.   Don't get that into your head, now. There's been no teacher there for years—and there won't be any teacher there, either. Cotton teaches these pickaninnies enough around here. Some of 'em's too smart as it is. The only reason I did have a teacher there once was to get you young ones o' Cora's educated. I gave you all a chance and I hope you appreciate it. [*He takes a long drink.*] Don't know why I did it. No other white man in these parts ever did it, as I know of. [*To* SAM] Get out of here! [*SAM exits left*] Guess I couldn't stand to see Cora's kids working around here dumb as the rest of these no-good darkies—need a dozen of 'em to chop one row of cotton, or to keep a house clean. Or maybe I didn't want Talbot eyeing you gals. [*Taking another drink*] Anyhow, I'm glad you and Bertha turned out right well. Yes, hum-m-m! [*Straightening up*] You know I tried to do something for those brothers of yours, too, but William's stupid as an ox—good for work, though—and that Robert's just an impudent, hardheaded, yellow young fool. I'm gonna break his damn neck for him if he don't watch out. Or else put Talbot on him.

SALLIE. [*Suddenly frightened*] Please, sir, don't put the overseer on Bert, Colonel Tom. He was the smartest boy at school, Bert was. On the football team, too. Please, sir, Colonel Tom. Let brother work here in the house, or somewhere else where Talbot can't mistreat him. He ain't used . . .

NORWOOD. [*Rising*] Telling me what to do, heh? [*Staring at her sternly*] I'll use the back of my hand across your face if you don't hush. [*He takes another drink. The noise of a Ford is heard outside.*] That's Bert now, I reckon. He's to take you to the railroad line, and while you're riding with him, you better put some sense into his head. And tell him I want to see him as soon as he gets back here. [*CORA enters left with a bundle and an umbrella.* SAM *and* WILLIAM *come downstairs with a big square trunk, and exit hurriedly, left.*]

SALLIE. Yes, sir, I'll tell him.

CORA. Colonel Tom, Sallie ain't got much time now. [*To the girl*] Come on, chile. Bert's here. Yo' big brother and Sam and Livonia and everybody's all waiting at de back door to say goodbye. And your baggage is being packed in. [*Noise of another car is heard outside.*] Who else is that there coming up de drive? [*CORA looks out the window.*] Mr. Higgins' car, Colonel Tom. Reckon he's coming to see you . . . Hurry up out o' this front room, Sallie. Here, take these things of your'n [*Hands her the bundle and parasol*] while I opens de door for Mr. Higgins. [*In a whisper*] Hurry up, chile! Get out! [*NORWOOD turns toward the front door as CORA goes to open it*]

SALLIE. [*Shyly to her father*] Goodbye, Colonel Tom.

NORWOOD. [*His eyes on the front door, scarcely noticing the departing SALLIE, he motions.*] Yes, yes goodbye! Get on now! [*CORA opens the front door as her daughter exits left.*] Well, well! Howdy do, Fred. Come in, come in! [*CORA holds the outer door of the vestibule wide as* FRED HIGGINS *enters with rheumatic dignity, supported on the arm of his chauffeur,* MOSE, *a very black Negro in a slouchy uniform.* CORA *closes the door and exits left hurriedly, following* SALLIE.]

NORWOOD. [*Smiling*] How's the rheumatiz today? Women or licker or heat must've made it worse—from the looks of your speed!

HIGGINS [*Testily, sitting down puffing and blowing in a big chair*] I'm in no mood for fooling, Tom, not now. [*To* MOSE] All right. [*The* CHAUFFEUR *exits front.* HIGGINS *continues angrily.*] Norwood, that damned yellow nigger buck of yours that drives that new Ford tried his best just now to push my car off the road, then got in front of me and blew dust in my face for the last mile coming down to your gate, trying to beat me in here—which he did. Such a deliberate piece of impudence I don't know if I've ever seen out of a nigger before in all the sixty years I've lived in this country. [*The noise of the Ford is heard going out the drive, and the cries of the* NEGROES *shouting farewells to* SALLIE.

HIGGINS listens indignantly.] What kind of crazy coons have you got on your place, anyhow? Sounds like a black Baptist picnic to me. [*Pointing to the window with his cane*] Tom, listen to that.

NORWOOD. [*Flushing*] I apologize to you, Fred, for each and every one of my darkies. [*SAM enters with more ice and another glass.*] Permit me to offer you a drink. I realize I've got to tighten down here.

HIGGINS. Mose tells me that was Cora's boy in that Ford—and that young black fool is what I was coming here to talk to you about today. That boy! He's not gonna be around here long—not the way he's acting. The white folks in town'll see to that. Knowing he's one of your yard niggers, Norwood, I thought I ought to come and tell you. The white folks at the Junction aren't intending to put up with him much longer. And I don't know what good the jail would do him once he got in there.

NORWOOD. [*Tensely*] What do you mean, Fred—jail? Don't I always take care of the folks on my plantation without any help from the Junction's police force? Talbot can do more with an unruly black buck than your marshal.

HIGGINS. Warn't lookin' at it that way, Tom. I was thinking how weak the doors   45
to that jail is. They've broke 'em down and lynched four niggers to my memory since it's been built. After what happened this morning, you better keep that yellow young fool out o' town from now on. It might not be safe for him around there—today, or no other time.

NORWOOD. What the hell? [*Perturbed*] He went in just now to take his sister to the depot. Damn it, I hope no ruffians'll break up my new Ford. What was it, Fred, about this morning?

HIGGINS. You haven't heard? Why, it's all over town already. He sassed out Miss Gray in the post office over a box of radio tubes that come by mail.

NORWOOD. He did, heh?

HIGGINS. Seems like the stuff was sent C.O.D. and got here all smashed up, so he wouldn't take it. Paid his money first before he saw the box was broke. Then wanted the money order back. Seems like the post office can't give money orders back—rule against it. Your nigger started to argue, and the girl at the window—Miss Gray—got scared and yelled for some of the mail clerks. They threw Bert out of the office, that's all. But that's enough. Lucky nothing more didn't happen. [*Indignantly*] That Bert needs a damn good beating—talking back to a white woman—and I'd like to give it to him myself, the way he kicked the dust up in my eyes all the way down the road coming out here. He was mad, I reckon. That's one yellow buck don't know his place, Tom, and it's your fault he don't—sending 'em off to be educated.

NORWOOD. Well, by God, I'll show him. I wish I'd have known it before he left   50
here just now.

HIGGINS. Well, he's sure got mighty aggravating ways for a buck his color to have. Drives down the main street and don't stop for nobody, white or black. Comes in my store and if he ain't waited on as quick as the white folks are, he walks out and tells the clerk his money's as good as a white man's any day. Said last week standing out on my store front that he wasn't *all* nigger no how; said his name was Norwood—not Lewis, like the rest of his family—and part of your plantation here would be his when you passed out—and all that kind of stuff, boasting to the walleyed coons listening to him.

NORWOOD. [*Astounded*] Well, I'll be damned!

HIGGINS. Now, Tom, you know that don't go 'round these parts 'o Georgia, nor nowhere else in the South. A darkie's got to keep in his place down here. Ruinous to other niggers hearing that talk, too. All this postwar propaganda on the radio about freedom and democracy—why the niggers think it's meant for them! And that Eleanor Roosevelt,° she ought to been muzzled. She's driving our niggers crazy—your boy included! Crazy! Talking about civil rights. Ain't been no race trouble in our country for three years—since the Deekin's lynching—but I'm telling you, Norwood, you better see that that buck of yours goes away from here. I'm speaking on the quiet, but I can see ahead. And what happened this morning about them radio tubes wasn't none too good.

NORWOOD.   [*Beside himself with rage*] A black ape! I—I . . .

HIGGINS.   You been too decent to your darkies, Norwood. That's what's the matter with you. And then the whole country suffers from a lot of impudent bucks who take lessons from your crowd. Folks been kicking about that, too. Guess you know it. Maybe that's the reason you didn't get that nomination for committeeman a few years back.

NORWOOD.   Maybe 'tis, Higgins. [*Rising and pacing the room*] God damn niggers! [*Furiously*] Everything turns on niggers, niggers, niggers! No wonder Yankees call this the Black Belt! [*He pours a large drink of whiskey.*]

HIGGINS.   [*Soothingly*] Well, let's change the subject. Hand me my glass, there, too.

NORWOOD.   Pardon me, Fred. [*He puts ice in his friend's glass and passes him the bottle.*]

HIGGINS.   Tom, you get excited too easy for warm weather . . . Don't ever show black folks they got you going, though. I think sometimes that's where you make your mistake. Keep calm, keep calm—and then you command. Best plantation manager I ever had never raised his voice to a nigger—and they were scared to death of him.

NORWOOD.   Have a smoke. [*Pushes cigars toward HIGGINS*]

HIGGINS.   You ought've married again, Tom—brought a white woman out here on this damn place o' yours. A woman could help you run things. Women have soft ways, but they can keep things humming. Nothing but blacks in the house—a man gets soft like niggers are inside. [*Puffing at cigar*] And living with a colored woman! Of course, I know we all have 'em—I didn't know you could make use of a white girl till I was past twenty. Thought too much o' white women for that—but I've given many a yellow gal a baby in my time. [*Long puff at cigar*] But for a man's own house you need a wife, not a black woman.

NORWOOD.   Reckon you're right, Fred, but it's too late to marry again now. [*Shrugging his shoulders*] Let's get off of darkies and women for awhile. How's crops? [*Sitting down*] How's politics going?

HIGGINS.   Well, I guess you know the Republicans is trying to stir up trouble for us in Washington. I wish the South had more men like Bilbo and Rankin° there. But, say, by the way, Lawyer Hotchkiss wants to see us both about that budget money next week. He's got some real Canadian stuff at his office, in his filing case, too—brought back from his vacation last summer. Taste better'n this old mountain juice we get around

---

53 *Eleanor Roosevelt:* Eleanor Roosevelt (1884–1962), the wife of President Franklin D. Roosevelt, was an outspoken champion of minority causes.   63 *Bilbo, Rankin:* Theodore Bilbo (1877–1947), senator from Mississippi from 1935 to 1947, and John Eliot Rankin (1882–1960), Mississippi Representative to the House from 1921 to 1953, were both noted advocates of white supremacy.

here. Not meaning to insult your drinks, Tom, but just remarking. I serve the same as you myself, label and all.

NORWOOD.   [*Laughing*] I'll have you know, sir, that this is prewar licker, sir!

HIGGINS.   Hum-m-m! Well, it's got me feelin' better'n I did when I come in   65
here—whatever it is. [*Puffs at his cigar*] Say, how's your cotton this year?

NORWOOD.   Doin' right well, specially down in the south field. Why not drive out that road when you leave and take a look at it? I'll ride down with you. I want to see Talbot, anyhow.

HIGGINS.   Well, let's be starting. I got to be back at the Junction by four o'clock. Promised to let that boy of mine have the car to drive over to Thomasville for a dance tonight.

NORWOOD.   One more shot before we go. [*He pours out drinks.*] The young ones must have their fling, I reckon. When you and I grew up down here it used to be a carriage and the best pair of black horses when you took the ladies out—now it's an automobile. That's a good lookin' new car of yours, too.

HIGGINS.   Right nice.

NORWOOD.   Been thinking about getting a new one myself, but money's been   70
kinder tight this year, and conditions are none too good yet, either. Reckon that's why everybody's so restless. [*He walks toward stairs calling.*] Cora! Oh, Cora! . . . If I didn't have a few thousand put away, I'd feel the pinch myself. [*As* CORA *appears on the stairs.*] Bring me my glasses up there by the side of my bed . . . Better whistle for Mose, hadn't I, Higgins? He's probably 'round back with some of his women. [*Winking*] You know I got some nice black women in this yard.

HIGGINS.   Oh, no, not Mose. I got my servants trained to stay in their places—right where I want 'em—while they're working for me. Just open the door and tell him to come in here and help me out. [NORWOOD *goes to the door and calls the* CHAUFEUR. MOSE *enters and assists his master out to the car.* CORA *appears with the glasses, goes to the vestibule and gets the* COLONEL'S *hat and cane which she hands him.*]

NORWOOD.   [*To* CORA] I want to see that boy o' yours soon as I get back. That won't be long, either. And tell him to put up that Ford of mine and don't touch it again.

CORA.   Yes, sir, I'll have him waiting here. [*In a whisper*] It's hot weather, Colonel Tom. Too much of this licker makes your heart upset. It ain't good for you, you know. [NORWOOD *pays her no attention as he exits toward the car. The noise of the departing motor is heard. Cora begins to tidy up the room. She takes a glass from a side table. She picks up a doily that was beneath the glass and looks at it long and lovingly. Suddenly she goes to the door left and calls toward the kitchen.*] William, you William! Com'ere, I want to show you something. Make haste, son. [*As* CORA *goes back toward the table, her eldest son,* WILLIAM *enters carrying a five-year-old boy.*] Look here at this purty doily yo' sister made this summer while she been here. She done learned all about sewing and making purty things at school. Ain't it nice, son?

WILLIAM.   Sho' is. Sallie takes after you, I reckon. She's a smart little crittur, ma. [*Sighs*] De Lawd knows, I was dumb at school. [*To his child*] Get down, Billy, you's too heavy. [*He puts the boy on the floor*] This here sewin's really fine.

BILLY.   [*Running toward the big upholstered chair and jumping up and down on the*   75
spring seat] Gityap! I's a mule driver. Haw! Gee!

CORA.   You Billy, get out of that chair 'fore I skins you alive. Get on into de kitchen, sah.

BILLY.   I'm playin' horsie, grandma. [*Jumps up in the chair*] Horsie! Horsie!

CORA.   Get! That's de Colonel's favorite chair. If he knows any little darkie's been jumpin' on it, he raise sand. Get on, now.

BILLY.   Ole Colonel's ma grandpa, ain't he? Ain' he ma white grandpa?

WILLIAM.   [*Snatching the child out of the chair*] Boy, I'm gonna fan your hide if you don't hush!

CORA.   Shs-ss-s! You Billy, hush yo' mouth! Chile, where you hear that? [*To her son*] Some o' you all been talking too much in front o' this chile. [*To the boy*] Honey, go on in de kitchen till yo' daddy come. Get a cookie from 'Vonia and set down on de back porch. [*Little BILLY exits left*]

WILLIAM.   Ma, you know it 'twarn't me told him. Bert's the one been goin' all over de plantation since he come back from Atlanta remindin' folks right out we's Colonel Norwood's chilluns.

CORA.   [*Catching her breath*] Huh!

WILLIAM.   He comes down to my shack tellin' Billy and Marybell they got a white man for grandpa. He's gonna get my chilluns in trouble sho'—like he got himself in trouble when Colonel Tom whipped him.

CORA.   Ten or 'leven years ago, warn't it?

WILLIAM.   And Bert's *sho'* in trouble now. Can't go back to that college like he could-a if he'd-a had any sense. You can't fool with white folks—an de Colonel ain't never really liked Bert since that there first time he beat him, either.

CORA.   No, he ain't. Leastwise, he ain't understood him. [*Musing sadly in a low voice*] Time Bert was 'bout seven, warn't it? Just a little bigger'n yo' Billy.

WILLIAM.   Yes.

CORA.   Went runnin' up to Colonel Tom out in de horse stables when de Colonel was showin' off his horses—I 'members so well—to fine white company from town. Lawd, that boy's always been foolish! He went runnin' up and grabbed a-holt de Colonel and yelled right in front o' de white folks' faces, "O, papa, Cora say de dinner's ready, papa!" Ain't never called him papa before, and I don't know where he got it from. And Colonel Tom knocked him right backwards under de horse's feet.

WILLIAM.   And when de company were gone, he beat that boy unmerciful.

CORA.   I thought sho' he were gonna kill ma chile that day. And he were mad at me, too, for months. Said I was teaching you chilluns who they pappy were. Up till then Bert had been his favorite little colored child round here.

WILLIAM.   Sho' had.

CORA.   But he never like him no more. That's why he sent him off to school so soon to stay, winter and summer, all these years. I had to beg and plead to have him home this summer—but I's sorry now I ever got that boy back here again.

WILLIAM.   He's sho' growed more like de Colonel all de time, ain't he? Bert thinks he's a real white man hisself now. Look at de first thing he did when he come home, he ain't seen de Colonel in six years—and Bert sticks out his hand fo' to shake hands with him!

CORA.   Lawd! That chile!

WILLIAM.   Just like white folks! And de Colonel turns his back and walks off. Can't blame him. He ain't used to such doings from colored folks. God knows what's got into Bert since he come back. He's acting like a fool—just like he was a boss man round here. Won't even say "Yes, sir" and "No, sir" no more to de white folks. Talbot asked him warn't he gonna work in de field this mornin'. Bert say "No!" and turn and walk away. White

man so mad, I could see him nearly foam at de mouth. If he warn't yo' chile, ma, he'd
been knocked in de head fo' now.

CORA. You's right.

WILLIAM. And you can't talk to him. I tried to tell him something the other day,
but he just laughed at me, and said we's all just scared niggers on this plantation. Says he
ain't no nigger, no how. He's a Norwood. He's half-white, and he's gonna act like it. [*In
amazement at his brother's daring*] And this is Georgia, too!

CORA. I's scared to death for de boy, William. I don't know what to do. De Colonel says he won't send him off to school no mo'. Says he's mo' sassy and impudent now
than any nigger he ever seed. Bert never has been like you was, and de girls, quiet and
sensible like you knowed you had to be. [*She sits down*] De Colonel say he's gonna make
Bert stay here now and work on this plantation like de rest of his niggers. He's gonna
show him what color he is. Like that time when he beat him for callin' him "papa." He
say he's gwine to teach him his place and make de boy know where he belongs. Seems
like me or you can't show him. Colonel Tom has to take him in hand, or these white
folks'll kill him around here and then—oh, My God!

WILLIAM. A nigger's just got to know his place in de South, that's all, ain't   100
he, ma?

CORA. Yes, son. That's all, I reckon.

WILLIAM. And ma brother's one damn fool nigger. Don't seems like he knows
nothin'. He's gonna ruin us all round here. Makin' it bad for everybody.

CORA. Oh, Lawd, have mercy! [*Beginning to cry*] I don't know what to do. De way
he's acting up can't go on. Way he's acting to de Colonel can't last. Somethin's gonna
happen to ma chile. I had a bad dream last night, too, and I looked out and seed de
moon all red with blood. I seed a path o' living blood across this house, I tell you, in my
sleep. Oh, Lawd, have mercy! [*Sobbing*] Oh, Lawd, help me in ma troubles. [*The noise of
the returning Ford is heard outside. CORA looks up, rises, and goes to the window.*] There's de
chile now, William. Run out to de back door and tell him I wants to see him. Bring him
in here where Sam and Livonia and de rest of 'em won't hear ever'thing we's sayin'. I
got to talk to ma boy. He's ma baby boy, and he don't know de way.

[*Exit WILLIAM through the door left. CORA is wiping her eyes and pulling herself together when the
front door is flung open with a bang and ROBERT enters.*]

ROBERT. [*Running to his mother and hugging her teasingly*] Hello, ma! Your daughter got off, and I've come back to keep you company in the parlor! Bring out the cookies
and lemonade. *Mister* Norwood's here!

CORA. [*Beginning to sob anew*] Take yo' hands off me, boy! Why don't you mind?   105
Why don't you mind me?

ROBERT. [*Suddenly serious, backing away*] Why, mamma, what's the matter? Did I
scare you? Your eyes are all wet! Has somebody been telling you 'bout this morning?

CORA. [*Not heeding his words*] Why don't you mind me, son? Ain't I told you and
told you not to come in that front door, never? [*Suddenly angry*] Will somebody have to
beat it into you? What's got wrong with you when you was away at that school? What am
I gonna do?

ROBERT. [*Carelessly*] Oh, I knew that the Colonel wasn't here. I passed him and
old man Higgins on the road down by the south patch. He wouldn't even look at me
when I waved at him. [*Half playfully*] Anyhow, isn't this my old man's house? Ain't I his
son and heir? [*Grandly, strutting around*] Am I not Mr. Norwood, Junior?

CORA.   [*Utterly serious*] I believe you goin' crazy, Bert. I believes you wants to get us all killed or run away or something awful like that. I believes . . . [*WILLIAM enters left*]

WILLIAM.   Where's Bert? He ain't come round back—[*Seeing his brother in the room*] How'd you get in here?

ROBERT.   [*Grinning*] Houses have front doors.

WILLIAM.   Oh, usin' de front door like de white folks, heh? You gwine do that once too much.

ROBERT.   Yes, like de white folks. What's a front door for, you rabbit-hearted coon?

WILLIAM.   Rabbit-hearted coon's better'n a dead coon any day.

ROBERT.   I wouldn't say so. Besides you and me's only half-coons, anyhow, big boy. And I'm gonna act like my white half, not my black half. Get me, kid?

WILLIAM.   Well, you ain't gonna act like it long here in de middle o' Georgy. And you ain't gonna act like it when de Colonel's around, either.

ROBERT.   Oh, no? My stay down here'll be short and sweet, boy, short and sweet. The old man won't send me away to college no more—so you think I'm gonna stick around and work in the fields? Like fun? I might stay here awhile and teach some o' you darkies to think like men, maybe—till it gets too much for the old Colonel—but no more bowing down to white folks for me—not Robert Norwood.

CORA.   Hush, son!

ROBERT.   Certainly not right on my own old man's plantation—Georgia or no Georgia.

WILLIAM.   [*Scornfully*] I hears you.

ROBERT.   *You* can do it if you want to, but I'm ashamed of you. I've been away from here six years. [*Boasting*] I've learned something, seen people in Atlanta, and Richmond, and Washington where the football team went—real colored people who don't have to take off their hats to white folks or let 'em go to bed with their sisters—like that young Higgins boy, asking me what night Sallie was comin' to town. A damn cracker! [*To CORA*] 'Scuse me, ma. [*Continuing*] Back here in these woods maybe Sam and Livonia and you and mama and everybody's got their places fixed for 'em, but not me. [*Seriously*] Nobody's gonna fix a place for me. I'm old man Norwood's son. Nobody fixed a place for him. [*Playfully again*] Look at me. I'm a 'fay boy. [*Pretends to shake his hair back*] See these gray eyes? I got the right to everything everybody else has. [*Punching his brother in the belly*], Don't talk to me, old slavery-time Uncle Tom.

WILLIAM.   [*Resentfully*] I ain't playin', boy. [*Pushes younger brother back with some force*] I ain't playin' a-tall.

CORA.   All right, chilluns, stop. Stop! And William, you take Billy and go on home. 'Vonia's got to get supper and she don't like no young-uns under her feet in de kitchen. I wants to talk to Bert in here now 'fore Colonel Tom gets back. [*Exit WILLIAM left. CORA continues to BERT*] Sit down, child, right here a minute and listen.

ROBERT.   [*Sitting down*] All right, ma.

CORA.   Hard as I's worked and begged and humbled maself to get de Colonel to keep you chilluns in school, you comes home wid yo' head full o' stubbornness and yo' mouth full o' sass for me an' de white folks an' everybody. You know can't no colored boy here talk like you's been doin' to no white folks, let alone to de Colonel and that old devil of a Talbot. They ain't gonna stand fo' yo' sass. Not only you, but I 'spects we's all gwine to pay fo' it, every colored soul on this place. I was scared to death today fo' yo' sister, Sallie, scared de Colonel warn't gwine to let her go back to school, neither, 'count o' yo' doins, but he did, thank Gawd—and then you come near makin' her miss de train. Did she have time to get her ticket and all?

CORA. [*Worried*] What's that?

ROBERT. The tubes was smashed when I got 'em, and I had already made out my money order, so the woman in the post office wouldn't give the three dollars back to me. All I did was explain to her that we could send the tubes back—but she got hot because there were two or three white folks waiting behind me to get stamps, I guess. So she yells at me to move on and not give her any of my "educated nigger talk." So I said, "I'm going to finish showing you these tubes before I move on"—and then she screamed and called the mail clerk working in the back, and told him to throw me out. [*Boasting*] He didn't do it by himself, though. Had to call all the white loafers out in the square to get me through that door.

CORA. [*Fearfully*] Lawd have mercy!

ROBERT. Guess if I hadn't-a had the Ford then, they'd've beat me half-to-death,   130
but when I saw how many crackers there was, I jumped in the car and beat it on away.

CORA. Thank God for that!

ROBERT. Not even a football man [*Half-boasting*] like me could tackle the whole junction. 'Bout a dozen colored guys standing around, too, and not one of 'em would help me—the dumb jiggaboos! They been telling me ever since I been here, [*Imitating darky talk*] "You can't argue wid whut folks, man. You better stay out o' this Junction. You must ain't got no sense, nigger! You's a fool" . . . Maybe I am a fool, ma—but I didn't want to come back here nohow.

CORA. I's sorry I sent for you.

ROBERT. Besides you, there ain't nobody in this country but a lot of evil white folks and cowardly niggers. [*Earnstly*] I'm no nigger, anyhow, am I, ma? I'm half-white. The Colonel's my father—the richest man in the county—and I'm not going to take a lot of stuff from nobody if I do have to stay here, not from the old man either. He thinks I ought to be out there in the sun working, with Talbot standing over me like I belonged in the chain gang. Well, he's got another thought coming! [*Stubbornly*] I'm a Norwood— not a field-hand nigger.

CORA. You means you ain't workin' no mo'?   135

ROBERT. [*Flaring*] No, I'm not going to work in the fields. What did he send me away to school for—just to come back here and be his servant, or pick his hills of cotton?

CORA. He sent you away to de school because *I* asked him and begged him, and got down on my knees to him, that's why. [*Quietly*] And now I just wants to make you see some sense, if you can. I knows, honey, you reads in de books and de papers, and you knows a lot more'n I do. But, chile, you's in Georgy—and I don't see how it is you don't know where you's at. This ain't up North—and even up yonder where we hears it's so fine, yo' sister has to pass for white to get along good.

ROBERT. [*Bitterly*] I know it.

CORA. She ain't workin' in no hotel kitchen like de Colonel thinks. She's in a office typewriting. And Sallie's studyin' de typewriter, too, at de school, but yo' pappy don't know it. I knows we ain't s'posed to study nothin' but cookin' and hard workin' here in Georgy. That's all I ever done, or knowed about. I been workin' on this very place all ma life—even 'fore I come to live in this Big House. When de Colonel's wife died, I come here, and borned you chilluns. And de Colonel's been real good to me in his way. Let you all sleep in this house with me when you was little, and sent you all off to school when you growed up. Ain't no white man in this county done that with his cullud chilluns before, far as I can know. But you—Robert, be awful, awful careful! When de Colonel comes back, in a few minutes, he wants to talk to you. Talk right to him, boy. Talk like you was colored, 'cause you ain't white.

ROBERT.   [*Angrily*] And I'm not black either. Look at me, mama. [*Rising and throwing up his arms*] Don't I look like my father? Ain't I as light as he is? Ain't my eyes gray like his eyes are? [*The noise of a car is heard outside*] Ain't this our house?

CORA.   That's him now. [*Agitated*] Hurry, chile, and let's get out of this room. Come on through yonder to the kitchen. [*She starts toward the door left.*] And I'll tell him you're here.

ROBERT.   I don't want to run into the kitchen. Isn't this our house? [*As CORA crosses hurriedly left, ROBERT goes toward the front door*] The Ford is parked out in front, anyway.

CORA.   [*At the door left to the rear of the house*] Robert! Robert! [*As ROBERT nears the front door, COLONEL NORWOOD enters, almost runs into the boy, stops at the threshold and stares unbelievingly at his son. CORA backs up against the door left.*]

NORWOOD.   Get out of here! [*He points toward the door to rear of the house where CORA is standing*].

ROBERT.   [*Half-smiling*] Didn't you want to talk to me?

NORWOOD.   Get out of here!

ROBERT.   Not that way. [*The COLONEL raises his cane to strike the boy. CORA screams. BERT draws himself up to his full height, taller than the old man and looking very much like him, pale and proud. The man and the boy face each other. NORWOOD does not strike.*]

NORWOOD.   [*In a hoarse whisper*] Get out of here. [*His hand is trembling as he points.*]

CORA.   Robert! Come on, son, come on! Oh, my God, come on. [*Opening the door left*]

ROBERT.   Not that way, ma. [*ROBERT walks proudly out the front door. NORWOOD, in an impotent rage, crosses the room to a small cabinet right, opens it nervously with a key from his pocket, takes out a pistol, and starts toward the front door. CORA overtakes him, seizes his arm, stops him.*]

CORA.   He's our son, Tom. [*She sinks slowly to her knees, holding his body.*] Remember, he's our son.

Curtain

ACT II

Scene 1

TIME.   *After supper. Sunset.*
SETTING.   *The same.*
ACTION.   *As the curtain rises, the stage is empty. Through the windows the late afternoon sun makes two bright paths toward the footlights. SAM, carrying a tray bearing a whiskey bottle and a bowl of ice, enters left and crosses toward the library. He stoops at the door right, listens a*

moment, knocks, then opens the door and goes in. In a moment SAM *returns. As he leaves the library, he is heard replying to a request of* NORWOOD'*s.*

SAM.   Yes, sah, Colonel! Sho' will, sah! Right away, sah! Yes, sah, I'll tell him. [*He closes the door and crosses the stage muttering to himself.*] Six o'clock. Most nigh that now. Better tell Cora to get that boy right in here. Can't nobody else do notin' with that fool Bert but Cora. [*He exits left. Can be heard calling*] Cora! You, Cora . . .

[*Again the stage is empty. Off stage, outside, the bark of a dog is heard, the sound of Negroes singing down the road, the cry of a child. The breeze moves the shadows of leaves and tree limbs across the sunlit paths from the windows. The door left opens and* CORA *enters, followed by* ROBERT.]

CORA.   [*Softly to* ROBERT *behind her in the dining room*] It's all right, son. He ain't come out yet, but it's nearly six, and that's when he said he wanted you, but I was afraid maybe you was gonna be late. I sent for you to come up here to de house and eat supper with me in de kitchen. Where'd you eat yo' vittuals at, chile?

ROBERT.   Down at Willie's house, ma. After the old man tried to hit me you still want me to hang around and eat up here?

CORA.   I wanted you to be here on time, honey, that's all. [*She is very nervous.*] I kinder likes to have you eat with me sometimes, too, but you ain't et up here more'n once this summer. But this evenin' I just wanted you to be here when de Colonel sent word for you, 'cause we's done had enough trouble today.

ROBERT.   He's not here on time, himself, is he?   5

CORA.   He's in de library. Sam couldn't get him to eat no supper tonight, and I ain't seen him a-tall.

ROBERT.   Maybe he wants to see me in the library, then.

CORA.   You know he don't 'low no colored folks in there 'mongst his books and things 'cept Sam. Some o' his white friends goes in there, but none o' us.

ROBERT.   Maybe he wants to see *me* in there, though.

CORA.   Can't you never talk sense, Robert? This ain't no time for foolin' and   10
jokin'. Nearly thirty years in this house and I ain't never been in there myself, not once, 'mongst de Colonel's papers. [*The clock strikes six.*] Stand over yonder and wait till he comes out. I's gwine on upstairs now, so's he can talk to you. And don't aggravate him no mo' for' God's sake. Agree to whatever he say. I's scared fo' you, chile, de way you been actin', and de fool tricks you done today, and de trouble about de post office besides. Don't aggravate him. Fo' yo' sake, honey, 'cause I loves you—and fo' all de po' colored folks on this place what has such a hard time when his humors get on him—agree to whatever he say, will you Bert?

ROBERT.   All right, ma. [*Voice rising*] But he better not start to hit me again.

CORA.   Shs-ss-s! He'll hear you. He's right in there.

ROBERT.   [*Sullenly*] This was the day I ought to have started back to school—like my sister. I stayed my summer out here, didn't I? Why didn't he keep his promise to me? You said if I came home I could go back to college again.

CORA.   Shs-ss-s! He'll be here now. Don't say nothin', chile, I's done all I could.

ROBERT.   All right, ma.   15

CORA.   [*Approaching the stairs*] I'll be in ma room, honey, where I can hear you when you goes out. I'll come down to de back door and see you 'fore you goes back to de shack. Don't aggravate him, chile.

[*She ascends the stairs. The boy sits down sullenly, left, and stares at the door opposite from which his father must enter. The clock strikes the quarter after six. The shadows of the window curtains have lengthened on the carpet. The sunshine has deepened to a pale orange, and the light paths grow less distinct across the floor. The boy sits up straight in his chair. He looks at the library door. It opens. NORWOOD enters. He is bent and pale. He looks across the room and sees the boy. Suddenly he straightens up. The old commanding look comes into his face. He strides directly across the room towad his son. The boy, half afraid, half defiant, yet sure of himself, rises. Now that ROBERT is standing, the white man turns, goes back to a chair near the table, right, and seats himself. He takes out a cigar, cuts off the end and lights it, and in a voice of mixed condescension and contempt, he speaks to his son. ROBERT remains standing near the chair.*]

NORWOOD.   I don't want to have to beat you another time as I did when you were a child. The next time I might not be able to control myself. I might kill you if I touched you again. I been runnin' this plantation for thirty-five years, and I never had to beat a Nigra as old as you are. I never had to beat one of Cora's children either—but you. The rest of 'em had sense 'nough to keep out of my sight, and to speak to me like they should . . . I don't have any trouble with my colored folks. Never have trouble. They do what I say, or what Mr. Talbot says, and that's all there is to it, I give 'em a chance. If they turn in their crops they get paid. If they're workin' for wages, they get paid. If they want to spend their money on licker, or buy an old car, or fix up their cabins, they can. Do what they choose long as they know their places and it don't hinder their work. And to Cora's young ones I give all the chances any colored folks ever had in these parts. More'n many a white child's had. I sent you all off to school. Let Bertha go on up North when she got grown and educated. Intend to let Sallie do the same. Gave your brother William that house he's living in when he got married, pay him for his work, help him out if he needs it. None of my darkies suffer. Sent you to college. Would have kept on, would have sent you back today, but I don't intend to pay for no darky, or white boy either if I had one, that acts the way you've been acting. And certainly for no black fool. Now I want to know what's wrong with you? I don't usually talk about what I'm going to do with anybody on this place. It's my habit to tell people *what to do*, not to discuss it with 'em. But I want to know what's the matter with you—whether you're crazy or not. In that case, you'll have to be locked up. And if you aren't, you'll have to change your ways a damn sight or it won't be safe for you here, and you know it—venting your impudence on white women, parking the car in front of my door, driving like mad through the Junction, and going, everywhere, just as you please. Now, I'm going to let you talk to me, but I want you to talk right.

ROBERT.   [*Still standing*] What do you mean, "talk right"?

NORWOOD.   I mean talk like a nigger should to a white man.

ROBERT.   Oh! But I'm not a nigger, Colonel Tom. I'm your son.

NORWOOD.   [*Testily*] You're Cora's boy.

ROBERT.   Women don't have children by themselves.

NORWOOD.   Nigger women don't know the fathers. You're a bastard.

[*ROBERT clenches his fist. NORWOOD turns toward the drawer where the pistol is, takes it out, and lays it on the table. The wind blows the lace curtains at the windows, and sweeps the shadows of falling leaves across the paths of sunlight on the floor.*]

ROBERT.   I've heard that before. I've heard it from Negroes, and I've heard it from white folks. Now I hear it from you. [*Slowly*] You're talking about my mother.

NORWOOD.   I'm talking about Cora, yes. Her children are bastards.   25

ROBERT.   [*Quickly*] And you're their father. [*Angrily*] How come I look like you, if you're not my father?

NORWOOD.   Don't shout at me, boy. I can hear you. [*Half-smiling*] How come your skin is yellow and your elbows rusty? How come they threw you out of the post office today for talking to a white woman? How come you're the crazy young buck you are?

ROBERT.   They had no right to throw me out. I asked for my money back when I saw the broken tubes. Just as you had no right to raise that cane today when I was standing at the door of this house where *you* live, while *I* have to sleep in a shack down the road with the field hands. [*Slowly*] But my mother sleeps with you.

NORWOOD.   You don't like it?   30

ROBERT.   No, I don't like it.

NORWOOD.   What can you do about it?

ROBERT.   [*After a pause*] I'd like to kill all the white men in the world.

NORWOOD.   [*Starting*] Niggers like you are hung to trees.

ROBERT.   I'm not a nigger.

NORWOOD.   You don't like your own race? [*ROBERT is silent*] Yet you don't like   35
white folks either?

ROBERT.   [*Defiantly*] You think I ought to?

NORWOOD.   You evidently don't like me.

ROBERT.   [*Boyishly*] I used to like you, when I first knew you were my father, when I was a little kid, before that time you beat me under the feet of your horses. [*Slowly*] I liked you until then.

NORWOOD.   [*A little pleased*] So you did, heh? [*Fingering his pistol*] A pickaninny calling me "papa." I should've broken your young neck for that first time. I should've broken your head for you today, too—since I didn't then.

ROBERT.   [*Laughing scornfully*] You should've broken my head?   40

NORWOOD.   Should've gotten rid of you before this. But you was Cora's child. I tried to help you. [*Aggrieved*] I treated you decent, schooled you. Paid for it. But tonight you'll get the hell off this place and stay off. Get the hell out of this county. [*Suddenly furious*] Get out of this state. Don't let me lay eyes on you again. Get out of here now. Talbot and the storekeeper are coming up here this evening to talk cotton with me. I'll tell Talbot to *see* that you go. That's all. [*NORWOOD motions toward the door, left.*] Tell Sam to come in here when you go out. Tell him to make a light here.

ROBERT.   [*Impudently*] Ring for Sam—I'm not going through the kitchen. [*He starts toward the front door*] I'm not your servant. You're not going to tell me what to do. You're not going to have Talbot run me off the place like a field hand you don't want to use any more.

NORWOOD.   [*Springing between his son and the front door, pistol in hand*] You black bastard! [*ROBERT goes toward him calmly, grasps his father's arm and twists it until the gun falls to the floor. The older man bends backward in startled fury and pain.*] Don't you dare put your . . .

ROBERT.   [*Laughing*] Why don't you shoot, papa? [*Louder*] Why don't you shoot?

NORWOOD.   [*Gasping as he struggles, fighting back*] . . . black . . . hands . . . on . . .   45
you . . .

ROBERT.   [*Hysterically, as he takes his father by the throat*] Why don't you shoot, papa? [*NORWOOD's hands claw the air helplessly. ROBERT chokes the struggling white man until his body grows limp*] Why don't you shoot! [*Laughing*] Why don't you shoot? Huh? Why?

[CORA *appears at the top of the stairs, hearing the commotion. She screams.*]

CORA.   Oh, my God! [*She rushes down.* ROBERT *drops the body of his father at her feet in a path of flame from the setting sun.* CORA *starts and stares in horror.*]

ROBERT.   [*Wildly*] Why didn't he shoot, mama? He didn't want *me* to live. Why didn't he shoot? [*Laughing*] He was the boss. Telling me what to do. Why didn't he shoot, then? He was the white man.

CORA.   [*Falling on the body*] Colonel Tom! Colonel Tom! Tom! Tom! [*Gazes across the corpse at her son*] He's yo' father, Bert.

ROBERT.   He's dead. The white man's dead. My father's dead. [*Laughing*] I'm living.

CORA.   Tom! Tom! Tom!

ROBERT.   Niggers are living. He's dead. [*Picks up the pistol*] This is what he wanted to kill me with, but he's dead. I can use it now. Use it on all the white men in the world, because they'll be coming looking for me now. [*Stuffs the pistol into his shirt*] They'll want me now.

CORA.   [*Rising and running toward her boy*] Quick, chile, out that way, [*Pointing toward the front door*] so they won't see you in de kitchen. Make for de swamp, honey. Cross de fields fo' de swamp. Go de crick way. In runnin' water, dogs can't smell no tracks. Hurry, chile!

ROBERT.   Yes, mama. I can go out the front way now, easy. But if I see they gonna get me before I can reach the swamp, I'm coming back here, mama, and [*Proudly*] let them take me out of my father's house—if they can. [*Pats the gun under his shirt*] They're not going to string me up to some roadside tree for the crackers to laugh at.

CORA.   [*Moaning aloud*] Oh, O-o-o! Hurry! Hurry, chile!

ROBERT.   I'm going, ma. [*He opens the door. The sunset streams in like a river of blood*]

CORA.   Run, chile!

ROBERT.   Not out of my father's house. [*He exits slowly, tall and straight against the sun.*]

CORA.   Fo' God's sake, hurry, chile! [*Glancing down the road*] Lawd have mercy! There's Talbot and de storekeeper in de drive. They sees my boy! [*Moaning*] They sees ma boy. [*Relieved*] But thank God, they's passin' him! [CORA *backs up against the wall in the vestibule. She stands as if petrified as* TALBOT *and the* STOREKEEPER *enter.*]

TALBOT.   Hello, Cora. What's the matter with you? Where's that damn fool boy o' your'n goin', coming out the front door like he owned the house? What's the matter with you, woman? Can't you talk? Can't you talk? Where's Norwood? Let's have some light in this dark place. [*He reaches behind the door and turns on the lights.* CORA *remains backed up against the wall, looking out into the twilight, watching* ROBERT *as he goes across the field*] Good God, Jim! Look at this! [*The* TWO WHITE MEN *stop in horror before the sight of* NORWOOD'S *body on the floor.*]

STOREKEEPER.   He's blue in the face. [*Bends over the body*] That nigger we saw walking out the door! [*Rising excitedly*] That nigger bastard of Cora's . . . [*Stooping over the body again*] Why the Colonel's dead!

TALBOT.   That nigger! [*Rushes toward the door*] He's running toward the swamp now . . . We'll get him . . . Telephone town—there, in the library. Telephone the sheriff. Get men, white men, after that nigger.

[*The* STOREKEEPER *rushes into the library. He can be heard talking excitedly on the phone.*]

STOREKEEPER. Sheriff! Sheriff! Is this the sheriff? I'm calling from Norwood's plantation. That nigger, Bert, has just killed Norwood—and run, headed for the swamp. Notify the gas station at the crossroads! Tell the boys at the sawmill to head him off at the creek. Warn everybody to be on the lookout. Call your deputies! Yes! Spread a dragnet. Get out the dogs. Meanwhile we'll start after him. [*He slams the phone down and comes back into the room.*] Cora, where's Norwood's car? In the barn? [CORA *does not answer.*]

TALBOT. Talk, you black bitch!

[*She remains silent.* TALBOT *runs, yelling and talking, out into the yard, followed by the* STORE-KEEPER. *Sounds of excited shouting outside, and the roar of a motor rushing down the drive. In the sky the twilight deepens into early night.* CORA *stands looking into the darkness.*]

CORA. My boy can't get to de swamp now. They's telephoned the white folks down that way. So he'll come back home now. Maybe he'll turn into de crick and follow de branch home directly. [*Protectively*] But they shan't get him. I'll make a place for to hide him. I'll make a place upstairs down under de floor, under ma bed. In a minute ma boy'll be runnin' from de white folks with their hounds and their ropes and their guns and everything they uses to kill po' colored folks with. [*Distressed*] Ma boy'll be out there runnin. [*Turning to the body on the floor*] Colonel Tom, you hear me? Our boy, out there runnin'. [*Fiercely*] *You* said he was ma boy—*ma* bastard boy. I heard you . . . but he's yours too . . . but yonder in de dark runnin'—runnin' from yo' people, from white people. [*Pleadingly*] Why don't you get up and stop 'em? He's *your* boy. His eyes is gray—like your eyes. He's tall like you's tall. He's proud like you's proud. And he's runnin'—runnin' from po' white trash what ain't worth de little finger o' nobody what's got your blood in 'em, Tom. [*Demandingly*] Why don't you get up from there and stop 'em, Colonel Tom? What's that you say? He ain't your chile? He's ma bastard chile? My yellow bastard chile? [*Proudly*] Yes, he's mine. But don't call him that. Don't you touch him. Don't you put your white hands on him. You's beat him enough, and cussed him enough. Don't you touch him now. He *is* ma boy and no white folks gonna touch him now. That's finished. I'm gonna make a place for him upstairs under ma bed. [*Backs away from the body toward the stairs*] He's ma chile. Don't you come in ma bedroom while he's up there. Don't you come to my bed no mo'. I calls you to help me now, and you just lays there. I calls you for to wake up, and you just lays there. Whenever you called me, in de night, I woke up. When you called for me to love, I always reached out ma arms fo' you. I borned you five chilluns and now one of 'em is out yonder in de dark runnin' from yo' people. Our youngest boy out yonder in de dark runnin'. [*Accusingly*] He's runnin' from you, too. You said he warn't your'n—he's just Cora's po' little yellow bastard. But he *is* your'n, Colonel Tom. [*Sadly*] And he's runnin' from you. You are out yonder in de dark, [*Points toward the door*] runnin' our chile, with de hounds and de gun in yo' hand, and Talbot's followin' 'hind you with a rope to hang Robert with. [*Confidently*] I been sleepin' with you too long, Colonel Tom, not to know that this ain't you layin' down there with yo' eyes shut on de floor. You can't fool me—you ain't never been so still like this before—you's out yonder runnin' ma boy through de fields in de dark, runnin' ma poor little helpless Bert through de fields in de dark to lynch him . . . Damn you, Colonel Norwood! [*Backing slowly up the stairs, staring at the rigid body below her*] Damn you, Thomas Norwood! God damn you!

Curtain

Scene 2

TIME.   *One hour later. Night.*
SETTING.   *The same.*
ACTION.   *As the curtain rises, the* UNDERTAKER *is talking to* SAM *at the outer door. All through this act the approaching cries of the man hunt are heard.*

UNDERTAKER.   Reckon there won't be no orders to bring his corpse back out here, Sam. None of us ain't seen Talbot or Mr. Higgins, but I'm sure they'll be having the funeral in town. The coroner told us to bring the body into the Junction. Ain't nothing' but niggers left out here now.

SAM.   [*Very frightened*] Yes, sah! Yes, sah! You's right, sah! Nothin' but us niggers, sah!

UNDERTAKER.   The Colonel didn't have no relatives far as you know, did he, Sam?

SAM.   No, sah. Ain't had none. No, sah! You's right, sah!

UNDERTAKER.   Well, you got everything o' his locked up around here, ain't you? Too bad there ain't no white folks about to look after the Colonel's stuff, but every white man that's able to walk's out with the posse. They'll have that young nigger swingin' before ten.

SAM.   [*Trembling*] Yes, sah, yes, sah! I 'spects so. Yes, sah!

UNDERTAKER.   Say, where's that woman the Colonel's been living with—where's that black housekeeper, Cora, that murderin's bastard's mother?

SAM.   She here, sah! She's up in her room.

UNDERTAKER.   [*Curiously*] I'd like to see how she looks. Get her down here. Say, how about a little drink before we start that ride back to town, for me and my partner out there with the body?

SAM.   Cora got de keys to all de licker, sah!

UNDERTAKER.   Well, get her down here then, double quick! [SAM *goes up the stairs. The* UNDERTAKER *leans in the front doorway talking to his partner outside in the wagon*] Bad business, a white man having saucy nigger children on his hands, and his black woman living in his own house.

VOICE OUTSIDE.   Damn right, Charlie.

UNDERTAKER.   Norwood didn't have a gang o' yellow gals, though, like Higgins and some o' these other big bugs. Just this one bitch far's I know, livin' with him damn near like a wife. Didn't even have much company out here. And they tell me ain't been a white woman stayed here overnight since his wife died when I was a baby. [SAM's *shuffle is heard on the stairs*] Here comes a drink, I reckon, boy. You needn't get down off the ambulance. I'll have Sam bring it out there to you. [SAM *descends followed by* CORA *who comes down the stairs. She says nothing. The* UNDERTAKER *looks up grinning at* CORA] Well, so you're the Cora that's got these educated nigger children? Hum-m! Well, I guess you'll see one of 'em swinging full of bullet holes when you wake up in the morning. They'll probably hang him to that tree down here by the Colonel's gate—'cause they tell me he strutted right out the front gate past that tree after the murder. Or maybe they'll burn him. How'd you like to see him swinging there roasted in the morning when you wake up, girlie?

CORA.   [*Calmly*] Is that all you wanted to say to me?

UNDERTAKER.   Don't get smart! Maybe you think there's nobody to boss you now. We gonna have a little drink before we go. Get out a bottle of rye.

CORA.   I takes ma orders from Colonel Norwood, sir.

UNDERTAKER.   Well, you'll take no more orders from him. He's dead out there in my wagon—so get along and get the bottle.

CORA.   He's out yonder with de mob, not in your wagon.

UNDERTAKER.   I tell you he's in my wagon!

CORA.   He's out there with de mob.   20

UNDERTAKER.   *God damn!* [*To his partner outside*] *I believe this black woman's gone crazy in here.* [*To* CORA] *Get the keys out for that licker, and be quick about it!* [CORA *does not move.* SAM *looks from one to the other, frightened.*]

VOICE OUTSIDE.   Aw, to hell with the licker, Charlie. Come on, let's start back to town. We want to get in on some of that excitement, too. They should've found that nigger by now—and I want to see 'em drag him out here.

UNDERTAKER.   All right, Jim. [*To* CORA *and* SAM] Don't you all go to bed until you see that bonfire. You niggers are getting besides yourselves around Polk County. We'll burn a few more of you if you don't be careful. [*He exits, and the noise of the dead-wagon going down the road is heard.*]

SAM.   Oh, Lawd, hab mercy on me! I prays, Lawd hab mercy! O, ma Lawd, ma Lawd, ma Lawd! Cora, is you a fool? *Is* you a fool? Why didn't you give de mens de licker, riled as these white folks is? In ma old age is I gonna be burnt by de crackers? Lawd, is I sinned? Lawd, what has I done? [*Suddenly stops moaning and becomes schemingly calm*] I don't have to stay here tonight, does I? I done locked up de Colonel's library, and he can't be wantin' nothin'. No, ma Lawd, he won't want nothin' now. He's with Jesus—or with de devil, one. [*To* CORA] I's gwine on away from here. Sam's gwine in town to his chilluns' house, and I ain't gwine by no road either. I gwine through de holler where I don't have to pass no white folks.   25

CORA.   Yes, Samuel, you go on. De Colonel can get his own drinks when he comes back tonight.

SAM.   [*Bucking his eyes in astonishment at* CORA] Lawd God Jesus!

[*He bolts out of the room as fast as his old legs will carry him.* CORA *comes down stairs, looks for a long moment out into the darkness, then closes the front door and draws the blinds. She looks down at the spot where the* COLONEL's *body lay.*]

CORA.   All de colored folks are runnin' from you tonight. Po' Colonel Tom, you too old now to be out with de mob. You got no business goin', but you had to go, I reckon. I 'members that time they hung Luke Jordon, you sent yo' dogs out to hunt him. The next day you killed all de dogs. You were kinder softhearted. Said you didn't like that kind of sport. Told me in bed one night you could hear them dogs howlin' in yo' sleep. But de time they burnt de courthouse when that po' little cullud boy was locked up in it cause they said he hugged a white girl, you was with 'em again. Said you had to go help 'em. Now you's out chasin' ma boy. [*As she stands at the window, she sees a passing figure.*] There goes yo' other woman, Colonel Tom, Livonia is runnin' from you too, now. She would've wanted you last night. Been wantin' you again ever since she got old and fat and you stopped layin' with her and put her in the kitchen to cook. Don't think I don't know, Colonel Tom. Don't think I don't remember them nights when you used to sleep in that cabin down by de spring. I knew 'Vonia was there with you. I ain't no fool, Colonel Tom. But she ain't bore you no chilluns. I'm de one that bore 'em. [*Musing*] White mens, and colored womens, and little bastard chilluns—that's de old way of de South—but it's ending now. Three of your yellow brothers yo' father had by Aunt Sallie Deal—what had to come and do your laundry to make her livin'—you got colored relatives scattered all over this county. Them de ways o' de South—mixtries, mixtries. [*WILLIAM enters left, silently, as his mother talks. She is sitting in a chair now. Without looking up*] Is that you, William?

WILLIAM. Yes, ma, it's me.

CORA. Is you runnin' from him, too?

WILLIAM. [*Hesitatingly*] Well, ma, you see . . . don't you think kinder . . . well, I reckon I ought to take Libby and ma babies on down to de church house with Reverend Martin and them, or else get 'long to town if I can hitch up them mules. They's scared to be out here, my wife and her ma. All de folks done gone from de houses down yonder by de branch, and you can hear de hounds a bayin' off yonder by de swamp, and cars is tearin' up that road, and de white folks is yellin' and hollerin' and carryin' on somethin' terrible over toward de brook. I done told Robert 'bout his foolishness. They's gonna hang him sure. Don't you think you better be comin' with us, ma. That is, do you want to? 'Course we can go by ourselves, and maybe you wants to stay here and take care o' de big house. I don't want to leave you, ma, but I . . . I . . .

CORA. Yo' brother'll be back, son, then I won't be by myself.

WILLIAM. [*Bewildered by his mothers sureness*] I thought Bert went . . . I thought he run . . . I thought . . .

CORA. No, honey. He went, but they ain't gonna get him out there. I sees him comin' back here now, to be with me. I's gwine to guard him 'till he can get away.

WILLIAM. Then de white folks'll come here, too.

CORA. Yes, de Colonel'll come back here sure. [*The deep baying of the hounds is heard at a distance through the night.*] Colonel Tom will come after his son.

WILLIAM. My God, ma! Come with us to town.

CORA. Go on, William, go on! Don't wait for them to get back. You never was much like neither one o' them—neither de Colonel or Bert—you's mo' like de field hands. Too much o' ma blood in you, I guess. You never liked Bert much, neither, and you always was afraid of de Colonel. Go on, son, and hide yo' wife and her ma and your chilluns. Ain't nothin' gonna hurt you. You never did go against nobody. Neither did I, till tonight. Tried to live right and not hurt a soul, white or colored. [*Addressing space*] I tried to live right, Lord. [*Angrily*] Tried to live right, Lord. [*Throws out her arms resentfully as if to say, "and this is what you give me."*] What's de matter, Lawd, you ain't with me?

[*The hounds are heard howling again.*]

WILLIAM. I'm gone, ma. [*He exits fearfully as his mother talks.*]

CORA. [*Bending over the spot on the floor where the COLONEL has lain. She calls.*] Colonel Tom! Colonel Tom! Colonel Tom! Look! Bertha and Sallie and William and Bert, all your chilluns, runnin' from you, and you layin' on de floor there, dead! [*Pointing*] Out yonder with the mob, dead. And when you come home, upstairs in my bed on top of my body, dead. [*Goes to the window, returns, sits down, and begins to speak as if remembering a far-off dream.*] Colonel Thomas Norwood! I'm just poor Cora Lewis, Colonel Norwood. Little black Cora Lewis, Colonel Norwood. I'm just fifteen years old. Thirty years ago, you put your hands on me to feel my breasts, and you say, "You a pretty little piece of flesh, ain't you? Black and sweet, ain't you?" And I lift up ma face, and you pull me to you, and we laid down under the trees that night, and I wonder if your wife'll know when you go back up the road into the big house. And I wonder if my mama'll know it, when I go back to our cabin. Mama said she nursed you when you was a baby, just like she nursed me. And I loved you in the dark, down there under that tree by de gate, afraid of you and proud of you, feelin' your gray eyes lookin' at me in de dark.

Then I cried and cried and told ma mother about it, but she didn't take it hard like I thought she'd take it. She said fine white mens like de young Colonel always took good care o' their colored womens. She said it was better than marryin' some black field hand and workin' all your life in de cotton and cane. Better even than havin' a job like ma had, takin' care o' de white chilluns. Takin' care o' you, Colonel Tom. [*As* CORA *speaks the sound of the approaching mob gradually grows louder and louder. Auto horns, the howling of dogs, the far-off shouts of men, full of malignant force and power, increase in volume.*] And I was happy because I liked you, 'cause you was tall and proud, 'cause you said I was sweet to you and called me purty. And when yo' wife died—de Mrs. Norwood [*Scornfully*] that never bore you any chilluns, the pale beautiful Mrs. Norwood that was like a slender pine tree in de winter frost . . . I knowed you wanted me. I was full with child by you then— William, it was—our first boy. And ma mammy said, go up there and keep de house for Colonel Tom, sweep de floors and make de beds, and by and by, you won't have to sweep de floors and make no beds. And what ma mammy said was right. It all come true. Sam and Rusus and 'Vonia and Lucy did de waitin' on you and me, and de washin' and de cleanin' and de cookin'. And all I did was a little sewin' now and then, and a little pre-servin' in de summer and a little makin' of pies and sweet cakes and things you like to eat on Christmas. And de years went by. And I was always ready for you when you come to me in de night. And we had them chilluns, your chilluns and mine, Tom Norwood, all of 'em! William, born dark like me, dumb like me, and then Baby John what died; then Bertha, white and smart like you; and then Bert with your eyes and your ways and your temper, and mighty nigh your color; then Sallie, nearly white, too, and smart, and purty. But Bert was yo' chile! He was always yo' child . . . Good-looking, and kind, and head-strong, and strange, and stubborn, and proud like you, and de one I could love most 'cause he needed de most lovin'. And he wanted to call you "papa," and I tried to teach him no, but he did it anyhow and [*Sternly*] you beat him, Colonel Thomas Norwood. And he growed up with de beatin' in his heart and your eyes in his head, and your ways, and your pride. And this summer he looked like you that time I first knowed you down by de road under them trees, young and fiery and proud. There was no touchin' Bert, just like there was no touchin' you. I could only love him, like I loved you. I could only love him. But I couldn't talk to him, because he hated you. He had your ways—and you beat him! After you beat that chile, then you died, Colonel Norwood. You died here in this house, and you been living dead a long time. You lived dead. [*Her voice rises above the nearing sounds of the mob.*] And when I said this evenin', "Get up! Why don't you help me?" You'd done been dead a long time—a long time before you laid down on this floor, here, with the breath choked out o' you—and Bert standin' over you living, living, living. That's why you hated him. And you want to kill him. Always, you wanted to kill him. Out there with de hounds and de torches and de cars and de guns, you want to kill ma boy. But you won't kill him! He's comin' home first. He's comin' home to me. He's comin' home! [*Outside the noise is tremendous now, the lights of autos flash on the window curtains, there are shouts and cries.* CORA *sits, tense, in the middle of the room.*] He's comin' home!

A MAN'S VOICE. [*Outside*] He's somewhere on this lot.   40

ANOTHER VOICE.   Don't shoot, men. We want to get him alive.

VOICE.   Close in on him. He must be in them bushes by the house.

FIRST VOICE.   Porch! Porch! Porch! There he is yonder—running to the door!

[*Suddenly shots are heard. The door bursts open and* ROBERT *enters, firing back into the dark-ness. The shots are returned by the mob, breaking the windows. Flares, lights, voices, curses, screams.*]

VOICES.   Nigger! Nigger! Nigger! Get the nigger!

[*CORA rushes toward the door and bolts it after her son's entrance.*]

CORA.   [*Leaning against the door*] I was waiting for you, honey. Yo' hiding place is all ready, upstairs, under ma bed, under de floor. I sawed a place there fo' you. They can't find you there. Hurry—before yo' father comes.

ROBERT.   [*Panting*] No time to hide, ma. They're at the door now. They'll be coming up the back way, too. [*Sounds of knocking and the breaking of glass*] They'll be coming in the windows. They'll be coming in everywhere. And only one bullet left, ma. It's for me.

CORA.   Yes, it's fo' you, chile. Save it. Go upstairs in mama's room. Lay on ma bed and rest.

ROBERT.   [*Going slowly toward the stairs with the pistol in his hand*] Goodnight, ma. I'm awful tired of running, ma. They been chasing me for hours.

CORA.   Goodnight, son.

[*CORA follows him to the foot of the steps. The door begins to give at the forcing of the mob. As ROBERT disappears above, it bursts open. A great crowd of white men pour into the room with guns, ropes, clubs, flashlights, and knives. CORA turns on the stairs, facing them quietly. TALBOT, the leader of the mob, stops.*]

TALBOT.   Be careful, men. He's armed. [*To CORA*] Where is that yellow bastard of yours—upstairs?

CORA.   Yes, he's going to sleep. Be quiet, you all. Wait. [*She bars the way with outspread arms.*]

TALBOT.   [*Harshly*] Wait, hell! Come on, boys, let's go. [*A single shot is heard upstairs.*] What's that?

CORA.   [*Calmly*] My boy . . . is gone . . . to sleep!

[*TALBOT and some of the men rush up the stairway, CORA makes a final gesture of love toward the room above. Yelling and shouting, through all the doors and windows, a great crowd pours into the room. The roar of the mob fills the house, the whole night, the whole world. Suddenly TALBOT returns at the top of the steps and a hush falls over the crowd.*]

TALBOT.   Too late, men. We're just a little too late.

[*A sigh of disappointment rises from the mob. TALBOT comes down the stairs, walks up to CORA and slaps her once across the face. She does not move. It is as though no human hand can touch her again.*]

Curtain

QUESTIONS

Act I

1.   Throughout the act—and the play—why are the children of Colonel Norwood and Cora referred to as just Cora's children?

2.   Why does the Colonel deny permission for Sallie's bags to be carried through the front door?

3. Throughout the act, what do we learn about Robert's attitudes toward his circumstances on the plantation? What do the Colonel and Higgins say about his attitude? Once Robert appears, what does he himself say about his situation?

4. What does the Colonel say about Sallie's ambition to start a nearby school? What does he advise her to do instead?

5. Who is Talbot? What does he represent? Why does he not appear until late in the second act?

6. What does Higgins report about how Robert has behaved in town? What does he tell Colonel Norwood to do about it?

7. As expressed in speech 61, what is Higgins's attitude toward black women? What does this attitude disclose about his character?

8. Describe the effect on both Robert and Colonel Norwood of the childhood incident when Robert called the Colonel "papa."

9. What has the Colonel decided to do about Robert? What are Cora's fears not only for Robert but for others?

Act II, Scene 1

10. What are the issues in the confrontation between Robert and Colonel Norwood?

11. What is Robert's dilemma (speech 35)? What has the Colonel now determined to do about Robert?

12. What is Robert's response to the Colonel's display of the gun, and his threat to use it?

13. What do Talbot and the storekeeper do once they learn that Colonel Norwood is dead? What chance does Robert have to escape?

14. Why does Cora speak so extensively over the Colonel's body?

Act II, Scene 2

15. Why are the undertaker and his companion introduced at this point? What are they like?

16. According to Cora (speech 27), what was the nature of the old "ways" of the south?

17. What is the purpose of Cora's second extensive monologue (speech 39)?

18. What finally happens to Robert? Why does Talbot slap Cora at the end?

GENERAL QUESTIONS

1. Describe *Mulatto* as a realistic play. Why is it important that the play contain many details about the plantation and the customs of the country?

2. What is the symbolism of the front door? The incident at the post office in town? Driving the Ford fast?

3. Describe Colonel Norwood. What characteristics of a southern plantation owner does he exhibit? What is shown about him by his having sent Robert and Sallie away to school? What does Cora say about him before and after he is dead?

4. Describe the character of Robert. What are his dominant traits? How politic is he in dealing with his circumstances? To what extent does he bring about his own destruction?

5. Describe Cora. What has her life been like? To what degree has she sacrificed her individuality to stay with Colonel Norwood? How does she try to protect her children? In her two major lengthy speeches, what seems to be happening to her?

6. In light of the historical time when the play was written and produced, could there have been any other outcome?

THORNTON WILDER, *THE HAPPY JOURNEY TO TRENTON AND CAMDEN*

The Happy Journey to Trenton and Camden, first published in 1931, is one of Thornton Wilder's early experiments in nonrealistic staging. He developed these techniques much more fully in later plays, including *Our Town* (1938) and *The Skin of Our Teeth* (1942), both of which were awarded the Pulitzer Prize. Wilder also wrote traditional realistic plays, including *The Merchant of Yonkers* (1938), which he later revised as *The Matchmaker* (1954). Ultimately, this play was adapted by Michael Stewart and Jerry Herman as the popular musical comedy *Hello, Dolly* (1964).

The set for *The Happy Journey to Trenton and Camden* is nonrealistic and is kept to a minimum. As the auto trip "progresses," Wilder's stage is basically empty, with no more props and scenery than a hat, some marbles, four chairs, a platform, a pea shooter, and a bed. He leaves it up to the characters themselves to bring the scenes and activities before our imaginations. Consequently we hear the children's excited reports of what they see as they look out the car windows; we visualize a funeral procession as Elmer Kirby stops the car to allow it to pass; we see the Stage Manager as a service station attendant kicking the car's tires and filling them with air; we imagine that the hot dogs are real as the family pantomimes the act of having a late afternoon snack (see speech 123 S.D.). Through these imaginative techniques Wilder calls our attention to the play's theatricality and to the nature of drama as a fictional representation of life.

The Happy Journey to Trenton and Camden also exemplifies Wilder's careful construction of plot and character. At one level, the plot is simple: it dramatizes the preparation for a trip, the trip itself, and the arrival at the destination. In a general way, these three actions progress through exposition, complication, crisis and catastrophe, and resolution. We learn about the Kirby family and their outlook on life, with special concentration on Kate Kirby—"Ma"— before the family gets in the car. Conflicts and hints of the formal crisis are developed during the trip. The play contains a submerged or hidden plot that deals with family life, death, and the ways in which people cope with loss and sorrow. These themes are brought into focus in the third phase of the action, which consists of the arrival at Camden and Ma's conversation with Beulah. Here we find both catastrophe and resolution as Ma characteristically deals with death and grief through love, care, faith, and attention to the details of daily living.

A vital additional dimension of the play results from its many geographical and cultural references, virtually from the beginning of the United States to the present day. The Kirby family is taking their "happy journey" in Revolutionary War territory. They "drive" south in their Chevrolet across New Jersey from Newark to Trenton—which was the site of one of the earliest Revolutionary victories under George Washington (speech 132)—and then to Camden, across the river from Philadelphia, which had been the capital of the Revolution. The song sung by Arthur, "The Trail of the Lonesome Pine" (speech 141), refers to Virginia, Washington's home state, and the family briefly discusses Washington's virtues.

In addition, the family's conversation is laden with references to current affairs of business, popular culture, and impending change—all matters that are integral to their thought. We learn that the elder Kirby daughter, Beulah (biblical), lives on Weyerhauser Street (American lumber) near an A & P (the national grocery chain). On their journey the family discusses steak (what could be more American than steak?) and observes road signs for spaghetti, men's clothing and suspenders, and a popular national brand of cigarettes. Their conversations produce references to a local newspaper, a national magazine, Longfellow, and Shakespeare. The dialogue also touches on the size of the U.S. population, the urban migration away from family farms, ethnic prejudice, the death of a (presumed) relative in war, and Protestant-Catholic religious diversity. The family joins together to sing the traditional "I've Been Working on the Railroad," and even demonstrates an early indulgence in fast food—perhaps the ultimate American character trait. Neither the adults nor the children say anything extraordinary about any of these topics, but their conversations unify them, and that is the point. As shown in Wilder's brief dramatization of the Kirby family, *The Happy Journey to Trenton and Camden* is a celebration of everyday American life, with an emphasis on familial relationships and personal stability.

THORNTON WILDER   (1897–1975)

The Happy Journey to Trenton and Camden _____ *1931*

CAST OF CHARACTERS

KATE KIRBY ("Ma"), *the Mother*   CAROLINE KIRBY, *the Younger Daughter*
ELMER KIRBY, *the Father*   ARTHUR KIRBY, *the Son*
BEULAH KIRBY, *the Older Daughter*   THE STAGE MANAGER

No scenery is required for this play. Perhaps a few dusty flats may be seen leaning against the brick wall at the back of the stage.

The five members of the KIRBY family and the STAGE MANAGER compose the cast. The STAGE MANAGER not only moves forward and withdraws the few properties that are required, but he reads from a typescript the lines of all the minor characters. He reads them clearly, but with little attempt at characterization, scarcely troubling himself to alter his voice, even when he responds in the person of a child or a woman.

As the curtain rises the STAGE MANAGER is leaning lazily against the proscenium pillar at the audience's left. He is smoking.

ARTHUR is playing marbles in the center of the stage.

CAROLINE is at the remote back right talking to some girls who are invisible to us. MA KIRBY is anxiously putting on her hat before an imaginary mirror.

MA.   Where's your pa? Why isn't he here? I declare we'll never get started.

ARTHUR.   Ma, where's my hat? I guess I don't go if I can't find my hat.

MA.   Go out into the hall and see if it isn't there. Where's Caroline gone to now, the plagued child?

ARTHUR.   She's out waitin' in the street talkin' to the Jones girls.—I just looked in the hall a thousand times, ma, and it isn't there. [*He spits for good luck before a difficult shot and mutters:*] Come on, baby

MA.   Go and look again, I say. Look carefully.

[*ARTHUR rises, runs to the right, turns around swiftly, returns to his game, flinging himself on the floor with a terrible impact, and starts shooting an aggie.*]

ARTHUR.   No, ma, it's not there.

MA.   [*Serenely.*] Well, you don't leave Newark without that hat, make up your mind to that. I don't go no journeys with a hoodlum.

ARTHUR.   Aw, ma!

[*MA comes down to the footlights and talks toward the audience as through a window.*]

MA.   Oh, Mrs. Schwartz!

THE STAGE MANAGER.   [*Consulting his script.*] Here I am, Mrs. Kirby. Are you going yet?

MA.   I guess we're going in just a minute. How's the baby?

THE STAGE MANAGER.   She's all right now. We slapped her on the back and she spat it up.

MA.   Isn't that fine!—Well now, if you'll be good enough to give the cat a saucer of milk in the morning and the evening, Mrs. Schwartz, I'll be ever so grateful to you.— Oh, good afternoon, Mrs. Hobmeyer!

THE STAGE MANAGER.   Good afternoon, Mrs. Kirby. I hear you're going away.

MA.   [*Modest.*] Oh, just for three days, Mrs. Hobmeyer, to see my married daughter, Beulah, in Camden. Elmer's got his vacation week from the laundry early this year, and he's just the best driver in the world.

[*CAROLINE comes "into the house" and stands by her mother.*]

THE STAGE MANAGER.   Is the whole family going?

MA.   Yes, all four of us that's here. The change ought to be good for the children. My married daughter was downright sick a while ago

THE STAGE MANAGER.   Tchk—Tchk—Tchk! Yes. I remember you tellin' us.

MA.   And I just want to go down and see the child. I ain't seen her since then. I just won't rest easy in my mind without I see her. [*To CAROLINE:*] Can't you say good afternoon to Mrs. Hobmeyer?

CAROLINE.   [*Blushes and lowers her eyes and says woodenly:*] Good afternoon, Mrs.   20
Hobmeyer.

THE STAGE MANAGER.   Good afternoon, dear.—Well, I'll wait and beat these rugs until after you're gone, because I don't want to choke you. I hope you have a good time and find everything all right.

MA.   Thank you, Mrs. Hobmeyer, I hope I will.—Well, I guess that milk for the cat is all, Mrs. Schwartz, if you're sure you don't mind. If anything should come up, the key to the back door is hanging by the ice box.

ARTHUR AND CAROLINE.   Ma! Not so loud. Everybody can hear yuh.

MA.   Stop pullin' my dress, children. [*In a loud whisper.*] The key to the back door I'll leave hangin' by the ice box and I'll leave the screen door unhooked.

THE STAGE MANAGER.   Now have a good trip, dear, and give my love to Loolie.°   25

MA.   I will, and thank you a thousand times. [*She returns "into the room."*] What can be keeping your pa?

ARTHUR.   I can't find my hat, ma.

[*Enter ELMER holding a hat.*]

ELMER.   Here's Arthur's hat. He musta left it in the car Sunday.

MA.   That's a mercy. Now we can start—Caroline Kirby, what you done to your cheeks?

CAROLINE.   [*Defiant-abashed.*] Nothin'.   30

MA.   If you've put anything on 'em, I'll slap you.

CAROLINE.   No, ma, of course I haven't. [*Hanging her head.*] I just rubbed'm to makem red. All the girls do that at High School when they're goin' places.

MA.   Such silliness I never saw. Elmer, what kep' you?

ELMER.   [*Always even-voiced and always looking out a little anxiously through his spectacles.*] I just went to the garage and had Charlie give a last look at it, Kate.

MA.   I'm glad you did. I wouldn't like to have no breakdown miles from any-   35
where. Now we can start. Arthur, put those marbles away. Anybody'd think you didn't want to go on a journey, to look at yuh.

[*They go out through the "hall," take the short steps that denote going downstairs, and find themselves in the street.*]

ELMER.   Here, you boys, you keep away from that car.

MA.   Those Sullivan boys put their heads into everything.

[*THE STAGE MANAGER has moved forward four chairs and a low platform. This is the automobile. It is in the center of the stage and faces the audience. The platform slightly raises the two chairs in the rear. PA's hands hold an imaginary steering wheel and continually shift gears. CAROLINE sits beside him. ARTHUR is behind him and MA behind CAROLINE.*]

25 *Loolie:*   a diminutive name for Beulah, the elder daughter.

CAROLINE. [*Self-consciously.*] Goodbye, Mildred. Goodbye, Helen.

THE STAGE MANAGER. Goodbye, Caroline. Goodbye, Mrs. Kirby. I hope y'have a good time.

MA. Goodbye, girls.

THE STAGE MANAGER. Goodbye, Kate. The car looks fine.

MA. [*Looking upward toward a window.*] Oh, goodbye, Emma! [*Modestly.*] We think it's the best little Chevrolet in the world.—Oh, goodbye, Mrs. Adler!

THE STAGE MANAGER. What, are you going away, Mrs. Kirby?

MA. Just for three days, Mrs. Adler, to see my married daughter in Camden.

THE STAGE MANAGER. Have a good time.

[*Now MA, CAROLINE, and THE STAGE MANAGER break out into a tremendous chorus of good-byes. The whole street is saying goodbye. Arthur takes out his pea shooter and lets fly happily into the air. There is a lurch or two and they are off.*]

ARTHUR. [*In sudden fright.*] Pa! Pa! Don't go by the school. Mr. Biedenbach might see us!

MA. I don't care if he does see us. I guess I can take my children out of school for one day without having to hide down back streets about it. [*ELMER nods to a passerby. MA asks without sharpness:*] Who was that you spoke to, Elmer?

ELMER. That was the fellow who arranges our banquets down to the Lodge, Kate.

MA. Is he the one who had to buy four hundred steaks? [*PA nods.*] I declare, I'm glad I'm not him.

ELMER. The air's getting better already. Take deep breaths, children.

[*They inhale noisily.*]

ARTHUR. Gee, it's almost open fields already. *"Weber and Heilbronner Suits for Well-dressed Men."* Ma, can I have one of them some day?

MA. If you graduate with good marks perhaps your father'll let you have one for graduation.

CAROLINE. [*Whining.*] Oh, Pa! do we have to wait while that whole funeral goes by?

[*PA takes off his hat. MA cranes forward with absorbed curiosity.*]

MA. Take off your hat, Arthur. Look at your father.—Why, Elmer, I do believe that's a lodge-brother of yours. See the banner? I suppose this is the Elizabeth branch. [*ELMER nods. MA sighs: Tchk—tchk—tchk. They all lean forward and watch the funeral in silence, growing momentarily more solemnized. After a pause, MA continues almost dreamily:*] Well, we haven't forgotten the one that he went on, have we? We haven't forgotten our good Harold. He gave his life for his country, we mustn't forget that. [*She passes her finger from the corner of her eye across her cheek. There is another pause.*] Well, we'll all hold up the traffic for a few minutes some day.

THE CHILDREN. [*Very uncomfortable.*] Ma!

MA. [*Without self-pity.*] Well I'm "ready," children. I hope everybody in this car is "ready." [*She puts her hand on PA's shoulder.*] And I pray to go first, Elmer. Yes. [*PA touches her hand.*]

THE CHILDREN. Ma, everybody's looking at you. Everybody's laughing at you.

MA. Oh, hold your tongues! I don't care what a lot of silly people in Elizabeth, New Jersey, think of me.—Now we can go on. That's the last.

[*There is another lurch and the car goes on.*]

CAROLINE. *"Fit-Rite Suspenders. The Working Man's Choice."* Pa, why do they spell Rite that way?

ELMER. So that it'll make you stop and ask about it, Missy.   60

CAROLINE. Papa, you're teasing me.—Ma, why do they say *"Three Hundred Rooms Three Hundred Baths"*?

ARTHUR. *"Miller's Spaghetti: The Family's Favorite Dish."* Ma, why don't you ever have spaghetti?

MA. Go along, you'd never eat it.

ARTHUR. Ma, I like it now.

CAROLINE. [*With gesture.*] Yum-yum. It looks wonderful up there. Ma, make some   65 when we get home?

MA. [*Dryly.*] "The management is always happy to receive suggestions. We aim to please."

[*The whole family finds this exquisitely funny.* THE CHILDREN *scream with laughter. Even* ELMER *smiles.* MA *remains modest.*]

ELMER. Well, I guess no one's complaining, Kate. Everybody knows you're a good cook.

MA. I don't know whether I'm a good cook or not, but I know I've had practice. At least I've cooked three meals a day for twenty-five years.

ARTHUR. Aw, Ma, you went out to eat once in a while.

MA. Yes. That made it a leap year.   70

[*This joke is no less successful than its predecessor. When the laughter dies down,* CAROLINE *turns around in an ecstasy of well-being and kneeling on the cushions says:*]

CAROLINE. Ma, I love going out in the country like this. Let's do it often, Ma.

MA. Goodness, smell that air will you! It's got the whole ocean in it.— Elmer, drive careful over that bridge. This must be New Brunswick we're coming to.

ARTHUR. [*Jealous of his mother's successes.*] Ma, when is the next comfort station?

MA. [*Unruffled.*] You don't want one. You just said that to be awful.

CAROLINE. [*Shrilly.*] Yes, he did, Ma. He's terrible. He says that kind of thing right   75 out in school and I want to sink through the floor, ma. He's terrible.

MA. Oh, don't get so excited about nothing, Miss Proper! I guess we're all yewman-beings in this car, at least as far as I know. And, Arthur, you try and be a gentle-man.—Elmer, don't run over that collie dog. [*She follows the dog with her eyes.*] Looked kinda peakèd to me. Needs a good honest bowl of leavings. Pretty dog, too. [*Her eyes fall on a billboard.*] That's a pretty advertisement for Chesterfield cigarettes, isn't it? Looks like Beulah, a little.

ARTHUR. Ma?

MA. Yes.

ARTHUR. [*"Route" rhymes with "out."*] Can't I take a paper route with the Newark Daily Post?

MA. No, you cannot. No, sir. I hear they make the paper boys get up at four-   80 thirty in the morning. No son of mine is going to get up at four-thirty every morning, not if it's to make a million dollars. Your *Saturday Evening Post* route on Thursday mornings is enough.

ARTHUR.   Aw, Ma.

MA.   No, sir. No son of mine is going to get up at four-thirty and miss the sleep God meant him to have.

ARTHUR.   [*Sullenly.*] Hhm! Ma's always talking about God. I guess she got a letter from him this morning. [*MA rises, outraged.*]

MA.   Elmer, stop that automobile this minute. I don't go another step with anybody that says things like that. Arthur, you get out of this car. Elmer, you give him another dollar bill. He can go back to Newark, by himself. I don't want him.

ARTHUR.   What did I say? There wasn't anything terrible about that.

ELMER.   I didn't hear what he said, Kate.

MA.   God has done a lot of things for me and I won't have him made fun of by anybody. Go away. Go away from me.

CAROLINE.   Aw, Ma,—don't spoil the ride.

MA.   No.

ELMER.   We might as well go on, Kate, since we've got started. I'll talk to the boy tonight.

MA.   [*Slowly conceding.*] All right, if you say so, Elmer. But I won't sit beside him. Caroline, you come, and sit by me.

ARTHUR.   [*Frightened.*] Aw, Ma, that wasn't so terrible.

MA.   I don't want to talk about it. I hope your father washes your mouth out with soap and water.—Where'd we all be if I started talking about God like that, I'd like to know! We'd be in the speak-easies and night-clubs and places like that, that's where we'd be.—All right, Elmer, you can go on now.

CAROLINE.   What did he say, Ma? I didn't hear what he said.

MA.   I don't want to talk about it.

[*They drive on in silence for a moment, the shocked silence after a scandal.*]

ELMER.   I'm going to stop and give the car a little water, I guess

MA.   All right, Elmer. You know best.

ELMER.   [*To a garage hand.*] Could I have a little water in the radiator—to make sure?

THE STAGE MANAGER.   [*In this scene alone he lays aside his script and enters into a role seriously.*] You sure can. [*He punches the tires.*] Air, all right? Do you need any oil or gas?

ELMER.   No, I think not. I just got fixed up in Newark.

MA.   We're on the right road for Camden, are we?

THE STAGE MANAGER.   Yes, keep straight ahead. You can't miss it. You'll be in Trenton in a few minutes. [*He carefully pours some water into the hood.*] Camden's a great town, lady, believe me.

MA.   My daughter likes it fine,—my married daughter.

THE STAGE MANAGER.   Ye'? It's a great burg all right. I guess I think so because I was born near there.

MA.   Well, well. Your folks still live there?

THE STAGE MANAGER.   No, my old man sold the farm and they built a factory on it. So the folks moved to Philadelphia.

MA.   My married daughter Beulah lives there because her husband works in the telephone company.—Stop pokin' me, Caroline!—We're all going down to see her for a few days.

THE STAGE MANAGER.   Ye'?

MA.   She's been sick, you see, and I just felt I had to go and see her. My husband and my boy are going to stay at the Y.M.C.A. I hear they've got a dormitory on the top floor that's real clean and comfortable. Had you ever been there?

THE STAGE MANAGER.   No. I'm Knights of Columbus myself.   110

MA.   Oh.

THE STAGE MANAGER.   I used to play basketball at the Y though. It looked all right to me. [*He has been standing with one foot on the rung of MA's chair. They have taken a great fancy to one another. He reluctantly shakes himself out of it and pretends to examine the car again, whistling.*] Well, I guess you're all set now, lady. I hope you have a good trip; you can't miss it.

EVERYBODY.   Thanks. Thanks a lot. Good luck to you. [*Jolts and lurches.*]

MA.   [*With a sigh.*] The world's full of nice people.—That's what I call a nice young man.

CAROLINE.   [*Earnestly.*] Ma, you oughtn't to tell'm all everything about yourself.   115

MA.   Well, Caroline, you do your way and I'll do mine.—He looked kinda thin to me. I'd like to feed him up for a few days. His mother lives in Philadelphia and I expect he eats at those dreadful Greek places.

CAROLINE.   I'm hungry. Pa, there's a hot dog stand. K'n I have one?

ELMER.   We'll all have one, eh, Kate? We had such an early lunch.

MA.   Just as you think best, Elmer.

ELMER.   Arthur, here's half a dollar.—Run over and see what they have. Not too   120
much mustard either. [*ARTHUR descends from the car and goes off stage right. MA and CAROLINE get out and walk a bit.*]

MA.   What's that flower over there?—I'll take some of those to Beulah.

CAROLINE.   It's just a weed, ma.

MA.   I like it.—My, look at the sky, wouldya! I'm glad I was born in New Jersey. I've always said it was the best state in the Union. Every state has something no other state has got.

[*They stroll about humming. Presently Arthur returns with his hands full of imaginary hot dogs which he distributes. He is still very much cast down by the recent scandal. He finally approaches his mother and says falteringly:*]

ARTHUR.   Ma, I'm sorry. I'm sorry for what I said.

[*He bursts into tears and puts his forehead against her elbow.*]

MA.   There. There. We all say wicked things at times. I know you didn't mean it   125
like it sounded. [*He weeps still more violently than before.*] Why, now, now! I forgive you, Arthur, and tonight before you go to bed you . . . [*She whispers.*] You're a good boy at heart, Arthur, and we all know it. [*CAROLINE starts to cry too. MA is suddenly joyously alive and happy.*] Sakes alive, it's too nice a day for us all to be cryin'. Come now, get in. You go up in front with your father, Caroline. Ma wants to sit with her beau. I never saw such children. Your hot dogs are all getting wet. Now chew them fine, everybody.—All right, Elmer, forward march.—Caroline, whatever are you doing?

CAROLINE.   I'm spitting out the leather, ma.

MA.   Then say: Excuse me.

CAROLINE.   Excuse me, please.

MA.   What's this place? Arthur, did you see the post office?

ARTHUR.   It said Lawrenceville.

MA.   Hhn. School kinda. Nice. I wonder what that big yellow house set back was.—Now it's beginning to be Trenton.

CAROLINE.   Papa, it was near here that George Washington crossed the Delaware. It was near Trenton, mama. He was first in war and first in peace, and first in the hearts of his countrymen.°

MA.   [*Surveying the passing world, serene and didactic.*] Well, the thing I like about him best was that he never told a lie. [*The CHILDREN are duly cast down. There is a pause.*] There's a sunset for you. There's nothing like a good sunset.

ARTHUR.   There's an Ohio license in front of us. Ma, have you ever been to Ohio?

MA.   No.

[*A dreamy silence descends upon them. CAROLINE sits closer to her father. MA puts her arm around ARTHUR.*]

ARTHUR.   Ma, what a lotta people there are in the world, ma. There must be thousands and thousands in the United States. Ma, how many are there?

MA.   I don't know. Ask your father.

ARTHUR.   Pa, how many are there?

ELMER.   There are a hundred and twenty-six million, Kate.°

MA.   [*Giving a pressure about ARTHUR's shoulder.*] And they all like to drive out in the evening with their children beside'm. [*Another pause.*] Why doesn't somebody sing something? Arthur, you're always singing something; what's the matter with you?

ARTHUR.   All right. What'll we sing? [*He sketches:*°]
"In the Blue Ridge mountains of Virginia,
On the trail of the lonesome pine . . ."°
No, I don't like that any more. Let's do:
"I been workin on de railroad
All de liblong day.
I been workin' on de railroad
Just to pass de time away."

[*CAROLINE joins in at once. Finally even MA is singing. Even PA is singing. MA suddenly jumps up with a wild cry:*]

MA.   Elmer, that signpost said Camden, I saw it.

ELMER.   All right, Kate, if you're sure.

[*Much shifting of gears, backing, and jolting.*]

---

132 *George Washington . . . countrymen:* In December, 1776 Washington's Revolutionary Army forces defeated Hessian troops at Trenton. After the victory many Americans rallied to the Revolutionary cause, and the Battle of Trenton was therefore a decisive turning point in the war. The phrase quoted by Caroline was written by Henry Lee (1756-1828) and is the most famous of the congressional resolutions passed in tribute to Washington upon his death in 1799.   139 *million:* The official figure of the 1930 census was 122,775,046.   141 *Sketches:* i.e., he sings fragments of music. "The Trail of the Lonesome Pine": a song by Harry Carroll (who also wrote the endlessly popular "Chopsticks") and Ballard MacDonald. "I've Been Working on the Railroad," which few Americans have not known or sung, is anonymous.

MA.   Yes, there it is. *Camden—five miles.* Dear old Beulah.—Now, children, you be good and quiet during dinner. She's just got out of bed after a big sorta operation, and we must all move around kinda quiet. First you drop me and Caroline at the door and just say hello, and then you men-folk go over to the Y.M.C.A. and come back for dinner in about an hour.

CAROLINE.   [*Shutting her eyes and pressing her fists passionately against her nose.*] I see   145
the first star. Everybody make a wish.

Star light, star bright,
First star I seen tonight.
I wish I may, I wish I might
Have the wish I wish tonight.

[*Then solemnly.*] Pins. Mama, you say "needles."

[*She interlocks little fingers with her mother.*]

MA.   Needles.
CAROLINE.   Shakespeare. Ma, you say "Longfellow."
MA.   Longfellow
CAROLINE.   Now it's a secret and I can't tell it to anybody. Ma, you make a wish.
MA.   [*With almost grim humor.*] No, I can make wishes without waiting for no star.   150
And I can tell my wishes right out loud too. Do you want to hear them?
CAROLINE.   [*Resignedly.*] No, ma, we know'm already. We've heard'm. [*She hangs her head affectedly on her left shoulder and says with unmalicious mimicry:*] You want me to be a good girl and you want Arthur to be honest-in-word-and-deed.
MA.   [*Majestically.*] Yes. So mind yourself.
ELMER.   Caroline, take out that letter from Beulah in my coat pocket by you and read aloud the places I marked with red pencil.
CAROLINE.   [*Working.*] "*A few blocks after you pass the two big oil tanks on your left . . .*"
EVERYBODY.   [*Pointing backward.*] There they are!   155
CAROLINE.   "*. . . you come to a corner where there's an A and P store on the left and a fire-house kitty-corner to it . . .*" [*They all jubilantly identify these landmarks.*] "*. . . turn right, go two blocks, and our house is Weyerhauser St. Number 471.*"
MA.   It's an even nicer street than they used to live in. And right handy to an A and P.
CAROLINE.   [*Whispering.*] Ma, it's better than our street. It's richer than our street.—Ma, isn't Beulah richer than we are?
MA.   [*Looking at her with a firm and glassy eye.*] Mind yourself, missy. I don't want to hear anybody talking about rich or not rich when I'm around. If people aren't nice I don't care how rich they are. I live in the best street in the world because my husband and children live there. [*She glares impressively at* CAROLINE *a moment to let this lesson sink in, then looks up, sees* BEULAH, *and waves.*] There's Beulah standing on the steps lookin' for us.

[BEULAH *has appeared and is waving. They all call out:*] Hello, Beulah—Hello. [*Presently they are all getting out of the car.* BEULAH *kisses her father long and affectionately.*]

BEULAH.   Hello, papa. Good old papa. You look tired, pa.—Hello, mama.—   160
Lookit how Arthur and Caroline are growing!
MA.   They're bursting all their clothes!—Yes, your pa needs a rest. Thank

Heaven, his vacation has come just now. We'll feed him up and let him sleep late. Pa has a present for you, Loolie. He would go and buy it.

BEULAH.   Why, pa, you're terrible to go and buy anything for me. Isn't he terrible?

MA.   Well, it's a secret. You can open it at dinner.

ELMER.   Where's Horace, Loolie?

BEULAH.   He was kep' over a little at the office. He'll be here any minute. He's   1
crazy to see you all.

MA.   All right. You men go over to the Y and come back in about an hour.

BEULAH.   [*As her father returns to the wheel, stands out in the street beside him.*] Go straight along, Pa, you can't miss it. It just stares at yuh. [*She puts her arm around his neck and rubs her nose against his temple.*] Crazy old Pa, goin' buyin' things! It's me that ought to be buyin' things for you, Pa.

ELMER.   Oh, no! There's only one Loolie in the world.

BEULAH.   [*Whispering, as her eyes fill with tears.*] Are you glad I'm still alive, Pa? [*She kisses him abruptly and goes back to the house steps. The* STAGE MANAGER *removes the automobile with the help of* ELMER *and* ARTHUR *who go off waving their goodbyes.*] Well, come on upstairs, Ma, and take off your things. Caroline, there's a surprise for you in the back yard.

CAROLINE.   Rabbits?   1

BEULAH.   No.

CAROLINE.   Chickins?

BEULAH.   No. Go and see. [*CAROLINE runs off stage. BEULAH and MA gradually go upstairs.*] There are two new puppies. You be thinking over whether you can keep one in Newark.

MA.   I guess we can. It's a nice house, Beulah. You just got a lovely home.

BEULAH.   When I got back from the hospital, Horace had moved everything into   1
it, and there wasn't anything for me to do.

MA.   It's lovely.

[*The* STAGE MANAGER *pushes out a bed from the left. Its foot is toward the right.* BEULAH *sits on it, testing the springs.*]

BEULAH.   I think you'll find the bed comfortable, Ma.

MA.   [*Taking off her hat.*] Oh, I could sleep on a heapa shoes, Loolie! I don't have no trouble sleepin'. [*She sits down beside her.*] Now let me look at my girl. Well, well, when I last saw you, you didn't know me. You kep' saying: When's Mama comin'? When's Mama comin'? But the doctor sent me away.

BEULAH.   [*Puts her head on her mother's shoulder and weeps.*] It was awful, mama. It was awful. She didn't even live a few minutes, mama. It was awful.

MA.   [*Looking far away.*] God thought best, dear. God thought best. We don't   1
understand why. We just go on, honey, doin' our business. [*Then almost abruptly— passing the back of her hand across her cheek.*] Well, now, what are we giving the men to eat tonight?

BEULAH.   There's a chicken in the oven.

MA.   What time didya put it in?

BEULAH.   [*Restraining her.*] Aw, Ma, don't go yet. I like to sit here with you this way. You always get the fidgets when we try and pet yuh, Mama.

MA.   [*Ruefully, laughing.*] Yes, it's kinda foolish. I'm just an old Newark bag-a-bones.

[*She glances at the backs of her hands.*]

BEULAH.   [*Indignantly.*] Why, Ma, you're good-lookin'! We always said you were   185
good-lookin.'—And besides, you're the best Ma we could ever have.

MA.   [*Uncomfortable.*] Well, I hope you like me. There's nothin' like being liked by
your family.—Now I'm going downstairs to look at the chicken. You stretch out here for
a minute and shut your eyes.—Have you got everything laid in for breakfast before the
shops close?

BEULAH.   Oh, you know! Ham and eggs.

[*They both laugh.*]

MA.   I declare I never could understand what men see in ham and eggs. I think
they're horrible.—What time did you put the chicken in?

BEULAH.   Five o'clock.

MA.   Well, now, you shut your eyes for ten minutes. [*BEULAH stretches out and shuts*   190
her eyes. MA descends the stairs absentmindedly singing:]
    "There were ninety and nine that safely lay
      In the shelter of the fold,
    But one was out on the hills away,
      Far off from the gates of gold. . . ."°

AND THE CURTAIN FALLS

---

190   *"The Ninety and Nine":* a hymn by Elizabeth Clephane (1830–1869), with music by David
Sankey (1840–1908). The hymn was well known and easily recognized in 1931, the year of *The
Happy Journey to Trenton and Camden.* See <http://tch.simplenet.com/htm/n/i/90_and_9.htm>.

QUESTIONS

Preparation for the Journey

1.   What expositional details are found in the opening stage direction? What additional exposition is established during the preparation for the journey?

2.   What do you learn about Ma during the preparation? How would you explain
her reaction to Arthur's missing hat and Caroline's red cheeks? Describe Ma's
relationship with her neighbors.

3.   What foreshadowing of the conclusion do you find in the exposition?

4.   How are Arthur and Caroline characterized initially? How does their behavior
on the trip reinforce or change these initial images?

5.   What is Elmer Kirby like? How would you characterize his relationship to Ma?

The Journey

6.   What is the effect of having the characters read the advertisements at the side of
the road?

7. How does Ma react to the funeral? How does she react to Arthur's remark that "Ma's always talking about God. I guess she got a letter from him this morning"? What does the remark reveal about Ma? What does her reaction reveal?

8. How does Ma relate to the garage attendant? What does this tell you about her?

9. How does Ma deal with Arthur's apology and tears?

10. What does Ma like about George Washington? Why is her opinion significant? What are Ma's wishes for her children, and what do these wishes tell you about her? Generally, what values does Ma represent?

11. Why is it significant that Ma spots the signpost to Camden and gets the car headed down the correct road?

The Arrival

12. What is Ma's reaction to Caroline's observation that the street Beulah lives on is "better than our street . . . richer than our street"?

13. What has happened to Beulah before the play opens? How has Ma dealt with this occurrence? Look up Isaiah 62:4 for an explanation of the name *Beulah*. Granted the biblical context, what symbolic significance might *Beulah* have in this play?

14. Why does the play end with Ma singing "The Ninety and Nine"? Of what significance is her selection of this hymn?

TOPICS FOR WRITING AND FURTHER DISCUSSION

1. What is the effect of having the Stage Manager perform all the "bit" parts (small roles for both men and women alike) and remain on stage even when he is not in a specific role?

2. How closely does this play follow the structural pattern of exposition, complication, crisis, catastrophe, and resolution? Where is the crisis? The catastrophe? How is the play resolved?

3. Who is the protagonist? Who or what are the antagonists? What are the conflicts? Which is central?

4. To what extent is Ma a stereotype or stock character? Is she round or flat? What evidence of her depth and variety of character does Wilder present? What negative quality or qualities does she possess?

5. How does Ma hold the Kirby family together? How does Wilder demonstrate this quality in her? How could one consider her a sentimentalized character (i.e., "too good to be true")?

6. What is Ma's attitude toward her own life? Her family? Her home? How realistically does she cope with day-to-day problems and the larger trials of the world?

7. Describe the meaning of the word "happy" in the title. In what ways is the journey happy, even if there is a minor family uproar during the trip?

TENNESSEE WILLIAMS, *THE GLASS MENAGERIE*

Tennessee Williams (1911-1983) grew up in Mississippi and Missouri, and many of his plays reflect the attitudes and customs that he encountered in his early years. Until he was eight, his family lived in genteel poverty, mostly in Columbus, Mississippi. In 1919 the family moved to a lower-class neighborhood in St. Louis. Williams, who was sickly and bookish, tried to escape from poverty and family conflicts by writing and going to the movies. One of his few companions during those years was his shy and withdrawn sister, Rose.

He entered the University of Missouri in 1931, but the Depression and family poverty forced him to drop out and go to work in a shoe warehouse. After two years of this work, he suffered a nervous collapse, but he finally finished college at the University of Iowa. He then began wandering the country, doing odd jobs and also writing. His first full-length play, *Battle of Angels*, was produced in 1940 but was unsuccessful. He continued to write, however, and was able to get *The Glass Menagerie* staged in 1945. The critical and popular success of this play marked the beginning of many good years in the theater. Along with Arthur Miller, during the 1940s and 1950s Williams dominated the American stage, going on to write many one-act plays and more than fifteen full-length dramas (many of which became successful films), including *A Streetcar Named Desire* (1947, Pulitzer Prize), *The Rose Tattoo* (1951), *Cat on a Hot Tin Roof* (1955, Pulitzer Prize), *Suddenly Last Summer* (1958), and *The Night of the Iguana* (1961).

The Glass Menagerie, written in 1944 and produced with favorable reviews in Chicago and New York in 1945, is a largely autobiographical play that explores the family dynamics, delusions, and personalities of the Wingfields. Williams originally developed his ideas for the play in a short story called "Portrait of a Girl in Glass" and then in a screenplay for Metro-Goldwyn-Mayer titled *The Gentleman Caller*. In these treatments as well as in *The Glass Menagerie*, Laura Wingfield is modeled after his sister, Rose Williams. The least competent member of the family, she is crippled by her own insecurity and her mother's expectations. At every opportunity, Laura withdraws into a world of glass figurines and old phonograph records left by her father when he abandoned the family. Amanda Wingfield is patterned after Williams's mother. She valiantly tries to hold the family together and provide for Laura's future, but her perspectives are skewed by her romanticized memories of a gracious southern past of plantations, formal dances, and "gentleman callers." Tom, a figure based on the playwright himself, is desperate to escape the trap of his impoverished family. He seeks to emulate the long-missing father and move out of the drab Wingfield apartment into adventure and experience.

The play offers a fascinating mixture of realistic and nonrealistic dramatic techniques. The realistic elements are the characters (excluding Tom when he narrates) and the language. This is especially true of Amanda's language, in which Williams skillfully recreates the diction and cadences characteristic of the deep south. As he points out in his production notes and stage directions, the play's structure and staging are nonrealistic. Williams employs various devices nonrealistically, including the narrator, music, lighting, and screen projections, to underscore the emotions of his characters and to explore ideas about family and personality.

One of Williams's most effective nonrealistic techniques in *The Glass Menagerie* is its structure as "a memory play," and therefore its illustration of how a first-person narrator can be used in a drama. The characters and the action are not real and they do not exist in the present. Rather, they represent Tom's memories and feelings about events that occurred approximately five years earlier, when America was in the grip of the Great Depression, when the Spanish Civil War had resulted in the imposition of a fascist dictatorship in Spain, and when World War II was beginning in Europe. As the narrator, Tom exists at the time of the action (1944), but the events he introduces are occurring in about 1939. When Tom becomes a character in the Wingfield household, he is the Tom of this earlier period, quite distinct from his identity as the present narrator. Thus, the action in the apartment is not strictly a realistic recreation of life. Instead, even though the actions and characters seem realistic, they are exaggerated and reshaped as Tom remembers them and regrets them.

TENNESSEE WILLIAMS   (1911–1983)

The Glass Menagerie _____ *1945*

THE CHARACTERS

Amanda Wingfield (*the mother*)
A little woman of great but confused vitality clinging frantically to another time and place. Her characterization must be carefully created, not copied from type. She is not paranoiac, but her life is paranoia. There is much to admire in Amanda, and as much to love and pity as there is to laugh at. Certainly she has endurance and a kind of heroism, and though her foolishness makes her unwittingly cruel at times, there is tenderness in her slight person.

Laura Wingfield (*her daughter*)
Amanda, having failed to establish contact with reality, continues to live vitally in her illusions, but Laura's situation is even graver. A childhood illness has left her crippled, one leg slightly shorter than the other, and held in a brace. This defect need not

be more than suggested on the stage. Stemming from this, Laura's separation increases till she is like a piece of her own glass collection, too exquisitely fragile to move from the shelf.

Tom Wingfield (*her son*)
And the narrator of the play. A poet with a job in a warehouse. His nature is not remorseless, but to escape from a trap he has to act without pity.

Jim O'Connor (*the gentleman caller*)
A nice, ordinary, young man.

PRODUCTION NOTES
Being a "memory play," *The Glass Menagerie* can be presented with unusual freedom of convention. Because of its considerably delicate or tenuous material, atmospheric touches and subtleties of direction play a particularly important part. Expressionism and all other unconventional techniques in drama have only one valid aim, and that is a closer approach to truth. When a play employs unconventional techniques, it is not, or certainly shouldn't be, trying to escape its responsibility of dealing with reality, or interpreting experience, but is actually or should be attempting to find a closer approach, a more penetrating and vivid expression of things as they are. The straight realistic play with its genuine Frigidaire and authentic ice-cubes, its characters who speak exactly as its audience speaks, corresponds to the academic landscape and has the same virtue of a photographic likeness. Everyone should know nowadays the unimportance of the photographic in art: that truth, life, or reality is an organic thing which the poetic imagination can represent or suggest, in essence, only through transformation, through changing into other forms than those which were merely present in appearance.

These remarks are not meant as a preface only to this particular play. They have to do with a conception of a new, plastic theatre which must take the place of the exhausted theatre of realistic conventions if the theatre is to resume vitality as a part of our culture.

THE SCREEN DEVICE: There is *only one important difference between the original and the acting version of the play* and that is the *omission* in the latter of the device that I tentatively included in my *original* script. This device was the use of a screen on which were projected magic-lantern slides bearing images or titles. I do not regret the omission of this device from the original Broadway production. The extraordinary power of Miss Taylor's° performance made it suitable to have the utmost simplicity in the physical production. But I think it may be interesting to some readers to see how this device was conceived. So I am putting it into the published manuscript. These images and legends, projected from behind, were cast on a section of wall between the front-room and dining-room areas, which should be indistinguishable from the rest when not in use.

The purpose of this will probably be apparent. It is to give accent to certain values in each scene. Each scene contains a particular point (or several) which is

Miss Taylor's: The role of Amanda was first played by the American actress Laurette Taylor (1884–1946).

structurally the most important. In an episodic play, such as this, the basic structure or narrative line may be obscured from the audience; the effect may seem fragmentary rather than architectural. This may not be the fault of the play so much as a lack of attention in the audience. The legend or image upon the screen will strengthen the effect of what is merely allusion in the writing and allow the primary point to be made more simply and lightly than if the entire responsibility were on the spoken lines. Aside from this structural value, I think the screen will have a definite emotional appeal, less definable but just as important. An imaginative producer or director may invent many other uses for this device than those indicated in the present script. In fact the possibilities of the device seem much larger to me than the instance of this play can possibly utilize.

THE MUSIC: Another extra-literary accent in this play is provided by the use of music. A single recurring tune, "The Glass Menagerie,"° is used to give emotional emphasis to suitable passages. This tune is like circus music, not when you are on the grounds or in the immediate vicinity of the parade, but when you are at some distance and very likely thinking of something else. It seems under those circumstances to continue almost interminably and it weaves in and out of your preoccupied consciousness; then it is the lightest, most delicate music in the world and perhaps the saddest. It expresses the surface vivacity of life with the underlying strain of immutable and inexpressible sorrow. When you look at a piece of delicately spun glass you think of two things: how beautiful it is and how easily it can be broken. Both of those ideas should be woven into the recurring tune, which dips in and out of the play as if it were carried on a wind that changes. It serves as a thread of connection and allusion between the narrator with his separate point in time and space and the subject of his story. Between each episode it returns as reference to the emotion, nostalgia, which is the first condition of the play. It is primarily Laura's music and therefore comes out most clearly when the play focuses upon her and the lovely fragility of glass which is her image.

THE LIGHTING: The lighting in the play is not realistic. In keeping with the atmosphere of memory, the stage is dim. Shafts of light are focused on selected areas or actors, sometimes in contradistinction to what is the apparent center. For instance, in the quarrel scene between Tom and Amanda, in which Laura has no active part, the clearest pool of light is on her figure. This is also true of the supper scene, when her silent figure on the sofa should remain the visual center. The light upon Laura should be distinct from the others, having a peculiar pristine clarity such as light used in early religious portraits of female saints or madonnas. A certain correspondence to light in religious paintings, such as El Greco's,° where the figures are radiant in atmosphere that is relatively dusky, could be effectively used throughout the play. (It will also permit a more effective use of the screen.) A free, imaginative use of light can be of enormous value in giving a mobile, plastic quality to plays of a more or less static nature.

Tennessee Williams

"*The Glass Menagerie*": Original music, including this recurrent theme, was composed for the play by Paul Bowles.   *El Greco:* Greek painter (ca. 1548–1614) who lived in Spain; typical paintings have elongated and distorted figures and extremely vivid foreground lighting set against a murky background.

Scene 1

The Wingfield apartment is in the rear of the building, one of those vast hive-like conglomerations of cellular living-units that flower as warty growths in overcrowded urban centers of lower middle-class population and are symptomatic of the impulse of this largest and fundamentally enslaved section of American society to avoid fluidity and differentiation and to exist and function as one interfused mass of automatism.

The apartment faces an alley and is entered by a fire escape, a structure whose name is a touch of accidental poetic truth, for all of these huge buildings are always burning with the slow and implacable fires of human desperation. The fire escape is part of what we see—that is, the landing of it and steps descending from it.

The scene is memory and is therefore nonrealistic. Memory takes a lot of poetic license. It omits some details; others are exaggerated, according to the emotional value of the articles it touches, for memory is seated predominantly in the heart. The interior is therefore rather dim and poetic.

At the rise of the curtain, the audience is faced with the dark, grim rear wall of the Wingfield tenement. This building is flanked on both sides by dark, narrow alleys which run into murky canyons of tangled clotheslines, garbage cans, and the sinister latticework of neighboring fire escapes. It is up and down these side alleys that exterior entrances and exits are made during the play. At the end of TOM's opening commentary, the dark tenement wall slowly becomes transparent° and reveals the interior of the ground-floor Wingfield apartment.

Nearest the audience is the living room, which also serves as a sleeping room for LAURA, the sofa unfolding to make her bed. Just beyond, separated from the living room by a wide arch or second proscenium with transparent faded portieres° (or second curtain), is the dining room. In an old-fashioned whatnot° in the living room are seen scores of transparent glass animals. A blown-up photograph of the father hangs on the wall of the living room, to the left of the archway. It is the face of a very handsome young man in a doughboy's° First World War cap. He is gallantly smiling, ineluctably smiling, as if to say "I will be smiling forever."

Also hanging on the wall, near the photograph, are a typewriter keyboard chart and a Gregg shorthand diagram. An upright typewriter on a small table stands beneath the charts.

The audience hears and sees the opening scene in the dining room through both the transparent fourth wall of the building and the transparent gauze portieres of the dining-room arch. It is during this revealing scene that the fourth wall slowly ascends, out of sight. This transparent exterior wall is not brought down again until the very end of the play, during TOM's final speech.

The narrator is an undisguised convention of the play. He takes whatever license with dramatic convention is convenient to his purposes.

TOM enters, dressed as a merchant sailor, and strolls across to the fire escape. There he stops and lights a cigarette. He addresses the audience.

TOM.   Yes, I have tricks in my pocket, I have things up my sleeve. But I am the opposite of a stage magician. He gives you illusion that has the appearance of truth. I give you truth in the pleasant disguise of illusion.

To begin with, I turn back time. I reverse it to that quaint period, the thirties, when the huge middle class of America was matriculating in a school for the blind. Their eyes had failed them, or they had failed their eyes, and so they were having their fingers pressed forcibly down on the fiery Braille alphabet of a dissolving economy.

---

transparent: The wall is painted on a scrim, a transparent curtain that is opaque when lit from the front and transparent when lit from behind.   *portieres:* curtains hung in a doorway; in production, these may also be painted on a scrim.   *whatnot:* a small set of shelves for ornaments.
doughboy: popular name for an American infantryman during World War I.

In Spain there was revolution. Here there was only shouting and confusion. In Spain there was Guernica.° Here there were disturbances of labor, sometimes pretty violent, in otherwise peaceful cities such as Chicago, Cleveland, Saint Louis . . . This is the social background of the play.

[*Music begins to play.*]

The play is memory. Being a memory play, it is dimly lighted, it is sentimental, it is not realistic. In memory everything seems to happen to music. That explains the fiddle in the wings.

I am the narrator of the play, and also a character in it. The other characters are my mother, Amanda, my sister, Laura, and a gentleman caller who appears in the final scenes. He is the most realistic character in the play, being an emissary from a world of reality that we were somehow set apart from. But since I have a poet's weakness for symbols, I am using this character also as a symbol; he is the long-delayed but always expected something that we live for.

There is a fifth character in the play who doesn't appear except in this larger-than-life-size photograph over the mantel. This is our father who left us a long time ago. He was a telephone man who fell in love with long distances; he gave up his job with the telephone company and skipped the light fantastic out of town . . .

The last we heard of him was a picture postcard from Mazatlan, on the Pacific coast of Mexico, containing a message of two words: "Hello—Goodbye!" and no address.

I think the rest of the play will explain itself. . . .

[*Amanda's voice becomes audible through the portieres.*]

[*Legend on screen:* "Où sont les neiges."°]

TOM *divides the portieres and enters the dining room.* AMANDA *and* LAURA *are seated at a drop-leaf table. Eating is indicated by gestures without food or utensils.* AMANDA *faces the audience.* TOM *and* LAURA *are seated profile. The interior has lit up softly and through the scrim we see* AMANDA *and* LAURA *seated at the table.*]

AMANDA.   [*calling*] Tom?
TOM.   Yes, Mother.
AMANDA.   We can't say grace until you come to the table!
TOM.   Coming, Mother. [*He bows slightly and withdraws, reappearing a few moments later in his place at the table.*]
AMANDA.   [*to her son*] Honey, don't *push* with your *fingers.* If you have to push with something, the thing to push with is a crust of bread. And chew—chew! Animals have secretions in their stomachs which enable them to digest food without mastication, but human beings are supposed to chew their food before they swallow it down. Eat food leisurely, son, and really enjoy it. A well-cooked meal has lots of delicate flavors that have to be held in the mouth for appreciation. So chew your food and give your salivary glands a chance to function!

[*Tom deliberately lays his imaginary fork down and pushes his chair back from the table.*]

Guernica: a Basque town that was destroyed in 1937 by German planes fighting on General Franco's side during the Spanish Civil War. The huge mural *Guernica,* painted by Pablo Picasso, depicts the horror of that bombardment (see p. 464).   1 S.D.: *"Où sont les neiges":* "Where are the snows (of yesteryear)," refrain from "The Ballade of Dead Ladies" by the French poet François Villon (ca. 1431–1463).

TOM.   I haven't enjoyed one bite of this dinner because of your constant directions on how to eat it. It's you that make me rush through meals with your hawklike attention to every bite I take. Sickening—spoils my appetite—all this discussion of—animals' secretion—salivary glands—mastication!

AMANDA.   [*lightly*] Temperament like a Metropolitan star.°

[*TOM rises and walks toward the living room.*]

You're not excused from the table.

TOM.   I'm getting a cigarette.

AMANDA.   You smoke too much.   10

[*LAURA rises.*]

LAURA.   I'll bring in the blanc mange.°

[*TOM remains standing with his cigarette by the portieres.*]

AMANDA.   [*rising*] No, sister, no, sister°—you be the lady this time and I'll be the darky.

LAURA.   I'm already up.

AMANDA.   Resume your seat, little sister—I want you to stay fresh and pretty—for gentlemen callers!

LAURA.   [*sitting down*] I'm not expecting any gentlemen callers.   15

AMANDA.   [*crossing out to the kitchenette, airily*] Sometimes they come when they are least expected! Why, I remember one Sunday afternoon in Blue Mountain°—

[*She enters the kitchenette.*]

TOM.   I know what's coming!

LAURA.   Yes. But let her tell it.

TOM.   Again?

LAURA.   She loves to tell it.   20

[*AMANDA returns with a bowl of dessert.*]

AMANDA.   One Sunday afternoon in Blue Mountain—your mother received—*seventeen!*—gentlemen callers! Why, sometimes there weren't chairs enough to accommodate them all. We had to send the nigger over to bring in folding chairs from the parish house.

TOM.   [*remaining at the portieres*] How did you entertain those gentlemen callers?

AMANDA.   I understood the art of conversation!

TOM.   I bet you could talk.

AMANDA.   Girls in those days *knew* how to talk, I can tell you.   25

TOM.   Yes?

[*Image on screen: AMANDA as a girl on a porch, greeting callers.*]

8 *Metropolitan star:* the Metropolitan Opera in New York City; opera stars are traditionally considered to be highly temperamental.   11 *blanc mange:* a bland molded pudding or custard.   12 *sister:* In the south of Amanda's youth, the oldest daughter in a family was frequently called "sister" by her parents and siblings.   16 *Blue Mountain:* an imaginary town in northwest Mississippi modeled after Clarksville, where Williams spent much of his youth. Blue Mountain (Clarksville) is at the northern edge of the Mississippi Delta, a large fertile plain that supports numerous plantations. This is the recollected world of Amanda's youth—plantations, wealth, black servants, and gentlemen callers who were the sons of cotton planters.

AMANDA.   They knew how to entertain their gentlemen callers. It wasn't enough for a girl to be possessed of a pretty face and a graceful figure—although I wasn't slighted in either respect. She also needed to have a nimble wit and a tongue to meet all occasions.

TOM.   What did you talk about?

AMANDA.   Things of importance going on in the world! Never anything coarse or common or vulgar.

[*She addresses* TOM *as though he were seated in the vacant chair at the table though he remains by the portieres. He plays this scene as though reading from a script.* °]

My callers were gentleman—all! Among my callers were some of the most prominent young planters of the Mississippi Delta—planters and sons of planters!

[TOM *motions for music and a spot of light on* AMANDA. *Her eyes lift, her face glows, her voice becomes rich and elegiac.*

[*Screen legend:* "Où sont les neiges d'antan?" °]

There was young Champ Laughlin who later became vice-president of the Delta Planters Bank. Hadley Stevenson who was drowned in Moon Lake and left his widow one hundred and fifty thousand in Government bonds. There were the Cutrere brothers, Wesley and Bates. Bates was one of my bright particular beaux! He got in a quarrel with that wild Wainwright boy. They shot it out on the floor of Moon Lake Casino. Bates was shot through the stomach. Died in the ambulance on his way to Memphis. His widow was also well provided-for, came into eight or ten thousand acres, that's all. She married him on the rebound—never loved her—carried my picture on him the night he died! And there was that boy that every girl in the Delta had set her cap for! That beautiful, brilliant young Fitzhugh boy from Greene County!

TOM.   What did he leave his widow?

AMANDA.   He never married! Gracious, you talk as though all of my old admirers had turned up their toes to the daisies!

TOM.   Isn't this the first you've mentioned that still survives?

AMANDA.   That Fitzhugh boy went North and made a fortune—came to be known as the Wolf of Wall Street! He had the Midas touch,° whatever he touched turned to gold! And I could have been Mrs. Duncan J. Fitzhugh, mind you! But—I picked your *father!*

LAURA.   [*rising*] Mother, let me clear the table.

AMANDA.   No, dear, you go in front and study your typewriter chart. Or practice your shorthand a little. Stay fresh and pretty!—It's almost time for our gentlemen callers to start arriving. [*She flounces girlishly toward the kitchenette.*] How many do you suppose we're going to entertain this afternoon?

[TOM *throws down the paper and jumps up with a groan.*]

LAURA.   [*alone in the dining room*] I don't believe we're going to receive any, Mother.

AMANDA.   [*reappearing airily*] What? No one?—not one? You must be joking!

29.1 *script:* Here Tom becomes both a character in the play and the stage manager.   29.2 *"Où sont les neiges d'antan?":* Where are the snows of yesteryear? See p. 1708n.   33 *Midas touch:* In Greek mythology, King Midas was given the power to turn everything he touched into gold.

[*LAURA nervously echoes her laugh. She slips in a fugitive manner through the half-open portieres and draws them gently behind her. A shaft of very clear light is thrown on her face against the faded tapestry of the curtains. Faintly the music of "The Glass Menagerie" is heard as she continues lightly:*]

Not one gentleman caller? It can't be true! There must be a flood, there must have been a tornado!

LAURA.   It isn't a flood, it's not a tornado, Mother. I'm just not popular like you were in Blue Mountain. . . .

[*TOM utters another groan. LAURA glances at him with a faint, apologetic smile. Her voice catches a little:*]

Mother's afraid I'm going to be an old maid.

[*The scene dims out with the "Glass Menagerie" music.*]

Scene 2

On the dark stage the screen is lighted with the image of blue roses. Gradually LAURA's figure becomes apparent and the screen goes out. The music subsides.

LAURA is seated in the delicate ivory chair at the small clawfoot table. She wears a dress of soft violet material for a kimono—her hair is tied back from her forehead with a ribbon. She is washing and polishing her collection of glass. AMANDA appears on the fire escape steps. At the sound of her ascent, LAURA catches her breath, thrusts the bowl of ornaments away, and seats herself stiffly before the diagram of the typewriter keyboard as though it held her spellbound. Something has happened to AMANDA. It is written in her face as she climbs to the landing: a look that is grim and hopeless and a little absurd. She has on one of those cheap or imitation velvety-looking cloth coats with imitation fur collar. Her hat is five or six years old, one of those dreadful cloche hats that were worn in the late Twenties, and she is clutching an enormous black patent-leather pocketbook with nickel clasps and initials. This is her full-dress outfit, the one she usually wears to the D.A.R.° Before entering she looks through the door. She purses her lips, opens her eyes very wide, rolls them upward and shakes her head. Then she slowly lets herself in the door. Seeing her mother's expression, LAURA touches her lips with a nervous gesture.

LAURA.   Hello, Mother, I was—[*She makes a nervous gesture toward the chart on the wall. AMANDA leans against the shut door and stares at LAURA with a martyred look.*]

AMANDA.   Deception? Deception? [*She slowly removes her hat and gloves, continuing the sweet suffering stare. She lets the hat and gloves fall on the floor—a bit of acting.*]

LAURA.   [*shakily*] How was the D.A.R. meeting?

[*AMANDA slowly opens her purse and removes a dainty white handkerchief which she shakes out delicately and delicately touches to her lips and nostrils.*]

Didn't you go to the D.A.R. meeting, Mother?

AMANDA.   [*faintly, almost inaudibly*] —No.—No. [*then more forcibly:*] I did not have the strength—to go to the D.A.R. In fact, I did not have the courage! I wanted to find a hole in the ground and hide myself in it forever! [*She crosses slowly to the wall and removes*

0.2 *D.A.R.:* Daughters of the American Revolution, a patriotic women's organization (founded in 1890) open only to women whose ancestors aided the American Revolution.

the diagram of the typewriter keyboard. *She holds it in front of her for a second, staring at it sweetly and sorrowfully—then bites her lips and tears it in two pieces.*]

LAURA.   [*faintly*] Why did you do that, Mother?   5

[AMANDA *repeats the same procedure with the chart of the Gregg Alphabet.*]

Why are you—

AMANDA.   Why? Why? How old are you, Laura?

LAURA.   Mother, you know my age.

AMANDA.   I thought you were an adult; it seems that I was mistaken. [*She crosses slowly to the sofa and sinks down and stares at LAURA.*]

LAURA.   Please don't stare at me, Mother.

[AMANDA *closes her eyes and lowers her head. There is a ten-second pause.*]

AMANDA.   What are we going to do, what is going to become of us, what is the   10
future?

[*There is another pause.*]

LAURA.   Has something happened, Mother?

[AMANDA *draws a long breath, takes out the handkerchief again, goes through the dabbing process.*]

Mother, has—something happened?

AMANDA.   I'll be all right in a minute, I'm just bewildered—[*She hesitates.*]—by
life. . . .

LAURA.   Mother, I wish that you would tell me what's happened!

AMANDA.   As you know, I was supposed to be inducted into my office at the D.A.R. this afternoon.

[*Screen image: A swarm of typewriters.*]

But I stopped off at Rubicam's Business College to speak to your teachers about your having a cold and ask them what progress they thought you were making down there.

LAURA.   Oh. . . .   1

AMANDA.   I went to the typing instructor and introduced myself as your mother. She didn't know who you were.

"Wingfield," she said, "We don't have any such student enrolled at the school!"

I assured her she did, that you had been going to classes since early in January.

"I wonder," she said, "if you could be talking about that terribly shy little girl who dropped out of school after only a few days' attendance?"

"No," I said, "Laura, my daughter, has been going to school every day for the past six weeks!"

"Excuse me," she said. She took the attendance book out and there was your name, unmistakably printed, and all the dates you were absent until they decided that you had dropped out of school.

I still said, "No, there must have been some mistake! There must have been some mix-up in the records!"

And she said, "No—I remember her perfectly now. Her hands shook so that she couldn't hit the right keys! The first time we gave a speed test, she broke down completely—was sick at the stomach and almost had to be carried into the wash room! After that morning she never showed up any more. We phoned the house but never got any answer"—While I was working at Famous-Barr,° I suppose, demonstrating those—

[*She indicates a brassiere with her hands.*]

Oh! I felt so weak I could barely keep on my feet! I had to sit down while they got me a glass of water! Fifty dollars' tuition, all of our plans—my hopes and ambitions for you— just gone up the spout, just gone up the spout like that.

[*LAURA draws a long breath and gets awkwardly to her feet. She crosses to the Victrola and winds it up.*°]

What are you doing?
    LAURA.   Oh! [*She releases the handle and returns to her seat.*]
    AMANDA.   Laura, where have you been going when you've gone out pretending that you were going to business college?
    LAURA.   I've just been going out walking.
    AMANDA.   That's not true.   20
    LAURA.   It is. I just went walking.
    AMANDA.   Walking? Walking? In winter? Deliberately courting pneumonia in that light coat? Where did you walk to, Laura?
    LAURA.   All sorts of places—mostly in the park.
    AMANDA.   Even after you'd started catching that cold?
    LAURA.   It was the lesser of two evils, Mother.   25

[*Screen image: Winter scene in a park.*]

I couldn't go back there. I—threw up—on the floor!
    AMANDA.   From half past seven till after five every day you mean to tell me you walked around the park, because you wanted to make me think that you were still going to Rubicam's Business College?
    LAURA.   It wasn't as bad as it sounds. I went inside places to get warmed up.
    AMANDA.   Inside where?
    LAURA.   I went in the art museum and the bird houses at the Zoo. I visited the penguins every day! Sometimes I did without lunch and went to the movies. Lately I've been spending most of my afternoons in the Jewel Box, that big glass house where they raise the tropical flowers.
    AMANDA.   You did all this to deceive me, just for deception? [*LAURA looks down.*]   30
Why?
    LAURA.   Mother, when you're disappointed, you get that awful suffering look on your face, like the picture of Jesus' mother in the museum!
    AMANDA.   Hush!
    LAURA.   I couldn't face it.

[*There is a pause. A whisper of strings is heard. Legend on screen: "The Crust of Humility."*]

16.8 *Famous-Barr:* a department store in St. Louis.   16.11 *winds it up:* Laura is using a spring-powered (rather than electric) phonograph that has to be rewound frequently. See p. 294n.

AMANDA. [*hopelessly fingering the huge pocketbook*] So what are we going to do the rest of our lives? Stay home and watch the parades go by? Amuse ourselves with the glass menagerie, darling? Eternally play those worn-out phonograph records your father left as a painful reminder of him? We won't have a business career—we've given that up because it gave us nervous indigestion! [*She laughs wearily.*] What is there left but dependency all our lives? I know so well what becomes of unmarried women who aren't prepared to occupy a position. I've seen such pitiful cases in the South—barely tolerated spinsters living upon the grudging patronage of sister's husband or brother's wife!—stuck away in some little mousetrap of a room—encouraged by one in-law to visit another—little birdlike women without any nest—eating the crust of humility all their life!

Is that the future that we've mapped out for ourselves? I swear it's the only alternative I can think of! [*She pauses.*] It isn't a very pleasant alternative, is it? [*She pauses again.*] Of course—some girls *do marry.*

[*LAURA twists her hands nervously.*]

Haven't you ever liked some boy?
    LAURA.   Yes. I liked one once. [*She rises.*] I came across his picture a while ago.
    AMANDA.   [*with some interest*] He gave you his picture?
    LAURA.   No, it's in the yearbook.
    AMANDA.   [*disappointed*] Oh—a high school boy.

[*Screen image: JIM as the high school hero bearing a silver cup.*]

    LAURA.   Yes. His name was Jim. [*She lifts the heavy annual from the claw-foot table.*] Here he is in *The Pirates of Penzance.*°
    AMANDA.   [*absently*] The what?
    LAURA.   The operetta the senior class put on. He had a wonderful voice and we sat across the aisle from each other Mondays, Wednesdays and Fridays in the Aud. Here he is with the silver cup for debating! See his grin?
    AMANDA.   [*absently*] He must have had a jolly disposition.
    LAURA.   He used to call me—Blue Roses.

[*Screen image: Blue roses.*]

    AMANDA.   Why did he call you such a name as that?
    LAURA.   When I had that attack of pleurosis—he asked me what was the matter when I came back. I said pleurosis—he thought that I said Blue Roses! So that's what he always called me after that. Whenever he saw me, he'd holler, "Hello, Blue Roses!" I didn't care for the girl that he went out with. Emily Meisenbach. Emily was the best-dressed girl at Soldan. She never struck me, though, as being sincere . . . It says in the Personal Section—they're engaged. That's—six years ago! They must be married by now.
    AMANDA.   Girls that aren't cut out for business careers usually wind up married to some nice man. [*She gets up with a spark of revival.*] Sister, that's what you'll do!

[*LAURA utters a startled, doubtful laugh. She reaches quickly for a piece of glass.*]

___

39 *The Pirates of Penzance:* a comic light opea (1879) by W.S. Gilbert and Arthur Sullivan.

LAURA.   But, Mother—
AMANDA.   Yes? [*She goes over to the photograph.*]
LAURA.   [*in a tone of frightened apology*] I'm—crippled!
AMANDA.   Nonsense! Laura, I've told you never, never to use that word.   50
Why, you're not crippled, you just have a little defect—hardly noticeable, even! When people have some slight disadvantage like that, they cultivate other things to make up for it—develop charm—and vivacity—and—*charm!* That's all you have to do! [*She turns again to the photograph.*] One thing your father had *plenty of*—was *charm!*

[*The scene fades out with music.*]

Scene 3

[*Legend on screen: "After the fiasco—"*

TOM *speaks from the fire escape landing.*]

TOM.   After the fiasco at Rubicam's Business College, the idea of getting a gentleman caller for Laura began to play a more and more important part in Mother's calculations. It became an obsession. Like some archetype of the universal unconscious, the image of the gentleman caller haunted our small apartment. . . .

[*Screen image: A young man at the door of a house with flowers.*]

An evening at home rarely passed without some allusion to this image, this specter, this hope. . . . Even when he wasn't mentioned, his presence hung in Mother's preoccupied look and in my sister's frightened, apologetic manner—hung like a sentence passed upon the Wingfields!

Mother was a woman of action as well as words. She began to take logical steps in the planned direction. Late that winter and in the early spring—realizing that extra money would be needed to properly feather the nest and plume the bird—she conducted a vigorous campaign on the telephone, roping in subscribers to one of those magazines for matrons called *The Homemaker's Companion*, the type of journal that features the serialized sublimations of ladies of letters who think in terms of delicate cuplike breasts, slim, tapering waists, rich, creamy thighs, eyes like wood smoke in autumn, fingers that soothe and caress like strains of music, bodies as powerful as Etruscan sculpture.

[*Screen image: The cover of a glamor magazine.*

AMANDA *enters with the telephone on a long extension cord. She is spotlighted in the dim stage.*]

AMANDA.   Ida Scott? This is Amanda Wingfield! We *missed* you at the D.A.R. last Monday! I said to myself: She's probably suffering with that sinus condition! How is that sinus condition?

Horrors! Heaven have mercy!—You're a Christian martyr, yes, that's what you are, a Christian martyr!

Well, I just now happened to notice that your subscription to the *Companion's* about to expire! Yes, it expires with the next issue, honey!—just when that wonderful new serial by Bessie Mae Hopper is getting off to such an exciting start. Oh, honey, it's something that you can't miss! You remember how *Gone with the Wind*° took everybody by storm? You simply couldn't go out if you hadn't read it. All everybody *talked* was Scarlett O'Hara. Well, this is a book that critics already compare to *Gone with the Wind*. It's the *Gone with the Wind* of the post-World-War generation!—What?—Burning?—Oh, honey, don't let them burn, go take a look in the oven and I'll hold the wire! Heavens— I think she's hung up!

[*The scene dims out.*]

[*Legend on screen: "You think I'm in love with Continental Shoemakers?"*]

[*Before the lights come up again, the violent voices of* TOM *and* AMANDA *are heard. They are quarreling behind the portieres. In front of them stands* LAURA *with clenched hands and panicky expression. A clear pool of light is on her figure throughout this scene.*]

TOM.   What in Christ's name am I—
AMANDA.   [*shrilly*] Don't you use that—
TOM.   —supposed to do!
AMANDA.   —expression! Not in my—
TOM.   Ohhh!
AMANDA.   —presence! Have you gone out of your senses?
TOM.   I have, that's true, *driven* out!
AMANDA.   What is the matter with you, you—big—big—IDIOT!
TOM.   Look!—I've got *no thing*, no single thing—
AMANDA.   Lower your voice!
TOM.   —in my life here that I can call my OWN! Everything is—
AMANDA.   Stop that shouting!
TOM.   Yesterday you confiscated my books! You had the nerve to—
AMANDA.   I took that horrible novel back to the library—yes! That hideous book
by that insane Mr. Lawrence.°

[*TOM laughs wildly.*]

I cannot control the output of diseased minds or people who cater to them—

[*TOM laughs still more wildly.*]

BUT I WON'T ALLOW SUCH FILTH BROUGHT INTO MY HOUSE! No, no, no, no, no!
TOM.   House, house! Who pays rent on it, who makes a slave of himself to—
AMANDA.   [*fairly screeching*] Don't you DARE to—
TOM.   No, no, *I* mustn't say things! *I've* got to just—
AMANDA.   Let me tell you—
TOM.   I don't want to hear any more!

[*He tears the portieres open. The dining-room area is lit with turgid smoky red glow. Now we see* AMANDA; *her hair is in metal curlers and she is wearing a very old bathrobe, much too large for her slight figure, a relic of the faithless Mr. Wingfield. The upright typewriter now stands on the drop-leaf table, along with a wild disarray of manuscripts. The quarrel was probably precipitated by*

2.3 *Gone with the Wind:* popular novel (1936) by Margaret Mitchell (1900–1949), set in the south before, during, and after the Civil War. Scarlett O'Hara was the heroine.   16 *Lawrence:* D. H. Lawrence (1885–1930), English poet and fiction writer, popularly known as an advocate of passion and sexuality. See "The Horse Dealer's Daughter," p. 500.

AMANDA's interruption of TOM's creative labor. A chair lies overthrown on the floor. Their gesticulating shadows are cast on the ceiling by the fiery glow.]

AMANDA. You *will* hear more, you—
TOM. No, I won't hear more, I'm going out!
AMANDA. You come right back in—
TOM. Out, out, out! Because I'm—   25
AMANDA. Come back here, Tom Wingfield! I'm not through talking to you!
TOM. Oh, go—
LAURA. [*desperately*]—Tom!
AMANDA. You're going to listen, and no more insolence from you! I'm at the end
of my patience!

[*He comes back toward her.*]

TOM. What do you think I'm at? Aren't I supposed to have any patience to reach   30
the end of, Mother? I know, I know. It seems unimportant to you, what I'm *doing*—what
I *want* to do—having a little *difference* between them! You don't think that—
AMANDA. I think you've been doing things that you're ashamed of. That's why
you act like this. I don't believe that you go every night to the movies. Nobody goes to
the movies night after night. Nobody in their right minds goes to the movies as often as
you pretend to. People don't go to the movies at nearly midnight, and movies don't let
out at two A.M. Come in stumbling. Muttering to yourself like a maniac! You get three
hours' sleep and then go to work. Oh, I can picture the way you're doing down there.
Moping, doping, because you're in no condition.
TOM. [*wildly*] No, I'm in no condition!
AMANDA. What right have you got to jeopardize your job? Jeopardize the security of us all? How do you think we'd manage if you were—
TOM. Listen! You think I'm crazy about the *warehouse?* [*He bends fiercely toward
her slight figure.*] You think I'm in love with the Continental Shoemakers? You think I
want to spend fifty-five *years* down there in that—*celotex interior!* with—*fluorescent—tubes!*
Look! I'd rather somebody picked up a crowbar and battered out my brains—than go
back mornings! I *go!* Every time you come in yelling that God damn *"Rise and Shine!"*
"Rise and Shine!" I say to myself, "How *lucky dead* people are!" But I get up. I *go!* For sixty-
five dollars a month I give up all that I dream of doing and being *ever! And you say self—
self's* all I ever think of. Why, listen, if self is what I thought of, Mother, I'd be where he
is—GONE! [*He points to his father's picture.*] As far as the system of transportation reaches!
[*He starts past her. She grabs his arm.*] Don't grab at me, Mother!
AMANDA. Where are you going?   35
TOM. I'm going to the *movies!*
AMANDA. I don't believe that lie!

[*TOM crouches toward her, overtowering her tiny figure. She backs away, gasping.*]

TOM. I'm going to opium dens! Yes, opium dens, dens of vice and criminals'
hangouts, Mother. I've joined the Hogan Gang,° I'm a hired assassin, I carry a tommy
gun in a violin case! I run a string of cat houses in the Valley! They call me Killer, Killer
Wingfield, I'm leading a double life, a simple, honest warehouse worker by day, by night

---

38 *Hogan Gang:* one of the major criminal organizations in St. Louis in the 1930s.

a dynamic *czar* of the *underworld, Mother.* I go to gambling casinos, I spin away fortunes on the roulette table! I wear a patch over one eye and a false mustache, sometimes I put on green whiskers. On those occasions they call me—*El Diablo!°* Oh, I could tell you many things to make you sleepless! My enemies plan to dynamite this place. They're going to blow us all sky-high some night! I'll be glad, very happy, and so will you! You'll go up, up on a broomstick, over Blue Mountain with seventeen gentlemen callers! You ugly—babbling old—*witch. . . .*

[*He goes through a series of violent, clumsy movements, seizing his overcoat, lunging to the door, pulling it fiercely open. The women watch him, aghast. His arm catches in the sleeve of the coat as he struggles to pull it on. For a moment he is pinioned by the bulky garment. With an outraged groan he tears the coat off again, splitting the shoulder of it, and hurls it across the room. It strikes against the shelf of LAURA's glass collection, and there is a tinkle of shattering glass. LAURA cries out as if wounded.*

Music.

Screen legend: "The Glass Menagerie."]

LAURA.   [*shrilly*] *My glass!*—menagerie. . . . [*She covers her face and turns away.*]

[*But AMANDA is still stunned and stupefied by the "ugly witch" so that she barely notices this occurrence. Now she recovers her speech.*]

AMANDA.   [*in an awful voice*] I won't speak to you—until you apologize!

[*She crosses through the portieres and draws them together behind her. TOM is left with LAURA. LAURA clings weakly to the mantel with her face averted. TOM stares at her stupidly for a moment. Then he crosses to the shelf. He drops awkwardly on his knees to collect the fallen glass, glancing at LAURA as if he would speak but couldn't.*

"The Glass Menagerie" music steals in as the scene dims out.]

Scene 4

The interior of the apartment is dark. There is a faint light in the alley. A deep-voiced bell in a church is tolling the hour of five.

TOM appears at the top of the alley. After each solemn boom of the bell in the tower, he shakes a little noisemaker or rattle as if to express the tiny spasm of man in contrast to the sustained power and dignity of the Almighty. This and the unsteadiness of his advance make it evident that he has been drinking. As he climbs the few steps to the fire escape landing light steals up inside. LAURA appears in the front room in a nightdress. She notices that TOM's bed is empty. TOM fishes in his pockets for his door key, removing a motley assortment of articles in the search, including a shower of movie ticket stubs and an empty bottle. At last he finds the key, but just as he is about to insert it, it slips from his fingers. He strikes a match and crouches below the door.

TOM.   [*bitterly*] One crack—and it falls through!

[*LAURA opens the door.*]

38 *El Diablo:* the devil.

LAURA.   Tom! Tom, what are you doing?

TOM.   Looking for a door key.

LAURA.   Where have you been all this time?

TOM.   I have been to the movies.   5

LAURA.   All this time at the movies?

TOM.   There was a very long program. There was a Garbo° picture and a Mickey Mouse and a travelogue and a newsreel and a preview of coming attractions. And there was an organ solo and a collection for the Milk Fund—simultaneously—which ended up in a terrible fight between a fat lady and an usher!

LAURA.   [*innocently*] Did you have to stay through everything?

TOM.   Of course! And, oh I forgot! There was a big stage show! The headliner on this stage show was Malvolio° the Magician. He performed wonderful tricks, many of them, such as pouring water back and forth between pitchers. First it turned to wine and then it turned to beer and then it turned to whisky. I know it was whisky it finally turned into because he needed somebody to come up out of the audience to help him, and I came up—both shows! It was Kentucky Straight Bourbon. A very generous fellow, he gave souvenirs. [*He pulls from his back pocket a shimmering rainbow-colored scarf.*] He gave me this. This is his magic scarf. You can have it, Laura. You wave it over a canary cage and you get a bowl of goldfish. You wave it over the goldfish bowl and they fly away canaries. . . . But the wonderfullest trick of all was the coffin trick. We nailed him into a coffin and he got out of the coffin without removing one nail. [*He has come inside.*] There is a trick that would come in handy for me—get me out of this two-by-four situation! [*He flops onto the bed and starts removing his shoes.*]

LAURA.   Tom—shhh!   10

TOM.   What're you shushing me for?

LAURA.   You'll wake up Mother.

TOM.   Goody, goody! Pay 'er back for all those "Rise an' Shines." [*He lies down, groaning.*] You know it don't take much intelligence to get yourself into a nailed-up coffin, Laura. But who in hell ever got himself out of one without removing one nail?

[*As if in answer, the father's grinning photograph lights up. The scene dims out.*]

[*Immediately following, the church bell is heard striking six. At the sixth stroke the alarm clock goes off in AMANDA's room, and after a few moments we hear her calling: "Rise and Shine! Rise and Shine! Laura, go tell your brother to rise and shine!"*]

TOM.   [*sitting up slowly*] I'll rise—but I won't shine.

[*The light increases.*]

AMANDA.   Laura, tell your brother his coffee is ready.   15

[*LAURA slips into the front room.*]

LAURA.   Tom!—It's nearly seven. Don't make Mother nervous.

[*He stares at her stupidly.*]

---

7 *Garbo:* Greta Garbo (1905–1990), Swedish star of American silent and early sound films.
9 *Malvolio:* the name, borrowed from a puritanical character in Shakespeare's *Twelfth Night,* means "malevolence" or "ill-will."

[*Beseechingly.*] Tom, speak to Mother this morning. Make up with her, apologize, speak to her!

TOM.   She won't to me. It's her that started not speaking.
LAURA.   If you just say you're sorry she'll start speaking.
TOM.   Her not speaking—is that such a tragedy?
LAURA.   Please—please!
AMANDA.   [*calling from the kitchenette*] Laura, are you going to do what I asked you to do, or do I have to get dressed and go out myself?
LAURA.   Going, going—soon as I get on my coat!

[*She pulls on a shapeless felt hat with a nervous, jerky movement, pleadingly glancing at* TOM. *She rushes awkwardly for her coat. The coat is one of* AMANDA*'s, inaccurately made-over, the sleeves too short for* LAURA.]

Butter and what else?
AMANDA.   [*entering from the kitchenette*] Just butter. Tell them to charge it.
LAURA.   Mother, they make such faces when I do that.
AMANDA.   Sticks and stones can break our bones, but the expression on Mr. Garfinkel's face won't harm us! Tell your brother his coffee is getting cold.
LAURA.   [*at the door*] Do what I asked you, will you, will you, Tom?

[*He looks sullenly away.*]

AMANDA.   Laura, go now or just don't go at all!
LAURA.   [*rushing out*] Going—going!

[*A second later she cries out.* TOM *springs up and crosses to the door.* TOM *opens the door.*]

TOM.   Laura?
LAURA.   I'm all right. I slipped, but I'm all right.
AMANDA.   [*peering anxiously after her*] If anyone breaks a leg on those fire-escape steps, the landlord ought to be sued for every cent he possesses! [*She shuts the door. Now she remembers she isn't speaking to* TOM *and returns to the other room.*]

[*As* TOM *comes listlessly for his coffee, she turns her back to him and stands rigidly facing the window on the gloomy gray vault of the areaway. Its light on her face with its aged but childish features is cruelly sharp, satirical as a Daumier print.*°

The music of "Ave Maria"° *is heard softly.*

TOM *glances sheepishly but sullenly at her averted figure and slumps at the table. The coffee is scalding hot; he sips it and gasps and spits it back in the cup. At his gasp,* AMANDA *catches her breath and half turns. Then she catches herself and turns back to the window.* TOM *blows on his coffee, glancing sidewise at his mother. She clears her throat.* TOM *clears his. He starts to rise, sinks back down again, scratches his head, clears his throat again.* AMANDA *coughs.* TOM *raises his cup in both hands to blow on it, his eyes staring over the rim of it at his mother for several moments. Then he slowly sets the cup down and awkwardly and hesitantly rises from the chair.*]

31.2 *Daumier print:* Honoré Daumier (1808–1879), French painter and engraver whose prints frequently satirized his society.   31.3 *"Ave Maria":* a Roman Catholic prayer to the Virgin Mary; the musical setting called for here is by Franz Schubert (1797–1828).

TOM.   [*hoarsely*] Mother. I—I apologize, Mother.

[*AMANDA draws a quick, shuddering breath. Her face works grotesquely. She breaks into childlike tears.*]

I'm sorry for what I said, for everything that I said, I didn't mean it.

AMANDA.   [*sobbingly*] My devotion has made me a witch and so I make myself hateful to my children!

TOM.   *No,* you *don't.*

AMANDA.   I worry so much, don't sleep, it makes me nervous!   35

TOM.   [*gently*] I understand that.

AMANDA.   I've had to put up a solitary battle all these years. But you're my right-hand bower!° Don't fall down, don't fail!

TOM.   [*gently*] I try, Mother.

AMANDA.   [*with great enthusiasm*] Try and you will *succeed!* [*The notion makes her breathless.*] Why, you—you're just *full* of natural endowments! Both of my children—they're *unusual* children! Don't you think I know it? I'm so—*proud!* Happy and—feel I've—so much to be thankful for but—promise me one thing, son!

TOM.   What, Mother?   40

AMANDA.   Promise, son, you'll—never be a drunkard!

TOM.   [*turns to her grinning*] I will never be a drunkard, Mother.

AMANDA.   That's what frightened me so, that you'd be drinking! Eat a bowl of Purina!

TOM.   Just coffee, Mother.

AMANDA.   Shredded wheat biscuit?   45

TOM.   No. No, Mother, just coffee.

AMANDA.   You can't put in a day's work on an empty stomach. You've got ten minutes—don't gulp! Drinking too-hot liquids makes cancer of the stomach. . . . Put cream in.

TOM.   No, thank you.

AMANDA.   To cool it.

TOM.   No! No, thank you, I want it black.   50

AMANDA.   I know, but it's not good for you. We have to do all that we can to build ourselves up. In these trying times we live in, all that we have to cling to is—each other. . . . That's why it's so important to—Tom, I—I sent out your sister so I could discuss something with you. If you hadn't spoken I would have spoken to you. [*She sits down.*]

TOM.   [*gently*] What is it, Mother, that you want to discuss?

AMANDA.   *Laura!*

[*TOM puts his cup down slowly.*]

[*Legend on screen "Laura." Music: "The Glass Menagerie."*]

TOM.   —Oh.—Laura . . .

AMANDA.   [*touching his sleeve*] You know how Laura is. So quiet but—still water   55
runs deep! She notices things and I think she—broods about them.

[*TOM looks up.*]

---

37 *right-hand bower* or *rightbower:* the Jack of trump in the card game *500*, the second-highest card (below the joker).

A few days ago I came in and she was crying.

TOM. What about?

AMANDA. You.

TOM. Me?

AMANDA. She has an idea that you're not happy here.

TOM. What gave her that idea?

AMANDA. What gives her any idea? However, you do act strangely. I—I'm not criticizing, understand *that!* I know your ambitions do not lie in the warehouse, that like everybody in the whole wide world—you've had to—make sacrifices, but—Tom—Tom— life's not easy, it calls for—Spartan endurance! There's so many things in my heart that I cannot describe to you! I've never told you but I—*loved* your father. . . .

TOM. [*gently*] I know that, Mother.

AMANDA. And you—when I see you taking after his ways! Staying out late—and— well, you *had* been drinking the night you were in that—terrifying condition! Laura says that you hate the apartment and that you go out nights to get away from it! Is that true, Tom?

TOM. No. You say there's so much in your heart that you can't describe to me. That's true of me, too. There's so much in my heart that I can't describe to *you!* So let's respect each other's—

AMANDA. But, why—*why*, Tom—are you always so *restless?* Where do you *go* to, nights?

TOM. I—go to the movies.

AMANDA. Why do you go to the movies so much, Tom?

TOM. I go to the movies because—I like adventure. Adventure is something I don't have much of at work, so I go to the movies.

AMANDA. But, Tom, you go to the movies *entirely* too *much!*

TOM. I like a lot of adventure.

[*AMANDA looks baffled, then hurt. As the familiar inquisition resumes, TOM becomes hard and impatient again. AMANDA slips back into her querulous attitude toward him.*

Image on screen: A sailing vessel with Jolly Roger.°]

AMANDA. Most young men find adventure in their careers.

TOM. Then most young men are not employed in a warehouse.

AMANDA. The world is full of young men employed in warehouses and offices and factories.

TOM. Do all of them find adventure in their careers?

AMANDA. They do or they do without it! Not everybody has a craze for adventure.

TOM. Man is by instinct a lover, a hunter, a fighter, and none of those instincts are given much play at the warehouse!

AMANDA. Man is by instinct! Don't quote instinct to me! Instinct is something that people have got away from! It belongs to animals! Christian adults don't want it!

TOM. What do Christian adults want, then, Mother?

AMANDA. Superior things! Things of the mind and the spirit! Only animals have to satisfy instincts! Surely your aims are somewhat higher than theirs! Than monkeys— pigs—

TOM. I reckon they're not.

70.2 *Jolly Roger:* the traditional flag of a pirate ship—a skull and crossbones on a field of black.

AMANDA.   You're joking. However, that isn't what I wanted to discuss.

TOM.   [*rising*] I haven't much time.

AMANDA.   [*pushing his shoulders*] Sit down.

TOM.   You want me to punch in red° at the warehouse, Mother?

AMANDA.   You have five minutes. I want to talk about Laura.   85

[*Screen legend: "Plans and Provisions."*]

TOM.   All right! What about Laura?

AMANDA.   We have to be making some plans and provisions for her. She's older than you, two years, and nothing has happened. She just drifts along doing nothing. It frightens me terribly how she just drifts along.

TOM.   I guess she's the type that people call home girls.

AMANDA.   There's no such type, and if there is, it's a pity! That is unless the home is hers, with a husband!

TOM.   What?   90

AMANDA.   Oh, I can see the handwriting on the wall as plain as I see the nose in front of my face! It's terrifying! More and more you remind me of your father! He was out all hours without explanation! —Then *left! Goodbye!* And me with the bag to hold. I saw that letter you got from the Merchant Marine. I know what you're dreaming of. I'm not standing here blindfolded. [*She pauses.*] Very well, then. Then *do* it! But not till there's somebody to take your place.

TOM.   What do you mean?

AMANDA.   I mean that as soon as Laura has got somebody to take care of her, married, a home of her own, independent—why, then you'll be free to go wherever you please, on land, on sea, whichever way the wind blows you! But until that time you've got to look out for your sister. I don't say me because I'm old and don't matter! I say for your sister because she's young and dependent.

I put her in business college—a dismal failure! Frightened her so it made her sick at the stomach. I took her over to the Young People's League at the church. Another fiasco. She spoke to nobody, nobody spoke to her. Now all she does is fool with those pieces of glass and play those worn-out records. What kind of a life is that for a girl to lead?

TOM.   What can I do about it?

AMANDA.   Overcome selfishness! Self, self, self is all that you ever think of!   95

[*TOM springs up and crosses to get his coat. It is ugly and bulky. He pulls on a cap with earmuffs.*]

Where is your muffler? Put your wool muffler on!

[*He snatches it angrily from the closet, tosses it around his neck and pulls both ends tight.*]

Tom! I haven't said what I had in mind to ask you.

TOM.   I'm too late to—

AMANDA.   [*catching his arm—very importunately; then shyly*] Down at the warehouse, aren't there some—nice young men?

TOM.   No!

AMANDA.   There *must* be—*some* . . .

---

84 *punch in red:* arrive late for work; the time clock stamps late arrival times in red on the time card.

TOM.   Mother— [*He gestures.*]

AMANDA.   Find out one that's clean-living—doesn't drink and ask him out for sister!

TOM.   What?

AMANDA.   For *sister!* To *meet!* Get *acquainted!*

TOM.   [*stamping to the door*] Oh, my go-osh!

AMANDA.   Will you? [*He opens the door. She says, imploringly:*] Will you?

[*He starts down the fire escape.*]

Will you? *Will* you, dear?

TOM.   [*calling back*] Yes!

[*AMANDA closes the door hesitantly and with a troubled but faintly hopeful expression.*

Screen image: The cover of a glamor magazine.

The spotlight picks up AMANDA on the phone.]

AMANDA.   Ella Cartwright? This is Amanda Wingfield! How are you honey? How is that kidney condition?

[*There is a five-second pause.*]

Horrors!

[*There is another pause.*]

You're a Christian martyr, yes, honey, that's what you are, a Christian martyr! Well, I just now happened to notice in my little red book that your subscription to the *Companion* has just run out! I knew that you wouldn't want to miss out on the wonderful serial starting in this new issue. It's by Bessie Mae Hopper, the first thing she's written since *Honeymoon for Three.* Wasn't that a strange and interesting story? Well, this one is even lovelier, I believe. It has a sophisticated, society background. It's all about the horsey set on Long Island!

[*The light fades out.*]

Scene 5

[*Legend on the screen: "Annunciation."*

Music is heard as the light slowly comes on.

It is early dusk of a spring evening. Supper has just been finished in the Wingfield apartment. AMANDA and LAURA, in light-colored dresses, are removing dishes from the table in the dining room, which is shadowy, their movements formalized almost as a dance or ritual, their moving forms as pale and silent as moths. TOM, in white shirt and trousers, rises from the table and crosses toward the fire escape.]

AMANDA.   [*as he passes her*] Son, will you do me a favor?

TOM.   What?

AMANDA.   Comb your hair! You look so pretty when your hair is combed!

[*TOM slouches on the sofa with the evening paper. Its enormous headline reads: "Franco Triumphs."°*]

There is only one respect in which I would like you to emulate your father.
TOM.   What respect is that?
AMANDA.   The care he always took of his appearance. He never allowed himself to   5
look untidy.

[*He throws down the paper and crosses to the fire escape.*]

Where are you going?
TOM.   I'm going out to smoke.
AMANDA.   You smoke too much. A pack a day at fifteen cents a pack. How much
would that amount to in a month? Thirty times fifteen is how much, Tom? Figure it out
and you will be astounded at what you could save. Enough to give you a night-school
course in accounting at Washington U.°! Just think what a wonderful thing that would
be for you, son!

[*TOM is unmoved by the thought.*]

TOM.   I'd rather smoke. [*He steps out on the landing, letting the screen door slam.*]
AMANDA.   [*sharply*] I know! That's the tragedy of it. . . . [*Alone, she turns to look at
her husband's picture.*]

[*Dance music: "The World Is Waiting for the Sunrise!"°*]

TOM.   [*to the audience*] Across the alley from us was the Paradise Dance Hall. On   10
evenings in spring the windows and doors were open and the music came outdoors.
Sometimes the lights were turned out except for a large glass sphere that hung from
the ceiling. It would turn slowly about and filter the dusk with delicate rainbow colors.
Then the orchestra played a waltz or a tango, something that had a slow and sensuous
rhythm. Couples would come outside, to the relative privacy of the alley. You could see
them kissing behind ash pits and telephone poles. This was the compensation for lives
that passed like mine, without any change or adventure. Adventure and change were
imminent in this year. They were waiting around the corner for all these kids.
Suspended in the mist over Berchtesgaden,° caught in the folds of Chamberlain's
umbrella. In Spain there was Guernica! But here there was only hot swing music and
liquor, dance halls, bars, and movies, and sex that hung in the gloom like a chandelier
and flooded the world with brief, deceptive rainbows. . . . All the world was waiting for
bombardments!

[*AMANDA turns from the picture and comes outside.*]

3.1 *"Franco Triumphs"*: Francisco Franco (1892–1975), dictator of Spain from 1939 until his death,
was the general of the victorious Falangist armies in the Spanish Civil War (1936–1939).
7 *Washington U*: Washington University, a highly competitive liberal arts school in St. Louis.
9.1 *"The World . . . Sunrise"*: popular song written in 1919 by Eugene Lockhart and Ernest Seitz.
10 *Berchtesgaden . . . Guernica*: The three names mentioned are all foreshadowings of World War II.
Berchtesgaden, a resort in the Bavarian Alps, was Adolf Hitler's favorite residence. Neville
Chamberlain was the British prime minister who signed the Munich Pact with Hitler in 1938,
allowing Nazi Germany to occupy parts of Czechoslovakia. Chamberlain, who always carried an
umbrella, declared that he had ensured "peace in our time." The bombardment of Guernica
during the Spanish Civil War made the name of the town synonymous with the horrors of war,
and especially the killing of civilian women and children. (See pp. 464, 1708.)

AMANDA.   [*sighing*] A fire escape landing's a poor excuse for a porch. [*She spreads a newspaper on a step and sits down, gracefully and demurely as if she were settling into a swing on a Mississippi veranda.*] What are you looking at?

TOM.   The moon.

AMANDA.   Is there a moon this evening?

TOM.   It's rising over Garfinkel's Delicatessen.

AMANDA.   So it is! A little silver slipper of a moon. Have you made a wish on it yet?

TOM.   Um-hum.

AMANDA.   What did you wish for?

TOM.   That's a secret.

AMANDA.   A secret, huh? Well, I won't tell mine either. I will be just as mysterious as you.

TOM.   I bet I can guess what yours is.

AMANDA.   Is my head so transparent?

TOM.   You're not a sphinx.°

AMANDA.   No, I don't have secrets. I'll tell you what I wished for on the moon. Success and happiness for my precious children! I wish for that whenever there's a moon, and when there isn't a moon, I wish for it, too.

TOM.   I thought perhaps you wished for a gentleman caller.

AMANDA.   Why do you say that?

TOM.   Don't you remember asking me to fetch one?

AMANDA.   I remember suggesting that it would be nice for your sister if you brought home some nice young man from the warehouse. I think that I've made that suggestion more than once.

TOM.   Yes, you have made it repeatedly.

AMANDA.   Well?

TOM.   We are going to have one.

AMANDA.   *What?*

TOM.   A gentleman caller!

[*The annunciation is celebrated with music.*

AMANDA rises.

Image on screen: A caller with a bouquet.]

AMANDA.   You mean you have asked some nice young man to come over?

TOM.   Yep. I've asked him to dinner.

AMANDA.   You really did?

TOM.   I did!

AMANDA.   You did, and did he—*accept?*

TOM.   He did!

AMANDA.   Well, well—well, well! That's—lovely!

TOM.   I thought that you would be pleased.

AMANDA.   It's definite then?

TOM.   Very definite.

AMANDA.   Soon?

---

22 *sphinx:* a mythological monster with the head of a woman and body of a lion, famous for her riddles. See p. 994.

TOM.   Very soon.

AMANDA.   For heaven's sake, stop putting on and tell me some things, will you?   45

TOM.   What things do you want me to tell you?

AMANDA.   *Naturally* I would like to know when he's *coming!*

TOM.   He's coming tomorrow.

AMANDA.   *Tomorrow?*

TOM.   Yep. Tomorrow.   50

AMANDA.   But, Tom!

TOM.   Yes, Mother?

AMANDA.   Tomorrow gives me no time!

TOM.   Time for what?

AMANDA.   Preparations! Why didn't you phone me at once, as soon as you asked   55
him, the minute that he accepted? Then, don't you see, I could have been getting ready!

TOM.   You don't have to make any fuss.

AMANDA.   Oh, Tom, Tom, Tom, of course I have to make a fuss! I want things nice,
not sloppy! Not thrown together. I'll certainly have to do some fast thinking, won't I?

TOM.   I don't see why you have to think at all.

AMANDA.   You just don't know. We can't have a gentleman caller in a pigsty! All
my wedding silver has to be polished, the monogrammed table linen ought to be laundered! The windows have to be washed and fresh curtains put up. And how about
clothes? We have to *wear* something, don't we?

TOM.   Mother, this boy is no one to make a fuss over!   60

AMANDA.   Do you realize he's the first young man we've introduced to your sister?
It's terrible, disgraceful that poor little sister has never received a single gentleman
caller! Tom, come inside! [*She opens the screen door.*]

TOM.   What for?

AMANDA.   I want to ask you some things.

TOM.   If you're going to make such a fuss, I'll call it off, I'll tell him not to come!

AMANDA.   You certainly won't do anything of the kind. Nothing offends people   65
worse than broken engagements. It simply means I'll have to work like a Turk! We won't
be brilliant, but we will pass inspection. Come on inside.

[*TOM follows her inside, groaning.*]

Sit down.

TOM.   Any particular place you would like me to sit?

AMANDA.   Thank heavens I've got that new sofa! I'm also making payments on a
floor lamp I'll have sent out! And put the chintz covers on, they'll brighten things up! Of
course I'd hoped to have these walls re-papered. . . . What is the young man's name?

TOM.   His name is O'Connor.

AMANDA.   That, of course, means fish°—tomorrow is Friday! I'll have that salmon
loaf—with Durkee's dressing! What does he do? He works at the warehouse?

TOM.   Of course! How else would I—   70

AMANDA.   Tom, he—doesn't drink?

TOM.   Why do you ask me that?

AMANDA.   Your father *did!*

TOM.   Don't get started on that!

---

69 *fish:* Amanda assumes that O'Connor is Catholic. Until the 1960s, Roman Catholics were
required by the church to abstain from meat on Fridays.

AMANDA.   He *does* drink, then?

TOM.   Not that I know of!

AMANDA.   Make sure, be certain! The last thing I want for my daughter's a boy who drinks!

TOM.   Aren't you being a little bit premature? Mr. O'Connor has not yet appeared on the scene!

AMANDA.   But will tomorrow. To meet your sister, and what do I know about his character? Nothing! Old maids are better off than wives of drunkards!

TOM.   Oh, my God!

AMANDA.   Be still!

TOM.   [*leaning forward to whisper*] Lots of fellows meet girls whom they don't marry!

AMANDA.   Oh, talk sensibly, Tom—and don't be sarcastic! [*She has gotten a hairbrush.*]

TOM.   What are you doing?

AMANDA.   I'm brushing that cowlick down! [*She attacks his hair with the brush.*] What is this young man's position at the warehouse?

TOM.   [*submitting grimly to the brush and the interrogation*] This young man's position is that of a shipping clerk, Mother.

AMANDA.   Sounds to me like a fairly responsible job, the sort of job *you* would be in if you just had more *get-up*. What is his salary? Have you any idea?

TOM.   I would judge it to be approximately eighty-five dollars a month.

AMANDA.   Well—not princely, but—

TOM.   Twenty more than I make.

AMANDA.   Yes, how well I know! But for a family man, eighty-five dollars a month is not much more than you can just get by on. . . .

TOM.   Yes, but Mr. O'Connor is not a family man.

AMANDA.   He might be, mightn't he? Some time in the future?

TOM.   I see. Plans and provisions.

AMANDA.   You are the only young man that I know of who ignores the fact that the future becomes the present, the present the past, and the past turns into everlasting regret if you don't plan for it!

TOM.   I will think that over and see what I can make of it.

AMANDA.   Don't be supercilious with your mother! Tell me some more about this—what do you call him?

TOM.   James D. O'Connor. The D. is for Delaney.

AMANDA.   Irish on *both* sides! *Gracious!* And he doesn't drink?

TOM.   Shall I call him up and ask him right this minute?

AMANDA.   The only way to find out about those things is to make discreet inquiries at the proper moment. When I was a girl in Blue Mountain and it was suspected that a young man drank, the girl whose attentions he had been receiving, if any girl *was*, would sometimes speak to the minister of his church, or rather her father would if her father was living, and sort of feel him out on the young man's character. That is the way such things are discreetly handled to keep a young woman from making a tragic mistake!

TOM.   Then how did you happen to make a tragic mistake?

AMANDA.   That innocent look of your father's had everyone fooled! He *smiled*— the world was *enchanted!* No girl can do worse than put herself at the mercy of a handsome appearance! I hope that Mr. O'Connor is not too good-looking.

TOM.   No, he's not too good-looking. He's covered with freckles and hasn't too much of a nose.

AMANDA.   He's not right-down homely, though?   105

TOM.   Not right-down homely. Just medium homely, I'd say.

AMANDA.   Character's what to look for in a man.

TOM.   That's what I've always said, Mother.

AMANDA.   You've never said anything of the kind and I suspect you would never give it a thought.

TOM.   Don't be so suspicious of me.   110

AMANDA.   At least I hope he's the type that's up and coming.

TOM.   I think he really goes in for self-improvement.

AMANDA.   What reason have you to think so?

TOM.   He goes to night school.

AMANDA.   [*beaming*] Splendid! What does he do, I mean study?   115

TOM.   Radio engineering and public speaking!

AMANDA.   Then he has visions of being advanced in the world! Any young man who studies public speaking is aiming to have an executive job some day! And radio engineering? A thing for the future! Both of these facts are very illuminating. Those are the sort of things that a mother should know concerning any young man who comes to call on her daughter. Seriously or—not.

TOM.   One little warning. He doesn't know about Laura. I didn't let on that we had dark ulterior motives. I just said, why don't you come and have dinner with us? He said okay and that was the whole conversation.

AMANDA.   I bet it was! You're eloquent as an oyster. However, he'll know about Laura when he gets here. When he sees how lovely and sweet and pretty she is, he'll thank his lucky stars he was asked to dinner.

TOM.   Mother, you mustn't expect too much of Laura.   120

AMANDA.   What do you mean?

TOM.   Laura seems all those things to you and me because she's ours and we love her. We don't even notice she's crippled any more.

AMANDA.   Don't say crippled! You know that I never allow that word to be used!

TOM.   But face facts, Mother. She is and—that's not all—

AMANDA.   What do you mean "not all"?   125

TOM.   Laura is very different from other girls.

AMANDA.   I think the difference is all to her advantage.

TOM.   Not quite all—in the eyes of others—strangers—she's terribly shy and lives in a world of her own and those things make her seem a little peculiar to people outside the house.

AMANDA.   Don't say peculiar.

TOM.   Face the facts. She is.   130

[*The dance hall music changes to a tango that has a minor and somewhat ominous tone.*]

AMANDA.   In what way is she peculiar—may I ask?

TOM.   [*gently*] She lives in a world of her own—a world of little glass ornaments, Mother. . . .

[*He gets up. AMANDA remains holding the brush, looking at him, troubled.*]

She plays old phonograph records and—that's about all—[*He glances at himself in the mirror and crosses to the door.*]

AMANDA. [*sharply*] Where are you going?

TOM. I'm going to the movies. [*He goes out the screen door.*]

AMANDA. Not to the movies, every night to the movies! [*She follows quickly to the screen door.*] I don't believe you always go to the movies!

[*He is gone. AMANDA looks worriedly after him for a moment. Then vitality and optimism return and she turns from the door, crossing to the portieres.*]

Laura! Laura!

[*LAURA answers from the kitchenette.*]

LAURA. Yes, Mother.

AMANDA. Let those dishes go and come in front!

[*LAURA appears with a dish towel. AMANDA speaks to her gaily.*]

Laura, come here and make a wish on the moon!

[*Screen image: The Moon.*]

LAURA. [*entering*] Moon—moon?

AMANDA. A little silver slipper of a moon. Look over your left shoulder, Laura, and make a wish!

[*LAURA looks faintly puzzled as if called out of sleep. AMANDA seizes her shoulders and turns her at an angle by the door.*]

Now! Now, darling, *wish!*

LAURA. What shall I wish for, Mother?

AMANDA. [*her voice trembling and her eyes suddenly filling with tears*] Happiness! Good fortune!

[*The sound of the violin rises and the stage dims out.*]

Scene 6

[*The light comes up on the fire escape landing. Tom is leaning against the grill, smoking. Screen image: The high school hero.*]

TOM. And so the following evening I brought Jim home to dinner. I had known Jim slightly in high school. In high school Jim was a hero. He had tremendous Irish good nature and vitality with the scrubbed and polished look of white chinaware. He seemed to move in a continual spotlight. He was a star in basketball, captain of the debating club, president of the senior class and the glee club and he sang the male lead in the annual light operas. He was always running or bounding, never just walking. He seemed always at the point of defeating the law of gravity. He was shooting with such velocity through his adolescence that you would logically expect him to arrive at nothing short of the White House by the time he was thirty. But Jim apparently ran into more interference after his graduation from Soldan. His speed had definitely slowed. Six years after he left high school he was holding a job that wasn't much better than mine.

[*Screen image: The Clerk.*]

He was the only one at the warehouse with whom I was on friendly terms. I was valuable to him as someone who could remember his former glory, who had seen him win basketball games and the silver cup in debating. He knew of my secret practice of retiring to a cabinet of the washroom to work on poems when business was slack in the warehouse. He called me Shakespeare. And while the other boys in the warehouse regarded me with suspicious hostility, Jim took a humorous attitude toward me. Gradually his attitude affected the others, their hostility wore off and they also began to smile at me as people smile at an oddly fashioned dog who trots across their path at some distance.

I knew that Jim and Laura had known each other at Soldan, and I had heard Laura speak admiringly of his voice. I didn't know if Jim remembered her or not. In high school Laura had been as unobtrusive as Jim had been astonishing. If he did remember Laura, it was not as my sister, for when I asked him to dinner, he grinned and said, "You know, Shakespeare, I never thought of you as having folks!"

He was about to discover that I did. . . .

[*Legend on screen: "The accent of a coming foot."*]

[*The light dims out on Tom and comes up in the Wingfield living room—a delicate lemony light. It is about five on a Friday evening of late spring which comes "scattering poems in the sky."*

AMANDA has worked like a Turk in preparation for the gentleman caller. The results are astonishing. The new floor lamp with its rose silk shade is in place, a colored paper lantern conceals the broken light fixture in the ceiling, new billowing white curtains are at the windows, chintz covers are on the chairs and sofa, a pair of new sofa pillows make their initial appearance. Open boxes and tissue paper are scattered on the floor.

LAURA stands in the middle of the room with lifted arms while AMANDA crouches before her, adjusting the hem of a new dress, devout and ritualistic. The dress is colored and designed by memory. The arrangement of LAURA's hair is changed; it is softer and more becoming. A fragile, unearthly prettiness has come out in LAURA: she is like a piece of translucent glass touched by light, given a momentary radiance, not actual, not lasting.]

AMANDA.   [*impatiently*] Why are you trembling?
LAURA.   Mother, you've made me so nervous!
AMANDA.   How have I made you nervous?
LAURA.   By all this fuss! You make it seem so important!   5
AMANDA.   I don't understand you, Laura. You couldn't be satisfied with just sitting home, and yet whenever I try to arrange something for you, you seem to resist it. [*She gets up.*] Now take a look at yourself. No, wait! Wait just a moment—I have an idea!
LAURA.   What is it now?

[*AMANDA produces two powder puffs which she wraps in handkerchiefs and stuffs in LAURA's bosom.*]

LAURA.   Mother, what are you doing?
AMANDA.   They call them "Gay Deceivers"!
LAURA.   I won't wear them!   10
AMANDA.   You will!
LAURA.   Why should I?
AMANDA.   Because, to be painfully honest, your chest is flat.
LAURA.   You make it seem like we were setting a trap.
AMANDA.   All pretty girls are a trap, a pretty trap, and men expect them to be.   15

[*Legend on screen: "A pretty trap."*]

Now look at yourself, young lady. This is the prettiest you will ever be! [*She stands back to admire* LAURA.] I've got to fix myself now! You're going to be surprised by your mother's appearance!

[AMANDA *crosses through the portieres, humming gaily.* LAURA *moves slowly to the long mirror and stares solemnly at herself. A wind blows the white curtains inward in a slow, graceful motion and with a faint, sorrowful sighing.*]

AMANDA. [*from somewhere behind the portieres*] It isn't dark enough yet.

[LAURA *turns slowly before the mirror with a troubled look.*

Legend on screen: "This is my sister: Celebrate her with strings!" Music plays.]

AMANDA. [*laughing, still not visible*] I'm going to show you something. I'm going to make a spectacular appearance!

LAURA. What is it, Mother?

AMANDA. Possess your soul in patience—you will see! Something I've resurrected from that old trunk! Styles haven't changed so terribly much after all. . . . [*She parts the portieres.*] Now just look at your mother! [*She wears a girlish frock of yellowed voile with a blue silk sash. She carries a bunch of jonquils—the legend of her youth is nearly revived. Now she speaks feverishly:*] This is the dress in which I led the cotillion. Won the cakewalk twice at Sunset Hill, wore one Spring to the Governor's Ball in Jackson!° See how I sashayed around the ballroom, Laura? [*She raises her skirt and does a mincing step around the room.*] I wore it on Sundays for my gentlemen callers! I had it on the day I met your father. . . . I had malaria fever all that Spring. The change of climate from East Tennessee to the Delta— weakened resistance. I had a little temperature all the time—not enough to be serious— just enough to make me restless and giddy! Invitations poured in—parties all over the Delta! "Stay in bed," said Mother, "you have a fever!"—but I just wouldn't. I took qui- nine° but kept on going, going! Evenings, dances! Afternoons, long, long rides! Picnics—lovely! So lovely, that country in May—all lacy with dogwood, literally flooded with jonquils! That was the spring I had the craze for jonquils. Jonquils became an absolute obsession. Mother said, "Honey, there's no more room for jonquils." And still I kept on bringing in more jonquils. Whenever, wherever I saw them, I'd say, "Stop! Stop! I see jonquils!" I made the young men help me gather the jonquils! It was a joke, Amanda and her jonquils. Finally there were no more vases to hold them, every available space was filled with jonquils. No vases to hold them? All right, I'll hold them myself! And then I—[*She stops in front of the picture. Music plays.*] met your father! Malaria fever and jonquils and then—this—boy. . . . [*She switches on the rose-colored lamp.*] I hope they get here before it starts to rain. [*She crosses the room and places the jonquils in a bowl on the table.*] I gave your brother a little extra change so he and Mr. O'Connor could take the service car home.

LAURA. [*with an altered look*] What did you say his name was?

AMANDA. O'Connor.

LAURA. What is his first name?

AMANDA. I don't remember. Oh, yes, I do. It was—Jim.

---

19 *Jackson:* capital of Mississippi. Amanda refers to the social events of her youth. A cotillion is a formal ball, often given for debutantes. The cakewalk is a strutting dance step.   *quinine:* long used as a standard drug to control malaria.

[*LAURA sways slightly and catches hold of a chair.*

Legend on screen: "Not Jim!"]

LAURA.   [*faintly*] Not—Jim!

AMANDA.   Yes, that was it, it was Jim! I've never known a Jim that wasn't nice!   25

[*The music becomes ominous.*]

LAURA.   Are you sure his name is Jim O'Connor?

AMANDA.   Yes. Why?

LAURA.   Is he the one that Tom used to know in high school?

AMANDA.   He didn't say so. I think he just got to know him at the warehouse.

LAURA.   There was a Jim O'Connor we both knew in high school—[*Then, with   30
effort.*] If that is the one that Tom is bringing to dinner—you'll have to excuse me, I won't come to the table.

AMANDA.   What sort of nonsense is this?

LAURA.   You asked me once if I'd ever liked a boy. Don't you remember I showed you this boy's picture?

AMANDA.   You mean the boy you showed me in the yearbook?

LAURA.   Yes, that boy.

AMANDA.   Laura, Laura, were you in love with that boy?   35

LAURA.   I don't know, Mother. All I know is I couldn't sit at the table if it was him!

AMANDA.   It won't be him! It isn't the least bit likely. But whether it is or not, you will come to the table. You will not be excused.

LAURA.   I'll have to be, Mother.

AMANDA.   I don't intend to humor your silliness, Laura. I've had too much from you and your brother, both! So just sit down and compose yourself till they come. Tom has forgotten his key so you'll have to let them in, when they arrive.

LAURA.   [*panicky*] Oh, Mother—*you* answer the door!   40

AMANDA.   [*lightly*] I'll be in the kitchen—busy!

LAURA.   Oh, Mother, please answer the door, don't make me do it!

AMANDA.   [*crossing into the kitchenette*] I've got to fix the dressing for the salmon. Fuss, fuss—silliness!—over a gentleman caller!

[*The door swings shut, LAURA is left alone.*

Legend on screen: "Terror!"

She utters a low moan and turns off the lamp—sits stiffly on the edge of the sofa, knotting her fingers together.

Legend on screen: "The Opening of a Door!"

TOM *and* JIM *appear on the fire escape steps and climb to the landing. Hearing their approach,* LAURA *rises with a panicky gesture. She retreats to the portieres. The doorbell rings.* LAURA *catches her breath and touches her throat. Low drums sound.*]

AMANDA.   [*calling*] Laura, sweetheart! The door!

[*LAURA stares at it without moving.*]

JIM.   I think we just beat the rain.

TOM.   Uh-huh. [*He rings again, nervously. JIM whistles and fishes for a cigarette.*]

AMANDA.   [*very, very gaily*] Laura, that is your brother and Mr. O'Connor! Will you let them in, darling?

[*LAURA crosses toward the kitchenette door.*]

LAURA.   [*breathlessly*] Mother—you go to the door!

[*AMANDA steps out of the kitchenette and stares furiously at LAURA. She points imperiously at the door.*]

LAURA.   Please, please!

AMANDA.   [*in a fierce whisper*] What is the matter with you, you silly thing?

LAURA.   [*desperately*] Please, you answer it, *please!*

AMANDA.   I told you I wasn't going to humor you, Laura. Why have you chosen this moment to lose your mind?

LAURA.   Please, please, please, you go!

AMANDA.   You'll have to go to the door because I can't.

LAURA.   [*despairingly*] I can't either!

AMANDA.   *Why?*

LAURA.   I'm *sick!*

AMANDA.   I'm sick, too—of your nonsense! Why can't you and your brother be normal people? Fantastic whims and behavior!

[*TOM gives a long ring.*]

Preposterous goings on! Can you give me one reason—[*She calls out lyrically.*] *Coming!* Just one second!—why you should be afraid to open a door? Now you answer it, Laura!

LAURA.   Oh, oh, oh . . . [*She returns through the portieres, darts to the Victrola, winds it frantically and turns it on.*]

AMANDA.   Laura Wingfield, you march right to that door!

LAURA.   *Yes—yes, Mother!*

[*A faraway, scratchy rendition of "Dardanella"° softens the air and gives her strength to move through it. She slips to the door and draws it cautiously open. TOM enters with the caller, JIM O'CONNOR.*]

TOM.   Laura, this is Jim. Jim, this is my sister, Laura.

JIM.   [*stepping inside*] I didn't know that Shakespeare had a sister!

LAURA.   [*retreating, stiff and trembling, from the door*] How—how do you do?

JIM.   [*heartily, extending his hand*] Okay!

[*LAURA touches it hesitantly with hers.*]

JIM.   Your hand's *cold*, Laura!

LAURA.   Yes, well—I've been playing the Victrola. . . .

61.2 *"Dardanella"*: a popular song and dance tune written in 1919 by Fred Fisher, Felix Bernard, and Johnny S. Black.

JIM.   Must have been playing classical music on it! You ought to play a little hot swing music to warm you up!

LAURA.   Excuse me—I haven't finished playing the Victrola. . . . [*She turns awkwardly and hurries into the front room. She pauses a second by the Victrola. Then she catches her breath and darts through the portieres like a frightened deer.*]

JIM.   [*grinning*] What was the matter?   70

TOM.   Oh—with Laura? Laura is—terribly shy.

JIM.   Shy, huh? It's unusual to meet a shy girl nowadays. I don't believe you ever mentioned you had a sister.

TOM.   Well, now you know. I have one. Here is the *Post Dispatch.*° You want a piece of it?

JIM.   Uh-huh.

TOM.   What piece? The comics?   75

JIM.   Sports! [*He glances at it.*] Ole Dizzy Dean° is on his bad behavior.

TOM.   [*uninterested*] Yeah? [*He lights a cigarette and goes over to the fire-escape door.*]

JIM.   Where are *you* going?

TOM.   I'm going out on the terrace.

JIM.   [*going after him*] You know, Shakespeare—I'm going to sell you a bill of   80
goods!

TOM.   What goods?

JIM.   A course I'm taking.

TOM.   Huh?

JIM.   In public speaking! You and me, we're not the warehouse type.

TOM.   Thanks—that's good news. But what has public speaking got to do with it?   85

JIM.   It fits you for—executive positions!

TOM.   Awww.

JIM.   I tell you it's done a helluva lot for me.

[*Image on screen: Executive at his desk.*]

TOM.   In what respect?

JIM.   In every! Ask yourself what is the difference between you an' me and men in   90
the office down front? Brains?—No!—Ability?—No! Then what? Just one little thing—

TOM.   What is that one little thing?

JIM.   Primarily it amounts to—social poise! Being able to square up to people and hold your own on any social level!

AMANDA.   [*from the kitchenette*] Tom?

TOM.   Yes, Mother?

AMANDA.   Is that you and Mr. O'Connor?   95

TOM.   Yes, Mother.

AMANDA.   Well, you just make yourselves comfortable in there.

TOM.   Yes, Mother.

AMANDA.   Ask Mr. O'Connor if he would like to wash his hands.

JIM.   Aw, no—no—thank you—I took care of that at the warehouse. Tom—   100

TOM.   Yes?

JIM.   Mr. Mendoza was speaking to me about you.

---

73 *Post Dispatch:* the *St. Louis Post Dispatch,* a newspaper.   76 *Dizzy Dean:* Jerome Herman (or Jay Hanna) Dean (1911–1974), outstanding pitcher with the St. Louis Cardinals (1932–1938).

TOM.   Favorably?

JIM.   What do you think?

TOM.   Well—

JIM.   You're going to be out of a job if you don't wake up.

TOM.   I am waking up—

JIM.   You show no signs.

TOM.   The signs are interior.

[*Image on screen: The sailing vessel with the Jolly Roger again.*]

TOM.   I'm planning to change. [*He leans over the fire escape rail, speaking with quiet exhilaration. The incandescent marquees and signs of the first-run movie houses light his face from across the alley. He looks like a voyager.*] I'm right at the point of committing myself to a future that doesn't include the warehouse and Mr. Mendoza or even a night-school course in public speaking.

JIM.   What are you gassing about?

TOM.   I'm tired of the movies.

JIM.   Movies!

TOM.   Yes, movies! Look at them—[*a wave toward the marvels of Grand Avenue*] All of those glamorous people—having adventures—hogging it all, gobbling the whole thing up! You know what happens? People go to the *movies* instead of *moving!* Hollywood characters are supposed to have all the adventures for everybody in America, while everybody in America sits in a dark room and watches them have them! Yes, until there's a war. That's when adventure becomes available to the masses! *Everyone's* dish, not only Gable's!° Then the people in the dark room come out of the dark room to have some adventures themselves—goody, goody! It's our turn now, to go to the South Sea Island— to make a safari—to be exotic, far-off! But I'm not patient. I don't want to wait till then. I'm tired of the *movies* and I am *about* to *move!*

JIM.   [*incredulously*] Move?

TOM.   Yes.

JIM.   When?

TOM.   Soon!

JIM.   Where? Where?

[*The music seems to answer the question, while* TOM *thinks it over. He searches in his pockets.*]

TOM.   I'm starting to boil inside. I know I seem dreamy, but inside—well, I'm boiling! Whenever I pick up a shoe, I shudder a little thinking how short life is and what I am doing! Whatever that means, I know it doesn't mean shoes—except as something to wear on a traveler's feet! [*He finds what he has been searching for in his pockets and holds out a paper to* JIM.] Look—

JIM.   What?

TOM.   I'm a member.

JIM.   [*reading*] The Union of Merchant Seamen.

TOM.   I paid my dues this month, instead of the light bill.

JIM.   You will regret it when they turn off the lights.

114 *Gable:* Clark Gable (1901–1960), popular American screen actor and matinee idol from the 1930s to his death.

TOM.   I won't be here.

JIM.   How about your mother?

TOM.   I'm like my father. The bastard son of a bastard! Did you notice how he's grinning in his picture in there? And he's been absent going on sixteen years!

JIM.   You're just talking, you drip. How does your mother feel about it?

TOM.   Shhh! Here comes Mother! Mother is not acquainted with my plans!   130

AMANDA.   [*coming through the portieres*] Where are you all?

TOM.   On the terrace, Mother.

[*They start inside. She advances to them. TOM is distinctly shocked at her appearance. Even JIM blinks a little. He is making his first contact with the girlish Southern vivacity and in spite of the night-school course in public speaking is somewhat thrown off the beam by the unexpected outlay of social charm. Certain responses are attempted by JIM but are swept aside by AMANDA's gay laughter and chatter. TOM is embarrassed but after the first shock JIM reacts very warmly. He grins and chuckles, is altogether won over.*

Image on screen: AMANDA as a girl.]

AMANDA.   [*coyly smiling, shaking her girlish ringlets*] Well, well, well, so this is Mr. O'Connor. Introductions entirely unnecessary. I've heard so much about you from my boy. I finally said to him, Tom—good gracious!—why don't you bring this paragon to supper? I'd like to meet this nice young man at the warehouse!—instead of just hearing him sing your praises so much! I don't know why my son is so stand-offish—that's not Southern behavior!

Let's sit down and—I think we could stand a little more air in here! Tom, leave the door open. I felt a nice fresh breeze a moment ago. Where has it gone to? Mmm, so warm already! And not quite summer, even. We're going to burn up when summer really gets started. However, we're having—we're having a very light supper. I think light things are better fo' this time of year. The same as light clothes are. Light clothes an' light food are what warm weather calls fo'. You know our blood gets so thick during th' winter—it takes a while fo' us to *adjust* ourselves!—when the season changes. . . . It's come so quick this year. I wasn't prepared. All of sudden—heavens! Already summer! I ran to the trunk an' pulled out this light dress—terribly old! Historical almost! But feels so good—so good an' co-ol, y'know. . . .

TOM.   Mother—

AMANDA.   Yes, honey?   135

TOM.   How about—supper?

AMANDA.   Honey, you go ask Sister if supper is ready! You know that Sister is in full charge of supper! Tell her you hungry boys are waiting for it. [*To JIM.*] Have you met Laura?

JIM.   She—

AMANDA.   Let you in? Oh, good, you've met already! It's rare for a girl as sweet an' pretty as Laura to be domestic! But Laura is, thank heavens, not only pretty but also very domestic. I'm not at all. I never was a bit. I never could make a thing but angel-food cake. Well, in the South we had so many servants. Gone, gone, gone. All vestige of gracious living! Gone completely! I wasn't prepared for what the future brought me. All of my gentlemen callers were sons of planters and so of course I assumed that I would be married to one and raise my family on a large piece of land with plenty of servants. But man proposes—and woman accepts the proposal! to vary that old, old saying a little but—I married no planter! I married a man who worked for the telephone company!

That gallantly smiling gentleman over there! [*She points to the picture.*] A telephone man who—fell in love with long-distance! Now he travels and I don't even know where! But what am I going on for about my—tribulations? Tell me yours—I hope you don't have any! Tom?

TOM.   [*returning*] Yes, Mother?

AMANDA.   Is supper nearly ready?

TOM.   It looks to me like supper is on the table.

AMANDA.   Let me look—[*She rises prettily and looks through the portieres.*] Oh lovely! But where is Sister?

TOM.   Laura is not feeling well and she says that she thinks she'd better not come to the table.

AMANDA.   What? Nonsense! Laura? Oh, Laura!

LAURA.   [*from the kitchenette, faintly*] Yes, Mother.

AMANDA.   You really must come to the table. We won't be seated until you come to the table! Come in, Mr. O'Connor. You sit over there and I'll. . . . Laura? Laura Wingfield! You're keeping us waiting, honey! We can't say grace until you come to the table!

[*The kitchenette door is pushed weakly open and LAURA comes in. She is obviously quite faint, her lips trembling, her eyes wide and staring. She moves unsteadily toward the table.*

Screen legend: "Terror!"

Outside a summer storm is coming on abruptly. The white curtains billow inward at the windows and there is a sorrowful murmur from the deep blue dusk.

LAURA suddenly stumbles; she catches at a chair with a faint moan.]

TOM.   Laura!

AMANDA.   Laura!

[*There is a clap of thunder.*

Screen legend: "Ah!"]

[*despairingly*] Why, Laura, you are ill, darling! Tom, help your sister into the living room, dear! Sit in the living room, Laura—rest on the sofa. Well! [*To JIM as TOM helps his sister to the sofa in the living room.*] Standing over the hot stove made her ill! I told her that it was just too warm this evening, but—

[*TOM comes back to the table.*]

Is Laura all right now?

TOM.   Yes.

AMANDA.   What is that? Rain? A nice cool rain has come up! [*She gives JIM a frightened look.*] I think we may—have grace—now . . . [*TOM looks at her stupidly.*] Tom, honey—you say grace!

TOM.   Oh . . . "For these and all thy mercies—"

[*They bow their heads, AMANDA stealing a nervous glance at JIM. In the living room LAURA, stretched on the sofa, clenches her hand to her lips, to hold back a shuddering sob.*]

God's Holy Name be praised—

[*The scene dims out.*]

Scene 7

[*It is half an hour later. Dinner is just being finished in the dining room, LAURA is still huddled upon the sofa, her feet drawn under her, her head resting on a pale blue pillow, her eyes wide and mysteriously watchful. The new floor lamp with its shade of rose-colored silk gives a soft, becoming light to her face, bringing out the fragile, unearthly prettiness which usually escapes attention. From outside there is a steady murmur of rain, but it is slackening and soon stops; the air outside becomes pale and luminous as the moon breaks through the clouds. A moment after the curtain rises, the lights in both rooms flicker and go out.*]

JIM.   Hey, there, Mr. Light Bulb!

[*AMANDA laughs nervously.*

Legend on screen: "Suspension of a public service."]

AMANDA.   Where was Moses when the lights went out? Ha-ha. Do you know the answer to that one, Mr. O'Connor?
JIM.   No, Ma'am, what's the answer?
AMANDA.   In the dark!

[*JIM laughs appreciatively.*]

Everybody sit still. I'll light the candles. Isn't it lucky we have them on the table? Where's a match? Which of you gentlemen can provide a match?
JIM.   Here.   5
AMANDA.   Thank you, Sir.
JIM.   Not at all, Ma'am!
AMANDA.   [*as she lights the candles*] I guess the fuse has burnt out. Mr. O'Connor, can you tell a burnt-out fuse? I know I can't and Tom is a total loss when it comes to mechanics. [*They rise from the table and go into the kitchenette, from where their voices are heard.*] Oh, be careful you don't bump into something. We don't want our gentleman caller to break his neck. Now wouldn't that be a fine howdy-do?
JIM.   Ha-ha! Where is the fuse-box?
AMANDA.   Right here next to the stove. Can you see anything?   10
JIM.   Just a minute.
AMANDA.   Isn't electricity a mysterious thing? Wasn't it Benjamin Franklin who tied a key to a kite? We live in such a mysterious universe, don't we? Some people say that science clears up all the mysteries for us. In my opinion it only creates more! Have you found it yet?
JIM.   No, Ma'am. All these fuses look okay to me.
AMANDA.   Tom!
TOM.   Yes, Mother?   15
AMANDA.   That light bill I gave you several days ago. That one I told you we got the notices about?

[*Legend on screen: "Ha!"*]

TOM.   Oh—yeah.
AMANDA.   You didn't neglect to pay it by any chance?
TOM.   Why, I—
AMANDA.   Didn't! I might have known it!   20

JIM.   Shakespeare probably wrote a poem on that light bill, Mrs. Wingfield.

AMANDA.   I might have known better than to trust him with it! There's such a high price for negligence in this world!

JIM.   Maybe the poem will win a ten-dollar prize.

AMANDA.   We'll just have to spend the remainder of the evening in the nineteenth century, before Mr. Edison made the Mazda lamp!°

JIM.   Candlelight is my favorite kind of light.

AMANDA.   That shows you're romantic! But that's no excuse for Tom. Well, we got through dinner. Very considerate of them to let us get through dinner before they plunged us into everlasting darkness, wasn't it, Mr. O'Connor?

JIM.   Ha-ha!

AMANDA.   Tom, as a penalty for your carelessness you can help me with the dishes.

JIM.   Let me give you a hand.

AMANDA.   Indeed you will not!

JIM.   I ought to be good for something.

AMANDA.   Good for something? [*Her tone is rhapsodic.*] You? Why, Mr. O'Connor, nobody, *nobody's* given me this much entertainment in years—as you have!

JIM.   Aw, now, Mrs. Wingfield!

AMANDA.   I'm not exaggerating, not one bit! But Sister is all by her lonesome. You go keep her company in the parlor! I'll give you this lovely old candelabrum that used to be on the altar at the Church of the Heavenly Rest. It was melted a little out of shape when the church burnt down. Lightning struck it one spring. Gypsy Jones was holding a revival at the time and he intimated that the church was destroyed because the Episcopalians gave card parties.

JIM.   Ha-ha.

AMANDA.   And how about you coaxing Sister to drink a little wine? I think it would be good for her! Can you carry both at once?

JIM.   Sure. I'm Superman!

AMANDA.   Now, Thomas, get into this apron!

[*JIM comes into the dining room, carrying the candelabrum, its candles lighted, in one hand and a glass of wine in the other. The door of the kitchenette swings closed on AMANDA's gay laughter; the flickering light approaches the portieres. LAURA sits up nervously as JIM enters. She can hardly speak from the almost intolerable strain of being alone with a stranger.*

Screen legend: "I don't suppose you remember me at all!"

At first, before JIM's warmth overcomes her paralyzing shyness, LAURA's voice is thin and breathless, as though she had just run up a steep flight of stairs. JIM's attitude is gently humorous. While the incident is apparently unimportant, it is to LAURA the climax of her secret life.]

JIM.   Hello there, Laura.

LAURA.   [*faintly*] Hello.

---

24 *Mazda lamp:* Thomas A. Edison (1847–1931) developed the first practical incandescent lamp in 1879.

[*She clears her throat.*]

JIM. How are you feeling now? Better?
LAURA. Yes. Yes, thank you.
JIM. This is for you. A little dandelion wine. [*He extends the glass toward her with extravagant gallantry.*]
LAURA. Thank you.
JIM. Drink it—but don't get drunk!   45

[*He laughs heartily.* LAURA *takes the glass uncertainly; she laughs shyly.*]

Where shall I set the candles?
LAURA. Oh—oh, anywhere . . .
JIM. How about here on the floor? Any objections?
LAURA. No.
JIM. I'll spread a newspaper under to catch the drippings. I like to sit on the floor. Mind if I do?
LAURA. Oh, no.   50
JIM. Give me a pillow?
LAURA. What?
JIM. A pillow!
LAURA. Oh . . . [*She hands him one quickly.*]
JIM. How about you? Don't you like to sit on the floor?   55
LAURA. Oh—yes.
JIM. Why don't you, then?
LAURA. I—will.
JIM. Take a pillow!

[*Laura does. She sits on the floor on the other side of the candelabrum.* JIM *crosses his legs and smiles engagingly at her.*] *I can't hardly see you sitting way over there.*

LAURA. I can—see you.
JIM. I know, but that's not fair, I'm in the limelight.   60

[*LAURA moves her pillow closer.*]

Good! Now I can see you! Comfortable?
LAURA. Yes.
JIM. So am I. Comfortable as a cow! Will you have some gum?
LAURA. No, thank you.
JIM. I think that I will indulge, with your permission. [*He musingly unwraps a stick*   65
of gum and holds it up.] Think of the fortune made by the guy that invented the first piece of chewing gum. Amazing, huh? The Wrigley Building° is one of the sights of Chicago— I saw it when I went up to the Century of Progress.° Did you take in the Century of Progress?
LAURA. No, I didn't.

65 *Wrigley Building:* Finished in 1924, this was one of the first skyscrapers in the United States. *Century of Progress:* a world's fair held in Chicago (1933–1934) to celebrate the city's centennial.

JIM.   Well, it was quite a wonderful exposition. What impressed me most was the Hall of Science. Gives you an idea of what the future will be in America, even more wonderful than the present time is! [*There is a pause. JIM smiles at her.*] Your brother tells me you're shy. Is that right—Laura?

LAURA.   I—don't know.

JIM.   I judge you to be an old-fashioned type of girl. Well, I think that's a pretty good type to be. Hope you don't think I'm being too personal—do you?

LAURA.   [*Hastily, out of embarrassment*] I believe I *will* take a piece of gum, if you—don't mind. [*clearing her throat*] Mr. O'Connor, have you—kept up with your singing?

JIM.   Singing? Me?

LAURA.   Yes. I remember what a beautiful voice you had.

JIM.   When did you hear me sing?

[*LAURA does not answer, and in the long pause which follows a man's voice is heard singing offstage.*]

VOICE:
>   O blow, ye winds, heigh-ho,
>   A-roving I will go!
>   I'm off to my love
>   With a boxing glove—
>   Ten thousand miles away!

JIM.   You say you've heard me sing?

LAURA.   Oh, Yes! Yes, very often . . . I—don't suppose—you remember me—at all?

JIM.   [*smiling doubtfully*] You know I have an idea I've seen you before. I had that idea soon as you opened the door. It seemed almost like I was about to remember your name. But the name that I started to call you—wasn't a name! And so I stopped myself before I said it.

LAURA.   Wasn't it—Blue Roses?

JIM.   [*springing up, grinning*] Blue Roses! My gosh, yes—Blue Roses! That's what I had on my tongue when you opened the door! Isn't it funny what tricks your memory plays? I didn't connect you with high school somehow or other. But that's where it was; it was high school. I didn't even know you were Shakespeare's sister! Gosh, I'm sorry.

LAURA.   I didn't expect you to. You—barely knew me!

JIM.   But we did have a speaking acquaintance, huh?

LAURA.   Yes, we—spoke to each other.

JIM.   When did you recognize me?

LAURA.   Oh, right away!

JIM.   Soon as I came in the door?

LAURA.   When I heard your name I thought it was probably you. I knew that Tom used to know you a little in high school. So when you came in the door—well, then I was—sure.

JIM.   Why didn't you *say* something, then?

LAURA.   [*breathlessly*] I didn't know what to say, I was—too surprised!

JIM.   For goodness' sakes! You know, this sure is funny!

LAURA.   Yes! Yes, isn't it, though . . .

JIM.   Didn't we have a class in something together?

---

74 *O blow . . . :* This is a simplified version of the refrain of "A Capital Ship" (1885), a song that Charles E. Carryl (1841–1920) wrote for the music of the early-nineteenth-century Irish sea shanty "Ten Thousand Miles Away."

LAURA.   Yes, we did.

JIM.   What class was that?

LAURA.   It was—singing—chorus!

JIM.   Aw!   95

LAURA.   I sat across the aisle from you in the Aud.

JIM.   Aw!

LAURA.   Mondays, Wednesdays, and Fridays.

JIM.   Now I remember—you always came in late.

LAURA.   Yes, it was so hard for me, getting upstairs. I had that brace on my leg—   100
it clumped so loud!

JIM.   I never heard any clumping.

LAURA.   [*wincing at the recollection*] To me it sounded like—thunder!

JIM.   Well, well, well, I never even noticed.

LAURA.   And everybody was seated before I came in. I had to walk in front of all
those people. My seat was in the back row. I had to go clumping all the way up the aisle
with everyone watching!

JIM.   You shouldn't have been self-conscious.   105

LAURA.   I know, but I was. It was always such a relief when the singing started.

JIM.   Aw, yes, I've placed you now! I used to call you Blue Roses. How was it that I
got started calling you that?

LAURA.   I was out of school a little while with pleurosis. When I came back you
asked me what was the matter. I said I had pleurosis—you thought that I said *Blue Roses.*
That's what you always called me after that!

JIM.   I hope you didn't mind.

LAURA.   Oh, no—I liked it. You see, I wasn't acquainted with many—people. . . .   110

JIM.   As I remember you sort of stuck by yourself.

LAURA.   I—I—never have had much luck at—making friends.

JIM.   I don't see why you wouldn't.

LAURA.   Well, I—started out badly.

JIM.   You mean being—   115

LAURA.   Yes, it sort of—stood between me—

JIM.   You shouldn't have let it!

LAURA.   I know, but it did, and—

JIM.   You were shy with people!

LAURA.   I tried not to be but never could—   120

JIM.   Overcome it?

LAURA.   No, I—I never could!

JIM.   I guess being shy is something you have to work out of kind of gradually.

LAURA.   [*sorrowfully*] Yes—I guess it—

JIM.   Takes time!   125

LAURA.   Yes—

JIM.   People are not so dreadful when you know them. That's what you have to
remember! And everybody has problems, not just you, but practically everybody has got
some problems. You think of yourself as having the only problems, as being the only
one who is disappointed. But just look around you and you will see lots of people as disappointed as you are. For instance, I hoped when I was going to high school that I would
be further along at this time, six years later, than I am now. You remember that wonderful write-up I had in *The Torch?*

LAURA.   Yes! [*She rises and crosses to the table.*]

JIM.   It said I was bound to succeed in anything I went into!

[*LAURA returns with the high school yearbook.*]

Holy Jeez! *The Torch!*

[*He accepts it reverently. They smile across the book with mutual wonder. LAURA crouches beside him and they begin to turn the pages. LAURA's shyness is dissolving in his warmth.*]

LAURA.   Here you are in *The Pirates of Penzance!*   1⁚

JIM.   [*wistfully*] I sang the baritone lead in that operetta.

LAURA.   [*raptly*] So—beautifully!

JIM.   [*protesting*] Aw—

LAURA.   Yes, yes—beautifully—beautifully!

JIM.   You heard me?   1⁙

LAURA.   All three times!

JIM.   No!

LAURA.   Yes!

JIM.   All three performances?

LAURA.   [*looking down*] Yes.   1⊿

JIM.   Why?

LAURA.   I—wanted to ask you to—autograph my program. [*She takes the program from the back of the yearbook and shows it to him.*]

JIM.   Why didn't you ask me to?

LAURA.   You were always surrounded by your own friends so much that I never had a chance to.

JIM.   You should have just—   14

LAURA.   Well, I—thought you might think I was—

JIM.   Thought I might think you was—what?

LAURA.   Oh—

JIM.   [*with reflective relish*] I was beleaguered by females in those days.

LAURA.   You were terribly popular!   1⁙

JIM.   Yeah—

LAURA.   You had such a—friendly way—

JIM.   I was spoiled in high school.

LAURA.   Everybody—liked you!

JIM.   Including you?   1⁙

LAURA.   I—yes, I—did, too— [*She gently closes the book in her lap.*]

JIM.   Well, well, well! Give me that program, Laura.

[*She hands it to him. He signs it with a flourish.*]

There you are—better late than never!

LAURA.   Oh, I—what a—surprise!

JIM.   My signature isn't worth very much right now. But some day—maybe—it will increase in value! Being disappointed is one thing and being discouraged is something else. I am disappointed but I am not discouraged. I'm twenty-three years old. How old are you?

LAURA.   I'll be twenty-four in June.   16

JIM.   That's not old age!

LAURA.   No, but—

JIM.   You finished high school?

LAURA.   [*with difficulty*] I didn't go back.

JIM.   You mean you dropped out?   165

LAURA.   I made bad grades in my final examinations. [*She rises and replaces the book and the program on the table. Her voice is strained.*] How is—Emily Meisenbach getting along?

JIM.   Oh, that kraut-head!

LAURA.   Why do you call her that?

JIM.   That's what she was.

LAURA.   You're not still—going with her?   170

JIM.   I never see her.

LAURA.   It was in the "Personal" section that you were—engaged!

JIM.   I know, but I wasn't impressed by that—propaganda!

LAURA.   It wasn't—the truth?

JIM.   Only in Emily's optimistic opinion!   175

LAURA.   Oh—

[*Legend: "What have you done since high school?"*

JIM lights a cigarette and leans indolently back on his elbows smiling at LAURA *with a warmth and charm which lights her inwardly with altar candles. She remains by the table, picks up a piece from the glass menagerie collection, and turns it in her hands to cover her tumult.*]

JIM.   [*after several reflective puffs on his cigarette*] What have you done since high school?

[*She seems not to hear him.*]

Huh?

[LAURA *looks up.*]

I said what have you done since high school, Laura?

LAURA.   Nothing much.

JIM.   You must have been doing something these six long years.

LAURA.   Yes.   180

JIM.   Well, then, such as what?

LAURA.   I took a business course at business college—

JIM.   How did that work out?

LAURA.   Well, not very—well—I had to drop out, it gave me—indigestion—

[*JIM laughs gently.*]

JIM.   What are you doing now?   185

LAURA.   I don't do anything—much. Oh, please don't think I sit around doing nothing! My glass collection takes up a good deal of time. Glass is something you have to take good care of.

JIM.   What did you say—about glass?

LAURA.   Collection I said—I have one—[*She clears her throat and turns away again, acutely shy.*]

JIM.   [*abruptly*] You know what I judge to be the trouble with you? Inferiority complex! Know what that is? That's what they call it when someone low-rates himself! I understand it because I had it too. Although my case was not so aggravated as yours seems to be. I had it until I took up public speaking, developed my voice, and learned that I had an aptitude for science. Before that time I never thought of myself as being outstanding in any way whatsoever! Now I've never made a regular study of it, but I have a friend who says I can analyze people better than doctors that make a profession of it. I don't claim that to be necessarily true, but I can sure guess a person's psychology. Laura! [*He takes out his gum.*] Excuse me, Laura. I always take it out when the flavor is gone. I'll use this scrap of paper to wrap it in. I know how it is to get it stuck on a shoe. [*He wraps the gum in paper and puts it in his pocket.*] Yep—that's what I judge to be your principal trouble. A lack of confidence in yourself as a person. You don't have the proper amount of faith in yourself. I'm basing that fact on a number of your remarks and also on certain observations I've made. For instance that clumping you thought was so awful in high school. You say that you even dreaded to walk into class. You see what you did? You dropped out of school, you gave up an education because of a clump, which as far as I know was practically nonexistent! A little physical defect is what you have. Hardly noticeable even! Magnified thousands of times by imagination! You know what my strong advice to you is? Think of yourself as *superior* in some way!

LAURA.   In what way would I think?

JIM.   Why, man alive, Laura! Just look about you a little. What do you see? A world full of common people! All of 'em born and all of 'em going to die! Which of them has one-tenth of your good points! Or mine! Or anyone else's, as far as that goes—gosh! Everybody excels in some one thing. Some in many! [*He unconsciously glances at himself in the mirror.*] All you've got to do is discover in *what!* Take me, for instance. [*He adjusts his tie at the mirror.*] My interest happens to lie in electro-dynamics. I'm taking a course in radio engineering at night school, Laura, on top of a fairly responsible job at the warehouse. I'm taking that course and studying public speaking.

LAURA.   Ohhhh.

JIM.   Because I believe in the future of television! [*turning his back to her*] I wish to be ready to go up right along with it. Therefore I'm planning to get in on the ground floor. In fact I've already made the right connections and all that remains is for the industry itself to get under way! Full steam—[*His eyes are starry.*] *Knowledge*—Zzzzzp! *Money*—Zzzzzp!—Power! That's the cycle democracy is built on!

[*His attitude is convincingly dynamic. LAURA stares at him, even her shyness eclipsed in her absolute wonder. He suddenly grins.*]

I guess you think I think a lot of myself!

LAURA.   No—o-o-o, I—

JIM.   Now how about you? Isn't there something you take more interest in than anything else?

LAURA.   Well, I do—as I said—have my—glass collection—

[*A peal of girlish laughter rings from the kitchenette.*]

JIM.   I'm not right sure I know what you're talking about. What kind of glass is it?

LAURA.   Little articles of it, they're ornaments mostly! Most of them are little animals made out of glass, the tiniest little animals in the world. Mother calls them a glass menagerie! Here's an example of one, if you'd like to see it! This one is one of the oldest. It's nearly thirteen.

[*Music: "The Glass Menagerie."*

He stretches out his hand.]

Oh, be careful—if you breathe, it breaks!

JIM.   I'd better not take it. I'm pretty clumsy with things.

LAURA.   Go, on, I trust you with him! [*She places the piece in his palm.*] There now—   200
you're holding him gently! Hold him over the light, he loves the light! You see how the light shines through him?

JIM.   It sure does shine!

LAURA.   I shouldn't be partial, but he is my favorite one.

JIM.   What kind of a thing is this one supposed to be?

LAURA.   Haven't you noticed the single horn on his forehead?

JIM.   A unicorn, huh?   205

LAURA.   Mmmm-hmmm!

JIM.   Unicorns—aren't they extinct in the modern world?

LAURA.   I know!

JIM.   Poor little fellow, he must feel sort of lonesome.

LAURA.   [*smiling*] Well, if he does, he doesn't complain about it. He stays on a   210
shelf with some horses that don't have horns and all of them seem to get along nicely together.

JIM.   How do you know?

LAURA.   [*lightly*] I haven't heard any arguments among them!

JIM.   [*grinning*] No arguments, huh? Well, that's a pretty good sign! Where shall I set him?

LAURA.   Put him on the table. They all like a change of scenery once in a while!

JIM.   Well, well, well, well—[*He places the glass piece on the table, then raises his arms*   215
and stretches.] Look how big my shadow is when I stretch!

LAURA.   Oh, oh, yes—it stretches across the ceiling!

JIM.   [*crossing to the door*] I think it's stopped raining. [*He opens the fire-escape door*
and the background music changes to a dance tune.] Where does the music come from?

LAURA.   From the Paradise Dance Hall across the alley.

JIM.   How about cutting the rug a little, Miss Wingfield?

LAURA.   Oh, I—   220

JIM.   Or is your program filled up? Let me have a look at it. [*He grasps an imagi-*
nary card.] Why, every dance is taken! I'll just have to scratch some out.

[*Waltz music: "La Golondrina"* °]

Ahh, a waltz! [*He executes some sweeping turns by himself, then holds his arms toward*
LAURA.]

LAURA.   [*breathlessly*] I—can't dance.

JIM.   There you go, that inferiority stuff!

LAURA.   I've never danced in my life!

JIM.   Come on, try!   225

220.2 *"La Golondrina":* a popular Mexican song (1883) written by Narciso Seradell (1843–1910).

LAURA.   Oh, but I'd step on you!

JIM.   I'm not made out of glass.

LAURA.   How—how—how do we start?

JIM.   Just leave it to me. You hold your arms out a little.

LAURA.   Like this?

JIM.   [*taking her in his arms*] A little bit higher. Right. Now don't tighten up, that's the main thing about it—relax.

LAURA.   [*laughing breathlessly*] It's hard not to.

JIM.   Okay.

LAURA.   I'm afraid you can't budge me.

JIM.   What do you bet I can't? [*He swings her into motion.*]

LAURA.   Goodness, yes, you can!

JIM.   Let yourself go, now, Laura, just let yourself go.

LAURA.   I'm—

JIM.   Come on!

LAURA.   —trying!

JIM.   Not so stiff—easy does it!

LAURA.   I know but I'm—

JIM.   Loosen th' backbone! There now, that's a lot better.

LAURA.   Am I?

JIM.   Lots, lots better! [*He moves her about the room in a clumsy waltz.*]

LAURA.   Oh, my!

JIM.   Ha-ha!

LAURA.   Oh, my goodness!

JIM.   Ha-ha-ha!

[*They suddenly bump into the table, and the glass piece on it falls to the floor. JIM stops the dance.*]

What did we hit?

LAURA.   Table.

JIM.   Did something fall off it? I think—

LAURA.   Yes.

JIM.   I hope that it wasn't the little glass horse with the horn!

LAURA.   Yes. [*She stoops to pick it up.*]

JIM.   Aw, aw, aw. Is it broken?

LAURA.   Now it is just like all the other horses.

JIM.   It's lost its—

LAURA.   Horn! It doesn't matter. Maybe it's a blessing in disguise.

JIM.   You'll never forgive me. I bet that that was your favorite piece of glass.

LAURA.   I don't have favorites much. It's no tragedy, Freckles. Glass breaks so easily. No matter how careful you are. The traffic jars the shelves and things fall off them.

JIM.   Still I'm awfully sorry that I was the cause.

LAURA.   [*smiling*] I'll just imagine he had an operation. The horn was removed to make him feel less—freakish!

[*They both laugh.*]

Now he will feel more at home with the other horses, the ones that don't have horns. . . .

JIM.   Ha-ha, that's very funny! [*Suddenly he is serious.*] I'm glad to see that you have a sense of humor. You know—you're—well—very different! Surprisingly different from anyone else I know! [*His voice becomes soft and hesitant with a genuine feeling.*] Do you mind me telling you that?

[*LAURA is abashed beyond speech.*]

I mean it in a nice way—

[*LAURA nods shyly, looking away.*]

You make me feel sort of—I don't know how to put it! I'm usually pretty good at expressing things, but—this is something that I don't know how to say!

[*LAURA touches her throat and clears it—turns the broken unicorn in her hands. His voice becomes softer.*]

Has anyone ever told you that you were pretty?

[*There is a pause, and the music rises slightly. LAURA looks up slowly, with wonder, and shakes her head.*]

Well, you are! In a very different way from anyone else. And all the nicer because of the difference, too.

[*His voice becomes low and husky. LAURA turns away, nearly faint with the novelty of her emotions.*]

I wish that you were my sister. I'd teach you to have some confidence in yourself. The different people are not like other people, but being different is nothing to be ashamed of. Because other people are not such wonderful people. They're one hundred times one thousand. You're one times one! They walk all over the earth. You just stay here. They're common as—weeds, but—you—well, you're—*Blue Roses!*

[*Image on screen: Blue Roses.*

The music changes.]

LAURA.   But blue is wrong for—roses. . . .
JIM.   It's right for you! You're—pretty!
LAURA.   In what respect am I pretty?
JIM.   In all respects—believe me! Your eyes—your hair—are pretty! Your hands are pretty! [*He catches hold of her hand.*] You think I'm making this up because I'm invited to dinner and have to be nice. Oh, I could do that! I could put on an act for you, Laura, and say lots of things without being very sincere. But this time I am. I'm talking to you sincerely. I happened to notice you had this inferiority complex that keeps you from feeling comfortable with people. Somebody needs to build your confidence up and make you proud instead of shy and turning away and—blushing. Somebody—ought to—*kiss* you, Laura!

[*His hand slips slowly up her arm to her shoulder as the music swells tumultuously. He suddenly turns about and kisses her on the lips. When he releases her, LAURA sinks on the sofa with a bright, dazed look. JIM backs away and fishes in his pocket for a cigarette.*

Legend on screen: "A souvenir."]

Stumblejohn!

265

[*He lights the cigarette, avoiding her look. There is a peal of girlish laughter from* AMANDA *in the kitchenette.* LAURA *slowly raises and opens her hand. It still contains the little broken glass animal. She looks at it with a tender, bewildered expression.*]

Stumblejohn! I shouldn't have done that—that was way off the beam. You don't smoke, do you?

[*She looks up, smiling, not hearing the question. He sits beside her rather gingerly. She looks at him speechlessly—waiting. He coughs decorously and moves a little further aside as he considers the situation and senses her feelings, dimly, with perturbation. He speaks gently.*]

Would you—care for a mint?

[*She doesn't seem to hear him but her look grows brighter even.*]

Peppermint? Life Saver? My pocket's a regular drugstore—wherever I go. . . . [*He pops a mint in his mouth. Then he gulps and decides to make a clean breast of it. He speaks slowly and gingerly.*] Laura, you know, if I had a sister like you, I'd do the same thing as Tom. I'd bring out fellows and—introduce her to them. The right type of boys—of a type to—appreciate her. Only—well—he made a mistake about me. Maybe I've got no call to be saying this. That may not have been the idea in having me over. But what if it was? There's nothing wrong about that. The only trouble is that in my case—I'm not in a situation to—do the right thing. I can't take down your number and say I'll phone. I can't call up next week and—ask for a date. I thought I had better explain the situation in case you—misunderstood it and—I hurt your feelings. . . .

[*There is a pause. Slowly, very slowly,* LAURA's *look changes, her eyes returning slowly from his to the glass figure in her palm.* AMANDA *utters another gay laugh in the kitchenette.*]

LAURA.   [*faintly*] You—won't—call again?
JIM.   No, Laura, I can't. [*He rises from the sofa.*] As I was just explaining, I've—got strings on me, Laura, I've—been going steady! I go out all the time with a girl named Betty. She's a home-girl like you, and Catholic, and Irish, and in a great many ways we—get along fine. I met her last summer on a moonlight boat trip up the river to Alton,° on the *Majestic.* Well—right away from the start it was—love!

[*Legend: Love!*

LAURA *sways slightly forward and grips the arm of the sofa. He fails to notice, now enrapt in his own comfortable being.*]

Being in love has made a new man of me!

[*Leaning stiffly forward, clutching the arm of the sofa,* LAURA *struggles visibly with her storm. But* JIM *is oblivious; she is a long way off.*]

The power of love is really pretty tremendous! Love is something that—changes the whole world, Laura!

[*The storm abates a little and* LAURA *leans back. He notices her again.*]

It happened that Betty's aunt took sick, she got a wire and had to go to Centralia.°

269.1 *Alton:* a city in Illinois about twenty miles north of St. Louis on the Mississippi River.
269.8 *Centralia:* a city in Illinois about sixty miles east of St. Louis.

So Tom—when he asked me to dinner—I naturally just accepted the invitation, not knowing that you—that he—that I—[He stops awkwardly.] Huh—I'm a stumblejohn!

[*He flops back on the sofa. The holy candles on the altar of* LAURA's *face have been snuffed out. There is a look of almost infinite desolation.* JIM *glances at her uneasily.*]

I wish that you would—say something.

[*She bites her lip which was trembling and then bravely smiles. She opens her hand again on the broken glass figure. Then she gently takes his hand and raises it level with her own. She carefully places the unicorn in the palm of his hand, then pushes his fingers closed upon it.*]

What are you—doing that for? You want me to have him? Laura?

[*She nods.*]

What for?

    LAURA.   A—souvenir. . . .   270

[*She rises unsteadily and crouches beside the Victrola to wind it up.*]

Legend on screen: *"Things have a way of turning out so badly!"* Or image: *"Gentleman caller waving goodbye—gaily."*

At this moment AMANDA *rushes brightly back into the living room. She bears a pitcher of fruit punch in an old-fashioned cut-glass pitcher, and a plate of macaroons. The plate has a gold border and poppies painted on it.*]

    AMANDA.   Well, well, well! Isn't the air delightful after the shower? I've made you children a little liquid refreshment. [*She turns gaily to* JIM.] Jim, do you know that song about lemonade?

"Lemonade, lemonade
Made in the shade and stirred with a spade—
Good enough for any old maid!"

    JIM.   [*uneasily*] Ha-ha! No—I never heard it.

    AMANDA.   Why, Laura! You look so serious!

    JIM.   We were having a serious conversation.

    AMANDA.   Good! Now you're better acquainted!   275

    JIM.   [*uncertainly*] Ha-ha! Yes.

    AMANDA.   You modern young people are much more serious-minded than my generation. I was so gay as a girl!

    JIM.   You haven't changed, Mrs. Wingfield.

    AMANDA.   Tonight I'm rejuvenated! The gaiety of the occasion, Mr. O'Connor! [*She tosses her head with a peal of laughter, spilling some lemonade.*] Oooo! I'm baptizing myself!

    JIM.   Here—let me—   280

    AMANDA.   [*setting the pitcher down*] There now. I discovered we had some maraschino cherries. I dumped them in, juice and all!

    JIM.   You shouldn't have gone to that trouble, Mrs. Wingfield.

    AMANDA.   Trouble, trouble? Why, it was loads of fun! Didn't you hear me cutting up in the kitchen? I bet your ears were burning! I told Tom how outdone with him I was for keeping you to himself so long a time! He should have brought you over much, much sooner! Well, now that you've found your way, I want you to be a very frequent caller! Not just occasional but all the time. Oh, we're going to have a lot of gay times together! I see them coming! Mmm, just breathe that air! So fresh, and the moon's so pretty! I'll skip back out—I know where my place is when young folks are having a— serious conversation!

JIM.   Oh, don't go out, Mrs. Wingfield. The fact of the matter is I've got to be going.

AMANDA.   Going, now? You're joking! Why, it's only the shank of the evening,° Mr. O'Connor!

JIM.   Well, you know how it is.

AMANDA.   You mean you're a young workingman and have to keep working-men's hours. We'll let you off early tonight. But only on the condition that next time you stay later. What's the best night for you? Isn't Saturday night the best night for you workingmen?

JIM.   I have a couple of time-clocks to punch, Mrs. Wingfield. One at morning, another one at night!

AMANDA.   My, but you *are* ambitious! You work at night, too?

JIM.   No, Ma'am, not work but—Betty!

[*He crosses deliberately to pick up his hat. The band at the Paradise Dance Hall goes into a tender waltz.*]

AMANDA.   Betty? Betty? Who's—Betty!

[*There is an ominous cracking sound in the sky.*]

JIM.   Oh, just a girl. The girl I go steady with!

[*He smiles charmingly. The sky falls.*

Legend: "The Sky Falls."]

AMANDA.   [*a long-drawn exhalation*] Ohhh . . . Is it a serious romance, Mr. O'Connor?

JIM.   We're going to be married the second Sunday in June.

AMANDA.   Ohhh—how nice! Tom didn't mention that you were engaged to be married.

JIM.   The cat's not out of the bag at the warehouse yet. You know how they are. They call you Romeo and stuff like that. [*He stops at the oval mirror to put on his hat. He carefully shapes the brim and the crown to give a discreetly dashing effect.*] It's been a ۱ on-derful evening, Mrs. Wingfield. I guess this is what they mean by Southern hospitality.

AMANDA.   It really wasn't anything at all.

JIM.   I hope it don't seem like I'm rushing off. But I promised Betty I'd pick her up at the Wabash depot, an' by the time I get my jalopy down there her train'll be in. Some women are pretty upset if you keep 'em waiting.

AMANDA.   Yes, I know—the tyranny of women! [*She extends her hand.*] Goodbye, Mr. O'Connor. I wish you luck—and happiness—and success! All three of them, and so does Laura! Don't you, Laura?

LAURA.   Yes!

285 *shank of the evening:* still early, the best part of the evening.

JIM. [*taking LAURA's hand*] Goodbye, Laura. I'm certainly going to treasure that souvenir. And don't you forget the good advice I gave you. [*He raises his voice to a cheery shout.*] So long, Shakespeare! Thanks again, ladies. Good night!

[*He grins and ducks jauntily out. Still bravely grimacing, AMANDA closes the door on the gentleman caller. Then she turns back to the room with a puzzled expression. She and LAURA don't dare to face each other. LAURA crouches beside the Victrola to wind it.*]

AMANDA. [*faintly*] Things have a way of turning out so badly. I don't believe that I would play the Victrola. Well, well—well! Our gentleman caller was engaged to be married? [*She raises her voice.*] Tom!

TOM. [*from the kitchenette*] Yes, Mother?

AMANDA. Come in here a minute. I want to tell you something awfully funny.

TOM. [*entering with a macaroon and a glass of the lemonade*] Has the gentleman 305
caller gotten away already?

AMANDA. The gentleman caller has made an early departure. What a wonderful joke you played on us!

TOM. How do you mean?

AMANDA. You didn't mention that he was engaged to be married.

TOM. Jim? Engaged?

AMANDA. That's what he just informed us. 310

TOM. I'll be jiggered! I didn't know about that.

AMANDA. That seems very peculiar.

TOM. What's peculiar about it?

AMANDA. Didn't you call him your best friend down at the warehouse?

TOM. He is, but how did I know? 315

AMANDA. It seems extremely peculiar that you wouldn't know your best friend was going to be married!

TOM. The warehouse is where I work, not where I know things about people!

AMANDA. You don't know things anywhere! You live in a dream; you manufacture illusions!

[*He crosses to the door.*]

Where are you going?

TOM. I'm going to the movies.

AMANDA. That's right, now that you've had us make such fools of ourselves. 320
The effort, the preparations, all the expense! The new floor lamp, the rug, the clothes for Laura! All for what? To entertain some other girl's fiancé! Go to the movies, go! Don't think about us, a mother deserted, an unmarried sister who's crippled and has no job! Don't let anything interfere with your selfish pleasure! Just go, go, go—to the movies!

TOM. All right, I will! The more you shout about my selfishness to me the quicker I'll go, and I won't go to the movies!

AMANDA. Go, then! Go to the moon—you selfish dreamer!

[*TOM smashes his glass on the floor. He plunges out on the fire escape, slamming the door. LAURA screams in fright. The dance-hall music becomes louder. TOM stands on the fire escape, gripping the rail. The moon breaks through the storm clouds, illuminating his face.*

Legend on screen: "And so goodbye . . ."

TOM's *closing speech is timed with what is happening inside the house. We see, as though through soundproof glass, that* AMANDA *appears to be making a comforting speech to* LAURA, *who is huddled upon the sofa. Now that we cannot hear the mother's speech, her silliness is gone and she has dignity and tragic beauty.* LAURA's *hair hides her face until, at the end of the speech, she lifts her head to smile at her mother.* AMANDA's *gestures are slow and graceful, almost dancelike, as she comforts her daughter. At the end of her speech she glances a moment at the father's picture—then withdraws through the portieres. At the close of* TOM's *speech,* LAURA *blows out the candles, ending the play.*]

TOM.   I didn't go to the moon, I went much further—for time is the longest distance between two places. Not long after that I was fired for writing a poem on the lid of a shoe-box. I left Saint Louis. I descended the steps of this fire escape for a last time and followed, from then on, in my father's footsteps, attempting to find in motion what was lost in space. I traveled around a great deal. The cities swept about me like dead leaves, leaves that were brightly colored but torn away from the branches. I would have stopped, but I was pursued by something. It always came upon me unawares, taking me altogether by surprise. Perhaps it was a familiar bit of music. Perhaps it was only a piece of transparent glass. Perhaps I am walking along a street at night, in some strange city, before I have found companions. I pass the lighted window of a shop where perfume is sold. The window is filled with pieces of colored glass, tiny transparent bottles in delicate colors, like bits of a shattered rainbow. Then all at once my sister touches my shoulder. I turn around and look into her eyes. Oh, Laura, Laura, I tried to leave you behind me, but I am more faithful than I intended to be! I reach for a cigarette, I cross the street, I run into the movies or a bar, I buy a drink, I speak to the nearest stranger—anything that can blow your candles out!

[LAURA *bends over the candles.*]

For nowadays the world is lit by lightning! Blow out your candles, Laura—and so goodbye. . . .

[*She blows the candles out.*]

QUESTIONS

1. What does the setting described in the opening stage direction tell you about the Wingfields? Consider especially the adjectives and the symbolism of the alley and the fire escape.

2. Who is the "fifth character" in the play, and how is his presence established? In what ways is Tom a parallel to this character?

3. What does Amanda reveal about her past in scene 1? How does Williams reveal that Amanda often dwells in the past?

4. What happened to Laura at Rubican's Business College? How can you account for her behavior? What plan of Amanda's did she upset?

5. What new plan for Laura's future does Amanda begin to develop in scene 2? Why is the plan impracticable? Why is the image of Jim introduced here?

6. Summarize the argument between Tom and Amanda in scene 3. What does Amanda assert about Tom? What does he claim about his life? Why is Laura spotlighted throughout the argument?

7. What sort of agreement does Amanda try to reach with Tom about Laura in scene 4?

8. How do Amanda and Laura react to the news of a gentleman caller? Describe Laura's feelings toward Jim during the conversation and the dancing in scene 7. Describe how he changes after the kiss.

9. Explain the symbolism of the unicorn (both whole and broken). Why does Laura give it to Jim as a souvenir?

10. What is Tom's situation at the end? To what degree has he achieved his dreams of escape and adventure?

11. Describe Amanda's and Laura's concluding situations. Why does Laura blow out the candles? What is the future for these women?

GENERAL QUESTIONS

1. Explain the most striking nonrealistic aspects of the play. What do these contribute to the play's meaning and impact? Which aspect is the most effective? Why?

2. Which characters in the play change significantly? To what extent do the characters succeed or fail? How do they try to escape the realities they face?

3. Consider Tom as character and narrator. Explain why his language changes as he shifts between narrator and character. What does the character dream about and strive for? What does the narrator learn about these dreams and strivings?

4. Explain why Laura cannot deal with reality. What does her glass menagerie symbolize?

5. Williams says that there is much to admire, pity, and laugh at in Amanda. What aspects of her character are admirable? Pitiable? Laughable? Which reaction is dominant for you at the close of the play? Why?

6. Tom calls Jim the play's "most realistic character." In what ways is Jim realistic? How are his dreams and goals more (or less) realistic than Tom's?

7. At the opening, Tom (as narrator) mentions the "social background," and he remarks on it throughout. Discuss how this background relates to the play, especially the events occurring in Europe.

8. Discuss the play's religious allusion and imagery, especially Malvolio the Magician, the "Ave Maria," the "Annunciation," the Paradise Dance Hall, and Laura's candles. How do these references affect the play's level of reality?

WRITING ABOUT REALISTIC
AND NONREALISTIC DRAMA

Your essay should take into account the traditional elements of drama—plot, character, language, setting, symbol, and theme. Conventional approaches to these elements are discussed in Chapter 26 (pp. 1277–80), and you may want to review this material. As you plan your essay, your overall concern should be to determine the relative degrees of realism or nonrealism with which the elements are presented and developed. Your discoveries here will enable you to describe the ways in which the play establishes its views and ideas about life and the world. In short, how do conventional aspects of dramatic structure, together with the degree of realism or nonrealism, create a perspective that is the unique property of the play?

Questions for Discovering Ideas

PLOT.   Does the play unfold in a chronological order that imitates reality, or does it mix past and present action? Is the action true to life or stylized? Are the conflicts resolved realistically, or does the playwright employ a conventional and perhaps improbable happy (or sad) ending? How does the realistic or nonrealistic development of these aspects affect the play's meaning and impact?

CHARACTER.   Are the characters realistic or symbolic, representative, or stereotyped? Are they round or flat? Are they motivated by lifelike considerations, like Amanda in *The Glass Menagerie,* who lives only in the past? Or are they motivated by the play's requirements, like the narrator, who has the artificial role of speaking directly to the audience? Are the characters consistent, or do they drop in and out of character? Is their clothing and makeup (as described in the stage directions) an imitation of real life, or is it theatrical and nonrealistic? Are all the characters developed in the same manner, or are there differences in the degree of realism you find in each? Is one character more or less realistic than any of the others? If so, why? Of what importance is this character to the play as a whole?

LANGUAGE.   Look carefully at the diction, style, and patterns of the dialogue. In realistic drama, what is the nature of the speeches? Is the language colloquial, formal, low? Is it appropriate for the characters? Is the dialogue normal or natural, granted the situation? Do the characters speak loudly? Do they whisper? Shout? Why? What pattern of consistency can you discover by studying how the characters speak? Within the confines of realistic drama, what normal or realistic variations occur? (For example, a letter is read aloud, a phone conversation occurs, a character is alone onstage and speaks to characters offstage as in O'Neill's *Before Breakfast* [Chapter 26], or a character speaks to characters who do not hear.) What proportion of the dialogue is ordinary two- or three-way conversation? How much variation occurs, and what kind is it? Why do you think the dramatists have varied the normal dialogue, and how do these variations shape your perception of the play?

In nonrealistic drama, some dialogue will be realistically normal or appear so, but much of it will be shaped by the play's nonrealistic premise. How do you identify nonrealistic speech? Do you find nonrealistic devices such as verse, song, or unnatural and patterned repetition? Does any character seem to be speaking in different voices? If so, why? Which characters seem to ignore other characters and speak instead to the air or to the audience? How extensive is such direct address? Does a single character do most of this talking? If so, what is he or she like? What does the character tell you about himself or herself? About the other characters in the play? The background? Plot? Action? Setting? Staging? How accurate and objective is this character? How does this direct address shape and control your responses?

In sum, how do all aspects of language determine the extent to which the play effectively communicates ideas and emotions to you? As you deal with language, also consider the significance of other aspects of sound indicated in the stage directions, such as sound effects or music.

SETTING. To what degree do the stage directions present the setting as realistic or nonrealistic? Do the directions call for the reproduction of an actual room or place? How much specific detail is included? If less than a fully realistic setting is described, how far does the playwright go in reducing the setting to the bare stage? How much of the physical theater (brick walls, pipes, wires, lights, backstage ropes) does the playwright indicate that he or she wants you to see or imagine? To what extent do you find symbolic, impressionistic, and nonrealistic devices such as transparent walls? How do the stage directions describe lighting? Is the lighting used realistically, to recreate natural illumination, or nonrealistically, to isolate and emphasize specific places, objects, characters, or actions? Most important, how do the setting and its degree of realism (or nonrealism) contribute to the impact and meaning of the play?

SYMBOLISM. Because symbols operate in life as they do in art, there is symbolism both in the realistic plays of Glaspell and Ibsen and in the relatively nonrealistic dramas of Miller and Williams. Are symbols introduced through realistic or logical techniques, or do they appear illogically and nonrealistically? You can focus your exploration directly on the symbol and its meaning (the water pollution in *An Enemy of the People*) or the nonrealistic methods through which it is established (the blue roses in *The Glass Menagerie*).

THEME.   What are the important concepts in the play, and how are they conveyed? Be sure to give special consideration to significantly realistic or non-realistic techniques. In considering realistic plays like *Trifles* or *Mulatto*, explore the ways in which realism in character, action, and setting contribute to the plays' ideas. Conversely, consider how Williams employs a strikingly nonrealistic device, such as the music or the screen projections, to convey and emphasize the themes of *The Glass Menagerie*.

Strategies for Organizing Ideas

Your central idea should show how realistic or nonrealistic elements affect part or all of the play. Try to connect the topic with its effect. For example, begin with sentences such as these: (1) "Tom as a nonrealistic narrator and realistic character unifies *The Glass Menagerie* and gives the play a coherent and subjective point of view." (2) "In *An Enemy of the People* [Chapter 31], the Mayor's threats of real-life economic reprisal bring out Dr. Stockmann's combativeness and moral strength."

The supporting details can be organized in any way that produces a logical and convincing essay. If you are writing about the ways in which nonrealistic devices emphasize meaning in *The Glass Menagerie*, for example, you might organize your essay around the setting, the lighting, and the screen device. When your essay focuses on only one element, you can organize your supporting details to reflect the order in which they occur in the play.

In your conclusion you might raise larger issues than you have already raised, or you might make broader connections not only about your topic but also about the play as a whole. You might also reconsider the significance of the play's general level of realistic or nonrealistic techniques.

DEMONSTRATIVE STUDENT ESSAY

Realism and Nonrealism in Tom's Triple Role in
The Glass Menagerie°

[1]   In The Glass Menagerie, Tennessee Williams combines realistic and non-realistic elements to explore the personalities and conflicts of the Wingfield family. One of his most effective nonrealistic elements in the play is his use of Tom in three different roles.* As a realistic character within the action, a nonrealistic

---

° See pp. 1703–54 for this play.
* Central idea.

stage manager of the action, and a nonrealistic narrator of the entire play, Tom combines three functions that significantly shape our perceptions.†

As a realistic character involved in the recollected action of the play, Tom is ensnared by the economic and emotional demands of his family and his job. In the opening description of the characters, Williams explains Tom's plight: "to escape from a trap he [Tom] has to act without pity." In addition, Tom himself dramatically expresses his need to escape from his stifling life at home. He discusses this need with his mother in scene 3, with Laura in scene 4, and, above all, with Jim in scene 6. Here, we see that Tom craves not only escape but also adventure. He tells Jim, "I'm planning a change." And he clearly expresses his desire to move out of the prison house of the family:

[2]

> It's our turn now, to go the South Sea Island—to make a safari--to be exotic, far off! But I'm not patient. I don't want to wait till then, I'm tired of the *movies* and I am *about* to *move!* (scene 6, speech 114)

> I'm starting to boil inside. I know I seem dreamy, but inside—well, I'm boiling. (scene 6, speech 120)

These expressions of his need to escape define a major line of the realistic thought and action in *The Glass Menagerie.*

Tom's realism as a character is undercut by his momentary role as a stage manager in scene 1. Here, he speaks with Amanda *"as though reading from a script."* In this same scene, "Tom *motions for music and a spot of light on* Amanda." Although this device is abandoned, the image of Tom [3] holding an imaginary script and giving cues to the musicians and the lighting technicians breaks any possible illusions that the play is imitating real life. The role as manager emphasizes the fact that *The Glass Menagerie* is a play designed for the stage and for live actors carrying out conventional stage roles.

Tom's part in shaping and unifying the play is most apparent in his nonrealistic function as narrator. In this role, he stands aside from the action occurring in the Wingfield apartment, and he also speaks directly to us. He introduces the characters, provides background, and supplies an ongoing commentary. In addition, he presents his own subjective views and also personifies the play's theme of escape. As the past character, the one actually [4] involved in the play's action, he represents a yearning for freedom and adventure. As the present narrator, he speaks truths that his character in its past role has not yet learned, and he thus recognizes that escape from the past is impossible. When the play closes, he tells us that he remains trapped (scene 7, speech 323), and thus he provides a final perspective on the central theme of escape.

The second striking aspect of Tom's function as narrator concerns his [5] complete control of the play. Because he is the narrator, the action in *The Glass Menagerie* represents Tom's memories of events, rather than the events

---

† Thesis sentence.

themselves. In the first speech of scene 1, he tells us, "The play is memory. Being a memory play, it is dimly lighted, it is sentimental, it is not realistic." Since the events from the past that occur onstage emerge from Tom's memory, it is he who provides an overriding unity and perspective. We see everything through his mind and from his point of view. As a nonrealistic narrator, he holds the stage action together and totally controls our responses.

[6]   Williams thus uses Tom in three distinct ways to create unity and perspective. As a realistic character aching to leave the confines of home, Tom embodies the theme of escape. As a nonrealistic stage manager, he illustrates the artificiality of the dramatic literary form and stresses the legendary nature of the action. As the play's narrator, he imposes a subjective but coherent control over the action and offers thematic resolution. The nonrealistic aspects of his roles mesh perfectly with other devices that Williams employs nonrealistically, especially the slides, music, and lighting.

[7]   Whether realistic or unrealistic, however, *The Glass Menagerie* is about life--its desires, its dreams, its need for independent action, its disappointments, and its poignancy. If Williams did not dramatize these issues, the technique alone would not make a great play. But he does dramatize them, and as a result the freedom of action and character he achieves through the combination of roles for Tom enables him to achieve a remarkable unity of topic, merging past with present and reality with unreality. Williams's use of Tom, then, is a major reason *The Glass Menagerie* is a great modern drama.

Commentary on the Essay

This essay shows how Williams's manipulation of Tom creates artistic and thematic unity in *The Glass Menagerie*. The primary focus is on character, but a number of distinct topics are taken up in connection with this element because the essay concerns Tom as a character, stage director, and narrator.

The body of the essay (paragraphs 2–5) takes up these three roles in the order listed in the introduction. Notice that this order does not reflect the sequence in which these roles occur in the play. Rather, they are organized to reflect a progression from the most realistic to the most nonrealistic aspects of Tom's three different functions. Thus, paragraph 2 discusses Tom as a realistic character and connects him to one of the play's central themes—entrapment and the desire to escape. Paragraphs 3, 4, and 5 shift to a consideration of Tom first as stage manager and second as narrator. These paragraphs explain the nonrealistic nature of these roles and explore the effects of Tom as the nonrealistic figure.

The concluding two paragraphs (6 and 7) provide a review and summary of the three roles Tom plays and the effects each produces in connection with theme and unity. In addition, they suggest a connection between the nonrealistic aspects of Tom's roles and the play's great power.

Throughout the body, direct quotation of dialogue or action as indicated in the stage directions is employed as supporting evidence. Quotations are used to validate specific points and are documented either within parentheses or in the body of discourse itself.

SPECIAL TOPICS FOR WRITING AND ARGUMENT ABOUT DRAMATIC REALITY AND NONREALITY

1. Compare the families of the Wingfields in *The Glass Menagerie,* the Kirbys in *The Happy Journey to Trenton and Camden,* and Colonel Norwood in *Mulatto* (to which you might wish to add the Helmers in *A Dollhouse* and the Wrights in *Trifles*). What concept of family do these plays present? What good and bad effects do the families create? Which type of effect predominates? How realistic is the internal family dissension? How serious? How essential to the various plots? What is unusual or illogical about the dissentions? How? Why?

2. Compare the sets of *The Happy Journey to Trenton and Camden* and *The Glass Menagerie.* What elements of realism or nonrealism are common to both? How? Why? What effects would the sets have on the audience? Why?

3. The screen device described in Williams's Production Notes (see p. 1705) is omitted from most productions of *The Glass Menagerie.* Why? Consider the advantages or disadvantages of referring to this device in the printed text. How do the screen images affect your reading?

4. Describe Hughes's symbolism in *Mulatto.* How does the symbolism bring out the black-white differences in the play? Which locations, objects, and actions are symbolic, and what do they symbolize? In what ways are the symbols realistic? If they were not realistic, would they be successful as symbols?

5. Consider any of the plays in this chapter, using a feminist approach (see Chapter 33 for a discussion of this approach). What elements of realism or nonrealism are relevant to such a discussion? To aid your discussion, you might use a study by Patricia R. Schroeder, *The Feminist Possibilities of Dramatic Realism* (Madison: Fairleigh Dickinson UP, 1996).

6. Write a research essay on the concept and practice of literary realism. To begin your research, you might wish to use books like Hugh S. Davies, *Realism in the Drama* (Cambridge, Cambridge UP, 1934); John B. Moore, *The Comic and the Realistic in English Drama* (New York: Russell & Russell, 1965); Harold H. Kolb, *The Illusion of Life: American Realism as a Literary Form* (Charlottesville: U of Virginia P, 1969); and Joseph P. Stern, *On Realism* (Boston: Routledge, 1973).

7. Write two separate versions of a scene of your own. (Some possible topics: a woman confronts her boyfriend upon learning that he has been seeing

someone else; a man has an interview with his boss and learns that he is being fired; an army lieutenant tells his platoon that they are about to be attacked; a woman realizes that she is the best salesperson in the firm.) In the first, aim for total reality; in the second, for total unreality. What differences do you think your intentions in each case require of you as a practicing dramatist? What different requirements are made on your dialogue, on your action, on your setting, and on your costuming and suggested makeup for your actors? What elements do you think are the most unrealistic in your unrealistic version, and why do you believe you make them so unrealistic? Does the lack of realism, in your judgment, make your scene either more or less dramatic? Write an introductory essay to your two versions explaining these and other principles of your dramatic composition.

Dramatic Vision and the Motion Picture Camera: Drama on the Silver (and Television) Screen

Film is the word most often used for motion pictures, although other common words are *picture, cinema,* and *movie.* It is a specialized type of drama, utilizing, like drama, the techniques of dialogue, monologue, and action. Also like drama, it employs movement and spectacle. For these reasons, film can be studied for aspects such as character, structure, tone, theme, and symbolism. Unlike drama, however, film embodies techniques from photography, film chemistry, sound, and editing. These techniques are so unique that they require special consideration.

A THUMBNAIL HISTORY OF FILM

Film arose out of technologies developed in the late nineteenth century. The first of these was the creation of a flexible substance—celluloid—that could accept the chemical emulsions that in the early years of photography could be applied only to glass. Other significant inventions were the motion picture camera and projector, together with screens coated with reflective silver iodide and on which the pictures were projected. Once these were in place, and once producers and directors decided to use the medium for full-length dramas, movies as we know them came into existence.

    Although the earliest filmmakers thought of motion pictures as private entertainment, it soon became apparent that the development of large film-making studios, national distribution, and a system of local movie theaters could become extremely lucrative. The history of film is hence just as much a history of the film business as of the art and development of film dramas and film acting. The enormous potential of the movie business was first realized with the production in 1915 of D. W. Griffith's landmark film *Birth of a Nation,* which realized an enormous profit on a small investment.

The first motion pictures were black and white and were silent. Producers realized that large profits required easily recognized actors with "big names," and so the "star system" made national figures out of actors such as Mary Pickford, Charlie Chaplin, and Rudolph Valentino. In 1928 the first talking picture, *Lights of New York,* was made. Film as we know it today was substantially established in 1932 with the first technicolor film, *La Cucaracha,* even though the use of color has undergone great refinement since then.

For a time after the end of World War II, the growth of television inhibited the power of the large studios. Soon, however, many films were developed specifically for television viewing, and popular pictures were released for television use. In the last decade, with the advent of videotape and laser technology, home viewing of films has become a normal feature of American life. Today, film rental outlets can be found in shopping districts everywhere, with the result that most of the movies ever made are within the reach of anyone with a television set and the proper playing equipment. Early dramatists dreamed of filling their theaters for a number of consecutive performances, thus reaching perhaps several thousand persons. Film writers today, however, reach millions in first-run movie houses and many millions more on television reruns, videocassettes, and DVD.

DVD TECHNOLOGY AND FILM STUDY

DVD technology (*digital video disk* or *digital versatile disk*), now becoming widely available, promises a flourishing future for students of film. The video resolution of DVD is greatly superior to that of tape and laser disk technology. DVD is also being used for many extra features that provide interesting background and sidelights. The DVD for Jonathan Demme's *The Silence of the Lambs* (1990) is exemplary. It includes the entire film itself, together with a wide variety of additional material. The disk contains an index that can be easily set up on a TV screen, and the various parts (chapters) of the film can be selected, played, stopped (the still pictures are of remarkably high quality), slowed, reversed, and enlarged as a viewer might wish. There are "voice-overs" by the principal actors, who comment on various scenes in which they figure prominently. There is also frequent voice-over commentary by the director, the screenwriter, and an FBI consultant. Additional features for study are selected scenes that were reduced or omitted in the final editing, together with reports of research into abnormal psychology that were made for the character development of the film's diabolical villain. In addition, many DVDs offer materials unobtainable elsewhere. The 1964 Richard Burton production of *Hamlet,* for example, is available only on DVD (in black and white). The DVD of Terry Gilliam's *Brazil* (1985) includes instructive interviews about the problems and controversies that preceded and followed the film's release.*

* Videocassettes still offer the most readily available means of seeing a film because the rental outlets for videocassettes are plentiful. The future of DVD technology may be inferred from the fact that in December 1999, in excess of 5,000 DVDs were available, with this number growing constantly. Many computer manufacturers have added DVD drives to their new models, so students may soon write their essays on the same machines they use to view the films.

STAGE PLAYS AND FILM

Although film is a form of drama, there are a number of important differences between film and stage productions. Plays can be produced many times, in many different places, with many different people. In bringing a play to life, the producer and director use not only actors but also artists, scene designers, carpenters, painters, lighting technicians, costume makers, choreographers, music directors, and musicians. For the actual performance of a play, however, the stage itself limits what can be done. In each theater production, the actors, setting, and effects are all physically confined to the stage.

The stage for makers of film, however, is virtually infinite, and the absence of restrictions permits the inclusion of any details whatever—car chases, underwater adventures, flying geese, wartime combat, legislative debates, executive discussions; scenes in living rooms, courtrooms, boxing rings, hotel rooms, football stadiums, kitchens; and locations in cities and countrysides anywhere—domestic or foreign, modern or ancient. If the setting is a desert island, the filmmaker can travel to such an island and film it in all its reality, complete with beach, palm trees, huts, and authentic natives-turned-actors. If the scene is a distant planet, the filmmaker can create an exotic planet location in the studio, with appropriate scenery, props, effects, lighting, and costumes for the space travelers. An additional freedom, sometimes too freely indulged, is offered by modern computerized special effects, which permit film scenes that were unimaginable for the greatest part of theater history. The freedom enjoyed by the filmmaker, in short, almost limitlessly exceeds the freedom of the play producer. Nothing is left to the audience's imagination.

The two types of dramatic productions—drama and film—are therefore greatly different. Each new production of a play is different from every other production, because not only the actors but also the appurtenances of the staging are unique. Shakespeare's play *Hamlet,* for example, has been produced innumerable times since Shakespeare's actors at the Globe Theatre first performed it at the beginning of the seventeenth century, and each subsequent production, including the various filmed versions, has been different from all the rest.

Paradoxically, this same variety cannot occur with films. Although the filmmaker has great freedom in producing each individual movie, this freedom also imposes its own limitations. Because of high production costs and also because films reach a mass audience through wide distribution, films are generally released in only one version, perhaps with "remakes" and dubbed versions for foreign audiences. Thus Orson Welles's *Citizen Kane* (1941) is in only one form, and although it was restored and reedited in 1991, it remains in this form even though it is frequently shown and seen. Interestingly, no person can ever claim to have seen all the productions of plays like *Hamlet,* but everyone who sees a film like *Citizen Kane* can claim to have seen it in its entirety.

THE AESTHETICS OF FILM

To the degree that film is confined to a screen, it can be compared visually with the art of the painter and the still photographer. It uses the language of visual art. One object in a painting can take on special relationships to others as the artist directs the eyes of the observer. A color used in one part can be balanced with the same color, or its complement, in another part. Painters and photographers can introduce certain colors and details as symbols and can suggest allegorical interpretations through the inclusion of mythical figures or universally recognized objects. Particular effects can be achieved with the use of the textures of paint or with control over shutter speed, focus, and various techniques of development. The techniques and effects are extensive.

The filmmaker is able to utilize most of the resources of the still photographer and many of those of the painter and can augment these with special effects. Artistically, the most confining aspect of film is the rectangular screen, but aside from that, film is unrestricted. Based in a dramatic text called a film script or shooting script, the film uses words and their effects, but it also employs the language of visual art and especially the particular vividness and power of moving pictures. When considering film, then, you should realize that film communicates not only with words but also with various visual techniques. The visual presentation is inseparable from the medium of film itself.

THE TECHNIQUES OF FILM

There are many techniques of film, and a full description and documentation of them can be—and has become—extensive.[1] In evaluating film, however, you need to familiarize yourself only with those aspects of technique that have an immediate bearing on your responses and interpretations.

Editing or Montage Is the Assembling of a Film out of Separate Parts

A finished film is a composite, not a continuous work filmed from start to end. The putting together of the film is the process of editing, or **montage** (assemblage, mounting, construction), which is, technically, a cutting and gluing. Depending on the flexibility of the film script, the various scenes of the film are planned before shooting begins, but the major task of montage is accomplished in a studio by editing specialists.

[1] See, for example, Louis D. Giannetti, *Understanding Movies,* 8th ed. (1999); Ephraim Katz, *The Film Encyclopedia,* 3rd ed., revised by Fred Klein and Ronald Dean Nolan (1998); *Halliwell's Film and Video Guide 1998,* John Walker ed. (1997); David Bleiler, *The Film and Video Guide: The Discerning Movie Lover's Guide 1998–1999* (1997); James Monaco et al., *The Encyclopedia of Film* (1991); James Monaco, *How to Read a Film,* rev. ed. (1998); James Monaco, *The Movie Guide* (1995); Roger Ebert, *Roger Ebert's Video Companion, 1998* (1997); Roger Ebert, *Roger Ebert's Movie Yearbook 2000* (1999); Daniel Talbot, ed., *Film: An Anthology* (Berkeley: U of California P, 1969); and John Wyver, *The Moving Image* (Oxford: Basil Blackwell, 1989).

If we again compare film with a stage play, we note that a theatrical production moves continuously, with pauses only for intermissions and scene changes. Your perception of the action is caused by your distance from the stage (perhaps aided by opera glasses or binoculars). Also, even as you move your eyes from one character to another, you still perceive the entire stage. In a film, however, the directors and editors *create* these continuous perceptions for you by piecing together different parts. The editors begin with many "takes" (separately filmed scenes, including many versions of the same scenes). What they select, or "mount," will be the film, and we never see the discarded scenes. Thus, it is editing that puts everything together.

MONTAGE CREATES NARRATIVE CONTINUITY.   The first use of montage, already suggested, is narrative continuity. For example, a climb up a steep cliff can be shown at the bottom, middle, and top (with backward slips and falls to show the danger of the climb and to make viewers catch their breath). All such narrative sequences result from the assembling of individual pieces, each one representing phases of the activity. A classic example of a large number of separate parts forming a narrative unit is the well-known shower murder in Alfred Hitchcock's *Psycho* (1959), where a forty-five-second sequence is made up of seventy-eight different shots (the woman in the shower, the murderer behind the curtain, the attack, the slumping figure, the running water, the dead woman's eye, the bathtub drain, etc.).

MONTAGE PROVIDES EXPLANATION OF CHARACTER AND MOTIVATION.   Montage is used in flashbacks to explain present, ongoing actions or characteristics; or in illustration of a character's thoughts and memories; or in brief examples from the unremembered past of a character suffering from amnesia. It also supplies direct visual explanation of character. A famous example occurs in Welles's *Citizen Kane* (the subject of the demonstrative student essay on p. 1782). The concluding scene shows overhead views of Kane's vast collection of statuary and mementos. At the very end, the camera focuses on a raging furnace, into which workmen have thrown his boyhood sled, which bears the brand name "Rosebud" (we have fleetingly seen Kane playing with the sled as a boy). Because "Rosebud" is Kane's last word, and everyone in the film is trying to decipher its meaning, this final scene reveals that Kane's dying thoughts were of his lost boyhood, before he was taken away from his parents, and that his unhappy life has resulted from his early rejection and personal pain.

MONTAGE FACILITATES DIRECTORIAL COMMENTARY.   Montage is also used symbolically as commentary, as in an early sequence in Charlie Chaplin's *Modern Times* (1936) that shows a large group of workers rushing to their factory jobs. Immediately following this scene is a view of a large, milling herd of sheep. By this symbolic montage, Chaplin suggests that the men are being herded and dehumanized by modern industry. Thus, montage and editorial statement go hand in hand.

Montage Is Used in Many Other Ways.   Montage can also produce other characteristics through camera work, development, and special effects. For example, filmmakers can reverse an action to emphasize its illogicality or ridiculousness. Editing can also speed up action (which makes even the most serious things funny) or slow things down. It can also blend one scene with another or juxtapose two or more actions in quick succession to show what people are doing while they are separated. The possibilities for creativity and innovation are extensive.

Film Utilizes Unique Visual Techniques

The Camera Is the Basic Tool of Film.   Whereas editing or montage is a finishing technique, the work of film begins with the camera, which permits great freedom in the presentation of characters and actions. In a film, the visual viewpoint can shift. Thus, a film can begin with a distant shot of the actors—a "long shot"—much like the view of actors onstage. Then the camera can zoom in to show a close-up or zoom out to present a wide and complete panorama. Usually a speaking actor will be the subject of a close-up, but the camera can also capture other actors' reactions in close-up. You must interpret the effects of close-ups and long shots yourself, but it should be plain that the frequent use of either—or of middle-distance views—is a means by which film directors control the perceptions of their characters and situations.

The camera can also move from character to character or from character to object. In this way, film can mark a series of reactions, concentrate your attention on a character's attitude, or comment visually on a character's actions. If a man and woman are in love, for example, the camera can shift, either directly or through montage, from the couple to flowers and trees, thus associating their love visually with objects of beauty and growth. Should the flowers be wilted and the trees leafless, however, the visual commentary might be that their love is doomed and hopeless.

The camera can also create unique effects. Slow motion, for example, can focus on a certain aspect of a person's character. The concentrated focus on a child running happily in a meadow (as in *The Color Purple* [1985] by Steven Spielberg) suggests the joy inherent in such movement. Surprisingly, speed is sometimes indicated by slow motion, which emphasizes strong muscular effort (as in the running scenes in Hugh Hudson's *Chariots of Fire* [1981]).

Many other camera techniques bear on action and character. The focus can be sharp at one point, indistinct at another. Moving a speaking character out of focus can suggest that listeners are bored. Sharp or blurred focus can also show that a character has seen things exactly or inexactly. In action sequences, the camera can be mounted in a moving vehicle to "track" or follow running human beings or horses, speeding bicycles and cars (as in Woody Allen's *Annie Hall*), or moving sailboats, canoes, speedboats, or rowboats. A camera operator on foot can also be the tracker, or the camera may track ground movement from an aircraft. Movement can also be captured by a rotating camera that follows a moving object or character. Alternatively, the camera can be fixed while a character or object moves from one side to the other.

THE PICTURES IN FILM INVOLVE LIGHT, SHADOW, AND COLOR.   As in the theater, the filmmaker uses light, shadow, and color to reinforce ideas and to create realistic and symbolic effects. A scene in sunshine, which brings out colors, and the same scene in rain and clouds or in twilight, all of which mute colors, create different moods. Characters in bright light are presumably open and frank, whereas characters in shadow may be hiding something, particularly in black-and-white films. Flashing or strobe lights might indicate a changeable or sinister character or situation.

Colors, of course, have much the same meaning that they have in any other artistic medium. Blue sky and clear light suggest happiness, while greenish light can indicate something ghoulish. A memorable control of color occurs midway through David O. Selznick's *Gone with the Wind* (1939) when Scarlett O'Hara reflects upon the devastation of her plantation home, Tara. She resolves never to be hungry again, and as she speaks she is silhouetted against a darkened orange sky—a background that suggests how totally the way of life she knew as a young woman has been burned away. As in this example, you may expect colors to complement the story of the film. Thus, lovers may wear clothing with the same or complementary colors, whereas people who are not "right" for each other may wear clashing colors.

Action Is the Essence of Film

The strength of film is direct action. Actions of all sorts—running, swimming, driving a car, fighting, embracing and kissing, or even just sitting; chases, trick effects, ambushes—all these and more create a sense of immediate reality, and all are tied (or should be) to narrative development. Scenes of action can run on for several minutes, with little or no accompanying dialogue, to carry on the story or to convey ideas about the interests and abilities of the characters.

Film Views of the Heads, Bodies, and Movements of Actors Are Related to a Film's Content

Closely related to the portrayal of action is the way in which film shows the human body (and animal bodies) together with bodily motion and gesture (or body language). The view or perspective that the filmmaker presents is particularly important. A torso shot of a character may stress no more than the content of that character's speech. A close-up shot, however, with the character's head filling the screen, may emphasize motives as well as content. The camera can also distort ordinary expectations of reality. Using wide-angle lenses and close-ups, for example, human subjects can be made to seem bizarre or grotesque, as are the faces in the crowd in Woody Allen's *Stardust Memories* (1980). Sometimes the camera creates other bodily distortions—for example, enlarging the limbs of the forest dweller in Ingmar Bergman's *Virgin Spring* (1959) or throwing into unnatural prominence a scolding mouth or a suspicious eye. Distortion invites interpretation: The filmmaker may be asserting that certain human beings, even supposedly normal ones, are odd, sinister, intimidating, or psychotic.

Sound Is Integral to the Presentation and Content of a Film

DIALOGUE AND MUSIC COMPLEMENT FILM DRAMATIZATIONS.   The first business of the sound track is the spoken dialogue, which is "mixed" in editing to be synchronized with the action. There are also many other elements in the sound track. Music, the most important, creates and augments moods. A melody in a major or minor key, or in a slow or fast tempo, can affect our perception of actions. If a character is thinking deeply, a complementary sound may be muted strings. But if the character is going insane, the music may become discordant and percussive.

Sometimes, music gives a film a special identity. Hudson's *Chariots of Fire,* for example, includes music by Vangelis Papathanassiou. Although this music is independently popular, it is always associated with the film. In addition, musical accompaniments can directly render dramatic statement, without dialogue. An example occurs in Welles's *Citizen Kane.* Beginning that portion of the narrative derived from the autobiography of a character who is now dead (the scene first focuses on his statue), the musical sound track by Bernard Herrmann quotes the *Dies Irae* theme from the Catholic mass for the dead. The instrumentation, however, makes the music funny, and we smile rather than grieve. Herrmann, incidentally, varies this theme elsewhere in the film, usually for comic effect.

FILM USES SPECIAL AND OFTEN INGENIOUS SOUND EFFECTS.   Special sound effects can also augment a film's action. The sound of a blow, for example, can be enhanced electronically to cause an impact similar to the force of the blow itself (as in the boxing scenes from the many *Rocky* films). At times some sounds, such as the noises of wailing people, squeaking or slamming doors, marching feet, or moving vehicles, are filtered electronically to create weird or ghostly effects. Often a character's words echo rapidly and sickeningly to show dismay or anguish. In a word, sound is a vital part of film.

FILM SCENES FOR STUDY

ORSON WELLES AND HERMAN J. MANKIEWICZ, SHOT 71 FROM THE SHOOTING SCRIPT OF *CITIZEN KANE*

Orson Welles (1915–1985) developed an early interest in the theater. As a youth he traveled extensively, even spending some time in Spain as a bullfighter. In 1937 he co-founded the Mercury Theater, specializing in hour-long Sunday

Still from *Citizen Kane*.

evening radio dramatizations. In October 1938 he achieved early immortality by acting in and directing a version of H. G. Wells's *The War of the Worlds*. This production created a near panic in the nation among listeners who did not understand they were hearing a dramatic production, not a real news broadcast about invaders from the planet Mars.

Within a few years Welles, along with Herman J. Mankiewicz, planned a film on a larger-than-life American figure. Their model was the newspaper magnate William Randolph Hearst. Mankiewicz produced a lengthy draft of the script, which was titled first *American* and then, a little later, *John Citizen, USA*. Welles changed the plot, rewrote many sections, and edited and shortened much of the original material. It was during this process of rewriting and editing that the title *Citizen Kane* was proposed and accepted. Soon, Welles began production with many of the actors of the Mercury Theater. Hearst, who quickly learned about the forthcoming film, sought a legal restraint on it, but *Citizen Kane* was successfully completed despite his efforts. The film reached the movie theaters with massive critical acclaim.

In 1958 a poll of international critics listed *Citizen Kane* as one of the twelve best films ever made. Its use of a format similar to *The March of Time* (a popular news feature series that ran regularly as a "selected short subject" in movie theaters), deep-focus camera work, unusual camera angles, contrasts of light and shadow, and its employment of four distinct points of view, together with its relentless insights into the major figure, all combined to make it a pioneering work in the history of film. Today, it is one of the touchstones in any discussion of movies, and its continued recognition justifies the claim that Welles was one of the great directors. After *Citizen Kane*, however, Welles struggled with personal and financial difficulties on each of his films, and he never again reached the heights of his first attempt.

The scene included here occurs about two-thirds of the way through the film. It is vital because it is a major indicator of Kane's personal decline. At first imbued with ideals for informing and reforming society, Kane (played by Welles) becomes publisher of a newspaper he has inherited, and he advances public-minded editorial policies. A high point in his career is his running for governor of the state, but he loses the election after his secret love affair is made public. The scene occurs right after the election loss. His most loyal supporter and co-worker, Jedediah "Jed" Leland (Joseph Cotten), confronts him and asks for a transfer to Chicago. The unspoken issue in the scene is that both men know that their friendship has been lost not because of the election but because of Kane's misperceptions of people and his desertion of his earlier ideals.

The scene is taken from the so-called shooting script, which in film most closely corresponds to a dramatic text; it is the full version, with copious directions for the actors. A comparison of this "shot," or scene, with the filmed version will show that some of the dialogue was trimmed for purposes of pacing and speed. The shortening indicates a major characteristic of film (and the production of plays), namely, to reduce speeches to no more than the essentials in order to keep the action moving and hold the audience's attention.

ORSON WELLES   (1915–1985)
AND HERMAN J. MANKIEWICZ   (1897–1953)

Shot 71 from the Shooting Script of Citizen Kane* _____ (1941)

RKO Radio Pictures. A Mercury Production. Producer and Director, Orson Welles. Photographer, Gregg Toland, Editor, Robert Wise. Art Director, Van Nest Polglase. Music, Bernard Herrmann. Special Effects, Vernon L. Walker.

Dissolve in.

71 Int. Kane's Office—"Inquirer"—Night—1916

[*KANE looks up from his desk as there is a knock on the door.*]

    KANE.   Come in.

[*LELAND enters.*]

    KANE.   [*Surprised*] I thought I heard somebody knock.
    LELAND.   [*A bit drunk*] I knocked. [*He looks at him defiantly*]
    KANE.   [*Trying to laugh it off*] Oh! An official visit of state, eh? [*Waves his hand*] Sit down, Jedediah.
    LELAND.   [*Sitting down angrily*] I'm drunk.

---

* The scene is gratefully reprinted from *The Citizen Kane Book* (Boston: Little, Brown & Co., 1971), pp. 228–231.

KANE. Good! It's high time—

LELAND. You don't have to be amusing.

KANE. All right. Tell you what I'll do. I'll get drunk, too.

LELAND. [*Thinks this over*] No. That wouldn't help. Besides, you never get drunk. [*Pauses*] I want to talk to you—about—about—[*He can't get it out*] 10

KANE. [*Looks at him sharply a moment*] If you've got yourself drunk to talk to me about Susan Alexander—I'm not interested.

LELAND. She's not important. What's much more important—[*He keeps glaring at Kane*]

KANE. [*As if genuinely surprised*] Oh! [*He gets up*] I frankly didn't think I'd have to listen to that lecture from you. [*Pauses*] I've betrayed the sacred cause of reform, is that it? I've set back the sacred cause of reform in this state twenty years. Don't tell me, Jed, *you—*

[*Despite his load,*° LELAND *manages to achieve a dignity about the silent contempt with which he looks at* KANE.]

KANE. [*An outburst*] What makes the sacred cause of reform so sacred? Why does the sacred cause of reform have to be exempt from all the other facts of life? Why do the laws of this state have to be executed by a man on a white charger?

[LELAND *lets the storm ride over his head.*]

KANE. [*Cont'd*] [*Calming down*] But, if that's the way they want it—they've made their choice. The people of this state obviously prefer Mr. Rogers to me. [*His lips tighten*] So be it. 15

LELAND. You talk about the people as though they belong to you. As long as I can remember you've talked about giving the people their rights as though you could make them a present of liberty—in reward for services rendered. You remember the working-man? You used to write an awful lot about the workingman. Well, he's turning into something called organized labor, and you're not going to like that a bit when you find out it means that he thinks he's entitled to something as his right and not your gift. [*He pauses*] And listen, Charles. When your precious underprivileged really do get together—that's going to add up to something bigger—than your privilege—and then I don't know what you'll do. Sail away to a desert island, probably, and lord it over the monkeys.

KANE. Don't worry about it too much, Jed. There's sure to be a few of them there to tell me where I'm wrong.

LELAND. You may not always be that lucky. [*Pauses*] Charlie, why can't you get to look at things less personally? Everything doesn't have to be between you and—the personal note doesn't always—

KANE. [*Violently*] The personal note is all there is to it. It's all there ever is to it. It's all there ever is to anything! Stupidity in our government—crookedness—even just complacency and self-satisfaction and an unwillingness to believe that anything done by a certain class of people can be wrong—you can't fight those things impersonally. They're not impersonal crimes against the people. They're being done by actual persons—with actual names and positions and—the right of the American people to their own country is not an academic issue, Jed, that you debate—and then the judges retire to return a verdict—and the winners give a dinner for the losers.

LELAND. You almost convince me, almost. The truth is, Charlie, you just don't care about anything except you. You just want to convince people that you love them so much that they should love you back. Only you want love on your own terms. It's

Load: i.e., a heavy amount of liquor.

something to be played your way—according to your rules. And if anything goes wrong and you're hurt—then the game stops, and you've got to be soothed and nursed, no matter what else is happening—and no matter who else is hurt!

[*They look at each other.*]

KANE.   [*Trying to kid him into a better humor*] Hey, Jedediah!

[*LELAND is not to be seduced.*]

LELAND.   Charlie, I wish you'd let me work on the Chicago paper—you said yourself you were looking for someone to do dramatic criticism there—
KANE.   You're more valuable here.

[*There is silence.*]

LELAND.   Well, Charlie, then I'm afraid there's nothing I can do but to ask you to accept—
KANE.   [*Harshly*] All right. You can go to Chicago.
LELAND.   Thank you.

[*There is an awkward pause.* KANE *opens a drawer of his desk and takes out a bottle and two glasses.*]

KANE.   I guess I'd better *try* to get drunk, anyway.

[*KANE hands JED a glass, which he makes no move to take.*]

KANE.   [*Cont'd*] But I warn you, Jedediah, you're not going to like it in Chicago. The wind comes howling in off the lake, and the Lord only knows if they've ever heard of lobster Newburg.
LELAND.   Will a week from Saturday be all right?
KANE.   [*Wearily*] Anytime you say.
LELAND.   Thank you.

[*KANE looks at him intently and lifts the glass.*]

KANE.   A toast, Jedediah—to love on *my* terms. Those are the only terms anybody knows—his own.

Dissolve

QUESTIONS

1.   What do you learn about the past and present relationship of Kane and Leland in this scene? What do Leland's speeches indicate about Kane's attitudes toward people? About Kane's shortcomings?

2.   Basing your conclusions on this scene, why do you think the film is named *Citizen Kane*, and not something like *The Life of an American Tycoon* or *The Perils of Wealth*?

3.   This scene is one of the revolutionary ones in the film because Welles and Toland (the principal photographer) shot it from floor height, emphasizing the distance from the camera to the heads of the characters. What effect do you think this vantage point has on viewers of the film? If you have seen the film, what do you think the camera angles and the lighting contribute to your perception of the characters?

ARTHUR LAURENTS, A SCENE FROM
THE TURNING POINT

Arthur Laurents is one of the most successful dramatists and screenplay writ-ers of the postwar period. Among his achievements in film are *The Snake Pit* (1948), *Anastasia* (1956), and *The Way We Were* (1973). His plays *West Side Story* (1957) and *Gypsy* (1959) had successful Broadway runs as musicals and also became successful films. His very first play, *Home of the Brave* (1946), was revived in 1999, and his *Time of the Cuckoo* (1952) was revived at Lincoln Center in New York in 2000. A recent work, *The Radical Mystique,* was produced in 1995 at the City Center. *The Turning Point* (1977), which Laurents also published as a novel, received the Golden Globe Award, the National Board of Review Best Picture, and the Writers Guild of America Award as the best film of the year.

   The Turning Point takes place against the background of ballet and the life of professional dancers. Deedee Rodgers (Shirley MacLaine) and Emma Jacklin (Anne Bancroft) had been close friends and rivals as young dancers with the American Ballet Theater. Deedee became pregnant and married before she had a chance to become a star, and after the birth of her daughter, Emilia, she left the stage entirely for family life. With her husband Wayne (Tom Skerrit), who had also earlier been a dancer, she moved to Oklahoma, had two more children, and established a successful ballet school.

   During the following seventeen years, Deedee has believed she could have gained stardom if she had not become a mother. She has also carried a grudge against Emma for having urged her to have the baby. In this way, Deedee believes, Emma pushed her aside when the two women had competed for the once-in-a-lifetime opportunity to dance in a new ballet. Emma, who won the role, went on to become famous as the company's prima ballerina. However, she has lived her life alone, her principal companions being the three dogs she keeps in her elegant apartment.

   As the film opens, the ballet company comes to perform in Oklahoma City. Deedee's first daughter, Emilia (Leslie Browne), is now a promising dancer, and with Emma's help and support she becomes a star with the com-pany during the following summer in New York. The scene included here occurs after a gala performance by the company, in which Emilia has brilliantly performed her first major solo dance, and in which Emma has been featured in a solo from *Anna Karenina,* perhaps for the last time.

   At the reception after the gala, Emma makes a show of acknowledging Emilia, a gesture that angers Deedee and leads her to conclude that for a number of months Emma has been trying to gain undue influence over Emilia. Shortly after this, the company's director, Adelaide (Martha Scott) asks Emma to create a new production of Tchaikowsky's *Sleeping Beauty* ballet, but *not* to dance in it. This request hits Emma with full force, for she now recognizes that she is getting old and is about to be pushed aside by dancers who, like Emilia, are young and strong. She rushes out and stops at the nearby bar, where she encounters Deedee. The scene, which is virtually a short play all by itself, then develops, as the long-pent-up frustration, apprehension, and guilt of both women emerge.

ARTHUR LAURENTS   (b. 1918)

A Scene from The Turning Point ———————————————— *1977*

Twentieth Century Fox. Producers, Herbert Ross and Arthur Laurents. Executive Producer, Nora Kaye. Photography, Robert Surtees. Film editor, William Reynolds. Music adapter, John Lanchbery. Director, Herbert Ross.

[SCENE] Interior Bar—Rainbow Room

[DEEDEE *is alone at the bar, drinking champagne. As* EMMA, *on her way to the Ladies' room, comes toward her,* DEEDEE *smiles and does a half-curtsy.* EMMA *stops and smiles back. Then she tosses her evening bag onto the bar.*]

    EMMA.   [*to the bartender*].   Champagne, please.

[*Declaration of war accepted. During the following, they both get refills, but they do not guzzle; there is no need for them to get drunk. Emotionally, each is ready to burst anyway. They (and we) are unaware of the bartender and he is unaware of them. For despite the lines, despite what each feels underneath, they are totally charming: two smiling, lovely, delightful friends having a chat.*]

    DEEDEE.   Remember the fairy tales we used to take turns reading to Emilia? Like the one about the two princesses? Every time one opened her mouth, out came diamonds and rubies. Every time the other opened her mouth, out came newts and hoptoads. Newts and hoptoads—[*taps her chest*]—coming out.

    EMMA.   One of those little toads has already made an appearance.

    DEEDEE.   Really! When?

    EMMA.   In my dressing room. When you said I shouldn't have bought Emilia that dress. Twice, you said it. Just before a performance. . . . I danced better tonight than I have in years.

    DEEDEE.   So I heard.

    EMMA.   Oh, another little toad! You've kept quite a few bottled up all these years, haven't you?

    DEEDEE.   Ohhh—embalmed, really.

    EMMA.   I think not. Why don't you let them out? I don't have a performance tomorrow.

[DEEDEE *looks at her, then accepts the challenge. She puts her glass down on the bar and holds out her hands with her fists clenched.*]

    DEEDEE.   Okay. Pick.

[EMMA puts her glass down and points to a fist. DEEDEE opens it.]

DEEDEE.   Ah, a tiny one. I'd practically forgotten him. *[Looks up now.]* Why'd you make your best pal doubt herself and her hubby, Emma? Why'd you take the chance of lousing up her marriage? Why'd you say: "You better have that baby. It's the only way you can hold on to Wayne." I'm just curious now.

EMMA.   You have a curious memory. but don't we all? As I remember, I said if you had an abortion, you might lose Wayne.

DEEDEE.   Sweet, but inaccurate. I've remembered your exact words for lo, these too many moons. I eventually figured out why you said 'em. Because you also said: "Forget Michael's ballet, there'll be others." You clever little twinkletoes! You knew a ballet like that comes once in a career. You wanted it real bad, so you lied to make sure you got what you wanted.

EMMA.   I've never had to lie to get what I wanted, Deedee. I'm too good.

DEEDEE.   Really?   15

EMMA.   Oh, yes.

DEEDEE.   Well, I suppose if you said "bullshit," you'd say it in French.

[Close shot.]

EMMA.   If that word came as naturally to me as it does to you, I'd have used it several times by now. In English. I think it's more appropriate that you say it—to yourself. For trying to blame *me* for what you did, for example. The choice was yours. It's much too late to regret it now, Deedee.

DEEDEE.   And the same to you, Emma me darlin'.

EMMA.   I certainly don't regret mine.   20

DEEDEE.   Then why are you trying to become a mother at your age?

EMMA.   Ooh, that's not a little toad. That's a rather large bullfrog. I don't want to be anybody's mother. I think of Emilia as a friend. And one reason I tried to help—stupid me!—I thought it would make you happy if your daughter became what you wanted to be and couldn't be.

DEEDEE.   Meaning you. It's so lovely to be you.

EMMA.   Obviously, you think so.

DEEDEE.   Oh, no no no no no no!   25

EMMA.   No no no no?

DEEDEE.   No; alas. And I doubt if Emilia could become you. Oh, she's as talented. She works as hard. But there's one thing, dearest friend, that you are that she, poor darling, is not.

EMMA.   And what, pray tell, is that?

DEEDEE.   A killer. You'll walk over anybody and still get a good night's sleep. That's what got you where you are, Emma.

[She is smiling adorably. EMMA smiles back, finishes her drink, pushes the glass to the bartender, keeps smiling until it is refilled, then picks it up. They are both smiling, almost laughing as EMMA looks at her drink, looks at DEEDEE, then throws the champagne in DEEDEE's face. A moment. Then DEEDEE sets down her glass.]

DEEDEE.   Good girl.   30

[She picks up her evening bag and starts out of the bar toward the exit and the elevators. The cool reaction infuriates EMMA. She puts down her glass and starts after DEEDEE.]

Interior corridor outside Rainbow Room

[*EMMA comes through the entrance to the Rainbow Room just as DEEDEE steps into an elevator.*]

EMMA.   Deedee!

[*She runs for the elevator and just gets in as the doors are closing.*]

Interior elevator—Rockefeller Center

EMMA.   I'm sick to death of your jealousy and resentment!
DEEDEE.   So am I.
EMMA.   Then stop blaming your goddamn life on me! You picked it!
DEEDEE.   You did. You took away the choice, you didn't give me the chance to   35
find out if I was good enough.
EMMA.   I can tell you now: you weren't.

[*The elevator doors open and DEEDEE strides out, EMMA after her.*]

Exterior Rockefeller Plaza—Night

[*EMMA is fast after DEEDEE, their heels clicking on the stone.*]

EMMA.   You knew it yourself. That's why you married Wayne!
DEEDEE [*whirls around*].   I loved him!
EMMA.   So much that you said to hell with your career!
DEEDEE.   Yes!   40
EMMA.   And got pregnant to prove you meant it!
DEEDEE.   Yes!
EMMA.   Lie to yourself, not to me. You got married because you knew you were
second-rate; you got pregnant because Wayne was a ballet dancer, and that meant queer!
DEEDEE.   *He wasn't!*
EMMA.   Still afraid someone will think he is? You were terrified then! You had to   4
prove he was a man! *That's* why you had a baby!
DEEDEE.   That's a goddamn lie!
EMMA.   It's the goddamn truth! You saddled him with a baby and blew his career!
And now she's grown up and better than you ever were and you're jealous!
DEEDEE.   You're certifiable! You'll use anything for an excuse.
EMMA.   What's that an excuse for?
DEEDEE.   Trying to take away my child!   5
EMMA.   I return the compliment: you're a liar!
DEEDEE.   And you're a user. You have been your whole life! Me, Michael—pre-
tending to love him!—Adelaide and now Emilia!
EMMA.   How Emilia?!
DEEDEE.   "How Emilia." That display five minutes ago: curtsy! Applause!
Embrace! For *you*, not her! You were using her so everyone'd say: "Emma's so gracious,
Emma's so wonderful!"
EMMA.   Untrue!   5
DEEDEE.   You *are* wonderful! You're amazing! It's incredible how you keep
going on. You're over the hill; you know it and *you're* terrified. All you've got are your

scrapbooks and your old toe shoes and those stupid, ridiculous dogs! What are you going to fill in with, Emma? Not my daughter. You keep your goddam hands off!

EMMA. I'm better for her than you are.

DEEDEE. Like hell!

EMMA. She came to me because her mother wasn't there. Her mother was too busy screwing her head off!

DEEDEE. You bitch! 60

[*She whacks EMMA with her evening bag. For a moment, EMMA is too startled to move. But as DEEDEE lifts her bag again, EMMA blocks it with one hand and with the other whacks DEEDEE with her evening bag. They both go at it: rarely hitting, ducking blows, slamming out blindly with their evening bags.*]

Exterior Rockefeller Center—Night

[*There they are, these two ladies in their evening gowns, each making a last pass, a last weak attempt to hit the other, and missing. They are panting, exhausted, and at last, they stop and just stand there, breathing hard.*]

[*Close shot—Their breath is coming back. DEEDEE smiles.*]

DEEDEE. If there'd been a photographer handy, you'd have a whole new career.

EMMA. I must look awful.

DEEDEE. No: beautiful. I don't know how you do it.

[*EMMA has taken out a mirror and is looking in it.*]

EMMA. If I can borrow your comb, I'll show you. Oh, I lost an earring.

DEEDEE [*handing her a comb*]. I'm sorry. 65

EMMA. I'm not.

DEEDEE. Really?

EMMA. Yes.

[*She returns the comb, and they start walking, looking for the lost earring. The following is very quiet:*]

DEEDEE. Jealousy is poison. Makes you a monster.

EMMA. Well, it does make one unfair. [*Smiles.*] Two. 70

DEEDEE. Two?

EMMA. Me, too.

DEEDEE [*a second, then laughs*]. Emma, you made a good joke!

EMMA. Yes, I did. . . . I'm really not so humorless.

DEEDEE. Listen, you got off some really good ones before. Oh, look! 75

[*She picks up the earring and gives it to EMMA.*]

EMMA. How did it get over here? Thank you.

DEEDEE. You also hit a couple of bull's-eyes before.

EMMA. So did you.

DEEDEE. Sit?

EMMA. Oh, please. 80

[*They sit on the rim of the fountain.*]

EMMA.   I don't really remember what I said about having the baby. But I do know I would have said anything to make sure I got that ballet. . . . I had to have it, Deedee. I just had to.

DEEDEE.   My God. Oh Emma. Emma, I didn't know how much all I wanted was for you to say just that. . . . Let's have a drink!

EMMA.   Absolutely!

[*They get up. EMMA links her arm through DEEDEE's as they start walking.*]

EMMA.   It's good.
DEEDEE.   You bet.
EMMA.   I'm glad Wayne's coming.
DEEDEE.   Me, too. . . . How's with Carter?
EMMA.   Ça va. . . . *That's* bullshit in French.

[*DEEDEE laughs and walks toward the street, to a taxi. But EMMA has stopped, turned toward the entrance to the party.*]

DEEDEE.   Not back to the party?
EMMA.   I have to.
DEEDEE [*nods, understands*].   Call me when you wake up.
EMMA.   If not before.

[*They smile—and walk in opposite directions.*]

QUESTIONS

1.   Despite the fact that the two women carry their anger so far as to strike each other, what does the scene show about the nature of friendship? What key admissions do the women make to effect their reconciliation?

2.   The film omits the last ten speeches of the script (concluding with "to say just that" in speech 82). Justify eliminating these last speeches.

3.   What is the effect of the fact that the locations of this scene move from the interior bar to the exterior plaza? Granted the actions of the two women, why can the scene not be in a single location (as it would necessarily be if written for the theater)? On the basis of your answers, what conclusions can you draw about the comparative freedoms and limitations of film and theater?

4.   View the film *The Turning Point,* and compare the details of the script with the final filmed version of the scene. Explain the purpose and nature of the changes in the film. If you had the freedom of a film director, what other liberties might you take in the performance? Why?

WRITING ABOUT FILM

Obviously the first requirement is to see the film, either in a theater, on video-cassette, or on DVD. No matter how you see it, you should go through it at least twice, making notes, because your discussion takes on value the more thoroughly you know the material. Include the names of the scriptwriter, director, composer, special effects editor, chief photographer, and major actresses and actors. If particular speeches are worth quoting, remember the general circumstances of the quotation and also, if possible, key words. Take notes on costume and color or (if the film is in black and white) on light and shade. You will need to rely on memory, but if you have videotape or DVD, you can easily check important details.

Questions for Discovering Ideas

ACTION

- How important is action? Is there much repetition of action, say, in slow motion or from different angles? Are actors (and animals) viewed closely or distantly? Why?
- What actions are stressed (chases, concealment, gun battles, lovemaking, etc.)? What does the type of action contribute to the film?
- What do close-ups (smiles and laughter, frowns, leers, anxious looks, etc.) show about character and motivation?
- What actions indicate seasonal conditions (cold by a character's stamping of feet, warmth by the character's removing a coat or shirt)? What connection do these actions have to the film's general ideas?
- Does the action show any changing of mood, say, from sadness to happiness or from indecision to decision?

CINEMATOGRAPHIC TECHNIQUES

- What notable techniques are used (colors, lighting, etc.)? What is their relationship to the film's characterizations and themes?
- What characterizes the use of the camera (tracking, close-ups, distant shots, camera angles, etc.)? How do the camera perspectives reinforce or detract from the film's theme and plot?
- How does the editing (the sequencing of scenes) reinforce or detract from story and theme?
- What scene or scenes best exemplify how the cinematographic techniques interact with the theme, plot, characters, setting, and so on? Why?

ACTING

- How well do the actors adapt to the medium of film? How convincing are their performances?
- How well do the actors control their facial expressions and body movement? Are they graceful? Awkward?
- What does their appearance lend to your understanding of their characters?
- Does it seem that the actors are genuinely creating their roles, or are they just reading through the parts?

Strategies for Organizing Ideas

Any of the organizing strategies discussed in the drama chapters are equally valid for an essay on a film, except that you will need to consider them in a visual context. For example, if you choose to discuss the effects of a character on the plot, you need to develop your argument using the evidence of camera techniques, montage, sound effects and the like.

When discussing film techniques, be sure to have good notes so that your supporting details are accurate. A good method is to concentrate on technique in only a few scenes. If you analyze the effects of montage, for example, you can use a videocassette recorder or DVD player to go over the scene a number of times.

In the conclusion of your essay, you might evaluate the effectiveness of the cinematic form to story and idea. Are all the devices of film used in the best possible way? Is anything overdone? Is anything underplayed? Is the film good, bad, or indifferent up to a point, and then does it change? How? Why?

DEMONSTRATIVE STUDENT ESSAY

Welles's *Citizen Kane:*° Whittling a Giant Down to Size

[1] *Citizen Kane* (1941) is a superbly crafted film in black and white. The script is by Herman Mankiewicz and Orson Welles, with photography by Gregg Toland, music by Bernard Herrmann, direction and production by Welles, and the leading role by Welles. It is the story of a wealthy and powerful man, Charles Foster Kane, who exemplifies the American Dream of economic self-sufficiency, self-determination, and self, period. The film does not explore the "greatness" of the hero, however, but rather exposes him as a misguided, unhappy person who tries to buy love and remake reality.* All aspects of the picture--characterization, structure, and technique--are focused on this goal.†

[2] At the film's heart is the deterioration of Kane, the newly deceased newspaper magnate and millionaire. He is not all bad, for he begins well before going tragically downward. For example, the view we see of him as a child, being taken away from home, invites sympathy. When we next see him as a young man, he idealistically takes over a daily newspaper, the *Inquirer*. This idealism makes him admirable but also makes his deterioration tragic. As he says to Thatcher in a moment of insight, he could have been a great person if he had not been wealthy. His corruption begins when he tries to alter the world to suit himself, as in his demented attempt to make an opera star out of his second wife, Susan, and his related attempt to shape critical praise for her. Even though he builds an opera house for her and also sponsors many performances, he cannot change reality. This tampering with truth indicates how completely he loses his youthful integrity.

°See pp. 1772–74 for this scene.
* Central idea.
† Thesis sentence.

[3]   The structure is progressively arranged to bring out such weaknesses. The film flows out of the opening obituary newsreel, from which we learn that Kane's dying word was the name "Rosebud" (the brand name of his boyhood sled, which is spoken at the beginning by a person [Kane] whose mouth is shown in close-up). The newsreel director, wanting to get the inside story, assigns a reporter named Thompson to learn about "Rosebud." Thompson's search unifies the rest of the film; he goes from place to place and person to person to collect materials and conduct interviews that disclose Kane's increasing strangeness and alienation. At the end, although the camera leaves Thompson to focus on the burning sled, he has been successful in uncovering the story of Kane's deterioration (even though he himself never learns what "Rosebud" means). Both the sled and the reporter therefore tie together the many aspects of the film.

[4]   It is through Thompson's searches that the film presents the flashback accounts of Kane's deterioration. The separate persons being interviewed (including Thatcher's handwritten account) each contribute something different to the narrative because their experiences with Kane have all been unique. As a result of these individual points of view, the story is quite intricate. For example, we learn in the Bernstein section that Jedediah proudly saves a copy of Kane's declaration about truth in reporting. We do not learn in Jedediah's interview, however, that he, Jedediah (Joseph Cotten), sends the copy back to Kane as an indictment of Kane's betrayal of principle. Rather, it is in *Susan's* account that we learn about the return, even though she herself understands nothing about it. This subtlety, so typical of the film, marks the ways in which the biography of Kane is progressively revealed.

[5]   Thus, the major importance of these narrating characters is to reveal and reflect Kane's disintegration. Jedediah is a man of principle who works closely with Kane, but after the lost election he rebels when he understands the falseness of Kane's personal life. He is totally alienated after Kane completes the unfinished attack on Susan's performance. Jedediah's change, or perhaps his assertion of principle, thus reveals Kane's increasing corruption. Susan, Kane's second wife (Dorothy Comingore), is naive, sincere, and warm, but her drinking, her attempted suicide, and her final separation show the harm of Kane's warped visions. Bernstein (Everett Sloane), the first person Thompson interviews, is a solitary figure who is uncritical of Kane, but it is he who first touches the theme about the mystery of Kane's motivations. Bernstein also takes on life when he speaks poignantly of his forty-five-year memory of the girl in white. Even though this revelation is brief, it suggests layers of feeling and longing.

[6]   In addition to these perceptive structural characterizations, *Citizen Kane* is a masterpiece of film technique. The camera images are sharp, with clear depth of field. In keeping with Kane's disintegration and mysteriousness, the screen is rarely bright. Instead, the film makes strong use of darkness and contrasts, almost to the point at times of blurring distinctions between people. Unique in Gregg Toland's camera work are the many shots taken from waist height or below, distorting the bodies of the characters by distancing their heads--suggesting that the characters are preoccupied with their own concerns and oblivious to normal perspectives. Nowhere is this distortion better exemplified than in the scene between Kane and Jedediah in the empty rooms after the lost election, when Jedediah asks permission to leave for Chicago.

[7]

As might be expected in a film so dominated by its central figure, the many symbols create strong statements about character. The most obvious is the sled, "Rosebud," the dominating symbol of the need for love and acceptance in childhood. Another notable symbol is glass and, in one scene, ice. In the party scene, two ice statues are in the foreground of the employees of the *Inquirer*. In another scene, a bottle looms large in front of Jedediah, who is drunk. In another, a pill bottle and drinking glass are in front of Susan, who has just used them in her suicide attempt. The suggestion of these carefully photographed symbols is that life is brittle and temporary. Particularly symbolic is the bizarre entertainment in the party scene. Because Kane joins the dancing and singing, the action suggests that he is doing no more than taking a role in life, never being himself or knowing himself. Symbols that frame the film are the wire fence and the "No Trespassing" sign at both beginning and end. These symbols suggest that even if we understand a little about Kane, or anyone else, there are boundaries we cannot pass, depths we can never reach.

[8]

There are also amusing symbols that suggest the diminution not only of Kane but also of the other characters. An example is Bernstein's high-backed chair, which makes him look like a small child. Similarly, the gigantic fireplace at Xanadu makes both Kane and Susan seem like pygmies--a symbol that great wealth dwarfs and dehumanizes people. Especially comic is Kane's picnic at Xanadu. In going into the country, Kane and his friends do not walk but ride in a long line of cars--more like a funeral procession than a picnic--and they stay overnight in a massive tent. Quite funny is the increasing distance between Kane and Emily, his first wife, in the rapid-fire shots that portray their developing separation. Even more comic is the vast distance at Xanadu between Kane and Susan when they discuss their life together. They are so far apart that they must shout to be heard. Amusing as these symbols of diminution and alienation are, however, they are also pathetic, because at first Kane finds closeness with both his wives.

[9]

In all respects, *Citizen Kane* is a superb film. This is not to say that the characters are likable or that the amusing parts make it a comedy. Instead, the film pursues truth, suggesting that greatness and wealth cannot give happiness. It is relentless in whittling away at its major figure. Kane is likable at times, and he is enormously generous (as shown when he sends Jedediah $25,000 in severance pay). But these high moments show the contrasting depths to which Kane falls, with the general point being that people who are powerful and great may deteriorate even at their height. The goal of the newsreel director at the beginning is to get at the "real story" behind the public man. There is more to any person than a two-hour film can reveal, but within its limits, *Citizen Kane* gets at the real story, and the real story is both sad and disturbing.

Commentary on the Essay

The major point of this essay is that the film diminishes the major figure, Kane. In this respect the essay illustrates the analysis of *character* (Chapter 4), and it therefore emphasizes how film can be considered as a form of literature.

Also shown in the essay are other methods of literary analysis: *structure* (Chapter 3) and *symbolism* (Chapter 9). Of these topics, only the use of symbols, because they are visually presented in the film, is unique to the medium of film as opposed to the medium of words.

Any one of the topics might be developed as a separate essay. There is more than enough about the character of Susan, for example, to sustain a complete essay, and the film's structure could be extensively explored. *Citizen Kane* itself as a repository of film techniques is rich enough for an exhaustive, book-length account.

Because the essay is about a film, the unique aspect of paragraph 1 is the opening brief description (stressing the medium of black and white) and the credits to the scriptwriters, principal photographer, composer, and director. Unlike works written by a single author, film is a collaborative medium, and therefore it is appropriate to recognize the separate efforts of the principal contributors.

Paragraph 2 begins the body and carries out a brief analysis of the major character. Paragraphs 3 to 5 discuss various aspects of the film's structure (the second topic announced in the thesis sentence) as they bear on Kane. Paragraph 3 explains the unifying importance of the sled and the reporter, Thompson. Paragraph 4 focuses on the film's use of flashback as a structural technique, while paragraph 5 discusses three of the flashback characters as they either intentionally or unintentionally reveal Kane's flaws. In paragraphs 6 to 8, the topic is film technique, the third and last topic of the thesis sentence. Paragraph 6 focuses on light, camera angles, and distortion; paragraph 7 treats visual symbols; paragraph 8 continues the topic of symbols but extends it to amusing ones. The final paragraph restates the central idea and also relates the theme of deterioration to the larger issue of how great wealth and power affect character. Thus, as a conclusion, this paragraph not only presents a summary but also notes the film's general ideas.

SPECIAL TOPICS FOR WRITING AND ARGUMENT ABOUT FILM

1. Select a single film technique, such as the use of color, the control of light, or the photographing of action, and write an essay describing how it is used in a film. For best results, use a DVD or a videocassette for your study. As much as possible, try to explain how the technique is used throughout the film. Determine constant and contrasting features, the relationship of the technique to the development of story and character, and so on.

2. Write an essay explaining how all the film techniques of a particular part or section are employed (i.e., camera angles, close-ups or long shots, tracking, on-camera and off-camera speeches, lighting, depth of field). For your study, you will have to rerun the section a number of times, trying to notice elements for the first time and also reinforcing your first observations. To add a research element to this question, you might consult the works by Giannetti, Halliwell, Katz, Monaco, Ebert, Talbot, and Wyver listed in the footnote on page 1766.

3. Pick out a news story and write a dramatic scene about it. Next, consider how to write the scene for a film, providing directions for actors and camera operators (e.g., "As Character A speaks, his face shows that he is lying; the camera zooms slowly in on his face, with a loss of focus," or "As Character A speaks, the camera focuses on Character B exchanging looks with Character C"). When you are done, write an explanation of how you intend your directions to bring out details about your story and characters.

A Career in Drama: Two Major Plays of Henrik Ibsen

The Norwegian playwright Henrik Johan Ibsen (1828–1906) is the acknowledged originator—the "father"—of modern drama. He deserves this recognition because of his pioneering selections of challenging and sometime shocking private and public issues. Today there are few restrictions on dramatists except success at the box office. Plays may range freely on almost any subject, such as the drug culture, sexual perversity, the right to commit suicide, the problems of real-estate dealers, the life of a go-go dancer, violence, family dissension, homosexuality, and the Vietnam war. If one includes film as drama, there is virtually no limit to the topics that dramatists can explore. It is well to stress that dramatists have not always been this free and that Ibsen was in the forefront of the struggle for free dramatic expression. A brief consideration of some of his major dramatic topics shows his originality and daring: the blinding and crippling effects of congenital syphilis, a woman's renunciation of a traditional protective marriage, suicide, the manipulations of people seeking personal benefits, the sacrifices of pursuing truth, the rejection of a child by a parent, and the abandonment of personal happiness in favor of professional interests.

IBSEN'S LIFE AND EARLY WORK

Ibsen was born in Skien (*shee-en*), Norway, a small town just seventy miles southwest of the capital, Christiana (now Oslo). Although his parents had been prosperous, they went bankrupt when he was only seven, and afterward the family struggled against poverty. When Ibsen was fifteen he was apprenticed to a pharmacist, and he seemed headed for a career in this profession even though he hated it. By 1849, however, when he wrote *Catiline*, his first play in verse, it was clear that the theater was to be his life. Largely through the efforts of the famous violinist Ole Bull, a new National Theater had been established in Bergen, and Ibsen was appointed its director. He stayed in Bergen for six years and then went to Christiana, where for the next five years he tried to fashion a genuine Norwegian national theater. His attempts proved fruitless, for the theater went bankrupt in 1862. After writing *The Pretenders* in 1864, he secured enough governmental travel money to enable him to leave Norway. For the next twenty-seven years he lived in Germany and Italy in what has been called a "self-imposed" exile.

Although this first part of Ibsen's theatrical career was devoted to many practical matters—production, management, directing, and finances—he was also constantly writing. His early plays were in verse and were mainly nationalist and romantic, as a few representative titles suggest: *Lady Inger of Oestraat* (1855), *The Feast of Solhaug* (1856), *Olaf Liljekrans* (1857). In his first ten years in Germany and Italy he finished four plays. The best known of these is *Peer Gynt* (1867), a fantasy play about a historical Norwegian hero, Peer Gynt, who is saved from spiritual emptiness by the love of the patient heroine Solveig. Today, *Peer Gynt* is best known because of the incidental music written for it by Norway's major composer, Edvard Grieg (1843–1907). Ibsen asked Grieg to compose the music for the initial performances in 1876. Grieg's response was enthusiastic and creative, and the result is enjoyed today by millions. Ibsen also supplied the poem for which Grieg composed one of his loveliest songs, "A Swan."

IBSEN'S MAJOR PROSE PLAYS

During the years when Ibsen was fighting poverty and establishing his career in the theater, Europe was undergoing great political and intellectual changes. Throughout the nineteenth century, Ibsen's home country, Norway, was trying to release itself from the domination of neighboring Sweden and to establish its own territorial and national integrity. In Ibsen's twentieth year, 1848, the "February Uprising" in Paris resulted in the deposition of the French king and the establishment of a new French republic. This same year also saw the publication of the *Communist Manifesto* of Karl Marx (1818–1883). In 1864, the year Ibsen left Norway, Marx's first socialist International was held in London. In addition, during the time Ibsen lived in Italy and Germany, both countries were going through the tenuous political processes of becoming true nation-states. In short, change was everywhere.

Ibsen also was changing and growing as a thinker and dramatist, driven by the idea that a forward and creative drama could bring about deeper and more permanent changes than could be effected by soldiers and politicians. Toward this end he developed the realistic *problem play*. Such a play posited a major personal, social, professional, or political problem that occasioned the play's dramatic conflicts and tensions. Each problem was timely, topical, and realistic, as were the characters, places, situations, and outcomes. In this vein Ibsen wrote the twelve major prose plays on which his reputation rests: *The Pillars of Society* (1877), *A Dollhouse* (1879), *Ghosts* (1881), *An Enemy of the People* (1882), *The Wild Duck* (1884), *Rosmersholm* (1886), *The Lady from the Sea* (1888), *Hedda Gabler* (1890), *The Master Builder* (1892), *Little Eyolf* (1894), *John Gabriel Borkman* (1896), and *When We Dead Awaken* (1899). He finished the first eight of these plays while living in Germany and Italy, the last four after returning to Norway in 1891.

In these major plays Ibsen dramatizes human beings breaking free from restrictions and inhibitions and trying to establish their individuality and freedom—freedom of self, inquiry, pursuit of truth, artistic dedication, and, above all, the freedom of love. In attempting to achieve these goals, Ibsen's dramatic characters find internal opposition in self-interest, self-indulgence, and self-denial, and external opposition in the personal and political influences and manipulations of others. Because the plays are designed to be realistic, Ibsen's characters fall short of their goals. At best they achieve a respite in their combat, as in *An Enemy of the People*, or begin a quest in new directions, as in *A Dollhouse*. They always make great sacrifices, sometimes losing life itself, as in *Hedda Gabler* and *John Gabriel Borkman*.

TWO MAJOR REALISTIC PLAYS

A Dollhouse (*Et Dukkehjem*, 1879)[1] and *An Enemy of the People* (*En Folkefiende*, 1882) are representative of Ibsen's major drama. They present believable people confronting virtually insoluble personal, marital, economic, and political problems. To make the problems seem real, Ibsen also specifies realistic locations: The setting for all three acts of *A Dollhouse* is the living room of the Helmer house, including piano, Christmas tree, carpeting, and wall engravings. In *An Enemy of the People* the settings are equally realistic, though more varied, changing from the Stockmann household to the print shop and the large home of Captain Horster. Ibsen is so scrupulous about stage realism in *An Enemy of the People* that a comparison of the Stockmann living room (Acts I and II) and the study (Act V) shows that the room arrangements and the placements of the doors correspond exactly, as though he had drawn a floor plan before he created his set directions.

---

[1] Ibsen's title *Et Dukkehjem* literally means the home (*hjem*) of a doll or puppet (*dukke*). *A Doll's House*, the traditional and most common English title of the play, is not an accurate rendering of *dukkehjem*, and, in addition, it is misleading because of some of the connotations of our word *doll*. Recent translators have used *A Doll House* as the title, but this form is not in regular use. Our English word for a toy house for dolls is listed in collegiate dictionaries as *dollhouse*, a one-word compound. *A Dollhouse* is therefore preferable to the other two titles because it accurately renders *Et Dukkehjem*, and it is also the form accepted in current dictionaries.

IBSEN'S PROBLEM PLAYS ARE INTEGRATED WITH EVENTS THAT HAVE HAPPENED BEFORE THE PLAYS BEGIN.   In addition to the realistic staging, Ibsen's realism includes the technique of presentation, particularly the exposition about the root causes of the problems that come to a head in the plays themselves. As *A Dollhouse* unfolds, we learn that years earlier, Nora Helmer had extended herself beyond her means to save Torvald from a near-fatal illness. We also learn that there had been an earlier relationship between Krogstad and Christine Linde. Similarly, in *An Enemy of the People*, we learn about Dr. Stockmann's earlier investigations into the problems of the water contamination, his indebtedness to his brother for his job, and the dangerous and criminal cutting of corners that occurred when the town's therapeutic spa was built. These details are logically and chronologically essential for our understanding of the problems and conflicts within both plays.

IBSEN'S PLAYS ARE HIGHLY SYMBOLIC.   Both *A Dollhouse* and *An Enemy of the People* are realistic, and they, like all the major plays, are replete with contextual symbolism. One of the later plays, for example, *John Gabriel Borkman*, dramatizes the freezing to death of the major character, an occurrence symbolizing what Borkman had done to himself much earlier by denying love. In *A Dollhouse*, one of the earliest of the great plays, the title itself symbolizes the dependent and dehumanized role of the wife within traditional middle-class marriages. (The Norwegian-Danish word for *doll* (*dukke*) can also mean "puppet" or "marionette.") In addition, the entire nation of Norway (cold, legal, male) is contrasted symbolically with Italy (warm, emotional, female). Ironically, the break in the Helmers' marriage is symbolically aligned with events that occur or have occurred in both locations. Other symbols in *A Dollhouse* are the Christmas tree, the children's presents, the death of Dr. Rank, and the mailbox. In *An Enemy of the People* the symbols are the town spa, the toxic wastes from the nearby tanneries, and the concepts of public opinion and the popular majority. Additional symbols are the Mayor's hat and stick, Evensen's horn, and the spring weather at the play's end. Perhaps the major symbol is the intrafamily antagonism of Dr. Thomas Stockmann and Mayor Peter Stockmann, for all the other conflicts stem from their personal alienation.

IBSEN AND THE "WELL-MADE PLAY"

The plot and structure of both *A Dollhouse* and *An Enemy of the People* show Ibsen's use of the conventions of the **well-made play** (*la pièce bien faite*), a form developed and popularized in nineteenth-century France by Eugène Scribe (1791–1861) and Victorien Sardou (1831–1908). Ibsen was familiar with well-made plays, having directed many of them himself at Bergen and Christiana (Oslo). The well-made play follows a rigid and efficient structure in which the drama begins at the story's climax. Usually the plot is built on a secret known by the audience and perhaps one or two of the characters. The well-made play thus begins in suspense and offers a pattern of increasing tension produced through exposition and the timely arrivals of new characters (like Krogstad and Vik) and threatening news or props like the Mayor's information about the last will and testament of Morten Kiil. In the course of action of the well-made play, the fortunes of the protagonist go from a low point, through a *peripeteia* or reversal (Aristotle's concept), to a high point at which the protagonist confronts and defeats the villain.

Although Ibsen makes use of many of the structural elements of the well-made play, he varies and departs from the pattern to suit his realistic purposes. Thus in *An Enemy of the People* his principal variations are his emphasis on the characterizations of the Stockmann brothers and also his introduction of *three* sets of villains confronting Dr. Stockmann in the fifth act (the Mayor, Morten Kiil, and Hovstad and Billing). In addition, because *An Enemy of the People* is a play about ideas and principles, Ibsen concludes the play on the new note of Dr. Stockmann's dedication to growth and the future. In *A Dollhouse* his variation is that Nora's confrontation with Krogstad, who is the apparent villain, does not lead to a satisfactory resolution but rather precipitates the more significant albeit intractable confrontation with her husband. In *A Dollhouse* and also in *An Enemy of the People* there is not a traditionally well-made victorious outcome; rather there are provisional outcomes—adjustments—in keeping with the realistic concept that as life goes on, problems continue.

IBSEN'S TIMELINESS AND DRAMATIC POWER

Ibsen's focus on real-life issues has given his plays continued timeliness and strength. *A Dollhouse*, for example, vividly portrays the totally dependant position of married women in the nineteenth century. Most notably, a woman could not borrow funds without a man's cosignature, and Nora had to violate the law to obtain the money to restore her husband's health. The mailbox, to which Torvald has the only key, symbolizes this limitation, and the ultimate disclosure of the box's contents, rather than freeing Nora and Torvald, highlights her dependency. Today's feminism has stressed the issues of female freedom and equality, together with many other issues vital to women, but the need for feminine individuality and independence has not been more originally and forcefully dramatized than in *A Dollhouse*.

In a remarkably prophetic vein, *An Enemy of the People* deals powerfully with the effects of pollution and the conflicts between preservers of the environment and proponents of business as usual. This issue emerges early in the play as soon as Dr. Stockmann learns about the toxic wastes contaminating the water of the town spa, on which the economic livelihood of the entire town depends.

At first the conflict resulting from Dr. Stockmann's discovery seems minor because his facts are so unassailable. But the issue is raised to a political level with the entry of the local newspaper editor and his publisher. Once Mayor Stockmann convinces these men that Dr. Stockmann is using his discoveries to suit his own political goals, the play enlarges into the opposition between the individual and society at large. As these conflicts develop, Ibsen creates two of the great moments in the history of drama—those scenes in Acts II and III in which Dr. Stockmann and his brother the Mayor argue over the issue of truth and individuality versus interest and collective public opinion. Their conflict comes to a head in Act IV, in which Ibsen, through Dr. Stockmann, establishes an individual's need and absolute right to pursue truth, wherever it may lead. The dramatic force of the emptied stage at the end of this act, with the cries and jeers of the angry mob reverberating loudly backstage, has not been equaled.

BIBLIOGRAPHIC STUDIES

Because of Ibsen's importance, there have been many translations and editions of the plays. The Modern Library Giant edition of Farquharson-Sharp's translations of *Eleven Plays by Henrik Ibsen* (introduction by H. L. Mencken) has been a mainstay for many decades. Rolf Fjelde published paperback translations in 1970 and followed these up with *The Complete Major Prose Plays* in 1978 (twelve plays). Michael Meyer's translations (sixteen plays in four paperback volumes, 1986) are of major significance. Other individual and collected plays have been translated by Peter Watts, Una Ellis-Fermor, James McFarlane, Christopher Hampton, Inger Lignell, Nicholas Rudall, William Archer, Christopher Fry, and Kenneth McLeish. These names by no means constitute a complete list. A short edition of Ibsen's poetry has been translated by Michael Feingold (1987).

The major biography of Ibsen is Halvdan Hoht, *Life of Ibsen*, translated and edited by Einar Haugen and A. E. Santaniello (New York: Blom, 1971). Significant critical and biographical studies include George Bernard Shaw, *The Quintessence of Ibsenism* (1891; rpt. 1957), the pioneering work of Ibsen criticism; Rolf Fjelde, *Ibsen: A Collection of Critical Essays* (Englewood Cliffs: Prentice Hall, 1965); Michael Meyer, *Henrik Ibsen: The Farewell to Poetry 1864–1882* (London: Hart-Davis, 1971); James Hurt, *Catiline's Dream: An Essay on Ibsen's Plays* (Urbana: U of Illinois P, 1972); Clela Allphin, *Women in the Plays of Henrik Ibsen* (New York: Revisionist, 1975); Harold Clurman, *Ibsen* (New York: Macmillan, 1977); Einar Haugen, *Ibsen's Drama: Author to Audience* (Minneapolis: U of Minnesota P, 1979); David Thomas, *Henrik Ibsen* (London, Macmillan, 1983); Yvonne Shafer, ed., *Approaches to Teaching Ibsen's* A Doll House (New York: MLA, 1985); Charles R. Lyons, ed., *Critical Essays on Henrik Ibsen* (Boston: Hall, 1987); Frederick Marker and Lise-Lone Marker, *Ibsen's Lively Art* (New York: Cambridge UP, 1989); Joan Templeton, "The *Doll House* Backlash: Criticism, Feminism, and Ibsen", *PMLA* 104 (1989): 28–40; Naomi Lebowitz, *Ibsen and the Great World* (Baton Rouge: Louisiana UP, 1990); Errol Durbach, A Doll's House: *Ibsen's Myth of Transformation* (Boston: Twayne,

1991); Brian Johnston, *The Ibsen Cycle: The Design of the Plays from* Pillars of Society *to* When We Dead Awaken (University Park: Pennsylvania State UP, 1992); and James McFarlane, ed., *The Cambridge Companion to Ibsen* (Cambridge: Cambridge UP, 1994).

HENRIK IBSEN   (1828–1906)

A Dollhouse (Et Dukkehjem) ———————————————— *1879*

Translated by R. Farquharson Sharp

CHARACTERS

Torvald Helmer, *a lawyer and bank manager*
Nora, *his wife*
Doctor Rank
Mrs. Christine Linde
Nils Krogstad, *a lawyer and bank clerk*
Ivar, Bob, *and* Emmy, the Helmers' *three young children*
Anne, *their nurse*
Helen, *a housemaid*
A Porter

The action takes place in HELMER'S *apartment.*

ACT 1

SCENE. *A room furnished comfortably and tastefully, but not extravagantly. At the back, a door to the right leads to the entrance hall, another to the left leads to* HELMER'S *study. Between the doors stands a piano. In the middle of the left-hand wall is a door, and beyond it a window. Near the window are a round table, armchairs and a small sofa. In the right-hand wall, at the farther end, another door; and on the same side, nearer the footlights, a stove, two easy chairs and a rocking-chair; between the stove and the door, a small table. Engravings on the walls; a cabinet with china and other small objects; a small book-case with well-bound books. The floors are carpeted, and a fire burns in the stove. It is winter.*

A bell rings in the hall; shortly afterwards the door is heard to open. Enter NORA, *humming a tune and in high spirits. She is in outdoor dress and carries a number of parcels; these she lays on the table to the right. She leaves the outer door open after her, and through it is seen a* PORTER *who is carrying a Christmas Tree and a basket, which he gives to the* MAID *who has opened the door.*

NORA.   Hide the Christmas Tree carefully, Helen. Be sure the children do not see it till this evening, when it is dressed. [*to the* PORTER, *taking out her purse.*] How much?
PORTER.   Sixpence.

NORA.   There is a shilling. No, keep the change. [*The* PORTER *thanks her, and goes out.* NORA *shuts the door. She is laughing to herself, as she takes off her hat and coat. She takes a packet of macaroons from her pocket and eats one or two; then goes cautiously to her husband's door and listens.*] Yes, he is in.

[*Still humming, she goes to the table on the right.*]

HELMER.   [*calls out from his room*] Is that my little lark twittering out there?

NORA.   [*busy opening some of the parcels*] Yes, it is!

HELMER.   Is my little squirrel bustling about?

NORA.   Yes!

HELMER.   When did my squirrel come home?

NORA.   Just now. [*puts the bag of macaroons into her pocket and wipes her mouth.*] Come in here, Torvald, and see what I have bought.

HELMER.   Don't disturb me. [*A little later, he opens the door and looks into the room, pen in hand.*] Bought, did you say? All these things? Has my little spendthrift been wasting money again?

NORA.   Yes, but, Torvald, this year we really can let ourselves go a little. This is the first Christmas that we have not needed to economise.

HELMER.   Still, you know, we can't spend money recklessly.

NORA.   Yes, Torvald, we may be a wee bit more reckless now, mayn't we? Just a tiny wee bit! You are going to have a big salary and earn lots and lots of money.

HELMER.   Yes, after the New Year; but then it will be a whole quarter before the salary is due.

NORA.   Pooh! we can borrow till then.

HELMER.   Nora! [*goes up to her and takes her playfully by the ear.*] The same little featherhead! Suppose, now, that I borrowed fifty pounds to-day, and you spent it all in the Christmas week, and then on New Year's Eve a slate fell on my head and killed me, and—

NORA.   [*putting her hands over his mouth*] Oh! don't say such horrid things.

HELMER.   Still, suppose that happened—what then?

NORA.   If that were to happen, I don't suppose I should care whether I owed money or not.

HELMER.   Yes, but what about the people who had lent it?

NORA.   They? Who would bother about them? I should not know who they were.

HELMER.   That is like a woman! But seriously, Nora, you know what I think about that. No debt, no borrowing. There can be no freedom or beauty about a home life that depends on borrowing and debt. We two have kept bravely on the straight road so far, and we will go on the same way for the short time longer that there need be any struggle.

NORA.   [*moving towards the stove*] As you please, Torvald.

HELMER.   [*following her*] Come, come, my little skylark must not droop her wings. What is this! Is my little squirrel out of temper? [*taking out his purse.*] Nora, what do you think I have got here?

NORA.   [*turning around quickly*] Money!

HELMER.   There you are. [*gives her some money*] Do you think I don't know what a lot is wanted for housekeeping at Christmas-time?

NORA.   [*counting*] Ten shillings—a pound—two pounds! Thank you, thank you, Torvald; that will keep me going for a long time.

HELMER.   Indeed it must.

NORA.   Yes, yes, it will. But come here and let me show you what I have bought. And all so cheap! Look, here is a new suit for Ivar, and a sword; and a horse and a trumpet for Bob; and a doll and dolly's bedstead for Emmy—they are very plain, but anyway she will soon break them in pieces. And here are dress-lengths and handkerchiefs for the maids; old Anne ought really to have something better.

HELMER.   And what is in this parcel?   30

NORA.   [*crying out*] No, no! you mustn't see that till this evening.

HELMER.   Very well. But now tell me, you extravagant little person, what would you like for yourself?

NORA.   For myself? Oh, I am sure I don't want anything.

HELMER.   Yes, but you must. Tell me something reasonable that you would particularly like to have.

NORA.   No, I really can't think of anything—unless, Torvald—   35

HELMER.   Well?

NORA.   [*playing with his coat buttons, and without raising her eyes to his*] If you really want to give me something, you might—you might—

HELMER.   Well, out with it!

NORA.   [*speaking quickly*] You might give me money, Torvald. Only just as much as you can afford; and then one of these days I will buy something with it.

HELMER.   But, Nora—   40

NORA.   Oh, do! dear Torvald; please, please do! Then I will wrap it up in beautiful gilt paper and hang it on the Christmas Tree. Wouldn't that be fun?

HELMER.   What are little people called that are always wasting money?

NORA.   Spendthrifts—I know. Let us do as you suggest, Torvald, and then I shall have time to think what I am most in want of. That is a very sensible plan, isn't it?

HELMER.   [*smiling*] Indeed it is—that is to say, if you were really to save out of the money I give you, and then really buy something for yourself. But if you spend it all on the housekeeping and any number of unnecessary things, then I merely have to pay up again.

NORA.   Oh but, Torvald—   45

HELMER.   You can't deny it, my dear little Nora. [*puts his arm round her waist*] It's a sweet little spendthrift, but she uses up a deal of money. One would hardly believe how expensive such little persons are!

NORA.   It's a shame to say that. I do really save all I can.

HELMER.   [*laughing*] That's very true—all you can. But you can't save anything!

NORA.   [*smiling quietly and happily*] You haven't any idea how many expenses we skylarks and squirrels have, Torvald.

HELMER.   You are an odd little soul. Very like your father. You always find some   50
new way of wheedling money out of me, and, as soon as you have got it, it seems to melt in your hands. You never know where it has gone. Still, one must take you as you are. It is in the blood; for indeed it is true that you can inherit these things, Nora.

NORA.   Ah, I wish I had inherited many of papa's qualities.

HELMER.   And I would not wish you to be anything but just what you are, my sweet little skylark. But, do you know, it strikes me that you are looking rather—what shall I say—rather uneasy to-day?

NORA.   Do I?

HELMER.   You do, really. Look straight at me.   55

NORA.   [*looks at him*] Well?

HELMER. [*wagging his finger at her*] Hasn't Miss Sweet-Tooth been breaking rules in town to-day?

NORA. No; what makes you think that?

HELMER. Hasn't she paid a visit to the confectioner's?

NORA. No, I assure you, Torvald—

HELMER. Not been nibbling sweets?

NORA. No, certainly not.

HELMER. Not even taken a bite at a macaroon or two?

NORA. No, Torvald, I assure you really—

HELMER. There, there, of course I was only joking.

NORA. [*going to the table on the right*] I should not think of going against your wishes.

HELMER. No, I am sure of that! besides, you gave me your word—[*going up to her*] Keep your little Christmas secrets to yourself, my darling. They will all be revealed to-night when the Christmas Tree is lit, no doubt.

NORA. Did you remember to invite Doctor Rank?

HELMER. No. But there is no need; as a matter of course he will come to dinner with us. However, I will ask him when he comes in this morning. I have ordered some good wine. Nora, you can't think how I am looking forward to this evening.

NORA. So am I! And how the children will enjoy themselves, Torvald!

HELMER. It is splendid to feel that one has a perfectly safe appointment, and a big enough income. It's delightful to think of, isn't it?

NORA. It's wonderful!

HELMER. Do you remember last Christmas? For a full three weeks beforehand you shut yourself up every evening till long after midnight, making ornaments for the Christmas Tree and all the other fine things that were to be a surprise to us. It was the dullest three weeks I ever spent!

NORA. I didn't find it dull.

HELMER. [*smiling*] But there was precious little result, Nora.

NORA. Oh, you shouldn't tease me about that again. How could I help the cat's going in and tearing everything to pieces?

HELMER. Of course you couldn't, poor little girl. You had the best of intentions to please us all, and that's the main thing. But it is a good thing that our hard times are over.

NORA. Yes, it is really wonderful.

HELMER. This time I needn't sit here and be dull all alone, and you needn't ruin your dear eyes and your pretty little hands—

NORA. [*clapping her hands*] No, Torvald, I needn't any longer, need I! It's wonderfully lovely to hear you say so! [*taking his arm*] Now I will tell you how I have been thinking we ought to arrange things, Torvald. As soon as Christmas is over—[*A bell rings in the hall.*] There's the bell. [*She tidies the room a little.*] There's someone at the door. What a nuisance!

HELMER. If it is a caller, remember I am not at home.

MAID. [*in the doorway*] A lady to see you, ma'am—a stranger.

NORA. Ask her to come in.

MAID. [*to HELMER*] The doctor came at the same time, sir.

HELMER. Did he go straight into my room?

MAID. Yes sir.

[*HELMER goes into his room. The* MAID *ushers in* MRS. *LINDE, who is in travelling dress, and shuts the door.*]

MRS. LINDE.   [*in a dejected and timid voice*] How do you do, Nora?

NORA.   [*doubtfully*] How do you do—

MRS. LINDE.   You don't recognise me, I suppose.

NORA.   No, I don't know—yes, to be sure, I seem to—[*suddenly*] Yes! Christine! Is it really you?

MRS. LINDE.   Yes, it is I.   90

NORA.   Christine! To think of my not recognising you! And yet how could I—[*in a gentle voice*] How you have altered, Christine!

MRS. LINDE.   Yes, I have indeed. In nine, ten long years—

NORA.   Is it so long since we met? I suppose it is. The last eight years have been a happy time for me, I can tell you. And so now you have come into the town, and have taken this long journey in winter—that was plucky of you.

MRS. LINDE.   I arrived by steamer this morning.

NORA.   To have some fun at Christmas-time, of course. How delightful! We will   95
have such fun together! But take off your things. You are not cold, I hope. [*helps her*] Now we will sit down by the stove, and be cosy. No, take this arm-chair; I will sit here in the rocking-chair. [*takes her hands*] Now you look like your old self again; it was only the first moment—You are a little paler, Christine, and perhaps a little thinner.

MRS. LINDE.   And much, much older, Nora.

NORA.   Perhaps a little older; very, very little; certainly not much. [*stops suddenly and speaks seriously*] What a thoughtless creature I am, chattering away like this. My poor, dear Christine, do forgive me.

MRS. LINDE.   What do you mean, Nora?

NORA.   [*gently*] Poor Christine, you are a widow.

MRS. LINDE.   Yes; it is three years ago now.   100

NORA.   Yes, I knew; I saw it in the papers. I assure you, Christine, I meant ever so often to write to you at the time, but I always put it off and something always prevented me.

MRS. LINDE.   I quite understand, dear.

NORA.   It was very bad of me, Christine. Poor thing, how you must have suffered. And he left you nothing?

MRS. LINDE.   No.

NORA.   And no children?   105

MRS. LINDE.   No.

NORA.   Nothing at all, then?

MRS. LINDE.   Not even any sorrow or grief to live upon.

NORA.   [*looking incredulously at her*] But, Christine, is that possible?

MRS. LINDE.   [*smiles sadly and strokes her hair*] It sometimes happens, Nora.   110

NORA.   So you are quite alone. How dreadfully sad that must be. I have three lovely children. You can't see them just now, for they are out with their nurse. But now you must tell me all about it.

MRS. LINDE.   No, no; I want to hear you.

NORA.   No, you must begin. I mustn't be selfish to-day; to-day I must only think of your affairs. But there is one thing I must tell you. Do you know we have just had a great piece of good luck?

MRS. LINDE.   No, what is it?

NORA.   Just fancy, my husband has been made manager of the Bank!

MRS. LINDE.   Your husband? What good luck!

NORA.   Yes, tremendous! A barrister's profession is such an uncertain thing, especially if he won't undertake unsavoury cases; and naturally Torvald has never been willing to do that, and I quite agree with him. You may imagine how pleased we are! He is to take up his work in the Bank at the New Year, and then he will have a big salary and lots of commissions. For the future we can live quite differently—we can do just as we like. I feel so relieved and so happy, Christine! It will be splendid to have heaps of money and not need to have any anxiety, won't it?

MRS. LINDE.   Yes, anyhow I think it would be delightful to have what one needs.

NORA.   No, not only what one needs, but heaps and heaps of money.

MRS. LINDE.   [*smiling*] Nora, Nora haven't you learnt sense yet? In our schooldays you were a great spendthrift.

NORA.   [*laughing*] Yes, that is what Torvald says now. [*wags her finger at her*] But "Nora, Nora" is not so silly as you think. We have not been in a position for me to waste money. We have both had to work.

MRS. LINDE.   You too?

NORA.   Yes; odds and ends, needlework, crochet-work, embroidery, and that kind of thing. [*dropping her voice*] And other things as well. You know Torvald left his office when we were married? There was no prospect of promotion there, and he had to try and earn more than before. But during the first year he overworked himself dreadfully. You see, he had to make money every way he could, and he worked early and late; but he couldn't stand it, and fell dreadfully ill, and the doctors said it was necessary for him to go south.

MRS. LINDE.   You spent a whole year in Italy didn't you?

NORA.   Yes. It was no easy matter to get away, I can tell you. It was just after Ivar was born; but naturally we had to go. It was a wonderfully beautiful journey, and it saved Torvald's life. But it cost a tremendous lot of money, Christine.

MRS. LINDE.   So I should think.

NORA.   It cost about two hundred and fifty pounds. That's a lot, isn't it?

MRS. LINDE.   Yes, and in emergencies like that it is lucky to have the money.

NORA.   I ought to tell you that we had it from papa.

MRS. LINDE.   Oh, I see. It was just about that time that he died, wasn't it?

NORA.   Yes; and, just think of it, I couldn't go and nurse him. I was expecting little Ivar's birth every day and I had my poor sick Torvald to look after. My dear, kind father—I never saw him again, Christine. That was the saddest time I have known since our marriage.

MRS. LINDE.   I know how fond you were of him. And then you went off to Italy?

NORA.   Yes; you see we had money then, and the doctors insisted on our going, so we started a month later.

MRS. LINDE.   And your husband came back quite well?

NORA.   As sound as a bell!

MRS. LINDE.   But—the doctor?

NORA.   What doctor?

MRS. LINDE.   I thought your maid said the gentleman who arrived here just as I did was the doctor?

NORA.   Yes, that was Doctor Rank, but he doesn't come here professionally. He is our greatest friend, and comes in at least once every day. No, Torvald has not had an hour's illness since then, and our children are strong and healthy and so am I. [*jumps up and claps her hands*] Christine! Christine! it's good to be alive and happy!—But how horrid of me; I am talking of nothing but my own affairs. [*Sits on a stool near her, and rests her arms on her knees*] You mustn't be angry with me. Tell me, is it really true that you did not love your husband? Why did you marry him?

MRS. LINDE.   My mother was alive then, and was bedridden and helpless, and I   140
had to provide for my two younger brothers; so I did not think I was justified in refusing his offer.

NORA.   No, perhaps you were quite right. He was rich at that time, then?

MRS. LINDE.   I believe he was quite well off. But his business was a precarious one; and, when he died, it all went to pieces and there was nothing left.

NORA.   And then?—

MRS. LINDE.   Well, I had to turn my hand to anything I could find—first a small shop, then a small school, and so on. The last three years have seemed like one long working-day, with no rest. Now it is at an end, Nora. My poor mother needs me no more, for she is gone; and the boys do not need me either; they have got situations and can shift for themselves.

NORA.   What a relief you must feel it—   145

MRS. LINDE.   No, indeed; I only feel my life unspeakably empty. No one to live for any more. [*gets up restlessly*] That was why I could not stand the life in my little back-water any longer. I hope it may be easier here to find something which will busy me and occupy my thoughts. If only I could have the good luck to get some regular work—office work of some kind—

NORA.   But, Christine, that is so frightfully tiring, and you look tired out now. You had far better go away to some watering-place.

MRS. LINDE.   [*walking to the window*] I have no father to give me money for a jour-ney, Nora.

NORA.   [*rising*] Oh, don't be angry with me.   150

MRS. LINDE.   [*going up to her*] It is you that must not be angry with me, dear. The worst of a position like mine is that it makes one so bitter. No one to work for, and yet obliged to be always on the look-out for chances. One must live, and so one becomes selfish. When you told me of the happy turn your fortunes have taken—you will hardly believe it—I was delighted not so much on your account as on my own.

NORA.   How do you mean?—Oh, I understand. You mean that perhaps Torvald could get you something to do.

MRS. LINDE.   Yes, that was what I was thinking of.

NORA.   He must, Christine. Just leave it to me; I will broach the subject very clev-erly—I will think of something that will please him very much. It will make me so happy to be of some use to you.

MRS. LINDE.   How kind you are, Nora, to be so anxious to help me! It is doubly   155
kind in you, for you know so little of the burdens and troubles of life.

NORA.   I—? I know so little of them?

MRS. LINDE.   [*smiling*] My dear! Small household cares and that sort of thing!—You are a child, Nora.

NORA.   [*tosses her head and crosses the stage*] You ought not to be so superior.

MRS. LINDE.   No?

NORA.   You are just like the others. They all think that I am incapable of anything   160
really serious—

MRS. LINDE.   Come, come—

NORA.   —that I have gone through nothing in this world of cares.

MRS. LINDE.   But, my dear Nora, you have just told me all your troubles.

NORA.   Pooh!—those were trifles. [*lowering her voice*] I have not told you the important thing.

MRS. LINDE.   The important thing? What do you mean?

NORA.   You look down upon me altogether, Christine—but you ought not to. You are proud, aren't you, of having worked so hard and so long for your mother?

MRS. LINDE.   Indeed, I don't look down on any one. But it is true that I am both proud and glad to think that I was privileged to make the end of my mother's life almost free from care.

NORA.   And you are proud to think of what you have done for your brothers.

MRS. LINDE.   I think I have the right to be.

NORA.   I think so, too. But now, listen to this; I too have something to be proud of and glad of.

MRS. LINDE.   I have no doubt you have. But what do you refer to?

NORA.   Speak low. Suppose Torvald were to hear! He mustn't on any account—no one in the world must know, Christine, except you.

MRS. LINDE.   But what is it?

NORA.   Come here. [*pulls her down on the sofa beside her*] Now I will show you that I too have something to be proud and glad of. It was I who saved Torvald's life.

MRS. LINDE.   "Saved"? How?

NORA.   I told you about our trip to Italy. Torvald would never have recovered if he had not gone there—

MRS. LINDE.   Yes, but your father gave you the necessary funds.

NORA.   [*smiling*] Yes, that is what Torvald and all the others think, but—

MRS. LINDE.   But—

NORA.   Papa didn't give us a shilling. It was I who procured the money.

MR. LINDE.   You? All that large sum?

NORA.   Two hundred and fifty pounds. What do you think of that?

MRS. LINDE.   But, Nora, how could you possibly do it? Did you win a prize in the Lottery?

NORA.   [*contemptuously*] In the Lottery? There would have been no credit in that.

MRS. LINDE.   But where did you get it from, then?

NORA.   [*humming and smiling with an air of mystery*] Hm, hm! Aha!

MRS. LINDE.   Because you couldn't have borrowed it.

NORA.   Couldn't I? Why not?

MRS. LINDE.   No, a wife cannot borrow without her husband's consent.

NORA.   [*tossing her head*] Oh, if it is a wife who has any head for business—a wife who has the wit to be a little bit clever—

MRS. LINDE.   I don't understand it at all, Nora.

NORA.   There is no need you should. I never said I had borrowed the money. I may have got it some other way. [*lies back on the sofa*] Perhaps I got it from some other admirer. When anyone is as attractive as I am—

MRS. LINDE.   You are a mad creature.

NORA.   Now, you know you're full of curiosity, Christine.

MRS. LINDE.   Listen to me, Nora dear. Haven't you been a little bit imprudent?

NORA.   [*sits up straight*] Is it imprudent to save your husband's life?

MRS. LINDE.   It seems to me imprudent, without his knowledge, to—

NORA.   But it was absolutely necessary that he should not know! My goodness, can't you understand that? It was necessary he should have no idea what a dangerous condition he was in. It was to me that the doctors came and said that his life was in danger, and that the only thing to save him was to live in the south. Do you suppose I didn't try, first of all, to get what I wanted as if it were for myself? I told him how much I should love to travel abroad like other young wives; I tried tears and entreaties with him; I told him that he ought to remember the condition I was in, and that he ought to be kind and indulgent to me; I even hinted that he might raise a loan. That nearly made him angry, Christine. He said I was thoughtless, and that it was his duty as my husband not to indulge me in my whims and caprices—as I believe he called them. Very well I thought, you must be saved— and that was how I came to devise a way out of the difficulty—

MRS. LINDE. And did your husband never get to know from your father that the money had not come from him?

NORA. No, never. Papa died just at that time. I had meant to let him into the   200
secret and beg him never to reveal it. But he was so ill then—alas, there never was any need to tell him.

MRS. LINDE. And since then have you never told your secret to your husband?

NORA. Good Heavens, no! How could you think so? A man who has such strong opinions about these things! And besides, how painful and humiliating it would be for Torvald, with his manly independence, to know that he owed me anything! It would upset our mutual relations altogether; our beautiful happy home would no longer be what it is now.

MRS. LINDE. Do you mean never to tell him about it?

NORA. [*meditatively, and with a half smile*] Yes—some day, perhaps, after many years, when I am no longer as nice-looking as I am now. Don't laugh at me! I mean of course, when Torvald is no longer as devoted to me as he is now; when my dancing and dressing-up and reciting have palled on him; then it may be a good thing to have some-thing in reserve—[*breaking off*] What nonsense! That time will never come. Now, what do you think of my great secret, Christine? Do you still think I am of no use? I can tell you, too, that this affair has caused me a lot of worry. It has been by no means easy for me to meet my engagements punctually. I may tell you that there is something that is called, in business, quarterly interest, and another thing called payment in instalments, and it is always so dreadfully difficult to manage them. I have had to save a little here and there, where I could, you understand. I have not been able to put aside much from my house-keeping money, for Torvald must have a good table. I couldn't let my children be shab-bily dressed; I have felt obliged to use up all he gave me for them, the sweet little darlings!

MRS. LINDE. So it has all had to come out of your own necessaries of life, poor   205
Nora?

NORA. Of course. Besides, I was the one responsible for it. Whenever Torvald has given me the money for new dresses and such things, I have never spent more than half of it; I have always bought the simplest and cheapest things. Thank Heaven, any clothes look well one me, and so Torvald has never noticed it. But it was often very hard on me, Christine—because it is delightful to be really well dressed, isn't it?

MRS. LINDE. Quite so.

NORA. Well, then I have found other ways of earning money. Last winter I was lucky enough to get a lot of copying to do; so I locked myself up and sat writing every evening until quite late at night. Many a time I was desperately tired; but all the same it was a tremendous pleasure to sit there working and earning money. It was like being a man.

MRS. LINDE. How much have you been able to pay off in that way?

NORA.   I can't tell you exactly. You see, it is very difficult to keep an account of a
business matter of that kind. I only know that I have paid every penny that I could scrape
together. Many a time I was at my wits' end. [*smiles*] Then I used to sit here and imagine
that a rich old gentleman had fallen in love with me—

MRS. LINDE.   What! Who was it?

NORA.   Be quiet!—that he had died; and that when his will was opened it contained, written in big letters, the instruction: "The lovely Mrs. Nora Helmer is to have all
I possess paid over to her at once in cash."

MRS. LINDE.   But, my dear Nora—who could the man be?

NORA.   Good gracious, can't you understand? There was no old gentleman at all;
it was only something that I used to sit here and imagine, when I couldn't think of any
way of procuring money. But it's all the same now; the tiresome old person can stay
where he is, as far as I am concerned; I don't care about him or his will either, for I am
free from care now. [*jumps up*] My goodness, it's delightful to think of, Christine! Free
from care! To be able to be free from care, quite free from care; to be able to play and
romp with the children; to be able to keep the house beautifully and have everything just
as Torvald likes it! And, think of it, soon the spring will come and the big blue sky!
Perhaps we shall be able to take a little trip—perhaps I shall see the sea again! Oh, it's a
wonderful thing to be alive and be happy. [*A bell is heard in the hall.*]

MRS. LINDE.   [*rising*] There is the bell; perhaps I had better go.

NORA.   No, don't go; no one will come in here; it is sure to be for Torvald.

SERVANT.   [*at the hall door*] Excuse me, ma'am—there is a gentleman to see the
master, and as the doctor is with him—

NORA.   Who is it?

KROGSTAD.   [*at the door*] It is I, Mrs. Helmer. [*MRS. LINDE starts, trembles, and turns to
the window.*]

NORA.   [*takes a step towards him, and speaks in a strained, low voice*] You? What is it?
What do you want to see my husband about?

KROGSTAD.   Bank business—in a way. I have a small post in the Bank, and I hear
your husband is to be our chief now—

NORA.   Then it is—

KROGSTAD.   Nothing but dry business matters, Mrs. Helmer; absolutely nothing
else.

NORA.   Be so good as to go into the study, then. [*She bows indifferently to him and
shuts the door into the hall; then comes back and makes up the fire in the stove.*]

MRS. LINDE.   Nora—who was that man?

NORA.   A lawyer, of the name of Krogstad.

MRS. LINDE.   Then it really was he.

NORA.   Do you know the man?

MRS. LINDE.   I used to—many years ago. At one time he was a solicitor's clerk in
our town.

NORA.   Yes, he was.

MRS. LINDE.   He is greatly altered.

NORA.   He made a very unhappy marriage.

MRS. LINDE.   He is a widower now, isn't he?

NORA.   With several children. There now, it is burning up.

[*Shuts the door of the stove and moves the rocking-chair aside.*]

MRS. LINDE.   They say he carries on various kinds of business.

NORA.   Really! Perhaps he does; I don't know anything about it. But don't let us think of business; it is so tiresome.

DOCTOR RANK.   [*comes out of HELMER'S study. Before he shuts the door he calls to him.*] No, my dear fellow, I won't disturb you; I would rather go into your wife for a little while. [*shuts the door and sees MRS. LINDE*] I beg your pardon; I am afraid I am disturbing you too.

NORA.   No, not at all. [*introducing him*] Doctor Rank, Mrs. Linde.

RANK.   I have often heard Mrs. Linde's name mentioned here. I think I passed you on the stairs when I arrived, Mrs. Linde?

MRS. LINDE.   Yes, I go up very slowly; I can't manage stairs well.   240

RANK.   Ah! some slight internal weakness?

MRS. LINDE.   No, the fact is I have been overworking myself.

RANK.   Nothing more than that? Then I suppose you have come to town to amuse yourself with our entertainments?

MRS. LINDE.   I have come to look for work.

RANK.   Is that a good cure for overwork?   245

MRS. LINDE.   One must live, Doctor Rank.

RANK.   Yes, the general opinion seems to be that it is necessary.

NORA.   Look here, Doctor Rank—you know you want to live.

RANK.   Certainly. However wretched I may feel, I want to prolong the agony as long as possible. All my patients are like that. And so are those who are morally diseased; one of them, and a bad case too, is at this very moment with Helmer—

MRS. LINDE.   [*sadly*] Ah!   250

NORA.   Whom do you mean?

RANK.   A lawyer of the name of Krogstad, a fellow you don't know at all. He suffers from a diseased moral character, Mrs. Helmer; but even he began talking of its being highly important that he should live.

NORA.   Did he? What did he want to speak to Torvald about?

RANK.   I have no idea; I only heard that it was something about the Bank.

NORA.   I didn't know this—what's his name—Krogstad had anything to do with   255
the Bank.

RANK.   Yes, he has some sort of appointment there. [*to MRS. LINDE*] I don't know whether you find also in your part of the world that there are certain people who go zealously snuffing about to smell out moral corruption, and, as soon as they have found some, put the person concerned into some lucrative position where they can keep their eye on him. Healthy natures are left out in the cold.

MRS. LINDE.   Still I think the sick are those who most need taking care of.

RANK.   [*shrugging his shoulders*] Yes, there you are. That is the sentiment that is turning Society into a sickhouse.

[*NORA, who has been absorbed in her thoughts, breaks out into smothered laughter and claps her hands.*]

RANK.   Why do you laugh at that? Have you any notion what Society really is?

NORA.   What do I care about tiresome Society? I am laughing at something quite   260
different, something extremely amusing. Tell me, Doctor Rank, are all the people who are employed in the Bank dependent on Torvald now?

RANK.   Is that what you find so extremely amusing?

NORA.   [*smiling and humming*] That's my affair! [*walking about the room*] It's perfectly glorious to think that we have—that Torvald has so much power over so many people. [*takes the packet from her pocket*] Doctor Rank, what do you say to a macaroon?

RANK.   What, macaroons? I thought they were forbidden here.

NORA.   Yes, but these are some Christine gave me.

MRS. LINDE.   What! I?—

NORA.   Oh, well, don't be alarmed! You couldn't know that Torvald had forbidden them. I must tell you that he is afraid they will spoil my teeth. But, bah!—once in a way— That's so, isn't it, Doctor Rank? By your leave? [*puts a macaroon into his mouth*] You must have one too, Christine. And I shall have one, just a little one—or at most two. [*walking about*] I am tremendously happy. There is just one thing in the world now that I should dearly love to do.

RANK.   Well, what is that?

NORA.   It's something I should dearly love to say, if Torvald could hear me.

RANK.   Well, why can't you say it?

NORA.   No, I daren't; it's so shocking.

MRS. LINDE.   Shocking?

RANK.   Well, I should not advise you to say it. Still, with us you might. What is it you would so much like to say if Torvald could hear you?

NORA.   I should just love to say—Well, I'm damned!

RANK.   Are you mad?

MRS. LINDE.   Nora, dear—!

RANK.   Say it, here he is!

NORA.   [*hiding the packet*] Hush! Hush! Hush!

[*HELMER comes out of his room, with his coat over his arm and his hat in his hands.*]

NORA.   Well, Torvald dear, have you got rid of him?

HELMER.   Yes, he has just gone.

NORA.   Let me introduce you—this is Christine, who has come to town.

HELMER.   Christine—? Excuse me, but I don't know—

NORA.   Mrs. Linde, dear; Christine Linde.

HELMER.   Of course. A school friend of my wife's, I presume?

MRS. LINDE.   Yes, we have known each other since then.

NORA.   And just think, she has taken a long journey in order to see you.

HELMER.   What do you mean?

MRS. LINDE.   No, really, I—

NORA.   Christine is tremendously clever at book-keeping, and she is frightfully anxious to work under some clever man, so as to perfect herself—

HELMER.   Very sensible, Mrs. Linde.

NORA.   And when she heard you had been appointed manager of the Bank—the news was telegraphed, you know—she travelled here as quick as she could. Torvald, I am sure you will be able to do something for Christine, for my sake, won't you?

HELMER.   Well, it is not altogether impossible. I presume you are a widow, Mrs. Linde?

MRS. LINDE.   Yes.

HELMER.   And have had some experience of book-keeping?

MRS. LINDE.   Yes, a fair amount.

HELMER.   Ah! well, it's very likely I may be able to find something for you—

NORA.   [*clapping her hands*] What did I tell you? What did I tell you?

HELMER.   You have just come at a fortunate moment, Mrs. Linde.

MRS. LINDE.   How am I to thank you?

HELMER.   There is no need. [*puts on his coat*] But to-day you must excuse me—

RANK.   Wait a minute; I will come with you.   300

[*Brings his fur coat from the hall and warms it at the fire.*]

NORA.   Don't be long away, Torvald dear.
HELMER.   About an hour, not more.
NORA.   Are you going too, Christine?
MRS. LINDE.   [*putting on her cloak*] Yes, I must go and look for a room.
HELMER.   Oh, well then, we can walk down the street together.   305
NORA.   [*helping her*] What a pity it is we are so short of space here: I am afraid it is
impossible for us—
MRS. LINDE.   Please don't think of it! Good-bye, Nora dear, and many thanks.
NORA.   Good-bye for the present. Of course you will come back this evening. And
you too, Dr. Rank. What do you say? If you are well enough? Oh, you must be! Wrap
yourself up well.

[*They go to the door all talking together. Children's voices are heard on the staircase.*]

NORA.   There they are. There they are! [*She runs to open the door. The NURSE comes
in with the children.*] Come in! Come in! [*stoops and kisses them*] Oh, you sweet blessings!
Look at them, Christine! Aren't they darlings?
RANK.   Don't let us stand here in the draught.   310
HELMER.   Come along, Mrs. Linde; the place will only be bearable for a mother
now!

[*RANK, HELMER and MRS. LINDE go downstairs. The NURSE comes forward with the children;
NORA shuts the hall door.*]

NORA.   How fresh and well you look! Such red cheeks!—like apples and roses.
[*The children all talk at once while she speaks to them.*] Have you had great fun? That's splendid! What, you pulled both Emmy and Bob along on the sledge?—both at once?—that
was good. You are a clever boy, Ivar. Let me take her for a little, Anne. My sweet little
baby doll! [*takes the baby from the MAID and dances it up and down*] Yes, yes, mother will
dance with Bob too. What! Have you been snowballing? I wish I had been there too! No,
no, I will take their things off, Anne; please let me do it, it is such fun. Go in now, you
look half frozen. There is some coffee for you on the stove.

[*The NURSE goes into the room on the left. NORA takes off the children's things and throws them
about, while they all talk to her at once.*]

NORA.   Really! Did a big dog run after you? But it didn't bite you? No, dogs don't
bite nice little dolly children. You mustn't look at the parcels, Ivar. What are they? Ah, I
daresay you would like to know. No, no—it's something nasty! Come, let us have a game!
What shall we play at? Hide and Seek? Yes, we'll play Hide and Seek. Bob shall hide first.
Must I hide? Very well, I'll hide first.

[*She and the children laugh and shout, and romp in and out of the room; at last NORA hides
under the table, the children rush in and look for her, but do not see her; they hear her smothered
laughter, run to the table, lift up the cloth and find her. Shouts of laughter. She crawls forward
and pretends to frighten them. Fresh laughter. Meanwhile there has been a knock at the hall door,
but none of them has noticed it. The door is half opened, and KROGSTAD appears. He waits a
little; the game goes on.*]

KROGSTAD.   Excuse me, Mrs. Helmer.

NORA.   [*with a stifled cry, turns round and gets up on to her knees*] Ah! what do you want?

KROGSTAD.   Excuse me, the outer door was ajar; I suppose someone forgot to shut it.

NORA.   [*rising*] My husband is out, Mr. Krogstad.

KROGSTAD.   I know that.

NORA.   What do you want here, then?

KROGSTAD.   A word with you.

NORA.   With me?—[*to the children, gently*] Go in to nurse. What? No, the strange man won't do mother any harm. When he has gone we will have another game. [*She takes the children into the room on the left, and shuts the door after them.*] You want to speak to me?

KROGSTAD.   Yes, I do.

NORA.   To-day? It is not the first of the month yet.

KROGSTAD.   No, it is Christmas Eve, and it will depend on yourself what sort of a Christmas you will spend.

NORA.   What do you want? To-day it is absolutely impossible for me—

KROGSTAD.   We won't talk about that till later on. This is something different. I presume you can give me a moment?

NORA.   Yes—yes, I can—although—

KROGSTAD.   Good. I was in Olsen's Restaurant and saw your husband going down the street—

NORA.   Yes?

KROGSTAD.   With a lady.

NORA.   What then?

KROGSTAD.   May I make so bold as to ask if it was a Mrs. Linde?

NORA.   It was.

KROGSTAD.   Just arrived in town?

NORA.   Yes, to-day.

KROGSTAD.   She is a great friend of yours, isn't she?

NORA.   She is. But I don't see—

KROGSTAD.   I knew her too, once upon a time.

NORA.   I am aware of that.

KROGSTAD.   Are you? So you know all about it; I thought as much. Then I can ask you, without beating about the bush—is Mrs. Linde to have an appointment in the Bank?

NORA.   What right have you to question me, Mr. Krogstad?—You, one of my husband's subordinates! But since you ask, you shall know. Yes, Mrs. Linde *is* to have an appointment. And it was I who pleaded her cause, Mr. Krogstad, let me tell you that.

KROGSTAD.   I was right in what I thought, then.

NORA.   [*walking up and down the stage*] Sometimes one has a tiny little bit of influence, I should hope. Because one is a woman, it does not necessarily follow that—. When anyone is in a subordinate position, Mr. Krogstad, they should really be careful to avoid offending anyone who—who—

KROGSTAD.   Who has influence?

NORA.   Exactly.

KROGSTAD.   [*changing his tone*] Mrs. Helmer, you will be so good as to use your influence on my behalf.

NORA.   What? What do you mean?

KROGSTAD.   You will be so kind as to see that I am allowed to keep my subordinate position in the Bank.

NORA.   What do you mean by that? Who proposes to take your post away from you?

KROGSTAD.   Oh, there is no necessity to keep up the pretence of ignorance. I can   350
quite understand that your friend is not very anxious to expose herself to the chance of rubbing shoulders with me; and I quite understand, too, whom I have to thank for being turned out.

NORA.   But I assure you—

KROGSTAD.   Very likely; but, to come to the point, the time has come when I should advise you to use your influence to prevent that.

NORA.   But, Mr. Krogstad, I *have* no influence.

KROGSTAD.   Haven't you? I thought you said yourself just now—

NORA.   Naturally I did not mean you to put that construction on it. I! What   355
should make you think I have any influence of that kind with my husband?

KROGSTAD.   Oh, I have known your husband from our student days. I don't suppose he is any more unassailable than other husbands.

NORA.   If you speak slightingly of my husband, I shall turn you out of the house.

KROGSTAD.   You are bold, Mrs. Helmer.

NORA.   I am not afraid of you any longer. As soon as the New Year comes, I shall in a very short time be free of the whole thing.

KROGSTAD.   [*controlling himself*] Listen to me, Mrs. Helmer. If necessary, I am pre-   360
pared to fight for my small post in the Bank as if I were fighting for my life.

NORA.   So it seems.

KROGSTAD.   It is not only for the sake of the money; indeed, that weighs least with me in the matter. There is another reason—well, I may as well tell you. My position is this. I daresay you know, like everybody else, that once, many years ago, I was guilty of an indiscretion.

NORA.   I think I have heard something of the kind.

KROGSTAD.   The matter never came into court; but every way seemed to be closed to me after that. So I took to the business that you know of. I had to do something; and, honestly, I don't think I've been one of the worst. But now I must cut myself free from all that. My sons are growing up; for their sake I must try and win back as much respect as I can in the town. This post in the Bank was like the first step up for me—and now your husband is going to kick me downstairs again into the mud.

NORA.   But you must believe me, Mr. Krogstad; it is not in my power to help you   365
at all.

KROGSTAD.   Then it is because you haven't the will; but I have means to compel you.

NORA.   You don't mean that you will tell my husband that I owe you money?

KROGSTAD.   Hm!—suppose I were to tell him?

NORA.   It would be perfectly infamous of you. [*Sobbing*] To think of his learning my secret, which has been my joy and pride, in such an ugly, clumsy way—that he should learn it from you! And it would put me in a horribly disagreeable position—

KROGSTAD.   Only disagreeable?   370

NORA.   [*impetuously*] Well, do it, then!—and it will be the worse for you. My husband will see for himself what a blackguard you are, and you certainly won't keep your post then.

KROGSTAD. I asked you if it was only a disagreeable scene at home that you were afraid of?

NORA. If my husband does get to know of it, of course he will at once pay you what is still owing, and we shall have nothing more to do with you.

KROGSTAD. [*coming a step nearer*] Listen to me, Mrs. Helmer. Either you have a very bad memory or you know very little of business. I shall be obliged to remind you of a few details.

NORA. What do you mean?

KROGSTAD. When your husband was ill, you came to me to borrow two hundred and fifty pounds.

NORA. I didn't know any one else to go to.

KROGSTAD. I promised to get you that amount—

NORA. Yes, and you did so.

KROGSTAD. I promised to get you that amount, on certain conditions. Your mind was so taken up with your husband's illness, and you were so anxious to get the money for your journey, that you seem to have paid no attention to the conditions of our bargain. Therefore it will not be amiss if I remind you of them. Now, I promised to get the money on the security of a bond which I drew up.

NORA. Yes, and which I signed.

KROGSTAD. Good. But below your signature there were a few lines constituting your father a surety for the money; those lines your father should have signed.

NORA. Should? He did sign them.

KROGSTAD. I had left the date blank; that is to say your father should himself have inserted the date on which he signed the paper. Do you remember that?

NORA. Yes, I think I remember—

KROGSTAD. Then I gave you the bond to send by post to your father. Is that not so?

NORA. Yes.

KROGSTAD. And you naturally did so at once, because five or six days afterwards you brought me the bond with your father's signature. And then I gave you the money.

NORA. Well, haven't I been paying it off regularly?

KROGSTAD. Fairly so, yes. But—to come back to the matter in hand—that must have been a very trying time for your, Mrs. Helmer?

NORA. It was, indeed.

KROGSTAD. Your father was very ill, wasn't he?

NORA. He was very near his end.

KROGSTAD. And died soon afterwards?

NORA. Yes.

KROGSTAD. Tell me, Mrs. Helmer, can you by any chance remember what day your father died?—on what day of the month, I mean.

NORA. Papa died on the 29th of September.

KROGSTAD. That is correct; I have ascertained it for myself. And, as that is so, there is a discrepancy [*taking a paper from his pocket*] which I cannot account for.

NORA. What discrepancy? I don't know—

KROGSTAD. The discrepancy consists, Mrs. Helmer, in the fact that your father signed this bond three days after his death.

NORA. What do you mean? I don't understand—

KROGSTAD. Your father died on the 29th of September. But, look here; your father has dated his signature the 2nd of October. It is a discrepancy, isn't it? [*NORA is silent.*] Can you explain it to me? [*NORA is still silent.*] It is a remarkable thing, too, that the words "2nd of October," as well as the year, are not written in your father's handwriting but in one that I think I know. Well, of course it can be explained; your father may have forgotten to date his signature, and someone else may have dated it haphazard before they knew of his death. There is no harm in that. It all depends on the signature of the name; and *that* is genuine, I suppose, Mrs. Helmer? It was your father himself who signed his name here?

NORA.   [*after a short pause, throws her head up and looks defiantly at him*] No, it was not. It was I that wrote papa's name.

KROGSTAD.   Are you aware that is a dangerous confession?

NORA.   In what way? You shall have your money soon.   405

KROGSTAD.   Let me ask you a question; why did you not send the paper to your father?

NORA.   It was impossible; papa was so ill. If I had asked him for his signature, I should have had to tell him what the money was to be used for; and when he was so ill himself I couldn't tell him that my husband's life was in danger—it was impossible.

KROGSTAD.   It would have been better for you if you had given up your trip abroad.

NORA.   No, that was impossible. That trip was to save my husband's life; I couldn't give that up.

KROGSTAD.   But did it never occur to you that you were committing a fraud on   410 me?

NORA.   I couldn't take that into account; I didn't trouble myself about you at all. I couldn't bear you, because you put so many heartless difficulties in my way, although you knew what a dangerous condition my husband was in.

KROGSTAD.   Mrs. Helmer, you evidently do not realise clearly what it is that you have been guilty of. But I can assure you that my one false step, which lost me all my reputation, was nothing more or nothing worse than what you have done.

NORA.   You? Do you ask me to believe that you were brave enough to run a risk to save your wife's life?

KROGSTAD.   The law cares nothing about motives.

NORA.   Then it must be a very foolish law.   415

KROGSTAD.   Foolish or not, it is the law by which you will be judged, if I produce this paper in court.

NORA.   I don't believe it. Is a daughter not to be allowed to spare her dying father anxiety and care? Is a wife not to be allowed to save her husband's life? I don't know much about law; but I am certain that there must be laws permitting such things as that. Have you no knowledge of such laws—you who are a lawyer? You must be a very poor lawyer, Mr. Krogstad.

KROGSTAD.   Maybe. But matters of business—such business as you and I have had together—do you think I don't understand that? Very well. Do as you please. But let me tell you this—if I lose my position a second time, you shall lose yours with me.

[*He bows, and goes out through the hall.*]

NORA.   [*appears buried in thought for a short time, then tosses her head*] Nonsense! Trying to frighten me like that!—I am not so silly as he thinks. [*begins to busy herself putting the children's things in order*] And yet—? No, it's impossible! I did it for love's sake.

THE CHILDREN.   [*in the doorway on the left*] Mother, the stranger man has gone out   420 through the gate.

NORA.   Yes, dears, I know. But, don't tell anyone about the stranger man. Do you hear? Not even papa.

CHILDREN.   No, mother; but will you come and play again?

NORA.   No, no—not now.

CHILDREN.   But, mother, you promised us.

NORA.   Yes, but I can't now. Run away in; I have such a lot to do. Run away in, my sweet little darlings. [*She gets them into the room by degrees and shuts the door on them; then sits down on the sofa, takes up a piece of needlework and sews a few stitches, but soon stops.*] No! [*throws down the work, gets up, goes to the hall door and calls out*] Helen! bring the Tree in. [*goes to the table on the left, opens a drawer, and stops again*] No, no! it is quite impossible!

MAID.   [*coming in with the Tree*] Where shall I put it, ma'am?

NORA.   Here, in the middle of the floor.

MAID.   Shall I get you anything else?

NORA.   No, thank you. I have all I want.   [*Exit* MAID.]

NORA.   [*begins dressing the tree*] A candle here—and flowers here—. The horrible man! It's all nonsense—there's nothing wrong. The Tree shall be splendid! I will do everything I can think of to please you, Torvald!—I will sing for you, dance for you— [HELMER *comes in with some papers under his arm*] Oh! are you back already?

HELMER.   Yes. Has anyone been here?

NORA.   Here? No.

HELMER.   That is strange. I saw Krogstad going out of the gate.

NORA.   Did you? Oh yes, I forgot, Krogstad was here for a moment.

HELMER.   Nora, I can see from your manner that he has been here begging you to say a good word for him.

NORA.   Yes.

HELMER.   And you were to appear to do it of your own accord; you were to conceal from me the fact of his having been here; didn't he beg that of you too?

NORA.   Yes, Torvald, but—

HELMER.   Nora, Nora, and you would be a party to that sort of thing? To have any talk with a man like that, and give him any sort of promise? And to tell me a lie into the bargain?

NORA.   A lie—?

HELMER.   Didn't you tell me no one had been here? [*shakes his finger at her*] My little song-bird must never do that again. A song-bird must have a clean beak to chirp with—no false notes! [*puts his arm round her waist*] That is so, isn't it? Yes, I am sure it is. [*lets her go*] We will say no more about it. [*sits down by the stove*] How warm and snug it is here!

[*Turns over his papers.*]

NORA.   [*after a short pause, during which she busies herself with the Christmas Tree*] Torvald!

HELMER.   Yes.

NORA.   I am looking forward tremendously to the fancy dress ball at the Stenborgs' the day after to-morrow.

HELMER.   And I am tremendously curious to see what you are going to surprise me with.

NORA.   It was very silly of me to want to do that.

HELMER.   What do you mean?

NORA.   I can't hit upon anything that will do; everything I think of seems so silly and insignificant.

HELMER.   Does my little Nora acknowledge that at last?

NORA.   [*standing behind his chair with her arms on the back of it*] Are you very busy, Torvald?   450

HELMER.   Well—

NORA.   What are all those papers?

HELMER.   Bank business.

NORA.   Already?

HELMER.   I have got authority from the retiring manager to undertake the nec-   455
essary changes in the staff and in the rearrangement of the work; and I must make use of the Christmas week for that, so as to have everything in order for the new year.

NORA.   Then that was why this poor Krogstad—

HELMER.   Hm!

NORA.   [*leans against the back of his chair and strokes his hair*] If you hadn't been so busy I should have asked you a tremendously big favour, Torvald.

HELMER.   What is that? Tell me.

NORA.   There is no one has such good taste as you. And I do so want to look nice   460
at the fancy-dress ball. Torvald, couldn't you take me in hand and decide what I shall go as, and what sort of a dress I shall wear?

HELMER.   Aha! so my obstinate little woman is obliged to get someone to come to her rescue?

NORA.   Yes, Torvald, I can't get along a bit without your help.

HELMER.   Very well, I will think it over, we shall manage to hit upon something.

NORA.   That *is* nice of you. [*goes to the Christmas Tree. A short pause.*] How pretty the red flowers look—. But, tell me, was it really something very bad that this Krogstad was guilty of?

HELMER.   He forged someone's name. Have you any idea what that means?   465

NORA.   Isn't it possible that he was driven to do it by necessity?

HELMER.   Yes; or, as in so many cases, by imprudence. I am not so heartless as to condemn a man altogether because of a single false step of that kind.

NORA.   No you wouldn't, would you, Torvald?

HELMER.   Many a man has been able to retrieve his character, if he has openly confessed his fault and taken his punishment.

NORA.   Punishment—?   470

HELMER.   But Krogstad did nothing of that sort; he got himself out of it by a cunning trick, and that is why he has gone under altogether.

NORA.   But do you think it would—?

HELMER.   Just think how a guilty man like that has to lie and play the hypocrite with everyone, how he has to wear a mask in the presence of those near and dear to him, even before his own wife and children. And about the children—that is the most terrible part of it all, Nora.

NORA.   How?

HELMER.   Because such an atmosphere of lies infects and poisons the whole life   475
of a home. Each breath the children take in such a house is full of the germs of evil.

NORA.   [*coming nearer him*] Are you sure of that?

HELMER.   My dear, I have often seen it in the course of my life as a lawyer. Almost everyone who has gone to the bad early in life has had a deceitful mother.

NORA.   Why do you only say—mother?

HELMER.   It seems most commonly to be the mother's influence, though naturally a bad father's would have the same result. Every lawyer is familiar with the fact. This Krogstad, now, has been persistently poisoning his own children with lies and dissimulation; that is why I say he has lost all moral character. [*holds out his hands to her*] That is why my sweet little Nora must promise me not to plead his cause. Give me your hand on it. Come, come, what is this? Give me your hand. There now, that's settled. I assure you it would be quite impossible for me to work with him; I literally feel physically ill when I am in the company of such people.

NORA.   [*takes her hand out of his and goes to the opposite side of the Christmas Tree*] How hot it is in here; and I have such a lot to do.

HELMER.   [*getting up and putting his papers in order*] Yes, and I must try and read through some of these before dinner; and I must think about your costume, too. And it is just possible I may have something ready in gold paper to hang up on the Tree. [*Puts his hand on her head.*] My precious little singing-bird!

[*He goes into his room and shuts the door after him.*]

NORA.   [*after a pause, whispers*] No, no—it isn't true. It's impossible; it must be impossible.

[*The NURSE opens the door on the left.*]

NURSE.   The little ones are begging so hard to be allowed to come in to mamma.

NORA.   No, no, no! Don't let them come in to me! You stay with them, Anne.

NURSE.   Very well, ma'am.

[*Shuts the door.*]

NORA.   [*pale with terror*] Deprave my little children? Poison my home? [*a short pause. Then she tosses her head.*] It's not true. It can't possibly be true.

ACT 2

THE SAME SCENE. *The Christmas Tree is in the corner by the piano, stripped of its ornaments and with burnt-down candle-ends on its dishevelled branches. NORA'S cloak and hat are lying on the sofa. She is alone in the room, walking about uneasily. She stops by the sofa and takes up her cloak.*

NORA.   [*drops the cloak*] Someone is coming now! [*goes to the door and listens*] No—it is no one. Of course, no one will come to-day, Christmas Day—nor tomorrow either. But, perhaps—[*opens the door and looks out*] No, nothing in the letter-box; it is quite empty. [*comes forward*] What rubbish! of course he can't be in earnest about it. Such a thing couldn't happen; it is impossible—I have three little children.

[*Enter the NURSE from the room on the left, carrying a big cardboard box.*]

NURSE.   At last I have found the box with the fancy dress.

NORA.   Thanks; put it on the table.

NURSE.   [*doing so*] But it is very much in want of mending.

NORA.   I should like to tear it into a hundred thousand pieces.

NURSE.   What an idea! It can easily be put in order—just a little patience.

NORA. Yes, I will go and get Mrs. Linde to come and help me with it.

NURSE. What, out again? In this horrible weather? You will catch cold, ma'am, and make yourself ill.

NORA. Well, worse than that might happen. How are the children?

NURSE. The poor little souls are playing with their Christmas presents, but— 10

NORA. Do they ask much for me?

NURSE. You see, they are so accustomed to have their mamma with them.

NORA. Yes, but, nurse, I shall not be able to be so much with them now as I was before.

NURSE. Oh well, young children easily get accustomed to anything.

NORA. Do you think so? Do you think they would forget their mother if she went 15
away altogether?

NURSE. Good heavens!—went away altogether?

NORA. Nurse, I want you to tell me something I have often wondered about—how could you have the heart to put your own child out among strangers?

NURSE. I was obliged to, if I wanted to be little Nora's nurse.

NORA. Yes, but how could you be willing to do it?

NURSE. What, when I was going to get such a good place by it? A poor girl who 20
has got into trouble should be glad to. Besides, that wicked man didn't do a single thing for me.

NORA. But I suppose your daughter has quite forgotten you.

NURSE. No, indeed she hasn't. She wrote to me when she was confirmed, and when she was married.

NORA. [*putting her arms round her neck*] Dear old Anne, you were a good mother to me when I was little.

NURSE. Little Nora, poor dear, had no other mother but me.

NORA. And if my little ones had no other mother, I am sure you would—What 25
nonsense I am talking! [*opens the box*] Go in to them. Now I must—. You will see to-morrow how charming I shall look.

NURSE. I am sure there will be no one at the ball so charming as you, ma'am.

[*Goes into the room on the left.*]

NORA. [*begins to unpack the box, but soon pushes it away from her*] If only I dared go out. If only no one would come. If only I could be sure nothing would happen here in the meantime. Stuff and nonsense! No one will come. Only I mustn't think about it. I will brush my muff. What, lovely gloves! Out of my thoughts, out of my thoughts! One, two, three, four, five, six—[*screams.*] Ah! there is someone coming—

[*Makes a movement towards the door, but stands irresolute.*]

[*Enter MRS. LINDE from the hall, where she has taken off her cloak and hat.*]

NORA. Oh, it's you, Christine. There is no one else out there, is there? How good of you to come!

MRS. LINDE. I heard you were up asking for me.

NORA. Yes, I was passing by. As a matter of fact, it is something you could help me 30
with. Let us sit down here on the sofa. Look here. To-morrow evening there is to be a fancy-dress ball at the Stenborgs', who live about us; and Torvald wants me to go as a Neapolitan fisher-girl, and dance the Tarantella that I learnt at Capri.

MRS. LINDE.   I see; you are going to keep up the character.

NORA.   Yes, Torvald wants me to. Look, here is the dress; Torvald had it made for me there, but now it is all so torn, and I haven't any idea—

MRS. LINDE.   We will easily put that right. It is only some of the trimming come unsewn here and there. Needle and thread? Now then, that's all we want.

NORA.   It *is* nice of you.

MRS. LINDE.   [*sewing*] So you are going to be dressed up to-morrow, Nora. I will tell you what—I shall come in for a moment and see you in your fine feathers. But I have completely forgotten to thank you for a delightful evening yesterday.

NORA.   [*gets up, and crosses the stages*] Well I don't think yesterday was a pleasant as usual. You ought to have come to town a little earlier, Christine. Certainly Torvald does understand how to make a house dainty and attractive.

MRS. LINDE.   And so do you, it seems to me; you are not your father's daughter for nothing. But tell me, is Doctor Rank always as depressed as he was yesterday?

NORA.   No; yesterday it was very noticeable. I must tell you that he suffers from a very dangerous disease. He has consumption of the spine, poor creature. His father was a horrible man who committed all sorts of excesses; and that is why his son was sickly from childhood, do you understand?

MRS. LINDE.   [*dropping her sewing*] But, my dearest Nora, how do you know anything about such things?

NORA.   [*walking about*] Pooh! When you have three children, you get visits now and then from—from married women, who know something of medical matters, and they talk about one thing and another.

MRS. LINDE.   [*goes on sewing. A short silence*] Does Doctor Rank come here every day?

NORA.   Every day regularly. He is Torvald's most intimate friend, and a great friend of mine too. He is just like one of the family.

MRS. LINDE.   But tell me this—is he perfectly sincere? I mean, isn't he the kind of man that is very anxious to make himself agreeable?

NORA.   Not in the least. What makes you think that?

MRS. LINDE.   When you introduced him to me yesterday, he declared he had often heard my name mentioned in this house; but afterwards I noticed that your husband hadn't the slightest idea who I was. So how could Doctor Rank—?

NORA.   That is quite right, Christine. Torvald is so absurdly fond of me that he wants me absolutely to himself, as he says. At first he used to seem almost jealous if I mentioned any of the dear folk at home, so naturally I gave up doing so. But I often talk about such things with Doctor Rank, because he likes hearing about them.

MRS. LINDE.   Listen to me, Nora. You are still very like a child in many things, and I am older than you in many ways and have a little more experience. Let me tell you this—you ought to make an end of it with Doctor Rank.

NORA.   What ought I to make an end of?

MRS. LINDE.   Of two things, I think. Yesterday you talked some nonsense about a rich admirer who was to leave you money—

NORA.   An admirer who doesn't exist, unfortunately! But what then?

MRS. LINDE.   Is Doctor Rank a man of means?

NORA.   Yes, he is.

MRS. LINDE.   And has no one to provide for?

NORA.   No, no one; but—

MRS. LINDE. And comes here every day? 55

NORA. Yes, I told you so.

MRS. LINDE. But how can this well-bred man be so tactless?

NORA. I don't understand you at all.

MRS. LINDE. Don't prevaricate, Nora. Do you suppose I don't guess who lent you the two hundred and fifty pounds?

NORA. Are you out of your senses? How can you think of such a thing! A friend 60
of ours, who comes here every day! Do you realise what a horribly painful position that would be?

MRS. LINDE. Then it really isn't he?

NORA. No, certainly not. It would never have entered into my head for a moment. Besides, he had no money to lend then; he came into his money afterwards.

MRS. LINDE. Well, I think that was lucky for you, my dear Nora.

NORA. No, it would never have come into my head to ask Doctor Rank. Although I am quite sure that if I had asked him—

MRS. LINDE. But of course you won't. 65

NORA. Of course not. I have no reason to think it could possibly be necessary. But I am quite sure that if I told Doctor Rank—

MRS. LINDE. Behind your husband's back?

NORA. I must make an end of it with the other one, and that will be behind his back too. I *must* make an end of it with him.

MRS. LINDE. Yes, that is what I told you yesterday, but—

NORA. [*walking up and down*] A man can put a thing like that straight much 70
easier than a woman—

MRS. LINDE. One's husband, yes.

NORA. Nonsense! [*standing still*] When you pay off a debt you get your bond back, don't you?

MRS. LINDE. Yes, as a matter of course.

NORA. And can tear it into a hundred thousand pieces, and burn it up—the nasty dirty paper!

MRS. LINDE. [*looks hard at her, lays down her sewing and gets up slowly*] Nora, you are 75
concealing something from me.

NORA. Do I look as if I were?

MRS. LINDE. Something has happened to you since yesterday morning. Nora, what is it?

NORA. [*going nearer to her*] Christine! [*listens*] Hush! there's Torvald come home. Do you mind going in to the children for the present? Torvald can't bear to see dressmaking going on. Let Anne help you.

MRS. LINDE. [*gathering some of the things together*] Certainly—but I am not going away from here till we have had it out with one another.

[*She goes into the room on the left, as HELMER comes in from the hall.*]

NORA. [*going up to HELMER*] I have wanted you so much, Torvald dear. 80

HELMER. Was that the dressmaker?

NORA. No, it was Christine; she is helping me to put my dress in order. You will see I shall look quite smart.

HELMER. Wasn't that a happy thought of mine, now?

NORA. Splendid! But don't you think it is nice of me, too, to do as you wish?

HELMER.   Nice?—because you do as your husband wishes? Well, well, you little rogue, I am sure you did not mean it in that way. But I am not going to disturb you; you will want to be trying on your dress, I expect.

NORA.   I suppose you are going to work.

HELMER.   Yes. [*shows her a bundle of papers*] Look at that. I have just been into the bank. [*Turns to go into his room.*]

NORA.   Torvald.

HELMER.   Yes.

NORA.   If your little squirrel were to ask you for something very, very prettily—?

HELMER.   What then?

NORA.   Would you do it?

HELMER.   I should like to hear what it is, first.

NORA.   Your squirrel would run about and do all her tricks if you would be nice, and do what she wants.

HELMER.   Speak plainly.

NORA.   Your skylark would chirp about in every room, with her song rising and falling—

HELMER.   Well, my skylark does that anyhow.

NORA.   I would play the fairy and dance for you in the moonlight, Torvald.

HELMER.   Nora—you surely don't mean that request you made of me this morning?

NORA.   [*going near him*] Yes, Torvald, I beg you so earnestly—

HELMER.   Have you really the courage to open up that question again?

NORA.   Yes, dear, you *must* do as I ask; you *must* let Krogstad keep his post in the Bank.

HELMER.   My dear Nora, it is his post that I have arranged Mrs. Linde shall have.

NORA.   Yes, you have been awfully kind about that; but you could just as well dismiss some other clerk instead of Krogstad.

HELMER.   This is simply incredible obstinacy! Because you chose to give him a thoughtless promise that you would speak for him, I am expected to—

NORA.   That isn't the reason, Torvald. It is for your own sake. This fellow writes in the most scurrilous newspapers; you have told me so yourself. He can do you an unspeakable amount of harm. I am frightened to death of him—

HELMER.   Ah, I understand; it is recollections of the past that scare you.

NORA.   What do you mean?

HELMER.   Naturally you are thinking of your father.

NORA.   Yes—yes, of course. Just recall to your mind what these malicious creatures wrote in the papers about papa, and how horribly they slandered him. I believe they would have procured his dismissal if the Department had not sent you over to inquire into it, and if you had not been so kindly disposed and helpful to him.

HELMER.   My little Nora, there is an important difference between your father and me. Your father's reputation as a public official was not above suspicion. Mine is, and I hope it will continue to be so, as long as I hold my office.

NORA.   You never can tell what mischief these men may contrive. We ought to be so well off, so snug and happy here in our peaceful home, and have no cares—you and I and the children, Torvald! That is why I beg you so earnestly—

HELMER.   And it is just by interceding for him that you make it impossible for me to keep him. It is already known at the Bank that I mean to dismiss Krogstad. Is it to get about now that the new manager has changed his mind at his wife's bidding—

NORA.   And what if it did?

HELMER.   Of course!—if only this obstinate little person can get her way! Do you   115
suppose I am going to make myself ridiculous before my whole staff, to let people think
that I am a man to be swayed by all sorts of outside influence? I should very soon feel the
consequences of it, I can tell you! And besides, there is one thing that makes it quite
impossible for me to have Krogstad in the Bank as long as I am manager.

NORA.   Whatever is that?

HELMER.   His moral failings I might perhaps have overlooked, if necessary—

NORA.   Yes, you could—couldn't you?

HELMER.   And I hear he is a good worker, too. But I knew him when we were
boys. It was one of those rash friendships that so often prove an incubus in after life. I
may as well tell you plainly, we were once on very intimate terms with one another. But
this tactless fellow lays no restraint on himself when other people are present. On the
contrary, he thinks it gives him the right to adopt a familiar tone with me, and every
minute it is "I say, Helmer, old fellow!" and that sort of thing. I assure you it is extremely
painful for me. He would make my position in the Bank intolerable.

NORA.   Torvald, I don't believe you mean that.   120

HELMER.   Don't you? Why not?

NORA.   Because it is such a narrow-minded way of looking at things.

HELMER.   What are you saying? Narrow-minded? Do you think I am narrow-
minded?

NORA.   No, just the opposite, dear—and it is exactly for that reason.

HELMER.   It's the same thing. You say my point of view is narrow-minded, so I   125
must be so too. Narrow-minded! Very well—I must put an end to this. [*Goes to the halldoor and calls.*] Helen!

NORA.   What are you going to do?

HELMER.   [*looking among his papers*] Settle it. [*Enter* MAID.] Look here; take this
letter and go downstairs with it at once. Find a messenger and tell him to deliver it, and
be quick. The address is on it, and here is the money.

Maid.   Very well, sir.

[*Exits with the letter.*]

HELMER.   [*putting his papers together*] Now then, little Miss Obstinate.

NORA.   [*breathlessly*] Torvald—what was that letter?   130

HELMER.   Krogstad's dismissal.

NORA.   Call her back, Torvald! There is still time. Oh Torvald, call her back! Do it
for my sake—for your own sake—for the children's sake! Do you hear me, Torvald? Call
her back!! You don't know what that letter can bring upon us.

HELMER.   It's too late.

NORA.   Yes, it's too late.

HELMER.   My dear Nora, I can forgive the anxiety you are in, although really it is   135
an insult to me. It is, indeed. Isn't it an insult to think that I should be afraid of a starving
quill-driver's vengeance? But I forgive you nevertheless, because it is such eloquent witness to your great love for me. [*takes her in his arms*] And that is as it should be, my own
darling Nora. Come what will, you may be sure I shall have both courage and strength if
they be needed. You will see I am man enough to take everything upon myself.

NORA.   [*in a horror-stricken voice*] What do you mean by that?

HELMER.   Everything, I say—

NORA.   [*recovering herself*] You will never have to do that.

HELMER.   That's right. Well, we will share it, Nora, as man and wife should. That is how it shall be. [*caressing her*] Are you content now? There! there!—not these frightened dove's eyes! The whole thing is only the wildest fancy!—Now, you must go and play through the Tarantella and practise with your tambourine. I shall go into the inner office and shut the door, and I shall hear nothing; you can make as much noise as you please. [*turns back at the door*] And when Rank comes, tell him where he will find me.

[*Nods to her, takes his papers and goes into his room, and shuts the door after him*]

NORA.   [*bewildered with anxiety, stands as if rooted to the spot, and whispers*] He is capable of doing it. He will do it. He will do it in spite of everything.—No, not that! Never, never! Anything rather than that! Oh, for some help, some way out of it! [*The door-bell rings.*] Doctor Rank! Anything rather than that—anything, whatever it is!

[*She puts her hands over her face, pulls herself together, goes to the door and opens it. RANK is standing without, hanging up his coat. During the following dialogue it begins to grow dark.*]

NORA.   Good-day, Doctor Rank. I knew your ring. But you mustn't go in to Torvald now; I think he is busy with something.

RANK.   And you?

NORA.   [*brings him in and shuts the door after him*] Oh, you know very well I always have time for you.

RANK.   Thank you. I shall make use of as much of it as I can.

NORA.   What do you mean by that? As much of it as you can?

RANK.   Well, does that alarm you?

NORA.   It was such a strange way of putting it. Is anything likely to happen?

RANK.   Nothing but what I have long been prepared for. But I certainly didn't expect it to happen so soon.

NORA.   [*gripping him by the arm*] What have you found out? Doctor Rank, you must tell me.

RANK.   [*sitting down by the stove*] It is all up with me. And it can't be helped.

NORA.   [*with a sigh of relief*] Is it about yourself?

RANK.   Who else? It is no use lying to one's self. I am the most wretched of all my patients, Mrs. Helmer. Lately I have been taking stock of my internal economy. Bankrupt! Probably within a month I shall lie rotting in the churchyard.

NORA.   What an ugly thing to say!

RANK.   The thing itself is cursedly ugly, and the worst of it is that I shall have to face so much more that is ugly before that. I shall only make one more examination of myself; when I have done that, I shall know pretty certainly when it will be that the horrors of dissolution will begin. There is something I want to tell you. Helmer's refined nature gives him an unconquerable disgust at everything that is ugly; I won't have him in my sick-room.

NORA.   Oh, but, Doctor Rank—

RANK.   I won't have him there. Not on any account. I bar my door to him. As soon as I am quite certain that the worst has come, I shall send you my card with a black cross on it, and then you will know that the loathsome end has begun.

NORA.   You are quite absurd to-day. And I wanted you so much to be in a really good humour.

RANK. With death stalking beside me?—To have to pay this penalty for another man's sin! Is there any justice in that? And in every single family, in one way or another, some such inexorable retribution is being exacted—

NORA. [*putting her hands over her ears*] Rubbish! Do talk of something cheerful.

RANK. Oh, it's a mere laughing matter, the whole thing. My poor innocent spine   160
has to suffer for my father's youthful amusements.

NORA. [*sitting at the table on the left*] I suppose you mean that he was too partial to asparagus and pâté de foie gras, don't you.

RANK. Yes, and to truffles.

NORA. Truffles, yes. And oysters too, I suppose?

RANK. Oysters, of course, that goes without saying.

NORA. And heaps of port and champagne. It is sad that all these nice things   165
should take their revenge on our bones.

RANK. Especially that they should revenge themselves on the unlucky bones of those who have not had the satisfaction of enjoying them.

NORA. Yes, that's the saddest part of it all.

RANK. [*with a searching look at her*] Hm!—

NORA. [*after a short pause*] Why did you smile?

RANK. No, it was you that laughed.   170

NORA. No, it was you that smiled, Doctor Rank!

RANK. [*rising*] You are a greater rascal than I thought.

NORA. I am in a silly mood to-day.

RANK. So it seems.

NORA. [*putting her hands on his shoulders*] Dear, dear Doctor Rank, death mustn't   175
take you away from Torvald and me.

RANK. It is a loss you would easily recover from. Those who are gone are soon forgotten.

NORA. [*looking at him anxiously*] Do you believe that?

RANK. People form new ties, and then—

NORA. Who will form new ties?

RANK. Both you and Helmer, when I am gone. You yourself are already on the   180
high road to it, I think. What did that Mrs. Linde want here last night?

NORA. Oho!—you don't mean to say you are jealous of poor Christine?

RANK. Yes, I am. She will be my successor in this house. When I am done for, this woman will—

NORA. Hush! don't speak so loud. She is in that room.

RANK. To-day again. There, you see.

NORA. She has only come to sew my dress for me. Bless my soul, how unreason-   185
able you are! [*sits down on the sofa*] Be nice now, Doctor Rank, and tomorrow you will see how beautifully I shall dance, and you can imagine I am doing it all for you—and for Torvald too, of course. [*takes various things out of the box*] Doctor Rank, come and sit down here, and I will show you something.

RANK. [*sitting down*] What is it?

NORA. Just look at those!

RANK. Silk stockings.

NORA. Flesh-coloured. Aren't they lovely? It is so dark here now, but to-morrow—. No, no, no! you must only look at the feet. Oh well, you may have leave to look at the legs too.

RANK. Hm!—   190

NORA.   Why are you looking so critical? Don't you think they will fit me?

RANK.   I have no means of forming an opinion about that.

NORA.   [*looks at him for a moment*] For shame! [*hits him lightly on the ear with the stockings*] That's to punish you. [*folds them up again*]

RANK.   And what other nice things am I to be allowed to see?

NORA.   Not a single thing more, for being so naughty. [*She looks among the things, humming to herself.*]

RANK.   [*after a short silence*] When I am sitting here, talking to you as intimately as this, I cannot imagine for a moment what would have become of me if I had never come into this house.

NORA.   [*smiling*] I believe you do feel thoroughly at home with us.

RANK.   [*in a lower voice, looking straight in front of him*] And to be obliged to leave it all—

NORA.   Nonsense, you are not going to leave it.

RANK.   [*as before*] And not be able to leave behind one the slightest token of one's gratitude, scarcely even a fleeting regret—nothing but an empty place which the first comer can fill as well as any other.

NORA.   And if I asked you now for a—? No!

RANK.   For what?

NORA.   For a big proof of your friendship—

RANK.   Yes, yes!

NORA.   I mean a tremendously big favour—

RANK.   Would you really make me so happy for once?

NORA.   Ah, but you don't know what it is yet.

RANK.   No—but tell me.

NORA.   I really can't, Doctor Rank. It is something out of all reason; it means advice, and help, and a favour—

RANK.   The bigger a thing it is the better. I can't conceive what it is you mean. Do tell me. Haven't I your confidence?

NORA.   More than anyone else. I know you are my truest and best friend, and so I will tell you what it is. Well, Doctor Rank, it is something you must help me to prevent. You know how devotedly, how inexpressibly deeply Torvald loves me; he would never for a moment hesitate to give his life for me.

RANK.   [*leaning towards her*] Nora—do you think he is the only one—?

NORA.   [*with a slight start*] The only one—?

RANK.   The only one who would gladly give his life for your sake.

NORA.   [*sadly*] Is that it?

RANK.   I was determined you should know it before I went away, and there will never be a better opportunity than this. Now you know it, Nora. And now you know, too, that you can trust me as you would trust no one else.

NORA.   [*rises, deliberately and quietly*] Let me pass.

RANK.   [*makes room for her to pass him, but sits still*] Nora!

NORA.   [*at the hall door*] Helen, bring in the lamp. [*goes over to the stove*] Dear Doctor Rank, that was really horrid of you.

RANK.   To have loved you as much as anyone else does? Was that horrid?

NORA.   No, but to go and tell me so. There was really no need—

RANK.   What do you mean? Did you know—? [*MAID enters with lamp, puts it down on the table, and goes out.*] Nora—Mrs. Helmer—tell me, had you any idea of this?

NORA.   Oh, how do I know whether I had or whether I hadn't? I really can't tell you— To think you could be so clumsy, Doctor Rank! We were getting on so nicely.

RANK.   Well, at all events you know now that you can command me, body and soul. So won't you speak out?

NORA.   [*looking at him*] After what happened?   225

RANK.   I beg you to let me know what it is.

NORA.   I can't tell you anything now.

RANK.   Yes, yes. You mustn't punish me in that way. Let me have permission to do for you whatever a man may do.

NORA.   You can do nothing for me now. Besides, I really don't need any help at all. You will find that the whole thing is merely fancy on my part. It really is so—of course it is! [*Sits down in the rocking-chair, and looks at him with a smile*] You are a nice sort of man, Doctor Rank!—don't you feel ashamed of yourself, now the lamp has come?

RANK.   Not a bit. But perhaps I had better go—for ever?   230

NORA.   No, indeed, you shall not. Of course you must come here just as before. You know very well Torvald can't do without you.

RANK.   Yes, but you?

NORA.   Oh, I am always tremendously pleased when you come.

RANK.   It is just that, that put me on the wrong track. You are a riddle to me. I have often thought that you would almost as soon be in my company as in Helmer's.

NORA.   Yes—you see there are some people one loves best, and others whom one   235
would almost always rather have as companions.

RANK.   Yes, there is something in that.

NORA.   When I was at home, of course I loved papa best. But I always thought it tremendous fun if I could steal down into the maid's room, because they never moralised at all, and talked to each other about such entertaining things.

RANK.   I see—it is *their* place I have taken.

NORA.   [*jumping up and going to him*] Oh, dear, nice Doctor Rank, I never meant that at all. But surely you can understand that being with Torvald is a little like being with papa—

[*Enter* MAID *from the hall*]

MAID.   If you please, ma'am. [*whispers and hands her a card*]   240

NORA.   [*glancing at the card*] Oh! [*puts it in her pocket*]

RANK.   Is there anything wrong?

NORA.   No, no, not in the least. It is only something—it is my new dress—

RANK.   What? Your dress is lying there.

NORA.   Oh, yes, that one; but this is another. I ordered it. Torvald mustn't know   245
about it—

RANK.   Oho! Then that was the great secret.

NORA.   Of course. Just go in to him; he is sitting in the inner room. Keep him as long as—

RANK.   Make your mind easy; I won't let him escape. [*goes into* HELMER'S *room*]

NORA.   [*to the* MAID] And he is standing waiting in the kitchen?

MAID.   Yes; he came up the back stairs.   250

NORA.   But didn't you tell him no one was in?

MAID.   Yes, but it was no good.

NORA.   He won't go away?

MAID.   No; he says he won't until he has seen you, ma'am.

NORA.   Well, let him come in—but quietly. Helen, you mustn't say anything about it to anyone. It is a surprise for my husband.

MAID.   Yes, ma'am, I quite understand. [*Exit.*]

NORA.   This dreadful thing is going to happen! It will happen in spite of me! No, no, no, it can't happen—it shan't happen!

[*She bolts the door of* HELMER'S *room. The* MAID *opens the hall door for* KROGSTAD *and shuts it after him. He is wearing a fur coat, high boots and a fur cap.*]

NORA.   [*advancing towards him*] Speak low—my husband is at home.

KROGSTAD.   No matter about that.

NORA.   What do you want of me?

KROGSTAD.   An explanation of something.

NORA.   Make haste then. What is it?

KROGSTAD.   You know, I suppose, that I have got my dismissal.

NORA.   I couldn't prevent it, Mr. Krogstad. I fought as hard as I could on your side, but it was no good.

KROGSTAD.   Does your husband love you so little, then? He knows that what I can expose you to, and yet he ventures—

NORA.   How can you suppose that he has any knowledge of the sort?

KROGSTAD.   I didn't suppose so at all. It would not be the least like our dear Torvald Helmer to show so much courage—

NORA.   Mr. Krogstad, a little respect for my husband, please.

KROGSTAD.   Certainly—all the respect he deserves. But since you have kept the matter so carefully to yourself, I make bold to suppose that you have a little clearer idea, than you had yesterday, of what it actually is that you have done?

NORA.   More than you could ever teach me.

KROGSTAD.   Yes, such a bad lawyer as I am.

NORA.   What is it you want of me?

KROGSTAD.   Only to see how you were, Mrs. Helmer. I have been thinking about you all day long. A mere cashier, a quill-driver, a—well, a man like me—even he has a little of what is called feeling, you know.

NORA.   Show it, then; think of my little children.

KROGSTAD.   Have you and your husband thought of mine? But never mind about that. I only wanted to tell you that you need not take this matter too seriously. In the first place there will be no accusation made on my part.

NORA.   No, of course not; I was sure of that.

KROGSTAD.   The whole thing can be arranged amicably; there is no reason why anyone should know anything about it. It will remain a secret between us three.

NORA.   My husband must never get to know anything about it.

KROGSTAD.   How will you be able to prevent it? Am I to understand that you can pay the balance that is owing?

NORA.   No, not just at present.

KROGSTAD.   Or perhaps that you have some expedient for raising the money soon?

NORA.   No expedient that I mean to make use of.

KROGSTAD.   Well, in any case, it would have been of no use to you now. If you stood there with ever so much money in your hand, I would never part with your bond.

NORA.   Tell me what purpose you mean to put it to.

KROGSTAD. I shall only preserve it—keep it in my possession. No one who is not 285
concerned in the matter shall have the slightest hint of it. So that if the thought of it
has driven you to any desperate resolution—

NORA. It has.

KROGSTAD. If you had it in your mind to run away from your home—

NORA. I had.

KROGSTAD. Or even something worse—

NORA. How could you know that? 290

KROGSTAD. Give up the idea.

NORA. How did you know I had thought of *that*?

KROGSTAD. Most of us think of that at first. I did, too—but I hadn't the courage.

NORA. [*faintly*] No more had I.

KROGSTAD. [*in a tone of relief*] No, that's it, isn't it—you hadn't the courage 295
either?

NORA. No, I haven't—I haven't.

KROGSTAD. Besides, it would have been a great piece of folly. Once the first storm
at home is over—. I have a letter for your husband in my pocket.

NORA. Telling him everything?

KROGSTAD. In as lenient a manner as I possibly could.

NORA. [*quickly*] He mustn't get the letter. Tear it up. I will find some means of 300
getting money.

KROGSTAD. Excuse me, Mrs. Helmer, but I think I told you just now—

NORA. I am not speaking of what I owe you. Tell me what sum you are asking
my husband for, and I will get the money.

KROGSTAD. I am not asking your husband for a penny.

NORA. What do you want, then?

KROGSTAD. I will tell you. I want to rehabilitate myself, Mrs. Helmer; I want to 305
get on; and in that your husband must help me. For the last year and a half I have not
had a hand in anything dishonourable, and all that time I have been struggling in most
restricted circumstances. I was content to work my way up step by step. Now I am turned
out, and I am not going to be satisfied with merely being taken into favour again. I want
to get on, I tell you. I want to get into the Bank again, in a higher position. Your husband
must make a place for me—

NORA. That he will never do!

KROGSTAD. He will; I know him; he dare not protest. And as soon as I am in there
again with him, then you will see! Within a year I shall be the manager's right hand. It
will be Nils Krogstad and not Torvald Helmer who manages the Bank.

NORA. That's a thing you will never see!

KROGSTAD. Do you mean that you will—?

NORA. I have courage enough for it now. 310

KROGSTAD. Oh, you can't frighten me. A fine, spoilt lady like you—

NORA. You will see, you will see.

KROGSTAD. Under the ice, perhaps? Down into the cold, coal-black water? And
then, in the spring, to float up to the surface, all horrible and unrecognisable, with your
hair fallen out—

NORA. You can't frighten me.

KROGSTAD. Nor you me. People don't do such things, Mrs. Helmer. Besides, what 315
use would it be? I should have him completely in my power all the same.

NORA. Afterwards? When I am no longer—

KROGSTAD.   Have you forgotten that it is I who have the keeping of your reputation? [*NORA stands speechlessly looking at him.*] Well, now, I have warned you. Do not do anything foolish. When Helmer has had my letter, I shall expect a message from him. And be sure you remember that it is your husband himself who has forced me into such ways as this again. I will never forgive him for that. Good-bye, Mrs. Helmer.

[*Exit through the hall*]

NORA.   [*goes to the hall door, opens it slightly and listens*] He is going. He is not putting the letter in the box. Oh no, no! that's impossible! [*opens the door by degrees*] What is that? He is standing outside. He is not going downstairs. Is he hesitating? Can he—

[*A letter drops into the box; then KROGSTAD's footsteps are heard, till they die away as he goes downstairs. NORA utters a stifled cry and runs across the room to the table by the sofa. A short pause.*]

NORA.   In the letter-box. [*steals across to the hall door*] There it lies—Torvald, Torvald, there is no hope for us now!

[*MRS. LINDE comes in from the room on the left, carrying the dress.*]

MRS. LINDE.   There, I can't see anything more to mend now. Would you like to try it on—?

NORA.   [*in a hoarse whisper*] Christine, come here.

MRS. LINDE.   [*throwing the dress down on the sofa*] What is the matter with you? You look so agitated!

NORA.   Come here. Do you see that letter? There, look—you can see it through the glass in the letter-box.

MRS. LINDE.   Yes, I see it.

NORA.   That letter is from Krogstad.

MRS. LINDE.   Nora—it was Krogstad who lent you the money!

NORA.   Yes, and now Torvald will know all about it.

MRS. LINDE.   Believe me, Nora, that's the best thing for both of you.

NORA.   You don't know all. I forged a name.

MRS. LINDE.   Good heavens—!

NORA.   I only want to say this to you, Christine—you must be my witness.

MRS. LINDE.   Your witness? What do you mean? What am I to—?

NORA.   If I should go out of my mind—and it might easily happen—

MRS. LINDE.   Nora!

NORA.   Or if anything else should happen to me—anything, for instance, that might prevent my being here—

MRS. LINDE.   Nora! Nora! you are quite out of your mind.

NORA.   And if it should happen that there were someone who wanted to take all the responsibility, all the blame, you understand—

MRS. LINDE.   Yes, yes—but how can you suppose—?

NORA.   Then you must be my witness, that it is not true, Christine. I am not out of my mind at all; I am in my right senses now, and I tell you no one else has known anything about it; I, and I alone, did the whole thing. Remember that.

MRS. LINDE.   I will, indeed. But I don't understand all this.

NORA.   How should you understand it? A wonderful thing is going to happen.

MRS. LINDE.   A wonderful thing?

NORA.   Yes, a wonderful thing!—But it is so terrible, Christine; it *mustn't* happen, not for all the world.

MRS. LINDE.   I will go at once and see Krogstad.

NORA.   Don't go to him; he will do you some harm.   345

MRS. LINDE.   There was a time when he would gladly do anything for my sake.

NORA.   He?

MRS. LINDE.   Where does he live?

NORA.   How should I know—? Yes [*feeling in her pocket*] here is his card. But the letter, the letter—!

HELMER.   [*calls from his room, knocking at the door*] Nora!   350

NORA.   [*cries out anxiously*] Oh, what's that? What do you want?

HELMER.   Don't be so frightened. We are not coming in; you have locked the door. Are you trying on your dress?

NORA.   Yes, that's it. I look so nice, Torvald.

MRS. LINDE.   [*who has read the card*] I see he lives at the corner here.

NORA.   Yes, but it's no use. It is hopeless. The letter is lying there in the box.   355

MRS. LINDE.   And your husband keeps the key?

NORA.   Yes, always.

MRS. LINDE.   Krogstad must ask for his letter back unread, he must find some pretence—

NORA.   But it is just at this time that Torvald generally—

MRS. LINDE.   You must delay him. Go in to him in the meantime. I will come back   360
as soon as I can.

[*She goes out hurriedly through the hall door.*]

NORA.   [*goes to* HELMER'S *door, opens it and peeps in*] Torvald!

HELMER.   [*from the inner room*] Well? May I venture at last to come into my own room again? Come along, Rank, now you will see— [*halting in the doorway*] But what is this?

NORA.   What is what, dear?

HELMER.   Rank led me to expect a splendid transformation.

RANK.   [*in the doorway*] I understood so, but evidently I was mistaken.   365

NORA.   Yes, nobody is to have the chance of admiring me in my dress until tomorrow.

HELMER.   But, my dear Nora, you look so worn out. Have you been practising too much?

NORA.   No, I have not practised at all.

HELMER.   But you will need to—

NORA.   Yes, indeed I shall, Torvald. But I can't get on a bit without you to help   370
me; I have absolutely forgotten the whole thing.

HELMER.   Oh, we will soon work it up again.

NORA.   Yes, help me, Torvald. Promise that you will! I am so nervous about it—all the people—. You must give yourself up to me entirely this evening. Not the tiniest bit of business—you mustn't even take a pen in your hand. Will you promise, Torvald dear?

HELMER.   I promise. This evening I will be wholly and absolutely at your service, you helpless little mortal. Ah, by the way, first of all I will just—

[*Goes towards the hall door*]

NORA.   What are you going to do there?

HELMER.   Only see if any letters have come.   375

NORA.   No, no! don't do that, Torvald!

HELMER.   Why not?

NORA.   Torvald, please don't. There is nothing there.

HELMER.   Well, let me look. [*Turns to go to the letter-box. NORA, at the piano, plays the first bars of the Tarantella. HELMER stops in the doorway.*] Aha!

NORA.   I can't dance to-morrow if I don't practise with you.

HELMER.   [*going up to her*] Are you really so afraid of it, dear.

NORA.   Yes, so dreadfully afraid of it. Let me practise at once; there is time now, before we go to dinner. Sit down and play for me, Torvald dear; criticise me, and correct me as you play.

HELMER.   With great pleasure, if you wish me to.

[*Sits down at the piano.*]

NORA.   [*takes out of the box a tambourine and a long variegated shawl. She hastily drapes the shawl round her. Then she springs to the front of the stage and calls out.*] Now play for me! I am going to dance!

[*HELMER plays and NORA dances. RANK stands by the piano behind HELMER and looks on.*]

HELMER.   [*as he plays*] Slower, slower!

NORA.   I can't do it any other way.

HELMER.   Not so violently, Nora!

NORA.   This is the way.

HELMER.   [*stops playing*] No, no—that is not a bit right.

NORA.   [*laughing and swinging the tambourine*] Didn't I tell you so?

RANK.   Let me play for her.

HELMER.   [*getting up*] Yes, do. I can correct her better then.

[*RANK sits down at the piano and plays. NORA dances more and more wildly. HELMER has taken up a position beside the stove, and during her dance gives her frequent instructions. She does not seem to hear him; her hair comes down and falls over her shoulders; she pays no attention to it, but goes on dancing. Enter MRS. LINDE.*]

MRS. LINDE.   [*standing as if spell-bound in the doorway*] Oh!—

NORA.   [*as she dances*] Such fun, Christine!

HELMER.   My dear darling Nora, you are dancing as if your life depended on it.

NORA.   So it does.

HELMER.   Stop, Rank; this is sheer madness. Stop, I tell you! [*RANK stops playing, and NORA suddenly stands still. HELMER goes up to her.*] I could never have believed it. You have forgotten everything I taught you.

NORA.   [*throwing away the tambourine*] There, you see.

HELMER.   You will want a lot of coaching.

NORA.   Yes, you see how much I need it. You must coach me up to the last minute. Promise me that, Torvald!

HELMER.   You can depend on me.

NORA.   You must not think of anything but me, either to-day or to-morrow; you mustn't open a single letter—not even open the letter-box—

HELMER.   Ah, you are still afraid of that fellow—

NORA.   Yes, indeed I am.

HELMER.   Nora, I can tell from your looks that there is a letter from him lying   405
there.

NORA.   I don't know; I think there is; but you must not read anything of that kind
now. Nothing horrid must come between us till this is all over.

RANK.   [*whispers to HELMER*] You mustn't contradict her.

HELMER.   [*taking her in his arms*] The child shall have her way. But to-morrow
night, after you have danced—

NORA.   Then you will be free.

[*MAID appears in the doorway to the right.*]

MAID.   Dinner is served, ma'am.   410

NORA.   We will have champagne, Helen.

MAID.   Very good, ma'am.   [*Exit.*]

HELMER.   Hullo!—are we going to have a banquet?

NORA.   Yes, a champagne banquet till the small hours. [*calls out*] And a few macaroons, Helen—lots, just for once!

HELMER.   Come, come, don't be so wild and nervous. Be my own little skylark,   415
as you used.

NORA.   Yes, dear, I will. But go in now and you too, Doctor Rank. Christine, you
must help me to do up my hair.

RANK.   [*whispers to HELMER as they go out*] I suppose there is nothing—she is not
expecting anything?

HELMER.   Far from it, my dear fellow; it is simply nothing more than this childish
nervousness I was telling you of.

[*They go into the right-hand room.*]

NORA.   Well!

MRS. LINDE.   Gone out of town.   420

NORA.   I could tell from your face.

MRS. LINDE.   He is coming home to-morrow evening. I wrote a note for him.

NORA.   You should have let it alone; you must prevent nothing. After all, it is
splendid to be waiting for a wonderful thing to happen.

MRS. LINDE.   What is it that you are waiting for?

NORA.   Oh, you wouldn't understand. Go in to them, I will come in a moment.   425
[*MRS. LINDE goes into the dining-room. NORA stands still for a little while, as if to compose herself.
Then she looks at her watch.*] Five o'clock. Seven hours till midnight; and then four-and
twenty hours till the next midnight. Then the Tarantella will be over. Twenty-four and
seven? Thirty-one hours to live.

HELMER.   [*from the doorway on the right*] Where's my little skylark?

NORA.   [*going to him with her arms outstretched*] Here she is!

ACT 3

THE SAME SCENE. *The table has been placed in the middle of the stage, with chairs round it.
A lamp is burning on the table. The door into the hall stands open. Dance music is heard in the
room above. MRS. LINDE is sitting at the table idly turning over the leaves of a book; she tries to*

read, but does not seem able to collect her thoughts. Every now and then she listens intently for a sound at the outer door.

MRS. LINDE.   [*looking at her watch*] Not yet—and the time is nearly up. If only he does not—. [*listens again*] Ah, there he is. [*Goes into the hall and opens the outer door carefully. Light footsteps are heard on the stairs. She whispers.*] Come in. There is no one here.

KROGSTAD.   [*in the doorway*] I found a note from you at home. What does this mean?

MRS. LINDE.   It is absolutely necessary that I should have a talk with you.

KROGSTAD.   Really? And is it absolutely necessary that it should be here?

MRS. LINDE.   It is impossible where I live; there is no private entrance to my rooms. Come in; we are quite alone. The maid is asleep, and the Helmers are at the dance upstairs.

KROGSTAD.   [*coming into the room*] Are the Helmers really at a dance to-night?

MRS. LINDE.   Yes, why not?

KROGSTAD.   Certainly—why not?

MRS. LINDE.   Now, Nils, let us have a talk.

KROGSTAD.   Can we two have anything to talk about?

MRS. LINDE.   We have a great deal to talk about.

KROGSTAD.   I shouldn't have thought so.

MRS. LINDE.   No, you have never properly understood me.

KROGSTAD.   Was there anything else to understand except what was obvious to all the world—a heartless woman jilts a man when a more lucrative chance turns up?

MRS. LINDE.   Do you believe I am as absolutely heartless as all that? And do you believe that I did it with a light heart?

KROGSTAD.   Didn't you?

MRS. LINDE.   Nils, did you really think that?

KROGSTAD.   If it were as you say, why did you write to me as you did at the time?

MRS. LINDE.   I could do nothing else. As I had to break with you, it was my duty also to put an end to all that you felt for me.

KROGSTAD.   [*wringing his hands*] So that was it. and all this—only for the sake of money!

MRS. LINDE.   You must not forget that I had a helpless mother and two little brothers. We couldn't wait for you, Nils; your prospects seemed hopeless then.

KROGSTAD.   That may be so, but you had no right to throw me over for any one else's sake.

MRS. LINDE.   Indeed I don't know. Many a time did I ask myself if I had the right to do it.

KROGSTAD.   [*more gently*] When I lost you, it was as if all the solid ground went from under my feet. Look at me now—I am a shipwrecked man clinging to a bit of wreckage.

MRS. LINDE.   But help may be near.

KROGSTAD.   It *was* near; but then you came and stood in my way.

MRS. LINDE.   Unintentionally, Nils. It was only to-day that I learnt it was your place I was going to take in the Bank.

KROGSTAD.   I believe you, if you say so. But now that you know it, are you not going to give it up to me?

MRS. LINDE.   No, because that would not benefit you in the least.

KROGSTAD.   Oh, benefit, benefit—I would have done it whether or no.

MRS. LINDE.   I have learnt to act prudently. Life, and hard, bitter necessity have taught me that.

KROGSTAD.   And life has taught me not to believe in fine speeches.

MRS. LINDE.   Then life has taught you something very reasonable. But deeds you must believe in?

KROGSTAD.   What do you mean by that?

MRS. LINDE.   You said you were like a shipwrecked man clinging to some wreckage.

KROGSTAD.   I had good reason to say so.

MRS. LINDE.   Well, I am like a shipwrecked woman clinging to some wreckage— 35 no one to mourn for, no one to care for.

KROGSTAD.   It was your own choice.

MRS. LINDE.   There was no other choice—then.

KROGSTAD.   Well, what now? 40

MRS. LINDE.   Nils, how would it be if we two shipwrecked people could join forces?

KROGSTAD.   What are you saying?

MRS. LINDE.   Two on the same piece of wreckage would stand a better chance than each on their own.

KROGSTAD.   Christine!

MRS. LINDE.   What do you suppose brought me to town? 45

KROGSTAD.   Do you mean that you gave me a thought?

MRS. LINDE.   I could not endure life without work. All my life, as long as I can remember, I have worked, and it has been my greatest and only pleasure. But now I am quite alone in the world—my life is so dreadfully empty and I feel so forsaken. There is not the least pleasure in working for one's self. Nils, give me someone and something to work for.

KROGSTAD.   I don't trust that. It is nothing but a woman's overstrained sense of generosity that prompts you to make such an offer of yourself.

MRS. LINDE.   Have you ever noticed anything of the sort in me?

KROGSTAD.   Could you really do it? Tell me—do you know all about my past life? 50

MRS. LINDE.   Yes.

KROGSTAD.   And do you know what they think of me here?

MRS. LINDE.   You seemed to me to imply that with me you might have been quite another man.

KROGSTAD.   I am certain of it.

MRS. LINDE.   Is it too late now? 55

KROGSTAD.   Christine, are you saying this deliberately? Yes, I am sure you are. I see it in your face. Have you really the courage, then—?

MRS. LINDE.   I want to be a mother to someone, and your children need a mother. We two need each other. Nils, I have faith in your real character—I can dare anything together with you.

KROGSTAD.   [*grasps her hands*] Thanks, thanks, Christine! Now I shall find a way to clear myself in the eyes of the world. Ah, but I forgot—

MRS. LINDE.   [*listening*] Hush! The Tarantella! Go, go!

KROGSTAD.   Why? What is it? 60

MRS. LINDE.   Do you hear them up there? When that is over, we may expect them back.

KROGSTAD.   Yes, yes—I will go. But it is all no use. Of course you are not aware what steps I have taken in the matter of the Helmers.

MRS. LINDE.   Yes. I know all about that.

KROGSTAD.   And in spite of that have you the courage to—?

MRS. LINDE.   I understand very well to what lengths a man like you might be driven by despair.

KROGSTAD.   If I could only undo what I have done!

MRS. LINDE.   You can. Your letter is lying in the letter-box now.

KROGSTAD.   Are you sure of that?

MRS. LINDE.   Quite sure, but—

KROGSTAD.   [*with a searching look at her*] Is that what it all means?—that you want to save your friend at any cost? Tell me frankly. Is that it?

MRS. LINDE.   Nils, a woman who has once sold herself for another's sake, doesn't do it a second time.

KROGSTAD.   I will ask for my letter back.

MRS. LINDE.   No, no.

KROGSTAD.   Yes, of course I will. I will wait here till Helmer comes; I will tell him he must give me my letter back—that it only concerns my dismissal—that he is not to read it—

MRS. LINDE.   No, Nils, you must not recall your letter.

KROGSTAD.   But, tell me, wasn't it for that very purpose that you asked me to meet you here?

MRS. LINDE.   In my first moment of fright, it was. But twenty-four hours have elapsed since then, and in that time I have witnessed incredible things in this house. Helmer must know all about it. This unhappy secret must be disclosed; they must have a complete understanding between them, which is impossible with all this concealment and falsehood going on.

KROGSTAD.   Very well, if you will take the responsibility. But there is one thing I can do in any case, and I shall do it at once.

MRS. LINDE.   [*listening*] You must be quick and go! The dance is over; we are not safe a moment longer.

KROGSTAD.   I will wait for you below.

MRS. LINDE.   Yes, do. You must see me back to my door.

KROGSTAD.   I have never had such an amazing piece of good fortune in my life.

[*Goes out through the outer door. The door between the room and the hall remains open.*]

MRS. LINDE.   [*tidying up the room and laying her hat and cloak ready*] What a difference! what a difference! Someone to work for and live for—a home to bring comfort into. That I will do, indeed. I wish they would be quick and come— [*listens*] Ah, there they are now. I must put on my things.

[*Takes up her hat and cloak. HELMER'S and NORA'S voices are heard outside; a key is turned, and HELMER brings NORA almost by force into the hall. She is in an Italian costume with a large black shawl round her; he is in evening dress and a black domino which is flying open.*]

NORA.   [*hanging back in the doorway, and struggling with him*] No, no, no!—don't take me in. I want to go upstairs again; I don't want to leave so early.

HELMER.   But, my dearest Nora—

NORA.   Please, Torvald dear—please, *please*—only an hour more.

HELMER.   Not a single minute, my sweet Nora. You know that was our agreement. Come along into the room; you are catching cold standing there.

[*He brings her gently into the room, in spite of her resistance.*]

MRS. LINDE.   Good evening.

NORA.   Christine!

HELMER.   You here, so late, Mrs. Linde?   90

MRS. LINDE.   Yes, you must excuse me; I was so anxious to see Nora in her dress.

NORA.   Have you been sitting here waiting for me?

MRS. LINDE.   Yes, unfortunately I came too late, you had already gone upstairs; and I thought I couldn't go away without having seen you.

HELMER.   [*taking off NORA's shawl*] Yes, take a good look at her. I think she is worth looking at. Isn't she charming, Mrs. Linde?

MRS. LINDE.   Yes, indeed she is.   95

HELMER.   Doesn't she look remarkably pretty? Everyone thought so at the dance. But she is terribly self-willed, this sweet little person. What are we to do with her? You will hardly believe that I had almost to bring her away by force.

NORA.   Torvald, you will repent not having let me stay, even if it were only for half an hour.

HELMER.   Listen to her, Mrs. Linde! She had danced her Tarantella, and it had been a tremendous success, as it deserved—although possibly the performance was a trifle too realistic—a little more so, I mean, than was strictly compatible with the limitations of art. But never mind about that! The chief thing is, she had made a success— she had made a tremendous success. Do you think I was going to let her remain there after that, and spoil the effect? No indeed! I took my charming little Capri maiden— my capricious little Capri maiden, I should say—on my arm; took one quick turn round the room; a curtsey on either side, and, as they say in novels, the beautiful apparition disappeared. An exit ought always to be effective, Mrs. Linde; but that is what I cannot make Nora understand. Pooh! this room is hot. [*throws his domino on a chair and opens the door of his room*] Hullo! it's all dark in here. Oh, of course—excuse me—.

[*He goes in and lights some candles.*]

NORA.   [*in a hurried and breathless whisper*] Well?

MRS. LINDE.   [*in a low voice*] I have had a talk with him.   100

NORA.   Yes, and—

MRS. LINDE.   Nora, you must tell your husband all about it.

NORA.   [*in an expressionless voice*] I knew it.

MRS. LINDE.   You have nothing to be afraid of as far as Krogstad is concerned; but you must tell him.

NORA.   I won't tell him.   105

MRS. LINDE.   Then the letter will.

NORA.   Thank you, Christine. Now I know what I must do. Hush—!

HELMER.   [*coming in again*] Well, Mrs. Linde, have you admired her?

MRS. LINDE.   Yes, and now I will say good-night.

HELMER.   What already? Is this yours, this knitting?   110

MRS. LINDE.   [*taking it*] Yes, thank you, I had very nearly forgotten it.

HELMER.   So you knit?

MRS. LINDE.   Of course.

HELMER.   Do you know, you ought to embroider.

MRS. LINDE.   Really? Why?   115

HELMER.   Yes, it's far more becoming. Let me show you. You hold the embroidery thus in your left hand, and use the needle with the right—like this—with a long, easy sweep. Do you see?

MRS. LINDE.   Yes, perhaps—

HELMER.   But in the case of knitting—that can never be anything but ungraceful; look here—the arms close together, the knitting-needles going up and down—it has a sort of Chinese effect—. That was really excellent champagne they gave us.

MRS. LINDE.   Well,—good-night, Nora, and don't be self-willed any more.

HELMER.   That's right, Mrs. Linde.

MRS. LINDE.   Good-night, Mr. Helmer.

HELMER.   [*accompanying her to the door*] Good-night, good-night. I hope you will get home all right. I should be very happy to—but you haven't any great distance to go. Good-night, good-night. [*She goes out; he shuts the door after her, and comes in again.*] Ah!—at last we have got rid of her. She is a frightful bore, that woman.

NORA.   Aren't you very tired, Torvald?

HELMER.   No, not in the least.

NORA.   Nor sleepy?

HELMER.   Not a bit. On the contrary, I feel extraordinarily lively. And you?—you really look both tired and sleepy.

NORA.   Yes, I am very tired. I want to go to sleep at once.

HELMER.   There, you see it was quite right of me not to let you stay there any longer.

NORA.   Everything you do is quite right, Torvald.

HELMER.   [*kissing her on the forehead*] Now my little skylark is speaking reasonably. Did you notice what good spirits Rank was in this evening?

NORA.   Really? Was he? I didn't speak to him at all.

HELMER.   And I very little, but I have not for a long time seen him in such good form. [*looks for a while at her and then goes nearer to her*] It is delightful to be at home by ourselves again, to be all alone with you—you fascinating, charming little darling!

NORA.   Don't look at me like that, Torvald.

HELMER.   Why shouldn't I look at my dearest treasure?—at all the beauty that is mine, all my very own?

NORA.   [*going to the other side of the table*] You mustn't say things like that to me to-night.

HELMER.   [*following her*] You have still got the Tarantella in your blood, I see. And it makes you more captivating than ever. Listen—the guests are beginning to go now. [*in a lower voice*] Nora—soon the whole house will be quiet.

NORA.   Yes, I hope so.

HELMER.   Yes, my own darling Nora. Do you know, when I am out at a party with you like this, why I speak so little to you, keep away from you, and only send a stolen glance in your direction now and then?—do you know why I do that? It is because I make believe to myself that we are secretly in love, and you are my secretly promised bride, and that no one suspects there is anything between us.

NORA.   Yes, yes—I know very well your thoughts are with me all the time.

HELMER.   And when we are leaving, and I am putting the shawl over your beautiful young shoulders—on your lovely neck—then I imagine that you are my young bride and that we have just come from the wedding, and I am bringing you for the first time into our home—to be alone with you for the first time—quite alone with my shy little darling! All this evening I have longed for nothing but you. When I watched the seductive figures of the Tarantella, my blood was on fire; I could endure it no longer, and that was why I brought you down so early—

NORA.   Go away, Torvald! You must let me go. I won't—

HELMER.   What's that? You're joking, my little Nora! You won't—you won't? Am I not your husband—?

[*A knock is heard at the outer door.*]

NORA.   [*starting*] Did you hear—?

HELMER.   [*going into the hall*] Who is it?

RANK.   [*outside*] It is I. May I come in for a moment?   145

HELMER.   [*in a fretful whisper*] Oh, what does he want now? [*aloud*] Wait a minute! [*unlocks the door*] Come, that's kind of you not to pass by our door.

RANK.   I thought I heard your voice, and felt as if I should like to look in. [*with a swift glance round*] Ah, yes!—these dear familiar rooms. You are very happy and cosy in here, you two.

HELMER.   It seems to me that you looked after yourself pretty well upstairs too.

RANK.   Excellently. Why shouldn't I? Why shouldn't one enjoy everything in this world?—at any rate as much as one can, and as long as one can. The wine was capital—

HELMER.   Especially the champagne.   150

RANK.   So you noticed that too? It is almost incredible how much I managed to put away!

NORA.   Torvald drank a great deal of champagne tonight, too.

RANK.   Did he?

NORA.   Yes, and he is always in such good spirits afterwards.

RANK.   Well, why should one not enjoy a merry evening after a well-spent day?   155

HELMER.   Well spent? I am afraid I can't take credit for that.

RANK.   [*clapping him on the back*] But I can, you know!

NORA.   Doctor Rank, you must have been occupied with some scientific investigation to-day.

RANK.   Exactly.

HELMER.   Just listen!—little Nora talking about scientific investigations!   160

NORA.   And may I congratulate you on the result?

RANK.   Indeed you may.

NORA.   Was it favourable, then?

RANK.   The best possible, for both doctor and patient—certainty.

NORA.   [*quickly and searchingly*] Certainty?   165

RANK.   Absolute certainty. So wasn't I entitled to make a merry evening of it after that?

NORA.   Yes, you certainly were, Doctor Rank.

HELMER.   I think so too, so long as you don't have to pay for it in the morning.

RANK.   Oh well, one can't have anything in this life without paying for it.

NORA.   Doctor Rank—are you fond of fancy-dress balls?   170

RANK.   Yes, if there is a fine lot of pretty costumes.

NORA.   Tell me—what shall we two wear at the next?

HELMER.   Little featherbrain!—are you thinking of the next already?

RANK.   We two? Yes, I can tell you. You shall go as a good fairy—

HELMER.   Yes, but what do you suggest as an appropriate costume for that?   175

RANK.   Let your wife go dressed just as she is in everyday life.

HELMER.   That was really very prettily turned. But can't you tell us what you will be?

RANK.   Yes, my dear friend, I have quite made up my mind about that.

HELMER.   Well?

RANK.   At the next fancy dress ball I shall be invisible.

HELMER.   That's a good joke!

RANK.   There is a big black hat—have you never heard of hats that make you invisible? If you put one on, no one can see you.

HELMER.   [*suppressing a smile*] Yes, you are quite right.

RANK.   But I am clean forgetting what I came for. Helmer, give me a cigar—one of the dark Havanas.

HELMER.   With the greatest pleasure. [*offers him his case*]

RANK.   [*takes a cigar and cuts off the end*] Thanks.

NORA.   [*striking a match*] Let me give you a light.

RANK.   Thank you. [*She holds the match for him to light his cigar.*] And now good-bye!

HELMER.   Good-bye, good-bye, dear old man!

NORA.   Sleep well, Doctor Rank.

RANK.   Thank you for that wish.

NORA.   Wish me the same.

RANK.   You? Well, if you want me to sleep well! And thanks for the light.

[*He nods to them both and goes out.*]

HELMER.   [*in a subdued voice*] He has drunk more than he ought.

NORA.   [*absently*] Maybe. [*HELMER takes a bunch of keys out of his pocket and goes into the hall.*] Torvald! what are you going to do there?

HELMER.   Empty the letter-box; it is quite full; there will be no room to put the newspaper in to-morrow morning.

NORA.   Are you going to work to-night?

HELMER.   You know quite well I'm not. What is this? Some one has been at the lock.

NORA.   At the lock—?

HELMER.   Yes, someone has. What can it mean? I should never have thought the maid—. Here is a broken hairpin. Nora, it is one of yours.

NORA.   [*quickly*] Then it must have been the children—

HELMER.   Then you must get them out of those ways. There, at last I have got it open. [*Takes out the contents of the letter-box, and calls to the kitchen.*] Helen!— Helen, put out the light over the front door. [*Goes back into the room and shuts the door into the hall. He holds out his hand full of letters.*] Look at that—look what a heap of them there are. [*turning them over*] What on earth is that?

NORA.   [*at the window*] The letter—No! Torvald, no!

HELMER.   Two cards—of Rank's.

NORA.   Of Doctor Rank's?

HELMER.   [*looking at them*] Doctor Rank. They were on the top. He must have put them in when he went out.

NORA.   Is there anything written on them?

HELMER.   There is a black cross over the name. Look there—what an uncomfortable idea! It looks as if he were announcing his own death.

NORA.   It is just what he is doing.

HELMER.   What? Do you know anything about it? Has he said anything to you?   210

NORA.   Yes. He told me that when the cards came it would be his leave-taking from us. He means to shut himself up and die.

HELMER.   My poor old friend. Certainly I knew we should not have him very long with us. But so soon! And so he hides himself away like a wounded animal.

NORA.   If it has to happen, it is best it should be without a word—don't you think so, Torvald?

HELMER.   [*walking up and down*] He had so grown into our lives. I can't think of him as having gone out of them. He, with his sufferings and his loneliness, was like a cloudy background to our sunlit happiness. Well, perhaps it is best so. For him, anyway. [*standing still*] And perhaps for us too, Nora. We two are thrown quite upon each other now. [*puts his arms round her*] My darling wife, I don't feel as if I could hold you tight enough. Do you know, Nora, I have often wished that you might be threatened by some great danger, so that I might risk my life's blood, and everything, for your sake.

NORA.   [*disengages herself, and says firmly and decidedly*] Now you must read your   215
letters, Torvald.

HELMER.   No, no; not to-night. I want to be with you, my darling wife.

NORA.   With the thought of your friend's death—

HELMER.   You are right, it has affected us both. Something ugly has come between us—the thought of the horrors of death. We must try and rid our minds of that. Until then—we will each go to our own room.

NORA.   [*hanging on his neck*] Good-night, Torvald—Good-night!

HELMER.   [*kissing her on the forehead*]. Good-night, my little singing-bird. Sleep   220
sound, Nora. Now I will read my letters through.

[*He takes his letters and goes into his room, shutting the door after him.*]

NORA.   [*gropes distractedly about, seizes* HELMER'S *domino, throws it round her, while she says in quick, hoarse, spasmodic whispers*] Never to see him again. Never! Never! [*puts her shawl over her head*] Never to see my children again either—never again. Never! Never!— Ah! the icy, black water—the unfathomable depths—If only it were over! He has got it now—now he is reading it. Good-by, Torvald and my children!

[*She is about to rush out through the hall, when* HELMER *opens his door hurriedly and stands with an open letter in his hand.*]

HELMER.   Nora!

NORA.   Ah!—

HELMER.   What is this? Do you know what is in this letter?

NORA.   Yes, I know. Let me go! Let me get out!   225

HELMER.   [*holding her back*] Where are you going?

NORA.   [*trying to get free*] You shan't save me, Torvald!

HELMER.   [*reeling*] True? Is this true, that I read here? Horrible! No, no—it is impossible that it can be true.

NORA.   It is true. I have loved you above everything else in the world.

HELMER.   Oh, don't let us have any silly excuses.   230

NORA.   [*taking a step towards him*] Torvald—!

HELMER.   Miserable creature—what have you done?

NORA.   Let me go. You shall not suffer for my sake. You shall not take it upon yourself.

HELMER.   No tragedy airs, please. [*locks the hall door*] Here you shall stay and give me an explanation. Do you understand what you have done? Answer me? Do you understand what you have done?

NORA.   [*looks steadily at him and says with a growing look of coldness in her face*] Yes, now I am beginning to understand thoroughly.

HELMER.   [*walking about the room*] What a horrible awakening! All these eight years—she who was my joy and pride—a hypocrite, a liar—worse, worse—a criminal! The unutterable ugliness of it all! For shame! For shame! [*NORA is silent and looks steadily at him. He stops in front of her.*] I ought to have suspected that something of the sort would happen. I ought to have foreseen it. All your father's want of principle—be silent!—all your father's want of principle has come out in you. No religion, no morality, no sense of duty—. How I am punished for having winked at what he did! I did it for your sake, and this is how you repay me.

NORA.   Yes, that's just it.

HELMER.   Now you have destroyed all my happiness. You have ruined all my future. It is horrible to think of! I am in the power of an unscrupulous man; he can do what he likes with me, ask anything he likes of me, give me any orders he pleases—I dare not refuse. And I must sink to such miserable depths because of a thoughtless woman!

NORA.   When I am out of the way, you will be free.

HELMER.   No fine speeches, please. Your father had always plenty of those ready, too. What good would it be to me if you were out of the way, as you say? Not the slightest. He can make the affair known everywhere; and if he does, I may be falsely suspected of having been a party to your criminal action. Very likely people will think I was behind it all—that it was I who prompted you! And I have to thank you for all this—you whom I have cherished during the whole of our married life. Do you understand now what it is you have done for me?

NORA.   [*coldly and quietly*] Yes.

HELMER.   It is so incredible that I can't take it in. But we must come to some understanding. Take off that shawl. Take it off, I tell you. I must try and appease him some way or another. The matter must be hushed up at any cost. And as for you and me, it must appear as if everything between us were just as before—but naturally only in the eyes of the world. You will still remain in my house, that is a matter of course. But I shall not allow you to bring up the children; I dare not trust them to you. To think that I should be obliged to say so to one whom I have loved so dearly, and whom I still—. No, that is all over. From this moment happiness is not the question; all that concerns us is to save the remains, the fragments, the appearance—

[*A ring is heard at the front-door bell.*]

HELMER.   [*with a start*] What is that? So late! Can the worst—? Can he—? Hide yourself, Nora. Say you are ill.

[*NORA stands motionless. HELMER goes and unlocks the hall door.*]

MAID.   [*half-dressed, comes to the door*] A letter for the mistress.

HELMER.   Give it to me. [*takes the letter, and shuts the door*] Yes, it is from him. You shall not have it; I will read it myself.

NORA.   Yes, read it.

HELMER.   [*standing by the lamp*] I scarcely have the courage to do it. It may mean ruin for both of us. No, I must know. [*tears open the letter, runs his eye over a few lines, looks at a paper enclosed and gives a shout of joy*] Nora! [*She looks at him questioningly.*] Nora!—No, I must read it once again—. Yes, it is true! I am saved! Nora, I am saved!

NORA.   And I?

HELMER.   You too, of course; we are both saved, both you and I. Look, he sends you your bond back. He says he regrets and repents—that a happy change in his life—never mind what he says! We are saved, Nora! No one can do anything to you. Oh, Nora, Nora!—no, first I must destroy these hateful things. Let me see—. [*takes a look at the bond*] No, no, I won't look at it. The whole thing shall be nothing but a bad dream to me. [*tears up the bond and both letters, throws them all into the stove, and watches them burn*] There—now it doesn't exist any longer. He says that since Christmas Eve you—. These must have been three dreadful days for you, Nora.

NORA.   I have fought a hard fight these three days.   250

HELMER.   And suffered agonies, and seen no way out but—. No, we won't call any of the horrors to mind. We will only shout with joy, and keep saying "It's all over! It's all over!" Listen to me, Nora. You don't seem to realise that it is all over. What is this?—such a cold, set face! My poor little Nora, I quite understand; you don't feel as if you could believe that I have forgiven you. But it is true, Nora, I swear it; I have forgiven you everything. I know that what you did, you did out of love for me.

NORA.   That is true.

HELMER.   You have loved me as a wife ought to love her husband. Only you had not sufficient knowledge to judge of the means you used. But do you suppose you are any the less dear to me, because you don't understand how to act on your own responsibility? No, no; only lean on me; I will advise you and direct you. I should not be a man if this womanly helplessness did not just give you a double attractiveness in my eyes. You must not think any more about the hard things I said in my first moment of consternation, when I thought everything was going to overwhelm me. I have forgiven you, Nora; I swear to you I have forgiven you.

NORA.   Thank you for your forgiveness.

[*She goes out through the door to the right.*]

HELMER.   No, don't go—. [*looks in*] What are you doing in there?   255

NORA.   [*from within*] Taking off my fancy dress.

HELMER.   [*standing at the open door*] Yes, do. Try and calm yourself, and make your mind easy again, my frightened little singing-bird. Be at rest, and feel secure; I have broad wings to shelter you under. [*walks up and down by the door*] How warm and cosy our home is, Nora. Here is shelter for you; here I will protect you like a hunted dove that I have saved from a hawk's claws. I will bring peace to your poor beating heart. It will come, little by little, Nora, believe me. Tomorrow morning you will look upon it all quite differently; soon everything will be just as it was before. Very soon you won't need me to assure you that I have forgiven you; you will yourself feel the certainty that I have done so. Can you suppose I should ever think of such a thing as repudiating you, or even reproaching you? You have no idea what a true man's heart is like, Nora. There is something so indescribably sweet and satisfying, to a man, in the knowledge that he has forgiven his wife—forgiven her freely, and with all his heart. It seems as if that had made her, as it were, doubly his own; he has given her a new life, so to speak; and she has in a way become both wife and child to him. So you shall be for me after this, my little scared, helpless darling. Have no anxiety about anything, Nora; only be frank and open with me, and I will serve as will and conscience both to you—. What is this? Not gone to bed? Have you changed your things?

NORA. [*in everyday dress*] Yes, Torvald, I have changed my things now.

HELMER. But what for?—so late as this.

NORA. I shall not sleep to-night.

HELMER. But, my dear Nora—

NORA. [*looking at her watch*] It is not so very late. Sit down here, Torvald. You and I have much to say to one another.

[*She sits down at one side of the table.*]

HELMER. Nora—what is this?—this cold, set face?

NORA. Sit down. it will take some time; I have a lot to talk over with you.

HELMER. [*sits down at the opposite side of the table*] You alarm me, Nora!—and I don't understand you.

NORA. No, that is just it. You don't understand me, and I have never understood you either—before to-night. No, you mustn't interrupt me. You must simply listen to what I say. Torvald, this is a settling of accounts.

HELMER. What do you mean by that?

NORA. [*after a short silence*] Isn't there one thing that strikes you as strange in our sitting here like this?

HELMER. What is that?

NORA. We have been married now eight years. Does it not occur to you that this is the first time we two, you and I, husband and wife, have had a serious conversation?

HELMER. What do you mean by serious?

NORA. In all these eight years—longer than that—from the very beginning of our acquaintance, we have never exchanged a word on any serious subject.

HELMER. Was it likely that I would be continually and for ever telling you about worries that you could not help me to bear?

NORA. I am not speaking about business matters. I say that we have never sat down in earnest together to try and get at the bottom of anything.

HELMER. But, dearest Nora, would it have been any good to you?

NORA. That is just it; you have never understood me. I have been greatly wronged, Torvald—first by papa and then by you.

HELMER. What! By us two—by us two, who have loved you better than anyone else in the world?

NORA. [*shaking her head*] You have never loved me. You have only thought it pleasant to be in love with me.

HELMER. Nora, what do I hear you saying?

NORA. It is perfectly true, Torvald. When I was at home with papa, he told me his opinion about everything, and so I had the same opinions; and if I differed from him I concealed the fact, because he would not have liked it. He called me his doll-child, and he played with me just as I used to play with my dolls. And when I came to live with you—

HELMER. What sort of an expression is that to use about our marriage?

NORA. [*undisturbed*] I mean that I was simply transferred from papa's hands into yours. You arranged everything according to your own taste, and so I got the same tastes as you—or else I pretended to, I am really not quite sure which—I think sometimes the one and sometimes the other. When I look back on it, it seems to me as if I had been living here like a poor woman—just from hand to mouth. I have existed merely to perform tricks for you, Torvald. But you would have it so. You and papa have committed a great sin against me. It is your fault that I have made nothing of my life.

HELMER.   How unreasonable and how ungrateful you are, Nora! Have you not been happy here?

NORA.   No, I have never been happy. I thought I was, but it has never really been so.

HELMER.   Not—not happy!   285

NORA.   No, only merry. And you have always been so kind to me. But our home has been nothing but a playroom. I have been your doll-wife, just as at home I was papa's doll-child; and here the children have been my dolls. I thought it great fun when you played with me, just as they thought it great fun when I played with them. That is what our marriage has been, Torvald.

HELMER.   There is some truth in what you say—exaggerated and strained as your view of it is. But for the future it shall be different. Playtime shall be over, and lesson-time shall begin.

NORA.   Whose lessons? Mine, or the children's?

HELMER.   Both yours and the children's, my darling Nora.

NORA.   Alas, Torvald, you are not the man to educate me into being a proper   290
wife for you.

HELMER.   And you can say that!

NORA.   And I—how am I fitted to bring up the children?

HELMER.   Nora!

NORA.   Didn't you say so yourself a little while ago—that you dare not trust me to bring them up?

HELMER.   In a moment of anger! Why do you pay any heed to that?   295

NORA.   Indeed, you were perfectly right. I am not fit for the task. There is another task I must undertake first. I must try and educate myself—you are not the man to help me in that. I must do that for myself. And that is why I am going to leave you now.

HELMER.   [*springing up*] What do you say?

NORA.   I must stand quite alone, if I am to understand myself and everything about me. It is for that reason that I cannot remain with you any longer.

HELMER.   Nora! Nora!

NORA.   I am going away from here now, at once. I am sure Christine will take me   300
in for the night—

HELMER.   You are out of your mind! I won't allow it! I forbid you!

NORA.   It is no use forbidding me anything any longer. I will take with me what belongs to myself. I will take nothing from you, either now or later.

HELMER.   What sort of madness is this!

NORA.   To-morrow I shall go home—I mean, to my old home. It will be easiest for me to find something to do there.

HELMER.   You blind, foolish woman!   305

NORA.   I must try and get some sense, Torvald.

HELMER.   To desert your home, your husband and your children! And you don't consider what people will say!

NORA.   I cannot consider that at all. I only know that it is necessary for me.

HELMER.   It's shocking. This is how you would neglect your most sacred duties.

NORA.   What do you consider my most sacred duties?   310

HELMER.   Do I need to tell you that? Are they not your duties to your husband and your children?

NORA.   I have other duties just as sacred.

HELMER.   That you have not. What duties could those be?

NORA.   Duties to myself.

HELMER.   Before all else, you are a wife and a mother.

NORA.   I don't believe that any longer. I believe that before all else I am a reasonable human being, just as you are—or, at all events, that I must try and become one.
I know quite well, Torvald, that most people would think you right, and that views of
that kind are to be found in books; but I can no longer content myself with what most
people say, or with what is found in books. I must think over things for myself and get to
understand them.

HELMER.   Can you not understand your place in your own home? Have you not a
reliable guide in such matters as that?—have you no religion?

NORA.   I am afraid, Torvald, I do not exactly know what religion is.

HELMER.   What are you saying?

NORA.   I know nothing but what the clergyman said when I went to be confirmed. He told us that religion was this, and that, and the other. When I am away from
all this, and am alone, I will look into that matter too. I will see if what the
clergyman said is true, or at all events if it is true for me.

HELMER.   This is unheard of in a girl of your age! But if religion cannot lead you
aright, let me try and awaken your conscience. I suppose you have some moral sense?
Or—answer me—am I to think you have none?

NORA.   I assure you, Torvald, that is not an easy question to answer. I really don't
know. The thing perplexes me altogether. I only know that you and I look at it in quite a
different light. I am learning, too, that the law is quite another thing from what I supposed; but I find it impossible to convince myself that the law is right. According to it a
woman has no right to spare her old dying father, or to save her husband's life. I can't
believe that.

HELMER.   You talk like a child. You don't understand the conditions of the world
in which you live.

NORA.   No, I don't. But now I am going to try. I am going to see if I can make out
who is right, the world or I.

HELMER.   You are ill, Nora; you are delirious; I almost think you are out of your
mind.

NORA.   I have never felt my mind so clear and certain as to-night.

HELMER.   And is it with a clear and certain mind that you forsake your husband
and your children?

NORA.   Yes, it is.

HELMER.   Then there is only one possible explanation.

NORA.   What is that?

HELMER.   You do not love me any more.

NORA.   No, that is just it.

HELMER.   Nora!—and you can say that?

NORA.   It gives me great pain, Torvald, for you have always been so kind to me,
but I cannot help it. I do not love you any more.

HELMER.   [*regaining his composure*] Is that a clear and certain conviction too?

NORA.   Yes, absolutely clear and certain. That is the reason why I will not stay
here any longer.

HELMER.   And can you tell me what I have done to forfeit your love?

NORA.   Yes, indeed I can. It was to-night, when the wonderful thing did not
happen; then I saw you were not the man I had thought you.

HELMER.   Explain yourself better—I don't understand you.

NORA.   I have waited so patiently for eight years; for, goodness knows, I knew very   340
well that wonderful things don't happen every day. Then this horrible misfortune came
upon me; and then I felt quite certain that the wonderful thing was going to happen at
last. When Krogstad's letter was lying out there, never for a moment did I imagine that
you would consent to accept this man's conditions. I was so absolutely certain that you
would say to him: Publish the thing to the whole world. And when that was done—

HELMER.   Yes, what then?—when I had exposed my wife to shame and disgrace?

NORA.   When that was done, I was so absolutely certain, you would come forward
and take everything upon yourself, and say: I am the guilty one.

HELMER.   Nora—!

NORA.   You mean that I would never have accepted such a sacrifice on your part?
No, of course not. But what would my assurances have been worth against yours? That
was the wonderful thing which I hoped for and feared; and it was to prevent that, that I
wanted to kill myself.

HELMER.   I would gladly work night and day for you, Nora—bear sorrow and want   345
for your sake. But no man would sacrifice his honour for the one he loves.

NORA.   It is a thing hundreds of thousands of women have done.

HELMER.   Oh, you think and talk like a heedless child.

NORA.   Maybe. But you neither think nor talk like the man I could bind myself to.
As soon as your fear was over—and it was not fear for what threatened me, but for what
might happen to you—when the whole thing was past, as far as you were concerned it
was exactly as if nothing at all had happened. Exactly as before, I was your little skylark,
your doll, which you would in future treat with doubly gentle care, because it was so brittle and fragile. [*getting up*] Torvald—it was then it dawned upon me that for eight years
I had been living here with a strange man, and had borne him three children—. Oh, I
can't bear to think of it! I could tear myself into little bits!

HELMER.   [*sadly*] I see, I see. An Abyss has opened between us—there is no denying it. But, Nora, would it not be possible to fill it up?

NORA.   As I am now, I am no wife for you.   350

HELMER.   I have it in me to become a different man.

NORA.   Perhaps—if your doll is taken away from you.

HELMER.   But to part!—to part from you! No, no, Nora, I can't understand that
idea.

NORA.   [*going out to the right*] That makes it all the more certain that it must be
done.

[*She comes back with her cloak and hat and a small bag which she puts on a chair by the table.*]

HELMER.   Nora, Nora, not now! Wait till to-morrow.   355

NORA.   [*putting on her cloak*] I cannot spend the night in a strange man's room.

HELMER.   But can't we live here like brother and sister—?

NORA.   [*putting on her hat*] You know very well that would not last long. [*puts the
shawl round her*] Good-bye, Torvald. I won't see the little ones. I know they are in better
hands than mine. As I am now, I can be of no use to them.

HELMER.   But some day, Nora—some day?   360

NORA.   How can I tell? I have no idea what is going to become of me.

HELMER.   But you are my wife, whatever becomes of you.

NORA.   Listen, Torvald. I have heard that when a wife deserts her husband's
house, as I am doing now, he is legally freed from all obligations towards her. In any

case I set you free from all your obligations. You are not to feel yourself bound in the slightest way, any more than I shall. There must be perfect freedom on both sides. See here is your ring back. Give me mine.

HELMER.   That too?

NORA.   That too.

HELMER.   Here it is.   36●

NORA.   That's right. Now it is all over. I have put the keys here. The maids know all about everything in the house—better than I do. To-morrow, after I have left her, Christine will come here and pack up my own things that I brought with me from home. I will have them sent after me.

HELMER.   All over! All over!—Nora, shall you never think of me again?

NORA.   I know I shall often think of you and the children and this house.

HELMER.   May I write to you, Nora?

NORA.   No—never. You must not do that.   37●

HELMER.   But at least let me send you—

NORA.   Nothing—nothing—

HELMER.   Let me help you if you are in want.

NORA.   No. I can receive nothing from a stranger.

HELMER.   Nora—can I never be anything more than a stranger to you?   37●

NORA.   [*taking her bag*] Ah, Torvald, the most wonderful thing of all would have to happen.

HELMER.   Tell me what that would be!

NORA.   Both you and I would have to be so changed that—. Oh, Torvald, I don't believe any longer in wonderful things happening.

HELMER.   But I will believe in it. Tell me? So changed that—?

NORA.   That our life together would be a real wedlock. Good-bye.   38●

[*She goes out through the hall.*]

HELMER.   [*sinks down on a chair at the door and buries his face in his hands*] Nora! Nora! [*looks round, and rises*] Empty. She is gone. [*A hope flashes across his mind.*] The most wonderful thing of all—?

[*The sound of a door slamming is heard from below.*]

QUESTIONS

Act I

1. What does the opening stage direction reveal about the Helmer family? About the time of year?

2. Explain the ways Nora and Torvald behave toward each other.

3. What does Torvald's refusal to consider borrowing and debt tell you about him (speech 22)? Where else in the play are these characteristics important?

4. What have the Helmer finances been like in the past? How is their situation about to change?

5. How are Mrs. Linde and Nora alike? Different? Why is it ironic that Nora helps Christine get a job at the bank? How will this affect Krogstad? Nora?

6. How does Ibsen show that Krogstad is a threat when he first appears?

7. Why should Nora's scene with her children in Act I not be cut in production? What does it show about Nora and the household?

8. What is Nora's secret "crime"? What is the explanation and justification for it? At the end of the act, what new problems does she face?

Act II

9. What is symbolized by the stripped Christmas tree?

10. What is implied about Nora's self perceptions when she calls herself "your little squirrel" and "your skylark"?

11. After sending Krogstad's dismissal, Torvald tells Nora that "You will see I am man enough to take everything upon myself" (speech 135). How does this speech conform to Nora's hopes? How is it ironic?

12. Why does Nora flirt with Dr. Rank? How and why does he distress her?

13. Why does Nora dance the Tarantella so wildly?

14. What is the "wonderful thing" that Nora is waiting for?

Act III

15. Explain Christine's past rejection of Krogstad. Why will she accept him now? How will their union differ from the Helmers' marriage?

16. What does Christine decide to do about Krogstad's letter? Why?

17. Explain the reactions of Torvald and Nora to the death of Dr. Rank.

18. Describe Torvald's reaction to Krogstad's first letter. How does Nora respond to Torvald? How do you respond to him? Why?

19. Explain what Nora learns about Torvald, herself, her marriage, and her identity as a woman as a result of Torvald's responses. Why does she decide to leave?

GENERAL QUESTIONS

1. Which elements and aspects of *A Dollhouse* are most and least realistic? Explain.

2. Consider Ibsen's symbolism, with reference to Dr. Rank, macaroons, the Christmas tree, the presents, the locked mailbox, the dance, Nora's black shawl, her change of clothing in Act III, and the door slam at the play's close.

3. Is Nora a victim of circumstances or a villain who brings about problems? What is Ibsen's view? What is yours? Why?

4. Describe the "role-playing" in the Helmer marriage. Does any evidence suggest that Nora knows she is playing a role? What degree of self-awareness, if any, characterizes Torvald's role-playing?

5. When Nora asks Torvald to restore Krogstad's job, Torvald refuses on the ground that he should not give in to his wife's pressure (Act II, speech 113). Later, he claims that their marriage is destroyed, but that they should keep up

the appearance of marital stability (Act III, speech 242). In the light of such statements, describe Torvald's character. What concerns him most about life and marriage?

6. A major theme in the play is that weakness and corruption are passed from generation to generation. Examine this theme in connection with Krogstad and his sons, Nora and her children, Nora and her father, and Dr. Rank.

7. Discuss the ideas about individual growth, marriage, and social convention in the play. How are these ideas developed and related? Which character most closely embodies Ibsen's ideas?

8. Write an essay about any or all of the following questions:

   a. Is *A Dollhouse* a comedy, a tragedy, or something in between?

   b. How do the play's characters change for the better (or worse)?

   c. How negative, or affirmative, is the conclusion? Why?

HENRIK IBSEN   (1828–1906)

An Enemy of the People (En Folkefiende) ——————————————— *1882*

Translated by Edgar V. Roberts

CHARACTERS

Dr. Thomas Stockmann, *a physician, and Chief Medical Officer of the town's Therapeutic Spa*
Mrs. Katrina Stockmann, *his wife*
Petra Stockmann, *their daughter, a young woman; a teacher*
Eilif Stockmann, *their thirteen-year-old son*
Morten Stockmann, *their ten-year-old son*
Peter Stockmann (The Mayor), *Dr. Stockmann's older brother, Principal Executive and Chief Constable of the local government, Chief Executive Officer of the Governing Board of the Spa, etc., etc.*
Morten Kiil, *owner of the tannery at the nearby town of Mølledal, and Mrs. Stockmann's stepfather*
Captain Horster, *a ship's captain, friendly to Dr. Stockmann and his family*
Hovstad, *editor-in-chief of the* People's Messenger
Billing, *assistant editor of the* Messenger
Aslaksen, *owner of a printing business, publisher of the* Messenger, *chair of the local Homeowners Association, and Secretary of the Temperance Union*
Vik, *a stout citizen; a shipowner, and Captain Horster's employer*

Workers, *seen in Aslaksen's print shop in Act III*
Local Townspeople, *men, women, and children—of all classes—who attend the meeting in Act IV. Three of these are named: Lamstad (2 Citizen); Pettersen, a drunken man; and Skipper Evensen, whose main task is to blow a horn. A number of the other citizens and workers have speaking lines. All react, demonstrate, and shout as a group.*

The location of the play is an unnamed town on the southern coast of Norway. The time and circumstances are those of 1882, the date of the play.

ACT I

SCENE. *Evening in the living room of DR. and MRS. STOCKMANN. The room is plainly but neatly furnished. At stage right are two doors, the upstage one leading to a hallway, the downstage one to DR. STOCKMANN's study. At upstage left, a door leads to the other family rooms. In the middle of the stage-left wall is a ceramic tile heating stove, and, farther downstage, a sofa with a mirror above and an oval coffee table in front. A lamp with a prominent lampshade is burning on the table. An open door in the back wall shows the dining room. BILLING is alone at the dining table, which also holds a lighted lamp. A napkin is tucked into his collar, and MRS. STOCKMANN is serving him from a platter of roast beef. The other chairs are empty, but the table has not yet been cleared of the plates, etc., of the diners who have left the table.*

MRS. STOCKMANN.   You see, Mr. Billing, if you come late, you have to settle for cold food.

BILLING   [*speaks while eating*].   This is good, thank you, really fine.

MRS. STOCKMANN.   My husband is very punctual about his meals, you know—

BILLING.   That's all right with me. In fact, I think I enjoy eating more when I'm alone.

MRS. STOCKMANN.   Well, since you feel that way—[*turns toward sounds at the hallway door.*] That's probably Mr. Hovstad.   5

BILLING.   You're right.

[*MAYOR PETER STOCKMANN enters, wearing an overcoat and his official hat and carrying a walking-stick.*]

THE MAYOR.   Good evening, Katrina.

MRS. STOCKMANN   [*enters the living room*].   Good evening. How are you? How nice of you to come over!

THE MAYOR.   I was just passing by, and so—[*Looks into the dining room*].   But I see you have another guest.

MRS. STOCKMANN   [*somewhat embarrassed*].   Oh, no, he came by quite by chance.   10
[*Speaks rapidly.*] Won't you have something to eat, too?

THE MAYOR.   Me? No, thank you. With my digestion, I can't eat hot meals at night.

MRS. STOCKMANN.   Not even just this once?

THE MAYOR.   No, my dear, no. I stick to my tea, bread, and butter, which is healthier for me—and cheaper, too.

MRS. STOCKMANN   [*smiles*].   Now, you can't say that Thomas and I are spendthrifts.

THE MAYOR.   No, not you, I'd never say that about *you*. [*Points to the doctor's study.*]   15
Is he in there?

MRS. STOCKMANN.   No, he went walking with the boys after dinner.

THE MAYOR.   I don't think that's a good idea. [*Listens.*] He may be coming now.

MRS. STOCKMANN.   No, not yet. [*A knock at the door.*] Come in! [*EDITOR HOVSTAD enters from the hallway.*] Oh, it's Mr. Hovstad!

HOVSTAD.   Yes. Please excuse me. I was delayed at the printer's. Mr. Mayor, good evening.

THE MAYOR   [*bows formally*].   Good evening. I suppose you're here on business?   20

HOVSTAD.   Yes, partly. It's about an article for the paper.

THE MAYOR.   As I thought. I understand my brother is a regular contributor to *The People's Messenger.*

HOVSTAD.   Yes, he writes for the *Messenger* on local matters.

MRS. STOCKMANN   [*to* HOVSTAD].   Would you like—[*Points to the dining room.*]

THE MAYOR.   Yes indeed. I'm sure *I* don't blame him for writing for a sympathetic audience. Besides that, Mr. Hovstad, I have nothing against your paper.

HOVSTAD.   No, I shouldn't think you did.

THE MAYOR.   On the whole, there's a beautiful sense of toleration in the town—genuine public spirit. And it all comes from our mutual interest—an interest that concerns to the highest degree all upright citizens—

HOVSTAD.   The Town Spa, yes.

THE MAYOR.   Precisely—our superb new Therapeutic Baths. Remember this, Mr. Hovstad, the Spa will bring us together. No question about it.

HOVSTAD.   Thomas says the same thing.

THE MAYOR.   Think of how the town has been reviving in the last year! People now have more money! There's life, and activity! Land and property values are soaring!

HOVSTAD.   Unemployment is going down.

THE MAYOR.   Yes, you're right. Tax rates for maintaining the poor are being lifted, and the middle class is relieved. Moreover, their relief will be greater if we have a good summer—huge crowds of visitors—and especially flocks of sick people, who will bring fame to our institution.

HOVSTAD.   I hear that the long-range weather forecasts are good.

THE MAYOR.   Things look favorable. We're getting inquiries and reservations for apartments every day.

HOVSTAD.   Well, the Doctor's article will be timely and relevant.

THE MAYOR.   Oh, he's written something new?

HOVSTAD.   This is something he wrote last winter—a commendation of the Spa and a description of its healthful benefits. But I held it for publication until now.

THE MAYOR.   Oh, was there some sort of problem?

HOVSTAD.   No, not that. I thought it better to hold it till now, in the spring, because it's now that people make their summer plans.

THE MAYOR.   Indeed, you're quite right, Mr. Hovstad.

MRS. STOCKMANN.   Yes, Thomas is a tireless booster of the Spa.

THE MAYOR.   Well, he's also one of the staff.

HOVSTAD.   Yes, and more, he was the first to create the idea of the Spa.

THE MAYOR.   Oh he did, did he? I hear that certain people think this, but nevertheless it seems to me that *I* also had a modest role in the undertaking.

MRS. STOCKMANN.   Yes, Thomas always says that.

HOVSTAD.   No one denies your share, Mr. Mayor. You got things going and made the Spa a reality. We all know that. I meant only that the Doctor got the idea first.

THE MAYOR.   Oh, yes, the *idea.* My brother has had lots of ideas—unfortunately. But when things get practical, you need different sorts of people, Mr. Hovstad. And I might have expected that here, in this house—

MRS. STOCKMANN.   But dear Brother—

HOVSTAD.   How could the Mayor—

MRS. STOCKMANN.   Please go in and have something to eat, Mr. Hovstad. My husband will be back soon.

HOVSTAD.   Perhaps just a little something, thank you. [*Goes to the dining room.*]

THE MAYOR   [*lowers his voice*].   Have you ever noticed that these country louts never have any manners?

MRS. STOCKMANN.   Now why should you bother yourself about that? Can't you and Thomas, as brothers, share the recognition?

THE MAYOR.   I would have thought so, but apparently not everyone seems satis- 55
fied with only a share.

MRS. STOCKMANN.   Come now—you and Thomas get along so well together. [*Listens to noises in the hallway.*] Here he comes now, I think. [*Goes to the hallway door and opens it.*]

DR. STOCKMANN [*speaks to various persons while entering amid general noise and laughter*].   Katrina, I've brought another guest. Isn't it great? Now then, Captain Horster, hang your coat on this rack. Oh, you're not wearing an overcoat? Katrina, just think, I met him on our walk and he almost didn't want to come along. [*CAPTAIN HORSTER, followed by DR. STOCKMANN, enters the room and greets MRS. STOCKMANN.*] In with you, boys. [*EILIF and MORTEN enter.*] The walk gave them a new appetite. Join us, Captain Horster, and have some roast beef.

[*He escorts HORSTER into the dining room. The boys follow them.*]

MRS. STOCKMANN.   But Thomas, do you see—

DR. STOCKMANN [*turns in the doorway.*]   Oh, Peter, it's you. [*Shakes hands with the MAYOR.*] This is really great!

THE MAYOR.   I was just leaving— 60

DR. STOCKMANN.   Nonsense. Stay for some hot toddy. You didn't forget the toddy, did you Katrina?

MRS. STOCKMANN.   Of course not. The water's just boiling.

[*She goes into the dining room.*]

THE MAYOR.   Hot toddy, too—!

DR. STOCKMANN.   Yes, have a seat so we can have it in comfort.

THE MAYOR.   No, thanks, I never stay at a drinking party. 65

DR. STOCKMANN.   But this isn't a party.

THE MAYOR.   It seems to me—[*Looks toward the dining room.*] It's amazing how they eat that much food.

DR. STOCKMANN [*rubs his hands*].   Yes, it's great to see young people eat. They never get filled up, and that's as it should be. They need the food to get strong, Peter, because they're the ones who'll be stirring things up in the future.

THE MAYOR.   And just what, as you put it, is going to need "stirring up"?

DR. STOCKMANN.   You'll have to ask the young people that—when the time 70
comes. But then, of course, old fogies like you and me won't be around to see it.

THE MAYOR.   Really! I'm not sure I like that expression.

DR. STOCKMANN.   Don't be so literal, Peter. You know that I'm quite happy. I'm glad to be alive here and now, and to be at the cutting edge. Everything is growing and coming to fruition, and it seems that an entire new world is emerging around me.

THE MAYOR.   You really think so?

DR. STOCKMANN.   Yes, but you can't see it the way I do. You've lived here all your life, and you're too used to things. But I was buried all those years up north; I never saw anyone with any new ideas. Well, to me, being here is the same as having flown into the middle of a bustling metropolitan center.

THE MAYOR.   A metropolitan center? 75

DR. STOCKMANN.   I know what you mean. Ours is a small town. But there's also life here—promise, and countless things to work and struggle for. That's the main thing. [*Calls.*] Katrina, did the mailman come today?

MRS. STOCKMANN   [*in the dining room*].   No, he didn't.

DR. STOCKMANN.   And then, Peter, to be well off! When you've lived at just a subsistence level, as we did, you value that.

THE MAYOR.   God forbid—

DR. STOCKMANN.   It's true. Up there we often lived close to the line. But now, we live like kings! We had roast beef today not only for dinner, but also for supper. Come and have some, or at least let me show it to you. Come here—

THE MAYOR.   No, no, it's unnecessary.

DR. STOCKMANN.   Well, come here, then. Do you see our new tablecloth?

THE MAYOR.   Yes, I noticed.

DR. STOCKMANN.   And we bought a lampshade. Do you see? Katrina had saved the money for it. It makes the room so cosy. Stand here—no, no, right here—yes, here. Do you see the way it focuses the light downward? I really think that's elegant. Right?

THE MAYOR.   Yes, if people can permit such luxury.

DR. STOCKMANN.   Oh yes, I can afford it. Katrina says I now make almost as much as we spend!

THE MAYOR.   Of course, almost!

DR. STOCKMANN.   Scientists like me are entitled to a better life, but even then I'm sure that most civil servants live better than I do.

THE MAYOR.   Well, yes, a chief officer, a superior court judge—

DR. STOCKMANN.   Well then, most businessmen, who spend two or three times more—

THE MAYOR.   Their circumstances are not the same as yours.

DR. STOCKMANN.   At any rate, I don't waste money. But I can't deny my need to entertain my friends. I was away from everything for so long, and I'm hungry for young, vital, ambitious associates with inquiring and active minds. That description fits everyone enjoying supper in there. You should really get to know Hovstad.

THE MAYOR.   By the way, Hovstad told me he was publishing one of your articles.

DR. STOCKMANN.   One of my articles?

THE MAYOR.   Yes, the one you wrote last winter about the Spa.

DR. STOCKMANN.   Oh yes, but I don't want that one printed just yet.

THE MAYOR.   Not yet? This seems to be a good time.

DR. STOCKMANN.   Well, yes, under normal circumstances. [*Paces.*]

THE MAYOR   [*looks at him closely*].   Is something wrong with the present circumstances?

DR. STOCKMANN   [*stops*].   To be frank, Peter, I can't say right now. There really could be some problems—but it's possible that there's no problem at all. It may be no more than my imagination.

THE MAYOR.   You're being very mysterious. Is something going on that I don't know about? You should know that I, as Chief Executive Officer of the Governing Board of the Baths—

DR. STOCKMANN.   And you should know that I——. But let's not lash out at each other, Peter.

THE MAYOR.   Of course not. I don't "lash out" at people, as you put it. But I must insist on orderly procedure, and that only the properly designated officials treat problems that may arise. I can't tolerate anyone going behind our backs.

DR. STOCKMANN.   Did I ever try to go behind anyone's back?

THE MAYOR.   Let's just say that you tend to do things in your own way, and that's   105
not very different. Individuals must subordinate their own interests to those of the community—or, to be more accurate, to the authorities who hold the community interest in trust.

DR. STOCKMANN.   I'm sure. But what in hell does this have to do with me?

THE MAYOR.   My good Thomas, this is what you never seem willing to learn. But look out, because some day, sooner or later, you'll have to pay for it. Now I've told you. Good-bye.

DR. STOCKMANN.   Are you crazy? You're on the wrong track!

THE MAYOR.   I'm usually not. Please excuse me now. [*Bows toward the dining room*]. Good night, Katrina. Good night, gentlemen. [*Leaves.*]

MRS. STOCKMANN   [*enters from the dining room*].   He's gone?   110

DR. STOCKMANN.   Yes, and in a foul mood.

MRS. STOCKMANN.   But dear Thomas, did you provoke him again?

DR. STOCKMANN.   No, not at all. And he can't make me give him any report before I'm ready.

MRS. STOCKMANN.   What are you making a report about?

DR. STOCKMANN.   Don't ask, Katrina.—But why hasn't the mailman come yet?   115

[*HOVSTAD, BILLING, and HORSTER enter from the dining room, followed by EILIF and MORTEN.*]

BILLING   [*stretches*].   Ah! A meal like that makes me feel like a new man, damn it.

HOVSTAD.   The mayor was not his usual sweet self, then?

DR. STOCKMANN.   It's just his bad digestion.

HOVSTAD.   I think that he couldn't stomach the two of us from the *Messenger.*

MRS. STOCKMANN.   I thought that you both carried it off well.   120

HOVSTAD.   Well, I think we have more of a truce than a peace.

BILLING.   Yes, that's the right word for it.

DR. STOCKMANN.   Let's not forget that Peter is all alone. He has no life, nothing but his job. And then think of the awful tea that he's always pouring into himself—! But now then, boys, sit down at the table. Can we have that hot toddy now, Katrina?

MRS. STOCKMANN   [*goes to the dining room*].   I'll have it right away!

DR. STOCKMANN.   Sit next to me, Captain Horster. We haven't seen you for a long   125
time—. Please sit down, friends.

[*They sit at the table. MRS. STOCKMANN carries in a tray with the appropriate glasses, bottles, etc.*]

MRS. STOCKMANN.   Here you are, gentlemen. This is arrack. This is rum. This is cognac. Just serve yourselves.

DR. STOCKMANN   [*takes a glass*].   Thank you, we will. [*They all pour drinks for themselves.*] And let's have cigars. Eilif, you know where they are. And Morten, bring me my pipe. [*The boys leave for the room on the right.*] I think Eilif takes a cigar once in a while, but I ignore it. [*Calls out.*] Morten, get my smoking-cap, too. Tell him where it is, Katrina. Ah, he has it. [*The boys bring the things.*] Now, friends. I'll stick with my pipe, you know. This one has seen many a day with me up north. [*They all touch glasses; cries of "Skoal," etc.*] Good health! Skoal! Ah, it's good to be warm and comfortable.

MRS. STOCKMANN   [*sits down and begins knitting*].   Do you sail soon, Captain Horster?

HORSTER.   Yes, I expect as early as next week,

MRS. STOCKMANN. To America, I suppose?   1₿

HORSTER. Yes, that's the schedule.

MRS. STOCKMANN. Then you can't vote in the next election?

HORSTER. Is there an election?

MRS. STOCKMANN. You didn't know?

HORSTER. No, I usually don't get involved.   1₿

MRS. STOCKMANN. You aren't concerned about public affairs?

HORSTER. No, I don't follow politics.

BILLING. Even so, people should vote.

HORSTER. Even if they don't know the issues?

BILLING. Don't know? What do you mean? Every community is like a large ship;   14
everyone should be ready to be a pilot.

HORSTER. That may be true on shore, but it won't work on a ship.

HOVSTAD. It's amazing that sailors have such small concern about what happens
on land.

BILLING. Yes, amazing.

DR. STOCKMANN. Sailors are like migratory birds, Hovstad; they find their homes
anywhere, north or south. And that's one more reason for our own vigilance. Mr.
Hovstad, is there anything of local interest in tomorrow's *Messenger*?

HOVSTAD. No, but I was planning to publish your article the day after tomorrow.   14

DR. STOCKMANN. My article, damn it all!—Listen, you'll have to hold that a bit
longer.

HOVSTAD. Really? We have the space, and it's just the right time—

DR. STOCKMANN. Yes, I understand, but wait just the same.

[*PETRA enters from the hallway, wearing a hat and coat, and carrying a stack of notebooks.*]

PETRA. Good evening.

DR. STOCKMANN. Good evening, Petra.   15

[*She greets everyone and removes her things and puts them on a chair near the door.*]

PETRA. I see that you've been having a good time while I've been working like a
slave.

DR. STOCKMANN. Well then, now it's your turn to enjoy.

BILLING. Can I get you a drink?

PETRA [*goes to the table*]. Thanks, I'll do it myself; you always make it too strong.
Oh, by the way, Father, I have a letter for you.

[*Goes to her things on the chair and removes a letter from her coat pocket.*]

DR. STOCKMANN. A letter? Who sent it?   15

PETRA. The mailman delivered it just as I was leaving—

DR. STOCKMANN [*gets up and goes to her*]. And you give it to me only now?

PETRA. I had no time to run upstairs again. Here you are.

DR. STOCKMANN [*grabs the letter and looks eagerly at it*]. Let's see, let's see. Yes,
this is it—!

MRS. STOCKMANN. Is this the one you've been expecting, Thomas?   16

DR. STOCKMANN. Yes. I have to go to go in. —Where's the lamp, Katrina? Is there
no light in my room again?

MRS. STOCKMANN.   Yes, it's lit and it's on your writing desk.

DR. STOCKMANN.   Good, good. Excuse me—just a few minutes— [*Goes into his study at the right.*]

PETRA.   What's this all about, Mother?

MRS. STOCKMANN.   I don't know. He's been asking about the mailman for the last few days.   165

BILLING.   Probably a report about an out-of-town patient.

PETRA.   Poor Dad, he may be working too hard. [*Mixes herself a drink.*] This looks so good!

HOVSTAD.   Were you teaching in the evening school too?

PETRA   [*speaks while holding the glass and drinking*].   Two hours.

BILLING.   And also four hours this morning?   170

PETRA.   Five hours.

MRS. STOCKMANN.   And you still have papers to grade?

PETRA.   A stack, yes.

HORSTER.   You seem overwhelmed with work.

PETRA.   Yes, but that's all right. I feel healthfully tired because of it.   175

BILLING.   You like that?

PETRA.   Yes, because I sleep so well.

MORTEN.   You must be really a bad person, Petra.

PETRA.   Bad?

MORTEN.   Yes, because you work so hard. Mr. Rørlund says work is punishment for our sins.   180

EILIF.   Pooh! What a dumbbell, to swallow garbage like that.

MRS. STOCKMANN.   Now then, Eilif!

BILLING   [*laughing*].   Kids, anyway!

HOVSTAD.   Don't you like working, Morten?

MORTEN.   Not on your life!   185

HOVSTAD.   Then what would you like to be?

MORTEN.   I'd like to be a Viking.

EILIF.   You'd have to be a heathen, then.

MORTEN.   Well, I could join the heathen church, couldn't I?

BILLING.   That's it, Morten. I agree completely.   190

MRS. STOCKMANN   [*signals negatively to BILLING*].   Now, Mr. Billing, you don't believe that.

BILLING.   Yes, damn it! I'm proud to be a heathen. We'll all be heathens before long.

MORTEN.   And then we'll be able to do anything we want?

BILLING.   Well, you see, Morten—

MRS. STOCKMANN.   Boys, you'll have to go to your rooms. You have studying to do for tomorrow.   195

EILIF.   But I want to stay here—

MRS. STOCKMANN.   No, no, off you go now.

[*The boys say good-night and leave through the doorway on the left.*]

HOVSTAD.   Do you think there's any harm in what I was saying?

MRS. STOCKMANN.   I'm not sure, but I don't like it.

PETRA.   But Mother, you're being foolish about this.   200

MRS. STOCKMANN.   You might be right, but I don't like it—not in our own house.

PETRA.   There's such great hypocrisy, both at home and at school. At home we can't speak, and at school we have to tell lies to the children.

HORSTER.   You tell lies?

PETRA.   Yes, don't you realize we have to teach all sorts of things we don't believe?

BILLING.   You're quite right.   20

PETRA.   If I had enough money I'd start my own school, where things would go differently.

BILLING.   Oh, just money—

HORSTER.   If you have ideas about a new school, Miss Stockmann, I'd be happy to offer you rooms. The house my father left me is empty, and there's a huge dining room downstairs.

PETRA   [*laughs*].   Why thank you, but nothing is likely to happen.

HOVSTAD.   No, I think Miss Petra is more likely to go into journalism. By the way,   21
have you been able to finish translating that English story you promised for us?

PETRA.   No, not yet, but soon, I hope.

[*DR. STOCKMANN enters from his study, with the open letter in hand.*]

DR. STOCKMANN   [*waves the letter*].   Well, the town is about to get some real news!

BILLING.   Real news?

MRS. STOCKMANN.   What do you mean?

DR. STOCKMANN.   A major discovery, Katrina.   2▮

HOVSTAD.   Truly?

MRS. STOCKMANN.   Your own discovery?

DR. STOCKMANN.   Yes, my own. [*Paces.*] Just let them accuse me of imagining things. [*Laughs.*] They'll have to be careful now about what they say.

PETRA.   Father, what is it?

DR. STOCKMANN.   All in due time. If only Peter were here now! It all shows how   22
human beings can go around and make judgments no better than the blindest of moles—

HOVSTAD.   Doctor, what are you saying?

DR. STOCKMANN   [*stands at the table*].   I ask, is it or is it not accepted opinion that our town is a healthy place?

HOVSTAD.   It is, yes.

DR. STOCKMANN.   A model for good health, in fact—a center to be accepted enthusiastically for those who are either ill or well?

MRS. STOCKMANN.   Yes, but Thomas, dear—   22

DR. STOCKMANN.   And we've touted it highly. I myself have written pamphlets and articles for the *Messenger*?

HOVSTAD.   Yes, and so?

DR. STOCKMANN.   And we've called our Spa "the artery of our town's blood" and "the center of the town's nervous system," and who the devil knows what other silly phrases—

BILLING.   In an extreme moment, I once said "the town's throbbing heart."

DR. STOCKMANN.   Right. Well, do you know the truth about these curative baths,   2▮
so marvellous, so magnificent, so highly eulogized—and so expensive? Do you know?

HOVSTAD.   No, but tell us.

MRS. STOCKMANN.   What are they?

DR. STOCKMANN.   The whole thing's a sewer!

PETRA. The Spa, Father?

MRS. STOCKMANN [*at the same time*]. Our baths? 235

HOVSTAD. But—

BILLING. Unbelievable!

DR. STOCKMANN. All the Spa buildings constitute a whited, polluted sepulcher—a threat to public health! All that poisoned runoff up at Mølledal, all that filth, is contaminating the water going to our reservoir! And the same damned, deadly effluent is also filtering out on our shore!

HORSTER. Do you mean at our Spa buildings, where our visitors take their treatments?

DR. STOCKMANN. Yes, right there. 240

HOVSTAD. But Doctor, how do you know all this?

DR. STOCKMANN. I've suspected something for quite a while, because last year some of the patients had unusual symptoms—typhoid, and gastrointestinal flu. Now I've studied things thoroughly.

MRS. STOCKMANN. You're right about those illnesses.

DR. STOCKMANN. At first we concluded that people were infected before they came here. But this winter I started thinking differently, and began analyzing our water.

MRS. STOCKMANN. So this is why you've been so busy. 245

DR. STOCKMANN. Yes, Katrina, I've been busy. But here we don't have much laboratory equipment, so I sent samples of the seawater and drinking water to the university for an exact chemical analysis.

HOVSTAD. Did they send you a report?

DR. STOCKMAN [*shows the letter*]. This is it. It shows conclusively that our water contains dangerously high levels of bacteria, both for drinking and bathing.

MRS. STOCKMANN. Thank heaven you found out now, before the summer season.

DR. STOCKMANN. Let's all be thankful. 250

HOVSTAD. What are you planning to do now, Doctor?

DR. STOCKMANN. Obviously, to make things right.

HOVSTAD. Is that possible?

DR. STOCKMANN. It must be possible, or else our Spa will be useless. But I have a plan.

MRS. STOCKMANN. But, dear Thomas, why did you keep this so quiet? 255

DR. STOCKMANN. Should I have chattered about it around town without conclusive evidence? I'm not that kind of idiot.

PETRA. But you could have told us.

DR. STOCKMANN. Not to you, not to anyone. But tomorrow you may go and tell the old Badger—

MRS. STOCKMANN. Now Thomas!

DR. STOCKMANN. All right, your stepfather. This will surprise him. He, along with 260
others, thinks I'm crazy, but now they'll see! [*Paces, rubbing his hands.*] This will really get the town stirred up, Katrina. Completely new water lines will have to be installed.

HOVSTAD [*rises*]. *All* the water lines—?

DR. STOCKMANN. Certainly. The intakes are too low; they'll need to be put on higher ground.

PETRA. So you were right all the time.

DR. STOCKMANN. You remember that, Petra? I wrote against the final plans before work was started. They paid no attention to me then, but they'll pay attention now! I've had a report ready for the Governing Board for the last week, and was only waiting for this. [*Waves the letter.*] I'll send it right away. [*Goes to his office, returning with papers.*] See here, all four sheets, along with an explanatory letter. A newspaper, Katrina, something for wrapping. That's fine. Now give it to—to—[*stamps his foot*]—what's her name? The maid, and tell her to take it to the Mayor.

[*MRS. STOCKMANN takes the package and leaves through the dining room.*]

PETRA.   Father, what will Uncle Peter say about this?   2€

DR. STOCKMANN.   What can he say? He should be glad that such important facts have been discovered.

HOVSTAD.   Would you consent to my publishing an article about this in the *Messenger*?

DR. STOCKMANN.   That would be excellent.

HOVSTAD.   The public should know, and the sooner the better.

DR. STOCKMANN.   Certainly.   27

MRS. STOCKMANN   [*returns*].   She's just gone off with it.

BILLING.   Doctor, you're the most important man in town.

DR. STOCKMANN   [*paces happily*].   Oh, come now! I've just been doing my civic duty. I was lucky enough to find the treasure. But just the same—

BILLING.   Hovstad, shouldn't the town give Dr. Stockmann some token of gratitude?

HOVSTAD.   Well, I'll certainly suggest one.   27

BILLING.   And I'll take up the matter with Aslaksen.

DR. STOCKMANN.   Dear friends, no nonsense. I won't hear of any ceremonies. And if the Governing Board should recommend a raise, I won't accept it. Katrina, I tell you, I'll turn it down.

MRS. STOCKMANN.   Thomas, you're right.

PETRA   [*raises her glass*].   Father, your health!

HOVSTAD AND BILLING.   Skoal, Doctor! Cheers!   28

HORSTER   [*clinks glasses with Dr. Stockmann*].   I hope this affair brings you endless good luck!

DR. STOCKMANN.   Thank you, dear friends, thank you. I'm so overwhelmingly glad! Oh what a blessing it is to realize that you've been able to serve your home town and fellow citizens. Hurrah, Katrina!

[*He embraces her and they do a whirling dance, with MRS. STOCKMANN laughingly protesting. Laughter, applause, and cheers for the DOCTOR. The boys poke their heads in at the door.*]

END OF THE FIRST ACT

ACT II

SCENE. *The same, the next morning. MRS. STOCKMANN, holding a letter, enters from the closed dining-room door. She calls toward the door of the DOCTOR'S study to announce herself.*

MRS. STOCKMANN.   Are you in there, Thomas?

DR. STOCKMANN   [*answers from within*].   Yes, I just came in. [*Enters.*] What have you got there?

MRS. STOCKMANN.   A letter from your brother. [*Gives it to him.*]

DR. STOCKMANN.   Ah, let's see. [*Opens the letter and reads.*] "Find enclosed the materials you sent me"— [*Reads on and mutters*].   Hmm!

MRS. STOCKMANN.   Well, what does he say?

DR. STOCKMANN   [*puts the papers in a pocket*].   Nothing more than that he will stop by to see us at about noon.

MRS. STOCKMANN.   Well then, be sure to be at home.

DR. STOCKMANN.   I will. I've already done my morning rounds.

MRS. STOCKMANN.   I wonder what he's going to say.

DR. STOCKMANN.   Most probably he'll be unhappy because he didn't discover the problem before I did.

MRS. STOCKMANN.   Doesn't that make you nervous?

DR. STOCKMANN.   No, he'll probably be broad-minded about things, but you know he gets damned anxious about anyone else invading his turf to do something good for the town.

MRS. STOCKMANN.   Well, I think you ought to share this with him. Why not let it be known that he was the one who got you going?

DR. STOCKMANN.   Fine. It's okay with me. I just want to put things right.

[*MORTEN KIIL peeks in from the hallway, looks around inquiringly, and chuckles.*]

MORTEN KIIL.   Is it—is it true?

MRS. STOCKMANN.   Father, how nice.

DR. STOCKMANN.   Father Kiil, good morning.

MRS. STOCKMANN.   Please come in.

MORTEN KIIL.   I'll come in if it's true, but I'm going if it's not.

DR. STOCKMANN.   If what is true?

MORTEN KIIL.   The crazy story about the water supply. Is it true?

DR. STOCKMANN.   It's true, but how did you hear about it?

MORTEN KIIL   [*enters*].   Petra flew by on her way to school.

DR. STOCKMANN.   Oh she did?

MORTEN KIIL.   Yes, and she says—. I thought she was kidding, but she wouldn't joke about a thing like that.

DR. STOCKMANN.   Certainly not; it's unthinkable.

MORTEN KIIL.   Well, if you believe everything people tell you, they'll make you a laughingstock before you know it. But it's true, then?

DR. STOCKMANN.   Absolutely true. But please sit down, Father. [*KIIL sits on the sofa.*] I think the town has been lucky—

MORTEN KIIL   [*stifles laughter*].   Luck for the town?

DR. STOCKMANN.   Yes, because my discovery was just in time.

MORTEN KIIL   [*still amused*].   Sure, sure, sure.—But I never would have believed that you'd play such hocus-pocus on your own brother.

DR. STOCKMANN.   Hocus-pocus?

MRS. STOCKMANN.   Now really, Father.

MORTEN KIIL   [*puts his hands and chin on the handle of his walking-cane, and winks at DR. STOCKMANN*].   Now, what's the story again? Some pernicious monsters have invaded the water intakes, right?

DR. STOCKMANN.   Right, infectious bacteria.

MORTEN KIIL.   And, as Petra says, there are hordes of these—huge hordes—right?

DR. STOCKMANN.   Right, millions and billions, in fact.

MORTEN KIIL.   But they're invisible, right?

DR. STOCKMANN.   Right.

MORTEN KIIL   [*laughs*].   Damn it all, I never heard anything better than this!

DR. STOCKMANN.   What are you saying?

MORTEN KIIL.   But Mayor Stockmann will never believe it.

DR. STOCKMANN.   We'll see about that.

MORTEN KIIL.   Do you think he's that big a fool—

DR. STOCKMANN.   My hope is that everyone in town will be such "fools," as you say.

MORTEN KIIL.   Everyone in town. It'd serve them right, too. They pressured me out of town government, they did. They think they know so much, but now they'll pay. Keep your magic spells going, Stockmann.

DR. STOCKMANN.   Now Mr. Kiil, really—

MORTEN KIIL.   Keep fooling them. [*Gets up.*] If you make the Mayor and his henchmen believe this, I'll give ten thousand to the poor—just like that.

DR. STOCKMANN.   Now this is very generous.

MORTEN KIIL.   Yes, I'm not wealthy, mind you, but if you pull this off, I'll remember the poor with five thousand—this next Christmas.

[*EDITOR HOVSTAD enters through the hallway door.*]

HOVSTAD.   Good morning. [*Sees MORTEN KIIL.*] Oh, I'm sorry.

DR. STOCKMANN.   Don't be. Come in.

MORTEN KIIL   [*chuckles*].   Aha! He's in on it too?

HOVSTAD.   What do you mean?

DR. STOCKMANN.   Yes, he knows everything.

MORTEN KIIL.   I'm not surprised. Get plenty of coverage about this in the papers. Make it big. I'll leave you to your work.

DR. STOCKMANN.   Can't you stay?

MORTEN KIIL.   No, I've got to go. Keep pushing this hocus-pocus, and, damn it all, you'll never be sorry, I promise you.

[*MORTEN KIIL leaves. MRS. STOCKMANN follows him out.*]

DR. STOCKMANN   [*laughs*].   Can you believe it? The old fellow doesn't believe the news about the water lines.

HOVSTAD.   Oh, so that's what all this was about.

DR. STOCKMANN.   Yes. Are you here about the same thing?

HOVSTAD.   I am. Can you spare me a few moments, Doctor?

DR. STOCKMANN.   Certainly, friend.

HOVSTAD.   Has the Mayor contacted you yet?

DR. STOCKMANN.   No, but he'll be coming by later.

HOVSTAD.   I've been thinking a lot about this.

DR. STOCKMANN.   And?

HOVSTAD.   Well you, as a doctor, see only one side of this, but there are lots of other considerations.

DR. STOCKMANN.   What do you mean? Let's sit. No, take the sofa. [*They sit, HOVSTAD on the sofa, DR. STOCKMANN on a chair next to the oval table.*] Now, you were telling me—

HOVSTAD.   Yesterday you said that the polluted water came from foul seepage through the ground.

DR. STOCKMANN. Absolutely—toxic seepage from the putrid swamp up at Mølledal.

HOVSTAD. With your leave, Doctor, I believe it's another kind of swamp.

DR. STOCKMANN. What do you mean? What kind of swamp?

HOVSTAD. The swamp on which our whole communal life stands and decays.

DR. STOCKMANN. In the devil's name, Mr. Hovstad, what sort of talk is this? 75

HOVSTAD. Piece by piece, the town has been taken over by a small clique of bureaucrats.

DR. STOCKMANN. Come now, the government is not large.

HOVSTAD. No, the government is just the tip of the iceberg. It's the town bigwigs, the ones with money, that have us in their clutches.

DR. STOCKMANN. Yes, but these are people with brains and dedication.

HOVSTAD. Where were their brains and dedication when the water lines were put 80
where they now lie?

DR. STOCKMANN. Well, I grant the stupidity of that, but things will soon be corrected.

HOVSTAD. Do you think this will be easy?

DR. STOCKMANN. At any rate, easy or not, it'll happen.

HOVSTAD. Yes, but only with the support of the press.

DR. STOCKMANN. But, friend, it won't be needed. I'm sure my brother— 85

HOVSTAD. Pardon me, Doctor. I have to tell you that I'm planning a series of editorials.

DR. STOCKMANN. In the paper?

HOVSTAD. Yes. When I first took over the *Messenger* my idea was to break up the ring of old bootlickers with all the power.

DR. STOCKMANN. Yes, but you told me you came close to bankruptcy because of this policy.

HOVSTAD. You're right; I admit it. It was inopportune to undermine public con- 90
fidence in those men then, because the whole Spa project depended on them. But now things are going well, and we can kiss these pompous crown princes goodbye.

DR. STOCKMANN. Even if they're replaced, they've done the town excellent service.

HOVSTAD. We'll give them their due. But a writer like me, with the advancement of the people as an objective, can't let this chance slide away to destroy the public's fairy-tale illusions of aristocratic infallibility.

DR. STOCKMANN. I agree with you there. Fairy tales must go.

HOVSTAD. I hesitate because the Mayor is your brother, but I'm sure that your priority is to the truth.

DR. STOCKMANN. That's self-evident. [*Bursts out.*] Yes, but— 95

HOVSTAD. You must realize that I see nothing to gain for myself in all this.

DR. STOCKMANN. My friend, who would ever think otherwise?

HOVSTAD. I was born poor, and that has enabled me to see what the lower classes need. And this is that the people themselves should have a role to play in government, because this, and only this, will bring out their abilities and intelligence and self-esteem—

DR. STOCKMANN. I understand your point.

HOVSTAD. You realize that dedicated journalists must take every opportunity in 100
the effort to liberate the masses, even though they might be called agitators or rabble rousers. For me, I'm willing to risk these accusations as long as my conscience is clear—

DR. STOCKMANN.   Just that, yes! Just that, My dear Mr. Hovstad, but all the same— [*A knocking at the door.*] The devil! Come in!

[*ASLAKSEN the printer enters, in a well-worn black suit and a wrinkled white scarf. He holds his hat and his gloves in his hands.*]

ASLAKSEN   [*bows*].   Doctor, please excuse my intrusion—

DR. STOCKMANN   [*rises*].   Well, hello! It's Mr. Aslaksen, the printer.

ASLAKSEN.   Yes, Doctor, you're right.

HOVSTAD   [*stands*].   Do you want me, Aslaksen?   1●

ASLAKSEN.   No, I didn't know you'd be here. I came to see the Doctor.

DR. STOCKMANN.   Well, then, what can I do for you?

ASLAKSEN.   Did I hear things right from Mr. Billing, that you plan to clean up our water systems?

DR. STOCKMANN.   That's right, the ones for the Spa.

ASLAKSEN.   Yes, I understand. Well, I want to give you my support on this.   1●

HOVSTAD   [*to DR. STOCKMANN*].   You see my point.

DR. STOCKMANN.   This is very kind of you, but—

ASLAKSEN.   It would be good to have us local tradesmen behind you. Together we make a solid majority in town, and it's always good to have the majority with you, Doctor.

DR. STOCKMANN.   You're certainly right, but this matter is so noncontroversial that it could never become a political issue—

ASLAKSEN.   Even so, support would be helpful. Our local politicians never like to   1●
do anything that someone else originates. That's why I think we might demonstrate a bit.

HOVSTAD.   He has a good point.

DR. STOCKMANN.   Demonstrate, you say? But how would you demonstrate?

ASLAKSEN.   Naturally, with great moderation, Doctor. I always do things moderately, for to me, moderation is a citizen's first obligation.

DR. STOCKMANN.   You are indeed well known for your moderation, Mr. Aslaksen.

ASLAKSEN.   I take pride in this. And this water-contamination business is impor-   1●
tant. The Spa can put the town on the map, and those of us in the trades, and those with rental property, can become rich. This is why we support you. You understand that I speak as Chair of the Homeowners Association—

DR. STOCKMANN.   Yes—?

ASLAKSEN.   And also as Secretary of the Temperance Union. You knew that this is one of my causes?

DR. STOCKMANN.   Oh yes, yes.

ASLAKSEN.   Well, you can see that I have many contacts, and with my reputation for moderation I have no small influence in town. You might say, in fact, that I have a certain degree of power.

DR. STOCKMANN.   Yes, Mr. Aslaksen, I know.   1●

ASLAKSEN.   So it would be relatively easy for me to initiate a testimonial.

DR. STOCKMANN.   A testimonial?

ASLAKSEN.   Yes, public recognition of your importance in an affair of such vital concern to the town. We would need, of course, a statement that would be judicious and moderate—something that would not be disagreeable to our local authorities. With care, I believe that we would not offend anyone.

HOVSTAD.   But even if someone were offended—

ASLAKSEN.   No, no, Mr. Hovstad, you don't get anywhere by insulting those who   130
have power over you. I once learned that the hard way. But no one can be put off by citizens expressing their views openly and moderately.

DR. STOCKMANN   [*shakes ASLAKSEN's hand*].   Your support is most gratifying, Mr.
Aslaksen. May I pour you some sherry?

ASLAKSEN.   No thanks, I never touch hard liquor.

DR. STOCKMANN.   Well, then, a glass of beer?

ASLAKSEN.   Nothing even like that so early in the day. I'm off now to see a few
landlords, to get things in motion.

DR. STOCKMANN.   This is quite kind of you, Mr. Aslaksen. But are all these cau-   135
tious steps necessary? Things seem so self-evident.

ASLAKSEN.   It's hard to get the authorities moving, Doctor, though sometimes I
understand their slowness—

HOVSTAD.   We're planning to stir things up in tomorrow's *Messenger*, Aslaksen.

ASLAKSEN.   But not too much, Mr. Hovstad. Without moderation, you'll get
nowhere; believe me, I've learned that. Well, thank you, Doctor. Be assured that we
small-business people stand behind you like a wall. The solid majority is with you, Doctor.

DR. STOCKMANN   [*shakes ASLAKSEN's hand*].   Good Mr. Aslaksen, I'm deeply grateful to you for this. Thank you. Goodbye.

ASLAKSEN   [*to HOVSTAD*].   I'm going to the print shop. Can you join me, Mr.   140
Hovstad?

HOVSTAD.   Later; I need to stay here a little while longer.

ASLAKSEN.   Good, I'll see you soon, then.

[*ASLAKSEN bows and leaves. DR. STOCKMANN accompanies him into the hallway, and then
returns.*]

HOVSTAD.   Well, Doctor, what do you think? Isn't it time to put a little courage
into such spineless fence-sitters?

DR. STOCKMANN.   You mean Aslaksen?

HOVSTAD.   Yes, I do. He's a fine enough fellow, but he can't take a decisive step,   145
and there are many just like him. They bend in the wind, this way and that way, and
finally they never accomplish anything.

DR. STOCKMANN.   Well, Aslaksen's heart seems in the right place.

HOVSTAD.   Yes, but if he were more decisive he'd be better.

DR. STOCKMANN.   I have to agree with you there.

HOVSTAD.   That's why the time is now so ripe. Public worship of authority must
end, and this official blunder with the water contamination must be brought home to
the voters.

DR. STOCKMANN.   Well, all right. The common good should be foremost. But   150
before more is done, I'll have to talk to my brother.

HOVSTAD.   In any event, I'll put together a feature article, and if the Mayor won't
listen to you—

DR. STOCKMANN.   You don't believe he won't listen?

HOVSTAD.   Anything is possible, and if it happens—

DR. STOCKMANN.   If it happens—if—you can publish my entire report—every last
word.

HOVSTAD.   Do I have your promise on that?   155

DR. STOCKMANN   [*gives HOVSTAD the report*].   Here, take it; there's no harm in your
reading it. You can return it later.

HOVSTAD.   Good; I will. Thank you, Doctor, and goodbye.

DR. STOCKMANN.   Goodbye. Everything is going to come out right, Mr. Hovstad, perfectly right.

HOVSTAD   [*bows and leaves*].   We'll see, we'll see.

DR. STOCKMANN   [*opens the dining-room door and calls*].   Katrina! Oh it's you, Petra.   1●

PETRA   [*enters*].   Yes, I just got home from school.

MRS. STOCKMANN   [*enters*].   Didn't Peter come yet?

DR. STOCKMANN.   No, but I've been talking to Hovstad about the broader significance of the water situation. He's quite excited, and has given me the freedom to publish about it in the *Messenger* whenever it's necessary.

MRS. STOCKMANN.   Will it be necessary?

DR. STOCKMANN.   No, not at all, but it's still gratifying to have support from the   1●
open-minded and independent press. Not only this, Katrina, but the Chair of the Homeowners Association has come to see me.

MRS. STOCKMANN.   Well, what was on his mind?

DR. STOCKMANN.   He promised his support, too, and everyone will support me if necessary. Katrina, do you know the support I have in back of me?

MRS. STOCKMANN.   No. What is it?

DR. STOCKMANN.   The solid majority.

MRS. STOCKMANN.   Is that really a good thing for you, Thomas?   1●

DR. STOCKMANN.   Yes, I believe so. [*Paces while rubbing his hands.*] Good Lord, how lucky it is to stand this way, as part of a family with one's fellow citizens!

PETRA.   And to be so right about things, father.

DR. STOCKMANN.   Beyond that, to do it for one's own hometown!

[*A doorbell rings.*]

MRS. STOCKMANN.   That was the doorbell.

DR. STOCKMANN.   It's him, then. [*A knock is heard at the door.*] Come in!   1●

THE MAYOR   [*enters from the hallway*].   Good morning.

DR. STOCKMANN.   Peter, I'm delighted to see you.

MRS. STOCKMANN.   How are you today, Peter?

THE MAYOR.   All right, thank you. [*To DR. STOCKMANN.*] Yesterday evening I received your report about the water condition at the Spa.

DR. STOCKMANN.   Did you finish it?   18●

THE MAYOR.   Yes, I did.

DR. STOCKMANN.   Well, what's your response to it?

THE MAYOR   [*looks at the women*].   Well—

MRS. STOCKMANN.   Come, Petra.

[*The women leave through the door at the left.*]

THE MAYOR   [*pauses briefly before he speaks.*]   Did you really need to do your studies   18●
behind my back?

DR. STOCKMANN.   Yes, because I had to be sure—

THE MAYOR.   Then you're sure now?

DR. STOCKMANN.   You must realize that I am.

THE MAYOR.   Do you plan to submit your study as an official report to the Governing Board of the Spa?

DR. STOCKMANN.   Yes. Something should be done right away.   19●

THE MAYOR.   In your usual manner, you make exaggerations in your report. I cite your claim that patients at our Baths are receiving perpetual poison.

DR. STOCKMANN.   Can you say it any other way, Peter? Our water, which we provide to the trusting souls who pay us huge fees to restore them to health, is poison for both drinking and bathing.

THE MAYOR.   And then you conclude that we must build diversionary drains for these so-called poisons from Mølledal, and also lay new intake mains?

DR. STOCKMANN.   Yes. Can you think of anything else? I can't.

THE MAYOR.   This morning I consulted with our Chief Engineer, and, in jest, as a   195
trial balloon, I asked him about possible costs for such proposals, just in the remote case they might be needed at some future time.

DR. STOCKMANN.   At some future time?

THE MAYOR.   Believe me, he was amused even at the suggestion. Do you have any idea what the new work would cost? His estimate is that the range could be anywhere from twenty-five to thirty million.

DR. STOCKMANN.   That much?

THE MAYOR.   Yes, and worse, the planning and construction would drag out for two years or more.

DR. STOCKMANN.   That long? Two whole years?   200

THE MAYOR.   Or more. And what could we do with the Spa facilities during this time? We'd need to close them. And even after the repairs, do you think anyone would come near them again, with the reputation that they'd been health hazards?

DR. STOCKMANN.   But Peter, they *are* hazardous.

THE MAYOR.   And all this is happening just as we're getting started. Nearby coastal towns have the same potential for therapeutic baths as ours. Don't you think their public relations people would work overtime to take our clientele? Where would that put us? We'd probably have to declare the whole extravagant thing a total loss, and then, Thomas, you would have brought your hometown to ruin.

DR. STOCKMANN.   Me? Ruin?

THE MAYOR.   The only viable future for this town is the Spa. You know that as well   205
as I do.

DR. STOCKMANN.   Well, what's your solution, then?

THE MAYOR.   I'm not persuaded by your report that the water is as bad as you make it seem.

DR. STOCKMANN.   Peter, it's worse, or at any rate it will be worse once the summer heat sets in.

THE MAYOR.   I told you that you exaggerate the danger. Surely a competent doctor can control noxious elements in the water, or neutralize them if they grow too plentiful.

DR. STOCKMANN.   And so? What else?   210

THE MAYOR.   We must acknowledge that current procedures for securing water cannot be substantially changed. But I believe that the Governing Board, if funding is available, might not be unwilling to institute certain improvements.

DR. STOCKMANN.   Do you believe that I can consent to this kind of underhanded scheme?

THE MAYOR.   An underhanded scheme?

DR. STOCKMANN.   Yes, an underhanded scheme, a lie, an outright crime against the town!

THE MAYOR.   As I've remarked, I've seen no persuasive evidence that the community is in any sort of danger.

DR. STOCKMANN.   Yes you have! There's no choice. You know my report is absolutely truthful, though you won't admit it. You're the one who insisted on the present locations of the intake mains and the Spa buildings, and it's this—your own damned blunder—that you won't admit. Bah! Do you imagine I don't see through you?

THE MAYOR.   Well, let's suppose, then, that you're right. I have the town's interests at heart, and without my present credibility I'm powerless to work for community betterment. For these reasons you must not submit your report. You must hold it back in the public interest. Then later, privately and quietly, we'll exert our best efforts. But for now, nothing—not a word—can be made public about this fatal affair.

DR. STOCKMANN.   My dear Peter, you may not be able to keep it quiet.

THE MAYOR.   It must be, and shall be.

DR. STOCKMANN.   You can't do it. Too many people already know.

THE MAYOR.   Know? Who? You can't mean that crew from the *Messenger?*

DR. STOCKMANN.   Yes, the open-minded and independent press will let you know your duty.

THE MAYOR   [*pauses before speaking*].   Thomas, you're a thoughtless and impetuous man. Have you considered what might happen to you because of all this?

DR. STOCKMANN.   To me?

THE MAYOR.   Yes, to you—and to your family.

DR. STOCKMANN.   What in the devil's name do you mean?

THE MAYOR.   As your older brother, have I not always been helpful to you?

DR. STOCKMANN.   Yes, and I'm thankful to you.

THE MAYOR.   Well, to a degree my own interests have coincided with yours. My hope has been that helping you better yourself financially would give me the power to hold you back on occasions.

DR. STOCKMANN.   You mean you did this for yourself?

THE MAYOR.   Yes, but only to a degree. Any public official is distressed when closest relatives do compromising things again and again.

DR. STOCKMANN.   You think I do compromising things?

THE MAYOR.   Yes, unfortunately, even when you don't mean to. You're naturally combative, Thomas, and you keep none of your thoughts private, whether they're plausible or implausible, but you publish them as soon as you get them either in short articles or whole pamphlets.

DR. STOCKMANN.   But isn't a citizen obligated to share new ideas with the public?

THE MAYOR.   The public has no need for new ideas. The public is best served by the good, old, recognized ideas they already have.

DR. STOCKMANN.   You really believe this?

THE MAYOR.   Yes, I do. And now I must speak frankly to you, which I have always avoided because you can be so irritable. The truth is, Thomas, you have no idea of how you hurt yourself by your thoughtless manner. You tear down politicians, and you denounce the government, by claiming that you are ignored or that you are victimized. But with such obstinacy, what else can you expect?

DR. STOCKMANN.   So, I'm obstinate, am I?

THE MAYOR.   Yes, you're an impossibly obstinate man to work with; I know. You place yourself above all consideration for others, and you have forgotten totally that I am the one you can thank for your position as Chief Medical Officer of the Spa—

DR. STOCKMANN.   But I was the natural one for this position—I and no one else! I   240
originated the idea that the town could become a thriving center for therapeutic baths,
and for many years, despite obstructions, I was the one who wrote vigorously to make the
Baths a reality.

THE MAYOR.   No doubt, but you were too early. Things were not yet right, but you
didn't think of that because you were locked away up north. It's a fact, however, that as
soon as things came together, I, along with others, took over, and—

DR. STOCKMANN.   And created the mess we have now. You fellows certainly did
things right!

THE MAYOR.   As far as I can see, this whole matter is just another of your habitual
ways of attacking people in authority. To you, rebelliousness is a personal way of life. But
I've told you, Thomas, that the very existence of the town is now the issue—not to mention my own reputation. And therefore I tell you, Thomas, that I'll be absolute about
the demand I'm going to make on you.

DR. STOCKMANN.   What's this?

THE MAYOR.   Now that you've spoken out when you should have kept quiet, the   245
matter can no longer be hushed up. Rumors will fly, and they'll be used against us. The
only thing to do is for you to issue a public denial.

DR. STOCKMANN.   Me? But how can I do that?

THE MAYOR.   We'll expect that further studies have shown you that things are not
as serious or dangerous as your first thoughts had led you to conclude.

DR. STOCKMANN.   You expect me to say this?

THE MAYOR.   Moreover, you must publicly express your confidence in the integrity of the Governing Board of the Spa, and in their willingness to remedy any possible
problems whatever.

DR. STOCKMANN.   But you can't set things right now just by cutting and pasting.   250
Peter, I'm giving you my professional judgment.

THE MAYOR.   Because you serve the Governing Board, you have no right to an
independent professional judgment.

DR. STOCKMANN   [*exclaims incredulously*].   No right?

THE MAYOR.   Privately, of course, you may think what you wish. But as an official
who must report to the Governing Board, you cannot make a public announcement
contrary to Board policy.

DR. STOCKMANN.   I've never—. As a doctor, as a scientist, I have no right—?

THE MAYOR.   This is not just a matter of science. It's complex, and there are fiscal   255
implications.

DR. STOCKMANN.   Complexity and fiscal implications can go to hell! I'm free to
speak out on any subject on earth!

THE MAYOR.   Be my guest! But not about the Spa. We forbid you that.

DR. STOCKMANN.   You forbid me? You? You pack of—

THE MAYOR.   I forbid you—I—the Chief Executive Officer of the Governing
Board. And when I forbid you, you *must* obey!

DR. STOCKMANN   [*suppresses rage*].   Peter, if we weren't brothers—   260

PETRA   [*enters*].   Father, he can't speak to you like this!

MRS. STOCKMANN   [*enters, trying to restrain PETRA*].   Petra, Petra—

THE MAYOR.   So you've been listening!

MRS. STOCKMANN.   You were so loud, we couldn't help hearing.

PETRA.   Yes, I listened!   265

THE MAYOR.   Well, actually, I'm glad—

DR. STOCKMANN.   You were talking about forbidding and obeying?

THE MAYOR.   Your insolence forced me to speak like that to you.

DR. STOCKMANN.   So I am to issue a lie publicly?

THE MAYOR.   You must make a statement—something like the one we spoke of.

DR. STOCKMANN.   And if I don't—obey?

THE MAYOR.   Then we ourselves will issue a statement of reassurance for the public.

DR. STOCKMANN.   If you do, I'll have to write against your position. I'll stand behind my conclusions. I'll prove you're wrong and I'm right. What will you do then?

THE MAYOR.   Then I won't be able to prevent your dismissal.

DR. STOCKMANN.   What—?

PETRA.   Father—dismissed!

MRS. STOCKMANN.   Fired!

THE MAYOR.   Dismissed as Chief Medical Officer of the Spa. I'll find myself in the position of giving you instant notice, and suspending you from your duties at the Spa.

DR. STOCKMANN.   You'd risk that!

THE MAYOR.   You're the one running the risks!

PETRA.   Uncle, this is shocking conduct toward a man like father!

MRS. STOCKMANN.   Petra, will you hold your tongue!

THE MAYOR   [*to* PETRA].   Oh, so we already speak out with no restraint. I might have expected it. [*To* MRS. STOCKMANN.]   My dear sister-in-law, you're the least impulsive person here. Use your influence over your husband to persuade him of the dangers he's running for the family and—

DR. STOCKMANN.   Family concerns are mine, and mine only!

THE MAYOR.   —for the family, I was saying, and for the town he lives in.

DR. STOCKMANN.   I'm the one who holds the good of the town foremost by trying to disclose the real dangers that face us. I'll show you who loves the town.

THE MAYOR.   You, who in blind defiance goes ahead to cut off the town's most important nourishment?

DR. STOCKMANN.   But what gives us our living gives poison to others! Are you insane? We live here by dealing in filth and corruption! Our thriving business life is nourished on lies!

THE MAYOR.   A fairy tale, or worse! Any person who can say such damaging things about his own hometown must be an enemy of society!

DR. STOCKMANN   [*confronts him*].   You dare—

MRS. STOCKMANN   [*stands between them to restrain them*].   Thomas!

PETRA   [*takes her father's arm*].   Father, control yourself!

THE MAYOR.   I will not be a party to violence! You've been warned; consider yourself—and your family! Goodbye! [*Leaves alone through the hallway.*]

DR. STOCKMANN   [*paces*].   Must I put up with this, Katrina, and in my own home?

MRS. STOCKMANN.   It's been both shameful and humiliating!

PETRA.   I'd like to tell him a thing or two—

DR. STOCKMANN.   I'm at fault for not baring my teeth at him sooner—and biting him. He suggested that I'm an enemy of the town! Me! I'm not going to take this!

MRS. STOCKMANN.   But dear Thomas, your brother has the power—

DR. STOCKMANN.   Yes, but I have the right.

MRS. STOCKMANN.   Yes, right, right. But what good is right without might?

PETRA.   Mother, how can you say that?   300

DR. STOCKMANN.   Don't be absurd, Katrina. When people are free, rightness always implies power. Besides, I have the open-minded and independent press in front of me, and the solid majority behind me. There's a good deal of power here, believe me.

MRS. STOCKMANN.   But God in heaven, Thomas, you don't plan to—

DR. STOCKMANN.   Don't plan to what?

MRS. STOCKMANN.   To set yourself against your brother?

DR. STOCKMANN.   What the hell else should I do? Shouldn't I follow what's true   305
and right?

PETRA.   Just what I wanted to say.

MRS. STOCKMANN.   You won't get anywhere. If they oppose you, they'll stop you from doing anything.

DR. STOCKMANN.   Katrina, just wait, and you'll see that I'll take the war to them.

MRS. STOCKMANN.   Yes, you'll drive yourself into your dismissal—that you'll do.

DR. STOCKMANN.   Whatever happens, I'll have fulfilled my obligations to the   310
public—and I have been called the enemy of society!

MRS. STOCKMANN.   But think of your family, Thomas—your home—those who depend on you.

PETRA.   Oh Mother, you always think of us first.

MRS. STOCKMANN.   Well, you may talk, but you could take care of yourself, if you had to. But think of the boys, Thomas, and of your own needs, and of me—

DR. STOCKMANN.   Katrina, you're talking nonsense. Do you think I could ever live with myself again if I had to go crawling—like a beaten coward—to Peter and his damned bootlickers?

MRS. STOCKMANN.   I don't know about that, but God help us from the sort of luck   315
we'll all have if you keep up your defiance. You'll be back at zero, with no job and no secure income. We've had our fill of that, Thomas. Think about it, and think of what can happen.

DR. STOCKMANN   [*squirms and clenches his fists*].   So much for being free but without power. Katrina, it's horrible.

MRS. STOCKMANN.   Yes, they're being horrible to you. it's true. But, God in heaven, there's so much unfairness that people have to endure in the world. [*EILIF and MORTEN, schoolbooks in their hands, enter while she is speaking.*] Think of our boys, Thomas, and what may happen to them. Surely you'd never—

DR. STOCKMANN   [*appears deeply moved*].   The boys—. [*With an effort, he becomes resolute.*] No, I'll never knuckle under, even if the world falls apart! [*Strides toward his office.*]

MRS. STOCKMANN   [*follows him*].   Thomas, what are you doing?

DR. STOCKMANN   [*turns at the door*].   I want the right to look my own boys in the   320
eyes when they're grown up and free! [*Leaves.*]

MRS. STOCKMANN   [*begins crying*].   God help and preserve us!

PETRA.   Father is marvelous! He'll never give in!

[*The boys are dumfounded, while* PETRA *cautions them to say nothing.*]

END OF THE SECOND ACT

ACT III

SCENE. *Afternoon. The editorial office of* THE PEOPLE'S MESSENGER. *On the rear wall, stage left, is the main outside door. At stage right, the rear wall contains the print-shop door, with glass windows through which the print shop can be seen. Several compositors are setting type, and one worker is operating a handpress. In the stage-right wall is another door. A long table in the middle of the room is spread out with papers, books, etc. There is a downstage window in the stage-left wall, in front of which there is a desk and a high stool where* HOVSTAD *is sitting and writing. Other chairs are at the table and along the walls. The office is generally drab and threadbare; all the furniture is old, nicked, stained, torn, and worn out.* BILLING *enters from the right, holding* DR. STOCKMANN's *manuscript.*

BILLING.   Now this is something!

HOVSTAD.   Did you finish reading it?

BILLING   [*puts the manuscript on the desk*].   I certainly did.

HOVSTAD.   The Doctor doesn't pull any punches.

BILLING.   None at all. His words are sledgehammer blows!

HOVSTAD.   You're right, but these people won't throw in the towel at the first hard punch.

BILLING.   I agree, and for this reason we have keep slugging away, blow after blow, until we knock out the whole establishment. As I was reading this I could see a dawning revolution.

HOVSTAD   [*turns toward the print shop*].   Shhh! Don't let Aslaksen hear you.

BILLING   [*lowers his voice*].   Aslaksen is scared of his own shadow. But you're the one in charge, right? You're printing the Doctor's article?

HOVSTAD.   Yes. Let's hope the mayor doesn't agree to go along with things first.

BILLING.   That would be damned awkward.

HOVSTAD.   Well, either way we come out ahead. If the Mayor doesn't get on board with the Doctor's suggestions, all the tradespeople and the Homeowners Association will be on his neck. And if he does get on board, he'll alienate most of the shareholders of the Baths, who up to now have been his prime supporters.

BILLING.   Yes, because they'll have to pay through the nose—

HOVSTAD.   You can bet on it. And then the ring will be broken. From then on, in paper after paper, we'll expose the incompetence of the Mayor on one thing or another, and make clear that the town's elective positions—all of them—should be taken over by people with fresh ideas.

BILLING.   You've pictured it! I see it! Damn it, we're at the beginning of a revolution!

[*A knock at the outside door.*]

HOVSTAD.   Shh! [*Calls.*] Come in! [*DR. STOCKMANN enters; HOVSTAD rises to greet him.*] Ah, Doctor, welcome!

DR. STOCKMANN.   Go ahead and print, Mr. Hovstad.

HOVSTAD.   You're sure.

BILLING.   Hurrah!

DR. STOCKMANN.   Print away. Yes, I'm sure. They'll have to take it. This town is going to see a knock-down, drag-out fight!

BILLING.   I hope we'll slit their throats, Doctor.

DR. STOCKMANN.   This article is only the start. I have ideas for four or five more already. Where is Aslaksen?

BILLING [*goes to the print-shop door and calls*].   Aslaksen, please come in for a moment.

HOVSTAD.   Did you say four or five articles, all about this?

DR. STOCKMANN.   No, not all on the same topic, but all of them stem out of the water-pollution issue. Things follow each other, just like fixing up an old house. It's just like that.   25

BILLING.   That's true, damn it. Once you start, you can't stop until you tear down the whole rickety structure.

ASLAKSEN [*enters*].   Tear down! The Doctor doesn't think the Bath Houses should be torn down?

HOVSTAD.   Not at all; don't worry.

DR. STOCKMANN.   We have something else in mind. Well, Mr. Hovstad, what's your response to my article?

HOVSTAD.   It's a masterpiece.   30

DR. STOCKMANN.   Honestly now? I'm very pleased.

HOVSTAD.   It's clear and to the point. It requires no special vocabulary or expertise. You'll rally all intelligent people.

ASLAKSEN.   And all prudent people, too?

BILLING.   Prudent, imprudent—the whole town.

ASLAKSEN.   Why then, we could certainly risk printing it.   35

DR. STOCKMANN.   Absolutely!

HOVSTAD.   Tomorrow's morning issue will have it.

DR. STOCKMANN.   Yes, in God's name, we shouldn't lose a single day. Mr. Aslaksen, would you please see to it personally that the printing goes right?

ASLAKSEN.   I'll do it gladly.

DR. STOCKMANN.   Treasure it carefully, as if it were gold—no typographic errors.   40
I'll come in later to read proof. I can't tell you how anxious I am to see the thing printed, and striking—

BILLING.   Striking—yes, like a flash of lightning—

DR. STOCKMANN.   —and meeting the approval of intelligent citizens. You won't believe what I've been through since morning. I've been insulted and menaced, and they've even threatened my basic human rights—

BILLING.   Your basic rights?

DR. STOCKMANN.   —they've tried to humiliate me, make me a coward, and set personal gain above my deepest, holiest convictions.

BILLING.   Damn it, this is unspeakable!   45

HOVSTAD.   Well, you can't expect anything else from this bunch.

DR. STOCKMANN.   But they haven't seen the end of me. With the *Messenger* as my power base, I'll put things in black and white, and every day I'll fire off one explosive article after another—

ASLAKSEN.   But, listen—

BILLING.   Hurrah! It's war! It's war!

DR. STOCKMANN.   I'll bring them to the ground! I'll crush them! I'll destroy their   50
fortress in the eyes of all right-thinking people!

ASLAKSEN.   But be moderate, good Doctor. Shoot, but with caution—

BILLING.   No, no, don't spare the dynamite!

DR. STOCKMANN [*goes on calmly*].   The issue is no longer just water pipes and sewers—No, our entire social structure needs cleansing and disinfecting—

BILLING.   Words of prophecy!

DR. STOCKMANN.   Everywhere, the bumbling incompetents should be put to pasture, and that means *all*. Today I've gotten a sense of a more perfect future—it's not clear yet, but it's taking shape in my mind. We need new standard-bearers, my friends, and new commanding officers at all our outposts.   55

BILLING.   Hear, hear!

DR. STOCKMANN.   To make it possible, we must all pull together. With unity, the revolution can be like a ship gliding smoothly from harbor. Am I right?

HOVSTAD.   My view is that we're close to getting municipal government into the right hands.

ASLAKSEN.   And there'll be no risk as long as we're moderate.

DR. STOCKMANN.   To hell with the risk! Everything I do, I do in the name of truth and because of my conscience.   60

HOVSTAD.   Doctor, you've earned our support.

ASLAKSEN.   Yes, our support. The Doctor is a true friend—a true benefactor of society.

BILLING.   Damn it, Aslaksen, Dr. Stockmann is a friend of the people!

ASLAKSEN.   I think the Homeowners Association will soon make use of that expression.

DR. STOCKMANN [*is moved, and shakes their hands*].   Thank you, thank you, dear friends. This phrase is so stirring; my own brother used a different one, but he'll regret it. I have to go and see a poor devil of a patient now, but I'll come back soon, as I said. Mr. Aslaksen, take care of the manuscript, and set the type carefully. Don't take out any exclamation points. You can add some, if you want. Good, good. For the moment, good-bye, goodbye!   65

[*They escort him to the main door, shaking hands, etc. He leaves.*]

HOVSTAD.   This man will be immensely useful.

ASLAKSEN.   Yes, but only with regard to the Spa. To follow him in other things might not be politic.

HOVSTAD.   Well, that depends—

BILLING.   You're always so damned afraid, Aslaksen.

ASLAKSEN.   Afraid? On local matters, Mr. Billing, I've learned to be cautious. I've learned this in the game of life. But put me in the area of national politics, even against the Government itself, and see how afraid I am.   70

BILLING.   You're right, I grant. But isn't this contradictory?

ASLAKSEN.   No, because I'm a man of conscience. Criticizing the national government is harmless, because the fellows up there don't notice, and they just stay put. But local politicians can be thrown out, and if you *do* get them out you might wind up with a bunch of incompetents—and really hurt not only the Homeowners but everyone.

HOVSTAD.   But don't you believe that the improved education of the populace is a necessary consequence of self-government?

ASLAKSEN.   Mr. Hovstad, when one's self-interests are at stake, other considerations are not as significant.

HOVSTAD.   I hope I'll never hold self-interest first!   7.

BILLING.   Hear, hear!

ASLAKSEN   [*smiles, and points to* HOVSTAD'S *desk*].   Mr. Sheriff Stensgaard preceded you at that desk.

BILLING   [*spits*].   He was a renegade!

HOVSTAD.   I'm not a turncoat, and I hope I never will be.

ASLAKSEN.   A politician should never say "never," Mr. Hovstad. And you, Mr.   80
Billing, you may need to pull in your sails a bit, since you've submitted your application for the Secretaryship of the Judicial Bench.

BILLING.   I—

HOVSTAD.   Is this true, Billing?

BILLING.   Well, yes, damn it, but you can understand my aim is to be a gadfly to the establishment.

ASLAKSEN.   This isn't my business. But if you imply that I'm afraid or contradictory, I remind you that the record of Aslaksen the printer is open. I've always been consistent, except for becoming more moderate. My heart is always with the people, but I won't deny that my mind goes with the authorities—the local ones, that is. [*Leaves through the print-shop door.*]

BILLING.   Hovstad, we've got to get him out.   85

HOVSTAD.   Have you got anyone else in mind to finance our paper and printing costs?

BILLING.   Damn it all that we don't have financial security.

HOVSTAD   [*sits at his desk*].   Yes, that would help—

BILLING.   Do you think that Dr. Stockmann—

HOVSTAD.   What's the use? He hasn't got anything.   90

BILLING.   No, but he may be close to a hot prospect. You know—old Morten Kiil, the one they call the "Badger."

HOVSTAD   [*speaks while writing*].   Do you know for sure that he's well fixed?

BILLING.   Yes, damn it! And the Stockmanns stand to inherit. At least the Stockmann children will get something.

HOVSTAD   [*faces* BILLING *directly*].   Are you counting on this?

BILLING.   Counting on it? Naturally, I never count on anything.   95

HOVSTAD.   You're right, and don't plan on the Secretaryship either. You're not on the final list.

BILLING.   You think I don't know that? Nothing could please me more. Losing the job will put me in fighting trim, and you need that here in the boondocks, where nothing ever happens to egg you on.

HOVSTAD   [*continues to write*].   Of course, of course.

BILLING.   But I'll make a mark yet!—Excuse me; I'm going to write the appeal to the Homeowners Association now. [*Leaves through the door on the right.*]

HOVSTAD   [*stays at his desk, chews the end of his pen, and talks slowly to himself*].   So,   100
this is how it is. [*A knock at the entrance door.*] Come in! [PETRA *enters.* HOVSTAD *rises.*] It's you, here? Why did you come?

PETRA.   Yes. Please excuse me—

HOVSTAD   [*offers her a chair*].   Please sit down.

PETRA.   No, thank you, I have to go right away.

HOVSTAD.   You have a word from your father, perhaps?

PETRA.   No, I'm here on my own. [*Takes a book out of her coat.*] This is the English   105
story.

HOVSTAD.   Why are you bringing it back?

PETRA.   I won't translate it.   1◗

HOVSTAD.   But you gave me your word—

PETRA.   I did, but then I hadn't read it. You haven't read it either?

HOVSTAD.   You know I don't read English, but—

PETRA.   Well, this is why you need something else. [*Puts the book on the table.*] You can't run this in the *Messenger.*

HOVSTAD.   Why not?

PETRA.   It contradicts everything you stand for.

HOVSTAD.   Well, but then—

PETRA.   You don't understand. The story's main theme is that a supernatural   11
power protects the so-called good people in the world and makes everything best for them in the end—and that all the so-called evil people get their punishment.

HOVSTAD.   But that's all right. It's what our readers demand.

PETRA.   Are you the one to give it to them? You know every single word is a fairy tale; things aren't like that in the real world.

HOVSTAD.   You're right. But realize that an editor is not totally free. If I want to lead my readers on the important political objectives of liberation and progress, I can't scare them off. A moral story like this one, on the back page, promotes their willingness to accept my editorial opinions on the front page; it makes them more confident.

PETRA.   Come now! You set such a web for your readers. You're not a spider!

HOVSTAD   [*smiles*].   No. I thank you for including me in your elevated simile,   12◗
but the strategy was really Billing's, not mine.

PETRA.   Billing's?

HOVSTAD.   Yes. In any event, he explained the idea the other day. It's Billing who wants the story. I don't know it myself.

PETRA.   But how can Billing, with his emancipated outlook—

HOVSTAD.   Well, Billing is many things to many people. I'm told he's also look-ing for a job in the magistrate's office.

PETRA.   I don't believe it. How could he make himself such a conformist?   12◗

HOVSTAD.   Ask him.

PETRA.   I would never have thought this of Billing.

HOVSTAD   [*looks at her intently*].   No? Is this so unexpected?

PETRA.   Yes. But maybe not. I'm really not sure—

HOVSTAD.   We journalists are not heroes, Miss.   13◗

PETRA.   You mean that?

HOVSTAD.   Sometimes I think so.

PETRA.   I can understand this about ordinary, everyday circumstances. But now, when you've taken a hand in this great cause—

HOVSTAD.   You mean this business with your father?

PETRA.   Yes. It seems to me that you must think of yourself as a person above most   13◗
others.

HOVSTAD.   Yes, I rather do feel that way today.

PETRA.   Of course you do. Why shouldn't you? You've really chosen a noble call-ing—to prepare the way for unrecognized truths and bold new ways of seeing—or even just to stand up without fear to support an injured man—

HOVSTAD.   Yes, especially when the injured man is—how should I say it—

PETRA.   You mean when he's so upright and honest?

HOVSTAD   [*softens his tone*].   Rather I mean when that man is your father.   14◗

PETRA   [*is suddenly struck*].   That?

HOVSTAD.   Yes, Miss Petra—Petra.

PETRA.   Is this what's first and foremost to you? Not principle, not truth, not the warmth of my father's great heart?

HOVSTAD.   Yes, of course, all that, too.

PETRA.   No, thanks, Hovstad. You're being dishonest, and I can't believe you any   145
more in anything.

HOVSTAD.   Can you be so angry at me when it's because of you—

PETRA.   I'm angry because you haven't been honest with Father. You talked to him as though truth and the common good were uppermost in your mind. You've made fools of both Father and me. You're not what you seem, and I'll never forgive you for that—never!

HOVSTAD.   You shouldn't be so spiteful, Miss Petra, not now, especially.

PETRA.   Why not now?

HOVSTAD.   Your father can't get anywhere without my help.   150

PETRA   [*stares at him in disgust*].   So you're also like that! Shame!

HOVSTAD.   No, I'm sorry. I just blurted that out. Don't believe what I said!

PETRA.   I know what to believe. Goodbye!

ASLAKSEN   [*hurries in from the print shop, trying to be secret*].   Hellfire and damnation, Mr. Hovstad!—[*Sees* PETRA.]   This is bad—

PETRA   [*points to the book on the desk, and walks toward the main door*].   That's the   155
book. Get someone else to translate it.

HOVSTAD   [*follows her*].   But Miss—

PETRA.   Goodbye! [*She leaves.*]

ASLAKSEN.   Listen, Mr. Hovstad—

HOVSTAD.   Yes, yes, what is it?

ASLAKSEN.   The Mayor is in the print shop.   160

HOVSTAD.   You say the Mayor?

ASLAKSEN.   Yes. He wants to talk with you. He came in the back way—I guess he didn't want to be seen.

HOVSTAD.   What's this about? No, wait, I'll go myself. [*Goes to the print-shop door and invites the* MAYOR *in. The* MAYOR *enters.*] Aslaksen, please see that no one—

ASLAKSEN.   I understand.   [*Goes into the print room*].

THE MAYOR.   You were not expecting me, Mr. Hovstad?   165

HOVSTAD.   I certainly wasn't.

THE MAYOR   [*looks around the room*].   You've made things cosy here. Quite nice.

HOVSTAD.   Well—

THE MAYOR.   And now I come here without an appointment to make a greater demands on your time.

HOVSTAD.   My pleasure, Mr. Mayor. I'm at your service. But let me take your   170
things. [*Puts the* MAYOR'S *hat and walking-stick on a stool.*] Won't you sit down?

THE MAYOR   [*sits beside the table*].   Thank you. [*HOVSTAD also sits at the table.*] Today, Mr. Hovstad, I've had a—an extremely distressing experience.

HOVSTAD.   Yes, with all the many duties of the Mayor's office—

THE MAYOR.   The one today concerns the Chief Medical Officer of the Spa.

HOVSTAD.   The Doctor?

THE MAYOR.   He has written a sort of report to the Governing Board, claiming   175
that there are supposed shortcomings at the Spa.

HOVSTAD.   No, he said this?

THE MAYOR.   Didn't he tell you? I understood him to say—

HOVSTAD.   Well, yes, it's true he let something drop about—

ASLAKSEN   [*enters from the print shop*].   I'll need that manuscript—

HOVSTAD   [*speaks brusquely*].   There—it's on the desk.

ASLAKSEN   [*finds it*].   Good.

THE MAYOR.   But see, that's it!

ASLAKSEN.   Yes, Mr. Mayor, this is the Doctor's article.

HOVSTAD.   Oh, is this the one you mean?

THE MAYOR.   The same. What do you think of it?

HOVSTAD.   Well, I'm not an expert, and I've only looked it over briefly.

THE MAYOR.   But you're still going to print it?

HOVSTAD.   I can't say no to a man with such impressive credentials—

ASLAKSEN.   Mr. Mayor, I have no say in the paper's policies.

THE MAYOR.   Certainly.

ASLAKSEN.   I only print the copy put in my hands.

THE MAYOR.   As well you should.

ASLAKSEN   [*walks toward the print shop*].   And therefore I must—

THE MAYOR.   But stay a moment, Mr. Aslaksen. [*ASLAKSEN remains.*] With your permission, Mr. Hovstad?

HOVSTAD.   By all means, Mr. Mayor.

THE MAYOR.   Mr. Aslaksen, you're a sober and deliberate man.

ASLAKSEN.   Your good opinion pleases me, sir.

THE MAYOR.   And a man with influence in many circles.

ASLAKSEN.   Well, it's mostly among the little people.

THE MAYOR.   The small taxpayers are the great majority—here and elsewhere.

ASLAKSEN.   Right.

THE MAYOR.   And I don't question that you know the common feelings of most of them. You follow me?

ASLAKSEN.   Yes, Mr. Mayor, I think I may safely say I do know them.

THE MAYOR.   Yes, and if there's such an admirable spirit of self-sacrifice among citizens of smaller means in our town, then—

ASLAKSEN.   What's this?

HOVSTAD.   Self-sacrifice?

THE MAYOR.   This is a beautiful token of public spirit—an overwhelmingly beautiful token. I almost said I didn't expect it. But you know these feelings more thoroughly than I do.

ASLAKSEN.   Yes, but Mr. Mayor—

THE MAYOR.   And the sacrifice the town will need to make will not be small.

HOVSTAD.   The town?

ASLAKSEN.   But I don't understand—It's the Spa—

THE MAYOR.   The first estimate for the changes recommended by the Chief Medical Officer are close to thirty million.

ASLAKSEN.   That's a huge sum, but—

THE MAYOR.   Naturally we'll need to float municipal bonds.

HOVSTAD   [*rises*].   This could never mean that the townspeople—

ASLAKSEN.   This can't come out of the town's property taxes—out of the empty pockets of the small taxpayers.

THE MAYOR.   Yes, my good Mr. Aslaksen, where else can we raise the money?

ASLAKSEN.   The people who own the Spa can do it.

THE MAYOR.   The shareholders can't extend themselves beyond where they've already gone.

ASLAKSEN.   Mr. Mayor, is this completely certain? 220

THE MAYOR.   I've assured myself of it. If we want these extensive changes, the town itself must pay for them.

ASLAKSEN.   But God damn it to hell—! I'm sorry, your Honor—this is something else!

HOVSTAD.   It certainly is!

THE MAYOR.   The worst part is that, for at least a couple of years, we'll have to close the Spa entirely.

HOVSTAD.   Closed? Entirely closed? 225

ASLAKSEN.   For two years?

THE MAYOR.   Yes, the work will take two years—at least.

ASLAKSEN.   But damn it all, Mr. Mayor, we can never put up with that! How can the Homeowners live?

THE MAYOR.   There's no easy answer, Mr. Aslaksen. But what can we do? Do you believe we'll get a single guest if someone goes around and paints the picture that our water is poisoned, that we live in a sewer, that the whole town—

ASLAKSEN.   And this is all just imagination? 230

THE MAYOR.   With all my best will, I've been able to reach no other conclusion about it.

ASLAKSEN.   Well, then, it's totally inexcusable of Dr. Stockmann—I beg your pardon, Mr. Mayor, but—

THE MAYOR.   What you're implying is regrettably true, Mr. Aslaksen. My brother has always been an impetuous man.

ASLAKSEN.   Mr. Hovstad, can you still support him after this?

HOVSTAD.   But who would have believed that—? 235

THE MAYOR.   I've prepared an impartial brief reviewing the conditions, and in it I've shown that any possible shortcomings may be addressed without shattering the current budget for the Spa.

HOVSTAD.   Do you have a copy, Mr. Mayor?

THE MAYOR [*reaches into a pocket*].   I do. I brought it along in case—

ASLAKSEN.   Oh my God, here he is!

THE MAYOR.   Who? My brother? 240

HOVSTAD.   Where? Where?

ASLAKSEN.   He's coming through the print shop!

THE MAYOR.   Unfortunate. I don't want a confrontation here, but I still have a few more things to tell you.

HOVSTAD [*directs him to the door on the right*].   Go in here for a time.

THE MAYOR.   But—? 245

HOVSTAD.   No one but Billing is there.

ASLAKSEN.   Quickly, Your Honor, he's here now!

THE MAYOR.   All right then, but be quick with him. [*Leaves through the door on the right. ASLAKSEN opens it and closes it for him.*]

HOVSTAD.   Make as though you're busy, Aslaksen.

[*HOVSTAD sits at his table and writes. ASLAKSEN works with papers on a chair at the right.*]

DR. STOCKMANN [*enters from the print shop*]. Here I am again. [*Puts down his hat and walking-stick.*]

HOVSTAD [*concentrates on his writing*]. Already, Doctor? Aslaksen, hurry up with the copy we spoke of. Time's getting tight for us.

DR. STOCKMANN [*to ASLAKSEN*]. I conclude the proofs aren't ready yet.

ASLAKSEN [*does not look up*]. No, the Doctor shouldn't expect them so soon.

DR. STOCKMANN. No, but I'm naturally impatient. I won't rest for a minute until I see everything in print.

HOVSTAD. Well, it'll take at least another hour. That's right, isn't it, Aslaksen?

ASLAKSEN. I'm afraid so.

DR. STOCKMANN. All right, dear friends. I'll come back again and again if I need to. When something so important as the welfare of the whole town is at stake, it's no time to be lazy. [*Begins to leave, but stops and comes back.*] Just one more thing—

HOVSTAD. Excuse me, but could we do it another time?

DR. STOCKMANN. I'll be done in a jiffy. It's just this: When people read my article tomorrow they'll also realize I've spent the whole winter working in the town's best interest—

HOVSTAD. Yes, but Doctor—

DR. STOCKMANN. I know what you'll say, that it was only my duty. Damn it all, any citizen would do the same. And I agree with you, but my fellow citizens out there—. God in heaven, think of their high opinion of me—!

ASLAKSEN. Yes, Doctor, the people have thought highly of you, up till now.

DR. STOCKMANN. And that's why I'm afraid that—. This is what I want to say: If my article creates an incentive, especially for the poor, to take a future share of town government into their own hands—

HOVSTAD [*rises, clears throat*]. Doctor, I won't hide this from you—

DR. STOCKMANN. Just as I thought; I knew it. But I won't have it. If anyone is setting something up—

HOVSTAD. Like what?

DR. STOCKMANN. Well, whatever—a demonstration, a testimonial dinner, a solicitation for a gift—then by all that's sacred, promise me to nip it in the bud. And you too, Mr. Aslaksen. Am I clear?

HOVSTAD. Doctor, pardon me, but we've got to tell you the plain truth.

[*MRS. STOCKMANN, in hat and coat, enters from the main outside door.*]

MRS. STOCKMANN [*sees the DOCTOR*]. I was right!

HOVSTAD [*walks toward her*]. You also, Mrs. Stockmann?

DR. STOCKMANN. Katrina, what the hell are you doing here?

MRS. STOCKMANN. You know what I'm doing.

HOVSTAD. Please sit down. Or perhaps—

MRS. STOCKMANN. Please, no thank you. And please don't mind my coming here for Stockmann, because, I want you to know, I'm the mother of three children.

DR. STOCKMANN. Claptrap! They know all that!

MRS. STOCKMANN. Well, it seems that you haven't been thinking of your wife and children lately, or else you wouldn't go on like this, leading us into disaster.

DR. STOCKMANN. But Katrina, this is insane! Does having a wife and children stop a man from proclaiming the truth—from being a good citizen—from serving his hometown?

MRS. STOCKMANN.   All these things, Thomas, but moderately.

ASLAKSEN.   I say that, too. Moderation in everything.

MRS. STOCKMANN.   And because of this, Mr. Hovstad, you are hurting us when   280
you coax my husband away from house and home and make him a dupe in all this.

HOVSTAD.   I'm not making anyone a dupe—

DR. STOCKMANN.   Dupe? Do you think I'm letting myself be used?

MRS. STOCKMANN.   You are. You're the most intelligent man in town, but,
Thomas, you're so easy to deceive. [*To* HOVSTAD.] And just think that he loses his position
at the Spa as soon as you publish his article—

ASLAKSEN.   What?

HOVSTAD.   Doctor, now see—   285

DR. STOCKMANN   [*laughs*].   Just let them try! They'll regret it, because the solid
majority is backing me!

MRS. STOCKMANN.   Yes, that's the problem, to have something as terrible as that
backing you!

DR. STOCKMANN.   Nonsense, Katrina! Go home and look after the house, and
leave the community to me. Why are you so afraid when I'm so confident and cheerful?
[*Paces, rubbing his hands.*] The people and the truth will be victorious, you can bet on it.
I can see it—all the open-minded middle classes forming a triumphant army—! [*Stops at
the chair where the* MAYOR *put his hat and stick.*] Now what the hell is this?

ASLAKSEN   [*sees the things*].   Oh, my God!

HOVSTAD   [*likewise*].   Ahem!   290

DR. STOCKMANN.   Here you see the highest authority!

[*Mockingly holds the* MAYOR'S *hat high in the air.*]

MRS. STOCKMANN.   The Mayor's hat!

DR. STOCKMANN.   And here's the crook of power, too. [*Displays the* MAYOR'S *walking
stick*]. How by all the fiends of hell did—

HOVSTAD.   Now, well—

DR. STOCKMANN.   Ah, I understand. He came here to harangue you. [*Laughs.*]   295
He sure came to the right place! And then he saw me in the print shop—. [*Bursts out
laughing.*] Did he run, Mr. Aslaksen?

ASLAKSEN   [*speaks rapidly*].   Oh yes, he ran, Doctor.

DR. STOCKMANN.   Ran away from both his stick and—. Ran away, my foot! Peter
doesn't run away from anything. But where the devil did you put him? Aha! In here,
naturally. Now you'll see, Katrina!

MRS. STOCKMANN.   Thomas, please—

ASLAKSEN.   Be careful, Doctor.

[*Still holding the stick,* DR. STOCKMANN *puts on the* MAYOR'S *hat. He goes to the door at the
right, opens it, and salutes as* THE MAYOR *enters in a rage.* BILLING *follows.*]

THE MAYOR.   What do you mean by this clowning?   300

DR. STOCKMANN   [*paces*].   Have respect, dear Peter. I'm the town's chief authority now!

MRS. STOCKMANN   [*on the verge of tears*].   Thomas, don't—

THE MAYOR   [*follows him*].   Give me my hat and stick!

DR. STOCKMANN   [*as before*].   *You* are only the constable, while *I* am the Mayor—
I am master of the whole town!

THE MAYOR.   Take off that hat! Remember, it's part of an official uniform!   30▪

DR. STOCKMANN.   Piffle! Do you think the people, waking up like a lion, are scared of uniforms? There'll be a revolution in town tomorrow; you'd better know that. You thought you could dismiss me, but I'll dismiss you—from all your posts. You think I can't? Well, listen: I've got the power of the people with me. Hovstad and Billing will thunder in the *People's Messenger,* and Aslaksen the Printer will lead the charge of the entire Homeowners Association—

ASLAKSEN.   I won't do it, Doctor.

DR. STOCKMANN.   But of course you will—

THE MAYOR.   Aha! Mr. Hovstad has perhaps decided to be part of this insurrection, then?

HOVSTAD.   No, Mr. Mayor.   31▪

ASLAKSEN.   No, Mr. Hovstad isn't such a fool as to wreck himself and his paper for no more than an insane idea!

DR. STOCKMANN   [*looks around the room*].   What does all this mean?

HOVSTAD.   You've put things in a false light, Doctor, and I can't support you any longer.

BILLING.   And in light of what the Mayor has just been telling me—

DR. STOCKMANN.   False? Let me worry about that. Just print the article, and I'll   31▪
justify it.

HOVSTAD.   I won't print it. I cannot, I will not, and I dare not print it!

DR. STOCKMANN.   Dare not? What talk is this? You're the editor, and it's the editors who make editorial decisions, I hope.

HOVSTAD.   No, it's the subscribers, Doctor.

THE MAYOR.   A good thing, too.

ASLAKSEN.   Public opinion—enlightened people—homeowners and such   32▪
people—they rule the papers.

DR. STOCKMANN   [*speaks calmly*].   And all this is now against me?

ASLAKSEN.   Yes, it is. Printing your article would ruin the community completely.

THE MAYOR.   My hat and stick, please. [*DR. STOCKMANN lays the things on the table. THE MAYOR takes them.*] Your tenure as the town's chief authority has ended abruptly.

DR. STOCKMANN.   No, it's not over yet. [*To HOVSTAD.*] Then it's quite impossible to publish my article in the *Messenger?*

HOVSTAD.   Quite impossible, and also because of your family.   32▪

MRS. STOCKMANN.   You needn't bother about the family, Mr. Hovstad.

THE MAYOR   [*takes a sheet of paper from his pocket, and offers it to HOVSTAD*].   If you put this in, it will be sufficient for the guidance of the public. It's an official explanation. Mr. Hovstad, would you please?

HOVSTAD   [*accepts the paper*].   Good. We'll print it right away.

DR. STOCKMANN.   But not mine! But you'll find that you can't suppress the truth so easily. Mr. Aslaksen, please publish my manuscript as a pamphlet—at my expense, and under my name. I'll have four hundred copies—no, five hundred! Make it six!

ASLAKSEN.   If you paid me its weight in gold, Doctor, I couldn't use my press for a   33▪
thing like this. I wouldn't dare, in the light of public opinion. No one in the whole town will print it!

DR. STOCKMANN.   Then give it back to me.

HOVSTAD   [*gives him the manuscript*].   Here you are.

DR. STOCKMANN   [*picks up his hat and stick*].   I'll make it public anyway. I'll call an open meeting, and all my fellow townspeople will come to hear me read the truth!

THE MAYOR.   No organization in town would let you rent their hall for this purpose.

ASLAKSEN.   Not a single one. I'm sure of it.   335

BILLING.   No, damn it, not one!

MRS. STOCKMANN.   This is a disgrace. Why is everyone turning against you?

DR. STOCKMANN   [*speaks in anger*].   I'll tell you why. All the men in this town are no better than old women—like you. They all think only of their families, and not of the community.

MRS. STOCKMANN   [*takes his arm*].   Then I'll show them an—old woman—acting for once as men of power should act. I'll stand with you, Thomas.

DR. STOCKMANN.   Bravely said, Katrina! On my soul, I'll make things public. If I   340 can't rent a hall, I'll hire a drummer to follow me all over town, and I'll shout out the truth at every corner!

THE MAYOR.   Certainly you're not such a prize idiot as all that!

DR. STOCKMANN.   Oh yes I am!

ASLAKSEN.   You won't find a single voter to back you up.

BILLING.   No, damn it, you won't!

MRS. STOCKMANN.   Don't give in, Thomas. I'll send the boys with you.   345

DR. STOCKMANN.   That's an inspired idea!

MRS. STOCKMANN.   Morten will love it, and Eilif will go along.

DR. STOCKMANN.   Yes, and Petra, and you too, Katrina.

MRS. STOCKMANN.   No, no, that's not for me. But I'll watch at the window and support you. That I can do.

DR. STOCKMANN   [*embraces her and kisses her*].   Thanks for this. Now, my good gen- 350 tlemen, we'll have a trial by combat! We'll see whether a pack of cowards can squelch a patriot trying to make the world a cleaner place!

[*He and* MRS. STOCKMANN *leave by the main door.*]

THE MAYOR   [*shakes his head reflectively*].   Now he's made her go crazy too!

END OF THE THIRD ACT

ACT IV

SCENE. *The following night. A large room in the home of* CAPTAIN HORSTER. *An anteroom at the back can be seen through opened folding doors. The entrance door is at the extreme rear. Three windows are in the wall at stage left, and lighted lamps at these windows illuminate the room. Downstage from these windows is a table, with candles and a chair. A small podium, on which there is a table with chair, candles, bell, water, and glass, is set at the middle of the stage-right wall. There is a door in this wall downstage from the podium, and some chairs are near it. The room is almost filled with an assortment of townspeople, including a few women and children, and at the curtain the townsfolk continue entering from the anteroom.*

1 CITIZEN   [*speaks to another citizen*].   Hello, Lamstad! You here too?

2 CITIZEN.   I always come to public meetings.

3 CITIZEN.   D'you have your whistle?

2 CITIZEN.   You bet. Got yours?

3 CITIZEN.   Right here! And old Skipper Evensen's bringin' a cow-horn!   5

2 CITIZEN.   He's a real joker, that Evensen!

[*General laughter and noise from the crowd.*]

4 CITIZEN [*meets the three citizens*].   What's going on here tonight?

2 CITIZEN.   Dr. Stockmann is speaking against the Mayor.

4 CITIZEN.   But my God, they're brothers!

1 CITIZEN.   So what? Dr. Stockmann ain't scared.

3 CITIZEN.   But he goofed up; I read that in the *Messenger.*

2 CITIZEN.   He's on the wrong side this time, because he couldn't rent the halls of the Homeowners Association or the Downtown Civic Club.

1 CITIZEN.   He couldn't even get the one at the Spa.

2 CITIZEN.   Not on your life, man.

5 CITIZEN.   Whose side are we on here?

6 CITIZEN.   Just watch Aslaksen, and follow his lead.

BILLING [*comes through the crowd, carrying a writing case*].   Excuse me please. Please let me through. I'm a reporter for the *Messenger.* [*Sits at the table on the left.*]

1 LABORER.   Who's that?

2 LABORER.   Oh, that's Billing. He works at Aslaksen's paper.

[*MRS. STOCKMANN and PETRA enter from the door at the right, escorted by CAPTAIN HORSTER. EILIF and MORTEN follow them.*]

HORSTER [*points to the chairs*].   Please sit here. Then, if things get out of hand, you can leave easily.

MRS. STOCKMANN.   You're not expecting any trouble?

HORSTER.   With a crowd like this you can't tell. But just sit tight here. You'll be fine!

MRS. STOCKMANN [*sits, along with PETRA*].   Letting my husband use the room was so kind.

HORSTER.   Well, since he couldn't get one elsewhere—

PETRA.   It was brave of you, Captain Horster.

HORSTER.   Oh, it was nothing.

[*HOVSTAD and ASLAKSEN enter amid the crowd: "Excuse me!" "Please!" etc.*]

ASLAKSEN [*goes to HORSTER*].   Is the Doctor here yet?

HORSTER.   He's in the next room.

[*Noise from the crowd at the anteroom door.*]

HOVSTAD.   Here's the Mayor!

BILLING.   Well I'll be damned, he's here after all!

[*THE MAYOR enters through the crowd, which parts for him. He bows and greets people as he goes, and takes a stand near the left wall. DR. STOCKMANN then enters from the door at the right, wearing a black frock coat and a white tie. A few townspeople applaud, but they are quickly restrained. Then perfect silence.*]

DR. STOCKMANN [*speaks quietly to MRS. STOCKMANN*].   Are you all right?

MRS. STOCKMANN.   Just fine, thanks. [*Lowers voice.*] Thomas, please don't lose your temper.

DR. STOCKMANN.   No, I'll control myself. [*Takes out his watch and looks at it. Steps to the podium and bows.*] It's quarter past—time to start. [*Takes his manuscript from his pocket.*]

ASLAKSEN   [*speaks loudly*].   First we should elect someone as Chair!   35
DR. STOCKMANN.   That won't be necessary.
VARIOUS VOICES IN THE CROWD.   Yes! Hear, hear! Elect a Chair! etc.
THE MAYOR.   I too think we should have a Chair!
DR. STOCKMANN.   But I called this meeting to give a lecture, Peter.
THE MAYOR   [*speaks to the crowd*].   This lecture may lead to controversy, however, and for that we need someone to chair.
VARIOUS VOICES.   A Chair! Elect someone! etc.   40
HOVSTAD.   It seems there is a consensus to elect a Chair!
DR. STOCKMANN   [*speaks resignedly*].   All right—let the majority rule.
ASLAKSEN.   Will the Mayor consent to serve?   [*Various townspeople applaud. Shouts of "Yes, Mr. Mayor!" "He should chair!" etc.*]
THE MAYOR.   You will all understand why I must ask to be excused from serving you. But we do have an acceptable candidate. I recommend to you the President of the Homeowner's Association, Mr. Aslaksen!
VARIOUS VOICES.   Yay, Aslaksen! Yes! Hurrah for Aslaksen! etc.   45

[*DR. STOCKMANN picks up his manuscript and leaves the podium.*]

ASLAKSEN.   As my fellow citizens have such confidence in me, I am not unwilling to accept—

[*Applause. Cheers. Whistles. etc. ASLAKSEN mounts the podium.*]

BILLING   [*writes*].   "Mr. Aslaksen was elected by acclamation."
ASLAKSEN.   As your newly elected Chair, permit me a few short words. You all know me as a peaceful and quiet person. I believe in sober moderation, and in—and in moderate sobriety!
VARIOUS TOWNSPEOPLE.   Yes, we know!   *Bravo!* etc.   [*Light applause.*]
ASLAKSEN.   I am a graduate of the school of hard knocks, and I've learned that   50
the most important virtue of a citizen is moderation—
THE MAYOR.   Hear, hear!
ASLAKSEN.   And furthermore, that discretion and moderation are essential to public service. Therefore I suggest to the distinguished man who has called this meeting that he exert all efforts to keep within the limits of moderation.
7 CITIZEN   [*stands near the door stage right*].   Let's hear it for the Moderation Party!
VARIOUS VOICES.   Be quiet! Shut your damn mouth! Shh! etc.
ASLAKSEN.   No demonstrations! Please keep order! Is there anyone who wishes   55
to speak?
THE MAYOR.   Mr. Chairman.
ASLAKSEN.   The Honorable Mayor Stockmann has the floor.
THE MAYOR.   Because I am the closest relative of the Chief Medical Officer of the Spa, you will understand my reticence in speaking. But out of my duty as the Chief Executive Officer, and out of my concern for the town, I must present a motion. I believe that no one here considers it in the town's interest to publicize unsubstantiated and dubious reports concerning the sanitary condition of our water supplies.
VARIOUS VOICES.   Absolutely not! No, no! No such reports! etc.
THE MAYOR.   Therefore I move that this assembly refuse to permit the Chief   60
Medical Officer to give his lecture or discuss it.   [*Voice of "Second the motion."*]
DR. STOCKMANN   [*angrily*].   Refuse permission?— What's all this?—
MRS. STOCKMANN   [*coughs*].   Ahem!

DR. STOCKMANN [*collects himself*]. Well, all right for now. Go ahead.

THE MAYOR. In my report printed in the *Messenger*, I laid out the facts so that all impartial citizens might draw their own conclusions. In it you have seen that the Chief Medical Officer's recommendations—in addition to being a direct vote of no confidence in the town's principal citizens—would require unacceptable tax increases for the town, to the extent of many millions.

[*Cries of indignation and many whistles and catcalls.*]

ASLAKSEN [*rings bell*]. Order, gentlemen. [*Stands.*] I rise to support the motion 6 of the Mayor. He's right that there's more to the Doctor's actions than meets the eye. He begins with the Spa, but his real motive is revolution—to get control of the town government. The Doctor of course is honest—no question of that. I too believe in self-government, with the proviso that it does not raise taxes. But higher taxes would result here, and therefore I'll see Dr. Stockmann in hell before I support him on this! Excuse my language, but some things have too high a cost. [*Vigorous approval from all sides.*]

HOVSTAD. My position also needs clarification. Dr. Stockmann's analysis at first seemed reasonable, and I judged him worthy of support. But we soon found cause to believe that we had been led astray by false conclusions—

DR. STOCKMANN. False—?

HOVSTAD. Well, not totally reliable conclusions, if you will. The Mayor's statement has established that. I think no one here doubts my devotion to freedom. The record of the *Messenger* on such important political issues is widely recognized. But from wiser and more experienced men I have learned that the paper should take cautious and prudent stands on local issues.

ASLAKSEN. I agree completely with the speaker.

HOVSTAD. And on this current issue, it's certain that there's now a consensus 7 against Dr. Stockmann. Is it not then, gentlemen, an editor's duty to work in tandem with popular sentiment? Is not an editor obligated to work diligently on behalf of the readers whose causes he accepts and reflects? Am I wrong in this?

VARIOUS VOICES. No! You're right! Well said! etc.

HOVSTAD. Personally, this public disagreement with Dr. Stockmann, in whose home I have been a guest, has caused me great agony. Till now he has deserved the unconditional respect of his fellow citizens. With so much virtue, his only flaw is his tendency to be ruled by his feelings rather than his judgment.

A SMALL NUMBER OF VOICES. True! Stockmann is okay! etc.

HOVSTAD. Nevertheless, my overriding concern for the public has directed me to make this break. In addition, there's another reason for which he should be deterred from his present course, and that is concern for his family—

DR. STOCKMANN. Just stick to water intakes and sewers! 7

HOVSTAD. —Concern for his wife and children, for whom he has made no security.

MORTEN. Does he mean us, Mother?

MRS. STOCKMANN. Shh!

ASLAKSEN. Gentlemen, are you ready to vote on the Mayor's motion?

DR. STOCKMANN. There's no need. This evening I don't wish to speak about the 8 filthiness of the Spa. No, you'll hear something different.

THE MAYOR [*aside*]. What's next?

PETTERSEN   [*he is drunk, and stands near the back door*].   I pay taxes, and I want to talk! My insolent—absolute—unacceptable comment is—

VARIOUS VOICES.   He's plastered! Shut him up! Put that lush out! What an idiot! Pipe down! etc. [*Pettersen is ejected.*]

DR. STOCKMANN.   May I speak?

ASLAKSEN   [*rings the bell*].   Dr. Stockmann has the floor.   85

DR. STOCKMANN.   Thank you. A few days ago, I would have allowed no one to silence me as has been done tonight. Like a lion, I would have defended my sacred right to speak. But now this doesn't matter to me, because I have more important things to say. [*The crowd, one of whom is* MORTEN KIIL, *moves closer to him.*] In the last few days I've been thinking things over a good deal, so much that my head was almost spinning—

THE MAYOR   [*coughs*].   Ahem!

DR. STOCKMANN.   —but I have put things in order, and that's why I'm in front of you this evening. I have a unique discovery to tell you about, my fellow citizens, a revelation far more significant than the pollution of our water and the contaminated ground at our Therapeutic Spa.

VARIOUS VOICES   [*shout*].   Not that! Out of order! Not about the Spa! We won't listen! etc.

DR. STOCKMANN.   No, my topic tonight is my great discovery of the last few days—   90 that it is our moral life that is polluted and that it is our communal assumptions that are built on contaminated ground.

VARIOUS VOICES   [*hushed*].   What's this about? What's he mean? etc.

THE MAYOR.   What kind of insinuation—!

ASLAKSEN   [*rings his bell*].   The speaker is cautioned to be moderate.

DR. STOCKMANN.   I was brought up in this town, and I have always loved it. When I had to leave it I was still not old, and in my exile I thought of it fondly almost as a place inhabited by angels. [*Brief applause in the crowd.*] In the depressing hell-hole up north where I practiced for so many years, the people lived far apart, here and there, among the rocks, and I sometimes thought that that they didn't need a physician like myself but rather a veterinarian.

BILLING   [*puts down his pen*].   Well, damn it, I never heard—   95

HOVSTAD.   You're insulting the common people!

DR. STOCKMANN.   Now wait! From what I've said, you'll agree that up north I didn't forget you. I was more like a brooding hen, and what I hatched was—the plan for our Therapeutic Spa! [*Applause and objections.*] When I was fortunate enough to return home I thought my life had reached fulfillment. But I had an ardent, relentless, burning wish, and that was to serve you and to be an asset to you.

THE MAYOR   [*looks at the ceiling*].   This is a strange way of doing it!

DR. STOCKMANN.   And so, blinded to reality, I was in bliss. However, yesterday morning—no, really the evening before—my blind eyes were opened, and the first thing I saw was the incredible stupidity of our authorities—

[*Consternation, objections, laughter.* MRS. STOCKMANN *coughs strongly.*]

THE MAYOR.   Mr. Chairman!   100

ASLAKSEN   [*rings his bell*].   The chair has authority to rule—

DR. STOCKMANN.   Let's not quibble about a word, Mr. Aslaksen. I only mean that I began to realize how bull-headed the town leaders had been about the Spa. Generally,

I find official types unbearable. They inhibit freedom at every turn. They're no better than goats among newly sprouted trees; they destroy everything. They frustrate a free person at every turn, and I don't see why they shouldn't be exterminated like any pest—

[*Uproar in the room.*]

THE MAYOR.   Mr. Chairman, can this be allowed?

ASLAKSEN   [*rings his bell*].   Doctor—!

DR. STOCKMANN.   I don't know why I didn't see the nature of the official types   10?
before—when each day I could see such a shining example right here in town—my brother Peter—dull in wit, inflexible in prejudice—

[*Laughter, uproar, whistles.* MRS. STOCKMANN *coughs continuously.* ASLAKSEN *rings his bell loudly, etc.*]

PETTERSEN   [*who has returned*].   Hey, is he talking about me? My name's Pettersen, but damn it to hell if I—

VARIOUS VOICES   [*shout in anger*].   Throw the drunk out! Through the door with 'im! etc. [*Pettersen is thrown out again.*]

THE MAYOR.   Who was that—individual?

1 CITIZEN.   I don't know, Mr. Mayor.

2 CITIZEN.   He has no business here.   11(

3 CITIZEN.   He's probably a lumberman over at—[*The rest cannot be heard.*]

ASLAKSEN.   Obviously that man's brain is drowned in beer! [*Laughter.*] Continue, Doctor, but be moderate.

DR. STOCKMANN.   So then, neighbors, I will say nothing more about our leading citizens. No one should claim that my main objective is to criticize them, for I take comfort that such parasites—living fossils of a passing age—are racing toward their own extinction. They don't need a doctor's help to hurry them along! No, *they're* not the danger; *they're* not the ones most active in poisoning our moral life and polluting the ground under us. No, *they're* not the worst enemies of truth and freedom.

VARIOUS VOICES   [*speaking from all sides*].   Who then? Who is it? Name them! etc.

DR. STOCKMANN.   Don't worry! I'll name them! This is the great discovery I made   115
yesterday. [*Raises his voice.*] The most dangerous enemy of truth and freedom among us is the solid majority. Yes, the damned, solid, popular majority! That's it! Now you know!

[*Tremendous uproar in the room. Most people are shouting, stamping their feet, whistling, booing, hissing, etc. A few older people look slyly at each other and appear to be enjoying themselves.* MRS. STOCKMANN *stands anxiously.* EILIF *and* MORTEN *begin quarrelling with some other boys who are demonstrating.* ASLAKSEN *rings his bell and pleads for order.* HOVSTAD *and* BILLING *try to speak, but are drowned out. Finally, things quiet down.*]

ASLAKSEN.   As Chair, I ask the speaker to withdraw his immoderate language and apologize to the body.

DR. STOCKMANN.   Not for the world, Mr. Aslaksen! It's the majority in our town who are denying me my free right to speak the truth.

HOVSTAD.   The majority always has right on its side.

BILLING.   And, damn it, it always has truth, too!

DR. STOCKMANN.   The majority is never right—never, I say! Majority rule is noth-   120
ing more than a fairy tale that all thinking people must oppose. Who forms the majority—the intelligent or the stupid? Is there any doubt that the stupid make up the landslide majority everywhere on earth? But you can throw me in hell if it's ever been

part of an eternal plan for the stupid to control the intelligent! [*Outcries, catcalls, disturbance.*] All right, you can shout me down, but you can't answer me. The majority does have *might*—more's the pity—but not *right*. *I* am right, along with a small number of others. It's the *minority* that's always right! [*More outcries, demonstrations, etc.*]

HOVSTAD   [*laughs*].   So in the last few days Dr. Stockmann has become an aristocrat!

DR. STOCKMANN.   I've said that I won't waste words on people like that shipwrecked crew of officials behind us. They're no longer even relevant. My thoughts are rather on the few who are creating new and exciting ideas. Such people are in the front ranks, beyond the shortsighted vision of the solid majority. *They* are leading the fight for ideas that are so new and rare that as yet they haven't recruited great numbers to their cause.

HOVSTAD.   Oh, so now the Doctor's a revolutionary!

DR. STOCKMANN.   Yes, in God's name, I am, Mr. Hovstad! I want to revolt against the fairy tale that truth belongs to the majority alone. What are the truths the majority usually flocks around? Old, worn-out, and disintegrating truths. And when a truth gets too old, gentlemen, it's close to being a lie. [*Laughter and scorn at him.*] Yes, believe as you wish, but truths don't live for 969 years, like Methuselah. An average truth can live no more than seventeen or eighteen, or at best twenty years. In fact, truths this old are fading and dying, but it's only then that the majority harvests them for the food of their moral life. As a doctor, I assure you that there's only moral starvation there. All these dead popular beliefs, which are no better than salted meat that's gone rotten, are the cause of our present epidemic of moral scurvy.

ASLAKSEN.   It seems to me that the speaker has wandered away from his text.   125

THE MAYOR.   I'm in agreement with the Chair.

DR. STOCKMANN.   Peter, you're crazy! I *am* staying on my subject, which is exactly this: It's the mass, the majority—the fiendish, solid majority—that's poisoning the sources of our moral life and passing its waste on the very ground we stand on.

HOVSTAD.   And the great open-minded majority does all this because they're reasonable enough to recognize only secure and sanctioned truths?

DR. STOCKMANN.   Ah, my good Mr. Hovstad, don't pretend to speak about truths! The truths that the mass accepts today are the truths secured by the advance guard at the time of our grandparents. Today's forward thinkers have gone far beyond them. I believe there's only one essential truth, and that is that no society can be healthy if it lives on outmoded, marrowless truths.

HOVSTAD.   Well, instead of standing there with your mind in the blue, why not   130 make it interesting and tell us what you mean by these "marrowless truths" we live on.

[*Support from various parts of the crowd.*]

DR. STOCKMANN.   Well, I could go on forever, but I might begin with one which is really an outrageous lie but which all the same feeds the *Messenger* and the *Messenger's* readers.

HOVSTAD.   And that is—?

DR. STOCKMANN.   It's the idea given to you from the past and which you transmit mindlessly at every opportunity. It's the falsehood that the crowd, the mass, the majority, form the kernel of the people—in fact, that they are the people—and that the common people, the most apathetic and worst prepared in society, have the same right to condemn and approve, to manage and advise, as those few people who are truly enlightened.

BILLING.   I hear this, damn it, but—

HOVSTAD [*shouts at the same time*]. Citizens, remember this!

VARIOUS VOICES. Aren't we the people! So only the aristocrats run things? etc.

1 LABORER. Down with him for talking like this!

2 LABORER. Yeah, throw 'im out!

3 CITIZEN [*shouts*]. Toot your horn, Evensen!

[*Sounds of a loud horn. Whistles and tremendous uproar in the room.*]

DR. STOCKMANN [*speaks when the noise subsides*]. Gentlemen, please listen. Can't you hear the truth for a change? I never expected that you'd all agree with me, but I thought that Mr. Hovstad might, at least after a while. He claims to be a freethinker—

VARIOUS VOICES [*in startled but hushed tones*]. He's a freethinker? What? Is Editor Hovstad a freethinker?

HOVSTAD [*shouts*]. Prove this, Dr. Stockmann! When did I say this in print?

DR. STOCKMANN [*pauses briefly*]. No, damn it, you're right—you've never been that honest. Well, I won't leave you dangling in the wind, Mr. Hovstad. [*To the crowd.*] Let *me* be the freethinker then. I'm going to persuade you logically that the *People's Messenger* misleads you shamelessly by telling you that you—the common folk, the masses—form what is called "The People." This is a lie, for common folk are only the raw material of the people. [*Grumbling, laughter, and commotion in the room.*] Well, consider the differences between thoroughbred and street animals. For instance, a farmyard hen is too scrawny for good eating. And its eggs? A common crow or raven does just as well. But with thoroughbred Spanish or Japanese hens, or well-nourished pheasants or turkeys, the story is different. As further evidence, consider the lives of dogs, which we human beings so closely resemble. Compare an ordinary street mongrel with a registered collie or setter which has been bred for many generations. Don't you think these thoroughbred dogs have better brains than the curs? You know the answer. The pups of the well-bred dogs take to training naturally, and do things that common mongrels could never learn. [*Uproar and disapproval all around.*]

9 CITIZEN [*shouts*]. So you think we're dogs?

10 CITIZEN. We're not animals, *Sir* Doctor!

DR. STOCKMANN. Yes, my friend, we really *are*, believe me—the highest animals on earth—but even among us there are just a few really good ones. Among people, there are wide differences between thoroughbreds and mongrels. And the funny thing is that Editor Hovstad totally agrees with me as long as the subject is four-footed creatures—

HOVSTAD. Yes, but they're in a different category.

DR. STOCKMANN. You see! When I apply the principle to us two-legged animals, he refuses the logic. He won't follow his ideas to their necessary conclusion, but rather turns everything upside down, and pontificates in the *Messenger* about the farmyard hens and mongrel curs being the best of the human menagerie! But it's always that way as long as popular bromides control the soul, and people don't free themselves to reach their own highest mental and spiritual distinction.

HOVSTAD. I don't claim distinction of any sort. I come from simple peasants, and I'm proud of my deep roots in the common people he's now insulting.

VARIOUS VOICES. Hurrah for Hovstad! Well said! etc.

DR. STOCKMANN. You recognize that common people are not confined to the lower economic levels. They yelp at our heels wherever we go, even in the highest circles and professions. I cite as an example His Honor, the Mayor. My brother Peter is just as common as anyone in two shoes—

[*Laughter and hisses.*]

THE MAYOR.   I protest these personal slurs!

DR. STOCKMANN   [*undisturbed*].   And he's common not because he is—as I am—a descendant of an old Pomeranian pirate. This is, I confess, our common origin—

THE MAYOR.   That family legend is not true!

DR. STOCKMANN.   But he is low because he uncritically accepts the opinions of his   155
superiors as his own. People like that are intellectual rabble, and this is why my statesmanlike brother Peter is so undistinguished and narrow-minded.

THE MAYOR.   Mr. Chairman—!

HOVSTAD.   So in this country people can be open-minded only if they're distinguished! This is certainly news!

DR. STOCKMANN.   Yes, that's *one* of my discoveries. Another is that open-mindedness is virtually the same as morality. This is why it's so indefensible for the *Messenger* to preach day in and day out that the people, the masses, the solid majority, are the guardians of understanding and morality, and that social and political evils are a residue of culture, just as the pollution of our Spa is a residue of the tannery wastes up at Mølledal. [*Uproar and interruptions. Unaffected, he laughs in his exhilaration.*] And yet the *Messenger* preaches on about elevating the masses to their higher destiny! But damn it all, if the *Messenger's* doctrines were right, then elevating the masses would do no more than drive them straight into the devil's hands! But fortunately this theory is only folklore. No, it's stupidity, poverty, and ugliness that make Old Nick prosper. A house that is not well cleaned and ventilated will soon make its inhabitants lose their moral judgment. Without the oxygen gained from constant cleansing, we lose our conscience. And I conclude that oxygen is lacking in many households here in town, because the popular majority have desensitized their consciences and are willing to build the town's wealth on a cesspool of lies and deceit.

ASLAKSEN.   Accusations like this, against the entire town, are outrageous!

10 CITIZEN.   I move that the Chair rule the speaker out of order.   160

VARIOUS VOICES.   Second! Hear, hear! Out of order! etc.

DR. STOCKMANN   [*becomes angry*].   If I can't speak here, I'll declare the truth in the streets! I'll write for papers in other towns! The entire country will see what's going on here!

HOVSTAD.   It seems that Dr. Stockmann is bent on ruining the town.

DR. STOCKMANN.   Yes, I love my hometown so much that I prefer its ruin to its living on lies.

ASLAKSEN.   Now you've *really* said it!   165

[*Uproar, shouts, catcalls, etc.* MRS. STOCKMANN *coughs, but* DR. STOCKMANN *no longer listens to her.*]

HOVSTAD   [*shouts over the noise.*]   Any person aiming to destroy the community is a public enemy!

DR. STOCKMANN   [*with rising anger*].   If the community lives on lies, what does its destruction matter? It ought to be pounded to rubble, or its pollution will infect other towns, and, finally, the entire country! And I say, with every fiber of my being, that if things go that far, may the country itself die, and may all its people be eliminated!

11 CITIZEN.   This is the talk of a real enemy of the people!

BILLING.   That voice—God damn it—that voice is the People's voice!

THE ENTIRE CROWD   [*shouts*].   He's an enemy of the people! He hates his coun-   17
try! He hates all the people! etc.

ASLAKSEN.   I'm deeply disturbed, both publicly and personally, at what we've
heard. Dr. Stockmann has revealed an unfortunate part of himself I would never have
dreamed possible. But the expression just voiced by one of you conveys the sense of this
meeting, and hence I would entertain the following resolution of censure: "This assembly declares that Dr. Thomas Stockmann, Chief Medical Officer of the Spa, is an enemy
of the people."

[*Cry of "So move" and "Second the motion." Tremendous applause and cheers, stamping of feet,
etc. A few men surround DR. STOCKMANN and hiss and menace him. MRS. STOCKMANN and
PETRA stand up. MORTEN and EILIF begin fighting other boys who have joined the hissing, but
they are separated by nearby adults.*]

DR. STOCKMANN   [*to those menacing him*].   You fools! I tell you—
ASLAKSEN   [*rings his bell*].   You no longer have the floor, Doctor. We'll take a vote,
but as a personal privilege for the Doctor, we'll do it by ballot and not by voice or hand.
Mr. Billing, do you have any paper?
BILLING.   Yes I do, both blue and white.
ASLAKSEN   [*walks to him*].   That's good, it will make the process easier. Cut it up;   17
yes, like that. [*To the crowd.*] Take blue for no; white for yes. I myself will collect your votes.

[*THE MAYOR leaves while ASLAKSEN and a few others put the ballots in their hats and distribute
them.*]

1 CITIZEN   [*to HOVSTAD*].   What should we think about the Doctor? Has he gone
off his rocker?
HOVSTAD.   You know he's always been headstrong.
2 CITIZEN   [*to BILLING*].   Billing, you've been at the house. Did you ever see him
drinking?
BILLING.   Well, I can't be sure, but there's always liquor on his table.
3 CITIZEN.   I think he goes around the bend at times.
1 CITIZEN.   Has there been any madness in the family?   18
BILLING.   I wouldn't be surprised.
4 CITIZEN.   No, it looks like pure spite to me; I think he's out to get someone.
BILLING.   Well, he did get turned down on his request for a raise.
THE FOUR CITIZENS   [*agree among themselves*].   Ah, we see it all now!
PETTERSEN   [*who has returned again*].   Gimme a blue one! And a white one too!   18
ANGRY VOICES.   There's that lush again! Out with him! etc.
MORTEN KIIL   [*speaks to DR. STOCKMANN*].   Well, Stockmann, do you see what your
hocus-pocus has done for you?
DR. STOCKMANN.   I've done my duty as I saw it.
MORTEN KIIL.   What did you say about the tanneries at Mølledal?
DR. STOCKMANN.   You understood me—that they're the source of the toxic waste.   19
MORTEN KIIL.   Including my tannery?
DR. STOCKMANN.   Yes, I'm sorry, but yours is the worst.
MORTEN KIIL.   Are you going to put this in the paper?
DR. STOCKMANN.   I won't hold anything back.
MORTEN KIIL.   That may cost you plenty, Stockmann. [*Leaves.*]   19
VIK   [*goes to HORSTER, ignoring the women*].   So, Captain, you permit your house to
be used by an enemy of the people.

HORSTER.   Mr. Vik, I have a right to do as I wish with my own property.

VIK.   Well, then, you can't object if I exercise the same right with mine.

HORSTER.   Sir, what are you saying?   200

VIK. You'll understand in the morning. [*Turns and walks away.*]

PETRA.   Captain Horster, wasn't he your shipowner?

HORSTER.   Yes, that was Mr. Vik.

ASLAKSEN   [*ballots in hand, he steps on the podium and rings his bell*].   Order, please!
Gentlemen, here are the results. All of you have voted but one—

12 CITIZEN   [*a young man*].   Yeah, that was the drunk!   205

ASLAKSEN.   And by a unanimous vote—except for a drunken man—this body of
citizens declares that Dr. Thomas Stockmann, Chief Medical Officer of the Spa, is an
enemy of the people! [*Applause, outcries.*] Let's have three cheers for our ancient and
noble community! [*Cheers.*] Let's also have three cheers for our honorable Mayor, who
has put our town above duty to family! [*More cheers.*] Our business is ended. Do I hear a
motion to adjourn? [*Cries of "So move," "Second."*] The meeting is now adjourned! [*Steps
down.*]

BILLING.   Long live our Chair!

THE ENTIRE CROWD.   Hurray for Aslaksen the Printer! etc.

DR. STOCKMANN.   Petra, my coat and hat. Captain, do you have space for passengers to the New World?

HORSTER.   Yes, Doctor, for you and yours I'll make room.   210

DR. STOCKMANN   [*as PETRA helps him with his coat*].   Katrina, boys, let's go. [*He
takes his wife's arm.*]

MRS. STOCKMANN   [*lowers her voice*].   Thomas, the back way.

DR. STOCKMANN.   There's no back way for me, Katrina. [*Raises his voice.*] You'll be
hearing from this enemy of the people again before he shakes the dust of this town from
his feet.° I cannot be as charitable as the person who said, "Forgive them, for they know
not what they do!"°

ASLAKSEN.   Dr. Stockmann, that's blasphemy!

BILLING.   Well, God d—. This is too much for a believing person!   215

13 CITIZEN   [*coarsely*].   So he's threatening us, is he?

ANGRY VOICES.   Smash his windows! Toss him in the fjord! etc.

3 CITIZEN   [*shouts*].   Blow your horn, Evensen! Toot, toot!

[*Loud horn calls, whistles, shouts, general turmoil.* HORSTER *leads* DR. STOCKMANN *and his
family toward the door at the rear.*]

THE WHOLE CROWD   [*howls, etc. at them*].   Enemy of the people! Enemy of the
people! Enemy of the people!

BILLING   [*gathers his notes*].   Well, damned if I'd go over and have a toddy with   220
the Stockmanns tonight!

[*The crowd pushes out the rear door. Their noise continues outside. From the street the receding
shouts continue: "Enemy of the people," "Enemy of the People!"*]

END OF THE FOURTH ACT

---

213 *he shakes . . . from his feet:* Mark 6:11.   *Forgive them . . . what they do:* Luke 23:34.

ACT V

SCENE. DR. STOCKMANN'S *study, the next morning. The room is in general disorder. At the walls are bookcases, along with cabinets containing various specimens. At the rear, a center door leads to the hallway. Downstage in the stage-left wall there is a door to the living room. The two windows in the stage-right wall are completely broken. In the middle of the room is the Doctor's desk, strewn with books, papers, etc.* DR. STOCKMANN, *in dressing gown, slippers, and smoking cap, is using an umbrella to scrape out broken glass and other debris from under a cabinet. Shortly after the curtain he produces a large stone.*

DR. STOCKMANN   [*calls through the living-room door*].   Here's another one, Katrina.
MRS. STOCKMANN   [*offstage*].   I'm sure you'll find more.
DR. STOCKMANN   [*adds the stone to a pile on the desk*].   These stones will be keepsakes. Eilif and Morten will see them every day, and will inherit them when they grow up. [*Rakes under another bookcase.*] Did what's-her-name get the glazier yet?
MRS. STOCKMANN   [*enters*].   Yes, but he wasn't sure he could make it today.
DR. STOCKMANN.   You'll soon see that he won't dare to come.
MRS. STOCKMANN.   Randina—the maid—thought the same. He's afraid because of the neighbors. [*Looks toward the door on the left, and calls.*] What is it, Randina. Yes, I'll take it. [*Leaves and returns immediately .*] It's a letter for you, Thomas.
DR. STOCKMANN.   Thank you. [*Takes the letter, opens it, and reads it quickly.*] Ah, as I expected.
MRS. STOCKMANN.   Who's it from?
DR. STOCKMANN.   Our landlord. It's a notice to leave.
MRS. STOCKMANN.   Can it be? He's such a nice man—
DR. STOCKMANN   [*looks at the letter*].   Says he doesn't dare do anything else. His fellow-citizens—public sentiment—dependent on others—can't offend superiors—no choice. You get the picture.
MRS. STOCKMANN.   But you see his reasons, Thomas.
DR. STOCKMANN.   Yes, I see. I see that the whole town is made up of cowards; they're all afraid of each other. [*Tosses the letter on the desk.*] But, Katrina, it's no matter. We'll sail to America, and then—
MRS. STOCKMANN.   Is this the best thing to do, Thomas?
DR. STOCKMANN.   Do you think we should stay here, where they've branded me as an enemy of the people, threatened me, and smashed my windows? And look, they've ripped my black trousers!
MRS. STOCKMANN.   Oh, dear! That's your best pair.
DR. STOCKMANN.   You should never battle for truth and freedom in your Sunday best! It isn't the trousers; you can sew them up again. It's rather the injustice that these scum dared to attack me as though they were my equals. I can never accept that.
MRS. STOCKMANN.   Certainly they treated you shabbily, Thomas, but does that justify leaving our own country permanently?
DR. STOCKMANN.   Don't you suppose the common mongrels are just as spiteful in other Norwegian towns we could live in? There's not much to choose from. But crap, their snapping at heels isn't the worst! The worst is that everyone in this country is a slave to party—though for that matter it's probably no different anywhere else. In the West, I'm sure, they have the same popular majority, the same pseudo-liberal public opinion, and all that devil's garbage. But, you see, things there are on a huge scale. They

may *kill* you, but they don't *torture* you with a thousand cuts, as they do here; they don't put your soul in a vise and squeeze the life out of you. If you need to, though, you can get away there. [*Paces.*] If only I knew of a bargain on an unexplored forest, or a tiny island in the South Seas—

MRS. STOCKMANN.   But what of the boys, Thomas?   20

DR. STOCKMANN   [*stops*].   You're so strange, Katrina! Do you want the boys to grow up in a society like ours? Last night you saw that half the people are crazy enough to be in straightjackets, and if the other half haven't lost their minds, it's because they're such blockheads they have nothing to lose.

MRS. STOCKMANN.   No, but Thomas, you speak so imprudently.

DR. STOCKMANN.   Well, isn't what I'm saying right? Don't they turn everything upside down? Don't they mix up right and wrong? Don't they call everything a lie that I know is the truth? But the most insane thing is that these grown people, who profess to support freedom, go around as a party and try to fool themselves and others into thinking that they're broad-minded and independent. Katrina, have you ever heard the like?

MRS. STOCKMANN.   Yes, it's wrong, but— [*PETRA enters from the living room.*] What, already back from school?

PETRA.   Yes. I've been dismissed.   25

MRS. STOCKMANN.   Dismissed?

DR. STOCKMANN.   You too, Petra?

PETRA.   Mrs. Busk gave me my walking papers, and I thought it best to go right away.

DR. STOCKMANN.   You did right.

MRS. STOCKMANN.   Who would have expected that Mrs. Busk was that sort of   30
person?

PETRA.   She isn't that sort, Mother. I could see how it hurt her. But she didn't dare do anything else, she said, and so I got fired.

DR. STOCKMANN   [*laughs and rubs his hands*].   She didn't dare either. How marvellous!

MRS. STOCKMANN.   Well, after the horrible scene last night—

PETRA.   That wasn't all. Father, just listen!

DR. STOCKMANN.   Well?   35

PETRA.   She showed me three letters she had got only this morning.

DR. STOCKMANN.   With no signatures, I assume?

PETRA.   Yes.

DR. STOCKMANN.   Because they didn't *dare* sign their names, Katrina.

PETRA.   And two of them reported that a man who had been a guest in our home   40
declared at the Club that I held dangerously liberated views on a number of things—

DR. STOCKMANN.   You didn't disavow them, I hope?

PETRA.   You know I didn't. Mrs. Busk herself, in private anyway, has liberated views, but because this is coming out about me, she didn't dare keep me.

MRS. STOCKMANN.   And one of our guests! That's what you get for your hospitality, Thomas!

DR. STOCKMANN.   We can't stay in this pig sty any longer. Pack our things right away, Katrina. The sooner we leave, the better.

MRS. STOCKMANN.   Shh! There's someone in the hall. Go see who it is, Petra.   45

PETRA   [*opens the living-room door*].   Oh, it's you, Captain Horster! Please come in.

HORSTER   [*enters*].   Good morning. I wanted to see how you're doing.

DR. STOCKMANN   [*shakes his hand*].   Thank you. You're so kind.

MRS. STOCKMANN.   And thank you again for protecting us from the mob, Captain Horster.

PETRA.   But how were you able to get back home again?   50

HORSTER.   Oh, I managed. I can take care of myself, and that crowd has more bark than bite.

DR. STOCKMANN.   Isn't their hangdog cowardice amazing? [*Shows the stones on the desk.*] Look, here are the stones they used to break our windows. Just look! No more than two in this pile have any class as rocks at all; the rest are gravel—just pebbles! And the crowd stood out there milling around, threatening to beat me to a pulp! But for action—action—you just don't see that in this town!

HORSTER.   This time, though, it was best for you, Doctor.

DR. STOCKMANN.   Your're right. But it still makes you mad, because if the country ever gets into a serious all-out fight, you'll see that public opinion will be to run away, Captain Horster, and the solid majority will be scared off like sheep. It's enough to make you sick. But hell, it's stupid to go on like this. They've called me the people's enemy, and so I'll *be* the people's enemy.

MRS. STOCKMANN.   You can never be that, Thomas.   55

DR. STOCKMANN.   Don't be too sure, Katrina. Being called such an ugly name is the same as being stabbed in the lung. That ghastly name is sitting in my stomach and gnawing at me like a cancer. No medicine can help this.

PETRA.   No, Father, you should just laugh at them.

HORSTER.   Doctor, one day they'll see things your way.

MRS. STOCKMANN.   Yes, as sure as you're standing here.

DR. STOCKMANN.   Sure, when it's too late. Well, they deserve it. Let them roll in   60
their own filth and regret that they once drove a patriot into exile. When do you sail, Captain Horster?

HORSTER.   Well, I came here to tell you—

DR. STOCKMANN.   Is something wrong with the ship?

HORSTER.   No, but what happened is that *I'm* not going along.

PETRA.   You haven't gotten your notice?

HORSTER   [*smiles*].   Yes, that's it.   65

PETRA.   You too!

MRS. STOCKMANN.   Thomas, do you see?

DR. STOCKMANN.   And all for the sake of truth! If I'd thought for one minute—

HORSTER.   Don't worry. I'll get a post from some shipping line or other out of town.

DR. STOCKMANN.   And here we have the estimable Mr. Vik—a man of wealth and   70
independence. What a God-damned farce!

HORSTER.   Oh, he's right-minded otherwise. He said he would've kept me, if he dared—

DR. STOCKMANN.   But he didn't dare? No, that goes without saying.

HORSTER.   He says it's not easy, being a party man and all—

DR. STOCKMANN.   Now here's a truth from on high! A party is like a meat grinder. It grinds everyone's brains together into a dead-level mash—fatheads and meatheads, all together.

MRS. STOCKMANN.   Thomas, really now!   75

PETRA   [*to* HORSTER].   If you hadn't taken us home, things might have been different for you.

HORSTER. I have no regrets.

PETRA [*extends her hand*]. Thank you for that!

HORSTER [*to* DR. STOCKMANN]. What I came to tell you is that I've another idea, if you're really resolved to leave—

DR. STOCKMANN. Excellent! The sooner the better— 80

[*A knock is heard offstage.*]

MRS. STOCKMANN. Shh! Someone's knocking.

PETRA. It must be Uncle.

DR. STOCKMANN. Ah! [*Calls.*] Come in!

MRS. STOCKMANN. Dear Thomas, please promise me—

[*The* MAYOR *enters from the hallway door.*]

THE MAYOR. You're busy. I can come back later— 85

DR. STOCKMANN. Not at all. Come in.

THE MAYOR. But I'd like to talk to you—just the two of us.

MRS. STOCKMANN. We'll go to the living room.

HORSTER. And I'll come back later.

DR. STOCKMANN. No, please, Captain, stay with them. I'd like to hear more— 90

HORSTER. I'll be glad to wait.

[*He follows* MRS. STOCKMANN *and* PETRA *into the living-room. The* MAYOR *says nothing but looks at the windows.*]

DR. STOCKMANN. You may find quite a draft here today. Why don't you put on your hat?

THE MAYOR. Thank you. [*Does so.*] I think I caught a cold last night. I stood and froze—

DR. STOCKMANN. You did? I thought it was rather warm.

THE MAYOR. I'm sorry I had no power to stop last night's excesses. 95

DR. STOCKMANN. Do you have anything else in particular to tell me?

THE MAYOR [*takes out a large envelope*]. This letter, from the Governing Board of the Spa.

DR. STOCKMANN. My notice?

THE MAYOR. Yes, bearing today's date. [*Puts the envelope on the desk.*] This is painful, but considering public opinion, we didn't dare do anything else.

DR. STOCKMANN [*smiles*]. Didn't dare? I keep hearing echoes today! 100

THE MAYOR. It's important for you to understand your present position. You can plan on no future medical practice here in town.

DR. STOCKMANN. The practice be damned to hell! But why are you so sure?

THE MAYOR. The Homeowners Association is circulating a petition from house to house recommending that responsible citizens stop using your services. I assure you that not a single family head will refuse to sign. Quite simply, no one will dare to refuse.

DR. STOCKMANN. I don't doubt you. But what then?

THE MAYOR. My advice is that you'd best leave town for a period. 105

DR. STOCKMANN. Yes, I've been thinking about that.

THE MAYOR. Good. And then after you've thought things out for a time—say half a year—after mature consideration you might find it fitting to write a brief apology admitting your mistake—

DR. STOCKMANN. You mean that I might get my post back?

THE MAYOR. Perhaps. It's not impossible.

DR. STOCKMANN. But what about public opinion? You wouldn't dare go against public opinion.

THE MAYOR. Public opinion is variable. And, frankly, it's especially important to us to have some sort of written apology from you.

DR. STOCKMANN. Oh, you're licking your chops for that! But for Christ's sake, don't you recall what I told you about such dirty tricks?

THE MAYOR. Things were different then. You believed the whole town was behind you—

DR. STOCKMANN. Yes, and now I believe the whole town's on my neck. [*Flares up.*] But even if the devil and his great-grandmother were on my neck—! Never! I say never!

THE MAYOR. Thomas, a family man can't behave as you do. You have no right, Thomas!

DR. STOCKMANN. No right? There's only one thing in the world that free persons have no right to do, and do you know what that is?

THE MAYOR. No.

DR. STOCKMANN. Naturally, but I'll tell you. Free persons have no right to get down and roll in filth—no right to lower themselves to the point where they're spitting in their own faces.

THE MAYOR. This has a jingle of plausibility, and it would explain your stubbornness if there were nothing else—. But there is—something else.

DR. STOCKMANN. What are you talking about?

THE MAYOR. You understand me very well. But as your brother, and as a man of perception, I advise you not to be too confident about prospects and hopes that may so easily fall through.

DR. STOCKMANN. Just what are you getting at?

THE MAYOR. Do you expect me to believe you know nothing about Mr. Kiil's will?

DR. STOCKMANN. Well, I know that his small estate will go to a foundation for old working people. But what does that have to do with me?

THE MAYOR. Well, first, the estate is not small. Mr. Tannerymaster Kiil is a rather wealthy man.

DR. STOCKMANN. I never had any idea!

THE MAYOR. Oh—truly? None? You also had no idea that a not insignificant amount of his wealth will go to your children, and that you and your wife will enjoy the interest for life? Didn't he ever tell you?

DR. STOCKMANN. No, never a blessed word! Rather the reverse. He always blasts away interminably about ridiculously high taxes. But you're sure of all this, Peter?

THE MAYOR. I have it on the best authority.

DR. STOCKMANN. Then, praise God, Katrina's secure—and the children too! I'll tell her right away. [*Calls.*] Katrina! Katrina!

THE MAYOR [*holds him back*]. Shh! Not a word yet!

MRS. STOCKMANN [*opens the door*]. What is it, Thomas?

DR. STOCKMANN. Not a thing. Wait inside a bit more. [*She closes the door. He begins pacing.*] Secure! And think—they're all secure, and for life. What a blessed feeling—to know you're secure!

THE MAYOR. Yes, but you're really not. Mr. Kiil the tanner can change his will whenever he wants.

DR. STOCKMANN. But, my good Peter, he won't. The old Badger is dancing for joy at the way I went after you and your precious cohorts.

THE MAYOR   [*starts, and looks intently at him*].   This puts things in a new light.

DR. STOCKMANN.   What things?

THE MAYOR.   This whole business was a coordinated maneuver. These wild and reckless slurs that you—in the name of truth—have aimed at our municipal leaders—

DR. STOCKMANN.   Were what?

THE MAYOR.   They were no more than an exchange for being named in that   140
revengeful old man's will.

DR. STOCKMANN   [*almost speechless*].   Peter, you're the most nauseating scum I've ever known!

THE MAYOR.   This is the end between us. Your dismissal is final, because we now have a weapon against you. [*Leaves.*]

DR. STOCKMANN.   Oh, my God! [*Calls toward the living room.*] Katrina, scrub the floor after him! Have her bring a pail—God damn it—what's-her-name, with the sooty nose—

MRS. STOCKMANN   [*at the living-room door*].   Thomas, hush, hush!

PETRA   [*also at the door*].   Father, Grandpa is here, and wants to speak with you   145
alone.

DR. STOCKMANN.   Why not? [*Goes to the door. PETRA and MRS. STOCKMANN leave. MORTEN KIIL enters and DR. STOCKMANN closes the door.*] Come in, Father. What is it? Please sit down.

MORTEN KIIL.   No, thank you. [*Looks around.*] You've made it look cosy here today, Stockmann.

DR. STOCKMANN.   Yes, doesn't it look that way?

MORTEN KIIL.   Really fine, and lots of fresh air. Today you have plenty of that oxee-gin you talked about yesterday. You have a clear conscience today, I suppose.

DR. STOCKMANN.   Yes, I have.   150

MORTEN KIIL.   I believe it. [*Pats his coat pocket.*] Do you know what I've got here?

DR. STOCKMANN.   A clear conscience too, I hope.

MORTEN KIIL.   Bah! Better than that. [*Takes out a leather folder, opens it, and shows a sheaf of papers.*]

DR. STOCKMANN   [*looks at him in surprise*].   Shares in the Spa?

MORTEN KIIL.   It wasn't hard to buy 'em today.   155

DR. STOCKMANN.   And you've been out snapping them up—

MORTEN KIIL.   All I could afford.

DR. STOCKMANN.   But, my good Father, the Spa is in such desperate condition!

MORTEN KIIL.   If only you return to sanity, you can put it back in tune soon enough.

DR. STOCKMANN.   Well, you yourself can see I'm doing all I can. But—everyone in   160
town is crazy.

MORTEN KIIL.   You said yesterday that the worst pollution came from my tannery. If that's true, then my grandfather and my father before me and I myself have all been poisoning the town for many years, like three angels of death. Do you believe I can live with that kind of shame?

DR. STOCKMANN.   Well, you'll have to get used to it.

MORTEN KIIL.   No, thanks. I prize my good name and reputation. I hear that people call me "the Badger," which is a sort of pig. But there's no way on earth they'll be right about this. I'm going to live and die with a clean reputation.

DR. STOCKMANN.   How do you plan to do that?

MORTEN KIIL.   You're going to make me clean, Stockmann.   165

DR. STOCKMANN. Me?

MORTEN KIIL. Do you know what money I used for the shares? No, you don't, but I'll tell you. It's the money that Katrina, Petra, and the boys will have when I'm gone. Yes, you see, I've been able to salt a little away, despite everything.

DR. STOCKMANN [*with rising anger*]. You've used Katrina's inheritance for that!

MORTEN KIIL. Yes. Everything is now sunk in the Spa. And now I'll find out, Stockmann, if you're a total lunatic! If you still say that tiny monsters and other such things come from my tannery, it's as though you're cutting wide strips of skin from the bodies of Katrina, and Petra, and the boys. A decent family man couldn't do that— unless he's totally crazy.

DR. STOCKMANN [*paces*]. But I am totally crazy—totally!   17●

MORTEN KIIL. You can't be so raving, foaming crazy that you'd destroy your wife and children.

DR. STOCKMANN [*stands in front of him*]. Why didn't you ask me before you bought all this trash?

MORTEN KIIL. Once something's done, it's best to finish it.

DR. STOCKMANN [*paces uneasily*]. If only I weren't so sure—. But I *am* sure! I'm absolutely positive!

MORTEN KIIL [*weighs the folder in his hand*]. If you hang on to your insane ideas,   17●
these will be worthless, you know. [*Returns the folder to his pocket.*]

DR. STOCKMANN. God damn it all! Researchers should be able to unearth a counteragent, some sort of antidote—

MORTEN KIIL. To kill the tiny monsters?

DR. STOCKMANN. Yes, or to make them harmless.

MORTEN KIIL. Couldn't you try rat poison?

DR. STOCKMANN. Don't be foolish. —But everyone says it's only my imagination.   18●
Well, let's have it their way—it's imagination. Didn't the short-sighted curs censure me as an enemy of the people—and weren't they howling to claw my clothes off, too?

MORTEN KIIL. And all the windows they smashed for you!

DR. STOCKMANN. And then there's my family responsibility. I'll take it up with Katrina. She's superb on these things.

MORTEN KIIL. Right, she's a sensible woman; listen to her.

DR. STOCKMANN [*turns toward him*]. But you, how could you mess things up so totally? To gamble with Katrina's inheritance, and leave me in such a painful bind? When I look at you, I think I'm seeing the devil himself.

MORTEN KIIL. I can see it's time to go. But I want an answer before two o'clock.   18●
Yes or *no*. With a "no," I'll will everything to my foundation before the day is over.

DR. STOCKMANN. And what does Katrina get then?

MORTEN KIIL. Not even a pinch of snuff.

[*The hall door opens, showing* HOVSTAD *and* ASLAKSEN *waiting to enter.*]

MORTEN KIIL. Well, look at this pair!

DR. STOCKMANN [*glares at them*]. What—? You dare come to see me?

HOVSTAD. Yes, of course.

ASLAKSEN. We've come to talk to you.   190●

MORTEN KIIL [*whispers to* DR. STOCKMANN]. "Yes" or "no," before two o'clock.

[*Leaves through the hallway door as* HOVSTAD *and* ASLAKSEN *enter.*]

ASLAKSEN [*glances at* HOVSTAD]. Oho!

DR. STOCKMANN. Well, what is it? And be quick!

HOVSTAD. I understand how you feel about our stand toward you last night— 195

DR. STOCKMANN. Oh, by all the devils in hell, you took a fine stand. You were as upright as a bent-over crone. "Spineless" is the right word to describe you.

HOVSTAD. Whatever you call it, we couldn't do anything else.

DR. STOCKMANN. You mean you didn't *dare* do anything else. Is that more like it?

HOVSTAD. Okay, say it your way.

ASLAKSEN. But why didn't you tell us in advance, just a small hint to Mr. Hovstad 200
or me?

DR. STOCKMANN. A hint? About what?

ASLAKSEN. About the idea behind it.

DR. STOCKMANN. I don't follow you.

ASLAKSEN [*nods confidentially*]. Oh I'm sure you do, Dr. Stockmann.

HOVSTAD. There's no reason to conceal things any longer. 205

DR. STOCKMANN [*stares from one to the other*]. What in the God-damn hell—?

ASLAKSEN. May I ask, isn't your father-in-law buying up shares in the Spa all over town?

DR. STOCKMANN. Yes, he's been buying shares today, but—?

ASLAKSEN. It would have been wiser to have someone else do it—someone not so closely related.

HOVSTAD. And you shouldn't have used your own name. No one needed to know 210
where the criticism about the Spa came from. You should have taken me in with you, Dr. Stockmann.

DR. STOCKMANN [*stares ahead blankly; a light seems to dawn for him, and he speaks as though struck from on high*]. Can this be possible? Can such things happen?

ASLAKSEN [*smiles*]. They can indeed. But only if you have a little—strategy—if you get my meaning.

HOVSTAD. And you should bring in others, because there's less risk for the individual when others are with you.

DR. STOCKMANN [*now composed*]. All right, gentlemen. What is it you want? 215

ASLAKSEN. Mr. Hovstad should—

HOVSTAD. No, *you* should explain, Aslaksen.

ASLAKSEN. Well, now that we understand how things are fitting together, we thought we could make the *Messenger* available to you.

DR. STOCKMANN. Would you dare that now? What of public opinion? Aren't you afraid of a storm of criticism?

HOVSTAD. We'll ride that out.

ASLAKSEN. And the Doctor must be ready to reverse positions quickly. As soon as 220
your attack has had its effect—

DR. STOCKMANN. As soon as Mr. Kiil and I have bought all the shares at panic prices, you mean—?

HOVSTAD. I presume that you have a—scientific purpose?—in wishing to control the Spa?

DR. STOCKMANN. Oh yes. It was for a *scientific purpose* that I brought the Old Badger in with me. And so we'll fiddle a bit with the intake pipes, and look professional while digging samples at the beach, and the town won't be out half a dollar. Doesn't that sound good?

HOVSTAD. I agree—particularly if you have the *Messenger* with you. 225

ASLAKSEN. In a free society the Press is powerful, Doctor.

DR. STOCKMANN.   Definitely, and so is public opinion. And you, Mr. Aslaksen, you will act as the conscience of the Homeowners Association?

ASLAKSEN.   Of both the Homeowners Association *and* the Temperance Society. Bank on it.

DR. STOCKMANN.   But gentlemen—I'm ashamed to ask about it, but what consideration for you—?

HOVSTAD.   You understand that we'd prefer to help you for nothing. But *The People's Messenger* is on wobbly legs. Things are not right, and I really don't want to close the paper now, when there's so much to work for in the larger political scene.

DR. STOCKMANN.   I agree. That would be hard for a *friend* of the people like you. *[Flares up.]* But I'm an *enemy* of the people! *[Searches around.]* Where did I put my stick? Where the hell's the stick?

HOVSTAD.   What's all this?

ASLAKSEN.   You'd never—?

DR. STOCKMANN *[stands]*.   Well, suppose I don't give you a dime's worth of my shares. Don't forget that the rich stay rich by hanging onto their money!

HOVSTAD.   Well, don't forget that your manipulation of shares can be reported in more than one way!

DR. STOCKMANN.   And you have just the talent for it! If I don't help the *Messenger*, you'll put a sinister turn on everything. You'll come howling after me and try to choke me the way a hound chokes a rabbit.

HOVSTAD.   That's nature's way; the strongest animals survive.

ASLAKSEN.   And take the nearest food, too.

DR. STOCKMANN *[while searching around]*.   Then go find yours in a gutter, damn it, because we're about to see which of the three of us is the strongest animal! *[Finds his umbrella and waves it.]* Here you go!

HOVSTAD.   You can't be violent!

ASLAKSEN.   Be careful with that umbrella!

DR. STOCKMANN.   Out the window with you, Mr. Hovstad!

HOVSTAD *[at the hallway door]*.   You're mad!

DR. STOCKMANN.   Out the window, Mr. Aslaksen! I tell you, jump! Distinguish yourself by being first for once!

ASLAKSEN *[dodges him at the desk]*.   Moderation, Doctor! I'm not strong! I can't do this! *[Shouts.]* Help! Help!

[MRS. STOCKMANN, PETRA, and HORSTER from the living room.]

MRS. STOCKMANN.   For the love of God! Thomas, what's going on here?

DR. STOCKMANN *[swings the umbrella]*.   Jump, I tell you! Into the gutter!

HOVSTAD.   This is an unprovoked attack! I call you as a witness, Captain Horster! *[Rushes out down the hall.]*

ASLAKSEN *[in confusion]*.   If only I knew the way out—*[Slips out through the living-room door.]*

MRS. STOCKMANN *[restrains DR. STOCKMANN]*.   Thomas, control yourself!

DR. STOCKMANN *[throws down the umbrella]*.   Damn, they got away after all!

MRS. STOCKMANN.   But what was it they wanted with you?

DR. STOCKMANN.   I'll tell you later; I've got to do something else right now. *[Goes to the desk and writes on a card.]* Katrina, what's written here?

MRS. STOCKMANN.   "No! No! No!" What does it mean?

DR. STOCKMANN.   I'll explain that later, too. [*Holds out the card.*] Petra, tell Soot-
face to run this over to the Badger as fast as she can. Hurry! [*PETRA takes the card and
leaves through the hallway door.*] Today I've been hounded by all devils of hell! But
now I'll use my pen to stab them! My ink will be venom and gall to poison them! My
inkpot will crack their skulls!

MRS. STOCKMANN.   Yes, but we're leaving the country, Thomas.   255

[*PETRA returns.*]

DR. STOCKMANN.   Well?

PETRA.   She took it.

DR. STOCKMANN.   Great!—Leaving, you say? No, I'll be damned if we leave! We're
staying where we are, Katrina.

PETRA.   We're staying?

MRS. STOCKMANN.   Here, in town?   260

DR. STOCKMANN.   Yes, here, absolutely. The battlefield is here; the fight will be
here; and I'll win here! But we've got to have a roof over our heads. Once you stitch up
my trousers, I'll go out to find another house.

HORSTER.   But you can share my house.

DR. STOCKMANN.   I can?

HORSTER.   Absolutely. I've got plenty of room, and I'm almost never home.

MRS. STOCKMANN.   Captain Horster, you're so sweet!   265

PETRA.   Thank you!

DR. STOCKMANN   [*shakes his hand*].   Thank you, thank you. Well, with that trouble
past I can begin things in earnest. There are hundreds of things to look into, Katrina,
and I'll be able to do it almost full-time—I meant to tell you earlier—because I've been
sacked at the Spa.

MRS. STOCKMANN   [*sighs*].   I expected that.

DR. STOCKMANN.   And they're taking away my practice, too. Well, so what? I still
have all the poor people, the ones who can't pay, and, God in Heaven, they're the ones
who need me most. Well, damn it, those little tyrants will have to listen to me! I'll preach
to them both in season and out of season, as it's written somewhere!

MRS. STOCKMANN.   But dearest Thomas, I think you've seen what comes from   270
preaching.

DR. STOCKMANN.   Katrina, don't be absurd! Should I let myself be destroyed by
public opinion and the solid majority and all that devilish drivel? No thanks! What I
want is plain and clear and simple. I only want to pound it into the skulls of these mongrels that the so-called progressive thinkers are the most treacherous enemies of freedom, that party policies wring the neck of every young and promising truth, that
political expediency turns morality and justice upside down, and that the result of all
this is that they're making life here a total nightmare. Don't you think, Captain Horster,
I can make people understand this?

HORSTER.   I'm sure you can. I don't know much about such things.

DR. STOCKMANN.   Well, you see; listen. The ones to be exterminated are the party
bigwigs. A party leader is like the dominant wolf in a pack. To stay on top, he has to keep
cutting down his rivals, or otherwise he's finished. Take Hovstad and Aslaksen, for example. How many rivals have they sent howling—or in any event clawed and bitten until
they can do nothing more than join the Homeowners Association or subscribe to the

People's Messenger? [*Sits at the edge of the desk.*] Come here, Katrina—. See the lovely sunlight streaming in. And breathe in that wonderfully fresh springtime air!

MRS. STOCKMANN.   If only we could live on sunshine and fresh air, Thomas!

DR. STOCKMANN.   I know, you'll have to pinch pennies for a while, but that's   27
minor; things will be all right. What worries me is that there's no one around with the dedication to *real* freedom of thought to take up my work after me.

PETRA.   Father, don't talk like that. You've lots of time. [*EILIF and MORTEN enter from the living room.*] Well hello, here come the boys already.

MRS. STOCKMANN.   Did you get a holiday?

MORTEN.   No. We had a fight with some other boys at recess.

EILIF.   They were the ones who started it!

MORTEN.   Right, and so Mr. Rørlund sent us home for a couple of days.   28

DR. STOCKMANN   [*snaps his fingers and jumps off the desk*].   That's it! By God, I've got it! You'll never set foot in school again!

BOTH BOYS.   Yay! No more school!

MRS. STOCKMANN.   But Thomas!

DR. STOCKMANN.   I said never! I'll be your teacher. I mean you'll never learn anything in God's creation—

MORTEN.   Hooray!   28.

DR. STOCKMANN.   —if I don't turn you into men of distinction and independent minds. Petra, you'll have to help me with this.

PETRA.   Father, count on me.

DR. STOCKMANN.   And I'll hold classes in the very room where they vilified me as an enemy of the people. But we need more; I'll need at least a dozen children to begin with.

MRS. STOCKMANN.   You won't get that kind in this town.

DR. STOCKMANN.   We can. [*To the boys.*] You must know some street kids—society's   29
real castaways?

MORTEN.   Sure thing, Father, I know loads of 'em!

DR. STOCKMANN.   Fine! Bring a few of them to me. This time I'm going to experiment with the mongrels themselves. There may be some remarkable minds there.

MORTEN.   And what will we do once we grow to be men of distinction and independent minds?

DR. STOCKMANN.   Boys, you'll drive all the wolves back into the wilderness!

[*EILIF looks skeptical; MORTEN jumps and cheers.*]

MRS. STOCKMANN.   Let's hope it's not the wolves who drive *you* away, Thomas.   29
DR. STOCKMANN.   Don't be foolish, Katrina! Drive me out?—Now, when I'm the strongest man in town?

MRS. STOCKMANN.   The strongest—now?

DR. STOCKMANN.   Yes, and I'll go so far to say that now I'm one of the strongest men in the whole world!

MORTEN.   Right on!

DR. STOCKMANN   [*lowers his voice*].   Shh! Don't say anything yet, but I've made another great discovery.

MRS. STOCKMANN.   Another one?

DR. STOCKMANN.   Yes, certainly, certainly. [*Gathers them around him, and speaks fervently.*] My discovery, you see, is that the strongest person in the world is the one who stands most alone.

MRS. STOCKMANN   [*smiles and shakes her head*].   Oh, Thomas!

PETRA   [*confidently takes his hands*].   Father!

END OF THE PLAY

QUESTIONS

Act I

1. Why does Ibsen introduce the Mayor before Dr. Stockmann?

2. What traits does the Mayor show in his conversations with Hovstad and Dr. Stockmann? In what ways are these traits important?

3. Why does Dr. Stockmann wish at first to hold back the publication of the paper he had written the previous winter?

4. Why does Ibsen include the casual conversation scenes before Petra's first entrance and after Dr. Stockmann leaves for his study? What do we learn about the various characters in these scenes?

5. What is Dr. Stockmann's discovery about the town spa? What is his view of the situation? To what degree is he naive about the effects of his discovery?

Act II

6. Describe Morten Kiil. What is his relationship with Dr. Stockmann? What does he know about science? What is ironic and comic about his promise to benefit the poor?

7. During his discussion with Dr. Stockmann, how does Hovstad escalate the issue of the water pollution? Why are these conversations important?

8. Who is Aslaksen? What does he represent? Why is he interesting? In what ways does he seem to be a flat character? Why does he refer to "moderation" here and throughout the play?

9. Describe the development of the scene between Dr. Stockmann and the Mayor. What are the Mayor's responses to Dr. Stockmann's discovery? How valid is the Mayor's position? If *you* lived in the town, what would you think about Dr. Stockmann's discovery?

10. Assume that speeches 200–225 represent a point when genuinely creative discussion and compromise might occur. In light of the characters of the brothers, why does the situation between them deteriorate, bringing about anger rather than understanding?

Act III

11. How do the opening references to boxing and military ordnance provide a theme for this act?

12. How are Dr. Stockmann's new views of the spa situation different from those he had in Act I? How has his conversation with the Mayor influenced his attitude?

13. What attitudes toward Dr. Stockmann are brought out in the conversations of Billing, Hovstad, and Aslaksen? What character traits of these men does Ibsen bring out?

14. Why does Petra return the English story to Hovstad? What is the meaning of the scene between them?

15. Describe the process by which the Mayor undermines Dr. Stockmann's report. Why does the Mayor attack Dr. Stockmann's character?

16. What is the effect on Dr. Stockmann of the entry of his wife? Characterize the relationship between them.

17. Explain the tension between Dr. Stockmann and the Mayor. How does the changing allegiance of Hovstad and Aslaksen contribute to this tension? How does Dr. Stockmann feel at the end of the act?

Act IV

18. Why does Horster offer Dr. Stockmann his home for the meeting and, later, for living and teaching (and earlier had offered the home to Petra for teaching)?

19. How does the Mayor, with Aslaksen, take over the meeting? How does this action contribute to the play's theme against the popular majority?

20. How do the Mayor and Aslaksen attack Dr. Stockmann's integrity? How does Dr. Stockmann overcome their maneuvers?

21. Describe Dr. Stockmann's speeches against the popular majority. What is the basis of his criticism? How are his ideas connected with Hovstad's ideas in Act II? What ideas are new (e.g., the majority-minority polarity, the analogy with animals, the need for exterminating corrupt societies)? Why does he include the Mayor in his attack?

22. Why are the appearances of Pettersen, the drunk, important? Why are the crowd responses important?

23. Explain Dr. Stockmann's assertions that truths can live for no more than eighteen to twenty years (speech 124).

24. What is the effect of Dr. Stockmann's quotations of the New Testament passages at the end of the act?

Act V

25. What is the physical state of Dr. Stockmann's study? Why is it in this condition?

26. Describe the effect of the verbal pattern "didn't dare not to" in the course of the act. Connect this pattern to the theme about public opinion and the popular majority.

27. Why does the Mayor describe the last will and testament of Morten Kiil? How does this news precipitate the final break between the two brothers?

28. Describe the attitudes of Hovstad and Aslaksen in this act. How have they changed? How are their speeches hypocritical? Why does Dr. Stockmann threaten them?

29. What choice does Morton Kiil offer Dr. Stockmann? How might this choice be taken as the crisis and climax of the play? How does his choice parallel the development of his attitudes in Act III?

30. Why does the play end on the news of Dr. Stockmann's latest discovery? How does this discovery reflect what has happened to him?

GENERAL QUESTIONS

1. Consider *An Enemy of the People* as a realistic drama. What particularly realistic devices does Ibsen utilize (e.g., time, place, the positions and relationships of scenery and properties, motivation)? How heavily does Ibsen rely upon sudden changes and unforeseen developments? What is the effect of such theatrical changes?

2. Trace the theme of the *friend/enemy of the people* in the course of the play. How does the term fit Dr. Stockmann, first as a friend, then as an enemy? How might the term be explained as ironic? What role is he playing at the play's end?

3. Characterize Dr. Stockmann. Consider things such as his idealism, pride, bravery, individuality, temper, political awareness, degree of cooperativeness, attitude toward his wife, general attitude toward his family, and the attitude of others toward him. How correct are the Mayor's opinions about him?

4. Defend the proposition that Dr. Stockmann's attack against the popular majority is more accurately explained as an attack against the *political and hypocritical manipulation* of the popular majority.

5. Explain the opposition in the play of minority versus majority rights. What is the connection between individual rights and Dr. Stockmann's insistence on, first, drawing, proclaiming, and publishing his own professional discoveries and opinions, and, later, educating young children to have "independent minds"? You might also consider the recurring references to public opinion and Dr. Stockmann's attack against political parties in Act V.

6. Explain the symbolic value of the Mølledal tanneries. What is the realistic meaning of the tanneries? How important are the tanneries in the play's development? Explain the use and meaning of other symbols in the play.

7. Describe the shortcomings and limitations of Dr. Stockmann's arguments in Act IV. Why do some of his ideas seem incorrect and even naïve?

8. What do you find in the play that is comic? Why do you think Ibsen included humor?

9. Write a character study of any of the major or minor characters in *An Enemy of the People.*

SPECIAL TOPICS FOR WRITING AND ARGUMENT ABOUT IBSEN

1. Ibsen's realism: places, situations, characters, conflicts, outcomes.

2. The permanence and importance of Ibsen's subject material: accuracy, comprehensiveness, insightfulness, and relevance then and now.

3. Organizational patterns in Ibsen's plays.

4. Ibsen's major characters: their natures, excellences, shortcomings.

5. The major antagonists in Ibsen: their interests, characteristics, and actions.

6. Ibsen's use of minor characters: their qualities, roundness or flatness, effects on major characters, and rewards or punishments.

7. The predicaments and dilemmas faced by Ibsen's major characters.

8. Ibsen's treatment of women: their nature, their relationships with men, their interests, their attempts to find identity and security.

9. Morality, ethics, and personal integrity in the makeup of Ibsen's characters and in the problems put forth in the plays.

10. The formal structures of Ibsen's plays.

11. Ibsen's use of symbols.

12. Ibsen's dialogue: the shorter speeches and their use; the situations in which he uses longer speeches, and their dramatic and ideological purposes.

13. Ibsen's use of humor and irony.

14. Law and legality as a force in the plays, whether for good or bad, reward or threat.

15. Ibsen's exposure of subterfuge and hypocrisy.

16. Problems in the staging of Ibsen's plays.

EDITED SELECTIONS FROM CRITICISM
OF IBSEN'S DRAMA

The following selected criticism is intended to supply details and ideas for essays on Ibsen's plays, particularly *A Dollhouse* and *An Enemy of the People*. For a more detailed bibliography, consult the "Bibliographic Sources" section (p. 1792), which may be augmented with your college library catalogue and the most recent volumes of the *MLA International Bibliography* available in your library's reference room. The bracketed page numbers refer to the original pagination of the sources included here. Footnotes, original Norwegian passages, and unnecessary references have been deleted here.

Freedom, Truth, and Society—Rhetoric and Reality*

During the night of 9 January 1871, a young Dane lay awake in his hospital bed in Rome   [68 writing. He was committing to paper a poem to which he had given the title 'To Henrik Ibsen'. He had recently received a letter from Ibsen—a letter carrying a powerful appeal to him to put himself at the head of the 'revolution of the human spirit' which the age cried out for. In the poem which formed his enthusiastic response, the young Dane—the critic Georg Brandes (1842–1927)—described how all those mendacious

*From Bjorn Hemmer, "Ibsen and the Realistic Problem Drama," in James McFarlane, ed., *The Cambridge Companion to Ibsen* (Cambridge: Cambridge UP, 1994).

and authoritarian forces of the contemporary age would be brought low when 'the intellectuals' made their revolt. And he raised the banner of freedom and progress with the words: 'Truth and Freedom are one and the same.'

Time after time in the years that followed, Ibsen was himself to raise this same revolutionary banner—with truth and freedom as the central watchwords. In later years these concepts could sound both abstract and ambiguous; nevertheless, within their historical context, they served as a battle cry in the struggle against the prevailing situation. 'Truth' alone—that truth of the new age such as a Brandes and an Ibsen saw it—could achieve liberation. Without truth there could be no change, no genuine 'freedom'. This was the ideological basis for that quartet of realistic social plays which Ibsen published in the years between 1877 and 1882: *Pillars of Society, A Doll's House, Ghosts* and *An Enemy of the People*. In both the first and the last of these plays the double-barrelled phrase 'truth and freedom' is used as a rallying cry and as a definition of what in the final instance the problematic reality of the day—'society'—lacked. This was the battleground on which Ibsen and Brandes found each other and where they could make common cause. However unlike they may have been, one thing they were agreed on: that *they* were conducting the case for progress and the future. They did nor stand alone, but they must be counted as the indisputable leaders in the campaign for a modern, radical and realistic literature in the cultural life of Scandinavia of this age. It was these two who most powerfully challenged the values of the existing middle-class society and who formulated the basic rights and liberties of the individual. [69]

In the November of the same year in which he wrote his poem to Ibsen, Brandes began a series of public lectures in Copenhagen on the literature of nineteenth-century Europe. These lectures provoked great attention and controversy, precisely because in them Brandes called upon writers to revolt. He did it in the light of an ideology of liberation which he himself linked directly to the ideas of freedom which underlay the French Revolution of 1789.

His main concern, Brandes declared, was not *political* opposition, for political liberty had very largely been assured. What was at stake was 'liberty of the spirit', 'liberty of thought and of the human condition'. The entire range of 'social values' would have to be changed radically by the younger generation before a new and vigorous literature could begin any new growth. But in Brandes's view it was surely the writers themselves who ought to take the lead in this work on behalf of progress.

What Brandes directs his criticism against is a conservative, stagnant society which 'under the mask of liberty has all the features of tyranny'. His target is Victorian society with its facade of false morality and its manipulation of public opinion. It is this same kind of society that Ibsen turns the searchlight on in his first realistic dramas. The people who live in such a society know the weight of 'public opinion' and of all those agencies which keep watch over society's 'law and order': the norms, the conventions and the traditions which in essence belong to the past but which continue into the present and there thwart individual liberty in a variety of ways. Not all see this as a problem. Consul Bernick, the bank manager Torvald Helmer and Pastor Manders have all accepted the premises for this kind of bourgeois living and have adapted to society's demands—without any awareness of the cost in human terms. In their own estimation, their task is to confirm the existing social structure—'pillars of society'.

The point that Ibsen and Brandes were making was that this kind of society could not satisfy the natural need of the individual for freedom. It all had to do with power, with status and with the role of the sexes. The repressive attitude of bourgeois society [70 towards everything that threatened its own position of power demonstrated only too clearly how far it had moved from the standpoint of the revolutionary citizens of 1789. The question of political and spiritual liberty had been thrust into the background by what had constantly been the motivating force in the life of the individual: economic freedom. Capital gave a position of power in society; and once those positions had been won, the bourgeois individual had acquired something which had to be defended. In this way, the bourgeois individual became a defender of the status quo and a traitor to his own officially expressed values. Official rhetoric was one thing; the realities on the other hand were something else.

It is this which forms the background to Ibsen's and Brandes's criticism of contemporary society. They found in their age a clear dichotomy between ideology and practice, a contradiction between the official and the private life of the bourgeois individual. Behind the splendour of the Victorian family facade there was to be found a much murkier reality. It was precisely these contradictions, this problematical element, in the bourgeois world that Ibsen made his special field as a realistic commentator on contemporary life. Both Ibsen and Brandes wanted to make the individual the sustaining element in society and thereby dethrone the bourgeois family as the central institution of society. From the perspective of the bourgeois individual the family is a micro-society which mirrors the nature of the macro-society and which is to bear witness to its health. In *Pillars of Society* the scoundrelly Consul Bernick is praised by the young teacher Rørlund for his 'exemplary family life'; and the consul's fellow-conspirator, the businessman Rummel, delivers himself of the following pronouncement: 'A man's home ought to be like a showcase'. But he himself recommends an *arranged* family tableau behind the glass walls.

In the spirit of liberalism, Ibsen lets the individual's status in the family stand as an illustration of his position in the wider society. The power structure within the walls of the domestic home reflects the hierarchical power structures which prevail in the wider world. But those who participate in public life also encounter other repressive forces. Consul Bernick eventually admits that he feels like an isolated tool of an uncomprehending and crippled society, controlled in all his actions.

The main social perspective in Ibsen's first realistic plays coincides with the perspective of Brandes's lecture series on 'Main Currents in Nineteenth Century Literature'. Here Brandes had presented a well-formulated programme for a new 'modern' literature. His challenge to his fellow authors was primarily that they should enter into [71 their own times and make contemporary concrete reality the subject of their writing: 'What shows a literature in our own day to be a living thing is the fact of its subjecting problems to debate . . . For a literature to submit nothing to debate is tantamount to its being in the process of losing all significance.

What sort of 'problems' he had in mind is illustrated by the examples he immediately adduces: marriage, religion, property rights, the relationships between the sexes, and social conditions. The objectives of his programme seem to have been both social and aesthetic. Brandes's idea was not that literature should become an instrument of abstract debate about prevailing social problems; his intention was to point out that if literature was to have any useful function at all, it had to come to grips with those conditions which invade and determine the concrete existence of the individual. Literature—as he put it—was to deal with 'our life', not with 'our dreams'.

If Ibsen's dramas in the period 1877 to 1882 have come to be designated as realistic *problem* plays, this has to be seen against the background of Brandes's formula-like statement. Some Ibsen scholars prefer the rubric 'critical realism'; others again have chosen to apply the term 'modern contemporary drama' to the whole series of works after 1877. Each of these different designations nevertheless has a bearing on one or other of the central elements in the kind of literary realism which Ibsen practised: on social problems, on critical perspective and contemporaneity. Indeed this last is often accepted as one of the defining characteristics of realism: '*Il faut être de temps.*'

Within the framework of these dramas, Ibsen concentrates on some phase in the contemporary situation where a latent crisis suddenly becomes visible. In this way he was able to embody contemporary social problems through the medium of an individual's destiny. This is another of realism's main tenets in the matter of individual characterization: the particular is to throw light on the general, and from one's response to a particular individual one should be able to glimpse the socially representative type. This, according to René Wellek, is an almost universal demand in theories of realism. It marks not only a polemical break with romantic characterization, but is also linked to realism's demand for objective reality and to its implicit didactic tendency. 'Truth' and 'sincerity' are concepts central to Linda Nochlin's account of the realists' own definition of where they stand. It may sound paradoxical to say that the realists combined on the one hand a wish for the objective presentation of reality with a didactic purpose on the other; but the paradox is illusory. A work of realism aspires to convey a moral message of general validity, and this is why the realist has need of the socially representative type. In [72] Ibsen this sometimes leads to a difficult balancing act between over-explicitness and caricatured characterization on the one hand, and on the other an objective evocation of plausible human types, where the author's presence is less evident. Viewed from a later standpoint in time, there are some things—particularly his treatment of selected male characters—that might prompt one to set a question mark against his 'realism'.

. . .

In his poetic practice, Ibsen demonstrates time after time that he conceives of truth as something individual and subjective. It is always the minority which is right. This [73] is why he lets Nora go out into the world alone both to find out who she really is and to be able to re-assess values and concepts. Ibsen has her sweep aside any doubts about what the problem is: 'I must try to discover who is right, society or me'. She admits her husband is right when he says she no longer understands the society they live in. As a dramatist, Ibsen must make it evident to his audience that Nora, as the drama moves towards its close, is truer and freer than before—and that her path is one of general validity. Helmer has mobilized the rhetoric of established society to keep Nora within the framework of the community and of the family. The reaction of the public was—and possibly still is—dependent on whether Nora's (and Ibsen's) use of an alternative rhetoric carries greater weight and conviction.

Nora's situation illustrates the pattern central to Ibsen's realistic problem dramas: the individual in opposition to a hostile society. The structure of the conflict is simple—and nobody can be in any doubt as to where the author's sympathies lie. Collective aberration about which ideals or values are true and which are false means that Ibsen sets in motion a process whereby concepts which are central to the bourgeois world are subject to re-definition. It is a striking feature of, for example, *Ghosts* that the reactionary Manders and the radical Helene Alving both make use of the concept of 'the ideal', despite their having totally contradictory views of the meaning of 'truth' and of individual 'freedom' in life. Ibsen clearly saw that the concepts of established bourgeois society needed a new content—something which he himself drew attention to in a letter to Brandes. In this same letter he writes of the need for 'a revolution of the human spirit', and claimed that the 1789 rallying-cry of 'Liberty, equality, fraternity' needed filling with new meaning.

Perhaps the battle-lines between the conservative bourgeoisie and the radical intelligentsia in Scandinavia in this age of Ibsen and Brandes were not as clearly drawn as all this might suggest. The literary history of Northern Europe has very largely been based on the premises of radicalism. The perspective may not entirely falsify history, but it does somewhat oversimplify it. There are distinctly conservative elements to be found in Ibsen's works of social criticism; and he gave clear acknowledgement of the part he played within the society he was attacking: 'One never stands totally without some share of responsibility or guilt in the society to which one belongs'. This is why he defines, in one and the same breath, the writing of poetry as the passing of judgement upon one's own self. Some of the phenomena he criticized were things he well knew from his own inner life. Honest introspection—what he was inclined to call 'self-anatomy'—had made [74 it clear to him that he too bore the stamp of the Victorian society of the day. Life and learning were not always the same, as he admitted in a speech to Norwegian students in Christiania in 1874, The irony directed at those who histrionically held high the banner of the ideal at no great cost to themselves lost none of its point when applied to himself and to fellow writers.

Nevertheless he stood distanced, an outsider, from the society he was criticizing. Like Brandes, he was marginalized in respect of the collective life of his own people—not least by the concrete fact of his own twenty-seven years in exile. It was a stance which gave Ibsen both a personal freedom as an artist and also the clarifying perspective of distance—something he always claimed as a necessity for himself as a writer.

It is something of a paradox that, in this socially critical phase of his authorship, he was able to create a large and broadly based market among the wider European public for his art. What he had to offer to this bourgeois public was a successive chronicling of their own vices and lies. Granted the setting of his works was Norwegian, but the perspective on Victorian morality was international enough when he allowed it to reveal its defects.

It is not to be wondered at that Ibsen's dramas provoked scandal and outrage. Yet at the same time he won a large following, including many of those whom he had attacked. Even a proportion of 'the pillars of society' found it worthwhile to listen to what this author had to say. This could well imply that bourgeois society had not entirely lost its sense of its past and of its own lost ideals. Even bourgeois society was ready to acknowledge that contemporary reality might have its problems—with socially destabilizing phenomena like industrialization, positivism, liberalism, secularization, political polarization and the like. Society in the 1870s was becoming increasingly fluid. Only the most conservative forces wished to defend its 'law and order' by neutralizing such 'enemies of the people' as Ibsen and Brandes. But strong resistance could be found—and this gave Ibsen an adversary and the stuff of conflict for his dramas. The opposition consisted of all those who wished to withdraw within the circle of their own little community, their small township or their family—there to defend their world against the threat from the new or larger world 'out there'. Ibsen himself in these years was a resident of this wider and freer European cultural scene. And he wrote about Norwegian provincial life. When for his first realistic problem drama he chose as its setting 'a small, Norwegian

coastal town', this was clearly connected to its being a milieu he was greatly familiar with from his childhood and early years. As an observant outsider he had lived in a small community of this kind—in Grimstad in the 1840s—and it was here he had first begun his career as a writer. Patterns and tensions—social, economic and psychological—pre-   [75]
sent themselves much more clearly in a small and easily surveyable community of this kind than in a larger and more pluralist society. For a dramatist, a society of this sort could nicely function as a social laboratory.

The Story Behind *An Enemy of the People**

The plot of *An Enemy of the People* had its origin in two actual incidents. Alfred Meisner, a young German poet whom Ibsen knew in Munich, had told him how, when his father had been medical officer at the spa of Teiplitz in the eighteen-thirties, there had occurred an outbreak of cholera which the Doctor felt it his duty to make known publicly. As a result the season was ruined and the citizens of Teiplitz became so enraged that they stoned the Doctor's house and forced him to flee the town.

Then there had been the case in Norway of a chemist named Harald Thaulow. For nearly ten years Thaulow had furiously attacked the Christiania Steam Kitchens for neglecting their duty towards the city's poor. He had delivered a violent speech on the subject in 1874, during Ibsen's visit to Norway; and on 23 February 1881, only a fortnight before he died, Thaulow had attempted to read a prepared speech at the annual general meeting of the Steam Kitchens. The chairman of the meeting tried to prevent him from speaking, and eventually the public forced him, amid commotion, to withdraw. Ibsen read a report of this meeting in *Aftenposten*, just at the time when his indignation at the reception of *Ghosts* was reaching its climax, and he must have recognised in the eccentric old chemist a spirit very kindred to its own. . . .

As with *The Pillars of Society*, an English Member of Parliament may also have con-   [312]
tributed something to the play. Charles Bradlaugh, having narrowly escaped imprisonment for his part in a pamphlet advocating birth control (he had actually been sentenced, but had escaped on appeal) had, been elected Radical M.P. for Northhampton in 1880, but had been barred from taking his seat on the ground that, since he was a confessed free-thinker, the oath would not bind him. New elections were held in Northampton, and he was returned each time, but was still excluded; in 1881, he was forcibly removed from the house by ten policemen. It was not until 1886 that a new Speaker granted him the right to take the oath and sit. 'You should hear Ibsen on Bradlaugh—he has the most vivid sympathy for him', wrote William Archer to his brother Charles on 14 March 1882, when Ibsen was about to start writing *An Enemy of the People;* and Bradlaugh has an obvious deal in common with Dr Stockman. . . . But, as Ibsen stated in his letter to Hegel of 9 September 1882, he himself was probably the chief model for the characters, at any rate in Act Four; and it is worth remembering that the house in Skien in which Ibsen had been born had been called Stockmannsgården. . . .

An Enemy of the People was published on 28 November 1882, in an edition (despite   [314]
the calamitous sales of *Ghosts*) of ten thousand copies. Its reception was mixed. Not surprisingly, Dr. Stockmann's hard remarks about political parties offended all the reviewers who belonged to either; a contemporary cartoon showed Ibsen chastising first the Liberals to the delight of the Tories, then the Tories to the delight of the Liberals, and

* From Michael Meyer, *Henrik Ibsen: The Farewell to Poetry 1864–1882* (London: Hart-Davis, 1971).

finally, in the person of Dr. Stockmann, both together. Henrik Jæger, fresh from lecturing against *Ghosts* round the country, declared in *Afterposten* that *An Enemy of the People* was 'personally the most likeable, psychologically the most interesting, and aesthetically the weakest of Ibsen's plays'. Arne Garborg, in *Nyt Tidsskrift* praised its technique but complained that 'there is a great deal of violent swearing', and that the public meeting in Act Four, which evidently nettled him, was 'rather detached and distant, almost as though portrayed from some other age but in a modern setting'. Erik Vullum in *Dagbladet* objected that, just as Bjørnson had been going round the country 'and even in America', holding meetings to proclaim his convictions about truth and justice, so 'now Ibsen comes and does exactly the same; he holds public meetings from town to town, and the public has to pay to attend them' . . . .

The theatres seized eagerly upon the play. The Christiania Theatre and the Royal [31 Theatres of Copenhagen and Stockholm, all of which had rejected *Ghosts* as unfit for [31 public presentation, immediately acquired production rights of *An Enemy of the People,* apparently unembarrassed by the fact that its theme was the unworthiness of those who 'do not dare'. Hans Schrøder, the director of the Christiania Theatre, telegraphed Ibsen for permission to give the first public performance of the play, and Ibsen agreed, stinging them for a lump payment of 4,000 crowns (£222); he had let them have *A Doll's House* for 2,500 crowns (£139). During December he wrote Schrøder three letters which have only recently come to light, and which are indispensable reading to any director attempting to stage the play:

Rome, 14 December 1882

Permit me to address to you a few lines concerning the forthcoming production of *An Enemy of the People.* It is not my intention or wish to attempt to influence *in absentio* either the staging or the casting; but the expression of certain feelings which I hold regarding various aspects of the play can do no harm.

I trust I may assume that Mrs. Wolf will play Mrs Stockmann . . . If for the role of Hovstad you have an otherwise suitable actor of not too heroic build, that is the kind of man you should choose. Hovstad is the son of poor people, has grown up in a dirty home on wretched and inadequate food, has frozen and toiled horribly throughout his childhood, and subsequently, as a poverty-stricken young man, has had to undergo considerable privation. Such living conditions leave their mark not only on a man's spirit but also on his outward appearance. Men of heroic exterior are an exception among the plebs. Whatever the circumstances Hovstad must always wear a depressed appearance, somewhat shrunken and stooping, and uncertain in his movements; all, of course, portrayed with complete naturalism.

Billing's lines are so worded that they require an east-coast and not e.g. a Bergen dialect. He is, essentially, an east-coast character.

Captain Horster has been ridiculously misunderstood by a Danish critic. He characterises Horster as an old man, Dr. Stockmann's old friend, etc. This is, of course, utterly wrong. Horster is a young man, one of the young people whose healthy appetite delights the Doctor, though he is an infrequent visitor at the house because he dislikes the company of Hovstad and Billing. Already in Act One, Horster's interest in Petra must subtly and delicately be indicated, and during the brief exchanges between him and her in Act Five we must sense that they stand at the threshold of a deep and passionate relationship.

Both the boys must be carefully instructed so that the difference in their characters is clearly established. And I must beg that in Act Four every possible actor at your disposal be used. The stage director must here enjoin the greatest possible naturalism and strictly forbid any caricaturing or exaggeration. The more realistic [317] characters you can work into the crowd the better.

Throughout the play the stage director must inexorably insist that none of the players alters his or her lines. They must be spoken exactly as they stand in the text. A lively tempo is desirable. When I was last at the Christiania Theatre the speech seemed to me to be very slow.

But above all, truthfulness to nature—the illusion that everything is real and that one is sitting and watching something that is actually taking place in real life. *An Enemy of the People* is not easy to stage. It demands exceptionally well-drilled ensemble playing, i.e. protracted and meticulously supervised rehearsals. But I rely upon the good-will of all concerned . . .

On 31 December Ibsen wrote again:

I fear I must once again trouble you with a few lines. From your kind letter which reached me yesterday I gather it is intended to have both the boys in my play acted by girls. This has somewhat disturbed me, since it seems to imply that sufficient attention has not been paid to the spirit in which this play was written and in which it requires to be staged. To allow boys' parts to be taken by women may sometimes be excusable in operetta, vaudeville, or the so-called romantic drama; for in these the prime requirement is unqualified illusion; every member of the audience is fully conscious throughout the evening that he is merely sitting in a theatre and watching a theatrical performance. But this should not be the case when *An Enemy of the People* is being acted. The spectator must feel as though he were invisibly present in Dr. Stockmann's living-room; everything here must seem real; the two boys included. Consequently they cannot be played by actresses dressed up in wigs and stays; their feminine figures will not be able to be concealed by their costume of shirt and trousers, and they will never make any spec- [318] tator believe that he is looking at real schoolboys from some small town. How in any case can a grown woman make herself look like a ten year old child? Both parts must therefore be played by children, at worst by a couple of small girls whose figures are not yet fully developed; and then damn the corsets and let them have big boys' boots on their legs. They must also, of course, be taught the way boys behave.

It is stated in the play that at the public meeting Dr. Stockmann is to be dressed in black; but his clothes must not be new or elegant, and his white cravat should sit a little crooked. . . .

An Enemy of the People is less frequently performed today than most of Ibsen's mature plays, for two principal reasons. One is, simply, the size of the cast. A crowd costs money, and without a crowd the great fourth act loses much of its impact (and a small crowd is almost worse than no crowd at all). The other problem is ideological. Some of the opinions expressed by Dr. Stockmann, especially his demand for 'aristocrats', contempt for the masses, and assertion that 'the minority is always right' strike an illiberal note in modern ears. On these points Ibsen was in fact expressing a commonly shared [319 attitude; Mill, Tocqueville, Dickens and most liberal thinkers of the time distrusted the tyranny of the commonplace majority. 'Those whose opinions go by the name of public opinion . . . are always a mass, that is to say, collective mediocrity', wrote Mill in his great essay *On Liberty*. 'No government by a democracy or a numerous aristocracy, either in its political acts or in the opinions, qualities, and tone of mind which it fosters, ever did or could rise above mediocrity, except in so far as the sovereign Many have let themselves be guided (which in their best times they always have done) by the counsels and influence of a more highly gifted and instructed One or Few. The initiation of all wise or noble things comes and must come from individuals; generally at first from some one individual.' That is precisely Dr. Stockmann's message. But it is an unfashionable viewpoint to put forward in an age of universal suffrage.

The play has, too, suffered worse than most from the dead hand of academic criticism. The kind of commentator that dismisses *Emperor and Galilean* as 'stone-cold', *Brand* as 'ambiguous' and *Little Eyolf* as 'a falling-off' (to quote from a recent and embarrassing English book intended as a vindication of Ibsen) has tended to reject *An Enemy of the People* as 'thin'. It lacks, indeed, the extra density and overtones of Ibsen's later works; but there are precious few other plays outside the Greeks, Shakespeare and Chekhov with which it need fear comparison. The truths it expresses have not dated, and are not likely to as long as there are town councils and politicians. Even adequately performed, it is one of the most accessible and compulsive of Ibsen's plays; and Dr. Stockmann is one of the half-dozen greatest male parts he wrote. . . .

. . . The historical importance of *An Enemy of the People* lies, as Erik Bøgh realised, [321 in that it is, except for *Danton's Death*, which no-one then knew about, the first political debate which succeeds in remaining a great play. It possesses, too, a wit and lightness which people do not usually associate with Ibsen, though he had both qualities at his command, as *Peer Gynt* and *The League of Youth* bear witness. It is the most Shavian of Ibsen's plays; and the last act is one of his finest. What, one might ask on finishing Act Four, *can* he write that will not seem an anti-climax after this? Yet when one has read or seen that final act, one wonders how else one could possibly have supposed that he would end the play—the surest test of dramatic inevitability.

Some months after the publication of *An Enemy of the People* Georg Brandes wrote to Ibsen apparently (the letter is lost) rebuking him for isolationism and not putting his shoulder to the progressive wheel. Ibsen replied (12 June 1883): 'You are of course right when you say that we must all try to spread our opinions. But I firmly believe that an intellectual pioneer can never gather a majority around him. In ten years the majority may have reached the point where Dr. Stockmann stood when the people held their meeting. But during those ten years the Doctor has not stood stationary; he is still at least ten years ahead of the others. The majority, the masses, the mob, will never catch him up; he can never rally them behind him. I myself feel a similarly unrelenting compulsion to keep pressing forward. A crowd now stands where I stood when I wrote my earlier books. But I myself am there no longer, I am somewhere else—far ahead of them—or so I hope.'

To the end of his literary career, which spanned fifty years, Ibsen was to keep moving relentlessly forward, never repeating the pattern of an earlier success. Just as, fifteen years previously, he had abandoned the epic form of poetic drama which had established him, so now he was to abandon the type of (to use a loose term) sociological drama which was to spread his fame throughout the western world, and with which his name is still principally and misleadingly linked. Having exposed the hollowness of a certain kind of left-wing politician in *The League of Youth,* he had gone on to expose the equal hollowness of their right-wing counterparts in *The Pillars of Society;* having questioned the sanctity of marriage in *A Doll's House,* he had questioned it yet further, together with several other equally sacred cows, in *Ghosts.* Then he had returned to the [322] field of politics, broadening his sights so as to include the ordinary voter in his line of fire. *An Enemy of the People* is an attack, not merely on those who lead people by the nose, but on those who allow themselves to be thus led. These four plays, for all their differences, shared one theme in common: the necessity of discovering who one really is and of trying to become that person. In his next play, he was to question even this belief.

Ibsen's Feminist Characters*

Anyone who claims that Ibsen thought of Nora as a silly, hysterical, or selfish woman is [34] either ignoring or misrepresenting the plain truth, present from the earliest to the most recent biographies, that Ibsen admired, even adored, Nora Helmer. Among all his characters, she was the one he liked best and found most real. While working on *A Doll House,* he announced to Suzannah Ibsen, his wife, "I've just seen Nora. She came right over to me and put her hand on my shoulder." The quick-witted Suzannah replied at once, "What was she wearing?" In a perfectly serious tone, Ibsen answered, "A simple blue woolen dress."

After *A Doll House* had made him famous, Ibsen was fond of explaining that his [35] heroine's "real" name was "Eleanora" but that she had been called "Nora" from childhood. Bergliot Bjornson Ibsen, the playwright's daughter-in-law, tells the story of how she and her husband, Sigurd, on one of the last occasions on which they saw Ibsen out of bed in the year he died, asked permission to name their newborn daughter "Eleanora." Ibsen was greatly moved. "God bless you, Bergliot," he said to her. He had, in fact, christened his own Nora with a precious gift, for both "Nora" and "Eleanora" were names given to the sister of Ole Schulerud, one of the few close friends of Ibsen's life, who in the early years of grinding poverty believed in Ibsen's genius and tirelessly hawked his first play to bookseller after bookseller, finally spending his small inheritance to pay for its publication.

Ibsen was inspired to write *A Doll House* by the terrible events in the life of his protégé Laura Petersen Kieler, a Norwegian journalist of whom he was extremely fond. Married to a man with a phobia about debt, she had secretly borrowed money to finance an Italian journey necessary for her husband's recovery from tuberculosis. She worked frantically to reimburse the loan, exhausting herself in turning out hackwork, and when her earnings proved insufficient, in desperation she forged a check. On discovering the crime, her husband demanded a legal separation on the grounds that she was an unfit mother and had her placed in an asylum, where she was put in the insane ward. Throughout the affair, Ibsen, her confidant and adviser, was greatly disturbed; he brooded on the wife, "forced to spill her heart's blood," as he wrote in a letter to her, and on the oblivious husband, allowing his wife to slave away on unworthy jobs, concerned neither about her physical welfare nor her work. Having done all for love, Laura Kieler was treated monstrously for her efforts by a husband obsessed with his standing in the eyes of the world. In Ibsen's working notes for *A Doll House* we find:

* From Joan Templeton, "The *Doll House* Backlash: Criticism, Feminism, and Ibsen." *PMLA* 104 (1989): 28–40.

She has committed forgery, and is proud of it; for she has done it out of love for her husband, to save his life. But this husband of hers takes his standpoint, conventionally honorable, on the side of the law, and sees the situation with male eyes.

The conflict between love and law, between heart and head, between feminine and masculine, is the moral center of *A Doll House.* But Ibsen would sharpen life's blurred edges to meet art's demand for plausibility. The heroine would be a housewife, not a writer, and the hackwork not bad novels but copying; her antagonist, the husband, would not be a cruel brute but a kind guardian: rather than put her into an asylum, he would merely denounce her as an unfit wife and mother, permitting her to receive bed and board, and then, once his reputation was safe, would offer to forgive her and take her back on the spot. The Helmers, in other words, would be "normal." And this normality would transform a sensational *fait divers* into a devastating picture of the ordinary relations between wife and husband and allow Ibsen to treat what he called, in a letter to Edmund Gosse, "the problems of married life." Moreover, he would reverse the ending: the original Nora, the career journalist, had begged to be taken back; his housewife would sadly, emphatically refuse to stay.

A year after *A Doll House* appeared, when Ibsen was living in Rome, a Scandinavian woman arrived there, who had left her husband and small daughter to run away with her lover. The Norwegian exile community considered her behavior unnatural and asked Ibsen what he thought. "It is not unnatural, only it is unusual" was Ibsen's opinion. The woman made it a point to speak with Ibsen, but to her surprise he treated her offhandedly. "Well, I did the same thing your Nora did," she said, offended. Ibsen replied quietly, "My Nora went alone."

A favorite piece of evidence in the argument that Ibsen was not interested in women's rights is his aversion to John Stuart Mill. It is popular to quote Ibsen's remark to Georg Brandes about Mill's declaration that he owed the best things in his writing to his wife, Harriet Taylor: "'Fancy!' [Ibsen] said smiling, 'if you had to read Hegel or Krause with the thought that you did not know for certain whether it was Mr. or Mrs. Hegel, Mr. or Mrs. Krause you had before you!'" But in fact, Brandes, one of Ibsen's closest associates and probably the critic who understood him best, reports this mot in a discussion of Ibsen's wholehearted support of the women's movement. He notes that Mill's assertion "seemed especially ridiculous to Ibsen, with his marked individualism," and explains that although Ibsen had at first little sympathy for feminism—perhaps, Brandes guesses, because of "irritation at some of the ridiculous forms the movement assumed"—this initial response gave way "to a sympathy all the more enthusiastic" when he saw that it was "one of the great rallying points in the battle of progress." [34]

A well-known, perhaps embarrassing fact about Ibsen, never brought up in discussions disclaiming his interest in women's rights, is that when he made the banquet speech denying that he had consciously worked for the movement, he was primarily interested in young women and annoyed by the elderly feminists who surrounded him. During the seventieth-birthday celebrations, Ibsen constantly exhibited his marked and, as Michael Meyer has it, "rather pathetic longing for young girls." He had already had several romantic friendships, including one that had caused a family scandal and threatened to wreck his marriage. In the light of this fully documented biographical information about the aging playwright, is his intention in *A Doll House* more likely to be revealed by what he said in irritation at a banquet or by what he wrote twenty years earlier in sketching out his play?

A woman cannot be herself in the society of today, which is exclusively a masculine society, with laws written by men, and with accusers and judges who judge feminine conduct from the masculine standpoint.

A Doll House is not about Everybody's struggle to find him- or herself but, according to its author, about Everywoman's struggle against Everyman.

A Doll House is a natural development of the play Ibsen had just written, the unabashedly feminist *Pillars of Society;* both plays reflect Ibsen's extremely privileged feminist education, which he shared with few other nineteenth-century male authors and which he owed to a trio of extraordinary women: Suzannah Thoresen Ibsen, his wife; Magdalen Thoresen, his colleague at the Norwegian National Theatre in Bergen, who was Suzannah's stepmother and former governess; and Camilla Wergeland Collett, Ibsen's literary colleague, valued friend, and the founder of Norwegian feminism.

Magdalen Thoresen wrote novels and plays and translated the French plays Ibsen put on as a young stage manager at the Bergen theater. She was probably the first "New Woman" he had ever met. She pitied the insolvent young writer, took him under her wing, and brought him home. She had passed her strong feminist principles on to her charge, the outspoken and irrepressible Suzannah, who adored her strong-minded stepmother and whose favorite author was George Sand. The second time Ibsen met Suzannah he asked her to marry him. Hjordis, the fierce shield-maiden of *The Vikings at Helgeland,* the play of their engagement, and Svanhild, the strong-willed heroine of *Love's Comedy,* the play that followed, owe much to Suzannah Thoresen Ibsen. Later, Nora's way of speaking would remind people of Suzannah's.

The third and perhaps most important feminist in Ibsen's life was his friend Camilla Collett, one of the most active feminists in nineteenth-century Europe and founder of the modern Norwegian novel. Fifteen years before Mill's *Subjection of Women,* Collett wrote *Amtmandens Døtre (The Governor's Daughters).* Faced with the choice of a masculine nom de plume or no name at all on the title page, Collett brought out her novel anonymously in two parts in 1854 and 1855, but she nonetheless became widely known as the author. Its main argument, based on the general feminist claim that women's feelings matter, is that women should have the right to educate themselves and to marry whom they please. In the world of the governor's daughters, it is masculine success that matters. Brought up to be ornaments and mothers, women marry suitable men and devote their lives to their husbands' careers and to their children. The novel, a cause célèbre, made Collett famous overnight.

Collett regularly visited the Ibsens in their years of exile in Germany, and she and Suzannah took every occasion to urge Ibsen to take up the feminist cause. They had long, lively discussions in the years preceding *A Doll House,* when feminism had become a strong movement and the topic of the day in Scandinavia. Collett was in Munich in 1877, when Ibsen was hard at work on *Pillars of Society,* and Ibsen's biographer Koht speculates that Ibsen may have deliberately prodded her to talk about the women's movement in order to get material for his dialogue. In any case, the play undoubtedly owes much to the conversations in the Ibsen household, as well as to the Norwegian suffragette Aasta Hansteen, the most notorious woman in the country. Deliberately provocative, Hansteen took to the platform wearing men's boots and carrying a whip to protect herself against the oppressor. A popular news item during the Ibsens' visit to Norway in 1874, Hansteen became the model for Lona Hessel, the shocking *raisonneuse* of *Pillars of Society.*

The play opens with a striking image of woman's place in the world: eight ladies participating in what has been, since antiquity, the most quintessentially female activity in literature—they are "busy sewing"—as they listen to the town schoolmaster read aloud from *Woman as the Servant of Society*. Lona Hessel bursts in, and when the ladies ask her how she can aid their "Society for the Morally Disabled," she suggests, "I can air it out." Returning from America, where she is rumored to have sung in saloons (even for money!), lectured, and written a book, Lona is the New Woman with a vengeance who teaches the others the truth. Lona had loved Bernick, but she packed her bags when he rejected her to marry for money. Bernick turns out not to have been much of a loss, however; he has reduced his wife, Betty, to an obedient cipher and made a personal servant of his sister, Martha, a paradigm of the nineteenth-century spinster who devotes her life to a male relative. Martha's story may have had its source in *The Governor's Daughters*. Like Collett's Margarethe, Martha had once loved a young man but, too modest to declare her feelings, suffered in silence. She now lives for her brother, who is insufferable when he speaks of her; she is a "nonentity," he explains, "who'll take on whatever comes along." It is in explaining Martha's exemplary function in life that Bernick speaks the line, "People shouldn't always be thinking of themselves first, especially women." Dina Dorf, Bernick's ward, disregards this happy maxim, and though she agrees to marry, she tells her husband-to-be, "But first I want to work, become something the way you have. I don't want to be a thing that's just taken along." Dina knows beforehand what Nora learns after eight years of marriage: "I have to try to educate myself. . . . I've got to do it alone."

Pillars of Society, little known and played outside Scandinavia and Germany, is one of the most radically feminist works of nineteenth-century literature. Ibsen took the old maid, the butt of society's ridicule, a figure of pity and contempt, and made her a heroine. Rejected as unfit to be a wife, Lona Hessel refuses to sacrifice herself to a surrogate family and escapes to the New World, where she leads an independent, authentic life. As *raisonneuse*, she summarizes his point of view for Bernick and the rest: "This society of yours is a bachelors' club. You don't see women."

It is simply not true, then, that Ibsen was not interested in feminism. It is also not true that "there is no indication that Ibsen was thinking of writing a feminist play when he first began to work seriously on *A Doll House* in the summer of 1879." In the spring of that year, while Ibsen was planning his play, a scandalous incident, easily available in the biographies, took place that proves not only Ibsen's interest in women's rights but his passionate support for the movement. Ibsen had made two proposals to the Scandinavian Club in Rome, where he was living: that the post of librarian be opened to women candidates and that women be allowed to vote in club meetings. In the debate on the proposal, he made a long, occasionally eloquent speech, part of which follows:

> Is there anyone in this gathering who dares assert that our ladies are inferior to us in culture, or intelligence, or knowledge, or artistic talent? I don't think many men would dare suggest that. Then what is it men fear? I hear there is a tradition here that women are cunning intriguers, and that therefore we don't want them. Well, I have encountered a good deal of male intrigue in my time.

Ibsen's first proposal was accepted, the second not, failing by one vote. He left the club in a cold rage. A few days later, he astonished his compatriots by appearing at a gala evening. People thought he was penitent. But he was planning a surprise: facing the ballroom and its dancing couples, he interrupted the music to make a terrible scene, haranguing the celebrants with a furious tirade. He had tried to bring them progress, he shouted, but their cowardly resistance had refused it. The women were especially contemptible, for it was for them he had tried to fight. A Danish countess fainted and had to be removed, but Ibsen continued, growing more and more violent. Gunnar Heiberg, who was present, later gave this account of the event:

> As his voice thundered it was as though he were clarifying his own thoughts, as his tongue chastised it was as though his spirit were scouring the darkness in search of his present spiritual goal—his poem [*A Doll House*]—as though he were personally bringing out his theories, incarnating his characters. And when he was done, he went out into the hall, took his overcoat and walked home.   [38]

In 1884, five years after *A Doll House* had made Ibsen a recognized champion of the feminist cause, he joined with H. E. Berner, president of the Norwegian Women's Rights League, and with his fellow Norwegian writers Bjornson, Lie, and Kielland, in signing a petition to the Storting, the Norwegian parliament, urging the passage of a bill establishing separate property rights for married women. When he returned the petition to Bjornson, Ibsen wryly commented that the Storting should not be interested in men's opinions: "To consult men in such a matter is like asking wolves if they desire better protection for the sheep." He also spoke of his fears that the current campaign for universal suffrage would come to nothing. The solution, which he despaired of seeing, would be the formation of a "strong, resolute progressive party" that would include in its goals "the statutory improvement of the position of woman."

It is foolish to apply the formalist notion that art is never sullied by argument to Ibsen's middle-period plays, written at a time when he was an outspoken and direct fighter in what he called the "mortal combat between two epochs." Ibsen was fiercely his own man, refusing all his life to be claimed by organizations or campaigns of many sorts, including the Women's Rights League and the movement to remove the mark of Sweden from the Norwegian flag. And he had a deeply conservative streak where manners were concerned (except when he lost his temper), for he was acutely suspicious of show. Temperamentally, Ibsen was a loner. But he was also, as Georg Brandes declared, "a born polemist." While it is true that Ibsen never reduced life to "ideas," it is equally true that he was passionately interested in the events and ideas of his day. He was as deeply anchored in his time as any writer has been before or since. Writing to his German translator a year after the publication of *A Doll House*, Ibsen offered one of the truest self-appraisals a writer has ever made:

> Everything that I have written is intimately connected with what I have lived through, even if I have not lived it myself. Every new work has served me as emancipation and catharsis; for none of us can escape the responsibility and the guilt of the society to which we belong.

A Marxist Approach to *A Doll House**

Theatrical production is a process that illuminates the dramatic text, and criticism is the   [76]
tool that enables theater artists to makes the most effective choices. This is the central premise of Drama 102 (Play Analysis), in which we discuss eight or so plays from a variety

*From Barry Witham and John Lutterbie, "A Marxist Approach to *A Doll House*," in Yvonne Shafer, ed., *Approaches to Teaching Ibsen's* A Doll House (New York: MLA, 1985).

of critical viewpoints. Although some of the plays lend themselves more readily to a particular kind of analysis (such as a Jungian reading of *The Emperor Jones*), we point out that this affinity should not exclude additional insights that can be gained from a structuralist or feminist reading. We stress that criticism is a preamble to production and that plays are complex and multifaceted. Moreover, we discourage the theatrical sleight of hand that frequently reduces plays to a single metaphor, and we encourage our students to view drama through the lenses of differing approaches.

In teaching *A Doll House* we first examine the text from a traditional point of view stressing historical and biographical considerations. We review Ibsen's commitment to women's rights and his interest in the career of Laura Kieler, who some critics believe was the model for Nora. Indeed, F. L. Lucas has stated that "one cannot fully understand Nora without knowing something of the strange, yet true story of Laura Kieler." By comparing the two women it is possible to watch Ibsen's heroine emerge from the despair and pain that characterized much of Kieler's life.

Still, the historical and biographical approach is limiting, and our next step is to explore the play through another lens. (The metaphor of the "lens" we have found to be particularly effective since it implies that there are no right or wrong interpretations but rather discoveries that can be made by studying a play from more than one vantage point.) The critical method that has stimulated many of our recent students—and that concerns us here—is a Marxist reading of the play. Marxist criticism is a complex topic, and, as the recent work of Fredric Jameson, Henri Arvon, and Raymond Williams exemplifies, critical methodologies vary widely. Moreover, many American students come to Marxist aesthetics with reluctance, conditioned partly by a distrust of all things Russian. Thus we try to emphasize specific issues on which critics agree, and we assign short readings from Terry Eagleton's *Marxism and Literary Criticism* as a point of departure.

It is important, of course, to review Marx's early writings with their humanistic focus and analysis of class structure. Notions of the dialectic and of human alienation are productive ways of introducing students to Marx since alienation seems to be a concept with which they can identify. This approach has the added value of breaking down some initial prejudices toward the subject matter. By stressing the human side of Marx's work, we can reduce student resistance and encourage a more objective view of the social [77 analysis that follows.

We then talk about the text of the play as an objectification of the author's idea, a process that is a creative act but that in dialectical terms is imperfect because it can never completely express Ibsen's vision or totally repress unconscious ideas that shape the text. Drawing on both Terry Eagleton and Louis Althusser (*Lenin and Philosophy*),we define ideology as a false consciousness, a system of beliefs and ideas that functions to disguise the inequities of a class-based society. Using this definition to examine the play, we stress the concept that ideology is shaped by both what is in the text (Torvald's domination of Nora) and by what is "absent" (Nora's relationship with her mother). One of the primary goals of any Marxist analysis is the investigation of ideological content, and the existence of this content allows Marxist critics to argue that all works of art are political. This is a highly controversial point with many students, and the discussions often become heated as we examine its implications.

We then focus on the economic realities of Ibsen's world. *A Doll House* is especially suited to this type of examination because the bank—an obvious and blatant symbol for money—stands at the center of the play. Torvald has just been appointed manager. Mrs. Linde wants to work there, as does Krogstad. And Nora's jubilation at the beginning of the play is directly related to the financial security ensured by Torvald's new job.

Moreover, an economic analysis quickly reveals how the consciousness of the characters is shaped and determined by their class and status. Even though Downs has argued that "except for three virtual supernumeraries, all the persons of the play belong to the educated middle class," it is clear that class differences do exist. Torvald stands for the moneyed elite—in this case the bank owners—while Mrs. Linde and Krogstad function as workers struggling to maintain a subsistence income.

A principal tenet of Marxist criticism is that human consciousness is a product of social conditions and that human relationships are often subverted by and through economic considerations. Mrs. Linde has sacrificed a genuine love to provide for her brothers, and Krogstad has committed a crime to support his children. Anne-Marie, the maid, has also been the victim of her economic background. Because she's "a girl who's poor and gotten in trouble," her relationship with her child has been interrupted and virtually destroyed. In each instance the need for money is linked with the ability to exist. But while the characters accept the social realities of their misfortunes, they do not appear to question how their human attitudes have been thoroughly shaped by socioeconomic considerations.

Once students begin to perceive how consciousness is affected by economics, a Marxist reading of Ibsen's play can illuminate a number of areas. Krogstad, for example, becomes less of a traditional villain when we realize that he is fighting for his job at the bank "as if it were life itself." And his realization of the senselessness of their lives is [78] poignantly revealed when he reflects on Mrs. Linde's past, "all this simply for money." Even Dr. Rank speaks about his failing health and imminent death in entirely financial terms. "These past few days I've been auditing my internal accounts. Bankrupt! Within a month I'll probably be laid out and rotting in the churchyard."

All these characters, however, serve as foils for the central struggle between Nora and Torvald and highlight the pilgrimage that Nora makes in the play. At the outset two things are clear: (1) Nora is enslaved by Torvald in economic terms, and (2) she equates personal freedom with the acquisition of wealth. The play begins joyfully not only because it is the holiday season but also because Torvald's promotion to bank manager will ensure "a safe, secure job with a comfortable salary." Nora is happy because she sees the future in wholly economic terms. "Won't it be lovely to have stacks of money and not a care in the world?"

What she learns, however, is that financial enslavement is symptomatic of other forms of enslavement—master-slave, male-female, sexual objectification, all of which characterize her relationship with Torvald—and that money is no guarantee of happiness. At the end of the play she renounces not only her marital vows but also her financial dependence because she has discovered that personal and human freedom are not measured in economic terms.

This discovery also prompts her to reexamine the society of which she is a part and leads us into a consideration of the ideology in the play. In what sense has Nora committed a criminal offense in forging her father's name? Is it indeed just that she should be punished for an altruistic act, one that cost her dearly both in terms of self-denial and the destruction of her family? Ibsen's defense of Nora is clear, of course, and his implicit indictment of a society that encourages this kind of injustice stimulates a discussion of the assumptions that created the law.

One of the striking things about *A Doll House* is how Anne-Marie accepts her alienation from her child as if it were natural, given the circumstances of class and money. It does not occur to her that laws were framed by other people and thus are capable of imperfection and susceptible to change. Nora broke a law that not only tries to stop thievery (the appropriation of capital) by outlawing forgery but also discriminates against anyone deemed a bad risk. Question leads to question as the class investigates why women were bad risks and why they had difficulty finding employment. It becomes obvious that the function of women in this society was not "natural" but artificial, a role created by their relationship to the family and by their subservience to men. In the marketplace they were a labor force expecting subsistence wages and providing an income to supplement that earned by their husbands or fathers. . . .   [79]

Viewing the play through the lens of Marxist aesthetics does make one thing clear. Nora's departure had ramifications for her society that went beyond the marriage bed. By studying the play within the context of its socioeconomic structure, we can see how the ideology in the text affects the characters and how they perpetuate the ideology. The conclusion of *A Doll House* was a challenge to the economic superstructures that had controlled and excluded the Noras of the world by manipulating their economic status and, by extension, their conscious estimation of themselves and their place in society.

The Character of Dr. Stockmann in *An Enemy of the People**

An Enemy of the People is at once the most high-spirited and the most overtly didactic of   [115]
Ibsen's major plays. Dr. Stockmann is a major comic creation, a courageous spokesman for Ibsen's ideas, which are presented explicitly by means of the public speech in Act IV. He is made even more attractive by his minor failings—his naiveté, his impetuousness, and his touches of vanity and self-indulgence. Ranged around him is a rogues' gallery of caricatures of Norwegian small-town types, from the tea-drinking Mayor down through representatives of the "free press" and the "compact majority" to the timid proletarian radical, Hovstad.

Ibsen wrote *An Enemy of the People* very quickly; he began it in March of 1882, at the height of the controversy over *Ghosts*, and completed it in June, less than three months later. It is true that he had been planning the play two years earlier and had laid his plans aside to write *Ghosts*. Nevertheless, the final version of the play seems to have   [116]
been influenced by the reception of *Ghosts*, especially the attacks from the liberal press in Norway, which particularly infuriated Ibsen. In January, just before beginning the play, for example, he had written to Brandes, using language very much like Stockmann's:

> And what can be said of the attitude assumed by the so-called liberal press—of those leaders of the people who speak and write of freedom of action and thought but who at the same time make themselves the slaves of the supposed opinions of their subscribers? I receive more and more proof that there is something demoralizing in engaging in politics and in joining parties. It will never, in any case, be possible to me to join a party that has the majority on its side. Bjoernson says, "The majority is always right." And as a practical politician he is bound, I suppose, to say so. I, on the contrary, must of necessity say, "The minority is always right." Naturally I am not thinking of that minority of standpatters who are left behind by the great middle party that we call liberal; I mean that minority which leads the van and pushes on to points the majority has not yet reached. I mean: that man is right who has allied himself most closely with the future.

*From James Hurt, *Catiline's Dream: An Essay on Ibsen's Plays* (Urbana: U of Illinois P, 1972).

These sentiments, and a number of similar ones from the letters written about this time, are repeated almost verbatim by Stockmann in his Act IV speech to the public meeting. Stockmann, like Ibsen, is anything but a democrat; he is a thoroughgoing aristocrat, though the aristocracy he calls for is one of the mind and spirit. Audiences, probably rightly, have generally chosen to emphasize less Stockmann's radical individualism than his courageous defiance of established authority, and have made *An Enemy of the People* into a "revolutionary" play in ways very far from Ibsen's intention.

Despite the similarity of Ibsen's and Stockmann's views, however, the doctor is much more than a mouthpiece for Ibsen, a portrait of the artist as a village radical. The comic irony with which Ibsen portrayed Stockmann is suggested in his comments in the letter he sent to his publisher along with the manuscript:

> I have the pleasure of sending you herewith the remainder of the manuscript of my new play. I have enjoyed writing this play, and I feel quite lost and lonely now that it is out of my hands. Dr. Stockmann and I got on so very well together; we agree on so many subjects. But the doctor is more muddle-headed than I am; and moreover he has other peculiarities that permit him to say things which would not be taken so well if I myself said them. I think you will agree with me when you have read the manuscript. [117]

There is something of Hjalmar Ekdal as well as of Gregers Werle in Dr. Stockmann's character. Like Hjalmar, he leaves the household to his quiet, competent wife, whom he often dismays with his habit of having guests in for meals they can ill afford. "Catherine says I earn almost as much as we spend," he proudly tells his brother. And like Hjalmar with his bread and butter, Stockmann is an inveterate snacker although, unlike Hjalmar, Stockmann enjoys seeing others eat, too. He is incredibly naive; as late as Act III he is still convinced that his discovery that the Baths are polluted will earn him the love and gratitude of his fellow citizens, and he modestly tells Hovstad that he must discourage any proposals for "a torchlight procession or a banquet or—a subscription for some little token of thanks." A comic irony envelops even the final tableau. "I've made a great discovery," he announces. "The strongest man in the world is he who stands most alone." But as he speaks, he is standing in the middle of an admiring group made up of his wife, his daughter, his two sons, and Captain Horster, who has donated his house to Stockmann. The actual last lines of the play are Mrs. Stockmann's loving, "Oh, Thomas—!" and Petra's "Father!" as she "warmly clasps his hands."

Much of the richness and complexity of character that make Stockmann more than a two-dimensional mouthpiece comes from the presence in the play of Ibsen's myth of the self. Stockmann—gregarious, outgoing, and impulsive—seems at the opposite pole from such lonely, introspective, and self-conscious characters as Brand and Mrs. Alving. And yet his inner experiences and his spiritual development have much in common with theirs. This psychological background also helps to account for the strange combination of traits in his character: his gullibility, his quick temper, his fierce individualism, his egotism, and his obstinacy. It helps to explain the psychological roots of his final slogan: "The strongest man in the world is he who stands most alone."

The original plan for the Baths came from Dr. Stockmann himself, although his brother Peter tries to claim equal credit for it. He has thought of the plan while working as a rural doctor in the north. He describes the circumstances in his fourth-act speech: [118]

DR. STOCKMANN.   For years I lived far up in the north. As I wandered among those people who lived scattered over the mountains, I often thought it would have been better for those poor degraded creatures if they'd had a vet instead of a man like me! . . . I sat there brooding like a duck on an egg; and the chick I hatched was—the plan for these Baths.

Once conceived, the idea has possessed Stockmann. At first it has met with indifference in the town, but he has persisted. "For years I fought alone for this idea! I wrote, and wrote—" he reminds his brother.

The plan for the Baths thus takes on the character of an obsessive project of the will, and the setting in which it is conceived is appropriate for such a project. Although the dominant settings for the myth of the self are "the valley," "the heights," and "the peaks," the cardinal compass points are sometimes subsumed into the pattern. The north is associated with the will and with projects of the will. Brand is a northerner, and he tells Ejnar that he was never "at home among you southerners." Gregers Werle, Rebecca West, and Ellida Wangel all conceive projects of the will in the isolated north. The south is associated with wholeness and the "joy of life." Nora has had a glimpse of these qualities on her trip to Italy and Oswald yearns for the sunlight and joy of Paris. Erhart Borkman's flight from the externally imposed duties of his northern home is toward the sunlight of Italy. The west, more rarely, is associated with freedom, as in *The Pillars of Society*, and the east, because the sun rises there, sometimes symbolizes transcendence and integration, as in *Emperor and Galilean*.

The plan for the Baths, desirable as it is for its own sake, is sufficiently ambiguous in its psychological meaning for Stockmann to explain his otherwise incredible blindness to reality at the beginning of the play. Obsessed by his project, he has built up a ludicrously idealistic conception of his fellow citizens. He believes that his self-centered and cynical brother will only regret that he was not the one to discover the pollution of [119] the Baths, he takes the representatives of the "free press" and the "compact majority" at their own evaluation, and he believes that the mass of his fellow townspeople will spontaneously offer him a torchlight procession for having revealed the truth, even though it is against their own interests. Most telling of all, he has a naive conception of his own motivations; he does not realize until the last scene how much of his own courage has been based on his presumed financial security.

Stockmann's project of the will, like all projects of the will in Ibsen, has led its creator into a position farther and farther removed from reality. The action of the play covers its gradual collapse, as one support after another is taken away from Stockmann: first his idealistic conception of his brother, then his illusions about the free press, the property owners, and the mass of citizens, and finally his illusions about his own motivations.

Stockmann's reaction to the loss of his defensive project is psychologically consistent with this interpretation of the project itself. Many of his attitudes and actions seem like distant echoes of Brand's lonely withdrawal into an inner world. Stockmann's ebullient self-confidence sometimes verges on messianism, as when he compares himself to Christ after the disastrous public meeting ("I'm not so forgiving as a certain person. I don't say, 'I forgive ye, for ye know not what ye do!'") and when he chooses twelve for the number of his pupil-disciples at the end of the play. His exaggerated respect for scientific facts to the neglect of any sympathetic understanding of their implications for his fellow citizens also indicates something of a defensive withdrawal into the world of his own mind. And most telling of all, the doctrine he enunciates at the public meeting can be read not only as a heroic battle-cry of individualism but also, in its celebration of the lonely, self-sufficient individual and its savage contempt for the "masses," as a defensive, schizoid "rising above" the threat of other people. There is a certain hysterical quality in Dr. Stockmann's cry for the whole town to be wiped out—"Let the whole land be laid waste! Let the whole people be exterminated!"—and in his scathing attacks on the "majority" as vermin," "short-winded sheep," and "filthy, ragged, common curs."

This ambiguous undercurrent in the public meeting scene continues through the [120] last act of the play, which is full of muted suggestions of the kind of mystic integration and rebirth associated with an "ascent to the peaks." When the act begins it appears that Stockmann has reached the lowest point in his fortunes. It is the morning after the tumultuous public meeting at which he was branded an "enemy of the people," Captain Horster has had to escort him and his family home in order to prevent their being physically assaulted, and the mob has broken out all the windows in the house. Stockmann has decided to emigrate to America with his family. A series of visitors—"the Devil's messengers"—however, disillusion him even more. First he learns that Horster has been fired by his shipowner. Then the Mayor arrives to deliver Stockmann's own letter of dismissal, tells him that his father-in-law's will leaves all his money to Stockmann, and accuses him of creating a scandal merely to please his embittered father-in-law. The father-in-law himself, Morten Kiil, is next; his pride has been hurt by the suggestion that his tanneries have poisoned the Baths, he has bought up most of the shares in the Baths, and he tells Stockmann that his wife will lose her inheritance if he does not recant. At this temptation, Stockmann wavers: "I must talk to Catherine. She knows about these things."

When Kiil leaves, Hovstad and Aslaksen arrive. They have heard of Morten Kiil's purchases of stock and assume that Stockmann has merely been trying to drive down the value of the stocks for personal profit. They threaten to expose him if he does not share his profits with them.

At this final straw, Stockmann loses his last illusion about his fellow townspeople that survived from his project of the will. He chases Hovstad and Aslaksen off with an umbrella and sends a note to Kiil refusing to recant. In a scene reminiscent of Brand's decision to "march under his own flag," he decides to remain in the town and start a school to build a new society of "free men and aristocrats." A hint of the mythic mountain peaks survives in the "glorious fresh spring air" blowing in through the shattered windows of Stockmann's study, as he gathers his family and friends around him and announces the birth of the new Stockmann—the "strongest man in the world" because he "stands alone."

SPECIAL
WRITING
TOPICS
ABOUT

LITERATURE

32
Writing and Documenting the Research Essay

Broadly, **research** is the act of systematic investigation, examination, and experimentation. It is the basic tool of intellectual inquiry for anyone engaged in any discipline—physics, chemistry, biology, psychology, anthropology, history, and literature, to name just a few disciplines. With research, our understanding and our civilization grow; without it, they die.

The beginning assumption of doing research is that the researcher is exploring new areas of knowledge. With each assignment the researcher acquires not only the knowledge gained from the particular task but also the skills needed to undertake further research and thereby to gain further knowledge. Some research tasks are elementary, such as using a dictionary to discover the meaning of a word and thereby aiding the understanding of an important passage. More involved research uses an array of resources: encyclopedias, biographies, introductions, critical studies, bibliographies, and histories. When you begin a research task you usually have little or no knowledge about your topic, but with such resources it is possible to acquire a good deal of expert knowledge in a relatively short time.

While research is the animating spark of all disciplines, our topic here is **literary research**—the systematic use of primary and secondary sources in studying a literary problem. In doing literary research, you consult not only individual works themselves (*primary sources*) but many other works that shed light on them and interpret them (*secondary sources*). Typical research tasks are to learn important facts about a work and about the period in which it was written; to learn about the lives, careers, and other works of authors; to discover and apply the comments and judgments of modern or earlier critics; to learn details that help explain the meaning of works; and to learn about critical and artistic taste.

SELECTING A TOPIC

In most instances, your instructor assigns a research essay on a specific topic. Sometimes, however, the choice of a topic is left entirely up to you. For such assignments, it is helpful to know the types of research essays you might find most congenial. Here are some possibilities.

1. *A particular work.* You might treat character (for example, "The Character of Bottom in Shakespeare's *A Midsummer Night's Dream*" or "The Question of Whether Willie Loman Is a Hero or an Antihero in Miller's *Death of a Salesman*") or tone, ideas, form, problems, and the like. A research paper on a single work is similar to an essay on the same work, except that the research paper takes into account more views and facts than those you are likely to have without the research.

2. *A particular author.* This essay is about an idea or some facet of style, imagery, setting, or tone of the author, tracing the origins and development of the topic through a number of different stories, poems, or plays. An example is "The Idea of the True Self as Developed by Frost in His Poetry before 1920." This type of essay is suitable if you are writing on a poet whose works are short, though a topic like "Shakespeare's Idea of the Relationships between Men and Women as Dramatized in *A Midsummer Night's Dream* and *Hamlet*" is also possible.

3. *Comparison and contrast* (see Chapter 35). There are two types:
   a. *An idea or quality common to two or more authors.* Here you show points of similarity or contrast, or else you show how one author's work can be taken to criticize another's. A possible subject is "The Theme of Ineffectuality in Eliot, Steinbeck, and Williams" or "Hughes's Antidiscrimination Poems in the Context of Twentieth-Century Race Relations."
   b. *Different critical views of a particular work or body of works.* Sometimes much is to be gained from an examination of differing critical opinions on topics like "The Meaning of Jackson's 'The Lottery,'" "Various Interpretations of Gray's *Elegy*," or "Hamlet's Views on Death." Such a study would attempt to determine the critical opinion and taste to which a work did or did not appeal, and it might also aim at conclusions about whether the work was in the advance or rear guard of its time.

4. *The influence of an idea, author, philosophy, political situation, or artistic movement on specific works of an author or authors.* An essay on influences can be specific and to the point, as in "Details of Early-Twentieth-Century Mexican-American Culture as Reflected in Parédes's 'The Hammon and the Beans,'" or else it can be more abstract and critical, as in "The Influence of Early-Twentieth-Century Oppression of Mexican-Americans on the Narrator of Parédes's 'The Hammon and the Beans.'"

5. *The origin of a particular work or type of work.* Such an essay might examine an author's biography to discover the germination and development of a work—for example, "'The Old Chief Mshlanga' as an Outgrowth of Lessing's Life in Rhodesia-Zimbabwe." Another way of discovering origins might be to relate a work to a particular type or tradition: "*Hamlet* as Revenge Tragedy" or "Molière's *Love Is the Doctor* and Its Relationship to the *Commedia dell'Arte.*"

If you consider these types, an idea of what to write may come to you. Perhaps you have particularly liked one author or several authors. If so, you might start to think along the lines of types 1, 2, and 3. If you are interested in influences or in origins, then types 4 or 5 may suit you better.

If you still cannot decide on a topic after rereading the works you have liked, then you should carry your search for a topic into your school library. Look up your author or authors in the computer or card catalogue. Your first goal should be to find a relatively recent book-length critical study published by a university press. Look for a title indicating that the book is a general one dealing with the author's major works rather than just one work. Study those chapters relevant to the work or works you have chosen. Most writers of critical studies describe their purpose and plan in their introductions or first chapters, so begin with the first part of the book. If there is no separate chapter on the primary text, use the index as your guide to the relevant pages. Reading in this way will give you enough knowledge about the issues and ideas raised by the work to enable you to select a promising topic. Once you make your decision, you are ready to develop a working bibliography.

SETTING UP A BIBLIOGRAPHY

The best way to develop a working bibliography of books and articles is to begin with major critical studies of the writer or writers. Again, go to the catalogue and find books that have been published by university presses. These books always contain comprehensive bibliographies. Be careful to read the chapters on your primary work or works and to look for the footnotes or endnotes, for often you can save time if you record the names of books and articles listed in these notes. Then refer to the bibliographies included at the ends of the books, and select likely looking titles. Now, look at the dates of publication of the scholarly books. Let us suppose that you have been looking at three, published in 1987, 1995, and 1999. Unless you are planning an extensive research assignment, you can safely assume that the writers of critical works will have done the selecting for you of important works published before the date of publication. These bibliographies will be reliable, and you can use them with confidence. Thus, the bibliography in a book published in 1999 will be complete up through about 1997–1998, for the writer will have completed the manuscript a year or two before the book was published. But such bibliographies will not go up to the present. For that, you will need to search for works published after the most recent of the books.

Consult Bibliographical Guides

Fortunately for students doing literary research, the Modern Language Association (MLA) of America has been providing a complete bibliography of literary studies for years, not only in English and American literatures but in the literatures of many foreign languages. This is the *MLA International Bibliography of Books and Articles on the Modern Languages and Literatures* (*MLA Bibliography*).The *MLA Bibliography* started achieving completeness in the late 1950s. By 1969 the project had grown so large that it was published in many parts, which are bound together in library editions. University and college libraries have sets of this bibliography on open shelves or tables. The *MLA Bibliography* is also published on CD-ROM and on the Internet.

There are many other bibliographies useful for students doing literary research, such as the *Essay and General Literature Index,* the *International Index,* the *Readers' Guide to Periodical Literature, A Bibliography of Literary Theory and Criticism* (available on the Internet at <http://fyl.unizar.es/filologia_inglesa/bibliography.html>) and various specific indexes. The *MLA Bibliography* is more than adequate, however, for most purposes. Remember that as you progress in your reading, the notes and bibliographies in the works you consult will also constitute an unfolding selective bibliography. For the demonstrative student research essay in this chapter, a number of entries were discovered not from bibliographies like those just listed but from the reference lists in critical books.

The *MLA Bibliography,* in the traditional book format, is conveniently organized by period and author. Should you be doing research about Gwendolyn Brooks, look her up in *Volume I: British and Irish, Commonwealth, English, Caribbean, and American Literatures,* where you will also find references to most other authors of works in English, such as Shakespeare, Wordsworth, and Kincaid. You will find most books and articles listed under the author's last name. In the *MLA Bibliography,* journal references are abbreviated, but a lengthy list explaining abbreviations appears at the beginning of the volume. Using the *MLA Bibliography* in the book format, begin with the most recent one and then go backward to your stopping point. If your library has machines dedicated to the electronic versions of the bibliography, you can do your searching by typing in the name of your author or subject. By whatever means you gain access to the bibliography, be sure to get the complete information, especially volume numbers and years of publication, for each article and book. You are now ready to find your sources and to take notes.

ONLINE LIBRARY SERVICES

Today, virtually all libraries have their own computerized catalogues. In addition, many libraries are connected with a vast array of local, national, and even international libraries, so that by using various online services, you can extend your research far beyond the capacities of your own library. You can even use a personal computer to gain access to the catalogues of large research libraries, provided that you punch in the correct entry information, are able and willing to follow the program codes, and are also patient and persistent. By using various "search engines" to gain access to sites on the World Wide Web, you can also discover special topics directly related to your subject—organizations devoted to making awards, for example, or clubs or other organizations that have been established in the home cities of particular authors, or works on topics inspired by various authors.

The ease with which you can gain access to the various libraries through a computer search is variable. Some library catalogues are friendly while others require a certain amount of trial and error.[1] In many cases you will need several tries to learn how to find what you are looking for, because the words some libraries use to categorize holdings are not immediately apparent. In all cases, practice with the various systems is essential, for you cannot expect to get the most out of an electronic search the first time you try.

After you have gained access, you can ask for books by specific authors, or for books about particular topics. If your author is Shakespeare, for example, you can ask for specific titles of his works or for books about him. A recent search for critical and interpretive works about Shakespeare in a large urban university library produced a list of 577 titles with accompanying bibliographical information. The same library listed 167 works dealing specifically with *Hamlet.* Another large library produced 2,412 titles on the criticism and interpretation of Shakespeare (not just in English but also in other languages). Once you have such materials on your screen, you can select and list only the titles that you think will be most useful to you.

Such a list comprises a fairly comprehensive search bibliography, which you can use when you physically enter the library to begin collecting and using materials. A major convenience is that many associated libraries, such as state colleges and urban public libraries, have pooled their resources. Thus, if you use the services of a network of nearby county libraries, you can go to another library to use materials that are not accessible at your own college or branch. If distances are great, however, and your own library does not have a book that you think is important to your project, you can ask a librarian to get the book for you through an interlibrary loan service. Usually, with time, the libraries will accommodate as many of your needs as they can.

---

[1] Libraries generally encourage access to their resources so proper entry instructions are often attached to computer terminals, particularly for internal use. When you are hooked into catalogues of distant libraries, you will find that the computer screen itself contains instructions about what you need to do to continue your search.

IMPORTANT CONSIDERATIONS ABOUT COMPUTER-AIDED RESEARCH

You must always keep in mind that online catalogues can give you only what has been entered into them. If one library classifies a work under "criticism and interpretation" and another classifies it under "characters," a search of "criticism and interpretation" at the first library will find the work but the same search at the second will not. Sometimes the inclusion of an author's life dates immediately following the name will throw off your search. Typographic errors in the system will cause additional search problems, although many programs try to forestall such difficulties by providing "nearby" entries to enable you to determine whether incorrectly entered topics may prove helpful to you. Also, if you use online services, be careful to determine the year when the computerization began. Many libraries have a recent commencement date—1978, for example, or 1985. For completeness, therefore, you would need assistance in finding catalogue entries for items published before these years.

Just a few years ago, the broadness of scope that electronic searches provide for most undergraduate students doing research assignments was not possible; today, it is commonplace. Even with the astounding possibilities of electronic resources, however, it is still necessary to take out actual books and articles—and read them and take notes on them—before you can begin and complete a research essay. The electronic services can help you locate materials, but they cannot do your reading, note taking, and writing. All that is still up to you, as it always has been.

TAKING NOTES AND PARAPHRASING MATERIAL

There are many ways of taking notes, but the consensus is that the best method is to use note cards. If you have never used cards before, you might profit from consulting any one of a number of handbooks and special workbooks on research.[2] The principal advantage of cards is that they can be classified; numbered and renumbered; shuffled; tried out in one place, rejected, and then used in another place (or thrown away); and arranged in order when you start to write.

Take Complete and Accurate Notes

WRITE THE SOURCE ON EACH CARD.   As you take notes, write the source of your information on each card. This may seem bothersome, but it is easier than going back to the library to locate the correct source after you have begun your essay. You can save time if you write all the data on one card—a "master card" for that source—and then create an abbreviation for the separate note cards you take from the source. Here is an example, which also includes the location where the reference was originally found (e.g., card catalogue, computer

---

[2] See, for example, Melinda G. Kramer, Glenn Leggett, and C. David Mead, *Prentice Hall Handbook for Writers*, 12th ed. (Englewood Cliffs: Prentice Hall, 1995), 501–05.

search, bibliography in a book, the *MLA Bibliography*, etc.). Observe that the author's last name goes first.

Donovan, Josephine, ed. 　　Feminist Literary Criticism: Explorations 　　in Theory. 2nd ed. Lexington: 　　UP of Kentucky, 1989. DONOVAN Card Catalogue, "Women"	PN 98 W64 F4

If you take many notes from this book, the name *Donovan* will serve as identification. Be sure not to lose your master cards because you will need them when you prepare your list of works cited. If possible, record the complete bibliographical data in a computer file.

RECORD THE PAGE NUMBER FOR EACH NOTE.　It would be hard to guess how much exasperation has been caused by the failure to record page numbers in notes. Be sure to write the page number down first, *before* you begin to take your note, and, to be doubly sure, write the page number again at the end of your note. If the detail goes from one page to the next in your source, record the exact spot where the page changes, as in this example:

> Heilbrun and Stimson, in DONOVAN, pp. 63–64
>
> [63] After the raising of the feminist consciousness it is necessary to develop / [64] "the growth of moral perception" through anger and the "amelioration of social inequities."

The reason for such care is that you may wish to use only a part of a note you have taken, and when there are two pages you will need to be accurate in locating what goes where.

RECORD ONLY ONE FACT OR OPINION ON A CARD.　Record only one major element on each card—one quotation, one paraphrase, one observation—*never two or more*. You might be tempted to fill up the entire card with many separate but unrelated details, but such a try at economy often gets you in trouble because you might want to use some of the details in other places. If you have only one entry per card, you will avoid such problems and also retain the freedom you need.

USE QUOTATION MARKS FOR ALL QUOTED MATERIAL. In taking notes it is extremely important to distinguish copied material from your own words. *Always put quotation marks around every direct quotation you copy verbatim from a source.* Make the quotation marks immediately, before you forget, so that you will always know that the words of your notes within quotation marks are the words of another writer.

Often, as you take a note, you may use some of your own words and some of the words from your source. In cases like this you should be even more cautious. Put quotation marks around *every word* that you take directly from the source, even if your note looks like a picket fence. Later, when you begin writing your essay, your memory of what is yours and not yours will be dim, and if you use another's words in your own essay without proper acknowledgment, you are risking the charge of plagiarism. Much of the time, plagiarism is caused not by deliberate deception but rather by sloppy note taking.

If Your Source Is Long, Make a Brief and Accurate Paraphrase

When you take notes, it is best to paraphrase the sources. A paraphrase is a restatement in your own words, and because of this it is actually a first step in the writing of the essay. In Chapter 2 you will find a full treatment of how to write a précis or abridgment (pp. 103-108). If you work on the techniques described there, you will be well prepared to write paraphrases when doing your research.

A big problem in paraphrasing is to capture the idea in the source without duplicating the words. The best way is to read and reread the passage you are noting. Turn over the book or journal and write out the idea *in your own words* as accurately as you can. Once you have this note, compare it with the original and make corrections to improve your thought and emphasis. Add a short quotation if you believe it is needed, but be sure to use quotation marks. If your paraphrase is too close to the original, *throw out the note and try again.* This effort may have its own reward because often you may be able to transfer some or even all of your note, word for word, directly to the appropriate place in your research essay.

To see the problems of paraphrasing, let us look at a paragraph of criticism and then see how a student doing research might take notes on it. The paragraph is by Maynard Mack, from an essay titled "The World of Hamlet," originally published in *The Yale Review* 41 (1952) and reprinted in *Twentieth Century Interpretations of Hamlet,* ed. David Bevington (Englewood Cliffs: Prentice Hall, 1968), p. 57.

The powerful sense of mortality in *Hamlet* is conveyed to us, I think, in three ways. First, there is the play's emphasis on human weakness, the instability of human purpose, the subjection of humanity to fortune—all that we might call the aspect of failure in man. Hamlet opens this theme in Act I, when he describes how from that single blemish, perhaps not even the victim's fault, a man's whole character may take corruption. Claudius dwells on it again, to an extent that goes far beyond the needs of the occasion, while engaged in seducing Laertes to step behind the arras of a seemer's world and dispose of Hamlet by a trick. Time qualifies everything, Claudius says, including love, including purpose. As for love—it has a "plurisy" in it and dies of its own too much. As for purpose—"That we would do, We should do when we would, for the 'would' changes. And hath abatements and delays as many As there are tongues, are hands, are accidents; And then this 'should' is like a spendthrift's sigh, That hurts by easing." The player-king, in his long speeches to his queen in the play within the play, sets the matter in a still darker light. She means these protestations of undying love, he knows, but our purposes depend on our memory, and our memory fades fast. Or else, he suggests, we propose something to ourselves in a condition of strong feeling, but then the feeling goes, and with it the resolve. Or else our fortunes change, he adds, and with these our loves: "The great man down, you mark his favorite flies." The subjection of human aims to fortune is a reiterated theme in *Hamlet,* as subsequently in *Lear.* Fortune is the harlot goddess in whose secret parts men like Rosencrantz and Guildenstern live and thrive; the strumpet who threw down Troy and Hecuba and Priam; the outrageous foe whose slings and arrows a man of principle must suffer or seek release in suicide. Horatio suffers them with composure: he is one of the blessed few "Whose blood and judgment are so well co-mingled That there are not a pipe for fortune's finger To sound what stop she please." For Hamlet the task is of a greater difficulty.

Because taking notes forces a shortening of this or any criticism, it also requires you to discriminate, judge, interpret, and select; good note taking is not easy. There are some things to guide you, however, when you go through the many sources you uncover.

THINK OF THE PURPOSE OF YOUR RESEARCH.   You may not know exactly what you are "fishing for" when you start to take notes, for you cannot prejudge what your essay will contain. Research is a form of discovery. But soon you will notice subjects and issues that your sources constantly explore. If you can accept one of these as your major topic, or focus of interest, you can use that as your guide in all further note taking.

For example, suppose you are taking notes on critical works about *Hamlet,* and after a certain amount of reading you have decided to focus on "Shakespeare's Tragic Views in *Hamlet.*" This decision would prompt you to take a note when you come to Mack's thought about mortality and death in the passage quoted above. In this instance, the following note would suffice:

Mack, in Bevington, 57   **Death and**
                                                              Mortality

Mack cites three ways in which <u>Hamlet</u> stresses death and mortality. The
first (57) is an emphasis on human shortcomings and "weakness." Corruption,
loss of memory and enthusiasm, bad luck, misery—all suit the sense of the
closeness of death to life.   **57**

Let us now suppose that you want a fuller note, in the expectation that
you need not just the topic but also some of Mack's detail. Such a note might
look like this:

Mack, in Bevington, 57   **Death and**
                                                              Mortality

The first of Mack's "three ways" in which a "powerful sense of mortality" is
shown in <u>Hamlet</u> is the illustration of human "weakness," "instability," and
helplessness before fate. In support, Mack refers to Hamlet's early speech on a
single fault leading to "corruption," also to Claudius's speech (in the scene
persuading Laertes to trick Hamlet). The player-king also talks about his
queen's forgetfulness and therefore inconstancy by default. As slaves to
fortune, Rosencrantz and Guildenstern are examples. Horatio is not a slave,
however. Hamlet's case is by far the worst of all.   **57**

In an actual essay, any part of this note would be useful. The words are almost
all the note taker's own, and the few quotations are within quotation marks.
Note that Mack, the critic, is properly recognized as the source of the criticism,
so that you could adapt the note easily when you are doing your writing. The
key here is that your taking of notes should be guided by your developing plan
for your essay.

Note taking is part of your thinking and composing process. You cannot
predict whether you will be able to use each of your notes, and you will therefore exclude many notes when you write your essay. You will always find, however, that taking notes is easier once you have determined your purpose.

TITLE EACH NOTE.   To help plan and develop the various parts of your
essay, write a title for each note in the upper right corner of the card, as in the
examples in this chapter. *This practice is a form of outlining that will help you immeasurably when you write your essay.* Let us assume that you have chosen to study the
importance of the Ghost in the play (the topic of the demonstrative student

essay on p. 1945). As you delve into your sources, you discover that there are conflicting views about how the Ghost should be understood. Here is a note about one of the questionable qualities of this character:

Negative, Devilish

Eleanor Prosser. <u>Hamlet and Revenge</u>. 2nd ed. Stanford: Stanford UP, 1971

[133] When describing his pain and suffering as a dead spirit, the Ghost is not specific but emphasizes the horror. He should, if a good spirit, try to use his suffering to urge repentance and salvation for Hamlet. [134] This emphasis is a sign that he is closer in nature to a devil than to a soul earning its way to redemption.

Notice that the title classifies the topic of the note. If you use such classifications while taking notes, a number of like-titled cards could form the substance of a section in your essay about the negative qualities of the Ghost in *Hamlet*. In addition, once you decide that "Negative, Devilish" is one of the topics you plan to explore, the topic itself will guide you in further study and note taking.

WRITE DOWN YOUR THOUGHTS, MARKING THEM AS YOUR OWN.   As you take your notes, you will be getting good thoughts of your own. Do not push these aside in your mind, on the chance of remembering them later, but write them down immediately. Often you may notice a detail that your source does not mention, or you may get a hint for an idea that the critic does not develop. Often, too, you may get thoughts that can serve as "bridges" between details in your notes or as introductions or concluding observations. Be sure to title your comment and also to mark it as your own thought. Here is such a note, which is related to the importance of the Ghost in the structure of *Hamlet*:

My Own   **Structure**

Shakespeare does an excellent job in creating and developing the Ghost. The Ghost shows many characteristics of a living human being, and he is fully integrated in the play's structure.

Observe that some of the ideas and language from this note are used in paragraphs 9 and 10 of the demonstrative student essay (p. 1948).

SORT YOUR CARDS INTO GROUPS. If you do a careful and thorough job of taking notes, your essay will have been forming in your mind already. The titles of your cards will suggest areas to be developed as you do your planning and initial drafting. Once you have assembled a stack of note cards derived from a reasonable number of sources (your instructor may have assigned an approximate number or a minimum number), you can sort them into groups according to the topics and titles. For the demonstrative research essay, after some shuffling and retitling, the cards were assembled in the following groups:

1. Importance in the play's action.
2. Importance in the play's themes.
3. Condition as a spirit.
   a. Good signs.
   b. Negative, devilish signs.
4. Human traits.
5. Importance in the play's structure.
6. Effect on other characters.

If you look at the major sections of the demonstrative student essay (on pp. 1945–50), you will see that the topics are closely adapted from these groups of cards. In other words, *the arrangement of the cards is an effective means of organizing and developing a research essay.*

ARRANGE THE CARDS IN EACH GROUP ACCORDING TO TOPICS AND IDEAS. There is still much to do with each group of cards. You cannot use the details as they fall randomly in your stack. You need to decide which notes are relevant. You might also need to retitle some cards and use them elsewhere. Those that remain will have to be arranged in a clear and logical order to be used in the essay.

Once you have your cards in order, you can write whatever comments or transitions are needed to move from detail to detail. Write this material directly on the cards, and be sure to use pencils or inks of different color, so that you can distinguish later between the original note and what you add now. Here is an example of such a "developed" note card.

Campbell, 127   Negative, Devilish

Shakespeare's Ghost reflects the general uncertainty at the time about how ghosts were to be interpreted. 127

This may be the best way to answer the questions about the Ghost's ambiguous nature. Moreover, Shakespeare may have been trying to be more lifelike than consistent with his Ghost.

By adding such commentary to your note cards, you will facilitate the actual writing of your first draft. In many instances, the note and the comment can be moved directly into the paper with only minor revision (material from this note and comment appears in paragraph 5 of the demonstrative essay).

BE CREATIVE AND ORIGINAL EVEN THOUGH YOU ARE DOING RESEARCH. You will not always transfer your notes directly into your essay. The major trap to avoid in a research paper is that your use of sources can become an end in itself and therefore a shortcut for your own thinking and writing. Often, students make the mistake of introducing details the way a master of ceremonies introduces performers in a variety show. This is unfortunate because it is the *student* whose essay will be judged, even though the sources, like the performers, do all the work. Thus, it is important to be creative and original in a research essay and to do your own thinking and writing, even though you are relying heavily on your sources. Here are four ways in which research essays may be original:

1. *Selection.* In each major section of your essay, you will include many details from your sources. To be creative you should select different but related details and avoid overlapping or repetition. Your final essay will be judged on the basis of the thoroughness with which you make your point with different details (which in turn will represent the completeness of your research). Even though you are relying on published materials and cannot be original on that score, your selection can be original because you bring these materials together for the first time, and because you emphasize some details and minimize others. Inevitably, your assemblage of details from your sources will be unique and therefore original.

2. *Development.* Your arrangement of your various points is an obvious area of originality: One detail seems naturally to precede another, and certain conclusions stem from certain details. As you present the details, conclusions, and arguments from your sources, you can also add an original stamp by introducing supporting

details different from those in the source material. You can also add your own emphasis to particular points—an emphasis that you do not find in your sources.

Naturally, the words that you use will be original. Your topic sentences, for example, will all be your own. As you introduce details and conclusions, you will need to write "bridges" to get yourself from point to point. These can be introductory remarks or transitions. In other words, as you write, you are not just stringing your notes together—you are actively tying thoughts together in a variety of creative ways. Your success in these efforts will constitute your greatest originality.

3. *Explanation of controversial views.* Closely related to your selection is that in your research you may have found conflicting or differing views on a topic. If you make a point to describe and distinguish these views, and explain the reasons for the differences, you are presenting material originally. To see how differing views can be handled, see paragraphs 4 and 5 of the demonstrative student essay (pp. 1946-47).

4. *Creation of your own insights and positions.* There are three possibilities here, all related to how well you have learned the primary texts on which your research in secondary sources is based:

   a. *Your own interpretations and ideas.* An important part of taking notes is to make your own points *precisely when they occur to you.* Often you can expand these as truly original parts of your essay. Your originality does not need to be extensive; it may consist of no more than a single insight. Here is such a card, which was written during the research on the ghost in *Hamlet:*

My Own   **FOR THE INTRODUCTION**

   The Ghost is minor in the action but major in the play. He is seen twice in scene 1, but this scene is really all about him. (Also about his appearances before the play opens.) In scene 4 of Act 1 he comes again and leads Hamlet off to scene 5—the biggest for him as an acting and speaking character. He speaks after this only from under the stage, and then a small appearance (but important) in III.4, and that's all. He is dominant because he sets everything in motion and therefore his presence is felt everywhere in the play.

The originality here is built around the idea of the small role but dominant significance of the Ghost. The discovery is not unusual or startling, but it nevertheless represents original thought about *Hamlet.* When modified and adapted (and put into full sentences with proper punctuation), the material of the card supplies much of the opening paragraph of the demonstrative student essay. You can see that the development of a "My Own" note card is important for a research essay.

b. *Gaps in the sources.* As you read your secondary sources, you may realize that an obvious conclusion is not made or that a certain detail is not stressed. Here is an area for you to develop on your own. Your conclusion can involve a particular interpretation or major point of comparison, or it can rest on a particularly important but underemphasized word or fact. In the demonstrative essay, for example, the writer discusses the idea that the Ghost's commands make it impossible for Hamlet to solve problems through negotiation—the way he might have chosen as prince and student. The commands force him instead into a plan requiring murder. Most critics observe that Hamlet's life is changed because of the Ghost but have not quite stressed this aspect of the change. Given such a critical "vacuum" (assuming that you cannot read all the articles about some of your topics, where your discovery may already have been published a number of times), it is right to begin filling it with your own insights. A great deal of scholarship is created in this way.

c. *Disputes with the sources.* Your sources may present certain arguments that you wish to dispute. As you develop your disagreement, you will be arguing originally, for the use you make of detail will be different from the use made by the critic or critics whom you are disputing. Also, your conclusions will be your own. This area of originality is similar to the laying out of controversial critical views, except that you furnish one of the opposing views yourself. The approach is limited because it is difficult to find many substantive points of interpretation on which there are not already clearly delineated opposing views. Paragraph 5 of the demonstrative essay shows a small point of disagreement (about whether Shakespeare was concerned with consistency in presenting the Ghost's spirit nature) but one that is nevertheless original.

DOCUMENTING YOUR WORK[3]

It is essential to acknowledge—to *document*—all sources from which you have *quoted or paraphrased* factual and interpretive information. If you do not give due acknowledgment, you run the risk of being challenged for presenting other people's work as your own. This is plagiarism, and it is a serious acadamic offense that can carry severe penalties. As the means of documentation, various reference systems use parenthetical references, footnotes, or endnotes. Whatever system is used, documentation almost always includes a carefully prepared list of works cited or a bibliography.

We will first discuss the list of works cited and then review the two major reference systems for use in a research paper. Parenthetical references, preferred by the Modern Language Association (MLA) since 1984, are described in Joseph Gibaldi's *MLA Handbook for Writers of Research Papers* (5th ed., 1999). Footnotes or endnotes are still required by many instructors.

---

[3] For the documentation of materials you find online and on the Internet, see Appendix I, "MLA Recommendations for Documenting Electronic Sources," (pp. 1993–96).

A List of Works Cited (Bibliography) Is a List of the Works You Have Used

The key to any reference system is a carefully prepared list of works cited that is included at the end of the essay. "Works cited" means exactly that; the list should include just those books and articles you have actually *used* in your essay. If, however, your instructor requires that you use footnotes or endnotes, you can extend your concluding list to be a complete bibliography both of works cited and also of works consulted but not actually used. *Always, always, always, follow your instructor's directions.*

The list of works cited should include the following information, in each entry, in the form indicated. If you are using a word processor with the capacity to make italics, you can italicize book and article titles, but be sure to notify your instructor in advance.

FOR A BOOK

1. The author's name, last name first, followed by first name and middle name or initial. Period.
2. The title, underlined (or italicized). Period.
3. The city of publication (not state or nation), colon; publisher (easily recognized abbreviations or key words can be used unless they seem awkward or strange; see the *MLA Handbook*, pp. 244–45), comma; year of publication. Period.

FOR AN ARTICLE

1. The author's name, last name first, followed by first name and middle name or initial. Period.
2. The title of the article, in quotation marks. Period.
3. The name of the journal or periodical, underlined or italicized, followed by volume number in Arabic (*not* Roman) numbers with no punctuation, then the year of publication within parentheses. Colon. For a daily paper or weekly magazine, omit the parentheses and cite the date in the British style followed by a colon (day, month, year, as in *29 Dec. 1999:*). Inclusive page numbers. Period (without any preceding *p.* or *pp.*).

The list of works cited should be arranged alphabetically by author, with unsigned articles listed by title. Bibliographical lists are begun at the left margin, with subsequent lines in hanging indentation, so that the key locating word—usually the author's last name—can be easily seen. Many unpredictable and complex combinations, including ways to describe works of art, musical or other performances, and films, are detailed extensively in the *MLA Handbook* (114–202). Here are two model entries:

BOOK: Alpers, Antony. *The Life of Katherine Mansfield.* New York: Viking, 1980.

ARTICLE: Hankin, Cheryl. "Fantasy and the Sense of an Ending in the Work of Katherine Mansfield." Modern Fiction Studies 24 (1978): 465–74.

Refer to Works Parenthetically as You Draw Details from Them

Within the text of your research essay, refer *parenthetically* to works from which you are using facts and conclusions. This parenthetical reference system is recommended in the *MLA Handbook* (204–29), and its principle is to provide documentation without asking readers to interrupt their reading to find footnotes or endnotes. Readers wanting to see the complete reference can easily find it in your list of works cited. With this system, you insert the author's last name and the relevant page number or numbers into the body of your essay. If the author's name is mentioned in the discussion, only the page number or numbers are given in parentheses. Here are two examples:

> Alexander Pope believed in the idea that the universe is a whole, a totally unified body, which provides a "viable benevolent system for the salvation of everyone who does good" (Kallich 24).

> Martin Kallich draws attention to Alexander Pope's belief in the idea that the universe is a whole, a totally unified body, which provides a "viable benevolent system for the salvation of everyone who does good" (24).

Footnotes and Endnotes Are Formal and Traditional Reference Formats

The most formal system of documentation still widely used is that of *footnotes* (references at the bottom of each page) or *endnotes* (references listed numerically at the end of the essay). If your instructor wants you to use one of these formats, do the following: Make a note the first time you quote or refer to a source, with the details ordered as outlined below.

FOR A BOOK

1. The author's name, first name or initials first, followed by middle name or initial, then last name. Comma.
2. The title, underlined or italicized for a book, no punctuation. If you are referring to a work in a collection (article, story, poem) use quotation marks for that, but underline the title of the book. No punctuation, but use a comma after the title if an editor, translator, or edition number follows.
3. The name of the editor or translator, if relevant. Abbreviate "editor" or "edited by" as *ed.*, "editors" as *eds.* Use *trans.* for "translator" or "translated by." No punctuation, but use a comma if an edition number follows.
4. The edition (if indicated), abbreviated thus: *2nd ed.*, *3rd ed.*, and so on. No punctuation.
5. The publication facts, within in parentheses, without any preceding or following punctuation, in the following order:
   a. City (but *not* the state or nation) of publication, colon.
   b. Publisher (clear abbreviations are acceptable and desirable), comma.
   c. Year of publication.

6.　The page number(s) with no *p.* or *pp.*, for example, *65, 6–10, 15–19, 295–307, 311–16.* Period. If you are referring to longer works, such as novels or longer stories that may have division or chapter numbers, include these numbers for readers who may be using an edition different from yours.

FOR AN ARTICLE

1.　The author, first name or initials first, followed by middle name or initial, then last name. Comma.

2.　The title of the article, in quotation marks. Comma.

3.　The name of the journal, underlined or italicized. No punctuation.

4.　The volume number, in Arabic letters. No punctuation.

5.　The year of publication in within parentheses. Colon. For newspaper and journal articles, omit the parentheses, and include day, month, and year (in the British style: *21 May 2000*). Colon.

6.　The page number(s) with no *p.* or *pp.*: *65, 6–10, 34–36, 98–102, 345–47.* Period.

For later notes to the same work, use the last name of the author as the reference unless you are referring to two or more works by the same author. Thus, if you refer to only one work by, say, Langston Hughes, the name *Hughes* will be enough for all later references. Should you be referring to other works by Hughes, however, you will also need to make a short reference to the specific works to distinguish them, such as *Hughes, "Mulatto,"* and *Hughes, "Let America Be America Again."*

Footnotes are placed at the bottom of each page, and endnotes are included on separate page(s) at the end of the essay. The first lines of both footnotes and endnotes should be paragraph indented, and continuing lines should be flush with the left margin. Both endnote and footnote numbers are positioned slightly above the line (as superior numbers) like this:[12]. You can single-space footnotes and endnotes and leave a line of space between them. Additionally, today's computer programs have specially designed and consecutively numbered footnote formats. These are generally acceptable, but be sure to consult your instructor. (For more detailed coverage of footnoting practices, see the *MLA Handbook*, 267–85.)

SAMPLE FOOTNOTES.　In the examples below, book titles and periodicals are shown <u>underlined</u>, as they would be in a typewritten or carefully handwritten essay.

[1] Blanche H. Gelfant, <u>Women Writing in America: Voices in Collage</u> (Hanover: UP of New England, for Dartmouth College, 1984) 110.

[2] Günter Grass, "Losses," <u>Granta</u> 42 (Winter 1992): 99.

[3] John O'Meara, "<u>Hamlet</u> and the Fortunes of Sorrowful Imagination: A Re-examination of the Genesis and Fate of the Ghost," <u>Cahiers Élisabéthains</u> 35 (1989): 21.

[4] Grass 104.　　[5] Gelfant 141.　　[6] O'Meara 17.

As a principle, you do not need to repeat in a note any material you have already mentioned in your own discourse. For example, if you recognize the author and title of your source, then the note should give no more than the data about publication. Here is an example:

> In <u>The Fiction of Katherine Mansfield</u>, Marvin Magalaner points out that Mansfield was as skillful in the development of epiphanies (that is, the use of highly significant though perhaps unobtrusive actions or statements to reveal the depths of a particular character) as James Joyce himself, the "inventor" of the technique.[9]
>
> 9 (Carbondale: Southern Illinois UP, 1971) 130.

Many Academic Disciplines Have Their Own Requirements for Documentation

Other reference systems and style manuals have been adopted by various disciplines (e.g., mathematics, medicine, psychology) to serve their own special needs. If you receive no instructions from your instructors in other courses, you can adapt the systems described here. If you need to use the documentation methods of other fields, however, use the *MLA Handbook*, 285–90, particularly 288–90, for guidance about what style manual to select.

Some Final Advice: When in Doubt, Consult Your Instructor

As long as all you want from a reference is the page number of a quotation or paraphrase, the parenthetical system described briefly here—and detailed fully in the *MLA Handbook*—is the most suitable and convenient one you can use. However, you may wish to use footnotes or endnotes if you need to add more details, provide additional explanations, or refer your readers to other materials that you are not using.

Whatever method you follow, *you must always acknowledge sources properly.* Remember that whenever you begin to write and make references, you might forget a number of specific details about documentation, and you will certainly discover that you have many questions. Be sure, then, to ask your instructor, who is your final authority.

STRATEGIES FOR ORGANIZING IDEAS IN YOUR RESEARCH ESSAY

In your research essay you may wish to expand your introduction more than usual because of the need to relate the problem of research to your topic. You may wish to bring in relevant historical or biographical information (see, for example, the introduction of the demonstrative student essay on pp. 1945–46). You may also wish to summarize critical opinion or describe critical problems about your topic. The idea is to lead your reader into your topic by providing interesting and significant materials that you have found.

Because of the greater length of most research essays, some instructors require a topic outline, which is in effect a brief table of contents. This pattern is observed in the demonstrative student essay. *Because the inclusion of an outline is a matter of instructor's choice, be sure to learn whether your instructor requires it.*

As you write the body and conclusion of your research essay, your development will be governed by your choice of topic. Consult the relevant chapters in this book about what to include for whatever approach or approaches you select (setting, idea, point of view, character, tone, or any other).

In length, the research essay can be anywhere from five to fifteen or more pages, depending on your instructor's assignment. Obviously, an essay on a single work will be shorter than one based on several. If you narrow the scope of your topic, as suggested in the approaches described at the beginning of this chapter, you can readily keep your essay within the assigned length. The following demonstrative student essay, for example, illustrates approach 1 (p. 1926) by being limited to only one character in one play. Were you to write on characters in a number of other plays by Shakespeare (approach 2), you could limit your total number of pages by stressing comparative treatments and by avoiding excessive detail about problems pertaining to only one work.

Although you limit your topic yourself in consultation with your instructor, you may encounter problems because you will be dealing not with one source alone but with many. Naturally the sources will provide you with details and also with many of your ideas. The problem is to handle the many strands without piling on too many details, and also without being led into digressions. It is important therefore to keep your central idea foremost; the constant stressing of your central idea will help you both to select relevant materials and to reject irrelevant ones.

It bears reemphasis that you need to distinguish between *your own work* and the *sources* you are using. Your readers will assume that everything you write is your own unless you indicate otherwise. Therefore, when blending your words with the ideas from sources, be clear about proper acknowledgments. Most commonly, if you are simply presenting details and facts, you can write straightforwardly and let parenthetical references suffice as your authority, as in the following sentence from the demonstrative student essay:

> Thus he is most emphatic that Hamlet should not kill her along with Claudius (Fisch 80), and he also voices concern about the reputation and future of Denmark (Gottschalk, "Scanning" 165).

Although the words belong to the writer of the essay, the parenthetical references clearly indicate that the idea for the sentence is derived from the two sources.

If you are using an interpretation unique to a particular writer, or if you are relying on a significant quotation from your source, you should make your acknowledgment an essential part of your discussion, as in this sentence:

> A. C. Bradley (126) suggests that these speeches indicate Shakespeare's master touch in the development of the Ghost's character.

Here the idea of the critic is singled out for special acknowledgment. If you indicate your sources in this way, no confusion can arise about how you have used your sources.

DEMONSTRATIVE STUDENT ESSAY

The Ghost in *Hamlet*°

OUTLINE

I. Introduction
    A. The Importance of the Ghost in *Hamlet*
    B. The Ghost's Influence on the Play's Themes
II. The Ghost's Status as a Spirit
III. The Ghost's Character
IV. The Ghost's Importance in the Structure of the Play
V. The Ghost's Effect
VI. Conclusion

(See pp. 1350–1453 for this play.)

I. INTRODUCTION

A. The Importance of the Ghost in <u>Hamlet</u>

[1]   <u>Even though the Ghost of Hamlet's father is present in only a few scenes of *Hamlet*, he is a dominating presence.</u>* He appears twice in the first scene, and this entire scene itself is about the meaning of these and earlier appearances. He enters again in the fourth scene of Act I, when he beckons to Hamlet and leads him offstage, in this way providing an early illustration of Hamlet's courage (Edgar 257). In the fifth scene of Act I he speaks for the first time, explaining how his brother Claudius murdered him and exhorting his son, Hamlet, to kill Claudius in retribution. Because this cry for revenge directly or

---

* Central idea.

indirectly causes the rest of the play's action, it is clear, as Marjorie Garber puts it, that "the dead man turned ghost is more powerful than he was when living" (304). After some words which the Ghost speaks from underground (i.e., under the stage), he does not enter again until the fourth scene of Act III, in the queen's closet or bedroom, when he reveals himself to Hamlet--but not to Gertrude--to reproach the Prince for not yet having killed Claudius. The Ghost is not present at the play's end, but the actions he sets in motion are concluded there, and hence his effect remains dominant.

B. The Ghost's Influence on the Play's Themes

[2]   Not only is the Ghost dominant over actions, but he is also directly linked to many of the play's themes. William Kerrigan calls the Ghost a "nightmind" who introduces the mental darkness of evil that dominates the play (42). In addition, the Ghost intensifies the play's "interior suffering" (Paris 85). This suffering is brought out in Hamlet's anguished soliloquies and also in the pain of Ophelia and Laertes (and even that of Claudius himself). Another theme is shown by the Ghost's commands to Hamlet--that of responsibility, whether personal, political, or conjugal (McFarland 15). Hamlet of course does not rush right out to kill Claudius, despite the Ghost's urgings, and hence the Ghost is indirectly responsible for the theme of hesitation--this great "Sphinx of modern Literature"--which has become one of the weaknesses cited most frequently about Hamlet's character (Jones 22). The Ghost's scary presence also poses questions about the power of superstition, terror, and fear (Campbell 211). Beyond these, deeply within the psychological realm, the Ghost has been cited as a "confirmation" of the influence of "psychic residues in governing and shaping human life" (McFarland 34), not to mention the significance of the Oedipus complex in the development of Hamlet's character.

[3]   Because the Ghost is so important, one hardly needs to justify studying him. His importance can be traced in his spirit nature, his influence on the play's structure, and his effect on Hamlet and therefore indirectly on all the major characters.†

II. THE GHOST AS A SPIRIT

[4]   To the play's characters, the Ghost is an apparition of questionable status. When Hamlet first sees the Ghost, he raises a question about whether the vision is "a spirit of health, or goblin damned" (I.4.40). Horatio adds that Hamlet is "desperate with imagination" (I.4.87), thus casting doubt upon the Ghost's reality even though he is seen by everyone onstage. When speaking with Hamlet, the Ghost is vague about his out-of-earth location, complaining that he is suffering hellish fires but intimating that he will do so only until his earthly sins are purged away. In the meanwhile, he says, he is able to walk the earth for a certain time, presumably only at night (but is his visit in Act III, scene 4, made in the daytime?). Surprising at it might seem, this detail about where ghosts spend their time reflects Renaissance religious controversies. Dramatizing a ghost returning from

---

† Thesis sentence.

purgatory might have been interpreted as a ratification of Catholic doctrine, and so it was apparently safest for Protestant writers like Shakespeare to show a ghost only of a person who was "freshly dead or on the point of death" (O'Meara 15) but to make the details vague.

[5]   The status and existence of ghosts therefore reflects uncertainties during the Elizabethan period. Lily Campbell offers a number of ways in which Elizabethans dealt with these uncertainties. First, James I of England (when still James VI of Scotland), in writing about departed spirits, emphasized that the devil himself could choose the shape of loved ones in order to deceive living persons and lead them to hell. It is this danger that Hamlet specifically describes. Second, as already mentioned, Elizabethan Catholic teaching held it possible for souls in purgatory to return to earth for a time to communicate with the living. Third, scientifically oriented thinkers interpreted ghostly appearances as a sign of madness or deep melancholia (Campbell 121) or what O'Meara calls "sorrowful imagination" (19). There were apparently a number of "tests" that might have enabled people to determine whether ghosts were authentic and not creations of the devil or products of a sick imagination. Most of these required that the spirit in question should demonstrate goodness of character and provide the living with comfort (Campbell 123).

[6]   The Ghost of King Hamlet both passes and fails these tests. He is not totally bad (Campbell 126), but he urges Hamlet to commit murder, something that no ghost trying to reach heaven would ever do (McFarland 36). Although the Ghost describes the pain of a soul in purgatory, he does so to create fear, not to urge Hamlet to seek salvation. Thus he indicates that he is more like the devil than a soul earning its way to redemption (Prossser 133-34; Frye 22). Another sign suggesting the Ghost's devilishness is that he withholds his appearance from Gertrude when he shows himself to Hamlet in Act III, scene 4 (Campbell 124). Hamlet creates his own test of the Ghost by getting the touring actors to perform *The Murder of Gonzago*. Once he sees the king's disturbance at the play, he concludes that the Ghost is real and not just a "figment of his melancholy imagination" (Harrison 883). However, perhaps the best answer to the conflicting signs about the Ghost is provided by Lily Campbell, who suggests that the ambiguity is a reflection of the general uncertainty about ghosts among Shakespeare's contemporaries (127). In other words, there was no unanimity about the nature and purposes of ghosts in Elizabethan times, and Shakespeare, if he was even concerned about theological issues of ghostly consistency, was reflecting common understanding and attitudes.

III. THE GHOST'S CHARACTER

[7]   Uncertainty aside, the Ghost is probably Shakespeare's rendering of what he thought a ghost would be like. He inherited a tradition of noisy, bloodthirsty ghosts from his sources--what Harold Fisch calls a "Senecan ghost" (91). There was also a tradition of "hungry ghosts," who were spirits prowling about the earth "searching for the life they were deprived of" (Austin 93). In this tradition, Shakespeare's Ghost is bloodthirsty, although ironically not as bloodthirsty as Hamlet himself becomes in the play (Gottschalk 166). The Ghost is surrounded by awe and horror (DeLuca 147) and is frightening, both to the soldiers at the

beginning of the play and also to Hamlet in Act III, scene 4 (Charney, <u>Style</u> 167–68). It would seem that horror is the main effect that Shakespeare was trying to create with the Ghost.

[8]   Although the Ghost is bloodthirsty and horrible, he has redeeming qualities (<u>Alexander 30</u>). He is toned down from a ghost in an anonymous and lost earlier play, perhaps a first version of *Hamlet* by Shakespeare himself (Bloom 383), which was described by Shakespeare's contemporary Thomas Lodge (1558–1625). Lodge talked about "ye ghost which cried so miserally [pitifully, sorrowfully] at ye theator . . . *Hamlet, reuenge"* [sic]. Shakespeare's Ghost also cries out for vengeance, but as former loving husband he is concerned about Hamlet's mother, Gertrude, directing his son to treat her kindly and help her (Fisch 80; Kerrigan 54). Also, as a former king, he voices concern about the reputation and future of Denmark (Gottschalk 165). Paul Gottschalk points to these redeeming qualilties to indicate that the Ghost is concerned with "restoration" as well as "retaliation" (166)--a view not shared by Norman Austin, who calls the Ghost "the spirit of ruin" (105).

[9]   Indeed, the Ghost has many qualities of a living human being. For example, he is witty, as Maurice Charney observes about the following interchange between the Ghost and Hamlet just at the beginning of the revelation speeches in Act I, scene 5, lines 6 –7:

HAMLET.   Speak, I am bound to hear.

GHOST.   So art thou to revenge, when thou shalt hear.

In other words, even though the Ghost may have come "with . . . airs from heaven, or blasts from hell" (I.4.41), he is still mentally alert enough to make a pun out of Hamlet's word "bound" (Charney, <u>Style</u> 118). To this quickness can be added his shrewd ability to judge his son's character. He knows that Hamlet may neglect duty, and hence his last words in Act I, scene 5, are "remember me," and his first words in Act III, scene 4 are "Do not forget." A. C. Bradley suggests that these speeches indicate Shakespeare's master touch in the development of the Ghost's character (126).

[10]   The Ghost also shows other human traits. He feels strong remorse about his lifelong crimes and "imperfections" for which his sudden death did not give him time to atone. It is this awareness that has made him bitter and vengeful. Also, he has a sense of appropriateness that extends to what he wears. Thus, at the beginning he appears on the parapets dressed in full armor. This battle uniform is in keeping with the location and also with his vengeful mission urging Hamlet to kill Claudius (Aldus 54). The armor is intimidating, a means of enforcing the idea that the Ghost in death has become a "spirit of hatred" (Austin 99). By contrast, in the closet scene he wears a dressing gown ("in his habit as he lived," [III.4.135]) as though he is prepared for ordinary palace activities of both business and leisure (Charney, <u>Style</u> 26).

IV. The GHOST'S IMPORTANCE IN THE STRUCTURE OF THE PLAY

[11]   Shakespeare's great strength as a dramatist is shown not only in his giving the Ghost such a round, full character, but also in his integrating the Ghost fully within the play's structure. According to Peter Alexander, the Ghost is "indispensable" in the plot as the source of communication to set things in motion (29). He is also a director and organizer as well as an informer--a figure who keeps the action moving until there is no stopping it (Aldus 100). A careful study of his speeches shows that he is a manipulator, playing upon his son's emotions to make him hurry the act of revenge. In addition, the Ghost is persistent, because his return to Hamlet in Act III, scene 4, to "whet thy almost blunted purpose" (line 111) is the mark of a manager who nervously intervenes when his directions are being neglected or delayed.

[12]   The Ghost is also significant as a part of one of the major structures of the play. During the imagined period when the events at Elsinore are taking place, Denmark is undergoing a national mobilization in preparation for war against Norway (Alexander 34). Structurally, the beginning and ending of Hamlet are marked by the fear of war and the political takeover by "Young Fortinbras" of Norway. Young Fortinbras is like Hamlet because King Hamlet, now the Ghost, had killed Old Fortinbras in single combat. Young Fortinbras is therefore as much an avenger as Hamlet (Honan 283), and the cause was King Hamlet, who now as a Ghost is prompting Hamlet to revenge. So strong is the Ghost's anger against Claudius that he insists on revenge even if it means the destabilization of his country in the face of impending war. Ironically, the Ghost in death is aiding in the fall of the kingdom he courageously defended in life.

[13]   There is an additional major structure involving the Ghost. Maurice Charney observes that the Ghost is significant in the "symmetrical" poison plots in the play (Style 39). The first of these plots, the poisoning of King Hamlet, is described by the Ghost himself in Act I, scene 5. The poisoning of the player king in Act III, scene 2, is a reenactment of the first murder, and it occurs in approximately the middle of the action. The final poisonings--of Gertrude, Laertes, Claudius, and finally Hamlet himself--occur in Act V, scene 2, the play's last scene. These actions have value as symbolic frames that measure the deterioration of the play's major characters.

V. THE GHOST'S EFFECT

[14]   Beyond the Ghost's practical and structural importance in the action, he has profound psychological influence, mainly negative, on the characters. Roy Walker describes him as a "prologue" to the "omen" of Hamlet himself, who is the agent of the "dread purpose" of vengeance (220). Because Hamlet is already suffering depression and melancholia, this murderous mission opens the wounds of his vulnerability (Campbell 127–28). Literally, Hamlet must give up everything he has ever learned, even "the movement of existence itself," so that he can carry out the Ghost's commandment (McFarland 32–33). In an invasive, overpowering manner, Hamlet's melancholy influences his love for Ophelia, his possible friendship with Laertes, and his relationship with his mother (Kott 49; Kirsch

31). No one escapes. The effects are like waves radiating outwardly, with the Ghost at the center as a relentless, destructive force. As Harold Bloom states, "everything in the play depends upon Hamlet's response to the Ghost" (387).

[15]   <u>This overwhelming ghostly force possesses Hamlet once the first encounter has occurred.</u> This possession is shown both literally and figuratively when the Ghost goes underground in Act I, scene 5, and hears Hamlet's conversation with Horatio and the guards. The Ghost thus represents "dimensions of reality" beyond what we see on the stage, a mysterious world "elsewhere" that dominates the very souls of living persons (Charney, "Asides" 127). As a result of this ever-present force, which as far as Hamlet is concerned might become visible at any moment, Hamlet is denied the healing that might normally occur after the death of a parent (Kirsch 26). The steady pressure to kill Claudius disrupts any movement to mental health and creates what Kirsch calls a "pathology of depression" (26) that inhibits Hamlet's actions (Bradley 123), causes his Oedipal preoccupation with the sexuality of his parents (Kirsch 22), and brings about his desire for the oblivion that suicide might bring (Kirsch 27).

[16]   <u>It is, finally, this power over his son that gives the Ghost the greatest influence in the play.</u> Once the Ghost has appeared, Hamlet can never be the same. He loses the dignity and composure that he has assumed as his right as a prince of Denmark and as a student in quest of knowledge (McFarland 38). The Ghost's commands make it impossible for Hamlet to solve problems through negotiation-- the way he might have chosen as prince and student. The commands force him instead into a plan requiring murder. What could be more normal than hesitation under such circumstances? Despite all Hamlet's reflections, however, the web of vengeance woven by the Ghost finally closes in on all those caught in it, both the deserving and undeserving. There is no solution but the final one--real death, which is the literal conclusion of the symbolic death represented by the Ghost when he first appears on the Elsinore battlements.

VI. CONCLUSION

[17]   The Ghost is real in terms of the play's action and structure. He is seen by the characters on the stage, and when he speaks we hear him. He is made round and full by Shakespeare, and his motivation is direct and clear, even though the signs of his status as a spirit are presented ambiguously. <u>But the Ghost is more.</u> He has been made a Ghost by the greed and envy of Claudius, and in this respect he becomes in the play either a conscious or an unwitting agent of the "unseen Fates or forces" of his own doom (Walker 220). What he brings is the unavoidable horror that seems somehow to be just beneath the surface of good, moral people, waiting for the chance to reach out and destroy. Once the forces are released, there is no holding them, and the tragedy is that there is no way to win against these odds.

WORKS CITED

Aldus, P. J. Mousetrap: Structure and Meaning in Hamlet. Toronto: U of Toronto P, 1977.

Alexander, Peter. Hamlet: Father and Son. Oxford: Clarendon, 1955.

Austin, Norman. "Hamlet's Hungry Ghost." Shenandoah 37.1 (1987): 78–105.

Bloom, Harold. Shakespeare: The Invention of the Human. New York: Riverhead, 1998.

Bradley, A. C. Shakespearean Tragedy. 1904. London: Macmillan, 1950.

Campbell, Lily B. Shakespeare's Tragic Heroes: Slaves of Passion. New York: Barnes & Noble, 1959.

Charney, Maurice. "Asides, Soliloquies, and Offstage Speech in Hamlet." Shakespeare and the Sense of Performance: Essays in the Tradition of Performance Criticism in Honor of Bernard Beckerman. Ed. Marvin and Ruth Thompson. Newark: U of Delaware P, 1989. 116–31.

---. Style in Hamlet. Princeton: Princeton UP, 1969.

DeLuca, Diana Macintyre. "The Movements of the Ghost in Hamlet." Shakespeare Quarterly 24 (1973): 147–54.

Edgar, Irving I. Shakespeare, Medicine, and Psychiatry. New York, Philosophical Library, 1970.

Fisch, Harold. Hamlet and the Word. New York: Ungar, 1971.

Frye, Roland Mushat. The Renaissance Hamlet: Issues and Responses in 1600. Princeton: Princeton UP, 1984.

Garber, Marjorie. "*Hamlet*: Giving Up the Ghost." William Shakespeare: Hamlet. Ed. Suzanne L. Wofford. Boston: Bedford, 1994: 297-331.

Gottschalk, Paul. "Hamlet and the Scanning of Revenge." Shakespeare Quarterly 24 (1973): 155–70.

Harrison, G. B., ed. Shakespeare: The Complete Works. 1948. New York: Harcourt, 1968.

Honan, Park. Shakespeare: A Life. Oxford: Oxford UP, 1998.

Jones, Ernest. Hamlet and Oedipus. 1949. New York: Doubleday, 1954.

Kerrigan, William. Hamlet's Perfection. Baltimore: Johns Hopkins UP, 1994.

Kirsch, Arthur. "Hamlet's Grief." ELH 48 (1981): 17–36.

Kott, Jan. Shakespeare, Our Contemporary. Trans. Boleslaw Taborski. 1967. London: Methuen, 1970.

McFarland, Thomas. Tragic Meanings in Shakespeare. New York: Random House, 1966.

O'Meara, John. "Hamlet and the Fortunes of Sorrowful Imagination: A Re-examination of the Genesis and Fate of the Ghost." Cahiers Élisabéthains 35 (1989): 15–25.

Paris, Jean. <u>Shakespeare</u>. Trans. Richard Seaver. New York: Grove, 1960.

Prosser, Eleanor. <u>Hamlet and Revenge</u>. 2nd ed. Stanford: Stanford UP, 1971.

Walker, Roy. "<u>Hamlet</u>: the Opening Scene." <u>Shakespeare: Modern Essays in Criticism</u>. Ed. Leonard F. Dean. New York: Oxford UP, 1961.

Commentary on the Essay

This essay illustrates an assignment requiring about twenty-five sources and about 2,500 words. The sources were located through an examination of library catalogues, the *MLA Bibliography,* library bookshelves, the Internet, and the bibliographies in some of the listed books. They represent the range of materials available in a college library with a selective, not exhaustive, set of holdings. Two of the sources (Austin and O'Meara) were obtained through interlibrary loan.

The writing itself is developed from the sources listed. Originality (see p. 1937) is provided by the structure and development of the essay, additional observations not existing in the sources, and transitions. The topic outline is placed appropriately at the beginning—a pattern you can follow unless your instructor asks for a more detailed outline, or, perhaps, for no outline at all.

Because the essay is concerned with only one work—and one subject about that work—it demonstrates approach 1 (p. 1926). The essay is eclectic, introducing discussions of ideas, character, style, and structure. These four topics fulfill the goal of covering the ground thoroughly, within the confines of the assignment. A shorter research assignment might deal with no more than, say, the Ghost's character, ignoring other topics. On the other hand, a longer essay might deal further with the philosophical and theological meanings of ghosts during the Elizabethan period, or a more detailed study of all the traits of the Ghost's character, and so on.

The central idea of the essay is stressed in paragraph 1, along with an assertion that the Ghost is a major influence in the play, together with a concession that the Ghost is only a minor character in the action. The research for this paragraph is derived primarily from a close reading of the play itself. Paragraph 2, continuing the exploration of the central idea, demonstrates that the Ghost figures in the major themes of *Hamlet.* Paragraph 3 is mainly functional, being used as the location of the thesis sentence.

Part II, containing paragraphs 4–6, deals with the Ghost's status as a spirit. Part III, with paragraphs 7–10, is concerned with the Ghost's human rather than spiritual characteristics. Part IV, with paragraphs 11–13, deals with the significance of the Ghost in the major structures that dominate the play. Part V, with three paragraphs, considers the Ghost's negative and inexorable influence over the major figures of *Hamlet,* the emphasis being the character of Hamlet as the transferring agent of the Ghost's destructive revenge. The concluding paragraph (17) sums up the essay with the final idea of how the Ghost affects the tragic nature of *Hamlet.*

The list of works cited is the basis of all parenthetical references in the essay, in accordance with the *MLA Handbook for Writers of Research Papers,* 5th ed. Using these references, an interested reader can consult the sources for a more detailed development of the ideas in the essay. The works cited can also serve as a springboard for expanded research.

33

Critical Approaches Important in the Study of Literature

A number of critical theories or approaches for understanding and interpreting literature are available to critics and students alike. Many of these were developed during the last hundred years to create a discipline of literary studies comparable with disciplines in the natural and social sciences. Literary critics have often borrowed liberally from other disciplines (e.g., history, psychology, anthropology) but have primarily aimed at developing literature as a study in its own right.

At the heart of the various critical approaches are many fundamental questions: What is literature? What does it do? Is its concern only to tell stories, or is it to express emotions? Is it private? Public? How does it get its ideas across? What more does it do than express ideas? How valuable was literature in the past, and how valuable is it now? What can it contribute to intellectual, artistic, and social history? To what degree is literature an art, as opposed to an instrument for imparting knowledge? How is literature used, and how and why is it misused? What theoretical and technical expertise may be invoked to enhance literary studies?

Questions such as these indicate that criticism is concerned not only with reading and interpreting stories, poems, and plays but also with establishing theoretical understanding. Because of such extensive aims, you will realize that a full explanation and illustration of the approaches would fill the pages of a long book. The following descriptions are therefore intended as no more than brief introductions. Bear in mind that in the hands of skilled critics, some of the approaches are so subtle, sophisticated, and complex that they are not only critical stances but also philosophies.

Although the various approaches provide divergent ways to study literature and literary problems, they reflect major tendencies rather than absolute straitjacketing. Not every approach is appropriate for every work, nor are the approaches always mutually exclusive. Even the most devoted practitioners of the methods do not pursue them rigidly. In addition, some of the approaches are more "user-friendly" than others for certain types of discovery. To a degree at least, most critics therefore take a particular approach but utilize methods that technically belong to one or more of the other approaches. A critic stressing the topical/historical approach, for example, might introduce the close study of a work that is associated with the method of the New Criticism. Similarly, a psychoanalytical critic might include details about archetypes. In short, a great deal of criticism is *pragmatic* or *eclectic* rather than rigid.

The approaches to be considered here are these: moral/intellectual, topical/historical, New Critical/formalist, structuralist, feminist, economic determinist/Marxist, psychological/psychoanalytic, archetypal/symbolic/ mythic, deconstructionist, and reader-response.

The object of learning about these approaches, like everything else in this book, is to help you develop your own reading and writing. Accordingly, following each of the descriptions is a brief paragraph showing how Hawthorne's story "Young Goodman Brown" (pp. 436–45) might be considered in the light of the particular approach. The paragraph following the discussion of structuralism, for example, shows how the structuralist approach can be applied to Goodman Brown and his story, and so also with the feminist approach, the economic determinist approach, and the others. Whenever you are doing your own writing about literature, you are free to use the various approaches as part or all of your assignment, if you believe the approach may help you.

(Victorians)?
Victorians - interested in
the moral value of
literature,
(Fighting fair, taking
care of the weak)

MORAL/INTELLECTUAL

The **moral/intellectual critical approach** is concerned with both content and values (see also Chapter 7). The approach is as old as literature itself, for literature is a traditional mode of imparting morality, philosophy, and religion. The concern in moral/intellectual criticism is not only to discover the meaning but also to determine whether works of literature are *true* and *significant* in addition.

To study literature from the moral/intellectual perspective is therefore to determine whether a work conveys a lesson or a message and whether it can help readers lead better lives and improve their understanding of the world: What ideas does the work contain? How strongly does the work bring forth its ideas? What application do the ideas have to the work's characters and situations? How can the ideas be evaluated intellectually? Morally? Discussions based on such questions do not imply that literature is primarily a medium of moral and intellectual exhortation. Ideally, moral/intellectual criticism should differ from sermonizing to the degree that readers should always be left with their own decisions about whether they wish to assimilate the content of a work and about whether this content is personally or morally acceptable.

Sophisticated critics have sometimes demeaned the moral/intellectual approach on the grounds that "message hunting" reduces a work's artistic value by treating it like a sermon or political speech; but the approach will be valuable as long as readers expect literature to be applicable to their own lives.

EXAMPLE

is amoral story, *written in the 1850's.*

"Young Goodman Brown" raises the issue of how an institution designed for human elevation, such as the religious system of colonial Salem, can be so *inmoralistic* ruinous. Does the failure result from the system itself or from the people who misunderstand it? Is what is true of religion as practiced by Brown also true of social and political institutions? Should any religious or political philosophy be given greater credence than good will and mutual trust? One of the major virtues of "Young Goodman Brown" is that it provokes questions like these but at the same time provides a number of satisfying answers. A particularly important one is that religious and moral beliefs should not be used to justify the condemnation of others. Another important answer is that attacks made from the refuge of a religion or group, such as Brown's puritanical judgment, are dangerous because the refuge enables the judge to condemn without thought and without personal responsibility.

TOPICAL/HISTORICAL

The traditional **topical/historical critical approach** stresses the relationship of literature to its historical period, and for this reason it has had a long life. Although much literature may be applicable to many places and times, much of it also directly reflects the intellectual and social worlds of the authors. When was the work written? What were the circumstances that produced it? What major issues does it deal with? How does it fit into the author's career? Keats's poem "On First Looking into Chapman's Homer" (p.777) for example, is his excited response to his reading of one of the major literary works of Western civilization. Hardy's "Channel Firing" (p. 703) is an acerbic response to continued armament and preparation for war during the last century.

The topical/historical approach investigates relationships of this sort, including the elucidation of words and concepts that today's readers may not immediately understand. Obviously, the approach requires the assistance of footnotes, dictionaries, library catalogues, histories, and handbooks.

A common criticism of the topical/historical approach is that in the extreme, it deals with background knowledge rather than with literature itself. It is possible, for example, for a topical/historical critic to describe a writer's life, the period of the writer's work, and the social and intellectual ideas of the time—all without ever considering the meaning, importance, and value of the work itself.

A reaction against such an unconnected use of historical details is the so-called New Historicism. This approach justifies the introduction of historical knowledge by integrating it with the understanding of particular texts. Readers of Arnold's "Dover Beach" (p. 693), for example, sometimes find it difficult fully to comprehend Arnold's statement "The Sea of Faith / Was once, too, at the full, . . ." If knowledge of the "Higher Criticism" of the Bible can be introduced, however, as a method established in Arnold's time, by which the Bible was considered as a historical document rather than the absolute uncontaminated word of God, then the sense of his idea can be clarified. Because the introduction of such historical material is designed to facilitate the reading of the poem—and also the reading of other literature of the period—the New Historicism represents an integration of knowledge and interpretation. As a principle, New Historicism entails the acquisition of as much historical information as possible, because our knowledge of the relationship of literature to its historical period can never be complete. The practitioner of New Historicism must always seek new information that will be relevant to literary works.

EXAMPLE (Salem witch trials of 1691.)

"Young Goodman Brown" is an allegorical story by Nathaniel Hawthorne (1804–1864), a New England writer who probed deeply into the relationships between religion and guilt. His ancestors had been involved in religious persecutions, including the Salem witch trials, and he, living 150 years afterward, wanted to analyze the weaknesses and uncertainties of the sin-dominated religion of the earlier period, a tradition of which he was a resentful heir. Not surprisingly, therefore, "Young Goodman Brown" takes place in Puritan colonial Salem, and Hawthorne's implied judgments are those of a severe critic of how the harsh old religion destroyed personal and family relationships. Although the immediate concerns of the story belong to a vanished age, Hawthorne's treatment is still valuable because it is still timely. historical reading of the story.

NEW CRITICAL/FORMALIST

New Criticism has been a dominant force in twentieth-century literary studies. To the degree that it focuses on literary texts as formal works of art, it departs from the traditional topical/historical approach. The objection raised by New Critics is that as topical/historical critics consider literary history, they evade direct contact with actual texts.

The inspiration for the **New Critical/formalist critical** approach was the French practice of *explication de texte*, a method that emphasizes detailed examination and explanation. The New Criticism is at its most brilliant in the formal analysis of smaller units such as entire poems and short passages. For the analysis of larger structures, the New Criticism also utilizes a number of techniques that form the basis for chapters in this book. Discussions of point of view, tone, plot, character, and structure, for example, are formal ways of looking at literature that are derived from the New Criticism.

The aim of the formalist study of literature is to provide readers not only with the means of explaining the content of works (What, specifically, does a work say?) but also with the insights needed for evaluating the artistic quality of individual works and writers (How well is it said?). A major aspect of New Critical thought is that content and form—including all ideas, ambiguities, subtleties, and even apparent contradictions—were originally within the conscious or subconscious control of the author. There are no accidents. It does not necessarily follow, however, that today's critic is able to define the author's intentions exactly, for such intentions require knowledge of biographical details that are irretrievably lost. Each literary work therefore takes on its own existence and identity, and the critic's work is to discover a reading or readings that explain the facts of the text. Note that the New Critic does not claim infallible interpretations and does not exclude the validity of multiple readings of the same work.

Dissenters from the New Criticism have noted a tendency by New Critics to ignore relevant knowledge that history and biography can bring to literary studies. In addition, the approach has been subject to the charge that stressing the explication of texts alone fails to deal with literary value and appreciation. In other words, the formalist critic, in explaining the meaning of literature, sometimes neglects the reasons for which readers find literature stimulating and valuable.

EXAMPLE

A major aspect of Hawthorne's "Young Goodman Brown" is that the details are so vague and dreamlike that many readers are uncertain about what is happening. The action is a nighttime walk by the protagonist, Young Goodman Brown, into a deep forest where he encounters a mysterious satanic ritual that leaves him bitter and misanthropic. This much seems clear, but the precise nature of Brown's experience is not clear, nor is the identity of the stranger (father, village elder, devil) who accompanies Brown as he begins his walk. At the story's end Hawthorne's narrator states that the whole episode may have been no more than a dream or nightmare. Yet when morning comes, Brown walks back into town as though returning from an overnight trip, and he recoils in horror from his fellow villagers, including his wife Faith (paragraph 70). Could his attitude result from nothing more than a nightmare?

Even at the story's end these uncertainties remain. For this reason one may conclude that Hawthorne deliberately creates the uncertainties to reveal how persons like Brown build defensive walls of judgment around themselves. The story thus implies that the real source of Brown's anger is as vague as his nocturnal walk, but he doesn't understand it in this way. Because Brown's vision and judgment are absolute, he rejects everyone around him, even if the cost is a life of bitter suspicion and spiritual isolation.

STRUCTURALIST

The principle of structuralism stems from the attempt to find relationships and connections among elements that appear to be separate and discrete. Just as physical science reveals unifying universal principles of matter such as gravity and the forces of electromagnetism (and is constantly searching for a "unified field theory"), the **structuralist critical approach** attempts to discover the forms unifying all literature. Thus a structural description of Maupassant's "The Necklace" (pp. 4–11) stresses that the main character, Mathilde, is an *active* protagonist who undergoes a *test* (or series of tests) and emerges with a victory, though not the kind she had originally hoped for. The same might be said of Mrs. Popov and Smirnov in Chekhov's *The Bear* (pp. 1625–34). If this same kind of structural view is applied to Bierce's "An Occurrence at Owl Creek Bridge" (pp. 257-63), the protagonist is defeated in the test. Generally, the structural approach applies such patterns to other works of literature to determine that certain protagonists are active or submissive, that they pass or fail their tests, or that they succeed or fail at other encounters. The key is that many apparently unrelated works reveal many common patterns or contain similar structures with important variations.

The structural approach is important because it enables critics to discuss works from widely separate cultures and historical periods. In this respect, critics have followed the leads of modern anthropologists, most notably Claude Lévi-Strauss (1908–1990). Along such lines, critics have undertaken the serious examination of folk and fairy tales. Some of the groundbreaking structuralist criticism, for example, was devoted to the structural principles underlying folktales of Russia. The method also bridges popular and serious literature, making little distinction between the two insofar as the description of the structures is concerned. Indeed, structuralism furnishes an ideal approach for comparative literature, and the method also enables critics to consolidate genres such as modern romances, detective tales, soap operas, and film.

Like the New Criticism, structuralism aims at comprehensiveness of description, and many critics would insist that the two are complementary and not separate. A distinction is that the New Criticism is at its best in dealing with smaller units of literature, whereas structuralism is best in the analysis of narratives and therefore larger units such as novels, myths, and stories. Because structuralism shows how fiction is organized into various typical situations, the approach merges with the archetypal approach, and at times it is difficult to find any distinctions between structuralism and archetypalism.

Structuralism, however, deals not just with narrative structures but also with structures of any type, wherever they occur. For example, structuralism makes great use of linguistics. Modern linguistic scholars have determined that there is a difference between "deep structures" and "surface structures" in language. A structuralist analysis of style, therefore, emphasizes how writers utilize such structures. The structuralist interpretation of language also perceives distinguishing types or "grammars" of language that are recurrent in various types of literature. Suppose, for example, that you encounter opening passages like the following:

> Once upon a time a young prince fell in love with a young princess. He decided to tell her of his love, and early one morning he left his castle on his white charger, riding toward her castle home high in the mountains.

> Early that morning, Alan had found himself thinking about Anne. He had believed her when she said she loved him, but his feelings about her were not certain, and his thinking had left him still unsure.

The words of these two passages create different and distinct frames of reference. One is a fairy tale of the past, the other a modern internalized reflection of feeling. The passages therefore demonstrate how language itself fits into predetermined patterns or structures. Similar uses of language structures can be associated with other types of literature.

EXAMPLE

> Young Goodman Brown is a hero who is passive, not active. He is a *witness*, a *receiver* rather than a *doer*. His only action—taking his trip in the forest—occurs at the story's beginning. After that point, he no longer acts but instead is acted upon, and what he sees puts his life's beliefs to a test. Of course, many protagonists undergo similar testing (such as rescuing victims and slaying particularly terrible dragons), and they emerge triumphant. Not so with Goodman Brown. He is a responder who allows himself to be victimized by his own perceptions—or misperceptions. Despite all his previous experiences with his wife and with the good people of his village, he generalizes too hastily. He lets the single disillusioning experience of his nightmare govern his entire outlook on others, and thus he fails his test and turns his entire life into failure.

FEMINIST

The **feminist critical approach** holds that most of our literature presents a masculine-patriarchal view in which the role of women is negated or at best minimized. As an adjunct of the feminist movement in politics, the feminist critique of literature seeks to raise consciousness about the importance and unique nature of women in literature.

Specifically, the feminist view attempts (1) to show that writers of traditional literature have ignored women and have also transmitted misguided and prejudiced views of them, (2) to stimulate the creation of a critical milieu that reflects a balanced view of the nature and value of women, (3) to recover the works of women writers of past times and to encourage the publication of present women writers so that the literary canon can be expanded to recognize women as thinkers and artists, and (4) to urge transformations in the language so as to eliminate inequities and inequalities that result from linguistic distortions.

In form, the feminist perspective requires the evaluation of literary works from the standpoint of the presentation of women. For works such as "The Necklace" (story), "Patterns" (poem, pp. 1174–76), and *The Bear* (play), a feminist critique focuses on how such works treat women and also on either the shortcomings or enlightenment of the author as a result of this treatment: How important are the female characters, how individual in their own right? Are they credited with their own existence and their own character? In their relationships with men, how are they treated? Are they given equal status? Ignored? Patronized? Demeaned? Pedestalized? How much interest do the male characters exhibit about women's concerns?   *Seneca falls meeting,*

EXAMPLE

> At the beginning of "Young Goodman Brown," Brown's wife, Faith, is only peripheral. In the traditional patriarchal spirit of wife-as-adjunct, she asks her husband to stay at home and take his journey at another time. Hawthorne does not give her the intelligence or dignity, however, to let her explain her concern (or might he not have been interested in what she had to say?), and she therefore remains in the background with her pink hair ribbon as her distinguishing characteristic. During the mid-forest satanic ritual she appears again and is given power, but only the power to cause her husband to go astray. Once she is led in as a novice in the practice of demonism, her husband falls right in step. Unfortunately, by following her, Brown can conveniently excuse himself from guilt by claiming that "she" had made him do it, just as Eve, in some traditional views of the fall of humankind, compelled Adam to eat the apple (Genesis 3:16–17). Hawthorne's attention to the male hero, in other words, permits him to distort the female's role.

ECONOMIC DETERMINIST/MARXIST   *money matters*

The concept of cultural and economic determinism is one of the major political ideas of the nineteenth century. Karl Marx (1818–1883) emphasized that the primary influence on life was economic, and he saw society as an opposition between the capitalist and working classes. The literature that emerged from this kind of analysis features individuals in the grips of the class struggle. Often called "proletarian literature," it emphasizes persons of the lower class—the poor and oppressed who spend their lives in endless drudgery and misery, and whose attempts to rise above their disadvantages usually result in renewed suppression.

Marx's political ideas were never widely accepted in the United States and have faded still more after the political breakup of the Soviet Union, but the idea of economic determinism (and the related term *Social Darwinism*) is still credible. As a result, much literature can be judged from an economic perspective: What is the economic status of the characters? What happens to them as a result of this status? How do they fare against economic and political odds?

What other conditions stemming from their class does the writer emphasize (e.g., poor education, poor nutrition, poor health care, inadequate opportunity)? To what extent does the work fail by overlooking the economic, social, and political implications of its material? In what other ways does economic determinism affect the work? How should readers consider the story in today's developed or underdeveloped world? Seemingly, Hawthorne's story "Young Goodman Brown," which we have used for analysis in these discussions, has no economic implications, but an **economic determinist/Marxist critical approach** might take the following turns:

"Young Goodman Brown" overlooks economic implication marixs story.

EXAMPLE

"Young Goodman Brown" is a fine story just as it is. It deals with the false values instilled by the skewed acceptance of sin-dominated religion, but it overlooks the economic implications of this situation. One suspects that the real story in the little world of Goodman Brown's Salem should be about survival and the disruption that an alienated member of society can produce. After Brown's condemnation and distrust of others forces him into his own shell of sick imagination, Hawthorne does not consider how such a disaffected character would injure the economic and public life of the town. Consider this, just for a moment: Why would the people from whom Brown recoils in disgust want to deal with him in business or personal matters? In town meetings, would they want to follow his opinions on crucial issues of public concern and investment? Would his preoccupation with sin and damnation make him anything more than a horror in his domestic life? Would his wife, Faith, be able to discuss household management with him, or how to take care of the children? All these questions of course are pointed toward another story—a story that Hawthorne did not write. They also indicate the shortcomings of Hawthorne's approach, because it is clear that the major result of Young Goodman Brown's selfish preoccupation with evil would be a serious disruption of the economic and political affairs of his small community.

Does not work from marxs point of view.

PSYCHOLOGICAL/PSYCHOANALYTIC

The scientific study of the mind is a product of psychodynamic theory as established by Sigmund Freud (1856–1939) and of the psychoanalytic method practiced by his followers. Psychoanalysis provided a new key to the understanding of character by claiming that behavior is caused by hidden and unconscious motives. It was greeted as a virtual revelation, and not surprisingly it had a profound effect on modern literature.

In addition, its popularity produced a **psychological/psychoanalytic approach** to criticism.[1] Some critics use the approach to explain fictional characters, as in the landmark interpretation by Freud and Ernest Jones that Shakespeare's Hamlet suffers from an Oedipus complex. Still other critics use it

---

[1] See also Chapter 4, "Characters: The People in Fiction".

successful initiation, Brown's initiation leads him into failure. In the private areas of life on which happiness depends, he falls short. He sees evil in his fellow villagers, condemns his minister, and shrinks even from his own family. His life is one of despair and gloom. His suspicions are those of a Puritan of long ago, but the timeliness of Hawthorne's story is that the archetype of misunderstanding and condemnation has not changed. Today's headlines of misery and war are produced by the same kind of intolerance that is exhibited by Goodman Brown.

DECONSTRUCTIONIST

The **deconstructionist critical approach**—which deconstructionists explain not as an approach but rather as a performance—was developed by the French critic Jacques Derrida (b. 1930). In the 1970s and 1980s it became a major but also controversial mode of criticism. As a literary theory, deconstructionism produces a type of analysis that stresses ambiguity and contradiction.

A major principle of deconstructionism is that Western thought has been *logocentric*; that is, Western philosophers have based their ideas on the assumption that central truth is knowable and entire (this view is incorrect, according to a deconstructionist). The deconstructionist view is instead that there is no central truth because circumstances and time, which are changeable and sometimes arbitrary, govern the world of the intellect. This analysis leads to the declaration "All interpretation is misinterpretation." That is, literary works cannot be encapsulated as organically unified entireties, and therefore there is not *one correct interpretation* but only *interpretations,* each one possessing its own validity.

In "deconstructing" a work, therefore, the deconstructionist critic raises questions about what other critics have claimed about the work: Is a poem accepted as a model of classicism? Then it also exhibits qualities of romanticism. Is a story about a young Native American's flight from school commonly taken as a criticism of modern urban life? Then it may also be taken as a story of the failure of youth. In carrying out such criticism, deconstructionist critics place heavy emphasis on the ideas contained in terms such as *ambivalence, discrepancy, enigma, uncertainty, delusion, indecision,* and *lack of resolution,* among others.

The deconstructionist attack on "correct," "privileged," or "accepted" readings is also related to the principle that language, and therefore literature, is unstable. "Linguistic instability" means that the understanding of words can never be exact or comprehensive because there is a never-ending *play* between the words in a text and their many shades of meaning, including possible future meanings. That is, the words do not remain constant and produce a definite meaning but instead call forth the possibility of "infinite substitutions" of meaning. Each work of literature is therefore ambiguous and uncertain because its full meaning is constantly *deferred.* This infinite play or semantic tension renders language unstable and makes correct or accepted readings impossible.

It is fair to state that deconstructionism, among all the literary theories, has received intense criticism that has sometimes bordered on discrediting the theory entirely. A number of critics find that the position is elusive and vague. They grant that literary works are often ambiguous, uncertain, and apparently contradictory, but they explain that the cause of these conditions is not linguistic instability but rather authorial intention. They also point out that the deconstructionist linguistic analysis is derivative, unoriginal, and incorrect. In addition, critics claim that the deconstructionist linguistic position simply does not support deconstructionist assertions about linguistic instability. Critics also draw attention to the contradiction that deconstructionism cannot follow its major premise about there being no "privileged readings" because it must recognize the privileged readings in order to invalidate or "subvert" them.

EXAMPLE

> There are many uncertainties in the details of "Young Goodman Brown." If one starts with the stranger on the path, one might conclude that he could be Brown's father, because he recognizes Brown immediately and speaks to him jovially. On the other hand, the stranger could be the devil (he is recognized as such by Goody Cloyse) because of his wriggling walking stick. After disappearing, the stranger also takes on the characteristics of an omniscient cult leader and seer, because at the satanic celebration he knows all the secret sins committed by Brown's neighbors and the community of greater New England. Additionally, he might represent a perverted conscience whose aim is to mislead and befuddle people by steering them into the holier-than-thou judgmentalism that Brown adopts. This method would be truly diabolical—to use religion in order to bring people to their own damnation. That the stranger is an evil force is therefore clear, but the pathways of his evil are not as clear. He seems to work his mission of damnation by reaching souls like that of Goodman Brown through means ordinarily attributed to conscience. If the stranger represents a satanic conscience, what are we to suppose that Hawthorne is asserting about what is considered real conscience?

READER-RESPONSE

The **reader-response critical approach** is rooted in *phenomenology*, a branch of philosophy that deals with the understanding of how things appear. The phenomenological idea of knowledge is that reality is to be found not in the external world itself but rather in the mental *perception* of externals. That is, all that we human beings can know—actual *knowledge*—is our collective and personal understanding of the world and our conclusions about it.

As a consequence of the phenomenological concept, reader-response theory holds that the reader is a necessary third party in the author-text-reader relationship that constitutes the literary work. The work, in other words, is not fully created until readers make a *transaction* with it by assimilating it and *actualizing* it in the light of their own knowledge and experience. The representative questions of the theory are these: What does this work mean to me, in my present intellectual and moral makeup? What particular aspects of my life can help me understand and appreciate the work? How can the work improve my understanding and widen my insights? How can my increasing understanding help me understand the work more deeply? The theory is that the free interchange or transaction that such questions bring about leads toward interest and growth so that readers can assimilate literary works and accept them as part of their lives.

As an initial way of reading, the reader-response method may be personal and anecdotal. In addition, by stressing response rather than interpretation, one of the leading exponents of the method (Stanley Fish) has raised the extreme question about whether texts, by themselves, have objective identity. These aspects have been cited as both a shortcoming and an inconsequentiality of the method.

It is therefore important to stress that the reader-response theory is *open.* It permits beginning readers to bring their own personal reactions to literature, but it also aims to increase the discipline and skills of readers. The more that readers bring to literature through their interests and disciplined studies, the more "competent" and comprehensive their responses will be. With cumulative experience, the disciplined reader will habitually adjust to new works and respond to them with increasing skill. If the works require special knowledge in fields such as art, politics, science, philosophy, religion, or morality, then competent readers will seek out such knowledge and utilize it in developing their responses. Also, because students experience many similar intellectual and cultural disciplines, it is logical to conclude that responses will tend not to diverge but rather to coalesce; agreements result not from personal but from cultural similarities. The reader-response theory, then, can and should be an avenue toward informed and detailed understanding of literature, but the initial emphasis is the *transaction* between readers and literary works.

EXAMPLE

"Young Goodman Brown" is worrisome because it shows so disturbingly that good intentions may cause harmful results. I think that a person with too high a set of expectations is ripe for disillusionment, just as Goodman Brown is. When people don't measure up to this person's standard of perfection, they can be thrown aside as though they are worthless. They may be good, but their past mistakes make it impossible for the person with high expectations to endure them. I have seen this situation occur among some of my friends and acquaintances, particularly in romantic relationships. Goodman Brown makes the same kind of misjudgment, expecting perfection and turning sour when he learns about flaws. It is not that he is not a good man, because he is shown at the start as a person of belief and stability. He uncritically accepts his nightmare revelation that everyone else is evil, however (including his parents), and he finally distrusts everyone because of this baseless suspicion. He cannot look at his neighbors without avoiding them like an "anathema," and he turns away from his own wife "without a greeting" (paragraph 70). Brown's problem is that he equates being human with being unworthy. By such a distorted standard of judgment all of us fail, and that is what makes the story so disturbing.

Taking Examinations on Literature

Succeeding on a literature examination is largely a result of intelligent and skill-ful preparation. Preparing means (1) studying the material assigned, in con-junction with the comments made in class by your instructor and by fellow students in discussion; (2) developing and reinforcing your own thoughts; (3) anticipating exam questions by creating and answering your own practice ques-tions; and (4) understanding the precise function of the test in your education.

First, realize that the test is not designed either to trap you or to hold down your grade. The grade you receive is a reflection of your achievement in the course. If your grades are low, you can improve them by studying diligently and systematically. Those students who can easily do satisfactory work might do supe-rior work if they improved their habits of preparation. From whatever level you begin, you can increase your achievement by improving your study methods.

Your instructor has three major concerns in evaluating your tests (assum-ing the correct use of English): (1) to assess the extent of your command over the subject material of the course (How good is your retention?); (2) to assess how well you respond to a question or deal with an issue (How well do you sep-arate the important from the unimportant?); and (3) to assess how well you draw conclusions about the material (How well are you educating yourself?).

FOCUSING DIRECTLY ON THE QUESTIONS ASKED

Many elements go into writing good answers on tests, but responsiveness is the most important. A major cause of low exam grades is that students really do not *answer* the questions asked. Does that failure seem surprising? The prob-lem is that some students do no more than retell a story or restate an argument; they never confront the issues in the question. This common problem has been treated throughout this book. Therefore, if you are asked, "Why does . . . ," be sure to emphasize the *why* and to use the *does* only to exemplify the *why*. If the question is about *organization*, focus on organization. If a *problem* has been raised, deal with the problem. In short, always *respond directly* to the question or instruction. Compare the following two answers to the same question:

Question: How is the setting of Bierce's "An Occurrence at Owl Creek Bridge" important in the story's development?

ANSWER A

The setting of Bierce's "An Occurrence at Owl Creek Bridge" is a major element in the development of the story. The first scene is on a railroad bridge in northern Alabama, and the action is that a man, Peyton Farquhar, is about to be hanged. He is a southerner who has been surrounded and captured by Union soldiers. They are ready to string him up and they have the guns and power, so he cannot escape. He is so scared that his own watch seems to sound loudly and slowly like a cannon. He also thinks about how he might escape once he is hanged, by freeing his hands and throwing off the noose that will be choking and killing him. The scene shifts to the week before, at Farquhar's plantation. A Union spy deceives Farquhar, thereby tempting him to try to sabotage the Union efforts to keep the railroad open. Because the spy tells Farquhar about the punishment, the reader assumes that Farquhar had tried the sabotage, was caught, and now is going to be hanged. The third scene is also at the bridge, but it is about what Farquhar sees and thinks in his own mind: He imagines that he has been hanged and then escapes. He thinks he falls into the creek, frees himself from the ropes, and makes it to shore, from which he makes the long walk home. His final thoughts are of his wife coming out of the house to meet him, with everything looking beautiful in the morning sunshine. Then we find out that all this was just in his mind, because we are back on the bridge, from which Farquhar is swinging, hanged, dead, with a broken neck.

ANSWER B

The setting of Bierce's "An Occurrence at Owl Creek Bridge" is a major element in the development of the story. The railroad bridge in northern Alabama, from which the doomed Peyton Farquhar will be hanged, is a frame for the story. The bridge, which begins as the real-life bridge in the first scene, becomes the bridge that the dying man imagines in the third. In between there is a brief scene at Farquhar's home, which took place a week before. The setting thus marks the progression of Farquhar's dying vision. He begins to distort and slow down reality—at the real bridge— when he realizes that there is no escape. The first indication of this distortion is that his watch seems to be ticking as slowly as a blacksmith's hammer. Once he is dropped from the bridge to be hanged, his perceptions slow down time so much that he imagines his complete escape before his death: falling into the water, freeing himself, being shot at, getting to shore, walking through a darkening forest, and returning home in beautiful morning sunshine. The final sentence brutally restores the real setting of the railroad bridge and makes clear that Farquhar is actually dead despite his imaginings. In all respects, therefore, the setting is essential to the story's development.

Answer A begins well and introduces important details of the story's setting, but it does not address the question because it does not show how the details figure into the story's development. On the other hand, answer B focuses directly on the connection between the locations and the changes in the protagonist's perceptions. Because of this emphasis, B is shorter than A; with the focus directly on the issue, there is no need for irrelevant narrative details. Thus, A is unresponsive and unnecessarily long, whereas B is responsive and includes details only if they exemplify the major points.

SYSTEMATIC PREPARATION

Your challenge is how best to prepare yourself to have a knowledgeable and ready mind at examination time. If you simply cram facts into your head for the test in the hope that you can adjust to the questions, you will likely flounder. You need a systematic approach.

Read and Reread the Material on Which You Are to Be Examined

Above all, recognize that your preparation should begin as soon as the course begins, not on the night before the exam. Complete each assignment by the date it is due, for you will understand the classroom discussion only if you know the material (see also the guides for study in Chapter 1, pp. 12–13). Then, about a week before the exam, review each assignment, preferably rereading everything completely. With this preparation, your study on the night before the exam will be fruitful and might be viewed as a climax of preparation, not the entire preparation.

Construct Your Own Questions: Go on the Attack

To prepare yourself fully for an exam, read *actively*, not passively. Read with a goal, and *go on the attack* by anticipating test conditions—creating and answering your own practice questions. Don't waste time trying to guess the questions you think your instructor might ask. Guessing correctly might happen (and wouldn't you be happy if it did?), but do not turn your study into a game of chance. Instead, arrange the subject matter by asking yourself questions that help you get things straight.

How can you construct your own questions? It is not as hard as you might think. Your instructor may have announced certain topics or ideas to be tested on the exam, and you might develop questions from these, or you might apply general questions to the specifics of your assignments, as in the following examples:

1. *Ideas about a character and the interactions of characters* (see also Chapter 4). What is *A* like? How does *A* grow or change in the work? What does *A* learn or not learn that brings about the conclusion? To what degree does *A* represent a type or an idea? How does *B* influence *A*? Does a change in *C* bring about any corresponding change in *A*?

2. *Ideas about technical and structural questions.* These can be broad, covering everything from *point of view* (Chapter 5) to prosody and rhyme (Chapter 19). The best guide here is to study those technical aspects that have been discussed in class, for it is unlikely that you will be asked to go beyond the levels considered in classroom discussion.

3. *Ideas about events or situations.* What relationship does episode *A* have to situation *B*? Does *C's* thinking about situation *D* have any influence on the outcome of event *E*?

4. *Ideas about a problem* (see also Chapter 27, pp. 1524–30). Why is character *A* or situation *X* this way and not that way? Is the conclusion justified by the ideas and events leading up to it?

Rephrase Your Notes as Questions

One of the best ways to construct questions is to adapt your classroom notes because notes are the fullest record you have about your instructor's views. As you work with your notes, refer to passages from the text that were studied by the class or stressed by your instructor. If there is time, memorize as many important phrases or lines as you can. Plan to incorporate these into your answers as evidence to support the points you make. Remember that it is useful to work not only with main ideas from your notes but also with matters such as style, imagery, and organization.

Obviously, you cannot make questions from all your notes, and you will therefore need to select from those that seem most important. As an example, here is a short note from a classroom discussion of Shakespeare's *Hamlet*: "In a major respect, a study in how private problems get public, how a court conspiracy can produce disastrous national and even international consequences." Notice how you can devise practice questions from this note:

1. In what ways is *Hamlet* not only about private problems but also about public ones?

2. Why should the consequences of Claudius's murder of Hamlet's father be considered disastrous?

The principle shown here is that exam questions should never be asked just about *what* but should rather get into the issues of *why*. Observe that the first question therefore adapts the words *in what ways* to the phrasing of the note. For the second, the word *why* has been adapted. Either question creates the need for you to study pointedly, and neither asks you merely to describe events. Question 1 requires you to consider the wider political effects of Hamlet's hostility toward Claudius, including Hamlet's murder of Polonius and the subsequent madness of Ophelia. Question 2, with its emphasis on disaster, leads you to consider not only the ruination of the hopes and lives of those in the play but also the importance of young Fortinbras and the eventual establishment of Norwegian control over Denmark after Claudius and Hamlet are gone. If you spent fifteen or twenty minutes writing practice answers to these questions, you could be confident in taking an examination on the material, for it is likely that you could adapt your study answers to any exam question about the personal and political implications of Claudius's murder of his brother.

Practice Writing Questions Even When Time Is Short

Whatever your subject, spend as much study time as possible making and answering your own questions. *Writing practice answers is one of the most important things you can do before an exam.* Remember also to work with your own remarks and the ideas you develop in the journal entries that you make when doing your regular assignments (see Chapter 1, pp. 13–14). Many of these will give you additional ideas for your own questions, which you can practice along with the questions you develop from your notes.

Obviously, with limited study time, you will not be able to create your own questions and answers indefinitely. Even so, don't neglect asking and answering your own questions. If time is too short for full practice answers, write out the main heads, or topics, of an answer. When the press of time (or the need for sleep) no longer permits you to make even such a brief outline answer, keep thinking of questions and their answers on the way to the exam. *Never read passively or unresponsively; always read with a creative, question-and-answer goal.* Think of studying as a preliminary step leading to writing.

The time you spend in this way will be valuable, for as you practice, you will develop control and therefore confidence. Often those who have difficulty with tests, or claim a phobia about them, prepare passively rather than actively. Your instructor's test questions compel responsiveness, organization, thought, and insight. But a passively prepared student is not ready for this challenge and therefore writes answers that are unresponsive and filled with summary. The grade for such a performance is low, and the student's fear of tests is reinforced. The best way to break such long-standing patterns of fear or uncertainty is active, creative study.

Study with a Classmate

Often the thoughts of another person can help you understand the material to be tested. Find a fellow student with whom you can work comfortably but also productively, for both of you together can help each other individually. In view of the need for steady preparation throughout a course, regular discussions about the material are a good idea. You might also make your joint study systematic by setting aside a specific evening or afternoon for work sessions. Many students have said that a major problem on the actual examination is their lack of familiarity with the way in which questions are phrased. Consequently, they need to interpret and understand every question before they begin answering it, and sometimes they misunderstanding the question entirely. If you work with a fellow student, however, and trade questions, you will be gaining experience (and confidence) in dealing with this basic difficulty about exams. Working with someone else can be extremely rewarding, just as it can also be stimulating and instructive. Make the effort.

TWO BASIC TYPES OF QUESTIONS ABOUT LITERATURE

Generally, there are two types of questions on literature exams. Keep them in mind as you prepare. The first type is *factual,* or *mainly objective;* and the second is *general, comprehensive, broad,* or *mainly subjective.* Except for multiple-choice questions, very few questions are purely objective in a literature course.

Anticipate the Kinds of Factual Questions That Might Be Asked

MULTIPLE-CHOICE QUESTIONS ASK YOU TO PICK THE MOST ACCURATE AND LIKELY ANSWERS. Multiple-choice questions are mainly factual. Your instructor will most likely use them for short quizzes, usually on days when an assignment is due, to make sure that you are keeping up with the reading. Multiple-choice questions test your knowledge of facts and your ingenuity in perceiving subtleties of phrasing. On a literature exam, however, this type of question is rare.

IDENTIFICATION QUESTIONS ASK FOR ACCURACY, EXPLANATION, AND A CERTAIN AMOUNT OF INTERPRETATION. Identification questions are interesting and challenging because they require you both to know details and also to develop thoughts about them. This type of question will frequently be used as a check on the depth and scope of your reading. In fact, an entire exam could be composed of only identification questions, each demanding perhaps five minutes to write. Here are some typical examples of what you might be asked to identify:

1. *A character.* To identify a character, it is necessary to describe briefly the character's position, main activity, and significance. Let us assume that Montresor is the character to be identified. Our answer should state that he is the narrator of Poe's "The Cask of Amontillado" (position) who invites Fortunato into his wine vaults on the pretext of testing the quality of some new Amontillado wine (main activity). He is therefore the major cause of the action, and he embodies one of the story's themes, that the desire for revenge makes human beings diabolically cruel (significance). Under the category of "significance," of course, you might develop as many ideas as you have time for, but the short example here is a general model for most examinations.

2. *Incidents or situations.* To identify an incident or a situation (for example, "A woman mourns the death of her husband"), first describe the circumstances and the principal character involved in them (Mrs. Popov's reaction to her widowhood in Chekhov's play *The Bear*), and then try to demonstrate its significance in the work. That is, in *The Bear*, Mrs. Popov is mourning the death of her husband, and in the course of the play Chekhov uses her feelings to show amusingly that life with real emotion is stronger than duty to the dead.

3. *Things, places, and dates.* Your instructor may ask you to identify a hair ribbon (Hawthorne's "Young Goodman Brown") or a beach (Arnold's "Dover Beach"), or the date of Lowell's "Patterns" (1916). For dates, you may be given a leeway of five or ten years. What is important about a date is not so much exactness as historical and intellectual perspective. The date of "Patterns," for example, was the third year of World War I, and the poem consequently reflects a reaction against the protracted and senseless loss of life in war (even though details of the poem itself suggest an eighteenth-century war). To claim "World War I" as the date of the poem would likely be acceptable as an answer if it happens that you cannot remember the exact date.

4. *Quotations.* You should remember enough of the text to identify a passage taken from it, or at least to make an informed guess. Generally, you should (1) locate the quotation, if you remember it, or else describe the probable location; (2) show the ways in which the quotation is typical of the content and style of the work you have read; and (3) describe the importance of the passage. If you suffer a momentary lapse of memory, write a reasoned and careful explanation of your guess. Even if your guess is wrong, the knowledge and cogency of your explanation should give you points.

TECHNICAL AND ANALYTICAL QUESTIONS AND PROBLEMS REQUIRE YOU TO RELATE KNOWLEDGE AND TECHNICAL UNDERSTANDING TO THE ISSUE. In a scale of ascending importance, the third and most difficult type of factual question relates to those matters of writing with which this book is concerned: technique, analysis, and problems. You might be asked to discuss the *setting, images, point of view,* or *important idea* of a work; you might be asked about the *tone* of a story or poem; or you might be asked to *explicate* a poem that may or may not be duplicated for your benefit (if it is not duplicated, woe to students who have not studied their assignments). Questions like these assume that you have technical knowledge, and they also ask you to examine the text within the limitations imposed by the terms.

Obviously, technical questions occur more frequently in advanced courses than in elementary ones, and the questions become more subtle as the courses become more advanced. Instructors of elementary courses may ask about ideas and problems but will likely not use many of the others unless they state their intentions to do so in advance or unless technical terms have been studied in class.

Questions of this type are fairly long, perhaps allowing from fifteen to twenty-five minutes for each. If you have two or more of these questions, try to space your time sensibly; do not devote eighty percent of your time to one question and leave only twenty percent for the rest.

Understand How Your Responses Will Be Judged and Graded

IDENTIFICATION QUESTIONS PROBE YOUR UNDERSTANDING AND APPLICATION OF FACTS. In all factual questions, your instructor is testing (1) your factual command and (2) your quickness in relating a part to the whole. Thus, suppose you are identifying the incident "a man kills a canary." It is correct to say that Glaspell's play *Trifles* (or her story "A Jury of Her Peers") is the location of the incident, that the murdered farmer John Wright is the killer, and that the canary belongs to his wife, Minnie Wright. Knowledge of these details clearly establishes that you know the facts. But a strong answer must go further. Even in the brief time you have for short answers, you should always connect the facts (1) to major causation in the work, (2) to an important idea or ideas, (3) to the development of the work, and (4) for a quotation, to the style. Time is short and you must be selective, but if you can make your answer move from facts to significance, you will always fashion superior responses. Along these lines, let us look at an answer identifying the action from *Trifles*:

> The action is from Glaspell's *Trifles*. The man who kills the bird is John Wright, and the owner is his wife, Minnie Wright. The killing is important because it is shown as the final indignity in Minnie Wright's desperate life, and it obviously makes her angry enough to strangle Wright in his sleep. It is thus the cause not only of the murder but also of the investigation bringing the officers and their wives onstage. In fact, the wringing of the bird's neck makes the play possible because it is the wives who discover the dead bird, and this discovery is the means by which Glaspell highlights them as the major characters in the play. Because the husband's brutal act shows how bleak the life of Minnie Wright actually was, it dramatizes the lonely plight of women in a male-dominated way of life like that on the Wright farm. The discovery also raises the issue of legality and morality, because the two wives decide to conceal the evidence, therefore protecting Minnie Wright from conviction and punishment.

Any of the points in this answer could be developed as a separate essay, but the paragraph is successful as a short answer because it goes beyond fact to deal with significance. Clearly, such answers are possible at the time of an exam only if you have devoted considerable thought beforehand to the works on which you will be tested. The more thinking and practicing you do before an exam, the better your answers will be. Remember this advice as an axiom: *You cannot write superior answers if you do not think extensively before the exam.* By ambitious advance study, you will be able to reduce surprise to an absolute minimum.

LONGER FACTUAL QUESTIONS PROBE YOUR KNOWLEDGE AND YOUR ABILITY TO ORGANIZE YOUR THOUGHTS. More extended factual questions also require more thoroughly developed organization. Remember that for these questions your skills in writing essays are important, because the quality of your composition will determine a major share of your instructor's evaluation of your answers. It is therefore best to take several minutes to gather your thoughts before you begin to write; *a ten-minute planned answer is preferable to a twenty-five-minute unplanned answer.* You do not need to write every possible fact on each particular question. Of greater importance is the use to which you put the facts that you know and the organization and development of your answer. Use a sheet of scratch paper to jot down the facts that you remember and your ideas about them in relation to the question. Then put them together, phrase a thesis sentence, and use your facts to exemplify and support your thesis.

It is always necessary to begin your answer pointedly, using key words or phrases from the question or direction if possible, so that your answer will have thematic shape. You should *never* begin an answer with "Because" and then go on from there without referring again to the question. To be most responsive during the short time available for an exam, you should use the question as your guide for your answer. Let us suppose that you have the following question on your test: "How does Glaspell use details in *Trifles* to reveal the character of Minnie Wright?" The most common way to go astray on such a question—and the easiest thing to do also—is to concentrate on Mrs. Wright's character rather than on how Glaspell uses detail to bring out her character. The word *how* makes a vast difference in the nature of the final answer, and hence a good method on the exam is to duplicate key phrases in the question to ensure that you make your major points clear. Here is an opening sentence that uses the key words and phrases (italicized here) from the question to direct thought and provide focus:

> Glaspell *uses details* of setting, marital relationships, and personal habits *to reveal the character of Minnie Wright* as a person of great but unfulfilled potential whom anger has finally overcome.

Because this sentence repeats the key phrases from the question and also because it promises to show *how* the details are to be focused on the character, it suggests that the answer to follow will be responsive.

General or Comprehensive Questions Require You to Connect a Number of Works to Broader Matters of Idea and Technique

General or comprehensive questions are particularly important on final examinations, when your instructor is testing your total comprehension of the course material. Considerable time is usually allowed for answering this type of question, which can be phrased in a number of ways:

1. A *direct question* asking about philosophy, underlying attitudes, main ideas, characteristics of style, backgrounds, and so on. Here are some possible questions in this category:

   What use do _____, _____, and _____ make of the topic of _____?

Define and characterize the short story as a genre of literature.

Explain the use of dialogue by the authors Hawthorne, Welty, and Maupassant. Contrast with the technique of point of view as used by _____, _____, and _____.

2. A *"comment"* question, often based on an extensive quotation, borrowed from a critic or written by your instructor for the occasion, asking about a broad class of writers, a literary movement, or the like. Your instructor may ask you to treat this question broadly (taking in many writers) or else to apply the quotation to a specific writer.

3. A *"suppose"* question, such as "What advice might Minnie Wright of *Trifles* give the speakers of Lowell's 'Patterns' and Keats's 'Bright Star'?" or "What might the speaker of Rossetti's poem 'Echo' say if she learned that her dead lover was Goodman Brown of Hawthorne's 'Young Goodman Brown'?" Although "suppose" questions might seem whimsical at first sight, they have a serious design and should prompt original and radical thinking. The first question, for example, should cause a test writer to bring out, from Minnie Wright's perspective, that the love of both speakers was not actual, but potential. She would likely sympathize with the speaker of "Patterns," but she might also say that the lost married life might not have been as ideal as the speaker assumes. For the speaker of "Bright Star," a male, Mrs. Wright might say that the steadfast love he seeks should be linked to kindness and toleration as well as passion.

Although "suppose" questions (and answers) are speculative, the need to respond to them requires a detailed consideration of the works involved, and in this respect the "suppose" question is a salutary means of learning. It is of course difficult to prepare for a "suppose" question, which you can therefore regard as a test not only of your knowledge but also of your inventiveness and ingenuity.

Understand How Your Responses to General and Comprehensive Questions Will Be Judged and Graded

When answering broad, general questions, you are dealing with an unstructured situation, and not only must you supply an *answer* but—equally important—you also must also create a *structure* within which your answer can have meaning. You might say that you make up your own specific question out of the original general question. If you were asked to consider the role of women as seen in works by Lowell, Maupassant, and Glaspell, for example, you would structure the question by focusing a number of clearly defined topics. A possible way to begin answering such a question might be this:

Lowell, Maupassant, and Glaspell present a view of female resilience by demonstrating the inner control, endurance, and power of adaptation of their major characters.

With this sort of focus, you would be able to proceed point by point, introducing supporting data as you form your answer.

As a general rule, the best method for answering a comprehensive question is comparison-contrast (see also Chapter 35). The reason is that in dealing with, say, a general question on Rossetti, Chekhov, and Keats, it is too easy to write *three* separate essays rather than *one*. Thus, you should try to create a topic such as "The treatment of real or idealized love" or "The difficulties in male-female relationships" and then to develop your answer point by point rather than writer by writer. By creating your answer in this way, you can bring in references to each or all of the writers as they become relevant. If you were to treat each writer separately, your comprehensive answer would lose focus and effectiveness, and it would be needlessly repetitive.

Remember that in judging your response to a general question, your instructor is interested in seeing (1) how effectively you perceive and explain the significant issues in the question, (2) how intelligently and clearly you organize your answer, and (3) how persuasively you use materials from the work as supporting evidence.

Bear in mind that in answering comprehensive questions, you do not have the freedom to write about anything at all. The freedom you do have, however, is the freedom to create your own organization and development in response to the questions your instructor has presented to you. The underlying idea of the comprehensive, general question is that you possess special knowledge and insights that cannot be discovered by more factual questions. You must therefore formulate your own responses to the material and introduce evidence that reflects your own insights and command of information.

Two final words: Good luck.

35

Comparison-Contrast and Extended Comparison-Contrast: Learning by Seeing Literary Works Together

A comparison-contrast essay is used to compare and contrast different authors or two or more works by the same author; different drafts of the same work; or characters, incidents, techniques, and ideas in the same work or in different works. The virtue of comparison-contrast is that it enables the study of works in perspective. No matter what works you consider together, the method helps you isolate and highlight individual characteristics, for the quickest way to get at the essence of one thing is to compare it with something else that is similar. Similarities are brought out by comparison; differences, by contrast. In other words, you can enhance your understanding of what a thing *is* by using comparison-contrast to determine what it *is not*.

For example, our understanding of Shakespeare's Sonnet 30; "When to the Sessions of Sweet Silent Thought" (p. 795) can be enhanced if we compare it with Christina Rossetti's poem "Echo" (p. 892). Both poems treat personal recollections of past experiences, told by a speaker to a listener who is not intended to be the reader. Both also refer to persons, now dead, with whom the speakers were closely involved. In these respects, the poems are comparable.

In addition to these similarities, there are important differences. Shakespeare's speaker numbers the dead persons as friends whom he laments generally, whereas Rossetti refers specifically to one person with whom the speaker was in love. Rossetti's topic is the sorrow of dead love, the irrevocability of the past, and the present loneliness of the speaker. Shakespeare includes his references to dead friends as a way of accounting for present sorrows, but then his speaker turns to the present and asserts that thinking about the "dear friend" being addressed enables him to restore past "losses" and end all "sorrows." In Rossetti's poem, there is no reconciliation of past and present; instead the speaker focuses entirely upon the sadness of the present moment. Although both poems are retrospective, Shakespeare's poem deals with the present while Rossetti's looks to the past. These differences show how the poems can be contrasted.

GUIDELINES FOR THE COMPARISON-CONTRAST METHOD

The preceding example, although brief, shows how the comparison-contrast method makes it possible to identify leading similarities and distinguishing differences in two works. Frequently you can overcome difficulty with one work by comparing and contrasting it with another work on a comparable subject. A few guidelines will help direct your efforts in writing comparison-contrast essays.

Clarify Your Intention

When planning a comparison-contrast essay, first decide on your goal, for you can use the method in a number of ways. One objective is the equal and mutual illumination of two (or more) works. For example, an essay comparing Hardy's "The Three Strangers" (pp. 436–45) with Hawthorne's "Young Goodman Brown" (pp. 133–47) might compare ideas, characters, or methods in these stories equally, without stressing or favoring either. If you wish to put just one of the works into particular focus, you might also use the comparison-contrast technique for that purpose. Thus you might emphasize "Young Goodman Brown" by using comparable material in "The Three Strangers" as a highlight for Hawthorne's story (and vice versa). You might also show your liking of a particular story, poem, or play at the expense of another, or emphasize a method or idea in one work that you do not find in the other work.

A first task, therefore, is to decide what to emphasize. The demonstrative student essay on pages 1985–87 gives equal time to both works being considered, without claiming the superiority of either. Unless you have a different rhetorical goal, this essay provides a suitable guide for most comparisons.

Find Common Grounds for Comparison

The second stage in preparing a comparison-contrast essay is to select and articulate a common ground for discussion. It is pointless to compare dissimilar things, for the resulting conclusions will not have much value. Instead, compare like with like: idea with idea, characterization with characterization, setting with setting, point of view with point of view, tone with tone. Nothing much can be learned from a comparison of Hardy's view of individuality and Chekhov's view of love; but a comparison of the relationship of individuality with identity and character in Hardy and Chekhov suggests common ground, with the promise of significant ideas to be developed through the examination of similarities and differences.

In seeking common ground, you will need to be inventive and creative. For instance, if you compare Maupassant's "The Necklace" (pp. 4–11) and Chekhov's *The Bear* (pp. 1625–34), these two works at first seem dissimilar. Yet common ground can be discovered, such as the treatment of self-deceit, the effects of chance on human affairs, and the authors' views of women. Although other works may seem even more dissimilar than these, it is usually possible to find a common ground for comparison and contrast. Much of your success in an essay of this type depends on your finding a workable basis—a common denominator—for comparison.

Integrate the Bases of Comparison

Let us assume that you have decided on your rhetorical purpose and on the basis or bases of your comparison. You have done your reading and taken notes, and you have a rough idea of what to say. The remaining problem is the treatment of your material.

One method is to make your points first about one work and then about the other. Unfortunately, such a comparison makes your paper seem like two separate lumps. ("Work 1" takes up one half of your paper, and "Work 2" takes up the other half.) Also, the method involves repetition because you must repeat many points when you treat the second subject.

Therefore, a better method is to treat the major aspects of your main idea and to refer to the two (or more) works as they support your arguments. Thus you refer constantly to *both* works, sometimes within the same sentence, and remind your reader of the point of your discussion. There are reasons for the superiority of this method: (1) You do not repeat your points needlessly, for you develop them as you raise them. (2) By constantly referring to the two works, you make your points without requiring a reader with a poor memory to reread previous sections.

As a model, here is a paragraph on "Natural References as a Basis of Comparison in Frost's 'Desert Places' and Shakespeare's Sonnet 73: 'That Time of Year Thou May'st in Me Behold.'"[1] The virtue of the paragraph is that it uses material from both poems simultaneously (as nearly as the time sequence of sentences allows) as the substance for the development of the ideas.

> (1) Both writers link their ideas to events occurring in the natural world. (2) Night as a parallel with death is common to both poems, with Frost speaking about it in his first line and Shakespeare introducing it in his seventh. (3) Along with night, Frost emphasizes the onset of winter and snow as a time of death and desolation. (4) With this natural description, Frost also symbolically refers to empty, secret, dead places in the inner spirit—crannies of the soul where bleak winter snowfalls correspond to selfishness and indifference. (5) By contrast, Shakespeare uses the fall season, with the yellowing and dropping of leaves and the migrations of birds, to stress the closeness of real death and therefore the need to love fully during the time remaining. (6) Both poems thus share a sense of gloom because both

[1] See pp. 912 and 877 for these poems.

present death as inevitable and final, just like the emptiness of winter. (7) Because Shakespeare's sonnet is addressed to a listener who is also a loved one, however, it is more outgoing than the more introspective poem of Frost. (8) Frost turns the snow, the night, and the emptiness of the universe inwardly in order to show the speaker's inner bleakness, and by extension, the bleakness of many human spirits. (9) Shakespeare instead uses the bleakness of seasons, night, and dying fires to state the need for loving "well." (10) The poems thus use common and similar references for different purposes and effects.

This paragraph links Shakespeare's references to nature to those of Frost. Five sentences speak of both authors together; three speak of Frost alone and two of Shakespeare alone, but all the sentences are unified topically. This interweaving of references indicates that the writer has learned both poems well enough to consider them together, and it also enables the writing to be more pointed and succinct than if the works were separately treated.

You can learn from this example: If you develop your essay by putting your two subjects constantly together, you will write economically and pointedly (not only for essays but also for tests). Beyond that, if you digest the material as successfully as this method indicates, you demonstrate that you are fulfilling a major educational goal—the assimilation and *use* of material. Too often, because you learn things separately (in separate works and courses, at separate times), you tend also to compartmentalize them. Instead, you should always try to relate them, to *synthesize* them. Comparison and contrast help in this process of putting together, of seeing things not as fragments but as parts of wholes.

Avoid the "Tennis-Ball" Method

As you make your comparison, do not confuse an interlocking method with a "tennis-ball" method, in which you bounce your subject back and forth constantly and repetitively, almost as though you were hitting observations back and forth over a net. The tennis-ball method is shown in the following example from a comparison of the characters Mathilde (Maupassant's "The Necklace") and Mrs. Popov (Chekhov's *The Bear*):

> Mathilde is a young married woman; Mrs. Popov is also young but a widow. Mathilde has at least some kind of social life, even though she doesn't have more than one friend; but Mrs. Popov chooses to lead a life of solitude. Mathilde's daydreams about wealth are responsible for her misfortune, and Mrs. Popov's dedication to the memory of her husband is capable of ruining her life. Mathilde is made unhappy because of her own shortcomings, but Mrs. Popov is rescued despite her shortcomings. In Mathilde's case the focus is on adversity not only causing trouble but also strengthening character. Similarly, in Mrs. Popov's case the focus is on a strong person realizing her strength regardless of her conscious decision to weaken herself.

Imagine the effect of an entire essay written in this boring "1, 2, 1, 2, 1, 2" order. Aside from the repetition and unvaried patterning of subjects, the tennis-ball method does not permit much illustrative development. You should not feel so constrained that you cannot take two or more sentences to develop a point about one writer or subject before you include comparative references to another. If you remember to interlock the two subjects of comparison, however, as in the paragraph about Frost and Shakespeare, your method will give you the freedom to develop your topics fully.

THE EXTENDED COMPARISON-CONTRAST ESSAY

For a longer essay about a number of works—such as a limited research paper, comprehensive exam questions, and the sort of extended essay required at the end of a semester—comparison-contrast is an essential method. You may wish to compare the works on the basis of elements such as ideas, plot, structure, character, metaphor, point of view, or setting. Because of the larger number of works, however, you will need to modify the way in which you employ comparison-contrast. Suppose you are dealing with not just two works but six, seven, or more. You need first to find a common ground to use as your central, unifying idea, just as you do for a comparison of only two works. Once you establish the common ground, you can classify or group your works on the basis of the similarities and differences they exemplify with regard to the topic. The idea is to get two *groups* for comparison, not just two works.

Let us assume that three or four works treat a topic in one way but that two or three do it in another (e.g., either criticism or praise of wealth and trade, the joys or sorrows of love, the enthusiasm of youth, or the disillusionment of age). In writing about these works, you might treat the topic itself in a straight-forward comparison-contrast method but use details from the works within the groupings as the material that you use for illustration and argument.

To make your essay as specific as possible, it is best to stress only a small number of works with each of your subpoints. Once you have established these points, there is no need to go into abundant detail with all the other works you are studying. Instead, you need to make no more than brief references to the other works, for your purpose should be to strengthen your points without creating more and more examples. Once you go to another subpoint, you use different works for illustration, so that by the end of your essay, you will have given due attention to each work in your assignment. In this way—by treating many works in small comparative groups—you can keep your essay reasonably brief, for there is no need to go into unproductive detail.

For illustration, the demonstrative student essay on pages 1988–90 shows how this grouping may be done. In the first part of the body of this essay, six works are used comparatively to show how private needs conflict with social, public demands. The next part shows how three works can be compared and contrasted on the basis of how they treat the topic of public concerns as expressed through law.

CITING REFERENCES IN A LONGER
COMPARISON-CONTRAST ESSAY

For the longer comparison-contrast essay, you may find a problem in making references to many different works. Generally you do not need to repeat full references. For example, if you refer to Louise of Chopin's "The Story of an Hour" or to Montresor of Poe's "The Cask of Amontillado," you should make the full references only once and then refer later just to the character, story, or author, according to your needs.

When you quote lines or passages or when you cite actions or characters in special ways, you should use parenthetical line, speech, or paragraph references, as in the demonstrative student essay on pages 1985–87. Be guided by the following principle: If you make a specific reference that you think your reader might want to examine in more detail, supply the line, speech, or paragraph number. If you refer to minor details that might easily be unnoticed or forgotten, also supply the appropriate number.

WRITING A COMPARISON-CONTRAST ESSAY

In planning your essay, you must first narrow and simplify your topic so that you can handle it conveniently. Should your subject be a comparison of two poets (as in the comparison-contrast of Lowell and Owen on pp. 1985–87), choose one or two of each poet's poems on the same or a similar topic, and write your essay about these.

Once you have found an organizing principle, along with the relevant works, begin to refine and to focus the direction of your essay. As you study each work, note common or contrasting elements and use these to form your central idea. At the same time, you can select the most illustrative works and classify them according to your topic, such as war, love, work, faithfulness, or self-analysis.

Strategies for Organizing Ideas

Begin by stating the works, authors, characters, or ideas that you are considering; then show how you have narrowed the topic. Your central idea should briefly highlight the principal grounds of comparison and contrast, such as that both works treat a common topic, exhibit a similar idea, use a similar form, or develop an identical attitude, and also that major or minor differences help make the works unique. You may also assert that one work is superior to the other, if you wish to make this judgment and defend it.

The body of your essay is governed by the works and your basis of comparison (ideas and essays, depictions of character, uses of setting, qualities of style, uses of point of view, and so on). For a comparison-contrast treatment on such a basis, your goal should be to shed light on both (or more) of the works you are treating. For example, you might examine a number of stories written in the first-person point of view (see Chapter 5). An essay on this topic might compare the ways in which each author uses the point of view to achieve similar or distinct effects; or it might compare a group of poems that employ similar images, symbols, or ironic methods. Sometimes, the process can be as simple as identifying female or male protagonists and comparing the ways in which their characters are developed. Another approach is to compare the *subjects,* as opposed to the *idea.* You might identify works dealing with general subjects such as love, death, youth, race, or war. Such groupings provide a basis for excellent comparisons and contrasts.

As you develop your essay, remember to keep comparison-contrast foremost. That is, your discussions of point of view, figurative language, or whatever should not so much explain these topics *as topics* but rather should explore *similarities and differences* of the works you are comparing. If your topic is an idea, for example, you need to explain the idea, but just enough to establish points of similarity or difference. As you develop such an essay, you might illustrate your arguments by referring to related uses of elements such as setting, characterization, rhythm, rhyme, symbolism, point of view, or metaphor. When you introduce these new subjects, you will be on target as long as you use them comparatively.

In concluding, you might reflect on other ideas or techniques in the works you have compared, make observations about similar qualities, or summarize briefly the grounds of your comparison. If there is a point you have considered especially important, you might stress that point again in your conclusion. Also, your comparison might have led you to conclude that one work—or group of works—is superior to another. Stressing that point again would make an effective conclusion.

DEMONSTRATIVE STUDENT ESSAY (TWO WORKS)

The Treatment of Responses to War in Lowell's "Patterns" and Owen's "Anthem for Doomed Youth"°

[1] Lowell's "Patterns" and Owen's "Anthem for Doomed Youth" are both powerful and unique condemnations of war.* Owen's short poem speaks broadly and generally about the ugliness of war and also about large groups of sorrowful people; Lowell's longer poem focuses on the personal grief of just one person. In a sense, Lowell's poem begins where Owen's ends, a fact that accounts for both the similarities and the differences between the two works. The antiwar themes can be compared on the basis of their subjects, their lengths, their concreteness, and their use of a common metaphor.†

[2] "Anthem for Doomed Youth" attacks war more directly than "Patterns." Owen's opening line "What passing-bells for those who die as cattle?" suggests that in war, human beings are depersonalized before they are slaughtered, like

° See pp. 1174 and 750 for these poems.
* Central idea.
† Thesis sentence.

so much meat, and his observations about the "monstrous" guns and the "shrill, demented" shells unambiguously condemn the horrors of war. By contrast, in "Patterns," warfare is far away, on another continent, intruding only when the messenger delivers the letter stating that the speaker's fiancé has been killed (lines 63-64). A comparable situation governs the last six lines of Owen's poem, quietly describing how those at home respond to the news that their loved ones have died in war. Thus the antiwar focus in "Patterns" is the contrast between the calm, peaceful life of the speaker's garden and the anguish of her responses. In "Anthem for Doomed Youth," the stress is more the external horrors of war that bring about the need for ceremonies honoring the dead.

[3]   Another major difference between the poems is their wide discrepancy in length. "Patterns" is an interior monologue or meditation of 107 lines, but it could not be shorter and still be convincing. In the poem the speaker thinks of the past and contemplates her future loneliness. Her final outburst, "Christ! What are patterns for?" could make no sense if she did not explain her situation as extensively as she does. "Anthem for Doomed Youth," however, is brief--a fourteen-line sonnet--because it is more general and less personal than "Patterns." Although Owen's speaker shows great sympathy, he or she views the sorrows of others distantly, unlike Lowell, who goes right into the mind and spirit of the grieving woman. Owen's use, in his last six lines, of phrases such as "tenderness of patient minds" and "drawing down of blinds" is a powerful representation of deep grief. He gives no further details even though thousands of individual stories might be told. In contrast, Lowell tells just one of these stories as she focuses on her solitary speaker's lost hopes and dreams. Thus the contrasting lengths of the poems are determined by each poet's treatment of the topic.

[4]   Despite these differences of approach and length, both poems are similarly concrete and real. Owen moves from the real scenes and sounds of far-off battlefields to the homes of the many soldiers who have been killed in battle, but Lowell's scene is a single place--the garden of her speaker's estate. The speaker walks on real gravel along garden paths that contain daffodils, squills, a fountain, and a lime tree. She thinks of her clothing and her ribboned shoes, and also of her fiancé's boots, sword hilts, and buttons. The images in Owen's poem are equally real but are not associated with individuals as in "Patterns." Thus Owen's images are those of cattle, bells, rifle shots, shells, bugles, candles, and window blinds. Although both poems reflect reality, Owen's details are more general and public; Lowell's are more personal and intimate.

[5]   Along with this concreteness, the poems share a major metaphor: that cultural patterns both control and frustrate human wishes and hopes. In "Patterns," this metaphor is shown in warfare itself (line 106), which is the pinnacle of organized human patterns of destruction. Further examples of the metaphor are found in details about clothing (particularly the speaker's stiff, confining gown in lines 5, 18, 21, 73, and 101, and also the lover's military boots in lines 46 and 49); the orderly, formal garden paths in which the speaker is walking (lines 1 and 93); her restraint at hearing about her lover's death; and her courtesy, despite her grief, in ordering refreshment for the messenger (line 69). Within such rigid patterns, her hopes for happiness have vanished, along with the sensuous spontaneity symbolized by her lover's hope to make love to her on a "shady seat" in the garden (lines 85-89). The metaphor of the constricting pattern is also seen in "Anthem for Doomed Youth," except that in this poem, the

pattern is the funeral, not love or marriage. Owen's speaker contrasts the calm, peaceful tolling of "passing-bells" (line 1) to the frightening sounds of war represented by the "monstrous anger of the guns," "the stuttering rifles' rapid rattle," and "the demented choirs of wailing shells" (lines 2-8). Thus, while Lowell uses the metaphor to reveal the irony of hope and desire being destroyed by war, Owen uses it to reveal the irony of war's negation of peaceful ceremonies.

Though in these ways the poems share topics and some aspects of treatment, they are distinct and individual. "Patterns" includes many references to visible things, whereas "Anthem for Doomed Youth" emphasizes sound (and silence). Both poems conclude on powerfully emotional although different notes. Owen's poem dwells on the pathos and sadness that war brings to many unnamed people, and Lowell's expresses the most intimate thoughts of a woman who is alone in the first agonies of grief. Although neither poem attacks the usual

[6] platitudes and justifications for war (the needs to mobilize, to sacrifice, to achieve peace through fighting, and so on), the attack is there by implication, for both poems make their appeal by stressing how war destroys the relationships that make life worth living. For this reason, despite their differences, both "Patterns" and "Anthem for Doomed Youth" are parallel anti-war poems, and both are strong expressions of feeling.

Commentary on the Essay

This demonstrative student essay shows how approximately equal attention can be given to the two works being studied. Words stressing similarity are *common, share, equally, parallel, both, similar,* and *also.* Contrasts are stressed by *while, whereas, different, dissimilar, contrast, although,* and *except.* Transitions from paragraph to paragraph are not different in this type of essay from those in other essays. Thus, the phrases *despite, along with this* and *in these ways,* which are used here, could be used anywhere for the same transitional purpose.

The central idea—that the poems mutually condemn war—is brought out in paragraph 1, together with the supporting idea that the poems blend into each other because both show responses to news of battle casualties.

Paragraph 2, the first in the body, discusses how each poem brings out its attack on warfare. Paragraph 3 explains the differing lengths of the poems as a function of differences in perspective. Because Owen's sonnet views war and its effects at a distance, it is brief; but because Lowell's interior monologue views death intimately, it needs more detail and greater length.

Paragraph 4, on the topic of concreteness and reality, shows that the two works can receive equal attention without the bouncing back and forth of the tennis-ball method. Three of the sentences in this paragraph (3, 4, and 6) are devoted exclusively to details in one poem or the other; but sentences 1, 2, 5, and 7 refer to both works, stressing points of broad or specific comparison. The scheme demonstrates that the two works are, in effect, interlocked within the paragraph.

Paragraph 5, the last in the body, considers the similar and dissimilar ways in which the poems treat the common metaphor of cultural patterns.

The conclusion, paragraph 6, summarizes the central idea, and it also stresses the ways in which the two poems, although similar, are distinct and unique.

DEMONSTRATIVE STUDENT ESSAY (EXTENDED COMPARISON-CONTRAST)

Literary Treatments of the Conflicts between Private and Public Life

[1]   The conflict between private or personal life, on the one hand, and public or civic and national life, on the other, is a topic common to many literary works.* Authors show that individuals try to maintain their personal lives and commitments even though they are tested and stressed by public and external forces. Ideally, individuals should have the freedom to follow their own wishes independently of the outside world. It is a fact, however, that living itself causes people to venture into the public world and therefore to encounter conflicts. Getting married, following a profession, observing the natural world, looking at a person's possessions, taking a walk--all these draw people into the public world in which rules, regulations, and laws override private wishes. To greater and lesser degrees, such conflicts are found in Arnold's "Dover Beach," Bierce's "An Occurrence at Owl Creek Bridge," Chekhov's *The Bear,* Glaspell's *Trifles,* Chopin's "The Story of an Hour," Hardy's "Channel Firing," Hawthorne's "Young Goodman Brown," Keats's "Bright Star," Layton's "Rhine Boat Trip," Lowell's "Patterns," Shakespeare's Sonnet 73: "That Time of Year Thou May'st in Me Behold," and Wordsworth's "Lines Written in Early Spring."° In these works, conflicts are shown between interests of individuals and those of the social, legal, and military public.†

[2]   One of the major private-public conflicts is created by the way in which characters respond to social conventions and expectations. In Chekhov's *The Bear,* for example, Mrs. Popov has given up her personal life to memorialize her dead husband. She wears black, stays in her house for a whole year, and swears eternal fidelity; and she does all this to exceed what she considers her public role as a grieving widow. Fortunately for her, Smirnov arrives on the scene and arouses her enough to make her give up this deadly pose. Not as fortunate is Hawthorne's Goodman Brown in "Young Goodman Brown." Brown's obligation is much less public and also more philosophical than Mrs. Popov's because his religiously inspired vision of evil creates a lifelong gloom in him. Although Mrs. Popov is easily moved from her position by the prospect of immediate life and vitality, Brown's fidelity to his vision of distrust locks him into a fear of evil from which not even his own faithful wife can shake him. The two characters therefore

---

* Central idea. See pp. 693, 257, 1625, 1244, 393, 703, 436, 779, 1169, 1174, 877, and 1048 for these works.
† Thesis sentence.

go in entirely different directions--one toward personal fulfillment, the other toward personal destruction.

[3]   Of particular note is that philosophical or religious difficulties such as those of Goodman Brown force a crisis in an individual life. In Arnold's "Dover Beach," for example, the speaker expresses regret about uncertainty and the loss of religious faith that wear away civilization just like surf beating on the stones of Dover Beach. This situation might make a person dreary and depressed, just like Goodman Brown. Arnold's speaker, however, in the lines "Ah, love, let us be true / To one another," finds power in personal fidelity and commitment (lines 29-30). In other words, the public world of "human misery" and the diminishing "Sea of Faith" is beyond control, and therefore all that is left is personal commitment. This is not to say that "Young Goodman Brown," as a story, is negative, for Hawthorne clearly implies that a positive personal life lies in the denial of choices like those made by Brown and in the acceptance of choices like those made by Mrs. Popov and Arnold's speaker.

[4]   To deny or to ignore the public world is a possible option that, under some circumstances, can be chosen. To a degree, for example, "Dover Beach" reflects a conscious decision to ignore the philosophic and religious uncertainty that the speaker finds in the intellectual and public world. Even more independent of such a public world, Shakespeare's "That Time of Year" and Keats's "Bright Star" bring out their ideas as reflections on purely personal situations. Shakespeare's speaker deals with the love between himself and the listener, whereas Keats's speaker, addressing a distant star, considers his need for steadfastness in his relationship with his "fair love." Louise in Chopin's "The Story of an Hour" embodies an interesting variation on the personal matters brought up in these two sonnets. At first, Louise is crushed by the news coming from the public world that her husband has been killed. Her first vision of herself is that of a grieving, private widow. As she thinks about things, however, she quickly begins to anticipate the liberation and freedom--to become free to explore the public world--that widowhood will give her. Ironically, it is the reappearance of her husband, who moves freely in the public world, that causes her sudden heart failure. What she looked forward to as the possibility of free choice to do and go where she wishes has suddenly been withdrawn from her by her renewed status within the publicly sanctioned system of marriage, and it is the abrupt loss of this possibility that produces the lethal shock to her system.

[5]   The complexity of the conflicts between private and public life is brought out in the way in which structures secure their power through law and legality. With immense power, the law sometimes acts as an arbitrary form of public judgment that disregards personal needs and circumstances. This idea is brought out on the most personal level in Glaspell's *Trifles,* in which the two major characters, both women, are faced urgently with the conflict between their personal identification with the accused woman, Minnie, and their public obligation to the law. One of the women, Mrs. Peters, is reminded that she is "married to the law" (speech 143); but she and Mrs. Hale suppress the evidence that they know would condemn Minnie, even though technically--by law, that is--their knowledge is public property. Their way of resolving the conflict therefore involves their rejection of public demands in favor of personal concerns.

[6]   The legal conflict can also be treated more generally and philosophically. For example, Wordsworth deals with the morality--or immorality--of the conflict in "Lines Written in Early Spring" when he says, "Have I not reason to lament / What man has made of man" (lines 15-16). "What man has made of man" in its most extreme form is legalized suppression and persecution, but Wordsworth does little more with the topic than to say that he laments it. Layton, however, in "Rhine Boat Trip," deals with the extremity of human cruelty. In this poem, Layton condemns the Nazi exterminations of "Jewish mothers" and "murdered rabbis" during the Holocaust of World War II. Ironically, the exterminations were carried out legally, for it has commonly been observed that the Nazis created laws to justify all their atrocities.

[7]   It is works about warfare that especially highlight how irreconcilable the conflicts between personal and public concerns can become. A comic but nevertheless real instance is dramatized by Thomas Hardy in "Channel Firing." In this poem, set in a church graveyard, the skeleton of "Parson Thirdly" views "gunnery practice out at sea" (line 10) as evidence that his "forty year" dedication to serving his church was a waste of time. His conclusion is that he would have been better off ignoring his public role and instead sticking "to pipes and beer." Although Thirdly is disillusioned, he has not been as deeply affected personally by warfare as the speaker of Lowell's "Patterns." Her fiancé, she learns, has been killed fighting abroad; and his death leads her to question--and by implication to doubt--the external "patterns" that destroy one's personal plans for life (line 107). Unlike both these characters, who are deeply touched by the effects of warfare, Peyton Farquhar, the main character in Bierce's "An Occurrence at Owl Creek Bridge," is actually killed by his commitment to a public concern--that of the south in the Civil War. As in "Channel Firing" and "Patterns," Farquhar's situation shows the absolute power of the public world over the private.

[8]   The works examined generally agree that, under ideal conditions, the private world should be supreme. They also demonstrate that in many ways, the public world invades the private world with a wide range of effects, from making people behave foolishly to destroying them utterly. Naturally, the tone of the works is shaped by the degree of seriousness of the conflict. Chekhov's *The Bear* is good-humored and farcical because the characters overcome the social roles in which they are cast. More sober are works such as "Dover Beach" and "Young Goodman Brown," in which characters are either overcome by public commitments or deliberately turn their backs on them. In the highest range of seriousness are works such as "Rhine Boat Trip," "Patterns," and "An Occurrence at Owl Creek Bridge," in which the individual is crushed by irresistible public forces. The works compared and contrasted here show varied and powerful conflicts between personal interests and public demands.

Commentary on the Essay

This demonstrative student essay, combining for discussion all three genres of fiction, poetry, and drama, is visualized as an assignment at the end of a unit of study. The expectation prompting the assignment is that a fairly large number of literary works can be profitably compared on the basis of a unifying subject, idea, or technique. For this essay, the works—seven poems, three stories, and two plays—are compared and contrasted on the common topic of private-public conflicts. It is obviously impossible to discuss all the works in detail in every paragraph. The essay therefore demonstrates that a writer may introduce a large number of works in a straightforward comparison-contrast method without a need for detailed comparison of each work with every other work on each of the major subtopics (social, legal, military).

Thus, the first section, consisting of paragraphs 2 to 4, treats six of the works. In paragraph 2, however, only two works are discussed, and in paragraph 3 one of these works is carried over for comparison with only one additional work. Paragraph 4 springs out of the second, utilizing one of the works discussed there and then bringing out comparisons with three additional works.

The same technique is used in the rest of the essay. Paragraph 5 introduces only one work; paragraph 6 introduces two additional works; and paragraph 7 introduces three works for comparison and contrast. Each of the twelve works is then eventually discussed at least once in terms of how it contributes to the major topic. One might note that the essay concentrates on a relatively small number of the works, such as Chekhov's *The Bear* and Hawthorne's "Young Goodman Brown," but that as newer topics are introduced, the essay goes on to works that are more closely connected to these topics.

The technique of extended comparison-contrast used in this way shows how the various works can be defined and distinguished in relation to the common idea. The concluding paragraph (8) summarizes these distinctions by suggesting a continuous line along which each of the works may be placed.

Even so, the treatment of so many texts might easily cause crowding and confusion. The division of the major topic into subtopics, as noted, is a major means of trying to make the essay easy to follow. An additional means is the introduction of transitional words and phrases such as *also, choose,* and *one of the major conflicts.*

An extended comparison-contrast essay cannot present a full treatment of each of the works. The works are unique, and there are many elements that do not yield to the comparison-contrast method. Ideas unique to Hardy's "Channel Firing," for example, are (1) that human beings need eternal rest and not eternal life, (2) that God is amused by—or indifferent to—human affairs, (3) that religious callings or vocations may be futile, and (4) that war itself is the supreme form of cruelty. All these topics would require separate treatment, but they are not particularly useful to the subject of the essay. A topic compatible with the general private-public topic is needed, and the connection is readily made (paragraph 7) through the character of Hardy's Parson Thirdly. Because the essay deals with the conflicts brought out by Thirdly's comments, Hardy's poem is linked to all the other works for comparative purposes. So it is with the other works, each of which could also be the subject of analysis from many standpoints other than comparison-contrast. The effect of the comparison of all the works collectively, however, is the enhanced understanding of each of the works separately. To achieve such an understanding and to explain it are the major goals of the extended comparison-contrast method.

SPECIAL TOPICS FOR WRITING AND ARGUMENT
ABOUT COMPARISON AND CONTRAST

1. The use of the speaker in Arnold's "Dover Beach" (p. 693) and Wordsworth's "Lines Written in Early Spring" (p. 1048).

2. The description of fidelity to love in Keats's "Bright Star" (p. 779) and Shakespeare's Sonnet 73: "That Time of Year Thou May'st in Me Behold" (p. 877), Arnold's "Dover Beach" (p. 693) or Lowell's "Patterns" (p. 1174).

3. The view of women in Chekhov's *The Bear* (p. 1625) and Maupassant's "The Necklace" (p. 4) or in Glaspell's *Trifles* (p. 1244) and Rossetti's "Echo" (p. 892).

4. The use of descriptive scenery in Hawthorne's "Young Goodman Brown" (p. 436) and Lowell's "Patterns" (p. 1174) or in Poe's "The Cask of Amontillado" (p. 563) and Bierce's "An Occurrence at Owl Creek Bridge" (p. 257).

5. Symbols of disapproval in Hardy's "Channel Firing" (p. 703) and Frost's "Desert Places" (p. 912).

6. The treatment of loss in Rossetti's "Echo" (p. 892) and Wagner's "The Boxes" (p. 1211).

7. Any of the foregoing topics applied to a number of separate works.

Appendix I
MLA Recommendations
for Documenting
Electronic Sources

ELECTRONIC SOURCES

Both students and instructors can now take advantage of the technology available to assist in research. While many libraries offer varied databases that enable researchers to locate information easily, the main thrust of technology is now the exploration of the World Wide Web (www). Through the use of various "search engines," you simply need to enter the name of an author, title, or topic for which you will be linked to a host of resources from all over the world—home pages of specific authors, literary organizations, works on various topics by contemporary writers—a good deal of what you're searching for. An important caveat is that many sources still remain in printed journals and magazines; they may or may not be on the Web. To make your searches thorough, therefore, *you must never neglect to search for printed information.*

This appendix provides general guidelines for making electronic source citations, and therefore it is intended to augment the section entitled "Documenting Your Work" in Chapter 32. For general information on citation recommendations by the Modern Language Association (MLA), see Joseph Gibaldi, *MLA Handbook for Writers of Research Papers,* 5th ed. (New York: MLA, 1999).

Because the available methods of obtaining electronic information are developing so rapidly, the printed style manuals have had difficulty keeping up with the changes. If you do a Web search looking for information on these styles, chances are the information you discover will vary from site to site. Therefore, you need to know the basics that are required for the citation of your sources.

When referring to electronic sources, it is vital to type every letter, number, symbol, dot, underline, and space accurately. Recovery systems are unforgiving, and mistakes or omissions *of any sort* make it impossible to retrieve your source. Electronic sources are often transitory because someone, somewhere, must maintain the sources (through the updating of information and the paying of fees). The sources therefore are not always reliable, so printing a copy of sources you plan to cite will make your citations both definite and accurate.

The style generally accepted in the "cyber" world, and the one recommended by the MLA, places angle brackets (< >) before and after Internet addresses and Uniform Resource Locators (URLs). If you see brackets around an address you want to use, do not use them as part of the address when you are seeking retrieval. Also, since a number of word-processing programs now support the use of italics, you can use either italics or underlines when needed. Each letter and symbol must be clearly identifiable, and italics can sometimes be ambiguous, so the use of underlines is generally more specific.[1] If in doubt about which to use, consult with your instructor.

MLA Style Guidelines

Many of the guidelines the MLA has authorized for the citation of electronic sources overlap with the MLA recommendations for printed sources, but to avoid ambiguity a number of recommendations bear repetition. Web sources are documented in basically the same style as printed sources. According to the MLA Web site,[2] the following items need to be included if they are available:

1. The name of the author, editor, compiler, or translator of the source (if available and relevant), reversed for alphabetizing (i.e., last name first), and followed by an abbreviation, such as *ed.*, if appropriate

2. If there is no author listed in the source, you should list the title first: The title of a poem, short story, article, or similar short work within a scholarly project, database, or periodical (in quotation marks); or the title of a posting to a discussion list or forum (taken from the subject line and enclosed by quotation marks), followed by the description *Online posting*

3. The title of a book (underlined or italicized)

4. The name of the editor, compiler, or translator of the text (if relevant and if not cited earlier), preceded by the appropriate abbreviation, such as *Ed.*

5. Publication information for any printed version of the source

6. The title of the scholarly project, database, periodical, or professional or personal site (underlined); or, for a professional or personal site with no title, a description such as *Home page*

---

[1] Angle brackets are not used currently in the system recommended by the American Psychological Association (APA); also, the APA prefers italics in the citation of addresses, whereas the MLA prefers the use of underlines.

[2] Source: Modern Language Association (MLA), <http://www.mla.org/main.stl.htm>.

7. The name of the editor of the scholarly project or database (if available)
8. The version number of the source (if not part of the title), or, for a journal, the volume number, issue number, or other identifying number
9. The date of electronic publication, of the latest update, or of posting
10. For a posting to a discussion list or forum, the name of the list or forum
11. The number range or total number of pages, paragraphs, or other sections, if they are numbered
12. The name of any institution or organization sponsoring or associated with the Web site
13. The date when the researcher accessed the source
14. The electronic address, or Uniform Resource Locator, of the source (in angle brackets < >)

EXAMPLES

For a Book

> Shaw, Bernard. <u>Pygmalion</u>. 1916. Bartleby.com, Inc. [Date of access] <http://www.bartleby.com/138/index.html>.

For a Poem

> Carroll, Lewis. "The Hunting of the Snark." 1876. <u>Project Gutenberg</u>. 8 Mar. 1992. Illinois Benedictine College. 14 Feb. 2000 <ftp://sunsite.unc.edu/pub/docs/books/gutenberg/etext91/snark12.txt>.

For a Journal Article

> Newbold, W. Webster. "Transactional Writing Instruction on the World Wide Web." <u>Kairos</u> 4.1 (Fall 1999): 16 secs. 14 Feb. 2000 <http://english.ttu.edu/kairos/4.1/binder.html?features/newbold/bridgenw.html>.

For a Magazine Article

> Simonson, Robert. "<u>Aida</u> Readies for Feb. 25 Bow at Broadway's Palace." <u>Playbill</u> 11 Feb. 2000. 14 Feb. 2000 <http://www.playbill.com/cgi-bin/plb/news?cmd=show&code=93462>.

Posting to a Discussion List

> Crowley, Paul. "The Death of Stratfordianism." Online posting. 5 Dec. 1999. Deja News. <humanities.lit.authors.shakespeare>.

For a Scholarly Project

> <u>Voice of the Shuttle: Web Page for Humanities Research</u>. Ed. Alan Liu. 14 Feb. 2000. University of California, Santa Barbara. 14 Feb. 2000 <http://vos.ucsb.edu/>.

For a Professional Site

> <u>The Nobel Foundation Official Website</u>. The Nobel Foundation. 2 Dec. 1999 <http://www.nobel.se/>.

For a Personal Site

> Barrett, Dan. The Gentle Giant Home Page. 14 Feb. 2000 <http://www.blazemonger.com/GG/index.html>.

For Synchronous Communications (such as MOOs, MUDs, and IRCs)

> Ghostly Presence. Group Discussion. Telnet. 8 Feb. 2000 <telnet://moo.du.org:8000/80anon/ anonview/14036#focus>.

For a Gopher Site

> Swift, Jonathan. "A Description of the Morning." 1709 <gopher://gopher.english.upenn.edu:70/00/ E-Text/PEAL/Swift/morning>.

Appendix II
Brief Biographies
of the Poets in Part III

Brian W. Aldiss (b. 1925) • Aldiss is best known as a writer of science fiction, but he has also written novels, dramas, reviews, and considerable poetry. He was educated in English private schools, and during World War II he served in the far east (Burma, Sumatra). After the war he worked for a time as a bookseller in Oxford, when he also began writing. His first published work was *The Brightfount Diaries* (1955), after which his output flourished. Among his many works are the companion novels *Frankenstein Unbound* (1973) and *Dracula Unbound* (1991). One of his poetry collections is *Homelife with Cats* (1992). Recent novels are *Somewhere East of Life* (1994) and *White Mars* (2000). He was the recipient of the British Science Fiction Award in 1972, and is a founding trustee of World Science Fiction (1982).

A. R. Ammons (Archie Randolph Ammons, b. 1926) • Ammons was educated in North Carolina and California. He began teaching at Cornell University in 1964, the year in which his second poetry collection was published. Among his honors are the Bollingen Prize (1973–74), a MacArthur Fellowship, and the Robert Frost medal from the Poetry Society of America. Some of his collections of poetry are *The Selected Poems: Expanded Edition* (1986), *Sumerian Vistas* (1987), *Garbage* (1993), and *Brink Road* (1996). He published a long poem, *Glare*, in 1997. "80–Proof" was included in *Diversifications* (1975).

Maya Angelou (b. 1928) • Born in St. Louis, Angelou acted and sang before becoming a writer. She is known as much for her fiction as for her poetry, and has also written plays. She achieved recognition with *I Know Why the Caged Bird Sings* (1970). *Just Give Me a Cool Drink of Water 'fore I Die* appeared in 1971, and she has published regularly since. Her national importance was recognized when she was chosen to read her poetry at the inauguration of President Clinton in January, 1993. Her collection of essays *Even the Stars Look Lonesome* appeared in 1997. Her collected work is *The Complete Collected Poems of Maya Angelou* (1994). In recent years she has spoken and sung on a number of public television productions.

Matthew Arnold (1822–1888) • One of the major Victorian poets, Arnold was brought up among books and learning, and eventually (1857) became Professor of Poetry at Oxford. In his Oxford lectures he described a loss of security and religious faith, and hence he stressed the need to recover absolutes—which to him was the major "function of criticism at the present time." "Dover Beach" is, along with "The Scholar Gypsy" and "Stanzas from the Grande Chartreuse," among his best-known poems.

Margaret Atwood (b. 1939) • For a brief biography, see p. 387.

W. H. Auden (Wystan Hugh Auden, 1907–1973) • Auden was born in England but became a permanent resident of the United States after the Spanish Civil War. A Marxist in his youth, he became a devout Christian in later years. He wrote prolifically, including collaborations with the dramatist Christopher Isherwood and the poet Louis MacNeice. Another notable collaboration is the libretto for Igor Stravinsky's opera *The Rake's Progress* (1951). He edited the *Oxford Book of Light Verse* (1938).

Imamu Amiri Baraka (LeRoi Jones, b. 1934) • Born in New Jersey, LeRoi Jones attended Rutgers, Howard, and Columbia Universities, and also the New School. After serving in the Air Force, he adopted the name Imamu Amiri Baraka. As a practical outgrowth of his devotion to African-American causes, he founded a community center—"Spirit House"—for African Americans in Newark, New Jersey. Among his many works are *Four Black Revolutionary Plays* (1969) and *African Revolution* (1973). He has appeared on television and on film, most notably as the character Rastaman in *Bullworth* (1998). His *Selected Poetry* appeared in 1979, and a full sampling of his work, including new poems, is in *The LeRoi Jones/Amiri Baraka Reader* (1999).

Wendell Berry (b. 1934) • One of the most popular poets in the United States, Berry is a resident of Kentucky, where he was brought up and educated and where he taught for many years. His output as a poet, essayist, and novelist has been voluminous. He has published many separate volumes of poetry, including *The Broken Ground* (1964), *Clearing* (1977), *The Wheel* (1982), *Entries* (1997), and *A Timbered Choir: The Sabbath Poems, 1979-1997* (1998). Readers may find some of his short fiction in *Fidelity: Five Stories* (1993). His *The Memory of Old Jack* (1999) is a recent novel. An early edition of his collected verse is *Collected Poems, 1957-1982* (1985).

Earle Birney (Alfred Earle Birney, 1904–1995) • One of the major modern Canadian writers, Birney was born in Calgary, Alberta, and received his higher education at the University of British Columbia. He was editor of *Twentieth Century Canadian Poetry* (1953). In 1975 McClelland and Stewart of Canada issued his collected poetry. By 1985 he had published more than a dozen collections of poetry in addition to his stories and plays.

Elizabeth Bishop (1911–1979) • Bishop was brought up by an aunt in Worcester, Massachusetts. She attended private schools and Vassar. During much of her life she lived in Brazil. She taught for a time at the University of Washington and then at Harvard. Her first collection of poems was *North and South* (1946), which she expanded in 1955 as *North and South—A Cold Spring,* for which she received the Pulitzer Prize in Poetry in 1956.

William Blake (1757–1827) • Blake was apprenticed to an engraver in London at the age of fourteen. Throughout his career he published his poems with his own engravings, and these original editions are now valuable collector's items. Blake was a revolutionary at heart who thought that humanity would flower if institutions were eliminated or at least redirected. *Songs of Experience,* from which "London" is taken, is a collection of poems on this theme, published in 1794, five years after the outbreak of the French Revolution. In this same year he published *Songs of Innocence,* from which "The Lamb" is taken.

Louise Bogan (1897–1970) • Born in Maine, Bogan spent most of her life in New York, writing regular reviews for *The New Yorker.* Her first volume of poems was *Body of This Death* (1923), in which "Women" appeared. Her *Collected Poems* (1954) was awarded the Bollingen Prize. Her major critical work was *Achievement in American Poetry, 1900–1950,* published in 1951. *Journey Around My Room* (1980) is a posthumous autobiographical work.

Arna Bontemps (1902–1973) • Born in Louisiana, Bontemps by profession was a librarian (at Fisk University). In addition to poetry, he published a number of novels and works of children's fiction. *One Hundred Years of Negro Freedom* (1961) is a widely heralded historical work.

Anne Bradstreet (1612–1672) • Bradstreet was born in England. She married early and came to the American colonies when she was eighteen. Her career was that of wife and mother, and she bore eight children. Nevertheless she managed to write poems regularly and kept them together in manuscript. In 1650 her brother-in-law had them published in London without her knowledge, and she was therefore unable to make corrections (see lines 3–6 of "The Author to Her Book"). The volume, titled *The Tenth Muse,* was the first poetic publication in England by anyone living in colonial America. A second and corrected edition was considered in about 1666, and "The Author to Her Book" was composed in this expectation, but the new edition did not appear until six years after her death.

Joseph Brodsky (Iosif Alexandrovich Brodsky, 1940–1996) • Brodsky, a native Russian, came to the United States after he was exiled in 1972 for what was then considered subversion of the Russian government (i.e., he declared that people should be free). As a new American he attempted to become a poet of English. Usually, however, he wrote in Russian and then translated his verse into English himself or with the aid of others. Professionally, he served as a poet in residence at a number of schools from Michigan to Massachusetts. His greatest recognition came with his receiving a MacArthur Foundation Fellowship and with his being named American Poet Laureate in 1991. His verse is collected in *To Urania: Selected Poems 1965–1985* (1988). His posthumous collection of poems, *So Forth,* was published in 1996.

Gwendolyn Brooks (b. 1917) • Brooks was born in Chicago, where she has spent most of her life. Winner of the Pulitzer Prize for Poetry in 1950 (for *Annie Allen,* 1949), she is concerned with race in both her fictional and poetic works. "We Real Cool" exemplified this emphasis. In 1967 she began directing her work toward African-American readers, and she has published a number of her poems in pamphlet form, of which *Primer for Blacks* (1980) is one. Recent works are *Blacks* (1991), *Maud Martha* (1993) and *Selected Poems* (1999).

Olga Broumas (b. 1949) • Broumas is a native of Greece. Coming to the United States, she received her B.A. from the University of Pennsylvania in 1970 and her M.F.A. from the University of Oregon in 1973. She has taught English and writing in Oregon and Idaho and now lives in Massachusetts. Some of her collections are *Caritas* (1976), *Pastoral Jazz* (1983), *Black Holes, Black Stockings* (prose poems, 1985), *Sappho's Gymnasium* (1995, with T. Begley), and *Rave: Poems 1975-1999* (1999). "Circe" was included in *Beginning with O* (1977).

Elizabeth Barrett Browning (1806–1861) • English born, Elizabeth Barrett suffered a crippling spinal injury when still a girl. Despite this adversity she had become a widely recognized poet when she married Robert Browning in 1846. Because of her condition and the English climate, the Brownings moved to Italy, where they remained until Elizabeth's death. During her lifetime, her reputation as a poet eclipsed Robert's. Her *Cry of the Children* (1843) was an early poetic protest against the industrial exploitation of children. In 1850 she published *Sonnets from the Portuguese,* which she presented as a gift to her husband.

Robert Browning (1812–1889) • In his twenties and early thirties, Browning wrote a number of versified plays for the stage, but these were unsuccessful, and he did not achieve fame in his native England until he was well into his fifties. Because of his experience with drama, he found his poetic voice within the medium of the dramatic monologue, which he perfected to a high degree. Both "My Last Duchess" and "Soliloquy of the Spanish Cloister" appeared in his *Dramatic Lyrics* of 1842, exactly during the time when he was also writing his plays.

Robert Burns (1759–1796) • The best known and loved poet of Scotland, Burns gave up farming and taught himself to read and write English, French, and Latin. He published his first volume, *Scots Poems Chiefly in the Scottish Dialect,* in 1786. His use of the down-to-earth idiom of Scots peasants, together with joyous irreverence and frank lustiness, made him instantly famous.

George Gordon, Lord Byron (1788–1824) • One of the major English Romantic poets, Byron created the so-called Byronic hero, a driven and solitary figure who is misunderstood by his fellow human beings. He published his semiautobiographical poem "Childe Harolde's Pilgrimage" in 1811. In 1815 he published *Hebrew Melodies* (1815), in which "The Destruction of Sennacherib" appeared. That year, he left England and never returned. He continued writing poetry as he traveled, including the 16,000-line unfinished poem *Don Juan.* He died at Missolonghi, in Greece, while fighting for Greek independence.

Thomas Campion (1567–1620) • English-born Campion was known in his day not only as a poet but also as a composer. He set many of his poems to music, including "Cherry Ripe." Two of his collections are *A Book of Airs* (1601) and *The Third and Fourth Books of Airs* (ca. 1617). His interest in the relationship of music and poetry prompted him to write a discourse on English metrics, *Observation in the Art of English Poesy* (1602).

Lewis Carroll (Charles L. Dodgson, 1832–1898) • Carroll is the pen name of English writer Charles L. Dodgson, who is famous for *Alice's Adventures in Wonderland* and *Through the Looking Glass.* Carroll was also a mathematician, lecturer, logician, and photographer. "Jabberwocky," from *Through the Looking Glass,* stems out of his interest in words. The word *chortle,* which he created in this poem (a blending of *chuckle* and *snort*), is now standard English.

Amy Clampitt (1920–1994) • Clampitt was a native of Iowa, receiving her education at Grinnell College and later at Columbia University. For many years she worked in the publishing field and also for the National Audubon Society. Although she wrote poetry during most of her lifetime, she was not published until she was in her sixties, her first volume being *The Kingfisher* (1983). During the remainder of her life she published regular volumes of poems, completing *What the Light was Like* (1985), *Archaic Figure* (1987), and *Westward* (1990). In 1994, the last year of her life, she published her final collection, *A Silence Opens.*

Lucille Clifton (b. 1936) • Clifton was born and educated in New York. Her productivity as a writer began in the 1970s and has been strong ever since. One of her earliest poetry collections was *An Ordinary Woman* (1974). She also published *Next: New Poems* (1987) and *Good Woman: Poems and a Memoir, 1969–1980* (1987). In addition to her poetry, she has written a number of stories and poems for children, such as *All Us Come Cross the Water* (1973), *The Book of Light* (1993), *Everett Anderson's Christmas Coming* (1993), and *The Lucky Stone* (1999). A collection of her poems is *Blessing the Boats: New and Selected Poems, 1988–2000* (2000).

Leonard Cohen (b. 1934) • Cohen is a native of Montreal, and he received his education at McGill University and also at Columbia. He traveled widely, spending years in Greece, England, New York, and California. He began writing poetry early. His first collections were *Let Us Compare Mythologies* (1956) and *The Spice Box of Earth* (1961). He also published two successful novels, *The Favorite Game* (1963) and *Beautiful Losers* (1966). Today he is best known for his featured television concerts and also for the many record albums and compact disc collections of his songs and music. Among the most recent of these are *The Future* (1992) and *Cohen Live* (1994). An anthology of his work is *The Concise Leonard Cohen* (1999).

Samuel Taylor Coleridge (1772–1834) • Coleridge was born in Devon, in southern England, and studied at Cambridge University but did not earn a degree. After a short stint as a soldier he fell into dire financial straits, from which he was rescued by the Wedgewood brothers (of ceramic fame), who provided him with an annuity so that he could devote himself to poetry. Wordsworth and he together published the *Lyrical Ballads* of 1798, a collection which is the benchmark of the English Romantic Movement (see also pp. 1034–35). Coleridge contributed "The Rime of the Ancient Mariner," his most famous poem, and also "Kubla Khan." After 1802 he wrote little poetry, but his *Biographia Literaria* of 1817 is one of the major works of literary criticism of the early nineteenth century.

Billy Collins (b. 1941) • A native of New York, Collins received degrees at Holy Cross and the University of California at Riverside. He lives in New York and is a professor of English at Lehman College. Among his collections of poetry are *The Apple that Astonished Paris* (1989), which includes "Schoolsville," *Questions about Angels* (1991), a winner in the National Poetry Series competition, *The Art of Drowning* (1996), and *Picnic, Lightning* (1998).

Frances Cornford (1886–1960) • Cornford, a granddaughter of Charles Darwin, lived most of her life in Cambridge, England. She published only a few volumes of verse, and her *Collected Poems* was published in 1954.

William Cowper (1731–1800) • Cowper is universally recognized because of his lines "God moves in a mysterious way / His wonders to perform." He received his education at an English private ("public") school, an institution that he attacked in his *Tirocinium* in 1785. He was qualified to practice law, but he never made a career of it. Although throughout his life he was troubled with depression and made at least two suicide attempts, he wrote a considerable amount of prose and much poetry. His most widely recognized long poem is *The Task* (1785), and his best lyric poems are to be found in the *Olney Hymns* (1775), which contained "God Moves in a Mysterious Way" and "Oh, for a Closer Walk with God."

Stephen Crane (1871–1900) • For a brief biography, see p. 115.

Richard Crashaw (1612–1649) • Crashaw left England when the English Civil War was beginning in 1642, and he spent the remainder of his life in Italy. He is best known as a religious and devotional poet, although he also wrote on so conventional a topic as "Wishes to His Supposed Mistress." In 1646 he published *Steps to the Temple*, which contained "On Our Crucified Lord." Other works (with Latin titles) were *A Book of Holy Epigrams* (1634) and the posthumous *Poems to Our God* (1652).

Countée Cullen (1903–1946) • Poet, novelist, and writer of children's books, Cullen studied at New York University and Harvard and became one of the leading figures in the Harlem Renaissance of the 1920s. Because he used an accent in spelling his first name, his friends gave him the nickname "Tay." He was a pioneer in dealing with the conditions and aspirations of African-Americans. His earliest book of poems was *Color* (1925), which included "Yet Do I Marvel." Among his later collections were *The Ballad of the Brown Girl* (1927) and *The Black Christ and Other Poems* (1929).

e. e. cummings (1894–1962) • Cummings studied at Harvard, receiving a master's degree there. During World War I, he served in the Ambulance Corps in France, and, as a result of false charges of treason, was imprisoned—an experience he wrote about in his first work, *The Enormous Room* (1922). He began publishing poetry shortly thereafter and continued doing so throughout his life. His collected poetry, consisting of more than a thousand poems, was published in 1992.

James Dickey (1923–1997) • Dickey was a native of Georgia. He served in World War II and afterwards spent a number of years writing advertising copy. After 1969 he became a full-time writer and teacher. During the 1980s he published three volumes of poetry. Usually his poems are narratives which touch on violence and tragedy. "The Performance," for example, demonstrates, on the one hand, the violence that characterizes Dickey's well-received novel *Deliverance* (1970), and on the other, the courageousness of a man insisting on his individuality and rights even against the greatest odds. One of his late novels was *To the White Sea*, published in 1993. A number of his works have been published posthumously in *The James Dickey Reader* (1999). His letters are included in *Crux: The Letters of James Dickey* (1999), and his poetry is collected in *James Dickey: The Selected Poems* (1998).

Emily Dickinson (1830-1886) • For a brief biography, see pp. 1060–66.

John Donne (ca. 1572–1631) • Donne was born into a Roman Catholic family at a time when the protestant reign of Elizabeth I was firmly established. In 1591 he enrolled at Lincoln's Inn in London to study science, philosophy, law, languages, and literature. In order to rise in English aristocratic circles, he changed his religion to Anglicanism. His hopes were ended in 1601, however, because of his elopement with Ann More, whose uncle accused him of a clandestine marriage (then a crime if the woman was an heiress) and had him jailed. Although the marriage was recognized in 1602, Donne could not regain political favor, and he and Ann struggled until he took a doctorate of divinity in 1616 (Ann died in 1617). He found favor and rose quickly to become Dean of St. Paul's Cathedral in London, where his sermons were well attended by the "nobility and gentry." He became widely known, publishing more than 130 of the sermons he delivered during his decade as dean. His poems, both religious and love poems, were not published during his lifetime but were circulated only privately in manuscript. They were first published two years after his death. For two centuries he was neglected, but in the twentieth century he has earned recognition as one of the greatest of English poets.

Michael Drayton (1563–1631) • Like his friend Shakespeare, Drayton was a native of Warwickshire. He became educated while serving in an aristocratic household. He was a versatile poet, writing not only sonnets but also topographic poetry (*England's Heroical Epistles,* 1599), epic (*Nymphidia,* 1627), and satire (*The Owl,* 1604), in addition to popular ballads, myths, and scriptural paraphrases. "Since There's No Help" appeared in his sonnet sequence *Idea, the Shepherd's Garland.*

John Dryden (1631–1700) • Poet Laureate from 1668 to 1688, Dryden was one of the foremost English poets and dramatists of the seventeenth century. His major poetic achievement was to fine-tune the heroic or neoclassic couplet, which he used for "To the Memory of Mr. Oldham." Nevertheless, he used blank verse for his best play, *All For Love* (1677), which deals with the same material as Acts IV and V of Shakespeare's *Antony and Cleopatra.* In 1688 he lost his official positions because he had been a supporter of the deposed James II. During the last twelve years of his life, therefore, he was forced to support himself mainly with translations, providing his contemporaries with poetic versions of Virgil, Ovid, Juvenal, and Chaucer.

Paul Laurence Dunbar (1872–1906) • Dunbar was born in Ohio, the son of former slaves. During his brief life he rose to prominence as a poet, dramatist, and novelist. His first two collections of poems, *Oak and Ivy* (1893) and *Majors and Minors* (1895), in which "Sympathy" appeared, were favorably reviewed by William Dean Howells. His collected poems were published posthumously in 1913.

Ray Durem (1915–1963) • Selected poems by Durem were printed in Dudley Randall's *The Black Poets: A New Anthology* (1971). Durem's collected verse appeared in *Take No Prisoners* (1962, 1971).

Richard (Ghormley) Eberhart (b. 1904) • Eberhart is a man of incredible longevity. The recipient of many awards, including the Pulitzer Prize in Poetry in 1966, he was born in Minnesota and received his higher education at Dartmouth and Cambridge. His many works include *Maine Poems* (1988), and *Collected Poems* of 1930, 1976, and 1988. In addition, *Long Reach: Uncollected Poems, 1948-1983* appeared in 1984, and *New and Selected Poems: 1930–1990,* was published in 1990. In 1982 the governor of New Hampshire, Eberhart's home state, proclaimed a Richard Eberhart Day in his honor.

T. S. Eliot (1888–1965) • Born in Missouri, Thomas Stearns Eliot moved to England in 1914 and became a British citizen in 1927. With *The Waste Land* in 1922, he electrified the literary world because of his poetic use of colloquial speech and frank subject matter. Though he is considered a hyper-serious poet, his lighter side is shown in *Old Possum's Book of Practical Cats* (1939). These poems achieved popular fame in 1983 in the Broadway musical *Cats,* which then began a record run of seventeen consecutive years, not closing until 2000.

Elizabeth Tudor, Queen Elizabeth I (1533–1603) • Queen of England from 1558 to 1603, Elizabeth was famed for her eloquence and wit. She is perhaps best remembered for the support she gave to Shakespeare and the acting company at the Globe Theater. She wrote a number of translations and left a small number of poems. Some other poems attributed to her are of doubtful authorship. Her works were edited and published in 1964.

James Emanuel (b. 1921) • Emanuel was born in Nebraska and attended Howard University. He earned his Ph.D. at Columbia in 1962 and joined the faculty of English at the City College of New York. Throughout his career, he has regularly written poetry, publishing poems in journals such as *Phylon* and *Negro Digest.* An early collection of his poems is *Panther Man* (1970). More recent collections are *Black Man Abroad: The Toulouse Poems* (1978), *A Chisel in the Dark* (1980), *The Broken Bowl* (1983), *Deadly James and Other Poems* (1987), and *Jazz: From the Haiku King* (1999). In 1967 he published a biography of Langston Hughes for the Twayne series of American authors.

Lynn Emanuel (b. 1949) • Emanuel is a native of New York and currently is director of the University of Pittsburgh's writing program. Her first two collections of poetry are *Hotel Fiesta* and *The Dig,* which have been reprinted together by the University of Illinois Press. Her most recent poetry collection is *Then, Suddenly* (1999).

John Engels (b. 1931) • Engels has published poetry regularly since the 1970s. Early collections are *Signals from the Safety Coffin* (1975) and *Blood Mountain* (1977). *Vivaldi in Early Fall* (1981) includes "Naming the Animals." Some of his later collections of verse are *Weather-Fear: New and Selected Poems, 1958–1982* (1983), *Cardinals in the Ice Age* (1987), *Big Water: Poems* (1995), and *Sinking Creek: Poems* (1998).

Abbie Huston Evans (1881–1983) • Evans was perhaps the longest-lived of all American or British poets, dying in 1983 at the age of 102. She began receiving recognition in the 1930s, and was granted an honorary Litt.D. degree from Bowdoin College in 1961. Her collections of poems are *Outcrop* (1928), *The Bright North* (1938), and *Fact of Crystal* (1961). The University of Pittsburgh Press published her *Collected Poems* in 1970. "The Iceberg Seven-Eighths Under" was first published in *Fact of Crystal.*

Mari Evans (b. 1923) • Evans has written fiction and criticism in addition to a major collection of poems, *I Am a Black Woman* (1970). *JD* (1975) is a collection of four stories about a young boy living in an urban housing project. Her *Black Women Writers (1950–1980): A Critical Evaluation* appeared in 1984. *A Dark and Splendid Mass* was published in 1992. Interest in social matters prompted her *Dear Corinne: Tell Somebody,* a fictional work about child abuse (1999). A collection of children's verse is *Sing My Black: Alternative Nursery Rhymes for Children* (1998).

Edward Field (b. 1924) • A native of Brooklyn, Field studied at New York University, and also, for a time, studied method acting at the Moscow Art Theatre. "Icarus" is taken from his first collection of poems, *Stand Up, Friend, with Me* (1963). Another of his collections is *Stars in My Eyes* (1979). In 1990 he edited *Head of a Sad Angel,* stories by Alfred Chester, with an introduction by Gore Vidal.

Carolyn Forché (b. 1950) • Forché is a native of Detroit. After her first volume of poems in the Yale Younger Poets series (*Gathering the Tribes* [1976]) she spent two years in El Salvador as a journalist for Amnesty International. In 1982 she translated Claribel Alegria's *Flowers for the Volcano* in an English-Spanish edition. Her next volume of poetry was *The Country Between Us* in 1982, which includes "Because One Is Always Forgotten." In 1993 she published *Against Forgetting: Twentieth-Century Poetry of Witness,* an anthology of poems protesting against repression and genocide. In 1995 she published a long poem, *The Angel of History.*

Robert (Churchill) Francis (1901–1987) • Francis received his higher education at Harvard and lived most of his life in Amherst, Massachusetts, not far from the home of Emily Dickinson. Some of his collections are *The Orb Weaver* (1980), *Come Out into the Sun* (1965), *Like Ghosts of Eagles* (1974), and *Butter Hill and Other Poems* (1984). His collected verse appeared in *Collected Poems 1936-1976* (1976). He received a number of distinctions, among them the Brandeis University Creative Arts Award in 1974.

Robert Frost (1874–1963) • For a brief biography, see pp. 1100–1105.

Isabella Gardner (1915–1981) • Isabella Gardner was born in Massachusetts. During her lifetime, she acted, edited *Poetry* magazine (1952–1956), taught, published four volumes of poems, and gave frequent poetry readings. She declared herself "a poet who is woman first and poet second." Two years before her death, she published much of her poetry in *Isabella Gardner: The Collected Poems.*

John Gay (1685–1732) • English poet and playwright John Gay was born and educated in Devon. As a young boy he was apprenticed to a silk mercer but freed himself to become a writer in London. For a time in the late 1720s, he was a gentleman-in-waiting to the young Duke of Cumberland, for whom he wrote his *Fables,* which were among the most popular poems in the eighteenth century. His most famous play is *The Beggar's Opera* (1728), which at a stroke created *ballad opera*—a form featuring spoken dialogue and songs sung to popular music. "Let Us Take the Road" is from this play, and the music is the March in the opera *Rinaldo* (1711) by Georg Friderich Handel.

Dan Georgakas (b. 1938) • A native of Detroit, Georgakas received degrees at Wayne State University and the University of Michigan. Since 1978 he has been a faculty member of New York's Empire State College, New York University, and Queens College. His publications are varied, dealing with the film industry, radical American publications, the International Workers of the World, and American Indians. His poetry collection *Happy Man* (1968) includes "Hiroshima Crewman." Also in 1968 he edited and published *Z: An Anthology of Revolutionary Poetry.* A coedited work, *Detroit: I Do Mind Dying: A Study in Urban Revolution* (1975) was reissued in 1998.

Chief Dan George (1899–1981) • In the early part of his life Chief Dan George took many jobs unrelated to writing. In 1947 he became chief of the Tse-lal-watt Sioux tribe, holding this post until 1959. In the 1960s he launched himself on an acting and writing career. His greatest success as an actor was in the film *Little Big Man* (1970), for which he received an Oscar nomination as best supporting actor. After this time he appeared in a number of films and television shows, and he spent much time campaigning for more Native American involvement in the film industry. His autobiography *You Call Me Chief* appeared in 1981, the last year of his life. His poem "My Heart Soars" is from *Sannichtoni* (1974).

Allen Ginsberg (1926–1997) • One of the major voices of the "beat generation" of the 1950s and 1960s, Ginsberg was born in New Jersey and lived in San Francisco for a time. For many years he was a distinguished professor at Brooklyn College. His landmark poetry collection was *Howl and Other Poems* (1956), which occasioned a court case when certain persons sued, unsuccessfully, to suppress it on the grounds of obscenity. Ironically, his collection of 1973, *The Fall of America: Poems of These States,* received a National Book Award. Among his later publications were *Cosmopolitan Greetings: Poems 1986–1992* (1994) and a four-CD/cassette box set titled *Holy Soul Jelly Roll: Poems and Songs 1949–1993* (available from Rhino Word Beat).

Nikki Giovanni (Yolande Cornelia Giovanni, Jr., b. 1943) • Giovanni, a poet whose reputation has coincided with the development of African-American consciousness and pride, was born in Tennessee. She has written poems for children and has also published interviews with James Baldwin and Alice Walker. Among her collections of poetry are *Black Feeling, Black Talk* (1968), *Black Judgment* (1968), and *Cotton Candy on a Rainy Day* (1978). Recent works are *Those Who Ride the Night Winds* (1983), *Sacred Cows—and Other Edibles* (1988), and *The Selected Poems of Nikki Giovanni* (1996).

Louise Glück (b. 1943) • A native of New York, Glück took her higher education at Sarah Lawrence and Columbia. She currently lives in Vermont and teaches at Williams College. Recent poetry collections are *Ararat* (1990), *The Wild Iris* (1992), *Meadowlands* (1996), and *Vita Nova: Poems* (1999). In 1985 she received the National Book Critics Circle Award.

Jorie Graham (b. 1951) • Graham is a person of international credentials. She is a native of New York but was brought up in Italy, studied in Paris, and received a degree in film from New York University. Later she studied writing at the University of Iowa, where she is a faculty member; she is also on the faculty of Harvard University. Her poetry is thoughtful—a number of critics have said difficult—reflective, and challenging. Among her collections are *The End of Beauty* (1987), *Region of Unlikeness* (1991), *Materialism* (1993, 1998), *The Dream of the Unified Field* (1995), *The End of Beauty* (1998), and *Swarm* (2000).

Robert Graves (1895–1985) • Graves fought in the British army in World War I and was badly wounded. His early autobiographical memoir, *Good-Bye to All That* (1929), deals in part with his war experiences. He became famous in the 1970s, when the BBC and PBS dramatized his historical novels about the life and times of the Roman Emperor Claudius. His studies of mythology, *The White Goddess* (1947) and *The Greek Myths* (1955), explained the meaning of ancient religion to a generation of students.

Thomas Gray (1716–1771) • Gray was professor of history at Cambridge University. His poetic output was small, but nevertheless in 1757 he was offered the honor of Poet Laureate, which he refused. The "Elegy Written in a Country Churchyard" has been called one of the most often quoted poems of the English language. Another of Gray's frequently quoted poems is the "Ode on a Distant Prospect of Eton College," which concludes with the familiar lines "Where ignorance is bliss / 'Tis folly to be wise."

Marilyn Hacker (b. 1942) • Hacker, a native of New York City, has been the recipient of a National Book Award (1975) and a Guggenheim Fellowship. Her collections of poems include *Presentation Piece* (1974), *Separations* (1976), *Taking Notice* (1980), which includes "Sonnet Ending with a Film Subtitle," and *Selected Poems* (1994). The year 1990 saw the publication of the collection *Going Back to the River,* and in the same year she included new and selected poems in *The Hang-Glider's Daughter.* *Squares and Courtyards* (2000) is her most recent collection. In 1989 the composer Dennis Riley set five of her poems to music for soprano and chamber ensemble. In 1995 she was awarded the Lenore Marshall Poetry Prize for her eighth book of poems, *Winter Numbers* (1994).

John Haines (b. 1936) • Born in Virginia, Haines served in the Navy during World War II, receiving a number of battle stars. He lives in Alaska, where at various times he has supported himself by working as a hunter, gardener, fisherman, and trapper, in addition to his writing. If any modern American writer can lay claim to being a poet of Nature and the frontier, it is Haines. He has published a number of collections, including *News from the Glacier: Selected Poems* (1982), New Poems 1980—88 (1990), *The Owl in the Mask of the Dreamer: Collected Poems* (1996), and *At the End of this Summer: Poems 1948–1954* (1997).

Donald Hall (b. 1928) • Hall was born in Connecticut. In addition to his devotion to poetry, he is a literary and art critic, a collector of literary anecdotes, and a student of baseball. He has published a number of poetry collections, including *The Alligator Bride* (1969), *Kicking the Leaves* (1978), *The Happy Man* (1986), *The Museum of Clear Ideas: New Poems* (1994), and *The Old Life* (1996). He is editor of *The Oxford Illustrated Book of American Children's Poems* (1999). His *The One Day* was the winning poetry collection of the National Book Critics Circle Award in 1988.

Daniel Halpern (b. 1945) • Halpern was born and raised in New York and is a professor in the graduate writing program of Columbia University. He has lived on both the east and west coasts and also has a residence in Morocco. He has produced a number of poetry volumes, including *Traveling on Credit* (1972), *Seasonal Rights* (1982), *Foreign Neon* (1991), *Selected Poems* (1994) and *Something Shining: Poems* (1999). He has also done work in editing and translating. Uniquely interesting about him is that he has coauthored a cookbook, *The Good Food: Soups, Stews, and Pastas* (1985). He has also written a tourist's guide to the "Essential Restaurants of Italy" (1990).

H. S. Hamod (b. 1936) • Sam Hamod is a Lebanese-American who was born in Indiana. He received a Ph.D. from the Writer's Workshop of the University of Iowa and has served as director of the National Communications Institute in Washington, D. C. He has published a large number of poetic volumes, including *Dying with the Wrong Name* (1980), from which "Leaves" is selected.

Thomas Hardy (1840–1928) • For a brief biography of Hardy, see p. 133.

Joy Harjo (b. 1951) • Harjo, who is Creek, Cherokee, and French, was born in Oklahoma. She received her B.A. from the University of New Mexico and her M.F.A. at the University of Iowa and has taught at a number of schools, including Arizona State University. In 1990 she received the American Indian Distinguished Achievement Award, and in 1991 she received the Josephine Miles Award for excellence in literature. She enjoys playing the saxophone, and has been involved in musical recordings. Her poetry collections are *The Last Song* (1975), *What Moon Drove Me to This?* (1980), *She Had Some Horses* (1983), *Secrets from the Center of the World* (1989), *In Mad Love and War* (1990), *The Woman Who Fell from the Sky* (1996, 1998), and *A Map to the Next World: Poems and Tales* (2000). She was a co-editor of *Reinventing the Enemy's Language: North American Native Women's Writing* (1997).

Frances E. W. Harper (1825–1911) • Although Harper was a native of Maryland, a slave state in 1825, she was born free. She ensured her continued freedom by eventually moving to the free state of Pennsylvania. Before the Civil War she lectured extensively against slavery and supported the Underground Railway. Early collections of her work were *Forest Leaves* (1845), *Eventide* (1854), and *Poems on Miscellaneous Subjects* (1854), the last containing a preface by William Lloyd Garrison. Her novel, *Iola Leroy, or Shadows Uplifted* (1892), was well received and was included as part of a collection of fiction by African-American writers. One of her better-known poetry collections is *Atlanta Offering: Poems* (1895). In 1970 and 1988 her reputation as a poet was permanently secured with the publications of complete editions of her poems.

Michael S. Harper (b. 1938) • Born in Brooklyn, the American poet Michael S. Harper should not be confused with the English writer Michael Harper. Harper has held distinguished visiting professorships at Carlton College and at Colgate and has received both a Guggenheim Fellowship and a National Endowment for the Arts Creative Writing Award. He currently teaches at Brown University. Some of his collections of poems are *Dear John, Dear Coltrane* (1970, 1985), *Images of Kin* (1977), *Nightmare Begins Responsibility* (1975), *Healing Song for the Inner Ear* (1984), and *Honorable Amendments* (1995). "Called" is from *Nightmare Begins Responsibility*.

Robert Hass (b. 1941) • A native of California, Hass is one of America's most distinguished poets. He was educated at Stanford. He taught at St. Mary's College and then became poet resident at the University of California at Berkeley. His first collection of poems, *Field Guide* (1973) received the Yale Series of Younger Poets Award. Among his many later collections are *Praise* (1979), *Twentieth Century Pleasures* (1984), *Human Wishes* (1989), and *Sun Under Wood* (1996). In 1995 he was appointed as the United States Poet Laureate.

Robert Hayden (1913–1980) • Born in Detroit and educated at the University of Michigan, Hayden became a professor of English at both Fisk and Michigan. His earliest collection of poems was *Heart-Shape in the Dust* (1940). He received a special prize for *A Ballad of Remembrance* at the World Festival of Negro Arts held in Senegal in 1962. His *Words in the Mourning Time* (1970) included laments for the assassinated leaders Martin Luther King and Robert Kennedy, together with poems opposing the Vietnamese war.

Seamus Heaney (b. 1939) • Heaney lives in Northern Ireland, which for many decades has been beset with Protestant-Catholic strife. Although the tensions of this situation have permeated some of his work, he has written broadly on many topics, as can be inferred from "The Otter," which is taken from his 1979 collection *Field Work*. Among Heaney's other collections of verse are *Wintering Out* (1972), *Seamus Heaney: Selected Poems, 1966–1987* (1990), and *The Spirit Level* (1996). His verse translation (1999) of the Old English poem *Beowulf* was well accepted both critically and commercially. The highlight of his many awards and distinctions is that he received the Nobel Prize for literature in 1995.

George Herbert (1593–1633) • Herbert, whose brother was an English lord, became a priest in 1630 after a career in government service. He died in 1633, leaving his poems to a friend, Nicholas Ferrar, who had them printed in 1633 as *The Temple*. The intricacy of Herbert's thought, illustrated in poems like "The Pulley" and "The Collar," has caused later critics to classify him as a "metaphysical" poet. In the twentieth century a large number of church-music composers have set many of his lyrics as choral anthems.

Robert Herrick (1591–1674) • Herrick attended Cambridge and became an Anglican priest in 1627. During the English Civil War he remained loyal to King Charles I, for which he was removed from service in 1647, but he resumed his duties after the Restoration of Charles II in 1660. His major collection of poems was *Hesperides,* published in 1648. A number of persons expressed disapproval because of his frank subject matter, but, as he said, though his muse was jocund, his spirit was chaste. "To the Virgins, to Make Much of Time" is one of the better-known poems in the *carpe diem* tradition.

William Heyen (b. 1940) • Heyen's father came to the United States from Germany in 1928. Two uncles who remained in Germany joined the Nazi party and were killed in combat when serving in the German army in World War II. Heyen's concern with the Holocaust is thus a complex product of his ethnic ties and his anguish over Nazi atrocities. "The Hair: Jacob Korman's Story" was published in *Erika: Poems of the Holocaust* (1984). Among his volumes of poems are *The City Parables* (1980), *Pterodactyl Rose: Poems of Ecology, and Ribbons: The Gulf War.* A collection of his poems titled *The Host: Selected Poems, 1965–1990* was published in 1994. This collection is also available in cassette form.

John Hollander (b. 1929) • Hollander was born in New York, received his Ph.D. from the University of Indiana, and has taught at Hunter College and Yale University. He is a remarkably energetic and diversified poet, writing shaped verse (such as "Swan and Shadow"), children's verse, and nonsense verse. His musical-critical study *The Untuning of the Sky: Ideas of Music in English Poetry, 1500–1700* appeared in 1961. In 1967 he published *Jiggery-Pokery: A Compendium of Double Dactyls,* in collaboration with Anthony Hecht. His *Rhyme's Reason* (1981) is a guide to the various forms of English verse, which he illustrates with his own examples. *Figurehead and Other Poems,* his most recent collection, was published in 1999.

A. D. Hope (Alec Derwent Hope, b. 1907) • Hope is a native Australian whose lyrics have been praised for their traditionalism, their clarity and directness, their satire, and their search for redemption in love, literature, and art. Collections are *Collected Poems* (1966), *Collected Poems, 1930–1970* (1972), *Antechinus: Poems 1975–1980* (1981), and *Selected Poems* (1992). A play, *Ladies from the Sea,* appeared in 1987. The Australian National University recognized Hope by granting him an honorary Litt.D. degree in 1972. A study of Hope by Robert Darling (*A. D. Hope*) was published in 1997 in the Twayne's English Authors Series.

Gerard Manley Hopkins (1844–1889) • Hopkins was an English poet gifted not only in poetry but also in music and art. At the age of twenty-two he converted to Roman Catholicism and became a Jesuit priest. Although he published the long poem *The Wreck of the Deutschland* in 1875, the poems linking his devotion to Nature, on which his reputation now rests, were not published until early in the twentieth century. Hopkins used the term "sprung rhythm" for his metrical system (see Glossary).

A. E. Housman (1859–1936) • Housman was a professor of classics at Cambridge University. He created one major book of verse, *A Shropshire Lad* (1896), a collection of poems stressing the brevity and fragility of youth and love. His major scholarly pursuit was a study of the ancient Latin writer Manilius, whose works he edited. His *More Poems* was published posthumously, and his *Complete Poems* was published in 1956.

Julia Ward Howe (1819–1910) • Julia Ward married Samuel Howe and together they edited the Boston *Commonwealth,* a journal devoted to humanitarian causes. She became an activist for women's liberation, world peace, and the abolition of slavery, and she was the first woman elected to the American Academy of Arts and Letters. According to tradition, she wrote the "Battle Hymn of the Republic" after watching troops marching to battle. The poem was immediately popular among Union soldiers, and since that time it has remained her most popular poem and one of America's representative patriotic songs (sung to the music of "John Brown's Body").

Langston Hughes (1902–1967) • See pp. 1663–66 for a short biography.

Randall Jarrell (1914–1965) • Jarrell was born in Tennessee. He received his B.A. and M.A. degrees from Vanderbilt University. He wrote poetry, criticism, a novel, and children's fiction. His 1945 collection of poems, *Little Friend, Little Friend*, which includes "The Death of the Ball Turret Gunner," resulted from his service in the Army Air Corps during World War II. He published a number of other verse collections, including *Selected Poems* (1955) and *The Woman at the Washington Zoo* (1960).

Robinson Jeffers (1887–1962) • Jeffers was born in Pittsburgh and spent most of his life in California. He used negative and often brutal subject matter in his poetry, for example fratricide in *Give Your Heart to the Hawks* (1933), betrayal in *Dear Judas, and Other Poems* (1929), and infidelity in *Thurso's Landing, and Other Poems* (1932). His adaptation of Euripides' *Medea* (1947), starring Judith Anderson in the title role, won him wide national recognition. "The Answer" and "The Purse-Seine" appeared in his *Selected Poetry* (1938).

Ben Jonson (1573–1637) • Jonson was raised in the household of his stepfather, a bricklayer, and young Ben began his working life in that trade. He was able to free himself to attend the Westminster School, where he began acquiring his immense store of knowledge. After brief service as a soldier, he embarked on a career as poet and playwright. After Shakespeare retired in 1611, Jonson was, in effect, the major practicing dramatist in England. In 1616 he published his nondramatic poems, *Epigrams* and *The Forrest*. He became England's first Poet Laureate in 1619.

Donald Justice (b. 1925) • Born in Florida, Justice received his B.A. from the University of Miami (1945). He received his Ph.D. from the University of Iowa and became a member of the faculty there. His collections of poetry include *The Summer Anniversaries* (1959), *Departures* (1973), *Selected Poems* (1979), for which he was awarded the Pulitzer Prize in 1980, *The Sunset Maker* (1987), and *New and Selected Poems* (1995). A generous selection of his work has been included in the recent publication, *A Donald Justice Reader*.

John Keats (1795–1821) • Keats is one of the major English Romantic poets. Both his parents died when he was still a child, and at the age of fifteen he was apprenticed to an apothecary-surgeon. In 1816 he received his license to practice medicine, but almost immediately he gave up that career in order to become a full-time poet. In the following five years he created a magnificent body of poetry. Mortally afflicted with tuberculosis, he went to Rome, where he took rooms in the building adjoining the Spanish Steps. He died in Rome at the age of 26 and is buried in the English Cemetery in Rome near the Pyramid of Sestus Sextus.

X. J. Kennedy (Joseph Charles Kennedy, b. 1929) • Kennedy is a New Jersey native. He received an M.A. from Columbia and a *Certificat* from the University of Paris (1956). His first book of verse was *Nude Descending a Staircase* (1961), which has been followed by many other major poetry collections. "Old Men Pitching Horseshoes" is from *Cross Ties* (1985), which received the *Los Angeles Times* Book Award for Poetry in 1985. "John While Swimming" is selected from the 1986 "juvenile" collection titled *Brats*.

Jane Kenyon (1947-1995) • Kenyon was a longtime resident of New Hampshire. She received fellowships from the National Endowment for the Arts and also from the Guggenheim Foundation. Collections of her poetry are *Room to Room* (1978), *The Boat of Quiet Hours* (1986), *Let Evening Come* (1990), and *Constance* (1993). *Otherwise: New and Selected Poems* (1996) is a posthumous collection, as is *A Hundred White Daffodils* (1999). Along with her husband, Donald Hall, she is the subject of a video interview by Bill Moyers for the *Films for the Humanities and Sciences* series (1994).

Henry King (1592–1669) • King became Bishop of Chichester in 1642 and held this position for the rest of his life. He had been a friend of John Donne and was likely one of Donne's early editors. During his lifetime he published two volumes of his own verse, one a poetic rendering of the Psalms and the other an edition of *Poems, Elegies, Paradoxes, and Sonnets* (1657). His collected poems were published in 1965.

Carolyn Kizer (b. 1925) • Born in Spokane, Washington, Kizer studied at the University of Washington with Theodore Roethke. During much of her life she has lived in California. One of her specialties is the adaptation of poems from China and Japan. "Night Sounds," from *Mermaids in the Basement* (1984), is an example. Since 1959 she has regularly published poetry collections, some of which are *Knock Upon Silence* (1965), *Midnight Was My Cry* (1971), *The Nearness of You* (1986), and *Harping On: Poems 1985–1995* (1996). In 1985 her collection of poems Yin (1984) received the Pulitzer Prize for Poetry.

Etheridge Knight (1931–1991) • Knight was born in Mississippi and educated himself in various jails and prisons. He was convicted of robbery and was sent to the Indiana State Prison (1960–1966). When there he was visited by Dudley Randall, who persuaded him that his salvation lay in the development of his power to write. One of the products was the set of haiku included in his first book, *Poems from Prison.* Knight went on to write and teach at the University of Pittsburgh. His collection *Belly Song and Other Poems* was published in 1973 and earned him a nomination for both the Pulitzer Prize and a National Book Award.

Maxine Kumin (Maxine Winokur Kumin, b. 1925) • Kumin was born in Philadelphia and has long been a resident of New Hampshire. She received B.A. and M.A. degrees at Radcliffe. In addition to her many volumes of poetry she has written novels, stories, children's books (two in collaboration with Anne Sexton), and essays. Her fourth collection of poetry, *Up Country: Poems of New England* (1972) received the 1973 Pulitzer Prize. *Our Ground Time Here Will Be Brief* appeared in 1982. Recently she has published a new collection, *Connecting the Dots* (1996).

Philip Larkin (1922–1985) • A novelist, editor, and reviewer as well as a poet, Larkin was born in northern England and attended Oxford. His first collection of verse was *The North Ship* (1946), followed nine years later by *The Less Deceived,* in which "Next Please" was printed. In 1964 he published *The Whitsun Weddings,* and in 1974 *High Windows.*

Irving Peter Layton (b. 1912) • Since 1945 Layton, one of Canada's major poets, has published more than fifty poem collections, included selected poetry in 1966, 1972, and 1986. A comprehensive selection of his poems, *A Wild Peculiar Joy: Selected Poems 1945–1982,* was published in 1983. *The Love Poems of Irving Layton and Dance with Desire: Love Poems* were published in 1984 and 1986. In 1982 and 1983 he was a nominee for the Nobel Prize in Literature.

Li-Young Lee (b. 1957) • Lee is a native of Indonesia and is acknowledged as a powerful voice among Asian Americans. He was the recipient of grants from the National Endowment for the Arts and from the Guggenheim Foundation. His major collections thus far are *Rose Poems* (1986) and *The City in Which I Love You* (1990), which was the Lamont Poetry Selection for 1990. In 1995 he published *The Winged Seed: A Remembrance,* an autobiographical memoir.

Denise Levertov (1923–1997) • Levertov was a native of England whose parents were Welsh and Jewish. She was educated at home and served as a nurse in World War II. After the war she married an American and left England to live in the United States. She began publishing poems in her twenties. Since her first poetry collection *The Double Image,* which appeared in 1946, she published at least two collections each decade. In the 1970s she published four. Her collections ranged from personal topics to deeply political ones, particularly *Light Up the Cave* (1981), which contains a number of poems on the Vietnam War. Some of her most recent poetry collections were *The Double Image* (1991), *Evening Train* (1992), and *Sands of the Well* (1996). The Academy of American Poets awarded her the 1995 Academy Fellowship. A posthumous collection of her poetry is *The Great Unknowing: Last Poems* (1999).

Philip Levine (b. 1928) • Levine's parents were Russian Jewish immigrants who settled in Detroit. He was educated there, and for higher education he went to Wayne University (now Wayne State University) and also the University of Iowa. For a long time he took industrial jobs, living in a number of cities before he became a professor at Fresno State in California. He is noted for his use of plain language and straightforward, simple syntax, in keeping with his pronounced sympathies for ordinary, working-class people. He has published many collections of poetry, including *They Feed, They Lion* (1972), *The Names of the Lost* (1976), *One for the Rose* (1981), *A Walk with Tom Jefferson* (1988), *What Work Is Like* (1991), *The Simple Truth* (1994), and *New Selected Poems* (1995). He has been honored with the American Book Award, the National Book Award, and the Pulitzer Prize for *The Simple Truth*.

C. Day Lewis (1904–1972) • Irish by birth, Cecil Day-Lewis was educated at Oxford and became politically active in the 1930s. Some of his poetic collections are *From Feathers to Iron* (1931), *The Gate* (1962), and *Selections from His Poetry* (1967). In addition to writing poems, he made translations from Latin and French and also wrote detective stories. In the 1950s he served as professor of poetry at Oxford and he became Poet Laureate in 1968.

Alan P. Lightman (b. 1948) • Lightman, a faculty member of the Massachusetts Institute of Technology, is a native of Tennessee. He received degrees from Princeton and the California Institute of Technology. He is well known for his scientific writings, such as *Great Ideas in Physics and Time for the Stars*. He has also written fiction. His novel *Good Benito* (1994), for example, describes the life and tribulations of a young scientist.

Liz Lochhead (b. 1947) • In addition to being a poet, Lochhead is also a writer of plays, translations, and television scripts. She is a native of Scotland, and she has taught at the Glasgow School of Art and the University of Glasgow. Her poetry collection *Memo For Spring* (1972) earned her a fellowship award from the Scottish Arts Council (1973). Some of her other poetry collections are *The Grimm Sisters* (1981), *Dreaming Frankenstein and Collected Poems* (1984), and *Bagpipe Muzak* (1991). She is a featured poet in the collection *Three Scottish Poets* of 1992.

William Wadsworth Longfellow (1807–1882) • Longfellow was acknowledged in his own time as one of the great United States poets. He was so popular, and his poetry sold so well, that he was able to live on the proceeds of his writing. After graduating from Bowdoin in 1825, he began mastering Spanish, French, Italian, German, and the Scandinavian languages. This mastery equipped him to accept a professorship in languages at Harvard in 1836. His translation of Dante's *Divine Comedy* appeared in 1867, and at this same time he composed a number of sonnets which he published in 1867 and 1875. Some of his best known works are *Ballads and Other Poems* (1842), *Evangeline* (1847), *The Song of Hiawatha* (1855), *The Children's Hour* (1860), and *Paul Revere's Ride* (1863).

Audre Lorde (1934–1992) • Lorde was a New Yorker whose parents were immigrants from Jamaica. She was educated at the National University of Mexico, Hunter College, and Columbia. Some of her poetry collections are *Chosen Poems Old and New* (1982), *Our Dead Behind Us* (1986), and *Undersong* (1992). *The Marvelous Arithmetics of Distance: Poems 1987-1992* (1993) was a posthumous collection.

Richard Lovelace (1618–ca. 1657) • One of the best-known "cavalier" poets of the early seventeenth century, Lovelace served King Charles I in the Civil Wars and was twice imprisoned by the Parliament side. Stripped of his wealth, he died obscurely and in poverty. A collection of his poems was published posthumously, and his collected works were published in 1925

Amy Lowell (1874–1925) • Lowell was a proponent of the imagist school of poetry early in the twentieth century. Her earliest collection of poems was *A Dome of Many-Colored Glass* (1912). Later collections were *Sword Blades and Poppy Seed* (1914) and *Legends* (1921). "Patterns" appeared in her collection *Men, Women, and Ghosts* (1916).

Thomas Lux (b. 1946) • A winner of the Kingsley Tufts poetry award, Lux was educated at the University of Iowa and has taught at Sarah Lawrence College for many years. His poetry has been characterized as an "ironic mingling of humor and sincerity." Some of his collections are *The Land Sighted* (1970), *The Drowned River: New Poems* (1990), *Pecked to Death by Swans* (1993), *Split Horizon* (1994), and *New and Selected Poems 1975–1995* (1997).

Gwendolyn MacEwen (1941–1987) • A major Canadian voice in poetry as well as the short story and the novel, MacEwen treats subjects such as birth, the passing of time, death, and the importance of the spiritual. From her first collection of poems in 1963 (*The Rising Sun*), she published regularly until her death in 1987. Some of her later collections are *Magic Animals* (1974), *The T. E. Lawrence Poems* (1982), *Earthlight* (1982), and *After Worlds* (1985).

Archibald MacLeish (1892–1982) • A native of Illinois, MacLeish graduated from Yale and had a varied public career during the years when he was also writing poetry. He received a Pulitzer Prize three times, twice for his poetry (1932, for *Conquistador,* and 1952, for *Collected Poems, 1917–1952*). In 1944 and 1945 he served President Franklin D. Roosevelt as an Assistant Secretary of State. Among his many poetry collections are *Songs for a Summer Day* (1915), *Songs for Eve* (1954), and *New and Collected Poems 1917–1976* (1976). "Ars Poetica" appeared in *Streets of the Moon* (1926).

Louis MacNeice (1907–1963) • A native of Ireland, MacNeice was a friend of W. H. Auden, D. Day Lewis, and other British writers during the 1930s and 40s. His poetic interests were less political than those of his friends, and more speculative and psychological. His first poetry collection was *Blind Fireworks* (1929). Later collections were *Holes in the Sky* (1948) and *The Burning Perch* (1961). His *Collected Poems* was published in 1966, three years after his death. "Snow" first appeared in his *Poems* of 1935.

Christopher Marlowe (1564–1593) • Marlowe is known as the major English dramatist before Shakespeare (*Tamberlaine the Great, Dr. Faustus, The Jew of Malta,* and *Edward II*), and he may have collaborated with Shakespeare in some of Shakespeare's earliest plays. Marlowe's unfinished poem *Hero and Leander* was completed by George Chapman and published in 1598. "Come Live with Me and Be My Love" was first published in 1599 in *The Passionate Pilgrim* and was republished with Sir Walter Raleigh's accompanying poem in *England's Helicon* in 1600. A definitive edition of Marlowe's poems appeared in 1968.

Andrew Marvell (1621–1678) • Marvel, one of the major metaphysical poets of the seventeenth century, was active during the unsettled period of the English Civil Wars of 1642–1649, the Commonwealth, and the Protectorate of Oliver Cromwell. The Restoration of King Charles II (1660) ushered in a period of relative calm in Marvell's life. During his long career, which he began as a tutor in an aristocratic household, he assisted Milton (who served as Latin Secretary for the English Commonwealth), and he also was a Member of Parliament. His poems were not published until three years after his death. A modern edition of his *Poems and Letters* was published in 1971.

John Masefield (1878–1967) • The English poet John Masefield, though not an academic, was a compulsive reader and writer. His youth was spent as a merchant seaman and worker at odd jobs in the United States. Eventually he published fifty volumes of poems, together with many plays and novels, and he became Poet Laureate of England in 1930. His two best-known poems are "I Must Go Down to the Sea Again," included in *Salt-Water Ballads* (1902), and "Cargoes," which appeared in *Ballads and Poems* (1910).

Heather McHugh (b. 1948) • McHugh is a native Californian who has taught in Washington, North Carolina, and Iowa, and lived in Maine. Her B.A. is from Radcliffe; her M.A. from Denver University. Her poetry was first collected in *Dangers* (1977) and *A World of Difference* (1981). Recent collections are *Broken English: Poetry and Partiality* (1993), *Hinge & Sign: Poems, 1968-1993* (1994), and *Father of the Predicaments* (1999).

Claude McKay (1890–1948) • McKay, one of the important voices in the Harlem Renaissance of the 1920s, was born in Jamaica, immigrated to the United States in 1912 and settled in Harlem in 1914. He wrote a number of novels, including *Home to Harlem* (1928), and short stories, published in *Gingertown* (1932). His poems were collected in *Songs of Jamaica* (1911), *Spring in New Hampshire and other Poems* (1920), and *Harlem Shadows* (1922), where we find "In Bondage" and "The White City."

James Merrill (1926–1995) • A native of New York City, Merrill lived variously in Connecticut and New York. Among his major awards were two Pulitzer Prizes (1971 and 1977), the Bollingen Prize, and two National Book Awards. *First Poems,* his earliest collection of poetry, was published in 1951, and he continued publishing collections throughout his life. His last collections were *Selected Poems* (1992) and *A Scattering of Salts* (1995). A man blessed with inherited wealth, Merrill supported the arts through the Ingram Merrill Foundation, which he set up to provide grants for writers and artists. "Laboratory Poem" was published in *The Country of a Thousand Years of Peace* (1959).

W. S. Merwin (William Stanley Merwin, b. 1927) • Merwin was born in New York and raised in New Jersey and Pennsylvania. He currently lives in Hawaii. He published *Selected Translations 1948–1968* in 1968 and was distinguished by a PEN translation prize for this work. In 1988 he published two collections of poems: *The Rain in the Trees* and *Selected Poems*. In 1996 he published *The Vixen,* a collection of poems about people and life in the southern part of France. Also in 1996 he published *Flower & Hand: Poems 1977–1983*. Three long poems make up his *The River Sound* (1999). He was awarded the Pulitzer Prize in Poetry for *The Carriers of Ladders* (1970). "Odysseus" appeared in one of his early collections, *The Drunk in the Furnace* (1960).

Edna St. Vincent Millay (1892–1950) • Known as a free spirit at Vassar, Millay matured quickly, receiving the Pulitzer Prize for Poetry—the first woman to do so—for *The Harp Weaver and Other Poems* (1923), which contained "What Lips My Lips Have Kissed." Her maturing concerns were reflected in *Make Bright the Arrows* (1940) and especially *The Murder of Lidice* (1942), which she wrote for radio presentation after the Nazi extermination of that Czech village. She published her *Collected Sonnets* in 1941. *Edna St. Vincent Millay: Collected Poems,* a centenary edition, was published in 1993.

John Milton (1608–1674) • Milton is acknowledged as one of the greatest English poets. His fame rests largely on the epic poem *Paradise Lost,* which he wrote in 1667, long after he became blind. He led a varied career and wrote extensively in both verse and prose, including many Latin poems. His most important political position was as Latin Secretary to Oliver Cromwell during the Interregnum (1649–1660). Latin at that time was the language of diplomacy, and a good Latinist like Milton was essential. Milton's Poems was published in 1645, and he issued a second edition in 1673.

Judith Minty (b. 1937) • Minty is of Finnish, Irish, and Mohawk descent. She has done a variety of things in addition to writing poetry, including working as a speech therapist, selling cosmetics, and serving to carry poetry to prisoners. She resides in Arcata,

California, and has taught at Humboldt State University and the University of California at Santa Cruz. Among her poetry collections are *Lake Songs and Other Fears* (1974), *In the Presence of Mothers* (1981), and *Counting the Losses, Jazz* (1986). A recent poetry collection is *Dancing the Fault.*

N. Scott Momaday (b 1934) • A member of the Kiowa Tribe, Momaday was educated at the University of New Mexico and Stanford University. He has taught at Stanford and the University of Arizona. His reputation as a novelist was gained by his *House Made of Dawn* (1968) and *The Way to Rainy Mountain* (1969). Despite his success as a novelist, he considers himself a poet. Some of his collections are *Angle of Geese and Other Poems* (1974), *The Gourd Dancer* (1976), and *In the Presence of the Sun: Stories and Poems 1961–1991* (1992).

Marianne Moore (1887–1972) • A native of Missouri, Moore graduated from Bryn Mawr. Her first poetry collection, *Poems,* was published without her knowledge in 1921. Later she published *Selected Poems* (1935), *Nevertheless* (1944), and *Collected Poems* (1951), for which she received a Pulitzer Prize. In 1967 she put together all the poems on which she wished her reputation to rest and published the collection as *Complete Poems.*

Lisel Mueller (b. 1924) • Lisel Neumann Mueller came to this country from Germany in 1939, just as World War II was intensifying in Europe. She studied at the University of Indiana and has taught at Goddard College. Even though English is not her first language, she has mastered the craft of English poetry and has made English translations of works by Marie Luise Kaschnitz. Her poetry volumes are *Dependencies* (1965), *The Private Life* (1976), *The Need to Hold Still* (1980), *Second Language: Poems* (1986), and *Waving from Shore: Poems* (1989). *Alive Together: New and Selected Poems* (1996) includes poems from each of these collections and adds a number of new poems. "Hope" was originally published in *The Private Life.*

Ogden Nash (1902–1971) • Nash is most closely associated with *The New Yorker,* which he served as an editor for many years. Wit, humor, and satire characterize his verse, with an emphasis on original and funny rhymes and rhythms. Students of music may remember his voice on a 1950s recording of Camille Saint-Saëns's *Carnival of the Animals.* His many poetry collections include *Free Wheeling* (1931), *The Bad Parents' Garden of Verse* (1936), *You Can't Get There from Here* (1957), *Everyone But Thee and Me* (1962), and *Bed Riddance* (1970).

Howard Nemerov (1920–1991) • Nemerov graduated from Harvard and served in World War II. After the war he taught at a number of colleges and began publishing his many essays, stories, plays, and poems. His poetry collections include *The Image and the Law* (1947), *The Western Approaches: Poems 1973–1975* (1975), and *Inside the Onion* (1985). The Library of Congress honored him as Poet Laureate from 1986 to 1988.

Jim Northrup (b. 1943) • Northrup is a Chippewa Indian and lives with his family on the Fond du Lac Reservation in Minnesota. He has published a number of stories, and his poems have been published mainly in magazines and journals. His major poetry collection, which also contains stories, is *Walking the Rez Road* (1993). His *The Rez Road Follies* was published in 1997. He writes a syndicated column and also works as an artist.

Naomi Shihab Nye (b. 1952) • Nye, a Palestinian American, is a native of Missouri but has lived for a time in Jerusalem. She is not only a poet but also a writer of children's books and, interestingly, a folk singer (with recordings to her credit). In her work as a teacher she has taught at the University of Hawaii and the University of Texas at Austin. She has published her poetry in a number of collections, including *Tatooed Feet* (1977), *Different Ways to Pray* (1980), *Hugging the Jukebox* (1982), *Yellow Glove* (1986), *Texas Poets in Concert: A Quartet* (1990, as one of four poets), *Red Suitcase* (1994), *Words Under the Words: Selected Poems* (1995), and *Fuel* (1998). A collection of her essays, *Never in a Hurry,* was published in 1996. She recently (1998) published *The Space between Our Footsteps: Poems and Paintings from the Middle East. Habibi* (1997, 1999) is an autobiographical novel for young people.

Frank O'Hara (1926–1966) • Both a poet and a playwright, O'Hara was a native of Baltimore but spent much of his life in New York City, where he worked for the Museum of Modern Art. In a freak accident in the summer of 1966, he was walking on a beach and was struck and killed by a dune buggy. During his short life he published a large number of poetry collections, including *A City, Winter, and Other Poems* (1952), *Meditations in an Emergency* (1957), from which "Poem" is taken, and *Love Poems* (1965). Posthumous collections are *In Memory of My Feelings: A Selection of Poems* (1967) and *The Collected Poems of Frank O'Hara* (1971).

Sharon Olds (b. 1942) • Born in San Francisco, Olds received her Ph.D. from Columbia in 1972 and has taught at New York University, Sarah Lawrence, Brandeis, and Columbia. In a recent informal survey among members of the Academy of American Poets, she was named most often as their favorite contemporary American poet. In 1998 she was named New York State Poet. Her early poetry collections are *Satan Says* (1980) and *The Dead and the Living* (1984), which contains "35/10." Recent collections are *The Gold Cell* (1987), *The Father* (1992), *The Wellspring* (1996), and *Blood, Tin, Straw* (1999). Although her poems are often physical and deeply personal, she remains, at heart, a private person.

Mary Oliver (b. 1935) • A native of Cleveland, Oliver took her higher education at Ohio State University and Vassar College. She is a longtime resident of Provincetown, Massachusetts, and is on the faculty of Bennington College. Her poetry collections have been regular and numerous, including *No Voyage and Other Poems* (1963), *Sleeping in the Forest* (1978), *American Primitive* (1983), *New and Selected Poems* (1992), *White Pine: Poems and Prose Poems* (1994), *Blue Pastures* (1995), *West Wind* (1997), and *Winter Hours: Poetry, Prose, and Essays* (1999). She is also the author of *A Poetry Handbook* (1994) and *Rules for the Dance: A Handbook for Writing and Reading Metrical Verse* (1998). She received the National Book Award and the Shelley Memorial Award, and in 1984 she was honored with the Pulitzer Prize for Poetry for *American Primitive*.

Michael Ondaatje (b. 1943) • Ondaatje was born in Ceylon (now Sri Lanka) and was educated in Ceylon, England, and Canada. He lives in Toronto, where he teaches and also pursues his hobby of raising and breeding dogs. He is best known for his widely acclaimed novel *The English Patient* (1992), which was made into a movie (1996) that received a number of best-picture awards and also won nine Oscars at the 1997 Academy Awards ceremony. Before this commercial success, Ondaatje had written plays and had also directed films. The interest he has in film is also shown in "Watching the Late Movies with Skyler." Among his ten volumes of poetry are *There's a Trick with a Knife I'm Learning to Do* (1979), *The Cinnamon Peeler* (1991), and *Handwriting: Poems* (1999). His newest novel is *Anil's Ghost* (2000).

Simon Ortiz (b. 1941) • Ortiz, of the Acoma Pueblo Indian Nation, was born in New Mexico. He attended the Universities of New Mexico and Iowa. His first volume of poetry was *Naked in the Wind* (1971). In 1991 he published the collection *After and Before the Lightning. Woven Stone*, a three-in-one volume of poems containing a memoir, appeared in 1992. His best-known collection of stories is *Howbah Indians* (1978). His most recent collection of stories is *Men on the Moon: Collected Short Stories* (1999).

Wilfred Owen (1893–1918) • A native of Shropshire, England, Owen became a British Army officer and was killed in France in 1918, just a week before the Armistice. He published only four poems in his lifetime, but after his death Siegfried Sassoon issued a collection of twenty-four poems (1920). Benjamin Britten used a number of Owen's poems, including "Anthem for Doomed Youth," as texts for his *War Requiem* (1962). The popular band 10,000 Maniacs recorded a version of both "Anthem for Doomed Youth" and "Dulce et Decorum Est" on their album *Hope Chest* (Elektra 9-60962-2).

P. K. Page (Patricia Kathleen Page Irwin, b. 1916) • Versatile as artist, fiction writer, and poet, Page was born in England and came to Canada with her parents in 1919. After completing school she did work in business, research, and radio. She married a diplomat, W. A. Irwin, who at various times served as Canadian ambassador to Australia, Brazil, and Mexico. One of her earliest works, a novel titled *The Sun and the Moon* (1944), was published under the pen name Judith Cape. Her earliest collection of poetry was *As Ten as Twenty* (1946). Among her many later collections are *The Metal and the Flower* (1954), *Evening Dance of the Grey Flies* (1981), *The Glass Air* (1985), *A Flask of Sea Water* (1989), and *The Hidden Room: Collected Poems* (1997).

Dorothy Parker (1893–1967) • Parker became legendary because of her many witty "one-liners" and also because of her often caustic book and drama reviews for *The New Yorker* in the period between the World Wars. Her first volume of poetry was *Enough Rope* (1926), which included "Resumé." "Penelope" was included in her comprehensive collection *Not So Deep as a Well* (1936). She wrote many short stories and served as a correspondent during the Spanish Civil War in the late 1930s.

Linda Pastan (b. 1932) • Pastan was born in New York. She received a B.A. from Radcliffe and an M.A. from Brandeis. Among her many volumes of verse are *A Perfect Circle of Sun* (1971), *Setting the Table* (1980), *Waiting for My Life* (1981), *PM/AM: New and Selected Poems* (1983), *A Fraction of Darkness* (1985), *An Early Afterlife* (1996), and *Carnival Evening: New and Selected Poems 1968–1998* (1998).

Marge Piercy (b. 1936) • A native of Detroit, Piercy received her B.A. from the University of Michigan (1957) and M.A. from Northwestern (1958). She now lives in Cape Cod. Among her novels are *Braided Lives* (1980) and *Fly Away Home* (1984). The first of her many poetry collections was *Breaking Camp* (1968). Others are *The Moon Is Always Female* (1980), in which "Will We Work Together" appeared, *Circles on the Water: Selected Poems* (1982), including "A Work of Artifice" and "The Secretary Chant," and *Available Light* (1988), which includes "Wellfleet Sabbath." Her most recent poetic volumes are *What Are Big Girls Made Of?* (1996), *Early Grrrl: The Early Poems of Marge Piercy* (1999), and *The Art of Blessing the Day: Poems with a Jewish Theme* (1999).

Robert Pinsky (b. 1940) • Poet, scholar, and translator, Pinsky was educated in his home state of New Jersey and also at Stanford. He has taught at the University of California, Boston University, and Harvard. Some of his poetry collections are *Sadness and Happiness* (1975), *An Explanation of America* (1979), *The Want Bone* (1990), and *The Figured Wheel: New and Collected Poems 1966-1996* (1996, 1997). *His Explanation of America* (1979) is a book-length poem. For a time he was poetry editor of the *New Republic*. In the 1990s he became Poet Laureate of the United States for three successive terms, the only person to be so honored. He has used the prestige of his position advantageously. He brought out a short book (*The Sounds of Poetry: A Brief Guide* [1998]), and he also has done much to put poetry before the public eye, appearing regularly on national television to read poems and to comment extensively on the subject of poetry. In this capacity he has become the most widely recognized person to serve as United States Poet Laureate. One of his important efforts for poetry has been the development of the favorite poems project. The result, which he worked on in collaboration with many persons from all walks of life, is *Americans' Favorite Poems* (1999). "Dying" is taken from his collection *History of My Heart* (1984, 1998).

Sylvia Plath (1932–1963) • One of the most confessional of poets, Plath was born in Massachusetts. After graduating from Smith College in 1955 she received a Fulbright Scholarship to England. She spent 1955–1956 in Cambridge, where she married Ted Hughes (1930-1999), who later became English Poet Laureate. The following years brought overpowering emotional distress, and she took her own life in 1963. Her poetry during these final years reflects the personal anguish that led to her suicide. Plath's *The Collected Poems* (1981) was awarded the 1982 Pulitzer Prize in Poetry.

Edgar Allan Poe (1809–1849) • See pp. 522–28 for a brief biography.

Katha Pollitt (b. 1949) • A native of New York, Pollitt received her B.A. at Radcliffe. She worked as an editor for the weekly magazine *The Nation* for many years and is an associate faculty member of the Bennington Writing Seminars Program. She has also achieved wide recognition as an essayist. Her first book of poems was *Antarctic Traveler* (1982). An important recent work is *Reasonable Creatures: Essays on Women and Feminism* (1995).

Alexander Pope (1688–1744) • Pope is the eminent eighteenth-century English poet, the acknowledged master of the neoclassic couplet. A childhood accident deformed his spine and retarded his physical growth, but it did not hinder his poetic gifts. Because his family was Roman Catholic, he was not sent to school but was educated at home. By age 23 he had completed *An Essay on Criticism* (1711), the leading English work of criticism in poetic form. After 1725 he devoted himself principally to writing satire, producing *The Dunciad* (1728, rev. 1743), the *Moral Essays* (1731–35), *An Epistle to Dr. Arbuthnot* (1735), and other satiric works, including the *Epilogues to the Satires* in dialogue form (1738). One of his life's plans was to publish a major philosophic work in poetry, but the only part he completed was the *Essay on Man* (1734).

Ezra Pound (1885–1972) • A native of Idaho, Pound was educated at the University of Pennsylvania and spent most of his life in Europe. He was the leading exponent of poetic imagism (see also Amy Lowell). During World War II he broadcast pro-Axis propaganda from Rome. After the war he was prosecuted for this, but was exonerated on the grounds of insanity. Pound is as much known for his influence on other poets as for his own poetry (T. S. Eliot acknowledged him as "the better maker" in the dedication to *The Waste Land*). He published many poetry collections, such as *Exultations* (1909), *Canzoni* (1911), and *Cathay* (1915), which contained his versions of Chinese poems (see p. 1188). His major work was the *Cantos,* which he worked on throughout his life after publishing the first portion in 1925.

Al Purdy (Alfred Wellington Purdy, 1918–2000) • Purdy was born in Ontario and spent considerable time as a factory worker, not coming to poetry until he was in his forties with his first collection, *Poems for all the Annettes* (1962; 1968). Since then he has published regularly, including *The Cariboo Horses* (1965), *Selected Poems* (1972), *The Stone Bird* (1981), *Piling Blood* (1984), *Collected Poems* (1986), *Rooms for Rent in the Outer Planets: Selected Poems 1962–1996* (1996), and *To Paris Never Again: New Poems* (1997).

Salvatore Quasímodo (1901–1968) • A native of Italy, Quasímodo's early work was part of the so-called Italian "hermetic" period prior to World War II. That is, his poetry was highly imagistic, personal, and nonpolitical. During the war he became militantly antifascist, and for this reason Mussolini sent him to prison. After the war he became deeply concerned with the conditions of common people. In addition, he translated many works into Italian. He was the recipient of the Nobel Prize for Literature in 1959. His *Complete Poems* was published in 1984.

Sir Walter Raleigh (ca. 1552–1618) • Raleigh was a courtier, explorer, and adventurer who alternately pleased and displeased Queen Elizabeth I. During the reign of James I he was imprisoned for thirteen years in the Tower of London. He was released to go on an expedition to South America, which proved disastrous. In 1618 he was executed for treason. Like many aristocrats he wrote extensively but circulated his poetry mostly in manuscript, with rare exceptions such as "The Nymph's Reply to the Shepherd." His collected poems were edited and published in 1951.

Dudley Randall (b. 1914) • A native of Washington, D. C., Randall spent five years working in the foundry at the Ford River Rouge plant in Michigan. He became a librarian after that and went on to the position of head librarian. In 1965 he founded the Broadside Press, an important and valuable publisher for African-American writers. One of the first poems from the press was "Ballad of Birmingham," which had earlier (1963) been set to music and made popular by the folk singer Jerry Moore. Randall's major poetry collections are *More to Remember: Poems of Four Decades* (1971) and *A Litany of Friends: New and Selected Poems* (1981, 1983).

John Crowe Ransom (1888–1974) • Along with Robert Penn Warren, Alan Tate, and Cleanth Brooks, Ransom was one of the important exponents of the New Criticism (see Chapter 33, p. 1957). He founded the Kenyon Review and edited it for twenty years. His major poetry collections are *Chills and Fever* (1924), *Two Gentlemen in Bonds* (1927), and *Selected Poems* (1945, revised in 1963 and 1969).

John Raven (b. 1936) • Raven's poems figured importantly in Dudley Randall's collection *The Black Poets: A New Anthology* (1971). His major collection of poems is *Blues for Momma* (1970).

Henry Reed (1914–1986) • Reed was English and received a degree from the University of Birmingham. He became best known in England for his translations and radio dramas. His major book of poems was *A Map of Verona* (1946), which contains "Naming of Parts." His radio plays were published in *The Streets of Pompeii* (1971, five plays in verse) and *Hilda Tablet and Others* (1971, four comedies in prose).

Adrienne Rich (b. 1929) • Rich is a native of Baltimore. She was educated at Radcliffe, studying writing with Robert Lowell. In 1986 she became a professor at Stanford. Her first collection of poetry, *A Change of World* (1951), received the Yale Series of Younger Poets Award. Since then she has published collections regularly, and she is acknowledged today as one of America's foremost poets. An advocate of women's rights and also lesbian rights, she is a major confessional poet, as may be inferred from the titles of two of her many collections: *Snapshots of a Daughter-in-Law* (1963) and *An Atlas of the Difficult World* (1991). Her most recent collection is *Midnight Salvage: Poems 1995–1998* (1999). She was offered the National Book Award for Poetry in 1974, but to show her unity with women she refused to accept for herself, accepting jointly with Audre Lorde "in the name of all women."

Anne Barbara Ridler (b. 1912) • Ridler is a writer not only of poems but also of plays, film plays, songs, and translations. She was an editor at the Oxford University Press, which published some of her poems, and also at Faber and Faber, where T. S. Eliot was an editor. Ridler published her first poetry collection, *Poems,* in 1939. Subsequent collections were *A Dream Observed and Other Poems* (1941), *The Golden Bird and Other Poems* (1951), *Selected Poems* (1961), *Some Time After and Other Poems* (1972), and *Collected Poems* (1994). She edited many collections, including an anthology of ghost stories. Most notable among her many other writings are English translations of the libretti of Mozart's operas *The Marriage of Figaro* and *Cosi fan Tutte.*

Edwin Arlington Robinson (1869–1935) • Robinson began his career inauspiciously with various jobs in New York City. The publication of *The Children of the Night* (1897) and *Captain Craig* (1902) impressed President Theodore Roosevelt, who arranged a position for him as clerk in the New York Customs House. After the publication of *The Town Down* *the River* in 1910, he was able to support himself with his poetry. "Tilbury Town," where many of his poetic characters reside, is modeled on Gardiner, Maine, the town where he grew up. He is particularly notable because he received the first Pulitzer Prize for poetry ever to be awarded (1922). He received the prize twice more, in 1924 and 1928.

Theodore Roethke (1908–1963) • Roethke was born in Saginaw, Michigan, where his father operated a greenhouse. His first collection of poems was *The Lost Son* (1948), which included "My Papa's Waltz." He achieved wide recognition before his death in 1963. In addition to distinguishing himself, he also taught other poets, numbering James Wright among his students at the University of Washington.

Christina Rossetti (1830–1894) • English-born Christina Rossetti's religious lyrics and ballads have made her a favorite with composers such as Gustav Holst and John Rutter. Painters of the Pre-Raphaelite Brotherhood, of whom her brother Dante Gabriel Rossetti was a leading figure, frequently called upon her to pose for their paintings. Ill health forced her to forsake a career as a governess, and after 1874 she became a virtual invalid. Some of her poetry collections are *Goblin Market and Other Poems* (1862), *The Prince's Progress and Other Poems* (1866), and *A Pageant and Other Poems* (1872). A modern edition of her *Complete Poems* was published in 1979.

Friedrich Rückert (1788–1866) • A younger contemporary of Goethe, Rückert became recognized in Germany as a poet who translated and popularized literature of the Orient. Some of his works are *Harnessed Sonnets* (1814), *The Wisdom of the Brahman* (1836), and the posthumous *Songs on the Death of Children* (1872). Today Rückert is known best because of the music that Gustav Mahler (1860–1911) set to his poems: *Songs on the Death of Children* (1902–1904) and *Five Rückert Songs* (1901–1902).

Muriel Rukeyser (1913–1980) • A *poète engagée*, Rukeyser was arrested in Alabama in the 1930s for demonstrating in favor of the Scottsboro Nine (see also Chapter 29, p. 1664). Later, she wrote on behalf of an imprisoned Korean poet in *The Gates* (1976). She published many collections, including *Theory of Flight* (1935), *Beast in View* (1944), *Body of Waking* (1958), and *Collected Poems* (1979).

Luis Omar Salinas (b. 1937) • Salinas was born in Texas. He attended Fresno State University from 1967 to 1972, and made his home in California. His first volume of poems was *Crazy Gypsy* (1970). In 1975 he was one of four poets included (along with Gary Soto) in *Entrance: Four Chicano Poets*. Since then he has been regularly productive. One of his major volumes was *The Sadness of Days: Selected and New Poems*, which appeared in 1987.

Sonia Sanchez (b. 1934) • Sanchez was born in Alabama. She received a B.A. from Hunter College in 1955, and for a time after that she worked for the Congress of Racial Equality. Her major teaching position was at Temple University. Early volumes of poetry were *Homecoming* (1969) and *We a BaddDDD People* (1970). More recently she published *homegirls & handgrenades* (1984), *Under a Soprano Sky* (1987), *Does Your House Have Lions* (1997), *Like the Singing Coming Off the Drums: Love Poems* (1998), and *Shake Loose My Skin: New and Selected Poems* (1999).

Carl Sandburg (1878–1967) • It is fair to say that Sandburg "knocked around" a good deal in his youth before working his way through Knox (then Lombard) College in Galesburg, Illinois, his home town. He published a volume of poetry in 1904 but did not gain recognition until 1914, when *Poetry* printed some of his poems. Later he published *Chicago Poems* (1916), *Smoke and Steel* (1920), *Selected Poems* (1926), and *Good Morning, America* (1928). He received the Pulitzer Prize in History (1939) for his biography of Abraham Lincoln and the Pulitzer Prize in Poetry (1951) for his *Complete Poems* of 1950.

May Sarton (Eleanor May Sarton, 1912–1995) • Sarton was born in Belgium and at the age of four came to the United States with her parents. Eventually she taught at both Harvard University and Wellesley College. Her first poetry volume appeared in 1937, when she was twenty-five (*Encounter in April*), and she published regularly after that, her final volume (*Coming into Eighty*), appearing in 1994, the year before her death. Her *Collected Poems, 1930–1970,* was published in 1974. An anthology of her work in all literary genres was edited by Bradford Daziel and published in 1991 as *Sarton Selected.*

Siegfried Sassoon (1886–1967) • Sassoon served as an officer in World War I, was wounded twice, and was awarded two medals for bravery (one of which he threw away). He is most widely recognized for his antiwar collections *The Old Huntsman* (1917) and *Counter-Attack and Other Poems* (1918), which contains "Dreamers." Neither of these books was well received. Later, Sassoon turned to spiritual subjects, as shown in *Vigils* (1935) and *Sequences* (1956). His *Collected Poems* was published in 1961.

Gjertrud Cecilia Schnackenberg (b. 1953) • Originally from Washington state, Schnackenberg now lives in Boston. She achieved great critical acclaim with the publication of her first volume of poems, *Portraits and Elegies* (1982, rev. ed. 1986). She later published *The Lamplit Answer* (1985) and *A Guildes Lapse of Time* (1992, 1994). She won the Rome Prize in literature for 1983–1984 and received an honorary doctorate degree from Mount Holyoke College, her alma mater, in 1985.

Virginia Scott (b. 1937) • Canadian born, Scott received her degrees at Boston University and Wisconsin. She created, edited, and managed the Sunbury Press, a small press, and received a national award for this work in 1980. She has published poetry widely in journals. Her collected poems appear in *The Witness Box* (1985) and *Toward Appomatox* (1992). She taught at Lehman College for many years.

Alan Seeger (1886–1916) • Seeger was born in New York and was educated at Harvard. When World War I began he joined the French Foreign Legion. He was killed in the Battle of the Somme in 1916. His war poems were published in *Collected Poems* (1916).

Brenda Serotte (b. 1946) • Serotte was born and educated in New York; she currently lives in Florida. For many years she worked as a secretary and received a Bachelor's degree from Lehman College. For a time she taught in a junior high school, and her experiences there have inspired many of her poems. Her background is that of Sephardic Jewry, her immediate forbears having left Turkey in 1918 to come to the United States. She describes life among Sephardic immigrants in "Turkish Days," published in the journal *Hopscotch* in 1999. Her poem "The Moor's Ring" won both the Edmond Jabès Prize and the Boas Prize. Currently she is completing a biographical memoir *Turkish Delights, and Other Fattening Recollections.*

Anne Sexton (1928–1974) • Massachusetts born, Sexton is one of the more personal confessional poets. *To Bedlam and Part Way Back* (1960), for example, developed out of a nervous breakdown, and her posthumous *The Awful Rowing Toward God* (1975) describes some of the feelings leading to her suicide in 1974. Her collection *Live or Die* (1966) was awarded the Pulitzer Prize in Poetry for 1967.

William Shakespeare (1564–1616) • For a brief biography, see pp. 1349–50.

Karl Shapiro (1913–2000) • Baltimore born, Shapiro has lived in Nebraska and California. He was recognized early in his distinguished career as a poet and critic—his *V-Letter and Other Poems* (1944) receiving the 1945 Pulitzer Prize. Among his many poetry collections are *Essay on Rime* (1945), *Poems of a Jew* (1958), *Selected Poems* (1968), *Selected Poems: 1940–1977* (1978) and *The Wild Card: Selected Poems Early and Late* (1998). He edited *Poetry* magazine for five years, *Prairie Schooner* for ten.

Percy Bysshe Shelley (1792–1822) • Shelley is one of the major English Romantic poets. He was a quintessential revolutionary and suffered expulsion from Oxford as a result of an early pamphlet titled *The Necessity of Atheism*. He married before he was twenty but within three years left his wife and went to Italy with Mary Godwin (1797–1851), the author of *Frankenstein*. The two were married in 1816. Throughout these years Shelley was writing his best-known short poems. He was working on his long philosophic poem *The Triumph of Life* in 1922 when he was drowned during a storm at sea. There are many excellent modern editions of his works, including the Houghton-Mifflin Cambridge edition and the Oxford edition.

Jane Shore (b. 1947) • Shore was born in New Jersey and took her M.A. at the University of Iowa in 1971. Her poems have been widely circulated in journals and magazines, and the general merit of her work is shown by frequent prizes and awards, including a grant from the National Endowment for the Arts. Her poetry collections are *Lying Down in the Olive Press* (1969), *Eye Level* (1977), *The Minute Hand* (1987), *Music Minus One: Poems* (1996, 1997), and *Happy Family: Poems* (1999).

Leslie Marmon Silko (b. 1948) • A Native American, Silko was brought up in Laguna Pueblo, New Mexico. She has taught at the University of Arizona and also at the University of New Mexico, and she has been honored with a MacArthur Foundation Fellowship. The topic in most of her works is the tradition of the Navajo People, which she treats with great love and understanding, as in "Where Mountain Lion Lay Down with Deer," which connects the individual with the past, the land, and Nature. A recent novel is *Gardens in the Dunes* (1999).

Dave Smith (b. 1942) • Smith, a native of Virginia, earned his B.A. from the University of Virginia in 1965 and for a time taught high school, including the coaching of football. He received his Ph.D. at Ohio University in 1976. He then taught at the University of Utah in Salt Lake City. Some of his collections are *Bull Island* (1970), *Goshawk, Antelope* (1979), and *The Roundhouse Voice: Poems 1970–1985* (1985), *Fate's Kite: Poems 1991–1995* (1995), *Floating on Solitude: Three Volumes of Poetry* (1996), and *The Wick of Memory: New and Selected Poems 1970-2000* (2000). "Bluejays" is from *Homage to Edgar Allan Poe* (1981).

Stevie Smith (Florence Margaret Smith, 1902–1971) • Smith was a native of Hull in Yorkshire. During her life she worked in publishing, and in addition she became well known as a radio personality because of her many poetry readings for the BBC. Some of her poetry collections were *A Good Time Was Had by All* (1937) and *Not Waving but Drowning* (1957). Posthumous collections of her work are *Scorpion and Other Poems* (1972) and *Collected Poems* (1975).

W. D. Snodgrass (b. 1926) • Snodgrass is a native of Pennsylvania. He received his B.A. from the University of Iowa and also did graduate study there. He taught at Wayne State University in Detroit (1959–1967) and was there when he published *Heart's Needle*, for which he received the 1960 Pulitzer Prize in Poetry. Among his other collections are *Gallows Songs of Christian Morgenstern* (1967), *After Experience* (1968), *If Birds Build with Your Hair* (1979), *Each in His Season* (1993) and *The Fuehrer Bunker: The Complete Cycle* (1995). *After Images: Autobiographical Sketches* (1999) is a collection of his essays.

Cathy Song (b. 1955) • A native of Honolulu, Cathy Song received her B.A. at Wellesley College and her M.A. from Boston University. She lives and teaches in Hawaii. Her first volume of verse was *Picture Bride* (1983), for which she received both the Yale Series of Younger Poets Award and a National Book Critics Circle Award. Her collection *School Figures* was published in 1994

Gary Soto (b. 1952) • Soto is a native of Fresno, California, and was educated in California. Since 1980 he has taught at Berkeley. Because of his native city he has sometimes been grouped with a "Fresno" school of poets. His first poetry collection was *The Elements of San Joaquin* (1977). Later collections are *The Tale of Sunlight* (1978), *Where Sparrows Work Hard* (1981), *Black Hair* (1985), *New and Selected Poems* (1995), *Junior College: Poems* (1997), and *A Natural Man* (1999). Soto is a prolific writer with many different interests, including works for young people. His book *Baseball in April* (1990), for example, was named a Best Book for Young Adults in 1990.

Stephen Spender (1909–1995) • Sir Stephen Spender, along with W. H. Auden, Christopher Isherwood, and Louis MacNeice, was one of the poets known as the Oxford Poets because they all attended Oxford in the late 1920s and early 1930s. After leaving Oxford, Spender lived for a time in Germany. He believed firmly in the need for poets to be politically engaged, and he joined the Communist Party for a few weeks in the 1930s, although he later renounced this affiliation (in *The God that Failed* [1950]). Along with editing journals and writing many prose works, he, with John Lehmann, wrote a five-act poetic play *Trial of a Judge,* based on circumstances in Germany at the time of Hitler. Spender's first poems were collected in a small book titled *Twenty Poems* in 1930. Later collections were *Poems of Dedication* (1947), *Edge of Being: Poems* (1949), and *Collected Poems* 1928–1953 (1955). He was knighted in 1962.

William E. Stafford (1914–1993) • Stafford, who published more than two dozen volumes of verse, was born in Kansas. He received his Ph.D. from Iowa State in 1955. In 1975 he was named Poet Laureate of Oregon, and at his death in 1993 he was a professor emeritus at Lewis and Clark College. For *Traveling through the Dark* (1962), his second volume of poetry, he won the National Book Award for Poetry in 1963. Among his many poetry collections are *Wyoming* (1985) and *An Oregon Message* (1987). With Marvin Bell, he published *Segues* in 1983. *Down in My Heart* (1994) is his autobiography of the years he spent in an internment camp for conscientious objectors in World War II.

Maura Stanton (b. 1946) • Stanton was born in Illinois. She took her B.A. at the University of Minnesota (1969) and her M.F.A. at the University of Iowa (1971). Since 1982 she has taught at the University of Indiana. Her major collections of poems are *Snow on Snow* (1975), which includes "The Conjurer," *Cries of Swimmers* (1984), *The Country I Come From* (1988), and *Life among the Trolls* (1998). Her major novel is *Molly Companion* (1977).

Gerald Stern (b. 1925) • Stern was born in Pittsburgh and became a faculty member of the University of Iowa's Writer's Workshop. He was honored by three grants from the National Endowment for the Arts and by a Guggenheim Fellowship. His *Lucky Life* (1977), which contains "Burying an Animal," received the Lamont Prize in Poetry in 1977. Most recently he published *Leaving Another Kingdom: Selected Poems* (1990), *Bread Without Sugar* (1992), *Odd Mercy* (1995), *Lucky Life* (1997), *This Time* (1998), and *Last Blue* (2000).

Wallace Stevens (1879–1955) • Stevens spent his professional life in business rather than academia. He wrote most of his poems after the age of fifty, but he included "The Emperor of Ice-Cream" and "Disillusionment of Ten O'Clock," both earlier poems, in the first edition of *Harmonium* in 1923. Some of his poetic collections are a second version of *Harmonium* (1931) and also *The Auroras of Autumn* (1950) and *Collected Poems* (1954).

Mark Strand (b. 1934) • Strand was born in Prince Edward Island, Canada. He studied at Antioch, Yale, and the University of Iowa, and taught at the University of Utah. He received many honors, including a particularly prized MacArthur Foundation Fellowship. In 1990 he was named United States Poet Laureate. Recent poetic collections are *The Continuous Life* (1990, 1992) and *Blizzard of One* (1999), for which he was awarded the Pulitzer Prize in poetry.

May Swenson (1919–1989) • Swenson was born in Utah and was of Swedish ancestry. She experimented constantly in her poetry, not only in content but also in form, as is shown in her work with shaped verse. Her *Iconographs* (1970) was a collection of formed poetry. The formed poem "Women" was included in her collection *New and Selected Things Taking Place* (1978). She also did translations from Swedish, as represented by *Windows and Stones* (1972).

Jonathan Swift (1667–1745) • Swift was born in Ireland. He became Dean of St. Patrick's Cathedral in Dublin, a position in which he served for thirty-one years. His most famous prose works are *A Tale of a Tub* (1704), *Gulliver's Travels* (1726), and *A Modest Proposal* (1729). Throughout his life, however, he constantly wrote poetry, and he devoted himself almost exclusively to poetry after 1730. His poems were edited by Harold Williams and published in three volumes in 1937.

James Tate (b. 1943) • Tate was born in Kansas City, earning degrees from the Universities of Kansas and Iowa. He taught English at the University of Massachusetts. Since his first collection, *The Lost Pilot*, published when he was only twenty-three, he has published a dozen volumes of verse. More recent works include *Viper Jazz* (1976), *Riven Doggeries* (1979), *Reckoner* (1986), *Distance from Loved Ones* (1990), *Selected Poems* (1991), for which he received the Pulitzer Prize for Poetry in 1992, and *Shroud of the Gnome* (1997, 1999). In 1994 he received the National Book Award for his new collection *Worshipful Company of Fletchers,* and in 1995 he was awarded the Tanning Prize— the largest annual literary prize in the United States—for his achievement as a poet. He was selected to edit *The Best American Poetry, 1997* (1997). "The Blue Booby" is from *The Oblivion Ha-Ha* (1970), his second major collection.

Alfred, Lord Tennyson (1809–1892) • One of the most popular of the Victorian poets, Tennyson became Poet Laureate in 1850. His earliest verse was published in collaboration with his brother, *Poems by Two Brothers* (1727). Some of his other collections were *Poems* (1842), *Locksley Hall* (1842), *The Princess* (1847), *Maud, and Other Poems* (1855) and *Idylls of the King* (1857–1891). He wrote *In Memoriam,* in which the well known phrase "nature red in tooth and claw" appears, from 1833 to 1850. A new collected and annotated edition of his poetry was published in 1969, but there are also many other useful editions.

Dylan Thomas (1914–1953) • A native of Wales, Thomas published his first collection, *Eighteen Poems*, in 1934. After World War II he became immensely popular in America as a speaker and lecturer because of the incantatory power with which he read his own poems. Fortunately, many of his readings survive on records available in college libraries. Thomas's *Collected Poems 1934–1952* was published in 1952 and was a commercial success. *The Poems of Dylan Thomas,* a definitive edition, was published in 1971. In the 1980s, the musician John Cale set "Do Not Go Gentle" to music as part of his *Falklands Suite* (found on Cale's *Words for the Dying,* Opal/Warner Bros. 9-26024-2).

Jean Toomer (1894–1967) • Toomer was born in Washington, D. C., studied at five colleges, and eventually settled in the African-American community in Sparta, Georgia. An important voice in the Harlem Renaissance, Toomer published his only book, *Cane,* a grouping of stories, poems, and a play, in 1923. A collection of his works may be found in *The Wayward and the Seeking* (1980).

Chase Twichell (b. 1950) • Twichell, born in Connecticut, received her B.A. from Trinity College in Hartford and her M.A. from the University of Iowa. For a time she did editorial work, and she now teaches at Princeton University. She has also taught at both the University of Alabama and Hampshire College. She has received a Guggenheim Fellowship and also a grant from the National Endowment for the Arts.

Among her poetry collections are *Northern Spy* (1981), *The Odds* (1986), *Perdido* (1991), *The Ghost of Eden* (1995, 1998), and *The Snow Watcher* (1998).

Peter Ulisse (b. 1944) • Ulisse lives in Connecticut, where he chairs the Humanities Department of Housatonic Community Technical College. He has written many poetry reviews for *Small Pond of Literature* and has served as editor of the *Connecticut River Review*. His first major poetry collection was *Vietnam Voices* (1990). In 1995 he published *Memory Is an Illusive State,* which includes "Odyssey: 20 Years Later."

Mona Van Duyn (b. 1921) • Van Duyn is a native of Iowa and received her college degrees there. She taught for a time at the University of Washington and has been considered a "Northwest" poet for this reason. Among her poetry collections are *Valentines to the Wide World* (1959), *Merciful Disguises* (1973), *Near Changes* (1990, 1992), and *Firefall* (1994).

Tino Villanueva (b. 1941) • Villanueva was born in San Marcos, Texas. He received his B.A. from Southwest Texas State University in 1969 and his M.A. from SUNY Buffalo in 1971. He has taught at Wellesley College. In addition to the works he has written in Spanish, he contributed to Philip Ortego's *We Are Chicanos: An Anthology of Mexican-American Literature* (1974). His most recent collection of poetry is *Scene from the Movie GIANT* (1993).

Judith Viorst (b. 1931) • Viorst is a native of New Jersey and received her degrees from Rutgers and the Washington Psychoanalytic Institute. She is known for her wry humor. Her first major volume was *It's Hard to Be Hip over Thirty and Other Tragedies of Married Life* in 1968. Among later works are *Necessary Losses* (1986) and *Forever Fifty and Other Negotiations* (1989, 1996). She also has written a considerable amount of fiction for young people.

Shelly Wagner (b. ca. 1948) • A resident of Virginia, Wagner received her B.A. from Old Dominion University, after which she worked as an interior designer and social worker. Her younger son Andrew drowned in 1984, and it was five years later that she began her cycle of elegiac poems, *The Andrew Poems,* including "Boxes," which was published in 1994. Before this she had published poetry in publications like *American Poetry Review and Poetry East.*

David Wagoner (b. 1926) • Wagoner was born in Ohio and studied at Pennsylvania State University and the University of Indiana. In 1954 he began teaching at the University of Washington, where he was a colleague, and later an editor, of Theodore Roethke. He has been extremely productive both as poet and novelist. A few of his many poetry collections are *Dry Sun, Dry Wind* (1953), *Staying Alive* (1966), *Collected Poems* (1976), *Landfall* (1981), *Through the Forest: New and Selected Poems* (1987), and *Walt Whitman Bathing* (1996).

Diane Wakoski (b. 1937) • Wakoski was born in California and graduated from Berkeley in 1960. Since 1967 she has been a member of the faculty of Michigan State University. Her selected collection of verse *Emerald Ice: Selected Poems, 1962–1988* (1988) indicates that by 1988 she had published more than twenty collections of verse, including *The George Washington Poems* (1967), *The Motorcycle Betrayal: Poems* (1971), and *Emerald Ice: Selected Poems 1962–1987* (1989).

Alice Walker (b. 1944) • For a brief biography, see p. 89.

Edmund Waller (1606–1687) • Waller, whom Dryden constantly praised for the quality and originality of his poetic couplets, was a Royalist during the English Civil Wars of 1642–1649, and for his efforts he was forced into exile. He returned in 1651 after swearing loyalty to Oliver Cromwell. After the Restoration, he supported King Charles II. His major collections of poetry were *Poems* (1645) and *Divine Poems* (1685).

Robert Penn Warren (1905–1989) • Three-time winner of the Pulitzer Prize (1947, 1957, 1978), and the first United States Poet Laureate (1985), Warren was one of the leaders of the New Criticism (see Chapter 33) and was also a leading exponent of southern literature and culture. With Cleanth Brooks, he wrote the *Understanding Poetry, Understanding Drama,* and *Understanding Fiction* series of textbooks that taught the techniques of New Criticism to a generation of graduate and undergraduate students His novel *All the King's Men* (1946) was made into a prize-winning motion picture in 1950. During his teaching career he taught at the University of Minnesota and then at Yale. Some of his poetry collections are *Thirty-Six Poems* (1935), *Promises* (1957), and *New and Selected Poems* (1985).

Charles H. Webb (b. 1952) • Webb is a native of Pennsylvania but grew up in Texas. He received degrees at Rice University, the University of Washington, and the University of Southern California. He teaches at California State University at Long Beach. Recent poetry collections are *Everyday Outrages* (1989) and *A Weeb for All Seasons* (1992). He has also published a novel, *The Wilderness Effect* (1982). Interestingly, before he took up teaching as a profession he had spent a decade as a rock guitarist and singer.

Phyllis Webb (b. 1927) • Webb is a native of British Columbia. She was educated at the University of British Columbia and also at McGill University. During her career she worked with the Canadian Broadcasting Company both as a program planner and a producer; she has also taught in various Canadian colleges and universities as a guest lecturer and professor. A major concern in her poetry has been the problem of maintaining personal integrity amid a world of "hate and broken things," to quote from one of her poems in *Trio* (1954). One of her interests has been to experiment with a form of Persian poetry, the ghazal, which consists of five couplets. Among her poetry collections are *Wilson's Bowl* (1980), *The Vision Tree* (1982), *Selected Poems* (1982), *Water and Light: Ghazals and Anti Ghazals* (1984), and *Hanging Fire* (1990).

Bruce Weigl (b. 1949) • Weigl, who teaches at Penn State, was born in Ohio. He took his B.A. at Oberlin (1974) and his Ph.D. at the University of Utah (1979). His poetry collections include *Like a Sack Full of Old Quarrels* (1976), *Executioner* (1977), *A Romance* (1979), *The Monkey Wars* (1984), *Song of Napalm* (1988), *What Saves Us* (1992), and *Sweet Lorain* (1996). His most recent collections are *Archaeology of the Circle: New and Selected Poems* (1998, 1999) and *After the Others* (1999).

Phillis Wheatley (ca. 1753–1784) • Wheatley was born in Africa. She was captured by slave traders and sold to John Wheatley, a Boston merchant, who treated her virtually as a daughter and saw to it that she was educated. When she published her *Poems on Various Subjects, Religious and Moral* (1773), however, the temper of the times made it necessary to include prefaces by Massachusetts men verifying that she was qualified to write poetry and that she had indeed written the poems in the collection. Although she wrote a second volume of poetry, she could not find a publisher for it during her lifetime. Her collected works were published in 1988.

Walt Whitman (1819–1892) • Whitman, who became a legend during his lifetime, is one of America's major poets. He was born in New York and lived with his family in both Long Island and Brooklyn. At various times he worked as a printer, teacher, reporter, and government bureaucrat. In addition, he served as a nurse during the Civil War. His major work was *Leaves of Grass*, which he first published as a collection of twelve poems in 1855, and to which he added as time went on. Many editions were published in his lifetime, the last one in 1892. *Drum Taps*, poems based on his Civil War experiences, was published in 1865; a second edition contained "When Lilacs Last in the Dooryard Bloom'd," his poem on the death of Lincoln.

Cornelius Whur (1782–1853) • Whur was a Methodist minister in Suffolk, England. In 1837 he published a poetry collection, *Village Musings on Moral and Religious Subjects,* which included "The First-Rate Wife." In his obituary notice he was recognized not only as a "distinguished" poet but also as a gardener.

Richard Wilbur (b. 1921) • Wilbur was born in New York. He has published a number of poetry collections, including *New and Collected Poems* (1988, 1989), for which he was awarded the Pulitzer Prize in poetry. He has also made a number of commercially successful translations of French drama. In 1988 he was distinguished as the second United States Poet Laureate (the first being Robert Penn Warren). His most recent collection is *Mayflies: New Poems and Translations* (2000).

C. K. Williams (Charles Kenneth Williams, b. 1936) • Williams is a native of New Jersey who graduated from Bucknell and the University of Pennsylvania. He taught at a number of schools and colleges and has become a permanent resident of France. He is known for his discursively long lines in the manner of Walt Whitman. Among his many volumes of poems are *Tar* (1983) and *Flesh and Blood* (1987), for which he was awarded the 1987 National Book Critics Circle Award; *Poems, 1963–1983* (1988); *A Dream of the Mind* (1992); and *Repair* (1999). Recently he has undertaken translations of Greek drama. "Dimensions" is taken from *Lies,* his collection of 1969.

William Carlos Williams (1883–1963) • Williams spent his career as a practicing pediatrician, but he early became friendly with Ezra Pound and Hilda Doolittle (H. D.). He developed a second career as a writer, producing poems, plays, stories, novels, and essays. He published poems throughout his life, beginning with *Poems* (1913) and *Tempers* (1913) and ending with *Pictures from Brueghel* (1963), for which he was posthumously awarded the Pulitzer Prize.

David Wojahn (b. 1953) • Wojahn is a native of Minnesota who received degrees from the Universities of Minnesota and Arizona. He teaches at the University of Arkansas, where he is also poetry editor of the journal *Crazy Horse*. His first volume of verse was *Icehouse Lights* (1981), which was distinguished by the Yale Series of Younger Poets Award. More recently he published *Mystery Train* (1990), which contains "It's Only Rock and Roll, But I Like It," *Late Empire* (1994), and *The Falling Hour* (1997).

William Wordsworth (1770–1850) • For a brief biography of Wordsworth, see pp. 1032–39.

James Wright (1927–1980) • Wright was born in Martins Ferry, Ohio, and received his Ph.D. at the University of Washington, where he was a student of Theodore Roethke. In 1966 he began teaching at Hunter College, and he remained there until his death in 1980. His first poetry collection, *The Green Wall,* appeared in 1957, and after that he published collections regularly, receiving the 1972 Pulitzer Prize in Poetry for his *Collected Poems* (1971). *This Journey* was published posthumously in 1982, and *Above the River: The Complete Poems* appeared in 1990.

Sir Thomas Wyatt (ca. 1503–1542) • Wyatt was a courtier in the service of King Henry VIII. He is credited with introducing the sonnet form into English as a result of his translations of the sonnets of the Italian sonneteer Petrarch. He circulated his poems in manuscript, although a number of them were anthologized after his death in *The Court of Venus* (1542) and *Seven Penitential Psalms* (1549). Modern editions of his poems were published in 1969, 1975, and 1978.

William Butler Yeats (1865–1939) • The foremost Irish poet of the twentieth century, Yeats was instrumental in the founding of the Abbey Theatre in Dublin in 1899. An unorthodox thinker, he developed his poems out of his vast reading and his special interest in spiritualism. He published many volumes of poems, including *The Green Helmet* (1910), *The Wild Swans at Coole* (1917), *The Winding Stair* (1929), and *The Collected Poems* (1932). He was awarded the Nobel Prize for Literature in 1923.

Paul Zimmer (b. 1934) • Zimmer, whose sister was the science-fiction writer Marion Zimmer Bradley, was born in Canton, Ohio, and received his B.A. from Kent State. He has managed bookstores and university presses, including the University of Iowa Press. Among his many volumes of poems are *A Seed on the Wind* (1960), *The Ribs of Death* (1967), *Family Reunion* (1983), and *Big Blue Train* (1993). His "Zimmer" poems are collected in *The Zimmer Poems* (1976), *Earthbound Zimmer* (1983), *The American Zimmer* (1984), *The Great Bird of Love* (1989), and *Crossing to Sunlight: Selected Poems* (1996).

Glossary
of Literary Terms

This glossary presents brief definitions of terms boldfaced in the text. Page references indicate where readers may find additional detail and illustration, together with discussions about how the concepts can be utilized in studying and writing about literature.

Abstract diction   Language describing qualities that are rarefied and theoretical (e.g., "good," "interesting," "neat," and so on); distinguished from *concrete diction*. 342, 720

Accentual rhythm   See *Sprung rhythm.*

Actions or **incidents**   The events or occurrences in a work. 3, 56, 62, 109, 1226

Allegory   A complete *narrative* that can also be applied to a parallel set of situations that may be political, moral, religious, or philosophical. See also *Parable.* 61, 62, 425–62, 1230

Alliteration   The repetition of identical consonant sounds (most often the sounds beginning words) in close proximity (e.g., "pensive poets," "grown grey"). 843, 852

Allusion   Unacknowledged references and quotations. Authors assume that readers will recognize the original sources, and relate their meaning to the new context. 430–31, 942, 963

Amphibrach   A three-syllable poetic *foot* consisting of a light, heavy, and light *stress.* 848

Amphimacer or **Cretic**   A three-syllable *foot* consisting of a heavy, light, and heavy stress. 848

Anagnorisis or **recognition**   Aristotle's term describing the point in a play, usually the *climax,* when a character experiences understanding. 1294

Analytical sentence outline   A scheme or plan for an essay, arranged according to topics (A, B, C, etc.) and with the topics expressed in sentences. 27

Analyzed rhyme   See *Inexact rhyme.*

Anapest   A three-syllable *foot* consisting of two light stresses climaxed by a heavy stress. 847

Anaphora   ("to carry again" or "repeat") The repetition of the same word or phrase throughout a work or a section of a work. The effect is to lend weight and emphasis. 779

Ancillary characters   Characters who set off or highlight the protagonist and who provide insight into the action. The *foil, choric figure,* and *raisonneur* are all ancillary characters. 1225

Antagonist   The person, idea, force, or general set of circumstances opposing the *protagonist,* an essential element of *plot.* 56, 174, 1225

Anticipation   See *Procatalepsis.*

Antimetabole   See *Chiasmus.*

Antithesis   A rhetorical device of opposition, in which one idea or word is established, and then the opposite idea or word is expressed, as in "I *burn* and *freeze*" and "I *love* and *hate*." 725, 898

Apostrophe   The addressing of a discourse to a real or imagined person who is not present; also, a speech to an abstraction. 779

Apron or **thrust stage**   A stage that projects into the auditorium area, thus increasing the space for action; a characteristic feature of Elizabethan theaters and many recent ones. 1232

Archetypal/symbolic/mythic critical approach   An interpretive approach explaining literature in terms of archetypal patterns (e.g., God's creation of human beings, the sacrifice of a hero, or the search for paradise). 1963

Archetype   A character, action, or situation that is a prototype or pattern of human life generally; a situation that occurs over and over again in literature, such as a quest, an initiation, or an attempt to overcome evil. Many *myths* are archetypes. 972

Archon, Eponymous   The Eponymous Archon was a leading magistrate in ancient Athens, after whom the year was named. He made arrangements for the tragedies and comedies to be performed at the yearly festivals in honor of the god Dionysus. 1290

Arena stage or **theater-in-the-round**   A theater arrangement, often outdoors, in which the audience totally surrounds the stage, with all actors entering and exiting along the same aisles used by the audience. 1232

Argument   The development of an idea, including the introduction of a hypothesis or major idea, supporting details, and logical conclusions. 15, 22, 29–33

Aside   A short speech delivered by a character to another character or to the audience, the convention being that the other characters on stage cannot hear it; the speaker usually reveals his or her thoughts or plans. 1348

Assertion   A sentence putting an *idea* (the subject) into operation (the predicate); necessary for both developing and understanding the idea. 465

Assonance   The repetition of identical vowel sounds in different words in close proximity, as in the d*ee*p gr*ee*n s*ea.* 843, 852

Atmosphere or **mood**   The emotional aura invoked by a work. 60, 289, 1229

Audience or **intended reader**   (1) The people attending a theatrical production. (2) The intended group of readers for whom a writer writes. 1234

Auditory images   References to sounds. 749

Authorial voice   The *voice* or *speaker* used by authors when seemingly speaking for themselves. The use of the term makes it possible to discuss a narration or presentation without identifying the ideas absolutely with those of the author. See also *Speaker, Point of view,* and *Third-person point of view.* 58, 174, 249

Bacchius or **Bacchic**   A three-syllable *foot* consisting of a light stress followed by two heavy stresses, as in "a new song." 848

Ballad, ballad measure   A narrative poem composed of *quatrains* in which lines of iambic tetrameter alternate with iambic trimeter, rhyming *x a x a*. 2, 670, 857, 900

Ballad opera   An eighteenth-century comic drama, originated by John Gay's *The Beggar's Opera* in 1728, featuring lyrics set to existing tunes. See also *Comic opera*. 1623

Beast fable   A fable featuring animals with human characteristics. 429

Beat or **accent**   A heavy stress or accent in a line of poetry. The number of beats in a line usually dictates the meter of the line (five beats in a *pentameter* line, etc.). 844

Blank verse   Unrhymed *iambic pentameter.* 2, 898

Blocking   In the performance of a play, the grouping and movement of characters on stage. 1231

Blocking agent   A person, circumstance, or attitude that obstructs the union of lovers. 1537

Box set   In the modern theater, a realistic setting of a single room from which the "fourth wall" is missing, so that the stage resembles a three-dimensional picture. 1231

Brainstorming   The exploration, discovery, and development of details to be used in a composition. 17

Breve   A mark in the shape of a bowl-like half circle (˘) to indicate a light stress or unaccented syllable. See *Schwa*. 845

Business or **stage business**   The gestures, expressions, and general activity (beyond *blocking*) of actors onstage. Usually, business is designed to create laughter. It is often spontaneous. 1231

Buskins   Elegantly laced boots (*kothorni* or *cothurni*) worn by the actors in ancient Greek tragedy. Eventually the buskins became elevator shoes to stress the royal status of actors by making them tall. 1301

Cacophony   Meaning "bad sound," the term *cacophony* refers to words combining sharp or harsh sounds; opposite of *euphony*. 853

Cadence group   A coherent word group spoken as a single rhythmical unit, such as a noun phrase ("our sacred honor") or prepositional phrase ("of parting day"). 848

Caesura, caesurae   The pause(s) separating phrases within lines of poetry, an important aspect of poetic *rhythm*. 848, 850–51

Carpe diem **poetry**   Poetry concerned with the shortness of life and the need to act in or enjoy the present. *Carpe diem* means "seize the day." 1007

Catastrophe   The "turning downward" of the dramatic *plot,* the fourth stage in the structure after the *climax.* The *dénouement* of a play, in which things are explained and put into place. 1228

Catharsis (purgation)   Aristotle's concept that tragedy, by arousing pity and fear (*eleos* and *phobos*), regularizes and shapes the emotions, and that therefore tragedy is essential in civilized society. 1293

Central idea   (1) The thesis or main idea of an essay. 000 (2) The *theme* of a literary work. 62

Character   An extended verbal representation of a human being, the inner self that determines thought, speech, and behavior. 3, 55–56, 62, 170–239, 686–714, 1224, 1661

Chiasmus or **antimetabole**   A rhetorical pattern in which words and ideas are repeated in the sequence *a b b a*, as in "I *lead* the life I *love;* I *love* the life I *lead.*" 725, 816

Choragos or *choregus*   The sponsor or financial backer of a classical Greek dramatic production. Often the *choragos* was honored by serving as the leader (*koryphaios*) of the chorus. 1297

Chòree See Trochee.

Choric figure A character who remains detached from the action and who provides commentary. See also *Raisonneur.* 1226

Chorus In ancient Athenian drama, the chorus was composed of fifteen young men in tragedies, and twenty-four in comedies, who chanted in unison and performed dance movements to a flute accompaniment. 1298

Chronology ("logic of time") The sequence of events in a work, with emphasis on the complex intertwining of cause and effect. 56, 1226

City Dionysia See *Dionysia.*

Clerihew A humorous closed-form poem in four lines, rhyming *a b a b,* usually about a famous real or literary person. 902

Cliché rhymes Trite and widely used rhymes, such as *moon* and *June* or *trees* and *breeze.* 854

Climax (Greek for "ladder") The high point of *conflict* and tension preceding the resolution or *dénouement* of a drama or story; the point of decision, of inevitability and no return. The climax is sometimes merged with the *crisis* in the consideration of dramatic and narrative structure. 112, 1228

Closed-form poetry Poetry written in specific and traditional patterns produced through control of *rhyme, meter,* line length, and line groupings. 897

Comedy A literary genre which, like *tragedy,* originated in the *Dionysia* festivals of ancient Athens. Derived from the Greek *komos* songs or "songs of merrymakers," the first comedies were wildly boisterous. Subsequently comedies became more subdued and realistic. In typical comedies today, confusions and doubts are resolved satisfactorily if not happily, and usually comedies are characterized by smiles and laughter. 1235

Comedy of the Absurd A modern form of comedy dramatizing the apparent pointlessness, ambiguity, uncertainty, and absurdity of existence. 1542

Comedy of manners A form of comedy, usually *regular* (five acts or three acts), in which attitudes and customs are examined and satirized in the light of high intellectual and moral standards. The *dialogue* is witty and sophisticated, and characters are often measured according to their linguistic and intellectual powers. 1541

Comic A pattern of action, including funny situations and language, that is solvable and correctible, and therefore satisfying. 1539

Comic opera An outgrowth of eighteenth-century *ballad operas,* but different from them in having music specially composed for the lyrics. 1623

Commedia dell'arte Broadly humorous farce developed in sixteenth-century Italy, featuring stock characters, stock situations, and much improvised *dialogue.* 1542

Commentary, analysis, or **interpretation** Passages of explanation and reflection about the meaning of actions, thoughts, dialogue, historical movements, and so on. 62

Commentator See *Raisonneur.*

Common ground of assent Those interests, concerns, and assumptions that the writer assumes in common with readers so that an effective and persuasive *tone* may be maintained. 812

Common measure A closed poetic quatrain, rhyming *a b a b,* in which lines of iambic tetrameter alternate with iambic trimeter. See also *Ballad measure.* 901

Comparison-contrast   A technique of analyzing two or more works in order to determine similarities and differences in topic, treatment, and quality. 1979–92

Complete   The second aspect of Aristotle's definition of *tragedy*, emphasizing the logic and wholeness of the play. 1295

Complex sentence   A sentence consisting of an independent clause together with a subordinate or dependent clause. 345

Complication   A stage of narrative and dramatic structure in which the major *conflicts* are brought out; the *rising action* of a *drama*. 112, 1227

Compound sentence   A sentence consisting of two simple sentences joined by a conjunction. 345

Compound-complex sentence   A sentence consisting of a compound sentence also integrating one or more dependent or subordinate clauses. Compound-complex sentences may become quite long and involved as more independent and subordinate clauses are added. 345

Concrete diction   Words that describe exact and particular conditions or qualities, such as *cold, sweet,* and *creamy* in reference to an ice-cream sundae. These words are *concrete,* while the application of *good* or *neat* to the sundae is *abstract.* See also *Abstract diction.* 58, 342, 720

Concrete poetry   Poetry depicting visual shapes in addition to ideas and emotions. 906

Conflict   The opposition between two characters, between large groups of people, or between *protagonists* and larger forces such as natural objects, ideas, modes of behavior, public opinion, and the like. Conflict may also be internal and psychological, involving choices facing a *protagonist.* It is the essence of *plot.* 56, 109, 1226

Connotation   The meanings that words suggest beyond their bare dictionary definitions. 343, 726

Consonant segments   Consonant sounds; sounds produced as a result of the touching or close proximity of the tongue or the lips in relation to the teeth or palate (e.g., *m, n, p, f, sh, ch*); contrasted with *vowel segments.* 842

Contextual symbol   A symbol that is derived not from common historical, cultural, or religious materials, but which is rather developed within the context of an individual work. See also *Cultural symbol.* 61, 427–28, 938, 963, 1230

Convention   An accepted feature of a genre, such as the *point of view* in a story, the *form* of a poem (e.g., *sonnet, ode*), the competence or brilliance of the detective in detective fiction, the impenetrability of disguise and concealment in a Shakespearean play, or the *chorus* in Greek drama. 19

Corpus Christi play   A type of medieval drama that enacts events from the Bible, such as the killing of Abel by Cain, the problems of Noah, the anger of Herod, and so on. The word is derived from the religious festival of Corpus Christi ("Christ's body"), held in the spring of each year. Also called *mystery plays.* See also *Cycle.* 1239

Cosmic irony (irony of fate)   *Situational irony* that is connected to a pessimistic or fatalistic view of life. 386, 1297

Costumes   The clothes worn by actors, designed to indicate historical periods, social status, economic levels, etc. 1234

Cothurni   See *Buskins.*

Counting   A way of determining qualities of *style* by counting numbers of words in sentences and paragraphs, average numbers of modifiers, average word lengths, etc. 344

Couplet   Two successive rhyming lines. 2, 898

Crisis   The point of uncertainty and tension—the *turning point*—that results from the *conflicts* and difficulties brought about through the complications of the *plot*. The crisis leads to the *climax*—that is, to the decision made by the *protagonist* to resolve the *conflict*. Sometimes the *crisis* and the *climax* are considered as two elements of the same stage of *plot* development. 112, 1228

Cultural (universal) symbol   A symbol recognized and shared as a result of a common social and cultural heritage. See also *Contextual symbol*. 61, 427, 938, 963, 1230

Cycle   (1) A group of closely related works. (2) In medieval religious drama, the complete set of plays performed during the Corpus Christi festival, from the creation of the world to the resurrection. As many as forty or fifty plays could make up the cycle. See also *Corpus Christi plays*. 1239

Dactyl   A three-syllable *foot* consisting of a heavy *stress* followed by two lights, as in *notable, parable,* and *terrible.* 847

Dactylic or **triple rhyme**   Rhyming *dactyls.* 855, 856

Deconstructionist critical approach   An interpretive literary approach that rejects absolute interpretations and stresses ambiguities and contradictions. 1965

Decorum   The convention or expectation that words and subjects should be exactly appropriate—*high* or *formal* words for serious subjects (e.g., *epic* poems, *tragedy*), and *low* or *informal* words for low subjects (e.g., *limericks, farce*). 723

Denotation   The standard dictionary meaning of a word. 343, 725

Dénouement ("untying") or **resolution**   The final stage of *plot* development, in which mysteries are explained, characters find their destinies, and the work is completed. Usually the dénouement is done as speedily as possible, for it occurs after all *conflicts* are ended. 113, 1228

Description   The exposition of scenes, actions, attitudes, and feelings. 60

Device   A *rhetorical figure* or strategy. 19

Deus ex machina   ("A god out of the machine"; *theos apo mechanes* in Greek) In ancient Greek drama, the entrance of a god to unravel the problems in a play. Today, the phrase *deus ex machina* refers to the artificial and illogical solution of problems. 1300

Dialect   The speech of a particular region or social group, usually characterized by unique words, expressions, and pronunciation. When a dialect becomes widespread in government, business, education, and literature, it is claimed as the standard of the particular language. 722

Dialogue   The speeches of two or more characters in a story, play, or poem. 3, 60, 62, 689, 1224

Diction   Word choice, types of words, and the level of language. 340, 719–45

Diction, formal or **high**   Proper, elevated, elaborate, and often polysyllabic language. 341, 720

Diction, informal or **low**   Relaxed, conversational, and familiar language, utilizing contractions and elisions, and sometimes employing *slang* and grammatical mistakes. 342, 721

Diction, neutral or **middle**   Correct language characterized by directness and simplicity. 341, 721

Digraph   Two alphabetical letters spelling one sound, as in *digraph,* where

<ph> spells the /f/ sound; *stick,* where <ck> spells the /k/ sound; and *thumb,* where <mb> spells the /m/ sound. 844

Dilemma Two choices facing a *protagonist,* usually in a tragic situation, with either choice being unacceptable or damaging; a cause of both internal and external *conflict.* 110, 1297

Dimeter A line of two metrical *feet.* 845

Dionysia The religious festivals of ancient Athens held to celebrate the god Dionysus. *Tragedy* developed as part of the Great, or City, Dionysia in March-April, and *comedy* developed as part of a shorter festival, the Lenaia. 1287, 1535

Dipody, dipodic foot, or **syzygy** The submergence of two normal *feet,* usually *iambs* or *trochees,* under a stronger beat, so that a "galloping" or "rollicking" *rhythm* results. 848

Director The person in charge of guiding and instructing all persons involved in a dramatic production. 1231

Discursive writing To be distinguished from imaginative writing, discursive writing is concerned with factual presentation and the development of reasonable and logical conclusions. 2–3

Dithyramb An ancient Athenian poetic form sung by choruses during the earliest *Dionysia.* The first *tragedies* originated from the dithyrambs. 1235, 1287

Donnée (French for "given") The given action or set of assumptions on which a work of literature is based, such as the unpredictability of love, the bleakness and danger of a postwar world, or the inescapability of guilt. See also *Postulate* or *Premise.* 54–55

Double dactyl A comic *closed-form* poem in two *quatrains,* written in dactylic *dimeter.* The second line must be a proper name, and the sixth or seventh a single word. 902

Double entendre ("double meaning") Deliberate ambiguity, often sexual and usually humorous. 385

Double plot Two different but related lines of *action,* most often in a play. 1226

Double rhyme See *Trochaic rhyme.*

Drama An individual play; also plays considered as a group; one of the three major *genres* of literature. 3, 1223–85

Dramatic convention See *Convention.*

Dramatic irony A special kind of *situational irony* in which a character perceives his or her plight in a limited way while the audience and one or more of the other characters understand it entirely. 61, 386, 815–16, 1229, 1298

Dramatic monologue A type of poem, derived from the theater, in which a speaker addresses an internal listener or the reader at length. The form is related to the *soliloquy.* 690

Dramatic (objective) point of view A third-person *narration* reporting speech and action, but excluding commentary on the actions and thoughts of the characters. 59, 246

Dying rhyme See *Falling rhyme.*

Dynamic character A character who undergoes adaptation, change, or growth, unlike the *static character,* who remains constant. In a *short story,* there is usually only one dynamic character, whereas in a *novel* there may be many. 174, 1225

Echoic words Words echoing the actions they describe, such as *buzz, bump,* and *slap;* important in the device of *onomatopoeia.* 852

Economic Determinist / Marxist critical approach An interpretive approach based on the theories of Karl Marx (1818–1883), stressing that literature is to be judged from an economic perspective. 1961

Editing See *Montage.*

Enclosing method See *Framing method.*

End-stopped line A line ending in a full pause, usually indicated with a period or semicolon. 850

English (Shakespearean) sonnet A sonnet form developed by Shakespeare, in *iambic pentameter,* composed of three *quatrains* and a *couplet,* rhyming *a b a b, c d c d, e f e f, g g.* 900

Enjambement or **run-on line** A line having no end punctuation but running over to the next line. 850

Epic A long narrative poem elevating character, speech, and action. 3, 51

Epigram A short and witty poem, usually in *couplets,* that makes a humorous or satiric point. 902

Episodia or **episode** An acting *scene* or section of Greek tragedy. Divisions separating the episodes were called *stasima,* or sections for the chorus. 62, 1303

Epitaph Lines composed to mark someone's death; a special type of *epigram.* 902

Euphony Meaning "good sound," *euphony* refers to word groups containing consonants that permit an easy and pleasant flow of spoken sound; opposite of *cacophony.* 853

Exact rhyme Rhyming words in which both the vowel and consonant sounds rhyme; also called *perfect rhyme.* It is important to note that rhymes result from *sound* rather than spelling; words do not have to be spelled the same way or look alike to rhyme. 853

Exodos The final episode in a Greek tragedy, occurring after the last choral ode. 1303

Explication A complete and detailed analysis of a work of literature, often word by word and line by line. 681-85, 1957

Exposition The stage of dramatic or narrative structure that introduces all things necessary for the development of the *plot.* 112

Eye rhyme Words that seem to rhyme because parts of them are spelled identically but pronounced differently (e.g., *bear, fear; fury, bury; stove, shove; wonder, yonder*). 856

Fable A brief *story* illustrating a moral truth, most often associated with the ancient Greek writer Aesop. 52, 429–30

Falling action See *Catastrophe.*

Falling rhyme *Trochaic rhymes,* such as *dying* and *crying,* and also *dactylic rhymes,* such as *flattery* and *battery.* 855

Fantasy The creation of events that are dreamlike or fantastic, departing from ordinary understanding of reality because of apparently illogical location, movement, causation, and *chronology.* 53

Farce A word derived from the Latin word *farsus,* meaning "stuffed," farce is an outlandish physical comedy overflowing with silly characters, improbable happenings, wild clowning, extravagant language, and bawdy jokes. 1542

Feminine rhyme See *Falling rhyme.*

Feminist critical approach An interpretive approach designed to raise consciousness about the importance and unique nature of women in literature. 1960

Fiction *Narratives* based in the imagination of the author, not in literal, reportorial facts; one of the three major *genres* of literature. 57–108

Figurative devices See *Figures of speech.*

Figurative language   See *Figures of speech.*

Figures, rhetorical   See *Figures of speech.*

Figures of speech   Organized patterns of comparison that deepen, broaden, extend, illuminate, and emphasize meaning, and also that conform to a particular patterns or forms such as *metaphor, simile,* and *parallelism.* 746–73.

Film   Motion pictures, movies. 1763–86

Film script   The written dramatic text on which a film is based, including directions for movement and expression. 1763

First-person point of view   The use of an "I," or first-person, *speaker* or *narrator* who tells about things that he/she has seen, done, spoken, heard, thought, and also learned about in other ways. 58, 62, 244, 248

Flashback   A method of *narration* in which past events are introduced into a present *action.* Also called *Selective recollection.* 114, 1660

Flat character   A character, usually minor, who is not individual but rather useful and structural, static and unchanging; distinguished from *round character.* 175, 1225

Foil   A character, usually minor, designed to highlight qualities of a major character. 1225

Foot   Measured combinations of heavy and light *stresses,* such as the *iamb,* that contain a light and a heavy stress. 844

Form, poetic   The various shapes and organizational modes of poetry. 897–936

Formal diction   See *Diction, formal* or *high.*

Formalist critical approach   See *New Critical/formalist critical approach.*

Formal substitution   See *Substitution.*

Framing (enclosing) method   The same features of topic or setting used at both the beginning and ending of a work so as to "frame" or "enclose" the work. 289

Free verse   Poetry based on the natural *rhythms* of phrases and normal pauses, not metrical *feet.* 3, 904

Freewriting   See *Brainstorming.*

French scene   A numbering system for a play in which a new scene is numbered whenever characters enter or leave the stage (as in Molière's *Love Is the Doctor*). 1605–22

Freytag pyramid   A diagram graphically showing the stages of dramatic *structure. Complication* and emotional intensity go upward like the side of a pyramid rising to its peak or point. Once the point is reached, intensity decreases just as the other side of the pyramid descends to its base. 1226

Gallery   The upper seats at the back and sides of a theater. 1299

General language   Words referring to broad classes of persons, objects, or phenomena; distinguished from *specific language.* 342, 720

Genre   A type of *literature,* such as *fiction* and *poetry;* also a type of work, such as detective fiction, epic poetry, tragedy, etc. 2–3

Graph, graphics (spelling)   Writing or spelling; the appearance of words on a page, as opposed to their actual sounds. 844

Great Dionysia   See *Dionysia.*

Gustatory images   References to impressions of taste. 751

Haiku   A poetic form derived from Japanese, traditionally containing three lines of 5, 7, and 5 syllables. 2, 902

Half rhyme   See *Inexact rhyme.*

Hamartia   The error or frailty that causes the downfall of a tragic *protagonist.* 1296

Heavy-stress rhyme   A *rhyme,* such as rhyming *iambs* or *anapests,* ending with a strong *stress.* 845

Heptameter or **the septenary**   A line consisting of seven metrical *feet.* 845

Hero, heroine   The major male and female *protagonists* in a narrative or drama; the terms are often used to describe leading characters in adventures and *romances.* 174

Heroic couplet   Also called the *neoclassic couplet.* Two successive rhyming lines of *iambic pentameter;* the second line is usually *end-stopped.* Couplets written between 1660 and 1800 are often called "heroic" regardless of their topic matter. 898

Hexameter   A line consisting of six metrical *feet.* 845

High comedy   Elegant comedies characterized by wit and sophistication, in which the complications grow out of character. See also *Comedy of manners.* 1541

Historical critical approach   See *Topical/historical critical approach.*

Hovering accent   See *Spondee.*

Hubris   Meaning "insolence, contemptuous violence," or pride, *hubris* defines the attitudes that lead tragic figures to commit their offenses. 1287

Humor   The capacity to cause laughter. 1539

Hymn   A religious song, consisting of one and usually many more replicating rhythmical *stanzas.* 901

Hyperbole   *Figurative language* in which emphasis is achieved through exaggeration. 385, 782

Hypocrites   (pronounced hip-POCK-rih-tayss) Meaning "one who plays a part," *hypocrites* was the ancient Athenian word for actor. 1289

Iamb   A two-syllable *foot* consisting of a light stress followed by a heavy stress (e.g., *the winds*). 845

Iambic pentameter   A line consisting of five iambic *feet.* 845

Idea   A concept, thought, opinion, or belief; in literature, a unifying, centralizing conception or *theme.* 57, 463–521, 1002–1031

Identical rhyme   The use of the same words in rhyming positions, such as *veil* and *veil* or *stone* and *stone.* 857

Idiom   Usage that produces unique words and phrases within regions, classes, or groups; e.g., standing *on* line or *in* line; carrying a *pail* or a *bucket;* drinking *pop* or *soda.* Also, the habits and structures of particular languages. 721

Image, imagery   Images are references that trigger the mind to fuse together memories of sights (*visual*), sounds (*auditory*), tastes (*gustatory*), smells (*olfactory*), motion (*kinesthetic* and *kinetic*), and sensations of touch (*tactile*). "Image" refers to a single mental creation. "Imagery" refers to images throughout a work or throughout the works of a writer or group of writers. Images may be *literal* (descriptive and pictorial) or *metaphorical* (figurative and suggestive). 3, 746–73

Imaginative literature   *Literature* based in the imagination of the writer, usually *fiction, poetry,* and *drama.* 2, *passim*

Imitation   The theory that literature is derived from life and is an imaginative duplication of experience; closely connected to *realism* and *verisimilitude.* 1294

Imperfect foot   A metrical *foot* consisting of a single syllable, either heavily or lightly stressed. 848

Incidents   See A*ctions.*

Incongruity   A discrepancy between what is ordinarily or normally expected and what is experienced. The resulting gap is a cause of amusement. 383

Inexact rhyme   *Rhymes* that are created out of words with similar but not identical sounds. In most of these instances, either the *vowel segments* are different while the *consonants* are the same, or vice versa. This type of rhyme is variously called *slant rhyme, near rhyme, half rhyme, off rhyme, analyzed rhyme,* or *suspended rhyme.* 856

Informal diction   See *Diction, informal* or *low.*

Inside speaker   The *speaker* of a poem presented in the *first-person point of view.* 687

Internal audience   See *Listener.*

Internal rhyme   The occurrence of rhyming words within a single line of verse. 854

Intrigue plot   The dramatic rendering of how a young woman and her lover, often aided by a maidservant or *soubrette,* usually foil the *blocking agent* of a parent or guardian. 1537

Invention   The process of discovering and determining materials to be included in a composition, whether an essay or an imaginative work; a vital phase of prewriting. 53

Ironic comedy   A form of comedy in which characters seem to be in the grips of uncontrollable, cosmic forces. The dominant tone is therefore ironic. 1542

Irony   Broadly, a means of indirection. Language that states the opposite of what is intended is *verbal irony.* The placement of characters in a state of ignorance is *dramatic irony,* while an emphasis on pow-

erlessness is *situational irony.* 61, 62, 382, 385–86, 813–16

Italian or **Petrarchan sonnet**   An *iambic pentameter* poem of fourteen lines, divided between the first eight lines (the *octave*) and the last six (the *sestet*). 900

Jargon   Words and phrases characteristic of a particular profession, trade, or pursuit, such as medicine, sociology, football, or the military. 723

Journal   A notebook or word-processor file for recording observations, here, about reading. 12

Kinesthetic images   Words describing human or animal motion and activity. 751

Kinetic images   Words describing general motion. 751

Kothorni   See *Buskins.*

Lenaia   See *Dionysia.*

Lighting   The general word describing the many types, positions, directions, and intensities of artificial lights used in the theater. 1233

Limerick   A five-line *closed-form poem* in which two lines of anapestic trimeter are followed by two in anapestic dimeter and a final line in trimeter, rhyming *a a b b a,* often used in comic and bawdy verse. 2, 902

Limited or **limited-omniscient point of view**   A third-person *narration* in which the actions and thoughts of the *protagonist* are the focus of attention. 59, 247

Line   The basic poetic unit of length, appearing as a row of words on a page, and containing phrases and sentences. Lines in the *closed poetic form* are composed of determinable numbers of metrical feet; lines in the *open poetic form* are variable, depending on content and rhythmical speech patterns. 897

Listener (internal audience) A character or characters imagined as the audience to whom a poem or story is spoken, and as a result one of the influences on the content of the work, as in Browning's "My Last Duchess." 689

Literature Written or oral compositions that tell stories, dramatize situations, express emotions, and analyze and advocate ideas. Literature is designed to engage readers emotionally as well as intellectually, with the major genres being *fiction, poetry, drama,* and *nonfiction prose,* and with many separate sub-forms. 1, *passim*

Long shot (film) A distant camera view, including not only characters but also their surroundings; distinguished from a *closeup.* 1768

Low comedy Crude, violent, and physical comedies and farces, characterized by sight gags, bawdy jokes, and outrageous situations. 1541

Lyric A short poem written in a repeating stanzaic form, often designed to be set to music; a *song.* 2, 901

Magnitude The third part of Aristotle's definition of tragedy, emphasizing that a play should be neither too long nor too short, so that artistic balance and proportion can be maintained. 1295

Main plot The central and major line of causation and action in a literary work. 1226

Major mover A major participant in a work's action, who either causes things to happen or is the subject of major events. If the first-person narrator is also a major mover, such as the *protagonist,* that fact gives firsthand authenticity to the narration. 241

Makeup The materials, such as cosmetics, wigs, and padding, applied to an actor to change appearance for a specific role, such as a youth, an aged person, or a hunchback. 1234

Malapropism The comic use of an improperly pronounced word, so that what comes out is another but incorrect word. Examples are *odorous* for *odious* (Shakespeare) or *pineapple* for *pinnacle* (Sheridan). The new word must be close enough to the correct word so that the resemblance is immediately recognized, along with the error. See also *Pun.* 383

Marxist critical approach See *Economic determinist/Marxist critical approach.*

Masculine rhyme See *Rising rhyme.*

Masks Masks were worn by ancient Athenian actors to illustrate and define the dramatic characters, such as youths, aged men, women, warriors, etc. 1301

Meaning That which is to be understood in a work; the total combination of ideas, actions, descriptions, and effects. 1002–1031

Mechanics of verse See *Prosody.*

Melodrama A sentimental dramatic form with an artificially happy ending. 1241

Metaphor ("carrying out a change") *Figurative language* that describes something as though it actually were something else, thereby enhancing understanding and insight. 3, 60, 774

Metaphorical language See *Figures of speech.*

Meter The number of *feet* within a line of traditional verse, such as *iambic pentameter* referring to a line containing five *iambs.* 845

Metonymy A *figure of speech* in which one thing is used as a substitute for another with which it is closely identified. 780

Metrical foot See *Foot.*

Metrics   See *Prosody.*

Middle Comedy   The Greek comedies written in the first two-thirds of the fourth century B.C.E. Middle Comedy lessened or eliminated the *chorus,* and did away with the exaggerated costumes of the Old Comedy. No Middle Comedies survive from antiquity. 1235, 1537

Mimesis   See *Representation.*

Miracle play   A medieval play dramatizing a miracle or miracles performed by a saint. An outgrowth of the earlier medieval *Corpus Christi play.* 1240

Monologue   A long speech spoken by a single character to himself or herself, to the audience, or to an off-stage character. 1224

Monometer   A line consisting of one metrical *Foot.* 845

Montage   The editing or assembling of the various camera "takes," or separate filmed scenes, to make a continuous film. 1766

Mood   See *Atmosphere.*

Moral/intellectual critical approach   An approach to the interpretation of literature that is concerned primarily with content and values. 1955

Morality play   A type of medieval and early Renaissance play that dramatizes the way to live a pious life. 1240

Motif   Meaning "something that moves," a *motif* is sometimes used in reference to a main *idea* or *theme* in a single work or in many works, such as a *carpe diem* theme, or a comparison of lovers to little worlds. See also *Archetype.* 1002

Motivation   The ideas and impulses that propel characters to a particular act or course of action. Motivation is the hallmark quality of *round characters.* 1225

Multiple plot   A work in which two or more stories are both contrasted and woven together, as in *A Midsummer Night's Dream.* 1226

Musical comedy   A modern prose play integrated with lyrics set to specially composed music. Usually, musical comedies are elaborately and expensively produced. 1623

Music of poetry   Broadly, the rhythms, sounds, and rhymes of poetry. See *Prosody.*

Muthos   See *Plot.*

Mystery plays   See *Corpus Christi plays.*

Myth, mythology, mythos   A *myth* is a story that deals with the relationships of gods to humanity or with battles among heroes. A myth may also be a set of beliefs or assumptions among societies. *Mythology* refers collectively to all the stories and beliefs, either of a single group or number of groups. A system of beliefs and religious or historical doctrine is a *mythos.* 2, 430, 969–1001

Mythical reader   See *Audience.*

Mythic critical approach   See *Archetypal/symbolic/mythic critical approach.*

Mythopoeic   The propensity to create *myths* and to live in terms of them. 970

Narration, narrative fiction   The relating or recounting of a sequence of events or actions. While a *narration* may be reportorial and historical, *narrative fiction* is primarily creative and imaginative. See also *Prose fiction.* 2, 51, 57, 62

Narrative ballad   A poem in *ballad measure* telling a story. 670

Narrative fiction   See *Prose fiction.*

Narrator   See *Speaker.*

Near rhyme   See *Inexact rhyme.*

Neoclassic couplet.   See *Heroic couplet.*

Neutral diction   See *Diction, neutral* or *middle.*

New comedy   The Greek comedy that developed at the end of the fourth century B.C.E., stressing wit, romanticism, and twists of plot. 1235, 1536

New Critical/formalist critical approach An approach to the interpretation of literature based on the French practice of *explication de texte,* stressing the form and details of literary works. 1957

Nonfiction prose   A *genre* consisting of essays, articles, and books that are concerned with real as opposed to fictional things; one of the major *genres* of literature. 2

Nonrealistic character   An undeveloped and often *symbolic character* without full *motivation* or individual identity. 1225

Nonrealistic drama   Dreamlike, fantastic, symbolic, and otherwise artificial plays that make no attempt to present an imitation of everyday reality. 1657, 1659–60

Novel   A long work of *prose fiction.* 2, 52

Objective point of view   See *Dramatic point of view.*

Octameter   A line of eight metrical *feet.* 845

Octave   The first eight lines of an *Italian sonnet,* unified by topic, *rhythm,* and *rhyme.* 900

Ode   A stanzaic poetic *form* (usually long, to contrast it with the *song*) with varying line lengths and sometimes intricate *rhyme* schemes. 901

Off rhyme   See *Inexact rhyme.*

Old comedy   The Athenian comedies of the fifth century B.C.E., featuring song, dance, ribaldry, satire, and invective. 1235, 1536

Olfactory imagery   *Images* referring to smell. 750

Omniscient point of view   A *third-person narrative* in which the *speaker* or *narrator,* with no apparent limitations, may describe intentions, actions, reactions, locations, and speeches of any or all of the characters, and may also describe their innermost thoughts (when necessary). 59, 246–47

Onomatopoeia   A blending of consonant and vowel sounds designed to imitate or suggest the activity being described. See also *Echoic words.* 852

Open-form poetry   Poems that avoid traditional structural patterns, such as *rhyme* or *meter,* in favor of other methods of organization. 904

Orchestra (theaters)   (1) In ancient Greek theaters, the *orchestra,* or dancing place, was the central circle where the chorus performed. (2) In modern *theaters,* the word now refers to the ground floor or first floor where the *audience* sits. 1299

Organic unity   The interdependence of all elements of a work, including character, actions, speeches, descriptions, thoughts, and observations. 56

Outside speaker   The speaker of a poem presented in a *third-person point of view.* 687

Overstatement   See *Hyperbole.*

Parable   A short *allegory* designed to illustrate a religious truth, most often associated with Jesus as recorded in the Gospels. 2, 52, 430

Parados   (1) A *parados* was either of the two aisles on each side of the *orchestra* in ancient Greek theaters, along which the performers could enter or exit. (2) The entry and first lyrical ode of the *chorus* in Greek tragedy, after the *prologue.* 1302

Paradox   A *figure of speech* embodying a contradiction that is nevertheless true. 778

Parallelism   A *figure of speech* in which the same grammatical forms are repeated. 345, 724, 898

Paranomasia   See *Pun.*

Paraphrase   A brief restatement, in one's own words, of all or part of a literary work; a *précis.* 679–81

Pathos   The "scene of suffering" in tragedy, which Aristotle defines as "a destructive or painful action, such as death on the stage, bodily agony, wounds, and the like." 1295

Pentameter   A line of five metrical *feet.* 845

Perfect rhyme   See *Exact rhyme.*

Performance   An individual production of a play, either for an evening or for an extended period, comprising acting, movement, lighting, sound effects, staging and scenery, ticket sales, and the accommodation of the audience. 1231

Peripeteia or **reversal**   Aristotle's term for a sudden reversal, when the action of a work, particularly a play, veers around quickly to its opposite. 1294

Persona   (Latin for "mask" [*prosopon* in Greek]) The *narrator* or *speaker* of a *story* or *poem.* See also *Speaker.* 58, 264, 686

Personification   A *figure of speech* in which human characteristics are attributed to nonhuman things or abstractions. 780

Perspective, dramatic   The *point of view* in drama, the way in which the dramatist focuses on major *characters* and on particular *problems.* 1228

Petrarchan sonnet   See *Italian sonnet.*

Phonetic, phonetics   The actual pronunciation of sounds, as distinguished from spelling or *graphics.* 844

Plausibility   See *Verisimilitude.*

Play   See *Drama.*

Plot   The plan or groundwork for a *story,* with the actions resulting from believable and authentic human responses to a *conflict.* It is causation, conflict, response, opposition, and interaction that make a *plot* out of a series of *actions.* Aristotle's word for plot is *muthos.* 56, 62, 109–10, 161–64, 1226, 1294

Poem, poet, poetry   A variable literary *genre* that is, foremost, characterized by the rhythmical qualities of language. While poems may be short (including *epigrams* and *haiku* of just a few lines) or long (*epics* of thousands of lines), the essence of poetry is compression, economy, and force, in contrast with the expansiveness of prose. There is no bar to the topics that poets may consider, and poems may range from the personal and lyric to the public and discursive. A *poem* is one poetic work. A *poet* is a person who writes poems. *Poetry* may refer to the poems of one writer, to poems of a number of writers, to all poems generally, or to the aesthetics of poetry considered as an art. 2, Chapters 13–25

Point of view   The *speaker, voice, narrator,* or *persona* of a work; the position from which details are perceived and related; a centralizing mind or intelligence; not to be confused with *opinion* or *belief.* 58–60, 240–84, 687, 1228

Point-of-view character   The central figure or *protagonist* in a *limited-point-of-view narration,* the *character* about whom events turn, the focus of attention in the *narration.* 247

Postulate or premise   The assumption on which a work of literature is based, such as a level of absolute, literal reality, or as a dreamlike, fanciful set of events. See also *Donnée.* 54

Précis   A shortening, or cutting down, of a narrative into its essential parts—

a synopsis, abridgment, paraphrase, condensation, or epitome. 102–107

Private symbol See *Contextual symbol.*

Probability or **plausibility** The standard that literature should be about what is probable, common, normal, and usual. 175

Problem A question or issue about the interpretation or understanding of a work. 1524

Problem play A type of *play* dealing with a problem, whether personal, social, political, environmental, or religious. 1241, 1788

Procatalepsis or **anticipation** A rhetorical strategy whereby the writer raises an objection and then answers it; the idea is to strengthen an argument by dealing with possible objections before a dissenter can raise them. 1525

Producer The person in charge of practical matters connected with a stage production, such as securing finances, arranging for theater use, furnishing materials, renting or making costumes and properties, guaranteeing payments, and so on. 1231

Prologue In Greek tragedy, the introductory action and speeches before the *parados,* or first entry, of the *chorus.* 1302

Props or **properties** The objects, furniture, and the like used on stage during a play. 1233

Proscenium, proscenium stage (1) See *proskenion.* (2) An arch that frames a *box set* and holds the curtain, thus creating the invisible fourth wall through which the *audience* sees the action of the *play.* 1231

Prose fiction *Imaginative* prose narratives (*short stories* and *novels*) that focus on one or a few *characters* who undergo a change or development as they interact with other characters and deal with their problems. 2, Chapters 2–12

Prose poem A short work, laid out to look like prose, but employing the methods of verse, such as *imagery,* for poetic ends. 904

Proskenion A raised stage built in front of the *skene* in ancient Greek theaters to separate the actors from the *chorus* and make them more prominent. 1299

Prosody The *sounds* and *rhythms* of poetry. 841–96

Protagonist The central character and focus of interest in a *narrative* or *drama.* 56, 62, 174, 1225

Psychological/psychoanalytic critical approach An interpretive literary approach stressing how psychology may be used in the explanation of both authors and literary works. 1962

Public mythology See *Universal mythology.*

Pun or **paranomasia** A witty word-play that reveals that words with different meanings have similar or even identical sounds. See also *Malapropism.* 781

Purgation See *Catharsis.*

Pyrrhic A metrical *foot* consisting of two unaccented *syllables.* 847

Quatrain (1) A four-line *stanza* or poetic unit. (2) In an *English* or *Shakespearean sonnet,* a group of four lines united by *rhyme.* 900, 957

Raisonneur A *character* who remains detached from the *action* and provides reasoned *commentary;* a *choric figure.* 1226

Reader-response critical approach An interpretive approach based on the proposition that literary works are not fully created until readers make *transactions* with them by *actualizing* them in the light of their own knowledge and experience. 1966

Realism or **verisimilitude** The use of true, lifelike, or probable situations and concerns. Also, the theory underlying the use of reality in literature. See also *Imitation.* 53, 288

Realistic character The accurate *imitation* of individualized men and women. 1225

Realistic comedy See *Ironic comedy.*

Realistic drama *Plays* that dramatize *characters* and situations similar to those in the world as we know it. 1657, 1658–59

Realistic setting A setting designed to resemble places that actually exist or that might exist. The settings of Ibsen's *A Dollhouse* are realistic. 1233

Recognition See *Anagnorisis.*

Regular play A *play,* usually of five acts, but often (recently) of three, that conforms to the various *rules of drama,* such as the *three unities.* 1227

Repetition See *Anaphora.*

Representation The Aristotelian idea that *drama* (*tragedy*) represents rather than duplicates history. Also called *mimesis.* 1294

Representative character A *flat character* with the qualities of all other members of a group (i.e., clerks, cowboys, detectives, etc.); a *stereotype.* 175

Research, literary The systematic use of primary and secondary sources for assistance in studying a literary *problem.* 1925–53

Resolution See *Dénouement.*

Response A reader's intellectual and emotional reactions to a literary work. 1966

Revenge tragedy A popular type of English Renaissance drama, developed by Thomas Kyd, in which a person is called upon (often by a ghost) to avenge the murder of a loved one. Shakespeare's *Hamlet* is in the tradition of revenge tragedy. 1349

Reversal See *Peripeteia.*

Rhetoric The art of persuasive writing; broadly, the art of all effective writing. 724

Rhetorical figures See *Figures of speech.*

Rhetorical substitution See *Substitution.*

Rhyme The repetition of identical concluding *syllables* in different words, most often at the ends of *lines.* 843, 853–58

Rhyme scheme The pattern of *rhyme,* usually indicated by assigning a letter of the alphabet to each rhyming sound. 857

Rhythm The varying speed, intensity, elevation, pitch, loudness, and expressiveness of speech, especially poetry. 844–51

Rising action The action in a play before the *climax.* 1227

Rising rhyme Rhymes produced with one-syllable words, like *sky* and *fly,* or with multisyllabic words in which the accent falls on the last syllable, such as *decline* and *confine.* 854

Romance (1) Lengthy Spanish and French stories of the sixteenth and seventeenth centuries. (2) Modern formulaic stories describing the growth of an enthusiastic love relationship. 2, 52

Romantic comedy Sympathetic comedy that presents the adventures of young lovers trying to overcome opposition and achieve a successful union. 1541

Romanticism The belief and assumption that reliance on emotion provides a valid and powerful means of knowing and also a reliable guide to ways of living. 1035–38

Round character A character who profits from experience and undergoes a change or development; usually but not necessarily the *protagonist.* 174, 1225

Rules of drama An important concept of dramatic composition, particularly during the neo-classic period. The rules were based on ancient practice and theory, particularly the use of the five-act pyramidal (*Freytag*) structure and the embodiment of the *three unities* of action, place, and time. See also *Regular play.* 1227

Run-on line See *Enjambement.*

Satire An attack on human follies or vices, as measured positively against a normative religious, moral, or social standard. 816–17

Satiric comedy A form of comedy designed to correct social and individual behavior by ridiculing human vices and follies. 1541

Satyr play A comic and burlesque play submitted by the ancient Athenian tragic dramatists along with their trilogies of tragedies. On each day of tragic performances, the satyr play was performed after the three tragedies. See also *Trilogy.* 1290

Scansion The act of determining the prevailing *rhythm* of a poem. 845

Scene (1) In a play, a part or division (of an act, as in *Hamlet,* or entire play, as in *Death of a Salesman*) in which there is a unity of subject, setting, and (often) actors. (2) In a film, a unit of continuous action in one location. 1232

Scenery The artificial environment created onstage to produce the illusion of a specific or generalized place and time. 1232

Schwa A middle vowel sound that in prosodic *scansion* occupies unstressed positions, even though the sound may be spelled as <a,e,i,o, or u>. 842

Scrim A stage curtain that becomes transparent when illuminated from upstage, permitting action to take place under various lighting conditions. 1233, 1707

Second-person point of view A *narration* in which a second-person listener ("you") is the *protagonist* and the speaker is someone with knowledge the protagonist does not possess or understand about his or her own actions (e.g., doctor, parent, rejected lover, etc.). 245, 249

Segment The smallest meaningful unit of sound, such as the *l, uh,* and *v* sounds making up the word "love." Segments are to be distinguished from spellings. 843

Selective recollection See *Flashback.*

Semivowel segments Midway between the consonant and vowel segments, the semivowel segments are *y, w,* and *h.* 843

Septenary See *Heptameter.*

Seriousness The first part of Aristotle's definition of *tragedy,* showing human character at its most elevated and significant. 1295

Sestet (1) A six-line stanza or unit of poetry. (2) The last six lines of an *Italian sonnet.* 900

Sets The physical objects used in a theatrical production. 1232

Setting The natural, manufactured, and cultural environment in which characters live and move, including all the artifacts they use in their lives. 285–339, 686–714

Shakespearean sonnet See *English sonnet.*

Shaped verse Poetry written so that the lines or words of the poem form a recognizable shape, such as a pair of wings or a geometrical figure. 906–908

Short story A compact, concentrated work of *narrative fiction* that may also contain description, dialogue, and commentary. Poe used the term "brief prose tale" for the short story and emphasized that it should create a major, unified impact. 2, 52, 53, Chapters 2–12

Sight rhyme   See *Eye rhyme.*

Simile   A figure of comparison, using *like* with nouns and as with clauses, as in "the trees were bent by the wind *like actors bowing after a performance.*" 775

Simple sentence   A complete sentence containing one subject and one verb, together with modifiers and complements. 345

Situational irony   A type of *irony* emphasizing that human beings are enmeshed in forces beyond their comprehension and control. 61, 62, 385, 813, 1229, 1297

Skene   In ancient Greek theaters, the skene ("tent," "hut") was a building in front of the orchestra that contained front and side doors from which actors could make entrances and exits. It served a variety of purposes, including the storage of costumes and props. 1299

Slang   *Informal diction* and substandard vocabulary. Some slang is a permanent part of the language (e.g., phrases like "I'll be damned," "Go jump in the lake," and our many four-letter words). Other slang is spontaneous, rising within a group (*jargon*), and often then being replaced when new slang emerges. 722

Slant rhyme   A *near rhyme*, in which the concluding consonant sounds, but not the vowel sounds, are identical, as in *should* and *food, slim* and *ham.* 843

Slapstick comedy   A type of low *farce* in which the humor depends almost entirely on physical actions and sight gags. 1542

Social drama   A type of *problem play* that deals with current social issues and the place of individuals in society. 1241

Soliloquy   A speech made by a character, alone on stage, directly to the audience, the convention being that the character is revealing thoughts and feelings. A soliloquy is to be distinguished from an *aside*, which is made to the audience (or confidentially to another character) when other characters are present. 1348

Song   A lyric poem with a number of repeating stanzas, written to be set to music. 2, 901, 1295

Sonnet   A poem of fourteen lines in *iambic pentameter.* 2, 900

Soubrette   Derived from *commedia dell'arte*, a soubrette is a maidservant, usually independent and saucy, who assists young lovers in overcoming the *blocking agent* represented by a parent or other relative. 1542

Sound   The phonetics of language, collectively and separately considered. See also *Prosody.* 843

Speaker   The *narrator* of a story or poem, the *point of view;* often an independent character who is completely imagined and consistently maintained by the author. In addition to narrating the essential events of the work (justifying status as the *narrator*), the speaker may introduce other aspects of his or her knowledge and may interject judgments and opinions. Often the character of the speaker is of as much interest as the *actions* or incidents. 58, 264

Specific language   Words referring to objects or conditions that may be perceived or imagined; distinguished from *general language.* 720

Speeches   See *Dialogue.*

Spondee   A two-syllable *foot* consisting of successive, equally heavy *accents* (e.g., *slow time, men's eyes*). 847

Sprung or **accentual rhythm**   A method of accenting, developed by Gerard

Manley Hopkins, in which major *stresses* are "sprung" from the poetic line. 849

Stage business See *Business.*

Stage convention See *Convention.*

Stage directions A playwright's instructions concerning lighting, scenery, blocking, tone of voice, action, entrances and exits, and the like. 1224

Stanza A group of poetic lines corresponding to paragraphs in prose; the *meters* and *rhymes* are usually repeating or systematic. 857, 897

Stasima (singular *stasimon*) Choral odes separating the episodes in Greek tragedies. 1303

Static character A character who undergoes no change; contrasted with a *dynamic character.* 175, 1225

Stereotype A character who is so ordinary and unoriginal that he/she seems to have been cast in a mold; a *representative character.* 175, 1225

Stichomythy In Greek tragedies, dialogue consisting of one-line speeches designed for rapid delivery. 1303

Stock character A *flat character* in a standard role with standard *traits,* such as the irate police captain, the bored hotel clerk, etc.; a *stereotype.* 175,1225

Stop sound The consonant sound produced by the momentary stoppage and release of breath either when the lips touch each other or when the tongue touches the teeth or palate. The stop sounds in English are *p, t,* and *k;* and *b, d,* and *g.* 842

Story A narrative, usually fictional, centering on a major character, and rendering a complete action. 2, 57–108

Stress The emphasis given to a syllable, either strong or light. See also *Beat.* 844

Strong-stress rhythm See *Heavy-stress rhythm.*

Structuralist critical approach An interpretive approach attempting to find relationships and connections among elements that appear to be separate and discrete. 1959

Structure The arrangement and placement of materials in a work. 56–57, 62, 111–14, 164–68, 1226

Style The manipulation of language; the placement of words in the service of content. 58, 340–79

Subject The topic that a literary work addresses, such as love, marriage, war, and death. 1230

Subplot A secondary line of *action* in a literary work that often comments directly or obliquely on the main *plot.* See also *Multiple plot.* 1226

Substitution *Formal substitution* is the use of an actual variant *foot* within a line, such as an *anapest* being used in place of an *iamb. Rhetorical substitution* is the manipulation of the *caesura* to create the effect of a series of differing *feet.* 849, 851

Suspended rhyme See *Inexact rhyme.*

Syllable A separately pronounced part of a word (e.g., the *eat* and *ing* parts of "eating") or, in some cases, a complete word (e.g., *the, when, screeched*). 844

Symbol, symbolism A specific word, idea, or object that may stand for ideas, values, persons, or ways of life. 60–62, 425–62, 937–68, 1230

Symbolic character A character whose primary function is symbolic, even though the character also retains normal or realistic qualities. 1226

Symbolic critical approach See *Archetypal/symbolic/mythic critical approach.*

Synecdoche   A *figure of speech* in which a part stands for a whole, or a whole for a part. 780

Synesthesia   A *figure of speech* uniting or fusing separate sensations or feelings; the description of one type of perception or thought with words that are appropriate to another. 782

Syntax   Word order and sentence structure. A mark of style is a writer's syntactical patterning (regular patterns and variations), depending on the rhetorical needs of the literary work. 724

Syzygy   See *Dipody*.

Tactile imagery   *Images* of touch and feeling. 751

Tenor (figurative language)   The sense, or meaning, of a *metaphor, symbol*, or other rhetorical figure. See *Vehicle*. 778

Tercet   A three-line unit or *stanza* of poetry, often rhyming *a a a* or *a b a*. 899

Terza rima   A three-line *stanza* form with the pattern *A–B–A, B–C–B*, etc. 899

Tetrameter   A line consisting of four metrical *feet*. 845

Theater of Dionysus   The ancient Athenian outdoor theater where Greek drama began. 1298

Theater in the Round   See *Arena stage*.

Theme   (1) The major or central idea of a work. (2) An essay, a short composition developing an interpretation or advancing an argument. (3) The main point or idea that a writer of an essay asserts and illustrates. 57,62, 465, 667,1002, 1230

Thesis statement or **thesis sentence**   An introductory sentence that names the topics to be developed in the body of an essay. 24

Third-person objective point of view   See *Dramatic point of view*.

Third-person point of view   A third-person method of *narration* (i.e., *she, he, it, they, them*, etc.), in which the *speaker* or *narrator* is not a part of the story, as with the *first-person point of view*. Because the third-person speaker may exhibit great knowledge and understanding, together with other qualities of character, he or she is often virtually identified with the author, but this identification is not easily decided. See also *Authorial voice, Omniscient point of view*. 246–47, 249

Three unities   Traditionally associated with Aristotle's descriptions of drama as expressed in the *Poetics*, the three unities are those of action, place, and time. The unities are a function of *verisimilitude*—the creation of literature as much like reality as possible. Therefore a play should dramatize a single major *action* that takes place in a single *place* during the approximate *time* it would take for completion, from beginning to end. During the Renaissance, some critics considered the unities to be essential aspects, or *rules, of* regular *drama*. Later critics considered the unity of action important, but minimized the unities of place and time. See *Regular drama*. 1304

Thrust stage   See *Apron stage*.

Tiring house   An enclosed area in an Elizabethan theater in which actors changed costumes and awaited their cues, and in which stage properties were kept. 1347

Tone   The techniques and modes of presentation that reveal or create attitudes. 61, 380–424, 808–40, 1229

Topic sentence   The sentence determining the subject matter of a paragraph. 25–26

Topical/historical critical approach   An interpretive approach that stresses the relationship of literature to its historical period. 1956

Traditional poetry See *Closed-form poetry.*

Tragedy A drama or other literary work that recounts the fall of an individual who, while undergoing suffering, deals responsibly with the situations and dilemmas that he or she faces, and who thus demonstrates the value of human effort. 1235, 1286–1534

Tragic flaw See *Hamartia.*

Tragicomedy A literary work—drama or story—containing a mixture of tragic and comic elements. 1241

Trait, traits A typical mode of behavior; the study of major traits provides a guide to the description of *character.* 170

Trilogy A group of three literary works, usually related or unified. For the ancient Athenian *Dionysia,* each competing tragic dramatist submitted a *trilogy* (three tragedies), together with *a satyr play.* 1290

Trimeter A line consisting of three metrical *feet.* 845

Triple rhyme See *Dactylic rhyme.*

Triplet See *Tercet.*

Trochaic (double) rhyme Rhyming *trochees* such as *flower* and *shower.* 855

Trochee, trochaic A two-syllable *foot* consisting of a heavy followed by a light *stress.* 846

Trope A short dramatic dialogue inserted into the church mass during the early Middle Ages. 1236

Tudor interlude Short tragedies, comedies, or historical plays performed by both professional actors and students during the reigns of Henry VII and Henry VIII (i.e., the first half of the sixteenth century). They sometimes featured abstract and allegorical characters and provided opportunities for both music and farcical action. 1345

Understatement Rhetorically, the deliberate underplaying or undervaluing of a thing to create emphasis. 385–782

Unities See *Three unities.*

Unit set A series of platforms, rooms, stairs, and exits that form the locations for all of a play's actions. A unit set enables scenes to change rapidly, without the drawing of a curtain and the placement of new sets. 1233

Universal (public) mythology Widely known mythic systems that have been well established over a long period of time, such as Greco-Roman mythology and Germanic mythology. 973

Universal symbol See *Cultural symbols.*

Value, values The expression of an idea or ideas that concurrently asserts their importance and desirability as goals, standards, and ideals. 465

Vehicle The image or reference of *figures of speech,* such as a *metaphor* or *simile;* it is the vehicle that carries or embodies the *tenor.* 778

Verbal irony Language stressing the importance of an idea by stating the opposite of what is meant. 61, 385, 813, 1229

Verisimilitude (i.e., "like truth") or realism A characteristic whereby the setting, circumstances, characters, dialogue, actions, and outcomes in a work are designed to seem true, lifelike, real, plausible, and probable. See also *Imitation.* 53, 175, 288, 1657

Versification See *Prosody.*

Villanelle A *closed-form poem* of nineteen lines, composed of five *tercets* and a concluding *quatrain.* The form requires that whole lines be repeated in a specific order and that only two rhyming sounds occur throughout. 2, 899

Virgule   A slash mark (/) used in *scansion* to mark the boundaries of poetic *feet*. 845

Visual image   Language describing visible objects. 748

Visual poetry   Poetry that draws much of its power from the appearance of the verse on the page. See also *Concrete poetry* and *Shaped verse*. 906–908

Voice   See *Speaker*.

Vowel rhyme   The use of vowels in rhyming positions, as in *day* and *sky*, or *key* and *play*. 857

Vowel sounds or **vowel segments** Continuant sounds produced by the resonation of the voice in the space between the tongue and the top of the mouth, such as the *ee* in *feel*, the *eh* in *bet*, and the *oo* in *cool*. See also *Consonant segments*. 842

Well-made play *(la pièce bien faite)*   A form developed and popularized in nineteenth-century France by Eugène Scribe (1791–1861) and Victorien Sardou (1831–1908). Typically, the well made play is built on both secrets and the timely arrivals of new characters and threats. The *protagonist* faces adversity and ultimately overcomes it. Ibsen's *A Dollhouse* exhibits many characteristics of a well-made play. 1790

Credits

Text

Brian Aldiss, "Flight 063" from *Isaac Asimov's Science Fiction* (December 1994). Copyright © 1984 by Brian Aldiss. Reprinted with the permission of the author and his agent, Robin Straus Agency, Inc.

A. R. Ammons, "80-Proof" from *Diversifications*. Copyright © 1964 by A. R. Ammons. Reprinted with the permission of W. W. Norton & Company, Inc.

Maya Angelou, "My Arkansas" from *And Still I Rise*. Copyright ©1978 by Maya Angelou. Reprinted with the permission of Random House, Inc.

Margaret Atwood, "Rape Fantasies" from *Dancing Girls*. Copyright © 1977, 1982 by O. W. Toad, Ltd. Available in an Anchor Books edition, Doubleday. Reprinted with the permission of the author and McClelland & Stewart Ltd., Toronto. "Siren Song" from *You Are Happy: Selected Poems 1965-1975*. Copyright © 1976 by Margaret Atwood. Reprinted with the permission of Houghton Mifflin Company and Oxford University Press, Canada. All rights reserved. "Variation on the Word *Sleep*" from *Selected Poems II: Poems Selected and New 1976-1986*. Copyright ©1987 by Margaret Atwood. Reprinted with the permission of Houghton Mifflin Company and Oxford University Press, Canada. All rights reserved.

W. H. Auden, "Musée des Beaux Arts" and "The Unknown Citizen" from *W. H. Auden: Collected Poems,* edited by Edward Mendelson. Copyright 1940, renewed © 1968 by W. H. Auden. Reprinted with the permission of Random House, Inc.

Toni Cade Bambara, "The Lesson" from *Gorilla, My Love*. Copyright © 1972 by Toni Cade Bambara. Reprinted with the permission of Random House, Inc.

Imamu Amiri Baraka (LeRoi Jones), "Ka 'Ba" from *Black Magic* (Indianapolis: The Bobbs-Merrill Company, 1969). Copyright © 1969 by Amiri Baraka. Reprinted with the permission of Sterling Lord Literistic, Inc.

Wendell Berry, "Through the Weeks of Deep Snow" from *Collected Poems*. Copyright © 1985 by Wendell Berry. Reprinted with the permission of North Point Press, a division of Farrar, Straus & Giroux, LLC.

Earle Birney, "Can. Lit." from *The Collected Poems of Earle Birney*. Copyright © 1975 by Earle Birney. Reprinted with the permission of McClelland & Stewart, Inc.

Elizabeth Bishop, "The Fish" and "One Art" from *The Complete Poems 1927-1979*. Copyright © 1979, 1983 by Alice Helen Methfessel. Reprinted with the permission of Farrar, Straus & Giroux, LLC.

Louise Bogan, "Women" from *The Blue Estuaries: Poems 1923-1968*. Copyright ©1968 by Louise Bogan, copyright renewed 1996 by Ruth Limmer. Reprinted with the permission of Farrar, Straus & Giroux, LLC.

Arna Bontemps, "A Black Man Talks of Reaping" from *Personals*. Copyright ©1963 by Arna Bontemps. Reprinted with the permission of Harold Ober Associates, Incorporated.

Gwendolyn Brooks, "We Real Cool" from *Blacks;* "Primer for Blacks" from *Primer for Blacks*. Both copyright ©1991 by Gwendolyn Brooks. Reprinted with the permission of the author.

Olga Broumas, "Circe" from *Beginning With O*. Copyright ©1977 by Olga Broumas. Reprinted with the permission of Yale University Press.

Robert Olen Butler, "Snow" from *A Good Scent from a Strange Mountain*. Copyright ©1992 by Robert Olen Butler. Reprinted with the permission of Henry Holt and Company, LLC.

Lynn Emanuel, "Like God" from *Then, Suddenl.* Copyright © 1999. Reprinted with the permission of the University of Pittsburgh Press.

John Engels, "Naming the Animals" from *Vivaldi in Early Fall.* Copyright © 1981. Reprinted with the permission of The University of Georgia Press.

Abbie Huston Evans, "The Iceberg Seven-Eighths Under" from *Collected Poems.* Copyright © 1970. Reprinted with the permission of the University of Pittsburgh Press.

Mari Evans, "I am a black woman" from *I Am A Black Woman* (New York: William Morrow & Company, 1970). Copyright © 1970 by Mari Evans. Reprinted with the permission of the author.

William Faulkner, "Barn Burning" from *Collected Stories of William Faulkner.* Copyright 1950 by Random House, Inc. Copyright © renewed 1971 by Jill Faulkner Summers. Reprinted with the permission of Random House, Inc.

Edward Field, "Icarus" from *Counting Myself Lucky: Selected Poems 1963-1992* (Santa Rosa, Calif.: Black Sparrow Press, 1992). Copyright © 1992 by Edward Field. Reprinted with the permission of the author.

Carolyn Forché, "Because One Is Always Forgotten" from *The Country Between Us.* Copyright © 1981 by Carolyn Forché. Reprinted with the permission of HarperCollins Publishers, Inc.

E. M. Forster, "The Point of It" from *The Eternal Moment, And Other Stories.* Copyright 1928 and renewed © 1956 by E. M. Forster. Reprinted with the permission of Harcourt, Inc.

Robert Francis, "Catch" from *The Orb Weaver* (Middletown, Conn.: Wesleyan University Press, 1960). Copyright © 1960 by Robert Francis. Reprinted with the permission of University Press of New England.

Robert Frost, "Stopping by Woods on a Snowy Evening," "Desert Places," "A Line-Storm Song," "Mending Wall," "Birches," "The Road Not Taken," "'Out, Out–'" "Fire and Ice," "Nothing Gold Can Stay," "Misgiving," "Acquainted with the Night," "Design," "The Strong Are Saying Nothing," "A Considerable Speck," "The Silken Tent," and "Choose Something Like a Star" from *The Poetry of Robert Frost,* edited by Edward Connery Lathem. Copyright 1936, 1942, 1951, 1956 by Robert Frost. Copyright © 1964, 1970 by Lesley Frost Ballantine. Copyright 1923, 1928, © 1969 by Henry Holt and Company, Inc. Reprinted with the permission of the publishers.

Ernest J. Gaines, "The Sky Is Gray" from *Bloodline.* Copyright © 1963 by Ernest Gaines. Reprinted with the permission of Doubleday, a division of Random House, Inc.

Isabella Gardner, "At a Summer Hotel," and "Collage of Echoes" from *The Collected Poems.* Copyright © 1990 by The Estate of Isabella Gardner. Reprinted with the permission of BOA Editions Ltd.

James W. Gargano, excerpt from "The Question of Poe's Narrators" from *The Recognition of Edgar Allen Poe: Selected Criticism Since 1829,* edited by Eric W. Carlson. Copyright © 1966. Reprinted with the permission of The University of Michigan Press.

Albert J. Gelpi, excerpt from *Emily Dickinson: The Mind of the Poet.* Copyright © 1966 by the President and Fellows of Harvard College. Reprinted with the permission of Harvard University Press.

Dan Georgakas, "Hiroshima Crewman" from *Happy Man.* Reprinted with the permission of the author.

Ellen Gilchrist, "The Songs of Songs" from *Light Can Be Both a Wave and a Particle* (Boston: Little, Brown and Company, 1989). Copyright © 1989 by Ellen Gilchrist. Reprinted with the permission of Don Congdon Associates, Inc.

Allen Ginsberg, "A Supermarket in California" from *Collected Poems 1947-1980.* Copyright © 1955 by Allen Ginsberg. Reprinted with the permission of HarperCollins Publishers, Inc.

Nikki Giovanni, "Nikki-Rosa" from *Black Feeling, Black Talk, Black Judgement.* Copyright © 1968, 1970 by Nikki Giovanni. "Woman" from *Cotton Candy on a Rainy Day.* Copyright © 1978 by Nikki Giovanni. Both reprinted with the permission of William Morrow & Company, Inc.

Louise Glück, "Snowdrops" from *The Wild Iris.* Copyright © 1992 by Louise Glück. "Penelope's Song" from *Meadowlands.* Copyright © 1996 by Louise Glück. Reprinted with the permission of HarperCollins Publishers, Inc.

Jorie Graham, "The Geese" from *The Dream of the Unified Field.* Copyright © 1980, 1983, 1987, 1991, 1993, 1995 by Jorie Graham. Reprinted with the permission of HarperCollins Publishers, Inc.

Robert Graves, "The Naked and the Nude" from *The Collected Poems of Robert Graves.* Copyright © 1958 by Robert Graves. Reprinted with the permission Oxford University Press, Inc.

Joanne Greenberg, "And Sarah Laughed" from *Rites of Passage* (New York: Henry Holt, 1972). Copyright © 1972 by Joanne Greenberg. Reprinted with the permission of The Wallace Literary Agency.

Robert Haas, "Museum" from *Human Wishes.* Copyright © 1989 by Robert Haas. Reprinted with the permission of HarperCollins Publishers, Inc.

Marilyn Hacker, "Sonnet Ending with a Film Subtitle" from *Taking Notice.* Copyright © 1976, 1978, 1979, 1980 by Marilyn Hacker. Reprinted with the permission of Frances Collin Literary Agent.

John Haines, "Little Cosmic Dust Poem" from *The Owl in the Mask of the Dreamer.* Copyright © 1993 by John Haines. Reprinted with the permission of Graywolf Press, Saint Paul, Minnesota.

Donald Hall, "Whip-poor-will" and "Scenic View" from *The Happy Man.* Copyright © 1981, 1982, 1983, 1984, 1986 by Donald Hall. Reprinted with the permission of Random House, Inc.

Photographs

Chapter 2:   page 59, The Metropolitan Museum of Art; p. 63, Marion Ettlinger; p. 67, courtesy Alfred A. Knopf, photo by Nancy Crampton; p. 89, AP/Wide World Photos; p. 95, Nancy Crampton.

Chapter 3:   page 111, Lauros-Giraudon; p. 115, Corbis; p. 148, Mariana Cook; p. 150, AP/Wide World Photos.

Chapter 4:   page 171, National Gallery of Art, Washington; p. 177, Culver Pictures, Inc.; p. 190, Corbis; p. 202, AP/Wide World Photos; p. 226, Robert Foothorap.

Chapter 5:   page 250, UPI/Corbis; p. 257, Culver Pictures, Inc.; p. 268, Erich Hartmann/Magnum Photos, Inc.; p. 274, Nancy Crampton.

Chapter 6:   page 286, The Trustees of the Wallace Collection; p. 287, Des Moines Art Center; p. 290, AP/Wide World Photos; p. 322, Monika Hilleary/Wallace Literary Agency; p. 331, Julius Ozick/Raines and Raines.

Chapter 7:   page 348, UPI/Corbis; p. 353, Jerry Bauer; p. 360, G. Paul Bishop/Alfred A. Knopf, Inc.; p. 366, Corbis; p. 369, UPI/Corbis.

Chapter 8:   page 381, National Gallery of Art, Washington; p. 387, UPI/Corbis; p. 393, Missouri Historical Society; p. 395, Tyler Hodgins/McClelland & Stewart, Inc.; p. 408, David Laurence.

Chapter 9:   page 426, Alinari/Art Resource, NY; p. 436, Corbis; p. 447, UPI/Corbis; p. 454, Arvind Garg/Globe Photos, Inc.

Chapter 10:   page 464, Giraudon/Art Resource, NY; p. 495, Corbis; p. 499, Corbis; p. 511, Gil Ihrig/Irene Zabytko.

Chapter 11:   page 522, Corbis.

Chapter 12:   page 589, Earl Perry/David Richmond/Earl G. Perry; p. 595, Witherspoon Associates; p. 617, Culver Pictures, Inc.; p. 628, Reuters/Corbis; p. 635, Corbis; p. 646, Leonda Finke; p. 651, UPI/Corbis.

Chapter 16:   page 748, Manchester City Art Galleries.

Chapter 20:   page 930, Foto Marburg/Art Resource, NY.

Chapter 22:   page 971, Ansel Adams/Ansel Adams Publishing Rights Trust; p. 994, Foto Marburg/Art Resource, NY.

Chapter 23:   page 1019, Alinari/Art Resource, NY.

Chapter 24:   page 1033, Culver Pictures, Inc.; p. 1061, Corbis; p. 1101, courtesy of the Herbert H. Lamson Library, Plymouth State College, Plymouth, New Hampshire.

Chapter 26:   page 1243, AP/Wide World Photos; p. 1265, Betty C. Keller; p. 1270, UPI/Corbis.

Chapter 27:   page 1299, Gian Berto Vanni/Art Resource, NY; p. 1300, D. A. Harissiadis/Benaki Museum, Athens, Photographic Archive; p. 1304, profile of statue of Sophocles. Museo Lateranense, Vatican Museums, Vatican State. Alinari/Art Resource, NY; p. 1346, Richard Kalina; p. 1349, Stock Montage, Inc./Historical Pictures Collection; p. 1454, AP/Wide World Photos; p. 1457, Billy Rose Theater Collection, The New York Public Library for the Performing Arts, Astor, Lenox, and Tilden Foundations.

Chapter 28:   page 1624, Corbis; p. 1634, William Morris Agency, Inc.

Chapter 29:   page 1663, UPI/Corbis; p. 1703, Billy Rose Theater Collection, New York Public Library for the Performing Arts, Astor, Lenox, and Tilden Foundations.

Chapter 30:   page 1771, Corbis.

Chapter 31:   page 1787, Corbis.

Insert III, rear: The stage, Shakespeare's Globe Theatre, London, England. Full-scale model used for the 1996 Prologue season. Designed by Pentagram Design Ltd. Copyright © photo by Franklin J. Hildy.

Index of Authors, Titles, and First Lines

The names of authors are printed in **bold type,** titles in *italic type,* and first lines in Roman type.

Index of Key Terms